ALMANACK OF WORLD FOOTBALL 2007

Guy Oliver

headline

The right of Guy Oliver to be identified as the Author of
the Work has been asserted by him in accordance with the
Copyright, Designs and Patents Act 1988.

First published in 2006
by HEADLINE PUBLISHING GROUP

1

Every effort has been made to fulfil requirements with regard to reproducing copyright material.
The author and publisher will be glad to rectify any omissions at the earliest opportunity.

A CIP catalogue record for this title is available from the British Library

10-digit ISBN 0 7553 1505 7 (hardback)
13-digit ISBN 978 0 7553 1505 5 (hardback)
10-digit ISBN 0 7553 1506 5 (trade paperback)
13-digit ISBN 978 0 7553 1506 2 (trade paperback)

Design: Guy Oliver
Design consultant: Peter Ward
Cover design: Head Design Ltd

Printed and bound in Great Britain by Mackays of Chatham PLC,
Chatham, Kent

Any views expressed in the Almanack of World Football do not necessarily reflect those of FIFA.
The data within the Almanack of World Football has been obtained from a variety of sources, official
and unofficial. Harpastum Publishing cannot vouch for the accuracy of the data in all cases
except for official data provided by FIFA, which is correct as of 9 July 2006.

Headline's policy is to use papers that are natural, renewable and recyclable products and
made from wood grown in sustainable forests. The logging and manufacturing processes
are expected to conform to the environmental regulations of the country of origin.

HEADLINE PUBLISHING GROUP
A division of Hachette Livre UK Ltd
338 Euston Road
London NW1 3BH

www.headline.co.uk
www.hodderheadline.com

CONTENTS

PART ONE – FIFA AND WORLD FOOTBALL

FIFA 13

PART TWO – THE ASSOCIATIONS

PART THREE – THE CONFEDERATIONS

AFC 872

CAF 915

CONCACAF 949

CONMEBOL 959

OFC 991

UEFA 996

FIFA ABBREVIATIONS

The table below shows the order in which the countries are listed within the Almanack. For an alphabetical listing of country names and their page number, please refer to the table on pages 7 and 8

	COUNTRY	PAGE		COUNTRY	PAGE
AFG	Afghanistan	154	CTA	Central African Republic	319
AIA	Anguilla	156	CUB	Cuba	321
ALB	Albania	158	CYP	Cyprus	324
ALG	Algeria	162	CZE	Czech Republic	328
AND	Andorra	166	DEN	Denmark	332
ANG	Angola	169	DJI	Djibouti	336
ANT	Netherlands Antilles	173	DMA	Dominica	338
ARG	Argentina	175	DOM	Dominican Republic	340
ARM	Armenia	182	ECU	Ecuador	342
ARU	Aruba	186	EGY	Egypt	346
ASA	American Samoa	188	ENG	England	351
ATG	Antigua and Barbuda	190	EQG	Equatorial Guinea	364
AUS	Australia	192	ERI	Eritrea	366
AUT	Austria	197	ESP	Spain	368
AZE	Azerbaijan	201	EST	Estonia	378
BAH	Bahamas	205	ETH	Ethiopia	382
BAN	Bangladesh	207	FIJ	Fiji	384
BDI	Burundi	210	FIN	Finland	386
BEL	Belgium	212	FRA	France	390
BEN	Benin	216	FRO	Faroe Islands	399
BER	Bermuda	218	GAB	Gabon	403
BFA	Burkina Faso	221	GAM	Gambia	406
BHR	Bahrain	224	GEO	Georgia	408
BHU	Bhutan	227	GER	Germany	412
BIH	Bosnia-Herzegovina	229	GHA	Ghana	421
BLR	Belarus	233	GNB	Guinea-Bissau	424
BLZ	Belize	237	GRE	Greece	426
BOL	Bolivia	239	GRN	Grenada	430
BOT	Botswana	243	GUA	Guatemala	432
BRA	Brazil	246	GUI	Guinea	436
BRB	Barbados	257	GUM	Guam	439
BRU	Brunei Darussalam	260	GUY	Guyana	441
BUL	Bulgaria	262	HAI	Haiti	443
CAM	Cambodia	266	HKG	Hong Kong	446
CAN	Canada	268	HON	Honduras	449
CAY	Cayman Islands	271	HUN	Hungary	453
CGO	Congo	273	IDN	Indonesia	457
CHA	Chad	276	IND	India	461
CHI	Chile	278	IRL	Republic of Ireland	465
CHN	China PR	283	IRN	Iran	469
CIV	Côte d'Ivoire	289	IRQ	Iraq	473
CMR	Cameroon	293	ISL	Iceland	477
COD	Congo DR	297	ISR	Israel	481
COK	Cook Islands	300	ITA	Italy	485
COL	Colombia	302	JAM	Jamaica	495
COM	Comoros	307	JOR	Jordan	498
CPV	Cape Verde Islands	309	JPN	Japan	501
CRC	Costa Rica	311	KAZ	Kazakhstan	510
CRO	Croatia	315	KEN	Kenya	513

ALPHABETICAL LISTING OF THE ASSOCIATIONS

As the 207 member associations of FIFA are organised in the Almanack according to their trigram and not alphabetically the following table provides a quick alphabetical reference to page numbers.

COUNTRY		PAGE	COUNTRY		PAGE
Afghanistan	AFG	154	Côte d'Ivoire	CIV	289
Albania	ALB	158	Croatia	CRO	315
Algeria	ALG	162	Cuba	CUB	321
American Samoa	ASA	188	Cyprus	CYP	324
Andorra	AND	166	Czech Republic	CZE	328
Angola	ANG	169	Denmark	DEN	332
Anguilla	AIA	156	Djibouti	DJI	336
Antigua and Barbuda	ATG	190	Dominica	DMA	338
Argentina	ARG	175	Dominican Republic	DOM	340
Armenia	ARM	182	Ecuador	ECU	342
Aruba	ARU	186	Egypt	EGY	346
Australia	AUS	192	El Salvador	SLV	738
Austria	AUT	197	England	ENG	351
Azerbaijan	AZE	201	Equatorial Guinea	EQG	364
Bahamas	BAH	205	Eritrea	ERI	366
Bahrain	BHR	224	Estonia	EST	378
Bangladesh	BAN	207	Ethiopia	ETH	382
Barbados	BRB	257	Faroe Islands	FRO	399
Belarus	BLR	233	Fiji	FIJ	384
Belgium	BEL	212	Finland	FIN	386
Belize	BLZ	237	France	FRA	390
Benin	BEN	216	Gabon	GAB	403
Bermuda	BER	218	Gambia	GAM	406
Bhutan	BHU	227	Georgia	GEO	408
Bolivia	BOL	239	Germany	GER	412
Bosnia-Herzegovina	BIH	229	Ghana	GHA	421
Botswana	BOT	243	Greece	GRE	426
Brazil	BRA	246	Grenada	GRN	430
British Virgin Islands	VGB	846	Guam	GUM	439
Brunei Darussalam	BRU	260	Guatemala	GUA	432
Bulgaria	BUL	262	Guinea	GUI	436
Burkina Faso	BFA	221	Guinea-Bissau	GNB	424
Burundi	BDI	210	Guyana	GUY	441
Cambodia	CAM	266	Haiti	HAI	443
Cameroon	CMR	293	Honduras	HON	449
Canada	CAN	268	Hong Kong	HKG	446
Cape Verde Islands	CPV	309	Hungary	HUN	453
Cayman Islands	CAY	271	Iceland	ISL	477
Central African Republic	CTA	319	India	IND	461
Chad	CHA	276	Indonesia	IDN	457
Chile	CHI	278	Iran	IRN	469
China PR	CHN	283	Iraq	IRQ	473
Chinese Taipei	TPE	802	Israel	ISR	481
Colombia	COL	302	Italy	ITA	485
Comoros	COM	307	Jamaica	JAM	495
Congo	CGO	273	Japan	JPN	501
Congo DR	COD	297	Jordan	JOR	498
Cook Islands	COK	300	Kazakhstan	KAZ	510
Costa Rica	CRC	311	Kenya	KEN	513

ACKNOWLEDGEMENTS

As with the first edition of the *Almanack of World Football*, a number of people have made significant contributions to this, the second edition. I am deeply indebted to Mark Gleeson for his expert analysis and round-ups of each of the countries in Africa and for helping to fill some of the inevitable gaps there. I am also much obliged to Daniel Fein for his statistical input with regard to the seasonal records of the 30 players short-listed for the FIFA World Player award.

There have been a number of significant improvements in this edition, notably in Part Three which deals with the confederations. Along with maps of each confederation we have included line ups and more detailed match information for the Champions League tournaments in Europe, Africa and Asia, along with the Copa Libertadores in South America. My thanks especially to Ravi Kumar at the AFC for his efforts on my behalf. Thanks also to Seamus Marten at the OFC and to the press department at UEFA for their help. A number of national associations, notably David Brand in American Samoa, have also readily provided data which is appreciated and I have made good use of the numerous websites run by many of the 207 associations affiliated to FIFA.

Once again Marius Schneider and his team at FIFA have been invaluable in answering my queries and providing the official data for the FIFA tournaments that have been played throughout the year. During the FIFA World Cup™ finals the official FIFAWorldCup.com website received over five billion page hits of which I was responsible for a good few. It is well worth visiting even now after the tournament has finished. Other websites that are invaluable for followers of the world game are the-afc.com, uefa.com, conmebol.com (which is now also available in English), concacaf.com and oceaniafootball.com, all of which provide detailed coverage of the game in their respective continents. Not forgetting FIFA.com with its full coverage of the game at international level and beyond.

I have once again relied on the hard work and dedication of the network of contributors to the rsssf.com and I can't praise highly enough the work they do and their passion for the game. My thanks also to Tom Lewis for his contribution to the China PR section and to Cris Freddi for putting me on the right track with regard to player caps and goals. Much appreciated. A huge thanks to Helen de Haan at FIFA. It has been a pleasure working with you. Also Lars Bretscher who became a dad on the day the Almanack was published in 2005. We must be coming up to Finn's first birthday! Thanks also to Andreas Herren for your support and goodwill.

I very much appreciate the efforts of Headline in getting the Almanack off the ground, especially Lorraine Jerram and David Wilson. Thanks also to Lucy Le Poidevin and, from a technical point of view, Rachel Geere. I couldn't hope to work with a better publisher. Thanks also to Paul Marsh and Camilla Ferrier for their efforts in spreading the word.

Last year in the rush to get the first edition completed, I forgot to thank a few key people, notably Michael Kirton for his generosity and advice in the early days. Thanks also to Marion, Liz, Barney, Christopher and Sava for unlocking the mysteries of excel spreadsheets which has made some of the tasks related to the Almanack much easier. Also to Helen Williams who was involved with the design of much of the earlier promotional material.

Finally, you would not be reading this without the invaluable contributions of the following: Tom Chittick for his brilliant and unquestioning support for the Almanack; Oliver Greenleaves for his expert skill in compiling significant amounts of data; Roger Lakin, wordsmith extraordinaire; my father Michael Oliver, wordsmith extraordinaire and self confessed grammar pedant who can spot a split infinitive a mile off - it's been a pleasure having you around - Dorothy Turner for being there for Ally and Archie and for doing the odd school run in the pouring rain; and finally to my family for being just brilliant - Ally and Archie you are just the best kids in the world and Sharyn, aside from your huge help inputting data, I just couldn't carry on doing this without your support, understanding and love.

Guy Oliver, Twickenham, August 2006

PART ONE

FIFA AND
WORLD FOOTBALL

FIFA

Fédération Internationale de Football Association

2005-06 was a busy year for FIFA with the staging of three major tournaments: the 2005 FIFA U-17 World Championship in Peru in September 2005; the first staging in its current format of the FIFA Club World Championship, in December 2005 in Japan; and of course the 2006 FIFA World Cup™ in Germany. Reports on all three tournaments can be found in part one of the Almanack on pages 33, 47 and 95 respectively. FIFA was rarely out of the headlines in the 2005-06 season, and not just because of the finals in Germany. Concerned about political interference in the running of football, FIFA suspended Yemen in August 2005 and action was also taken against a number of other associations, including Greece, whose defence of their European crown was threatened briefly by suspension in July 2006. Fortunately, it didn't take long for the politicians to come to their senses. At the first ever FIFA Congress in Africa, held in Marrakech in September 2005, Comoros and Timor-Leste were elected as the 206th and 207th members of FIFA. The Marrakech Congress also saw the creation of the FIFA Task Force for the Good of the Game, established to provide a framework for looking into and dealing with issues concerning financial matters, political matters and competitions. One of the task force's biggest challenges will be striking the right balance between

THE FIFA BIG COUNT OF 2000

	Male	Female		Male	Female
Registered players	12 487 938	491 296	Referees	678 011	41 833
Non registered players	82 214 931	9 188 610	Officials	3 218 480	428 828
Youth players	15 793 467	2 204 348	Total involved	220 496 336	21 884 254
Children & Occasional	110 000 000	10 000 000	in football	246 747 742	
Professionals	125 304	2 160	Number of clubs	305 060	
Total players	242 380 590		Number of teams	1 548 146	

club and international football, an issue highlighted by the Charleroi court case involving Abdelmajid Oulmers, who was injured on national team duty with Morocco. Racism, most notably in Spain, blighted the 2005-06 season in Europe, and so the Executive Committee of FIFA approved a change to article 55 of the FIFA Disciplinary Code to allow strict sanctions to be imposed on clubs associated with racist acts. Measures include the imposition of a three point deduction for a first offence, six points for a second offence and relegation if problems persist. FIFA also came down hard on Turkey for the incidents following its play-off defeat at the hands of Switzerland in November. In addition to suspensions for the players involved, the national side was forced to play three competitive home matches either behind closed doors or on neutral territory. At the FIFA World Player Gala in December 2005, Ronaldinho and Birgit Prinz scooped the main prizes; the football community of Iquitos in Peru won the FIFA Fair Play Award for their hospitality during the FIFA U-17 World Championship in Peru; and referee, Anders Frisk, won the Presidential Award. Frisk was subject to appalling harassment after officiating in the UEFA

Fédération Internationale de Football Association (FIFA)
FIFA-Strasse 20, PO Box, 8044 Zürich, Switzerland
Tel +41 43 222 7777   Fax +41 43 222 7878
contact@fifa.org
www.fifa.com
www.fifaworldcup.com
President: BLATTER Joseph S.
General Secretary: LINSI Urs   Deputy General Secretary: SCHALLART Michael
Delegate of the President for Special Affairs: CHAMPAGNE Jérôme

FIFA EXECUTIVE COMMITTEE

President: BLATTER Joseph S. SUI   Senior Vice-President: GRONDONA Julio ARG   Vice-President: WILL David H. SCO

Vice-President: JOHANSSON Lennart SWE   Vice-President: HAYATOU Issa CMR   Vice-President: CHUNG Mong Joon, Dr KOR

Vice-President: WARNER Jack A. TRI   Vice-President: VILLAR LLONA Angel Maria ESP

ORDINARY MEMBERS OF THE EXECUTIVE COMMITTEE

D'HOOGHE Michel, Dr BEL	SASSO SASSO Isaac David CRC	TEIXEIRA Ricardo Terra BRA
BIN HAMMAM Mohamed QAT	ERZIK Senes TUR	BLAZER Chuck USA
MAKUDI Worawi THA	LEOZ Nicolás, Dr PAR	TBD
DIAKITE Amadou MLI	KOLOSKOV Viacheslav, Dr RUS	MAYER-VORFELDER Gerhard GER
PLATINI Michel FRA	FUSIMALOHI 'Ahongalu TGA	OGURA Junji JPN
CHIBOUB Slim TUN	Observer: TEMARII Reynald TAH	General Secretary: LINSI Urs, Dr SUI

Champions League match between Chelsea and Barcelona and he subsequently quit the game. His award was intended as a strong signal to players and fans alike to respect match officials. January 2006 saw UN Secretary-General Kofi Annan visit FIFA House to promote projects like "Red Card to Child Labour" and to foster further cooperation between the two bodies. In March, the main focus of the meeting of the International Football Association Board (IFAB) was to approve a series of modifications to the Laws of the Game and to endorse instructions to referees and assistant referees to clamp down on time-wasting, reckless play, simulation, and gamesmanship in general. The IFAB also gave the green light for further tests on goal-line technologies, with the proviso that any system would have to give an immediate indication to the referee so as not to disrupt games. Also in March, FIFA approved its 100th GOAL project in Africa, and Timor-Leste, Libya, Jamaica, Mexico, Canada, New Caledonia, Iceland and Wales were all given the go-ahead for first-time projects, bringing to 181 the number of countries to have benefited from the programme. In April, FIFA announced a surplus of 214 million Swiss Francs in its 2005 accounts. The future stability of the governing body, which moved into its new headquarters opposite the city zoo in May 2006, looks assured after the restructuring of its sponsorship strategy. A new top tier of six FIFA partners have been signed up for the period 2007- 2014, with Emirates Airline signing a deal in April for $195m thus joining Hyundai, Sony and Visa who had already joined the programme. The sixth partner, Coca-Cola, is committed until 2022. At the FIFA Congress in Munich in June 2006 a new Ethics Committee was approved to tackle illegal betting, manipulation, bribery and other illegal practices. FIFA also amended its statutes to bring it into line with the World Anti-Doping Agency code, while retaining the right to use individual case management. Finally, the FIFA Coca-Cola World Ranking system was revised with the main change being to determine countries' positions based on results over the last four, rather than eight years.

OTHER FIFA COMMITTEES

	Chairman	Organising Committee for...	Chairman
Emergency Committee	BLATTER Joseph S.	The FIFA World Cup™	JOHANSSON Lennart
Finance Committee	GRONDONA Julio H.	The FIFA Confederations Cup	BLAZER Chuck
Internal Audit Committee	CARRARO Franco, Dr	The Olympic Football Tournaments	HAYATOU Issa
Referees' Committee	VILLAR LLONA Angel Maria	The FIFA World Youth Championship	WARNER Jack A.
Technical & Development Committee	PLATINI Michel	The U-17 World Championship	WARNER Jack A.
Sports Medical Committee	D'HOOGHE Michel, Dr	The FIFA Club World Championship	KOLOSKOV Viacheslav, Dr
Players' Status Committee	MAYER-VORFELDER Gerhard	Women's Football and FIFA Women's World Cup	MAKUDI Worawi
Legal Committee	WILL David H.	The U-20 and U-17 Women's World Cups	BALZER Chuck
Committee for Ethics and Fair Play	ERZIK Senes	The FIFA Club World Cup	KOLOSKOV Viacheslav
Media Committee	MAYER-VORFELDER Gerhard	Futsal and Beach Soccer Committee	TEIXEIRA Ricardo Terra
Associations Committee	KOLOSKOV Viacheslav, Dr	Marketing and Television Advisory Board	GRONDONA Julio H.
Football Committee	VILLAR LLONA Angel Maria	FIFA Club Task Force	MAYER-VORFELDER Gerhard
Strategic Study Committee	BLATTER Joseph S.	FIFA Medical Assessment and Research Centre	D'HOOGHE Michel, Dr
Goal Bureau	BIN HAMMAM Mohamed	Doping Control Sub-Committee	D'HOOGHE Michel, Dr
Disciplinary Committee	MATHIER Marcel, Me.	Appeal Committee	SALGUERO Rafael
FIFA Club Task Force	CHIBOUB Slim		

FIFA TOURNAMENTS

FIFA WORLD CUP™

Year	Host Country	Winners	Score	Runners-up	Venue
1930	Uruguay	Uruguay	4-2	Argentina	Centenario, Montevideo
1934	Italy	Italy	2-1	Czechoslovakia	PNF, Rome
1938	France	Italy	4-2	Hungary	Colombes, Paris
1950	Brazil	Uruguay	2-1	Brazil	Maracanã, Rio de Janeiro
1954	Switzerland	Germany FR	3-2	Hungary	Wankdorf, Berne
1958	Sweden	Brazil	5-2	Sweden	Råsunda, Stockholm
1962	Chile	Brazil	3-1	Czechoslovakia	Estadio Nacional, Santiago
1966	England	England	4-2	Germany FR	Wembley, London
1970	Mexico	Brazil	4-1	Italy	Azteca, Mexico City
1974	Germany FR	Germany FR	2-1	Netherlands	Olympiastadion, Munich
1978	Argentina	Argentina	3-1	Netherlands	Monumental, Buenos Aires
1982	Spain	Italy	3-1	Germany FR	Bernabeu, Madrid
1986	Mexico	Argentina	3-2	Germany FR	Azteca, Mexico City
1990	Italy	Germany FR	1-0	Argentina	Olimpico, Rome
1994	USA	Brazil	0-0 3-2p	Italy	Rose Bowl, Pasadena
1998	France	France	3-0	Brazil	Stade de France, Paris
2002	Korea Rep/Japan	Brazil	2-0	Germany	International Stadium, Yokohama
2006	Germany	Italy	1-1 5-3p	France	Olympiastadion, Berlin

The FIFA World Cup™ is the most popular single sports event in the world and ranks alongside the Olympic Games as the focus of sporting attention in the years that the two sporting festivals are held. When FIFA was founded in 1904 it reserved the right to organise a world championship for its members. However, it took more than a quarter of a century for that aim to become reality and it wasn't until the Barcelona Congress of 1929 that a resolution was passed paving the way for the first tournament to be held the following year in Uruguay. The reason the World Cup was such a long time in coming was due to the huge appeal of the Football Tournament of the Olympic Games, the winners of which were regarded as world champions. The Olympic tournament had first been officially organised in 1908 but by the late 1920s there was growing disquiet amongst the members of FIFA that, because of the amateur ethos and the surge of professionalism after 1925, especially within central Europe, the best players were no longer eligible to compete. Although FIFA was responsible for organising the Olympic Football Tournament, the then FIFA President Jules Rimet realised that the best way forward was to organise a separate tournament that was open to anyone. Just 13 teams entered the first tournament, a figure that has risen to over 200 today. It may be the dream of every footballer to take part in the FIFA World Cup™ but only a very select club of players and nations have won the coveted prize – seven nations and 274 players to be precise. Staged every four years, the finals have been hosted by 15 countries with Mexico, Italy, France and Germany each having been granted the honour twice. For many years the hosting would alternate between the Americas and Europe but in 2002 Asia welcomed the tournament for the first time and in 2010 South Africa will entertain as each continent is given a chance on a rotational basis. Much of the excitement of the FIFA World Cup™ can also be found in the qualifying tournaments, which in some parts of the world are now spread over two years. The 32 places in the finals are decided on a continental basis with the hosts, but no longer the holders, qualifying automatically. For the 2006 tournament South America had four guaranteed places, Europe 13, Africa five, Asia four and Central and North America three, with the final two places decided via a series of play-offs between all the Confederations bar Europe and Africa. For many just making it to the finals is achievement enough although for the elite the aim remains focused on winning the Cup itself. Not that the trophy is actually a cup anymore. For the first eight tournaments it was possible to celebrate by drinking champagne from the Jules Rimet trophy, but since 1974 the solid gold trophy is in the form of a globe, held aloft by two athletes at the moment of victory.

FIFA WOMEN'S WORLD CUP

Year	Host Country	Winners	Score	Runners-up	Venue
1991	China PR	USA	2-1	Norway	Tianhe, Guangzhou
1995	Sweden	Norway	2-0	Germany	Råsunda, Stockholm
1999	USA	USA	0-0 5-4p	China PR	Rose Bowl, Pasadena
2003	USA	Germany	2-1	Sweden	Home Depot Centre, Carson

With the rapid growth of women's football since the 1970s it was a logical step for FIFA to organise a World Cup for women in 1991 to replace the growing number of unofficial tournaments that were being staged around the world. As early as 1970, 40,000 fans in the Stadio Communale in Turin watched Denmark beat Italy to win the Coppa del Mondo while the following year the Danes won the Mundial 1971 in front of 110,000 fans in Mexico City's Azteca Stadium, beating the hosts in the final of a tournament that had been played to packed stadia throughout. The surge in interest in women's football in the Far East and in the Americas in the late 1980s convinced FIFA that the time was right to get involved in the women's game. In 1988 they organised the FIFA Women's Invitation Tournament in China PR. The event, won by Norway, who beat Sweden in the final in Guangzhou, was a huge success although it isn't counted as part of the FIFA Women's World Cup record. The first official tournament was held three years later, in 1991, and again hosted by China PR. The winners were the United States, a major player in the popularisation of the women's game thanks to the seven million women and girls involved with football there. Two of the tournaments since then have been held in the USA although the 2003 tournament should have been held in China but was switched to the States due to the SARS outbreak in the Far East. Many expected the hosts to win the Cup for a third time but the Germans surprised everyone by becoming the third nation to be crowned world champions after the USA and Norway. Played every four years the tournament has firmly established itself as the pinnacle of the women's game. The next edition will be held in China PR in September 2007.

FIFA CLUB WORLD CUP

Year	Host Country	Winners	Score	Runners-up	Venue
2000	Brazil	Corinthians, BRA	0-0 4-3p	Vasco da Gama, BRA	Maracana, Rio de Janeiro
2005	Japan	São Paulo FC, BRA	1-0	Liverpool, ENG	Yokohama International, Tokyo

Rarely has there been more controversy engendered by a tournament than the furore surrounding the FIFA Club World Championship; yet the logic behind the tournament is incontrovertible. Every Confederation has a championship for national teams and club sides yet for decades the only world championship has been for national teams. Fans around the world have been denied the chance to watch their teams play against clubs from different Confederations and vie for the title of world champions. European critics railed against FIFA when the FIFA Club World Championship was introduced in 2000 citing an overcrowded fixture list. The argument was put on hold following the bankruptcy of FIFA's marketing partners ISL in 2001 which meant a five year gap before the second edition could be organised. Once again the top European clubs complained, even threatening to boycott the tournament but after taking on their concerns, FIFA announced that the second Club World Championship would take place in Tokyo in December 2005, replacing the annual Toyota Cup played between the European and South American club champions and that it would be held annually thereafter. Club fears of a fixture overload were resolved by adopting a straight knock-out format with the Asian, African, Central and North American and Oceania teams playing a preliminary round with the European and South American champions joining in for the semi-finals. To win the first title in 2000, Brazilian club Corinthians had to play four games over nine days, but it took just two games for their compatriots São Paulo FC to be crowned champions in 2005. In December 2004 FC Porto were the final winners of the Toyota Cup, ending a 44 year chapter of European and South American competition and ushering in a new and long overdue era in club football in which the champions of all six confederations can battle for the mantle of world champions.

MEN'S OLYMPIC FOOTBALL TOURNAMENT

Year	Host City	Winners	Score	Runners-up	Venue
1896	Athens	Demonstration sport			
1900	Paris	Demonstration sport			
1904	St Louis	Demonstration sport			
1906	Athens	Demonstration sport			
1908	London	England	2-0	Denmark	White City, London
1912	Stockholm	England	4-2	Denmark	Stockholms Stadion, Stockholm
1916	Berlin	Games cancelled			
1920	Antwerp	Belgium	2-0	Czechoslovakia	Olympisch Stadion, Antwerp
1924	Paris	Uruguay	3-0	Switzerland	Colombes, Paris
1928	Amsterdam	Uruguay	1-1 2-1	Argentina	Olympisch Stadion, Amsterdam
1932	Los Angeles	No football tournament played			
1936	Berlin	Italy	2-1	Austria	Olympiastadion, Berlin
1940	Tokyo/Helsinki	Games cancelled			
1944	London	Games cancelled			
1948	London	Sweden	3-1	Yugoslavia	Wembley, London
1952	Helsinki	Hungary	2-0	Yugoslavia	Olympiastadion, Helsinki
1956	Melbourne	Soviet Union	1-0	Yugoslavia	Melbourne Cricket Ground
1960	Rome	Yugoslavia	3-1	Denmark	Flaminio, Rome
1964	Tokyo	Hungary	2-1	Czechoslovakia	National Stadium, Tokyo
1968	Mexico City	Hungary	4-1	Bulgaria	Azteca, Mexico City
1972	Munich	Poland	2-1	Hungary	Olympiastadion, Munich
1976	Montreal	German DR	3-1	Poland	Olympic Stadium, Montreal
1980	Moscow	Czechoslovakia	1-0	German DR	Centralny, Moscow
1984	Los Angeles	France	2-0	Brazil	Rose Bowl, Pasadena
1988	Seoul	Soviet Union	2-1	Brazil	Olympic Stadium, Seoul
1992	Barcelona	Spain	3-2	Poland	Camp Nou, Barcelona
1996	Atlanta	Nigeria	3-2	Argentina	Sanford Stadium, Athens
2000	Sydney	Cameroon	2-2 5-4p	Spain	Olympic Stadium, Sydney
2004	Athens	Argentina	1-0	Paraguay	Olympic Stadium, Athens

The history of the Men's Olympic Football Tournament can be divided into three broad phases. Before the introduction of the FIFA World Cup™ in 1930 the winners were lauded as world champions, an honour won twice by Uruguay and England (playing under the banner of Great Britain) and once by Belgium. After 1928 the tournament remained amateur in a world increasingly dominated by professionalism, a situation exploited by countries from the communist bloc who were professionals in all but name. From 1952 until 1980 teams from behind the Iron Curtain walked off with every title, notably the Hungarians, winners in 1952, 1964 and 1968. For the 1984 and 1988 tournaments the amateur restrictions were relaxed with all players who had not taken part in a World Cup eligible to compete, but in 1992 the third major phase began when it became an age-restricted tournament for under-23s although three over-age players were also permitted in the team. Sixteen nations have won Olympic football gold although it is a competition that has been dominated by Europe with only four nations from elsewhere winning the prize. After the legendary triumphs of Uruguay in the 1920s it wasn't until 2004 that another South American team – Argentina – won and the Olympic title remains the only major title not yet won by Brazil. In 1996 Nigeria broke the duck for Africa and that was followed in Sydney four years later by Cameroon. Four previous winners no longer exist as countries – the Soviet Union, East Germany, Czechoslovakia and Yugoslavia while there is also some confusion as to the inaugural winners. The team representing Great Britain was the famous pre-World War One England amateur team that was so instrumental in spreading the game across Europe, hence the listing as England rather than Great Britain. As with the FIFA World Cup™ the finalists for the Olympics are decided by continental qualifying competitions which in 2004 resulted in four finalists from Africa and Europe (including hosts Greece), three from Asia, two from South America, two from the rest of the Americas and one from Oceania.

WOMEN'S OLYMPIC FOOTBALL TOURNAMENT

Year	Host City	Winners	Score	Runners-up	Venue
1996	Atlanta	USA	2-1	China	Sanford Stadium, Athens
2000	Sydney	Norway	3-2	USA	Sydney Football Stadium, Sydney
2004	Athens	USA	2-1	Brazil	Karaiskaki, Piraeus

Women's football is a very recent addition to the list of Olympic sports but in conjunction with the FIFA Women's World Cup it now provides the sport with a second championship of world repute, as, unlike the men's Olympic Football Tournament, the full national teams can enter. The 1996 games in Atlanta were the perfect launch pad for the Women's Olympic Football Tournament with the final between the USA and China witnessed by 76,489 in the Sanford Stadium in Athens, Georgia, while the average for all games was 39,362. The United States have remained the predominant force since winning the first final against China, losing to Norway in Sydney and then winning again in 2004 against Brazil. Whereas the participants for the 1996 tournament qualified by finishing amongst the top eight in the 1995 Women's World Cup, there is now a qualifying tournament run along continental lines.

FIFA CONFEDERATIONS CUP

Year	Host Country	Winners	Score	Runners-up	Venue
1992	Saudi Arabia	Argentina	3-1	Saudi Arabia	King Fahd, Riyadh
1995	Saudi Arabia	Denmark	2-0	Argentina	King Fahd, Riyadh
1997	Saudi Arabia	Brazil	6-0	Australia	King Fahd, Riyadh
1999	Mexico	Mexico	4-3	Brazil	Azteca, Mexico City
2001	Korea/Japan	France	1-0	Japan	International Stadium, Yokohama
2003	France	France	1-0	Cameroon	Stade de France, Paris
2005	Germany	Brazil	4-1	Argentina	Waldstadion, Frankfurt

Conceived in 1992, the Confederations Cup's purpose was to bring together the continental champions from around the world. Initially known as the King Fahd Cup, it was later rebranded the FIFA Confederations Cup in 1997 when it came under FIFA's control. Riyadh in Saudi Arabia staged the first three editions, but from 1999 other countries were give the opportunity to host the tournament in an effort to broaden its appeal and before the 2002 and 2006 FIFA World Cups™ it was used as a timely trial run in Korea Republic and Japan in 2001 and in Germany in 2005. After drawing criticism from within Europe, especially among the big clubs who complained of fixture overcrowding, FIFA responded by switching the tournament from a two year to a four year cycle. As in 2001 and 2005 it will now be used as a trial run before each FIFA World Cup™ with the next edition in South Africa in 2009.

FIFA FUTSAL WORLD CHAMPIONSHIP

Year	Host Country	Winners	Score	Runners-up	Venue
1989	Netherlands	Brazil	2-1	Netherlands	Rotterdam
1992	Hong Kong	Brazil	4-1	United States	Hong Kong
1996	Spain	Brazil	6-4	Spain	Barcelona
2000	Guatemala	Spain	4-3	Brazil	Guatemala City
2004	Chinese Taipei	Spain	2-1	Italy	Taipei City

Futsal, the five-a-side indoor version of football, has become an increasingly important part of FIFA's work and since 1989 there have been five FIFA Futsal World Championships. The first three were won by Brazil, the major power in the game, though that position has been challenged by Spain, who have won the past two titles. Via a series of continental qualifiers, most of which double up as continental championships, 16 teams qualify for the finals. Games consist of two periods of 20 minutes and any of seven substitutes may be brought on or taken off throughout the game as many times as desired.

FIFA U-20 WORLD CUP

Year	Host Country	Winners	Score	Runners-up	Final Venue
1977	Tunisia	Soviet Union	2-2 9-8p	Mexico	El Menzah, Tunis
1979	Japan	Argentina	3-1	Soviet Union	National Stadium, Tokyo
1981	Australia	Germany FR	4-0	Qatar	Sydney Cricket Ground
1983	Mexico	Brazil	1-0	Argentina	Azteca, Mexico City
1985	Soviet Union	Brazil	1-0	Spain	Centralny, Moscow
1987	Chile	Yugoslavia	1-1 5-4p	Germany FR	Estadio Nacional, Santiago
1989	Saudi Arabia	Portugal	2-0	Nigeria	King Fahd, Riyadh
1991	Portugal	Portugal	0-0 4-2p	Brazil	Da Luz, Lisbon
1993	Australia	Brazil	2-1	Ghana	Sydney Football Stadium, Sydney
1995	Qatar	Argentina	2-0	Brazil	Khalifa, Doha
1997	Malaysia	Argentina	2-1	Uruguay	Shahalam Stadium, Shah Alam
1999	Nigeria	Spain	4-0	Japan	Surulere, Lagos
2001	Argentina	Argentina	3-0	Ghana	Jose Amalfitani, Buenos Aires
2003	UAE	Brazil	1-0	Spain	Zayed Sports City, Abu Dhabi
2005	Netherlands	Argentina	2-1	Nigeria	Galgenwaard, Utrecht
2007	Canada				Toronto

As well as the Football Tournament of the Olympic Games, FIFA organises three other major age-restricted championships. The longest established of these is the FIFA World Youth Championship, competed for by players under the age of 20. Starting with the 2007 edition to be held in Canada, the tournament will be known by a new name, the FIFA U-20 World Cup. Since its inception in 1977 in Tunisia, the tournament has been held every two years and countries from all six Confederations have hosted the event at least once. The winners of the FIFA World Youth Championship have all hailed from either Europe or South America, with Argentina having won five titles and Brazil four - double the number of their nearest rivals, Portugal. At first, many were sceptical of the value of a youth tournament, especially with the problems associated with over-aged players. But it seems that this issue has died down, largely thanks to the harsh penalties handed out to those caught cheating. The FIFA World Youth Championship is now seen in most countries as a vital step in the education of the top young footballers, where they can encounter high pressure tournament conditions and different styles of play early in their careers - experiences that benefit both their clubs, and, later on, their full national teams. Clubs in some countries still prefer their younger players to not take part, but it is surely no coincidence that countries like Brazil, Argentina and Spain, where support for the tournament is strong, are producing young players of a very high calibre consistently. The first tournament, in 1977, was also the first global tournament to take place in Africa, with the Soviet Union beating Mexico 9-8 on penalties in Tunis. Through the years, many great players have graced the tournament, none more so than in 1979 when Diego Maradona lead his team to a title that was celebrated in Argentina almost as much as the FIFA World Cup™ win the year before. Germany's only title came two years later in Australia, when they beat Qatar, the smallest nation ever to appear in a FIFA final. Then it was the turn of Brazil, who won the 1983 and 1985 tournaments with players such as current national team coach, Carlos Dunga, and the 1994 FIFA World Cup™ winners Claudio Taffarel, Jorginho and Bebeto. One of the most famous triumphs came in Chile in 1987, when a European team won a FIFA tournament on South American soil for the first and, so far, only time. The triumphant Yugoslav side contained great names such as Zvonimir Boban, Robert Prosinecki and Davor Suker. The next two tournaments, in 1989 and 1991, saw back-to-back wins for Portugal with a group of players that were soon to become known as the 'Golden Generation,' notably Luis Figo, João Pinto, Paulo Sousa and Rui Costa. In the 1990s, Argentina rose to prominence again, winning in 1995, 1997 and 2001 under the guidance of coach Jose Pekerman, and then again in 2005 to seal a record five titles. In-between, Spain won a first title in 1999 in Nigeria, the first time a FIFA tournament had been played in sub-Saharan Africa. The 2007 tournament in Canada, which kicks off on Saturday 30 June, will be held in six cities: Edmonton (Group A), Burnaby (B), Toronto (C), Montreal (D), Ottawa (E) and Victoria (F). The final will be held on July 22 in the new soccer stadium in Toronto.

FIFA U-17 WORLD CHAMPIONSHIP

Year	Host Country	Winners	Score	Runners-up	Final Venue
1985	China	Nigeria	2-0	Germany FR	Workers' Stadium, Beijing
1987	Canada	Soviet Union	1-1 3-1p	Nigeria	Varsity Stadium, Toronto
1989	Scotland	Saudi Arabia	2-2 5-4p	Scotland	Hampden Park, Glasgow
1991	Italy	Ghana	1-0	Spain	Comunale, Florence
1993	Japan	Nigeria	2-1	Ghana	National Stadium, Tokyo
1995	Ecuador	Ghana	3-2	Brazil	Monumental, Guayaquil
1997	Egypt	Brazil	2-1	Ghana	National Stadium, Cairo
1999	New Zealand	Brazil	0-0 8-7p	Australia	North Harbour, Auckland
2001	Trinidad	France	3-0	Nigeria	Hasely Crawford, Port of Spain
2003	Finland	Brazil	1-0	Spain	Töölö, Helsinki
2005	Peru	Mexico	3-0	Brazil	Estadio Nacional, Lima
2007	Korea Republic				

The second of the FIFA age-restricted tournaments to be introduced was the FIFA U-17 World Championship, now known as the FIFA U-17 World Cup. It has been held every two years since 1985 and countries from all six Confederations have hosted the event at least once. Brazil is the most successful nation in the history of the tournament with three titles, all won in a six year period between 1997 and 2003. Competition has been much more open than in the U-20 event, with African, Asian and North American sides all challenging the supremacy of the South Americans and Europeans by winning tournaments. Right from the start, Nigeria beat Germany 2-0 in Beijing in the final of the inaugural 1985 tournament to become the first African world champions at any level. The Nigerians reached the final again in Toronto two years later, but were beaten on penalties by the Soviet Union. In the third tournament, Saudi Arabia were the surprise winners, beating Scotland in another final decided on penalties to give Asia its first world championship. By reaching the final, the Scots were the first and so far only host nation to make it that far. African supremacy at this level was then confirmed in Italy in 1991, Japan in 1993 and in Ecuador in 1995, with Ghana appearing in all three finals, winning in 1991 and 1995 and losing to Nigeria in Tokyo in 1993. In the late 1990s, Brazil, rather belatedly, began to flex their muscles with Ronaldinho inspiring his country to its first triumph in the 1997 finals in Egypt - a title successfully defended two years later in New Zealand. France was the first European winner for 14 years when they beat Nigeria in the 2001 final in Trinidad and Tobago, but overall the European record has been poor with only France and Spain reaching the final since the start of the 1990s. Spain's first appearance in the final came in 2003, in Finland, but they were beaten by a Brazil team winning a record third title. In the 2005 final in Peru, Mexico beat Brazil to win a first world championship for the CONCACAF region, the only confederation until then, apart from Oceania, not to have won the trophy.

FIFA U-20 WOMEN'S WORLD CUP

Year	Host Country	Winners	Score	Runners-up	Final Venue
2002	Canada	United States	1-0	Canada	Commonwealth, Edmonton
2004	Thailand	Germany	2-0	China PR	Rajamangala National, Bangkok
2006	Russia				Lokomotiv, Moscow

In 2002, due to the growing interest in women's football, the third of FIFA's youth tournaments was launched, the FIFA U-19 Women's World Championship. After two editions, the tournament was changed to an U-20 contest to bring it in line with the men's event, while 2008 will see the launch of the FIFA U-17 Women's World Cup which will complete the line-up of FIFA's age-restricted tournaments. The two editions of the U-19 event were played in Canada and Thailand, and the rise in standards has surprised even those involved in the women's game. The USA and Germany have dominated, with the Americans winning the inaugural event and then losing in the semi-finals to Germany in 2004; Germany going on to beat China PR in the final.

FIFA WORLD PLAYER 2005

FIFA WORLD PLAYER 2005

Rank	Player	Club	Nat	1st	x5	2nd	x3	3rd	x1	Total
1	RONALDINHO	Barcelona	BRA	159	795	46	138	23	23	956
2	LAMPARD Frank	Chelsea	ENG	25	125	45	135	46	46	306
3	ETO'O Samuel	Barcelona	CMR	15	75	29	87	28	28	190
4	HENRY Thierry	Arsenal	FRA	11	55	34	102	15	15	172
5	ADRIANO	Internazionale	BRA	17	85	21	63	22	22	170
6	SHEVCHENKO Andriy	Milan	UKR	16	80	18	54	19	19	153
7	GERRARD Steven	Liverpool	ENG	11	55	19	57	19	19	131
8	KAKA	Milan	BRA	10	50	12	36	15	15	101
9	MALDINI Paolo	Milan	ITA	7	35	11	33	8	8	76
10	DROGBA Didier	Chelsea	CIV	3	15	12	36	14	14	65
11	BALLACK Michael	Bayern München	GER	6	30	8	24	10	10	64
12	RONALDO	Real Madrid	BRA	7	35	7	21	7	7	63
13	ZIDANE Zinedine	Real Madrid	FRA	5	25	8	24	6	6	55
14	IBRAHIMOVIC Zlatan	Juventus	SWE	1	5	5	15	16	16	36
15	DECO	Barcelona	POR	1	5	4	12	7	7	24
16	RIQUELME Juan Román	Villarreal	ARG	1	5	3	9	6	6	20
17	ROBINHO	Real Madrid	BRA	0	0	5	15	4	4	19
18	BECKHAM David	Real Madrid	ENG	1	5	3	9	3	3	17
	ROONEY Wayne	Manchester United	ENG	0	0	3	9	8	8	17
20	CRISTIANO RONALDO	Manchester United	POR	1	5	1	3	5	5	13
21	VAN NISTELROOY Ruud	Manchester United	NED	1	5	1	3	3	3	11
	ESSIEN Michael	Chelsea	GHA	1	5	1	3	3	3	11
23	RAUL	Real Madrid	ESP	0	0	0	0	8	8	8
	NEDVED Pavel	Juventus	CZE	0	0	2	6	2	2	8
25	ROBBEN Arjen	Chelsea	NED	1	5	0	0	0	0	5
26	CAFU	Milan	BRA	0	0	1	3	0	0	3
	OKOCHA Jay-Jay	Bolton Wanderers	NGA	0	0	1	3	0	0	3
	NESTA Alessandro	Milan	ITA	0	0	0	0	3	3	3
	ROBERTO CARLOS	Real Madrid	BRA	0	0	1	3	0	0	3
30	BUFFON Gianluigi	Juventus	ITA	0	0	0	0	1	1	1

Each first placing earns five points • Each second placing earns three points • Each third placing earns one point

FIFA WOMEN'S WORLD PLAYER 2005

Rank	Player	Club	Nat	1st	x5	2nd	x3	3rd	x1	Total
1	PRINZ Birgit	1.FFC Frankfurt	GER	75	375	39	117	21	21	513
2	MARTA	Umeå IK	BRA	55	275	43	129	25	25	429
3	BOXX Shannon	University of Notre Dame	USA	25	125	27	81	29	29	235
4	LJUNGBERG Hanna	Umeå IK	SWE	20	100	29	87	19	19	206
5	LINGOR Renate	1.FFC Frankfurt	GER	19	95	20	60	15	15	170
6	DOMINGUEZ Maribel	Barcelona	MEX	13	65	13	39	11	11	115
7	GULBRANDSEN Solveig	Kolbotn	NOR	15	75	5	15	7	7	97
	MINNERT Sandra	07 Bad Neuenahr	GER	11	55	10	30	12	12	97
9	WELSH Christie	University of Penn State	USA	4	20	15	45	13	13	78
10	SMITH Kelly	Arsenal	ENG	5	25	7	21	14	14	60
11	MOSTROM Malin	Umeå IK	SWE	4	20	6	18	9	9	47
12	GEORGES Laura	Boston College	FRA	3	15	5	15	14	14	44
13	NKWOCHA Perpetua	Tianjin Huisen	NGA	2	10	7	21	10	10	41
14	HO Sun Hui		PRK	2	10	8	24	3	3	37
15	SAWA Homare		JPN	1	5	5	15	15	15	35
16	SINCLAIR Christine	University of Portland	CAN	0	0	4	12	14	14	26
17	NORDBY Bente	Asker	NOR	2	10	2	6	6	6	22
18	PARK Eun Sun		KOR	1	5	4	12	3	3	20
	STANGELAND Ane	Kolbotn	NOR	1	5	4	12	3	3	20
20	KALMARI Laura	Djurgården/Alvsjö	FIN	1	5	3	9	4	4	18
	MODISE Portia	Soweto Ladies	RSA	1	5	3	9	4	4	18
22	MARKLUND Hanna	Umeå IK	SWE	1	5	2	6	5	5	16
23	KUNNAS Satu	United	FIN	0	0	0	0	2	2	2
	PAASKE SORENSEN Cathrine	Brøndby	DEN	0	0	0	0	2	2	2

Each first placing earns five points • Each second placing earns three points • Each third placing earns one point

FIFA WORLD PLAYER 2005 – HOW THEY VOTED

Coach	1st	2nd	3rd	Captain	1st	2nd	3rd
AIA Ben Davies	Ronaldinho	Adriano	C. Ronaldo	no vote	none	none	none
ALB Hans Peter Briegel	Ronaldinho	Lampard	Kaká	Igli Tare	Maldini	Kaká	Ronaldinho
ALG Ighil Ali Meziane	Lampard	Ballack	Eto'o	Hickem Mezair	Lampard	Ronaldinho	Ballack
AND David Rodrigo	Robben	Shevchenko	Ronaldinho	Justo Ruiz	Adriano	Lampard	Gerrard
ARG José Nestor Pekerman	Ronaldo	Eto'o	Lampard	Juan Pablo Sorín	Maldini	Gerrard	Drogba
ARM Henk Wisman	Ronaldinho	Lampard	Henry	Hovsepyan Sargis	Adriano	Eto'o	Deco
ASA invalid votes	-	-	-	no vote	-	-	-
ATG Veron Edwards	Ronaldinho	Shevchenko	Kaká	Verton Harris	Drogba	Ronaldinho	Lampard
AUS Guus Hiddink	invalid vote	Ronaldinho	Kaká	Mark Viduka	Ronaldinho	Henry	Shevchenko
AUT Willi Rutensteiner	Ballack	Ibrahimovic	Ronaldinho	Andreas Ivanschitz	Ronaldinho	Shevchenko	Gerrard
AZE Vagif Sadigov	Ronaldinho	Gerrard	Adriano	Rashad Sadigov	Ronaldinho	Kaká	Shevchenko
BAH Gary White	Ronaldinho	Gerrard	Maldini	Cameron Hepple	Ronaldinho	Rooney	Robinho
BAN Diego Andres Cruciani	Ronaldinho	Henry	Riquelme	Arif Khan Joy	Ronaldo	Henry	Lampard
BEL Aimé Anthuenis	Ronaldinho	Kaká	Ibrahimovic	Bart Goor	Ronaldinho	Eto'o	Ibrahimovic
BER Kyle Lightbourne	Ronaldinho	Lampard	Adriano	Maurice Lowe	Ronaldinho	Eto'o	Lampard
BFA Bernard Simondi	Eto'o	Ronaldinho	Lampard	no vote	-	-	-
BHU Kharey Basnet	Henry	Drogba	Gerrard	Pasang Tshering	Ronaldo	Henry	Gerrard
BIH Blaz Sliskovic	Riquelme	Ibrahimovic	Lampard	Sergej Barbarez	Ballack	Ronaldinho	Nesta
BLR Anatoli Baidachny	Shevchenko	Ronaldinho	Drogba	Sergey Shtaniuk	Shevchenko	Ronaldinho	V. Nistelrooy
BLZ Ian Mork	Ronaldinho	Maldini	Shevchenko	Shane Orio	Eto'o	Henry	Ronaldinho
BOL Ovidio Messa	Ronaldinho	Beckham	Raúl	Ronald Raldes	Ronaldinho	Beckham	Raúl
BOT Veselin Jelusic	Drogba	Adriano	Ronaldinho	Tshepiso Molwantwa	Eto'o	Drogba	Kaká
BRA Carlos Alberto Parreira	Zidane	V. Nistelrooy	Gerrard	Cafú	C. Ronaldo	Zidane	Maldini
BRB Mark Doherty	Gerrard	Essien	Eto'o	John Parris	Essien	Eto'o	Gerrard
BUL Hristo Stoitchkov	Ronaldinho	Deco	Shevchenko	Stiliyan Petrov	Lampard	Ronaldinho	Shevchenko
CAN Frank Yallop	Adriano	Lampard	Ronaldinho	Dwayne de Rosario	Adriano	Henry	Ronaldinho
CAY Marcos A. Tinoco	Ronaldinho	Kaká	Zidane	Frederick Wilks	Lampard	Ronaldinho	Zidane
CGO Gaston Tschiangana	Ronaldinho	Drogba	Eto'o	Barthélemy Ngatsono	Ronaldinho	Eto'o	Drogba
CHI Nelson Acosta Lopez	Ronaldinho	Nedved	Eto'o	Luis Fuentes	Ronaldinho	Eto'o	Henry
CHN Zhu Guanghu	Shevchenko	Maldini	Kaká	Li Weifeng	Shevchenko	Maldini	Kaká
CIV Henri Michel	Ronaldinho	Lampard	Gerrard	Cyrille Domoraud	Ronaldinho	Henry	Adriano
COK Tim Jerks	Ronaldinho	Henry	V. Nistelrooy	Joseph Chambers	Henry	Maldini	Ronaldinho
COL Reinaldo Rueda Rivera	Ronaldinho	Eto'o	Lampard	Ivan Ramiro Cordoba	Lampard	Ronaldinho	Maldini
COM Mohamed Chamuté	Ronaldinho	Zidane	Ballack	Salihi Maoulida	Zidane	Ronaldo	Lampard
CPV Alexandre Alhinho	Ballack	Lampard	Ronaldinho	Claudio Aguiar	Gerrard	Ronaldinho	Deco
CRC Alexandre Guinmares	Ronaldinho	Lampard	Eto'o	Luis Marin Murillo	Ronaldinho	Adriano	Eto'o
CRO Zlatko Kranjcar	Ronaldinho	Robinho	Kaká	Niko Kovac	Lampard	Ronaldinho	Buffon
CUB William Barracks	Ronaldinho	Ronaldo	Eto'o	Daniel Benmudez	Ronaldinho	Ronaldo	Kaká
CYP Angelos Anastasiadis	Ronaldinho	Eto'o	Drogba	Nikos Panayiotou	Ronaldinho	Adriano	Ibrahimovic
CZE Karel Brückner	Ronaldinho	Gerrard	Henry	Tomas Galasek	Ronaldinho	Lampard	Henry
DEN Morten Olsen	Adriano	Ibrahimovic	Ronaldinho	Thomas Helveg	Ronaldinho	Lampard	Adriano
DJI Mohamed Omar Ali	Ronaldinho	Gerrard	Adriano	Baycal Farah	Ronaldinho	Lampard	Shevchenko
DMA Clifford Celaire	Beckham	Deco	Raúl	Delbert Daley	Ronaldinho	Beckham	Shevchenko
DOM Juan Emilio Mojica	Ronaldinho	Adriano	Eto'o	Ramon Odalis Garcia	Ronaldinho	Adriano	Eto'o
ECU Luis Fernando Suarez	Lampard	Eto'o	Robinho	Ivan Hurtado Angulo	Ronaldinho	Cafú	Ronaldo
EGY Hasan Shehata	Ronaldinho	Henry	Drogba	Ahmed Hasan	Ronaldinho	Henry	Drogba
ENG Sven Göran Eriksson	Ronaldinho	Adriano	Ibrahimovic	David Beckham	Ronaldo	Ronaldinho	Ibrahimovic
EQG Antonio Dumas	Adriano	Ronaldo	V. Nistelrooy	Angel Nding Ondo	Adriano	Okocha	Riquelme
ERI Negash Teklit Negassi	Ronaldinho	Adriano	Lampard	Haile Goitom	Ronaldinho	Lampard	Kaká
ESP Luis Aragones Suarez	Eto'o	Henry	Ronaldo	Raúl Gonzales Blanco	Maldini	Henry	Eto'o
EST Jelle Goes	Gerrard	Eto'o	Lampard	Martin Reim	Lampard	Ronaldinho	Eto'o
ETH Sewenet Bishow	Ronaldinho	Eto'o	Gerrard	Mulugetta Hihret	Eto'o	Ronaldinho	Lampard
FIJ Lee Sterrey	Deco	Eto'o	Kaká	Esala Masi	Ronaldinho	Ronaldo	Henry
FIN Jyrki Heliskoski	Adriano	Ronaldinho	Gerrard	Sami Hyypiä	Shevchenko	Lampard	Ronaldinho
FRA Raymond Domenech	Maldini	Drogba	Rooney	Zinedine Zidane	Drogba	Maldini	Raúl
FRO Jogvan Martin Olsen	Eto'o	Lampard	Adriano	Oli Johannesen	Ronaldinho	Zidane	Lampard
GAB Nzamba Rapa	Ronaldinho	Henry	Eto'o	Msi Ahue	Henry	Eto'o	Ronaldinho
GEO Gaioz Dazsadze	Ronaldinho	Gerrard	Maldini	Kakha Kaladze	Ronaldinho	Shevchenko	Lampard
GER Jürgen Klinsmann	Lampard	Ronaldinho	Adriano	Michael Ballack	Kaká	Ibrahimovic	Eto'o
GHA Ratomir Dujkovic	Ronaldinho	Lampard	Drogba	no vote	-	-	-
GNB Baciro Candé	Ronaldinho	Eto'o	C. Ronaldo	Braima Injai	Lampard	Zidane	Drogba
GRE Otto Rehhagel	Ronaldinho	Adriano	Lampard	Theodoros Zagorakis	Kaká	Lampard	Ronaldinho
GUA Ramon Maradiaga	Ronaldinho	Lampard	Kaká	Gonzalo Romero	Ronaldinho	Riquelme	Adriano
GUM Morio Tsukitata	Ballack	Ronaldinho	Gerrard	no vote	-	-	-

FIFA WORLD PLAYER 2005 – HOW THEY VOTED

	Coach	1st	2nd	3rd	Captain	1st	2nd	3rd
HKG	Sun Cheung Lai	Eto'o	Ronaldinho	Ibrahimovic	Pei Tak Man	Ronaldinho	Kaká	Shevchenko
HON	José de la Paz Herrera	Ronaldinho	Eto'o	Henry	Wilmer Velásquez	Ronaldo	Maldini	Riquelme
HUN	Lothar Matthäus	Ronaldinho	Lampard	Adriano	Zoltan Gera	Ronaldinho	Lampard	Gerrard
IND	Syed Naeemuddin	Adriano	Riquelme	Lampard	S. Venkatesch	Lampard	Ronaldinho	Rooney
IRL	Don Givens	Ronaldinho	Lampard	Henry	no votes	-	-	-
IRN	invalid votes	-	-	-	invalid votes	-	-	-
ISL	Asgeir Sigurvinsson	Kaká	Ronaldinho	Lampard	Eidur Gudjohnsen	Ronaldinho	Adriano	Lampard
ISR	Abraham Grant	Ronaldinho	Shevchenko	Ballack	Avi Nimni	Ronaldinho	Eto'o	Lampard
ITA	Marcello Lippi	Lampard	Ronaldinho	Ibrahimovic	Fabio Cannavaro	Ibrahimovic	Ronaldinho	Raúl
JAM	Wendell Downswell	Ronaldinho	Ronaldo	Shevchenko	Ricardo Gardner	Ronaldinho	Shevchenko	Kaká
JOR	Mahmoud El-Gohary	Ronaldinho	Eto'o	Ballack	Faisal Ibrahim	Ronaldinho	Henry	Zidane
JPN	Zico	Adriano	Lampard	Ballack	Miyamoto Tsuneyasu	Adriano	Kaká	Lampard
KAZ	Sergey Timofeyev	Shevchenko	Ronaldinho	Henry	Nurbol Zhumaskaliyev	Gerrard	Ronaldinho	Ronaldo
KGZ	Nematjan Zakirov	Eto'o	Drogba	Ronaldo	Zakir Djalilov	Ronaldinho	Shevchenko	Drogba
KOR	Dick Advocaat	V. Nistelrooy	Lampard	Ronaldinho	Lee Woon-Jae	Shevchenko	Ronaldinho	Lampard
KSA	Gabriel Calderon	Ronaldo	Eto'o	Adriano	Sami Al Jaber	Lampard	Ronaldinho	Gerrard
KUW	Mihai Stochita	Ronaldinho	Shevchenko	Gerrard	Bashar Abdullah	Ronaldinho	Henry	Eto'o
LBY	Ilija Loncarenc	Ronaldinho	Maldini	Lampard	Taib Tarek	Eto'o	Ronaldinho	Ronaldo
LCA	Carson Millar	Lampard	Ronaldinho	Eto'o	Jean Zarl	Gerrard	Ballack	Kaká
LIE	Matin Andermatt	Kaká	Lampard	Robinho	Daniel Hasler	Kaká	Shevchenko	Lampard
LTU	Algimantas Liubinskas	Ronaldinho	Eto'o	Gerrard	Aurelijus Skarbalius	Ballack	Lampard	Ronaldinho
LUX	Guy Hellers	Ronaldinho	Deco	Ibrahimovic	Remy Sebastien	Ronaldinho	Zidane	Nedved
LVA	Jurijs Andrejevs	Ronaldinho	Gerrard	Shevchenko	Vitalijs Astafjevs	Shevchenko	Ronaldinho	Lampard
MAD	Auguste Raux	Lampard	Gerrard	Henry	Fidele Randriamalala	Ballack	Lampard	Ronaldinho
MAR	Philippe Troussier	Ronaldinho	Ballack	Lampard	Talal Karkori	Ronaldinho	Henry	Eto'o
MAS	Norijan bin Bakak	Ronaldinho	Robinho	Ronaldo	Paozh Saari	Ronaldinho	Robinho	Ronaldo
MDA	Victor Pasulko	Shevchenko	Ronaldinho	Adriano	Valeriu Catinsus	Shevchenko	Ronaldinho	Adriano
MDV	Lim Kim Chon	Ronaldinho	Gerrard	Shevchenko	no vote	-	-	-
MEX	Ricardo La Volpe	Lampard	Shevchenko	Deco	Pavel Pardo	Lampard	Adriano	Shevchenko
MGL	Ishdorj Otgonbayar	Henry	Rooney	C. Ronaldo	Lumbengarav Donrov	Henry	Rooney	C. Ronaldo
MKD	Boban Babunski	Ronaldinho	Ballack	Kaká	Petar Milosevski	Eto'o	Lampard	Raúl
MLI	Mory Goita	Ronaldinho	Drogba	Lampard	Boubacar S. Kone	Ronaldinho	Drogba	Lampard
MLT	Horst Heese	Adriano	Maldini	Ibrahimovic	Gilbert Agius	Adriano	Maldini	Ibrahimovic
MSR	Ottley Laborde	Ronaldinho	Henry	Lampard	Elton E. Williams	Ronaldinho	Henry	Lampard
MTN	Mohamed Ould Messoud	Henry	Eto'o	Ballack	Ahmed Mohamed	Henry	Eto'o	Ballack
MWI	Michael Hennigan	Eto'o	Drogba	Essien	James Chilapondwa	Ronaldinho	Kaká	Eto'o
MYA	Ivan Venkov Kolev	Ronaldinho	Lampard	Ibrahimovic	Soe Myat Min	Ronaldinho	Adriano	Lampard
NAM	Seth Boois	Adriano	Robinho	Rooney	invalid votes	-	-	-
NCA	Mauricio Cruz	Ronaldinho	Adriano	Deco	Carlos R. Alonso	Lampard	Adriano	Henry
NED	Marco van Basten	Ronaldinho	Adriano	Gerrard	Edwin van der Saar	Lampard	Ronaldinho	Rooney
NGA	Austine Eguanon	Lampard	Ronaldinho	Gerrard	Jay-Jay Okocha	Kaká	Riquelme	Ronaldinho
NIR	Lawrie Sanchez	Ronaldinho	Gerrard	Lampard	Aaron Hughes	Ronaldinho	Zidane	Lampard
NOR	Aage Hareide	Ronaldinho	Lampard	Adriano	Thomas Myhre	Ronaldinho	Gerrard	Lampard
NZL	Ricki Herbert	Ronaldinho	Lampard	Gerrard	Danny Hay	Eto'o	Lampard	Ronaldinho
OMA	Srecko Juricic	Kaká	Ronaldinho	Lampard	no vote	none	none	none
PAK	U. F. Tariq Lutfi	Ronaldinho	Adriano	Henry	Jaffar Khan	Ronaldinho	Henry	Deco
PAL	Azmi Nassar	Ronaldinho	Drogba	Deco	Jendeya Saeb	Ronaldinho	Deco	Raúl
PAN	José Hernandez	Henry	Eto'o	Kaká	no vote	-	-	-
PAR	Anibal Ruiz	Zidane	Ronaldinho	Riquelme	Carlos Alberto Gamarra	Ronaldinho	Ronaldo	Shevchenko
PER	Freddy Ternero	Shevchenko	Kaká	Lampard	Jorge Soto	Henry	Lampard	Ronaldinho
PHI	José Arsiton Caslib	Ronaldinho	Ballack	Shevchenko	Emelio A. Caligdong	Ronaldinho	Ballack	Shevchenko
POL	Pawel Janas	Ronaldinho	Lampard	Eto'o	Tomasz Klos	Lampard	Ronaldinho	Maldini
POR	Luiz Felipe Scolari	Kaká	Lampard	Ibrahimovic	Luis Figo	Maldini	Henry	Ibrahimovic
PUR	Ricardo Romano	Ronaldinho	Ballack	Henry	Christopher Bores	Ronaldinho	Henry	Lampard
QAT	Dzemaludin Musovic	Ronaldinho	Zidane	Shevchenko	Saad Al-Shammari	Ronaldinho	Shevchenko	Adriano
ROU	Victor Piturca	Ronaldinho	Lampard	Ibrahimovic	Christian Chivu	Ronaldinho	Lampard	Ibrahimovic
RUS	Yury Semin	Shevchenko	Ronaldinho	Lampard	Alexey Smertin	Lampard	Shevchenko	Ronaldinho
SCG	Ilija Petkovic	Lampard	Ronaldinho	Adriano	Savo Milosevic	Ronaldinho	Eto'o	Maldini
SCO	Walter Smith	Ronaldinho	Lampard	Ballack	Barry Ferguson	Ronaldinho	Lampard	Rooney
SEN	Sarr Abdoulaye	Ronaldinho	Henry	Eto'o	Lamine Diatta	Ronaldinho	Henry	Eto'o
SEY	Raoul Shongu	Ronaldinho	Henry	Eto'o	Denis Barber	Ronaldinho	Adriano	Lampard
SIN	Radojko Avramovic	Ronaldinho	Lampard	Shevchenko	Aide Iskandar	Ronaldinho	Eto'o	Rooney
SLE	John Jeboh Sherrington	Ronaldinho	Ballack	Eto'o	Sidique Mamasaray	Ronaldinho	Shevchenko	Eto'o
SLV	Miguel Aguilar Ovando	Ronaldinho	Shevchenko	Henry	Victor Velasquez Molina	Ronaldinho	Lampard	Drogba

FIFA WORLD PLAYER 2005 – HOW THEY VOTED

	Coach	1st	2nd	3rd	Captain	1st	2nd	3rd
SMR	Giampaolo Mazza	Shevchenko	Ronaldinho	Nesta	Andy Selva	Ronaldo	Ronaldinho	Maldini
SOM	invalid votes	-	-	-	invalid votes	-	-	-
SRI	Sampath Perera	Adriano	Kaká	Riquelme	Dudley Stainwall	Adriano	Kaká	Riquelme
STP	Edson Braganca Dias	Ronaldinho	Drogba	Lampard	Yorcelan Sousa Baía	Ronaldinho	Drogba	Lampard
SUD	Ahmed Babiker Elfaki	Ronaldinho	Henry	Adriano	Haitham Mustafa	Ronaldinho	Adriano	Henry
SUI	Jakob Kuhn	Ronaldinho	Henry	Shevchenko	Johann Vogel	Shevchenko	Gerrard	Ronaldinho
SVK	Dusan Galis	Ronaldinho	Lampard	Zidane	Miroslav Karhan	Ronaldinho	C. Ronaldo	Adriano
SVN	Branko Oblak	Ronaldinho	Lampard	Eto'o	Aleksander Knaus	Ronaldinho	Ibrahimovic	Henry
SWE	Lars Lagerbäck	Shevchenko	Maldini	Raúl	Olof Mellberg	Lampard	Eto'o	Maldini
SWZ	Nyanga Hlophe	Ronaldinho	Zidane	Beckham	Sipho Dvuba	Kaká	Lampard	Eto'o
SYR	Miloslav Radenovic	Gerrard	Eto'o	Adriano	Al Said	Ronaldinho	Gerrard	Ibrahimovic
TAN	Dr. Mshindo Msolla	Ronaldinho	Drogba	Gerrard	Mecky Maxime	Ronaldinho	Henry	Rooney
TCA	Paul F. Crosbie	Eto'o	Maldini	Lampard	no vote	-	-	-
TGA	Milan Jankovic	Gerrard	Adriano	Drogba	Kilifi Uele	Adriano	Ronaldinho	Ballack
THA	Chanvit Polchivin	Ronaldinho	Gerrard	Zidane	Kosin Hathairattankool	Ronaldinho	Gerrard	Zidane
TKM	Rahim Kurbanmamedov	Gerrard	Henry	C. Ronaldo	Durdiyev Kurbangeldi	Gerrard	Adriano	Rooney
TRI	Leo Beenhakker	Eto'o	Lampard	Deco	Dwight Yorke	Ronaldinho	Lampard	Adriano
TUN	Roger Lemerre	Zidane	Henry	Essien	Khaled Badra	Ronaldinho	Adriano	Drogba
TUR	Fatih Terim	Shevchenko	Kaká	Eto'o	Rüstü Reçber	Gerrard	Henry	Ronaldinho
UAE	Juma Rabec	Ronaldinho	Gerrard	Shevchenko	Muhsin Musabeh	Ronaldinho	Gerrard	Ballack
UGA	Sam B. Ssimbwa	Henry	Ronaldinho	Nedved	Andrew Mwesingwa	Ronaldinho	Henry	Lampard
UKR	Oleg Blokhin	Lampard	Kaká	Ronaldinho	Andriy Shevchenko	Kaká	Ronaldinho	Nesta
URU	Jorge Fossati	Ronaldinho	Roberto Carlos	Adriano	Paolo Montero	Zidane	Nedved	Adriano
USA	Bruce Arena	Ronaldinho	Shevchenko	Lampard	Claudio Reyna	Ronaldinho	Shevchenko	Eto'o
UZB	Bob Houghton	Maldini	Gerrard	Lampard	Mirdjaiai Kasimov	Ronaldinho	Shevchenko	Beckham
VEN	Richard Paèz	Ronaldinho	Lampard	Eto'o	Luis Vera	Ronaldinho	Henry	Robinho
VIE	Alfred Riedl	Henry	Ronaldinho	Gerrard	Phan Van Tai Em	Ronaldinho	Gerrard	Adriano
VIR	Felix St. Rose	Ronaldinho	Henry	Beckham	Dwight Ferguson	Ronaldinho	Henry	Lampard
WAL	John Toshak	Maldini	Ronaldinho	Lampard	no vote	-	-	-
ZAM	Kalusha Bwalya	Ronaldinho	Eto'o	Lampard	Misheck Lungu	Ronaldinho	Eto'o	Drogba
ZIM	C. Mhlauri	Eto'o	Shevchenko	Drogba	P. Ndlovu	Gerrard	Robinho	Essien

FIFA WOMEN'S WORLD PLAYER 2005 – HOW THEY VOTED

	Coach	1st	2nd	3rd	Captain	1st	2nd	3rd
AIA	Colin Johnson	Marta	Prinz	Welsh	Melesa Anderson	Prinz	Ljungberg	Marta
ALG	Azzedine Chih	Prinz	Boxx	Sinclair	Naïma Laouadi	Prinz	Stangeland	Boxx
AND	Yavier Roura	Marta	Prinz	Dominguez	no vote	-	-	-
ARG	José Carlos Borrello	Ljungberg	Marta	Dominguez	Marisa Isabel Gerez	Ljungberg	Prinz	Marta
ARM	Mher Miqaelyan	Prinz	Lingor	Gulbrandsen	Gayane Konstanyan	Prinz	Lingor	Gulbrandsen
ATG	Rowan Benjamin	Prinz	Marta	Ljungberg	Kayla Simon	Marta	Prinz	Minnert
AUS	Tom Sermanni	Boxx	Sawa	Marta	Cheryl Salisbury	Ljungberg	Boxx	Sawa
AUT	Ernst Weber	Ljungberg	Marta	Smith	Gertrud Stallinger	Ljungberg	Smith	Moström
AZE	Boris Tibilov	Marta	Boxx	Lingor	Kifayat Osmanova	Marta	Boxx	Lingor
BAH	Matthew Green	Prinz	Marta	Sinclair	Talitha Wood	Marta	Prinz	Sinclair
BAN	Abu Yusuf	Ljungberg	Minnert	Boxx	Ayesha Akter	Boxx	Ljungberg	Sun Hui Ho
BEL	Anne Noë	Prinz	Ljungberg	Marta	Femke Maes	Marta	Ljungberg	Gulbrandsen
BER	Vance Brown	Minnert	Marta	Ljungberg	Naquita Dill	Marta	Boxx	Nordby
BFA	Marguerite Karama	Minnert	Welsh	Nkwocha	Diane Kankyono	Minnert	Nkwocha	Modise
BHR	Ghazi Al Majed	Georges	Sun Hui Ho	Sinclair	Reem Butabah	Marta	Sun Hui Ho	Sawa
BIH	Dzevad Bekic	Dominguez	Ljungberg	Minnert	Sabina Pehic	Boxx	Minnert	Sinclair
BLR	Aleh Volakh	Ljungberg	Gulbrandsen	Prinz	Natalia Ryzhevich	Prinz	Minnert	Ljungberg
BLZ	Ian Mork	Marta	Dominguez	Prinz	Denise van Stuivenberg	Boxx	Dominguez	Marta
BOL	Maitte Zamorano	Georges	Marta	Boxx	Lili Rocabado	Georges	Marta	Boxx
BRA	Luiz Antonio Fereira	Marklund	Boxx	Prinz	Maurine Gonçalves	Eun Sun Park	Dominguez	Sawa
BUL	Emil Dimitrov	Prinz	Ljungberg	Nordby	Deiana Petrakieva	Prinz	Ljungberg	Stangeland
CAN	Even Pellerud	Boxx	Prinz	Marta	Charmaine Hooper	Prinz	Sawa	Lingor
CAY	Thiago da Cunha	Marta	Prinz	Boxx	Wanda Sue Nixon	Prinz	Marta	Welsh
CGO	Jean-Paul M'Pilla	Prinz	Marta	Smith	Rachelle Nzoungani	Marta	Nkwocha	Boxx
CHI	Osvaldo Hurtado	Marta	Prinz	Dominguez	Alejandra Aviles	Marta	Prinz	Dominguez
CHN	Pei Encai	Marta	Prinz	Boxx	Zhang Ouying	Marta	Prinz	Boxx
CMR	Charles Kamdem	Prinz	Ljungberg	Nkwocha	Rolande Belemgato	Boxx	Marta	Modise
COK	Tim Jerks	Marta	Prinz	Boxx	Mii Piri	Marta	Prinz	Sinclair

FIFA WOMEN'S WORLD PLAYER 2005 – HOW THEY VOTED

Coach	1st	2nd	3rd	Captain	1st	2nd	3rd
COL Julio Valdivieso	Marta	Dominguez	Boxx	Monica Johana Castillo	Marta	Dominguez	Boxx
COM Itoubou	Stangeland	Minnert	Marta	Celine Ahmed	Moström	Boxx	Georges
CRC Ricardo Rodriguez	Marta	Prinz	Ljungberg	Monica Salasar-Carrillo	Prinz	Marta	Marklund
CRO Damir Ruhek	Smith	Marta	Prinz	Renata Pirsa	Prinz	Kalmari	Ljungberg
CUB Rufino Sotolongo Reyes	Dominguez	Welsh	Minnert	Yohania Ocampo	Dominguez	Welsh	Minnert
CYP no vote	-	-	-	no vote	-	-	-
CZE Dusan Zovinec	Prinz	Moström	Marta	Eva Smeralova	Dominguez	Prinz	Marta
DEN Peter Bonde	Gulbrandsen	Boxx	Lingor	Katrine Pedersen	Gulbrandsen	Prinz	Smith
DJI Mahmoud Ismael	Prinz	Moström	Gulbrandsen	Kourecha Ali Gueni	Ljungberg	Marta	Prinz
DMA Hypolite Robertson	Lingor	Marta	Prinz	Nicola Jean-Jacques	Prinz	Sinclair	Marta
DOM José Luis Elejarde	Boxx	Dominguez	Minnert	Ana Odaliz Diaz	Boxx	Dominguez	Minnert
ECU Garys Estupiñan	Marta	Prinz	Sinclair	Yolinna Ruiz	Smith	Marta	Sawa
EGY Mohamed El Siagy	Prinz	Sinclair	Boxx	Dina Abdel Halim	Prinz	Sinclair	Boxx
ENG Hope Powell	Marta	Lingor	Boxx	Faye White	Gulbrandsen	Lingor	Moström
EQG Sebastian Jangue Enga	Boxx	Nkwocha	Smith	Candida Esono Angué	Boxx	Minnert	Georges
ERI Negash Teklit Negassi	Prinz	Marta	Ljungberg	Merhawit Tekeste	Prinz	Marta	Ljungberg
ESP Ignacio Quereda Laviña	Marta	Prinz	Moström	Maider Castillo	Prinz	Marta	Lingor
EST Juri Saar	Prinz	Ljungberg	Marta	Elis Meetua	Marta	Ljungberg	Prinz
ETH Abraham Mebratu	Boxx	Lingor	Nkwocha	Harna Turga	Nkwocha	Boxx	Lingor
FIN Michael Käld	Marta	Lingor	Nordby	Sanna Valkonen	Marta	Nordby	Lingor
FRA Elisabeth Loisel	Gulbrandsen	Boxx	Marta	Sonia Bompastor	Lingor	Marta	Ljungberg
FRO Alvur Hansen	Gulbrandsen	Lingor	Marta	Bara Skaale Klakstein	Ljungberg	Marta	Gulbrandsen
GAB Do Casta	Marta	Prinz	Nkwocha	M. Berenger	Marta	Prinz	Nkwocha
GEO Maia Japaridze	Prinz	Welsh	Nordby	Bela Gogsatze	Prinz	Ljungberg	Smith
GER Silvia Neid	Marta	Stangeland	Moström	Birgit Prinz	Gulbrandsen	Smith	Stangeland
GHA Bashir Kweku Hayford	Welsh	Sun Hui Ho	Nkwocha	no vote	-	-	-
GNB Sana Cassama	Dominguez	Prinz	Marta	Eudalice da Veiga	Boxx	Nkwocha	Ljungberg
GRE Dimitrios Batsilas	Prinz	Marta	Ljungberg	Eftichia Michaelidou	Marta	Boxx	Prinz
GUA Antonio Garcia Gamboa	Lingor	Prinz	Marta	Maria Fernanda Rossell	Prinz	Ljungberg	Sinclair
GUM Norio Tsukitate	Marta	Welsh	Sawa	no vote	-	-	-
HKG Chi Kwong Chu	Boxx	Welsh	Sawa	Wing Kam Ho	Boxx	Welsh	Eun Sun Park
HON Miguel Escalante	Lingor	Dominguez	Sawa	Amaya Waleska	Lingor	Dominguez	Sawa
HUN Andras Telek	Prinz	Ljungberg	Smith	Aranka Paraoanu	Prinz	Kalmari	Smith
IND Hartinder Singh	Prinz	Welsh	Boxx	Sradhanjali Samantaray	Nkwocha	Smith	Welsh
IRL Noel King	Prinz	Welsh	Georges	Ciara Grant	Marta	Prinz	Welsh
IRN Shahrzad Mozafar	Lingor	Georges	Marklund	Leila Vaghari	Smith	Minnert	Prinz
ISL Jorundur Aki Sveinsson	Marta	Prinz	Lingor	Asthildur Helgadottir	Marta	Lingor	Prinz
ISR Alon Schraier	Dominguez	Prinz	Marta	Dagan Mital	Dominguez	Boxx	Smith
ITA Pietro Ghedin	Gulbrandsen	Boxx	Lingor	Patrizia Panico	Gulbrandsen	Boxx	Lingor
JAM Vin Blaine	Ljungberg	Georges	Smith	Stacy Johnson	Prinz	Ljungberg	Minnert
JPN Hiroshi Ohashi	Marta	Prinz	Boxx	Hiromi Isozaki	Marta	Prinz	Boxx
KAZ Aitpay Jamantayev	Prinz	Ljungberg	Sinclair	Natalya Ivanova	Prinz	Ljungberg	Georges
KGZ Gulbara Umatalieva	Nordby	Prinz	Smith	Svetlana Pokachalova	Sawa	Ljungberg	Sun Hui Ho
KOR Ahn Jong Kwan	Sun Hui Ho	Sawa	Welsh	Yoo Soung Sil	Sun Hui Ho	Sawa	Welsh
KSA invalid votes	-	-	-	no vote	-	-	-
KUW invalid votes	-	-	-	no vote	-	-	-
LAO no vote	-	-	-	invalid votes	-	-	-
LCA Trevor Anderson	Moström	Ljungberg	P. Sörensen	Angela Mathurin	Welsh	Lingor	Georges
LTU Vytautas Tutlys	Prinz	Ljungberg	Welsh	Justina Lavrenovaite	Ljungberg	Marta	Kunnas
LUX Jean Romain	Prinz	Sun Hui Ho	Ljungberg	Barbara Agostino	Prinz	Georges	Lingor
LVA Agris Bandolis	Prinz	Marta	Ljungberg	Katrine Verreva	Marta	Prinz	Georges
MAD Herihaja Andriatianasasoa	Marta	Prinz	Boxx	Cynthia Antoasy	Prinz	Marta	Boxx
MAR invalid votes	-	-	-	no vote	-	-	-
MAS Ibrahim Mohd	Boxx	Ljungberg	Welsh	Damelia	Boxx	Ljungberg	Welsh
MDA Evghenii Pusicov	Ljungberg	Minnert	Stangeland	Elena Turcan	Gulbrandsen	Lingor	Marklund
MDV Lim Kim Chon	Prinz	Ljungberg	Smith	no vote	-	-	-
MEX Leonardo Cuellar	Prinz	Boxx	Minnert	Monica Gonzalez	Gulbrandsen	Boxx	Ljungberg
MGL Ishdorj Otgonbayar	Minnert	Eun Sun Park	Sawa	no vote	-	-	-
MKD Dobrislav Dimovski	Lingor	Gulbrandsen	P. Sörensen	Marija Stankovska	Lingor	Minnert	Nordby
MLI Kouyale Aissata	Boxx	Stangeland	Lingor	N'Daye Diaty	Boxx	Lingor	Prinz
MLT Pierre Brincat	Ljungberg	Marta	Prinz	Rebecca D'Agostino	Prinz	Ljungberg	Minnert
MSR invalid votes	-	-	-	invalid votes	-	-	-
MTN invalid votes	-	-	-	invalid votes	-	-	-
MWI Stuart Mbolembole	Ljungberg	Boxx	Minnert	Margreat Chombo	Ljungberg	Boxx	Minnert

FIFA WOMEN'S WORLD PLAYER 2005 – HOW THEY VOTED

	Coach	1st	2nd	3rd	Captain	1st	2nd	3rd
MYA	U Aye Maung	Prinz	Shannon Box	Marta	San San Maw	Prinz	Boxx	Marta
NAM	Gabriel Freyer	Modise	Nkwocha	Moström	invalid votes	-	-	-
NCA	Edward Miguel Urroz	Prinz	Marta	Dominguez	Gretchen Vianney Reyes	Prinz	Marta	Georges
NED	Vera Pauw	Gulbrandsen	Boxx	Prinz	Marlen Wissink	Gulbrandsen	Marta	Moström
NGA	Mr. Rolanson	Minnert	Modise	Sinclair	Kikelomo Ajayi	Smith	Minnert	Modise
NIR	Alfie Wylie	Lingor	Gulbrandsen	Prinz	Aine McGovern	Minnert	Lingor	Georges
NOR	Bjarne Berntsen	Lingor	Boxx	Welsh	Ane Stangeland	Boxx	Marta	Lingor
NZL	John Herdman	Prinz	Marta	Kalmari	Maia Jackman	Prinz	Boxx	Marta
PAK	U. F. Tariq Lufti	Nordby	Marklund	Boxx	Kiran Ilyas Ghouri	Boxx	Nordby	Marklund
PAL	Azmi Nassar	Lingor	Minnert	Sun Hui Ho	Haya Morsi	Minnert	Prinz	Moström
PAN	Ezequiel Fernandez	Boxx	Dominguez	Sinclair	Laura Fuente	Dominguez	Welsh	Prinz
PAR	Esteban von Lücken	Marta	Welsh	Dominguez	Silvia Getto	Marta	Welsh	Sawa
PER	Lizandro Barbaran Pinedo	Marta	Welsh	Prinz	Adriana Davila	Prinz	Marta	Smith
PHI	Marlon M. Maro	Prinz	Eun Sun Park	Sawa	Josephine D. Loren	Prinz	Eun Sun Park	Sawa
POL	Jan Stepczak	Lingor	Marta	Kunnas	Maria Makowska	Ljungberg	Lingor	Marta
POR	José Augusto	Boxx	Welsh	Prinz	Carla Correia	Lingor	Prinz	Ljungberg
PUR	Jorge Oscar Rosa	Welsh	Dominguez	Prinz	Nancy Pagan	Marta	Welsh	Dominguez
ROU	Gheorghe Staicu	Ljungberg	Prinz	Lingor	Daniela Pufulete	Lingor	Prinz	Ljungberg
RUS	Yuri Bystritsky	Prinz	Georges	Marta	Tatiana Skotnikova	Prinz	Kalmari	Sawa
SCG	Perica Krstic'	Minnert	Gulbrandsen	Kalmari	Zorana Stancijevic	Minnert	Gulbrandsen	Kalmari
SCO	Anna Signeul	Prinz	Lingor	Gulbrandsen	Julie Fleeting	Boxx	Sawa	Smith
SEN	Diaby Bassouaré	Marta	Ljungberg	Kalmari	Seyni Ndir Seek	Ljungberg	Lingor	Nkwocha
SEY	Jason Damoo	Prinz	Marta	Ljungberg	Diane Lablache	Prinz	Marta	Ljungberg
SIN	Li Jing	Boxx	Sun Hui Ho	Georges	Norsuria Bte Damsuri	Ljungberg	Boxx	Welsh
SLV	José Ricardo Herrera	Dominguez	Boxx	Lingor	Elena Cristina Caceres	Marta	Dominguez	Boxx
SOM	invalid votes	-	-	-	invalid votes	-	-	-
SRI	invalid votes	-	-	-	invalid votes	-	-	-
STP	Gustavo Clement	Marta	Nkwocha	Prinz	Zaninae Vaz	Marta	Nkwocha	Prinz
SUD	invalid votes	-	-	-	invalid votes	none	none	none
SUI	Béatrice von Siebenthal	Moström	Lingor	Marta	Prisca Steinegger	Lingor	Marta	Boxx
SUR	Kenneth Jaliens	Minnert	Sinclair	Welsh	Smil Aisa	Prinz	Smith	Dominguez
SVK	Frantisek Urvay	Gulbrandsen	Georges	Ljungberg	Jana Hanzelova	Gulbrandsen	Ljungberg	Marta
SVN	Zoran Zirkvencic	Prinz	Ljungberg	Georges	Karmen Vais	Ljungberg	Prinz	Welsh
SWE	Marika Domanski Lyfors	Marta	Boxx	Gulbrandsen	Malin Andersson	Marta	Lingor	none
SYR	Fajer Ibrahim	Gulbrandsen	Lingor	Marklund	Hana Jannoud	Marta	Moström	Boxx
TCA	Paul Crosbie	Prinz	Boxx	Ljungberg	Sonia Bien-Aime	Prinz	Ljungberg	Boxx
TGA	Mailan Jankovic	Dominguez	Marta	Moström	Adelaide Tuivailala	Marta	Boxx	Sinclair
THA	Suphon Yapapha	Marta	Prinz	Sinclair	Sunisa Kongpipat	Marta	Prinz	Sinclair
TPE	Tai-Ying Chou	Lingor	Sun Hui Ho	Eun Sun Park	Yu-Chen Huang	Lingor	Sun Hui Ho	Eun Sun Park
TRI	Jamaal Shabazz	Marta	Smith	Boxx	J. James	Prinz	Marta	Moström
TUR	Ali Kilzilet	Prinz	Smith	Georges	Nihan Su	Prinz	Stangeland	Boxx
UGA	Catherine Adipo	Prinz	Eun Sun Park	Nkwocha	Fatumah Luwedde	Marta	Prinz	Nkwocha
UKR	Vladimir Kulaev	Prinz	Ljungberg	Boxx	Elena Mazurenko	Prinz	Ljungberg	Boxx
URU	Juan Duarte	Dominguez	Marta	Georges	Stefania Maggionini	Dominguez	Marta	Georges
USA	Greg Ryan	Lingor	Prinz	Marta	Kristine Lilly	Moström	Lingor	Smith
UZB	Kim Mariman	Prinz	Moström	Sawa	Nargiza Abdurasulova	Prinz	Moström	Sawa
VEN	Ivan Haldonado	Prinz	Marta	Dominguez	Yunelis Gonzalez	Prinz	Sun Hui Ho	Dominguez
VIE	Mai Duc Chung	Kalmari	Marta	Minnert	Doan Thi Kim Chi	Minnert	Smith	Dominguez
VIN	invalid votes	none	none	none	invalid votes	-	-	-
VIR	Yohannes Worede	Smith	Dominguez	Marta	no vote	-	-	-
WAL	Andrew Beattie	Prinz	Marta	Boxx	Jayne Ludlow	Lingor	Moström	Prinz
ZAM	Ephesania Banda	Boxx	Lingor	Nordby	Annie Namkunga	Welsh	Modise	Georges
ZIM	V. Bauers	Prinz	Modise	Nkwocha	P. Mpaca	Dominguez	Marta	Modise

PAST WINNERS OF THE FIFA WOMEN'S WORLD PLAYER AWARD

WOMEN'S WORLD PLAYER 2001

		Votes
HAMM Mia	USA	154
SUN Wen	CHN	79
MILBRETT Tiffeny	USA	47
PRINZ Birgit	GER	40
FITSCHEN Doris	GER	37
SISSI	BRA	35
LJUNBERG Hanna	SWE	29
WIEGMANN Bettina	GER	17
RIISE Hege	NOR	16
MELLGREN Dagny	NOR	13

WOMEN'S WORLD PLAYER 2002

		Votes
HAMM Mia	USA	161
PRINZ Birgit	GER	96
SUN Wen	CHN	58
MILBRETT Tiffeny	USA	45
PICHON Marinette	FRA	42
SINCLAIR Christine	CAN	38
JONES Steffi	GER	19
RIISE Hege	NOR	17
SISSI	BRA	14
BAI Jie	CHN	13

WOMEN'S WORLD PLAYER 2003

		Votes
PRINZ Birgit	GER	268
HAMM Mia	USA	133
LJUNGBERG Hanna	SWE	84
SVENSSON Victoria	SWE	82
MEINERT Maren	GER	69
WIEGMANN Bettina	GER	49
MOSTROEM Malin	SWE	23
KATIA	BRA	14
LINGOR Renate	GER	14
MARTA	BRA	13

WOMEN'S WORLD PLAYER 2004

		Votes
PRINZ Birgit	GER	376
HAMM Mia	USA	286
MARTA	BRA	281
WAMBACH Abby	USA	126
LILLY Kristine	USA	109
LJUNGBERG Hanna	SWE	109
BOXX Shannon	USA	102
SVENSSON Victoria	SWE	89
LINGOR Renate	GER	89
CRISTIANE	BRA	80

WOMEN'S WORLD PLAYER 2005

		Votes
PRINZ Birgit	GER	513
MARTA	BRA	429
BOXX Shannon	USA	235
LJUNGBERG Hanna	SWE	206
LINGOR Renate	GER	170
DOMINGUEZ Maribel	MEX	115
GULBRANDSEN Solveig	NOR	97
MINNERT Sandra	GER	97
WELSH Christie	USA	78
SMITH Kelly	ENG	60

PAST WINNERS OF THE FIFA WORLD PLAYER AWARD

FIFA WORLD PLAYER 1991

		Votes
MATTHÄUS Lothar	GER	128
PAPIN Jean-Pierre	FRA	113
LINEKER Gary	ENG	40
PROSINECKI Robert	YUG	38
VAN BASTEN Marco	NED	23
BARESI Franco	ITA	12
ZAMORANO Ivan	CHI	10
BREHME Andreas	GER	9
VIALLI Gianluca	ITA	8
SCIFO Enzo	BEL	7

FIFA WORLD PLAYER 1992

		Votes
VAN BASTEN Marco	NED	151
STOICHKOV Hristo	BUL	88
HÄSSLER Thomas	GER	61
PAPIN Jean-Pierre	FRA	46
LAUDRUP Brian	DEN	44
SCHMEICHEL Peter	DEN	44
BERGKAMP Dennis	NED	29
RIJKAARD Frank	NED	23
PELE Abedi	GHA	10
BARESI Franco	ITA	10

FIFA WORLD PLAYER 1993

		Votes
VAN BASTEN Marco	NED	151
STOICHKOV Hristo	BUL	88
HÄSSLER Thomas	GER	61
PAPIN Jean-Pierre	FRA	46
LAUDRUP Brian	DEN	44
SCHMEICHEL Peter	DEN	44
BERGKAMP Dennis	NED	29
RIJKAARD Frank	NED	23
PELE Abedi	GHA	10
BARESI Franco	ITA	10

FIFA WORLD PLAYER 1994

		Votes
ROMARIO	BRA	346
STOICHKOV Hristo	BUL	100
BAGGIO Roberto	ITA	80
HAGI Gheorghe	ROU	50
MALDINI Paolo	ITA	40
BEBETO	BRA	16
BERGKAMP Dennis	NED	11
DUNGA Carlos	BRA	9
BARESI Franco	ITA	7
BROLIN Tomas	SWE	7

FIFA WORLD PLAYER 1995

		Votes
WEAH George	LBR	170
MALDINI Paolo	ITA	80
KLINSMANN Jürgen	GER	58
ROMARIO	BRA	50
BAGGIO Roberto	ITA	49
STOICHKOV Hristo	BUL	37
ZAMORANO Ivan	CHI	36
JUNINHO	BRA	28
SAMMER Matthias	GER	23
LAUDRUP Michael	DEN	20

FIFA WORLD PLAYER 1996

		Votes
RONALDO	BRA	329
WEAH George	LBR	140
SHEARER Alan	ENG	123
SAMMER Matthias	GER	109
KLINSMANN Jürgen	GER	54
KANU Nwankwo	NGA	32
MALDINI Paolo	ITA	25
SUKER Davor	CRO	24
BATISTUTA Gabriel	ARG	19
ROMARIO	BRA	13

FIFA WORLD PLAYER 1997

		Votes
RONALDO	BRA	480
ROBERTO CARLOS	BRA	65
BERGKAMP Dennis	NED	62
ZIDANE Zinedine	FRA	62
RAÚL	ESP	51
DEL PIERO Alessandro	ITA	27
SUKER Davor	CRO	20
BATISTUTA Gabriel	ARG	16
SHEARER Alan	ENG	16
LEONARDO	BRA	14

FIFA WORLD PLAYER 1998

		Votes
ZIDANE Zinedine	FRA	518
RONALDO	BRA	164
SUKER Davor	CRO	108
OWEN Michael	ENG	43
BATISTUTA Gabriel	ARG	40
RIVALDO	BRA	37
BERGKAMP Dennis	NED	33
DAVIDS Edgar	NED	26
DESAILLY Marcel	FRA	23
THURAM Lillian	FRA	14

FIFA WORLD PLAYER 1999

		Votes
RIVALDO	BRA	538
BECKHAM David	ENG	194
BATISTUTA Gabriel	ARG	79
ZIDANE Zinedine	FRA	68
VIERI Christian	ITA	39
FIGO Luis	POR	35
SHEVCHENKO Andriy	UKR	34
RAÚL	ESP	31
COLE Andy	ENG	24
YORKE Dwight	TRI	19

FIFA WORLD PLAYER 2000

		Votes
ZIDANE Zinedine	FRA	370
FIGO Luis	POR	329
RIVALDO	BRA	263
BATISTUTA Gabriel	ARG	57
SHEVCHENKO Andriy	UKR	48
BECKHAM David	ENG	41
HENRY Thierry	FRA	35
NESTA Alessandro	ITA	23
KLUIVERT Patrick	NED	22
TOTTI Francesco	ITA	14

FIFA WORLD PLAYER 2001

		Votes
FIGO Luis	POR	250
BECKHAM David	ENG	238
RAÚL	ESP	96
ZIDANE Zinedine	FRA	94
RIVALDO	BRA	92
VERON Juan Sebastian	ARG	71
KAHN Oliver	GER	65
OWEN Michael	ENG	61
SHEVCHENKO Andriy	UKR	46
TOTTI Francesco	ITA	40

FIFA WORLD PLAYER 2002

		Votes
RONALDO	BRA	387
KAHN Oliver	GER	171
ZIDANE Zinedine	FRA	148
ROBERTO CARLOS	BRA	114
RIVALDO	BRA	92
RAÚL	ESP	90
BALLACK Michael	GER	82
BECKHAM David	ENG	51
HENRY Thierry	FRA	38
OWEN Michael	ENG	34

FIFA WORLD PLAYER 2003

		Votes
ZIDANE Zinedine	FRA	264
HENRY Thierry	FRA	186
RONALDO	BRA	176
NEDVED Pavel	CZE	158
ROBERTO CARLOS	BRA	105
VAN NISTELROOY Ruud	NED	86
BECKHAM David	ENG	74
RAÚL	ESP	39
MALDINI Paolo	ITA	37
SHEVCHENKO Andriy	UKR	26

FIFA WORLD PLAYER 2004

		Votes
RONALDINHO	BRA	620
HENRY Thierry	FRA	552
SHEVCHENKO Andriy	UKR	253
NEDVED Pavel	CZE	178
ZIDANE Zinedine	FRA	150
ADRIANO	BRA	98
DECO	POR	96
RONALDO	BRA	96
VAN NISTELROOY Ruud	NED	67
KAKA & ROONEY Wayne		64

FIFA WORLD PLAYER 2005

		Votes
RONALDINHO	BRA	956
LAMPARD Frank	ENG	306
ETO'O Samuel	CMR	190
HENRY Thierry	FRA	172
ADRIANO	BRA	170
SHEVCHENKO Andriy	UKR	153
GERRARD Steven	ENG	131
KAKA	BRA	101
MALDINI Paolo	ITA	76
DROGBA Didier	CIV	65

RECORDS OF THE 30 PLAYERS SELECTED FOR THE 2005 AWARD

1 – RONALDINHO

21-03-1980 Porto Alegre, BRA (1.80/76)

		League		Sth Am/Europe		BRA	
1998	Grêmio	14	1	SA 8	10 1 CL qf		
1999	Grêmio	17	5	SA 18	5 2 MS gE	10	7
2000	Grêmio	11	8	SA 10	4 1 MS gB	7	1
2001	Grêmio	0	0	SA 5		4	1
01-02	PSG	28	9	L1 4	6 2 UC r3	9	3
02-03	PSG	27	8	L1 11	4 1 UC r3	9	2
03-04	Barcelona	32	15	PD 2	7 4 UC r4	5	2
04-05	Barcelona	35	9	PD 1	7 4 CL r2	16	11
05-06	Barcelona	29	19	PD 1	17 8 CL W	8	0

Honours: CA 1999, WC 2002, CC 2005; CL 2006 Lge 2005 2006,
Cup 2001; Brazil debut: 26-06-1999 v LVA

2 – LAMPARD, FRANK

21-06-1978 Romford, ENG (1.83/79)

		League		Europe		ENG	
95-96	West Ham Utd	2	0	PL 10			
95-96	Swansea City	9	1	D3 22			
96-97	West Ham Utd	13	0	PL 14			
97-98	West Ham Utd	31	4	PL 8			
98-99	West Ham Utd	38	5	PL 5			
99-00	West Ham Utd	34	7	PL 9	4 1 UC r2	1	0
00-01	West Ham Utd	30	7	PL 15		1	0
01-02	Chelsea	37	5	PL 6	4 1 UC r2	5	0
02-03	Chelsea	38	6	PL 4	2 1 UC r1	4	0
03-04	Chelsea	38	10	PL 2	14 4 CL sf	12	5
04-05	Chelsea	38	13	PL 1	12 4 CL sf	9	3
05-06	Chelsea	35	16	PL 1	8 2 CL r2	13	3

Honours: Lge 2005 2006; LCup 2005
England debut: 10-10-1999 v BEL

3 – ETO'O, SAMUEL
10-03-1981 Nkon, CMR (1.80/75)

Season	Club	League				Europe				CMR
97-98	Leganés	28	3	D2	13					
98-99	Real Madrid	1	0	PD	-					
98-99	Espanyol	0	0	PD	7					
99-00	Real Madrid	2	0	PD	-	3	0	CL	W	
99-00	Mallorca	13	6	PD	10					
00-01	Mallorca	28	11	PD	3					
01-02	Mallorca	30	6	PD	16	9	3	C/U	r3	
02-03	Mallorca	30	14	PD	9					
03-04	Mallorca	32	17	PD	11	7	4	UC	r4	
04-05	Barcelona	37	24	PD	1	7	4	CL	r2	Total
05-06	Barcelona	34	27	PD	1	11	6	CL	W	66 24

Honours: CN 2000 2002, Olympic Gold 2000; Lge 2005 2006, Cup 2003 • Cameroon debut: 9-08-1997 v ZAM

4 – HENRY, THIERRY
17-08-1977 Paris, FRA (1.87/81)

Season	Club	League				Europe				FRA
94-95	Monaco	8	3	L1	6					
95-96	Monaco	18	3	L1	3	1	0	UC	r1	
96-97	Monaco	36	9	L1	1	9	1	UC	sf	
97-98	Monaco	30	4	L1	3	9	7	CL	sf	9 3
98-99	Monaco	13	1	L1	-	5	0	UC	r3	
98-99	Juventus	16	3	SA	6					2 0
99-00	Arsenal	31	17	PL	2	12	8	C/U	F	10 5
00-01	Arsenal	35	17	PL	2	14	4	CL	qf	8 2
01-02	Arsenal	33	24	PL	1	11	7	CL	r2	9 2
02-03	Arsenal	37	24	PL	2	12	7	CL	r2	13 10
03-04	Arsenal	37	30	PL	1	10	5	CL	qf	12 5
04-05	Arsenal	32	25	PL	2	8	5	CL	r2	7 1
05-06	Arsenal	32	27	PL	4	11	5	CL	F	15 8

Honours: WC 1998, EC 2000, CC 2003; Lge 1997 2002 2004, Cup 2002 2003 • France debut: 11-10-1997 v RSA

5 – ADRIANO
17-02-1982 Rio de Janeiro, BRA (1.89/87)

Season	Club	League				Europe				BRA
1999	Flamengo	0	0	SA	12					
2000	Flamengo	19	7	SA	15					1 0
2001	Flamengo	17	6	SA	24					
01-02	Internazionale	8	1	SA	-	5	0	UC	qf	
01-02	Fiorentina	15	6	SA	17					
02-03	Parma	28	15	SA	6	2	2	UC	r2	5 3
03-04	Parma	9	8	SA	-	2	1	UC	r3	
03-04	Internazionale	16	9	SA	4					8 7
04-05	Internazionale	30	16	SA	3	9	10	CL	qf	11 7
05-06	Internazionale	30	13	SA	3	11	6	CL	qf	11 8

Honours: CA 2004, CC 2005; Cup 2005
Brazil debut: 15-11-2000 v COL • 60 caps • 27 goals

6 – SHEVCHENKO, ANDRIY
29-09-1976 Dvirkivshchyna, UKR (1.83/73)

Season	Club	League				Europe				UKR
94-95	Dynamo Kyiv	16	1	PL	1	2	1	CL	g	2 0
95-96	Dynamo Kyiv	31	16	PL	1	3	2	CL	g	2 1
96-97	Dynamo Kyiv	20	6	PL	1					6 2
97-98	Dynamo Kyiv	23	19	PL	1	10	6	CL	qf	3 2
98-99	Dynamo Kyiv	28	18	PL	1	14	10	CL	sf	9 1
99-00	Milan	32	24	SA	3	6	1	CL	g	7 3
00-01	Milan	34	24	SA	6	14	9	CL	r2	7 5
01-02	Milan	29	14	SA	4	6	3	UC	sf	6 5
02-03	Milan	24	5	SA	3	11	4	CL	W	6 2
03-04	Milan	32	24	SA	1	9	4	CL	qf	4 1
04-05	Milan	29	17	SA	2	10	6	CL	F	8 5
05-06	Milan	28	19	SA	2	12	9	CL	sf	9 4

Honours: CL 2003, Lge 1995 1996 1997 1998 1999 2004, Cup 1996 1998 1999 2003 • Ukraine debut: 25-03-1995 v CRO

7 – GERRARD, STEVEN
30-05-1980 Whiston, ENG (1.87/78)

Season	Club	League				Europe				ENG
97-98	Liverpool	0	0	PL	3					
98-99	Liverpool	12	0	PL	7	1	0	UC	r1	
99-00	Liverpool	29	1	PL	4					2 0
00-01	Liverpool	33	7	PL	3	9	2	UC	W	3 0
01-02	Liverpool	28	3	PL	2	14	1	CL	qf	5 1
02-03	Liverpool	34	5	PL	5	11	0	C/U	qf	8 2
03-04	Liverpool	34	4	PL	4	8	2	UC	r4	10 1
04-05	Liverpool	30	7	PL	5	10	4	CL	W	6 2
05-06	Liverpool	32	10	PL	3	11	6	CL	r2	13 3

Honours: CL 2005, UC 2001, Cup 2001 2006, LCup 2001 2003
England debut: 31-05-2000 v UKR

8 – KAKA
22-04-1982 Brasilia, BRA (1.83/73)

Season	Club	League				Europe				BRA
2000	São Paulo	0	0	SA						
2001	São Paulo	26	12	SA	qf					
2002	São Paulo	20	8	SA	qf					4 1
2003	São Paulo	10	2	SA	-					1 0
03-04	Milan	30	10	SA	1	10	2	CL	qf	11 3
04-05	Milan	36	7	SA	2	8	2	CL	F	11 4
05-06	Milan	35	14	SA	2	12	5	CL	sf	16 4

Honours: WC 2002, CC 2005; Lge 2004 • Debut: 31-01-2002 v BOL

9 – MALDINI, PAOLO
26-06-1968 Milan, ITA (1.87/85)

Season	Club	League				Europe				ITA
84-85	Milan	1	0	SA	5					
85-86	Milan	27	1	SA	7	6	0	UC	r3	
86-87	Milan	29	1	SA	5					
87-88	Milan	26	2	SA	1	2	0	UC	r2	7 0
88-89	Milan	26	0	SA	3	7	0	CL	W	7 0
89-90	Milan	30	1	SA	2	11	0	CL	W	12 0
90-91	Milan	26	4	SA	2	6	0	CL	qf	6 0
91-92	Milan	31	3	SA	1					8 0
92-93	Milan	31	2	SA	1	10	1	CL	F	7 2
93-94	Milan	30	1	SA	1	13	1	CL	W	11 0
94-95	Milan	29	2	SA	4	13	0	CL	F	6 0
95-96	Milan	30	3	SA	1	8	0	UC	qf	7 1
96-97	Milan	26	1	SA	11	6	0	CL	gD	10 2
97-98	Milan	30	0	SA	10					12 1
98-99	Milan	31	1	SA	1					9 1
99-00	Milan	27	1	SA	3	6	0	CL	gH	9 0
00-01	Milan	31	1	SA	6	14	0	CL	r2	8 0
01-02	Milan	15	1	SA	4	4	0	UC	sf	7 0
02-03	Milan	29	2	SA	3	19	0	CL	W	
03-04	Milan	30	0	SA	1	11	0	CL	qf	
04-05	Milan	33	0	SA	2	13	1	CL	F	
05-06	Milan	14	2	SA	2	9	0	CL	sf	

Honours: CL 1989 1990 1994 2003, Lge 1988 1992 1993 1994 1996 1999 2004, Cup 2003
Italy debut: 31-03-1988 v YUG • 126 caps • 7 goals

10 – DROGBA, DIDIER

11-03-1978 Abidjan, CIV (1.83/86)

Season	Club	League				Europe				CIV	
98-99	Le Mans	2	0	D2	17						
99-00	Le Mans	30	6	D2	8						
00-01	Le Mans	11	0	D2	14						
01-02	Le Mans	21	5	D2	5						
01-02	Guingamp	11	3	L1	16						
02-03	Guingamp	34	17	L1	7						
03-04	Oly. Marseille	35	18	L1	7	10	6	C/U	F		
04-05	Chelsea	26	10	PL	1	9	5	CL	sf	Total	
05-06	Chelsea	29	12	PL	1	7	1	CL	r2	34	24

Honours: Lge 2005 2006, LCup 2005
Côte d'Ivoire debut: 8-09-2002 v RSA

11 – BALLACK, MICHAEL

26-09-1976 Chemnitz, GER (1.89/80)

Season	Club	League				Europe				GER	
95-96	Chemnitzer FC	15	0	B2	15						
96-97	Chemnitzer FC	34	10	D3	4						
97-98	Kaiserslautern	16	0	BL	1						
98-99	Kaiserslautern	30	4	BL	5	6	0	CL	qf	1	0
99-00	Bayer Leverkusen	23	3	BL	2	2	2	UC	r3	8	0
00-01	Bayer Leverkusen	27	7	BL	4	5	2	CL	g	8	3
01-02	Bayer Leverkusen	29	17	BL	2	16	6	CL	F	11	6
02-03	Bayern München	26	10	BL	1	7	1	CL	g	5	3
03-04	Bayern München	28	7	BL	2	8	0	CL	r2	11	8
04-05	Bayern München	27	13	BL	1	9	2	CL	qf	13	8
05-06	Bayern München	26	14	BL	1	6	1	CL	r2	13	3

Honours: Lge 1998 2003 2005 2006, Cup 2003 2005 2006
Germany debut: 28-04-1999 v SCO

12 – RONALDO

22-09-76 Bento Ribeiro, BRA (1.83/82)

Season	Club	League				Europe				BRA	
1994	Cruzeiro	14	12	SA	15					3	1
94-95	PSV Eindhoven	33	30	ED	3	2	3	UC	r1	6	1
95-96	PSV Eindhoven	13	12	ED	2	5	6	UC	qf	1	2
96-97	Barcelona	37	34	PD	2	7	5	CW	W	17	15
97-98	Internazionale	32	25	SA	2	11	6	UC	W	17	11
98-99	Internazionale	19	14	SA	8	6	1	CL	qf	7	6
99-00	Internazionale	7	3	SA	4					3	1
00-01	Internazionale	0	0	SA	5					0	0
01-02	Internazionale	10	7	SA	3	5	0	UC	sf	10	9
02-03	Real Madrid	31	23	PD	1	11	6	CL	sf	5	2
03-04	Real Madrid	32	24	PD	4	9	4	CL	qf	10	6
04-05	Real Madrid	34	21	PD	2	10	3	CL	r2	8	3
05-06	Real Madrid	23	14	PD	2	2	0	CL	r2	10	6

Honours: WC 1994 2002, CC 1997, CA 1997 1999; CW 1997, UC 1998, Lge 2003, Cup 1993 1996 • Brazil debut: 23-03-1994 v ARG

13 – ZIDANE, ZINEDINE

23-06-1972 Marseille, FRA (1.85/78)

Season	Club	League				Europe				FRA	
88-89	Cannes	2	0	L1							
89-90	Cannes	0	0	L1							
90-91	Cannes	28	1	L1							
91-92	Cannes	31	5	L1		4	0	UC	r3		
92-93	Bordeaux	35	10	L1							
93-94	Bordeaux	34	6	L1	4	6	2	UC	r3		
94-95	Bordeaux	37	6	L1	7	4	1	UC	r2	3	2
95-96	Bordeaux	33	6	L1	16	10	1	UC	F	14	3
96-97	Juventus	29	5	SA	1	13	2	CL	F	9	1
97-98	Juventus	32	7	SA	1	11	3	CL	F	13	5
98-99	Juventus	25	2	SA	6	10	0	CL	sf	6	0
99-00	Juventus	32	4	SA	2	10	0	U/C	r4	14	5
00-01	Juventus	33	6	SA	2	4	0	CL	gE	7	2
01-02	Real Madrid	31	7	PD	3	9	3	CL	W	1	1
02-03	Real Madrid	33	9	PD	1	14	3	CL	sf	7	3
03-04	Real Madrid	33	7	PD	4	10	3	CL	qf	11	4
04-05	Real Madrid	29	6	PD	2	10	0	CL	r2		
05-06	Real Madrid	29	9	PD	2	4	0	CL	r2	15	5

Honours: WC 1998; EC 2000; CL 2002, Lge 1997 1998 2003
France debut: 17-08-1994 v CZE

14 – IBRAHIMOVIC, ZLATAN

3-10-1981 Malmö, SWE (1.92/84)

Season	Club	League				Europe				SWE	
1999	Malmö FF	6	1	AS	13						
2000	Malmö FF	26	12	D2	2						
2001	Malmö FF	8	3	AS	9					3	0
01-02	Ajax	24	6	ED	1	6	1	C/U	r2	9	1
02-03	Ajax	25	13	ED	2	13	5	CL	qf	4	3
03-04	Ajax	22	13	ED	1	8	2	CL	g	11	5
04-05	Ajax	3	3	ED	-						
04-05	Juventus	35	16	SA	1	10	0	CL	qf	6	6
05-06	Juventus	35	7	SA	1	9	3	CL	qf	8	3

Honours: Lge 2002 2004 2005 2006, Cup 2002
Sweden debut: 31-01-2001 v FRO

16 – RIQUELME, JUAN ROMAN

24-06-1978 Buenos Aires, ARG (1.80/76)

Season	Club	League				Sth Am/Europe				ARG	
96-97	Boca Juniors	22	4	PD	10/9	2	0	SC	r1		
97-98	Boca Juniors	19	0	PD	2/6	6	0	CM	qf	1	0
98-99	Boca Juniors	37	10	PD	1/1	5	0	CM	r1	5	0
99-00	Boca Juniors	24	4	PD	3/7	11	3	CL	W		
00-01	Boca Juniors	27	10	PD	1/3	12	3	CL	W		
01-02	Boca Juniors	22	10	PD	3/3	4	0	CL	qf	1	0
02-03	Barcelona	30	3	PD	6	11	2	CL	r2	3	1
03-04	Villarreal	33	8	PD	8	12	4	UC	sf	2	0
04-05	Villarreal	35	15	PD	3	9	2	UC	qf	12	5
05-06	Villarreal	25	12	PD	7	14	2	CL	sf	12	2

Honours: CL 2000 2001, Lge 1999x2 2001
Argentina debut: 16-11-1997 v COL

15 – DECO

27-08-1977 São Bernardo do Campo, BRA (1.74/75)

Season	Club	League				Europe				POR	
1997	Corinthians	0	0	SA	17						
97-98	Alverca	32	13	D2	3						
98-99	Salgueiros	12	2	D1	-						
98-99	Porto	6	0	SL	1						
99-00	Porto	23	1	SL	2	11	3	CL	qf		
00-01	Porto	31	6	SL	2	10	0	C/U	qf		
01-02	Porto	30	13	SL	3	15	6	CL	r2		
02-03	Porto	30	10	SL	1	12	1	UC	W	4	1
03-04	Porto	28	2	SL	1	12	2	CL	W	15	0
04-05	Barcelona	35	8	PD	1	7	2	CL	r2	10	1
05-06	Barcelona	29	3	PD	1	11	2	CL	W	10	1

Honours: CL 2004 2006, UC 2003, Lge 1999 2003 2004 2005 2006, Cup 2000 2001 2003 • Portugal debut: 29-03-2003 v BRA

17 - ROBINHO

25-01-1984 São Vicente, BRA (1.72/60)

		League				Europe				BRA	
2002	Santos	24	7	SA	1						
2003	Santos	32	9	SA	2	14	4	CL	F	5	0
2004	Santos	37	21	SA	1	8	4	CL	qf		
2005	Santos	11	7	SA		9	6	CL	qf	12	4
05-06	Real Madrid	37	8	PD	2	8	0	CL	r2	10	1

Honours: CC 2005; Lge 2002 2004
Brazil debut: 13-07-2003 v MEX

18 - ROONEY, WAYNE

24-10-1985 Liverpool, ENG (1.80/76)

		League				Europe				ENG	
02-03	Everton	33	6	PL	7					5	0
03-04	Everton	34	9	PL	17					12	9
04-05	Manchester Utd	29	11	PL	3	6	3	CL	r2	6	0
05-06	Manchester Utd	36	16	PL	2	5	1	CL	r1	10	2

Honours: LCup 2006
England debut: 12-02-2003 v AUS

20 - CRISTIANO RONALDO

5-02-1985 Funchal, POR (1.84/78)

		League				Europe				POR	
02-03	Sporting CP	25	3	SL	3	3	0	CL	r1		
03-04	Manchester Utd	29	4	PL	3	5	0	CL	r2	13	2
04-05	Manchester Utd	33	5	PL	3	8	0	CL	r2	10	7
05-06	Manchester Utd	33	9	PL	2	8	1	CL	r1	15	3

Honours: Cup 2004, LCup 2006
Portugal debut: 20-08-2001 v KAZ

18 - BECKHAM, DAVID

2-05-1975 Leytonstone, ENG (1.82/74)

		League				Europe				ENG	
94-95	Manchester Utd	4	0	PL		1	1	CL	r1		
94-95	Preston NE	5	2	D4	5						
95-96	Manchester Utd	33	7	PL	1	2	0	UC	r1		
96-97	Manchester Utd	36	8	PL	1	10	2	CL	sf	9	0
97-98	Manchester Utd	37	9	PL	2	8	0	CL	qf	9	1
98-99	Manchester Utd	34	6	PL	1	12	2	CL	W	5	0
99-00	Manchester Utd	31	6	PL	1	13	2	CL	qf	11	0
00-01	Manchester Utd	31	9	PL	1	12	0	CL	qf	8	3
01-02	Manchester Utd	28	11	PL	3	13	4	CL	sf	12	3
02-03	Manchester Utd	31	6	PL	1	13	3	CL	qf	6	4
03-04	Real Madrid	32	3	PD	4	7	1	CL	qf	12	2
04-05	Real Madrid	30	4	PD	2	8	0	CL	r2	9	3
05-06	Real Madrid	31	3	PD	2	7	1	CL	r2	13	1

Honours: CL 1999; Lge 1996 1997 1999 2000 2001 2003, Cup 1996 1999 • England debut: 1-09-1996 v MDA

21 - VAN NISTELROOY, RUUD

1-07-1976 Oss, NED (1.88/80)

		League				Europe				NED	
93-94	Den Bosch	2	0	D2	11						
94-95	Den Bosch	15	3	D2	18						
95-96	Den Bosch	21	2	D2	3						
96-97	Den Bosch	31	12	D2	7						
97-98	Heerenveen	31	13	ED	6						
98-99	PSV Eindhoven	34	31	ED	3	7	6	CL	r1	5	1
99-00	PSV Eindhoven	23	29	ED	1	8	3	CL	r1	5	0
00-01	PSV Eindhoven	9	2	ED	1					2	0
01-02	Manchester Utd	32	23	ED	3	14	10	CL	SF	6	4
02-03	Manchester Utd	34	25	PL	1	11	14	CL	qf	7	3
03-04	Manchester Utd	32	20	PL	3	7	4	CL	r2	13	7
04-05	Manchester Utd	17	6	PL	3	7	8	CL	r2	6	4
05-06	Manchester Utd	35	21	PL	2	8	2	CL	r1	10	6

Honours: Lge 2000 2001 2003, Cup 2004, LCup 2006
Netherlands debut: 18-11-1998 v GER

21 - ESSIEN, MICHAEL

3-12-1982 Accra, GHA (1.80/77)

		League				Europe				GHA	
99-00	Liberty										
00-01	Bastia	13	1	L1	8						
01-02	Bastia	24	4	L1	11						
02-03	Bastia	29	6	L1	12						
03-04	Oly. Lyonnais	34	3	L1	1	8	0	CL	qf		
04-05	Oly. Lyonnais	37	4	L1	1	10	5	CL	qf	Total	
05-06	Chelsea	31	2	PL	1	6	0	CL	r2	20	4

Honours: Lge 2004 2005 2006
Ghana debut: 21-01-2002 v MAR

23 - NEDVED, PAVEL

30-08-1972 Cheb, CZE (1.77/70)

		League				Europe				CZE	
91-92	Dukla Praha	19	3	D1	11						
92-93	Sparta Praha	18	0	D1	1	5	0	UC	qf		
93-94	Sparta Praha	23	3	D1	1	4	0	CL	r2	1	0
94-95	Sparta Praha	27	6	D1	1	2	0	CL	pr	0	0
95-96	Sparta Praha	27	14	D1	4	8	5	UC	r3	13	1
96-97	Lazio	32	7	SA	4	3	2	UC	r2	6	1
97-98	Lazio	26	11	SA	7	11	2	UC	F	7	2
98-99	Lazio	21	1	SA	2	8	4	CC	W	8	1
99-00	Lazio	28	5	SA	1	13	1	CL	qf	11	4
00-01	Lazio	31	9	SA	3	10	3	CL	r2	9	3
01-02	Juventus	32	4	SA	1	7	0	CL	r2	7	3
02-03	Juventus	29	9	SA	1	15	5	CL	F	8	1
03-04	Juventus	30	6	SA	3	6	2	CL	r2	13	1
04-05	Juventus	27	7	SA	1	10	3	CL	qf	0	0
05-06	Juventus	33	5	SA	3	8	2	CL	qf	6	1

Honours: Lge 1993 1994 1995 2000 2002 2003 2005 2006,
Cup 1993 1996 1998 2000 • Czech Republic debut: 5-06-1994 v IRL

23 - RAUL

27-06-1977 Madrid, ESP (1.80/68)

		League				Europe				ESP	
94-95	Real Madrid	28	9	PD	1						
95-96	Real Madrid	40	19	PD	6	8	6	CL	qf		
96-97	Real Madrid	42	20	PD	1					7	1
97-98	Real Madrid	35	10	PD	4	11	2	CL	W	9	2
98-99	Real Madrid	37	25	PD	2	8	3	CL	qf	7	10
99-00	Real Madrid	34	17	PD	5	15	10	CL	W	12	4
00-01	Real Madrid	36	24	PD	1	12	7	CL	sf	11	4
01-02	Real Madrid	35	14	PD	3	12	6	CL	W	9	7
02-03	Real Madrid	31	16	PD	1	12	9	CL	sf	8	4
03-04	Real Madrid	35	11	PD	4	9	2	CL	qf	12	6
04-05	Real Madrid	32	9	PD	2	10	4	CL	r2	10	3
05-06	Real Madrid	26	5	PD	2	6	2	CL	r2	14	3

Honours: CL 1998 2000 2002, Lge 1995 1997 2001 2003
Spain debut: 9-10-1996 v CZE

25 - ROBBEN, ARJEN

23-01-1984 Bedum, NED (1.80/75)

Season	Club	League				Europe				NED	
00-01	Groningen	18	2	ED	14						
01-02	Groningen	28	6	ED	15						
02-03	PSV Eindhoven	33	12	ED	1	4	1	CL	r1	1	0
03-04	PSV Eindhoven	23	5	ED	2	8	2	CL	qf	9	2
04-05	Chelsea	18	7	PL	1	5	1	CL	sf	4	2
05-06	Chelsea	28	6	PL	1	6	0	CL	r2	9	3

Honours: Lge 2003 2005 2006, LCup 2005
Netherlands debut: 30-04-2003 v POR

26 - CAFU

7-06-1970 São Paulo, BRA (1.76/74)

Season	Club	League				Sth Am/Europe				BRA	
1989	São Paulo	3	0	SA	2						
1990	São Paulo	17	1	SA	2					3	0
1991	São Paulo	20	1	SA	1					9	0
1992	São Paulo	21	1	SA	6	14	0	CL	W	2	0
1993	São Paulo	18	1	SA	4	8	2	CL	W	12	1
1994	São Paulo	16	2	SA	6	2	0	CL	-	7	2
94-95	Real Zaragoza	16	0	PD	7			CW	W		
1995	Palmeiras	19	0	SA	5	2	2	CL	qf	5	0
1996	Palmeiras	16	0	SA	qf					3	0
1997	Palmeiras	0	0	SA	-					12	0
97-98	Roma	31	1	SA	4					17	0
98-99	Roma	20	1	SA	5	6	0	UC	qf	11	0
99-00	Roma	28	2	SA	6	5	0	UC	r4	11	2
00-01	Roma	31	1	SA	1	5	0	UC	r4	6	0
01-02	Roma	27	0	SA	2	10	2	CL	r2	14	0
02-03	Roma	26	0	SA	8	12	0	CL	r2	4	0
03-04	Milan	28	1	SA	1	11	0	CL	qf	11	0
04-05	Milan	33	1	SA	2	12	0	CL	F	7	0
05-06	Milan	19	1	SA	2	5	0	CL	sf	9	0

Honours: WC 1994 2002, CA 1997 1999, CC 1997; CL 1992 1993, CW 1995, Lge 1991 2001 2004 • Brazil debut: 12-09-1990 v ESP

26 - ROBERTO CARLOS

10-04-1973 Garça, BRA (1.68/70)

Season	Club	League				Europe				BRA	
1992	União São João									7	0
1993	Palmeiras	20	1	SA	1					5	0
1994	Palmeiras	24	2	SA	1						
1995	Palmeiras	23	3	SA	5					11	1
95-96	Internazionale	30	5	SA	7	2	1	UC	r1	2	0
96-97	Real Madrid	37	4	PD	1					12	2
97-98	Real Madrid	35	4	PD	4	7	2	CL	W	16	1
98-99	Real Madrid	35	5	PD	2	8	0	CL	qf	9	1
99-00	Real Madrid	35	4	PD	5	17	4	CL	W	10	1
00-01	Real Madrid	36	5	PD	1	11	4	CL	sf	4	1
01-02	Real Madrid	31	3	PD	3	12	1	CL	W	15	1
02-03	Real Madrid	37	5	PD	1	15	1	CL	qf	4	0
03-04	Real Madrid	32	5	PD	4	8	2	CL	qf	9	1
04-05	Real Madrid	34	3	PD	2	10	1	CL	r2	1	0
05-06	Real Madrid	35	5	PD	2	7	0	CL	r2	10	1

Honours: WC 2002, CC 1997, CA 1997 1999; CL 1998 2000 2002, Lge 1993 1994 1997 2001 2003 • Brazil debut: 26-02-1992 v USA

26 - NESTA, ALESSANDRO

19-03-1976 Milan, ITA (1.87/79)

Season	Club	League				Europe				ITA	
93-94	Lazio	2	0	SA	4						
94-95	Lazio	11	0	SA	2						
95-96	Lazio	23	0	SA	3	3	0	UC	r2		
96-97	Lazio	25	0	SA	4	4	0	UC	r2	5	0
97-98	Lazio	30	0	SA	7	10	1	UC	F	10	0
98-99	Lazio	20	1	SA	2	4	0	CW	W	5	0
99-00	Lazio	28	0	SA	1	10	0	CL	qf	11	0
00-01	Lazio	29	0	SA	3	8	0	CL	r2	7	0
01-02	Lazio	25	0	SA	6	6	0	CL	r1	8	0
02-03	Milan	29	1	SA	3	14	0	CL	W	7	0
03-04	Milan	26	0	SA	1	7	0	CL	qf	9	0
04-05	Milan	29	0	SA	2	12	0	CL	F	5	0
05-06	Milan	30	1	SA	2	10	0	CL	sf	10	0

Honours: WC 2006; CL 2003, CW 1999, Lge 2000 2004, Cup 1998 2000 2003; Italy debut: 5-10-1996 v MDA

26 - OKOCHA, JAY-JAY

14-08-1973 Enugu, NGA (1.87/85)

Season	Club	League				Europe				NGA	
92-93	Eint. Frankfurt	20	2	BL	3	3	0	UC	r2		
93-94	Eint. Frankfurt	19	2	BL	5	4	2	UC	qf		
94-95	Eint. Frankfurt	27	7	BL	9	7	0	UC	qf		
95-96	Eint. Frankfurt	24	7	BL	17						
96-97	Fenerbahçe	33	16	SL	3	8	1	CL	r1		
97-98	Fenerbahçe	30	14	SL	2	2	0	UC	r1		
98-99	PSG	25	4	L1	9	2	1	CW	r1		
99-00	PSG	23	2	L1	2						
00-01	PSG	16	2	L1	9	6	1	CL	r1		
01-02	PSG	20	4	L1	4	3	0	UC	r3		
02-03	Bolton Wand.	31	7	PL	17						
03-04	Bolton Wand.	35	0	PL	8						
04-05	Bolton Wand.	31	6	PL	6					Total	
05-06	Bolton Wand.	27	1	PL	8	7	0	UC	r3	74	

Honours: None
Nigeria debut: 2-05-1993 v CIV

30 - BUFFON, GIANLUIGI

28-01-1978 Carrara, ITA (1.90/88)

Season	Club	League				Europe				ITA	
95-96	Parma	9	-	SA	5						
96-97	Parma	27	-	SA	2	1	-	UC	r1		
97-98	Parma	32	-	SA	6	8	-	CL	r1	2	-
98-99	Parma	34	-	SA	4	11	-	UC	W	7	-
99-00	Parma	32	-	SA	5	9	-	C/U	r4	6	-
00-01	Parma	34	-	SA	4	7	-	U	r4	5	-
01-02	Juventus	34	-	SA	1	10	-	CL	r2	10	-
02-03	Juventus	32	-	SA	1	15	-	CL	F	8	-
03-04	Juventus	32	-	SA	3	6	-	CL	r2	11	-
04-05	Juventus	37	-	SA	1	11	-	CL	qf	8	-
05-06	Juventus	18	-	SA	1	4	-	CL	qf	10	-

Honours: UC 1999, Lge 2002 2003 2005, Cup 1999
Italy debut: 29-10-1997 v RUS

KEY

WC = FIFA World Cup™ • EC = UEFA European Championship • CC = FIFA Confederations Cup • OG = Olympic gold • CA = Copa America • CN = Africa Cup of Nations • CL = UEFA Champions League or Copa Libertadores • UC = UEFA Cup • CW = Cup Winners Cup • C/U = UEFA Champions League then the UEFA Cup • LGE = Domestic League championship • CUP = Domestic Cup • LCUP = League Cup • AS = Allsvenskan (Sweden) • BL = Bundesliga (Germany) • B2 = Bundesliga 2 (Germany) • ED = Eredivisie (Netherlands) • L1 = Ligue 1 (France) • PD = Primera Division (Argentina & Spain) • PL = Premier League (England) • SA = Serie A (Brazil and Italy) • SL = Superliga (Portugal & Turkey) • The first line for each player gives the following information - date and place of birth, nationality, height in meters, weight in kilogrammes • The columns for each table read as follows - season, club, league appearances, league goals, name of the league, final position; continental appearances, continental goals, competition, round reached; international appearances, international goals

FIFA U–17 WORLD CHAMPIONSHIP PERU 2005

The 11th edition of the FIFA U-17 World Championship saw the tournament come to South America for only the second time, Ecuador having hosted the competition ten years earlier. Up for grabs was the chance for a European nation to win a FIFA tournament on the continent for only the second time. That was never going to be an easy challenge with Brazil, victorious in three of the previous four tournaments, feeling very much at home. But, in a competition full of surprises, the winners came from an entirely unexpected source - not from Europe, South America or even Africa, but from CONCACAF, in the shape of Mexico. Never before had Central or North America produced a world champion, but Mexico's Under-17 side beat Brazil comprehensively 3-0 in the final, and in Carlos Vela they had the tournament's top scorer. Although Brazil boasted a talented team, including the Golden Ball winner Anderson, the final was not their only defeat in the competition. In the first round they lost 3-1 to Gambia, a nation making its first appearance in a FIFA tournament and one that had qualified largely thanks to hosting the African championship. Gambia then went on to beat Qatar but were cruelly denied a place in the quarter-finals on goal difference after losing their final game to the Netherlands - both teams and Brazil all finishing on six points. The other big talking point of the opening group stage was the elimination of Italy by Korea DPR, reviving memories of the 1966 FIFA World Cup™ in England, although in the final match of the group stage between the two in Peru, a draw was enough to see the Koreans through. Another feature of the group stage was that CONCACAF provided two of the four group winners, neither of which was Mexico, although both - Costa Rica and the USA - crashed out in the quarter-finals to Mexico and the Netherlands respectively. The Dutch along with Turkey provided the main European challenge, but both were then eliminated in the semi-finals. The Dutch crashed out 4-0 to Mexico, while the Turks lost an absolute thriller against Brazil that was decided by an injury time Igor goal with the Turks having fought back from being 3-0 down. In the final, Brazil missed the talents of Anderson but it was Mexico's day as the nation celebrated a first world title.

FIFA U-17 WORLD CHAMPIONSHIP PERU 2005

First round groups	Pts	Quarter-final groups		Semi-finals		Final	
Costa Rica	5						
China PR	5	Mexico	3				
Ghana	3	Costa Rica	1				
Peru	1						
				Mexico	4		
	Pts			Netherlands	0		
Turkey	9						
Mexico	6	USA	0				
Australia	3	Netherlands	2				
Uruguay	0						
						Mexico	3
	Pts					Brazil	0
USA	7						
Korea DPR	4	Turkey	5				
Italy	4	China	1				
Côte d'Ivoire	1						
				Turkey	3		
	Pts			Brazil	4		
Brazil	6						
Netherlands	6	Korea DPR	1			3rd Place Play-off	
Gambia	6	Brazil	3			Netherlands	2
Qatar	0					Turkey	1

	GROUP A	PL	W	D	L	F	A	GD	PTS	CRC	CHN	GHA	PER
1	Costa Rica	3	1	2	0	4	2	+2	5		1-1	1-1	2-0
2	China PR	3	1	2	0	3	2	+1	5	1-1		1-1	1-0
3	Ghana	3	0	3	0	3	3	=	3	1-1	1-1		1-1
4	Peru	3	0	1	2	1	4	-3	1				

Mansiche, Trujillo, 16-09-2005
17:00, 18 000, Kamikawa JPN, Hiroshima JPN, Komaleeswaran IND

CHN   1   1   CRC

Tang Naixin [17]   Carrillo [10]

CHINA PR			COSTA RICA		
1	WANG Dalei		QUESADA Alfonso	1	
3	TANG Naixin		MYRIE Dave	2	88
5	GU Cao	80	(c) DAWSON Rudy	3	
9	GU Jinjin	46	JIMENEZ Brayan	4	
10	ZHU Yifan		CARRILLO Roberto	7	
13	LI Zhuangfei (c)		BORGES Celso	8	
14	DU Longquan	59	CORDERO Luis	10	69
16	DENG Zhuoxiang		SOLORZANO Jean	11	
18	YANG Xu		RODRIGUEZ Esteban	12	
19	HUANG Jie	81	PANIAGUA Fernando	14	
20	WANG Weilong		RAMOS Leslie	16	
	Tr: ZHANG Ning		Tr: ALFARO Geovanny		
4	LI Linfeng	81	RECINOS Ariel	9	88
7	YU Dabao	46	ELIZONDO Cesar	17	69
12	WANG Gang	59			

Mansiche, Trujillo, 16-09-2005
20:00, 21 100, De Bleeckere BEL, Simons BEL, Hermans BEL

PER   1   1   GHA

Chavez [12p]   Cardenas OG [62]

PERU			GHANA		
12	CASTELLANOS GianFranco		BONSU Nana	19	
2	RAMOS Christian (c)		TAGOE James	4	
4	LAURA Christian	70	DANSO Ernest	5	
5	PEIXOTO Kerwin		TELFER David	6	
8	ESPEJO Gianfranco		WAKASO Mubarak	10	
9	ESPEJO Gianfranco	59	OPPONG Samad	8	
13	ZAMBRANO Carlos		AGYEMANG Opoku	9	
14	REY Jesus	63	BUKARI Sadat	10	
15	CARDENAS Miguel	86	(c) ANSONG Emmanuel	12	
16	FLORES Carlos		BOATENG Charles	17	
17	BALLON Josepmir		APPIAH George	18	18
	Tr: PAVONI Jose		Tr: DUNCAN David		
9	MESARINA Jose	70	QUARTEY Jonathan	11	18
10	ELIAS Carlos	86	ABUBAKAR Awudu	15	59
11	CARNERO Javier	63			

Mansiche, Trujillo, 19-09-2005
15:30, 15 000, Larrionda URU, Rial URU, Fandino URU

GHA   1   1   CRC

Quartey [58]   Borges [47]

GHANA			COSTA RICA		
19	BONSU Nana		QUESADA Alfonso	1	
4	TAGOE James		MYRIE Dave	2	
5	DANSO Ernest		(c) DAWSON Rudy	3	
6	TELFER David		JIMENEZ Brayan	4	
8	OPPONG Samad	62	CARRILLO Roberto	7	71
9	AGYEMANG Opoku		BORGES Celso	8	
11	QUARTEY Jonathan		SOLORZANO Jean	11	
12	ANSONG Emmanuel (c)		RODRIGUEZ Esteban	12	
16	ABUBAKAR Awudu		PANIAGUA Fernando	14	
17	BOATENG Charles	87	RAMOS Leslie	16	
18	APPIAH George	22	ELIZONDO Cesar	17	
	Tr: DUNCAN David		Tr: ALFARO Geovanny		
14	ADARKWA Anthony	62	CALVO David	6	87
			CORDERO Luis	10	71
			GUARDIA Guillermo	19	22

Mansiche, Trujillo, 19-09-2005
18:15, 20 000, Ruiz COL, Navia COL, Tamayo ECU

PER   0   1   CHN

    Deng Zhuoxiang [13]

PERU			CHINA PR		
12	CASTELLANOS GianFranco	94	WANG Dalei	1	
2	RAMOS Christian (c)	58	CUI Nanri	2	
4	LAURA Christian	64	TANG Naixin	3	
5	PEIXOTO Kerwin	77	GU Jinjin	9	
8	ESPEJO Gianfranco	76	ZHU Yifan	10	
9	CHAVEZ Daniel		(c) LI Zhuangfei	13	
13	ZAMBRANO Carlos		DU Longquan	14	
14	REY Jesus		DENG Zhuoxiang	16	
15	CARDENAS Miguel		YANG Xu	18	
16	FLORES Carlos	90	HUANG Jie	19	
17	BALLON Josepmir	86	WANG Weilong	20	
	Tr: PAVONI Jose		Tr: ZHANG Ning		
7	MESARINA Jose	64	LI Lifeng	4	58
10	ELIAS Carlos	76	CAI Yaohui	6	77
11	CARNERO Javier	90	WANG Gang	12	90

Max Augustin, Iquitos, 22-09-2005
18:15, 25 000, Shield AUS, Gibson AUS, Wilson AUS

CRC   2   0   PER

Solorzano [46+], Elizondo [77]

COSTA RICA			PERU		
1	QUESADA Alfonso		CASTELLANOS GianFranco	12	
2	MYRIE Dave		(c) RAMOS Christian	2	
3	DAWSON Rudy (c)		LAURA Christian	4	70
4	JIMENEZ Brayan		PEIXOTO Kerwin	5	
6	CALVO David		ESPEJO Gianfranco	8	
7	CARRILLO Roberto	35	CHAVEZ Daniel	9	
8	BORGES Celso		ZAMBRANO Carlos	13	
11	SOLORZANO Jean	89	REY Jesus	14	65
12	RODRIGUEZ Esteban		CARDENAS Miguel	15	
14	PANIAGUA Fernando		FLORES Carlos	16	
19	GUARDIA Guillermo	70	BALLON Josepmir	17	57
	Tr: ALFARO Geovanny		Tr: PAVONI Jose		
9	RECINOS Ariel	89	ELIAS Carlos	10	57
10	CORDERO Luis	35	CARNERO Javier	11	65
17	ELIZONDO Cesar	70	PORTUGAL Walter	18	70

Miguel Grau, Piura, 22-09-2005
18:15, 15 320, Hamer LUX, Texier FRA, Crelo LUX

GHA   1   1   CHN

Bukari [56]   Wang Xuanhong [60]

GHANA			CHINA PR		
19	BONSU Nana		CHI Wenyi	17	
4	TAGOE James		TANG Naixin	3	
5	DANSO Ernest	68	LI Linfeng	4	
6	TELFER David	46	YANG Jian	8	79
7	WAKASO Mubarak		GU Jinjin	9	
9	AGYEMANG Opoku		(c) LI Zhuangfei	13	
10	BUKARI Sadat		WANG Xuanhong	15	76
11	QUARTEY Jonathan		DENG Zhuoxiang	16	
12	ANSONG Emmanuel (c)		YANG Xu	18	
17	BOATENG Charles		HUANG Jie	19	
18	APPIAH George	21	WANG Weilong	20	
	Tr: DUNCAN David		Tr: ZHANG Ning		
2	APPIAH George	46	CUI Nanri	2	68
			CAI Yaohui	6	79
			DU Longquan	14	76

	GROUP B	PL	W	D	L	F	A	GD	PTS	TUR	MEX	AUS	URU
1	Turkey	3	3	0	0	6	3	3	9		2-1	1-0	3-2
2	Mexico	3	2	0	1	6	2	4	6			3-0	2-0
3	Australia	3	1	0	2	2	5	-3	3				2-1
4	Uruguay	3	0	0	3	3	7	-4	0				

Nacional, Lima, 16-09-2005
14:15, 8 000, Hamer LUX, Texier FRA. Crelo LUX

URU 0 2 MEX

Vela 47, Villaluz 54

#	URUGUAY			MEXICO	#
1	IRRAZABAL Yonatan			ARIAS Sergio	1
2	KAGELMACHER Gary	46		(c) ARAUJO Patricio	2
3	DIAZ Martin (c)			VALDEZ Efrain	3
4	SUAREZ Damian			SANCHEZ Christian	4
5	GONZALEZ Alejandro			MORENO Hector	5
8	ROMAN Marcel			ESPARZA Omar	6
9	FIGUEROA Elias	71		HERNANDEZ Jorge	7
10	VONDER PUTTEN Gerardo	56		DOS SANTOS Giovani	8
14	ARISMENDI Hugo	88		VELA Carlos	9
15	PAZ Cristian			ALDRETE Adrian	16
19	ALFARO Emiliano	83 86		VILLALUZ Cesar	18
	Tr: FERRIN Gustavo			Tr: RAMIREZ Jesus	
7	ACOSTA Michel	46 86		GALLEGOS Mario	11
11	SCORZA Enzo	56 88		ANDRADE Edgar	13
17	ALVAREZ Santiago	83 71		VALVERDE Pedro	17

Nacional, Lima, 16-09-2005
17:00, 14 200, Stott USA, Stricland USA, BARKEY USA

TUR 1 0 AUS

Dahin Nuri 84

#	TURKEY			AUSTRALIA	#
1	BABACAN Volkan			VRTESKI Alex	1
4	FERIN Erkan (c)			CUMMING Jamie	2
5	KESCI Serdar		69	D APUZZO David	3
6	KARADAS Harun	73		OOSTENDORP Wade	4
7	YILMAZ Deniz			SPIRANOVIC Matthew	5
8	ERKIN Caner	87		ALLWRIGHT Joel	7
9	KOSE Tevfik		62	KRUSE Robbie	8
10	SAHIN Nuri			(c) PATAFTA Kaz	10
11	OZCAN Ozgurcan	56		BURNS Nathan	14
18	DURUER Murat			JAMIESON Scott	16
19	DEMIR Aykut	83		BROXHAM Leigh	17
	Tr: AVCI Abdullah			Tr: POSTECOGLOU Ange	
3	BIKMAZ Ferhat	73	83	MULLEN Matthew	6
14	YILMAZ Aydin	56	62	MILLER Daniel	11
16	BERISHA Ergun	87	69	PARK Matthew	19

Nacional, Lima, 19-09-2005
15:30, 6 000, Elizondo ARG, Garcia, ARG, Otero ARG

MEX 3 0 AUS

Esparza 20, Vela 2 43 79

#	MEXICO			AUSTRALIA	#
1	ARIAS Sergio			VRTESKI Alex	1
2	ARAUJO Patricio (c)			CUMMING Jamie	2
3	VALDEZ Efrain	76		D APUZZO David	3
4	SANCHEZ Christian			OOSTENDORP Wade	4
5	MORENO Hector			SPIRANOVIC Matthew	5
6	ESPARZA Omar			ALLWRIGHT Joel	7
8	DOS SANTOS Giovani	84		KRUSE Robbie	8
9	VELA Carlos	81		(c) PATAFTA Kaz	10
13	ANDRADE Edgar	67		BURNS Nathan	14
16	ALDRETE Adrian	39		JAMIESON Scott	16
18	VILLALUZ Cesar	46		BROXHAM Leigh	17
	Tr: RAMIREZ Jesus			Tr: POSTECOGLOU Ange	
7	HERNANDEZ Jorge	67	46	MULLEN Matthew	6
10	GUZMAN Ever	84	39	MILLER Daniel	11
20		81	76	PARK Matthew	19

Nacional, Lima, 19-09-2005
18:15, 4 000, Daami TUN, Dante MLI, Ndoye SEN

URU 2 3 TUR

Duruer Murat OG 28, Figueroa 75

#	URUGUAY			TURKEY	#
1	IRRAZABAL Yonatan			BABACAN Volkan	1
2	KAGELMACHER Gary			(c) FERIN Erkan	4
3	DIAZ Martin (c)			KESCI Serdar	5
4	SUAREZ Damian	57		KARADAS Harun	6
5	GONZALEZ Alejandro			YILMAZ Deniz	7
8	ROMAN Marcel			ERKIN Caner	8
9	FIGUEROA Elias			KOSE Tevfik	9
10	VONDER PUTTEN Gerardo			SAHIN Nuri	10
11	SCORZA Enzo		85	YILMAZ Aydin	14
14	ARISMENDI Hugo	71	78	DURUER Murat	18
15	PAZ Cristian	57		DEMIR Aykut	19
	Tr: FERRIN Gustavo			Tr: AVCI Abdullah	
7	ACOSTA Michel	57	57	BIKMAZ Ferhat	3
19	ALFARO Emiliano	71	78	OZCAN Ozgurcan	11
			85	BERISHA Ergun	16

Elias Aguirre, Chiclayo, 22-09-2005
15:30, 11 100, Damon RSA, Molefe RSA, Yeboah GHA

AUS 2 1 URU

Burns 20, Kruse 83 — Figueroa 38

#	AUSTRALIA			URUGUAY	#
1	VRTESKI Alex			GOICOECHEA Mauro	12
2	CUMMING Jamie		46	KAGELMACHER Gary	2
3	D APUZZO David			(c) DIAZ Martin	3
4	OOSTENDORP Wade		85	SUAREZ Damian	4
5	SPIRANOVIC Matthew			GONZALEZ Alejandro	5
6	MULLEN Matthew	46	73	ACOSTA Michel	7
7	ALLWRIGHT Joel			ROMAN Marcel	8
8	KRUSE Robbie	89		FIGUEROA Elias	9
10	PATAFTA Kaz (c)			VONDER PUTTEN Gerardo	10
14	BURNS Nathan			SCORZA Enzo	11
16	JAMIESON Scott	86		ARISMENDI Hugo	14
	Tr: POSTECOGLOU Ange			Tr: FERRIN Gustavo	
13	TRIFIRO Jason	89	73	PAZ Cristian	15
17	BROXHAM Leigh	46	46	GONZALEZ Marcelo	16
20	MARONEY Brendan	86	85	ALVAREZ Santiago	17

Miguel Grau, Piura, 22-09-2005
15:30, 14 560, Kamikawa JPN, Hiroshima JPN, Komaleeswaran IND

MEX 1 2 TUR

Guzman 11 — Yilmaz Deniz 28, Erkin Caner 91+

#	MEXICO			TURKEY	#
1	ARIAS Sergio			KIVRAK Onur	12
2	ARAUJO Patricio (c)	46		YILMAZ Mehmet	2
3	VALDEZ Efrain			BIKMAZ Ferhat	3
5	MORENO Hector			YILMAZ Deniz	7
7	HERNANDEZ Jorge			ERKIN Caner	8
10	GUZMAN Ever			SAHIN Nuri	10
11	GALLEGOS Mario		65	(c) OZCAN Ozgurcan	11
13	ANDRADE Edgar			BALAK Emre	13
15	SILVA Carlos		56	YILMAZ Aydin	14
17	VALVERDE Pedro	46	82	BERISHA Ergun	16
20	ESQUEDA Alejandro	62		COBAN Cengiz	17
4	SANCHEZ Christian	46	56	KOSE Tevfik	9
6	ESPARZA Omar	46	65	TASDEMIR Anil	15
14	BELTRAN Heriberto	62	82	DURUER Murat	18

	GROUP C	PL	W	D	L	F	A	GD	PTS	USA	PRK	ITA	CIV
1	USA	3	2	1	0	7	4	3	7		3-2	3-1	1-1
2	Korea DPR	3	1	1	1	6	4	2	4			1-1	3-0
3	Italy	3	1	1	1	6	7	-1	4				4-3
4	Côte d'Ivoire	3	0	1	2	4	8	-4	1				

Elias Aguirre, Chiclayo, 17-09-2005
10:00, 14 800, Mohd Salleh MAS, Saeed MDV, Ishak MAS

CIV 3 4 ITA

Diomande [27], Fofana [53],
Kouassi.K [87]

Tiboni 2 [21] [32], Mandorlini [86]
Foti [89]

	COTE D'IVOIRE			ITALY	
1	TAHOUROU Ikossie			ALFONSO Enrico	1
2	KEITA Ali			BRIVIO Davide	2
3	KOUAKOU Irenee		(c)	DE SILVESTRI Lorenzo	3
4	BOSSON Romaric (c)			CREMONESI Michele	5
6	AGOUSSI Jules			GRECO Daniele	6
7	YAO Martial	46	46	D ATTOMA Tommaso	7
8	KOUASSI Pacome	46		PALERMO Simone	8
9	KOUASSI Koffi		56	TIBONI Christian	9
10	DIOMANDE Alassane			FOTI Salvatore	11
12	KOUADIO Serge	92		MANDORLINI Matteo	15
18	BAMBA Siaka			MANCOSU Marco	18
	Tr: BOHE Francois			Tr: ROCCA Francesco	
11	FOFANA Ismael	46	46	ANGELUCCI Manuel	4
14	ABDUL Moustapha	92	46	RUSSOTTO Andrea	10
15	VAMARA Diarra	46	76	DALLA COSTA Marco	19

Elias Aguirre, Chiclayo, 17-09-2005
12:45, 15 200, Damon RSA, Molefe RSA, Yeboah GHA

PRK 2 3 USA

Choe Myong Ho [24], Kim Kuk Jin [86]

Soroka [13], Nakazawa [43]
Zimmerman [72]

	KOREA DPR			USA	
1	JU Kwang Min			RUECKNER Bryant	1
5	PAK Nam Chol			IGWE Amaechi	2
7	YUN Yong Il			ALSTON Kevin	3
9	CHOE Myong Ho		(c)	SARKODIE Ofori	5
10	RI Hung Ryong	72		KIRK Quavas	6
11	PAK Chol Min			NAKAZAWA Kyle	8
12	KIM Kuk Jin			ZIMMERMAN Preston	9
13	JON Kwang Ik (c)		62	ARVIZU David	10
14	KIM Chol Ung		87	SOROKA Ryan	11
16	PIN Sok Chol			WAGNER Blake	13
19	KIM Kyong Il		71	FARFAN Mike	19
	Tr: JO Tong Sop			Tr: HACKWORTH John	
18	JONG Chol Min	72	87	SUBOTIC Neven	14
			62	BESAGNO Nik	16
			71	HALL Jeremy	17

Elias Aguirre, Chiclayo, 20-09-2005
15:30, 15 240, Shield AUS, Gibson AUS, Wilson AUS

ITA 1 3 USA

Russotto [74]

Sarkodie [47], Nakazawa [67]
Soroka [90]

	ITALY			USA	
1	ALFONSO Enrico			RUECKNER Bryant	1
2	BRIVIO Davide			ALSTON Kevin	3
3	DE SILVESTRI Lorenzo (c)		(c)	SARKODIE Ofori	5
4	ANGELUCCI Manuel	74	71	KIRK Quavas	6
5	CREMONESI Michele			NAKAZAWA Kyle	8
6	GRECO Daniele	65		ZIMMERMAN Preston	9
7	D ATTOMA Tommaso	57		ARVIZU David	10
8	PALERMO Simone			SOROKA Ryan	11
9	TIBONI Christian			WAGNER Blake	13
11	FOTI Salvatore	60	66	BESAGNO Nik	16
18	MANCOSU Marco		83	FARFAN Mike	19
	Tr: ROCCA Francesco			Tr: HACKWORTH John	
10	RUSSOTTO Andrea	65	66	IGWE Amaechi	2
16	SCOZZARELLA Matteo	74	71	ALTIDORE Josmer	4
17	CIA Michael	57	83	SUBOTIC Neven	14

Elias Aguirre, Chiclayo, 20-09-2005
18:45, 14 500, De Bleeckere BEL, Simons BEL, Hermans BEL

CIV 0 3 PRK

Choe Myong Ho 2 [9p] [38]
Kim Kyong Il [44]

	COTE D'IVOIRE			KOREA DPR	
1	TAHOUROU Ikossie	46		JU Kwang Min	1
2	KEITA Ali			PAK Nam Chol	5
3	KOUAKOU Irenee			YUN Yong Il	7
4	BOSSON Romaric (c)			RI Chol Myong	8
5	GNABOUYOU Marius		88	CHOE Myong Ho	9
6	AGOUSSI Jules			RI Hung Ryong	10
9	KOUASSI Koffi		83	PAK Chol Min	11
10	DIOMANDE Alassane	64		KIM Kuk Jin	12
11	FOFANA Ismael		41	JON Kwang Ik (c)	13
12	KOUADIO Serge	59		PIN Sok Chol	16
18	BAMBA Siaka			KIM Kyong Il	19
	Tr: BOHE Francois			Tr: JO Tong Sop	
16	ANDY Yves	46	88	PAK Chol Ryong	4
14	ABDUL Moustapha	59	41	MUN Kyong Nam	17
15	VAMARA Diarra	64	83	JONG Chol Min	18

Nacional, Lima, 23-09-2005
15:30, 12 000, Ruiz COL, Navia COL, Tamayo ECU

USA 1 1 CIV

Hall [4]

Bamba [87]

	USA			COTE D'IVOIRE	
1	RUECKNER Bryant			ANDY Yves	16
2	IGWE Amaechi	84	60	KEITA Ali	2
5	SARKODIE Ofori (c)			KOUAKOU Irenee	3
8	NAKAZAWA Kyle		(c)	BOSSON Romaric	4
9	ZIMMERMAN Preston	77		GNABOUYOU Marius	5
10	ARVIZU David	88		AGOUSSI Jules	6
12	FARFAN Gabe		75	DIOMANDE Alassane	10
13	WAGNER Blake			FOFANA Ismael	11
15	KELLY Dan			DIABATE Zie	13
17	HALL Jeremy		46	VAMARA Diarra	15
19	FARFAN Mike	64		BAMBA Siaka	18
	Tr: HACKWORTH John			Tr: BOHE Francois	
7	GONZALEZ Omar	77	75	KOUASSI Pacome	8
11	SOROKA Ryan	64	60	KOUASSI Koffi	9
14	SUBOTIC Neven	88	46	KOUADIO Serge	12

Mansiche, Trujillo, 23-09-2005
15:30, 10 000, Daami TUN, Dante MLI, Ndoye SEN

ITA 1 1 PRK

Palermo [92+]

Kim Kuk Jin [22]

	ITALY			KOREA DPR	
1	ALFONSO Enrico			JU Kwang Min	1
2	BRIVIO Davide			PAK Nam Chol	5
3	DE SILVESTRI Lorenzo (c)			YUN Yong Il	7
5	CREMONESI Michele			RI Chol Myong	8
7	D ATTOMA Tommaso		89	CHOE Myong Ho	9
8	PALERMO Simone		83	RI Hung Ryong	10
14	MAURI Stefano	46	51	PAK Chol Min	11
15	MANDORLINI Matteo	46	72	KIM Kuk Jin	12
16	SCOZZARELLA Matteo			JON Kwang Ik	13
17	CIA Michael			PIN Sok Chol	16
19	DALLA COSTA Marco	57		KIM Kyong Il	19
	Tr: ROCCA Francesco			Tr: JO Tong Sop	
6	GRECO Daniele	57	83	KIM Chol Ung	14
10	RUSSOTTO Andrea	46	89	MYONG In Ho	15
18	MANCOSU Marco	46	51	JONG Chol Min	18

GROUP D		PL	W	D	L	F	A	GD	PTS	BRA	NED	GAM	QAT
1	Brazil	3	2	0	1	9	4	5	6		2-1	1-3	6-0
2	Netherlands	3	2	0	1	8	5	3	6			2-0	5-3
3	Gambia	3	2	0	1	6	4	2	6				3-1
4	Qatar	3	0	0	3	4	14	-10	0				

Miguel Grau, Piura, 17-09-2005
15:15, 20 800, Shield AUS, Gibson AUS, Wilson AUS

NED 5 3 QAT

Emnes 2 [6] [84], Buijs [30p],   Ali Yahya [11p], Yusef Ali [31]
Van der Kooij [58], Goossens [65]   Al Khalfan [83]

NETHERLANDS				QATAR	
1	KRUL Tim			AL MOHANNADI Ghaith	1
3	MARCELLIS Dirk (c)			AL QUTATTI Marzouq	2
4	BUIJS Jordy			SOLAIMAN Ali	3
6	VORMER Ruud	82		(c) AL KAABI Johar	5
7	ZAALMAN Melvin	57		AL SULAITI Abdulaziz	6
8	SARPONG Jeffrey		46	AL SHUAIBI Faisal	7
10	ANITA Vurnon			YAHYA Ali	9
11	GOOSSENS John		72	AL YAZIDI Mohammed	10
12	VORTHOREN Niels	57		AL ABDULLA Khalid	11
14	VAN DER KOOIJ Mike		82	ALI Yusef	15
17	EMNES Marvin			AL YAZIDI Hamood	16
	Tr: KAISER Ruud			Tr: RUIJS Tini	
5	VAN DER LAAN Martijn	57	72	AL KUWARI Abdulla	8
9	BISESWAR Diego	57	46	AL KHALFAN Khalfan	14
18	ROORDA Geert-Arend	82	82	AL MARRI Jaralla	19

Miguel Grau, Piura, 20-09-2005
15:30, 18 424, Mohd Salleh MAS, Saeed MDV, Ishak MAS

QAT 1 3 GAM

Yusef Ali [32]   Ceesay [24], Jallow [78p], Jagne [92+]

QATAR				GAMBIA	
1	AL MOHANNADI Ghaith			SUSO Babucarr	16
2	AL QUTATTI Marzouq	68		SONKO Ousman	3
4	AL EMAIS Ahmed			NGUM Alagie	4
5	AL KAABI Johar (c)			CONTEH Lamin	5
6	AL SULAITI Abdulaziz	57		BOJANG Mandou	6
9	YAHYA Ali			COLE George	8
10	AL YAZIDI Mohammed	46	81	CEESAY Momodou	9
11	AL ABDULLA Khalid			MANSALLY Abdoulie	12
14	AL KHALFAN Khalfan			NYASSI Sainey	14
15	ALI Yusef		68	JAITEH Tijan	15
16	AL YAZIDI Hamood			(c) JALLOW Ousman	20
	Tr: RUIJS Tini			Tr: OSAM-DUODU Fred	
7	AL SHUAIBI Faisal	57	81	JAGNE Pa Modou	13
8	AL KUWARI Abdulla	46	68	NYASSI Sanna	17
12	AL SULAITI Khalid	68 [71]			

Nacional, Lima, 23-09-2005
18:15, 17 000, Larrionda URU, Rial URU, Fandino URU

GAM 0 2 NED

Goossens [33], Marcellis [72]

GAMBIA			NETHERLANDS	
16	SUSO Babucarr		KRUL Tim	1
3	SONKO Ousman		HIARIEJ Tom	2
4	NGUM Alagie		(c) MARCELLIS Dirk	3
5	CONTEH Lamin		BUIJS Jordy	4
6	BOJANG Mandou	70	VORMER Ruud	6
8	COLE George	64	ZAALMAN Melvin	7
9	CEESAY Momodou		SARPONG Jeffrey	8
12	MANSALLY Abdoulie		BISESWAR Diego	9
14	NYASSI Sainey	87	ANITA Vurnon	10
17	NYASSI Sanna		GOOSSENS John	11
20	JALLOW Ousman (c)	76	VAN DER KOOIJ Mike	14
	Tr: OSAM-DUODU Fred		Tr: KAISER Ruud	
13	JAGNE Pa Modou	87 70	VORTHOREN Niels	12
		76	PIETERS Erik	15
		64	EMNES Marvin	17

Miguel Grau, Piura, 17-09-2005
18:00, 22 300, Rodriguez MEX, Leal CRC, Camargo MEX

BRA 1 3 GAM

Igor [23]   Mansally [27], Ceesay [45], Jallow [74p]

BRAZIL				GAMBIA	
1	FELIPE			SUSO Babucarr	16
2	LEYRIELTON		87	SONKO Ousman	3
3	SIDNEI			NGUM Alagie	4
4	SAMUEL			BOJANG Mandou	6
5	ROBERTO			CEESAY Momodou	9
6	MARCELO	[50]	[80]	SOHNA Ebrima	[11]
7	DENILSON (c)	71	78	MANSALLY Abdoulie	12
9	IGOR	71		NYASSI Sainey	[14]
10	RAMON			JAITEH Tijan	15
11	MEZENGA		[93]	LEIGH Saja	[18]
18	RENATO	77	87	(c) JALLOW Ousman	20
	Tr: RODRIGUES Nelson			Tr: OSAM-DUODU Fred	
13	VINICIUS	71	87	GOMEZ Pierre	2
19	CELSO	77 [80]	87	CONTEH Lamin	[5]
20	JOSE CLAUDIO	71	78	NYASSI Sanna	17

Miguel Grau, Piura, 20-09-2005
18:15, 20 749, Stott USA, Strickland USA, Barkey USA

NED 1 2 BRA

Sidnei OG [28]   Igor [8], Ramon [60]

NETHERLANDS				BRAZIL	
1	KRUL Tim			FELIPE	1
3	MARCELLIS Dirk (c)			LEYRIELTON	2
4	BUIJS Jordy	21		SIDNEI	[3]
5	VAN DER LAAN Martijn	53	79	SAMUEL	4
6	VORMER Ruud			ROBERTO	[5]
8	SARPONG Jeffrey			(c) DENILSON	7
9	BISESWAR Diego			ANDERSON	8
10	ANITA Vurnon			IGOR	9
11	GOOSSENS John			RAMON	10
15	PIETERS Erik		79	VINICIUS	13
19	SCHET Mitchell	62	84	RENATO	18
	Tr: KAISER Ruud			Tr: RODRIGUES Nelson	
2	HIARIEJ Tom	21	79	SIMOES	14
14	VAN DER KOOIJ Mike	53	79	MAURICIO	16
17	EMNES Marvin	62	84	TACIO	17

Mansiche, Trujillo, 23-09-2005
18:15, 15 000, De Bleevkere BEL, Simons BEL, Hermans BEL

QAT 0 6 BRA

Ramon 2 [13] [47+], Denilson [39]
Roberto [57], Renato [58], Anderson [74]

QATAR				BRAZIL	
1	AL MOHANNADI Ghaith			FELIPE	1
3	SOLAIMAN Ali	[73]	2	LEYRIELTON	2
4	AL EMAIS Ahmed	[70]		SIDNEI	[3]
5	AL KAABI Johar			ROBERTO	5
6	AL SULAITI Abdulaziz (c)			(c) DENILSON	7
8	AL KUWARI Abdulla			ANDERSON	8
9	YAHYA Ali			IGOR	9
10	AL YAZIDI Mohammed	46	77	RAMON	[10]
11	AL ABDULLA Khalid	82		VINICIUS	13
15	ALI Yusef			SIMOES	14
16	AL YAZIDI Hamood		86	RENATO	18
	Tr: RUIJS Tini			Tr: RODRIGUES Nelson	
13	AL EIDH Abdulla	82	86	MAURICIO	16
14	AL KHALFAN Khalfan	46	77	TACIO	17
			77	JOSE CLAUDIO	20

QUARTER-FINALS

Miguel Grau, Piura, 25-09-2005
16:00, 14 724, Mohd Salleh MAS, Saeed MDV, Ishak MAS

CRC 1 3 MEX

Valdez OG 67

Valdez 88, Guzman 92, Vela 105

#	COSTA RICA			MEXICO	#
1	QUESADA Alfonso			ARIAS Sergio	1
2	MYRIE Dave	94		(c) ARAUJO Patricio	2
3	DAWSON Rudy (c)			VALDEZ Efrain	3
4	JIMENEZ Brayan		77	SANCHEZ Christian	4
6	CALVO David			MORENO Hector	5
7	CARRILLO Roberto	46	107	ESPARZA Omar	6
8	BORGES Celso		60	HERNANDEZ Jorge	7
9	RECINOS Ariel	82		DOS SANTOS Giovani	8
11	SOLORZANO Jean			VELA Carlos	9
12	RODRIGUEZ Esteban			ALDRETE Adrian	16
14	PANIAGUA Fernando			VILLALUZ Cesar	18
	Tr: ALFARO Geovanny			Tr: RAMIREZ Jesus	
5	CHACON Carlos	94	77	GUZMAN Ever	10
10	CORDERO Luis	46	60	ANDRADE Edgar	13
17	ELIZONDO Cesar	82	107	VALVERDE Pedro	17

Max Augustin, Iquitos, 25-09-2005
19:00, 24 000, Rodriguez MEX, Leal CRC, Camargo MEX

TUR 5 1 CHN

Kose Tevfik 2 10 88, Erkin Caner 2 33 91+, Sahin Nuri 54

Gu Jinjin 57

#	TURKEY			CHINA PR	#
1	BABACAN Volkan			WANG Dalei	1
2	YILMAZ Mehmet			TANG Naixin	3
3	BIKMAZ Ferhat			GU Cao	5
4	FERIN Erkan (c)			GU Jinjin	9
5	KESCI Serdar	46		ZHU Yifan	10
6	KARADAS Harun	76		(c) LI Zhuangfei	13
7	YILMAZ Deniz	80	59	WANG Xuanhong	15
8	ERKIN Caner			DENG Zhuoxiang	16
9	KOSE Tevfik			YANG Xu	18
10	SAHIN Nuri	89		HUANG Jie	19
11	OZCAN Ozgurcan	63		WANG Weilong	20
	Tr: AVCI Abdullah			Tr: ZHANG Ning	
14	YILMAZ Aydin	63	76	CAI Yaohui	6
16	BERISHA Ergun	80	59	YU Dabao	7
18	DURUER Murat	89	46	YANG Jian	8

Mansiche, Trujillo, 26-09-2005
16:00, 9 000, Elizondo ARG, Garcia ARG, Otero ARG

USA 0 2 NED

Sarpong 2 46+ 84

#	USA			NETHERLANDS	#
1	RUECKNER Bryant			(c) KRUL Tim	1
3	ALSTON Kevin	16		HIARIEJ Tom	2
5	SARKODIE Ofori (c)		78	BUIJS Jordy	4
6	KIRK Quavas			VORMER Ruud	6
8	NAKAZAWA Kyle			SARPONG Jeffrey	8
9	ZIMMERMAN Preston			BISESWAR Diego	9
10	ARVIZU David	85		ANITA Vurnon	10
11	SOROKA Ryan		82	GOOSSENS John	11
13	WAGNER Blake			VAN DER KOOIJ Mike	14
14	SUBOTIC Neven	73	46	PIETERS Erik	15
19	FARFAN Mike	79	54	EMNES Marvin	17
	Tr: HACKWORTH John			Tr: KAISER Ruud	
4	ALTIDORE Josmer	79	46	VAN DER LAAN Martijn	5
7	GONZALEZ Omar	85	54	ZAALMAN Melvin	7
17	HALL Jeremy	16	82	ROORDA Geert-Arend	18

Max Augustin, Iquitos, 26-09-2005
19:00, 25 000, Hamer LUX, Texier FRA, Crelo LUX

BRA 3 1 PRK

Ramon 48, Celso 97, Igor 120

Kim Kyong II 82

#	BRAZIL			KOREA DPR	#
1	FELIPE			JU Kwang Min	1
2	LEYRIELTON			PAK Nam Chol	5
3	SIDNEI			YUN Yong II	7
5	ROBERTO			RI Chol Myong	8
7	DENILSON (c)		102	CHOE Myong Ho	9
8	ANDERSON	77	63	RI Hung Ryong	10
9	IGOR			PAK Chol Min	11
10	RAMON		69	(c) JON Kwang Ik	13
13	VINICIUS	80		PIN Sok Chol	16
14	SIMOES			MUN Kyong Nam	17
18	RENATO		54	KIM Kyong II	19
	Tr: Rodrigues Nelson			Tr: JO Tong Sop	
16	MAURICIO	54	69	KIM Chol Ung	14
17	TACIO	80	102	MYONG In Ho	15
19	CELSO	77	63	JONG Chol Min	18

SEMI-FINALS

Elias Aguirre, Chclayo, 29-09-2005
16:00, 16 800, Shield AUS, Gibson AUS, Wilson AUS

MEX 4 0 NED

Villaluz 2 33 61, Moreno 50, Guzman 90

#	MEXICO			NETHERLANDS	#
1	ARIAS Sergio			(c) KRUL Tim	1
2	ARAUJO Patricio (c)			HIARIEJ Tom	2
3	VALDEZ Efrain	88		VAN DER LAAN Martijn	5
4	SANCHEZ Christian			VORMER Ruud	6
5	MORENO Hector			ZAALMAN Melvin	7
6	ESPARZA Omar			SARPONG Jeffrey	8
7	HERNANDEZ Jorge		66	BISESWAR Diego	9
8	DOS SANTOS Giovani	75		ANITA Vurnon	10
9	VELA Carlos	91		GOOSSENS John	11
16	ALDRETE Adrian		57	VORTHOREN Niels	12
18	VILLALUZ Cesar		4	VAN DER KOOIJ Mike	14
	Tr: RAMIREZ Jesus			Tr: KAISER Ruud	
10	GUZMAN Ever	75	4	PIETERS Erik	15
11	GALLEGOS Mario	91	57	ROORDA Geert-Arend	18
13	ANDRADE Edgar	88	66	SCHET Mitchell	19

Mansiche, Trujillo, 29-09-2005
19:00, 19 000, De Bleeckere BEL, Simons BEL, Hermans BEL

TUR 3 4 BRA

Erkin Caner 47, Kose Tevfik 70, Sahin Nuri 76

Celso 1, Anderson 26, Marcelo 32, Igor 90

#	TURKEY				BRAZIL	#
1	BABACAN Volkan				FELIPE	1
2	YILMAZ Mehmet				LEYRIELTON	2
3	BIKMAZ Ferhat				SAMUEL	4
4	FERIN Erkan (c)	45			ROBERTO	5
5	KESCI Serdar	92			MARCELO	6
6	KARADAS Harun	46			(c) DENILSON	7
7	YILMAZ Deniz				ANDERSON	8
8	ERKIN Caner	94			IGOR	9
9	KOSE Tevfik	73			RAMON	10
10	SAHIN Nuri				SIMOES	14
14	YILMAZ Aydin	46		93	CELSO	19
	Tr: AVCI Abdullah				Tr: Rodrigues Nelson	
11	OZCAN Ozgurcan	46	94	94	VINICIUS	13
18	DURUER Murat	46	73		MAURICIO	16
				93	TACIO	17

U-17 2005 Final　　　　　　**Estadio Nacional, Lima**　　　　　　**2-10-2005**

Kick-off: 18:00　　　　　　　　　　　　　　　　　　Attendance: 40 000

MEX　　　　3　0　　　　BRA

Carlos Vela [31], Omar Esparza [33], Ever Guzman [86]

MEXICO				MATCH STATS		BRAZIL			
1	GK	ARIAS Sergio				FELIPE	GK	1	
2	DF	ARAUJO Patricio (c)		20	Shots	18	LEYRIELTON	DF	2
3	DF	VALDEZ Efrain		7	Shots on Goal	11	SIDNEI	DF	3
4	DF	SANCHEZ Christian		26	Fouls Committed	20	ROBERTO	MF	5
5	DF	MORENO Hector	75	4	Corner Kicks	2	MARCELO	DF	6
6	MF	ESPARZA Omar		1	Offside	0	64	(c) DENILSON	MF	7
7	MF	HERNANDEZ Jorge		44	Possession %	56	16	ANDERSON	FW	8
8	FW	DOS SANTOS Giovani	79				IGOR	FW	9
9	FW	VELA Carlos	92+	MATCH OFFICIALS		RAMON	MF	10
16	MF	ALDRETE Adrian		REFEREE		82	SIMOES	DF	14
18	MF	VILLALUZ Cesar		DE BLEECKERE Frank BEL		CELSO	MF	19
		Tr: RAMIREZ Jesus		ASSISTANTS		Tr: Rodrigues Nelson			
		Substitutes		SIMONS Mark BEL		Substitutes			
12	GK	GALLARDO Alejandro		HERMANS Peter BEL		LUIZ CARLOS	GK	12
19	GK	FLORES Cristian		4TH OFFICIAL		JOAO	GK	15
10	FW	GUZMAN Ever	79	SHIELD Mark AUS		SAMUEL	DF	4
11	MF	GALLEGOS Mario				64	MEZENGA	FW	11
13	MF	ANDRADE Edgar				VINICIUS	DF	13
14	FW	BELTRAN Heriberto				16	MAURICIO	MF	16
15	MF	SILVA Carlos	92+				TACIO	MF	17
17	DF	VALVERDE Pedro	75				RENATO	MF	18
20	FW	ESQUEDA Alejandro				82	JOSE CLAUDIO	FW	20

In spite of the scoreline, it was not an easy game. I didn't expect such a resounding victory as Brazil are a good side. I'm thrilled to have won this tournament. My players were fantastic and played as a team. That made the difference.

Jesus Ramírez

I'm so proud to have won this tournament and to have created history. I never would have thought we would win this final by three goals. The key to our success was, first and foremost, that we're a very close-knit group of players and have been for a long time.

Carlos Vela

We started well enough but the game got away from us after the first goal. Renato was injured and then we lost Anderson right at the start. We made countless mistakes but the loss of Anderson changed the course of the game.

Nelson Rodrígues

I'm upset because we didn't have a single chance to win this tonight. We never really got into the match, especially after we conceded the first goal. We were never able to play our normal game. I think the loss against Gambia in our first game damaged our morale.

Ramon

MATCH REPORT

The substitution of Brazilian striker Anderson, who went off with an ankle injury after just 16 minutes, was a decisve moment in the match and came after Brazil had dominated possession in the early stages. Without the player of the tournament Brazil lacked direction up front although before Mexico took the lead Celso had hit the bar from a free kick. The first goal, two minutes later, came thanks to two of the stars of the tournament. Barcelona's Giovanni Dos Santos received the ball from a throw-in and beat two defenders to cross the ball into the penalty area for Carlos Vela to head home. A couple of miniutes later they were two up thanks to an absolutely stunning half volley from Omar Esparza. He ran onto a fabulous through ball from Cesar Villaluz in midfield to beat the Brazilian keeper Felipe from well outside of the area. In the second half Mexico allowed the Brazilians more possession but sealed the match just before the end when Guman found himself unmarked from a free kick to round Felipe to score - despite losing the ball in the process.

Third Place Play-Off, Nacional, Lima, 2-10-2005

15:00, 35 000, Larrionda URU, Rial URU, Fandino URU

NED   2   1   TUR

Goossens 2 [13] [88]   Sahin Nuri [90]

NETHERLANDS			TURKEY	
1	KRUL Tim (c)		(c) BABACAN Volkan	1
2	HIARIEJ Tom	73	YILMAZ Mehmet	2
4	BUIJS Jordy		BIKMAZ Ferhat	3
5	VAN DER LAAN Martijn	46	YILMAZ Deniz	7
6	VORMER Ruud	73 [92]	ERKIN Caner	8
7	ZAALMAN Melvin	59	KOSE Tevfik	9
8	SARPONG Jeffrey		SAHIN Nuri	10
10	ANITA Vurnon		BERISHA Ergun	16
11	GOOSENS John		COBAN Cengiz	17
15	PIETERS Erik		DURUER Murat	18
17	EMNES Marvin	68	DEMIR Aykut	19
	Tr: KAISER Ruud		Tr: AVCI Abdullah	
9	BISESWAR Diego	59 73	BALAK Emre	13
12	VORTHOREN Niels	68 46	YILMAZ Aydin	14
18	ROORDA Geert-Arend	73		

ADIDAS GOLDEN BALL

1	ANDERSON	BRA
2	DOS SANTOS Giovani	MEX
3	SAHIN Nuri	TUR

ADIDAS GOLDEN SHOE

			Goals	Assists
1	VELA Carlos	MEX	5	-
2	SAHIN Nuri	TUR	4	3
3	KOSE Tevfik	TUR	4	2

FIFA FAIR PLAY AWARD

1	Korea DPR
2	Netherlands
3	Costa Rica

AUS – AUSTRALIA FIFA U–17 WORLD CHAMPIONSHIP PERU 2005

No	Pos	Name	Shirt Name	DoB	Club	Cms	Kg	Games	Mins	Goals	Y	R
1	GK	VRTESKI Alex	VRTESKI	28-09-1988	Sorrento	194	104	3	270	-		
2	DF	CUMMING Jamie	CUMMING	19-08-1988	Victorian IoS	182	72	3	270		2	
3	DF	D APUZZO David	DAPUZZO	05-09-1988	Blacktown City Demons	179	73	3	235		1	
4	DF	OOSTENDORP Wade	OOSTENDORP	20-04-1988	Sydney FC	183	82	3	270		1	
5	DF	SPIRANOVIC Matthew	SPIRANOVIC	27-06-1988	Victorian IoS	188	84	3	270		1	
6	MF	MULLEN Matthew	MULLEN	24-02-1989	South Australian SI	183	72	3	97		1	
7	MF	ALLWRIGHT Joel	ALLWRIGHT	04-03-1988	South Australian SI	178	68	3	270			
8	FW	KRUSE Robbie	KRUSE	05-10-1988	Queensland AoS	180	66	3	241	1	1	
10	MF	PATAFTA Kaz	PATAFTA	25-10-1988	Australian IoS	172	64	3	270		1	
11	FW	MILLER Daniel	MILLER	29-01-1988	Preston Lions	183	82	2	79			
12	GK	IRELAND Daniel	IRELAND	20-01-1989	New South Wales IoS	190	83	0	0			
13	MF	TRIFIRO Jason	TRIFIRO	03-06-1988	Westfields Sports High	172	68	1	1			
14	FW	BURNS Nathan	BURNS	07-05-1988	Westfields Sports High	170	70	3	270	1	1	
15	DF	CHARITY Blake	CHARITY	27-02-1988	Queensland AoS	190	84	0	0			
16	MF	JAMIESON Scott	JAMIESON	13-10-1988	Bolton Wanderers	175	65	3	215		1	
17	MF	BROXHAM Leigh	BROXHAM	13-01-1988	Victorian IoS	169	66	3	173			
18	GK	LANCINI Shanon	LANCINI	05-08-1988	Queensland AoS	178	80	0	0			
19	MF	PARK Matthew	PARK	22-04-1988	Victorian IoS	189	72	2	35			
20	MF	MARONEY Brendan	MARONEY	06-05-1988	Blacktown City Demons	170	68	1	4			

IoS = Institute of Sport • AoS = Academy of Sport • SI = Sports Institute

---

BRA – BRAZIL FIFA U–17 WORLD CHAMPIONSHIP PERU 2005

No	Pos	Name	Shirt Name	DoB	Club	Cms	Kg	Games	Mins	Goals	Y	R
1	GK	FELIPE	FELIPE	10-01-1988	Santos	192	83	6	570			
2	DF	LEYRIELTON	LEYRIELTON	22-06-1988	Goias	171	64	6	557		1	
3	DF	SIDNEI	SIDNEI	23-08-1989	Internacional	182	80	5	480		4	
4	DF	SAMUEL	SAMUEL	07-03-1988	Atlético Mineiro	185	73	3	259			
5	MF	ROBERTO	ROBERTO	24-04-1988	Guarani	176	74	6	570	1	2	
6	DF	MARCELO	MARCELO	12-05-1988	Fluminense	173	72	3	229	1		2
7	MF	DENILSON	DENILSON	16-02-1988	São Paulo	178	70	6	525	1	1	
8	FW	ANDERSON	ANDERSON	13-04-1988	Gremio	174	77	5	363	2		
9	FW	IGOR	IGOR	14-06-1988	Corinthians	176	72	6	550	4		
10	MF	RAMON	RAMON	24-05-1988	Atlético Mineiro	180	68	6	540	4	2	
11	FW	MEZENGA	MEZENGA	08-08-1988	Flamengo	183	79	2	116			
12	GK	LUIZ CARLOS	LUIZ CARLOS	24-05-1988	Internacional	190	82	0	0			
13	DF	VINICIUS	VINICIUS	07-01-1988	Palmeiras	181	70	5	269			
14	DF	SIMOES	SIMOES	04-07-1988	Botafogo	182	80	5	393	1		
15	GK	JOAO	JOAO	06-04-1988	Atlético Paranaense	191	84	0	0			
16	MF	MAURICIO	MAURICIO	21-10-1988	Corinthians	180	70	5	172			
17	MF	TACIO	TACIO	21-01-1988	Vitoria	172	66	4	60			
18	MF	RENATO	RENATO	08-02-1988	Flamengo	185	82	4	301	1		
19	MF	CELSO	CELSO	25-08-1988	Portuguesa	177	68	4	234	2	2	1
20	FW	JOSE CLAUDIO	CLAUDIO	28-07-1989	Palmeiras	179	69	3	40			

CHN – CHINA PR FIFA U-17 WORLD CHAMPIONSHIP PERU 2005

No	Pos	Name	Shirt Name	DoB	Club	Cms	Kg	Games	Mins	Goals	Y	R
1	GK	WANG Dalei	D L WANG	10-01-1989	Dalian Shide	185	75	3	269			1
2	DF	CUI Nanri	N R CUI	27-01-1988	Jilin Aodong	171	65	2	80			
3	DF	TANG Naixin	N X TANG	29-04-1988	Liaoning	184	71	4	360	1		
4	DF	LI Linfeng	L F LI	09-01-1988	Shandong Luneng	186	78	3	109			
5	DF	GU Cao	C GU	31-05-1988	Shanghai Shenhua	183	80	2	170		1	1
6	MF	CAI Yaohui	Y H CAI	08-01-1988	Guangdong	176	71	3	38			
7	MF	YU Dabao	D B YU	18-04-1988	Shandong Luneng	181	73	2	75		1	
8	MF	YANG Jian	J YANG	04-10-1988	Liaoning	177	66	2	123			
9	FW	GU Jinjin	J J GU	14-04-1989	Tianjin Teda	174	68	4	303	1	3	
10	MF	ZHU Yifan	Y F ZHU	01-03-1988	Beijing Hyundai	177	69	3	226			
11	GK	ZHANG Xu	X ZHANG	19-05-1988	Shandong Luneng	175	67	0	0			
12	FW	WANG Gang	G WANG	17-02-1989	Tianjin Teda	187	69	2	32			
13	MF	LI Zhuangfei	ZH F LI	24-01-1988	Shandong Luneng	177	72	4	346			
14	MF	DU Longquan	L Q DU	29-05-1988	Liaoning	180	70	3	163			
15	MF	WANG Xuanhong	X H WANG	24-07-1989	Liaoning	178	73	2	135	1	1	
16	DF	DENG Zhuoxiang	ZH X DENG	24-10-1988	Wuhan Huanghelou	178	70	4	360	1	1	
17	GK	CHI Wenyi	W Y CHI	18-02-1988	Jilin Aodong	181	75	1	90		1	
18	FW	YANG Xu	X YANG	12-02-1988	Liaoning	188	76	4	360			
19	MF	HUANG Jie	J HUANG	07-02-1989	Shanghai Shenhua	179	72	4	350		1	
20	DF	WANG Weilong	W L WANG	24-02-1988	Shandong Luneng	184	73	4	360			

CIV – COTE D'IVOIRE FIFA U-17 WORLD CHAMPIONSHIP PERU 2005

No	Pos	Name	Shirt Name	DoB	Club	Cms	Kg	Games	Mins	Goals	Y	R
1	GK	TAHOUROU Ikossie	TAHOUROU	25-12-1989	Academy Mimos-Sifcom	178	69	2	136		1	
2	DF	KEITA Ali	KEITA	01-10-1988	CFDC	172	64	3	240			
3	MF	KOUAKOU Irenee	KOUAKOU	20-03-1988	Academy Mimos-Sifcom	176	60	3	270			
4	DF	BOSSON Romaric	BOSSON	12-04-1988	Stella Club	178	70	3	270		1	
5	DF	GNABOUYOU Marius	GNABOUYOU	08-12-1988	Academy Mimos-Sifcom	177	62	2	180			
6	DF	AGOUSSI Jules	AGOUSSI	19-09-1990	OCF	179	64	3	270			
7	MF	YAO Martial	YAO	04-10-1989	Academy Mimos-Sifcom	172	65	1	46			
8	MF	KOUASSI Pacome	KOUASSI	25-12-1988	Academy Mimos-Sifcom	177	66	2	61			
9	FW	KOUASSI Koffi	KOFFI	17-11-1989	CFDC	164	64	3	210	1		
10	FW	DIOMANDE Alassane	DIOMANDE	28-11-1988	Stella Club	174	71	3	229	1		
11	FW	FOFANA Ismael	FOFANA	08-09-1988	Academy Mimos-Sifcom	180	68	3	224	1		
12	FW	KOUADIO Serge	KOUADIO	31-12-1988	Academy Mimos-Sifcom	177	83	3	192			
13	DF	DIABATE Zie	DIABATE	02-03-1989	IFER	177	65	1	90			
14	FW	ABDUL Moustapha	ABDUL MOUSTAPHA	09-06-1988	Academy Mimos-Sifcom	180	66	2	32			
15	MF	VAMARA Diarra	DIARRA	16-02-1989	Stella Club	176	72	3	116		1	
16	GK	ANDY Yves	ANDY	12-08-1988	Academy Mimos-Sifcom	182	81	2	134			
17	FW	KOUADIO Gilbert	AHOUTOU	17-12-1988	EFYM	168	61	0	0			
18	DF	BAMBA Siaka	BAMBA	24-08-1989	OCF	175	64	3	270	1	1	
19	FW	KOUROUMA Boua	BOUA	26-04-1988	CFDC	169	67	0	0			
20	GK	KONE Ibrahim	KONE	05-12-1989	CF Excellence	190	76	0	0			

CRC – COSTA RICA FIFA U-17 WORLD CHAMPIONSHIP PERU 2005

No	Pos	Name	Shirt Name	DoB	Club	Cms	Kg	Games	Mins	Goals	Y	R
1	GK	QUESADA Alfonso	QUESADA	15-03-1988	LD Alajuelense	186	78	4	390		1	
2	DF	MYRIE Dave	MYRIE	1-06-1988	Libre	182	65	4	362			
3	DF	DAWSON Rudy	DAWSON	8-05-1988	LD Alajuelense	180	70	4	390		1	
4	DF	JIMENEZ Brayan	JIMENEZ	15-03-1988	Deportivo Saprissa	180	68	4	390			
5	DF	CHACON Carlos	CHACON	3-06-1988	Barrio Mexico	175	64	1	26			
6	DF	CALVO David	CALVO	3-10-1988	LD Alajuelense	165	64	3	213			
7	DF	CARRILLO Roberto	CARRILLO	1-01-1988	Deportivo Saprissa	171	64	4	242	1		
8	MF	BORGES Celso	BORGES	27-05-1988	Deportivo Saprissa	181	74	4	390	1		
9	FW	RECINOS Ariel	RECINOS	1-05-1988	Brujas	178	66	3	85		1	
10	MF	CORDERO Luis	CORDERO	21-05-1988	Deportivo Saprissa	173	58	4	217			
11	FW	SOLORZANO Jean	SOLORZANO	8-01-1988	LD Alajuelense	179	66	4	389	1		
12	MF	RODRIGUEZ Esteban	RODRIGUEZ	25-01-1988	Libre	165	59	4	390			
13	DF	WASTOM Kendall	WASTOM	1-01-1988	Deportivo Saprissa	195	84	0	0			
14	MF	PANIAGUA Fernando	PANIAGUA	9-09-1988	Deportivo Saprissa	175	74	4	390			
15	DF	VARGAS Alonso	VARGAS	5-04-1988	LD Alajuelense	173	66	0	0			
16	DF	RAMOS Leslie	RAMOS	25-01-1988	LD Alajuelense	176	68	2	177		1	
17	MF	ELIZONDO Cesar	ELIZONDO	10-02-1988	Deportivo Saprissa	172	63	4	101	1		
18	GK	VENEGAS Armando	VENEGAS	24-01-1988	Deportivo Saprissa	185	72	0	0			
19	FW	GUARDIA Guillermo	GUARDIA	24-04-1988	LD Alajuelense	176	71	2	138			
20	GK	THOMPSON Giancarlo	THOMPSON	19-02-1988	Libre	175	73	0	0			

GAM - GAMBIA FIFA U-17 WORLD CHAMPIONSHIP PERU 2005

No	Pos	Name	Shirt Name	DoB	Club	Cms	Kg	Games	Mins	Goals	Y	R
1	GK	NJIE Abdoulie	A.B. Njie	01-03-1988	Steve Biko	176	70	0	0			
2	DF	GOMEZ Pierre	P. GOMEZ	03-05-1989	Banjul Hawks	186	75	1	3			
3	DF	SONKO Ousman	O. SONKO	02-10-1988	Gambia Ports Authority	169	63	3	267		1	
4	DF	NGUM Alagie	A. NGUM	18-10-1988	Gamtel	174	64	3	270			
5	DF	CONTEH Lamin	L. CONTEH	22-08-1989	Sait Matty	182	65	3	183		1	
6	DF	BOJANG Mandou	M. BOJANG	18-11-1988	Gambia Ports Authority	185	75	3	270			
7	FW	FAYE Edi	E.S. FAYE	14-07-1989	Sait Matty	177	74	0	0			
8	DF	COLE George	COLE	11-08-1989	Wallidan	172	64	2	180	1		
9	FW	CEESAY Momodou	M. CEESAY	24-12-1988	Wallidan	195	84	3	261	2	1	
10	MF	MBYE Omar	O. MBYE	28-12-1989	Gamtel	172	65	0	0			
11	DF	SOHNA Ebrima	E. SOHNA	14-12-1988	Wallidan	184	65	1	80		1	1
12	MF	MANSALLY Abdoulie	A. MANSALLY	27-01-1989	Sait Matty	175	70	3	258	1	1	
13	FW	JAGNE Pa Modou	M. JAINE	26-12-1989	Gambia Ports Authority	175	70	2	12	1		
14	MF	NYASSI Sainey	SAINEY	31-01-1989	Gambia Ports Authority	173	60	3	267	1		
15	MF	JAITEH Tijan	T. JAITEH	31-12-1988	Gambia Ports Authority	185	70	2	158			
16	GK	SUSO Babucarr	B. SUSO	11-09-1989	Sait Matty	183	75	3	270			
17	MF	NYASSI Sanna	SANNA	31-01-1989	Gambia Ports Authority	170	60	3	124	2		
18	DF	LEIGH Saja	S. LEIGH	24-11-1988	Sait Matty	182	64	1	89			1
19	GK	ALLEN Christopher	C. ALLEN	19-12-1989	Gamtel	180	70	0	0			
20	FW	JALLOW Ousman	O. JALLOW	21-10-1988	Wallidan	181	72	3	267	2	1	

GHA - GHANA FIFA U-17 WORLD CHAMPIONSHIP PERU 2005

No	Pos	Name	Shirt Name	DoB	Club	Cms	Kg	Games	Mins	Goals	Y	R
1	GK	SOWAH Ernest	SOWAH	31-03-1988	Mercenaries	180	65	0	0			
2	DF	ADJETEY Emmanuel	ADJETEY	15-12-1988	Ashgold	168	60	1	44			
3	FW	SALIFU Razak	SALIFU	01-10-1988	Midtjylland	173	60	0	0			
4	DF	TAGOE James	TAGOE	06-07-1988	Chance for Children	171	65	3	270			
5	DF	DANSO Ernest	DANSO	25-11-1989	Nania	183	60	3	270	1		
6	DF	TELFER David	TELFER	01-12-1988	Ashanti Gold	171	61	3	226			
7	DF	WAKASO Mubarak	WAKASO	25-07-1990	Ashanti Gold	171	66	2	100			1
8	DF	OPPONG Samad	OPPONG	21-07-1988	Corners Babies	171	55	2	121			
9	FW	AGYEMANG Opoku	AGYEMANG	07-06-1989	Ashanti Gold	174	62	3	270	1		
10	FW	BUKARI Sadat	BUKARI	12-04-1989	Heart of Lions	177	64	2	180	1		
11	DF	QUARTEY Jonathan	QUARTEY	02-06-1988	Heart of Lions	186	65	3	252	1	1	
12	DF	ANSONG Emmanuel	ANSONG	22-10-1989	Great Olympics	168	55	3	270			
13	MF	SOGBE Francis	SOGBE	08-03-1988	Inter Allies	177	65	0	0			
14	MF	ADARKWA Anthony	ADARKWA	15-08-1989	Nungua	171	62	1	28			
15	FW	ABUBAKAR Awudu	ABUBAKAR	16-10-1988	State Envoys	168	64	2	121			
16	GK	OBODAI Seth	OBODAI	11-07-1989	Winneba Academy	168	65	0	0			
17	MF	BOATENG Charles	BOATENG	14-12-1989	Nania	174	60	3	270			
18	FW	APPIAH George	APPIAH	13-08-1989	Liberty	177	60	3	129		1	
19	GK	BONSU Nana	BONSU	01-12-1988	Zaytuna	174	60	3	270	1		
20	FW	ASANTE Ernest	ASANTE	06-11-1988	Feyenoord Academy	171	60	0	0			

ITA - ITALY FIFA U-17 WORLD CHAMPIONSHIP PERU 2005

No	Pos	Name	Shirt Name	DoB	Club	Cms	Kg	Games	Mins	Goals	Y	R
1	GK	ALFONSO Enrico	ALFONSO	04-05-1988	Chievo Verona	191	83	3	270			
2	DF	BRIVIO Davide	BRIVIO	17-03-1988	Atalanta Bergamo	185	78	3	270			
3	DF	DE SILVESTRI Lorenzo	DE SILVESTRI	23-05-1988	Lazio Rome	187	79	3	270	2		
4	DF	ANGELUCCI Manuel	ANGELUCCI	18-01-1988	Ternana	183	68	2	108	1		
5	DF	CREMONESI Michele	CREMONESI	15-04-1988	Cremonese	184	78	3	270	1		
6	MF	GRECO Daniele	GRECO	27-04-1988	Lazio Rome	173	57	3	188	2		
7	MF	D ATTOMA Tommaso	D ATTOMA	15-04-1988	Lumezzane	180	73	3	193			
8	MF	PALERMO Simone	PALERMO	17-08-1988	AS Rome	181	70	3	270	1		
9	FW	TIBONI Christian	TIBONI	06-04-1988	Atalanta Bergamo	189	78	2	146	2		
10	FW	RUSSOTTO Andrea	RUSSOTTO	25-05-1988	Treviso	174	67	3	99	1	2	
11	FW	FOTI Salvatore	FOTI	08-08-1988	Sampdoria Genoa	192	75	2	150	1	1	1
12	GK	TORNAGHI Paolo	TORNAGHI	21-06-1988	Internazionale	192	74	0	0			
13	DF	FRANCESCHINI Fabio	FRANCESCHINI	08-05-1988	Lecce	185	69	0	0			
14	MF	MAURI Stefano	MAURI	11-02-1988	Atalanta Bergamo	182	64	1	46			
15	MF	MANDORLINI Matteo	MANDORLINI	22-10-1988	Parma	178	66	2	136	1		
16	MF	SCOZZARELLA Matteo	SCOZZARELLA	05-06-1988	Atalanta Bergamo	171	57	2	106			
17	MF	CIA Michael	CIA	03-08-1988	Suedtirol / Alto Adige	174	69	2	123	1		
18	MF	MANCOSU Marco	MANCOSU	22-08-1988	Cagliari	182	72	3	224			
19	FW	DALLA COSTA Marco	DALLA COSTA	25-03-1988	Internazionale	188	73	2	71			
20	GK	SANTARELLI Simone	SANTARELLI	07-09-1988	Lazio Rome	183	83	0	0			

MEX – MEXICO FIFA U-17 WORLD CHAMPIONSHIP PERU 2005

No	Pos	Name	Shirt Name	DoB	Club	Cms	Kg	Games	Mins	Goals	Y	R
1	GK	ARIAS Sergio	S. ARIAS	27-02-1988	Guadalajara	190	79	6	570		1	
2	DF	ARAUJO Patricio	P. ARAUJO	30-01-1988	Guadalajara	174	77	6	526		2	
3	DF	VALDEZ Efrain	E. VALDEZ	22-02-1988	Pumas UNAM	178	65	6	568	1	2	
4	DF	SANCHEZ Christian	C. SANCHEZ	04-04-1988	Atlas	178	71	6	481			
5	DF	MORENO Hector	H. MORENO	17-01-1988	Pumas UNAM	180	81	6	555	1	2	
6	MF	ESPARZA Omar	O. ESPARZA	21-05-1988	Guadalajara	180	81	6	511	2	1	
7	MF	HERNANDEZ Jorge	J. HERNANDEZ	22-02-1988	Atlas	185	70	6	424			
8	FW	DOS SANTOS Giovani	G. DOS SANTOS	11-05-1989	FC Barcelona	170	71	5	448		1	
9	FW	VELA Carlos	C. VELA	01-03-1989	Guadalajara	172	71	5	467	5	1	
10	FW	GUZMAN Ever	E. GUZMAN	15-03-1988	Monarcas Morelia	173	65	5	165	4		
11	MF	GALLEGOS Mario	M. GALLEGOS	15-04-1988	Atlas	170	66	3	95			
12	GK	GALLARDO Alejandro	A. GALLARDO	16-01-1988	Atlas	178	56	0	0			
13	MF	ANDRADE Edgar	E. ANDRADE	02-03-1988	Cruz Azul	175	78	5	221			
14	FW	BELTRAN Heriberto	H. BELTRAN	03-03-1988	Pachuca	170	66	1	28			
15	MF	SILVA Carlos	C. SILVA	06-02-1988	America	168	69	2	91		1	
16	MF	ALDRETE Adrian	A. ALDRETE	14-06-1988	Monarcas Morelia	180	70	5	480		2	
17	DF	VALVERDE Pedro	P. VALVERDE	06-04-1988	Cruz Azul	169	65	4	93			
18	MF	VILLALUZ Cesar	C. VILLALUZ	18-07-1988	Cruz Azul	165	68	5	476	3	1	
19	GK	FLORES Cristian	C. FLORES	30-04-1988	Atlas	172	71	0	0			
20	FW	ESQUEDA Alejandro	A. ESQUEDA	19-04-1988	America	180	70	2	71			

NED – NETHERLANDS FIFA U-17 WORLD CHAMPIONSHIP PERU 2005

No	Pos	Name	Shirt Name	DoB	Club	Cms	Kg	Games	Mins	Goals	Y	R
1	GK	KRUL Tim	KRUL	03-04-1988	Newcastle Utd.	190	75	6	540			
2	DF	HIARIEJ Tom	HIARIEJ	25-07-1988	Groningen	171	72	5	429			
3	DF	MARCELLIS Dirk	MARCELLIS	13-04-1988	PSV Eindhoven	177	75	3	270	1		
4	DF	BUIJS Jordy	BUYS	28-12-1988	Feyenoord Rotterdam	185	78	5	369	1	1	1
5	DF	VAN DER LAAN Martijn	VAN DER LAAN	29-07-1988	Groningen	175	76	5	310		1	
6	MF	VORMER Ruud	VORMER	11-05-1988	Alkmaar	176	73	6	495		1	
7	FW	ZAALMAN Melvin	ZAALMAN	17-06-1988	Sparta Rotterdam	165	62	5	306			
8	MF	SARPONG Jeffrey	SARPONG	03-08-1988	Ajax Amsterdam	173	67	6	540	2	1	
9	FW	BISESWAR Diego	BISESWAR	08-03-1988	Feyenoord Rotterdam	173	72	6	400		1	
10	MF	ANITA Vurnon	ANITA	04-04-1989	Ajax Amsterdam	167	63	6	540			
11	FW	GOOSSENS John	GOOSSENS	25-07-1988	Ajax Amsterdam	176	66	6	532	4	2	
12	MF	VORTHOREN Niels	VORTHOREN	21-02-1988	Willem II	185	79	4	156			
13	GK	VERHOEFF Koen	VERHOEFF	06-03-1988	Ajax Amsterdam	178	79	0	0			
14	DF	VAN DER KOOIJ Mike	VAN DER KOOY	30-01-1989	Utrecht	183	78	5	297	1		
15	DF	PIETERS Erik	PIETERS	07-08-1988	Utrecht	183	80	5	326		2	
16	GK	SKVERER Nicholas	SKVERER	14-01-1988	Nijmegen	179	70	0	0			
17	FW	EMNES Marvin	EMNES	27-05-1988	Sparta Rotterdam	174	66	5	266	2		
18	MF	ROORDA Geert-Arend	ROORDA	02-03-1988	Heerenveen	188	78	4	66			
19	FW	SCHET Mitchell	SCHET	28-01-1988	Feyenoord Rotterdam	176	68	2	86		1	
20	MF	VAN DER HEIJDEN Jan-Arie	VAN DER HEYDEN	03-03-1988	Ajax Amsterdam	182	70	0	0			

PER – PERU FIFA U-17 WORLD CHAMPIONSHIP PERU 2005

No	Pos	Name	Shirt Name	DoB	Club	Cms	Kg	Games	Mins	Goals	Y	R
1	GK	CABALLERO Wilfredo	CABALLERO	14-05-1988	Universitario	186	78	0	0			
2	DF	RAMOS Christian	RAMOS	04-11-1988	Sporting Cristal	182	72	3	270		2	
3	DF	URIBE Ricardo	URIBE	09-10-1988	Alianza Lima	164	62	0	0			
4	DF	LAURA Christian	LAURA	13-02-1988	Sporting Cristal	174	70	3	204			
5	DF	PEIXOTO Kerwin	PEIXOTO	21-02-1988	Alianza Lima	182	75	3	270			
6	MF	GALLIQUIO Luis	GALLIQUIO	22-08-1988	Sporting Cristal	171	74	0	0			
7	MF	MESARINA Jose	MESARINA	15-11-1988	Alianza Lima	168	66	2	46			
8	MF	ESPEJO Gianfranco	ESPEJO	04-03-1988	Sporting Cristal	185	79	3	256		1	
9	FW	CHAVEZ Daniel	CHAVEZ	08-01-1988	Academia Dep. Cantolao	175	72	3	270	1		
10	FW	ELIAS Carlos	ELIAS	23-03-1988	Alianza Lima	174	78	3	51			
11	FW	CARNERO Javier	CARNERO	13-07-1988	Sporting Cristal	165	69	3	56			
12	GK	CASTELLANOS Gian Franco	CASTELLANOS	08-04-1988	Sporting Cristal	187	84	3	270			
13	MF	ZAMBRANO Carlos	ZAMBRANO	10-07-1989	Academia Dep. Cantolao	183	71	3	245		1	
14	FW	REY Jesus	REY	09-02-1988	Universitario	172	61	3	243			
15	MF	CARDENAS Miguel	CARDENAS	31-05-1988	Alianza Lima	172	73	3	266		1	
16	MF	FLORES Carlos	FLORES	09-01-1988	Alianza Lima	174	70	3	270			
17	MF	BALLON Josepmir	BALLON	21-03-1988	Academia Dep. Cantolao	178	68	3	233		1	
18	MF	PORTUGAL Walter	PORTUGAL	09-03-1988	Alianza Lima	168	71	1	20			
19	GK	ENRIQUEZ Bruno	ENRIQUEZ	13-05-1988	Alianza Lima	180	71	0	0			
20	DF	ZAVALA Jose	ZAVALA	14-12-1988	Academia Dep. Cantolao	184	80	0	0			

PRK – KOREA DPR FIFA U-17 WORLD CHAMPIONSHIP PERU 2005

No	Pos	Name	Shirt Name	DoB	Club	Cms	Kg	Games	Mins	Goals	Y	R
1	GK	JU Kwang Min	JU K M	20-05-1990	Kigwancha	187	70	4	390			
2	DF	YUN Myong Song	YUN M S	21-04-1988	Rimyongsu	169	63	0	0			
3	DF	PAK In Gol	PAK I G	29-01-1988	Sobaeksu	183	72	0	0			
4	MF	PAK Chol Ryong	PAK C R	03-11-1988	Kigwancha	170	61	1	2			
5	DF	PAK Nam Chol	PAK N C	03-10-1988	Amrokgang	182	75	4	390	1		
6	GK	KIM Hyon Chol	KIM H C	15-02-1989	Kimilsung Univ.	170	63	0	0			
7	DF	YUN Yong Il	YUN Y I	31-07-1988	Wolmido	169	59	4	390			
8	MF	RI Chol Myong	RI C M	18-02-1988	Muyok	172	64	3	300			
9	MF	CHOE Myong Ho	CHOE M H	03-07-1988	Kyonggongop	172	65	4	369	3	1	
10	FW	RI Hung Ryong	RI H R	22-09-1988	Kimilsung Univ.	167	60	4	308			
11	FW	PAK Chol Min	PAK C M	10-12-1988	Rimyongsu	166	60	4	344			
12	MF	KIM Kuk Jin	KIM K J	05-01-1989	Pyongyang	173	65	3	252	2		1
13	DF	JON Kwang Ik	JON K I	05-04-1988	Amrokgang	169	64	4	290			
14	MF	KIM Chol Ung	KIM C U	05-05-1988	Kyonggongop	180	60	3	148			
15	FW	MYONG In Ho	MYONG I H	15-06-1988	Sobaeksu	170	65	2	19			
16	DF	PIN Sok Chol	BIN S C	22-08-1988	Kigwancha	176	63	4	390			
17	DF	MUN Kyong Nam	MUN K N	08-04-1989	Amrokgang	179	67	2	169		1	
18	FW	JONG Chol Min	JONG C M	29-10-1988	Rimyongsu	176	68	4	121			
19	MF	KIM Kyong Il	KIM K I	11-12-1988	Rimyongsu	173	64	4	390	2	1	
20	GK	PAK Kyong Il	PAK K I	01-01-1988	April 25 Sports Group	181	73	0	0			

QAT – QATAR FIFA U-17 WORLD CHAMPIONSHIP PERU 2005

No	Pos	Name	Shirt Name	DoB	Club	Cms	Kg	Games	Mins	Goals	Y	R
1	GK	AL MOHANNADI Ghaith	ALMOHANNADI	02-11-1988	Al Khor	175	68	3	270			
2	DF	AL QUTATTI Marzouq	MARZOUQ	22-05-1988	Al Gharrafa	173	66	2	158			
3	DF	SOLAIMAN Ali	ALI S	09-02-1988	Al Ahli (QAT)	176	62	2	163			1
4	DF	AL EMAIS Ahmed	AHMED A	06-07-1988	Al Ahli (QAT)	179	73	2	160		1	1
5	DF	AL KAABI Johar	ALKAABI	09-06-1988	Al Arabi	180	70	3	270	1		
6	MF	AL SULAIRI Abdulaziz	ALSULAIRI	11-06-1988	Al Arabi	180	59	3	237			
7	MF	AL SHUAIBI Faisal	ALSHUAIBI	16-06-1988	Al Wakra	167	57	2	79			
8	MF	AL KUWARI Abdulla	AL-KUWARI	16-04-1988	Qatar Sports	165	65	3	152	1		
9	FW	YAHYA Ali	ALI A.	20-01-1988	Al Sadd	173	62	3	270	1	1	
10	MF	AL YAZIDI Mohammed	ALYAZIDI	30-10-1988	Al Sadd	168	50	3	164			
11	MF	AL ABDULLA Khalid	ALABDULLA	07-01-1988	Al Arabi	168	57	3	262			
12	DF	AL SULAITI Khalid	AL-SULAITI K.	26-04-1988	Al Arabi	175	61	1	3			1
13	DF	AL EIDH Abdulla	ALEIDH	22-03-1988	Rayyan	177	71	1	8			
14	MF	AL KHALFAN Khalfan	AL-KHALFAN	18-02-1988	Al Sadd	167	57	3	178	1	1	
15	FW	ALI Yusef	YUSEF A.	14-10-1988	Al Sadd	179	66	3	262	2	2	
16	MF	AL YAZIDI Hamood	ALYAZIDI	28-05-1988	Al Sadd	173	62	3	270			
17	GK	SHANA Amro	AMRO	28-03-1988	Al Arabi	178	77	0	0			
18	FW	AL KUWARI Abdulaziz	AL-KUWARI A.	17-05-1988	Qatar Sports	170	59	0	0			
19	FW	AL MARRI Jaralla	AL-MARRI	03-04-1988	Rayyan	179	67	1	8			
20	GK	ESSA Jabor	J. ESSA	05-07-1988	Al Sadd	186	93	0	0			

TUR – TURKEY FIFA U-17 WORLD CHAMPIONSHIP PERU 2005

No	Pos	Name	Shirt Name	DoB	Club	Cms	Kg	Games	Mins	Goals	Y	R
1	GK	BABACAN Volkan	VOLKAN	11-08-1988	Fenerbahce	192	82	5	450			
2	DF	YILMAZ Mehmet	MEHMET	26-03-1988	Bursaspor	182	75	4	343			
3	DF	BIKMAZ Ferhat	FERHAT	06-07-1988	Hanover 96	180	75	6	410	2		
4	DF	FERIN Erkan	ERKAN	20-03-1988	Galatasaray	174	74	4	316	1	1	
5	DF	KESCI Serdar	SERDAR	18-01-1988	Galatasaray	171	64	4	359	3	1	
6	DF	KARADAS Harun	HARUN	14-01-1988	Galatasaray	171	65	4	266	2		
7	MF	YILMAZ Deniz	DENIZ	26-02-1988	Bayern Munich	183	75	6	487	2		
8	MF	ERKIN Caner	CANER	04-10-1988	Vestel Manisaspor	177	74	6	536	4	1	1
9	FW	KOSE Tevfik	TEVIK	12-07-1988	Bayer Leverkusen	180	65	6	484	4	1	
10	MF	SAHIN Nuri	NURI	05-09-1988	Borussia Dortmund	179	71	6	539	4		
11	FW	OZCAN Ozgurcan	OZGURCAN	10-04-1988	Galatasaray	185	85	5	244	1		1
12	GK	KIVRAK Onur	ONUR RECEP	01-01-1988	Karsiyaka	186	79	1	90			
13	DF	BALAK Emre	EMRE	11-08-1988	Samsunspor	178	72	2	107			
14	MF	YILMAZ Aydin	AYDIN	29-01-1988	Galatasaray	175	66	6	292	1		
15	DF	TASDEMIR Anil	ANIL	01-01-1988	Goztepspor	172	65	1	25			
16	DF	BERISHA Ergun	ERGUN	24-06-1988	Grasshopper-Club	180	65	5	189	1		
17	DF	COBAN Cengiz	CENGIZ	20-01-1988	Trabzonspor	176	72	2	180	1		
18	MF	DURUER Murat	MURAT	15-01-1988	Ankaragucu	178	66	6	311	1		
19	DF	DEMIR Aykut	AYKUT	22-10-1988	Breda	180	67	3	270	1		
20	GK	BIRNICAN Eray	ERAY	20-07-1988	Yildirim Bosnaspor	188	83	0	0			

URU - URUGUAY FIFA U-17 WORLD CHAMPIONSHIP PERU 2005

No	Pos	Name	Shirt Name	DoB	Club	Cms	Kg	Games	Mins	Goals	Y	R
1	GK	IRRAZABAL Yonatan	IRRAZABAL	12-02-1988	Defensor Sporting	180	75	2	180			
2	MF	KAGELMACHER Gary	KAGELMACHER	21-04-1988	Danubio	183	80	3	182	1		
3	DF	DIAZ Martin	DIAZ	17-03-1988	Defensor Sporting	187	79	3	270			
4	DF	SUAREZ Damian	SUAREZ	27-04-1988	Defensor Sporting	172	65	3	265	1		
5	DF	GONZALEZ Alejandro	A. GONZALEZ	23-03-1988	Penarol	182	78	3	270	2		
6	DF	ARIAS Alvaro	ARIAS	03-10-1988	Penarol	183	79	0	0			
7	MF	ACOSTA Michel	ACOSTA	14-02-1988	Paysandu	187	84	3	150	1		
8	FW	ROMAN Marcel	ROMAN	07-02-1988	Danubio	175	69	3	270			
9	FW	FIGUEROA Elias	FIGUEROA	26-01-1988	Liverpool (URU)	187	81	3	270	2		
10	FW	VONDER PUTTEN Gerardo	VONDER PUTTEN	28-02-1988	Danubio	175	70	3	236			
11	MF	SCORZA Enzo	SCORZA	01-03-1988	Danubio	166	63	3	214	1		
12	GK	GOICOECHEA Mauro	GOICOECHEA	27-03-1988	Danubio	184	81	1	90			
13	FW	FLORES Carlos	FLORES	04-02-1988	Defensor Sporting	173	68	0	0			
14	DF	ARISMENDI Hugo	ARISMENDI	25-01-1988	Nacional	189	77	3	251			
15	MF	PAZ Cristian	PAZ	28-01-1988	Nacional	189	84	3	164	1		
16	MF	GONZALEZ Marcelo	M. GONZALEZ	18-07-1988	Danubio	172	70	1	44			
17	FW	ALVAREZ Santiago	ALVAREZ	29-06-1989	Racing (URU)	183	74	2	12			
18	FW	OLIVERA Vicente	OLIVERA	27-07-1988	Danubio	175	74	0	0			
19	MF	ALFARO Emiliano	ALFARO	28-04-1988	Liverpool (URU)	173	69	2	102			
20	GK	ROLERO Mathias	ROLERO	10-09-1988	Basanez	184	78	0	0			

USA - USA FIFA U-17 WORLD CHAMPIONSHIP PERU 2005

No	Pos	Name	Shirt Name	DoB	Club	Cms	Kg	Games	Mins	Goals	Y	R
1	GK	RUECKNER Bryant	RUECKNER	20-01-1988	PSG California	183	71	4	360			
2	DF	IGWE Amaechi	IGWE	20-05-1988	Santa Clara Sporting	183	75	3	198		1	
3	DF	ALSTON Kevin	ALSTON	05-05-1988	Potomac Cougars	170	63	3	196			
4	FW	ALTIDORE Josmer	ALTIDORE	06-11-1989	Boca Juniors (USA)	177	68	2	30			
5	MF	SARKODIE Ofori	SARKODIE	18-06-1988	Chicago Magic	175	77	4	360	1		
6	FW	KIRK Quavas	KIRK	13-04-1988	Chicago Magic	186	75	3	251			
7	FW	GONZALEZ Omar	GONZALEZ	11-10-1988	Dallas Texans	195	89	2	18			
8	MF	NAKAZAWA Kyle	NAKAZAWA	16-03-1988	ISC Strikers	177	60	4	360	2		
9	FW	ZIMMERMAN Preston	ZIMMERMAN	21-11-1988	Crossfire Premier	181	78	4	347	1		
10	FW	ARVIZU David	ARVIZU	19-04-1988	Pateadores	167	59	4	325		1	
11	MF	SOROKA Ryan	SOROKA	05-03-1988	Delco	169	62	4	293	2		
12	MF	FARFAN Gabe	G. FARFAN	23-06-1988	La Jolla Nomads	178	64	1	90			
13	DF	WAGNER Blake	WAGNER	29-01-1988	HC United	175	64	4	360		1	
14	DF	SUBOTIC Neven	SUBOTIC	10-12-1988	Manatee Magic	193	79	4	85			1
15	MF	KELLY Dan	KELLY	29-03-1989	Tennessee Futbol Club	179	71	1	90			
16	MF	BESAGNO Nik	BESAGNO	15-11-1988	Real Salt Lake	185	79	2	94			
17	MF	HALL Jeremy	HALL	11-09-1988	HC United	175	68	3	183	1		
18	GK	RESTREPO Diego	RESTREPO	25-02-1988	Team Boca	183	82	0	0			
19	MF	FARFAN Mike	M. FARFAN	23-06-1988	La Jolla Nomads	176	62	4	297		1	
20	GK	PERK Brian	PERK	21-07-1989	Pateadores	179	75	0	0			

FIFA INTERACTIVE WORLD CUP 2005

It had been just under 40 years in coming but England finally won a second World Cup thanks to the unlikely figure of 18-year-old Chris Bullard. The Englishman won the second edition of the FIFA Interactive World Cup, played on EA Sports FIFA 06 and XBox, at the final tournament held in London on December 18th at The Brewery.

FIFA INTERACTIVE WORLD CUP 2005

Regional semis	Regional finals	Quarter-final groups	Semi-finals	Final
London, 15-10-2005				
Michael Barratt, ENG				
Mike Douglas, UK	**Michael Barratt, UK**			
Andreas Plachetta, GER	Ryan Cullender, UK			
Ryan Cullender, UK				
São Paulo, 22-10-2005				
Bruno de Carriço, BRA				
Felipe Martins, BRA	**Bruno de Carriço, BRA**			
Abilio Fabiano, BRA	Thiago Countinho, BRA			
Thiago Countinho, BRA				
		Chris Bullard, ENG		
		Gabor Mokos, HUN		
Seoul, 30-10-2005		Bruno de Carriço, BRA		
Yoon Seo Park, KOR		Yoon Seo Park, KOR		
Yang Shi Chao, CHN	**Yoon Seo Park, KOR**	Tahir Latif, AUS		
Kim Sung Jae, KOR	Maxi Qing, CHN			
Maxi Qing, CHN				
			Chris Bullard, ENG	
			Ruben Morales, MEX	
Johannesburg, 12-11-2005				
David Letsoala, RSA				
Gary Hatfield, ENG	**David Letsoala, RSA**			
Chris Gardener, RSA	Itumeleng Modise, RSA			
Itumeleng Modise, RSA				
				Chris Bullard, ENG
				Gabor Mokos, HUN
Los Angeles, 19-11-2005				
Ruben Morales, MEX				
Isidro Situates, USA	**Ruben Morales, MEX**			
Ali Elabari, USA	Filip Stoynev, USA			
Filip Stoynev, USA				
			Javier Devis Lara, ESP	
			Gabor Mokos, HUN	
Sydney, 26-11-2005				
Tahir Latif, AUS				
Antony Zmire, AUS	**Tahir Latif, AUS**			
Prayas Pradhan, NEP	Giovanni Fichera, AUS	Javier Devis Lara, ESP		
Giovanni Fichera, AUS		Ruben Morales, MEX		
		Manuel Voltolina, ITA		
Cologne, 4-12-2005		Michael Barratt, UK		
Gabor Makos, HUN		David Letsoalo, RSA		
Philipp Rodowski, GER	**Gabor Makos, HUN**			
Oezden Fedagar, SUI	Alex Holzhammer, GER			
Alex Holzhammer, GER				
			Xbox Live Finals	
Paris, 10-12-2005			Chris Bullard, ENG	
Javier Devis Lara, ESP			Robin Fitters, BEL	Bullard and Voltolina
Franck Mandry, FRA	**Javier Devis Lara, ESP**		Christian Wind Bøglund, DEN	qualified to join the eight
Tom Van Rousselt, BEL	Matija Biljeskovic, USA		**Manuel Voltolina, ITA**	regional qualifiers in the
Matija Biljeskovic, USA				final

FIFA CLUB WORLD CHAMPIONSHIP 2005

São Paulo FC returned to Japan as South American champions for the third time and, as in 1992 when they beat Barcelona, and in 1993 when they beat Milan, they once again triumphed over one of the great European sides. This time they defeated Liverpool to win the competition played for the first time in its new format. From 1960 to 1980 the South American and European champions met annually on a home and away basis for the Intercontinental Cup. In 1981, a second era for the tournament was launched when, under the sponsorship of Toyota, the two champions met in a single game played in Tokyo - a system that lasted for 24 years. Two important differences were introduced when the third era was launched in 2005, though continuity was provided by Tokyo remaining the venue and Toyota maintaining its sponsorship. The first change saw FIFA take over the organisation and the second was to invite the four other continental club champions to take part. Rather than play the tournament in groups, the number of games was kept to a minimum by playing a simple knock-out format with São Paulo and Liverpool joining the competition after the first round. Of the six entrants, only Sydney FC lacked any real international experience. Despite being able to call on the guile of coach, Pierre Littbarski, a FIFA World Cup™ winner with West Germany in 1990, and striker Dwight Yorke, a UEFA Champions League winner with Manchester United in 1999, they were beaten in the first round by Costa Rica's Deportivo Saprissa. The other first round tie saw African champions Al Ahly from Egypt, take on Saudi's Al Ittihad, fresh from winning the Asian Champions League in successive years. Despite an unbeaten run stretching back 55 matches, and dominating for much of the match, Al Ahly were beaten by their Arab neighbours. In the semi-finals, two goals from Peter Crouch helped Liverpool beat Saprissa comfortably while Al Ittihad provided tough competition for São Paulo. In an entertaining game, goalkeeper Rogerio Ceni scored a penalty to help the Brazilians win 3-2 to set up a final against Liverpool. Once again Ceni was the hero as São Paulo won the final 1-0 to be crowned world champions.

FIFA CLUB WORLD CHAMPIONSHIP TOYOTA CUP JAPAN 2005

Quarter-finals			Semi-finals			Final		
São Paulo FC	BRA	Bye						
			São Paulo FC	BRA	3			
			Al Ittihad	KSA	2			
Al Ahly	EGY	0						
Al Ittihad	KSA	1						
						São Paulo FC	BRA	1
						Liverpool	ENG	0
Deportivo Saprissa	CRC	1						
Sydney FC	AUS	0						
			Deportivo Saprissa	CRC	0			
			Liverpool	ENG	3			
Liverpool	ENG	Bye						

Fifth Place Play-off			Third Place Play-off		
Sydney FC	AUS	2	Deportivo Saprissa	CRC	3
Al Ahly	EGY	1	Al Ittihad	KSA	2

First Round	National Stadium, Tokyo	11-12-2005
Kick-off: 19:20		Attendance: 28 281

AL ITTIHAD   1   0   AL AHLY

Mohammed Noor [78]

		AL ITTIHAD			MATCH STATS					AL AHLY		
1	GK	ZAID Mabrouk							EL HADARY Essam	GK	1
2	DF	AL DOSARI Ahmed Dukhi		10	Shots	7	71		EL SHATER Islam	DF	2
3	FW	KALLON Mohammed		9	Shots on Goal	3			EL SAYED Ahmed	DF	5
4	DF	TUKAR Redha		25	Fouls Committed	18			GOMAA Wael	DF	6
7	MF	HAIDAR Mohammed	64	6	Corner Kicks	4			(C) MOHAMED Shady	MF	7
8	MF	ABUSHGEER Manaf	94	2	Offside	0			BARAKAT Mohamed	MF	8
11	MF	TCHECO		43	Possession %	57			MOTAB Emad	FW	9
14	MF	KHARIRI Saud					46		GILBERTO	MF	12
18	MF	NOOR Mohammed (C)			MATCH OFFICIALS				MOUSTAFA Hassan	MF	14
20	DF	FALATAH Adnan			REFEREE				SHAWKY Mohamed	MF	17
21	DF	AL MONTASHARI Hamad			POLL Graham ENG				ABOUTRIKA Mohamed	FW	22
		Tr: IORDANESCU Anghel			ASSISTANTS				Tr: DE JESUS Manuel Jose		
		Substitutes			TURNER Glenn ENG				Substitutes		
5	DF	AL GARNI Ali	94		SHARP Philip ENG		71		ASHOUR Hossam	MF	13
17	MF	SOWED Ibrahim	64		4TH OFFICIAL		46	84	ABOU MOSALEM Ahmed	DF	15
					SIMON Carlos BRA		84		HOSNI Osama	FW	18

To be fair, we didn't play well in the first 45 minutes. In the second period we tried to build up our game with possession and we created more problems for our opponents. I think we deserved to win but if they had scored in the first half, which they deserved to do, then the result could well have been different.

Anghel Iordanescu

They got the goal at the right moment. In the second half they pressed much more and we became nervous and failed to move the ball around. Instead we hit long balls which was easy for their tall defenders. We lacked aggression and creativity. One day we had to lose. It was the wrong moment but that's life.

Manuel Jose

First Round	Toyota Stadium, Toyota	12-12-2005
Kick-off: 19:20		Attendance: 28 538

SYDNEY FC   0   1   DEPORTIVO SAPRISSA

Christian Bolanos [47]

		SYDNEY FC			MATCH STATS					DEPORTIVO SAPRISSA		
1	GK	BOLTON Clint							(C) PORRAS Jose	GK	1
2	DF	FYFE Iain		10	Shots	11			BOLANOS Christian	MF	2
3	DF	CECCOLI Alvin	81	4	Shots on Goal	7			CORDERO Victor	DF	3
10	MF	CORICA Steve	83	21	Fouls Committed	9			GONZALEZ Ronald	DF	4
11	FW	MIURA Kazu		9	Corner Kicks	2			DRUMMOND Jervis	DF	5
12	MF	CARNEY David		1	Offside	3	89		CENTENO Walter	MF	8
14	MF	PACKER Andrew	61	56	Possession %	44			GOMEZ Ronald	FW	11
15	MF	MC FLYNN Terry	61				93		SABORIO Alvaro	FW	12
16	DF	MILLIGAN Mark			MATCH OFFICIALS				BADILLA Gabriel	DF	16
19	FW	YORKE Dwight (C)			REFEREE				AZOFEIFA Randall	MF	19
22	FW	PETROVSKI Sasho			KAMIKAWA Toru JPN		83		BENNETT Tray	DF	23
		Tr: LITTBARSKI Pierre			ASSISTANTS				Tr: MEDFORD Hernan		
		Substitutes			HIROSHIMA Yoshikazu JPN				Substitutes		
4	DF	RUDAN Mark	61		KIM Dae Young KOR		89		PARKS Reynaldo	DF	6
9	FW	ZDRILIC David	83		4TH OFFICIAL		83		LOPEZ Jose Luis	MF	17
21	FW	BUONAVOGLIA Gianpaolo	61		GUEZZAZ Mohamed MAR		93		DRUMMOND Gerold	FW	20

We are 12 months old and we played against a team with history. It was a good performance from Sydney against a team that have been champions of their country 23 times. Their goal came at the wrong moment for us. We tried to come back but were hit by the red card. I'm glad we fought right until the end.

Pierre Littbarski

I'm very happy because Saprissa made history tonight. It was a tight game just as we thought. Sydney are good and know how to defend and attack. They are not a one man side (Dwight Yorke). The people of Costa Rica have the right to celebrate, just as we will.

Hernan Medford

Semi-final	National Stadium, Tokyo	14-12-2005
Kick-off: 19:20		Attendance: 31 510

AL ITTIHAD   2   3   SAO PAULO FC

Mohammed Noor [33], Hamad Al Montashari [68]   Amoroso 2 [16] [47], Rogerio Ceni [57p]

		AL ITTIHAD			MATCH STATS			SAO PAULO FC		
1	GK	ZAID Mabrouk						(C) ROGERIO CENI	GK	1
2	DF	AL DOSARI Ahmed Dukhi	67	11	Shots	13		CICINHO	DF	2
3	FW	KALLON Mohammed		4	Shots on Goal	5		FABAO	DF	3
4	DF	TUKAR Redha		20	Fouls Committed	24		EDCARLOS	DF	4
8	MF	ABUSHGEER Manaf		5	Corner Kicks	3		LUGANO Diego	DF	5
11	MF	TCHECO		2	Offside	4		JUNIOR	DF	6
14	MF	KHARIRI Saud		50	Possession %	50		MINEIRO	MF	7
17	MF	SOWED Ibrahim	64					JOSUE	MF	8
18	MF	NOOR Mohammed (C)			MATCH OFFICIALS			DANILO	MF	10
20	DF	FALATAH Adnan			REFEREE			AMOROSO	FW	11
21	DF	AL MONTASHARI Hamad			SARS Alain FRA	89		ALOISIO	FW	14
		Tr: IORDANESCU Anghel			ASSISTANTS			Tr: AUTUORI Paulo		
		Substitutes			ARNAULT Frederic FRA			Substitutes		
7	MF	HAIDAR Mohammed	64		TEXIER Vincent FRA	89		GRAFITE	FW	9
13	DF	AL HARBI Osama	67		4TH OFFICIAL					
					KAMIKAWA Toru JPN					

It was a good quality game, a good show for the fans. There were many opportunities for both sides to score. We didn't start the game well, maybe because in the mind of the players we were playing against a team from the country who are world champions. We just needed a little more courage.

Anghel Iordanescu

It was very surprising, a very difficult game especially in the first half. They closed us down a lot and marked us tightly. After scoring we sat back and relaxed instead of pressing. The second half was different. We had more of the ball and the second goal was a beautiful move.

Paulo Autuori

Semi-final	International Stadium, Yokohama	15-12-2005
Kick-off: 19:20		Attendance: 43 902

DEPORTIVO SAPRISSA   0   3   LIVERPOOL

Peter Crouch 2 [3] [58], Steven Gerrard [32]

		DEPORTIVO SAPRISSA			MATCH STATS			LIVERPOOL		
1	GK	PORRAS Jose (C)						REINA Jose Manuel	GK	12
2	MF	BOLANOS Christian		12	Shots	14	72	HYYPIA Sami	DF	4
3	DF	CORDERO Victor		5	Shots on Goal	6		RIISE John Arne	DF	6
4	DF	GONZALEZ Ronald		16	Fouls Committed	12	64	(C) GERRARD Steven	MF	8
5	DF	DRUMMOND Jervis		7	Corner Kicks	5		CISSE Djibril	FW	9
8	MF	CENTENO Walter		6	Offside	3	79	XABI ALONSO	MF	14
11	FW	GOMEZ Ronald	76	47	Possession %	53		CROUCH Peter	FW	15
12	FW	SABORIO Alvaro	83					JOSEMI	DF	17
16	DF	BADILLA Gabriel			MATCH OFFICIALS			TRAORE Djimi	DF	21
19	MF	AZOFEIFA Randall			REFEREE			SISSOKO Momo	MF	22
23	DF	BENNETT Tray	46		CHANDIA Carlos CHI			CARRAGHER Jamie	DF	23
		Tr: MEDFORD Hernan			ASSISTANTS			Tr: BENITEZ Rafael		
		Substitutes			JULIO Cristian CHI			Substitutes		
7	FW	ALEMAN Allan	83		VARGAS Mario CHI	72		GARCIA Luis	MF	10
10	MF	SOLIS Alonso	46		4TH OFFICIAL	64		SINAMA PONGOLLE Florent	FW	11
20	FW	DRUMMOND Gerold	76		GUEZZAZ Mohamed MAR	79		HAMANN Didi	MF	16

We've had a very tough match because their players are physically very strong. It was more difficult than we expected but they have got very good forwards, with people like Crouch, who is incredibly tall. How are you supposed to defend against a player like that?

Ronald Gonzalez

Getting a very early goal was the key to the game and, as I always say, you can never score early enough. We thought it would be easier from that moment on, but we couldn't relax until we got the third. By then our aim was to keep a clean sheet and set a new record (of 11) for the club.

Rafa Benitez

Match for 5th Place	National Stadium, Tokyo	16-12-2005
Kick-off: 20:00		Attendance: 15 951

AL AHLY   1   2   SYDNEY FC

Emad Motab [45]

Dwight Yorke [35], David Carney [66]

AL AHLY					MATCH STATS				SYDNEY FC		
21	GK	EL SAYED Nader							BOLTON Clint	GK	1
3	DF	ABDEL WAHAB Mohamed	76	15	Shots	3			FYFE Iain	DF	2
4	DF	EL NAHHAS Emad	63	4	Shots on Goal	2			RUDAN Mark	DF	4
5	DF	EL SAYED Ahmed		18	Fouls Committed	16	78		TALAY Ufuk	MF	6
6	DF	GOMAA Wael		6	Corner Kicks	0			BINGLEY Matt	DF	8
8	MF	BARAKAT Mohamed		3	Offside	4	64		CORICA Steve	MF	10
9	FW	MOTAB Emad		61	Possession %	39			MIURA Kazu	FW	11
13	MF	ASHOUR Hossam							CARNEY David	MF	12
17	MF	SHAWKY Mohamed			MATCH OFFICIALS				MILLIGAN Mark	DF	16
18	FW	HOSNI Osama (C)	46		REFEREE				(C) YORKE Dwight	FW	19
22	FW	ABOUTRIKA Mohamed			KAMIKAWA Toru JPN		89		PETROVSKI Sasho	FW	22
		Tr: DE JESUS Manuel Jose			ASSISTANTS				Tr: LITTBARSKI Pierre		
		Substitutes			HIROSHIMA Yoshikazu JPN				Substitutes		
2	DF	EL SHATER Islam	46		KIM Dae Young KOR		89		ZDRILIC David	FW	9
7	MF	MOHAMED Shady	63		4TH OFFICIAL		64		PACKER Andrew	MF	14
23	FW	FLAVIO	76		SARS Alain FRA		78		MC FLYNN Terry	MF	15

*This just wasn't our tournament. The first game
spoiled things for us but today we played the football
we are known for. We made two mistakes and they
scored two goals. We could have scored four or five
but in the end we scored just one - but that's football!
I'm happy with my players.*

Manuel Jose

*Unfortunately one team has to lose. Al Ahly played
some beautiful football and we were a bit lucky to
win, but I've been a long time in the game to know
that it's the result that counts. Dwight is the heart of
the team. He's become our leader and is motivating
the others to perform.*

Pierre Littbarski

Match for 3rd Place	International Stadium, Yokohama	18-12-2005
Kick-off: 16:20		Attendance:

AL ITTIHAD   2   3   DEPORTIVO SAPRISSA

Mohammed Kallon [28], Joseph-Desire Job [53p]

Alvaro Saborio 2 [13] [85p], Ronald Gomez [89]

AL ITTIHAD					MATCH STATS				DEPORTIVO SAPRISSA		
1	GK	ZAID Mabrouk							(C) PORRAS Jose	GK	1
3	FW	KALLON Mohammed		15	Shots	11			BOLANOS Christian	MF	2
4	DF	TUKAR Redha	69	7	Shots on Goal	6	80		GONZALEZ Ronald	DF	4
8	MF	ABUSHGEER Manaf		22	Fouls Committed	18			PARKS Reynaldo	DF	6
10	FW	JOB Joseph-Desire		3	Corner Kicks	4			CENTENO Walter	MF	8
11	MF	TCHECO		1	Offside	6	64		SOLIS Alonso	MF	10
13	DF	AL HARBI Osama		56	Possession %	44			SABORIO Alvaro	FW	12
14	MF	KHARIRI Saud							ESQUIVEL Juan	DF	13
18	MF	NOOR Mohammed (C)	87		MATCH OFFICIALS				BADILLA Gabriel	DF	16
20	DF	FALATAH Adnan			REFEREE				LOPEZ Jose Luis	MF	17
21	DF	AL MONTASHARI Hamad	87		GUEZZAZ Mohamed MAR		90		DRUMMOND Gerold	FW	20
		Tr: IORDANESCU Anghel			ASSISTANTS				Tr: MEDFORD Hernan		
		Substitutes			ENDENG Zogo CMR				Substitutes		
6	DF	AL KAHTANI Mesfr	69		TEXIER Vincent FRA		90		CORDERO Victor	DF	3
9	FW	FALLATAH Hamzah	87		4TH OFFICIAL		80		ALEMAN Allan	FW	7
					POLL Graham ENG		64		GOMEZ Ronald	FW	11

*We contrived to lose third place in the championship
in the last five minutes. We didn't start well but we
managed to get back into the game. At 2-1 we had
chances to increase our lead and should have closed
it out. Hopefully we can do better if we return again
next year.*

Anghel Iordanescu

*We're very satisfied as we've made history with this
third place finish. I have to congratulate my boys,
who have done a great job. We played a great game
and are even more delighted to have beaten a great
opponent like Al Ittihad. Our great victory in Japan
shows just how competitive we are.*

Hernan Medford

Final	International Stadium, Yokohama	18-12-2005
Kick-off: 19:20		Attendance: 66 821

SAO PAULO FC   1 0   LIVERPOOL

Mineiro [27]

SAO PAULO FC			MATCH STATS			LIVERPOOL		
1	GK	ROGERIO CENI (C)				REINA Jose Manuel	GK	12
2	DF	CICINHO	4	Shots	21	79 WARNOCK Stephen	DF	2
3	DF	FABAO	2	Shots on Goal	8	FINNAN Steve	DF	3
4	DF	EDCARLOS	15	Fouls Committed	17	HYYPIA Sami	DF	4
5	DF	LUGANO Diego	0	Corner Kicks	17	KEWELL Harry	MF	7
6	DF	JUNIOR	2	Offside	7	(C) GERRARD Steven	MF	8
7	MF	MINEIRO	46	Possession %	54	GARCIA Luis	MF	10
8	MF	JOSUE				XABI ALONSO	MF	14
10	MF	DANILO		MATCH OFFICIALS	85	MORIENTES Fernando	FW	19
11	FW	AMOROSO		REFEREE	79	SISSOKO Momo	MF	22
14	FW	ALOISIO		ARCHUNDIA Benito MEX		CARRAGHER Jamie	DF	23
		Tr: AUTUORI Paulo		ASSISTANTS		Tr: BENITEZ Rafael		
		Substitutes		VERGARA Hector CAN		Substitutes		
22	GK	BOSCO		VELAZQUEZ Arturo MEX		DUDEK Jerzy	GK	1
23	GK	FLAVIO KRETZER		4TH OFFICIAL		CARSON Scott	GK	13
9	FW	GRAFITE		KAMIKAWA Toru JPN	79	RIISE John Arne	DF	6
12	FW	CHRISTIAN				CISSE Djibril	FW	9
13	DF	ALEX			79	SINAMA PONGOLLE Florent	FW	11
15	MF	DENILSON			85	CROUCH Peter	FW	15
16	DF	FABIO SANTOS				HAMANN Didi	MF	16
17	MF	RENAN				JOSEMI	DF	17
18	DF	FLAVIO DONIZETE				TRAORE Djimi	DF	21
19	FW	THIAGO						
20	MF	RICHARLYSON						
21	MF	SOUZA						

We deserved to win. The statistics show that we had 21 shots, 17 corners, we hit the crossbar twice and had three goals disallowed. What more can you do? In the last 10 minutes we played inside their box. I'm disappointed with the result but very happy with my players.
Rafa Benitez

We were the better side. We've let a title slip out of our hands and it's the kind of competition you usually only get one chance at.
Pepe Reina

In the last eight months we've won the two greatest trophies of our history. We know how to win when we need to.
Rogerio Ceni

The most important thing in football is the final score. It was very important to pressurise Liverpool and I was happy about how we started the match. Our team has played more than 80 games this season. We deserved the title and beat a great team.
Paulo Autuori

MATCH REPORT

The match stats tell the story as wave after wave of Liverpool attacks were thwarted by the sturdy São Paulo defence and the inspirational Rogerio Ceni in goal. Liverpool came into the match on the back of a club record run of 11 games without having conceded a goal and that record looked safe despite the Brazilians dominating the early possession. A speculative Cicinho lob from the halfway line that just cleared the bar was one of the highlights of the first half but just before the half hour a lovely pass from Aloisio split the Liverpool defence and found Mineiro who side footed home to score the only goal of the game. From then on it was almost all Liverpool. Luis Garcia hit the bar a minute later, Gerrard shot wide whilst Garcia and Sami Hyypia forced saves from the goalkeeper. In the second half Ceni was again the saviour saving well from Gerrard, Kewell and Luis Garcia again. Liverpool twice had the ball in the back of the net but Garcia and Florent Sinama Pongolle had their efforts ruled out for offside. Unsurprisingly Rogerio Ceni was voted Man of the Match as the Brazilians celebrated becoming club world champions.

AL AHLY – FIFA CLUB WORLD CHAMPIONSHIP 2005

No	Pos	Name	Shirt Name	DoB	Nationality	Cms	Kg	Games	Mins	Goals	Y	R
1	GK	EL HADARY Essam	E. HADARY	15-01-1973	EGY	188	87	1	90			
2	DF	EL SHATER Islam	I EL SHATER	16-11-1976	EGY	178	70	2	116			
3	DF	ABDEL WAHAB Mohamed	M.A. EL WAHAB	1-10-1983	EGY	174	75	1	76			
4	DF	EL NAHHAS Emad	E. NAHHAS	15-02-1976	EGY	184	71	1	63			
5	DF	EL SAYED Ahmed	A. SAYED	30-10-1980	EGY	181	76	2	180			
6	DF	GOMAA Wael	W. GOMAA	3-08-1975	EGY	183	79	2	180		1	
7	MF	MOHAMED Shady	SHADI	29-11-1977	EGY	180	79	2	117		1	
8	MF	BARAKAT Mohamed	BARAKAT	7-09-1976	EGY	172	63	2	180			
9	FW	MOTAB Emad	EMAD	20-02-1983	EGY	176	74	2	180	1	1	
10	MF	REYAD Wael	W. RIAD	2-08-1982	EGY	166	60	0	0			
11	MF	HASSAN Ahmed	A. HASSAN	12-04-1979	EGY	167	74	0	0			
12	MF	GILBERTO	JELBERTO	21-09-1982	ANG	176	70	1	45			
13	MF	ASHOUR Hossam	H. ASHOUR	9-03-1986	EGY	173	64	2	109		1	
14	MF	MOUSTAFA Hassan	H. MOSTAFA	20-11-1979	EGY	172	71	1	90			
15	DF	ABOU MOSALEM Ahmed	A. ABOU MOSLEM	25-07-1981	EGY	170	70	1	39			
16	DF	ADEL Rami	R. ADEL	18-08-1979	EGY	183	82	0	0			
17	MF	SHAWKY Mohamed	M. SHAWKY	5-10-1981	EGY	181	75	2	180			
18	FW	HOSNI Osama	O. HOSNY	18-06-1982	EGY	174	70	2	51			
19	GK	ABDELHAMID Amir	A. A. EL HAMID	24-04-1979	EGY	180	80	0	0			
20	MF	KHASHABA Hady	HADY	19-12-1972	EGY	180	79	0	0			
21	GK	EL SAYED Nader	NADER	31-12-1972	EGY	184	84	1	90			
22	FW	ABOUTRIKA Mohamed	ABOU TARIKA	7-11-1978	EGY	182	79	2	180			
23	FW	FLAVIO	FLAVIO	30-12-1979	ANG	173	73	1	14			

AL ITTIHAD – FIFA CLUB WORLD CHAMPIONSHIP 2005

No	Pos	Name	Shirt Name	DoB	Nationality	Cms	Kg	Games	Mins	Goals	Y	R
1	GK	ZAID Mabrouk	ZAID	11-02-1976	KSA	185	68	3	270			
2	DF	AL DOSARI Ahmed Dukhi	DOKY	25-10-1976	KSA	175	68	2	157		2	
3	FW	KALLON Mohammed	KALLON	6-10-1979	SLE	178	63	3	270	1	1	
4	DF	TUKAR Redha	TAKAR	29-11-1975	KSA	188	81	3	249		1	
5	DF	AL GARNI Ali	AL GARNI	19-09-1978	KSA	167	63	1	1			
6	DF	AL KAHTANI Mesfr	AL KAHTANI	15-01-1984	KSA	170	64	1	21			
7	MF	HAIDAR Mohammed	HAIDAR	29-04-1980	KSA	168	60	2	90			
8	MF	ABUSHGEER Manaf	ABOSHGAIR	5-02-1980	KSA	165	56	3	269			
9	FW	FALLATAH Hamza	HAMZAH	8-10-1972	KSA	178	66	1	3			
10	FW	JOB Joseph-Desire	JOB	1-12-1977	CMR	180	62	1	90	1		
11	MF	TCHECO	TCHECO	11-04-1976	BRA	173	65	3	270			
12	MF	HAKAMI Abdoh	HAKAMI	14-07-1983	KSA	180	60	0	0			
13	DF	AL HARBI Osama	OSAMA	16-05-1984	KSA	187	80	2	113		2	
14	MF	KHARIRI Saud	KHARIRI	8-07-1980	KSA	180	68	3	270		2	
17	MF	SOWED Ibrahim	SOWED	21-07-1974	KSA	172	60	2	90			
18	MF	NOOR Mohammed	NOOR	26-02-1978	KSA	172	61	3	267	2		
20	DF	FALATAH Adnan	ADNAN	20-10-1983	KSA	168	64	3	270		1	
21	DF	AL MONTASHARI Hamad	AL MONTASHARI	22-06-1982	KSA	186	74	3	267	1	1	1
22	GK	AL SADIG Hussain	AL SADIG	15-10-1973	KSA	182	78	0	0			
23	GK	AL ANTAIF Tisir	AL ANTAIF	16-02-1974	KSA	183	80	0	0			
15		PEDRINHO	Not entitled to play		BRA							
16		MARCAO	Not entitled to play		BRA							
19		LIMA	Not entitled to play		BRA							

DEPORTIVO SAPRISSA – FIFA CLUB WORLD CHAMPIONSHIP 2005

No	Pos	Name	Shirt Name	DoB	Nationality	Cms	Kg	Games	Mins	Goals	Y	R
1	GK	PORRAS Jose	PORRAS	08-11-1970	CRC	184	81	3	270		1	
2	MF	BOLANOS Christian	BOLANOS	17-05-1984	CRC	178	67	3	270	1		
3	DF	CORDERO Victor	V CORDERO	09-11-1973	CRC	183	75	3	181			
4	DF	GONZALEZ Ronald	GONZALEZ	08-08-1970	CRC	181	80	3	260		2	
5	DF	DRUMMOND Jervis	JERVIS	08-09-1976	CRC	172	66	2	180			
6	DF	PARKS Reynaldo	PARKS	04-12-1974	CRC	174	75	2	91			
7	FW	ALEMAN Allan	ALEMAN	29-07-1983	CRC	164	60	2	17			
8	MF	CENTENO Walter	PATE	06-10-1974	CRC	174	70	3	269		1	
9	MF	BRENES Pablo	BRENES	04-08-1982	CRC	173	61	0	0			
10	MF	SOLIS Alonso	SOLIS	14-10-1978	CRC	178	68	2	109			
11	FW	GOMEZ Ronald	RONALD	24-01-1975	CRC	183	80	3	192	1	1	
12	FW	SABORIO Alvaro	SABO	25-03-1982	CRC	183	77	3	262	2		
13	DF	ESQUIVEL Juan	ESQUIVEL	12-08-1980	CRC	171	69	1	90			
14	DF	NUNEZ Andres	NUNEZ	27-07-1976	CRC	176	71	0	0			
15	MF	PHILLIPS Saul	PHILLIPS	03-10-1984	CRC	178	77	0	0			
16	DF	BADILLA Gabriel	GABRIEL	30-06-1984	CRC	180	73	3	270		1	
17	MF	LOPEZ Jose Luis	LOPEZ	31-03-1981	CRC	178	74	2	97			
18	GK	GONZALEZ Fausto	FAUSTO	13-09-1978	CRC	180	78	0	0			
19	MF	AZOFEIFA Randall	AZOFEIFA	30-12-1984	CRC	183	77	2	180		1	
20	FW	DRUMMOND Gerold	GERALD	08-09-1976	CRC	172	71	3	104			
21	GK	NAVAS Keylor	NAVAS	15-12-1986	CRC	184	75	0	0			
22	DF	FONSECA Jose	FONSECA	25-11-1973	CRC	170	77	0	0			
23	DF	BENNETT Tray	BENNETT	05-08-1975	CRC	174	71	2	128			

LIVERPOOL – FIFA CLUB WORLD CHAMPIONSHIP 2005

No	Pos	Name	Shirt Name	DoB	Nationality	Cms	Kg	Games	Mins	Goals	Y	R
1	GK	DUDEK Jerzy	DUDEK	23-03-1973	POL	188	80	0	0			
2	DF	WARNOCK Stephen	WARNOCK	12-12-1981	ENG	175	74	1	79			
3	DF	FINNAN Steve	FINNAN	20-04-1976	IRL	183	77	1	90			
4	DF	HYYPIA Sami	HYYPIA	7-10-1973	FIN	193	87	2	162			
6	DF	RIISE John Arne	RIISE	24-09-1980	NOR	185	89	2	101			
7	MF	KEWELL Harry	KEWELL	22-09-1978	AUS	180	79	1	90			
8	MF	GERRARD Steven	GERRARD	30-05-1980	ENG	183	79	2	154	1		
9	FW	CISSE Djibril	CISSE	12-08-1981	FRA	185	83	1	90			
10	MF	GARCIA Luis	LUIS GARCIA	24-06-1978	ESP	178	66	2	108			
11	FW	SINAMA PONGOLLE Florent	SINAMA	20-10-1984	FRA	176	72	2	37			
12	GK	REINA Jose Manuel	REINA	31-08-1982	ESP	188	94	2	180			
13	GK	CARSON Scott	CARSON	3-09-1985	ENG	191	88	0	0			
14	MF	XABI ALONSO	ALONSO	25-11-1981	ESP	183	77	2	169			
15	FW	CROUCH Peter	CROUCH	30-01-1981	ENG	200	84	2	95	2		
16	MF	HAMANN Didi	HAMANN	27-08-1973	GER	191	83	1	11			
17	DF	JOSEMI	JOSEMI	15-11-1979	ESP	183	80	1	90			
19	FW	MORIENTES Fernando	MORIENTES	5-04-1976	ESP	182	78	1	85			
21	DF	TRAORE Djimi	TRAORE	1-03-1980	MLI	191	79	1	90			
22	MF	SISSOKO Momo	SISSOKO	22-01-1985	MLI	191	80	2	169			
23	DF	CARRAGHER Jamie	CARRAGHER	28-01-1978	ENG	185	81	2	180			
5		O'DONNELL Danny	Did not travel		ENG							
18		POTTER Darren	Did not travel		IRL							
20		RAVEN David	Did not travel		ENG							

SAO PAULO FC – FIFA CLUB WORLD CHAMPIONSHIP 2005

No	Pos	Name	Shirt Name	DoB	Nationality	Cms	Kg	Games	Mins	Goals	Y	R
1	GK	ROGERIO CENI	ROGERIO	22-01-1973	BRA	188	88	2	180	1	1	
2	DF	CICINHO	CICINHO	24-06-1980	BRA	171	72	2	180			
3	DF	FABAO	FABAO	15-06-1976	BRA	187	85	2	180			
4	DF	EDCARLOS	EDCARLOS	10-05-1985	BRA	183	80	2	180			
5	DF	LUGANO Diego	LUGANO	2-11-1980	URU	188	87	2	180		2	
6	DF	JUNIOR	JUNIOR	20-06-1973	BRA	173	70	2	180			
7	MF	MINEIRO	MINEIRO	2-08-1975	BRA	169	66	2	180	1	1	
8	MF	JOSUE	JOSUE	19-07-1979	BRA	169	63	2	180			
9	FW	GRAFITE	GRAFITE	2-04-1979	BRA	189	83	2	16			
10	MF	DANILO	DANILO	11-06-1979	BRA	186	84	2	180	1		
11	FW	AMOROSO	AMOROSO	5-07-1974	BRA	180	71	2	180	2	1	
12	FW	CHRISTIAN	CHRISTIAN	23-04-1975	BRA	186	83	0	0			
13	DF	ALEX	ALEX	9-05-1982	BRA	189	86	0	0			
14	FW	ALOISIO	ALOISIO	27-01-1975	BRA	186	86	2	164			
15	MF	DENILSON	DENILSON	16-02-1988	BRA	178	73	0	0			
16	DF	FABIO SANTOS	F. SANTOS	16-09-1985	BRA	179	75	0	0			
17	MF	RENAN	RENAN	29-03-1985	BRA	181	80	0	0			
18	DF	FLAVIO DONIZETE	F. DONIZETE	16-01-1984	BRA	183	87	0	0			
19	FW	THIAGO	THIAGO	24-02-1986	BRA	184	74	0	0			
20	MF	RICHARLYSON	RICHARLYSON	27-12-1982	BRA	176	72	0	0			
21	MF	SOUZA	SOUZA	4-02-1979	BRA	176	65	0	0			
22	GK	BOSCO	BOSCO	14-11-1974	BRA	184	80	0	0			
23	GK	FLAVIO KRETZER	F. KRETZER	10-02-1979	BRA	196	97	0	0			

SYDNEY FC – FIFA CLUB WORLD CHAMPIONSHIP 2005

No	Pos	Name	Shirt Name	DoB	Nationality	Cms	Kg	Games	Mins	Goals	Y	R
1	GK	BOLTON Clint	BOLTON	22-08-1975	AUS	188	95	2	180			
2	DF	FYFE Iain	FYFE	03-04-1982	AUS	185	83	2	180			
3	DF	CECCOLI Alvin	CECCOLI	05-08-1974	AUS	178	79	1	81			1
4	DF	RUDAN Mark	RUDAN	27-08-1975	AUS	191	90	2	119		1	
6	MF	TALAY Ufuk	TALAY	26-03-1976	AUS	178	76	1	78			
7	MF	MIDDLEBY Robert	MIDDLEBY	09-08-1975	AUS	173	74	0	0			
8	DF	BINGLEY Matt	BINGLEY	16-08-1971	AUS	183	82	1	90			
9	FW	ZDRILIC David	ZDRILIC	13-04-1974	AUS	182	81	2	8			
10	MF	CORICA Steve	CORICA	24-03-1973	AUS	174	71	2	147			
11	FW	MIURA Kazu	KAZU	26-02-1967	JPN	178	68	2	180			
12	MF	CARNEY David	CARNEY	30-11-1983	AUS	181	78	2	180	1		
13	MF	WELLS Dustin	WELLS	31-05-1983	AUS	197	80	0	0			
14	MF	PACKER Andrew	PACKER	16-06-1980	AUS	180	78	2	87		1	
15	MF	MC FLYNN Terry	MC FLYNN	27-03-1981	NIR	174	76	2	73		1	
16	DF	MILLIGAN Mark	MILLIGAN	04-08-1985	AUS	178	78	2	180		1	
17	DF	TIMPANO Jacob	TIMPANO	03-01-1986	AUS	189	86	0	0			
18	DF	OOSTENDORP Wade	OOSTENDORP	20-04-1988	AUS	183	76	0	0			
19	FW	YORKE Dwight	YORKE	03-11-1971	TRI	179	79	2	180	1	1	
20	GK	PASFIELD Justin	PASFIELD	30-05-1985	AUS	189	78	0	0			
21	FW	BUONAVOGLIA Gianpaolo	BUONAVOGLIA	19-10-1975	AUS	165	63	1	29			
22	FW	PETROVSKI Sasho	PETROVSKI	05-03-1975	AUS	181	80	2	179			
23	GK	BLOWES Mitchell	BLOWES	25-02-1981	AUS	180	85	0	0			
5		ZATKOVICH Ruben	Not entitled to play		AUS							

2006 FIFA WORLD CUP™ QUALIFIERS

QUALIFYING MATCHES PLAYED IN ASIA

Preliminary Round			

First Group Stage			

Final Group Stage			

Group 1		Pts
Iran	IRN	15
Jordan	JOR	12
Qatar	QAT	9
Laos	LAO	0

Group 2		Pts
Uzbekistan	UZB	16
Iraq	IRQ	11
Palestine	PAL	7
Chinese Taipei	TPE	0

Group 3		Pts
Japan	JPN	18
Oman	OMA	10
India	IND	4
Singapore	SIN	3

Bangladesh	BAN	0	0
Tajikistan	TJK	2	2
Turkmenistan	TKM	11	2
Afghanistan	AFG	0	0
Chinese Taipei	TPE	3	3
Macao	MAC	0	1
Pakistan	PAK	0	0
Kyrgyzstan	KGZ	2	4
Laos	LAO	0	0
Sri Lanka	SRI	0	3
Mongolia	MGL	0	0
Maldives	MDV	1	12
Guam - withdrew	GUM		
Nepal - withdrew	NEP		

Laos qualified as best loser after the withdrawl of Guam and Nepal.

Group 4		Pts
Kuwait	KUW	15
China PR	CHN	15
Hong Kong	HKG	6
Malaysia	MYS	0

Group 5		Pts
Korea DPR	PRK	11
United Arab Emirates	UAE	10
Thailand	THA	7
Yemen	YEM	5

Group 6		Pts
Bahrain	BHR	14
Syria	SYR	8
Tajikistan	TJK	7
Kyrgyzstan	KGZ	4

Group 7		Pts
Korea Republic	KOR	14
Lebanon	LIB	11
Vietnam SR	VIE	4
Maldives	MDV	4

Group 8		Pts
Saudi Arabia	KSA	18
Turkmenistan	TKM	7
Indonesia	IDN	7
Sri Lanka	SRI	2

Group A		Pts
Saudi Arabia	KSA	14
Korea Republic	KOR	10
Kuwait	KUW	5
Uzbekistan	UZB	4

Group B		Pts
Japan	IRN	15
Iran	JPN	13
Bahrain	BHR	4
Korea DPR	PRK	3

Saudi Arabia, Korea Republic, Iran and Japan qualified for the finals in Germany. Kuwait and Bahrain play off with the Bahrain meeting the fourth-placed team from CONCACAF, Trinidad and Tobago.

Details of FIFA World Cup™ qualifiers played in Asia before August 2005 can be found in the *Almanack of World Football 2006* on pages 76-97

THIRD PHASE GROUP A

Pakhtakor, Tashkent		
17-08-2005, 18:05, 40 000, Mohd Salleh MAS		

UZB   **3**   **2**   **KUW**

Djeparov [41p], Shatskikh [51]
Soliev [76]

Al Mutwa [15], Abdulaziz [30]

UZBEKISTAN			KUWAIT		
1 SAFONOV Evgeni			KANKUNE Shehab	1	
4 KASIMOV Mirdjalal			ABDULLAH Yaqoub	2	
5 ALIKULOV Asror			JARRAGH Mohamad	3	
8 DJEPAROV Srver			AL SHAMMARI Nohayer	5	
10 KARPENKO Victor	83	82	ZADAH Khaled	7	
15 GEYNRIKH Alexander	46		ABDULAZIZ Bashar	9	
16 SHATSKIKH Maksim			AL SHUWAYE Nawaf	14	
17 NIKOLAEV Alexey			AL SHAMMARI Khaled	16	
18 KADADAZE Timur			AL MUTWA Bader	17	
20 DAVLETOV Fevzi	52		AL ATAIQI Jarah	18	
22 SHIRSHOV Nikolai		59	AL HAMAD Fahad	20	
Tr: HOUGHTON Bob			Tr: STOICHITA Mihai		
9 SOLIEV Anvarjon	46	59	AL SHAMMARI Husain	8	
13 BIKMOEV Marat	52	82	AL AZEMI Ahmad	19	
14 KIRYAN Vladislav	83				

World Cup Stadium, Seoul		
17-08-2005, 20:05, 61 586, Kunsuta THA		

KOR   **0**   **1**   **KSA**

Al Anbar [4]

KOREA REPUBLIC			SAUDI ARABIA		
1 LEE Woon Jae			ZAID Mabrouk	1	
2 YOU Kyoung Youl			FALLATHA Redha	3	
4 KIM Jin Kyu			ALQADI Naif Ali	5	
5 KIM Young Chul		70	HAIDAR Mohammed	7	
6 BAEK Ji Hoon	60	90	AL ABDULLHA Saheb	8	
8 KIM Do Heon	75		AL BAHRI Ahmed	15	
10 PARK Chu Young			AL THAKER Khaled	16	
11 CHA Du Ri	55		AL SAQRI Saleh	19	
12 LEE Young Pyo			AL MOWALAD Zaid	25	
13 KIM Dong Jin	75		AL ANBAR Mohammed	26	
19 AHN Jung Hwan		57	AL MESHAL Saeed	29	
Tr: BONFRERE Jo			Tr: CALDERON Gabriel		
15 KIM Jung Woo	60	57	AL JASSAM Taisser	6	
16 CHUNG KYyung Ho	55	70	MAJRASHI Naji	9	
18 CHO Jae Jin	75	90	JAHDALI Walid	14	

THIRD PHASE GROUP A	PL	W	D	L	F	A	PTS	KSA	KOR	UZB	KUW
1 **Saudi Arabia**	6	4	2	0	10	1	14		2-0	3-0	3-0
2 **Korea Republic**	6	3	1	2	9	5	10	0-1		2-1	2-0
3 **Uzbekistan**	6	1	2	3	7	11	5	1-1	1-1		3-2
4 **Kuwait**	6	1	1	4	4	13	4	0-0	0-4	2-1	

Saudi Arabia and Korea Republic qualified for the finals • Uzbekistan qualified for a play-off against Bahrain

THIRD PHASE GROUP B

International Stadium, Yokohama
17-08-2005, 19:30, 66 098, Shaban KUW

JAP 2 1 IRN

Kaji [28], Oguro [76]   Daei [79]

JAPAN			IRAN	
23 KAWAGUCHI Yoshikatsu			MIRZAPOUR Ebrahim	1
2 TANAKA Makoto			GOLMOHAMMADI Yahya	4
4 ENDO Yasuhito	84		NEKOUNAM Javad	6
5 MIYAMOTO Tsuneyasu			DAEI Ali	10
8 OGASAWARA Mitsuo		73	VAHEDI Alireza	11
14 SANTOS Alessandro			KABEI Hossein	13
15 FUKUNISHI Takashi			ALAVI Seyed	15
16 OGURO Masashi		46	JABARI Mojtaba	17
21 KAJI Akira			KAMELI Jalal	19
22 NAKAZAWA Yuji			NOSRATI Mohammad	20
28 TAMADA Keiji	88	46	BORHANI Arash	25
Tr: Zico			Tr: IVANKOVIC Branko	
26 KONNO Yasuyuki	84	46	KAZEMEYAN Javad	7
30 ABE Yuki	88	46	MOBALI Eman	23
		73	MANIEI Meysam	28

National Stadium, Manama
17-08-2005, 19:35, 3 000, Maidin SIN

BHR 2 3 PRK

Isa [49], Ahmed [54]   Choe Chol Man [28], Kim Chol Ho [43]
                                                  An Chol Hyok [89]

BAHRAIN			KOREA DPR	
1 ALI Hassan			KIM Myong Gil	23
5 MOHAMED Abdulla	68		HWANG Myong Chol	3
9 AHMED Husain			SO Hyok Chol	5
12 BASHEER Mohamed		86	KIM Chol Ho	7
13 MOHAMED Talal			HAN Sun Li	11
14 ISA Salman			HAN Song Chol	14
15 FARHAN Saleh		76	KIM Yong Jun	15
18 MAKKI Husain	46	29	CHOE Chol Man	17
19 NOROOZ Hasan Ali			KIM Song Chol	18
29 HUBAIL Mohammed			PAK Chol Jin	20
30 MOSHKHAS Ebrahim	88		AN Chol Hyok	22
Tr: PERUZOVIC Luka			Tr: KIM Myong Song	
4 YUSUF AL HUJAIRI Ahmed	88	29	KIM Myong Chol	9
10 SALMEEN Mohamed	46	76	AN Jong Ho	10
16 MOHAMED ADNAN Sayed	68	86	RI Yong Gwang	12

THIRD PHASE GROUP B	PL	W	D	L	F	A	PTS	JPN	IRN	BHR	PRK
1 Japan	6	5	0	1	9	4	15		2-1	1-0	2-1
2 Iran	6	4	1	1	7	3	13	2-1		1-0	1-0
3 Bahrain	6	1	1	4	4	7	4	0-1	0-0		2-3
4 Korea DPR	6	1	0	5	5	11	3	0-2	0-2	1-2	

Japan and Iran qualified for the finals • Bahrain qualified for a play-off against Uzbekistan

QUALIFYING MATCHES PLAYED IN AFRICA

Preliminary Round

Congo	CGO	1	1
Sierra Leone	SLE	0	1
Seychelles	SEY	0	1
Zambia	ZAM	4	1
Equatorial Guinea	EQG	1	0
Togo	TOG	0	2
Gambia	GAM	2	0
Liberia	LBR	0	3
Guinea-Bissau	GNB	1	0
Mali	MLI	2	2
Burkina Faso	BFA	w-o	
Central African Republic	CTA		
Ghana	GHA	5	2
Somalia	SOM	0	0
Swaziland	SWZ	1	0
Cape Verde Islands	CPV	1	3
Uganda	UGA	3	1
Mauritius	MRI	0	3
Madagascar	MAD	1	2
Benin	BEN	1	3
Sudan	SUD	3	0
Eritrea	ERI	0	0
São Tomé e Príncipe	STP	0	0
Libya	LBY	1	8
Niger	NIG	0	0
Algeria	ALG	1	6
Chad	CHA	3	0
Angola	ANG	1	2
Burundi	BDI	0	1
Gabon	GAB	0	4
Zimbabwe	ZIM	3	1
Mauritania	MTN	0	2
Rwanda	RWA	3	1
Namibia	NAM	0	1
Tanzania	TAN	0	0
Kenya	KEN	0	3
Guinea	GUI	1	4
Mozambique	MOZ	0	3
Ethiopia	ETH	1	0
Malawi	MWI	3	0
Botswana	BOT	4	0
Lesotho	LES	1	0

Group Stage

Group 1		Pts
Togo	TOG	23
Senegal	SEN	21
Zambia	ZAM	19
Congo	CGO	10
Mali	MLI	8
Liberia	LBR	4

Group 2		Pts
Ghana	GHA	21
Congo DR	COD	16
South Africa	RSA	16
Burkina Faso	BFA	13
Cape Verde Islands	CPV	10
Uganda	UGA	8

Group 3		Pts
Côte d'Ivoire	CIV	22
Cameroon	CMR	21
Egypt	EGY	17
Libya	LBY	12
Sudan	SUD	6
Benin	BEN	5

Group 4		Pts
Angola	ANG	21
Nigeria	NGA	21
Zimbabwe	ZIM	15
Gabon	GAB	10
Algeria	ALG	8
Rwanda	RWA	5

Group 5		Pts
Tunisia	TUN	21
Morocco	MAR	20
Guinea	GUI	17
Kenya	KEN	10
Botswana	BOT	9
Malawi	MWI	6

The African qualifying system involved a preliminary knock-out round for 42 teams. The 21 winners joined the nine seeded teams - Cameroon, Nigeria, South Africa, Senegal, Tunisia, Morocco, Egypt, Côte d'Ivoire and Congo DR - in the group stage with the five group winners qualifying for the finals.

Details of FIFA World Cup™ qualifiers played in Africa before August 2005 can be found in the *Almanack of World Football 2006* on pages 99-126

GROUP 1

Chililabombwe, Chililabombwe
3-09-2005, 15:00, 20 000, Abd El Fatah EGY

ZAM 0 1 SEN

Diouf 57

No	ZAMBIA		
16	MWEENE Kennedy		
2	CHILEMBI Laughter		
4	NKETANI Kennedy		
5	TANA Elijah		86
7	KATONGO Christopher		
8	CHANSA Isaac	76	
9	MBESUMA Collins	62	
13	LUNGU Mishek		
14	NUMBA Mumamba	65	
15	CHALWE Linos	71	80
17	SINKALA Andrew		
	Tr: BWALYA Kalusha		
10	KALABA Rainford	76	80
12	MULENGA Clifford	65	62
19	MWAPE Davies	71	86

		SENEGAL	No
		SYLVA Tony	1
		DAIKHATE Pape	4
		DIAWARA Souleymane	5
86		DIOUF EL Hadji	11
		FAYE Amdy	12
		DIATTA Lamine	13
62		MENDY Frederic	14
		BA Issa	15
		COLY Ferdinand	17
80		NIANG Mamadou	18
		BEYE Habib	21
		Tr: SARR Abdoulaye	
80		CAMARA Souleymane	3
62		KAMARA Diomansy	9
86		NDAW Guirane	19

Stade du 26 mars, Bamako
3-09-2005, 18:00, 10 000, Mbera GAB

MLI 2 0 CGO

Demba 48, Sissoko 51

No	MALI		
1	TANGARA Fousseni		
3	DIAWARA Fousseiny	76	
4	COULIBALY Adama		46
5	KONE Boubacar		
7	SIDIBE Mamady	52	67
9	KEITA Sidi Yaya	31	
11	TRAORE Dramane		
12	KEITA Seydou		
13	DEMBA Abdoulai Demba		75
15	TRAORE Djimi		
18	SISSOKO Momo		
	Tr: LECHANTRE Pierre		
8	KEITA Alphousseyni	31	46
14	DIAMOUTENE Souleymane	76	75
17	COULIBALY Dramane	52	67

		CONGO	No
		MOUKO Barel	1
		NGO Patrick	3
46		OPONGA Camille	4
		KIMBEMBE Christel	5
67		TSOUMOU Denis	6
		EWOLO Oscar	7
		FILANCKEMBO Nancy	10
		BHEBEY Rudy	11
75		MAMOUNA-OSSILA Armel	12
		ONTSONDO Bienvenu	17
		LEONCE Andzouana	18
		Tr: TCHIANGANA Gaston	
46		DE BUISSON Michel	9
75		BOUITY Bertrand	13
67		LAKOU Belisaire	14

Kegue, Lome
4-09-2005, 15:30, 28 000, Abdel Rahman SUD

TOG 3 0 LBR

Adebayor 2 52 93+, Mamam 69

No	TOGO		
16	AGASSA Kossi		
3	ABALO Yaovi		
5	ATTE-OUDEYI Zanzan		
6	AZIAWONOU Yao		
10	MAMAM Cherif- Toure		
12	AKOTO Eric	48	
13	MATHIAS Emmanuel	58	
14	OLUFADE Adekanmi	48	
15	ROMAO Jacques	33	35
17	COUBADJA Abdel		
18	SENAYA Junior	50	
	Tr: KESHI Stephen		
4	ADEBAYOR Sheyi	48	48
7	SALIFOU Moustapha	50	35
9	SOULIEMANE Robert	33	58

		LIBERIA	No
		SWEN Saylee	1
		KPOTO Varmah	4
		PENIE Aloysius	6
		BARLEE Shelton	7
		TEAH Robert	8
48		ZEO Gardiehbey	9
58		TONDO Isaac	10
		WESSEH Solomon	11
		GARWO Prince	14
		LEWIS Eic	17
		DORBOR Gizzie	18
		Tr: SAYON Joseph	
48		GRANUE Patrick	5
35		WILSON Edward	13
58		DUKULY Chris	15

Antoinette Tubman, Monrovia
1-10-2005, 16:00, 0, Evehe CMR

LBR 0 5 ZAM

Lwipa 2 50 82, Mweetwa 2 51 63
Numba 61

No	LIBERIA		
1	SWEN Saylee		
4	KPOTO Varmah		
6	PENIE Aloysyni	56	
7	BARLEE Shelton		
8	TEAH Robert		
9	DOE Sackie		
10	TONDO Isaac	46	46
14	GARWO Prince	87	80
15	DUKULY Chris		
17	LEWIS Eric	66	
18	DORBOR Gizzie		
	Tr: SAYON Joseph		
2	KICMETT Melvin	87	80
12	POPO Isaac	56	66
13	WILSON Edward	46	46

		ZAMBIA	No
		MWEENE Kennedy	16
		HACHILESA Clive	3
		MUSONDA Joseph	4
		NKETANI Kennedy	5
		PHIRI Lawrence	6
		NJOVU Lameck	8
80		CHANDA Boyd	9
		KAPOSA Owen	12
		MWABA Crispin	13
66		NUMBA Mumamba	14
		MWEETWA Nchimunya	15
		Tr: BWALYA Kalusha	
80		SINYANGWE Mark	7
		MWANDILA Noel	10
66		LWIPA Ignatius	17

Stade Léopold Sedar Senghor, Dakar
8-10-2005, 15:00, 30 000, Maillet SEY

SEN 3 0 MLI

Camara 2 18 65, Diouf 23

No	SENEGAL		
1	SYLVA Tony		
4	DAIKHATE Pape		
7	CAMARA Henri		
10	BA Issa		
11	DIOUF EL Hadji	75	
12	FAYE Amdy	69	
13	DIATTA Lamine		
14	MENDY Frederic	8	
17	DRAME Boukary		
19	DIOP Bouba		
21	BEYE Habib		
	Tr: SARR Abdoulaye		
5	NDAW Guirane	69	64
6	RAHMANE Barry	8	53
9	KAMARA Diomansy	75	76

		MALI	No
		TANGARA Fousseni	1
64		DIAWARA Fousseiny	3
		COULIBALY Soumaila	4
		KONE Boubacar	7
		KEITA Alphousseyni	9
		KEITA Seydou	12
76		DIALLO Mamadou	13
		DIAMOUTENE Souleymane	14
		TRAORE Djimi	15
53		SISSOKO Momo	18
		KANOUTE Frederic	19
		Tr: LECHANTRE Pierre	
64		TOURE Bassala	8
53		TRAORE Dramane	11
76		DEMBA Abdoulai Demba	17

Stade Alphonse Massamba, Brazzaville
8-10-2005, 16:00, 20 000, Shelmani LBY

CGO 2 3 TOG

Bouity 26, Mamouna-Ossila 56
Adebayor 40, Coubadja 2 60 70

No	CONGO		
3	NGO Patrick		
5	KOUVOUAMA Jean		
6	TSOUMOU Denis		
8	DJIMBI Landry	45	
9	MAKITA-PASSY Fabry		
10	FILANCKEMBO Nancy	59	
12	MAMOUNA-OSSILA Armel	85	
13	BOUITY Bertrand		
14	SITA Luriel		
16	KOUSIATAMA Bilolo		
17	ONTSONDO Bienvenu		
	Tr: TCHIANGANA Gaston		
2	MAKOUNDOURAFFET R.	85	58
4	OCKAKAS Otolo	45	
11	BHEBEY Rudy	59	

		TOGO	No
		AGASSA Kossi	16
		NIBOMBE Dare	2
		ABALO Jean-Paul	3
		ADEBAYOR Emmanuel	4
		ATTE-OUDEYI Mohama	5
		AZIAWONOU Yao	6
		MAMAH Abdul	9
58		MAMAM Cherif-Toure	10
		ROMAO Jaques	15
		COUBADJA Abdel	17
		SENAYA Junior	18
		Tr: KESHI Stephen	
58		SALIFOU Moustapha	8

SECOND PHASE GROUP 1	PL	W	D	L	F	A	PTS	TOG	SEN	ZAM	CGO	MLI	LBR
1 Togo	10	7	2	1	20	8	23		3-1	4-1	2-0	1-0	3-0
2 Senegal	10	6	3	1	21	8	21	2-2		1-0	2-0	3-0	6-1
3 Zambia	10	6	1	3	16	10	19	1-0	0-1		2-0	2-1	1-0
4 Congo	10	3	1	6	10	14	10	2-3	0-0	2-3		1-0	3-0
5 Mali	10	2	2	6	11	14	8	1-2	2-2	1-1	2-0		4-1
6 Liberia	10	1	1	8	3	27	4	0-0	0-3	0-5	0-2	1-0	

Togo qualified for the finals

GROUP 2

SECOND PHASE GROUP 2	PL	W	D	L	F	A	PTS	GHA	COD	RSA	BFA	CPV	UGA
1 Ghana	10	6	3	1	17	4	21		0-0	3-0	2-1	2-0	2-0
2 Congo DR	10	4	4	2	14	10	16	1-1		1-0	3-2	2-1	4-0
3 South Africa	10	5	1	4	12	14	16	0-2	2-2		2-0	2-1	2-1
4 Burkina Faso	10	4	1	5	14	13	13	1-0	2-0	3-1		1-2	2-0
5 Cape Verde Islands	10	3	1	6	8	15	10	0-4	1-1	1-2	1-0		1-0
6 Uganda	10	2	2	6	6	15	8	1-1	1-0	0-1	2-2	1-0	

Ghana qualified for the finals

Stade du 4 aout, Ouagadougou
3-09-2005, 18:00, 25 000, Codjia BEN

BFA 3   1 RSA

Cisse 2 [32 47], Kebe [39]   Zuma [75]

BURKINA FASO			SOUTH AFRICA	
16	SOULAMA Abdulaye		VONK Hans	1
2	OUATTARA Moussa	45	RAMMILE Thabiso	3
4	TASSEMBEDO Soumaila		MOKOENA Aaron	4
6	BARRO Tanguy		MABIZELA Mbulelo	5
8	KERE Mahamoudou	66	62	MORRIS Nasief	6
9	KEBE Yahia	81		BARTLETT Shaun	9
12	PANANDETIGUIRI Saidou		PIENAAR Steven	10
13	OUATTARA Boureima		VAN HEERDEN Elrio	11
15	ROUAMBA Florent		MHLONGO Benson	12
17	NIKIEMA Abdoul Aziz	88	61	NOMVETHE Siyabonga	14
18	CISSE Abdoulaye		MC CARTHY Benedict	17
	Tr: BERNARD Simondi		Tr: BAXTER Stuart	
7	COULIBALY Amadou	66	62	LEKGWATHI Lucky	2
11	KABORE Ibrahim	88	45	KATZA Ricardo	7
14	MINOUNGOU Dieubonne	81	61	ZUMA Sibusiso	15

Stade de Martyrs, Kinshasa
4-09-2005, 15:30, 75 000, Guezzaz MAR

COD 2   1 CPV

Mubiala [21], Mputu [49]   Morais [24]

CONGO DR			CAPE VERDE ISLANDS	
1	KALEMBA Lukoki		MONTEIRO Jose	1
3	NSUMBU Dituabanza		ALMEIDA Rui	2
5	MBALA Mbuta	88	BARROS Jose	3
6	MILAMBO Mutamba		VEIGA Nelson	5
8	MPUTU Mabi	70	BORGES Victor	7
9	LUALUA Lomana	60	GOMES Arlindo	9
10	NONDA Shabani		AGUIAR Claudio	11
11	MUBIALA Kitambala	91	GOMES Janicio	14
14	ILONGO Ngasanya		DA LUZ Emerson	17
15	ILUNGA Herita	92	MORAIS Carlos	18
18	GLADYS Bokede	89	DA VEIGA Jose	19
	Tr: LE ROY Claude		Tr: ALHINHO Alexandre	
12	MATUMDNA Zola	88	60	FERNANDES P. GOMES	10
17	FUAMBA Kinkela	70	89	BAPTISTA Joao	15
		92	MEDINA PIRES Gerson	21

Baba Yara, Kumasi
4-09-2005, 16:30, 45 000, Hicuburundi BDI

GHA 2   0 UGA

Essien [10], Amoah [15]

GHANA			UGANDA	
1	ADJEI Sammy		ONYANGO Denis	18
4	PANTSIL John		MASABA Simon	2
5	MENSAH John		BATABAIRE Timothy	4
6	PAPPOE Emmanuel		NSEREKO Stephen	5
7	LARYEA Kingston	53	KASULE Noah	7
8	ESSIEN Michael	63	MASSA Geofrey	11
10	APPIAH Stephen	67	MAWEJJE Tony	12
11	ISSAH Gabriel		LAWRENCE Segawa	13
14	AMOAH Matthew		MWESIGWA Andrew	14
15	ASAMOAH Frimpong	37	BALYEJJUSA Emmanuel	16
17	EDUSEI Daniel	55	SERUNKUMA Geofrey	17
	Tr: DUJKOVIC Ratomir		Tr: ABBAS Mohammed	
12	BOAKYE Isaac	37	67	KAYIZI Vincent	9
13	HAMZA Mohammed	53	55	MUWANGA Martin	10
18	YAHUZA Abubakar	63			

Estadio da Varzea, Praia
8-10-2005, 14:00, 6 500, Daami TUN

CPV 0   4 GHA

Asamoah [5], Muntari [35], Gyan [75]
Attram [87]

CAPE VERDE ISLANDS			GHANA	
1	MONTEIRO Jose		ADJEI Sammy	1
3	BARROS Jose		PANTSIL John	4
5	VEIGA Nelson		MENSAH John	5
7	BORGES Victor		PAPPOE Emmanuel	6
8	GOMES Domingos		LARYEA Kingston	7
9	GOMES Arlindo	68	ESSIEN Michael	8
10	GOMES Eduardo	72	ASAMOAH Frimpong	9
11	AGUIAR Claudio		APPIAH Stephen	10
15	NEVES Fernando	61	64	MUNTARI Sulley	11
16	MENDES Sandrom	46	83	AMOAH Matthew	14
19	DA VEIGA Jose		ISSAH Gabriel	17
	Tr: ALHINHO Alexandre		Tr: DUJKOVIC Ratomir	
4	DA MOURA Jose	68	64	GYAN Asamoah	3
13	BAPTISTA Joao	46	72	ATTRAM Godwin	12
17	EVORA Hugo	61	83	EDUSEI Daniel	15

Absa Park, Durban
8-10-2005, 17:00, 35 000, Mbera GAB

RSA 2 2 CGO

Zuma 2 5 52
Mputu 11, Nonda 44

SOUTH AFRICA			CONGO DR		
1	VONK Hans			KALEMBA Lukoki	1
4	MOKOENA Aaron			MUBIALA Kitambala	2
5	EVANS Philip			NSUMBU Dituabanza	3
6	MORRIS Nasief			MILAMBO Mutamba	6
7	KATZA Ricardo	82	82	MPUTU Mabi	8
10	PIENAAR Steven	72	72	KABAMBA Musasa	9
11	VAN HEERDEN Elrio	80	80	NONDA Shabani	10
12	PHIRI Alfred			MBAJO Kibemba	11
13	TAU Jimmy			LUBANZADJO Mayasistlua	13
15	ZUMA Sibusiso	69	69	ILONGO Ngasanya	14
18	ZWANE Arthur	16		KASONGO Dandu	15
	Tr: BAXTER Stuart			Tr: LE ROY Claude	
9	NHZOKO Nkosinathi	80	69	KAMUDIMBA Jean-Paul	4
14	NOMVETHE Siyabonga	16	82	MBALA Mbuta	5
			72	LELO Mbele	7

Nelson Mandela Stadium, Kampala
8-10-2005, 18:00, 1 433, Benouza ALG

UGA 2 2 BFA

Masaba 30, Serunkuma 71
Kebe 15, Rouamba 75

UGANDA			BURKINA FASO		
1	KALYESUBULA Hannington			SOULAMA Abdulaye	16
2	MASABA Simon			OUATTARA Moussa	2
4	BATABAIRE Timothy	65	65	KABORE Ibrahim	3
5	NSEREKO Stephen			TASSEMBEDO Soumaila	4
6	SEKAGYA Ibrahim			HABOUNA Bamogo	5
7	KASULE Noah			ROUAMBA Florent	6
10	OCHAMA Morley	87		KERE Mahamoudou	8
12	MAWEJJE Tony	52		DAGANO Moumouni	9
13	LAWRENCE Segawa			PANANDETIGUIRI Saidou	12
15	SERUNKUMA Geofrey			KEBE Yahia	15
20	MUBIRU Hassan	68	88	NIKIEMA Abdoul Aziz	17
	Tr: ABBAS Mohammed			Tr: BERNARD Simondi	
3	BONGOLE Anthony	87	88	MINOUNGOU Dieubonne	14
11	MASSA Geofrey	68	65	TOURE Amadou	18
16	BALYEJJUSA Emmanuel	52			

GROUP 3

El Meriekh, Omdurman
17-08-2005, 20:30, 12 000, Maillet SEY

SUD 1 0 BEN

Tambal 20

SUDAN			BENIN		
18	ABDALLA Elmuez			CHITOU Rachad	1
6	LADO Richard			CHITOU Charaf	2
7	ALADIN Ahmed			OLOU Oscar	3
8	KARAR Haitham			HOUNTONTO De Gaulle	4
10	TAMBAL Haytham	88		MOUSSA Traore	5
12	ABDALLA Bader			AMOUSSOU Sevi	10
13	EL BASHIR Hamouda	70	74	AGBESSI Coffi	12
14	BAKHEBT Omer			NASSIROU Youssouf	13
15	DAMAR Amir		54	OMOTOYOSSI Razak	15
16	ALI Khalid			TCHOMOGO Seidath	18
17	AGAB SIDO Faisal	82		COREA Jaures	19
	Tr: AHMED Mohamed			Tr: ATTUQUAYEFIO Cecil	
5	HADO Alaa Eldin	70	54	TOCLOMITI Stanislas	8
9	IBRAHIM Kamal	88	74	BABATUNDE Bello	20
11	AMARI Abdel	82			

11 June, Tripoli
2-09-2005, 19:00, 20 000, Pare BFA

LBY 0 0 SUD

LIBYA				SUDAN	
12	ALEJANDRO Ruben			ABDALLA Elmuez	18
3	SHUSHAN Naji			HADO Alaa Eldin	5
6	SULIMAN Marei			LADO Richard	6
7	ALHAMALI Akram	75	46	KATOUL Alaadin	7
9	MASLI Ahmed Frag	46	85	AHMED Haitham	8
10	OSMAN Ahmed			TAMBAL Haytham	10
15	KARA Nader		66	ABDALLA Bader	12
18	HAMADI Osama			BAKHEBT Omer	14
19	BOUBAKR Abdul Salam			DAMAR Amir	15
22	OSMAN Walid			ALI Khalid	16
23	AL SHIBANI Younus			AGAB SIDO Faisal	17
	Tr: LONCAREVIC Ilija			Tr: AHMED Mohamed	
13	ESNANI Mohamed	46	46	ABDEL Amar	3
24	ZUWAY Ahmed	75	85	KAMAL SAYED Ibrahim	9
			66	EL BASHIR Hamouda	13

Houphouet-Boigny, Abidjan
4-09-2005, 16:00, 34 500, Daami TUN

CIV 2 3 CMR

Drogba 2 38 47
Webo 3 30 47 85

COTE D'IVOIRE			CAMEROON		
16	GNANHOUAN Gerard			SOULEYMANOU Hamidou	16
3	BOKA Etienne			WOME Pierre	3
4	TOURE Abib			SONG Rigobert	4
5	ZOKORA Didier			GEREMI	8
7	GUEL Tchiressoa	45		ETOO Samuel	9
8	KALOU Bonadventure			MAKOUN Jean	12
11	DROGBA Didier			SAIDOU Alioum	14
13	ZORO Marc	57		WEBO Achille	15
15	DINDANE Aruna			DOUALA Rudolphe	18
17	DOMORAUD Cyrille			OLEMBE Salomon	20
18	TIENE Siaka	84		KALLA Raymond	21
	Tr: MICHEL Henri			Tr: JORGE Artur	
2	FAE Emerse	45		ATOUBA Thimothee	2
6	DEMEL Guy	84		MEYONG ZE Albert	11
12	MEITE Abdoulaye	57		DJEMBA DJEMBA Eric	19

Arab Contractors, Cairo
4-09-2005, 20:30, 5000, Buenkadila COD

EGY 4 1 BEN

Zaki 3 12 15 84, Hossam Mido 71
Sessegnon 60

EGYPT			BENIN		
1	EL SAYED Abdel			CHITOU Rachad	1
4	EL-NAHHAS Emad			CHITOU Charaf	2
5	EL SAQUA Abdel			OLOU Oscar	3
7	FATHI Ahmed	56		HOUNTONTO De Gaulle	4
8	ABD RABO Hosni			MOUSSA Traore	5
9	HOSSAM MIDO Ahmed	75		BALOGOUN Emmanuel	8
10	MOTAB Emad			OGUNBIYI Muri	11
11	SHAWKY Mohamed		40	NASSIROU Youssouf	13
13	EL SAYED Tarek	53		SEKA Noel	15
17	HASSAN Ahmed		83	SESSEGNON Stephane	17
19	ZAKI Amr			MAIGA Abou	18
	Tr: TARDELLI Marco			Tr: CODJO Edme	
14	GHALI Hossam	56	83	OROU Ibdoga	12
18	HOSNI Osama	75	40	COREA Jaures	19
21	RAGAB Abdalla	53			

Stade Omnisport, Yaoundé
8-10-2005, 16:00, 38 750, Coulibaly MLI

CMR 1 1 EGY

Douala [20]   Shawky [79]

CAMEROON			EGYPT	
16	SOULEYMANOU Hamidou		EL HADRY Essam	1
3	WOME Pierre	64	ABDEL WAHAB Mohamed	3
4	SONG Rigobert		EL SAQUA Abdel	5
5	KALLA Raymond		FATHI Ahmed	7
6	ANGBWA Benoit	82	ABD RABO Hosni	8
9	ETOO Samuel	83	MOTAB Emad	10
14	SAIDOU Alioum		SHAWKY Mohamed	11
15	WEBO Achille	63	GHALI Hossam	14
18	DOUALA Rudolphe	71	HASSAN Ahmed	17
20	OLEMBE Salomon		ZAKI Amr	19
21	MAKOUN Jean	85	GOMAA Wael	20
Tr: JORGE Artur			Tr: SHEHATA Hassan	
7	KOME Daniel	85 63	ZIDAN Mohamed	9
11	NDIEFI Pius	71 64	EL SAYED Tarek	13
13	FEUTCHINE Guy	82 83	ABOUTRIKA Mohamed	22

El Meriekh, Omdurman
8-10-2005, 18:00, 20 000, Damon RSA

SUD 1 3 CIV

Tambal [89]   Akale [22], Dindane 2 [51 73]

SUDAN			COTE D'IVOIRE	
1	MOHAMED Abu		BARRY Boubacar	1
5	HADO Alaa Eldin	90	AKALE Kanga	2
6	LADO Richard	68	EBOUE Emmanuel	3
7	HASSAN Hassan	57	TOURE Abib	4
8	KARAR Haitham		ZOKORA Alain	5
10	SAEED James	55	KOUASSI Blaise	6
12	ABDALLA Bader		DJIRE Aboulaye	7
14	BAKHEBT Omer		YAPI Gilles	10
15	DAMAR Amir		DROGBA Didier	11
16	ALI Khalid	60	MEITE Abdoulaye	12
17	AGAB Sido Faisal	79	DINDANE Aruna	15
Tr: AHMED Mohamed			Tr: MICHEL Henri	
2	ABDEL Elnazeir	57 90	KONE Arouna	9
11	AMARI Abdel	79 68	DOUMBIA Almamy	13
13	TAMBAL Haytham	55 60	SAIKA Tiene	18

Stade Rene Pleven, Cotonou
9-10-2005, 16:00, 1 880, Mususa ZIM

BEN 1 0 LBY

Chitou [60]

BENIN			LIBYA	
1	CHITOU Rachad		DE AGUSTINI Luis	12
2	CHITOU Charaf		SHUSHAN Naji	3
4	HOUNTONTO De Gaulle		AL HAMALI Akram	7
7	BOCO Romualde	57	GUMA KKARA Nader	15
8	TOCLOMITI Stanislas	57	SAFTAR Mahmud	17
11	MAIGA Abou	76	HAMADI Osama	18
12	SALOMON Michel	56 71	BOUBAKR Abdul Salam	19
15	ADJAMONSI Anicet		ELTREKI Emad	22
17	SESSEGNON Stephane		AL SHIBANI Younus	23
18	TCHOMOGO Seidath		ZUWAY Ahmed M.	24
19	OMOTOYOSSI Razak		OSMAN Walid	26
Tr: CODJO Edme			Tr: LONCAREVIC Ilija	
10	BALOGOUN Emmanuel	76 71	JALAL Walid	2
13	NASSIROU Youssouf	56 57	SLIL Abdunaser	8
		57	MASOUD Munir	20

SECOND PHASE GROUP 3	PL	W	D	L	F	A	PTS	CIV	CMR	EGY	LBY	SUD	BEN
1 Côte d'Ivoire	10	7	1	2	20	7	22		2-3	2-0	2-0	5-0	3-0
2 Cameroon	10	6	3	1	18	10	21	2-0		1-1	1-0	2-1	2-1
3 Egypt	10	5	2	3	26	15	17	1-2	3-2		4-1	6-1	4-1
4 Libya	10	3	3	4	8	10	12	0-0	0-0	2-1		0-0	4-1
5 Sudan	10	1	3	6	6	22	6	1-3	1-1	0-3	0-1		1-0
6 Benin	10	1	2	7	9	23	5	0-1	1-4	3-3	1-0	1-1	

Ghana qualified for the finals

GROUP 4

SECOND PHASE GROUP 4	PL	W	D	L	F	A	PTS	ANG	NGA	ZIM	GAB	ALG	RWA
1 Angola	10	6	3	1	12	6	21		1-0	1-0	3-0	2-1	1-0
2 Nigeria	10	6	3	1	21	7	21	1-1		5-1	2-0	1-0	2-0
3 Zimbabwe	10	4	3	3	13	14	15	2-0	0-3		1-0	1-1	3-1
4 Gabon	10	2	4	4	11	13	10	2-2	1-1	1-1		0-0	3-0
5 Algeria	10	1	5	4	8	15	8	0-0	2-5	2-2	0-3		1-0
6 Rwanda	10	1	2	7	6	16	5	0-1	1-1	0-2	3-1	1-1	

Angola qualified for the finals

National Stadium, Harare
4-09-2005, 15:00, 55 000, Ssegona UGA

ZIM 3 1 **RWA**

Kaondera [4], Mwaruwari [43], Rambanapasi [78]   Makonese OG [30]

ZIMBABWE			RWANDA	
1 MURAMBADORO Energy			NDORI Jean Claude	18
2 MPOFU Dumisani			NDIKUMANA Hamadi	3
3 NYANDORO Esrom			GASANA Philipe	4
4 MWANJALE Method			FRITZ Emeran	6
6 MAKONESE Zvenyika			MULISA Jimmy	7
9 MWARUWARI Beniamin			DUKUZE Abdul	8
10 KAONDERA Shingayi		81	ELIAS Joao Rafael	9
11 YOHANE Charles		75	BOBO Bola	10
12 NDLOVU Peter	79		UWIMANA Abdoul	11
15 SIBANDA Ronald	53		KIZITO Manfred	15
18 LUPAHLA Joel	88		YOSSAM Mikey	16
Tr: MHLAURI Charles			Tr: PALMGREN Roger	
5 CHANDIDA Francis	79	81	NDAYIRAGIJE Claude	14
8 RAMBANAPASI Ashley	53	75	LOMAMI John	17
17 BADZA Brian	88			

Cidadela, Luanda
4-09-2005, 15:00, 35 000, Coulibaly MLI

ANG 3 0 **GAB**

Mantorras [44], Ze Kalanga [89]   Nsi-Akoue OG [25]

ANGOLA			GABON	
1 JOAO PEREIRA			OVONO Didier	1
3 JAMBA			AMBOUROUET Georges	2
4 LEBO LEBO			OKOGO Saturnin	3
6 YAMBA ASHA			NSI-AKOUE Rene	5
7 FIGUEIREDO			MOUYOUMA Dieudonne	6
8 ANDRE			ZUE Theodore	7
9 MANTORRAS			NGUEMA Stephane	10
10 AKWA		76	LONDO Dieudonne	12
11 GILBERTO			DJISSIKADIE Alain	18
13 LOCO			MBANANGOYE Zita	21
14 MENDONCA		53	ANTCHOUET Henri	26
Tr: DE OLIVEIRA GONCALVES Luis			Tr: JAIRZINHO	
16 FLAVIO		76	AUBAME Catilina	11
17 ZE KALANGA		85	LARY Yannick	15
18 LOVE		53	AKIEREMY Georges	20

Ahmed Zabana, Oran
4-09-2005, 20:30, 11 000, Shelmani LBY

ALG 2 5 **NGA**

Yacef [48], Mansour [58]   Martins 3 [20p 88 90], Utaka [42] Obodo [81]

ALGERIA			NIGERIA	
1 MEZAIR Hicham			ENYEAMA Vincent	1
3 BELHADJ Nadir	70		YOBO Joseph	2
4 MADOUNI Ahmed	46		TAIWO Taye	3
5 MENIRI Mehdi			ODIAH Chidi	5
6 MANSOURI Yazid	85		ENAKAHIRE Joseph	6
7 YACEF Hanza		55	UTAKA John	7
10 SAIFI Rafik		89	MARTINS Obafemi	9
11 BOUTABOUT Mansour			AYILA Yussuf	13
15 ZIANI Karim	68	70	ORUMA Wilson	16
22 BOUGHERRA Madjid			OBODO Chris	18
23 BRAHAMI Mohamed		69	AYODELE Makinwa	19
Tr: MEZIANE Ighil			Tr: EGUAVOEN Augustine	
12 ARRACHE Salim	85	69	KANU Nwankwo	4
17 ACHIOU Hocine	46	89	AIYEGBENI Yakubu	8
19 MAMOUNI Maamar	70	70	OLOFINJANA Seyi	14

Abuja National Stadium, Abuja
8-10-2005, 15:00, 45 000, Pare BFA

NGA 5 1 **ZIM**

Martins 2 [35 75p], Ayila [62] Kanu [80p], Odemwingie [89]   Mwaruwari [70]

NIGERIA			ZIMBABWE	
1 ENYEAMA Vincent			MURAMBADORO Energy	1
2 YOBO Joseph			MWANJALE Method	4
3 TAIWO Taye			MAKONESE Zvenyika	6
5 ODIAH Chidi			GOMBAMI Honour	7
9 MARTINS Obafemi	86		RAMBANAPASI Ashley	8
13 AYILA Yussuf	79		MWARUWARI Beniamin	9
16 ORUMA Wilson		86	KAONDERA Shingayi	10
18 OBODO Chris			YOHANE Charles	11
19 AYODELE Makinwa	68	67	NDLOVU Peter	12
20 ODEMWINGIE Peter			MATOLA James	14
21 NWANERI Obinna		64	LUPAHLA Joel	18
Tr: EGUAVOEN Augustine			Tr: MHLAURI Charles	
4 KANU Nwankwo	68	86	MATAWU Clemence	3
14 OLOFINJANA Seyi	79	67	CHANDIDA Francis	5
17 AGHAHOWA Julius	86	64	BADZA Brian	17

Pierre Claver Divounguy, Port-Gentil
8-10-2005, 15:30, 37 000, Diouf SEN

GAB 0 0 **ALG**

GABON			ALGERIA	
1 BIDONGA Yann			MEZAIR Hicham	1
2 AMBOUROUET Georges			BOUGHERRA Madjid	2
5 MOUYOUMA Thierry	27		ZAOUI Samir	5
7 ZUE Theodore	62		ABDESSLAM Cherif	6
10 NGUEMA Stephane		89	YACEF Hanza	7
12 MOUNDOUNGA Rodrigue			KRAOUCHE Nasreddine	8
15 NSI-AKOUE Rene		76	SAIFI Rafik	10
16 MOUBAMBA Cedric			BOUTABOUT Mansour	11
20 MBANANGOYE Zita			BRAHAMI Mohamed	14
21 DJISSIKADIE Alain		88	METREF Hocine	18
26 ANTCHOUET Henri	56		ZIANI Antar	21
Tr: NZAMBA-NZAMBA Raphael			Tr: MEZIANE Ighil	
6 ONTSIGUI Nazaire	27 83	89	FENIER Hocine	15
8 MBOUSSY Waldi	62	88	BENATTIA Abdelmadjid	17
17 MVE-MINTSA Claude-Cedric	56	76	HADI-AISSA Lazhar	20

Stade Amahoro, Kigali
8-10-2005, 16:00, 25 000, Guezzaz MAR

RWA 0 1 **ANG**

Akwa [79]

RWANDA			ANGOLA	
18 NKUNZINGOMA Ramadhani			JOAO PEREIRA	1
3 NDIKUMANA Hamadi			JACINTO	2
6 GASERUKA Alua			JAMBA	3
7 MULISA Jimmy	68		LEBO LEBO	4
8 SIBOMANA Abdul			YAMBA ASHA	6
10 GATETE Jean Michel		68	FIGUEIREDO	7
11 KAREKEZI Olivier			ANDRE	8
13 NTAGANDA Elias			AKWA	10
14 SAID Abedi	78		GILBERTO	11
16 KABONGO Honore	70	55	MENDONCA	14
17 FRITZ Emeran		60	FLAVIO	16
Tr: PALMGREN Roger			Tr: DE OLIVEIRA GONCALVES Luis	
5 HATEGEKIMANA B'venture	78	60	MANTORRAS	9
9 BOBO Bola	68	55	MAURITO	15
12 UWIMANA Abdoul	70	68	ZE KALANGA	17

GROUP 5

Stade 7 Novembre, Tunis
17-08-2005, 20:45, 60 000, Evehe CMR

TUN 1 0 KEN

Guemamdia 2

#	TUNISIA					KENYA	#
1	BOUMNIJEL Ali					OTIENO Arnold	1
3	HAGUI Karim					MUKENYA Edwin	2
6	TRABELSI Hatem					ORODI Evans	3
9	GUEMAMDIA Haykel	62				AMANAKA Zablon Davies	5
10	GHODHBANE Kaies	59				SHABAN Adan	6
11	SANTOS	83				MULAMA Titus	7
12	MNARI Jawhar					ABDALLA Ali Mohamed	8
13	BOUAZIZI Riadh					SIRENGO Mark	9
14	CHADLI Adel					MARIAGA Macdonald	10
15	JAIDI Radhi			62		MWALALA Bernard	15
20	CLAYTON					MAMBO Robert	17
	Tr: LEMERRE Roger					Tr: KHERI Mohammed	
17	JOMAA Issam	59	62	62		BARASA John	11
18	BENACHOUR Slim	62					
24	ZITOUNI Ali	83					

Moi International Sports Centre, Nairobi
3-09-2005, 16:00, Sowe GAM

KEN 0 2 TUN

Guemamdia 2, Jomaa 85

#	KENYA					TUNISIA	#
1	OTIENO Arnold					BOUMNIJEL Ali	1
2	MUKENYA Edwin	46				HAGUI Karim	3
4	OTIENO Musa					TRABELSI Hatem	6
5	AMANAKA Zablon Davies			63		NAMOUCHI Hamed	8
6	ANTHONY Ivan			88		GUEMAMDIA Haykel	9
7	MULAMA Titus					GHODHBANE Kaies	10
8	MOHAMMED Ali	46				BOUAZIZI Riadh	13
10	MARIAGA Macdonald			72		BEN SAADA Chaouki	14
11	MARUTI Bonaventure	74				BENACHOUR Slim	18
12	GITAU Moses	50				CLAYTON	20
17	MAMBO Robert					SAIDI Karim	21
	Tr: KHERI Mohammed					Tr: LEMERRE Roger	
9	SIRENGO Mark	74		88		BENWANNES Radhouene	2
15	MWALALA Bernard	46		63		MHADHEBI Imed	7
19	OWINO Julius	50		72		JOMAA Issam	17

Prince Moulay Abdellah, Rabat
3-09-2005, 20:00, 25 000, Benouza ALG

MAR 1 0 BOT

El Karkouri 56

#	MOROCCO					BOTSWANA	#
1	LAMYAGHRI Nadir					TSHELAMETSI Kagiso	1
2	REGRAGUI Hoalid					MOTLHABANE Khumo	3
5	EL KARKOURI Talal					MOGALADI Michael	4
8	BENASKAR Aziz			80		GABOLWELWE Nelson	6
13	KHARJA Houssine	66				MOTLHABANKWE Tshepo	8
14	AHNAFOUF Abdelaziz	54				MOATLHAPING Moemedi	10
15	SAFRI Youssef			89		SELOLWANE Diphetogo	11
16	MOKHTARI Youssef	83				MOLWANTWA Tshepiso	12
17	BOUKHARI Nouredine					AMOS Ernest	14
20	HADJI Youssef			59		GABANAKGOSI Seabo	15
21	EL KADDOURI Badr					THUMA Mompati	18
	Tr: BADOU Zaki					Tr: JELUSIC Veselin	
9	BOU Saboun Abdelali	54	59	59		LETSHOLATHEBE Ndiapo	2
10	SEKTIOUI Tarik	66	80	80		MOTHUSI Tebogo	7
11	EL YAAGOUBI Mohammed	83	89	89		MATSHAMEKO Alex	9

Stade du 28 septembre, Conakry
4-09-2005, 16:30, 2 518, Mana NGA

GUI 3 1 MWI

Feindouno 12, Kaba 36
Bangoura.S 67

Mkandawire 37

#	GUINEA					MALAWI	#
16	CAMARA Kemoko					SANUDI Swadic	1
2	FEINDOUNO Pascal	81				KONDOWE Fisher	2
3	CAMARA Ibrahima					CHAVULA Moses	3
4	JABI Daouda					CHILAPONOWA James	4
5	BALDE Dianbobo					NDHOLVU Wisdom	5
6	THIAM Pablo	15				MPONDA Peter	7
7	MANSARE Fode	83				ZAKAZAKA Jimmy	9
14	CAMARA Ousmane					MKANDAWIRE Noel	10
15	KALABANE Oumar					KAMANGA Allan	13
19	KABA Diawara	60				KAMWENDO Joseph	14
20	BANGOURA Ibrahima	86				NGAMBI Robert	15
	Tr: NEVEU Patrice					Tr: CHIMODZI Young	
9	BANGOURA Sambegou	60	81	81		MBISA Tendai	6
17	DIALLO Mamadou	15	83	83		WADAEWA Peter	17
21	CORRIA Victor	86					

Kamuzu, Blantyre
8-10-2005, 15:00, 12 000, Codjia BEN

MWI 3 0 KEN

Zakazaka 6, Mkandawire 2 49 61

#	MALAWI					KENYA	#
1	KAPUZA Semion					ONYISO Francis	16
2	KONDOWE Fisher	30				SHABAN Adan	6
3	MSOWOYA Maupo					ORODI Evans	5
4	CHILAPONOWA James	59		66		SIMIYU Sammy Wanyonyi	7
5	NDHOLVU Wisdom	57				ECHESA Hillary	8
7	MPONDA Peter					SIRENGO Mark	9
9	ZAKAZAKA Jimmy	77				ABDURAZAK Hussein	10
10	KAMWENDO Joseph					OCHIENG Edgar	12
12	KAFOTEKA Elvis					OWINO George	13
14	MKANDAWIRE Noel	92				OWINO Julius	14
15	NGAMBI Robert	87				MWALALA Bernard	15
	Tr: CHIMODZI Young					Tr: KHERI Mohammed	
6	KAMANGA Allan	92	30	30		HUSSEIN Mohamed	3
11	WADAEWA Peter	77	66	66		TIEGO Collins	4
13	CHIPATALA Emmanuel	59	57	57		NYONGESA Levy	18

National Stadium, Gaborone
8-10-2005, 16:00, 16 800, Sowe GAM

BOT 1 2 GUI

Molwantwa 35

Bangoura.O 2 73 76

#	BOTSWANA					GUINEA	#
1	TSHELAMETSI Kagiso					CAMARA Kemoko	22
3	THUMA Mompati			45		CAMARA Ibrahima	3
4	MOGALADI Michael					JABI Daouda	4
8	MOTLHABANKWE Tshepo					BALDE Dianbobo	5
10	MOATLHAPING Moemedi	86	84			MANSARE Fode	7
11	SELOLWANE Diphetogo					SYLLA Kanfory	8
12	MOLWANTWA Tshepiso					SYLLA Abdoulkarim	10
14	AMOS Ernest			45		YOULA Souleymane	11
15	GABANAKGOSI Seabo					CAMARA Ousmane	14
17	MATSHAMEKO Alex	82				KABA Hamadi	18
18	GABONAMONG Mogogi					KABA Diawara	19
	Tr: JELUSIC Veselin					Tr: NEVEU Patrice	
5	NTSHINGANE Masego	82	84	84		CISSE Morlaye	12
7	MOTHUSI Tebogo	86	45	45		BANGOURA Ousmane	13
				45		BANGOURA Ibrahima	15

Stade 7 Novembre, Tunis
8-10-2005, 20:45, 60 000, Abd El Fatah EGY

TUN   2   2   MAR

Clayton [18], Chadli [69]   Chamarh [3], El Karkouri [42]

TUNISIA				MOROCCO
1	BOUMNIJEL Ali			LAMYAGHRI Nadir 22
3	HAGUI Karim			REGRAGUI Hoalid 2
5	JAZIRI Ziad			OUADDOU Abdeslem 4
6	TRABELSI Hatem			El KARKOURI Talal 5
8	NAMOUCHI Hamed		72	BOUKHARI Nouredine 8
11	SANTOS	68		KHARJA Houssine 13
13	BOUAZIZI Riadh			BENASKAR Aziz 14
14	CHADLI Adel		58	SAFRI Youssef 15
15	JAIDI Radhi			CHAMARH Marouane 17
18	BENACHOUR Slim	63	88	HADJI Youssef 20
20	CLAYTON	51		EL KADDOURI Badr 21
	Tr: LEMERRE Roger			Tr: BADOU Zaki
4	YAHIA Alaeddine	51	88	BOU SABOUN Abdelali 9
9	GUEMAMDIA Haykel	68	72	EL YAAGOUBI Mohammed 11
12	MNARI Jawhar	63	58	HDIOUAD Mourad 18

SECOND PHASE GROUP 5	PL	W	D	L	F	A	PTS	TUN	MAR	GUI	KEN	BOT	MWI
1	Tunisia	10	6	3	1	25	9	21		2-2	2-0	1-0	4-1	7-0
2	Morocco	10	5	5	0	17	7	20	1-1		1-0	5-1	1-0	4-1
3	Guinea	10	5	2	3	15	10	17	2-1	1-1		1-0	4-0	3-1
4	Kenya	10	3	1	6	8	17	10	0-2	0-0	2-1		1-0	3-2
5	Botswana	10	3	0	7	10	18	9	1-3	0-1	1-2	2-1		2-0
6	Malawi	10	1	3	6	12	26	6	2-2	1-1	1-1	3-0	1-3	

Tunisia qualified for the finals

QUALIFYING MATCHES PLAYED IN CENTRAL AMERICA, NORTH AMERICA AND THE CARIBBEAN

First Preliminary Round				Second Preliminary Round				First Group Stage			Final Group Stage	

First Preliminary Round

Grenada	GRN	5	3
Guyana	GUY	0	1
Bermuda	BER	13	7
Montserrat	MSR	0	0
Haiti	HAI	5	2
Turks and Caicos Isl.	TCA	0	0
British Virgin Islands	VGB	0	0
St Lucia	LCA	1	9
Cayman Islands	CAY	1	0
Cuba	CUB	2	3
Aruba	ARU	1	1
Surinam	SUR	2	8
Antigua and Barbuda	ATG	2	0
Netherlands Antilles	ANT	0	3
Dominica	DMA	1	3
Bahamas	BAH	1	1
US Virgin Islands	VIR	0	0
St Kitts and Nevis	SKN	4	7
Dominican Republic	DOM	0	6
Anguilla	AIA	0	0

Second Preliminary Round

Grenada	GRN	3	3
USA	USA	0	2
Bermuda	BER	1	2
El Salvador	SLV	2	2
Haiti	HAI	1	0
Jamaica	JAM	1	3
St Lucia	LCA	0	0
Panama	PAN	4	3
Cuba	CUB	2	1
Costa Rica	CRC	2	1
Surinam	SUR	1	1
Guatemala	GUA	1	3
Netherlands Antilles	ANT	1	0
Honduras	HON	2	4
Canada	CAN	4	4
Belize	BLZ	0	0
Dominica	DMA	0	0
Mexico	MEX	10	8
St Kitts and Nevis	SKN	2	3
Barbados	BRB	0	2
Dominican Republic	DOM	0	0
Trinidad & Tobago	TRI	2	4
Nicaragua	NCA	2	1
St Vincent/Grenadines	VIN	2	4

First Group Stage

Group 1	Pts
USA	12
Panama	8
Jamaica	7
El Salvador	4

Group 2	Pts
Costa Rica	10
Guatemala	10
Honduras	7
Canada	5

Group 3	Pts
Mexico	18
Trinidad & Tobago	12
St Vincent/Grenadines	6
St Kitts and Nevis	0

Final Group Stage

Final Group	Pts
USA	22
Mexico	22
Costa Rica	16
Trinidad & Tobago	13
Guatemala	11
Panama	2

The top three from the final group stage qualified for the finals in Germany. The fourth-placed team, Trinidad and Tobago qualified after a play-off against an Asian side, Bahrain. The preliminary rounds consisted of 12 groups, 10 of which had three teams. The seeded team in each group received a bye into the second preliminary round and faced the winners from the first preliminary round.

Details of FIFA World Cup™ qualifiers played in North, Central America and the Caribbean before August 2005 can be found in the *Almanack of World Football 2006* on pages 128-146

Rentschler, Hartford
17-08-2005, 20:00, 25 500, Rodriguez MEX

USA 1 0 TRI

McBride 2

USA				TRINIDAD & TOBAGO	
18	KELLER Kasey			JACK Kelvin	21
3	BERHALTER Gregg		44	CHARLES Atiba	2
4	ALBRIGHT Chris			JOHN Avery	3
5	O BRIEN John	46		ANDREWS Marvin	4
7	LEWIS Eddie		40	LAWRENCE Dennis	6
10	REYNA Claudio			BIRCHALL Christopher	7
15	CONVEY Bobby	88		WHITLEY Aurtis	9
19	RALSTON Steve	71	54	JOHN Stern	14
20	MC BRIDE Brian	82		SPANN Silvio	16
21	DONOVAN Landon			YORKE Dwight	19
22	ONYEWU Oguchi		44	SAMUEL Colin	20
	Tr: ARENA Bruce			Tr: BEENHAKER Leo	
9	QUARANTA Santino	71	44	SANCHO Brent	5
13	TWELLMAN Taylor	82	44	SEALY Scott	8
14	ARMAS Chris	46	54	JONES Kenwyne	15

Mateo Flores, Guatemala City
17-08-2005, 20:00, 24 000, Sibrian SLV

GUA 2 1 PAN

Romero 93, Baloy OG 70   Dely 19

GUATEMALA				PANAMA	
1	KLEE Miguel			PENEDO Jaime	1
3	MELGAR Pablo			RIVERA Carlos	2
8	ROMERO Gonzalo		72	MORENO Luis	3
9	GARCIA Freddy			TORRES Jose Anthony	4
12	FIGUEROA Carlos	46		BALOY Felipe	5
14	PONCIANO Elmer	60		DELY VALDES Jorge	7
15	PLATA Juan Carlos	77		BLANCO Alberto	8
16	GIRON Julio	67	47	MEDINA Julio	10
18	PONCIANO Selvin			PHILLIPS Ricardo	15
20	RUIZ Carlos		76	TEJADA Luis	18
26	SANABRIA Angel			MITRE Engin	20
	Tr: MARADIAGA Ramon			Tr: HERNANDEZ Jose	
7	THOMPSON Fredy	46	76	BROWN Roberto	11
10	VILLATORO Roberto	67	72	TORRES Roman	14
24	DAVILA Maynor	77	60	RODRIGUEZ Luis	21

Azteca, Mexico City
17-08-2005, 21:00, 27 000, Pineda HON

MEX 2 0 CRC

Borgetti 63, Fonseca 86

MEXICO				COSTA RICA	
1	SANCHEZ Oswaldo			PORRAS Jose	18
2	RODRIGUEZ Francisco			DRUMMOND Jervis	2
3	SALCIDO Carlos			UMANA Michael	4
4	MARQUEZ Rafael	60		MARTINEZ Gilberto	5
5	OSORIO Ricardo			FONSECA Danny	6
6	TORRADO Gerardo	46		WANCHOPE Paulo	9
7	ZINHA	67		CENTENO Walter	10
8	PARDO Pavel			GOMEZ Ronald	11
9	BORGETTI Jared			GONZALEZ Leonardo	12
17	FONSECA Jose			CORDERO Victor	13
20	GALINDO Gerardo			BOLANOS Christian	16
	Tr: LA VOLPE Ricardo			Tr: GUIMARAES Alexandre	
10	BRAVO Omar	67	75	ROJAS Oscar	7
11	MORALES Ramon	46	69	SOTO Jafet	22
14	PINEDA Gonzaio	60			

Hasely Crawford Stadium, Port of Spain
3-09-2005, 16:30, 15 000, Archundia MEX

TRI 3 2 GUA

Latapy 48, John 2 85 86   Andrews OG 3, Romero 61

TRINIDAD & TOBAGO				GUATEMALA	
21	JACK Kelvin			KLEE Miguel	1
3	JOHN Avery			CABRERA Gustavo	6
4	ANDREWS Marvin			THOMPSON Fredy	7
5	SANCHO Brent			ROMERO Gonzalo	8
7	BIRCHALL Christopher	46	56	GARCIA Freddy	9
9	WHITLEY Aurtis			RAMIREZ Guillermo	11
10	LATAPY Russel			PONCIANO Elmer	14
11	EDWARDS Carlos	73		GIRON Julio	16
14	JOHN Stern			PONCIANO Selvin	18
16	SPANN Silvio			RUIZ Carlos	20
19	YORKE Dwight			SANABRIA Angel	26
	Tr: BEENHAKER Leo			Tr: MARADIAGA Ramon	
8	SEALY Scott		56	FIGUEROA Carlos	12
13	COX Ian	88			
20	SCOTLAND Jason	88 46			

Columbus Crew Stadium, Columbus
3-09-2005, 19:30, 24 685, Batres GUA

USA 2 0 MEX

Ralston 53, Beasley 57

USA				MEXICO	
18	KELLER Kasey			SANCHEZ Oswaldo	1
2	HEJDUK Frankie		59	RODRIGUEZ Francisco	2
3	BERHALTER Gregg			SALCIDO Carlos	3
7	LEWIS Eddie			MARQUEZ Rafael	4
10	REYNA Claudio			DAVINO Duilio	5
14	ARMAS Chris			TORRADO Gerardo	6
17	BEASLEY DaMarcus	69		ZINHA	7
19	RALSTON Steve	78		BORGETTI Jared	9
20	MC BRIDE Brian	90		MORALES Ramon	11
21	DONOVAN Landon	72	58	FONSECA Jose	17
22	ONYEWU Oguchi			GALINDO Gerardo	20
	Tr: ARENA Bruce			Tr: LA VOLPE Ricardo	
11	CUNNINGHAM Jeff	90	69	BRAVO Omar	10
23	QUARANTA Santino	78	59	MENDEZ Mario	16
25	MASTROENI Pablo	72	58	MEDINA Alberto	22

Estadio Rommel Fernandez, Panama City
3-09-2005, 20:00, 21 000, Stott USA

PAN 1 3 CRC

Tejada 90   Saborio 44, Centeno 51, Gomez 73

PANAMA				COSTA RICA	
1	PENEDO Jaime			PORRAS Jose	18
2	RIVERA Carlos			DRUMMOND Jervis	2
3	MORENO Luis			MARIN Luis	3
4	TORRES Jose Anthony			MARTINEZ Gilberto	5
5	BALOY Felipe		40	BOLANOS Christian	7
6	GOMEZ Gabriel			SOLIS Mauricio	8
7	DELY VALDES Jorge			CENTENO Walter	10
8	BLANCO Alberto			GOMEZ Ronald	11
15	PHILLIPS Ricardo			MILLER Roy	16
18	TEJADA Luis		73	SABORIO Alvaro	20
21	RODRIGUEZ Luis	61	65	SOTO Jafet	22
	Tr: HERNANDEZ Jose			Tr: GUIMARAES Alexandre	
9	DELY VALDESJulio	61	40	UMANA Michael	4
			65	FONSECA Danny	6
			73	PARKS Winston	21

Ricardo Saprissa, San Jose
7-09-2005, 20:00, 17 000, Batres GUA

CRC 2 0 TRI

Saborio [15], Centeno [50]

COSTA RICA				TRINIDAD & TOBAGO	
18 PORRAS Jose				JACK Kelvin	21
2 DRUMMOND Jervis				ANDREWS Marvin	4
3 MARIN Luis				LAWRENCE Dennis	6
5 MARTINEZ Gilberto				BIRCHALL Christopher	7
8 SOLIS Mauricio		59		WHITLEY Aurtis	9
9 WANCHOPE Paulo				LATAPY Russel	10
10 CENTENO Walter				EDWARDS Carlos	11
11 GOMEZ Ronald				COX Ian	13
16 MILLER Roy	71			JOHN Stern	14
17 SOLIS Alonso	56	70		SPANN Silvio	16
19 SABORIO Alvaro	63			YORKE Dwight	19
Tr: MENDEZ Cesar				Tr: BEENHAKER Leo	
4 UMANA Michael	71	70		SEALY Scott	8
7 BOLANOS Christian	56	59		SCOTLAND Jason	20
20 SEQUEIRA Douglas	63				

Mateo Flores, Guatemala City
7-09-2005, 20:00, 27 000, Rodriguez MEX

GUA 0 0 USA

GUATEMALA				USA	
1 KLEE Miguel				HAHNEMANN Marcus	1
3 MELGAR Pablo				VANNEY Greg	3
7 THOMPSON Fredy	70			ALBRIGHT Chris	6
8 ROMERO Gonzalo		87		DEMPSEY Clint	8
11 RAMIREZ Guillermo	45	57		CUNNINGHAM Jeff	11
14 PONCIANO Elmer				CONRAD James	12
15 PLATA Juan Carlos	77			TWELLMAN Taylor	13
16 GIRON Julio				CONVEY Bobby	15
18 PONICIANO Selvin				MARSHALL Chad	22
23 ACEVEDO Mario		64		QUARANTA Santino	23
26 SANABRIA Angel				MASTROENI Pablo	25
Tr: MARADIAGA Ramon				Tr: ARENA Bruce	
10 VILLATORO Roberto	77	57		JOHNSON Ed	9
12 FIGUEROA Carlos	70	64		DONOVAN Landon	10
24 DAVILA Maynor	45	87		RALSTON Steve	19

Azteca, Mexico City
7-09-2005, 21:00, 40 000, Hall USA

MEX 5 0 PAN

Perez [31], Marquez [54], Borgetti [59]
Fonseca [75], Pardo [76]

MEXICO				PANAMA	
1 SANCHEZ Oswaldo				PENEDO Jaime	1
2 RODRIGUEZ Francisco				RIVERA Carlos	2
3 SALCIDO Carlos				TORRES Jose Anthony	4
4 MARQUEZ Rafael		82		BALOY Felipe	5
7 ZINHA	71			GOMEZ Gabriel	6
8 PARDO Pavel		69		DELY VALDES Jorge	7
9 BORGETTI Jared		83		MEDINA Julio	10
11 MORALES Ramon	46	78		PHILLIPS Ricardo	15
14 PINEDA Gonzalo				AVILA Gustavo	19
23 PEREZ Luis	69	46		RODRIGUEZ Luis	21
Tr: LA VOLPE Ricardo				Tr: HERNANDEZ Jose	
15 MORALES Carlos	69	46		DELY VALDES Julio	9
17 FONSECA Jose	71	69		BROWN Roberto	11
22 MEDINA Alberto	46	83		GUARDIA Ubaldo	16

Ricardo Saprissa, San Jose
8-10-2005, 19:00, 18 000, Archundia MEX

CRC 3 0 USA

Wanchope [34], Hernandez 2 [60] [88]

COSTA RICA				USA	
18 PORRAS Jose				HOWARD Tim	1
2 DRUMMOND Jervis		75		BOCANEGRA Carlos	4
3 MARIN Luis		61		ALBRIGHT Chris	5
5 MARTINEZ Gilberto				LEWIS Eddie	7
8 SOLIS Mauricio	59			CHING Brian	9
9 WANCHOPE Paulo	76			CONVEY Bobby	15
10 CENTENO Walter				BEASLEY Da Marcus	17
11 GOMEZ Ronald				TWELLMAN Taylor	20
12 GONZALEZ Leonardo				ONYEWU Oguchi	22
15 WALLACE Harold				POPE Eddie	23
19 SABORIO Alvaro	59			MASTROENI Pablo	25
Tr: GUIMARAES Alexandre				Tr: ARENA Bruce	
16 HERNANDEZ Carlos	59	75		MARTINO Kyle	10
20 SEQUEIRA Douglas	59	61		QUARANTA Santino	21
21 PARKS Winston	76				

Potosino Alfonso Lastras, San Luis Potosi
8-10-2005, 20:00, 30 000, Prendergast JAM

MEX 5 2 GUA

Franco [19], Fonseca 4 [48] [51] [62] [66]

MEXICO				GUATEMALA	
1 CORONA Jose				KLEE Miguel	1
2 RODRIGUEZ Francisco				MELGAR Pablo	3
4 OSORIO Ricardo		78		THOMPSON Fredy	7
5 LOPEZ Israel				ROMERO Gonzalo	8
6 TORRADO Gerardo	55			RAMIREZ Guillermo	11
10 FRANCO Guillermo				PONCIANO Elmer	14
14 PINEDA Gonzalo	64			GIRON Julio	16
16 MENDEZ Mario				PONICIANO Selvin	18
17 FONSECA Jose		55		RODRIGUEZ Mario	19
19 LOZANO Jaime	58	74		RUIZ Carlos	20
23 PEREZ Luis				SANABRIA Angel	26
Tr: LA VOLPE Ricardo				Tr: MARADIAGA Ramon	
3 HUIQUI Joel	58	74		CABRERA Gustavo	6
7 ROJAS Oscar	55	78		GARCIA Freddy	9
18 MORALES Carlos	64	55		ACEVEDO Mario	23

Estadio Rommel Fernandez, Panama City
8-10-2005, 20:00, 1 000, Navarro CAN

PAN 0 1 TRI

John [61]

PANAMA				TRINIDAD & TOBAGO	
1 PENEDO Jaime				JACK Kelvin	21
2 SOLANILLA Joel				JOHN Avery	3
3 MORENO Luis				ANDREWS Marvin	4
8 GUARDIA Ubaldo				LAWRENCE Dennis	6
5 TORRES Roman				BIRCHALL Christopher	7
6 GOMEZ Gabriel		87		LATAPY Russel	10
8 BROWN James	85			EDWARDS Carlos	11
10 MEDINA Julio				JOHN Stern	14
11 LOMBARDO Angel				SPANN Silvio	16
18 BASILE Anthony	67	61		THEOBALD Densil	18
19 TORRES Gabriel	77			YORKE Dwight	19
Tr: HERNANDEZ Jose				Tr: BEENHAKER Leo	
7 DELY VALDES Jorge	77	87		WHITLEY Aurtis	9
13 OLIVARES Miguel	85	61		JONES Kenwyne	15
17 AGUILAR Edwin	67				

Mateo Flores, Guatemala City
12-10-2005, 18:00, 23 912, Hall USA

GUA 3 1 CRC

Ponciano 2, Garcia 16, Ruiz 30 | Myre 60

GUATEMALA				COSTA RICA		
1	KLEE Miguel			MESEN Alvaro	1	
3	MELGAR Pablo		45	MARIN Luis	3	
7	THOMPSON Fredy			UMANA Michael	4	
8	ROMERO Gonzalo			FONSECA Danny	6	
9	GARCIA Freddy	72		SOTO Jafet	10	
14	PONCIANO Elmer		77	VIQUEZ Mario	12	
16	GIRON Julio			BADILLA Cristian	16	
18	PONCIANO Selvin			MYRE Roy	17	
20	RUIZ Carlos	88	66	SABORIO Alvaro	19	
23	ACEVEDO Mario	89		SEQUEIRA Douglas	20	
26	SANABRIA Angel			PARKS Winston	21	
	Tr: MARADIAGA Ramon			Tr: GUIMARAES Alexandre		
11	RAMIREZ Guillermo	72	77	SOLIS Alonso	7	77
15	PLATA Juan Carlos	88	66	DIAZ Minor	14	66
17	PEZZAROSSI Dwight	89	45	AZOFEIFA Randall	22	45

Hasely Crawford Stadium, Port of Spain
12-10-2005, 20:00, 23 000, Pineda HON

TRI 2 1 MEX

John 2 43 69 | Lozano 38

TRINIDAD & TOBAGO				MEXICO		
21	JACK Kelvin	46		CORONA Jose	1	
3	JOHN Avery			RODRIGUEZ Francisco	2	
4	ANDREWS Marvin			HUIQUI Joel	3	67
5	GRAY Cyd			LOPEZ Israel	5	
6	LAWRENCE Dennis			ROJAS Oscar	7	
7	BIRCHALL Christopher		67	FRANCO Guillermo	10	74
9	WHITLEY Aurtis	80		SANCHEZ Hugo	15	
10	LATAPY Russel			FONSECA Jose	17	
11	EDWARDS Carlos			MORALES Carlos	18	
14	JOHN Stern			LOZANO Jaime	19	
19	YORKE Dwight		46	PEREZ Luis	23	
	Tr: BEENHAKER Leo			Tr: LA VOLPE Ricardo		
1	HISLOP Shaka	46	46	BRISENO Omar	11	
18	THEOBALD Densil	80	80	MENDEZ Mario	16	67
				RODRIGUEZ Juan Pablo	20	74

Gillette Stadium, Boston
12-10-2005, 20:07, 2 500, Alcala MEX

USA 2 0 PAN

Martino 51, Twellman 57

USA			PANAMA		
1	HOWARD Tim		PENEDO Jaime	1	
2	DEMPSEY Clint		SOLANILLA Joel	2	
5	ALBRIGHT Chris		MORENO Luis	3	
8	SPECTOR Jonathan		GUARDIA Ubaldo	4	
10	MARTINO Kyle	67	BALOY Felipe	5	
12	CALIFF Danny		GOMEZ Gabriel	6	
16	CARROLL Brian		DELY VALDES Jorge	7	
19	MAPP Justin	57	BROWN James	8	61
20	TWELLMAN Taylor	74	DELY VALDES Julio	9	
21	QUARANTA Santino		LOMBARDO Angel	10	61
22	MARSHALL Chad		GALLARDO Luis	11	61
	Tr: ARENA Bruce		Tr: HERNANDEZ Jose		
9	CHING Brian	74	TORRES Roman	13	61
13	CLARK Ricardo	67	BASILE Anthony	18	61
14	RALSTON Steve	57	TORRES Gabriel	19	61

	FINAL GROUP	PL	W	D	L	F	A	PTS	USA	MEX	CRC	TRI	GUA	PAN
1	USA	10	7	1	2	16	6	22		2-0	3-0	1-0	2-0	2-0
2	Mexico	10	7	1	2	22	9	22	2-0		2-0	2-0	5-2	5-0
3	Costa Rica	10	5	1	4	15	14	16	3-0	1-2		2-0	3-2	2-1
4	Trinidad and Tobago	10	4	1	5	10	15	13	1-2	2-1	0-0		3-2	2-0
5	Guatemala	10	3	2	5	16	18	11	0-0	0-2	3-1	5-1		2-1
6	Panama	10	0	2	8	4	21	2	0-3	1-1	1-3	0-1	0-0	

USA, Mexico and Costa Rica qualified for the finals • Trinidad and Tobago qualified for a play-off against Bahrain

QUALIFYING MATCHES PLAYED IN SOUTH AMERICA

Qualification for the 2006 FIFA World Cup™ from South America involved all 10 members of CONMEBOL playing each other home and away. The top four teams in the group qualified automatically whilst the fifth team had to play off against the winners from Oceania.

Hernando Siles, La Paz
3-09-2005, 15:00, 8 434, Baldassi ARG

BOL 1 2 ECU

Vaca 41 / Delgado 2 8 49

#	BOLIVIA	m	m		#	ECUADOR	m
1	ARIAS Carlos				12	MORA Cristian	
3	JAUREGUI Sergio				3	HURTADO Ivan	
4	ALVAREZ Lorgio				4	DE LA CRUZ Ulises	
8	GOMEZ Jesus		45		5	VALENCIA Luis	45
9	MENDEZ Limberg	54			6	AMBROSSI Paul	
12	FLORES Walter	66			8	MENDEZ Edison	
15	VACA Doyle				11	DELGADO Agustin	
16	RALDES Ronald		89		15	AYOVI Marlon	89
20	BOTERO Joaquin				17	ESPINOZA Giovanny	
24	GALINDO Gonzalo		63		18	REASCO Neicer	63
26	PACHI Danner	54			20	TENORIO Edwin	
	Tr: MESA Ovidio					Tr: SUAREZ Luis	
10	VACA Joselito	54	45		7	SALAS Franklin	45
11	PAZ Lider	54	63		10	LARA Christian	63
17	ARCE Juan Carlos	66	89		14	CASTILLO Segundo	89

Defensores del Chaco, Asuncion
3-09-2005, 17:00, 32 000, Simon BRA

PAR 1 0 ARG

Santa Cruz 14

#	PARAGUAY	m	m		ARGENTINA	#
1	VILLAR Justo				ABBONDANZIERI Roberto	1
2	NUNEZ Jorge				AYALA Roberto	2
4	GAMARRA Carlos				SORIN Juan	3
5	CACERES Julio Cesar				COLOCCINI Fabricio	4
8	BARRETO Edgar				HEINZE Gabriel	6
10	ACUNA Roberto				ZABALETA Pablo	7
13	PAREDES Carlos	71			RIQUELME Juan	8
18	HAEDO VALDEZ Nelson				FARIAS Ernesto	9
19	DOS SANTOS Julio	87	80		DELGADO Cesar	11
21	CANIZA Denis				GONZALEZ Luis	16
24	SANTA CRUZ Roque	45			CAMBIASSO Esteban	19
	Tr: RUIZ Anibal				Tr: PEKERMAN Jose	
9	CABANAS Salvador	45	71		D ALESSANDRO Andres	15
23	CUEVAS Nelson	87	80		MESSI Lionel	18

Pachenricho Romero, Maracaibo
3-09-2005, 19:00, 6 000, Rezende BRA

VEN 4 1 PER

Maldonado 17, Arango 68 / Farfan 63
Torrealba 2 73 79

#	VENEZUELA	m	m		m	PERU	#
1	ANGELUCCI Gilberto					DELGADO Erick	1
6	CICHERO Alejandro					VILLALTA Miguel	2
8	VERA Luis				45	VILCHEZ Walter	6
9	MALDONADO Giancarlos	72				VARGAS Juan	7
10	URDANETA Gabriel					GUERRERO Jose	9
11	PAEZ Ricardo				76	COMINGES Juan	10
13	VIELMA Leonel					HUAMAN Jorge	15
16	MORAN Ruberth	58				GUADALUPE Luis	16
17	ROJAS Jorge					FARFAN Jefferson	17
18	ARANGO Juan	81			91	LA ROSA Juan Carlos	20
20	GONZALEZ Hector					PEREZ Edwin	25
	Tr: PAEZ Richard					Tr: TERNERO Freddy	
14	JIMENEZ Leopoldo	81	91		91 76	MOSTTO Miguel	11
15	TORREALBA Jose	72			45	ALVA NIEZEN Piero	23
19	GONZALEZ Andree	58					

Estadio Mane Garrincha, Brasilia
4-09-2005, 16:00, 39 000, Amarilla PAR

BRA 5 0 CHI

Juan 11, Robinho 21
Adriano 3 27 29 92

#	BRAZIL	m		CHILE	#
1	DIDA			TAPIA Nelson	1
2	CAFU			ALVAREZ Cristian	2
3	LUCIO			MALDONADO Claudio	3
4	JUAN	59		CONTRERAS Pablo	5
5	EMERSON	59		RUBIO Eduardo	7
6	ROBERTO CARLOS	66		PIZARRO David	8
7	ADRIANO	59		PINILLA Mauricio	15
8	KAKA			ROJAS Ricardo	16
9	RONALDO	45		MELENDEZ Rodrigo	18
10	ROBINHO			FUENTES Luis	22
11	ZE ROBERTO	59		TELLO Rodrigo	25
	Tr: PARREIRA Carlos Alberto			Tr: ACOSTA Nelson	
15	GILBERTO SILVA	59 59		PEREZ Rodrigo	4
16	JUNINHO PERNAMBUCANO	66 59		ACUNA Jorge	6
17	RICARDINHO	45 59		JIMENEZ Luis	10

Centenario, Montevideo
4-09-2005, 18:20, 60 000, Elizondo ARG

URU 3 2 COL

Zalayeta 3 42 51 86 / Soto 79, Angel 82

#	URUGUAY	m	m		m	COLOMBIA	#
1	CARINI Fabian					CALERO Miguel	1
2	RODRIGUEZ Guillermo					CORDOBA Ivan	2
4	MONTERO Paolo					OROZCO Andres	7
5	GARCIA Pablo					ANGEL Juan Pablo	9
6	LOPEZ Diego					MORENO Malher	10
7	VARELA Gustavo	83				SOTO Elkin	13
9	RECOBA Alvaro	78				PEREA Luis	14
15	PEREZ Diego				60	VIAFARA John	15
17	ZALAYETA Marcelo				82	REY Luis	18
18	MORALES Richard	69	90		20	BEDOYA Gerardo	20
21	FORLAN Diego					RESTREPO John	21
	Tr: FOSSATI Jorge					Tr: RUEDA Reinaldo	
8	SOSA Marcelo	69 87			60	VARGAS Fabian	6
13	ESTOYANOFF Fabian	78	90		90	OVIEDO Frankie	8
22	SANCHEZ Vicente	83	82		82	ARZUAGA Martin	16

Estadio Olimpico Atahualpa, Quito
8-10-2005, 16:00, 37 270, Rezende BRA

ECU 0 0 URU

#	ECUADOR	m		URUGUAY	#	m
12	MORA Cristian			CARINI Fabian	1	
3	HURTADO Ivan			LUGANO Diego	2	
4	DE LA CRUZ Ulises			RODRIGUEZ Dario	3	
5	VALENCIA Luis	56		GARCIA Pablo	5	
6	AMBROSSI Paul			LOPEZ Diego	6	
8	MENDEZ Edison			VARELA Gustavo	7	
9	BORJA Felix	76		RODRIGUEZ Guillermo	8	
11	DELGADO Agustin			RECOBA Alvaro	9	82
15	AYOVI Marlon			REGUEIRO Mario	11	69
17	ESPINOZA Giovanny			POUSO Omar	15	
20	TENORIO Edwin			MORALES Richard	18	
	Tr: SUAREZ Luis			Tr: FOSSATI Jorge		
10	LARA Christian	56 76		SILVA Dario	10	76
22	MINA Roberto	76 69		NUNEZ Richard	20	69
		82		FORLAN Diego	21	82

Metropolitano Roberto Melendez, Barranquilla
8-10-2005, 16:00, 22 380, Souza BRA

COL 1 1 CHI

Rey 24 — Rojas 64

COLOMBIA

1	CALERO Miguel		
2	CORDOBA Ivan		
3	YEPES Mario		
4	PALACIO Haider		
6	VARGAS Fabian	71	
7	PACHECO Victor	63	
9	ANGEL Juan Pablo		57
16	SOTO Elkin		
18	REY Luis	66	80
20	BEDOYA Gerardo		
21	RESTREPO John		
	Tr: RUEDA Reinaldo		
8	FERREIRA David	71	57
17	PATINO Jairo	63	57
24	ARZUAGA Martin	66	80

CHILE

		Player	No.
		BRAVO Claudio	12
		MALDONADO Claudio	3
		PEREZ Rodrigo	4
57		CONTRERAS Pablo	5
		ACUNA Jorge	6
		PIZARRO David	8
57		JIMENEZ Luis	10
		VILLARROEL Moises	14
80		PINILLA Mauricio	15
		ROJAS Francisco	16
		FUENTES Luis	22
		Tr: ACOSTA Nelson	
57		NAVIA Reinaldo	9
57		MIROSEVIC Milovan	17
80		VALDIVIA Jorge	21

Pachenricho Romero, Maracaibo
8-10-2005, 17:00, 13 272, Elizondo ARG

VEN 0 1 PAR

Haedo Valdez 64

VENEZUELA

1	ANGELUCCI Gilberto		
3	REY Jose Manuel		
6	CICHERO Alejandro		
8	VERA Luis		
9	MALDONADO Giancarlos	74	
10	URDANETA Gabriel	69	
11	PAEZ Ricardo		88
16	MORAN Ruberth	55	
17	ROJAS Jorge		78
18	ARANGO Juan		
20	GONZALEZ Hector		
	Tr: PAEZ Richard		
7	TORREALBA Jose	55	78
15	MORENO Alejandro	74	88
19	GONZALEZ Andree	69	86

PARAGUAY

		Player	No.
		GOMEZ Derlis	12
		NINEZ Jorge	2
		GAMARRA Carlos	4
		CACERES Julio Cesar	5
		FATECHA Cristian	6
		ACUNA Roberto	10
88		GAVILAN Diego	16
86		HAEDO VALDEZ Nelson	18
78		DOS SANTOS Julio	19
		CANIZA Denis	21
		SANTA CRUZ Roque	24
		Tr: RUIZ Anibal	
78		MONTIEL Jose	11
88		DA SILVA Paulo	14
86		CUEVAS Nelson	23

Hernando Siles, La Paz
9-10-2005, 16:00, 22 725, Larrionda URU

BOL 1 1 BRA

Castillo 49 — Juninho Pernambucano 25

BOLIVIA

1	ARIAS Carlos		
3	JAUREGUI Sergio		
7	CRISTALDO Luis		
10	BALDIVIESO Julio		
14	HOYOS Miguel	46	
15	VACA Doyle		
16	RALDES Ronald		
20	BOTERO Joaquin	76	
21	ANGULO Carmelo		
24	GALINDO Gonzalo		
27	GUTIERREZ Limberg	46	58
	Tr: MESA Ovidio		
11	PAZ Lider	76	58
18	CASTILLO Jose	46	58
26	PACHI Danner	46	79

BRAZIL

		JULIO CESAR	1
		CICINHO	2
		LUISAO	3
		ROQUE JUNIOR	4
58		GILBERTO SILVA	5
		GILBERTO	6
		ROBINHO	7
79		JUNINHO PERNAMBUCANO	8
		ADRIANO	9
		RICARDINHO	10
		RENATO	11
		Tr: PARREIRA Carlos Alberto	
58		GUSTAVO NERY	14
58		ALEX	15
79		JULIO BAPTISTA	16

Monumental, Buenos Aires
9-10-2005, 19:10, 36 977, Torres PAR

ARG 2 0 PER

Riquelme 81p, Guadalupe OG 90

ARGENTINA

1	ABBONDANZIERI Roberto	
2	AYALA Roberto	
3	SORIN Juan	
4	COLOCCINI Fabricio	
5	BATTAGLIA Sebastian	
6	MILITO Gabriel	
8	RIQUELME Juan	79
9	CRESPO Hernan	
18	GONZALEZ Cristian	58
19	MESSI Lionel	
20	GONZALEZ Luis	
	Tr: PEKERMAN Jose	
11	TEVEZ Carlos	58 80
15	SANTANA Mario	79 82

PERU

		GARCIA Julio	25
		SOTO Jorge	4
		HIDALGO Martin	5
		TORRES Rainer	8
		GUERRERO Jose	9
		GUADALUPE Luis	16
		FARFAN Jefferson	17
		CIURLIZZA Marco	19
78		BUTRON Leao	21
		GALLIQUIO John	22
		RODRIGUEZ Alberto	24
		Tr: TERNERO Freddy	
80		DELGADO Erick	1
82		COMINGES Juan	10
89		ROSS Douglas	11

Modelo, Tacna
12-10-2005, 20:00, 14 774, Sequeira ARG

PER 4 1 BOL

Vassallo 11, Acasiete 38
Farfan 2 45 82 — Gutierrez 66

PERU

1	DELGADO Erick		
2	ACASIETE Santiago		
4	SOTO Jorge		
5	HIDALGO Martin	63	
8	TORRES Rainer	46	
10	COMINGES Juan	83	
16	GUADALUPE Luis		
17	FARFAN Jefferson		
18	VASSALLO Gustavo	63	
19	CIURLIZZA Marco	74	
22	GALLIQUIO John	46	
	Tr: TERNERO Freddy		
6	MENDOZA Jose	46	63
11	ROSS Douglas	63	83
25	GARCIA Julio	83	

BOLIVIA

		Player	No.
		ARIAS Carlos	1
		JAUREGUI Sergio	3
63		GOMEZ Jesus	8
46		BALDIVIESO Julio	10
		VACA Doyle	15
		RALDES Ronald	16
		CASTILLO Jose	18
		BOTERO Joaquin	20
		ANGULO Carmelo	21
		GALINDO Gonzalo	24
		PACHI Danner	26
		Tr: MESA Ovidio	
63		PAZ Lider	11
83		VACA Joselito	22
74	46	GUTIERREZ Limberg	27

Defensores del Chaco, Asuncion
12-10-2005, 20:30, 12 374, Rezende BRA

PAR 0 1 COL

Rey 7

PARAGUAY

1	VILLAR Justo		
2	NUNEZ Jorge	61	
3	MANZUR Julio		
5	CACERES Julio Cesar		
6	FATECHA Cristian		
9	CABANAS Salvador	63	
10	ACUNA Roberto		
17	MONTIEL Jose		
19	DOS SANTOS Julio	75	
21	CANIZA Denis		
23	CUEVAS Nelson		
	Tr: RUIZ Anibal		
7	LOPEZ Dante	63	
15	CACERES Juan Daniel	61	74
20	CARDOZO Jose	75	80

COLOMBIA

		Player	No.
		CALERO Miguel	1
		CORDOBA Ivan	2
		YEPES Mario	3
89		ANGEL Juan Pablo	9
74		MORENO Malher	10
		PASSO Oscar	13
		PEREA Luis	14
		VIAFARA John	15
		SOTO Elkin	16
80		REY Luis	18
		RESTREPO John	21
		Tr: RUEDA Reinaldo	
89		VANEGAS Samuel	5
74		VARGAS Fabian	6
80		RENTERIA Wason	11

Mangueirao, Belem
12-10-2005, 21:30, 47 000, Baldassi ARG

BRA	**3**	**0**	**VEN**

Adriano [28], Ronaldo [51]
Roberto Carlos [61]

BRAZIL			VENEZUELA		
1	DIDA		DUDAMEL Rafael	22	
2	CAFU		VALLENILLA Luis	2	
3	LUCIO		REY Jose Manuel	3	
4	JUAN		HERNANDEZ Jonay	4	
5	EMERSON		CICHERO Alejandro	6	
6	ROBERO CARLOS	70	MALDONADO Giancarlos	9	
7	ADRIANO	64	61 URDANETA Gabriel	10	
8	KAKA		50 PAEZ Ricardo	11	
9	RONALDO		VIELMA Leonel	13	
10	RONALDINHO	64	JIMENEZ Leopoldo	14	
11	ZE ROBERTO	68	ARANGO Juan	18	
	Tr: PARREIRA Carlos Alberto		Tr: PAEZ Richard		
16	JUNINHO PERNAMBUCANO	68	70 TORREALBA Jose	7	
17	ALEX	64	61 ROJAS Jorge	17	
18	ROBINHO	64	50 GONZALEZ Hector	20	

Nacional, Santiago
12-10-2005, 21:30, 49 530, Elizondo ARG

CHI	**0**	**0**	**ECU**

CHILE			ECUADOR		
12	BRAVO Claudio		VILLAFUERTE Edwin	1	
3	MALDONADO Claudio		GUAGUA Jorge	2	
4	PEREZ Rodrigo	69	LARA Christian	8	
8	PIZARRO David	89	BORJA Felix	9	
9	NAVIA Reinaldo		CASTILLO Segundo	14	
10	JIMENEZ Luis	68	SARITAMA Luis	16	
14	VILLARROEL Moises	59	ESPINOZA Giovanny	17	
16	ROJAS Ricardo		REASCO Neicer	18	
18	MELENDEZ Rodrigo	57	CORTEZ Jose	19	
21	VALDIVIA Jorge	54	TENORIO Edwin	20	
22	FUENTES Luis		CAICEDO Luis	21	
	Tr: ACOSTA Nelson		Tr: SUAREZ Luis		
17	MIROSEVIC Milovan	59	57 DE LA CRUZ Ulises	4	
19	FERNANDEZ Matias	68	69 AMBROSSI Paul	6	
26	SUAZO Humbero	54	89 MINA Roberto	22	

Centenario, Montevideo
12-10-2005, 22:30, 55 000, Souza BRA

URU	**1**	**0**	**ARG**

Recoba [46]

URUGUAY			ARGENTINA		
1	CARINI Fabian		ABBONDANZIERI Roberto	1	
2	LUGANO Diego		AYALA Roberto	2	
3	RODRIGUEZ Dario		SORIN Juan	3	
4	MONTERO Paolo		PONZIO Leonardo	4	
5	GARCIA Pablo		BATTAGLIA Sebastian	5	
7	VARELA Gustavo		SAMUEL Walter	6	
8	DIOGO Carlos		RIQUELME Juan	8	
9	RECOBA Alvaro	75	80 CRESPO Hernan	9	
17	ZALAYETA Marcelo	65	TEVEZ Carlos	11	
18	MORALES Richard		65 GONZALEZ Luis	15	
21	FORLAN Diego	89	65 GONZALEZ Cristian	18	
	Tr: FOSSATI Jorge		Tr: PEKERMAN Jose		
6	LOPEZ Diego	89	65 DELGADO Cesar	7	
13	ESTOYANOFF Fabian	75	80 AIMAR Pablo	16	
15	POUSO Omar	65	65 MESSI Lionel	19	

		PL	W	D	L	F	A	PTS	BRA	ARG	ECU	PAR	URU	COL	CHI	VEN	PER	BOL
1	Brazil	18	9	7	2	35	17	34		3-1	1-0	4-1	3-3	0-0	5-0	3-0	1-0	3-1
2	Argentina	18	10	4	4	29	17	34	3-1		1-0	0-0	4-2	1-0	2-2	3-2	2-0	3-0
3	Ecuador	18	8	4	6	23	19	28	1-0	2-0		5-2	0-0	2-1	2-0	2-0	0-0	3-2
4	Paraguay	18	8	4	6	23	23	28	0-0	1-0	2-1		4-1	0-1	2-1	1-0	1-1	4-1
5	Uruguay	18	6	7	5	23	28	25	1-1	1-0	1-0	1-0		3-2	2-1	0-3	1-3	5-0
6	Colombia	18	6	6	6	24	16	24	1-2	1-1	3-0	1-1	5-0		1-1	0-1	5-0	1-0
7	Chile	18	5	7	6	18	22	22	1-1	0-0	0-0	0-1	1-1	0-0		2-1	2-1	3-1
8	Venezuela	18	5	3	10	20	28	18	2-5	0-3	3-1	0-1	1-1	0-0	0-1		4-1	2-1
9	Peru	18	4	6	8	20	28	18	1-1	1-3	2-2	4-1	0-0	0-2	2-1	0-0		4-1
10	Bolivia	18	4	2	12	20	37	14	1-1	1-2	1-2	2-1	0-0	4-0	0-2	3-1	1-0	

Brazil, Argentina, Ecuador and Paraguay qualified for the finals • † Uruguay qualified for a play-off against Australia

Details of FIFA World Cup™ qualifiers played in South America before August 2005 can be found in the *Almanack of World Football 2006* on pages 147-159

QUALIFYING MATCHES PLAYED IN OCEANIA

Preliminary Round		

Group 1		Pts
Solomon Islands	SOL	10
Tahiti	TAH	8
New Caledonia	NCL	7
Tonga	TGA	3
Cook Islands	COK	0

Group 2		Pts
Vanuatu	VAN	10
Fiji	FIJ	9
Papua New Guinea	PNG	7
Samoa	SAM	3
American Samoa	ASA	0

Group Stage		

		Pts
Australia	AUS	13
Solomon Islands	SOL	10
New Zealand	NZL	9
Fiji	FIJ	4
Tahiti	TAH	4
Vanuatu	VAN	3

Play-off		

Australia	AUS	2	7
Solomon Islands	SOL	1	0

Australia qualified to meet Uruguay
in a play-off

FINAL ROUND

Stadium Australia, Sydney
3-09-2005, 19:30, 16 000, Mohd Salleh MAS

AUS 7 0 SOL

Culina [20], Viduka 2 [36] [43], Cahill [57],
Chipperfield [64], Thompson [68], Emerton [89]

AUSTRALIA			SOLOMON ISLANDS	
1	SCHWARZER Mark		ARUWAFU Francis	20
2	NEILL Lucas		LEO Leslie	2
5	VIDMAR Tony		HOUKARAWA Mahlon	3
6	POPOVIC Tony	57	**53** KILIFA Nelson **6**	
7	EMERTON Brett		46 MAEMAE Alick	7
8	SKOKO Josip	71	BILLY Kidston	9
9	VIDUKA Mark		42 SURI Batram	10
10	CAHILL Tim		LUI George	13
12	CHIPPERFIELD Scott		OMOKIRIO Gideon	17
15	ALOISI John	62	FAARODO Henry	18
19	CULINA Jason		59 WASI Francis	19
	Tr: HIDDINK Guus		Tr: ANDRIOLI Ayrton	
13	GRELLA Vince	71	42 SURI George	5
14	THOMPSON Archie	62	59 ANISUA Richard	12
23	BRESCIANO Marco	57	46 WAITA Stanley	16

Lawson Tama, Honiara
6-09-2005, 13:00, 16 000, Maidin SIN

SOL 1 2 AUS

Faarodo [49]   Thompson [19], Emerton [58]

SOLOMON ISLANDS			AUSTRALIA	
1	RAY Felix		KALAC Zeljko **18**	
2	LEO Leslie	79	NEILL Lucas **2**	
3	HOUKARAWA Mahlon		MCKAIN Jon **6**	
5	SURI George		EMERTON Brett	7
10	SURI Batram	65	46 VIDUKA Mark	9
11	MENAPI Commins		46 CAHILL Tim	10
13	LUI George	**47**	67 CHIPPERFIELD Scott	12
16	WAITA Stanley	84	GRELLA Vince **13**	
17	OMOKIRIO Gideon		THOMPSON Archie	14
18	FAARODO Henry		CULINA Jason	19
19	WASI Francis		BRESCIANO Marco **23**	
	Tr: ANDRIOLI Ayrton		Tr: HIDDINK Guus	
8	INIGA Abraham	65	67 LAZARIDIS Stan	11
12	ANISUA Richard	79	46 ELRICH Ahmad	21
14	SAMANI Jack	84	46 WILKSHIRE Luke	22

Details of FIFA World Cup™ qualifiers played in Oceania before August 2005 can be found in the *Almanack of World Football 2006* on pages 160-166

QUALIFYING MATCHES PLAYED IN EUROPE

Group 1		Pts	Group 2		Pts	Group 3		Pts	Group 4		Pts
Netherlands	NED	32	Ukraine	UKR	25	Portugal	POR	30	France	FRA	20
Czech Republic	CZE	27	Turkey	TUR	23	Slovakia	SVK	23	Switzerland	SUI	18
Romania	ROU	25	Denmark	DEN	22	Russia	RUS	23	Israel	ISR	18
Finland	FIN	16	Greece	GRE	21	Estonia	EST	17	Rep of Ireland	IRL	17
Macedonia FYR	MKD	9	Albania	ALB	13	Latvia	LVA	15	Cyprus	CYP	4
Armenia	ARM	7	Georgia	GEO	10	Liechtenstein	LIE	8	Faroe Islands	FRO	1
Andorra	AND	5	Kazakhstan	KAZ	1	Luxembourg	LUX	0			

Group 5		Pts	Group 6		Pts	Group 7		Pts	Group 8		Pts
Italy	ITA	23	England	ENG	25	Serbia/Montenegro	SCG	22	Croatia	CRO	24
Norway	NOR	18	Poland	POL	24	Spain	ESP	20	Sweden	SWE	24
Scotland	SCO	13	Austria	AUT	15	Bosnia-Herzegovina	BIH	16	Bulgaria	BUL	15
Slovenia	SVN	12	Northern Ireland	NIR	9	Belgium	BEL	12	Hungary	HUN	14
Belarus	BLR	10	Wales	WAL	8	Lithuania	LTU	10	Iceland	ISL	4
Moldova	MDA	5	Azerbaijan	AZE	3	San Marino	SMR	0	Malta	MLT	3

Play-offs		
Norway	NOR	0 0
Czech Republic	CZE	1 1
Switzerland	SUI	2 2
Turkey	TUR	0 4
Spain	ESP	5 1
Slovakia	SVK	1 1

The group winners and the two second-placed teams with the best records qualified for the finals. The remaining six second-placed teams qualified for a single knock-out round to determine the final three places. Second-placed teams were ranked according to their record against the first, third, fourth, fifth and sixth-placed teams in their groups

The Netherlands, Czech Republic, Ukraine, Portugal, France, Switzerland, Italy, England, Poland, Serbia and Montenegro, Spain, Croatia and Sweden qualified for the finals

Details of FIFA World Cup™ qualifiers played in Europe before August 2005 can be found in the *Almanack of World Football 2006* on pages 167-198

GROUP 1

City Stadium, Skopje			
17-08-2005, 20:00, 6 800, Messias ENG			
MKD	**0**	**3**	**FIN**

Eremenko 2 [8] [45], Roiha [87]

MACEDONIA FYR			FINLAND		
1	MADZOVSKI Filip		JAASKELAINEN Jussi	1	
2	POPOV Goran		PASANEN Petri	2	
3	NOVESKI Nikolce		HYYPIA Sami	4	
4	SEDLOSKI Goce		TIHINEN Hannu	5	
5	VASOSKI Aleksandar	65	TAINIO Teemu	8	
6	MITRESKI Aleksandar	61	FORSSELL Mikael	9	
7	PETROV Robert		KUQI Shefki	18	
8	SUMOLIKOSKI Velice		KALLIO Toni	19	
9	PANDEV Goran	32	84	EREMENKO Alexei Jun.	20
10	MAZNOV Goran	57	HEIKKINEN Markus	23	
11	MAZNOV Goran	79	LAGERBLOM Pekka	25	
	Tr: SANTRAC Slobodan		Tr: HELISKOSKI Jyrki		
15	POPOV Robert	65	84	SAARINEN Janne	3
16	NALIMI Ilami	32	79	LITMANEN Jari	10
17	GROZDANOVSKI Vlatko	57	61	ROIHA Paulus	22

Gheorghe Hagi, Constanta			
17-08-2005, 21:30, 8 200, Jakov ISR			
ROU	**2**	**0**	**AND**

Mutu 2 [29] [41]

ROMANIA			ANDORRA		
1	LOBONT Bogdan		ALVAREZ Jesus	1	
2	CONTRA Cosmin		AYALA Josep	2	
3	RAT Razvan	79	46	ESCURA Jordi	3
4	TAMAS Gabriel		SONEJEE Oscar	4	
5	CHIVU Cristian		SIVERA Antoni	5	
6	COCIS Razvan		LIMA Ildefons	6	
7	PETRE Florentin	76	90	RODRIGUEZ Albert	7
8	MUNTEANU Dorinel	46	80	RIERA Gabriel	9
9	NICULESCU Claudiu		BERNAUS Marc	10	
10	MUTU Adrian		SILVA Fernando	11	
11	DICA Nicolae		PUJOL Marc	20	
	Tr: PITURCA Victor		Tr: RODRIGO David		
13	PASCOVICI Mihai	79	46	MARTIN SANCHEZ Xavi	14
14	TARARACHE Mihai	46	90	GARCIA Genis	15
15	BALAN Tiberiu	76	80	MORENO Sergi	16

Comunal, Andorra la Vella
3-09-2005, 16:00, 860, Ver Eecke BEL

AND 0 0 FIN

ANDORRA			FINLAND	
1 ALVAREZ Jesus			KAVEN Mikko	1
2 ESCURA Jordi			SAARINEN Janne	3
3 MARTIN SANCHEZ Xavi			HYYPIA Sami	4
4 SONEJEE Oscar			TIHINEN Hannu	5
5 LIMA Antoni			TAINIO Teemu	8
6 LIMA Ildefons		73	FORSSELL Mikael	9
7 SIVERA Antoni			KUIVASTO Toni	14
8 PUJOL Marc	84	46	KOPTEFF Peter	17
9 MORENO Sergi	71		KUQI Shefki	18
10 JIMENEZ Manel			KALLIO Toni	19
11 RUIZ Justo	87	64	EREMENKO Alexei Jun.	20
Tr: RODRIGO David			Tr: HELISKOSKI Jyrki	
14 RIERA Gabriel	71	73	SJOLUND Daniel	15
16 GARCIA Genis	84	64	RIIHILAHTI Aki	16
18 FERNANDEZ Juli	87	46	LAGERBLOM Pekka	25

Gheorghe Hagi, Constanta
3-09-2005, 21:00, 7 000, Hauge NOR

ROU 2 0 CZE

Mutu 2 [28] [56]

ROMANIA			CZECH REPUBLIC	
1 LOBONT Bogdan			CECH Petr	1
2 CONTRA Cosmin			GRYGERA Zdenek	2
3 RAT Razvan			POLAK Jan	3
4 TAMAS Gabriel		59	BOLF Rene	5
5 CHIVU Cristian		14	JANKULOVSKI Marek	6
6 PETRE Ovidiu			SMICER Vladimir	7
7 PETRE Florentin	53		POBORSKY Karel	8
8 MUNTEANU Dorinel	72		KOLLER Jan	9
9 MAZILU Ionut			BAROS Milan	15
10 MUTU Adrian	88	75	HEINZ Marek	18
11 COCIS Razvan			UJFALUSI Tomas	21
Tr: PITURCA Victor			Tr: BRUCKNER Karel	
13 BADOI Vali	53	59	SIVOK Tomas	12
16 CODREA Paul	72	75	JUN Tomas	19
18 BUCUR Gheorghe	88	14	POSPECH Zdenek	20

Republican, Yerevan
3-09-2005, 22:00, 1 747, Dougal SCO

ARM 0 1 NED

Van Nistelrooij [64]

ARMENIA			NETHERLANDS	
1 BEREZOVSKI Roman			VAN DER SAR Edwin	1
3 DOKHOYAN Karen		63	KROMKAMP Jan	2
4 HOVSEPYAN Sargis			BOULAHROUZ Khalid	3
5 ARZUMANYAN Robert			OPDAM Barry	4
6 KHACHATRYAN Romik			VAN BRONCKHORST Gio	5
8 MKRTCHYAN Aghvan			MADURO Hedwiges	6
9 MELKONYAN Samvel	84		KUYT Dirk	7
10 MANUCHARYAN Edgar	17	51	LANDZAAT Denny	8
11 HAKOBYAN Aram	80		VAN NISTELROOIJ Ruud	9
15 ALEKSANYAN Karen			COCU Phillip	10
18 TATEOSIAN Alexander		75	VAN PERSIE Robin	11
Tr: WISMAN Hendrik			Tr: VAN BASTEN Marco	
2 ALEKSANYAN Valeri	84	51	SNEIJDER Wesley	14
7 HAKOBYAN Ara	17	75	VAN DER VAART Rafael	15
14 VOSKANYAN Aram	80	63	HESSELINK Jan	17

Andruv, Olomouc
7-09-2005, 17:30, 12 015, Hansson SWE

CZE 4 1 ARM

Heinz [47], Polak 2 [52] [76], Baros [58] Hakobyan [85]

CZECH REPUBLIC			ARMENIA	
16 BLAZEK Jaromir			BEREZOVSKI Roman	1
2 GRYGERA Zdenek			DOKHOYAN Karen	3
3 POLAK Jan			HOVSEPYAN Sargis	4
4 GALASEK Tomas			ARZUMANYAN Robert	5
8 POBORSKY Karel		71	KHACHATRYAN Romik	6
9 KOLLER Jan			HAKOBYAN Ara	7
13 SKACEL Rudolf	46		MKRTCHYAN Aghvan	10
15 BAROS Milan	80	57	HAKOBYAN Aram	11
18 HEINZ Marek			ALEKSANYAN Karen	15
21 UJFALUSI Tomas			ALEKSANYAN Valeri	16
22 ROZEHNAL David	70	64	TATEOSIAN Alexander	18
Tr: BRUCKNER Karel			Tr: WISMAN Hendrik	
7 SMICER Vladimir	46	64	MELIKYAN Eghishe	2
12 SIVOK Tomas	70	71	TIGRANYAN Armen	13
19 JUN Tomas	80	57	PETROSYAN Galust	17

Ratina Stadium, Tampere
7-09-2005, 19:00, 6 467, Jakobsson ISL

FIN 5 1 MKD

Forssell 3 [10] [12] [61], Tihinen [41]
Eremenko [54] Maznov [48]

FINLAND			MACEDONIA	
1 KAVEN Mikko			JOVCEV Gogo	1
2 PASANEN Petri			POPOV Robert	2
3 SAARINEN Janne	52		NOVESKI Nikolce	3
5 TIHINEN Hannu			LAZAREVSKI Vlade	4
8 TAINIO Teemu	80		BOZINOVSKI Vasko	5
9 FORSSELL Mikael			MITRESKI Aleksandar	6
14 KUIVASTO Toni		57	GROZDANOVSKI Vlatko	7
16 RIIHILAHTI Aki	71	46	SUMOLIKOSKI Velice	8
19 KALLIO Toni			PANDEV Goran	9
20 EREMENKO Alexei Jun.			MUSTAFI Nebi	10
23 HEIKKINEN Markus		80	MAZNOV Goran	11
Tr: HELISKOSKI Jyrki			Tr: BABUNSKI Boban	
13 NYMAN Ari	52	80	NUHIJI Ardijan	14
17 KOPTEFF Peter	71	57	IGNATOV Stojan	17
21 JOHANSSON Jonathan	80	46	POPOV Goran	18

Philips Stadion, Eindhoven
7-09-2005, 20:30, 34 000, Hanacsek HUN

NED 4 0 AND

Van Der Vaart [23], Cocu [27]
Van Nistelrooij 2 [43] [89]

NETHERLANDS			ANDORRA	
1 VAN DER SAR Edwin			ALVAREZ Jesus	1
2 LUCIUS Theo	67		AYALA Josep	2
3 BOULAHROUZ Khalid			MARTIN SANCHEZ Xavi	3
4 OPDAM Barry			FERNANDEZ Juli	4
5 DE CLER Tim			LIMA Antoni	5
6 COCU Phillip		38	SONEJEE Oscar	6
7 VAN PERSIE Robin			SIVERA Antoni	7
8 SNEIJDER Wesley	78	76	JIMENEZ Manel	8
9 VAN NISTELROOIJ Ruud		54	SILVA Fernando	9
10 VAN DER VAART Rafael			BERNAUS Marc	10
11 ROBBEN Arjen		30	RUIZ Justo	11
Tr: VAN BASTEN Marco			Tr: RODRIGO David	
14 MADURO Hedwiges	78	76	SANCHEZ Juli	12
17 HESSELINK Jan	67	54	RIERA Gabriel	14
		30	ESCURA Jordi	18

Olympic Stadium, Helsinki
8-10-2005, 17:00, 11 500, Guenov BUL

FIN 0 1 ROU

Mutu 41p

FINLAND			ROMANIA	
1 JAASKELAINEN Jussi			LOBONT Bogdan	1
3 SAARINEN Janne	75	54	CONTRA Cosmin	2
4 HYYPIA Sami			RAT Razvan	3
8 TAINIO Teemu			TAMAS Gabriel	4
9 FORSSELL Mikael	73		IENCSI Adrian	5
13 NYMAN Ari	62		PETRE Ovidiu	6
14 KUIVASTO Toni			PETRE Florentin	7
19 KALLIO Toni			MUNTEANU Dorinel	8
20 EREMENKO Alexei Jun.		90	MAZILU Ionut	9
23 HEIKKINEN Markus		82	MUTU Adrian	10
25 LAGERBLOM Pekka			COCIS Razvan	11
Tr: HELISKOSKI Jyrki			Tr: PITURCA Victor	
15 SJOLUND Daniel	73	54	BADOI Vali	13
17 KOPTEFF Peter	75	90	NICULAE Daniel	17
21 JOHANSSON Jonathan	62	82	ROSU Laurentiu	18

Toyota Arena, Prague
8-10-2005, 20:30, 17 478, Sars FRA

CZE 0 2 NED

Van Der Vaart 31, Opdam 38

CZECH REPUBLIC			NETHERLANDS	
1 CECH Petr			VAN DER SAR Edwin	1
2 GRYGERA Zdenek	84		KROMKAMP Jan	2
3 POLAK Jan	67	57	BOULAHROUZ Khalid	3
4 GALASEK Tomas			OPDAM Barry	4
8 POBORSKY Karel			VAN BRONCKHORST Gio	5
9 STAJNER Jiri	76		MADURO Hedwiges	6
10 ROSICKY Tomas			KUYT Dirk	7
13 JIRANEK Martin	44		LANDZAAT Denny	8
15 BAROS Milan			VAN NISTELROOIJ Ruud	9
21 UJFALUSI Tomas			VAN DER VAART Rafael	10
22 ROZEHNAL David	76		ROBBEN Arjen	11
Tr: BRUCKNER Karel			Tr: VAN BASTEN Marco	
7 SMICER Vladimir	44	84	DE JONG Nigel	12
12 JAROLIM David	76	57	VLAAR Ron	13
18 HEINZ Marek	67	76	VAN PERSIE Robin	17

Comunal, Andorra la Vella
12-10-2005, 16:00, 430, Stokes IRL

AND 0 3 ARM

Sonejee OG 40, Hakobyan Aram 52
Hakobyan Ara 62

ANDORRA			ARMENIA	
1 ALVAREZ Jesus			KASPAROV Gevorg	1
2 AYALA Josep			MELIKYAN Eghishe	2
3 MARTIN SANCHEZ Xavi			DOKHOYAN Karen	3
4 SONEJEE Oscar			ARZUMANYAN Robert	5
5 LIMA Antoni			KHACHATRYAN Romik	6
6 LIMA Ildefons	44		HAKOBYAN Ara	7
7 SIVERA Antoni	19	83	MKHITARYAN Romik	9
8 VIEIRA Marcio	57	81	HAKOBYAN Aram	11
9 RIERA Gabriel	83		ALEKSANYAN Karen	15
10 BERNAUS Marc		78	ALEKSANYAN Valeri	16
11 RUIZ Justo			TATEOSIAN Alexander	18
Tr: RODRIGO David			Tr: WISMAN Hendrik	
12 SANCHEZ Juli	19	83	VOSKANYAN Artur	8
14 CLEMENTE Ludovic	57	78	MELKONYAN Samvel	10
17 JIMENEZ Manel	83	81	VOSKANYAN Aram	14

Olympic Stadium, Helsinki
12-10-2005, 18:30, 11 234, Mejuto Gonzalez ESP

FIN 0 3 CZE

Jun 6, Rosicky 51, Heinz 58

FINLAND			CZECH REPUBLIC	
1 JAASKELAINEN Jussi			CECH Petr	1
3 SAARINEN Janne	12		GRYGERA Zdenek	2
4 HYYPIA Sami			GALASEK Tomas	4
8 TAINIO Teemu			MARES Pavel	6
11 KOLKKA Joonas	61		SMICER Vladimir	7
14 KUIVASTO Toni			POBORSKY Karel	8
15 SJOLUND Daniel	63	86	ROSICKY Tomas	10
19 KALLIO Toni			HEINZ Marek	18
21 JOHANSSON Jonathan	73		JUN Tomas	19
23 HEIKKINEN Markus			UJFALUSI Tomas	21
25 LAGERBLOM Pekka	58		ROZEHNAL David	22
Tr: HELISKOSKI Jyrki			Tr: BRUCKNER Karel	
9 FORSSELL Mikael	63	61	POLAK Jan	3
13 NYMAN Ari	58	73	KOVAC Radoslav	5
17 KOPTEFF Peter	12	86	STAJNER Jiri	9

Amsterdam ArenA, Amsterdam
12-10-2005, 19:30, 50 000, Farina ITA

NED 0 0 MKD

NETHERLANDS			MACEDONIA FYR	
1 VAN DER SAR Edwin			MILOSEVSKI Petar	1
2 DE JONG Nigel			NOVESKI Nikolce	2
3 BOULAHROUZ Khalid	53		POPOV Goran	3
4 OPDAM Barry			SEDLOSKI Goce	4
5 VAN BRONCKHORST Gio			MITRESKI Igor	5
6 MADURO Hedwiges	63		VASOSKI Aleksandar	6
7 KUYT Dirk			MEGLEHSKI Tohi	7
8 LANDZAAT Denny	46		MASEV Danco	8
9 VAN NISTELROOIJ Ruud	70		TASEVSKI Darko	10
10 VAN DER VAART Rafael	90		NAUMOSKI Ilco	11
11 VAN PERSIE Robin	85		PANDEV Goran	19
Tr: VAN BASTEN Marco			Tr: BABUNSKI Boban	
14 SNEIJDER Wesley	46	90	HRISTOV Georgi	9
15 DAVIDS Edgar	63	70	STOJKOV Aco	17
17 BABEL Ryan	85	53	SUMOLIKOSKI Velice	18

GROUP 1	PL	W	D	L	F	A	PTS	NED	CZE	ROU	FIN	MKD	ARM	AND
1 Netherlands	12	10	2	0	27	3	32		2-0	2-0	3-1	0-0	2-0	4-0
2 Czech Republic	12	9	0	3	35	12	27	0-2		1-0	4-3	6-1	4-1	8-1
3 Romania	12	8	1	3	20	10	25	0-2	2-0		2-1	2-1	3-0	2-0
4 Finland	12	5	1	6	21	19	16	0-4	0-3	0-1		5-1	3-1	3-0
5 Macedonia FYR	12	2	3	7	11	24	9	2-2	0-2	1-2	0-3		3-0	0-0
6 Armenia	12	2	1	9	9	25	7	0-1	0-3	1-1	0-2	1-2		2-1
7 Andorra	12	1	2	9	4	34	5	0-3	0-4	1-5	0-0	1-0	0-3	

Netherlands qualified for the finals • Czech Republic qualified for a play-off against Norway

GROUP 2

Central Stadium, Almaty
17-08-2005, 18:00, 9 000, Havrilla SVK

KAZ   **1 2**   **GEO**

Kenzhekhanov [23]   Demetradze 2 [50] [82]

KAZAKHSTAN				GEORGIA	
1 LORIYA David				LOMAIA George	1
5 KUCHMA Alexandr				MENTESAHSHVILI Zurab	2
6 BAIZHANOV Maxat				KALADZE Kakha	4
7 IRISMETOV Farkhadbek				KANKAVA Jaba	6
8 TRAVIN Andrey				TSIKITISHVILI Levan	7
10 KHOHLOV Nikita				GAKHOKIDZE Georgi	8
14 KENZHEKHANOV Daniyar	65	67		IASHVILI Alexander	9
15 FAMILTSEV Alexander				KOBIASHVILI Levan	10
17 LARIN Sergey	82	90		DEMETRADZE George	11
19 ZHUNASKALIYEV Nurbol				KHIZANISHVILI Zurab	13
20 AZOVSKIY Maxim	58	78		ALADASHVILI Kakhaber	17
Tr: TIMOFEYEV Sergei				Tr: DARSADZE Gaioz	
11 NIZOVTSEV Maxim	58	67		MUJIRI David	15
16 CHICHULIN Anton	82	90		GANUGRAVA George	16
21 KROKHMAL Alexandr	65	78		ODIKADZE David	18

Qemal Stafa, Tirana
3-09-2005, 20:00, 3 000, Slupik POL

ALB   **2 1**   **KAZ**

Myrtaj [53], Bogdani [56]   Nizovtsev [62]

ALBANIA				KAZAKHSTAN	
1 LIKA Ilion				LORIYA David	1
2 BEQIRI Elvin				IRISMETOV Farkhadbek	2
5 CANA Lorik		70		KENZHEKHANOV Daniyar	3
6 HASI Besnik				KUCHMA Alexandr	5
7 MURATI Edvin		53		BAIZHANOV Maxat	6
9 MYRTAJ Florian	90			SMAKOV Samat	8
13 SKELA Ervin				BALTIYEV Ruslan	14
14 LALA Altin				TRAVIN Andrey	15
15 JUPI Redi		66		ZHUNASKALIYEV Nurbol	16
22 BOGDANI Erion	85			LARIN Sergey	17
23 HAXHI Altin	46			KHOHLOV Nikita	19
Tr: BRIEGEL Hans-Peter				Tr: TIMOFEYEV Sergei	
8 BUSHAJ Alban	85	66		KARPOVICH Andrey	9
10 AGOLLI Amsi	46	70		LITVINENKO Oleg	10
21 KAPLLANI Edmond	90	53		NIZOVTSEV Maxim	11

Lokomotivi, Tbilisi
3-09-2005, 20:15, 0, Ovrebo NOR

GEO   **1 1**   **UKR**

Gakhokidze [89]   Rotan [43]

GEORGIA				UKRAINE	
1 LOMAIA George				SHOVKOVSKI Alexandr	1
2 MENTESAHSHVILI Zurab	78			NESMACHNY Andriy	2
4 KALADZE Kakha				FEDOROV Sergyi	3
7 TSIKITISHVILI Levan				TYMOSHYUK Anatoliy	4
8 GAKHOKIDZE Georgi				YEZERSKI Vladimir	5
9 KANKAVA Jaba				RUSOL Andrey	6
10 KOBIASHVILI Levan	78			SHEVCHENKO Andriy	7
11 DEMETRADZE George				ROTAN Ruslan	8
13 KHIZANISHVILI Zurab		75		VORONIN Andrey	10
16 ASATIANI Malkhaz	87	68		SHYSHCHENKO Sermiy	11
18 ODIKADZE David				GUSIN Andrei	14
Tr: DARSADZE Gaioz				Tr: BLOKHIN Oleg	
6 ASHVETIA Mikhail	87	68		REBROV Sergiy	15
14 GOGUA Gogita	78	75		NAZARENKO Sergey	18
15 MUJIRI David	78				

Besiktas Inönü, Istanbul
3-09-2005, 21:00, 29 721, Mejuto Gonzalez ESP

TUR   **2 2**   **DEN**

Buruk [47], Metin [81]   Jensen [40], Larsen [93+]

TURKEY				DENMARK	
1 DEMIREL Volkan				SORENSEN Thomas	1
4 OZALAN Alpay				POULSEN Christian	2
6 OZAT Umit		46		PRISKE Brian	3
8 SAHIN Selcuk				AGGER Daniel	4
9 TEKKE Fatih		85		JENSEN Niclas	5
10 BASTURK Yildiray	46			HELVEG Thomas	6
11 SAS Hasan	46			GRAVESEN Thomas	7
17 METIN Tumer				JENSEN Claus	8
19 TORAMAN Ibrahim				TOMASSON Jon Dahl	9
20 SUKUR Hakan		78		JORGENSEN Martin	10
22 ALTINTOP Hamit				ROMMEDAHL Dennis	11
Tr: TERIM Fatih				Tr: OLSEN Morten	
7 BURUK Okan	46	46		GRAVGAARD Michael	13
15 CIMSIR Huseyin	46	78		GRONKJAER Jesper	15
		85		LARSEN Soren	18

Central Stadium, Almaty
7-09-2005, 19:00, 18 000, Tudor ROU

KAZ 1 2 GRE

Zhalmagambetov 53 — Giannakopoulos 78, Lymperopoulos 94+

#	KAZAKHSTAN			GREECE	#
1	LORIYA David			NIKOPOLIDIS Antonios	1
3	KHOHLOV Nikita			SEITARIDIS Giourkas	2
4	AZOVSKIY Maxim	52		BASINAS Angelos	6
5	KUCHMA Alexandr			ZAGORAKIS Theo	7
7	AVDEYEV Igor			GIANNAKOPOULOS Stelios	8
8	SMAKOV Samat			CHARISTEAS Angelos	9
9	KARPOVICH Andrey	86	76	FYSSAS Panagiotis	14
10	LITVINENKO Oleg		54	VRYZAS Zisis	15
15	FAMILTSEV Alexander	78		KAPSIS Mihalis	19
16	RADIONOV Denis	94		KARAGOUNIS Georgios	20
19	ZHALMAGAMBETOV Maxim	80	60	KATSOURANIS Konst'inos	21
	Tr: TIMOFEEV Sergei			Tr: REHHAGEL Otto	
2	LARIN Sergey	52	60	KAFES Pantelis	16
14	BALTIYEV Ruslan	80	76	GEKAS Theofanis	17
17	TRAVIN Andrey	78	54	LYMPEROPOULOS Nikos	33

Olympic Stadium, Kyiv
7-09-2005, 19:15, 67 000, Sars FRA

UKR 0 1 TUR

— Metin 55

#	UKRAINE			TURKEY	#
1	SHOVKOVSKI Alexandr			DEMIREL Volkan	1
2	NESMACHNY Andriy			OZALAN Alpay	4
3	FEDOROV Sergyi			OZAT Umit	6
4	TYMOSHYUK Anatoliy	91		BURUK Okan	7
5	VASHCHUK Vladislav			SAHIN Selcuk	8
6	RUSOL Andrey	82		TEKKE Fatih	9
8	ROTAN Ruslan	67		METIN Tumer	17
9	HUSYEV Oleh			TORAMAN Ibrahim	19
10	VORONIN Andrey	83		SUKUR Hakan	20
11	BYELIK Olekcii			ALTINTOP Hamit	22
16	SHELAEV Oleg	80	46	KARADENIZ Gokdeniz	25
	Tr: BLOKHIN Oleg			Tr: TERIM Fatih	
14	GUSIN Andrei	83	82	SAS Hasan	11
15	SHYSHCHENKO Sermiy	80	46	CIMSIR Huseyin	15
19	VENGLINSKI Oleg	67	91	AKIN Serhat	24

Parken, Copenhagen
7-09-2005, 20:00, 27 177, Bozinovski MKD

DEN 6 1 GEO

Jensen 10, Poulsen 30, Agger 43, Tomasson 55, Larsen 2 80 84 — Demetradze 37

#	DENMARK			GEORGIA	#
1	SORENSEN Thomas			LOMAIA George	1
2	POULSEN Christian	60		MENTESAHSHVILI Zurab	2
3	GRAVGAARD Michael			KALADZE Kakha	4
4	AGGER Daniel		82	TSIKITISHVILI Levan	7
5	JENSEN Niclas			GAKHOKIDZE Georgi	8
6	HELVEG Thomas			KOBIASHVILI Levan	10
7	GRAVESEN Thomas		69	DEMETRADZE George	11
8	JENSEN Claus	63	20	KHIZANISHVILI Zurab	13
9	TOMASSON Jon Dahl	69		GOGUA Gogita	14
10	JORGENSEN Martin			ASATIANI Malkhaz	16
11	ROMMEDAHL Dennis		60	ODIKADZE David	18
	Tr: OLSEN Morten			Tr: DARSADZE Gaioz	
12	KAHLENBERG Thomas	60	82	SALUKVADZE Lasha	3
17	PEREZ Kenneth	69	60	GANUGRAVA George	5
18	LARSEN Soren	63	69	MUJIRI David	15

Meteor, Dnepropetrovsk
8-10-2005, 19:15, 24 000, Verbist BEL

UKR 2 2 ALB

Shevchenko 45, Rotan 86 — Bogdani 2 75 83

#	UKRAINE			ALBANIA	#
1	SHOVKOVSKI Alexandr			LIKA Ilion	1
3	FEDOROV Sergyi			BEQIRI Elvin	2
4	TYMOSHYUK Anatoliy			DALLKU Armend	4
5	SHELAEV Oleg			CANA Lorik	5
6	RUSOL Andrey			HASI Besnik	6
7	SHEVCHENKO Andriy	59		ALIAJ Ardian	11
8	ROTAN Ruslan			SKELA Ervin	13
9	HUSYEV Oleh			LALA Altin	14
10	VORONIN Andrey		70	TARE Igli	17
16	NAZARENKO Sergey	71		BOGDANI Erion	22
18	SEHVCHUK Vyacheslav		83	HAXHI Altin	23
	Tr: BLOKHIN Oleg			Tr: BRIEGEL Hans-Peter	
11	VOROBEY Andriy	71	83	MURATI Edvin	7
17	BYELIK Olekcii	59	70	KAPLLANI Edmond	21

Boris Paichadze, Tbilisi
8-10-2005, 20:00, 0, Hyytia FIN

GEO 0 0 KAZ

#	GEORGIA			KAZAKHSTAN	#
1	REVISHVILI Nukri			LORIYA David	1
2	MJAVANADZE Kakhaber			ZHUNASKALIYEV Nurbol	2
3	SALUKVADZE Lasha			AZOVSKIY Maxim	4
4	KALADZE Kakha		52	KUCHMA Alexandr	5
5	GANUGRAVA George			IRISMETOV Farkhadbek	7
8	KANKAVA Jaba			SMAKOV Samat	8
9	ASHVETIA Mikhail	86		TRAVIN Andrey	9
10	KOBIASHVILI Levan			NIZOVTSEV Maxim	11
11	DEMETRADZE George			MUKANOV Daniyar	16
15	MUJIRI David		54	LARIN Sergey	17
16	ASATIANI Malkhaz		66	KENZHEKHANOV Daniyar	19
	Tr: DARSADZE Gaioz			Tr: TIMOFEEV Sergei	
18	TSINAMDZGHVRISHVILI Rati	86			
			54	KHOHLOV Nikita	3
			66	LITVINENKO Oleg	10
			52	FAMILTSEV Alexander	15

Parken, Copenhagen
8-10-2005, 20:00, 42 099, De Bleeckere BEL

DEN 1 0 GRE

Gravgaard 40

#	DENMARK			GREECE	#
1	SORENSEN Thomas			NIKOPOLIDIS Antonios	1
2	POULSEN Christian			SEITARIDIS Giourkas	2
3	GRAVGAARD Michael			BASINAS Angelos	6
4	NIELSEN Per			ZAGORAKIS Theo	7
5	JENSEN Niclas			GIANNAKOPOULOS Stelios	8
6	PRISKE Brian		77	VRYZAS Zisis	15
7	GRAVESEN Thomas			KAPSIS Mihalis	19
8	JENSEN Claus	86		KARAGOUNIS Georgios	20
9	TOMASSON Jon Dahl			KATSOURANIS Konst'inos	21
10	JORGENSEN Martin			KYRGIAKOS Sotirios	25
11	ROMMEDAHL Dennis	72	62	LYMPEROPOULOS Nikos	33
	Tr: OLSEN Morten			Tr: REHHAGEL Otto	
15	GRONKJAER Jesper	72	62	KAFES Pantelis	16
18	LARSEN Soren	86	77	GEKAS Theofanis	17
			46	SALPINGIDIS Dimitrios	22

Qemal Stafa, Tirana
12-10-2005, 18:00, 8 000, Dauden Ibanez ESP

ALB   0   1   TUR

Metin [58]

ALBANIA			TURKEY	
1 LIKA Ilion			DEMIREL Volkan	23
2 BEQIRI Elvin			OZALAN Alpay	4
4 DALLKU Armend	63		OZAT Umit	6
5 CANA Lorik		46	BURUK Okan	7
6 HASI Besnik		46	BASTURK Yildiray	10
11 ALIAJ Ardian			CIMSIR Huseyin	15
13 SKELA Ervin			SAHIN Selcuk	16
14 LALA Altin			METIN Tumer	17
17 TARE Igli	73		TORAMAN Ibrahim	19
22 BOGDANI Erion		92	ALTINTOP Halil	21
23 HAXHI Altin	50		ALTINTOP Hamit	22
Tr: BRIEGEL Hans-Peter			Tr: TERIM Fatih	
7 MURATI Edvin	50	46	BELOZOGLU Emre	5
15 JUPI Redi	63	46	KAHVECI Nihat	8
21 KAPLLANI Edmond	73	92	ATES Necati	18

Karaiskaki Stadium, Athens
12-10-2005, 19:00, 28 186, Trefoloni ITA

GRE   1   0   GEO

Papadopoulos [17]

GREECE			GEORGIA	
1 NIKOPOLIDIS Antonios			REVISHVILI Nukri	1
2 SEITARIDIS Giourkas			MJAVANADZE Kakhaber	2
5 DELLAS Traianos	63	46	SALUKVADZE Lasha	3
6 BASINAS Angelos			KALADZE Kakha	4
7 ZAGORAKIS Theo	53		GANUGRAVA George	5
11 PAPADOPOULOS Dimitrios			KANKAVA Jaba	8
18 GOUMAS Ioannis			KOBIASHVILI Levan	10
19 KAPSIS Mihalis		86	DEMETRADZE George	11
21 KATSOURANIS Konst'inos			KHIZANISHVILI Zurab	13
22 SALPINGIDIS Dimitrios			GOGUA Gogita	14
26 MANTZIOS Evangelos	46		MUJIRI David	15
Tr: REHHAGEL Otto			Tr: DARSADZE Gaioz	
15 VRYZAS Zisis	46	86	GOTSIRIDZE Revaz	6
16 KAFES Pantelis	53	46	TSINAMDZGHVRISHVILI Rati	9
32 ANATOLAKIS Georgos	63			

Central Stadium, Almaty
12-10-2005, 22:00. 8 050, Trivkovic CRO

KAZ   1   2   DEN

Kuchma [86]   Gravgaard [46], Tomasson [49]

KAZAKHSTAN			DENMARK	
1 NOVIKOV Yuriy		46	SORENSEN Thomas	1
2 IRISMETOV Farkhadbek	66		POULSEN Christian	2
5 KUCHMA Alexandr			GRAVGAARD Michael	3
6 KHOHLOV Nikita			NIELSEN Per	4
7 AVDEYEV Igor		87	JENSEN Niclas	5
8 SMAKOV Samat			PRISKE Brian	6
9 KARPOVICH Andrey			JENSEN Daniel	7
10 LITVINENKO Oleg	50		LARSEN Soren	8
15 FAMILTSEV Alexander	56		TOMASSON Jon Dahl	9
16 MUKANOV Daniyar			JORGENSEN Martin	10
19 ZHUNASKALIYEV Nurbol		46	ROMMEDAHL Dennis	11
Tr: TIMOFEEV Sergei			Tr: OLSEN Morten	
3 TRAVIN Andrey	66	87	HELVEG Thomas	12
11 KENZHEKHANOV Daniyar	50	46	KAHLENBERG Thomas	14
17 LARIN Sergey	56	46	CHRISTIANSEN Jesper	16

GROUP 2	PL	W	D	L	F	A	PTS	UKR	TUR	DEN	GRE	ALB	GEO	KAZ
1 Ukraine	12	7	4	1	18	7	25		0-1	1-0	1-1	2-2	2-0	2-0
2 Turkey	12	6	5	1	23	9	23	0-3		2-2	0-0	2-0	1-1	4-0
3 Denmark	12	6	4	2	24	12	22	1-1	1-1		1-0	3-1	6-1	3-0
4 Greece	12	6	3	3	15	9	21	0-1	0-0	2-1		2-0	1-0	3-1
5 Albania	12	4	1	7	11	20	13	0-2	0-1	0-2	2-1		3-2	2-1
6 Georgia	12	2	4	6	14	25	10	1-1	2-5	2-2	1-3	2-0		0-0
7 Kazakhstan	12	0	1	11	6	29	1	1-2	0-6	1-2	1-2	0-1	1-2	

Ukraine qualified for the finals • Turkey qualified for a play-off against Switzerland

GROUP 3

Skonto, Riga
17-08-2005, 18:00, 10 000, Poll ENG

LVA 1 1 RUS

Astafjevs [6]   Arshavin [24]

	LATVIA			RUSSIA		
1	KLOINKO Alexandrs			AKINFEEV Igor	1	
2	STEPANOVS Igors			BEREZUTSKY Alexei	2	
3	ASTAFJEVS Vitalijs			SENNIKOV Dmitri	3	
4	SMIRNOVS Maris			EVSEEV Vadim	4	
5	LAIZANS Juris	59		KARYAKA Andrei	5	
6	ZIRNIS Dzintars			IGNASHEVICH Sergei	6	
8	BLEIDELIS Imants	67		KHOKHLOV Dmitry	7	
9	VERPAKOVSKIS Maris			ALDONIN Evgeni	8	
10	RUBINS Andrejs			ARSHAVIN Andrei	9	
11	RIMKUS Vits	76	84	BILYALETDINOV Dinyar	10	
17	KORABLOVS Igors			KERZHAKOV Alexander	11	
	Tr: ANDREJEVS Jurijs			Tr: SYOMIN Yuri		
14	PROHORENKOVS Andrejs	76	59	BYSTROV Vladimir	14	
			67	SEMSHOV Igor	17	
			84	KIRICHENKO Dmitri	18	

Rheinpark, Vaduz
17-08-2005, 20:15, 1 150, Layec FRA

LIE 0 0 SVK

	LIECHTENSTEIN			SLOVAKIA		
1	JEHLE Peter			CONTOFALSKY Kamil	1	
2	TELSER Martin		80	GRESKO Vratislav	2	
3	STOCKLASA Michael	89		ZABAVNIK Radoslav	3	
4	BUCHEL Martin			KRATOCHVIL Roman	4	
5	WOLFINGER Mario		46	HLINKA Peter	5	
6	STOCKLASA Martin			KARHAN Miroslav	6	
7	BECK Roger			KISEL Karol	7	
8	BUCHEL Ronny		46	JAKUBKO Martin	8	
9	BECK Thomas			HAD Marian	9	
10	ROHRER Raphael	65		MINTAL Marek	10	
11	VOGT Franz-Josef	75		VITTEK Robert	11	
	Tr: MEIER Urs			Tr: GALIS Dusan		
14	RITZBERGER Marco	89	80	SLOVAK Samuel	14	
16	ALABOR Claudio	65	46	SNINSKY Dusan	15	
17	FRICK Daniel	75	46	REITER Lubomir	17	

A. Le Coq Arena, Tallinn
3-09-2005, 18:00, 8 970, Undiano Mallenco ESP

EST 2 1 LVA

Oper [11], Smirnov [71]   Laizans [90]

	ESTONIA			LATVIA		
1	KOTENKO Artur			KLOINKO Alexandrs	1	
2	JAAGER Enar			STEPANOVS Igors	2	
3	STEPANOV Andrei			ASTAFJEVS Vitalijs	3	
4	PIIROJA Raio			SMIRNOVS Maris	4	
5	KRUGLOV Dmitri			LAIZANS Juris	5	
6	LEETMA Liivo		86	ZIRNIS Dzintars	6	
7	SMIRNOV Maksim	78	81	BLEIDELIS Imants	8	
8	DMITRIJEV Aleksandr			VERPAKOVSKIS Maris	9	
9	VILKMAE Kristen	57		RUBINS Andrejs	10	
10	OPER Andres		75	RIMKUS Vits	11	
11	TEREKHOV Sergei			KORABLOVS Igors	17	
	Tr: GOES Jelle			Tr: ANDREJEVS Jurijs		
17	TEEVER Ingemar	78	81	SOLONICINS Genadijs	13	
18	NEEMELO Tarmo	57	75	PROHORENKOVS Andrejs	13	
			86	MOROZS Viktors	16	

Lokomotiv, Moscow
3-09-2005, 19:00, 18 123, Hyytia FIN

RUS 2 0 LIE

Kerzhakov 2 [27 66]

	RUSSIA			LIECHTENSTEIN		
1	AKINFEEV Igor			JEHLE Peter	1	
2	BEREZUTSKY Alexei			TELSER Martin	2	
3	BEREZUTSKY Vassili			STOCKLASA Michael	3	
4	SMERTIN Alexei			D'ELIA Fabio	5	
5	ANYUKOV Aleksandr			STOCKLASA Martin	6	
6	IGNASHEVICH Sergei		46	VOGT Franz-Josef	7	
7	IZMAILOV Marat		70	BUCHEL Ronny	8	
8	PAVLUCHENKO Roman	66	85	BECK Thomas	9	
9	ARSHAVIN Andrei	75		FRICK Mario	10	
10	BILYALETDINOV Dinyar			BURGMEIER Franz	11	
11	KERZHAKOV Alexander	82		BUCHEL Martin	15	
	Tr: SYOMIN Yuri			Tr: ANDERMATT Martin		
13	ALDONIN Evgeni	66	46	ROHRER Raphael	14	
17	TITOV Egor	75	85	FRICK Daniel	16	
18	KIRICHENKO Dmitri	82	70	FISCHER Benjamin	18	

Algarve, Faro-Loule
3-09-2005, 21:15, 25 300, Van Egmond NED

POR 6 0 LUX

Jorge [24], Ricardo Carvalho [30]
Pauleta 2 [38 57], Simao Sabrosa 2 [80 85]

	PORTUGAL			LUXEMBOURG		
1	RICARDO			OBERWEIS Marc	1	
2	PAULO FERREIRA			HOFFMANN Eric	2	
4	JORGE ANDRADE		40	LANG Benoit	3	
6	COSTINHA			HEINZ Tim	4	
7	LUIS FIGO			REITER Claude	5	
9	PAULETA			LEWECK Fons	6	
14	NUNO VALENTE			STRASSER Jeff	7	
16	RICARDO CARVALHO		68	REMY Sebastien	8	
17	CRISTIANO RONALDO	62		FEDERSPIEL Ben	9	
18	MANICHE	46		COLLETTE Dan	10	
20	DECO	68	62	PACE Carlo	11	
	Tr: SCOLARI Luiz Felipe			Tr: HELLERS Guy		
11	SIMAO SABROSA	62	40	SCHNELL Tom	15	
23	HELDER POSTIGA	68	68	SABOTIC Ernad	16	
36	JOAO MOUTINHO	46	62	SAGRAMOLA Chris	17	

Lokomotiv, Moscow
7-09-2005, 19:00, 28 800, Merk GER

RUS 0 0 POR

	RUSSIA			PORTUGAL		
1	AKINFEEV Igor			RICARDO	1	
2	BEREZUTSKY Vassili			PAULO FERREIRA	2	
3	BEREZUTSKY Alexei			JORGE ANDRADE	4	
4	SMERTIN Alexei	44		COSTINHA	6	
5	SENNIKOV Dmitri			LUIS FIGO	7	
6	IGNASHEVICH Sergei		68	PAULETA	9	
7	IZMAILOV Marat	73		NUNO VALENTE	14	
8	ALDONIN Evgeni			RICARDO CARVALHO	16	
9	BILYALETDINOV Dinyar			CRISTIANO RONALDO	17	
10	ARSHAVIN Andrei	88	85	MANICHE	18	
11	KERZHAKOV Alexander		75	DECO	20	
	Tr: SYOMIN Yuri			Tr: SCOLARI Luiz Felipe		
17	SEMAK Sergei	73	75	SIMAO SABROSA	11	
18	ANYUKOV Aleksandr	88	68	HELDER POSTIGA	23	
			85	JOAO MOUTINHO	36	

Skonto, Riga
7-09-2005, 19:00, 8 800, Plautz AUT

LVA 1 1 SVK

Laizans 74 — Vittek 35

#	LATVIA			SLVOAKIA	#
1	KLOINKO Alexandrs			CONTOFALSKY Kamil	1
2	ZAKRESEVSKIS Arturs			GRESKO Vratislav	2
3	ASTAFJEVS Vitalijs			ZABAVNIK Radoslav	3
5	LAIZANS Juris			KRATOCHVIL Roman	4
6	ZIRNIS Dzintaris			SKRTEL Martin	5
7	ISAKOVS Aleksandrs			KARHAN Miroslav	6
8	BLEIDELIS Imants		85	VALACHOVIC Jozef	7
9	VERPAKOVSKIS Maris	77		HOLOSKO Filip	8
10	RUBINS Andrejs			HAD Marian	9
11	RIMKUS Vits	70	64	MINTAL Marek	10
17	KORABLOVS Igors	24	77	VITTEK Robert	11
	Tr: ANDREJEVS Jurijs			Tr: GALIS Dusan	
16	MOROZS Viktors	70	85	VARGA Stanislav	14
18	ZAVORONKOVS Vladimirs	24	64	HLINKA Peter	15
			77	KISEL Karol	16

Rheinpark, Vaduz
7-09-2005, 19:30, 2 300, Skomina SVN

LIE 3 0 LUX

Frick 38, Fischer 77, Beck 92+

#	LIECHTENSTEIN			LUXEMBOURG	#
1	JEHLE Peter			OBERWEIS Marc	1
2	TELSER Martin			SCHNELL Tom	2
3	STOCKLASA Michael			REITER Claude	3
4	BUCHEL Martin	75		HOFFMANN Eric	4
5	D'ELIA Fabio			FEDERSPIEL Ben	5
6	STOCKLASA Martin			LEWECK Charles	6
7	FISCHER Benjamin			STRASSER Jeff	7
8	BUCHEL Ronny	83	59	JOACHIM Aurelien	9
9	BECK Thomas	80		COLLETTE Dan	10
10	FRICK Mario	89	69	SAGRAMOLA Chris	11
11	BURGMEIER Franz	61		REMY Sebastien	16
	Tr: ANDERMATT Martin			Tr: HELLERS Guy	
14	ROHRER Raphael	75	80	PACE Carlo	8
16	FRICK Daniel	89	61	SABOTIC Ernad	15
17	BECK Roger	83	69	DA LUZ Claudio	17

Tehelné Pole, Bratislava
8-10-2005, 17:00, 12 800, Allaerts BEL

SVK 1 0 EST

Hlinka 72

#	SLVOAKIA			ESTONIA	#
1	CONTOFALSKY Kamil			KOTENKO Artur	1
2	HAD Marian	70		JAAGER Enar	2
3	SKRTEL Martin			STEPANOV Andrei	3
4	KRATOCHVIL Roman			PIIROJA Raio	4
5	HLINKA Peter			KRUGLOV Dmitri	5
6	ZABAVNIK Radoslav	87	87	LEETMA Liivo	6
7	KISEL Karol			SMIRNOV Maksim	7
8	NEMETH Szilard			DMITRIJEV Aleksandr	8
9	SESTAK Stanislav	46	37	VILKMAE Kristen	9
10	HODUR Ivan	77		OPER Andres	10
11	VITTEK Robert	74	74	TEREKHOV Sergei	11
	Tr: GALIS Dusan			Tr: GOES Jelle	
14	HOLOSKO Filip	46	87	RAHN Taavi	15
15	SAPARA Marek	77	74	LINDPERE Joel	17
17	REITER Lubomir	70	37	NEEMELO Tarmo	18

Lokomotiv, Moscow
8-10-2005, 19:00, 20 000, Tudor ROU

RUS 5 1 LUX

Izmailov 6, Kerzhakov 17, Pavluchenko 69, Kirichenko 2 74 93 — Reiter 51

#	RUSSIA			LUXEMBOURG	#
1	AKINFEEV Igor			GILLET Stephane	1
2	BEREZUTSKY Vassili			SCHNELL Tom	2
3	BEREZUTSKY Alexei			MUTSCH Mario	3
5	SENNIKOV Dmitri			HOFFMANN Eric	4
9	IZMAILOV Marat	57		REITER Claude	5
10	ARSHAVIN Andrei	61	75	LEWECK Charles	6
11	KERZHAKOV Alexander	67		PETERS Rene	7
20	SEMSHOV Igor			LEWECK Fons	8
22	ANYUKOV Aleksandr		86	MANNON Paul	9
24	GUSEV Rolan		78	COLLETTE Dan	10
				REMY Sebastien	16
	Tr: SYOMIN Yuri			Tr: HELLERS Guy	
17	SEMAK Sergei	57	75	FEDERSPIEL Ben	11
18	KIRICHENKO Dmitri	67	86	DA LUZ Claudio	13
19	PAVLUCHENKO Roman	61	78	SABOTIC Ernad	14

Aveiro, Aveiro
8-10-2005, 21:15, 29 000, Gilewski POL

POR 2 1 LIE

Pauleta 48, Nuno Gomes 85 — Fischer 32

#	PORTUGAL			LIECHTENSTEIN	#
1	RICARDO			JEHLE Peter	1
2	PAULO FERREIRA			TELSER Martin	2
4	JORGE ANDRADE			STOCKLASA Michael	3
7	LUIS FIGO			HASLER Daniel	4
8	PETIT			D'ELIA Fabio	5
9	PAULETA			STOCKLASA Martin	6
11	SIMAO SABROSA	74	87	BECK Thomas	7
14	NUNO VALENTE			BUCHEL Ronny	8
16	RICARDO CARVALHO	55	55	FISCHER Benjamin	9
17	CRISTIANO RONALDO	84		FRICK Mario	10
18	MANICHE	71	51	BURGMEIER Franz	11
	Tr: SCOLARI Luiz Felipe			Tr: ANDERMATT Martin	
19	TIAGO	71	87	ROHRER Raphael	14
21	NUNO GOMES	84	55	FRICK Daniel	16
30	HUGO VIANA	74	51	BECK Roger	17

Dragao, Porto
12-10-2005, 19:30, 35 000, Frojdfeldt SWE

POR 3 0 LVA

Pauleta 2 20 22, Hugo Viana 86

#	PORTUGAL			LATVIA	#
12	QUIM			KLOINKO Alexandrs	1
4	JORGE ANDRADE			STEPANOVS Igors	2
7	LUIS FIGO	80		ASTAFJEVS Vitalijs	3
9	PAULETA	57		ZAKRESEVSKIS Arturs	4
13	MIGUEL			MOROZS Viktors	5
15	CANEIRA			ZIRNIS Dzintaris	6
17	CRISTIANO RONALDO	46		ISAKOVS Aleksandrs	7
18	MANICHE		57	SOLONICINS Genadijs	8
19	TIAGO		73	VERPAKOVSKIS Maris	9
20	DECO			RUBINS Andrejs	10
29	FERNANDO MEIRA	57		RIMKUS Vits	11
	Tr: SCOLARI Luiz Felipe			Tr: ANDREJEVS Jurijs	
21	NUNO GOMES	46	57	VISNAKOVS Aleksejs	14
23	HELDER POSTIGA	57	57	KALNINS Gatis	15
30	HUGO VIANA	80	73	BLANKS Kristaps	17

Josy-Barthel, Luxembourg		
12-10-2005, 20:15, 2 010, Dereli TUR		
LUX	**0 2**	**EST**

Oper 2 [7 78]

	LUXEMBOURG			ESTONIA	
1	GILLET Stephane			KOTENKO Artur	1
2	KINTZIGER Kim			JAAGER Enar	2
3	MUTSCH Mario	72		STEPANOV Andrei	3
4	HOFFMANN Eric			PIIROJA Raio	4
5	REITER Claude			KRUGLOV Dmitri	5
6	LEWECK Charles	77	61	RAHN Taavi	6
7	PETERS Rene		61	TEREKHOV Sergei	7
8	LEWECK Fons			DMITRIJEV Aleksandr	8
9	MANNON Paul	56		NEEMELO Tarmo	9
10	COLLETTE Dan			OPER Andres	10
16	REMY Sebastien			KLAVAN Ragnar	11
	Tr: HELLERS Guy			Tr: GOES Jelle	
11	FEDERSPIEL Ben	72	61	SMIRNOV Maksim	15
13	DA LUZ Claudio	77	61	REIM Martin	16
18	KITENGE Joel	56			

Tehelné Pole, Bratislava		
12-10-2005, 20:30, 22 317, Rosetti ITA		
SVK	**0 0**	**RUS**

	SLOVAKIA			RUSSIA	
1	CONTOFALSKY Kamil			AKINFEEV Igor	1
2	HAD Marian			BEREZUTSKY Vassili	2
3	SKRTEL Martin			BEREZUTSKY Alexei	3
4	KRATOCHVIL Roman			SMERTIN Alexei	4
5	HLINKA Peter			SENNIKOV Dmitri	5
6	KARHAN Miroslav	67		IZMAILOV Marat	7
7	ZABAVNIK Radoslav			LOSKOV Dmitri	9
8	NEMETH Szilard	82		ARSHAVIN Andrei	10
9	VALACHOVIC Jozef		67	KERZHAKOV Alexander	11
10	HODUR Ivan	57	56	BILYALETDINOV Dinyar	15
11	VITTEK Robert		81	ANYUKOV Aleksandr	22
	Tr: GALIS Dusan			Tr: SYOMIN Yuri	
14	HOLOSKO Filip	57	56	SEMAK Sergei	17
15	DURICA Jan	82	67	KIRICHENKO Dmitri	18
16	KISEL Karol	67	81	PAVLUCHENKO Roman	19

GROUP 3	PL	W	D	L	F	A	PTS	POR	SVK	RUS	EST	LVA	LIE	LUX
1 Portugal	12	9	3	0	35	5	30		2-0	7-1	4-0	3-0	2-1	6-0
2 Slovakia	12	6	5	1	24	8	23	1-1		0-0	1-0	4-1	7-0	3-1
3 Russia	12	6	5	1	23	12	23	0-0	1-1		4-0	2-0	2-0	5-1
4 Estonia	12	5	2	5	16	17	17	0-1	1-2	1-1		2-1	2-0	4-0
5 Latvia	12	4	3	5	18	21	15	0-2	1-1	1-1	2-2		1-0	4-0
6 Liechtenstein	12	2	2	8	13	23	8	2-2	0-0	1-2	1-2	1-3		3-0
7 Luxembourg	12	0	0	12	5	48	0	0-5	0-4	0-4	0-2	3-4	0-4	

Portugal qualified for the finals • Slovakia qualified for a play-off against Spain

GROUP 4

Toftir, Toftir		
17-08-2005, 19:00, 2 720, Johannesson SWE		
FRO	**0 3**	**CYP**

Konstantinou 2 [39 77]
Krassas [95+]

	FAROE ISLANDS			CYPRUS	
1	KNUDSEN Jens			MORPHIS Michael	1
2	OLSEN Suni	15	81	THEODOTOU Georgios	2
3	HANSEN Johan	79		MAKRIDIS Konstantinos	7
4	DANIELSEN Atli			KRASSAS Asimakis	8
5	JACOBSEN Jon Roi			OKKAS Ioannis	9
6	JACOBSEN Rogvi			CHARALAMPIDIS Konst.	10
8	JORGENSEN Claus Bech		88	KONSTANTINOU Michael	11
9	BORG Jakup			MICHAIL Chrysostomos	13
10	JONSSON Todi	46		LOUKA Loukas	17
11	FLOTUM Andrew		63	GARPOZIS Alexandros	22
13	JOHANNESEN Oli		45	ELEFTHERIOU Lefteris	24
	Tr: LARSEN Henrik			Tr: ANASTASIADIS Angelos	
7	LAKJUNI Hedin	79	81	CHARALAMBOUS Elias	5
12	JACOBSEN Christian	46	63	OKKARIDES Stelios	6
18	HORG Mortan	15	88	YIASOUMI Yiasoumis	18

St Jakob-Park, Basel		
3-09-2005, 17:30, 30 000, Rosetti ITA		
SUI	**1 1**	**ISR**

Frei [6]   Keisi [20]

	SWITZERLAND			ISRAEL	
1	ZUBERBUEHLER Pascal			DAVIDOVITCH Nir	1
3	MAGNIN Ludovic	89		HARAZI Alon	2
6	VOGEL Johann			BEN HAIM Tal	3
9	FREI Alexander			BENADO Arik	4
10	YAKIN Hakan	65		KEISI Adoram	6
16	BARNETTA Tranquillo		71	NIMNI Avi	8
20	MUELLER Patrick			BADEER Valeed	10
21	GYGAX Daniel			TAL Idan	11
22	VONLANTHEN Johan	82	94	BENAYOUN Yossi	15
24	SENDEROS Philippe		65	KATAN Yaniv	20
26	DEGEN Philipp			SABAN Klemi	21
	Tr: KUHN Koebi			Tr: GRANT Avraham	
7	CABANAS Ricardo	65	65	GOLAN Omer	12
17	SPYCHER Christoph	89	94	SWAN Abbas	17
30	LUSTRINELLI Mauro	82	71	ZAUDBERG Michael	18

Felix Bollaert, Lens
3-09-2005, 21:00, 40 126, Jara CZE

FRA 3 – 0 FRO

Cisse 2 (14, 76), Olsen 18 OG

#	FRANCE			FAROE ISLANDS	#
23	COUPET Gregory			MIKKELSEN Jakup	1
2	BOUMSONG Jean-Alain			OLSEN Suni	2
4	VIEIRA Patrick		56	HORG Mortan	3
5	GALLAS William			JACOBSEN Jon Roi	5
6	MAKELELE Claude			BENJAMINSEN Frodi	7
7	MALOUDA Florent		76	JORGENSEN Claus Bech	8
9	CISSE Djibril			BORG Jakup	9
10	ZIDANE Zinedine	59	67	JONSSON Todi	10
12	HENRY Thierry	67		FLOTUM Andrew	11
15	THURAM Lilian	76		JOHANNESEN Oli	13
19	SAGNOL Willy			HOJSTED Ingi	14
	Tr: DOMENECH Raymond			Tr: LARSEN Henrik	
11	WILTORD Sylvain	67	67	JACOBSEN Rogvi	6
17	SQUILACI Sebastien	76	56	JACOBSEN Christian	12
22	DHORASOO Vikash	59	76	LAKJUNI Hedin	17

Torsvollur, Tórshavn
7-09-2005, 18:00, 2 240, Vink NED

FRO 0 – 2 ISR

Nimni 54, Katan 79

#	FAROE ISLANDS			ISRAEL	#
1	MIKKELSEN Jakup			DAVIDOVITCH Nir	1
2	OLSEN Suni			HARAZI Alon	2
3	HORG Mortan			BEN HAIM Tal	3
5	JACOBSEN Jon Roi			BENADO Arik	4
6	JACOBSEN Rogvi			KEISI Adoram	6
7	BENJAMINSEN Frodi		66	BALILI Pini	7
8	JORGENSEN Claus Bech	85		NIMNI Avi	8
9	BORG Jakup	69		BADEER Valeed	10
12	JACOBSEN Christian			BENAYOUN Yossi	15
13	JOHANNESEN Oli			SWAN Abbas	17
14	HOJSTED Ingi	62	86	KATAN Yaniv	20
	Tr: LARSEN Henrik			Tr: GRANT Avraham	
11	FLOTUM Andrew	62	66	TAL Idan	11
15	SAMUELSEN Simun	85	86	BITON Moshe	14
17	LAKJUNI Hedin	69			

Lansdowne Road, Dublin
7-09-2005, 19:55, 36 000, Fandel GER

IRL 0 – 1 FRA

Henry 68

#	IRELAND REPUBLIC			FRANCE	#
1	GIVEN Shay			COUPET Gregory	23
2	CARR Stephen			BOUMSONG Jean-Alain	2
3	O SHEA John			VIEIRA Patrick	4
4	CUNNINGHAM Kenny			GALLAS William	5
5	DUNNE Richard			MAKELELE Claude	6
6	KEANE Roy			ZIDANE Zinedine	10
7	REID Andy			WILTORD Sylvain	11
8	KILBANE Kevin	80		HENRY Thierry	12
9	MORRISON Clinton	80		THURAM Lilian	15
10	KEANE Robbie			SAGNOL Willy	19
11	DUFF Damien			DHORASOO Vikash	22
	Tr: KERR Brian			Tr: DOMENECH Raymond	
14	HARTE Ian	80	70	MALOUDA Florent	7
17	DOHERTY Gary	80	76	CISSE Djibril	9
			90	GIVET Gael	21

G.S.P, Nicosia
7-09-2005, 21:15, 2 561, Ivanov RUS

CYP 1 – 3 SUI

Aloneftis 35 — Frei 15, Senderos 71, Gygax 84

#	CYPRUS			SWITZERLAND	#
1	MORPHIS Michael			ZUBERBUEHLER Pascal	1
2	LOUKA Loukas			VOGEL Johann	6
5	CHARALAMBOUS Elias			WICKY Raphael	8
6	OKKARIDES Stelios	46	73	FREI Alexander	9
7	ALONEFTIS Efstathios		90	BARNETTA Tranquillo	16
8	KRASSAS Asimakis	64		SPYCHER Christoph	17
9	OKKAS Ioannis			MUELLER Patrick	20
10	CHARALAMPIDIS Konst.			GYGAX Daniel	21
11	KONSTANTINOU Michael		82	VONLANTHEN Johan	22
13	MICHAIL Chrysostomos	82		SENDEROS Philippe	24
19	ILIA Marios			DEGEN Philipp	26
	Tr: DIMITRAKOPOULOS Leonidas			Tr: KUHN Koebi	
3	NIKOLAOU Nikos	64	73	YAKIN Hakan	10
4	LAMBROU Lambros	46	90	COLTORTI Fabio	14
18	YIASOUMI Yiasoumis	82	82	LUSTRINELLI Mauro	30

G.S.P, Nicosia
8-10-2005, 20:00, 13 546, Kassai HUN

CYP 0 – 1 IRL

Elliott 6

#	CYPRUS			IRELAND REPUBLIC	#
1	PANAYIOTOU Nicos			GIVEN Shay	1
2	LOUKA Loukas			CARR Stephen	2
4	LAMBROU Lambros			O SHEA John	3
7	MAKRIDIS Konstantinos			CUNNINGHAM Kenny	4
8	ALONEFTIS Efstathios			DUNNE Richard	5
9	OKKAS Ioannis	69		KAVANAGH Graham	6
10	CHARALAMPIDIS Konst.		46	FINNAN Steve	7
11	KONSTANTINOU Michael			KILBANE Kevin	8
13	MICHAIL Chrysostomos	29		ELLIOTT Stephen	9
17	GARPOZIS Alexandros		85	KEANE Robbie	10
19	ILIA Marios	73	60	DUFF Damien	11
	Tr: ANASTASIADIS Angelos			Tr: KERR Brian	
15	MARAGKOS Christakis	73	60	REID Steven	13
16	KRASSAS Asimakis	29	46	HOLLAND Matt	15
18	YIASOUMI Yiasoumis	69	85	CONNOLLY David	17

Stade de Suisse, Berne
8-10-2005, 20:45, 31 400, Hauge NOR

SUI 1 – 1 FRA

Magnin 80 — Cisse 53

#	SWITZERLAND			FRANCE	#
1	ZUBERBUEHLER Pascal			COUPET Gregory	23
3	MAGNIN Ludovic			VIEIRA Patrick	4
6	VOGEL Johann			GALLAS William	5
7	CABANAS Ricardo			MAKELELE Claude	6
8	WICKY Raphael	83	90	MALOUDA Florent	7
9	FREI Alexander			BOUMSONG Jean-Alain	8
16	BARNETTA Tranquillo	90		ZIDANE Zinedine	10
20	MUELLER Patrick			WILTORD Sylvain	11
22	VONLANTHEN Johan	60		REVEILLERE Anthony	13
24	SENDEROS Philippe		46	DHORASOO Vikash	14
26	DEGEN Philipp			THURAM Lilian	15
	Tr: KUHN Koebi			Tr: DOMENECH Raymond	
21	GYGAX Daniel	60	46	CISSE Djibril	9
30	LUSTRINELLI Mauro	83	90	GOVOU Sidney	22
34	BEHRAMI Valon	90			

Ramat Gan, Tel Aviv
8-10-2005, 21:10, 31 857, Brugger AUT

ISR 2 1 FRO

Benayoun [1], Zaudberg [91+]

Samuelsen [93+]

ISRAEL			FAROE ISLANDS	
1	DAVIDOVITCH Nir		MIKKELSEN Jakup	1
2	HARAZI Alon		HORG Mortan	3
3	BEN HAIM Tal	15	HANSEN Johan	4
4	BENADO Arik		JACOBSEN Jon Roi	5
6	KEISI Adoram		JACOBSEN Rogvi	6
8	NIMNI Avi		BENJAMINSEN Frodi	7
10	BADEER Valeed	80	JACOBSEN Christian	9
12	GOLAN Omer	67	JORGENSEN Claus Bech	10
15	BENAYOUN Yossi	67	FLOTUM Andrew	11
17	SWAN Abbas	46	JOHANNESEN Oli	13
20	KATAN Yaniv	73	HOJSTED Ingi	14
	Tr: GRANT Avraham		Tr: LARSEN Henrik	
7	BALILI Pini	73	15 DANIELSEN Atli	2
14	ARBITMAN Shlomi	67	67 FREDERIKSBERG Jonhard	12
18	ZAUDBERG Michael	46	80 SAMUELSEN Simun	15

Lansdowne Road, Dublin
12-10-2005, 19:45, 35 944, Merk GER

IRL 0 0 SUI

IRELAND REPUBLIC			SWITZERLAND	
1	GIVEN Shay		ZUBERBUEHLER Pascal	1
2	CARR Stephen		MAGNIN Ludovic	3
3	HARTE Ian		VOGEL Johann	6
4	CUNNINGHAM Kenny		CABANAS Ricardo	7
5	DUNNE Richard		WICKY Raphael	8
6	HOLLAND Matt		FREI Alexander	9
7	REID Andy	79	87 BARNETTA Tranquillo	16
8	O SHEA John		MUELLER Patrick	20
9	MORRISON Clinton	86	53 VONLANTHEN Johan	22
10	KEANE Robbie	65	SENDEROS Philippe	24
11	KILBANE Kevin		DEGEN Philipp	26
	Tr: KERR Brian		Tr: KUHN Koebi	
13	REID Steven	79	53 STRELLER Marco	11
17	ELLIOTT Stephen	65	87 GYGAX Daniel	21
18	DOHERTY Gary	86		

Stade de France, Paris
12-10-2005, 20:45, 78 864, Stark GER

FRA 4 0 CYP

Zidane [29], Wiltord [32]
Dhorasoo [44], Giuly [84]

FRANCE			CYPRUS	
23	COUPET Gregory		MORPHIS Michael	12
2	BOUMSONG Jean-Alain		LOUKA Loukas	2
4	VIEIRA Patrick	25	LAMBROU Lambros	4
5	GALLAS William		CHARALAMBOUS Elias	5
9	CISSE Djibril	79	MAKRIDIS Konstantinos	7
10	ZIDANE Zinedine		ALONEFTIS Efstathios	8
11	WILTORD Sylvain	60	CHARALAMPIDIS Konst.	10
14	DHORASOO Vikash		KRASSAS Asimakis	16
15	THURAM Lilian	46	GARPOZIS Alexandros	17
19	SAGNOL Willy	61	YAISOUMI Yiasoumis	18
22	GOVOU Sidney	91	ILIA Marios	19
	Tr: DOMENECH Raymond		Tr: ANASTASIADIS Angelos	
8	GIULY Ludovic	60	79 NIKOLAOU Marios	3
18	DIARRA Alou	25	46 MARAGKOS Christakis	15
21	JURIETTI Franck	91	61 FILANIOTIS Petros	21

GROUP 4	PL	W	D	L	F	A	PTS	FRA	SUI	ISR	IRL	CYP	FRO
1 France	10	5	5	0	14	2	20		0-0	0-0	0-0	4-0	3-0
2 Switzerland	10	4	6	0	18	7	18	1-1		1-1	1-1	1-0	6-0
3 Israel	10	4	6	0	15	10	18	1-1	2-2		1-1	2-1	2-1
4 Republic of Ireland	10	4	5	1	12	5	17	0-1	0-0	2-2		3-0	2-0
5 Cyprus	10	1	1	8	8	20	4	0-2	1-3	1-2	0-1		2-2
6 Faroe Islands	10	0	1	9	4	27	1	0-2	1-3	0-2	0-2	0-3	

France qualified for the finals • Switzerland qualified for a play-off against Turkey

GROUP 5

Hampden Park, Glasgow
3-09-2005, 17:30, 50 185, Michel SVK

SCO 1   1 ITA

Miller [13]   Grosso [75]

SCOTLAND			ITALY	
1 GORDON Craig			PERUZZI Angelo	1
2 MC NAMARA Jackie	46		ZACCARDO Cristian	2
3 WEBSTER Andy			ZAMBROTTA Gianluca	3
4 DAILLY Christian			GATTUSO Gennaro	4
5 WEIR David			CANNAVARO Fabio	5
6 FERGUSON Barry			NESTA Alessandro	6
7 FLETCHER Darren	60		DE ROSSI Daniele	7
8 GRAHAM Alexander			PIRLO Andrea	8
9 MILLER Kenny			VIERI Christian	9
10 HARTLEY Paul			TOTTI Francesco	10
11 QUASHIE Nigel	71		IAQUINTA Vincenzo	11
Tr: SMITH Walter			Tr: LIPPI Marcello	
15 BEATTIE Craig	46		GROSSO Fabio	14
18 MC CANN Neil	60		CAMORANESI Mauro	15
	71		TONI Luca	18

Republican Stadium, Chisinau
3-09-2005, 19:00, 5 000, Duhamel FRA

MDA 2   0 BLR

Rogaciov 2 [17] [49]

MOLDOVA			BELARUS	
1 HMARUC Evgheni			ZHAUNOU Yury	1
2 OLEXICI Ghenadie			KULCHY Aleksandr	2
3 SAVINOV Alexei			YASKOVICH Sergei	3
4 REBEJA Radu			OMELYANCHUK Sergei	4
5 CATINSUS Valerii			SHTANYUK Sergei	5
6 PRIGANIUC Iurie			GURENKO Sergei	6
7 COVALCIUC Serghei	86	69	KORYTKO Vladimir	7
8 IVANOV Stanislav			BELKEVICH Valentin	8
9 ROGACIOV Serghei	80	56	KALACHEV Timofei	9
10 BORET Vadim	46		HLEB Aleksandr	10
11 DADU Serghei			KUTUZOV Vitaly	11
Tr: PASULKO Viktor			Tr: BAIDACHNY Anatoly	
13 BORDIAN Vitalie	46	69	HLEB Vyacheslav	13
16 POPOVICI Alexander	80	56	BULYGA Vitaly	17
17 FRUNZA Viorel	86			

Petrol Arena, Celje
3-09-2005, 20:45, 10 055, Medina Cantalejo ESP

SVN 2   3 NOR

Cimirotic 4, Zlogar 83   Carew 3, Lundekvam [23]
                                  Pedersen [92+]

SLOVENIA			NORWAY	
1 MAVRIC Borut			MYHRE Thomas	1
3 FILEKOVIC Suad	60		BERGDOLMO Andre	2
4 MAVRIC Matej			HAGEN Erik	3
5 CESAR Bostjan			LUNDEKVAM Claus	4
6 KNAVS Aleksander			HOILAND Jon	5
10 CEH Nastja	67		SOLLI Jan	6
11 KOMAC Andrej			HAESTAD Kristofer	7
13 ZLOGAR Anton			GRINDHEIM Christian	8
14 CIMIROTIC Sebastijan			PEDERSEN Morten	9
16 RODIC Aleksandar			CAREW John	10
18 ACIMOVIC Milenko	56	11	IVERSEN Steffen	11
Tr: OBLAK Branko			Tr: HAREIDE Age	
8 KOREN Robert	60	67	ANDRESEN Martin	15
17 LAVRIC Klemen	56	10 82	BRAATEN Daniel	16
		82	ARST Ole	18

Ullevaal, Oslo
7-09-2005, 19:00, 24 904, Hamer LUX

NOR 1   2 SCO

Arst 89   Miller 2 [20] [30]

NORWAY			SCOTLAND	
1 MYHRE Thomas			GORDON Craig	1
2 BERGDOLMO Andre			MC NAMARA Jackie	2
3 RISETH Vidar			WEBSTER Andy	3
4 LUNDEKVAM Claus			PRESSLEY Steven	4
5 RIISE John Arne			WEIR David	5
6 SOLLI Jan	46		FERGUSON Barry	6
7 ANDRESEN Martin			FLETCHER Darren	7
8 GRINDHEIM Christian			GRAHAM Alexander	8
9 OSTENSTAD Egil	46	40	MILLER Kenny	9
10 CAREW John			HARTLEY Paul	10
11 VALENCIA Alex	46	72	MC FADDEN James	11
Tr: HAREIDE Age			Tr: SMITH Walter	
14 HAESTAD Kristofer	46	72	BEATTIE Craig	15
16 BRAATEN Daniel	46	40	MC CANN Neil	18
18 ARST Ole	46			

Dynamo, Minsk
7-09-2005, 20:00, 30 299, Temmink NED

BLR 1   4 ITA

Kutuzov 4   Toni 3 [6] [13] [55]
                                   Camoranesi 45

BELARUS			ITALY	
1 ZHAUNOU Yury			PERUZZI Angelo	1
2 KULCHY Aleksandr	79		ZACCARDO Cristian	2
3 YASKOVICH Sergei	32		GROSSO Fabio	3
4 OMELYANCHUK Sergei			GATTUSO Gennaro	4
5 SHTANYUK Sergei			CANNAVARO Fabio	5
6 LAVRIK Andrei			NESTA Alessandro	6
7 KOVBA Denis		83	CAMORANESI Mauro	7
8 BELKEVICH Valentin			PIRLO Andrea	8
9 BULYGA Vitaly		56	GILARDINO Alberto	9
10 HLEB Aleksandr			TOTTI Francesco	10
11 KUTUZOV Vitaly	75	65	TONI Luca	11
Tr: BAIDACHNY Anatoly			Tr: LIPPI Marcello	
13 HLEB Vyacheslav	75	83	BARZAGLI Andrea	13
14 TARLOVSKY Igor	32	56	BARONE Simone	16
17 KORYTKO Vladimir	79	65	IAQUINTA Vincenzo	18

Republican Stadium, Chisinau
7-09-2004, 21:15, 7 200, Baskakov RUS

MDA 1   2 SVN

Rogaciov 31   Lavric 47, Mavric 58

MOLDOVA			SLOVENIA	
1 HMARUC Evgheni			HANDANOVIC Samir	12
2 OLEXICI Ghenadie		46	FILEKOVIC Suad	3
3 SAVINOV Alexei			MAVRIC Matej	4
4 REBEJA Radu			CESAR Bostjan	5
5 CATINSUS Valerii			KNAVS Aleksander	6
6 PRIGANIUC Iurie			KOREN Robert	8
7 COVALCIUC Serghei	89		CEH Nastja	10
8 IVANOV Stanislav			ZLOGAR Anton	13
9 ROGACIOV Serghei	89	46	CIMIROTIC Sebastijan	14
10 BORDIAN Vitalie		88	RODIC Aleksandar	16
11 DADU Serghei	83		SESLAR Simon	19
Tr: PASULKO Viktor			Tr: OBLAK Branko	
16 POPOVICI Alexander	89	46	PECNIK Andrej	2
17 FRUNZA Viorel	83	88	SUKALO Goran	7
18 IEPUREANU Serghei	89	46	LAVRIC Klemen	17

Hampden Park, Glasgow
8-10-2005, 15:00, 51 105, Szabo HUN

SCO 0 1 BLR

Kutuzov [5]

#	SCOTLAND				BELARUS	#
1	GORDON Craig				KHOMUTOVSKY Vasily	1
2	GRAHAM Alexander				KULCHY ALeksandr	2
3	MURRAY Ian				TARLOVSKY Igor	3
4	PRESSLEY Steven				OSTROVSKY Andrei	4
5	WEIR David				KORYTKO Vladimir	5
6	FERGUSON Barry				LAVRIK Andrei	6
7	FLETCHER Darren				KOVBA Denis	7
8	DAILLY Christian	88			BULYGA Vitaly	8
9	MILLER Kenny				KALACHEV Timofei	9
10	HARTLEY Paul				HLEB Aleksandr	10
11	MC CULLOCH Lee				KUTUZOV Vitaly	11
	Tr: SMITH Walter				Tr: BAIDACHNY Anatoly	
		88	88		SASHCHEKA Dzianis	16

Ullevaal, Oslo
8-10-2005, 20:15, 23 409, Bennett RSA

NOR 1 0 MDA

Rushfeldt [50]

#	NORWAY				MOLDOVA	#
1	MYHRE Thomas				HMARUC Evgheni	1
2	BERGDOLMO Andre				LASCENCOV Serghei	2
3	HAGEN Erik				SAVINOV Alexei	3
4	HANGELAND Brede				OLEXICI Ghenadie	4
5	RIISE John Arne				CATINSUS Valerii	5
6	JOHNSEN Marius	64			PRIGANIUC Iurie	6
7	HAESTAD Kristofer				COVALCIUC Serghei	7
8	GRINDHEIM Christian	81			IVANOV Stanislav	8
9	PEDERSEN Morten				ROGACIOV Serghei	9
10	RUSHFELDT Sigurd	83	69		BORDIAN Vitalie	10
11	IVERSEN Steffen	91	72		DADU Serghei	11
	Tr: HAREIDE Age				Tr: PASULKO Viktor	
16	SOLLI Jan	64	81		GATCAN Alexandr	16
17	HELSTAD Thorstein	91	72		POPOVICI Alexander	17
18	BRAATEN Daniel	83	69		BORET Vadim	18

Renzo Barbera, Palermo
8-10-2005, 21:00, 19 123, Poulat FRA

ITA 1 0 SVN

Zaccardo [78]

#	ITALY				SLOVENIA	#
1	PERUZZI Angelo				MAVRIC Borut	1
2	ZAMBROTTA Gianluca				FILEKOVIC Suad	3
3	GROSSO Fabio				MAVRIC Matej	4
4	GATTUSO Gennaro				CESAR Bostjan	5
5	CANNAVARO Fabio				KNAVS Aleksander	6
6	NESTA Alessandro				KOREN Robert	8
7	CAMORANESI Mauro				KOMAC Andrej	11
8	PIRLO Andrea	81			ZLOGAR Anton	13
9	TONI Luca	87	46		POKORN Jalen	15
10	TOTTI Francesco	84			RODIC Aleksandar	16
11	GILARDINO Alberto	60			ACIMOVIC Milenko	18
	Tr: LIPPI Marcello				Tr: OBLAK Branko	
13	ZACCARDO Cristian	60	84		SILJAK Ermin	9
16	DE ROSSI Daniele	81	46		CIMIROTIC Sebastijan	14
19	VIERI Christian	87				

Via del Mare, Lecce
12-10-2005, 20:30, 28 160, Benquerenca POR

ITA 2 1 MDA

Viera [70], Gilardino [85]   Gatcan [76]

#	ITALY				MOLDOVA	#
1	DE SANCTIS Morgan				PASCENCO Serghei	1
2	ZACCARDO Cristian				LASCENCOV Serghei	2
3	GROSSO Fabio	61			SAVINOV Alexei	3
4	DE ROSSI Daniele				OLEXICI Ghenadie	4
5	BONERA Daniele	45			CATINSUS Valerii	5
6	MATERAZZI Marco				PRIGANIUC Iurie	6
7	DIANA Aimo				COVALCIUC Serghei	7
8	BARONE Simone				GATCAN Alexandr	8
9	VIERI Christian	86			ROGACIOV Serghei	9
10	DEL PIERO Alessandro				BORET Vadim	10
11	IAQUINTA Vincenzo	67			DADU Serghei	11
	Tr: LIPPI Marcello				Tr: PASULKO Viktor	
13	ZAMBROTTA Gianluca	61	86		MITEREV Iurie	14
15	BLASI Manuele	45				
19	GILARDINO Alberto	67				

Petrol Arena, Celje
12-10-2005, 20:30, 9 100, Temmink NED

SVN 0 3 SCO

Fletcher [4], McFadden [47]
Hartley [84]

#	SLOVENIA				SCOTLAND	#
1	HANDANOVIC Samir				GORDON Craig	1
4	MAVRIC Matej	25			DAILLY Christian	2
5	CESAR Bostjan				GRAHAM Alexander	3
6	KNAVS Aleksander		46		PRESSLEY Steven	4
8	KOREN Robert				WEIR David	5
10	CEH Nastja				WEBSTER Andy	6
11	KOMAC Andrej				FLETCHER Darren	7
13	ZLOGAR Anton	72			QUASHIE Nigel	8
14	CIMIROTIC Sebastijan		46		MILLER Kenny	9
16	RODIC Aleksandar	54			HARTLEY Paul	10
18	ACIMOVIC Milenko				MC FADDEN James	11
	Tr: OBLAK Branko				Tr: SMITH Walter	
2	PECNIK Andrej	58 25	72		CALDWELL Steven	13
9	SILJAK Ermin	54	46		CALDWELL Gary	14
20	ILIC Branko	58	46		O CONNER Garry	16

Dynamo, Minsk
12-10-2005, 21:30, 13 222, Plautz AUT

BLR 0 1 NOR

Helstad [70]

#	BELARUS				NORWAY	#
1	KHOMUTOVSKY Vasily				MYHRE Thomas	1
2	KULCHY ALeksandr				HOILAND Jon	2
3	OSTROVSKY Andrei		80		HAGEN Erik	3
4	OMELYANCHUK Sergei				HANGELAND Brede	4
5	SHTANYUK Sergei				RIISE John Arne	5
6	TARLOVSKY Igor		73		SOLLI Jan	6
7	KOVBA Denis	58			STROMSTAD Fredrik	7
8	BULYGA Vitaly				GRINDHEIM Christian	8
9	KALACHEV Timofei				PEDERSEN Morten	9
10	SASHCHEKA Dzianis	62	46		RUSHFELDT Sigurd	10
11	KUTUZOV Vitaly				IVERSEN Steffen	11
	Tr: BAIDACHNY Anatoly				Tr: HAREIDE Age	
14	KIRILCHIK Pavel	58	80		BORGENSEN Bard	14
16		62	46		HELSTAD Thorstein	17
			73		GASHI Ardian	18

GROUP 5		PL	W	D	L	F	A	PTS	ITA	NOR	SCO	SVN	BLR	MDA
1	Italy	10	7	2	1	17	8	23		2-1	2-0	1-0	4-3	2-1
2	Norway	10	5	3	2	12	7	18	0-0		1-2	3-0	1-1	1-0
3	Scotland	10	3	4	3	9	7	13	1-1	0-1		0-0	0-1	2-0
4	Slovenia	10	3	3	4	10	13	12	1-0	2-3	0-3		1-1	3-0
5	Belarus	10	2	4	4	12	14	10	1-4	0-1	0-0	1-1		4-0
6	Moldova	10	1	2	7	5	16	5	0-1	0-0	1-1	1-2	2-0	

Italy qualified for the finals • Norway qualified for a play-off against the Czech Republic

GROUP 6

Millennium, Cardiff
3-09-2005, 15:00, 70 715, Ivanov RUS

WAL	0 1	ENG

Joe Cole [54]

	WALES				ENGLAND	
1	COYNE Danny				ROBINSON Paul	1
2	DUFFY Richard				YOUNG Luke	2
3	RICKETTS Samuel				COLE Ashley	3
4	GABBIDON Danny		84		GERRARD Steven	4
5	PAGE Robert	65			FERDINAND Rio	5
6	PARTRIDGE David				CARRAGHER Jamie	6
7	FLETCHER Carl				BECKHAM David	7
8	ROBINSON Carl	54			LAMPARD Frank	8
9	HARTSON John				ROONEY Wayne	9
10	DAVIES Simon	70	68		WRIGHT-PHILLIPS Shaun	10
11	GIGGS Ryan		77		COLE Joe	11
	Tr: TOSHACK John				Tr: ERIKSON Sven Goran	
12	COLLINS James	65	77		HARGREAVES Owen	15
17	KOUMAS Jason	54	84		RICHARDSON Kieran	16
18	EARNSHAW Rob	70	68		DEFOE Jermain	17

Windsor Park, Belfast
3-09-2005, 15:00, 12 000, Stanisic SCG

NIR	2 0	AZE

Elliott [60], Feeney [84]

	NORTHERN IRELAND				AZERBAIJAN	
1	TAYLOR Maik				KRAMARENKO Dmitriy	1
2	BAIRD Chris				AMIRBAYOV Rafael	2
3	CAPALDI Tony				HAJIYEV Altandil	3
5	CRAIGAN Stephen				GULIYEV Emin	5
6	DAVIS Steve		64		GURBANOV Makhmud	7
7	GILLESPIE Keith				KERIMOV Aslan	8
8	JOHNSON Damien		75		ALIYEV Samir	11
9	HEALY David	79			SADIGOV Rashad	14
10	QUINN James	30			MUZIKOR Yuriy	15
11	ELLIOTT Stuart	89			IMAMALIEV Emin	19
18	HUGHES Michael		83		TAGIZADE Zaur	20
	Tr: SANCHEZ Lakrie				Tr: SADIKOV Vagif	
13	ROBINSON Stephen	89	64		PANAMARYOV Anotoliy	10
14	FEENEY Warren	30	83		NABIYER Nadir	18
15	JONES Steve	79	75		SHUKUROV Mohir	21

Slaski, Chorzow
3-09-2005, 20:30, 40 000, De Santis ITA

POL	3 2	AUT

Smolarek [13], Kosowski [22]
Zurawski [67]

Linz 2 [61] [80]

	POLAND				AUSTRIA	
1	BORUC Artur				SCHRANZ Andreas	1
2	KLOS Tomasz				HIEBLINGER Mario	2
3	RZASA Tomasz				STRANZL Martin	3
4	BASZCZYNSKI Marcin				POGATETZ Emanuel	4
5	KOSOWSKI Kamil	87	80		EHMANN Anton	5
6	BAK Jacek				AUFHAUSER Rene	6
7	SOBOLEWSKI Radoslaw		80		SCHOPP Markus	7
8	SMOLAREK Ebi	72			KUEHBAUER Dietmar	8
9	ZURAWSKI Maciej		46		STANDFEST Joachim	9
10	SZYMKOWIAK Miroslav	83			IVANSCHITZ Andreas	10
11	RASIAK Grzegorz				MAYRLEB Christian	11
	Tr: JANAS Pawel				Tr: KRANKL Hans	
13	MILA Sebastian	72	80		KIESENEBNER Markus	15
14	ZEWLAKOW Michal	87	80		KULJIC Sanel	17
16	RADOMSKI Arkadiusz	83	46		LINZ Roland	18

Windsor Park, Belfast
7-09-2005, 19:45, 14 069, Busacca SUI

NIR	1 0	ENG

Healy [73]

	NORTHERN IRELAND				ENGLAND	
1	TAYLOR Maik				ROBINSON Paul	1
2	BAIRD Chris				YOUNG Luke	2
3	CAPALDI Tony				COLE Ashley	3
5	CRAIGAN Stephen		75		GERRARD Steven	4
6	DAVIS Steve				FERDINAND Rio	5
7	GILLESPIE Keith				CARRAGHER Jamie	6
8	JOHNSON Damien				BECKHAM David	7
9	HEALY David	85	80		LAMPARD Frank	8
10	QUINN James	78			ROONEY Wayne	9
11	ELLIOTT Stuart	92			OWEN Michael	10
18	HUGHES Aaron		53		WRIGHT-PHILLIPS Shaun	11
	Tr: SANCHEZ Lakrie				Tr: ERIKSON Sven Goran	
15	FEENEY Warren	78	80		HARGREAVES Owen	15
16	SPROULE Ivan	85	53		COLE Joe	16
17	DUFF Mike	92	75		DEFOE Jermain	17

Wojska Polskiego, Warsaw
7-09-2005, 20:30, 13 500, Larsen DEN

POL	1	0	WAL

Zurawski [52]

	POLAND			WALES	
1	BORUC Artur			COYNE Danny	1
2	JOP Mariusz	46		EDWARDS Rob	2
3	RZASA Tomasz			RICKETTS Samuel	3
4	BASZCZYNSKI Marcin			GABBIDON Danny	4
5	KOSOWSKI Kamil	80		COLLINS James	5
6	BAK Jacek			PARTRIDGE David	6
7	SOBOLEWSKI Radoslaw			FLETCHER Carl	7
8	SMOLAREK Ebi	87	69	KOUMAS Jason	8
9	ZURAWSKI Maciej		82	EARNSHAW Rob	9
10	SZYMKOWIAK Miroslav			DAVIES Simon	10
11	RASIAK Grzegorz	65		GIGGS Ryan	11
	Tr: JANAS Pawel			Tr: TOSHACK John	
14	ZEWLAKOW Michal	87	46	DUFFY Richard	15
15	FRANKOWSKI Tomas	65	69	DAVIES Craig	16
16	RADOMSKI Arkadiusz	80	82	LEDLEY Joseph	17

Tofik Bakhramov, Baku
7-09-2005, 21:00, 2 800, Verbist BEL

AZE	0	0	AUT

	AZERBAIJAN			AUSTRIA	
1	KRAMARENKO Dmitriy			SCHRANZ Andreas	1
2	AMIRBAYOV Rafael			IBERTSBERGER Andreas	2
3	HAJIYEV Altandil		50	STRANZL Martin	3
4	AKHMEDOV Tarlan			POGATETZ Emanuel	4
5	GULIYEV Emin		81	GERCALIV Ronald	5
6	GULIYEV Kamal			MORZ Michael	6
8	KERIMOV Aslan		61	MAYRLEB Christian	7
9	GURBANOV Gurban	89		KIESENEBNER Markus	8
13	SHUKUROV Mohir			LINZ Roland	9
15	MUZIKOR Yuriy	79		IVANSCHITZ Andreas	10
22	TAGIZADE Zaur	88		AMERHAUSER Martin	11
	Tr: SADIKOV Vagif			Tr: KRANKL Hans	
17	ALIYEV Samir	89	50	HIEBLINGER Mario	13
18	BAKHSHIYEV Elmar	79	81	SAEUMEL Juergen	16
21	NABIYER Nadir	88	61	KULJIC Sanel	17

Windsor Park, Belfast
8-10-2005, 14:00, 13 451, Bossen NED

NIR	2	3	WAL

Duff [47], Davis [50]

Davies [27], Robinson [37]
Giggs [81]

	NORTHERN IRELAND			WALES	
1	TAYLOR Maik			JONES Paul	1
2	DUFF Mike	82		DELANEY Mark	2
3	CAPALDI Tony		87	RICKETTS Samuel	3
4	MURDOCK Colin			FLETCHER Carl	4
5	CRAIGAN Stephen		51	COLLINS James	5
6	DAVIS Steve			PARTRIDGE David	6
7	GILLESPIE Keith		77	EARNSHAW Rob	7
8	JOHNSON Damien			ROBINSON Carl	8
9	HEALY David			HARTSON John	9
10	QUINN James			DAVIES Simon	10
11	ELLIOTT Stuart	65		GIGGS Ryan	11
	Tr: SANCHEZ Lawrie			Tr: TOSHACK John	
16	JONES Steve	82	87	COLLINS Daniel	15
17	BRUNT Chris	65	77	VAUGHAN David	16
			51	DUFFY Richard	17

Old Trafford, Manchester
8-10-2005, 16:00, 64 822, Medina Cantalejo ESP

ENG	1	0	AUT

Lampard [24]

	ENGLAND			AUSTRIA	
1	ROBINSON Paul			MACHO Juergen	1
2	YOUNG Luke			DOBER Andreas	2
3	CARRAGHER Jamie			STRANZL Martin	3
4	GERRARD Steven			SCHARNER Paul	4
5	TERRY John		80	IBERTSBERGER Andreas	5
6	CAMPBELL Sol	65		AUFHAUSER Rene	6
7	BECKHAM David	58	65	SCHOPP Markus	7
8	LAMPARD Frank			KIESENEBNER Markus	8
9	CROUCH Peter			LINZ Roland	9
10	OWEN Michael	80		IVANSCHITZ Andreas	10
11	COLE Joe	62	45	WEISSENBERGER Markus	11
	Tr: ERIKSSON Sven Goran			Tr: RUTTENSTEINER Willibald	
12	KING Ledley	62	45	SARIYAR Yuksul	15
14	FERDINAND Rio	65	80	LASNIK Andreas	17
16	RICHARDSON Kieran	80	65	KULJIC Sanel	18

Old Trafford, Manchester
12-10-2005, 19:45, 65 467, Nielsen DEN

ENG	2	1	POL

Owen [44], Lampard [81]

Frankowski [45]

	ENGLAND			POLAND	
1	ROBINSON Paul			BORUC Artur	1
2	YOUNG Luke			JOP Mariusz	2
3	CARRAGHER Jamie			BASZCZYNSKI Marcin	4
4	KING Ledley			KOSOWSKI Kamil	5
5	FERDINAND Rio			BAK Jacek	6
6	TERRY John		79	SOBOLEWSKI Radoslaw	7
7	WRIGHT-PHILLIPS Shaun	67	46	SMOLAREK Ebi	8
8	LAMPARD Frank		39	ZURAWSKI Maciej	9
9	ROONEY Wayne			LEWANDOWSKI Mariusz	10
10	OWEN Michael	84		RASIAK Grzegorz	11
11	COLE Joe	87		ZEWLAKOW Michal	14
	Tr: ERIKSSON Sven Goran			Tr: JANAS Pawel	
14	JENAS Jermaine	84	79	RADOMSKI Arkadiusz	16
15	SMITH Alan	87	39	FRANKOWSKI Tomas	17
16	CROUCH Peter	67	46	KRZYNOWEK Jacek	18

Millennium, Cardiff
12-10-2005, 19:45, 32 628, Hansson SWE

WAL	2	0	AZE

Giggs 2 [3] [51]

	WALES			AZERBAIJAN	
1	JONES Paul			KRAMARENKO Dmitriy	1
2	DUFFY Richard		79	AGHAYER Emin	2
3	COLLINS Daniel	53		AMIRBAYOV Rafael	3
4	FLETCHER Carl	68		GULIYEV Vugar	6
5	COLLINS James			KERIMOV Aslan	8
6	GABBIDON Danny			SHUKUROV Mohir	13
7	VAUGHAN David			SADIGOV Rashad	14
8	ROBINSON Carl			MUZIKOR Yuriy	15
9	HARTSON John		68	ISMAYLOV Farrukh	16
10	DAVIES Simon		88	IMAMALIEV Emin	19
11	GIGGS Ryan	73		TAGIZADE Zaur	22
	Tr: TOSHACK John			Tr: SADIKOV Vagif	
14	COTTERILL David	73	79	BAKHSHIYEV Elmar	5
17	RICKETTS Samuel	53	88	POLADOV Ruslan	10
18	CROFTS Andrew	68	68	ALIYEV Samir	17

Ernst Happel Stadion, Vienna
12-10-2005, 20:30, 12 500, Briakos GRE

AUT　　2　　0　　NIR

Aufhauser 2 [44] [90]

AUSTRIA				NORTHERN IRELAND
1	MACHO Juergen			TAYLOR Maik 1
2	DOBER Andreas	46		BAIRD Chris 2
3	STRANZL Martin			MURDOCK Colin 3
4	SCHARNER Paul			DUFF Mike 4
5	POGATETZ Emanuel	74		CRAIGAN Stephen 5p
6	AUFHAUSER Rene			DAVIS Steve 6
7	SCHOPP Markus	54		GILLESPIE Keith 7
8	KIESENEBNER Markus		74	JOHNSON Damien 8
9	LINZ Roland		70	HEALY David 9
10	IVANSCHITZ Andreas		57	QUINN James 10
11	WALLNER Roman	77	75	BRUNT Chris 11
	Tr: RUTTENSTEINER Willibald			Tr: SANCHEZ Lawrie
13	GERCALIV Ronald	77	70	JONES Steve 14
14	STANDFEST Joachim	54	57	FEENEY Warren 15
15	IBERTSBERGER Andreas	46	75	ELLIOTT Stuart 16

GROUP 6		PL	W	D	L	F	A	PTS	ENG	POL	AUT	NIR	WAL	AZE
1	England	10	8	1	1	17	5	25		2-1	1-0	4-0	2-0	2-0
2	Poland	10	8	0	2	27	9	24	1-2		3-2	1-0	1-0	8-0
3	Austria	10	4	3	3	15	12	15	2-2	1-3		2-0	1-0	2-0
4	Northern Ireland	10	2	3	5	10	18	9	1-0	0-3	3-3		2-3	2-0
5	Wales	10	2	2	6	10	15	8	0-1	2-3	0-2	2-2		2-0
6	Azerbaijan	10	0	3	7	1	21	3	0-1	0-3	0-0	0-0	1-1	

Italy qualified for the finals • Norway qualified for a play-off against the Czech Republic

GROUP 7

Bilino Polje, Zenica
3-09-2005, 20:15, 12 000, Benquerenca POR

BIH　　1　　0　　BEL

Barbarez 62

BOSNIA-HERZEGOVINA				BELGIUM
1	HASAGIC Kenan			PROTO Silvio 1
2	BERBEROVIC Dzemal			SIMONS Timmy 3
3	MUSIC Vedin			VAN BUYTEN Daniel 4
4	SPAHIC Emir			DESCHACHT Olivier 5
5	BAJRAMOVIC Zlatan			VANDERHAEGHE Yves 6
6	PAPAC Sasa		67	BUFFEL Thomas 10
7	BOLIC Elvir	72		MPENZA Mbo 11
8	MILENKOVIC Ninoslav	77		PIERONI Luigi 16
9	BARBAREZ Sergej		78	VAN DAMME Jelle 19
10	GRUJIC Vladan		78	VANDENBORRE Anthony 20
11	BARTOLOVIC Mladen	88		KOMPANY Vincent 27
	Tr: SLISKOVIC Blaz			Tr: ANTHUENIS Aime
15	JAKIROVIC Sergej	88	78	DAERDEN Koen 7
17	MISIMOVIC Zvjezdan	72	78	GARAERTS Karel 14
18	HRGOVIC Mirko	77	67	VANDENBERGH Kevin 18

FK Crvena Zvezda, Belgrade
3-09-2005, 20:30, 20 203, Nielsen DEN

SCG　　2　　0　　LTU

Kezman 18, Ilic 74

SERBIA/MONTENEGRO				LITHUANIA
1	JEVRIC Dragoslav			KARCHEMARSKAS Zh'nas 1
3	DRAGUTINOVIC Ivica			SEMBERAS Deividas 2
4	DULJAJ Igor		84	DZIAUKSTAS Rolandas 3
5	VIDIC Nemanja			PAULAUSKAS Gediminas 4
6	GAVRANCIC Goran			SKERLA Andrius 5
8	KEZMAN Mateja	76		SKARBALIUS Aurelijus 7
9	MIOLSEVIC Savo	60		CESNAUSKIS Edgaras 8
10	STANKOVIC Dejan			JANKAUSKAS Edgaras 9
11	DJORDJEVIC Predrag		70	PREIKSAITIS Aidas 10
20	KRSTAJIC Mladen		67	MIKOLIUNAS Saulius 11
22	ILIC Sasa		89	CESNAUSKIS Deividas 18
	Tr: PETKOVIC Ilija			Tr: LIUBINSKAS Algimantas
7	KOROMAN Ognjen	60	84	ZUTAUTAS Darius 13
18	VUKIC Zvonimir	89	70	SAVENAS Mantas 14
19	ZIGIC Nikola	76	67	RADZINEVICIUS Andrius 16

Vilnius, Vilnius
7-09-2005, 20:00, 4 000, Kassai HUN

LTU 0 1 BIH

Barbarez [28]

#	LITHUANIA			#	BOSNIA/HERZEGOVINA	
1	KARCHEMARSKAS Zh'nas				HASAGIC Kenan	1
2	SEMBERAS Deividas				BERBEROVIC Dzemal	2
3	DZIAUKSTAS Rolandas	60			MUSIC Vedin	3
4	STANKEVICIUS Marius				BAJIC Branimir	4
5	CESNAUSKIS Deividas	66			BAJRAMOVIC Zlatan	5
6	ZVIRGZDAUSKAS Tomas				PAPAC Sasa	6
7	SKARBALIUS Aurelijus	46	64		BOLIC Elvir	7
8	CESNAUSKIS Edgaras	76			MILENKOVIC Ninoslav	8
9	JANKAUSKAS Edgaras				BARBAREZ Sergej	9
10	DANILEVICIUS Tomas				GRUJIC Vladan	10
11	POSKUS Robertas		82		BESLIJA Mirsad	14
	Tr: LIUBINSKAS Algimantas				Tr: SLISKOVIC Blaz	
14	SAVENAS Mantas	46	64		JAKIROVIC Sergej	15
16	MIKOLIUNAS Saulius	66	60		BARTOLOVIC Mladen	16
			82		MISIMOVIC Zvjezdan	17

Stedelijk, Antwerp
7-09-2005, 20:30, 8 207, Stokes IRL

BEL 8 0 SMR

Simons [34p], Daerden 2 [39 67], Buffel [44]
Mpenza 2 [52 71], Vandenbergh [53], Van Buyten [83]

#	BELGIUM			#	SAN MARINO	
1	PROTO Silvio				CECCOLI Michele	1
3	SIMONS Timmy		33		VALENTINI Carlo	2
4	VAN BUYTEN Daniel				ANDREINI Matteo	3
5	DESCHACHT Olivier		77		CRESCENTINI Federico	4
6	VANDERHAEGHE Yves	69			DELLA VALLE Alessandro	5
8	GOOR Bart				BACCIOCCHI Simone	6
10	BUFFEL Thomas		61		MAIANI Giacomo	7
11	MPENZA Mbo				DOMENICONI Marco	8
18	VANDENBERGH Kevin				GASPERONI Alex	9
20	VANDENBORRE Anthony	69			SELVA Andy	10
27	KOMPANY Vincent	12	70		MORETTI Michele	11
	Tr: ANTHUENIS Aime				Tr: MAZZA Gianpaolo	
7	DAERDEN Koen	12	70		CIACCI Nicola	13
13	HOEFKENS Carl	69	77		NANNI Luca	17
17	BISCONTI Roberto	69	61		SELVA Roberto	18

Vicente Calderon, Madrid
7-09-2005, 22:00, 51 491, Poll ENG

ESP 1 1 SCG

Raul [19]   Kezman [68]

#	SPAIN			#	SERBIA/MONTENEGRO	
1	IKER CASILLAS				JEVRIC Dragoslav	1
2	SALGADO Michel				DRAGUTINOVIC Ivica	3
3	ASIER		90		DULJAJ Igor	4
4	MARCHENA Carlos				VIDIC Nemanja	5
5	PUYOL				GAVRANCIC Goran	6
6	XAVI		85		KOROMAN Ognjen	7
7	RAUL				KEZMAN Mateja	8
9	FERNANDO TORRES	53			STANKOVIC Dejan	10
11	VICENTE	75			DJORDJEVIC Predrag	11
14	XABI ALONSO				KRSTAJIC Mladen	20
17	JOAQUIN	67	46		ILIC Sasa	22
	Tr: ARAGONES Luis				Tr: PETKOVIC Ilija	
16	LUIS GARCIA	67	85		MARIC Milos	15
19	LUQUE	75	90		KOVACZVIC Nenad	16
21	TAMUDO Raul	53	46 90		ZIGIC Nikola	19

Vilnius, Vilnius
8-10-2005, 20:00, 1 500, Wegereef NED

LTU 0 2 SCG

Kezman [44], Vukic [85]

#	LITHUANIA			#	SERBIA/MONTENEGRO	
1	KARCHEMARSKAS Zh'nas				JEVRIC Dragoslav	1
2	STANKEVICIUS Marius				VIDIC Nemanja	5
3	DZIAUKSTAS Rolandas				GAVRANCIC Goran	6
4	PAULAUSKAS Gediminas	77			NADJ Albert	7
5	SKERLA Andrius		88		KEZMAN Mateja	8
6	PREIKSAITIS Aidas		10		STANKOVIC Dejan	10
7	SAVENAS Mantas				DJORDJEVIC Predrag	11
8	CESNAUSKIS Deivida				LUKOVIC Aleksandar	13
9	JANKAUSKAS Edgaras				VUKIC Zvonimir	18
10	MIKOLIUNAS Saulius	59	56 90		ZIGIC Nikola	19
11	DANILEVICIUS Tomas	86			KRSTAJIC Mladen	20
	Tr: LIUBINSKAS Algimantas				Tr: PETKOVIC Ilija	
13	LAURISAS Aivaras	77	10		MLADENOVIC Dragan	4
17	MORINAS Igoris	59	88		MILOSEVIC Savo	9
18	RADZINEVICIUS Tomas	86	56		LJUBOJA Danijel	21

Bilino Polje, Zenica
8-10-2005, 20:00, 8 500, Hamer LUX

BIH 3 0 SMR

Bolic 3 [46 75 82]

#	BOSNIA-HERZEGOVINA			#	SAN MARINO	
1	TOLJA Almir				CECCOLI Michele	1
2	BERBEROVIC Dzemal				ANDREINI Matteo	2
3	MUSIC Vedin				VANNUCCI Damiano	3
4	SPAHIC Emir		71		CRESCENTINI Federico	4
5	BAJIC Branimir				DELLA VALLE Alessandro	5
6	CRLIC Ivica				NANNI Luca	6
7	BOLIC Elvir		90		DOMENICONI Marco	7
8	GRUJIC Vladan	81			GASPERONI Alex	8
9	BARBAREZ Sergej	77	81		MARANI Manuel	9
10	SALIHAMIDZIC Hasan	69			SELVA Andy	10
11	BARTOLOVIC Mladen				MARANI Michele	11
	Tr: SLISKOVIC Blaz				Tr: MAZZA Gianpaolo	
16	HRGOVIC Mirko	69	90		MORETTI Michele	15
17	MISIMOVIC Zvjezdan	77	81		MONTAGNA Paolo	16
18	PELAK Albin	81	71		PALAZZI Mirco	18

King Baudouin, Brussels
8-10-2005, 20:45, 40 300, Michel SVK

BEL 0 2 ESP

Fernando Torres 2 [56 66]

#	BELGIUM			#	SPAIN	
1	PROTO Silvio				IKER CASILLAS	1
3	SIMONS Timmy				SALGADO Michel	2
4	VAN BUYTEN Daniel				MARCHENA Carlos	4
5	DESCHACHT Olivier				PUYOL	5
6	VANDERHAEGHE Yves				ALBELDA	6
8	GOOR Bart				RAUL	7
9	MPENZA Emile		70		FERNANDO TORRES	9
10	BUFFEL Thomas	63			XAVI	10
11	MPENZA Mbo	76	55		VICENTE	11
13	HOEFKENS Carl				ANTONIO	12
20	VANDENBORRE Anthony	63	55		JOAQUIN	17
	Tr: ANTHUENIS Aime				Tr: ARAGONES Luis	
2	DEFLANDRE Eric	63	70		BARAJA	8
15	WALASIAK Jonathan	63	55		REYES	14
16	PIERONI Luigi	76	55		VILLA David	21

FK Crvena Zvezda, Belgrade
12-10-2005, 20:30, 46 305, Vassaras GRE

SCG	1	0	BIH

Kezman [7]

SERBIA/MONTENEGRO			BOSNIA-HERZEGOVINA	
1	JEVRIC Dragoslav		HASAGIC Kenan	1
5	VIDIC Nemanja	84	BERBEROVIC Dzemal	2
6	GAVRANCIC Goran	66	MUSIC Vedin	3
7	KOROMAN Ognjen		SPAHIC Emir	4
8	KEZMAN Mateja	87	BAJRAMOVIC Zlatan	5
11	DJORDJEVIC Predrag		MILENKOVIC Ninoslav	6
15	DULJAJ Igor	71	BOLIC Elvir	7
17	NADJ Albert	74 46	GRLIC Ivica	8
18	VUKIC Zvonimir	67	BARBAREZ Sergej	9
19	ZIGIC Nikola		SALIHAMIDZIC Hasan	10
20	KRSTAJIC Mladen		JAKIROVIC Sergej	11
Tr: PETKOVIC Ilija			Tr: SLISKOVIC Blaz	
4	MLADENOVIC Dragan	67 66	BESLIJA Mirsad	14
13	LUKOVIC Aleksandar	87 71	MISIMOVIC Zvjezdan	16
22	ILIC Sasa	74 46	BARTOLOVIC Mladen	17

Stadio Olimpico, Serravalle
12-10-2005, 20:30, 3 426, Meyer GER

SMR	0	6	ESP

            Antonio Lopez [1], Fernando Torres 3 [11 78 89p]
            Sergio Ramos 2 [31 48]

SAN MARINO			SPAIN	
1	GASPERONI Federico		IKER CASILLAS	1
2	ANDREINI Matteo	84	ALBELDA	6
3	VANNUCCI Damiano	72	RAUL	7
4	NANNI Luca		FERNANDO TORRES	9
5	DELLA VALLE Alessandro		ANTONIO LOPEZ	12
6	BACCIOCCHI Simone	68	REYES	14
7	DOMENICONI Marco		SERGIO RAMOS	15
8	GASPERONI Alex		DE LA PENA Ivan	18
9	MONTAGNA Paolo	71	JUANITO	20
10	MARANI Manuel	87 58	VILLA David	21
11	MARANI Michele		PABLO	22
Tr: MAZZA Gianpaolo			Tr: ARAGONES Luis	
14	MASI Mattia	71 58	BARAJA	8
16	NANNI Federico	87 68	VICENTE	11
18	PALAZZI Mirco	84 72	MISTA	19

Vilnius, Vilnius
12-10-2005, 21:30, 1 500, Riley ENG

LTU	1	1	BEL

Deschacht OG [82]   Garaerts [20]

LITHUANIA			BELGIUM	
1	KARCHEMARSKAS Zh'nas		PROTO Silvio	1
2	SEMBERAS Deividas	83	DEFLANDRE Eric	2
3	DZIAUKSTAS Rolandas		SIMONS Timmy	3
4	STANKEVICIUS Marius	90	DESCHACHT Olivier	5
5	SKERLA Andrius		VANDERHAEGHE Yves	6
6	PREIKSAITIS Aidas		GARAERTS Karel	7
7	SAVENAS Mantas		GOOR Bart	8
8	PAULAUSKAS Gediminas		MPENZA Emile	9
9	DANILEVICIUS Tomas		MPENZA Mbo	11
11	MORINAS Igoris	81	HOEFKENS Carl	13
13	ZUTAUTAS Darius		WALASIAK Jonathan	15
Tr: LIUBINSKAS Algimantas			Tr: ANTHUENIS Aime	
10	MIKOLIUNAS Saulius	81 45	MAERTENS Birger	17
17	RADZINEVICIUS Tomas	90 45	VANDENBORRE Anthony	20

	GROUP 7	PL	W	D	L	F	A	PTS	SCG	ESP	BIH	BEL	LTU	SMR
1	Serbia & Montenegro	10	6	4	0	16	1	22		0-0	1-0	0-0	2-0	5-0
2	Spain	10	5	5	0	19	3	20	1-1		1-1	2-0	0-1	5-0
3	Bosnia-Herzegovina	10	4	4	2	12	9	16	0-0	1-1		1-0	1-1	3-0
4	Belgium	10	3	3	4	16	11	12	0-2	0-2	4-1		1-1	8-0
5	Lithuania	10	2	4	4	8	9	10	0-2	0-0	0-1	1-1		4-0
6	San Marino	10	0	0	10	2	40	0	0-3	0-6	1-3	1-2	0-1	

Serbia and Montenegro qualified for the finals • Spain qualified for a play-off against Slovakia

GROUP 8

	GROUP 8	PL	W	D	L	F	A	PTS	CRO	SWE	BUL	HUN	ISL	MLT
1	Croatia	10	7	3	0	21	5	24		1-0	2-2	3-0	4-0	3-0
2	Sweden	10	8	0	2	30	4	24	0-1		3-0	3-0	3-1	6-0
3	Bulgaria	10	4	3	3	17	17	15	1-3	0-3		2-0	3-2	4-1
4	Hungary	10	4	2	4	13	14	14	0-0	0-1	1-1		3-2	4-0
5	Iceland	10	1	1	8	14	27	4	1-3	1-4	1-3	2-3		4-1
6	Malta	10	0	3	7	4	32	3	1-1	0-7	1-1	0-2	0-0	

Croatia and Sweden qualified for the finals

Rasunda, Stockholm
3-09-2005, 17:15, 35 000, De Bleeckere BEL

SWE 3 0 BUL

Ljungberg [60], Mellberg [75]
Ibrahimovic [90]

	SWEDEN			BULGARIA	
1	ISAKSSON Andreas			IVANKOV Dimitar	27
2	OSTLUND Alexander			KISHISHEV Radostin	2
3	MELLBERG Olof			PETKOV Ivaylo	4
4	LUCIC Teddy			ILIEV Valentin	5
5	EDMAN Erik		48	GEORGIEV Blagoy	7
6	LINDEROTH Tobias		78	YANKOV Chavdar	8
7	WILHELMSSON Christian	80	78	LAZAROV Zdravko	11
8	KALLSTROM Kim	72		PETROV Martin	17
9	LJUNGBERG Fredrik	91		PETROV Stilian	19
10	IBRAHIMOVIC Zlatan		58	IVANOV Georgi	20
11	LARSSON Henrik			TOPUZAKOV Elin	21
	Tr: LAGERBACK Lars			Tr: STOICHKOV Hristo	
14	ALEXANDERSSON Niclas	72	78	KAMBUROV Martin	14
15	ANDERSSON Daniel	91	78	ILIEV Georgi	18
17	JONSON Mattias	80	58	GARGOROV Emil	23

Laugardalsvollur, Reykjavík
3-09-2005, 18:05, 5 520, Stark GER

ISL 1 3 CRO

Gudjohnsen [24]   Balaban 2 [56] [61], Srna [82]

	ICELAND			CROATIA	
1	ARASON Arni			PLETIKOSA Stipe	1
2	SIGURDSSON Kristjan			SRNA Darijo	2
3	SIGURDSSON Indridi	44		SIMUNIC Josip	3
4	GUNNARSSON Brynjar			KOVAC Robert	4
5	HELGASON Audun	79		TUDOR Igor	5
6	GISLASON Stefan			SIMIC Dario	7
7	HREIDARSSON Hermann			BABIC Marko	8
8	EINARSSON Gylfi		84	PRSO Dado	9
9	GUDJOHNSEN Eidur			KOVAC Niko	10
10	STEINSSON Gretar			KRANJCAR Niko	19
11	HELGUSON Heidar	25		BALABAN Bosko	21
	Tr: OLAFSSON/SIGURVINSSON			Tr: KRANJCAR Zlatko	
14	ARNASON Kari	79	84	BOSNJAK Ivan	14
15	VIDARSSON Arnar	44			
17	THORVALDSSON Gunnar	25			

Ferenc Puskas Stadium, Budapest
3-09-2005, 20:45, 5 900, Godulyan UKR

HUN 4 0 MLT

Torghelle [34], Said OG [55]
Takacs [64], Rajczi [85]

	HUNGARY			MALTA	
1	KIRALY Gabor			HABER Justin	1
2	BODNAR Laszlo		56	SCICLUNA Kenneth	2
3	HALMOSI Peter			WELLMAN Steve	3
4	JUHASZ Roland			BRIFFA Roderick	4
5	VANCZAK Vilmos			SAID Brian	5
6	TAKACS Akos		68	GRIMA Massimo	6
7	BOOR Zoltan	57		PULLICINO Peter	7
8	HAJNAL Tamas		85	MATTOCKS Claude	8
9	TORGHELLE Sandor			COHEN Andrew	9
10	GERA Zoltan	76		WOODS Ivan	10
11	KENESEI Krisztian	69		ANONAM Orosco	11
	Tr: MATTHAEUS Lothar			Tr: HEESE Horst	
15	HUSZTI Szabolcs	57	85	CIANTAR Ian	13
16	BUZSAKY Akos	76	68	SAMMUT Kevin	17
17	RAJCZI Peter	69	56	ZAHRA Antoine	18

Ta'Qali National Stadium, Ta'Qali
7-09-2005, 18:45, 916, Briakos GRE

MLT 1 1 CRO

Wellman [74]   Kranjcar [19]

	MALTA			CROATIA	
1	HABER Justin			PLETIKOSA Stipe	1
2	PULLICINO Peter			SRNA Darijo	2
3	WELLMAN Steve			SIMUNIC Josip	3
4	BRIFFA Roderick		80	SIMIC Dario	7
5	SAID Brian			BABIC Marko	8
6	SCICLUNA Kenneth	46		PRSO Dado	9
7	AGIUS Gilbert			KOVAC Niko	10
8	MATTOCKS Claude	72	92	TOKIC Mario	11
9	COHEN Andrew	89		KRANJCAR Niko	19
10	WOODS Ivan		68	SERIC Anthony	20
11	ANONAM Orosco		68	BALABAN Bosko	21
	Tr: HEESE Horst			Tr: KRANJCAR Zlatko	
13	CIANTAR Ian	72	68	BOSNJAK Ivan	14
16	GRIMA Massimo	89	68	LEKO Ivan	16
17	SAMMUT Kevin	46	80	KLASNIC Ivan	17

Vasilij Levski, Sofia
7-09-2005, 19:00, 18 000, Demirlek TUR

BUL 3 2 ISL

Berbatov [21], Iliev [69]   Steinsson [9], Hreidarsson [16]
Petrov [86]

	BULGARIA			ICELAND	
27	IVANKOV Dimitar			ARASON Arni	1
2	KISHISHEV Radostin			SIGURDSSON Kristjan	2
4	PETKOV Ivaylo			SIGURDSSON Indridi	3
5	ILIEV Valentin			GUNNARSSON Brynjar	4
8	YANKOV Chavdar	45		HELGASON Audun	5
9	BERBATOV Dimitar			GISLASON Stefan	6
11	LAZAROV Zdravko	76		HREIDARSSON Hermann	7
17	PETROV Martin		75	ARNASON Kari	8
19	PETROV Stilian			GUDJOHNSEN Eidur	9
20	TOPUZAKOV Elin			STEINSSON Gretar	10
23	GARGOROV Emil	91		HELGUSON Heidar	11
	Tr: STOICHKOV Hristo			Tr: OLAFSSON/SIGURVINSSON	
15	GENKOV Tsvetan	76	75	VIDARSSON Arnar	15
18	ILIEV Georgi	45			
22	KARASLAVOV Assen	91			

Ferenc Puskas Stadium, Budapest
7-09-2005, 20:45, 20 161, Farina ITA

HUN 0 1 SWE

                                        Ibrahimovic [91+]

	HUNGARY			SWEDEN	
1	KIRALY Gabor			ISAKSSON Andreas	1
2	BODNAR Laszlo			OSTLUND Alexander	2
3	VANCZAK Vilmos			MELLBERG Olof	3
4	JUHASZ Roland	46		LUCIC Teddy	4
5	EGER Lazlo			ANDERSSON Christoffer	5
6	TAKACS Akos			LINDEROTH Tobias	6
7	BOOR Zoltan	87		ALEXANDERSSON Niclas	7
8	HAJNAL Tamas	90		WILHELMSSON Christian	8
9	TORGHELLE Sandor			LJUNGBERG Fredrik	9
10	GERA Zoltan		93	IBRAHIMOVIC Zlatan	10
11	HUSZTI Szabolcs			LARSSON Henrik	11
	Tr: MATTHAEUS Lothar			Tr: LAGERBACK Lars	
13	GYEPES Gabor	46	93	ALLBACK Marcus	16
16	HALMOSI Peter	87			
18	KEREKES Zsombor	90			

Vasilij Levski, Sofia
8-10-2005, 18:00, 4 652, Delevic SCG

BUL   2   0   HUN

Berbatov [29], Lazarov [55]

BULGARIA		HUNGARY	
27 IVANKOV Dimitar		KIRALY Gabor	1
2 KISHISHEV Radostin		BODNAR Laszlo	2
5 ILIEV Valentin		VANCZAK Vilmos	3
8 YANKOV Chavdar	74	JUHASZ Roland	4
9 BERBATOV Dimitar		STARK Peter	5
11 LAZAROV Zdravko	62	BALOG Zoltan	6
13 VENKOV Mihail		46 HALMOSI Peter	7
17 PETROV Martin		78 BUZSAKY Akos	8
18 ILIEV Georgi		90 TORGHELLE Sandor	9
19 PETROV Stilian	46	HAJNAL Tamas	10
21 TOPUZAKOV Elin		HUSZTI Szabolcs	11
Tr: HUBCHEV Petar		Tr: MATTHAEUS Lothar	
7 GEORGIEV Blagoy	62	78 KOVACS Zoltan	17
14 KAMBUROV Martin	46	46 KEREKES Zsombor	18
23 GARGOROV Emil	74		

Maksimir, Zagreb
8-10-2005, 20:15, 34 015, De Santis ITA

CRO   1   0   SWE

Srna [55]

CROATIA		SWEDEN	
1 BUTINA Tomislav		ISAKSSON Andreas	1
2 SRNA Darijo		OSTLUND Alexander	2
3 SIMUNIC Josip		MELLBERG Olof	3
4 KOVAC Robert		LUCIC Teddy	4
5 TUDOR Igor		EDMAN Erik	5
8 BABIC Marko		66 LINDEROTH Tobias	6
9 PRSO Dado	92	ALEXANDERSSON Niclas	7
10 KOVAC Niko		71 SVENSSON Anders	8
13 TOMAS Stjepan		LJUNGBERG Fredrik	9
17 KLASNIC Ivan	70	66 JONSON Mattias	10
19 KRANJCAR Niko		LARSSON Henrik	11
Tr: KRANJCAR Zlatko		Tr: LAGERRBACK Lars	
7 SIMIC Dario	92	66 WILHELMSSON Christian	15
14 BOSNJAK Ivan	70	71 KALLSTROM Kim	16
		66 ELMANDER Johan	18

Ta'Qali National Stadium, Ta'Qali
12-10-2005 19:00, 2 844, Godulyan UKR

MLT   1   1   BUL

Zahra [79]   Yankov [67]

MALTA		BULGARIA	
1 HABER Justin		KOLEV Stoyan	12
2 CIANTAR Ian		87 KISHISHEV Radostin	2
3 AZZOPARDI Ian	65	ILIEV Valentin	5
4 BRIFFA Roderick		YANKOV Chavdar	8
5 SAID Brian		BERBATOV Dimitar	9
6 DIMECH Luke		63 BOJINOV Valeri	10
7 WELLMAN Steve		VENKOV Mihail	13
8 PULLICINO Peter		46 PETROV Martin	17
9 COHEN Andrew	89	ILIEV Georgi	18
10 WOODS Ivan	71	TOPUZAKOV Elin	21
11 MALLIA George		GARGOROV Emil	23
Tr: HEESE Horst		Tr: HUBCHEV Petar	
14 BARBARA Etienne	71	63 GEORGIEV Blagoy	7
17 GRIMA Massimo	89	46 LAZAROV Zdravko	11
18 ZAHRA Antoine	65	87 KAMBUROV Martin	14

Ujpesti, Budapest
12-10-2005, 19:30, 6 979, Larsen DEN

HUN   0   0   CRO

HUNGARY		CROATIA	
1 KIRALY Gabor		BUTINA Tomislav	1
2 BODNAR Laszlo		SRNA Darijo	2
3 VANCZAK Vilmos		KOVAC Robert	4
4 GYEPES Gabor		TUDOR Igor	5
5 STARK Peter		VRANJES Jurica	6
6 KORSOS Gyorgy		BABIC Marko	8
7 BARANYOS Zsolt	76	TOKIC Mario	11
8 BOOR Zoltan		TOMAS Stjepan	13
9 KOVACS Zoltan	42	LEKO Ivan	15
10 HAJNAL Tamas	62	KLASNIC Ivan	17
11 HUSZTI Szabolcs		BALABAN Bosko	21
Tr: MATTHAEUS Lothar		Tr: KRANJCAR Zlatko	
16 BUZSAKY Akos	76	89 SIMIC Dario	7
		62 89 BOSNJAK Ivan	14
		42 LEKO Jerko	16

Rasunda, Stockholm
12-10-2005, 19:30, 33 716, Ivanov.V RUS

SWE   3   1   ISL

Ibrahimovic [29]
Larsson [42], Kallstrom [91+]   Arnason [11]

SWEDEN		ICELAND	
1 ISAKSSON Andreas		ARASON Arni	1
2 OSTLUND Alexander		SIGURDSSON Kristjan	2
3 MELLBERG Olof		SIGURDSSON Indridi	3
4 LUCIC Teddy		84 GUNNARSSON Brynjar	4
5 EDMAN Erik		HELGASON Audun	5
6 LINDEROTH Tobias		GISLASON Stefan	6
7 WILHELMSSON Christian	66	JONSSON Solvi	7
8 SVENSSON Anders	74	70 ARNASON Kari	8
9 LJUNGBERG Fredrik		74 THORVALDSSON Gunnar	9
10 IBRAHIMOVIC Zlatan	74	STEINSSON Gretar	10
11 LARSSON Henrik		HELGUSON Heidar	11
Tr: LAGERBACK Lars		Tr: OLAFSSON/SIGURVINSSON	
14 ALEXANDERSSON Niclas	66	70 EINARSSON Gylfi	14
16 KALLSTROM Kim	74	84 VIDARSSON Arnar	15
17 ALLBACK Marcus	74	74 SIGURDSSON Hannes	17

EUROPEAN PLAY-OFFS

Ullevaal, Oslo
12-11-2005, 19:30, 24 264, Busacca SUI

NOR 0 1 CZE

Smicer [31]

	NORWAY			CZECH REPUBLIC	
1	MYHRE Thomas			CECH Petr	1
2	BERGDOLMO Andre			GRYGERA Zdenek	2
3	HAGEN Erik			GALASEK Tomas	4
4	HANGELAND Brede			JANKULOVSKI Marek	6
5	RIISE John Arne		79	SMICER Vladimir	7
6	SOLLI Jan	45		POBORSKY Karel	8
7	HAESTAD Kristofer		88	ROSICKY Tomas	10
8	GRINDHEIM Christian	87		NEDVED Pavel	11
9	PEDERSEN Morten		61	BAROS Milan	15
10	CAREW John			UJFALUSI Tomas	21
11	IVERSEN Steffen	79		ROZEHNAL David	22
	Tr: HAREIDE Age			Tr: BRUCKNER Karel	
15	STROMSTAD Fredrik	87	61	POLAK Jan	14
16	BRAATEN Daniel	45	79	HEINZ Marek	18
18	ARST Ole	79	88	JAROSIK Jiri	20

Toyota Arena, Prague
16-11-2005, 20:15, 17 464, Poll ENG

CZE 1 0 NOR

Rosicky [35]

	CZECH REPUBLIC			NORWAY	
1	CECH Petr			MYHRE Thomas	1
2	GRYGERA Zdenek			HOILAND Jon	2
6	JANKULOVSKI Marek			HAGEN Erik	3
7	SMICER Vladimir	75		HANGELAND Brede	4
8	POBORSKY Karel		88	RIISE John Arne	5
10	ROSICKY Tomas	67	57	HELSTAD Thorstein	6
11	NEDVED Pavel			HAESTAD Kristofer	7
14	POLAK Jan			STROMSTAD Fredrik	8
15	BAROS Milan	90		PEDERSEN Morten	9
21	UJFALUSI Tomas			CAREW John	10
22	ROZEHNAL David		46	IVERSEN Steffen	11
	Tr: BRUCKNER Karel			Tr: HAREIDE Age	
5	KOVAC Radoslav	67	88	JOHNSEN Marius	15
9	JAROSIK Jiri	75	46	SOLLI Jan	16
17	PLASIL Jaroslav	90	57	ARST Ole	18

Stade de Suisse, Berne
12-11-2005, 20:45, 31 130, Michel SVK

SUI 2 0 TUR

Senderos [41], Behrami [86]

	SWITZERLAND			TURKEY	
1	ZUBERBUEHLER Pascal			DEMIREL Volkan	23
3	MAGNIN Ludovic			OZALAN Alpay	4
6	VOGEL Johann			OZAT Umit	6
7	CABANAS Ricardo		45	KAHVECI Nihat	8
9	FREI Alexander			BALCI Serkan	14
11	STRELLER Marco	77		CIMSIR Huseyin	15
16	BARNETTA Tranquillo	83		SAHIN Selcuk	16
20	MUELLER Patrick			METIN Tumer	17
21	GYGAX Daniel			TORAMAN Ibrahim	19
24	SENDEROS Philippe			SUKUR Hakan	20
26	DEGEN Philipp		83	SANLI Tuncay	25
	Tr: KUHN Koebi			Tr: TERIM Fatih	
22	VONLANTHEN Johan	77	45	BURUK Okan	7
34	BEHRAMI Valon	83	83	PENBE Ergun	13
			77	ALTINTOP Hamit	21

Sükrü Saracoglu, Istanbul
16-11-2005, 20:15, 42 000, De Bleeckere BEL

TUR 4 2 SUI

Sanli 3 [22] [36] [89], Ates [52p]   Frei [2p], Streller [84]

	TURKEY			SWITZERLAND	
23	DEMIREL Volkan			ZUBERBUEHLER Pascal	1
2	SEYHAN Tolga			VOGEL Johann	6
4	OZALAN Alpay			CABANAS Ricardo	7
5	BELOZOGLU Emre			WICKY Raphael	8
13	PENBE Ergun			FREI Alexander	9
16	SAHIN Selcuk			BARNETTA Tranquillo	16
18	ATES Necati			SPYCHER Christoph	17
20	SUKUR Hakan			MUELLER Patrick	20
22	ALTINTOP Hamit		33	GYGAX Daniel	21
24	AKIN Serhat			SENDEROS Philippe	24
25	SANLI Tuncay		46	DEGEN Philipp	26
	Tr: TERIM Fatih			Tr: KUHN Koebi	
9	TEKKE Fatih		33 86	STRELLER Marco	11
10	BASTURK Yildiray		86	HUGGEL Benjamin	14
17	METIN Tumer		46	BEHRAMI Valon	34

Vicente Calderon, Madrid
12-11-2005, 22:00, 47 210, De Santis ITA

ESP 5 1 SVK

Luis Garcia 3 [10] [18] [75], Fernando Torres [65], Morientes [79]   Nemeth [49]

	SPAIN			SLOVAKIA	
1	IKER CASILLAS			CONTOFALSKY Kamil	1
2	SALGADO Michel			PETRAS Martin	2
3	ASIER			SKRTEL Martin	3
4	XAVI			KRATOCHVIL Roman	4
5	PUYOL		63	HAD Marian	5
6	ALBELDA	65	72	KARHAN Miroslav	6
7	RAUL			HLINKA Peter	7
9	FERNANDDO TORRES		46	HOLOSKO Filip	8
17	REYES	55		ZABAVNIK Radoslav	9
21	LUIS GARCIA	76	66	HODUR Ivan	10
22	PABLO			VITTEK Robert	11
	Tr: ARAGONES Luis			Tr: GALIS Dusan	
10	MORIENTES Fernando	76	72	JANOCKO Vladimir	14
11	VICENTE	55	66	GRESKO Vratislav	15
14	XABI ALONSO	65	46	NEMETH Szilard	17

Tehelné Pole, Bratislava
16-11-2005, 20:15, 23 587, Merk GER

SVK 1 1 ESP

Holosko [50]   Villa [71]

	SLOVAKIA			SPAIN	
1	CONTOFALSKY Kamil			IKER CASILLAS	1
2	GRESKO Vratislav	78		SALGADO Michel	2
3	SKRTEL Martin		74	XAVI	4
4	KRATOCHVIL Roman			PUYOL	5
5	DURICA Jan		65	RAUL	7
6	ZABAVNIK Radoslav			BARAJA	8
7	HLINKA Peter		61	FERNANDDO TORRES	9
8	NEMETH Szilard	83		VICENTE	11
9	KRAJCIK Matej			ANTONIO LOPEZ	12
10	HODUR Ivan	46		XABI ALONSO	14
11	VITTEK Robert			PABLO	22
	Tr: PETRAS Ladislav			Tr: ARAGONES Luis	
14	HOLOSKO Filip	46	65	MORIENTES Fernando	10
15	FODREK Branislav	83	74	SERGIO RAMOS	15
16	CECH Marek	78	61	VILLA David	16

ASIAN PLAY-OFF

Pakhtakor, Tashkent
8-10-2005, 17:05, 55 000, Busacca SUI

UZB 1 1 BHR

Shatskikh 19   Mohamed Talal 17

No	UZBEKISTAN	min		min	BAHRAIN	No
1	SAFONOV Evgeni				ALI Hassan	1
2	RADKEVICH Vladimir				MARZOOQ Abdulla	3
3	FEDOROV Andrei	62		62	JALAL Sayed	7
4	KASIMOV Mirdjalal	81		81	AHMED Husain	9
5	ALIKULOV Asror				SALMEEN Mohamed	10
8	DJEPAROV Server				BASHEER Mohamed	12
9	SOLIEV Anvarjon	46			MOHAMED Talal	13
10	KARPENKO Victor	61			GHULOOM Salman Isa	14
16	SHATSKIKH Maksim				MOHAMED ADNAN Sayed	16
17	NIKOLAEV Alexey			84	BABA Hussain	17
18	KADADAZE Timur				HUBAIL Mohammed	29
	Tr: HOUGHTON Bob				Tr: PERUZOVIC Luka	
13	BIKMOEV Marat	61		62	ABDUL RAHMAN Rashed	8
15	GEYNRIKH Alexander	46		84	FARHAN Saleh	15
				81	HUBAIL Alaa	30

National Stadium, Manama
12-10-2005, 22:00, 25 000, Poll ENG

BHR 0 0 UZB

No	BAHRAIN	min		min	UZBEKISTAN	No
1	ALI Hassan				SAFONOV Evgeni	1
3	MARZOOQ Abdulla				RADKEVICH Vladimir	2
7	JALAL Sayed	63			FEDOROV Andrei	3
9	AHMED Husain				KASIMOV Mirdjalal	4
10	SALMEEN Mohamed	70			ALIKULOV Asror	5
12	BASHEER Mohamed				DJEPAROV Server	8
13	MOHAMED Talal	82	70	70	SOLIEV Anvarjon	9
14	GHULOOM Salman Isa	63		63	KARPENKO Victor	10
16	MOHAMED ADNAN Sayed				GEYNRIKH Alexander	15
17	BABA Hussain				NIKOLAEV Alexey	17
29	HUBAIL Mohammed				KADADAZE Timur	18
	Tr: PERUZOVIC Luka				Tr: HOUGHTON Bob	
8	ABDUL RAHMAN Rashed	63	70	70	KHOLMURADOV Zafar	11
15	FARHAN Saleh	70	63	63	BIKMOEV Marat	13
30	HUBAIL Alaa	82				

ASIA – CONCACAF PLAY-OFF

Hasely Crawford, Port of Spain
12-11-2005, 18:30, 24 991, Shield AUS

TRI 1 1 BHR

Birchall 76   Ghuloom 72

No	TRINIDAD & TOBAGO	min		min	BAHRAIN	No
21	JACK Kelvin				ALI Hassan	1
3	JOHN Avery				MARZOOQ Abdulla	3
4	ANDREWS Marvin				JALAL Sayed	7
6	LAWRENCE Dennis				ABDUL RAHMAN Rashed	8
7	BIRCHALL Christopher	46		46	AHMED Husain	9
8	WHITLEY Aurtis				SALMEEN Mohamed	10
10	LATAPY Russel	67		77	MOHAMED Talal	13
11	EDWARDS Carlos			90	GHULOOM Salman Isa	14
14	JOHN Stern	81			MAHFOODH Sayed	16
16	SPANN Silvio				BABA Hussain	17
19	YORKE Dwight				HUBAIL Mohammed	29
	Tr: BEENHAKER Leo				Tr: PERUZOVIC Luka	
15	JONES Kenwyne	81		77	TALEB Ahmed	20
20	SCOTLAND Jason	67		90	AAISH Fouzi Mubarak	26
				46	HUBAIL Alaa	30

National Stadium, Manama
16-11-2005, 19:00, 35 000, Ruiz COL

BHR 0 1 TRI

Lawrence 49

No	BAHRAIN	min		min	TRINIDAD & TOBAGO	No
1	ALI Hassan				JACK Kelvin	21
7	JALAL Sayed				JOHN Avery	3
8	ABDUL RAHMAN Rashed				ANDREWS Marvin	4
9	AHMED Husain				LAWRENCE Dennis	6
12	BASHEER Mohamed			21	BIRCHALL Christopher	7
13	MOHAMED Talal				WHITLEY Aurtis	8
14	GHULOOM Salman Isa	80		82	EDWARDS Carlos	11
16	MAHFOODH Sayed				JOHN Stern	14
17	BABA Hussain	[92]		78	JONES Kenwyne	15
29	HUBAIL Mohammed				YORKE Dwight	19
30	HUBAIL Alaa				GRAY Cyd	24
	Tr: PERUZOVIC Luka				Tr: BEENHAKER Leo	
26	AAISH Fouzi Mubarak	80		82	COX Ian	2
				78	LATAPY Russel	10
				21	SPANN Silvio	16

OCEANIA – SOUTH AMERICA PLAY-OFFS

Centenario, Montevideo
12-11-2005, 18:00, 55 000, Larsen DEN

URU 1 0 AUS

Dario Rodriguez 37

No	URUGUAY	min		min	AUSTRALIA	No
1	CARINI Fabian				SCHWARZER Mark	1
3	RODRIGUEZ Dario				NEILL Lucas	2
4	MONTERO PAOLO				CHIPPERFIELD Scott	3
5	GARCIA Pablo				VIDMAR Tony	5
6	LOPEZ Diego	64			POPOVIC Tony	6
8	DIOGO Carlos				EMERTON Brett	7
9	RECOBA Alvaro	80			VIDUKA Mark	9
15	PEREZ Diego				KEWELL Harry	10
17	ZALAYETA Marcelo	64			GRELLA Vince	13
18	MORALES Richard			52	THOMPSON Archie	14
21	FORLAN Diego	19			CULINA Jason	19
	Tr: FOSSATI Jorge				Tr: HIDDINK Guus	
2	RODRIGUEZ Guillermo	64	80	80	ALOISI John	15
10	SILVA Dario	19	52	52	BRESCIANO Marco	23
13	ESTOYANOFF Fabian	64				

Telstra, Sydney
16-11-2005, 20:00, 82 698, Medina Cantalejo ESP

AUS 1 0 URU

Bresciano 35   Australia won 4-2 on penalties

No	AUSTRALIA	min		min	URUGUAY	No
1	SCHWARZER Mark				CARINI Fabian	1
2	NEILL Lucas				LUGANO Diego	2
3	CHIPPERFIELD Scott				RODRIGUEZ Dario	3
4	CAHILL Tim	81			MONTERO PAOLO	4
5	VIDMAR Tony				GARCIA Pablo	5
6	POPOVIC Tony	31			RODRIGUEZ Guillermo	6
7	EMERTON Brett	110			VARELA Gustavo	7
9	VIDUKA Mark				DIOGO Carlos	8
13	GRELLA Vince			72	RECOBA Alvaro	9
19	CULINA Jason	72		97	REGUEIRO Mario	11
23	BRESCIANO Marco	96			MORALES Richard	18
	Tr: HIDDINK Guus				Tr: FOSSATI Jorge	
8	SKOKO Josip	110	97	97	ESTOYANOFF Fabian	13
10	KEWELL Harry	31	81	81	SOSA Marcelo	14
15	ALOISI John	96	72	72	ZALAYETA Marcelo	17

2006 FIFA WORLD CUP GERMANY™

History dictated that, going into the 2006 FIFA World Cup™ finals in Germany, one thing was for sure: Argentina, Brazil, Germany or Italy would make it to the final. Never before in the tournament had there been a FIFA World Cup™ final without one of that quartet present and Germany 2006 turned out to be no exception. Few, however, would have predicted that of the four, it would be Italy. Most pundits looked no further than Brazil: this was going to be the Ronaldinho show, with a supporting cast of Kaka, Adriano and Ronaldo. Some even wondered why anyone else was bothering to turn up, such was the formality of the occasion. Thankfully, football is more unpredictable than that, and the corporate juggernaut that is now the Brazil team failed to get out of second gear in their first five games then crashed off the road against France in the quarter-finals. Argentina's star burned more brightly in the first round, but they too came unstuck in the quarter-finals against a German team that had, over the course of the tournament, captured the hearts of the German public. The success of the hosts helped make the atmosphere in Germany during June and July truly outstanding. Has there ever been a better organised or supported tournament? But even the revitalised Germans fell short of the final, leaving Italy to maintain the historical record.

With Italian football in the midst of the most serious scandal ever to affect the game in the country, few gave Italy a chance at the start of the tournament. Thirteen of the squad were with clubs under the threat of relegation but, in the face of adversity, the national team found a strength and unity that may not otherwise have been there. The Italians have been unspectacular at times but, as ever, the 2006 team was based on a solid defence that conceded just two goals all tournament - one an own goal and the other a contentious penalty. They also rode their luck, especially against Australia when Fabio Grosso conned the referee into giving a decisive penalty deep into injury-time. Perhaps we should have known this was going to be Italy's year; after all they make it to the final every 12 years and the last time they won, in 1982, their triumph was played out against the backdrop of a major betting and match fixing scandal.

This wasn't just Italy's tournament though. The overall consensus was that Germany 2006 provided many entertaining games – mostly in the first round group stage - and numerous surprises, such as Ecuador's qualification from group A, Trinidad and Tobago's draw with Sweden, and the outstanding Cote d'Ivoire team, so unlucky to be drawn in the toughest group of all. Also unexpected was Ghana's elimination of the Czech Republic, ranked number two in the world; Australia's never say die attitude and, perhaps the biggest surprise of all, that Togo actually made it onto the pitch given the internal wrangling over bonuses and who was going to coach the team.

There were also points of concern - notably the ridiculous spectacle of players falling over at the slightest contact - but these were largely overshadowed in the memory by spectacular goals, starting with the very first of the tournament by Germany's Philipp Lahm in the sixth minute of the opening game; Joe Cole's long-range effort for England against Sweden; and the brilliant volley by Maxi Rodrigues that settled Argentina's last-sixteen tie with Mexico. The best, perhaps, was the team effort scored by Argentina's Esteban Cambiasso, finishing off a 24-pass move against Serbia and Montenegro. The tournament also saw Ronaldo become the highest scorer in the history of the finals with his goal against Ghana.

The tension of the knock-out stage saw the entertainment value decline as goals became scarcer, although France did buck the trend, gaining a new lease of life after a group stage from which they only just managed to qualify. Spain, Brazil and Portugal were brushed aside on the way to the final in Berlin and central to their resurgence was the pivotal figure of Zinedine Zidane. A shame then that the lasting image of the 2006 FIFA World Cup™ will always be of Zidane head-butting Marco Materazzi in the chest in extra-time in the final. Whatever the provocation, it was an extraordinary end to the career of one of the all-time greats. Instead, the glory was Italy's. Germany had spoiled their party in 1990 and, 16 years on, the tables were turned as the most successful European nation of all-time won the tournament for the fourth time. The Italians have now won the trophy on Italian, French, Spanish and German soil. What price another Italian triumph in 12 years time, should the FIFA World Cup™ return to Europe again in 2018?

GROUP A	PL	W	D	L	F	A	GD	PTS	GER	ECU	POL	CRC
1 Germany	3	3	0	0	8	2	+6	9		3-0	1-0	4-2
2 Ecuador	3	2	0	1	5	3	+2	6			2-0	3-0
3 Poland	3	1	0	2	2	4	-2	3				2-1
4 Costa Rica	3	0	0	3	3	9	-6	0				

GROUP B	PL	W	D	L	F	A	GD	PTS	ENG	SWE	PAR	TRI
1 England	3	2	1	0	5	2	+3	7		2-2	1-0	2-0
2 Sweden	3	1	2	0	3	2	+1	5			1-0	0-0
3 Paraguay	3	1	0	2	2	2	=	3				2-0
4 Trinidad and Tobago	3	0	1	2	0	4	-4	1				

GROUP C	PL	W	D	L	F	A	GD	PTS	ARG	NED	CIV	SCG
1 Argentina	3	2	1	0	8	1	+7	7		0-0	2-1	6-0
2 Netherlands	3	2	1	0	3	1	+2	7			2-1	1-0
3 Côte d'Ivoire	3	1	0	2	5	6	-1	3				3-2
4 Serbia and Montenegro	3	0	0	3	2	10	-8	0				

GROUP D	PL	W	D	L	F	A	GD	PTS	POR	MEX	ANG	IRN
1 Portugal	3	3	0	0	5	1	+4	9		2-1	1-0	2-0
2 Mexico	3	1	1	1	4	3	+1	4			0-0	3-1
3 Angola	3	0	2	1	1	2	-1	2				1-1
4 Iran	3	0	1	2	2	6	-4	1				

GROUP E	PL	W	D	L	F	A	GD	PTS	ITA	GHA	CZE	USA
1 Italy	3	2	1	0	5	1	+4	7		2-0	2-0	1-1
2 Ghana	3	2	0	1	4	3	+1	6			2-0	2-1
3 Czech Republic	3	1	0	2	3	4	-1	3				3-0
4 USA	3	0	1	2	2	6	-4	1				

GROUP F	PL	W	D	L	F	A	GD	PTS	BRA	AUS	CRO	JPN
1 Brazil	3	3	0	0	7	1	+6	9		2-0	1-0	4-1
2 Australia	3	1	1	1	5	5	=	4			2-2	3-1
3 Croatia	3	0	2	1	2	3	-1	2				0-0
4 Japan	3	0	1	2	2	7	-5	1				

GROUP G	PL	W	D	L	F	A	GD	PTS	SUI	FRA	KOR	TOG
1 Switzerland	3	2	1	0	4	0	+4	7		0-0	2-0	2-0
2 France	3	1	2	0	3	1	+2	5			1-1	2-0
3 Korea Republic	3	1	1	1	3	4	-1	4				2-1
4 Togo	3	0	0	3	1	6	-5	0				

GROUP H	PL	W	D	L	F	A	GD	PTS	ESP	UKR	TUN	KSA
1 Spain	3	3	0	0	8	1	+7	9		4-0	3-1	1-0
2 Ukraine	3	2	0	1	5	4	+1	6			1-0	4-0
3 Tunisia	3	0	1	2	3	6	-3	1				2-2
4 Saudi Arabia	3	0	1	2	2	7	-5	1				

2006 FIFA WORLD CUP GERMANY™

First round groups	Pts	Round of Sixteen		Quarter-finals		Semi-finals		Final	
Germany	9								
Ecuador	6	**Italy**	1						
Poland	3	Australia	0						
Costa Rica	0								
				Italy	3				
	Pts			Ukraine	0				
England	7								
Sweden	5	Switzerland	0 0p						
Paraguay	3	**Ukraine**	0 3p						
Trinidad & Tob	1								
						Italy	2		
	Pts					Germany	0		
Argentina	7								
Netherlands	7	**Argentina**	2						
Côte d'Ivoire	3	Mexico	1						
Serbia & Mont.	0								
				Argentina	1 2p				
	Pts			**Germany**	1 4p				
Portugal	9								
Mexico	4	Sweden	0						
Angola	2	**Germany**	2						
Iran	1								
								Italy	1 5p
	Pts							France	1 3p
Italy	7								
Ghana	6	**Portugal**	1						
Czech Republic	3	Netherlands	0						
USA	1								
				Portugal	0 3p				
	Pts			England	0 1p				
Brazil	9								
Australia	4	Ecuador	0						
Croatia	2	**England**	1						
Japan	1								
						Portugal	0		
	Pts					**France**	1		
Switzerland	7								
France	5	**Brazil**	3						
Korea Republic	4	Ghana	0						
Togo	0								
				Brazil	0				
	Pts			**France**	1				
Spain	9								
Ukraine	6	Spain	1						
Tunisia	1	**France**	3						
Saudi Arabia	1								

First Round Group A	FIFA World Cup Stadium, Munich	Friday, 9-06-2006
Kick-off: 18:00		Attendance: 66 000

GERMANY 4 2 COSTA RICA

Philipp Lahm [6], Miroslav Klose 2 [17 61], Torsten Frings [87]   Paulo Wanchope 2 [12 73]

		GERMANY			MATCH STATS				COSTA RICA		
1	GK	LEHMANN Jens		21	Shots	4		PORRAS Jose	GK	18
3	DF	FRIEDRICH Arne		10	Shots on Goal	2		(C) MARIN Luis	DF	3
7	MF	SCHWEINSTEIGER Bastian		11	Fouls Committed	15	66	UMANA Michael	DF	4
8	MF	FRINGS Torsten		7	Corner Kicks	3		MARTINEZ Gilberto	DF	5
11	FW	KLOSE Miroslav (†)	79	3	Caught offside	3		FONSECA Danny	MF	6
16	DF	LAHM Philipp		63	Possession %	37	78	SOLIS Mauricio	MF	8
17	DF	MERTESACKER Per		(C)Captain † Man of the Match				WANCHOPE Paulo	FW	9
18	MF	BOROWSKI Tim	72					CENTENO Walter	MF	10
19	MF	SCHNEIDER Bernd (C)	91+		MATCH OFFICIALS		91+	GOMEZ Ronald	FW	11
20	FW	PODOLSKI Lukas			REFEREE			GONZALEZ Leonardo	DF	12
21	DF	METZELDER Christoph		ELIZONDO Horacio ARG				SEQUEIRA Douglas	MF	20
		Tr: KLINSMANN Jurgen			ASSISTANTS				Tr: GUIMARAES Alexandre		
		Substitutes		GARCIA Dario ARG				Substitutes		
5	MF	KEHL Sebastian	72	OTERO Rodolfo ARG			66	DRUMMOND Jervis	DF	2
10	FW	NEUVILLE Oliver	79		4TH OFFICIAL		78	BOLANOS Christian	MF	7
22	MF	ODONKOR David	91+	CHANDIA Carlos CHI			91+	AZOFEIFA Randall	MF	14

It was a very open game. We were a little nervous before and during the match and because of that we made a couple of mistakes. Costa Rica's goals came from some pretty basic errors. I'd like to thank the crowd who were right behind us and urged us on when we were struggling.

Jurgen Klinsmann

Two of their goals were absolutely brilliant. I wasn't surprised two of ours came through the middle of the German defence. We knew exactly where to attack and we capitalised on that brilliantly. Germany dealt us psychological blows at key times. Everytime we scored they came straight back and did the same.

Alexandre Guimaraes

First Round Group A	FIFA World Cup Stadium, Gelsenkirchen	Friday, 9-06-2006
Kick-off: 21:00		Attendance: 52 000

POLAND 0 2 ECUADOR

Carlos Tenorio [24] ,Augustin Delgado [80]

		POLAND			MATCH STATS				ECUADOR		
1	GK	BORUC Artur		7	Shots	10	69	MORA Cristian	GK	12
2	DF	JOP Mariusz		3	Shots on Goal	6		(C) HURTADO Ivan	DF	3
4	DF	BASZCZYNSKI Marcin		9	Fouls Committed	15		DE LA CRUZ Ulises	DF	4
6	DF	BAK Jacek (C)		11	Corner Kicks	2	83	MENDEZ Edison	MF	8
7	MF	SOBOLEWSKI Radoslaw	67	3	Caught offside	2		† DELGADO Agustin	FW	11
8	MF	KRZYNOWEK Jacek	78	56	Possession %	44		CASTILLO Segundo	MF	14
9	FW	ZURAWSKI Maciej	83	(C)Captain † Man of the Match				VALENCIA Luis	MF	16
10	MF	SZYMKOWIAK Miroslav						ESPINOZA Giovanny	DF	17
14	DF	ZEWLAKOW Michal			MATCH OFFICIALS			REASCO Neicer	DF	18
15	MF	SMOLAREK Ebi			REFEREE			TENORIO Edwin	MF	20
16	MF	RADOMSKI Arkadiusz		KAMIKAWA Toru JPN			65	TENORIO Carlos	FW	21
		Tr: JANAS Pawel			ASSISTANTS				Tr: SUAREZ Luis		
		Substitutes		HIROSHIMA Yoshikazu JPN				Substitutes		
5	MF	KOSOWSKI Kamil	78	KIM Dae Young KOR			69	GUAGUA Jorge	DF	2
21	FW	JELEN Ireneusz	67		4TH OFFICIAL		83	URRUTIA Patricio	MF	6
23	FW	BROZEK Pawel	83	MICHEL Lubos SVK			65	KAVIEDES Ivan	FW	10

We made a mistake and were punished for it. The first goal threw us and it reminded me of Korea in 2002 because after we conceded the first goal we lost our focus, our communication and our organisation. Football is a game of mistakes and we were punished for ours.

Michal Zewlakow

We're very tired as it was a really physical game. The players were very focused. I notice people criticise us for only ever winning at high altitude but this stadium was more suited to Poland, so everyone knows we can win in other conditions. We mustn't get carried away, though, as this was just the first step.

Luis Suarez

First Round Group A	Westfalenstadion, Dortmund	Wednesday, 14-06-2006
Kick-off: 21:00		Attendance: 65 000

GERMANY   1 0   POLAND

Neuville Oliver 91+

		GERMANY			MATCH STATS				POLAND		
1	GK	LEHMANN Jens		16	Shots	5		BORUC Artur	GK	1
3	DF	FRIEDRICH Arne	64	8	Shots on Goal	3		BASZCZYNSKI Marcin	DF	4
7	MF	SCHWEINSTEIGER Bastian	77	21	Fouls Committed	17	75	(C) BAK Jacek	DF	6
8	MF	FRINGS Torsten		10	Corner Kicks	4	77	SOBOLEWSKI Radoslaw	MF	7
11	FW	KLOSE Miroslav		6	Caught offside	2		KRZYNOWEK Jacek	MF	8
13	MF	BALLACK Michael (C)		58	Possession %	42	83	ZURAWSKI Maciej	FW	9
16	DF	LAHM Philipp †		(C) Captain † Man of the Match				ZEWLAKOW Michal	DF	14
17	DF	MERTESACKER Per		MATCH OFFICIALS				SMOLAREK Ebi	MF	15
19	MF	SCHNEIDER Bernd		REFEREE				RADOMSKI Arkadiusz	MF	16
20	FW	PODOLSKI Lukas	71	MEDINA CANTALEJO Luis ESP		91+		BOSACKI Bartosz	MF	19
21	DF	METZELDER Christoph		ASSISTANTS				JELEN Ireneusz	FW	21
		Tr: KLINSMANN Jurgen		GIRALDEZ Victoriano ESP				Tr: JANAS Pawel		
		Substitutes		MEDINA Pedro ESP		83		Substitutes		
10	FW	NEUVILLE Oliver	71	4TH OFFICIAL				DUDKA Dariusz	DF	17
18	MF	BOROWSKI Tim	77	AL GHAMDI Khalil KSA		91+	77	LEWANDOWSKI Mariusz	DF	18
22	MF	ODONKOR David	64				91+	BROZEK Pawel	FW	23

We had so many chances but the ball just didn't seem to want to go in. We kept up the tempo throughout the matchbut the longer you go on without scoring, the more nervous you feel. The substitutions were designed to give us more pace. You can't write the Germans off until the final whistle blows.

Jurgen Klinsmann

We weren't able to put our tactical plan into action. We played a lot better in a number of areas, and it was an improved performance overall, but at the end of the day it wasn't to be. We were down to ten men at the end and very tired so we were unable to resist the enormous pressure the Germans put us under.

Pawel Janas

First Round Group A	FIFA World Cup Stadium, Hamburg	Thursday, 15-06-2006
Kick-off: 15:00		Attendance: 50 000

ECUADOR   3 0   COSTA RICA

Carlos Tenorio 8, **Agustin Delgado** 54, **Ivan Kaviedes** 92+

		ECUADOR			MATCH STATS				COSTA RICA		
12	GK	MORA Cristian		14	Shots	12		PORRAS Jose	GK	18
3	DF	HURTADO Ivan (C)		7	Shots on Goal	4		(C) MARIN Luis	DF	3
4	DF	DE LA CRUZ Ulises		18	Fouls Committed	22	29	UMANA Michael	DF	4
8	MF	MENDEZ Edison		3	Corner Kicks	4		FONSECA Danny	MF	6
11	FW	DELGADO Agustin †		3	Caught offside	2		SOLIS Mauricio	MF	8
14	MF	CASTILLO Segundo		51	Possession %	49	84	WANCHOPE Paulo	FW	9
16	MF	VALENCIA Luis	73	(C) Captain † Man of the Match				CENTENO Walter	MF	10
17	DF	ESPINOZA Giovanny	69	MATCH OFFICIALS				GOMEZ Ronald	FW	11
18	DF	REASCO Neicer		REFEREE		56		GONZALEZ Leonardo	DF	12
20	MF	TENORIO Edwin		CODJIA Coffi BEN				WALLACE Harold	DF	15
21	FW	TENORIO Carlos	46	ASSISTANTS				SEQUEIRA Douglas	MF	20
		Tr: SUAREZ Luis		NTAGUNGIRA Celestin RWA				Tr: GUIMARAES Alexandre		
		Substitutes		ADERODJOU Aboudou BEN		84		Substitutes		
2	DF	GUAGUA Jorge	69	4TH OFFICIAL		56		BERNARD Kurt	FW	13
6	MF	URRUTIA Patricio	73	GUEZZAZ Mohamed MAR		29		HERNANDEZ Carlos	MF	16
10	FW	KAVIEDES Ivan	46					SABORIO Alvaro	FW	19

People back in Ecuador will be delighted and so they should be, because this is a day for celebration. The one thing that we have got going for us is that we are solid at the back. Everything we do in the match is based on that. Today we achieved our goal - to play one more match than at the last World Cup.

Luis Suarez

They scored an early goal from a situation that didn't look very threatening and from that point we were always chasing the game. In the second half they scored early on again and we had to take risks without ever having a lot of possession. That played right into Ecuador's hands.

Alexandre Guimaraes

First Round Group A	Olympiastadion, Berlin	Tuesday, 20-06-2006
Kick-off: 16:00		Attendance: 72 000

ECUADOR   0   3   GERMANY

Miroslav Klose 2 [4] [44], Lukas Podolski [57]

		ECUADOR			MATCH STATS			GERMANY		
12	GK	MORA Cristian		7	Shots	15		LEHMANN Jens	GK	1
2	DF	GUAGUA Jorge		2	Shots on Goal	9		FRIEDRICH Arne	DF	3
4	DF	DE LA CRUZ Ulises		22	Fouls Committed	18		HUTH Robert	DF	4
8	MF	MENDEZ Edison		5	Corner Kicks	2	66	SCHWEINSTEIGER Bastian	MF	7
9	FW	BORJA Felix	46	0	Caught offside	3	66	FRINGS Torsten	MF	8
10	FW	KAVIEDES Ivan		57	Possession %	43		KLOSE Miroslav	FW	11
13	DF	AMBROSSI Paul						† (C) BALLACK Michael	MF	13
15	MF	AYOVI Marlon (C)	68	(C)Captain †Man of the Match				LAHM Philipp	DF	16
16	MF	VALENCIA Luis	63	MATCH OFFICIALS				MERTESACKER Per	DF	17
17	DF	ESPINOZA Giovanny		REFEREE			73	SCHNEIDER Bernd	MF	19
20	MF	TENORIO Edwin		IVANOV Valentin RUS				PODOLSKI Lukas	FW	20
		Tr: SUAREZ Luis		ASSISTANTS				Tr: KLINSMANN Jurgen		
		Substitutes		GOLUBEV Nikolay RUS				Substitutes		
6	MF	URRUTIA Patricio	68	VOLNIN Evgueni RUS			66	NEUVILLE Oliver	FW	10
7	MF	LARA Christian	63	4TH OFFICIAL			73	ASAMOAH Gerald	FW	14
23	FW	BENITEZ Christian	46	STOTT Kevin			66	BOROWSKI Tim	MF	18

We found ourselves a goal down right from the off and on the day the opposition were quite simply stronger, quicker and played better football than we did. I'm disappointed because that really wasn't a good performannce. Every team has to lose at some point but it's the manner of the defeat.

Luis Suarez

It's great for our self-confidence and also because we're growing as a team. The game was different in style from the one against Poland. It was played in really high temperatures and Ecuador wanted to keep things slow. Miroslav Klose is in his prime and is unbelievably hungry for goals.

Jurgen Klinsmann

First Round Group A	FIFA World Cup Stadium, Hanover	Tuesday, 20-06-2006
Kick-off: 16:00		Attendance: 43 000

COSTA RICA   1   2   POLAND

Ronald Gomez [25]   Bartosz Bosacki 2 [33] [66]

		COSTA RICA			MATCH STATS			POLAND		
18	GK	PORRAS Jose		12	Shots	10		BORUC Artur	GK	1
2	DF	DRUMMOND Jervis	70	5	Shots on Goal	7		BASZCZYNSKI Marcin	DF	4
3	DF	MARIN Luis (C)		12	Fouls Committed	20		(C) BAK Jacek	DF	6
4	DF	UMANA Michael		2	Corner Kicks	8	46	KRZYNOWEK Jacek	MF	7
7	MF	BOLANOS Christian	78	4	Caught offside	1		ZURAWSKI Maciej	FW	9
8	MF	SOLIS Mauricio		49	Possession %	51		SZYMKOWIAK Miroslav	MF	10
9	FW	WANCHOPE Paulo		(C)Captain †Man of the Match				ZEWLAKOW Michal	DF	14
10	MF	CENTENO Walter		MATCH OFFICIALS			85	SMOLAREK Ebi	MF	15
11	FW	GOMEZ Ronald	82	REFEREE			64	RADOMSKI Arkadiusz	MF	16
12	DF	GONZALEZ Leonardo		MAIDIN Shamsul SIN				† BOSACKI Bartosz	MF	19
17	DF	BADILLA Gabriel		ASSISTANTS				JELEN Ireneusz	FW	21
		Tr: GUIMARAES Alexandre		PERMPANICH Prachya THA				Tr: JANAS Pawel		
		Substitutes		GHULOUM Eisa UAE				Substitutes		
15	DF	WALLACE Harold	70	4TH OFFICIAL			85	RASIAK Grzegorz	FW	11
16	MF	HERNANDEZ Carlos	82	DAMON Jerome RSA			64	LEWANDOWSKI Mariusz	DF	18
19	FW	SABORIO Alvaro	78				46	BROZEK Pawel	FW	23

We had a very bad game against Ecuador but against Germany and today we played really well. The situation is not as bad as many in the media say. What is important is to be calm and to take the right decisions. If we keep coming to the World Cup the moment will come when our football level will improve.

Luis Marin

The players did what they could. I am happy about the performance here. The temperature was very high and I am glad that we played so well.

Pawel Janas

Our earlier games cost us the chance of going through. If we'd had a different result against Ecuador...

Bartosz Bosacki

First Round Group B	Waldstadion, Frankfurt	Saturday, 10-06-2006
Kick-off: 15:00		Attendance: 48 000

ENGLAND 1 0 PARAGUAY

Carlos Gamarra OG [3]

		ENGLAND			MATCH STATS					PARAGUAY		
1	GK	ROBINSON Paul					8		VILLAR Justo	GK	1
2	DF	NEVILLE Gary		13	Shots	7	82		TOLEDO Delio	DF	3
3	DF	COLE Ashley		5	Shots on Goal	2		(C)	GAMARRA Carlos	DF	4
4	MF	GERRARD Steven		13	Fouls Committed	13			CACERES Julio Cesar	DF	5
5	DF	FERDINAND Rio		6	Corner Kicks	1	68		BONET Carlos	MF	6
6	DF	TERRY John		4	Caught offside	3			SANTA CRUZ Roque	FW	9
7	MF	BECKHAM David (C)		53	Possession %	47			ACUNA Roberto	MF	10
8	MF	LAMPARD Frank †		(C)Captain †Man of the Match					PAREDES Carlos	MF	13
10	FW	OWEN Michael	56	MATCH OFFICIALS					RIVEROS Cristian	MF	16
11	MF	COLE Joe	83	REFEREE					VALDEZ Nelson	FW	18
21	FW	CROUCH Peter		RODRIGUEZ Marco MEX					CANIZA Denis	DF	21
	Tr: ERIKSSON Sven-Goran			ASSISTANTS					Tr: RUIZ Anibal		
		Substitutes		CAMARGO Jose Luis MEX					Substitutes		
16	MF	HARGREAVES Owen	83	LEAL Leonel CRC			82		NUNEZ Jorge	DF	2
20	MF	DOWNING Stewart	56	4TH OFFICIAL			8		BOBADILLA Aldo	GK	22
				CODJIA Coffi BEN			68		CUEVAS Nelson	FW	23

In the first half until about 35-40 minutes I think we did well and played the football we should have. For a long time in the second half we struggled to keep the ball and to come out as a team and we gave a lot of possession to Paraguay. The heat knocked us out a little but they didn't have many chances.

Sven-Goran Eriksson

After the surprise of the early goal, I think we managed to control a very strong team who could go all of the way to the final although we could have done more in the second half. I told the players in the dressing room that they have played a good game - but not a great game as we didn't win.

Anibal Ruiz

First Round Group B	Westfalenstadion, Dortmund	Saturday, 10-06-2006
Kick-off: 18:00		Attendance: 62 959

TRINIDAD & TOBAGO 0 0 SWEDEN

		TRINIDAD AND TOBAGO			MATCH STATS				SWEDEN		
1	GK	HISLOP Shaka						SHAABAN Rami	GK	23
3	DF	JOHN Avery	46	6	Shots	18		(C) MELLBERG Olof	DF	3
5	DF	SANCHO Brent		2	Shots on Goal	6		LUCIC Teddy	DF	4
6	DF	LAWRENCE Dennis		10	Fouls Committed	9		EDMAN Erik	DF	5
7	MF	BIRCHALL Christopher		1	Corner Kicks	8	78	LINDEROTH Tobias	MF	6
8	DF	GRAY Cyd		1	Caught offside	2		ALEXANDERSSON Niclas	MF	7
11	MF	EDWARDS Carlos		40	Possession %	60	62	SVENSSON Anders	MF	8
12	FW	SAMUEL Collin	52	(C)Captain †Man of the Match				LJUNGBERG Freddie	MF	9
14	FW	JOHN Stern		MATCH OFFICIALS				IBRAHIMOVIC Zlatan	FW	10
18	MF	THEOBALD Densill	66	REFEREE				LARSSON Henrik	FW	11
19	FW	YORKE Dwight (C) †		MAIDIN Shamsul SIN			78	WILHELMSSON Christian	MF	21
	Tr: BEENHAKKER Leo			ASSISTANTS				Tr: LAGERBACK Lars		
		Substitutes		PERMPANICH Prachya THA				Substitutes		
9	MF	WHITLEY Aurtis	66	GHULOUM UAE			78	KALLSTROM Kim	MF	16
13	FW	GLEN Cornell	52	4TH OFFICIAL			78	JONSON Mattias	FW	18
				RUIX Oscar COL			62	ALLBACK Marcus	FW	20

We ground out a result today and we fought hard all of the way. We had some bad luck with the red card so early in the second half but we stayed together and played as a team and got a result when no-one gave us a chance. We earned some respect and made some friends all over the world with this game.

Stern John

It's just one of those matches that happens now and again. We controlled the play and created many more chances than our opponents but the ball didn't want to go into the net. We were not sharp enough in front of goal and also the Trinidad goalkeeper, Shaka Hislop, had a brilliant game.

Lars Lagerback

First Round Group B	Frankenstadion, Nuremerg	Thursday, 15-06-2006
Kick-off: 18:00		Attendance: 41 000

ENGLAND   2   0   TRINIDAD & TOBAGO

Peter Crouch [83], Steven Gerrard [91+]

		ENGLAND			MATCH STATS				TRINIDAD AND TOBAGO		
1	GK	ROBINSON Paul							HISLOP Shaka	GK	1
3	DF	COLE Ashley		23	Shots	7			SANCHO Brent	DF	5
4	MF	GERRARD Steven		8	Shots on Goal	3			LAWRENCE Dennis	DF	6
5	DF	FERDINAND Rio		15	Fouls Committed	19			BIRCHALL Christopher	MF	7
6	DF	TERRY John		7	Corner Kicks	3			GRAY Cyd	DF	8
7	MF	BECKHAM David (C) †		2	Caught offside	2			WHITLEY Aurtis	MF	9
8	MF	LAMPARD Frank		62	Possession %	38			EDWARDS Carlos	MF	11
10	FW	OWEN Michael	58	(C) Captain † Man of the Match					JOHN Stern	FW	14
11	MF	COLE Joe	75	MATCH OFFICIALS			70		JONES Kenwyne	FW	15
15	DF	CARRAGHER Jamie	58	REFEREE			85		THEOBALD Densill	MF	18
21	FW	CROUCH Peter		KAMIKAWA Toru JPN					(C) YORKE Dwight	FW	19
	Tr: ERIKSSON Sven-Goran			ASSISTANTS				Tr: BEENHAKKER Leo			
	Substitutes			HIROSHIMA Yoshikazu JPN					Substitutes		
9	FW	ROONEY Wayne	58	KIM Dae Young			70		GLEN Cornell	FW	13
19	MF	LENNON Aaron	58	4TH OFFICIAL			85		WISE Evans	MF	16
20	MF	DOWNING Stewart	75	STOTT Kevin USA							

We had a lot of chances in the first 80 minutes and we were unlucky not to take them. Trinidad and Tobago defended with eight, nine or ten men behind the ball and made things very difficult for us. They showed great discipline and great strength but we showed great patience too.

Sven-Goran Eriksson

We are disappointed. My players played with a lot of courage and a lot of passion - that's the only way they can play. It was very hard to see the first goal go in. As the minutes tick by and the game goes on, your hopes build and you get more excited. After that I wasn't surprised to see England score a second.

Leo Beenhakker

First Round Group B	Olympiastadion, Berlin	Thursday, 15-06-2006
Kick-off: 21:00		Attendance: 72 000

SWEDEN   1   0   PARAGUAY

Freddie Ljungberg [89]

		SWEDEN			MATCH STATS				PARAGUAY		
1	GK	ISAKSSON Andreas							BOBADILLA Aldo	GK	22
3	DF	MELLBERG Olof (C)		17	Shots	16			NUNEZ Jorge	DF	2
4	DF	LUCIC Teddy		10	Shots on Goal	3			(C) GAMARRA Carlos	DF	4
5	DF	EDMAN Erik		19	Fouls Committed	15			CACERES Julio Cesar	DF	5
6	MF	LINDEROTH Tobias		6	Corner Kicks	3	81		BONET Carlos	MF	6
7	MF	ALEXANDERSSON Niclas		3	Caught offside	1	63		SANTA CRUZ Roque	FW	9
9	MF	LJUNGBERG Freddie †		57	Possession %	43			ACUNA Roberto	MF	10
10	FW	IBRAHIMOVIC Zlatan	46	(C) Captain † Man of the Match					PAREDES Carlos	MF	13
11	FW	LARSSON Henrik		MATCH OFFICIALS			62		RIVEROS Cristian	MF	16
16	MF	KALLSTROM Kim	86	REFEREE					VALDEZ Nelson	FW	18
21	MF	WILHELMSSON Christian	68	MICHEL Lubos SVK					CANIZA Denis	DF	21
	Tr: LAGERBACK Lars			ASSISTANTS				Tr: RUIZ Anibal			
	Substitutes			SLYSKO SVK					Substitutes		
17	FW	ELMANDER Johan	86	BALKO Martin SVK			81		BARRETO Edgar	MF	8
18	FW	JONSON Mattias	68	4TH OFFICIAL			62		DOS SANTOS Julio	MF	19
20	FW	ALLBACK Marcus	46	DAMON Jerome RSA			63		LOPEZ Dante	FW	20

It's always frustrating when you are sitting on the bench and so many chances are being wasted, but it would have been worse if we weren't playing well and weren't creating any chances. It was a really good team effort from us tonight. I have a lot of respect for the Paraguay team but we created more chances.

Lars Lagerback

We came here with a big dream and now we are going home with nothing. It is very difficult to explain what happened. The team is sad because we feel that we have done enough in the game. We weren't bad in either game. The players' confidence was there. We are really disappointed.

Roque Santa Cruz

First Round Group B	FIFA World Cup Stadium, Cologne	Tuesday, 20-06-2006
Kick-off: 21:00		Attendance: 45 000

SWEDEN 2 2 ENGLAND

Marcus Allback [51], Henrik Larsson [90]　　　　　　　　　　Joe Cole [34], Steven Gerrard [85]

		SWEDEN			MATCH STATS				ENGLAND		
1	GK	ISAKSSON Andreas		9	Shots	14		ROBINSON Paul	GK	1
3	DF	MELLBERG Olof (C)		6	Shots on Goal	8	56	COLE Ashley	DF	3
4	DF	LUCIC Teddy		18	Fouls Committed	13		FERDINAND Rio	DF	5
5	DF	EDMAN Erik		12	Corner Kicks	6		TERRY John	DF	6
6	MF	LINDEROTH Tobias	91+	0	Caught offside	1		(C) BECKHAM David	MF	7
7	MF	ALEXANDERSSON Niclas		45	Possession %	55		LAMPARD Frank	MF	8
9	MF	LJUNGBERG Freddie		(C) Captain † Man of the Match			69	ROONEY Wayne	FW	9
11	FW	LARSSON Henrik					4	OWEN Michael	FW	10
16	MF	KALLSTROM Kim		MATCH OFFICIALS				† COLE Joe	MF	11
18	FW	JONSON Mattias	54	REFEREE				CARRAGHER Jamie	DF	15
20	FW	ALLBACK Marcus	75	BUSACCA Massimo SUI				HARGREAVES Owen	MF	16
		Tr: LAGERBACK Lars		ASSISTANTS				Tr: ERIKSSON Sven-Goran		
		Substitutes		BURAGINA Francesco SUI				Substitutes		
17	FW	ELMANDER Johan	75	ARNET Matthias SUI			69	GERRARD Steven	MF	4
19	MF	ANDERSSON Daniel	91+	4TH OFFICIAL			56	CAMPBELL Sol	DF	12
21	MF	WILHELMSSON Christian	54	AL GHAMDI Khalil KSA			4	CROUCH Peter	FW	21

We had problems in the first half - England played well but we were too ambitious. We lost too many one v ones. At half-time I told them to be a little more cool. I wasn't surprised that we put them under pressure towards the end. This has happened so often that I'm not surprised by my players' character.

Lars Lagerback

We did very well in the first half but started badly in the second. We let them play a lot of long balls into our box. We must defend better at set pieces. We scored two fantastic goals but it was a little annoying to concede two from set pieces. The important thing was to win the group, which we've done.

Sven-Goran Eriksson

First Round Group B	Fritz-Walter-Stadion, Kaiserslautern	Tuesday, 20-06-2006
Kick-off: 21:00		Attendance: 46 000

PARAGUAY 2 0 TRINIDAD & TOBAGO

Brent Sancho OG [25], Nelson Cuevas [86]

		PARAGUAY			MATCH STATS				TRINIDAD AND TOBAGO		
22	GK	BOBADILLA Aldo		16	Shots	9		JACK Kelvin	GK	21
2	DF	NUNEZ Jorge		9	Shots on Goal	2	31	JOHN Avery	DF	3
4	DF	GAMARRA Carlos (C)		18	Fouls Committed	21		SANCHO Brent	DF	5
5	DF	CACERES Julio Cesar	77	7	Corner Kicks	1		LAWRENCE Dennis	DF	6
8	MF	BARRETO Edgar		3	Caught offside	3	67	BIRCHALL Christopher	MF	7
9	FW	SANTA CRUZ Roque		53	Possession %	47		WHITLEY Aurtis	MF	9
10	MF	ACUNA Roberto		(C) Captain † Man of the Match				EDWARDS Carlos	MF	11
13	MF	PAREDES Carlos					41	GLEN Cornell	FW	13
18	FW	VALDEZ Nelson	66	MATCH OFFICIALS				JOHN Stern	FW	14
19	MF	DOS SANTOS Julio †		REFEREE				THEOBALD Densill	MF	18
21	DF	CANIZA Denis	89	ROSETTI Roberto ITA				(C) YORKE Dwight	FW	19
		Tr: RUIZ Anibal		ASSISTANTS				Tr: BEENHAKKER Leo		
		Substitutes		COPELLI Cristiano ITA				Substitutes		
14	DF	DA SILVA Paulo	89	STAGNOLI Alessandro ITA			67	LATAPY Russell	FW	10
15	DF	MANZUR Julio	77	4TH OFFICIAL			31	JONES Kenwyne	FW	15
23	FW	CUEVAS Nelson	66	DE BLEECKERE Frank BEL			41	WISE Evans	MF	16

We had asked the players to try and lift their spirits after the Sweden defeat. We knew that it wasn't easy, because that was a harsh blow but it was important to get up for this game and play for pride and honour. The boys showed that they are a classy team. We can leave the tournament in the right way.

Anibal Ruiz

It was an open game and we had some chances, but that's football. Before the tournament started people were expecting us to lose 6-0, 8-0. For that reason I'm disappointed to be out of the competition. I'm very satisfied with the effort my players put in. They played with pride and passion.

Leo Beenhakker

| First Round Group C | FIFA World Cup Stadium, Hamburg | Saturday, 10-06-2006 |
| Kick-off: 21:00 | | Attendance: 49 480 |

ARGENTINA 2 1 COTE D'IVOIRE

Hernan Crespo [24], Javier Saviola [38]   Didier Drogba [82]

ARGENTINA				MATCH STATS			COTE D'IVOIRE		
1	GK	ABBONDANZIERI Roberto					TIZIE Jean-Jacques	GK	1
2	DF	AYALA Roberto		9	Shots	13	62	AKALE Kanga	MF	2
3	DF	SORIN Juan (C)		4	Shots on Goal	4		BOKA Arthur	DF	3
5	MF	CAMBIASSO Esteban		15	Fouls Committed	17		TOURE Kolo	DF	4
6	DF	HEINZE Gabriel		3	Corner Kicks	6		ZOKORA Didier	MF	5
7	FW	SAVIOLA Javier †	75	6	Caught offside	0	55	KALOU Bonaventure	FW	8
8	MF	MASCHERANO Javier		49	Possession %	51		(C) DROGBA Didier	FW	11
9	FW	CRESPO Hernan	64	(C)Captain †Man of the Match				MEITE Abdoulaye	DF	12
10	MF	RIQUELME Juan	93+	MATCH OFFICIALS			77	KEITA Kader	MF	18
18	MF	RODRIGUEZ Maxi		REFEREE				TOURE Yaya	MF	19
21	DF	BURDISSO Nicolas		DE BLEECKERE Frank BEL				EBOUE Emmanuel	DF	21
		Tr: PEKERMAN Jose		ASSISTANTS				Tr: MICHEL Henri		
		Substitutes		HERMANS Peter BEL				Substitutes		
14	FW	PALACIO Rodrigo	64	VROMANS Walter BEL			77	KONE Arouna	FW	9
16	MF	AIMAR Pablo	93+	4TH OFFICIAL			62	KONE Bakary	FW	14
22	MF	GONZALEZ Luis	75	POULAT Eric FRA			55	DINDANE Aruna	FW	15

We defended when we had to defend, we created openings and we took our chances when they came. We were up against very tough opponents who did not perform like a team making their first World Cup appearance but like a team capable of achieving real success here.

Jose Pekerman

I am a little disappointed. We created a lot of goalscoring opportunities but we couldn't take them. We paid a very heavy price for our lack of experience and at this level any mistakes you make are invariably punished. We played a good deal better in the second half but we weren't clinical enough.

Henri Michel

| First Round Group C | Zentralstadion, Leipzig | Sunday, 11-06-2006 |
| Kick-off: 15:00 | | Attendance: 37 216 |

SERBIA/MONTENEGRO 0 1 NETHERLANDS

                                                                                      Arjen Robben [18]

SERBIA AND MONTENEGRO				MATCH STATS			NETHERLANDS		
1	GK	JEVRIC Dragoslav					(C) VAN DER SAR Edwin	GK	1
3	DF	DRAGUTINOVIC Ivica		11	Shots	12	86	MATHIJSEN Joris	MF	4
4	MF	DULJAJ Igor		4	Shots on Goal	6		VAN BRONCKHORST Giovanni	DF	5
6	DF	GAVRANCIC Goran		15	Fouls Committed	23		COCU Phillip	FW	8
8	FW	KEZMAN Mateja	67	6	Corner Kicks	4	69	VAN NISTELROOIJ Ruud	FW	9
9	FW	MILOSEVIC Savo (C)	46	2	Caught offside	3		† ROBBEN Arjen	MF	11
10	MF	STANKOVIC Dejan		39	Possession %	61		OOIJER Andre	DF	13
11	MF	DJORDJEVIC Predrag		(C)Captain †Man of the Match				HEITINGA John	DF	14
14	DF	DJORDJEVIC Nenad	43	MATCH OFFICIALS				VAN PERSIE Robin	MF	17
17	MF	NADJ Albert		REFEREE			60	VAN BOMMEL Mark	MF	18
20	DF	KRSTAJIC Mladen		MERK Marcus GER				SNEIJDER Wesley	DF	20
		Tr: PETKOVIC Ilija		ASSISTANTS				Tr: VAN BASTEN Marco		
		Substitutes		SCHRAER Christian GER				Substitutes		
7	MF	KOROMAN Ognjen	43	SALVER Jan-Hendrik GER			86	BOULAHROUZ Khalid	DF	3
19	FW	ZIGIC Nikola	46	4TH OFFICIAL			60	LANDZAAT Denny	DF	6
21	FW	LJUBOJA Danijel	67	GUEZZAZ Mohamed MAR			69	KUYT Dirk	MF	7

It's a real shame that we lost the way we did. Congratulations to the Dutch, even though we were the one who had the better chances. We played really cautiously, we didn't want our defence to be opened up, but unfortunately our attack didn't work well today.

Ilija Petkovic

We knew before the game that it would be difficult. We started well and controlled the game well at times, but our opponents also had their chances. The early lead helped us and we can be very satisfied when you take the heat into account. We slowed down a little in the second half.

Arjen Robben

First Round Group C | **FIFA World Cup Stadium, Gelsenkirchen** | **Friday, 16-06-2006**
Kick-off: 15:00 | | Attendance: 52 000

ARGENTINA　　6　0　SERBIA/MONTENEGRO

Maxi Rodriguez 2 [6] [41], Esteban Cambiasso [31],
Hernan Crespo [78], Carlos Tevez [84], Lionel Messi [88]

		ARGENTINA			MATCH STATS			SERBIA AND MONTENEGRO		
1	GK	ABBONDANZIERI Roberto						JEVRIC Dragoslav	GK	1
2	DF	AYALA Roberto		11	Shots	4		DULJAJ Igor	MF	4
3	DF	SORIN Juan (C)		9	Shots on Goal	1		GAVRANCIC Goran	DF	6
6	DF	HEINZE Gabriel		14	Fouls Committed	22		KOROMAN Ognjen	MF	7
7	FW	SAVIOLA Javier	59	3	Corner Kicks	4		KEZMAN Mateja	FW	8
8	MF	MASCHERANO Javier		3	Caught offside	0	70	(C) MILOSEVIC Savo	FW	9
9	FW	CRESPO Hernan		58	Possession %	42		STANKOVIC Dejan	MF	10
10	MF	RIQUELME Juan †		(C) Captain † Man of the Match				DJORDJEVIC Predrag	MF	11
18	MF	RODRIGUEZ Maxi	75	MATCH OFFICIALS				DUDIC Milan	DF	15
21	DF	BURDISSO Nicolas		REFEREE		46		NADJ Albert	MF	17
22	MF	GONZALEZ Luis	17	ROSETTI Roberto ITA				KRSTAJIC Mladen	DF	20
		Tr: PEKERMAN Jose		ASSISTANTS				Tr: PETKOVIC Ilija		
		Substitutes		COPELLI Cristiano ITA				Substitutes		
5	MF	CAMBIASSO Esteban	17	STAGNOLI Alessandro ITA		46		ERGIC Ivan	MF	2
11	FW	TEVEZ Carlos	59	4TH OFFICIAL		70		VUKIC Zvonimir	MF	18
19	FW	MESSI Lionel	75	ABD EL FATAH Essam EGY		50		LJUBOJA Danijel	FW	21

We have to be happy but also calm. All three areas of the team played well - in attack as well as defending. Today we played good football and that's the most important thing. The Euphoria? It's difficult to stop it, especially amongst the fans but the big players have to take charge and calm everyone else down.

Javier Saviola

It's an absolutely terrible result - the worst in our history and I've got to take responsibility for it. Time will tell if they played a great game or we played a bad one. I don't want to point the finger at any player in particular. We made some errors for sure but the buck stops with me.

Ilija Petkovic

First Round Group C | **Gottlieb-Daimler-Stadion, Stuttgart** | **Friday, 16-06-2006**
Kick-off: 18:00 | | Attendance: 52 000

NETHERLANDS　　2　1　COTE D'IVOIRE

Robin van Persie [23], Ruud van Nistelrooij [27]　　　　　　　　　**Bakary Kone [38]**

		NETHERLANDS			MATCH STATS			COTE D'IVOIRE		
1	GK	VAN DER SAR Edwin (C)						TIZIE Jean-Jacques	GK	1
4	DF	MATHIJSEN Joris		9	Shots	16		BOKA Arthur	DF	3
5	DF	VAN BRONCKHORST Giovanni		8	Shots on Goal	9		TOURE Kolo	DF	4
8	MF	COCU Phillip		24	Fouls Committed	15		ZOKORA Didier	MF	5
9	FW	VAN NISTELROOIJ Ruud	73	3	Corner Kicks	8	73	KONE Arouna	FW	9
11	FW	ROBBEN Arjen †		6	Caught offside	4		(C) DROGBA Didier	FW	11
13	DF	OOIJER Andre		51	Possession %	49		MEITE Abdoulaye	DF	12
14	DF	HEITINGA John	46	(C) Captain † Man of the Match		62		KONE Bakary	FW	14
17	FW	VAN PERSIE Robin		MATCH OFFICIALS				TOURE Yaya	MF	19
18	MF	VAN BOMMEL Mark		REFEREE		62		EBOUE Emmanuel	DF	21
20	MF	SNEIJDER Wesley	50	RUIZ Oscar COL		62		ROMARIC	MF	22
		Tr: VAN BASTEN Marco		ASSISTANTS				Tr: MICHEL Henri		
		Substitutes		TAMAYO Fernando ECU				Substitutes		
3	DF	BOULAHROUZ Khalid	46	NAVIA Jose COL		73		AKALE Kanga	MF	2
6	MF	LANDZAAT Denny	73	4TH OFFICIAL		62		YAPI YAPO Gilles	MF	10
10	MF	VAN DER VAART Rafael	50	RODRIGUEZ Marco MEX		62		DINDANE Aruna	FW	15

We were very good for the first half-hour and created any number of chances but we eased off after Côte d'Ivoire scored their goal. After that we all saw how good they were if you let them play. In fact they were so good in the second half we had no option but to defend. We're just overjoyed about getting through.

Marco van Basten

The pattern has basically been the same in both our matches. We've been forced to chase a two goal deficit because on both occasions we've been unable to contain our opponents. It's always going to be difficult turning it around against class sides like these. We simply lack experience.

Henri Michel

First Round Group C	Waldstadion, Frankfurt	Wednesday, 21-06-2006
Kick-off: 21:00		Attendance: 48 000

NETHERLANDS   0   0   ARGENTINA

		NETHERLANDS			MATCH STATS				ARGENTINA		
1	GK	VAN DER SAR Edwin (C)							ABBONDANZIERI Roberto	GK	1
2	DF	JALIENS Kew		9	Shots	10			(C) AYALA Roberto	DF	2
3	DF	BOULAHROUZ Khalid		3	Shots on Goal	3			CAMBIASSO Esteban	MF	5
7	FW	KUYT Dirk		23	Fouls Committed	17			MASCHERANO Javier	MF	8
8	MF	COCU Phillip		7	Corner Kicks	10		80	RIQUELME Juan	MF	10
9	FW	VAN NISTELROOIJ Ruud	56	1	Caught offside	4			† TEVEZ Carlos	FW	11
10	MF	VAN DER VAART Rafael		53	Possession %	47			MILITO Gabriel	DF	15
13	DF	OOIJER Andre		(C) Captain † Man of the Match					CUFRE Leandro	DF	17
15	DF	DE CLER Tim			MATCH OFFICIALS				RODRIGUEZ Maxi	MF	18
17	FW	VAN PERSIE Robin	67		REFEREE		70		MESSI Lionel	FW	19
20	MF	SNEIJDER Wesley	86	MEDINA CANTAEJO Luis ESP			24		BURDISSO Nicolas	DF	21
		Tr: VAN BASTEN Marco			ASSISTANTS				Tr: PEKERMAN Jose		
		Substitutes		GIRALDEZ Victoriano ESP					Substitutes		
6	MF	LANDZAAT Denny	67	MEDINA Pedro ESP			24		COLOCCINI Fabricio	DF	4
16	MF	MADURO Hedwiges	86		4TH OFFICIAL		80		AIMAR Pablo	MF	16
21	FW	BABEL Ryan	56	CHANDIA Carlos CHI			70		CRUZ Julio	FW	20

We can be pleased with the result. Argentina are a sensational team and we should be proud of getting a draw against them. You could see that from the way we had to work really hard to stay on equal terms. We needed to be cautious because Sunday match is more important than today's.

Marco van Basten

It was a very closely contested game against quality opponents and we could have won because we created more clear-cut opportunities. It's true that both sides had already qualified so the level of intensity could have been higher. The defences were solid and that made for a close, competitive game.

Jose Pekerman

First Round Group C	FIFA World Cup Stadium, Munich	Wednesday, 21-06-2006
Kick-off: 21:00		Attendance: 66 000

COTE D'IVOIRE   3   2   SERBIA/MONTENEGRO

Aruna Dindane 2 [37p 67], Bonaventure Kalou [86p]   Nikola Zigic [10], Sasa Ilic [20]

		COTE D'IVOIRE			MATCH STATS				SERBIA AND MONTENEGRO		
23	GK	BARRY Boubacar							JEVRIC Dragoslav	GK	1
2	MF	AKALE Kanga	60	20	Shots	6			ERGIC Ivan	MF	2
3	DF	BOKA Arthur		10	Shots on Goal	3			DULJAJ Igor	MF	4
5	MF	ZOKORA Didier		13	Fouls Committed	22			GAVRANCIC Goran	DF	6
6	DF	KOUASSI Blaise		9	Corner Kicks	1			(C) STANKOVIC Dejan	MF	10
9	FW	KONE Arouna		7	Caught offside	1			DJORDJEVIC Predrag	MF	11
15	FW	DINDANE Aruna †		68	Possession %	32			DJORDJEVIC Nenad	DF	14
17	DF	DOMORAUD Cyrille (C)	92+	(C) Captain † Man of the Match					DUDIC Milan	DF	15
18	MF	KEITA Kader	73		MATCH OFFICIALS		67		ZIGIC Nikola	FW	19
19	MF	TOURE Yaya			REFEREE		16		KRSTAJIC Mladen	DF	20
21	DF	EBOUE Emmanuel		RODRIGUEZ Marco MEX					ILIC Sasa	MF	22
		Tr: MICHEL Henri			ASSISTANTS				Tr: PETKOVIC Ilija		
		Substitutes		CAMARGO Jose Luis MEX					Substitutes		
8	FW	KALOU Bonaventure	73	LEAL Leonel CRC			67		MILOSEVIC Savo	FW	9
14	FW	KONE Bakary	60		4TH OFFICIAL		46+	16	NADJ Albert	MF	17
				GUEZZAZ Mohamed MAR							

There is a weakness in this team. We need a lot of opportunities to get one or two goals and at this level that's not good enough. I think they have a lot of potential, but that's nothing new. They have a good future ahead of them. They need to go back to work quickly to qualify for the next World Cup in 2010.

Henri Michel

Hopefully we can come back and leave a better impression than we have here. Football keeps getting better and it will continue to improve. Everyone will remember this World Cup and so will we. Côte d'Ivoire were outstanding but they were also unfortunate because they could have finished second in this group.

Ilija Petkovic

First Round Group D | **Frankenstadion, Nuremberg** | **Sunday, 11-06-2006**

Kick-off: 18:00 — Attendance: 41 000

MEXICO 3 1 IRAN

Omar Bravo 2 ²⁸ ⁷⁶, Zinha ⁷⁹

Yahya Golmohammadi ³⁶

		MEXICO				MATCH STATS				IRAN		
1	GK	SANCHEZ Oswaldo							MIRZAPOUR Ebrahim	GK	1
3	DF	SALCIDO Carlos		7	Shots	7		MAHDAVIKIA Mehdi	MF	2
4	DF	MARQUEZ Rafael (C)		4	Shots on Goal	5		GOLMOHAMMADI Yahya	DF	4
5	DF	OSORIO Ricardo		25	Fouls Committed	21		REZAEI Rahman	DF	5
6	MF	TORRADO Gerardo	46	6	Corner Kicks	5		NEKOUNAM Javad	MF	6
8	MF	PARDO Pavel		1	Caught offside	2	63	KARIMI Ali	MF	8
9	FW	BORGETTI Jared	52	53	Possession %	47		HASHEMIAN Vahid	FW	9
10	FW	FRANCO Guillermo	46	(C) Captain † Man of the Match				(C) DAEI Ali	FW	10
14	DF	PINEDA Gonzalo		MATCH OFFICIALS				KAABI Hossein	DF	13
16	DF	MENDEZ Mario		REFEREE				TEYMOURIAN Andranik	MF	14
19	FW	BRAVO Omar †		ROSETTI Roberto ITA			81	NOSRATI Mohammad	DF	20
		Tr: LA VOLPE Ricardo		ASSISTANTS				Tr: IVANKOVIC Branko		
		Substitutes		COPELLI Cristiano ITA				Substitutes		
7	MF	ZINHA	46	STAGNOLI Alessandro ITA			81	BORHANI Arash	FW	15
17	FW	FONSECA Jose	52	4TH OFFICIAL			63	MADANCHI Mehrzad	MF	21
23	MF	PEREZ Luis	46	DAMON Jerome RSA						

We kept the ball better in the second half which settled us. The two changes in the second half were the key to victory.
Ricardo La Volpe

I know my father was watching me from heaven and I thank the team for the flowers before the game.
Oswaldo Sanchez

Mexico were not a superior team. We were equal to them. The most disappointing thing is that we made two mistakes that lead to goals.
Ali Daei

We played too defensively in the second half, mainly due to the fact that Ali Karimi went off injured.
Vahid Hashemian

First Round Group D | **FIFA World Cup Stadium, Cologne** | **Sunday, 11-06-2006**

Kick-off: 21:00 — Attendance: 45 000

ANGOLA 0 1 PORTUGAL

Pauleta ⁴

		ANGOLA				MATCH STATS				PORTUGAL		
1	GK	JOAO RICARDO							RICARDO	GK	1
3	DF	JAMBA		11	Shots	16		FERNANDO MEIRA	DF	5
5	DF	KALI		3	Shots on Goal	8		† (C) LUIS FIGO	MF	7
7	MF	FIGUEIREDO	80	29	Fouls Committed	20	72	PETIT	MF	8
8	MF	ANDRE		2	Corner Kicks	5		PAULETA	FW	9
10	FW	AKWA (C)	60	1	Caught offside	0		SIMAO SABROSA	MF	11
11	MF	MATEUS		42	Possession %	58		MIGUEL	MF	13
14	MF	MENDONCA		(C) Captain † Man of the Match				NUNO VALENTE	MF	14
17	MF	ZE KALANGA	70	MATCH OFFICIALS				RICARDO CARVALHO	FW	16
20	DF	LOCO		REFEREE			60	CRISTIANO RONALDO	MF	17
21	DF	DELGADO		LARRIONDA Jorge URU			83	TIAGO	FW	19
		Tr: DE OLIVEIRA GONCALVES Luis		ASSISTANTS						
		Substitutes		RIAL Walter URU				Substitutes		
6	MF	MILOY	80	FANDINO Pablo URU			60	COSTINHA	MF	6
9	FW	MANTORRAS	60	4TH OFFICIAL			83	HUGO VIANA	FW	10
13	MF	EDSON	70	STOTT Kevin USA			72	MANICHE	FW	18

I don't think Portugal played badly; I think that Angola played well. We are the underdogs in this group and what we want to do is make things difficult for our opponents. We tried to keep their key players quiet and I think we were largely successful - apart from the goal.
Luis Oliveira Goncalves

It was a difficult game, but that's what we expected. Getting an early goal helped us settle and we created three or four chances, if not more. Angola got better in the second half and at times played better than we did. That's why I put on an extra midfielder. There are no easy games at this World Cup.
Luiz Felipe Scolari

First Round Group D	FIFA World Cup Stadium, Hanover	Friday, 16-06-2006
Kick-off: 21:00		Attendance: 43 000

MEXICO　　　　0　0　　　　ANGOLA

		MEXICO			MATCH STATS				ANGOLA		
1	GK	SANCHEZ Oswaldo							† JOAO RICARDO	GK	1
3	DF	SALCIDO Carlos		13	Shots	8			JAMBA	DF	3
4	DF	MARQUEZ Rafael (C)		8	Shots on Goal	1			KALI	DF	5
5	DF	OSORIO Ricardo		20	Fouls Committed	22	73		FIGUEIREDO	MF	7
6	MF	TORRADO Gerardo		6	Corner Kicks	5	79		ANDRE	MF	8
7	MF	ZINHA	52	0	Caught offside	8			(C) AKWA	FW	10
8	MF	PARDO Pavel		54	Possession %	46	68		MATEUS	MF	11
10	FW	FRANCO Guillermo	74	(C) Captain † Man of the Match					MENDONCA	MF	14
14	DF	PINEDA Gonzalo	78	MATCH OFFICIALS			83		ZE KALANGA	MF	17
16	DF	MENDEZ Mario		REFEREE					LOCO	DF	20
19	FW	BRAVO Omar		MAIDIN Shamsul SIN					DELGADO	DF	21
	Tr: LA VOLPE Ricardo			ASSISTANTS				DE OLIVEIRA GONCALVES Luis			
	Substitutes			PERMPANICH Prachya THA					Substitutes		
11	FW	MORALES Ramon	78	GHULOUM Eisa UAE			83		MILOY	MF	6
17	FW	FONSECA Jose	74	4TH OFFICIAL			68		MANTORRAS	FW	9
21	FW	ARELLANO Jesus	52	CHANDIA Carlos CHI			73		RUI MARQUES	DF	15

There was only one team out there and that was Mexico. The problem is, when the ball doesn't want to go in, it doesn't go in. Some games are like that and the Angola keeper put in an extraordinary performnce. Angola played just as we expected them to and were very defensive.

Ricardo La Volpe

It's our first World Cup and after two games we've already got a point. The whole country celebrated the the performance against Portugal and they'll obviously be celebrating this point against Mexico even more. It was a good performance. Mexico are very strong and it's not easy to play against them.

Luis Oliveira Goncalves

First Round Group D	Waldstadion, Frankfurt	Saturday, 17-06-2006
Kick-off: 15:00		Attendance: 48 000

PORTUGAL　　　　2　0　　　　IRAN

Deco [63], Cristiano Ronaldo [80p]

		PORTUGAL			MATCH STATS				IRAN		
1	GK	RICARDO							MIRZAPOUR Ebrahim	GK	1
5	DF	FERNANDO MEIRA		18	Shots	5			MAHDAVIKIA Mehdi	MF	2
6	MF	COSTINHA		10	Shots on Goal	1	88		(C) GOLMOHAMMADI Yahya	DF	4
7	FW	LUIS FIGO (C)	88	19	Fouls Committed	18			REZAEI Rahman	DF	5
9	FW	PAULETA		13	Corner Kicks	31	65		NEKOUNAM Javad	MF	6
13	DF	MIGUEL		4	Caught offside	3			KARIMI Ali	MF	8
14	DF	NUNO VALENTE		63	Possession %	37			HASHEMIAN Vahid	FW	9
16	DF	RICARDO CARVALHO		(C) Captain † Man of the Match					KAABI Hossein	DF	13
17	FW	CRISTIANO RONALDO		MATCH OFFICIALS					TEYMOURIAN Andranik	MF	16
18	MF	MANICHE	67	REFEREE					NOSRATI Mohammad	DF	20
20	MF	DECO †	80	POULAT Eric FRA			66		MADANCHI Mehrzad	MF	21
	Tr: SCOLARI Luiz Felipe			ASSISTANTS				Tr: IVANKOVIC Branko			
	Substitutes			DAGORNE Lionel FRA					Substitutes		
8	MF	PETIT	67	TEXIER Vincent FRA			88		BAKHTIARIZADEH Sohrab	DF	3
11	FW	SIMAO SABROSA	88	4TH OFFICIAL			65		ZANDI Ferydoon	MF	7
19	FW	TIAGO	80	GUEZZAZ Mohamed MAR			66		KHATIBI Rasoul	FW	11

This was the best performance by my team in the last seven or eight games. We were very strong in the first half but we just couldn't score so we continued the same way in the second half and then we scored. I like the Iranian team. They are physically very strong and very tall.

Luiz Felipe Scolari

It was an even game. We started to see more mistakes from the Portugal side and we wanted to take dvantage. I was trying to make a substitution then right at this moment Deco scored this wonderful goal. Because Portugal were so strong it was hard for us and they made it difficult for us to score.

Branko Ivankovic

First Round Group D   **FIFA World Cup Stadium, Gelsenkirchen**   **Wednesday, 21-06-2006**

Kick-off: 16:00   Attendance: 52 000

PORTUGAL   2   1   MEXICO

Maniche [6], Simao Sabrosa [24p]   Jose Fonseca [29]

PORTUGAL				MATCH STATS			MEXICO		
1	GK	RICARDO		11	Shots	14	SANCHEZ Oswaldo	GK	1
3	DF	CANEIRA		5	Shots on Goal	6	SALCIDO Carlos	DF	3
5	DF	FERNANDO MEIRA		29	Fouls Committed	18	(C) MARQUEZ Rafael	DF	4
7	FW	LUIS FIGO (C)	80	4	Corner Kicks	5	OSORIO Ricardo	DF	5
8	MF	PETIT		1	Caught offside	2	69	PARDO Pavel	MF	8
11	FW	SIMAO SABROSA		50	Possession %	50	80	PINEDA Gonzalo	DF	14
13	DF	MIGUEL	61	(C)Captain † Man of the Match			MENDEZ Mario	DF	16
16	DF	RICARDO CARVALHO		MATCH OFFICIALS			† FONSECA Jose	FW	17
18	MF	MANICHE		REFEREE			BRAVO Omar	FW	19
19	MF	TIAGO		MICHEL Lubos SVK		46	RODRIGUEZ Francisco	DF	22
23	FW	HELDER POSTIGA	69			61	PEREZ Luis	MF	23
		Tr: SCOLARI Luiz Felipe		ASSISTANTS			Tr: LA VOLPE Ricardo		
		Substitutes		SLYSKO Roman SVK			Substitutes		
2	DF	PAULO FERREIRA	61	BALKO Martin SVK		46	ZINHA	MF	7
15	FW	BOA MORTE	80	4TH OFFICIAL		80	FRANCO Guillermo	FW	10
21	FW	NUNO GOMES	69	ABD EL FATAH Essam EGY		69	CASTRO Jose Antonio	DF	15

The players that came in did their job well. Today, I liked the result best as it puts us in an ideal position. My major concern was from the 15th to 30th minute of the second half when we were a man up and should have dominated. We should have passed the ball around more but we made many small mistakes.

Luiz Felipe Scolari

We are creating chances but we're not converting them. When you have control you need to score and we even missed a penalty. I think we've played well in the games. I've watched us on video and we're controlling games. There are few teams that meet our standard when it comes to playing the ball.

Ricardo La Volpe

First Round Group D   **Zentralstadion, Leipzig**   **Wednesday, 21-06-2006**

Kick-off: 16:00   Attendance: 38 000

IRAN   1   1   ANGOLA

Sohrab Bakhtiarizadeh [75]   Flavio [60]

IRAN				MATCH STATS			ANGOLA		
1	GK	MIRZAPOUR Ebrahim		18	Shots	15	JOAO RICARDO	GK	1
2	MF	MAHDAVIKIA Mehdi		13	Shots on Goal	7	JAMBA	DF	3
3	DF	BAKHTIARIZADEH Sohrab		19	Fouls Committed	23	KALI	DF	5
5	DF	REZAEI Rahman		3	Corner Kicks	6	73	MILOY	MF	6
7	MF	ZANDI Ferydoon		2	Caught offside	5	51	FIGUEIREDO	MF	7
9	FW	HASHEMIAN Vahid	39	55	Possession %	45	23	(C) AKWA	FW	10
10	FW	DAEI Ali (C)		(C)Captain † Man of the Match			MATEUS	MF	11
13	DF	KAABI Hossein	67	MATCH OFFICIALS			MENDONCA	MF	14
14	MF	TEYMOURIAN Andranik		REFEREE			† ZE KALANGA	MF	17
20	DF	NOSRATI Mohammad	13	SHIELD Mark AUS			LOCO	DF	20
21	MF	MADANCHI Mehrzad					DELGADO	DF	21
		Tr: IVANKOVIC Branko		ASSISTANTS			Tr: DE OLIVEIRA GONCALVES Luis		
		Substitutes		GIBSON Nathan AUS			Substitutes		
11	FW	KHATIBI Rasoul	39	WILSON Ben AUS		73	RUI MARQUES	DF	15
15	FW	BORHANI Arash	67	4TH OFFICIAL		51	FLAVIO	FW	16
23	MF	SHOJAEI Masoud	13	SIMON Carlos BRA		23	LOVE	FW	18

We felt we could win right until the very end and I must congratulate the players for giving it their all. Luck was not on our side. We created a lot more opportunities than Angola and we desrved to win the game. We've not enjoyed much good fortune over the three matches to be honest.

Branko Ivankovic

When we scored I thought we could go on and win the game but we just didn't have it in us to get a second. I'm very, very proud of the way my team has performed and we can leave Germany with our heads held high. That's the most important thing about our whole World Cup experience.

Luis Oliveira Goncalves

First Round Group E	FIFA World Cup Stadium, Hanover	Monday, 12-06-2006
Kick-off: 21:00		Attendance: 43 000

ITALY   2   0   GHANA

Andrea Pirlo [40], Vincenzo Iaquinta [83]

ITALY				MATCH STATS				GHANA		
1	GK	BUFFON Gianluigi						KINGSTON Richard	GK	22
2	DF	ZACCARDO Cristian		18	Shots	14	89	GYAN Asamoah	FW	3
3	DF	GROSSO Fabio		13	Shots on Goal	4		KUFFOUR Samuel	DF	4
4	MF	DE ROSSI Daniele		8	Fouls Committed	22		MENSAH John	DF	5
5	DF	CANNAVARO Fabio (C)		12	Corner Kicks	4	46	PAPPOE Emmanuel	DF	6
9	FW	TONI Luca	82	3	Caught offside	3		ESSIEN Michael	MF	8
10	MF	TOTTI Francesco	56	47	Possession %	53		(C) APPIAH Stephen	MF	10
11	FW	GILARDINO Alberto	64	(C)Captain †Man of the Match				MUNTARI Sulley	MF	11
13	DF	NESTA Alessandro		MATCH OFFICIALS			68	AMOAH Matthew	FW	14
20	MF	PERROTTA Simone		REFEREE				PANTSIL John	DF	15
21	MF	PIRLO Andrea †		SIMON Carlos BRA				ADDO Eric	MF	18
		Tr: LIPPI Marcello		ASSISTANTS				Tr: DUJKOVIC Ratomir		
		Substitutes		TAVARES Aristeu BRA				Substitutes		
7	FW	DEL PIERO Alessandro	82	CORONA Ednilson BRA			46	SHILLA Illiasu	DF	7
15	FW	IAQUINTA Vincenzo	64	4TH OFFICIAL			89	TACHIE-MENSAH Alex	FW	12
16	MF	CAMORANESI Mauro	56	AL GHAMDI Khalil KSA			68	PIMPONG Razak	FW	19

It was an entertaining game; we got a good result and played well. I'm happy for the squad, who haven't had things easy recently. We did our homework and Ghana played just as we expected. They're physically powerful, skilful and quick on the break, but we knew we could exploit some of their weaker points.

Marcello Lippi

Had the marking on Andrea Pirlo been tighter when he scored the first goal, the match could have gone very differently. The second goal was just a simple defensive error. I'm happy with the way my players performed, they played well. Congratulations to Italy, who did well today.

Ratomir Dujkovic

First Round Group E	FIFA World Cup Stadium, Gelsenkirchen	Monday, 12-06-2006
Kick-off: 18:00		Attendance: 52 000

USA   0   3   CZECH REPUBLIC

Jan Koller [5], Tomas Rosicky 2 [36] [76]

USA				MATCH STATS				CZECH REPUBLIC		
18	GK	KELLER Kasey						CECH Petr	GK	1
4	DF	MASTROENI Pablo	46	6	Shots	10		GRYGERA Zdenek	DF	2
6	DF	CHERUNDOLO Steve	46	1	Shots on Goal	5		(C) GALASEK Tomas	MF	4
7	DF	LEWIS Eddie		15	Fouls Committed	19		JANKULOVSKI Marek	DF	6
10	MF	REYNA Claudio (C)		2	Corner Kicks	5	82	POBORSKY Karel	MF	8
15	MF	CONVEY Bobby		0	Caught offside	9	45	KOLLER Jan	FW	9
17	MF	BEASLEY DaMarcus		55	Possession %	45	86	† ROSICKY Tomas	MF	10
20	FW	MC BRIDE Brian	77	(C)Captain †Man of the Match				NEDVED Pavel	MF	11
21	MF	DONOVAN Landon		MATCH OFFICIALS				PLASIL Jaroslav	MF	20
22	DF	ONYEWU Oguchi		REFEREE				UJFALUSI Tomas	DF	21
23	DF	POPE Eddie		AMARILLA Carlos PAR				ROZEHNAL David	DF	22
		Tr: ARENA Bruce		ASSISTANTS				Tr: BRUCKNER Karel		
		Substitutes		ANDINO Amelio PAR				Substitutes		
5	MF	O BRIEN John	46	BERNAL Manuel PAR			45	LOKVENC Vratislav	FW	12
9	FW	JOHNSON Eddie	46	4TH OFFICIAL			86	STAJNER Jiri	MF	17
16	FW	WOLFF Josh	77	CHANDIA Carlos CHI			82	POLAK Jan	MF	19

I'm very disappointed in the performance of a number of our players over 90 minutes. The better team won today. Give them credit. They punished us for every mistake we made. At 1-0 we had a chance. Claudio hits the post, they come back and get an absolutely great goal by Rosicky.

Bruce Arena

The injury to Jan Koller was the only negative thing from this match. He did a great job today. I'm very proud of all of my players. They were very disciplined, they were quite good in the defensive phase and especially in these, let's say, not very easy climatic conditions.

Karel Bruckner

First Round Group E	Fritz-Walter-Stadion, Kaiserslautern	Saturday, 17-06-2006
Kick-off: 21:00		Attendance: 46 000

ITALY   1   1   USA

Alberto Gilardino [22]   Cristian Zaccardo OG [27]

		ITALY	
1	GK	BUFFON Gianluigi	
2	DF	ZACCARDO Cristian	54
4	MF	DE ROSSI Daniele	28
5	DF	CANNAVARO Fabio (C)	
9	FW	TONI Luca	61
10	MF	TOTTI Francesco	35
11	FW	GILARDINO Alberto	
13	DF	NESTA Alessandro	
19	DF	ZAMBROTTA Gianluca	
20	MF	PERROTTA Simone	
21	MF	PIRLO Andrea	
		Tr: LIPPI Marcello	
		Substitutes	
7	FW	DEL PIERO Alessandro	54
8	MF	GATTUSO Gennaro	35
15	FW	IAQUINTA Vincenzo	61

MATCH STATS

10	Shots	8	
3	Shots on Goal	0	45
13	Fouls Committed	24	
7	Corner Kicks	3	62
11	Caught offside	1	
54	Possession %	46	52

(C)Captain † Man of the Match

MATCH OFFICIALS

REFEREE

LARRIONDA Jorge URU   47

ASSISTANTS

RIAL Walter URU

FANDINO Pablo   52

4TH OFFICIAL

AL GHAMDI Khalil KSA   62

	USA		
† KELLER Kasey	GK	18	
BOCANEGRA Carlos	DF	3	
MASTROENI Pablo	DF	4	
CHERUNDOLO Steve	DF	6	
DEMPSEY Clint	MF	8	
(C) REYNA Claudio	MF	10	
CONVEY Bobby	MF	15	
MC BRIDE Brian	FW	20	
DONOVAN Landon	MF	21	
ONYEWU Oguchi	DF	22	
POPE Eddie	DF	23	
Tr: ARENA Bruce			
Substitutes			
CONRAD Jimmy	DF	13	
BEASLEY DaMarcus	MF	17	

We made mistakes and didn't keep the ball. The equaliser that deflected off Zaccardo was bad luck but we weren't good enough to take advantage of the two sendings off. Am I angry with De Rossi? He made a serious mistake but that's something we will deal with in-house. We struggled tonight.

Marcelo Lippi

The team were fantastic tonight playing with nine men against ten. Keller was our hero tonight - he made some outstanding saves. Bobby Convey also had an excellent game. After tonight I know I've got a fantastic bunch of players. I don't want to talk about the red cards.

Bruce Arena

First Round Group E	FIFA World Cup Stadium, Cologne	Saturday, 17-06-2006
Kick-off: 18:00		Attendance: 45 000

CZECH REPUBLIC   0   2   GHANA

                                         Asamoah Gyan [2], Sulley Muntari [82]

		CZECH REPUBLIC	
1	GK	CECH Petr	
2	DF	GRYGERA Zdenek	
4	MF	GALASEK Tomas (C)	46
6	DF	JANKULOVSKI Marek	
8	MF	POBORSKY Karel	56
10	MF	ROSICKY Tomas	
11	MF	NEDVED Pavel	
12	FW	LOKVENC Vratislav	
20	MF	PLASIL Jaroslav	68
21	DF	UJFALUSI Tomas	65
22	DF	ROZEHNAL David	
		Tr: BRUCKNER Karel	
		Substitutes	
7	MF	SIONKO Libor	68
17	MF	STAJNER Jiri	56
19	MF	POLAK Jan	46

MATCH STATS

14	Shots	20	85
4	Shots on Goal	8	
16	Fouls Committed	22	
6	Corner Kicks	7	
4	Caught offside	10	
50	Possession %	50	

(C)Captain † Man of the Match

MATCH OFFICIALS

REFEREE

ELIZONDO Horacio ARG   46

ASSISTANTS

GARCIA Dario ARG

OTERO Rodolfo ARG   80

4TH OFFICIAL

DAMON Jerome RSA   85

	GHANA		
KINGSTON Richard	GK	22	
GYAN Asamoah	FW	3	
MENSAH John	DF	5	
SHILLA Illiasu	DF	7	
† ESSIEN Michael	MF	8	
(C) APPIAH Stephen	MF	10	
MUNTARI Sulley	MF	11	
MOHAMED Habib	DF	13	
AMOAH Matthew	FW	14	
PANTSIL John	DF	15	
ADDO Otto	MF	20	
Tr: DUJKOVIC Ratimir			
Substitutes			
BOATENG Derek	MF	9	
ADDO Eric	MF	18	
PIMPONG Razak	FW	19	

Congratulations to the Ghana team. We don't take injury and tiredness as excuses for our defeat because our opponents played splendid attacking football today. We made defensive errors and our rivals looked constantly dangerous with their excellent midfielders.

Karel Bruckner

We played good football today and it was Czech goalkeeper Petr Cech who saved his team from conceding more goals.

Ratomir Dujkovic

We felt no fear before the game. The win was very important for African football.

Michael Essien

First Round Group E	FIFA World Cup Stadium, Hamburg	Thursday, 22-06-2006
Kick-off: 16:00		Attendance: 50 000

CZECH REPUBLIC   0   2   ITALY

Marco Materazzi [26], Filippo Inzaghi [87]

		CZECH REPUBLIC			MATCH STATS				ITALY		
1	GK	CECH Petr		11	Shots	14		BUFFON Gianluigi	GK	1
2	DF	GRYGERA Zdenek		8	Shots on Goal	6		GROSSO Fabio	DF	3
5	MF	KOVAC Radoslav	78	18	Fouls Committed	17		(C) CANNAVARO Fabio	DF	5
6	DF	JANKULOVSKI Marek		4	Corner Kicks	5		GATTUSO Gennaro	MF	8
8	MF	POBORSKY Karel	46	1	Caught offside	1	60	TOTTI Francesco	MF	10
10	MF	ROSICKY Tomas		48	Possession %	52	17	GILARDINO Alberto	FW	11
11	MF	NEDVED Pavel (C)		(C)Captain † Man of the Match			74	NESTA Alessandro	DF	13
15	FW	BAROS Milan	64					CAMORANESI Mauro	MF	16
19	MF	POLAK Jan	47+	**MATCH OFFICIALS**				ZAMBROTTA Gianluca	DF	19
20	MF	PLASIL Jaroslav		**REFEREE**				PERROTTA Simone	MF	20
22	DF	ROZEHNAL David		ARCHUNDIA Benito MEX				PIRLO Andrea	MF	21
		Tr: BRUCKNER Karel		**ASSISTANTS**				Tr: LIPPI Marcello		
		Substitutes		RAMIREZ Jose MEX				Substitutes		
14	MF	JAROLIM David	64	VERGARA Hector CAN			74	BARONE Simone	MF	17
17	MF	STAJNER Jiri	46	**4TH OFFICIAL**			60	INZAGHI Filippo	FW	18
18	FW	HEINZ Marek	78	RUIZ Oscar COL			17	† MATERAZZI Marco	DF	23

I'm very sad and disappointed to be going home. The Italians were not that good. They didn't have too many chances.

Tomas Rosicky

Italy played a typical Italian game, very strong in defence and it was too difficult for us with ten players.

David Jarolim

I've been asked a lot whether the team has been distracted by things happening at home in Italy at the moment but that's not the case. The only pressure the players feel comes from the big match nerves. We have a solid close knit squad. They know this is a unique opportunity to achieve something.

Marcello Lippi

First Round Group E	Frankenstadion, Nuremberg	Thursday, 22-06-2006
Kick-off: 16:00		Attendance: 41 000

GHANA   2   1   USA

Haminu Draman [22], Stephen Appiah [47+p]   Clint Dempsey [43]

		GHANA			MATCH STATS				USA		
22	GK	KINGSTON Richard		9	Shots	7		KELLER Kasey	GK	18
5	DF	MENSAH John		4	Shots on Goal	3	61	BOCANEGRA Carlos	DF	3
7	DF	SHILLA Illiasu		32	Fouls Committed	16	74	CHERUNDOLO Steve	DF	6
8	MF	ESSIEN Michael		2	Corner Kicks	7		LEWIS Eddie	DF	7
9	MF	BOATENG Derek	46	8	Caught offside	6	40	DEMPSEY Clint	MF	8
10	MF	APPIAH Stephen (C) †		48	Possession %	52		(C) REYNA Claudio	MF	10
13	DF	MOHAMED Habib		(C)Captain † Man of the Match				CONRAD Jimmy	DF	13
14	FW	AMOAH Matthew	59	**MATCH OFFICIALS**				BEASLEY DaMarcus	MF	17
15	DF	PANTSIL John		**REFEREE**				MC BRIDE Brian	FW	20
19	FW	PIMPONG Razak		MERK Markus GER				DONOVAN Landon	MF	21
23	MF	DRAMANI Haminu	80	**ASSISTANTS**				ONYEWU Oguchi	DF	22
		Tr: DUJKOVIC Ratomir		SCHRAER Christian GER				Tr: ARENA Bruce		
		Substitutes		SALVER Jan-Hendrik GER				Substitutes		
12	FW	TACHIE-MENSAH Alex	80	**4TH OFFICIAL**			61	JOHNSON Eddie	FW	9
18	MF	ADDO Eric	59	KAMIKAWA Toru JPN			40	OLSEN Ben	MF	14
20	MF	ADDO Otto	46				74	CONVEY Bobby	MF	15

We didn't play as usual. They're a strong, great team and they were pushing forward trying to beat us. That's why we didn't play as before. This is a piece of history for this group of players, for myself, because for the first time we are in the last 16 of the World Cup. In Ghana I can imagine what's happening in the streets.

Ratomir Dujkovic

I feel sorry for our team. We played a very good game. We're certainly at fault in the second half for not doing better with our attacking play to get that second goal. But having said that, to be in a position to have to chase the game on the penalty call was disappointing.

??

First Round Group F	Fritz-Walter-Stadion, Kaiserslautern	Monday, 12-06-2006
Kick-off: 15:00		Attendance: 46 000

AUSTRALIA 3 1 JAPAN

Tim Cahill 2 [84] [89], John Aloisi [92+]   Shunsuke Nakamura [26]

		AUSTRALIA			MATCH STATS					JAPAN		
1	GK	SCHWARZER Mark							KAWAGUCHI Yoshikatsu	GK	23
2	DF	NEILL Lucas		20	Shots	6			KOMANO Yuichi	DF	3
3	DF	MOORE Craig	61	12	Shots on Goal	2		(C)	MIYAMOTO Tsuneyasu	DF	5
5	MF	CULINA Jason		22	Fouls Committed	11			NAKATA Hidetoshi	MF	7
7	MF	EMERTON Brett		5	Corner Kicks	3			TAKAHARA Naohiro	FW	9
9	FW	VIDUKA Mark (C)		5	Caught offside	3			NAKAMURA Shunsuke	MF	10
10	FW	KEWELL Harry		52	Possession %	48		79	YANAGISAWA Atsushi	FW	13
13	MF	GRELLA Vince		(C)Captain † Man of the Match					SANTOS Alessandro	DF	14
14	DF	CHIPPERFIELD Scott		MATCH OFFICIALS					FUKUNISHI Takashi	MF	15
20	MF	WILKSHIRE Luke	75	REFEREE				56	TSUBOI Keisuke	DF	19
23	MF	BRESCIANO Marco	53	ABD EL FATAH Essam EGY					NAKAZAWA Yuji	DF	22
		Tr: HIDDINK Guus		ASSISTANTS					Tr: Zico		
		Substitutes		DANTE Dramane MLI					Substitutes		
4	MF	CAHILL Tim †	53	NDOYE Mamadou SEN			56	91+	MONIWA Teruyuki	DF	2
15	FW	ALOISI John	75	4TH OFFICIAL			91+		OGURO Masashi	FW	16
19	FW	KENNEDY Joshua	61	POULAT Eric FRA			79		ONO Shinji	MF	18

It was a dramatic match. We always knew we had the ability but time was running out. I think mentally and physically Japan were very drained and we had a bit left. One thing the other team doesn't have is Aussie spirit.

Lucas Neill

I'm still in shock after what happened during this match. We played great, we led for so long and yet we ended up being beaten. It was very hot today, but that just meant that both teams had to work hard. I have to congratulate Tim Cahill. He was brilliant and turned the match on its head.

Yoshikatsu Kawaguchi

First Round Group F	Olympiastadion, Berlin	Tuesday, 13-06-2006
Kick-off: 21:00		Attendance: 72 000

BRAZIL 1 0 CROATIA

Kaka [44]

		BRAZIL			MATCH STATS					CROATIA		
1	GK	DIDA							PLETIKOSA Stipe	GK	1
2	DF	CAFU (C)		13	Shots	9			SRNA Darijo	MF	2
3	DF	LUCIO		6	Shots on Goal	3			SIMUNIC Josip	DF	3
4	DF	JUAN		20	Fouls Committed	20			KOVAC Robert	DF	4
5	MF	EMERSON		5	Corner Kicks	7			TUDOR Igor	DF	5
6	DF	ROBERTO CARLOS		3	Caught offside	4			SIMIC Dario	DF	7
7	FW	ADRIANO		50	Possession %	50			BABIC Marko	MF	8
8	MF	KAKA †		(C)Captain † Man of the Match					PRSO Dado	FW	9
9	FW	RONALDO	69	MATCH OFFICIALS					(C) KOVAC Niko	MF	10
10	MF	RONALDINHO		REFEREE			41		KLASNIC Ivan	FW	17
11	MF	ZE ROBERTO		ARCHUNDIA Benito MEX			56		KRANJCAR Niko	MF	19
		Tr: PARREIRA Carlos Alberto		ASSISTANTS					Tr: KRANJCAR Zlatko		
		Substitutes		RAMIREZ Jose MEX					Substitutes		
23	FW	ROBINHO	69	VERGARA Hector CAN			41		LEKO Jerko	MF	16
				4TH OFFICIAL			56		OLIC Ivica	FW	18
				GUEZZAZ Mohamed MAR							

The challenge is not the first game. In addition to the fact that the team hasn't played much together, we faced an adversary that was very good and marking very well, with energy. I think the game was balanced - we had more shots on goal but we had a certain difficulty imposing our own rhythm.

Carlos Alberto Parreira

Brazil made a goal from just one chance. This defeat won't stop us from going further but they do have fantastic players in their side with the likes of Kaka.

Zlatko Kranjcar

First Round Group F	FIFA World Cup Stadium, Munich	Sunday, 18-06-2006
Kick-off: 18:00		Attendance: 66 000

BRAZIL   2   0   AUSTRALIA

Adriano [49], Fred [90]

		BRAZIL			MATCH STATS					AUSTRALIA		
1	GK	DIDA								SCHWARZER Mark	GK	1
2	DF	CAFU (C)		16	Shots	14			NEILL Lucas	DF	2
3	DF	LUCIO		6	Shots on Goal	4	69		MOORE Craig	DF	3
4	DF	JUAN		9	Fouls Committed	25	56		CAHILL Tim	MF	4
5	MF	EMERSON	72	7	Corner Kicks	4			CULINA Jason	MF	5
6	DF	ROBERTO CARLOS		5	Caught offside	1	41		POPOVIC Tony	DF	6
7	FW	ADRIANO	88	54	Possession %	46			EMERTON Brett	MF	7
8	MF	KAKA			(C)Captain † Man of the Match				(C) VIDUKA Mark	FW	9
9	FW	RONALDO	72		MATCH OFFICIALS				GRELLA Vince	MF	13
10	MF	RONALDINHO			REFEREE				CHIPPERFIELD Scott	DF	14
11	MF	ZE ROBERTO †			MERK Markus GER				STERJOVSKI Mile	MF	21
		Tr: PARREIRA Carlos Alberto			ASSISTANTS				Tr: HIDDINK Guus		
		Substitutes			SCHRAER Christian GER				Substitutes		
17	MF	GILBERTO SILVA	72		SALVER Jan-Hendrik GER		56		KEWELL Harry	FW	10
21	FW	FRED	88		4TH OFFICIAL		69		ALOISI John	FW	15
23	FW	ROBINHO	72		RODRIGUEZ Marco MEX		41		BRESCIANO Marco	MF	23

The Australians marked us very tightly in the first half but after the break the heat took its toll and we were able to find enough space to score our goals. We had to play a patient game. The team is evolving and we are growing together in every way. Brazil's quality is there for all to see.

Kaka

We created some chances but didn't quite have the luck we needed. We really pushed forwards towards the end but we couldn't quite turn pressure into goals.

Scott Chipperfield

We're really frustrated and disappointed but we played very well.

Lucas Neill

First Round Group F	Frankenstadion, Nuremberg	Sunday, 18-06-2006
Kick-off: 15:00		Attendance: 41 000

JAPAN   0   0   CROATIA

		JAPAN			MATCH STATS					CROATIA		
23	GK	KAWAGUCHI Yoshikatsu								PLETIKOSA Stipe	GK	1
5	DF	MIYAMOTO Tsuneyasu (C)		12	Shots	16	87		SRNA Darijo	MF	2
7	MF	NAKATA Hidetoshi †		5	Shots on Goal	6			SIMUNIC Josip	DF	3
8	MF	OGASAWARA Mitsuo		19	Fouls Committed	18			KOVAC Robert	DF	4
9	FW	TAKAHARA Naohiro	85	5	Corner Kicks	11	70		TUDOR Igor	DF	5
10	MF	NAKAMURA Shunsuke		1	Caught offside	6			SIMIC Dario	DF	7
13	FW	YANAGISAWA Atsushi	61	56	Possession %	44			BABIC Marko	MF	8
14	DF	SANTOS Alessandro			(C)Captain † Man of the Match				PRSO Dado	FW	9
15	MF	FUKUNISHI Takashi	46		MATCH OFFICIALS				(C) KOVAC Niko	MF	10
21	DF	KAJI Akira			REFEREE				KLASNIC Ivan	FW	17
22	DF	NAKAZAWA Yuji			DE BLEECKERE Frank BEL		78		KRANJCAR Niko	MF	19
		Tr: ZICO			ASSISTANTS				Tr: KRANJCAR Zlatko		
		Substitutes			HERMANS Peter BEL				Substitutes		
16	FW	OGURO Masashi	85		VROMANS Walter BEL		78		MODRIC Luka	MF	14
17	MF	INAMOTO Junichi	46		4TH OFFICIAL		70		OLIC Ivica	FW	18
20	FW	TAMADA Keiji	61		STOTT Kevin USA		87		BOSNJAK Ivan	FW	22

It was very difficult to play at this time because of the heat and we have done this twice in succession. The players have suffered but they did so well. We didn't create a lot of opportunities and when we did we felt too much pressure. It was a very equal game. We didn't lose so we are still in the competition.

Zico

We dominated, created a lot of chances, but unfortunately we were out of luck. I thought it was the correct decision to award the penalty and I thought it was a truly wonderful save from Japan's goalkeeper. If you look at the game as a whole, we were better organised and we created the better chances.

Zlatko Kranjcar

First Round Group F	Westfalenstadion, Dortmund	Thursday, 22-06-2006
Kick-off: 21:00		Attendance: 65 000

JAPAN   1   4   BRAZIL

Keiji Tamada [34]   Ronaldo 2 [46+] [81], Juninho Pernambuco [53], Gilberto [59]

		JAPAN			MATCH STATS				BRAZIL		
23	GK	KAWAGUCHI Yoshikatsu					82	(C) DIDA	GK	1
7	MF	NAKATA Hidetoshi		9	Shots	21		LUCIO	DF	3
8	MF	OGASAWARA Mitsuo	56	3	Shots on Goal	14		JUAN	DF	4
10	MF	NAKAMURA Shunsuke		9	Fouls Committed	6	71	KAKA	MF	8
11	FW	MAKI Seiichiro	60	3	Corner Kicks	11		† RONALDO	FW	9
14	DF	SANTOS Alessandro		4	Caught offside	0	71	RONALDINHO	MF	10
17	MF	INAMOTO Junichi		40	Possession %	60		CICINHO	DF	13
19	DF	TSUBOI Keisuke		(C)Captain † Man of the Match				GILBERTO	DF	16
20	FW	TAMADA Keiji		MATCH OFFICIALS				GILBERTO SILVA	MF	17
21	DF	KAJI Akira		REFEREE				JUNINHO PERNAMBUCANO	MF	19
22	DF	NAKAZAWA Yuji (C)		POULAT Eric FRA				ROBINHO	FW	23
		Tr: ZICO		ASSISTANTS				Tr: PARREIRA Carlos Alberto		
		Substitutes		DAGORNE Lionel FRA				Substitutes		
6	DF	NAKATA Koji	56	TEXIER Vincent FRA			82	ROGERIO CENI	GK	12
9	FW	TAKAHARA Naohiro	66 60	4TH OFFICIAL			71	ZE ROBERTO	MF	11
16	FW	OGURO Masashi	66	DAMON Jerome RSA			71	RICARDINHO	MF	20

If we had not conceded just before half-time it would have been different. Instead they came out full of confidence. Our passing wasn't the best perhaps because we were too anxious. Japan has had only ten years of professional football and there is some way to go before we can be equal to the great powers.

Zico

We've been out of Brazil for 35-40 days and things may have got monotonous but now we have found our spark. All the new players did well - we have no doubts about them. Today we played more like Brazilians as we kept the ball for longer periods. Ronaldo is back. We believe he is special!

Carlos Alberto Parreira

First Round Group F	Gottlieb-Daimler-Stadion, Stuttgart	Thursday, 22-06-2006
Kick-off: 21:00		Attendance: 52 000

CROATIA   2   2   AUSTRALIA

Darijo Srna [2], Niko Kovac [56]   Craig Moore [38p], Harry Kewell [79]

		CROATIA			MATCH STATS				AUSTRALIA		
1	GK	PLETIKOSA Stipe						KALAC Zeljko	GK	18
2	MF	SRNA Darijo		8	Shots	12		NEILL Lucas	DF	2
3	DF	SIMUNIC Josip	93+	3	Shots on Goal	7		MOORE Craig	DF	3
5	DF	TUDOR Igor		21	Fouls Committed	25		CAHILL Tim	MF	4
7	DF	SIMIC Dario	85	4	Corner Kicks	9		CULINA Jason	MF	5
8	MF	BABIC Marko		2	Caught offside	1	87	EMERTON Brett	MF	7
9	FW	PRSO Dado		44	Possession %	56		(C) VIDUKA Mark	FW	9
10	MF	KOVAC Niko (C)		(C)Captain † Man of the Match				† KEWELL Harry	FW	10
13	DF	TOMAS Stjepan	83	MATCH OFFICIALS			63	GRELLA Vince	MF	13
18	FW	OLIC Ivica	74	REFEREE			75	CHIPPERFIELD Scott	DF	14
19	MF	KRANJCAR Niko	65	POLL Graham ENG			71	STERJOVSKI Mile	MF	21
		Tr: KRANJCAR Zlatko		ASSISTANTS				Tr: HIDDINK Guus		
		Substitutes		SHARP Philip ENG				Substitutes		
14	MF	MODRIC Luka	74	TURNER Glenn ENG			63	ALOISI John	FW	15
16	MF	LEKO Jerko	65	4TH OFFICIAL			75	KENNEDY Joshua	FW	19
17	FW	KLASNIC Ivan	83	STOTT Kevin USA			71	BRESCIANO Marco	MF	23

We couldn't consolidate our early lead. We sat back too deep and invited the Australians onto us. It was a very intense and physical game. Igor Tudor had the goal at his mercy just before the end but the ball just wouldn't go in. I'm very disappointed. The team gave everything but it was a disasterous result for us.

Zlatko Kranjcar

The match was an emotional rollercoaster ride. We came back from behind twice and it was a fantastic match for the fans. We showed character after their early goal and kept going forward. My team showed they have hearts like lions. The ace up our sleeve today was Harry Kewell. He made the difference.

Guus Hiddink

First Round Group G	Gottlieb-Daimler-Stadion, Stuttgart	Tuesday, 13-06-2006
Kick-off: 18:00	Temperature:	Attendance: 52 000

FRANCE   0 0   SWITZERLAND

FRANCE				MATCH STATS		SWITZERLAND		
16	GK	BARTHEZ Fabien				ZUBERBUEHLER Pascal	GK	1
3	DF	ABIDAL Eric		9 Shots 7		MAGNIN Ludovic	DF	3
4	MF	VIEIRA Patrick		3 Shots on Goal 4		SENDEROS Philippe	DF	4
5	DF	GALLAS William		18 Fouls Committed 18		(C) VOGEL Johann	MF	6
6	MF	MAKELELE Claude †		4 Corner Kicks 1		CABANAS Ricardo	MF	7
10	MF	ZIDANE Zinedine (C)		5 Caught offside 0	82	WICKY Raphael	MF	8
11	FW	WILTORD Sylvain	84	51 Possession % 49		FREI Alexander	FW	9
12	FW	HENRY Thierry		(C)Captain † Man of the Match	56	STRELLER Marco	FW	11
15	DF	THURAM Lilian		MATCH OFFICIALS		BARNETTA Tranquillo	MF	16
19	DF	SAGNOL Willy		REFEREE	75	MUELLER Patrick	DF	20
22	MF	RIBERY Frank	70	IVANOV Valentin RUS		DEGEN Philipp	DF	23
		Tr: DOMENECH Raymond		ASSISTANTS		Tr: KUHN Koebi		
		Substitutes		GOLUBEV Nikolay RUS		Substitutes		
8	MF	DHORASOO Vikash	84	VOLNIN Evgueni RUS	75	DJOUROU Johan	DF	2
14	FW	SAHA Louis	70	4TH OFFICIAL	82	MARGAIRAZ Xavier	MF	5
				STOTT Kevin USA	56	GYGAX Daniel	FW	10

It's become a habit with the Swiss. That's the tihrd time we've played them without scoring, which proves how well they defend. But we didn't concede either which proves we can defend well too. I felt my players were a little too impatient. We saw a lot less of the ball in the second half.

Raymond Domenech

We have to be pleased with that. France dominated, especially in the first 45 minutes and we were far too nervous, losing too many balls. In those circumstances it was hard to expect any more from the game. I'm very content with the overall performance of my team.

Koebi Kuhn

First Round Group G	Waldstadion, Frankfurt	Tuesday, 13-06-2006
Kick-off: 15:00	Temperature:	Attendance: 48 000

KOREA REPUBLIC   2 1   TOGO

Lee Chun Soo [54], Ahn Jung Hwan [72]

Mohamed Kader [31]

KOREA REPUBLIC				MATCH STATS		TOGO		
1	GK	LEE Woon Jae (C)				AGASSA Kossi	GK	16
2	DF	KIM Young Chul		16 Shots 9		NIBOMBE Dare	DF	2
4	DF	CHOI Jin Cheul		6 Shots on Goal 3	53	(C) ABALO Jean-Paul	DF	3
6	DF	KIM Jin Kyu	46	16 Fouls Committed 17		ADEBAYOR Emmanuel	FW	4
7	MF	PARK Ji Sung		3 Corner Kicks 4		TCHANGAI Massamasso	DF	5
12	DF	LEE Young Pyo		2 Caught offside 4	86	SALIFOU Moustapha	FW	7
13	MF	LEE Eul Yong	68	64 Possession % 36		MAMAM Cherif Toure	MF	10
14	FW	LEE Chun Soo		(C)Captain † Man of the Match		ROMAO Alaixys	MF	15
17	MF	LEE Ho		MATCH OFFICIALS		MOHAMED KADER	FW	17
19	FW	CHO Jae Jin	83	REFEREE	55	SENAYA Yao Junior	FW	18
22	DF	SONG Chong Gug		POLL Graham ENG	62	ASSEMOASSA Ludovic	DF	19
		Tr: ADVOCAAT Dick		ASSISTANTS		Tr: PFISTER Otto		
		Substitutes		SHARP Phillip ENG		Substitutes		
5	MF	KIM Nam Il	68	TURNER Glenn ENG	86	AZIAWONOU Yao	MF	6
9	FW	AHN Jung Hwan †	46	4TH OFFICIAL	62	FORSON Richmond	FW	13
18	DF	KIM Sang Sik	83	DAMON Jerome RSA	55	TOURE Assimiou	DF	23

Even though we were behind we didn't panic and had enough belief in ourselves to keep playing to our strengths. When Ahn Jung Hwan came on as a substitute we all expected a lot from him. He has a lot of experience and that can tip the scales in a match and we saw that with his excellent goal.

Park Ji Sung

The first half was good but the second half was very tough, especially after our captain had been sent off. The substitution we had to make due to injury also had a negative effect on our team. We're a bit lacking in experience for an event like this. The debate about the manager's job didn't affect us though.

Kossi Agassa

First Round Group G — Zentralstadion, Leipzig — Sunday, 18-06-2006

Kick-off: 21:00 — Attendance: 43 000

FRANCE 1 1 KOREA REPUBLIC

Thierry Henry [9]

Park Ji Sung [81]

FRANCE				MATCH STATS			KOREA REPUBLIC			
16	GK	BARTHEZ Fabien		15	Shots	5	(C) LEE Woon Jae	GK	1	
3	DF	ABIDAL Eric		4	Shots on Goal	2	KIM Young Chul	DF	2	
4	MF	VIEIRA Patrick		20	Fouls Committed	10	KIM Dong Jin	DF	3	
5	DF	GALLAS William		6	Corner Kicks	2	CHOI Jin Cheul	DF	4	
6	MF	MAKELELE Claude		4	Caught offside	1	KIM Nam Il	MF	5	
7	MF	MALOUDA Florent	88	52	Possession %	48	† PARK Ji Sung	MF	7	
10	MF	ZIDANE Zinedine (C)	91+	(C)Captain † Man of the Match			LEE Young Pyo	DF	12	
11	FW	WILTORD Sylvain	60	MATCH OFFICIALS		46	LEE Eul Yong	MF	13	
12	FW	HENRY Thierry		REFEREE		72	LEE Chun Soo	FW	14	
15	DF	THURAM Lilian		ARCHUNDIA Benito MEX		69	LEE Ho	MF	17	
19	DF	SAGNOL Willy		ASSISTANTS			CHO Jae Jin	FW	19	
Tr: DOMENECH Raymond				RAMIREZ Jose MEX			Tr: ADVOCAAT Dick			
Substitutes				VERGARA Hector CAN		72	Substitutes			
8	MF	DHORASOO Vikash	88	4TH OFFICIAL		46	AHN Jung Hwan	FW	9	
20	FW	TREZEGUET David	91+	ABD EL Fatah EGY		69	SEOL Ki Hyeon	FW	11	
22	MF	RIBERY Frank	60				KIM Sang Sik	DF	18	

I'm disappointed with the result because we played some high-quality football and gave it our all. We decided to be adventurous right from the word go but it was a very physical game and that takes its toll. The team struggled in the second half but we weren't in any danger until the move leading up to the goal.

Raymond Domenech

It was a miraculous performance to come back from a goal down to get a draw against France. I decided to change the tactics by putting on an extra wide man in the second half and it worked a treat. We were lucky to only concede one goal in the first half and that helped us get back in the game.

Dick Advocaat

First Round Group G — Westfalenstadion, Dortmund — Monday, 19-06-2006

Kick-off: 15:00 — Attendance: 65 000

TOGO 0 2 SWITZERLAND

Alexander Frei [16], Tranquillo Barnetta [88]

TOGO				MATCH STATS			SWITZERLAND			
16	GK	AGASSA Kossi		10	Shots	15	ZUBERBUEHLER Pascal	GK	1	
2	DF	NIBOMBE Dare		7	Shots on Goal	9	MAGNIN Ludovic	DF	3	
4	FW	ADEBAYOR Emmanuel		18	Fouls Committed	14	SENDEROS Philippe	DF	4	
5	DF	TCHANGAI Massamasso (C)		4	Corner Kicks	8	(C) VOGEL Johann	MF	6	
8	MF	AGBOH Kuami	25	6	Caught offside	5	CABANAS Ricardo	MF	7	
9	MF	DOSSEVI Thomas	69	50	Possession %	50	WICKY Raphael	MF	8	
10	MF	MAMAM Cherif Toure	87	(C)Captain † Man of the Match		77	† FREI Alexander	FW	9	
13	FW	FORSON Richmond		MATCH OFFICIALS		87	GYGAX Daniel	FW	10	
15	MF	ROMAO Alaixys		REFEREE		46	BARNETTA Tranquillo	MF	16	
17	FW	MOHAMED KADER		AMARILLA Carlos PAR			MUELLER Patrick	DF	20	
23	DF	TOURE Assimiou		ASSISTANTS			DEGEN Philipp	DF	23	
Tr: PFISTER Otto				ANDINO Amelio PAR			Tr: KUHN Koebi			
Substitutes				BERNAL Manuel PAR		77	Substitutes			
7	FW	SALIFOU Moustapha	25	4TH OFFICIAL		87	STRELLER Marco	FW	11	
11	FW	MALM Robert	87	GUEZZAZ Mohamed MAR		46	LUSTRINELLI Mauro	FW	18	
18	FW	SENAYA Yao Junior	69				YAKIN Hakan	FW	22	

If you are faced with disputes for weeks like the ones we've had then that's bound to affect you deep down. When you take the circumstances into account, I think we played really well. Switzerland played with one up front. We tried to exploit that by packing the midfield but we couldn't put our chances away.

Otto Pfister

Now all of Germany knows what a passionate race the Swiss are. What the fans did was simply fantastic. We didn't play tremendously well in the first half and gave the ball away too much. But we didn't lose faith in ourselves. Our objective was to win by more than one goal and we succeeded in doing that.

Marco Streller

First Round Group G	FIFA World Cup Stadium, Cologne	Friday, 23-06-2006
Kick-off: 21:00		Attendance: 45 000

TOGO   0 2   FRANCE

Patrick Vieira [55], Thierry Henry [61]

		TOGO			MATCH STATS				FRANCE		
16	GK	AGASSA Kossi							BARTHEZ Fabien	GK	16
2	DF	NIBOMBE Dare		8	Shots	17	81	† (C) VIEIRA Patrick	MF	4
3	DF	ABALO Jean-Paul (C)		2	Shots on Goal	9		GALLAS William	DF	5
4	FW	ADEBAYOR Emmanuel	75	22	Fouls Committed	12		MAKELELE Claude	MF	6
5	DF	TCHANGAI Massamasso		1	Corner Kicks	9	74	MALOUDA Florent	MF	7
6	MF	AZIAWONOU Yao		3	Caught offside	5		HENRY Thierry	FW	12
7	FW	SALIFOU Moustapha		44	Possession %	56		SILVESTRE Mikael	DF	13
10	MF	MAMAM Cherif Toure	59	(C)Captain †Man of the Match				THURAM Lilian	DF	15
13	FW	FORSON Richmond		MATCH OFFICIALS				SAGNOL Willy	DF	19
17	FW	MOHAMED KADER		REFEREE				TREZEGUET David	FW	20
18	FW	SENAYA Yao Junior		LARRIONDA Jorge URU			77	RIBERY Frank	MF	22
		Tr: Pfister Otto		ASSISTANTS				Tr: DOMENECH Raymond		
		Substitutes		RIAL Walter URU				Substitutes		
9	MF	DOSSEVI Thomas	75	FANDINO Pablo URU			77	GOVOU Sidney	FW	9
14	FW	OLUFADE Adekanmi	59	4TH OFFICIAL			74	WILTORD Sylvain	FW	11
				CHANDIA Carlos CHI			81	DIARRA Alou	MF	18

You have to remember that we were playing against the former world champions. There are players with a lot of class in that side. It was the immense talent of those players that made the difference. We defended our goal well and even created two great chances but it got tougher as time went on.

Otto Pfister

At half-time, we told ourselves one thing - push forward, keep pushing and push even more. I'm happy for the players. They never gave up and fought hard in adversity. We had to get past this obstacle and now we've done that we can afford to breathe a little. They made it hard for us as they did for the Swiss and Koreans.

Raymond Domenech

First Round Group G	FIFA World Cup Stadium, Hanover	Friday, 23-06-2006
Kick-off: 21:00		Attendance: 43 000

SWITZERLAND   2 0   KOREA REPUBLIC

Philippe Senderos [23], Alexander Frei [77]

		SWITZERLAND			MATCH STATS				KOREA REPUBLIC		
1	GK	ZUBERBUEHLER Pascal							(C) LEE Woon Jae	GK	1
4	DF	SENDEROS Philippe	53	12	Shots	15		KIM Dong Jin	DF	3
6	MF	VOGEL Johann (C)		6	Shots on Goal	8		CHOI Jin Cheul	DF	4
7	MF	CABANAS Ricardo		8	Fouls Committed	20		KIM Nam Il	MF	5
8	MF	WICKY Raphael	88	8	Corner Kicks	6		KIM Jin Kyu	DF	6
9	FW	FREI Alexander †		3	Caught offside	3		PARK Ji Sung	MF	7
16	MF	BARNETTA Tranquillo		46	Possession %	54	66	PARK Chu Young	FW	10
17	DF	SPYCHER Christoph		(C)Captain †Man of the Match			63	LEE Young Pyo	DF	12
20	DF	MUELLER Patrick		MATCH OFFICIALS				LEE Chun Soo	FW	14
22	FW	YAKIN Hakan	71	REFEREE				LEE Ho	MF	17
23	DF	DEGEN Philipp		ELIZONDO Horacio ARG				CHO Jae Jin	FW	19
		Tr: KUHN Koebi		ASSISTANTS				Tr: ADVOCAAT Dick		
		Substitutes		GARCIA Dario ARG				Substitutes		
2	DF	DJOUROU Johan	53	OTERO Rodolfo ARG			63	AHN Jung Hwan	FW	9
5	MF	MARGAIRAZ Xavier	71	4TH OFFICIAL			66	SEOL Ki Hyeon	FW	11
19	MF	BEHRAMI Valon	88	ABD EL FATAH Essam EGY						

It was a very intense match tonight against a team that had already proven themselves. I think we were a bit lucky in the end but I also think it was a deserved result. I would really like to congratulate my defence for not conceding a goal in the first round. We have reached our first objective.

Koebi Kuhn

We were too polite early in the game. They controlled the game in the first period but in the second half we pressurised them and we deserved more than the nothing we got. The Korean team did very well pointwise. Four points is a big haul and we have nothing to be ashamed of.

Dick Advocaat

First Round Group H	Zentralstadion, Leipzig	Wednesday, 14-06-2006
Kick-off: 15:00	Temperature:	Attendance: 43 000

SPAIN 4 0 UKRAINE

Xabi Alonso [13], David Villa 2 [17 48p], Fernando Torres [81]

SPAIN				MATCH STATS			UKRAINE		
1	GK	CASILLAS Iker (C)					SHOVKOVSKIY Oleksandr	GK	1
3	DF	PERNIA Mariano		19	Shots	5	NESMACHNIY Andriy	DF	2
5	DF	PUYOL Carlos		10	Shots on Goal	2	TYMOSCHUK Anatoliy	MF	4
8	MF	XAVI †		11	Fouls Committed	14	YEZERSKIY Vladimir	DF	5
9	FW	TORRES Fernando		7	Corner Kicks	1	RUSOL Andriy	DF	6
11	FW	GARCIA Luis	77	0	Caught offside	8	(C) SHEVCHENKO Andriy	FW	7
14	MF	XABI ALONSO	55	54	Possession %	46	46	GUSEV Oleg	MF	9
15	DF	RAMOS Sergio		(C)Captain †Man of the Match			VORONIN Andriy	FW	10
16	MF	MARCOS SENNA		MATCH OFFICIALS		46	GUSIN Andriy	MF	14
21	FW	VILLA David	55	REFEREE		47	VASHCHUK Vladislav	DF	17
22	DF	PABLO		BUSACCA Massimo SUI		64	ROTAN Ruslan	MF	21
Tr: ARAGONES Luis				ASSISTANTS			Tr: BLOKHIN Oleg		
Substitutes				BURAGINA Francesco SUI			Substitutes		
6	MF	ALBELDA David	55	ARNET Matthias SUI		46	SHELAYEV Oleg	MF	8
7	FW	RAUL	55	4TH OFFICIAL		64	REBROV Serhiy	MF	11
18	MF	FABREGAS Cesc	77	ROSETTI Roberto ITA		46	VOROBEY Andriy	FW	16

There is a tremendous amount of quality in our midfield and we are very strong physically. The fact is we dominated as soon as we got possession and their heads went down when we scored the second. I didn't expect such a convincing result and I honestly thought they would make it tougher for us.

Luis Aragones

I'm extremely disappointed. We weren't disciplined at all and the players failed to follow the instructions the coaching team gave them. I'm not so disappointed about the result as the attitude of the players. It's embarrasing for all of us. Sadly, we've been the worst European team in the competition so far.

Oleg Blokhin

First Round Group H	FIFA World Cup Stadium, Munich	Wednesday, 14-06-2006
Kick-off: 18:00	Temperature:	Attendance: 66 000

TUNISIA 2 2 SAUDI ARABIA

Zied Jaziri [23], Radhi Jaidi [92+] Yasser Al Kahtani [57], Sami Al Jaber [84]

TUNISIA				MATCH STATS			SAUDI ARABIA		
1	GK	BOUMNIJEL Ali					ZAID Mabrouk	GK	21
3	DF	HAGGUI Karim		6	Shots	13	DOKHI Ahmed	DF	2
5	FW	JAZIRI Zied †		2	Shots on Goal	5	TUKAR Redha	DF	3
6	DF	TRABELSI Hatem		17	Fouls Committed	12	AL MONTASHARI Hamad	DF	4
9	FW	CHIKHAOUI Yassine	82	3	Corner Kicks	4	AL GHAMDI Omar	MF	6
12	MF	MNARI Jaouhar		1	Caught offside	1	75	NOOR Mohammed	MF	8
13	MF	BOUAZIZI Riadh (C)	55	49	Possession %	51	(C) SULIMANI Hussein	DF	13
14	MF	CHEDLI Adel	69	(C)Captain †Man of the Match			KHARIRI Saud	MF	14
15	DF	JAIDI Radhi		MATCH OFFICIALS			AZIZ Khaled	MF	16
18	DF	JEMMALI David		REFEREE		67	AL TEMYAT Nawaf	MF	18
20	MF	NAMOUCHI Hamed		SHIELD Mark AUS		82	AL KAHTANI Yaser	FW	20
Tr: LEMERRE Roger				ASSISTANTS			Tr: PAQUETA Marcos		
Substitutes				GIBSON Nathan AUS			Substitutes		
2	FW	ESSEDIRI Karim	82	WILSON Ben AUS		75	AMEEN Mohammed	MF	7
8	MF	NAFTI Mehdi	55	4TH OFFICIAL		82	AL JABER Sami	FW	9
10	MF	GHODHBANE Kaies	69	CHANDIA Carlos CHI		67	AL HAWSAWI Malek	FW	23

It was a point gained for me. We controlled the game well despite being a little nervous. The goal gave us a bit more confidence, but it wasn't enough. Then we started to concentrate too much on holding onto the lead. But I'm still happy that my players found the strength to go in search of the equaliser at the end.

Roger Lemerre

In the first half we were very nervous and made lots of mistakes. At half-time, I told my players to express themselves a bit more and to attack down the wings. They realised what they had to do and rectified the situation in the second half. Our defence played well in my opinion, even though we conceded two goals.

Marcos Paqueta

First Round Group H	Gottlieb-Daimler-Stadion, Stuttgart	Monday, 19-06-2006
Kick-off: 21:00		Attendance: 52 000

SPAIN 3 1 TUNISIA

Raul [71], Fernando Torres 2 [76] [91+p]   Jaouhar Mnari [8]

SPAIN				MATCH STATS			TUNISIA		
1	GK	CASILLAS Iker (C)					BOUMNIJEL Ali	GK	1
3	DF	PERNIA Mariano		24	Shots	4	HAGGUI Karim	DF	3
5	DF	PUYOL Carlos		10	Shots on Goal	3	JAZIRI Zied	FW	5
8	MF	XAVI		9	Fouls Committed	24	TRABELSI Hatem	DF	6
9	FW	TORRES Fernando		12	Corner Kicks	1	NAFTI Mehdi	MF	8
11	FW	GARCIA Luis		1	Caught offside	6	MNARI Jaouhar	MF	12
14	MF	XABI ALONSO †		66	Possession %	34	(C) BOUAZIZI Riadh	MF	13	57
15	DF	RAMOS Sergio	46	(C)Captain †Man of the Match			CHEDLI Adel	MF	14	80
16	MF	MARCOS SENNA	46	MATCH OFFICIALS			JAIDI Radhi	DF	15
21	FW	VILLA David	57	REFEREE			AYARI Anis	DF	19	57
22	DF	PABLO		SIMON Carlos BRA			NAMOUCHI Hamed	MF	20
		Tr: ARAGONES Luis		ASSISTANTS			Tr: LEMERRE Roger		
		Substitutes		TAVARES Aristeu BRA			Substitutes		
7	FW	RAUL	46	CORONA Ednilson		57	YAHIA Alaeddine	DF	4
17	MF	JOAQUIN	57	4TH OFFICIAL		80	GUEMAMDIA Haykel	FW	7
18	MF	FABREGAS Cesc	46	CHANDIA Carlos CHI		57	GHODHBANE Kaies	MF	10

This win was very hard to come by. The Tunisians caused us problems with their counter-attacking style. In the second half we played our quick technical game and created danger. Raul is fast and has great technique. Bringing him and Cesc Fabregas on worked out very well.

Luis Aragones

We have to accept it but it's a disappointment because we were within sight of victory. The team didn't fall apart in the second half and Spain only put two significant moves together but the circumstances of the match meant that the result switched around very quickly.

Roger Lemerre

First Round Group H	FIFA World Cup Stadium, Hamburg	Monday, 19-06-2006
Kick-off: 18:00		Attendance: 50 000

SAUDI ARABIA 0 4 UKRAINE

Andriy Rusol [4], Serhiy Rebrov [36], Andriy Shevchenko [46]
Maksym Kalinichenko [84]

SAUDI ARABIA				MATCH STATS			UKRAINE		
21	GK	ZAID Mabrouk					SHOVKOVSKIY Oleksandr	GK	1
2	DF	DOKHI Ahmed	55	6	Shots	19	NESMACHNIY Andriy	DF	2
3	DF	TUKAR Redha		0	Shots on Goal	9	TYMOSCHUK Anatoliy	MF	4
4	DF	AL MONTASHARI Hamad		24	Fouls Committed	25	RUSOL Andriy	DF	6
6	MF	AL GHAMDI Omar		2	Corner Kicks	6	(C) SHEVCHENKO Andriy	FW	7	86
7	MF	AMEEN Mohammed	55	0	Caught offside	0	SHELAYEV Oleg	MF	8
8	MF	NOOR Mohammed	77	50	Possession %	50	GUSEV Oleg	MF	9
13	DF	SULIMANI Hussein (C)		(C)Captain †Man of the Match			VORONIN Andriy	FW	10	79
14	MF	KHARIRI Saud		MATCH OFFICIALS			REBROV Serhiy	MF	11	71
16	MF	AZIZ Khaled		REFEREE			† KALINICHENKO Maksim	MF	19
20	FW	AL KAHTANI Yaser		POLL Graham ENG			SVIDERSKIY Vyacheslav	DF	22
		Tr: PAQUETA Marcos		ASSISTANTS			Tr: BLOKHIN Oleg		
		Substitutes		SHARP Philip ENG			Substitutes		
9	FW	AL JABER Sami	77	TURNER Glenn ENG		79	GUSIN Andriy	MF	14
12	DF	KHATHRAN Abdulaziz	55	4TH OFFICIAL		86	MILEVSKIY Artem	FW	15
23	FW	AL HAWSAWI Malek	55	KAMIKAWA Toru JPN		71	ROTAN Ruslan	MF	21

We suffered what Ukraine suffered against Spain in the first game -two goals in the first half and one right at the beginning of the second half that created havoc with the team. It was wet, the ball was greasy on the turf and we struggled with that. We don't have a lot of rain in Saudi Arabia.

Marcos Paqueta

Our plan was to prevent them getting the ball in the midfield and for the most part we succeeded in doing that and were able to counter-attack really quickly. In their game against Tunisia we saw they had problems with dead-ball situations. We were able to take advantage because of Kalinichenko's great delivery.

Oleg Blokhin

First Round Group H	Fritz-Walter-Stadion, Kaiserslautern	Friday, 23-06-2006
Kick-off: 16:00		Attendance: 46 000

SAUDI ARABIA 0 1 SPAIN

Juanito [36]

SAUDI ARABIA				MATCH STATS			SPAIN			
21	GK	ZAID Mabrouk					CANIZARES Santiago	GK	19
2	DF	DOKHI Ahmed		7	Shots	19	SALGADO Michel	DF	2
3	DF	TUKAR Redha		4	Shots on Goal	13	MARCHENA Carlos	DF	4
4	DF	AL MONTASHARI Hamad		22	Fouls Committed	22	ALBELDA David	MF	6
8	MF	NOOR Mohammed		4	Corner Kicks	10	46	(C) RAUL	FW	7
9	FW	AL JABER Sami (C)	68	5	Caught offside	0	70	REYES Jose Antonio	MF	10
11	FW	AL HARTHI Saad		41	Possession %	59	LOPEZ Antonio	DF	12
12	DF	KHATHRAN Abdulaziz		(C)Captain †Man of the Match			INIESTA	MF	13
13	DF	SULIMANI Hussein	81	MATCH OFFICIALS			JOAQUIN	MF	17
14	MF	KHARIRI Saud		REFEREE		66	FABREGAS Cesc	MF	18
16	MF	AZIZ Khaled	13	CODJIA Coffi BEN			† JUANITO	DF	20
		Tr: PAQUETA Marcos		ASSISTANTS			Tr: ARAGONES Luis		
		Substitutes		NTAGUNGIRA Celestin RWA			Substitutes		
18	MF	AL TEMYAT Nawaf	13	ADERODJOU Aboudou BEN		66	XAVI	MF	8
19	MF	MASSAD Mohammed	81	4TH OFFICIAL		70	TORRES Fernando	FW	9
23	FW	AL HAWSAWI Malek	68	GUEZZAZ Mohamed MAR		46	VILLA David	FW	21

Playing in the World Cup has been a grat experience for Saudi Arabia. It's a wonderful opportunity for the younger players to face strong teams. We're going home with great memories of this tournament and the fans. We enjoyed a good qualifying campaign but we came up short in terms of international experience here.

Marcos Paqueta

We've picked up nine points and the World Cup starts now. We're happy but not overconfident. The second half wasn't so impressive because we lost our shape and we let them get on top of us. The first half was a different story. I wasn't surprised by Saudi Arabia. I liked what I saw.

Luis Aragones

First Round Group H	Olympiastadion, Berlin	Friday, 23-06-2006
Kick-off: 16:00		Attendance: 72 000

UKRAINE 1 0 TUNISIA

Andriy Shevchenko [70p]

UKRAINE				MATCH STATS			TUNISIA			
1	GK	SHOVKOVSKIY Oleksandr					BOUMNIJEL Ali	GK	1
2	DF	NESMACHNIY Andriy		9	Shots	9	HAGGUI Karim	DF	3
4	MF	TYMOSCHUK Anatoliy †		6	Shots on Goal	3	46+	JAZIRI Zied	FW	5
6	DF	RUSOL Andriy		18	Fouls Committed	24	TRABELSI Hatem	DF	6
7	FW	SHEVCHENKO Andriy (C)	88	3	Corner Kicks	3	91+	NAFTI Mehdi	MF	8
8	MF	SHELAYEV Oleg		2	Caught offside	5	MNARI Jaouhar	MF	12
9	MF	GUSEV Oleg		47	Possession %	53	79	(C) BOUAZIZI Riadh	MF	13
10	FW	VORONIN Andriy		(C)Captain †Man of the Match		79	CHEDLI Adel	MF	14
11	MF	REBROV Serhiy	55	MATCH OFFICIALS			JAIDI Radhi	DF	15
19	MF	KALINICHENKO Maksim	75	REFEREE			AYARI Anis	DF	19
22	DF	SVIDERSKIY Vyacheslav		AMARILLA Carlos PAR			NAMOUCHI Hamed	MF	20
		Tr: BLOKHIN Oleg		ASSISTANTS			Tr: Lemerre Roger		
		Substitutes		ANDINO Amelio PAR			Substitutes		
14	MF	GUSIN Andriy	75	BERNAL Manuel PAR		91+	GHODHBANE Kaies	MF	10
15	FW	MILEVSKIY Artem	88	4TH OFFICIAL		79	SANTOS	FW	11
16	FW	VOROBEY Andriy	55	RODRIGUEZ Marco MEX		79	BEN SAADA Chaouki	FW	17

Today we saw that everybody was nervous. In the first half we didn't allow the Tunisians to do anything but the dismissal of the Tunisian player was not good for us. We lost our discipline. Let me congratulate the team. We wanted to make it to the round of 16 and now we have made it.

Oleg Blokhin

Every four years we do the same thing. Even with the little we showed in this tournament there is no doubt that we had the ability to get past the first round. Today we thought we could do it with 11 against 11 but with ten men it was always going to be hard. I don't think the red card was justified.

Mehdi Nafti

Round of Sixteen	FIFA World Cup Stadium, Munich	Saturday, 24-06-2006
Kick-off: 17:00		Attendance: 66 000

GERMANY 2 0 SWEDEN

Lukas Podolski 2 [4] [12]

GERMANY				MATCH STATS				SWEDEN		
1	GK	LEHMANN Jens		MATCH STATS				ISAKSSON Andreas	GK	1
3	DF	FRIEDRICH Arne		26	Shots	5		(C) MELLBERG Olof	DF	3
7	MF	SCHWEINSTEIGER Bastian	72	11	Shots on Goal	2	35	LUCIC Teddy	DF	4
8	MF	FRINGS Torsten	85	16	Fouls Committed	20		EDMAN Erik	DF	5
11	FW	KLOSE Miroslav †		4	Corner Kicks	4		LINDEROTH Tobias	MF	6
13	MF	BALLACK Michael (C)		3	Caught offside	2		ALEXANDERSSON Niclas	MF	7
16	DF	LAHM Philipp		63	Possession %	37		LJUNGBERG Freddie	MF	9
17	DF	MERTESACKER Per		(C)Captain † Man of the Match			72	IBRAHIMOVIC Zlatan	FW	10
19	MF	SCHNEIDER Bernd		MATCH OFFICIALS				LARSSON Henrik	FW	11
20	FW	PODOLSKI Lukas	74	REFEREE			39	KALLSTROM Kim	MF	16
21	DF	METZELDER Christoph		SIMON Carlos BRA			52	JONSON Mattias	FW	18
		Tr: KLINSMANN Jurgen		ASSISTANTS				Tr: LAGERBACK Lars		
		Substitutes		TAVARES Aristeu BRA				Substitutes		
5	MF	KEHL Sebastian	85	CORONA Ednilson BRA			39	HANSSON Petter	DF	13
10	FW	NEUVILLE Oliver	74	4TH OFFICIAL			72	ALLBACK Marcus	FW	20
18	MF	BOROWSKI Tim	72	MAIDIN Shamsul SIN			52	WILHELMSSON Christian	MF	21

Watching this Germany team was a true delight, especially in the first 30 minutes. I can't remember the last time Germany played football like that. Our tactics were perfect. We scored our goals early on and kept creating chances. Strangely enough, we weren't as good when Sweden had a man sent off.

Jurgen Klinsmann

They were really very good today. We were far too passive at the start. We were second to every ball. We lost to a combination of back luck, a good German team and the early goals. It's difficult enough against Germany with 11 men and even more difficult when you're down to ten.

Lars Lagerback

Round of Sixteen	Zentralstadion, Leipzig	Saturday, 24-06-2006
Kick-off: 21:00		Attendance: 43 000

ARGENTINA 2 1 MEXICO

Hernan Crespo [10], Maxi Rodriguez [98]   Rafael Marquez [6]

ARGENTINA				MATCH STATS				MEXICO		
1	GK	ABBONDANZIERI Roberto		MATCH STATS				SANCHEZ Oswaldo	GK	1
2	DF	AYALA Roberto		11	Shots	12		SALCIDO Carlos	DF	3
3	DF	SORIN Juan (C)		5	Shots on Goal	3		(C) MARQUEZ Rafael	DF	4
5	MF	CAMBIASSO Esteban	76	23	Fouls Committed	28		OSORIO Ricardo	DF	5
6	DF	HEINZE Gabriel		6	Corner Kicks	5	38	PARDO Pavel	MF	8
7	FW	SAVIOLA Javier	84	8	Caught offside	2		BORGETTI Jared	FW	9
8	MF	MASCHERANO Javier		51	Possession %	49	74	MORALES Ramon	FW	11
9	FW	CRESPO Hernan	75	(C)Captain † Man of the Match				CASTRO Jose Antonio	DF	15
10	MF	RIQUELME Juan		MATCH OFFICIALS				MENDEZ Mario	DF	16
13	DF	SCALONI Lionel		REFEREE				FONSECA Jose	FW	17
18	MF	RODRIGUEZ Maxi †		BUSACCA Massimo SUI			66	GUARDADO Andres	DF	18
		Tr: PEKERMAN Jose		ASSISTANTS				Tr: LA VOLPE Ricardo		
		Substitutes		BURAGINA Francesco SUI				Substitutes		
11	FW	TEVEZ Carlos	75	ARNET Matthias SUI			38	TORRADO Gerardo	MF	6
16	MF	AIMAR Pablo	76	4TH OFFICIAL			74	ZINHA	MF	7
19	FW	MESSI Lionel	84	AL GHAMDI Khalil KSA			66	PINEDA Gonzalo	DF	14

We had our problems, but that was down to our opponents who denied us possession and made us work hard to get it back. Football is a combination of tactical discipline, mental stability, a winning mentality and the ability of the players at key times and overall I thought we were worthy winners.

Jose Pekerman

It was an even game, just as I expected it to be, and it was a magnificent individual goal that decided it. Having said that, Mexico gave a good account of themselves. Once again, though, we didn't achieve what we came to do, which was to reach the quarter-finals at least.

Ricardo La Volpe

Round of Sixteen	Gottlieb-Daimler-Stadion, Stuttgart	Sunday, 25-06-2006
Kick-off: 17:00		Attendance: 52 000

ENGLAND   1   0   ECUADOR

David Beckham [60]

		ENGLAND			MATCH STATS				ECUADOR		
1	GK	ROBINSON Paul							MORA Cristian	GK	12
3	DF	COLE Ashley		8	Shots	9		(C) HURTADO Ivan	DF	3
4	MF	GERRARD Steven	92+	4	Shots on Goal	3		DE LA CRUZ Ulises	DF	4
5	DF	FERDINAND Rio		13	Fouls Committed	24		MENDEZ Edison	MF	8
6	DF	TERRY John †		5	Corner Kicks	7		DELGADO Agustin	FW	11
7	MF	BECKHAM David (C)	87	3	Caught offside	6		CASTILLO Segundo	MF	14
8	MF	LAMPARD Frank		49	Possession %	51		VALENCIA Luis	MF	16
9	FW	ROONEY Wayne		(C)Captain † Man of the Match				ESPINOZA Giovanny	DF	17
11	MF	COLE Joe	77	MATCH OFFICIALS				REASCO Neicer	DF	18
16	MF	HARGREAVES Owen		REFEREE		69		TENORIO Edwin	MF	20
18	MF	CARRICK Michael		DE BLEECKERE Frank BEL		72		TENORIO Carlos	FW	21
		Tr: ERIKSSON Sven-Goran		ASSISTANTS				Tr: SUAREZ Luis		
		Substitutes		HERMANS Peter BEL				Substitutes		
15	DF	CARRAGHER Jamie	77	VROMANS Walter BEL		69		LARA Christian	MF	7
19	MF	LENNON Aaron	87	4TH OFFICIAL		72		KAVIEDES Ivan	FW	10
20	MF	DOWNING Stewart	92+	RUIZ Oscar COL						

I think it's about time we got a bit of luck in a game. Yes, we could have scored more goals but in the end we had to rely on Beckham. He's a player who attracts criticism but he showed again today that he is capable of deciding a match. The team is getting better and Rooney is improving with every game.
Sven-Goran Eriksson

It was an intense game, very nervy for both teams and it was only ever going to be resolved by a stroke of genius. I'm very proud of my players. I don't know what would have happened if Carlos Tenorio had taken that chance. Our performance in the tournament was very good - our aim was to get past the group stage.
Luis Suarez

Round of Sixteen	Frankenstadion, Nuremberg	Sunday, 25-06-2006
Kick-off: 21:00		Attendance: 41 000

PORTUGAL   1   0   NETHERLANDS

Maniche [23]

		PORTUGAL			MATCH STATS				NETHERLANDS		
1	GK	RICARDO							(C) VAN DER SAR Edwin	GK	1
5	DF	FERNANDO MEIRA		10	Shots	20	63		BOULAHROUZ Khalid	DF	3
6	MF	COSTINHA	46+	6	Shots on Goal	9	56		MATHIJSEN Joris	MF	4
7	FW	LUIS FIGO (C)	84	10	Fouls Committed	15	95+		VAN BRONCKHORST Giovanni	DF	5
9	FW	PAULETA	46	3	Corner Kicks	5			KUYT Dirk	MF	7
13	DF	MIGUEL		4	Caught offside	2	84		COCU Phillip	FW	8
14	DF	NUNO VALENTE		38	Possession %	62			ROBBEN Arjen	MF	11
16	DF	RICARDO CARVALHO		(C)Captain † Man of the Match					OOIJER Andre	DF	13
17	FW	CRISTIANO RONALDO	34	MATCH OFFICIALS					VAN PERSIE Robin	MF	17
18	MF	MANICHE †		REFEREE		67			VAN BOMMEL Mark	MF	18
20	MF	DECO	78	IVANOV Valentin RUS					SNEIJDER Wesley	DF	20
		Tr: SCOLARI Luiz Felipe		ASSISTANTS					Tr: VAN BASTEN Marco		
		Substitutes		GOLUBEV Nikolay RUS					Substitutes		
8	MF	PETIT	46	VOLNIN Evgueni RUS		56			VAN DER VAART Rafael	MF	10
11	FW	SIMAO SABROSA	34	4TH OFFICIAL		67			HEITINGA John	DF	14
19	MF	TIAGO	83	RODRIGUEZ Marco MEX		84			VENNEGOOR OF HESSELINK Jan	FW	19

What I saw today from this group of players hasn't been seen in Portugal for many years. I have never seen anybody fight so much and do so much for Portugal. In spite of the odd moment of excess on the part of both teams, it was an intense, controversial and difficult game.
Luiz Felipe Scolari

It's a shame there wasn't much football played in the second half. At half-time we told the players to be careful because if there's one red card, then more usually follow. Portugal are an experienced side and I think that was the main difference. They used all the tricks in the book and knew how to waste time.
Marco Van Basten

Round of Sixteen	Fritz-Walter-Stadion, Kaiserslautern	Monday, 26-06-2006
Kick-off: 17:00		Attendance: 46 000

ITALY 1 0 AUSTRALIA

Francesco Totti 95+p

		ITALY			MATCH STATS			AUSTRALIA		
1	GK	BUFFON Gianluigi †					SCHWARZER Mark	GK	1
3	DF	GROSSO Fabio		11	Shots	8	NEILL Lucas	DF	2
5	DF	CANNAVARO Fabio (C)		6	Shots on Goal	4	MOORE Craig	DF	3
7	FW	DEL PIERO Alessandro	75	17	Fouls Committed	26	CAHILL Tim	MF	4
8	MF	GATTUSO Gennaro		2	Corner Kicks	2	CULINA Jason	MF	5
9	FW	TONI Luca	56	2	Caught offside	2	(C) VIDUKA Mark	FW	9
11	FW	GILARDINO Alberto	46	41	Possession %	59	GRELLA Vince	MF	13
19	DF	ZAMBROTTA Gianluca		(C)Captain †Man of the Match			CHIPPERFIELD Scott	DF	14
20	MF	PERROTTA Simone		MATCH OFFICIALS			WILKSHIRE Luke	MF	20
21	MF	PIRLO Andrea		REFEREE		81	STERJOVSKI Mile	MF	21
23	DF	MATERAZZI Marco	50	MEDINA CANTALEJO Luis ESP			BRESCIANO Marco	MF	23
		Tr: LIPPI Marcello		ASSISTANTS			Tr: HIDDINK Guus		
		Substitutes		GIRALDEZ Victoriano ESP			Substitutes		
6	DF	BARZAGLI Andrea	56	MEDINA Pedro ESP		81	ALOISI John	FW	15
10	MF	TOTTI Francesco	75	4TH OFFICIAL					
15	FW	IAQUINTA Vincenzo	46	POULAT Eric FRA					

We were concerned about their high-tempo game and their tireless running. We contained them very well in the first half and carved out three clear chances for ourselves. After the break we went down to ten men. The quality of our organisation and our spirit saw us through.

Marcello Lippi

I'm very proud of the way my players performed through-out the tournament and particularly against Italy. We wanted to avoid penalty-kicks but as things unfolded we would have taken them. We wanted to play attractive spectacular football but in contrast to the Italians we weren't lethal enough in front of goal.

Guus Hiddink

Round of Sixteen	FIFA World Cup Stadium, Cologne	Monday, 26-06-2006
Kick-off: 21:00		Attendance: 45 000

SWITZERLAND 0 0 UKRAINE
0 ^P_S_O 3

		SWITZERLAND			MATCH STATS			UKRAINE		
1	GK	ZUBERBUEHLER Pascal					† SHOVKOVSKIY Oleksandr	GK	1
2	DF	DJOUROU Johan	34	12	Shots	10	NESMACHNIY Andriy	DF	2
3	DF	MAGNIN Ludovic		6	Shots on Goal	2	TYMOSCHUK Anatoliy	MF	4
6	MF	VOGEL Johann (C)		24	Fouls Committed	20	(C) SHEVCHENKO Andriy	FW	7
7	MF	CABANAS Ricardo		5	Corner Kicks	6	SHELAYEV Oleg	MF	8
8	MF	WICKY Raphael		0	Caught offside	1	GUSEV Oleg	MF	9
9	FW	FREI Alexander	117	55	Possession %	45	VORONIN Andriy	FW	10
16	MF	BARNETTA Tranquillo		(C)Captain †Man of the Match		111	GUSIN Andriy	MF	14
20	DF	MUELLER Patrick		MATCH OFFICIALS		94	VOROBEY Andriy	FW	16
22	FW	YAKIN Hakan	64	REFEREE			VASHCHUK Vladislav	DF	17
23	DF	DEGEN Philipp		ARCHUNDIA Benito MEX		75	KALINICHENKO Maksim	MF	19
		Tr: KUHN Koebi		ASSISTANTS			Tr: BLOKHIN Oleg		
		Substitutes		RAMIREZ Jose MEX			Substitutes		
11	FW	STRELLER Marco	64	VERGARA Hector CAN		94	REBROV Serhiy	FW	11
13	DF	GRICHTING Stephane	34	4TH OFFICIAL		111	MILEVSKIY Artem	FW	15
18	FW	LUSTRINELLI Mauro	117	DAMON Jerome RSA		75	ROTAN Ruslan	MF	21

I expected Ukraine to play like this. It was no surprise, but despite that, we couldn't take advantage. We wanted to prove that our young team was capable of standing on its own two feet and we showed that. We played some good football in Germany and our fans had a great time.

Koebi Kuhn

I don't think that anyone believed in us, most people had written us off. Today we proved that we could play decent football. We play for results. We have fought so hard and come so far. We made a lot of stupid mistakes and could have let a goal in because Switzerland played very well.

Oleg Blokhim

Round of Sixteen	Westfalenstadion, Dortmund	Tuesday, 27-06-2006
Kick-off: 17:00		Attendance: 65 000

BRAZIL 3 0 GHANA

Ronaldo [5], Adriano [46+], Ze Roberto [84]

		BRAZIL			MATCH STATS					GHANA		
1	GK	DIDA								KINGSTON Richard	GK	22
2	DF	CAFU (C)		11	Shots	18	81			GYAN Asamoah	FW	3
3	DF	LUCIO		10	Shots on Goal	7				MENSAH John	DF	5
4	DF	JUAN		18	Fouls Committed	24				PAPPOE Emmanuel	DF	6
5	MF	EMERSON	46	3	Corner Kicks	4				SHILLA Illiasu	DF	7
6	DF	ROBERTO CARLOS		5	Caught offside	4				(C) APPIAH Stephen	MF	10
7	FW	ADRIANO	61	48	Possession %	52				MUNTARI Sulley	MF	11
8	MF	KAKA	83	(C)Captain †Man of the Match		70				AMOAH Matthew	FW	14
9	FW	RONALDO			MATCH OFFICIALS					PANTSIL John	DF	15
10	MF	RONALDINHO			REFEREE		60			ADDO Eric	MF	18
11	MF	ZE ROBERTO †			MICHEL Lubos SVK					DRAMANI Haminu	MF	23
		Tr: PARREIRA Carlos Alberto			ASSISTANTS					Tr: DUJKOVIC Ratomir		
		Substitutes			SLYSKO Roman SVK					Substitutes		
17	MF	GILBERTO SILVA	46		BALKO Martin SVK		60			BOATENG Derek	MF	9
19	MF	JUNINHO PERNAMBUCANO	61		4TH OFFICIAL		70			TACHIE-MENSAH Alex	FW	12
20	MF	RICARDINHO	83		SHIELD Mark AUS							

The scoreline was deceptive because it was a very difficult match. Our big problem was that our passing went astray. We played more with haste than speed. Our passing was sloppy. It's not as though we didn't put the effort in but rather that we were surprised by Ghana's good performanace.

Carlos Alberto Parreira

The Absence of Michael Essien was crucial, no doubt about it. He controls our play right up to the final third of the pitch. The chances that we missed were also crucial in the outcome of the game. If you give them a fraction of a second they can kill you off, just as they did today.

Ratomir Dujkovic

Round of Sixteen	FIFA World Cup Stadium, Hanover	Tuesday, 27-06-2006
Kick-off: 21:00		Attendance: 43 000

SPAIN 1 3 FRANCE

David Villa [28p] Frank Ribery [41], Patrick Vieira [83], Zinedine Zidane [92+]

		SPAIN			MATCH STATS					FRANCE		
1	GK	CASILLAS Iker								BARTHEZ Fabien	GK	16
3	DF	PERNIA Mariano		7	Shots	9				ABIDAL Eric	DF	3
5	DF	PUYOL Carlos		2	Shots on Goal	5				† VIEIRA Patrick	MF	4
7	FW	RAUL (C)	54	29	Fouls Committed	23				GALLAS William	DF	5
8	MF	XAVI	72	8	Corner Kicks	5				MAKELELE Claude	MF	6
9	FW	TORRES Fernando		2	Caught offside	8	74			MALOUDA Florent	MF	7
14	MF	XABI ALONSO		61	Possession %	39				(C) ZIDANE Zinedine	MF	10
15	DF	RAMOS Sergio		(C)Captain †Man of the Match		88				HENRY Thierry	FW	12
18	MF	FABREGAS Cesc			MATCH OFFICIALS					THURAM Lilian	DF	15
21	FW	VILLA David	54		REFEREE					SAGNOL Willy	DF	19
22	DF	PABLO			ROSSETI Roberto ITA					RIBERY Frank	MF	22
		Tr: ARAGONES Luis			ASSISTANTS					Tr: DOMENECH Raymond		
		Substitutes			COPELLI Cristiano ITA					Substitutes		
11	FW	GARCIA Luis	54		STAGNOLI Alessandro ITA		74			GOVOU Sidney	FW	9
16	MF	MARCOS SENNA	72		4TH OFFICIAL		88			WILTORD Sylvain	FW	11
17	MF	JOAQUIN	54		MERK Markus GER							

It was a very even game. We had more possession in the first half and created more opportunities. We gave as good as we got against France and we still lost. Their equaliser hit us badly but I don't think the final scoreline was an accurate reflection. We've got a young side and they gave everything.

Luis Aragones

We won because we were patient, worked hard, stuck together and were intelligent. We started slowly but were in top gear by the end. We made the most of Spain's anxiety and stopped them from playing their game. We had some difficult moments but the players used their heads and their intelligence.

Raymond Domenech

Quarter-final	Olympiastadion, Berlin	Friday, 30-06-2006
Kick-off: 17:00		Attendance: 72 000

GERMANY 1 1 ARGENTINA

Miroslav Klose [80]   4 $\overset{P}{\underset{O}{S}}$ 2   Roberto Ayala [49]

		GERMANY			MATCH STATS					ARGENTINA		
1	GK	LEHMANN Jens						71		ABBONDANZIERI Roberto	GK	1
3	DF	FRIEDRICH Arne		10	Shots	12				AYALA Roberto	DF	2
7	MF	SCHWEINSTEIGER Bastian	74	5	Shots on Goal	5				(C) SORIN Juan	DF	3
8	MF	FRINGS Torsten		23	Fouls Committed	32				COLOCCINI Fabricio	DF	4
11	FW	KLOSE Miroslav	86	4	Corner Kicks	6				HEINZE Gabriel	DF	6
13	MF	BALLACK Michael (C) †		3	Caught offside	3				MASCHERANO Javier	MF	8
16	MF	HITZLSPERGER Thomas		42	Possession %	58		79		CRESPO Hernan	FW	9
17	DF	LAHM Philipp		(C)Captain †Man of the Match				72		RIQUELME Juan	MF	10
19	MF	SCHNEIDER Bernd	62	MATCH OFFICIALS						TEVEZ Carlos	FW	11
20	FW	PODOLSKI Lukas		REFEREE						RODRIGUEZ Maxi	MF	18
21	DF	METZELDER Christoph		MICHEL Lubos SVK						GONZALEZ Luis	MF	22
		Tr: KLINSMANN Jurgen		ASSISTANTS						Tr: PEKERMAN Jose		
		Substitutes		SLYSKO Roman SVK						Substitutes		
10	FW	NEUVILLE Oliver	86	BALKO Martin SVK				71		FRANCO Leonardo	GK	12
18	MF	BOROWSKI Tim	74	4TH OFFICIAL				72		CAMBIASSO Esteban	MF	5
22	MF	ODONKOR David	62	BUSACCA Massimo SUI				79		CRUZ Julio	FW	20

The whole game was on a knife-edge but we had the better of the chances and were more efficient in front of goal so overall we deserved to win. Today was a match up between the two best teams in the tournament so far. I had every confidence in the players taking the penalties and obviously in Jens Lehmann.

Jurgen Klinsmann

We were pretty much on top throughout the match and my players gave their all. I always felt that we were better than Germany but that's not always enough to get the win. All I can say is that Argentina played good attractive football and won the fans over. We haven't made the progress we were hoping for.

Jose Pekerman

Quarter-final	FIFA World Cup Stadium, Hamburg	Friday, 30-06-2006
Kick-off: 21:00		Attendance: 50 000

ITALY 3 0 UKRAINE

Gianluca Zambrotta [6], Luca Toni 2 [59 69]

		ITALY			MATCH STATS					UKRAINE		
1	GK	BUFFON Gianluigi								SHOVKOVSKIY Oleksandr	GK	1
3	DF	GROSSO Fabio		10	Shots	13				NESMACHNIY Andriy	DF	2
5	DF	CANNAVARO Fabio (C)		7	Shots on Goal	7				TYMOSCHUK Anatoliy	MF	4
6	DF	BARZAGLI Andrea		15	Fouls Committed	31		47+		RUSOL Andriy	DF	6
8	MF	GATTUSO Gennaro †	77	1	Corner Kicks	3				(C) SHEVCHENKO Andriy	FW	7
9	FW	TONI Luca		2	Caught offside	2				SHELAYEV Oleg	MF	8
10	MF	TOTTI Francesco		41	Possession %	59				GUSEV Oleg	MF	9
16	MF	CAMORANESI Mauro	68	(C)Captain †Man of the Match						GUSIN Andriy	MF	14
19	DF	ZAMBROTTA Gianluca		MATCH OFFICIALS				72		MILEVSKIY Artem	FW	15
20	MF	PERROTTA Simone		REFEREE						KALINICHENKO Maksim	MF	19
21	MF	PIRLO Andrea	68	DE BLEECKERE Frank BEL				20		SVIDERSKIY Vyacheslav	DF	22
		Tr: LIPPI Marcello		ASSISTANTS						Tr: BLOKHIN Oleg		
		Substitutes		HERMANS Peter BEL						Substitutes		
2	DF	ZACCARDO Cristian	77	VROMANS Walter BEL				20		VOROBEY Andriy	FW	16
17	MF	BARONE Simone	68	4TH OFFICIAL				47+		VASHCHUK Vladislav	DF	17
22	DF	ODDO Massimo	68	KAMIKAWA Toru JPN				72		BYELIK Oleksiy	FW	20

Their attack was very dangerous but we managed to keep them out. They're a very physical team and we suffered a bit because of that.

Fabio Cannavaro

Everybody played well. We were very determined this evening and we didn't let our concentartion slip.

Gianluca Zambrotta

I'm very disappointed. I don't think the scoreline is a fair reflection of the match. Italy's opening goal meant that we were forced to attack and, even though we came up against a good defence, we still managed to create several chances to equalise when we were losing 1-0.

Oleg Blokhin

Quarter-final	FIFA World Cup Stadium, Gelsenkirchen	Saturday, 1-07-2006
Kick-off: 17:00		Attendance: 52 000

ENGLAND 0 0 PORTUGAL
1 P S O 3

ENGLAND				MATCH STATS			PORTUGAL		
1	GK	ROBINSON Paul		9	Shots	20	RICARDO	GK	1
2	DF	NEVILLE Gary		4	Shots on Goal	9	FERNANDO MEIRA	DF	5
3	DF	COLE Ashley		21	Fouls Committed	10	86 (C) LUIS FIGO	MF	7
4	MF	GERRARD Steven		6	Corner Kicks	4	63 PETIT	MF	8
5	DF	FERDINAND Rio		0	Caught offside	3	PAULETA	FW	9
6	DF	TERRY John		43	Possession %	57	MIGUEL	MF	13
7	MF	BECKHAM David (C)	52	(C)Captain † Man of the Match			NUNO VALENTE	MF	14
8	MF	LAMPARD Frank		MATCH OFFICIALS			RICARDO CARVALHO	FW	16
9	FW	ROONEY Wayne	62	REFEREE			CRISTIANO RONALDO	MF	17
11	MF	COLE Joe	65	ELIZONDO Horacio ARG		74	MANICHE	FW	18
16	MF	HARGREAVES Owen †		ASSISTANTS			TIAGO	FW	19
		Tr: Eriksson Sven-Goran		GARCIA Dario ARG			Tr: SCOLARI Luiz Felipe		
		Substitutes		OTERO Rodolfo ARG		74	Substitutes		
15	DF	CARRAGHER Jamie	119	4TH OFFICIAL		63	HUGO VIANA	FW	10
19	MF	LENNON Aaron	119 52	CODJIA Coffi BEN		86	SIMAO SABROSA	MF	11
21	FW	CROUCH Peter	65				HELDER POSTIGA	DF	23

*Even after the red card we still played well and creat-
ed good chances. But losing on penalties is not good
enough. I thought the players showed a lot of character.
It remained an equal game even with 10 against 11.
With a squad of this quality we should have got to at
least the semi-finals, if not further.*

Sven-Goran Eriksson

*It was a wonderful match, with everything a World
Cup match could want - chances, passion, drama - it
was electrifying. Only penalties could separate the
teams. They played an incredible match with only ten
players. We are progressing because we have added
a new warrior spirit.*

Luiz Felipe Scolari

Quarter-final	Waldstadion, Frankfurt	Saturday, 1-07-2006
Kick-off: 21:00		Attendance: 48 000

BRAZIL 0 1 FRANCE

Thierry Henry [57]

BRAZIL				MATCH STATS			FRANCE		
1	GK	DIDA		7	Shots	9	BARTHEZ Fabien	GK	16
2	DF	CAFU (C)	76	1	Shots on Goal	5	ABIDAL Eric	DF	3
3	DF	LUCIO		22	Fouls Committed	17	VIEIRA Patrick	MF	4
4	DF	JUAN		5	Corner Kicks	7	GALLAS William	DF	5
6	DF	ROBERTO CARLOS		2	Caught offside	5	MAKELELE Claude	MF	6
8	MF	KAKA	79	55	Possession %	45	81 MALOUDA Florent	MF	7
9	FW	RONALDO		(C)Captain † Man of the Match			86 † (C) ZIDANE Zinedine	MF	10
10	MF	RONALDINHO		MATCH OFFICIALS			HENRY Thierry	FW	12
11	MF	ZE ROBERTO		REFEREE			THURAM Lilian	DF	13
17	MF	GILBERTO SILVA		MEDINA CANTALEJO Luis ESP		77	SAGNOL Willy	DF	19
19	MF	JUNINHO PERNAMBUCANO	63	ASSISTANTS			RIBERY Frank	MF	22
		Tr: PARREIRA Carlos Alberto		GIRALDEZ Victoriano ESP			Tr: DOMENECH Raymond		
		Substitutes		MEDINA Pedro ESP		77	Substitutes		
7	FW	ADRIANO	63	4TH OFFICIAL		81	GOVOU Sidney	FW	9
13	DF	CICINHO	76	SHIELD Mark AUS		86	WILTORD Sylvain	FW	11
23	FW	ROBINHO	79				SAHA Louis	FW	14

*We started the game well and our passing was sharp.
But our attackers always found it difficult because
France, just like other teams that we have played, got
all of their men behind the ball. Our defence marked
tightly, so much so that their goal came from a
set-piece. The French team played with a lot of spirit.*

Carlos Alberto Parreira

*We had an overall strategy for playing against Brazil
as well as individual plans for dealing with their
players. I wouldn't say we dominated but we did keep
the necessary control. The victory belongs to the
whole squad. It wasn't so much Zidane followed by
the others but rather Zidane together with the others.*

Raymond Domenech

Semi-final	Westfalenstadion, Dortmund	Tuesday, 4-07-2006
Kick-off: 21:00		Attendance: 65 000

GERMANY 0 2 ITALY

Fabio Grosso [119], **Alessandro Del Piero** [121+]

		GERMANY			MATCH STATS				ITALY		
1	GK	LEHMANN Jens		13	Shots	15			BUFFON Gianluigi	GK	1
3	DF	FRIEDRICH Arne		2	Shots on Goal	10			GROSSO Fabio	DF	3
5	MF	KEHL Sebastian		21	Fouls Committed	19		(C)	CANNAVARO Fabio	DF	5
11	FW	KLOSE Miroslav	111	4	Corner Kicks	12	74		GATTUSO Gennaro	MF	8
13	MF	BALLACK Michael (C)		2	Caught offside	11			TONI Luca	FW	9
16	DF	LAHM Philipp		43	Possession %	57	91		TOTTI Francesco	MF	10
17	DF	MERTESACKER Per		(C) Captain † Man of the Match					CAMORANESI Mauro	MF	16
18	MF	BOROWSKI Tim	73				104		ZAMBROTTA Gianluca	DF	19
19	MF	SCHNEIDER Bernd	83		MATCH OFFICIALS				PERROTTA Simone	MF	20
20	FW	PODOLSKI Lukas			REFEREE				† PIRLO Andrea	MF	21
21	DF	METZELDER Christoph			ARCHUNDIA Benito MEX				MATERAZZI Marco	DF	23
		Tr: KLINSMANN Jurgen			ASSISTANTS				Tr: LIPPI Marcello		
		Substitutes			RAMIREZ Jose MEX				Substitutes		
7	MF	SCHWEINSTEIGER Bastian	73		VERGARA Hector CAN		104		DEL PIERO Alessandro	FW	7
10	FW	NEUVILLE Oliver	111		4TH OFFICIAL		74		GILARDINO Alberto	FW	11
22	MF	ODONKOR David	83		KAMIKAWA Toru JPN		91		IAQUINTA Vincenzo	FW	15

We're obviously very, very disappointed. That's to be expected when there is so much emotion involved and when it turns out that a dream has died. It really hurts when the other side delivers a knockout punch right before the final whistle - that takes some coming to terms with. Congratulations to Italy.

Jurgen Klinsmann

It would have been unfair if we hadn't won or if it had gone to penalties. Our game was on a higher level to Germany's tonight - we hit the post and the bar and we had the better of the play. The hosts can have no complaints. We had a lot more of the possession overall and that gave us a certain confidence.

Marcello Lippi

Quarter-finalSemi-final	FIFA World Cup Stadium, Munich	Wednesday, 5-07-2006
Kick-off: 21:00		Attendance: 66 000

PORTUGAL 0 1 FRANCE

Zinedine Zidane [33p]

		PORTUGAL			MATCH STATS				FRANCE		
1	GK	RICARDO		12	Shots	5			BARTHEZ Fabien	GK	16
5	DF	FERNANDO MEIRA		5	Shots on Goal	4			ABIDAL Eric	DF	3
6	MF	COSTINHA	75	18	Fouls Committed	11			VIEIRA Patrick	MF	4
7	FW	LUIS FIGO (C)		8	Corner Kicks	3			GALLAS William	DF	5
9	FW	PAULETA	68	4	Caught offside	0			MAKELELE Claude	MF	6
13	DF	MIGUEL	62	59	Possession %	41	69		MALOUDA Florent	MF	7
14	DF	NUNO VALENTE		(C) Captain † Man of the Match			85	(C)	ZIDANE Zinedine	MF	10
16	DF	RICARDO CARVALHO							HENRY Thierry	FW	12
17	FW	CRISTIANO RONALDO			MATCH OFFICIALS				† THURAM Lilian	DF	15
18	MF	MANICHE			REFEREE				SAGNOL Willy	DF	19
20	MF	DECO			LARRIONDA Jorge URU		72		RIBERY Frank	MF	22
		Tr: SCOLARI Luiz Felipe			ASSISTANTS				Tr: DOMENECH Raymond		
		Substitutes			RIAL Walter URU				Substitutes		
2	DF	PAULO FERREIRA	62		FANDINO Pablo URU		72		GOVOU Sidney	FW	9
11	FW	SIMAO SABROSA	68		4TH OFFICIAL		69		WILTORD Sylvain	FW	11
23	FW	HELDER POSTIGA	75		SHIELD Mark AUS		85		SAHA Louis	FW	14

It was an even game but I reckon a draw ending in a penalty shoot-out would have been fairer. We're a small country and it's hard to get this far. If France got a penalty then Ronaldo should have got one as well. This team is fantastic and they played well right from the start of the competition.

Luis Felipe Scolari

I salute Portugal for making us suffer, but there had to be a winner. It was clearly our toughest match and they were the side that caused us most problems - more than Brazil, but in a different context. This France team showed their ability to endure pressure, buckle down, stick together and hold out.

Raymond Domenech

Third Place Play-off	Gottlieb-Daimler-Stadion, Stuttgart	Saturday, 8-07-2006
Kick-off: 21:00		Attendance: 52 000

GERMANY 3 1 PORTUGAL

Bastian Schweinsteiger 2 [56] [78], Petit OG [60]   Nuno Gomes [88]

GERMANY

12	GK	KAHN Oliver (C)	
2	DF	JANSEN Marcell	
5	MF	KEHL Sebastian	
6	DF	NOWOTNY Jens	
7	MF	SCHWEINSTEIGER Bastian †	79
8	MF	FRINGS Torsten	
11	FW	KLOSE Miroslav	65
16	DF	LAHM Philipp	
19	MF	SCHNEIDER Bernd	
20	FW	PODOLSKI Lukas	71
21	DF	METZELDER Christoph	
		Tr: KLINSMANN Jurgen	

Substitutes			
9	FW	HANKE Mike	71
10	FW	NEUVILLE Oliver	65
15	MF	HITZLSPERGER Thomas	79

MATCH STATS

12	Shots	13
5	Shots on Goal	8
15	Fouls Committed	15
2	Corner Kicks	7
1	Caught offside	3
43	Possession %	57

(C)Captain †Man of the Match

MATCH OFFICIALS
REFEREE
KAMIKAWA Toru JPN
ASSISTANTS
HIROSHIMA Yoshikazu JPN
KIM Dae Young KOR
4TH OFFICIAL
CODJIA Coffi BEN

PORTUGAL

RICARDO	GK	1	
PAULO FERREIRA	DF	2	
RICARDO COSTA	DF	4	
FERNANDO MEIRA	DF	5	
COSTINHA	MF	6	46
PAULETA	FW	9	77
SIMAO SABROSA	MF	11	
NUNO VALENTE	MF	14	69
CRISTIANO RONALDO	MF	17	
MANICHE	FW	18	
DECO	DF	20	
Tr: SCOLARI Luiz Felipe			

Substitutes			
LUIS FIGO	MF	7	77
PETIT	MF	8	46
NUNO GOMES	DF	21	69

It's impossible to put into words what happened here this evening. You can't top that. The fans were fantastic and the team played like men possessed. I'm so incredibly proud that the team managed to put in such an excellent performance. We're going to celebrate this all night long.

Jurgen Klinsmann

There was nothing to chose between the two teams in the first half, but in the second, we let two goals in one after the other, the first from a swerving shot and the second when Petit deflected a free-kick. Germany's third goal was a beauty though. We had chances ourselves but just couldn't put them away.

Luiz Felipe Scolari

ADIDAS GOLDEN BALL

1 ZIDANE Zinedine, France
2 CANNAVARO Fabio, Italy
3 PIRLO Andrea, Italy

ADIDAS GOLDEN SHOE

			Goals	Assists
1	KLOSE Miroslav	GER	5	1
2	CRESPO Hernan	ARG	3	1
2	RONALDO	BRA	3	1

FIFA FAIR PLAY AWARD

1 Brazil
1 Spain

PENALTY SHOOT-OUTS AT THE 2006 FIFA WORLD CUP™ GERMANY

PENALTY SHOOT-OUT

Ukraine First		Switzerland Second	
SHEVCHENKO Andriy	✗	STRELLER Marco	✗
MILEVSKIY Artem	✔	BARNETTA Tranquillo	✗
REBROV Serhiy	✔	CABANAS Ricardo	✗
GUSEV Oleg	✔		

Ukraine qualified for the quarter-finals 3-0 on penalties

PENALTY SHOOT-OUT

Germany First		Argentina Second	
NEUVILLE Oliver	✔	CRUZ Julio	✔
BALLACK Michael	✔	AYALA Roberto	✗
PODOLSKI Lukas	✔	RODRIGUEZ Maxi	✔
BOROWSKI Tim	✔	CAMBIASSO Esteban	✗

Germany qualified for the semi-finals 4-2 on penalties

PENALTY SHOOT-OUT

Portugal First		England Second	
SIMAO SABROSA	✔	LAMPARD Frank	✗
HUGO VIANO	✗	HARGREAVES Owen	✔
PETIT	✗	GERRARD Steven	✗
HELDER POSTIGA	✔	CARRAGHER Jamie	✗
CRISTIANO RONALDO	✔		

Portugal qualified for the semi-finals 3-1 on penalties

PENALTY SHOOT-OUT

Italy First		France Second	
PIRLO Andrea	✔	WILTORD Sylvain	✔
MATERAZZI Marco	✔	TREZEGUET David	✗
DE ROSSI Daniele	✔	ABIDAL Eric	✔
DEL PIERO Alessandro	✔	SAGNOL Willy	✔
GROSSO Fabio	✔		

Italy win the FIFA World Cup™ 5-3 on penalties

Final	Olympiastadion, Berlin	Sunday, 9-07-2006
Kick-off: 20:00		Attendance: 69 000

ITALY 1 1 FRANCE

Marco Materazzi [19] **5** P S O **3** Zinedine Zidane [7p]

ITALY

1	GK	BUFFON Gianluigi	
3	DF	GROSSO Fabio	
5	DF	CANNAVARO Fabio (C)	
8	MF	GATTUSO Gennaro	
9	FW	TONI Luca	
10	MF	TOTTI Francesco	61
16	MF	CAMORANESI Mauro	86
19	DF	ZAMBROTTA Gianluca	
20	MF	PERROTTA Simone	61
21	MF	PIRLO Andrea †	
23	DF	MATERAZZI Marco	

Tr: LIPPI Marcello

Substitutes

12	GK	PERUZZI Angelo	
14	GK	AMELIA Marco	
2	DF	ZACCARDO Cristian	
4	MF	DE ROSSI Daniele	61
6	DF	BARZAGLI Andrea	
7	FW	DEL PIERO Alessandro	86
11	FW	GILARDINO Alberto	
13	DF	NESTA Alessandro	
15	FW	IAQUINTA Vincenzo	61
17	MF	BARONE Simone	
18	FW	INZAGHI Filippo	
22	DF	ODDO Massimo	

MATCH STATS

5	Shots	13
3	Shots on Goal	5
17	Fouls Committed	24
5	Corner Kicks	7
4	Caught offside	2
55	Possession %	45

(C) Captain † Man of the Match

MATCH OFFICIALS
REFEREE
ELIZONDO Horacio ARG

ASSISTANTS
GARCIA Dario ARG
OTERO Rodolfo ARG

4TH OFFICIAL
MEDINA CANTALEJO Luis ESP

FRANCE

	BARTHEZ Fabien	GK	16
	ABIDAL Eric	DF	3
56	VIEIRA Patrick	MF	4
	GALLAS William	DF	5
	MAKELELE Claude	MF	6
	MALOUDA Florent	MF	7
110	(C) ZIDANE Zinedine	MF	10
107	HENRY Thierry	FW	12
	THURAM Lilian	DF	15
	SAGNOL Willy	DF	19
100	RIBERY Frank	MF	22

Tr: DOMENECH Raymond

Substitutes

	LANDREAU Mickael	GK	1
	COUPET Gregory	GK	23
	BOUMSONG Jean-Alain	DF	2
	DHORASOO Vikash	MF	8
	GOVOU Sidney	FW	9
107	WILTORD Sylvain	FW	11
	SILVESTRE Mikael	DF	13
	SAHA Louis	FW	14
	GIVET Gael	DF	17
56	DIARRA Alou	MF	18
100	TREZEGUET David	FW	20
	CHIMBONDA Pascal	DF	21

It was a special game, starting with that penalty, then an equaliser and a general drop in tension. The further we progressed in this tournament the more we realised we could win it. How do I feel right now? I'm a world champion!

Marcello Lippi

The team got stronger and that was all part of the plan. You could see that in how we were a notch above our opponents in extra-time. I don't know what Materazzi said, but he's the man of the match not Pirlo. I'm sad for Zidane.

Raymond Domenech

MATCH HIGHLIGHTS

7′ Zidane scores a 'Panenka' style penalty. 19′ Materazzi scores with a header from a corner. 28′ Materazzi goes close from another corner. 36′ Toni heads against the crossbar from yet another corner. 46′ Henry breaks through the defence but Buffon saves. 62′ Toni heads a goal but it is disallowed for offside. 63′ Another good chance for Henry. 99′ Ribery shoots just wide. 104′ Zidane's header is saved by Buffon. 110′ Zidane is sent off for headbutting Materazzi.

MATCH REPORT

There was little to chose between the two teams before the start of the match and absolutely nothing by the end. Both goals came early in the first half, the first a penalty from Zidane that came off the underside of the bar to just creep over the line, after Marco Materazzi was adjudged to have fouled Florent Malouda. Materazzi made up for it 12 minutes later when he exploited the weakness of the French defence in the air at corners. Italy dominated for much of the rest of the first half, with Luca Toni heading against the bar from another corner, but it was the French who were the better side in the second half with Henry twice going close early on. Zidane had the best chance in extra time but was then sent off for an extraordinary headbutt on Materazzi. Italy was superb in the penalty shoot-out scoring all five of theirs which left David Trezeguet to rue his miss.

ANG – ANGOLA SQUAD 2006 FIFA WORLD CUP™

No	Pos	Name	Shirt Name	DoB	Club	Cms	Kg	Games	Mins	Goals	Y	R	Cap	Gls
1	GK	JOAO RICARDO	JOÃO RICARDO	07-01-1970	no club affiliation	180	76	3	270		1		29	0
2	DF	MARCOS AIROSA	AIROSA	06-08-1984	Barreirense	178	75	0	0				2	0
3	DF	JAMBA	JAMBA	10-07-1977	Atlético Aviação	182	78	3	270		1		38	0
4	DF	LEBO LEBO	LEBO LEBO	29-05-1977	Petro Atlético	187	79	0	0				15	0
5	DF	KALI	KALI	11-10-1978	Barreirense	187	80	3	270				24	0
6	MF	MILOY	MILOY	27-05-1981	Interclube	182	84	3	107				14	0
7	MF	FIGUEIREDO	FIGUEIREDO	28-11-1972	Varzim	170	77	3	226				25	2
8	MF	ANDRE	ANDRÉ MACANGA	14-05-1978	Al Kuwait SC	175	72	2	169		1	1	35	0
9	FW	MANTORRAS	MANTORRAS	18-03-1982	Benfica	178	77	2	52				13	3
10	FW	AKWA	AKWÁ	30-05-1977	no club affiliation	180	81	3	201				80	36
11	MF	MATEUS	MATEUS	18-06-1984	Gil Vicente	174	72	3	181				7	2
12	GK	LAMA	LAMÁ	01-02-1981	Petro Atlético	187	93	0	0				9	0
13	MF	EDSON	EDSON	02-03-1980	Paços Ferreira	175	69	1	20				8	0
14	MF	MENDONCA	MENDONCA	09-10-1982	Varzim	172	70	3	270		1		37	3
15	DF	RUI MARQUES	RUI MARQUES	03-09-1977	Hull City	185	79	2	34				3	0
16	FW	FLAVIO	FLÁVIO	30-12-1979	Al Ahly Cairo	173	73	1	39	1			47	14
17	MF	ZE KALANGA	ZÉ KALANGA	12-10-1983	Petro Atlético	175	70	3	243		2		26	4
18	FW	LOVE	CABUNGULA	14-01-1979	Atlético Aviação	178	78	1	67				36	6
19	FW	ANDRE TITI BUENGO	TITI BUENGO	11-02-1980	Clermont	189	87	0	0				2	0
20	DF	LOCO	LOCÓ	25-12-1984	Primeiro de Agosto	180	79	3	270		2		14	0
21	DF	DELGADO	DELGADO	01-11-1979	Petro Atlético	178	78	3	270		1		20	0
22	GK	MARIO	MÁRIO	01-06-1985	Interclube	184	80	0	0				1	0
23	DF	MARCO ABREU	MARCO ABREU	08-12-1974	Portimonense	180	79	0	0				3	0

ARG – ARGENTINA SQUAD 2006 FIFA WORLD CUP™

No	Pos	Name	Shirt Name	DoB	Club	Cms	Kg	Games	Mins	Goals	Y	R	Cap	Gls
1	GK	ABBONDANZIERI Roberto	ABBONDANZIERI	19-08-1972	Boca Juniors	186	89	5	461				27	0
2	DF	AYALA Roberto	AYALA	14-04-1973	Valencia	177	75	5	510	1			105	7
3	DF	SORIN Juan	SORIN	05-05-1976	Villarreal	173	65	4	420		2		75	11
4	DF	COLOCCINI Fabricio	COLOCCINI	22-01-1982	Deportivo La Coruña	183	78	2	186				25	1
5	MF	CAMBIASSO Esteban	CAMBIASSO	18-08-1980	Internazionale	178	73	5	377	1	1		27	2
6	DF	HEINZE Gabriel	HEINZE	19-04-1978	Manchester United	178	78	4	420		2		33	1
7	FW	SAVIOLA Javier	SAVIOLA	11-12-1981	Sevilla	169	62	3	218	1	1		34	10
8	MF	MASCHERANO Javier	MASCHERANO	08-06-1984	Corinthians	171	66	5	510		2		20	0
9	FW	CRESPO Hernan	CRESPO	05-07-1975	Chelsea	184	78	4	308	3	1		59	32
10	MF	RIQUELME Juan	RIQUELME	24-06-1978	Villarreal	182	75	5	451				36	8
11	FW	TEVEZ Carlos	TEVEZ	05-02-1984	Corinthians	168	67	4	286	1			25	4
12	GK	FRANCO Leonardo	FRANCO	20-05-1977	Atlético Madrid	188	79	1	49				4	0
13	DF	SCALONI Lionel	SCALONI	16-05-1978	West Ham United	182	80	1	120				7	0
14	FW	PALACIO Rodrigo	PALACIO	05-02-1982	Boca Juniors	175	66	1	26				3	0
15	DF	MILITO Gabriel	MILITO	07-09-1980	Real Zaragoza	177	78	1	90				16	0
16	MF	AIMAR Pablo	AIMAR	03-11-1979	Valencia	170	62	3	55				43	7
17	DF	CUFRE Leandro	CUFRE	09-05-1978	Roma	177	76	2	90			1	3	0
18	MF	RODRIGUEZ Maxi	RODRIGUEZ	02-01-1981	Atlético Madrid	173	73	5	495	3	1		18	6
19	FW	MESSI Lionel	MESSI	24-06-1987	Barcelona	170	65	3	121	1			10	2
20	FW	CRUZ Julio	CRUZ	10-10-1974	Internazionale	190	78	2	61		1		17	3
21	DF	BURDISSO Nicolas	BURDISSO	12-04-1981	Internazionale	174	77	3	204				11	0
22	MF	GONZALEZ Luis	GONZALEZ	19-01-1981	Porto	185	75	3	152		1		30	5
23	GK	USTARI Oscar	USTARI	03-07-1986	Independiente	184	82	0	0				0	0

AUS – AUSTRALIA SQUAD 2006 FIFA WORLD CUP™

No	Pos	Name	Shirt Name	DoB	Club	Cms	Kg	Games	Mins	Goals	Y	R	Cap	Gls
1	GK	SCHWARZER Mark	SCHWARZER	06-10-1972	Middlesbrough	196	86	3	270				40	0
2	DF	NEILL Lucas	NEILL	09-03-1978	Blackburn Rovers	185	80	4	360				29	0
3	DF	MOORE Craig	MOORE	12-12-1975	Newcastle United	186	80	4	310	1	1		37	3
4	MF	CAHILL Tim	CAHILL	06-12-1979	Everton	180	69	4	273	2	2		20	11
5	MF	CULINA Jason	CULINA	05-08-1980	PSV Eindhoven	175	75	4	360		1		17	1
6	FW	POPOVIC Tony	POPOVIC	04-07-1973	Crystal Palace	193	90	1	41				57	7
7	MF	EMERTON Brett	EMERTON	22-02-1979	Blackburn Rovers	185	85	3	267		1	1	51	11
8	MF	SKOKO Josip	SKOKO	10-12-1975	Stoke City	177	77	0	0				46	9
9	FW	VIDUKA Mark	VIDUKA	09-10-1975	Middlesbrough	188	91	4	360				37	6
10	FW	KEWELL Harry	KEWELL	22-09-1978	Liverpool	183	85	3	214	1			23	7
11	MF	LAZARIDIS Stan	LAZARIDIS	16-08-1972	Birmingham City	175	76	0	0				59	0
12	GK	COVIC Ante	COVIC	13-06-1975	Hammarby IF	192	89	0	0				1	0
13	MF	GRELLA Vince	GRELLA	05-10-1979	Parma	183	79	4	333		2		21	0
14	DF	CHIPPERFIELD Scott	CHIPPERFIELD	30-12-1975	Basel	180	70	4	345				50	11
15	FW	ALOISI John	ALOISI	05-02-1976	Alaves	188	83	4	72	1			45	24
16	DF	BEAUCHAMP Michael	BEAUCHAMP	08-03-1981	Central Coast Mariners	191	85	0	0				2	0
17	FW	THOMPSON Archie	THOMPSON	23-10-1978	PSV Eindhoven	171	70	0	0				20	21
18	GK	KALAC Zeljko	KALAC	16-12-1972	Milan	202	91	1	90				53	0
19	FW	KENNEDY Joshua	KENNEDY	20-08-1982	Dynamo Dresden	192	82	2	44				3	1
20	MF	WILKSHIRE Luke	WILKSHIRE	02-10-1981	Bristol City	177	80	2	165		1		10	0
21	MF	STERJOVSKI Mile	STERJOVSKI	27-05-1979	Basel	180	79	3	242				25	4
22	DF	MILLIGAN Mark	MILLIGAN	04-08-1985	Sydney FC	178	78	0	0				1	0
23	MF	BRESCIANO Marco	BRESCIANO	11-02-1980	Parma	182	73	4	211				28	7

BRA – BRAZIL SQUAD 2006 FIFA WORLD CUP™

No	Pos	Name	Shirt Name	DoB	Club	Cms	Kg	Games	Mins	Goals	Y	R	Cap	Gls
1	GK	DIDA	DIDA	07-10-1973	Milan	195	85	5	442				91	0
2	DF	CAFU	CAFU	07-06-1970	Milan	176	75	4	346		2		142	5
3	DF	LUCIO	LÚCIO	08-05-1978	Bayern München	188	81	5	450		1		55	2
4	DF	JUAN	JUAN	01-02-1979	Bayer Leverkusen	182	73	5	450		2		43	2
5	MF	EMERSON	EMERSON	04-04-1976	Juventus	184	84	3	207		1		73	6
6	DF	ROBERTO CARLOS	R.CARLOS	10-04-1973	Real Madrid	168	70	4	360				125	11
7	FW	ADRIANO	ADRIANO	17-02-1982	Internazionale	189	86	4	266	2	1		36	25
8	MF	KAKA	KAKÁ	22-04-1982	Milan	183	73	5	413	1			43	14
9	FW	RONALDO	RONALDO	22-09-1976	Real Madrid	183	82	5	411	3	2		97	62
10	MF	RONALDINHO	RONALDINHO	21-03-1980	Barcelona	178	70	5	431				68	27
11	MF	ZE ROBERTO	ZÉ ROBERTO	06-07-1974	Bayern München	172	71	5	379	1			84	6
12	GK	ROGERIO CENI	R. CENI	22-01-1973	Sao Paulo FC	188	88	1	8				16	0
13	DF	CICINHO	CICINHO	24-06-1980	Real Madrid	172	72	2	104				12	1
14	DF	LUISAO	LUISÃO	13-02-1981	Benfica	192	81	0	0				19	1
15	DF	CRIS	CRIS	03-06-1977	Olympique Lyonnais	183	77	0	0				16	1
16	DF	GILBERTO	GILBERTO	25-04-1976	Hertha Berlin	180	78	1	90	1	1		10	1
17	MF	GILBERTO SILVA	G.SILVA	07-10-1976	Arsenal	191	78	4	243				40	3
18	MF	MINEIRO	MINEIRO	02-08-1975	Sao Paulo FC	169	69	0	0				2	0
19	MF	JUNINHO PERNAMBUCANO	JUNINHO	30-01-1975	Olympique Lyonnais	178	71	3	182	1			40	6
20	MF	RICARDINHO	RICARDINHO	23-05-1976	Corinthians	176	73	2	26				21	1
21	FW	FRED	FRED	03-10-1983	Olympique Lyonnais	185	75	1	2	1			4	3
22	GK	JULIO CESAR	JULIO CESAR	03-09-1979	Internazionale	186	79	0	0				11	0
23	FW	ROBINHO	ROBINHO	25-01-1984	Real Madrid	172	60	4	140		1		27	5

CIV – COTE D'IVOIRE SQUAD 2006 FIFA WORLD CUP™

No	Pos	Name	Shirt Name	DoB	Club	Cms	Kg	Games	Mins	Goals	Y	R	Cap	Gls
1	GK	TIZIE Jean-Jacques	TIZIE	07-09-1972	Esperance	183	80	2	180				26	0
2	MF	AKALE Kanga	AKALE	07-03-1981	Auxerre	178	73	3	139				25	3
3	DF	BOKA Arthur	BOKA	02-04-1983	RC Strasbourg	166	67	3	270		1		26	1
4	DF	TOURE Kolo	TOURE K.	19-03-1981	Arsenal	183	76	2	180				44	1
5	MF	ZOKORA Didier	ZOKORA	14-12-1980	Saint-Etienne	183	78	3	270		1		41	0
6	DF	KOUASSI Blaise	KOUASSI	02-02-1975	Troyes	182	75	1	90				37	0
7	MF	FAE Emerse	FAE	24-01-1984	Nantes	174	71	0	0				14	1
8	FW	KALOU Bonaventure	KALOU	12-01-1978	Paris St-Germain	182	77	2	72	1			51	12
9	FW	KONE Arouna	KONE A.	11-11-1983	PSV Eindhoven	182	85	3	176				21	2
10	MF	YAPI YAPO Gilles	YAPI	30-01-1982	Young Boys Berne	171	63	1	28				27	2
11	FW	DROGBA Didier	DROGBA	11-03-1978	Chelsea	180	84	2	180	1	2		34	24
12	DF	MEITE Abdoulaye	MEITE	06-10-1980	Olympique Marseille	185	82	2	180				20	0
13	DF	ZORO Marc	ZORO	27-12-1983	Messina	182	75	0	0				13	0
14	FW	KONE Bakary	KONE B.	17-09-1981	Nice	163	61	3	120	1			19	4
15	FW	DINDANE Aruna	DINDANE	26-11-1980	RC Lens	174	76	3	153	2	1		37	13
16	GK	GNANHOUAN Gerard	GNANHOUAN	12-02-1979	Montpellier	182	77	0	0				6	0
17	DF	DOMORAUD Cyrille	DOMORAUD	22-07-1971	Creteil	180	80	1	89			1	51	0
18	MF	KEITA Kader	KEITA	06-08-1981	Lille	184	78	2	150		1		28	6
19	MF	TOURE Yaya	TOURE Y.	13-05-1983	Olympiacos	189	79	3	270				17	2
20	MF	DEMEL Guy	DEMEL	13-06-1981	Hamburger SV	191	83	0	0				7	0
21	DF	EBOUE Emmanuel	EBOUE	04-06-1983	Arsenal	178	72	3	270		1		14	0
22	MF	ROMARIC	ROMARIC	04-06-1983	Le Mans	187	88	1	62				9	0
23	GK	BARRY Boubacar	BARRY	30-12-1979	Beveren	180	69	1	90				7	0

CRC – COSTA RICA SQUAD 2006 FIFA WORLD CUP™

No	Pos	Name	Shirt Name	DoB	Club	Cms	Kg	Games	Mins	Goals	Y	R	Cap	Gls
1	GK	MESEN Alvaro	MESEN A.	24-12-1972	CS Herediano	180	80	0	0				38	0
2	DF	DRUMMOND Jervis	DRUMMOND J.	08-09-1976	Deportivo Saprissa	172	66	2	94				58	1
3	DF	MARIN Luis	MARIN L.	10-08-1974	LD Alajuelense	180	76	3	270		2		123	5
4	DF	UMANA Michael	UMAÑA M.	16-07-1982	Brujas Escazú	178	73	3	270		1		21	0
5	DF	MARTINEZ Gilberto	MARTINEZ G.	01-10-1979	Brescia	174	76	1	66				58	0
6	MF	FONSECA Danny	FONSECA D.	07-11-1979	CS Cartagines	179	77	2	119		1		24	2
7	MF	BOLANOS Cristian	BOLAÑOS C.	17-05-1984	Deportivo Saprissa	178	67	2	90				18	1
8	MF	SOLIS Mauricio	SOLIS M.	13-12-1972	Comunicaciones	177	78	3	258		1		110	6
9	FW	WANCHOPE Paulo	WANCHOPE P.	31-07-1976	CS Herediano	182	83	3	270	2			72	45
10	MF	CENTENO Walter	CENTENO W.	06-10-1974	Deportivo Saprissa	174	69	3	264				96	15
11	FW	GOMEZ Ronald	GOMEZ R.	24-01-1975	Deportivo Saprissa	183	80	3	261	1	1		83	24
12	DF	GONZALEZ Leonardo	GONZALEZ L.	21-11-1980	CS Herediano	186	74	3	236				39	0
13	FW	BERNARD Kurt	BERNARD K.	08-12-1977	Puntarenas	185	85	1	6				4	0
14	MF	AZOFEIFA Randall	AZOFEIFA R.	30-12-1984	Deportivo Saprissa	182	83	1	1				6	0
15	DF	WALLACE Harold	WALLACE H.	07-09-1975	LD Alajuelense	175	72	2	110				80	1
16	MF	HERNANDEZ Carlos	HERNANDEZ C.	09-04-1982	LD Alajuelense	170	70	2	42				19	6
17	MF	BADILLA Gabriel	BADILLA G.	30-06-1984	Deportivo Saprissa	181	73	1	90		1		8	0
18	GK	PORRAS Jose	PORRAS J.	08-11-1970	Deportivo Saprissa	184	81	3	270				19	0
19	FW	SABORIO Alvaro	SABORIO A.	25-03-1982	Deportivo Saprissa	183	82	2	73				25	7
20	MF	SEQUEIRA Douglas	SEQUEIRA D.	23-08-1977	Real Salt Lake	186	81	2	180				31	2
21	FW	NUNEZ Victor	NUÑEZ V.	15-04-1980	CS Cartagines	178	81	0	0				3	0
22	DF	RODRIGUEZ Michael	RODRIGUEZ M.	30-12-1981	LD Alajuelense	174	76	0	0				3	0
23	GK	ALFARO Wardy	ALFARO W.	31-12-1977	LD Alajuelense	180	66	0	0				2	0

CRO – CROATIA SQUAD 2006 FIFA WORLD CUP™

No	Pos	Name	Shirt Name	DoB	Club	Cms	Kg	Games	Mins	Goals	Y	R	Cap	Gls
1	GK	PLETIKOSA Stipe	PLETIKOSA	08-01-1979	Hajduk Split	193	88	3	270		1		52	0
2	MF	SRNA Darijo	SRNA	01-05-1982	Shakhtar Donetsk	182	78	3	267	1	1		38	9
3	DF	SIMUNIC Josip	SIMUNIC	18-02-1978	Hertha Berlin	195	89	3	269			1	44	3
4	DF	KOVAC Robert	R. KOVAC	06-04-1974	Juventus	182	78	2	180		2		58	0
5	DF	TUDOR Igor	TUDOR	16-04-1978	Siena	193	90	3	250		2		53	3
6	MF	VRANJES Jurica	VRANJES	31-01-1980	Werder Bremen	184	70	0	0				24	0
7	DF	SIMIC Dario	SIMIC	12-11-1975	Milan	180	76	3	265			1	82	3
8	MF	BABIC Marko	BABIC	28-01-1981	Bayer Leverkusen	186	74	3	270				35	3
9	FW	PRSO Dado	PRSO	05-11-1974	Rangers	187	76	3	270				31	9
10	MF	KOVAC Niko	N. KOVAC	15-10-1971	Hertha Berlin	178	75	3	221	1	1		60	8
11	DF	TOKIC Mario	TOKIC	23-07-1975	FK Austria Vienna	180	77	0	0				28	0
12	GK	DIDULICA Joe	DIDULICA	14-10-1977	FK Austria Vienna	191	78	0	0				4	0
13	DF	TOMAS Stjepan	TOMAS	06-03-1976	Galatasaray	186	82	1	83				48	1
14	MF	MODRIC Luka	MODRIC	09-09-1985	Dinamo Zagreb	173	65	2	28				6	0
15	MF	LEKO Ivan	I. LEKO	07-02-1978	Club Brugge	179	77	0	0				13	0
16	MF	LEKO Jerko	J. LEKO	09-04-1980	Dynamo Kyiv	186	77	2	74				37	2
17	FW	KLASNIC Ivan	KLASNIC	29-01-1980	Werder Bremen	186	79	3	153				22	7
18	FW	OLIC Ivica	OLIC	14-09-1979	CSKA Moskva	183	81	3	128				38	6
19	MF	KRANJCAR Niko	KRANJCAR	13-08-1984	Hajduk Split	185	80	3	233				23	3
20	MF	SERIC Anthony	SERIC	15-01-1979	Panathinaikos	181	75	0	0				14	0
21	FW	BALABAN Bosko	BALABAN	15-10-1978	Club Brugge	180	78	0	0				27	9
22	FW	BOSNJAK Ivan	BOSNJAK	06-02-1979	Dinamo Zagreb	178	70	1	3				14	1
23	GK	BUTINA Tomislav	BUTINA	30-03-1974	Club Brugge	191	88	0	0				28	0

CZE – CZECH REPUBLIC SQUAD 2006 FIFA WORLD CUP™

No	Pos	Name	Shirt Name	DoB	Club	Cms	Kg	Games	Mins	Goals	Y	R	Cap	Gls
1	GK	CECH Petr	CECH	20-05-1982	Chelsea	197	87	3	270				44	0
2	DF	GRYGERA Zdenek	GRYGERA	14-05-1980	Ajax	185	78	3	270		1		43	1
3	DF	MARES Pavel	MARES	18-01-1976	Zenit St Peterburg	185	77	0	0				10	0
4	MF	GALASEK Tomas	GALASEK	15-01-1973	Ajax	180	77	2	135				51	1
5	MF	KOVAC Radoslav	KOVAC	27-11-1979	Spartak Moskva	188	77	1	78				7	0
6	DF	JANKULOVSKI Marek	JANKULOVSKI	09-05-1977	Milan	183	82	3	270				51	8
7	FW	SIONKO Libor	SIONKO	01-02-1977	Rangers	175	70	1	22				18	1
8	MF	POBORSKY Karel	POBORSKY	30-03-1972	Ceske Budejovice	175	70	3	183				118	8
9	FW	KOLLER Jan	KOLLER	30-03-1973	Borussia Dortmund	202	100	1	45	1			69	43
10	MF	ROSICKY Tomas	ROSICKY	04-10-1980	Borussia Dortmund	175	67	3	266	2	1		57	17
11	MF	NEDVED Pavel	NEDVED	30-08-1972	Juventus	175	73	3	270				90	18
12	FW	LOKVENC Vratislav	LOKVENC	27-09-1973	Austria Salzburg	196	88	2	135		2		74	14
13	DF	JIRANEK Martin	JIRANEK	25-05-1979	Spartak Moskva	183	77	0	0				24	0
14	MF	JAROLIM David	JAROLIM	17-05-1979	Hamburger SV	172	69	1	26				4	0
15	FW	BAROS Milan	BAROS	28-10-1981	Aston Villa	181	77	1	64				50	27
16	GK	BLAZEK Jaromir	BLAZEK	29-12-1972	Sparta Praha	188	82	0	0				11	0
17	MF	STAJNER Jiri	STAJNER	27-05-1976	Hannover 96	185	82	3	83				24	3
18	FW	HEINZ Marek	HEINZ	04-08-1977	Galatasaray	188	75	1	12				28	5
19	MF	POLAK Jan	POLAK	14-03-1981	1.FC Nürnberg	181	77	3	100			1	21	5
20	MF	PLASIL Jaroslav	PLASIL	05-01-1982	Monaco	183	71	3	248				17	1
21	DF	UJFALUSI Tomas	UJFALUSI	24-03-1978	Fiorentina	185	76	2	155			1	50	2
22	DF	ROZEHNAL David	ROZEHNAL	05-07-1980	Paris St-Germain	191	79	3	270		1		25	0
23	GK	KINSKY Antonin	KINSKY	31-05-1975	Saturn Moskva	187	83	0	0				5	0

ECU – ECUADOR SQUAD 2006 FIFA WORLD CUP™

No	Pos	Name	Shirt Name	DoB	Club	Cms	Kg	Games	Mins	Goals	Y	R	Cap	Gls
1	GK	VILLAFUERTE Edwin	E. VILLAFUERTE	12-03-1979	Deportivo Quito	186	80	0	0				15	0
2	DF	GUAGUA Jorge	J. GUAGUA	28-09-1981	El Nacional	179	75	3	132				21	1
3	DF	HURTADO Ivan	I. HURTADO	16-08-1974	Al Arabi	180	77	3	249		1		133	5
4	DF	DE LA CRUZ Ulises	U. DE LA CRUZ	08-02-1974	Aston Villa	178	74	4	360		2		88	5
5	DF	PERLAZA Jose	J. L. PERLAZA	06-10-1981	Olmedo	193	77	0	0				3	0
6	MF	URRUTIA Patricio	P. URRUTIA	15-10-1977	LDU Quito	178	65	3	46				9	0
7	MF	LARA Christian	C. LARA	27-04-1980	El Nacional	162	60	2	48				21	3
8	MF	MENDEZ Edison	E. MENDEZ	16-03-1979	LDU Quito	175	68	4	360		1		68	10
9	FW	BORJA Felix	F. BORJA	02-04-1983	El Nacional	180	70	1	45				7	1
10	FW	KAVIEDES Ivan	I. KAVIEDES	24-10-1977	Argentinos Juniors	182	71	4	178	1			48	14
11	FW	DELGADO Agustin	A. DELGADO	23-12-1974	LDU Quito	187	83	3	263	2			71	31
12	GK	MORA Cristian	C. MORA	26-08-1979	LDU Quito	185	73	4	360		1		12	0
13	DF	AMBROSI Paul	P. AMBROSI	14-10-1980	LDU Quito	177	70	1	90				25	0
14	MF	CASTILLO Segundo	S. CASTILLO	15-05-1982	El Nacional	180	76	3	270		1		14	1
15	MF	AYOVI Marlon	M. AYOVI	27-09-1971	Deportivo Quito	174	76	1	68				75	5
16	MF	VALENCIA Luis	A. VALENCIA	04-08-1985	Recreativo Huelva	180	77	4	316		2		21	3
17	DF	ESPINOZA Giovanny	G. ESPINOZA	12-04-1977	LDU Quito	184	85	4	339				60	2
18	DF	REASCO Neicer	N. REASCO	23-07-1977	LDU Quito	170	73	3	270				34	0
19	MF	SARITAMA Luis	F. SARITAMA	20-10-1983	Deportivo Quito	175	70	0	0				15	0
20	MF	TENORIO Edwin	E. TENORIO	16-06-1976	Barcelona (ECU)	172	64	4	339				72	0
21	FW	TENORIO Carlos	C. TENORIO	14-05-1979	Al Sadd	182	78	3	182	2	1		32	7
22	GK	LANZA Damian	D. LANZA	10-04-1982	Aucas	186	89	0	0				5	0
23	FW	BENITEZ Cristian	C. BENITEZ	01-05-1986	El Nacional	168	68	1	45				6	0

ENG – ENGLAND SQUAD 2006 FIFA WORLD CUP™

No	Pos	Name	Shirt Name	DoB	Club	Cms	Kg	Games	Mins	Goals	Y	R	Cap	Gls
1	GK	ROBINSON Paul	ROBINSON	15-10-1979	Tottenham Hotspur	193	90	5	480		1		26	0
2	DF	NEVILLE Gary	G. NEVILLE	18-02-1975	Manchester United	178	72	2	210				81	0
3	DF	COLE Ashley	A. COLE	20-12-1980	Arsenal	170	67	5	480				51	0
4	MF	GERRARD Steven	GERRARD	30-05-1980	Liverpool	188	78	5	410	2	1		47	9
5	DF	FERDINAND Rio	FERDINAND	07-11-1978	Manchester United	188	76	5	446				52	1
6	DF	TERRY John	TERRY	07-12-1980	Chelsea	182	74	5	480		2		29	1
7	MF	BECKHAM David	BECKHAM	02-05-1975	Real Madrid	182	74	5	409	1			94	17
8	MF	LAMPARD Frank	LAMPARD	20-06-1978	Chelsea	177	78	5	480		1		45	11
9	FW	ROONEY Wayne	ROONEY	24-10-1985	Manchester United	178	78	4	253			1	33	11
10	FW	OWEN Michael	OWEN	14-12-1979	Newcastle United	172	67	3	118				80	36
11	MF	COLE Joe	J. COLE	08-11-1981	Chelsea	175	69	5	390	1			37	6
12	DF	CAMPBELL Sol	CAMPBELL	18-09-1974	Arsenal	188	91	1	34				69	1
13	GK	JAMES David	JAMES	01-08-1970	Manchester City	193	94	0	0				34	0
14	DF	BRIDGE Wayne	BRIDGE	05-08-1980	Fulham	177	68	0	0				23	1
15	DF	CARRAGHER Jamie	CARRAGHER	28-01-1978	Liverpool	182	76	4	162		1		29	0
16	MF	HARGREAVES Owen	HARGREAVES	20-01-1981	Bayern München	180	73	4	307		2		34	0
17	MF	JENAS Jermaine	JENAS	18-02-1983	Tottenham Hotspur	180	70	0	0				15	0
18	MF	CARRICK Michael	CARRICK	28-07-1981	Tottenham Hotspur	182	74	1	90				7	0
19	MF	LENNON Aaron	LENNON	16-04-1987	Tottenham Hotspur	165	63	3	102				4	0
20	MF	DOWNING Stewart	DOWNING	22-07-1984	Middlesbrough	182	69	3	50				5	0
21	FW	CROUCH Peter	CROUCH	30-01-1981	Liverpool	198	69	4	321	1	1		11	6
22	GK	CARSON Scott	CARSON	03-09-1985	Liverpool	190	89	0	0				0	0
23	FW	WALCOTT Theo	WALCOTT	16-03-1989	Arsenal	176	68	0	0				1	0

ESP – SPAIN SQUAD 2006 FIFA WORLD CUP™

No	Pos	Name	Shirt Name	DoB	Club	Cms	Kg	Games	Mins	Goals	Y	R	Cap	Gls
1	GK	CASILLAS Iker	CASILLAS	20-05-1981	Real Madrid	184	80	3	270				61	0
2	DF	SALGADO Michel	M. SALGADO	22-10-1975	Real Madrid	173	73	1	90				51	0
3	DF	PERNIA Mariano	M. PERNIA	04-05-1977	Getafe	177	78	3	270		1		4	1
4	DF	MARCHENA Carlos	C. MARCHENA	31-07-1979	Valencia	182	75	1	90				28	1
5	DF	PUYOL Carles	PUYOL	13-04-1978	Barcelona	178	78	3	270		2		50	1
6	MF	ALBELDA David	ALBELDA	01-09-1977	Valencia	181	77	2	125				35	0
7	FW	RAUL	RAUL	27-06-1977	Real Madrid	180	68	4	179	1			99	44
8	MF	XAVI	XAVI	25-01-1980	Barcelona	170	68	4	276				40	1
9	FW	TORRES Fernando	F. TORRES	20-03-1984	Atlético Madrid	181	78	4	290	3			34	13
10	MF	REYES Jose Antonio	REYES	01-09-1983	Arsenal	175	71	1	70		1		20	4
11	FW	GARCIA Luis	LUIS GARCIA	24-06-1978	Liverpool	176	64	3	158				13	3
12	DF	LOPEZ Antonio	A. LOPEZ	13-09-1981	Atlético Madrid	173	65	1	90				11	1
13	MF	INIESTA	A. INIESTA	11-05-1984	Barcelona	169	64	1	90				4	0
14	MF	XABI ALONSO	ALONSO	25-11-1981	Liverpool	183	75	3	235	1			29	1
15	DF	RAMOS Sergio	SERGIO RAMOS	30-03-1986	Real Madrid	183	73	3	270				14	2
16	MF	MARCOS SENNA	SENNA	17-07-1976	Villarreal	177	73	3	154				6	0
17	MF	JOAQUIN	JOAQUIN	21-07-1981	Betis Sevilla	179	75	3	159				40	4
18	MF	FABREGAS Cesc	CESC	04-05-1987	Arsenal	175	70	4	213		1		8	0
19	GK	CANIZARES Santiago	CAÑIZARES	18-12-1969	Valencia	181	81	1	90				46	0
20	DF	JUANITO	JUANITO	23-07-1976	Betis Sevilla	179	70	1	90	1			16	1
21	FW	VILLA David	DAVID VILLA	03-12-1981	Valencia	175	69	4	211	3			12	5
22	DF	PABLO	PABLO	03-08-1981	Atlético Madrid	192	80	3	270				14	0
23	GK	REINA Jose Manuel	REINA	31-08-1982	Liverpool	187	85	0	0				3	0

FRA – FRANCE SQUAD 2006 FIFA WORLD CUP™

No	Pos	Name	Shirt Name	DoB	Club	Cms	Kg	Games	Mins	Goals	Y	R	Cap	Gls
1	GK	LANDREAU Mickael	LANDREAU	14-05-1979	Nantes	184	84	0	0				3	0
2	DF	BOUMSONG Jean-Alain	BOUMSONG	14-12-1979	Newcastle United	190	84	0	0				19	1
3	DF	ABIDAL Eric	ABIDAL	11-09-1979	Olympique Lyonnais	180	75	6	570		2		14	0
4	MF	VIEIRA Patrick	VIEIRA	23-06-1976	Juventus	193	83	7	587	2	1		94	6
5	DF	GALLAS William	GALLAS	17-08-1977	Chelsea	181	72	7	660				47	1
6	MF	MAKELELE Claude	MAKELELE	18-02-1973	Chelsea	174	70	7	660		2		50	0
7	MF	MALOUDA Florent	MALOUDA	13-06-1980	Olympique Lyonnais	184	73	6	506		1		19	2
8	MF	DHOROSOO Vikash	DHOROSOO	10-10-1973	Paris St-Germain	168	63	2	8				18	1
9	FW	GOVOU Sidney	GOVOU	27-07-1979	Olympique Lyonnais	175	72	4	60				23	3
10	MF	ZIDANE Zinedine	ZIDANE	23-06-1972	Real Madrid	185	78	6	559	3	3	1	108	31
11	FW	WILTORD Sylvain	WILTORD	10-05-1974	Olympique Lyonnais	173	72	7	205				87	26
12	FW	HENRY Thierry	HENRY	17-08-1977	Arsenal	188	83	7	636	3			85	36
13	DF	SILVESTRE Mikael	SILVESTRE	09-08-1977	Manchester United	183	86	1	90				40	2
14	FW	SAHA Louis	SAHA	08-08-1978	Manchester United	184	75	3	29		2		12	2
15	DF	THURAM Lilian	THURAM	01-01-1972	Juventus	185	80	7	660		1		121	2
16	GK	BARTHEZ Fabien	BARTHEZ	28-06-1971	Olympique Marseille	182	76	7	660				87	0
17	DF	GIVET Gael	GIVET	09-10-1981	Monaco	181	78	0	0				11	0
18	MF	DIARRA Alou	DIARRA	15-07-1981	RC Lens	190	79	2	73				11	0
19	DF	SAGNOL Willy	SAGNOL	18-03-1977	Bayern München	180	78	7	660		3		45	0
20	FW	TREZEGUET David	TREZEGUET	15-10-1977	Juventus	187	75	3	111				66	32
21	FW	CHIMBONDA Pascal	CHIMBONDA	21-02-1979	Wigan Athletic	182	75	0	0				1	0
22	MF	RIBERY Frank	RIBERY	07-04-1983	Olympique Marseille	175	72	7	516	1	1		10	1
23	GK	COUPET Gregory	COUPET	31-12-1972	Olympique Lyonnais	181	80	0	0				18	0

GER – GERMANY SQUAD 2006 FIFA WORLD CUP™

No	Pos	Name	Shirt Name	DoB	Club	Cms	Kg	Games	Mins	Goals	Y	R	Cap	Gls
1	GK	LEHMANN Jens	LEHMANN	10-11-1969	Arsenal	190	87	6	600				38	0
2	DF	JANSEN Marcell	JANSEN	04-11-1985	B. Mönchengladbach	190	88	1	90				8	0
3	DF	FRIEDRICH Arne	FRIEDRICH	29-05-1979	Hertha Berlin	185	78	6	574		1		42	0
4	DF	HUTH Robert	HUTH	18-08-1984	Chelsea	191	88	1	90				17	2
5	MF	KEHL Sebastian	KEHL	13-02-1980	Borussia Dortmund	186	80	4	233				31	3
6	DF	NOWOTNY Jens	NOWOTNY	11-01-1974	Bayer Leverkusen	184	87	1	90				47	1
7	MF	SCHWEINSTEIGER Bastian	SCHWEINSTEIGER	01-08-1984	Bayern München	180	76	7	529	2	1		35	9
8	MF	FRINGS Torsten	FRINGS	22-11-1976	Werder Bremen	182	80	6	541	1	2		58	8
9	FW	HANKE Mike	HANKE	05-11-1983	VfL Wolfsburg	184	75	1	19				7	1
10	FW	NEUVILLE Oliver	NEUVILLE	01-05-1973	B. Mönchengladbach	171	64	7	138	1			62	9
11	FW	KLOSE Miroslav	KLOSE	09-06-1978	Werder Bremen	182	74	7	587	5			62	29
12	GK	KAHN Oliver	KAHN	15-06-1969	Bayern München	188	88	1	90				86	0
13	MF	BALLACK Michael	BALLACK	26-09-1976	Bayern München	189	80	5	510		1		70	31
14	FW	ASAMOAH Gerald	ASAMOAH	03-10-1978	Schalke 04	180	85	1	17				41	6
15	MF	HITZLSPERGER Thomas	HITZLSPERGER	05-04-1982	VfB Stuttgart	183	77	1	11				16	0
16	DF	LAHM Philipp	LAHM	11-11-1983	Bayern München	170	62	7	690	1			25	2
17	DF	MERTESACKER Per	MERTESACKER	29-09-1984	Hannover 96	196	85	6	600				29	1
18	MF	BOROWSKI Tim	BOROWSKI	02-05-1980	Werder Bremen	194	84	6	246		2		26	2
19	MF	SCHNEIDER Bernd	SCHNEIDER	17-11-1973	Bayer Leverkusen	176	74	7	577				71	1
20	FW	PODOLSKI Lukas	PODOLSKI	04-06-1985	1.FC Köln	180	81	7	636	3	1		32	15
21	DF	METZELDER Christoph	METZELDER	05-11-1980	Borussia Dortmund	193	84	6	600		2		28	0
22	MF	ODONKOR David	ODONKOR	21-02-1984	Borussia Dortmund	174	74	4	122		2		5	0
23	GK	HILDEBRAND Timo	HILDEBRAND	05-04-1979	VfB Stuttgart	185	77	0	0				3	0

GHA – GHANA SQUAD 2006 FIFA WORLD CUP™

No	Pos	Name	Shirt Name	DoB	Club	Cms	Kg	Games	Mins	Goals	Y	R	Cap	Gls
1	GK	ADJEI Sammy	ADJEI	01-09-1980	Ashdod	186	80	0	0				31	0
2	DF	SARPEI Hans	SARPEI	28-06-1976	VfL Wolfsburg	178	68	0	0				7	0
3	FW	GYAN Asamoah	ASAMOAH	22-11-1985	Modena	186	77	3	255	1	2	1	16	9
4	DF	KUFFOUR Samuel	KUFFOUR	03-09-1976	Roma	178	75	1	90				59	3
5	DF	MENSAH John	MENSAH	29-11-1982	Stade Rennais	177	72	4	360		1		37	0
6	DF	PAPPOE Emmanuel	PAPPOE	03-03-1981	Hapoel Kfar Saba	177	78	2	135				29	0
7	DF	SHILLA Illiasu	ALHASSAN	26-10-1982	Asante Kotoko	188	81	4	315		1		6	0
8	MF	ESSIEN Michael	ESSIEN	03-12-1982	Chelsea	180	77	3	270		2		20	4
9	MF	BOATENG Derek	BOATENG D.	02-05-1983	AIK Stockholm	185	78	3	120		1		14	3
10	MF	APPIAH Stephen	S. APPIAH	24-12-1980	Fenerbahçe	178	77	4	360	1	2		46	12
11	MF	MUNTARI Sulley	MUNTARI	27-08-1984	Udinese	180	76	3	270	1	3		19	6
12	FW	TACHIE-MENSAH Alex	TACHIE MENSAH	15-02-1977	St Gall	178	75	3	31				8	0
13	DF	MOHAMED Habib	HABIB	10-12-1983	King Faisal	178	69	2	180		1		3	0
14	FW	AMOAH Matthew	AMOAH	24-10-1980	Borussia Dortmund	175	66	4	277				20	7
15	DF	PANTSIL John	PAINTSIL	15-06-1981	Hapoel Tel-Aviv	178	80	4	360		1		25	0
16	GK	OWU George	OWU	07-07-1982	AshantiGold	179	70	0	0				6	0
17	DF	QUAYE Daniel	QUAYE	25-12-1980	Hearts	178	68	0	0				7	0
18	MF	ADDO Eric	E. ADDO	12-11-1978	PSV Eindhoven	182	68	4	191		1		10	0
19	FW	PIMPONG Razak	PIMPONG	30-12-1982	FC København	173	72	3	117				7	0
20	MF	ADDO Otto	O. ADDO	09-06-1975	Mainz 05	188	80	2	90		1		15	1
21	DF	ISSAH Ahmed	ISSAH	24-05-1982	Randers FC	185	80	0	0				10	0
22	GK	KINGSON Richard	KINGSON	13-06-1978	Ankaraspor	182	83	4	360				37	0
23	MF	DRAMAN Haminu	DRAMAN	01-04-1986	Crvena Zvezda	173	70	2	170	1			9	1

IRN – IRAN SQUAD 2006 FIFA WORLD CUP™

No	Pos	Name	Shirt Name	DoB	Club	Cms	Kg	Games	Mins	Goals	Y	R	Cap	Gls
1	GK	MIRZAPOUR Ebrahim	E.MIRZAPOUR	16-09-1978	Foolad Ahvaz	192	85	3	270				67	0
2	MF	MAHDAVIKIA Mehdi	M.MAHDAVIKIA	24-07-1977	Hamburger SV	176	73	3	270				92	11
3	DF	BAKHTIARIZADEH Sohrab	S.BAKHTIARIH	11-09-1977	Saba Battery Tehran	185	76	2	92	1			33	3
4	DF	GOLMOHAMMADI Yahya	Y.GOLMOHAMMADI	19-03-1971	Saba Battery Tehran	178	76	2	178	1	1		71	5
5	DF	REZAEI Rahman	R.REZAEI	20-02-1975	Messina	178	72	3	270				46	3
6	MF	NEKOUNAM Javad	J.NEKOUNAM	07-09-1980	Al Sharjah	180	78	2	180		2		73	12
7	MF	ZANDI Ferydoon	F.ZANDI	26-04-1979	1.FC Kaiserslautern	184	80	2	115	1			12	1
8	MF	KARIMI Ali	A.KARIMI	08-11-1978	Bayern München	178	79	2	128				92	33
9	FW	HASHEMIAN Vahid	V.HASHEMIAN	21-07-1976	Hannover 96	182	78	3	219				31	11
10	FW	DAEI Ali	A.DAEI	21-03-1969	Saba Battery Tehran	192	80	2	180				149	109
11	FW	KHATIBI Rasoul	R.PAKIKHATIBI	22-09-1978	Pas Tehran	172	71	2	75				14	1
12	GK	ROUDBARIAN Hassan	H.ROUDBARIAN	06-07-1978	Pas Tehran	182	80	0	0				3	0
13	DF	KAABI Hossein	H.KAEBI	23-09-1985	Foolad Ahvaz	167	63	3	247		1		47	1
14	MF	TEYMOURIAN Andranik	ANDERANIK T.	06-03-1983	AbooMoslem	180	73	3	270		1		10	1
15	FW	BORHANI Arash	A.BORHANI	14-09-1983	Pas Tehran	175	72	2	32				22	8
16	FW	ENAYATI Reza	R.ENAYATI	23-09-1976	Esteghlal Tehran	178	75	0	0				15	4
17	FW	KAZEMEIAN Javad	J.KAZEMIAN	23-04-1981	Pirouzi	174	69	0	0				25	0
18	MF	NAVIDKIA Moharram	M.NAVIDKIA	01-11-1982	Sepahan Isfahan	181	72	0	0				24	1
19	DF	SADEQI Amir Hossein	A.SADEGHI	06-09-1981	Esteghlal Ahvaz	180	78	0	0				1	0
20	DF	NOSRATI Mohammad	M.NOSRATI	11-01-1982	Pas Tehran	180	78	3	184				47	3
21	MF	MADANCHI Mehrzad	M.MADANCHI	10-01-1985	Pirouzi	180	74	3	183		2		3	0
22	GK	TALEBLOO Vahid	V.TALEBLOO	26-05-1982	Esteghlal Tehran	185	75	0	0				1	0
23	MF	SHOJAEI Masoud	M.SOLEIMANI	09-06-1984	Saipa Karadj	184	73	1	77				4	0

ITA – ITALY SQUAD 2006 FIFA WORLD CUP™

No	Pos	Name	Shirt Name	DoB	Club	Cms	Kg	Games	Mins	Goals	Y	R	Cap	Gls
1	GK	BUFFON Gianluigi	BUFFON	28-01-1978	Juventus	190	83	7	690				67	0
2	DF	ZACCARDO Cristian	ZACCARDO	21-12-1981	Palermo	184	77	3	157				15	1
3	DF	GROSSO Fabio	GROSSO	28-11-1977	Palermo	190	82	6	600	1		1	23	2
4	MF	DE ROSSI Daniele	DE ROSSI	24-07-1983	Roma	182	80	3	177		1	1	20	3
5	DF	CANNAVARO Fabio	CANNAVARO	13-09-1973	Juventus	175	72	7	690				100	1
6	DF	BARZAGLI Andrea	BARZAGLI	08-05-1981	Palermo	186	79	2	124				10	0
7	FW	DEL PIERO Alessandro	DEL PIERO	09-11-1974	Juventus	173	73	5	169	1			79	27
8	MF	GATTUSO Gennaro	GATTUSO	09-01-1978	Milan	177	77	6	552			2	47	1
9	FW	TONI Luca	TONI	26-05-1977	Fiorentina	194	89	6	483	2			24	9
10	MF	TOTTI Francesco	TOTTI	27-09-1976	Roma	180	82	7	467	1	1		58	9
11	FW	GILARDINO Alberto	GILARDINO	05-07-1982	Milan	185	78	5	305	1			20	8
12	GK	PERUZZI Angelo	PERUZZI	16-02-1970	Lazio	181	88	0	0				31	0
13	DF	NESTA Alessandro	NESTA	19-03-1976	Milan	187	79	3	197				77	0
14	GK	AMELIA Marco	AMELIA	02-04-1982	Livorno	190	88	0	0				1	0
15	FW	IAQUINTA Vincenzo	IAQUINTA	21-11-1979	Udinese	186	77	5	188	1			17	1
16	MF	CAMORANESI Mauro	CAMORANESI	04-10-1976	Juventus	174	70	5	353			2	26	1
17	MF	BARONE Simone	BARONE	30-04-1978	Palermo	180	75	2	38				15	1
18	FW	INZAGHI Filippo	INZAGHI	09-08-1973	Milan	181	74	1	30	1			50	22
19	DF	ZAMBROTTA Gianluca	ZAMBROTTA	19-02-1977	Juventus	181	76	6	600	1	3		58	2
20	MF	PERROTTA Simone	PERROTTA	17-09-1977	Roma	178	72	7	615				31	1
21	MF	PIRLO Andrea	PIRLO	19-05-1979	Milan	177	65	7	668	1			31	5
22	GK	ODDO Massimo	ODDO	14-06-1976	Lazio	183	75	1	22				21	0
23	DF	MATERAZZI Marco	MATERAZZI	19-08-1973	Internazionale	193	82	4	363	2		1	32	2

JPN – JAPAN SQUAD 2006 FIFA WORLD CUP™

No	Pos	Name	Shirt Name	DoB	Club	Cms	Kg	Games	Mins	Goals	Y	R	Cap	Gls
1	GK	NARAZAKI Seigo	NARAZAKI	15-04-1976	Nagoya Grampus Eight	185	76	0	0				50	0
2	DF	MONIWA Teruyuki	MONIWA	08-09-1981	FC Tokyo	181	77	1	35				10	1
3	DF	KOMANO Yuichi	KOMANO	25-07-1981	Sanfrecce Hiroshima	171	71	1	90				9	0
4	MF	ENDO Yasuhito	ENDO	28-01-1980	Gamba Osaka	177	75	0	0				40	3
5	DF	MIYAMOTO Tsuneyasu	MIYAMOTO	07-02-1977	Gamba Osaka	176	72	2	180		2		70	3
6	DF	NAKATA Koji	K. NAKATA	09-07-1979	Basel	182	74	1	34				56	2
7	MF	NAKATA Hidetoshi	NAKATA	22-01-1977	Bolton Wanderers	175	72	3	270				77	11
8	MF	OGASAWARA Mitsuo	OGASAWARA	05-04-1979	Kashima Antlers	173	72	2	146				53	7
9	FW	TAKAHARA Naohiro	TAKAHARA	04-06-1979	Hamburger SV	180	74	3	181		1		44	17
10	MF	NAKAMURA Shunsuke	NAKAMURA	24-06-1978	Celtic	178	69	3	270	1			63	16
11	FW	MAKI Seiichiro	MAKI	07-08-1980	JEF United Chiba	184	77	1	60				11	3
12	GK	DOI Yoichi	DOI	25-07-1973	FC Tokyo	184	83	0	0				4	0
13	FW	YANAGISAWA Atsushi	YANAGISAWA	27-05-1977	Kashima Antlers	177	75	2	140				58	17
14	DF	SANTOS Alessandro	ALEX	20-07-1977	Urawa Reds	178	69	3	270				75	5
15	MF	FUKUNISHI Takashi	FUKUNISHI	01-09-1976	Jubilo Iwata	181	74	2	135				64	7
16	FW	OGURO Masashi	OGURO	04-05-1980	Grenoble	177	71	3	30				21	5
17	MF	INAMOTO Junichi	INAMOTO	18-09-1979	West Bromwich Albion	180	76	2	135				65	4
18	MF	ONO Shinji	ONO	27-09-1979	Urawa Reds	175	74	1	11				55	6
19	DF	TSUBOI Keisuke	TSUBOI	16-09-1979	Urawa Reds	179	67	2	146				35	0
20	FW	TAMADA Keiji	TAMADA	11-04-1980	Nagoya Grampus Eight	173	63	2	119	1			41	9
21	DF	KAJI Akira	KAJI	13-01-1980	Gamba Osaka	175	67	2	180			1	44	1
22	DF	NAKAZAWA Yuji	NAKAZAWA	25-02-1978	Yokohama F Marinos	187	78	3	270				52	9
23	GK	KAWAGUCHI Yoshikatsu	KAWAGUCHI	15-08-1975	Jubilo Iwata	179	78	3	270				92	0

KOR – KOREA REPUBLIC SQUAD 2006 FIFA WORLD CUP™

No	Pos	Name	Shirt Name	DoB	Club	Cms	Kg	Games	Mins	Goals	Y	R	Cap	Gls
1	GK	LEE Woon Jae	WOONJAE	26-04-1973	Suwon Bluewings	182	82	3	270				100	0
2	DF	KIM Young Chul	YOUNGCHUL	30-06-1976	S'nam Ilhwa Chunma	183	80	2	180			1	14	1
3	DF	KIM Dong Jin	DONGJIN	29-01-1982	FC Seoul	183	72	2	180	1			36	2
4	DF	CHOI Jin Cheul	JINCHEUL	26-03-1971	Chonbuk Hyundai	187	80	3	270				65	4
5	MF	KIM Nam II	NAMIL	14-03-1977	Suwon Bluewings	180	75	3	202				69	1
6	DF	KIM Jin Kyu	JINKYU	16-02-1985	Jubilo Iwata	184	80	2	135			1	25	3
7	MF	PARK Ji Sung	JISUNG	25-02-1981	Manchester United	178	70	3	270	1			63	6
8	MF	KIM Do Heon	DOHEON	14-07-1982	S'nam Ilhwa Chunma	175	67	0	0				32	5
9	FW	AHN Jung Hwan	JUNGHWAN	27-01-1976	MSV Duisburg	177	71	3	90	1		1	64	16
10	FW	PARK Chu Young	CHUYOUNG	10-07-1985	FC Seoul	182	70	1	66	1			19	5
11	FW	SEOL Ki Hyeon	KIHYEON	08-01-1979	Wolverhampton	184	73	2	69				69	13
12	MF	LEE Young Pyo	YOUNGPYO	23-04-1977	Tottenham Hotspur	176	66	3	243				88	5
13	MF	LEE Eul Yong	EULYONG	08-09-1975	Trabzonspor	176	69	2	113				49	3
14	FW	LEE Chun Soo	CHUNSOO	09-07-1981	Ulsan Hyundai	175	65	3	252	1	2		65	7
15	MF	BAEK Ji Hoon	JIHOON	28-02-1985	FC Seoul	174	60	0	0				12	0
16	FW	CHUNG Kyung Ho	KYUNGHO	22-05-1980	Gwangju Sangmu	179	70	0	0				40	5
17	MF	LEE Ho	HO	22-10-1984	Ulsan Hyundai	182	76	3	249			1	14	0
18	DF	KIM Sang Sik	SANGSIK	17-12-1976	S'nam Ilhwa Chunma	184	72	2	28				44	2
19	FW	CHO Jae Jin	JAEJIN	09-07-1981	Shimizu S-Pulse	185	81	3	263				24	5
20	FW	KIM Yong Dae	YONGDAE	11-10-1979	S'nam Ilhwa Chunma	186	73	0	0				15	0
21	GK	KIM Young Kwang	YOUNGKWANG	28-06-1983	Chunnam Dragons	184	80	0	0				6	0
22	DF	SONG Chong Gug	CHONGGUG	20-02-1979	Suwon Bluewings	175	71	1	90				52	3
23	DF	CHO Won Hee	WONHEE	17-04-1983	Suwon Bluewings	177	72	0	0				13	1

KSA – SAUDI ARABIA SQUAD 2006 FIFA WORLD CUP™

No	Pos	Name	Shirt Name	DoB	Club	Cms	Kg	Games	Mins	Goals	Y	R	Cap	Gls
1	GK	AL DEAYEA Mohammed	ALDEAYEA	02-08-1972	Al Hilal	188	77	0	0				181	0
2	DF	DOKHI Ahmed	DOKHI	25-10-1976	Al Ittihad	175	72	3	235		1		70	4
3	DF	TUKAR Redha	TUKER	29-11-1975	Al Ittihad	179	81	3	270				39	6
4	DF	AL MONTASHARI Hamad	ALMONTASHARI	22-06-1982	Al Ittihad	181	72	3	270				34	6
5	DF	AL QADI Naif	N. ALQADI	03-04-1979	Al Ahli	176	74	0	0				28	2
6	MF	AL GHAMDI Omar	OMAR	11-04-1979	Al Hilal	170	68	2	180		1		40	5
7	MF	AMEEN Mohammed	AMEEN	29-04-1980	Al Ittihad	175	66	2	70				18	7
8	MF	NOOR Mohammed	NOOR	26-02-1978	Al Ittihad	186	70	3	242				65	22
9	FW	AL JABER Sami	ALJABER	11-12-1972	Al Hilal	176	72	3	89	1		1	162	44
10	MF	AL SHLHOUB Mohammad	ALSHALHOUB	08-12-1980	Al Hilal	163	59	0	0				48	15
11	FW	AL HARTHI Saad	SAAD	03-02-1984	Al Nasr	178	64	1	90				15	12
12	DF	KHATHRAN Abdulaziz	ALKHATHRAN	31-07-1973	Al Hilal	169	61	2	125				20	0
13	DF	SULIMANI Hussein	SULAIMANI	21-01-1977	Al Ahli	174	70	3	261				99	3
14	MF	KARIRI Saud	KARIRI	08-07-1980	Al Ittihad	184	68	3	270		1		36	12
15	DF	AL BAHRI Ahmed	ALBAHRI	18-09-1980	Al Shabab	178	68	0	0				11	3
16	MF	AZIZ Khaled	AZIZ	14-07-1981	Al Hilal	172	72	3	193				16	2
17	DF	AL BISHI Mohamed	ALBISHI	03-05-1987	Al Ahli	183	83	0	0				0	0
18	MF	AL TEMYAT Nawaf	N. ALTEMYAT	28-06-1976	Al Hilal	176	70	2	144		1		57	13
19	MF	MASSAD Mohammed	MASSAD	17-02-1983	Al Ahli	176	62	1	9				5	0
20	FW	AL KAHTANI Yasser	YASSER	10-10-1982	Al Hilal	166	65	2	172	1			47	33
21	GK	ZAID Mabrouk	ZAID	11-02-1979	Al Ittihad	185	62	3	270				35	0
22	GK	KHOJAH Mohammad	KHOJAH	15-03-1982	Al Shabab	189	86	0	0				8	0
23	FW	AL HAWSAWI Malek	MALEK	10-08-1981	Al Ahli	178	68	3	80				7	0

MEX – MEXICO SQUAD 2006 FIFA WORLD CUP™

No	Pos	Name	Shirt Name	DoB	Club	Cms	Kg	Games	Mins	Goals	Y	R	Cap	Gls
1	GK	SANCHEZ Oswaldo	O. SANCHEZ	21-09-1973	Guadalajara	184	79	4	390				74	0
2	DF	SUAREZ Claudio	C. SUAREZ	17-12-1968	Chivas USA	181	75	0	0				178	6
3	DF	SALCIDO Carlos	C. SALCIDO	02-04-1980	Guadalajara	174	70	4	390		1		36	2
4	DF	MARQUEZ Rafael	R. MARQUEZ	13-02-1979	Barcelona	182	74	4	390	1	2		69	8
5	DF	OSORIO Ricardo	R. OSORIO	30-03-1980	Cruz Azul	173	68	4	390				43	1
6	MF	TORRADO Gerardo	G. TORRADO	30-04-1979	Cruz Azul	172	66	3	217	2			59	2
7	MF	ZINHA	A. NAELSON	23-05-1976	Toluca	163	66	4	188	1	1		36	5
8	MF	PARDO Pavel	P. PARDO	26-07-1976	América	174	69	4	308				129	5
9	FW	BORGETTI Jared	J. BORGETTI	14-08-1973	Bolton Wanderers	182	78	2	172				77	38
10	FW	FRANCO Guillermo	G. FRANCO	03-11-1976	Villarreal	184	77	3	129				10	2
11	FW	MORALES Ramon	R. MORALES	10-10-1975	Guadalajara	168	62	2	86				48	5
12	GK	CORONA Jose	J. DE J. CORONA	26-01-1981	Tecos UAG	181	82	0	0				6	0
13	GK	OCHOA Guillermo	G. OCHOA	13-07-1985	América	185	73	0	0				1	0
14	DF	PINEDA Gonzalo	G. PINEDA	19-10-1982	Guadalajara	177	67	4	291		1		34	1
15	DF	CASTRO Jose Antonio	J.A. CASTRO	11-08-1980	América	177	63	2	141		1		14	0
16	DF	MENDEZ Mario	M. MENDEZ	01-06-1979	Monterrey	175	67	4	380				36	0
17	FW	FONSECA Jose	F. FONSECA	02-10-1979	Cruz Azul	184	79	4	264	1	1		33	20
18	DF	GUARDADO Andres	A. GUARDADO	28-09-1986	Atlas	169	61	1	66				8	0
19	FW	BRAVO Omar	O. BRAVO	04-03-1980	Guadalajara	174	71	3	270	2			36	9
20	MF	GARCIA Rafael	R. GARCIA	14-08-1974	Atlas	175	66	0	0				52	3
21	FW	ARELLANO Jesus	J. ARELLANO	08-05-1973	Monterrey	171	65	1	38				70	7
22	DF	RODRIGUEZ Francisco	F. J. RODRIGUEZ	20-10-1981	Guadalajara	191	80	1	45		1		33	1
23	MF	PEREZ Luis	L. PEREZ	12-01-1981	Monterrey	170	70	2	106			1	54	8

NED – NETHERLANDS SQUAD 2006 FIFA WORLD CUP™

No	Pos	Name	Shirt Name	DoB	Club	Cms	Kg	Games	Mins	Goals	Y	R	Cap	Gls
1	GK	VAN DER SAR Edwin	VAN DER SAR	29-10-1970	Manchester United	197	84	4	360				113	0
2	DF	JALIENS Kew	JALIENS	15-09-1978	AZ Alkmaar	183	68	1	90				2	0
3	DF	BOULAHROUZ Khalid	BOULAHROUZ	28-12-1981	Hamburger SV	191	86	4	202	1	1		14	0
4	DF	MATHIJSEN Joris	MATHIJSEN	05-04-1980	AZ Alkmaar	182	72	3	232	1			11	0
5	DF	VAN BRONCKHORST Giovanni	V. BRONCKHORST	05-02-1975	Barcelona	178	76	3	269	1	1		60	3
6	MF	LANDZAAT Denny	LANDZAAT	06-05-1976	AZ Alkmaar	178	70	3	70				26	1
7	FW	KUYT Dirk	KUYT	22-07-1980	Feyenoord	184	77	3	201	1			22	4
8	MF	COCU Phillip	COCU	29-10-1970	PSV Eindhoven	182	74	4	354				101	10
9	FW	VAN NISTELROOIJ Ruud	V. NISTELROOY	01-07-1976	Manchester United	188	80	3	198	1			54	28
10	MF	VAN DER VAART Rafael	VAN DER VAART	11-02-1983	Hamburger SV	175	70	3	164	1			38	6
11	FW	ROBBEN Arjen	ROBBEN	23-01-1984	Chelsea	181	80	3	270	1	1		23	7
12	DF	KROMKAMP Jan	KROMKAMP	17-08-1980	Liverpool	184	83	0	0				11	0
13	DF	OOIJER Andre	OOIJER	11-07-1974	PSV Eindhoven	185	74	4	360				23	2
14	DF	HEITINGA John	HEITINGA	15-11-1983	Ajax	180	75	3	158	1			21	2
15	DF	DE CLER Tim	DE CLER	08-11-1978	AZ Alkmaar	179	69	1	90				4	0
16	MF	MADURO Hedwiges	MADURO	13-02-1985	Ajax	185	79	1	4				12	0
17	FW	VAN PERSIE Robin	V. PERSIE	06-08-1983	Arsenal	183	71	4	337	1			14	2
18	MF	VAN BOMMEL Mark	V. BOMMEL	22-04-1977	Barcelona	187	80	3	217		2		40	7
19	FW	VENNEGOOR of HESSELINK Jan	VENNEGOOR	07-11-1978	PSV Eindhoven	190	88	1	6				8	0
20	MF	SNEIJDER Wesley	SNEIJDER	09-06-1984	Ajax	170	72	4	316	1			27	5
21	FW	BABEL Ryan	BABEL	19-12-1986	Ajax	185	79	1	34				7	3
22	GK	TIMMER Henk	TIMMER	03-12-1971	AZ Alkmaar	188	90	0	0				2	0
23	GK	STEKELENBURG Maarten	STEKELENBURG	22-09-1982	Ajax	197	92	0	0				2	0

PAR – PARAGUAY SQUAD 2006 FIFA WORLD CUP™

No	Pos	Name	Shirt Name	DoB	Club	Cms	Kg	Games	Mins	Goals	Y	R	Cap	Gls
1	GK	VILLAR Justo	VILLAR	30-06-1977	Newells Old Boys	180	83	1	8				40	0
2	DF	NUNEZ Jorge	NUÑEZ	22-01-1978	Estudiantes LP	176	78	3	188		1		18	1
3	DF	TOLEDO Delio	TOLEDO	10-02-1976	Real Zaragoza	182	78	1	82				31	4
4	DF	GAMARRA Carlos	GAMARRA	17-02-1971	Palmeiras	180	86	3	270				109	12
5	DF	CACERES Julio Cesar	CÁCERES	05-10-1979	River Plate	181	77	3	257				35	2
6	MF	BONET Carlos	BONET	02-10-1977	Libertad	176	76	2	149				31	1
7	MF	CABANAS Salvador	CABAÑAS	05-08-1980	Jaguares Chiapas	173	82	0	0				15	1
8	MF	BARRETO Edgar	BARRETO	15-07-1984	NEC Nijmegen	178	81	2	99		1		17	0
9	FW	SANTA CRUZ Roque	SANTACRUZ	16-08-1981	Bayern München	191	86	3	243				46	13
10	MF	ACUNA Roberto	ACUÑA	25-03-1972	Deportivo La Coruña	175	82	3	270		1		96	5
11	MF	GAVILAN Diego	GAVILAN	01-03-1980	Newells Old Boys	176	75	0	0				39	0
12	GK	GOMEZ Derlis	GOMEZ	02-11-1972	Sportivo Luqueño	181	86	0	0				5	0
13	MF	PAREDES Carlos	PAREDES	16-07-1976	Reggina	179	82	3	270		2		71	10
14	DF	DA SILVA Paulo	DA SILVA	01-02-1980	Toluca	184	83	1	1				34	0
15	DF	MANZUR Julio	MANZUR	22-01-1981	Santos	187	83	1	13				14	0
16	MF	RIVEROS Cristian	RIVEROS	16-10-1982	Libertad	179	77	2	152				11	0
17	MF	MONTIEL Jose	MONTIEL	19-03-1988	Olimpia Asuncion	175	71	0	0				6	0
18	FW	VALDEZ Nelson	H. VALDEZ	28-11-1983	Werder Bremen	178	71	3	246		1		14	4
19	MF	DOS SANTOS Julio	DOS SANTOS	07-05-1983	Bayern München	190	85	2	118		1		19	5
20	FW	LOPEZ Dante	DANTE	16-08-1983	Genoa	185	81	1	27				8	3
21	DF	CANIZA Denis	CAÑIZA	29-08-1974	Cruz Azul	174	73	3	269		1		77	1
22	GK	BOBADILLA Aldo	BOBADILLA	20-04-1976	Libertad	192	88	3	262				8	0
23	FW	CUEVAS Nelson	CUEVAS	10-01-1980	Pachuca	174	69	2	46	1			37	6

POL – POLAND SQUAD 2006 FIFA WORLD CUP™

No	Pos	Name	Shirt Name	DoB	Club	Cms	Kg	Games	Mins	Goals	Y	R	Cap	Gls
1	GK	BORUC Artur	BORUC	20-02-1980	Celtic	192	85	3	270		2		20	0
2	DF	JOP Mariusz	JOP	03-08-1978	FK Moskva	188	81	1	90				13	0
3	DF	GANCARCZYK Seweryn	GANCARCZYK	22-11-1981	Metalist Kharkiv	181	71	0	0				2	0
4	DF	BASZCZYNSKI Marcin	BASZCZYNSKI	07-06-1977	Wisla Krakow	183	70	3	270		1		35	1
5	MF	KOSOWSKI Kamil	KOSOWSKI	30-08-1977	Southampton	186	78	1	12				46	4
6	DF	BAK Jacek	BAK	24-03-1973	Al Rayyan	187	78	3	270		1		75	2
7	MF	SOBOLEWSKI Radoslaw	SOBOLEWSKI	13-12-1976	Wisla Krakow	182	79	2	142		1	1	21	1
8	MF	KRZYNOWEK Jacek	KRZYNOWEK	15-05-1976	Bayer Leverkusen	180	73	3	245		1		61	9
9	FW	ZURAWSKI Maciej	ZURAWSKI	12-09-1976	Celtic	180	74	3	218				53	15
10	MF	SZYMKOWIAK Miroslaw	SZYMKOWIAK	12-11-1976	Trabzonspor	179	72	2	180				31	3
11	FW	RASIAK Grzegorz	RASIAK	12-01-1979	Southampton	190	84	1	5				31	8
12	GK	KUSZCZAK Tomasz	KUSZCZAK	20-03-1982	West Bromwich Albion	190	84	0	0				4	0
13	MF	MILA Sebastian	MILA	10-07-1982	FK Austria Vienna	178	67	0	0				27	6
14	DF	ZEWLAKOW Michal	ZEWLAKOW	22-04-1976	RSC Anderlecht	183	78	3	263				59	1
15	MF	SMOLAREK Ebi	SMOLAREK	09-01-1981	Borussia Dortmund	176	66	3	265		1		16	4
16	MF	RADOMSKI Arkadiusz	RADOMSKI	27-06-1977	FK Austria Vienna	180	81	3	244		1		23	0
17	DF	DUDKA Dariusz	DUDKA	09-12-1983	Wisla Krakow	182	78	1	7				8	0
18	DF	LEWANDOWSKI Mariusz	LEWANDOWSKI	18-05-1979	Shakhtar Donetsk	185	83	2	39				27	1
19	DF	BOSACKI Bartosz	BOSACKI	20-12-1975	Lech Poznan	189	81	2	180	2			13	2
20	MF	GIZA Piotr	GIZA	28-02-1980	Cracovia	179	75	0	0				4	0
21	FW	JELEN Ireneusz	JELEN	09-04-1981	Wisla Plock	184	74	3	202				11	2
22	GK	FABIANSKI Lukasz	FABIANSKI	18-04-1985	Legia Warsaw	190	83	0	0				2	0
23	FW	BROZEK Pawel	BROZEK	21-04-1983	Wisla Krakow	180	72	3	53				7	1

POR – PORTUGAL SQUAD 2006 FIFA WORLD CUP™

No	Pos	Name	Shirt Name	DoB	Club	Cms	Kg	Games	Mins	Goals	Y	R	Cap	Gls
1	GK	RICARDO	RICARDO	11-02-1976	Sporting CL	188	80	7	660		1		56	0
2	DF	PAULO FERREIRA	P.FERREIRA	18-01-1979	Chelsea	181	76	3	147		1		33	0
3	DF	CANEIRA	CANEIRA	09-02-1979	Sporting CL	178	75	1	90				15	0
4	DF	RICARDO COSTA	R.COSTA	16-05-1981	Porto	183	80	1	90				4	0
5	DF	FERNANDO MEIRA	F.MEIRA	05-06-1978	VfB Stuttgart	192	81	7	660				37	2
6	MF	COSTINHA	COSTINHA	01-12-1974	Dynamo Moskva	180	74	5	286		2	1	49	2
7	FW	LUIS FIGO	FIGO	04-11-1972	Internazionale	180	75	7	531		1		127	32
8	MF	PETIT	PETIT	25-09-1976	Benfica	178	68	6	394		2		42	4
9	FW	PAULETA	PAULETA	28-04-1973	Paris St-Germain	181	79	6	434	1	1		88	47
10	MF	HUGO VIANA	H.VIANA	15-01-1983	Valencia	179	77	2	53				23	1
11	FW	SIMAO SABROSA	SIMÃO	31-10-1979	Benfica	170	64	7	407	1			50	10
12	GK	QUIM	QUIM	13-11-1975	Benfica	184	76	0	0				24	0
13	DF	MIGUEL	MIGUEL	04-01-1980	Valencia	175	64	6	513		1		34	1
14	DF	NUNO VALENTE	N.VALENTE	12-09-1974	Everton	182	78	6	549		2		29	1
15	FW	BOA MORTE	BOA MORTE	04-08-1977	Fulham	180	79	1	10				25	1
16	DF	RICARDO CARVALHO	R.CARVALHO	18-05-1978	Chelsea	183	79	6	570		2		30	1
17	FW	CRISTIANO RONALDO	C.RONALDO	05-02-1985	Manchester United	184	75	6	484	1	1		38	12
18	MF	MANICHE	MANICHE	11-11-1977	Chelsea	179	77	7	565	2	2		38	6
19	MF	TIAGO	TIAGO	02-05-1981	Olympique Lyonnais	183	79	5	263				27	0
20	MF	DECO	DECO	27-08-1977	Barcelona	176	73	4	338	1	1	1	39	3
21	FW	NUNO GOMES	NUNO GOMES	05-07-1976	Benfica	181	76	2	42	1	1		55	24
22	GK	PAULO SANTOS	P. SANTOS	11-12-1972	Sporting Braga	184	86	0	0				1	0
23	FW	HELDER POSTIGA	H.POSTIGA	02-08-1982	Saint-Etienne	182	79	3	118				27	9

SCG - SERBIA AND MONTENEGRO SQUAD 2006 FIFA WORLD CUP™

No	Pos	Name	Shirt Name	DoB	Club	Cms	Kg	Games	Mins	Goals	Y	R	Cap	Gls
1	GK	JEVRIC Dragoslav	JEVRIC	08-07-1974	Ankaraspor	186	82	3	270				43	0
2	MF	ERGIC Ivan	ERGIC	21-01-1981	Basel	185	84	2	135				3	0
3	DF	DRAGUTINOVIC Ivica	DRAGUTINOVIC	13-11-1975	Sevilla	184	86	1	90		1		27	0
4	MF	DULJAJ Igor	DULJAJ	29-10-1979	Shakhtar Donetsk	175	72	3	270		1		40	2
5	DF	VIDIC Nemanja	VIDIC	21-10-1981	Manchester United	188	83	0	0				20	1
6	DF	GAVRANCIC Goran	GAVRANCIC	02-08-1978	Dynamo Kyiv	191	84	3	270		2		28	0
7	MF	KOROMAN Ognjen	KOROMAN	19-09-1978	Portsmouth	179	71	2	97		2		27	1
8	FW	KEZMAN Mateja	KEZMAN	12-04-1979	Atlético Madrid	180	71	2	132			1	49	17
9	FW	MILOSEVIC Savo	MILOSEVIC	02-09-1973	Osasuna	187	81	3	138				101	35
10	MF	STANKOVIC Dejan	STANKOVIC	11-09-1978	Internazionale	181	75	3	270		1		61	11
11	MF	DJORDJEVIC Predrag	P. DJORDJEVIC	04-08-1972	Olympiakos	184	75	3	270				37	1
12	GK	KOVACEVIC Oliver	KOVACEVIC	29-10-1974	CSKA Sofia	186	88	0	0				3	0
13	DF	BASTA Dusan	BASTA	18-08-1984	Crvena Zvezda	183	72	0	0				2	0
14	DF	DJORDJEVIC Nenad	N. DJORDJEVIC	07-08-1979	Partizan	183	76	2	133				17	1
15	DF	DUDIC Milan	DUDIC	01-11-1979	Crvena Zvezda	183	77	2	180		1		13	0
16	DF	PETKOVIC Dusan	PETKOVIC	13-06-1974	OFK Beograd	188	80	0	0				12	1
17	MF	NADJ Albert	NADJ	29-10-1974	Partizan	174	72	3	165		1	1	45	3
18	MF	VUKIC Zvonimir	VUKIC	19-07-1979	Partizan	182	72	1	20				26	6
19	FW	ZIGIC Nikola	ZIGIC	25-09-1980	Crvena Zvezda	202	96	2	112	1			13	4
20	DF	KRSTAJIC Mladen	KRSTAJIC	04-03-1974	Schalke 04	191	81	3	196		1		48	2
21	FW	LJUBOJA Danijel	LJUBOJA	04-09-1978	VfB Stuttgart	187	80	2	63				17	1
22	MF	ILIC Sasa	ILIC	30-12-1977	Galatasaray	178	72	1	90	1			33	6
23	GK	STOJKOVIC Vladimir	STOJKOVIC	28-07-1983	Crvena Zvezda	195	92	0	0				0	0

SUI - SWITZERLAND SQUAD 2006 FIFA WORLD CUP™

No	Pos	Name	Shirt Name	DoB	Club	Cms	Kg	Games	Mins	Goals	Y	R	Cap	Gls
1	GK	ZUBERBUEHLER Pascal	ZUBERBÜHLER	08-01-1971	Basel	197	98	4	390				44	0
2	DF	DJOUROU Johan	DJOUROU	18-01-1987	Arsenal	192	89	3	86		1		5	0
3	DF	MAGNIN Ludovic	MAGNIN	20-04-1979	VfB Stuttgart	185	76	3	300		1		33	2
4	DF	SENDEROS Philippe	SENDEROS	14-02-1985	Arsenal	190	87	3	233	1	1		15	3
5	MF	MARGAIRAZ Xavier	MARGAIRAZ	07-01-1984	FC Zurich	185	80	2	27				5	0
6	MF	VOGEL Johann	VOGEL	08-03-1977	Milan	175	70	4	390		1		89	2
7	MF	CABANAS Ricardo	CABANAS	17-01-1979	1.FC Köln	173	70	4	377		1		41	4
8	MF	WICKY Raphael	WICKY	26-04-1977	Hamburger SV	178	75	4	380		1		71	1
9	FW	FREI Alexander	FREI	15-07-1979	Stade Rennais	180	73	4	384	2	1		49	27
10	FW	GYGAX Daniel	GYGAX	28-08-1981	Lille	179	73	2	79				24	5
11	FW	STRELLER Marco	STRELLER	18-06-1981	1.FC Köln	195	82	3	125		1		13	3
12	GK	BENAGLIO Diego	BENAGLIO	08-09-1983	Nacional Funchal	193	83	0	0				1	0
13	DF	GRICHTING Stephane	GRICHTING	30-03-1979	Auxerre	184	80	1	86				7	0
14	FW	DEGEN David	DAVID DEGEN	15-02-1983	Basel	183	76	0	0				3	0
15	MF	DZEMAILI Blerim	DZEMAILI	12-04-1986	FC Zurich	179	73	0	0				3	0
16	MF	BARNETTA Tranquillo	BARNETTA	22-05-1985	Bayer Leverkusen	176	62	4	390	1	1		17	3
17	DF	SPYCHER Christoph	SPYCHER	30-03-1978	Eintracht Frankfurt	174	78	1	90		1		22	0
18	FW	LUSTRINELLI Mauro	LUSTRINELLI	26-02-1976	Sparta Praha	173	66	2	6				7	0
19	MF	BEHRAMI Valon	BEHRAMI	19-04-1985	Lazio	184	71	1	2				7	1
20	DF	MUELLER Patrick	MUELLER	17-12-1976	Olympique Lyonnais	182	69	4	375				68	3
21	GK	COLTORTI Fabio	COLTORTI	03-12-1980	Grasshopper-Club	197	98	0	0				2	0
22	MF	YAKIN Hakan	YAKIN	22-02-1977	Young Boys	180	79	3	180		1		49	14
23	DF	DEGEN Philipp	PHILIPP DEGEN	15-02-1983	Borussia Dortmund	184	78	4	390				19	0

SWE - SWEDEN SQUAD 2006 FIFA WORLD CUP™

No	Pos	Name	Shirt Name	DoB	Club	Cms	Kg	Games	Mins	Goals	Y	R	Cap	Gls
1	GK	ISAKSSON Andreas	ISAKSSON	03-10-1981	Stade Rennais	199	88	3	270				42	0
2	DF	NILSSON Mikael	NILSSON	24-06-1978	Panathinaikos	182	75	0	0				27	3
3	DF	MELLBERG Olof	MELLBERG	03-09-1977	Aston Villa	184	82	4	360				68	2
4	DF	LUCIC Teddy	LUCIC	15-04-1973	BK Häcken	187	75	4	305		1	1	85	0
5	DF	EDMAN Erik	EDMAN	11-11-1978	Stade Rennais	179	78	4	360				41	1
6	MF	LINDEROTH Tobias	LINDEROTH	21-04-1979	FC København	177	73	4	347		1		62	1
7	MF	ALEXANDERSSON Niclas	ALEXANDERSSON	29-12-1971	IFK Göteborg	181	73	4	360		1		91	7
8	MF	SVENSSON Anders	A. SVENSSON	17-07-1976	Elfsborg IF	177	82	1	62				67	13
9	MF	LJUNGBERG Fredrik	LJUNGBERG	16-04-1977	Arsenal	176	73	4	360	1	1		61	13
10	FW	IBRAHIMOVIC Zlatan	IBRAHIMOVIC	03-10-1981	Juventus	192	90	3	207				41	18
11	FW	LARSSON Henrik	LARSSON	20-09-1971	Barcelona	177	74	4	360	1	1		93	36
12	GK	ALVBAGE John	ALVBÅGE	10-08-1982	Viborg	187	83	0	0				2	0
13	DF	HANSSON Petter	HANSSON	14-12-1976	SC Heerenveen	186	84	1	51				14	0
14	DF	STENMAN Fredrik	STENMAN	02-06-1983	Bayer Leverkusen	187	82	0	0				1	0
15	DF	SVENSSON Karl	K. SVENSSON	21-03-1984	IFK Göteborg	189	82	0	0				1	0
16	MF	KALLSTROM Kim	KÄLLSTRÖM	24-08-1982	Stade Rennais	181	79	4	227				38	4
17	FW	ELMANDER Johan	ELMANDER	27-05-1981	Brøndby IF	188	79	2	19				20	7
18	FW	JONSON Mattias	JONSON	16-01-1974	Djurgårdens IF	178	76	4	140	1			57	9
19	MF	ANDERSSON Daniel	ANDERSSON	28-08-1977	Malmo	178	79	1	1				48	0
20	FW	ALLBACK Marcus	ALLBÄCK	05-07-1973	FC København	180	77	4	166	1	2		60	24
21	MF	WILHELMSSON Christian	WILHELMSSON	08-12-1979	RSC Anderlecht	177	67	4	220				33	2
22	FW	ROSENBERG Markus	ROSENBERG	27-09-1982	Ajax	184	81	0	0				8	3
23	GK	SHAABAN Rami	SHAABAN	30-06-1975	Fredrikstad FK	193	93	1	90				2	0

TOG - TOGO SQUAD 2006 FIFA WORLD CUP™

No	Pos	Name	Shirt Name	DoB	Club	Cms	Kg	Games	Mins	Goals	Y	R	Cap	Gls
1	GK	TCHAGNIROU Ouro-Nimini	TCHAGNIROU	31-12-1977	Djoliba	190	85	0	0				9	0
2	DF	NIBOMBE Dare	NIBOMBE	16-06-1980	Mons	196	91	3	270				19	1
3	DF	ABALO Jean-Paul	ABALO	26-06-1975	Apoel Nicosia	177	75	2	143		1		67	1
4	FW	ADEBAYOR Emmanuel	ADEBAYOR	26-02-1984	Arsenal	190	70	3	255	1			32	12
5	DF	TCHANGAI Massamasso	TCHANGAI	08-08-1978	Benevento	183	73	3	270	1			37	5
6	MF	AZIAWONOU Yao	AZIAWONOU	30-11-1979	Young Boys Bern	185	82	2	94	1			34	1
7	FW	SALIFOU Moustapha	SALIFOU M.	01-06-1983	Stade Brestois	180	76	3	241		2		37	4
8	MF	AGBOH Kuami	AGBOH	28-12-1977	Beveren	177	72	1	25				5	0
9	MF	DOSSEVI Thomas	DOSSEVI	06-03-1979	Valenciennes	183	82	2	84		1		12	1
10	MF	MAMAM Cherif Toure	T. CHERIF	13-01-1983	Metz	182	81	3	236	1			42	7
11	FW	MALM Robert	MALM	21-08-1973	Stade Brestois	179	77	1	3				2	0
12	DF	AKOTO Eric	AKOTO	20-07-1980	Admira	192	83	0	0				32	1
13	FW	FORSON Richmond	FORSON R.	23-05-1980	JA Poire sur Vie	180	70	3	208				11	0
14	FW	OLUFADE Adekanmi	OLUFADE	07-01-1980	Al Sailiya	170	70	1	31				25	0
15	MF	ROMAO Alaixys	ROMAO	18-01-1984	Louhans-Cuiseaux	180	74	2	180		2		13	0
16	GK	AGASSA Kossi	AGASSA	02-07-1978	Metz	190	85	3	270				52	0
17	FW	MOHAMED KADER	C. KADER-TOURE	08-04-1979	Guingamp	174	74	3	270	1			49	14
18	FW	SENAYA Yao Junior	J- SENAYA	19-04-1984	YF Juventus	167	70	3	166				19	2
19	DF	ASSEMOASSA Ludovic	ASSEMOASSA	18-09-1980	Ciudad Murcia	184	83	1	62				6	0
20	MF	ERASSA Affo	ERASSA	19-02-1983	Moulins	190	78	0	0				6	0
21	MF	ATSOU Franck	ATSOU	01-08-1978	Al Hilal	188	84	0	0				13	0
22	GK	OBILALE Kodjovi	OBILALE K.	08-10-1984	Etoile Filante	193	87	0	0				0	0
23	DF	TOURE Assimiou	A. TOURE	01-01-1988	Bayer Leverkusen	180	78	2	125				3	0

TRI - TRINIDAD AND TOBAGO SQUAD 2006 FIFA WORLD CUP™

No	Pos	Name	Shirt Name	DoB	Club	Cms	Kg	Games	Mins	Goals	Y	R	Cap	Gls
1	GK	HISLOP Shaka	HISLOP	22-02-1969	West Ham United	193	91	2	180		1		26	0
2	DF	COX Ian	COX	25-03-1971	Gillingham	183	77	0	0				16	0
3	DF	JOHN Avery	A. JOHN	18-06-1975	New England Rev.	183	77	2	77		1		59	0
4	DF	ANDREWS Marvin	ANDREWS	22-12-1975	Rangers	187	82	0	0				98	10
5	DF	SANCHO Brent	SANCHO	13-03-1977	Gillingham	185	84	3	270		1		43	0
6	DF	LAWRENCE Dennis	LAWRENCE	01-08-1974	Wrexham	201	76	3	270				66	4
7	MF	BIRCHALL Christopher	BIRCHALL	05-05-1984	Port Vale	175	82	3	270				22	3
8	DF	GRAY Cyd	GRAY	21-11-1976	San Juan Jabloteh	173	74	2	180		1		41	1
9	MF	WHITLEY Aurtis	WHITLEY	01-05-1977	San Juan Jabloteh	180	82	3	181		2		27	1
10	FW	LATAPY Russell	LATAPY	02-08-1968	Falkirk	183	76	1	23				67	28
11	MF	EDWARDS Carlos	EDWARDS	24-10-1978	Luton Town	180	73	3	270				54	1
12	FW	SAMUEL Collin	SAMUEL	27-08-1981	Dundee United	175	76	1	52				19	3
13	FW	GLEN Cornell	GLEN	21-10-1980	Los Angeles Galaxy	175	73	3	99				38	11
14	FW	JOHN Stern	S. JOHN	30-10-1976	Coventry City	180	84	3	270				98	65
15	FW	JONES Kenwyne	JONES	05-10-1984	Southampton	188	78	2	129	1			31	2
16	FW	WISE Evans	WISE	23-11-1973	Waldhof Mannheim	175	64	2	54				18	3
17	DF	CHARLES Atiba	CHARLES	29-09-1977	Williams Connection	188	84	0	0				19	0
18	MF	THEOBALD Densill	THEOBALD	27-06-1982	Falkirk	181	78	3	241	1			41	1
19	FW	YORKE Dwight	YORKE	03-11-1971	Sydney FC	182	75	3	270				57	15
20	FW	SCOTLAND Jason	SCOTLAND	18-02-1979	St. Johnstone	175	74	0	0				25	5
21	GK	JACK Kelvin	JACK	29-04-1976	Dundee FC	193	91	1	90				33	0
22	GK	INCE Clayton	INCE	13-07-1972	Coventry City	191	85	0	0				63	0
23	MF	WOLFE Anthony	WOLFE	23-12-1983	San Juan Jabloteh	180	72	0	0				4	0

TUN - TUNISIA SQUAD 2006 FIFA WORLD CUP™

No	Pos	Name	Shirt Name	DoB	Club	Cms	Kg	Games	Mins	Goals	Y	R	Cap	Gls
1	GK	BOUMNIJEL Ali	BOUMNIJEL	13-04-1966	Club Africain	188	80	3	270				50	0
2	FW	ESSEDIRI Karim	ESSEDIRI	29-07-1979	Rosenborg BK	185	81	1	8				8	0
3	DF	HAGGUI Karim	HAGGUI	20-01-1984	RC Strasbourg	188	82	3	270		1		28	4
4	DF	YAHIA Alaeddine	YAHIA	26-09-1981	Saint-Etienne	186	81	1	33				14	0
5	FW	JAZIRI Zied	JAZIRI	12-07-1978	Troyes	171	71	3	226	1	1	1	63	14
6	DF	TRABELSI Hatem	TRABELSI	25-01-1977	Ajax	180	74	3	270		1		58	0
7	FW	GUEMAMDIA Haykel	GUEMAMDIA	22-12-1981	RC Strasbourg	182	71	1	10		1		14	5
8	MF	NAFTI Mehdi	NAFTI	28-11-1978	Birmingham City	178	76	3	214		1		31	1
9	FW	CHIKHAOUI Yassine	CHIKHAOUI	22-09-1986	Etoile du Sahel	187	80	1	82		1		2	0
10	MF	GHODHBANE Kaies	GHODBANE	07-01-1976	Konyaspor	183	78	3	55				91	6
11	FW	SANTOS	DOS SANTOS	20-03-1979	Toulouse	172	68	1	11				28	18
12	MF	MNARI Jaouhar	MNARI	08-11-1976	1.FC Nürnberg	183	83	3	270	1	1		39	2
13	MF	BOUAZIZI Riadh	BOUAZIZI	08-04-1973	Erciyesspor	186	76	3	191		2		87	4
14	MF	CHEDLI Adel	CHEDLI	16-09-1976	1.FC Nürnberg	176	70	3	228	1			40	4
15	DF	JAIDI Radhi	JAIDI	30-08-1975	Bolton Wanderers	192	89	3	270	1	2		91	6
16	GK	NEFZI Adel	NEFZI	16-03-1974	US Monastir	183	86	0	0				0	0
17	FW	BEN SAADA Chaouki	BEN SAADA	01-07-1984	Bastia	170	65	1	11				11	0
18	DF	JEMMALI David	JEMMALI	13-12-1974	Girondins Bordeaux	188	80	1	90				3	0
19	DF	AYARI Anis	AYARI	16-02-1982	Samsunspor	181	75	2	147		1		25	1
20	MF	NAMOUCHI Hamed	NAMOUCHI	14-02-1984	Rangers	183	74	3	270				16	1
21	DF	SAIDI Karim	SAIDI	24-03-1983	Lecce	184	76	0	0				15	0
22	GK	KASRAOUI Hamdi	KASRAOUI	18-01-1983	Esperance	192	87	0	0				6	0
23	MF	MELLITI Sofiane	MELLITI	18-08-1978	Gaziantepspor	178	80	0	0				14	1

UKR – UKRAINE SQUAD 2006 FIFA WORLD CUP™

No	Pos	Name	Shirt Name	DoB	Club	Cms	Kg	Games	Mins	Goals	Y	R	Cap	Gls
1	GK	SHOVKOVSKYI Oleksandr	SHOVKOVSKYI	02-01-1975	Dynamo Kyiv	191	86	5	480				73	0
2	DF	NESMACHNYI Andriy	NESMACHNYI	28-02-1979	Dynamo Kyiv	182	72	5	480		1		54	0
3	DF	IATSENKO Oleksandr	IATSENKO	24-02-1985	Kharkiv	180	75	0	0				1	0
4	MF	TYMOSCHUK Anatoliy	TYMOSCHUK	30-03-1979	Shakhtar Donetsk	181	70	5	480		1		59	1
5	DF	YEZERSKYI Vladimir	YEZERSKYY	15-11-1976	Dnipro Dnipropetrovsk	183	77	1	90		1		25	1
6	DF	RUSOL Andriy	RUSOL	16-01-1983	Dnipro Dnipropetrovsk	182	75	4	317	1	2		27	2
7	FW	SHEVCHENKO Andriy	SHEVCHENKO	29-09-1976	Milan	183	73	5	474	2			69	31
8	MF	SHELAYEV Oleg	SHELAYEV	05-11-1976	Dnipro Dnipropetrovsk	181	74	5	435		1		24	0
9	MF	GUSEV Oleg	GUSIEV	25-04-1983	Dynamo Kyiv	179	73	5	435				30	1
10	FW	VORONIN Andriy	VORONIN	21-07-1979	Bayer Leverkusen	179	75	4	370				36	4
11	MF	REBROV Serhiy	REBROV	03-06-1974	Dynamo Kyiv	175	80	4	178	1			74	15
12	GK	PYATOV Andriy	PYATOV	28-06-1984	Vorskla Poltava	190	78	0	0				1	0
13	DF	CHIGRYNSKYI Dmytro	CHYGRYNSKYY	07-11-1986	Shakhtar Donetsk	190	81	0	0				0	0
14	MF	GUSIN Andriy	GUSIN	11-12-1972	CSK VVS Samara	188	79	5	281				69	9
15	FW	MILEVSKIY Artem	MILEVSKYI	12-01-1985	Dynamo Kyiv	190	78	4	87		1		4	0
16	FW	VOROBEY Andriy	VOROBYEY	29-11-1978	Shakhtar Donetsk	178	70	4	244				57	7
17	DF	VASHCHUK Vladyslav	VASHCHUK	02-01-1975	Dynamo Kyiv	180	72	3	210			1	61	1
18	MF	NAZARENKO Serhiy	NAZARENKO	16-02-1980	Dnipro Dnipropetrovsk	176	69	0	0				15	2
19	MF	KALINICHENKO Maksym	KALINICHENKO	26-01-1979	Spartak Moskva	176	67	4	330	1	2		25	4
20	FW	BELIK Oleksiy	BELIK	15-02-1981	Shakhtar Donetsk	184	76	1	18				16	4
21	MF	ROTAN Ruslan	ROTAN	29-10-1981	Dynamo Kyiv	176	69	3	128				22	3
22	DF	SVIDERSKYI Vyacheslav	SVIDERSKYY	01-01-1979	Arsenal Kyiv	185	80	3	200		3		9	0
23	GK	SHUST Bohdan	SHUST	04-03-1986	Shakhtar Donetsk	189	83	0	0				2	0

USA – USA SQUAD 2006 FIFA WORLD CUP™

No	Pos	Name	Shirt Name	DoB	Club	Cms	Kg	Games	Mins	Goals	Y	R	Cap	Gls
1	GK	HOWARD Tim	HOWARD	06-03-1979	Manchester United	187	90	0	0				16	0
2	DF	ALBRIGHT Chris	ALBRIGHT	14-01-1979	Los Angeles Galaxy	185	83	0	0				20	1
3	DF	BOCANEGRA Carlos	BOCANEGRA	25-05-1979	Fulham	184	77	2	180				42	6
4	DF	MASTROENI Pablo	MASTROENI	29-08-1976	Colorado Rapids	178	78	2	90		1		50	0
5	MF	O BRIEN John	O'BRIEN	29-08-1977	Chivas USA	178	73	1	45				32	3
6	DF	CHERUNDOLO Steve	CHERUNDOLO	19-02-1979	Hannover 96	168	66	3	196				38	1
7	DF	LEWIS Eddie	LEWIS	17-05-1974	Leeds United	181	71	2	164		1		71	8
8	MF	DEMPSEY Clint	DEMPSEY	09-03-1983	New England Rev	185	77	2	152	1			23	6
9	FW	JOHNSON Eddie	JOHNSON	31-03-1984	Kansas City Wizards	187	77	2	74				20	9
10	MF	REYNA Claudio	REYNA	20-07-1973	Manchester City	178	72	3	220		1		112	8
11	FW	CHING Brian	CHING	24-05-1978	Houston Dynamo	182	83	0	0				20	4
12	GK	BERHALTER Gregg	BERHALTER	01-08-1973	Energie Cottbus	186	76	0	0				44	0
13	DF	CONRAD Jimmy	CONRAD	12-02-1977	Kansas City Wizards	188	84	2	128				17	0
14	MF	OLSEN Ben	OLSEN	03-05-1977	Washington DC Utd	173	68	1	50				35	6
15	MF	CONVEY Bobby	CONVEY	27-05-1983	Reading	173	68	3	158				42	1
16	FW	WOLFF Josh	WOLFF	25-02-1977	Kansas City Wizards	175	72	1	13				48	9
17	MF	BEASLEY DaMarcus	BEASLEY	24-05-1982	PSV Eindhoven	170	64	3	208				61	12
18	GK	KELLER Kasey	KELLER	29-11-1969	B. Mönchengladbach	188	86	3	270				96	0
19	GK	HAHNEMANN Marcus	HAHNEMANN	15-06-1972	Reading	192	99	0	0				6	0
20	FW	MC BRIDE Brian	McBRIDE	19-06-1972	Fulham	185	77	3	257				95	30
21	MF	DONOVAN Landon	DONOVAN	04-03-1982	Los Angeles Galaxy	173	67	3	270				84	25
22	DF	ONYEWU Oguchi	ONYEWU	13-05-1982	Standard Liege	192	91	3	270		1		17	1
23	DF	POPE Eddie	POPE	24-12-1973	Real Salt Lake	183	80	2	137			1	82	8

KEY

No = Shirt number • Pos = position (GK = goalkeeper • DF = defender • MF = midfielder • FW = forward) • Shirt name = the name that appears on the players shirt • DoB = date of birth • Club = player's club • Cms = height of the player in centimetres • Kg = weight of the player in kilogrammes • Games = games played during the 2006 FIFA World Cup™ finals • Mins = minutes played during the finals • Goals = goals scored during the finals • Y = Yellow cards received during the finals • R = red cards received during the finals (the award of two yellows in a match is considered as one red. See the games played for the distinction between a sending off for two yellows cards or for a straight red) • Cap = number of appearances made by the player in all international matches as of July 10, 2006 • Gls = number of goals scored by the player in all international matches as of July 10, 2006

REVIEW OF WOMEN'S FOOTBALL

FIFA WOMEN'S WORLD RANKING 2004 TO 2006

Country	Code	03-2004	06-2004	08-2004	12-2004	03-2005	06-2005	09-2005	12-2005	03-2006	05-2006
Algeria	ALG	96	96	74	78	78	79	78	78	80	79
Angola	ANG	87	86	87	92	92	93	93	93	95	96
Netherlands Antilles	ANT										128
Argentina	ARG	38	37	37	37	37	37	37	36	37	36
Armenia	ARM	103	103	104	109	109	109	109	108	109	110
Aruba	ARU										127
Antigua and Barbuda	ATG										122
Australia	AUS	16	16	15	15	15	15	15	16	15	15
Austria	AUT	47	47	46	47	47	47	47	45	45	44
Bahamas	BAH	101	101	102	106	106	106	106	105	106	106
Belgium	BEL	28	28	27	27	27	28	30	31	31	34
Bermuda	BER	111	111					119	117	117	117
Bosnia-Herzegovina	BIH	79	81	82	85	85	86	86	85	87	90
Belarus	BLR	43	42	41	40	40	41	42	42	41	39
Belize	BLZ	115	115	116	120	120	121	123	122	124	126
Bolivia	BOL	81	80	81	86	86	87	87	86	88	88
Botswana	BOT	107	107	109	114	114	115	115	114	114	
Brazil	BRA	6	6	4	4	4	4	4	4	4	4
Bulgaria	BUL	48	48	48	48	48	48	48	48	48	47
Canada	CAN	11	11	12	11	11	12	12	13	12	11
Cayman Islands	CAY	114	114	115	119	119	120	122	121	122	124
Congo	CGO			105	110	110	110	110	109	110	112
Chile	CHI	51	51	51	51	51	51	51	51	51	51
China PR	CHN	5	5	6	6	9	9	9	9	8	8
Cameroon	CMR	80	79	80	82	83	84	84	83	85	85
Congo DR	COD	89	89	91	96	96	97	97	96	97	99
Cook Islands	COK	94	94	96	101	101	101	101	100	101	102
Colombia	COL	35	36	36	36	35	35	38	38	38	38
Costa Rica	CRC	45	45	45	45	45	46	46	46	46	46
Croatia	CRO	44	44	44	44	44	44	45	47	47	48
Cyprus	CYP	109	109	111	116	116	117	117	115	115	115
Czech Republic	CZE	22	20	20	22	22	22	23	21	21	21
Denmark	DEN	8	9	9	7	7	9	8	8	9	9
Dominica	DMA	83	83	84	88	88	89	89	89	91	93
Dominican Republic	DOM	99	99	100	104	104	104	104	102	103	105
Ecuador	ECU	52	52	52	52	52	52	53	52	52	52
Egypt	EGY						59	59	58	61	75
England	ENG	13	14	14	14	14	14	14	12	13	12
Equatorial Guinea	EQG								119	119	89
Spain	ESP	20	21	21	20	20	20	20	20	20	20
Estonia	EST	78	78	79	84	84	85	85	84	86	87
Ethiopia	ETH	112	112	113	107	107	107	107	106	107	108
Fiji	FIJ	69	70	70	72	72	73	73	74	75	74
Finland	FIN	19	18	18	16	16	16	14	16	16	16
France	FRA	9	7	7	9	5	5	5	7	5	6
Faroe Islands	FRO				70	70	70	71	71	72	71
Gabon	GAB	109	109	111	116	116	117	117	115	115	115
Germany	GER	1	1	1	1	1	1	1	1	1	1
Ghana	GHA	49	49	49	50	50	50	50	50	50	50
Greece	GRE	57	53	53	53	53	53	52	55	55	54
Guatemala	GUA	75	75	76	80	80	81	81	81	83	82
Guinea	GUI				103	107	107	107	106	107	109
Guam	GUM	66	68	68	69	69	72	72	72	73	72
Haiti	HAI	56	57	57	57	57	58	57	56	56	55
Hong Kong	HKG	64	64	64	65	65	66	67	66	67	67
Honduras	HON	85	85	86	90	90	91	91	91	93	95
Hungary	HUN	26	28	27	27	28	32	31	35	35	37
Indonesia	IDN	60	60	60	62	62	65	64	64	65	64
India	IND	58	58	58	58	58	57	57	56	56	55
Republic of Ireland	IRL	36	35	35	35	34	34	35	32	32	32
Iceland	ISL	17	17	17	18	18	18	17	19	19	18
Israel	ISR	69	69	69	71	71	71	69	67	68	65
Italy	ITA	10	10	10	10	10	10	10	10	10	10
Jamaica	JAM	73	73	73	76	76	77	77	76	78	81
Japan	JPN	14	13	13	13	13	12	11	11	11	13
Kazakhstan	KAZ	61	61	61	64	64	63	65	63	64	68

Country	Code	03-2004	06-2004	08-2004	12-2004	03-2005	06-2005	09-2005	12-2005	03-2006	05-2006
Korea Republic	KOR	24	24	26	26	26	26	22	23	23	23
St Lucia	LCA	92	92	94	98	98	99	99	98	99	111
Lebanon	LIB										119
Lithuania	LTU				60	60	61	61	60	60	60
Latvia	LVA				61	61	62	62	61	61	61
Morocco	MAR	53	53	54	54	54	54	54	58	58	59
Malaysia	MAS	71	71	71	74	74	76	76	75	77	78
Moldova	MDA	88	87	88	93	93	94	94	92	94	97
Maldives	MDV				100	100	111	111	110	111	113
Mexico	MEX	25	26	25	25	25	25	26	26	26	26
Macedonia FYR	MKD							121	119	121	121
Mali	MLI	72	72	72	79	79	80	79	79	76	76
Malta	MLT	97	97	98	103	103	103	103	103	104	107
Mozambique	MOZ	107	107	109	114	114	115	115	120	123	125
Myanmar	MYA	46	46	46	46	46	45	44	44	44	43
Namibia	NAM	113	113	114	118	118	119	120	118	118	118
Nicaragua	NCA	100	100	101	105	105	105	105	103	104	101
Netherlands	NED	15	15	16	17	17	17	18	17	17	17
Nigeria	NGA	27	25	23	24	23	24	25	24	24	24
Northern Ireland	NIR	77	77	78	83	82	83	83	77	79	77
Norway	NOR	3	3	3	3	3	3	3	3	3	3
New Zealand	NZL	21	22	22	21	20	21	21	22	22	22
Panama	PAN	62	62	62	63	63	64	63	62	63	63
Paraguay	PAR	65	65	65	66	66	67	66	65	66	66
Peru	PER	39	38	38	38	38	38	34	34	34	32
Philippines	PHI	76	76	77	81	81	81	81	81	83	84
Papua New Guinea	PNG	59	59	59	59	59	60	60	59	59	58
Poland	POL	32	32	32	32	32	31	32	27	27	30
Portugal	POR	34	34	34	34	36	36	36	40	41	45
Korea DPR	PRK	7	8	8	8	8	7	7	6	7	7
Puerto Rico	PUR	105	105	107	112	112	113	113	112	113	114
Romania	ROU	33	33	33	33	33	33	33	33	33	31
South Africa	RSA	63	63	63	73	73	74	74	72	73	72
Russia	RUS	12	12	11	12	13	13	13	14	14	14
Samoa	SAM	98	98	99	102	102	102	102	101	102	104
Serbia & Montenegro	SCG	30	30	31	31	31	30	28	30	30	29
Scotland	SCO	31	31	30	29	29	29	29	29	29	27
Senegal	SEN	102	102	90	94	94	95	95	94	80	79
Singapore	SIN	86	88	89	90	90	92	92	88	90	92
St Kitts and Nevis	SKN										122
El Salvador	SLV	91	91	93	97	97	98	98	97	98	103
Switzerland	SUI	29	27	29	30	30	27	27	27	28	28
Surinam	SUR	83	83	84	88	88	89	89	89	91	93
Slovakia	SVK	37	40	42	42	42	43	39	43	43	42
Slovenia	SVN				75	75	75	75	70	71	62
Sweden	SWE	4	4	5	6	6	6	6	6	5	5
Swaziland	SWZ	104	104	106	111	111	111	111	110	111	
Tahiti	TAH	93	93	95	99	99	100	100	99	100	100
Tanzania	TAN			117	121	121	122	124	123	125	129
Tonga	TGA	54	54	55	55	55	55	55	53	53	53
Thailand	THA	41	41	40	41	41	40	40	41	40	41
Chinese Taipei	TPE	23	23	24	23	23	23	24	25	25	25
Trinidad and Tobago	TRI	40	39	39	39	39	39	41	39	39	40
Tunisia	TUN										86
Turkey	TUR	68	67	67	68	68	69	70	69	70	70
Ukraine	UKR	18	19	19	19	19	19	19	18	18	19
Uruguay	URU	67	66	66	67	67	68	68	68	69	69
USA	USA	2	2	2	1	2	2	2	2	2	2
Uzbekistan	UZB	50	50	50	49	49	49	49	49	49	49
Vanuatu	VAN	82	82	83	87	87	88	88	87	89	91
Venezuela	VEN	74	74	74	77	77	78	80	80	82	83
Vietnam	VIE	42	42	43	43	43	42	43	36	36	35
St Vincent/Grenadines	VIN	95	95	97							
Wales	WAL	55	55	56	56	56	56	56	54	54	57
Zambia	ZAM	106	106	108	113	113	114	114	113	120	120
Zimbabwe	ZIM	90	90	92	95	95	96	96	95	96	98

INTERNATIONALS PLAYED SINCE THE FIFA WOMEN'S WORLD CUP 2003

2003	Venue		Score		Comp
12-10	LAGOS	Nigeria B	3-1	Mali	AAG
12-10	CAMPINA	Romania	2-0	Bosnia-H'govina	ECq
12-10	KADUNA	South Africa	3-1	Cameroon	AAG
15-10	KADUNA	Cameroon	1-0	Mali	AAG
15-10	SINGAPORE	Singapore	1-1	Hong Kong	Fr
16-10	ABUJA	Nigeria B	1-0	South Africa	AAG
17-10	KILKIS	Greece	4-3	Serbia & Mont'gro	Fr
18-10	MOGILEV	Belarus	1-1	Israel	ECq
18-10	BELISCE	Croatia	2-3	Romania	ECq
18-10	ODENSE	Denmark	3-0	Netherlands	ECq
19-10	KRAVARE	Czech Republic	2-0	Scotland	ECq
19-10	AXIOUPOLI	Greece	2-2	Serbia & Mont'gro	Fr
20-10	SINGAPORE	Hong Kong	4-1	Singapore	Fr
21-10	MOSCOW	Russia	2-2	England	Fr
21-10	SINGAPORE	Singapore	0-5	Thailand	Fr
22-10	TA'QALI	Malta	0-9	Republic of Ireland	ECq
22-10	KANSAS CITY	USA	2-2	Italy	Fr
24-10	TEGUCIGALPA	Honduras	2-2	Guatemala	Fr
25-10	LIVADIA	Greece	7-0	Armenia	ECq
25-10	PRETORIA	South Africa	13-0	Namibia	OGq
26-10	KUMASI	Ghana	2-0	Congo DR	OGq
26-10	TEGUCIGALPA	Honduras	1-1	Guatemala	Fr
26-10	HARARE	Zimbabwe	0-0	Angola	OGq
28-10	THIVA	Armenia	0-9	Greece	ECq
28-10	SWANSEA	Wales	1-1	Portugal	Fr
30-10	LLANELLI	Wales	1-0	Portugal	Fr
31-10	SAN CRISTOBAL	Dominican Rep.	0-7	Haiti	OGq
31-10	GUATEMALA CITY	Guatemala	0-2	Honduras	Fr
31-10	KUALA LUMPUR	Malaysia	0-4	Philippines	Fr
31-10	KUALA LUMPUR	Thailand	6-0	Indonesia	Fr
02-11	ANITGUA	Guatemala	1-1	Honduras	Fr
02-11	SAN CRISTOBAL	Haiti	3-2	Dominican Rep.	OGq
02-11	KUALA LUMPUR	Malaysia	3-1	Indonesia	Fr
02-11	KUALA LUMPUR	Thailand	4-1	Philippines	Fr
02-11	DALLAS	USA	3-1	Mexico	Fr
04-11	GUATEMALA CITY	Guatemala	0-2	Mexico	Fr
04-11	KUALA LUMPUR	Malaysia	0-4	Thailand	Fr
04-11	KUALA LUMPUR	Philippines	5-0	Indonesia	Fr
06-11	ANTIGUA	Guatemala	0-5	Mexico	Fr
06-11	SINGAPORE	Singapore	2-1	Philippines	Fr
08-11	LUANDA	Angola	1-0	Zimbabwe	OGq
08-11	WINDHOEK	Namibia	1-13	South Africa	OGq
08-11	PANAMA CITY	Panama	1-3	Mexico	Fr
09-11	KINSHASA	Congo DR	1-2	Ghana	OGq
09-11	PARAMARIBO	Surinam	0-2	Trinidad & Tobago	OGq
12-11	PARAMARIBO	Trinidad & Tobago	4-2	Surinam	OGq
13-11	PRESTON	England	5-0	Scotland	Fr
14-11	PANAMA CITY	Panama	4-1	Honduras	Fr
15-11	QUIMPER	France	7-1	Poland	ECq
15-11	REUTLINGEN	Germany	13-0	Portugal	ECq
15-11	DRAMA	Greece	3-1	Slovakia	ECq
15-11	BELGRADE	Serbia & Mont'gro	0-4	Sweden	ECq
16-11	LAS ROZAS	Spain	0-2	Norway	ECq
16-11	TA'QALI	Malta	1-4	Croatia	ECq
16-11	PANAMA CITY	Panama	4-2	Honduras	Fr
19-11	GUATEMALA CITY	Belize	0-18	Guatemala	OGq
21-11	GUATEMALA CITY	Panama	15-2	Belize	OGq
21-11	EINDHOVEN	Netherlands	3-0	Belgium	ECq
23-11	GUATEMALA CITY	Guatemala	1-1	Panama	OGq
29-11	NAOUSSA	Greece	0-2	Austria	ECq
02-12	HAI PHONG	Philippines	0-0	Malaysia	SEA
02-12	NAM DINH	Thailand	2-4	Myanmar	SEA

2003	Venue		Score		Comp
02-12	HAI PHONG	Vietnam	6-0	Indonesia	SEA
04-12	HAI PHONG	Indonesia	1-1	Philippines	SEA
04-12	HAI PHONG	Malaysia	1-3	Vietnam	SEA
04-12	NAM DINH	Myanmar	3-0	Singapore	SEA
05-12	GEORGETOWN	Jamaica	3-0	Cayman Islands	OGq
06-12	NAM DINH	Indonesia	2-2	Malaysia	SEA
06-12	POMBAL	Portugal	0-1	Czech Republic	ECq
06-12	NAM DINH	Singapore	0-2	Thailand	SEA
06-12	HAI PHONG	Vietnam	3-0	Philippines	SEA
07-12	GEORGETOWN	Cayman Islands	0-1	Jamaica	OGq
08-12	HAI PHONG	Myanmar	8-0	Malaysia	SEA
08-12	HAI PHONG	Vietnam	3-1	Thailand	SEA
10-12	TEGUCIGALPA	Nicaragua	0-1	Honduras	OGq
11-12	HAI PHONG	Thailand	6-1	Malaysia	SEA
11-12	HAI PHONG	Vietnam	2-1	Myanmar	SEA
12-12	TEGUCIGALPA	Mexico	8-0	Nicaragua	OGq
14-12	TEGUCIGALPA	Honduras	0-6	Mexico	OGq
2004					
15-01	ATHENS	Greece	1-1	Scotland	Fr
17-01	ATHENS	Greece	0-3	Scotland	Fr
21-01	ATHENS	Greece	0-3	Italy	Fr
30-01	SHENZHEN	China PR	2-1	Canada	Fr
30-01	SHENZHEN	USA	3-0	Sweden	Fr
31-01	IBADAN	Nigeria	1-1	Ghana	OGq
01-02	SHENZHEN	China PR	0-0	USA	Fr
01-02	JOHANNESBURG	South Africa	6-2	Angola	OGq
01-02	SHENZHEN	Sweden	3-1	Canada	Fr
03-02	SHENZHEN	China PR	2-2	Sweden	Fr
03-02	SHENZHEN	USA	2-0	Canada	Fr
07-02	ALBUFEIRA	Portugal	0-11	Germany	ECq
14-02	LUANDA	Angola	3-2	South Africa	OGq
14-02	ACCRA	Ghana	1-1	Nigeria	OGq
17-02	VIAREGGIO	Italy	2-1	Netherlands	Fr
18-02	BRISBANE	Australia	2-0	New Zealand	Fr
18-02	BRISBANE	China PR	0-3	Korea DPR	Fr
18-02	SETE	France	1-1	Scotland	Fr
19-02	PORTSMOUTH	England	2-0	Denmark	Fr
20-02	ATHENS	Greece	0-2	Russia	Fr
21-02	BRISBANE	Australia	-	Korea DPR	Fr
21-02	MONTPELLIER	France	6-3	Scotland	Fr
21-02	BRISBANE	New Zealand	0-3	China PR	Fr
22-02	ATHENS	Greece	1-1	Russia	Fr
24-02	BRISBANE	Australia	0-0	China PR	Fr
24-02	BRISBANE	Korea DPR	11-0	New Zealand	Fr
25-02	SAN JOSE	Mexico	5-0	Haiti	OGq
25-02	SAN JOSE	Trinidad & Tobago	0-7	USA	OGq
26-02	HEREDIA	Canada	6-0	Jamaica	OGq
26-02	HEREDIA	Costa Rica	6-1	Panama	OGq
27-02	HEREDIA	Haiti	0-8	USA	OGq
27-02	HEREDIA	Trinidad & Tobago	1-8	Mexico	OGq
28-02	SAN JOSE	Canada	6-0	Panama	OGq
28-02	SAN JOSE	Costa Rica	1-0	Jamaica	OGq
29-02	ALGINET	Spain	9-1	Belgium	ECq
29-02	SAN JOSE	Haiti	2-6	Trinidad & Tobago	OGq
29-02	SAN JOSE	USA	2-0	Mexico	OGq
01-03	HEREDIA	Costa Rica	1-2	Canada	OGq
01-03	HEREDIA	Jamaica	0-3	Panama	OGq
02-03	BA	Fiji	0-2	Papua N. Guinea	OGq
03-03	SAN JOSE	Canada	1-2	Mexico	OGq
03-03	SAN JOSE	USA	4-0	Costa Rica	OGq
04-03	BA	Australia	10-0	Papua N. Guinea	OGq
04-03	FURTH	Germany	0-1	China PR	Fr

INTERNATIONALS PLAYED SINCE THE FIFA WOMEN'S WORLD CUP 2003

2004	Venue		Score		Comp
05-03	HEREDIA	Canada	4-0	Costa Rica	OGq
05-03	HEREDIA	Mexico	2-3	USA	OGq
06-03	BA	Fiji	0-7	Australia	OGq
07-03	BRUSSELS	Belgium	1-6	Norway	ECq
07-03	SCHWANDORF	China PR	1-0	Czech Republic	Fr
10-03	LEIDEN	Netherlands	6-0	Republic of Ireland	Fr
12-03	PRETORIA	South Africa	2-2	Nigeria	OGq
13-03	REYKJAVIK	Iceland	5-1	Scotland	Fr
14-03	FERREIRAS	Denmark	0-1	Sweden	ALG
14-03	FARO	Greece	1-0	Wales	ALG
14-03	GUIA	Italy	1-0	China PR	ALG
14-03	GUIA	Norway	4-1	Finland	ALG
14-03	FARO	Portugal	2-0	Northern Ireland	ALG
14-03	FERREIRAS	USA	5-1	France	ALG
16-03	QUARTEIRA	Denmark	0-1	USA	ALG
16-03	OLHAO	Finland	0-4	China PR	ALG
16-03	ALBUFEIRA	Northern Ireland	0-2	Greece	ALG
16-03	OLHAO	Norway	3-0	Italy	ALG
16-03	ALBUFEIRA	Portugal	2-3	Wales	ALG
16-03	QUARTEIRA	Sweden	0-3	France	ALG
18-03	SILVES	Denmark	0-1	France	ALG
18-03	LAGOS	Finland	1-2	Italy	ALG
18-03	SILVES	Norway	0-0	China PR	ALG
18-03	GUIA	Portugal	3-0	Greece	ALG
18-03	LAGOS	Sweden	3-1	USA	ALG
18-03	GUIA	Wales	3-1	Northern Ireland	ALG
20-03	OLHAO	China PR	1-1	Sweden	ALG
20-03	FERREIRAS	Finland	4-0	Wales	ALG
20-03	FARO	Italy	3-3	France	ALG
20-03	MONTECHORO	Northern Ireland	0-2	Greece	ALG
20-03	LOULE	Portugal	0-1	Denmark	ALG
20-03	FARO	USA	4-1	Norway	ALG
21-03	LA RODA	Spain	0-0	Netherlands	ECq
30-03	ABUJA	Nigeria	1-0	South Africa	OGq
31-03	ALBENA	Bulgaria	0-3	Kazakhstan	Fr
31-03	BOZEN	Italy	0-1	Germany	Fr
31-03	ALBENA	Romania	0-5	Russia	Fr
03-04	SETUBAL	Portugal	1-2	Ukraine	ECq
04-04	ALBENA	Russia	5-0	Kazakhstan	Fr
06-04	ALBENA	Bulgaria	1-1	Romania	Fr
09-04	BASEL	Switzerland	0-0	Belgium	Fr
10-04	DUBLIN	Republic of Ireland	8-1	Croatia	ECq
10-04	SIMFEROPOL	Ukraine	1-0	Scotland	ECq
11-04	MAPUTO	Mozambique	3-1	Swaziland	Fr
11-04	BASEL	Switzerland	1-0	Belgium	Fr
18-04	HIROSHIMA	China PR	11-0	Myanmar	OGq
18-04	LUCENA	Spain	0-1	Denmark	ECq
18-04	TOKYO	Japan	7-0	Vietnam	OGq
18-04	HIROSHIMA	Korea Republic	7-0	Guam	OGq
18-04	HIROSHIMA	Korea DPR	5-0	Chinese Taipei	OGq
18-04	HIROSHIMA	Singapore	0-2	Hong Kong	OGq
20-04	HIROSHIMA	Guam	0-9	China PR	OGq
20-04	HIROSHIMA	Hong Kong	0-9	Korea DPR	OGq
20-04	HIROSHIMA	Myanmar	0-7	Korea Republic	OGq
20-04	HIROSHIMA	Chinese Taipei	5-0	Singapore	OGq
20-04	TOKYO	Vietnam	0-0	Thailand	OGq
22-04	HIROSHIMA	China PR	3-0	Korea Republic	OGq
22-04	READING	England	0-3	Nigeria	Fr
22-04	HIROSHIMA	Guam	0-2	Myanmar	OGq
22-04	HIROSHIMA	Hong Kong	1-3	Chinese Taipei	OGq
22-04	HIROSHIMA	Korea DPR	8-0	Singapore	OGq
22-04	TOKYO	Thailand	0-6	Japan	OGq
24-04	OTTENSHEIM	Austria	1-2	Greece	ECq
24-04	HIROSHIMA	China PR	1-0	Korea Republic	OGq
24-04	REIMS	France	6-0	Hungary	ECq
24-04	ANDRIA	Italy	1-1	Finland	ECq
24-04	TOKYO	Korea DPR	0-3	Japan	OGq
24-04	SOLOTHURN	Switzerland	0-2	Sweden	ECq
24-04	BIRMINGHAM, AL	USA	5-1	Brazil	Fr
25-04	LEUVEN	Belgium	0-3	Netherlands	ECq
26-04	HIROSHIMA	Japan	0-1	China PR	OGq
26-04	HIROSHIMA	Korea DPR	5-1	Korea Republic	OGq
28-04	OLDENBURG	Germany	6-0	Ukraine	ECq
29-04	SENEC	Slovakia	2-2	Greece	ECq
01-05	DUNAUJVAROS	Hungary	2-2	Poland	ECq
01-05	BUCHAREST	Romania	1-1	Republic of Ireland	ECq
02-05	MONS	Belgium	2-0	Spain	ECq
02-05	LIVINGSTON	Scotland	1-3	Germany	ECq
08-05	LEOPOLDSDORF	Austria	3-0	Slovakia	ECq
08-05	HAMRUN	Malta	0-8	Romania	ECq
08-05	KWIDZYN	Poland	1-1	Russia	ECq
09-05	SARAJEVO	Bosnia-H'govina	1-4	Republic of Ireland	ECq
09-05	UH'SKE HRADISTE	Czech Republic	5-1	Portugal	ECq
09-05	TEL AVIV	Israel	12-1	Estonia	ECq
09-05	ALBUQUERQUE	USA	3-0	Mexico	Fr
12-05	VAXJO	Sweden	5-1	Serbia & Mont'gro	ECq
14-05	PETERBOROUGH	England	1-0	Iceland	Fr
15-05	LAHTI	Finland	4-0	Serbia & Mont'gro	ECq
16-05	SLAVONSKI BROD	Croatia	6-0	Bosnia-H'govina	ECq
16-05	SELYATINO	Russia	0-3	France	ECq
22-05	FARUM	Denmark	2-0	Spain	ECq
22-05	TRAPANI	Italy	0-0	Switzerland	ECq
22-05	MR WEZEP	Netherlands	0-2	Norway	ECq
23-05	LIVINGSTON	Scotland	2-1	Portugal	ECq
25-05	ASTANA	Kazakhstan	0-2	Belarus	ECq
27-05	ODENSE	Denmark	2-1	Norway	ECq
29-05	SZEKESFEHERVAR	Hungary	0-5	Iceland	ECq
29-05	DAR ES SAALAM	Tanzania	4-0	Eritrea	CN
30-05	MALABO	Equatorial Guinea	2-2	Congo	CN
30-05	HERZLIYYA	Israel	3-1	Kazakhstan	ECq
02-06	REYKJAVIK	Iceland	0-3	France	ECq
05-06	ROUDNICE	Czech Republic	4-1	Ukraine	ECq
05-06	PETROYSA DRAMA	Greece	1-0	Serbia & Mont'gro	Fr
06-06	LOUISVILLE	USA	1-1	Japan	Fr
07-06	KALABAKI DRAMA	Greece	3-3	Serbia & Mont'gro	Fr
12-06	BRAZZAVILLE	Congo	2-0	Equatorial Guinea	CN
12-06	ASMARA	Eritrea	1-1	Tanzania	CN
25-06	DUBLIN	Republic of Ireland	5-0	Malta	ECq
26-06	BENEVENTO	Italy	2-1	Sweden	ECq
30-06	BEIJING	China PR	0-2	Australia	Fr
01-07	BEIJING	China PR	1-1	Australia	Fr
03-07	NASHVILLE	USA	1-0	Canada	Fr
06-07	ATHENS	Greece	0-1	Russia	Fr
08-07	MEXICO CITY	Mexico	1-2	Australia	Fr
10-07	DAKAR	Senegal	2-8	Nigeria	CN
11-07	BRAZZAVILLE	Congo	0-2	Cameroon	CN
11-07	CONAKRY	Guinea	0-13	Ghana	CN
11-07	GUADALAJARA	Mexico	2-0	Australia	Fr
11-07	BAMAKO	Mali	2-2	Algeria	CN
11-07	BLANTYRE	Malawi	0-4	Ethiopia	CN
11-07	DAR ES SAALAM	Tanzania	0-3	Zimbabwe	CN
21-07	HOFFENHEIM	Germany	0-1	Norway	Fr
21-07	BLAINE	USA	3-1	Australia	Fr
23-07	BLIDA	Algeria	1-0	Mali	CN

INTERNATIONALS PLAYED SINCE THE FIFA WOMEN'S WORLD CUP 2003

2004	Venue		Score		Comp	2004	Venue		Score		Comp
24-07	OFFENBACH	Germany	3-1	Nigeria	Fr	24-09	PRETORIA	South Africa	1-2	Ethiopia	CN
24-07	ACCRA	Ghana	9-0	Guinea	CN	25-09	JOHANNESBURG	Algeria	1-3	Cameroon	CN
24-07	WARRI	Nigeria	4-1	Senegal	CN	25-09	PRIBRAM	Czech Republic	0-5	Germany	ECq
24-07	UDEVALLA	Sweden	0-4	Norway	Fr	25-09	PRETORIA	Nigeria	3-0	Mali	CN
25-07	YAOUNDE	Cameroon	0-0	Congo	CN	25-09	NIS	Serbia & Mont'gro	1-2	Italy	ECq
25-07	ADDIS ABEBA	Ethiopia	5-0	Malawi	CN	25-09	ROCHESTER, NY	USA	4-3	Iceland	Fr
25-07	HARARE	Zimbabwe	4-0	Tanzania	CN	26-09	AALBORG	Denmark	6-0	Belgium	ECq
30-07	TOKYO	Japan	3-0	Canada	Fr	26-09	DIJON	France	2-5	Russia	ECq
31-07	ODRANCI	Slovenia	0-2	Czech Republic	Fr	28-09	JOHANNESBURG	Ghana	0-1	Cameroon	CN
01-08	HARTFORD	USA	3-1	China PR	Fr	28-09	JOHANNESBURG	Nigeria	4-0	Ethiopia	CN
06-08	ATHENS	Australia	1-0	Mexico	Fr	29-09	KATWIJK	Netherlands	1-5	Denmark	ECq
06-08	ZEIST	Netherlands	0-2	Japan	Fr	29-09	KRUSEVAC	Serbia & Mont'gro	1-0	Switzerland	ECq
11-08	THESSALONIKI	Brazil	1-0	Australia	OGr1	29-09	PITTSBURGH	USA	3-0	Iceland	Fr
11-08	PATRAS	Germany	8-0	China PR	OGr1	30-09	HO CHI MINH CITY	Indonesia	1-0	Philippines	Fr
11-08	HERAKLIO	Greece	0-3	USA	OGr1	01-10	JOHANNESBURG	Ghana	0-0	Ethiopia	CN
11-08	VOLOS	Sweden	0-1	Japan	OGr1	01-10	HO CHI MINH CITY	Myanmar	17-0	Maldives	Fr
14-08	PATRAS	China PR	1-1	Mexico	OGr1	02-10	VAASA	Finland	1-1	Sweden	ECq
14-08	HERAKLIO	Greece	0-1	Australia	OGr1	02-10	PORSGRUNN	Norway	2-0	Spain	ECq
14-08	ATHENS	Japan	0-1	Nigeria	OGr1	02-10	HO CHI MINH CITY	Philippines	2-1	Singapore	Fr
14-08	THESSALONIKI	USA	2-0	Brazil	OGr1	02-10	BUCHAREST	Romania	10-0	Croatia	ECq
15-08	SZAMOTULY	Poland	0-2	Finland	Fr	03-10	JOHANNESBURG	Cameroon	0-5	Nigeria	CN
17-08	ATHENS	Germany	2-0	Mexico	OGr1	03-10	RISHON LEZION	Israel	0-2	Belarus	ECq
17-08	PATRAS	Greece	0-7	Brazil	OGr1	03-10	OPOLE	Poland	1-5	France	ECq
17-08	VOLOS	Sweden	2-1	Nigeria	OGr1	03-10	SELYATINO	Russia	4-0	Hungary	ECq
17-08	THESSALONIKI	USA	1-1	Australia	OGr1	03-10	PORTLAND	USA	5-0	New Zealand	Fr
19-08	BRISTOL	England	1-2	Russia	Fr	04-10	HO CHI MINH CITY	Singapore	1-0	Indonesia	Fr
19-08	DINGWALL	Scotland	6-0	Switzerland	Fr	04-10	HO CHI MINH CITY	Vietnam	14-0	Maldives	Fr
20-08	PATRAS	Germany	2-1	Nigeria	OGqf	05-10	HO CHI MINH CITY	Vietnam	1-1	Myanmar	Fr
20-08	UKMERGE	Lithuania	4-1	Latvia	Fr	07-10	HO CHI MINH CITY	Myanmar	7-0	Indonesia	Fr
20-08	HERAKLIO	Mexico	0-5	Brazil	OGqf	09-10	HO CHI MINH CITY	Vietnam	4-1	Indonesia	Fr
20-08	VOLOS	Sweden	2-1	Australia	OGqf	10-10	CINCINNATI	USA	6-0	New Zealand	Fr
20-08	THESSALONIKI	USA	2-1	Japan	OGqf	12-10	KLAKSVIK	Faroe Islands	1-2	Republic of Ireland	Fr
21-08	UKMERGE	Latvia	0-5	Estonia	Fr	14-10	BERLIN	Germany	0-0	Netherlands	Fr
21-08	SENEC	Slovakia	2-3	Austria	ECq	16-10	PIETARSAARI	Finland	1-0	Russia	ECq
22-08	REYKJAVIK	Iceland	0-2	Russia	ECq	16-10	KANSAS CITY	USA	1-0	Mexico	Fr
22-08	UKMERGE	Lithuania	2-2	Estonia	Fr	20-10	MOSCOW	Russia	1-3	Finland	ECq
23-08	PATRAS	Sweden	0-1	Brazil	OGsf	20-10	CHICAGO	USA	5-1	Republic of Ireland	Fr
23-08	HERAKLIO	USA	2-1	Germany	OGsf	23-10	HOUSTON	USA	5-0	Republic of Ireland	Fr
25-08	MINSK	Belarus	8-1	Kazakhstan	ECq	03-11	EAST RUTHERFORD	USA	1-1	Denmark	Fr
26-08	ATHENS	Germany	1-0	Sweden	OG3p	06-11	Philadelphia	USA	1-3	Denmark	Fr
26-08	ATHENS	USA	2-1	Brazil	OGf	10-11	REYKJAVIK	Iceland	2-7	Norway	ECq
28-08	ST. JOHN'S	Antigua/Barbuda	1-0	Anguilla	Fr	13-11	BATTICE	Belgium	5-1	Hungary	ECq
29-08	ST. JOHN'S	Antigua/Barbuda	0-1	Anguilla	Fr	13-11	CROTONE	Italy	2-1	Czech Republic	ECq
29-08	PARNU	Estonia	1-3	Belarus	ECq	13-11	OSLO	Norway	2-1	Iceland	ECq
04-09	BERGEN	Norway	3-1	Italy	Fr	13-11	HO CHI MINH CITY	Vietnam	3-0	Hong Kong	Fr
04-09	VISP	Switzerland	0-2	Italy	Fr	27-11	CASLAV	Czech Republic	0-3	Italy	ECq
05-09	TA'QALI	Malta	0-2	Bosnia-H'govina	ECq	01-12	SINGAPORE	Singapore	2-0	Guam	Fr
05-09	DINGWALL	Scotland	3-2	Czech Republic	ECq	08-12	CARSON	USA	5-0	Mexico	Fr
08-09	SLAGELSE	Denmark	2-3	France	Fr	18-12	TOKYO	Japan	11-0	Chinese Taipei	Fr
18-09	HEERHUGOWAARD	Netherlands	1-2	England	Fr	2005					
18-09	PRETORIA	South Africa	0-3	Ghana	CN	28-01	QUANZHOU	China PR	3-1	Russia	Fr
18-09	PRETORIA	Zimbabwe	1-1	Ethiopia	CN	28-01	QUANZHOU	Germany	0-1	Australia	Fr
19-09	VOGOSCA	Bosnia-H'govina	0-0	Romania	ECq	30-01	QUANZHOU	China PR	3-0	Australia	Fr
19-09	JOHANNESBURG	Cameroon	2-2	Mali	CN	30-01	QUANZHOU	Germany	1-0	Russia	Fr
19-09	ASTANA	Kazakhstan	0-0	Estonia	ECq	01-02	QUANZHOU	China PR	0-2	Germany	Fr
19-09	JOHANNESBURG	Nigeria	4-0	Algeria	CN	01-02	QUANZHOU	Russia	0-5	Australia	Fr
21-09	JOHANNESBURG	Ghana	2-1	Ethiopia	CN	04-02	YIWU	China PR	0-0	Denmark	Fr
21-09	JOHANNESBURG	Zimbabwe	2-1	South Africa	CN	04-02	DUBAI	Czech Republic	4-0	Romania	Fr
22-09	JOHANNESBURG	Algeria	3-0	Mali	CN	07-02	YIWU	China PR	1-1	Denmark	Fr
22-09	JOHANNESBURG	Cameroon	2-2	Nigeria	CN	15-02	LAS PALMAS G.C.	Spain	2-2	Finland	Fr
22-09	TUITJENHOORN	Netherlands	0-1	England	Fr	17-02	MILTON KEYNES	England	4-1	Italy	Fr
24-09	JOHANNESBURG	Ghana	2-0	Zimbabwe	CN	17-02	LAS PALMAS G.C.	Spain	0-0	Netherlands	Fr

INTERNATIONALS PLAYED SINCE THE FIFA WOMEN'S WORLD CUP 2003

2005	Venue		Score		Comp
18-02	LAS PALMAS G.C.	Netherlands	0-1	Finland	Fr
19-02	LA MANGA	Norway	0-2	France	Fr
22-02	LA MANGA	Norway	0-1	France	Fr
23-02	SANTA MARIA	Portugal	0-2	Italy	Fr
07-03	SIMFEROPOL	Ukraine	1-2	Russia	Fr
09-03	FERREIRAS	Denmark	4-1	Finland	ALG
09-03	PADERNE	England	4-0	Northern Ireland	ALG
09-03	FERREIRAS	France	0-1	USA	ALG
09-03	LAGOS	Norway	2-1	China PR	ALG
09-03	QUARTEIRA	Portugal	1-2	Mexico	ALG
09-03	LAGOS	Sweden	1-2	Germany	ALG
11-03	SILVES	China PR	0-2	Sweden	ALG
11-03	GUIA	Denmark	1-2	France	ALG
11-03	FARO	England	4-0	Portugal	ALG
11-03	SILVES	Germany	4-0	Norway	ALG
11-03	FARO	Mexico	2-0	Northern Ireland	ALG
11-03	GUIA	USA	3-0	Finland	ALG
12-03	CORK	Republic of Ireland	2-0	Belgium	Fr
13-03	ALVOR	China PR	0-2	Germany	ALG
13-03	LAGOS	England	5-0	Mexico	ALG
13-03	LOULE	Finland	1-2	France	ALG
13-03	LAGOS	Northern Ireland	2-1	Portugal	ALG
13-03	LOULE	Sweden	1-1	Norway	ALG
13-03	VILA REAL	USA	4-0	Denmark	ALG
15-03	GUIA	England	0-0	China PR	ALG
15-03	FARO-LOULE	Germany	0-1	USA	ALG
15-03	QUARTEIRA	Mexico	1-1	Finland	ALG
15-03	MONTECHORO	Northern Ireland	1-3	Portugal	ALG
15-03	FARO	Norway	2-1	Denmark	ALG
15-03	FARO-LOULE	Sweden	2-3	France	ALG
17-03	TAPOLCA	Hungary	0-3	Poland	Fr
19-03	TAPOLCA	Hungary	0-4	Poland	Fr
25-03	ARLON	Belgium	2-1	Switzerland	Fr
26-03	SYDNEY	Australia	0-2	Japan	Fr
27-03	ETHE	Belgium	0-4	Switzerland	Fr
29-03	MIRANDA	Australia	2-1	Japan	Fr
03-04	ALBENA	Bulgaria	2-0	Kazakhstan	Fr
05-04	VARNA	Korea DPR	6-1	Romania	Fr
09-04	VARNA	Bulgaria	0-5	Korea DPR	Fr
09-04	VARNA	Kazakhstan	2-2	Romania	Fr
12-04	MALE DVORNIKY	Slovakia	2-1	Hungary	Fr
13-04	MONTBELIARD	France	0-0	Netherlands	Fr
13-04	GYOR	Hungary	2-0	Slovakia	Fr
13-04	GENOA	Italy	1-0	Denmark	Fr
19-04	APELDOORN	Netherlands	1-1	Canada	Fr
21-04	TRANMERE	England	2-1	Scotland	Fr
21-04	OSNABRUECK	Germany	3-1	Canada	Fr
24-04	HILDESHEIM	Germany	3-2	Canada	Fr
25-04	CAIRO	Egypt	1-0	Algeria	Fr
27-04	VILDBJERG	Denmark	7-2	Switzerland	Fr
27-04	STRASBOURG	France	0-2	Canada	Fr
27-04	FLUGGI	Italy	0-0	Finland	Fr
30-04	VAXJO	Sweden	0-0	Denmark	Fr
03-05	TRELLEBORG	Sweden	2-0	Netherlands	Fr
06-05	BARNSLEY	England	1-0	Norway	Fr
18-05	VENICE	Italy	2-0	Republic of Ireland	Fr
20-05	TURKU	Finland	2-0	Scotland	Fr
21-05	TOKYO	Japan	6-0	New Zealand	Fr
21-05	KUALA LUMPUR	Malaysia	1-6	Philippines	Fr
21-05	GARIC	Slovenia	7-1	Macedonia FYR	Fr
23-05	KUALA LUMPUR	Philippines	0-5	Myanmar	Fr
24-05	ZALAEGERSZEG	Hungary	2-0	Slovenia	Fr

2005	Venue		Score		Comp
25-05	COPENHAGEN	Denmark	3-4	Canada	Fr
25-05	KUALA LUMPUR	Malaysia	0-16	Myanmar	Fr
25-05	PERTH	Scotland	0-2	Iceland	Fr
26-05	WALSALL	England	4-1	Czech Republic	Fr
26-05	SHELKOVO	Russia	2-4	Japan	Fr
28-05	MOSCOW	Russia	0-2	Japan	Fr
28-05	STOCKHOLM	Sweden	3-1	Canada	Fr
30-05	SINGAPORE	Singapore	0-1	Philippines	Fr
31-05	SARPSBORG	Norway	3-0	Canada	Fr
05-06	MANCHESTER	England	3-2	Finland	ECr1
05-06	BLACKPOOL	Sweden	1-1	Denmark	ECr1
06-06	PRESTON	France	3-1	Italy	ECr1
06-06	WARRINGTON	Germany	1-0	Norway	ECr1
06-06	DUBLIN	Republic of Ireland	2-1	Faroe Islands	Fr
08-06	BLACKBURN	Denmark	2-1	England	ECr1
08-06	BLACKPOOL	Sweden	0-0	Finland	ECr1
09-06	WARRINGTON	France	1-1	Norway	ECr1
09-06	PRESTON	Italy	0-4	Germany	ECr1
11-06	BLACKBURN	England	0-1	Sweden	ECr1
11-06	BLACKPOOL	Finland	2-1	Denmark	ECr1
12-06	WARRINGTON	Germany	3-0	France	ECr1
12-06	HANOI	Guam	0-10	India	ACq
12-06	PRESTON	Norway	5-3	Italy	ECr1
12-06	HANOI	Vietnam	6-1	Philippines	ACq
13-06	HANOI	Indonesia	0-0	Singapore	ACq
13-06	HANOI	Maldives	0-6	Uzbekistan	ACq
14-06	HANOI	India	1-2	Chinese Taipei	ACq
14-06	HANOI	Philippines	1-4	Myanmar	ACq
15-06	PRESTON	Germany	4-1	Finland	ECsf
15-06	HANOI	Singapore	1-5	Thailand	ACq
15-06	HANOI	Uzbekistan	3-0	Hong Kong	ACq
16-06	HANOI	Myanmar	0-1	Vietnam	ACq
16-06	WARRINGTON	Norway	3-2	Sweden	ECsf
16-06	HANOI	Chinese Taipei	11-0	Guam	ACq
17-06	HANOI	Hong Kong	4-0	Maldives	ACq
17-06	HANOI	Thailand	4-0	Indonesia	ACq
19-06	BLACKBURN	Germany	3-1	Norway	ECf
19-06	HANOI	Chinese Taipei	3-0	Singapore	ACq
19-06	HANOI	Vietnam	4-1	Hong Kong	ACq
20-06	HANOI	India	2-3	Thailand	ACq
20-06	HANOI	Myanmar	2-1	Uzbekistan	ACq
26-06	VIRGINIA BEACH	USA	2-0	Canada	Fr
09-07	MOSCOW	Russia	5-1	Republic of Ireland	WCq
10-07	PORTLAND	USA	7-0	Ukraine	Fr
12-07	CUNNINGSBURGH	Bermuda	0-3	Faroe Islands	Fr
16-07	TIANJIN	China PR	1-2	Australia	Fr
19-07	TIANJIN	China PR	2-0	Australia	Fr
22-07	LECZNA	Poland	1-2	Ukraine	Fr
23-07	TOKYO	Japan	4-2	Australia	Fr
24-07	STEZYCA	Poland	0-4	Ukraine	Fr
24-07	CARSONES	USA	3-0	Iceland	Fr
26-07	JEONJU	Korea Republic	0-0	Australia	Fr
28-07	JEONJU	Korea Republic	3-0	Australia	Fr
31-07	PERTH	Scotland	2-1	Northern Ireland	Fr
01-08	JEONJU	Korea Republic	2-0	China PR	Fr
01-08	JEONJU	Korea DPR	1-0	Japan	Fr
03-08	DAEJEON	China PR	0-0	Japan	Fr
04-08	JEONJU	Korea Republic	1-0	Korea DPR	Fr
06-08	DAEGU	China PR	0-1	Korea DPR	Fr
06-08	DAEGU	Korea Republic	0-0	Japan	Fr
07-08	SEDIBENG	South Africa	12-0	Mozambique	Fr
09-08	SEDIBENG	South Africa	4-0	Mozambique	Fr

INTERNATIONALS PLAYED SINCE THE FIFA WOMEN'S WORLD CUP 2003

2005 Venue		Score		Comp	2005 Venue		Score		Comp
13-08 PEREIRA	Colombia	3-1	Bolivia	BG	05-10 QUANG NINH	Chinese Taipei	2-1	India	Fr
13-08 PEREIRA	Peru	5-1	Venezuela	BG	07-10 QUANG NINH	Vietnam	2-1	India	Fr
14-08 ARMENIA	Colombia	3-1	Venezuela	BG	10-10 QUANG NINH	Vietnam	2-0	Chinese Taipei	Fr
14-08 MONTENEGRO	Peru	4-0	Ecuador	BG	12-10 ZWOLLE	Netherlands	6-0	Switzerland	Fr
15-08 PEREIRA	Colombia	0-2	Peru	BG	16-10 FULLERTON	USA	0-0	Australia	Fr
15-08 PEREIRA	Ecuador	3-1	Bolivia	BG	19-10 EL PASO	Mexico	0-2	Australia	Fr
16-08 ARMENIA	Ecuador	0-0	Venezuela	BG	20-10 BAYREUTH	Germany	4-0	Scotland	WCq
16-08 GOYANG CITY	Korea Republic	0-2	Korea DPR	Fr	23-10 CHARLESTON	USA	3-0	Mexico	Fr
16-08 MONTENEGRO	Peru	2-0	Bolivia	BG	27-10 TAPOLCA	Hungary	0-13	England	WCq
17-08 ARMENIA	Bolivia	2-1	Venezuela	BG	29-10 KAPFENBERG	Austria	0-1	Netherlands	WCq
17-08 MONTENEGRO	Colombia	5-0	Ecuador	BG	29-10 SLAVONSKI BROD	Croatia	2-0	Bosnia/H'govina	WCq
19-08 ARMENIA	Colombia	1-0	Ecuador	BG	29-10 DRAMA	Greece	0-2	Serbia & Mont'gro	WCq
19-08 ARMENIA	Peru	3-0	Bolivia	BG	29-10 BERGEN	Norway	1-0	Italy	WCq
20-08 PEREIRA	Colombia	0-3	Peru	BG	29-10 MOGOSOAIA	Romania	3-2	Northern Ireland	WCq
20-08 PEREIRA	Ecuador	3-2	Bolivia	BG	30-10 HEVERLEE	Belgium	2-3	Poland	WCq
20-08 OULU	Finland	4-0	Netherlands	Fr	30-10 HELSINKI	Finland	0-1	Spain	WCq
20-08 KOSZALIN	Poland	0-3	Switzerland	Fr	01-11 ALCOCHETE	Portugal	1-4	Sweden	WCq
20-08 SENEC	Slovakia	2-1	Romania	WCq	02-11 BAGNAROLA	Italy	6-0	Serbia & Mont'gro	WCq
21-08 PARNU	Estonia	2-5	Israel	WCq	05-11 LANGENROHR	Austria	1-3	France	WCq
21-08 REYKJAVIK	Iceland	3-0	Belarus	WCq	05-11 MADRID	Spain	3-2	Belgium	WCq
26-08 CAMPINA	Romania	4-1	Kazakhstan	WCq	05-11 LISBON	Portugal	0-3	Czech Republic	WCq
27-08 MINSK	Belarus	1-1	Czech Republic	WCq	05-11 SABAC	Serbia & Mont'gro	0-4	Ukraine	WCq
27-08 LILLESTROM	Norway	4-1	Ukraine	WCq	06-11 KRSKO	Slovenia	4-1	Malta	WCq
27-08 SLUPSK	Poland	1-5	Denmark	WCq	09-11 BLOIS	France	2-0	Hungary	WCq
28-08 MOSCOW	Russia	6-0	Scotland	WCq	09-11 KAVALA	Greece	1-3	Ukraine	WCq
28-08 KRSKO	Slovenia	2-0	Bosnia-H'govina	WCq	10-11 MADRID	Spain	2-2	Denmark	WCq
28-08 KARLSKOGA	Sweden	2-2	Iceland	WCq	10-11 RISHON LEZION	Israel	2-0	Moldova	WCq
31-08 STROMBEEK	Belgium	0-3	Finland	WCq	10-11 BALLYMENA	Northern Ireland	2-1	Slovakia	WCq
31-08 ASTANA	Kazakhstan	0-4	Slovakia	WCq	12-11 ULM	Germany	4-0	Switzerland	WCq
01-09 AMSTETTEN	Austria	1-4	England	WCq	17-11 ZWOLLE	Netherlands	0-1	England	WCq
01-09 VANCOUVER	Canada	1-3	Germany	Fr	22-11 MARIKINA CITY	Indonesia	1-2	Thailand	SEA
01-09 ZUG	Switzerland	0-2	Russia	WCq	22-11 MARIKINA CITY	Myanmar	1-0	Vietnam	SEA
04-09 EDMONTON	Canada	3-4	Germany	Fr	24-11 MARIKINA CITY	Indonesia	0-5	Myanmar	SEA
06-09 TA'QALI	Malta	1-4	Croatia	WCq	24-11 MARIKINA CITY	Philippines	0-1	Thailand	SEA
07-09 SENS	France	6-0	Republic of Ireland	Fr	25-11 GOSFORD	Australia	0-0	China PR	Fr
07-09 ZWOLLE	Netherlands	0-2	Italy	Fr	26-11 MARIKINA CITY	Philippines	2-0	Indonesia	SEA
14-09 SINGAPORE	Singapore	2-0	Malaysia	Fr	26-11 MARIKINA CITY	Thailand	0-1	Vietnam	SEA
18-09 AMMAN	Jordan	6-1	Bahrain	Fr	28-11 TUMBI UMBI	Australia	3-1	China PR	Fr
23-09 AMMAN	Iran	5-0	Syria	WAC	28-11 MARIKINA CITY	Myanmar	2-1	Thailand	SEA
23-09 AMMAN	Jordan	9-0	Palestine	WAC	28-11 MARIKINA CITY	Philippines	1-5	Vietnam	SEA
24-09 SLAVONSKI BROD	Croatia	3-5	Slovenia	WCq	30-11 MARIKINA CITY	Philippines	1-3	Myanmar	SEA
24-09 KRAVARE	Czech Republic	1-0	Iceland	WCq	30-11 MARIKINA CITY	Vietnam	8-0	Indonesia	SEA
24-09 VAASA	Finland	3-1	Poland	WCq	03-12 SYDNEY	Australia	0-0	China PR	Fr
24-09 ANGERS	France	0-1	Netherlands	WCq	03-12 MARIKINA CITY	Myanmar	0-1	Vietnam	SEA
24-09 BUK	Hungary	0-3	Austria	WCq	03-12 OGHARA	Nigeria	1-0	South Africa	Fr
24-09 MONZA	Italy	3-1	Ukraine	WCq	30-12 PHUKET	Thailand	1-0	Vietnam	Fr
24-09 CHISINAU	Moldova	3-1	Estonia	WCq	2006				
24-09 LAZAREVAC	Serbia & Mont'gro	0-4	Norway	WCq	06-01 ALEXANDRIA	Egypt	0-0	Algeria	Fr
24-09 SKELLEFTEA	Sweden	6-0	Belarus	WCq	18-01 GUANGZHOU	China PR	1-1	France	Fr
25-09 FARUM	Denmark	3-0	Belgium	WCq	18-01 GUANGZHOU	USA	3-1	Norway	Fr
25-09 SIEGEN	Germany	5-1	Russia	WCq	20-01 GUANGZHOU	China PR	3-1	Norway	Fr
25-09 AMMAN	Jordan	9-0	Bahrain	WAC	20-01 GUANGZHOU	USA	0-0	France	Fr
25-09 LAGOS	Nigeria	1-0	Cameroon	Fr	22-01 GUANGZHOU	China PR	0-2	USA	Fr
25-09 AMMAN	Palestine	0-4	Syria	WAC	22-01 GUANGZHOU	Norway	1-1	France	Fr
25-09 PERTH	Scotland	0-0	Republic of Ireland	WCq	05-02 MASPALOMAS	Finland	0-1	Netherlands	Fr
27-09 AMMAN	Bahrain	0-7	Iran	WAC	07-02 LARNACA	England	0-0	Sweden	Fr
27-09 AMMAN	Syria	0-6	Jordan	WAC	08-02 MASPALOMAS	Finland	0-0	Netherlands	Fr
29-09 AMMAN	Palestine	0-7	Iran	WAC	09-02 ACHNAS	England	1-0	Sweden	Fr
29-09 KUTNO	Poland	3-2	Spain	WCq	18-02 SHIZUOKA	Japan	2-0	Russia	Fr
29-09 AMMAN	Syria	2-1	Bahrain	WAC	19-02 UNKNOWN (BEN)	Benin	1-0	Malawi	WCq
01-10 AMMAN	Bahrain	1-1	Palestine	WAC	19-02 UNKNOWN (MOZ)	Mozambique	9-0	Namibia	WCq
01-10 AMMAN	Iran	1-2	Jordan	WAC	19-02 UNKNOWN (SEN)	Senegal	4-0	Central Af. Rep.	WCq

INTERNATIONALS PLAYED SINCE THE FIFA WOMEN'S WORLD CUP 2003

2006	Venue		Score		Comp
19-02	UNKNOWN (STP)	Sao Tome e Pr.	0-3	Togo	WCq
23-02	MEXICALI	Canada	3-1	Mexico	Fr
23-02	ALMERE	Netherlands	0-0	China PR	Fr
25-02	PALM SPRINGS	Canada	1-1	Mexico	Fr
25-02	BELLINZONA	Switzerland	2-3	Denmark	Fr
26-02	UNKNOWN (MWI)	Malawi	0-0	Benin	Fr
26-02	UNKNOWN (TOG)	Togo	6-0	Sao Tome e Pr.	WCq
01-03	VANCOUVER	Canada	1-0	Netherlands	Fr
01-03	HOMBURG	Germany	0-1	China PR	Fr
04-03	VICTORIA	Canada	3-1	Netherlands	Fr
07-03	SENEC	Slovakia	3-2	Hungary	Fr
08-03	GYOR	Hungary	1-0	Slovakia	Fr
08-03	ISERNIA	Italy	4-0	Scotland	Fr
09-03	NORWICH	England	1-0	Iceland	Fr
09-03	FARO	France	2-2	Denmark	ALG
09-03	LOULE	Germany	5-0	Finland	ALG
09-03	LOULE	Norway	0-0	Sweden	ALG
09-03	ALVOR	Portugal	0-1	Republic of Ireland	ALG
09-03	FARO	USA	0-0	China PR	ALG
10-03	AGNONE	Japan	4-0	Scotland	Fr
11-03	LOULE	China PR	0-1	France	ALG
11-03	LUBUMBASHI	Congo DR	3-0	Zambia	WCq
11-03	QUARTEIRA	Denmark	0-5	USA	ALG
11-03	ALVOR	Finland	0-0	Norway	ALG
11-03	VILA REAL	Republic of Ireland	0-0	Mexico	ALG
11-03	RABAT	Morocco	0-2	Mali	WCq
11-03	PRETORIA	South Africa	6-2	Mozambique	WCq
11-03	UNKNOWN (SEN)	Senegal	7-0	Guinea	WCq
11-03	LOULE	Sweden	0-3	Germany	ALG
12-03	LUANDA	Angola	3-2	Equatorial Guinea	WCq
12-03	COTONOU	Benin	1-1	Cote d'Ivoire	WCq
12-03	BRIDGETOWN	Barbados	0-1	Antigua/Barbuda	Fr
12-03	BRAZZAVILLE	Congo	9-0	Togo	WCq
12-03	VENAFRO	Italy	1-0	Japan	Fr
13-03	LAGOS	Denmark	0-6	China PR	ALG
13-03	FARO	Germany	1-0	Norway	ALG
13-03	SILVES	Portugal	0-6	Mexico	ALG
13-03	LAGOS	Sweden	4-1	Finland	ALG
13-03	FARO	USA	4-1	France	ALG
14-03	BRIDGETOWN	Barbados	0-1	Antigua/Barbuda	Fr
15-03	ALBUFEIRA	China PR	0-1	Norway	ALG
15-03	FARO	France	0-1	Sweden	ALG
15-03	LAGOA	Ireland Republic	0-4	Denmark	ALG
15-03	FERREIRAS	Mexico	3-4	Finland	ALG
15-03	KLOTEN	Switzerland	3-2	Wales	Fr
15-03	FARO	USA	0-0	Germany	ALG
18-03	UNKNOWN (ATG)	Antigua/Barbuda	0-0	Barbados	Fr
18-03	GEORGETOWN	Cayman Islands	1-2	Neth. Antilles	Fr
25-03	CURACAO	Neth. Antilles	1-0	Cayman Islands	Fr
25-03	ST. JOHN'S	Antigua/Barbuda	2-0	St. Vincent/Gr.	Fr
25-03	SARAJEVO	Bosnia/H'govina	1-0	Malta	WCq
25-03	ATHENS	Greece	0-3	Norway	WCq
25-03	ANDRASHIDA	Hungary	0-5	Netherlands	WCq
25-03	BIENNE	Switzerland	2-0	Republic of Ireland	WCq
26-03	ST. JOHN'S	Antigua/Barbuda	3-1	St. Vincent/Gr.	Fr
26-03	ATH	Belgium	0-2	Denmark	WCq
26-03	UNKNOWN (CIV)	Cote d'Ivoire	1-1	Benin	WCq
26-03	BLACKBURN	England	0-0	France	WCq
26-03	UNKNOWN (EQG)	Equatorial Guinea	3-1	Angola	WCq
26-03	CONAKRY	Guinea	1-5	Senegal	WCq
26-03	NAIROBI	Kenya	7-0	Djibouti	WCq
26-03	BAMAKO	Mali	4-1	Morocco	WCq
26-03	MAPUTO	Mozambique	1-6	South Africa	WCq
26-03	UNKNOWN (TOG)	Togo	1-3	Congo	WCq
26-03	NEWTOWN	Wales	3-0	Moldova	WCq
26-03	NDOLA	Zambia	2-3	Congo DR	WCq
29-03	VRBOVEC	Croatia	1-0	Malta	WCq
29-03	AVERSA	Italy	2-0	Greece	WCq
30-03	ARANDA	Spain	7-0	Poland	WCq
30-03	SENEC	Slovakia	2-0	Northern Ireland	WCq
30-03	CARDIFF	Wales	1-1	Israel	WCq
01-04	VIRGIN GORDA	British Virgin Isl.	1-3	US Virgin Islands	WCq
02-04	VARNA	Bulgaria	4-2	Kazakhstan	Fr
04-04	VARNA	Bulgaria	1-0	Romania	Fr
04-04	VARNA	Ukraine	4-1	Kazakhstan	Fr
06-04	VARNA	Kazakhstan	1-7	Romania	Fr
08-04	VARNA	Bulgaria	1-2	Ukraine	Fr
08-04	MUTENICE	Czech Republic	2-1	Slovenia	Fr
09-04	ST. THOMAS	US Virgin Islands	5-0	British Virgin Isl.	WCq
10-04	VARNA	Romania	1-1	Ukraine	Fr
12-04	ZWOLLE	Netherlands	2-1	Iceland	Fr
15-04	LAJKOVAC	Serbia & Mont'gro	3-1	Greece	WCq
19-04	ALEXANDRIA	Algeria	12-0	Lebanon	ARC
20-04	ALEXANDRIA	Egypt	2-1	Tunisia	ARC
20-04	GILLINGHAM	England	4-0	Austria	WCq
20-04	ALEXANDRIA	Syria	2-1	Palestine	ARC
21-04	ALEXANDRIA	Algeria	0-0	Morocco	ARC
22-04	BRUSSELS	Belgium	2-4	Spain	WCq
22-04	KLADNO	Czech Republic	2-3	Sweden	WCq
22-04	ALEXANDRIA	Egypt	6-0	Syria	ARC
22-04	ATHENS	Greece	0-5	Italy	WCq
22-04	DUNAUJVAROS	Hungary	0-5	France	WCq
22-04	DUBLIN	Republic of Ireland	2-0	Switzerland	WCq
22-04	CASTRIES	St. Lucia	6-1	St. Vincent/Gr.	Fr
22-04	LURGAN	Northern Ireland	1-0	Kazakhstan	WCq
22-04	ALEXANDRIA	Palestine	0-4	Tunisia	ARC
22-04	JAWORZNO	Poland	1-5	Finland	WCq
23-04	ALEXANDRIA	Lebanon	0-8	Morocco	ARC
23-04	RHYL	Wales	0-0	Estonia	WCq
24-04	ALEXANDRIA	Egypt	9-0	Palestine	ARC
24-04	CASTRIES	St. Lucia	2-2	St. Vincent/Gr.	Fr
24-04	ALEXANDRIA	Tunisia	10-0	Syria	ARC
26-04	ALEXANDRIA	Algeria	3-0	Tunisia	ARC
26-04	ALEXANDRIA	Egypt	2-4	Morocco	ARC
26-04	CORRADINO	Malta	1-3	Slovenia	WCq
26-04	PERTH	Scotland	1-0	Switzerland	WCq
27-04	VIBORG	Denmark	5-0	Spain	WCq
29-04	ALEXANDRIA	Algeria	1-0	Morocco	ARC
29-04	SAN SALVADOR	El Salvador	2-3	Guatemala	Fr
29-04	ALEXANDRIA	Tunisia	2-1	Egypt	ARC
30-04	SAN SALVADOR	El Salvador	0-1	Guatemala	Fr
03-05	ORANJESTAD	Surinam	7-1	Neth. Antilles	WCq
04-05	SANTO DOMINGO	Bermuda	4-0	Turks and Caicos	WCq
04-05	SANTO DOMINGO	Dominican Rep.	3-1	US Virgin Islands	WCq
05-05	ORANJESTAD	Aruba	1-2	Neth. Antilles	WCq
06-05	MINSK	Belarus	1-2	Iceland	WCq
06-05	SANTO DOMINGO	Dominican Rep.	5-0	Turks and Caicos	WCq
06-05	TAMPERE	Finland	3-0	Belgium	WCq
06-05	DUBLIN	Republic of Ireland	0-2	Scotland	WCq
06-05	LVOV	Ukraine	2-1	Serbia & Mont'gro	WCq
06-05	SANTO DOMINGO	US Virgin Islands	1-4	Bermuda	WCq
07-05	ORANJESTAD	Aruba	0-3	Surinam	WCq
07-05	SARAJEVO	Bosnia-H'govina	1-6	Slovenia	WCq
07-05	COPENHAGEN	Denmark	3-1	Poland	WCq

INTERNATIONALS PLAYED SINCE THE FIFA WOMEN'S WORLD CUP 2003

2006	Venue		Score		Comp
07-05	HERTZELIYA	Israel	1-0	Estonia	WCq
07-05	KUMAMOTO	Japan	1-3	USA	Fr
07-05	CHISINAU	Moldova	0-3	Wales	WCq
07-05	TRELLEBORG	Sweden	5-1	Portugal	WCq
08-05	SANTO DOMINGO	Dominican Rep.	3-1	Bermuda	WCq
08-05	KINGSTON	Jamaica	5-0	St. Lucia	WCq
08-05	KINGSTON	St. Kitts & Nevis	3-2	Antigua/Barbuda	WCq
08-05	SANTO DOMINGO	US Virgin Islands	2-0	Turks and Caicos	WCq
09-05	OSAKA	Japan	0-1	USA	Fr
10-05	COTTBUS	Germany	1-0	Republic of Ireland	WCq
10-05	KINGSTON	Jamaica	10-0	Antigua/Barbuda	WCq
10-05	KINGSTON	St. Lucia	3-2	St. Kitts & Nevis	WCq
10-05	MERIDA	Mexico	9-0	Nicaragua	WCq
10-05	SANDEFJORD	Norway	3-0	Serbia & Mont'gro	WCq
11-05	SOUTHAMPTON	England	2-0	Hungary	WCq
11-05	POZOBLANCO	Spain	0-0	Finland	WCq
11-05	CHISINAU	Moldova	0-1	Israel	WCq
11-05	BEJA	Portugal	0-1	Belarus	WCq
11-05	SENEC	Slovakia	2-0	Kazakhstan	WCq
12-05	KINGSTON	Antigua/Barbuda	1-2	St. Lucia	WCq
12-05	KINGSTON	Jamaica	11-0	St. Kitts & Nevis	WCq
12-05	MERIDA	Nicaragua	2-1	El Salvador	WCq
13-05	ZWOLLE	Netherlands	0-2	France	WCq
14-05	MERIDA	Mexico	8-0	El Salvador	WCq
14-05	KRSKO	Slovenia	3-0	Croatia	WCq
19-05	MALABAR	Trinidad/Tobago	10-0	Grenada	WCq
19-05	MALABAR	St. Vincent/Gr.	2-0	Dominica	WCq
20-05	ZENICA	Bosnia/H'govina	2-1	Croatia	WCq
20-05	LONDONDERRY	Northern Ireland	1-4	Romania	WCq
21-05	MALABAR	Dominica	2-2	Grenada	WCq
21-05	PROVIDENCIALES	Turks and Caicos	0-4	Cayman Islands	Fr
21-05	MALABAR	Trinidad/Tobago	4-1	St. Vincent/Gr.	WCq
23-05	MALABAR	Grenada	0-5	St. Vincent/Gr.	WCq
23-05	MALABAR	Trinidad/Tobago	6-0	Dominica	WCq
24-05	PANAMA CITY	Guatemala	2-1	Costa Rica	WCq
24-05	PERTH	Scotland	0-4	Russia	WCq
25-05	MELBOURNE	Australia	2-1	Mexico	Fr
26-05	PANAMA CITY	Panama	2-0	Costa Rica	WCq
27-05	PARAMARIBO	Surinam	0-3	Haiti	WCq
28-05	ALBERT PARK	Australia	3-0	Mexico	Fr
28-05	PANAMA CITY	Panama	3-0	Guatemala	WCq
29-05	COTONOU	Benin	2-3	Equatorial Guinea	Fr
29-05	HO CHI MINH	Myanmar	2-3	Thailand	Fr
29-05	HO CHI MINH	Vietnam	1-0	Chinese Taipei	Fr
30-05	PORT M'BOURNE	Australia	4-0	Mexico	Fr
31-05	HO CHI MINH	Myanmar	0-3	Chinese Taipei	Fr
31-05	HO CHI MINH	Vietnam	3-2	Thailand	Fr
02-06	HO CHI MINH	Chinese Taipei	1-1	Thailand	Fr
02-06	HO CHI MINH	Vietnam	1-0	Myanmar	Fr
04-06	ROUDNICE	Czech Republic	6-0	Portugal	WCq
07-06	CORRADINO	Malta	1-1	Bosnia/H'govina	WCq
08-06	UNKNOWN (SEN)	Senegal	1-1	South Africa	Fr
10-06	UNKNOWN (SEN)	Senegal	1-1	South Africa	Fr
12-06	BANGKOK	Thailand	6-0	Singapore	Fr
16-06	SHANGHAI	China PR	2-1	Australia	Fr
17-06	DUBLIN	Republic of Ireland	0-2	Russia	WCq
17-06	ALMATY	Kazakhstan	1-1	Northern Ireland	WCq
17-06	MARIUPOL	Ukraine	2-1	Italy	WCq
18-06	MINSK	Belarus	0-6	Sweden	WCq
18-06	VALGA	Estonia	3-2	Moldova	WCq
18-06	REYKJAVIK	Iceland	3-0	Portugal	WCq
19-06	SHANGHAI	China PR	2-0	Australia	Fr

2006	Venue		Score		Comp
20-06	HALDEN	Norway	4-0	Greece	WCq
21-06	BELGRADE	Serbia & Mont'gro	0-7	Italy	WCq
22-06	MOGOSOAIA	Romania	2-3	Slovakia	WCq
23-06	MARIUPOL	Ukraine	6-0	Greece	WCq
25-06	TORONTO	Canada	2-1	Italy	Fr

Fr = Friendly • AAG = All Africa Games • EC = UEFA European Women's Championship • OG = Olympic Games • SEA = Southeast Asian Games ALG = Algarve Cup • CN = CAF African Women's Championship WAC = West Asian Championship • ARC = Arab Championship BG = Bolivarian Games • WCq = FIFA Women's Cup qualifier

q = qualifier • r1 = final tournament first round group • qf = quarter-final • sf = semi-final • f = final

CHINA PR 2005 SUPER LEAGUE

	Pl	W	D	L	F	A	Pts
Shanghai SVA	14	10	4	0	30	11	34
Tianjin Huisen	14	7	3	4	17	13	24
Beijing Chengjian	14	6	5	3	16	11	23
Jiangsu Huatai	14	5	7	2	12	9	22
Dalian Shide	14	7	1	6	18	10	22
Hebei Huayao	14	3	3	8	13	22	12
Guangdong Haiyin	14	2	4	8	6	14	10
Army	14	1	3	10	5	27	6

CZECH REPUBLIC 2005-06 FIRST DIVISION

	Pl	W	D	L	F	A	Pts
Sparta Praha	16	15	1	0	62	8	46
Slavia Praha	16	12	2	2	59	14	38
Otrokovice	16	10	2	4	41	19	32
Hradec Králóve	16	6	4	6	25	22	22
Brno	16	7	1	8	34	27	22
Plzen	16	3	5	8	13	31	14
Krásná Studánka	16	3	5	8	9	29	14
Sobedruhy	16	2	2	12	13	51	8
Hlucín	16	2	2	12	12	57	8

DENMARK 2005-06 FIRST DIVISION

	Pl	W	D	L	F	A	Pts
Brøndby	21	19	1	1	81	8	58
Fortuna Hjørring	21	17	2	2	73	16	53
Skovlunde	21	12	4	5	43	22	40
Skovbakken	21	7	5	9	29	41	26
Varde	21	6	1	14	18	55	19
Team Viborg	21	5	2	14	15	46	17
Vejle	21	4	4	13	25	48	16
OB	21	3	3	15	12	60	12

ENGLAND 2005-06 PREMIER LEAGUE

	Pl	W	D	L	F	A	Pts
Arsenal LFC	18	16	2	0	83	20	50
Everton LFC	18	14	2	2	46	20	44
Charlton Athletic LFC	18	12	3	3	41	13	39
Doncaster Rov. Belles	18	7	2	9	32	34	23
Bristol Rovers WFC	18	4	8	6	19	29	20
Birmingham City LFC	18	6	2	10	24	40	20
Leeds United LFC	18	4	6	8	27	36	18
Fulham FC Ladies	18	4	2	12	24	45	14
Sunderland	18	3	4	11	22	57	13
Chelsea	18	3	3	12	22	46	12

Cup Final: Arsenal LFC 5-0 Leeds United LFC

HUNGARY 2005-06 FIRST DIVISION

	Pl	W	D	L	F	A	Pts
1.FC Femina	24	19	3	2	133	17	60
MTK Budapest	23	17	3	3	98	17	54
WHC Viktória	24	16	4	4	84	22	52
Györ ETO	24	10	3	11	48	49	33
IRIS Hungarokábel	23	7	1	15	39	88	22
Debreceni VSC	24	6	0	18	23	80	18
ASI Renova	24	0	2	22	10	162	2

FINLAND 2005 FIRST DIVISION

	Pl	W	D	L	F	A	Pts
HJK Helsinki	18	14	3	1	51	12	45
FC Espoo	18	13	2	3	51	14	41
FC United Pietarsaari	18	12	3	3	53	17	39
Honka	18	11	2	5	57	27	35
KMF	18	10	2	6	35	28	32
SCR Raisio	18	9	1	8	33	31	28
Sport	18	4	4	10	19	31	16
TiPS Vantaa	18	4	2	12	16	37	14
Ilves Tampere	18	1	3	14	13	47	6
MPS Helsinki	18	0	2	16	9	93	2

Cup Final: FC United Pietarsaari 1-0 FC Espoo

FRANCE 2005-06 DIVISION 1

	Pl	W	D	L	F	A	Pts
FCF Juvisy	22	21	0	1	83	15	85
Montpellier HSC	22	17	3	2	68	15	76
Olympique Lyonnais	22	10	8	4	34	12	60
Toulouse FC	22	11	4	7	38	18	59
CNFE FF	22	10	4	8	42	31	56
ASJ Soyaux	22	10	4	8	40	30	56
FCF Hénin-Beaumont	22	9	2	11	27	51	51
Paris St-Germain	22	8	3	11	26	32	49
USCCO Compiègne	22	5	6	11	23	41	43
ESOF La Roche	22	5	2	15	19	54	39
FC Vendeheim	22	2	5	15	13	53	33
St Memmie Olympique	22	3	1	18	15	76	32

Cup Final: Montpellier HSC 1-1 4-3p Olympique Lyonnais

GERMANY 2005-06 FIRST DIVISION

	Pl	W	D	L	F	A	Pts
FFC Turbine Potsdam	22	19	2	1	115	13	59
FCR 2001 Duisburg	22	17	4	1	91	11	55
1. FFC Frankfurt	22	17	1	4	97	25	52
SC 07 Bad Neuenahr	22	14	2	6	61	40	44
Hamburger SV	22	10	3	9	42	40	33
SG Essen-Schönebeck	22	9	3	10	44	49	30
SC Freiburg	22	9	5	8	45	48	29
FC Bayern München	22	8	3	11	41	48	27
FFC Heike Rheine	22	5	5	12	39	56	20
FFC Brauweiler Pulheim	22	3	4	15	24	79	13
VfL Sindelfingen	22	2	5	15	19	72	11
FSV Frankfurt	22	0	1	21	5	142	1

Cup Final: 1.FFC Turbine Potsdam 2-0 1.FFC Frankfurt

ICELAND 2005 FIRST DIVISION

	Pl	W	D	L	F	A	Pts
Breidablik	14	13	1	0	47	9	40
Valur Reykjavík	14	12	0	2	60	13	36
IBV Vestmannæyjar	14	8	0	6	41	30	24
KR Reykjavík	14	7	1	6	39	24	22
Keflavík	14	6	0	8	31	35	18
Stjarnan	14	5	0	9	18	36	15
FH Hafnarfjördur	14	3	1	10	10	46	10
IA Akranes	14	0	1	13	10	63	1

Cup Final: Breidablik 4-1 KR Reykjavík

ITALY 2005-06
FIRST DIVISION

	Pl	W	D	L	F	A	Pts
Fiammamonza	22	17	5	0	47	17	56
Bardolino	22	15	3	4	64	20	48
Torino	22	14	4	4	60	25	46
Torres Terra Sarda	22	11	5	6	50	18	38
Vigor Senigallia	22	11	2	9	40	27	35
Milan	22	8	7	7	38	21	31
Aircargo Agliana	22	8	3	11	31	33	27
Monti del Matese	22	7	6	9	25	36	27
Tavagnacco	22	6	6	10	32	30	24
Reggiana	22	6	4	12	26	30	22
Atalanta	22	5	3	14	39	45	18
Atletico Oristano	22	0	0	22	4	154	0

Cup Final: Bardolino 4-1 Aircargo Agliana

JAPAN 2005
L.LEAGUE

	Pl	W	D	L	F	A	Pts
NTV Beleza	21	18	3	0	84	5	57
TASAKI Perule FC	21	16	3	2	68	13	51
Iga FC Kunoichi	21	11	6	4	29	26	39
TEPCO Mareeze	21	11	1	9	33	30	34
Urawa Reds Ladies	21	10	3	8	40	38	33
Okayama Yunogo	21	5	0	16	20	49	15
Speranza Takatsuki	21	3	1	17	14	64	10
Takarazuka Bunny's	21	1	1	19	12	75	4

27th All Japan Women's Football Championship Final 2006
NTV Belaza 4-1 TASAKI Perule

NORWAY 2005
FIRST DIVISION

	Pl	W	D	L	F	A	Pts
Kolbotn	18	14	3	1	72	15	45
Team Strømmen	18	12	3	3	44	22	39
Fløya	18	10	3	5	49	27	33
Trondheim/Orn	18	10	3	5	31	17	33
Klepp	18	8	5	5	39	24	29
Røa	18	9	1	8	36	28	28
Asker	18	7	3	8	34	30	24
Sandviken	18	4	3	11	25	58	15
Liungen	18	2	1	15	19	76	7
Kattem	18	1	1	16	20	72	4

RUSSIA 2005
FIRST DIVISION

	Pl	W	D	L	F	A	Pts
Rossiyanka MO	20	14	6	0	64	17	48
Lada Togliatti	20	13	3	4	59	24	42
Nadezhda Noginsk	20	9	6	5	39	20	33
FK Tyazan VDV	20	8	5	7	54	26	29
Spartak Moskva	20	11	3	6	58	23	36
Prialit Reutov	20	7	3	10	36	48	24
Chertanovo Moskva	20	5	0	15	18	87	15
Neva Sankt Peterburg	20	0	0	20	11	94	0

Cup Final: Rossiyanka 2-1 Spartak Moskva

SCOTLAND 2005-06
FIRST DIVISION

	Pl	W	D	L	F	A	Pts
Hibernian LFC	22	20	2	0	107	17	62
Glasgow City LFC	22	19	2	1	69	18	59
Kilmarnock	21	15	3	3	54	22	48
Newburgh LFC	22	12	5	5	44	28	41
Hamilton Academical	22	12	3	7	44	30	39
Raith Rovers	22	6	5	11	37	58	23
Forfar Farmington	22	6	2	14	33	59	20
Whitehill Welfare	21	5	4	12	26	45	19
Aberdeen LFC	22	4	7	11	31	53	19
Arsenal North LFC	22	4	3	15	22	55	15
Cove Rangers LFC	20	3	5	12	29	73	14
Queen's Park LFC	22	3	3	16	23	70	12

Cup Final: Glasgow City 5-1 Aberdeen LFC

SPAIN 2005-06
FIRST DIVISION

	Pl	W	D	L	F	A	Pts
Espanyol	24	20	0	4	80	25	60
Sevilla	24	19	3	2	78	37	60
Levante	24	17	4	3	64	15	55
Rayo Vallecano	24	15	3	6	58	36	48
Athletic Bilboko	24	13	2	9	52	46	41
Puebla	24	11	1	12	36	52	34
Estudiantes	24	9	5	10	45	38	32
Barcelona	24	8	4	12	39	51	28
Lagunak	24	8	2	14	34	47	26
Torrejón	24	7	4	13	47	55	25
Oviedo	24	6	4	14	41	59	22
T. Alcaine	24	5	3	16	31	67	18
Gijón	24	0	1	23	19	96	1

SWITZERLAND 2005-06
LIGUE NATIONALE A

	Pl	W	D	L	F	A	Pts
SC LUwin.ch	21	13	6	2	58	14	45
FFC Zuchwil 05	21	12	4	5	63	30	40
FC Schwerzenbach	21	11	4	6	37	27	37
FFC Bern	21	8	4	9	36	37	28
FFC Zürich Seebach	21	8	4	9	33	35	28
FC Rapid Lugano	21	6	4	11	32	55	22
FC Rot-Schwarz Thun	21	5	4	12	32	69	19
Ruggell-Liechtenstein	21	4	4	13	22	46	16

Cup Final: SC LUwin.ch 5-0 SV Seebach Zürich

SWEDEN 2005
DAMALLSVENSKAN

	Pl	W	D	L	F	A	Pts
Umeå IK	22	21	1	0	94	11	64
Malmö FF DFF	22	18	2	2	72	16	56
Djurgården/Alvsjö	22	13	3	6	41	21	42
Linköpings FC	22	11	3	8	41	28	36
Kopparbergs/Göteborg	22	9	5	8	38	32	32
Sunnanå SK	22	9	3	10	36	37	30
KIF Orebro DFF	22	8	6	8	35	43	30
Mallbackens IF	22	6	4	12	28	49	22
Hammarby IF DFF	22	5	5	12	26	43	20
QBIK	22	5	1	16	19	60	16
AIK Solna	22	4	3	15	17	59	15
Själevads	22	3	4	15	19	67	13

Cup Final: Djurgården/Alvsjö 3-1 Umeå IK

USA 2006
W-LEAGUE

Central Conference Atlantic Division

	Pl	W	D	L	F	A	Pts
Charlotte Lady Eagles†	14	10	0	4	32	14	30
Cocoa Expos Women	14	9	1	4	17	16	28
Richmond Kickers†	14	9	1	4	31	13	28
Central Florida Crush	14	7	2	5	25	21	23
Atlanta Silverbacks	14	6	1	7	23	17	19
Hampton Roads	14	5	1	8	18	28	16
Bradenton Athletics	14	2	5	7	12	27	11
Carolina Dynamo	14	1	3	10	7	29	6

Central Conference Midwest Division

	Pl	W	D	L	F	A	Pts
Michigan Hawks†	14	10	2	2	41	13	32
Minnesota Lightening†	14	9	2	3	34	19	29
Cleveland Internationals	14	9	1	4	36	22	28
Chicago Gaels	14	7	3	4	29	19	24
Cincinnati Ladyhawks	14	5	3	6	33	33	18
London Gryphons	14	4	1	9	28	45	13
Fort Wayne Fever	14	3	2	9	16	37	11
West Michigan Firewomen	14	2	0	12	9	38	6

Conference play-off semi-finals: **Charlotte** 1-1 5-4p Minnesota **Richmond** 2-0 Michigan
Final: **Charlotte** 1-0 Richmond

Eastern Conference Northeast Division

	Pl	W	D	L	F	A	Pts
New Jersey Wildcats†	14	14	0	0	61	3	42
Western Mass Pioneers†	14	10	1	3	43	10	31
Boston Renegades†	14	9	2	3	52	16	29
Long Island Riders†	14	7	2	5	28	17	23
Nth Virginia Majestics†	14	5	0	9	28	28	15
New York Magic	14	4	2	8	20	26	14
South Jersey Banshees	14	2	1	11	10	50	7
N. Hampshire Phantoms	14	0	2	12	4	96	2

Eastern Conference Northern Division

	Pl	W	D	L	F	A	Pts
Ottawa Fury†	12	10	1	1	38	7	31
Toronto Lynx†	12	7	4	1	37	4	25
Laval Comets	12	6	3	3	30	13	21
Hamilton Avalanche	12	6	1	5	20	25	19
Vermont Voltage	12	4	1	7	12	24	13
Rochester Rhinos	12	4	0	8	22	30	12
Sudbury Canadians	12	0	0	12	2	58	0

Conference play-off first round: **Long Island** 1-0 Boston; **Western Mass** 1-0 Nth Virginia; **Ottawa** 3-2 Toronto
Semi-finals: **Ottawa** 3-0 Western Mass; **New Jersey** 1-0 Long Island
Final: **Ottawa** 3-2 New Jersey

Western Conference

	Pl	W	D	L	F	A	Pts
Vancouver Whitecaps†	12	11	1	0	38	7	34
Seattle Sounders†	12	5	3	4	21	18	18
Mile High Edge†	12	4	2	6	22	23	14
Real Colorado Cougars	12	3	5	4	25	27	14
Fort Collins Force	12	3	2	7	15	25	11
San Diego Gauchos	12	2	3	7	14	35	9

Conference semi-final: **Seattle** 1-0 Mile High;

Championship Finals

Semi-finals: **Vancouver** 5-0 Seattle; **Ottawa** 2-1 Charlotte
Third place: Seattle 1-0 Charlotte
Final: **Vancouver** 3-0 Ottawa
Vancouver Whitecaps are the 2006 W-League champions
† Qualified for the play-offs • ‡ Qualified for the finals

USA 2006
WPSL

West Conference

	Pl	W	D	L	F	A	Pts
Ajax America†	12	11	0	1	40	8	33
San Diego Sea Lions	12	10	1	1	31	8	31
California Storm	14	10	1	3	47	15	31
Sonoma County Sol	14	9	1	4	25	12	28
Lamorinda East Bay	14	5	0	9	26	28	15
San Fran. Nighthawks	14	3	2	9	16	34	11
Sacramento Pride	14	1	2	11	10	52	5
Las Vegas Tabagators	14	1	1	12	12	40	1

Southwest Conference

	Pl	W	D	L	F	A	Pts
Denver Diamonds	5	4	1	0	10	1	13
Colorado Springs Sabers	6	2	0	4	3	12	6
Utah Spiders	2	0	0	2	1	4	0

West/Southwest play-off: **San Diego** † 1-0 Denver

Midwest Conference

	Pl	W	D	L	F	A	Pts
River Cities	12	9	2	1	23	5	29
Tennessee Lady Blues	10	7	0	3	24	13	21
FC Indiana	10	5	3	2	25	9	18
Memphis Mercury	10	3	1	6	15	19	10
Michigan Phoenix	10	3	0	7	11	27	9
FC St Louis	10	1	1	8	7	27	3

South Conference

	Pl	W	D	L	F	A	Pts
Tampa Bay Elite	10	10	0	0	28	5	30
Central Florida Strikers	13	6	2	5	27	25	20
Palm Beach United	9	4	1	4	12	17	13
Orlando Falcons	9	4	0	5	6	17	12
Ft. Lauderdale Fusion	8	2	0	6	12	16	6
Miami Revolution	7	0	0	7	0	9	0

Midwest/South play-off: **River Cities** † 3-1 Tampa Bay Elite

Eastern Conference North Division

	Pl	W	D	L	F	A	Pts
Adirondack Lynx	10	7	0	3	22	15	21
Long Island Fury	10	6	2	2	30	8	20
New England Mutiny	10	6	1	3	24	13	19
Massachusetts Stingers	10	5	2	3	16	14	17
Bay State Select	10	5	0	5	19	25	15
New York AC	10	4	1	5	13	19	13
Boston Aztecs	10	2	6	2	11	11	12
Rhode Island Rays	8	1	0	7	9	25	3

Eastern Conference South Division

	Pl	W	D	L	F	A	Pts
Atlantic City Diablos	10	8	1	1	19	5	25
Northampton Laurels	10	6	2	2	17	11	20
FC Virginia	10	6	1	3	22	11	19
Philadelphia Pirates	10	3	2	5	6	16	11
Maryland Pride	9	2	0	7	6	10	6
Central Delaware SA	9	1	1	7	4	13	4

Eastern Conference semi-finals: **Long Island** 2-1 Atlantic City; **Adirondack** 3-2 Northampton
Final: **Long Island** † 2-0 Adirondack

Championship Finals

Semi-finals: **Long Island** 2-0 San Diego; **Rivers Cities** 2-1 Ajax America • Third place: San Diego 3-3 4-3p Ajax
Final: **Long Island** 1-0 River Cities
Long Island Fury are the 2006 WPSL champions
† Qualified for the finals

PART TWO

THE
ASSOCIATIONS

AFG – AFGHANISTAN

NATIONAL TEAM RECORD
JULY 1ST 2002 TO JULY 9TH 2006

PL	W	D	L	F	A	%
14	2	2	10	8	44	21.4

FIFA/COCA-COLA WORLD RANKING

1993	1994	1995	1996	1997	1998	1999	2000	2001	2002	2003	2004	2005	High	Low
-	-	-	-	-	-	-	-	-	-	196	200	189	**189** 12/05	204 01/03

	2005–2006										
08/05	09/05	10/05	11/05	12/05	01/06	02/06	03/06	04/06	05/06	06/06	07/06
200	200	199	198	189	189	189	189	188	188	-	173

Despite the huge popularity of football and the many games being played throughout the country, Afghanistan suffers from the lack of an organised domestic championship; this despite strenuous efforts being made to establish the game on a firm footing. As a result the focus of attention remains the national team. After the fiasco of the tour to Italy, where nine players went missing only to be subsequently arrested, the side was rebuilt and in December 2005 Afghanistan entered the South Asian Football Federation Championship in Karachi. Having lost a warm up international against Tajikistan 4-0, worse was to follow in the tournament with a 9-1 thrashing in their opening

INTERNATIONAL HONOURS
None

match. Remarkably, however, coach Mohamed Kargar managed to turn things around. A narrow defeat against the hosts Pakistan was then followed by a 2-1 win over Sri Lanka, a team ranked over 50 places above them in the FIFA/Coca-Cola World Ranking. It was only the second time since their first international match in 1941 that the national side had managed a victory. In April 2006 the team then took part in the first AFC Challenge Cup, held in Bangladesh, and although there was no victory to celebrate, Afghanistan drew their final two games to chalk up another historic first - never before had the team gone two games without defeat. Progress indeed.

THE FIFA BIG COUNT OF 2000

	Male	Female		Male	Female
Registered players	3 000	0	Referees	75	0
Non registered players	3 000	0	Officials	50	0
Youth players	5 600	0	Total involved	11 725	
Total players	11 600		Number of clubs	440	
Professional players	0	0	Number of teams	450	

Afghanistan Football Federation (AFF)
PO Box 5099, Kabul, Afghanistan
Tel +93 75 2023770   Fax +93 75 2023770
e-mail aff.kabul@gmail.com   www. none
President: KARAMUDDIN Karim   General Secretary: FARID Esmail
Vice-President: MUZAFARI Sayed Zia   Treasurer: RUSTAMI Mukhtar   Media Officer: WADEED Mohammad Nadir
Men's Coach: KARGAR Mohamed   Women's Coach: None
AFF formed: 1933   AFC: 1954   FIFA: 1948
Red shirts with white trimmings, Red shorts, Red socks or white shirts with red trimmings, White shorts, White socks

RECENT INTERNATIONALS PLAYED BY AFGHANISTAN

2002	Opponents	Score	Venue	Comp	Scorers	Att	Referee
No international matches played in 2002							
2003							
10-01	Sri Lanka	L 0-1	Dhaka	SAFr1			
12-01	India	L 0-4	Dhaka	SAFr1			
14-01	Pakistan	L 0-1	Dhaka	SAFr1			
16-03	Kyrgyzstan	W 2-1	Kathmandu	ACq	Sayeed Tahir [26], Farid Azimi [76]		
18-03	Nepal	L 0-4	Kathmandu	ACq			
19-11	Turkmenistan	L 0-11	Ashgabat	WCq		12 000	Busurmankulov KGZ
23-11	Turkmenistan	L 0-2	Kabul	WCq		6 000	Khan PAK
2004							
No international matches played in 2004							
2005							
9-11	Tajikistan	L 0-4	Dushanbe	Fr			
7-12	Maldives	L 1-9	Karachi	SAFr1	Sayed Maqsood [39]		
9-12	Pakistan	L 0-1	Karachi	SAFr1			
11-12	Sri Lanka	W 2-1	Karachi	SAFr1	Hafizullah Qadami [35], Abdul Maroof Gullistani [41]		
2006							
1-04	India	L 0-2	Chittagong	CCr1		2 500	Al Ghatrifi OMA
3-04	Chinese Taipei	D 2-2	Chittagong	CCr1	Hafizullah Qadami 2 [20 23]	2 500	Lee Gi Young KOR
5-04	Philippines	D 1-1	Chittagong	CCr1	Sayed Maqsood [26]	3 000	Mujghef JOR

SAF = South Asian Football Federation Cup • AC = Asian Cup • CC = AFC Challenge Cup • WC = FIFA World Cup™
q = qualifier • r1 = first round group

AFGHANISTAN NATIONAL TEAM RECORDS AND RECORD SEQUENCES

Records			Sequence records			
Victory	2-1	KYR 2003, SRI 2005	Wins	1	2003, 2005	Clean sheets	1	
Defeat	0-11	TKM 2003	Defeats	12	1948-1975	Goals scored	3	1954-59, 1979
Player Caps	n/a		Undefeated	2	2006	Without goal	6	1941-1951
Player Goals	n/a		Without win	26	1941-2003	Goals against	21	1948-1984

RECENT LEAGUE AND CUP RECORD

Championship		Cup	
Year	Champions		Winners
No championship has been organised in Afghanistan since the 1970s			

AFGHANISTAN COUNTRY INFORMATION

Capital	Kabul	Independence	1919 from the UK	GDP per Capita	$700
Population	28 513 677	Status	Islamic Republic of Afghanistan	GNP Ranking	109
Area km²	647 500	Language	Pushtu, Dari	Dialling code	+93
Population density	44 per km²	Literacy rate	36%	Internet code	.af
% in urban areas	20 %	Main religion	Sunni Muslim 80%	GMT +/-	+4.5
Towns/Cities ('000)	Kabul 3 043; Kandahar 391; Mazar-e-Sharif 303; Herat 272; Jalabad 200; Kunduz 161; Ghazni 143; Bamiyan 125; Balkh 114; Baglan 108; Ghardez 103; Khost 96; Maymaneh 79				
Neighbours (km)	Iran 936; Turkmenistan 744; Uzbekistan 137; Tajikistan 1 206; China 76; Pakistan 2 430				
Main stadia	Kabul National Stadium – Kabul 25 000				

AIA – ANGUILLA

NATIONAL TEAM RECORD
JULY 1ST 2002 TO JULY 9TH 2006

PL	W	D	L	F	A	%
3	0	1	2	1	8	16.7

FIFA/COCA-COLA WORLD RANKING

1993	1994	1995	1996	1997	1998	1999	2000	2001	2002	2003	2004	2005	High		Low	
-	-	-	-	190	197	202	197	194	196	198	197	198	**189**	06/97	**202**	02/00

2005–2006											
08/05	09/05	10/05	11/05	12/05	01/06	02/06	03/06	04/06	05/06	06/06	07/06
197	197	197	197	198	198	198	1998	199	199	-	-

Few of the smaller member nations of FIFA have done more to develop the women's game than Anguilla and the tiny Caribbean island can now boast a successful league - the AFFL - with fully autonomous clubs taking part. In the near future the League will also benefit from the construction of the new national stadium on the grounds of the James Ronald Webster Park Annex. After a number of delays the groundbreaking ceremony was finally held on October 31, 2005. The stadium will provide a 1,100 capacity floodlit venue for all football on the island as well as serving as a technical and administrative centre for the Anguilla Football Association. In 2005 the

INTERNATIONAL HONOURS
None

AFFL was won by Shining Stars while the men's league was won for the fourth time in five years by Roaring Lions. They finished top ahead of Spartans International in the regular season but in April 2006, in the play-offs, they faced Attackers in the final, a match they won 1-0. The only national team in action was the women's U-19 team who entered the qualifiers for the FIFA U-20 Women's World Championship for the first time. They put in an heroic performance in a group staged in Surinam, finishing as runners-up to the hosts. Having beaten the Netherlands Antilles 5-2 in their first match, they then drew against Surinam but then lost the final match to Dominica.

THE FIFA BIG COUNT OF 2000

	Male	Female		Male	Female
Registered players	140	0	Referees	15	0
Non registered players	100	0	Officials	20	0
Youth players	320	200	Total involved	805	
Total players	760		Number of clubs	4	
Professional players	0	0	Number of teams	9	

Anguilla Football Association (AFA)
PO Box 1318, The Valley, Anguilla
Tel +1 264 497 7323   Fax +1 264 497 7324
axafa@yahoo.com   www. none
President: GUISHARD Raymond   General Secretary: HUGHES Damian
Vice-President: CARTY Diana D.   Treasurer: TBD   Media Officer: HUGHES Damian
Men's Coach: HODGE Vernon   Women's Coach: JOHNSON Colin
AFA formed: 1990   CONCACAF: 1996   FIFA: 1996
Colours: Turquoise & white shirts, Turquoise shorts, Turquoise socks or Orange & blue shirts, Orange shorts, Orange socks

RECENT INTERNATIONALS PLAYED BY ANGUILLA

2002	Opponents	Score		Venue	Comp	Scorers	Att	Referee
6-07	British Virgin Islands	L	1-2	Tortola	Fr			
2003								
No international matches played in 2003								
2004								
19-03	Dominican Republic	D	0-0	Santo Domingo	WCq		400	Mattus CRC
21-03	Dominican Republic	L	0-6	Santo Domingo	WCq		850	Porras CRC
2005								
No international matches played in 2005								
2006								
No international matches played in 2006 before August								

Fr = Friendly match • WC = FIFA World Cup™ • q = qualifier

ANGUILLA NATIONAL TEAM RECORDS AND RECORD SEQUENCES

Records			Sequence records					
Victory	4-1	MSR 2001	Wins	1		Clean sheets	1	
Defeat	0-14	GUY 1998	Defeats	17	1991-1998	Goals scored	5	2000-2002
Player Caps	n/a		Undefeated	1		Without goal	7	1991-1994
Player Goals	n/a		Without win	18	1991-1998	Goals against	27	1991-2002

RECENT LEAGUE AND CUP RECORD

	Championship	Cup
Year	Champions	Winners
1998	Spartans International	No tournament played
1999	Attackers	No tournament played
2000	No tournament played	No tournament played
2001	Roaring Lions	No tournament played
2002	Roaring Lions	No tournament played
2003	Roaring Lions	No tournament played
2004	Spartans International	No tournament played
2005	Roaring Lions	No tournament played

ANGUILLA COUNTRY INFORMATION

Capital	The Valley	Independence		GDP per Capita	$8 600
Population	13 008	Status	Overseas territory of the UK	GDP Ranking	n/a
Area km²	102	Language	English	Dialling code	+1 264
Population density	128 per km²	Literacy rate	95%	Internet code	.ai
% in urban areas	n/a	Main religion	Christian 88%	GMT +/–	-4
Towns/Cities ('000)	North Side 1; The Valley 1; Stoney Ground 1; The Quarter 1				
Neighbours (km)	Caribbean Sea 61				
Main stadia	Ronald Webster Park Annex – The Valley 1 100				

ALB – ALBANIA

ALBANIA NATIONAL TEAM RECORD
JULY 1ST 2002 TO JULY 9TH 2006

PL	W	D	L	F	A	%
33	11	5	17	42	54	40.9

FIFA/COCA-COLA WORLD RANKING

1993	1994	1995	1996	1997	1998	1999	2000	2001	2002	2003	2004	2005		High	Low
92	100	91	116	116	106	83	72	96	93	89	86	82		65 07/06	124 08/97

2005–2006											
08/05	09/05	10/05	11/05	12/05	01/06	02/06	03/06	04/06	05/06	06/06	07/06
87	86	85	85	82	83	82	88	86	85	-	65

In the four years from the end of the 2002 FIFA World Cup™ there have been encouraging signs for the Albanian national team, and the fifth place finish in their 2006 FIFA World Cup™ qualifying group was not as bad as might at first sight appear. It was the toughest of all the qualifying groups and points were taken off both European champions Greece as well as Ukraine. Preparations for UEFA Euro 2008™ got off to a poor start, however, when coach Hans-Peter Briegel resigned in May 2006 due to a dispute over a new contract. Drawn in a group with the Netherlands, Romania, Belarus, Slovenia, Luxembourg and Bulgaria, there was the genuine prospect of a highest ever finish in a qualifying

INTERNATIONAL HONOURS
Balkan Cup 1946

group, but Briegel will be a tough act for the new coach Otto Baric to follow. The Championship saw a reversal of the top two places from the previous season with Elbasani winning only their second championship - 22 years after the first which was won under the name of Labinoti. A 3-2 away win against Tirana in the penultimate round, thanks to a late penalty by goalkeeper Elvis Kotorri, saw Elbasani clinch the title, proving that good organisation can be enough to match the big Tirana clubs. SK Tirana made up for their disappointment by winning the Cup four days later when they beat Vllaznia 1-0, thanks to a second half Klodian Duro free kick.

THE FIFA BIG COUNT OF 2000

	Male	Female		Male	Female
Registered players	9 000	0	Referees	1 000	0
Non registered players	30 000	0	Officials	1 000	0
Youth players	9 000	0	Total involved	50 000	
Total players	48		Number of clubs	400	
Professional players	0	0	Number of teams	900	

The Football Association of Albania (FSHF)
Federata Shqiptare e Futbolit, Rruga Labinoti, Pallati perballe Shkolles, "Gjuhet e Huaja", Tirana, Albania
Tel +355 43 46601   Fax +355 43 46 609
fshf@albaniaonline.net   www.fshf.org
President: DUKA Armand   General Secretary: BICI Arben
Vice-President: KASMI Bujar   Treasurer: KASMI Bujar   Media Officer: NURISHMI Lysien
Men's Coach: BARIC Otto   Women's Coach: None
FSHF formed: 1930   UEFA: 1954   FIFA: 1932
Red shirts with black trimming, Black shorts, Red socks or White shirts with red and black trimming, black shorts, White socks

RECENT INTERNATIONALS PLAYED BY ALBANIA

2002	Opponents	Score		Venue	Comp	Scorers	Att	Referee
12-10	Switzerland	D	1-1	Tirana	ECq	Murati [79]	15 000	Erdemir TUR
16-10	Russia	L	1-4	Volgograd	ECq	Duro.K [13]	18 000	Sundell SWE
2003								
12-02	Vietnam	W	5-0	Bastia Umbra - ITA	Fr	Bushi [16], Myrtaj 2 [21 38], Dragusha [53], Pinari [85]		Nikoluci ITA
29-03	Russia	W	3-1	Shkoder	ECq	Rraklli [20], Lala [79], Tare [82]	16 000	Allaerts BEL
2-04	Republic of Ireland	D	0-0	Tirana	ECq		20 000	Farina ITA
30-04	Bulgaria	L	0-2	Sofia	Fr		9 325	Vidlak CZE
7-06	Republic of Ireland	L	1-2	Dublin	ECq	Skela [8]	33 000	Mikulski POL
11-06	Switzerland	L	2-3	Geneva	ECq	Lala [23], Skela [86p]	26 000	Bennett ENG
20-08	Macedonia	L	1-3	Prilep	Fr	Skela [74]	3 000	Mihajlevic SCM
6-09	Georgia	L	0-3	Tbilisi	ECq		18 000	Vollquartz DEN
10-09	Georgia	W	3-1	Tirana	ECq	Hasi [52], Tare [54], Bushi [80]	10 500	Salomir ROM
11-10	Portugal	L	3-5	Lisbon	Fr	Aliaj 2 [13 59], Tare [43]	5 000	Garibian FRA
15-11	Estonia	W	2-0	Tirana	Fr	Aliaj [26], Bushi [81]	5 000	Douros GRE
2004								
18-02	Sweden	W	2-1	Tirana	Fr	Skela [69], Aliaj [75]	15 000	Paparesta ITA
31-03	Iceland	W	2-1	Tirana	Fr	Aliaj [42], Bushi [78]	12 000	Bertini ITA
28-04	Estonia	D	1-1	Tallinn	Fr	Aliaj [51]	1 500	Sipailo LVA
18-08	Cyprus	L	1-2	Nicosia	Fr	Rraklli [64]	200	Kapitanis CYP
4-09	Greece	W	2-1	Tirana	WCq	Murati [2], Aliaj [11]	15 800	Gonzalez ESP
8-09	Georgia	L	0-2	Tbilisi	WCq		20 000	Courtney NIR
9-10	Denmark	L	0-2	Tirana	WCq		14 500	Baskarov RUS
13-10	Kazakhstan	W	1-0	Almaty	WCq	Bushi [61]	12 300	Stuchlik AUT
2005								
9-02	Ukraine	L	0-2	Tirana	WCq		12 000	Bennett ENG
26-03	Turkey	L	0-2	Istanbul	WCq		32 000	Plautz AUT
30-03	Greece	L	0-2	Piraeus	WCq		31 700	Layec FRA
29-05	Poland	L	0-1	Szczecin	Fr		14 000	Weiner GER
4-06	Georgia	W	3-2	Tirana	WCq	Tare 2 [5 56], Skela [33]	BCD	Tudor ROM
8-06	Denmark	L	1-3	Copenhagen	WCq	Bogdani [73]	26 366	Frojdfeldt SWE
17-08	Azerbaijan	W	2-1	Tirana	Fr	Bushi [37], Cana [72]	7 300	
3-09	Kazakhstan	W	2-1	Tirana	WCq	Myrtaj [53], Bogdani [56]	3 000	Slupik POL
8-10	Ukraine	D	2-2	Dnepropetrovsk	WCq	Bogdani 2 [75 83]	24 000	Verbist BEL
12-10	Turkey	L	0-1	Tirana	WCq		8 000	Dauden Ibanez ESP
2006								
1-03	Lithuania	L	1-2	Tirana	Fr	Aliaj [38p]		Pieri ITA
22-03	Georgia	D	0-0	Tirana	Fr			

Fr = Friendly match • EC = UEFA EURO 2004 • WC = FIFA World Cup™ • q = qualifier • BCD = behind closed doors

ALBANIA NATIONAL TEAM RECORDS AND RECORD SEQUENCES

Records			Sequence records					
Victory	5-0	VIE 2003	Wins	4	1999-2000	Clean sheets	3	Three times
Defeat	0-12	HUN 1950	Defeats	10	1989-1991	Goals scored	7	1973-1980
Player Caps	73	STRAKOSHA Foto	Undefeated	4	Four times	Without goal	6	1987-88, 1990-91
Player Goals	14	BUSHI Alban	Without win	25	1985-1991	Goals against	14	1988-1991

ALBANIA COUNTRY INFORMATION

Capital	Tirana (Tiranë)	Independence	1912	GDP per Capita	$4 500
Population	3 544 808	Status	Republic	GNP Ranking	118
Area km²	28 748	Language	Albanian	Dialling code	+355
Population density	123 per km²	Literacy rate	86%	Internet code	.al
% in urban areas	37%	Main religion	Muslim 70%	GMT + / –	+1
Towns/Cities ('000)	Tirana 374; Durrës 122; Elbasan 100; Shkodër 89; Vlorë 89; Fier 59; Korçë 58; Berat 47				
Neighbours (km)	Greece 282; Macedonia 151; Serbia and Montenegro 287				
Main stadia	Qemal Stafa – Tirana 19 500; Loro Boriçi – Shkodër 16 000; Tomori – Berat 14 500; Ruzhdi Bizhuta – Elbasan 13 000; Selman Stermasi – Tirana 12 500				

ALBANIA NATIONAL TEAM PLAYERS AND COACHES

Record Caps			Record Goals			Recent Coaches	
STRAKOSHA Foto	1990-'05	73	BUSHI Alban	1995-'06	14	RRELI Shyqri	1988-'90
RRAKLLI Altin	1992-'05	63	RRAKLLI Altin	1992-'05	11	SHULA Argon	1990
TARE Igli	1997-'06	63	KUSHTA Sokol	1987-'06	10	BIRCE Bejkush	1990-'94
VATA Rudi	1990-'01	59	TARE Igli	1997-'06	9	BAJKO Neptun	1994-'96
BUSHI Alban	1995-'06	59	ALIAJ Ardian	2002-'06	8	HAFIZI Astrit	1996-'99
HAXHI Altin	1995-'06	51	BOGDANI Erion	1996-'06	7	ZHEGA Medin	2000-'01
LALA Altin	1998-'06	49	BORICI Loro	1946-'58	6	DEMOLLARI Sulejman	2001-'02
XHUMBA Arben	1994-'02	48	KOLA Bledar	1994-'01	6	DOSSENA Giuseppe	2002
DEMOLLARI Sulejman	1983-'95	45	SKELA Ervin	2000-'06	6	BRIEGEL Hans-Peter	2002-'06
SHULKU Ilir	1992-'00	41				BARIC Otto	2006-

CLUB DIRECTORY

Club	Town/City	Stadium	Capacity	www.	Lge	Cup
KS Besa	Kavaje	Besa	8 000		0	0
KS Dinamo	Tiranë	Qemal Stafa	19 500		16	13
KS Elbasani	Elbasan	Ruzhdi Bizhuda	8 000		1	2
KS Lushnja	Lushnjë	Roza Haxhiu	12 000		0	0
FK Partizani	Tiranë	Qemal Stafa	19 500		15	15
KS Shkumbini	Peqin	Fusha Sportive	5 000		0	0
KS Skënderbeu	Korçë	Skënderbeu	8 000		1	0
KS Teuta	Durrës	Niko Dovana	12 000		1	3
SK Tirana	Tiranë	Selman Stërmasi	12 500	sktirana.com	22	13
KS Vllaznia	Shkodër	Loro Borici	16 000		9	5

RECENT LEAGUE AND CUP RECORD

	Championship						Cup		
Year	Champions	Pts	Runners-up	Pts	Third	Pts	Winners	Score	Runners-up
1990	Dinamo Tiranë	50	Partizani Tiranë	49	Flamurtari Vlorë	39	Dinamo Tiranë	1-1 4-2p	Flamurtari Vlorë
1991	Flamurtari Vlorë	54	Partizani Tiranë	48	Vllaznia Shkodër	45	Partizani Tiranë	1-1 4-3p	Flamurtari Vlorë
1992	Vllaznia Shkodër	44	Partizani Tiranë	38	Teuta Durrës	33	SK Elbasani	2-1	Besa Kavajë
1993	Partizani Tiranë	43	Teuta Durrës	38	Besa Kavajë	37	Partizani Tiranë	1-0	Albpetrol Patosi
1994	Teuta Durrës	37	SK Tirana	33	Flamurtari Vlorë	30	SK Tirana	0-0 1-0	Teuta Durrës
1995	SK Tirana	44	Teuta Durrës	32	Partizani Tiranë	32	Teuta Durrës	0-0 4-3p	SK Tirana
1996	SK Tirana	55	Teuta Durrës	54	Partizani Tiranë	46	SK Tirana	1-1 4-3p	Flamurtari Vlorë
1997	SK Tirana	46	Vllaznia Shkodër	43	Flamurtari Vlorë	41	Partizani Tiranë	2-2 4-3p	Flamurtari Vlorë
1998	Vllaznia Shkodër	72	SK Tirana	65	Partizani Tiranë	64	Apolonia Fier	1-0	Lushnjë
1999	SK Tirana	61	Vllaznia Shkodër	60	Bylis Ballshi	59	SK Tirana	0-0 3-0p	Vllaznia Shkodër
2000	SK Tirana	52	Tomori Berat	52	Teuta Durrës	49	Teuta Durrës	0-0 5-4p	Lushnjë
2001	Vllaznia Shkodër	56	SK Tirana	54	Dinamo Tiranë	52	SK Tirana	5-0	Teuta Durrës
2002	Dinamo Tiranë	63	SK Tirana	62	Partizani Tiranë	46	SK Tirana	1-0	Dinamo Tiranë
2003	SK Tirana	60	Vllaznia Shkodër	49	Partizani Tiranë	46	Dinamo Tiranë	1-0	Teuta Durrës
2004	SK Tirana	80	Dinamo Tiranë	71	Vllaznia Shkodër	68	Partizani Tiranë	1-0	Dinamo Tiranë
2005	SK Tirana	84	SK Elbasani	79	Dinamo Tiranë	62	Teuta Durrës	0-0 6-5p	SK Tirana
2006	KF Elbasani	72	SK Tirana	62	Dinamo Tiranë	61	SK Tirana	1-0	Vllaznia Shkodër

ALBANIA 2005-06

KATEGORIA SUPERIORE

	Pl	W	D	L	F	A	Pts	Elbasani	SK Tirana	Dinamo	Partizani	Besa	Vllaznia	Shkumbini	Teuta	Skënderbeu	Lushnja
KF Elbasani †	36	21	10	5	50	22	73		1-0 1-0	3-0 1-1	0-1 1-1	1-0 2-1	2-0 1-0	2-0 2-0	2-1 2-0	3-1 2-1	4-0 1-0
SK Tirana ‡	36	17	11	8	54	33	62	1-1 2-3		1-1 3-0	1-0 1-0	1-1 1-1	2-0 2-1	4-4 3-1	2-1 0-1	3-0 2-0	1-0 1-0
Dinamo Tiranë ‡	36	17	10	9	53	35	61	0-0 1-1	3-3 1-1		1-2 3-0	2-2 3-2	3-0 2-1	3-1 0-0	4-0 2-0	3-1 1-0	3-0 0-1
Partizani Tiranë	36	18	6	12	51	35	60	1-0 2-0	1-0 2-2	2-1 1-0		1-1 3-1	2-0 2-2	1-0 3-0	3-0 4-1	3-0 3-1	2-0 3-0
Besa Kavajë	36	13	7	16	49	42	46	0-1 **0-2**	1-1 0-2	3-0 0-1	4-1 2-1		0-1 1-0	2-1 2-0	1-0 1-4	4-0 2-0	0-0 6-0
Vllaznia Shkodër	36	13	6	17	39	45	45	0-0 3-2	1-2 0-2	1-1 0-2	1-0 1-0	0-3 5-2		5-0 0-0	3-1 1-1	2-1 1-0	3-0 1-0
Shkumbini Peqin	36	12	7	17	31	49	43	1-2 0-0	1-1 0-1	0-2 0-1	2-1 2-0	1-0 1-0	0-0 1-0		2-1 **0-2**	2-1 2-1	1-0 2-1
Teuta Durrës	36	11	9	16	32	45	42	1-1 0-0	1-0 0-4	0-1 1-0	1-2 1-0	0-2 2-1	3-0 3-1	2-1 0-0		1-1 1-1	1-0 1-1
Skënderbeu Korçë	36	12	6	18	33	50	42	1-0 0-0	4-3 1-0	0-1 1-0	2-1 0-0	2-0 0-0	1-0 2-1	3-0 0-2	1-0 1-0		1-1 2-1
KS Lushnja	36	5	10	21	22	58	25	0-2 2-4	**0-1** 0-0	2-2 1-4	2-1 1-1	1-1 1-0	1-3 0-1	3-2 0-1	0-0 0-0	2-1 1-1	

27/08/2005 - 20/05/2006 • † Qualified for the UEFA Champions League • ‡ Qualified for the UEFA Cup • Matches in bold awarded 2-0
Top scorers: Hamdi SALIHI, SK Tirana, 28; El Hadji GOUDJABI, Dinamo, 16; Vioresin SINANI, Vllaznia, 13

ALBANIA 2005-06
KATEGORIA E PARE (2)

	Pl	W	D	L	F	A	Pts
Flamurtari Vlorë	26	20	1	5	52	16	61
Apolonia Fier	26	16	7	3	47	20	55
Kastrioti Krujë	26	15	7	4	35	14	52
Luftëtari Gjirokastër	26	15	3	8	37	25	48
Pogradeci	26	14	5	7	34	28	47
Tomori Berat	26	11	4	11	42	40	37
Turbina Cërrik	26	9	8	9	30	29	35
Erzeni Shijak	26	9	6	11	29	34	33
Minatori Tepelenë	26	8	5	13	27	31	29
Ada Velipojë	26	9	2	15	25	40	29
Laçi	26	7	7	12	16	23	28
Besëlidhja Lezhë	26	7	7	12	31	27	28
Egnatia Rrogozhinë	26	8	4	14	27	38	28
Butrinti Sarandë	26	1	0	25	10	77	3

10/09/2005 - 13/05/2006

KUPA E SHQIPERISE 2005-06

Round of 16

SK Tirana	1	5
Apolonia Fier *	0	2
Kastrioto Krujë *	1	0
Partizani Tiranë	0	3
Lushnja	1	3
Luftëtari Gjirokastër *	0	1
Skënderbeu Korçë *	0	1
Dinamo Tiranë	2	6
Elbasani	0	5
Pogradeci *	2	1
Flamurtari Vlorë *	0	1
Teuta Durrës	2	1
Shkumbini Peqin	0	4
Butrinti Sarandë *	1	0
Besa Kavajë *	1	1
Vllaznia Shkodër	1	2

Quarter-finals

SK Tirana	3	1
Partizani Tiranë *	2	1
Lushnja *	0	0
Dinamo Tiranë	2	4
Elbasani	3	3
Teuta Durrës *	3	1
Shkumbini Peqin *	0	0
Vllaznia Shkodër	2	1

Semi-finals

SK Tirana *	4	0
Dinamo Tiranë	2	1
Elbasani	0	2
Vllaznia Shkodër *	2	1

Final

| SK Tirana ‡ | 1 |
| Vllaznia Shkodër | 0 |

CUP FINAL

Roza Haxhiu, Lushnjë
10-05-2006, Ref: Farina ITA

Scorer - Klodian Duro 65 for SK Tirana

* Home team in the first leg • ‡ Qualified for the UEFA Cup

ALG – ALGERIA

NATIONAL TEAM RECORD
JULY 1ST 2002 TO JULY 9TH 2006

PL	W	D	L	F	A	%
38	11	15	12	43	44	48.7

FIFA/COCA-COLA WORLD RANKING

1993	1994	1995	1996	1997	1998	1999	2000	2001	2002	2003	2004	2005		High		Low
35	57	48	49	59	71	86	82	75	68	62	73	80		30	09/93	88	11/99

					2005–2006						
08/05	09/05	10/05	11/05	12/05	01/06	02/06	03/06	04/06	05/06	06/06	07/06
81	83	82	82	80	80	81	85	87	87	-	93

There can be no hiding the bitter disappointment felt in Algeria over the steady decline of the national team which has now sunk to near an all-time low in the FIFA/Coca-Cola World Ranking. The FIFA World Cup™ qualifying campaign ended with a whimper and without even a place in the Nations Cup finals in Egypt. With ten coaches in the past five years, guiding the team has become one of the least enviable jobs on the continent. The latest incumbent, Frenchman Jean-Michel Cavalli, has the task of leading the Desert Warriors to the Nations Cup finals in Ghana from a group containing Guinea, Gambia and Cape Verde. Jeunesse Sportive Kabylie won a second title

INTERNATIONAL HONOURS
Qualified for the FIFA World Cup™ finals 1982 1986 CAF African Cup of Nations 1990
CAF Youth Cup 1979 All Africa Games 1978 African Champions League Mouloudia Alger 1976, JS Kabylie 1981 1990

in three years in the Algerian league, although, had their main rivals USM Alger not walked off after the first half of a match between the two early in the season, USM would have won the title, even if they had lost the abandoned match. The three point deduction imposed on them made all the difference in the final standings. USM were also runners-up in the Cup after losing in the final against local rivals MC Alger. In front of a packed stadium in the capital, Mouloudia won the Cup for the first time in ten years with Nourredine Deham scoring both of their goals in a 2-1 victory. It was the first time since 1972 that the big two clubs from Algiers had met in the final.

THE FIFA BIG COUNT OF 2000

	Male	Female		Male	Female
Registered players	125 260	976	Referees	530	38
Non registered players	225 600	104	Officials	20 505	310
Youth players	58 900	0	Total involved	432 223	
Total players	410 840		Number of clubs	252	
Professional players	260	0	Number of teams	2 329	

Fédération Algérienne de Football (FAF)
Chemin Ahmed Ouaked, Case Postale 39, Dely-Ibrahim, Alger, Algeria
Tel +213 21 372929   Fax +213 21 367266
FAFFOOT@yahoo.fr   www.faf.org.dz
President: HADDADJ Hamid   General Secretary: BOUCHEMLA Mourad
Vice-President: KHELAIFIA Mohamed   Treasurer: MECHRARA Mohamed   Media Officer: HADDADJ Hamid
Men's Coach: CAVALLI Jean-Michel   Women's Coach: CHIH Azzedine
FAF formed: 1962   CAF: 1964   FIFA: 1963
Green shirts, White shorts, Green socks or White shirts, Green shorts, White socks

RECENT INTERNATIONALS PLAYED BY ALGERIA

2002	Opponents	Score		Venue	Comp	Scorers	Att	Referee
20-08	Congo DR	D	1-1	Blida	Fr	Haddou [61p]		Benaissa ALG
7-09	Namibia	W	1-0	Windhoek	CNq	OG [4]	13 000	Tangawarima ZIM
24-09	Uganda	D	1-1	Annaba	Fr	Amaouche [46]		Benaissa ALG
11-10	Chad	W	4-1	Annaba	CNq	Akrour 2 [26 72p], Belmadi 2 [54 69]	20 000	El Beltagy EGY
2003								
25-01	Uganda	W	1-0	Kampala	Fr	Ammour [64]	5 000	Aouuby UGA
12-02	Belgium	L	1-3	Annaba	Fr	Belmadi [89]	40 000	Baraket TUN
29-03	Angola	D	1-1	Luanda	Fr	Akrour [85]	8 000	Mavunza ANG
24-04	Madagascar	W	3-1	Amiens	Fr	Fellahi [26], Belkaid [60], Cherrad [76]	1 000	Garibian FRA
29-05	Burkina Faso	L	0-1	Avion	Fr		1 050	Gannard FRA
20-06	Namibia	W	1-0	Blida	CNq	Kraouche [5]	30 000	Auda EGY
6-07	Chad	D	0-0	N'Djamena	CNq			
4-09	Qatar	W	1-0	Dinard	Fr	Cherrad [26]	400	
24-09	Gabon	D	2-2	Algiers	Fr	Fellahi [51], Achiou [59]. W 4-3p	2 000	Zekrini ALG
26-09	Burkina Faso	D	0-0	Algiers	Fr	W 4-3p	1 500	Benouza ALG
11-10	Niger	W	1-0	Niamey	WCq	Boutabout [63]	20 126	Coulibaly MLI
14-11	Niger	W	6-0	Algiers	WCq	Cherrad 2 [16 22], Boutabout 2 [42 70], Mamouni [45], Akrour [82]	50 000	El-Arjoun MOR
2004								
15-01	Mali	L	0-2	Algiers	Fr		7 000	Zehmoun TUN
25-01	Cameroon	D	1-1	Sousse	CNr1	Zafour [51]	20 000	Codjia BEN
29-01	Egypt	W	2-1	Sousse	CNr1	Mamouni [13], Achiou [85]	15 000	Hamer LUX
3-02	Zimbabwe	L	1-2	Sousse	CNr1	Achiou [72]	10 000	Maillet SEY
8-02	Morocco	L	1-3	Sfax	CNqf	Cherrad [83]	20 000	Shelmani LBY
28-04	China PR	L	0-1	Clermont-Ferrand	Fr		1 600	Poulat FRA
30-05	Jordan	D	1-1	Annaba	Fr	Cherrad [60]	20 000	Zahmoul TUN
5-06	Angola	D	0-0	Annaba	WCq		55 000	Daami TUN
20-06	Zimbabwe	D	1-1	Harare	WCq	Cherrad [3]	65 000	Ntambidila COD
3-07	Nigeria	L	0-1	Abuja	WCq		35 000	Hisseine CHA
17-08	Burkina Faso	D	2-2	Blida	Fr	Tahraoui [33], Arrache [54]	15 000	Tahri MAR
5-09	Gabon	L	0-3	Annaba	WCq		51 000	Ndoye SEN
9-10	Rwanda	D	1-1	Kigali	WCq	Bourahli [14]	20 000	Abdel Rahmen SUD
17-11	Senegal	L	1-2	Toulon	Fr	Daoud [77]	4 000	Bata FRA
2005								
9-02	Burkina Faso	W	3-0	Algiers	Fr	Saifi 2 [29 42], Sofiane [72]	5 000	Benaissa ALG
27-03	Rwanda	W	1-0	Oran	WCq	Boutabout [48]	20 000	Abd El Fatah EGY
5-06	Angola	L	1-2	Luanda	WCq	Boutabout [63]	27 000	Hicuburundi BDI
12-06	Mali	L	0-3	Arles	Fr			
19-06	Zimbabwe	D	2-2	Oran	WCq	Yahia [17], Daoud [48]	15 000	Pare BFA
4-09	Nigeria	L	2-5	Oran	WCq	Yacef [48], Boutabout [58]	11 000	Shelmani LBY
8-10	Gabon	D	0-0	Port-Gentil	WCq		37 000	Diouf SEN
2006								
28-02	Burkina Faso	D	0-0	Rouen	Fr		2 000	Duhamel FRA

Fr = Friendly match • CN = CAF African Cup of Nations • WC = FIFA World Cup™ • q = qualifier • r1 = first round group • qf = quarter-final

ALGERIA NATIONAL TEAM RECORDS AND RECORD SEQUENCES

Records			Sequence records				
Victory	15-1	YEM 1973	Wins	10	1957-1963	Clean sheets	4	Five times
Defeat	0-5	BFA 1975, GDR 1976	Defeats	5	1974	Goals scored	16	2000-2001
Player Caps	n/a		Undefeated	15	1989-1991	Without goal	5	1989
Player Goals	n/a		Without win	11	2004	Goals against	9	2000-2001

ALGERIA COUNTRY INFORMATION

Capital	Algiers (Alger)	Independence	1962	GDP per Capita	$6 000
Population	32 129 324	Status	Republic	GNP Ranking	47
Area km²	2 381 740	Language	Arabic	Dialling code	+213
Population density	13 per km²	Literacy rate	60%	Internet code	.dz
% in urban areas	56%	Main religion	Muslim 99%	GMT +/–	+1
Towns/Cities ('000)	Algiers 1 980; Oran 646; Constantine 450; Batna 280; Bab Azwar 277; Setif 226; Al Jilfah 213; Annaba 206; Biskra 196; Sidi Bel Abbès 191; Tibissah 182; Tiyarat 176; Al Buni 171				
Neighbours (km)	Tunisia 965; Libya 982; Niger 956; Mali 1 376; Mauritania 463; Western Sahara 42; Morocco 1 559; Mediterranean Sea 998				
Main stadia	Stade 5 Juillet – Algiers 66 000; Stade 19 Mai – Annaba 50 000; Ahmed Zabana - Oran 50 000; Stade 24 Février – Sidi Bel Abbes 50 000; Frères Brakni – Blida 35 000				

RECENT NATIONAL TEAM COACHES

	Years
ZOUBA / KERIMALI	2001
MADJER Rabah	2001-'02
ZOUBA Hamid	2002-'03
LEEKENS George	2003
SAADANE Rabah	2003-'04
WASEIGE Robert	2004
FERGANI Ali	2004-'05
IGHIL Meziane	2005-'06
CAVALLI Jean-Michel	2006-

CLUB DIRECTORY

Club	Town/City	Stadium	Capacity	www.	Lge	Cup	CL
CR Belouizdad	Algiers	20 Août 1955	20 000	chabab-belcourt.com	6	5	0
CS Constantine	Constantine	Chahid Hamlaoui	40 000		1	0	0
ES Setif	Setif	8 Mai 1945	25 000		2	6	0
GC Mascara	Mascara	Unité Africaine	5 000		1	0	0
JS Kabylie	Tizi Ouzou	1 Novembre 1954	25 000	js-kabylie.com	13	4	2
MC Alger	Algiers	5 Juillet 1962	80 000	mcalger.com	6	5	1
MC Oran	Oran	Ahmed Zabana	50 000	mouloudia.com	4	4	0
NA Hussein Dey	Algiers	Frères Zioui	7 000	nasria.com	1	1	0
USM Algiers	Algiers	Omar Hammadi	15 000	usma-alger.com	5	7	0
WA Tlemcen	Tlemcen	Frères Zerga	6 000	watlemcen.com	0	2	0

CR = Chabab Riadhi • CS = Club Sportif • ES = Entente Sportive • GC = Ghali Club • JS = Jeunesse Sportive • MC = Mouloudia Chaabia (Alger) • MC = Mouloudia Club (Oran) • NA = Nasr Athletic • USM = Union Sportive Madinet • WA = Widad Athletic

RECENT LEAGUE AND CUP RECORD

	Championship						Cup		
Year	Champions	Pts	Runners-up	Pts	Third	Pts	Winners	Score	Runners-up
1990	JS Kabylie	40	MC Oran	36	MC Alger	34	Tournament not held		
1991	MO Constantine	38	AS Ain Mlila	36	ASM Oran	36	USM Bel Abbés	2-0	JS Kabylie
1992	MC Oran	39	USM El Harrach	35	WA Tlemcen	35	JS Kabylie	1-0	ASO Chlef
1993	MC Oran	38	NA Hussein Dey	37	US Chaouia	36	Tournament not held		
1994	US Chaouia	35	JS Kabylie	35	JS Bordj Menaiel	35	JS Kabylie	1-0	AS Ain Mlila
1995	JS Kabylie	40	MC Oran	35	USM Blida	33	CR Belouizdad	2-1	OM Médéa
1996	USM Algiers	60	MC Oran	58	WA Tlemcen	51	MC Oran	1-0	Ittihad Blida
1997	CS Constantine	56	MC Oran	55	USM Algiers	49	USM Algiers	1-0	CA Batna
1998	USM El Harrach	3-2	USM Algiers				WA Tlemcen	1-0	MC Oran
1999	MC Alger	1-0	JS Kabylie				USM Alger	2-0	JS Kabylie
2000	CR Belouizdad	47	MC Oran	38	MC Constantine	38	MC Ouargla	2-1	WA Tlemcen
2001	CR Belouizdad	62	USM Algiers	55	JS Kabylie	52	USM Alger	1-0	CR Méchria
2002	USM Alger	57	JS Kabylie	52	WA Tlemcen	51	WA Tlemcen	1-0	MC Oran
2003	USM Alger	58	USM Blida	51	NA Hussein Dey	51	USM Alger	2-1	CR Belouizdad
2004	JS Kabylie	61	USM Alger	58	NA Hussein Dey	49	USM Alger	0-0 5-4p	JS Kabylie
2005	USM Alger	67	JS Kabylie	54	MC Alger	49	ASO Chlef	1-0	USM Sétif
2006	JS Kabylie	58	USM Alger	57	ASO Chlef	52	MC Alger	2-1	USM Alger

ALGERIA 2005-06

PREMIERE DIVISION

	Pl	W	D	L	F	A	Pts	JS Kabylie	USM Alger	ASO Chlef	ES Sétif	CA Bordj	MC Alger	CR Bel'dad	Paradou AC	CA Batna	USM Blida	NAHD	MC Oran	WA Tlemcen	CS Con'tine	USM Annaba	US Biskra
JS Kabylie †	30	17	7	6	47	21	58		3-0	0-1	4-2	2-0	2-1	1-2	3-0	1-0	3-0	3-0	3-1	0-0	2-2	4-1	5-0
USM Alger §3 †	30	18	6	6	50	30	57	1-0		1-0	2-0	4-1	1-0	2-1	3-2	3-0	3-2	2-1	5-2	1-0	2-1	1-0	3-1
ASO Chlef	30	15	7	8	45	25	52	0-1	0-0		2-2	1-1	1-0	2-0	4-0	4-0	2-1	2-0	1-0	1-0	3-1	5-2	1-0
ES Sétif	30	14	5	11	30	26	47	0-0	2-1	2-1		0-0	2-0	1-0	2-1	1-0	2-0	2-1	0-0	2-0	2-0	2-1	1-0
CA Bordj Bou Arréridj	30	13	7	10	22	24	46	0-0	1-0	1-1	1-0		1-2	1-0	0-0	1-0	1-0	1-0	2-0	1-0	3-1	1-0	1-0
MC Alger	30	13	5	12	42	35	44	1-1	1-1	1-3	2-1	3-1		0-1	2-0	3-2	1-0	2-0	3-0	2-1	3-0		
CR Bélouizdad	30	11	7	12	30	31	40	1-0	1-3	0-0	1-0	0-1	1-2		1-1	1-0	2-1	0-0	1-0	2-1	2-0	3-1	3-2
Paradou AC	30	11	7	12	36	38	40	3-0	1-3	1-0	1-0	0-0	1-3	2-1		2-1	2-0	0-1	3-2	1-0	2-0	0-0	2-1
CA Batna	30	11	5	14	32	35	38	0-1	3-1	2-1	2-0	0-1	1-0	2-2	3-2		0-1	1-2	0-0	3-1	1-1	1-0	2-0
USM Blida	30	10	8	12	26	30	38	1-0	0-0	0-3	1-0	2-0	2-1	2-1	1-1	0-0		3-0	1-0	2-0	1-0	1-0	0-1
NA Hussein Dey	30	10	8	12	27	35	38	0-1	2-1	2-0	1-0	1-1	2-2	0-0	1-1	3-2	0-0		2-1	1-2	1-0	2-0	2-1
MC Oran	30	10	7	13	35	42	37	3-1	1-1	0-0	0-1	1-0	1-3	2-1	2-6	1-0	1-1	4-0		2-0	1-1	3-2	1-0
WA Tlemcen	30	10	7	13	25	33	37	1-3	0-0	2-1	2-2	1-0	3-2	1-0	1-0	1-2	2-0	1-0	1-0		1-0	2-0	1-1
CS Constantine	30	10	6	14	27	36	36	0-1	2-1	1-2	1-0	2-0	2-1	0-0	0-0	0-1	2-1	1-0	2-0	1-1		2-0	0-0
USM Annaba	30	10	5	15	33	40	35	0-0	2-2	3-0	1-0	2-0	1-0	2-1	2-1	1-3	1-0	1-1	1-2	2-0	4-1		2-0
US Biskra	30	3	11	16	13	39	20	0-1	0-2	1-1	0-1	1-0	0-0	1-1	0-0	0-0	0-0	0-0	0-0	2-2	1-0	0-2	

25/08/2005 - 25/05/2006 • † Qualified for the CAF Champions League • Match in bold awarded 3-0 • §3 = three points deducted

ALGERIA 2005-06
SECONDE DIVISION (2)

	Pl	W	D	L	F	A	Pts
OMR El Anasser	34	21	7	6	65	23	70
JSM Béjaïa	34	19	8	7	48	18	65
ASM Oran	34	15	13	6	62	40	58
RC Kouba	34	15	9	10	50	33	54
MO Béjaïa	34	15	7	12	38	31	52
USM El Harrach	34	14	9	11	47	29	51
MC Saïda	34	14	9	11	48	51	51
MO Constantine	34	13	11	10	40	39	50
MC El Eulma	34	13	9	12	35	32	48
Bou Saada	34	12	11	11	33	40	47
JSM Tiaret	34	14	5	15	40	48	47
AS Khroub	34	12	8	14	53	49	44
MSP Batna	34	11	10	13	39	44	43
WA Boufarik	34	12	7	15	32	40	43
SA Mohamadia	34	12	7	15	31	41	43
US Chaouia	34	9	12	13	32	46	39
GC Mascara	34	7	5	22	30	62	26
IRB Sidi Aïssa	34	3	3	28	11	68	12

26/08/2005 - 26/05/2006

COUPE D'ALGERIE 2005-06

Round of 16
MC Alger *	2
CRB Dar El Beida	0
US Biskra	1
ES Sétif *	3
ASM Oran *	1
MC El Eulma	1
CS Constantine *	0
WA Tlemcen	1
JS Kabylie	1
ES Guelma *	0
AS Khroub *	0
NA Hussein Dey	2
RC Kouba	1
CA Bordj Bou Arréridj *	0
USM Annaba	0
USM Alger *	2

Quarter-finals
MC Alger	2
ES Sétif *	1
ASM Oran	1
WA Tlemcen *	2
JS Kabylie	1 4p
NA Hussein Dey *	1 2p
RC Kouba *	0 1p
USM Alger	0 4p

Semi-finals
MC Alger	3
WA Tlemcen	1
JS Kabylie	0 2p
USM Alger	0 4p

Final
MC Alger ‡	2
USM Alger	1

CUP FINAL
Stade du 5 Juillet, Algiers
15-06-2006, Att. 70 000, Ref: Haimoudi

Scorers - Nourredine Deham 2 42 50p for MCA; Doukouré 85 for USMA

* Home team • ‡ Qualified for the CAF Confederation Cup

AND – ANDORRA

NATIONAL TEAM RECORD
JULY 1ST 2002 TO JULY 9TH 2006

PL	W	D	L	F	A	%
25	1	3	21	5	65	10

FIFA/COCA-COLA WORLD RANKING

1993	1994	1995	1996	1997	1998	1999	2000	2001	2002	2003	2004	2005	2006	High		Low	
-	-	-	187	185	171	145	145	140	137	147	138	125		125	12/05	188	06/97

2005–2006											
08/05	09/05	10/05	11/05	12/05	01/06	02/06	03/06	04/06	05/06	06/06	07/06
134	125	128	127	125	126	126	127	128	129	-	131

Just nine defeats in 12 FIFA World Cup™ qualifying games represents a major breakthrough for the Andorran national team. The aim for long standing coach David Rodrigo is not to revert to type in the qualifiers for UEFA Euro 2008™. It won't be easy with games against England, Israel, Croatia, Russia, Macedonia and Estonia as they search for a first ever point in the competition. The one thing the Andorrans have in their favour is that there can't be a team in European or world football where the majority of team members have played together for so long and under the same coach. For the second year running there was a first time winner in the Andorran league with last

INTERNATIONAL HONOURS
None

year's runners-up Ranger's gaining revenge over Sant Julià. There was no repeat of the titanic duel of the previous season between the two, however, with Ranger's losing just one game all season and finishing 12 points ahead of their rivals. Ranger's only defeat of the season was against Sant Julià - the only team to have beaten them in the League or Cup during the past two seasons. Although Ranger's didn't lose in the Cup, they didn't manage to win it either as, for the first time, the final was decided on penalties and Ranger's were the unlucky losers. For their opponents Santa Coloma, an injury-time equaliser paved the way to a fourth successive Cup triumph.

THE FIFA BIG COUNT OF 2000

	Male	Female		Male	Female
Registered players	623	0	Referees	24	3
Non registered players	700	0	Officials	86	4
Youth players	386	23	Total involved	1 849	
Total players		1 732	Number of clubs	19	
Professional players	0	0	Number of teams	35	

Federació Andorrana de Fútbol (FAF)
Avinguda Carlemany 67, 3° pis, Apartado postal 65 AD, Escaldes-Engordany, Principat d'Andorra
Tel +376 805830   Fax +376 862006
administracio@fedanfut.com   www.fedanfut.com
President: AMAT ESCOBAR Francesc   General Secretary: GEA Tomas
Vice-President: MORALES Antonio   Treasurer: GARCIA Josep   Media Officer: GARCIA Adolfo
Men's Coach: RODRIGO David   Women's Coach: RODRIGO David
FAF formed: 1994   UEFA: 1996   FIFA: 1996
Blue shirts with yellow and red trimmings, Blue shorts, Blue socks or Red shirts with yellow and black trimmings, Blue shorts, Blue socks

RECENT INTERNATIONALS PLAYED BY ANDORRA

2002	Opponents	Score		Venue	Comp	Scorers	Att	Referee
21-08	Iceland	L	0-3	Rejkjavik	Fr		2 900	Isaksen FRO
12-10	Belgium	L	0-1	Andorra la Vella	ECq		700	Nalbandyan ARM
16-10	Bulgaria	L	1-2	Sofia	ECq	Lima.A 80	42 000	Richards WAL
2003								
2-04	Croatia	L	0-2	Varazdin	ECq		8 500	Salomir ROM
30-04	Estonia	L	0-2	Andorra la Vella	ECq		500	Aydin TUR
7-06	Estonia	L	0-2	Tallinn	ECq		3 500	Juhos HUN
11-06	Belgium	L	0-3	Gent	ECq		12 000	Shmolik BLR
13-06	Gabon	L	0-2	Andorra la Vella	Fr			
6-09	Croatia	L	0-3	Andorra la Vella	ECq		800	Liba CZE
10-09	Bulgaria	L	0-3	Andorra la Vella	ECq		1 000	Mikulski POL
2004								
14-04	China PR	D	0-0	Peralada	Fr			
28-05	France	L	0-4	Montpellier	Fr		27 750	Daami TUN
5-06	Spain	L	0-4	Getafe	Fr		14 000	Trefolini ITA
4-09	Finland	L	0-3	Tampere	WCq		7 437	Siric CRO
8-09	Romania	L	1-5	Andorra la Vella	WCq	Pujol 28p	1 100	Kircher GER
13-10	FYR Macedonia	W	1-0	Andorra la Vella	WCq	Bernaus 60	350	Podeschi SMR
17-11	Netherlands	L	0-3	Andorra la Vella	WCq		2 000	Yefet ISR
2005								
9-02	FYR Macedonia	D	0-0	Skopje	WCq		5 000	Verbist BEL
26-03	Armenia	L	1-2	Yerevan	WCq	Silva 56	2 100	Attard MLT
30-03	Czech Republic	L	0-4	Andorra la Vella	WCq		900	Messner AUT
4-06	Czech Republic	L	1-8	Liberec	WCq	Riera 36	9 520	Dereli TUR
17-08	Romania	L	0-2	Constanta	WCq		8 200	Jakov ISR
3-09	Finland	D	0-0	Andorra la Vella	WCq		860	Ver Eecke BEL
7-09	Netherlands	L	0-4	Eindhoven	WCq		34 000	Hanacsek HUN
12-10	Armenia	L	0-3	Andorra la Vella	WCq		430	Stokes IRL
2006								

No international matches played in 2006 before July

Fr = Friendly match • EC = UEFA EURO 2004™ • WC = FIFA World Cup™ • q = qualifier

ANDORRA NATIONAL TEAM PLAYERS AND COACHES

Record Caps			Record Goals			Recent Coaches	
SONEJEE Oscar	1997-'05	59	LIMA Ildefons	1997-'05	3	CODINA Isidrea	1996
ALVAREZ Jesus Luis 'Koldo'	1998-'05	55	LUCENDO Jesus Julian	1996-'03	3	MILOIE Manuel	1997-'99
TXEMA Josep	1997-'05	55	LIMA Antoni	1997-'05	2	RODRIGO David	1999-
RUIZ Justo	1998-'05	54	GONZALEZ Emiliano	1998-'03	2		
SANCHEZ Juli	1996-'05	53	RUIZ Justo	1998-'05	2		
LIMA Antoni	1997-'05	46	SANCHEZ Juli	1996-'05	2		

ANDORRA NATIONAL TEAM RECORDS AND RECORD SEQUENCES

Records			Sequence records				
Victory	2-0	BLR 2000, ALB 2002	Wins	1		Clean sheets	2	2000
Defeat	1-7	POR 2001	Defeats	11	2002-2003	Goals scored	2	Three times
Player Caps	59	SONEJEE Oscar	Undefeated	3	2000	Without goal	11	2003-2004
Player Goals	3	LIMA I, LUCENDO	Without win	23	1996-2000	Goals against	11	2000-02, 2002-03

ANDORRA COUNTRY INFORMATION

Capital	Andorra la Vella	Independence	1278	GDP per Capita	$19 000
Population	69 865	Status	Principality	GNP Ranking	150
Area km²	468	Language	Catalan (official), French	Dialling code	+376
Population density	149 per km²	Literacy rate	99%	Internet code	.ad
% in urban areas	63%	Main religion	Christian 94%	GMT + / –	+1
Towns/Cities ('000)	Andorra la Vella 22; Les Escaldes 13; Encamp 9				
Neighbours (km)	France 56; Spain 63				
Main stadia	Comunal – Andorra la Vella 1 140				

ANDORRA 2005–06

LLIGA ANDORRANA PRIMERA DIVISIO

	Pl	W	D	L	F	A	Pts	Ranger's	Sant Julià	S. Coloma	Lusitans	Inter	Athlètic	Principat	Extremenya
Ranger's FC ‡	20	16	3	1	73	12	51		1-3 2-1	2-0 1-1	2-0 3-1	4-0	7-0	6-0	7-1
Sant Julià	20	12	3	5	61	19	39	0-2 1-1		2-0 1-0	3-1 5-1	1-2	5-0	2-0	10-0
Santa Coloma	20	11	3	6	47	17	36	0-1 1-2	2-2 2-0		0-2 1-0	3-1	2-1	5-0	9-0
Lusitans	20	9	1	10	30	41	28	1-7 0-2	1-6 1-0	1-3 1-1		0-1	2-1	3-1	6-1
Inter Escaldes	20	11	3	6	36	28	36	1-4	2-2	0-5	0-1		0-0 2-2	5-1 2-1	3-1 3-0
Athlètic Escaldes	20	8	4	8	21	27	28	0-0	1-3	0-2	0-1	0-1 1-0		0-0 2-0	2-0 3-0
CE Principat	20	3	2	15	18	55	11	1-5	0-5	0-2	2-4	1-4 0-3	0-1 1-2		5-2 1-0
Extremenya	20	0	1	19	11	98	1	0-14	0-9	0-8	2-3	0-2 1-4	1-4 0-1	1-1 1-3	

25/09/2005 - 30/04/2006 • ‡ Qualified for the UEFA Cup • Match in bold awarded 3-0

ANDORRA 2005–06 SEGONA DIVISIO (2)

	Pl	W	D	L	F	A	Pts
Encamp	18	14	4	0	64	12	46
Engordany	18	11	1	6	44	35	34
Benfica	18	7	4	7	26	29	25
Santa Coloma B	18	7	3	8	33	30	24
Sporting Escaldes	12	3	2	7	14	36	11
TRI Principat	12	2	1	9	11	30	7
Lusitans B	12	2	1	9	8	28	7

24/09/2005 - 30/04/2006

COPA CONSTITUCIO 2005–06

Quarter-finals		Semi-finals		Final	
Santa Coloma	w-o				
Extremenya		Santa Coloma	1		
Engordany	0	Sant Julià	0		
Sant Julià	5			Santa Coloma	1 5p
Lusitans	0 7p			Ranger's	1 3p
Athlètic Escaldes	0 6p	Lusitans	0 2p	14-05-2006	
Inter Escaldes	2	Ranger's	0 4p	Scorers - Leo 90 for Santa Coloma;	
Ranger's	3			Alex Pareja 61 for Ranger's	

RECENT LEAGUE AND CUP RECORD

	Championship							Cup		
Year	Champions	Pts	Runners-up	Pts	Third	Pts		Winners	Score	Runners-up
1997	Principat	61	Veterans d'Andorra	59	Encamp	41		Principat	7-0	Sant Julia
1998	Principat	56	Santa Coloma	55	Encamp	38		Principat	4-3	Santa Coloma
1999	Principat	62	Santa Coloma	54	Encamp	43		Principat	3-1	Santa Coloma
2000	Constelació	64	Santa Coloma	28	Inter d'Escaldes	20		Constelació	6-0	Encamp
2001	Santa Coloma	24	Sant Julia	22	Inter d'Escaldes	12		Lusitans	2-0	Inter d'Escaldes
2002	Encamp	44	Sant Julia	43	Santa Coloma	42		Santa Coloma	5-3	Sant Julia
2003	Santa Coloma	49	Encamp	48	Sant Julia	38		Santa Coloma	1-0	Sant Julia
2004	Santa Coloma	45	Sant Julia	43	Ranger's	34		Santa Coloma	2-1	Sant Julia
2005	Sant Julia	54	Ranger's	51	Santa Coloma	37		Santa Coloma	1-1 5-3p	Ranger's
2006	Ranger's	51	Sant Julia	39	Santa Coloma	36				

ANG – ANGOLA

NATIONAL TEAM RECORD
JULY 1ST 2002 TO JULY 9TH 2006

PL	W	D	L	F	A	%
48	19	15	14	61	50	55.2

FIFA/COCA-COLA WORLD RANKING

1993	1994	1995	1996	1997	1998	1999	2000	2001	2002	2003	2004	2005	High	Low
102	106	80	70	58	50	52	55	55	76	83	72	61	**45** 07/00	**124** 06/94

2005–2006											
08/05	09/05	10/05	11/05	12/05	01/06	02/06	03/06	04/06	05/06	06/06	07/06
71	65	60	62	61	63	60	60	58	57	-	55

There may never be another year quite like the one just experienced by Angolan fans as their national team made an historic and unlikely first appearance at the finals of the FIFA World Cup™. Many predicted an embarrassing outcome to the adventure, especially after their meek exit in the first round at the Nations Cup in Egypt. But despite also going home after the first round in Germany, the Palancas Negras more than held their own, drawing with Mexico and Iran and only narrowly going down against Portugal. Assuming that the revenues from the tournament are spent wisely there is no reason why Angola shouldn't be at finals in the future, although qualifying from

INTERNATIONAL HONOURS
Qualified for the FIFA World Cup™ 2006   CAF Youth Championship 2001   COSAFA Cup 1999 2001 2004

Africa is likely to become ever more competitive. Angola also sent out a strong message from the finals that African teams can suceed without foreign coaches. At home the championship went right down to the wire with a first title for Sagrada Esperança, only the fifth club to win the League since independence. The final game of the season saw the top two, level on points, face each other in a winner takes all tie in which Sagrada beat Petro Atlético 1-0 thanks to a Lebo Lebo goal after 35 seconds. Defending champions Atlético Avaição would have won the title had that match been a draw but they did beat Inter Clube to win the Cup for only the second time - their first for 11 years.

THE FIFA BIG COUNT OF 2000

	Male	Female		Male	Female
Registered players	5000	0	Referees	250	0
Non registered players	35 000	0	Officials	1 900	0
Youth players	3 000	0	Total involved	45 150	
Total players	43 000		Number of clubs	100	
Professional players	0	0	Number of teams	500	

Federaçao Angolana de Futebol (FAF)
Compl. da Cidadela Desportiva, Luanda - 3449, Angola
Tel +244 2 264948   Fax +244 2 260566
fafutebol@ebonet.net   www.fafutebol.com
President: FERNANDES Justino Dr   General Secretary: PEREIRA DA SILVA Augusto
Vice-President: MANGUEIRA Antonio   Treasurer: GOMES FURTADO Antonio   Media Officer: MACEDO Arlindo
Men's Coach: DE OLIVEIRA GONCALVES Luis   Women's Coach: NZUZI Andre
FAF formed: 1979   CAF: 1996   FIFA: 1980
Red shirts with black trimmings, Black shorts, Red socks

RECENT INTERNATIONALS PLAYED BY ANGOLA

2003	Opponents	Score		Venue	Comp	Scorers	Att	Referee
20-04	Zimbabwe	L	0-1	Harare	CCr1		20 000	Nkuna ZAM
21-06	Nigeria	D	2-2	Benin City	CNq	Figueiredo [9], Akwa [55]		
6-07	Malawi	W	5-1	Luanda	CNq	Msowoya [2], Akwa [3], Flavio [33], Stopirra [76], Chinho [89]	10 000	
20-08	Congo DR	L	0-2	Luanda	Fr			
7-09	Namibia	W	2-0	Luanda	Fr	Delgado [44], Flavio [63]	5 000	De Sousa ANG
20-09	Namibia	W	3-1	Windhoek	Fr	Jaburu, Avelino Lopes, Akwa [80]		
12-10	Chad	L	1-3	N'Djamena	WCq	Bruno Mauro [49]	30 000	Nahi CIV
16-11	Chad	W	2-0	Luanda	WCq	Akwa [42], Bruno Mauro [57]	30 000	Buenkadila COD
2004								
31-03	Morocco	L	1-3	Casablanca	Fr	Norberto [84]	7 000	Helal EGY
28-04	Ghana	D	1-1	Accra	Fr	Fofana [55]		Kotey GHA
9-05	Namibia	W	2-1	Luanda	CCr1	Love 2 [26 67]	4 000	Ngcamphalala SWZ
23-05	Congo DR	W	3-1	Kinshasa	Fr	Gilberto [8], Bruno Mauro [40], Maurito [89]	60 000	
5-06	Algeria	D	0-0	Annaba	WCq		55 000	Daami TUN
20-06	Nigeria	W	1-0	Luanda	WCq	Akwa [84]	40 000	Nkole ZAM
3-07	Gabon	D	2-2	Libreville	WCq	Akwa [19], Marco Paulo [81]	20 000	Louzaya CGO
18-07	Botswana	D	1-1	Luanda	CCqf	Flavio [3]. W 5-3p	6 000	Phomane LES
5-09	Rwanda	W	1-0	Luanda	WCq	Freddy [52]	30 000	Damon RSA
19-09	Mozambique	W	1-0	Maputo	CCsf	Flavio [68]	50 000	Jovinala MWI
10-10	Zimbabwe	W	1-0	Luanda	WCq	Flavio [53]	17 000	Lwanja MWI
20-11	Zambia	D	0-0	Lusaka	CCf	W 5-4p		Lwanja MWI
2005								
22-02	Congo	W	2-0	Brazzaville	Fr			
27-03	Zimbabwe	L	0-2	Harare	WCq			Codjia BEN
27-05	Tunisia	L	1-4	Tunis	Fr	Flavio [77p]	4 000	
3-06	Algeria	W	2-1	Luanda	WCq	Flavio [50], Akwa [58]	27 000	Hicuburundi BDI
17-06	Nigeria	D	1-1	Kano	WCq	Figueiredo [60]	17 000	Abd El Fatah EGY
9-08	Botswana	D	0-0	Johannesburg	Fr			
10-08	Botswana	D	0-0	Johannesburg	Fr			
13-08	Zimbabwe	L	1-2	Mmabatho	CCsf	Love [52]		Kapanga MWI
17-08	Cape Verde Islands	W	2-1	Lisbon	Fr	Mantorras [46], Love [86]		
4-09	Gabon	W	3-0	Luanda	WCq	OG [25], Mantorras [44], Ze Kalanga [89]	35 000	Coulibaly MLI
8-10	Rwanda	W	1-0	Kigali	WCq	Akwa [79]	25 000	Guezzaz MAR
16-11	Japan	L	0-1	Tokyo	Fr		52 406	
2006								
17-01	Morocco	D	2-2	Marrakech	Fr	Akwa [41] Mantorras [74p]		
21-01	Cameroon	L	1-3	Cairo	CNr1	Flavio [31p]	8 000	Guezzaz MAR
25-01	Congo DR	D	0-0	Cairo	CNr1		2 000	Diatta SEN
29-01	Togo	W	3-2	Cairo	CNr1	Flavio 2 [9 39], Maurito [86]	4 000	El Arjoun MAR
1-03	Korea Republic	L	0-1	Seoul	Fr		63 255	Supian MAS
29-04	Mauritius	W	5-1	Maseru	CCr1	Akwa 3 [3 28 55], Mateus [59], Love [89]		Moeketsi LES
30-04	Lesotho	W	3-1	Maseru	CCr2	Mateus [47], Ze Kalanga 2 [50 61]		Mlangeni SWZ
30-05	Argentina	L	0-2	Salerno	Fr		7 000	Farina ITA
2-06	Turkey	L	2-3	Arnhem	Fr	Akwa [32], Love [83]	1 200	Wegereef NED
11-06	Portugal	L	0-1	Cologne	WCr1		45 000	Larrionda URU
16-06	Mexico	D	0-0	Hanover	WCr1		43 000	Maidin SIN
21-06	Iran	D	1-1	Leipzig	WCr1	Flavio [60]	38 000	Shield AUS

Fr = Friendly match • CN = CAF African Cup of Nations • CC = COSAFA Castle Cup • WC = FIFA World Cup™
q = qualifier • r1 = first round group • qf = quarter-final • sf = semi-final • f = final

ANGOLA NATIONAL TEAM RECORDS AND RECORD SEQUENCES

Records			Sequence records					
Victory	7-1	SWZ 2000	Wins	3	Four times	Clean sheets	5	2004-2005
Defeat	0-6	POR 1989	Defeats	6	1989-1990	Goals scored	11	2001
Player Caps	n/a		Undefeated	12	2004-2005	Without goal	3	1980-1981
Player Goals	n/a		Without win	13	1980-1982	Goals against	8	1989-90, 1998-91

ANGOLA COUNTRY INFORMATION

Capital	Luanda	Independence	1975	GDP per Capita	$1 900
Population	10 978 552	Status	Republic	GNP Ranking	102
Area km²	1 246 700	Language	Portuguese	Dialling code	+244
Population density	9 per km²	Literacy rate	45%	Internet code	.ao
% in urban areas	32%	Main religion	Christian 90%	GMT + / –	+1
Towns/Cities ('000)	Luanda 2 776; Huambo 226; Lobito 207; Benguela 151; Kuito 113; Lubango 102; Malanje 87
Neighbours (km)	Congo 201; Congo DR 2 511; Zambia 1 110; Namibia 1 376; Atlantic Ocean 1 600
Main stadia	Cidadela – Luanda 60 000; Do Santos – Viana 17 000; Nossa Senhora do Monte – Lubango 14 000

CLUB DIRECTORY

Club	Town/City	Stadium	Capacity	Lge	Cup
Académica Petróleo do Kwanda	Soyo	Soyo	5 000	0	0
Atlético Petróleos do Namibe (prev Sonangol)	Namibe	Joaquim Morais	5 000	0	0
Atlético Sport Aviação (ASA)	Luanda	Joaquim Dinis	10 000	3	2
SL Benfica Luanda	Luanda	São Paulo	4 000	0	0
SL Benfica Lubango	Lubango	Nossa Senhora do Monte	14 000	0	0
Clube Desportivo Huíla	Lubango	Nossa Senhora do Monte	14 000	0	0
GD Inter Clube Luanda	Luanda	Coqueiros	12 000	0	2
Onze Bravos Maqui	Huambo	Cacilhas	5 000	0	0
Petro Atlético (Petróleos Luanda)	Luanda	Coqueiros	12 000	13	8
Primeiro de Agosto	Luanda	Coqueiros	12 000	8	3
Primeiro de Maio	Benguela	Municipal	4 000	2	2
Progresso Sambizanga	Luanda	Cidadela	60 000	0	1
Sagrada Esperança	Malanje	Municipal 1° de Maio	3 000	1	2
Sporting Cabinda	Cabinda	Tafe	9 000	0	0

RECENT LEAGUE AND CUP RECORD

	Championship						Cup		
Year	Champions	Pts	Runners-up	Pts	Third	Pts	Winners	Score	Runners-up
1990	Petro Atlético	42	Primeiro de Maio	39	Primeiro de Agosto	35	Primeiro de Agosto	1-0	Petro Atlético
1991	Primeiro de Agosto		Sagrada Esperança		Petro Atlético		Primeiro de Agosto	2-1	Petro Atlético
1992	Primeiro de Agosto		Atlético Aviação	40	Petro Atlético	40	Petro Atlético	3-2	Primeiro de Agosto
1993	Petro Atlético	32	Primeiro de Maio	29	Desportivo EKA	26	Petro Atlético	2-1	Atlético Aviação
1994	Petro Atlético		Primeiro de Maio		Independente		Petro Atlético	0-0 2-1	Independente
1995	Petro Atlético						Atlético Aviação	3-1	Independente
1996	Primeiro de Agosto						Prog. Sambizanga	1-0	Primeiro de Maio
1997	Petro Atlético						Petro Atlético	2-1	Primeiro de Agosto
1998	Primeiro de Agosto	62	Petro Atlético	58	Atlético Aviação	50	Petro Atlético	4-1	Primeiro de Agosto
1999	Primeiro de Agosto	59	Académica Lobito	51	Inter Clube	49	Sagrada Esperança	1-0	Atlético Aviação
2000	Petro Atlético	63	Atlético Aviação	44	Petro Huambo	42	Petro Atlético	1-0	Inter Clube
2001	Petro Atlético	57	Atlético Aviação	50	Petro Huambo	42	Sonangol	3-2	Sporting Cabinda
2002	Atlético Aviação	57	Primeiro de Agosto	53	Petro Atlético	51	Petro Atlético	3-0	Desportivo Huíla
2003	Atlético Aviação	53	Petro Atlético	52	Petro Huambo	46	Inter Clube	1-0	Sagrada Esperança
2004	Atlético Aviação	56	Sagrada Esperança	53	Inter Clube	51	Sonangol	2-0	Primeiro de Agosto
2005	Sagrada Esperança	51	Atlético Aviação	50	Petro Atlético	48	Atlético Aviação	1-0	Inter Clube

ANGOLA 2005

CAMPEONATO NACIONAL XXVII GIRABOLA 1° DIVISAO

	Pl	W	D	L	F	A	Pts	Sagrada	ASA	Petro At.	1° Agosto	1° Maio	Benfica	Cabinda	Namibe	Inter	Progresso	Huíla	Petro H'bo	Lobito	Sporting Bié
Sagrada Esperança †	26	15	6	5	34	19	51		0-0	1-0	2-1	2-2	2-0	0-1	3-0	0-0	1-0	3-1	1-0	2-1	3-1
Atlético Aviação †	26	14	8	4	37	20	50	1-2		2-0	1-0	1-0	0-2	2-1	2-3	1-1	3-1	2-0	2-0	2-1	4-0
Petro Atlético ‡	26	14	6	6	28	17	48	1-0	2-3		1-0	3-1	1-0	1-1	1-1	1-0	1-0	2-0	2-1	1-0	1-0
Primeiro de Agosto	26	11	8	7	36	21	41	3-0	1-1	1-2		1-1	1-1	1-0	5-2	0-0	4-1	3-1	1-1	3-1	3-0
Primeiro de Maio	26	9	10	7	26	25	37	1-1	2-2	0-0	2-1		1-0	1-1	4-2	2-1	2-1	1-0	0-1	1-0	1-0
Benfica Luanda	26	10	7	9	28	19	37	0-1	1-2	2-1	0-0	0-0		4-0	2-0	2-0	0-0	0-0	2-0	2-0	2-1
Sporting Cabinda	26	9	6	11	23	31	33	2-1	0-0	1-1	1-2	0-1	1-0		1-0	1-2	3-1	1-0	1-0	2-1	0-0
At. Petróleos Namibe	26	8	9	9	25	31	33	0-2	1-0	0-2	0-0	1-0	2-2	2-0		0-0	0-0	1-1	1-0	0-0	4-0
Inter Clube	26	8	9	9	27	28	33	0-1	0-2	1-0	1-1	2-1	2-1	0-2	2-2		2-2	1-0	2-0	1-1	2-1
Progresso Sambizanga	26	7	11	8	23	26	32	0-1	1-1	0-2	1-0	0-0	1-1	2-2	1-1	3-1		0-0	0-0	0-0	1-0
Desportivo Huíla	26	7	10	9	22	25	31	1-1	1-1	0-0	0-1	1-1	2-1	3-0	1-0	2-1	0-2		2-1	0-0	3-0
Petro Huambo	26	8	6	12	13	19	30	1-0	0-0	1-0	0-1	0-0	1-0	2-1	2-0	0-0	0-1	0-1		1-0	1-0
Académica Lobito	26	6	7	13	20	29	25	1-1	0-1	1-1	1-0	2-0	0-2	1-0	0-1	2-1	1-3	1-1	1-0		2-0
Sporting Petróleos Bié	26	3	3	20	13	45	12	1-3	0-1	0-1	0-2	2-1	0-1	3-0	0-1	0-4	0-1	1-1	0-0	3-2	

19/02/2005 - 23/10/2005 • † Qualified for CAF Champions League • ‡ Qualified for CAF Confederation Cup • Matches in bold awarded 3-0

ANGOLA 2005 2° DIVISAO

Zona A

	Pl	W	D	L	F	A	Pts
Académica Soyo	14	11	1	2	24	7	34
Kabuscorp Palanca	14	11	1	2	45	9	34
Santos	14	9	3	2	25	9	30
Polivalente Palanca	13	5	4	4	11	13	19
21 de Janeiro	11	2	4	5	11	23	10
Atlético Brilhantes	11	1	3	7	4	27	6
Benfica Milunga	13	1	2	10	12	20	5
Construtores	10	0	2	8	1	25	2

Zona B

	Pl	W	D	L	F	A	Pts
Benfica Lubango	10	8	0	2	14	7	24
Recreativo Caála	10	6	1	3	11	6	19
Benfica Huambo	9	5	3	1	19	4	18
Desportivo Kakuvas	7	2	1	4	6	16	7
Desportivo Chibia	7	0	2	5	0	11	2
Ferroviário Huíla	7	0	1	6	3	9	1

9/07/2005 - 23/10/2005

Zona C

	Pl	W	D	L	F	A	Pts
Onze Bravos Maqui	10	5	4	1	24	6	19
Ritondo Malanje	10	6	3	1	13	2	21
Inter Clube 4° Junho	10	6	2	2	9	5	20
Heróis da Baixa	9	3	0	6	4	11	9
Lacrau Army	9	2	2	5	6	10	8
Desportivo Cuca	8	0	1	7	0	22	1

TACA NACIONAL 2005

Round of 16

Atlético Aviação	1
Benfica Luanda	0
Sporting Petróleos Bié	
Académica Kwanda	†
Primeiro de Maio	1
At. Petróleos Namibe	0
Petro Huambo	0
Primeiro de Agosto	1
Sagrada Esperança	1 4p
Petro Atlético	1 3p
Polivalente Palanca	0
Sporting Cabinda	2
Progresso Sambizanga	1
Académica Lobito	0
Desportivo Huíla	0
Inter Clube	4

Quarter-finals

Atlético Aviação	1 3p
Académica Kwanda	1 2p
Primeiro de Maio	0 1p
Primeiro de Agosto	0 3p
Sagrada Esperança	2
Sporting Cabinda	1
Progresso Sambizanga	1
Inter Clube	4

Semi-finals

Atlético Aviação	1
Primeiro de Agosto	0
Sagrada Esperança	0 7p
Inter Clube	0 8p

Final

Atlético Aviação	1
Inter Clube ‡	0

CUP FINAL

Estádio dos Coqueiros, Luanda
11-11-2005, Ref: Domingos

Scorer - Kadima 83 for ASA

* Home team • † Awarded 3-0 • ‡ Qualified for CAF Confederation Cup

ANT – NETHERLANDS ANTILLES

NATIONAL TEAM RECORD
JULY 1ST 2002 TO JULY 9TH 2006

PL	W	D	L	F	A	%
12	5	2	5	19	17	50

FIFA/COCA-COLA WORLD RANKING

1993	1994	1995	1996	1997	1998	1999	2000	2001	2002	2003	2004	2005		High		Low
128	152	125	142	156	156	167	175	183	177	188	163	168		118	07/95	188 12/03

					2005–2006						
08/05	09/05	10/05	11/05	12/05	01/06	02/06	03/06	04/06	05/06	06/06	07/06
166	166	166	166	168	168	168	169	170	170	-	176

With no activity on the international front, the focus for football has been on the local championships in Curacão and in Bonaire, although fans of the latter had their season disrupted by a dispute involving four of the top clubs - ATC, Estrellas, Juventus and Vitesse - which brought the league to a standstill. The final of the Curacão championship was also delayed, but thankfully only by four days after Jong Colombia unsuccessfully complained that Deportivo Barber had used an ineligible player during the semi-final group stage. Over the course of the season Deportivo Barber had shown they merited their place in the final, having comfortably won the 18 match first stage

INTERNATIONAL HONOURS
None

and the six team second stage, from which four clubs qualified for the semi-final group. They didn't win the final, however. Against Union Deportivo Banda Abou (Undeba), after a goalless 90 minutes, they lost to a Luigison Doran goal in extra-time to bring to an end their four year reign as champions of Curacão. Earlier in the season Centro Barber had won the Kopa Antiano, a competition played over three weeks which is the closest the country has to a national championship. After winning the four team first round group, they played second placed Victory Boys in the final, which they won 2-1 thanks to goals from Oscar Molina and Ivendell Meulens.

THE FIFA BIG COUNT OF 2000

	Male	Female		Male	Female
Registered players	600	0	Referees	38	0
Non registered players	2 200	0	Officials	306	0
Youth players	740	0	Total involved	3 884	
Total players	3 540		Number of clubs	36	
Professional players	0	0	Number of teams	71	

Nederlands Antilliaanse Voetbal Unie (NAVU)
Bonamweg 49, Curaçao
Tel +599 97365040   Fax +599 97365047
navusoccer@interneeds.net   www.navusoccer.com
President: FRANCISCA Rignaal   General Secretary: SEALY Aubrey
Vice-President: TBD   Treasurer: MARIA Nelson   Media Officer: None
Men's Coach: VERBEEK Peter   Women's Coach: None
NAVU formed: 1921   CONCACAF: 1961   FIFA: 1932
White shirts with blue trimmings, Blue shorts, Red socks or Blue shirts, White shorts, Blue socks

RECENT INTERNATIONALS PLAYED BY NETHERLANDS ANTILLES

2002	Opponents	Score		Venue	Comp	Scorers	Att	Referee
28-07	Guyana	L	1-2	Georgetown	GCq	Muzo [14]		
11-08	Guyana	W	1-0	Willemstad	GCq	Martis [43], W 3-2p		Villar Polo ARU
20-11	Antigua and Barbuda	D	1-1	Port-au-Prince	GCq	Forbuis [88]		Bowen CAY
22-11	Haiti	L	0-3	Port-au-Prince	GCq			Bowen CAY
2003								
No international matches played in 2003								
2004								
10-01	Surinam	D	1-1	Paramaribo	Fr	Forbuis [38]		Jol NED
17-01	Surinam	W	2-0	Willemstad	Fr	Silberie, Christina		
28-01	Aruba	W	6-1	Willemstad	Fr			
18-02	Antigua and Barbuda	L	0-2	St John's	WCq		1 500	Navarro CAN
31-03	Antigua and Barbuda	W	3-0	Willemstad	WCq	Siberie [27], Martha [46], Hose [48]	9 000	Piper TRI
27-04	Dominican Republic	W	3-1	Willemstad	Fr	Bernardus 2 [6 32], Cicilia [7]		Faneite ANT
12-06	Honduras	L	1-2	Willemstad	WCq	Hose [75]	12 000	McArthur GUY
19-06	Honduras	L	0-4	San Pedro Sula	WCq		30 000	Alcala MEX
2005								
No international matches played in 2005								
2006								
No international matches played in 2006 before July								

Fr = Friendly match • GC = CONCACAF Gold Cup™ • WC = FIFA World Cup™ • q = qualifier

NETHERLANDS ANTILLES NATIONAL TEAM RECORDS AND RECORD SEQUENCES

Records			Sequence records					
Victory	15-0	PUR 1959	Wins	5	Three times	Clean sheets	3	1961-1962, 1966
Defeat	0-8	NED 1962, MEX 1973	Defeats	6	1973-1980	Goals scored	30	1926-1948
Player Caps	n/a		Undefeated	9	1959-1961	Without goal	3	Four time
Player Goals	n/a		Without win	17	1969-1980	Goals against	19	1968-1980

RECENT LEAGUE AND CUP RECORD

Kopa Antiano				Curacao Champions				Bonaire Champions		
Year	Winners	Score	Runners-up	Winners	Score	Runners-up	Winners	Score	Runners-up
2000	No competition			Jong Colombia	2-1	Centro Barber	Estrellas	4-1	Uruguay
2001	Jong Colombia	3-0	Juventus		-		Estrellas	2-0	Real Rincon
2002	Centro Barber	2-1	SUBT	Centro Barber	2-1	SUBT	Estrellas	1-0	Real Rincon
2003	Centro Barber	2-1	Jong Colombia	Centro Barber	1-0	Jong Colombia	Real Rincon	3-0	Juventus
2004				Centro Barber	1-0	Victory Boys	Real Rincon	0-0 1-0	Estrellas
2005	Centro Barber	2-1	Victory Boys	Centro Barber	4-1	Victory Boys	Juventus	1-0	Estrellas
2006				Undeba	1-0	Centro Barber			

NETHERLANDS ANTILLES COUNTRY INFORMATION

Capital	Willemstad	Independence	Part of the Netherlands with		GDP per Capita	$11 400
Population	218 126	Status	autonomy in internal affairs		GNP Ranking	n/a
Area km²	960	Language	Dutch		Dialling code	+599
Population density	227 per km²	Literacy rate	96%		Internet code	.an
% in urban areas	n/a	Main religion	Christian		GMT + / –	-4
Towns/Cities ('000)	Willemstad (Curaçao) 97; Princess Quarter (Sint Maarten) 13; Kraleendijk (Bonaire) 3;					
Neighbours (km)	Netherlands Antilles is a group of Caribbean islands consisting of Bonaire, Curaçao, Saba, Sint Eustatius & Sint Maarten					
Main stadia	Ergilio Hato – Willemstad 15 000; Municipal – Kralendijk 3 000					

ARG - ARGENTINA

NATIONAL TEAM RECORD
JULY 1ST 2002 TO JULY 9TH 2006

PL	W	D	L	F	A	%
55	33	12	10	105	58	70.9

After so much hope and promise it all ended in tears for Argentina at the 2006 FIFA World Cup™ with a penalty shoot-out defeat at the hands of hosts Germany. It's a memory that will haunt Esteban Cambiasso, who missed the vital last kick, because it was within Argentina's capability to win the tournament. Individually full of craft and guile they were also gifted as a team unit. Their 6-0 demolition of Serbia and Montenegro - a team that had conceded just one goal in qualification - will remain a classic for years to come, whilst Cambiasso's goal in that game, the result of a 24 pass build-up, will feature high on the list of all-time greats. Central to the team was midfielder Juan Roman Riquelme who had an eventful season with Villarreal in Spain, taking them to the semi-finals of the UEFA Champions League, but there was class throughout the side. The belief amongst players and fans alike was that this was their best shot at winning the tournament since 1986. At the end of the penalty shoot-out, the sheer anguish of the moment saw an unsightly melee on the pitch prompted by the disappointed Argentines. The defeat also signalled the end for coach Jose Pekerman, three times a world champion with Argentina as their youth coach, who quit after

INTERNATIONAL HONOURS
FIFA World Cup™ 1978 1986

Olympic Gold 2004   **FIFA World Youth Championship** 1979 1995 1997 2001 2005

Copa América 1910 1921 1925 1927 1929 1937 1941 1945 1946 1947 1955 1957 1959 1991 1993

Sudamericana Sub-20 1967 1997 1999 2003   **Sudamericana Sub-17** 1985 2003

Copa Toyota Libertadores Independiente 1964 1965 1972 1973 1974 1975 1984, Racing Club 1967, Estudiantes 1968 1969 1970, Boca Juniors 1977 1978 2000 2001 2003, Argentinos Juniors 1985, River Plate 1986 1996, Vélez Sarsfield 1994

the game. At home the Argentine championship was dominated by Boca Juniors, who won both the Apertura and Clausura, the first team since River Plate in the 1999-2000 season to achieve that feat. They were gifted the Apertura title when leaders Gimnasia La Plata could only draw their final two matches, having won their previous eight, leaving the La Plata side still looking for their first title since 1929. Boca's Clausura campaign got off to a poor start with two defeats in their first five games but those were the only games they lost, culminating in a run of seven wins, to finish the season comfortably clear of Lanus. There was further cheer for coach Alfio Basile when Boca retained the Copa Sudamericana in December by beating Mexico's UNAM Pumas on penalties in the final. Boca had failed to qualify for the 2006 Copa Libertadores but Argentina still had three representatives in the quarter-finals with Vélez Sarsfield, Estudiantes and River Plate. River have a history of reaching the final when the year ends in a six, but not this time around as none of the trio made it through to the semi-finals.

Asociación del Fútbol Argentino (AFA)
Viamonte 1366/76, Buenos Aires - 1053
Tel +54 11 43727900   Fax +54 11 43754410
gerencia@afa.org.ar   www.afa.org.ar
President: GRONDONA Julio H.   General Secretary: MEISZNER Jose Luis
Vice-President: AGUILAR Jose Maria   Treasurer: PORTELL Carlos   Media Officer: TBD
Men's Coach: BASILE Alfio   Women's Coach: BORRELO Jose Carlos
AFA formed: 1893   CONMEBOL: 1916   FIFA: 1912
Light blue and white striped shirts, Black shorts, White socks or Dark blue shirts, Black shorts, White socks

RECENT INTERNATIONAL MATCHES PLAYED BY ARGENTINA

2004	Opponents	Score	Venue	Comp	Scorers	Att	Referee
30-03	Ecuador	W 1-0	Buenos Aires	WCq	Crespo [60]	55 000	Vazquez URU
28-04	Morocco	W 1-0	Casablanca	Fr	Kily Gonzalez [52]	60 000	Ndoye SEN
2-06	Brazil	L 1-3	Belo Horizonte	WCq	Sorin [81]	50 000	Ruiz COL
6-06	Paraguay	D 0-0	Buenos Aires	WCq		43 000	Simon BRA
27-06	Colombia	L 0-2	New York	Fr			Terry USA
30-06	Peru	W 2-1	New York	Fr	Kily Gonzalez [25p], Saviola [72]	41 013	Stott USA
7-07	Ecuador	W 6-1	Chiclayo	CAr1	Kily Gonzalez [5p], Saviola 3 [64 74 79], D'Alessandro [84] Gonzalez.L [90]	24 000	Amarilla PAR
10-07	Mexico	L 0-1	Chiclayo	CAr1		25 000	Rezende BRA
13-07	Uruguay	W 4-2	Piura	CAr1	Kily Gonzalez [19p], Figueroa 2 [20 89], Ayala [80]	24 000	Selman CHI
17-07	Peru	W 1-0	Chiclayo	CAqf	Tevez [60]	25 000	Amarilla PAR
20-07	Colombia	W 3-0	Lima	CAsf	Tevez [32], Gonzalez.L [51], Sorin [80]	22 000	Hidalgo PER
25-07	Brazil	D 2-2	Lima	CAf	Kily Gonzalez [21p], Delgado [87]	43 000	Amarilla PAR
18-08	Japan	W 2-1	Shizuoka	Fr	Galletti [4], Santana [40]	45 000	Lu CHN
4-09	Peru	W 3-1	Lima	WCq	Rosales [14], Coloccini [66], Sorin [92]	28 000	Simon BRA
9-10	Uruguay	W 4-2	Buenos Aires	WCq	Gonzalez.L [6], Figueroa 2 [32 54], Zanetti [44]	50 000	Souza BRA
13-10	Chile	D 0-0	Santiago	WCq		57 671	Amarilla PAR
16-11	Venezuela	W 3-2	Buenos Aires	WCq	Rey OG [3], Riquelme [46+], Saviola [65]	30 000	Hidalgo PER
2005							
9-02	Germany	D 2-2	Dusseldorf	Fr	Crespo 2 [40p 81]	52 000	Farina ITA
9-03	Mexico	D 1-1	Los Angeles	Fr	Zarate [67]	51 345	Hall USA
26-03	Bolivia	W 2-1	La Paz	WCq	Figueroa [57], Galletti [63]	25 000	Larrionda URU
30-03	Colombia	W 1-0	Buenos Aires	WCq	Crespo [65]	40 000	Amarilla PAR
4-06	Ecuador	L 0-2	Quito	WCq		37 583	Selman CHI
8-06	Brazil	W 3-1	Buenos Aires	WCq	Crespo 2 [3 40], Riquelme [18]	49 497	Mendez URU
15-06	Tunisia	W 2-1	Köln	CCr1	Riquelme [33p], Saviola [57]	28 033	Rosetti ITA
18-06	Australia	W 4-2	Nürnberg	CCr1	Figueroa 3 [12 53 89], Riquelme [31p]	25 618	Maidin SIN
21-06	Germany	D 2-2	Nürnberg	CCr1	Riquelme [33], Cambiasso [74]	42 088	Michel SVK
26-06	Mexico	D 1-1	Hanover	CCsf	Figueroa [110]	40 718	Rosetti ITA
29-06	Brazil	L 1-4	Frankfurt	CCf	Aimar [65]	45 591	Michel SVK
17-08	Hungary	W 2-1	Budapest	Fr	Rodriguez.M [19], Heinze [62]	27 000	Merk GER
3-09	Paraguay	L 0-1	Asuncion	WCq		32 000	Simon BRA
9-10	Peru	W 2-0	Buenos Aires	WCq	Riquelme [81p], OG [90]	36 977	Torres PAR
12-10	Uruguay	L 0-1	Montevideo	WCq		55 000	Souza BRA
12-11	England	L 2-3	Geneva	Fr	Crespo [34], Samuel [54]	29 000	Leuba SUI
16-11	Qatar	W 3-0	Doha	Fr	Riquelme [70], Cruz [72], Ayala [73]		Al Fadhli KUW
2006							
1-03	Croatia	L 2-3	Basel	Fr	Tevez [4], Messi [6]	13 138	Nobs SUI
30-05	Angola	W 2-0	Salerno	Fr	Rodriguez.M [28], Sorin [36]	7 000	Farina ITA
10-06	Côte D'Ivoire	W 2-1	Hamburg	WCr1	Crespo [24], Saviola [38]	49 480	De Bleeckere BEL
16-06	Serbia & Montenegro	W 6-0	Gelsenkirchen	WCr1	Rodriguez.M 2 [6 41], Cambiasso [31], Crespo [78] Tevez [84], Messi [88]	52 000	Rosetti ITA
21-06	Netherlands	D 0-0	Frankfurt	WCr1		48 000	Medina Cantalejo ESP
24-06	Mexico	W 2-1	Leipzig	WCr2	Crespo [10], Rodriguez.M [98]	43 000	Busacca SUI
30-06	Germany	D 1-1	Berlin	WCqf	Ayala [49], L 2-4p	72 000	Michel SVK

Fr = Friendly match • KC = Kirin Cup • CA = Copa América • CC = FIFA Confederations Cup • WC = FIFA World Cup™
q = qualifier • r1 = 1st round • qf = quarter-final • sf = semi-final • f = final

ARGENTINA NATIONAL TEAM RECORDS AND RECORD SEQUENCES

Records			Sequence records				
Victory	12-0	ECU 1942	Wins	9	1941-1942	Clean sheets	8	1998
Defeat	1-6	CZE 1958	Defeats	4	1911-1912	Goals scored	42	1942-1954
Player Caps	106	SIMEONE Diego	Undefeated	31	1991-1993	Without goal	8	1989-1990
Player Goals	56	BATISTUTA Gabriel	Without win	10	1989-1990	Goals against	13	1906-1910

ARGENTINA COUNTRY INFORMATION

Capital	Buenos Aires	Independence	1816	GDP per Capita	$11 200
Population	39 144 753	Status	Republic	GNP Ranking	18
Area km²	2 766 890	Language	Spanish	Dialling code	+54
Population density	14 per km²	Literacy rate	96%	Internet code	.ar
% in urban areas	88%	Main religion	Christian 92%	GMT + / −	-3
Towns/Cities ('000)	Buenos Aires 11 548; Cordoba 1 441; Rosario 1 218; Mendoza 973; Tucuman 828; La Plata 684; Mar del Plata 645; Salta 548; San Juan 469; Santa Fe 456; Resistencia 406				
Neighbours (km)	Bolivia 832; Paraguay 1 880; Brazil 1 224; Uruguay 579; Chile 5 150; Atlantic Ocean 4 989				
Main stadia	Monumental – Buenos Aires 66 449; Cilindro – Buenos Aires 64 161; La Bombonera – Buenos Aires 60 245; Independiente – Buenos Aires 57 901; Jose Amalfitani – Buenos Aires 49 747				

ARGENTINA NATIONAL TEAM PLAYERS AND COACHES

Record Caps			Record Goals			Recent Coaches	
SIMEONE Diego	1988-'02	106	BATISTUTA Gabriel	1991-'02	56	PIZZUTI Juan Jose	1970-'72
AYALA Roberto	1994-'06	105	MARADONA Diego	1977-'94	34	SIVORI Omar	1972-'73
ZANETTI Javier	1994-'05	102	CRESPO Hernan	1995-'06	32	CAP Vladislao	1974
RUGGERI Oscar	1983-'94	97	ARTIME Luis	1961-'67	24	MENOTTI Cesar Luis	1974-'82
MARADONA Diego	1977-'94	91	LUQUE Leopoldo	1975-'81	22	BILARDO Carlos	1983-'90
ORTEGA Ariel	1993-'03	86	PASSARELLA Daniel	1976-'86	22	BASILE Alfio	1990-'94
BATISTUTA Gabriel	1991-'02	78	MASANTONIO Herminio	1935-'42	21	PASSARELLA Daniel	1994-'98
SORIN Juan	1995-'06	75	SANFILLIPO Jose	1956-'62	21	BIELSA Marcelo	1999-'04
GALLEGO America	1975-'82	73	KEMPES Mario	1973-'82	20	PEKERMAN Jose	2004-'06
PASSARELLA Daniel	1976-'86	70				BASILE Alfio	2006-

CLUB DIRECTORY

Club	Town/City	Stadium	Capacity	www.	Lge	CL
Argentinos Juniors	Buenos Aires	Diego Maradona	24 800	argentinosjuniors.com.ar	2	1
Arsenal	Buenos Aires	Viaducto	16 300	None	0	0
Banfield	Buenos Aires	Florencio Sola	33 351	clubabanfield.com.ar	0	0
Boca Juniors	Buenos Aires	La Bombonera	57 395	bocajuniors.com.ar	26	5
Colón	Santa Fe	Cementerio Elefantes	32 500	None	0	0
Estudiantes	La Plata	Luis Jorge Hirsch	20 000	estudiantesdelp.com.ar	4	3
Gimnasia y Esgrima	La Plata	Bosque	33 000	gelp.com.ar	1	0
Independiente	Buenos Aires	Doble Visera	57 901	independiente.co.ar	16	7
Instituto	Cordoba	Monumental	26 535	None	0	0
Lanús	Buenos Aires	La Fortaleza	44 000	lanusclubatletico.com.ar	0	0
Newell's Old Boys	Rosario	El Coloso	42 000	pasionrojinegra.com.ar	5	0
Olimpo	Bahía Blanca	Roberto Carminatti	15 000	aurinegro.com.ar	0	0
Quilmes	Buenos Aires	Centenario	33 000	quilmesac.com	2	0
Racing Club	Buenos Aires	Cilindro	64 161	racingclub.com	16	1
River Plate	Buenos Aires	Monumental	76 687	cariverplate.com.ar	33	2
Rosario Central	Rosario	Gigante de Arroyito	41 654	rosariocentral.com	4	0
San Lorenzo	Buenos Aires	Nuevo Gasometro	43 480	sanlorenzo.com.ar	12	0
Vélez Sarsfield	Buenos Aires	El Fortin	49 540	velezsarsfield.com.ar	6	1

FIFA/COCA-COLA WORLD RANKING

1993	1994	1995	1996	1997	1998	1999	2000	2001	2002	2003	2004	2005		High	Low
8	10	7	22	17	5	6	3	2	5	5	3	4		2	24 08/96

2005–2006											
08/05	09/05	10/05	11/05	12/05	01/06	02/06	03/06	04/06	05/06	06/06	07/06
2	3	4	4	4	4	4	4	8	9	-	3

THE FIFA BIG COUNT OF 2000

	Male	Female		Male	Female
Registered players	140 000	3 000	Referees	3 255	5
Non registered players	1 100 000	15 000	Officials	34 283	400
Youth players	245 467	2 000	Total involved	1 543 410	
Total players	1 505 467		Number of clubs	2 994	
Professional players	2 500	0	Number of teams	17 826	

ARGENTINA 2005–06

PRIMERA DIVISION — TORNEO APERTURA

	Pl	W	D	L	F	A	Pts	Boca	Gim.LP	Vélez	Indep'te	Banfield	River	Estud.	Arg.Jun.	S.Lorenzo	Colón	Racing	Olimpo	Lanús	Arsenal	Rosario C.	Newell's	Quilmes	Gimnasia J.	Tiro Federal	Instituto
Boca Juniors	19	12	4	3	36	17	40			2-0	2-0		1-0				0-1	2-0				2-2	2-1		4-1	2-1	3-0
Gimnasia La Plata	19	11	4	4	28	19	37	0-2				0-6	3-0			3-2	1-0	3-1		1-0			0-0			4-1	1-1
Vélez Sarsfield	19	10	3	6	26	16	33							0-2	0-1		2-1	1-0	2-0			0-2	1-0			1-0	2-2
Independiente	19	8	8	3	34	22	32						1-0		1-1		1-1	4-0	4-0			2-2	2-0			1-0	3-0
Banfield	19	5	13	1	25	15	28	1-1	1-1	0-0	2-2		4-1			5-0	2-0			1-1				0-0			
River Plate	19	8	4	7	31	22	28	0-0	1-3	0-1	3-1			5-1	3-2			4-1					2-1	1-1		2-0	
Estudiantes La Plata	19	8	4	7	23	22	28	1-3	1-0			1-1	2-0		1-0		0-1					2-2	3-1			2-0	
Argentinos Juniors	19	8	4	7	19	20	28	0-1				1-1	1-0	2-1			1-0		0-0	1-0				1-2	1-2		1-0
San Lorenzo	19	8	4	7	33	39	28	3-2		3-2	1-1			1-3				1-4	2-1		1-1			4-2		1-1	5-3
Colón Santa Fe	19	7	5	7	28	27	26							2-1	2-0					0-2	2-0	0-0	2-0	1-1		4-3	1-1
Racing Club	19	7	4	8	28	27	25					0-0	1-1	3-1		3-0			2-2		3-1	0-1		4-1	3-3		2-3
Olimpo	19	5	8	6	19	23	23	1-2	2-1					2-2	2-1	3-0	1-1			1-1	0-0		1-0				
Lanús	19	5	8	6	21	31	23	1-1		0-4	2-4			1-1			3-1	1-0			1-1				2-1	0-2	1-1
Arsenal	19	5	7	7	23	24	22	4-1	1-1	0-1	2-4	1-1	1-0		1-2				1-2				1-3				
Rosario Central	19	5	7	7	20	29	22	0-3								0-0	0-3	1-1			0-4		1-1		1-1	2-1	3-2
Newell's Old Boys	19	5	5	9	25	27	20					2-2			3-2	3-0					0-1	0-1		1-3	2-1	2-1	5-0
Quilmes	19	4	7	8	20	27	19	0-4	0-1	1-1	1-1					2-0	4-2				0-1		1-1			2-2	1-2
Gimnasia y Es. Jujuy	19	3	9	7	23	30	18			1-2				1-1	1-2	0-0	0-1	2-2			2-1		1-1	2-0			
Tiro Federal	19	4	3	12	22	31	15	0-1				0-1	1-4				1-2	1-1			0-2	4-0			0-0		2-1
Instituto Córdoba	19	2	9	8	11	27	15	0-1				0-0	1-4	0-0		2-0		0-0			0-2	0-0			0-0	0-0	

5/08/2005 – 14/12/2005 • Top scorers: Javier CAMPORA, Tiro Federal, 13; Jose CALDERON, Estudiantes, 10, Rodrigo PALACIO, Boca Juniors, 10; Leonardo PISCULICHI, Argentinos Juniors, 10; Gonzalo VARGAS, Gimnasia LP, 10

ARGENTINA 2005–06

PRIMERA DIVISION — TORNEO CLAUSURA

	Pl	W	D	L	F	A	Pts	Boca	Lanús	River	Gim.J	Gim.LP	Newell's	Banfield	S.Lorenzo	Olimpo	Vélez	Estud.	Indep'te	Rosario C.	Arg.Jun.	Arsenal	Colón	Quilmes	Racing	Instituto	Tiro Federal
Boca Juniors †‡	19	13	4	2	37	14	43		3-0	1-1			3-0		2-1	1-2	2-0	4-0					1-0		3-1		
Lanús ‡	19	10	5	4	26	15	35			4-1		2-1			0-2	2-0	2-1	1-1		2-0			3-0			2-0	
River Plate †‡	19	9	7	3	39	23	34				2-0		3-1		3-0		3-1	2-0	2-2	3-1						0-2	3-1
Gimnasia Y Esg. Jujuy	19	10	3	6	26	16	33	2-1	1-0			0-0		0-1			1-0	3-1		2-1	1-0	0-1	2-0	2-1			
Gimnasia La Plata †‡	19	9	5	5	31	22	32			3-3				0-2		3-1	1-1			3-0	4-3	0-0		4-0		2-0	
Newell's Old Boys	19	8	7	4	27	18	31	1-1	1-2	3-1	3-1	2-3		1-1		1-0		2-0						0-0	2-0		
Banfield †‡	19	10	1	8	28	22	31				2-1				2-2		0-1		1-0	2-0	3-1	0-1		3-0	2-0	2-1	
San Lorenzo ‡	19	7	7	5	15	14	28				0-0			2-2		1-0			2-0		1-2		0-0		0-2	0-0	1-1
Olimpo Bahía Blanca	19	7	5	7	22	22	26			1-0		0-2		2-2			0-2	0-0	4-1		1-0			3-0	2-0	3-0	
Vélez Sarsfield †‡	19	5	10	4	21	18	25	**0-3**	0-0	1-1	0-0	2-1						1-0	1-0		0-2			0-0	2-0		
Estudiantes La Plata	19	6	6	7	25	31	24					0-4		2-1			2-2		1-1	1-1	2-2	1-2		2-1	4-1	0-3	
Independiente	19	6	5	8	18	18	23	0-2	0-0	1-1	0-0	0-1								1-2	1-0		0-3		0-2	0-0	
Rosario Central	19	5	8	6	15	17	23	1-2				0-0			1-0		2-0				1-1		2-0	1-1	1-0	3-0	
Argentinos Juniors	19	5	7	7	26	28	22	1-2	1-1	1-1				0-1			0-0	2-1				1-0		2-0		4-0	
Arsenal	19	5	7	7	17	20	22				1-1			0-0				1-2	1-1		1-1		1-0	1-1	0-3		
Colón Santa Fe	19	5	5	9	19	26	20	1-2	1-3	2-2		0-2			1-0		4-2	0-1		0-3	1-1			1-0			
Quilmes	19	5	5	9	15	28	20	**0-3**				3-1			1-1		1-0				1-1	2-1	1-0		0-3	3-1	
Racing Club	19	5	4	10	14	24	19	0-3	0-0			0-1	1-1		1-0		0-2		0-2				2-2				2-0
Instituto Córdoba	19	3	4	12	16	37	13	1-1	2-1			1-2			1-1		0-5		0-1		2-1				1-0		3-4
Tiro Federal	19	3	3	13	15	39	12	0-0	0-1	0-5		0-2	2-1		0-1				3-3		0-2				0-1	1-1	

27/01/2006 – 14/05/2006 • † Qualified for Copa Libertadores 2007 • ‡ Qualified for Copa Sudamericana 2006 • Matches in bold awarded 3-0
Relegation decided on three year record • Relegation play-offs: Hurácan BA 1-1 2-2 **Argentinos Juniors**; Belgrano Córdoba 2-1 2-1 Olimpo
Top scorers: Gonzalo VARGAS, Gimnasia LP, 12; Martin PALERMO, Boca, 11; Ernesto FARIAS, River, 11; Ignacio SCOCCO, Newell's 9; Sergio AGUERO, Independiente, 9; Silvio CARRARIO, Quilmes, 8

ARGENTINA 2005-06 NACIONAL B (2) APERTURA

	Pl	W	D	L	F	A	Pts
Godoy Cruz †	19	12	4	3	29	14	40
Almagro	19	10	5	4	28	17	35
Chacarita Juniors	19	9	7	3	23	9	34
Huracán BA	19	10	4	5	26	16	34
Defensa y Justicia	19	7	9	3	19	13	30
Ferro Carril Oeste	19	8	5	6	15	15	29
Belgrano Córdoba	19	7	6	6	19	20	27
Tigre	19	4	12	3	16	13	24
Ben Hur	19	6	6	7	20	19	24
Unión Santa Fe	19	5	9	5	29	29	24
Huracán Tres Arroyos	19	5	8	6	20	24	23
San Martín San Juan	19	4	10	5	15	15	22
Talleres Córdoba	19	4	10	5	18	19	22
Atlético Rafaela	19	5	7	7	19	25	22
CA Infantiles	19	4	9	6	20	22	21
Juventud Antoniana	19	5	6	8	13	16	21
Nueva Chicago	19	2	13	4	23	25	19
Aldosivi	19	5	4	10	19	29	19
El Porvenir	19	4	4	11	18	30	16
San Martín Mendoza	19	3	4	12	13	32	13

4/08/2005 - 4/12/2005 • † Qualified for the championship play-off as Apertura winner

ARGENTINA 2005-06 NACIONAL B (2) CLAUSURA

	Pl	W	D	L	F	A	Pts
Nueva Chicago †	19	10	5	4	30	20	35
Belgrano Córdoba ‡	19	11	2	6	29	19	35
San Martín San Juan‡	19	9	6	4	23	15	33
Talleres Córdoba ‡	19	9	6	4	27	20	33
Atlético Rafaela	19	8	7	4	27	21	31
Tigre	19	8	7	4	13	13	31
San Martín Mendoza	19	9	3	7	27	25	30
Aldosivi	19	9	2	8	20	21	29
Chacarita Juniors ‡	19	6	8	5	24	18	26
Juventud Antoniana	19	8	2	9	23	20	26
Ben Hur	19	6	8	5	17	16	26
El Porvenir	19	7	3	9	14	23	24
Godoy Cruz	19	5	8	6	20	21	23
CA Infantiles	19	6	5	8	19	25	23
Huracán BA ‡	19	6	4	9	27	29	22
Unión Santa Fe	19	4	10	5	16	19	22
Defensa y Justicia	19	6	3	10	28	25	21
Almagro	19	3	8	8	14	24	17
Huracán Tres Arroyos	19	4	4	11	15	26	16
Ferro Carril Oeste	19	3	5	11	15	28	14

8/12/2005 - 11/05/2006 • † Qualified for the championship play-off as Clausura winner • ‡ Qualified for play-offs on season record

Championship play-off: Neuva Chicago 1-1 1-3 **Godoy Cruz** • Godoy Cruz are Nacional B champions and are promoted • Nueva Chicago meet the team with the best overall record, Belgrano Córdoba, for the second promtion place play-off.
Second Promotion Place Play-off: **Nueva Chicago** 3-1 3-3 Belgrano Córdoba • Nueva Chicago promoted • Belgrano play-off against Olimpo.
The four teams with the next best season records play-off in the Reducido for the right to meet Argentinos Juniors.
Reducido semi-finals: Talleres 0-2 0-0 Chacarita Juniors; San Martín 3-2 0-3 Huracán BA • Reducido final: Huracán BA 3-0 0-2 Chacarita Juniors. Huracán BA meet Argentinos .

RECENT LEAGUE RECORD

	Torneo Clausura					Torneo Apertura		
Year	Champions	Pts	Runners-up	Pts	Champions	Pts	Runners-up	Pts
1990					Newell's Old Boys	28	River Plate	26
1991	Boca Juniors	32	San Lorenzo	27	River Plate	31	Boca Juniors	24
1992	Newell's Old Boys	29	Vélez Sarsfield	27	Boca Juniors	27	River Plate	25
1993	Vélez Sarsfield	27	Independiente	24	River Plate	24	Vélez Sarsfield	23
1994	Independiente	26	Huracán	25	River Plate	31	San Lorenzo	26
1995	San Lorenzo	30	Gimnasia LP	29	Vélez Sarsfield	41	Racing Club	35
1996	Vélez Sarsfield	40	Gimnasia LP	39	River Plate	46	Independiente	37
1997	River Plate	41	Colón Santa Fé	35	River Plate	45	Boca Juniors	44
1998	Vélez Sarsfield	46	Lanús	40	Boca Juniors	45	Gimnasia LP	36
1999	Boca Juniors	44	River Plate	37	River Plate	44	Rosario Central	43
2000	River Plate	42	Independiente	36	Boca Juniors	41	River Plate	37
2001	San Lorenzo	47	River Plate	41	Racing Club	42	River Plate	41
2002	River Plate	43	Gimnasia LP	37	Independiente	43	Boca Juniors	40
2003	River Plate	43	Boca Juniors	39	Boca Juniors	39	San Lorenzo	36
2004	River Plate	40	Boca Juniors	36	Newell's Old Boys	36	Vélez Sarsfield	34
2005	Vélez Sarsfield	39	Banfield	33	Boca Juniors	40	Gimnasia LP	37
2006	Boca Juniors	43	Lanús	35				

The system of two leagues in a year - the Apertura and Clausura - was adopted in mid 1990 • Newell's beat Boca in a play-off in 1991 but there have been no play-offs since • The season runs from August to July with the Apertura played at the end of the calendar year and the Clausura at the beginning of the calendar year

BOCA JUNIORS 2005–06

Date	Opponents	Score		Comp	Scorers
7-08-2005	Gimnasia y Esgrima Jujuy	W 4-1	H	TAP	Palacio 2 [9 82], Palermo [10], Diaz [13]
14-08-2005	Rosario Central	D 2-2	H	TAP	Bilos [78], Barros Schelotto [92+]
21-08-2005	Lanús	D 1-1	A	TAP	Bilos [35]
28-08-2005	Instituto Córdoba	W 30	H	TAP	Palermo 2 [31 68], Cardozo [35]
7-09-2005	San Lorenzo	L 2-3	A	TAP	Delgado [23], Palermo [59]
11-09-2005	Argentinos Juniors	W 1-0	H	TAP	Palacio [78]
18-09-2005	Gimnasia y Esgrima La Plata	W 2-0	A	TAP	Palacio [31], Insúa [56]
21-09-2005	Cerro Porteño - PAR	D 2-2	A	CSr2	Cardozo [2], Palacio [12]
25-09-2005	Racing Club	W 2-0	H	TAP	Diaz [20], Palacio [40]
29-09-2005	Cerro Porteño - PAR	W 5-1	H	CSr2	Krupoviesa [9], Palermo [66], Barros Schelotto [75], Cardozo [87], Insúa [89]
2-10-2005	Quilmes	W 4-0	A	TAP	Palermo 2 [11p 43], Palacio 2 [53 87]
5-10-2005	Tiro Federal	W 2-1	H	TAP	Bilos 2 [48 64]
16-10-2005	River Plate	D 0-0	A	TAP	
19-10-2005	Internacional - BRA	L 0-1	A	CSqf	
29-10-2005	Newell's Old Boys	W 2-1	H	TAP	Insúa [34], Palacio [70]
7-11-2005	Banfield	D 1-1	A	TAP	Palacio [82]
10-11-2005	Internacional - BRA	W 4-1	H	CSqf	Palacio 3 [6 77 90], Palermo [75]
13-11-2005	Colón Santa Fe	L 0-1	H	TAP	
17-11-2005	Arsenal	L 1-4	A	TAP	Insúa [35]
20-11-2005	Vélez Sarsfield	W 2-0	H	TAP	Insúa 2 [59 88]
23-11-2005	Universidad Católica - CHI	D 2-2	H	CSsf	Insúa [70], Palermo [83]
27-11-2005	Estudiantes La Plata	W 3-1	A	TAP	Ledesma [3], Palacio [42], Barros Schelotto [80]
1-12-2005	Universidad Católica - CHI	W 1-0	A	CSsf	Schiavi [59]
6-12-2005	Pumas UNAM - MEX	D 1-1	A	CSf	Palacio [30]
11-12-2005	Independiente	W 2-0	H	TAP	Palermo [59], Insúa [89]
14-12-2005	Olimpo	W 2-1	A	TAP	Diaz [10], Insúa [41]
18-12-2005	Pumas UNAM - MEX	D 1-1	H	CSf	Palermo [31]. W 4-3p
29-01-2006	Gimnasia y Esrima Jujuy	L 1-2	A	TCL	Palermo [47]
1-02-2006	Rosario Central	W 2-1	A	TCL	Palermo [25], Palacio [39]
5-02-2006	Lanús	W 3-0	H	TCL	Silvestre [18], Palermo [52], Palacio [85]
12-02-2006	Instituto Córdoba	D 1-1	A	TCL	Silvestre [55]
19-02-2006	San Lorenzo	L 1-2	H	TCL	Insúa [90]
26-02-2006	Argentinos Juniors	W 2-1	A	TCL	Delgado [35], Krupoviesa [58]
1-03-2006	Gimnasia y Esgrima La Plata	W 3-0	H	TCL	Bilos [26], Palermo [64], Delgado [88]
5-03-2006	Racing Club	W 3-0	A	TCL	Palermo [48], Insúa [67], Delgado [81]
12-03-2006	Quilmes	W 3-1	H	TCL	Díaz [17], Insúa [27], Palermo [81]
19-03-2006	Tiro Federal	D 0-0	A	TCL	
26-03-2006	River Plate	D 1-1	H	TCL	Palermo [90p]
29-03-2006	Newell's Old Boys	D 1-1	A	TCL	Palacio [68]
2-04-2006	Banfield	W 2-1	H	TCL	Galarza OG [16], Ibarra [90]
9-04-2006	Colón Santa Fe	W 2-1	A	TCL	Ameli OG [10], Palacio [25]
16-04-2006	Arsenal	W 1-0	H	TCL	Palermo [73]
23-04-2006	Vélez Sarsfield	W 3-2	A	TCL	Palermo 2 [27 89], Silvestre [40]. Abandoned 89'. Awarded 3-0 to Boca
30-04-2006	Estudiantes La Plata	W 4-0	H	TCL	Insúa 2 [21 79], Palacio [57], Barros Schelotto [88]
7-05-2006	Independiente	W 2-0	A	TCL	Palacio [37], Palermo [47]
14-05-2006	Olimpo	W 2-0	H	TCL	Silvestre [18], Palacio [60]

TAP = Torneo Apertura • CS = Copa Sudamericana • TCL = Torneo Clausura
r2 = second round • qf = quarter-final • sf = semi-final • f = final • H = Salta

RIVER PLATE 2005–06

Date	Opponents	Score		Comp	Scorers
7-08-2005	Tiro Federal	W 2-0	H	TAP	Gallardo [8], Farías [90]
14-08-2005	Gimnasia y Esgrima Jujuy	D 0-0	A	TAP	
21-08-2005	Newell's Old Boys	W 2-1	H	TAP	Barrado [22], Santana [85]
28-08-2005	Banfield	L 1-4	A	TAP	Gallardo [4]
7-09-2005	Colón Santa Fe	W 3-2	H	TAP	Santana [60], Gallardo [80], Oberman [84]
11-09-2005	Arsenal	L 0-1	A	TAP	
14-09-2005	Corinthians - BRA	D 0-0	A	CSr2	
18-09-2005	Vélez Sarsfield	L 0-1	H	TAP	
25-09-2005	Estudiantes LP	L 0-1	A	TAP	
28-09-2005	Corinthians - BRA	D 1-1	H	CSr2	
2-10-2005	Independiente	W 3-1	H	TAP	Montenegro [24], Garcia 2 [45] [46]
5-10-2005	Olimpo	L 1-2	A	TAP	Garcia [64]
16-10-2005	Boca Juniors	D 0-0	H	TAP	
30-10-2005	Rosario Central	W 3-0	A	TAP	Gallardo [16p], Domínguez [28], Farías [50p]
9-11-2005	Lanús	W 4-1	H	TAP	Garcia 2 [2 73], Farías [19], Montenegro [90]
13-11-2005	Instituto Córdoba	W 4-1	H	TAP	Farías 3 [37 51 60], Gallardo [86]
17-11-2005	San Lorenzo	W 5-1	H	TAP	Gallardo 2 [2p 7], Talamonti [44], Garcia 2 [86 90]
20-11-2005	Argentinos Juniors	L 0-1	A	TAP	
27-11-2005	Gimnasia y Esgrima La Plata	L 1-3	H	TAP	Fernandez [82]
4-12-2005	Racing Club	D 1-1	A	TAP	Farías [7]
11-12-2005	Quilmes	D 1-1	H	TAP	Santana [33]
26-01-2006	Oriente Petrolero - BOL	W 6-0	H	CLpr	Santana [20], Montenegro [37], Gallardo 2 [39p 57p], Farías [34], San Martín [46]
29-01-2006	Tiro Federal	W 5-0	A	TCL	Montenegro 2 [2 40], Patino [13], Santana [19], Farías [63]
2-02-2006	Oriente Petrolero - BOL	W 2-0	A	CLpr	Toja [15], Vaca OG [23]
5-02-2006	Newell's Old Boys	L 1-3	A	TCL	Montenegro [16]
8-02-2006	Gimnasia y Esgrima Jujuy	W 2-0	H	TCL	Domínguez [36], Farías [57]
12-02-2006	Banfield	W 3-1	H	TCL	Figueroa [39], Higuain [54], Gallardo [84]
16-02-2006	Libertad - PAR	L 0-2	A	CLg8	
19-02-2006	Colón Santa Fe	D 2-2	A	TCL	Figueroa 2 [24 60]
25-02-2006	Arsenal	W 3-1	H	TCL	Farías 2 [31 82], Talamonti [51]
1-03-2006	Vélez Sarsfield	D 1-1	A	TCL	Domínguez [73]
5-03-2006	Estudiantes LP	W 3-1	H	TCL	Higuain [18], Tula [48], Farías [90]
8-03-2006	El Nacional - ECU	W 4-3	H	CLg8	Farías [4], Santana [68], Montenegro [79], Gallardo [82]
12-03-2006	Independiente	D 1-1	A	TCL	Zapata [45]
16-03-2006	Paulista - BRA	W 4-1	H	CLg8	Santana [10], Montenegro 2 [13 51], Aban [82]
19-03-2006	Olimpo	W 3-0	H	TCL	Higuain 2 [23 41], Montenegro [65]
26-03-2006	Boca Juniors	D 1-1	A	TCL	Farías [39]
29-03-2006	Rosario Central	W 2-0	H	TCL	Farías 2 [18 37]
2-04-2006	Lanús	L 1-4	A	TCL	Farías [51]
5-04-2006	Paulista - BRA	L 1-2	A	CLg8	Patiño [18]
9-04-2006	Instituto Córdoba	W 3-1	H	TCL	Zapata [13], Farías 2 [61p 72]
12-04-2006	El Nacional - ECU	L 0-2	A	CLg8	
16-04-2006	San Lorenzo	D 0-0	A	TCL	
20-04-2006	Libertad - PAR	W 1-0	H	CLg8	Zapata [68]
23-04-2006	Argentinos Juniors	D 2-2	H	TCL	Patiño [46], Gallardo [80]
26-04-2006	Corinthians - BRA	W 3-2	H	CLr2	Farías [25], Ferrari [30], Santana [80]
30-04-2006	Gimnasia y Esgrima La Plata	D 3-3	A	TCL	Higuain [22], Sambueza [53p], Morales Neumann [81]
4-05-2006	Corinthians - BRA	W 3-1	A	CLr2	Dyego Coelho OG [56], Higuain 2 [71 81]
7-05-2006	Racing Club	L 0-2	H	TCL	
11-05-2006	Libertad - PAR	D 2-2	H	CLqf	Montenegro [76], Farías [81]
14-05-2006	Quilmes	W 3-1	A	TCL	Gallardo 2 [21 30], Gerlo [34]. Abandoned at 67'. Awarded 3-0 to River
18-07-2006	Libertad - PAR	L 1-3	A	CLqf	Farías [76]

TAP = Torneo Apertura • CS = Copa Sudamericana • TCL = Torneo Clausura
pr = preliminary round • g8 = Group 8 • r2 = second round • qf = quarter-final

ARM – ARMENIA

NATIONAL TEAM RECORD
JULY 1ST 2002 TO JULY 9TH 2006

PL	W	D	L	F	A	%
29	6	4	19	23	55	27.6

FIFA/COCA-COLA WORLD RANKING

1993	1994	1995	1996	1997	1998	1999	2000	2001	2002	2003	2004	2005	High		Low	
-	141	113	106	105	100	85	90	95	107	113	119	108	79	09/00	159	07/94

2005–2006											
08/05	09/05	10/05	11/05	12/05	01/06	02/06	03/06	04/06	05/06	06/06	07/06
120	115	109	110	108	108	108	109	109	109	-	105

It was more of the same in Armenian domestic football in the 2005–06 season with Pyunik winning a fifth consecutive championship and Mika Ashtarak retaining the Cup, their fifth triumph in seven seasons. The one difference, perhaps, was that Pyunik were just a little less invincible than before. There were no repeats of their record breaking unbeaten run of the previous season and they finished just four points ahead of Mika. There was some measure of revenge for Mika when the two met in the Cup Final with Armen Shahgeldian scoring the only goal of the game to win it for Mika. Not since 2000 has a team other than these two won a trophy in Armenia. On the international

INTERNATIONAL HONOURS
None

front Armenia's woes continued as they only just managed to avoid the wooden spoon in their FIFA World Cup™ qualifying group - thanks to two wins over minnows Andorra. Those two wins were the only wins during the past two seasons and with difficult fixtures in their UEFA Euro 2008™ qualifying group against the likes of Portugal, Belgium, Serbia and Poland, new coach Samvel Darbinyan has a tough job ahead of him. The 2005-06 season got off to an uninspired start with a 0-0 draw against Jordan and ended with a last place finish in the Cyprus international tournament, and after just a year in charge Dutchman Henrik Wisman was sacked as coach.

THE FIFA BIG COUNT OF 2000

	Male	Female		Male	Female
Registered players	1 600	100	Referees	64	10
Non registered players	35 000	100	Officials	140	20
Youth players	2 550	160	Total involved	39 744	
Total players	39 510		Number of clubs	56	
Professional players	550	0	Number of teams	78	

Football Federation of Armenia (FFA)

Khanjyan str. 27, Yerevan 375 010, Armenia
Tel +374 1 568 883 Fax +374 1 539 517
ffarm@arminco.com www.ffa.am
President: HAYRAPETYAN Ruben General Secretary: MINASYAN Armen
Vice-President: TBD Treasurer: PAPIKYAN Gevorg Media Officer: MANUKYAN Arayik
Men's Coach: DARBINYAN Samvel Women's Coach: MIKAYELYAN Mher
FFA formed: 1992 UEFA: 1993 FIFA: 1992
Red shirts with white trimmings, Blue shorts, Orange socks or White shirts with blue trimmings, Blue shorts, White socks

RECENT INTERNATIONALS PLAYED BY ARMENIA

2002	Opponents		Score	Venue	Comp	Scorers	Att	Referee
7-09	Ukraine	D	2-2	Yerevan	ECq	Petrosyan.Art [73], Sargsyan [90p]	9 000	Vuorela FIN
16-10	Greece	L	0-2	Athens	ECq		6 000	Ceferin SVN
2003								
12-02	Israel	L	0-2	Tel Aviv	Fr		8 000	Trentlange ITA
29-03	Northern Ireland	W	1-0	Yerevan	ECq	Petrosyan.Art [86]	10 321	Beck LIE
2-04	Spain	L	0-3	Leon	ECq		13 500	Yefet ISR
7-06	Ukraine	L	3-4	Lviv	ECq	Sargsyan 2 [14p 52], Petrosyan.Art [74]	35 000	Albrecht GER
6-09	Greece	L	0-1	Yerevan	ECq		6 500	Temmink NED
10-09	Northern Ireland	W	1-0	Belfast	ECq	Karamyan.Arm [29]	8 616	Stredak SVK
11-10	Spain	L	0-4	Yerevan	ECq		15 000	Meier SUI
2004								
18-02	Hungary	L	0-2	Paphos	Fr		400	Gerasimou CYP
19-02	Kazakhstan	D	3-3	Paphos	Fr	Petrosyan.G [52], Karamyan.Art 2 [73 80] L 2-3p	100	
21-02	Georgia	W	2-0	Nicosia	Fr	Karamyan.Arm [42], Karamyan.Art [52]		
28-04	Turkmenistan	W	1-0	Yerevan	Fr	Ara Hakobyan [68]	7 500	
18-08	FYR Macedonia	L	0-3	Skopje	WCq		4 375	Guenov BUL
8-09	Finland	L	0-2	Yerevan	WCq		2 864	Malzinskas LTU
9-10	Finland	L	1-3	Tampere	WCq	Shahgeldyan [32]	7 894	Fandel GER
13-10	Czech Republic	L	0-3	Yerevan	WCq		3 205	Granat POL
17-11	Romania	D	1-1	Yerevan	WCq	Dokhoyan [62]	1 403	De Bleeckere BEL
2005								
18-03	Kuwait	L	1-3	Al Ain	Fr	Mkhitaryan [87p]		
26-03	Andorra	W	2-1	Yerevan	WCq	Ara Hakobyan [30], Khachatryan.R [73]	2 100	Attard MLT
30-03	Netherlands	L	0-2	Eindhoven	WCq		35 000	Trefoloni ITA
4-06	FYR Macedonia	L	1-2	Yerevan	WCq	Manucharyan [55]	2 870	Mikulski POL
8-06	Romania	L	0-3	Constanta	WCq		5 146	Briakos GRE
17-08	Jordan	D	0-0	Amman	Fr			
3-09	Netherlands	L	0-1	Yerevan	WCq		1 747	Dougal SCO
7-09	Czech Republic	L	1-4	Olomouc	WCq	Hakobyan [85]	12 015	Hansson SWE
12-10	Andorra	W	3-0	Andorra la Vella	WCq	OG [40], Aram Hakobyan [52], Ara Hakobyan [62]	430	Stoks IRL
2006								
28-02	Romania	L	0-2	Nicosia	Fr		1 000	Tsacheilidis GRE
1-03	Cyprus	L	0-2	Limassol	Fr			

Fr = Friendly match • EC = UEFA EURO 2004™ • WC = FIFA World Cup™ • q = qualifier

ARMENIA NATIONAL TEAM RECORDS AND RECORD SEQUENCES

Records			Sequence records				
Victory	3-0	ALB 1997, AND x2	Wins	2	2004	Clean sheets	2	2004
Defeat	0-7	CHI 1997, GEO 1997	Defeats	5	1995-1996	Goals scored	6	1999-2000
Player Caps	78	HOVSEPYAN Sargis	Undefeated	3	Four times	Without goal	7	1999
Player Goals	11	PETROSYAN Artur	Without win	10	1996-1997	Goals against	13	1994-1996

ARMENIA COUNTRY INFORMATION

Capital	Yerevan	Independence	1991	GDP per Capita	$3 500
Population	2 991 360	Status	Republic	GNP Ranking	136
Area km²	29 800	Language	Armenian	Dialling code	+374
Population density	100 per km²	Literacy rate	99%	Internet code	.am
% in urban areas	69%	Main religion	Christian 98%	GMT + / –	+4
Towns/Cities ('000)	Yerevan 1 093; Gyumri 148; Vanadzor 101; Vagharshapat 49; Hrazdan 40; Abovyan 35				
Neighbours (km)	Georgia 164; Azerbaijan 787; Iran 35; Turkey 268				
Main stadia	Razdan – Yerevan 48 250; Hanrapetakan – Yerevan 14 968; Kotayk – Abovyan 5 500				

ARMENIA NATIONAL TEAM PLAYERS AND COACHES

Record Caps			Record Goals			Recent Coaches	
HOVSEPYAN Sargis	1992-'06	78	PETROSYAN Artur	1992-'04	11	DARBINYAN Samvel	1995-'96
PETROSYAN Artur	1992-'04	69	SHAHGELDYAN Armen	1992-'05	6	HOVANNISYAN Khoren	1996-'98
VARDANYAN Harutyun	1994-'04	62	YESAYAN Tigran	1996-'99	4	BARSEGYAN Suren	1998-'99
BEREZOVSKI Roman	1996-'06	45	HAKOBYAN Ara	1998-'06	4	SUKIASYAN Varuzhan	1999-'01
SHAHGELDYAN Armen	1992-'05	44	KARAMYAN Arman	2000-'05	4	ADAMYAN Andravik	2002
KHACHATRYAN Romik	1997-'05	43	ASSADOURYAN Eric	1996-'98	3	LOPEZ Oscar	2002
MKHITARYAN Hamlet	1994-'06	42	SARGSYAN Albert	1997-'05	3	STOICHITA Mihai	2003-'04
SUKIASYAN Yervand	1994-'01	36	KARAMYAN Artavzad	2000-'05	3	CASONI Bernard	2004-'05
DOKHOYAN Karen	1999-'05	34				WISMAN Hendrik	2005-'06

CLUB DIRECTORY

Club	Town/City	Stadium	Capacity	www.	Lge	Cup
Ararat	Yerevan	Razdan	48 250	fcararat.com	1	4
Banants	Yerevan	Kotayk, Abovyan	5 500	fcbanants.com	0	1
Gandzasar	Kapan				0	0
Kilikia	Yerevan	Razdan	48 250		0	0
MIKA	Ashtarak	Vardanank	12 000		0	5
Pyunik	Yerevan	Razdan	48 250		7	3
Shirak	Gyumri	Ozanyan	3 020	fcshirak.8m.net	3	0
Ulysses (ex Dinamo-Zenit)	Yerevan	Kasakh, Ashtarak	3 000		0	0

RECENT LEAGUE AND CUP RECORD

	Championship							Cup		
Year	Champions	Pts	Runners-up	Pts	Third	Pts		Winners	Score	Runners-up
1992	Shirak Kumajri*	37	Homenetmen*	37	Banants Kotiak	36		Banants Aboyan	2-0	Homenetmen
1993	Ararat Yerevan	51	Shirak Gyumri	49	Banants Kotiak	48		Ararat Yerevan	3-1	Shirak Gyumri
1994	Shirak Gyumri	52	AOSS Yerevan	47	Ararat Yerevan	47		Ararat Yerevan	1-0	Shirak Gyumri
1995								Ararat Yerevan	4-2	Kotayk Abovyan
1996	Pyunik Yerevan	60	Shirak Gyumri	51	FK Yerevan	44		Pyunik Yerevan	3-2	Kotayk Abovyan
1997	Pyunik Yerevan	59	Ararat Yerevan	52	FK Yerevan	50		Ararat Yerevan	1-0	Pyunik Yerevan
1998	Tsement Ararat	64	Shirak Gyumri	61	FK Yerevan	48		Tsement Ararat	3-1	FK Yerevan
1999	Shirak Gyumri	73	Ararat Yerevan	72	Tsement Ararat	71		Tsement Ararat	3-2	Shirak Yerevan
2000	Araks Ararat	61	Ararat Yerevan	59	Shirak Gyumri	58		Mika Ashtarak	2-1	Zvarnots Yerevan
2001	Pyunik Yerevan	53	Zvarnots Yerevan	48	Spartak Yerevan	48		Mika Ashtarak	1-1 4-3p	Ararat Yerevan
2002	Pyunik Yerevan	59	Shirak Gyumri	51	Banants Yerevan	50		Pyunik Yerevan	2-0	Zvarnots Yerevan
2003	Pyunik Yerevan	74	Banants Yerevan	66	Shirak Gyumri	53		Mika Ashtarak	1-0	Banants Yerevan
2004	Pyunik Yerevan	71	Mika Ashtarak	55	Banants Yerevan	43		Pyunik Yerevan	0-0 6-5p	Banants Yerevan
2005	Pyunik Yerevan	39	Mika Ashtarak	35	Banants Yerevan	33		Mika Ashtarak	2-0	Kilikia Yerevan
2006								Mika Ashtarak	1-0	Pyunik Yerevan

*Championship shared • Due to a change in the calendar season there was a spring championship in 1995 won by Shirak & Ararat • In 1997 there was an autumn championship won by FK Yerevan • Tsement Ararat changed their name to Araks Ararat and then Spartak Yerevan. They merged with Banants to become Banants Yerevan in 2002 • Pyunik previously known as Homenetmen and AOSS.

ARMENIA 2005

PREMIER LEAGUE

	Pl	W	D	L	F	A	Pts	Pyunik	Mika	Banants	Esteghlal	Kilikia	Dinamo	Ararat	Shirak	Lernayin
Pyunik Yerevan †	20	11	6	3	35	15	39		1-0 1-1	0-0 2-2	1-1 0-1	1-0 2-1	4-1 5-0	5-0	3-1	3-1
Mika Ashtarak ‡	20	9	8	3	30	16	35	0-0 1-2		4-4 4-1	1-1 1-0	2-2 0-0	2-1 1-2	1-0	3-0	2-0
Banants Yerevan ‡	20	9	6	5	31	27	33	2-5 2-1	0-2 1-2		1-0 4-1	2-0 1-3	3-1 1-0	4-1	1-0	3-0
Esteghlal-Kotayk	20	8	7	5	22	19	31	0-0 2-1	0-0 0-2	1-1 0-0		2-2 2-0	1-0 1-0	1-1	3-0	3-0
Kilikia Yerevan	20	4	5	11	20	32	17	0-3 1-4	0-2 0-0	0-1 0-1	4-3 0-1		0-0 3-1	5-0	4-2	1-0
Dinamo-Zenit Yerevan	20	2	2	16	12	41	8	0-1 0-1	0-2 0-3	0-0 1-4	1-3 0-2	4-2 0-2		0-1	2-1	3-2
Ararat Yerevan	18	4	2	12	11	39	14	0-3	0-1	1-2	1-3	0-5	0-4		1-0 1-0	0-2
Shirak Gyumri	18	3	3	12	19	36	12	0-0	1-2	0-5	1-2	3-1	3-3	2-0 1-1		1-4
Lernayin Yerevan	16	3	0	13	14	37	9	0-2	1-3	2-3	1-4	0-3	1-0	0-3	0-3	

12/04/2005 - 6/11/2005 • † Qualified for the UEFA Champions League • ‡ Qualified for the UEFA Cup • Lernayin withdrew after 11 matches. Their matches in bold were awarded 3-0 to their opponents • After 16 rounds the top six play-off for the title taking only their records against each other with them • Ararat and Shirak played two further rounds against each other • Relegation play-off: Shirak 5-1 Gandzasar Kapan • Gandzasar were promoted despite losing • Top Scorer: Nshan ERZRUMIAN, Kilikia, 18

ARMENIA 2005
SECOND DIVISION

	Pl	W	D	L	F	A	Pts
Pyunik-2 Yerevan	24	18	3	3	82	15	57
Ararat-2 Yerevan	24	18	2	4	72	18	56
Gandzasar Kapan	24	16	3	5	62	24	51
Yerevan United §3	24	16	5	3	64	22	50
Mika-2 Ashtarak	24	14	8	2	64	16	50
Banants-2 Yerevan	24	12	4	8	57	38	40
Esteghlal-Kotayk-2	24	9	4	11	39	45	31
Vagharshapat	24	8	4	12	38	59	28
FIMA Yerevan	24	7	4	13	27	43	25
Dinamo Yerevan §3	24	6	3	15	26	56	18
Lori Vanadzor	24	6	0	18	39	77	18
FA Abovian	24	2	0	22	13	125	6
Zenit Charentsavan §6	24	4	0	20	12	57	6
Araks Ararat		Withdrew after 7 matches					
Banant-3 Yerevan		Withdrew after 8 matches					

19/04/2005 - 8/10/2005 • § points deducted • Zenit withdrew after 15 rounds. Their remaining fixtures were awarded 3-0

FFA CUP 2006

First round			Quarter-finals		Semi-finals		Final	
Mika Ashtarak	Bye							
			Mika Ashtarak					
Mika-2 Ashtarak	1	0	Gandzasar Kapan *					
Gandzasar Kapan *	3	4			Mika Ashtarak *	3 1		
Banants-2 Yerevan	0	3			Kilikia Yerevan	0 0		
Pyunik-2 Yerevan *	1	0	Banants-2 Yerevan	1 1 3p				
			Kilikia Yerevan *	1 1 4p				
Kilikia Yerevan	Bye						Mika Ashtarak ‡	1
Banants Yerevan	Bye						Pyunik Yerevan	0
			Banants Yerevan	0 2				
Hay Ari Yerevan	1	0	Shirak Gyumri *	0 1				
Shirak Gyumri *	0	2			Banants Yerevan	0 2		
Ararat Yerevan	4	3			Pyunik Yerevan *	1 1		
Ararat-2 Yerevan *	0	1	Ararat Yerevan	1 1 5p				
			Pyunik Yerevan *	1 1 6p				
Pyunik Yerevan	Bye							

* Home team in the first leg • ‡ Qualified for the UEFA Cup

CUP FINAL

Hanrapetakan, Yerevan
9-05-2006, Att: 1 400, Ref: Nalbandian

Scorer - Armen Shahgeldian 28 for Mika

ARU – ARUBA

NATIONAL TEAM RECORD
JULY 1ST 2002 TO JULY 9TH 2006

PL	W	D	L	F	A	%
5	0	0	5	3	24	0

FIFA/COCA-COLA WORLD RANKING

1993	1994	1995	1996	1997	1998	1999	2000	2001	2002	2003	2004	2005	High	Low
165	173	171	181	177	180	191	184	185	189	195	198	200	**164** 02/94	**201** 04/06

2005–2006											
08/05	09/05	10/05	11/05	12/05	01/06	02/06	03/06	04/06	05/06	06/06	07/06
199	199	199	200	200	200	200	200	201	201	-	196

With no international matches played since March 2004, the ten team Division di Honor provided the focus for the action in Aruba. The first stage of the tournament, from which the top four qualified, was won by SV Dakota from the capital Oranjestad, who with 15 titles remain the most successful club in the country although only one of those titles has come in the past 20 years. Deportivo Nacional, three times champions since the turn of the century and Racing Club, champions in 2002, were the two major casualties of the first round, both finishing agonizingly close outside of the top four. Qualifying along with Dakota were Estrella, defending champions

INTERNATIONAL HONOURS
None

Britannia and La Fama. The second round saw the four teams play each other twice with the top two then contesting the championship final. That turned out to be Estrella and Britannia. The final then went to three matches with Estrella winning the first 1-0, losing the second 4-1 and then winning the decider 2-1, on June 6, to claim the title for the 12th time. Britannia may have missed out on a second championship the year after their first, but their title in 2005 meant that they qualified for the CONCACAF Champions' Cup. Drawn against Surinam's Robinhood they played two games in Trinidad but lost them both.

THE FIFA BIG COUNT OF 2000

	Male	Female		Male	Female
Registered players	2 200	0	Referees	24	3
Non registered players	900	0	Officials	130	10
Youth players	3 200	0	Total involved	6 467	
Total players	6 300		Number of clubs	54	
Professional players	0	0	Number of teams	127	

Arubaanse Voetbal Bond (AVB)
Ferguson Street Z/N, PO Box 376, Oranjestad, Aruba
Tel +297 829550   Fax +297 829550
avbaruba@setarnet.aw   www.avbaruba.aw
President: KELLY Rufo   General Secretary: LACLE Egbert
Vice-President: FARO Bernardo A   Treasurer: CROES Adrian   Media Officer: CROES Adrian
Men's Coach: MUNOZ Marcelo   Women's Coach: None
AVB formed: 1932   CONCACAF: 1961   FIFA: 1988
Yellow shirts, Blue shorts, Yellow and Blue socks

RECENT INTERNATIONALS PLAYED BY ARUBA

2002	Opponents	Score		Venue	Comp	Scorers	Att	Referee
28-07	Surinam	L	0-2	Oranjestad	GCq			Faneijte ANT
11-08	Surinam	L	0-6	Paramaribo	GCq		2 500	Mercera ANT
2003								
No international matches played in 2003								
2004								
28-01	Netherlands Antilles	L	1-6	Willemstad	Fr			
28-02	Surinam	L	1-2	Oranjestad	WCq	Escalona.M [89]	2 108	Moreno PAN
27-03	Surinam	L	1-8	Paramaribo	WCq	Escalona.M [24]	4 000	Prendergast JAM
2005								
No international matches played in 2005								
2006								
No international matches played in 2006 before July								

Fr = Friendly match • GC = CONCACAF Gold Cup™ • WCq = FIFA World Cup™ • q = qualifier

ARUBA NATIONAL TEAM RECORDS AND RECORD SEQUENCES

Records			Sequence records					
Victory	4-1	CUB 1953	Wins	1		Clean sheets	1	
Defeat	1-8	SUR 2004	Defeats	11	1953-1996	Goals scored	9	1944-1953
Player Caps	n/a		Undefeated	3	1944-1953	Without goal	5	1991-1992
Player Goals	n/a		Without win	12	1953-1996	Goals against	24	1934-1997

RECENT LEAGUE AND CUP RECORD

	Championship			Cup
Year	Champions	Score	Runners-up	Winners
1998	Estrella	2-1	Dakota	No tournament held
1999	Estrella	2-1	Nacional	No tournament held
2000	Nacional	1-1 1-1 1-0	Dakota	No tournament held
2001	Nacional	3-1 1-0	Racing Club	No tournament held
2002	Racing Club	†	Nacional	No tournament held
2003	Nacional	1-0 2-1	Estrella	No tournament held
2004	No tournament due to season readjustment			No tournament held
2005	Britannia	2-1 1-0	Racing Club	No tournament held
2006	Estrella	1-0 1-4 2-1	Britannia	No tournament held

† Played on a league basis

ARUBA COUNTRY INFORMATION

Capital	Oranjestad	Independence	Part of the Netherlands with	GDP per Capita	$28 000
Population	71 218	Status	autonomy in internal affairs	GNP Ranking	n/a
Area km²	193	Language	Dutch	Dialling code	+297
Population density	369 per km²	Literacy rate	97%	Internet code	.aw
% in urban areas	n/a	Main religion	Christian 90%	GMT +/−	-5
Towns/Cities ('000)	Oranjestad 29; Sint Nicolaas 17; Druif; Santa Cruz; Barcadera;				
Neighbours (km)	Caribbean Sea 68				
Main stadia	Guillermo Trinidad – Oranjestad 5 500				

ASA – AMERICAN SAMOA

NATIONAL TEAM RECORD
JULY 1ST 2002 TO JULY 9TH 2006

PL	W	D	L	F	A	%
4	0	0	4	1	34	0

FIFA/COCA-COLA WORLD RANKING

1993	1994	1995	1996	1997	1998	1999	2000	2001	2002	2003	2004	2005		High		Low	
-	-	-	-	-	193	199	203	201	201	202	204	205		192	10/98	205	12/05

2005–2006											
08/05	09/05	10/05	11/05	12/05	01/06	02/06	03/06	04/06	05/06	06/06	07/06
205	205	205	205	205	205	205	205	205	205	-	196

With no international matches played since the FIFA World Cup™ qualifiers in May 2004 there has been no opportunity for the national team to escape the stigma of being officially the worst in the world. However, the revision in the way the FIFA/Coca-Cola World Ranking is calculated, introduced in July 2006, did mean that American Samoa was joined at the bottom by a host of other teams. If ever there was an idea for a tournament... Central to the progress of football on this tiny Pacific island will be the new facilities at Pago Park. The delayed project finally got underway in mid 2006 and is scheduled for completion in early 2007. Financed by the FIFA Goal project and the

INTERNATIONAL HONOURS
None

Oceania Football Confederation, it will provide the country with international standard football pitches, a new headquarters for the ASFA as well as a technical centre. Organising football properly in the past without these facilities has proved to be a challenging task. League tournaments have been sporadic and none have been played for the past two years. The association has indicated that its major task is to get both the men's and women's national teams to a competitive level in Oceania and as a first step there are plans to send both to the South Pacific Games in Samoa in 2007. The new facilities will also enable new leagues to kick-off later in 2007, for both men and women.

THE FIFA BIG COUNT OF 2000

	Male	Female		Male	Female
Registered players	1 000	0	Referees	50	0
Non registered players	400	0	Officials	100	0
Youth players	1 000	0	Total involved	2 550	
Total players	2 400		Number of clubs	30	
Professional players	0	0	Number of teams	100	

American Samoa Football Association (ASFA)
ASFA Normalisation Committee, PO Box 999413, Pago Pago, American Samoa
Tel +684 6998160   Fax +689 6998161
asfa@blueskynet.as   www.none
President: BRAND David   General Secretary: TBC
Vice-President: TBC   Treasurer: TBC   Media Officer: None
Men's Coach: None   Women's Coach: None
ASFA formed: 1984   OFC: 1994   FIFA: 1998
Navy blue shirts, White shorts, Red socks

RECENT INTERNATIONALS PLAYED BY AMERICAN SAMOA

2002	Opponents	Score	Venue	Comp	Scorers	Att	Referee
No international matches played in 2002							
2003							
No international matches played in 2003							
2004							
10-05	Samoa	L 0-4	Apia	WCq		500	Afu SOL
12-05	Vanuatu	L 1-9	Apia	WCq	Natia 39	400	Fox NZL
15-05	Fiji	L 0-11	Apia	WCq		300	Fox NZL
17-05	Papua New Guinea	L 0-10	Apia	WCq		150	Afu SOL
2005							
No international matches played in 2005							
2006							
No international matches played in 2006 before July							

WC = FIFA World Cup™ • q = qualifier

AMERICAN SAMOA NATIONAL TEAM RECORDS AND RECORD SEQUENCES

Records			Sequence records					
Victory	3-0	Wallis/Futuna 1983	Wins	1		Clean sheets	1	
Defeat	0-31	AUS 2001	Defeats	28	1983-	Goals scored	3	1983, 1994
Player Caps	n/a		Undefeated	1		Without goal	5	2001-2002
Player Goals	n/a		Without win	28	1983-	Goals against	28	1983-

RECENT LEAGUE AND CUP RECORD

	Championship		Cup
Year	Champions		Winners
1996	No tournament held		No tournament held
1997	Fat Boys		No tournament held
1998	No tournament held		No tournament held
1999	Konica Machine		No tournament held
2000	PanSa & Wild Wild West		No tournament held
2001	PanSa		No tournament held
2002	PanSa		No tournament held
2003	No tournament held		No tournament held
2004	PanSa		No tournament held
2005	No tournament held		No tournament held
2006	No tournament held		No tournament held

AMERICAN SAMOA COUNTRY INFORMATION

Capital	Pago Pago	Independence	Unincorporated territory of the USA	GDP per Capita	$8 000
Population	57 902	Status		GNP Ranking	n/a
Area km²	199	Language	Samoan	Dialling code	+684
Population density	291 per km²	Literacy rate	97%	Internet code	.as
% in urban areas	n/a	Main religion	Christian	GMT +/-	-10
Towns/Cities ('000)	Tafuna 11; Nu'uuli 5; Pago Pago 4; Leone 4; Faleniu 3; Ili'ili 3				
Neighbours (km)	South Pacific Ocean 116				
Main stadia	Veterans Memorial – Pago Pago 10 000				

ATG – ANTIGUA AND BARBUDA

NATIONAL TEAM RECORD
JULY 1ST 2002 TO JULY 9TH 2006

PL	W	D	L	F	A	%
19	5	2	12	21	37	31.6

FIFA/COCA-COLA WORLD RANKING

1993	1994	1995	1996	1997	1998	1999	2000	2001	2002	2003	2004	2005	High	Low
117	136	137	145	159	137	147	144	157	155	170	153	154	**116** 02/94	**170** 01/04

2005–2006											
08/05	09/05	10/05	11/05	12/05	01/06	02/06	03/06	04/06	05/06	06/06	07/06
154	153	154	155	154	155	155	155	158	160	-	145

After a number of years pushing for the title, Hitachi Centre Sap finally won the Cingular Wireless Premier League and they did it in convincing fashion. Defending champions Bassa were trying to emulate English Harbour and Empire by winning a hat-trick of titles but they finished third, eight points adrift of Sap who clinched the title with a game to go thanks to a 4-1 victory over Liberta. Prime Minister Baldwin Spencer was on hand to present captain Tyio Simon with the trophy. It turned out to be a great year for the club with the women's team winning both the League and the FA Cup. In the men's FA Cup there were surprise winners, however, when Freeman's Ville, who

INTERNATIONAL HONOURS
None

had just secured promotion to the Premier League, beat Bassa on penalties after the match had ended 1-1 at the Yasco Sports Complex. They won a 'best of three' shoot out 2-1 to secure the Cup. On the international front it was a quiet year for new coach Derrick 'Pretty Boy' Edwards (everyone in Antigua has a nickname!) with just three matches - all of which were lost. Hungary provided a first ever taste of European opposition with a match in Fort Lauderdale which was lost 3-0. Then after the end of the Championship an inexperienced national team played a rain delayed two match series in Guyana, both of which were won by the hosts.

THE FIFA BIG COUNT OF 2000

	Male	Female		Male	Female
Registered players	1 000	0	Referees	30	0
Non registered players	700	0	Officials	100	0
Youth players	1 000	0	Total involved	2 830	
Total players	2 700		Number of clubs	15	
Professional players	0	0	Number of teams	50	

Antigua and Barbuda Football Association (ABFA)
Suite 19, Vendors Mall, PO Box 773, St John's, Antigua
Tel +1 268 5626012   Fax +1 268 5626016
abfa@candw.ag   www.antiguafootball.org
President: RICHARDS Mervyn   General Secretary: DERRICK Gordon
Vice-President: GATESWORTH James   Treasurer: GARDNER Dwight   Media Officer: DERRICK Gordon
Men's Coach: EDWARDS Derrick   Women's Coach: None
ABFA formed: 1928   CONCACAF: 1980   FIFA: 1970
Red shirts with black, yellow and white trimmings, Black shorts, Black socks

RECENT INTERNATIONALS PLAYED BY ANTIGUA AND BARBUDA

2002	Opponents	Score		Venue	Comp	Scorers	Att	Referee
29-10	St Kitts and Nevis	D	1-1	St John's	Fr			
8-11	St Lucia	L	1-2		Fr			
18-11	Haiti	L	0-1	Port-au-Prince	GCq			Bowen CAY
20-11	Netherlands Antilles	D	1-1	Port-au-Prince	GCq	Jeffers [77]		Bowen CAY
2003								
26-03	Trinidad and Tobago	L	0-2	Port of Spain	GCq			James GUY
28-03	Cuba	L	0-2	Macoya	GCq			James GUY
30-03	Guadeloupe	L	0-2	Marabella	GCq			Callender BRB
2004								
31-01	St Kitts and Nevis	W	1-0		Fr			
18-02	Netherlands Antilles	W	2-0	St John's	WCq	Roberts [42], Clarke [89]	1 500	Navarro CAN
21-03	St Kitts and Nevis	W	3-2	Basseterre	Fr			
31-03	Netherlands Antilles	L	0-3	Willemstad	WCq		9 000	Piper TRI
2-11	Montserrat	W	5-4	Basseterre	GCq	OG [30], Frederick [53], Gonsalves [67 82], Thomas [72]		Phillip GRN
4-11	St Kitts and Nevis	L	0-2	Basseterre	GCq			Phillip GRN
6-11	St Lucia	L	1-2	Basseterre	GCq	Dublin [65]		Bedeau GRN
2005								
12-01	Trinidad and Tobago	W	2-1	St John's	Fr	Byers [48], Isaac [57]	2 000	
6-02	Barbados	L	2-3	Bridgetown	Fr	Thomas [2], Byers [74]	4 000	
18-12	Hungary	L	0-3	Fort Lauderdale	Fr			
2006								
24-02	Guyana	L	1-2	Linden	Fr	Skepples [77]		James GUY
26-02	Guyana	L	1-4	Georgetown	Fr	Julian [76]		Lancaster GUY

Fr = Friendly match • GC = CONCACAF Gold Cup™ • WCq = FIFA World Cup™ • q = qualifier

ANTIGUA AND BARBUDA NATIONAL TEAM RECORDS AND RECORD SEQUENCES

Records			Sequence records				
Victory	8-0	MSR 1994	Wins	3	1992, 1997, 2004	Clean sheets	3	1992, 1999
Defeat	1-11	TRI 1972	Defeats	7	1972-1984	Goals scored	8	1995-97, 1998
Player Caps	n/a		Undefeated	6	2000	Without goal	3	1990, 2003
Player Goals	n/a		Without win	8	2002-2003	Goals against	12	2000-2001

ANTIGUA AND BARBUDA 2005-06 PREMIER LEAGUE

	Pl	W	D	L	F	A	Pts
Sap	18	13	3	2	33	15	42
Hoppers	18	11	2	5	33	16	35
Bassa	18	10	4	4	41	20	34
Empire	18	10	2	6	37	27	32
Parham	18	7	4	7	16	15	25
Villa Lions	18	7	3	8	21	23	24
Liberta	18	6	5	7	17	16	23
Old Road	18	6	2	10	27	41	20
Wadadli	18	5	2	11	17	34	17
West Ham	18	1	1	16	14	49	4

31/08/2005 - 8/01/2006

RECENT LEAGUE RECORD

	Championship				
Year	Champions	Pts	Runners-up	Pts	Third	Pts
1998	Empire	32	English Harbour	29	Sap	29
1999	Empire		Parham			
2000	Empire	2-0	English Harbour			
2001	Empire	58	Bassa	37	Sap	33
2002	Parham	57	Empire	53	Sap	37
2003	Parham	38	Sap	37	Hoppers	35
2004	Bassa	34	Sap	28	Parham	23
2005	Bassa	43	Hoppers	43	Empire	39
2006	Sap	42	Hoppers	35	Bassa	34

ANTIGUA AND BARBUDA COUNTRY INFORMATION

Capital	St John's	Independence	1981	GDP per Capita	$11 000
Population	68 320	Status	Commonwealth	GNP Ranking	164
Area km²	443	Language	English	Dialling code	+1 268
Population density	154 per km²	Literacy rate	95%	Internet code	.ag
% in urban areas	36%	Main religion	Christian 96%	GMT +/–	-4.5
Towns/Cities ('000)	St John's 25; All Saints 2; Liberta 1; Potters Village 1				
Neighbours (km)	Caribbean Sea & North Atlantic Ocean 153				
Main stadia	Recreation Ground – St John's 18 000; Police Ground – St George's 3 000				

AUS – AUSTRALIA

AUSTRALIA NATIONAL TEAM RECORD
JULY 1ST 2002 TO JULY 9TH 2006

PL	W	D	L	F	A	%
40	24	6	10	106	40	67.5

2005–06 was a seminal season for Australian football by any standards with qualification for a first FIFA World Cup™ appearance in 32 years the undoubted highlight. There was also the ground-breaking move from the Oceania Football Confederation to the Asian Football Confederation but perhaps the event with the biggest long-term significance was the launch of the new Hyundai A-League, won by Sydney FC. All three events should have a beneficial impact on the game in Australia as it strives to compete with cricket, rugby league, rugby union, Aussie rules and even swimming and tennis, in a country where sport has a profile largely unmatched anywhere in the world - both from the point of view of participation as well as interest from the general public. The scenes that greeted Australia's dramatic qualification for the finals in Germany were impressive with wild celebrations into the night following the penalty shoot-out victory against Uruguay. Much of the credit went to Dutch coach Guus Hiddink, who took over following the poor display at the FIFA Confederations Cup in Germany. Despite the problems with the time difference, big crowds gathered in the small hours to watch Australia in the FIFA World Cup™ finals, with seven

INTERNATIONAL HONOURS
Qualified for the FIFA World Cup™ 1974 2006
Oceania Nations Cup 1980 1996 2000 2004   Oceania Women's Championship 1995 1998 2003
Oceania Youth Cup 1978 1982 1985 1987 1988 1990 1994 1996 1998 2001 2003
Oceania U-17 1983 1986 1989 1991 1993 1995 1999 2001 2003
Oceania Champions Cup Adelaide City 1987, South Melbourne 1999, Wollongong Wolves 2001, Sydney FC 2005

million tuning in for the historic triumph over Japan, a record audience for a late night programme. In the event, Australia had a tournament that exceeded all expectations and they were desperately unlucky not to make it to the quarter-finals. It took a highly debatable Italian penalty deep into injury time to beat them, but deep down the players knew the game should have been won by then. Prime Minister John Howard got into the mood of things by suggesting that Australia should even put in a bid to host the finals in the future. In the meantime Australia took a big step at improving standards by joining the Asian Football Confederation on January 1, 2006 and in February played a first AFC Asian Cup qualifier, securing a 3-0 victory over Bahrain in Manama. Seven months earlier in August 2005, the Hyundai A-League had been launched amidst a blaze of publicity. Dwight Yorke signed for Sydney FC and led them to the championship with a 1-0 victory over Central Coast Mariners before a crowd of 41,689 in the final. The belief is that the A-League can provide a good grounding for young players breaking into the game, attract Australian players back from Europe, and even begin to rival the J.League as a destination for foreign players.

Football Federation Australia Limited (FFA)
Suite 701 Level 7, 26 College Street, Locked Bag A4071, Sydney South, NSW 2000 1235, Australia
Tel +61 2 83545555   Fax +61 2 83545590
info@footballaustralia.com.au   www.footballaustralia.com.au
President: LOWY Frank   General Secretary: O'NEILL John
Vice-President: SCHWARTZ Brian   Treasurer: WALKER Mark   Media Officers: HODGE Stuart & SMITH Peter
Men's Coach: HIDDINK Guus   Women's Coach: SERMANNI Tom
FFA formed: 1961   OFC: 1966-72 & 1978-2005   AFC: 2006   FIFA: 1963
Yellow shirts with green trimmings, Green shorts, Yellow socks

RECENT INTERNATIONALS PLAYED BY AUSTRALIA

2003	Opponents	Score		Venue	Comp	Scorers	Att	Referee
12-02	England	W	3-1	London	Fr	Popovic [17], Kewell [42], Emerton [84]	34 590	Gonzalez ESP
19-08	Republic of Ireland	L	1-2	Dublin	Fr	Viduka [49]	37 200	Vidlak CZE
7-09	Jamaica	W	2-1	Reading	Fr	Bresciano [19], Kewell [58]	8 050	D'Urso ENG
2004								
18-02	Venezuela	D	1-1	Caracas	Fr	Agostino [18]	12 000	Ruiz COL
30-03	South Africa	W	1-0	London	Fr	Bresciano [19]	16 108	Halsey ENG
21-05	Turkey	L	1-3	Sydney	Fr	Bresciano [49p]	28 326	Kamikawa JPN
24-05	Turkey	L	0-1	Melbourne	Fr		28 953	Rugg NZL
9-05	New Zealand	W	1-0	Adelaide	WCq	Bresciano [40]	12 100	Larsen DEN
31-05	Tahiti	W	9-0	Adelaide	WCq	Cahill 2 [14 47], Skoko [43], OG [44], Sterjovski 3 [51 61 74] Zdrilic [85], Chipperfield [89]	1 200	Attison VAN
2-06	Fiji	W	6-1	Adelaide	WCq	Madaschi 2 [6 50], Cahill 3 [39 66 75], Elrich [89]	2 200	Gonzalez ESP
4-06	Vanuatu	W	3-0	Adelaide	WCq	Aloisi 2 [25 85], Emerton [81]	4 000	Ariiotima TAH
6-06	Solomon Islands	D	2-2	Adelaide	WCq	Cahill [50], Emerton [52]	1 500	Gonzalez ESP
9-10	Solomon Islands	W	5-1	Honaria	OCf	Skoko 2 [5 28], Milicic [19], Emerton [44], Elrich [79]	21 000	O'Leary NZL
12-10	Solomon Islands	W	6-0	Sydney	OCf	Milicic [5], Kewell [9], Vidmar.T [60], Thompson [79] Elrich [80], Emerton [89]	19 208	Rakaroi FIJ
16-11	Norway	D	2-2	London	Fr	Cahill [45], Skoko [58]	7 364	Styles ENG
2005								
9-02	South Africa	D	1-1	Durban	Fr	Chipperfield [70]	25 000	Lim Kee Chong MRI
26-03	Iraq	W	2-1	Sydney	Fr	Bresciano [22], Elrich [72]	30 258	O'Leary NZL
29-03	Indonesia	W	3-0	Perth	Fr	Milicic 2 [25 57], Zdrilic [85]	13 719	Yamanishi JPN
9-06	New Zealand	W	1-0	London	Fr	Colosimo [86]	9 023	Dean ENG
15-06	Germany	L	3-4	Frankfurt	CCr1	Skoko [21], Aloisi 2 [31 92+]	46 466	Amarilla PAR
18-06	Argentina	L	2-4	Nürnberg	CCr1	Aloisi 2 [61p 70]	25 618	Maidin SIN
21-06	Tunisia	L	0-2	Leipzig	CCr1		23 952	Chandia CHI
3-09	Solomon Islands	W	7-0	Sydney	WCq	Culina [20], Viduka 2 [36 43], Cahill [57], Chipperfield [64], Thompson [68], Emerton [89]	16 000	Mohd Salleh MAS
6-09	Solomon Islands	W	2-1	Honiara	WCq	Thompson [19], Emerton [58]	16 000	Maidin SIN
9-10	Jamaica	W	5-0	London	Fr	Bresciano [2], Thompson [27], Viduka [47], Aloisi [59], Griffiths [84]	6 570	Riley ENG
12-11	Uruguay	L	0-1	Montevideo	WCpo		55 000	Larsen DEN
16-11	Uruguay	W	1-0	Sydney	WCpo	Bresciano [35]. W 4-2p	82 698	Medina Cantalejo ESP
2006								
22-02	Bahrain	W	3-1	Manama	ACq	Thompson [53], Skoko [79], Elrich [87p]	2 500	Mohd Salleh MAS
25-05	Greece	W	1-0	Melbourne	Fr	Skoko [16]	95 103	Riley ENG
4-06	Netherlands	D	1-1	Rotterdam	Fr	Cahill [41]	49 000	Dean ENG
7-06	Liechtenstein	W	3-1	Ulm	Fr	Sterjovski [19], Kennedy [74], Aloisi [82]	5 872	Star GER
12-06	Japan	W	3-1	Kaiserslautern	WCr1	Cahill 2 [84 89], Aloisi [92+]	46 000	Abd El Fatah EGY
18-06	Brazil	L	0-2	Munich	WCr1		66 000	Merk GER
22-06	Croatia	D	2-2	Stuttgart	WCr1	Moore [38p], Kewell [79]	52 000	Poll ENG
26-06	Italy	L	0-1	Kaiserslautern	WCr2		46 000	Medina Cantalejo ESP

Fr = Friendly match • OC = OFC Oceania Nations Cup • CC = FIFA Confederations Cup • WC = FIFA World Cup™
q = qualifier • r1 = first round group • sf = semi-final • f = final

AUSTRALIA NATIONAL TEAM RECORDS AND RECORD SEQUENCES

Records			Sequence records					
Victory	31-0	ASA 2001	Wins	14	1996-1997	Clean sheets	6	2000, 2001
Defeat	0-8	RSA 1955	Defeats	5	1955	Goals scored	31	1924-1954
Player Caps	87	TOBIN Alex	Undefeated	20	1996-1997	Without goal	4	Three times
Player Goals	29	MORI Damian	Without win	6	Five times	Goals against	11	1936-1947

AUSTRALIA COUNTRY INFORMATION

Capital	Canberra	Independence	1901 from the UK	GDP per Capita	$29 000
Population	19 913 144	Status	Commonwealth	GNP Ranking	15
Area km²	7 686 850	Language	English	Dialling code	+61
Population density	2 per km²	Literacy rate	99%	Internet code	.au
% in urban areas	85%	Main religion	Christian 76%	GMT +/–	+10
Towns/Cities ('000)	Sydney 4 394; Melbourne 3 730; Brisbane 1 843; Perth 1 446; Adelaide 1 074; Gold Coast 501; Newcastle 497; Canberra 324; Wollongong 260; Hobart 204; Cairns 154; Geelong 150				
Neighbours (km)	Indian Ocean and the South Pacific Ocean 25 760				
Main stadia	Telstra Stadium – Sydney 83 500; Energy Australia – Newcastle 28 000; Members Equity – Perth 18 450; Hindmarsh – Adelaide 15 000				

AUSTRALIA NATIONAL TEAM PLAYERS AND COACHES

Record Caps			Record Goals			Recent Coaches	
TOBIN Alex	1988-'98	87	MORI Damian	1992-'02	29	SHOULDER Jim	1976-'78
WADE Paul	1986-'96	84	ABONYI Attila	1967-'77	25	GUTENDORF Rudi	1979-'81
VIDMAR Tony	1991-'05	75	KOSMINA John	1977-'88	25	SCHEINFLUG Les	1981-'83
WILSON Peter	1970-'77	64	ALOISI John	1997-'06	24	AROK Frank	1983-'98
ABONYI Attila	1967-'77	61	ZDRILIC David	1997-'06	21	THOMSON Eddie	1990-'96
KOSMINA John	1977-'88	60	THOMPSON Archie	2001-'06	21	BLANCO Raul	1996
IVANOVIC Milan	1991-'98	59	ARNOLD Graham	1985-'97	19	VENABLES Terry	1997-'98
LAZARIDIS Stan	1993-'06	59	BAARTZ Ray	1967-'74	18	BLANCO Raul	1998
ROONEY Jimmy	1970-'80	57	VIDMAR Aurelio	1991-'01	17	FARINA Frank	1999-'05
POPOVIC Tony	1995-'06	57				HIDDINK Guus	2005-'06

CLUB DIRECTORY

Club	City	Stadium	Capacity	www.	Lge	CL
Adelaide United FC	Adelaide	Hindmarsh Stadium	15 000	adelaideunited.com.au	0	0
Central Coast Mariners	Gosford	Central Coast Stadium	20 000	ccmariners.com.au	0	0
New Zealand Knights FC	Albany	North Harbour Stadium	25 000	knightsfc.com	0	0
Melbourne Victory	Melbourne	Olympic Park	20 000	melbournevictory.com.au	0	0
Newcastle United Jets	Newcastle	Energy Australia Stadium	27 000	nufc.com.au	0	0
Perth Glory FC	Perth	Members Equity Stadium	18 450	perthglory.com.au	0	0
Queensland Roar FC	Brisbane	Suncorp Stadium	52 579	qldroar.com.au	0	0
Sydney FC	Sydney	Aussie Stadium	40 792	sydneyfc.com	1	1

FIFA/COCA-COLA WORLD RANKING

1993	1994	1995	1996	1997	1998	1999	2000	2001	2002	2003	2004	2005		High		Low	
49	58	51	50	35	39	89	73	48	50	82	58	48		31	07/97	92	06/00

2005–2006											
08/05	09/05	10/05	11/05	12/05	01/06	02/06	03/06	04/06	05/06	06/06	07/06
57	50	54	49	48	48	48	44	44	42	-	33

THE FIFA BIG COUNT OF 2000

	Male	Female		Male	Female
Registered players	60 000	6 000	Referees	3 000	50
Non registered players	250 000	8 000	Officials	4 000	400
Youth players	60 000	5 000	Total involved	396 450	
Total players	389 000		Number of clubs	1 200	
Professional players	200	0	Number of teams	12 000	

AUSTRALIA 2005–06

HYUNDAI A-LEAGUE

	Pl	W	D	L	F	A	Pts	Adelaide	Sydney	Mariners	Jets	Glory	Roar	Victory	Knights
Adelaide United †	21	13	4	4	33	25	43		3-2	1-1 1-1	2-4	2-4	0-0 4-2	1-0 1-0	1-0
Sydney FC †	21	10	6	5	35	28	36	2-1 2-1		2-3 1-1	1-1 0-0	0-0	1-0	1-1 2-1	2-0
Central Coast Mariners ‡	21	8	8	5	35	28	32	1-2	1-5		1-1 4-1	4-0	2-2	1-2 3-1	0-2 1-0
Newcastle Jets ‡	21	9	4	8	27	29	31	0-1 1-2	2-1	1-0		1-5 1-3	0-1 0-5	1-0	4-0 3-0
Perth Glory	21	8	5	8	34	29	29	1-2 1-2	1-2 1-2	0-1 2-2	0-1		2-1 0-2	2-1	3-0
Queensland Roar	21	7	7	7	27	22	28	1-2	1-3 2-1	1-1 2-2	0-1	0-0		1-1 0-1	2-0 1-1
Melbourne Victory	21	7	5	9	26	24	26	0-1	5-0	0-2	1-0 0-0	2-2 2-2	0-1		3-0 2-1
New Zealand Knights	21	1	3	17	15	47	6	1-2 1-1	1-3 2-2	1-3	2-4	0-1 1-4	0-2	2-3	

26/08/2005 - 5/02/2006 • † Qualified for the Major Semi-final • ‡ Qualified for the Minor Semi-final

A-LEAGUE PLAY-OFFS

Major Semi-final

Sydney FC	2	2
Adelaide United	2	1

Grand Final

Sydney FC	1
Central Coast Mariners	0

Preliminary Final

Adelaide United	0
Central Coast Mariners	1

Minor Semi-final

Newcastle Jets	0	1
Central Coast Mariners	1	1

10/02/2006 - 5/03/2006 • The loser of the Major Semi-final automatically meets the winner of the Minor Semi-final in the Preliminary Final

GRAND FINAL 2006

Aussie Stadium, Sydney, 5-03-2006, Att: 41 689, Referee: Shield

Sydney FC   1   Corica [62]

Central Coast Mariners   0

Sydney - Clint BOLTON - Alvin CECCOLI, Mark RUDAN (Ian FYFE 72), Matthew BINGLEY, Steve CORICA, Sasho PETROVSKI (Robbie MIDDLEBY 90), David CARNEY, Andrew PACKER, Terry MCFLYNN, Jacob TIMPANO (Ruben ZADKOVICH 81), Dwight YORKE. Tr: Pierre LITTBARSKI

Mariners - Danny VUKOVIC - Wayne O'SULLIVAN, Noel SPENCER, Michael BEAUCHAMP, Andre GUMPRECHT, Dean HEFFERNAN, Tom PONDELJAK, Damien BROWN (Matthew OSMAN 68), Stewart PETRIE (Adam KWASNIK 73), Andrew CLARK, Alex WILKINSON (Paul O'GRADY 84). Tr: Lawrie MCKINNA

RECENT LEAGUE RECORD

Championship/Regular Season						Grand Final		
Year	Champions/First	Pts	Second	Pts	Third	Pts	Champions	Score	Runners-up
1990	Marconi Fairfield	38	South Melbourne	36	Melbourne CSC	35	Sydney Olympic	2-0	Marconi Fairfield
1991	Melbourne CSC	37	South Melbourne	34	Adelaide City	33	South Melbourne	1-1 5-4p	Melbourne CSC
1992	Melbourne CSC	35	Sydney Olympic	34	South Melbourne	31	Adelaide City	0-0 4-2p	Melbourne CSC
1993	South Melbourne	58	Marconi Fairfield	53	Adelaide City	41	Marconi Fairfield	1-0	Adelaide City
1994	Melbourne Knights	53	South Melbourne	47	Sydney United	46	Adelaide City	1-0	Melbourne Knights
1995	Melbourne Knights	70	Adelaide City	69	Sydney United	68	Melbourne Knights	2-0	Adelaide City
1996	Marconi Fairfield	60	Melbourne Knights	59	Sydney Olympic	59	Melbourne Knights	2-1	Marconi Fairfield
1997	Sydney United	56	Brisbane Strikers	47	South Melbourne	46	Brisbane Strikers	2-0	Sydney United
1998	South Melbourne	48	Carlton	45	Adelaide City	43	South Melbourne	2-1	Carlton
1999	Sydney United	58	South Melbourne	57	Perth Glory	53	South Melbourne	3-2	Sydney United
2000	Perth Glory	64	Wollongong Wolves	60	Carlton Blues	58	Wollongong Wolves	3-3 7-6p	Perth Glory
2001	South Melbourne	69	Wollongong Wolves	61	Perth Glory	61	Wollongong Wolves	2-1	South Melbourne
2002	Perth Glory	55	Newcastle United	42	Sydney Olympic	40	Sydney Olympic	1-0	Perth Glory
2003	Sydney Olympic	51	Perth Glory	50	Parramatta Power	40	Perth Glory	2-0	Olympic Sharks
2004	Perth Glory	57	Parramatta Power	51	Adelaide United	40	Perth Glory	1-0	Parramatta Power
2005	No tournament								
2006	Adelaide United	43	Sydney FC	36	Central Coast Mar's	32	Sydney FC	1-0	Central Coast Mar's

From 1987 the season was split into a regular season from which the top clubs qualified for the play-offs, culminating in a Grand Final to determine the champions • Eastern Suburbs became Sydney City • Fitzroy became Heidelberg United • Melbourne CSC became Melbourne Knights

SYDNEY FC 2005–06

Date	Opponents	Score		Comp	Scorers	
31-05-2005	Auckland City	W	3-2	N	OCCr1	Ceccoli [32], Talay [47], Corica [93+]	
2-06-2005	Sobou FC	W	9-2	N	OCCr1	Fyfe [5], Petrovski 3 [14 43 71], Zdrilic 3 [19 40 42], Brodie [79], Salazar [82]	
4-06-2005	AS Pirea	W	6-0	A	OCCr1	Zdrilic 4 [11 25 35 39], Buonavoglia [43], Carney [85]	
7-06-2005	Tafea FC	W	6-0	N	OCCsf	Petrovski [26], Zdrilic [39], Bingley [44p], Corica 2 [65 90], Salazar [87]	
10-06-2005	AS Magenta	W	2-0	N	OCCf	Bingley [16], Zdrilic [59]	
28-08-2005	Melbourne Victory	D	1-1	H	HAL	Yorke [44]	25 208
2-09-2005	New Zealand Knights	W	3-1	A	HAL	Rudan [24], Bingley [73], Middleby [94+]	9 827
11-09-2005	Newcastle Jets	L	1-2	A	HAL	Yorke [77]	9 127
16-09-2005	Central Coast Mariners	L	2-3	H	HAL	Packer [13], Yorke [72]	15 614
23-09-2005	Queensland Roar	W	3-1	A	HAL	Corica 2 [5 67], McFlynn [72]	23 142
1-10-2005	Perth Glory	W	2-1	H	HAL	Petrovski [48], Yorke [65]	13 157
9-10-2005	Adelaide United	W	2-1	H	HAL	Carney [53], Petrovski [87]	18 276
16-10-2005	Melbourne Victory	L	0-5	H	HAL		18 206
21-10-2005	New Zealand Knights	W	2-0	H	HAL	Petrovski [10], Carney [30]	11 836
30-10-2005	Newcastle Jets	D	1-1	H	HAL	Carney [71]	9 132
5-11-2005	Central Coast Mariners	W	5-1	A	HAL	Yorke [9p], Talay [14], Petrovski 3 [23 68 83]	10 529
13-11-2005	Queensland Roar	W	1-0	H	HAL	Zdrilic [54]	13 030
19-11-2005	Perth Glory	D	0-0	H	HAL		16 242
27-11-2005	Adelaide United	L	2-3	A	HAL	Miura 2 [33 76]	14 068
3-12-2005	Melbourne Victory	W	2-1	H	HAL	Corica [24], Carney [81]	17 272
12-12-2005	Deportivo Saprissa	L	0-1	N	CWCqf		28 538
16-12-2005	Al Ahly - EGY	W	2-1	N	CWC5p	Yorke [35], Carney [66]	15 951
30-12-2005	New Zealand Knights	D	2-2	A	HAL	Carney [6], Yorke [45p]	4 212
6-01-2006	Newcastle Jets	D	0-0	H	HAL		15 211
14-01-2006	Central Coast Mariners	D	1-1	H	HAL	Carney [61]	15 977
21-01-2006	Queensland Roar	L	1-2	A	HAL	Petrovski [85]	13 302
29-01-2006	Perth Glory	W	2-1	A	HAL	Rudan [14], Zadkovich [23]	12 796
3-02-2006	Adelaide United	W	2-1	H	HAL	Yorke [47p], Ceccoli [71]	25 557
12-02-2006	Adelaide United	D	2-2	A	HALsf	Corica [9], Petrovski [39]	15 104
19-02-2006	Adelaide United	W	2-1	H	HALsf	Petrovski [29], Rudan [76]	30 377
5-03-2006	Central Coast Mariners	W	1-0	H	HALf	Corica [62]	41 689

HAL = Hyundai A-League • OCC = OFC Oceania Champions Cup • CWC = FIFA Club World Championship
r1 = First round group • qf = quarter-finals • 5p = fifth place play-off • sf = semi-final • f = final • po = end of season play-offs

ADELAIDE UNITED 2005–06

Date	Opponents	Score		Comp	Scorers	
26-08-2005	Newcaste Jets	W	1-0	A	HAL	Veart [19]	13 160
2-09-2005	Queensland Roar	D	0-0	H	HAL		11 020
9-09-2005	Melbourne Victory	W	1-0	H	HAL	Brain [I]	8 785
17-09-2005	Perth Glory	W	2-1	A	HAL	Aloisi.R [32], Shengqing [65]	8 052
25-09-2005	Central Coast Mariners	D	1-1	H	HAL	Valkanis [34]	7 013
2-10-2005	New Zealand Knights	W	2-1	A	HAL	Dodd [33], Shengqing [78]	3 558
9-10-2005	Sydney FC	L	1-2	A	HAL	Valkanis [50]	18 276
14-10-2005	Newcastle Jets	L	2-4	H	HAL	Valkanis [38], Corbo OG [67]	13 182
22-10-2005	Queensland Roar	W	2-1	A	HAL	Rech [58], Pantelis [89]	15 181
28-10-2005	Melbourne Victory	W	1-0	A	HAL	Veart [83]	16 201
6-11-2005	Perth Glory	L	2-4	H	HAL	Veart [13p], Rees [53]	10 868
13-11-2005	Central Coast Mariners	W	2-1	A	HAL	Dodd [85], Rech [91+]	5 467
20-11-2005	New Zealand Knights	W	1-0	H	HAL	Shengqing [38]	9 676
27-11-2005	Sydney FC	W	3-2	H	HAL	Rech 2 [4 84], Veart [14]	14 068
2-12-2005	Newcaste Jets	W	2-1	A	HAL	Veart [75], Brain [79]	10 132
1-01-2006	Queensland Roar	W	4-2	H	HAL	Veart [29], Shengqing [30], Rech 2 [40 63]	8 426
5-01-2006	Melbourne Victory	W	1-0	H	HAL	Dodd [14]	13 427
12-01-2006	Perth Glory	W	2-1	A	HAL	Shengqing [3], Aloisi [71]	5 033
20-01-2006	Central Coast Mariners	D	1-1	H	HAL	Veart [50p]	13 008
28-01-2006	New Zealand Knights	D	1-1	A	HAL	Brain [21]	3 079
3-02-2006	Sydney FC	L	1-2	A	HAL	Shengqing [51]	25 557
12-02-2006	Sydney FC	D	2-2	H	HALsf	Dodd [31], Rech [33]	15 104
19-02-2006	Sydney FC	L	1-2	A	HALsf	Shengqing [60]	30 377
26-02-2006	Central Coast Mariners	L	0-1	H	HALpo		11 405

HAL = Hyundai A-League • sf = semi-final • po = play-off

AUT – AUSTRIA

NATIONAL TEAM RECORD
JULY 1ST 2002 TO JULY 9TH 2006

PL	W	D	L	F	A	%
32	10	9	13	46	47	45.3

FIFA/COCA-COLA WORLD RANKING

1993	1994	1995	1996	1997	1998	1999	2000	2001	2002	2003	2004	2005	High		Low	
36	49	39	34	25	22	28	44	56	65	67	83	69	17	05/99	90	09/04

2005–2006											
08/05	09/05	10/05	11/05	12/05	01/06	02/06	03/06	04/06	05/06	06/06	07/06
71	79	74	72	69	71	70	75	76	79	-	60

The Viennese revival continued in the 2005–06 season with FK Austria Wien winning the Bundesliga and then beating SV Mattersburg in the Cup Final to secure their second double in four seasons and their tenth overall. They were pushed all the way by SV Austria Salzburg playing under new owner Dietrich Mateschitz, the billionaire founder of the Red Bull drinks empire. Known locally as Red Bull Salzburg the team are part of a growing sports empire that consists of the Red Bull F1 racing team and the newly aquired MetroStars in the USA's MLS. If there is a threat to the recent success of clubs in Vienna, there can be little doubt that this is where it will

INTERNATIONAL HONOURS
Qualified for the FIFA World Cup™ 1934 1954 1958 1978 1982 1990 1998 **International Cup** 1932

FIFA Junior Tournament 1950 **UEFA Junior Tournament** 1957 **Mitropa Cup** SK Rapid 1930, First Vienna 1931, FK Austria 1933 1936

come from. The hope is that the Bundesliga as a whole will benefit as Austrian football strives to regain former glories that once saw it amongst the most feared on the continent. With UEFA Euro 2008™ to be jointly hosted with Switzerland, the opportunity is there for the national team to contribute to this revival, but unlike the Swiss, Austria missed out on the FIFA World Cup™ finals, finishing third in their group behind England and Poland. Without any competitive matches before the Euro finals, new coach Josef Hickersberger faces a tough task in preparing a team capable of making an impact - even with the advantage of being hosts.

THE FIFA BIG COUNT OF 2000

	Male	Female		Male	Female
Registered players	290 360	4 200	Referees	2 400	18
Non registered players	250 000	10 000	Officials	390 000	200
Youth players	90 100	2 800	Total involved	1 040 078	
Total players	647 460		Number of clubs	4 497	
Professional players	360	0	Number of teams	10 535	

Osterreichischer Fussball-Bund (OFB)

Ernst Happel Stadion, Sektor A/F, Postfach 340, Meiereistrasse 7, Wien 1021, Austria

Tel +43 1 727180   Fax +43 1 7281632

office@oefb.at   www.oefb.at

President: STICKLER Friedrich   General Secretary: LUDWIG Alfred

Vice-President: EHRENBERGER Kurt   Treasurer: TALOS Rudolf, HR Mag   Media Officer: GOLLATZ Ronald

Men's Coach: KRANKL Hans   Women's Coach: WEBER Ernst

OFB formed: 1904   UEFA: 1954   FIFA: 1907

Red shirts, White shorts, Red socks or White shirts, Black shorts, White socks

RECENT INTERNATIONALS PLAYED BY AUSTRIA

2002	Opponents	Score		Venue	Comp	Scorers	Att	Referee
21-08	Switzerland	L	2-3	Basle	Fr	Wallner 2 [11 81]	23 500	Rosetti ITA
7-09	Moldova	W	2-0	Vienna	ECq	Herzog 2 [4p 30p]	18 300	Dougal SCO
12-10	Belarus	W	2-0	Minsk	ECq	Schopp [57], Akagunduz [90]	15 000	Poulat FRA
16-10	Netherlands	L	0-3	Vienna	ECq		46 300	Collina ITA
20-11	Norway	L	0-1	Vienna	Fr		15 800	Abraham HUN
2003								
26-03	Greece	D	2-2	Graz	Fr	Schopp [52], Haas [81]	8 500	Ovrebo NOR
2-04	Czech Republic	L	0-4	Prague	ECq		20 000	Nieto ESP
30-04	Scotland	W	2-0	Glasgow	Fr	Kirchler [28], Haas [34]	12 189	Vollquartz DEN
7-06	Moldova	L	0-1	Tiraspol	ECq		10 000	Silva POR
11-06	Belarus	W	5-0	Innsbruck	ECq	Aufhauser [33], Haas [47], Kirchler [52], Wallner [62], Cerny [70]	8 100	Frojdfeldt SWE
20-08	Costa Rica	W	2-0	Vienna	Fr	Glieder [34p], Wallner [70]	16 000	Hamer LUX
6-09	Netherlands	L	1-3	Rotterdam	ECq	Pogatetz [34]	47 000	Poulat FRA
11-10	Czech Republic	L	2-3	Vienna	ECq	Haas [51], Ivanschitz [77]	32 350	Kasnaferis GRE
2004								
31-03	Slovakia	D	1-1	Bratislava	Fr	Kollmann [90]	4 500	Vidlak CZE
28-04	Luxembourg	W	4-1	Innsbruck	Fr	Kirchler [5], Kiesenebner [9], Haas [85], Kollmann [88]	9 400	Skomina SVN
25-05	Russia	D	0-0	Graz	Fr		9 600	Vuorela FIN
18-08	Germany	L	1-3	Vienna	Fr	Amerhauser [10]	37 900	Collina ITA
4-09	England	D	2-2	Vienna	WCq	Kollmann [71], Ivanschitz [72]	48 000	Lubos SVK
8-09	Azerbaijan	W	2-0	Vienna	WCq	Stranzl [23], Kollmann [44]	26 400	Sammut MLT
9-10	Poland	L	1-3	Vienna	WCq	Schopp [30]	46 100	Batista POR
13-10	Northern Ireland	D	3-3	Belfast	WCq	Schopp 2 [14 72], Mayrleb [59]	11 810	Shield AUS
2005								
8-02	Cyprus	D	1-1	Limassol	Fr	Kirchler [43]. L 4-5p	300	Hyytia FIN
9-02	Latvia	D	1-1	Limassol	Fr	Sariyar [41]	50	Theodotou CYP
26-03	Wales	W	2-0	Cardiff	WCq	Vastic [81], Stranzl [85]	47 760	Allaerts BEL
30-03	Wales	W	1-0	Vienna	WCq	Aufhauser [87]	29 500	Mejuto Gonzalez ESP
17-08	Scotland	D	2-2	Graz	Fr	Ibertsberger [83], Standfest [87]	13 800	Dereli TUR
3-09	Poland	L	2-3	Chorzow	WCq	Linz 2 [61 80]	40 000	De Santis ITA
7-09	Azerbaijan	D	0-0	Baku	WCq		2 800	Verbist BEL
8-10	England	L	0-1	Manchester	WCq		64 822	Medina Cantalejo ESP
12-10	Northern Ireland	W	2-0	Vienna	WCq	Aufhauser 2 [44 90]	12 500	Briakos GRE
2006								
1-03	Canada	L	0-2	Vienna	Fr		9 000	Van Egmond NED
23-05	Croatia	L	1-4	Vienna	Fr	Ivanschitz [14]	22 000	Fandel GER

Fr = Friendly match • EC = UEFA EURO 2004™ • WC = FIFA World Cup™ • q = qualifier

AUSTRIA NATIONAL TEAM RECORDS AND RECORD SEQUENCES

Records			Sequence records					
Victory	9-0	MLT 1977	Wins	7	1933-1934	Clean sheets	5	1931, 1996
Defeat	1-11	ENG 1908	Defeats	6	1946-1947	Goals scored	28	1931-1934
Player Caps	103	HERZOG Andreas	Undefeated	14	1931-1932	Without goal	3	
Player Goals	44	POLSTER Anton	Without win	9	1973-1974	Goals against	17	1919-22, 1954-56

AUSTRIA COUNTRY INFORMATION

Capital	Vienna (Wien)	Independence	1918	GDP per Capita	$30 000
Population	8 174 762	Status	Republic	GNP Ranking	22
Area km²	83 870	Language	German	Dialling code	+
Population density	97 per km²	Literacy rate	99%	Internet code	.at
% in urban areas	56%	Main religion	Christian 83%	GMT + / –	+1
Towns/Cities ('000)	Vienna 1 569; Graz 222; Linz 181; Salzburg 145; Innsbruck 112; Klagenfurt 90; Villach 58; Wels 57; Sankt Pölten 49; Dornbirn 43; Steyr 39; Wiener Neustadt 38; Bregenz 26				
Neighbours (km)	Czech Republic 362; Slovakia 91; Hungary 366; Slovenia 330; Italy 430; Switzerland 164; Liechtenstein 35; Germany 784				
Main stadia	Ernst Happel – Vienna 44 844; Linzer – Linz 21 328; Salzburg – Salzburg 18 686; Gerhard Hanappi – Vienna 18 456; Tivoli Neu – Innsbruck 17 400; Arnold Schwarzenegger – Graz 15 400				

AUSTRIA NATIONAL TEAM PLAYERS AND COACHES

Record Caps			Record Goals			Recent Coaches	
HERZOG Andreas	1988-'03	103	POLSTER Toni	1982-'00	44	HICKERSBERGER Josef	1988-'90
POLSTER Toni	1982-'00	95	KRANKL Hans	1973-'85	34	RIEDL Alfred	1990-'91
HANAPPI Gerhard	1948-'62	93	HOF Erich	1957-'69	28	CONSTANTINI Dietmar	1991
KOLLER Karl	1952-'65	86	HORVATH Hans	1924-'34	28	HAPPEL Ernst	1992
KONCILLA Friedl	1970-'85	84	SCHALL Toni	1927-'34	28	CONSTANTINI Dietmar	1992
PEZZEY Bruno	1975-'90	84	SINDELAR Matthias	1926-'37	27	PROHASKA Herbert	1993-'99
PROHASKA Herbert	1974-'89	83	HERZOG Andreas	1988-'03	26	BARIC Otto	1999-'01
KRANKL Hans	1973-'85	69	ZISCHEK Karl	1931-'45	24	KRANKL Hans	2002-'05
WEBER Heribert	1976-'89	68	SCHACHNER Walter	1976-'94	23	HERZOG Andreas	2005
STOGER Peter	1988-'99	65	WAGNER Theo	1946-'57	22	HICKERSBERGER Josef	2006-

CLUB DIRECTORY

Club	Town/City	Stadium	Capacity	www.	Lge	Cup
VfB Admira/Wacker	Mödling	Südstadt	12 000	admirazone.com	8	5
FK Austria	Wien	Franz-Horr-Stadion	11 800	fk-austria.at	22	24
Grazer AK	Graz	Graz-Liebenau	15 428	gak.at	1	4
SV Mattersburg	Mattersburg	Pappelstadion	19 700	svm.at	0	0
SV Pasching	Pasching	Waldstadion	5 650	fcsuperfund.at	0	0
SK Rapid	Wien	Gerhard-Hanappi-Stadion	19 600	skrapid.at	31	14
SV Ried	Reid im innkreis	Waldstadion	7 870	fcsuperfund.at	0	0
SV Austria Salzburg	Salzburg	Wals-Siezenheim	18 686	redbulls.com	3	0
SK Sturm	Graz	Graz-Liebenau	15 428	sksturm.at	2	3
FC Wacker Tirol	Innsbruck	Tivoli Neu	17 400	fc-wacker-tirol.at	10	7

RECENT LEAGUE AND CUP RECORD

	Championship							Cup		
Year	Champions	Pts	Runners-up	Pts	Third	Pts		Winners	Score	Runners-up
1990	FC Tirol Innsbruck	38	FK Austria Wien	31	Admira-Wacker	29		FK Austria Wien	3-1	SK Rapid Wien
1991	FK Austria Wien	36	FC Tirol Innsbruck	35	SK Sturm Graz	32		SV Stockerau	2-1	SK Rapid Wien
1992	FK Austria Wien	33	SV Austria Salzburg	33	FC Tirol Innsbruck	33		FK Austria Wien	1-0	Admira-Wacker
1993	FK Austria Wien	36	SV Austria Salzburg	36	Admira-Wacker	28		Wacker Innsbruck	3-1	SK Rapid Wien
1994	SV Austria Salzburg	51	FK Austria Wien	49	Admira-Wacker	44		FK Austria Wien	4-0	FC Linz
1995	SV Austria Salzburg	47	SK Sturm Graz	47	SK Rapid Wien	46		SK Rapid Wien	1-0	DSV Leoben
1996	SK Rapid Wien	73	SK Sturm Graz	67	FC Tirol Innsbruck	62		SK Sturm Graz	3-1	Admira-Wacker
1997	SV Austria Salzburg	69	SK Rapid Wien	66	SK Sturm Graz	55		SK Sturm Graz	2-1	First Vienna FC
1998	SK Sturm Graz	81	SK Rapid Wien	70	Grazer AK	61		SV Ried	3-1	SK Sturm Graz
1999	SK Sturm Graz	73	SK Rapid Wien	70	Grazer AK	65		SK Sturm Graz	1-1 4-2	LASK Linz
2000	FC Tirol Innsbruck	74	SK Sturm Graz	74	SK Rapid Wien	66		Grazer AK	2-2 4-3p	SV Austria Salzburg
2001	FC Tirol Innsbruck	68	SK Rapid Wien	60	Grazer AK	57		FC Kärnten	2-1	FC Tirol Innsbruck
2002	FC Tirol Innsbruck	75	SK Sturm Graz	65	Grazer AK	63		Grazer AK	3-2	SK Sturm Graz
2003	FK Austria Wien	70	Grazer AK	57	SV Austria Salzburg	56		FK Austria Wien	3-0	FC Kärnten
2004	Grazer AK	72	FK Austria Wien	71	SV Pasching	63		Grazer AK	3-3 5-4p	FK Austria Wien
2005	SK Rapid Wien	71	Grazer AK	70	FK Austria Wien	69		FK Austria Wien	3-1	SK Rapid Wien
2006	FK Austria Wien	67	SV Austria Salzburg	63	SV Pasching	58		FK Austria Wien	3-0	SV Mattersburg

AUSTRIA 2005-06

T-MOBILE BUNDESLIGA

	Pl	W	D	L	F	A	Pts	FK Austria	Salzburg	Pasching	Ried	SK Rapid	GAK	Mattersburg	SK Sturm	Wacker	Admira
FK Austria Wien †	36	19	10	7	51	33	**67**		2-0 2-2	0-2 1-1	2-0 3-0	0-2 3-1	3-2 2-1	3-0 1-0	2-1 0-0	0-0 2-1	2-1 4-4
SV Austria Salzburg †	36	20	3	13	62	42	**63**	1-0 3-0		1-0 1-2	2-0 3-0	0-2 2-0	1-0 5-0	4-0 3-1	3-0 3-2	2-0 5-2	3-2 0-1
SV Pasching ‡	36	16	10	10	43	32	**58**	0-1 2-0	1-0 0-0		0-0 0-1	2-0 1-0	1-0 1-0	2-0 2-0	2-2 3-1	2-3 1-1	5-0 0-3
SV Ried	36	13	13	10	48	47	**52**	0-0 0-0	2-0 2-1	0-0 1-2		2-2 0-0	2-1 2-1	3-2 2-2	2-1 2-0	0-0 3-0	4-0 2-0
SK Rapid Wien	36	13	10	13	51	41	**49**	3-1 0-3	2-3 0-1	3-0 3-1	2-2 6-0		3-2 2-0	1-2 2-0	2-3 3-1	2-0 2-1	0-1 0-1
Grazer AK	36	13	6	17	47	48	**45**	1-0 0-0	3-1 3-1	0-0 1-2	2-2 1-4	1-1 3-1		1-0 3-0	2-0 2-3	1-1 0-1	4-1 3-0
SV Mattersburg ‡	36	12	8	16	40	54	**44**	1-2 0-2	0-1 2-1	0-0 1-2	4-3 3-1	0-0 0-0	3-1 1-0		1-1 1-1	0-0 2-2	3-1 3-2
SK Sturm Graz	36	10	12	14	44	51	**42**	0-0 1-3	0-0 4-0	2-0 1-1	3-1 1-0	2-2 0-0	0-2 0-0	0-2 0-1		0-0 2-3	2-1 1-1
FC Wacker Tirol	36	10	12	14	44	55	**42**	2-2 0-2	3-0 3-2	2-2 1-0	1-1 0-1	0-3 0-0	0-1 1-3	4-2 2-0	0-2 2-4		1-0 4-0
VfB Admira/Wacker	36	9	6	21	42	69	**33**	1-2 0-1	0-4 0-3	1-2 2-1	2-2 0-0	1-1 2-1	1-2 2-0	1-2 0-1	2-3 2-0	5-2 1-1	

12/07/2005 - 13/05/2006 • † Qualified for the UEFA Champions League • ‡ Qualified for the UEFA Cup
Top scorers: Sanel KULJIC, Reid, 15; Roland LINZ, FK Austria, 15; Mario BAZINA, GAK/Rapid, 11; Marc JANKO, Salzburg, 11; Marek KINCL, Rapid, 11; Michael MORZ, Mattersburg, 11

AUSTRIA 2005-06
ERSTE LIGA (2)

	Pl	W	D	L	F	A	Pts
SC Rheindorf Altach	33	19	6	8	58	33	**63**
SC Austria Lustenau	33	16	10	7	49	28	**58**
LASK Linz	33	16	9	8	46	30	**57**
FK Austria Wien (Am)	33	15	10	8	54	34	**55**
FC Kärnten	33	14	6	13	50	44	**48**
FC Gratkorn	33	12	11	10	40	38	**47**
DSV Leoben	33	12	8	13	52	47	**44**
Kapfenburger SV	33	9	8	16	43	62	**35**
SC Schwanenstadt	33	9	6	18	31	49	**33**
FC Kufstein	33	4	4	25	22	80	**16**

8/07/2005 - 12/05/2006

OFB POKAL 2005-06

Round of sixteen		Quarter-finals		Semi-finals		Final	
FK Austria Wien	2						
FC Wacker Tirol	0	**FK Austria Wien**	1				
LASK Linz	0	SV Kapfenberg	0				
SV Kapfenberg	2			**FK Austria Wien**	4		
FC Gratkorn	2			SV Ried	0		
SKN St Polten	1	FC Gratkorn	1				
FK Austria Wien (Am)	0	**SV Ried**	2				
SV Ried	5					**FK Austria Wien**	3
SV Pasching	3					SV Mattersburg ‡	0
Grazer AK	1	**SV Pasching**	3				
SK Sturm Graz	0	SC Rheindorf Altach	2				
SC Rheindorf Altach	2			SV Pasching	2		
SK Rapid Wien	1 4p			**SV Mattersburg**	3		
SC Austria Lustenau	1 2p	SK Rapid Wien	0				
SC Schwanenstadt	0	**SV Mattersburg**	1				
SV Mattersburg	3			‡ Qualified for the UEFA Cup			

CUP FINAL

Ernst-Happel-Stadion, Vienna
9-05-2006, 20 100, Ref: Hofmann

Scorers - Sebo 27, Rushfeldt 45, Troansky 82
for FK Austria

AZE – AZERBAIJAN

NATIONAL TEAM RECORD
JULY 1ST 2002 TO JULY 9TH 2006

PL	W	D	L	F	A	%
40	4	15	21	25	71	28.7

FIFA/COCA-COLA WORLD RANKING

1993	1994	1995	1996	1997	1998	1999	2000	2001	2002	2003	2004	2005	High	Low
-	147	141	125	123	99	97	115	113	113	119	113	114	**97** 06/99	**170** 07/94

	2005–2006										
08/05	09/05	10/05	11/05	12/05	01/06	02/06	03/06	04/06	05/06	06/06	07/06
116	114	114	113	114	114	114	114	112	112	-	109

An extraordinary eight match winning run, in which they didn't concede a single goal, saw FK Baku win the Azeri title for the first time. Founded in 2004 when businessman Khafiz Mamedov bought Dinamo Baku, the club have had a successful start to life having won the Cup in 2005. Baku had looked out of sorts for much of the campaign and sacked coach Asker Abdullayev after a defeat against Karvan Yevlakh in March, but new coach Beyukaga Gadzhiev turned things around to steal the title from Karvan right at the death. Going into the final match a point ahead of Karvan, Baku beat Inter 1-0 with a goal from Emin Imamaliyev to secure the title. A draw between Karvan and

INTERNATIONAL HONOURS
None

Neftchi in the penultimate round had effectively put paid to the challenge of both clubs. Karvan's Côte d'Ivoire striker Yacouba Bamba was the top scorer in a league which manages to attract a number of foreign players thanks to the oil industry which dominates the country and especially the capital. It was a regional team, however, who won the Cup when Karabakh Agdam consigned Karvan to yet another runners-up spot, Samir Musayev scoring a late winner in a 2-1 victory. On the international front Vagif Sadykov was replaced as national team coach by Sahin Diniyev in preparation for the UEFA Euro 2008™ qualifiers.

THE FIFA BIG COUNT OF 2000

	Male	Female		Male	Female
Registered players	1 146	85	Referees	90	15
Non registered players	75 000	155	Officials	320	16
Youth players	158	60	Total involved	77 045	
Total players	76 604		Number of clubs	76	
Professional players	650	0	Number of teams	512	

Association of Football Federations of Azerbaijan (AFFA)

37 Khojali Avenue, Baku AZ 1025, Azerbaijan
Tel +994 12 908308   Fax +994 12 989393
affa@azeronline.com   www.none
President: MIRZAYEV Ramiz   General Secretary: ASADOV Fuad
Vice-President: NASIROV Elshad   Treasurer: JAFAROV Lativ   Media Officer: GULIEV Mikail
Men's Coach: DINIYEV Sahin   Women's Coach: TIBILOV Boris
AFFA formed: 1992   UEFA: 1994   FIFA: 1994
White shirts, Blue shorts, White socks or Blue shirts, White shorts, Blue socks

RECENT INTERNATIONALS PLAYED BY AZERBAIJAN

2002 Opponents		Score	Venue	Comp	Scorers	Att	Referee
3-07	Estonia	D 0-0	Kuressaare	Fr		2 200	Vollquartz DEN
6-07	Latvia	D 0-0	Riga	Fr		2 000	Miezelis LTU
8-08	Iran	D 1-1	Tabriz	Fr	Ismailov [16]	25 000	Rahimi Moghadam IRN
21-08	Uzbekistan	W 2-0	Baku	Fr	Aliyev.S [39], Ismaelov [79]	7 000	Abdullayev AZE
7-09	Italy	L 0-2	Baku	ECq		37 000	Vassaras GRE
12-10	Finland	L 0-3	Helsinki	ECq		11 853	Hamer LUX
20-11	Wales	L 0-2	Baku	ECq		8 000	Huyghe BEL
2003							
12-02	Serbia & Montenegro	D 2-2	Podgorica	ECq	Gurbanov.G 2 [59 78]	8 000	Granat POL
29-03	Wales	L 0-4	Cardiff	ECq		72 500	Leuba SUI
11-06	Serbia & Montenegro	W 2-1	Baku	ECq	Gurbanov.G [86p], Ismailov [90]	5 000	Fisker DEN
6-09	Finland	L 1-2	Baku	ECq	Ismailov [89]	7 500	Hrinak SVK
11-10	Italy	L 0-4	Reggio Calabria	ECq		30 000	Dougal SCO
14-12	United Arab Emirates	D 3-3	Dubai	Fr	Nabiyev 2 [35 90], Kerimov [85]		Mohamed UAE
18-12	Oman	L 0-1	Muscat	Fr			
20-12	Saudi Arabia	L 0-1	Riyadh	Fr			
2004							
18-02	Israel	L 0-6	Tel Aviv	Fr		13 250	Paraty POR
31-03	Moldova	L 1-2	Chisinau	Fr	Gurbanov.G [20]	5 500	Godulyan UKR
28-04	Kazakhstan	W 3-2	Almaty	Fr	Nabiyev [31], Guliev [57], Sadigov [80]	20 000	Chynybekov KGZ
28-05	Uzbekistan	W 3-1	Baku	Fr	Gurbanov.G [31], Gurbanov.I [64], Guliev [75]	12 000	
6-06	Latvia	D 2-2	Riga	Fr	Guliev [55], Gurbanov.G [74p]	8 000	Maisonlahti FIN
18-08	Jordan	D 1-1	Amman	Fr	Ponomarev [23]	4 000	
4-09	Wales	D 1-1	Baku	WCq	Sadigov [55]	8 000	Trivkovic CRO
8-09	Austria	L 0-2	Vienna	WCq		26 400	Sammut MLT
9-10	Northern Ireland	D 0-0	Baku	WCq		6 460	Hanacsek HUN
13-10	England	L 0-1	Baku	WCq		17 000	Hamer LUX
17-11	Bulgaria	D 0-0	Baku	Fr		10 000	Sipailo LVA
2005							
21-01	Trinidad and Tobago	L 0-1	Port of Spain	Fr		500	
23-01	Trinidad and Tobago	L 0-2	Marabella	Fr		1 000	Gordon TRI
9-02	Moldova	D 0-0	Baku	Fr		3 000	
26-03	Poland	L 0-8	Warsaw	WCq		9 000	Vollquartz DEN
30-03	England	L 0-2	Newcastle	WCq		49 046	Costa POR
29-05	Iran	L 1-2	Tehran	Fr	Gurbanov.G [67]		
4-06	Poland	L 0-3	Baku	WCq		10 458	Undiano Mallenco ESP
17-08	Albania	L 1-2	Tirana	Fr	Tagizade [2]	7 300	
3-09	Northern Ireland	L 0-2	Belfast	WCq		12 000	Stanisic SCG
7-09	Austria	D 0-0	Baku	WCq		2 800	Verbist BEL
12-10	Wales	L 0-2	Cardiff	WCq		32 628	Hansson SWE
2006							
28-02	Ukraine	D 0-0	Baku	Fr			Sipailo LVA
12-04	Turkey	D 1-1	Baku	Fr			Paniashvili GEO
18-05	Moldova	D 0-0	Chisinau	Fr			

Fr = Friendly match • EC = UEFA EURO 2004™ • WCq = FIFA World Cup™ • q = qualifier

AZERBAIJAN NATIONAL TEAM RECORDS AND RECORD SEQUENCES

Records			Sequence records					
Victory	4-0	LIE 1999	Wins	2	1998, 2004	Clean sheets	2	
Defeat	0-10	FRA 1995	Defeats	11	1994-1995	Goals scored	6	2004
Player Caps	73	AKHMEDOV Tarlan	Undefeated	4	2002	Without goal	9	1999-2000, 2004-05
Player Goals	12	GURBANOV Gurban	Without win	21	2004-20066	Goals against	19	2002-2004

AZERBAIJAN COUNTRY INFORMATION

Capital	Baku	Independence	1991	GDP per Capita	$3 400
Population	7 868 385	Status	Republic	GNP Ranking	111
Area km²	86 600	Language	Azerbaijani	Dialling code	+994
Population density	90 per km²	Literacy rate	96%	Internet code	.az
% in urban areas	56%	Main religion	Muslim 93%	GMT +/–	+5
Towns/Cities ('000)	Baku 1 116; Gäncä 303; Sumgayit 265; Mingäçevir 95; Qaraçuxur 72; Ali Bayramli 70				
Neighbours (km)	Iran 179; Turkey 9; Armenia 787; Georgia 322; Russia 284				
Main stadia	Tofik Bakhramov – Baku 29 858; Mehdi Huseyn-zade – Sumqayit 16 000				

AZERBAIJAN NATIONAL TEAM PLAYERS AND COACHES

Record Caps			Record Goals			Recent Coaches	
AKHMEDOV Tarlan	1994-'05	73	GURBANOV Gurban	1992-'05	12	SADYKOV Vagif	1996-'98
AGAEV Emin	1994-'05	65	TAGIZADE Zaur	1997-'05	6	ALEKSEROV Akhmed	1998-'99
GURBANOV Gurban	1992-'05	65	RZAEV Vidadi	1992-'01	5	ABDULLAYEV Asgar	1999-'00
GURBANOV Makhmud	1994-'05	63	SULEYMANOV Nazim	1992-'98	5	PONOMAREV Igor	2000-'02
KERIMOV Aslan	1994-'06	60	ISMAILOV Farrukh	1998-'05	5	TUAEV Kazbek	2002
GULIYEV Kamal	2000-'05	46	LICHKIN Vyacheslav	1995-'01	4	SADYKOV Vagif	2002-'03
LICHKIN Vyacheslav	1995-'01	45	ABUSHEV Rasim	1993-'99	3	ABDULLAYEV Asgar	2003
ASADOV Arif	1994-'02	43	GULIYEV Emin	2000-'05	3	CARLOS ALBERTO TORRES	2003-'05
GULIYEV Emin	2000-'05	42	NABIEV Nadir	2002'-05	3	SADYKOV Vagif	2005
ABUSHEV Rasim	1993-'99	40				DINIYEV Sahin	2005-

CLUB DIRECTORY

Club	Town/City	Stadium	Capacity	www.	Lge	Cup
FK Baku	Baku	Tofik Bakhramov	29 858		1	1
FK Gança (ex Kapaz)	Gança	Sahar	9 300		3	4
Genclerbirliyi	Sumgayit	Mehdi Huseyinzade	16 000		0	0
FK Geyazan	Gazakh				0	0
FK Inter	Baku	Zabrat	3 000		0	0
FK Karabakh Agdam	Baku	Tofik Ismailov	9 300		1	2
FK Karvan	Yevlakh	Yevlakh	5 000	karvan.az	0	0
FK Khazar	Lenkoran	Rasim Kara			0	0
MOIK	Baku				0	0
MTK-Araz	Imisli	Habio Halilov			0	0
PFC Neftchi	Baku	Tofik Bakhramov	29 858	neftchi.com	5	5
FK Olimpik (ex AMMK)	Baku				0	0
FK Shahdag-Samur	Khusar	Sovket Orduhanov			0	0
PFK Turan	Tovuz	Shehar	5 000		1	0

RECENT LEAGUE AND CUP RECORD

Championship						Cup		
Year	Champions	Pts	Runners-up	Pts	Third	Pts	Winners	Score	Runners-up
1992	Neftchi Baku	62	Khazar Sumgayit	57	Turan Tovuz	56	Inshaatchi Baku	2-1	Kur Mingäçevir
1993	Karabakh Agdam	1-0	Khazar Sumgayit				Karabakh Agdam	1-0	Insh. Sabirabad
1994	Turan Tovuz	50	Karabakh Agdam	49	Kapaz Gança	47	Kapaz Gança	2-0	Khazar Lenkoran
1995	Kapaz Gança	42	Turan Tovuz	40	Neftchi Baku	38	Neftchi Baku	1-0	Kur-Nur
1996	Neftchi Baku	36	Khazri Buzovna	33	Kapaz Gança	32	Neftchi Baku	3-0	Karabakh Agdam
1997	Neftchi Baku	74	Karabakh Agdam	71	Khazri Buzovna	66	Kapaz Gança	1-0	Khazri Buzovna
1998	Kapaz Gança	70	Dinamo Baku	54	Shamkir	54	Kapaz Gança	2-0	Karabakh Agdam
1999	Kapaz Gança	58	Karabakh Agdam	54	Dinamo Baku	52	Neftchi Baku	0-0 5-4p	Shamkir
2000	Shamkir	55	Kapaz Gança	44	Neftchi Baku	43	Kapaz Gança	2-1	Karabakh Agdam
2001	Shamkir	51	Neftchi Baku	51	Vilash Masalli	38	Shafa Baku	2-1	Neftchi Baku
2002	Championship abandoned with eight rounds to play						Neftchi Baku	W-0	Shamkir
2003	No championship played						No tournament played		
2004	Neftchi Baku	69	Shamkir	64	Karabakh Agdam	60	Neftchi Baku	1-0	Shamkir
2005	Neftchi Baku	78	Khazar Lenkoran	78	Karvan Yevlakh	76	FK Baku	2-1	Inter Baku
2006	FK Baku	58	Karvan Yevlakh	57	Neftchi Baku	54	Karabakh Agdam	2-1	Karvan Yevlakh

AZERBAIJAN 2005-06

YUKSAK LIGA (1)

	Pl	W	D	L	F	A	Pts	Baku	Karvan	Neftchi	Inter	Karabakh	Turan	Khazar	Shahdag	MTK-Araz	Ganja	Gen'birliyi	Olimpik	MOIK	Geyazan
FK Baku †	26	18	4	4	42	12	58		1-0	2-2	1-0	2-1	1-0	1-1	0-1	3-0	0-0	2-0	2-0	3-0	3-0
Karvan Yevlakh ‡	26	17	6	3	50	9	57	1-0		0-0	0-0	1-0	1-0	1-0	3-0	1-0	7-1	3-1	1-0	5-0	5-0
Neftchi Baku	26	15	9	2	51	16	54	0-1	0-0		1-1	2-0	1-0	2-2	1-1	1-2	1-1	0-0	4-0	6-0	
Inter Baku	26	14	8	4	35	14	50	0-1	2-1	0-1		2-0	1-0	2-0	2-1	1-0	5-0	0-0	1-0	3-0	1-0
Karabakh Agadam ‡	26	12	4	10	32	32	40	2-4	0-0	2-2	1-0		1-0	2-1	0-1	2-1	0-0	1-1	3-2	2-1	2-1
Turan Tovuz	26	11	5	10	27	21	38	0-1	0-0	0-2	0-1	2-1		1-0	2-3	3-1	2-1	1-0	1-0	5-1	1-0
Khazar Lenkoran	26	9	9	8	27	18	36	0-1	0-0	0-1	1-1	1-0	1-0		1-2	0-0	1-1	0-0	1-0	6-0	2-0
Shahdag Khusar	26	10	5	11	26	36	35	0-3	1-2	1-4	0-2	3-1	0-0	0-2		1-1	0-0	2-0	0-0	1-0	1-0
MTK-Araz Imishli	26	9	8	9	31	36	35	2-1	1-3	0-5	2-2	1-0	0-1	2-1	3-0		3-1	1-1	0-0	3-1	2-0
FK Ganca	26	7	7	12	35	46	28	0-2	1-0	0-5	2-2	1-2	0-0	1-2	3-1	5-0		0-2	0-1	5-1	3-0
Genclerbirliyi Sumgayit	26	6	9	11	25	36	27	0-2	0-3	1-2	1-2	0-2	2-0	0-1	3-2	2-3	2-2		1-3	1-0	2-0
Olimpik Baku	26	5	8	13	15	27	23	0-1	0-5	1-3	0-0	1-2	0-0	0-0	0-0	0-0	1-0	0-1		0-1	2-0
MOIK Baku	26	2	3	21	13	67	9	0-4	0-5	0-1	0-3	0-2	1-2	0-0	0-1	0-3	0-3	1-1	0-2		1-0
Geyazan Gazakh	26	0	9	17	14	52	9	1-1	0-2	0-1	1-1	1-3	1-4	0-0	1-1	1-1	2-2	1-1	2-2	2-2	

12/08/2005 - 30/05/2006 • † Qualified for the UEFA Champions League • ‡ Qualified for the UEFA Cup
Top scorers: Yacouba BAMBA, Karvan, 16; Ahmed TIJANI, Shahdag, 15; Pathe BANGOURA, Genclerbirliyi, 12; Nadir NABIYEV, Neftchi, 12

AZERBAIJAN 2005-06 BIRINCI DASTA (2)

	Pl	W	D	L	F	A	Pts
Gilan Khanlar	30	22	6	2	72	14	72
Khazar-2 Lenkoran	30	22	3	5	60	18	69
Simurq Zaqatala	30	19	8	3	67	14	65
ANSAD-Petrol	30	20	2	8	56	30	62
Adliyye Baku	30	16	8	6	63	30	56
Bakili Baku	30	16	8	6	32	23	56
ABN Barda	30	13	9	8	50	30	48
Rote Fahne Tovuz	30	13	6	11	49	46	45
Neftchi-2 Baku	30	12	4	14	29	34	40
Energetik Mingaçevir	30	10	5	15	41	52	35
Genclerbirliyi-2	30	9	5	16	35	53	32
Shahdag-2 Khusar	30	6	10	14	37	80	28
Azerbaijan U-17	30	6	4	20	33	52	22
Yeni Yevlakh	30	5	6	19	26	54	21
Vilas Masalli	30	4	6	20	30	71	18
Sarur Baku	30	2	2	26	12	91	8

21/09/2005 - 25/05/2006

FFA CUP 2005-06

Round of 16

Karabakh Agdam	0	2
Khazar-2 Lenkoran *	0	1
Olimpik Baku *	0	0
FK Baku	0	3
Turan Tovuz	0	1
Gilan Khanlar *	0	0
Genclerbirliyi Sumgayit	2	0
Neftchi Baku *	1	2
Khazar Lenkoran	2	1
Shahdag Khusar *	0	0
Bakili Baku	1	0
MTK-Araz Imishli *	5	2
Inter Baku	1	1
Geyazan Gazakh *	1	0
FK Ganca *	1	1
Karvan Yevlakh	3	1

Quarter-finals

Karabakh Agdam *	3	0
FK Baku	2	0
Turan Tovuz	0	0
Neftchi Baku *	3	0
Khazar Lenkoran	1	0
MTK-Araz Imishli *	0	0
Inter Baku	1	1
Karvan Yevlakh *	1	4

Semi-finals

Karabakh Agdam	0	1
Neftchi Baku *	0	0
Khazar Lenkoran *	1	0
Karvan Yevlakh	0	3

Final

Karabakh Agdam ‡	2
Karvan Yevlakh	1

* Home team in the first leg • ‡ Qualified for the UEFA Cup

CUP FINAL
Safa, Baku
3-06-2006, Att: 5 000, Ref: Aliyev
Scorers - Vasif Haqverdiyev [45], Samir Musayev [87] for Karabakh; Roman Akhalkatsi [1] for Karvan

BAH – BAHAMAS

NATIONAL TEAM RECORD
JULY 1ST 2002 TO JULY 9TH 2006

PL	W	D	L	F	A	%
3	0	1	2	2	10	16.7

FIFA/COCA-COLA WORLD RANKING

1993	1994	1995	1996	1997	1998	1999	2000	2001	2002	2003	2004	2005	High		Low	
167	-	-	-	-	-	189	178	184	187	193	192	193	166	08/93	197	03/99

				2005–2006							
08/05	09/05	10/05	11/05	12/05	01/06	02/06	03/06	04/06	05/06	06/06	07/06
192	192	192	192	193	193	193	193	194	194	-	193

Caledonia Celtic once again confirmed their position as the top club in the Bahamas when they retained the New Providence Football League title in a close race with Bears FC. The twelve game tournament, played between November and May, saw the top two pull away from Gunite Pool Sharks and Peter Kemp Strikers early on. Team Toyota had a miserable season, losing all nine matches they played before withdrawing from the League just as United FC had earlier done. The decisive game between the top two came right at the end of the season when Celtic beat Bears 3-0 to win the Championship by three points. There was consolation for Bears when they beat Sharks

INTERNATIONAL HONOURS
None

9-3 in the final of the New Providence Cup at the BFA National Centre for Football Development, with Wesley Williams scoring four in the 12 goal thriller. In the traditionally weaker Grand Bahama Football League, Brita Red Bulls won the championship with Lions finishing second. Historically there has been a play-off between the winners of the two leagues but only once has a team from Grand Bahama ever won it - Freeport in 1996 - and the staging of the play-off has become rather haphazard in recent years. There has been little activity on the international front with the national team inactive since the FIFA World Cup™ qualifiers played in 2004.

THE FIFA BIG COUNT OF 2000

	Male	Female		Male	Female
Registered players	396	242	Referees	21	9
Non registered players	2 000	250	Officials	45	20
Youth players	850	160	Total involved	3 993	
Total players	3 898		Number of clubs	30	
Professional players	0	0	Number of teams	104	

Bahamas Football Association (BFA)
Plaza on the Way, West Bay Street, PO Box N-8434, Nassau, NP, Bahamas
Tel +1 242 3225897   Fax +1 242 3225898
lehaven@bahamas.net.bs   www.bahamasfootballassoc.com
President: SEALEY Anton   General Secretary: HAVEN Lionel E.
Vice-President: LUNN Fred   Treasurer: LAFLEUR Pierre   Media Officer: HAVEN Lionel E.
Men's Coach: WHITE Gary   Women's Coach: GREEN Matthew
BFA formed: 1967   CONCACAF: 1981   FIFA: 1968
Yellow shirts with sky blue trimmings, Black shorts, Yellow socks

RECENT INTERNATIONAL MATCHES PLAYED BY BAHAMAS

2002	Opponents	Score	Venue	Comp	Scorers	Att	Referee
No international matches played in 2002							
2003							
27-12	Haiti	L 0-6	Miami	Fr			
2004							
26-03	Dominica	D 1-1	Nassau	WCq	Casimir 88	800	Forde BRB
28-03	Dominica	L 1-3	Nassau	WCq	Jean 67	900	Pineda HON
2005							
No international matches played in 2005							
2006							
No international matches played in 2006 before July							

Fr = Friendly match • WC = FIFA World Cup™ • q = qualifier

BAHAMAS NATIONAL TEAM RECORDS AND RECORD SEQUENCES

Records			Sequence records					
Victory	3-0	TCA 1999	Wins	2	2000	Clean sheets	2	1999
Defeat	0-9	HAI 2000	Defeats	4	1999, 2000-2003	Goals scored	2	2000, 2004
Player Caps	n/a		Undefeated	2	1999, 2000	Without goal	4	2000-2003
Player Goals	n/a		Without win	6	2000-present	Goals against	12	1999-present

RECENT LEAGUE RECORD

	New Providence Championship					Grand Bahama	New Prov. Cup	National
Year	Champions	Pts	Runners-up	Pts	3rd Place	Pts	Champions	Winners	Winners
2000	Cavalier FC						Abacom United	Cavalier FC	Abacom United
2001	Cavalier FC	42	Gunite Pool Sharks	33	Team Toyota	33	Abacom United	Cavalier FC	Cavalier FC
2002	Bears FC	19	Team Toyota	18	United FC	15	Abacom United	Khaki Superstars	Not played
2003	Bears FC	23	United FC	22	Team Toyota	19	Abacom United	Bears FC	Bears FC
2004	Bears FC	29	Caledonia Celtic	26	Caledonia Celtic	23	Haitian Superstars	Bears FC	Not played
2005	Caledonia Celtic	27	RCA Racing Blue	21	Bears FC	18		Bears FC	
2006	Caledonia Celtic	29	Bears FC	26	Gunite Pool Sharks	17	Brita Red Bulls	Bears FC	

The National Championship is played between the champions of New Providence and the champions of Grand Bahama

BAHAMAS COUNTRY INFORMATION

Capital	Nassau	Independence	1973	GDP per Capita	$16 700
Population	299 697	Status	Commonwealth	GNP Ranking	117
Area km²	13 940	Language	English	Dialling code	+1 242
Population density	21 per km²	Literacy rate	96%	Internet code	.bs
% in urban areas	87%	Main religion	Christian 94%	GMT +/–	-5
Towns/Cities ('000)	Nassau 227; Freeport 46; Coppers Town 8; Marsh Harbour 5; Freetown 4; High Rock 3				
Neighbours (km)	North Atlantic Ocean 3 542				
Main stadia	Thomas A. Robinson – Nassau 9 100; Grand Bahama – Freeport 3 100				

BAN – BANGLADESH

NATIONAL TEAM RECORD
JULY 1ST 2002 TO JULY 9TH 2006

PL	W	D	L	F	A	%
22	10	5	7	26	27	56.8

FIFA/COCA-COLA WORLD RANKING

1993	1994	1995	1996	1997	1998	1999	2000	2001	2002	2003	2004	2005		High		Low	
116	130	138	136	141	157	130	151	146	159	151	167	160		110	04/96	170	11/05

2005–2006										
08/05	09/05	10/05	11/05	12/05	01/06	02/06	03/06	04/06	05/06	06/06	07/06
168	168	169	170	160	143	143	143	141	140	-	143

It was a decidedly mixed year for the Bangladesh national team. In December they travelled to Pakistan to defend their South Asian Football Federation Cup title and after easily negotiating the first round group stage, faced a potentially difficult semi-final against the hosts. It took a penalty just before half-time by Mohamad Sujan to secure a third consecutive appearance in the final. Once again, however, they were undone by India in the final, losing 2-0. The national team also got off to a poor start in the AFC Asian Cup qualifiers but with the inaugural AFC Challenge Cup taking place at home, there was the real prospect of continental silverware for the first time. Reserved for

INTERNATIONAL HONOURS
Qualified for AFC Asian Cup Finals 1980   Represented in the Football Tournament of the Asian Games 1978 1982 1986 1990
South Asian Federation Games 1999   South Asian Football Federation Cup 2003

nations considered to be in the lower tier of Asian football, Bangladesh qualified easily from their first round group but there was huge disappointment at the heavy defeat against Tajikistan in the quarter-finals. Domestically Brothers Union retained their Dhaka Premier League title thanks to a Sujan goal in a play-off against Mohammedan, following a very tight three-horse race. In the National Football League play-offs, however, they lost to Mohammedan in the semi-finals, who then went on to defeat Abahani in the final to become the first club to win the title twice.

THE FIFA BIG COUNT OF 2000

	Male	Female		Male	Female
Registered players	95 350	0	Referees	2 950	0
Non registered players	5 000 000	0	Officials	64 000	32 000
Youth players	135 000	0	Total involved	5 329 800	
Total players	5 230 850		Number of clubs	3 800	
Professional players	0	0	Number of teams	7 000	

Bangladesh Football Federation (BFF)
BFF House, Motijheel, Dhaka 1000, Bangladesh
Tel +880 2 7161582   Fax +880 2 7160270
bffbd@citechco.net   www.bffonline.com
President: SULTAN S.A.   General Secretary: HUQ Anwarul
Vice-President: AHMED Monir   Treasurer: ALAM CHOWDHURY Shah   Media Officer: AL FATAH Ahmed Sayed
Men's Coach: CRUCIANI Diego   Women's Coach: MOSHARAF Badal
BFF formed: 1972   AFC: 1974   FIFA: 1974
Green with black and red trimmings, Green shorts, Red socks or White shirts with black and red trimmings, White shirts, White socks

RECENT INTERNATIONAL MATCHES PLAYED BY BANGLADESH

2003	Opponents		Score	Venue	Comp	Scorers	Att	Referee
11-01	Nepal	W	1-0	Dhaka	SAr1	Ahmed Alfaz [30]		Kunsuta THA
13-01	Maldives	W	1-0	Dhaka	SAr1	Arif Khan [89]		Vidanagamage SRI
15-01	Bhutan	W	3-0	Dhaka	SAr1	Ariful Kabir Farhad 2 [4 54], Rukunuzzaman Kanchan [79]		Balu IND
18-01	India	W	2-1	Dhaka	SAsf	Rukunuzzaman Kanchan [78], Matiur Munna [98 GG]		Kunsuta THA
20-01	Maldives	D	1-1	Dhaka	SAf	Rukunuzzaman Kanchan [14] W 5-3p		Vidanagamage SRI
27-03	Laos	L	1-2	Hong Kong	ACq	Ariful Kabir Farhad [90]		Liu Sung Ho TPE
30-03	Hong Kong	D	2-2	Hong Kong	ACq	Mahmud Hossein Titu [66], Hossein Monwar [78]		
26-11	Tajikistan	L	0-2	Dhaka	WCq		6 000	Khanthachai THA
30-11	Tajikistan	L	0-2	Dushanbe	WCq		12 000	Pereira IND
2004								

No international matches played in 2004

2005								
8-12	Bhutan	W	3-0	Karachi	SAr1	Ariful Kabir Farhad 2 [42 58], Zahid Hasan Ameli [85]		
10-12	Nepal	W	2-0	Karachi	SAr1	Rokonuzzaman Kanchan 2 [27 87]		
12-12	India	D	1-1	Karachi	SAr1	Zahid Hasan Ameli [77]		
14-12	Pakistan	W	1-0	Karachi	SAsf	Mohammad Sujan [44p]		
17-12	India	L	0-2	Karachi	SAf			
22-12	Pakistan	D	0-0	Dhaka	ACq			
26-12	Pakistan	W	1-0	Karachi	ACq	Firaj Mahmud Hossain [84]		
2006								
22-02	Uzbekistan	L	0-5	Uzbekistan	ACq		12 000	Ebrahim BHR
1-03	Hong Kong	L	0-1	Dhaka	ACq		1 000	Sarkar IND
1-04	Cambodia	W	2-1	Dhaka	CCr1	Alfaz Ahmed [31], Hasan Ameli [64]	35 000	Tan Hai CHN
3-04	Guam	W	3-0	Dhaka	CCr1	Hasan Ameli [49], Abdul Hossain 2 [83 85]	18 000	U Ein Cho MYA
5-04	Palestine	D	1-1	Dhaka	CCr1	Mahadi Tapu [55]	22 000	Mombini IRN
10-04	Tajikistan	L	1-6	Dhaka	CCqf	Alfaz Ahmed [17]	15 000	AK Nema IRQ

SA = South Asian Football Federation Cup • AC = AFC Asian Cup • CC = AFC Challenge Cup • WCq = FIFA World Cup™
q = qualifier • r1 = first round group • sf = semi-final • f = final • GG = Golden Goal

BANGLADESH NATIONAL TEAM RECORDS AND RECORD SEQUENCES

Records			Sequence records					
Victory	8-0	MDV 1985	Wins	4	2003	Clean sheets	3	1984, 1999, 2003
Defeat	0-9	KOR 1979	Defeats	7	1979-1981	Goals scored	8	1984, 2001-2003
Player Caps	n/a		Undefeated	6	2001-2003	Without goal	5	1980-82, 2000-01
Player Goals	n/a		Without win	19	1973-1979	Goals against	34	1973-1983

RECENT LEAGUE RECORD

Dhaka League						National Championship		
Year	Champions	Pts	Runners-up	Pts	Third	Pts	Winners	Score	Runners-up

Year	Champions	Pts	Runners-up	Pts	Third	Pts
1992	Abahani	37	Mohammedan	33	Brothers Union	27
1993	Mohammedan	30	Abahani	29	Brothers Union	23
1994	Abahani	28	Muktijoddha	25	Mohammedan	25
1995	Abahani	43	Mohammedan	42	Muktijoddha	33
1996	Mohammedan	48	Abahani	43	Muktijoddah	33
1997	No championship due to a readjustment in the timings of the season					
1998	Muktijoddha	52	Mohammedan	50	Abahani	42
1999	Mohammedan	40	Abahani	37	Muktijoddha	34
2000	Muktijoddha	40	Abahani	37	Mohammedan	33
2001	Abahani	41	Mohammedan	27	Rahmatganj	18
2002	Mohammedan	33	Abahani	31	Muktijoddha	29
2003	No championship due to a readjustment in the timings of the season					
2004	Brothers Union	40	Sheikh Russell	38	Abahani	33
2005	Brothers Union ‡	39	Mohammedan	39	Abahani	38

Winners	Score	Runners-up
Abahani	†	Mohammedan
	Not played	
Mohammedan	0-0 6-5p	Abahani
Muktijoddha	1-1 3-2p	Mohammedan
Brothers Union	0-0 4-2p	Muktijoddha
Mohammedan	2-0	Abahani

† played on a league system • ‡ Play-off in 2005: Brothers Union 1-0 Mohammedan

BANGLADESH COUNTRY INFORMATION

Capital	Dhaka	Independence	1971		GDP per Capita	$1 900
Population	141 340 476	Status	Republic		GNP Ranking	51
Area km²	144 000	Language	Bengali		Dialling code	+880
Population density	98 per km²	Literacy rate	40%		Internet code	.bd
% in urban areas	18%	Main religion	Muslim 87%		GMT +/−	+6
Towns/Cities ('000)	Dhaka 6 493; Chittagong 3 672; Khulna 1 342; Rajshahi 700; Comilla 389; Tungi 337; Mymensingh 330; Sylhet 326; Rangpur 285; Narsinghdi 281; Barisal 280;					
Neighbours (km)	India 4 053; Burma 193; Bay of Bengal 580					
Main stadia	Bangabandhu – Dkaka 36 000; Sher-e-Bangla Mirpur – Dhaka 30 000					

BANGLADESH 2005

5TH NATIONAL FOOTBALL LEAGUE

First Stage Group A

	Pl	W	D	L	F	A	Pts	Brothers U	Nobanabin	Army	Kacharipara	Khulna
Brothers Union †	4	2	2	0	6	0	8		0-0	4-0	0-0	2-0
Nobanabin Somabesh †	4	2	1	1	5	4	7	1-2		1-0	3-2	
Army †	4	2	1	1	3	5	7				1-0	0-0
Kacharipara Jamalpur	4	1	1	2	2	4						1-0
Khulna Town Club	4	0	1	3	2	6	1					

First Stage Group B

	Pl	W	D	L	F	A	Pts	Abahani	Muktijo'dha	Moham'dan	Feni	Moham'dan
Abahani †	4	3	1	0	11	1	10		0-0	1-0	5-1	5-0
Muktijoddha †	4	2	2	0	7	0	8			0-0	3-0	4-0
Mohammedan †	4	2	1	1	6	3	7				4-1	2-1
Feni	4	1	0	3	7	12	3					5-0
Mohammedan Rangamati	4	0	0	4	1	16	0					

Second Stage (in Dhaka)

	Pl	W	D	L	F	A	Pts	Abahani	Brothers U	Moham'dan	Muktij'dha	Army	Nobanabin
Abahani †	5	3	2	0	9	3	11		2-2	*1-0**	*0-0**	1-0	6-1
Brothers Union †	5	2	3	0	3	2	9			0-0	1-0	*4-0**	*0-0**
Mohammedan Dhaka †	5	2	2	1	8	1	8				*0-0**	6-0	2-1
Muktijoddha †	5	2	2	1	9	3	8					4-0	5-2
Army	5	1	0	4	0	11	3						*2-1**
Nobanabin Somabesh	5	0	1	4	4	13	1						

24/11/2005 - 3/01/2006 • † Teams qualifying for the next stage • 6 regional qualifiers were played to determine the final 10 teams • Abahani, Brothers Union, Mohammedan Dhaka and Muktijoddha were given byes to the first round • * Teams took records against first stage qualifiers into the second stage

CHAMPIONSHIP PLAY-OFFS

Semi-finals		Final	
Mohammedan	1	8-01-2006, Bangabandhu, 25000	
Brothers Union	0	**Mohammedan**	2
Muktijoddha	1	Abahani	0
Abahani	2	Scorers - Chibiuka 48, Alfaz 90	

BANGLADESH 2005

DHAKA PREMIER LEAGUE

	Pl	W	D	L	F	A	Pts	Brothers U	Moham'dan	Abahani	Muktijo'dha	Sh. Russell	Farashganj	Arambagh	Wanderers	Fakirerpool	Dipali
Brothers Union	18	12	3	3	42	17	39		0-0	2-1	1-2	2-2	1-0	2-1	5-0	3-0	2-1
Mohammedan	18	11	6	1	33	13	39	1-1		0-1	1-0	2-1	3-1	6-1	3-1		4-1
Abahani	18	11	5	2	38	15	38	3-0	1-1		0-2	2-0	0-0	0-0	4-1	2-1	3-1
Muktijoddha	18	11	1	6	34	23	34	1-3	0-2	1-2		0-4	2-0	4-3	2-1	1-2	2-0
Sheikh Russell	18	7	6	5	33	18	27	0-2	0-0	1-2	0-0		0-1	2-0	3-1	10-0	2-0
Farashganj	18	6	5	7	18	19	23	2-4	0-1	0-0	2-3	0-1		0-0	1-1	2-1	2-1
Arambagh	18	4	8	6	23	24	20	1-0	2-2	1-1	0-2	2-2	0-0		1-3	3-1	4-0
Dhaka Wanderers	18	2	7	9	18	43	13	1-3	1-1	0-5	1-6	1-1	1-2	0-0		1-1	1-1
Fakirerpool YMC	18	3	3	12	20	50	12	1-4	1-2	1-6	1-3	2-2	0-1	0-2	0-0		4-3
Dipali	18	0	2	16	20	57	2	0-7	1-3	3-5	0-3	2-3	1-4	2-2	1-3	2-3	

28/05/2005 - 9/09/2005 • Championship play-off: Brothers Union 1-0 Mohammeden (12-09-2005, Bangabandhu, Ref: Azad, Scorer: Sujan 22p)

BDI – BURUNDI

NATIONAL TEAM RECORD
JULY 1ST 2002 TO JULY 9TH 2006

PL	W	D	L	F	A	%
21	4	5	12	18	37	30.9

FIFA/COCA-COLA WORLD RANKING

1993	1994	1995	1996	1997	1998	1999	2000	2001	2002	2003	2004	2005		High		Low	
101	126	146	137	152	141	133	126	139	135	145	152	147		96	08/93	160	07/98

2005–2006											
08/05	09/05	10/05	11/05	12/05	01/06	02/06	03/06	04/06	05/06	06/06	07/06
143	142	142	143	147	148	148	148	149	150	-	157

The tiny East African country is one of almost half of the Confederation of African Football's membership who were confined to the international wilderness after losing out in the preliminaries of the 2006 FIFA World Cup™ qualifiers. Save for participation in the annual East and Central African Senior Challenge Cup, it has meant a hiatus for the national side 'Intamba'. Burundi played just four internationals in 2005, drawing one and losing three of them at the CECAFA tournament in neighbouring Rwanda. Inter Stars represented the country in the 2006 CAF Champions League and made it through to the second round, but only after a technicality. They had

INTERNATIONAL HONOURS
None

lost on the away goals rule to CAPS United of Zimbabwe but were restored to the event after CAPS United had been disqualified for using improperly registered players. In the second round, they won 2-1 against the formidable Raja Casablanca of Morocco, but that was only after they had lost the first leg 0-7. Inter Stars had won the championship in November. Infrastructure progress in the country, being rebuilt after civil war, is reflected in the start of construction of a new stadium at Kanyosha in the capital Bujumbura. The country's national team and league were also recipients of a major sponsorship deal from a brewing company.

THE FIFA BIG COUNT OF 2000

	Male	Female		Male	Female
Registered players	4 582	384	Referees	399	13
Non registered players	17 000	400	Officials	9 134	86
Youth players	6 151	102	Total involved	38 251	
Total players	28 619		Number of clubs	165	
Professional players	0	0	Number of teams	189	

Fédération de Football du Burundi (FFB)
Building Nyogozi, Boulevard de l'Uprona, Case postale 3426, Bujumbura, Burundi
Tel +257 928762   Fax +257 242892
lydiansekera@yahoo.fr   www.none
President: NSEKERA Lydia   General Secretary: TBD
Vice-President: SAMUGABO Mustapha   Treasurer: NDEBERI Robert   Media Officer: None
Men's Coach: NIYONZIMA Dominique   Women's Coach: HAKIZIMANA Kebe
FFB formed: 1948   CAF: 1972   FIFA: 1972
Red shirts with white trimmings, White shorts, Green socks

RECENT INTERNATIONAL MATCHES PLAYED BY BURUNDI

2003	Opponents	Score		Venue	Comp	Scorers	Att	Referee
30-03	Côte d'Ivoire	L	0-1	Bujumbura	CNq			Gasingwa RWA
8-06	Côte d'Ivoire	L	1-6	Abidjan	CNq	Shabani [88]	50 000	Monteiro Duarte CPV
6-07	South Africa	L	0-2	Bujumbura	CNq		8 000	Teshome ETH
12-10	Gabon	D	0-0	Bujumbura	WCq		10 000	Itur KEN
15-11	Gabon	L	1-4	Libreville	WCq	Nzeyimana [90]	15 000	Ndoye SEN
2004								
11-12	Ethiopia	L	1-2	Addis Abeba	CCr1	Hakizimana [75p]		
13-12	Rwanda	W	3-1	Addis Abeba	CCr1	Hakizimana [51p], Ntibazonkizia [54], Nzohabonayo [83]		
15-12	Tanzania	W	2-0	Addis Abeba	CCr1	Kubis 2 [46 90]		
17-12	Zanzibar †	W	2-1	Addis Abeba	CCr1	Nahimana [43], Hakizimana [78p]		
22-12	Sudan	W	2-1	Addis Abeba	CCsf	Ntibazonkizia [22], Kubis [75]		
25-12	Ethiopia	L	0-3	Addis Abeba	CCf			
2005								
28-11	Tanzania	L	1-2	Kigali	CCr1			
2-12	Eritrea	D	0-0	Kigali	CCr1			
4-12	Rwanda	L	0-2	Kigali	CCr1			
2006								
No international matches played in 2006 before July								

Fr = Friendly match • CN = CAF African Cup of Nations qualifier • CC = CECAFA Cup • WCq = FIFA World Cup™
q = qualifier • r1 = 1st round • † Not a full international

BURUNDI NATIONAL TEAM RECORDS AND RECORD SEQUENCES

Records			Sequence records					
Victory	6-2	RWA 1976	Wins	5	1996-1998	Clean sheets	6	1993-1998
Defeat	1-6	CIV 2003	Defeats	4	1999	Goals scored	9	1982-1992
Player Caps	n/a		Undefeated	8	1993-1998	Without goal	3	1982, 1993
Player Goals	n/a		Without win	14	2001-2004	Goals against	10	1975-1981

RECENT LEAGUE AND CUP RECORD

Year	Champions	Cup Winners
1996	Fantastique	Vital'O
1997	Maniema	Vital'O
1998	Vital'O	Elite
1999	Vital'O	Vital'O
2000	Vital'O	Atletico Olympique
2001	Prince Louis	
2002	Muzinga	
2003	Championship abandoned	
2004	Atletico Olympique	Bafalo Muramvya
2005	Inter Stars	

BURUNDI COUNTRY INFORMATION

Capital	Bujumbura	Independence	1962	GDP per Capita	$600
Population	6 231 221	Status	Republic	GNP Ranking	161
Area km²	27 830	Language	Kirundi/French	Dialling code	+257
Population density	224 per km²	Literacy rate	45%	Internet code	.bi
% in urban areas	8%	Main religion	Muslim 43%	GMT +/-	+2
Towns/Cities ('000)	Bujumbura 330; Muyinga 71; Ruyigi 38; Gitega 23; Ngozi 21; Rutana 20; Bururi 19;				
Neighbours (km)	Rwanda 290, Tanzania 451, Congo DR 233. Burundi also borders Lake Tanganyika				
Main stadia	Prince Louis Rwagasore – Bujumbura 22 000				

BEL – BELGIUM

NATIONAL TEAM RECORD
JULY 1ST 2002 TO JULY 9TH 2006

PL	W	D	L	F	A	%
32	13	9	10	48	43	54.7

FIFA/COCA-COLA WORLD RANKING

1993	1994	1995	1996	1997	1998	1999	2000	2001	2002	2003	2004	2005	High		Low	
25	24	24	42	41	35	33	27	20	17	16	45	55	**16**	01/03	**56**	05/06

2005–2006										
08/05	09/05	10/05	11/05	12/05	01/06	02/06	03/06	04/06	05/06	06/06	07/06
52	47	49	52	55	55	54	50	56	56	-	57

A quite awful year for Belgian football; there is no other way to describe it. Hoping for a seventh consecutive appearance in the finals of the FIFA World Cup™, the national team finished a miserable fourth in their qualifying group whilst the domestic scene was thrown into chaos by a match fixing scandal that went to the very heart of the game. With the huge opportunities opened up by internet betting, the Belgian league was targeted as a soft touch by Far East syndicates, with the activities of Chinese betting syndicates attracting particular interest from the Belgian police. In all more than 50 players were suspected of fixing matches although the figure could turn out to be much higher.

INTERNATIONAL HONOURS
Qualified for the FIFA World Cup™ finals 1930 1934 1938 1954 1970 1982 1986 1990 1994 1998 2002 **Olympic Gold** 1920

Remaining free from scandal, the 'big three' lived up to their name for once with Standard maintaining their recent revival, although they were denied a first championship in 23 years by Anderlecht. The two met in Brussels with three weeks of the season left and a 2-0 victory for Anderlecht saw them overtake Standard. They then clinched their 28th League title on the final weekend. Zulte Waregem were the surprise winners of the Belgian Cup. Founded in 2001 through the merger of KSV Waregem and Zultse VV, they had beaten Club Brugge in the first round and in the final against Mouscron they won thanks to an injury time winner from Tim Matthys.

THE FIFA BIG COUNT OF 2000

	Male	Female		Male	Female
Registered players	84 816	3 772	Referees	6 378	158
Non registered players	125 000	800	Officials	77 478	3 618
Youth players	240 119	8 096	Total involved	550 235	
Total players	462 603		Number of clubs	2 002	
Professional players	386	0	Number of teams	16 780	

Union Royale Belge des Sociétés de Football Association / Koninklijke Belgische Voetbalbond (URBSFA/KBVB)
145 Avenue Houba de Strooper, Bruxelles 1020, Belgium
Tel +32 2 4771211   Fax +32 2 4782391
urbsfa.kbvb@footbel.com   www.footbel.com
President: DE KEERSMAECKER Francois   General Secretary: HOUBEN Jean-Paul
Vice-President: VANDEN STOCK Roger   Treasurer: LANDSHEERE Germain   Media Officer: CORNU Nicolas
Men's Coach: VANDEREYCKEN Rene   Women's Coach: NOE-HAESENDONCK Anne
URBSFA/KBVB formed: 1895   UEFA: 1954   FIFA: 1904
Red shirts with black trimmings, Red shorts, Red socks or Black shirts with red trimmings, Black shorts, Black socks

RECENT INTERNATIONAL MATCHES PLAYED BY BELGIUM

2002	Opponents	Score		Venue	Comp	Scorers	Att	Referee
21-08	Poland	D	1-1	Szczecin	Fr	Sonck [42]	19 000	Ingvarsson SWE
7-09	Bulgaria	L	0-2	Brussels	ECq		20 000	Hauge NOR
12-10	Andorra	W	1-0	Andorra La Vella	ECq	Sonck [61]	700	Nalbandyan ARM
16-10	Estonia	W	1-0	Tallinn	ECq	Sonck [2]	2 500	Riley ENG
2003								
12-02	Algeria	W	3-1	Annaba	Fr	Mpenza.E 2 [2 57], Sonck [7]	40 000	Baraket TUN
29-03	Croatia	L	0-4	Zagreb	ECq		25 000	Fandel GER
30-04	Poland	W	3-1	Brussels	Fr	Sonck [28], Buffel [56], Soetaers [86]	27 000	McDonald SCO
7-06	Bulgaria	D	2-2	Sofia	ECq	OG [31], Clement [56]	42 000	Collina ITA
11-06	Andorra	W	3-0	Gent	ECq	Goor 2 [20 68], Sonck [44]	12 000	Shmolik BLR
20-08	Netherlands	D	1-1	Brussels	Fr	Sonck [39]	38 000	Fandel GER
10-09	Croatia	W	2-1	Brussels	ECq	Sonck 2 [34 42]	35 000	Poll ENG
11-10	Estonia	W	2-0	Liege	ECq	OG [45], Buffel [61]	26 000	Busacca SUI
2004								
18-02	France	L	0-2	Brussels	Fr		43 160	Halsey ENG
31-03	Germany	L	0-3	Cologne	Fr		46 500	Wegereef NED
28-04	Turkey	L	2-3	Brussels	Fr	Sonck [33], Dufer [85]	25 000	Van Egmond NED
29-05	Netherlands	W	1-0	Eindhoven	Fr	Goor [77p]	32 500	Colombo FRA
18-08	Norway	D	2-2	Oslo	Fr	Buffel 2 [25 34]	16 669	Stupik POL
4-09	Lithuania	D	1-1	Charleroi	WCq	Sonck [61]	19 218	Loizou CYP
9-10	Spain	L	0-2	Santander	WCq		17 000	Nielsen DEN
17-11	Serbia & Montenegro	L	0-2	Brussels	WCq		28 350	Frojdfeldt SWE
2005								
9-02	Egypt	L	0-4	Cairo	Fr		5 000	Beltagi EGY
26-03	Bosnia-Herzegovina	W	4-1	Brussels	WCq	Mpenza.E 2 [15 54], Daerden [44], Buffel [77]	36 700	Hrinak SVK
30-03	San Marino	W	2-1	Serravalle	WCq	Simons [18p], Van Buyten [65]	871	Kasnaferis GRE
4-06	Serbia & Montenegro	D	0-0	Belgrade	WCq		16 662	Ivanov.V RUS
17-08	Greece	W	2-0	Brussels	Fr	Mpenza.E [19], Mpenza.M [24]	20 000	Berntsen NOR
3-09	Bosnia-Herzegovina	L	0-1	Zenica	WCq		12 000	Benquerenca POR
7-09	San Marino	W	8-0	Antwerp	WCq	Simons [34p], Daerden 2 [39 67], Buffel [44], Mpenza.M 2 [52 71], Vandenbergh [53], Van Buyten [83]	8 207	Stokes IRL
8-10	Spain	L	0-2	Brussels	WCq		40 300	Michel SVK
12-10	Lithuania	D	1-1	Vilnius	WCq	Garaerts [20]	1 500	Riley ENG
2006								
1-03	Luxembourg	W	2-0	Luxembourg	Fr	Vandenbergh [42], Pieroni [61]. Abandoned 65 mins		Einwaller AUT
11-05	Saudi Arabia	W	2-1	Sittard	Fr	Caluwe [3], Vanden Borre [55]		Bossen NED
20-05	Slovakia	D	1-1	Trnava	Fr	Geraerts [76]	4 174	Kassai HUN
24-05	Turkey	D	3-3	Genk	Fr	OG [28], Sonck [43], Hoefkens [90]	15 000	Stuchlik AUT

Fr = Friendly match • EC = UEFA EURO 2004™ • WCq = FIFA World Cup™ • q = qualifier

BELGIUM NATIONAL TEAM RECORDS AND RECORD SEQUENCES

Records			Sequence records					
Victory	10-1	SMR 2001	Wins	7	1979-1980	Clean sheets	5	1972-1973, 1989
Defeat	2-11	ENG 1909	Defeats	7	1927-1928	Goals scored	21	1937-1945
Player Caps	96	CEULEMANS Jan	Undefeated	11	1988-1989	Without goal	5	1999
Player Goals	30	VAN HIMST & VOORHOOF	Without win	13	1933-1935	Goals against	38	1928-1933

BELGIUM COUNTRY INFORMATION

Capital	Brussels	Independence	1830	GDP per Capita	$29 100
Population	10 348 276	Status	Kingdom	GNP Ranking	20
Area km²	30 528	Language	Flemish/French	Dialling code	+32
Population density	339 per km²	Literacy rate	99%	Internet code	.be
% in urban areas	97%	Main religion	Christian 90%	GMT + / –	+1
Towns/Cities ('000)	Brussels 1 019; Antwerp 459; Ghent 231; Charleroi 200; Liège 182; Brugge 116; Namur 106; Leuven 92; Mons 91; Aalst 77; Mechelen 77; La Louvière 76; Kortrijk 73; Hasselt 69				
Neighbours (km)	Netherlands 450; Germany 167; Luxembourg 148; France 620; North Sea 66				
Main stadia	Roi Baudouin (Heysel) – Brussels 50 000; Jan Breydel – Brugge 29 975; Sclessin – Liège 29 173				

BELGIUM NATIONAL TEAM PLAYERS AND COACHES

Record Caps			Record Goals			Recent Coaches	
CEULEMANS Jan	1977-'91	96	VOORHOOF Bernard	1928-'40	30	GOETHALS Raymond	1968-'76
GERETS Eric	1975-'91	86	VAN HIMST Paul	1960-'74	30	THYS Guy	1976-'89
VAN DER ELST Franky	1984-'98	86	WILMOTS Marc	1994-'02	28	MEEUWS Walter	1989-90
SCIFO Enzo	1984-'98	84	MERMANS Jeff	1945-'56	27	THYS Guy	1990-'91
VAN HIMST Paul	1960-74	81	DE VEEN Robert	1906-'13	26	VAN HIMST Paul	1991-'96
GRUN Georges	1984-'95	77	BRAINE Raymond	1925-'39	26	VAN MOER Wilfred	1996-'97
STAELENS Lorenzo	1990-'00	70	CEULEMANS Jan	1977-'91	23	LEEKENS Georges	1997-'99
WILMOTS Marc	1994-'02	70	DEGRYSE Marc	1984-'96	23	WASIEGE Robert	1999-'02
MEES Vic	1949-'60	68	COPPENS Rik	1949-'59	21	ANTHUENIS Aime	2002-'05
HEYLENS Georges	1961-'73	67				VANDEREYCKEN Rene	2006-

CLUB DIRECTORY

Club	Town/City	Stadium	Capacity	www.	Lge	Cup
RSC Anderlecht	Brussels	Vanden Stock	28 063	rsca.be	27	8
KSK Beveren	Antwerp	Freethiel	13 290	kskbeveren.be	2	2
FC Brussels	Brussels	Machtens	15 266	fcmbs.be	1	0
KSV Cercle Brugge	Brugge	Jan Breydel	29 268	cerclebrugge.be	3	2
Club Brugge KV	Brugge	Jan Breydel	29 268	clubbrugge.be	13	9
RSC Charleroi	Charleroi	Pays de Charleroi	20 000	rcsc.be	0	0
Excelsior Mouscron	Mouscron	Le Canonnier	10 692	excelsior.be	0	0
KRC Genk	Genk	Feniksstadion	22 989	krcgenk.be	2	2
KAA Gent	Gent	Ottenstadion	18 215	kaagent.be	0	2
Germinal Beerschot	Antwerp	Olympic Stadion	12 500	germinal-beerschot.be	0	1
Lierse SK	Lier	Vanderpoorten	14 538	lierse.com	4	2
KSC Lokeren	Lokeren	Daknam	12 000	sporting.be	0	0
K Sint-Truidense VV	Sint-Truiden	Staaien	12 861	stvv.com	0	0
R Standard Liège	Liège	Sclessin	30 000	standardliege.com	8	5
KVC Westerlo	Westerlo	't Kuipipe	10 278	kvcwesterlo.be	0	1
SV Zulte Waregem	Waregem	Regenboogstadion	8 5000	SVZW.be	0	1

RECENT LEAGUE AND CUP RECORD

	Championship						Cup		
Year	Champions	Pts	Runners-up	Pts	Third	Pts	Winners	Score	Runners-up
1990	Club Brugge	57	RSC Anderlecht	53	KV Mechelen	50	RFC Liège	2-1	Germinal Ekeren
1991	RSC Anderlecht	53	KV Mechelen	50	Club Brugge	47	Club Brugge	3-1	KV Mechelen
1992	Club Brugge	53	RSC Anderlecht	49	Standard Liège	46	Royal Antwerp FC	2-2 9-8p	KV Mechelen
1993	RSC Anderlecht	58	Standard Liège	45	KV Mechelen	42	Standard CL	2-0	RSC Charleroi
1994	RSC Anderlecht	55	Club Brugge	53	RFC Seraing	43	RSC Anderlecht	2-0	Club Brugge
1995	RSC Anderlecht	52	Standard Liège	51	Club Brugge	49	Club Brugge	3-1	Germinal Ekeren
1996	Club Brugge	81	RSC Anderlecht	71	Germinal Ekeren	53	Club Brugge	2-1	Cercle Brugge
1997	Lierse SK	73	Club Brugge	71	Excelsior Mouscron	61	Germinal Ekeren	4-2	RSC Anderlecht
1998	Club Brugge	84	KRC Genk	66	Germinal Ekeren	58	KRC Genk	4-0	Club Brugge
1999	KRC Genk	73	Club Brugge	71	RSC Anderlecht	70	Lierse SK	3-1	Standard Liège
2000	RSC Anderlecht	75	Club Brugge	67	KAA Gent	63	KRC Genk	4-1	Standard Liège
2001	RSC Anderlecht	83	Club Brugge	78	Standard Liège	60	KVC Westerlo	1-0	KFC Lommelse
2002	KRC Genk	72	Club Brugge	72	RSC Anderlecht	66	Club Brugge	3-1	Excelsior Mouscron
2003	Club Brugge	79	RSC Anderlecht	71	KSC Lokeren	60	La Louvière	3-1	Sint-Truidense
2004	RSC Anderlecht	81	Club Brugge	72	Standard Liège	65	Club Brugge	4-2	KSK Beveren
2005	Club Brugge	79	RSC Anderlecht	76	Standard Liège	70	Germinal Beerschot	2-1	Club Brugge
2006	RSC Anderlecht	70	Standard Liège	65	Club Brugge	64	Zulte Waregem	2-1	Excelsior Mouscron

BELGIUM 2005-06

LIGUE JUPILER

	Pl	W	D	L	F	A	Pts	Anderlecht	Stabdard	Brugge	Gent	Genk	Beerschot	Waregem	Lokeren	Westerlo	Brussels	Charleroi	Roeselare	Mouscron	Cercle	St Truiden	Beveren	Lierse	Louvière
RSC Anderlecht †	34	20	10	4	72	27	70		2-0	2-2	3-0	4-1	3-1	3-0	1-1	5-0	2-0	3-1	5-1	3-1	2-2	3-0	4-0	3-0	6-0
Standard Club Liège †	34	19	8	7	51	28	65	2-0		2-0	0-2	1-0	3-1	1-2	2-1	1-0	1-0	1-0	0-0	2-1	7-1	2-0	1-3	3-1	1-1
Club Brugge ‡	34	18	10	6	51	33	64	0-2	1-1		2-1	3-0	2-0	2-1	0-1	2-1	3-0	2-1	1-0	2-0	2-0	2-1	1-0	3-1	4-0
KAA Gent	34	18	7	9	48	34	61	0-0	2-1	4-1		2-0	2-1	1-3	1-2	0-1	2-1	2-2	1-2	0-0	1-0	1-0	3-0	1-1	3-0
KRC Genk	34	16	9	9	52	38	57	3-3	0-1	2-2	2-1		1-0	3-1	2-2	2-0	1-0	0-0	4-1	1-0	3-1	2-0	2-0	1-0	1-0
Germinal Beerschot	34	14	7	13	50	45	49	2-0	2-2	1-1	2-1	2-2		2-0	2-1	0-1	0-1	0-1	2-2	1-0	0-0	4-0	3-1	4-0	1-1
Zulte Waregem ‡	34	14	7	13	51	49	49	1-2	1-2	2-1	1-2	1-0	2-1		1-1	1-2	0-0	3-0	2-1	4-1	3-1	1-5	2-2	0-1	0-0
KSC Lokeren	34	12	11	11	48	49	47	2-2	0-0	2-0	1-2	1-1	1-2	2-3		3-2	1-0	3-2	2-2	1-1	2-1	1-2	1-2	1-0	3-2
KVC Westerlo	34	13	7	14	42	48	46	2-1	0-2	0-0	0-1	1-1	1-3	2-2	1-1		3-0	1-1	3-2	0-5	2-0	2-1	4-1	0-0	2-1
FC Brussels	34	12	10	12	30	30	46	1-1	3-1	1-1	0-1	1-0	0-1	1-1	1-1	1-0		2-2	1-0	0-1	1-2	0-0	3-1	2-1	0-0
RSC Charleroi	34	11	12	11	39	39	45	1-1	0-0	3-3	2-0	2-1	2-0	2-0	3-1	2-1	1-0		1-1	1-0	0-1	0-1	4-0	0-1	0-2
KSV Roeselare ‡ (FP)	34	10	11	13	44	42	41	0-2	0-0	1-1	1-1	1-2	5-1	0-3	4-0	0-2	0-1	2-0		5-0	1-0	1-1	1-0	2-0	4-1
Excelsior Mouscron	34	11	4	18	43	43	37	0-1	2-1	0-1	1-2	0-1	0-1	1-1	0-1	0-1	0-1	1-0	0-1		6-0	3-0	1-3	5-0	2-1
Cercle Brugge	34	10	7	17	38	61	37	0-2	0-3	0-1	1-2	1-1	3-0	2-4	1-0	2-2	0-1	2-0	2-2	1-0		2-1	1-1	3-0	1-0
Sint-Truiden VV	34	8	10	16	36	49	34	3-0	0-0	2-2	1-1	2-2	1-2	2-0	1-2	0-1	0-1	1-1	1-0	3-6	1-1		1-0	1-1	1-3
KSK Beveren	34	9	6	19	35	55	33	0-1	0-2	0-1	0-1	0-2	0-0	2-1	1-3	3-1	0-2	1-1	1-1	1-0	5-1	4-1		4-1	1-0
Lierse SK	34	8	8	18	22	52	32	0-0	0-2	1-1	1-3	1-2	0-2	2-1	2-1	1-1	0-0	1-0	2-0	0-4	1-0	2-0			0-0
RAA Louvieroise	34	4	14	16	26	56	26	0-0	2-3	0-1	1-1	2-3	1-1	2-2	1-1	0-3	0-3	2-2	0-0	0-0	0-0	0-2	2-0	1-0	

5/08/2005 - 5/05/2006 • † Qualified for the UEFA Champions League • ‡ Qualified for the UEFA Cup • Top scorers: Tosin DOSUNMU, Beerschot, 18; Mohammed TCHITE, Standard CL, 16; Aristide BANCE, Lokeren, 15; Bosko BALABAN, Club Brugge, 13; Kevin VANDENBERGH, Genk, 12

BELGIUM 2005-06
TWEEDE CLASSE (2)

	Pl	W	D	L	F	A	Pts
RAEC Mons	32	18	9	5	58	29	63
KVSK United ‡	32	17	10	5	59	35	61
Verbroedering Geel ‡	32	16	6	10	43	29	54
Red Star Waasland	32	14	11	7	55	45	53
KV Kortrijk	32	14	10	8	50	40	52
Oud-Heverlee Leuven	32	14	8	10	48	36	50
Royal Antwerp	32	14	7	11	53	50	49
AS Eupen	32	12	8	12	46	47	44
VW Hamme ‡	32	12	7	13	48	47	43
KV Oostende	32	10	11	11	44	46	41
KSK Ronse	32	11	6	15	47	60	39
AFC Tubize	32	11	5	16	42	48	38
KV Mechelen	32	9	9	14	38	44	36
Excelsior Virton	32	8	12	12	27	39	36
Union St Gilloise	32	8	9	15	37	53	33
Dessel Sport	32	8	7	17	33	48	31
KMSK Deinze	32	6	5	21	33	65	23
Beringen-H.-Zolder			Withdrew after 23 rounds				

31/08/2005 - 7/05/2006 • ‡ Qualified for play-offs

BELGIUM 2005-06
TWEEDE CLASSE PLAY-OFFS

	Pl	W	D	L	F	A	Pts	Lierse	United	Hamme	Geel
Lierse SK	6	4	0	2	13	7	12		2-1	2-0	5-0
KVSK United	6	3	1	2	11	9	10	2-1		3-1	2-1
VW Hamme	6	3	0	3	8	9	9	2-0	2-1		2-1
Verbroedering Geel	6	1	1	4	8	15	4	2-3	1-2	2-1	

COUPE DE BELGIQUE 2005-06

Eighth-finals		Quarter-finals			Semi-finals			Final	
SV Zulte-Waregem	1								
Verbroedering Geel *	0	SV Zulte-Waregem *	3	1					
Lierse SK *	2	KVC Westerlo	0	3					
KVC Westerlo	2				SV Zulte-Waregem	2	0		
KAA Gent *	1 5p				Standard Club Liège *	1	1		
Cercle Brugge	1 3p	KAA Gent *	2	2					
Germinal Beerschot	0	Standard Club Liège	1	4					
Standard Club Liège *	1							SV Zulte-Waregem ‡	2
RSC Charleroi	2							Excelsior Mouscron	1
Oud-Heverlee Leuven	0	RSC Charleroi	0	1					
KRC Genk	1	Sint-Truiden VV *	0	0					
Sint Truiden VV *	2				RSC Charleroi *	0	1		
KSK Beveren *	5				Excelsior Mouscron	1	1		
KSC Lokeren	1	KSK Beveren	0	0					
RAEC Mons	1	Excelsior Mouscron *	0	2					
Excelsior Mouscron *	2								

CUP FINAL
Roi Baudouin, Brussels
13-05-2006, 35 000

Scorers - Leleu [11], Matthys [90] for Waregem; Custovic [62] for Mouscron

* Home team/home team in 1st leg • ‡ Qualified for the UEFA Cup

BEN – BENIN

NATIONAL TEAM RECORD
JULY 1ST 2002 TO JULY 9TH 2006

PL	W	D	L	F	A	%
38	9	7	22	36	65	32.9

FIFA/COCA-COLA WORLD RANKING

1993	1994	1995	1996	1997	1998	1999	2000	2001	2002	2003	2004	2005		High		Low
130	143	161	143	137	127	140	148	152	146	121	122	113		106 07/06		165 07/96

	2005–2006									
08/05	09/05	10/05	11/05	12/05	01/06	02/06	03/06	04/06	05/06	06/06	07/06
125	126	118	115	113	113	113	113	114	114	-	106

Benin have battled to come to terms with reality after the heady heights of participation at the 2004 African Nations Cup finals in Tunisia, where they made their debut performance on the continental stage. The tiny West African country, who have never broken into the top 100 of the FIFA/Coca-Cola World Ranking, had lost their tag of whipping boys with their surprise place among the 16 finalists at the 2004 Nations Cup, but they lost all three matches and since have managed just two wins in 18 matches. 'Les Ecureuils' only success came in a friendly against Burkina Faso and in the final group game in their 2006 FIFA World Cup™ qualifying group, where they beat Libya 1-0.

INTERNATIONAL HONOURS
None

It was not enough, however, to prevent them from finishing bottom of their six-team group. It has been a time of transition for the national side, who turned to the bulk of the players who had played in the under-20 side at the FIFA World U-20 Championship in the Netherlands in June and July 2005. It was Benin's first foray at a FIFA competition and they were far from overwhelmed with draws against Australia and Japan before a narrow 0-1 loss to their Dutch hosts saw them eliminated at the first hurdle. At home the Championship resumed after two years of disruption and was won by Mogas 90 from the capital Porto-Novo in a close contest with Dragons and Buffles.

THE FIFA BIG COUNT OF 2000

	Male	Female		Male	Female
Registered players	4 500	0	Referees	200	0
Non registered players	15 000	0	Officials	1 400	0
Youth players	2 500	0	Total involved	23 600	
Total players	22 000		Number of clubs	100	
Professional players	0	0	Number of teams	400	

Fédération Béninoise de Football (FBF)
Stade René Pleven d'Akpakpa, Case Postale 965, Cotonou 01, Benin
Tel +229 330537   Fax +229 330537
www.none
President: ANJORIN Moucharafou   General Secretary: DIDAVI Bruno Arthur
Vice-President: AKPLOGAN Firmin   Treasurer: AHOUANVOEBLA Augustin   Media Officer: None
Men's Coach: DODJO Edme   Women's Coach: None
FBF formed: 1962   CAF: 1969   FIFA: 1962
Green shirts with yellow and red trimmings, Yellow shorts, Red socks

RECENT INTERNATIONAL MATCHES PLAYED BY BENIN

2003	Opponents	Score		Venue	Comp	Scorers	Att	Referee
11-10	Madagascar	D	1-1	Antananarivo	WCq	Adjamonsi [74]	5 131	Maillet SEY
16-11	Madagascar	W	3-2	Cotonou	WCq	Tchomogo.O 3 [33p 62 90+2]	20 000	Imiere NGA
2004								
14-01	Tunisia	L	0-2	Djerba	Fr		6 000	
17-01	Tunisia	L	1-2	Tunis	Fr	Ahoueya [60]	25 000	
27-01	South Africa	L	0-2	Sfax	CNr1		12 000	Coulibaly MLI
31-01	Morocco	L	0-4	Sfax	CNr1		20 000	Maillet SEY
4-02	Nigeria	L	1-2	Sfax	CNr1	Latoundji [90]	15 000	Abd El Fatah EGY
20-05	Togo	L	0-1	Cotonou	Fr			
23-05	Togo	D	1-1	Lome	Fr	Amoussou [9]		
26-05	Burkina Faso	W	1-0	Cotonou	Fr	Maiga [75]		
6-06	Cameroon	L	1-2	Yaoundé	WCq	Tchomogo.S [11]	40 000	Mbera GAB
13-06	Burkina Faso	L	2-4	Ouagadougou	Fr	Amoussou [33], Adjamonsi [44p]		
20-06	Sudan	D	1-1	Cotonou	WCq	Ogunbiyi [30]	20 000	Guezzaz MAR
4-07	Egypt	D	3-3	Cotonou	WCq	Tchomogo.O [8p], Ahoueya [46], Ogunbiyi [68]	15 000	Chukwujekwu NGA
3-09	Libya	L	1-4	Tripoli	WCq	Osseni [12]	30 000	Kidane Tesfu ERI
3-10	Gabon	L	0-2	Libreville	Fr			
10-10	Côte d'Ivoire	L	0-1	Cotonou	WCq		25 000	Sowe GAM
2005								
27-03	Côte d'Ivoire	L	0-3	Abidjan	WCq		35 000	Guirat TUN
4-06	Cameroon	L	1-4	Cotonou	WCq	Agbessi [81]	20 000	El Arjoun MAR
17-08	Sudan	L	0-1	Omdurman	WCq		12 000	Maillet SEY
4-09	Egypt	L	1-4	Cairo	WCq	Sessegnon [60]	5 000	Buenkadila COD
23-09	United Arab Emirates	D	0-0	Dubai	Fr			
9-10	Libya	W	1-0	Cotonou	WCq	Chitou [60]	1 880	Mususa ZIM
2006								
26-02	Equatorial Guinea	L	0-1	Cotonou	Fr			
29-03	Equatorial Guinea	L	0-2	Bata	Fr			

Fr = Friendly match • CN = CAF African Cup of Nations • WCq = FIFA World Cup™ • q = qualifier • r1 = first round group

BENIN NATIONAL TEAM RECORDS AND RECORD SEQUENCES

Records			Sequence records					
Victory	6-2	CHA 1963	Wins	3	2003	Clean sheets	3	2003
Defeat	1-10	NGA 1959	Defeats	9	1991-1993	Goals scored	7	1963-1965, 2004
Player Caps	n/a		Undefeated	7	1963-1965	Without goal	5	1988-1990, 1991
Player Goals	n/a		Without win	24	1984-1991	Goals against	14	1963-1969

RECENT LEAGUE AND CUP RECORD

	Championship						Coupe de l'Independence		
Year	Champions	Pts	Runners-up	Pts	Third	Pts	Winners	Score	Runners-up
2001	No championship held						Buffles Borgou	1-0	Dragons
2002	Dragons	15	Requins	15	Postel	13	Jeunesse Pobe	0-0 1-1 4-3p	Mogas 90
2003	Dragons	21	Buffles Borgou	19	Postel	14	Mogas 90	1-0	Soleil
2004	Championship unfinished						Mogas 90	1-0	Requins
2005	No championship held						No competition		
2006	Mogas 90	34	Dragons	33	Buffles Borgou	32			

BENIN COUNTRY INFORMATION

Capital	Porto-Novo	Independence	1960	GDP per Capita	$1 100
Population	7 250 033	Status	Republic	GNP Ranking	135
Area km²	112 620	Language	French, Fon, Yoruba	Dialling code	+229
Population density	64 per km²	Literacy rate	40%	Internet code	.bj
% in urban areas	31%	Main religion	Indigenous 50%	GMT +/−	+1
Towns/Cities ('000)	Cotonou 690; Abomey 385; Porto Novo 234; Djougou 202; Parakou 163; Bohicon 125				
Neighbours (km)	Niger 226; Nigeria 773; Togo 644; Burkina Faso 306; Atlantic Ocean (Bight of Benin) 121				
Main stadia	Stade de l'Amitié – Cotonou 35 000; Stade Municipale – Porto Novo 20 000				

BER – BERMUDA

NATIONAL TEAM RECORD
JULY 1ST 2002 TO JULY 9TH 2006

PL	W	D	L	F	A	%
18	5	3	10	37	33	36.1

FIFA/COCA-COLA WORLD RANKING

1993	1994	1995	1996	1997	1998	1999	2000	2001	2002	2003	2004	2005		High	Low
84	102	140	167	176	185	163	153	166	172	183	157	161		**78** 08/93	**185** 12/98

2005–2006											
08/05	09/05	10/05	11/05	12/05	01/06	02/06	03/06	04/06	05/06	06/06	07/06
157	158	159	158	161	161	161	161	162	162	-	160

The Holy Grail for football clubs in Bermuda remains winning the triple crown of Premier League, FA Cup and Friendship Trophy. Vasco were the last team to achieve it, in 1998, following on from Somerset Trojans in 1968, 1969 and 1970, Pembroke Hamilton Club (PHC) in 1971 and North Village in 1978. After a 28 year gap North Village did it again, thanks to two Cup victories over Dandy Town and an impressive display in the League which saw them beaten just once, by Devonshire Cougars. In Cup competitions North Village made it seven wins in seven finals since 1994 against the luckless Dandy Town. In the FA Cup a Keishen Bean hat-trick helped seal the

INTERNATIONAL HONOURS
None

triple crown but the match went to extra time and wasn't settled until the closing stages. For Kentoine Jennings it meant joining an exclusive club of footballers to have won more than one triple crown, having been part of the 1998 Vasco team. There was some consolation for Dandy Town with their 1-0 victory over Somerset Trojans in the less important Martonmere Cup final. With no international matches since May 2005 the focus has been on domestic issues but May 2006 saw the career of one of Bermuda's finest internationals end on a high when Shaun Goater hung up his boots after helping Southend win the League One Championship in England.

THE FIFA BIG COUNT OF 2000

	Male	Female		Male	Female
Registered players	1 804	180	Referees	30	2
Non registered players	700	0	Officials	200	10
Youth players	1 500	30	Total involved	4 456	
Total players	4 214		Number of clubs	47	
Professional players	4	0	Number of teams	95	

Bermuda Football Association (BFA)
48 Cedar Avenue, Hamilton, HM 12, Bermuda
Tel +1 441 2952199   Fax +1 441 2950773
bfa@northrock.bm   www.bfa.bm
President: MUSSENDEN Larry   General Secretary: SABIR David
Vice-President: FURBERT Chris   Treasurer: O'BRIEN Delroy   Media Officer: None
Men's Coach: LIGHTBOURNE Kyle   Women's Coach: BROWN Vance
BFA formed: 1928   CONCACAF: 1966   FIFA: 1966
Blue shirts with red and white trimmings, Blue shorts, Blue socks

RECENT INTERNATIONAL MATCHES PLAYED BY BERMUDA

2002	Opponents		Score	Venue	Comp	Scorers	Att	Referee
No international matches played in 2002								
2003								
26-12	Barbados	L	1-2	Hamilton	Fr	Nusum [79]		Mouchette BER
2004								
1-01	Barbados	L	0-4	Hamilton	Fr			Raynor BER
10-02	Trinidad and Tobago	L	0-1	Hamilton	Fr		3 000	Raynor BER
12-02	Trinidad and Tobago	D	2-2	Hamilton	Fr	Smith.C [36], Simons [76]		Crockwell BER
29-02	Montserrat	W	13-0	Hamilton	WCq	Ming 3 [5 20 50], Nusum 3 [15 54 60], Smith.K [36], Bean.R 2 [41 52], Steede [43], Wade [77], Simons [83], Burgess [87]	3 000	Kennedy USA
21-03	Montserrat	W	7-0	Plymouth	WCq	Hill [15], Nusum 2 [21 44], Bean.R [39], Smith.K 2 [45 46], Ming [76]	250	Charles DOM
31-03	Nicaragua	W	3-0	Hamilton	Fr	Goater 2 [33 65p], Simons [90]		Crockwell BER
2-04	Nicaragua	W	2-1	Hamilton	Fr	Nusum 2 [47 67]		Raynor BER
28-04	Panama	L	1-4	Panama City	Fr	Ashwood [14]		
30-04	Nicaragua	L	0-2	Diriamba	Fr		800	
2-05	Nicaragua	L	0-2	Esteli	Fr			
13-06	El Salvador	L	1-2	San Salvador	WCq	Nusum [30]	12 000	Campos NCA
20-06	El Salvador	D	2-2	Hamilton	WCq	Burgess [5p], Nusum [21]	4 000	Whittaker CAY
24-11	Cayman Islands	W	2-1	Kingstown	GCq	Smith.K [4], Hill [34]	200	Mathews SKN
26-11	St Vincent/Grenadines	D	3-3	Kingstown	GCq	Smith.K [42], Lowe [82], Ming [90p]		
28-11	British Virgin Islands	L	0-2	Kingstown	GCq		400	Mathews SKN
2005								
25-05	Trinidad and Tobago	L	0-4	Port of Spain	Fr		400	
27-05	Trinidad and Tobago	L	0-1	Marabella	Fr			
2006								
No international matches played in 2006 before July								

Fr = Friendly match • GC = 2005 CONCACAF Gold Cup™ • WC = FIFA World Cup™ • q = qualifier

BERMUDA NATIONAL TEAM RECORDS AND RECORD SEQUENCES

Records			Sequence records					
Victory	13-0	MSR 2004	Wins	4	2004	Clean sheets	3	2004
Defeat	0-6	DEN 1969, CAN 1983	Defeats	6	1968-1969	Goals scored	17	1990-1992
Player Caps	n/a		Undefeated	7	1990-1991	Without goal	2	
Player Goals	n/a		Without win	10	1964-1969	Goals against	12	1968-1971

BERMUDA COUNTRY INFORMATION

Capital	Hamilton	Independence	British Crown Colony	GDP per Capita	$36 000
Population	64 935	Status		GNP Ranking	n/a
Area km²	53.3	Language	English	Dialling code	+1 441
Population density	1 218 per km²	Literacy rate	99%	Internet code	.bm
% in urban areas	100%	Main religion	Christian	GMT +/-	-4
Towns/Cities ('000)	Hamilton 1; St George 1				
Neighbours (km)	North Atlantic Ocean				
Main stadia	National Stadium – Hamilton 8 500; White Hill – Sandys				

BERMUDA 2005-06

PREMIER DIVISION

	Pl	W	D	L	F	A	Pts	North Village	Trojans	Dandy Town	Cougars	Zebras	Blazers	Colts	Rangers
North Village	14	11	2	1	44	10	35		2-0	2-1	2-0	1-1	3-1	2-0	7-2
Somerset Trojans	14	8	4	2	26	15	28	0-0		1-0	3-2	2-1	0-0	3-0	3-3
Dandy Town	14	9	1	4	29	22	28	0-3	0-4		3-2	4-1	1-0	4-3	1-0
Devonshire Cougars	14	8	1	5	37	20	25	2-0	4-2	2-3		5-0	3-4	1-0	2-0
PHC Zebras	14	4	3	7	28	31	15	1-3	2-2	1-3	1-4		4-2	5-0	6-0
Boulevard Blazers	14	4	2	8	22	33	14	1-7	0-1	1-4	0-5	2-2		1-2	3-0
Devonshire Colts	14	2	2	10	12	33	8	1-3	0-1	2-2	1-1	0-2	0-3		3-2
Ireland Rangers	14	2	1	11	16	50	7	0-9	1-4	0-3	1-4	1-0	1-4	3-0	

30/09/2005 - 5/03/2006 • Top scorers: Aljame ZUILL, Cougars, 11; Raynell LIGHTBOURNE, Zebras, 9; Carlos SMITH, Dandy Town, 9

FRIENDSHIP TROPHY 2005-06

Quarter-finals		Semi-finals		Final	
North Village	3				
Somerset Trojans	0	North Village	5		
Ireland Rangers †	1	Devonshire Colts	1		
Devonshire Colts	0			North Village	2
PHC Zebras	4			Dandy Town	1
Boulevard Blazers	0	PHC Zebras	1		
Devonshire Cougars	0	Dandy Town	3	National Sports Centre, 12-03-2006	
Dandy Town	1	† Rangers disqualified		Scorers - Bean, Smith for Village; Anderson for Town	

FA CUP 2005-06

Round of sixteen		Quarter-finals		Semi-finals		Final	
North Village	1						
Paget Lions	0	North Village	4				
Crossroads	0	Prospect United	1				
Prospect United	1			North Village	9		
Southampton Rangers	2			Hamilton Parish	0		
Young Mens SC	0	Southampton Rangers	1				
St George's Colts	1	Hamilton Parish	2				
Hamilton Parish	4					North Village	4
Devonshire Cougars	1					Dandy Town	1
Devonshire Colts	0	Devonshire Cougars	2				
Somerset Eagles	1	Ireland Rangers	0				
Ireland Rangers	3			Devonshire Cougars	2		
PHC Zebras	6			Dandy Town	3		
St George's Allstars	0	PHC Zebras	1				
Wolves	0	Dandy Town	2				
Dandy Town	3						

CUP FINAL

National Sports Centre, Hamilton
9-04-2006, Ref: Mouchette

Scorers - Keishan Bean 3, Kerntoine
Jennings for North Village; Ottis Stede for
Dandy Town

RECENT LEAGUE AND CUP RECORD

	Championship						FA Cup		
Year	Champions	Pts	Runners-up	Pts	Third	Pts	Winners	Score	Runners-up
1997	Devonshire Colts	41	Vasco da Gama	34	Dandy Town	31	Boulevard Blazers	3-2	Wolves
1998	Vasco da Gama		Dandy Town		Boulevard Blazers		Vasco da Gama	2-1	Devonshire Colts
1999	Vasco da Gama	41	Dandy Town	33	North Village	32	Devonshire Colts	1-0	Dandy Town
2000	PHC Zebras	39	North Village	37	Dandy Town	32	North Village	2-1	Devonshire Colts
2001	Dandy Town	29	North Village	28	Devonshire Colts	26	Devonshire Colts	3-1	North Village
2002	North Village	27	Dandy Town	23	Devonshire Cougars	22	North Village	3-0	Dandy Town
2003	North Village	29	Devonshire Cougars	23	Boulevard Blazers	20	North Village	5-1	Prospect
2004	Dandy Town	31	Devonshire Cougars	30	Boulevard Blazers	25	Dandy Town	3-3 2-1	Devonshire Cougars
2005	Devonshire Cougars	32	Dandy Town	30	PHC Zebras	26	North Village	2-0	Hamilton Parish
2006	North Village	35	Somserset Trojans	28	Dandy Town	28	North Village	4-1	Dandy Town

BFA – BURKINA FASO

NATIONAL TEAM RECORD
JULY 1ST 2002 TO JULY 9TH 2006

PL	W	D	L	F	A	%
40	13	9	18	42	49	43.7

FIFA/COCA-COLA WORLD RANKING

1993	1994	1995	1996	1997	1998	1999	2000	2001	2002	2003	2004	2005	2006	High	Low
127	97	101	107	106	75	71	69	78	75	78	84	87		62 08/98	127 12/93

2005–2006											
08/05	09/05	10/05	11/05	12/05	01/06	02/06	03/06	04/06	05/06	06/06	07/06
91	89	88	89	87	87	87	90	89	89	-	74

Failure to qualify for the African Nations Cup finals in Egypt came as a disappointment to 'Les Etalons' (the Stallions) but Burkina Faso remain a testy opponent on the African circuit. Fourth place in their 2006 FIFA World Cup™ qualifying group denied the Burkinabe a trip to Egypt and led to a clean out of their coaching staff. The departure of Frenchman Bernard Simondi has seen the Burkina football federation recall one of the legends of the local game, Idrissa 'Saboteur' Traore. Simondi, whose contract was only scheduled to run out at the end of 2007, said he was going home to France on holiday in May and never returned. It was the coaching acumen of Traore

INTERNATIONAL HONOURS
None

that ensured qualification for Les Etalons for the 1996 African Nations Cup finals, which marked the transition for the country from perennial whipping boys on the African stage to a much respected side. Traore has come on board again with a talented generation of youth players awaiting promotion to the top ranks of a national side still dominated by European-based players. ASFA Yenenga and Etoile Filante continue to keep up their traditional rivalry with both claiming the main honours for the season. Despite losing two of their last three matches, ASFA clung on to win the League whilst Etoile continued their good record in the Cup beating Racing Club 3-2 in the final.

THE FIFA BIG COUNT OF 2000

	Male	Female		Male	Female
Registered players	1 065	400	Referees	92	5
Non registered players	40 500	1 700	Officials	2 100	200
Youth players	555	350	Total involved	46 967	
Total players	44 570		Number of clubs	87	
Professional players	10	0	Number of teams	775	

Fédération Burkinabé de Foot-Ball (FBF)
Centre Technique National, Ouaga 2000, 01 Casa Postale 57, Ouagadougou 01, Burkina Faso
Tel +226 50 396864   Fax +226 50 396866
febefoo@fasonet.bf   www.fasofoot.com
President: DIAKITE Seydou   General Secretary: ZANGREYANOGHO Joseph
Vice-President: KABORE Salif   Treasurer: TRAORE SOME Clemence   Media Officer: BARRY Alpha
Men's Coach: TRAORE Idrissa   Women's Coach: None
FBF formed: 1960   CAF: 1964   FIFA: 1964
Green shirts with red and white trimmings, Green shorts, Green socks

RECENT INTERNATIONAL MATCHES PLAYED BY BURKINA FASO

2003	Opponents	Score		Venue	Comp	Scorers	Att	Referee
24-09	Benin	W	1-0	Algiers	Fr	Balbone [57]		
26-09	Algeria	D	0-0	Algiers	Fr	L 3-4p	1 500	Benouza ALG
23-10	Zimbabwe	L	1-4	Hyderabad	AAG	Samba [16]		
25-10	Uzbekistan	L	0-1	Hyderabad	AAG			
27-10	Iran	W	2-1	Hyderabad	AAG			
8-11	Gabon	D	0-0	Moanda	Fr			
15-11	Morocco	L	0-1	Meknes	Fr		25 000	Boukhtir TUN
2004								
17-01	Egypt	D	1-1	Port Said	Fr	Dagano [35]	8 000	
20-01	Guinea	L	0-1	Sainte-Maxime	Fr			
26-01	Senegal	D	0-0	Tunis	CNr1		2 000	Guezzaz MAR
30-01	Mali	L	1-3	Tunis	CNr1	Minoungou [50]	1 500	Shelmani LBY
2-02	Kenya	L	0-3	Bizerte	CNr1		4 550	Sowe GAM
26-05	Benin	L	0-1	Cotonou	Fr			
30-05	Libya	W	3-2	Ouagadougou	Fr	Kone.Y [11], Kabore.I [34], Diabate [70]		
5-06	Ghana	W	1-0	Ouagadougou	WCq	Zongo [79]	25 000	Chukwujekwu NGA
13-06	Benin	W	4-2	Ouagadougou	Fr	Toure.A [41], Coulibaly.A [55], Dagano [89], Ouedraogo.A [90]		
20-06	Congo DR	L	2-3	Kinshasa	WCq	Toure.A [26], Dagano [85]	75 000	Djaoupe TOG
3-07	South Africa	L	0-2	Johannesburg	WCq		25 000	Ramanampamonjy MAD
17-08	Algeria	D	2-2	Blida	Fr	Zongo [50p], Ouedraogo.H [67]	15 000	Tahri MAR
4-09	Uganda	W	2-0	Ouagadougou	WCq	Dagano [34], Nikiema [79]	30 000	Lemghambodj MTN
9-10	Cape Verde Islands	L	0-1	Praia	WCq		6 000	Aziaka TOG
17-11	Morocco	L	0-4	Rabat	Fr		5 000	Keita.M MLI
2005								
9-02	Algeria	L	0-3	Algiers	Fr		3 000	Benaissa ALG
20-03	Korea Republic	L	0-1	Dubai	Fr			
26-03	Cape Verde Islands	L	1-2	Ouagadougou	WCq	Dagano [71]	27 500	Evehe CMR
29-05	Togo	L	0-1	Lome	Fr			
5-06	Ghana	L	1-2	Kumasi	WCq	Dagano [30]	11 920	Abd El Fatah EGY
18-06	Congo DR	W	2-0	Ouagadougou	WCq	Panandetiguiri [3], Dagano [68]	25 000	Shelmani LBY
3-09	South Africa	W	3-1	Ouagadougou	WCq	Cisse 2 [32 47], Kebe [39]	25 000	Codjia BEN
8-10	Uganda	D	2-2	Kampala	WCq	Kebe [15], Rouamba [75]	1 433	Benouza ALG
2006								
28-02	Algeria	D	0-0	Rouen	Fr		2 000	Duhamel FRA

Fr = Friendly match • CN = CAF African Cup of Nations • AAG = Afro-Asian Games • WC = FIFA World Cup™ • q = qualifier, r1 = first round group

BURKINA FASO NATIONAL TEAM RECORDS AND RECORD SEQUENCES

Records			Sequence records					
Victory	4-0	MOZ 2003	Wins	6	1988	Clean sheets	6	2003
Defeat	0-7	ALG 1981	Defeats	10	1976-1981	Goals scored	24	1998-2000
Player Caps	n/a		Undefeated	7	1999	Without goal	4	Three times
Player Goals	n/a		Without win	13	1976-82, 1994-96	Goals against	13	1960-1967

BURKINA FASO COUNTRY INFORMATION

Capital	Ouagadougou	Independence	1960	GDP per Capita	$1 100
Population	13 574 820	Status	Republic	GNP Ranking	133
Area km²	274 200	Language	French	Dialling code	+226
Population density	49 per km²	Literacy rate	26%	Internet code	.bf
% in urban areas	27%	Main religion	Muslim 50%	GMT +/–	0
Towns/Cities ('000)	Ouagadougou 1 031; Bobo-Dioulasso 370; Koudougou 86; Banfora 63; Ouahigouya 61				
Neighbours (km)	Mali 1,000; Niger 628; Benin 306; Togo 126; Ghana 549; Côte d'Ivoire 584				
Main stadia	Stade du 4 Août – Ouagadougou 40 000; Stade Municipal – Bobo-Dioulasso 30 000				

BURKINA FASO 2005-06

PREMIERE DIVISION

	Pl	W	D	L	F	A	Pts	ASFA/Y	RCK	USO	EFO	USFA	CFO	RCB	USCO	ASEC-K	ASFB	SONABEL	Santos	USFRAN	JCB
ASFA/Yennenga †	26	16	5	5	43	16	53		2-0	0-0	**1-0**	2-1	2-1	2-0	1-2	1-0	2-0	2-0	2-0	3-0	2-0
Rail Club Kadiogo	26	16	4	6	39	22	52	4-1		0-3	**0-3**	1-2	2-0	1-1	1-0	2-0	0-0	3-1	2-1	2-0	3-0
US Ouagadougou	26	13	11	2	38	15	50	0-0	1-3		0-0	0-0	2-2	1-0	0-0	1-0	0-0	1-0	1-1	3-1	2-1
Etoile Filante	26	15	3	8	44	27	48	2-1	3-2	1-4		1-1	0-1	2-1	1-0	0-1	2-0	0-1	2-2	6-1	2-0
US Forces Armées	26	11	7	8	44	31	40	1-6	0-2	0-1	3-0		2-1	3-2	3-0	1-1	4-0	1-1	1-1	6-0	5-1
Commune FC	26	11	6	9	24	26	39	0-3	0-2	0-2	0-2	2-1		2-1	0-1	2-1	0-0	0-0	0-2	1-0	1-1
Racing Club B-D	26	8	11	7	26	19	35	2-0	0-0	0-0	0-1	2-1	1-2		2-0	1-0	0-0	1-1	3-1	1-0	0-0
US Comoé	26	8	11	7	21	22	35	0-0	1-0	0-0	0-2	0-0	0-1	1-1		2-1	0-0	1-0	0-0	0-0	3-1
ASEC Koudougou	26	9	6	11	19	24	33	1-0	1-2	0-2	2-1	1-0	0-1	1-1	1-1		1-0	1-0	1-1	1-0	1-0
ASF Bobo-Dioulasso	26	7	10	9	24	31	31	2-5	0-1	2-2	1-2	1-1	0-3	0-0	3-3	0-0		2-0	0-1	2-1	2-0
AS SONABEL	26	6	12	8	22	26	30	0-0	0-0	2-1	0-2	3-2	0-0	0-0	2-0	2-2	2-4		1-1	0-0	3-0
Santos	26	6	8	12	29	39	26	0-3	2-4	0-2	3-1	0-1	1-3	0-3	0-2	2-0	1-2	2-2		3-0	2-2
USFRAN	26	2	8	16	11	50	14	0-0	0-1	0-4	1-6	1-2	0-0	0-3	2-2	1-0	0-2	0-0	1-0		0-0
Jeunesse Club B-D	26	0	6	20	12	48	6	0-2	0-1	2-5	1-2	1-2	0-1	0-0	0-2	0-1	0-1	0-1	0-2	2-2	

17/12/2005 - 17/06/2006 • † Qualified for the CAF Champions League • Matches in bold were awarded • Top scorer: Moctar OUEDRAOGO, USFA, 15

COUPE NATIONALE DU FASO 2005-06

Round of 16	Quarter-finals	Semi-finals	Final
Etoile Filante			
	Etoile Filante 4		
	Rail Club Kadiogo 1		
Rail Club Kadiogo		Etoile Filante 2	
Centre Formation B-D		ASFA/Yennenga 1	
	Centre Formation B-D 1 1p		
	ASFA/Yennenga 1 2p		
ASFA/Yennenga			Etoile Filante ‡ 3
ASEC Koudougou			Racing Club B-D 2
	ASEC Koudougou 2		
	Secteur 21 B-D 1		
Secteur 21 B-D		ASEC Koudougou 0	
US Ouagadougou		Racing Club B-D 2	
	US Ouagadougou 2		
	Racing Club B-D 3		
Racing Club B-D			

CUP FINAL
Stade de 4 Août, Ouagadougou
30-07-2006
Scorers - Herve Oussale [80], Valery Sanou [103], Amadou Ousmane [110] for EFO; Oumarou Nebie [40], Youssouf Ouattarta [115] for RCB

* Home team • † Bye • ‡ Qualified for the CAF Confederation Cup

RECENT LEAGUE AND CUP RECORD

	Championship					Cup		
Year	Champions	Pts	Runners-up	Pts	Third	Pts	Winners	Score	Runners-up

Year	Champions	Pts	Runners-up	Pts	Third	Pts	Winners	Score	Runners-up
1990	Etoile Filante	64	ASFA Yennega	61	Rail Club Kadiogo	61	Etoile Filante	2-1	ASFA Yennega
1991	Etoile Filante	60	US Cheminots	52	Rail Club Kadiogo	51	ASFA Yennega		
1992	Etoile Filante	53	ASFA Yennega	53	AS Fonctionnaire	49	Etoile Filante	2-1	Rail Club Kadiogo
1993	Etoile Filante	55	Racing Club B-D	54	Rail Club Kadiogo	49	Etoile Filante	2-0	ASF Bobo-Dioulasso
1994	Etoile Filante						Rail Club Kadiogo	1-0	Racing Club B-D
1995	ASFA Yennega						Racing Club B-D		ASFA Yennega
1996	Racing Club B-D						Etoile Filante		
1997	Racing Club B-D						ASF Bobo-Dioulasso		
1998	US Forces Armées						ASF Bobo-Dioulasso	0-0 7-6p	US Forces Armées
1999	ASFA Yennega	53	Etoile Filante	47	US Forces Armées	43	Etoile Filante	3-2	US Forces Armées
2000	US Forces Armées	44	Etoile Filante	41	ASFA Yennega	39	Etoile Filante	3-1	US Ouagadougou
2001	Etoile Filante	51	ASFA Yennega	49	US Forces Armées	41	Etoile Filante	3-1	ASF Bobo-Dioulasso
2002	ASFA Yennega	49	US Forces Armées	44	Etoile Filante	39	US Forces Armées	2-0	ASF Bobo-Dioulasso
2003	ASFA Yennega	51	US Ouagadougou	47	Etoile Filante	45	Etoile Filante	0-0 5-4p	ASFA Yennega
2004	ASFA Yennega	43	US Ouagadougou	40	Etoile Filante	39	ASF Bobo-Dioulasso	0-0 3-2p	US Forces Armées
2005	Rail Club Kadiogo	57	US Ouagadougou	50	US Forces Armées	50	US Ouagadougou	2-0	ASF Bobo-Dioulasso
2006	ASFA Yennega	53	Rail Club Kadiogo	52	US Ouagadougou	50	Etoile Filante	3-2	Racing Club B-D

BHR – BAHRAIN

BAHRAIN NATIONAL TEAM RECORD
JULY 1ST 2002 TO JULY 9TH 2006

PL	W	D	L	F	A	%
65	26	19	20	108	83	54.6

FIFA/COCA-COLA WORLD RANKING

1993	1994	1995	1996	1997	1998	1999	2000	2001	2002	2003	2004	2005	2006	High		Low	
78	73	99	118	121	119	136	138	110	105	64	49	52		44	09/04	138	12/00

					2005–2006						
08/05	09/05	10/05	11/05	12/05	01/06	02/06	03/06	04/06	05/06	06/06	07/06
50	53	55	53	52	52	52	54	54	54	-	94

With the unprecedented fourth place finish at the AFC Asian Cup in China fresh in the mind, there was genuine hope in Bahrain that the national team could break their FIFA World Cup™ duck and qualify for the finals in Germany; and what's more they nearly did it. In the event though, they fell at the final hurdle having done the hard work. By finishing third in their second round group, Bahrain qualified to meet Uzbekistan in a play-off, where thanks to an error by the referee, an original 1-0 defeat in Tashkent was replayed to a draw, a result that ultimately saw Bahrain through to another play-off, this time against Trinidad. A 1-1 draw away in Trinidad seemed the ideal result

INTERNATIONAL HONOURS
Qualified for the AFC Asian Cup finals 1988 2004 Represented at the Asian Games 1974 1978 1986 1994 2002

to take back to Bahrain but a Dennis Lawrence header just after half-time saw Trinidad qualify instead, to the utter despair of the Bahraini fans. The failure to qualify cast a long shadow over the rest of the season and the national team got off to a poor start in the AFC Asian Cup qualifiers, losing to Australia. In the League there was a three horse race between Muharraq, Al Ahli and Riffa which was only decided on the last day when Muharraq won 1-0 against Setra to clinch their 28th title - 19 more than their nearest rivals Riffa. There was a new name on the Cup, however, after Al Najma beat Manama rivals Al Ahli 1-0 in the final.

THE FIFA BIG COUNT OF 2000

	Male	Female		Male	Female
Registered players	770	0	Referees	98	0
Non registered players	1 650	0	Officials	616	0
Youth players	2 970	0	Total involved	6 104	
Total players		5 390	Number of clubs	44	
Professional players	0	0	Number of teams	110	

Bahrain Football Association (BFA)
Bahrain National Stadium, PO Box 5464, Manama, Bahrain
Tel +973 17 689569   Fax +973 17 781188
bhrfa@batelco.com.bh   www.bahrainfootball.org
President: AL-KHALIFA Sheik Salman Bin Ibrahim   General Secretary: JASSEM Ahmed Mohammed
Vice-President: AL-KHALIFA Sheik Ali Bin Khalifa   Treasurer: AL NA'AMI Ahmed Abdulla   Media Officer: AL BASHA Ali Abdullah
Men's Coach: BRIEGEL Hans-Peter   Women's Coach: SHAMLAN Mohamed
BFA formed: 1957   AFC: 1970   FIFA: 1966
Red shirts with white trimmings, Red shorts, Red socks or White shirts with red trimmings, White shorts, White socks

RECENT INTERNATIONAL MATCHES PLAYED BY BAHRAIN

2004	Opponents	Score		Venue	Comp	Scorers	Att	Referee
9-06	Kyrgyzstan	W	5-0	Muharraq	WCq	Hubail.A 3 [12 45 60], Ali Ahmed.H [66], Duaij [82]	2 800	Al Saeedi UAE
5-07	Thailand	W	2-0	Bangkok	Fr	Hubail.A, Ali Ahmed.H		
10-07	Korea Republic	L	0-2	Gwangju	Fr		35 241	Fong HKG
17-07	China PR	D	2-2	Beijing	ACr1	Hubail.M [41], Ali Ahmed.H [89]	40 000	Mohd Salleh MAS
21-07	Qatar	D	1-1	Beijing	ACr1	Hubail.M [90]		Kamizawa JPN
25-07	Indonesia	W	3-1	Jinan	ACr1	Ali Ahmed.H [43], Hubail.A [57], Yousuf [82]	20 000	Codjia BEN
30-07	Uzbekistan	D	2-2	Chengdu	ACqf	Hubail.A 2 [71 76]	18 000	Kwon KOR
3-08	Japan	L	3-4	Jinan	ACsf	Hubail.A 2 [6 71], Duaij [85]		Maidin SIN
6-08	Iran	L	2-4	Beijing	AC3p	Yousuf [48], Farhan [57]		Al Marzouqi UAE
26-08	Kuwait	D	0-0	Muharraq	Fr			
2-09	Palestine	W	1-0	Muharraq	Fr	Hussain Ali [86]		
8-09	Kyrgyzstan	W	2-1	Bishkek	WCq	Hussain Ali [23], Hubail.M [58]	10 000	Rungklay THA
13-10	Syria	D	2-2	Damascus	WCq	Mahfoodh [27], Mohamed.T [90+2]	35 000	Moradi IRN
17-11	Tajikistan	W	4-0	Manama	WCq	Mohamed.T [9], Mohamed.H [40], Hubail.M 2 [42 77]	15 000	Sun CHN
1-12	Finland	L	1-2	Manama	Fr	Hussain Ali [6]	10 000	
3-12	Latvia	D	2-2	Manama	Fr	Mohammed.S [2], Hussain Ali [72]. W 4-2p	2 000	Al Hilali OMA
11-12	Yemen	D	1-1	Doha	GCr1	Yousuf [25]		
14-12	Kuwait	D	1-1	Doha	GCr1	Hussain Ali [45]		
17-12	Saudi Arabia	W	3-0	Doha	GCr1	Al Marzouki [54], Ghuloom [78], Yousef [90]		
20-12	Oman	L	2-3	Doha	GCsf	Jalal [51], Duaij [77]		
23-12	Kuwait	W	3-1	Doha	GC3p	Nada OG [31], Hubail.A [56], Duaij [90]		
2005	Opponents							
25-01	Norway	L	0-1	Manama	Fr			
2-02	Lebanon	W	2-1	Doha	Fr	Salem, Hussain Ali		
9-02	Iran	D	0-0	Manama	WCq		25 000	Mohd Salleh MAS
25-03	Korea DPR	W	2-1	Pyongyang	WCq	Hussain Ali 2 [7 58]	50 000	Rungklay THA
30-03	Japan	L	0-1	Saitama	WCq		67 549	Irmatov UZB
27-05	Saudi Arabia	D	1-1	Riyadh	Fr	Mahfoodh [18p]		
3-06	Japan	L	0-1	Manama	WCq		32 000	Mohd Salleh MAS
8-06	Iran	L	0-1	Tehran	WCq		80 000	Kwon Jong Chul KOR
3-08	Turkmenistan	W	5-0	Manama	Fr	Al Marzooki [7], Mahfoodh [35], Hussain Ali [63], Farhan [82p], Al Dakeel [84]		
7-08	Iraq	D	2-2	Manama	Fr	Mahfoodh [27], Hussain Ali [86]		
17-08	Korea DPR	L	2-3	Manama	WCq	Ghuloom [49], Hussain Ali [54]	3 000	Maidin SIN
8-10	Uzbekistan	D	1-1	Tashkent	WCpo	Mohamed.T [17]	55 000	Busacca SUI
12-10	Uzbekistan	D	0-0	Manama	WCpo		25 000	Poll ENG
27-10	Panama	W	5-0	Manama	Fr	Al Dakeel [44], Al Hejeri [82], Abbas [83], Al Marzooki [88], Mubarak [89]		
12-11	Trinidad and Tobago	D	1-1	Port of Spain	WCpo	Ghuloom [72]	24 991	Shield AUS
16-11	Trinidad and Tobago	L	0-1	Manama	WCpo		35 000	Ruiz COL
2006								
30-01	Syria	D	1-1	Manama	Fr	Fawzi Ayesh [60]		
16-02	Palestine	L	0-2	Muharraq	Fr			
22-02	Australia	L	1-3	Manama	ACq	Hussain Ali [35]	2 500	Mohd Salleh MAS
1-03	Kuwait	D	0-0	Kuwait City	ACq		16 000	Moradi IRN

Fr = Friendly match • AR = Arab Cup • AC = AFC Asian Cup • GC = Gulf Cup • WC = FIFA World Cup™
q = qualifier • r1 = first round group • qf = quarter-final • sf = semi-final • f = final • 3p = third place play-off

BAHRAIN NATIONAL TEAM RECORDS AND RECORD SEQUENCES

Records			Sequence records		
Victory	6-0	SRI 1991	Wins	5	2001
			Clean sheets	5	1988
Defeat	1-10	IRQ 1966	Defeats	9	1974-1975
			Goals scored	11	2004
Player Caps	n/a		Undefeated	6	1993, 2001
			Without goal	7	1988-1990
Player Goals	n/a		Without win	12	1988-1990
			Goals against	12	1974-1976

BAHRAIN COUNTRY INFORMATION

Capital	Manama	Independence	1971	GDP per Capita	$16 900
Population	677 886	Status	Kingdom	GNP Ranking	101
Area km²	665	Language	Arabic	Dialling code	+973
Population density	1 019 per km²	Literacy rate	89%	Internet code	.bh
% in urban areas	90%	Main religion	Muslim 100%	GMT + / –	+3
Towns/Cities ('000)	Manama 147; Al-Muharraq 97; Al-Riffa 94; Madinat 65; Al-Wusta 51; Ali 55; Issa 38				
Neighbours (km)	Persian Gulf 161				
Main stadia	National Stadium – Manama 30 000; Issa Town – Issa 20 000; Al Muharraq – Muharraq 10 000				

BAHRAIN 2005–06

FIRST DIVISION

	Pl	W	D	L	F	A	Pts	Muharraq	Ahli	Riffa	Najma	Setra	Malikiya	East Riffa	Busaiteen	Shabab	Bahrain
Muharraq †	18	11	5	2	29	17	38		1-1	1-3	1-0	2-1	2-0	2-0	0-0	2-2
Al Ahli	18	10	7	1	47	20	37	1-1		1-3	2-2	2-2	4-2	2-2	3-1	8-0	5-0
Riffa	18	9	6	3	36	17	33	0-0	2-3		3-1	3-0	0-0	4-1	0-1	1-1	5-0
Al Najma	18	7	4	7	29	28	25	1-2	2-4	1-1		2-4	2-1	1-0	1-2	2-1	0-0
Setra	18	6	4	8	25	33	22	1-3	1-4	2-1	0-2		1-2	2-2	0-0	1-2	3-2
Malikiya	18	5	5	8	27	23	20	0-1	0-0	1-2	2-3	4-0		1-1	1-1	4-0	0-1
East Riffa	18	5	5	8	29	36	20	1-3	0-1	0-4	3-1	1-1	1-1		3-1	0-1	5-4
Busaiteen	18	5	5	8	19	29	20	1-2	1-1	2-2	1-4	0-2	2-1	1-4		2-2	2-0
Al Shabab	18	5	3	10	21	39	18	2-5	0-1	1-5	2-1	2-3	0-1	3-4	0-1		2-0
Bahrain Club	18	3	4	11	16	36	13	0-1	0-4	1-1	0-0	0-2	2-5	3-1	1-0	0-2	

7/10/2005 - 15/04/2006 • † Qualified for the AFC Cup • Play-off: **Al Shabab** 4-2 3-0 Manama

BAHRAIN 2005–06 SECOND DIVISION

	Pl	W	D	L	F	A	Pts
Al Hala	14	11	3	0	35	9	36
Manama	14	10	3	1	26	6	33
Al Sahel	14	5	4	4	16	14	19
Essa Town	14	4	5	4	12	11	17
Al Ittihad	14	2	6	5	8	18	12
Al Ittifaq	14	2	5	6	9	16	11
Al Tadamun	14	1	6	7	9	22	9
Budaia	14	0	6	8	4	23	6

17/10/2005 - 8/05/2006

KINGS CUP 2006

Quarter-finals		Semi-finals		Final	
Al Najma	2				
Busaiteen	0	**Al Najma**	2		
Al Shabab	3	Al Hala	1		
Al Hala	5			**Al Najma**	1
Muharraq	2			Al Ahli	0
East Riffa	1	Muharraq	1		
Riffa	1	**Al Ahli**	3	26-05-2006
Al Ahli	2			Scorer - Rashed Jamal 25

CROWN PRINCE CUP 2005

Semi-finals		Final	
Muharraq	2		
Al Najma	1	**Muharraq**	2
Al Ahli	1	Riffa	1
Riffa	2	21-05-2006

Played between the top four in the League

FA CUP 2005

Semi-finals		Final	
Muharraq	4		
Al Ahli	2	**Muharraq**	2
Bahrain Club	1	Busaiteen	1
Busaiteen	3	22-12-2005

The first round consisted of three groups of six teams

RECENT LEAGUE AND CUP RECORD

	Championship						King's Cup		
Year	Champions	Pts	Runners-up	Pts	Third	Pts	Winners	Score	Runners-up
1998	West Riffa	45	Muharraq	38	East Riffa	36	West Riffa	2-1	Budaia
1999	Muharraq	39	Al Ahli	30	West Riffa	28	East Riffa	1-0	Al-Hala
2000	West Riffa	4-0	East Riffa				East Riffa	3-1	Qadisiya
2001	Muharraq	52	Besaiteen	45	West Riffa	40	Al Ahli	1-0	Essa Town
2002	Muharraq	46	Al Ahli	46	Riffa	36	Muharraq	0-0 4-2p	Al Ahli
2003	Riffa	40	Muharraq	34	Al Ahli	32	Al Ahli	2-1	Muharraq
2004	Muharraq	48	Riffa	36	Al Ahli	30	Al Shabab	2-1	Busaiteen
2005	Riffa	40	Muharraq	36	Al Ahli	33	Muharraq	1-0	Al Shabab
2006	Muharraq	38	Al Ahli	37	Riffa	33	Al Najma	1-0	Al Ahli

BHU – BHUTAN

NATIONAL TEAM RECORD
JULY 1ST 2002 TO JULY 9TH 2006

PL	W	D	L	F	A	%
17	1	2	14	7	49	11.8

FIFA/COCA-COLA WORLD RANKING

1993	1994	1995	1996	1997	1998	1999	2000	2001	2002	2003	2004	2005	High		Low	
-	-	-	-	-	-	-	201	202	199	187	187	190	187	12/03	202	05/01

2005–2006											
08/05	09/05	10/05	11/05	12/05	01/06	02/06	03/06	04/06	05/06	06/06	07/06
189	189	189	189	190	190	190	190	190	190	-	187

A busy year by Bhutan standards saw the national team end an 11-match losing streak when they drew 0-0 with Brunei in the inaugural AFC Challenge Cup in Bangladesh. It was the second tournament entered in the space of five months, but in both, Bhutan finished bottom of their first round group. There was just one goal to celebrate - by striker Bikash Pradhan in a 1-3 defeat at the hands of Nepal in the South Asian Federation Cup in Pakistan in December. With the advent of the AFC Challenge Cup for the 'emerging nations' within Asia, Bhutan did not enter the AFC Asian Cup and so as one of the few nations that didn't enter the FIFA World Cup™ Bhutan have

INTERNATIONAL HONOURS
None

effectively taken themselves out of the top echelon of world competition. As such there are unlikely to be any repeats of the 20-0 defeat suffered at the hands of Kuwait in 2000. There were also welcome developments in club football in Bhutan when 2004 champions Transport United entered the inaugural AFC President's Cup, the first time any club from Bhutan had taken part in official continental competition. Three first round defeats in the tournament held in Nepal were not surprising but there were no embarrassing scorelines. Encouraged by their efforts, Transport United went on to defend their domestic title, edging out Druk Pol and Yedzin by a point in the final table.

THE FIFA BIG COUNT OF 2000

	Male	Female		Male	Female
Registered players	500	0	Referees	50	0
Non registered players	1 000	0	Officials	100	0
Youth players	500	0	Total involved	2 150	
Total players	2 000		Number of clubs	30	
Professional players	0	0	Number of teams	60	

Bhutan Football Federation (BFF)
PO Box 365, Thimphu, Bhutan
Tel +975 2 322350   Fax +975 2 321131
bff@druknet.net.bt   www.none
President: WANGCHUK Lyonpo Khandu HE   General Secretary: WANGCHUK Ugyen
Vice-President: TSHERING Dasho Gyom   Treasurer: DORJI B.T.   Media Officer: None
Men's Coach: BASNET Khare   Women's Coach: None
BFF formed: 1983   AFC: 1993   FIFA: 2000
Yellow shirts with red trimmings, Yellow shorts, Yellow socks or Red shirts with yellow trimmings, Red shorts, Red socks

RECENT INTERNATIONAL MATCHES PLAYED BY BHUTAN

2002	Opponents	Score		Venue	Comp	Scorers	Att	Referee
No international matches played in 2002 after June								
2003								
11-01	Maldives	L	0-6	Dhaka	SAr1			Vidanagamage SRI
13-01	Nepal	L	0-2	Dhaka	SAr1		25 000	Magheshwaran IND
15-01	Bangladesh	L	0-3	Dhaka	SAr1		15 000	Magheshwaran IND
23-04	Guam	W	6-0	Thimphu	ACq	Wangay Dorji 2 [31] [33], Dinesh Chetri [59], Passang Tshering [76p], Pema Chophel [88] Yeshey Nedup [89]		
27-04	Mongolia	D	0-0	Thimphu	ACq			
6-10	Indonesia	L	0-2	Jeddah	ACq			
8-10	Saudi Arabia	L	0-6	Jeddah	ACq			
10-10	Yemen	L	0-8	Jeddah	ACq			
13-10	Indonesia	L	0-2	Jeddah	ACq			
15-10	Saudi Arabia	L	0-4	Jeddah	ACq			
17-10	Yemen	L	0-4	Jeddah	ACq			
2004								
No international matches played in 2004								
2005								
8-12	Bangladesh	L	0-3	Karachi	SAr1			
10-12	India	L	0-3	Karachi	SAr1			
12-12	Nepal	L	1-3	Karachi	SAr1	Pradhan [47]		
2006								
2-04	Nepal	L	0-2	Chittagong	CCr1		3 500	Gosh BAN
4-04	Sri Lanka	L	0-1	Chittagong	CCr1			Saidov UZB
6-04	Brunei Darussalam	D	0-0	Chittagong	CCr1		2 000	Al Ghatrifi OMA

SAF = South Asian Football Federation Cup • AC = AFC Asian Cup • CC = AFC Challenge Cup • q = qualifier • r1 = first round group

BHUTAN NATIONAL TEAM RECORDS AND RECORD SEQUENCES

Records			Sequence records					
Victory	6-0	GUM 2003	Wins	1		Clean sheets	2	2003
Defeat	0-20	KUW 2000	Defeats	15	1984-2001	Goals scored	3	2000-2002
Player Caps	n/a		Undefeated	2	2003	Without goal	9	2003-2005
Player Goals	n/a		Without win	15	1984-2001	Goals against	15	1984-2001

RECENT LEAGUE AND CUP RECORD

	Championship		Cup
Year	Champions		Winners
2001	Druk Pol		No tournament played
2002	Druk Star		No tournament played
2003	Druk Pol		No tournament played
2004	Transport United		Druk Pol
2005	Transport United		Druk Pol

BHUTAN COUNTRY INFORMATION

Capital	Thimphu	Independence	1949	GDP per Capita	$1 300
Population	2 185 569	Status	Kingdom	GNP Ranking	170
Area km²	47 000	Language	Dzongkha	Dialling code	+975
Population density	46 per km²	Literacy rate	44%	Internet code	.bt
% in urban areas	6%	Main religion	Buddhist 70%	GMT +/–	+6
Towns/Cities ('000)	Thimphu 66; Phuntsholing 65; Punakha 18; Samdrup Jongkhar 14; Geylegphug 7; Jakar 4				
Neighbours (km)	China 470; India 605				
Main stadia	Changlimithang – Thimphu 15 000; PSA Phuntsholing – Phuntsholing 6 000				

BIH – BOSNIA-HERZEGOVINA

NATIONAL TEAM RECORD
JULY 1ST 2002 TO JULY 9TH 2006

PL	W	D	L	F	A	%
30	10	9	11	31	37	48.3

FIFA/COCA-COLA WORLD RANKING

1993	1994	1995	1996	1997	1998	1999	2000	2001	2002	2003	2004	2005		High		Low
-	-	-	152	99	96	75	78	69	87	59	79	65		**43**	07/06	**173** 09/96

2005–2006											
08/05	09/05	10/05	11/05	12/05	01/06	02/06	03/06	04/06	05/06	06/06	07/06
78	67	69	65	65	64	65	64	63	63	-	43

It was another encouraging year all round for football in Bosnia-Herzegovina, most notably with the national team putting in a spirited effort to qualify for the FIFA World Cup™ finals. In the event they finished third in their group, tucked in just behind Serbia and Spain. Defending champions Greece, Turkey and Norway will be the teams to beat in the UEFA Euro 2008™ qualifiers if Bosnia are to qualify for a final tournament for the first time. However, with many of the established stars now the wrong side of 30, coach Blaz Sliskovic's main task will be to blend the old with the new. There was also an encouraging run by Siroki Brijeg in the UEFA Cup, with wins

INTERNATIONAL HONOURS
None

over Albania's Teuta and Serbia's Zeta, before they bowed out to FC Basel in the first round proper. Neither Zepce or Zrinjski managed to get past the first preliminary round of either the UEFA Cup or Champions League respectively. It was a good year all round for Siroki Brijeg with a second Championship in three years, won with relative ease from Sarajevo and defending champions Zrinjski, and they came close to achieving the double. In the Cup Final against Orasje they drew the first leg 0-0 at home but then lost the second leg 3-0. That meant a first trophy for the small northern town of Orasje on the tenth anniversary of the formation of their club.

THE FIFA BIG COUNT OF 2000

	Male	Female		Male	Female
Registered players	12 290	162	Referees	776	0
Non registered players	37 000	800	Officials	11 990	510
Youth players	30 430	109	Total involved	94 067	
Total players	80 791		Number of clubs	775	
Professional players	420	0	Number of teams	1 980	

Football Federation of Bosnia-Herzegovina (FFBH/NSBiH)
Nogometni/Fudbalski Savez Bosne i Hercegovine, Ferhadija 30, Sarajevo - 71000, Bosnia-Herzegovina
Tel +387 33 276660   Fax +387 33 444332
nsbih@bih.net.ba   www.nfsbih.ba
President: DOMINKOVIC Iljo   General Secretary: USANOVIC Munib
Vice-President: COLAKOVIC Sulejman   Treasurer: KURES Miodrag   Media Officer: PECIKOZA Slavica
Men's Coach: SLISKOVIC Blaz   Women's Coach: BEKIC Dzevad
FFBH formed: 1992   UEFA: 1996   FIFA: 1996
White shirts with blue trimmings, Blue shorts, White socks or Blue shirts with white trimmings, White shorts, Blue socks

RECENT INTERNATIONAL MATCHES PLAYED BY BOSNIA-HERZEGOVINA

2002 Opponents		Score	Venue	Comp	Scorers	Att	Referee
21-08 Yugoslavia	L	0-2	Sarajevo	Fr		9 000	Siric CRO
7-09 Romania	L	0-3	Sarajevo	ECq		4 000	Batista POR
11-10 Germany	D	1-1	Sarajevo	Fr	Baljic [21]	5 000	De Santis ITA
16-10 Norway	L	0-2	Oslo	ECq		24 169	Benes CZE
2003							
12-02 Wales	D	2-2	Cardiff	Fr	Baljic [5], Barbarez [64]	25 000	Malcolm NIR
29-03 Luxembourg	W	2-0	Zenica	ECq	Bolic [53], Barbarez [79]	10 000	Hyytia FIN
2-04 Denmark	W	2-0	Copenhagen	ECq	Barbarez [23], Baljic [29]	30 845	Stredak SVK
7-06 Romania	L	0-2	Craiova	ECq		36 000	Bossen NED
6-09 Norway	W	1-0	Zenica	ECq	Bajramovic [86]	18 000	Bre FRA
10-09 Luxembourg	W	1-0	Luxembourg	ECq	Barbarez [36]	3 500	Kapitanis CYP
11-10 Denmark	D	1-1	Sarajevo	ECq	Bolic [39]	35 500	Barber ENG
2004							
18-02 Macedonia FYR	L	0-1	Skopje	Fr		8 000	Vrajkov BUL
31-03 Luxembourg	W	2-1	Luxembourg	Fr	Misimovic [63], Bolic [71]	2 000	Rogalla SUI
28-04 Finland	W	1-0	Zenica	Fr	Misimovic [88]	20 000	Bozinovski MKD
18-08 France	D	1-1	Rennes	Fr	Grlic [37]	26 527	McDonald SCO
8-09 Spain	D	1-1	Zenica	WCq	Bolic [79]	14 380	De Santis ITA
9-10 Serbia & Montenegro	D	0-0	Sarajevo	WCq		22 440	Veissiere FRA
2005							
2-02 Iran	L	1-2	Tehran	Fr	Bolic [17]	15 000	
26-03 Belgium	L	1-4	Brussels	WCq	Bolic [1]	36 700	Hrinak SVK
30-03 Lithuania	D	1-1	Sarajevo	WCq	Misimovic [21]	6 000	Baskakov RUS
4-06 San Marino	W	3-1	Serravalle	WCq	Salihamidzic 2 [17 38], Barbarez [75]	750	Demirlek TUR
8-06 Spain	D	1-1	Valencia	WCq	Misimovic [39]	38 041	Bennett ENG
17-08 Estonia	L	0-1	Tallinn	Fr		4 000	Fojdfeldt SWE
3-09 Belgium	W	1-0	Zenica	WCq	Barbarez [62]	12 000	Benquerenca POR
7-09 Lithuania	W	1-0	Vilnius	WCq	Barbarez [28]	4 000	Kassai HUN
8-10 San Marino	W	3-0	Zenica	WCq	Bolic 3 [46 75 82]	8 500	Hamer LUX
12-10 Serbia & Montenegro	L	0-1	Belgrade	WCq		46 305	Vassaras GRE
2006							
28-02 Japan	D	2-2	Dortmund	Fr	Misimovic [56p], Spahic [67]	10 000	Wack GER
26-05 Korea Republic	L	0-2	Seoul	Fr		64 836	Cheung Yim Yau HKG
31-05 Iran	L	2-5	Tehran	Fr	Misimovic [4], Barbarez [17]		Mohd Salleh MAS

Fr = Friendly match • EC = UEFA EURO 2004™ • WC = FIFA World Cup™ • q = qualifier

BOSNIA-HERZEGOVINA NATIONAL TEAM RECORDS AND RECORD SEQUENCES

Records				Sequence records				
Victory	5-0	LIE 2001	Wins	3	1999-2000, 2005	Clean sheets	3	2005
Defeat	0-5	ARG 1998	Defeats	3	Four times	Goals scored	10	1998-1999
Player Caps	51	BOLIC Elvir	Undefeated	4	1997, 2004	Without goal	3	Three times
Player Goals	22	BOLIC Elvir	Without win	7	2002-2003	Goals against	7	2002-2003

BOSNIA-HERZEGOVINA COUNTRY INFORMATION

Capital	Sarajevo	Independence	1992	GDP per Capita	$6 100
Population	4 007 608	Status	Republic	GNP Ranking	114
Area km²	51 129	Language	Bosnian, Croatian, Serbian	Dialling code	+387
Population density	78 per km²	Literacy rate	93%	Internet code	.ba
% in urban areas	49%	Main religion	Christian 46%, Muslim 40%	GMT + / −	+1
Towns/Cities ('000)	Sarajevo 696; Banja Luka 221; Zenica 164; Tuzla 142; Mostar 104; Bihac 75; Bugojno 41; Brcko 38; Bijeljina 37; Prijedor 36, Trebinje 33; Travnik 31; Doboj 27; Cazin 21;				
Neighbours (km)	Croatia 932; Serbia and Montenegro 527; Adriatic Sea 20				
Main stadia	Olimpijski Kosevo – Sarajevo 37 500; Bijeli Brijeg – Mostar 20 000				

BOSNIA-HERZEGOVINA NATIONAL TEAM PLAYERS AND COACHES

Record Caps			Record Goals			Recent Coaches	
BOLIC Elvir	1996-'05	51	BOLIC Elvir	1996-'05	22	MUZUROVIC Fuad	1995-'98
BARBAREZ Sergej	1998-'06	44	BARBAREZ Sergej	1998-'06	15	MUSOVIC Dzemaludin	1998-'99
SALIHAMIDZIC Hasan	1996-'05	42	BALJIC Elvir	1996-'05	14	HADZIBEGIC Faruk	1999
MUSIC Vedin	1995-'06	39	SALIHAMIDZIC Hasan	1996-'05	6	SMAJLOVIC Drago	1999-'01
BALJIC Elvir	1996-'05	39	MISIMOVIC Zvjezdan	2004-'06	5	SLISKOVIC Blaz	2002-
KONJIC Muhamed	1995-'04	38	KODRO Meho	1996-'00	3		
HIBIC Mirsad	1997-'04	36	KONJIC Muhamed	1995-'04	3		
SABIC Nermin	1996-'04	32					
BESLIJA Mirsad	2001-'06	27					

CLUB DIRECTORY

Club	Town/City	Stadium	Capacity	www.	Lge	Cup
FK Buducnost	Banovici	Gradski	5 000	buducnost.net	0	0
NK Celik	Zenica	Bilino Polje	16 000		3	2
NK Jedinstvo	Bihac	Jedinstvo	10 000		0	0
FK Leotar	Trebinje	Police	8 500		1	0
FK Modrica Maxima	Modrica	Modrica	2 500		0	1
NK Orasje	Orasje	Goal	3 000		0	1
NK Posusje	Posusje	Mokri Dolac	4 000	nkposusje.com	0	0
FK Radnik	Bijeljina	Gradski	5 000		0	0
FK Sarajevo	Sarajevo	Olimpijski Kosevo	37 500	fcsarajevo.com	0 - 2 †	4
NK Siroki Brijeg	Siroki Brijeg	Pecara	6 000	nk-siroki.brijeg.com	1	0
FK Slavija	Sarajevo-Lukavica	Slavija Lukavica	5 000		0	0
FK Sloboda	Tuzla	Tusanj	7 000	fcsloboda.com	0	0
NK Travnik	Travnik	Pirota	3 500	nktravnik.com.ba	0	0
FK Zeljeznicar	Sarajevo	Grbavica	15 000	nk.zeljeznicar.co.ba	3 - 1 ‡	3
NK Zepce	Zepce	Zepce	2 000	nk_zepce.com	0	0
NK Zrinjski	Mostar	Bijeli brijeg	10 000	zrinjski.max.net.ba	1	0

† Sarajevo won two championships in the former Yugoslavia • ‡ Zeljeznicar won one championship in the former Yugoslavia

RECENT LEAGUE AND CUP RECORD

	Championship						Cup		
Year	Champions	Pts	Runners-up	Pts	Third	Pts	Winners	Score	Runners-up
1995	Celik Zenica	9	Sarajevo	4	Bosna Visoko	3	Celik Zenica		
1996	Celik Zenica	68	Lukavac	64	Sloboda Tuzla	63	Celik Zenica	2-1	Sloboda Tuzla
1997	Celik Zenica	58	Sarajevo	56	Bosna Visoko	54	Sarajevo	2-0	Zeljeznicar
1998	Zeljeznicar	1-0	Sarajevo				Sarajevo	1-0	Sloboda Tuzla
1999	No overall winner	†					Bosna Visoko	1-0	Sarajevo
2000	Brotnjo Citluk	‡	Buducnost Banovici				Zeljeznicar	3-1	Sloboda Tuzla
2001	Zeljeznicar	91	Brotnjo Citluk	84	Sarajevo	81	Zeljeznicar	3-2	Sarajevo
2002	Zeljeznicar	62	Siroki Brijeg	51	Brotnjo Citluk	47	Sarajevo	2-1	Zeljeznicar
2003	Leotar Trebinje	85	Zeljeznicar	82	Sarajevo	69	Zeljeznicar	0-0 2-0	Leotar Trebinje
2004	Siroki Brijeg	61	Zeljeznicar	59	Sarajevo	56	Modrica Maksima	1-1 4-2p	Borac Banja Luka
2005	Zrinjski Mostar	61	Zeljeznicar	51	Siroki Brijeg	45	Sarajevo	1-0 1-1	Siroki Brijeg
2006	Siroki Brijeg	63	Sarajevo	60	Zrinjski Mostar	54	Orasje	0-0 3-0	Siroki Brijeg

From 1995 to 1997 the NSBiH controlled only the Muslim league • From 1998 to 2000 the winners of the Muslim and Croat leagues took part in a play-off • From 2001 to 2002 there was a combined Muslim and Croat league • Since 2003 with the inclusion of the Serbian league there has been a unified structure in the country • † Sarajevo and Posusje, the winners of the Muslim and Croat league did not play-off for the national title • ‡ Brotnjo won on away goals after 1-1 0-0 draws

BOSNIA-HERZEGOVINA 2005-06

PREMIJER LIGA

	Pl	W	D	L	F	A	Pts	Siroki	Sarajevo	Zrinjski	Modrica	Slavija	Zeljeznicar	Jedinstvo	Zepce	Leotar	Posusje	Sloboda	Orasje	Radnik	Celik	Travnik	Buducnost
Siroki Brijeg †	30	19	6	5	38	19	63		2-1	1-0	2-1	3-0	2-0	1-0	0-1	3-0	1-1	1-0	2-1	2-1	2-0	3-0	1-0
Sarajevo ‡	30	18	6	6	57	26	60	3-0		1-0	2-1	1-1	0-0	2-0	2-0	1-0	3-0	2-0	5-1	4-1	6-1	3-0	2-1
Zrinjski Mostar	30	17	3	10	47	29	54	0-0	3-1		1-0	3-0	1-1	2-0	2-1	1-0	1-0	4-1	1-0	4-0	2-1	3-1	2-0
Modrica Maxima	30	17	2	11	53	30	53	1-0	2-0	3-0		1-0	1-1	3-2	4-0	2-1	1-0	2-0	1-3	4-1	1-0	4-0	4-1
Slavija Istocno Sarajevo	30	12	5	13	41	47	41	1-1	1-1	2-1	3-1		1-4	0-1	1-0	1-0	4-0	1-0	3-0	0-0	2-1	3-2	3-0
Zeljeznicar Sarajevo	30	11	7	12	38	33	40	0-1	0-1	3-1	1-2	4-2		2-1	2-1	0-2	3-0	5-1	2-1	0-0	0-0	1-0	3-1
Jedinstvo Bihac	30	13	1	16	38	40	40	0-2	1-0	1-3	1-3	5-0	2-0		3-0	2-1	3-0	2-1	2-0	2-0	4-1	1-0	2-0
Zepce Limorad	30	11	7	12	29	40	40	0-0	1-3	2-0	0-0	1-1	3-1	1-0		2-0	1-0	0-0	1-3	1-0	1-0	1-0	2-1
Leotar Trebinje	30	12	3	15	43	48	39	3-1	1-1	2-1	2-1	3-2	1-0	2-0	5-1		5-2	1-0	4-2	1-3	1-0	1-1	1-3
Posusje	30	12	3	15	38	46	39	1-2	0-1	2-1	2-0	4-1	1-0	1-1	4-1	4-2		3-2	1-0	0-0	3-0	1-0	1-0
Sloboda Tuzla	30	11	6	13	31	40	39	0-0	1-3	2-1	0-4	1-0	1-1	3-1	1-0	3-2			0-0	3-0	3-0	1-0	3-0
Orasje	30	12	2	16	50	51	38	1-3	1-1	1-2	1-0	4-1	1-0	4-1	2-0	3-0	2-3	4-1		6-1	3-2	3-0	1-0
Radnik Bijeljina	30	11	5	14	37	52	38	0-1	0-3	1-3	5-4	1-0	3-1	3-0	1-1	2-1	4-1	0-0	1-0		3-0	2-1	2-0
Celik Zenica	30	10	5	15	33	45	35	2-0	2-1	0-2	1-0	1-4	0-0	3-0	1-1	3-1	2-1	0-0	4-1	1-0		1-1	3-0
Travnik	30	10	4	16	33	41	34	0-1	2-0	0-0	1-0	2-0	0-2	2-0	1-1	3-1	1-0	2-0	4-2	3-2	0-2		5-0
Buducnost Banovici	30	10	3	17	29	48	33	0-0	3-3	1-0	1-0	1-3	2-1	1-0	0-2	1-1	0-1	3-1	5-0	2-1	1-0		

6/08/2005 - 13/05/2006 • † Qualified for the UEFA Champions League • ‡ Qualified for the UEFA Cup
Top scorers: Petar JELIC, Modrica, 19; Damir TOSUNOVIC, Orasje, 12; Mirza MESIC, Zepce, 12; Domagoj ABRAMOVIC, Siroki Brijeg, 11

BOSNIA 2005-06 PRVA LIGA FBIH (2)

	Pl	W	D	L	F	A	Pts
Velez Mostar	30	19	7	4	52	21	64
Rudar Kakanj	30	15	5	10	48	27	50
Brotnjo Citluk	30	15	3	12	58	33	48
MIS Kresevo	30	15	3	12	42	41	48
SASK Napredak	30	14	5	11	38	23	47
Troglav Livno	30	13	8	9	45	42	47
Gradina Srebrenik	30	14	4	12	56	39	46
GOSK Gabela	30	14	4	12	37	29	46
Bosna Visoko	30	14	4	12	39	38	46
Mramor	30	15	1	14	30	37	46
Radnicki Lukavac	30	14	3	13	29	29	45
Vitez FIS	30	12	7	11	33	33	43
Iskra Bugojno	30	12	6	12	36	34	42
Podgrmec Sanski Most	30	9	4	17	31	51	31
Olimpik Sarajevo	30	6	7	17	28	48	25
Ljubuski	30	3	1	26	9	86	10

6/08/2005 - 13/05/2006

BOSNIA 2005-06 PRVA LIGA FBIH (2)

	Pl	W	D	L	F	A	Pts
Borac Banja Luka	30	19	5	6	50	19	62
Ljubic Prnjavor	30	16	5	9	45	28	53
Drina Zvornik	30	15	5	10	39	28	50
Kozara Gradiska	30	14	5	11	37	33	47
BSK Crni Djordje	30	14	5	11	34	36	47
Rudar Prijedor	30	14	2	14	36	39	44
Rudar Ugljevik	30	12	7	11	40	34	43
Sloga Doboj	30	13	4	13	37	31	43
Glasinac Sokolac	30	12	7	11	32	28	43
Mladost Gacko	30	14	1	15	39	43	43
Jedinstvo Brcko	30	11	7	12	38	38	40
Sloboda Novi Grad	30	11	6	13	36	49	40
Famos Vojkoviei	30	11	6	13	32	35	39
Laktasi	30	12	3	15	44	49	39
Sloga Trn	30	9	7	14	27	37	34
Nikos Kanbera	30	4	4	22	18	57	16

6/08/2005 - 13/05/2006

KUP BIH 2005-06

Round of sixteen

Orasje *	2	0
Buducnost Banovici	1	0
Zrinjski Mostar *	3	0
Modrica Maxima	1	2
MIS Kresevo	3	0
Igman Konjic	0	1
Posusje *	0	0
Zepce Limorad	0	1
Zeljeznicar *	2	0
Rudar Ugljevik	0	1
Borac Banja Luka	0	1
Sarajevo *	4	3
Slavija Istocno Sarajevo	1	4
SASK Napredak *	0	0
Rudar Kakanj	0	1
Siroki Brijeg *	2	0

Quarter-finals

Orasje	5	1
Modrica Maxima *	0	1
MIS Kresevo	0	2
Zepce Limorad *	1	2
Zeljeznicar	1	†
Sarajevo *	1	†
Slavija Istocno Sarajevo	0	1
Siroki Brijeg *	4	1

Semi-finals

Orasje *	2	1
Zepce Limorad	1	1
Zeljeznicar *	1	0
Siroki Brijeg	0	2

Final

Orasje ‡	0	3
Siroki Brijeg	0	0

CUP FINAL
1st leg. 19-04-2006
2nd leg. 3-05-2006
Scorers - Pejic 2 [54] [90], Kobas [79] for Orasje

† Sarajevo expelled from Cup
* Home team in the 1st leg • ‡ Qualified for the UEFA Cup

BLR – BELARUS

NATIONAL TEAM RECORD
JULY 1ST 2002 TO JULY 9TH 2006

PL	W	D	L	F	A	%
37	15	7	15	53	56	50

FIFA/COCA-COLA WORLD RANKING

1993	1994	1995	1996	1997	1998	1999	2000	2001	2002	2003	2004	2005		High	Low
137	121	88	90	110	104	95	96	85	74	90	69	61		**59** 11/05	**142** 07/94

2005–2006											
08/05	09/05	10/05	11/05	12/05	01/06	02/06	03/06	04/06	05/06	06/06	07/06
61	71	70	59	61	61	63	63	64	65	-	73

It proved to be a very disappointing FIFA World Cup™ qualifying campaign for Belarus after they had shown some promise at the start. A defeat at the hands of Moldova in Chisinau was followed shortly after by a 1-0 win against a resurgent Scotland at Hampden Park, but the team still finished one off the bottom of the qualifying group. If coach Anatoly Baidachny can instil some consistency into the team, their UEFA Euro 2008™ qualifying group does offer the potential to challenge for a place in the finals. One team in Belarus that didn't suffer from inconsistency were first time champions Shakhtyor Soligorsk, a team with the backing of the state oil company. Their title was

INTERNATIONAL HONOURS
None

never really in doubt and they remained undefeated for the first 24 games of the Championship. Their run finally came to an end against defending champions Dinamo Minsk in the penultimate game of the season - a Sergei Pavlyukovich goal seven minutes from time ending their dream of becoming the first team to go through a season unbeaten. With the Cup Final played in the June of the following year, Shakhter had to wait to see if they could do the double and although they reached the final, their hopes were dashed by two extra time goals in a 3-1 defeat by BATE Borisov, winners of the Cup for the first time.

THE FIFA BIG COUNT OF 2000

	Male	Female		Male	Female
Registered players	7 880	286	Referees	1 032	10
Non registered players	110 000	94	Officials	1 090	48
Youth players	11 550	100	Total involved	132 090	
Total players	129 910		Number of clubs	80	
Professional players	1 380	106	Number of teams	418	

Belarus Football Federation (BFF)
Prospekt Pobeditelei 20/3 Minsk 222 020, Belarus
Tel +375 172 545600   Fax +375 172 544483
info@bff.by   www.bff.by
President: NEVYGLAS Gennady   General Secretary: DMITRANITSA Leonid
Vice-President: VERGEENKO Mikhail   Treasurer: KOLTOVICH Valentina   Media Officer: LESHCHIK Alexander
Men's Coach: PUNTUS Yuri   Women's Coach: VOLOKH Oleg
BFF formed: 1989   UEFA: 1993   FIFA: 1992
Red shirts with green trimmings, Green shorts, Red socks or White shirts, White shorts, White socks

RECENT INTERNATIONAL MATCHES PLAYED BY BELARUS

2002	Opponents	Score	Venue	Comp	Scorers	Att	Referee
21-08	Latvia	W 4-2	Riga	Fr	Kutuzov [16], Kulchy [30], Romaschenko.Ma 2 [64 86]	4 200	Kaasik EST
7-09	Holland	L 0-3	Eindhoven	ECq		34 000	Barber ENG
12-10	Austria	L 0-2	Minsk	ECq		15 000	Poulat FRA
16-10	Czech Republic	L 0-2	Teplice	ECq		12 850	Fleischer GER
2003							
29-03	Moldova	W 2-1	Minsk	ECq	Kutuzov [43], Gurenko [58]	7 500	Verbist BEL
2-04	Uzbekistan	D 2-2	Minsk	Fr	Tsygalko [26], Rozhkov [52]	4 000	Lauks LVA
30-04	Uzbekistan	W 2-1	Tashkent	Fr	Shuneiko [15], Kutuzov [55]	4 000	Kolpakov KGZ
7-06	Holland	L 0-2	Minsk	ECq		28 000	Ovrebo NOR
11-06	Austria	L 0-5	Innsbruck	ECq		8 100	Frojdfeldt SWE
20-08	Iran	W 2-1	Minsk	Fr	Romaschenko.Ma [10p], Shtanyuk [41]	10 000	Ivanov.N RUS
6-09	Czech Republic	L 1-3	Minsk	ECq	Bulyga [14]	11 000	McCurry SCO
10-09	Moldova	L 1-2	Tiraspol	ECq	Vasilyuk [89p]	7 000	Selevic SCM
2004							
14-02	Estonia	L 1-2	Valletta	Fr	Tarasenko [89]	200	Casha MLT
16-02	Moldova	W 1-0	Valletta	Fr	Hleb.V [39]	40	Attard MLT
18-02	Malta	W 4-0	Valletta	Fr	Kornilenko [12], Tsygalko [30], Biahanski [71], Lashankou [85]		Kaldma EST
18-02	Cyprus	W 2-0	Achnas	Fr	Romaschenko.Ma 2 [56 70]	500	Kalis CYP
21-02	Latvia	W 4-1	Limassol	Fr	Bulyga [20], Romaschenko.Ma 3 [73p 87p 90]	100	
28-04	Lithuania	W 1-0	Minsk	Fr	Blizniuk [75]	8 000	Ivanov RUS
18-08	Turkey	W 2-1	Denizli	Fr	Hleb.V [67], Kouba [90]	18 000	Mrkovic BIH
8-09	Norway	D 1-1	Oslo	WCq	Kutuzov [77]	25 272	Gomes Costa POR
9-10	Moldova	W 4-0	Minsk	WCq	Omelyanchuk [45], Kutuzov [65], Bulyga [75], Romashchenko.Ma [90]	21 000	Dereli TUR
13-10	Italy	L 3-4	Parma	WCq	Romashchenko 2 [52 88], Bulyga [76]	19 833	Megia Davila ESP
22-11	United Arab Emirates	W 3-2	Dubai	Fr	Shkabara [44], Kovel [60], Kulchy [90]	600	Al Delawar BHR
2005							
9-02	Poland	W 3-1	Warsaw	Fr	Hleb.A [8], Hleb.V [84], Lavrik [92+]	6 000	Zuta LTU
30-03	Slovenia	D 1-1	Celje	WCq	Kulchy [49]	6 450	Al Ghamdi KSA
4-06	Slovenia	D 1-1	Minsk	WCq	Belkevich [18]	29 042	Hansson SWE
8-06	Scotland	D 0-0	Minsk	WCq		28 287	Benquerenca POR
17-08	Lithuania	L 0-1	Vilnius	Fr		2 500	Sipailo LVA
3-09	Moldova	L 0-2	Chisinau	WCq		5 000	Duhamel FRA
7-09	Italy	L 1-4	Minsk	WCq	Kutuzov [4]	30 299	Temmink NED
8-10	Scotland	W 1-0	Glasgow	WCq	Kutuzov [5]	51 105	Szabo HUN
12-10	Norway	L 0-1	Minsk	WCq		13 222	Plautz AUT
12-11	Latvia	W 3-1	Minsk	Fr	Kortyko [26], Kornilenko 2 [52 90]	8 300	Egorov RUS
2006							
28-02	Greece	L 0-1	Limassol	Fr		3 000	Salomir ROU
1-03	Finland	D 2-2	Larnaca	Fr	Kornilenko [34], Shkabara [53]. L 4-5p	120	Krajnic SVN
30-05	Tunisia	L 0-3	Radès/Tunis	Fr			
2-06	Libya	D 1-1	Radès/Tunis	Fr	L 1-3p		

Fr = Friendly match • EC = UEFA EURO 2004™ • WC = FIFA World Cup™ • q = qualifier

BELARUS NATIONAL TEAM RECORDS AND RECORD SEQUENCES

Records			Sequence records			
Victory	5-0	LTU 1998	Wins	6	2004	
Defeat	0-5	AUT 2003	Defeats	8	1997	
Player Caps	78	GURENKO Sergei	Undefeated	8	2004	
Player Goals	13	ROMASHCHENKO Maxym	Without win	14	1998-2000	
			Clean sheets	3	1998, 2004	
			Goals scored	17	2003-2005	
			Without goal	3	Four times	
			Goals against	13	2002-2004	

BELARUS COUNTRY INFORMATION

Capital	Minsk	Independence	1991	GDP per Capita	$6 100
Population	10 310 520	Status	Republic	GNP Ranking	81
Area km²	207 600	Language	Belorussian	Dialling code	+375
Population density	49 per km²	Literacy rate	99%	Internet code	.by
% in urban areas	71%	Main religion	Christian 80%	GMT + / –	+2
Towns/Cities ('000)	Minsk 1 742; Gomel 480; Mogilev 365; Vitebsk 342; Grodno 317; Brest 300				
Neighbours (km)	Russia 959; Ukraine 891; Poland 407; Lithuania 502; Latvia 141				
Main stadia	Dinamo – Minsk 42 375; Neman – Grodno 15 000; Dinamo – Brest 15 000				

NATIONAL TEAM PLAYERS AND COACHES

Record Caps			Record Goals			Recent Coaches	
GURENKO Sergei	1994-'05	78	ROMASHCHENKO Maxym	1998-'06	13	VERGEYENKO Mikhail	1992-'93
SHTANYUK Sergei	1995-'06	62	BELKEVICH Valentin	1992-'05	10	BOROVSKIY Sergei	1994-'97
BELKEVICH Valentin	1992-'05	56	KUTUZOV Vitaly	2002-'06	9	VERGEYENKO Mikhail	1997-'99
KULCHIY Alexandr	1996-'06	56	GERASIMETS Sergei	1992-'99	7	BOROVSKIY Sergei	1999-'00
OSTROVSKIY Andrei	1994-'05	52	VASILYUK Roman	2000-'03	7	MALOFEYEV Eduard	2000-'03
ROMASHCHENKO Maxym	1998-'06	48	KACHURO Petr	1994-'02	5	BAIDACHNY Anatoliy	2003-'05
KHATSKEVICH Alexandr	1993-'05	39	KULCHIY Alexandr	1996-'06	5	PUNTUS Yuri	2006-
LAVRIK Andre	1997-'05	37	KHATSKEVICH Alexandr	1993-'05	4		
YAKHIMOVICH Erik	1993-'01	34	MAKOVSKIY Vladimir	1995-'06	4		
TUMILOVICH Gennadiy	1998-'04	32	BULYGA Vitaly	2003-'06	4		

CLUB DIRECTORY

Club	Town/City	Stadium	Capacity	www.	Lge	Cup
FC BATE Borisov	Borisov	City	5 500	fcbate.by	2	1
Belshina Bobruisk	Bobruisk	Spartak	4 800		1	3
Darida Mikashevichi	Zhdanovichi	Darida	1 500		0	0
Dinamo Brest	Brest	Sportkomplex Brestskiy	3 000	dinamobrest.dax.ru	0	0
Dinamo Minsk	Minsk	Dinamo	42 375	dinamo-minsk.com	7 - 1 †	3
Dnepr-Transmash	Mogilev	Spartak	11 200	fcdnepr.com	1	0
FC Gomel	Gomel	Luch	5 000		1	1
Lokomotiv Minsk	Minsk	Lokomotiv	2 000	skvich.com	0	0
Lokomotiv Vitebsk	Vitebsk	Dinamo	5 000		0	1
MTZ-RIPO Minsk	Minsk	Traktor	17 600		0	1
Naftan Novopolotsk	Novopolotsk	Atlant	6 500		0	0
Neman Grodno	Grodno	Neman	14 000	neman.boom.ru	0	1
Shakhter Soligorsk	Soligorsk	Stroitel	5 000	fcshakhter.by	1	1
Torpedo Zhodino	Zhodino	Torpedo	5 000		0	0

† Dinamo Minsk won a Soviet championship

RECENT LEAGUE AND CUP RECORD

	Championship						Cup		
Year	Champions	Pts	Runners-up	Pts	Third	Pts	Winners	Score	Runners-up
1992	Dinamo Minsk	25	Dnepr Mogilev	24	Dinamo Brest	19	Dinamo Minsk	6-1	Dnepr Mogilev
1993	Dinamo Minsk	57	KIM Vitebsk	47	Belarus Minsk	46	Neman Grodno	2-1	Vedrich Rechitsa
1994	Dinamo Minsk	52	Dinamo-93 Minsk	43	KIM Vitebsk	43	Dinamo Minsk	3-1	Fandok Bobruisk
1995	Dinamo Minsk	48	Dvina Minsk	45	Dinamo-93 Minsk	42	Dinamo-93 Minsk	1-1 7-6p	Torpedo Mogilev
1995	Dinamo Minsk	38	MPKC Mozyr	36	Dinamo-93 Minsk	32	-		
1996	MPKC Mozyr	76	Dinamo Minsk	75	Belshina Bobruisk	63	MPKC Mozyr	4-1	Dinamo Minsk
1997	Dinamo Minsk	70	Belshina Bobruisk	66	Lokomotiv Vitebsk	59	Belshina Bobruisk	2-0	Dinamo-93 Minsk
1998	Dnepr-Transmash	67	BATE Borisov	58	Belshina Bobruisk	57	Lokomotiv Vitebsk	2-1	Dinamo Minsk
1999	BATE Borisov	77	Slavija Mozyr	65	FC Gomel	63	Belshina Bobruisk	1-1 4-2p	Slavija Mozyr
2000	Slavija Mozyr	74	BATE Borisov	64	Dinamo Minsk	62	Slavija Mozyr	2-1	Torpedo-SKA Minsk
2001	Belshina Bobruisk	56	Dinamo Minsk	53	BATE Borisov	51	Belshina Bobruisk	1-0	Slavija Mozyr
2002	BATE Borisov	56	Neman Grodno	56	Shakhtyor Soligorsk	51	FC Gomel	2-0	BATE Borisov
2003	FC Gomel	74	BATE Borisov	66	Dinamo Minsk	64	Dinamo Minsk	2-0	Lokomotiv Minsk
2004	Dinamo Minsk	75	BATE Borisov	70	Shakhtyor Soligorsk	65	Shakhtyor Soligorsk	1-0	FC Gomel
2005	Shakhtyor Soligorsk	63	Dinamo Minsk	50	MTZ-RIPO Minsk	49	MTZ-RIPO Minsk	2-1	BATE Borisov
2006							BATE Borisov	3-1	Shakhtyor Soligorsk

Slavija Mozyr previously known as MPKC • Lokomotiv Vitebsk previously known as KIM and then Dvina

BELARUS 2005

PREMIER LEAGUE

	Pl	W	D	L	F	A	Pts	Shakhter	Dinamo	MTZ-RIPO	Torpedo	BATE	Dnepr	Gomel	Brest	Naftan	Darida	Lokomotiv	Neman	Zvezda	Slavija
Shakhtyor Soligorsk †	26	19	6	1	59	14	63		1-1	3-1	4-0	2-2	3-0	1-0	4-0	2-2	3-1	1-0	3-0	3-1	0-0
Dinamo Minsk ‡	26	15	5	6	50	26	50	1-0		3-1	2-0	2-2	5-2	3-1	2-0	3-2	0-1	4-0	0-1	3-0	1-0
MTZ-RIPO Minsk	26	16	1	9	43	30	49	1-1	0-1		1-0	0-1	2-1	3-1	0-4	1-0	5-1	1-0	1-0	3-1	2-0
Torpedo Zhodino	26	14	5	7	40	25	47	0-1	2-2	3-1		1-1	3-0	1-0	0-2	1-0	0-0	3-1	3-2	0-0	6-1
BATE Borisov ‡	26	12	11	3	42	27	47	0-2	1-0	0-1	0-1		2-1	1-1	2-1	3-0	1-1	1-0	2-0	4-0	2-0
Dnepr-Transmash	26	12	7	7	48	36	43	1-1	0-0	2-1	1-0	1-1		1-0	2-2	1-1	3-3	5-1	6-0	4-0	0-0
FC Gomel	26	12	3	11	34	32	39	0-3	2-1	1-0	2-1	2-3	1-2		2-1	1-2	3-1	0-1	3-0	4-2	2-1
Dinamo Brest	26	11	3	12	39	33	36	0-1	1-1	1-0	0-1	1-2	2-1	1-0		1-0	0-2	1-2	4-1	3-0	2-0
Naftan Novopolotsk	26	10	3	13	43	44	33	1-4	3-2	2-3	0-2	1-2	3-4	0-2	2-1		3-2	4-0	3-0	3-1	3-1
Darida Mikashevichi	26	7	8	11	30	36	29	0-2	0-1	1-3	0-3	1-1	4-1	1-1	1-0	0-0		0-0	0-1	1-2	1-2
Lokomotiv Minsk	26	7	5	14	30	43	26	0-2	3-2	2-3	2-3	3-3	0-1	0-1	3-2	0-2	0-0		4-1	0-0	5-0
Neman Grodno	26	7	3	16	20	50	24	0-3	1-2	0-2	0-2	1-1	1-3	1-2	2-2	1-0	1-3	2-0		1-0	1-0
Zvezda-BGU Minsk	26	3	5	18	24	60	14	1-3	2-4	1-2	2-2	2-2	0-2	0-1	1-4	5-3	0-4	1-1	0-1		1-2
Slavija Minsk	26	2	5	19	14	60	11	1-6	0-4	0-5	0-2	2-2	0-3	1-1	1-3	1-3	0-1	0-2	1-1	0-1	

16/04/2005 - 5/11/2005 • † Qualified for the UEFA Champions League • ‡ Qualified for the UEFA Cup
Top scorers: Valeriy STRIPEIKIS, Naftan, 16; Igor CHUMACHENKO, Naftan, 14; Alexandr KLIMENKO, Shakhter, 14

BELARUS 2005
SECOND DIVISION

	Pl	W	D	L	F	A	Pts
Belshina Bobruisk	30	23	4	3	61	19	73
Lokomotiv Vitebsk	30	21	7	2	76	23	70
FC Smorgon	30	15	9	6	57	35	54
ZLIN Gomel	30	14	12	4	35	17	54
Smena Minsk	30	14	8	8	31	23	50
Granit Mikashevichi	30	13	7	10	39	35	46
Khimik Svetlogorsk	30	14	3	13	42	34	45
Vedrich-97 Rechitsa	30	11	6	13	37	41	39
FC Baranovichi	30	11	5	14	38	43	38
FC Lida	30	10	7	13	41	43	37
Veras Nesvizh	30	9	10	11	31	33	37
Torpedo-Kadino Mogilev	30	7	8	15	22	45	29
Kommunalnik Slonim	30	8	4	18	35	43	28
FC Bereza	30	8	4	18	36	58	28
FC Orsha	30	6	6	18	33	74	24
Dnepr Rogachev	30	4	4	22	22	70	16

16/04/2005 - 6/11/2005

BFF CUP 2006

Round of sixteen

BATE Borisov *	2 12p
Slavija Mozyr	2 11p
Lokomotiv Minsk	0
Dinamo Brest *	2
FC Baranovichi *	2
FK Polatsk	1
Neman Grodno	1
Zvezda-BGU Minsk *	3
FC Gomel *	1
Torpedo Zhodino	0
Veras Nesvizh	0
Khimik Svetlogorsk *	1
Dinamo Minsk	4
Naftan Novopolotsk *	0
MTZ-RIPO Minsk *	2
Shakhtyor Soligorsk	3

Quarter-finals

BATE Borisov	0	1
Dinamo Brest †	0	0
FC Baranovichi	1	0
Zvezda-BGU Minsk †	4	2
FC Gomel *	5	0
Khimik Svetlogorsk	1	0
Dinamo Minsk *	0	0
Shakhtyor Soligorsk	1	1

Semi-finals

BATE Borisov *	3	4
Zvezda-BGU Minsk	1	0
FC Gomel	0	1
Shakhtyor Soligorsk *	0	1

Final

BATE Borisov ‡	3
Shakhtyor Soligorsk	1

‡ Qualified for the UEFA Cup
* Home team/home team in the 1st leg • † Both legs played in Minsk

CUP FINAL

Dinamo Stadium, Minsk
27-05-2006, Att: 5 200, Ref: Shmolik
Scorers - Dimitrij Molosh [26], Dimitrij Platonau [115], Henadz Bliznyuk [117] for BATE; Alexandr Klimenka [65] for Shakhter

BLZ - BELIZE

NATIONAL TEAM RECORD
JULY 1ST 2002 TO JULY 9TH 2006

PL	W	D	L	F	A	%
5	0	0	5	0	15	0

FIFA/COCA-COLA WORLD RANKING

1993	1994	1995	1996	1997	1998	1999	2000	2001	2002	2003	2004	2005		High		Low	
-	-	173	182	179	186	190	186	167	158	174	181	180		157	05/02	196	07/07

2005–2006											
08/05	09/05	10/05	11/05	12/05	01/06	02/06	03/06	04/06	05/06	06/06	07/06
180	180	182	181	180	180	180	180	180	180	-	196

With just five matches played in the 2006 FIFA World Cup™ cycle, Belize have found it difficult to garner the necessary experience to haul themselves off the bottom rung of the international football ladder. All five of those games were lost and not a single goal scored. It has to be remembered that Belize did not join FIFA until 1986 but there is a determination to improve standards. In time the football academy in Belmopan, opened in 2002, will provide the players needed to help Belize raise standards to those of their Central American neighbours, whilst club football is also slowly becoming more established. The 10-1 aggregate defeat suffered by Placencia

INTERNATIONAL HONOURS
None

Pirates at the hands of Costa Rica's Alajuelense in the CONCACAF Champions Cup does, however, give a fair indication of the level of football in Belize. The League is becoming better organised and is very competitive with most of the major towns represented. The 2006 RFG Insurance Cup, the main competition in the country, was won by New Site Erei from Dangriga. They beat Boca on penalties in the two-legged final having topped their first round group before going on to beat Kremandala and then FC Belize in the play-offs. Defending champions Juventus did not have a good year, withdrawing from their first round group after just four games.

THE FIFA BIG COUNT OF 2000

	Male	Female		Male	Female
Registered players	1 436	0	Referees	60	1
Non registered players	2 000	500	Officials	400	50
Youth players	471	0	Total involved	4 918	
Total players	4 407		Number of clubs	22	
Professional players	236	0	Number of teams	116	

Football Federation of Belize (FFB)

26 Hummingbird Highway, Belmopan, PO Box 1742, Belize City
Tel +501 822 3410   Fax +501 822 3377
info@belizefootball.bz   www.belizefootball.bz
President: CHIMILIO Bertie Dr   General Secretary: HULSE Marguerite
Vice-President: DAVIS Ray   Treasurer: BAXTER Matthews   Media Officer: None
Men's Coach: TBD   Women's Coach: TBD
FFB formed: 1980   CONCACAF: 1986   FIFA: 1986
Red shirts with white and blue trimmings, Red shorts, Red socks

RECENT INTERNATIONAL MATCHES PLAYED BY BELIZE

2002	Opponents	Score		Venue	Comp	Scorers	Att	Referee
No international matches played after June 2002								
2003								
No international matches played in 2003								
2004								
13-06	Canada	L	0-4	Kingston, Ontario	WCq		8 245	Batres GUA
16-06	Canada	L	0-4	Kingston, Ontario	WCq		5 124	Gordon TRI
2005								
19-02	Guatemala	L	0-2	Guatemala City	GCq		10 000	Quesada CRC
21-02	Honduras	L	0-4	Guatemala City	GCq		3 000	Campos NCA
23-02	Nicaragua	L	0-1	Guatemala City	GCq		3 000	Campos NCA
2006								
No international matches played in 2006 before July								

GC = CONCACAF Gold Cup™ • WC = FIFA World Cup™ • q = qualifier

BELIZE NATIONAL TEAM RECORDS AND RECORD SEQUENCES

Records			Sequence records					
Victory	7-1	NCA 2002	Wins	3	2001-2002	Clean sheets	2	2000-2001
Defeat	0-7	CRC 1999	Defeats	6	1997-2000	Goals scored	5	2001-2002
Player Caps	n/a		Undefeated	3	2000-01, 2001-02	Without goal	5	2004-2005
Player Goals	n/a		Without win	12	1995-2000	Goals against	11	1995-2000

RECENT LEAGUE RECORD

Year	Winners	Score	Runners-up
1998	Juventus	2-0 6-1	Acros
1999	Juventus	2-1 1-1	La Victoria Dolphins
2000	Sagitún	0-2 2-0 3-0	Grigamandala
2001	Kulture Yabra	1-0 2-0	Belmopan Bandits
2002	Kulture Yabra	1-1 4-2p 2-1	Juventus
2003	Not played		
2004	Not played		
2005	Juventus	1-0 1-0	Sagitún
2006	New Site Erei	0-0 1-1 5-4p	Boca FC

In 2002 the leading clubs of the BPFL withdrew from the Football Federation of Belize and set up a rival league

2002	Sagitún	1-1 1-1 3-2p	Belmopan Bandits
2003	Kulture Yabra	2-0 2-1	Belmopan Bandits
2004	Sagitún	0-2 3-2 1-0	Juventus

BELIZE COUNTRY INFORMATION

Capital	Belmopan	Independence	1981	GDP per Capita	$4 900
Population	272 945	Status	Commonwealth	GNP Ranking	159
Area km²	22 966	Language	English	Dialling code	+501
Population density	11 per km²	Literacy rate	75%	Internet code	.bz
% in urban areas	47%	Main religion	Christian 77%	GMT + / –	-6
Towns/Cities ('000)	Belize City 61; San Ignacio 16; Orange Walk 15; Belmopan 13; Dangriga 10; Corozal 8				
Neighbours (km)	Mexico 250; Guatemala 266; Caribbean Sea 386				
Main stadia	People's Stadium – Orange Walk 3 000; MCC Grounds – Belize City 2 500				

BOL – BOLIVIA

NATIONAL TEAM RECORD
JULY 1ST 2002 TO JULY 9TH 2006

PL	W	D	L	F	A	%
27	6	4	17	27	50	29.6

FIFA/COCA-COLA WORLD RANKING

1993	1994	1995	1996	1997	1998	1999	2000	2001	2002	2003	2004	2005	High	Low
58	44	53	39	24	61	61	65	70	92	99	94	96	18 07/97	114 08/03

2005–2006											
08/05	09/05	10/05	11/05	12/05	01/06	02/06	03/06	04/06	05/06	06/06	07/06
100	100	96	96	96	97	98	101	101	102	-	85

There can be no hiding the fact that the past four years have been hugely disappointing for the Bolivian national team. Qualification for USA'94 was seen by some as the launch pad to even greater feats, especially with the Tahuichi Academy receiving worldwide acclaim. Since then, however, it has been all downhill, culminating with the embarrassing last place finish in the South American qualifying group for the 2006 FIFA World Cup™. Without the huge advantage of altitude for the home games played in La Paz, the situation might have even been worse, but as it was, of their nine games played there, three were lost. Politically it was a turbulent year for the country

INTERNATIONAL HONOURS
Qualified for the FIFA World Cup™ finals 1930 1950 1994 Copa América 1963

with mass street protests culminating in the presidential elections in December and the championship was even suspended for three weeks at one stage. Bolivian clubs were not exempt from the turmoil, and when Bolívar failed to pay their players for over six months, they were forced to play a crucial match with their youth team. Remarkably for a club in such trouble, they had previously won the opening championship of the year, and were in the running to win the closing before they were ordered by FIFA to have three points deducted for failure to pay former coach Gustavo Huerta. That let in Blooming to win the title, their first since 1999.

THE FIFA BIG COUNT OF 2000

	Male	Female		Male	Female
Registered players	14 698	1 080	Referees	480	30
Non registered players	210 000	0	Officials	95	20
Youth players	30 240	0	Total involved	256 643	
Total players	256 018		Number of clubs	809	
Professional players	360	0	Number of teams	999	

Federación Boliviana de Fútbol (FBF)
Av. Libertador Bolivar 1168, Cochabamba, Bolivia
Tel +591 4 4244982   Fax +591 4 4282132
fbfcba@entelnet.bo   www.fbf.com.bo
President: CASTEDO Walter   General Secretary: REINOSO Mario
Vice-President: MENDEZ Mauricio   Treasurer: JIMENEZ Pedro   Media Officer: SILVER Javier
Men's Coach: MESA Ovidio   Women's Coach: MELGAR Herman
FBF formed: 1925   CONMEBOL: 1926   FIFA: 1926
Green shirts, White shorts, Green socks

RECENT INTERNATIONAL MATCHES PLAYED BY BOLIVIA

2002	Opponents		Score	Venue	Comp	Scorers	Att	Referee
21-08	Venezuela	L	0-2	Caracas	Fr		25 000	Ibarra VEN
2003								
19-03	Mexico	L	0-2	Dallas	Fr		40 000	Terry USA
10-06	Portugal	L	0-4	Lisbon	Fr		10 000	Kenan ISR
31-08	Panama	W	3-0	La Paz	Fr	Mendez [21], Ricaldi [51], Gutierrez.L [84]	8 000	Ortube BOL
7-09	Uruguay	L	0-5	Montevideo	WCq		45 000	Hidalgo PER
10-09	Colombia	W	4-0	La Paz	WCq	Baldivieso [12p], Botero 3 [27 48 58]	30 000	Oliveira BRA
11-10	Honduras	W	1-0	Washington	Fr	Pena.JM [89]	20 000	Kennedy USA
15-11	Argentina	L	0-3	Buenos Aires	WCq		30 042	Hidalgo PER
18-11	Venezuela	L	1-2	Maracaibo	WCq	Botero [60]	25 000	Reinoso ECU
2004								
30-03	Chile	L	0-2	La Paz	WCq		42 000	Martin ARG
1-06	Paraguay	W	2-1	La Paz	WCq	Cristaldo [8], Suarez.R [72]	23 013	Rezende BRA
5-06	Ecuador	L	2-3	Quito	WCq	Gutierrez.L [58], Castillo [75]	30 020	Brand VEN
6-07	Peru	D	2-2	Lima	CAr1	Botero [36], Alvarez [57]	45 000	Baldassi ARG
9-07	Colombia	L	0-1	Lima	CAr1		35 000	Ramos ECU
12-07	Venezuela	D	1-1	Trujillo	CAr1	Galindo [32]	25 000	Mattus CRC
5-09	Brazil	L	1-3	Sao Paulo	WCq	Cristaldo [48]	60 000	Baldassi ARG
9-10	Peru	W	1-0	La Paz	WCq	Botero [56]	23 729	Reinoso ECU
12-10	Uruguay	D	0-0	La Paz	WCq		24 349	Rezende BRA
13-11	Guatemala	L	0-1	Washington DC	Fr		22 000	Prus USA
17-11	Colombia	L	0-1	Barranquilla	WCq		25 000	Torres PAR
2005								
26-03	Argentina	L	1-2	La Paz	WCq	Castillo [49]	25 000	Larrionda URU
29-03	Venezuela	W	3-1	La Paz	WCq	Cichero OG [2], Castillo [25], Vaca [84]	7 908	Lecca PER
4-06	Chile	L	1-3	Santiago	WCq	Castillo [83p]	46 729	Rezende BRA
8-06	Paraguay	L	1-4	Asuncion	WCq	Galindo [30]	5 534	Brand VEN
3-09	Ecuador	L	1-2	La Paz	WCq	Vaca [41]	8 434	Baldassi ARG
9-10	Brazil	D	1-1	La Paz	WCq	Castillo [49]	22 725	Larrionda URU
12-10	Peru	L	1-4	Tacna	WCq	Gutierrez.L [66]	14 774	Sequeira ARG
2006								

No international matches played in 2006 before July

Fr = Friendly match • CA = Copa América • WC = FIFA World Cup™ • q = qualifier • r1 = first round group

BOLIVIA NATIONAL TEAM RECORDS AND RECORD SEQUENCES

Records			Sequence records					
Victory	9-2	HAI 2000	Wins	5	1963, 1993, 1998	Clean sheets	3	1998, 1999
Defeat	1-10	BRA 1949	Defeats	9	1926-1930	Goals scored	15	1995-1996
Player Caps	93	SANDY Marco Antonio	Undefeated	9	1997	Without goal	7	1994
Player Goals	16	UGARTE Víctor Agustín	Without win	19	1945-1948	Goals against	18	1977-1980

BOLIVIA COUNTRY INFORMATION

Capital	Sucre; La Paz	Independence	1825	GDP per Capita	$2 400
Population	8 724 156	Status	Republic	GNP Ranking	95
Area km²	1 098 580	Language	Spanish	Dialling code	+591
Population density	8 per km²	Literacy rate	87%	Internet code	.bo
% in urban areas	61%	Main religion	Christian	GMT + / –	-4
Towns/Cities ('000)	Santa Cruz 1 342; Cochabamba 900; El Alto 834; La Paz 812; Sucre 224; Oruro 208; Tarija 159; Potosi 141; Montero 88; Trinidad 84; Yacuiba 82; Riberalta 74; Guayaramerin 36				
Neighbours (km)	Brazil 3 400; Paraguay 750; Argentina 832; Chile 861; Peru 900				
Main stadia	Hernando Siles – La Paz 42 000; Ramón Tahuichi Aguilera – Santa Cruz 38 000; Felix Capriles – Cochabamba 32 000; Olimpico Patria – Sucre 30 000				

NATIONAL TEAM PLAYERS AND COACHES

Record Caps			Record Goals				Recent Coaches	
SANDY Marco Antonio	1993-'03	93	UGARTE Victor Agustin	1947-'63	16	VIERA Hector		1998
CRISTALDO Luis Héctor	1989-'05	92	ARAGONES Carlos	1977-'81	15	LOPEZ Antonio		1999
MELGAR José Milton	1980-'97	89	BALDIVIESO Julio César	1991-'05	15	ARAGONES Carlos		2000-'01
BORJA Carlos Fernando	1979-'95	88	SANCHEZ Erwin	1989-'05	15	HABEGGER Jorge		2001
BALDIVIESO Julio César	1991-'05	85	ALCOCER Máximo	1957-'36	13	TRUCCO Carlos Leonel		2001-'02
RIMBA Miguel Angel	1989-'00	80	ETCHEVERRY Marco Antonio	1989-'02	13	ROCHA		2003
SANCHEZ Oscar	1994-'05	77	BOTERO Joaquín	1999-'05	12	GIOVAGNOLI Dalcio		2003
PENA Juan Manuel	1991-'04	76	AGUILAR Miguel	1977-'83	10	ACOSTA Nelson		2003-'04
ETCHEVERRY Marco Antonio	1989-'03	71	RAMALLO Luis William	1989-'97	9	BLACUT Ramiro		2004-'05
MORENO Jaime	1991-'00	63	MEZZA Ovidio	1972-'83	8	MESA Ovidio		2005-

CLUB DIRECTORY

Club	Town/City	Stadium	Capacity	www.	Lge	CL
Aurora	Cochabamba	Tahuichi	40 000	clunaurora.com.bo	1	0
Blooming	Santa Cruz	Tahuichi	40 000		4	0
Bolívar	La Paz	Hernando Siles	55 000	clubbolivar.com	17	0
Jorge Wilsterman	Cochabamba	Felix Capriles	35 000		9	0
La Paz FC	La Paz	Hernando Siles	55 000		0	0
Oriente Petrolero	Santa Cruz	Tahuichi	40 000		5	0
Real Potosi	Potosi	Guzman	15 000	clubrealpotosi.com	0	0
Real Santa Cruz	Santa Cruz	Camba	12 000		0	0
San Jose	Oruro	Monumental	33 000		1	0
The Strongest	La Paz	Achumani	40 000	thestrongest.com.bo	8	0
Universidad Iberoamericana	La Paz	Libertador Bolivar	30 000		0	0
Union Central	Tarija	Centenario	20 000		0	0

RECENT LEAGUE RECORD

	Championship Play-off		
Year	Champions	Score	Runners-up
1994	Bolívar	‡	Jorge Wilstermann
1995	San Jose	†	
1996	Bolívar	3-1	Oriente Petrolero
1997	Bolívar	‡	Oriente Petrolero
1998	Blooming	3-0 1-0	Jorge Wilsterman
1999	Blooming	3-2 3-2	The Strongest
2000	Jorge Wilsterman	4-1 0-4 2-2 4-3p	Oriente Petrolero
2001	Oriente Petrolero	1-4 4-3 2-0	Bolívar
2002	Bolívar	†	

Torneo Apertura					Torneo Clausura			
Year	Champions	Pts	Runners-up	Pts	Champions	Pts	Runners-up	Pts
2003	The Strongest	46	Bolívar	45	The Strongest	13	Jorge Wilstermann	10
2004	Bolívar	53	Aurora	38	The Strongest	27	Oriente Petrolero	27
2005	Bolívar	44	The Strongest	43	Blooming	19	Bolívar	14

The system of Apertura and Clausura was adopted at the start of 1994 with a play-off between the winners to determine the champions • † Won both stages so no play-off • ‡ Play-off held on a league system • From 2003 the winners of both the Apertura and Clausura were champions in their own right

BOLIVIA 2005

TORNEO APERTURA

	Pl	W	D	L	F	A	Pts	Bolívar	Strongest	Oriente	Aurora	Blooming	Wilstermann	La Paz	San José	Real Potosí	Destroyers	Unión	Ibero.
Bolívar †	22	13	5	4	55	20	44		0-0	3-0	4-3	5-0	1-0	0-1	2-0	8-2	6-1	0-1	2-0
The Strongest †	22	13	4	5	45	19	43	2-1		2-0	0-1	6-0	2-0	3-2	1-1	4-0	4-0	2-0	3-1
Oriente Petrolero †	22	12	5	5	39	27	41	2-1	1-0		3-3	4-2	0-3	2-1	1-1	3-1	1-1	5-1	2-0
Aurora	22	10	5	7	37	32	35	1-1	2-0	0-3		3-1	2-1	0-0	2-1	1-1	2-0	4-0	4-0
Blooming	22	11	2	9	27	37	35	0-2	1-0	2-1	2-0		0-0	1-0	2-0	1-0	1-0	3-2	3-2
Jorge Wilstermann	22	10	4	8	34	24	34	0-3	2-3	1-1	2-0	3-1		2-1	3-1	2-0	2-0	3-0	3-0
La Paz	22	10	3	9	35	33	33	1-3	2-1	1-3	2-2	3-1	1-1		2-1	0-1	6-1	2-0	2-0
San José	22	8	6	8	48	36	30	2-2	1-1	1-2	6-0	3-0	3-2	6-3		2-2	7-2	2-0	2-1
Real Potosí	22	7	6	9	31	42	27	0-4	2-2	2-1	1-0	2-1	1-0	1-3	3-3		4-0	6-0	1-1
Destroyers	22	6	3	13	29	54	21	1-1	2-3	1-3	2-3	1-4	2-0	4-0	4-3	1-0		3-1	2-0
Unión Central	22	5	4	13	20	42	19	2-2	0-2	0-1	2-1	0-0	2-4	0-1	1-0	4-0	0-0		3-0
Univ. Iberoamericana	22	1	5	16	11	45	8	1-4	0-4	0-0	0-3	0-1	0-0	0-1	0-2	1-1	3-1	1-1	

5/03/2005 - 24/07/2005 • † Qualified for the 2006 Copa Libertadores
Top scorers: Ruben AGUILERA, San José, 21; Luis SILLERO, Jorge Wilstermann, 14

BOLIVIA 2005

TORNEO CLAUSURA 1ST STAGE

Group A

	Pl	W	D	L	F	A	Pts	Blooming	San José	Strongest	Wilstermann	Destroyers	Ibero.	Bolívar	La Paz	Oriente	Potosí	Aurora	Unión
Blooming ‡	12	8	2	2	34	13	26		3-0	0-0	2-3	3-0	10-0			2-1			
San José ‡	12	7	1	4	22	17	22	5-1		0-3	2-1	3-1	4-0				2-1		
The Strongest ‡	12	6	3	3	22	10	21	0-1	2-0		1-0	6-0	6-1	2-2					
Jorge Wilstermann	12	5	2	5	21	13	17	1-2	0-1	0-0		5-2	2-0					1-2	
Destroyers	12	5	1	6	26	26	16	1-2	3-2	3-1	0-0		6-0						6-0
Univ. Iberoamericana	12	0	0	12	6	52	0	1-7	1-2	0-1	0-6	1-3		1-2					

Group B

	Pl	W	D	L	F	A	Pts	Blooming	San José	Strongest	Wilstermann	Destroyers	Ibero.	Bolívar	La Paz	Oriente	Potosí	Aurora	Unión
Bolívar ‡	12	9	3	0	32	13	30			3-0					3-1	4-0	3-1	3-2	4-0
La Paz ‡	12	5	4	3	17	15	19					3-1		2-2		3-0	0-0	1-0	1-1
Oriente Petrolero ‡	12	5	3	4	15	17	18	1-1						1-2	4-1		2-1	1-0	2-1
Real Potosí	12	2	6	4	20	19	12		1-1					2-2	2-1	1-1		2-2	6-0
Aurora	12	2	4	6	11	15	10			1-2				0-1	0-0	1-1	1-1		0-1
Unión Central	12	3	1	8	14	30	10				3-1			2-3	1-2	0-1	4-2	1-2	

20/08/2005 - 5/11/2005 • ‡ Qualified for the 2nd stage

TORNEO CLAUSURA 2ND STAGE

	Pl	W	D	L	F	A	Pts	Blooming	Bolívar	Oriente	La Paz	Strongest	San José
Blooming †	10	6	1	3	20	20	19		4-2	1-0	2-1	4-1	2-1
Bolívar §3 ‡	10	5	2	3	22	17	14	4-2		3-0	4-3	2-2	1-1
Oriente Petrolero	10	4	1	5	11	16	13	3-1	2-1		2-0	1-1	1-0
La Paz	10	3	3	4	17	14	12	5-0	1-2	3-1		1-1	1-1
The Strongest	10	3	3	4	14	18	12	2-3	1-3	1-0	1-2		3-2
San José	10	2	4	4	12	11	10	1-1	1-0	5-1	0-0	0-1	

12/11/2005 - 14/12/2005 • † Qualified for the 2007 Copa Libertadores • ‡ Qualified for the 2006 Copa Sudamericana • § = points deducted
Top scorers: Juan Matias FISCHER, Bolívar, 16; Gualberto MOJICA, Blooming, 13; Dayson de Jesus GUALE, La Paz, 13
Universidad Iberoamericana relegated on overall season record • Copa Simon Bolívar final: Guabira 0-2 1-6 Universitario Sucre. Universitario promoted to the top level • Guabira entered a play-off against Destroyers: Destroyers 1-0 5-1 Guabira. Destroyers remain at the top level.

BOT – BOTSWANA

NATIONAL TEAM RECORD
JULY 1ST 2002 TO JULY 9TH 2006

PL	W	D	L	F	A	%
45	9	20	16	31	41	42.2

FIFA/COCA-COLA WORLD RANKING

1993	1994	1995	1996	1997	1998	1999	2000	2001	2002	2003	2004	2005		High		Low	
140	145	155	161	162	155	165	150	153	136	112	102	101		**96**	09/05	**165**	02/00

2005–2006											
08/05	09/05	10/05	11/05	12/05	01/06	02/06	03/06	04/06	05/06	06/06	07/06
101	96	99	99	101	99	100	102	103	103	-	104

Botswana's steady progress culminated in victory in May 2006 over neighbours South Africa in the group phase of the Cosafa Castle Cup. The penalty shootout win at the National stadium over the powerhouse of the region sent the town's citizens onto the streets of the normally placid Gaborone to celebrate a first-ever success over Bafana Bafana. Success for the national side, the Zebras, had been on cards with their obvious progress over the previous 12 months. Botswana won a first-ever FIFA World Cup™ qualifier away from home with a 3-1 triumph over against Malawi last June and in friendly matches had proven their mettle against the likes of Angola, the

INTERNATIONAL HONOURS
None

Democratic Republic of Congo and Zambia. Much of the credit went to the steady hand of youthful Serbian coach Vesselin Jelusic, but he has since left his post at the helm of the Zebras to take on a new task of developing youth football in the southern African country. There was also progress at club level as Township Rollers reached the third round of the CAF Confederation Cup with a rare win over Zambian opposition. Rollers had qualified for the competion after wining the Cup in 2005 with a 3-1 triumph over Botswana Defence Force XI in the final. Police XI, coached by Sthando Mogwadi, secured the League title in May with the soldiers again in the bridesmaids' role.

THE FIFA BIG COUNT OF 2000

	Male	Female		Male	Female
Registered players	6 000	0	Referees	200	0
Non registered players	8 000	0	Officials	800	0
Youth players	3 000	0	Total involved	18 000	
Total players	17 000		Number of clubs	50	
Professional players	0	0	Number of teams	400	

Botswana Football Association (BFA)
PO Box 1396, Gaborone, Botswana
Tel +267 3900279   Fax +267 3900280
bfa@info.bw   www.bfa
President: MAKGALEMELE Dikgang Philip   General Secretary: NTSHINOGANG Thabo
Vice-President: RAMOTLHWA Segolame   Treasurer: KANDJII David   Media Officer: NTSHINOGANG Thabo
Men's Coach: JELUSIC Veselin   Women's Coach: None
BFA formed: 1970   CAF: 1976   FIFA: 1978
Blue shirts with white and black stripes, Blue shorts, Blue socks

RECENT INTERNATIONAL MATCHES PLAYED BY BOTSWANA

2003	Opponents	Score		Venue	Comp	Scorers	Att	Referee
7-09	Swaziland	D	0-0	Gaborone	CNq			Moeketsi RSA
13-10	Congo DR	L	0-2	Kinshasa	CNq			Mandzioukouta CGO
14-12	Zambia	W	1-0	Gaborone	Fr	Selolwane [20]		
2003								
9-03	Lesotho	L	0-1	Gaborone	Fr			
16-03	Namibia	W	1-0	Windhoek	CCr1	Molwantwa [4]		Fakudze SWZ
30-03	Libya	D	0-0	Tripoli	CNq			Lassina Pare BFA
16-05	Lesotho	W	2-1	Maseru	Fr	Ntshingane 2		
25-05	Malawi	D	1-1	Gaborone	CCqf	Ntshingane [21], L 1-3p	25 000	Infante MOZ
7-06	Libya	L	0-1	Gaborone	CNq			Nunkoo MRI
10-06	Trinidad and Tobago	D	0-0	Gaborone	Fr		5 000	
22-06	Swaziland	L	2-3	Mbabane	CNq	Mogaladi [41], Kolagano [56]	10 000	
5-07	Congo DR	D	0-0	Gaborone	CNq			
6-09	Swaziland	W	3-0	Mbabane	Fr			
11-10	Lesotho	W	4-1	Gaborone	WCq	Molwantwa [7], Gabolwelwe [44], Selolwane 2 [50] [53]	10 000	Manuel Joao ANG
16-11	Lesotho	D	0-0	Maseru	WCq		9 000	Shikapande ZAM
13-12	Zimbabwe	L	0-2	Selibe-Phikwe	Fr		7 000	
2004								
29-02	Lesotho	D	0-0	Maseru	CCr1	W 11-10p	10 000	Mufeti NAM
28-04	Namibia	D	0-0	Windhoek	Fr		1 500	
26-05	Mozambique	D	0-0	Maputo	Fr		2 000	
5-06	Tunisia	L	1-4	Tunis	WCq	Selolwane [65]	2 844	Abdel Rahman SUD
19-06	Malawi	W	2-0	Gaborone	WCq	Selolwane [7], Gabolwelwe [25]	15 000	Awuye UGA
3-07	Morocco	L	0-1	Gaborone	WCq		22 000	Dlamini SWZ
18-07	Angola	D	1-1	Luanda	CCqf	Motlhabankwe [25], L 3-5p	6 000	Phomane LES
18-08	Zimbabwe	L	0-2	Bulawayo	Fr		5 000	
5-09	Guinea	L	0-4	Conakry	WCq		25 000	Agbenyega GHA
9-10	Kenya	W	2-1	Gaborone	WCq	Molwantwa [51], Selolwane [58]	16 500	Colembi ANG
15-12	Lesotho	D	1-1	Maseru	Fr			
2005								
26-02	Zambia	D	0-0	Gaborone	Fr			
16-03	Zimbabwe	D	1-1	Harare	Fr	Moathiaping [72]	3 000	
26-03	Kenya	L	0-1	Nairobi	WCq		15 000	Buenkadila COD
16-04	Namibia	D	1-1	Windhoek	CCr1	Moathiaping [90]		Sentso LES
17-04	Zimbabwe	L	0-2	Windhoek	CCr1			Mavunza ANG
4-06	Tunisia	L	1-3	Gaborone	WCq	Gabonamong [13]	20 000	Mana NGA
18-06	Malawi	W	3-1	Blantyre	WCq	Molwantwa [10], Selolwane [40], Motlhabankwe [87]	20 000	Evehe CMR
1-07	Congo DR	D	0-0	Gaborone	Fr			
9-08	Angola	D	0-0	Johannesburg	Fr			
10-08	Angola	D	0-0	Johannesburg	Fr			
3-09	Morocco	L	0-1	Rabat	WCq		25 000	Benouza ALG
8-10	Guinea	L	1-2	Gaborone	WCq	Molwantwa [35]	16 800	Sowe GAM
2006								
14-05	Zambia	D	0-0	Gaborone	Fr	W 5-4p		
20-05	Madagascar	W	2-0	Gaborone	CCr1	Mothiaping [66], Mothibane [68]		
21-05	South Africa	D	0-0	Gaborone	CCr1	W 6-5p		
6-07	Malawi	L	1-2	Lilongwe	Fr	Pontsho Moloi		
8-07	Malawi	D	0-0	Blantyre	Fr			

Fr = Friendly match • CN = CAF African Cup of Nations • CC = COSAFA Cup • WC = FIFA World Cup™ • q = qualifier • r1 = first round group • qf = quarter-final

BOTSWANA NATIONAL TEAM RECORDS AND RECORD SEQUENCES

Records			Sequence records					
Victory	6-2	SWZ 2002	Wins	4	2001-2002	Clean sheets	3	Three times
Defeat	1-8	MWI 1968	Defeats	8	1968-1986	Goals scored	4	Three times
Player Caps	n/a		Undefeated	5	2001-2002	Without goal	6	1990-91, 2002
Player Goals	n/a		Without win	24	1994-1999	Goals against	14	1983-1995

BOTSWANA COUNTRY INFORMATION

Capital	Gaborone	Independence	1966	GDP per Capita	$9000
Population	1 561 973	Status	Republic	GDP Ranking	
Area km²	600 370	Language	English, Setswana	Dialling code	+267
Population density	2 per km²	Literacy rate	74%	Internet code	.bw
% in urban areas	28%	Main religion	Indigenous 85%	GMT + / –	+2
Towns/Cities ('000)	Gaborone 208; Francistown 89; Molepolole 63; Selibe Phikwe 53; Maun 49; Serowe 47				
Neighbours (km)	Zimbabwe 813; South Africa 1,840; Namibia 1,360				
Main stadia	National Stadium – Gaborone 22,500				

BOTSWANA 2005-06 PREMIER LEAGUE

	Pl	W	D	L	F	A	Pts
Police †	30	20	6	4	54	25	66
Defence Force	30	14	9	7	47	34	51
Bot. Meat Commission	30	14	9	7	36	24	51
ECCO City Green	30	13	10	7	62	48	48
Nico United	30	13	8	9	37	37	47
Prisons XI	30	13	6	11	39	34	45
Township Rollers	30	11	12	7	38	36	45
Notwane FC	30	12	6	12	47	40	42
TASC	30	11	9	10	35	35	42
Centre Chiefs	30	11	7	12	41	34	40
Gaborone United	30	10	8	12	41	38	38
FC Satmos	30	8	12	10	40	52	36
Lobtrans Gunners	30	9	8	13	34	40	35
Mogoditshane Fighters	30	10	4	16	33	38	34
Naughty Boys	30	7	6	17	31	50	27
Mosquito	30	1	6	23	27	77	9

14/10/2005 - 18/06/2006

† Qualified for the CAF Champions League
Top scorers: Malepa BOLELANG, ECCO City Green, 22; Mpho MABOGO, BDF, 19; Relegation play-offs: Fighters 0-1 Comets; Stone Breakers 1-0 Comets; Stone Breakers 1-3 Fighters; Comets 1-1 Fighters; Fighters 0-2 Stone Breakers; Comets 1-0 Stone Breakers • Comets top the group and are promoted • Mogoditshane Fighters finished bottom and are relegated

COCA-COLA CUP 2005

Round of 16		Quarter-finals		Semi-finals		Final	
Township Rollers	3						
Police	2	Township Rollers	2				
Jwaneng Comets	2 4p	Centre Chiefs	0				
Centre Chiefs	2 5p			Township Rollers	3		
Lobtrans Gunners				Boteti Young Fighters	1		
Prisons		Lobtrans Gunners	0				
Santos	0	Boteti Young Fighters	1				
Boteti Young Fighters	1					Township Rollers ‡	3
Nico United	3					Defence Force	1
Satmos	2	Nico United	2				
Motlakase	1	Notwane	1				
Notwane	3			Nico United	1 2p		
TASC	2 4			Defence Force	1 3p		
TAFIC	2 2	TASC	0 3p				
Red Sparks	0	Defence Force	0 4p				
Defence Force	2						

CUP FINAL
27-08-2005

Scorers - Moathaping 2 [7] [110], Mongala [111] for Township Rollers; Tobega [21p] for BDF

* Home Team • ‡ Qualified for the CAF Confederation Cup

RECENT LEAGUE AND CUP RECORD

	Championship						Cup		
Year	Champions	Pts	Runners-up	Pts	Third	Pts	Winners	Score	Runners-up
1999	Mogoditshane	25	Defence Force	21	Centre Chiefs	21	Mogodishane	3-0	Satmos
2000	Mogoditshane	42	Centre Chiefs	40	Defence Force	37	Mogodishane	1-1 5-4p	Gaborone United
2001	Mogoditshane	45	Defence Force	44	Police XI	43	TASC	2-0	Extension Gunners
2002	Defence Force	47	Mogoditshane	38	Centre Chiefs	36	Tafic	0-0 6-5p	TASC
2003	Mogoditshane	2-1	Police XI				Mogodishane	1-0	Township Rollers
2004	Defence Force		Police XI		TASC	39	Defence Force	2-1	Mogodishane
2005	Township Rollers	52	Police XI	51	Centre Chiefs	45	Township Rollers	3-1	Defence Force
2006	Police XI	66	Defence Force	51	Meat Commission	51			

BRA – BRAZIL

NATIONAL TEAM RECORD
JULY 1ST 2002 TO JULY 9TH 2006

PL	W	D	L	F	A	%
60	33	17	10	122	47	66.7

Not since 1990 have Brazil been knocked out so early in the finals of the FIFA World Cup™. The defeat in Germany in the quarter-finals was greeted with dismay and the usual finger wagging, but as Ronaldinho said after the finals, "We can't win it every time!" and it would have been uncharted territory if Brazil had made it to a fourth consecutive final. In recent years France have had the Indian Sign over Brazil and so it was no surprise that for the third time in six tournaments they were responsible for Brazil's exit. The expectation placed on the national team was perhaps unrealistic and it's worth noting that in the 60 games played by Brazil since the final in Yokohama in 2002, only just over half of them were won, with ten ending in defeat. Only once before - from 1962 to 1966 - have Brazil lost so many matches from World Cup to World Cup. For Ronaldinho, the disappointment will have been tempered by the fact that he was a large part of the inspiration behind Barcelona's triumph in the UEFA Champions League. There was one world championship to celebrate, when São Paulo won the FIFA Club World Championship in Tokyo in December, proving that there is life in the Brazilian league yet. Indeed the story of the season in Serie A was

INTERNATIONAL HONOURS
FIFA World Cup™ 1958 1962 1970 1994 2002   **FIFA Confederations Cup** 1997 2005
FIFA World Youth Championship 1983 1985 1993 2003   **FIFA U-17 World Championship** 1997 1999 2003
Copa América 1919 1922 1949 1989 1997 1999 2004   **South American Women's Championship** 1991 1995 1998 2003
Sudamericana Sub-20 1974 1983 1985 1988 1991 1992 1995 2001   **Sudamericana Sub-17** 1988 1991 1995 1997 1999 2001
FIFA Club World Championship Corínthians 2000   **Copa Toyota Libertadores** Santos 1962 1963 Cruzeiro 1976 1997
Flamengo 1981 Grêmio 1983 1995 São Paulo 1992 1993 2005 Vasco da Gama 1998 Palmeiras 1999 Internacional 2006

the rebirth of Corinthians backed by the MSI millions. With close to 50 million dollars invested in the club, notably with the signing of Argentine Star Carlos Tevez, Corinthians duly won the title in 2005, although their triumph was controversial. Allegations of match fixing meant that a number of games had to be replayed but had the original results stood, the title would have gone to Internacional instead. Internacional put the disappointment behind them, however, with a great Copa Libertadores campaign in 2006. They reached the final for the first time in their history, where they met defending champions São Paulo. It was the second all-Brazilian final in a row and despite being the underdogs, Internacional beat São Paulo 4-3 on aggregate to claim the title. Perhaps the surprise of the season was the mini-revival of football in Rio de Janeiro witnessed during the Copa do Brasil. The city boasted half of the teams in the quarter-finals; three of the four semi-finalists and both finalists in Vasco da Gama and Flamengo and it was Flamengo who won their first major trophy at home since 1992.

Confederação Brasileira de Futebol (CBF)
Rua Victor Civita 66, Bloco 1 - Edificio 5 - 5 Andar, Barra da Tijuca, Rio de Janeiro 22.775-040, Brazil
Tel +55 21 35359610   Fax +55 21 35359611
CBF@cbffutebol.com.br   www.cbfnews.com.br
President: TEIXEIRA Ricardo Terra   General Secretary: TEIXEIRA Marco Antonio
Vice-President: BASTOS Jose Sebastiao   Treasurer: OSORIO LOPES DA COSTA Antonio   Media Officer: PAIVA Rodrigo
Men's Coach: DUNGA Carlos   Women's Coach: FERREIRA Luiz
CBF formed: 1914   CONMEBOL: 1916   FIFA: 1923
Yellow shirts with green trimmings, Blue shorts, White socks or Blue shirts with white trimmings, White shorts, White socks

RECENT INTERNATIONAL MATCHES PLAYED BY BRAZIL

2003	Opponents	Score		Venue	Comp	Scorers	Att	Referee
19-11	Uruguay	D	3-3	Curitiba	WCq	Kaka [19], Ronaldo 2 [29 87]	30 000	Elizondo ARG
2004								
18-02	Republic of Ireland	D	0-0	Dublin	Fr		44 000	Frisk SWE
31-03	Paraguay	D	0-0	Asuncion	WCq		40 000	Ruiz COL
28-04	Hungary	W	4-1	Budapest	Fr	Kaka [33], Luis Fabiano 2 [36 45], Ronaldinho [76]	45 000	De Santis ITA
20-05	France	D	0-0	Paris	FIFA		79 344	Gonzalez ESP
2-06	Argentina	W	3-1	Belo Horizonte	WCq	Ronaldo 3 [16p 67p 90p]	50 000	Ruiz COL
6-06	Chile	D	1-1	Santiago	WCq	Luis Fabiano [15]	62 503	Elizondo ARG
8-07	Chile	W	1-0	Arequipa	CAr1	Luis Fabiano [89]	35 000	Rodriguez MEX
11-07	Costa Rica	W	4-1	Arequipa	CAr1	Adriano 3 [45 54 68], Juan [49]	12 000	Baldassi ARG
14-07	Paraguay	L	1-2	Arequipa	CAr1	Luis Fabiano [35]	8 000	Hidalgo PER
18-07	Mexico	W	4-0	Piura	CAqf	Alex [26p], Adriano 2 [65 78], Ricardo Oliveira [87]	22 000	Ruiz COL
21-07	Uruguay	D	1-1	Lima	CAsf	Adriano [46] W 5-3p	10 000	Rodriguez MEX
25-07	Argentina	D	2-2	Lima	CAf	Luisao [45], Adriano [90]	43 000	Amarilla PAR
18-08	Haiti	W	6-0	Port-au-Prince	Fr	Roger 2 [17 40], Ronaldinho 3 [33 70 80], Nilmar [89]	15 000	Oliveira BRA
5-09	Bolivia	W	3-1	Sao Paulo	WCq	Ronaldo [1], Ronaldinho [12p], Adriano [44]	60 000	Baldassi ARG
8-09	Germany	D	1-1	Berlin	Fr	Ronaldinho [9]	74 315	Meier SUI
9-10	Venezuela	W	5-2	Maracaibo	WCq	Kaka 2 [5 34], Ronaldo 2 [48 50], Adriano [75]	26 133	Chandia CHI
13-10	Colombia	D	0-0	Maceio	WCq		20 000	Larrionda URU
16-11	Ecuador	L	0-1	Quito	WCq		38 308	Ruiz COL
2005								
9-02	Hong Kong	W	7-1	Hong Kong	Fr	Lucio [19], Roberto Carlos [30], Ricardo Oliveira 2 [45 57], Ronaldinho [49], Robinho [77], Alex [79p]	23 425	Zhou Weixin CHN
27-03	Peru	W	1-0	Goiania	WCq	Kaka [74]	49 163	Amarilla PAR
30-03	Uruguay	D	1-1	Montevideo	WCq	Emerson [67]	60 000	Baldassi ARG
27-04	Guatemala	W	3-0	Sao Paulo	Fr	Anderson [4], Romario [16], Grafite [65]	36 235	Vazquez URU
5-06	Paraguay	W	4-1	Porto Alegre	WCq	Ronaldinho 2 [32p 41p], Ze Roberto [70], Robinho [82]	45 000	Vazquez URU
8-06	Argentina	L	1-3	Buenos Aires	WCq	Roberto Carlos [71]	49 497	Mendez URU
16-06	Greece	W	3-0	Leipzig	CCr1	Adriano [41], Robinho [46], Juninho Pernambuco [81]	42 507	Michel SVK
19-06	Mexico	L	0-1	Hanover	CCr1		43 677	Rosetti ITA
22-06	Japan	D	2-2	Köln	CCr1	Robinho [10], Ronaldinho [32]	44 922	Daami TUN
26-06	Germany	W	3-2	Nürnberg	CCsf	Adriano 2 [21 76], Ronaldinho [43p]	42 187	Breeze AUS
29-06	Argentina	W	4-1	Frankfurt	CCf	Adriano 2 [11 63], Kaka [16], Ronaldinho [47]	45 591	Michel SVK
17-08	Croatia	D	1-1	Split	Fr	Ricardinho [41]	30 000	Meyer GER
4-09	Chile	W	5-0	Brasilia	WCq	Juan [11], Robinho [21], Adriano 3 [27 29 92+]	39 000	Amarilla PAR
9-10	Bolivia	D	1-1	La Paz	WCq	Juninho Pernambuco [25]	22 725	Larrionda URU
12-10	Venezuela	W	3-0	Belem	WCq	Adriano [28], Ronaldo [51], Roberto Carlos [61]	47 000	Baldassi ARG
12-11	United Arab Emirates	W	8-0	Abu Dhabi	Fr	Kaka [20], Adriano [52], Fred 2 [57 84], Lucio [54], Juninho Pernambuco 2 [70 79], Cicinho [90]	50 000	Abd El Fatah EGY
2006								
1-03	Russia	W	1-0	Moscow	Fr	Ronaldo [15]	19 000	Busacca SUI
4-06	New Zealand	W	4-0	Geneva	Fr	Ronaldo [43], Adriano [51], Kaká [86], Juninho P'buco [90]	32 000	Laperriere SUI
13-06	Croatia	W	1-0	Berlin	WCr1	Kaká [44]	72 000	Archundia MEX
18-06	Australia	W	2-0	Munich	WCr1	Adriano [49], Fred [90]	66 000	Merk GER
22-06	Japan	W	4-1	Dortmund	WCr1	Ronaldo 2 [46+ 81], Juninho P'buco [53], Gilberto [59]	65 000	Poulat FRA
27-06	Ghana	W	3-0	Dortmund	WCr2	Ronaldo [5], Adriano [46+], Ze Roberto [84]	65 000	Michel SVK
1-07	France	L	0-1	Frankfurt	WCqf		48 000	Medina Cantalejo ESP

Fr = Friendly match • CC = FIFA Confederations Cup • GC = CONCACAF Gold Cup • CA = Copa America • WC = FIFA World Cup™
FIFA = FIFA Centennial celebration match • q = qualifier • r1 = 1st round • r2 = second round • qf = quarter-final • sf = semi-final • f = final

BRAZIL NATIONAL TEAM RECORDS AND RECORD SEQUENCES

Records			Sequence records				
Victory	10-1	BOL 1949	Wins	14	1997	Clean sheets	8	1989
Defeat	0-6	URU 1920	Defeats	4	2001	Goals scored	47	1994-1997
Player Caps	126	CAFU	Undefeated	45	1993-1997	Without goal	5	1990
Player Goals	77	PELE	Without win	7	1983-84, 1990-91	Goals against	24	1937-1944

BRAZIL COUNTRY INFORMATION

Capital	Brasilia	Independence	1822 from Portugal	GDP per Capita	$7 600
Population	184 101 109	Status	Republic	GNP Ranking	1
Area km²	8 511 965	Language	Portuguese	Dialling code	+55
Population density	21 per km²	Literacy rate	84%	Internet code	.br
% in urban areas	78%	Main religion	Christian 95%	GMT + / –	-3

Towns/Cities ('000)	São Paulo 19 091; Rio de Janeiro 11 719; Belo Horizonte 4 919; Porto Alegre 3 762; Recife 3 540; Salvador 3 415; Fortaleza 3 131; Curitiba 3 042; Brasilia 2 207; Belém 2 252; Brasilia 2 207; Goiânia 1 855; Santos 1 664; Manaus 1 598; Vitória 1 512; Campinas 1 443; São Luis 1 224; Natal 1 172, Maceió 1 064; Teresina 1 014; João Pessoa 975; Ribeirão Preto 840; Florianópolis 790
Neighbours (km)	Venezuela 2 200; Guyana 1 119; Surinam 597; French Guiana 673; Uruguay 985; Argentina 1 224; Paraguay 1 290; Bolivia 3 400; Peru 1 560; Colombia 1 643; Atlantic Ocean 7 491
Main stadia	Maracanã – Rio 103 045; Mineirão – Belo Horizonte 81 987; Morumbi – São Paulo 80 000; Castelão – São Luis 75 000; Castelão – Fortaleza 69 000; Fonte Nova – Salvador 66 000

BRAZIL NATIONAL TEAM PLAYERS AND COACHES

Record Caps			Record Goals			Recent Coaches	
CAFU	1990-'05	142	PELE	1957-'71	77	LAZARONI Sebastião	1989-'90
ROBERTO CARLOS	1992-'06	125	RONALDO	1994-'06	62	FALCAO Roberto	1990-'01
CLAUDIO TAFFAREL	1987-'98	102	ROMARIO	1987-'05	56	PAULO Ernesto	1991
DJALMA SANTOS	1952-'68	100	ZICO	1971-'89	52	PARREIRA Carlos Alberto	1991-'94
RONALDO	1994-'06	97	BEBETO	1985-'98	39	ZAGALLO Mario	1994-'98
GILMAR	1953-'69	95	RIVALDO	1993-'03	36	LUXEMBURGO Wanderlay	1998-'00
ROBERTO RIVELINO	1965-'78	92	JAIRZINHO	1963-'82	36	LEAO Emerson	2000-'01
PELE	1957-'71	91	TOSTAO	1966-'72	32	SCOLARI Luis Felipe	2001-'02
CARLOS DUNGA	1982-'98	91	ADEMIR DE MENEZES	1945-'53	31	PARREIRA Carlos Alberto	2002-'06
DIDA	1995-'06	91	CARECA	1982-'93	29	DUNGA Carlos	2006-

FIFA/COCA-COLA WORLD RANKING

1993	1994	1995	1996	1997	1998	1999	2000	2001	2002	2003	2004	2005		High	Low	
3	1	1	1	1	1	1	1	3	1	1	1	1		1	8	08/93

2005–2006											
08/05	09/05	10/05	11/05	12/05	01/06	02/06	03/06	04/06	05/06	06/06	07/06
1	1	1	1	1	1	1	1	1	1	-	1

THE FIFA BIG COUNT OF 2000

	Male	Female		Male	Female
Registered players	275 000	4 000	Referees	3 000	46
Non registered players	5 500 000	30 000	Officials	40 000	1 000
Youth players	1 222 828	2 000	Total involved	7 077 874	
Total players	7 033 828		Number of clubs	6 000	
Professional players	14 709	152	Number of teams	20 000	

BRAZIL 2005

SERIE A

Team	Pl	W	D	L	F	A	Pts	Corinth'ns	Inter	Goiás	Palmeiras	Flu	Atlético PR	Paraná	Cruzeiro	Botafogo	Santos	São Paulo	Vasco	Fortaleza	Juventude	Flamengo	Fig'ense	Caetano	Ponte P.	Coritiba	Atlético MG	Paysandu	Brasiliense
Corinthians †	42	24	9	9	87	59	81		1-1	1-1	3-1	0-1	2-0	1-0	4-3	3-3	7-1	1-5	1-1	3-0	2-2	4-2	2-1	0-2	3-1	3-0	1-1	3-2	3-2
Internacional †	42	23	9	10	72	49	78	0-0		2-3	2-1	2-2	3-2	0-2	4-1	0-2	0-1	3-0	3-1	1-0	5-2	1-1	3-0	2-1	2-1	**3-2**	1-1	1-0	1-0
Goiás †	42	22	8	12	68	51	74	3-2	0-1		2-1	1-2	4-2	1-1	1-0	4-0	3-4	3-0	4-3	2-1	1-0	2-0	0-0	0-0	4-1	2-1	3-1	4-1	1-3
Palmeiras †	42	20	10	12	81	65	70	1-1	3-2	3-1		3-2	1-1	1-2	2-1	4-1	2-1	2-1	5-2	1-2	3-2	0-1	2-2	2-1	2-1	2-1	1-1	1-0	5-3
Fluminense ‡	42	19	11	12	79	70	68	0-2	3-0	1-1	2-2		4-1	0-1	2-1	3-2	4-3	2-1	3-2	2-0	1-2	2-2	2-0	0-1	4-3	2-4	0-2	5-2	**1-1**
Atlético Paranaense‡	42	18	7	17	76	67	61	1-2	1-3	1-0	4-0	3-2		2-1	5-4	2-0	3-3	4-7	2-0	0-2	2-2	0-0	0-2	2-0	0-1	1-0	2-0	3-2	4-0
Paraná ‡	42	17	10	15	59	51	61	2-3	3-1	0-2	1-3	6-1	2-0		2-0	2-0	1-1	0-4	0-0	3-0	0-1	3-0	1-3	1-1	3-2	1-0	2-0	4-1	
Cruzeiro ‡	42	17	9	16	73	72	60	2-1	3-2	3-1	2-0	2-6	1-2	0-1		**2-2**	3-2	3-3	3-0	0-0	4-0	0-1	3-1	2-2	2-2	2-1	4-3	1-0	1-1
Botafogo ‡	42	17	8	17	57	56	59	3-1	0-1	3-1	1-2	1-2	2-0	2-0	2-1		3-3	1-1	2-2	3-0	2-0	0-1	1-0	4-2	2-0	2-1	2-0	1-1	
Santos ‡	42	16	11	15	68	71	59	**2-3**	0-4	1-2	1-1	2-1	1-1	1-2	1-1	1-0		2-3	2-4	1-2	0-0	2-0	2-0	1-3	1-3	3-1	3-1	3-0	2-0
São Paulo †	42	16	10	16	77	67	58	**1-1**	1-3	0-1	3-3	1-3	1-1	1-1	1-1	1-0	1-2		4-2	3-2	3-1	2-0	4-1	3-2	1-0	2-2	4-1	1-1	1-2
Vasco da Gama	42	15	11	16	74	84	56	2-3	4-1	2-0	0-2	0-2	1-3	1-3	3-1	**0-1**	3-3	1-0		0-0	5-2	2-1	**3-3**	3-2	0-0	2-2	2-1	4-0	1-0
Fortaleza	42	16	7	19	58	64	55	2-1	1-2	1-1	1-1	5-1	1-4	2-2	3-1	3-1	0-0	1-0	4-2		2-0	2-1	5-2	5-2	2-1	0-1	1-4	1-2	2-0
Juventude	42	15	10	17	66	72	55	1-0	2-1	2-1	1-2	**3-4**	1-1	4-1	2-0	0-0	0-0	0-1	1-1	3-1		4-1	**2-0**	2-2	3-1	1-3	0-1	3-2	2-1
Flamengo	42	14	13	15	56	60	55	1-4	1-1	1-0	0-0	0-0	0-1	1-1	1-1	1-6	1-1	0-3	0-4	3-0	3-4		2-2	2-0	1-0	2-1	1-2	2-1	3-4
Figueirense	42	14	11	17	65	72	53	2-3	1-2	3-0	1-4	1-1	2-0	2-0	0-0	1-0	1-3	1-5	1-1	0-4	3-0	1-0		2-0	4-0	0-0	0-1	3-3	2-2
São Caetano	42	14	10	18	54	60	52	1-0	1-1	0-1	2-2	2-2	3-2	1-0	1-0	1-1	3-0	1-1	2-2	1-1	1-1	0-0	0-1		2-1	1-1	3-1	1-2	2-0
Ponte Preta	42	15	6	21	63	80	51	3-5	1-1	2-0	2-6	2-1	0-2	1-0	2-3	0-1	2-1	**2-0**	4-2	2-1	3-2	2-2	2-1	1-0		0-3	3-3	2-0	3-1
Coritiba	42	13	10	19	51	60	49	0-1	0-0	2-1	0-0	1-2	2-1	0-3	0-3	2-1	3-4	2-0	2-0	2-1	3-2	4-1	2-2	2-1			1-0	3-1	1-1
Atlético Mineiro	42	13	8	21	54	59	47	0-1	1-1	1-2	1-3	1-2	2-3	0-1	0-1	0-2	3-0	0-0	0-2	3-1	3-1	4-1	2-3	1-0	1-0			2-2	0-1
Paysandu	42	12	5	25	63	92	41	0-2	1-2	1-0	2-1	1-2	2-1	3-4	**4-1**	2-0	2-3	2-2	0-2	1-2	3-0	1-4	3-1	3-2	2-2	2-1	0-2		2-1
Brasiliense	42	10	11	21	47	67	41	2-4	0-0	1-2	3-0	3-2	1-1	0-1	0-2	3-1	1-0	2-1	0-2	3-0	2-1	1-4	0-1	1-1	1-4	0-1	1-1	1-2	

23/04/2005 - 4/12/2005 • † Qualied for the Copa Libertadores 2006 • ‡ Qualified for the Copa Sudamericana 2006
Top scorers: ROMARIO, Vasco da Gama, 22; ROBSON, Paysandu 21; Carlos TEVEZ, Corinthians, 20; RAFAEL SOBIS, Internacional, 20
Matches in bold were replayed as the original games had been refereed by Edilson P. Carvalho. The original results were - Vasco 0-1 Botafogo;
Ponte Preta 1-0 São Paulo; Paysandu 1-2 Cruzeiro; Juventude 1-4 Figueirense; Santos 4-2 Corinthians; Vasco 2-1 Figueirense; Cruzeiro 4-1
Botafogo; Juventude 2-0 Fluminense; Internacional 3-2 Coritiba; São Paulo 3-2 Corinthians; Fluminense 3-0 Brasiliense

BRAZIL 2005 — SERIE B PRIMEIRA FASE

Team	Pl	W	D	L	F	A	Pts
Santa Cruz †	21	12	5	4	32	21	41
Marília †	21	11	2	8	38	28	35
Guarani †	21	10	5	6	30	23	35
Grêmio †	21	9	8	4	32	26	35
Santo André †	21	10	4	7	34	25	34
Portuguesa †	21	10	4	7	35	27	34
Náutico †	21	10	3	8	35	34	33
Avaí †	21	10	2	9	34	28	32
Vila Nova	21	10	2	9	28	29	32
Ituano	21	9	4	8	33	26	31
Ceará	21	8	5	8	27	22	29
CRB	21	8	5	8	28	37	29
Gama	21	8	4	9	28	33	28
São Raimundo	21	8	4	9	22	28	28
Paulista	21	7	7	7	39	35	28
Sport Recife	21	8	3	10	29	32	27
Vitória	21	7	6	8	35	35	27
Bahia	21	7	4	10	28	33	25
Anapolina	21	7	4	10	23	31	25
Barbarense	21	6	6	9	20	24	24
Criciúma	21	6	1	14	24	45	19
Caxias	21	4	4	13	19	33	16

23/04/2005 - 10/09/2005 • † Qualified for semi-final stage

SERIE B FASE SEMI-FINAL — Group A

Team	Pl	W	D	L	F	A	Pts	SC	Grêm	SA	Avaí
Santa Cruz †	6	4	1	1	13	5	13		1-0	3-0	5-1
Grêmio †	6	4	0	2	8	4	12	2-0		0-2	2-0
Santo André	6	3	1	2	7	5	10	1-1	0-1		3-0
Avaí	6	0	0	6	3	17	0	1-3	1-3	0-1	

16/09/2005 - 14/10/2005 • † Qualified for final stage

SERIE B FASE SEMI-FINAL — Group B

Team	Pl	W	D	L	F	A	Pts	Náut	Port	Maril	Guar
Náutico †	6	4	0	2	13	7	12		0-1	3-0	1-0
Portuguesa †	6	3	1	2	7	6	10	1-2		2-0	1-0
Marília	6	3	0	3	10	13	9	4-3	3-1		3-2
Guarani	6	1	1	4	6	10	4	1-4	1-1	2-0	

17/09/2005 - 15/10/2005 • † Qualified for final stage

SERIE B FASE FINAL — Group A

Team	Pl	W	D	L	F	A	Pts	Grêm	SC	Náut	Port
Grêmio	6	3	3	0	8	4	12		2-0	1-0	2-2
Santa Cruz	6	3	1	2	7	8	10	1-1		1-0	2-1
Náutico	6	2	0	4	6	6	6	0-1	0-2		4-1
Portuguesa	6	1	2	3	9	12	5	1-1	4-1	0-2	

22/10/2005 - 26/11/2005

COPA DO BRASIL 2006

First Round

Team	Leg 1	Leg 2
Flamengo	1	2
ASA *	1	1
Parnahyba *	0	1
ABC	1	5
Potiguar *	2	2
Santo André	0	1
Estrela do Norte *	1	0
Guarani	1	3
Fortaleza	3	
Vilhena *	1	
Bahia	0	1
Ceilândia *	0	2
Mineiros *	3	2
Americano	1	4
Atlétco Herman Aichunger *	0	
Atlético Mineiro	3	
Santos	0	3
Sergipe *	0	0
Londrina	2	1
URT *	3	1
Remo	0	4
Itabaiana *	0	1
São Raimundo *	0	
Brasiliense	2	
Náutico	1	4
Rio Branco *	0	1
ICADA *	0	1
Coritiba	0	3
Botafogo (RJ)	2	5
Operário *	1	1
Serra *	1	
Ipatinga	3	
Fluminense	3	3
Operário (MT) *	2	1
Treze	1	1
CENE *	2	3
Paysandu	2	
Colinas *	0	
Grêmio Coariense *	2	
Vila Nova	5	
Vitória	1	5
Imperatriz *	1	2
Vila Aurora *	0	0
Santa Cruz	0	1
CRB	1	3
São José *	0	0
Nacional *	2	
Cruzeiro	5	
Volta Redonda *	2	1 7p
América (MG)	1	2 6p
Moto Clube *	1	
Atlético Paranaense	3	
Grêmio	2	4
Piauí *	1	0
Noroeste	1	2
15 de Novembro *	4	0
Criciúma	2	2
Novo Hamburgo *	2	1
Cabofriense *	1	1
São Caetano	1	4
Iraty	4	
Ulbra *	2	
Botafogo (PB) *	1	0
Vasco da Gama	1	7

Second Round

Team	Leg 1	Leg 2
Flamengo	1	4
ABC *	0	0
Potiguar *	0	
Guarani	4	
Fortaleza	1	3
Ceilândia *	1	1
Mineiros *	3	1
Atlético Mineiro	2	4
Santos	3	
URT *	1	
Remo	1	0
Brasiliense *	3	1
Náutico *	2	0
Coritiba	0	0
Botafogo (RJ)	0	1
Ipatinga *	3	3
Fluminense	5	
CENE *	3	
Paysandu	1	1
Vila Nova *	3	0
Vitória	2	3
Santa Cruz *	2	2
CRB *	0	
Cruzeiro	2	
Volta Redonda *	2	0
Atlético Paranaense	1	0
Grêmio	0	1 5p
15 de Novembro *	1	0 6p
Criciúma	1	4
São Caetano *	4	0
Iraty *	2	1
Vasco da Gama	2	5

Third Round

Team	Leg 1	Leg 2
Flamengo *	5	0
Guarani	1	1
Fortaleza	2	1
Atlético Mineiro *	0	3
Santos *	2	1
Brasiliense	1	1
Náutico	1	1
Ipatinga *	3	3
Fluminense	2	4
Vila Nova *	2	0
Vitória *		
Cruzeiro		
Volta Redonda *	1	1
15 de Novembro	0	2
Criciúma *	1	0
Vasco da Gama	2	1

If the away team wins the first leg by two goals in the first or second round no second leg is played

COPA DO BRASIL 2006

Quarter-finals **Semi-finals** **Final**

BRAZILIAN CUP FINAL

1st leg. Maracanã, Rio de Janeiro
19-07-2006, Att: 43 955, Ref: Gaciba

Scorer - Obina 2 [60] [62]

Flamengo - Diego - Renato Silva (Obina),
Fernando, Ronaldo Angelim∗ - Leonardo Moura,
Jônatas, Toró (Júnior∗), Renato Augusto
(Rodrigo Arroz), Renato, Juan - Luizão.
Tr: Ney Franco
Vasco - Cássio - Wagner Diniz, Fábio Braz,
Jorge Luiz, Diego - Ives∗, Andrade∗, Morais,
Ramon∗ (Abedi) - Edilson, Valdiram.
Tr: Renato Gaúcho

Flamengo *	4	0
Atlético Mineiro	1	0

Flamengo	1	2
Ipatinga *	1	1

Santos *	1	1 3p
Ipatinga	1	1 5p

Flamengo *	2	1
Vasco da Gama	0	0

Fluminense	3	1
Cruzeiro *	2	0

Fluminense *	0	1
Vasco da Gama	1	1

BRAZILIAN CUP FINAL

2nd leg. Maracanã, Rio de Janeiro
26-07-2006, Att: 44 660, Ref: Simon

Scorer - Juan [27]

Flamengo - Diego - Renato Silva, Fernando∗,
Rodrigo Arroz - Leonardo Moura, Toró∗ (Obina),
Jônatas, Renato, Juan - Renato Augusto∗
(Peralta), Luizão∗ (Léo).
Tr: Ney Franco
Vasco - Cássio - Wagner Diniz∗, Fabio Braz,
Jorge Luiz, Diego - Ygor, Andrade (Abedi∗),
Ramon (Valdiram), Morais∗ (Ernane) - Valdir
Papel∗, Edilson.
Tr: Renato Gaúcho

Volta Redonda *	0	1
Vasco da Gama	0	2

* Home team in the first leg

BRAZIL STATE CHAMPIONSHIPS 2006

CAMPEONATO PAULISTA SERIE A1

	Pl	W	D	L	F	A	Pts	Santos	São Paulo	Palmeiras	Noroeste	S. Caetano	Corinthians	Rio Branco	Juventus	Ituano	América	São Bento	Paulista	Ponte Preta	Bragantino	S. André	Marília	Guarani	Portuguesa	P. Santista	Mogi Mirim
Santos	19	14	1	4	33	19	43						1-0		1-0					1-0	3-1	3-0	3-2		2-0		2-0
São Paulo FC	19	13	3	3	46	21	42	3-1				4-2	1-1	2-1		0-1	2-0		5-1				3-3	3-1			3-0
Palmeiras	19	11	3	5	37	28	36					4-0	1-1	0-2	4-3	2-1	1-4	1-0		4-2	1-1						4-0
Noroeste	19	10	4	5	34	26	34						1-3		1-0			2-2		1-1	4-2	4-0	2-1	1-0	3-2		
São Caetano	19	9	5	5	26	23	32	2-3					1-0		2-1	1-0		2-0		1-2				2-0	1-0	1-1	1-1
Corinthians	19	9	4	6	43	24	31	0-1	1-2							2-1			5-0	2-2		4-1	4-1	1-1	2-2		5-1
Rio Branco	19	9	3	7	34	28	30		2-4			3-1			1-4		1-1	0-0		1-2	2-1		5-2			2-0	
Juventus	19	8	3	8	31	28	27	1-2				3-1	0-1						3-2			0-1	1-1	1-1	1-2	2-0	
Ituano	19	7	6	6	27	23	27	0-2					1-1	2-3			3-0		2-1	4-1		2-2		2-1		1-0	3-0
América	19	8	1	10	25	30	25	2-3						2-3	0-0	2-1		0-2	1-3			1-2	0-2				3-1
São Bento	19	7	4	8	23	27	25	1-1	2-0				1-1	3-2					0-1			1-1	1-1	1-0	1-0		
Paulista	19	7	4	8	28	33	25	3-1				3-0	1-3			2-0	1-1	1-2				1-2	2-1	2-2			2-1
Ponte Preta	19	6	7	6	24	24	25		1-2					1-3	1-0	1-1	1-1		2-0			1-2	2-2				1-0
Bragantino	19	6	6	7	24	26	24	3-3						2-3		3-0			1-1	0-1		0-2	0-1	0-0			2-0
Santo André	19	6	3	10	26	38	21	1-0	1-3					1-3	1-3	2-0			3-2		0-2		0-2	1-1			2-1
Marília	19	5	5	9	25	34	20	0-2	1-2					2-3			0-2	2-1				0-1		3-1	2-2	1-0	
Guarani	19	4	7	8	24	31	19	2-1						1-1	1-1				3-2		1-2	0-1	1-2		2-2	2-0	0-0
Portuguesa	19	5	3	11	21	30	18						1-2			2-1	0-2	1-0	3-1	0-2	5-2	1-1	1-2	3-2			
AA Portuguesa Santista	19	5	2	12	22	38	17	2-1	0-5							2-3			0-1			3-1	2-2	4-1	2-1		2-1
Mogi Mirim	19	2	4	13	18	40	10				1-2	1-2	1-5	3-5	1-4		4-1	1-0		2-2			0-2	0-0			

11/01/2006 - 9/04/2006 • Top scorers: NILMAR, Corinthians, 18; THIAGO, São Paulo, 10

BRAZIL STATE CHAMPIONSHIPS 2006

CAMPEONATO CARIOCA 2006 RESULTS

	Botafogo	Mad'eira	América	C'friense	Am'cano	Frib'ense	Volta R.	Flu	Vasco	Iguaçu	Fla	P'guesa
Botafogo		0-2	1-1		3-0					5-3	1-1	
Madureira	1-2		0-3		1-0		2-1			3-1		0-0
América				1-1	2-1		1-2			2-1	2-2	
Cabofriense			0-0			5-2			2-0	1-2	2-1	2-1
Americano	2-2	2-1		3-2			2-1	2-2		3-2		
Friburgense				3-2	1-0			1-1			3-3	3-1
Volta Redonda	3-2	3-1		3-1		1-2			1-2	2-1		
Fluminense	2-2			2-0	0-1	1-4			2-2		3-2	4-0
Vasco da Gama			3-1		2-2		2-1					2-2
Nova Iguaçu			0-2		5-1			0-6	2-4			3-2
Flamengo	3-2	2-3			4-2		0-0		1-2	0-1		
Portuguesa	0-2		0-3		0-2		2-1				2-2	

Clubs listed according to overall position • Taça Guanabara results in shaded boxes • Taça Rio results in unshaded boxes

TAÇA GUANABARA

Group A	Pl	W	D	L	F	A	Pts
Americano †	5	3	1	1	12	10	10
Cabofriense †	5	3	0	2	7	7	9
Nova Igaçu	5	3	0	2	5	11	9
Fluminense	5	2	2	1	14	5	8
Flamengo	5	1	2	2	9	9	5
Portuguesa	5	0	1	4	5	13	1

Group B	Pl	W	D	L	F	A	Pts
América †	5	3	0	2	10	6	9
Botafogo †	5	3	0	2	12	9	9
Volta Redonda	5	3	0	2	10	8	9
Vasco da Gama	5	2	1	2	10	7	7
Friburgense	5	2	1	2	6	8	7
Madureira	5	1	0	4	4	11	3

14/01/2006 - 12/02/2006 • † Qualified for the semis
Semi-finals: Botafogo 2-1 Americano; América 1-1 5-4p Cabofriense • Final: Botafogo 3-1 América

CARIOCA FINAL

(Played between the winners of the Taça Guanabara and Taça Rio)

1st leg. Maracana, Rio de Janeiro
2-04-2006, 31 176, Ref: Beltrami

Botafogo 2-0 Madureira

Scorers - Reinaldo 67, Macedo 27

2nd leg. Maracana, Rio de Janeiro
9-04-2006, 44 550, Ref: Azevedo

Botafogo 3-1 Madureira

Scorers - Ricardo Lucas 2 38 50, Reinaldo 85 for Botafogo; Fabio Junior for Madureira

TAÇA RIO

Group A	Pl	W	D	L	F	A	Pts
Cabofriense †	6	2	3	1	10	7	9
Americano †	6	2	2	2	9	9	8
Fluminense	6	2	2	2	10	11	8
Flamengo	6	1	3	2	11	12	6
Portuguesa	6	1	2	3	5	11	5
Nova Igaçu	6	1	1	4	10	13	4

Group B	Pl	W	D	L	F	A	Pts
América †	6	3	2	1	10	6	11
Madureira †	6	3	2	1	9	6	11
Friburgense	6	3	1	2	14	15	10
Vasco da Gama	6	2	3	1	12	11	9
Volta Redonda	6	2	1	3	8	8	7
Botafogo	6	1	4	1	10	9	7

18/02/2006 - 19/03/2006 • † Qualified for the semis
Semi-finals: Americano 3-1 América; Madureira 1-1 4-3p Cabofriense • Final: Madureira 1-0 Americano

CLUB DIRECTORY

Club	Town/City	Stadium	Capacity	www.	Lge	Cup	SC	CL
Atlético Mineiro	Belo Horizonte	Mineirão	81 987	atletico.com.br	1	0	38	0
Atlético Paranaense	Curitiba	Arena da Baixada	32 000	atleticopr.com.br	1	0	21	0
Botafogo	Rio de Janeiro	Arena Petrobrás	30 000	botafogonocoracao.com.br	1	0	18	0
Corinthians	São Paulo	São Jorge	12 000	sccorinthians.com.br	4	2	25	0
Coritiba	Curitiba	Pinheirão	56 793	coritiba.com.br	1	0	32	0
Criciúma	Criciúma	Heribelto Hulse	28 749	criciumaec.com.br	0	1	7	0
Cruzeiro	Belo Horizonte	Mineirão	81 987	cruzeiro.com.br	1	4	34	2
Figueirense	Florianópolis	Orlando Scarpelli	21 069	figueirense.com.br	0	0	13	0
Flamengo	Rio de Janeiro	Arena Petrobrás	30 000	flamengo.com.br	4	1	28	1
Fluminense	Rio de Janeiro	Raulino de Oliveira	20 000	fluminense.com.br	1	0	29	0
Goiás	Goiânia	Serra Dourada	54 048	goiasesporteclube.com.br	0	0	21	0
Grêmio	Porto Alegre	Olímpico	51 081	gremio.com.br	2	4	34	2
Guarani	Campinas	Brinco de Ouro	30 988	guaranifc.com.br	1	0	2	0
Internacional	Porto Alegre	Beira Rio	58 306	internacional.com.br	3	1	36	0
Juventude	Caxias do Sul	Alfredo Jaconi	30 519	juventude.com.br	0	1	1	0
Palmeiras	São Paulo	Parque Antartica	32 000	palmeiras.com.br	4	1	21	1
Paraná	Curitiba	Vila Capanema	22 500	paranaclube.com.br	0	0	7	0
Paysandu	Belém	Mangueirão	12 000	paysandu.com.br	0	0	41	0
Ponte Preta	Campinas	Moisés Lucarelli	20 080	pontepretaesportes.com.br	0	0	0	0
Santos	Santos	Vila Belmiro	28 120	Santosfc.com.br	2	0	16	2
São Caetano	São Caetano do Sul	Municipal	22 738	adsaocaetano.com.br	0	0	1	0
São Paulo	São Paulo	Morumbi	80 000	spfc.com.br	3	0	21	3
Vasco da Gama	Rio de Janeiro	São Januário	35 000	crvascodagama.com	3	0	22	1
Vitória	Salvador	Barradão	35 000	ecvitoria.com.br	0	0	23	0

Lge = National Championship since the first tournament in 1971 • Cup = Copa do Brasil since the first tournament in 1989 • SC = State Championship • Clubs in Rio also use the Maracanã (103 045) for the bigger games • Clubs in São Paulo also use the Pacaembu (45 000)

2006 STATE CHAMPIONSHIPS

State	Winners	Score	Runners-up
Acre	Adesg	‡	
Alagoas	Coruripe	1-0 0-1 6-5p	CSA
Amapá	São José	0-0 1-1 10-9p	Amapá
Amazonas	São Raimundo	1-1	Fast
Bahia	Colo Colo	‡	
Ceará	Ceará	1-0 1-0	Fortaleza
Distrito Federal	Brasiliense	†	Gama
Espírito Santo	Vitória	1-1 3-1	Estrela do Norte
Goiás	Goiás	0-0 1-0	Atlético Goianiense
Maranhão			
Mato Grosso	Operário	2-0 2-1	Barra do Garças
Mato Grosso Sul	Coxim	0-0 0-0	Chapadão
Minas Gerais	Cruzeiro	1-1 1-0	Ipatinga
Pará	Paysandu	2-1 2-3 4-1p	Ananindeua

State	Winners	Score	Runners-up
Paraíba			
Paraná	Paraná Clube	3-0 1-1	Adap
Pernambuco	Sport Recife	2-1 0-1 5-4p	Santa Cruz
Piauí	Ríver	0-0 2-1	Flamengo
Rio de Janeiro	Botafogo	2-0 3-1	Madureira
Rio Grande Nor.	Baraúnas	2-0 1-3	Potiguar
Rio Grande Sul	Grêmio	0-0 1-1	Internacional
Rondônia	ULBRA Ji-Paraná	1-0 0-1	VEC
Roraima	Baré	‡	
Santa Catarina	Figueirense	1-2 3-0	Joinville
São Paulo	Santos	†	São Paulo FC
Sergipe			
Tocantins	Araguaína	2-1 2-2	Tocantinópolis

‡ Won both stages so no final needed. † Played on a league basis

RECENT LEAGUE AND CUP RECORD

	National Championship				Cup		
Year	Champions	Score/Runners-up	Runners-up/Third		Winners	Score	Runners-up
1989	Vasco da Gama	1-0	São Paulo FC		Grêmio	0-0 2-1	Sport Recife
1990	Corinthians	1-0 1-0	São Paulo FC		Flamengo	1-0 0-0	Goiás
1991	São Paulo FC	1-0 0-0	Bragantino		Criciúma	1-1 0-0	Grêmio
1992	Flamengo	3-0 2-2	Botafogo		Internacional	1-2 1-0	Fluminense
1993	Palmeiras	1-0 2-0	Vitória		Cruzeiro	0-0 2-1	Grêmio
1994	Palmeiras	3-1 1-1	Corinthians		Grêmio	0-0 1-0	Ceará
1995	Botafogo	2-1 1-1	Santos		Corinthians	2-1 1-0	Grêmio
1996	Grêmio	0-2 2-0	Portuguesa		Cruzeiro	1-1 2-1	Palmeiras
1997	Vasco da Gama	0-0 0-0	Palmeiras		Grêmio	0-0 2-2	Flamengo
1998	Corinthians	2-2 1-1 2-0	Cruzeiro		Palmeiras	0-1 2-0	Cruzeiro
1999	Corinthians	2-3 2-0 0-0	Atlético Mineiro		Juventude	2-1 0-0	Botafogo
2000	Vasco da Gama	1-1 3-1	São Caetano		Cruzeiro	0-0 2-1	São Paulo FC
2001	Atlético Paranaense	4-2 1-0	São Caetano		Grêmio	2-2 3-1	Corinthians
2002	Santos	2-0 3-2	Corinthians		Corinthians	2-1 1-1	Brasiliense
2003	Cruzeiro	100	Santos 87	São Paulo FC 78	Cruzeiro	1-1 3-1	Flamengo
2004	Santos	89	Atlético Paranaense 86	São Paulo FC 82	Santo André	2-2 2-0	Flamengo
2005	Corinthians	81	Internacional 78	Goiás 74	Paulista	2-0 0-0	Fluminense
2006					Flamengo	2-0 1-0	Vasco da Gama

CORINTHIANS 2005-06

Date	Opponents	Score	H/A	Comp	Scorers	Att
20-04-2005	Figueirense	W 2-0	H	CBr3	Tevez [45], Marcelo Mattos [67]	33 343
24-04-2005	Juventude	D 2-2	H	SA	Tevez [10], Marcelo Mattos [43]	17 431
1-05-2005	Botafogo	L 1-3	A	SA	Gil [32]	
4-05-2005	Figueirense	L 0-2	A	CBr3	L 2-3p	16 401
8-05-2005	São Paulo	L 1-5	H	SA	Carlos Alberto [88]	17 490
15-05-2005	Atlético Paranaense	W 2-1	A	SA	Bobô [49], Marcelo Mattos [54]	16 373
22-05-2005	Figueirense	W 2-1	H	SA	Tevez [26], Roger [54]	8 031
29-05-2005	Atlético Mineiro	W 1-0	A	SA	Tevez [26]	15 845
12-06-2005	Flamengo	W 4-2	H	SA	Jô 2 [23][83], Abuda [52], Roger [77]	
18-06-2005	Brasiliense	W 4-2	A	SA	Carlos Alberto [25], Ronny [52], Gustavo Nery [63], Edson [87]	20 216
26-06-2005	Fluminense	L 0-1	H	SA		
3-07-2005	Fortaleza	L 1-2	A	SA	Abuda [4]	33 516
10-07-2005	Palmeiras	W 3-1	H	SA	Gustavo Nery [52], Rosinei 2 [61][66]	39 629
16-07-2005	Paraná	W 3-2	A	SA	Marinho [37], Tevez [54], Dinelson [77]	13 746
21-07-2005	Paysandu	W 3-2	H	SA	Bobô [68], Dinelson [70], Jô [86]	31 658
24-07-2005	Vasco da Gama	W 3-2	A	SA	Gustavo Nery [11], Marcelo Mattos [33], Abuda [83]	3 243
27-07-2005	Cruzeiro	W 4-3	H	SA	Roger [12], Rosinei 2 [60][62] Tevez [74]	32 713
3-08-2005	Coritiba	W 3-0	H	SA	Tevez 2 [4][24], Bobô [89]	27 813
6-08-2005	São Caetano	L 0-2	H	SA		32 007
10-08-2005	Internacional	D 0-0	A	SA		12 502
14-08-2005	Ponte Preta	W 5-3	A	SA	Tevez 2 [14][69], Roger 2 [48][50], Sebá [74]	11 029
17-08-2005	Goiás	W 2-0	A	CSr1	Dinelson [18], Fabrício [35]	13 328
21-08-2005	Goiás	D 1-1	H	SA	Marcelo Mattos [85]	32 000
24-08-2005	Juventude	L 0-1	A	SA		3 909
28-08-2005	Botafogo	D 3-3	H	SA	Jô [18], Roger [29], Rosinei [59]	20 742
31-08-2005	Goiás	D 1-1	H	CSr1	Ronny [25]	
11-09-2005	Atlético Paranaense	W 2-0	H	SA	Marcelo Mattos [58], Carlos Alberto [86]	13 150
14-09-2005	River Plate	D 0-0	H	CSr2		6 098
18-09-2005	Figueirense	W 3-2	A	SA	Nilmar [16], Gustavo Nery [55], Eduardo [69]	6 613
22-09-2005	Atlético Mineiro	D 1-1	H	SA	Hugo [37]	20 045
25-09-2005	Flamengo	W 3-1	A	SA	Nilmar [7], Tevez 2 [66][75]	8 186
28-09-2005	River Plate	D 1-1	A	CSr2	Marinho [91+]	
2-10-2005	Brasiliense	W 3-2	H	SA	Roger [33], Wescley [36], Rosinei [42]	32 000
5-10-2005	Fluminense	W 2-0	A	SA	Gustavo Nery 2 [1][47]	2 553
8-10-2005	Fortaleza	W 3-0	H	SA	Rosinei 2 [44][50], Carlos Alberto [63]	20 357
13-10-2005	Santos	W 3-2	A	SA	Betão [35], Nilmar [72], Carlos Alberto [87p]	13 041
16-10-2005	Palmeiras	D 1-1	A	SA	Tevez [20]	34 282
19-10-2005	Pumas UNAM	W 2-1	H	CSqf	Hugo [34], Bobô [70]	5 163
22-10-2005	Paraná	W 1-0	H	SA	Tevez [13]	32 000
24-10-2005	São Paulo	D 1-1	A	SA	Carlos Alberto [41]	26 994
27-10-2005	Paysandu	W 2-0	H	SA	Tevez [4], Rosinei [70]	32 250
30-10-2005	Vasco da Gama	D 1-1	H	SA	Tevez [71]	22 214
2-11-2005	Cruzeiro	L 1-2	A	SA	Nilmar [46]	22 874
6-11-2005	Santos	W 7-1	H	SA	Rosinei [1], Tevez 3 [20][36][53], Nilmar 2 [57][77], Marcelo Mattos [90]	21 918
9-11-2005	Pumas UNAM	L 0-3	A	CSqf		
13-11-2005	Coritiba	W 1-0	A	SA	Carlos Alberto [23]	28 936
16-11-2005	São Caetano	L 0-1	A	SA		11 650
20-11-2005	Internacional	D 1-1	H	SA		32 935
27-11-2005	Ponte Preta	W 3-1	H	SA	Gustavo Nery [37], Coelho [86], Carlos Alberto [93+]	64 937
4-12-2005	Goiás	L 2-3	A	SA	Tevez [50], Coelho [57]	43 000
11-01-2006	EC Noroeste	L 0-1	A	SP		17 692
15-01-2006	Portuguesa Santista	W 5-1	H	SP	Rafael Moura [6], Nilmar 3 [8][47][88], Elton [86]	7 614
19-01-2006	Juventus	W 2-1	H	SP	Rafael Moura 2 [48][89]	12 683
22-01-2006	Portuguesa	L 1-2	A	SP	Tevez [4]	15 991
29-01-2006	Rio Branco	W 4-1	A	SP	Nilmar 2 [30][71], Tevez [48], Carlos Alberto [86]	10 636
1-02-2006	São Bento	W 5-0	H	SP	Tevez 3 [13][58][69], Ricardinho [32], Marcelo Mattos [63]	20 022
4-02-2006	Bragantino	W 4-1	H	SP	Nilmar 2 [28][88], Tevez [74], Rafael Moura [89]	28 364
8-02-2006	São Caetano	L 1-2	A	SP	Rafael Moura [31]	9 523
12-02-2006	Santos	L 0-1	H	SP		33 450
15-02-2006	Deportivo Cali - COL	W 1-0	A	CLg4	Ricardinho [79]	
19-02-2006	Mogo Mirim	W 5-1	A	SP	Nilmar 4 [19][41][43][64], Rafael Moura [40]	7 851
22-02-2006	Universidad Católica - CHI	D 2-2	H	CLg4	Roger [21], Nilmar [61]	
25-02-2006	Santo Andre	W 4-1	H	SP	Nilmar 2 [37][73], Rafael Moura [39], Carlos Alberto [80]	11 096
2-03-2006	Ituano	W 3-2	A	SP	Nilmar 2 [64][81], Roger [85]	9 581
5-03-2006	Marilia	D 1-1	H	SP	Nilmar [42]	14 960
9-03-2006	Tigres UNAL - MEX	L 0-2	A	CLg4		27 500

CORINTHIANS 2005–06 (CONT'D)

Date	Opponents	Score		Comp	Scorers	Att
12-03-2006	São Paulo FC	L 1-2	H	SP	Nilmar [76]	42 376
19-03-2006	América	W 2-1	A	SP	Marcelo Mattos [15], Carlao [33]	12 405
22-03-2006	Tigres UNAL - MEX	W 1-0	H	CLg4	Tevez [27]	
26-03-2006	Palmeiras	D 1-1	A	SP	Nilmar [8]	18 989
30-03-2006	Guarani	D 2-2	H	SP	Marcos [48], Rafael Moura [72]	1962
2-04-2006	Ponte Preta	W 1-0	A	SP	Renato [83]	4 409
6-04-2006	Universidad Católica - CHI	W 3-2	A	CLg4	Tevez [23], Nilmar 2 [37 60]	17 578
9-04-2006	Paulista	D 2-2	H	SP	Rafael Akai [1], Elton [47]	1 701
16-04-2006	Grêmio	L 0-2	A	SA		
19-04-2006	Deportivo Cali - COL	W 3-0	H	CLg4	Marcus Vinicius [6], Tevez [28], Nilmar [81]	33 918
2-04-2006	São Caetano	W 3-0	H	SA		17 648
26-04-2006	River Plate - ARG	L 2-3	A	CLr2	Tevez [15], Xavier [90]	38 910
30-04-2006	Ponte Preta	L 2-3	A	SA		7 668
4-05-2006	River Plate - ARG	L 1-3	H	CLr2	Nilmar [39]	32 089
7-05-2006	São Paulo	L 1-3		SA		20 857
14-05-2006	Paraná	W 2-1	A	SA		7 809

SP = Campeonato Paulista • CB = Copa do Brasil • SA = Serie A • CS = Copa Sudamericana • r1 = first round • r2 = second round • qf = quarter-finals • H = Pacaembu • **H** = Morumbi • *H* = Mogi Mirim • H̲ = Limeira • **A** = Pacaembu • *A* = Morumbi

SAO PAULO 2005–06

Date	Opponents	Score		Comp	Scorers	Att
20-01-2005	Ituano	W 4-2	H	SP	Diego Tardelli [26], Lugano [62], Rodrigo [70], Grafite [88]	6 527
23-01-2005	América	W 4-3	A	SP	Diego Tardelli [8], Danilo [31], Rogério Ceni [69], Cicinho [76]	11 830
27-01-2005	Inter de Limeira	W 2-0	H	SP	Diego Tardelli 2 [29 46]	5 947
30-01-2005	União São João	W 2-1	H	SP	Cicinho [18], Diego Tardelli [45]	11 367
5-02-2005	União Barbarense	D 2-2	A	SP	Josué [5], Diego Tardelli [27]	7 891
9-02-2005	São Caetano	W 4-3	A	SP	Diego Tardelli [10], Marco Antônio [85], Grafite [88], Josué [92+]	8 096
12-02-2005	Atlético Sorocaba	W 4-1	H	SP	Grafite 3 [13 28 61], Josué [33]	16 333
20-02-2005	Palmeiras	W 3-0	A	SP	Diego Tardelli [5], Rogério Ceni [75], Luizão [86]	36 772
24-02-2005	Portuguesa Santista	W 5-0	H	SP	Cicinho [44], Renan [57], Diego Tardelli 2 [51 87], Luizão [69]	7 502
27-02-2005	Corinthians	W 1-0	H	SP	Danilo [51]	50 708
3-03-2005	The Strongest	D 3-3	A	CLg3	Danilo [21], Luizão [57], Grafite [97+]	
6-03-2005	Paulista	D 2-2	A	SP	Luizão [38], Josué [79]	8 779
9-03-2005	Universidad de Chile	W 4-2	H	CLg3	Lugano [2], Rogério Ceni [20], Cicinho [45], Grafite [64]	
12-03-2005	Rio Branco	W 1-0	H	SP	Rogério Ceni [73]	11 572
16-03-2005	Quilmes	D 2-2	A	CLg3	Diego Tardelli [47], Grafite [68]	
19-03-2005	Marília	W 6-0	H	SP	Júnior [1], Danilo 2 [33 45], Marco Antônio [51], Grafite [66], Rogério Ceni [70]	12 552
23-03-2005	Guarani	W 2-1	A	SP	Marco Antônio [60], Grafite [70]	10 953
26-03-2005	Santo André	W 3-1	H	SP	Diego Tardelli 2 [4 52], Rogério Ceni [42]	30 375
31-03-2005	Portuguesa	L 1-2	A	SP	Júnior [40]	34 933
3-04-2005	Santos	D 0-0	A	SP		12 382
9-04-2005	Ponte Preta	L 1-2	H	SP	Luizão [5]	21 317
13-04-2005	Quilmes	W 3-1	H	CLg3	Diego Tardelli 2 [32 55], Cicinho [83]	38 703
17-04-2005	Mogi Mirim	W 2-1	A	SP	Grafite [39], Souza [64]	4 306
21-04-2005	Universidad de Chile	D 1-1	A	CLg3	Luizão [27]	
24-04-2005	Fluminense	L 1-2	A	SA	Souza [76]	13 719
30-04-2005	Paraná	D 1-1	H	SA	Lugano [90]	3 623
8-05-2005	Corinthians	W 5-1	A	SA	Rogério Ceni [3p], Luizão 2 [12 47], Danilo [16], Cicinho [73]	17 490
11-05-2005	The Strongest	W 3-0	H	CLg3	Edcarlos [30], Luizão [38], Grafite [52]	
14-05-2005	Coritiba	W 1-0	H	SA	Fabão [68]	6 401
18-05-2005	Palmeiras	W 1-0	A	CLr2	Cicinho [59]	
22-05-2005	Vasco da Gama	L 1-3	A	SA	Danilo [2]	1 399
25-05-2005	Palmeiras	W 2-0	H	CLr2	Rogério Ceni [81p], Cicinho [89]	60 395
28-05-2005	Cruzeiro	D 1-1	H	SA	Rogério Ceni [43p]	7 371
1-06-2005	Tigres	W 4-0	H	CLqf	Rogério Ceni 2 [30 58], Luizão [39], Souza [61]	42 903
12-06-2005	Paysandu	D 2-2	A	SA	Rogério Ceni [18], Roger [65]	19 584
15-06-2005	Tigres	L 1-2	A	CLqf	Souza [87]	
19-06-2005	Botafogo	W 1-0	H	SA	Paulo Matos [76]	4 180
22-06-2005	River Plate	W 2-0	H	CLsf	Danilo [76], Rogério Ceni [89]	61 078
25-06-2005	Internacional	L 1-3	H	SA	Souza [35]	3 509
29-06-2005	River Plate	W 3-2	A	CLsf	Danilo [11], Amoroso [59], Fabão [80]	58 956
6-07-2005	Atlético Paranaense	D 1-1	A	CLf	Durval OG [52]	
9-07-2005	Flamengo	W 2-0	H	SA	Júnior Baiano OG [15], Hernanes [90]	4 123
14-07-2005	Atlético Paranaense	W 4-0	H	CLf	Amoroso [16], Fabão [52], Luizão [70], Diego Tardelli [89]	71 986

SAO PAULO 2005–06 (CONT'D)

Date	Opponents	Score			Comp	Scorers	Att
17-07-2005	Santos	L	1-2	A	SA	Hernanes [37]	8 648
20-07-2005	Brasiliense	D	3-3	A	SA	Diego Tardelli [6], Danilo [21], Rogério Ceni [51]	22 579
23-07-2005	São Caetano	L	0-1	H	SA		7 819
27-07-2005	Atlético Mineiro	D	0-0	A	SA		14 330
31-07-2005	Juventude	L	1-2	A	SA	Lugano [79]	5 835
4-08-2005	Palmeiras	D	3-3	H	SA	Amoroso 2 [32][34], Danilo [41]	14 810
7-08-2005	Goiás	L	0-1	H	SA		7 009
10-08-2005	Figueirense	L	1-3	A	SA	Amoroso [22]	6 614
14-08-2005	Fortaleza	W	3-2	H	SA	Mineiro [2], Amoroso [57], Josué [68]	22 724
17-08-2005	Internacional	L	1-2	A	CSr1	Mineiro [39]	
20-08-2005	Atlético Paranaense	L	2-4	A	SA	Christian [30], Amoroso [91+p]	20 396
24-08-2005	Fluminense	D	1-1	H	SA	Amoroso [82]	11 984
28-08-2005	Paraná	W	4-0	A	SA	Rogério Ceni [31], Lugano [36], Amoroso [51], Aderaldo OG [75]	12 782
1-09-2005	Internacional	D	1-1	H	CSr1	Souza [41]	
11-09-2005	Coritiba	W	4-1	A	SA	Rogério Ceni [20p], Christian [81], Hernanes [83], Cicinho [85]	16 979
18-09-2005	Vasco da Gama	W	4-2	H	SA	Amoroso 2 [4][38], Christian [11], Rogério Ceni [93+]	15 417
21-09-2005	Cruzeiro	W	3-2	A	SA	Flávio [57], Christian [61], Rogério Ceni [71p]	23 787
24-09-2005	Paysandu	W	4-1	H	SA	Danilo 2 [11][90], Christian [51], Lugano [60]	18 612
2-10-2005	Botafogo	D	1-1	A	SA	Christian [17]	2 574
5-10-2005	Internacional	L	0-3	A	SA		12 407
11-10-2005	Ponte Preta	W	3-2	H	SA	Mineiro [8], Christian [10], Júnior [86]	5 285
16-10-2005	Flamengo	W	6-1	A	SA	Edcarlos 2 [3][24], Amoroso [43], Thiago [87], Mineiro [90], Souza [91+]	1 864
19-10-2005	Ponte Preta	L	0-2	A	SA		14 000
22-10-2005	Santos	L	1-2	H	SA	Amoroso [71]	4 607
24-10-2005	Corinthians	D	1-1	H	SA	Amoroso [52p]	26 994
27-10-2005	Brasiliense	L	1-2	H	SA	Cicinho [4]	2 170
30-10-2005	São Caetano	W	1-0	A	SA	Neto OG [61]	3 944
2-11-2005	Atlético Mineiro	D	2-2	H	SA	Roger [27], Rogério Ceni [54]	2 992
5-11-2005	Juventude	W	3-1	H	SA	Christian [17], Mineiro [23], Roger [53]	8 801
12-11-2005	Palmeiras	L	1-2	A	SA	Richarlysson [61]	5 252
16-11-2005	Goiás	L	0-3	A	SA		12 526
19-11-2005	Figueirense	W	4-2	H	SA	Fábio Santos [6], Thiago 3 [23][68][85]	3 908
27-11-2005	Fortaleza	L	0-1	A	SA		55 461
4-12-2005	Atlético Paranaense	W	3-1	H	SA	Lugano 2 [10][21], Rogério Ceni [34]	23 565
14-12-2005	Al Ittihad - KSA	W	3-2	N	CWCsf	Amoroso 2 [16][47], Rogério Ceni [57p]	31 510
18-12-2005	Liverpool - ENG	W	1-0	N	CWCf	Mineiro [27]	66 821
18-01-2006	Santa André	L	0-1	A	SP		5 929
21-01-2006	São Caetano	W	2-1	H	SP	Grafite [7], Mineiro [56]	8 307
25-01-2006	Juventus	L	0-1	H	SP		15 477
29-01-2006	Guarani	D	3-3	H	SP	Thiago [30], Souza [46], Roger [64]	4 420
1-02-2006	Marilia	W	2-0	A	SP	Junior [22], Roger [89]	13 257
5-02-2006	Palmeiras	W	4-2	H	SP	Danilo [44], Thiago 2 [70][79], Mineiro [89]	30 570
9-02-2006	Portuguesa	W	3-1	H	SP	Alex Dias [8], Danilo [13], Josue [71]	10 877
12-02-2006	Portuguesa Santista	W	5-0	A	SP	Thiago [20], Danilo 2 [34][51], Fabao [45], Richarlyson [89]	9 349
15-02-2006	Bragantino	D	3-3	A	SP	Danilo [17], Thiago 2 [59][89]	6 375
18-02-2006	Paulista	W	5-1	H	SP	Danilo [12], Souza [27], Alex Dias 2 [30][73], Rogério Ceni [68]	19 963
22-02-2006	Mogi Mirim	W	3-0	H	SP	Mineiro [52], Souza [55], Rogério Ceni [79]	9 675
25-02-2006	Ponte Preta	W	2-1	A	SP	Danilo [58], Andre Dias [88]	7 331
1-03-2006	Caracas FC - VEN	W	2-1	A	CLg1	Danilo [35], Aloisio [62]	2 450
5-03-2006	São Bento	L	0-2	A	SP		12 787
8-03-2006	Cienciano - PER	W	4-1	H	CLg1	Fabao [2], Alex Dias [20], Thiago [66], Souza [77]	
12-03-2006	Corinthians	W	2-1	A	SP	Danilo [29], Andre Dias [76]	42 376
18-03-2006	Noroeste	D	1-1	H	SP	Thiago [55]	25 155
21-03-2006	Chivas Guadalajara - MEX	L	1-2	A	CLg1	Danilo [25]	21 512
26-03-2006	Rio Branco	W	4-2	A	SP	Fabao [22], Leandro [52], Thiago [55], Rogério Ceni [89]	8 701
29-03-2006	América	W	2-0	H	SP	Alex Dias 2 [54][69]	4 457
2-04-2006	Santos	W	3-1	H	SP	Rogério Ceni [44], Thiago [73], Alex Dias [89]	51 520
5-04-2006	Chivas Guadalajara - MEX	L	1-2	A	CLg1	Aloisio [30]	44 648
9-04-2006	Ituano	W	2-0	A	SP	Thiago [3], Rogério Ceni [4]	8 646
12-04-2006	Cienciano - PER	W	2-0	A	CLg1	Aloisio [21], Mineiro [42]	
20-04-2006	Caracas FC - VEN	W	2-0	H	CLg1	Danilo [57], Rogério Ceni [92+]	21 854
26-04-2006	Palmeiras - BRA	D	1-1	A	CLr2	Aloisio [23]	
3-05-2006	Palmeiras - BRA	W	2-1	H	CLr2	Aloisio [13], Rogério Ceni [86]	55 080
10-05-2006	Estudiantes LP	L	0-1	A	CLqf		21 677

SP = Campeonato Paulista • CL = Copa Libertadores • SA = Serie A • CS = Copa Sudamericana • CWC = FIFA Club World Championship • r1 = first round • r2 = second round • qf = quarter-finals • sf = semi-finals • f = final • H = São Caetano • A = Morumbi • A = Mogi Mirim

BRB – BARBADOS

NATIONAL TEAM RECORD
JULY 1ST 2002 TO JULY 9TH 2006

PL	W	D	L	F	A	%
27	11	6	10	39	36	51.9

FIFA/COCA-COLA WORLD RANKING

1993	1994	1995	1996	1997	1998	1999	2000	2001	2002	2003	2004	2005		High		Low
114	107	103	110	113	121	113	104	107	99	124	121	115		93	06/00	152 07/06

2005–2006										
08/05	09/05	10/05	11/05	12/05	01/06	02/06	03/06	04/06	05/06	06/06 07/06
120	121	119	119	115	115	115	117	118	119	- 152

In 2005 Notre Dame continued their domination of the League by winning their seventh title in nine years, finishing a healthy eight points clear of Barbados Defence Force in second place. Their only defeat during the season came early in the campaign against leaders Eden Stars. There was no repeat of their double celebrations from the previous year, however, with defeat in the quarter-finals of the Cup to perennial rivals Paradise, who then went on to beat Barbados Defence Force 3-1 in the final. Off the field it was an eventful year with FIFA temporarily suspending Barbados in June 2005 after a dispute over the September 2004 football association elections. The dispute

INTERNATIONAL HONOURS
None

also affected relations between the clubs and the BFA and the 2005 League season ground to a halt for two months as a result. Since the ban on fielding international teams was lifted, only the senior women's team has seen any action, although they failed to even make the preliminary group stage of the Women's Caribbean Cup, which was used as a regional qualifying tournament for the FIFA Women's World Cup. There was two major surprises in the 2006 League campaign with Youth Milan winning the title and the relegation of Paradise. It was the first time since 1995 that a team other than Notre Dame or Paradise had won the title.

THE FIFA BIG COUNT OF 2000

	Male	Female		Male	Female
Registered players	2 500	0	Referees	70	0
Non registered players	2 600	0	Officials	400	0
Youth players	2 500	0	Total involved	8 070	
Total players	7 600		Number of clubs	80	
Professional players	0	0	Number of teams	200	

Barbados Football Association (BFA)
Richmond Welches, PO Box 1362, Bridgetown, St Michael, BB 11000, Barbados
Tel +1 246 2281707   Fax +1 246 2286484
bdosfootball@caribsurf.com   www.barbadossoccer.com
President: JONES Ronald   General Secretary: BECKLES Patrick
Vice-President: BARROW Keith   Treasurer: HUNTE Curtis   Media Officer: BECKLES Patrick
Men's Coach: DOHERTY Mark   Women's Coach: DOHERTY Mark
BFA formed: 1910   CONCACAF: 1968   FIFA: 1968
Royal blue shirts with gold trimmings, Gold shorts, White socks

RECENT INTERNATIONAL MATCHES PLAYED BY BARBADOS

2002	Opponents		Score	Venue	Comp	Scorers	Att	Referee
25-07	Trinidad & Barbados	D	0-0	Basseterre	Fr		700	
27-07	St Kitts & Nevis	L	0-3	Basseterre	Fr			
6-10	St Lucia	W	3-2	Bridgetown	Fr	Valencius, Xavier, Forde.M		
9-11	Jamaica	D	1-1	St George's	GCq	Goodridge [88]	3 000	Murray TRI
11-11	Grenada	W	2-0	St George's	GCq	Lucas [66], Goodridge [90]	2 500	Murray TRI
13-11	Guadeloupe	L	0-1	St George's	GCq		3 250	Brizan TRI
2003								
12-01	Jamaica	W	1-0	Bridgetown	Fr	Williams [61]	7 500	
26-01	Finland	D	0-0	Bridgetown	Fr			Bynoe TRI
12-02	Martinique	D	3-3	Bridgetown	Fr	Lucas [5], Williams [9], Straker [48]		
23-03	Jamaica	L	1-2	Kingston	Fr	Cox [59]		Bowen CAY
26-12	Bermuda	W	2-1	Hamilton	Fr	Lovell 2 [39 43]		Mouchette BER
2004								
1-01	Bermuda	W	4-0	Hamilton	Fr	Parris [6], Riley [51], Goodridge 2 [74 76]		Raynor BER
11-01	Grenada	W	2-0	Bridgetown	Fr	Forde.N [35], Riley [58]	2 000	Small BRB
18-01	Canada	L	0-1	Bridgetown	Fr			Forde BRB
31-01	Grenada	W	1-0	St George's	Fr	Riley [70]		
15-02	Guyana	L	0-2	Bridgetown	Fr		1 200	Small BRB
12-03	Dominica	W	2-1	Bridgetown	Fr	OG [28], Burrowes [85]	46	
30-05	Northern Ireland	D	1-1	Bridgetown	Fr	Skinner [40]	8 000	Brizan TRI
13-06	St Kitts & Nevis	L	0-2	Bridgetown	WCq		3 700	Alfaro SLV
19-06	St Kitts & Nevis	L	2-3	Basseterre	WCq	Skinner [33], Goodridge [45]	3 500	Pineda HON
2005								
23-01	Guyana	W	3-0	Bridgetown	Fr	Forde.M [41], OG [53], Goodridge [58],		
30-01	St Vincent/Grenadines	W	3-1	Bridgetown	Fr	Riley 2 [47 82], Goodridge [80]	3 000	
6-02	Antigua & Barbuda	W	3-2	Bridgetown	Fr	Forde.M [10], Stanford [40], Goodridge [57]	4 000	
13-02	Guyana	D	3-3	Bridgetown	Fr	Forde.N [5], Lucas [29], James [56]	6 000	Callender BRB
20-02	Cuba	L	0-3	Bridgetown	GCq		5 000	Prendergast JAM
22-02	Jamaica	L	0-1	Bridgetown	GCq			Brizan TRI
24-02	Trinidad & Tobago	L	2-3	Bridgetown	GCq	Forde.N [32], Lucas [86]	3 000	Prendergast JAM
2006								

No international matches played in 2006 before July

Fr = Friendly match • GC = CONCACAF Gold Cup • WC = FIFA World Cup™ • q = qualifier

BARBADOS NATIONAL TEAM RECORDS AND RECORD SEQUENCES

Records			Sequence records					
Victory	6-1	CAY 1993	Wins	3	Five times	Clean sheets	3	1990, 1996
Defeat	0-7	USA 2000	Defeats	5	2000	Goals scored	8	1998-99, 2000
Player Caps	n/a		Undefeated	8	2000	Without goal	3	Three times
Player Goals	n/a		Without win	10	1976-88	Goals against	15	2000-01

BARBADOS COUNTRY INFORMATION

Capital	Bridgetown	Independence	1966 from the UK	GDP per Capita	$15 700
Population	278 289	Status	Commonwealth	GNP Ranking	132
Area km²	431	Language	English	Dialling code	+1 246
Population density	645 per km²	Literacy rate	98%	Internet code	.bb
% in urban areas	47%	Main religion	Christian 71%	GMT +/–	-4
Towns/Cities ('000)	Bridgetown 98; Speightstown 3; Oistins 2, Bathsheba 1; Holetown 1; Bulkeley 1; Crane 1				
Neighbours (km)	Barbados is an island bordered by the Caribbean Sea and the Atlantic Ocean				
Main stadia	Waterford National Stadium – Bridgetown 15 000				

BARBADOS 2005

PREMIER DIVISION

	Pl	W	D	L	F	A	Pts	Notre Dame	BDF	Silver Sands	Paradise	Eden Stars	Youth Milan	Beverly Hills	Gall Hill	Pinelands	Oxley United
Notre Dame	18	12	5	1	44	11	41		0-0	1-1	1-1	4-1	4-1	3-0	4-0	2-1	7-0
Barbados Defence F.	18	10	3	5	32	18	33	0-1		2-3	1-2	1-0	4-1	1-1	3-0	4-2	1-0
Silver Sands	18	9	5	4	38	18	32	0-2	0-2		0-3	1-0	2-2	0-0	2-0	7-2	9-1
Paradise	18	8	6	4	36	20	30	0-2	0-2	0-0		0-0	3-1	4-2	1-2	6-2	2-1
Eden Stars	18	9	3	6	29	27	30	1-0	1-0	1-0	2-2		2-4	2-5	2-1	2-1	2-1
Youth Milan	18	7	7	4	44	30	28	1-1	4-0	1-1	0-0	3-3		1-1	1-2	5-1	6-1
Beverly Hills	18	5	6	7	29	33	21	2-5	1-3	0-1	4-2	0-2	2-2		0-1	2-1	3-1
Gall Hill	18	5	2	11	18	30	17	0-3	1-1	0-0	1-1	0-0	0-1	0-3		1-2	4-0
Pinelands	18	3	2	13	24	59	11	2-2	0-2	1-8	0-5	3-1	2-3	1-1	2-1		1-3
Oxley United	18	2	1	15	17	65	7	0-2	1-5	0-1	0-5	1-6	1-5	2-2	0-4	4-0	

6/03/2005 - 2/10/2005 • Top scorers: Peter STOUTE, Silver Sands, 21; Travis COPPIN, Pinelands, 12

BARBADOS 2006

PREMIER DIVISION

	Pl	W	D	L	F	A	Pts	Youth Milan	Notre Dame	Silver Sands	BDF	Eden Stars	Gall Hill	Britons Hill	Tudor Bridge	Beverley Hills	Paradise
Youth Milan	18	11	4	3	33	20	37		1-3	2-2	0-2	1-0	1-1	2-1	0-1	2-0	1-0
Notre Dame	18	10	6	2	32	13	36	0-3		0-0	1-1	3-1	3-0	1-1	1-0	3-1	1-0
Silver Sands	18	7	9	2	33	21	30	0-2	2-2		4-1	2-2	2-0	3-1	0-0	2-2	2-0
Barbados Defence F.	18	7	6	5	23	23	27	1-3	0-4	0-0		1-2	3-1	1-1	3-0	2-2	1-0
Eden Stars	18	5	6	7	29	34	21	4-4	1-1	3-3	0-0		0-2	2-0	0-1	3-2	4-1
Gall Hill	18	5	5	8	21	26	20	0-1	0-0	1-1	1-2	5-0		2-0	2-0	3-6	1-1
Brittons Hill	17	5	5	7	21	29	20	1-4	2-1	1-4	0-0	2-1	2-1		1-1	2-5	**3-0**
Tudor Bridge	18	5	5	8	14	24	20	2-2	0-2	2-1	2-1	0-2	0-1	1-1		2-1	0-1
Beverley Hills	18	5	5	8	21	37	19	1-2	0-4	1-3	1-2	2-2	2-2	4-0	0-2		1-0
Paradise	17	2	4	11	13	27	10	1-2	0-2	1-2	1-2	4-2	0-0	-	1-1	2-2	

12/02/2006 - 9/07/2006 • Top scorers: Dwayne STANFORD, Beverley Hills, 17; Dwayne Gale, Notre Dame, 13 • Match in bold was awarded

FA CUP 2005

Round of sixteen		Quarter-finals		Semi-finals		Final	
Paradise	6						
Ellerton	0	Paradise	3				
Haggatt Hall	1	Notre Dame	2				
Notre Dame	3			Paradise	4		
Wales	3			Fairy Valley	0		
Jackson	0	Wales	0				
Grazettes	1 0p	Fairy Valley	1				
Fairy Valley	1 3p					Paradise	3
Brittons Hill	3					Barbados Defence F.	1
Silver Sands	1	Brittons Hill	2				
Police	1	Eden Stars	0				
Eden Stars	2			Brittons Hill	0	**CUP FINAL**	
Youth Milan	3			Barbados Defence F.	3		
Tudor Hill	2	Youth Milan	1			YMCA, Bridgetown	
Gall Hall	1	Barbados Defence F.	3			9-10-2005	
Barbados Defence F.	4						

RECENT LEAGUE AND CUP RECORD

	Championship						Cup		
Year	Champions	Pts	Runners-up	Pts	Third	Pts	Winners	Score	Runners-up
2000	Notre Dame	35	Paradise	31	Youth Milan		Paradise	2-1	Notre Dame
2001	Paradise	43	Youth Milan	41	Notre Dame	35	Notre Dame	1-0	Youth Milan
2002	Notre Dame	44	Paradise	32	Youth Milan	30	Youth Milan	2-1	Notre Dame
2003	Paradise	*	BDF				Paradise	1-0	Weymouth Wales
2004	Notre Dame	52	Beverly Hills	42	Youth Milan	40	Notre Dame	3-2	Silver Sands
2005	Notre Dame	41	BDF	33	Silver Sands	32	Paradise	3-1	BDF
2006	Youth Milan	37	Notre Dame	36	Silver Sands	30			

* Paradise beat Barbados Defence Force 4-1 on penalties in the Championship final

BRU – BRUNEI DARUSSALAM

NATIONAL TEAM RECORD
JULY 1ST 2002 TO JULY 9TH 2006

PL	W	D	L	F	A	%
5	1	2	2	3	8	40

FIFA/COCA-COLA WORLD RANKING

1993	1994	1995	1996	1997	1998	1999	2000	2001	2002	2003	2004	2005	High	Low
151	165	167	170	178	183	185	193	189	194	194	199	199	145 08/93	199 12/04

2005–2006											
08/05	09/05	10/05	11/05	12/05	01/06	02/06	03/06	04/06	05/06	06/06	07/06
198	198	198	199	199	199	199	199	193	193	-	178

The domestic season in Brunei was marred by the withdrawal of defending champions DPMM in September after having played 12 of the 16 rounds in the B-League. DPMM withdrew to take part in the Malaysian second division - the Premier League - and the defection caused a three month hiatus in the season. DPMM had only lost one game, to long time leaders AH United, a game that was later annulled. The decision cost AH United the title which went instead to QAF who beat Armed Forces in a crucial game in the penultimate round. There was some measure of recompense for AH United when they beat Armed Forces on penalties in the delayed Cup Final after the match

INTERNATIONAL HONOURS
None

had finished 2-2. They had twice led through Brian Iman and Asrul Sahdon only to be pegged back before Zulkifli Abu Bakar scored the winning penalty. With hindsight the decision by DPMM was a good one as in June 2006 they won promotion to the top flight of Malaysian football, the Super League. After the end of the season at home, there was a rare foray by the Brunei national team into the international arena when they entered the inaugural AFC Challenge Cup in Bangladesh. The team performed with some credit, most notably in the surprise 2-1 victory over Nepal which ended a run of 23 games without a win.

THE FIFA BIG COUNT OF 2000

	Male	Female		Male	Female
Registered players	300	0	Referees	30	0
Non registered players	1 000	0	Officials	100	0
Youth players	500	0	Total involved	1 930	
Total players	1 800		Number of clubs	20	
Professional players	0	0	Number of teams	40	

The Football Association of Brunei Darussalam (BAFA)
PO Box 2010, Bandar Seri Begawan, BS 8674, Brunei Darussalam
Tel +673 2 382761   Fax +673 2 382760
bruneifasg@yahoo.com   www.bafa.org.bn
President: HUSSAIN YUSSOFF Pehin Dato Haji   General Secretary: MATUSIN MATASAN Pengiran Haji
Vice-President: HASSAN ABAS Pengiran Haji   Treasurer: PANG Jeffery   Media Officer: None
Men's Coach: YUNOS Haji   Women's Coach: None
BAFA formed: 1959   AFC: 1970   FIFA: 1969
Yellow shirts, Black shorts, Black socks

RECENT INTERNATIONAL MATCHES PLAYED BY BRUNEI DARUSSALAM

2002 Opponents	Score	Venue	Comp	Scorers	Att	Referee
No international matches played in 2002						
2003						
21-03 Maldives	D 1-1	Male	ACq	Faldin [89]		
23-03 Myanmar	L 0-5	Male	ACq			
2004						
No international matches played in 2004						
2005						
No international matches played in 2005						
2006						
2-04 Sri Lanka	L 0-1	Chittagong	CCr1		2 000	Saidov UZB
4-04 Nepal	W 2-1	Chittagong	CCr1	Safari [47], Sallehuddin [70]	2 500	Al Ghatrifi OMA
6-04 Bhutan	D 0-0	Chittagong	CCr1		2 000	Al Ghatrifi OMA

AC = AFC Asian Cup • q = qualifier

BRUNEI DARUSSALAM NATIONAL TEAM RECORDS AND RECORD SEQUENCES

Records			Sequence records				
Victory	2-0	PHI 1980, PHI 1989	Wins	2	1980	Clean sheets	1	
Defeat	0-12	UAE 2001	Defeats	12	1972-80, 1999-01	Goals scored	4	1998-1999
Player Caps	n/a		Undefeated	2		Without goal	11	1999-2001
Player Goals	n/a		Without win	23	1999-2006	Goals against	26	1982-1987

BRUNEI 2005-06

B-LEAGUE

	Pl	W	D	L	F	A	Pts	QAF	ABDB	AH United	Wijaya	NBT	Kasuka	Jerudong	Indera	Bandaran	DPMM
QAF	16	13	2	1	69	26	41		1-1	1-4	2-2	3-1	6-2	3-1	4-3	9-4	1-2
ABDB Armed Forces	16	12	3	1	67	20	39	2-3		1-1	5-0	10-0	1-0	4-0	6-2	8-0	0-3
AH United	16	12	2	2	65	17	38	2-3	2-3		2-0	4-0	3-1	3-1	10-1	6-2	2-0
Wijaya	16	8	5	3	33	21	29	3-4	0-0	1-1		2-1	6-1	1-0	2-1	6-1	-
NBT Berakas	16	6	1	9	26	35	19	0-2	2-3	1-2	1-2		2-1	2-1	3-1	4-1	0-5
Kasuka Tutong	16	4	3	9	23	50	15	1-9	0-5	0-6	1-1	1-0		2-1	2-2	2-2	-
Jerudong	16	3	2	11	23	45	11	0-3	2-4	1-6	0-0	2-2	0-5		2-0	4-3	-
Indera	16	3	1	12	25	70	10	0-9	3-8	0-8	0-5	0-4	3-0	6-3		2-4	0-6
Bandaran	16	1	1	14	27	74	4	0-7	4-6	1-5	1-2	0-3	3-4	1-5	0-1		0-9
DPMM Jerudong	DPMM withrew after 12 games							6-0	-	1-0	-	7-0	9-1	5-0	-	-	

13/05/2005 - 6/02/2006 • All games played involving DPMM were annulled

RECENT LEAGUE AND CUP RECORD

Championship						Cup		
Year	Champions	Pts	Runners-up	Pts	Third	Pts	Winners	Score	Runners-up
2002	DPMM	19	ABDB Armed Forces	16	Kasuka	9	Wijaya	1-0	ABDB Armed Forces
2003	Wijaya	25	DPMM	22	ABDB Armed Forces	21	ABDB Armed Forces	3-0	Kota Ranger
2004	DPMM	52	AH United	42	ABDB Armed Forces	37	DPMM	0-0 3-1p	ABDB Armed Forces
2005	QAF	41	ABDB Armed Forces	39	AH United	38	AH United	2-2 4-3p	ABDB Armed Forces

BRUNEI DARUSSALAM COUNTRY INFORMATION

Capital	Bandar Seri Begawan	Independence	1984 from the UK	GDP per Capita	$18 600
Population	365 251	Status	Sultanate	GNP Ranking	97
Area km²	5 770	Language	Malay	Dialling code	+673
Population density	63 per km²	Literacy rate	90%	Internet code	.bn
% in urban areas	70%	Main religion	Muslim 67%	GMT +/-	+8
Towns/Cities ('000)	Bandar Seri Begawan 64; Kuala Belait 31; Pekan Seria 30; Tutong 19; Bangar 3				
Neighbours (km)	Malaysia 381; South China Sea 161				
Main stadia	Sultan Hassal Bolkiah – Bandar Ser Begawan 30 000				

BUL – BULGARIA

NATIONAL TEAM RECORD
JULY 1ST 2002 TO JULY 9TH 2006

PL	W	D	L	F	A	%
42	20	11	11	66	52	60.7

FIFA/COCA-COLA WORLD RANKING

1993	1994	1995	1996	1997	1998	1999	2000	2001	2002	2003	2004	2005		High		Low
31	16	17	15	36	49	37	53	51	42	34	37	39		8	06/95	58 08/02

	2005–2006										
08/05	09/05	10/05	11/05	12/05	01/06	02/06	03/06	04/06	05/06	06/06	07/06
46	45	46	39	39	39	40	39	38	37	-	37

A comfortable mid-table finish was all the Bulgarian national team could achieve in the FIFA World Cup™ qualifiers and at no point did they threaten the runaway leaders Croatia and Sweden in the campaign. With an embarrassment of attacking riches in the team, shoring up the defence will be a priority if Bulgaria are to make an impact in a UEFA Euro 2008™ qualifying group in which the Netherlands and Romania will start as favourites. With just five international matches played during the season, most attention has been focused on domestic competition with Levski Sofia and CSKA Sofia once again sharing the honours. The season got off to a poor start when Pirin

INTERNATIONAL HONOURS
European Youth Tournament 1959 1969 1974, **Balkan Cup** 1932 1935 1976

Blagoevgrad were expelled from the top flight after two rounds for financial reasons, but it was business as usual with CSKA and Levski taking a firm grip on the League. By the winter break CSKA had established a seven point lead at the top. Their first defeat came at the end of March against Lokomotiv Plovdiv but it heralded a major collapse which allowed Levski to overtake them. By the time Levski lost only their second match of the season, on the final day, they already had the title in the bag. Levski also revived past memories with a great European run, reaching the quarter-finals of the UEFA Cup before losing to Schalke.

THE FIFA BIG COUNT OF 2000

	Male	Female		Male	Female
Registered players	32 024	143	Referees	2 989	25
Non registered players	80 000	150	Officials	1 835	45
Youth players	10 632	25	Total involved	127 868	
Total players	122 974		Number of clubs	541	
Professional players	960	0	Number of teams	1 418	

Bulgarian Football Union (BFU)
Bulgarski Futbolen Soius, 26 Tzar Ivan Assen II Str., Sofia - 1124, Bulgaria
Tel +359 2 9426202   Fax +359 2 9426200
bfu@bfunion.bg   www.bfunion.bg
President: MIHAILOV Borislav   General Secretary: KAPRALOV Stefan
Vice-President: KASSABOV Michail   Treasurer: PEEV Todor   Media Officer: KARAIVANOV Atanas
Men's Coach: STOITCHKOV Hristo   Women's Coach: DIMITROV Lachezar
BFU formed: 1923   UEFA: 1954   FIFA: 1924
White shirts with green trimmings, Green shorts, White socks or Red shirts, Green, White

RECENT INTERNATIONAL MATCHES PLAYED BY BULGARIA

2002	Opponents		Score	Venue	Comp	Scorers	Att	Referee
21-08	Germany	D	2-2	Sofia	Fr	Berbatov 21, Balakov 50p	10 000	Bre FRA
7-09	Belgium	W	2-0	Brussels	ECq	Jankovic 17, Petrov.S	20 000	Hauge NOR
12-10	Croatia	W	2-0	Sofia	ECq	Petrov.S 22, Berbatov 37	43 000	Frisk SWE
16-10	Andorra	W	2-1	Sofia	ECq	Chilikov 37, Balakov 58	42 000	Richards WAL
20-11	Spain	L	0-1	Granada	Fr		20 000	Coue FRA
2003								
12-02	Hungary †	W	1-0	Laranaca	Fr	Jancovic 36. Abandoned after 45' due to weather	200	Theodotou CYP
27-03	Serbia & Montenegro	W	2-1	Kruševac	Fr	Petrov.S 14, Todorov 56	10 000	Lazarevski MKD
2-04	Estonia	D	0-0	Tallinn	ECq		4 000	Plautz AUT
30-04	Albania	W	2-0	Sofia	Fr	Berbatov 2 3 34	9 325	Vidlak CZE
7-06	Belgium	D	2-2	Sofia	ECq	Berbatov 52, Todorov 72p	42 000	Collina ITA
20-08	Lithuania	W	3-0	Sofia	Fr	Dimitrov 2 25p 45, Berbatov 33	2 000	Bolognino ITA
6-09	Estonia	W	2-0	Sofia	ECq	Petrov.M 16, Berbatov 67	25 128	Wack GER
10-09	Andorra	W	3-0	Andorra la Vella	ECq	Berbatov 2 10 23, Hristov 58	1 000	Mikulski POL
11-10	Croatia	L	0-1	Zagreb	ECq		37 000	Veissiere FRA
18-11	Korea Republic	W	1-0	Seoul	Fr	Manchev 19	38 257	Saleh MAS
2004								
18-02	Greece	L	0-2	Athens	Fr		6 000	Poll ENG
31-03	Russia	D	2-2	Sofia	Fr	Berbatov 2 15 66	14 938	Garcia POR
28-04	Cameroon	W	3-0	Sofia	Fr	Berbatov 2 7 54p, Lazarov 56	13 987	Verbist BEL
2-06	Czech Republic	L	1-3	Prague	Fr	Petkov.M 90	6 627	Stredak SVK
14-06	Sweden	L	0-5	Lisbon	ECr1		31 652	Riley ENG
18-06	Denmark	L	0-2	Braga	ECr1		22 000	Cortez Batista POR
22-06	Italy	L	1-2	Guimaraes	ECr1	Petrov.M 45p	16 002	Ivanov RUS
18-08	Republic of Ireland	D	1-1	Dublin	Fr	Bojinov 70	31 887	Brines SCO
4-09	Iceland	W	3-1	Reykjavik	WCq	Berbatov 35 49, Yanev 62	5 014	Hamer LUX
9-10	Croatia	D	2-2	Zagreb	WCq	Petrov.M 77, Berbatov 86	31 565	Collina ITA
13-10	Malta	W	4-1	Sofia	WCq	Berbatov 2 43 55, Yanev 47, Yankov 88	16 800	Richards WAL
17-11	Azerbaijan	D	0-0	Baku	Fr		3 000	Sipailo LVA
29-11	Egypt	D	1-1	Cairo	Fr	Gargorov 90		
2005								
9-02	Serbia & Montenegro	D	0-0	Sofia	Fr		2 957	Genov BUL
26-03	Sweden	L	0-3	Sofia	WCq		42 530	Fandel GER
30-03	Hungary	D	1-1	Budapest	WCq	Petrov.S 51	11 586	Wegereef NED
4-06	Croatia	L	1-3	Sofia	WCq	Petrov.M 72	35 000	Nielsen DEN
17-08	Turkey	W	3-1	Sofia	Fr	Berbatov 2 24 43, Petrov.M 38	25 000	Zografos GRE
3-09	Sweden	L	0-3	Stockholm	WCq		35 000	De Bleeckere BEL
7-09	Iceland	W	3-2	Sofia	WCq	Berbatov 21, Iliev.G 69, Petrov.M 86	18 000	Demirlek TUR
8-10	Hungary	W	2-0	Sofia	WCq	Berbatov 29, Lazarov 55	4 652	Delevic SCG
12-10	Malta	D	1-1	Ta'Qali	WCq	Yankov 67	2 844	Godulyan UKR
12-11	Georgia	W	6-2	Sofia	Fr	Yankov 2 2 28, Berbatov 2 35 47, Todorov 2 63 90p		
16-11	Mexico	W	3-0	Phoenix	Fr	Valkanov 4, Bojinov 34, Berbatov 80	35 526	Hall USA
2006								
1-03	FYR Macedonia	W	1-0	Skopje	Fr	Petrov.M 38	8 000	
9-05	Japan	W	2-1	Osaka	Fr	Todorov.S 1, Yanev 90	44 851	Megia Davila ESP
11-05	Scotland	L	1-5	Kobe	Fr	Todorov.Y 26	5 780	Kamikawa JPN

Fr = Friendly match • EC = UEFA EURO 2004™ • WC = FIFA World Cup™ • q = qualifier • r1 = first round group • † Not a full international

BULGARIA NATIONAL TEAM RECORDS AND RECORD SEQUENCES

Records			Sequence records					
Victory	7-0	NOR 1957, MLT 1982	Wins	5	1983 & 1987	Clean sheets	4	1963
Defeat	0-13	ESP 1933	Defeats	7	1924-1927	Goals scored	18	1934-1938
Player Caps	102	MIKHAILOV Borislav	Undefeated	11	1972-1973	Without goal	4	1984 & 1998
Player Goals	47	BONEV Hristo	Without win	16	1977-1978	Goals against	24	1924-1932

BULGARIA COUNTRY INFORMATION

Capital	Sofia	Independence	1908 from Ottoman Empire	GDP per Capita	$7 600
Population	7 517 973	Status	Republic	GNP Ranking	79
Area km²	110 910	Language	Bulgarian	Dialling code	+359
Population density	67 per km²	Literacy rate	98%	Internet code	.bg
% in urban areas	71%	Main religion	Christian 85%	GMT + / –	+2
Towns/Cities ('000)	Sofia 1 044; Plovdiv 324; Varna 304; Burgas 186; Ruse 156; Pleven 128				
Neighbours (km)	Romania 608; Turkey 240; Greece 494; Macedonia FYR 148; Serbia & Montenegro 318; Black Sea 354				
Main stadia	Plovdiv Stadion – Plovdiv 48 000; Vassil Levski – Sofia 43 384; Hristo Botev – Vratza 32 000				

BULGARIA NATIONAL TEAM PLAYERS AND COACHES

Record Caps			Record Goals				Recent Coaches	
MIKHAILOV Borislav	1983-'98	102	BONEV Christo	1967-'79	47	VOUTSOV Ivan		1982-'86
BONEV Christo	1967-'79	96	STOITCHKOV Hristo	1987-'99	37	MLADENOV Hristo		1986-'88
BALAKOV Krasimir	1988-'03	92	BERBATOV Dimitar	1999-'06	31	ANGUELOV Boris		1988-'89
PENEV Dimitar	1965-'74	90	KOSTADINOV Emil	1988-'98	26	VOUTSOV Ivan		1989-'91
STOITCHKOV Hristo	1986-'99	83	JEKOV Petar	1963-'72	25	PENEV Dimitar		1991-'96
SIRAKOV Nasko	1983-'96	81	KOLEV Ivan	1950-'63	25	BONEV Christo		1996-'99
SADKOV Anyo	1981-'91	80	SIRAKOV Nasko	1983-'97	23	DIMITROV Dimitar		1999
YANKOV Zlatko	1989-'99	79	MILANOV Dimitar	1948-'59	20	MLADENOV Stoicho		1999-'01
DIMITROV Georgi	1978-'87	77	ASPAROUKHOV Georgi	1962-'70	19	MARKOV Plamen		2002-'04
IVANOV Trifon	1988-'98	76	DERMENDJIEV Dinko	1966-'77	19	STOITCHKOV Hristo		2004-

CLUB DIRECTORY

Club	Town/City	Stadium	Capacity	www.	Lge	Cup
Belasitza Petrich	Petrich	Tsar Samuil	12 000	rondia-bg.com	0	0
Beroe Stara Zagora	Stara Zagora	Beroe	17 800		1	0
Botev	Plovdiv	Hristo Bonev	21 000		2	
Cherno More Varna	Varna	Ticha	12 000		0	0
CSKA Sofia	Sofia	Bulgarska Armia	24 000	cska.bg	30	10
Koneliano	German, Sofia	Vasil Levski	43 384		0	0
Levski Sofia	Sofia	Georgi Asparukhov	29 698	levski.bg	24	11
Litex Lovech	Lovech	Lovech	7 000	fclitex-lovech.bg	2	2
Lokomotiv Plovdiv	Plovdiv	Lokomotiv	20 000	lokopd.com	1	0
Lokomotiv Sofia	Sofia	Lokomotiv	25 000		3	1
Marek Dupnitza	Dupnitza	Bonchuk	12 500	marek.matrix-bg.net	0	0
Rilski sportist	Samokov	Iskar	7 000		0	0
Rodopa Smolian	Smolian	Septemvri	6 000		0	0
Spartak Varna	Varna	Spartak	7 500		0	0
Slavia Sofia	Sofia	Slavia	28 000	pfcslavia.com	7	1
Vihren	Sandanski	Gradski	5 000		0	0

RECENT LEAGUE AND CUP RECORD

Championship						Cup		
Year	Champions	Pts	Runners-up	Pts	Third	Pts	Winners	Score	Runners-up
1990	CSKA Sofia	47	Levski Sofia	36	Slavia Sofia	36	Sliven	2-0	CSKA Sofia
1991	Etar Veliko Tarnovo	44	CSKA Sofia	37	Slavia Sofia	37	Levski Sofia	2-1	Botev Plovdiv
1992	CSKA Sofia	47	Levski Sofia	45	Botev Plovdiv	37	Levski Sofia	5-0	Pirin Blagoevgrad
1993	Levski Sofia	50	CSKA Sofia	42	Botev Plovdiv	38	CSKA Sofia	1-0	Botev Plovdiv
1994	Levski Sofia	71	CSKA Sofia	54	Botev Plovdiv	50	Levski Sofia	1-0	Pirin Blagoevgrad
1995	Levski Sofia	79	Lokomotiv Sofia	68	Botev Plovdiv	60	Lokomotiv Sofia	4-2	Botev Plovdiv
1996	Slavia Sofia	67	Levski Sofia	62	Lokomotiv Sofia	58	Slavia Sofia	1-0	Levski Sofia
1997	CSKA Sofia	71	Neftohimik Burgas	67	Slavia Sofia	57	CSKA Sofia	3-1	Levski Sofia
1998	Liteks Lovech	69	Levski Sofia	64	CSKA Sofia	61	Levski Sofia	5-0	CSKA Sofia
1999	Liteks Lovech	73	Levski Sofia	71	Levski Kjustendil	57	CSKA Sofia	1-0	Litex Lovech
2000	Levski Sofia	74	CSKA Sofia	64	Velbazhd	55	Levski Sofia	2-0	Neftohimik Burgas
2001	Levski Sofia	69	CSKA Sofia	62	Velbazhd	57	Litex Lovech	1-0	Velbazhd
2002	Levski Sofia	65	Litex Lovech	55	Lokomotiv Plovdiv	53	Levski Sofia	3-1	CSKA Sofia
2003	CSKA Sofia	66	Levski Sofia	60	Litex Lovech	55	Levski Sofia	2-1	Litex Lovech
2004	Lokomotiv Plovdiv	75	Levski Sofia	72	CSKA Sofia	65	Litex Lovech	2-2 4-3p	CSKA Sofia
2005	CSKA Sofia	79	Levski Sofia	76	Lokomotiv Plovdiv	58	Levski Sofia	2-1	CSKA Sofia
2006	Levski Sofia	68	CSKA Sofia	65	Litex Lovech	60	CSKA Sofia	3-1	Cherno More Varna

BULGARIA 2005–06

'A' PFG

	Pl	W	D	L	F	A	Pts	Levski	CSKA	Litx	Lok Sofia	Lok Plovdiv	Belasitsa	Slavia	Cherno More	Vihren	Beroe Stara	Marek	Rodopa	Botev	Pirin 1922	Naftex	Pirin
Levski Sofia †	28	21	5	2	71	23	68	-	1-1	1-1	3-1	4-0	2-0	5-0	3-1	2-0	2-0	2-0	6-1	4-1	3-0	6-0	-
CSKA Sofia ‡	28	20	5	3	73	22	65	0-1	-	2-1	3-2	4-3	2-2	2-1	3-0	6-0	7-0	1-1	7-0	1-0	2-0	3-0	-
Litex Lovech ‡	28	18	6	4	51	22	60	1-0	1-1	-	3-1	3-1	2-1	2-1	5-2	4-1	1-0	4-0	3-0	2-0	0-2	1-0	-
Lokomotiv Sofia ‡	28	18	0	10	49	29	54	0-2	1-2	1-0	-	4-2	0-1	2-1	2-1	2-0	4-1	4-0	3-1	1-0	5-0	3-0	-
Lokomotiv Plovdiv	28	11	7	10	43	42	40	2-4	1-0	1-2	1-2	-	1-2	3-0	2-0	2-1	2-1	2-0	3-1	0-0	3-1	3-1	-
Belasitsa Petrich	28	11	6	11	33	33	39	2-1	1-5	1-2	0-1	1-1	-	2-0	0-0	2-0	4-0	1-0	0-1	4-1	1-0	2-1	-
Slavia Sofia	28	12	3	13	33	34	39	2-2	1-2	0-0	2-0	0-1	1-0	-	1-0	1-2	4-2	1-0	3-0	2-1	3-1	1-0	2-0
Cherno More Varna	28	10	7	11	29	27	37	0-1	0-0	1-1	0-2	0-0	4-0	1-0	-	3-1	0-0	2-0	0-1	2-0	3-1	1-0	-
Vihren Sandanski	28	10	2	16	35	55	32	1-2	1-3	1-5	2-0	1-1	2-0	0-2	2-1	-	3-1	3-2	2-1	3-2	1-1	2-0	-
Beroe Stara Zagora	28	8	8	12	36	53	32	4-4	1-4	3-1	1-2	1-1	2-1	3-2	0-4	2-1	-	0-0	3-0	2-0	3-0	2-1	-
Marek Dupnitsa	28	8	7	13	23	37	31	2-3	1-4	0-0	0-2	3-1	1-3	1-0	1-1	2-1	1-0	-	1-0	3-0	0-0	2-0	-
Rodopa Smolian	28	7	4	17	23	52	25	1-2	1-0	0-1	2-1	1-2	2-1	1-3	0-1	1-2	2-2	0-0	-	0-0	2-1	1-2	-
Botev Plovdiv	28	4	12	12	20	38	24	1-2	1-4	0-0	1-0	1-0	0-0	0-0	0-0	3-1	2-2	1-0	1-0	-	0-0	3-3	-
Pirin 1922 Blagoevgrad	28	5	8	15	23	46	23	1-1	0-3	1-3	0-2	3-2	1-1	0-1	0-1	3-1	0-0	1-2	2-2	0-0	-	2-0	-
Naftex Burgas	28	4	6	18	14	43	18	0-2	0-1	0-2	0-1	1-1	0-0	1-0	1-0	1-0	0-0	0-0	0-1	1-1	1-2	-	
Pirin Blagoevgrad	Expelled after two rounds							-	-	-	-	-	-	-	0-1	-	-	-	-	-	-	-	

6/08/2005 - 31/05/2006 • † Qualified for the UEFA Champions League • ‡ Qualified for the UEFA Cup • Matches in bold annulled

BULGARIA 2005–06
'B' PFG

	Pl	W	D	L	F	A	Pts
Rilski Sp. Samokov	26	20	3	3	54	25	63
Koneliano German	26	19	5	2	54	15	62
Spartak Pleven	26	19	2	5	58	18	59
Vidima Rakovski	26	12	7	7	39	26	43
Beli Orli Pleven	26	11	5	10	34	32	38
Pirin Gotse Delchev	26	10	6	10	39	27	36
Hebar Pazardzhik	26	10	3	13	35	35	33
Etar Veliko Tarnovo	26	9	3	14	31	39	30
Minyor Bobov Dol	26	8	5	13	34	37	29
Lokomotiv Mezdra	26	7	6	13	25	46	27
Montana	26	6	8	12	23	47	26
Minyor Pernik	26	6	6	14	25	43	24
Yantra Gabrovo	26	5	7	14	23	52	22
Balkan Botevgrad	26	5	4	17	11	43	19

13/08/2005 - 31/05/2006

BFU CUP 2005–06

Round of 16

CSKA Sofia *	1
Litex Lovech	0
Vidima Rakovski *	0
Beroe Stara Zagora	1
Pirin 1922 Blagoevgrad	2
Rodopa Smolian *	0
Arkus Lyaskovets *	0
Naftex Burgas	4
Shumen 2001 *	2
Spartak Pleven	0
AKB Minyor Radnevo	0
Rilski Sp. Samokov	5
Vihren Sandanski *	2
Marek Dupnitsa	1
Levski Sofia	2
Cherno More Varna *	3

Quarter-finals

CSKA Sofia *	4
Beroe Stara Zagora	1
Pirin 1922 Blagoevgrad*	1 3p
Naftex Burgas	1 4p
Shumen 2001 *	2
Rilski Sp. Samokov	1
Vihren Sandanski *	0
Cherno More Varna	2

Semi-finals

CSKA Sofia *	4
Naftex Burgas	1
Shumen 2001 *	1
Cherno More Varna	2

Final

CSKA Sofia ‡	3
Cherno More Varna	1

CUP FINAL

Vasil Levski, Sofia
24-05-2005, Att: 7 216
Scorers - Emil Gargorov 2 12 28, Guillaume Dah Zadi 34 for CSKA; Moke 94+p for Cherno More

* Home team • ‡ Qualified for the UEFA Cup

CAM – CAMBODIA

NATIONAL TEAM RECORD
JULY 1ST 2002 TO JULY 9TH 2006

PL	W	D	L	F	A	%
13	2	0	11	11	53	15.4

FIFA/COCA-COLA WORLD RANKING

1993	1994	1995	1996	1997	1998	1999	2000	2001	2002	2003	2004	2005		High		Low
-	-	180	186	170	162	168	169	169	176	178	184	188		**156** 07/98		**188** 03/06

2005–2006											
08/05	09/05	10/05	11/05	12/05	01/06	02/06	03/06	04/06	05/06	06/06	07/06
186	186	185	185	188	188	188	188	184	184	-	183

The creation of the AFC Challenge Cup and the AFC President's Cup has brought a new lease of life to the Cambodian national team and to Cambodian club sides with the prospect of regular international competition for both. Until now the national team has had to rely on the biennial Tiger Cup played by the nations of southeast Asia for fixtures but all three games at the inaugural AFC Challenge Cup in Nepal came against opponents from other parts of Asia. While the win against Guam was not wholly unexpected, it did end a run of seven consecutive defeats. With more international experience the hope is that the national team will enter the qualifiers for the 2010

INTERNATIONAL HONOURS
None

FIFA World Cup™ and improve upon a record of two draws and ten defeats in the tournament. There was also encouraging news at club level. The 2005 champions Khemera qualified for the second edition of the AFC President's Cup in Malaysia where they reached the semi-finals after winning their first round group. There they lost 3-0 to the 2005 runners-up, Kyrgyzstan's Dordoi-Dynamo, but it was only the second time that a club from Cambodia had entered an Asian competition and their first round wins over Transport United from Bhutan and Tatung from Chinese Taipei were the first games ever won - a small piece of history to celebrate.

THE FIFA BIG COUNT OF 2000

	Male	Female		Male	Female
Registered players	1 000	0	Referees	64	0
Non registered players	5 000	0	Officials	150	0
Youth players	500	0	Total involved	6 714	
Total players		6 500	Number of clubs	60	
Professional players	0	0	Number of teams	400	

Cambodian Football Federation (CFF)
Chaeng Maeng Village Rd, Kab Srov, Sangkat Samrong Krom, Khan Dangkor, Phnom Penh, Cambodia
Tel +855 23 364889   Fax +855 23 222670
the-cff@yahoo.com   www.none
President: KHEK Ravy   General Secretary: CHHEANG Yean
Vice-President: KEO Sarin   Treasurer: CHAN Soth   Media Officer: None
Men's Coach: O'DONELL Scott   Women's Coach: None
CFF formed: 1933   AFC: 1957   FIFA: 1953
Blue shirts, Blue shorts, Blue socks

RECENT INTERNATIONAL MATCHES PLAYED BY CAMBODIA

2002	Opponents	Score		Venue	Comp	Scorers	Att	Referee
11-12	Malaysia	L	0-5	Kuala Lumpur	Fr			
15-12	Vietnam SR	L	2-9	Jakarta	TCr1	Hok Sochetra [27], Ung Kanyanith [53]	5 000	Nagalingham SIN
17-12	Indonesia	L	2-4	Jakarta	TCr1	Hok Sochetra 2 [10 44]	20 000	Khantachai THA
19-12	Myanmar	L	0-5	Jakarta	TCr1		2 000	Ebrahim BHR
21-12	Philippines	W	1-0	Jakarta	TCr1	Ung Kanyanith [90]	2 500	Napitupulu IDN
2003								
No international matches played in 2003								
2004								
9-12	Vietnam SR	L	1-9	Ho Chi Minh City	TCr1	Hang Sokunthea [44]	8 000	Supian MAS
11-12	Laos	L	1-2	Ho Chi Minh City	TCr1	Hing Darith [27]	20 000	Kwon Jong Chul KOR
13-12	Indonesia	L	0-8	Ho Chi Minh City	TCr1		17 000	Sun Baojie CHN
15-12	Singapore	L	0-3	Ho Chi Minh City	TCr1		2 000	Ebrahim BHR
2005								
11-10	Singapore	L	0-2	Phnom Penh	Fr			
2006								
1-04	Bangladesh	L	1-2	Dhaka	CCr1	Chan Rithy [68]	35 000	Tan Hai CHN
3-04	Palestine	L	0-4	Dhaka	CCr1		2 500	AK Nema IRQ
6-04	Guam	W	3-0	Dhaka	CCr1	Sok Buntheang [37], Keo Kosal [40], Kouch Sokumpheak [63]	500	U Win Cho MYA

Fr = Friendly match • TC = ASEAN Tiger Cup • CC = AFC Challenge Cup • r1 = first round group

CAMBODIA NATIONAL TEAM RECORDS AND RECORD SEQUENCES

Records			Sequence records					
Victory	11-0	YEM 1966	Wins	1		Clean sheets	1	
Defeat	0-10	IDN 1995	Defeats	10	1995-1997	Goals scored	3	1997
Player Caps	n/a		Undefeated	1		Without goal	5	1996-1997
Player Goals	n/a		Without win	17	1998-2002	Goals against	20	1997-2000

RECENT LEAGUE RECORD

Year	Champions
1996	Body Guards Club
1997	Body Guards Club
1998	Royal Dolphins
1999	Royal Dolphins
2000	National Police
2001	No tournament played
2002	Samart United
2003	No tournament played
2004	No tournament played
2005	Khemera

CAMBODIA COUNTRY INFORMATION

Capital	Phnom Penh	Independence	1953	GDP per Capita	$1 900
Population	13 363 421	Status	Kingdom	GNP Ranking	127
Area km²	181 040	Language	Khmer	Dialling code	+855
Population density	73 per km²	Literacy rate	66%	Internet code	.kh
% in urban areas	21%	Main religion	Buddhist 95%	GMT +/−	+7
Towns/Cities ('000)	Phnom Penh 1 573; Preah Sihanouk 157; Bat Dambang 150; Siem Reab 148				
Neighbours (km)	Laos 541; Vietnam 1,228; Thailand 803; Gulf of Thailand 443				
Main stadia	National Olympic − Phnom Penh 50 000				

CAN – CANADA

NATIONAL TEAM RECORD
JULY 1ST 2002 TO JULY 9TH 2006

PL	W	D	L	F	A	%
30	10	3	17	33	49	38.3

FIFA/COCA-COLA WORLD RANKING

1993	1994	1995	1996	1997	1998	1999	2000	2001	2002	2003	2004	2005		High		Low
44	63	65	40	66	101	81	63	92	70	87	90	84		**40**	12/96	**101**	12/98

2005–2006											
08/05	09/05	10/05	11/05	12/05	01/06	02/06	03/06	04/06	05/06	06/06	07/06
84	84	86	87	84	84	85	85	84	83	-	54

After a number of years in the doldrums, soccer in Canada is beginning to stage something of a comeback. With the hosting of the FIFA U-20 World Cup in July 2007, the game is back on the agenda with fixtures scheduled for Montreal, Ottawa, Toronto, Edmonton, Vancouver and Victoria. In preparation the U-20 team has been very active and in May 2006 a crowd of 14,250 saw them beat Brazil 2-1, the first victory over the South Americans by any male Canadian team. The other major news of the year was the awarding of a MLS franchise to Toronto for the 2007 season. The team will play in the newly-constructed venue which will host the FIFA U-20 World Cup final with

INTERNATIONAL HONOURS
Qualified for the FIFA World Cup™ 1986 Qualified for the FIFA Women's World Cup 1995 1999 2003 Olympic Gold 1904 (Unofficial)
CONCACAF Gold Cup 2000 CONCACAF Women's Gold Cup 1998 CONCACAF U-20 Championship 1986 1996

top level club football returning to the country for the first time since the days of the NASL. The Canadian flag was also flown by Montreal Impact in the American USL. They finished top of the table in the regular season but then lost to Seattle Sounders in the semi-finals. Vancouver Whitecaps also reached the play-offs but lost in the quarter-finals in what is effectively the second division of football in the USA behind MLS. There was disappointment on the national team front with the resignation of Frank Yallop in June 2006. He left to take over as head coach of LA Galaxy.

THE FIFA BIG COUNT OF 2000

	Male	Female		Male	Female
Registered players	62 100	35 000	Referees	7 000	6 000
Non registered players	400 000	200 000	Officials	100 000	50 000
Youth players	418 000	235 000	Total involved	1 513 100	
Total players	1 350 100		Number of clubs	5 900	
Professional players	100	0	Number of teams	51 000	

The Canadian Soccer Association (CSA)
Place Soccer Canada, 237 Metcalfe Street, Ottawa, Ontario, K2P 1R2, Canada
Tel +1 613 2377678   Fax +1 613 2371516
info@soccercan.ca   www.canadasoccer.com
President: LINFORD Colin   General Secretary: PIPE Kevan
Vice-President: MONTAGLIANI Victor   Treasurer: URSINI Vincent   Media Officer: COCHRANE Earl
Men's Coach: TBC   Women's Coach: PELLERUD Even
CSA formed: 1912   CONCACAF: 1978   FIFA: 1912-28, 1946
Red shirts with white trimmings, Red shorts, Red socks or White shirts with red trimmings, White shorts, White socks

RECENT INTERNATIONAL MATCHES PLAYED BY CAMBODIA

2002	Opponents	Score		Venue	Comp	Scorers	Att	Referee
15-10	Scotland	L	1-3	Edinburgh	Fr	De Rosario [9p]	16 207	Huyghe BEL
2003								
18-01	USA	L	0-4	Fort Lauderdale	Fr		6 549	Sibrian SLV
12-02	Libya	W	4-2	Tripoli	Fr	McKenna [18], Brennan [34], Stalteri [47], Canizalez [81]	45 000	
29-03	Estonia	L	1-2	Tallinn	Fr	Stalteri [47]	2 500	Hansson SWE
1-06	Germany	L	1-4	Wolfsburg	Fr	McKenna [20]	24 000	Poulat FRA
12-07	Costa Rica	W	1-0	Foxboro	GCr1	Stalteri [59]	33 652	Piper TRI
14-07	Cuba	L	0-2	Foxboro	GCr1		8 780	Prendergast JAM
11-10	Finland	L	2-3	Tampere	Fr	Radzinski [75], De Rosario [85]	5 350	
15-11	Czech Republic	L	1-5	Teplice	Fr	Radzinski [89]	8 343	Sundell SWE
18-11	Republic of Ireland	L	0-3	Dublin	Fr		23 000	Whitby WAL
2004								
18-01	Barbados	W	1-0	Bridgetown	Fr	Corazzin [10]		Ford BRB
30-05	Wales	L	0-1	Wrexham	Fr		10 805	McKeon IRE
13-06	Belize	W	4-0	Kingston	WCq	Peschisolido [39], Radzinski [55], McKenna [75], Brennan [83]	8 245	Batres GUA
16-06	Belize	W	4-0	Kingston	WCq	Radzinski [45], De Rosario 2 [63 73], Brennan [85]	5 124	Gordon TRI
18-08	Guatemala	L	0-2	Vancouver	WCq		6 725	Sibrian SLV
4-09	Honduras	D	1-1	Edmonton	WCq	De Vos [82]	9 654	Archundia MEX
8-09	Costa Rica	L	0-1	San Jose	WCq		13 000	Ramdhan TRI
9-10	Honduras	D	1-1	San Pedro Sula	WCq	Hutchinson [73]	42 000	Stott USA
13-10	Costa Rica	L	1-3	Vancouver	WCq	De Rosario [12]	4 728	Prendergast JAM
17-11	Guatemala	W	1-0	Guatemala City	WCq	De Rosario [57]	18 000	Rodriguez MEX
2005								
9-02	Northern Ireland	W	1-0	Belfast	Fr	Occean [31]	11 156	Attard MLT
26-03	Portugal	L	1-4	Barcelos	Fr	McKenna [85]	13 000	Ishchenko UKR
2-07	Honduras	L	1-2	Vancouver	Fr	McKenna [70]	4 105	Valenzuela USA
7-07	Costa Rica	L	0-1	Seattle	GCr1		15 831	Prendergast JAM
9-07	USA	L	0-2	Seattle	GCr1		15 109	Brizan TRI
12-07	Cuba	W	2-1	Foxboro	GCr1	Gerba [69], Hutchinson [87]	15 211	Moreno PAN
3-09	Spain	L	1-2	Santander	Fr	Grande [73]	11 978	Colombo FRA
16-11	Luxembourg	W	1-0	Hesperange	Fr	Hume [69]		Gomes Costa POR
2006								
22-01	USA	D	0-0	San Diego	Fr		6 077	Archundia MEX
1-03	Austria	W	2-0	Vienna	Fr	Brennan [65], Reda [71]	9 000	Van Egmond NED

Fr = Friendly match • GC = CONCACAF Gold Cup • WC = FIFA World Cup™ • q = qualifier • r1 = first round group

CANADA NATIONAL TEAM RECORDS AND RECORD SEQUENCES

Records			Sequence records					
Victory	7-0	USA 1904	Wins	6	2000	Clean sheets	5	1996
Defeat	0-8	MEX 1993	Defeats	9	1974-1976	Goals scored	10	1980-1983 & 1985
Player Caps	82	SAMUEL Randy	Undefeated	15	1999-2000	Without goal	5	1986 & 2000
Player Goals	19	CATLIFF & MITCHELL	Without win	12	1974-1976	Goals against	17	1988-1992

CANADA COUNTRY INFORMATION

Capital	Ottawa	Independence	1867	GDP per Capita	$29 800
Population	32 507 874	Status	Commonwealth	GNP Ranking	8
Area km²	9 984 670	Language	English/French	Dialling code	+1
Population density	3 per km²	Literacy rate	99%	Internet code	.ca
% in urban areas	77%	Main religion	Christian 82%	GMT + / –	-3.5 / -8
Towns/Cities ('000)	Toronto 4 612; Montreal 3 268; Vancouver 1 837; Calgary 968; Ottawa 874; Edmonton 822; Hamilton 653; Quebec 645; Winnipeg 632; Kitchener 409; London 346; Victoria 289				
Neighbours (km)	USA 8 893; Arctic Ocean, Atlantic Ocean & Pacific Ocean 202 020				
Main stadia	Commonwealth Stadium – Edmonton 60 217; York University – Toronto 25 000 (from 2007)				

CANADA NATIONAL TEAM PLAYERS AND COACHES

Record Caps			Record Goals			Recent Coaches	
SAMUEL Randy	1983-'97	82	CATLIFF John	1984-'94	19	WAITERS Tony	1983-'87
WATSON Mark	1991-'04	72	MITCHELL Dale	1980-'93	19	BEARPARK Bob	1986-'87
HOOPER Lyndon	1986-'97	66	BUNBURY Alex	1986-'97	16	TAYLOR Tony	1988
BUNBURY Alex	1986-'97	65	VRABLIC Igor	1984-'86	11	LENARDUZZI Bob	1989
DASOVIC Nick	1992-'04	63	CORAZZIN Carlo	1994-'04	11	WAITERS Tony	1990-'91
SWEENEY Mike	1980-'93	61	PESCHISOLIDO Paul	1992-'04	10	LENARDUZZI Bob	1992-'97
MILLER Colin	1983-'97	61	MCKENNA Kevin	2000-'06	8	TWAMLEY Bruce	1998
CORAZZIN Carlo	1994-'04	58	DE ROSARIO Dwayne	2000-'06	7	OSIECK Holger	1999-'03
WILSON Bruce	1974-'86	57	PARSONS Les	1972-'80	7	MILLER Colin	2003
FORREST Craig	1988-'01	56	RADZINSKI Tomasz	1995-'04	7	YALLOP Frank	2003-'06

CLUB DIRECTORY

Club	Town/City	Stadium	Capacity	www.	League
Montreal Impact	Montreal	Claude Robillard	14 000	impactmontreal.com	USL A-League
Toronto Lynx	Toronto	Centennial Stadium	3 500	lynxsoccer.com	USL A-League
Vancouver Whitecaps	Vancouver	Swangard, Burnaby	6 100	whitecapsfc.com	USL A-League

CAY – CAYMAN ISLANDS

NATIONAL TEAM RECORD
JULY 1ST 2002 TO JULY 9TH 2006

PL	W	D	L	F	A	%
9	2	0	7	4	20	22.2

FIFA/COCA-COLA WORLD RANKING

1993	1994	1995	1996	1997	1998	1999	2000	2001	2002	2003	2004	2005		High	Low
154	150	131	148	164	153	148	159	165	164	181	176	181		**127** 11/95	**184** 03/04

2005–2006										
08/05	09/05	10/05	11/05	12/05	01/06	02/06	03/06	04/06	05/06	06/06	07/06
177	177	177	176	181	181	181	182	182	182	-	175

After finishing as runners-up in the previous two seasons, Scholars won back the Fosters National League title from Money Express. Both clubs won their respective divisions in the regular season, Scholars in the West Zone and Money Express - who had changed their name for the start of the season from Western Union - in the East Zone. The top two in each zone qualified for the Final Four semi-finals and with Scholars and Money Express kept apart, they were expected to make the final. That didn't happen, however, with Scholars facing George Town instead, a match they won 2-1, to win their fourth title in ten years. It also meant a second double in four seasons as the

INTERNATIONAL HONOURS
None

previous weekend they had beaten Money Express 2-0 in the FA Cup Final. There was some consolation for Money Express with their triumph earlier in the year in the other major knock-out tournament ,the CIFA Digicel Cayman Cup. They beat George Town 2-0 in the final at the George Town Annex with both goals scored by Sheldon Hoppins. With relatively little action on the international front, the football association has made the development of club football a priority, with the bold step of clubs collecting gate revenues introduced for the first time in the 2005-06 season. The hope is for clubs to identify more with their local communities and to raise standards.

THE FIFA BIG COUNT OF 2000

	Male	Female		Male	Female
Registered players	592	224	Referees	48	3
Non registered players	1 000	0	Officials	180	16
Youth players	540	140	Total involved	2 743	
Total players	2 496		Number of clubs	39	
Professional players	0	0	Number of teams	48	

Cayman Islands Football Association (CIFA)

Truman Bodden Sports Complex, Olympic Way, Off Walkers Road, PO Box 178, GT, Grand Cayman, Cayman Islands

Tel +1 345 9495775   Fax +1 345 9457673

cifa@candw.ky   www.caymanfootball.ky

President: WEBB Jeffrey   General Secretary: BLAKE Bruce

Vice-President: FREDERICK David   Treasurer: WATSON Canover   Media Officer: MORGAN Kenisha

Men's Coach: TINOCO Marcos   Women's Coach: CUNHA Thiago

CIFA formed: 1966   CONCACAF: 1993   FIFA: 1992

Red shirts, Blue shorts, White socks or White shirts, White shorts, Red socks

RECENT INTERNATIONAL MATCHES PLAYED BY THE CAYMAN ISLANDS

2002	Opponents		Score	Venue		Scorers	Att.	Referee
17-11	Nicaragua	L	0-1	Grand Cayman	Fr			
27-11	Cuba	L	0-5	Grand Cayman	GCq			Prendergast JAM
29-11	Dominican Republic	W	1-0	Grand Cayman	GCq	Forbes 27		Grant HAI
1-12	Martinique	L	0-3	Grand Cayman	GCq			Prendergast JAM
2003								
No international matches played in 2003								
2004								
22-02	Cuba	L	1-2	Grand Cayman	WCq	Elliot 72	1 789	Sibrian SLV
27-03	Cuba	L	0-3	Havana	WCq		3 500	Rodriguez MEX
24-11	Bermuda	L	1-2	Kingstown	GCq	Berry 48	200	Matthew SKN
26-11	British Virgin Islands	W	1-0	Kingstown	GCq	Whittaker 49		
28-11	St Vincent/Grenadines	L	0-4	Kingstown	GCq		850	Prendergast JAM
2005								
No international matches played in 2005								
2006								
No international matches played in 2006 before July								

Fr = Friendly match • GC = CONCACAF Gold Cup • WC = FIFA World Cup™ • q = qualifier

CAYMAN ISLANDS NATIONAL TEAM RECORDS AND RECORD SEQUENCES

Records			Sequence records					
Victory	5-0	VGB 1994	Wins	3	1994	Clean sheets	2	1994, 1995
Defeat	2-9	TRI 1995	Defeats	8	1991-1993	Goals scored	5	1993-94, 2000
Player Caps	n/a		Undefeated	4	1994-1995	Without goal	5	2000
Player Goals	n/a		Without win	9	1991-93, 1995-98	Goals against	10	1991-1993

RECENT LEAGUE AND CUP RECORD

	Championship				Cup		
Year	Champions	Score	Runners-up		Winners	Score	Runners-up
1998	Scholars International				George Town		
1999	George Town						
2000	Western Union						
2001	Scholars International	†	George Town		Bodden Town		
2002	George Town	2-1	Future		George Town	4-0	Scholars International
2003	Scholars International	3-1	Sunset		Scholars International	2-1	Bodden Town
2004	Latinos	3-2	Scholars International		Latinos	2-1	George Town
2005	Western Union	0-0 3-2p	Scholars International		Western Union	2-0	Scholars International
2006	Scholars International	2-1	George Town		Scholars International	2-0	Money Express

† Played on a league system

CAYMAN ISLANDS COUNTRY INFORMATION

Capital	George Town	Independence		GDP per Capita	$35 000
Population	43 103	Status	British Crown Colony	GNP Ranking	n/a
Area km²	262	Language	English	Dialling code	+1 345
Population density	164 per km²	Literacy rate	98%	Internet code	.ky
% in urban areas	%	Main religion	Christian	GMT +/–	-5
Towns/Cities ('000)	George Town 27; West Bay 10; Bodden Town 6; East End 1; North Side 1				
Neighbours (km)	The Cayman Islands consist of three islands in the Caribbean Sea				
Main stadia	Truman Boden – George Town 7 000; ED Bush – West Bay 2 500				

CGO – CONGO

NATIONAL TEAM RECORD
JULY 1ST 2002 TO JULY 9TH 2006

PL	W	D	L	F	A	%
32	9	9	14	26	37	42.2

FIFA/COCA-COLA WORLD RANKING

1993	1994	1995	1996	1997	1998	1999	2000	2001	2002	2003	2004	2005	High	Low
103	114	119	100	101	112	94	86	94	97	108	117	110	85 11/00	139 04/96

	2005–2006										
08/05	09/05	10/05	11/05	12/05	01/06	02/06	03/06	04/06	05/06	06/06	07/06
111	113	112	111	110	111	111	111	111	111	-	108

A sudden dearth of playing talent and a host of coaching changes have seen the effectiveness of Congo's 'Diables Rouges' (Red Devils) dissipated in recent years, culminating in a disappointing FIFA World Cup™ qualifying campaign. The Congolese, who were on the cusp of qualification for the 1998 finals in France and competitive in the 2002 campaign, made it through to the group phase of the 2006 qualifiers but were never really in contention. In 2005, they managed just one win and one draw in five qualifying matches and it was on their home pitch in Brazzaville that opponents Togo were able to clinch a place in the finals in Germany. Congo started 2005 on the back foot with

INTERNATIONAL HONOURS
CAF African Cup of Nations 1972 African Games 1965 CAF Champions League CARA Brazzaville 1974

the departure of their French coach Christian Letard, thrusting Gaston Tchiangana back into the coaching hot seat. They have since procured another French coach in Noel Tosi, who takes charge of their bid to qualify for the 2008 African Nations Cup finals. Limited infrastructure and financial resources in the country mean that the League was again divided into four groups, cutting down on the number of matches and subsequent travel bills. Brazzaville's Diables Noirs and Saint Michel d'Ouenzé reached the final but their decider was abandoned because of crowd rioting three minutes from time, leading FECOFOOT to decide not to award a title.

THE FIFA BIG COUNT OF 2000

	Male	Female		Male	Female
Registered players	5 625	250	Referees	125	10
Non registered players	25 000	150	Officials	625	30
Youth players	2 400	115	Total involved	34 300	
Total players	33 540		Number of clubs	266	
Professional players	0	0	Number of teams	278	

Fédération Congolaise de Football (FECOFOOT)
80 Rue Eugene Etienne, Centre Ville Brazzaville, Case postale 11, Brazzaville, Congo
Tel +242 811563   Fax +242 812524
fecofoot@yahoo.fr   www.none
President: IBOVI Antoine   General Secretary: TSIKA Joseph
Vice-President: BAKALA MAYINDA Thomas   Treasurer: NDENGUET Lylian   Media Officer: BAKANDILA Joseph
Men's Coach: TCHIANGANA Gaston   Women's Coach: KAYA Gilbert
FECOFOOT formed: 1962   CAF: 1966   FIFA: 1962
Green shirts, Yellow shorts, Red socks

RECENT INTERNATIONAL MATCHES PLAYED BY CONGO

2002	Opponents	Score	Venue	Comp	Scorers	Att	Referee
25-08	Congo DR	L 1-3	Brazzaville	Fr			
1-09	Gabon	D 0-0	Brazzaville	Fr			
8-09	Burkina Faso	D 0-0	Brazzaville	CNq		60 000	Itur KEN
13-10	Mozambique	W 3-0	Maputo	CNq	Tsoumou [49], Nguie [70], Bakouma [73]		Lwanja MWI
2003							
9-03	Congo DR	L 0-3	Kinshasa	Fr			
4-05	Central African Rep.	W 2-1	Brazzaville	CNq	Embingou [6], Owolo [52]		
8-06	Central African Rep.	D 0-0	Bangui	CNq			Hissene CHA
21-06	Burkina Faso	L 0-3	Ouagadougou	CNq		36 000	Mana NGA
6-07	Mozambique	D 0-0	Brazzaville	CNq			
12-10	Sierra Leone	W 1-0	Brazzaville	WCq	Mvoubi [89p]	4 800	Mana NGA
16-11	Sierra Leone	D 1-1	Freetown	WCq	Nguie [67]	20 000	Monteiro Lopez CPV
5-12	Gabon	W 3-2	Brazzaville	CMr1	Ayessa [25], Ndey [56], Beaulia [67]		Tchoumba CMR
9-12	Gabon	D 1-1	Brazzaville	CMr1	Ayessa [56]		
10-12	Cameroon	L 0-2	Brazzaville	CMsf			Mbera GAB
13-12	Gabon	W 1-0	Brazzaville	CM3p			
2004							
5-06	Senegal	L 0-2	Dakar	WCq		18 000	Benouza ALG
20-06	Liberia	W 3-0	Brazzaville	WCq	Bouanga [52], Mamouna-Ossila [55], Batota [66]	25 000	Lemghambodj MTN
4-07	Mali	W 1-0	Brazzaville	WCq	Mamouna-Ossila [30]	20 000	Evehe CMR
5-09	Togo	L 0-2	Lome	WCq		20 000	Mbera GAB
10-10	Zambia	L 2-3	Brazzaville	WCq	Bouanga [75], Mamouna-Ossila [81]	20 000	Yacoubi TUN
2005							
5-02	Central African Rep.	W 1-0	Libreville	CMr1	Bhebey [10]		
8-02	Gabon	L 0-1	Libreville	CMr1			
12-02	Gabon	L 1-2	Libreville	CM3p	Lakou [35]		
22-02	Angola	L 0-2	Brazzaville	Fr			
19-03	Gabon	D 0-0	Libreville	Fr			
26-03	Zambia	L 0-2	Chililabombwe	WCq		20 000	Maillet SEY
5-06	Senegal	D 0-0	Brazzaville	WCq		40 000	Damon RSA
19-06	Liberia	W 2-0	Paynesville	WCq	Bhebey 2 [3 73]	5 000	Sillah GAM
3-09	Mali	L 0-2	Bamako	WCq		10 000	Mbera GAB
8-10	Togo	L 2-3	Brazzaville	WCq	Bouity [26], Mamouna-Ossila [56]	20 000	Shelmany LBY
2006							
4-03	Equatorial Guinea	L 1-2	Bata	CMr1			
8-03	Chad	D 0-0	Bata	CMr1			

Fr = Friendly match • CN = African Cup of Nations • CM = CEMAC Cup • WC = FIFA World Cup™
q = qualifier • r1 = first round group • sf = semi-final • 3p = third place play-off

CONGO NATIONAL TEAM RECORDS AND RECORD SEQUENCES

Records			Sequence records				
Victory	11-0	STP 1976	Wins	5	1983	Clean sheets	4	1983, 1998-1999
Defeat	1-8	MAD 1960	Defeats	5	1968, 1973, 1993	Goals scored	11	1975-1977
Player Caps	n/a		Undefeated	8	1963-1965	Without goal	7	1992-1993
Player Goals	n/a		Without win	9	2001-2002	Goals against	14	1965-1968

CONGO COUNTRY INFORMATION

Capital	Brazzaville	Independence	1960 from France	GDP per Capita	$700
Population	2 998 040	Status	Republic	GNP Ranking	137
Area km²	342 000	Language	French	Dialling code	+242
Population density	8 per km²	Literacy rate	77%	Internet code	.cg
% in urban areas	59%	Main religion	Christian 50%	GMT + / −	+1
Towns/Cities ('000)	Brazzaville 1 115; Pointe-Noire 628; Loubomo 70; Nkayi 70; Loandjili 26; Madingou 22				
Neighbours (km)	Central African Republic 467; Congo DR 2 410; Angola 201; Gabon 1 903; Cameroon 523; Atlantic Ocean 169				
Main stadia	Stade de la Révolution – Brazzaville 50 000				

CHAMPIONNAT NATIONALE 2005

Quarter-finals		Semi-finals		Final	
St Michel Ouenzé	4				
La Mancha	1	St Michel Ouenzé	3		
JS Bougainvillées	0	Club 57	2		
Club 57	1			St Michel Ouenzé	2
AS Police	2			Diables Noirs	2
Vita Club Mokanda	0	AS Police	1 3p	2-10-2005	
Patronage Sainte Anne	0 3p	Diables Noirs	1 5p	Stade de la Révolution, Brazzaville	
Diables Noirs	0 4p			Scorers - Litsingui 2 for SMO; Mvoula, Bamba-Kalifa for Diables Noirs	

Final abandoned after 87 minutes due to crowd trouble. The title was not awarded to either team

COUPE DU CONGO 2005

Round of 16		Quarter-finals		Semi-finals		Final	
Diables Noirs	4						
Inter Club	0	Diables Noirs	1 1				
Inter Club Dolisie	0 5p	JS Bougainvillées	0 0				
JS Bougainvillées	0 3p			Diables Noirs	1 1		
St Michel Ouenzé	1 4p			Vita Club Mokanda	0 1		
Cheminots	1 2p	St Michel Ouenzé	0 1				
Olympic		Vita Club Mokanda	2 1				
Vita Club Mokanda	†					Diables Noirs	1 4p
Léopards	3					Patronage Sainte Anne	1 2p
La Mancha	2	Léopards	1 2				
Sonad'eau	0	Munisport	1 0			CUP FINAL	
Munisport	6			Léopards	1 0		
CARA Brazzaville	2			Patronage Sainte Anne	2 4		
Etoile du Congo	1	CARA Brazzaville	0 0			15-08-2005	
Patronage Kinkala	0	Patronage Sainte Anne	2 2				
Patronage Sainte Anne	4	† Vita won the replay after the first match was abandoned at 2-2					

RECENT LEAGUE AND CUP RECORD

	Championship				Cup		
Year	Champions	Score	Runners-up		Winners	Score	Runners-up
1994	Etoile du Congo	2-0	Inter Club		EPB Pointe Noire		Inter Club
1995	AS Cheminots	1-0	Patronage Sainte Anne		Etoile du Congo	1-0	Inter Club
1996	Munisport				Vita Club Mokanda		
1997	Munisport				Tournament not played		
1998	Vita Club Mokanda	1-0	Etoile du Congo		Tournament not played		
1999	Vita Club Mokanda				Tournament not played		
2000	Etoile du Congo	†			Etoile du Congo	5-1	Vita Club Mokanda
2001	Etoile du Congo	1-0	La Mancha		AS Police	1-0	Etoile du Congo
2002	AS Police	2-1	Etoile du Congo		Etoile du Congo	2-1	FC Abeilles
2003	St Michel Ouenzé	0-0	La Mancha		Diables Noirs	0-0 3-2p	Vita Club Mokanda
2004	Diables Noirs	2-1	AS Police		Munisport	0-0 3-0p	Vita Club Mokanda
2005	Final abandoned. Neither St Michel nor Diables Noirs awarded title				Diables Noirs	1-1 4-2p	Patronage Sainte Anne

† Played on a league system

CHA – CHAD

NATIONAL TEAM RECORD
JULY 1ST 2002 TO JULY 9TH 2006

PL	W	D	L	F	A	%
16	4	6	6	18	25	43.7

FIFA/COCA-COLA WORLD RANKING

1993	1994	1995	1996	1997	1998	1999	2000	2001	2002	2003	2004	2005		High	Low
166	175	180	188	184	178	166	163	176	173	152	168	159		**128** 07/06	**190** 09/97

2005–2006											
08/05	09/05	10/05	11/05	12/05	01/06	02/06	03/06	04/06	05/06	06/06	07/06
157	157	158	158	159	160	160	160	159	159	-	128

For the past three years Chad has been one of the numerous African countries whose footballing expeditions have been few and far between remaining stuck in a competitive vacuum. The national team last played in a competitive international in November 2003 at the start of the 2006 FIFA World Cup™ qualifiers, where they gave Angola a surprise but eventually lost on the away goals rule after a 3-3 aggregate draw. Participation in the regional CEMAC tournament has given them some added practice, and twice they have reached the semi-finals, but it is the new cycle of African football, starting in late 2006, that will afford Chad an opportunity to write a new chapter in their

INTERNATIONAL HONOURS
None

football history. They have been drawn with Congo, South Africa and Zambia in their qualifying group for the 2008 African Nations Cup finals in Ghana. The country had displayed some ambition with the appointment of the gold-medal winning Cameroon Olympic coach Jean-Paul Akono four years ago. He left after the FIFA World Cup™ qualifying exit, but it did show Chad's desire to improve their status and competitiveness. By reaching the semi-finals of the past two editions of the CEMAC Cup, Chad saw their position in the FIFA/Coca-Cola World Ranking soar to a highest ever placing of 128, thanks largely to the new system used to calculate the positions.

THE FIFA BIG COUNT OF 2000

	Male	Female		Male	Female
Registered players	5 000	0	Referees	200	0
Non registered players	20 000	0	Officials	1 500	0
Youth players	2 500	0	Total involved	29 200	
Total players	27 500		Number of clubs	100	
Professional players	0	0	Number of teams	500	

Fédération Tchadienne de Football (FTF)
Case postale 886, N'Djamena, Chad
Tel +235 518740   Fax +235 523806
ftfa@intnet.td   www.none
President: MAHAMAT Saleh Issa   General Secretary: RAMADANE Daouda
Vice-President: BANAYE Hisseine   Treasurer: RAMADANE Daouda   Media Officer: ZOUTANE DABA Martin
Men's Coach: TIGABE Ousman   Women's Coach: None
FTF formed: 1962   CAF: 1962   FIFA: 1988
Blue shirts, Yellow shorts, Red socks

RECENT INTERNATIONAL MATCHES PLAYED BY CHAD

2002	Opponents	Score		Venue	Comp	Scorers	Att	Referee
26-07	Sudan	L	0-2	Khartoum	Fr			Abdel Rahman SUD
28-07	Ethiopia	W	3-2	Khartoum	Fr			Rassas Lebrato SUD
30-07	Uganda	L	0-2	Khartoum	Fr			Salih SUD
11-10	Algeria	L	1-4	Annaba	CNq	Naay 70	20 000	El Beltagy EGY
2003								
30-03	Namibia	W	2-0	N'Djamena	CNq	Hissein 2 57 89p		Dimanche CTA
7-06	Namibia	L	1-2	Windhoek	CNq	Hissein 35	5 000	Colembi ANG
6-07	Algeria	D	0-0	N'Djamena	CNq			
12-10	Angola	W	3-1	N'Djamena	WCq	Oumar 3 53 74 83	30 000	Nahi CIV
16-11	Angola	L	0-2	Luanda	WCq		30 000	Buenkadila COD
2004								
No international matches played in 2004								
2005								
8-02	Equatorial Guinea	D	0-0	Libreville	CMr1			
10-02	Gabon	W	3-2	Libreville	CMsf	Djenet 3, Doumbe 8, Nguembaye 56		
22-05	Sudan	L	1-4	Khartoum	Fr			
27-05	Sudan	D	1-1	Khartoum	Fr			
2006								
6-03	Equatorial Guinea	D	1-1	Bata	CMr1			
8-03	Congo	D	0-0	Bata	CMr1			
11-03	Cameroon †	L	0-1	Bata	CMsf			
14-03	Gabon	D	2-2	Bata	CM3p	Mahamat 20p, Doumbé 52		

Fr = Friendly match • CN = African Cup of Nations • CM = CEMAC Cup • WC = FIFA World Cup™
q = qualifier • r1 = first round group • sf = semi-final • † Not an official international

CHAD NATIONAL TEAM RECORDS AND RECORD SEQUENCES

Records			Sequence records				
Victory	5-0	STP 1976	Wins	3	1999	Clean sheets	2	1986, 1999
Defeat	2-6	BEN 1963	Defeats	7	1991-1997	Goals scored	4	Three times
Player Caps	n/a		Undefeated	4	1984-85, 2005-06	Without goal	5	1992-1997
Player Goals	n/a		Without win	12	1976-86, 1991-99	Goals against	9	1978-86, 1991-98

RECENT LEAGUE RECORD

Year	Champions
1996	AS Coton Chad
1997	Tourbillon
1998	AS Coton Chad
1999	Renaissance
2000	Tourbillon
2001	Tourbillon
2002	No tournament
2003	No tournament
2004	No tournament
2005	

CHAD COUNTRY INFORMATION

Capital	N'Djamena	Independence	1960 from France	GDP per Capita	$1 200
Population	9 538 544	Status	Republic	GNP Ranking	145
Area km²	1 284 000	Language	French, Arabic	Dialling code	+235
Population density	7 per km²	Literacy rate	47%	Internet code	.td
% in urban areas	21%	Main religion	Muslim 51%, Christian 35%	GMT +/-	+1
Towns/Cities ('000)	N'Djamena 721; Moundou 135; Sarh 102; Abeche 74; Kelo 42; Koumra 36; Pala 35				
Neighbours (km)	Libya 1 055; Sudan 1 360; Central African Republic 1 197; Cameroon 1 094; Nigeria 87; Niger 1 175				
Main stadia	Stade National - N'Djamena 30 000				

CHI – CHILE

NATIONAL TEAM RECORD
JULY 1ST 2002 TO JULY 9TH 2006

PL	W	D	L	F	A	%
37	13	13	11	42	40	52.7

FIFA/COCA-COLA WORLD RANKING

1993	1994	1995	1996	1997	1998	1999	2000	2001	2002	2003	2004	2005	High		Low	
55	47	36	26	16	16	23	19	39	84	80	74	64	**8**	04/98	**84**	12/02

2005–2006											
08/05	09/05	10/05	11/05	12/05	01/06	02/06	03/06	04/06	05/06	06/06	07/06
73	76	72	63	64	64	66	67	67	64	-	46

With just one appearance in the finals of the FIFA World Cup™ since 1982, the national team in Chile has long been a source of disappointment for fans in the country, and it was no different in the qualifying tournament for the finals in Germany. Chile finished three points adrift of the play-off position, seemingly unable to maintain their former role as one of the second tier powers on the South American continent. At club level there was a return to former glories for Union Española, champions for the first time since 1977 when they beat Coquimbo Unido 4-2 on aggregate in the 2005 Apertura final. Universidad Catolica had won the most points in the group stage - as they also

INTERNATIONAL HONOURS
Qualified for the FIFA World Cup™ 1930 1950 1962 1966 1974 1982 1998   **Copa Libertadores** Colo Colo 1991

did in the Clausura - but lost in the play-offs on penalties to Huachipato. Catolica made no mistake in the Clausura, beating eternal rivals Universidad de Chile in the final, although it did take another penalty shoot-out to separate the two. On route, their Argentine keeper Jose Maria Buljubasich went a record 1,352 minutes unbeaten as Catolica played the first 14 games without conceding. He missed out on Danny Verlinden's world record by just 38 minutes. Colo Colo finished trophyless for the third year following their financial collapse in 2002, but in June 2005 they became the first South American club to float on the stock market and promptly went on to win the 2006 Apertura.

THE FIFA BIG COUNT OF 2000

	Male	Female		Male	Female
Registered players	519 983	950	Referees	5 002	0
Non registered players	400 000	0	Officials	14 500	200
Youth players	264 293	1 000	Total involved	1 205 928	
Total players	1 186 226		Number of clubs	4 931	
Professional players	1 125	0	Number of teams	29 498	

Federación de Fútbol de Chile (FFCH)
Avenida Quilin No. 5635, Comuna Peñalolén, Casilla No. 3733, Central de Casillas, Santiago de Chile, Chile
Tel +56 2 3975000   Fax +56 2 2843510
ffch@chile.cl   www.anfp.cl
President: SARATE Jose Abdalah   General Secretary: LAFRENTZ Jorge
Vice-President: JELVEZ Sergio   Treasurer: OLIVARES ESCOBAR Claudio   Media Officer: ARAYA Sergio
Men's Coach: ACOSTA Nelson   Women's Coach: PRIETO Ignacio
FFCH formed: 1895   CONMEBOL: 1916   FIFA: 1913
Red shirts with blue and white trimmings, Blue shorts, White socks or White shirts, White shorts, Blue socks

RECENT INTERNATIONAL MATCHES PLAYED BY CHILE

2003 Opponents	Score	Venue	Comp	Scorers	Att	Referee
20-08 China	D 0-0	Tianjin	Fr		20 000	Huang CHN
6-09 Argentina	D 2-2	Buenos Aires	WCq	Mirosevic [60], Navia [77]	38 000	Aquino PAR
9-09 Peru	W 2-1	Santiago	WCq	Pinilla [35], Norambuena [70]	60 000	Elizondo ARG
15-11 Uruguay	L 1-2	Montevideo	WCq	Melendez [20]	60 000	Martin ARG
18-11 Paraguay	L 0-1	Santiago	WCq		63 000	Mendez URU
2004						
18-02 Mexico	D 1-1	Carson	Fr	Navia [46]	20 173	Cruz USA
30-03 Bolivia	W 2-0	La Paz	WCq	Villarroel [38], Gonzalez.M [60]	42 000	Martin ARG
28-04 Peru	D 1-1	Antofagasta	Fr	Fuentes [56]	23 000	Amarilla PAR
1-06 Venezuela	W 1-0	San Cristobal	WCq	Pinilla [84]	30 000	Torres PAR
6-06 Brazil	D 1-1	Santiago	WCq	Navia [89p]	65 000	Elizondo ARG
8-07 Brazil	L 0-1	Arequipa	CAr1		35 000	Rodriguez MEX
11-07 Paraguay	D 1-1	Arequipa	CAr1	Gonzalez.S [71]	35 000	Mendez URU
14-07 Costa Rica	L 1-2	Tacna	CAr1	Olarra [40]	20 000	Ortube BOL
5-09 Colombia	D 0-0	Santiago	WCq		62 523	Souza BRA
10-10 Ecuador	L 0-2	Quito	WCq		27 956	Ortube BOL
13-10 Argentina	D 0-0	Santiago	WCq		57 671	Amarilla PAR
17-11 Peru	L 1-2	Lima	WCq	Gonzalez.S [91+]	39 752	Baldassi ARG
2005						
9-02 Ecuador	W 3-0	Vina del Mar	Fr	Maldonado [25], Gonzalez.M [35], Pinilla [83]	15 000	Favale ARG
26-03 Uruguay	D 1-1	Santiago	WCq	Mirosevic [47]	55 000	Ruiz COL
30-03 Paraguay	L 1-2	Asuncion	WCq	Pinilla [72]	10 000	Elizondo ARG
4-06 Bolivia	W 3-1	Santiago	WCq	Fuentes 2 [8 34], Salas [66]	46 729	Rezende BRA
8-06 Venezuela	W 2-1	Santiago	WCq	Jimenez 2 [31 60]	35 506	Torres PAR
17-08 Peru	L 1-3	Tachna	Fr	Fuentes [37]		Ortube BOL
4-09 Brazil	L 0-5	Brasilia	WCq		39 000	Amarilla PAR
8-10 Colombia	D 1-1	Barranquilla	WCq	Rojas [64]	22 380	Souza BRA
12-10 Ecuador	D 0-0	Santiago	WCq		49 350	Elizondo ARG
2006						
25-04 New Zealand	W 4-1	Rancagua	Fr	Suazo [36], OG [39], Roco [61], Rubio [67]	8 000	Osorio CHI
27-04 New Zealand	W 1-0	La Calera	Fr	Rubio [35]		Acosta CHI
24-05 Republic of Ireland	W 1-0	Dublin	Fr	Iturra [49]	41 200	Ingvarsson SWE
30-05 Côte d'Ivoire	D 1-1	Vittel	Fr	Suazo [77p]		Lamarre FRA
2-06 Sweden	D 1-1	Stockholm	Fr	Suazo [51]	34 735	Stark GER

Fr = Friendly match • CA = Copa América • WC = FIFA World Cup™ • q = qualifier • r1 = first round group

CHILE NATIONAL TEAM PLAYERS AND COACHES

Record Caps			Record Goals			Recent Coaches	
SANCHEZ Leonel	1955-'68	84	SALAS Marcelo	1994-'05	35	ARAVENA Orlendo	1987-'89
TAPIA Nelson	1994-'05	73	ZAMORANO Ivan	1987-'01	34	SALAH Arturo	1990-'93
FOUILLOUX Alberto	1960-'72	70	CASZELY Carlos	1969-'85	29	JOZIC Mirko	1994
ESTAY Fabian	1990-'01	69	SANCHEZ Leonel	1955-'68	23	AZKARGORTA Xavier	1995-'96
ZAMORANO Ivan	1987-'01	69	ARAVENA Jorge	1983-'89	22	ACOSTA Nelson	1996-'00
SALAS Marcelo	1994-'05	64	LETELIER Juan Carlos	1979-'89	18	GARCIA Pedro	2001
MARGAS Javier	1990-'00	63	HORMAZABAL Enrique	1950-'63	17	GARCES Jorge	2001
RAMIREZ Miguel	1991-'03	62	RAMIREZ BANDA Jaime	1954-'66	12	VACCIA Cesar	2002
ACUNA Clarence	1995-'04	61	RUBIO Hugo	1985-'92	12	OLMOS Juvenal	2003-'05
LETELIER Juan Carlos	1979-'89	57	TORO Raul	1936-'41	12	ACOSTA Nelson	2005-

CHILE NATIONAL TEAM RECORDS AND RECORD SEQUENCES

Records			Sequence records					
Victory	7-0	VEN 1979	Wins	5	1950-1952	Clean sheets	8	1983-1985
Defeat	0-7	BRA 1959	Defeats	10	1922-1924	Goals scored	18	1995-1997
Player Caps	84	SANCHEZ Leonel	Undefeated	10	1995-1996	Without goal	4	Three times
Player Goals	35	SALAS Marcelo	Without win	33	1910-1924	Goals against	41	1910-1928

CHILE COUNTRY INFORMATION

Capital	Santiago	Independence	1818 from Spain	GDP per Capita	$9 900
Population	15 823 957	Status	Republic	GNP Ranking	43
Area km²	756 950	Language	Spanish	Dialling code	+56
Population density	20 per km²	Literacy rate	95%	Internet code	.cl
% in urban areas	84%	Main religion	Christian 99%	GMT + / –	-4
Towns/Cities ('000)	Santiago 4 837; Puente Alto 510; Antofagasta 309; Vina del Mar 294; Valparaiso 282; Talcahuano 282; San Bernardo 249; Temuco 238; Iquique 227; Concepción 215; Rancagua 212				
Neighbours (km)	Peru 160; Bolivia 861; Argentina 5 150; South Pacific Ocean 6 435				
Main stadia	Estadio Nacional – Santiago 77 000; Monumental – Santiago 62 500; Municipal – Concepción 35 000; Estadio Regional – Antofagasta 26 339; Santa Laura – Santiago 25 000				

CLUB DIRECTORY

Club	Town/City	Stadium	Capacity	www.	Lge	CL
Antogagasta	Antofagasta	Regional	26 339		0	0
Audax Italiano	Santiago	Municipal La Florida	8 500	audax.cl	4	0
Cobreloa	Calama	Municipal	20 180	cdcobreloa.cl	8	0
Cobresal	El Salvador	El Cobre	20 752		0	0
Colo Colo	Santiago	Monumental	62 500	colocolo.cl	24	1
Coquimbo Unido	Coquimbo	Sanchez Rumoroso	15 000		0	0
Everton	Viña del Mar	Sausalito	18 037		3	0
Huachipato	Talcahuano	Las Higueras	10 000	cdhuachipato.cl	1	0
La Serena	La Serena	La Portada	18 000		0	0
O'Higgins	Rancagua	El Teniente	25 000		0	0
Palestino	Santiago	La Cisterna	12 000	palestino.cl	2	0
Puerto Montt	Puerto Montt	Chinquihue	10 000		0	0
Rangers	Talca	Fiscal	17 020	rangers.cl	0	0
Universidad Católica	Santiago	San Carlos	20 000	lacatolica.cl	9	0
Universidad Concepción	Concepción	Municipal	35 000	udeconcefutbol.cl	0	0
Universidad de Chile	Santiago	Nacional	77 000		12	0
Unión Española	Santiago	Santa Laura	25 000		6	0
Santiago Morning	Santiago	Santiago Bueras	8 000		1	0
Santiago Wanderers	Valparaíso	Playa Ancha	19 000	santiagowanderers.cl	3	0

RECENT LEAGUE AND CUP RECORD (1990–2001)

Championship						Cup		
Year	Champions	Pts	Runners-up	Pts	Third	Pts	Winners	Score	Runners-up
1990	Colo Colo	46	Univ. Católica	38	Unión Española	37	Colo Colo	3-2	Univ. Católica
1991	Colo Colo	44	Coquimbo Unido	39	Univ. Católica	38	Univ. Católica	1-0	Cobreloa
1992	Cobreloa	44	Colo Colo	42	Univ. Católica	41	Unión Española	3-1	Colo Colo
1993	Colo Colo	44	Cobreloa	40	Univ. Católica	37	Unión Española	3-1	Cobreloa
1994	Univ. de Chile	49	Univ. Católica	48	O'Higgins	39	Colo Colo	1-1 4-2p	O'Higgins
1995	Univ. de Chile	62	Univ. Católica	60	Colo Colo	52	Univ. Católica	4-2	Cobreloa
1996	Colo Colo	63	Univ. Católica	59	Cobreloa	51	Colo Colo	0-0 1-0	Rangers
1997	Univ. Católica	37	Colo Colo	37	Univ. de Chile	30	Tournament not held		
1997	Colo Colo	35	Univ. Católica	30	Audax Italiano	29	Tournament not held		
1998	Colo Colo	64	Univ. de Chile	63	Univ. Católica	53	Univ. de Chile	1-1 2-0	Audax Italiano
1999	Univ. de Chile	47	Univ. Católica	44	Cobreloa	40	Tournament not held		
2000	Univ. de Chile	61	Cobreloa	52	Colo Colo	49	Univ. de Chile	2-1	Santiago Morning
2001	Santiago Wanderers	66	Univ. Católica	60	Univ. de Chile	57	Tournament discontinued		

RECENT LEAGUE RECORD (FROM 2002)

Apertura				Clausura			
Year	Champions	Score	Runners-up	Winners	Score	Runners-up
2002	Univ. Católica	1-1 4-0	Rangers	Colo Colo	2-0 3-2	Univ. Católica
2003	Cobreloa	0-0 4-0	Colo Colo	Cobreloa	2-2 2-1	Colo Colo
2004	Univ. de Chile	0-0 1-1 4-2p	Cobreloa	Cobreloa	3-1 0-0	Unión Española
2005	Unión Española	1-0 3-2	Coquimbo Unido	Univ. Católica	1-0 1-2 5-4p	Univ. de Chile
2006	Colo Colo	2-1 0-1 4-2p	Univ. de Chile			

Chile adopted the format of two Championships per year in 2002

CHILE 2005
PRIMERA DIVISIÓN APERTURA

Grupo 1	Pl	W	D	L	F	A	Pts
Colo Colo †	19	9	5	5	34	24	32
Huachipato †	19	10	1	8	31	28	31
Unión San Felipe	19	5	3	11	16	26	18
Deportes Melipilla	19	4	5	10	14	30	17
Audax Italiano	19	3	7	9	22	32	16

Grupo 2	Pl	W	D	L	F	A	Pts
Cobreloa †	19	10	3	6	35	29	33
Coquimbo Unido ‡	19	9	2	8	27	29	29
La Serena	19	7	5	7	28	35	26
Santiago Wanderers	19	7	2	10	28	30	23
Puerto Montt	19	5	3	11	30	36	18

Grupo 3	Pl	W	D	L	F	A	Pts
Unión Española †	19	7	5	7	32	31	26
Deportes Concepción ‡	19	6	7	6	20	21	25
Univ. Concepción	19	6	4	9	23	31	22
Palestino	19	6	3	10	21	28	21
Deportes Temuco	19	3	8	8	24	31	17

Grupo 4	Pl	W	D	L	F	A	Pts
Univ. Católica †	19	14	2	3	39	13	44
Univ. de Chile †	19	12	3	4	36	19	39
Cobresal ‡	19	9	5	5	32	25	32
Everton ‡	19	8	6	5	32	27	30
Rangers	19	7	7	5	24	23	28

† Qualified for the play-offs • ‡ Qualified for the repechaje

CHILE 2005
PRIMERA DIVISIÓN CLAUSURA

Grupo 1	Pl	W	D	L	F	A	Pts
Univ. Católica †	19	15	4	0	33	3	49
Huachipato †	19	10	4	5	31	20	34
Deportes Concepción ‡	19	9	6	4	28	24	33
Unión San Felipe	19	6	5	8	24	33	23
Puerto Montt	19	5	3	11	17	31	18

Grupo 2	Pl	W	D	L	F	A	Pts
Univ. de Chile †	19	11	5	3	34	24	38
La Serena ‡	19	6	6	7	24	24	24
Everton	19	5	8	6	23	22	23
Santiago Wanderers	19	6	5	8	17	23	23
Deportes Temuco	19	6	1	12	17	39	19

Grupo 3	Pl	W	D	L	F	A	Pts
Cobresal †	19	8	4	7	30	24	28
Cobreloa ‡	19	6	5	8	23	21	23
Palestino	19	4	8	7	24	28	20
Audax Italiano	19	4	6	9	24	32	18
Rangers	19	4	6	9	24	32	18

Grupo 4	Pl	W	D	L	F	A	Pts
Colo Colo †	19	13	5	1	47	17	44
Univ. Concepción †	19	8	3	8	27	28	27
Unión Española	19	6	6	7	30	34	24
Deportes Melipilla	19	6	2	11	17	23	20
Coquimbo Unido	19	3	6	10	18	30	15

† Qualified for the play-offs • ‡ Qualified for the repechaje

APERTURA PLAY-OFFS 2005

Repechaje

Coquimbo Unido	2-1	Everton
Dep. Concepción	4-3	Cobresal

Quarter-finals		Semi-finals		Final	
Unión Española *	1 1 3p				
Univ. de Chile	2 0 2p	Unión Española *	0 1 10p		
Dep. Concepción*	1 1	Univ. Católica	0 1 9p		
Univ. Católica	2 4			Unión Española *	1 3
Huachipato *	4 1			Coquimbo Unido	0 2
Colo Colo	0 0	Huachipato	1 1		
Cobreloa	0 1	Coquimbo Unido*	2 1		
Coquimbo Unido*	1 1				

* At home in the first leg • Unión Española won the Apertura and qualified for the Copa Libertadores 2006 • Top Apertura scorers: Joel ESTAY, Everton, 13; Alvaro SARABIA, Puerto Montt, 13; Héctor MANCILLA, Huachipato, 13; José Luis VILLANUEVA, Univ. Católica, 12; Marcelo CORRALES, Coquimbo Unido, 11

RELEGATION/PROMOTION PLAY-OFFS

Home team first leg	Scores	Home team second leg
O'Higgins	1-0 3-3	Deportes Melipilla
Provincial Osorno	0-1 2-1 5-3p	Puerto Montt

Unión San Felipe and Deportes Temuco relegated automatically based on their record over three seasons • Puerto Mont retained their top flight status • Melipilla relegated • Santiago Morning, Antofagasta and O'Higgins promoted

CLAUSURA PLAY-OFFS 2005

Repechaje

Cobreloa	5-0	Dep. Concepción

Quarter-finals		Semi-finals		Final	
Univ. Católica	1 2				
Cobreloa *	1 1	Univ. Católica	3 1		
Colo Colo	1 3 1p	La Serena *	3 0		
La Serena *	1 3 4p			Univ. Católica	1 1 5p
Cobresal *	2 1			Univ. de Chile *	0 2 4p
Huachipato	1 1	Cobresal *	2 2		
Univ. Concepción*	1 0	Univ. de Chile	1 4		
Univ. de Chile	2 0				

* At home in the first leg • † Universidad Católica won the Clausura and qualified for the Copa Libertadores 2006 • Top Clausura scorers: César DIAZ, Cobresal, 13; Gonzalo FIERRO, Colo Colo, 13; Cristian MONTECINOS, Deportes Concepción, 13

PRIMERA DIVISION RESULTS 2005

Apertura results are listed in the shaded boxes

	Audax	Cobreloa	Cobresal	Colo Colo	Concep.	Coquimbo	Everton	Huachip.	La Serena	Melipilla	Palestino	P. Montt	Rangers	Temuco	Española	S. Felipe	Católica	Concep.	U de Ch.	Wanderers
Audax Italiano		3-0	3-2	1-1	6-0	0-0	1-1	1-0	0-0	1-3	0-2	3-3	2-2	1-2	4-5	1-1	0-4	1-1	1-1	1-1
Cobreloa	1-2		2-1	0-1	2-1	4-0	1-1	2-1	5-0	3-1	1-0	4-3	1-1	5-4	4-1	1-1	0-2	2-0	1-1	3-0
Cobresal	2-1	3-1		2-2	0-1	2-1	2-2	2-0	0-1	2-0	1-1	3-0	2-0	4-1	4-3	3-0	0-0	1-0	2-4	1-2
Colo Colo	3-0	2-0	2-2		2-1	2-0	2-1	1-0	1-1	2-2	4-1	2-0	4-1	4-0	4-2	5-0	0-0	0-1	1-1	1-1
Dep. Concepción	0-2	1-0	1-0	2-0		3-0	2-1	1-1	2-1	0-0	2-0	1-1	1-1	3-1	2-1	1-1	1-1	1-0	1-2	3-1 2-1
Coquimbo Unido	1-0	2-2	1-1	2-4	2-0		2-2	0-1	1-2	2-1	2-1	4-1	0-0	3-0	1-1	1-0	0-3	3-1	1-3	3-1
Everton	2-1	1-0	3-1	1-3	1-1	0-1		1-3	3-1	1-1	0-0	3-2	1-3	3-0	0-0	3-1	1-2	1-1	3-2	0-1
Huachipato	2-0	5-4	0-2	2-2	3-1	3-2	3-1		4-1	3-0	0-0	1-4	0-1	5-1	3-1	2-0	0-0	2-0	1-0	2-1
La Serena	1-1	1-0	2-3	3-7	2-2	2-2	0-0	2-3		1-0	4-0	2-0	0-1	2-0	1-1	1-1	0-1	2-0	2-3	2-3
Dep. Melipilla	1-0	0-1	1-2	2-3	1-0	0-1	0-3	1-0	1-0		1-3	1-0	4-1	0-0	1-2	0-1	1-2	1-1		0-1
Palestino	4-0	1-1	0-0	1-0	0-2	3-1	1-1	2-3	3-4	0-0		0-3	3-1	1-0	2-3	1-2	0-1	1-2	1-1	4-0
Puerto Montt	2-2	1-0	1-0	0-3	1-1	1-0	0-1	0-1	3-0	0-1	2-0		1-2	1-1	2-1	1-0	1-2	1-2	0-1	3-1
Rangers	2-0	0-1	2-3	3-2	1-1	0-1	1-1	1-1	1-2	1-1	2-2	3-0		5-1	0-0	2-1	1-3	1-1	1-3	0-2
Temuco	1-0	2-1	1-1	1-2	1-1	2-1	0-3	1-2	1-1	1-0	1-1	4-1	1-1		1-2	1-0	1-2	1-2	1-2	1-0
Unión Española	3-3	1-0	2-1	1-3	1-2	4-2	2-2	2-1	1-2	2-1	4-1	4-1	2-1	1-1		0-1	0-0	3-2	0-2	0-1
Unión San Felipe	2-0	1-1	1-2	2-3	3-1	2-1	0-2	2-3	0-0	2-0	1-1	1-0	0-1	1-0	2-1		0-2	2-1	4-1	3-2
Univ. Católica	2-1	4-1	1-0	1-0	0-0	1-0	1-2	2-0	3-0	5-0	3-0	1-0	3-0	2-0	1-1	5-1		5-2	2-1	3-0
Univ. Concepción	3-0	0-1	4-1	1-2	3-3	1-1	2-1	2-0	1-3	1-2	0-2	4-3	2-1	3-3	0-0	2-0	0-1		0-3	1-0
Univ. de Chile	3-1	0-0	1-1	1-0	3-0	1-1	2-1	1-3	2-1	2-0	4-2	1-2	3-2	5-3	2-0	2-1	1-0			3-0
Santiago Wanderers	0-2	1-2	1-3	1-1	1-1	2-0	4-1	2-0	0-0	3-0	1-2	3-1	1-1	0-1	1-1	3-1	0-2	3-0	0-1	

CHILE 2006 PRIMERA DIVISION APERTURA

Grupo 1
	Pl	W	D	L	F	A	Pts
Univ. Concepción †	18	9	6	3	31	23	33
Audax Italiano †	18	9	5	4	32	22	32
Universidad Católica ‡	18	9	5	4	27	20	32
Cobresal	18	6	4	8	26	32	22
Santiago Wanderers	18	5	2	11	16	30	17

Grupo 2
	Pl	W	D	L	F	A	Pts
Universidad de Chile †	18	10	5	3	27	20	35
Deportes La Serena ‡	18	5	7	6	32	31	22
Everton	18	5	6	7	20	27	21
Coquimbo Unido	18	3	8	7	16	26	17
Santiago Morning	18	2	6	10	15	31	12

Grupo 3
	Pl	W	D	L	F	A	Pts
Colo Colo †	18	13	1	4	54	22	40
Cobreloa †	18	9	3	6	32	24	30
Unión Española ‡	18	8	4	6	24	21	28
Antofagasta	18	5	6	7	26	31	21
Puerto Montt	18	4	5	9	33	32	17

Grupo 4
	Pl	W	D	L	F	A	Pts
Huachipato †	18	11	3	4	32	19	36
O'Higgins ‡	18	5	6	7	20	25	21
Palestino	18	4	4	10	22	35	16
Rangers	18	4	4	10	26	40	16
Deportes Concepción				Withdrew			

† Qualified for the play-offs • ‡ Qualified for the repechaje

CHILE 2005 PRIMERA B (2)

	Pl	W	D	L	F	A	BP	Pts
Santiago Morning	26	16	4	6	60	34	10	62
Antofagasta	26	15	6	5	43	20	7	58
Provincial Osorno	26	11	10	5	51	39	9	52
Nublense	26	13	5	8	53	44	5	49
O'Higgins	26	9	8	9	41	35	9	44
Deportes Arica	26	11	5	10	42	39	5	43
Deportes Ovalle §4	26	11	7	8	44	43	5	41
Lota Schwager	26	11	2	13	46	53	5	40
San Luis	26	9	9	8	42	47	3	39
Magallanes	26	9	5	12	42	46	4	36
Unión La Calera	26	10	2	14	41	47	3	35
Fernández Vial	26	8	5	13	34	57	3	32
Deportes Copiapó §3	26	3	7	16	26	51	3	16
Naval §23	26	5	7	14	43	53	8	7

6/05/2005 - 30/10/2005 • § = points deducted • BP = bonus points from first stage • Play-offs: O'Higgins 1-0 3-3 Dep Melipilla; Osorno 0-1 2-1 3-5p Puerto Montt

APERTURA PLAY-OFFS 2006

Repechaje
Unión Española ‡	2-2	Deportes Serena
Univ. Católica ‡	1-1	O'Higgins

Quarter-finals
Colo Colo	4	5
Unión Española *	0	0
Audax Italiano *	2	0
Univ. Concepción	1	2
Huachipato	1	4
Cobreloa *	3	0
Univ. Católica *	2	1
Univ. de Chile	2	3

Semi-finals
Colo Colo	3	0
Univ. Concepción *	4	2
Huachipato	1	2
Univ. de Chile *	6	2

Final
Colo Colo †	2 0	4p
Univ. de Chile	1 1	2p

* At home in the first leg • Both legs of the final played at the Estadio Nacional, Santiago • ‡ Qualified on better season record • † Colo Colo won the Apertura
Top scorers: Humberto SUAZO, Colo Colo, 19; Matías FERNÁNDEZ, Colo Colo, 14

CHN – CHINA PR

NATIONAL TEAM RECORD
JULY 1ST 2002 TO JULY 9TH 2006

PL	W	D	L	F	A	%
47	21	12	14	71	47	57.4

Early elimination from the FIFA World Cup™ meant that China's only serious competition came at the start of the season in the East Asian Football Federation Championship. Coach Zhu Guanghu blooded some new talent such as forward Gao Lin, midfielder Hao Junmin, and defenders Zhang Yaokun and Ji Mingyi, and after beating Korea DPR, and drawing with Japan and hosts Korea Republic, China were victorious for the first time in the short history of the tournament. But inconsistency, and especially a lack of fire-power, has hampered the national team. A poor defeat to Iraq in the Asian Cup qualifiers, and a series of losses to club and regional teams on a tour of Spain were somewhat balanced by gritty friendly performances against Germany and France. However, until Zhu can find some reliable forwards, China will remain among the also-rans in Asian football. Much effort is now going into the under-20 team in the hope they will make an impression at the Beijing Olympics. The game in China certainly needs a lift, with fans largely unimpressed by the fare on offer in the Chinese Super League. Dalian far outdistanced their main rivals Shanghai Shenhua and Shandong to take their eighth title since the beginning of profession-

INTERNATIONAL HONOURS
Qualified for the FIFA World Cup™ 2002
AFC Asian Women's Championship 1986 1989 1991 1993 1995 1997 1999
Asian U-19 Championship 1985   Asian U-17 Championship 1992 2004
AFC Asian Champions League Liaoning 1990

alism in 1994 and they went on to complete only their second double, beating Shandong in the FA Cup final. With no relegation to fear, teams like Chongqing and Shenyang fielded large numbers of junior players while there was alarm at the increase in gambling and the involvement of Chinese businessmen in betting scandals in both Belgium and Finland. Once again, foreigners dominated the scoring lists. Beijing's Bosnian striker Branko Jelic hit a record 21 goals during the season, while Wuhan, Dalian and Shandong all relied on bought-in talent. Newly promoted Wuhan provided the most encouraging story. Expected to struggle, they were up amongst the leaders throughout the first half of the league campaign, and ended up with silverware after winning the CSL Cup. However, the malaise in the domestic game was summed up by the tale of Sichuan. The Chengdu-based club were one of the most popular in the country a decade ago, averaging crowds of 40,000. But changes of ownership have left them little more than Dalian's farm team, and a move to a spectacular, but remote, stadium in the Chengdu suburbs alienated fans. With crowds sometimes barely touching a thousand, they folded at the end of the season.

Football Association of the People's Republic of China (CFA)
2 Tiyuguan Road, Beijing 100763, China PR
Tel +86 10 67117019   Fax +86 10 67142533
li_chen@fa.org.cn   www.fa.org.cn
President: YUAN Weimin   General Secretary: YALONG Xie
Vice-President: YALONG Xie   Treasurer: NAN Yong   Media Officer: LU Ting & DONG Hua
Men's Coach: ZHU Guanghu   Women's Coach: MA Liangxing
CFA formed: 1924   AFC: 1974   FIFA: 1931-58 & 1974
White shirts with red trimmings, White shorts, White socks or Red shirts with white trimmings, Red shorts, Red socks

RECENT INTERNATIONAL MATCHES PLAYED BY CHINA PR

2003	Opponents	Score		Venue	Comp	Scorers	Att	Referee
4-12	Japan	L	0-2	Tokyo	EAC		41 742	Nagalingam SIN
7-12	Korea Republic	L	0-1	Saitama	EAC		27 715	Abdul Hamid MAS
10-12	Hong Kong	W	3-1	Yokohama	EAC	Zhao Xuri [20], Liu Jindong [21], Yang Chen [44]	17 400	Piromya THA
2004								
27-01	FYR Macedonia	D	0-0	Shanghai	Fr		24 000	Lu Jun CHN
29-01	FYR Macedonia	W	1-0	Shanghai	Fr	Zheng Zhi [88]	17 500	Yang Zhiqiang CHN
3-02	Finland	W	2-1	Guangzhou	Fr	Zhang Yuning [42], Hao Haidong [53]		
7-02	Finland	W	2-1	Shenzhen	Fr	Zhang Yuning [8], Zheng Zhi [41]		
18-02	Kuwait	W	1-0	Guangzhou	WCq	Hao Haidong [75]	50 000	Roman UZB
17-03	Myanmar	W	2-0	Guangzhou	Fr	Zheng Zhi [16], Xu Yunlong [29]		
31-03	Hong Kong	W	1-0	Hong Kong	WCq	Hao Haidong [71]	9 000	Rungklay THA
14-04	Andorra	D	0-0	Peralada	Fr			
28-04	Algeria	W	1-0	Clermont-Ferrand	Fr	Xiao Zhanbo [26]	1 600	Poulat FRA
1-06	Hungary	W	2-1	Beijing	Fr	Zhou Haibin [44], Zheng Zhi [88p]	18 000	Chiu HKG
9-06	Malaysia	W	4-0	Tianjin	WCq	Hao Haidong [43], Sun Jihai [62], Li Xiaopeng 2 [66 76]	35 000	Park Sang Gu KOR
3-07	Lebanon	W	6-0	Chongqing	Fr	Li Jinyu 2 [15 50], Yan Song [61], Li Ming [69], Zhang Shuo [79], Li Yi [86]		
10-07	United Arab Emirates	D	2-2	Hohhot	Fr	Zheng Zhi 2 [63 90p]		
17-07	Bahrain	D	2-2	Beijing	ACr1	Zheng Zhi [58], Li Jinyu [66p]	40 000	Subkhiddin MAS
21-07	Indonesia	W	5-0	Beijing	ACr1	Shao Jiayi 2 [24 65], Hao Haidong [39], Li Ming [51], Li Yi [80]		Talaat LIB
25-07	Qatar	W	1-0	Beijing	ACr1	Xu Yunlong [78]	60 000	Moradi IRN
30-07	Iraq	W	3-0	Beijing	ACqf	Hao Haidong [8], Zheng Zhi 2 [79p 90p]	60 000	Maidin SIN
3-08	Iran	D	1-1	Beijing	ACsf	Shao Jiayi [19] W 4-3p	51 000	Talaat LIB
7-08	Japan	L	1-3	Beijing	ACf	Li Ming [31]	62 000	Al Fadhi KUW
8-09	Malaysia	W	1-0	Penang	WCq	Li Jinyu [67]	14 000	Karim BHR
13-10	Kuwait	L	0-1	Kuwait City	WCq		10 000	Kunsuta THA
17-11	Hong Kong	W	7-0	Guangzhou	WCq	Li Jinyu 2 [8 47], Shao Jiayi 2 [42 44], Xu Yunlong [49], Yu Genwei [88], Li Weifeng [90+2]	20 300	Lee Jong Kuk KOR
2005								
26-03	Spain	L	0-3	Salamanca	Fr		17 000	Batista POR
29-03	Republic of Ireland	L	0-1	Dublin	Fr		35 222	Casha MLT
19-06	Costa Rica	D	2-2	Changsa	Fr	Zhang Yaokun [27], Sun Xiang [79]	20 000	Lee Gi Young KOR
22-06	Costa Rica	W	2-0	Guangzhou	Fr	Zheng Zhi [44p], Xie Hui [54]	15 000	Yu Byung Seob KOR
31-07	Korea Republic	D	1-1	Daejon	EAC	Sun Xiang [52]	25 374	Nishimura JPN
3-08	Japan	D	2-2	Daejon	EAC	Li Jinyu [37], Zhang Yonghai [43]	1 827	
7-08	Korea DPR	W	2-0	Daegu	EAC	Li Yan [14], Xie Hui [67]		
12-10	Germany	L	0-1	Hamburg	Fr		48 734	Batista POR
13-11	Serbia & Montenegro	L	0-2	Nanjing	Fr		30 000	
2006								
12-02	Honduras	L	0-1	Guangzhou	Fr		20 000	Supian MAS
22-02	Palestine	W	2-0	Guangzhou	ACq	Du Wei [23], Li Weifeng [62]	16 500	Kwon Jong Chul KOR
1-03	Iraq	L	1-2	Al Ain	ACq	Tao Wei [54]	7 700	Al Saeedi UAE
3-06	Switzerland	L	1-4	Zurich	Fr	Dong Fangzhuo [91+]	16 000	Stokes IRL
7-06	France	L	1-3	St Etienne	Fr	Zheng Zhi [69p]	34 147	Davila ESP

Fr = Friendly match • EAC = East Asian Championship • AC = AFC Asian Cup • WC = FIFA World Cup™
q = qualifier • r1 = first round group • qf = quarter-final • sf = semi-final • f = final

CHINA PR NATIONAL TEAM RECORDS AND RECORD SEQUENCES

Records			Sequence records					
Victory	19-0	GUM 2000	Wins	10	1919-1930	Clean sheets	8	1998-2000
Defeat	0-5	USA 1992	Defeats	5	1982, 2002	Goals scored	20	1915-1934
Player Caps	115	HAO Haidong	Undefeated	19	2003-2004	Without goal	5	2002
Player Goals	41	HAO Haidong	Without win	7	1996, 2000-2001	Goals against	9	1934-1957

Includes records dating back to the Far-Eastern Games of 1913-1934

CHINA PR COUNTRY INFORMATION

Capital	Beijing	Independence	221BC	GDP per Capita	$5 000
Population	1 298 847 624	Status	Republic	GNP Ranking	6
Area km²	9 596 960	Language	Mandarin	Dialling code	+86
Population density	135 per km²	Literacy rate	90%	Internet code	.cn
% in urban areas	30%	Main religion	Atheist	GMT +/-	+8

Towns/Cities ('000)	Shanghai 12 762; Beijing 7 490; Wuhan 4 191; Chengdu 3 999; Chongqing 3 975; Xian 3 959; Tianjin 3 791; Shenyang 3 519; Harbin 3 234; Guangzhou 3 146; Nanjing 3 095; Taiyuan 2 727; Changchun 2 541; Changsha 2 074; Jinan 2 073; Tangshan 2 057; Dalian 2 039
Neighbours (km)	Mongolia 4 677; Russia 3 645; Korea DPR 1 416; Vietnam 1 281; Laos 423; Burma 2 185; Bhutan 470; Nepal 1 236; India 3 380; Pakistan 523; Tajikistan 414; Kyrgyzstan 858; Kazakhstan 1 533; Afghanistan 76; Yellow Sea & South and East China Seas 14 500
Main stadia	Guangdong Olympic – Guangzhou 80 012; Shanghai Stadium – Shanghai 80 000; Worker's Stadium – Beijing 72 000; Wulihe Stadium – Shenyang 65 000; Wuhan Stadium – Wuhan 60 000; Qingdao Yizhong Center – Qingdao 60 000

CLUB DIRECTORY

Club	Town/City	Stadium	Capacity	Lge	Cup	CL
Beijing Hyundai	Beijing	Fengtai	33 000	5	4	0
Changchun Yatai	Changchun	Changchun	38 000	0	0	0
Chongqing Lifan	Chongqing	Yanghe	58 680	0	1	0
Dalian Shide	Dalian	Jinzhou	31 000	8	3	0
Liaoning	Anshan & Fushun	City & Lei Feng	30 000	8	2	1
Qingdao Zhongneng	Qingdao	Yizhong	60 000	0	1	0
Shandong Luneng	Ji'nan	Provincial	43 700	1	3	0
Shanghai Liancheng	Shanghai	Yuanshen	20 000	0	0	0
Shanghai Shenhua	Shanghai	Hongkou	35 000	4	3	0
Shenyang Ginde	Shenyang	Wulihe	65 000	0	0	0
Shenzhen Kingway	Shenzhen	City	33 000	1	0	0
Tianjin Teda	Tianjin	Minyuan 20 000 & Teda 36 000		3	1	0
Wuhan Guanggu	Wuhan	Xinhualu	36 000	0	0	0
Xi'an Chanba	Xi'an	Coca-Cola	30 000	0	0	0
Xiamen Lanshi	Xiamen	City	30 000	0	0	0

Sichuan folded • Shanghai International moved to Xi'an and renamed Xi'an Chanba • Shanghai Zobon and Shanghai Jiucheng merged to become Shanghai Liancheng (Shanghai United)

FIFA/COCA-COLA WORLD RANKING

1993	1994	1995	1996	1997	1998	1999	2000	2001	2002	2003	2004	2005	High	Low
53	40	66	76	55	37	88	75	54	63	86	54	72	37 12/98	89 07/06

2005–2006											
08/05	09/05	10/05	11/05	12/05	01/06	02/06	03/06	04/06	05/06	06/06	07/06
54	60	65	69	72	73	75	71	66	68	-	89

THE FIFA BIG COUNT OF 2000

	Male	Female		Male	Female
Registered players	75 000	490	Referees	4 713	56
Non registered players	7 000 000	40 000	Officials	2 548	420
Youth players	125 000	3 851	Total involved	7 252 078	
Total players	7 244 341		Number of clubs	2 347	
Professional players	1 492	256	Number of teams	16 536	

CHINA PR 2005

CSL (CHINESE SUPER LEAGUE)

	Pl	W	D	L	F	A	Pts	Dalian	Shanghai S	Shandong	Tianjin	Wuhan	Beijing	Qingdao	Shanghai I	Sichuan	Liaoning	Shanghai Z	Shenzhen	Shenyang	Chongqing
Dalian Shide †	26	21	2	3	57	18	65		1-2	3-0	1-0	2-0	2-1	2-1	1-0	3-0	5-0	1-0	2-0	1-0	2-2
Shanghai Shenhua †	26	15	8	3	41	23	53	2-1		0-0	2-2	1-1	1-0	2-0	1-0	1-0	1-0	3-0	1-1	6-1	3-0
Shandong Luneng T.	26	15	7	4	47	30	52	1-1	2-2		2-1	2-1	4-2	0-0	2-1	2-0	4-1	3-1	0-0	1-0	4-1
Tianjin Teda	26	14	7	5	48	26	49	2-1	1-1	1-3		3-0	2-1	2-0	2-0	3-0	5-1	1-1	3-1	2-1	1-1
Wuhan Huanghelou	26	11	9	6	34	26	42	0-1	2-2	3-2	2-2		3-2	1-1	3-2	1-0	1-0	2-0	0-0	3-0	3-1
Beijing Hyundai	26	12	4	10	46	32	40	3-4	4-0	4-0	0-1	1-0		4-1	3-1	3-1	0-0	3-1	1-1	2-2	2-0
Qingdao Zhongneng	26	9	7	10	26	31	34	0-2	1-0	2-3	1-4	2-0	1-0		0-1	3-1	1-0	0-0	0-0	2-1	2-1
Shanghai International	26	8	7	11	30	32	31	1-2	1-2	2-0	2-2	0-0	0-2	0-2		1-1	0-0	3-0	1-1	2-1	2-1
Sichuan Guancheng	26	8	5	13	28	45	29	0-4	0-1	0-3	1-3	1-3	2-1	1-1	1-3		1-0	3-2	2-0	4-2	2-1
Liaoning	26	7	8	11	34	42	29	2-4	0-1	2-2	1-0	1-1	3-2	3-4	1-1	2-2		1-1	5-1	1-1	2-1
Shanghai Zobon	26	5	7	14	18	35	22	0-1	1-0	0-1	1-2	0-0	1-2	1-0	1-2	0-0	1-3		2-1	1-0	1-0
Shenzhen Jianlibao	26	4	10	12	22	42	22	1-5	2-	2-2	0-2	0-0	0-1	2-1	0-3	0-2	1-3	2-1		2-3	3-0
Shenyang Ginde	26	4	6	16	19	43	18	0-1	1-2	0-3	1-0	0-3	1-1	0-0	0-0	1-2	0-2	1-1	0-1		1-0
Chongqing Lifan	26	2	7	17	16	41	13	0-4	1-2	0-1	1-1	0-1	0-1	0-0	3-1	1-1	1-0	0-0	0-1	0-1	

2/04/2005 - 5/11/2005 • † Qualified for the AFC Champions League • No relegation • Top scorers: Branko JELIC - BIH, Beijing 21; ZOU Jie, Dalian, 15; GILSON - BRA, Wuhan, 14; XIE Hui, Shanghai Shenhua, 14; Zoran JANKOVIC - BUL, Dalian, 13; YU Genwei, Tianjin, 12

CHINA PR 2005

CHINA LEAGUE (2)

	Pl	W	D	L	F	A	Pts	Xiamen	Changchun	Zhejiang	Guangzhou	Jiangsu	Qingdao	Nanjing	Yanbian	Shanghai	Henan	Chengdu	Hunan	Dalian	Harbin
Xiamen Lanshi	26	20	4	2	61	23	64		1-0	1-1	3-1	0-1	3-1	2-0	2-0	3-1	3-2	3-2	5-1	3-0	3-0
Changchun Yatai	26	20	4	2	71	22	64	2-2		3-1	4-2	1-1	0-1	4-1	3-2	2-1	3-1	6-0	2-0	9-0	3-0
Zhejiang Lucheng	26	17	4	5	50	23	55	0-3	1-3		1-0	2-1	2-0	2-0	5-1	1-1	3-2	3-0	4-0	3-0	3-0
Guangzhou Rizhiquan	26	15	7	4	50	22	52	0-1	1-1	1-1		2-1	2-1	3-2	0-0	5-1	4-0	4-0	2-0	1-0	3-0
Jiangsu Shuntian	26	13	8	5	43	21	47	1-1	1-2	1-1	1-1		1-0	2-2	2-0	0-0	1-0	2-0	3-1	2-0	3-0
Qingdao Hisense	26	12	5	9	35	32	41	3-2	0-4	1-0	0-0	2-2		1-0	2-0	1-1	0-1	3-0	3-0	1-1	3-0
Nanjing Yoyo	26	10	6	10	43	38	36	1-2	2-2	1-0	0-2	2-0	0-1		2-1	3-2	0-0	4-2	5-1	2-0	3-0
Yanbian	26	10	3	13	43	41	33	1-2	1-3	1-2	0-2	1-1	3-0	1-1		4-2	1-0	2-1	3-2	6-1	3-0
Shanghai Jiucheng	26	7	8	11	47	55	29	2-4	1-3	0-2	2-2	1-6	5-2	1-1	2-0		1-1	2-1	5-0	1-1	3-0
Henan Jianye	26	7	6	13	28	37	27	0-1	1-2	1-3	1-4	1-0	2-2	1-0	3-2	1-2		0-1	1-2	1-0	3-0
Chengdu Wuniu	26	8	2	16	40	57	26	2-4	2-0	0-3	1-2	0-1	1-3	3-1	3-3	5-3	4-3		2-1	2-0	3-0
Hunan Xiangjun	26	5	4	17	24	56	19	0-0	0-1	0-2	0-2	0-3	0-2	2-4	0-2	3-3	1-1	2-1		2-0	3-0
Dalian Changbo	26	4	7	15	23	53	19	1-4	1-2	1-3	2-2	0-1	0-1	3-1	1-3	1-1	1-1	1-0	1-1		3-0
Harbin Guoli ‡	26	0	0	26	0	78	0	0-3	0-3	0-3	0-3	0-3	0-3	0-3	0-3	0-3	0-3	0-3	0-3	0-3	

4/03/2005 - 22/10/2005 • ‡ All Harbin's games were awarded as 0-3 defeats • Top scorer: Lin Jiuke, Guangzhou Rizhiquan, 15

RECENT LEAGUE AND CUP RECORD

Championship

Year	Champions	Pts	Runners-up	Pts	Third	Pts
1994	Dalian	33	Guangzhou	27	Shanghai Shenhua	26
1995	Shanghai Shenhua	46	Beijing	42	Dalian	42
1996	Dalian	46	Shanghai Shenhua	39	August 1st	35
1997	Dalian	51	Shanghai Shenhua	40	Beijing	34
1998	Dalian	62	Shanghai Shenhua	45	Beijing	43
1999	Shandong	48	Liaoning	47	Sichuan	45
2000	Dalian	56	Shanghai Shenhua	50	Sichuan	44
2001	Dalian	53	Shanghai Shenhua	48	Liaoning	48
2002	Dalian	57	Shenzhen	52	Beijing	52
2003	Shanghai Shenhua	55	Shanghai Int'l	54	Dalian	53
2004	Shenzhen	42	Shandong	36	Shanghai Int'l	32
2005	Dalian	65	Shanghai Shenhua	53	Shandong	52

FA Cup

Winners	Score	Runners-up
No Tournament		
Jinan	2-0	Shanghai Shenhua
Beijing	4-1	Jinan
Beijing	2-1	Shanghai Shenhua
Shanghai Shenhua	2-1 2-1	Liaoning
Shandong	2-1 2-1	Dalian
Chongqing	0-1 4-1	Beijing
Dalian	1-0 2-1	Beijing
Qingdao	1-3 2-0	Liaoning
Beijing	3-0	Dalian
Shandong	2-1	Sichuan
Dalian	1-0	Shandong

LANDI FA CUP 2005

First Round		Round of 16		Quarter-finals		Semi-finals		Final	
Dalian Shide	3								
Yanbian	0	**Dalian Shide**	3 5						
Tianjin Kangshifu	4 3p	Qingdao Hisense *	1 0						
Qingdao Hisense	4 4p			**Dalian Shide** *	6 0				
Henan Jianye	3			Shenzhen Jianlibao	2 1				
Shanghai Zobon	2	Henan Jianye *	1 0						
		Shenzhen Jianlibao	0 4						
Shenzhen Jianlibao	Bye					**Dalian Shide** *	1 5		
						Xiamen Lanshi	1 0		
Liaoning	0 1p	**Liaoning** *	1 2						
Harbin Guoli †	0 3p	Dalian Changbo	0 0						
Qingdao Zhongneng	0 3p			**Liaoning** *	0 1				
Dalian Changbo	0 4p			**Xiamen Lanshi**	1 2			**Dalian Shide**	1
		Sichuan Guancheng	0 6					Shandong Luneng Taishan	0
Sichuan Guancheng	Bye	**Xiamen Lanshi** *	3 3						
Jiangsu Shuntian	0								
Xiamen Lanshi	2								
Beijing Hyundai	1	**Beijing Hyundai** *	1 1						
Nanjing Yoyo	0	Wuhan Huanghelou	0 1						
Shanghai Jiucheng	1			**Beijing Hyundai** *	2 1				
Wuhan Huanghelou	2			Shanghai Shenhua	0 2				
Zhejiang Lucheng	1 7p	Zhejiang Lucheng *	2 0						
Chongqing Lifan	1 6p	**Shanghai Shenhua**	2 0						
						Beijing Hyundai *	1 3		
Shanghai Shenhua	Bye					**Shandong Luneng Taishan**	3 4		
Shanghai International *	1	**Shanghai International** *	5 4						
Chengdu Wuniu	0	Hunan Xiangjun	1 0						
Shenyang Ginde	0			Shanghai International *	1 2				
Hunan Xiangjun	2			**Shandong Luneng Taishan**	2 2				
Guangzhou Rizhiquan	2	Guangzhou Rizhiquan *	1 2						
Changchun Yatai	0	**Shandong Luneng Taishan**	2 5						
Shandong Luneng Taishan	Bye								

CUP FINAL

Teda Stadium, Tianjin, 20-11-2005

Scorer – Mai Shuai 69

* Home team/home team in the first leg • † Harbin expelled from China League and FA Cup

DALIAN SHIDE 2005

Date	Opponents	Score		Comp	Scorers
26-03-2005	Yanbian	W 3-0	H	FACr1	Zou Jie [67], Jankovic [73p], Zhu Ting [78]
2-04-2005	Sichuan Guangcheng	W 3-0	H	CSL	Zou Jie [33], Jankovic [48], Wang Sheng [64]
10-04-2005	Liaoning	W 4-2	A	CSL	Jankovic 3 [4 20 35], Pantelic [81]
14-04-2005	Shanghai International	W 1-0	H	CSL	Quan Lei [14]
17-04-2005	Shanghai Zobon	W 1-0	A	CSL	Zou Jie [28]
24-04-2005	Chongqing Lifan	D 2-2	H	CSL	Zou Jie [61], Jankovic [90p]
30-04-2005	Shandong Luneng Taishan	D 1-1	A	CSL	Jankovic [90p]
4-05-2005	Tianjin Teda	W 1-0	H	CSL	Yan Song [36]
8-05-2005	Shenzhen Jianlibao	W 2-0	H	CSL	Zou Jie [5], Zhao Xuri [50]
14-05-2005	Shenyang Ginde	W 1-0	A	CSL	Li Ming [43]
17-05-2005	Qingdao Zhongneng	W 1-0	H	SLCr1	Wang Sheng [35]
22-05-2005	Shanghai Shenhua	L 1-2	H	CSL	Jankovic [41p]
29-05-2005	Qingdao Zhongneng	L 3-4	H	SLCr1	Yan Song [7], Ji Mingyi [12], Zou Jie [75]
18-06-2005	Qingdao Hisense	W 3-1	A	FACr2	Ma Shuai 2 [50 88], Jankovic [85p]
26-06-2005	Qingdao Hisense	W 5-0	H	FACr2	Zou Jie [56], Ji Mingyi [60], Ma Shuai 2 [62 79], Jankovic [72]
2-07-2005	Wuhan Huanghelou	W 1-0	A	CSL	Wang Sheng [12]
6-07-2005	Qingdao Zhongneng	W 2-1	H	CSL	Jankovic [23], Qin Sheng OG [47]
10-07-2005	Beijing Hyundai	W 4-3	A	CSL	Jankovic [17], Pantelic [36], Zou Jie [51], Ma Shuai [65]
17-07-2005	Sichuan Guangcheng	W 4-0	A	CSL	Quan Lei [23], Pantelic 2 [50 63], Jankovic [88]
20-07-2005	Liaoning	W 5-0	H	CSL	Zou Jie 3 [45 50 81], Jankovic [46], Adilson [66]
24-07-2005	Shenzhen Jianlibao	W 6-2	H	FACqf	Pantelic [7], Zou Jie 2 [18 62], Jankovic [55], Yan Song [72]
10-08-2005	Shenzhen Jianlibao	L 0-1	A	FACqf	
14-08-2005	Shanghai International	W 2-1	A	CSL	Jankovic [30], Zou Jie [63]
20-08-2005	Shanghai Zobon	W 1-0	H	CSL	Yang Lin OG [35]
27-08-2005	Chongqing Lifan	W 4-0	A	CSL	Zou Jie 2 [4 64], Anderson [50], Wang Sheng [78]
31-08-2005	Shandong Luneng Taishan	W 3-0	H	CSL	Zou Jie 2 [35 46], Hu Zhaojun [61]
4-09-2005	Tianjin Teda	L 1-2	A	CSL	Zou Jie [40]
9-09-2005	Shenzhen Jianlibao	W 5-1	H	CSL	Ma Shuai 2 [17 45], Yan Song [36], Quan Lei [80], Zou You [85]
18-09-2005	Shenyang Ginde	W 1-0	H	CSL	Hu Zhaojun [47]
25-09-2005	Shanghai Shenhua	L 1-2	A	CSL	Yan Song [53]
2-10-2005	Xiamen Lanshi	D 1-1	H	FACsf	Li Ming [89p]
5-10-2005	Xiamen Lanshi	W 5-0	A	FACsf	Zou Jie 3 [12 48 83], Zhu Ting [73], Hu Zhaojun [74]
23-10-2005	Wuhan Huanghelou	W 2-0	H	CSL	Jankovic [60], Zhao Xuri [69]
30-10-2005	Qingdao Zhongneng	W 2-0	A	CSL	Ma Shuai 2 [42 90]
5-11-2005	Beijing Hyundai	W 2-1	H	CSL	Zou Jie [64], Yan Song [86]
20-11-2005	Shandong Luneng Taishan	W 1-0	N	FACf	Ma Shuai [69]

FAC = FA Cup • CSL = Chinese Super League • SLC = Super League Cup
r1 = first round • r2 = second round • qf = quarter-final • sf = semi-final • f = final • N = Teda Stadium, Tianjin

SUPER LEAGUE CUP 2005

First round		Quarter-finals		Semi-finals		Final	
Wuhan Huanghelou *	1 0 6p						
Tianjin Teda	0 1 5p	**Wuhan Huanghelou**	1 4				
Dalian Shide	1 3	Qingdao Zhongneng *	4 0				
Qingdao Zhongneng *	0 4			**Wuhan Huanghelou** *	1 1 4p		
Beijing Hyundai *	1 1			Shandong Luneng	1 1 3p		
Shanghai Int'l	0 2	Beijing Hyundai *	2 2				
		Shandong Luneng T.	2 3				
Shandong Luneng T.	Bye						
Shanghai Shenhua	4 3					**Wuhan Huanghelou**	1 2
Shanghai Zobon *	1 1	**Shanghai Shenhua**	2 2			Shenzhen Jianlibao *	1 0
Sichuan Guangcheng	1 3	Chongqing Lifan *	0 1				
Chongqing Lifan *	5 3			Shanghai Shenhua *	0 2		
Liaoning	3 0			**Shenzhen Jianlibao**	1 2		
Shenyang Ginde *	1 0	Liaoning *	1 2				
		Shenzhen Jianlibao	4 3				
Shenzhen Jianlibao	Bye						

Open to Super League clubs only • * Home team in the first leg

CUP FINAL

1st leg. Shenzhen, 12-11-2005
Scorers - Zhang Yonghai [40] for Shenzhen;
Cai Xi [47] for Wuhan

2nd leg. Wuhan
Scorers - Gilson [66], Vincent [68] for Wuhan

CIV – COTE D'IVOIRE

NATIONAL TEAM RECORD
JULY 1ST 2002 TO JULY 9TH 2006

PL	W	D	L	F	A	%
39	21	8	10	67	40	64.1

FIFA/COCA-COLA WORLD RANKING

1993	1994	1995	1996	1997	1998	1999	2000	2001	2002	2003	2004	2005	High		Low	
33	25	20	51	52	44	53	51	44	64	70	40	42	**20**	12/95	**75**	05/04

2005–2006											
08/05	09/05	10/05	11/05	12/05	01/06	02/06	03/06	04/06	05/06	06/06	07/06
44	50	48	41	42	42	32	32	32	32	-	20

The Ivorians enthralled the viewing public with the tempo and charisma of their debut performance at the FIFA World Cup™ finals but did not make it past the first round. Indeed, they were effectively eliminated after their first two matches at the tournament in Germany, before winning 3-2 against Serbia and Montenegro in their final match for a well-deserved consolation. It remains, however, the cherry on top of a great 12 months for the Elephants, who emerged by the narrowest of margins to qualify for the finals and then verified their credentials with a storming performance at the 2006 African Nations Cup finals. In Egypt, the Ivorians reached the Nations Cup final for

INTERNATIONAL HONOURS
Qualified for the FIFA World Cup™ finals 2006   **African Cup of Nations** 1992   **CAF African Champions League** ASEC Mimosas 1998

only the second time and could have won the game in regular time had it not been for some glaring misses by captain Didier Drogba, ironically also their best player over the last year. Instead they lost on post-match penalties to the hosts but emerged as the future of an African continent who will host the next FIFA World Cup™ finals in 2010. Drogba was unlucky to lose out to Samuel Eto'o in the polling for the African Footballer of the Year, the margin of two votes making it the tightest race to date. ASEC Abidjan won a fifth successive title and completed the League and Cup double to continue their dominance of the domestic scene.

THE FIFA BIG COUNT OF 2000

	Male	Female		Male	Female
Registered players	11 000	0	Referees	500	0
Non registered players	75 000	0	Officials	3 500	0
Youth players	10 000	0	Total involved	100 000	
Total players	96 000		Number of clubs	200	
Professional players	50	0	Number of teams	1 200	

Fédération Ivoirienne de Football (FIF)
01 Case postale 1202, Abidjan 01, Côte d'Ivoire
Tel +225 21240027   Fax +225 21259552
fifci@aviso.ci   www.fif.ci
President: ANOUMA Jacques   General Secretary: DIABATE Sory
Vice-President: KESSE Feh Lambert   Treasurer: ABINAN Pascal   Media Officer: None
Men's Coach: TBD   Women's Coach: None
FIF formed: 1960   CAF: 1960   FIFA: 1960
Orange shirts with white trimmings, White shorts, Green socks

RECENT INTERNATIONAL MATCHES PLAYED BY COTE D'IVOIRE

2002	Opponents	Score		Venue	Comp	Scorers	Att	Referee
8-09	South Africa	D	0-0	Abidjan	CNq		30 000	Coulibaly MLI
2003								
11-02	Cameroon	W	3-0	Chateauroux	Fr	Guel [37], Drogba [45], Kalou [83p]	3 000	Ennjini FRA
30-03	Burundi	W	1-0	Bujumbura	CNq	Bakari [57]		Gasingwa RWA
30-04	Morocco	W	1-0	Rabat	Fr	Kalou [83p]	20 000	El Arjoun MAR
8-06	Burundi	W	6-1	Abidjan	CNq	Drogba 3 [7 27 32], Bakari 2 [56 78], Dindane [70]	50 000	Monteiro Duarte CPV
22-06	South Africa	L	1-2	Johannesburg	CNq	Kalou [41]	35 000	Maillet SEY
10-09	Tunisia	L	2-3	Tunis	Fr	Dindane [88], Kalou [90p]	17 000	Djaballah ALG
15-11	Senegal	L	0-1	Dakar	Fr		50 000	Daami TUN
2004								
31-03	Tunisia	W	2-0	Tunis	Fr	Drogba 2 [34 65]	10 000	Haimoudi ALG
28-04	Guinea	W	4-2	Aix-les-Bains	Fr	Drogba [8], Toure [32], Kalou [45], Bakari [68]	2 000	
6-06	Libya	W	2-0	Abidjan	WCq	Dindane [35], Drogba [63p]	40 827	Colembi ANG
20-06	Egypt	W	2-1	Alexandria	WCq	Dindane [22], Drogba [75]	13 000	Guirat TUN
4-07	Cameroon	L	0-2	Yaounde	WCq		80 000	Guezzaz MAR
18-08	Senegal	W	2-1	Avignon	Fr	Boka [32], Dindane [68]	5 000	
5-09	Sudan	W	5-0	Abidjan	WCq	Drogba [12p], Dindane 2 [15 64], Yapi [25], Bakary Kone [56]	20 000	Mana NGA
10-10	Benin	W	1-0	Cotonou	WCq	Dindane [48]	25 000	Sowe GAM
2005								
8-02	Congo DR	D	2-2	Rouen	Fr	Dindane [39], Kalou [88p]	4 000	Duhamel FRA
27-03	Benin	W	3-0	Abidjan	WCq	Kalou [7], Drogba 2 [19 59]	35 000	Guirat TUN
3-06	Libya	D	0-0	Tripoli	WCq		45 000	Lim Kee Chong MRI
19-06	Egypt	W	2-0	Abidjan	WCq	Drogba 2 [41 49]	30 000	Damon RSA
17-08	France	L	0-3	Montpellier	Fr		31 457	Bertini ITA
4-09	Cameroon	L	2-3	Abidjan	WCq	Drogba 2 [38 47]	34 500	Daami TUN
8-10	Sudan	W	3-1	Omdurman	WCq	Akale [22], Dindane 2 [51 73]	20 000	Damon RSA
12-11	Romania	W	2-1	Le Mans	Fr	Arouna Kone [48], Bakary Kone [91+]	5 377	Fautrel FRA
16-11	Italy	D	1-1	Geneva	Fr	Drogba [71]	18 500	Bertolini SUI
2006								
17-01	Jordan	W	2-0	Abu Dhabi	Fr	Drogba [30], Akale [80]		
21-01	Morocco	W	1-0	Cairo	CNr1	Drogba [38]	8 000	Damon RSA
24-01	Libya	W	2-1	Cairo	CNr1	Drogba [10], Yaya Toure [74]	42 000	Maidin SIN
28-01	Egypt	L	1-3	Cairo	CNr1	Arouna Kone [43]	74 000	Maillet SEY
4-02	Cameroon	D	1-1	Cairo	CNqf	Bakary Kone [91], W 12-11p	4 000	Sowe GAM
7-02	Nigeria	W	1-0	Alexandria	CNsf	Drogba [47]	20 000	Damon RSA
10-02	Egypt	D	0-0	Cairo	CNf	L 2-4p	74 000	Daami TUN
1-03	Spain	L	2-3	Valladolid	Fr	Akale [12], Kalou [47]	30 000	Rodomonti ITA
27-05	Switzerland	D	1-1	Basel	Fr	Fae [47]	22 000	Vuorela FIN
30-05	Chile	D	1-1	Vittel	Fr	Dindane [71p]		Lamarre FRA
4-06	Slovenia	W	3-0	Every-Bondoufle	Fr	Drogba 2 [35 36], Akale [70]	8 000	
10-06	Argentina	L	1-2	Hamburg	WCr1	Drogba [82]	49 480	De Bleeckere BEL
16-06	Netherlands	L	1-2	Stuttgart	WCr1	Bakary Kone [38]	52 000	Ruiz COL
21-06	Serbia & Montenegro	W	3-2	Munich	WCr1	Dindane 2 [37p 67], Kalou [86p]	66 000	Rodriguez MEX

Fr = Friendly match • CN = African Cup of Nations • WC = FIFA World Cup™ • q = qualifier

COTE D'IVOIRE NATIONAL TEAM RECORDS AND RECORD SEQUENCES

Records			Sequence records				
Victory	6-0	Four times	Wins	7	1984	Clean sheets	9	1991
Defeat	2-6	GHA 1971	Defeats	6	1977-1979	Goals scored	15	1983-1984
Player Caps	n/a		Undefeated	16	1987-1989	Without goal	3	1985, 1989
Player Goals	n/a		Without win	7	1985	Goals against	11	1980-1983

COTE D'IVOIRE COUNTRY INFORMATION

Capital	Yamoussoukro	Independence	1960	GDP per Capita	$1 400
Population	17 327 724	Status	Republic	GNP Ranking	85
Area km²	322 460	Language	French	Dialling code	+225
Population density	53 per km²	Literacy rate	43%	Internet code	.ci
% in urban areas	44%	Main religion	Traditional 40%	GMT + / –	0
Towns/Cities ('000)	Abidjan 3 692; Bouaké 572; Daloa 217; Yamoussoukro 200; San Pedro 195; Korhogo 172				
Neighbours (km)	Mali 532; Burkina Faso 584; Ghana 668; Liberia 716; Guinea 610; Atlantic Ocean 515				
Main stadia	Houphouët-Boigny – Abidjan 45 000; Robert Champroux – Abidjan 20 000				

CLUB DIRECTORY

Club	Town/City	Stadium	Capacity	www.	Lge	Cup	CL
Africa Sports National	Abidjan	Houphouët-Boigny	45 000		14	13	0
ASEC Mimosas	Abidjan	Houphouët-Boigny	45 000	asec.ci	21	14	1
AS Denguélé Sports d'Odienné	Odienne	Mamadou-Coulibal	10 000		0	0	0
Entente Sportive de Bingerville	Bingerville	Municipal	4 000		0	0	0
Issia Wazi FC	Gagnoa	Victor-Biaka-Boda	12 000		0	0	0
Jeunesse Club d'Abidjan	Abidjan	Robert-Champroux	20 000		0	0	0
Lakota FC	Lakota				0	0	0
Réveil Club de Daloa	Daloa	Municipal	4 000		0	1	0
Sabé Sports de Bouna	Bouna	Bouna	3 000		0	0	0
Séwé Sport de San Pedro	San Pedro	Auguste-Demise	8 000		0	0	0
Sporting Club de Gagnoa	Gagnoa	Victor-Biaka-Boda	12 000		1	0	0
Stade d'Abidjan	Abidjan	Robert-Champroux	20 000		5	5	1
Stella Club d'Adjamé	Abidjan	Parc des Sports	10 000		3	2	0
Centre de Formation Yéo Martial	Abidjan	Houphouët-Boigny	45 000		0	0	0

RECENT LEAGUE AND CUP RECORD

	Championship						Cup		
Year	Champions	Pts	Runners-up	Pts	Third	Pts	Winners	Score	Runners-up
1990	ASEC Mimosas						ASEC Mimosas	2-0	SC Gagnoa
1991	ASEC Mimosas	57	Africa Sports	54	SC Gagnoa	34	No final played		
1992	ASEC Mimosas						No final played		
1993	ASEC Mimosas						Africa Sports	2-1	ASC Bouaké
1994	ASEC Mimosas	18	Africa Sports	18	SO Armée	9	Stade Abidjan	4-2	Africa Sports
1995	ASEC Mimosas	23	SO Armée	18	Africa Sports	15	ASEC Mimosas	2-0	Stade Abidjan
1996	Africa Sports						SO Armée	0-0 10-9p	Africa Sports
1997	ASEC Mimosas	26	SO Armée	15	Africa Sports	12	ASEC Mimosas	4-0	Africa Sports
1998	ASEC Mimosas	24	FC Man	16	Africa Sports	13	Africa Sports	3-0	Stade Abidjan
1999	Africa Sports	28	ASEC Mimosas	23	Stade Abidjan	16	ASEC Mimosas	5-0	Séwé San Pedro
2000	ASEC Mimosas	21	Sabé Bouna	16	Africa Sports	16	Stade Abidjan	2-1	ASEC Mimosas
2001	ASEC Mimosas	55	Satellite FC	45	Africa Sports	41	Alliance Bouaké	2-0	ASC Bouaké
2002	ASEC Mimosas	22	Jeunesse Abidjan	18	Satellite FC	16	Africa Sports	2-0	Renaissance
2003	ASEC Mimosas	21	Africa Sports	19	Stella Adjamé	15	ASEC Mimosas	1-1 4-2p	Africa Sports
2004	ASEC Mimosas	68	Africa Sport	48	Stella Adjamé	43	CO Bouaflé	2-1	Stade Abidjan
2005	ASEC Mimosas	66	Africa Sport	55	Jeunesse Abidjan	45	ASEC Mimosas	1-0	Séwé San Pedro

COTE D'IVOIRE 2005

PREMIERE DIVISION

	Pl	W	D	L	F	A	Pts	ASEC	Africa Sport	JCA	Issia	Séwé	Gagnoa	Stade	Stella	Denguélé	Réveil	Bingerville	Sabé	Bouaflé	Satellite
ASEC Mimosas †	26	21	3	2	39	9	66		0-1	3-2	1-0	0-0	1-2	1-0	1-0	2-1	2-0	2-0	1-0	2-0	4-1
Africa Sport †	26	15	10	1	32	10	55	0-1		2-0	0-0	0-0	2-2	1-1	2-0	2-0	2-0	1-0	2-0	2-0	1-0
Jeunesse Abidjan ‡	26	14	3	9	32	22	45	0-1	0-1		1-3	0-1	2-1	2-1	2-0	2-1	1-0	0-1	2-0	0-1	3-0
Issia Wazi	26	13	5	8	35	24	44	0-0	0-2	0-0		1-0	2-1	0-1	2-1	2-0	2-1	3-0	1-2	1-0	1-1
Séwé San Pedro	26	10	12	4	31	22	42	0-2	1-1	2-2	1-0		0-1	4-1	2-0	2-2	2-1	1-0	1-0	1-0	2-0
Sporting Gagnoa	26	12	4	10	35	36	40	0-1	1-1	0-1	2-1	2-1		0-2	1-0	2-1	1-1	3-2	3-2	**3-0**	6-2
Stade Abidjan	26	9	8	9	25	27	35	0-0	1-1	0-0	2-3	1-1	3-0		1-0	1-2	0-2	1-0	1-1	1-0	1-0
Stella Adjamé	26	8	8	10	35	29	32	0-2	0-0	1-0	3-2	3-3	1-1	1-1		1-2	2-3	4-1	5-1	2-2	2-0
Denguélé Odienné	26	7	8	11	29	29	29	0-1	1-1	1-3	2-3	1-1	4-0	1-0	0-0		0-0	0-0	1-1	3-0	0-1
Réveil Daloa	26	7	6	13	28	37	27	1-2	2-3	2-3	0-4	1-1	1-0	1-1	0-2	2-1		2-2	0-1	2-1	3-0
Entente Bingerville	26	6	8	12	17	30	26	0-2	0-2	0-1	1-0	1-1	0-1	2-0	1-1	1-1	1-0		1-1	1-0	2-1
Sabé Sports Bouna	26	5	8	13	19	34	23	0-2	1-1	0-2	1-1	1-1	0-1	1-2	0-0	0-1	1-0	0-0		0-0	3-2
CO Bouaflé	26	6	3	17	14	34	21	0-3	0-1	0-2	1-2	0-1	2-0	0-2	1-0	1-0	1-1	2-0	1-2		1-0
Satellite FC	26	4	4	18	19	47	16	1-2	0-0	0-1	0-1	1-1	3-1	0-3	1-3	0-3	1-2	0-0	2-1	2-0	

19/02/2005 - 2/10/2005 • † Qualified for the CAF Champions League • ‡ Qualified for the CAF Confederation Cup • Match in bold was awarded • The top six at the end of May 2005 qualified for the Coupe Nationale along with 10 teams from the second and third levels • EFYM and Lakota promoted

COUPE NATIONALE 2005

Round of sixteen		Quarter-finals		Semi-finals		Final	
ASEC Mimosas	1						
Jeunesse Abidjan	0	ASEC Mimosas	2				
Adzopé	1 2p	Lakota	0				
Lakota	1 4p			ASEC Mimosas	4		
ASC Cocody	1			Africa Sports	0		
Ouragahio	0	ASC Cocody	1				
Agnéby Agboville	0	Africa Sports	4				
Africa Sports	1					ASEC Mimosas	1
EFYM	1 5p					Séwé San Pedro ‡	0
Sikensi	1 4p	EFYM					
Toumodi	1	Ban FC					
Ban FC	2			EFYM	0		
Sporting Club Gagnoa	2			Séwé San Pedro	1		
Issia Wazi	0	Sporting Club Gagnoa	0				
USC Bassam	0	Séwé San Pedro	1				
Séwé San Pedro	1	‡ Qualified for the CAF Confederation Cup					

CUP FINAL

Stade Houphouët-Boigny, Abidjan
31-07-2005. Ref: Chicoto

Scorer - Doumbia Mamadou [18]

CMR – CAMEROON

NATIONAL TEAM RECORD
JULY 1ST 2002 TO JULY 9TH 2006

PL	W	D	L	F	A	%
36	17	10	9	46	35	61.1

FIFA/COCA-COLA WORLD RANKING

1993	1994	1995	1996	1997	1998	1999	2000	2001	2002	2003	2004	2005	High		Low	
23	31	37	56	53	41	58	39	38	16	14	23	23	12	07/03	62	04/97

2005–2006											
08/05	09/05	10/05	11/05	12/05	01/06	02/06	03/06	04/06	05/06	06/06	07/06
28	22	23	22	23	23	16	15	15	15	-	12

The width of the post denied Cameroon their perennial place at the FIFA World Cup™ finals in a dramatic reversal for the Indomitable Lions. Cameroon had been involved in a neck-and-neck battle with Cote d'Ivoire for a place among the 32 finalists in Germany and looked to be in the driving seat after forcing a dramatic win away in Abidjan in September. They needed only a win against Egypt at home in their final match to qualify for the FIFA World Cup finals for an African record breaking sixth time. But the Pharaohs proved a stubborn opponent and the game was tied at 1-1 deep into stoppage time when Cameroon were awarded a fortuitous penalty. Successful

INTERNATIONAL HONOURS
Qualified for the FIFA World Cup™ finals 1982 1990 1994 1998 2002 **African Cup of Nations** 1984 1988 2000 2002 **African Games** 1991 1999 2003 **African Youth** 1995 **African U-17** 2003 **CAF African Champions League** Oryx Doula 1965, Canon Yaounde 1971 1978 1980, Union Douala 1979

conversion, thereof, would have ensured a trip to the FIFA World Cup™ finals and although defender Pierre Wome's fierce shot sent the opposing goalkeeper the wrong way, it hit the outside of the post. Samuel Eto'o won the African Footballer of the Year award for a record-equalling third time but he and his team mates proved disappointing at the African Nations Cup finals in Egypt where the Ivorians eliminated them, in another penalty heartbreak, at the quarter-final stage. A third successive title for Coton Sport from Garoua saw them again fly the flag in the 2006 CAF Champions League while second division Impots FC from Yaoundé were unlikely Cup winners.

THE FIFA BIG COUNT OF 2000

	Male	Female		Male	Female
Registered players	12 450	500	Referees	2 000	30
Non registered players	75 000	1 000	Officials	5 000	0
Youth players	10 000	0	Total involved	105 980	
Total players	98 950		Number of clubs	720	
Professional players	450	0	Number of teams	3 000	

Fédération Camerounaise de Football (FECAFOOT)
Avenue du 27 aout 1940, Tsinga-Yaoundé, Case Postale 1116, Yaoundé, Cameroon
Tel +237 2210012   Fax +237 7991393
fecafoot@fecafootonline.com   www.fecafootonline.com
President: IYA Mohammed   General Secretary: PRECHEUR Patrick
Vice-President: ATANGANA Jean Rene   Treasurer: ALIOUM Alhadji Hamadou   Media Officer: ABDOURAMAN M.
Men's Coach: TBD   Women's Coach: KAMDEM Charles
FECAFOOT formed: 1959   CAF: 1963   FIFA: 1962
Green shirts with yellow trimmings, Red shorts, Yellow socks or Red shirts, Green shorts, Yellow socks

RECENT INTERNATIONAL MATCHES PLAYED BY CAMEROON

2002 Opponents		Score	Venue	Comp	Scorers	Att	Referee
No international matches played after in 2002 after June							
2003							
11-02 Côte d'Ivoire	L	0-3	Chateauroux	Fr		3 000	Ennjini FRA
27-03 Madagascar	W	2-0	Tunis	Fr	Eto'o [15], Job [43]		Zahmoul TUN
30-03 Tunisia	L	0-1	Tunis	Fr			Guezzaz MAR
19-06 Brazil	W	1-0	Paris	CCr1	Eto'o [83]	46 719	Ivanov RUS
21-06 Turkey	W	1-0	Paris	CCr1	Geremi [90p]	43 743	Amarilla PAR
23-06 United States	D	0-0	Lyon	CCr1		19 206	Shield AUS
26-06 Colombia	W	1-0	Lyon	CCsf	N'Diefi [9]	12 352	Merk GER
29-06 France	L	0-1	Paris	CCf		51 985	Ivanov RUS
19-11 Japan	D	0-0	Oita	Fr		38 627	Lu CHN
7-12 Central African Rep.	D	2-2	Brazzaville	CM r1	Mokake [60]		
9-12 Central African Rep.	L	0-1	Brazzaville	CMr1			
10-12 Congo	W	2-0	Brazzaville	CMsf	Ambassa [45], Abada [90]		Youssouf GAB
13-12 Central African Rep.	W	3-2	Brazzaville	CMf	Mevengue [16p], Mokake.M [69], Mokake.E [78]		Bantsimba CGO
2004							
25-01 Algeria	D	1-1	Sousse	CNr1	Mboma [44]	20 000	Codjia BEN
29-01 Zimbabwe	W	5-3	Sfax	CNr1	Mboma 3 [31 44 64], Mbami 2 [39 66]	15 000	Aboubacar CIV
3-02 Egypt	D	0-0	Monastir	CNr1		20 000	Bujsaim UAE
8-02 Nigeria	L	1-2	Monastir	CNqf	Eto'o [42]	18 000	Guezzaz MAR
28-04 Bulgaria	L	0-3	Sofia	Fr		13 987	Verbist BEL
6-06 Benin	W	2-1	Yaoundé	WCq	Eto'o [42], Song [45]	40 000	Mbera GAB
18-06 Libya	D	0-0	Misurata	WCq		7 000	Lim Kee Chong MRI
4-07 Côte d'Ivoire	W	2-0	Yaoundé	WCq	Eto'o [80], Feutchine [82]	80 000	Guezzaz MAR
5-09 Egypt	L	2-3	Cairo	WCq	Tchato [88], Eto'o [90]	25 000	Lim Kee Chong MRI
9-10 Sudan	D	1-1	Omdurman	WCq	Job [90+2]	30 000	Buenkadila COD
17-11 Germany	L	0-3	Leipzig	Fr		4 200	De Santis ITA
2005							
9-02 Senegal	W	1-0	Creteil	Fr	Geremi [87]	8 000	Lhermite FRA
27-03 Sudan	W	2-1	Yaoundé	WCq	Geremi [34], Webo [90]	30 000	Diatta SEN
4-06 Benin	W	4-1	Cotonou	WCq	Song [19], Webo [51], Geremi [64], Eto'o [69]	20 000	El Arjoun MAR
19-06 Libya	W	1-0	Yaoundé	WCq	Webo [37]	36 000	Coulibaly MLI
4-09 Côte d'Ivoire	W	3-2	Abidjan	WCq	Webo 3 [30 47 85]	34 500	Daami TUN
8-10 Egypt	D	1-1	Yaounde	WCq	Douala [20]	38 750	Coulibaly MLI
15-11 Morocco	D	0-0	Clairefontaine	Fr			
2006							
21-01 Angola	W	3-1	Cairo	CNr1	Eto'o 3 [21 39 78]	8 000	Guezzaz MAR
25-01 Togo	W	2-0	Cairo	CNr1	Eto'o [68] ,Meyong Ze [86]	3 000	Sowe GAM
29-01 Congo DR	W	2-0	Cairo	CNr1	Geremi [31], Eto'o [33]	5 000	Coulibaly MLI
4-02 Côte d'Ivoire	D	1-1	Cairo	CNqf	Meyong Ze [96], L 11-12p	4 000	Sowe GAM
27-05 Netherlands	L	0-1	Rotterdam	Fr		46 228	Plautz AUT

Fr = Friendly match • CC = FIFA Confederations Cup • CN = African Cup of Nations • CM = CEMAC Championship • WC = FIFA World Cup™
q = qualifier • r1 = 1st round • qf = quarter-final • sf = semi-final • f = final

CAMEROON NATIONAL TEAM RECORDS AND RECORD SEQUENCES

Records			Sequence records				
Victory	9-2	SOM 1960	Wins	7	2002	Clean sheets	7	2002
Defeat	1-6	NOR 1990, RUS 1994	Defeats	3	Five times	Goals scored	24	1967-1972
Player Caps	103	SONG Rigobert	Undefeated	16	1981-1983	Without goal	4	1981, 2001
Player Goals	33	MBOMA Patrick	Without win	9	1994-1995	Goals against	11	1969-1972

CAMEROON COUNTRY INFORMATION

Capital	Yaoundé	Independence	1960 from UN Trusteeship	GDP per Capita	$1 800
Population	16 063 678	Status	Republic	GNP Ranking	91
Area km²	475 440	Language	French, English	Dialling code	+237
Population density	33 per km²	Literacy rate	72%	Internet code	.cm
% in urban areas	45%	Main religion	Indigenous 40% Christian 40%	GMT + / –	+1
Towns/Cities ('000)	Douala 1 338; Yaoundé 1 299; Garoua 436; Kousseri 435; Bamenda 393; Bafoussam 290				
Neighbours (km)	Central African Republic 797; Chad 1 094; Congo 523; Equatorial Guinea 189; Gabon 298; Nigeria 1,690				
Main stadia	Amadou Ahidjo – Yaoundé 80 000; Stade de la Réunification – Douala 30 000				

CLUB DIRECTORY

Club	Town/City	Stadium	Capacity	Lge	Cup	CL
Bamboutos	Mbouda	Stade Municipal	11 000	0	0	0
Botafogo	Buéa	Moliko Stadium	8 000	0	0	0
Canon Sportif	Yaoundé	Stade Ahmadou Ahidjo	80 000	10	12	3
Cintra	Yaoundé	Stade Ahmadou Ahidjo	80 000	0	0	0
Cotonsport	Garoua	Stade Omnisport Poumpoum Rey	22 000	6	2	0
Espérance	Guider	Stade Municipal	10 000	0	0	0
Fovu Club	Baham	Stade Municipal	7 000	1	1	0
Kadji Sport Academy	Douala	Stade de la Reunification	30 000	0	0	0
Mount Cameroun FC	Buéa	Moliko Stadium	8 000	0	1	0
Ngaoundéré University FC	Ngaoundéré	Stade Municipal	10 000	0	0	0
PWD (Public Works Dept)	Bamenda	Stade Municipal	10 000	0	0	0
Racing Club	Bafoussam	Stade Municipal de Bamendzi	5 000	4	1	0
Renaissance	Ngoumou	Stade Ahmadou Ahidjo	80 000	0	0	0
Sable	Batié	Stade de la Reunification	30 000	1	0	0
Tonnerre Kalara Club	Yaoundé	Stade Ahmadou Ahidjo	80 000	5	5	0
Union Sportive	Douala	Stade de la Reunification	30 000	4	5	1
Unisport	Bafang	Stade Municipal	5 000	1	0	0
Victoria United	Limbe	Stade Municipal	12 000	0	0	0

RECENT LEAGUE AND CUP RECORD

	Championship						Cup		
Year	Champions	Pts	Runners-up	Pts	Third	Pts	Winners	Score	Runners-up
1990	Union Douala	59	Prévoyance Yaoundé	47	Panthère Bangangté	47	Prévoyance Yaoundé	1-1 6-5p	Tonnerre Yaoundé
1991	Canon Yaoundé	43	Diamant Yaoundé	34	Racing Bafoussam	32	Tonnerre Yaoundé	1-0	Racing Bafoussam
1992	Racing Bafoussam						Olympique Mvolyé	1-0	Diamant Yaoundé
1993	Racing Bafoussam	44	Unisport Bafang	43	Union Douala	38	Canon Yaoundé	2-0	Léopards Douala
1994	Aigle Nkongsamba	42	Cotonsport Garoua	38	Union Douala	36	Olympique Mvolyé	1-0	Tonnerre Yaoundé
1995	Racing Bafoussam	52	Léopard Douala	48	Unisport Bafang	48	Canon Yaoundé	1-0	Océan Kribi
1996	Unisport Bafang	56	Cotonsport Garoua	47	Canon Yaoundé	47	Racing Bafoussam	1-0	Stade Banjoun
1997	Cotonsport Garoua	62	Stade Bandjoun	60	Union Douala	55	Union Douala	2-1	Ports FC Douala
1998	Cotonsport Garoua	54	Canon Yaoundé	53	Tonnerre Yaoundé	51	Dynamo Douala	1-0	Canon Yaoundé
1999	Sable Batié	58	Cotonsport Garoua	56	Racing Bafoussam	49	Canon Yaoundé	2-1	Cotonsport Garoua
2000	Fovu Baham	59	Cotonsport Garoua	53	Union Douala	51	Kumbo Strikers	1-0	Unisport Bafang
2001	Cotonsport Garoua	58	Tonnerre Yaoundé	53	Fovu Baham	50	Fovu Baham	3-2	Cintra Yaoundé
2002	Canon Yaoundé	55	Cotonsport Garoua	53	Bamboutos Mbouda	50	Mt Cameroun	2-1	Sable Batié
2003	Cotonsport Garoua	62	Canon Yaoundé	51	PWD Bamenda	51	Cotonsport Garoua	2-1	Sable Batié
2004	Cotonsport Garoua	30	Racing Bafoussam	28	Union Douala	26	Cotonsport Garoua	1-0	Union Douala
2005	Cotonsport Garoua	71	Aigle Royal Menoua	53	Astres Douala	51	Impôts Yaoundé	1-0	Unisport Bafang

CAMEROON 2005

PREMIERE DIVISION

	Pl	W	D	L	F	A	Pts	Cotonsport	Aigle Royal	Les Astres	Fovu	Sahel	Foudre	Canon	Sable	Espérance	Bamboutos	Racing	Kadji	Union	M Cameroon	PWD	Tonnerre	Ngaoundéré	Unisport
Cotonsport Garoua †	34	20	11	3	47	18	71		3-1	1-0	1-0	1-1	3-1	2-0	1-0	1-1	2-1	5-0	2-0	3-2	1-0	3-0	1-0	1-0	1-0
Aigle Royal Menoua †	34	15	8	11	36	29	53	2-1		0-1	0-1	2-1	1-0	1-1	1-3	2-0	1-1	2-0	2-1	2-0	0-0	2-0	1-0	1-0	3-0
Les Astres Douala ‡	34	14	9	11	47	41	51	1-3	0-0		1-1	0-1	1-2	2-1	2-4	3-1	1-0	3-1	2-2	0-0	3-1	2-1	1-2	3-1	3-0
Fovu Baham	34	13	12	9	38	33	51	1-1	1-0	2-2		**4-0**	3-2	1-1	2-1	1-0	1-1	0-0	2-0	2-0	0-1	0-1	1-0	1-1	1-0
Sahel Maroua §2	34	15	7	12	38	37	50	1-1	1-2	0-0	1-0		0-1	1-3	2-1	1-0	0-0	1-2	1-0	0-0	1-2	2-3	2-0	5-0	2-0
Foudre Akonolinga	34	14	8	12	43	33	50	0-0	1-0	1-2	0-1	1-2		3-2	1-1	1-0	0-0	1-0	2-1	4-2	0-0	4-0	2-0	4-1	1-1
Canon Yaoundé §2	34	13	12	9	38	29	49	1-1	1-1	3-0	2-0	5-0	0-0		2-1	0-1	0-0	2-0	0-0	1-0	1-0	0-1	0-0	1-1	3-1
Sable Batie	34	12	13	9	37	29	49	1-1	1-0	1-1	0-0	2-0	0-2	0-1		2-0	1-1	1-1	2-1	2-0	1-0	0-0	1-1	2-0	1-0
Espérance Guider	34	12	9	13	30	34	45	1-3	1-1	2-0	2-0	0-1	1-0	1-1	0-0		2-1	1-0	8-0	1-0	0-0	0-0	1-0	0-1	1-0
Bamboutos Mbouda	34	12	8	14	31	27	44	1-0	1-0	3-0	3-0	2-0	1-0	1-2	0-2	0-0		0-0	1-0	1-4	0-1	2-0	3-0	1-0	1-0
Racing Bafoussam	34	11	11	12	23	30	44	0-1	0-1	1-0	1-1	1-0	1-0	3-1	0-0	0-0	1-0		2-2	2-1	2-0	0-0	0-1	1-0	1-0
Kadji Sport Douala	34	12	7	15	45	52	43	0-1	3-2	0-3	2-1	1-2	1-2	2-1	3-1	5-1	0-2	1-2		2-1	0-0	4-2	1-0	2-1	2-2
Union Douala	34	11	8	15	43	43	41	5-1	1-1	1-2	5-2	2-0	0-0	0-1	2-1	2-0	**2-0**	1-0	2-3		2-1	3-1	1-1	0-0	5-1
Mount Cameroon	34	9	14	11	27	27	41	1-0	0-0	0-0	1-1	2-2	2-1	2-2	0-1	0-0	1-0	2-0	0-0	0-1		1-1	1-0	1-0	0-1
PWD Bamenda	34	9	13	12	22	37	40	0-0	1-0	0-3	0-0	1-0	1-1	0-1	1-1	**0-1**	1-0	0-0	0-1	1-1	1-0		1-1	2-0	1-1
Tonnerre Yaoundé §1	34	10	9	15	32	40	38	0-1	4-1	2-2	**0-3**	0-1	3-1	0-1	1-0	3-0	3-2	1-0	0-4	1-1	2-2	0-0		1-2	2-1
Univ. Ngaoundéré	34	7	12	15	23	40	33	0-0	0-0	2-1	2-2	1-1	1-0	**3-0**	0-0	1-2	1-0	0-0	0-1	2-1	1-1	0-1	2-0		0-0
Unisport Bafang	34	6	11	17	27	48	29	0-0	0-2	1-2	1-2	1-1	1-4	0-0	1-1	4-1	1-0	1-1	2-1	1-1	0-1	2-0	1-1	2-1	

13/03/2005 - 13/11/2005 • † Qualified for the CAF Champions League • ‡ Qualified for the Confederation Cup • Union Douala and Mount Cameroon took part in the Tournoi Inter Poules but retained their top flight status • §2 = two points deducted • §1 = one point deducted • Matches in bold were awarded

CAMEROON 2005
TOURNOI INTER POULES (2)

Pool A - in Douala	Pl	W	D	L	F	A	Pts
Fédéral Noun	5	3	1	1	9	6	10
Mount Cameroon	5	3	1	1	9	2	10
Lakers Kumba	5	3	0	2	11	9	9
Danaï Yagoua	5	2	2	2	4	5	5
Yong Academy	5	1	1	3	6	10	4
Renaissance	5	1	1	3	2	9	4

Pool B - in Buea	Pl	W	D	L	F	A	Pts
Impôts Yaoundé	5	3	2	0	7	1	11
Union Douala	5	3	1	1	5	2	10
AS Douala-2	5	3	1	1	4	2	10
Union Abong-Mbang	5	2	1	2	6	6	7
Pilote Garoua	5	1	0	4	3	6	4
Epervier Ebolowa	5	0	1	4	3	11	1

COUPE DE CAMEROUN 2005

Round of 16			Quarter-finals			Semi-finals		Final	
Impôts Yaoundé *	3	4							
Aigle Royal Menoua	0	2	**Impôts Yaoundé**	1	1				
Fovu Baham	0	0	Les Astres Douala *	0	1				
Les Astres Douala *	3	0				**Impôts Yaoundé**	2		
Sable Batié	2	1				Sahel Maroua †	0		
Bamboutos Mbouda *	0	0	Sable Batié	1	1				
Canon Yaoundé *	1	0	**Sahel Maroua ***	2	3				
Sahel Maroua	1	0						**Impôts Yaoundé ‡**	1
Cotonsport Garoua†	0							Unisport Bafang	0
Foudre Akonolinga † *	0		**Cotonsport Garoua**	1	1				
BAO Edéa	0	2	Univ. Ngaoundéré *	1	0				
Univ. Ngaoundéré *	3	0				Cotonsport Garoua	1	1	
Union Douala	0	5				**Unisport Bafang**	2	0	
Renaissance *	1	1	Union Douala *	0	1				
Kadji Sports Douala	0	1	**Unisport Bafang**	3	0	† withdrew			
Unisport Bafang *	1	2	* Home team in the first leg • ‡ Qualified for the CAF Confederation Cup						

CUP FINAL

Stade Ahmadou Ahidjo, Yaoundé
22-12-2005, Ref: Dongo

Scorer - Enama Okouda [35]

COD – CONGO DR

NATIONAL TEAM RECORD
JULY 1ST 2002 TO JULY 9TH 2006

PL	W	D	L	F	A	%
46	14	18	14	61	62	50

FIFA/COCA-COLA WORLD RANKING

1993	1994	1995	1996	1997	1998	1999	2000	2001	2002	2003	2004	2005	High		Low	
71	68	68	66	76	62	59	70	77	65	56	78	77	51	09/03	81	07/01

2005–2006											
08/05	09/05	10/05	11/05	12/05	01/06	02/06	03/06	04/06	05/06	06/06	07/06
79	72	75	76	77	78	73	74	70	69	-	67

The undoubted potential of one of Africa's biggest countries was again given a rare airing at the 2006 African Nations Cup finals where the Democratic Republic of Congo made it to the last eight of the tournament in Egypt. After a calamity in Tunisia at the 2004 African Nations Cup finals, the Congolese, who are now again nicknamed the 'Leopards', came back strongly in Egypt. Coach Claude LeRoy, who was given more resources and opportunity to work with his side than many of his predecessors, harnessed the undoubted potential and served notice that if football in DR Congo is allowed to develop consistently in future, the national side could well return to their previous

INTERNATIONAL HONOURS
Qualified for the FIFA World Cup™ finals 1974
African Cup of Nations 1968 1974 **CAF Champions League** TP Mazembe 1967 1968 AS Vita Club 1973

pre-eminent position in the African rankings. The Leopards finished second in their FIFA World Cup™ qualifying group, making a strong finish which saw just one defeat in their last nine qualifiers. Domestic honours went to Daring Club Motema Pembe, who won the national championship play-off group with a one point advantage over FC St Eloi Lupopo from the country's second city of Lubumbashi. DCMP peaked late in the season after finishing third in the regional Kinshasa league from which they just qualified for the national play-offs.

THE FIFA BIG COUNT OF 2000

	Male	Female		Male	Female
Registered players	25 000	0	Referees	1 000	0
Non registered players	150 000	0	Officials	7 000	0
Youth players	20 000	0	Total involved	203 000	
Total players	195 000		Number of clubs	700	
Professional players	0	0	Number of teams	3 000	

Fédération Congolaise de Football-Association (FECOFA)
31 Avenue de la Justice, c/Gombe, Case postale 1284, Kinshasa 1, Congo DR
Tel +243 81 9049788   Fax +243 81 3013527
nzilafanan@hotmail.com   www.none
President: SELEMANI Omari   General Secretary: TSHIHIYOKA Bashige
Vice-President: TSHIMANGA MWAMBA Donatien   Treasurer: BONDEMBE Bokanyanga   Media Officer: NZILA Fanan
Men's Coach: LE ROY Claude   Women's Coach: BONGANYA Polycarpe
FECOFA formed: 1919   CAF: 1973   FIFA: 1962
Blue shirts with yellow trimmings, Blue shorts, Blue socks or Yellow shirts with blue trimmings, Blue shorts, Yellow socks

RECENT INTERNATIONAL MATCHES PLAYED BY CONGO DR

2003	Opponents	Score		Venue	Comp	Scorers	Att	Referee
22-02	Malawi	D	1-1	Blantyre	Fr			
23-02	Malawi	W	3-2	Lilongwe	Fr			
5-03	Sudan	W	3-1	Khartoum	Fr			
9-03	Congo	W	3-0	Kinshasa	Fr			
16-03	Lesotho	D	2-2	Maseru	Fr			
30-03	Swaziland	D	1-1	Mbabane	CNq	Musasa 65		Katjimune NAM
8-06	Swaziland	W	2-0	Kinshasa	CNq	Mpiana 18, Musasa 71	60 000	Ravelotslam MRI
22-06	Libya	W	2-1	Kinshasa	CNq	Masudi 29, Mpiana 83		
5-07	Botswana	D	0-0	Gaborone	CNq			
20-08	Angola	W	2-0	Luanda	Fr	Massaro 46, Mbotale 52		
2004								
14-01	Egypt	D	2-2	Port Said	Fr	Dinzey 52, Mbala 70	10 000	Kamal EGY
25-01	Guinea	L	1-2	Tunis	CNr1	Masudi 30	3 000	Aboubacar CIV
28-01	Tunisia	L	0-3	Tunis	CNr1		20 000	Damon RSA
1-02	Rwanda	L	0-1	Bizerte	CNr1		700	Ndoye SEN
23-05	Angola	L	1-3	Kinshasa	Fr	Kalulika 30p	60 000	Ntambidila COD
6-06	Uganda	L	0-1	Kampala	WCq		45 000	Maillet SEY
20-06	Burkina Faso	W	3-2	Kinshasa	WCq	Mbajo 12, Mbala 75, Bageta 88p	75 000	Djaoupe TOG
3-07	Cape Verde Islands	D	1-1	Praia	WCq	Kaluyitu 1	3 800	Nahi CIV
18-08	Mali	L	0-3	Paris	Fr			Derrien FRA
5-09	South Africa	W	1-0	Kinshasa	WCq	Kabamba 86	85 000	Hicuburundi BDI
10-10	Ghana	D	0-0	Kumasi	WCq		30 000	Coulibaly MLI
2005								
8-02	Côte d'Ivoire	D	2-2	Rouen	Fr	Makondele 44, Nonda 92+p	4 000	Duhamel FRA
27-03	Ghana	D	1-1	Kinshasa	WCq	Nonda 50	80 000	Sowe GAM
5-06	Uganda	W	4-0	Kinshasa	WCq	Nonda 2 2 69p, Ilongo 58, Matumona 78	80 000	Daami TUN
18-06	Burkina Faso	L	0-2	Ouagadougou	WCq		25 000	Shelmani LBY
1-07	Botswana	D	0-0	Gaborone	Fr			
16-08	Guinea	W	3-1	Paris	Fr	Mbala 37, LuaLua 62, Mputu 79		
4-09	Cape Verde Islands	W	2-1	Kinshasa	WCq	Mubiala 21, Mputu 49	75 000	Guezzaz MAR
25-09	Zambia	D	2-2	Chililabombwe	Fr	Bokese 54, Matumona 65		
27-09	Zambia	D	0-0	Lubumbashi	Fr			
8-10	South Africa	D	2-2	Durban	WCq	Mputu 11, Nonda 44	35 000	Mbera GAB
11-11	Tunisia	D	2-2	Paris	Fr	Mputu 16, Lutula 57		Garibian FRA
16-11	Libya	L	1-2	Paris	Fr	Mbokane 47		
11-12	Zambia	D	1-1	Lubumbashi	Fr	OG 28		
14-12	Zambia	L	1-4	Chingola	Fr	Ilingo 55		
2006								
9-01	Morocco	L	0-3	Rabat	Fr			
14-01	Senegal	D	0-0	Dakar	Fr			Sowe GAM
21-01	Togo	W	2-0	Cairo	CNr1	Mputu 42, LuaLua 61	6 000	Daami TUN
25-01	Angola	D	0-0	Cairo	CNr1		2 000	Diatta SEN
29-01	Cameroon	L	0-2	Cairo	CNr1		5 000	Coulibaly MLI
3-02	Egypt	L	1-4	Cairo	CNqf	OG 45	74 000	Sowe GAM
12-05	Mexico	L	1-2	Mexico City	Fr	Mbokani 51	75 000	Flores MEX

Fr = Friendly match • CN = CAF African Cup of Nations • WC = FIFA World Cup™ • q = qualifier • r1 = first round group

CONGO DR NATIONAL TEAM RECORDS AND RECORD SEQUENCES

Records			Sequence records				
Victory	10-1	ZAM 1969	Wins	5	1973-1974	Clean sheets	4	Four times
Defeat	0-9	YUG 1974	Defeats	5	2004	Goals scored	38	1976-1985
Player Caps	n/a		Undefeated	12	2002-2004	Without goal	4	1990
Player Goals	n/a		Without win	9	2005-2006	Goals against	13	1964-1966

CONGO DR COUNTRY INFORMATION

Capital	Kinshasa	Independence	1960 from Belgium	GDP per Capita	$700
Population	58 317 930	Status	Republic	GNP Ranking	120
Area km²	2 345 410	Language	French	Dialling code	+243
Population density	24 per km²	Literacy rate	65%	Internet code	.zr
% in urban areas	29%	Main religion	Christian 70%	GMT + / –	+1
Towns/Cities ('000)	Kinshasa 7 787; Lubumbashi 1 374; Kolwezi 910; Mbuji-Mayi 874; Kisangani 539; Kananga 463; Likasi 422; Boma 344; Tshikapa 267; Bukavu 225; Mwene-Ditu 189; Kikwit 186				
Neighbours (km)	Congo 2 410; Central African Republic 1 577; Sudan 628; Uganda 765; Rwanda 217; Burundi 233; Tanzania 459; Zambia 1 930; Angola 2 511; Atlantic Ocean 37				
Main stadia	Stade des Martyrs – Kinshasa 80 000; Stade Municipal – Lubumbashi 35 000; Stade Municipal – Kinshasa 20 000; Stade de Virunga – Goma 8 000				

CONGO DR 2005

LIGUE NATIONAL DE FOOTBALL FINAL ROUND

	Pl	W	D	L	F	A	Pts	DCMP	St Eloi	Mazembe	Vita	Virunga	Tshinkunku
DC Motema Pembe †	10	6	1	3	20	12	19		3-2	0-0	2-1	1-0	9-1
FC St Eloi Lupopo †	10	5	3	2	11	5	18	2-0		1-0	0-0	0-0	2-0
TP Mazembe ‡	10	5	2	3	20	8	17	4-1	0-1		2-0	1-0	9-0
AS Vita Club	10	4	2	4	8	10	14	0-2	0-3	2-0		1-0	2-0
DC Virunga	10	3	4	3	8	5	13	2-0	2-0	1-1	0-0		1-1
FC Tshinkunku	10	0	2	8	5	32	2	0-2	0-0	2-3	0-2	0-2	

29/05/2005 - 4/10/2005 • † Qualified for the CAF Champions League • ‡ Qualified for the CAF Confederation Cup

CONGO DR 2005 KINSHASA LEAGUE (EPFKIN)

	Pl	W	D	L	F	A	Pts
AS Vita Club §3	30	18	6	6	52	23	57
SC Inter	30	15	8	7	37	18	53
DC Motema Pembe §6	30	16	4	10	34	25	46
Olympic Club	30	12	9	9	34	22	45
AS Dragons §3	30	12	10	8	37	27	43
Les Stars	30	9	14	7	26	24	41
Style du Congo	30	9	14	7	21	21	41
SC Malaika	30	11	7	12	26	33	40
FC Okinawa	30	9	12	9	28	29	39
AJ Vainquers	30	9	11	10	26	33	38
Canon Buromeca	30	10	7	13	30	31	37
Bel 'Or	30	8	12	10	30	32	36
AS Manuilu	30	10	5	15	33	46	35
FC Pharmagros	30	8	10	12	23	36	34
FC Tornado	30	6	11	13	16	33	29
FC Nzakimuena	30	5	6	19	17	37	21

17/03/2004 - 25/10/2004 • §3 = Three points deducted • §6 = Six points deducted

CONGO DR 2005 COUPE DU CONGO (XXII) FINAL ROUND

Poule A

	Pl	W	D	L	F	A	Pts		
SC Cilu Lukala †	2	1	1	0	5	1	4	4-0	1-1
FC Simba Kolwezi	2	1	0	1	2	5	3		2-1
OC Muungano	2	0	1	1	2	3	1		

Poule B

	Pl	W	D	L	F	A	Pts		
AS Vita Kabasha †	2	2	0	0	5	2	6	3-1	2-1
FC Banaco Kananga	2	1	0	1	3	4	3		2-1
AS Canon Buromeca	2	0	0	2	2	4	0		

14/11/2004 - 21/11/2004 • † Qualified for the final • Played in Kinshasa

Final: **Vita Kabasha** 1-1 4-2p SC Cilu Lukala

Scorers - Masudi [63] for Vita; Lusadisu [59] for Cilu • Vita Kabasha qualify for the CAF Confederation Cup

RECENT LEAGUE AND CUP RECORD

	Championship						Cup		
Year	Champions	Pts	Runners-up	Pts	Third	Pts	Winners	Score	Runners-up
1997	AS Vita Club	†	DC Motema Pembe				AS Dragons	2-1	AS Vita Club
1998	DC Motema Pembe	13	AS Vita Club	8	SM Sanga Balende	6	AS Dragons	1-0	AS Sucrière
1999	DC Motema Pembe		TP Mazembe		AS Vita Club		AS Dragons	3-2	AS Paulino
2000	TP Mazembe	16	SM Sanga Balende	8	AS Vita Club	5	TP Mazembe	2-0	AS St-Luc Kananga
2001	TP Mazembe	†	FC St-Eloi Lupopo				AS Vita Club	3-0	AS Veti Matadi
2002	FC St-Eloi Lupopo	25	TP Mazembe	23	AS Vita Club	18	US Kenya	2-1	SM Sanga Balende
2003	AS Vita Club	27	SC Cilu	18	FC St-Eloi Lupopo	17	DC Motema Pembe	2-0	TP Mazembe
2004	DC Motema Pembe	14	TP Mazembe	11	FC St-Eloi Lupopo	6	CS Cilu Lukala	1-0	AS St Luc Kananga
2005	DC Motema Pembe	19	FC St-Eloi Lupopo	18	TP Mazembe	17	AS Vita Kabasha	1-1 4-2p	CS Cilu Lukala

† Knock-out format • Toute Puissant Mazembe beat FC Saint-Eloi Lupopo 1-1 3-1 in the 2001 final

COK – COOK ISLANDS

NATIONAL TEAM RECORD
JULY 1ST 2002 TO JULY 9TH 2006

PL	W	D	L	F	A	%
5	0	1	4	1	17	10

FIFA/COCA-COLA WORLD RANKING

1993	1994	1995	1996	1997	1998	1999	2000	2001	2002	2003	2004	2005		High	Low
-	-	-	188	192	173	182	170	179	182	190	190	194		**169** 07/00	**195** 05/06

2005–2006											
08/05	09/05	10/05	11/05	12/05	01/06	02/06	03/06	04/06	05/06	06/06	07/06
192	193	193	194	194	194	194	194	195	195	-	194

With three championships since the turn of the century, Nikao Sokattack are rapidly establishing themselves as the top club in the Cook Islands, and after successfully defending their national title in 2005 they qualified once again for the preliminary stage of the OFC Club Championship, played at Govind Park in Fiji in February 2006. Hoping for a first ever win for the country in the competition, Nikao led at half-time in their first two matches before conceding late goals against both Tuanaimato Breeze of Samoa and Lotoha'apai of Tonga. Against hosts Nokia Eagles, who won the preliminary round to qualify for the finals, they did manage a first ever point with a 0-0

INTERNATIONAL HONOURS
None

draw. Fans of rivals Tupapa would say that their team won three points at the 2001 tournament, but that was due to a game being awarded to them. Nikao's Steve Willis even managed to add to his goal from the 2005 tournament to become the all-time leading scorer from the Cook Islands in the competition! There was no national team activity at any level during the season thanks to the withdrawal of the women's U-19 team from the qualifying tournament of the FIFA U-20 Women's World Championship, although the senior women's team are scheduled to take part of the OFC Women's Championship in 2007.

THE FIFA BIG COUNT OF 2000

	Male	Female		Male	Female
Registered players	700	250	Referees	60	20
Non registered players	150	50	Officials	70	0
Youth players	900	300	Total involved	2 500	
Total players	2 350		Number of clubs	35	
Professional players	0	0	Number of teams	113	

Cook Islands Football Association (CIFA)
Matavora Main Road, PO Box 29, Tupapa, Rarotonga, Cook Islands
Tel +682 28980   Fax +682 28981
cifa@cisoccer.org.ck   www.none
President: HARMON Lee   General Secretary: ELIKANA Tingika
Vice-President: PARKER Allen   Treasurer: NUMANGA Jake   Media Officer: TONGA Vainga
Men's Coach: JERKS Tim   Women's Coach: TILLOTSON Maurice
CIFA formed: 1971   OFC: 1994   FIFA: 1994
Green shirts with white sleeves, Green shorts, White socks

RECENT INTERNATIONAL MATCHES PLAYED BY COOK ISLANDS

2002 Opponents	Score	Venue	Comp	Scorers	Att	Referee
No international matches played in 2002						
2003						
No international matches played in 2003						
2004						
5-05 Samoa	D 0-0	Auckland	Fr			
10-05 Tahiti	L 0-2	Honiara	WCq		12 000	Singh FIJ
12-05 Solomon Islands	L 0-5	Honiara	WCq		14 000	Fred VAN
15-05 Tonga	L 1-2	Honiara	WCq	Pareanga 59	15 000	Sosongan PNG
17-05 New Caledonia	L 0-8	Honiara	WCq		400	Singh FIJ
2005						
No international matches played in 2005						
2006						
No international matches played in 2006 before July						

Fr = Friendly match • WC = FIFA World Cup™ • q = qualifier

COOK ISLANDS NATIONAL TEAM RECORDS AND RECORD SEQUENCES

Records			Sequence records				
Victory	3-0	ASA 2000	Wins	2	1998, 2000	Clean sheets	1	
Defeat	0-30	TAH 1971	Defeats	6	2000-2001	Goals scored	4	1996-1998
Player Caps	n/a		Undefeated	3	1998	Without goal	5	2001-2004
Player Goals	n/a		Without win	11	2000-	Goals against	16	1971-2000

RECENT LEAGUE AND CUP RECORD

	Championship		Cup		
Year	Champions	Winners	Score	Runners-up
1996	Avatiu FC	Avatiu FC		
1997	Avatiu FC	Avatiu FC		
1998	No Tournament	Teau-o-Tonga		
1999	Tupapa FC	Tupapa FC		
1999	Avatiu FC	Avatiu FC	3-1	Tupapa FC
2000	Nikao Sokattacck	Avatiu FC	3-1	Nikao Sokattack
2001	Tupapa FC	Tupapa FC	5-1	Avatiu FC
2002	Tupapa FC	Nikao Sokattack	3-2	Tupapa FC
2003	Tupapa FC	Nikao Sokattack	3-1	Tupapa FC
2004	Nikao Sokattack	Tupapa FC	3-3 3-1p	Nikao Sokattack
2005	Nikao Sokattack	Nikao Sokattack		

COOK ISLANDS COUNTRY INFORMATION

Capital	Avarua	Independence	Self-governing in free asso-	GDP per Capita	$5 000
Population	21 200	Status	ciation with New Zealand	GNP Ranking	n/a
Area km²	240	Language	English, Maori	Dialling code	+682
Population density	88 per km²	Literacy rate	95%	Internet code	.ck
% in urban areas	n/a	Main religion	Christian	GMT +/–	-10
Towns/Cities ('000)	Avarua 13; Mangaia; Amuri; Omoka; Atiu; Mauke				
Neighbours (km)	South Pacific Ocean 120				
Main stadia	National Stadium – Avarua 3 000				

COL – COLOMBIA

NATIONAL TEAM RECORD
JULY 1ST 2002 TO JULY 9TH 2006

PL	W	D	L	F	A	%
52	17	19	16	55	48	50.9

FIFA/COCA-COLA WORLD RANKING

1993	1994	1995	1996	1997	1998	1999	2000	2001	2002	2003	2004	2005	High	Low
21	17	15	4	10	34	25	15	5	37	39	26	24	4 12/96	41 03/04

2005–2006											
08/05	09/05	10/05	11/05	12/05	01/06	02/06	03/06	04/06	05/06	06/06	07/06
24	26	23	25	24	24	27	30	27	27	-	21

Failure to qualify for a second successive FIFA World Cup™ finals was a huge disappointment for fans in Colombia, but after a terrible start to the campaign, it had always been on the cards. Failure to beat Chile at home in the penultimate round cost Colombia dear as they finished a point behind Uruguay in the play-off spot. There was also little joy on the international scene for Colombian clubs in either the 2005 Copa Sudamericana or in the 2006 Copa Libertadores, with none of the entrants getting past the round of sixteen. The Copa Libertadores title won by Once Caldas in 2004 now seems a distant memory. At home, the 2005 season saw a number of surprises, notably the

INTERNATIONAL HONOURS
Qualified for the FIFA World Cup™ finals 1962 1990 1994 1998 Copa América 2001 Juventud de América 1987 2005 South America U-17 1993
Copa Toyota Libertadores Atlético Nacional Medellín 1989 Once Caldas 2004

return to form of Independiente Santa Fe, a team without a championship since 1975. They reached the final of the Apertura - the first club from Bogota to reach a final since the new system was adopted in 1997 - but they lost to Atlético Nacional. In the Clausura, newly promoted Real Cartagena were the surprise finalists, but they too then lost to Deportivo Cali, themselves champions for the first time in eight years. The biggest surprise of all, however, was a first ever title for Deportivo Pasto, who beat Deportivo Cali in the 2006 Apertura final.

THE FIFA BIG COUNT OF 2000

	Male	Female		Male	Female
Registered players	80 000	1 000	Referees	2 000	0
Non registered players	1 300 000	10 000	Officials	12 000	400
Youth players	150 000	1 000	Total involved	1 556 400	
Total players	1 542 000		Number of clubs	2 500	
Professional players	2 500	0	Number of teams	7 000	

Federación Colombiana de Fútbol (COLFUTBOL)
Avenida 32, No. 16-22 Piso 4°, Apdo Aéreo 17602, Bogotá, Colombia
Tel +57 1 2889838   Fax +57 1 2889559
info@colfutbol.org   www.colfutbol.org
President: ASTUDILLO Oscar Dr   General Secretary: SIERRA Celina
Vice-President: YUNIS Hernan   Treasurer: MORENO Gustavo   Media Officer: ROSAS Victor
Men's Coach: RUEDA Reinaldo   Women's Coach: SILVA Jose
COLFUTBOL formed: 1924   CONMEBOL: 1940   FIFA: 1936
Yellow shirts with blue and red trimmings, Blue shorts, Red socks or Blue shirts,

RECENT INTERNATIONAL MATCHES PLAYED BY COLOMBIA

2003	Opponents	Score		Venue	Comp	Scorers	Att	Referee
7-09	Brazil	L	1-2	Barranquilla	WCq	Angel [38]	47 600	Elizondo ARG
10-09	Bolivia	L	0-4	La Paz	WCq		23 200	Oliveira BRA
15-11	Venezuela	L	0-1	Barranquilla	WCq		20 000	Chandia CHI
19-11	Argentina	D	1-1	Barranquilla	WCq	Angel [47]	19 034	Simon BRA
2004								
18-02	Honduras	D	1-1	Tegucigalpa	Fr	Herrera [58]	8 000	Alfaro SLV
31-03	Peru	W	2-0	Lima	WCq	Grisales [30], Oviedo [42]	29 325	Rezende BRA
28-04	El Salvador	W	2-0	Washington	Fr	Rey [52], Oviedo [61]	21 000	Vaughan USA
2-06	Ecuador	L	1-2	Quito	WCq	Oviedo [57]	31 484	Baldassi ARG
6-06	Uruguay	W	5-0	Barranquilla	WCq	Pacheco 2 [17 31], Moreno [20], Restrepo [81], Herrera [86]	7 000	Carlos PAR
27-06	Argentina	W	2-0	Miami	Fr	Moreno [21], Herrera [75]	32 415	Terry USA
6-07	Venezuela	W	1-0	Lima	CAr1	Moreno [22p]	45 000	Rezende BRA
9-07	Bolivia	W	1-0	Lima	CAr1	Perea [90]	35 000	Ramos ECU
12-07	Peru	D	2-2	Trujillo	CAr1	Congo [34], Aguilar [52]	25 000	Rodriguez MEX
17-07	Costa Rica	W	2-0	Trujillo	CAqf	Aguilar [41], Moreno [45p]	18 000	Mendez URU
20-07	Argentina	L	0-3	Lima	CAsf		22 000	Hidalgo PER
24-07	Uruguay	L	1-2	Cusco	CA3p	Herrera [70]	35 000	Ortube BOL
5-09	Chile	D	0-0	Santiago	WCq		62 523	Souza BRA
9-10	Paraguay	D	1-1	Barranquilla	WCq	Grisales [17]	25 000	Elizondo ARG
13-10	Brazil	D	0-0	Maceio	WCq		20 000	Larrionda ARG
17-11	Bolivia	W	1-0	Barranquilla	WCq	Yepes [18]	25 000	Torres PAR
2005								
15-01	Korea Republic	W	2-1	Los Angeles	Fr	Castillo [41p], Perea [75]	20 000	Fris
17-01	Guatemala	D	1-1	Los Angeles	Fr	Hurtado [80]	15 000	Vaughn USA
23-02	Mexico	D	1-1	Culiacan	Fr	Perea [58]	10 000	Gasso MEX
9-03	USA	L	0-3	Fullerton	Fr		7 086	Moreno MEX
26-03	Venezuela	D	0-0	Maracaibo	WCq		18 000	Simon BRA
30-03	Argentina	L	0-1	Buenos Aires	WCq		40 000	Amarilla PAR
31-05	England	L	2-3	New Jersey	Fr	Yepes [45], Ramirez.A [78]	58 000	Hall USA
4-06	Peru	W	5-0	Barranquilla	WCq	Rey [29], Soto [55], Angel [58], Restrepo [75], Perea [78]	15 000	Torres PAR
8-06	Ecuador	W	3-0	Barranquilla	WCq	Moreno 2 [5 9], Arzuaga [70]	20 402	Simon BRA
6-07	Panama	L	0-1	Miami	GCr1		10 311	Batres GUA
10-07	Honduras	L	1-2	Miami	GCr1	Moreno [30p]	17 292	Hall USA
12-07	Trinidad and Tobago	W	2-0	Miami	GCr1	Aguilar [77], Hurtado [79]	11 000	Rodriguez MEX
17-07	Mexico	W	2-1	Houston	GCqf	Castrillón [58], Aguilar [74]	60 050	Sibrian SLV
21-07	Panama	L	2-3	New Jersey	GCsf	Patiño 2 [62 88]	41 721	Sibrian SLV
4-09	Uruguay	L	2-3	Montevideo	WCq	Soto [79], Angel [82]	60 000	Elizondo ARG
8-10	Chile	D	1-1	Barranquilla	WCq	Rey [24]	22 380	Souza BRA
12-10	Paraguay	W	1-0	Asuncion	WCq	Rey [7]	12 374	Rezende BRA
2006								
1-03	Venezuela	D	1-1	Maracaibo	Fr	Soto [70]	15 000	Carpio ECU
24-05	Ecuador	D	1-1	East Rutherford	Fr	Soto [54]	52 425	Vaughn USA
27-05	Romania	D	0-0	Chicago	Fr		15 000	Hall USA
30-05	Poland	W	2-1	Chorzow	Fr	Murillo [19], Martinez [64]	40 000	Szabo HUN
2-06	Germany	L	0-3	Mönchengladbach	Fr		45 600	Hauge NOR
4-06	Morocco	W	2-0	Barcelona	Fr	Rodallega [41p], Soto [86]	11 000	Segura Garcia ESP

Fr = Friendly match • CC = FIFA Confederations Cup • GC = CONCACAF Gold Cup • CA = Copa América • WC = FIFA World Cup™
q = qualifier • r1 = first round group • qf = quarter-final • sf = semi-final • 3p = third place play-off

COLOMBIA NATIONAL TEAM RECORDS AND RECORD SEQUENCES

Records			Sequence records				
Victory	5-0	ARG 1993, URU 2004	Wins	7	1988-1989	Clean sheets	6	2001
Defeat	0-9	BRA 1957	Defeats	7	1947-1949	Goals scored	15	1995-1997
Player Caps	111	VALDERRAMA Carlos	Undefeated	27	1992-1994	Without goal	6	2002-2003
Player Goals	25	IGUARAN Arnoldo	Without win	15	1947-1957	Goals against	14	1938-46, 1961-63

COLOMBIA COUNTRY INFORMATION

Capital	Bogotá	Independence	1810 from Spain	GDP per Capita	$6 300
Population	42 310 775	Status	Republic	GNP Ranking	40
Area km²	1 138 910	Language	Spanish	Dialling code	+57
Population density	37 per km²	Literacy rate	91%	Internet code	.co
% in urban areas	73%	Main religion	Christian	GMT + / –	-5
Towns/Cities ('000)	Bogotá 7 102; Cali 2 392; Medellin 2 000; Barranquilla 1 380; Cartagena 952; Cúcuta 721; Bucaramanga 571; Pereira 440; Santa Marta 431; Ibagué 421; Pasto 382; Manizales 357				
Neighbours (km)	Venezuela 2 050; Brazil 1 643; Peru 1 496; Ecuador 590; Panama 225; North Pacific Ocean 1 448; Caribbean Sea 1 760				
Main stadia	Metropolitano – Barranquilla 58 000; Atanasio Giradot – Medellin 52 700; El Campin – Bogotá 48 600; Pascual Guerrero – Cali 45 000; Centenario – Armenia 29 000				

COLOMBIA NATIONAL TEAM PLAYERS AND COACHES

Record Caps			Record Goals			Recent Coaches	
VALDERRAMA Carlos	1985-'98	111	IGUARAN Arnoldo	1979-'93	25	GARCIA Luis	1991
ALVAREZ Leonel	1985-'97	101	ASPRILLA Faustino	1993-'01	20	ORTIZ Humberto	1992
RINCON Freddy	1990-'01	84	RINCON Freddy	1990-'01	17	MATURANA Francisco	1993-'94
PEREA Luis	1987-'94	78	ARISTIZABAL Victor	1993-'03	15	GOMEZ Hernán Dario	1995-'98
CORDOBA Oscar	1993-'03	71	VALENCIA José	1992-'98	14	ALVAREZ Javier	1999
IGUARAN Arnoldo	1979-'93	68	DE AVILA Anthony	1983-'98	13	GARCIA Luis	2000-'01
HIGUITA René	1987-'99	68	VALENCIANO Iván	1991-'00	13	MATURANA Francisco	2001
MENDOZA Alexis	1987-'97	67	ORTIZ Willington	1973-'85	12	RUEDA Reynaldo	2002
ARISTIZABAL Victor	1993-'03	66	VALDERRAMA Carlos	1985-'98	11	MATURANA Francisco	2002-'03
HERRERA Luis	1987-'96	62				RUEDA Reynaldo	2004-

CLUB DIRECTORY

Club	Town/City	Stadium	Capacity	www.	Lge	CL
América	Cali	Pascual Guerrero	45 000	america.com.co	12	0
Atlético Bucaramanga	Bucaramanga	Alfonso Lopez	33 000		0	0
Deportivo Cali	Cali	Pascual Guerrero	45 000	deporcali.com	8	0
Chicó	Bogotá	Alfonso Lopez	12 000	chicofc.com	0	0
Envigado	Envigado	Polideportivo Sur	12 000	envigadofutbolclub.com	0	0
Atlético Huila	Neiva	Guillermo Alcid	15 000	elatleticohuila.com	0	0
Atlético Junior	Barranquilla	Metropolitano	58 000		5	0
Independiente Medellin	Medellin	Atanasio Girardot	52 700	dim.com.co	4	0
Millonarios	Bogota	El Campin	48 600	millonarios.com.co	13	0
Atlético Nacional	Medellin	Atanasio Girardot	52 700	atlnacional.com.co	8	1
Once Caldas	Manizales	Palogrande	33 000	oncecaldas.com.co	2	1
Deportivo Pasto	Pasto	Libertad	14 000	deporpasto.com	1	0
Deportivo Pereira	Pereira	Olimpico	34 000	clubdeportivopereira.com	0	0
Deportes Quindio	Armenia	Centenario	29 000		1	0
Independiente Santa Fe	Bogotá	El Campin	48 600	independientesantafe.com	6	0
Deportes Tolima	Ibagué	Manuel Toro	19 000	deportestolima.com	1	0
Corporación Tuluá	Tuluá	12 de Octubre	12 000	cortulua.com.co	0	0
Unión Magdalena	Santa Marta	Eduardo Santos	23 000		1	0

RECENT LEAGUE AND CUP RECORD

Championship Play-off/Apertura from 2002				Clausura		
Year	Champions	Score	Runners-up	Winners	Score	Runners-up
1997	América Cali	1-0 2-0	Atlético Bucaramanga			
1998	Deportivo Cali	4-0 0-0	Once Caldas			
1999	Atlético Nacional	1-1 0-0 4-2p	América Cali			
2000	América Cali	‡	Atlético Junior			
2001	América Cali	1-0 2-0	Independiente Medellin			
2002	América Cali	2-1 1-0	Independiente Medellín	Independiente Medellín	2-0 1-1	Deportivo Pasto
2003	Once Caldas	0-0 1-0	Atlético Junior	Deportes Tolima	2-0 1-3 4-2p	Deportivo Cali
2004	Independiente Medellin	2-1 0-0	Atlético Nacional	Atlético Junior	3-0 2-5 5-4p	Atlético Nacional
2005	Atlético Nacional	0-0 2-0	Independiente Santa Fe	Deportivo Cali	2-0 1-0	Real Cartagena
2006	Deportivo Pasto	1-0 1-1	Deportivo Cali			

Colombia adopted the format of two Championships per year in 2002 • ‡ Final tournament played as a league

COLOMBIA 2005
DIMAYOR TORNEO APERTURA

	Pl	W	D	L	F	A	Pts
Atlético Nacional †	18	10	6	2	36	20	36
Indep. Santa Fe †	18	7	7	4	20	16	28
Indep. Medellín †	18	8	3	7	22	23	27
Envigado †	18	7	6	5	33	24	27
Deportivo Cali †	18	7	6	5	24	18	27
Atlético Huila †	18	7	6	5	16	12	27
Deportes Tolima †	18	6	9	3	21	14	27
Once Caldas †	18	6	8	4	21	17	26
Deportivo Pasto	18	6	8	4	22	21	26
Atlétici Junior	18	7	4	7	26	23	25
Real Cartagena	18	7	3	8	18	20	24
América Cali	18	6	6	6	24	26	24
Boyacá Chicó	18	6	4	8	18	19	22
Millonarios	18	4	9	5	25	33	21
Atlético Bucaramanga	18	5	5	8	14	18	20
Unión Magdalena	18	4	4	10	11	22	16
Deportes Quindío	18	4	4	10	14	32	16
Deportes Pereira	18	2	8	8	15	22	14

12/02/2005 - 15/05/2005 • † Qualified for the second stage

TORNEO CLAUSURA SECOND STAGE

Group A	Pl	W	D	L	F	A	Pts			
Deportivo Cali †	6	3	2	1	10	6	11		2-0	3-1	0-0
Atlético Junior	6	3	1	2	7	8	10	3-2		1-0	2-1
Once Caldas	6	2	0	4	7	9	6	0-1	2-0		2-1
América Cali	6	1	3	2	8	9	6	2-2	1-1	3-2	

Group B	Pl	W	D	L	F	A	Pts			
Real Cartagena †	6	3	1	2	9	6	10		1-0	4-0	3-2
Indep. Medellín	6	3	1	2	9	7	10	2-0		0-2	2-1
Indep. Santa Fe	6	2	2	2	6	8	8	1-1	1-1		2-1
Deportes Pereira	6	2	0	4	8	11	6	1-0	2-4	1-0	

12/11/2005 - 11/12/2005 • † Qualified for the final

TORNEO CLAUSURA FINAL

Home team first leg	Score	Home team second leg
Real Cartagena	0-2 0-1	**Deportivo Cali**

COLOMBIA 2005
PRIMERA B (2) FIRST ROUND

	Pl	W	D	L	F	A	Pts
Cúcuta Deportivo †	34	17	10	7	45	24	61
Patriotas Tunja †	34	17	10	7	51	33	61
Corporación Tuluá †	34	16	10	8	45	32	58
Valledupar †	34	16	9	9	44	32	57
Academica Bogotá †	34	15	9	10	49	37	54
Pumas de Casanare †	34	15	9	10	46	35	54
Deportivo Rionegro †	34	14	11	9	54	38	53
Bajo Cauca †	34	14	11	9	54	43	53
CD La Equidad Bogotá	34	13	12	9	35	35	51
Florida SC Medellín	34	13	7	14	37	51	46
Expreso Rojo	34	12	10	12	46	34	46
Bogotá FC	34	11	8	15	50	45	41
Centauros Villavicencio	34	10	9	15	38	56	39
Barranquilla FC	34	8	12	14	39	47	36
Bello FC	34	8	11	15	34	51	35
Alianza Petrolera	34	6	15	13	30	49	33
Depor FC Cartajo	34	6	10	18	33	53	28
Girardot FC	34	4	9	21	24	59	21

† Qualified for the second round

TORNEO APERTURA SECOND STAGE

Group A	Pl	W	D	L	F	A	Pts			
Atlético Nacional †	6	4	2	0	11	5	14		4-1	2-1	0-0
Deportes Tolima	6	4	1	1	13	9	13	1-1		3-1	3-1
Indep. Medellín	6	2	0	4	11	15	6	1-2	2-4		4-3
Deportivo Cali	6	0	1	5	6	12	1	1-2	0-1	1-2	

Group B	Pl	W	D	L	F	A	Pts			
Indep. Santa Fe †	6	4	0	2	8	5	12		0-2	4-2	2-0
Envigado	6	3	2	1	9	6	11	0-1		2-1	2-1
Atlético Huila	6	1	3	2	10	12	6	1-0	2-2		2-2
Once Caldas	6	0	3	3	6	10	3	0-1	1-1	2-2	

18/05/2005 - 19/06/2005 • † Qualified for the final

TORNEO APERTURA FINAL

Home team first leg	Score	Home team second leg
Independiente Santa Fé	0-0 0-2	**Atlético Nacional Medellín**

COLOMBIA 2005
DIMAYOR TORNEO CLAUSURA

	Pl	W	D	L	F	A	Pts
Deportivo Cali †	18	8	6	4	30	23	30
Indep. Medellín †	18	9	2	7	28	23	29
América Cali †	18	9	2	7	24	20	29
Deportes Pereira †	18	9	2	7	27	26	29
Atlético Junior †	18	9	2	7	22	27	29
Real Cartagena †	18	8	5	5	26	19	29
Once Caldas †	18	8	5	5	25	21	29
Indep. Santa Fe †	18	8	5	5	20	17	29
Deportes Tolima	18	8	3	7	24	18	27
Atlético Bucaramanga	18	7	6	5	24	16	27
Atlético Nacional	18	6	8	4	22	16	26
Deportivo Pasto	18	7	4	7	20	18	25
Deportes Quindío	18	7	4	7	18	19	25
Millonarios	18	7	3	8	22	21	24
Envigado	18	5	6	7	20	22	21
Atlético Huila	18	4	4	10	18	32	16
Boyacá Chicó	18	3	6	9	12	24	15
Unión Magdalena	18	0	7	11	15	35	7

10/07/2005 - 6/11/2005 • † Qualified for the second stage

PRIMERA B SECOND STAGE

Group A	Pl	W	D	L	F	A	Pts			
Cúcuta Deportivo †	6	4	1	1	9	5	13		2-1	3-1	2-0
Corporación Tuluá	6	3	1	2	9	7	10	2-0		2-0	2-2
Academica Bogotá	6	2	1	3	5	6	7	0-0	3-0		1-0
Deportivo Rionegro	6	1	1	4	4	9	4	1-2	0-2	1-0	

Group B	Pl	W	D	L	F	A	Pts			
Bajo Cauca †	6	3	2	1	10	7	11		2-0	3-3	2-0
Patriotas Tunja	6	3	1	2	9	4	10	2-0		1-0	5-0
Valledupar	6	1	3	2	8	10	6	2-2	2-1		1-3
Pumas de Casanare	6	1	2	3	3	9	5	0-1	0-0	0-0	

† Qualified for the final

PRIMERA B FINAL

Home team first leg	Score	Home team second leg
Bajo Cauca	1-1 0-1	**Cúcuta Deportivo**

Cúcuta Deportivo promoted to replace Unión Magdalena

COLOMBIA 2005 LIGA DIMAYOR REGULAR SEASON RESULTS

PRIMERA A

	América	Bucaramanga	Cali	Cartagena	Boyacá Chicó	Envigado	Huila	Junior	Magdalena	Medellín	Millonarios	Nacional	Once Caldas	Pasto	Pereira	Quindío	Santa Fe	Tolima
América Cali	—	1-2	0-0 2-0	2-1	1-1	1-0	2-1	4-1	2-1	3-2	1-1	1-0	1-1	1-0	0-1	2-2	2-2	0-2
Atlético Bucaramanga	0-2	—	1-1	0-1 2-1	1-1	0-0	2-0	0-2	2-1	4-0	2-2	2-1	1-1	2-0	0-1	2-0	3-0	0-0
Deportivo Cali	2-0 1-2	2-0	—	2-2	1-0	1-1	2-0	4-1	4-2	0-1	4-2	3-3	3-0	2-2	3-0	3-0	1-1	1-2
Real Cartagena	2-1	1-0 3-0	0-1	—	2-1	0-1	1-1	3-1	2-1	1-3	3-1	1-3	3-0	1-0	1-1	1-0	0-2	2-1
Boyacá Chicó	1-0	2-0	0-0	1-2	—	1-0	1-0	2-0	1-0	2-1	0-2	0-0	1-1	3-4 0-2	2-1	0-2	0-1	0-0
Envigado	1-1	2-2	0-0	1-1	1-2	—	1-1	3-0	2-1	3-3	4-1	2-4	1-2	2-0	2-1	3-0	2-1	2-0
Atlético Huila	3-0	0-3	2-0	2-2	3-0	2-1	—	1-2	0-0	1-0	1-0	0-0	3-3	0-4	1-2	2-0	0-0	0-0 2-1
Atlético Junior	5-3	0-0	3-1	0-0	2-1	3-2	1-0	—	0-1 2-1	2-3	4-3	2-0	1-0	1-0	2-0	3-1	1-1	1-0
Unión Magdalena	1-3	0-2	2-0	0-1	2-2	1-3	0-1	1-0 1-2	—	0-2	1-1	2-2	1-1	2-0	1-1	0-1	1-1	0-0
Indep. Medellín	3-1	0-1	0-1	2-1	1-0	1-1	4-1	1-0	5-0	—	2-1	0-4 1-1	1-0	2-1	2-0	4-0	1-0	0-2
Millonarios	0-1	1-1	1-2	2-1	2-2	2-1	2-0	0-0	1-0	1-0	—	0-0	2-1	1-0	0-0	3-0	1-0 0-3 1-3	2-0
Atlético Nacional	2-1	3-2	5-0	1-1	2-0	1-0	1-2	0-1	2-0	3-1 3-2	1-1	—	2-1	1-0	0-0	3-0	1-1	1-3
Once Caldas	1-0	0-0	1-1	1-0	2-1	2-2	1-0	2-1	4-0	3-0	2-1	1-2	—	1-0	1-0 3-3	1-0	0-0	1-2
Deportivo Pasto	2-0	1-0	1-0	1-1	1-0 1-1	2-1	3-1	2-1	1-1	0-1	1-0	1-0	1-1	—	0-0	1-0	1-1	2-1
Deportivo Pereira	1-2	1-0	0-2	1-0	2-0	1-1	0-0	2-1	3-0	3-0	0-2	1-1	2-2 0-2	5-3	—	1-1	0-1	2-0
Deportes Quindío	1-0	2-1	1-1	1-0	1-4	2-0	0-1	3-1	2-0	0-0	3-3	1-1	0-1	1-1	3-2	—	0-0	1-0
Indep. Santa Fe	2-5	0-0	1-3	1-0	1-0	0-0	1-0	1-0	0-0	2-1	0-1 1-0	1-2	1-0	2-0	4-2	3-1	—	0-2
Deportes Tolima	0-0	1-0	2-0	1-2	1-1	4-1	1-2 2-0	1-1	1-1	0-0	3-3	1-1	3-1	1-1	2-0	3-0	2-1	—

Apertura results are in the shaded boxes • Local rivals play each other four times in the regular season. In this instance Apertura results are listed first

---

COLOMBIA 2006 DIMAYOR TORNEO APERTURA

	Pl	W	D	L	F	A	Pts
Once Caldas †	18	10	7	1	31	15	37
Cúcuta Deportivo †	18	11	4	3	29	14	37
Deportes Tolima †	18	9	5	4	36	19	32
Atlético Nacional †	18	9	3	6	27	19	30
Deportes Pereira †	18	7	8	3	20	15	29
Millonarios †	18	7	7	4	27	23	28
Deportivo Cali †	18	8	4	6	20	17	28
Deportivo Pasto †	18	7	6	5	28	21	27
Deportes Quindío	18	8	3	7	18	17	27
América Cali	18	8	3	7	20	25	27
Envigado	18	5	7	6	20	22	22
Atlético Bucaramanga	18	6	3	9	17	23	21
Boyacá Chicó	18	4	8	6	19	22	20
Indep. Santa Fe	18	5	5	8	24	32	20
Atlético Huila	18	6	2	10	17	33	20
Atlético Junior	18	4	5	9	22	29	17
Indep. Medellín	18	3	5	10	15	28	14
Real Cartagena	18	2	1	15	14	30	7

4/02/2006 - 21/05/2006 • † Qualified for the second stage

TORNEO APERTURA SECOND STAGE

Group A	Pl	W	D	L	F	A	Pts	DC	DT	OC	DP
Deportivo Cali †	6	3	3	0	11	6	12		2-2	2-1	4-1
Deportes Tolima	6	2	3	1	9	8	9	0-0		4-0	2-1
Once Caldas	6	2	1	3	7	10	7	0-1	1-1		3-1
Deportes Pereira	6	1	1	4	10	13	4	2-2	4-0	1-2	

Group B	Pl	W	D	L	F	A	Pts	DP	CD	AN	Mi
Deportivo Pasto †	6	4	1	1	9	5	13		2-0	2-1	1-1
Cúcuta Deportivo	6	3	1	2	8	8	10	0-1		2-1	2-1
Atlético Nacional	6	2	0	4	9	10	6	1-3	2-3		2-0
Millonarios	6	1	2	3	5	8	5	2-0	1-1	0-2	

31/05/2006 - 18/06/2006 • † Qualified for the final

TORNEO APERTURA FINAL

Home team first leg	Score	Home team second leg
Deportivo Cali	0-1 1-1	**Deportivo Pasto**

COM – COMOROS

NATIONAL TEAM RECORD
JULY 1ST 2002 TO JULY 9TH 2006

PL	W	D	L	F	A	%
0	0	0	0	0	0	0

FIFA/COCA-COLA WORLD RANKING

1993	1994	1995	1996	1997	1998	1999	2000	2001	2002	2003	2004	2005	High	Low
-	-	-	-	-	-	-	-	-	-	-	-	-	-	-

2005–2006											
08/05	09/05	10/05	11/05	12/05	01/06	02/06	03/06	04/06	05/06	06/06	07/06
-	-	-	-	-	-	-	-	-	-	-	-

There was an emotive burst of applause in Cairo in January when the Comoros Islands became the 53rd member of the Confederation of African Football and collected their flag from the main stage at the organisation's congress, as a symbol of their welcome to the world's footballing family. Just weeks later, the island nation's first ever international football match saw a spirited performance from their league champions Coin Nord Mitsamiouli, but they succumbed to an extra time goal and were eliminated from the CAF Champions League. Mitsamiouli lost 1-0 away to AS Port Louis 2000 in Curepipe, Mauritius in a one-off tie in the first round. The lack of adequate playing facilities in the

INTERNATIONAL HONOURS
None

Comoros meant that the tie was decided over just one match and it proved a gutsy first outing although a slip of concentration just four minutes from time ended the possibility of a fairytale start. The Comoros also entered a side in the CAF Confederation Cup but there was a similar disappointment for Elan Club whose one-off tie away at Ferroviario Beira ended in a 2-0 defeat. A first full international for the island archipelago's national side is still some way off as they did not enter the qualifiers for the 2008 African Nations Cup. The Comoros did play in the past in the Indian Ocean Island games but the matches are not recognised as full internationals because Comoros were not FIFA members then.

THE FIFA BIG COUNT OF 2000

	Male	Female		Male	Female
Registered players	n/a	n/a	Referees	n/a	n/a
Non registered players	n/a	n/a	Officials	n/a	n/a
Youth players	n/a	n/a	Total involved	n/a	
Total players		n/a	Number of clubs	n/a	
Professional players	n/a	n/a	Number of teams	n/a	

Fédération Comorienne de Football (FFC)
Case Postale 798, Moroni, Comoros
Tel +269 733179   Fax +269 733236
dhl@snpt.km   www.none
President: FAKRIDINE Mahamoud   General Secretary: ABDOU CHAKOUR Mariata
Vice-President: TOURQUI Salim   Treasurer: TBD   Media Officer: None
Men's Coach: none   Women's Coach: none
FFC formed: 1979   CAF: 1986   FIFA: 2005

RECENT INTERNATIONAL MATCHES PLAYED BY COMOROS

2002 Opponents	Score	Venue	Comp	Scorers	Att	Referee
No international matches played in 2002						
2003						
30-08 Reunion †	L 0-1	Flacq	IOr1		103	Labrosse SEY
2-09 Reunion †	L 0-4	Flacq	IOr1			
4-09 Mauritius †	L 0-5	Curepipe	IOsf		4 500	Labrosse SEY
6-09 Seychelles †	L 0-2	Curepipe	IO3p			
2004						
No international matches played in 2004						
2005						
No international matches played in 2005						
2006						
No international matches played in 2006 before July						

IO = Indian Ocean Games • r1 = first round group • sf = semi-final • 3p = third place play-off • † Not regarded as full internationals because Comoros was not yet a member of FIFA

COMOROS NATIONAL TEAM RECORDS AND RECORD SEQUENCES

Records			Sequence records					
Victory	2-1	REU 1979	Wins	1	1979, 1990	Clean sheets	1	1990
Defeat	1-6	REU 1979	Defeats	10	1990-	Goals scored	3	1979
Player Caps	n/a		Undefeated	1	1979, 1985, 1990	Without goal	8	1993-
Player Goals	n/a		Without win	10	1990	Goals against	10	1990-

Comoros joined FIFA in 2005 and have yet to play an official international. The above data relates to games played in the Indian Ocean Games

RECENT LEAGUE AND CUP RECORD

	Comoros	Grande Comore	Anjouan	Mwali	Cup
Year	Champions	Champions	Champions	Champions	Winners
2003		Volcan Club		Belle Lumière	Coin Nord
2004		Elan Club	Etoile d'Or	Belle Lumière	
2005	Coin Nord	Coin Nord	Chirazienne	Belle Lumière	
2006					

COMOROS COUNTRY INFORMATION

Capital	Moroni	Independence	1975 from France	GDP per Capita	$700
Population	671 247	Status	Republic	GNP Ranking	155
Area km²	2 170	Language	Arabic, French, Shikomoro	Dialling code	+269
Population density	309 per km²	Literacy rate	56.5%	Internet code	.km
% in urban areas	34%	Main religion	Muslim 98%	GMT +/−	+3
Towns/Cities ('000)	Moroni 42 (Grande Comore/Njazidja); Mutsamudu 14 (Anjouan/Nzwani); Fomboni 14 (Moheli/Mwali)				
Neighbours (km)	Indian Ocean 340				
Main stadia	Stade de Beaumer, Moroni				

CPV – CAPE VERDE ISLANDS

NATIONAL TEAM RECORD
JULY 1ST 2002 TO JULY 9TH 2006

PL	W	D	L	F	A	%
23	7	3	13	25	35	36.9

FIFA/COCA-COLA WORLD RANKING

1993	1994	1995	1996	1997	1998	1999	2000	2001	2002	2003	2004	2005	High	Low
147	161	144	155	171	167	177	156	159	154	143	129	118	119 05/05	182 04/00

2005–2006											
08/05	09/05	10/05	11/05	12/05	01/06	02/06	03/06	04/06	05/06	06/06	07/06
123	122	123	120	118	119	120	122	122	123	-	102

At the halfway point in the 2006 FIFA World Cup™ preliminaries in June 2005, the tiny island archipelago found itself within one win from an unlikely place at the top of the qualifying group and with dreams of a potential trip to the finals in Germany. But after losing at home to South Africa, their hopes faded and in the end they had to settle for second-last place in the group, losing their last four matches. The end of the campaign also marked the end of the coaching career of Alexandre Alhinho, whose tutelage had seen the Cape Verdians climb to the brink of a place in the top 100 of the FIFA/Coca-Cola World Ranking. Alhinho, brother of the former Portuguese international Carlos, had

INTERNATIONAL HONOURS
Copa Amilcar Cabral 2000

done much to convince Portuguese players of Cape Verdian descent to throw in their international futures with the island state. As a result, the team's competitiveness had been greatly enhanced by the likes of Cafu, Nene and in particular, Sandro, the Vitoria Setubal midfielder and team captain. Alhinho's assistant Jose Rui, a former professional in Portugal, has taken over at the helm of the side. League success went to Sporting Praia, who beat Academico Sal 3-2 on aggregate in the championship play-off, winning 1-0 away in the first leg and drawing 2-2 in the return in the capital. Financial constraints kept Cape Verdian clubs from participating in the annual African club competitions.

THE FIFA BIG COUNT OF 2000

	Male	Female		Male	Female
Registered players	6 350	0	Referees	191	2
Non registered players	5 200	0	Officials	550	0
Youth players	2 810	0	Total involved	15 103	
Total players	14 360		Number of clubs	89	
Professional players	600	0	Number of teams	154	

Federação Caboverdiana de Futebol (FCF)
Praia Cabo Verde, FCF CX, Case postale 234, Praia, Cape Verde Islands
Tel +238 2 611362   Fax +238 2 611362
fcf@cvtelecom.cv   www.fcf.cv
President: SEMEDO Mario   General Secretary: REZENDE Jose João
Vice-President: ALMEIDA Fernando   Treasurer: REZENDE Jose João   Media Officer: None
Men's Coach: ZE RUI Carlos   Women's Coach: none
FCF formed: 1982   CAF: 1986   FIFA: 1986
Blue shirts, Blue shorts, Blue socks or White shirts, White shorts, Red socks

RECENT INTERNATIONAL MATCHES PLAYED BY THE CAPE VERDE ISLANDS

2002 Opponents	Score		Venue	Comp	Scorers	Att	Referee
6-09 Mauritania	W	2-0	Nouakchott	CNq	Litos [44], Toni [60]		Sillah GAM
13-10 Kenya	L	0-1	Praia	CNq			Aboubacar CIV
20-11 Luxembourg	D	0-0	Hesperange	Fr		2 750	Leduntu FRA
2003							
29-03 Togo	W	2-1	Praia	CNq	Duka [64], Calo [75p]		Nandigna GNB
31-05 Senegal	L	1-2	Dakar	Fr	Calo [38]	20 000	Carlos Santos GNB
8-06 Togo	L	2-5	Lome	CNq	Lito [7], Calo [27]		Pare BFA
21-06 Mauritania *	W	3-0	Praia	CNq	Lito [58], Calo 2 [72p 73]		
5-07 Kenya	L	0-1	Nairobi	CNq		35 000	
12-10 Swaziland	D	1-1	Mbabane	WCq	Calo [59]	5 000	Teshome ERI
16-11 Swaziland	W	3-0	Praia	WCq	Cafu 2 [51 65], Calo [89]	6 000	Aboubacar CIV
2004							
5-06 South Africa	L	1-2	Bloemfontein	WCq	Janicio [78]	30 000	Tessema ETH
13-06 Senegal	L	1-3	Praia	Fr	Gabei [76]	10 000	
19-06 Uganda	W	1-0	Praia	WCq	Cafu [42]	5 000	Coulibaly MLI
3-07 Congo DR	D	1-1	Praia	WCq	Modeste [26]	3 800	NAHI CIV
5-09 Ghana	L	0-2	Kumasi	WCq		35 000	Tamuni LBY
9-10 Burkina Faso	W	1-0	Praia	WCq	Cafu [2]	6 000	Aziaka TOG
2005							
26-03 Burkina Faso	W	2-1	Ouagadougou	WCq	Calo 2 [48 87]	27 500	Evehe CMR
4-06 South Africa	L	1-2	Praia	WCq	Gomes [77]	6 000	Benouza ALG
18-06 Uganda	L	0-1	Kampala	WCq		5 000	Kidane ERI
17-08 Angola	L	1-2	Lisbon	Fr	Lito [26]		
4-09 Congo DR	L	1-2	Kinshasa	WCq	Cafu [24]	75 000	Guezzaz MAR
8-10 Ghana	L	0-4	Praia	WCq		6 500	Daami TUN
2006							
27-05 Portugal	L	1-4	Evora	Fr	OG [21]		

Fr = Friendly match • CN = CAF African Cup of Nations • WC = FIFA World Cup™
q = qualifier • * Abandoned after 85 minutes when Mauritania were reduced to six players - the result stood

CAPE VERDE ISLANDS NATIONAL TEAM RECORDS AND RECORD SEQUENCES

Records			Sequence records				
Victory	3-0	GNB 81, MTN 03, SWZ 03	Wins	3	2000	Clean sheets	3	2000
Defeat	2-5	SEN 1981	Defeats	4	1982-83, 1985-87	Goals scored	7	2000
Player Caps	n/a		Undefeated	7	2000	Without goal	5	1985-87, 1998-2000
Player Goals	n/a		Without win	9	1997-2000	Goals against	9	1988-1989

RECENT LEAGUE RECORD

	Championship						Championship Play-off		
Year	Champions	Pts	Runners-up	Pts	Third	Pts	Champions	Score	Runners-up
2000	Derby São Vicente						Derby São Vicente	1-1 1-0	Académica B'vista
2001	Onze Unidos	14	Académica do Sal	13	Botafogo	11			
2002	Sporting da Praia	19	Batuque	19	Académica Fogo	16			
2003	Académico do Sal						Académico do Sal	3-1 3-2	FC Ultramarina
2004	Sal-Rei SC						Sal-Rei SC	2-0 1-2	Académica Praia
2005	Derby São Vicente						Derby São Vicente	1-1 4-3	Sporting da Praia
2006	Sporting da Praia						Sporting da Praia	1-0 2-2	Académica do Sal

CAPE VERDE ISLANDS COUNTRY INFORMATION

Capital	Praia	Independence	1975 from Portugal	GDP per Capita	$1 400
Population	415 294	Status	Republic	GNP Ranking	166
Area km²	4 033	Language	Portuguese	Dialling code	+238
Population density	102 per km²	Literacy rate	76%	Internet code	.cv
% in urban areas	54%	Main religion	Christian	GMT +/-	-1
Towns/Cities ('000)	Praia 111; Mindelo 69; Santa Maria 16; Pedra Badejo 9; São Filipe 8; Assomada 7				
Neighbours (km)	Cape Verde consists of a group of 13 islands in the North Atlantic Ocean				
Main stadia	Estadio da Varzea – Praia 8 000; Estadio Municipal Adérito Sena – Midelo 5 000				

CRC – COSTA RICA

NATIONAL TEAM RECORD
JULY 1ST 2002 TO JULY 9TH 2006

PL	W	D	L	F	A	%
60	24	10	26	86	87	48.3

FIFA/COCA-COLA WORLD RANKING

1993	1994	1995	1996	1997	1998	1999	2000	2001	2002	2003	2004	2005		High		Low
42	65	78	72	51	67	64	60	30	21	17	27	21		17	05/03	93 07/96

	2005–2006										
08/05	09/05	10/05	11/05	12/05	01/06	02/06	03/06	04/06	05/06	06/06	07/06
21	19	20	21	21	21	25	25	26	26	-	45

Qualification for the finals of the 2006 FIFA World Cup™ was the crowning moment for a golden generation of players from Costa Rica. The likes of Luis Marin and Paulo Wanchope have been mainstays of the national team for the best part of a decade, during which time Costa Rica have qualified for consecutive finals. There was no getting over the fact, however, that after a bright first game against Germany, the Costa Ricans had a disappointing tournament, especially the 3-0 defeat at the hands of Ecuador. Earlier in the year Deportivo Saprissa had finished as 'best of the rest'

INTERNATIONAL HONOURS

Qualified for the FIFA World Cup™ finals 1990 2002 2006 Central American Championship 1941 1946 1948 1953 1955 1960 1961 1963
UNCAF Championship 1991 1997 1999 2003 2005 CONCACAF U-20 Championship 1954 1960 1988 CONCACAF U-17 Championship 1994
CONCACAF Club Championship LD Alajuelense 1986 2004 Deportivo Saprissa 1993 1995 2005 CS Cartiginés 1995

behind Europe and South America in the 2005 FIFA Club World Championship in Tokyo. Having lost to Liverpool in the semi-finals, they then beat Al Ittihad to take third place. They couldn't defend their continental title, however, as both they and LD Alajuelense lost in the semi-finals to Mexico's Toluca and América respectively. Saprissa did win back their domestic title from LD Alajuelense. They won both stages of the championship, beating Perez Zeledon in the final of the Apertura on penalties, and LD Alajuelense in the Clausura, so no play-off was needed.

THE FIFA BIG COUNT OF 2000

	Male	Female		Male	Female
Registered players	2 740	1 200	Referees	120	5
Non registered players	35 000	1 500	Officials	1 500	20
Youth players	28 248	0	Total involved	70 333	
Total players		68 688	Number of clubs	128	
Professional players	1 040	0	Number of teams	5 760	

Federación Costarricense de Fútbol (FEDEFUTBOL)
Costado Norte Estatua, León Cortés, Sabana Este, San José 670-1000, Costa Rica
Tel +506 2221544   Fax +506 2552674
ejecutivo@fedefutbol.com   www.fedefutbol.com
President: NAVARRO Hermes   General Secretary: CASTRO Milton
Vice-President: ORLANDO Moreira   Treasurer: RODRIGO Gonzalez   Media Officer: HIDALGO Marvin
Men's Coach: TBD   Women's Coach: RODRIGUEZ Ricardo
FEDEFUTBOL formed: 1921   CONMEBOL: 1962   FIFA: 1927
Red shirts, Blue shorts, White socks or White shirts, White shorts, Red socks

RECENT INTERNATIONAL MATCHES PLAYED BY COSTA RICA

2004	Opponents	Score		Venue	Comp	Scorers	Att	Referee
31-03	Mexico	L	0-2	Carson	Fr		27 000	Stott USA
4-06	Nicaragua	W	5-1	San Carlos	Fr	Scott [19], Ledezma [30], Parks.W 2 [46 57], Solis.A [90]	BCD	
12-06	Cuba	D	2-2	Havana	WCq	Sequeira [12], Saborio [42]	18 500	Archundia MEX
20-06	Cuba	D	1-1	Alajuela	WCq	Gomez [31]	12 000	Prendergast JAM
8-07	Paraguay	L	0-1	Arequipa	CAr1		30 000	Ruiz COL
11-07	Brazil	L	1-4	Arequipa	CAr1	Marin [81]	12 000	Baldassi ARG
14-07	Chile	W	2-1	Tacna	CAr1	Wright [59], Herron [90]	20 000	Ortube BOL
17-07	Colombia	L	0-2	Trujillo	CAqf		18 000	Mendez URU
18-08	Honduras	L	2-5	Alajuela	WCq	Herron 2 [20 36]	14 000	Rodriguez MEX
5-09	Guatemala	L	1-2	Guatemala City	WCq	Solis [24]	27 460	Stott USA
8-09	Canada	W	1-0	San Jose	WCq	Wanchope [46]	13 000	Ramdhan TRI
9-10	Guatemala	W	5-0	San Jose	WCq	Hernandez.C [19], Wanchope 3 [36 62 69], Fonseca [83]	18 000	Archundia MEX
13-10	Canada	W	3-1	Vancouver	WCq	Wanchope [49], Sunsing [81] Hernandez.C [87]	4 000	Prendergast JAM
17-11	Honduras	D	0-0	San Pedro Sula	WCq		18 000	Sibrian SLV
2005								
12-01	Haiti	D	3-3	San Jose	Fr	Centeno [2], Scott [10], Herron [13p]		Porras CRC
9-02	Mexico	L	1-2	San Jose	WCq	Wanchope [38]	22 000	Batres GUA
16-02	Ecuador	L	1-2	Heredia	Fr	Alfaro [46]	1 000	Duran CRC
21-02	El Salvador	W	2-1	Guatemala City	GCq	Wilson [75], Myrie [90]	3 000	Batres GUA
23-02	Panama	W	1-0	Guatemala City	GCq	Myrie [83]	3 000	Archundia MEX
25-02	Guatemala	W	4-0	Guatemala City	GCq	Segura [9], Sequeira [22], Wilson [41], Scott [61]	11 159	Archundia MEX
27-02	Honduras	D	1-1	Guatemala City	GCq	Wilson [68], W 7-6p	1 491	Batres GUA
26-03	Panama	W	2-1	San Jose	WCq	Wilson [40p], Myre [91+]	8 000	Rodriguez MEX
30-03	Trinidad and Tobago	D	0-0	Port of Spain	WCq		8 000	Navarro CAN
24-05	Norway	L	0-1	Oslo	Fr		21 251	Van Egmond NED
4-06	USA	L	0-3	Salt Lake City	WCq		40 586	Batres GUA
8-06	Guatemala	W	3-2	San Jose	WCq	Hernandez.C [34], Gomez [65], Wanchope [92+]	BCD	Archundia MEX
19-06	China PR	D	2-2	Changsha	Fr	Solis [57], Gomez [75]	20 000	Lee Gi Young KOR
22-06	China PR	L	0-2	Guangzhou	Fr		15 000	Yu Byung Seob KOR
7-07	Canada	W	1-0	Seattle	GCr1	Soto.J [30p]	15 831	Prendergast JAM
9-07	Cuba	W	3-1	Seattle	GCr1	Brenes 2 [61 85p], Soto.J [81p]	15 109	Archundia MEX
12-07	USA	D	0-0	Foxboro	GCr1		15 211	Archundia MEX
16-07	Honduras	L	2-3	Foxboro	GCqf	Bolaños [39], Ruíz [81]	22 108	Archundia MEX
17-08	Mexico	L	0-2	Mexico City	WCq		27 000	Pineda HON
3-09	Panama	W	3-1	Panama City	WCq	Saborio [44], Centeno [51], Gomez [73]	21 000	Stott USA
7-09	Trinidad and Tobago	W	2-0	San Jose	WCq	Saborio [15], Centeno [50]	17 000	Batres GUA
8-10	USA	W	3-0	San Jose	WCq	Wanchope [34], Hernandez.C 2 [60 88]	18 000	Archundia MEX
12-10	Guatemala	L	1-3	Guatemala City	WCq	Myre [60]	23 912	Hall USA
9-11	France	L	2-3	Fort-de-France	Fr	Saborio [14], Fonseca [41]	16 216	Pineda MEX
2006								
11-02	Korea Republic	W	1-0	Oakland	Fr	Saborio [40p]		Vaughn USA
1-03	Iran	L	2-3	Tehran	Fr	Hernandez.C [43], Fonseca [60]	25 000	Al Marzouqi UAE
28-05	Ukraine	L	0-4	Kyiv	Fr		25 000	Ivanov.N RUS
30-05	Czech Republic	L	0-1	Jablonec	Fr		14 500	Bede HUN
9-06	Germany	L	2-4	Munich	WCr1	Wanchope 2 [12 73]	66 000	Elizondo ARG
15-06	Ecuador	L	0-3	Hamburg	WCr1		50 000	Codjia BEN
20-06	Poland	L	1-2	Hanover	WCr1	Gomez [25]	43 000	Maidin SIN

Fr = Friendly match • GC = CONCACAF Gold Cup • CA = Copa América • WC = FIFA World Cup™
q = qualifier • r1 = first round group • qf = quarter-finals • BCD = behind closed doors

COSTA RICA NATIONAL TEAM RECORDS AND RECORD SEQUENCES

Records			Sequence records					
Victory	12-0	PUR 1946	Wins	11	1960-1961	Clean sheets	5	1961, 2001-2002
Defeat	0-7	MEX 1975	Defeats	6	2006	Goals scored	28	1935-1946
Player Caps	123	MARIN Luis	Undefeated	12	1965	Without goal	4	1980-1983
Player Goals	45	WANCHOPE Paulo	Without win	8	1997	Goals against	12	Three times

COSTA RICA COUNTRY INFORMATION

Capital	San José	Independence	1821 from Spain	GDP per Capita	$9 100
Population	3 956 507	Status	Republic	GNP Ranking	74
Area km²	51 100	Language	Spanish	Dialling code	+506
Population density	77 per km²	Literacy rate	96%	Internet code	.cr
% in urban areas	50%	Main religion	Christian 92%	GMT +/–	-6
Towns/Cities ('000)	San José 335; Limón 63; San Francisco 55; Alajuela 47; Liberia 45; Paraiso 39				
Neighbours (km)	Nicaragua 309; Panama 330; Caribbean Sea & Pacific Ocean 1 290				
Main stadia	Alejandro Soto – Alajuela 22 500; Ricardo Saprissa – San José 21 260				

COSTA RICA NATIONAL TEAM PLAYERS AND COACHES

Record Caps			Record Goals		
MARIN Luis	1993-'06	123	WANCHOPE Paulo	1996-'06	45
SOLIS Mauricio	1993-'06	110	FONSECA Rolando	1992-'05	42
FONSECA Rolando	1992-'05	96	ULLOA Juan		27
CENTENO Walter	1995-'06	96	GOMEZ Ronald	1993-'06	24
MEDFORD Hernán	1987-'02	84	MONGE Jorge		23
GOMEZ Ronald	1993-'06	83	MEDFORD Hernán	1987-'02	18
WALLACE Harold	1995-'06	80	CENTENO Walter	1995-'06	15
LONNIS Erick	1992-'02	76	MADRIGAL Rafael		15
LOPEZ Wilmer	1995-'03	76	HERRERA Rodolfo		14
WANCHOPE Paulo	1996-'06	72	SAENZ Roy		12

CLUB DIRECTORY

Club	Town/City	Stadium	Capacity	www.	Lge	CL
Liga Deportiva Alajuelense	Alajuela	Alejandro Morera Soto	22 500	ldacr.org	24	2
AD Belén	Heredia	Polideportivo Belén	10 500		0	0
Brujas Escazú FC	San José	Nicolas Macis	4 500		0	0
AD Carmelita	Alajuela	Carlos Alvarado	4 000		0	0
Club Sport Cartaginés	Cartago	Fello Meza	18 000	cartagines.co.cr	3	1
Club Sport Herediano	Heredia	Eladio Rosabal Cordero	8 144	herediano.com	21	0
Municipal Liberia	Liberia	Edgardo Baltodano	5 000		0	0
AD Pérez Zeledón	San Isidro	Municipal	5 500		0	0
Puntarenas FC	Puntarenas	Lito Pérez	8 700		0	0
AD Ramonense	Alajuela	Guillermo Vargas	5 000		0	0
Santos de Guápiles	Guápiles	Ebal Rodrigues	3 000		0	0
Deportivo Saprissa	San José	Ricardo Saprissa	21 260	saprissa.co.cr	24	3

RECENT LEAGUE RECORD

Year	Winners	Score	Runners-up
1990	Championship not awarded		
1991	Liga Deportiva Alajuelense	2-1 1-0	Deportivo Saprissa
1992	Liga Deportiva Alajuelense		Deportivo Saprissa
1993	CS Herediano	2-0	CS Cartaginés
1994	Deportivo Saprissa	2-0 1-2	Liga Deportiva Alajuelense
1995	Deportivo Saprissa	3-1 0-1	Liga Deportiva Alajuelense
1996	Liga Deportiva Alajuelense	3-1 1-1	CS Cartaginés
1997	Liga Deportiva Alajuelense	3-2 1-1	Deportivo Saprissa
1998	Deportivo Saprissa	0-1 2-0	Liga Deportiva Alajuelense
1999	Deportivo Saprissa	†	
2000	Liga Deportiva Alajuelense	†	
2001	Liga Deportiva Alajuelense	0-1 3-0	CS Herediano
2002	Liga Deportiva Alajuelense	2-2 4-0	Santos de Guápiles
2003	Liga Deportiva Alajuelense	†	
2004	Deportivo Saprissa	1-1 2-1	CS Herediano
2005	Liga Deportiva Alajuelense	3-1 1-0	AD Pérez Zeledón
2006	Deportivo Saprissa	†	

† Won both Apertura and Clausura so automatic champions

COSTA RICA 2005-06 — TORNEO APERTURA

Group A	Pl	W	D	L	F	A	Pts
LD Alajuelense	16	9	5	2	29	9	32
Municipal Puntarenas	16	8	4	4	23	15	28
CS Herediano	16	8	4	4	23	16	28
Santacruceña	16	6	2	8	17	19	20
Municipal Liberia	16	2	2	12	9	33	8
AD Ramonense	16	0	3	13	7	32	3

Group B	Pl	W	D	L	F	A	Pts
Deportivo Saprissa	16	11	4	1	28	12	37
AD Pérez Zeledón	16	7	5	4	21	18	26
CS Cartaginés	16	7	4	5	30	22	25
Brujas Escazú FC	16	6	7	3	16	12	25
Santos de Guápiles	16	5	6	5	22	23	21
AD Carmelita	16	2	4	10	11	25	10

30/07/2005 - 4/12/2005 • † Qualified for the play-offs

COSTA RICA 2005-06 — TORNEO CLAUSURA

Group A	Pl	W	D	L	F	A	Pts
Municipal Puntarenas	16	11	4	1	29	12	37
Deportivo Saprissa	16	10	3	3	22	16	33
Municipal Liberia	16	10	2	4	28	18	32
CS Herediano	16	7	2	7	19	18	23
AD Ramonense	16	6	1	9	16	19	19
Santacruceña	16	2	1	13	9	29	7

Group B	Pl	W	D	L	F	A	Pts
Brujas Escazú FC	16	7	3	6	19	17	24
LD Alajuelense	16	7	2	7	20	15	23
AD Pérez Zeledón	16	6	4	6	20	16	22
AD Carmelita	16	5	4	7	18	19	19
CS Cartaginés	16	4	5	7	15	22	17
Santos de Guápiles	16	4	3	9	15	29	15

14/01/2006 - 2/04/2006 • † Qualified for the play-offs

APERTURA PLAY-OFFS

Semi-finals

Deportivo Saprissa	0	4
Mun'pal Puntarenas	2	1

LD Alajuelense	0	1	4p
AD Pérez Zeledón	1	0	5p

Final

Deportivo Saprissa	1 1	4p
AD Pérez Zeledón	1 1	2p

Final 1st leg, 28-12-2005, San Isidro; Scorers - Gonzalez.B 69 for PZ; Drummond.G 40 for DS • 2nd leg, 31-12-2005, San José; Scorers - Gómez.R 94+ for DS; Cunnhingan 24 for PZ

CLAUSURA PLAY-OFFS

Semi-finals

Deportivo Saprissa	1	2
Brujas Escazú FC	0	1

Mun'pal Puntarenas	0	1
LD Alajuelense	2	1

Final

Deportivo Saprissa	1	2
LD Alajuelense	1	1

Final 1st leg, 17-04-2006, Alajuela; Scorers - Fonseca.R 56 for LDA; Saborio 86 for DS • 2nd leg, 31-12-2005, San José; Scorers - Centeno.W 2 8 42 for DS; Hernandez.C 19 for LDA

COSTA RICA 2005-06 — PRIMERA DIVISION CHAMPIONSHIP FINAL

Home team first leg   Score   Home team second leg

Deportivo Saprissa won both the Apertura and Clausura so no play-off needed

COSTA RICA RESULTS 2005-06

	LDA	Brujas	Carmelita	Cartaginés	Herediano	Liberia	Pérez Zeledón	Puntarenas	Ramonense	Santa'ceña	Santos	Saprissa
LD Alajuelense		1-3	2-1	2-1	4-0 1-0	4-0 1-2	1-0 3-0	1-0	2-0	0-0 1-0	0-0 3-0	1-1
Brujas Escazú FC	0-0 2-1		1-0 0-0	1-2 1-1	0-0	0-1	1-0 1-0	1-1	0-1	1-0	2-2 0-1	0-1
AD Carmelita	1-1 0-3	1-1 2-0			0-3 1-1	1-2	1-1 0-1	1-2	2-1	1-0	1-2 5-2	0-2
CS Cartaginés	3-2 1-0	1-2 0-1	4-2 2-1		0-2	5-1	0-1 2-0	1-3	2-1	1-0	3-1 0-0	0-1
CS Herediano	1-2	1-0	1-0	3-2		2-1 2-0	4-0	1-1 2-2	2-0 1-0	3-2 2-0	2-0	0-1 0-1
Municipal Liberia	2-5	5-3	0-1	1-1	0-1 4-1		2-1	1-1 0-1	0-0 1-0	0-2 3-0	2-1	0-1 2-1
AD Pérez Zeledón	1-1	1-1 0-1	2-1 1-1	2-2 2-0	2-1	4-1		1-0	3-0	5-0	2-0 3-0	1-1 2-1
Mun. Puntarenas	1-0 1-0	0-0	1-0	3-0	1-1 2-1	3-1 2-2	2-1		4-1 2-1	2-1 3-0	3-1	3-0
AD Ramonense	0-3 1-0	0-2	0-1	0-0	0-3 3-2	0-1 0-2	1-1	2-3 0-1		2-2 3-1	1-2	0-1
Santacruceña	0-3	1-2	2-0	2-0	1-0 2-0	1-0 1-2	1-2	0-1 0-0	1-0 0-1		0-2	1-2 1-2
Santos de Guápiles	2-1	0-0 0-4	2-0 2-0	2-2 2-2	1-1	3-0	1-1 0-0	2-1	1-2	2-3		2-3 1-2
Deportivo Saprissa	0-0	3-4 2-0	1-1 1-1	1-3 2-0	0-0	1-0	3-0	2-1 2-1	2-0 3-2	2-1	3-0	

Clausura matches listed in bold

CRO – CROATIA

NATIONAL TEAM RECORD
JULY 1ST 2002 TO JULY 9TH 2006

PL	W	D	L	F	A	%
49	22	16	11	74	48	61.2

FIFA/COCA-COLA WORLD RANKING

1993	1994	1995	1996	1997	1998	1999	2000	2001	2002	2003	2004	2005		High	Low
122	62	41	24	19	4	9	18	19	32	20	23	20		3 01/99	125 03/94

2005–2006											
08/05	09/05	10/05	11/05	12/05	01/06	02/06	03/06	04/06	05/06	06/06	07/06
20	24	19	20	20	20	23	19	24	23	-	23

Having topped their 2006 FIFA World Cup™ qualification group unbeaten, there was real hope amongst Croatian fans that their national team could come close to emulating the exploits of the 1998 squad that finished third in France. Those expectations were heightened after a very good performance against Brazil in the opening match, a game the Croats were unlucky to lose, but poor displays against Japan and then Australia saw the team crash out in the first round, leaving many back home wondering just how the current team came to be compared with the team of '98. One survivor from 1998, Dario Simic, will certainly remember the 2006 tournament. In the match

INTERNATIONAL HONOURS
Qualified for the FIFA World Cup™ finals 1998 2002 2006

against Australia he became the first player to receive three yellow cards in the finals while at the same time winning a record 82nd cap for his country. In the Croatian championship, Dinamo Zagreb won a record eighth title as Hajduk Split fell fell short in their attempt to win a hat-trick of titles. NK Rijeka did, however, manage to retain the Cup, and they did it in dramatic fashion. They won the first leg of the final at home against Varteks Varazdin 4-0, but it was only an away goal in a 5-1 defeat in the return that saved the day for them, after Varteks very nearly pulled off one of the most spectacular comebacks of all time.

THE FIFA BIG COUNT OF 2000

	Male	Female		Male	Female
Registered players	28 322	430	Referees	2 802	15
Non registered players	210 000	0	Officials	14 975	85
Youth players	458 204	0	Total involved	714 833	
Total players	696 956		Number of clubs	1 186	
Professional players	605	0	Number of teams	3 205	

Croatian Football Federation (HNS)
Hrvatski nogometni savez, Rusanova 13, Zagreb 10 000, Croatia
Tel +385 1 2361555   Fax +385 1 2441501
info@hns-cff.hr   www.hns-cff.hr
President: MARKOVIC Vlatko   General Secretary: SREBRIC Zorislav
Vice-President: ZEC Vlado   Treasurer: BAJRIC Ruzica   Media Officer: ROTIM Ivan
Men's Coach: BILIC Slaven   Women's Coach: RUHEK Damir
HNS formed: 1912   UEFA: 1993   FIFA: 1992
Red and white chequered shirts, White shorts, Blue socks or Blue shirts, Blue shorts, Blue socks

RECENT INTERNATIONAL MATCHES PLAYED BY CROATIA

2003	Opponents	Score		Venue	Comp	Scorers	Att	Referee
20-08	England	L	1-3	Ipswich	Fr	Mornar [77]	28 700	Larsen DEN
6-09	Andorra	W	3-0	Andorra-la-Vella	ECq	Kovac [4], Simunic [16], Rosso [71]	800	Liba CZE
10-09	Belgium	L	1-2	Brussels	ECq	Simic [35]	35 000	Poll ENG
11-10	Bulgaria	W	1-0	Zagreb	ECq	Olic [48]	37 000	Veissiere FRA
15-11	Slovenia	D	1-1	Zagreb	ECpo	Prso [5]	35 000	Merk GER
19-11	Slovenia	W	1-0	Ljubljana	ECpo	Prso [61]	9 000	Meier SUI
2004								
18-02	Germany	L	1-2	Split	Fr	Neretljak [86]	15 000	Frojdfeldt SWE
31-03	Turkey	D	2-2	Zagreb	Fr	Sokota [2], Srna [76]	12 000	Ferreira POR
28-04	FYR Macedonia	W	1-0	Skopje	Fr	Klasnic [33]	15 000	Arzuman TUR
29-05	Slovakia	W	1-0	Rijeka	Fr	Olic [29]	5 000	Kassai HUN
5-06	Denmark	W	2-1	Copenhagen	Fr	Sokota [27], Olic [39]	30 843	Stuchlik AUT
13-06	Switzerland	D	0-0	Leiria	ECr1		24 000	Cortez Batista POR
17-06	France	D	2-2	Leiria	ECr1	Rapajic [48p], Prso [52]	28 000	Milton Nielsen DEN
21-06	England	L	2-4	Lisbon	ECr1	Kovac.N [5], Tudor [73]	62 000	Collina ITA
18-08	Israel	W	1-0	Zagreb	Fr	Simunic [29]	10 000	Granat POL
4-09	Hungary	W	3-0	Zagreb	WCq	Prso 2 [31 54], Gyepes OG [80]	20 853	Riley ENG
8-09	Sweden	W	1-0	Gothenburg	WCq	Srna [64]	40 023	Dauden Ibanez ESP
9-10	Bulgaria	D	2-2	Zagreb	WCq	Srna 2 [15 31]	31 565	Collina ITA
16-11	Republic of Ireland	L	0-1	Dublin	Fr		33 200	Orrason ISL
2005								
9-02	Israel	D	3-3	Jerusalem	Fr	Klasnic 2 [15 78], Srna [55p]	4 000	Kailis CYP
26-03	Iceland	W	4-0	Zagreb	WCq	Kovac.N 2 [38 75], Simunic [70], Prso [91+]	17 912	Damon RSA
30-03	Malta	W	3-0	Zagreb	WCq	Prso 2 [22 35], Tudor [79]	15 510	Kapitanis CYP
4-06	Bulgaria	W	3-1	Sofia	WCq	Babic [19], Tudor [57], Kranjcar [80]	35 000	Nielsen DEN
17-08	Brazil	D	1-1	Split	Fr	Kranjcar [32]	30 000	Meyer GER
3-09	Iceland	W	3-1	Reykjavik	WCq	Balaban 2 [56 61], Srna [82]	5 520	Stark GER
7-09	Malta	D	1-1	Ta'Qali	WCq	Kranjcar [19]	916	Briakos GRE
8-10	Sweden	W	1-0	Zagreb	WCq	Srna [55]	34 015	De Santis ITA
12-10	Hungary	D	0-0	Budapest	WCq		6 979	Larsen DEN
12-11	Portugal	L	0-2	Coimbra	Fr		15 000	Nielsen DEN
2006								
29-01	Korea Republic	L	0-2	Hong Kong	Fr		16 841	Fong Yau Fat HKG
1-02	Hong Kong	W	4-0	Hong Kong	Fr	Knezevic [16], OG [30], Da Silva [64], Bosnjak [72]	13 971	Iemoto JPN
1-03	Argentina	W	3-2	Basel	Fr	Klasnic [3], Srna [52], Simic [92+]	13 138	Nobs SUI
23-05	Austria	W	4-1	Vienna	Fr	Klasnic 2 [11 35], Babic [54], Balaban [69]	22 000	Fandel GER
28-05	Iran	D	2-2	Osijek	Fr	Prso [31], Babic [97+]	19 500	Siric CRO
3-06	Poland	L	0-1	Wolfsburg	Fr		8 000	Meyer GER
7-06	Spain	L	1-2	Geneva	Fr	OG [14]	15 000	Lannoy FRA
13-06	Brazil	L	0-1	Berlin	WCr1		72 000	Archundia MEX
18-06	Japan	D	0-0	Nuremberg	WCr1		41 000	De Bleeckere BEL
22-06	Australia	D	2-2	Stuttgart	WCr1	Srna [2], Kovac.N [56]	52 000	Poll ENG

Fr = Friendly match • EC = UEFA EURO 2004™ • WC = FIFA World Cup™
q = qualifier • po = play-off • r1 = first round group

CROATIA NATIONAL TEAM RECORDS AND RECORD SEQUENCES

Records			Sequence records					
Victory	7-0	AUS 1998	Wins	5	1994-95, 1995-96	Clean sheets	4	1994, 2002
Defeat	1-5	GER 1941, GER 1942	Defeats	2	Four times	Goals scored	21	1996-1998
Player Caps	82	SIMIC Dario	Undefeated	12	2000-2001	Without goal	3	2005-2006
Player Goals	45	SUKER Davor	Without win	6	1999, 2006	Goals against	8	1996-1997

CROATIA COUNTRY INFORMATION

Capital	Zagreb	Independence	1991 from Yugoslavia	GDP per Capita	$10 600	
Population	4 496 869	Status	Republic	GNP Ranking	63	
Area km²	56 542	Language	Croatian	Dialling code	+385	
Population density	79 per km²	Literacy rate	98%	Internet code	.hr	
% in urban areas	64%	Main religion	Christian 92%	GMT + / –	+1	
Towns/Cities ('000)	Zagreb 698; Split 176; Rijeka 141; Osijek 88; Zadar 71; Slavonski Brod 60; Pula 59					
Neighbours (km)	Slovenia 670; Hungary 329; Serbia & Montenegro 266; Bosnia & Herzegovina 932; Adriatic Sea 1 777					
Main stadia	Poljud – Split 39 941; Maksimir – Zagreb 38 923; Gradski – Osijek 19 500					

COSTA RICA NATIONAL TEAM PLAYERS AND COACHES

Record Caps			Record Goals			Recent Coaches	
SIMIC Dario	1996-'06	82	SUKER Davor	1990-'02	45	JERKOVIC Drazen	1990-'91
JARNI Robert	1990-'02	81	VLAOVIC Goran	1992-'02	15	POKLEPOVIC Stanko	1992
SUKER Davor	1990-'02	69	BOBAN Zvonimir	1990'-99	12	MARKOVIC Vlatko	1992-'93
ASANOVIC Aljosa	1990-'00	62	WOLFL Franjo	1940-'44	12	BLAZEVIC Miroslav	1994-'00
SOLDO Zvonimir	1994-'02	61	BOKSIC Alen	1993-'02	10	JOZIC Mirko	2000-'02
KOVAC Niko	1996-'06	60	PROSINECKI Robert	1993-'02	10	Baric Otto	2002-'04
LADIC Drazen	1990-'99	59	BALABAN Bosko	2000-'06	9	KRANJCAR Zlatko	2004-'06
KOVAC Robert	1999-'06	58	SRNA Dario	2002-'06	9	BILIC SLAVEN	2006-
STIMAC Igor	1992-'02	53	PRSO Dado	2003-'06	9		
TUDOR IGOR	1997-'06	53					

CLUB DIRECTORY

Club	Town/City	Stadium	Capacity	www.	Lge	Cup
NK Dinamo Zagreb	Zagreb	Maksimir	38 923	nk-dinamo.hr	8 - 4	7 - 7
HNK Hajduk Split	Split	Poljud	39 941	hnkhajduk.hr	6 - 9	4 - 9
NK Inter Zapresic	Zapresic	Inter	8 000	nk-inter.com	0	1
NK Kamen Ingrad	Velika	Kamen Ingrad	4 000		0	0
NK Medimurje	Cakovec	Mladost	4 000		0	0
NK Osijek	Osijek	Gradski Vrt	19 500		0	1
NK Pula 1856	Pula	Gradski	7 000		0	0
HNK Rijeka	Rijeka	Kantrida	10 275	nk-rijeka.hr	0	2 - 2
NK Slaven Belupo	Koprivnica	Gradski	3 054	nk-slaven-belupo	0	0
NK Varteks	Varazdin	Varteksa	9 300	nk-varteks.hr	0	0
NK Zadar	Zadar	Stanovi	8 000		0	0
NK Zagreb	Zagreb	Kranjceviceva	12 000		1	0

Where two figures are shown in the League and Cup column, the second indicates trophies won in the Yugoslav League and Cup

RECENT LEAGUE AND CUP RECORD

	Championship						Cup		
Year	Champions	Pts	Runners-up	Pts	Third	Pts	Winners	Score	Runners-up
1992	Hajduk Split	36	NK Zagreb	33	NK Osijek	27	Inker Zapresic	1-1 1-0	HASK Gradjanski
1993	Croatia Zagreb	49	Hajduk Split	42	NK Zagreb	40	Hjaduk Split	4-1 1-2	Croatia Zagreb
1994	Hajduk Split	50	NK Zagreb	49	Croatia Zagreb	48	Croatia Zagreb	2-0 0-1	NK Rijeka
1995	Hajduk Split	65	Croatia Zagreb	64	NK Osijek	59	Hajduk Split	3-2 1-0	Croatia Zagreb
1996	Croatia Zagreb	26	Hajduk Split	26	Varteks Varazdin	24	Croatia Zagreb	2-0 1-0	Varteks Varazdin
1997	Croatia Zagreb	81	Hajduk Split	60	Dragovoljac Zagreb	49	Croatia Zagreb	2-1	NK Zagreb
1998	Croatia Zagreb	49	Hajduk Split	36	NK Osijek	32	Croatia Zagreb	1-0 2-1	Varteks Varazdin
1999	Croatia Zagreb	45	NK Rijeka	44	Hajduk Split	39	NK Osijek	2-1	Cibalia Vinkovici
2000	Dinamo Zagreb	75	Hajduk Split	61	NK Osijek	53	Hajduk Split	2-0 0-1	Dinamo Zagreb
2001	Hajduk Split	66	Dinamo Zagreb	65	NK Osijek	57	Dinamo Zagreb	2-0 1-0	Hajduk Split
2002	NK Zagreb	67	Hajduk Split	65	Dinamo Zagreb	59	Dinamo Zagreb	1-1 1-0	Varteks Varazdin
2003	Dinamo Zagreb	78	Hajduk Split	70	Varteks Varazdin	57	Hajduk Spit	1-0 4-0	Uljanik Pula
2004	Hajduk Split	78	Dinamo Zagreb	76	NK Rijeka	42	Dinamo Zagreb	1-1 0-0†	Varteks Varazdin
2005	Hajduk Split	56	Inter Zapresic	54	NK Zagreb	50	Rijeka	2-1 1-0	Hajduk Split
2006	Dinamo Zagreb	76	NK Rijeka	65	Varteks Varazdin	47	Rijeka	4-0 1-5	Varteks Varazdin

Dinamo Zagreb previously known as HASK Gradjanski and then as Croatia Zagreb • † Dinamo won on away goals

CROATIA 2005–06
PRVA HNL OZUJSKO (1)

	Pl	W	D	L	F	A	Pts	Dinamo	Rijeka	Varteks	Osijek	Hajduk	Kamen	Pula Staro	Slaven	Cibalia	Zagreb	Medimurje	Inter
Dinamo Zagreb †	32	24	4	4	78	21	76		5-1 1-2	1-0 2-1	3-1 1-0-0	1-0	5-0 2-0	1-0	4-1	1-0	4-1	3-0	0-0
NK Rijeka ‡	32	20	5	7	61	36	65	0-1 2-2		3-1 2-1 4-1 3-1	1-0 1-1 3-1 3-0	2-2	4-2	4-1	0-0	4-1	0-0		
Varteks Varazdin ‡	32	15	2	15	51	48	47	2-5 3-5 1-4 1-0			0-1 3-0 0-1 2-0 1-3 1-2	2-0	2-2	4-0	3-1	3-2	2-0		
NK Osijek	32	13	5	14	31	48	44	1-0 0-0 0-1 0-2 2-0 0-2		1-1 2-1 1-0 1-0		1-0	4-2	1-1	1-0	1-1	1-0		
Hajduk Split	32	10	10	12	40	35	40	0-1 1-0 0-1 0-4 3-0 2-2 6-0 3-0					1-2 4-1	1-1	1-1	1-1	3-1	1-0	3-2
Kamen Ingrad Velika	32	11	5	16	33	47	38	1-5 1-3 0-1 1-0 0-1 0-1 2-0 1-2 2-1 1-0					2-1	0-0	2-0	1-2	2-2	0-1	
Pula Staro cesko	32	13	6	13	44	36	45	2-1	3-0	0-1	2-2	2-0	1-2		1-0 2-0 2-3 0-2 2-0 4-1 4-0 1-0 3-0 2-1				
Slaven Belupo	32	10	11	11	46	48	41	0-2	1-3	4-3	3-1	0-0	1-1 1-1 2-2			4-2 1-0 1-0 3-0 1-1 0-0 3-0 1-1			
Cibalia Vinkovci	32	9	10	13	33	47	37	0-4	4-0	1-0	3-1	1-0	1-1 0-2 0-0 1-0 1-1				1-1 2-1 0-2 0-0 1-0 1-1		
NK Zagreb	32	11	4	17	26	43	37	0-4	2-0	0-1	0-1	1-2	2-1	2-0 1-0 3-1 0-0 0-0				1-0 1-0 1-0 3-1	
Medimurje Cakovec	32	9	9	14	40	51	36	1-5	2-4	1-4	1-0	1-1	0-3	2-0 2-0 2-0 3-4 3-4	4-0 0-0				1-2 2-2
Inter Zapresic	32	8	7	17	30	53	31	0-6	0-2	1-2	2-3	2-2	0-0	2-0 1-4 2-1 1-2	1-0 4-3	1-0 1-0	1-0 3-0	1	

20/07/2005 – 13/05/2006 • † Qualified for the UEFA Champions League • ‡ Qualified for the UEFA Cup • Each team plays each other twice before the top six play each other twice in the Championship group and the bottom six play each other twice in the relegation group • This system is also used in the Second Division

CROATIA 2005–06
GRUPA SJEVER (2)

	Pl	W	D	L	F	A	Pts
NK Belisce †	32	18	7	7	52	27	61
Graficar Vodovod Osijek	32	15	9	8	57	39	54
Metalac Osijek	32	14	10	8	46	26	52
NK Koprivnica	32	14	8	10	45	36	50
NK Bjelovar	32	14	6	12	39	39	48
HNK Vukovar '91	32	13	5	14	41	32	44
Marsonia Slavonski Brod	32	16	6	10	51	41	54
NK Cakovec	32	13	10	9	59	47	49
Granicar Zupanja	32	11	6	15	45	40	39
Slavonija Pozega	32	10	8	14	53	62	38
Dilj Vinkovci	32	8	6	18	37	75	30
Mladost Molve	32	3	5	24	32	93	14

20/08/2005 – 14/05/2006 • † play-off versus Jug winner •
Play-off: Not held. Sibenik promoted

CROATIA 2005–06
GRUPA JUG (2)

	Pl	W	D	L	F	A	Pts
NK Sibenik †	32	21	6	5	71	38	69
Croatia Sesvete	32	18	5	9	61	42	59
Pomorac Kostrena	32	15	13	4	65	31	58
NK Novalja	32	13	6	13	49	44	45
NK Imotski	32	10	10	12	36	43	40
Naftas Ivanic-Grad	32	8	8	16	38	62	32
NK Zadar	32	15	6	11	52	34	51
Hrvatski dragovoljac	32	13	9	10	48	39	48
Solin Grada	32	13	6	13	60	50	45
Mosor Zrnovnica	32	9	9	14	30	53	36
Segesta Sisak	32	9	4	19	34	59	31
NK Karlovac	32	4	6	22	21	70	18

21/08/2005 – 13/05/2006 • † play-off versus Sjever winner

HRVATSKOG NOGOMETNOG KUPA 2005–06

Round of sixteen		Quarter-finals		Semi-finals		Final	
NK Rijeka *	3						
Medimurje Cakovec	1	NK Rijeka	2 8				
Moslavina Kutina	2						
Vinogradar Mladina *	3	Vinogradar Mladina *	1 0	NK Rijeka	1 1		
NK Osijek *	2			Hajduk Split *	1 0		
Inter Zapresic	0	NK Osijek *	1 1				
Segesta Sisak	1	Hajduk Split	1 2				
Hajduk Split	2					NK Rijeka ‡	4 1
Kamen Ingrad Velika	3					Varteks Varazdin	0 5
Cibalia Vinkovci *	1	Kamen Ingrad Velika	0 4				
ZET Zagreb	0	Slaven Belupo *	1 1	Kamen Ingrad Velika	3 1		
Slaven Belupo *	5			Varteks Varazdin *	3 2		
Naftas Ivanic-Grad *	3	Naftas Ivanic Grad	1 1				
Dinamo Zagreb	2	Varteks Varazdin *	4 1				
Hrvatski dragovoljac *	0						
Varteks Varazdin	2	* Home team/home team in the first leg • ‡ Qualified for the UEFA Cup					

CUP FINAL
1st leg, Rijeka, 26-04-2006
2nd leg, Varazdin, 3-05-2006

CTA – CENTRAL AFRICAN REPUBLIC

NATIONAL TEAM RECORD
JULY 1ST 2002 TO JULY 9TH 2006

PL	W	D	L	F	A	%
14	2	4	8	12	23	28.6

FIFA/COCA-COLA WORLD RANKING

1993	1994	1995	1996	1997	1998	1999	2000	2001	2002	2003	2004	2005	High		Low	
157	174	180	183	188	192	175	176	182	179	177	180	183	**153**	08/93	**197**	10/99

2005–2006											
08/05	09/05	10/05	11/05	12/05	01/06	02/06	03/06	04/06	05/06	06/06	07/06
183	183	183	183	183	183	183	181	181	181	-	172

The Central African Republic have been handed a forum for more regular international competition with the creation of the regional CEMAC Cup in central Africa, in which they have now competed for the last three years. They were runners-up in the inaugural edition in 2003 but did not make an impression in 2005 or 2006 after failing to win a game. The Central African Republic is arguably one of few countries on the African continent where football is not the most popular sport, coming a distant second to basketball. The basketball team have been African champions in the past and much of the sporting resources make their way to them, leaving football as a poor cousin. The

INTERNATIONAL HONOURS
None

Central African Republic was one of just a handful of nations who did not play in the qualifiers for the 2006 World Cup™ finals, withdrawing from their preliminary round tie against Burkina Faso, and they also have not entered the field for the upcoming 2008 African Nations Cup qualifiers. Two clubs were entered into continental competition in 2006 with Anges de Fatima proving a credible opponent, before being eliminated by Daring Club Motema Pembe of the Democratic Republic of Congo in the first round of the CAF Champions League. TP USCA Bangui lost to Astres Douala from nearby Cameroon in the CAF Confederation Cup.

THE FIFA BIG COUNT OF 2000

	Male	Female		Male	Female
Registered players	4 500	350	Referees	150	10
Non registered players	10 000	800	Officials	1 500	300
Youth players	500	110	Total involved	18 220	
Total players	16 260		Number of clubs	263	
Professional players	0	0	Number of teams	263	

Fédération Centrafricaine de Football (RCA)
Avenue de Martyrs, Case Postale 344, Bangui, Central African Republic
Tel +236 619545   Fax +236 615660
dameca@intnet.cf   www.none
President: KAMACH Thierry   General Secretary: GBATE Jeremie
Vice-President: SAKILA Jean-Marie   Treasurer: MABOGNA Patrick   Media Officer: NDOTAH Christian
Men's Coach: YANGUERE Francois Cesar   Women's Coach: NGBANGANDIMBO Camille
RCA formed: 1961   CAF: 1965   FIFA: 1963
Blue shirts, White shorts, Blue socks

RECENT INTERNATIONAL MATCHES PLAYED BY THE CENTRAL AFRICAN REPUBLIC

2002	Opponents	Score		Venue	Comp	Scorers	Att	Referee
9-09	Mozambique	D	1-1	Bangui	CNq	Tamboula [72]		Ndong EQG
12-10	Burkina Faso	L	1-2	Ouagadougou	CNq	Ouefio [38]	25 000	Camara GUI
2003								
4-05	Congo	L	1-2	Brazzaville	CNq	Makita [84]		
8-06	Congo	D	0-0	Bangui	CNq			Hissene CHA
22-06	Mozambique	L	0-1	Maputo	CNq		15 000	
6-07	Burkina Faso	L	0-3	Bangui	CNq			
7-12	Cameroon	D	2-2	Brazzaville	CMr1	Oroko [10], Sandjo [30]		Mbera GAB
9-12	Cameroon	W	1-0	Brazzaville	CMr1	Sandjo [85]		Mandioukouta CGO
11-12	Gabon	W	2-0	Brazzaville	CMsf			
13-12	Cameroon	L	2-3	Brazzaville	CMf	Oroko [63], Destin [74]		Bansimba CGO
2004								
No international matches played in 2004								
2005								
3-02	Gabon	L	0-4	Libreville	CMr1			
5-02	Congo	L	0-1	Libreville	CMr1			
2006								
6-03	Cameroon †	L	0-2	Malabo	CMr1			
8-03	Gabon	D	2-2	Malabo	CMr1			

CN = CAF African Cup of Nations • CM = CEMAC Cup • q = qualifier • r1 = first round group • sf = semi-final • f = final
† Not an official international

CENTRAL AFRICAN REPUBLIC NATIONAL TEAM RECORDS AND RECORD SEQUENCES

Records			Sequence records					
Victory	4-0	CHA 1999	Wins	2	1976, 1999, 2003	Clean sheets	2	2003
Defeat	1-7	CMR 1984	Defeats	9	1985-1987	Goals scored	7	1990-1999
Player Caps	n/a		Undefeated	3	2003	Without goal	4	1988-1989
Player Goals	n/a		Without win	16	1976-1987	Goals against	19	1976-1988

RECENT LEAGUE AND CUP RECORD

	League		Cup		
Year	Champions		Winners	Score	Runners-up
1996	Tempête Mocaf				
1997	Tempête Mocaf		USCA de Bangui	2-0	Anges de Fatima
1998	Championship not finished		Anges de Fatima	3-0	AS Petroca
1999	Tempête Mocaf		Olympique Réal		
2000	Olympique Réal		Anges de Fatima	2-1	Olympique Réal
2001	Olympique Réal		Stade Centrafricain	2-1	Tempête Mocaf
2002	Championship annulled				
2003	Tempête Mocaf		Tempête Mocaf	8-0	Ouham Pendé
2004	Olympique Réal		Tempête Mocaf	2-0	SCAF
2005	Anges de Fatima		USCA de Bangui		Lobaye

CENTRAL AFRICAN REPUBLIC COUNTRY INFORMATION

Capital	Bangui	Independence	1960 from France	GDP per Capita	$1100
Population	3 742 482	Status	Republic	GNP Ranking	154
Area km²	622 984	Language	French	Dialling code	+236
Population density	6 per km²	Literacy rate	42%	Internet code	.cf
% in urban areas	39%	Main religion	Christian 50%	GMT +/−	+1
Towns/Cities ('000)	Bangui 684; Carnot 83; Kaga-Bandoro 82; Mbaiki 76; Berbérati 59; Bouar 55; Bouar 55				
Neighbours (km)	Sudan 1 165; Congo DR 1 577; Congo 467; Cameroon 797; Chad 1 197				
Main stadia	Barthelemy Boganda – Bangui 35 000				

CUB – CUBA

NATIONAL TEAM RECORD
JULY 1ST 2002 TO JULY 9TH 2006

PL	W	D	L	F	A	%
27	15	6	6	44	29	66.7

FIFA/COCA-COLA WORLD RANKING

1993	1994	1995	1996	1997	1998	1999	2000	2001	2002	2003	2004	2005	High	Low
159	175	96	68	88	107	77	77	76	71	75	76	75	**51** 08/96	**175** 12/94

					2005–2006							
08/05	09/05	10/05	11/05	12/05	01/06	02/06	03/06	04/06	05/06	06/06	07/06	
74	73	76	75	75	75	77	78	79	80	-	96	

Languishing in-between CONCACAF Gold Cup and FIFA World Cup™ tournaments, it was a quiet season on the international front for the Cuban national team, even for the women, who didn't enter the qualifying tournaments for either the 2006 FIFA Women's U-20 Championship in Russia or the FIFA Women's World Cup in 2007. Even in club football there was no international action with 2004 champions Villa Clara failing to enter the 2005-06 CONCACAF Champions Cup. Instead the focus during the season was on the 91st Campeonato de Fútbol, played between September and January. There was a surprise right from the start when Villa Clara, finalists in four

INTERNATIONAL HONOURS
Qualified for the FIFA World Cup™ finals 1938
CONCACAF U-17 Championship 1988   Central American and Caribbean Games 1930 1974 1978 1986

of the past five seasons and all-time record title holders, failed to get past the first round group and qualify for the ten team final group. The format of the tournament was changed with the title decided solely on a league basis without a championship play-off. The new format brought with it a first time winner as the race went down to the final weekend. Two teams from the far south-east of the island, Holguín and Santiago de Cuba, neither of whom had ever won the championship, met in a winner takes all tie, although the resulting 0-0 draw was enough for Holguín to secure the title.

THE FIFA BIG COUNT OF 2000

	Male	Female		Male	Female
Registered players	26 220	200	Referees	199	0
Non registered players	1 000 000	0	Officials	5 000	0
Youth players	12 000	100	Total involved	1 043 719	
Total players	1 038 520		Number of clubs	338	
Professional players	0	0	Number of teams	1 470	

Asociación de Fútbol de Cuba (AFC)
Calle 41 No. 4109 e/ 44 y 46, La Habana, Cuba
Tel +53 7 2076440   Fax +53 7 2043563
futbol@inder.co.cu   www.none
President: HERNANDEZ Luis   General Secretary: GARCES Antonio
Vice-President: ARAGON Victor   Treasurer: CAMINO Otto Fernandez   Media Officer: PEREIRA LEON Jesus
Men's Coach: TRIANA Gonzalez   Women's Coach: SOTOLONGO Rufino
AFC formed: 1924   CONCACAF: 1961   FIFA: 1932
Red shirts with white trimmings, Red shorts, Red socks or White shirts, White shorts, White socks

RECENT INTERNATIONAL MATCHES PLAYED BY CUBA

2002	Opponents	Score		Venue	Comp	Scorers	Att	Referee
27-11	Cayman Islands	W	5-0	Grand Cayman	GCq	Driggs [21], Moré 2 [23 77], Dalcourt [80], Galindo [86]		Prendergast JAM
29-11	Martinique	W	2-1	Grand Cayman	GCq	Moré [38], Dalcourt [60]		Prendergast JAM
1-12	Dominican Republic	W	2-1	Grand Cayman	GCq	OG [63], Prado [67]		Grant HAI
2003								
11-03	Jamaica	D	0-0	Havana	Fr		10 000	
13-03	Jamaica	W	1-0	Havana	Fr	Galindo [43]	15 000	Hernandez CUB
26-03	Guadeloupe	W	3-2	Port of Spain	GCq	Galindo 2 [17 83], Dalcourt [30]	6 000	Callendar BRB
28-03	Antigua and Barbuda	W	2-0	Macoya	GCq	Moré 2 [65 78]	4 000	James GUY
30-03	Trinidad and Tobago	W	3-1	Marabella	GCq	Ramirez [26], Moré [72], Galindo [77]	5 000	James GUY
27-06	Panama	L	0-2	Panama City	Fr			Moreno PAN
29-06	Panama	L	0-1	Panama City	Fr			Vidal PAN
6-07	Jamaica	W	2-1	Kingston	Fr	Fernandez [20], Marquez [38]	8 500	Bowen CAY
14-07	Canada	W	2-0	Foxboro	GCr1	Moré 2 [15 46]	8 780	Prendergast JAM
16-07	Costa Rica	L	0-3	Foxboro	GCr1		10 361	Archundia MEX
19-07	USA	L	0-5	Foxboro	GCqf		15 627	Prendergast JAM
19-11	Trinidad and Tobago	L	1-2	Port of Spain	Fr	Galindo [47]	8 000	
2004								
22-02	Cayman Islands	W	2-1	Grand Cayman	WCq	Moré [53], Marten [89]	1 789	Sibrian SLV
16-03	Panama	D	1-1	Havana	Fr	Moré [33]		Rojas Corbeas CUB
18-03	Panama	W	3-0	Havana	Fr	Colome [36], Galindo [49], Moré [55]		Yero Rodriguez CUB
27-03	Cayman Islands	W	3-0	Havana	WCq	Moré 3 [7 50 66]	3 500	Rodriguez MEX
20-05	Grenada	D	2-2	Havana	Fr	Galindo [15], Faife [23]		
12-06	Costa Rica	D	2-2	Havana	WCq	Moré 2 [24 75]	18 500	Archundia MEX
20-06	Costa Rica	D	1-1	Alajuela	WCq	Cervantes [46+]	12 000	Prendergast JAM
2005								
9-01	Haiti	W	1-0	Port-au-Prince	GCq	Galindo [51]	15 000	Minyetti DOM
16-01	Haiti	D	1-1	Havana	GCq	Marquez [112]		Brizan TRI
20-02	Barbados	W	3-0	Bridgetown	GCq	Moré 2 [24 71], Galindo [90]	7 000	Prendergast JAM
22-02	Trinidad and Tobago	W	2-1	Bridgetown	GCq	Moré 2 [23 48]	2 100	Lancaster GUY
24-02	Jamaica	L	0-1	Bridgetown	GCq		3 000	Brizan TRI
7-07	USA	L	1-4	Seattle	GCr1	Moré [18]	15 831	Pineda HON
9-07	Costa Rica	L	1-3	Seattle	GCr1	Galindo [72]	15 109	Archundia MEX
12-07	Canada	L	1-2	Foxboro	GCr1	Cervantes [90]	15 211	Moreno PAN
2006								

No international matches played in 2006 before July

Fr = Friendly match • GC = CONCACAF Gold Cup • WC = FIFA World Cup™ • q = qualifier • r1 = first round group

CUBA NATIONAL TEAM RECORDS AND RECORD SEQUENCES

Records			Sequence records					
Victory	9-0	PUR 1995	Wins	7	1998-1999	Clean sheets	7	1996
Defeat	0-8	SWE 1938	Defeats	18	1949-1960	Goals scored	12	2003-2005
Player Caps	n/a		Undefeated	11	1981-83, 2004-05	Without goal	4	1957, 1983, 2002
Player Goals	n/a		Without win	20	1949-1960	Goals against	26	1949-1961

CUBA COUNTRY INFORMATION

Capital	Havana	Independence	1902 from Spain	GDP per Capita	$2 900
Population	11 308 764	Status	Republic	GNP Ranking	69
Area km²	110 860	Language	Spanish	Dialling code	+53
Population density	102 per km²	Literacy rate	97%	Internet code	.cu
% in urban areas	76%	Main religion	None	GMT +/–	-5
Towns/Cities ('000)	Havana 2 163; Santiago 555; Camagüey 347; Holguín 319; Guantánamo 272; Santa Clara 250				
Neighbours (km)	North Atlantic Ocean, Caribbean Sea and the Gulf of Mexico 3 735				
Main stadia	Estadio Panamericano – Havana 34 000; Pedro Marrero – Havana 28 000				

CUBA 2005
CAMPEONATO NACIONAL FIRST ROUND

Group A	Pl	W	D	L	F	A	Pts
Ciudad de La Habana †	8	5	2	1	17	8	17
La Habana †	8	4	1	3	14	10	13
Matanzas †	8	3	2	3	10	9	11
Pinar de Río	8	3	2	3	9	12	11
Isla de la Juventud	8	0	3	5	5	16	3

Group B	Pl	W	D	L	F	A	Pts
Cienfuegos †	7	4	2	1	9	6	14
Camagüey †	8	4	1	3	6	13	13
Sancti Spíritus †	7	2	3	2	6	6	9
Villa Clara	8	2	2	4	9	7	8
Ciego de Avila	8	1	4	3	11	9	7

3/09/2005 - 12/10/2005 • † Clubs qualifying for the Second Round

CUBA 2005
CAMPEONATO NACIONAL FIRST ROUND

Group C	Pl	W	D	L	F	A	Pts
Granma †	7	4	2	1	11	8	14
Santiago de Cuba †	8	3	3	2	11	10	12
Holguín †	8	3	2	3	12	8	11
Guantanamo †	8	3	2	3	12	12	11
Las Tunas	7	0	3	4	6	14	3

3/09/2005 - 12/10/2005 • † Clubs qualifying for the Second Round

CUBA 2005
CAMPEONATO NACIONAL SECOND ROUND

	Pl	W	D	L	F	A	Pts	Holguín	Ciudad LH	Santiago	Cienfuegos	Granma	Matanzas	La Habana	Camagüey	Guant'amo	Sancti Sp.
Holguín	18	9	5	4	15	13	32		1-1	0-1	1-0	1-0	0-1	2-0	2-0	1-0	1-0
Ciudad de La Habana	18	8	6	4	25	15	30	5-0		0-1	1-2	1-0	3-0	1-1	1-0	2-1	2-2
Santiago de Cuba	18	8	5	5	23	10	29	0-0	3-1		0-1	0-0	1-1	1-1	0-2	6-0	5-0
Cienfuegos	18	7	6	5	21	11	27	1-1	0-1	0-1		1-2	4-1	3-0	5-0	1-0	0-0
Granma	18	6	7	5	16	13	25	0-0	1-1	0-2	0-0		0-0	2-0	1-1	0-0	2-0
Matanzas	18	6	6	6	17	20	24	2-0	0-0	1-0	1-0	3-4		1-1	1-2	1-2	1-1
La Habana	18	4	8	6	16	21	20	0-1	1-3	1-0	0-0	1-0	0-1		1-1	3-1	3-1
Camagüey	18	5	5	8	12	20	20	0-1	1-0	1-0	1-1	0-2	0-1	1-1		1-2	1-0
Guantanamo	18	5	5	8	14	23	20	0-1	0-0	1-1	0-1	2-1	1-0	1-1	1-0		1-1
Sancti Spíritus	18	1	9	8	13	26	12	2-2	1-2	0-1	1-1	0-1	1-1	1-1	0-0	2-1	

23/10/2005 - 14/01/2006

CLUB DIRECTORY

Club	Town/City	Stadium	Lge
Camagüey	Camagüey	Terreno de Futbol de Florida	0
Ciego de Avila	Ciego de Avila	CVD Deportivo	3
Cienfuegos	Cienfuegos		2
Ciudad de La Habana	Havana	Pedro Marrero	6
Granma	Bayamo	Conrado Benitez	0
Holguín	Holguín	Turcio Lima	1
Industriales	Havana	Campo Armada	4
Las Tunas	Victoria de Las Tunas	Ovidio Torres	0
Matanzas	Matanzas	Terreno de Futbol de Colon	0
Pinar del Río	Pinar del Río	La Bombonera	6
Santiago de Cuba	Santiago de Cuba	Antonio Maceo	0
Villa Clara	Santa Clara	Camilo Cienfuegos	10

RECENT LEAGUE RECORD

Year	Winners	Score	Runners-up
1996	Villa Clara	2-3 4-0	Cienfuegos
1997	Villa Clara	1-2 2-0	Pinar del Río
1998	Ciudad de La Habana	2-1 1-0	Villa Clara
1999	No championship due to season readjustment		
2000	Pinar del Río	0-1 2-1†	Ciudad de La Habana
2001	Ciudad de La Habana	2-1 0-0	Villa Clara
2002	Ciego de Avila	1-0 0-0	Granma Bayamo
2003	Villa Clara	1-0 2-0	Ciudad de La Habana
2003	Ciego de Avila	1-1 2-0	Villa Clara
2004	Villa Clara	0-1 3-0	Pinar del Río
2005	Holguín	‡	Ciudad de La Habana

† Won on away goals • ‡ Played on a league basis

CYP – CYPRUS

NATIONAL TEAM RECORD
JULY 1ST 2002 TO JULY 9TH 2006

PL	W	D	L	F	A	%
34	10	6	18	35	55	38.2

FIFA/COCA-COLA WORLD RANKING

1993	1994	1995	1996	1997	1998	1999	2000	2001	2002	2003	2004	2005		High		Low
72	67	73	78	82	78	63	62	79	80	97	108	96		**58**	02/99	**113** 03/05

2005–2006											
08/05	09/05	10/05	11/05	12/05	01/06	02/06	03/06	04/06	05/06	06/06	07/06
105	103	103	97	96	97	98	98	100	100	-	92

Football in Cyprus may not make many headlines around the world, but the country is experiencing something of a football revolution. After years of being tagged as the poor relations of European football, that no longer rings true, especially with regard to the national team. If evidence was needed that the changes are affecting club football too, it came in the second preliminary round of the UEFA Champions League. Champions Anorthosis Famagusta were drawn against Turkey's Trabzonspor in the first ever meeting of the two nations in European club competition. The 3-1 home victory in the first leg, watched by a crowd of 14,613 in Nicosia, was made all the more

INTERNATIONAL HONOURS
None

memorable by the fact that Anorthosis have been homeless since 1974, the year Turkish troops invaded the north of the island and occupied Famagusta. The League in Cyprus has become more competitive in recent years and the three-way chase between Apollon, Omonia and APOEL went down to the last weekend. With just two points separating the teams, all three won, which meant a first title for Apollon since 1994. The triumph was dedicated to their 31-year-old Hungarian forward Gabor Zavadszky, who died in January. APOEL won the Cup after beating AEK Larnaca 3-2, the winner coming from Sasa Jovanovic at the start of the second period of extra-time.

THE FIFA BIG COUNT OF 2000

	Male	Female		Male	Female
Registered players	33 250	104	Referees	162	1
Non registered players	10 487	0	Officials	1 869	75
Youth players	7 000	74	Total involved	53 022	
Total players	50 915		Number of clubs	321	
Professional players	450	1	Number of teams	506	

Cyprus Football Association (CFA)

1 Stasinos Street, Engomi, PO Box 25071, Nicosia 2404, Cyprus
Tel +357 22 590960   Fax +357 22 590544
cfa@cytanet.com.cy   www.none
President: KOUTSOKOUMNIS Costakis   General Secretary: GEORGIADES Chris
Vice-President: KATSIKIDES Tassos   Treasurer: MARANGOS Spyros   Media Officer: GIORGALIS Kyriakos
Men's Coach: ANASTASIADIS Angelos   Women's Coach: IAKOVOU Pepis
CFA formed: 1934   UEFA: 1962   FIFA: 1948
Blue shirts with white trimmings, White shorts, Blue socks or White shirts with blue trimmings, White shorts, White socks

RECENT INTERNATIONAL MATCHES PLAYED BY CYPRUS

2002	Opponents		Score	Venue	Comp	Scorers	Att	Referee
21-08	Northern Ireland	D	0-0	Belfast	Fr		6 922	Jones WAL
7-09	France	L	1-2	Nicosia	ECq	Okkas [15]	10 000	Fandel GER
20-11	Malta	W	2-1	Nicosia	ECq	Rauffmann [50], Okkas [74]	5 000	Guenov BUL
2003								
29-01	Greece	L	1-2	Larnaca	Fr	Konstantinou.M [28p]	2 000	Loizou CYP
12-02	Russia	L	0-1	Limassol	Fr		300	Efthimiadis GRE
13-02	Slovakia	L	1-3	Larnaca	Fr	Rauffmann [40]	250	Kapitanis CYP
29-03	Israel	D	1-1	Limassol	ECq	Rauffmann [61]	8 500	McCurry SCO
2-04	Slovenia	L	1-4	Ljubljana	ECq	Konstantinou.M [10]	5 000	Costa POR
30-04	Israel	L	0-2	Palermo	ECq		1 000	Benes CZE
7-06	Malta	W	2-1	Ta'Qali	ECq	Konstantinou.M 2 [22p 53]	3 000	Brugger AUT
6-09	France	L	0-5	Paris	ECq		55 000	Irvine NIR
11-10	Slovenia	D	2-2	Limassol	ECq	Georgiou.S [74], Yiasoumi [84]	2 346	Ovrebo NOR
2004								
18-02	Belarus	L	0-2	Achnas	Fr		500	Kailis CYP
19-02	Georgia	W	3-1	Nicosia	Fr	Charalampidis 2 [44 55], Ilia [73]	200	Kapitanis CYP
21-02	Kazakhstan	W	2-1	Larnaca	Fr	Charalampidis [3], Michail.C [8]	300	Lajuks LVA
19-05	Jordan	D	0-0	Nicosia	Fr		2 500	Loizou CYP
18-08	Albania	W	2-1	Nicosia	Fr	Konstantinou.M 2 [13p 48]	200	Kapitanis CYP
4-09	Republic of Ireland	L	0-3	Dublin	WCq		36 000	Paniashvili GEO
8-09	Israel	L	1-2	Tel Aviv	WCq	Konstantinou.M [59]	21 872	Shmolik BLR
9-10	Faroe Islands	D	2-2	Nicosia	WCq	Konstantinou.M [15], Okkas [81]	1 400	Gadiyev AZE
13-10	France	L	0-2	Nicosia	WCq		3 319	Larsen DEN
17-11	Israel	L	1-2	Nicosia	WCq	Okkas [45]	1 624	Kaldma EST
2005								
8-02	Austria	D	1-1	Limassol	Fr	Charalampidis [90]. W 5-4p	300	Hyytia FIN
9-02	Finland	L	1-2	Nicosia	Fr	Michail.C [24]	300	Lajuks LVA
26-03	Jordan	W	2-1	Larnaca	Fr	Charalampidis [9], Okkas [28]	200	Kapitanis CYP
30-03	Switzerland	L	0-1	Zurich	WCq		16 066	Dougal SCO
13-08	Iraq	W	2-1	Limassol	Fr	Yiasoumi 2 [63 79]	500	
17-08	Faroe Islands	W	3-0	Toftir	WCq	Konstantinou 2 [39 77], Krassas [95+]	2 720	Johannesson SWE
7-09	Switzerland	L	1-3	Nicosia	WCq	Aloneftis [35]	2 561	Ivanov.N RUS
8-10	Republic of Ireland	L	0-1	Nicosia	WCq		13 546	Kassai HUN
12-10	France	L	0-4	Paris	WCq		78 864	Stark GER
16-11	Wales	W	1-0	Limassol	Fr	Michail.C [43p]	1 000	Jakov ISR
2006								
28-02	Slovenia	L	0-1	Larnaca	Fr		1 000	Tsacheilidis GRE
1-03	Armenia	W	2-0	Limassol	Fr	Okkas [18], Michail.C [61]		

Fr = Friendly match • EC = UEFA EURO 2004™ • WC = FIFA World Cup™ • q = qualifier

CYPRUS NATIONAL TEAM RECORDS AND RECORD SEQUENCES

Records			Sequence records					
Victory	5-0	AND 2000	Wins	3	1992, 1998, 2000	Clean sheets	2	1992-93, 1994,1996
Defeat	0-12	GER 1969	Defeats	19	1973-1978	Goals scored	7	1997-1998
Player Caps	82	PITTAS Pambos	Undefeated	6	1997-1998	Without goal	6	1975, 1987-1988
Player Goals	19	KONSTANTINOU Michael	Without win	39	1984-1992	Goals against	36	1973-1981

CYPRUS COUNTRY INFORMATION

Capital	Nicosia	Independence	1960 from the UK	GDP per Capita	$19 200
Population	775 927	Status	Republic	GNP Ranking	89
Area km²	9 250	Language	Greek, Turkish	Dialling code	+357
Population density	83 per km²	Literacy rate	97%	Internet code	.cy
% in urban areas	54%	Main religion	Christian 82%	GMT + / −	+2
Towns/Cities ('000)	Nicosia 242; Limassol 154; Larnaka 48; Gazimagusa 42; Paphos 35; Girne 26; Güzelyurt 14				
Neighbours (km)	Mediterranean Sea 648				
Main stadia	Neo GSP (Pancypria) − Nicosia 23 400; Tsirion − Limassol 13 152; Zenon − Larnaca 13 032				

CYPRUS NATIONAL TEAM PLAYERS AND COACHES

Record Caps			Record Goals			Recent Coaches	
PITTAS Pambos	1987-'99	82	KONSTANTINOU Michalis	1998-'05	21	IOAKOVOU Panikos	1984-'87
PANAYIOTOU Nikos	1994-'05	74	OKKAS Yiannakis	1997-'06	13	CHARALAMBOUS Takis	1987
YIANGOUDAKIS Yiannakis	1980-'94	68	AGATHOKLEOUS Mariojos	1994-'03	10	IOAKOVOU Panikos	1988-'91
OKKAS Yiannakis	1997-'06	67	GOGIC Sinisa	1994-'99	8	MICHAILIDIS Andreas	1991-'96
CHARALAMBOUS Marios	1991-'02	60	SOTIRIOU Andros	1991-'99	8	PAPADOPOULOS Stavros	1997
THEODOTOU Gheorghios	1996-'02	58	VRAHIMIS Phivos	1977-'82	8	GEORGIOU Panikos	1997-'99
IOANNOU Dimitris	1991-'01	50	ENGOMITIS Panayiotis	1994-'03	7	PAPADOPOULOS Stavros	1999-'01
KONSTANTINOU Michalis	1998-'05	48	PITTAS Pambos	1987-'99	7	CHARALAMBOUS Takis	2001
SAVVIDES George	1982-'95	47	KAIAFAS Sotiris	1975-'80	6	VUKOTIC Momcilo	2001-'04
PANTZIARAS Nikos	1975-'87	46	IOANNOU Yiannakis	1991-'99	6	ANASTASIADIS Angelos	2004-

CLUB DIRECTORY

Club	Town/City	Stadium	Capacity	Lge	Cup
AEK	Larnaca	Zenon	13 032	0	1
AEL	Limassol	Tsirion	13 152	5	6
AEP	Paphos	Paphiako	11 000	0	0
Anorthosis	Larnaca	Andonis Papadopoulos	9 500	12	9
APOEL	Nicosia	Pancypria	23 400	18	18
Apollon	Limassol	Tsirion	13 152	3	5
Aris	Limassol	Tsirion	13 152	0	0
Ayia Napa	Ayia Napa	Municipal	2 000	0	0
Digenis	Nicosia	Makarion	16 000	0	0
ENP	Paralimni	Municipal	8 000	0	0
Ethnikos	Achna	Dasaki	4 000	0	0
Nea Salamina	Larnaca	Ammochostos	8 000	0	1
Olympiakos	Nicosia	Pancypria	23 400	3	1
Omonia	Nicosia	Pancypria	23 400	19	12

RECENT LEAGUE AND CUP RECORD

	Championship							Cup		
Year	Champions	Pts	Runners-up	Pts	Third	Pts		Winners	Score	Runners-up
1990	APOEL Nicosia	41	Omonia Nicosia	35	Pezoporikos	31		NEA Salamina	3-2	Omonia Nicosia
1991	Apollon Limassol	44	Anorthosis F'gusta	41	APOEL Nicosia	35		Omonia Nicosia	1-0	Olympiakos Nicosia
1992	APOEL Nicosia	60	Anorthosis F'gusta	58	Apollon Limassol	53		Apollon Limassol	1-0	Omonia Nicosia
1993	Omonia Nicosia	59	Apollon Limassol	57	NEA Salamina	48		APOEL Nicosia	4-1	Apollon Limassol
1994	Apollon Limassol	63	Anorthosis F'gusta	61	APOEL Nicosia	56		Omonia Nicosia	1-0	Anorthosis F'gusta
1995	Anorthosis F'gusta	73	Omonia Nicosia	67	NEA Salamina	57		APOEL Nicosia	4-2	Apollon Limassol
1996	APOEL Nicosia	64	Anorthosis F'gusta	55	Omonia Nicosia	53		APOEL Nicosia	2-0	AEK Larnaca
1997	Anorthosis F'gusta	65	Apollon Limassol	52	Omonia Nicosia	46		APOEL Nicosia	2-0	Omonia Nicosia
1998	Anorthosis F'gusta	66	Omonia Nicosia	62	Apollon Limassol	55		Anothosis F'gusta	3-1	Apollon Limassol
1999	Anorthosis F'gusta	67	Omonia Nicosia	67	APOEL Nicosia	59		APOEL Nicosia	2-0	Anorthosis F'gusta
2000	Anorthosis F'gusta	65	Omonia Nicosia	59	APOEL Nicosia	46		Omonia Nicosia	4-2	APOEL Nicosia
2001	Omonia Nicosia	57	Olympiakos	54	AEL Limassol	52		Apollon Limassol	1-0	NEA Salamina
2002	APOEL Nicosia	59	Anorthosis F'gusta	58	AEL Limassol	54		Anorthosis F'gusta	1-0	Ethnikos Achnas
2003	Omonia Nicosia	60	Anorthosis F'gusta	59	APOEL Nicosia	55		Anorthosis F'gusta	0-0 5-3p	AEL Limassol
2004	APOEL Nicosia	65	Omonia Nicosia	62	Apollon Limassol	49		AEK Larnaca	2-1	AEL Limassol
2005	Anorthosis F'gusta	62	APOEL Nicosia	58	Omonia Nicosia	47		Omonia Nicosia	2-0	Digenis Morfu
2006	Apollon Limassol	64	Omonia Nicosia	63	APOEL Nicosia	62		APOEL Nicosia	3-2	AEK Larnaca

CYPRUS 2005-06
DIVISION A

	PI	W	D	L	F	A	Pts	Apollon	Omonia	APOEL	Anorthosis	ENP	Salamina	AEL	AEK	Ethnikos	Digenis	Olympiakos	APOP	APEP	THOI
Apollon Limassol †	26	19	7	0	68	24	64		0-0	1-1	3-1	3-0	5-1	2-0	3-0	2-1	3-2	4-0	4-0	5-1	4-0
Omonia Nicosia ‡	26	20	3	3	59	20	63	1-1		1-0	2-2	0-1	6-2	2-0	3-1	3-2	3-0	1-0	4-0	2-1	2-1
APOEL Nicosia ‡	26	19	5	2	63	22	62	2-2	2-1		5-3	2-0	5-3	2-0	3-0	1-0	1-0	2-2	5-0	2-0	5-1
Anorthosis Famagusta	26	15	8	3	55	26	53	1-1	2-1	2-2		0-0	2-0	5-0	1-0	2-0	1-0	1-0	1-1	6-1	1-0
ENP Paralimni	26	12	7	7	40	28	43	1-1	0-1	2-1	0-1		2-2	3-5	1-0	3-3	2-2	1-1	4-0	6-1	1-0
Nea Salamina	26	12	5	9	53	48	41	2-2	0-1	0-2	2-5	0-2		2-1	3-2	2-1	4-1	5-1	2-1	5-0	3-1
AEL Limassol	26	10	5	11	44	48	35	1-4	1-2	1-1	3-0	2-1	0-3		1-1	2-3	3-0	2-2	4-3	4-0	3-2
AEK Larnaca	26	9	4	13	39	37	31	2-3	2-3	1-2	1-1	1-0	0-0	2-0		3-0	1-1	3-0	5-0	3-1	2-0
Ethnikos	26	8	4	14	42	43	28	1-2	0-1	1-2	0-5	0-1	2-4	0-0	2-1		4-2	4-0	2-0	4-0	1-1
Digenis Morfu	26	7	7	12	33	45	28	2-3	0-4	0-1	1-1	0-2	2-1	2-2	1-0	2-0		0-1	1-1	3-3	1-0
Olympiakos Nicosia	26	6	9	11	40	50	27	2-3	1-3	1-3	1-2	1-1	1-1	3-2	1-1	1-3			3-2	8-0	0-1
APOP	26	5	3	18	35	65	18	1-2	0-1	1-2	0-1	0-2	1-1	1-3	1-2	3-2	1-1	1-3		3-1	7-1
APEP	26	1	5	20	17	72	8	1-2	0-5	0-3	0-1	0-2	1-3	1-2	2-1	0-2	1-2	0-0	1-2		1-1
THOI Lakatamia	26	1	4	21	15	75	7	1-4	0-5	0-7	0-6	0-1	1-2	1-2	1-4	0-6	1-1	0-2	0-3	0-0	

27/08/2005 - 6/05/2006 • † Qualified for the UEFA Champions League • ‡ Qualified for the UEFA Cup • Top scorer: Lukasz SOSIN, Apollon, 28

CYPRUS 2005-06
DIVISION B

	PI	W	D	L	F	A	Pts
AEP Paphos	26	17	6	3	69	23	57
Aris Limassol	26	18	2	6	66	36	56
Ayia Napa	26	14	6	6	48	27	48
Alki Larnaca	26	12	5	9	48	34	41
Omonia Aradippou	26	9	10	7	33	29	37
MEAP Nisou	26	9	9	8	38	36	36
Doxa Katokopia	26	8	11	7	37	30	35
Halkanoras Dhaliou	26	9	7	10	37	35	34
Anagennisis Yermasoyia	26	9	5	12	39	47	32
Onisilos Sotiras	26	8	8	10	33	42	32
Iraklis Yerolakkou	26	8	7	11	33	50	29
Elpida Xylofagou	26	8	3	15	27	44	27
Ethikos Ashia	26	7	5	14	41	50	26
SEK Athanasiou	26	1	6	19	19	85	9

17/09/2005 - 7/05/2006

COCA-COLA CUP 2005-06

Group Stage

Group A	Pts
Anorthosis F'gusta	14
AEP Paphos	11
Digenis Morfou	6
THOI Lakatamia	1

Group B	Pts
APOEL Nicosia	15
Apollon Limassol	13
APEP	5
ASIL Lysi	1

Group C	Pts
Olympiakos	13
Nea Salamina	13
AEL Limassol	5
Ethnikos Ashia	3

Group D	Pts
Omonia Nicosia	15
AEK Larnaca	9
ENP Parailmni	9
Aris Limassol	3

Quarter-finals

APOEL Nicosia	1	4
Nea Salamina *	2	0
Apollon Limassol *	0	0
Omonia Nicosia	2	0
AEP Paphos *	2	1
Olympiakos	0	2
Anorthosis F'gusta	0	3
AEK Larnaca *	2	1

Semi-finals

APOEL Nicosia *	3	3
Omonia Nicosia	3	1
AEP Paphos *	1	0
AEK Larnaca	1	0

Final

APOEL Nicosia ‡	3
AEK Larnaca	2

CUP FINAL

Zenon, Larnaca
13-05-2006

Scorers - Marios Neophytou [15p], Alxandros Kaklamanos [17], Sasa Jovanovic [107] for APOEL;
Jatto Cisse [19], Narcis Raducan [42p] for AEK

* Home team in the first leg • ‡ Qualified for the UEFA Cup

CZE – CZECH REPUBLIC

NATIONAL TEAM RECORD
JULY 1ST 2002 TO JULY 9TH 2006

PL	W	D	L	F	A	%
48	34	5	9	116	41	76

FIFA/COCA-COLA WORLD RANKING

1993	1994	1995	1996	1997	1998	1999	2000	2001	2002	2003	2004	2005	High	Low
-	34	14	5	3	8	2	5	14	15	6	4	2	2	67 03/94

2005–2006											
08/05	09/05	10/05	11/05	12/05	01/06	02/06	03/06	04/06	05/06	06/06	07/06
4	4	3	2	2	2	2	2	2	2	-	10

It all ended in tears for Czech football at the end of a season that had promised so much. Going into the FIFA World Cup™ finals, the national team was ranked second in the world and were actively being touted as dark horses for the title, talk that was bolstered after a fine 3-0 opening win against the USA. The injury to Koller in that match, however, was to prove critical as lack of firepower saw the team lose 2-0 against Ghana, and then by the same result to Italy, to go crashing out at the first stage. It was a huge disappointment for a nation making its first appearance in the finals without the Slovaks. Earlier, the end of the championship had been tainted with yet more

INTERNATIONAL HONOURS
Qualified for the FIFA World Cup™ finals 2006   UEFA U-21 Championship 2002

corruption as match fixing claims came back to haunt Czech football. Two contentious penalties had been given in Mlada Bloeslav's 3-2 win at champions Slovan Liberec, a result that qualified Mlada for the UEFA Champions League, while Viktoria Plzen's 3-1 win away against Sparta Praha, also thanks to two dubious penalties, saw them avoid relegation. Sparta only narrowly avoided missing out on qualifying for Europe for the first time in 24 years thanks to a penalty shoot-out victory in the Cup Final. After a goalless draw against the previous year's winners, Baník Ostrava, Sparta held their nerve to win 4-2.

THE FIFA BIG COUNT OF 2000

	Male	Female		Male	Female
Registered players	241 235	2 984	Referees	3 600	5
Non registered players	100 000	3 000	Officials	8 000	200
Youth players	236 988	3 038	Total involved	599 050	
Total players	587 245		Number of clubs	2 000	
Professional players	1 208	0	Number of teams	3 940	

Football Association of Czech Republic (CMFS)

Ceskomoravsky Fotbalovy Svaz, Diskarska 100, Praha 6 - 16017, Czech Republic
Tel +420 2 33029111   Fax +420 2 33353107
cmfs@fotbal.cz   www.fotbal.cz
President: MOKRY Pavel   General Secretary: FOUSEK Petr
Vice-President: KOSTAL Vlastimil   Treasurer: FISCHER Jiri   Media Officer: MACHO Daniel
Men's Coach: BRUCKNER Karel   Women's Coach: ZOVINEC Dusan
CMFS formed: 1901   UEFA: 1954   FIFA: 1907 & 1994
Red shirts with blue and white trimmings, White shorts, Blue socks or White shirts, White shorts, White socks

RECENT INTERNATIONAL MATCHES PLAYED BY THE CZECH REPUBLIC

2003	Opponents	Score	Venue	Comp	Scorers	Att	Referee
12-02	France	W 2-0	Paris	Fr	Grygera [7], Baros [62]	57 366	Stark GER
29-03	Netherlands	D 1-1	Rotterdam	ECq	Koller [68]	51 180	Nielsen DEN
2-04	Austria	W 4-0	Prague	ECq	Nedved [19], Koller 2 [32 62], Jankulovski [56p]	20 000	Nieto ESP
30-04	Turkey	W 4-0	Teplice	Fr	Rosicky [2], Koller [21], Smicer [27], Baros [38]	14 156	Szabo HUN
11-06	Moldova	W 5-0	Olomouc	ECq	Smicer [41], Koller [73p], Stajner [82], Lokvenc 2 [88 90]	12 097	Jakobsson ISL
6-09	Belarus	W 3-1	Minsk	ECq	Nedved [37], Baros [54], Smicer [85]	11 000	McCurry SCO
10-09	Netherlands	W 3-1	Prague	ECq	Koller [15p], Poborsky [38], Baros [90]	18 356	Batista POR
11-10	Austria	W 3-2	Vienna	ECq	Jankulovski [27], Vachousek [79], Koller [90]	32 350	Kasnaferis GRE
15-11	Canada	W 5-1	Teplice	Fr	Jankulovski [26p], Heinz [49], Poborsky [55], Sionko [63], Skacel [82]	8 343	Sundell SWE
2004							
18-02	Italy	D 2-2	Palermo	Fr	Stajner [42], Rosicky [89]	20 935	Braamhaar NED
31-03	Republic of Ireland	L 1-2	Dublin	Fr	Baros [81]	42 000	Fisker DEN
28-04	Japan	L 0-1	Prague	Fr		11 802	McKeon IRE
2-06	Bulgaria	W 3-1	Prague	Fr	Baros [54], Plasil [74], Rosicky [81]	6 627	Stredak SVK
6-06	Estonia	W 2-0	Teplice	Fr	Baros 2 [6 22]	11 873	Bruggwer AUT
15-06	Latvia	W 2-1	Aveiro	ECr1	Baros [73], Heinz [85]	21 744	Veissiere FRA
19-06	Netherlands	W 3-2	Aveiro	ECr1	Koller [23], Baros [71], Smicer [88]	29 935	Gonzalez ESP
23-06	Germany	W 2-1	Lisbon	ECr1	Heinz [30], Baros [77]	46 849	Hauge NOR
27-06	Denmark	W 3-0	Porto	ECqf	Koller [49], Baros 2 [63 65]	41 092	Ivanov RUS
1-07	Greece	L 0-1	Porto	ECsf		42 449	Collina ITA
18-08	Greece	D 0-0	Prague	Fr		15 050	Dougal SCO
8-09	Netherlands	L 0-2	Amsterdam	WCq		48 488	Merk GER
9-10	Romania	W 1-0	Prague	WCq	Koller [36]	16 028	Rosetti ITA
13-10	Armenia	W 3-0	Yerevan	WCq	Koller 2 [3 75]	3 205	Granat POL
17-11	FYR Macedonia	W 2-0	Skopje	WCq	Lokvenc [88], Koller [90]	7 000	Meier SUI
2005							
9-02	Slovenia	W 3-0	Celje	Fr	Koller [10], Jun [47], Polak [79]	4 000	Strahonja CRO
26-03	Finland	W 4-3	Teplice	WCq	Baros [7], Rosicky [34], Polak [58], Lokvenc [87]	16 200	Larsen DEN
30-03	Andorra	W 4-0	Andorra la Vella	WCq	Jankulovski [31p], Baros [40], Lokvenc [53], Rosicky [92+p]	900	Messner AUT
4-06	Andorra	W 8-1	Liberec	WCq	Lokvenc 2 [12 92], Koller [30], Smicer [37], Galasek [52], Baros [79], Rosicky [84], Polak [86]	9 520	Dereli TUR
8-06	FYR Macedonia	W 6-1	Teplice	WCq	Koller 4 [41 45 48 52], Rosicky [73p], Baros [87]	14 150	Dauden Ibanez ESP
17-08	Sweden	L 1-2	Gothenburg	Fr	Koller [22p]	23 117	Bennett ENG
3-09	Romania	L 0-2	Constanta	WCq		7 000	Hauge NOR
7-09	Armenia	W 4-1	Olomouc	WCq	Heinz [47], Polak 2 [52 76], Baros [58]	12 015	Hansson SWE
8-10	Netherlands	L 0-2	Prague	WCq		17 478	Sars FRA
12-10	Finland	W 3-0	Helsinki	WCq	Jun [6], Rosicky [51], Heinz [58]	11 234	Mejuto Gonzalez ESP
12-11	Norway	W 1-0	Oslo	WCpo	Smicer [31]	24 264	Busacca SUI
16-11	Norway	W 1-0	Prague	WCpo	Rosicky [35]	17 464	Poll ENG
2006							
1-03	Turkey	D 2-2	Izmir	Fr	Poborsky [21p], Stajner [63]	58 000	Meyer GER
26-05	Saudi Arabia	W 2-0	Innsbruck	Fr	Baros [15], Jankulovski [90p]	4 000	Einwaller AUT
30-05	Costa Rica	W 1-0	Jablonec	Fr	Lokvenc [82]	14 500	Bede HUN
3-06	Trinidad and Tobago	W 3-0	Prague	Fr	Koller 2 [6 40], Nedved [22]	15 910	Johansson SWE
12-06	USA	W 3-0	Gelsenkirchen	WCr1	Koller [5], Rosicky 2 [36 76]	52 000	Amarilla PAR
17-06	Ghana	L 0-2	Cologne	WCr1		45 000	Elizondo ARG
22-06	Italy	L 0-2	Hamburg	WCr1		50 000	Archundia MEX

Fr = Friendly match • EC = UEFA EURO 2004™ • WC = FIFA World Cup™ • q = qualifier • r1 = first round group • qf = quarter-final • sf = semi-final

CZECH REPUBLIC NATIONAL TEAM RECORDS AND RECORD SEQUENCES

Records			Sequence records					
Victory	6-0	MLT 1996, BUL 2001	Wins	7	2003	Clean sheets	4	Three times
Defeat	0-3	SUI 1994	Defeats	3	2000	Goals scored	17	2002-2004
Player Caps	118	POBORSKY Karel	Undefeated	20	2002-2004	Without goal	3	2004
Player Goals	43	KOLLER Jan	Without win	3	Four times	Goals against	8	1999-2000, 2003-04

CZECH REPUBLIC COUNTRY INFORMATION

Capital	Prague (Praha)	Independence	1993 split from Slovakia	GDP per Capita	$15 700
Population	10 246 178	Status	Republic	GNP Ranking	45
Area km²	78 866	Language	Czech	Dialling code	+420
Population density	129 per km²	Literacy rate	99%	Internet code	.cz
% in urban areas	65%	Main religion	Christian 43%, Atheist 40%	GMT + / −	+1
Towns/Cities ('000)	Praha 1 154; Brno 377; Ostrava 317; Plzen 165; Olomouc 102; Liberec 99; Ceske Budejovice 97				
Neighbours (km)	Poland 658; Slovakia 215 Austria 362; Germany 646				
Main stadia	Strahov – Praha 20 565; Na Stinadlech – Teplice 18 428; Andruv – Olomouc 12 119				

CZECH REPUBLIC NATIONAL TEAM PLAYERS AND COACHES

Record Caps			Record Goals			Recent Coaches	
POBORSKY Karel	1994-'06	118	KOLLER Jan	1999-'06	43	JEZEK Vaclav	1993
KUKA Pavel	1990-'01	87	KUKA Pavel	1990-'01	29	UHRIN Dusan	1994-'97
NEDVED Pavel	1994-'06	90	BAROS Milan	2001-'06	27	CHOVANEC Jozef	1998-'01
NEMEC Jiri	1990-'01	83	SMICER Vladimir	1993-'05	27	BRUECKNER Karel	2001-
SMICER Vladimir	1993-'05	81	BERGER Patrick	1993-'01	18		
LOKVENC Vratislav	1995-'06	74	NEDVED Pavel	1994-'06	18		
KOLLER Jan	1999-'06	69	SKUHRAVY Tomas	1985-'95	17		
KADLEC Miroslav	1987-'97	64	ROSICKY Tomas	2000-'06	15		

Appearances for Czechoslovakia:
Kuka 24 of 87, Nemec 40 of 84, Kadlec 38 of 64

Goals for Czechoslovakia:
Kuka 7 of 29, Skuhravy 14 of 17

CLUB DIRECTORY

Club	Town/City	Stadium	Capacity	www.	Lge	Cup
FC Baník Ostrava	Ostrava	Bazaly	18 020	fcb.cz	1 - 3	1 - 3
FK Chmel Blsany	Blsany	Chmel	2 300	fkblsany.cz	0	0
1.FC Brno	Brno	Na Srbské	12 500	1fcbrno.cz	0 - 1	0
SK Dynamo	Ceské Budéjovice	Na Steleckem Ostrove	6 129	dynamocb.cz	0	0
1.FK Drnovice	Drnovice	Drnovice	6 400	fkdrnovice.cz	0	0
FK Jablonec 97	Jablonec nad Nisou	Strelnice	15 577	fkjablonec97.cz	0	1 - 0
FK Marila Pribram	Pribram	Marila	8 000	fkmarila.cz	0	0
FK Mladá Boleslav	Mladá Boleslav	Mestsky	4 280	fk-mladaboleslav.cz	0	0
SFC Opava	Opava	Mestsky	17 687	sfc.cz	0	0
SK Sigma Olomouc	Olomouc	Andruv	12 119	sigmafotbal.cz	0	0
SK Slavia Praha	Prague	Evzena Rosickeho	19 336	slavia.cz	5 - 9	3 - 15
1.FC Slovácko	Uherské Hradiste	Mestsky Futbalovy	8 121	fc.synot.cz	0	0
FC Slovan Liberec	Liberec	U Nisy	9 090	fcslovanliberec.cz	2 - 0	1 - 0
AC Sparta Praha	Prague	Strahov (Toyota Arena)	20 565	sparta.cz	11 - 19	3 - 22
FK Teplice	Teplice	Na Stinadlech	18 428	fkteplice.cz	0	1 - 0
FC Tescoma Zlín	Zlín	Letná	4 541	fctescomazlin.cz	0	0

Where there are two figures in the League or Cup column, the first shows titles won in Czech tournaments, the second in Czechoslovakian tournaments

RECENT LEAGUE AND CUP RECORD

	Championship						Cup		
Year	Champions	Pts	Runners-up	Pts	Third	Pts		Winners	Score	Runners-up
1990								Dukla Praha	5-3	Uherske Hradiste
1991								Baník Ostrava	4-2	Dy. Ceske Budejovice
1992								Sparta Praha	2-1	Baník Ostrava
1993								Sparta Praha	2-0	FC Boby Brno
1994	Sparta Praha	45	Slavia Praha	39	Baník Ostrava	36		Viktoria Zizkov	2-2 6-5p	Sparta Praha
1995	Sparta Praha	70	Slavia Praha	64	Boby Brno	54		SK Hradec Kralové	0-0 3-1p	Viktoria Zizkov
1996	Slavia Praha	70	Sigma Olomouc	61	Jablonec nad Nisou	53		Sparta Praha	4-0	Petra Drnovice
1997	Sparta Praha	65	Slavia Praha	61	Jablonec nad Nisou	56		Slavia Praha	1-0	Dukla Praha
1998	Sparta Praha	71	Slavia Praha	59	Sigma Olomouc	55		FK Jablonec	2-1	Petra Drnovice
1999	Sparta Praha	60	FK Teplice	55	Slavia Praha	55		Slavia Praha	1-0	Slovan Liberec
2000	Sparta Praha	76	Slavia Praha	68	FK Drnovice	48		Slovan Liberec	2-1	Baník Ratiskovice
2001	Sparta Praha	68	Slavia Praha	52	Sigma Olomouc	52		Viktoria Zizkov	2-1	Sparta Praha
2002	Slovan Liberec	64	Sparta Praha	63	Viktoria Zizkov	63		Slavia Praha	2-1	Sparta Praha
2003	Sparta Praha	65	Slavia Praha	64	Viktoria Zizkov	50		FK Teplice	1-0	FK Jablonec
2004	Baník Ostrava	63	Sparta Praha	58	Sigma Olomouc	55		Sparta Praha	2-1	Baník Ostrava
2005	Sparta Praha	64	Slavia Praha	53	FK Teplice	53		Baník Ostrava	2-1	1.FC Slovácko
2006	Slovan Liberec	59	Mladá Boleslav	54	Slavia Praha	54		Sparta Praha	0-0 4-2p	Baník Ostrava

Prior to 1994 clubs played in the Czechoslovakian League, whilst the winners of the Czech Cup played the winners of the Slovak Cup

CZECH REPUBLIC 2005-06

I. GAMBRINUS LIGA

	Pl	W	D	L	F	A	Pts	Slovan	Mladá	Slavia	Teplice	Sparta	Baník	Slovácko	Jablonec	Sigma	Siad	Tescoma	Brno	Marila	Viktoria	Vysocina	Chmel
Slovan Liberec †	30	16	11	3	43	22	59		2-3	3-3	1-1	2-0	1-0	2-0	2-0	2-0	1-1	1-0	0-0	1-0	2-0	0-0	2-0
Mladá Boleslav †	30	16	6	8	50	36	54	2-4		4-1	0-2	2-0	2-1	1-0	2-1	2-0	1-0	2-0	2-1	0-0	2-2	4-0	4-1
Slavia Praha ‡	30	15	9	6	56	34	54	1-3	2-1		1-1	4-1	4-0	2-0	3-2	2-1	3-0	1-0	3-1	1-0	1-1	1-1	0-0
FK Teplice	30	12	16	2	38	24	52	0-0	1-1	1-0		2-1	0-2	0-0	1-1	1-0	4-3	2-1	1-1	2-1	2-1	3-1	2-1
Sparta Praha ‡	30	13	6	11	43	39	45	1-2	4-2	2-1	0-0		0-2	1-0	3-0	1-2	2-1	1-0	1-1	1-1	1-3	2-0	5-2
Baník Ostrava	30	10	10	10	35	32	40	1-1	1-3	1-3	0-0	0-2		2-0	2-1	4-1	0-0	4-1	1-1	0-1	6-0	1-0	0-0
1.FC Slovácko	30	9	11	10	29	28	38	1-2	1-1	0-0	1-1	2-0	0-0		1-0	2-2	2-1	2-0	1-1	2-0	1-0	1-0	2-0
FK Jablonec 97	30	10	7	13	35	39	37	1-0	1-1	0-2	0-0	2-1	1-2	2-1		1-2	3-0	2-0	0-2	3-1	3-1	0-0	2-0
Sigma Olomouc	30	10	7	13	34	44	37	1-0	2-3	4-3	0-0	1-2	1-0	1-1	0-2		1-1	0-0	3-2	2-1	1-1	1-2	3-2
SIAD Most	30	10	6	14	34	41	36	1-2	1-0	0-3	2-1	0-3	4-0	3-2	3-0	0-2		0-0	3-3	1-0	1-0	2-1	3-1
Tescoma Zlin	30	8	11	11	27	33	35	1-1	2-0	2-2	0-0	3-2	1-0	3-1	3-1	1-0	1-1		2-0	1-0	0-0	1-1	0-1
1.FC Brno	30	7	14	9	35	36	35	0-1	4-2	1-0	1-2	1-1	1-1	0-0	1-1	1-0	1-1	1-0		1-1	1-3	1-2	1-0
Marila Pribram	30	8	10	12	36	36	34	2-2	1-2	2-2	1-1	2-2	2-2	1-1	2-2	1-1	1-2	3-0	1-0		3-0	2-1	1-1
Viktoria Plzen	30	7	10	13	30	43	31	1-1	0-1	1-1	3-3	1-2	0-0	0-2	1-2	1-0	2-1	1-1	2-1	2-1		0-0	2-0
Vysocina Jihlava	30	6	11	13	20	36	29	0-2	0-0	0-3	0-4	0-1	0-1	1-0	1-1	3-0	1-0	0-0	0-0	0-2	2-3		0-0
Chmel Blsany	30	5	11	14	22	44	26	0-0	1-0	1-3	0-0	0-0	1-1	1-1	1-0	0-2	0-1	3-2	2-2	1-0	0-3	2-2	

5/08/2005 - 13/05/2006 • † Qualified for the UEFA Champions League • ‡ Qualified for the UEFA Cup • Top scorer: Milan IVANA, Slovácko, 11

CZECH REPUBLIC 2005-06
II. LIGA

	Pl	W	D	L	F	A	Pts
SK Kladno	30	17	6	7	45	21	57
Dy. Ceske Budejovice	30	17	4	9	55	26	55
MFK Ustí nad Labem	30	14	7	9	47	39	49
FC Hradec Králové	30	13	10	7	31	28	49
Viktoria Zizkov	30	12	10	8	42	33	46
HFK Olomouc	30	9	14	7	27	32	41
Xaverov H. Pocerince	30	11	7	12	40	35	40
Hanácká S. Kromeriz	30	10	9	11	32	36	39
FC Vitkovice	30	9	9	12	26	33	36
Hlucín	30	10	6	14	31	47	36
FK Kunovice	30	9	8	13	35	43	35
AS Pardubice	30	9	7	14	35	38	34
Sparta Praha 'B'	30	8	10	12	32	37	34
Sigma Olomouc 'B'	30	9	7	14	33	40	34
1.FK Drnovice	30	7	13	10	24	40	34
1.FC Brno 'B'	30	7	11	12	24	32	32

5/08/2005 - 11/06/2006

POHAR CMFS 2005-06

Round of 16

Sparta Praha	2
SK Kladno *	0
Chmel Blsany	2 3p
Viktoria Zizkov	2 4p
1.FC Slovácko *	2
FK Teplice	0
Ustí nad Labem *	0
1.FC Brno	1
FC Hradec Králové *	2
HFK Olomouc	1
FC Vítkovice *	0
Slavia Praha	1
FK Kunovice *	1
Dynamo Ceské B'jovice	0
Marila Príbram *	1
Baník Ostrava	2

Quarter-finals

Sparta Praha *	2
Viktoria Zizkov	0
1.FC Slovácko *	0 1p
1.FC Brno	0 4p
FC Hradec Králové *	1
Slavia Praha	0
FK Kunovice *	0
Baník Ostrava	2

Semi-finals

Sparta Praha *	2
1.FC Brno	0
FC Hradec Králové	0
Baník Ostrava *	2

Final

Sparta Praha ‡	0 4p
Baník Ostrava	0 2p

CUP FINAL

U Nisy, Liberec
19-05-2006, Att: 4 464, Ref: Damková

* Home team • ‡ Qualified for the UEFA Cup

DEN – DENMARK

NATIONAL TEAM RECORD
JULY 1ST 2002 TO JULY 9TH 2006

PL	W	D	L	F	A	%
46	25	13	8	82	45	68.5

FIFA/COCA-COLA WORLD RANKING

1993	1994	1995	1996	1997	1998	1999	2000	2001	2002	2003	2004	2005		High		Low	
6	14	9	6	8	19	11	22	18	12	13	14	13		3	05/97	27	05/98

	2005–2006										
08/05	09/05	10/05	11/05	12/05	01/06	02/06	03/06	04/06	05/06	06/06	07/06
18	14	14	13	13	13	14	14	11	11	-	17

Morten Olsen's Danish national team may have missed out on the finals of the FIFA World Cup™ but there were enough encouraging signs to bode well for the UEFA Euro 2008™ qualifiers. Indeed it wasn't until the final match of the season, against France, that Denmark lost, a run that included a comprehensive victory over England and seven straight wins. Danish clubs, however, continue to struggle in European club competition, with Brøndby failing yet again to qualify for the group stage of the Champions League, although the introduction of the Royal League has added an extra dimension to Scandinavian club football. Danish clubs have done well, particularly FC

INTERNATIONAL HONOURS
Qualified for the FIFA World Cup™ finals 1986 1998 2002 Qualified for the FIFA Women's World Cup finals 1991 1995 1999
UEFA European Championship 1992

København, who retained their title in 2006 thanks to a 1-0 victory over Norway's Lillestrøm in the final at the Parken in Copenhagen. København then went on to win the Danish League to complete a miserable year for runners-up Brøndby, whose coach Michael Laudrup quit at the end of the season. It was a good year, though, for Second Division Randers. Not only did they win promotion, but they also won the Cup with a 1-0 win over Esbjerg. Karsten Johansen scored the only goal but was promptly sent-off for taking his shirt off, having already been booked.

THE FIFA BIG COUNT OF 2000

	Male	Female		Male	Female
Registered players	175 000	25 285	Referees	4 450	20
Non registered players	80 000	20 000	Officials	8 000	200
Youth players	70 000	25 000	Total involved	407 955	
Total players	395 285		Number of clubs	1 000	
Professional players	940	15	Number of teams	1 599	

Dansk Boldspil-Union (DBU)
DBU Allé 1, Brøndby 2605, Denmark
Tel +45 43 262222   Fax +45 43 262245
dbu@dbu.dk   www.dbu.dk
President: HANSEN Allan   General Secretary: HANSEN Jim
Vice-President: MOLLER Jesper   Treasurer: MOGENSEN Torben   Media Officer: BERENDT Lars
Men's Coach: OLSEN Morten   Women's Coach: HEINER-MOLLER Kenneth
DBU formed: 1889   UEFA: 1954   FIFA: 1904
Red shirts with white trimmings, White shorts, Red socks or White shirts with red trimmings, Red shorts, White socks

RECENT INTERNATIONAL MATCHES PLAYED BY DENMARK

2003	Opponents	Score	Venue	Comp	Scorers	Att	Referee
1-02	Iran	L 0-1	Hong Kong	Fr		15 100	Chiu Sin Chuen HKG
12-02	Egypt	W 4-1	Cairo	Fr	Jensen.C 3 [31 68 70], Tomasson [59]	30 000	El Fatah EGY
29-03	Romania	W 5-2	Bucharest	ECq	Rommedahl 2 [9 90], Gravesen [53], Tomasson [72], OG [74]	55 000	Gonzalez ESP
2-04	Bosnia-Herzegovina	L 0-2	Copenhagen	ECq		30 845	Stredak SVK
30-04	Ukraine	W 1-0	Copenhagen	Fr	Gravesen [37]	14 599	Mikulski POL
7-06	Norway	W 1-0	Copenhagen	ECq	Gronkjaer [5]	41 824	Poll ENG
11-06	Luxembourg	W 2-0	Luxembourg	ECq	Jensen.C [22], Gravesen [50]	6 869	Baskakov RUS
20-08	Finland	D 1-1	Copenhagen	Fr	Gonkjaer [42]	14 882	McCurry SCO
10-09	Romania	D 2-2	Copenhagen	ECq	Tomasson [35p], Lauresen [90]	42 049	Meier SUI
11-10	Bosnia-Herzegovina	D 1-1	Sarajevo	ECq	Jorgensen.M [12]	35 500	Barber ENG
15-11	England	W 3-2	Manchester	Fr	Jorgensen.M 2 [8 30p], Tomasson [82]	64 159	Hrinak SVK
2004							
18-01	USA	D 1-1	Carson	Fr	Larsen [28p]	10 461	Moreno MEX
18-02	Turkey	W 1-0	Adana	Fr	Jorgensen.M [32]	15 000	Wack GER
31-03	Spain	L 0-2	Gijon	Fr		18 600	Costa POR
28-04	Scotland	W 1-0	Copenhagen	Fr	Sand [61]	22 485	Ingvarsson SWE
30-05	Estonia	D 2-2	Tallinn	Fr	Tomasson [28], Perez [80]	3 000	Bossen HOL
5-06	Croatia	L 1-2	Copenhagen	Fr	Sand [56]	30 843	Stuchlik AUT
14-06	Italy	D 0-0	Guimaraes	ECr1		19 595	Gonzalez ESP
18-06	Bulgaria	W 2-0	Braga	ECr1	Tomasson [44], Gronkjaer [90]	24 131	Baptista POR
22-06	Sweden	D 2-2	Porto	ECr1	Tomasson 2 [28 66]	26 115	Merk GER
27-06	Czech Republic	L 0-3	Porto	ECqf		41 092	Ivanov RUS
18-08	Poland	W 5-1	Poznan	Fr	Madsen 3 [23 30 90], Gaardsoe [51], Jensen.C [86]	4 500	Bebek CRO
4-09	Ukraine	D 1-1	Copenhagen	WCq	Jorgensen.M [9]	36 335	Meier SUI
9-10	Albania	W 2-0	Tirana	WCq	Jorgensen.M [52], Tomasson [72]	14 500	Baskakov RUS
13-10	Turkey	D 1-1	Copenhagen	WCq	Tomasson [27p]	41 331	De Santis ITA
17-11	Georgia	D 2-2	Tbilisi	WCq	Tomasson 2 [7 64]	20 000	Ceferin SVN
2005							
9-02	Greece	L 1-2	Athens	WCq	Rommedahl [46+]	32 430	Collina ITA
26-03	Kazakhstan	W 3-0	Copenhagen	WCq	Moller.P 2 [10 48], Poulsen [33]	20 980	Gilewski POL
30-03	Ukraine	L 0-1	Kyiv	WCq		60 000	Michel SVK
2-06	Finland	W 1-0	Tampere	Fr	Silberhauser [90]	9 238	Wegereef NED
8-06	Albania	W 3-1	Copenhagen	WCq	Larsen.S 2 [5 47], Jorgensen.M [55]	26 366	Frojdfeldt SWE
17-08	England	W 4-1	Copenhagen	Fr	Rommedahl [60], Tomasson [63], Gravgaard [67], Larsen [92+]	41 438	Ovrebro NOR
3-09	Turkey	D 2-2	Istanbul	WCq	Jensen [40], Larsen [93+]	29 721	Mejuto Gonzalez ESP
7-09	Georgia	W 6-1	Copenhagen	WCq	Jensen [10], Poulsen [30], Agger [43], Tomasson [55], Larsen 2 [80 84]	27 177	Bozinovski MKD
8-10	Greece	W 1-0	Copenhagen	WCq	Gravgaard [40]	42 099	De Bleeckere BEL
12-10	Kazakhstan	W 2-1	Almaty	WCq	Gravgaard [46], Tomasson [49]	8 050	Trivkovic CRO
2006							
26-01	Singapore	W 2-1	Singapore	Fr	Bech 2 [58 67]	10 392	Srinivasan IND
29-01	Hong Kong	W 3-0	Hong Kong	Fr	Berg [19], Augustinussen [39], Due [51]	16 841	Iemoto JPN
1-02	Korea Republic	W 3-1	Hong Kong	Fr	Jacobsen [43], Bech [65], Silberbauer [88]	13 971	Fong Yau Fat HKG
1-03	Israel	W 2-0	Tel Aviv	Fr	Perez [3], Skoubo [18]	15 762	Sippel GER
27-05	Paraguay	D 1-1	Aarhus	Fr	Tomasson [51]	20 047	Bennett ENG
31-05	France	L 0-2	Lens	Fr		39 000	Kelly IRL

Fr = Friendly match • EC = UEFA EURO 2004™ • WC = FIFA World Cup™ • q = qualifier • r1 = first round group • qf = quarter-final

DENMARK NATIONAL TEAM RECORDS AND RECORD SEQUENCES

Records			Sequence records				
Victory	17-1	FRA 1908	Wins	11	1912-1916	Clean sheets	4	1993, 1995
Defeat	0-8	GER 1937	Defeats	7	1970-1971	Goals scored	26	1942-1948
Player Caps	129	SCHMEICHEL Peter	Undefeated	12	1992-93, 2005-06	Without goal	7	1970-1971
Player Goals	52	NIELSEN Poul	Without win	14	1969-1971	Goals against	21	1939-1946

DENMARK COUNTRY INFORMATION

Capital	Copenhagen	Independence	950 as a unified state	GDP per Capita	$31 100
Population	5 413 392	Status	Kingdom	GNP Ranking	25
Area km²	43 094	Language	Danish	Dialling code	+45
Population density	125 per km²	Literacy rate	99%	Internet code	.dk
% in urban areas	85%	Main religion	Christian 98%	GMT + / –	+1
Towns/Cities ('000)	København 1 089; Aarhus 226; Odense 145; Aalborg 122; Esbjerg 72; Randers 55				
Neighbours (km)	Germany 68; North Sea & Baltic Sea 7 314				
Main stadia	Parken – Copenhagen 41 781; Brøndby – Copenhagen 29 000; Idrætspark – Aarhus 21 000				

DENMARK NATIONAL TEAM PLAYERS AND COACHES

Record Caps			Record Goals			Recent Coaches	
SCHMEICHEL Peter	1987-'01	129	NIELSEN Poul	1912-'25	52	WILLIAMS Charles	1908-'10
LAUDRUP Michael	1982-'98	104	JØRGENSEN Pauli	1925-'39	44	ANDERSEN BYRVAL Axel	1913-'18
OLSEN Morten	1970-'89	102	MADSEN Ole	1958-'69	42	SØRENSEN Arne	1956-'61
HELVEG Thomas	1994-'05	100	TOMASSON Jon Dahl	1997-'06	39	PETERSEN Poul	1962-'66
SIVEBAEK John	1982-'92	87	ELKJAER-LARSEN Preben	1977-'88	38	STRITTICH Rudi	1970-'75
HEINTZE Jan	1987-'02	86	LAUDRUP Michael	1982-'98	35	NIELSEN Kurt	1976-'79
OLSEN Lars	1986-'96	84	ENOKSEN Henning	1958-'66	29	PIONTEK Sepp	1979-'90
LAUDRUP Brian	1987-'98	82	ROHDE Michael	1915-'31	22	MØLLER-NIELSEN Richard	1990-'96
TOMASSON Jon Dahl	1997-'06	81	SAND Ebbe	1998-'04	22	JOHANSSON Bo	1996-'00
VILFORT KIM	1983-'96	77				OLSEN Morten	2000-

CLUB DIRECTORY

Club	Town/City	Stadium	Capacity	www.	Lge	Cup
AaB	Aalborg	Aalborg	16 000	ab-fodbold.dk	2	2
AGF	Aarhus	Aarhus Idrætspark	21 000	agf.co.dk	5	9
Brøndby IF	København	Brøndby	29 000	brondby.com	10	5
Esbjerg FB	Esbjerg	Esbjerg Idrætspark	14 500	efb.dk	5	2
Herfølge BK	Herfølge	Herfølge	7 500	hb.dk	1	0
FC København	København	Parken	41 781	fck.dk	5	3
FC Midtjylland	Herning	SAS Arena	12 500	fc-mj.dk	0	0
FC Nordsjælland	Farum	Farum Park	10 000	fcnfodbold.dk	0	0
OB	Odense	Odense	15 633	ob.dk	3	4
Randers FC	Randers	Randers	18 000	randersfc.dk	0	4
Silkeborg IF	Silkeborg	Silkeborg	9 800	sif-support.dk	1	1
Viborg FF	Viborg	Viborg	9 796	vff.dk	0	1

KB won 15 championships and one Cup whilst B1903 won seven Championships and two Cups before the clubs merged in 1992 to form FC København

RECENT LEAGUE AND CUP RECORD

	Championship						Cup		
Year	Champions	Pts	Runners-up	Pts	Third	Pts		Winners	Score	Runners-up
1990	Brøndby IF	42	B 1903 København	31	Ikast FS	30		Lyngby BK	0-0 6-1	AGF Aarhus
1991	Brøndby IF	26	Lyngby BK	24	AGF Aarhus	20		OB Odense	0-0 4-3p	AaB Aalborg
1992	Lyngby BK	32	B 1903 København	29	Frem København	26		AGF Aarhus	3-0	B 1903 København
1993	FC København	32	OB Odense	31	Brøndby IF	30		OB Odense	2-0	AaB Aalborg
1994	Silkeborg IF	31	FC København	29	Brøndby IF	27		Brøndby IF	0-0 3-1p	Naestved IF
1995	AaB Aalborg	31	Brøndby IF	29	Silkeborg IF	24		FC København	5-0	Akademisk
1996	Brøndby IF	67	AGF Aarhus	66	OB Odense	60		AGF Aarhus	2-0	Brøndby IF
1997	Brøndby IF	68	Vejle BK	54	AGF Aarhus	52		FC København	2-0	Ikast FS
1998	Brøndby IF	76	Silkeborg IF	63	FC København	61		Brøndby IF	4-1	FC København
1999	AaB Aalborg	64	Brøndby IF	61	Akademisk	56		Akademisk	2-1	AaB Aalborg
2000	Herfølge BK	56	Brøndby IF	54	Akademisk	52		Viborg FF	1-0	AaB Aalborg
2001	FC København	63	Brøndby IF	58	Silkeborg IF	56		Silkeborg IF	4-1	Akademisk
2002	Brøndby IF	69	FC København	69	FC Midtjylland	57		OB Odense	2-1	FC København
2003	FC København	61	Brøndby IF	56	Farum BK	51		Brøndby IF	3-0	FC Midtjylland
2004	FC København	68	Brøndby IF	67	Esbjerg FB	62		FC København	1-0	AaB Aalborg
2005	Brøndby IF	69	FC København	57	FC Midtjylland	57		Brøndby IF	3-2	FC Midtjylland
2006	FC København	73	Brøndby IF	67	OB Odense	58		Randers FC	1-0	Esbjerg FB

DENMARK 2005–06

SAS LIGAEN

	Pl	W	D	L	F	A	Pts	København	Brøndby	OB	Viborg	AaB	Esbjerg	Midtjylland	Silkeborg	Nordsjælland	Horsens	Sønderjyske	AGF
FC København †	33	22	7	4	62	27	73		0-0	1-1	2-1 3-1	1-0	5-1 2-1	3-1 2-0	2-0 2-3	3-3	2-0 1-0	4-1	1-1 1-1
Brøndby IF ‡	33	21	4	8	60	34	67	1-1 3-0		1-0	1-0 3-1	4-3 3-0	3-0 5-0	2-0 3-1	2-1 3-1	4-1	3-0	1-2	4-0
OB Odense	33	17	7	9	49	28	58	0-2 1-0	1-3 0-1		3-0	2-1 0-2	1-0	0-1	3-1 2-1	0-0 2-0	3-0	2-3 3-0	3-1
Viborg FF	33	15	9	9	62	43	54	0-1	3-1	2-0 1-2		2-2 2-0	2-0 1-0	1-1	2-3	3-1 4-1	1-1	3-1 1-1	2-2
AaB Aalborg	33	11	12	10	48	44	45	0-1 0-2	3-0	0-0	1-1		2-0 1-0	1-1 2-2	1-1	1-0 1-1	2-4	2-2 3-2	2-2 1-1
Esbjerg FB	33	12	6	15	43	45	42	3-1	2-3	0-0 2-2	1-0	4-3		2-1 2-0	4-0 2-0	4-0 0-0	1-1 3-2	0-1	1-3
FC Midtjylland	33	10	11	12	42	52	41	1-3	2-0	0-1 1-2	1-1 0-1	2-4	2-1		0-0 1-0	0-2 1-1	2-1 0-0	2-2 3-3	2-0
Silkeborg IF	33	11	6	16	33	50	39	0-3	2-0	1-0	1-1 1-3	1-4 2-1	0-0	1-1		2-0 0-1	2-1 3-2	0-1 2-1	1-0
FC Nordsjælland	33	9	11	13	49	55	38	1-2 1-1	0-2 0-3	1-3	0-1	2-0	0-2	3-2	2-2		5-0 3-0	1-1 4-2	3-1
AC Horsens	33	8	13	12	29	41	37	0-1	0-0 4-1	0-0 0-0	3-3 1-0	0-0 1-0	3-4	0-0	0-0	2-0		1-1	2-1
Sønderjyske	33	6	8	19	41	72	26	0-1 1-4	1-2 2-4	0-4	2-2	0-1	1-3 2-4	0-2	2-0	2-2	1-3 1-1		2-1 1-0
AGF Aarhus	33	4	10	19	36	63	22	0-4	3-0 0-2	0-4 1-3	0-2 0-1	2-3	3-3 1-1	2-4	1-1	2-2	1-2	2-0	

19/07/2005 – 14/05/2006 • † Qualified for the UEFA Champions League • ‡ Qualified for the UEFA Cup • Top scorers: Steffen HØJER, Viborg, 16; Mads JUNKER, Nordsjælland, 15; ALVARO SANTOS, København, 15; Marcus ALLBACK, København, 15; Fredrik BERGLUND, Esbjerg 14

DENMARK 2005–06
1. DIVISION (2)

	Pl	W	D	L	F	A	Pts
Vejle BK	30	19	6	5	62	32	**63**
Randers FC	30	19	4	7	64	30	**61**
Lyngby BK	30	18	5	7	68	44	**59**
Køge	30	17	8	5	59	35	**59**
Fremad Amager	30	15	4	11	54	55	**49**
Kolding FC	30	14	4	12	50	50	**46**
FC Frederica	30	12	5	13	48	40	**41**
Olstykke	30	12	5	13	41	40	**41**
Herfølge BK	30	11	7	12	51	41	**40**
Frem København	30	11	7	12	47	42	**40**
Hellerup IK	30	9	11	10	44	44	**38**
Akademisk Boldclub	30	11	4	15	43	54	**37**
Brabrand	30	10	5	15	32	54	**35**
Nykøbing Alliancen	30	9	7	14	51	53	**34**
Skjold	30	4	6	20	27	75	**18**
Brønshøj	30	1	8	21	28	80	**11**

30/07/2005 – 18/06/2006

DONG CUP 2005–06

Round of 16		Quarter-finals		Semi-finals		Final	
Randers FC *	2						
AC Horsens	0	Randers FC *	3				
Viborg FF	2 5p	Frem København	0				
Frem København *	2 6p			Randers FC *	0 1		
OB Odense	1 6p			AaB Aalborg	0 1		
Kolding FC *	1 5p	OB Odense	2 6p				
FC Midtjylland	1	AaB Aalborg *	2 7p			Randers FC ‡	1
AaB Aalborg *	2					Esbjerg FB	0
Brøndby IF *	2						
Silkeborg IF	1	Brøndby IF *	1				
Slagelse BK&IF *	2 4p	FC København	0				
FC København	2 5p			Brøndby IF	2 1		
B 1909 Odense *	5			Esbjerg FC *	5 0		
Herfølge BK	2	B 1909 Odense *	1				
Lyngby BK *	0 4p	Esbjerg FC	3				
Esbjerg FC	0 5p						

CUP FINAL

Parken, Copenhagen
11-05-2006, Att: 23 825, Ref: KM Nielsen

Scorer - Karsten Johansen 114 for Randers

* Home team/home team in the first leg • ‡ Qualified for the UEFA Cup

DJI – DJIBOUTI

NATIONAL TEAM RECORD
JULY 1ST 2002 TO JULY 9TH 2006

PL	W	D	L	F	A	%
4	0	0	4	2	18	0

FIFA/COCA-COLA WORLD RANKING

1993	1994	1995	1996	1997	1998	1999	2000	2001	2002	2003	2004	2005		High		Low	
-	169	177	185	189	191	195	189	193	195	197	201	200		169	12/94	201	12/04

2005–2006											
08/05	09/05	10/05	11/05	12/05	01/06	02/06	03/06	04/06	05/06	06/06	07/06
201	201	201	201	200	200	200	200	200	200	-	196

Floundering at the bottom of the African football rankings, the tiny East African state will soon be treading unfamiliar waters as they participate in the qualifiers for the 2008 African Nations Cup finals. Djibouti, who have never gone above 169 in the FIFA/Coca-Cola World Ranking, have entered the preliminaries for the first time in six years. It is only the third time they have entered the qualifiers for the biennial championship but the opportunity of more regular international competition should serve the side well. That they have been paired at home with FIFA World Cup™ finalists Cote d'Ivoire can be seen as either a blessing or burden but the chance to rub shoulders

INTERNATIONAL HONOURS
None

with the likes of Didier Drogba and Bonaventure Kalou will certainly serve as inspiration to the 'Red Sea' players. At the end of 2005, Djibouti were heavily trounced in the four matches they played at the annual CECAFA Cup tournament, held in 2005 in Kigali, Rwanda. There was even a 2-1 defeat by traditional foes Somalia, whose infrastructure circumstances are far worse than that in the former French colony. The experience was the first international outing in four years for Djibouti and it is becoming increasingly apparent that the small state is now seeking to play a more regular role in international competition.

THE FIFA BIG COUNT OF 2000

	Male	Female		Male	Female
Registered players	900	132	Referees	70	0
Non registered players	2 000	0	Officials	400	0
Youth players	996	0	Total involved	4 498	
Total players	4 028		Number of clubs	40	
Professional players	0	0	Number of teams	90	

Fédération Djiboutienne de Football (FDF)
Centre Technique National, Case postale 2694, Djibouti
Tel +253 353599   Fax +253 353588
fdf-1979@yahoo.fr   www.none
President: DABAR Houssein Fadoul   General Secretary: KAMIL Hasan
Vice-President: YONIS Mohamed Yacin   Treasurer: HASSAN Ziad Moussa   Media Officer: None
Men's Coach: KAMIL Hasan   Women's Coach: KAMIL Hasan
FDF formed: 1979   CAF: 1986   FIFA: 1994
Green shirts, White shorts, Blue socks

RECENT INTERNATIONAL MATCHES PLAYED BY DJIBOUTI

2002	Opponents	Score	Venue	Comp	Scorers	Att	Referee
No international matches played in 2002							
2003							
No international matches played in 2003							
2004							
No international matches played in 2004							
2005							
27-11	Somalia	L 1-2	Kigali	CCr1	Abdoul Rahman Okishi		
30-11	Uganda	L 1-6	Kigali	CCr1	Abdirahman Okieh		
3-12	Ethiopia	L 0-6	Kigali	CCr1			
5-12	Sudan	L 0-4	Kigali	CCr1			
2006							
No international matches played in 2006 before July							

CC = CECAFA Cup • r1 = First round group

DJIBOUTI NATIONAL TEAM RECORDS AND RECORD SEQUENCES

Records			Sequence records					
Victory	4-1	YEM 1988	Wins	1		Clean sheets	1	
Defeat	1-10	UGA 2001	Defeats	7	1994-1999	Goals scored	6	1998-2000
Player Caps	n/a		Undefeated	1		Without goal	2	1994-1998, 2000
Player Goals	n/a		Without win	22	1994-2006	Goals against	20	1983-2000

RECENT LEAGUE AND CUP RECORD

	League		Cup		
Year	Champions	Winners	Score	Runners-up
1996	Force Nationale de Police	Balbala		
1997	Force Nationale de Police	Force Nationale de Police		
1998	Force Nationale de Police	Force Nationale de Police		
1999	Force Nationale de Police	Balbala		
2000	CDE Djibouti			
2001	Force Nationale de Police	Chemin de Fer		
2002	AS Borreh	Jeunesse Espoir		Chemin de Fer
2003	Gendarmerie Nationale	AS Borreh	1-1 5-4p	AS Ali-Sabieh
2004	Gendarmerie Nationale	Chemin de Fer	6-2	AS Borreh
2005	CDE Djibouti	Poste de Djibouti	2-0	AS Port

DJIBOUTI COUNTRY INFORMATION

Capital	Djibouti	Independence	1977 from France	GDP per Capita	$1 300
Population	768 200	Status	Republic	GNP Ranking	167
Area km²	23 000	Language	Arabic, French	Dialling code	+253
Population density	20 per km²	Literacy rate	49%	Internet code	.dj
% in urban areas	83%	Main religion	Muslim 94%	GMT +/−	+3
Towns/Cities ('000)	Djibouti 623; Ali Sabieh 40; Tadjoura 22; Obock 17; Dikhil 12				
Neighbours (km)	Somalia 58; Ethiopia 349; Eritrea 109; Red Sea & Gulf of Aden 314				
Main stadia	Stade du Ville – Djibouti 10 000				

DMA – DOMINICA

NATIONAL TEAM RECORD
JULY 1ST 2002 TO JULY 9TH 2006

PL	W	D	L	F	A	%
10	4	1	5	13	29	45

FIFA/COCA-COLA WORLD RANKING

1993	1994	1995	1996	1997	1998	1999	2000	2001	2002	2003	2004	2005	High		Low	
-	-	158	138	139	133	149	152	161	174	185	165	172	129	7/98	185	12/03

2005–2006											
08/05	09/05	10/05	11/05	12/05	01/06	02/06	03/06	04/06	05/06	06/06	07/06
167	167	167	169	172	172	172	173	174	174	-	183

In the end, the DFA CLICO Premiere Division Championship came down to the final match of the season, in March, between Harris Paints Harlem United from Newtown and Indian Inn River Bombers from Portsmouth. Bombers went into the match at the Geneva Playing Field two points ahead of Harlem United and twice they led in the match. They went ahead through Clayton Morvan only for Len Walters to equalise, but by half-time Malcolm Leblanc had restored the lead. In the second half United's coach Don Leogal brought on substitutes Junior Emanuel and Kerry Alleyne, both of whom went on to score to win the match for Harlem United. It was Harlem's seventh title

INTERNATIONAL HONOURS
None

in ten years, much to the delight of the majority of the thousand fans watching the game. The only action for the national team came in a short two game tour of Guyana during which both matches were lost 3-0. The women's national team entered the FIFA Women's World Cup qualifiers but after being drawn in a strong four team group played in Trinidad, they only just managed to avoid the wooden spoon on goal difference from Grenada, having lost to both St Vincent and Trinidad and Tobago. The under-19's fared better in their FIFA U-20 Women's World Championship qualifiers, managing a win against Anguilla, but they still didn't make it out of their group.

THE FIFA BIG COUNT OF 2000

	Male	Female		Male	Female
Registered players	463	30	Referees	35	0
Non registered players	500	0	Officials	21	0
Youth players	652	0	Total involved	1 701	
Total players	1 645		Number of clubs	15	
Professional players	0	0	Number of teams	19	

Dominica Football Association (DFA)
Bath Estate, PO Box 372, Roseau, Dominica
Tel +1 767 4487577   Fax +1 767 4487587
domfootball@cwdom.dm   www.none
President: FRANCIS Dexter   General Secretary: CELAIRE Clifford
Vice-President: PANDENQUE Mervin   Treasurer: GREENAWAY P. Walter   Media Officer: FRAMPTON Ferdinand
Men's Coach: LEOGAL Don   Women's Coach: ROBERTSON Hypolite
DFA formed: 1970   CONMEBOL: 1994   FIFA: 1994
Emerald shirts, Black shorts, Green socks

RECENT INTERNATIONAL MATCHES PLAYED BY DOMINICA

2002	Opponents	Score		Venue	Comp	Scorers	Att	Referee
No international matches played in 2002								
2003								
No international matches played in 2003								
2004								
28-01	British Virgin Islands	W	1-0	Tortola	Fr	Cuffy [34]		Matthew SKN
31-01	US Virgin Islands	W	5-0	St Thomas	Fr	OG [12], Marshall [42], Dangler [68], Casimir [87], George [90]		Matthew SKN
1-02	British Virgin Islands	W	2-1	Tortola	Fr	Marshall [44], Peters [70]		Charles DMA
12-03	Barbados	L	1-2	Bridgetown	Fr	Peters [88]	46	
26-03	Bahamas	D	1-1	Nassau	WCq	Casimir [88]	800	Forde BRB
28-03	Bahamas	W	3-1	Nassau	WCq	Casimir 2 [39 86], Peters [85]	900	Pineda HON
19-06	Mexico	L	0-10	San Antonio, USA	WCq		36 451	Callender BRB
27-06	Mexico	L	0-8	Aguascalientes	WCq		17 000	Stott USA
10-11	Martinique †	L	1-5	Fort de France	GCq	Peltier [42]		Arthur LCA
12-11	Guadeloupe †	L	0-7	Rivière-Pilote	GCq			Arthur LCA
14-11	French Guyana †	L	0-4	Fort de France	GCq		5 800	Fenus LCA
2005								
30-09	Guyana	L	0-3	Linden	Fr			
2-10	Guyana	L	0-3	Georgetown	Fr			
2006								
No international matches played in 2006 before July								

Fr = Friendly match • WC = FIFA World Cup™ • q = qualifier • † Not a full international

DOMINICA NATIONAL TEAM RECORDS AND RECORD SEQUENCES

Records			Sequence records					
Victory	6-1	VGB 1997	Wins	3	1997, 1999, 2004	Clean sheets	2	1997 2004
Defeat	0-10	MEX 2004	Defeats	5	1998-99, 2001-02	Goals scored	8	1999-2000
Player Caps	n/a		Undefeated	4	1998	Without goal	3	1994-1995, 2001
Player Goals	n/a		Without win	8	2001-2002	Goals against	17	1997-1999

RECENT LEAGUE AND CUP RECORD

	Championship						Cup		
Year	Champions	Pts	Runners-up	Pts	Third	Pts	Winners	Score	Runners-up
1997	Harlem United	22	Black Rocks	19	Pointe Michel	12	Harlem Bombers	1-0	Black Rocks
1998	Pointe Michel						Pointe Michel	1-0	ACS Zebians
1999	Harlem United	46	Superwoods United						
2000	Harlem United	13	Dublanc Strikers	13					
2001	Harlem United	22	Dublanc Strikers	22	South East	19			
2002	St Joseph	12	ACS Zebians	12	Harlem Bombers	10	South East	1-0	Antilles Kensbro
2003	Harlem United	†	ACS Zebians				Harlem United		
2004	Harlem United						Harlem United	3-0	ACS Zebians
2005	Dublanc Strikers	31	Pointe Michel	29	South East	29	South East	2-0	Harlem United
2006	Harlem United	29	River Bombers	28					

† Harlem United beat Zebians in the final

DOMINICA COUNTRY INFORMATION

Capital	Roseau	Independence	1978 from the UK	GDP per Capita	$5 400
Population	69 278	Status	Republic/Commonwealth	GNP Ranking	181
Area km²	754	Language	English	Dialling code	+1767
Population density	91 per km²	Literacy rate	94%	Internet code	.dm
% in urban areas	69%	Main religion	Christian 92%	GMT +/–	-4
Towns/Cities ('000)	Roseau 16; Berekua 3; Portsmouth 3; Marigot 2; Atkinson 2; La Plaine 2; Mahaut 2				
Neighbours (km)	Caribbean Sea and the North Atlantic 148				
Main stadia	Windsor Park – Roseau 6 000				

DOM – DOMINICAN REPUBLIC

NATIONAL TEAM RECORD
JULY 1ST 2002 TO JULY 9TH 2006

PL	W	D	L	F	A	%
10	3	1	6	19	18	35

FIFA/COCA-COLA WORLD RANKING

1993	1994	1995	1996	1997	1998	1999	2000	2001	2002	2003	2004	2005		High		Low
153	164	159	130	144	152	155	157	160	149	171	170	174		116 05/96	186	07/06

2005–2006											
08/05	09/05	10/05	11/05	12/05	01/06	02/06	03/06	04/06	05/06	06/06	07/06
172	172	173	173	174	174	174	174	175	175	-	186

There is no doubt as to who were the heroes of the past season in the Dominican Republic. In their FIFA U-20 Women's World Championship qualifier, the Dominican Republic scored an incredible 25 goals without reply against the British Virgin Islands, a record score for a women's game anywhere in the world. Osana Valerio reached double figures, scoring 10 of the 25 goals. Having already beaten the US Virgin Islands 8-0, hopes were high for the final match against neighbours Haiti, but that was lost 2-1 and their campaign was at an end. The senior women's team also hosted a qualifying group, this time for the FIFA Women's World Cup, but despite winning it and thereby

INTERNATIONAL HONOURS
None

qualifying for the Women's Caribbean Cup finals, and potentially the CONCACAF Women's Gold Cup, it remains a long and difficult route for Caribbean nations to make it to the world finals. In contrast to the women, the men's national team has been inactive since mid 2004 following their withdrawal from the 2005 Caribbean Cup, and there has also been little activity amongst the clubs. Indeed, if the Dominican Republic is to succeed internationally, the presence of a regular and strong domestic league is a prerequisite. The Liga Mayor was supposed to do just that, but the competition has yet to follow a regular schedule.

THE FIFA BIG COUNT OF 2000

	Male	Female		Male	Female
Registered players	607	200	Referees	30	10
Non registered players	80 000	1 000	Officials	200	20
Youth players	15 002	600	Total involved	97 669	
Total players	97 409		Number of clubs	495	
Professional players	7	0	Number of teams	710	

Federación Dominicana de Fútbol (FEDOFUTBOL)
Centro Olimpico Juan Pablo Duarte, Ensanche Miraflores, Apartado postal 1953, Santo Domingo, Dominican Republic
Tel +1 809 5426923   Fax +1 809 3812734
fedofutbol.f@codetel.net.do   www.fedofutbol.org
President: GUZMAN Osiris   General Secretary: MIRANDA Angel Rolando
Vice-President: OGANDO Isaac   Treasurer: LEDESMA Felix   Media Officer: SANCHEZ CABRERA Angel
Men's Coach: CRNOKRAK Ljubomir   Women's Coach: ELEJALDE G. Jose
FEDOFUTBOL formed: 1953   CONCACAF: 1964   FIFA: 1958
Navy blue shirts, White shorts, Red socks

RECENT INTERNATIONAL MATCHES PLAYED BY THE DOMINICAN REPUBLIC

2002 Opponents	Score	Venue	Comp	Scorers	Att	Referee
16-08 US Virgin Islands	W 6-1	Santo Domingo	GCq	Zapata [16], Contreras [28], Almanza [33], Mejia 2 [38 67], Odalis.R [62]		Forde BRB
18-08 US Virgin Islands	W 5-1	Santo Domingo	GCq	Lopez [12], Zapata [14], Sanchez [43], Valenzuela [67], Mejia [88]		Jean-Lesley HAI
27-11 Martinique	L 0-4	Grand Cayman	GCq			Grant HAI
29-11 Cayman Islands	L 0-1	Grand Cayman	GCq			Grant HAI
1-12 Cuba	L 1-2	Grand Cayman	GCq	Marino [20]		Grant HAI
2003						
No international matches played in 2003						
2004						
19-03 Anguilla	D 0-0	Santo Domingo	WCq		400	Mattus CRC
21-03 Anguilla	W 6-0	Santo Domingo	WCq	Zapata [15], Severino 2 [38 61], Contrera 2 [57 90], Casquez [77]	850	Porras CRC
27-04 Netherlands Antilles	L 1-3	Willemstad	Fr	Zapata [9]		Faneijte ANT
13-06 Trinidad and Tobago	L 0-2	Santo Domingo	WCq		2 500	Moreno PAN
20-06 Trinidad and Tobago	L 0-4	Marabella	WCq		5 500	Pinas SUR
2005						
No international matches played in 2005						
2006						
No international matches played in 2006 before July						

Fr = Friendly match • GC = CONCACAF Gold Cup • WC = FIFA World Cup™ • q = qualifier

DOMINICAN REPUBLIC NATIONAL TEAM RECORDS AND RECORD SEQUENCES

Records		Sequence records			
Victory	6-0 AIA 2004	Wins	4	1999-2000	Clean sheets 3 1999-2000
Defeat	0-8 HAI 1967, TRI 1996	Defeats	5	1974-1976	Goals scored 5 1987-91, 1991-93
Player Caps	n/a	Undefeated	4	1999-2000	Without goal 3 Three times
Player Goals	n/a	Without win	16	1987-1992	Goals against 15 1991-1996

RECENT LEAGUE AND CUP RECORD

	Championship					Cup		
Year	Champions	Pts	Runners-up	Pts	Third	Pts	Winners	Score Runners-up
1997	San Cristóbal	21	Moca	17	Bancredicard	15		
1998	No tournament played							
1999	FC Don Bosco							
2000	No tournament played							
2001	CD Pantoja	21	Baninter Jarabacoa	19	Bancredicard	13	Domingo Savio	2-2 5-4p CD Pantoja
2002	Baninter Jarabacoa	25	Moca	19	Bancredicard	14	Bancredicard	1-0 Cañabrava
2003	Baninter Jarabacoa	31	Bancredicard	26	Moca	23		
2004	No tournament played							
2005	Deportivo Pantoja	40	Barcelona	39	Don Bosco	39		

Bancredicard renamed Barcelona

DOMINICAN REPUBLIC COUNTRY INFORMATION

Capital	Santo Domingo	Independence	1865	GDP per Capita	$6 000
Population	8 833 634	Status	Republic	GNP Ranking	67
Area km²	48 730	Language	Spanish	Dialling code	+1 809
Population density	181 per km²	Literacy rate	84%	Internet code	.do
% in urban areas	65%	Main religion	Christian 95%	GMT + / –	-4
Towns/Cities ('000)	Santo Domingo 2 240; Santiago 505; La Romana 171; San Pedro de Macorís 152; Puerto Plata 135				
Neighbours (km)	Haiti 360; Atlantic Ocean & Caribbean Sea 1 288				
Main stadia	Olimpico – Santo Domingo 35 000; Quisqueya – Santo Domingo 30 000				

ECU – ECUADOR

NATIONAL TEAM RECORD
JULY 1ST 2002 TO JULY 9TH 2006

PL	W	D	L	F	A	%
53	19	12	22	61	71	47.2

FIFA/COCA-COLA WORLD RANKING

1993	1994	1995	1996	1997	1998	1999	2000	2001	2002	2003	2004	2005		High		Low
48	55	55	33	28	63	65	54	37	31	37	39	37		26	05/98	76 06/95

2005–2006											
08/05	09/05	10/05	11/05	12/05	01/06	02/06	03/06	04/06	05/06	06/06	07/06
33	33	36	37	37	38	38	38	39	39	-	28

The finals of the 2006 FIFA World Cup™ surpassed all expectations for Ecuador with few predicting that the national team would progress beyond the group stages. And yet they did; and with some style, handsomely beating Poland 2-0 in their opening match, and Costa Rica 3-0 in the second, a result which saw them qualify for the knock-out stage. A team that is a match for anyone at the altitude of Quito finally proved that it could compete away from home. After losing to hosts Germany, the Ecuadorians then faced another major European power, England, and but for a shot against the bar by Carlos Tenorio and a superb free kick goal from David Beckham, Ecuador may

INTERNATIONAL HONOURS
Qualified for the FIFA World Cup™ finals 2002 2006

well have progressed further, but they proved to South America, and the rest of the world, that they are an emerging power that should be taken seriously. The country has a strong league and LDU Quito are showing that Ecuadorian clubs can also compete successfully at international level. The 2004 Copa Sudamericana semi-finalists reached the knock-out stage of the Copa Libertadores for the third year running before losing to Internacional of Brazil in the quarter-finals. At home LDU had to share the honours with local rivals El Nacional as the federation experimented with two champions in 2005, although the Apertura and Clausura winners will play-off for the title in 2006.

THE FIFA BIG COUNT OF 2000

	Male	Female		Male	Female
Registered players	11 639	300	Referees	276	14
Non registered players	1 000 000	1 300	Officials	657	200
Youth players	8 934	200	Total involved	1 023 520	
Total players	1 022 373		Number of clubs	1 000	
Professional players	9 656	26	Number of teams	3 361	

Federación Ecuatoriana de Fútbol (FEF)
Avenida las Aguas y Calle, Alianza, PO Box 09-01-7447, Guayaquil 593, Ecuador
Tel +593 42 880610   Fax +593 42 880615
fef@gye.satnet.net   www.ecuafutbol.org
President: CHIRIBOGA Luis   General Secretary: ACOSTA Francisco
Vice-President: VILLACIS Carlos   Treasurer: MORA Hugo   Media Officer: MESTANZA Victor
Men's Coach: SUAREZ Luis   Women's Coach: ESTUPINAN Garis
FEF formed: 1925   CONMEBOL: 1930   FIFA: 1926
Yellow shirts with blue and red trimmings, Blue shorts, Red socks

RECENT INTERNATIONAL MATCHES PLAYED BY ECUADOR

2003	Opponents	Score		Venue	Comp	Scorers	Att	Referee
6-09	Venezuela	W	2-0	Quito	WCq	Espinoza.G [5], Tenorio.C [72]	14 997	Selman CHI
10-09	Brazil	L	0-1	Manaus	WCq		36 601	Solorzano VEN
15-11	Paraguay	L	1-2	Asuncion	WCq	Mendez [58]	12 000	Paniagua BOL
19-11	Peru	D	0-0	Quito	WCq		34 361	Gonzalez PAR
2004								
10-03	Mexico	L	1-2	Tuxtla Gutierrez	Fr	Mendez [33p]	20 000	Batres GUA
30-03	Argentina	L	0-1	Buenos Aires	WCq		55 000	Vazquez URU
28-04	Honduras	D	1-1	Fort Lauderdale	Fr	Ordonez [81]	15 000	Saheli USA
2-06	Colombia	W	2-1	Quito	WCq	Delgado [3], Salas [66]	31 484	Baldassi ARG
5-06	Bolivia	W	3-2	Quito	WCq	Soliz OG [27], Delgado [32], De la Cruz [38]	32 020	Brand VEN
7-07	Argentina	L	1-6	Chiclayo	CAr1	Delgado [62]	24 000	Amarilla PAR
10-07	Uruguay	L	1-2	Chiclayo	CAr1	Salas [73]	25 000	Brand VEN
13-07	Mexico	L	1-2	Piura	CAr1	Delgado [71]	21 000	Lecca PER
5-09	Uruguay	L	0-1	Montevideo	WCq		28 000	Hidalgo PER
10-10	Chile	W	2-0	Quito	WCq	Kaviedes [49], Mendez.E [54]	27 956	Ortube BOL
14-10	Venezuela	L	1-3	San Cristobal	WCq	Ayovi.M [41p]	13 800	Lecca PER
20-10	Jordan	L	0-3	Tripoli	Fr			
22-10	Nigeria	D	2-2	Tripoli	Fr	Poroso [65], W 5-4p		
27-10	Mexico	L	1-2	New Jersey	Fr	Calle [80]		Prus USA
17-11	Brazil	W	1-0	Quito	WCq	Mendez.E [77]	38 308	Ruiz COL
2005								
26-01	Panama	W	2-0	Ambato	Fr	Tenorio.O [88] [91+]	5 000	Vasco ECU
29-01	Panama	W	2-0	Babahoyo	Fr	Kaviedes [45], Tenorio.O [56]		
9-02	Chile	L	0-3	Vina del Mar	Fr		15 000	Favale ARG
16-02	Costa Rica	W	2-1	Heredia	Fr	Ayovi [60p], Guagua [86]	1 000	Duran CRC
27-03	Paraguay	W	5-2	Quito	WCq	Valencia 2 [32] [49], Mendez 2 [47+] [47], Ayovi [77p]	32 449	Mendez URU
30-03	Peru	D	2-2	Lima	WCq	De la Cruz [4], Valencia [45]	40 000	Chandia CHI
4-05	Paraguay	W	1-0	East Rutherford	Fr	Mendez [51]	26 491	
4-06	Argentina	W	2-0	Quito	WCq	Lara [53], Delgado [89]	37 583	Selman CHI
8-06	Colombia	L	0-3	Barranquilla	WCq		20 402	Simon BRA
11-06	Italy	D	1-1	East Rutherford	Fr	Ayovi [18p]	27 583	Vaughn USA
17-08	Venezuela	W	3-1	Loja	Fr	Borja [7], Lara 2 [40] [67]	10 000	Vasco ECU
3-09	Bolivia	W	2-1	La Paz	WCq	Delgado 2 [8] [49]	8 434	Baldassi ARG
8-10	Uruguay	D	0-0	Quito	WCq		37 270	Rezende BRA
12-10	Chile	D	0-0	Santiago	WCq		49 530	Elizondo ARG
13-11	Poland	L	0-3	Barcelona	Fr		6 000	Delgado ESP
29-12	Uganda	L	1-2	Cairo	Fr	Kaviedes [1]		
2006								
25-01	Honduras	W	1-0	Guayaquil	Fr	Caicedo [67]	10 000	Ramos ECU
1-03	Netherlands	L	0-1	Amsterdam	Fr		35 000	Benquerenca POR
30-03	Japan	L	0-1	Oita	Fr		36 507	Maidin ECU
24-05	Colombia	D	1-1	East Rutherford	Fr	Castillo [51]	52 425	Vaughn USA
28-05	FYR Macedonia	L	1-2	Madrid	Fr	Tenorio.C [25]	4 000	
9-06	Poland	W	2-0	Gelsenkirchen	WCr1	Tenorio.C [24]	52 000	Kamikawa JPN
15-06	Costa Rica	W	3-0	Hamburg	WCr1	Tenorio.C [8], Delgado [54], Kaviedes [92+]	50 000	Codjia BEN
20-06	Germany	L	0-3	Berlin	WCr1		72 000	Ivanov.V RUS
25-06	England	L	0-1	Stuttgart	WCr2		52 000	De Bleeckere BEL

Fr = Friendly match • CA = Copa América • WC = FIFA World Cup™ • q = qualifier • r1 = first round group

ECUADOR NATIONAL TEAM RECORDS AND RECORD SEQUENCES

Records			Sequence records				
Victory	6-0	PER 1975	Wins	6	1996	Clean sheets	3	Five times
Defeat	0-12	ARG 1942	Defeats	18	1938-1945	Goals scored	16	1991-1993
Player Caps	133	HURTADO Iván	Undefeated	8	1996, 2000-2001	Without goal	5	1985-1987
Player Goals	31	DELGADO Augustín	Without win	34	1938-1949	Goals against	28	1953-1963

ECUADOR COUNTRY INFORMATION

Capital	Quito	Independence	1822 from Spain	GDP per Capita	$3 300
Population	13 212 742	Status	Republic	GNP Ranking	77
Area km²	283 560	Language	Spanish	Dialling code	+593
Population density	46 per km²	Literacy rate	92%	Internet code	.ec
% in urban areas	58%	Main religion	Christian	GMT + / −	-5
Towns/Cities ('000)	Guayaquil 1 952; Quito 1 399, Cuenca 276; Santo Domingo 200; Machala 198; Manta 183				
Neighbours (km)	Colombia 590; Peru 1 420; Pacific Ocean 2 237				
Main stadia	Monumental – Guayaquil 59 283; La Casa Blanca – Quito 41 596				

ECUADOR NATIONAL TEAM PLAYERS AND COACHES

Record Caps			Record Goals		
HURTADO Iván	1992-'06	133	DELGADO Agustín	1994-'06	31
AGUINAGA Alex	1987-'04	109	HURTADO Eduardo	1992-'00	26
CAPURRO Luis	1985-'03	100	AGUINAGA Alex	1987-'04	23
DE LA CRUZ Ulises	1995-'06	88	AVILES Raúl	1987-'93	16
CHALA Cléber	1992-'04	86	GRAZIANI Ariel	1997-'00	15
CEVALLOS José	1994-'05	77	KAVIEDES Iván	1998-'06	14
FERNANDEZ Angel	1991-'04	77	FERNANDEZ Angel	1991-'04	12
AYOVI Marlon	1998-'06	75	MENDEZ Edison	2000-'06	10
HURTADO Eduardo	1992-'00	74	RAFFO Carlos	1959-'63	10
TENORIO Edwin	1998-'06	72	BENITEZ Hermen	1984-'89	8

CLUB DIRECTORY

Club	Town/City	Stadium	Capacity	www.	Lge
Aucas	Quito	Chillogallo	21 489	aucas.com	0
Barcelona	Guayaquil	Monumental	59 283	barcelonaac.com	13
Deportivo Cuenca	Cuenca	Alejandro Aguilar	18 830		1
Deportivo Olmedo	Riobamba	Olimpico Riobamba	18 936		1
Deportivo Quevedo	Quevedo	7 de Octubre	16 000		0
Deportivo Quito	Quito	Olimpico Atahualpa	40 948	sdquito.com	2
Emelec	Guayaquil	George Capwell	18 222	csemelec.com	10
LDU de Loja	Loja	Reina de Cisne	14 935		0
LDU de Quito	Quito	Casablanca	41 596	clubldu.com	8
El Nacional	Quito	Olimpico Atahualpa	40 948	elnacional.com	12

RECENT LEAGUE RECORD

Championship						Championship Play-off		
Year	Champions	Pts	Runners-up	Pts	Third	Pts	Champions	Score	Runners-up
1990	LDU Quito	7	Barcelona	6	Emelec	6			
1991	Barcelona	10	Valdez	5	El Nacional	5			
1992	El Nacional	15	Barcelona	15	Emelec	13	El Nacional	2-1 1-1	Barcelona
1993	Emelec	19	El Nacional	18	Barcelona	18			
1994	Emelec	14	El Nacional	13.5	Barcelona	11			
1995	Barcelona						Barcelona	2-0 1-0	Espoli
1996	El Nacional						El Nacional	2-1 2-0	Emelec
1997	Barcelona	19	Deportivo Quito	19	Emelec	15			
1998	LDU Quito						LDU Quito	0-1 7-0	Emelec
1999	El Nacional	20	LDU Quito	19	Emelec	18			
2000	Olmedo	23	El Nacional	20	Emelec	20			
2001	Emelec	22	El Nacional	21	Olmedo	20			
2002	Emelec	20	Barcelona	19	El Nacional	18			
2003	LDU Quito	26	Barcelona	23	El Nacional	20			
2004	Deportivo Cuenca	19.5	Olmedo	19	LDU Quito	18			
2005	LDU Quito						LDU Quito	0-1 3-0	Barcelona
2005	El Nacional	25	Deportivo Cuenca	20	LDU Quito	17			

Although Ecuador has long used the Apertura and Clausura system popular across the Americas, until 2005 there has always been an end of season tournament to decide the overall champions. In 1995, 1996, 1998 and the 2005 Apertura this involved a grand final and not the traditional liguilla format. A play-off happened in 1992 after El Nacional and Barcelona finished equal on points.

ECUADOR 2005

SERIE A TORNEO APERTURA

	Pl	W	D	L	F	A	Pts	LDU Quito	Nacional	Barcelona	Cuenca	LDU Loja	Dep. Quito	Aucas	Olmedo	Emelec	Quevedo
LDU Quito	18	13	2	3	48	22	41		7-0	4-0	4-1	3-1	2-1	1-0	6-3	1-0	5-0
El Nacional	18	9	6	3	41	27	33	4-1		4-0	1-1	4-1	1-1	2-0	0-1	5-2	1-1
Barcelona	18	7	5	6	19	31	26	1-0	1-1		2-1	2-1	1-0	2-0	1-1	2-2	1-0
Deportivo Cuenca	18	7	4	7	26	28	25	5-1	2-2	0-0		2-1	0-4	0-1	2-0	3-0	2-1
LDU de Loja	18	7	4	7	35	38	25	1-1	2-5	2-0	5-2		3-1	1-1	2-1	3-1	5-3
Deportivo Quito	18	7	3	8	36	23	24	0-4	3-3	5-0	1-2	5-0		0-2	1-1	4-0	3-0
Aucas	18	7	3	8	22	27	24	2-3	0-3	3-0	1-0	2-2	0-5		2-2	1-0	3-2
Olmedo	18	6	5	7	22	25	23	1-2	2-4	3-1	2-0	0-1	0-1	1-0		0-0	1-0
Emelec	18	5	5	8	24	31	20	0-2	2-0	1-2	1-1	3-2	2-0	2-1	0-0		5-1
Deportivo Quevedo	18	2	3	13	22	43	9	0-1	0-1	3-3	1-2	2-2	2-1	1-3	2-3	3-1	

12/02/2005 - 2/07/2005 • Top scorers: Wilson SEGURA, LDU de Loja, 21; Ariel José GRAZIANI, LDU Quito, 16; Gabriel GARCIA, LDU Quito, 13; Felix BORJA, Nacional, 11

APERTURA PLAY-OFFS

Quarter-finals			Semi-finals			Final		
LDU Quito	1	5						
Olmedo	1	1	LDU Quito	1	3			
LDU de Loja	1	3	Dep. Cuenca	2	1			
Dep. Cuenca	1	3				LDU Quito †	0	3
El Nacional	0	4				Barcelona	1	0
Aucas	0	0	El Nacional	1	1			
Dep. Quito	2	0	Barcelona	1	2			
Barcelona	0	2	† Qualified for the Copa Libertadores 2006					

ECUADOR 2005

SERIE A TORNEO CLAUSURA STAGE ONE

	Pl	W	D	L	F	A	Pts	Nacional	Aucas	Olmedo	Cuenca	LDU Quito	Barcelona	Espoli	Dep. Quito	Emelec	LDU Loja
El Nacional	18	9	4	5	42	27	31		2-4	2-1	0-0	2-3	4-1	4-3	1-2	3-0	2-1
Aucas	18	9	2	7	28	21	29	0-3		0-0	2-3	2-1	2-0	1-2	0-1	2-1	4-0
Olmedo	18	7	6	5	25	23	27	2-0	0-1		1-1	0-3	1-1	2-2	2-2	2-0	3-2
Deportivo Cuenca	18	6	9	3	19	19	27	1-1	2-1	0-1		0-0	0-0	1-0	1-1	1-0	3-2
LDU Quito	18	7	5	6	25	20	26	2-1	0-3	1-2	2-0		3-0	3-2	1-1	0-0	3-0
Barcelona	18	7	5	6	26	25	26	3-3	2-0	2-1	5-2	1-0		0-1	2-0	1-1	2-0
Espoli	18	7	2	9	29	31	23	1-3	0-2	2-3	0-0	2-0	2-1		5-0	4-1	1-0
Deportivo Quito	18	5	8	5	21	27	23	2-4	1-1	1-0	1-1	1-1	2-3	2-0		2-2	1-1
Emelec	18	5	6	7	20	25	21	0-0	2-1	1-1	0-1	1-0	2-1	6-1	2-0		1-1
LDU de Loja	18	2	5	11	22	39	11	1-7	1-2	2-3	2-2	2-2	1-1	2-1	0-1	4-0	

29/07/2005 - 6/11/2005 • Top scorers (inc Liguilla): Omar GUERRA, Aucas, 17; Felix BORJA, Nacional, 15; Pablo PALACIOS, Aucas, 13

ECUADOR 2005 SERIE A TORNEO CLAUSURA LIGUILLA

	Pl	W	D	L	F	A	Pts	Na	DC	LDU	Au	Ol	Ba
El Nacional † §3	10	7	1	2	23	9	25		2-0	2-3	5-1	2-1	2-0
Deportivo Cuenca †	10	6	2	2	12	10	20	2-1		0-0	2-1	1-0	2-0
LDU Quito	10	5	2	3	20	13	17	1-3	1-1		4-1	5-1	4-1
Aucas §2	10	3	1	6	17	24	12	1-4	5-2	3-1		1-1	1-2
Olmedo §1	10	2	2	6	7	15	9	0-2	0-1	1-0	1-2		1-1
Barcelona	10	2	2	6	6	14	8	0-0	0-1	0-1	2-1	0-1	

16/11/2005 - 21/12/2005 • † Qualified for the 2006 Copa Libertadores • § = Bonus points from the first stage

ECUADOR 2005 SERIE B APERTURA LIGUILLA

	Pl	W	D	L	F	A	Pts	Es	Ma	LP	TU
Espoli §1	6	3	2	1	16	10	12		6-2	3-2	3-0
Manta FC §0.5	6	3	1	2	10	13	10.5	4-2		2-1	1-0
LDU de Portoviejo	6	2	2	2	8	7	8	1-1	0-0		2-0
Técnico Universitario	6	1	1	4	6	10	4	1-1	4-1	1-2	

11/06/2005 - 9/07/2005 • Espoli promoted to Serie A for the Clausura

ECUADOR 2005 SERIE B CLAUSURA LIGUILLA

	Pl	W	D	L	F	A	Pts	Ma	UC	Ma	TU
Macará §1	6	4	2	0	12	5	15		3-2	4-2	1-0
Univ. Católica §0.5	6	4	1	1	11	4	13.5	0-0		5-0	1-0
Manta FC	6	1	2	3	6	13	5	1-1	0-1		1-1
Técnico Universitario	6	0	1	5	3	10	1	0-3	1-2	1-2	

5/11/2005 - 10/12/2005 • Macará promoted to Serie A for 2006 Apertura

EGY – EGYPT

NATIONAL TEAM RECORD
JULY 1ST 2002 TO JULY 9TH 2006

PL	W	D	L	F	A	%
60	36	12	12	118	50	70

Success in both the African Nations Cup finals and in the CAF Champions League made it arguably the most successful 12 month period ever for Egyptian football. The national side, the Pharaohs, overcame a jittery start and a pessimistic public to triumph at the tournament in January and February, which the country hosted with aplomb. The win on penalties over Cote d'Ivoire in the final put the seal on a dramatic three weeks of competition where the Egyptians grew in competence and confidence with each passing performance. Such was the level of pessimism at the start, that at the opening game, a 3-0 win over Libya in the newly renovated Cairo International Stadium, the venue was only half full, but the crowds increased dramatically with each Egyptian success. The fans were also witness to one of the most public fall outs in world football when coach Hassan Shehata substituted Premier League star Mido in the semi-final against Senegal. Mido took none to kindly to the decision, berating his coach on the touchline. Shehata had the last laugh, however, as his substitute Amr Zaki scored the winner within a minute after coming on. That's one way to settle an argument and unsurprisingly Mido didn't take part in the final. In truth Egypt could

INTERNATIONAL HONOURS
Qualified for the FIFA World Cup™ finals 1934 1990
CAF African Cup of Nations 1957 1959 1986 1998 2006   **African Games** 1987 1991
CAF African Youth Championship 1981 1991 2003 **CAF African U-17 Championship** 1997
CAF African Champions League Ismaili 1969, Al Ahly 1982 1987 2001 2006, Zamalek 1984 1986 1993 1996 2002

have done with him in what turned out to be an edgy and nervous performance against the Ivorians. In the event it was goalkeeper Essam El Hadary who was the star of the shoot-out as the Egyptians won the trophy for a record fifth time. Just one month before the kick off of the Nations Cup, Al Ahly had won the CAF Champions League with predictable dominance, beating Etoile du Sahel of Tunisia 3-0 in the second leg of the final after a goalless draw in the first leg in Sousse. Midfielder Mohamed Barakat, who went on to star in the Nations Cup tournament, was voted the Champions League's best player. Al Ahly lost their 18-month 55 match unbeaten record in Japan at the FIFA Club World Championship in December where they disappointingly lost to the champions of both Asia and Oceania. But this was a minor setback as the Cairo giants romped home to the Egyptian title by finishing unbeaten for a second successive season. They drew just three of their 26 matches to finish a massive 14 points clear of arch rivals Zamalek, who they then also beat convincingly 3-0 in the Cup Final. Without a single defeat in domestic football for over two years following their Cup Final loss against Mokawloon on July 2, 2004, the current Al Ahly side have certainly built a reputation as one of the all-time greats of African football.

Egyptian Football Association (EFA)
5 Gabalaya Street, Gezira, El Borg Post Office, Cairo, Egypt
Tel +20 2 7351793   Fax +20 2 7367817
www.efa.com.eg
President: ZAHER Samir   General Secretary: WAHAB Farouk Abdel
Vice-President: SHOUBEIR Ahmed   Treasurer: ABBAS Mamdouh   Media Officer: EL SAFEI Mandouh
Men's Coach: SHEHATA Hassan   Women's Coach: None
EFA formed: 1921   CAF: 1957   FIFA: 1923
Red shirts with white trimmings, White shorts, White socks

RECENT INTERNATIONAL MATCHES PLAYED BY EGYPT

2003	Opponents	Score		Venue	Comp	Scorers	Att	Referee
10-10	Senegal	W	1-0	Cairo	Fr	Hossam Mido [58]	20 000	
15-11	South Africa	W	2-1	Cairo	Fr	Abdel Hady [73], Hossam Mido [90]	10 000	Salim LBY
18-11	Sweden	W	1-0	Cairo	Fr	Belal [10]	15 000	Abdalla LBY
12-12	Kenya	W	1-0	Manama	Fr	El Sayed [8]		
15-12	Bahrain	W	1-0	Manama	Fr	Youssef [90]	20 000	
18-12	Iraq	W	2-0	Manama	Fr	Belal 2 [21 50]		
2004								
25-01	Zimbabwe	W	2-1	Sfax	CNr1	Abdel Hamid [58], Barakat [62]	22 000	Lassina Pare BFA
29-01	Algeria	L	1-2	Sousse	CNr1	Belal [26]	15 000	Hamer LUX
3-02	Cameroon	D	0-0	Monastir	CNr1		20 000	Bujsaim UAE
31-03	Trinidad and Tobago	W	2-1	Cairo	Fr	Aboutraika [60], Abdelhalim Ali [65]	5 000	El Beltagy EGY
24-05	Zimbabwe	W	2-0	Cairo	Fr	Aboutraika [73], Hosni [83]	10 000	
29-05	Gabon	W	2-0	Cairo	Fr	Hossam Hassan 2 [90 95]	15 000	Auda EGY
6-06	Sudan	W	3-0	Khartoum	WCq	Abdelhalim Ali [6], Aboutraika [53], Abdel Wahab [88]	10 000	Kidane Tesfu ERI
20-06	Côte d'Ivoire	L	1-2	Alexandria	WCq	Aboutraika [55]	13 000	Guirat TUN
4-07	Benin	D	3-3	Cotonou	WCq	Ahmed Hassan [66], Aboutraika [75], Moustafa.H [80]	15 000	Chukwujekwu NGA
5-09	Cameroon	W	3-2	Cairo	WCq	Shawky [45], Ahmed Hassan [74p], El Sayed [86]	25 000	Lim Kee Chong MRI
8-10	Libya	L	1-2	Tripoli	WCq	Zaki [57]	40 000	Haimoudi ALG
29-11	Bulgaria	D	1-1	Cairo	Fr	Moteab [85]		
2005								
8-01	Uganda	W	3-0	Cairo	Fr	Zaki 2 [38 67p], Shawky [63]		
4-02	Korea Republic	W	1-0	Seoul	Fr	Moteab [14]	16 054	
9-02	Belgium	W	4-0	Cairo	Fr	Moteab 2 [39 50], Abdelmalk [52], Hosni [80]	5 000	El Beltagy EGY
14-03	Saudi Arabia	W	1-0	Dammam	Fr	Moteab [64]		
27-03	Libya	W	4-1	Cairo	WCq	Hossam Mido [55] Moteab 2 [56 80], Ahmed Hassan [76]	30 000	Poulat FRA
27-05	Kuwait	W	1-0	Kuwait City	Fr	Ahmed Hassan [52]		
5-06	Sudan	W	6-1	Cairo	WCq	Abdelhalim Ali 2 [8 31], Zaki 2 [28 50], El Sayed [62], Abdelmalk [71]	20 000	Mususa ZIM
19-06	Côte d'Ivoire	L	0-2	Abidjan	WCq		30 000	Damon RSA
29-07	Qatar	W	5-0	Geneva	Fr	Aboutraika 2 [59 84], Hosni [66], Zaki 2 [70 88]		
31-07	United Arab Emirates	D	0-0	Geneva	Fr	W 5-4p		
17-08	Portugal	L	0-2	Ponta Delgada	Fr		20 000	Granat POL
4-09	Benin	W	4-1	Cairo	WCq	Zaki 3 [12 15 84], Hossam Mido [71]	5 000	Buenkadila COD
8-10	Cameroon	D	1-1	Yaounde	WCq	Shawky [79]	38 750	Coulibaly MLI
16-11	Tunisia	L	1-2	Cairo	Fr	Hossam Mido [49]		
27-12	Uganda	W	2-0	Cairo	Fr	Amr Zaki 2 [45 66]		
2006								
5-01	Zimbabwe	W	2-0	Alexandria	Fr	Abdelhalim Ali 2 [33 78]		
14-01	South Africa	L	1-2	Cairo	Fr	Zaki [24p]		
20-01	Libya	W	3-0	Cairo	CNr1	Hossam Mido [18], Aboutraika [22], Ahmed Hassan [78]	65 000	Pare BFA
24-01	Morocco	D	0-0	Cairo	CNr1		75 000	Codjia BEN
28-01	Côte d'Ivoire	W	3-1	Cairo	CNr1	Moteab 2 [8 69], Aboutraika [61]	74 000	Mailett SEY
3-02	Congo DR	W	4-1	Cairo	CNqf	Ahmed Hassan 2 [33p 89], Hossam Hassan [41], Moteab [58]	74 000	Sowe GAM
7-02	Senegal	W	2-1	Cairo	CNsf	Ahmed Hassan [36p], Zaki [80]	74 000	Evehe CMR
10-02	Côte d'Ivoire	D	0-0	Cairo	CNf	W 4-2p	74 000	Daami TUN
3-06	Spain	L	0-2	Elche	Fr		38 000	Farina ITA

Fr = Friendly match • CN = CAF African Cup of Nations • WC = FIFA World Cup™ • q = qualifier • r1 = first round group

EGYPT NATIONAL TEAM RECORDS AND RECORD SEQUENCES

Records			Sequence records				
Victory	15-0	LAO 1963	Wins	9	2003-2004	Clean sheets	10	1989
Defeat	3-11	ITA 1928	Defeats	4	1990	Goals scored	22	1963-1964
Player Caps	170	HASSAN Hossam	Undefeated	15	1963-64, 2000-01	Without goal	4	1985, 1990
Player Goals	69	HASSAN Hossam	Without win	9	1981-1983	Goals against	13	1972-1973

EGYPT COUNTRY INFORMATION

Capital	Cairo	Independence	1936	GDP per Capita	$4 000
Population	76 117 421	Status	Republic	GNP Ranking	37
Area km²	1 001 450	Language	Arabic	Dialling code	+20
Population density	76 per km²	Literacy rate	57%	Internet code	.eg
% in urban areas	45%	Main religion	Muslim 94%	GMT + / –	+2
Towns/Cities ('000)	Cairo 7 836; Alexandria 3 865; Giza 2 468; Shubra 1 005; Port Said 546; Suez 497; Mehalla al Kubra 434; Luxor 430; Assiout 429; Mansoura 425; Tanta 408; El Faiyum 311; Ismailya 288; El Zagazig 286; Kafr el Dauwar 271; Aswan 243; Qena 243; Menia 229; Damanhoor 229				
Neighbours (km)	Gaza Strip 11; Israel 266; Sudan 1 273; Libya 1 115; Mediterranean Sea & Red Sea 2 450				
Main stadia	International – Cairo 74 100; Port Said – Port Said 22 000; Alexandria – Alexandria 25 000				

CLUB DIRECTORY

Club	Town/City	Stadium	Capacity	Lge	Cup	CL
Al Ahly (National)	Cairo	Ahly Sports Club	25 000	31	34	4
ENPPI (Petroleum)	Cairo	Osman Ahmed Osman	60 000	0	1	0
Ghazl	Al Mehalla	Al Mehalla	20 000	0	0	0
Ismaily	Ismailya	Ismailiya Stadium	16 500	3	2	1
Ittihad (Unity)	Alexandria	Alexandria Stadium	20 000	0	6	0
Al Jaish (Army Club)	Cairo	Military Academy	28 500	0	0	0
Al Masry	Port Said	Port Said Stadium	22 000	0	1	0
Mokawloon (Arab Contractors)	Cairo	Osman Ahmed Osman	60 000	1	3	0
Sawahel (Border Guards)	Alexandria	Harras El-Hedoud	22 000	0	0	0
Suez Cement	Suez	Suez	25 000	0	0	0
Zamalek	Cairo	Zamalek	25 000	11	20	5

FIFA/COCA-COLA WORLD RANKING

1993	1994	1995	1996	1997	1998	1999	2000	2001	2002	2003	2004	2005		High		Low	
26	22	23	28	32	28	38	33	41	39	32	34	32		**17**	05/98	**44**	05/03

2005–2006											
08/05	09/05	10/05	11/05	12/05	01/06	02/06	03/06	04/06	05/06	06/06	07/06
26	31	32	33	32	32	17	17	18	17	-	29

THE FIFA BIG COUNT OF 2000

	Male	Female		Male	Female
Registered players	13 768	223	Referees	1 731	0
Non registered players	250 000	0	Officials	102	0
Youth players	6 648	0	Total involved	272 472	
Total players	270 639		Number of clubs	545	
Professional players	350	0	Number of teams	6 000	

EGYPT 2005-06

PREMIER LEAGUE

	Pl	W	D	L	F	A	Pts	Ahly	Zamalek	ENPPI	Ismaily	Sawahel	Jaish	Ittihad	Masry	Mokawloon	Suez	Ghazl	Assiout	Aluminium	Koroum
Al Ahly †	26	23	3	0	57	6	72		0-0	1-0	2-0	4-2	2-0	1-0	2-0	2-0	4-0	2-2	1-0	1-0	2-0
Zamalek †	26	18	4	4	48	22	58	0-2		1-0	2-1	1-0	1-1	1-1	0-1	3-1	4-1	3-0	2-0	5-0	1-1
ENPPI Cairo ‡	26	13	7	6	32	18	46	0-1	0-1		2-2	1-0	1-0	1-1	3-0	2-1	0-2	3-0	1-0	2-1	3-1
Ismaily	26	12	3	11	33	32	39	0-4	1-2	0-2		2-1	2-0	1-0	0-0	2-0	1-0	4-0	2-0	1-0	
Sawahel	26	11	5	10	35	25	38	0-1	5-0	0-0	2-1		3-2	1-0	0-0	1-0	1-1	2-1	0-0	2-0	2-0
Al Jaish	26	10	4	12	28	31	34	0-3	1-4	0-1	1-0	2-0		2-1	1-1	1-0	3-1	0-1	2-1	1-0	2-0
Ittihad	26	8	8	10	19	28	32	0-6	0-3	0-0	1-1	1-0	2-1		2-1	2-2	1-1	1-0	1-0	2-0	2-0
Al Masry	26	8	7	11	27	30	31	0-2	3-1	0-1	1-2	1-1	1-0	1-0		2-0	2-2	5-0	0-0	0-0	2-0
Mokawloon	26	8	4	14	26	34	28	1-3	0-1	1-0	1-2	1-2	2-0	1-0	5-2		0-1	3-0	3-2	1-0	0-0
Suez Cement	26	6	10	10	28	45	28	0-0	1-3	1-1	3-2	0-4	0-4	0-0	1-0	2-0		0-0	1-3	5-1	1-1
Ghazl Al Mehalla	26	6	9	11	21	34	27	1-3	0-1	2-2	1-0	2-0	0-1	0-0	2-0	2-0	2-2		1-1	1-1	1-0
Assiout Cement	26	6	8	12	26	36	26	0-3	2-3	1-1	3-4	2-1	1-0	1-0	1-1	1-2	2-2	2-1		0-0	1-2
Aluminium NH	26	6	7	13	16	36	25	0-2	0-2	0-3	3-0	0-4	1-1	2-0	1-0	0-0	2-0	0-0	0-0		2-1
Koroum	26	5	5	16	22	41	20	0-3	0-3	1-2	1-0	2-1	2-2	0-1	2-3	3-1	3-0	1-1	0-2	1-2	

12/08/2005 - 22/05/2006 • † Qualified for the 2007 CAF Champions League • ‡ Qualified for the 2007 CAF Confederation Cup

CUP 2005-06

Round of 16			Quarter-finals		Semi-finals		Final	
Al Ahly *	1							
Ittihad	0		Al Ahly *	3				
Aluminium	1 5p		Suez Cement	0				
Suez Cement *	1 6p				Al Ahly	1		
Al Masry *	2				Sawahel	0		
Al Tersana	1		Al Masry	1				
Mostqabal	1		Sawahel *	2			Al Ahly	3
Sawahel *	5						Zamalek	0
Ismaily *	1							
Koroum	0		Ismaily *	1			**CUP FINAL**	
Dekernes	1		Kafr Al Sheikh	0				
Kafr Al Sheikh *	3				Ismaily	1 2p	16-06-2006	
ENPPI *	3				Zamalek	1 4p		
Al Jaish	1		ENPPI *	1			Scorers - Emad Moteab 2 [20 70], Emad El	
Mokawloon	2		Zamalek	2			Nahhas [37] for Al Ahly	
Zamalek *	5							

* Home team

RECENT LEAGUE AND CUP RECORD

	Championship							Cup		
Year	Champions	Pts	Runners-up	Pts	Third	Pts		Winners	Score	Runners-up
1990	Unfinished due to Egypt's participation in the 1990 FIFA World Cup™							Mokawloon	2-1	Suez Canal
1991	Ismaily	51	Al Ahly	51	Zamalek	50		Al Ahly	1-0	Aswan
1992	Zamalek	40	Ismaily	37	Ghazl Al Mehalla	33		Al Ahly	2-1	Zamalek
1993	Zamalek	45	Al Ahly	39	Ghazl Al Mehalla	31		Al Ahly	3-2	Ghazl Al Mehalla
1994	Al Ahly	39	Ismaily	39	Zamalek	35		Not held		
1995	Al Ahly	58	Zamalek	50	Ismaili	43		Mokawloon	2-0	Ghazl Al Mehalla
1996	Al Ahly	70	Zamalek	66	Ismaili	52		Al Ahly	3-1	Mansoura
1997	Al Ahly	69	Zamalek	60	Mansoura	49		Ismaily	1-0	Al Ahly
1998	Al Ahly	68	Zamalek	62	Mokawloon	54		Al Masry	4-3	Mokawloon
1999	Al Ahly	68	Zamalek	41	Ismaily	40		Zamalek	3-1	Ismaily
2000	Al Ahly	60	Ismaily	54	Zamalek	52		Ismaily	4-0	Mokawloon
2001	Zamalek	65	Al Ahly	57	Al Masry	46		Al Ahly	2-0	Ghazl Al Mehalla
2002	Ismaily	66	Al Ahly	64	Zamalek	53		Zamalek	1-0	Baladeyet Mehalla
2003	Zamalek	67	Al Ahly	66	Ismaily	46		Al Ahly	1-1 4-3p	Ismaily
2004	Zamalek	68	Al Ahly	59	Ismaily	51		Mokawloon	2-1	Al Ahly
2005	Al Ahly	74	ENPPI	43	Sawahel	39		ENPPI	1-0	Ittihad
2006	Al Ahly	72	Zamalek	58	ENPPI	46		Al Ahly	3-0	Zamalek

AL AHLY 2005–06

Date	Opponents	Score		Comp	Scorers
26-06-2005	Raja Casablanca - MAR	W 1-0	H	CLgA	Shawki [57]
10-07-2005	Enyimba - NGR	W 1-0	A	CLgA	Moteab [12]
22-07-2005	Ajax Cape Town - RSA	W 2-0	H	CLgA	Ahmed El Sayed [8], Moteab [90+]
7-08-2005	Ajax Cape Town - RSA	D 0-0	A	CLgA	
13-08-2005	Koroum	W 2-0	H	Lge	Gilberto [45], Moteab [60]
20-08-2005	Raja Casablanca - MAR	D 1-1	A	CLgA	Moteab [90+]
26-08-2005	Assiout Cement	W 1-0	H	Lge	Aboutraika [59]
30-08-2005	Ghazl Al Mehalla	W 3-1	A	Lge	Flavio [16], El Nahhas [85], Barakat [95+]
11-09-2005	Enyimba - NGR	W 2-1	H	CLgA	Hosni 2 [39 81]
15-09-2005	ENPPI	W 1-0	H	Lge	Barakat [72]
10-09-2005	Aluminium	W 1-0	H	Lge	Moteab [45]
25-09-2005	Zamalek - EGY	W 2-1	A	CLsf	Moteab [37], Barakat [44]
16-10-2005	Zamalek - EGY	W 2-0	H	CLsf	Barakat 2 [62 71]
20-10-2005	Al Jaish	W 3-0	A	Lge	Barakat [53], Hosni [59], Wael Reyadh [74]
29-10-2005	Etoile du Sahel - TUN	D 0-0	A	CLf	
4-11-2005	Ittihad	W 6-0	A	Lge	El Nahhas 3 [8p 30 68], Barakat 2 [45 46], Aboutraika [92+]
12-11-2005	Etoile du Sahel - TUN	W 3-0	H	CLf	Aboutraika [20], Hosni [51], Barakat [90]
19-11-2005	Suez Cement	W 4-0	H	Lge	El Nahhas [15], Hosni [23], Barakat 2 [52 60p]
25-11-2005	Al Masry	W 2-0	H	Lge	Aboumesallem [28], Hosni [41]
27-11-2005	Mokawloon	W 3-1	A	Lge	Aboutraika 3 [1 51p 56]
11-12-2005	Al Ittihad - KSA	L 0-1	N	CWCr1	
16-12-2005	Sydney FC - AUS	L 1-2	N	CWC5p	Moteab [45]
18-02-2006	Koroum	W 3-0	A	Lge	Abdel Wahab [7], Aboutraika 2 [78 90]
28-02-2006	Ghazl Mehalla	D 2-2	H	Lge	Aboutraika 2 [54p 83p]
4-03-2006	Zamalek	D 0-0	H	Lge	
9-03-2006	ENPPI	W 1-0	A	Lge	Abdel Wahab [32]
13-03-2006	Sawahel	W 1-0	A	Lge	Barakat [35]
18-03-2006	Tusker - KEN	W 2-0	A	CLr1	
24-03-2006	Aluminium	W 2-0	A	Lge	El Nahhas [33p], Aboutraika [66]
28-03-2006	Al Jaish	W 2-0	H	Lge	Moteab [6], Aboutraika [61]
31-03-2006	Tusker - KEN	W 3-0	H	CLr1	
5-04-2006	Ismaily	W 2-0	H	Lge	El Nahhas [45p], Wael Gomaa [91+]
9-04-2006	Al Masry	W 2-0	A	Lge	Hassan Moustafa 2 [38 58]
13-04-2006	Ittihad	W 1-0	H	Lge	Shawki [46]
17-04-2006	Assiout Cement	W 3-0	A	Lge	Aboutraika 2 [48 88], Ashour [93+]
23-04-2006	Renacimiento - EQG	D 0-0	A	CLr1	
28-04-2006	Suez Cement	D 0-0	A	Lge	
2-05-2006	Bani Suef Telephones	W 1-0	A	CUPr2	Ahmed Hassan [13]
6-05-2006	Renacimiento - EQG	W 4-0	H	CLr2	
10-05-2006	Mokawloon	W 2-0	H	Lge	Ahmed El Sayed [4], Aboutraika [48p]
14-05-2006	Zamalek	W 2-0	A	Lge	Moteab [7], Aboutraika [10]
18-05-2006	Sawahel	W 4-2	H	Lge	El Nahhas [19p], Aboutraika [33], Moteab [62], Hassan Moustafa [77]
22-05-2006	Ismaily	W 4-0	A	Lge	Barakat [5], Aboutraika 2 [44p 52p], Abdel Wahab [93+]
6-06-2006	Ittihad	W 1-0	H	CUPr3	Aboutraika [27p]
9-06-2006	Suez Cement	W 3-0	H	CUPqf	Abdel Wahab [20], Moteab 2 [32 72]
13-06-2006	Sawahel	W 1-0	H	CUPsf	Abdel Wahab [43]
16-06-2006	Zamalek	W 3-0	N	CUPf	Moteab 2 [20 70], El Nahhas [37]

Lge = Egyptian League • Cup = Egyptian Cup • CL = CAF Champions League • CWC = FIFA Club World Championship
r1 = first round • r2 = second round • r3 = third round • 5p = fifth place play-off • N = National Stadium, Tokyo •

ENG – ENGLAND

NATIONAL TEAM RECORD
JULY 1ST 2002 TO JULY 9TH 2006

PL	W	D	L	F	A	%
47	30	10	7	89	44	74.5

England and penalty kicks. The two just don't mix. Since 1990 the national team has been knocked out of five major tournaments on penalties and Germany 2006 was another chapter in this particular horror story. From being touted as potential winners, England never really got out of first gear at the tournament, their preparations and progress overshadowed by Wayne Rooney's broken toe, Michael Owen's lack of fitness and the inclusion of 17 year old Theo Walcott who had yet to make his debut for Arsenal - all of which left England's attacking options look decidedly thin on the ground. Add into the mix the searing heat, which precluded the team from playing its usual high tempo game, and England never looked like potential winners. In the end they bowed out for the third tournament running in the quarter-finals against opposton coached by Luiz Felipe Scolari. This time Portugal provided an insurmountable barrier, especially after Argentine referee Horacio Elizondo had sent Wayne Rooney off in the second half. No wonder the Football Association had tried to tempt Scolari with the England job to replace Sven-Goran Eriksson after the finals. He declined and the job went instead to Eriksson's assistant Steve McClaren, fresh from taking his

INTERNATIONAL HONOURS
FIFA World Cup™ 1966
Qualified for the FIFA World Cup™ 1950 1954 1958 1962 1966 1970 1982 1986 1990 1998 2002 2006 **Qualified for the FIFA Women's World Cup** 1995
European U-21 Championship 1982 1984   **European Junior Championship** 1948 1963 1964 1971 1972 1973 1975 1980 1993
UEFA Champions League Manchester United 1968 1999 Liverpool 1977 1978 1981 1984 2005 Nottingham Forest 1979 1980 Aston Villa 1982

club side Middlesbrough to the UEFA Cup final. McClaren was the only Englishman on the short list to have actually won a trophy but he couldn't add a second as Middlesbrough lost 4-0 to Sevilla in the UEFA Cup final. Domestically there was little that any of the clubs could do to stop the Chelsea bandwagon as Jose Mourinho's side comfortably defended their League title. They won their first nine League matches and although Manchester United put in a challenge when Chelsea went through a poor spell late on, the title was never really in doubt. The UEFA Champions League threw up a rematch against Barcelona in the first knock-out round for Chelsea, but this year they came off second best and it was down to Arsenal to fly the English flag in the competition. Based on a defence that didn't concede a goal in ten consecutive matches, they made it to the final for the first time with a very young team guided by the experienced Thierry Henry, but once again Barcelona destroyed English hopes with two late goals giving them a 2-1 victory in Paris. Liverpool and Manchester United were the other trophy winners during the season, with Liverpool winning a thrilling FA Cup final against West Ham United on penalties, whilst Manchester United beat Wigan Athletic comfortably in the League Cup Final.

The Football Association (The FA)
25 Soho Square, London W1D 4FA, United Kingdom
Tel +44 20 77454545   Fax +44 20 77454546
info@TheFA.com   www.TheFA.com
President: THOMPSON Geoffrey   General Secretary: BARWICK Brian
Vice-President: DEIN David   Treasurer: WILLIAMS Steve   Media Officer: BEVINGTON Adrian
Men's Coach: MCCLAREN Steve   Women's Coach: POWELL Hope
The FA formed: 1863   UEFA: 1954   FIFA: 1905-20 & 1945
White shirts with red trimmings, Navy blue shorts, White socks or Red shirts with white trimmings, White shorts, Red socks

RECENT INTERNATIONAL MATCHES PLAYED BY ENGLAND

2003 Opponents	Score		Venue	Comp	Scorers	Att	Referee
29-03 Liechtenstein	W	2-0	Vaduz	ECq	Owen [28], Beckham [53]	3 548	Kasnaferis GRE
2-04 Turkey	W	2-0	Sunderland	ECq	Vassell [76], Beckham [90p]	47 667	Meier SUI
22-05 South Africa	W	2-1	Durban	Fr	Southgate [1], Heskey [64]	48 000	Chong MRI
3-06 Serbia & Montenegro	W	2-1	Leicester	Fr	Gerrard [35], Cole.J [82]	30 900	Allaerts BEL
11-06 Slovakia	W	2-1	Middlesbrough	ECq	Owen 2 [62p 73]	35 000	Stark GER
20-08 Croatia	W	3-1	Ipswich	Fr	Beckham [9p], Owen [51], Lampard [80]	28 700	Larsen DEN
6-09 Macedonia	W	2-1	Skopje	ECq	Rooney [53], Beckham [63p]	20 500	De Bleeckere BEL
10-09 Liechtenstein	W	2-0	Manchester	ECq	Owen [46], Rooney [52]	64 931	Fisker DEN
11-10 Turkey	D	0-0	Istanbul	ECq		45 000	Collina ITA
16-11 Denmark	L	2-3	Manchester	Fr	Rooney [5], Cole.J [9]	64 159	Hrinak SVK
2004							
18-02 Portugal	D	1-1	Faro	Fr	King [48]	27 000	Kassai HUN
31-03 Sweden	L	0-1	Gothenburg	Fr		40 464	Ovrebo NOR
1-06 Japan	D	1-1	Manchester	Fr	Owen [22]	38 581	Rosetti ITA
5-06 Iceland	W	6-1	Manchester	Fr	Lampard [25], Rooney 2 [27 38], Vassell 2 [57 77], Bridge [68]	43 500	Wegereef NED
13-06 France	L	1-2	Lisbon	ECr1	Lampard [38]	62 487	Merk GER
17-06 Switzerland	W	3-0	Coimbra	ECr1	Rooney 2 [23 75], Gerrard [82]	28 214	Ivanov RUS
21-06 Croatia	W	4-2	Lisbon	ECr1	Scholes [40], Rooney 2 [45 68], Lampard [79]	57 047	Collina ITA
24-06 Portugal	D	2-2	Lisbon	ECqf	Owen [3], Lampard [115]. L 5-6p	62 564	Meier SUI
18-08 Ukraine	W	3-0	Newcastle	Fr	Beckham [28], Owen [50], Wright-Phillips [70]	35 387	McCurry SCO
4-09 Austria	D	2-2	Vienna	WCq	Lampard [24], Gerrard [63]	48 500	Lubos SVK
8-09 Poland	W	2-1	Chorzow	WCq	Defoe [37], Glowacki OG [58]	38 000	Farina ITA
9-10 Wales	W	2-0	Manchester	WCq	Lampard [4], Beckham [76]	65 224	Hauge NOR
13-10 Azerbaijan	W	1-0	Baku	WCq	Owen [22]	15 000	Hamer LUX
17-11 Spain	L	0-1	Madrid	Fr		48 000	Kasnaferis GRE
2005							
9-02 Netherlands	D	0-0	Birmingham	Fr		40 705	Frojdfeldt SWE
26-03 Northern Ireland	W	4-0	Manchester	WCq	Cole.J [47], Owen 2 [52], Baird OG [54], Lampard [62]	62 239	Stark GER
30-03 Azerbaijan	W	2-0	Newcastle	WCq	Gerrard [51], Beckham [62]	49 046	Costa POR
28-05 USA	W	2-1	Chicago	Fr	Richardson 2 [4 44]	47 637	Archundia MEX
31-05 Colombia	W	3-2	New Jersey	Fr	Owen 3 [35 44 58]	58 000	Hall USA
17-08 Denmark	L	1-4	Copenhagen	Fr	Rooney [87]	41 438	Ovrebro NOR
3-09 Wales	W	1-0	Cardiff	WCq	Cole.J [53]	70 795	Ivanov.V RUS
7-09 Northern Ireland	L	0-1	Belfast	WCq		14 069	Busacca SUI
8-10 Austria	W	1-0	Manchester	WCq	Lampard [25p]	64 822	Medina ESP
12-10 Poland	W	2-1	Manchester	WCq	Owen [43], Lampard [80]	65 467	Nielsen DEN
12-11 Argentina	W	3-2	Geneva	Fr	Rooney [38], Owen 2 [87 90]	29 000	Leuba SUI
2006							
1-03 Uruguay	W	2-1	Liverpool	Fr	Crouch [75], Cole.J [93+]	40 013	Farina ITA
30-05 Hungary	W	3-1	Manchester	Fr	Gerrard [47], Terry [51], Crouch [83]	56 323	Vink NED
3-06 Jamaica	W	6-0	Manchester	Fr	Lampard [11], Taylor OG [17], Crouch 3 [29 65 89], Owen [32]	70 373	Plautz AUT
10-06 Paraguay	W	1-0	Frankfurt	WCr1	Gamarra OG [3]	48 000	Rodriguez MEX
15-06 Trinidad and Tobago	W	2-0	Nuremburg	WCr1	Crouch [83], Gerrard [91+]	41 000	Kamikawa JPN
20-06 Sweden	D	2-2	Cologne	WCr1	Cole.J [34], Gerrard [85]	45 000	Busacca SUI
25-06 Ecuador	W	1-0	Stuttgart	WCr2	Beckham [60]	52 000	De Bleeckere BEL
1-07 Portugal	D	0-0	Gelsenkirchen	WCqf	L 1-3p	52 000	Elizondo ARG

Fr = Friendly match • EC = UEFA EURO 2004™ • WC = FIFA World Cup™ • q = qualifier • r1 = first round group • qf = quarter-final

ENGLAND NATIONAL TEAM RECORDS AND RECORD SEQUENCES

Records			Sequence records				
Victory	15-0	FRA 1906	Wins	10	1908-1909	Clean sheets	7	1908-1909
Defeat	1-7	HUN 1954	Defeats	3	Six times	Goals scored	53	1884-1901
Player Caps	125	SHILTON Peter	Undefeated	20	1889-1896	Without goal	4	1981
Player Goals	49	CHARLTON Bobby	Without win	7	1958	Goals against	13	1873-81, 1959-60

The 15-0 victory over France was achieved by the England Amateur team. The FA do not regard it as a full international although the match is part of the official French records • The England Amateurs won a world record 17 consecutive matches from 1906-1909

ENGLAND COUNTRY INFORMATION

Capital	London	Independence	Part of the United Kingdom	GDP per Capita	$29 600
Population	49 561 800	Status	Kingdom	GNP Ranking	4
Area km²	130 439	Language	English	Dialling code	+44
Population density	380 per km²	Literacy rate	99%	Internet code	.uk
% in urban areas	89%	Main religion	Christian	GMT +/-	0
Metropolitan areas ('000)	London 7 489; West Midlands (Birmingham) 2 555; Greater Manchester 2 482; West Yorkshire (Leeds, Bradford) 2 079; Merseyside (Liverpool) 1 362; South Yorkshire (Sheffield) 1 266; Tyne & Wear (Newcastle, Sunderland) 1 075				
Towns/Cities ('000)	London 7 489; Birmingham 986; Liverpool 468; Leeds 457; Sheffield 448, Bristol 432, Manchester 395, Leicester 341; Coventry 309, Kingston upon Hull 302; Bradford 300; Stoke-on-Trent 260; Wolverhampton 252; Southampton 249; Plymouth 247; Reading 246				
Neighbours (km)	Scotland 164; Wales 468				
Main stadia	Wembley – London 90 000; Old Trafford – Manchester 68 174; Emirates Stadium – London 60 000; St James' Park – Newcastle 52 142; Anfield – Liverpool 45 362; Villa Park – Birmingham 43 275				

ENGLAND NATIONAL TEAM PLAYERS AND COACHES

Record Caps			Record Goals			Recent Coaches	
SHILTON Peter	1970-'90	125	CHARLTON Bobby	1958-'70	49	REVIE Don	1974-'77
MOORE Bobby	1962-'73	108	LINEKER Gary	1984-'92	48	GREENWOOD Ron	1977-'82
CHARLTON Bobby	1958-'70	106	GREAVES Jimmy	1959-'67	43	ROBSON Bobby	1982-'90
WRIGHT Billy	1946-'59	105	OWEN Michael	1998-'06	36	TAYLOR Graham	1990-'93
BECKHAM David	1996-'06	94	FINNEY Tom	1946-'58	30	VENABLES Terry	1994-'96
ROBSON Bryan	1980-'91	90	LOFTHOUSE Nat	1950-'58	30	HODDLE Glenn	1996-'99
SANSOM Kenny	1979-'88	86	SHEARER Alan	1992-'00	30	WILKINSON Howard	1999
WILKINS Ray	1976-'86	84	WOODWARD Vivian †	1903-'11	29	KEEGAN Kevin	1999-'00
NEVILLE Gary	1995-'06	81	BLOOMER Steve	1895-'07	28	TAYLOR Peter	2000
LINEKER Gary	1984-'92	80	PLATT David	1989-'96	27	ERIKSSON Sven Goran	2000-'06
OWEN Michael	1998-'06	80	† also scored 44 goals for England amateurs			McCLAREN Steve	2006-

FIFA/COCA-COLA WORLD RANKING

1993	1994	1995	1996	1997	1998	1999	2000	2001	2002	2003	2004	2005		High		Low	
11	18	21	12	4	9	12	17	10	7	8	8	9		4	12/97	27	02/96

2005–2006											
08/05	09/05	10/05	11/05	12/05	01/06	02/06	03/06	04/06	05/06	06/06	07/06
7	11	9	9	9	9	9	9	10	10	-	5

THE FIFA BIG COUNT OF 2000

	Male	Female		Male	Female
Registered players	1 502 500	18 200	Referees	33 000	450
Non registered players	1 000 000	17 000	Officials	34 800	500
Youth players	750 000	23 000	Total involved	3 379 450	
Total players	3 310 700		Number of clubs	42 000	
Professional players	2 500	0	Number of teams	64 850	

ENGLAND 2005-06

BARCLAYS PREMIERSHIP

	Pl	W	D	L	F	A	Pts	Chelsea	Man Utd	Liverpool	Arsenal	Spurs	Blackburn	Newcastle	Bolton	West Ham	Wigan	Everton	Fulham	Charlton	Midd'boro	Man City	Villa	Portsmouth	B'ham City	WBA	Sunderland
Chelsea †	38	29	4	5	72	22	91		3-0	2-0	1-0	2-1	4-2	3-0	5-1	4-1	1-0	3-0	3-2	1-1	1-0	2-0	2-1	2-0	2-1	4-0	2-0
Manchester United †	38	25	8	5	72	34	83	1-0		1-0	2-0	1-1	1-2	2-0	4-1	1-0	4-0	1-1	4-2	4-0	0-0	1-1	1-0	3-0	3-0	3-0	0-0
Liverpool †	38	25	7	6	57	25	82	1-4	0-0		1-0	1-0	1-0	2-0	1-0	2-0	3-0	3-1	5-1	0-0	2-0	1-0	3-1	3-0	1-1	1-0	1-0
Arsenal †	38	20	7	11	68	31	67	0-2	0-0	2-1		1-1	3-0	2-0	1-1	2-3	4-2	2-0	4-1	3-0	7-0	1-0	5-0	4-0	1-0	3-1	3-1
Tottenham Hotspur ‡	38	18	11	9	53	38	65	0-2	1-2	0-0	1-1		3-2	2-0	1-0	1-1	2-2	2-0	1-0	2-1	2-0	2-1	0-0	3-1	2-0	2-1	3-2
Blackburn Rovers ‡	38	19	6	13	51	42	63	1-0	4-3	0-1	1-0	0-0		0-3	0-0	3-2	1-1	0-2	2-1	4-1	3-2	2-0	2-0	2-1	2-0	2-0	2-0
Newcastle United	38	17	7	14	47	42	58	1-0	0-2	1-3	1-0	3-1	0-1		3-1	0-0	3-1	2-0	1-1	0-0	2-2	1-0	1-1	2-0	1-0	3-0	3-2
Bolton Wanderers	38	15	11	12	49	41	56	0-2	1-2	2-2	2-0	1-0	0-0	2-0		4-1	1-1	0-2	1-1	4-1	1-1	2-0	1-1	1-0	1-0	2-0	2-0
West Ham United ‡	38	16	7	15	52	55	55	1-3	1-2	1-2	0-0	2-1	3-1	2-4	1-2		0-2	2-2	2-1	0-0	0-1	1-1	0-4	0-2	4-3	3-0	1-0
Wigan Athletic	38	15	6	17	45	52	51	0-1	1-2	0-1	2-3	1-2	0-3	1-0	2-1	1-2		1-1	1-0	3-0	1-1	4-3	3-2	1-2	1-1	0-1	1-0
Everton	38	14	8	16	34	49	50	1-1	0-2	1-3	0-1	1-0	1-0	1-0	0-4	1-2	0-1		3-1	3-1	1-0	1-0	4-1	0-1	0-0	2-2	2-2
Fulham	38	14	6	18	48	58	48	1-0	2-3	2-0	0-4	1-0	2-1	1-2	1-0	2-1	2-1	1-0		2-1	1-0	2-1	3-3	1-3	0-6	1-2	1-1
Charlton Athletic	38	13	8	17	41	55	47	0-2	1-3	2-0	0-1	2-3	0-2	3-1	0-1	2-1	0-0	0-1	2-1		2-5	0-2	1-2	5-0	0-2	2-0	
Middlesbrough	38	12	9	17	48	58	45	3-0	4-1	0-0	2-1	3-3	0-2	1-2	4-3	2-0	2-3	0-1	3-2	0-3		0-0	0-4	1-1	1-0	2-2	0-2
Manchester City	38	13	4	21	43	48	43	0-1	3-1	0-1	1-3	0-2	0-0	3-0	0-1	2-1	0-1	2-0	1-2	3-2	0-1		3-1	2-1	4-1	0-0	2-1
Aston Villa	38	10	12	16	42	55	42	1-1	0-2	0-2	0-0	1-1	1-0	1-2	2-1	2-0	4-0	0-0	1-0	2-3	0-1	1-0		3-1	0-0	2-1	
Portsmouth	38	10	8	20	37	62	38	0-2	1-3	1-3	1-1	0-2	2-2	0-0	1-1	1-0	2-1	0-1	1-2	1-0	1-2	1-1	1-1		1-1	1-0	2-1
Birmingham City	38	8	10	20	28	50	34	0-0	2-2	2-2	0-2	0-2	2-1	0-0	1-0	1-2	2-0	0-1	1-0	0-1	0-3	1-2	0-1	5-0		1-1	1-0
West Bromwich Albion	38	7	9	22	31	58	30	1-2	1-2	0-2	1-2	1-1	0-2	0-3	0-0	0-1	1-2	4-0	0-0	1-2	0-2	2-0	1-2	2-1	2-3		0-1
Sunderland	38	3	6	29	26	69	15	1-2	1-3	0-2	0-3	1-1	0-1	1-4	0-0	1-1	0-1	0-1	2-1	1-3	0-3	1-2	1-3	1-4	0-1	1-1	

13/08/2005 - 7/05/2006 • † Qualified for the UEFA Champions League • ‡ Qualified for the UEFA Cup
Top scorers: Thierry HENRY, Arsenal, 27; Ruud VAN NISTELROOIJ, Manchester United, 21; Darren BENT, Charlton Athletic, 18; Robbie KEANE, Tottenham Hotspur, 16; Frank LAMPARD, Chelsea, 16; Wayne ROONEY, Manchester United 16; Marlon HAREWOOD, West Ham United 14

ENGLAND 2005-06

COCA-COLA FOOTBALL LEAGUE CHAMPIONSHIP (2)

	Pl	W	D	L	F	A	Pts	Reading	Sheff Utd	Watford	PNE	Leeds Utd	Palace	Wolves	Coventry	Norwich	Luton	Cardiff	South'ton	Stoke	Plymouth	Ipswich	Leicester	Burnley	Hull	Sheff Wed	Derby	QPR	Crewe	Millwall	Brighton
Reading	46	31	13	2	99	32	106		2-1	0-0	2-1	1-1	3-2	1-1	2-0	4-0	3-0	5-1	2-0	3-1	1-2	2-0	2-0	2-1	3-1	2-0	5-0	2-1	1-0	5-0	5-1
Sheffield United	46	26	12	8	76	46	90	1-1		1-4	2-1	1-1	1-0	1-0	2-1	1-3	4-0	0-0	3-0	2-1	2-0	0-4	1-3	0-3	2-1	2-3	0-0	2-2	3-1		
Watford ‡	46	22	15	9	77	53	81	0-0	2-3		1-2	0-1	2-3	1-4	2-0	2-1	1-1	2-1	3-1	4-0	0-0	3-2	1-0	2-2	2-1	2-3	1-2	2-2	3-1		
Preston North End ‡	46	20	20	6	59	30	80	0-3	0-0	1-1		2-0	2-0	2-0	5-1	2-1	1-1	0-1	0-0	3-1	0-0	0-0	0-0	1-1	1-1	1-0	2-0	0-0			
Leeds United ‡	46	21	15	10	57	38	78	1-1	1-1	2-1	0-0		0-1	2-0	3-1	2-2	2-1	0-1	2-1	0-0	0-0	0-2	2-1	2-0	3-0	3-1	2-0	1-0	2-1	3-3	
Crystal Palace ‡	46	21	12	13	67	48	75	1-1	1-2	3-3	1-1	1-2		1-1	2-2	2-1	1-2	2-1	2-0	2-0	2-0	2-0	2-1	2-1	2-1	1-1					
Wolverhampton W.	46	16	19	11	50	42	67	0-2	0-0	1-1	1-0	1-1	1-4	2-0		2-2	1-0	2-1	2-0	0-0	0-0	1-1	1-0	0-0	1-0	1-3	1-1	3-1	1-1	1-2	1-0
Coventry City	46	16	15	15	62	65	63	1-1	2-0	3-1	0-1	1-1	1-4	2-0		2-2	1-0	3-1	1-1	1-1	1-0	0-2	2-1	6-1	3-0	1-1	1-0	2-0			
Norwich City	46	18	8	20	56	65	62	0-1	2-1	2-0	3-0	1-1	1-1	1-2	1-1		2-0	1-0	3-1	1-1	1-1	1-0	0-2	2-1	6-1	3-0	1-1	1-1	1-2	1-0	
Luton Town	46	17	10	19	66	67	61	3-2	1-1	1-2	3-0	0-0	2-0	1-1	1-2	4-2		3-3	3-2	2-3	1-1	1-0	2-2	3-2	2-2	1-0	2-0	4-1	2-1	3-0	
Cardiff City	46	16	12	18	58	59	60	2-5	0-1	1-3	2-2	2-1	1-0	2-2	0-0	1-2		2-1	3-0	0-2	1-1	3-0	1-0	0-0	0-0	6-1	1-1	1-1			
Southampton	46	13	19	14	49	50	58	0-0	0-1	1-3	0-0	3-4	0-0	0-0	1-1	1-0	1-3	3-2		2-0	0-0	2-1	0-0	1-1	1-3	0-0	1-1	2-0	0-0		
Stoke City	46	17	7	22	54	63	58	0-1	1-0	3-0	0-0	1-1	1-3	1-3	0-1	3-1	2-1	0-3	1-2		0-0	2-2	3-2	1-0	0-3	0-0	1-2	2-0	3-0		
Plymouth Argyle	46	13	17	16	39	46	56	0-2	0-0	3-3	0-0	0-3	2-0	2-0	0-3	1-1	1-2	0-1	2-1	2-1		1-0	1-1	0-2	3-1	1-2	2-3	1-1	1-1	1-2	
Ipswich Town	46	14	14	18	53	66	56	0-3	1-1	0-1	0-4	1-1	0-2	1-1	2-2	0-1	1-0	0-2	1-4	3-1		2-0	2-1	1-1	2-2	2-1	1-1	1-2			
Leicester City	46	13	15	18	51	59	54	1-1	4-2	2-2	1-2	1-2	1-0	1-0	0-2	1-0	1-1	2-1	2-0	4-2	1-0	0-0		0-1	3-2	2-0	2-2	1-2	1-1	1-1	0-0
Burnley	46	14	12	20	46	54	54	0-3	1-2	4-1	0-2	1-2	0-0	0-0	3-1	3-2	1-0	2-1	1-3	3-1	0-1	0-0		1-0	2-2	1-0	3-0	2-1	1-1		
Hull City	46	12	16	18	49	55	52	1-1	1-3	1-2	1-1	0-1	2-3	1-2	1-0	1-1	0-1	1-0	1-0	2-0	1-0	1-0		2-1	0-0	1-0	1-2			
Sheffield Wednesday	46	13	13	20	39	52	52	1-1	1-2	1-1	2-0	1-0	0-0	0-2	3-2	1-0	0-2	1-3	0-1	0-2	0-0	0-1	2-1	0-0	1-1		2-1	1-1	3-0	1-2	1-1
Derby County	46	10	20	16	53	67	50	2-2	0-1	1-2	1-1	0-0	1-3	1-4	2-0	1-2	2-2	2-1	1-0	3-3	1-3	1-0	0-0	1-0	1-2	2-3		1-1			
Queens Park Rangers	46	12	14	20	50	65	50	1-2	2-1	1-2	0-2	0-1	1-3	0-0	0-1	3-0	1-0	1-0	1-2	1-2	2-3	1-1	2-2	0-0	1-1		1-2	1-0	1-1		
Queens Park Rangers data / Crewe Alexandra	46	9	15	22	57	86	42	3-4	1-3	0-0	0-2	1-0	2-2	0-4	4-1	1-2	3-1	1-1	1-1	1-2	1-2	2-2	2-1	2-2	2-0	1-1	3-4			4-2	2-1
Millwall	46	8	16	22	35	62	40	2-2	0-1	1-2	0-3	1-2	1-0	1-0	1-0	1-1	0-1	1-0	1-0	0-1	1-1	1-2	0-3		0-2				1-1	1-3	0-2
Brighton & Hove Alb.	46	7	17	22	39	71	38	0-2	0-1	0-1	0-0	2-1	2-3	1-1	2-2	1-3	1-1	1-2	0-2	1-5	2-0	1-1	1-2	0-0	2-1	0-2	0-0	2-1	0-2	2-2	

6/08/2005 - 30/04/2006 • ‡ Qualified for the play-offs • Top scorers: Marlon King, Watford, 21; Dave KITSON, Reading, 18; Cameron JEROME, Cardiff City, 18; Kevin DOYLE, Reading, 18; Andrew JOHNSON, Crystal Palace, 15; Ade AKINBIYI, Sheffield Utd, 15, Gary McSHEFFREY, Coventry City 15
Play-off semi-finals: Crystal Palace 0-3 0-0 **Watford**; Leeds United 1-1 2-0 **Preston North End**; Play-off final: **Watford** 3-0 Leeds United

ENGLAND 2005-06

COCA-COLA FOOTBALL LEAGUE ONE (3)

	Pl	W	D	L	F	A	Pts
Southend United	46	23	13	10	72	43	82
Colchester United	46	22	13	11	58	40	79
Brentford ‡	46	20	16	10	72	52	76
Huddersfield Town‡	46	19	16	11	72	59	73
Barnsley ‡	46	18	18	10	62	44	72
Swansea City ‡	46	18	17	11	78	55	71
Nottingham Forest	46	19	12	15	67	52	69
Doncaster Rovers	46	20	9	17	55	51	69
Bristol City	46	18	11	17	66	62	65
Oldham Athletic	46	18	11	17	58	60	65
Bradford City	46	14	19	13	51	49	61
Scunthorpe United	46	15	15	16	68	73	60
Port Vale	46	16	12	18	49	54	60
Gillingham	46	16	12	18	50	64	60
Yeovil Town	46	15	11	20	54	62	56
Chesterfield	46	14	14	18	63	73	56
Bournemouth	46	12	19	15	49	53	55
Tranmere Rovers	46	13	15	18	50	52	54
Blackpool	46	12	17	17	56	64	53
Rotherham United	46	12	16	18	52	62	52
Hartlepool	46	11	17	18	44	59	50
Milton Keynes Dons	46	12	14	20	45	66	50
Swindon Town	46	11	15	20	46	65	48
Walsall	46	11	14	21	47	70	47

6/08/2005 - 6/05/2006 • ‡ Qualified for the play-offs • Top scorers: Freddy EASTWOOD, Southend United, 23; Billy SHARPE, Scunthorpe United, 23; Lee TRUNDLE, Swansea City, 20; James HAYTER, Bournemouth, 20; Dean WINDASS, Bradford City, 16
Play-off semi-finals: **Barnsley** 0-1 3-1 Huddersfield Town; **Swansea City** 1-1 2-0 Brentford; Play-off final: **Barnsley** 2-2 4-3p Swansea City

ENGLAND 2005-06

COCA-COLA FOOTBALL LEAGUE TWO (4)

	Pl	W	D	L	F	A	Pts
Carlisle United	46	25	11	10	84	42	86
Northampton Town	46	22	17	7	63	37	83
Leyton Orient	46	22	15	9	67	51	81
Grimsby Town ‡	46	22	12	12	64	44	78
Cheltenham Town ‡	46	19	15	12	65	53	72
Wycombe Wand's ‡	46	18	17	11	72	56	71
Lincoln City ‡	46	15	21	10	65	53	66
Darlington	46	16	15	15	58	52	63
Peterborough Utd	46	17	11	18	57	49	62
Shrewsbury Town	46	16	13	17	55	55	61
Boston United	46	15	15	16	50	60	60
Bristol Rovers	46	17	9	20	59	67	60
Wrexham	46	15	14	17	61	54	59
Rochdale	46	14	14	18	66	69	56
Chester City	46	14	12	20	53	59	54
Mansfield Town	46	13	15	18	59	66	54
Macclesfield Town	46	12	18	16	60	71	54
Barnet	46	12	18	16	44	57	54
Bury	46	12	17	17	45	57	53
Torquay United	46	13	13	20	53	66	52
Notts County	46	12	16	18	48	63	52
Stockport County	46	11	19	16	57	78	52
Oxford United	46	11	16	19	43	57	49
Rushden & Diamonds	46	11	12	23	44	76	45

6/08/2005 - 6/05/2006 • ‡ Qualified for the play-offs • Top scorers: Karl HAWLEY, Carlisle United, 23; Richard LAMBERT, Rochdale, 22; Richard WALKER, Bristol Rovers, 20; Richard BARKER, Mansfield Town, 18; Scott McGLEISH, Northampton Town, 17; Tommy MOONEY, Wycombe, 17
Play-off semi-finals: Wycombe 1-2 0-0 **Cheltenham Town**; Lincoln City 0-1 1-2 **Grimsby Town**; Play-off final: **Cheltenham Town** 1-0 Grimsby Town

ENGLAND 2005–06

NATIONWIDE CONFERENCE (5)

	Pl	W	D	L	F	A	Pts
Accrington Stanley	42	28	7	7	76	45	**91**
Hereford United ‡	42	22	14	6	59	33	**80**
Grays Athletic ‡	42	21	13	8	94	55	**76**
Halifax Town ‡	42	21	12	9	55	40	**75**
Morecambe ‡	42	22	8	12	68	41	**74**
Stevenage Borough	42	19	12	11	62	47	**69**
Exeter City	42	18	9	15	65	48	**63**
York City	42	17	12	13	63	48	**63**
Burton Albion	42	16	12	14	50	52	**60**
Dagenham & Red'ge	42	16	10	16	63	59	**58**
Woking	42	14	14	14	58	47	**56**
Cambridge United	42	15	10	17	51	57	**55**
Aldershot	42	16	6	20	61	74	**54**
Canvey Island	42	13	12	17	47	58	**51**
Kidderminster Har.	42	13	11	18	39	55	**50**
Gravesend & N'fleet	42	13	10	19	45	57	**49**
Crawley Town	42	12	11	19	48	55	**47**
Southport	42	10	10	22	36	68	**40**
Forest Green	42	8	14	20	49	62	**38**
Tamworth	42	8	14	20	32	63	**38**
Scarborough	42	9	10	23	40	66	**37**
Altrincham	42	10	11	21	40	71	**23**

Results grid (column headers, left→right): Accrington, Gereford, Grays, Halifax, Morecambe, Stevenage, Exeter, York, Burton, Dagenham, Woking, Cambridge, Aldershot, Canvey Isl, Kidd'ster, Gravesend, Crawley, Southport, For. Green, Tamworth, Scarb'gh, Altrincham

	Acc	Ger	Gra	Hal	Mor	Ste	Exe	Yor	Bur	Dag	Wok	Cam	Ald	Can	Kid	Gra	Cra	Sou	For	Tam	Sca	Alt
Accrington Stanley	—	2-1	2-3	1-1	2-0	1-1	1-2	2-1	2-1	1-0	2-1	1-0	3-2	1-0	2-0	1-1	4-2	4-0	2-0	2-1	1-0	1-0
Hereford United	2-2	—	0-2	1-0	1-0	2-0	0-2	1-0	2-0	1-4	0-3	0-2	1-1	0-1	1-0	1-1	2-1	1-1	1-1	1-0	4-0	0-0
Grays Athletic	1-2	2-2	—	1-1	1-2	2-2	3-0	1-1	2-3	0-4	2-2	5-3	2-1	1-2	2-2	6-1	1-0	1-1	2-2	5-0	5-0	1-1
Halifax Town	2-2	2-1	2-1	—	0-0	1-1	2-0	1-0	1-0	3-0	1-0	1-0	1-1	0-2	0-0	2-0	2-2	2-1	1-1	0-4	0-1	0-2
Morecambe	3-2	2-3	0-1	1-0	—	4-1	2-2	2-0	3-1	2-0	3-1	0-1	5-2	1-0	2-0	3-0	3-0	0-0	3-2	0-0	3-2	3-0
Stevenage Borough	3-1	0-0	0-1	1-0	1-0	—	2-0	1-2	3-2	1-1	1-3	2-1	3-0	3-0	1-2	0-1	0-4	5-0	0-0	3-0	1-3	1-2
Exeter City	1-3	1-2	1-2	4-2	2-0	0-2	—	1-3	1-2	3-1	1-1	4-0	0-0	2-1	0-1	4-0	5-0	0-0	3-0	1-1	3-1	
York City	2-4	1-3	1-2	0-2	1-1	0-1	4-2	—	0-1	1-1	2-1	1-1	0-3-2	2-1	2-2	1-0	0-0	0-0	5-1	2-1	3-1	5-0
Burton Albion	0-2	0-1	1-1	1-1	2-0	4-3	1-2	0-0	—	2-2	1-2	0-1	2-1	2-1	0-0	3-0	1-0	0-1	0-1	1-2	1-1	0-0
Dagenham & Red'ge	1-2	0-1	1-2	1-0	3-1	2-2	2-2	0-2	3-1	—	1-3	1-0	2-0	2-2	3-0	1-2	0-3	3-3	1-1	2-1	0-2	2-4
Woking	0-1	1-1	1-1	2-2	0-1	1-3	2-2	2-0	0-2	2-0	—	0-1	1-2	1-1	0-1	1-3	0-0	1-0	2-1	5-0	4-0	3-1
Cambridge United	3-1	2-1	1-1	1-1	1-2	2-1	0-2	1-2	0-2	2-1	1-2	—	0-2	3-1	0-2	1-1	2-1	2-1	2-2	2-1	2-1	4-0
Aldershot	1-4	0-1	0-3	3-1	2-0	2-1	0-2	1-1	3-1	1-1	1-3	—	—	2-2	1-0	3-2	3-2	2-2	0-2	1-0	2-0	1-0
Canvey Island	0-2	1-1	2-1	0-1	3-3	1-1	1-1	1-2	0-2	2-1	2-1	—	—	2-1	1-2	2-1	1-1	1-1	1-1	1-2	1-1	4-0
Kidderminster Har.	2-0	1-1	0-5	0-1	1-0	0-0	1-0	0-0	0-1	3-1	2-1	1-0	1-4	3-2	—	—	0-2	1-0	1-1	1-3	0-1	2-1
Gravesend & N'fleet	1-3	1-2	1-3	4-0	1-0	0-2	2-2	2-0	1-1	3-2	0-0	0-0	3-2	0-1	2-1	—	1-1	2-2	2-0	2-0	0-0	2-0
Crawley Town	0-1	0-2	1-3	2-2	1-3	1-2	0-0	1-1	1-0	0-2	2-1	0-3	1-2	0-1	2	2-0	—	1-0	3-0	2-0	2-0	
Southport	2-0	1-2	1-4	0-2	0-3	3-2	0-3	1-4	3-2	1-2	1-0	2-2	0-1	2-0	1-4	1-0	0-2	—	3-1	1-1	0-2	1-1
Forest Green	1-1	2-1	2-2	1-2	0-2	0-0	1-2	1-0	0-3	0-3	1-0	4-2	1-2	0-0	0-0	2-2	1-2	—	—	1-3	5-1	5-0
Tamworth	1-2	0-1	2-2	1-2	0-3	2-0	1-1	0-3	1-1	2-2	0-1	1-1	2-1	1-0	0-0	0-0	0-0	0-0	—		0-1	1-1
Scarborough	2-2	0-1	2-7	2-0	0-1	1-1	0-1	2-2	3-0	0-1	1-1	1-2	2-2	1-2	1-3	1-1	3-1	2-0	1-1	0-0	—	1-2
Altrincham	2-0	1-0	0-2	1-2	2-0	1-1	1-1	0-3	1-2	0-5	0-4	2-1	5-1	0-1	3-0	2-2	1-1	1-0	2-1	2-0	1-1	—

6/08/2005 - 6/05/2006 • ‡ Qualified for the play-offs
Play-off semi-finals: Morecambe 1-1 2-3 **Hereford United**; Halifax Town 3-2 2-2 Grays Athletic; Play-off final: **Hereford United** 3-2 Halifax Town

CLUB DIRECTORY

Club	Town/City	Stadium	Capacity	www.	Lge	Cup	LCup	CL
Arsenal	London	Emirates Stadium	60 000	arsenal.com	13	10	2	0
Aston Villa	Birmingham	Villa Park	42 573	avfc.co.uk	7	7	5	1
Blackburn Rovers	Blackburn	Ewood Park	31 367	rovers.co.uk	3	6	1	0
Bolton Wanderers	Bolton	The Reebok	27 879	bwfc.co.uk	0	4	0	0
Charlton Athletic	London	The Valley	26 875	cafc.co.uk	0	1	0	0
Chelsea	London	Stamford Bridge	42 449	chelseafc.com	3	3	3	0
Everton	Liverpool	Goodison Park	40 565	evertonfc.com	9	5	0	0
Fulham	London	Craven Cottage	22 400	fulhamfc.com	0	0	0	0
Liverpool	Liverpool	Anfield	45 362	liverpoolfc.tv	18	7	7	5
Manchester City	Manchester	City of Manchester	48 000	mcfc.co.uk	2	4	2	0
Manchester United	Manchester	Old Trafford	76 000	manutd.com	15	11	2	2
Middlesbrough	Middlesbrough	The Riverside	35 120	mfc.co.uk	0	0	1	0
Newcastle United	Newcastle	St James' Park	52 193	nufc.co.uk	4	6	0	0
Portsmouth	Portsmouth	Fratton Park	20 228	pompeyfc.co.uk	2	1	0	0
Reading	Reading	Madejski	24 200	readingfc.co.uk	0	0	0	0
Sheffield United	Sheffield	Bramall Lane	28 000	sufc.co.uk	1	4	0	0
Tottenham Hotspur	London	White Hart Lane	36 252	spurs.co.uk	2	8	3	0
Watford	London	Vicarage Road	19 500	watfordfc.com	0	0	0	0
West Ham United	London	Upton Park	34 500	whufc.co.uk	0	3	0	0
Wigan Athletic	Wigan	JJB Stadium	25 000	wiganathletic.tv	0	0	0	0

RECENT LEAGUE AND CUP RECORD

	Championship						Cup		
Year	Champions	Pts	Runners-up	Pts	Third	Pts	Winners	Score	Runners-up
1993	Manchester United	84	Aston Villa	74	Norwich City	72	Arsenal	1-1 2-1	Sheffield Wed'day
1994	Manchester United	92	Blackburn Rovers	84	Newcastle United	77	Manchester United	4-0	Chelsea
1995	Blackburn Rovers	89	Manchester United	88	Nottingham Forest	77	Everton	1-0	Manchester United
1996	Manchester United	82	Newcastle United	78	Liverpool	71	Manchester United	1-0	Liverpool
1997	Manchester United	75	Newcastle United	68	Arsenal	68	Chelsea	2-0	Middlesbrough
1998	Arsenal	78	Manchester United	77	Liverpool	65	Arsenal	2-0	Newcastle United
1999	Manchester United	79	Arsenal	78	Chelsea	75	Manchester United	2-0	Newcastle United
2000	Manchester United	91	Arsenal	73	Leeds United	69	Chelsea	1-0	Aston Villa
2001	Manchester United	80	Arsenal	70	Liverpool	69	Liverpool	2-1	Arsenal
2002	Arsenal	87	Liverpool	80	Manchester United	77	Arsenal	2-0	Chelsea
2003	Manchester United	83	Arsenal	78	Newcastle United	69	Arsenal	1-0	Southampton
2004	Arsenal	90	Chelsea	79	Manchester United	75	Manchester United	3-0	Millwall
2005	Chelsea	95	Arsenal	83	Manchester United	77	Arsenal	0-0 5-4p	Manchester United
2006	Chelsea	91	Manchester United	83	Liverpool	82	Liverpool	3-3 3-1p	West Ham United

CARLING LEAGUE CUP 2005-06

Third Round		Fourth Round		Quarter-finals		Semi-finals		Final	
Manchester United *	4								
Barnet	1	Manchester United *	3						
Fulham *	2	West Bromwich Albion	1						
West Bromwich Albion	3			Manchester United	3				
Millwall	3			Birmingham City *	1				
Mansfield *	2	Millwall *	2 3p						
Norwich City	1	Birmingham City	2 4p			Manchester United	1 2		
Birmingham City *	2					Blackburn Rovers *	1 1		
Middlesbrough	1	Middlesbrough *	2						
Everton *	0	Crystal Palace	1						
Liverpool	1			Middlesbrough *	0				
Crystal Palace *	2			Blackburn Rovers	1				
Charlton Athletic	1 5p	Charlton Athletic *	2						
Chelsea *	1 4p	Blackburn Rovers	3					Manchester United	4
Leeds United	0							Wigan Athletic	0
Blackburn Rovers *	3								
Arsenal	3	Arsenal *	3						
Sunderland *	0	Reading	0						
Sheffield United	0			Arsenal	2 3p				
Reading *	2			Doncaster Rovers *	2 1p				
Aston Villa *	1	Aston Villa	0						
Burnley	0	Doncaster Rovers *	3						
Gillingham	0					Arsenal	0 2		
Doncaster Rovers *	2					Wigan Athletic *	1 1		
Bolton Wanderers *	1	Bolton Wanderers *	2						
West Ham United	0	Leicester City	1						
Cardiff City *	0			Bolton Wanderers	0				
Leicester City	1			Wigan Athletic *	2				
Newcastle United	1	Newcastle United	0						
Grimsby Town *	0	Wigan Athletic *	1						
Watford	0								
Wigan Athletic *	3								

* Home team/home team in the first leg of the semi-finals

CARLING CUP FINAL

Millenium Stadium, Cardiff
26-02-2006, Att. 66 866, Ref. Wiley
Scorers - Rooney 2 33 61, Saha 55, Ronaldo 59

Man Utd - Van der Sar - Neville, G. Brown (Vidic 83),
Ferdinand, Silvestre (Evra 83) - Ronaldo (Richardson
73), O'Shea, Giggs, Park - Saha, Rooney. Tr- Ferguson
Wigan - Pollitt (Filan 14) - Chimbonda, De Zeeuw,
Henchoz (McCulloch 62), Baines - Bullard, Kavanagh
(Ziegler 72), Scharner, Teale - Camara, Roberts.
Tr- Jewell

FA CUP 2005-06

Third Round		Fourth Round		Fifth Round	
Liverpool	5				
Luton Town *	3	Liverpool	2		
Ipswich Town *	0	Portsmouth *	1		
Portsmouth	1			Liverpool *	1
Wolverhampton Wanderers *	1			Manchester United	0
Plymouth Argyle	0	Wolverhampton Wanderers *	0		
Burton Albion *	0 0	Manchester United	3		
Manchester United	0 5				
Stoke City *	0 1 5p				
Tamworth	0 1 4p	Stoke City *	2		
Barnsley *	1 0	Walsall	1		
Walsall	1 2			Stoke City *	0
Reading	1 3			Birmingham City	1
West Bromwich Albion *	1 2	Reading *	1 1		
Torquay United *	0 0	Birmingham City	1 2		
Birmingham City	0 2				
Newcastle United *	1				
Mansfield Town	0	Newcastle United	2		
Chester City	2 0	Cheltenham Town *	0		
Cheltenham Town *	2 1			Newcastle United *	1
Leicester City *	3			Southampton	0
Tottenham Hotspur	2	Leicester City *	0		
Milton Keynes Dons	3	Southampton	1		
Southampton *	4				
Colchester United	2				
Sheffield United *	1	Colchester United *	3		
Burnley	1	Derby County	1		
Derby County *	2			Colchester United	1
Everton	1 1			Chelsea *	3
Millwall *	1 0	Everton *	1 1		
Huddersfield Town	1	Chelsea	1 4		
Chelsea *	2				
Middlesbrough	1 5				
Nuneaton Borough *	1 2	Middlesbrough	1 1		
Brighton & Hove Albion *	0	Coventry City *	1 0		
Coventry City	1			Middlesbrough	2
Crystal Palace *	4			Preston North End *	0
Northampton Town	1	Crystal Palace	1 1		
Crewe Alexandra	1	Preston North End *	1 2		
Preston North End *	2				
Brentford	3				
Stockport County	2	Brentford *	2		
Northwich Victoria	0	Sunderland	1		
Sunderland *	3			Brentford	1
Leyton Orient	2			Charlton Athletic *	3
Fulham *	1	Leyton Orient	1		
Sheffield Wednesday *	2	Charlton Athletic *	2		
Charlton Athletic	4				
Manchester City *	3				
Scunthorpe United	1	Manchester City *	1		
Leeds United	1 3 2p	Wigan Athletic	0		
Wigan Athletic *	1 3 4p			Manchester City	1 2
Port Vale *	2			Aston Villa *	1 1
Doncaster Rovers	1	Port Vale	1		
Hull City *	0	Aston Villa *	3		
Aston Villa	1				
Bolton Wanderers	3				
Watford *	0	Bolton Wanderers *	1		
Cardiff City	1	Arsenal	0		
Arsenal *	2			Bolton Wanderers *	0 1
Blackburn Rovers *	3			West Ham United	0 2
Queens Park Rangers	0	Blackburn Rovers	2		
Norwich City *	1	West Ham United *	4		
West Ham United	2				

* Home team

FA CUP 2005–06

Quarter-finals   **Semi-finals**   **Final**

Liverpool	7
Birmingham City *	0

Liverpool †	2
Chelsea	1

Newcastle United	0
Chelsea *	1

Liverpool	3 3p
West Ham United ‡‡	3 1p

Middlesbrough	0 4
Charlton Athletic *	0 2

Middlesbrough	0
West Ham United ‡	1

Manchester City *	1
West Ham United	2

FA CUP FINAL 2006

Millennium Stadium, Cardiff, 13-05-2005, 15:00, Att: 71 140, Ref: Wiley

Liverpool   3   3p   Cisse [32], Gerrard 2 [54] [90]

West Ham United   3   1p   Carragher OG [21], Ashton [28], Konchesky [64]

Liverpool - Jose REINA - Jamie CARRAGHER, Steve FINNAN, Sami HYYPIA, Xabi ALONSO (Jan KROMKAMP 67), Steven GERRARD, Harry KEWELL (Fernando MORIENTES 48), John Arne RIISE, Mohamed SISSOKO, Djibril CISSE, Peter CROUCH (Dietmar HAMANN 71). Tr: Rafa BENITEZ

West Ham - Shaka HISLOP - Anton FERDINAND, Daniel GABBIDON, Paul KONCHESKY, Yossi BENAYOUN, Matthew ETHERINGTON (Teddy SHERINGHAM 85), Carl FLETCHER (Christian DAILLY 77), Nigel REO-COKER, Lionel SCALONI, Dean ASHTON (Bobby ZAMORA 71), Marlon HAREWOOD. Tr: Alan PARDEW

Penalties: Hamann ✓, Zamora ✗, Hyypia ✗, Sheringham ✓, Gerrard ✓, Konchesky ✗, Riise ✓, Ferdinand ✗

† Played at Old Trafford, Manchester
‡ Played at Villa Park, Birmingham
‡‡ Qualified for the UEFA Cup

CHELSEA 2005–06

Date	Opponents	Score		Comp	Scorers	Att
7-08-2005	Arsenal	W 2-1	N	CS	Drogba 2 [8 57]	58 014
14-08-2005	Wigan Athletic	W 1-0	A	PL	Crespo [90]	23 575
21-08-2005	Arsenal	W 1-0	H	PL	Drogba [73]	42 136
24-08-2005	West Bromwich Albion	W 4-0	H	PL	Lampard 2 [23 80], Cole [43], Drogba [68]	41 201
27-08-2005	Tottenham Hotspur	W 2-0	A	PL	Del Horno [39], Duff [71]	36 077
10-09-2005	Sunderland	W 2-0	H	PL	Geremi [54], Drogba [82]	41 969
13-09-2005	RSC Anderlecht	W 1-0	H	CLgG	Lampard [19]	29 575
17-09-2005	Charlton Athletic	W 2-0	A	PL	Crespo [55], Robben [60]	27 111
24-09-2005	Aston Villa	W 2-1	H	PL	Lampard 2 [45 75p]	42 146
28-09-2005	Liverpool	D 0-0	A	CLgG		42 743
2-10-2005	Liverpool	W 4-1	A	PL	Lampard [27p], Duff [43], Cole [63], Geremi [82]	44 235
15-10-2005	Bolton Wanderers	W 5-1	H	PL	Drogba 2 [52 61], Lampard 2 [55 59], Gudjohnsen [74]	41 775
19-10-2005	Real Betis - ESP	W 4-0	H	CLgG	Drogba [24], Carvalho [44], Cole [59], Crespo [64]	36 457
23-10-2005	Everton	D 1-1	A	PL	Lampard [50]	36 042
26-10-2005	Charlton Athletic	D 1-1	H	LCr3	L 4-5p. Terry [41]	42 198
29-10-2005	Blackburn Rovers	W 4-2	H	PL	Drogba [10], Lampard 2 [14p 62], Cole [74]	41 553
1-11-2005	Real Betis	L 0-1	A	CLgG		55 000
6-11-2005	Manchester United	L 0-1	H	PL		67 864
19-11-2005	Newcastle United	W 3-0	H	PL	Cole [47], Crespo [51], Duff [90]	42 268
23-11-2005	RSC Anderlect - BEL	W 2-0	A	CLgG	Crespo [8], Carvalho [15]	21 070
26-11-2005	Portsmouth	W 2-0	A	PL	Crespo [27], Lampard [67p]	20 182
3-12-2005	Middlesbrough	W 1-0	H	PL	Terry [62]	41 666
6-12-2005	Liverpool	D 0-0	H	CLgG		41 598
10-12-2005	Wigan Athletic	W 1-0	H	PL	Terry [67]	42 060
18-12-2005	Arsenal	W 2-0	H	PL	Robben [39], Cole [73]	38 347
26-12-2005	Fulham	W 3-2	H	PL	Gallas [3], Lampard [24], Crespo [74]	42 313
28-12-2005	Manchester City	W 1-0	H	PL	Cole [79]	46 587
31-12-2005	Birmingham City	W 2-0	H	PL	Crespo [25], Robben [43]	40 652
2-01-2006	West Ham United	W 3-1	A	PL	Lampard [25], Crespo [61], Drogba [80]	34 758
7-01-2006	Huddersfield Town	W 2-1	H	FACr3	Cole [12], Gudjohnsen [82]	41 650
15-01-2006	Sunderland	W 2-1	H	PL	Crespo [28], Robben [69]	32 420
22-01-2006	Charlton Athletic	D 1-1	H	PL	Gudjohnsen [19]	41 355
28-01-2006	Everton	D 1-1	A	FACr4	Lampard [73]	29 742
1-02-2006	Aston Villa	D 1-1	A	PL	Robben [14]	38 562
5-02-2006	Liverpool	W 2-0	H	PL	Gallas [35], Crespo [68]	42 316
8-02-2006	Everton	W 4-1	H	FACr4	Robben [22], Lampard [36p], Crespo [39], Terry [74]	39 301
11-02-2006	Middlesbrough	L 0-3	A	PL		31 037
19-02-2006	Colchester United	W 3-1	H	FACr5	Ferreira [37], Cole 2 [79 91+]	41 810
22-02-2006	Barcelona - ESP	L 1-2	H	CLr2	Motta OG [59]	39 521
25-02-2006	Portsmouth	W 2-0	H	PL	Lampard [65], Robben [78]	42 254
4-03-2006	West Bromwich Albion	W 2-1	A	PL	Drogba [51], Cole [74]	26 581
7-03-2006	Barcelona - ESP	D 1-1	A	CLr2	Lampard [93+]	98 436
11-03-2006	Tottenham Hotspur	W 2-1	H	PL	Essien [14], Gallas [92+]	42 243
19-03-2006	Fulham	L 0-1	A	PL		22 486
22-03-2006	Newcastle United	W 1-0	H	FACqf	Terry [4]	42 279
25-03-2006	Manchester City	W 2-0	H	PL	Drogba 2 [30 33]	42 321
1-04-2006	Birmingham City	D 0-0	A	PL		26 364
9-04-2006	West Ham United	W 4-1	H	PL	Drogba [28], Crespo [31], Terry [54], Gallas [69]	41 919
15-04-2006	Bolton Wanderers	W 2-0	A	PL	Terry [44], Lampard [59]	27 266
17-04-2006	Everton	W 3-0	H	PL	Lampard [28], Drogba [62], Essien [74]	41 765
22-04-2006	Liverpool	L 1-2	N	FACsf	Drogba [70]	64 575
29-04-2006	Manchester United	W 3-0	H	PL	Gallas [5], Cole [61], Carvalho [73]	42 219
2-05-2006	Blackburn Rovers	L 0-1	A	PL		20 243
7-05-2006	Newcastle United	L 0-1	A	PL		52 309

PL = FA Premier League (Barclays Premiership) • CL = UEFA Champions League • FAC = FA Cup • LC = Carling League Cup
gH = Group H • r3 = 3rd round • r4 = 4th round • r5 = 5th round • qf = quarter-final • sf = semi-final • f = final • N = Millennium Stadium •
N = Old Trafford, Manchester

MANCHESTER UNITED 2005–06

Date	Opponents	Score			Scorers	Att
9-08-2005	Debreceni VSC - HUN	W 3-0	H	CLpr3	Rooney [7], Van Nistelrooij [49], Ronaldo [63]	51 701
13-08-2005	Everton	W 2-0	A	PL	Van Nistelrooij [43], Rooney [46]	38 610
20-08-2005	Aston Villa	W 1-0	H	PL	Van Nistelrooij [66]	67 934
24-08-2005	Debreceni VSC - HUN	W 3-0	A	CLpr3	Heinze 2 [20 61], Richardson [65]	27 000
28-08-2005	Newcastle United	W 2-0	A	PL	Rooney [66], Van Nistelrooij [90]	52 327
10-09-2005	Manchester City	D 1-1	H	PL	Van Nistelrooij [45]	67 839
14-09-2005	Villarreal - ESP	D 0-0	H	CLgD		19 550
18-09-2005	Liverpool	D 0-0	A	PL		44 917
24-09-2005	Blackburn Rovers	L 1-2	H	PL	Van Nistelrooij [67]	67 765
27-09-2005	Benfica - POR	W 2-1	H	CLgD	Giggs [39], Van Nistelrooij [85]	66 112
1-10-2005	Fulham	W 3-2	A	PL	Van Nistelrooij 2 [17 45], Rooney [18]	21 862
15-10-2005	Sunderland	W 3-1	A	PL	Rooney [40], Van Nistelrooij [76], Rossi [87]	39 085
18-10-2005	Lille OSC - FRA	D 0-0	H	CLgD		60 626
22-10-2005	Tottenham Hotspur	D 1-1	H	PL	Silvestre [7]	67 856
26-10-2005	Barnet	W 4-1	H	LCr3	Miller [4], Richardson [19], Rossi [51], Ebanks-Blake [89]	43 673
29-10-2005	Middlesbrough	L 1-4	A	PL	Ronaldo [90]	30 579
2-11-2005	Lille OSC - FRA	L 0-1	A	CLgD		66 470
6-11-2005	Chelsea	W 1-0	H	PL	Fletcher [31]	67 864
19-11-2005	Charlton Athletic	W 3-1	A	PL	Smith [37], Van Nistelrooij 2 [70 85]	26 730
22-11-2005	Villarreal - ESP	D 0-0	H	CLgD		67 471
27-11-2005	West Ham United	W 2-1	A	PL	Rooney [47], O'Shea [56]	34 755
30-11-2005	West Bromwich Albion	W 3-1	H	LCr4	Ronaldo [12p], Saha [16], O'Shea [56]	48 924
3-12-2005	Portsmouth	W 3-0	H	PL	Scholes [20], Rooney [80], Van Nistelrooij [84]	67 684
7-12-2005	Benfica - POR	L 1-2	A	CLgD	Scholes [6]	62 174
11-12-2005	Everton	D 1-1	H	PL	Giggs [15]	67 831
14-12-2005	Wigan Athletic	W 4-0	H	PL	Ferdinand [30], Rooney 2 [35 55], Van Nistelrooij [70]	67 793
17-12-2005	Aston Villa	W 2-0	A	PL	Van Nistelrooij [10], Rooney [51]	37 128
20-12-2005	Birmingham City	W 3-1	H	LCqf	Saha 2 [46 63], Park [50]	20 454
26-12-2005	West Bromwich Albion	W 3-0	H	PL	Scholes [35], Ferdinand [45], Van Nistelrooij [63]	67 972
28-12-2005	Birmingham City	D 2-2	A	PL	Van Nistelrooij [5], Rooney [54]	28 459
31-12-2005	Bolton Wanderers	W 4-1	H	PL	N'Gotty OG [8], Saha [44], Ronaldo 2 [68 90]	67 858
3-01-2006	Arsenal	D 0-0	A	PL		38 313
8-01-2006	Burton Albion	D 0-0	A	FACr3		6 191
11-01-2006	Blackburn Rovers	D 1-1	A	LCsf	Saha [30]	24 348
14-01-2006	Manchester City	L 1-3	A	PL	Van Nistelrooij [76]	47 192
18-01-2006	Burton Albion	W 5-0	H	FACr3	Saha [7], Rossi 2 [23 90], Richardson [52], Giggs [68]	53 564
22-01-2006	Liverpool	W 1-0	H	PL	Ferdinand [90]	67 874
25-01-2006	Blackburn Rovers	W 2-1	H	LCsf	Van Nistelrooij [8], Saha [51]	61 637
29-01-2006	Wolverhampton Wanderers	W 3-0	H	FACr4	Richardson 2 [5 51], Saha [44]	28 333
1-02-2006	Blackburn Rovers	L 3-4	A	PL	Saha [37], Van Nistelrooij 2 [63 68]	25 484
4-02-2006	Fulham	W 4-2	H	PL	Park [6], Ronaldo 2 [14 86], Saha [23]	67 844
11-02-2006	Portsmouth	W 3-1	A	PL	Van Nistelrooij [18], Ronaldo 2 [38 45]	20 206
18-02-2006	Liverpool	L 0-1	A	FACr5		44 039
26-02-2006	Wigan Athletic	W 4-0	N	LCf	Rooney 2 [34 63], Saha [58], Ronaldo [61]	66 866
6-03-2006	Wigan Athletic	W 2-1	A	PL	Ronaldo [74], Chimbonda OG [90]	23 574
12-03-2006	Newcastle United	W 2-0	H	PL	Rooney 2 [8 12]	67 858
18-03-2006	West Bromwich Albion	W 2-1	A	PL	Saha 2 [16 64]	27 623
26-03-2006	Birmingham City	W 3-0	H	PL	Taylor OG [2], Giggs [16], Rooney [83]	69 070
29-03-2006	West Ham United	W 1-0	H	PL	Van Nistelrooij [45]	69 522
1-04-2006	Bolton Wanderers	W 2-1	A	PL	Saha [33], Van Nistelrooij [79]	27 718
9-04-2006	Arsenal	W 2-0	H	PL	Rooney [54], Park [78]	70 908
14-04-2006	Sunderland	D 0-0	H	PL		72 519
17-04-2006	Tottenham Hotspur	W 2-1	A	PL	Rooney 2 [7 35]	36 141
29-04-2006	Chelsea	L 0-3	A	PL		42 219
1-05-2006	Middlesbrough	D 0-0	H	PL		69 531
7-05-2006	Charlton Athletic	W 4-0	H	PL		73 006

CS = Community Shield • PL = FA Premier League (Barclays Premiership) • CL = UEFA Champions League • FAC = FA Cup • LC = Carling League Cup
gD = Group D • r3 = 3rd round • r4 = 4th round • r5 = 5th round • qf = quarter-final • sf = semi-final • f = final • N = Millennium Stadium

LIVERPOOL 2005-06

Date	Opponents	Score			Scorers	Att
13-07-2005	TNS Llansantffraid - WAL	W 3-0	H	CLpr1	Gerrard 3 [8 21 90]	44 760
19-07-2005	TNS Llansantffraid - WAL	W 3-0	N	CLpr1	Cisse [26], Gerrard 2 [85 86]	8 009
26-07-2005	FBK Kaunas - LTU	W 3-1	A	CLpr2	Cisse [26], Carragher [29], Gerrard [54]	6 747
2-08-2005	FBK Kaunas - LTU	W 2-0	H	CLpr2	Gerrard [77], Cisse [86]	43 717
10-08-2005	CSKA Sofia - BUL	W 3-1	A	CLpr3	Cisse [24], Morientes 2 [30 58]	16 553
13-08-2005	Middlesbrough	D 0-0	A	PL		31 908
20-08-2005	Sunderland	W 1-0	H	PL	Alonso [24]	44 913
23-08-2005	CSKA Sofia - BUL	L 0-1	H	CLpr3		42 175
26-08-2005	CSKA Moskva - RUS	W 3-1	N	USC	Cisse 2 [82 103], Garcia [119]	
10-09-2005	Tottenham Hotspur	D 0-0	A	PL		36 148
13-09-2005	Real Betis - ESP	W 2-1	A	CLgG	Pongolle [2], Garcia [13]	34 862
18-09-2005	Manchester United	D 0-0	H	PL		44 917
24-09-2005	Birmingham City	D 2-2	A	PL	Garcia [67], Cisse [83]	27 733
28-09-2005	Chelsea - ENG	D 0-0	H	CLgG		42 743
2-10-2005	Chelsea	L 1-4	H	PL	Gerrard [36]	44 325
15-10-2005	Blackburn Rovers	W 1-0	H	PL	Cisse [75]	44 697
19-10-2005	RSC Anderlecht - BEL	W 1-0	A	CLgG	Cisse [20]	21 824
22-10-2005	Fulham	L 0-2	A	PL		22 480
25-10-2005	Crystal Palace	L 1-2	A	LCr3	Gerrard [40]	19 673
29-10-2005	West Ham United	W 2-0	H	PL	Alonso [18], Zenden [82]	44 537
1-11-2005	RSC Anderlecht - BEL	W 3-0	H	CLgG	Morientes [33], Garcia [60], Cisse [89]	42 607
5-11-2005	Aston Villa	W 2-0	A	PL	Gerrard [84], Alonso [89]	42 551
19-11-2005	Portsmouth	W 3-0	H	PL	Zenden [23], Cisse [38], Morientes [79]	44 394
23-11-2005	Real Betis - ESP	D 0-0	H	CLgG		42 077
26-11-2005	Manchester City	W 1-0	A	PL	Riise [60]	47 105
30-11-2005	Sunderland	W 2-0	A	PL	Garcia [30], Gerrard [45]	32 697
3-12-2005	Wigan Athletic	W 3-0	H	PL	Crouch 2 [19 42], Garcia [70]	44 098
6-12-2005	Chelsea - ENG	D 0-0	A	CLgG		41 598
10-12-2005	Middlesbrough	W 2-0	H	PL	Morientes 2 [71 77]	43 510
15-12-2005	Deportivo Saprissa - CRC	W 3-0	N	CWCsf	Crouch 2 [3 58], Gerrard [32]	43 902
18-12-2005	São Paulo FC - BRA	L 0-1	N	CWCf		66 821
26-12-2005	Newcastle United	W 2-0	H	PL	Gerrard [14], Crouch [43]	44 197
28-12-2005	Everton	W 3-1	A	PL	Crouch [11], Gerrard [18], Cisse [47]	40 158
31-12-2005	West Bromwich Albion	W 1-0	H	PL	Crouch [51]	44 192
2-01-2006	Bolton Wanderers	D 2-2	A	PL	Gerrard [67p], Garcia [82]	27 604
7-01-2006	Luton Town	W 5-3	A	FACr3	Gerrard [15], Pongolle 2 [61 73], Alonso 2 [68 90]	10 170
14-01-2006	Tottenham Hotspur	W 1-0	H	PL	Kewell [58]	44 983
22-01-2006	Manchester United	L 0-1	A	PL		67 874
29-01-2006	Portsmouth	W 2-1	A	FACr4	Gerrard [36], Riise [40]	17 247
1-02-2006	Birmingham City	D 1-1	H	PL	Gerrard [62]	43 851
5-02-2006	Chelsea	L 0-2	A	PL		42 316
8-02-2006	Charlton Athletic	L 0-2	A	PL		27 111
11-02-2006	Wigan Athletic	W 1-0	A	PL	Hyypia [30]	25 023
14-02-2006	Arsenal	W 1-0	H	PL	Garcia [87]	44 065
18-02-2006	Manchester United	W 1-0	H	FACr5	Crouch [18]	44 039
21-02-2006	Benfica - POR	L 0-1	A	CLr2		63 702
26-02-2006	Manchester City	W 1-0	H	PL	Kewell [40]	44 121
4-03-2006	Charlton Athletic	D 0-0	H	PL		43 892
8-03-2006	Benfica - POR	L 0-2	H	CLr2		42 744
12-03-2006	Arsenal	L 1-2	A	PL	Garcia [75]	38 221
15-03-2006	Fulham	W 5-1	H	PL	Fowler [16], Brown OG [34], Morientes [70], Crouch [89], Warnock [90]	42 293
19-03-2006	Newcastle United	W 3-1	A	PL	Crouch [10], Gerrard [35], Cisse [52]	52 302
21-03-2006	Birmingham City	W 7-0	A	FACqf	Hyypia [1], Crouch 2 [4 38], Morientes [59], Riise [70], Tebily OG [77], Cisse [89]	27 378
25-03-2006	Everton	W 3-1	H	PL	Neville OG [45], Garcia [47], Kewell [84]	44 923
1-04-2006	West Bromwich Albion	W 2-0	A	PL	Fowler [7], Cisse [38]	27 576
9-04-2006	Bolton Wanderers	W 1-0	H	PL	Fowler [45]	44 194
16-04-2006	Blackburn Rovers	W 1-0	H	PL	Fowler [29]	29 142
22-04-2006	Chelsea	W 2-1	N	FACsf	Riise [21], Garcia [53]	64 471
26-04-2006	West Ham United	W 2-1	A	PL	Cisse 2 [19 54]	34 852
29-04-2006	Aston Villa	W 3-1	H	PL	Morientes [5], Gerrard 2 [60 66]	44 479
7-05-2006	Portsmouth	W 3-1	A	PL	Fowler [51], Crouch [83], Cisse [88]	20 240
13-05-2006	West Ham United	D 3-3	N	FACf	Cisse [32], Gerrard 2 [54 90]. W 3-1p	71 140

PL = FA Premier League (Barclays Premiership) • CL = UEFA Champions League • FAC = FA Cup • LC = Carling League Cup • USC = UEFA Super Cup
pr3 = third preliminary round • gA = Group A • r3 = 3rd round • r4 = 4th round • r5 = 5th round • qf = quarter-final • sf = semi-final • f = final
N = Racecourse Ground, Wrexham • **N** = Stade Louis II, Monaco • *N* = Yokohama International, Yokohama • <u>N</u> = Old Trafford, Manchester • <u>*N*</u> = Millennium
Stadium, Cardiff

ARSENAL 2005-06

Date	Opponents	Score			Scorers	Att
7-08-2005	Chelsea	L	1-2	N	CS	Fabregas [65]	58 014
14-08-2005	Newcastle United	W	2-0	H	PL	Henry [81], Van Persie [87]	38 072
21-08-2005	Chelsea	L	0-1	A	PL		42 136
24-08-2005	Fulham	W	4-1	H	PL	Cygan 2 [32 90], Henry 2 [53 82]	37 866
10-09-2005	Middlesbrough	L	1-2	A	PL	Reyes [90]	28 075
14-09-2005	FC Thun - SUI	W	2-1	H	CLgB	Gilberto [51], Bergkamp [90]	34 498
19-09-2005	Everton	W	2-0	H	PL	Campbell 2 [11 30]	38 121
24-09-2005	West Ham United	D	0-0	A	PL		34 742
27-09-2005	Ajax - NED	W	2-1	A	CLgB	Ljungberg [2], Pires [68p]	43 250
2-10-2005	Birmingham City	W	1-0	H	PL	Clemence OG [81]	37 891
15-10-2005	West Bromwich Albion	L	1-2	A	PL	Senderos [18]	26 604
18-10-2005	Sparta Praha - CZE	W	2-0	H	CLgB	Henry 2 [21 74]	12 128
22-10-2005	Manchester City	W	1-0	H	PL	Pires [61p]	38 189
25-10-2005	Sunderland	W	3-0	A	LCr3	Eboue [61], Van Persie 2 [67p 87]	47 366
29-10-2005	Tottenham Hotspur	D	1-1	A	PL	Pires [77]	36 154
2-11-2005	Sparta Praha - CZE	W	3-0	H	CLgB	Henry [23], Van Persie 2 [81 86]	35 115
5-11-2005	Sunderland	W	3-1	H	PL	Van Persie [12], Henry 2 [36 82]	38 210
19-11-2005	Wigan Athletic	W	3-2	A	PL	Van Persie [11], Henry 2 [21 41]	25 004
22-11-2005	FC Thun - SUI	W	1-0	A	CLgB	Pires [88]	31 330
26-11-2005	Blackburn Rovers	W	3-0	H	PL	Fabregas [4], Henry [45], Van Persie [90]	38 192
29-11-2005	Reading	W	3-0	H	LCr4	Reyes [12], Van Persie [42], Lupoli [65]	36 137
3-12-2005	Bolton Wanderers	L	0-2	A	PL		26 792
7-12-2005	Ajax - NED	D	0-0	H	CLgB		35 376
10-12-2005	Newcastle United	L	0-1	A	PL		52 297
18-12-2005	Chelsea	L	0-2	H	PL		38 347
21-12-2005	Doncaster Rovers	D	2-2	A	LCqf	Owusu-Abeyle [63], Gilberto [120], W 3-1p	10 006
26-12-2005	Charlton Athletic	W	1-0	A	PL	Reyes [58]	27 111
28-12-2005	Portsmouth	W	4-0	H	PL	Bergkamp [7], Reyes [13], Henry 2 [36 42p]	38 223
31-12-2005	Aston Villa	D	0-0	A	PL		37 114
3-01-2006	Manchester United	D	0-0	H	PL		38 313
7-01-2006	Cardiff City	W	2-1	H	FACr3	Pires 2 [6 18]	36 552
10-01-2006	Wigan Athletic	L	0-1	A	LCsf		12 181
14-01-2006	Middlesbrough	W	7-0	H	PL	Henry 3 [20 30 68], Senderos [22], Pires [45], Gilberto [59], Hleb [84]	38 186
21-01-2006	Everton	L	0-1	A	PL		36 920
24-01-2006	Wigan Athletic	W	2-1	H	LCsf	Henry [65], Van Persie [108]	34 692
28-01-2006	Bolton Wanderers	L	0-1	A	FACr4		13 326
1-02-2006	West Ham United	L	2-3	H	PL	Henry [45], Pires [89]	38 216
4-02-2006	Birmingham City	W	2-0	A	PL	Adebayor [21], Henry [63]	27 075
11-02-2006	Bolton Wanderers	D	1-1	H	PL	Gilberto [90]	38 193
14-02-2006	Liverpool	L	0-1	A	PL		44 065
21-02-2006	Real Madrid - ESP	W	1-0	A	CLr2	Henry [47]	74 000
25-02-2006	Blackburn Rovers	L	0-1	A	PL		22 504
4-03-2006	Fulham	W	4-0	A	PL	Henry 2 [31 77], Adebayor [35], Fabregas [86]	22 397
8-03-2006	Real Madrid - ESP	D	0-0	H	CLr2		35 487
12-03-2006	Liverpool	W	2-1	H	PL	Henry 2 [21 84]	38 221
18-03-2006	Charlton Athletic	W	3-0	H	PL	Pires [13], Adebayor [32], Hleb [49]	38 223
28-03-2006	Juventus - ITA	W	2-0	H	CLqf	Fabregas [40], Henry [69]	35 472
1-04-2006	Aston Villa	W	5-0	H	PL	Adebayor [18], Henry 2 [25 46], Van Persie [72], Diaby [81]	38 183
5-04-2006	Juventus - ITA	D	0-0	A	CLqf		46 031
9-04-2006	Manchester United	L	0-2	A	PL		70 908
12-04-2006	Portsmouth	D	1-1	A	PL	Henry [37]	20 230
15-04-2006	West Bromwich Albion	W	3-1	H	PL	Hleb [44], Pires [76], Bergkamp [89]	38 167
19-04-2006	Villarreal - ESP	W	1-0	H	CLsf	Toure [41]	35 438
22-04-2006	Tottenham Hotspur	D	1-1	H	PL	Henry [84]	38 326
25-04-2006	Villarreal - ESP	D	0-0	A	CLsf		23 000
1-05-2006	Sunderland	W	3-0	A	PL	Collins OG [28], Fabregas [40], Henry [43]	44 003
4-05-2006	Manchester City	W	3-1	A	PL	Ljungberg [30], Reyes 2 [78 84]	41 875
7-05-2006	Wigan Athletic	W	4-2	H	PL	Pires [8], Henry 3 [35 56 76p]	38 359
17-05-2006	Barcelona - ESP	L	1-2	N	CLf		79 500

CS = Community Shield • PL = FA Premier League (Barclays Premiership) • CL = UEFA Champions League • FAC = FA Cup • LC = Carling League Cup
gB = Group B • r2 = 2nd round • r3 = 3rd round • r4 = 4th round • r5 = 5th round • qf = quarter-final • sf = semi-final • f = final
N = Millennium Stadium, Cardiff • **N** = Stade de France, Paris

EQG – EQUATORIAL GUINEA

NATIONAL TEAM RECORD
JULY 1ST 2002 TO JULY 9TH 2006

PL	W	D	L	F	A	%
15	6	3	6	13	21	50

FIFA/COCA-COLA WORLD RANKING

1993	1994	1995	1996	1997	1998	1999	2000	2001	2002	2003	2004	2005		High		Low
-	-	-	-	-	195	188	187	190	192	160	171	171		95	07/06	195 12/98

					2005–2006						
08/05	09/05	10/05	11/05	12/05	01/06	02/06	03/06	04/06	05/06	06/06	07/06
171	171	171	171	171	173	173	165	161	154	-	95

Teams from Equatorial Guinea have emerged as the shock packages of African football over the last 12 months, notably champions Renacimiento who left a trail of destruction in their wake in 2006. Admittedly the club from Malabo is packed with imported players from Cameroon, Liberia and Senegal, and coached by the Cameroonian Alain Wabo, but they have been blazing a new trail for the tiny nation. The progress to the third round of the CAF Champions League in 2006 was the furthest a side from Equatorial Guinea has ever gone. Along the way they beat both Africa Sports from Cote d'Ivoire and Stade Malien from Mali, before defeat at the hands of defending champions

INTERNATIONAL HONOURS
CEMAC Cup 2006

Al Ahly of Egypt. But dropping down to the CAF Confederation Cup, they picked up where they left off with an incredulous 5-0 thumping of Nigeria's Iwuanyanwu Nationale to qualify for the group phase. The national side, known as 'Zalang Nacional', has also contributed to the upswing in fortunes. In March 2006 they were the host team at the CEMAC tournament held in Bata. Coached by the Brazilian Antonio Dumas they topped their first round group ahead of Congo and Chad and in the semi-finals beat Gabon on penalties to reach the final for the first time. It took another penalty shoot-out but they beat Cameroon's B team to win the trophy.

THE FIFA BIG COUNT OF 2000

	Male	Female		Male	Female
Registered players	1 000	200	Referees	70	4
Non registered players	3 000	150	Officials	40	0
Youth players	1 000	0	Total involved	5 464	
Total players	5 350		Number of clubs	30	
Professional players	0	0	Number of teams	68	

Federación Ecuatoguineana de Fútbol (FEGUIFUT)

Apartado de correo numero 1017, Malabo, Equatorial Guinea
Tel +240 9 1874   Fax +240 9 1874
feguifut@wanadoo.gq   www.none
President: MANGA OBIANG Bonifacio   General Secretary: MARTIN PEDRO Ndong
Vice-President: ESONO MELCHOR Edjo   Treasurer: MANUEL Nsi Nguema   Media Officer: BORABOFA Clemente
Men's Coach: DUMAS Antonio   Women's Coach: EKANG Jose Davio
FEGUIFUT formed: 1960   CAF: 1986   FIFA: 1986
Red shirts, Red shorts, Red socks

RECENT INTERNATIONAL MATCHES PLAYED BY EQUATORIAL GUINEA

2002	Opponents	Score		Venue	Comp	Scorers	Att	Referee
8-09	Sierra Leone	L	1-3	Malabo	CNq	Mavidi [82]		Tavares Neto STP
13-10	Morocco	L	0-5	Rabat	CNq			Boukthir TUN
2003								
29-03	Gabon	L	0-4	Libreville	CNq			Tavares Neto STP
8-06	Gabon	W	2-1	Malabo	CNq	Mba [22], Mangongo [50]		Buenkadila COD
22-06	Sierra Leone	L	0-2	Freetown	CNq			
6-07	Morocco	L	0-1	Malabo	CNq			
11-10	Togo	W	1-0	Bata	WCq	Barila [25p]	25 000	Evehe CMR
12-11	São Tomé e Príncipe	W	3-1	Malabo	Fr			
16-11	Togo	L	0-2	Lome	WCq		12 000	Mandzioukouta CGO
2004								
No international matches played in 2004								
2005								
5-02	Cameroon †	L	0-3	Libreville	CMr1			
8-02	Chad	D	0-0	Libreville	CMr1			
2006								
26-02	Benin	W	1-0	Cotonou	Fr			
4-03	Congo	W	2-1	Bata	CMr1			
6-03	Chad	D	1-1	Bata	CMr1			
11-03	Gabon	D	0-0	Bata	CMsf	W 4-2p		
14-03	Cameroon †	D	1-1	Bata	CMf	W 4-2p		
29-03	Benin	W	2-0	Bata	Fr	Ivan Zarandona [18], Armando Justice [44]		

Fr = Friendly match • CN = CAF African Cup of Nations • CM = CEMAC Cup • WC = FIFA World Cup™
q = qualifier • r1 = first round group • sf = semi-final • f = final • † Not a full international

EQUATORIAL GUINEA NATIONAL TEAM RECORDS AND RECORD SEQUENCES

Records			Sequence records					
Victory	4-2	CAR 1999	Wins	2	2003	Clean sheets	1	
Defeat	0-6	CGO 1990	Defeats	9	1999-2003	Goals scored	2	
Player Caps	n/a		Undefeated	6	2005-2006	Without goal	2	Five times
Player Goals	n/a		Without win	22	1984-1999	Goals against	22	1988-2003

RECENT LEAGUE AND CUP RECORD

Year	Champions	Cup Winners
1996	Cafe Bank Sportif Malabo	FC Akonangui
1997	Deportivo Mongomo	Union Vesper
1998	CD Ela Nguema	Union Vesper
1999	FC Akonangui	CD Unidad
2000	CD Ela Nguema	CD Unidad
2001	FC Akonangui	Atlético Malabo
2002	CD Ela Nguema	FC Akonangui
2003	Atlético Malabo	Deportivo Mongomo
2004	Renacimiento	CD Ela Nguema
2005	Renacimiento	

EQUATORIAL GUINEA COUNTRY INFORMATION

Capital	Malabo	Independence	1968 from Spain	GDP per Capita	$2 700
Population	523 051	Status	Republic	GNP Ranking	175
Area km²	28 051	Language	Spanish	Dialling code	+240
Population density	18 per km²	Literacy rate	80%	Internet code	.gq
% in urban areas	42%	Main religion	Christian	GMT +/−	+1
Towns/Cities ('000)	Malabo 101; Bata 82; Ebebiyin 13; Mbini 12; Luba 7				
Neighbours (km)	Cameroon 189; Gabon 350; Bight of Biafra 296. Malabo is on the island of Bioko in the Atlantic				
Main stadia	Internacional – Malabo 6 000				

ERI – ERITREA

NATIONAL TEAM RECORD
JULY 1ST 2002 TO JULY 9TH 2006

PL	W	D	L	F	A	%
16	2	3	11	10	25	21.8

FIFA/COCA-COLA WORLD RANKING

1993	1994	1995	1996	1997	1998	1999	2000	2001	2002	2003	2004	2005	High		Low	
-	-	-	-	-	189	169	158	171	157	155	169	169	153	11/03	189	12/98

2005–2006											
08/05	09/05	10/05	11/05	12/05	01/06	02/06	03/06	04/06	05/06	06/06	07/06
169	170	172	172	169	169	169	170	171	171	-	177

Eritrea's participation in the CECAFA Cup at the end of 2005 marked an end to a 24-month hiatus in international competition for the small Red Sea state, embroiled in conflict with neighbours Ethiopia. Football development has had to take a back seat in the country as the low-intensity conflict dominates civil priorities. But Eritrea have entered the qualifiers for the 2008 African Nations Cup finals in Ghana, putting them back into a competitive frame of mind. Their performance in the regional tournament in Kigali saw them return home with just one point from their four matches played but they did take their Rwanda hosts close in a 2-3 defeat. Eritrea did not compete

INTERNATIONAL HONOURS
None

in the 2004 edition of the event and, as a result, have now amassed an unwanted winless streak of nine matches, their last victory having been in the 2004 African Nations Cup qualifiers at home to the Seychelles. Eritrea have only been FIFA members since 1998 and can only boast of a high of 153 in the FIFA/Coca-Cola World Ranking. Red Sea FC from Asmara won the 14-team Championship in 2005 finishing a point ahead of Denden in a close race. In a League reduced to eight clubs in 2006, they were beaten into second place by Adulis Club of Asmara and were also knocked out in the first round of the CAF Champions League by Kenya's Tusker.

THE FIFA BIG COUNT OF 2000

	Male	Female		Male	Female
Registered players	2 700	150	Referees	214	0
Non registered players	180 000	70 000	Officials	850	10
Youth players	1 267	300	Total involved	255 491	
Total players	254 417		Number of clubs	15	
Professional players	0	0	Number of teams	204	

Eritrean National Football Federation (ENFF)
Sematat Avenue 29-31, PO Box 3665, Asmara, Eritrea
Tel +291 1 120335   Fax +291 1 126821
enff@tse.co.er   www.none
President: SIUM Solomon   General Secretary: GHEBREMARIAM Yemane
Vice-President: GEBREYESUS Tesfaye   Treasurer: GEUSH Tikue   Media Officer: LIJAM Amamel
Men's Coach: TBD   Women's Coach: TBD
ENFF formed: 1996   CAF: 1998   FIFA: 1998
Blue shirts, Red shorts, Green socks

RECENT INTERNATIONAL MATCHES PLAYED BY ERITREA

2002	Opponents	Score		Venue	Comp	Scorers	Att	Referee
8-09	Seychelles	L	0-1	Victoria	CNq			
12-10	Zimbabwe	L	0-1	Asmara	CNq			
1-12	Burundi	D	1-1	Arusha	CCr1	Yonnas Tesfaye [87]		
4-12	Sudan	W	2-1	Arusha	CCr1	Elias Dedesaye [14], Aram Negash [45]		
6-12	Kenya	L	1-4	Arusha	CCr1	Berhane Aergaye [78]		
8-12	Tanzania	D	1-1	Arusha	CCr1	Dinyen Pasemaye [45]		
2003								
30-03	Mali	L	0-2	Asmara	CNq			
7-06	Mali	L	0-1	Bamoko	CNq			
21-06	Seychelles	W	1-0	Asmara	CNq	Yonnas Fessehaye [62]		
5-07	Zimbabwe	L	0-2	Harare	CNq			
12-10	Sudan	L	0-3	Khartoum	WCq		18 000	Tamuni LBY
16-11	Sudan	D	0-0	Asmara	WCq		12 000	Abdulle Ahmed SOM
30-11	Uganda	L	1-2	Kassala	CCr1	Ghirmay Shinash [70]		
2-12	Kenya	L	2-3	Kassala	CCr1	Tesfaldet Goitom 2 [30 48]		
2004								
No international matches played in 2004								
2005								
28-11	Zanzibar †	L	0-3	Kigali	CCr1			
30-11	Rwanda	L	2-3	Kigali	CCr1	Suleiman Muhamoul 2		
2-12	Burundi	D	0-0	Kigali	CCr1			
4-12	Tanzania	L	0-1	Kigali	CCr1			
2006								
No international matches played in 2006 before July								

CN = CAF African Cup of Nations • CC = CECAFA Cup • WC = FIFA World Cup™ • q = qualifier • r1 = first round group • † Not a full international

ERITREA NATIONAL TEAM RECORDS AND RECORD SEQUENCES

Records			Sequence records					
Victory	2-0	KEN 1994	Wins	2	1994	Clean sheets	3	1994
Defeat	0-5	GHA 1999	Defeats	3	1994-98, 2001-02	Goals scored	4	2002
Player Caps	n/a		Undefeated	3	1994	Without goal	6	1999-2000
Player Goals	n/a		Without win	10	2000-2002	Goals against	9	2001-2003

RECENT LEAGUE AND CUP RECORD

Year	Champions	Cup Winners
1998	Red Sea FC Asmara	Hintsa Asmara
1999	Red Sea FC Asmara	
2000	Red Sea FC Asmara	
2001	Hintsa Asmara	
2002	Red Sea FC Asmara	
2003	Anseba Sports Club Keren	
2004	Adulis Club Asmara	
2005	Red Sea FC Asmara	
2006	Adulis Club Asmara	

ERITREA COUNTRY INFORMATION

Capital	Asmara	Independence	1993	GDP per Capita	$700
Population	4 447 307	Status	Transitional	GNP Ranking	162
Area km²	121 320	Language	Tigrinya, Arabic	Dialling code	+291
Population density	36 per km²	Literacy rate	80%	Internet code	.er
% in urban areas	17%	Main religion	Christian, Muslim	GMT +/–	+3
Towns/Cities ('000)	Asmara 563; Assab 78; Keren 58; Mitsiwa 39; Addi Ugri 17; Barentu 15; Addi Keyih 13				
Neighbours (km)	Djibouti 109; Ethiopia 912; Sudan 605; Red Sea 2 234				
Main stadia	ChicChero – Asmara 12 000				

ESP – SPAIN

NATIONAL TEAM RECORD
JULY 1ST 2002 TO JULY 9TH 2006

PL	W	D	L	F	A	%
49	32	14	3	97	27	79.6

In the four years from the end of the FIFA World Cup™ in 2002, to the end of the finals in Germany, Spain lost just three international matches, a record that only France could match. Yet despite this fine run of results, two of those defeats came at critical times in major competitions, leaving the Spanish wondering if they will ever get it right when it really matters. At Euro 2004 in Portugal, a first round defeat at the hands of the hosts saw the Spaniards knocked out in the group stage, whilst in Germany, fine performances in the first round were followed by an unlucky defeat against the French in the second round in what was perhaps the match of the tournament. Coach Luis Aragones was one of the few to survive the now customary post tournament cull of coaches, and he is building a young team that may well have the potential to win tournaments in future years. Central to those plans is likely to be Cesc Fabregas who became the youngest Spaniard ever to appear in the finals, having celebrated his 19th birthday just before the tournament. Fabregas also had a sensational season at Arsenal, helping them to the final of the UEFA Champions League, a final won of course by his boyhood club, Barcelona. Rarely has there been such an outstanding

INTERNATIONAL HONOURS
Qualified for the FIFA World Cup™ finals 1934 1950 1962 1966 1978 1982 (hosts) 1986 1990 1994 1998 2002 2006

Olympic Gold 1992   **FIFA Futsal World Championship** 2000 2004

FIFA World Youth Championship 1999   **FIFA Junior Tournament** 1952 1954

UEFA U-21 Championship 1986 1998 **UEFA U-19 Championship** 1995 2002 2004 2006 **UEFA U-17 Championship** 1986 1988 1991 1997 1999 2001

UEFA Champions League Real Madrid 1956 1957 1958 1959 1960 1966 1998 2000 2002 Barcelona 1992 2006

favourite in the competition at the start, and rarely have those favourites so comprehensively gone on to dominate as Barcelona did, or with such style. Ronaldinho was the show-stopper, but the supporting cast of Samuel Eto'o, Lionel Messi, Deco, Carlos Puyol et al was as strong as one could hope for. Having gained revenge over Chelsea in the first knock-out round they then beat Milan in the San Siro in the semis to book their place in the final in Paris. There it was unsung hero Henrik Larsson who stole the show to give Barcelona only their second European Cup. Their progress to the Spanish title was equally as regal, leaving rivals Real Madrid trailing in their wake, and trophyless, for an unprecedented third season running. Barca's 3-0 demolition of Real in the Bernabeu even prompted an ovation for Ronaldinho from the home crowd. Espanyol had a roller-coaster season, winning the Copa del Rey, but it took an injury-time winner from Ferran Corominas in their last game, against Real Sociedad, to save them from relegation. Sevilla may have missed out on Champions League qualification to Osasuna, but having just celebrated their first trophy since 1948 by winning the UEFA Cup, there wasn't a single sad face in the red half of the city.

Real Federación Española de Fútbol (RFEF)
Ramon y Cajal s/n, Apartado postale 385, Las Rozas 28230, Madrid, Spain

Tel +34 91 4959800   Fax +34 91 4959801

rfef@rfef.es   www.rfef.es

President: VILLAR LLONA Angel Maria   General Secretary: PEREZ Jorge

Vice-President: PADRON Juan   Treasurer: LARREA Juan   Media Officer: NUNEZ Rogelio

Men's Coach: ARAGONES Luis   Women's Coach: QUEREDA Ignacio

RFEF formed: 1913   UEFA: 1954   FIFA: 1904

Red shirts with yellow trimmings, Blue shorts, Blue socks or White shirts with red trimmings, White shorts, White socks

RECENT INTERNATIONAL MATCHES PLAYED BY SPAIN

2003	Opponents	Score		Venue	Comp	Scorers	Att	Referee
12-02	Germany	W	3-1	Palma	Fr	Raúl 2 [31 76p], Guti [82]	20 000	Riley ENG
29-03	Ukraine	D	2-2	Kyiv	ECq	Raúl [83], Etxeberria [87]	82 000	Riley ENG
2-04	Armenia	W	3-0	Leon	ECq	Diego Tristan [62], Helguera [68], Joaquin [90]	13 500	Yefet ISR
30-04	Ecuador	W	4-0	Madrid	Fr	De Pedro [15], Morientes 3 [21 23 64]	35 000	Kvaratskhelia GEO
7-06	Greece	L	0-1	Zaragoza	ECq		32 000	Sars FRA
11-06	Northern Ireland	D	0-0	Belfast	ECq		11 365	Larsen DEN
6-09	Portugal	W	3-0	Lisbon	Fr	Etxeberria [11], Joaquin [64], Diego Tristan [76]	21 176	Salomir ROU
10-09	Ukraine	W	2-1	Elche	ECq	Raúl 2 [59 71]	38 000	Hauge NOR
11-10	Armenia	W	4-0	Yerevan	ECq	Valeron [7], Raúl [76], Reyes 2 [87 90]	15 000	Meier SUI
15-11	Norway	W	2-1	Valencia	ECpo	Raúl [20], Berg OG [85]	53 000	Poll ENG
19-11	Norway	W	3-0	Oslo	ECpo	Raúl [34], Vicente [49], Etxeberria [55]	25 106	Collina ITA
2004								
18-02	Peru	W	2-1	Barcelona	Fr	Etxeberria [30], Baraja [32]	23 580	Layec FRA
31-03	Denmark	W	2-0	Gijon	Fr	Morientes [22], Raúl [60]	18 600	Almeida Costa POR
28-04	Italy	D	1-1	Genoa	Fr	Torres [53]	30 300	Poll ENG
5-06	Andorra	W	4-0	Getafe	Fr	Morientes [25], Baraja [45], Cesar [65], Valeron [89]	14 000	Trefolini ITA
12-06	Russia	W	1-0	Faro-Loule	ECr1	Valeron [60]	28 100	Meier SUI
16-06	Greece	D	1-1	Porto	ECr1	Morientes [28]	25 444	Michel SVK
20-06	Portugal	L	0-1	Lisbon	ECr1		52 000	Frisk SWE
18-08	Venezuela	W	3-2	Las Palmas	Fr	Morientes [40], Tamudo 2 [56 67]	32 500	Rodomonti ITA
3-09	Scotland	D	1-1	Valencia	Fr	Raúl [56p]. Abandoned 59' after floodlight failure	11 000	Bre FRA
8-09	Bosnia-Herzegovina	D	1-1	Zenica	WCq	Vicente [65]	14 380	De Santis ITA
9-10	Belgium	W	2-0	Santander	WCq	Luque [60], Raúl [65]	17 000	Nielsen DEN
13-10	Lithuania	D	0-0	Vilnius	WCq		9 114	Pouat FRA
17-11	England	W	1-0	Madrid	Fr	Del Horno [9]	70 000	Kasnaferis GRE
2005								
9-02	San Marino	W	5-0	Almeria	WCq	Joaquin [15], Torres [32], Raúl [42], Guti [61], Del Horno [75]	12 580	Clark SCO
26-03	China	W	3-0	Salamanca	Fr	Torres [3p], Xavi [32], Joaquin [53]	17 000	Cortes POR
30-03	Serbia & Montenegro	D	0-0	Belgrade	WCq		48 910	Busacca SUI
4-06	Lithuania	W	1-0	Valencia	WCq	Luque [68]	25 000	Farina ITA
8-06	Bosnia-Herzegovina	D	1-1	Valencia	WCq	Marchena [96+]	38 041	Bennett ENG
17-08	Uruguay	W	2-0	Gijon	Fr	OG [24], Vicente [38p]	23 348	Benquerenca POR
3-09	Canada	W	2-1	Santander	Fr	Tamudo [7], Morientes [69]	11 978	Colombo FRA
7-09	Serbia & Montenegro	D	1-1	Madrid	WCq	Raul [19]	51 491	Poll ENG
8-10	Belgium	W	2-0	Brussels	WCq	Fernando Torres 2 [56 66]	40 300	Michel SVK
12-10	San Marino	W	6-0	Serravalle	WCq	Antonio Lopez [1], Fernando Torres 3 [11 78 89p], Sergio Ramos 2 [31 48]	3 426	Meyer GER
12-11	Slovakia	W	5-1	Madrid	WCpo	Luis Garcia 3 [10 18 75], Fernando Torres [65], Morientes [79]	47 210	De Santis ITA
16-11	Slovakia	D	1-1	Bratislava	WCpo	Villa [71]	23 587	Merk GER
2006								
1-03	Côte d'Ivoire	W	3-2	Valladolid	Fr	Villa [22], Reyes [74], Juanito [85]	30 000	Rodomonti ITA
27-05	Russia	D	0-0	Albacete	Fr		15 000	Ferreira POR
3-06	Egypt	W	2-0	Elche	Fr	Raul [14], Reyes [57]	38 000	Farina ITA
7-06	Croatia	W	2-1	Geneva	Fr	Pernia [62], Fernando Torres [92+]	15 000	Lannoy FRA
14-06	Ukraine	W	4-0	Leipzig	WCr1	Xabi Alonso [13], Villa 2 [17 48p], Fernando Torres [81]	43 000	Busacca SUI
19-06	Tunisia	W	3-1	Stuttgart	WCr1	Raul [71], Fernando Torres 2 [76 91+]	52 000	Simon BRA
23-06	Saudi Arabia	W	1-0	Kaiserslautern	WCr1	Juanito [36]	46 000	Codjia BEN
27-06	France	L	1-3	Hanover	WCr2	Villa [28p]	43 000	Rosetti ITA

Fr = Friendly match • EC = UEFA EURO 2004™ • WC = FIFA World Cup™ • q = qualifier • po = play-off • r1 = first round group

SPAIN NATIONAL TEAM RECORDS AND RECORD SEQUENCES

Records			Sequence records				
Victory	13-0	BUL 1933	Wins	9	1924-1927	Clean sheets	7	1992
Defeat	1-7	ITA 1928, ENG 1931	Defeats	3	Five times	Goals scored	20	1947-1951
Player Caps	126	ZUBIZARRETA Andoni	Undefeated	30	1994-1997	Without goal	3	1985, 1992
Player Goals	44	Raúl	Without win	10	1980	Goals against	11	1952 1955

SPAIN COUNTRY INFORMATION

Capital	Madrid	Independence	1492	GDP per Capita	$22 000
Population	40 280 780	Status	Kingdom	GNP Ranking	9
Area km²	504 782	Language	Spanish	Dialling code	+34
Population density	79 per km²	Literacy rate	97%	Internet code	.es
% in urban areas	76%	Main religion	Christian	GMT + / –	+1
Towns/Cities ('000)	Madrid 3 102; Barcelona 1 570; Valencia 769; Sevilla 686; Zaragoza 635; Málaga 557; Murcia 410; Palma 378; Las Palmas 365; Bilbao 349; Alicante 327, Valladolid 315; Córdoba 311; Vigo 286, Gijón 262; Granada 248; La Coruña 236; Elche 227; Vitoria 224; Oviedo 198				
Neighbours (km)	France 623; Andorra 63; Gibraltar 1; Portugal 1 214; Morocco 15; Mediterranean Sea & North Atlantic Ocean 4 964				
Main stadia	Camp Nou – Barcelona 98 934; Bernabeu – Madrid 80 354; La Cartuja – Sevilla 72 000; Mestalla – Valencia 53 000; San Mamés – Bilbao 39 750; Romareda – Zaragoza 34 700				

SPAIN NATIONAL TEAM PLAYERS AND COACHES

Record Caps			Record Goals			Recent Coaches	
ZUBIZARRETA Andoni	1985-'98	126	RAUL	1996-'06	44	Committee	1969
RAUL	1996-'06	99	HIERRO Fernando	1989-'02	29	KUBALA Ladislao	1969-'80
HIERRO Fernando	1989-'02	89	BUTRAGUENO Emilio	1984-'92	26	SANTAMARIA José	1980-'82
CAMACHO José Antonio	1975-'88	81	MORIENTES Fernando	1998-'05	25	MUNOZ Miguel	1982-'88
GORDILLO Rafael	1978-'88	75	DI STEFANO Alfredo	1957-'61	23	SUAREZ Luis	1988-'91
BUTRAGUENO Emilio	1984-'92	69	SALINAS Julio	1986-'96	22	MIERA Vicente	1991-'92
ARCONADA Luis	1977-'85	68	MICHEL	1985-'29	21	CLEMENTE Javier	1992-'98
MICHEL	1985-'92	66	ZARRA	1945-'51	20	CAMACHO José Antonio	1998-'02
LUIS ENRIQUE	1991-'02	62	LANGARA Isidrio	1932-'36	17	SAEZ Iñaki	2002-'04
NADAL Miguel Angel	1991-'02	62	PIRRI & REGUEIRO Luis		16	ARAGONES Luis	2004-

FIFA/COCA-COLA WORLD RANKING

1993	1994	1995	1996	1997	1998	1999	2000	2001	2002	2003	2004	2005		High		Low	
5	2	4	8	11	15	4	7	7	3	3	5	5		2	12/94	25	03/98

2005–2006											
08/05	09/05	10/05	11/05	12/05	01/06	02/06	03/06	04/06	05/06	06/06	07/06
8	8	8	6	5	5	6	6	5	5	-	7

THE FIFA BIG COUNT OF 2000

	Male	Female		Male	Female
Registered players	117 438	10 307	Referees	553	7
Non registered players	1 700 000	150 000	Officials	60 000	2 000
Youth players	478 884	1 025	Total involved	2 520 214	
Total players	2 457 654		Number of clubs	33 555	
Professional players	1 362	0	Number of teams	101 906	

SPAIN 2005-06

PRIMERA DIVISION

	Pl	W	D	L	F	A	Pts	Barcelona	Real Madrid	Valencia	Osasuna	Sevilla	Celta	Villarreal	Deportivo	Getafe	Atlético	Zaragoza	Athletic	Mallorca	Betis	Espanyol	Sociedad	Santander	Alavés	Cádiz	Málaga
Barcelona †	38	25	7	6	80	35	82		1-1	2-2	3-0	2-1	2-0	1-0	3-2	3-1	1-3	2-2	2-1	2-0	5-1	2-0	5-0	4-1	2-0	1-0	2-0
Real Madrid †	38	20	10	8	70	40	70	0-3		1-2	1-1	4-2	2-3	3-3	4-0	1-0	2-1	1-0	3-1	2-0	0-0	4-0	1-1	1-2	3-0	3-1	2-1
Valencia †	38	19	12	7	58	33	69	1-0	0-0		2-0	0-2	2-0	1-1	2-2	1-1	1-1	2-2	1-1	3-0	1-0	4-0	2-1	1-1	3-0	5-3	2-1
Osasuna †	38	21	5	12	49	43	68	2-1	0-1	2-1		1-0	2-0	2-1	1-2	0-4	2-1	1-1	3-2	1-0	0-2	2-0	2-0	1-1	3-2	2-0	1-1
Sevilla ‡	38	20	8	10	54	39	68	3-2	4-3	1-0	0-1		1-0	2-0	0-2	3-0	0-0	1-1	2-1	1-1	1-0	1-1	3-2	1-0	2-0	0-0	3-1
Celta Vigo ‡	38	20	4	14	45	33	64	0-1	1-2	0-1	2-0	2-1		1-0	0-3	1-0	2-1	4-0	0-1	2-0	2-1	1-0	1-0	0-0	1-2	1-2	0-2
Villarreal	38	14	15	9	50	39	57	0-2	0-0	1-0	2-1	1-1	1-2		1-1	2-1	1-1	0-0	3-1	3-0	1-2	4-0	0-2	2-0	3-2	1-1	2-1
Deportivo La Coruña	38	15	10	13	47	45	55	3-3	3-1	0-1	0-1	0-0	0-2	0-2		1-0	1-0	1-1	1-2	2-1	1-1	1-2	0-1	2-0	0-2	1-0	2-1
Getafe	38	15	9	14	54	49	54	1-3	1-1	2-1	0-0	1-0	1-1	1-1	1-2		0-3	5-2	1-1	1-1	1-0	5-0	2-1	1-2	2-2	3-1	3-2
Atlético Madrid	38	13	13	12	45	37	52	2-1	0-3	0-0	0-1	0-1	0-3	1-1	3-2	0-1		0-0	1-0	0-1	1-1	1-1	1-0	2-1	1-1	3-0	5-0
Real Zaragoza	38	10	16	12	46	51	46	0-2	1-1	2-2	3-1	0-2	1-0	0-1	1-1	1-2	0-2		3-2	3-1	4-3	1-1	0-1	1-1	3-0	1-2	1-1
Athletic Bilbao	38	11	12	15	40	46	45	3-1	0-2	0-3	1-0	0-1	1-1	1-1	1-2	1-0	1-1	1-0		1-1	2-0	1-1	3-0	0-0	0-2	1-0	1-2
RCD Mallorca	38	10	13	15	37	51	43	0-3	2-1	2-1	0-1	1-1	1-0	0-1	1-1	1-2	2-3	1-0	1-1		1-1	0-5	2-0	0-0	1-0	1-4	
Real Betis	38	10	12	16	34	51	42	1-4	0-2	0-2	1-0	2-1	0-2	2-3	0-1	1-0	1-0	0-0	1-1	2-1		0-0	2-0	1-0	3-0	1-1	1-1
RCD Espanyol ‡	38	10	11	17	36	56	41	1-2	1-0	1-3	2-4	5-0	2-0	1-2	1-2	0-2	1-1	1-2	2-1	1-1	2-0		1-0	0-2	0-0	0-2	3-1
Real Sociedad	38	11	7	20	48	65	40	0-2	2-2	1-2	1-2	1-2	2-2	1-3	2-0	3-0	3-2	1-3	3-3	2-1	1-1	0-1		1-0	2-1	2-0	3-0
Racing Santander	38	9	13	16	36	49	40	2-2	2-3	2-1	2-1	2-3	0-1	1-0	0-3	1-3	0-1	0-0	0-1	0-0	1-1	2-2			1-2	0-1	1-1
Deportivo Alavés	38	9	12	17	35	54	39	0-0	0-3	1-1	2-1	1-0	1-1	1-0	3-4	0-1	0-2	0-0	0-3	2-0	1-1	3-1	2-2			0-0	3-2
Cádiz	38	8	12	18	36	52	36	1-3	1-2	0-1	1-3	0-4	1-1	1-1	1-1	1-0	1-1	1-2	1-0	1-2	1-1	2-0	2-2	1-1	0-0		5-0
Málaga	38	5	9	24	36	68	24	0-0	0-2	0-0	1-2	0-2	0-2	0-0	1-1	1-2	0-2	0-1	2-1	0-2	5-0	1-2	3-1	2-3	0-0	0-2	

27/08/2005 – 20/05/2006 • † Qualified for the UEFA Champions League • ‡ Qualified for the UEFA Cup • Top scorers: Samuel ETO'O, Barcelona, 26; David VILLA, Valencia, 25; RONALDINHO, Barcelona, 17; Diego MILITO, Zaragoza, 15; RONALDO, Real Madrid, 14

SPAIN 2005-06

SEGUNDA DIVISION A (2)

	Pl	W	D	L	F	A	Pts	Recreativo	Gimnàstic	Levante	C. Murcia	Lorca	Almería	Xerez	Numancia	Gijón	Valladolid	RM B	Castellón	Albacete	Elche	Ejido	R. Murcia	Hércules	Tenerife	Lleida	RC Ferrol	Malaga B	Eibar
Recreativo Huelva	42	22	12	8	67	32	78		3-0	4-1	1-0	2-1	2-0	1-2	1-1	0-0	2-0	4-1	2-2	1-1	2-0	2-2	1-0	1-0	3-1	3-2	3-0	0-0	0-0
Gimnàstic Tarragona	42	23	7	12	48	38	76	0-0		1-0	2-0	2-0	1-0	0-3	1-0	0-4	3-2	0-1	1-1	4-1	1-0	2-0	3-1	1-1	0-0	0-2	1-2	3-2	1-0
Levante	42	20	14	8	53	39	74	1-3	1-1		6-0	0-0	2-4	2-3	1-0	0-0	2-1	3-0	2-1	1-1	0-2	0-1	0-2	0-1	0-2	0-2	2-1	2-3	1-0
Ciudad de Murcia	42	20	12	10	53	42	72	3-1	2-0	2-1		1-0	0-0	2-6	0-1	1-0	0-2	2-1	0-0	4-0	1-1	0-1	1-0	3-0	3-1	2-1	5-0	0-2	
Lorca Deportiva	42	19	12	11	56	39	69	2-1	1-0	1-1	2-2		1-1	1-1	1-1	1-0	2-0	2-1	3-2	3-2	1-0	0-0	1-4	0-1	1-1	2-1	1-1	0-1	0
Almería	42	20	7	15	54	43	67	2-1	0-1	5-1	1-0	1-0		3-0	1-2	3-0	2-1	3-2	2-1	1-2	2-0	1-2	2-0	1-0	2-0	3-1	2-1	2-1	1-1
Xerez	42	18	13	11	60	46	67	1-1	0-0	0-1	0-3	0-0	0-0		1-1	0-0	0-0	2-1	1-2	1-0	1-1	2-1	0-1	0-3	1-0	1-2	0-4	2-2	1-0
Numancia	42	18	9	15	50	55	63	0-3	0-1	0-1	1-1	0-3	0-1	1-0		1-0	3-2	3-2	2-1	1-0	3-1	1-2	0-0	0-2	0-1	0-1	1-2	1-1	2
Sporting Gijón	42	13	17	12	41	34	56	1-1	0-1	0-2	2-2	1-0	1-0	1-1	1-0		1-1	1-1	2-0	2-0	2-2	1-1	1-1	0-1	1-2	2-2	0-3	1-0	0-1
Real Valladolid	42	14	13	15	54	54	55	0-1	0-2	3-3	0-2	1-1	0-3	1-3	1-1	1-3		1-0	1-0	0-1	2-0	1-0	1-1	1-1	3-2	3-3	1-1	0-0	
Real Madrid B	42	16	7	19	55	50	53	1-2	1-0	0-0	1-1	2-0	1-4	3-1	1-1	1-2-3		1-2	3-0	4-0	2-0	1-0	0-3	0-3	1-2	0-0	4-1	1-0	
Castellón	42	14	12	16	46	50	54	2-0	0-2	0-0	1-0	2-0	3-2	0-1	1-0	0-0-3		0-0		1-1	2-1	2-1	1-2	1-0	0-0	3-1	0-2	2-2	0
Albacete	42	14	12	16	44	57	54	1-0	1-4	1-1	2-1	0-3	1-2	0-0	0-1	0-2	3-1	0-1	1-1		1-2	1-0	0-0	2-0	3-2	1-0	1-2	0-1	2-1
Elche	42	13	14	15	47	54	53	1-1	1-0	0-1	0-0	1-3	0-0	1-0	4-1	0-0	0-0	2-2	1-1	2-4-3		2-0	1-1	1-1	2-3	2-1	0-0	2-1	
Polideportivo Ejido	42	15	8	19	43	50	53	0-0	2-0	0-0	2-3	0-1	4-1	0-1	1-0	1-1	0-3	0-2	2-0	2-1		0-3	3-1	2-0	1-4	2-1	2-0	1	
Real Murcia	42	13	13	16	41	40	52	0-2	0-1	0-0	0-0	1-1	0-0	1-3	1-1	0-2	0-2	1-1	4-1	2-0	1-0	0-0		3-1	2-2	0-2	1-4	4-1	1-0
Hércules	42	13	13	16	39	49	52	0-2	0-1	3-0	2-1	0-2	2-2	0-3	4-0	3-2	2-0	0-1	1-0	2-1	0-0	1-0	1-0		1-0	2-1	1-1	1-1	1-1
Tenerife	42	13	12	17	53	60	51	1-0	3-1	0-1	0-1	2-3	2-1	3-1	2-1	1-3	2-0	1-1	1-1	1-0	0-2	2-1	3-1	0-0		2-2	1-2	3-2	1-1
Lleida	42	12	10	20	43	53	46	0-4	1-2	0-1	1-2	2-1	0-0	1-5	0-0	1-0	4-2	1-1	0-3	0-0	0-0	1-0	1-0	1-2-1		1-1	0-0	0-0	
Racing Club Ferrol	42	7	16	19	44	63	37	0-3	1-1	2-1	1-0	3-1	1-1	1-1	3-0	0-0	1-0	1-2-3	2-1	0-1	2-2	1-1	2-3-0	0			2-1	4-0	
Malaga B	42	8	12	22	42	68	36	0-2	1-2	0-0	0-1	2-1	3-1	0-0	5-4	1-0	2-1	0-1	1-2	1-1	1-3	0-1	2-0	1-1	4-0	1-0	1		1-1
Eibar	42	6	17	19	28	45	35	2-1	0-1	1-1	0-0	0-3	0-1	0-1	1-2	0-1	0-1	1-3	2-0	1-1	1-2	3-1	0-0	0-1	0-1	1-1	1-1	1-1	

27/08/2005 – 18/06/2006

COPA DEL REY 2005-06

Third Round   **Fourth Round**   **Round of Sixteen**

Third Round		Fourth Round		Round of Sixteen		
				Espanyol	1	3
Lleida	1			Getafe *	0	3
Logroñés *	0	Lleida *	2			
Rayo Vallecano *	1	**Getafe**	4			
Getafe	2					
				Sevilla	2	0
Burgos *	1			**Cádiz ***	3	0
Racing Santander	0	Burgos *	0			
Albacete *	1	**Cádiz**	2			
Cádiz	3					
				Valencia	2	1
				Villarreal *	0	0
				Osasuna	0	2
				Deportivo La Coruña *	3	1
				Real Madrid	1	4
Hospitalet *	4			Athletic Bilbao *	0	0
Nastic	3	Hospitalet *	1			
Real Unión Irún *	0	**Athletic Bilbao**	3			
Athletic Bilbao	1					
Celta Vigo	3					
Tenisca *	1	**Celta Vigo**	1			
Málaga	1 2p	Baza *	0			
Baza *	1 4p			Celta Vigo *	1	0
				Real Betis	1	0
				Barcelona	3	6
Eibar *	1			Zamora *	1	0
Deportivo Aláves	0	Eibar	1 3p			
Real Sociedad	1 0p	**Zamora ***	1 4p			
Zamora *	1 2p					
Atlético Madrid	1					
Las Palmas *	0	**Atlético Madrid**	1			
RCD Mallorca	1	Alcoyano *	0			
Alcoyano *	4			Atlético Madrid *	0	2
Xerez *	3			**Real Zaragoza**	1	2
Numancia	2	Xerez *	2 6p			
Alicante *	1 5p	**Real Zaragoza**	2 7p			
Real Zaragoza	1 6p					

* Home team/home team in the first leg

COPA DEL REY 2005-06

Quarter-finals   **Semi-finals**   **Final**

Espanyol	2	2
Cádiz *	0	0

Espanyol *	2	0
Deportivo La Coruña	1	0

Valencia	0	1
Deportivo La Coruña *	1	1

Espanyol ‡	4
Real Zaragoza	1

Real Madrid	1	1
Real Betis *	0	0

Real Madrid	1	4
Real Zaragoza *	6	0

Barcelona	2	2
Real Zaragoza *	4	2

COPA DEL REY FINAL 2006

Bernabeu, Madrid, 12-04-2006, Att: 78 500, Ref: Carballo

Espanyol	4	Tamudo [2], Luis Garcia 2 [33] [86], Coro [71]
Real Zaragoza	1	Ewerthon [28]

Espanyol - Carlos KAMENI - Pablo ZABALETA, Alberto LOPO, Daniel JARQUE●, David GARCIA, Antonio Alvarez ITO● (Ferrán Corominas CORO 60), FREDSON (MOISES 60), Eduardo COSTA, Ivan DE LA PENA, Luis GARCIA, Raúl TAMUDO● (Walter PANDIANI 76). Tr: Miguel Angel LOTINA

Zaragoza - César SANCHEZ●●●74 - Leonardo PONZIO, ALVARO Luiz, Gabriel MILITO●, Delio César TOLEDO (Raúl VALBUENA 75), Oscar GONZALEZ● (SAVIO 50), Alberto ZAPATER, Albert CELADES● (José María MOVILLA 65), Rubén García CANI, EWERTHON, Diego MILITO. Tr: Victor MUNOZ

‡ Qualified for the UEFA Cup

SPAIN 2004-05
SEGUNDA DIVISION B (3) PLAY-OFFS

First Round			Second Round			Promoted Clubs
Salamanca	3	3				
Gramenet *	2	1	Salamanca	0	1	Salamanca promoted to
Pontevedra	2	0	Sevilla B *	0	0	Segunda Division A
Sevilla B *	0	3				
Ponferradina *	3	2				
Universidad Palmas	2	1	Ponferradina *	1	1	Ponferradina promoted to
Aguilas	1	0	Alicante	1	0	Segunda Division A
Alicante *	2	0				
Las Palmas *	1	1				
Real Sociedad B	0	2	Las Palmas	2	1	Las Palmas promoted to
Badalona	0	2	Linares *	2	0	Segunda Division A
Linares *	2	3				
Vecindario *	2	1				
Cartagena	2	0	Vecindario *	2	1	Vecindario promoted to
Burgos *	0	0	Levante B	0	2	Segunda Division A
Levante B	1	1	* Home team in the first leg			

CLUB DIRECTORY

Club	Town/City	Stadium	Capacity	www.	Lge	Cup	CL
Deportivo Alavés	Vitoria	Mendizorroza	19 841	alaves.com	0	0	0
Athletic Club	Bilbao	San Mamés	39 750	athletic-club.net	8	23	0
Atlético Madrid	Madrid	Vicente Calderón	54 851	clubatleticodemadrid.com	9	9	0
Barcelona	Barcelona	Camp Nou	98 260	fcbarcelona.com	18	24	2
Real Betis	Sevilla	Ruiz de Lopera	52 500	realbetisbalompie.es	1	2	0
Cádiz	Cádiz	Ramón de Caranza	20 000	cadizcf.com	0	0	0
Real Club Celta	Vigo	Balaídos	31 800	celtavigo.net	0	0	0
RC Deportivo	La Coruña	Riazor	34 178	canaldeportivo.com	1	2	0
Espanyol	Barcelona	Olímpic de Montjuïc	55 000	rcdespanyo.com	0	4	0
Getafe	Madrid	Coliseum	14 400	getafecf.com	0	0	0
Málaga	Málaga	La Rosaleda	22 800	malagacf.es	0	0	0
RCD Mallorca	Palma	Son Moix	24 142	rcdmallorca.es	0	1	0
Osasuna	Pamplona	El Sadar	19 980	osasuna.es	0	0	0
Racing	Santander	El Sardinero	22 500	realracingclub.es	0	0	0
Real Madrid	Madrid	Santiago Bernabeu	80 000	realmadrid.com	29	17	9
Real Sociedad	San Sebastiăn	Anoeta	32 082	realsociedad.com	2	2	0
Sevilla	Sevilla	Sánchez Pizjuán	43 000	sevillafc.es	1	3	0
Valencia	Valencia	Mestalla	55 000	valenciacf.es	6	6	0
Villarreal	Villarreal	El Madrigal	23 500	villarrealcf.es	0	0	0
Real Zaragoza	Zaragoza	La Romareda	34 596	realzaragoza.com	0	6	0

RECENT LEAGUE AND CUP RECORD

	Championship						Cup		
Year	Champions	Pts	Runners-up	Pts	Third	Pts	Winners	Score	Runners-up
1990	Real Madrid	62	Valencia	53	Barcelona	51	Barcelona	2-0	Real Madrid
1991	Barcelona	57	Atlético Madrid	47	Real Madrid	46	Atlético Madrid	1-0	Mallorca
1992	Barcelona	55	Real Madrid	54	Atlético Madrid	53	Atlético Madrid	2-0	Real Madrid
1993	Barcelona	58	Real Madrid	57	Deportivo	54	Real Madrid	2-0	Real Zaragoza
1994	Barcelona	56	Deportivo	56	Real Zaragoza	46	Real Zaragoza	0-0 5-4p	Celta Vigo
1995	Real Madrid	55	Deportivo	51	Real Betis	46	Deportivo	2-1	Valencia
1996	Atlético Madrid	87	Valencia	83	Barcelona	80	Atlético Madrid	1-0	Barcelona
1997	Real Madrid	92	Barcelona	90	Deportivo	77	Barcelona	3-2	Real Betis
1998	Barcelona	74	Athletic Bilbao	65	Real Sociedad	63	Barcelona	1-1 4-3p	Mallorca
1999	Barcelona	79	Real Madrid	68	Mallorca	66	Valencia	3-0	Atlético Madrid
2000	Deportivo	69	Barcelona	64	Valencia	64	Espanyol	2-1	Atlético Madrid
2001	Real Madrid	80	Deportivo	73	Mallorca	71	Real Zaragoza	3-1	Celta Vigo
2002	Valencia	75	Deportivo	68	Real Madrid	66	Deportivo	2-1	Real Madrid
2003	Real Madrid	78	Real Sociedad	76	Deportivo	72	Mallorca	3-0	Recreativo Huelva
2004	Valencia	77	Barcelona	72	Deportivo	71	Real Zaragoza	3-2	Real Madrid
2005	Barcelona	84	Real Madrid	80	Villarreal	65	Real Betis	2-1	Osasuna
2006	Barcelona	82	Real Madrid	70	Valencia	69	Espanyol	4-1	Real Zaragoza

BARCELONA 2005-06

Date	Opponents	Score		Comp	Scorers	Att
13-08-2005	Real Betis	W 3-0	A	SC	Giuly [47], Eto'o [52], Ronaldinho [63]	30 000
20-08-2005	Real Betis	L 1-2	H	SC	Eto'o [14]	80 000
27-08-2005	Alavés	D 0-0	A	PD		17 047
11-09-2005	Mallorca	W 2-0	H	PD	Eto'o 2 [26 32]	71 948
14-09-2005	Werder Bremen - GER	W 2-0	A	CLgC	Deco [13], Ronaldinho [77p]	42 466
18-09-2005	Atlético Madrid	L 1-2	A	PD	Eto'o [6]	48 000
21-09-2005	Valencia	D 2-2	H	PD	Giuly [44], Deco [75]	77 458
24-09-2005	Real Betis	W 4-1	A	PD	Van Bommel [19], Eto'o 2 [57 77], Ezquerro [89]	45 000
27-09-2005	Udinese - ITA	W 4-1	H	CLgC	Ronaldinho 3 [12 31 89p], Deco [40]	74 730
1-10-2005	Real Zaragoza	D 2-2	H	PD		73 926
15-10-2005	Deportivo La Coruña	D 3-3	A	PD	Eto'o [40], Ronaldinho 2 [45 51p]	34 000
18-10-2005	Panathinaikos - GRE	D 0-0	A	CLgC		56 804
22-10-2005	Osasuna	W 3-0	H	PD	Eto'o 2 [46 53], Giuly [88]	63 802
26-10-2005	Málaga	W 2-0	H	PD	Ronaldinho [81p], Larsson [88]	61 634
30-10-2005	Real Sociedad	W 5-0	H	PD	Van Bommel [18], Ronaldinho 2 [35 59], Puyol [75], Larsson [85]	81 050
2-11-2005	Panathinaikos - GRE	W 5-0	H	CLgC	Van Bommel [1], Eto'o 3 [14 40 65], Messi [34]	64 321
6-11-2005	Getafe	W 3-1	A	PD	Eto'o [1], Giuly [62], Thiago [72]	16 400
19-11-2005	Real Madrid	W 3-0	A	PD	Eto'o [15], Ronaldinho 2 [59 77]	78 000
22-11-2005	Werder Bremen - GER	W 3-1	H	CLgC	Gabri [14], Ronaldinho [26], Larsson [71]	67 273
27-11-2005	Racing Santander	W 4-1	H	PD	Eto'o [30], Messi [51], Ronaldinho [56p], Silvinho [65]	57 422
4-12-2005	Villarreal	W 2-0	A	PD	Peña OG [24], Deco [63]	23 000
7-12-2005	Udinese - ITA	W 2-0	A	CLgC	Ezquerro [86], Iniesta [90]	33 570
11-12-2005	Sevilla	W 2-1	H	PD	Eto'o [65], Ronaldinho [77]	61 840
17-12-2005	Cadíz	W 3-1	A	PD	Giuly [31], Eto'o 2 [45p 48]	22 087
20-12-2005	Celta Vigo	W 2-0	H	PD	Eto'o 2 [37 56]	61 994
3-01-2006	Zamora	W 3-1	A	CDRr5	Van Bronckhorst [36], Marquez [80], Giuly [84]	11 000
7-01-2006	Espanyol	W 2-1	A	PD	Deco [43], Eto'o [47]	28 190
11-01-2006	Zamora	W 6-0	H	CDRr5	Ezquerro [1], Larsson 2 [19 20], Thiago [34], Van Bommel [51], Lopez [80p]	16 242
15-01-2006	Athletic Bilbao	W 2-1	H	PD	Ronaldinho [38p], Messi [51]	67 911
22-01-2006	Alavés	W 2-0	H	PD	Larsson [46], Messi [80]	72 081
26-01-2006	Real Zaragoza	L 2-4	A	CDRqf	Larsson [36], Ronaldinho [62p]	33 000
29-01-2006	Mallorca	W 3-0	H	PD	Giuly [39], Messi 2 [76 81]	20 500
1-02-2006	Real Zaragoza	W 2-1	H	CDRqf	Messi [42], Larsson [92+]	56 200
5-02-2006	Atlético Madrid	L 1-3	H	PD	Larsson [64]	78 784
12-02-2006	Valencia	L 0-1	A	PD		50 000
18-02-2006	Real Betis	W 5-1	H	PD	Larsson [17], Melli OG 2 [29 59], Ronaldinho [59], Messi [85]	81 294
22-02-2006	Chelsea - ENG	W 2-1	A	CLr2	Terry OG [72], Eto'o [80]	39 521
25-02-2006	Real Zaragoza	W 2-0	A	PD	Ronaldinho [79p], Larsson [82]	32 000
4-03-2006	Deportivo La Coruna	W 3-2	H	PD	Ronaldinho [2], Larsson [33], Eto'o [62]	77 113
7-03-2006	Chelsea - ENG	D 1-1	H	CLr2	Ronaldinho [78]	98 436
12-03-2006	Osasuna	L 1-2	A	PD	Larsson [71]	18 537
18-03-2006	Real Sociedad	W 2-0	H	PD	Larsson [8], Eto'o [51]	38 472
21-03-2006	Getafe	W 3-1	H	PD	Matellan OG [22], Eto'o 2 [52 69]	67 592
25-03-2006	Málaga	D 0-0	A	PD		25 000
28-03-2006	Benfica - POR	D 0-0	A	CLqf		65 000
1-04-2006	Real Madrid	D 1-1	H	PD	Ronaldinho [22p]	98 295
5-04-2006	Benfica - POR	W 2-0	H	CLqf	Ronaldinho [19], Eto'o [89]	89 475
9-04-2006	Racing Santander	D 2-2	A	PD	Larsson [17], Eto'o [32]	20 670
14-04-2006	Villarreal	W 1-0	H	PD	Eto'o [10]	77 024
18-04-2006	Milan - ITA	W 1-0	A	CLsf	Giuly [57]	76 883
26-04-2006	Milan - ITA	D 0-0	H	CLsf		95 661
29-04-2006	Cádiz	W 1-0	H	PD	Ronaldinho [9]	72 357
3-05-2006	Celta Vigo	W 1-0	A	PD	Eto'o [55]	20 000
6-05-2006	Espanyol	W 2-0	H	PD	Jarque OG [19], Ronaldinho [51]	87 952
13-05-2006	Sevilla	L 2-3	A	PD	Ezquerro [40], Sylvinho [41]	44 000
17-05-2006	Arsenal - ENG	W 2-1	N	CLf	Eto'o [76], Belletti [81]	79 500
20-05-2006	Athletic Bilbao	L 1-3	A	PD	Eto'o [35]	39 000

SC = Supercopa • PD = Primera División • CL = UEFA Champions League • CDR = Copa del Rey
gC = Group C • r2 = second round • r5 = fifth round • qf = quarter-final • sf = semi-final • f = final • N = Stade de France, Paris

REAL MADRID 2005-06

Date	Opponents	Score			Comp	Scorers	Att
28-08-2005	Cadíz	W	2-1	A	PD	Ronaldo 4, Raúl 85	20 500
10-09-2005	Celta Vigo	L	2-3	H	PD	Ronaldo 37p, Baptista 44	80 000
13-09-2005	Olympique Lyonnais - FRA	L	0-3	A	CLgF		40 309
18-09-2005	Espanyol	L	0-1	A	PD		38 950
22-09-2005	Athletic Bilbao	W	3-1	H	PD	Robinho 52, Gonzalez 2 64 68	70 000
25-09-2005	Alavés	W	3-0	A	PD	Ronaldo 2 59 83, Guti 90	14 596
28-09-2005	Olympiacos - GRE	W	2-1	H	CLgF	Raúl 8, Soldado 86	64 327
2-10-2005	Mallorca	W	4-0	H	PD	Ronaldo 33, Roberto Carlos 2 45 65, Baptista 77	72 140
15-10-2005	Atlético Madrid	W	3-0	A	PD	Ronaldo 2 8p 60, Perea OG 90	60 000
19-10-2005	Rosenborg BK - NOR	W	4-1	H	CLgF	Woodgate 48, Raúl 52, Helguera 68, Beckham 82	64 870
23-10-2005	Valencia	L	1-2	H	PD	Raúl 36	77 321
26-10-2005	Deportivo La Coruña	L	1-3	A	PD	Raúl 86	33 000
29-10-2005	Real Betis	W	2-0	A	PD	Robinho 30, Mejia 79	45 000
1-11-2005	Rosenborg BK - NOR	W	2-0	A	CLgF	Dorsin OG 26, Guti 41	21 270
6-11-2005	Real Zaragoza	W	1-0	H	PD	Roberto Carlos 78p	78 000
19-11-2005	Barcelona	L	0-3	H	PD		78 000
23-11-2005	Olympique Lyonnais - FRA	D	1-1	A	CLgF	Guti 41	67 304
27-11-2005	Real Sociedad	D	2-2	A	PD	Bravo 87, Zidane 88	23 393
3-12-2005	Getafe	W	1-0	H	PD	Ronaldo 18	72 204
6-12-2005	Olympiacos - GRE	L	1-2	A	CLgF	Ramos 7	30 496
11-12-2005	Málaga	W	2-0	A	PD	Ramos 34, Robinho 38	23 000
18-12-2005	Osasuna	D	1-1	H	PD	Soldado 83	70 000
21-12-2005	Racing Santander	L	1-2	H	PD	Ronaldo 68	50 000
3-01-2006	Athletic Bilbao	W	1-0	A	CDRr5	Beckham 70	38 000
8-01-2006	Villarreal	D	0-0	A	PD		23 000
12-01-2006	Athletic Bilbao	W	4-0	H	CDRr5	Robinho 2 30 90, Ramos 66, Soldado 87	60 000
15-01-2006	Sevilla	W	4-2	H	PD	Guti 7, Zidane 3 58p 61 94+	60 000
18-01-2006	Real Betis	W	1-0	A	CDRqf	Cassano 64	50 000
21-01-2006	Cadíz	W	3-1	H	PD	Roberto Carlos 68, Beckham 71, Robinho 83	80 000
25-01-2006	Real Betis	W	1-0	H	CDRqf	Robinho 44	62 000
29-01-2006	Celta Vigo	W	2-1	A	PD	Robinho 16, Cicinho 56	30 000
4-02-2006	Espanyol	W	4-0	H	PD	Guti 14, Zidane 2 43 51, Ronaldo 47	75 000
8-02-2006	Real Zaragoza	L	1-6	A	CDRsf	Baptista 38	32 000
11-02-2006	Athletic Bilbao	W	2-0	A	PD	Robinho 5, Raul Bravo 90	37 000
14-02-2006	Real Zaragoza	W	4-0	H	CDRsf	Cicinho 1, Robinho 5, Ronaldo 10, Roberto Carlos 60	80 000
18-02-2006	Alavés	W	3-0	H	PD	Guti 6, Robinho 11, Cicinho 77	71 000
21-02-2006	Arsenal - ENG	L	0-1	H	CLr2		74 000
26-02-2006	Mallorca	L	1-2	A	PD	Sergio Ramos 31	18 000
4-03-2006	Atlético Madrid	W	2-1	H	PD	Cassano 4, Julio Baptista 40	75 000
8-03-2006	Arsenal - ENG	D	0-0	A	CLr2		35 487
11-03-2006	Valencia	D	0-0	A	PD		50 000
19-03-2006	Real Betis	D	0-0	H	PD		75 000
22-03-2006	Real Zaragoza	D	1-1	A	PD	Ronaldo 90	30 000
26-03-2006	Deportivo La Coruña	W	4-0	H	PD	Hector OG 9, Ronaldo 37, Sergio Ramos 70, Julio Baptista 82	70 000
1-04-2006	Barcelona	D	1-1	H	PD	Ronaldo 37	98 295
8-04-2006	Real Sociedad	D	1-1	H	PD	Ronaldo 25	65 000
16-04-2006	Getafe	D	1-1	A	PD	Julio Baptista 61	15 000
23-04-2006	Málaga	W	2-1	H	PD	Zidane 67p, Sergio Ramos 90	70 000
30-04-2006	Osasuna	W	1-0	A	PD	Julio Baptista 51p	18 789
4-05-2006	Racing Santander	W	3-2	A	PD	Roberto Carlos 33p, Soldado 61, Robinho 71	17 307
7-05-2006	Villarreal	D	3-3	H	PD	Julio Baptista 2 22 88, Zidane 66	78 000
16-05-2006	Sevilla	L	3-4	A	PD	Beckham 2 15 26, Zidane 72	42 000

PD = Primera División • CL = UEFA Champions League • CDR = Copa del Rey
gF = Group F • r2 = second round • r5 = fifth round • qf = quarter-final • sf = semi-final

VALENCIA 2005-06

Date	Opponents	Score		Comp	Scorers	Att
17-07-2005	AA Gent - BEL	D 0-0	A	ITCr3		8 430
23-07-2005	AA Gent - BEL	W 2-0	H	ITCr3	Villa [6], Kluivert [78]	22 100
27-07-2005	Roda JC Kerkrade - NED	W 4-0	H	ITCsf	Rufete 3 [36 41 50], Moretti [83]	24 800
3-08-2005	Roda JC Kerkrade - NED	D 0-0	A	ITCsf		3 300
9-08-2005	Hamburger SV - GER	L 0-1	A	ITCf		55 386
23-08-2005	Hamburger SV - GER	D 0-0	H	ITCf		36 250
27-08-2005	Real Betis	W 1-0	H	PD	Aimar [53]	48 000
11-09-2005	Real Zaragoza	D 2-2	A	PD	Angulo [2], Villa [81]	32 000
17-09-2005	Deportivo La Coruña	D 2-2	H	PD	Villa [50p], Miguel [80]	45 000
21-09-2005	Barcelona	D 2-2	A	PD	Villa 2 [53p 54]	77 500
24-09-2005	Real Sociedad	W 2-1	H	PD	Aimar [37], Villa [47]	45 000
1-10-2005	Getafe	L 1-2	A	PD	Villa [29]	14 500
16-10-2005	Malaga	W 2-1	H	PD	Ayala [8], Vicente [55]	45 000
23-10-2005	Real Madrid	W 2-1	A	PD	Baraja [22], Villa [39p]	77 321
27-10-2005	Sevilla	L 0-2	H	PD		45 000
30-10-2005	Racing Santander	D 1-1	H	PD	Albelda [11]	45 000
5-11-2005	Villarreal	L 0-1	A	PD		18 000
20-11-2005	Cadíz	W 1-0	A	PD	Vicente [81]	19 000
26-11-2005	Celta Vigo	W 2-0	H	PD	Villa [72], Fábio Aurelio [79]	40 000
4-12-2005	Espanyol	W 3-1	A	PD	Angulo [15], Villa [42], Aimar [61]	21 220
10-12-2005	Athletic Bilbao	D 1-1	H	PD	Villa [75]	45 000
18-12-2005	Alavés	W 1-0	A	PD	Albiol [7]	14 131
21-12-2005	Mallorca	W 3-0	H	PD	Albelda [46], Villa [64], Fábio Aurelio [80]	35 000
4-01-2006	Villarreal	W 2-0	A	CDRr5	Regueiro [54], Villa [67p]	18 000
8-01-2006	Atlético Madrid	D 0-0	A	PD		35 000
11-01-2006	Villarreal	W 1-0	H	CDRr5	Garcia [59]	35 000
14-01-2006	Osasuna	W 2-0	H	PD	Regueiro [47], Villa [51]	40 000
19-01-2006	Deportivo La Coruña	L 0-1	A	CDRqf		20 000
22-01-2006	Real Betis	W 2-0	A	PD	Villa 2 [35 78]	35 000
25-01-2006	Deportivo La Coruña	D 1-1	H	CDRqf	Villa [44]. Abandoned 44' at 1-0. Match finished on 1-02-2006	0*
29-01-2006	Real Zaragoza	D 2-2	H	PD	Kluivert [82], Aimar [88]	45 000
4-02-2006	Deportivo La Coruña	W 1-0	A	PD	Villa [23]	28 000
12-02-2006	Barcelona	W 1-0	H	PD	Villa [44]	50 000
19-02-2006	Real Sociedad	W 2-1	A	PD	Regueiro 2 [69 89]	20 000
26-02-2006	Getafe	D 1-1	H	PD	Navarro [78]	30 000
5-03-2006	Málaga	D 0-0	A	PD		20 000
11-03-2006	Real Madrid	D 0-0	H	PD		50 000
19-03-2006	Racing Santander	L 1-2	A	PD	Villa [75]	15 604
22-03-2006	Villarreal	D 1-1	H	PD	Baraja [37]	51 000
26-03-2006	Sevilla	L 0-1	A	PD		45 000
2-04-2006	Cádiz	W 5-3	H	PD	Villa 2 [2 65], Angulo 2 [33 57], Navarro [35]	40 000
8-04-2006	Celta Vigo	W 1-0	A	PD	Angulo [29]	16 000
16-04-2006	Espanyol	W 4-0	H	PD	Villa [39p], Ayala [66], Mista [70], Baraja [86]	40 000
23-04-2006	Athletic Bilbao	W 3-0	A	PD	Villa 3 [81 84 86]	39 000
30-04-2006	Alavés	W 3-0	H	PD	Baraja [24], Aimar [32], Villa [50p]	40 000
3-05-2006	RCD Mallorca	L 1-2	A	PD	Angulo [16]	19 000
6-05-2006	Atlético Madrid	D 1-1	H	PD	Villa [11p]	40 000
16-05-2006	Osasuna	L 1-2	A	PD	Villa [93+]	19 517

ITC = Intertoto Cup • PD = Primera División • CDR = Copa del Rey
• r3 = third round • r5 = fifth round • qf = quarter-final • sf = semi-final • f = final
* Played behind closed doors

EST – ESTONIA

NATIONAL TEAM RECORD
JULY 1ST 2002 TO JULY 9TH 2006

PL	W	D	L	F	A	%
56	15	14	27	52	80	39.3

FIFA/COCA-COLA WORLD RANKING

1993	1994	1995	1996	1997	1998	1999	2000	2001	2002	2003	2004	2005		High	Low
109	119	129	102	100	90	70	67	83	60	68	81	76		**60** 12/02	**135** 02/96

	2005–2006										
	08/05	09/05	10/05	11/05	12/05	01/06	02/06	03/06	04/06	05/06	06/06	07/06
	82	81	81	77	76	76	77	79	79	77	-	82

TVMK Tallinn were the team of the seaon in Estonia, winning the League for the first time in November and then the Cup in the following May; but the top four of TVMK, Levadia, Trans Narva and Flora were in a completely different class to the rest of the clubs in the League. Between them they lost just two games all season against the six clubs that finished below them and dropped just two points in total against the bottom four. The competition resembled a mini-tournament between the top four in which TVMK's only defeat came away to Levadia. They chalked up a staggerring 138 goals in the campaign, 41 of which were scored by Teemo Neemelo, a new record

INTERNATIONAL HONOURS
Baltic Cup 1929 1931 1938

for the Estonian championship. The Cup Final, played midway through the following season, saw Flora try stop the TVMK bandwagon and win their first Cup since 1998, but a late goal from Latvian winger Vladislavs Gabovs was enough to win the trophy for TVMK before a disappointing crowd of just 350 in Tallinn. On the international front, Estonia will be hoping to build on an excellent FIFA World Cup™ qualifying campaign that saw them win five of their games to finish a respectable fourth in their group. With four of the squad having reached 100 caps and two more within touching distance, experience is the national team's key weapon.

THE FIFA BIG COUNT OF 2000

	Male	Female		Male	Female
Registered players	2 764	103	Referees	152	3
Non registered players	14 000	500	Officials	400	20
Youth players	2 770	64	Total involved	20 776	
Total players	20 201		Number of clubs	163	
Professional players	110	0	Number of teams	264	

Estonian Football Association (EFA)
Eesti Jalgpalli Liit, A.Le Coq Arena, Asula 4c, Tallinn 11312, Estonia
Tel +372 6 279960   Fax +372 6 279969
efa@jalgpall.ee   www.jalgpall.ee
President: TBD   General Secretary: SIREL Tonu
Vice-President: POHLAK Aivar   Treasurer: TBD   Media Officer: UIBOLEHT Mihkel
Men's Coach: GOES Jelle   Women's Coach: SAAR Juri
EFA formed: 1921   UEFA: 1992   FIFA: 1923-43 & 1992
Blue shirts with white trimmings, Black shorts, White socks or White shirts with black trimmings, Black shorts, Blue socks

RECENT INTERNATIONAL MATCHES PLAYED BY ESTONIA

2002	Opponents	Score		Venue	Comp	Scorers	Att	Referee
3-07	Lithuania	L	1-5	Valga	BC	Sirel [57]	800	Ingvarsson SWE
5-07	Latvia	D	0-0	Tallinn	BC			Ingvarsson SWE
20-08	Poland	L	1-2	Tallinn	Fr	Lemsalu [90]	4 500	Johannesson SWE
6-09	Bulgaria	L	0-2	Sofia	ECq		25 128	Wack GER
11-10	Belgium	L	0-2	Liege	ECq		26 000	Busacca SUI
15-11	Albania	L	0-2	Tirana	Fr		5 000	Douros GRE
19-11	Hungary	W	1-0	Budapest	Fr	Rooba.M [86]	1 200	Sedivy CZE
17-12	Saudi Arabia	D	1-1	Dammam	Fr	Zahhovaiko [40]	1 500	Al-Mehannah KSA
20-12	Oman	L	1-3	Muscat	Fr	Zelinski [45]	1 000	Al-Harrassi OMA
2004								
14-02	Belarus	W	2-1	Ta'Qali	Fr	Rooba.M [13], Lemsalu [45]	200	Casha MLT
16-02	Malta	L	2-5	Ta'Qali	Fr	Zahhovaiko [16], Piiroja [44]		Orlic MDA
18-02	Moldova	W	1-0	Ta'Qali	Fr	Lindpere [58]	100	Sammut MLT
31-03	Northern Ireland	L	0-1	Tallinn	Fr		2 900	Petteri FIN
28-04	Albania	D	1-1	Tallinn	Fr	Viikmäe [80]	1 500	Sipailo LVA
27-05	Scotland	L	0-1	Tallinn	Fr		4 000	Poulsen DEN
30-05	Denmark	D	2-2	Tallinn	Fr	Viikmäe [77], Lindpere [90]	3 000	Bossen NED
6-06	Czech Republic	L	0-2	Teplice	Fr		11 873	Brugger AUT
11-06	Macedonia FYR	L	2-4	Tallinn	Fr	Zahhovaiko [54], Teever [65]	2 200	Frojdfeldt SWE
18-08	Liechtenstein	W	2-1	Vaduz	WCq	Viikmäe [34], Lindpere [80]	912	Bozinovski MKD
4-09	Luxembourg	W	4-0	Tallinn	WCq	Teever [7], Schauls OG [41], Oper [61], Viikmäe [67]	3 000	Kelly IRL
8-09	Portugal	L	0-4	Leiria	WCq		27 214	Demirlek TUR
13-10	Latvia	D	2-2	Riga	WCq	Oper [72], Teever [79]	8 500	Meyer GER
17-11	Russia	L	0-4	Krasnodar	WCq		29 000	Busacca SUI
30-11	Thailand	D	0-0	Bangkok	Fr	L 3-4p	35 000	Mat Amin MAS
2-12	Hungary	L	0-5	Bangkok	Fr		800	Tongkhan THA
2005								
9-02	Venezuela	L	0-3	Maracaibo	Fr		8 000	Vasco Villacis ECU
26-03	Slovakia	L	1-2	Tallinn	WCq	Oper [57]	3 051	Frojdfeldt SWE
30-03	Russia	D	1-1	Tallinn	WCq	Terekhov [63]	8 850	Paparesta ITA
20-04	Norway	L	1-2	Tallinn	Fr	Saharov [81]	2 500	Vink NED
4-06	Liechtenstein	W	2-0	Tallinn	WCq	Stepanov [27], Oper [57]	3 000	Whitby WAL
8-06	Portugal	L	0-1	Tallinn	WCq		10 280	Riley ENG
17-08	Bosnia-Herzegovina	W	1-0	Tallinn	Fr	Viikmäe 35	4 000	Frojdfeldt SWE
3-09	Latvia	W	2-1	Tallinn	WCq	Oper [11], Smirnov [71]	8 970	Undiano Mallenco ESP
8-10	Slovakia	L	0-1	Bratislava	WCq		12 800	Allaerts BEL
12-10	Luxembourg	W	2-0	Luxembourg	WCq	Oper 2 [7 78]	2 010	Dereli TUR
12-11	Finland	D	2-2	Helsinki	Fr	Kruglov [62p], Lindpere [85]	1 900	Gilewski POL
16-11	Poland	L	1-3	Ostrowiec	Fr	Teever [68]	8 500	Hyytia FIN
2006								
1-03	Northern Ireland	L	0-1	Belfast	Fr		13 600	Vink NED
28-05	Turkey	D	1-1	Hamburg	Fr	Neemelo [87]	6 000	Weiner GER
31-05	New Zealand	D	1-1	Tallinn	Fr	Klavan [3]	3 500	Rasmussen DEN

Fr = Friendly match • EC = UEFA EURO 2004™ • BC = Baltic Cup • WC = FIFA World Cup™ • q = qualifier

ESTONIA NATIONAL TEAM RECORDS AND RECORD SEQUENCES

Records			Sequence records					
Victory	6-0	LTU 1928	Wins	3	2000	Clean sheets	3	1999, 2000, 2003
Defeat	2-10	FIN 1922	Defeats	13	1994-1995	Goals scored	13	1928-30, 1999-00
Player Caps	147	REIM Martin	Undefeated	6	Three times	Without goal	11	1994-1995
Player Goals	30	OPER Andreas	Without win	34	1993-1996	Goals against	19	1934-1937

ESTONIA COUNTRY INFORMATION

Capital	Tallinn	Independence	1991 from the Soviet Union	GDP per Capita	$12 300
Population	1 341 664	Status	Republic	GNP Ranking	110
Area km²	425 226	Language	Estonian	Dialling code	+372
Population density	3 per km²	Literacy rate	99%	Internet code	.ee
% in urban areas	73%	Main religion	Christian	GMT + / –	+2
Towns/Cities ('000)	Tallinn 394; Tartu 101; Narva 66; Kothla-Järve 46; Pärnu 44; Viljandi 20; Rakvere 16				
Neighbours (km)	Russia 294; Latvia 339; Baltic Sea & Gulf of Finland 3 794				
Main stadia	A. Le Coq Arena – Tallinn 10 300				

ESTONIA NATIONAL TEAM PLAYERS AND COACHES

Record Caps			Record Goals			Recent Coaches	
REIM Martin	1992-'06	147	OPER Andreas	1995-'06	30	PIIR Uno	1992-'93
KRISTAL Marko	1991-'05	143	ZELINSKI Indrek	1994-'06	26	UBAKIVI Roman	1994-'95
POOM Mart	1991-'06	104	ELLMAN-EELMA Eduard	1921-'35	21	SARAP Aavo	1995
ZELINSKI Indrek	1994-'06	101	PIHLAK Arnold	1920-'31	17	THORDARSON Teitur	1996-'99
VIIKMAE Kristen	1997-'06	100	KUREMAA Richard	1933-'39	16	RUUTLI Tarmo	1999-'00
OPER Andreas	1995-'06	99	REIM Martin	1992-'06	14	LILLEVERE Aivar	2000
TEREHOV Sergei	1997-'06	85	SIIMENSON Georg	1932-'39	14	PIJPERS Arno	2000-'04
LEMSALU Marek	1991-'04	84	VIIKMAE Kristen	1997-'05	14	GOES Jelle	2004-
KIRS Urmas	1991-'00	80	KRISTAL Marko	1991-'05	9		
ALONEN Viktor	1992-'01	71					

CLUB DIRECTORY

Club	Town/City	Stadium	Capacity	Lge	Cup
FC Ajax	Lasnamäe			0	0
FC Flora	Tallinn	A. Le Coq Arena	8 700	7	2
FC Levadia	Tallinn	Kadriorg Staadion	4 700	3	4
JK Maag (ex Merkuur)	Tartu	Tamme Stadion	700	0	0
JK Tammeka	Tartu	Tamme Stadion	700	0	0
JK Trans	Narva	Kreenholmi Staadion	3 000	0	1
FC TVMK	Tallinn	Kalevi Keskstaadion	12 000	1	2
JK Vaprus	Pärnu	Pärnu Kalevi Staadion	1 900	0	0
JK Tulevik	Viljandi	Linnastaadion	2 506	0	0
FC Warrior (ex FC Valga)	Valga	Valga Keskstaadion	2 500	0	0

RECENT LEAGUE AND CUP RECORD

	Championship						Cup		
Year	Champions	Pts	Runners-up	Pts	Third	Pts	Winners	Score	Runners-up
1992	Norma Tallinn	12	EP Jõhvi	10	TVMV Tallinn	8			
1993	Norma Tallinn	42	Flora Tallinn	34	Nikol Tallinn	33	Nikol Tallinn	0-0 4-2p	Norma Tallinn
1994	Flora Tallinn	36	Norma Tallinn	36	Nikol-Marlekor	33	Norma Tallinn	4-1	Trans Narva
1995	Flora Tallinn	41	Lantana-Marlekor	40	Trans Narva	26	Flora Tallinn	2-0	Lantana-Marlekor
1996	Lantana Tallinn	37	Flora Tallinn	31	Tevalte-Marlekor	31	Tallinna Sadam	2-0	EP Jõhvi
1997	Lantana Tallinn	41	Flora Tallinn	38	Tallinna Sadam	24	Tallinna Sadam	3-2	Lantana Tallinn
1998	Flora Tallinn	42	Tallinna Sadam	32	Lantana Tallinn	25	Flora Tallinn	3-2	Lantana Tallinn
1998	Flora Tallinn	35	Tallinna Sadam	34	Lantana Tallinn	25			
1999	Levadia Maardu	73	Tulevik Viljandi	53	Flora Tallinn	47	Levadia Maardu	3-2	Tulevik Viljandi
2000	Levadia Maardu	74	Flora Tallinn	55	TVMK Tallinn	48	Levadia Maardu	2-0	Tulevik Viljandi
2001	Flora Tallinn	68	TVMK Tallinn	56	Levadia Maardu	55	Trans Narva	1-0	Flora Tallinn
2002	Flora Tallinn	64	Levadia Maardu	62	TVMK Tallinn	53	Levadia Tallinn	2-0	Levadia Maardu
2003	Flora Tallinn	76	TVMK Tallinn	65	Levadia Maardu	49	TVMK Tallinn	2-2 4-1p	Flora Tallinn
2004	Levadia Tallinn	69	TVMK Tallinn	63	Flora Tallinn	58	Levadia Tallinn	3-0	TVMK Tallinn
2005	TVMK Tallinn	95	Levadia Tallinn	89	Trans Narva	75	Levadia Tallinn	1-0	TVMK Tallinn
2006							TVMK Tallinn	1-0	TVMK Tallinn

Play-off in 1994: Flora 5-2 Norma • Levadia Tallinn known as Levadia Maardu until 2003 • The orginal Levadia Tallinn sold its license to Merkuur Tartu • Tevalte-Marlekor became TVMK in 1998 and are unrelated to the original TVMK who became TVMV in 1993 then Nikol, Nikol-Marlekor, Lantana-Marlekor and finally Lantana Tallinn before being disbanded in 2000

ESTONIA 2005

MEISTRILIIGA

	Pl	W	D	L	F	A	Pts	TVMK	Levadia	Trans	Flora	Tulevik	Merkuur	Tammeka	Valga	Kuressaare	Dünamo
TVMK Tallinn †	36	30	5	1	138	21	95		2-2 0-0	0-0 0-0	4-2 4-2	1-1 2-0	2-1 8-1	9-0 5-0	5-0 3-0	3-1 6-1	5-1 9-1
Levadia Tallinn ‡	36	28	5	3	97	25	89	2-1 1-2		1-1 3-0	0-2 2-0	2-0 2-1	4-0 8-0	5-2 1-0	3-0 3-0	2-0 4-0	5-0 3-1
Trans Narva	36	23	6	7	99	34	75	0-3 0-2	3-1 0-4		2-2 2-0	1-2 **4-0**	6-2 4-0	5-1 6-0	3-1 3-0	4-1 3-0	7-3 7-0
Flora Tallinn ‡	36	21	6	9	81	36	69	1-3 0-1	0-2 1-3	2-1 0-0		3-0 0-1	0-0 1-0	3-0 3-1	2-0 1-0	6-0 7-0	3-1 7-0
Tulevik Viljandi	36	12	11	13	46	48	47	0-2 0-3	2-2 1-3	0-2 0-0	1-1 3-2		0-0 **5-1**	1-1 3-1	0-2 2-0	1-0 1-0	4-1 1-1
Merkuur Tartu	36	11	7	18	52	86	40	1-6 1-3	2-2 2-3	2-3 0-7	1-1 0-6	2-0 2-1		3-0 0-1	2-1 2-1	5-0 2-0	3-1 4-0
Tammeka Tartu	36	8	5	23	50	88	29	0-2 0-3	0-2 1-2	0-3 0-3	0-2 1-3	2-2 2-4	2-2 2-0		3-4 2-1	3-1 2-2	9-0 3-0
Valga	36	8	4	24	38	78	28	0-5 0-1	0-3 0-4	1-2 0-2	1-3 0-4	1-2 1-5	1-1 2-1	1-0 1-1		0-1 2-4	2-1 5-0
Kuressaare	36	7	6	23	40	96	27	1-6 1-8	0-2 1-3	2-5 1-3	1-3 1-1	1-1 1-1	1-2 1-1	1-0 2-1	1-0 0-0 0-3		2-0 8-1
Dünamo Tallinn	36	3	3	30	28	157	12	0-7 0-12	0-4 0-4	0-6 0-5	0-3 0-2	0-0 2-0	1-6 2-1	2-7 1-2	3-6 1-1	1-0 3-4	

6/03/2005 - 6/11/2005 • † Qualified for the UEFA Champions League • ‡ Qualified for the UEFA Cup • Relegation play-off: Ajax 1-0 1-2 Kuressaare • Top scorers: Tarmo NEEMELO, TVMK, 41; Maksim GRUZNOV, Trans Narva, 26; Vjatseslav ZAHOVAIKO, Flora, 19; Ingemar TEEVER, TVMK, 19 • Matches in bold were later awarded as wins for Tulevik

ESTONIA 2005
ESILIIGA (2)

	Pl	W	D	L	F	A	Pts
Vaprus Pärnu	36	26	6	4	92	39	84
Levadia Tallinn II	36	26	4	6	104	31	82
Ajax Lasnamäe	36	23	8	5	111	30	77
Tallinna Kalev	36	18	9	9	85	71	63
Tervis Pärnu	36	14	8	14	73	53	50
TVMK II Tallinn	36	12	5	19	51	80	41
FC Elva	36	10	6	20	42	71	36
Lelle SK	36	11	1	24	49	100	34
Tallinna JK	36	9	4	23	38	100	30
Merkuur-Juunior Tartu	36	3	5	28	27	97	14

5/03/2005 - 5/11/2005 • Levadia ineligible for promotion

EFA CUP 2005-06

Round of sixteen

TVMK Tallinn *	2
Levadia Tallinn	1
Merkuur-Junior Tartu	0
Warrior Valga *	4
Dünamo Tallinn *	5
Järva-Jaani	2
Tallinna Kuradid *	0
Trans Narva	9
Maag Tartu *	3
Lelle SK	0
Kaitseliit Kalev *	4
FC Kuressaare	5
Tallinna Kalev	8
Hansa United *	0
Tulevik Viljandi	1
Flora Tallinn *	2

Quarter-finals

TVMK Tallinn	2
Warrior Valga *	1
Dünamo Tallinn	1
Trans Narva *	4
Maag Tartu *	7
FC Kuressaare	0
Tallinna Kalev *	0
Flora Tallinn	5

Semi-finals

TVMK Tallinn	3
Trans Narva *	2
Maag Tartu *	0
Flora Tallinn	2

Final

TVMK Tallinn	1
Flora Tallinn ‡	0

CUP FINAL

Kadriorg, Tallinn
17-05-2006, Att: 350

Scorer - Gabrovs 86 for TVMK

* Home team • ‡ Qualified for the UEFA Cup

ETH – ETHIOPIA

NATIONAL TEAM RECORD
JULY 1ST 2002 TO JULY 9TH 2006

PL	W	D	L	F	A	%
29	12	6	11	40	34	51.7

FIFA/COCA-COLA WORLD RANKING

1993	1994	1995	1996	1997	1998	1999	2000	2001	2002	2003	2004	2005	High	Low
96	115	105	108	126	145	142	133	155	138	130	151	112	**90** 10/93	**155** 12/01

2005–2006											
08/05	09/05	10/05	11/05	12/05	01/06	02/06	03/06	04/06	05/06	06/06	07/06
127	128	128	128	112	112	112	112	113	112	-	101

Victory in the annual CECAFA Cup at the end of 2005 ensured a second successive title in the regional championship for Ethiopia but the question over whether they can translate that form onto a bigger stage remains to be answered. Andualem Negussie scored the goal that ensured a 1-0 win over hosts Rwanda in the final in Kigali in December. Ethiopia had looked impressive throughout the event with wins over Sudan, Djibouti and Somalia and 4-0 thumping of Zanzibar in the semi-finals. The result has meant that coach Sewnet Bishaw has been kept on in his job despite the clamour for a foreign coach for the 2008 African Nations Cup qualifying campaign. It has also

INTERNATIONAL HONOURS
CAF African Cup of Nations 1962   **CECAFA Cup** 1987 2001 2004 2005

meant that Ethiopia are on the brink of again breaking into the top 100 of the FIFA/Coca-Cola World Rankings, where their high of 90 was achieved over a decade ago. The country has had no other competition, besides the annual regional event, after they missed out on the group phase of the 2006 FIFA World Cup™ qualifiers. They were eliminated in the preliminary round in 2003 by Malawi. St George were crowned champions in 2006, retaining their title and confirming their dominant position in the domestic game. The army team, Mekelakey, won their first Cup since 1990, for a record eleventh triumph overall.

THE FIFA BIG COUNT OF 2000

	Male	Female		Male	Female
Registered players	19 000	0	Referees	1 000	0
Non registered players	180 000	0	Officials	7 000	0
Youth players	10 000	0	Total involved	217 000	
Total players	209 000		Number of clubs	500	
Professional players	0	0	Number of teams	3 000	

Ethiopian Football Federation (EFF)
Addis Abeba Stadium, PO Box 1080, Addis Abeba, Ethiopia
Tel +251 115 514321   Fax +251 115 515899
eff@telecom.net.et   www.none
President: WOLDEGIORGIS Ashebir Dr   General Secretary: EJIGU Ashenafi
Vice-President: TBD   Treasurer: YADEITA Abu   Media Officer: None
Men's Coach: BISHAW Sewnet   Women's Coach: MELESE Shale
EFF formed: 1943   CAF: 1957   FIFA: 1953
Green shirts, Yellow shorts, Red socks

RECENT INTERNATIONAL MATCHES PLAYED BY ETHIOPIA

2003	Opponents	Score		Venue	Comp	Scorers	Att	Referee
8-06	Liberia	L	0-1	Monrovia	CNq		14 000	Aguidissou BEN
22-06	Niger	W	2-0	Addis Abeba	CNq	Azad OG [15], Kidanu [51]	25 000	
6-07	Guinea	L	0-3	Conakry	CNq			
12-10	Malawi	L	1-3	Addis Abeba	WCq	Getu [81p]	20 000	Abd El Fatah EGY
15-11	Malawi	D	0-0	Lilongwe	WCq		20 000	Abdel Rahman SUD
2004								
11-12	Burundi	W	2-1	Addis Abeba	CCr1	Sebsebe Shegere [20], Tefera [22]		
15-12	Rwanda	D	0-0	Addis Abeba	CCr1		20 000	
17-12	Tanzania	W	2-0	Addis Abeba	CCr1	Alamerew [55], Tesfaye [90]		
19-12	Zanzibar †	W	3-0	Addis Abeba	CCr1	Tefera [50], Girma [54], Mensur [64]		
22-12	Kenya	D	2-2	Addis Abeba	CCsf	Alamerew [24], Tesfaye [58]. W 5-4p	50 000	Ssegonga UGA
25-12	Burundi	W	3-0	Addis Abeba	CCf	Negussie [25], Tesfaye [32], Alamerew [49]	30 000	
2005								
12-03	Sudan	L	1-3	Khartoum	Fr			
24-11	Sudan	W	5-1	Khartoum	Fr	Teffera, Tesfaye, Shegere, Demeke, Feleke		
27-11	Uganda	D	0-0	Kigali	CCr1			
1-12	Sudan	W	3-1	Kigali	CCr1	Sebsebe Shegere 3		
3-12	Djibouti	W	6-0	Kigali	CCr1	Mebrati [12], Shegere [40], Atten, Sesela [68], Pegpathen [86], Pirman [87]		
5-12	Somalia	W	3-1	Kigali	CCr1			
8-12	Zanzibar †	W	4-0	Kigali	CCsf	Girma [14], Teferrah 3 [46 48 82]		
10-12	Rwanda	W	1-0	Kigali	CCf	Negussie [59]		
2006								

No international matches played in 2006 before July

Fr = Friendly match • CN = CAF African Cup of Nations • CC = CECAFA Cup • WC = FIFA World Cup™
q = qualifier • r1 = first round group • sf = semi-final • f = final • † Not an official International

ETHIOPIA NATIONAL TEAM RECORDS AND RECORD SEQUENCES

Records			Sequence records					
Victory	8-1	DJI 1983	Wins	5	1967-1968, 2005	Clean sheets	3	1984
Defeat	0-13	IRQ 1992	Defeats	4	Five times	Goals scored	1	1995-97, 2000-02
Player Caps	n/a		Undefeated	11	1984-1988	Without goal	5	1995
Player Goals	n/a		Without win	9	1996-1999	Goals against	18	1956-1962

RECENT LEAGUE AND CUP RECORD

	Championship						Cup		
Year	Champions	Pts	Runners-up	Pts	Third	Pts	Winners	Score	Runners-up
1999	St George	47	Awassa City	39	Ethiopian Coffee	33	St George		
2000	St George	46	EEPCO Mebrat Hail	39	Ethiopian Coffee	38	Ethiopian Coffee	2-1	Awassa City
2001	EEPCO Mebrat Hail	59	St George	49	Ethiopian Coffee	48	EEPCO Mebrat Hail	2-1	Guna Trading
2002	St George	61	Ethiopian Coffee	50	EEPCO Mebrat Hail	45	Medhin	6-3p	EEPCO Mebrat Hail
2003	St George	56	Arba Minch Textile	55	Ethiopian Coffee	44	Ethiopian Coffee	2-0	EEPCO Mebrat Hail
2004	Awassa City	48	Ethiopian Coffee	46	Trans Ethiopia	45	Banks	1-0	Ethiopian Coffee
2005	St George	64	Trans Ethiopia	46	Awassa City	44	Awassa City	2-2 wop	Muger Cement
2006	St George	56	Ethiopian Coffee	52	EEPCO Mebrat Hail		Mekelakeya	1-0	Ethiopian Coffee

ETHIOPIA COUNTRY INFORMATION

Capital	Addis Abeba	Independence	Occupied by Italy 1936-41	GDP per Capita	$700
Population	67 851 281	Status	Republic	GNP Ranking	103
Area km²	1 127 127	Language	Amharic	Dialling code	+251
Population density	60 per km²	Literacy rate	42%	Internet code	.et
% in urban areas	13%	Main religion	Muslim 45%, Christian 40%	GMT +/−	+3
Towns/Cities ('000)	Addis Abeba 2 757; Dire Dawa 252; Nazret 214; Bahir Dar 168; Gondar 153; Mek'ele 151; Dese 136; Awassa 133; Jimma 128; Debre Zeyit 104; Kembolcha 93; Harer 90				
Neighbours (km)	Eritrea 912; Djibouti 349; Somalia 1 600; Kenya 861; Sudan 1 606				
Main stadia	Addis Abeba Stadium – Addis Abeba 35 000; Awassa Kenema – Awassa 25 000				

FIJ – FIJI

NATIONAL TEAM RECORD
JULY 1ST 2002 TO JULY 9TH 2006

PL	W	D	L	F	A	%
18	10	2	6	33	28	61.1

FIFA/COCA-COLA WORLD RANKING

1993	1994	1995	1996	1997	1998	1999	2000	2001	2002	2003	2004	2005		High	Low
107	120	139	157	146	124	135	141	123	140	149	135	135		**94** 07/94	**161** 09/98

2005–2006											
08/05	09/05	10/05	11/05	12/05	01/06	02/06	03/06	04/06	05/06	06/06	07/06
137	139	137	136	135	135	135	138	140	142	-	134

With the establishment of the OFC Club Championship, domestic football in Fiji is undergoing something of a transformation. Started in 2005, the Club Franchise League acts as a qualifying tournament for the Oceania event instead of the long established League Championship, which is competed for by regional teams. At stake is the potential of qualifying for the FIFA Club World Championship, greatly enhanced since Australia's move to the Asian confederation. The second edition was won by Nokia Eagles from Nadi who beat 2005 champions 4R Electric from Ba 5-4 on penalties in the final after the match ended scoreless. Only one other team - General Machinery

INTERNATIONAL HONOURS
Melanesian Cup 1988 1989 1992 1998 2000 **South Pacific Games** 1991 2003

from Lautoka - took part in the competition. The Eagles then won a four team tournament in the preliminary round of the OFC Club Championship, to qualify for the finals in New Zealand where they managed to reach the semi-finals before losing 9-1 to the eventual winners Auckland City. The main focus of domestic football does, however, remain the regional tournaments. In 2005 Ba won two of the titles on offer - the League and the FA Cup - but it was Lautoka who won the long established Inter-District Competition, a tournament first organised in 1937. The only national team action saw Fiji host India for two friendly internationals, both of which were won.

THE FIFA BIG COUNT OF 2000

	Male	Female		Male	Female
Registered players	9 838	303	Referees	90	0
Non registered players	5 000	0	Officials	2 500	50
Youth players	15 000	710	Total involved	33 491	
Total players	30 851		Number of clubs	300	
Professional players	0	0	Number of teams	1 775	

Fiji Football Association (FFA)
73 Knolly Street, PO Box 2514, Suva, Fiji
Tel +679 3300453   Fax +679 3304642
bobkumar@fijifootball.com.fj   www.fijifootball.com
President: SAHU KHAN Muhammad Dr   General Secretary: KUMAR Bob Sant
Vice-President: KEWAL Hari Dr   Treasurer: TBD   Media Officer: None
Men's Coach: BUESNEL Tony   Women's Coach: None
FFA formed: 1938   OFC: 1966   FIFA: 1963
White shirts, Blue shorts, Blue socks

RECENT INTERNATIONAL MATCHES PLAYED BY FIJI

2002	Opponents		Score	Venue	Comp	Scorers	Att	Referee
6-07	New Caledonia	W	2-1	Auckland	OCr1	Toma.Ve [23], Bukaudi [49]	1 000	Rugg NZL
8-07	Vanuatu	L	0-1	Auckland	OCr1		800	Sosognan PNG
10-07	Australia	L	0-8	Auckland	OCr1		1 000	Sosognan PNG
2003								
30-06	Vanuatu	D	0-0	Suva	SPr1			Taga VAN
7-07	Solomon Islands	W	2-1	Lautoka	SPr1	Veresa Toma [4], Esala Masi [13]	6 000	Ariiotima TAH
9-07	Tahiti	W	2-1	Lautoka	SPsf	Waqa [9], Veresa Toma [106]	8 000	Attison VAN
11-07	New Caledonia	W	2-0	Suva	SPf	Manoa Masi [30], Esala Masi [63]	10 000	Attison VAN
2004								
12-05	Papua New Guinea	W	4-2	Apia	WCq	Rabo [24], Veresa Toma [48+], Gataurua [78], Rokotakala [90]	400	Diomis AUS
15-05	American Samoa	W	11-0	Apia	WCq	Veresa Toma 3 [7 11 16], Vulivulu [24], Rokotakala 2 [32 38], Sabutu 2 [46+ 81], Esala Masi [60], Gataurua 2 [75 77]	300	Fox NZL
17-05	Samoa	W	4-0	Apia	WCq	Veresa Toma [17], Sabutu [52], Esala Masi [82], Rokotakala [84]	450	Diomis AUS
19-05	Vanuatu	L	0-3	Apia	WCq		200	Breeze AUS
29-05	Tahiti	D	0-0	Adelaide	WCq		3 000	Farina ITA
31-05	Vanuatu	W	1-0	Adelaide	WCq	Veresa Toma [73]	500	Ariiotima TAH
2-06	Australia	L	1-6	Adelaide	WCq	Gataurua [19]	2 200	Iturralde Gonzalez ESP
4-06	Solomon Islands	L	1-2	Adelaide	WCq	Veresa Toma [21]	1 500	Attison VAN
6-06	New Zealand	L	0-2	Adelaide	WCq		300	Larsen DEN
2005								
12-08	India	W	1-0	Lautoka	Fr	Esala Masi [14p]	10 000	Fox NZL
14-08	India	W	2-1	Suva	Fr	Luke Vidovi [25], Esala Masi [61]	11 000	O'Leary NZL
2006								

No international matches played in 2006 before July

OC = Oceania Nations Cup • SP = South Pacific Games • WC = FIFA World Cup™ • q = qualifier • r1 = first round group • sf = semi-final • f = final

FIJI NATIONAL TEAM RECORDS AND RECORD SEQUENCES

Records			Sequence records					
Victory	15-1	GUM 1991, COK 1971	Wins	6	2003-2004	Clean sheets	4	1992, 1989-90
Defeat	0-13	NZL 1981	Defeats	8	1985-1986	Goals scored	15	1985-1989
Player Caps	n/a		Undefeated	13	1989-1991	Without goal	5	1985
Player Goals	n/a		Without win	12	1983-1988	Goals against	13	1983-1988

RECENT LEAGUE AND CUP RECORD

	League	Inter-District Competition			Battle of the Giants			FA Cup		
Year	Winners	Winners	Score	Finalist	Winners	Score	Finalist	Winners	Score	Finalist
1997	Suva	Ba	2-0	Nadi	Labasa	1-0	Nadi	Labasa	0-0	Ba
1998	Nadi	Nadi	3-1	Lautoka	Ba	1-0	Nadi	Ba	3-0	Nadi
1999	Ba	Nadi	1-0	Ba	Ba	1-0	Tavua	Labasa	2-1	Lautoka
2000	Nadi	Ba	1-0	Nadi	Ba	2-0	Labasa	Lautoka	2-0	Nadroga
2001	Ba	Rewa	1-0	Ba	Ba	2-0	Lautoka	Nadroga	1-1 7-6p	Labasa
2002	Ba	Nadi	1-1 4-2p	Rewa	Nadroga	2-1	Labasa	Lautoka	1-1 3-2p	Nasinu
2003	Ba	Ba	1-0	Nadi	Rewa	1-0	Ba	Navua	1-0	Rewa
2004	Ba	Ba	3-0	Rewa	Rewa	2-0	Nadi	Ba	2-0	Suva
2005	Ba	Lautoka	2-0	Ba	Navua	1-0	Rewa	Ba	1-0	Nadi
2006								Ba	3-0	Labasa

FIJI COUNTRY INFORMATION

Capital	Suva	Independence	1970 from the UK	GDP per Capita	$5 800
Population	880 874	Status	Republic	GNP Ranking	141
Area km²	18 270	Language	English, Fijian	Dialling code	+679
Population density	48 per km²	Literacy rate	93%	Internet code	.fj
% in urban areas	41%	Main religion	Christian 52%, Hindu 38%	GMT + / −	+12
Towns/Cities ('000)	Suva 199; Nadi 53; Lautoka 49; Labasa 33; Nausori 32; Lami 21; Ba 20; Sigatoka 12				
Neighbours (km)	Fiji consists of two large islands, Viti Levu and Vanua Levu, along with 880 islets in the South Pacific				
Main stadia	National Stadium – Suva 5 000; Govind Park – Ba 4 000; Churchill Park – Lautoka 2 000				

FIN – FINLAND

NATIONAL TEAM RECORD
JULY 1ST 2002 TO JULY 9TH 2006

PL	W	D	L	F	A	%
50	19	10	21	64	64	48

FIFA/COCA-COLA WORLD RANKING

1993	1994	1995	1996	1997	1998	1999	2000	2001	2002	2003	2004	2005		High		Low	
45	38	44	79	60	55	56	59	46	43	40	43	46		**36**	03/05	**79**	12/96

2005–2006											
08/05	09/05	10/05	11/05	12/05	01/06	02/06	03/06	04/06	05/06	06/06	07/06
43	40	44	45	46	46	46	48	49	49	-	70

After the promise of the qualifying campaign for the 2002 FIFA World Cup™, there was no hiding the disappointment following the lacklustre performance in the qualifiers for Germany 2006 which saw the national team finish way off the pace behind the Netherlands, the Czech Republic and Romania. Englishman Roy Hodgson was brought in to give new direction for the UEFA Euro 2008™ qualifiers, but under his charge the team failed to win any of the six matches played in 2006. There was celebration in the women's camp, however, following the decision to award UEFA Women's Euro 2009™ to the country after the team's successful run to the semi-finals in

INTERNATIONAL HONOURS
None

England in 2005. There were first time champions in the men's Veikkausliiga, with MyPa-47 from the town of Anjalankoski finally managing to win the title after finishing second on five occasions since being promoted in 1992. The Second Division was won by FC Honka whose promotion means that Finland's second city of Espoo will have a first ever representative in the top flight. Haka beat TPS Turku 4-1 to win the Cup for a record 12th time but the season was scarred by match fixing allegations and Allianssi's involvement with the betting syndicate implicated in the Belgian match fixing scandal. In May 2006 the club folded.

THE FIFA BIG COUNT OF 2000

	Male	Female		Male	Female
Registered players	17 112	964	Referees	2 303	230
Non registered players	83 000	7 000	Officials	10 500	3 000
Youth players	64 265	12 540	Total involved	200 914	
Total players	184 881		Number of clubs	1 865	
Professional players	325	0	Number of teams	4 365	

Suomen Palloliitto (SPL/FBF)
Urheilukatu 5, PO Box 191, Helsinki 00251, Finland
Tel +358 9 742151   Fax +358 9 74215200
firstname.lastname@palloliitto.fi   www.palloliitto.fi
President: HAMALAINEN Pekka   General Secretary: HOLOPAINEN Teuvo
Vice-President: GUSTAFSSON Jukka   Treasurer: HOLOPAINEN Teuvo   Media Officer: TERAVA Sami
Men's Coach: HODGSON Roy   Women's Coach: KALD Michael
SPL/FBF formed: 1907   UEFA: 1954   FIFA: 1908
White shirts with blue trimmings, Blue shorts, White socks or Blue shirts with white trimmings, White shorts, Red socks

RECENT INTERNATIONAL MATCHES PLAYED BY FINLAND

2003	Opponents	Score		Venue	Comp	Scorers	Att	Referee
12-02	Northern Ireland	W	1-0	Belfast	Fr	Hyypia [49]	6 137	McDonald SCO
29-03	Italy	L	0-2	Palermo	ECq		34 074	Ivanov RUS
30-04	Iceland	W	3-0	Helsinki	Fr	Litmanen [55p], Forssell [57], Johansson.J [79]	4 005	Frojdfeldt SWE
22-05	Norway	L	0-2	Oslo	Fr		13 436	Clark SCO
7-06	Serbia & Montenegro	W	3-0	Helsinki	ECq	Hyypia [19], Kolkka [45], Forssell [56]	17 343	Colombo FRA
11-06	Italy	L	0-2	Helsinki	ECq		36 850	Siric CRO
20-08	Denmark	D	1-1	Copenhagen	Fr	Riihilahti [88]	14 882	McCurry SCO
6-09	Azerbaijan	W	2-1	Baku	ECq	Tainio [52], Nurmela [76]	8 000	Hrinak SVK
10-09	Wales	D	1-1	Cardiff	ECq	Forssell [79]	72 500	Dauden Ibanez ESP
11-10	Canada	W	3-2	Tampere	Fr	Forssell [14], Kolkka [16], Tainio [32]	5 350	Richmond SCO
16-11	Honduras	W	2-1	Houston	Fr	Tainio [60], Hakanpaa [68]	26 000	Hall USA
19-11	Costa Rica	L	1-2	San Jose	Fr	Nurmela [61p]	11 000	Batres CRC
2004								
3-02	China	L	1-2	Guangzhou	Fr	Eremenko [51]	15 000	Lee Gi Young KOR
7-02	China	L	1-2	Shenzhen	Fr	Kopteff [37]	18 000	Bae Jae Young KOR
31-03	Malta	W	2-1	Ta'Qali	Fr	Eremenko [51], Litmanen [86]	1 100	Trefoloni ITA
28-04	Bosnia-Herzegovina	L	0-1	Zenica	Fr		20 000	Bozinovski MKD
28-05	Sweden	L	1-3	Tammerfors	Fr	Litmanen [8p]	16 500	Undiano Mallenco ESP
18-08	Romania	L	1-2	Bucharest	WCq	Eremenko [90+3]	17 500	Gilewski POL
4-09	Andorra	W	3-0	Tampere	WCq	Eremenko 2 [42 64], Riihhilahti [58]	7 437	Siric CRO
8-09	Armenia	W	2-0	Yerevan	WCq	Forssell [24], Eremenko [67]	2 864	Malzinskas LTU
9-10	Armenia	W	3-1	Tampere	WCq	Kuqi 2 [9 87], Eremenko [28]	7 894	Fandel GER
13-10	Netherlands	L	1-3	Amsterdam	WCq	Tainio [13]	50 000	Bennett ENG
17-11	Italy	L	0-1	Messina	Fr		7 043	Tudor ROU
1-12	Bahrain	W	2-1	Manama	Fr	Pohja [9], Huusko [67]	10 000	Najm LIB
3-12	Oman	D	0-0	Manama	Fr	L 3-4p	3 000	Masoudi IRN
2005								
8-02	Latvia	W	2-1	Nicosia	Fr	Johansson.J [31], Huusko [72]	102	Kailis CYP
9-02	Cyprus	W	2-1	Nicosia	Fr	Roiha 2 [66 70]	1 502	Romans LVA
12-03	Kuwait	W	1-0	Kuwait City	Fr	Kuqi.N [16]	1 500	Al Shatti KUW
18-03	Saudi Arabia	W	4-1	Dammam	Fr	Kuivasto [4], Kuqi.N 2 [71 78], Nurmela [76]	8 000	Al Amri KSA
26-03	Czech Republic	L	3-4	Teplice	WCq	Litmanen [46], Riihilahti [73], Johansson.J [79]	16 200	Larsen DEN
2-06	Denmark	L	0-1	Tampere	Fr		9 238	Wegereef NED
8-06	Netherlands	L	0-4	Helsinki	WCq		37 786	Hamer LUX
17-08	FYR Macedonia	W	3-0	Skopje	WCq	Eremenko 2 [8 45], Roiha [87]	6 800	Messias ENG
3-09	Andorra	D	0-0	Andorra la Vella	WCq		860	Van Eecke BEL
7-09	FYR Macedonia	W	5-1	Tampere	WCq	Forssell 3 [10 12 61], Tihinen [41], Eremenko [54]	6 467	Jakobsson ISL
8-10	Romania	L	0-1	Helsinki	WCq		11 500	Guenov BUL
12-10	Czech Republic	L	0-3	Helsinki	WCq		11 234	Mejuto Gonzalez ESP
12-11	Estonia	D	2-2	Helsinki	Fr	Sjolund [7], Arkivuo [59]	1 900	Gilewski POL
2006								
21-01	Saudi Arabia	D	1-1	Riyadh	Fr	Roiha [87]	3 000	Al Anzi KUW
25-01	Korea Republic	L	0-1	Riyadh	Fr		800	Al Jerman KSA
18-02	Japan	L	0-2	Shizuoka	Fr		40 702	Lee Gi Young KOR
28-02	Kazakhstan	D	0-0	Larnaca	Fr	L 1-3p	100	Trattos CYP
1-03	Belarus	D	2-2	Larnaca	Fr	Riihilahti [82], Forssell [90]. W 5-4p	120	Krajnic SVN
25-05	Sweden	D	0-0	Gothenburg	Fr		25 754	Gilewski POL

Fr = Friendly match • EC = UEFA EURO 2004™ • WC = FIFA World Cup™ • q = qualifier

FINLAND NATIONAL TEAM RECORDS AND RECORD SEQUENCES

Records				Sequence records			
Victory	10-2	EST 1922	Wins	4	2005	Clean sheets	3	1924, 1993
Defeat	0-13	GER 1940	Defeats	14	1967-1969	Goals scored	14	1925-1927
Player Caps	102	LITMANEN Jari	Undefeated	10	2001-2002	Without goal	5	1937, 1971-1972
Player Goals	25	LITMANEN Jari	Without win	27	1939-1949	Goals against	44	1936-1949

FINLAND COUNTRY INFORMATION

Capital	Helsinki	Independence	1917 from Russia	GDP per Capita	$27 400
Population	5 214 512	Status	Republic	GNP Ranking	29
Area km²	338 145	Language	Finnish	Dialling code	+358
Population density	15 per km²	Literacy rate	99%	Internet code	.fi
% in urban areas	63%	Main religion	Christian 90%	GMT + / –	+2
Towns/Cities ('000)	Helsinki 558; Espoo 229; Tampere 202; Vantaa 188; Turku 175; Oulu 128; Lahti 98				
Neighbours (km)	Norway 736; Russia 1 340; Sweden 614; Baltic Sea, Gulf of Bothnia & Gulf of Finland 1 250				
Main stadia	Olympiastadion – Helsinki 42 062; Lahden – Lahti 14 500; Finnair – Helsinki 10 770				

FINLAND NATIONAL TEAM PLAYERS AND COACHES

Record Caps			Record Goals			Recent Coaches	
LITMANEN Jari	1989-'06	102	LITMANEN Jari	1989-'06	25	RYTKONEN Aulis	1975-'78
HJELM Ari	1983-'96	100	HJELM Ari	1983-'96	20	MALM Esko	1979-'81
PETAJA Erkka	1983-'94	83	PAATELAINEN Mika-Matti	1986-'00	18	KUUSELA Martti	1982-'87
TOLSA Arto	1964-'81	76	EKLOF Verner	1919-'27	17	VAKKILA Jukka	1988-'92
HYYPIA Sami	1992-'06	75	FORSSELL Mikael	1999-'06	16	LINDHOLM Tommy	1993-'94
PAATELAINEN Mika-Matti	1986-'00	70	KOPONEN Aulis	1924-'35	16	IKALAINEN Jukka	1994-'96
JOHANSSON Jonatan	1996-'06	69	ASTROM Gunnar	1923-'37	16	MØLLER NIELSEN Richard	1996-'99
RANTA Esko	1971-'80	69	KANERVA William	1922-'38	13	MUURINEN Antti	2000-'05
PELTONEN Juhani	1955-'70	68	VAIHELA Jorma	1947-'54	13	HELISKOSKI Jyrki	2005
KOLKKA Joonas	1994-'06	67				HODGSON Roy	2006-

CLUB DIRECTORY

Club	City/Town	Stadium	Capacity	www.	Lge	Cup
FC Haka	Valkeakoski	Tehtaan kenttä	6 400	fchaka.fi	9	12
HJK	Helsinki	Finnair Stadion	10 770	hjk.fi	21	8
FC Honka	Espoo	Hagalunds Idrottspark	3 000	fchonka.fi	0	0
IFK	Mariehamn	Idrottsparken	1 500	ifkmariehamn.com	0	0
FC Inter	Turku	Veritas Stadion	9 000	fcinter.com	0	0
FF Jaro	Pietarsaari	Keskuskenttä	5 000	ffjaro.fi	0	0
FC KooTeePee	Kotka	Arto Tolsa Areena	4 780	fckooteepee.fi	0	0
KuPS	Kuopio	Väinölänniemi	9 800	kups.fi	5	2
FC Lahti	Lahti	Lahden Stadion	14 500	fclahti.fi	0	0
MyPa-47	Anjalankoski	Jalkapallokenttä	4 067	mypa.fi	1	3
Tampere United	Tampere	Ratina Stadion	16 850	tampereunited.com	3	2
TPS	Turku	Veritas Stadion	9 000	tps.fi	8	2
VPS	Vaasa	Hietalahti	4 300	vps-vaasa.fi	2	0

RECENT LEAGUE AND CUP RECORD

Championship						Cup		
Year	Champions	Pts	Runners-up	Pts	Third	Pts	Winners	Score	Runners-up
1991	Kuusysi Lahti	59	MP Mikkeli	58	Haka Valkeakoski	54	TPS Turku	0-0 5-3p	Kuusysi Lahti
1992	HJK Helsinki	66	Kuusysi Lahti	63	Jazz Pori	63	MyPa-47	2-0	Jaro Pietarsaari
1993	Jazz Pori	41	MyPa-47	54	HJK Helsinki	49	HJK Helsinki	2-0	RoPS Rovaniemi
1994	TVP Tampere	52	MyPa-47	50	HJK Helsinki	43	TPS Turku	2-1	HJK Helsinki
1995	Haka Valkeakoski	59	MyPa-47	53	HJK Helsinki	52	MyPa-47	1-0	FC Jazz Pori
1996	FC Jazz Pori	47	MyPa-47	45	TPS Turku	44	HJK Helsinki	0-0 4-3p	TPS Turku
1997	HJK Helsinki	58	VPS Vaasa	48	FinnPa Helsinki	39	Haka Valkeakoski	2-1	TPS Turku
1998	Haka Valkeakoski	48	VPS Vaasa	45	PK-35 Helsinki	44	HJK Helsinki	3-2	PK-35 Helsinki
1999	Haka Valkeakoski	67	HJK Helsinki	65	MyPa-47	47	Jokerit Helsinki	2-1	FF Jaro Pietarsaari
2000	Haka Valkeakoski	66	Jokerit Helsinki	62	MyPa-47	61	HJK Helsinki	1-0	KTP Kotka
2001	Tampere United	68	HJK Helsinki	67	MyPa-47	62	Atlantis Helsinki	1-0	Tampere United
2002	HJK Helsinki	65	MyPa-47	60	Haka Valkeakoski	52	Haka Valkeakoski	4-1	FC Lahti
2003	HJK Helsinki	57	Haka Valkeakoski	53	Tampere United	47	HJK Helsinki	2-1	Allianssi Vantaa
2004	Haka Valkeakoski	59	Allianssi Vantaa	48	Tampere United	47	MyPa-47	2-1	Hämeenlinna
2005	MyPa-47	56	HJK Helsinki	52	Tampere United	51	Haka Valkeakoski	4-1	TPS Turku

Jokerit Helsinki known as PK-35 from 1999 to 2004 when they became Klubi-04 Helsinki

FINLAND 2005

VEIKKAUSLIIGA (1)

	Pl	W	D	L	F	A	Pts	MyPa-47	HJK	Tampere	Haka	Inter	Lahti	Allianssi	KooTeePee	TPS	KuPS	Jaro	IFK	RoPS	TP-47
MyPa-47 Anjalankoski†	26	17	5	4	51	18	56		1-1	3-0	2-3	1-1	3-1	0-0	2-1	1-0	3-0	0-2	2-1	5-1	5-0
HJK Helsinki‡	26	15	7	4	43	26	52	1-0		0-2	1-0	2-1	2-1	2-2	2-2	3-1	0-1	1-0	0-0	7-0	2-0
Tampere United	26	15	6	5	38	21	51	0-1	1-1		0-0	1-0	3-1	2-0	2-0	2-2	0-0	3-0	2-1	3-3	4-0
Haka Valkeakoski‡	26	13	11	2	47	19	50	1-0	2-0	1-3		1-1	0-0	8-0	1-1	6-0	1-0	2-1	3-1	4-0	2-0
Inter Turku	26	12	8	6	38	20	44	1-4	0-0	0-1	0-1		4-0	0-0	2-0	2-0	3-2	2-2	4-0	2-0	1-0
FC Lahti	26	11	5	10	39	36	38	1-4	1-2	3-1	0-0	1-0		4-1	1-1	1-0	2-1	4-0	3-0	4-1	1-4
Allianssi Vantaa	26	8	10	8	33	41	34	1-3	1-2	1-0	2-2	2-3	3-1		1-2	3-3	1-1	1-2	3-1	1-1	1-0
KooTeePee Kotka	26	9	6	11	35	42	33	2-2	5-3	3-0	3-3	0-2	2-0	1-2		1-0	0-2	2-0	3-1	0-0	0-3
TPS Turku	26	8	6	12	30	35	30	0-2	0-1	0-1	0-0	1-3	0-1	0-0	3-1		3-1	2-0	4-1	3-0	1-0
KuPS Kuopio	26	8	5	13	32	45	29	0-3	1-2	0-2	0-0	0-3	1-4	1-2	2-1	1-1		1-0	2-2	2-1	3-1
Jaro Pietarsaari	26	6	8	12	21	31	26	0-0	0-0	1-3	0-1	0-0	0-0	1-1	6-1	1-0	2-1		0-0	2-0	0-2
IFK Mariehamn	26	6	5	15	27	43	23	0-1	3-4	0-0	0-1	0-2	2-0	0-0	2-0	0-1	2-4	3-1		1-0	4-2
RoPS Rovaniemi	26	3	8	15	18	50	17	0-2	0-2	0-1	2-2	0-0	1-1	1-3	0-1	0-0	3-4	1-0	1-0		0-0
TP-47 Tornio	26	4	4	18	22	47	16	0-1	1-2	0-1	2-2	1-1	0-3	0-1	0-2	3-5	3-1	0-0	0-2	0-2	

28/04/2005 - 15/10/2005 • † Qualified for the UEFA Champions League • ‡ Qualified for the UEFA Cup • Allianssi refused license for 2006 season
Relegation play-off: VPS 0-0 1-1 RoPS. RoPS relegated on away goals • Top scorers: Juho MAKELA, HJK, 16; David CARLSSON, IFK, 14; RAFAEL, Lahti, 14

FINLAND 2005
YKKONEN (2)

	Pl	W	D	L	F	A	Pts
Honka Espoo	26	17	6	3	57	17	57
VPS Vaasa	26	17	2	7	49	23	53
PK-35 Helsinki	26	12	9	5	28	21	45
KPV Kokkola	26	13	2	11	36	29	41
Rakuunat Lappeenranta	26	12	5	9	34	36	41
Viikingit Helsinki	26	11	4	11	43	34	37
Atlantis Helsinki	26	9	7	10	39	35	34
PP-70 Tampere	26	9	5	12	32	39	32
MP Mikkeli	26	9	5	12	31	42	32
AC Oulu	26	8	7	11	32	33	31
FC Hämeenlinna	26	8	6	12	26	39	30
VG-62 Naantali	26	8	5	13	29	41	29
OLS Oulu	26	8	4	14	23	42	28
P-Iirot Rauma	26	6	3	17	25	53	21

4/05/2005 - 1/10/2005 • OLS replaced the bankrupt Jazz
Pori at the start of the season • Relegation play-offs:
SalPa 0-4 1-3 Hämeenlinna. No change in divisions
Klubi-04 Helsinki 2-1 2-3 VG-62. VG relegated on away goals

SUOMEN CUP 2005

Round of 16		Quarter-finals		Semi-finals		Final	
Haka Valkeakoski	5						
FC Kuusankoski *	2	Haka Valkeakoski *	4				
TP Seinäjoki *	0	Tampere United	1				
Tampere United	1			Haka Valkeakoski	1		
PK-35 Helsinki	2			Honka Espoo *	0		
PS Kemi *	1	PK-35 Helsinki	1				
JJK Jyväskylä	0	Honka Espoo *	4				
Honka Espoo *	2					Haka Valkeakoski ‡	4
FC Lahti	2					TPS Turku	1
City Stars *	0	FC Lahti	1				
Klubi-04 Helsinki *	0	MyPa-47 Anjalankoski*	0				
MyPa-47 Anjalankoski	2			FC Lahti	1 3p		
TP-47 Tornio	7			TPS Turku *	1 5p		
FC Espoo *	2	TP-47 Tornio *	1				
Jaro Pietarsaari *	0	TPS Turku	2				
TPS Turku	2						

* Home team • ‡ Qualified for the UEFA Cup

CUP FINAL
Finnair Stadium, Helsinki, 29-10-2005
Scorers - Popovich [40], Fowler [50],
Innanen [59], Mattila [90] for Haka;
Auremaa [83] for TPS

FRA – FRANCE

NATIONAL TEAM RECORD
JULY 1ST 2002 TO JULY 9TH 2006

PL	W	D	L	F	A	%
56	37	16	3	109	26	80.4

The designers of the French kit were agonisingly close to being called upon to put a second star above the cockerel on the national team badge, but the dream of winning a second FIFA World Cup™ evaporated when Zidane's head met Materazzi's chest with just ten minutes of the final remaining. To lose on penalties was hard for the French to take as they had enjoyed the better of the final, especially in the second half and in extra-time before Zidane's departure. Zidane cited extreme provocation as the reason for his assault and the French public readily forgave him, and rightly so given his unique contribution in helping establish France as one of the major powers of world football. The French had started the finals slowly, drawing against Switzerland and Korea and were struggling against Togo until Patrick Vieira's goal early in the second half eased their way into the knock-out round. Zidane had missed the Togo game due to suspension and there was even talk that he should be dropped for the match against Spain. He wasn't and suddenly France sprang to life, beating Spain, Brazil and then Portugal to reach the final, with Zidane, Vieira and Henry at the heart of everything, although Zidane's virtuoso performance against Brazil was one of the highlights

INTERNATIONAL HONOURS

FIFA World Cup™ 1998   **Qualified for the FIFA Women's World Cup finals** 2003
Qualified for the FIFA World Cup™ finals 1930 1934 1938 1954 1958 1966 1978 1982 1986 1998 2002 2006
FIFA Junior Tournament 1949   **FIFA U-17 World Championship** 2001   **UEFA European Championship** 1984 2000
UEFA U-21 Championship 1988   **UEFA U-19 Championship** 1983 1996 1997 2000   **UEFA U-17 Championship** 2004
UEFA Champions League Olympique Marseille 1993

of the tournament. There were chances to win the final - from Henry at the start of the second half to Zidane's header in extra time - but in the end it was David Trezeguet's penalty miss that was the difference between the French and the Italians. The fact remains though, that France have lost just three games since the finals in Japan and Korea, a record that no other team in the world can better - not even Italy or Brazil. Domestically there was a change of coach for Lyon, with the appointment of Gerard Houllier, but the change only reinforced their domination of the League. By winning a fifth consecutive title they matched the achievements of the great Marseille team of the early 1990s and the aim is now to win an unprecedented sixth in a row. Not bad for a club that at the start of 2002 had never even won a championship. Many had tipped them to win the Champions League and they were just minutes away from knocking Milan out in the quarter-finals before conceding twice in the last five minutes. PSG salvaged some pride for the long suffering Parisian fans with a 2-1 victory over Marseille at the Stade de France in the Cup Final, whilst Nancy celebrated winning their first silverware for 28 years when they beat Nice in the League Cup Final.

Fédération Française de Football (FFF)
60 Bis Avenue d'Iéna, Paris 75116, France
Tel +33 1 44317300   Fax +33 1 47208296
webmaster@fff.fr   www.fff.fr
President: ESCALETTES Jean-Pierre   General Secretary: LAMBERT Jacques
Vice-President: THIRIEZ Frederic   Treasurer: DESUMER Bernard   Media Officer: LE HUEDE Jean-Yves
Men's Coach: DOMENECH Raymond   Women's Coach: LOISEL Elisabeth
FFF formed: 1919   UEFA: 1954   FIFA: 1904
Blue shirts with white trimmings, White shorts, Red socks or White shirts with blue trimmings, Blue shorts, Red socks

RECENT INTERNATIONAL MATCHES PLAYED BY FRANCE

2003	Opponents	Score		Venue	Comp	Scorers	Att	Referee
20-08	Switzerland	W	2-0	Geneva	Fr	Wiltord [13], Marlet [55]	30 000	Allaerts BEL
6-09	Cyprus	W	5-0	Paris	ECq	Trezeguet 2 [7 80], Wiltord 2 [19 40], Henry [59]	50 132	Irvine NIR
10-09	Slovenia	W	2-0	Ljubljana	ECq	Trezeguet [9], Dacourt [71]	8 000	Messina ITA
11-10	Israel	W	3-0	Paris	ECq	Henry [9], Trezeguet [25], Boumsong [43]	57 009	Bolognino ITA
15-11	Germany	W	3-0	Gelsenkirchen	Fr	Henry [21], Trezeguet 2 [54 81]	53 574	Farina ITA
2004								
18-02	Belgium	W	2-0	Brussels	Fr	Govou [46], Saha [76]	43 160	Halsey ENG
31-03	Netherlands	D	0-0	Rotterdam	Fr		52 000	Stark GER
20-05	Brazil	D	0-0	Paris	FIFA		79 334	Mejuto Gonzalez ESP
28-05	Andorra	W	4-0	Montpellier	Fr	Wiltord 2 [44 56], Saha [68], Marlet [73]	27 753	Daami TUN
6-06	Ukraine	W	1-0	Paris	Fr	Zidane [87]	66 646	Ceferin SVN
13-06	England	W	2-1	Lisbon	ECr1	Zidane 2 [90 90+3]	65 272	Merk GER
17-06	Croatia	D	2-2	Leiria	ECr1	Tudor OG [22], Trezeguet [64]	29 160	Nielsen DEN
21-06	Switzerland	W	3-1	Coimbra	ECr1	Zidane [20], Henry 2 [76 84]	28 111	Michel SVK
25-06	Greece	L	0-1	Lisbon	ECqf		45 390	Frisk SWE
18-08	Bosnia-Herzegovina	D	1-1	Rennes	Fr	Luyindula [7]	26 527	McDonald SCO
4-09	Israel	D	0-0	Paris	WCq		43 527	Temmink NED
8-09	Faroe Islands	W	2-0	Tórshavn	WCq	Giuly [32], Cisse [73]	5 917	Thomson SCO
9-10	Ireland Republic	D	0-0	Paris	WCq		78 863	Dauden Ibañez ESP
13-10	Cyprus	W	2-0	Nicosia	WCq	Wiltord [38], Henry [72]	3 319	Larsen DEN
17-11	Poland	D	0-0	Paris	Fr		50 480	Benquerença POR
2005								
9-02	Sweden	D	1-1	Paris	Fr	Trezeguet [35]	56 923	Rodriguez Santiago ESP
26-03	Switzerland	D	0-0	Paris	WCq		79 373	De Santis ITA
30-03	Israel	D	1-1	Tel Aviv	WCq	Trezeguet [50]	32 150	Merk GER
31-05	Hungary	W	2-1	Metz	Fr	Cisse [10], Malouda [35]	26 000	Allaerts BEL
17-08	Côte d'Ivoire	W	3-0	Montpellier	Fr	Gallas [28], Zidane [62], Henry [66]	31 457	Bertini ITA
3-09	Faroe Islands	W	3-0	Lens	WCq	Cisse 2 [14 76], Olsen OG [18]	40 126	Jara CZE
7-09	Republic of Ireland	W	1-0	Dublin	WCq	Henry [68]	36 000	Fandel GER
8-10	Switzerland	D	1-1	Berne	WCq	Cisse [53]	31 400	Hauge NOR
12-10	Cyprus	W	4-0	Paris	WCq	Zidane [29], Wiltord [32], Dhorasoo [44], Giuly [84]	78 864	Stark GER
9-11	Costa Rica	W	3-2	Fort-de-France	Fr	Anelka [49], Cisse [80], Henry [87]	16 000	Alcala MEX
12-11	Germany	D	0-0	Paris	Fr		58 889	Bennett ENG
2006								
1-03	Slovakia	L	1-2	Paris	Fr	Wiltord [75p]	55 000	Thomson FRA
27-05	Mexico	W	1-0	Paris	Fr	Malouda [45]	80 000	Daami TUN
31-05	Denmark	W	2-0	Lens	Fr	Henry [13], Wiltord [76p]	39 000	Kelly IRL
7-06	China PR	W	3-1	St Etienne	Fr	Trezeguet [30], OG [89], Henry [92+]	34 147	Megia Davila ESP
13-06	Switzerland	D	0-0	Stuttgart	WCr1		52 000	Ivanov RUS
18-06	Korea Republic	D	1-1	Leipzig	WCr1	Henry [9]	43 000	Archundia MEX
23-06	Togo	W	2-0	Cologne	WCr1	Vieira [55], Henry [61]	45 000	Larrionda URU
27-06	Spain	W	3-1	Hanover	WCr2	Ribery [41], Vieira [83], Zidane [92+]	48 000	Medina Cantalejo ESP
1-07	Brazil	W	1-0	Frankfurt	WCqf	Henry [57]	48 000	Medina Cantalejo ESP
5-07	Portugal	W	1-0	Munich	WCsf	Zidane [33p]	66 000	Larrionda URU
9-07	Italy	D	1-1	Berlin	WCf	Zidane [7p]. L 3-5p	69 000	Elizondo ARG

Fr = Friendly match • EC = UEFA EURO 2004™ • FIFA = FIFA Centennial match • WC = FIFA World Cup™
q = qualifier • r1 = first round group • qf = quarter-final • sf = semi-final • f = final

FRANCE NATIONAL TEAM RECORDS AND RECORD SEQUENCES

Records			Sequence records					
Victory	10-0	AZE 1995	Wins	14	2003-2004	Clean sheets	11	2003-2004
Defeat	1-17	DEN 1908	Defeats	12	1908-1911	Goals scored	17	1999-2000
Player Caps	121	THURAM Lilian	Undefeated	30	1994-1996	Without goal	4	1924-1925, 1986
Player Goals	41	PLATINI Michel	Without win	15	1908-1911	Goals against	24	1905-1912

FRANCE COUNTRY INFORMATION

Capital	Paris	Independence	France unified in 486	GDP per Capita	$27 600
Population	60 424 213	Status	Republic	GNP Ranking	5
Area km²	547 030	Language	French	Dialling code	+33
Population density	110 per km²	Literacy rate	99%	Internet code	.r
% in urban areas	73%	Main religion	Christian	GMT + / −	+1

Towns/Cities ('000)	Paris 2 110; Marseille 792; Lyon 463; Toulouse 411; Nice 341; Nantes 284; Strasbourg 273; Montpellier 238, Bordeaux 219; Rennes 213; Reims 192; Lille 189; Le Havre 188; Saint-Etienne 170; Angers 158; Grenoble 154, Toulon 154; Dijon 153; Brest 150, Le Mans 147
Neighbours (km)	Belgium 620; Luxembourg 73; Germany 451; Switzerland 573; Italy 488; Monaco 4; Spain 623; Andorra 56; North Atlantic & Mediterranean Sea 3 427
Main stadia	Stade de France − Saint-Denis, Paris 79 959; Vélodrome − Marseille 60 031; Parc des Princes − Paris 48 712; Gerland − Lyon 41 184; De la Beaujoire − Nantes 38 486;

FRANCE NATIONAL TEAM PLAYERS AND COACHES

Record Caps			Record Goals			Recent Coaches	
THURAM Lilian	1994-'06	121	PLATINI Michel	1976-'87	41	BOULOGNE Georges	1969-'73
DESAILLY Marcel	1993-'04	116	HENRY Thierry	1997-'06	36	KOVACS Stefan	1973-'75
ZIDANE Zinedine	1994-'06	108	TREZEGUET David	1998-'06	32	HIDALGO Michel	1976-'84
DESCHAMPS Didier	1989-'00	103	ZIDANE Zinedine	1994-'06	31	MICHEL Henri	1984-'88
BLANC Laurent	1989-'00	97	FONTAINE Just	1953-'60	30	PLATINI Michel	1988-'92
LIZARAZU Bixente	1992-'04	97	PAPIN Jean-Pierre	1986-'95	30	HOULLIER Gérard	1992-'93
VIEIRA Patrick	1997-'05	94	DJORKAEFF Youri	1993-'02	28	JACQUET Aimé	1994-'98
WILTORD Sylvian	1999-'06	87	WILTORD Sylvian	1999-'06	26	LEMERRE Roger	1998-'02
BARTHEZ Fabien	1994-'06	87	VINCENT Jean	1953-'61	22	SANTINI Jacques	2002-'04
HENRY Thierry	1997-'06	85	NICOLAS Jean	1933-'38	21	DOMENECH Raymond	2004-

FIFA/COCA-COLA WORLD RANKING

1993	1994	1995	1996	1997	1998	1999	2000	2001	2002	2003	2004	2005		High		Low	
15	19	8	3	6	2	3	2	1	2	2	2	5		1	05/01	25	04/98

2005–2006											
08/05	09/05	10/05	11/05	12/05	01/06	02/06	03/06	04/06	05/06	06/06	07/06
9	6	5	5	5	5	5	8	7	8	-	4

THE FIFA BIG COUNT OF 2000

	Male	Female		Male	Female
Registered players	795 596	13 338	Referees	25 606	100
Non registered players	1 100 000	21 000	Officials	60 000	500
Youth players	1 042 830	21 659	Total involved	3 080 629	
Total players	2 994 423		Number of clubs	19 835	
Professional players	1 331	0	Number of teams	142 600	

FRANCE 2005-06

LIGUE 1 ORANGE

	Pl	W	D	L	F	A	Pts	Lyon	Bordeaux	Lille	Lens	Marseille	Auxerre	Rennes	Nice	PSG	Monaco	Le Mans	Nancy	St Etienne	Nantes	Sochaux	Toulouse	Troyes	Ajaccio	Strasbourg	Metz
Olympique Lyonnais †	38	25	9	4	73	31	84		0-0	1-3	1-1	2-1	1-1	1-4	2-1	2-0	2-1	8-1	1-0	4-0	3-1	1-0	1-1	2-1	3-2	1-0	4-0
Girondins Bordeaux †	38	18	15	5	43	25	69	1-1		1-0	1-0	1-1	1-1	1-0	2-0	1-0	0-2	1-0	2-2	1-0	0-0	0-0	1-1	2-0	2-0	1-0	2-1
Lille OSC †	38	16	14	8	56	31	62	4-0	3-2		0-0	0-0	1-1	1-0	4-0	0-0	0-1	4-0	1-0	2-0	2-0	3-0	0-0	1-2	2-0	2-0	3-1
RC Lens ‡	38	14	18	6	48	34	60	1-1	1-1	4-2		2-0	7-0	0-0	2-2	1-1	1-1	2-0	1-2	2-1	3-1	2-1	1-0	1-0	1-0	2-1	0-0
Olympique Marseille	38	16	12	10	44	35	60	1-1	0-2	1-1	1-1		1-0	1-0	1-0	1-0	2-1	1-1	6-0	2-0	2-1	0-0	0-0	2-1	1-1	2-2	3-1
AJ Auxerre	38	17	8	13	50	39	59	0-2	1-0	3-2	1-0	1-2		2-0	2-0	2-0	2-1	0-0	0-1	0-0	4-0	3-0	2-0	3-0	2-0	4-0	1-1
Stade Rennais	38	18	5	15	48	49	59	1-3	2-2	2-2	4-1	3-2	3-1		1-0	1-1	1-3	1-0	0-2	0-1	0-2	2-1	4-1	2-0	3-0	2-1	2-1
OGC Nice	38	16	10	12	36	31	58	1-1	0-1	2-0	0-0	1-1	0-2	1		1-0	2-0	1-0	1-0	0-1	1-1	1-2	2-1	1-1	1-0	3-1	2-1
Paris Saint-Germain ‡	38	13	13	12	44	38	52	0-1	3-1	2-1	3-4	0-0	4-1	2-0	1-2		0-0	0-1	1-0	2-2	2-0	3-1	2-0	2-1	2-4	1-0	4-1
AS Monaco	38	13	13	12	42	36	52	2-1	0-1	0-1	0-0	1-0	0-2	0-2	0-0	1-1		2-0	2-2	1-0	1-1	4-1	1-0	1-1	3-0	1-1	3-0
Le Mans UC 72	38	13	13	12	33	36	52	1-2	1-0	1-1	0-0	3-0	0-2	4-0	2-0	0-0	0-0		0-0	0-1	0-2	1-1	1-1	1-0	1-0	2-0	2-0
AS Nancy-Lorraine ‡	38	12	12	14	35	37	48	0-2	0-0	0-0	1-2	1-1	1-3	6-0	0-0	1-0	1-1	1-0		2-0	0-0	0-3	2-0	2-1	0-0	1-2	1-1
AS Saint-Etienne	38	11	14	13	29	39	47	0-0	1-1	0-2	2-0	2-1	1-1	0-0	0-1	3-0	1-1	3-0	0-2		1-0	0-0	1-3	1-1	0-0	0-2	2-0
FC Nantes	38	11	12	15	37	41	45	0-1	0-1	1-1	2-0	1-3	3-2	2-0	0-0	0-0	0-0	1-0	3-0	1-1		3-1	2-0	1-1	0-2	4-3	0-0
FC Sochaux	38	11	11	16	34	47	44	0-4	0-3	0-0	1-1	0-1	1-0	1-0	1-1	0-1	2-1	0-0	0-2	4-0	1-0		0-1	1-1	3-1	1-1	1-1
Toulouse FC	38	10	11	17	36	47	41	0-1	1-0	0-0	1-1	1-0	2-0	0-1	0-2	1-0	3-3	0-2	1-1	1-1	1-0	1-2		2-1	3-0	1-2	2-0
ES Troyes AC	38	9	12	17	37	47	39	0-1	1-1	1-0	1-1	0-1	1-1	2-1	1-2	1-1	1-2	1-3	0-1	0-0	1-0	2-1	3-1		3-0	1-1	0-0
AC Ajaccio	38	8	9	21	27	53	33	1-3	0-2	3-3	0-0	3-1	1-0	0-1	0-3	1-1	1-0	0-0	1-0	3-1	0-2	0-1	1-0	0-1		0-0	0-1
RC Strasbourg	38	5	14	19	33	56	29	0-4	0-0	2-2	1-1	0-0	0-0	0-0	1-0	0-0	1-1	1-2	1-2	1-3	0-1	0-1	0-0	2-4	2-0		2-1
FC Metz	38	6	11	21	26	59	29	0-4	0-1	0-2	0-1	1-0	1-2	0-1	1-0	1-0	2-1	0-0	0-0	0-1	1-4	0-1	2-2	2-4	2-0	0-0	

29/07/2005 - 13/05/2006 • † Qualified for the UEFA Champions League • ‡ Qualified for the UEFA Cup
Top scorers: PAULETA, Paris Saint-Germain, 21; FRED, Olympique Lyonnais, 14; Peter ODEMWINGIE, Lille, 14; Daniel COUSIN, RC Lens, 13

FRANCE 2005-06

LIGUE 2 ORANGE

	Pl	W	D	L	F	A	Pts	Valenc'nes	Sedan	Lorient	Caen	Dijon	Bastia	Le Havre	Créteil	Guingamp	Grenoble	Gueugnon	Montpellier	Istres	Reims	Chât'roux	Amiens	Brest	Clermont	Laval	Sète
Valenciennes FC	38	21	11	6	51	28	74		1-1	1-0	2-1	2-1	0-1	0-1	1-1	2-0	2-0	0-0	2-1	1-0	1-0	2-0	0-1	1-3	0-2	1-2	2-1
CS Sedan Ardennes	38	19	14	5	50	32	71	0-3		1-0	1-1	0-2	1-1	2-1	2-1	2-0	2-1	2-0	2-0	3-1	1-1	1-1	1-1	2-2	3-0	1-1	2-1
FC Lorient	38	18	12	8	49	26	66	1-1	0-0		1-3	1-0	1-0	0-0	0-0	2-1	1-2	2-0	3-0	1-1	3-1	2-1	1-1	5-0	0-2	2-1	3-1
SM Caen	38	18	12	8	56	35	66	0-2	1-1	1-0		1-4	4-1	3-1	0-0	1-1	1-0	0-0	1-0	1-3	2-1	3-0	3-1	2-1	2-1	1-0	
Dijon FCO	38	16	12	10	47	32	60	2-0	0-1	0-0	0-2		0-2	1-2	1-1	1-2	0-0	3-0	2-2	2-2	0-0	2-1	2-1	1-1	1-1	3-1	3-0
SC Bastia	38	16	10	12	47	40	58	1-0	1-1	1-1	0-2	0-2		1-1	1-1	2-2	0-0	3-0	0-0	1-4	2-0	4-1	4-0	3-0	1-0		
Le Havre AC	38	13	16	9	48	41	55	3-0	0-2	0-0	2-0	1-2	2-2		1-1	4-1	2-1	1-0	0-0	1-0	0-3	1-1	2-0	2-1	4-0	1-0	
US Créteil-Lusitanos	38	13	15	10	46	33	54	1-1	0-1	1-1	3-2	1-2	1-1	1-1		2-1	1-0	4-0	3-0	4-1	0-2	1-1	0-0	3-1	3-1	3-0	
En Avant Guingamp	38	12	14	12	32	32	50	0-2	1-1	1-0	0-0	0-0	1-1	1-0	0-0		0-1	0-0	1-0	2-0	0-1	6-0	1-0	3-1	3-1	0-1	
Grenoble Foot 38	38	12	12	14	42	45	48	2-3	1-3	1-0	0-2	1-2	5-1	1-1	0-0	0-0		3-0	2-2	0-0	1-0	2-1	3-0	1-2	2-0	1-0	
FC Gueugnon	38	11	15	12	29	37	48	2-0	1-0	0-1	2-2	0-0	2-0	1-0	0-0	1-0	1-1		3-1	2-0	0-0	2-1	0-0	0-1	2-0	1-1	3-3
Montpellier-Hérault	38	12	11	15	34	43	47	0-0	0-1	0-3	1-3	2-0	1-1	2-1	0-0	0-0	1-1	3-1		3-1	0-0	2-1	2-1	1-1	1-0	1-2	2-1
FC Istres	38	12	11	15	33	45	47	1-4	2-2	2-1	0-0	1-1	1-0	1-0	1-0	0-2	1-1	0-1	1-0		3-0	2-1	1-0	1-1	0-1	1-2	1-0
Stade de Reims	38	10	15	13	32	31	45	0-0	1-2	1-2	2-0	0-1	0-2	1-0	0-0	0-0	0-0	0-1	0-0	1-0		3-0	0-0	1-0	4-1	3-1	2-0
LB Châteauroux	38	10	14	14	48	48	44	1-1	0-1	0-1	1-1	1-1	1-1	3-0	0-2	1-3	1-1	2-1	4-3	1-0		0-0	0-3	3-3	2-3	1-0	
Amiens SFC	38	9	16	13	32	44	43	1-2	0-0	1-1	1-1	1-2	0-1	0-0	0-1	0-2	1-0	0-1	1-1		1-0	0-3		2-0	2-1	1-1	
Stade Brestois	38	9	15	14	34	48	42	1-1	4-1	0-1	2-1	0-4	0-2	2-2	0-2	2-3	1-0	0-0	0-0	1-1	1-0	0-1		2-0	2-2	1-1	
Clermont Foot	38	10	8	20	35	59	38	1-2	1-0	0-3	0-3	3-3	2-0	2-2	2-0	3-2	1-0	0-1	1-0	0-0	0-2	2-0	0-1		1-0	0-0	
Stade Lavallois	38	9	8	21	38	59	35	0-2	0-2	0-1	1-0	0-1	1-2	0-0	2-1	2-0	0-1	1-0	0-2	1-2	2-1	1-2	1-1	1-0	2-1		2-0
FC Sète 34	38	4	11	23	31	60	23	1-2	0-1	0-2	1-1	0-0	1-0	0-3	1-1	1-2	1-3	2-0	2-0	1-2	1-2	2-4	4-1	1-1	1-3	3-2	

29/07/2005 - 12/05/2006

COUPE DE FRANCE 2005-06

Round of 64		Round of 32		Round of 16	
Paris Saint-Germain	4				
Vermelles US §	0	Paris Saint-Germain *	1		
Noisy le Sec *	0	AJ Auxerre	0		
AJ Auxerre	1			Paris Saint-Germain	3
RC Strasbourg *	4			Lyon Duchere *	0
AS Nancy-Lorraine	0	RC Strasbourg	0 4p		
Toulouse	1	Lyon Duchere *	0 5p		
Lyon Duchere *	2				
Vitre	1				
Fontenay LCVF *	0	Vitre *	3		
SM Caen	4	Longuenesse	1		
Longuenesse *	0			Vitre §§	0
Lorient	2			Lille OSC	2
Vannes *	1	Lorient *	0		
AS Saint-Etienne *	0	Lille OSC	1		
Lille OSC	1				
Calais *	3				
Troyes AC	2	Calais	1		
Mulhouse	0	St Genevieve *	0		
St Genevieve *	5			Calais *	1
Amiens SC *	2			Stade Brestois	0
Plabennec	0	Amiens SC	0		
OGC Nice	0	Stade Brestois *	2		
Stade Brestois *	3				
Dijon FCO *	2				
Forbach	1	Dijon FCO *	1		
FC Istres	3 3p	Moulins	0		
Moulins *	3 5p			Dijon FCO	0
Boisguillaume	0 5p			FC Nantes *	3
Brive *	0 4p	Boisguillaume *	0		
US Valenciennes	1	FC Nantes	2		
FC Nantes *	2				
Stade Rennais	3				
Corte 2 *	2	Stade Rennais *	1		
Le Mans *	0	RC Lens	0		
RC Lens	1			Stade Rennais	4
AS Monaco	6			Colmar *	1
Rhone Vallees *	0	AS Monaco	0		
St Louis Neuweg *	1	Colmar *	1		
Colmar	2				
Girondins Bordeaux	3				
Wasquehal *	1	Girondins Bordeaux *	2		
St Pryve *	0	Entente SSG	1		
Entente SSG	6			Girondins Bordeaux	0
Roye *	1			Montpellier HSC *	1
Alencon US	0	Roye	1		
Hyeres	1	Montpellier HSC *	6		
Montpellier HSC *	2				
Olympique Lyonnais	4				
Grenoble *	0	Olympique Lyonnais	2		
Saint Lo *	0	AC Ajaccio *	1		
AC Ajaccio	2			Olympique Lyonnais *	1
Agde RCO	1 4p			SC Bastia	0
AS Cannes *	1 3p	Agde RCO	0		
Louhans	3 1p	SC Bastia *	2		
SC Bastia	3 3p				
Sochaux-Montbéliard	2				
Oissel *	1	Sochaux-Montbéliard	2		
Yzeure	0	Châteauroux *	1		
Châteauroux *	2			Sochaux-Montbéliard	0
FC Metz	4			Olympique Marseille *	2
Jeanne d'Arc *	0	FC Metz	0		
Le Havre AC	0	Olympique Marseille *	2		
Olympique Marseille *	4				

* Home team • §§ Played in Rennes

COUPE DE FRANCE 2005-06

Quarter-finals　　　　　　　　**Semi-finals**　　　　　　　**Final**

| Paris Saint-Germain * | 2 |
| Lille OSC | 1 |

| Paris Saint-Germain | 2 |
| FC Nantes * | 1 |

| Calais § | 0 |
| FC Nantes | 1 |

| Paris Saint-Germain ‡ | 2 |
| Olympique Marseille | 1 |

| Stade Rennais * | 5 |
| Montpellier HSC | 3 |

| Stade Rennais | 0 |
| Olympique Marseille * | 3 |

| Olympique Lyonnais * | 1 |
| Olympique Marseille | 2 |

COUPE DE FRANCE FINAL 2006

Stade de France, Saint-Denis, Paris, 29-04-2006, 20:45, 80 000, Ref: Duhamel

Paris Saint-Germain　　2　　Kalou [6], Dhorasoo [49]

Olympique Marseille　　1　　Maoulida [67]

PSG - Lionel LETIZI◦ - Sylvain ARMAND◦, Bernard MENDY, David ROZEHNAL, Mario YEPES - Edouard CISSE, Vikash DHORASOO, Modeste MBAMI◦, Jérôme ROTHEN - Pedro PAULETA◦, Bonaventure KALOU. Tr: Guy LACOMBE
OM - Fabien BARTHEZ - Taye Ismailia TAIWO◦, Habib BEYE (Samir NASRI 80), Renato CIVELLI, Frédéric DEHU - Lorik CANA, Sabri LAMOUCHI, Franck RIBERY - Mamadou NIANG, Mickaël PAGIS (Wilson ORUMA◦ 38), Toifilou MAOULIDA. Tr: Jean FERNANDEZ

§ Played in Lens • ‡ Qualified for the UEFA Cup

COUPE DE LA LIGUE 2005–06

Round of 16		Quarter-finals		Semi-finals		Final	
AS Nancy-Lorraine *	1						
Lorient	0	**AS Nancy-Lorraine ***	1				
Montpellier HSC *	0	AJ Ajaccio	0				
AJ Ajaccio	1			**AS Nancy-Lorraine ***	2		
En Avant Guingamp *	2			Le Mans	0		
SM Caen	0	En Avant Guingamp *	1 2p				
AJ Auxerre *	1 1p	**Le Mans**	1 3p				
Le Mans	1 4p					**AS Nancy-Lorraine ‡**	2
AS Monaco *	1					OGC Nice	1
Lille OSC	0	**AS Monaco**	2				
Paris Saint-Germain	0	Toulouse *	0				
Toulouse *	2			AS Monaco *	0	**LEAGUE CUP FINAL**	
Girondins Bordeaux *	3			**OGC Nice**	1	Stade de France, St-Denis, Paris	
FC Nantes	1	Girondins Bordeaux	1			22-04-2006, 20:50, 76 830, Ref: Layec	
CS Sedan Ardennes	0	**OGC Nice ***	2			Scorers - Zerka [22], Kim [65] for Nancy;	
OGC Nice *	2					Vahirua [48] for Nice	

* Home team • ‡ Qualified for the UEFA Cup

CLUB DIRECTORY

Club	Town/City	Stadium	Capacity	www.	Lge	Cup	CL
AJ Auxerre	Auxerre	Abbé-Deschamps	23 493	aja.fr	1	4	0
Girondins Bordeaux	Bordeaux	Chaban-Delmas	34 198	girondins.com	5	3	0
Racing Club Lens	Lens	Felix-Bollaert	41 233	rclens.fr	1	0	0
Le Mans UC 72	Le Mans	Omnisports Léon-Bollée	17 801	muc72.fr	0	0	0
Lille OSC	Lille	Métropole	18 086	losc.fr	2	5	0
FC Lorient	Lorient	Le Moustoir	18 696	fcl-lorient.com	0	1	0
Olympique Lyonnais	Lyon	Stade Gerland	41 044	olweb.fr	5	3	0
Olympique Marseille	Marseille	Stade Velodrome	60 013	om.net	9	10	1
AS Monaco	Monaco	Stade Louis II	18 521	asm-fc.com	7	5	0
AS Nancy-Lorraine	Nancy	Marcel-Picot	20 087	asnl.net	0	1	0
FC Nantes Atlantique	Nantes	Stade Beaujoire	38 373	fcna.fr	8	3	0
OGC Nice	Nice	Stade du Ray	18 696	ogcnice.com	4	3	0
Paris Saint-Germain	Paris	Parc des Princes	48 527	psg.fr	2	7	0
Stade Rennais	Rennes	Parc des Sports	31 127	staderennais.com	0	2	0
AS Saint-Etienne	Saint-Etienne	Geoffroy-Guichard	35 616	asse.fr	10	6	0
CS Sedan Ardennes	Sedan	Louis-Dugauguez	23 189	cssedan.com	0	2	0
FC Sochaux	Montbeliard	Stade Bonal	20 005	fcsochaux.fr	2	1	0
Toulouse FC	Toulouse	Municipal	36 508	tfc.info	0	0	0
ES Troyes	Troyes	Stade de l'Aube	21 877	estac.fr	0	0	0
Valenciennes FC	Valenciennes	Nungesser	11 316	va-fc.com	0	0	0

RECENT LEAGUE AND CUP RECORD

	Championship						Cup		
Year	Champions	Pts	Runners-up	Pts	Third	Pts	Winners	Score	Runners-up
1990	Olympique Marseille	53	Girondins Bordeaux	51	AS Monaco	46	SCP Montpellier	2-1	Racing Club Paris
1991	Olympique Marseille	55	AS Monaco	51	AJ Auxerre	48	AS Monaco	1-0	Olympique Marseille
1992	Olympique Marseille	58	AS Monaco	52	Paris St-Germain	47	Unfinished due to Bastia disaster		
1993	Olympique Marseille	55	Paris St-Germain	51	AS Monaco	51	Paris St-Germain	3-0	FC Nantes
1994	Paris St-Germain	59	Olympique Marseille	51	AJ Auxerre	46	AJ Auxerre	3-0	Montpellier HSC
1995	FC Nantes	79	Olympique Lyonnais	69	Paris St-Germain	67	Paris St-Germain	1-0	RC Strasbourg
1996	AJ Auxerre	72	Paris St-Germain	68	AS Monaco	68	AJ Auxerre	2-1	Nîmes Olympique
1997	AS Monaco	79	Paris St-Germain	67	FC Nantes	64	OGC Nice	1-1 4-3p	Guingamp
1998	Racing Club Lens	68	FC Metz	68	AS Monaco	59	Paris St-Germain	2-1	Racing Club Lens
1999	Girondins Bordeaux	72	Olympique Marseille	71	Olympique Lyonnais	63	FC Nantes	1-0	CS Sedan Ardennes
2000	AS Monaco	65	Paris St-Germain	58	Olympique Lyonnais	56	FC Nantes	2-1	Calais
2001	FC Nantes	68	Olympique Lyonnais	64	Lille OSC	59	RC Strasbourg	0-0 5-4p	Amiens SC
2002	Olympique Lyonnais	66	Racing Club Lens	64	AJ Auxerre	59	FC Lorient	1-0	SC Bastia
2003	Olympique Lyonnais	68	AS Monaco	67	Olympique Marseille	65	AJ Auxerre	2-1	Paris St-Germain
2004	Olympique Lyonnais	79	Paris St-Germain	76	AS Monaco	75	Paris St-Germain	1-0	Châteauroux
2005	Olympique Lyonnais	79	Lille OSC	67	AS Monaco	63	AJ Auxerre	2-1	CS Sedan
2006	Olympique Lyonnais	84	Girondins Bordeaux	69	Lille OSC	62	Paris St-Germain	2-1	Olympique Marseille

OLYMPIQUE LYONNAIS 2005-06

Date	Opponents	Score				Scorers	Att
27-07-2005	Auxerre	W	4-1	A	SC	Ben Arfa [3p], Carew 3 [34 68 73]	10 967
31-07-2005	Le Mans	W	2-1	A	Lge	Wiltord [37], Carew [58]	13 197
7-08-2005	RC Strasbourg	W	1-0	H	Lge	Carew [26]	37 680
14-08-2005	Olympique Marseille	D	1-1	A	Lge	Carew [35]	57 609
20-08-2005	Nancy-Lorraine	W	1-0	H	Lge	Caçapa [90]	39 938
28-08-2005	Auxerre	W	2-0	A	Lge	Diarra [6], Juninho [45]	14 276
10-09-2005	Monaco	W	2-1	H	Lge	Fred 2 [5 49]	39 043
13-09-2005	Real Madrid - ESP	W	3-0	H	CLgF	Carew [21], Juninho [26], Wiltord [31]	40 309
17-09-2005	Girondins Bordeaux	D	1-1	A	Lge	Wiltord [64]	32 020
22-09-2005	RC Lens	D	1-1	H	Lge	Tiago [38]	36 337
25-09-2005	Nantes	W	1-0	A	Lge	Fred [80]	33 289
28-09-2005	Rosenborg BK - NOR	W	1-0	A	CLgF	Cris [45]	20 620
2-10-2005	Stade Rennais	W	3-1	A	Lge	Juninho [53], Tiago [74], Wiltord [88]	28 998
16-10-2005	Ajaccio	W	3-2	H	Lge	Fred [30], Juninho [50], Wiltord [69]	36 347
19-10-2005	Olympiacos - GRE	W	2-1	H	CLgF	Juninho [4], Govou [89]	38 093
22-10-2005	Metz	W	4-0	A	Lge	Carew [23], Juninho [36], Wiltord [44], Malouda [51]	19 333
25-10-2005	Nantes	D	1-1	A	LCr2	Govou [90], L 3-4p	28 025
29-10-2005	Sochaux	W	1-0	H	Lge	Malouda [54]	40 117
1-11-2005	Olympiacos - GRE	W	4-1	A	CLgF	Juninho [41], Carew 2 [43 57], Diarra [55]	30 848
5-11-2005	Toulouse	W	1-0	A	Lge	Govou [9]	28 254
19-11-2205	Troyes	W	2-1	H	Lge	Cris 2 [27 76]	37 940
23-11-2005	Real Madrid - ESP	D	1-1	A	CLgF	Carew [72]	67 304
26-11-2005	OGC Nice	D	1-1	A	Lge	Govou [76]	12 849
3-12-2005	Paris Saint Germain	W	2-0	H	Lge	Fred [5], Carew [90]	38 134
6-12-2005	Rosenborg BK - NOR	W	2-1	H	CLgF	Benzema [33], Fred [93+]	40 425
11-12-2005	Saint Etienne	D	0-0	A	Lge		35 352
16-12-2005	OSC Lille	L	1-3	H	Lge	Govou [69]	37 677
4-01-2006	RC Strasbourg	W	4-0	A	Lge	Wiltord 3 [6 56 74], Berthod [42]	19 375
8-01-2006	Grenoble	W	4-0	A	CDFr9	Benzema 2 [23 29], Diarra [51], Ben Arfa [76]	14 000
11-01-2006	Olympique Marseille	W	2-1	H	Lge	Tiago [54], Govou [83]	38 912
14-01-2006	Nancy-Lorraine	W	2-0	A	Lge	Caçapa [49], Fred [83]	19 126
22-01-2006	Auxerre	D	1-1	H	Lge	Diarra [43]	37 958
1-02-2006	Ajaccio	W	2-1	A	CDFr10	Cris [107], Govou [113]	4 000
5-02-2006	Girondins Bordeaux	D	0-0	H	Lge		39 354
11-02-2006	RC Lens	D	1-1	A	Lge	Wiltord [90]	40 037
17-02-2006	Nantes	W	3-1	H	Lge	Juninho [9], Diarra [35], Fred [56]	38 393
21-02-2006	PSV Eindhoven - NED	W	1-0	A	CLr2	Juninho [65]	35 000
25-02-2006	Stade Rennais	L	1-4	H	Lge	Juninho [38p]	39 168
4-03-2006	Ajaccio	W	3-1	A	Lge	Juninho [61], Fred [79], Benzema [89]	4 037
8-03-2006	PSV Eindhoven - NED	W	4-0	H	CLr2	Tiago 2 [26 45], Wiltord [71], Fred [90]	37 901
11-03-2006	Metz	W	4-0	H	Lge	Malouda 2 [13 34], Carew [16], Muller [90]	37 000
18-03-2006	Sochaux	W	4-0	A	Lge	Wiltord 2 [26 52], Pedretti [45], Malouda [58]	18 770
21-03-2006	Bastia	W	1-0	H	CDFr11	Juninho [56]	29 026
25-03-2006	Toulouse	D	1-1	H	Lge	Carew [49]	39 794
29-03-2006	Milan - ITA	D	0-0	H	CLqf		39 500
1-04-2006	Troyes	W	1-0	A	Lge	Tiago [77]	17 835
4-04-2006	Milan - ITA	L	1-3	A	CLqf	Diarra [31]	78 894
8-04-2006	OGC Nice	W	2-1	H	Lge	Fred [23], Malouda [51]	38 545
11-04-2006	Olympique Marseille	L	1-2	H	CDFqf	Fred [21]	38 885
16-04-2006	Paris Saint-Germain	W	1-0	A	Lge	Fred [24]	43 128
30-04-2006	Saint-Etienne	W	4-0	H	Lge	Hellebuyck OG [8], Fred [40], Juninho [56p], Pedretti [81]	39 081
6-05-2006	Lille OSC	L	0-4	A	Lge		17 143
13-05-2006	Le Mans	W	8-1	H	Lge	Fred 3 [19 40 77], Cris [27], Wiltord [30], Juninho [43], Govou [86], Tiago [88]	40 426

SC = Trophée des champions • Lge = Ligue 1 • CDF = Coupe de France • LC = Coupe de la Ligue • CL = UEFA Champions League
gF = Group D • r1 = first round • r2 = second round • r3 = third round • qf = quarter-final

PARIS SAINT-GERMAIN 2005-06

Date	Opponents		Score			Scorers	Att
29-05-2005	Metz	W	4-1	H	Lge	Kalou [5], Cissé [37], Rothen [49], Landrin [80]	42 844
6-08-2005	Sochaux	W	1-0	A	Lge	Cissé [52]	17 543
13-08-2005	Toulouse	W	2-0	H	Lge	Pauleta 2 [43 61]	41 341
21-08-2005	Troyes	D	1-1	A	Lge	Pauleta [36]	17 507
27-08-2005	OGC Nice	L	1-2	H	Lge	Pauleta [2]	43 475
10-09-2005	RC Strasbourg	W	1-0	H	Lge	Kalou [28]	40 748
18-09-2005	Saint-Etienne	L	0-3	A	Lge		27 771
21-09-2005	Lille OSC	W	2-1	H	Lge	Pauleta 2 [12 55]	35 889
24-09-2005	Le Mans	D	0-0	A	Lge		14 728
1-10-2005	Nantes	W	2-0	H	Lge	Yepes [67], Pauleta [75]	41 164
16-10-2005	Olympique Marseille	L	0-1	A	Lge		54 260
22-10-2005	Nancy-Lorraine	W	1-0	H	Lge	Kalou [53]	40 140
26-10-2005	Troyes	W	4-1	H	LCr2	Cissé [8], Pauleta 2 [47 58], Badiane [73]	20 399
30-10-2005	Auxerre	L	0-2	A	Lge		19 980
6-11-2005	Monaco	D	0-0	H	Lge		43 555
20-11-2005	Girondins Bordeaux	W	2-0	A	Lge	Yepes [35], Pauleta [50]	32 204
27-11-2005	RC Lens	L	3-4	H	Lge	Pauleta 2 [5 89], Yepes [92+]	40 895
3-12-2005	Olympique Lyonnais	L	0-2	A	Lge		38 134
10-12-2005	Stade Rennais	W	2-0	H	Lge	Pauleta 2 [39 63]	37 747
17-12-2005	Ajaccio	D	1-1	A	Lge	Kalou [42]	3 672
21-12-2005	Toulouse	L	0-2	A	LCr3		17 132
4-01-2006	Sochaux	W	3-1	H	Lge	Landrin [26], Pancrate [57], Pauleta [74]	36 806
7-01-2006	Vermelles	W	4-0	A	CDFr9	Pauleta [8], Armand [51], Bueno [78], Rodriguez [83]	15 311
12-01-2006	Toulouse	L	0-1	A	Lge		19 609
15-01-2006	Troyes	W	2-1	H	Lge	Pauleta [45], Pancrate [90]	35 118
21-01-2006	OGC Nice	L	0-1	A	Lge		11 941
1-02-2006	Auxerre	W	1-0	H	CDFr10	Pauleta [73]	16 301
4-02-2006	Saint-Etienne	D	2-2	H	Lge	Pauleta [31], Pancrate [82]	43 026
8-02-2006	RC Strasbourg	D	1-1	A	Lge	Pauleta [31]	17 732
12-02-2006	Lille OSC	D	0-0	A	Lge		13 392
18-02-2006	Le Mans	L	0-1	H	Lge		39 663
25-02-2006	Nantes	D	0-0	A	Lge		32 691
5-03-2006	Olympique Marseille	D	0-0	H	Lge		43 906
11-03-2006	Nancy-Lorraine	D	1-1	A	Lge	Kalou [77]	17 631
14-03-2006	Lyon La Duchère	W	3-0	A	CDFr11	Bueno [30], Pauleta 2 [74 76]	9 000
19-03-2006	Auxerre	W	4-1	H	Lge	Kalou 2 [26 57], Pauleta 2 [36 55]	35 528
26-03-2006	Monaco	D	1-1	A	Lge	Paulo Cesar [16]	11 668
2-04-2006	Girondins Bordeaux	W	3-1	H	Lge	Pauleta 3 [6 37 42]	41 913
8-04-2006	RC Lens	D	1-1	A	Lge	Kalou [77]	39 513
11-04-2006	Lille OSC	W	2-1	H	CDFqf	Kalou [40], Pauleta [57]	21 345
16-04-2006	Olympique Lyonnais	L	0-1	H	Lge		43 128
20-04-2006	Nantes	W	2-1	A	CDFsf	Pancrate [68], Pauleta [86]	35 000
29-04-2006	Olympique Marseille	W	2-1	N	CDFf	Kalou [6], Dhorasoo [49]	80 000
3-05-2006	Stade Rennais	D	1-1	A	Lge	Kalou [90]	28 425
6-05-2006	Ajaccio	L	2-4	H	Lge	Yepes [30], Pauleta [52]	41 361
13-05-2006	Metz	L	0-1	A	Lge		15 807

Lge = Ligue 1 • CDF = Coupe de France • LC = Coupe de la Ligue • gD = Group D • r2 = second round • r3 = third round • r9 = ninth round • r10 = tenth round • r11 = eleventh round • qf = quarter-final • sf = semi-final • f = final • N = Stade de France

LEAGUE CUP FINALS

Year	Winners	Score	Runners-up
1995	Paris St-Germain	2-0	SC Bastia
1996	FC Metz	0-0 5-4p	Olympique Lyonnais
1997	RC Strasbourg	0-0 6-5p	Girondins Bordeaux
1998	Paris St-Germain	2-2 4-2p	Girondins Bordeaux
1999	RC Lens	1-0	FC Metz
2000	Gueugnon	2-0	Paris St-Germain
2001	Olympique Lyonnais	2-1	AS Monaco
2002	Girondins Bordeaux	3-0	FC Lorient
2003	AS Monaco	4-1	FC Sochaux
2004	FC Sochaux	1-1 5-4p	FC Nantes
2005	RC Strasbourg	2-1	SM Caen
2006	AS Nancy-Lorraine	2-1	OGC Nice

FRO – FAROE ISLANDS

NATIONAL TEAM RECORD
JULY 1ST 2002 TO JULY 9TH 2006

PL	W	D	L	F	A	%
25	4	2	19	22	64	20

FIFA/COCA-COLA WORLD RANKING

1993	1994	1995	1996	1997	1998	1999	2000	2001	2002	2003	2004	2005	High		Low	
115	133	120	135	117	125	112	117	117	114	126	131	132	**104**	07/99	**169**	07/06

2005–2006											
08/05	09/05	10/05	11/05	12/05	01/06	02/06	03/06	04/06	05/06	06/06	07/06
126	134	134	131	132	132	132	135	137	139	-	169

The Faroe Islands have been one of the nations worst affected by the change in the way the FIFA/Coca-Cola World Ranking is calculated, falling 30 places to 169th in July 2006 when the changes came into effect. It was perhaps no surprise given the poor FIFA World Cup™ qualifying campaign, a campaign that saw the national team finish with just a single point, from an away game in Cyprus. Oddly enough, the facilities for football in the Faroes have improved dramatically in the last few years, but that obviously doesn't necessarily lead to better results. There was, however, great excitement in the League with a four-way race for the title between Tórshavn rivals B'36 and

INTERNATIONAL HONOURS
None

HB, along with Skála and NSI Runavík. Going into the last day, there was a winner-takes-all tie between B'36 and HB although if that had been a draw and Skála had beaten GI, Skála would have been crowned champions. In the event B'36 won 2-1 to win their seventh title. There was also joy for B'36 earlier in the season when they knocked Iceland's IBV out of the UEFA Cup in the first preliminary round before losing to Denmark's Midtjylland. The Cup Final, usually played each year on the national Olaifest holiday, which falls just after the UEFA deadline for European entries, was delayed until later in the season.

THE FIFA BIG COUNT OF 2000

	Male	Female		Male	Female
Registered players	1 406	208	Referees	97	0
Non registered players	1 800	200	Officials	865	125
Youth players	3 317	954	Total involved	8 972	
Total players	7 885		Number of clubs	40	
Professional players	0	0	Number of teams	309	

The Faroe Islands' Football Association (FSF)
Gundadalur, PO Box 3028, Tórshavn 110, Faroe Islands
Tel +298 351979   Fax +298 319079
fsf@football.fo   www.football.fo
President: HOLM Oli   General Secretary: MIKLADAL Isak
Vice-President: A LIDARENDA Niklas   Treasurer: TBD   Media Officer: MIKLADAL Isak
Men's Coach: OLSEN Jogvan   Women's Coach: HANSEN Alvur
FSF formed: 1979   UEFA: 1988   FIFA: 1988
White shirts with blue trimmings, Blue shorts, White socks or Blue shirts with white trimmings, White shorts, White socks

RECENT INTERNATIONAL MATCHES PLAYED BY THE FAROE ISLANDS

2002	Opponents	Score		Venue	Comp	Scorers	Att	Referee
21-08	Liechtenstein	W	3-1	Tórshavn	Fr	Jacobsen.JR [70], Benjaminsen [75], Johnsson.J [84]	3 200	Orrason ISL
7-09	Scotland	D	2-2	Toftir	ECq	Petersen.J 2 [7 13]	4 000	Granat POL
12-10	Lithuania	L	0-2	Kaunas	ECq		2 500	Delevic YUG
16-10	Germany	L	1-2	Hannover	ECq	Friedrich OG [45]	36 628	Koren ISR
2003								
27-04	Kazakhstan	W	3-2	Toftir	Fr	Borg [17p], Petersen.J [45], Lakjuni [49]	420	Jakobsson ISL
29-04	Kazakhstan	W	2-1	Tórshavn	Fr	Flotum [65], Johnsson.J [75]	800	Bergmann ISL
7-06	Iceland	L	1-2	Reykjavik	ECq	Jacobsen.R [62]	6 038	Liba CZE
11-06	Germany	L	0-2	Tórshavn	ECq		6 130	Wegereef NED
20-08	Iceland	L	1-2	Toftir	ECq	Jacobsen.R [65]	3 416	Iturralde Gonzalez ESP
6-09	Scotland	L	1-3	Glasgow	ECq	Johnsson.J [35]	40 901	Ceferin SVN
10-09	Lithuania	L	1-3	Toftir	ECq	Olsen [43]	2 175	Trivkovic CRO
2004								
21-02	Poland	L	0-6	San Fernando	Fr		100	Cascales ESP
1-06	Netherlands	L	0-3	Lausanne	Fr		3 200	Leuba SUI
18-08	Malta	W	3-2	Toftir	Fr	Borg [20], Petersen.J [35], Benjaminsen [77]	1 932	Laursen DEN
4-09	Switzerland	L	0-6	Basel	WCq		11 880	Tudor ROU
8-09	France	L	0-2	Tórshavn	WCq		5 917	Thomson SCO
9-10	Cyprus	D	2-2	Nicosia	WCq	Jorgensen.CB [21], Jacobsen.R [43]	1 400	Gadiyev AZE
13-10	Ireland Republic	L	0-2	Dublin	WCq		36 000	Lajuks LVA
2005								
4-06	Switzerland	L	1-3	Toftir	WCq	Jacobsen.R [70]	2 047	Gumienny BEL
8-06	Ireland Republic	L	0-2	Tórshavn	WCq		5 180	Guenov BUL
17-08	Cyprus	L	0-3	Toftir	WCq		2 720	Johannesson SWE
3-09	France	L	0-3	Lens	WCq		40 126	Jara CZE
7-09	Israel	L	0-2	Tórshavn	WCq		2 240	Vink NED
8-10	Israel	L	1-2	Tel Aviv	WCq	Samuelsen [93+]	31 857	Brugger AUT
2006								
14-05	Poland	L	0-4	Wronki	Fr		4 000	Prus USA

Fr = Friendly match • EC = UEFA EURO 2004™ • WC = FIFA World Cup™ • q = qualifier

FAROE ISLANDS NATIONAL TEAM RECORDS AND RECORD SEQUENCES

Records			Sequence records					
Victory	3-0	SMR 1995	Wins	2	1997, 2002, 2003	Clean sheets	1	
Defeat	0-9	ISL 1985	Defeats	13	1992-1995	Goals scored	5	1986
Player Caps	77	JOHANNESEN Oli	Undefeated	3	2002	Without goal	7	1991-1992
Player Goals	9	JONSSON Todi	Without win	26	1990-1995	Goals against	26	1990-1995

FAROE ISLANDS COUNTRY INFORMATION

Capital	Tórshavn	Independence	Self governing division of	GDP per Capita	$22 000
Population	46 662	Status	the Kingdom of Denmark	GNP Ranking	n/a
Area km²	1 399	Language	Faroese, Danish	Dialling code	+298
Population density	33 per km²	Literacy rate	99%	Internet code	.fo
% in urban areas	n/a	Main religion	Christian	GMT + / −	0
Towns/Cities ('000)	Tórshavn 13; Klaksvik 4; Hoyvik 2; Argir 1; Fuglafjørdur 1; Vágur 1; Tvøroyri 1				
Neighbours (km)	North Atlantic Ocean 1 117				
Main stadia	Svangaskard − Toftir 7 000; Gundadalur − Tórshavn 8 020; Tórsvøllur − Tórshavn 7 000				

FAROE ISLANDS NATIONAL TEAM PLAYERS AND COACHES

Record Caps			Record Goals			Recent Coaches	
JOHANNESEN Oli	1992-'06	77	JONSSON Todi	1991-'05	9	GUDLAUGSSON Páll	1993
KNUDSEN Jens-Martin	1988-'06	65	ARGE Uni	1992-'02	8	NORDBUD Jogvan	1993
JOHNSSON Julian	1995-'05	61	PETERSEN John	1995-'04	6	SIMONSEN Allan	1994-'02
PETERSEN John	1995-'04	57	JACOBSEN Rógvi	1999-'05	6	LARSEN Henrik	2002-
MORKORE Allan	1990-'01	54	JOHNSSON Julian	1995-'05	4		
HANSEN Ossur	1992-'02	51	MULLER Jan Allan	1988-'98	4		
JONSSON Todi	1991-'05	45	MORKORE Kurt	1988-'01	3		
HANSEN Jens Kristian	1994-'02	44	HANSEN Jens Kristian	1994-'02	3		
BORG Jákup	1998-'06	43					
MIKKELSEN Jákup	1995-'06	42					

CLUB DIRECTORY

Club	Town/City	Stadium	Capacity	www.	Lge	Cup
B'36 (Fótbóltsfelagid B'36)	Tórshavn	Gundadalur	8 020	b36.fo	7	3
EB/Streymur	Oyrabakki	Molini	1 000	eb-streymur.fo	0	0
GI (Gøtu Itróttarfelag)	Gøtu	Serpugerdi	3 000	gigotu.fo	6	6
HB (Havnar Bóltfelag)	Tórshavn	Gundadalur	8 020	hb.fo	18	14
IF (Itróttarfelag Fuglarfjørdur)	Fuglafjørdur	Fuglafjørdur	3 000	if.fo	1	0
KI (Klaksvikar Itróttarfelag)	Klaksvik	Klaksvik	4 000	ki-klaksvik.fo	16	4
NSI (Nes Soknar Itróttarfelag)	Runavik	Runavik	2 000	nsi.fo	0	2
Skála	Skali	Skali	1 000		0	0
TB (Tvøroyrar Bóltfelag)	Tvøroyri	Sevmyri	3 000	tb.fo	8	4
VB (Vágs Bóltfelag)	Vágur	Vestri a Eidinum	3 000	vb1905.fo	1	1

RECENT LEAGUE AND CUP RECORD

	Championship						Cup		
Year	Champions	Pts	Runners-up	Pts	Third	Pts	Winners	Score	Runners-up
1990	HB Tórshavn	24	B'36 Tórshavn	20	MB Midvagur	19	KI Klaksvik	6-1	GI Gøtu
1991	KI Klaksvík	24	B'36 Tórshavn	24	GI Gøtu	23	B'36 Tórshavn	3-0	HB Tórshavn
1992	B'68 Toftir	27	GI Gøtu	25	KI Klaksvík	23	HB Tórshavn	1-0	KI Klaksvík
1993	GI Gøtu	28	HB Tórshavn	25	KI Klaksvík	23	B'71 Sandur	1-1 2-1	HB Tórshavn
1994	GI Gøtu	32	HB Tórshavn	30	B'71 Sandur	24	KI Klaksvik	2-1	B'71 Sandur
1995	GI Gøtu	41	HB Tórshavn	33	B'68 Tórshavn	30	HB Tórshavn	3-1	B'68 Toftir
1996	GI Gøtu	39	KI Klaksvik	39	HB Tórshavn	32	GI Gøtu	2-2 5-3	HB Tórshavn
1997	B'36 Tórshavn	48	HB Tórshavn	41	GI Gøtu	35	GI Gøtu	6-0	VB Vágur
1998	HB Tórshavn	45	KI Klaksvík	38	B'36 Tórshavn	37	HB Tórshavn	2-0	KI Klaksvík
1999	KI Klaksvik	41	GI Gøtu	39	B'36 Tórshavn	38	KI Klaksvik	3-1	B'36 Tórshavn
2000	VB Vágur	40	HB Tórshavn	38	B'68 Toftir	31	GI Gøtu	1-0	HB Tórshavn
2001	B'36 Tórshavn	46	GI Gøtu	42	B'68 Toftir	31	B'36 Tórshavn	1-0	KI Klaksvík
2002	HB Tórshavn	41	NSI Runavík	36	KI Klaksvik	33	NSI Runavik	2-1	HB Tórshavn
2003	HB Tórshavn	41	B'36 Tórshavn	37	B'68 Toftir	35	B'36 Tórshavn	3-1	GI Gøtu
2004	HB Tórshavn	41	B'36 Tórshavn	34	Skála	30	HB Tórshavn	3-1	NSI Runavik
2005	B'36 Tórshavn	54	Skála	50	HB Tórshavn	50	GI Gøtu	4-1	IF Fuglafyørdur

FAROE ISLANDS 2005

1. DEILD

Team	Pl	W	D	L	F	A	Pts	B'36	Skála	HB	NSI	EB	IF	KI	VB	GI	TB
B'36 Tórshavn †	27	15	9	3	38	17	54		2-2	0-0 2-1	0-1 2-0	1-0 0-1	1-1	2-1 0-0	1-0	3-0 3-1	0-0
Skála ‡	27	13	11	3	55	30	50	1-1 2-2		4-3 1-1	3-1	1-1	3-3 2-1	4-0	0-1 3-1	2-2	5-1 2-0
HB Tórshavn	27	15	5	7	66	35	50	1-1	1-2		3-1	2-1	4-0 3-0	6-0 9-0	2-1 2-1	3-1 4-1	3-1 4-1
NSI Runavík	27	14	8	5	58	44	50	1-0	1-0	3-3 2-1		2-5	1-1 4-1	1-0	5-1 3-1	1-1	1-1 2-0
EB/Streymur Eidi	27	11	10	6	48	35	43	1-2	0-0 0-1	4-0	2-2		2-2	2-2 1-1	1-0	1-1 6-1	1-1 3-0
IF Fuglafjørdur	27	6	9	12	32	57	27	0-2 0-2	0-0	1-1	1-2	2-3		0-3 3-0	3-3	4-3 1-3	1-0 0-0
KI Klaksvík	27	7	4	16	40	52	25	0-2 0-2	0-0	4-3	2-3	3-5	6-0-1 2-4		0-2	1-1 5-1	1-2 6-1
VB Vágur	27	6	6	15	36	57	24	0-3 1-2	1-5	1-0	2-2 2-3	1-1	0-1 3-2	5-1		0-1 0-3	0-1 5-1
GI Gøtu	27	6	5	16	35	58	23	1-2	2-3 1-4	0-2	0-0 1-5	1-2	1-5 3-0	1-2	1-2 1-1		2-1
TB Tvøroyri	27	5	7	15	26	49	22	0-0	1-2	1-0 1-2	4-4	3-0 1-1	0-1 0-0	1-2	0-2 3-0	3-1	

28/03/2005 - 22/10/2005 • † Qualified for the UEFA Champions League • ‡ Qualified for the UEFA Cup • Relegation play-off: GI 3-0 4-1 B'71 •
Top scorers: Christian JACOBSEN, NSI, 18; Sorin ANGHEL, EB/Streymur, 16; Jonhard FREDERIKSBERG, Skála, 13; Bogi GREGERSEN, Skála, 12

FAROE ISLANDS 2005
2. DEILD

Team	Pl	W	D	L	F	A	Pts
B'68 Toftir	18	14	3	1	71	16	45
B'71 Sandur	18	13	2	3	66	20	41
FS Vágar	18	12	2	4	51	18	38
AB Argir	18	12	2	4	55	33	38
HB Tórshavn 2	18	7	1	10	40	44	22
LIF Leirvík	18	6	3	9	45	48	21
Royn Hvalba	18	6	2	10	27	52	20
Sumba	18	6	1	11	35	68	19
B'36 Tórshavn 2	18	4	3	11	21	47	15
GI Gøtu 2	18	0	1	17	18	83	1

30/04/2005 - 22/10/2005
Relegation play-off: KI Klaksvík 2 2-1 5-2 B'36 Tórshavn 2

FAROE ISLANDS 2005
3. DEILD

Team	Pl	W	D	L	F	A	Pts
SI Sorvágur	16	11	2	3	70	31	35
KI Klaksvík 2	16	6	6	4	39	24	24
B'68 Toftir	16	7	2	7	22	26	23
NSI Runavík 2	16	7	2	7	28	36	23
IF Fuglafjørdur 2	16	6	4	6	42	49	22
Fram Tórshavn	16	5	5	6	27	27	20
EB/Streymur Eidi 2	16	6	1	9	40	48	19
Skála 2	16	5	3	8	26	34	18
HB Tórshavn 3	16	5	3	8	30	49	18
VB Vágur							Excluded

1/05/2005 - 1/10/2005

GAB – GABON

NATIONAL TEAM RECORD
JULY 1ST 2002 TO JULY 9TH 2006

PL	W	D	L	F	A	%
38	11	13	14	48	41	46.1

FIFA/COCA-COLA WORLD RANKING

1993	1994	1995	1996	1997	1998	1999	2000	2001	2002	2003	2004	2005	High		Low	
60	64	67	46	63	82	74	89	102	121	111	109	104	**45**	01/96	**125**	05/03

2005–2006										
08/05	09/05	10/05	11/05	12/05	01/06	02/06	03/06	04/06	05/06	06/06	07/06
98	105	102	102	104	104	104	105	106	105	-	96

Just four points from their last five matches in the FIFA World Cup™ qualifiers proved a major disappointment to the ambitions of Gabon, who were hoping for at least a third place finish in the qualifying tournament and a place at the African Nations Cup finals in Egypt. Instead the central African country finished fourth, five points behind nearest rivals Zimbabwe. It cost the former FIFA World Cup™ winner, Brazilian Jairzinho his job. He was replaced by another ex-FIFA World Cup™ star in diminutive Frenchman Alain Giresse, who arrived just in time to see Azingo Nationale finish in third place at the CEMAC tournament in Bata, Equatorial Guinea. The

INTERNATIONAL HONOURS
None

Gabonese played with a home-based side but will be much stronger when they start the qualifying campaign for the 2008 African Nations Cup finals. Mangasport won the League and Cup double in 2005, finishing three points clear of US Bitam and beating Sogea 2-0 in the Cup Final. Gabon's hopes of being hosts of the 2010 African Nations Cup finals received a boost at around the same time as the country withdrew from the hosting of the 2006 African women's championship. A joint bid from Gabon and Equatorial Guinea made it to the final list of four to be considered by the Confederation of African Football.

THE FIFA BIG COUNT OF 2000

	Male	Female		Male	Female
Registered players	5 000	0	Referees	100	0
Non registered players	5 000	0	Officials	800	0
Youth players	2 500	0	Total involved	13 400	
Total players	12 500		Number of clubs	50	
Professional players	0	0	Number of teams	200	

Fédération Gabonaise de Football (FGF)
Case postale 181, Libreville, Gabon
Tel +241 774862   Fax +241 564199
fegafoot@internetgabon.com   www.none
President: ABABE Leon   General Secretary: BOUASSA MOUSSADJI Barthelemy
Vice-President: OSSAMY NDJOUBI Alain   Treasurer: NZE NGUEMA Jean   Media Officer: SALA Ngouahbeaud
Men's Coach: GIRESSE Alain   Women's Coach: None
FGF formed: 1962   CAF: 1967   FIFA: 1963
Green shirts, Blue shorts, White socks or Yellow shirts, Yellow shorts, White socks

RECENT INTERNATIONAL MATCHES PLAYED BY GABON

2002	Opponents	Score		Venue	Comp	Scorers	Att	Referee
25-08	Angola	L	0-1	Luanda	Fr		10 000	
1-09	Congo	D	0-0	Brazzaville	Fr			
7-09	Morocco	L	0-1	Libreville	CNq		30 000	Evehe Devine CMR
12-10	Sierra Leone	L	0-2	Freetown	CNq			Ekoue-Toulan TOG
2003								
29-03	Equatorial Guinea	W	4-0	Libreville	CNq	Moulengui [9], Yannick 2 [39 48], Bito'o [67p]		Tavares Neto STP
8-06	Equatorial Guinea	L	1-2	Malabo	CNq	Dissikadie [43]		Buenkadila COD
13-06	Andorra	W	2-0	Andorra la Vella	Fr			Ledentu FRA
20-06	Morocco	L	0-2	Rabat	CNq		15 000	Shelmani LBY
6-07	Sierra Leone	W	2-0	Libreville	CNq	Mbanangoye [33], Mintsa		
24-09	Algeria	D	2-2	Algiers	Fr	Nguéma [21], Moubamba [83]. L 3-4p	2 000	Zekkini ALG
26-09	Benin	W	4-0	Algiers	Fr	Mockom [17], Mintsa [44], Nguéma 2 [65 74]		
12-10	Burundi	D	0-0	Bujumbura	WCq		10 000	Itur KEN
8-11	Burkina Faso	D	0-0	Moanda	Fr			
15-11	Burundi	W	4-1	Libreville	WCq	Nzigou [2], Mwinyi OG [16], Nguéma 2 [38 80]	15 000	Ndoye SEN
5-12	Congo	L	2-3	Brazzaville	CMr1	Nguéma [40], Edou [63]		Tchoumba CMR
9-12	Congo	D	1-1	Brazzaville	CMr1			
11-12	Central African Rep	L	0-2	Brazzaville	CMsf			
13-12	Congo	L	0-1	Brazzaville	CM3p			
2004								
29-05	Egypt	L	0-2	Cairo	Fr		15 000	Auda EGY
5-06	Zimbabwe	D	1-1	Libreville	WCq	Zue [52]	25 000	Quartey GHA
19-06	Rwanda	L	1-3	Kigali	WCq	Zue [20]	16 325	Abdulkadir TAN
3-07	Angola	D	2-2	Libreville	WCq	Issiemou [44], Zue [49]	20 000	Louzaya CGO
5-09	Algeria	W	3-0	Annaba	WCq	Aubame [56], Akieremy [73], Bito'o [84]	51 000	Ndoye SEN
3-10	Benin	W	2-0	Libreville	Fr	Djissikadie, Nguéma		
9-10	Nigeria	D	1-1	Libreville	WCq	Issiemou [29]	26 000	Yameogo BFA
2005								
3-02	Central African Rep	W	4-0	Libreville	CMr1	Akoué [32p], Nguéma [42], Yinda 2 [52 82]		
8-02	Congo	W	1-0	Libreville	CMr1	Poaty [38]		
10-02	Chad	L	2-3	Libreville	CMsf	Akoué [58p], Mabiala [69]		
12-02	Congo	W	2-1	Libreville	CM3p	Yembi, Akoué		
19-03	Congo	D	0-0	Libreville	Fr			
26-03	Nigeria	L	0-2	Port Harcourt	WCq		16 489	Hicuburundi BDI
5-06	Zimbabwe	L	0-1	Harare	WCq		55 000	Ssegonga UGA
18-06	Rwanda	W	3-0	Libreville	WCq	Djissikadie [10], Londo [55], Zue [60]	10 000	El Arjoun MAR
4-09	Angola	L	0-3	Luanda	WCq			
8-10	Algeria	D	0-0	Port-Gentil	WCq			
2006								
4-03	Cameroon †	D	0-0	Malabo	CMr1			
8-03	Central African Rep	D	2-2	Malabo	CMr1			
11-03	Equatorial Guinea	D	0-0	Bata	CMsf	L 2-4p		
14-03	Chad	D	2-2	Bata	CM3p	W 7-6p		

Fr = Friendly match • CN = CAF African Cup of Nations • CM = CEMAC Cup • WC = FIFA World Cup™
q = qualifier • r1 = first round group • sf = semi-final • 3p = third place play-off • † Not a full international

GABON NATIONAL TEAM RECORDS AND RECORD SEQUENCES

Records			Sequence records					
Victory	7-0	BEN 1995	Wins	4	1985, 1992	Clean sheets	5	1986-87, 1988
Defeat	1-6	GUI 1967	Defeats	5	1967-1971	Goals scored	14	1998-1999
Player Caps	n/a		Undefeated	11	1996	Without goal	4	2002
Player Goals	n/a		Without win	20	1977-1984	Goals against	11	1996-1997

GABON COUNTRY INFORMATION

Capital	Libreville	Independence	1960 from France	GDP per Capita	5 500
Population	1 355 246	Status	Republic	GNP Ranking	121
Area km²	267 667	Language	French	Dialling code	+241
Population density	5 per km²	Literacy rate	63%	Internet code	.ga
% in urban areas	%	Main religion	Christian 75%	GMT + / –	+1
Towns/Cities ('000)	Libreville 578; Port-Gentil 109; Masuku 42; Oyem 30; Moanda 30; Mouila 22; Lambaréné 20				
Neighbours (km)	Equatorial Guinea 350; Cameroon 298; Congo 1 903				
Main stadia	Stade Omar Bongo – Libreville 40 000				

GABON 2005
CHAMPIONNAT NATIONAL FINAL STAGE

	Pl	W	D	L	F	A	Pts	Ma	USB	So	DT	105	Mi
Mangasport Moanda †	10	7	2	1	16	6	23		1-1	2-1	2-0	1-0	2-0
US Bitam	10	6	2	2	12	10	20	2-1		2-1	1-1	2-1	1-0
Sogéa	9	4	1	4	11	9	13	0-2	1-0		-	2-1	0-0
Delta Téléstar	8	2	3	3	9	10	9	1-2	0-1	2-1		-	2-2
FC 105 Libreville	9	2	2	5	8	11	8	1-1	3-0	0-2	0-2		0-0
Missiles Libreville	10	0	4	6	5	15	4	0-2	1-2	0-3	1-1	1-2	

24/08/2005 - 13/11/2005 • † Qualified for the 2006 CAF Champions League • TP Akwembé and USM Libreville relegated after finishing bottom of their first round groups

COUPE DU GABON INTERCLUBS 2005

Round of 16			Quarter-finals		Semi-finals		Final	
Mangasport Moanda	0	5p						
USM Libreville	0	4p	Mangasport Moanda	2				
Cercle Mbérie Sportif	1		Delta Téléstar	0				
Delta Téléstar	2				Mangasport Moanda	0 4p		
US Bitam	2				Wongosport	0 3p		
Stade Mandji	1		US Bitam	0				
Jeunesse Libreville	0		Wongosport	2			Mangasport Moanda	2
Wongosport	2						Sogéa ‡	0
Missiles Libreville	3							
Stade d'Akébé	1		Missiles Libreville	w-o				
Munadji 76 Tchibanga	2	3p	FC 105 Libreville		Missiles Libreville	1		
FC 105 Libreville	2	4p			Sogéa	2		
TP Akwembé	2		TP Akwembé	0				
Ogooué Maritime	0							
US Oyem	0		Sogéa	2				
Sogéa	1							

‡ Qualified for the CAF Confederation Cup

CUP FINAL
Stade Omar Bongo, Libreville, 31-07-2005

Scorers - Humel Yinda [37], Seydou Barro [57] for Mangasport

RECENT LEAGUE AND CUP RECORD

	Championship						Cup		
Year	Champions	Pts	Runners-up	Pts	Third	Pts	Winners	Score	Runners-up
1999	Petrosport †	63	FC 105	52	USM Libreville	46	US Bitam	2-1	Aigles Verts
2000	Mangasport	30	AO Evizo	30	FC 105	22	AO Evizo		
2001	FC 105	62	Mangasport	59	TP Akwembé	59	Mangasport	1-0	TP Akwembé
2002	USM Libreville	54	FC 105	49	Mangasport	39	USM Libreville	1-1 4-2p	Jeunesse
2003	US Bitam	45	FC 105	45	Wongosport	37	US Bitam	1-1 4-3p	USM Libreville
2004	Mangasport	32	Téléstar	31	US Bitam	26	FC 105	3-2	Mangasport
2005	Mangasport	23	US Bitam	20	Sogéa	13	Mangasport	2-0	Sogéa

† Championship abandoned in 1999 - FC 105 were later awarded the title

GAM – GAMBIA

NATIONAL TEAM RECORD
JULY 1ST 2002 TO JULY 9TH 2006

PL	W	D	L	F	A	%
11	5	1	5	15	10	50

FIFA/COCA-COLA WORLD RANKING

1993	1994	1995	1996	1997	1998	1999	2000	2001	2002	2003	2004	2005		High		Low
125	117	112	128	132	135	151	155	148	143	138	154	164		101 09/94		166 05/06

2005–2006											
08/05	09/05	10/05	11/05	12/05	01/06	02/06	03/06	04/06	05/06	06/06	07/06
160	160	161	161	164	164	164	166	166	166	-	158

Gambia's participation at the FIFA U-17 World Championship in Peru last September exposed the tiny west African country to a new level of competition and held out the promise of a much brighter footballing future for one of the continent's smallest countries, especially given the heroic performances during the tournament. Gambia were winners of the African under-17 championship on home soil in 2005 and in Peru they caused a sensation by beating Brazil and Qatar in the first two matches they played. They then lost to the Netherlands in the third, a result that unbelievably saw them fail to make the knock-out stage. The young players have not had the opportunity to

INTERNATIONAL HONOURS
CAF African U-17 Championship 2005

graduate up into the country's senior side, the Hawks, which has played just once over the last three years.The team will be back into a cycle of competition, however, with the qualifiers for the 2008 African Nations Cup finals. Wallidan won a second successive championship but could not complete a League and Cup double when they were beaten 4-1 by Bakau United in the Cup Final. Both sides did qualify for African competition in 2006 but after entering the CAF Champions League and CAF Confederation Cup they then withdrew because of financial constraints, exposing themselves to three year bans from the Confederation of African Football.

THE FIFA BIG COUNT OF 2000

	Male	Female		Male	Female
Registered players	2 500	0	Referees	100	0
Non registered players	2 500	0	Officials	600	0
Youth players	1 000	0	Total involved	6 700	
Total players	6 000		Number of clubs	50	
Professional players	0	0	Number of teams	200	

Gambia Football Association (GFA)
Independence Stadium, Bakau, PO Box 523, Banjul, The Gambia
Tel +220 4496980   Fax +220 4494802
info@gambiafa.org   www.gambiafa.org
President: KINTEH Seedy   General Secretary: BOJANG Jammeh
Vice-President: TAMBA Lang Tombong Lt Col   Treasurer: CEESSAY Kemo   Media Officer: SAIWE Pap
Men's Coach: NDONG Sang   Women's Coach: PASUWAREH Faye
GFA formed: 1952   CAF: 1962   FIFA: 1966
Red shirts, Red shorts, Red socks or Blue shirts, Blue shorts, Blue socks

RECENT INTERNATIONAL MATCHES PLAYED BY GAMBIA

2002	Opponents	Score		Venue	Comp	Scorers	Att	Referee
25-08	Sierra Leone	W	1-0	Banjul	Fr	Samba [58]		
1-09	Guinea	W	1-0	Banjul	Fr	Jatta [70]		
12-10	Lesotho	W	6-0	Banjul	CNq	Nyang 2 [7 40], Sarr [45], Ceesay 2 [55 88], Soli	25 000	Ba MTN
2003								
16-02	Nigeria	L	0-1	Banjul	Fr		30 000	
30-03	Senegal	D	0-0	Banjul	CNq		30 000	Djingarey NIG
31-05	Mauritania	W	4-1	Banjul	Fr			
7-06	Senegal	L	1-3	Dakar	CNq	Sillah [63]		Guirat TUN
6-07	Lesotho	L	0-1	Maseru	CNq		10 000	
12-10	Liberia	W	2-0	Bakau	WCq	Njie [64], Sonko [79]	20 000	Codjia BEN
16-11	Liberia	L	0-3	Monrovia	WCq		10 000	Coulibaly MLI
2004								
No international matches played in 2004								
2005								
12-06	Sierra Leone	L	0-1	Freetown	Fr			
2006								
No international matches played in 2006 before July								

Fr = Friendly match • CN = CAF African Cup of Nations • WC = FIFA World Cup™ • q = qualifier

GAMBIA NATIONAL TEAM RECORDS AND RECORD SEQUENCES

Records			Sequence records					
Victory	6-0	LES 2002	Wins	3	2002	Clean sheets	3	1991, 2002
Defeat	0-8	GUI 1972	Defeats	9	1968-1977	Goals scored	7	1962-1971
Player Caps	n/a		Undefeated	4	Four times	Without goal	7	1998-2000
Player Goals	n/a		Without win	17	1997-2001	Goals against	16	1962-1979

RECENT LEAGUE AND CUP RECORD

	Championship						Cup		
Year	Champions	Pts	Runners-up	Pts	Third	Pts	Winners	Score	Runners-up
1997	Real Banjul						Real Banjul	1-0	Banjul Hawks
1998	Real Banjul						Wallidan	1-1 4-3p	Ports Authority
1999	Ports Authority						Wallidan	1-1 4-3p	Mass Sosseh
2000	Real Banjul	35	Banjul Hawks	34	Wallidan	30	Steve Biko	1-1 4-2p	Wallidan
2001	Wallidan	38	Steve Biko	32	Real Banjul	27	Wallidan	3-0	Blackpool
2002	Wallidan	37	Real Banjul	34	Banjul Hawks	33	Wallidan	1-0	Real Banjul
2003	Armed Forces						Wallidan	1-0	Banjul Hawks
2004	Wallidan	38	Banjul Hawks	35	Ports Authority	28	Wallidan	1-1 9-8p	Armed Forces
2005	Wallidan	29	GAMTEL	29	Banjul Hawks	29	Bakau United	4-1	Wallidan

GAMBIA COUNTRY INFORMATION

Capital	Banjul	Independence	1965 from the UK	GDP per Capita	$1 700
Population	1 546 848	Status	Republic	GNP Ranking	172
Area km²	11 300	Language	English	Dialling code	+220
Population density	136 per km²	Literacy rate	33%	Internet code	.gm
% in urban areas	26%	Main religion	Muslim 90%	GMT +/–	0
Towns/Cities ('000)	Serekunda 218; Brikama 101; Bakau 47; Farafenni 36; Banjul 34; Lamin 16; Sukuta 15				
Neighbours (km)	Senegal 740; Atlantic Ocean 80				
Main stadia	Independence Stadium – Bakau 20 000; Brikama – Banjul 15 000				

GEO – GEORGIA

NATIONAL TEAM RECORD
JULY 1ST 2002 TO JULY 9TH 2006

PL	W	D	L	F	A	%
35	7	7	21	35	71	30

FIFA/COCA-COLA WORLD RANKING

1993	1994	1995	1996	1997	1998	1999	2000	2001	2002	2003	2004	2005	High		Low	
-	92	79	95	69	52	66	66	58	90	93	104	104	**42**	09/98	**156**	04/94

					2005–2006						
08/05	09/05	10/05	11/05	12/05	01/06	02/06	03/06	04/06	05/06	06/06	07/06
103	104	100	100	104	105	105	104	101	101	-	87

After winning the first ten League titles after independence, Dinamo Tbilisi are finding life just a touch more difficult nowadays and in the past seven seasons they have been champions just twice. The latest teams to challenge the established order are Sioni from the town of Bolnisi near the Armenian border and Ameri from the capital Tbilisi. They both won their first honours in 2006 with Sioni the unlikely winners of the Championship following a close fought battle with WIT Georgia in the expanded 16 team tournament. The race went down to the last match of the season with Sioni beating Torpedo 4-0 whilst WIT could only draw with Dinamo Batumi. The following

INTERNATIONAL HONOURS
None

Saturday Ameri met Zestafoni in their first Cup Final - just four years after their formation. It went to penalties but they consigned Zestafoni to the runners-up spot for the second year running. It was all change for the national team with experienced German coach Klaus Toppmoller brought in to resuscitate an ailing side that had experienced a very poor qualifying campaign for the 2006 FIFA World Cup™, a campaign that saw just two wins in the 12 games played. Georgia conceded five goals at home to Turkey and six away in Copenhagen while the 0-0 draw at home to Kazakhstan rather embarrassingly gave their opponents a first point after 13 consecutive defeats.

THE FIFA BIG COUNT OF 2000

	Male	Female		Male	Female
Registered players	2 700	100	Referees	87	0
Non registered players	110 000	150	Officials	1 000	0
Youth players	21 100	100	Total involved	135 237	
Total players	134 150		Number of clubs	127	
Professional players	900	0	Number of teams	728	

Georgian Football Federation (GFF)
76a Chavchavadze Avenue, Tbilisi 0162, Georgia
Tel +995 32 912680   Fax +995 32 001128
gff@gff.ge   www.gff.ge
President: AKHALKATSI Nodar   General Secretary: UGULAVA Ucha
Vice-President: KAVTARADZE Gogi ·   Treasurer: CHKHIKVADZE Nargiza   Media Officer: TZONBILADZE Alexander
Men's Coach: TOPPMOLLER Klaus   Women's Coach: JAPARIDZE Maia
GFF formed: 1990   UEFA: 1992   FIFA: 1992
White shirts with red trimmings, White shorts, White socks or Red shirts with white trimmings, Red shorts, Red socks

RECENT INTERNATIONAL MATCHES PLAYED BY GEORGIA

2002	Opponents	Score	Venue	Comp	Scorers	Att	Referee
21-08	Turkey	L 0-3	Trabzon	Fr		15 000	Agelakis GRE
8-09	Switzerland	L 1-4	Basle	ECq	Arveladze.S [62]	20 500	Hrinak SVK
2003							
12-02	Moldova	D 2-2	Tbilisi	Fr	Chaladze [61], Ashvetia [83]	7 000	Hovanisyan ARM
29-03	Republic of Ireland	L 1-2	Tbilisi	ECq	Kobiashvili [62]	15 000	Vassaras GRE
2-04	Switzerland	D 0-0	Tbilisi	ECq		10 000	Trivkovic CRO
30-04	Russia	W 1-0	Tbilisi	ECq	Asatiani [11]	11 000	Wack GER
11-06	Republic of Ireland	L 0-2	Dublin	ECq		36 000	Iturralde Gonzalez ESP
6-09	Albania	W 3-0	Tbilisi	ECq	Arveladze.S 2 [9 44], Ashvetia [18]	18 000	Vollquartz DEN
10-09	Albania	L 1-3	Tirana	ECq	Arveladze.S [63]	10 500	Salomir ROU
11-10	Russia	L 1-3	Moscow	ECq	Iashvili [5]	30 000	Plautz AUT
2004							
18-02	Romania	L 0-3	Larnaca	Fr		200	Lajuks LVA
19-02	Cyprus	L 1-3	Nicosia	Fr	Gabidauri [56]		Kapitanis CYP
21-02	Armenia	L 0-2	Nicosia	Fr		200	Loizou CYP
27-05	Israel	L 0-1	Tbilisi	Fr		24 000	Oriekhov UKR
18-08	Moldova	L 0-1	Tiraspol	Fr		8 000	Godulyan UKR
4-09	Turkey	D 1-1	Trabzon	WCq	Asatiani [85]	10 169	Medina Cantalejpo ESP
8-09	Albania	W 2-0	Tbilisi	WCq	Iashvili [15], Demetradze [90+1]	20 000	Courtney NIR
13-10	Ukraine	L 0-2	Lviv	WCq		28 000	Stark GER
17-11	Denmark	D 2-2	Tbilisi	WCq	Demetradze [33], Asatiani [76]	20 000	Ceferin SVN
2005							
9-02	Lithuania	W 1-0	Tbilisi	Fr	Ashvetia [57]	1 000	Gadiyev AZE
26-03	Greece	L 1-3	Tbilisi	WCq	Asatiani [22]	23 000	Rosetti ITA
30-03	Turkey	L 2-5	Tbilisi	WCq	Amisulashvili [13], Iashvili [40]	10 000	Hauge NOR
4-06	Albania	L 2-3	Tirana	WCq	Burduli [85], Kobiashvili [94+]	BCD	Tudor ROU
17-08	Kazakhstan	W 2-1	Almaty	WCq	Demetradze 2 [50 82]	9 000	Havrilla SVK
3-09	Ukraine	D 1-1	Tbilisi	WCq	Gakhokidze [89]	BCD	Ovrebo NOR
7-09	Denmark	L 1-6	Copenhagen	WCq	Demetradze [37]	27 177	Bozinovski MKD
8-10	Kazakhstan	D 0-0	Tbilisi	WCq		BCD	Hyytia FIN
12-10	Greece	L 0-1	Athens	WCq		28 186	Trefoloni ITA
12-11	Bulgaria	L 2-6	Sofia	Fr	Jakobia [83], Gogua [90]		
16-11	Jordan	W 3-2	Tbilisi	Fr	Demetradze 2 [3 64], Arveladze.S [73]		
2006							
27-02	Moldova	L 1-5	Ta'Qali	Fr	Tskitishvili [18p]	330	Casha MLT
1-03	Malta	W 2-0	Ta'Qali	Fr	Martsvaladze [8], Kankava [18]	1 100	Banari MDV
22-03	Albania	D 0-0	Tirana	Fr			Dondarini ITA
27-05	New Zealand	L 1-3	Altenkirchen	Fr	Arveladze.S [41]	1 000	
31-05	Paraguay	L 0-1	Dornbirn	Fr		2 000	Gangle AUT

Fr = Friendly match • EC = UEFA EURO 2004™ • WC = FIFA World Cup™ • q = qualifier • BCD = Behind closed doors

GEORGIA NATIONAL TEAM RECORDS AND RECORD SEQUENCES

Records			Sequence records				
Victory	7-0	ARM 1997	Wins	5	1997-1998	Clean sheets	3	1997
Defeat	0-5	ROM 1996	Defeats	7	2003-2004	Goals scored	10	2001-2002
Player Caps	69	NEMSADZE Giorgi	Undefeated	8	1997-1998	Without goal	3	Four times
Player Goals	20	ARVELADZE Shota	Without win	8	1999, 2003-2004	Goals against	11	1998-1999

GEORGIA COUNTRY INFORMATION

Capital	Tbilisi	Independence	1991 from the Soviet Union	GDP per Capita	$2 500
Population	4 693 892	Status	Republic	GNP Ranking	130
Area km²	69 700	Language	Georgian	Dialling code	+995
Population density	67 per km²	Literacy rate	99%	Internet code	.ge
% in urban areas	58%	Main religion	Christian 83%	GMT + / –	+4
Towns/Cities ('000)	Tbilisi 1 049; Kutaisi 178; Batumi 118; Rustavi 109; Sukhumi 81; Zugdidi 73; Gori 46				
Neighbours (km)	Russia 723; Azerbaijan 322; Armenia 164; Turkey 252; Black Sea 310				
Main stadia	Boris Paichadze – Tbilisi 74 380; Mikheil Meshki – Tbilisi 27 223; Tsentral – Batumi 18 600				

GEORGIA NATIONAL TEAM PLAYERS AND COACHES

Record Caps				Record Goals				Recent Coaches	
NEMSADZE Giorgi	1992-'04	69		ARVELADZE Shota	1992-'05	20		CHIVADZE Aleksandre	1993-'96
JAMARAULI Gocha	1994-'04	62		KETSBAIA Temur	1994-'03	17		KIPIANI David	1997
KOBIASHVILI Levan	1996-'06	60		IASHVILI Aleksander	1998-'05	9		GUTSAEV Vladimir	1998-'99
ARVELADZE Shota	1992-'05	54		KAVELASHVILI Mikheil	1994-'02	9		BOSKAMP Johan	1999
KINKLADZE Giorgi	1992-'05	54		DEMETRADZE Giorgi	1996-'05	9		KIPIANI, DZODZUASHVILI	1999-'01
KETSBAIA Temur	1994-'03	52		KINKLADZE Giorgi	1992-'05	8		CHIVADZE Aleksandre	2001-'03
KALADZE Kakha	1996-'05	50		ARVELADZE Archil	1994-'02	6		SUSAK Ivo	2003
KAVELASHVILI Mikheil	1994-'02	46		JAMARAULI Gocha	1994-'04	6		GIRESSE Alain	2004-'05
DEMETRADZE Giorgi	1996-'05	43		ASHVETIA Mikheil	1996-'05	5		TOPPMOLLER Klaus	2005-
TSKITISHVILI Levan	1995-'06	39							

CLUB DIRECTORY

Club	Town/City	Stadium	Capacity	www.	Lge	Cup
FC Ameri	Tbilisi	Ameri	1 000	fcameri.ge	0	1
FC Dinamo Batumi	Batumi	Central	19 600		0	1
FC Borjomi	Borjomi	Zeinklishvili	5 000	fcborjomi.com	0	0
FC Chikhura Sachkhere	Sachkhere				0	0
FC Dila Gori	Gori	Burjanadze	8 230		0	0
FC Dinamo Tbilisi	Tbilisi	Boris Paichadze	20 500	fcdinamo.ge	12	8
FC Kakheti Telavi	Telavi	Givi Chokheli	17 000		0	0
FC Torpedo Kutaisi	Kutaisi	Torpedo	19 400		3	2
FC Lokomotivi Tbilisi	Tbilisi	Lokomotivi	24 500		0	3
FC Merani Tbilisi	Tbilisi	Sinatle	2 500		0	0
FC Kolkheti-1913	Poti	Phazisi 6 000	6 000		0	0
FC Sioni Bolnisi	Bolnisi	Temur Stapania	3 000		1	0
FC Tbilisi	Tbilisi	Olimpi	2 000	fctbilisi.ge	0	0
FC Tskhinvali	Gori	Kartli Gori	2 000		0	0
FC WIT-Georgia	Tbilisi	Mtskheta Central	2 000	witgeorgia.ge	1	0
FC Zestafoni	Zestafoni	Central	5 000	fczestafoni.ge	0	0

RECENT LEAGUE AND CUP RECORD

	Championship						Cup		
Year	Champions	Pts	Runners-up	Pts	Third	Pts	Winners	Score	Runners-up
1990	Iberia Tbilisi	78	Guria Lanchkhuti	72	Gorda Rustavi	69	Guria Lanchkhuti	1-0	Tskhumi Sukhumi
1991	Iberia Tbilisi	47	Guria Lanchkhuti	46	FC Kutaisi	35	No tournament played		
1992	Dinamo Tbilisi	87	Tskhumi Sukhumi	76	Gorda Rustavi	75	Dinamo Tbilisi	3-1	Tskhumi Sukhumi
1993	Dinamo Tbilisi	77	Shevardeni 1906	64	Alazani Gurdzhaani	63	Dinamo Tbilisi	4-2	FC Batumi
1994	Dinamo Tbilisi	48	Kolkheti 1913 Poti	44	Torpedo Kutaisi	31	Dinamo Tbilisi	1-0	Metalurgi Rustavi
1995	Dinamo Tbilisi	78	Samtredia	74	Kolkheti 1913 Poti	63	Dinamo Tbilisi	1-0	Dinamo Batumi
1996	Dinamo Tbilisi	79	Margveti Zestafoni	68	Kolkheti 1913 Poti	68	Dinamo Tbilisi	1-0	Dinamo Batumi
1997	Dinamo Tbilisi	81	Kolkheti 1913 Poti	67	Dinamo Batumi	62	Dinamo Tbilisi	1-0	Dinamo Batumi
1998	Dinamo Tbilisi	71	Dinamo Batumi	61	Kolkheti 1913 Poti	57	Dinamo Batumi	2-1	Dinamo Tbilisi
1999	Dinamo Tbilisi	77	Torpedo Kutaisi	67	Lokomotivi Tbilisi	64	Torpedo Kutaisi	0-0 4-2p	Samgurali
2000	Torpedo Kutaisi	46	WIT Georgia Tbilisi	41	Dinamo Tbilisi	41	Lokomotivi Tbilisi	0-0 4-2p	Torpedo Kutaisi
2001	Torpedo Kutaisi	44	Lokomotivi Tbilisi	41	Dinamo Tbilisi	38	Torpedo Kutaisi	0-0 4-3p	Lokomotivi Tbilisi
2002	Torpedo Kutaisi	48	Lokomotivi Tbilisi	47	Dinamo Tbilisi	44	Lokomotivi Tbilisi	2-0	Torpedo Kutaisi
2003	Dinamo Tbilisi	48	Torpedo Kutaisi	46	WIT Georgia Tbilisi	41	Dinamo Tbilisi	3-1	Sioni Bolnisi
2004	WIT Georgia Tbilisi	41	Sioni Bolnisi	41	Dinamo Tbilisi	40	Dinamo Tbilisi	2-1	Torpedo Kutaisi
2005	Dinamo Tbilisi	75	Torpedo Kutaisi	70	FC Tbilisi	69	Lokomotivi Tbilisi	2-0	FC Zestafoni
2006	Sioni Bolnisi	73	WIT Georgia Tbilisi	68	Dinamo Tbilisi	64	Ameri Tbilisi	2-2 4-3p	FC Zestafoni

GEORGIA 2005-06

UMAGLESI LIGA

	Pl	W	D	L	F	A	Pts	Sioni	WIT	Dinamo	Zestafoni	Borjomi	Batumi	Ameri	Lokom'vi	Kakheti	Kolkheti	Dila	Torpedo	FC Tbilisi	Tskhinvali	Sukhumi	Spartaki
Sioni Bolnisi †	30	23	4	3	57	17	73		1-0	1-0	1-0	1-0	2-2	3-0	4-0	4-1	2-0	2-0	3-1	1-0	6-1	1-0	4-0
WIT Georgia Tbilisi ‡	30	21	5	4	53	17	68	2-1		1-0	1-2	4-0	0-0	3-1	2-0	1-0	3-0	2-0	1-0	2-1	3-0	2-2	2-0
Dinamo Tbilisi	30	20	4	6	61	22	64	3-0	0-0		2-2	1-2	3-1	1-2	1-0	1-0	5-0	4-1	2-1	1-0	1-0	4-0	3-0
FC Zestafoni	30	18	7	5	44	22	61	0-0	0-4	1-0		0-0	0-0	1-0	3-0	4-0	3-0	2-0	1-1	2-1	3-1	4-1	1-0
FC Borjomi	30	19	2	9	50	26	59	1-0	1-0	4-2	1-0		0-1	2-1	2-0	2-1	1-0	4-3	1-0	2-0	4-0	3-0	5-0
Dinamo Batumi	30	17	7	6	42	21	58	0-1	1-1	1-2	2-2	1-0		1-0	0-1	1-0	2-0	3-1	2-0	1-0	0-0	4-0	5-0
Ameri Tbilisi ‡	30	15	4	11	32	26	49	0-1	1-2	1-1	2-0	1-0	0-1		4-1	0-0	1-0	1-0	5-1	0-2	1-0	1-0	1-0
Lokomotivi Tbilisi	30	11	4	15	41	48	37	1-1	1-2	0-3	0-0	2-1	1-2	3-0		3-0	2-0	2-1	2-3	1-4	3-0	1-0	3-1
Kakheti Telavi	30	10	4	16	33	46	34	0-2	0-1	1-3	1-0	1-0	1-3	1-2	4-3		3-2	3-0	1-0	1-1	4-0	3-1	1-0
Kolkheti 1913 Poti	30	9	5	16	26	36	32	0-1	1-0	0-0	1-2	0-0	0-1	0-1	4-1	2-2		2-1	1-0	2-1	3-0	4-0	1-0
Dila Gori	30	9	4	17	35	44	31	0-2	1-3	0-2	0-1	2-0	2-0	0-1	0-0	4-2	1-0		2-0	3-0	4-2	5-0	1-0
Torpedo Kutaisi	30	8	6	16	28	42	30	0-4	2-2	0-2	2-3	0-2	0-1	0-1	0-0	1-0	0-0	0-0		1-0	4-1	4-2	1-0
FC Tbilisi	30	9	2	19	29	44	29	1-2	0-1	2-3	0-1	2-3	0-1	0-5	1-3	0-0	0-2	3-0	1-0		2-0	4-3	1-0
FC Tskhinvali	30	8	3	19	30	61	27	1-3	0-3	0-2	0-2	1-2	1-2	1-0	2-1	0-1	1-3	2-2	0-0	3-0		4-3	2-0
Dinamo Sukhumi	30	5	3	22	26	70	18	1-2	0-1	1-6	0-1	1-3	2-1	0-3	4-1	2-0	1-0	1-1	0-3	0-2	0-2		0-0
Spartaki Tbilisi	30	3	6	21	12	57	15	1-1	1-4	0-3	1-3	3-2	0-0	1-1	0-6	0-0	0-0	1-0	1-2	1-0	1-3	0-1	

30/07/2005 - 9/05/2006 • † Qualified for the UEFA Champions League • ‡ Qualified for the UEFA Cup

Top scorers: Jaba DVALI, Dinamo Tbilisi, 21; Koka MIKUCHADZE, Sioni, 19; Zurabi IONANIDZE, Zestafoni, 17

GEORGIA 2005-06 PIRVELI LIGA (2)

	Pl	W	D	L	F	A	Pts
Chikhura Sachkhere	34	24	6	4	87	34	78
Merani Tbilisi	34	23	5	6	59	27	74
FC Gagra	34	19	11	4	49	22	68
Dinamo-2 Tbilisi	34	18	8	8	57	27	62
Meshakre Agara	34	18	5	11	46	32	59
Meskheti Akhaltsikhe	34	17	6	11	50	30	57
Ameri-2 Tbilisi	34	14	9	11	40	29	51
FC Rustavi	34	13	10	11	50	37	49
Guria Lanchkhuti	34	14	5	15	50	47	47
WIT Georgia-2 Tbilisi	34	13	6	15	43	45	45
FC Tbilisi-2	34	12	8	14	34	40	44
FC Zugdidi	34	12	7	15	24	33	43
Meshakhte Tqibuli	34	11	9	14	38	40	42
Magharoeli Chiatura	34	10	7	17	38	56	37
FC Zestafoni-2	34	9	9	16	23	44	36
FC Sagarejo	34	7	10	17	28	44	31
Imedi Tbilisi	34	6	2	26	22	85	20
Liakhvi Tamarasheni	34	4	1	29	24	90	13

11/08/2005 - 10/05/2006

GEORGIAN CUP 2005-06

Round of 16

Ameri Tbilisi *	4	0
FC Gagra	1	0
Dinamo Batumi *	0	0
Kolkheti 1913 Poti	2	1
FC Borjomi *	2	2
Dinamo Sukhumi	0	1
Meskheti Akhaltsikhe	0	1
Sioni Bolnisi *	2	1
WIT Georgia Tbilisi *	1	5
Torpedo Kutaisi	0	0
FC Tbilisi	0	0
Lokomotivi Tbilisi *	1	1
Dinamo Tbilisi *	0	2
Chikhura Sachkhere	0	0
Spartak Tbilisi *	0	1
FC Zestafoni	4	3

Quarter-finals

Ameri Tbilisi *	0	1
Kolkheti 1913 Poti	0	0
FC Borjomi	0	0
Sioni Bolnisi *	1	1
WIT Georgia Tbilisi *	3	1
Lokomotivi Tbilisi	1	0
Dinamo Tbilisi	0	0
FC Zestafoni *	1	0

Semi-finals

Ameri Tbilisi	0	1
Sioni Bolnisi *	0	0
WIT Georgia Tbilisi *	1	1
FC Zestafoni	2	3

Final

Ameri Tbilisi	2	4p
FC Zestafoni	2	3p

CUP FINAL

Mikheil Meskhi, Tbilisi
13-05-2006, Att: 10 000, Ref: Vadachkoria

Scorers - Davitashvili [10], Tsinamdzghvrishvili [50] for Ameri; Ionanidze [29], Ghonghadze [90] for Zestafoni

* Home team in first leg • ‡ Qualified for the UEFA Cup

GER – GERMANY

NATIONAL TEAM RECORD
JULY 1ST 2002 TO JULY 9TH 2006

PL	W	D	L	F	A	%
59	31	15	13	121	72	64.4

Because the German national team came so close to doing what no-one before the FIFA World Cup™ believed was possible, the disappointment at being knocked-out in the semi-finals of their own tournament didn't seem to be the disaster that surely in years past it would have been considered. Jurgen Klinsmann had been mocked and criticised by the press in Germany, not least because he continued to base himself in America, but he stuck to his attacking principles and that paid handsome dividends in the end. His team started off with four convincing wins, albeit against teams that posed little threat. But the manner of victory won the fans over and brought the whole tournament to life, with the fan fests enticing millions of Germans onto the streets to watch matches, and not just those involving Germany. In the quarter-finals Germany faced Argentina, their first opponents of real class. The tie was won in spectacular fashion on penalties after the Germans fought back to draw 1-1. The reward was a semi-final against Italy, a team with the Indian Sign over Germany. And so it proved again. Without a win against a top ranked nation since the 1-0 victory over England in 2001, Germany extended that unwanted record by losing to the Italians for the third

INTERNATIONAL HONOURS

FIFA World Cup™ 1954 1974 1990   **FIFA Women's World Cup** 2003

Olympic Gold 1976 (GDR)   **FIFA World Youth Championship** 1981   **FIFA Women's U-19 Championship** 2004

UEFA European Championship 1972 1980 1996   **UEFA Women's European Championship** 1989 1991 1995 1997 2001 2005

UEFA U-19 Championship 1981 1986 (GDR)   **UEFA U-17 Championship** 1984 1992   **UEFA Women's U-19 Championship** 2000 2001 2002 2006

UEFA Champions League Bayern München 1974 1975 1976 2001, Hamburger SV 1983, Borussia Dortmund 1997

time in the FIFA World Cup™ finals, following on from 1970 and 1982, although it took two goals right at the end of extra-time to do it. It was an heroic defeat which had former critics calling for Klinsmann to carry on, but after the third place victory over Portugal, he stepped down and was replaced by his assistant Joachim Loew. The hope is that the successful hosting of the finals will give the Bundesliga the boost it needs. The general perception is that it is falling behind the big three leagues of Spain, England and Italy, even though the Bundesliga has the highest average attendance in the world. Once again Bayern dominated to the near exclusion of every other team. They opened their campaign with six successive wins, which along with the nine consecutive wins at the end of the previous campaign, set a new Bundesliga record. With three defeats all season, two of them against Hamburg, a 20th title was never in doubt and for the first time in the history of German football, Bayern also won consecutive doubles, after beating Eintracht Frankfurt 1-0 in a rather uninspired Cup Final. It was Bayern's fourth double since the turn of the century, illustrating the huge gap that has developed between the Bavarian giants and the rest of the Bundesliga.

Deutscher Fussball-Bund (DFB)

Im Weller 14, Postfach 71 02 65, Nürnberg 90482, Germany

Tel +49 69 67880   Fax +49 69 6788266

info@dfb.de   www.dfb.de

President: MAYER-VORFELDER Gerhard, ZWANZIGER Theo Dr   General Secretary: SCHMIDT Horst R.

Vice-President: NELLE Engelbert   Treasurer: SCHMIDHUBER Heinrich   Media Officer: STENGER Harald

Men's Coach: LOEW Joachim   Women's Coach: NEID Silvia

DFB formed: 1900   UEFA: 1954   FIFA: 1904

White shirts with black trimmings, Black shorts, White socks or Red shirts with black trimmings, White shorts, White socks

RECENT INTERNATIONAL MATCHES PLAYED BY GERMANY

2004	Opponents	Score		Venue	Comp	Scorers	Att	Referee
18-02	Croatia	W	2-1	Split	Fr	Klose [34], Ramelow [90]	15 000	Frojdfeldt SWE
31-03	Belgium	W	3-0	Cologne	Fr	Kuranyi [45], Hamann [55], Ballack [81]	46 500	Wegereef NED
28-04	Romania	L	1-5	Bucharest	Fr	Lahm [88]	12 000	Rosetti ITA
27-05	Malta	W	7-0	Freiburg	Fr	Ballack 4 [15 17 59 86], Nowotny [33], Frings [42], Bobic [90]	22 000	Stredlak SVK
2-06	Switzerland	W	2-0	Basel	Fr	Kuranyi 2 [62 84]	30 000	Messina ITA
6-06	Hungary	L	0-2	Kaiserslautern	Fr		36 590	Bennett ENG
15-06	Netherlands	D	1-1	Porto	ECrl	Frings [30]	52 000	Frisk SWE
19-06	Latvia	D	0-0	Porto	ECrl		22 344	Riley ENG
23-06	Czech Republic	L	1-2	Lisbon	ECrl	Ballack [21]	46 849	Hauge NOR
18-08	Austria	W	3-1	Vienna	Fr	Kuranyi 3 [2 61 73]	37 900	Collina ITA
8-09	Brazil	D	1-1	Berlin	Fr	Kuranyi [17]	74 315	Meier SUI
9-10	Iran	W	2-0	Tehran	Fr	Ernst [5], Bdaric [53]	110 000	Mane KUW
17-11	Cameroon	W	3-0	Leipzig	Fr	Kuranyi [71], Klose 2 [78 88]	44 200	De Santis ITA
16-12	Japan	W	3-0	Yokohama	Fr	Klose 2 [54 90], Ballack [69]	61 805	Shield AUS
19-12	Korea Republic	L	1-3	Busan	Fr	Ballack [24]	45 775	Mohd Salleh MAS
21-12	Thailand	W	5-1	Bangkok	Fr	Kuranyi 2 [34 38], Podolski 2 [73 89], Asamoah [84]	15 000	Maidin SIN
2005								
9-02	Argentina	D	2-2	Dusseldorf	Fr	Frings [28p], Kuranyi [45]	52 000	Farina ITA
26-03	Slovenia	W	1-0	Celje	Fr	Podolski [27]	8 500	Poll ENG
4-06	Northern Ireland	W	4-1	Belfast	Fr	Asamoah [17], Ballack 2 [62 66p], Podolski [81]	14 000	Richmond SCO
8-06	Russia	D	2-2	Mönchengladbach	Fr	Schweinsteiger 2 [30 69]	46 228	Plautz AUT
15-06	Australia	W	4-3	Frankfurt/Main	CCrl	Kuranyi [17], Mertesacker [23], Ballack [60p], Podolski [88]	46 466	Amarilla PAR
18-06	Tunisia	W	3-0	Cologne	CCrl	Ballack [74p], Schweinsteiger [80], Hanke [88]	44 377	Prendergast JAM
21-06	Argentina	D	2-2	Nuremberg	CCrl	Kuranyi [29], Asamoah [51]	42 088	Michel SVK
25-06	Brazil	L	2-3	Nuremberg	CCsf	Podolski [23], Ballack [48+p]	42 187	Chandia CHI
29-06	Mexico	W	4-3	Leipzig	CC3p	Podolski [37], Schweinsteiger [41], Huth [79], Ballack [97]	43 335	Breeze AUS
17-08	Netherlands	D	2-2	Rotterdam	Fr	Ballack [49], Asamoah [81]	41 000	Hauge NOR
3-09	Slovakia	L	0-2	Bratislava	Fr		9 276	Braamhaar NED
7-09	South Africa	W	4-2	Bremen	Fr	Podolski 3 [12 48 55], Borowski [47]	28 100	Gilewski POL
8-10	Turkey	L	1-2	Istanbul	Fr	Neuivle [90]	25 000	Messina ITA
12-10	China PR	W	1-0	Hamburg	Fr	Frings [51p]	48 734	Batista POR
12-11	France	D	0-0	Paris	Fr		58 889	Bennett ENG
2006								
1-03	Italy	L	1-4	Florence	Fr	Huth [82]	28 317	Iturralde ESP
22-03	USA	W	4-1	Dortmund	Fr	Schweinsteiger [46], Neuville [73], Klose [75], Ballack [79]	64 500	Fröjdfeldt SWE
27-05	Luxembourg	W	7-0	Freiburg	Fr	Klose 2 [5 59], Frings [19p], Podolski 2 [36 65p], Neuville 2 [90 90]	23 000	Rogallo SUI
30-05	Japan	D	2-2	Leverkusen	Fr	Klose [75], Schweinsteiger [80]	22 500	Vassaras GRE
2-06	Colombia	W	3-0	Mönchengladbach	Fr	Ballack [20], Schweinsteiger [37], Borowski [69]	45 000	Hauge NOR
9-06	Costa Rica	W	4-2	Munich	WCr1	Lahm [6], Klose 2 [17 61], Frings [87]	66 000	Elizondo ARG
14-06	Poland	W	1-0	Dortmund	WCr1	Neuville [91+]	65 000	Medina Cantalejo ESP
20-06	Ecuador	W	3-0	Berlin	WCr1	Klose 2 [4 44], Podolski [57]	72 000	Ivanov RUS
24-06	Sweden	W	2-0	Munich	WCr2	Podolski 2 [4 12]	66 000	Simon BRA
30-06	Argentina	D	1-1	Berlin	WCqf	Klose [80]	72 000	Michel SVK
4-07	Italy	L	0-2	Dortmund	WCsf		65 000	Archundia MEX
8-07	Portugal	W	3-1	Stuttgart	WC3p	Schweinsteiger 2 [56 78], Petit OG [60]	52 000	Kamikawa JPN

Fr = Friendly match • EC = UEFA EURO 2004™ • CC = FIFA Confederations Cup • q = qualifier
r1 = first round group • sf = semi-final • 3p = third place play-off • f = final

GERMANY NATIONAL TEAM RECORDS AND RECORD SEQUENCES

Records			Sequence records					
Victory	16-0	RUS 1912	Wins	12	1979-1980	Clean sheets	6	1966
Defeat	0-9	ENG 1909	Defeats	7	1912-1913	Goals scored	33	1940-1952
Player Caps	150	MATTHAUS Lothar	Undefeated	23	1978-1980	Without goal	3	1985
Player Goals	68	MULLER Gerd	Without win	10	1912-1920	Goals against	15	1910-1912

GERMANY COUNTRY INFORMATION

Capital	Berlin	Independence	Unified in 1871, 1991	GNP per Capita	$27 600
Population	82 424 609	Status	Federal Republic	GNP Ranking	3
Area km²	357 021	Language	German	Dialling code	+49
Population density	230 per km²	Literacy rate	99%	Internet code	.de
% in urban areas	85%	Main religion	Christian 68%	GMT + / -	+1
Towns/Cities ('000)	Berlin 3 398; Hamburg 1 733; München 1 246; Köln 968; Frankfurt 648; Dortmund 594; Stuttgart 591; Düsseldorf 577; Essen 576; Bremen 546; Hannover 519; Duisberg 505; Nürnberg 497; Leipzig 492; Dresden 480; Bochum 387; Wuppertal 363; Bielefeld 327				
Neighbours (km)	Denmark 68; Poland 456; Czech Republic 646; Austria 784; Switzerland 334; France 451; Luxembourg 138; Belgium 167; Netherlands 577; North Sea & Baltic Sea 2 389				
Main stadia	Westfalenstadion – Dortmund 82 678; Olympiastadion – Berlin 76 065; Allianz Arena – München 66 000; Arena AufSchalke – Gelsenkirchen 61 027				

GERMANY NATIONAL TEAM PLAYERS AND COACHES

Record Caps			Record Goals			Recent Coaches	
MATTHAUS Lothar	1980-'00	150	MULLER Gerd	1966-'74	68	NERZ Otto	1926-'36
KLINSMANN Jürgen	1987-'98	108	STREICH Joachim - GDR	1969-'84	53	HERBERGER Sepp	1936-'63
KOHLER Jürgen	1986-'98	105	VOLLER Rudi	1982-'94	47	SCHON Helmut	1963-'78
BECKENBAUER Franz	1965-'77	103	KLINSMANN Jürgen	1987-'98	47	DERWALL Jupp	1978-'84
HABLER Thomas	1988-'00	101	RUMMENIGGE Karl-Heinz	1976-'86	45	BECKENBAUER Franz	1984-'90
STREICH Joachim - GDR	1969-'84	98	SEELER Uwe	1954-'70	43	VOGTS Bertie	1990-'98
DORNER Hans-Jürgen - GDR	1969-'85	96	BIERHOFF Oliver	1996-'02	37	RIBBECK Erich	1998-'00
VOGTS Bertie	1967-'78	96	WALTER Fritz	1940-'58	33	VOLLER Rudi	2000-'04
MAIER Sepp	1966-'79	95	FISCHER Klaus	1977-'82	32	KLINSMANN Jürgen	2004-'06
RUMMENIGGE Karl-Heinz	1976-'86	95	BALLACK Michael	1999-'06	31	LOEW Joachim	2006-

FIFA/COCA-COLA WORLD RANKING

1993	1994	1995	1996	1997	1998	1999	2000	2001	2002	2003	2004	2005		High		Low
1	5	2	2	2	3	5	11	12	4	12	19	16		1	08/93	22	03/06

2005–2006											
08/05	09/05	10/05	11/05	12/05	01/06	02/06	03/06	04/06	05/06	06/06	07/06
11	15	15	16	16	17	19	22	19	19	-	9

THE FIFA BIG COUNT OF 2000

	Male	Female		Male	Female
Registered players	1 318 250	84 050	Referees	78 67	1 567
Non registered players	2 281 614	533 832	Officials	52 752	1 000
Youth players	1 829 518	208 905	Total involved	6 390 155	
Total players	6 256 169		Number of clubs	26 697	
Professional players	870	0	Number of teams	172 716	

GERMANY 2005-06

1. BUNDESLIGA

	Pl	W	D	L	F	A	Pts	Bayern	Werder	HSV	Schalke	Leverkusen	Hertha	Dortmund	Nürnberg	Stuttgart	Gladbach	Mainz	Hannover	Arminia	Eintracht	Wolfsburg	Kaiserslautern	Köln	Duisburg
Bayern München †	34	22	9	3	67	32	75		3-1	1-2	3-0	1-0	3-0	3-3	2-1	3-1	3-0	2-1	1-0	2-0	5-2	2-0	2-1	2-2	4-0
Werder Bremen †	34	21	7	6	79	37	70	3-0		1-1	0-0	2-1	0-3	3-2	6-2	1-1	2-0	4-2	5-0	5-2	4-1	6-1	0-2	6-0	2-0
Hamburger SV †	34	21	5	8	53	30	68	2-0	1-2		1-0	0-2	2-1	2-4	3-0	2-2	2-0	1-0	1-1	2-1	1-1	0-1	3-0	3-1	2-0
Schalke 04 ‡	34	16	13	5	47	31	61	1-1	2-1	0-2		7-4	0-0	0-0	2-0	3-2	1-1	1-0	2-0	3-1	2-0	2-2	2-1	1-1	3-0
Bayer Leverkusen ‡	34	14	10	10	64	49	52	2-5	1-1	0-1	1-1		1-2	2-1	2-2	1-1	2-1	1-2	0-0	1-1	2-1	4-0	5-1	2-1	3-2
Hertha BSC Berlin	34	12	12	10	52	48	48	0-0	1-2	4-2	1-2	1-5		0-0	1-1	2-0	2-2	3-1	1-1	1-0	2-0	3-0	3-0	2-4	3-2
Borussia Dortmund	34	11	13	10	45	42	46	1-2	0-1	1-1	1-2	1-2	2-0		2-1	0-0	2-1	1-1	0-2	2-0	1-1	3-2	2-1	2-1	2-0
1.FC Nürnberg	34	12	8	14	49	51	44	1-2	3-1	2-1	1-1	1-1	2-1	1-2		0-1	5-2	3-0	1-1	2-3	0-1	1-0	3-2	2-1	3-0
VfB Stuttgart	34	9	16	9	37	39	43	0-0	0-0	1-2	2-0	0-2	3-3	0-0	1-0		1-1	2-1	2-2	1-1	0-2	2-1	1-0	2-3	0-1
Bor. Mönchengladbach	34	10	12	12	42	50	42	1-3	2-1	0-0	0-0	1-1	2-2	2-1	0-1	1-1		1-0	2-2	2-0	4-3	1-1	4-1	2-0	2-1
1.FSV Mainz 05	34	9	11	14	46	47	38	2-2	0-2	1-3	1-0	3-1	2-2	1-1	4-1	1-2	3-0		0-0	1-1	2-2	5-1	0-2	4-2	1-1
Hannover 96	34	7	17	10	43	47	38	1-1	0-0	2-1	1-2	2-2	2-2	1-2	1-1	3-3	1-1	2-2		0-1	2-0	2-4	5-1	1-0	1-1
Arminia Bielefeld	34	10	7	17	32	47	37	1-2	0-1	0-2	0-1	1-0	3-0	1-0	0-0	2-1	0-2	2-0	4-1		1-0	0-1	0-0	3-2	0-2
Eintracht Frankfurt ‡	34	9	9	16	42	51	36	0-1	0-1	1-2	0-1	1-4	1-1	2-0	1-0	0-1	3-0		1-1	2-2		3-0	1-1	6-3	5-2
VfL Wolfsburg	34	7	13	14	33	55	34	0-0	1-1	0-1	0-0	2-1	1-1	2-1	1-1	2-1	1-0	2-0	0-3	2-1	0-0		1-0	2-2	1-1
1.FC Kaiserslautern	34	8	9	17	47	71	33	1-1	1-5	0-3	0-2	2-2	0-2	3-3	1-3	1-1	3-0	0-2	1-0	2-0	1-2	3-2		2-2	5-3
1.FC Köln	34	7	9	18	49	71	30	1-2	1-4	0-1	2-2	0-3	0-1	0-0	3-4	0-0	2-1	1-0	1-4	4-2	1-1	3-0	2-3		3-1
MSV Duisburg	34	5	12	17	34	63	27	1-3	3-5	0-2	1-1	1-3	2-1	1-1	0-1	1-1	1-0	0-0	0-1	1-0	1-1	0-2	1-1		

5/08/2005 - 13/05/2006 • † Qualified for the UEFA Champions League • ‡ Qualified for the UEFA Cup • Top scorers: Miroslav KLOSE, Werder, 25; Dimitar BERBATOV, Leverkusen, 21; Halil ALTINTOP, Kaiserslautern, 20; Roy MAKAAY, Bayern, 17; Robert VITTEK, Nürnberg, 16; Ivan KLASNIC, Werder, 15; Michael BALLACK, Bayern, 14; Ebi SMOLAREK, Dortmund, 13

GERMANY 2005-06

2. BUNDESLIGA

	Pl	W	D	L	F	A	Pts	Bochum	Alemannia	Cottbus	Freiburg	Fürth	Karlsruher	Aue	Burghausen	Paderborn	Hansa	Offenbach	Braunschweig	TSV 1860	Unterhaching	Dynamo	Saarbrücken	Ahlen	Siegen
VfL Bochum	34	19	9	6	55	26	66		1-4	2-2	4-0	1-1	2-3	1-0	1-2	1-1	1-0	0-1	4-0	1-0	1-0	1-0	3-0	3-0	3-1
Alemannia Aachen	34	20	5	9	61	36	65	0-2		0-0	0-1	0-1	2-1	3-1	2-0	2-1	3-2	0-1	2-1	1-0	1-0	2-0	4-0	6-2	3-0
Energie Cottbus	34	16	10	8	49	33	58	0-1	5-1		2-1	1-2	0-0	1-0	4-1	1-2	2-0	1-2	2-1	3-1	2-0	1-0	3-1	0-0	2-2
SC Freiburg	34	16	8	10	41	33	56	0-0	0-2	4-1		1-0	0-0	2-0	2-1	1-0	2-2	2-0	1-0	2-1	3-2	1-0	3-1	3-0	2-2
SpVgg Greuther Fürth	34	15	9	10	51	42	54	1-3	0-0	1-1	1-2		3-1	1-3	6-2	1-1	2-0	2-0	0-1	2-2	2-0	3-1	0-0	2-0	1-0
Karlsruher SC	34	15	8	11	55	45	53	1-1	2-1	2-2	1-0	1-0		5-2	0-1	2-3	1-0	1-1	7-0	1-2	0-1	2-1	2-1	3-1	2-0
Erzgebirge Aue	34	13	9	12	38	36	48	0-1	2-1	2-2	1-0	1-0	0-0		1-1	1-2	1-0	0-0	2-0	3-0	0-1	2-0	2-0	0-0	0-2
Wacker Burghausen	34	12	11	11	45	49	47	0-4	1-1	0-1	2-1	2-2	1-1	1-1		5-1	1-0	1-2	1-0	1-1	1-0	1-1	2-0	1-3	1-0
Paderborn 07	34	13	7	14	46	40	46	1-3	3-1	0-0	1-1	1-2	2-0	0-2	1-3		3-0	4-1	3-0	0-1	1-1	0-2	5-0	1-0	4-0
Hansa Rostock	34	13	4	17	44	49	43	1-3	0-0	1-0	0-1	2-1	1-0	1-0	2-0	1-2		2-3	4-1	3-3	4-2	1-3	3-0	1-2	2-0
Offenbacher Kickers	34	12	7	15	42	53	43	0-0	2-4	2-0	2-1	2-1	1-3	2-1	1-1	1-1	5-1		2-0	2-5	4-1	0-0	2-3	0-3	1-1
Eint. Braunschweig	34	13	4	17	37	48	43	0-0	0-1	0-1	0-0	3-0	1-0	0-1	1-2	2-0	4-1	2-0		3-3	3-0	1-0	1-2	3-1	1-0
TSV 1860 München	34	11	9	14	41	44	42	0-1	0-0	2-3	0-1	2-2	2-0	1-1	1-1	4-1	1-1	1-0	4-1		1-4	1-2	1-0	0-0	3-0
SpVgg Unterhaching	34	12	6	16	42	48	42	0-1	2-2	1-2	0-2	6-2	1-2	0-4	1-4	4-1	1-1	1-1	3-0	0-1		2-0	1-0	0-1	2-0
Dynamo Dresden	34	11	8	15	39	45	41	0-0	1-3	1-1	2-0	1-2	3-2	1-4	1-2	0-2	0-1	4-1	1-1	2-0	2-3		2-0	3-1	1-0
1.FC Saarbrücken	34	11	5	18	37	63	38	0-4	2-5	1-3	2-1	1-0	1-2	1-1	1-0	0-2	0-4	2-0	0-0	5-3	5-1			1-0	0-3
LR Ahlen	34	9	8	17	36	50	35	2-2	0-2	0-1	0-0	1-2	2-3	3-1	2-2	1-3	1-0	3-0	1-2	1-0	0-0	3-1			0-1
Sportfreunde Siegen	34	8	7	19	35	54	31	3-0	2-2	2-4	1-0	1-3	0-0	0-1	2-0	1-2	1-1	1-1	1-4	4-0	2-2	0-4	0-3		

6/08/2005 - 14/05/2006 • Top scorers: Christian EIGLER, Fürth, 18; Giovanni FEDERICO, Karlsruher, 14; Marek KREJCI, Burghausen, 14

DFB POKAL 2005–06

First Round

Team	Score
Bayern München	4
MSV 1919 Neuruppin *	0
VfL Bochum II *	2
Erzgebirge Aue	3
Bayer Leverkusen	8
Rot-Weiss Erfurt II *	0
Stuttgarter Kickers *	1
Hamburger SV	5
1.FC Kaiserslautern	3
Eintracht Trier *	0
LR Ahlen	1
Rot-Weiß Erfurt *	2
VfL Osnabrück *	2 10p
SpVgg Greuther Fürth	2 9p
Hansa Rostock II *	0
FSV Mainz 05	3
Werder Bremen	3
SG Wattenscheid 09 *	1
SC Paderborn 07 *	0
VfL Wolfsburg	2
Alenannia Aachen	3
SSV Jahn Regensburg *	1
1.FC Köln II *	0
Hannover 96	4
Hertha BSC Berlin	3
TuS Koblenz *	2
FC Kutzhof *	0
Borussia Mönchengladbach	3
VfL Bochum	6
Tennis Borussia Berlin *	0
Wacker Burghausen	2
Sankt Pauli *	3
Arminia Bielefeld	3
Magdeburger SV *	0
Rot-Weiss Essen *	2 4p
Energie Cottbus	2 5p
1.FC Saarbrücken	1 5p
FC Ingolstadt *	1 4p
Holstein Kiel *	0
SpVgg Unterhaching	2
Hansa Rostock	5
FC 08 Villingen *	2
TSG Hoffenheim *	3
VfB Stuttgart	4
Karlsruher SC	3
FSV Mainz II *	0
1.FC Köln	1
Kickers Offenbach *	3
TSV 1860 München	2
Wuppertaler SV *	1
VfL Wolfsburg II *	0
MSV Duisberg	1
Eintracht Braunschweig *	2
Borussia Dortmund	1
Spfr. Siegen *	0
SC Freiburg	1
1.FC Nürnberg	4
1.FC Eschborn *	0
FC Sachsen Leipzig *	1 3p
Dynamo Dresden	1 5p
Schalke 04	3
FC Bremerhaven *	0
Rot-Weiß Oberhausen *	1
Eintracht Frankfurt	2

Second Round

Team	Score
Bayern München	1
Erzgebirge Aue *	0
Bayer Leverkusen	2
Hamburger SV *	3
1.FC Kaiserslautern	4
Rot-Weiß Erfurt *	2
VfL Osnabrück *	2 2p
FSV Mainz 05	2 4p
Werder Bremen *	2 5p
VfL Wolfsburg	2 4p
Alemannia Aachen *	1
Hannover 96	2
Hertha BSC Berlin *	3
Borussia Mönchengladbach	0
VfL Bochum	0
Sankt Pauli *	4
Arminia Bielefeld *	2
Energie Cottbus	1
1.FC Saarbrücken	1
SpVgg Unterhaching *	2
Hansa Rostock *	3
VfB Stuttgart	2
Karlsruher SC	1
Kickers Offenbach *	2
TSV 1860 München *	3
MSV Duisburg	2
Eintracht Braunschweig	1
SC Freiburg *	4
1.FC Nürnberg *	3
Dynamo Dresden	0
Schalke 04	0
Eintracht Frankfurt *	6

Third Round

Team	Score
Bayern München *	1
Hamburger SV	0
1.FC Kaiserslautern *	1 3p
FSV Mainz 05	1 4p
Werder Bremen	4
Hannover 96 *	1
Hertha BSC Berlin	3
Sankt Pauli	4
Arminia Bielefeld *	2
SpVgg Unterhaching	0
Hansa Rostock	1 3p
Kickers Offenbach	1 4p
TSV 1860 München	3
SC Freiburg *	1
1.FC Nürnberg	1 4p
Eintracht Frankfurt *	1 1p

DFB POKAL 2005-06

Quarter-finals   **Semi-finals**   **Final**

Bayern München *	3
FSV Mainz 05	2

Bayern München	3
Sankt Pauli *	0

Werder Bremen	1
Sankt Pauli *	3

Bayern München	1
Eintracht Frankfurt ‡	0

Arminia Bielefeld *	1 4p
Kickers Offenbach	1 2p

Arminia Bielefeld	0
Eintracht Frankfurt *	1

DFB POKAL FINAL 2006

Olympiastadion, Berlin, 29-04-2006, 20:00, 74 349, Ref: Fandel

Bayern München	1	Pizarro 59
Eintracht Frankfurt	0	

TSV 1860 München *	1
Eintracht Frankfurt	3

Bayern - Oliver KAHN - Willy SAGNOL●, LUCIO, Valerien ISMAEL, Philipp LAHM● - Hasan SALIHAMIDZIC (ZE ROBERTO 46), Martin DEMICHELIS, Michael BALLACK●, Owen HARGREAVES (Jens JEREMIES 82) - Roy MAKAAY (Mehmet SCHOLL 90), Claudio PIZARRO. Tr: Felix MAGATH
Eintracht - Oka NIKOLOV - Marko REHMER (Daniyel CIMEN 34) (Markus WEISSENBERGER 82), Marco RUSS, Aleksandar VASOSKI● - Patrick OCHS, Benjamin HUGGEL, Christoph SPYCHER - Stefan LEXA (Francisco COPADO 72), Alexander MEIER, Benjamin KOHLER - Ioannis AMANATIDIS. Tr: Friedhelm FUNKEL

GERMANY 2005–06
REGIONALLIGA NORD

	Pl	W	D	L	F	A	Pts
Rot-Weiss Essen	36	23	7	6	67	34	76
Carl Zeiss Jena	36	22	6	8	58	32	72
VfB Lübeck	36	20	9	7	60	36	69
Holstein Kiel	36	19	9	8	64	42	66
Fortuna Düsseldorf	36	18	9	9	62	47	63
FC St. Pauli	36	17	10	9	53	38	61
Hertha BSC Berlin II	36	16	7	13	54	44	55
Wuppertaler SV	36	13	12	11	42	42	51
Kickers Emden	36	14	7	15	50	45	49
VfL Osnabrück	36	14	7	15	56	58	49
Bayer Leverkusen II	36	13	5	18	56	64	44
Werder Bremen II	36	11	10	15	46	47	43
Hamburger SV II	36	12	7	17	45	48	43
Rot-Weiß Erfurt	36	11	9	16	40	48	42
Preußen Münster	36	12	6	18	37	49	42
SG Wattenscheid 09	36	10	9	17	50	65	39
Rot-Weiß Oberhausen	36	10	9	17	30	53	39
1. FC Köln II	36	6	8	22	39	74	26
Chemnitzer FC	36	5	6	25	35	78	21

29/07/2005 - 27/05/2006

GERMANY 2005–06
REGIONALLIGA SUD

	Pl	W	D	L	F	A	Pts
FC Augsburg	34	23	7	4	73	26	76
TuS Koblenz	34	18	12	4	55	31	66
SV Wehen	34	17	6	11	63	46	57
TSG Hoffenheim	34	17	5	12	47	34	56
SV Darmstadt 98	34	16	6	12	57	44	54
VfR Aalen	34	15	9	10	43	33	54
VfB Stuttgart II	34	14	11	9	50	43	53
Stuttgarter Kickers	34	12	12	10	46	39	48
SV Elversberg	34	12	12	10	40	37	48
SpVgg Bayreuth	34	11	13	10	51	54	46
Karlsruher SC II	34	12	6	16	41	51	42
Bayern München II	34	11	9	14	34	44	42
1. FC Kaiserslautern II	34	12	5	17	39	44	41
SC Pfullendorf	34	10	10	14	30	34	40
TSV 1860 München II	34	9	10	15	39	51	37
Eintracht Trier	34	9	9	16	41	58	36
SSV Jahn Regensburg	34	7	11	16	37	48	32
1. FC Eschborn	34	1	7	26	15	84	10

5/08/2005 - 27/05/2006

CLUB DIRECTORY

Club	Town/City	Stadium	Capacity	www.	Lge	Cup	CL
TSV Alemannia Aachen	Aachen	Tivoli Stadion	24 816	alemannia-aachen.de	0	0	0
Hertha BSC Berlin	Berlin	Olympiastadion	76 065	herthabsc.de	2	0	0
Arminia Bielefeld	Bielefeld	Schüco Arena	26 601	arminia-bielefeld.de	0	0	0
VfL Bochum	Bochum	Ruhrstadion	32 645	vfl-bochum.de	0	0	0
Werder Bremen	Bremen	Weserstadion	35 800	werder-online.de	4	5	0
FC Energie Cottbus	Cottbus	Stadion der Freundschaft	22 450	fcenergie.de	0	0	0
Borussia Dortmund	Dortmund	Signal Iduna (Westfalenstadion)	81 264	borussia-dortmund.de	6	2	1
Eintracht Frankfurt	Frankfurt	Commerzbank-Arena	61 146	eintracht.de	1	4	0
Schalke 04	Gelsenkirchen	Veltins Arena (Arena AufSchalke)	61 010	schalke04.de	7	4	0
Hamburger SV	Hamburg	AOL Arena	55 000	hsv.de	6	3	1
Hannover 96	Hanover	AWD Arena	49 000	hannover96.de	2	1	0
Bayer Leverkusen	Leverkusen	BayArena	22 500	bayer04.de	0	1	0
1.FSV Mainz 05	Mainz	Stadion am Bruchweg	18 600	mainz05.de	0	0	0
Borussia Mönchengladbach	Mönchengladbach	Borussia-Park	53 148	borussia.de	5	3	0
Bayern München	Munich	Allianz-Arena	66 000	fcbayern.de	20	13	4
1.FC Nürnberg	Nuremburg	Frankenstadion	44 833	fcn.de	9	3	0
VfB Stuttgart	Stuttgart	Gottlieb-Daimler	54 088	vfb-stuttgart.de	4	3	0
VfL Wolfsburg	Wolfsburg	Volkswagen-Arena	30 000	vfl-wolfsburg.de	0	0	0

RECENT LEAGUE AND CUP RECORD

Year	Champions	Pts	Runners-up	Pts	Third	Pts
1990	Bayern München	49	1.FC Köln	43	Eintracht Frankfurt	43
1991	1.FC Kaiserslautern	48	Bayern München	45	Werder Bremen	42
1992	VfB Stuttgart	52	Borussia Dortmund	52	Eintracht Frankfurt	50
1993	Werder Bremen	48	Bayern München	47	Eintracht Frankfurt	42
1994	Bayern München	44	1.FC Kaiserslautern	43	Bayer Leverkusen	39
1995	Borussia Dortmund	49	Werder Bremen	48	SC Freiburg	46
1996	Borussia Dortmund	68	Bayern München	62	Schalke 04	56
1997	Bayern München	71	Bayer Leverkusen	69	Borussia Dortmund	63
1998	1.FC Kaiserslautern	68	Bayern München	66	Bayer Leverkusen	55
1999	Bayern München	78	Bayer Leverkusen	63	Hertha BSC Berlin	62
2000	Bayern München	73	Bayer Leverkusen	73	Hamburger SV	59
2001	Bayern München	63	Schalke 04	62	Borussia Dortmund	58
2002	Borussia Dortmund	70	Bayer Leverkusen	69	Bayern München	68
2003	Bayern München	75	VfB Stuttgart	59	Borussia Dortmund	58
2004	Werder Bremen	74	Bayern München	68	Bayer Leverkusen	65
2005	Bayern München	77	Schalke 04	63	Werder Bremen	59
2006	Bayern München	75	Werder Bremen	70	Hamburger SV	68

	Cup	
Winners	Score	Runners-up
1.FC Kaiserslautern	3-2	Werder Bremen
Werder Bremen	1-1 4-3p	1.FC Köln
Hannover 96	0-0 4-3p	B. Mönchengladbach
Bayer Leverkusen	1-0	Hertha Berlin (Am)
Werder Bremen	3-1	Rot-Weiss Essen
B. Mönchengladbach	3-0	VfL Wolfsburg
1.FC Kaiserslautern	1-0	Karlsruher SC
VfB Stuttgart	2-0	Energie Cottbus
Bayern München	2-1	MSV Duisberg
Werder Bremen	1-1 5-4p	Bayern München
Bayern München	3-0	Werder Bremen
Schalke 04	2-0	1.FC Union Berlin
Schalke 04	4-2	Bayer Leverkusen
Bayern München	3-1	1.FC Kaiserslautern
Werder Bremen	3-2	Alemannia Aachen
Bayern München	2-1	Schalke 04
Bayern München	1-0	Eintracht Frankfurt

FC BAYERN MUNCHEN 2005-06

Date	Opponents	Score		Comp	Scorers	Att
26-07-2005	VfB Stuttgart	L 1-2	H	LPsf	Makaay [18]	50 000
5-08-2005	Borussia Mönchengladbach	W 3-0	H	BL	Hargreaves [28], Makaay 2 [86 89]	66 000
13-08-2005	Bayer Leverkusen	W 5-2	A	BL	Ballack [3], Makaay 3 [11 57 60], Karimi [35]	22 500
21-08-2005	MSV Neuruppin	W 4-0	A	DPr1	Ismael [9], Scholl 2 [49 84], Ottl [69]	33 189
27-08-2005	Hertha BSC Berlin	W 3-0	H	BL	Ballack [47], Scholl [85], Makaay [87]	66 000
10-09-2005	1.FC Nürnberg	W 2-1	A	BL	Guerrero [21], Ballack [60]	46 939
14-09-2005	SK Rapid Wien - AUT	W 1-0	A	CLgA	Guerrero [60]	47 540
17-09-2005	Hannover 96	W 1-0	H	BL	Demichelis [9]	66 000
20-09-2005	Eintracht Frankfurt	W 1-0	A	BL	Guerrero [72]	51 000
24-09-2005	Hamburger SV	L 0-2	A	BL		55 800
27-09-2005	Club Brugge - BEL	W 1-0	H	CLgA	Demichelis [32]	66 000
1-10-2005	VfL Wolfsburg	W 2-0	H	BL	Santa Cruz [67], Lucio [91+]	66 000
15-10-2005	Schalke 04	D 1-1	A	BL	Santa Cruz [19]	61 524
18-10-2005	Juventus - ITA	W 2-1	H	CLgA	Deisler [32], Demichelis [39]	66 000
22-10-2005	MSV Duisberg	W 4-0	H	BL	Ballack [27], Zé Roberto [33], Santa Cruz [59], Pizarro [91+]	66 000
26-10-2005	Erzgebirge Aue	W 1-0	A	DPr2	Ballack [80]	16 500
29-10-2005	1.FC Köln	W 2-1	A	BL	Lucio [55], Ballack [74]	50 000
2-11-2005	Juventus - ITA	L 1-2	A	CLgA	Deisler [66]	16 076
5-11-2005	Werder Bremen	W 3-1	H	BL	Schweinsteiger [3], Pizarro [34], Makaay [44]	66 000
19-11-2005	Arminia Bielefeld	W 2-1	A	BL	Pizarro 2 [82 93+]	26 601
22-11-2005	SK Rapid Wien - AUT	W 4-0	H	CLgA	Deisler [21], Karimi [54], Makaay 2 [72 77]	66 000
26-11-2005	FSV Mainz 05	W 2-1	H	BL	Pizarro 2 [28 54]	66 000
3-12-2005	VfB Stuttgart	D 0-0	A	BL		57 000
7-12-2005	Club Brugge - BEL	D 1-1	A	CLgA	Pizarro [21]	27 860
11-12-2005	1.FC Kaiserslautern	W 2-1	H	BL	Ballack [26], Makaay [54p]	66 000
17-12-2005	Borussia Dortmund	W 2-1	A	BL	Karimi [52], Pizarro [73]	81 000
21-12-2005	Hamburger SV	W 1-0	H	DPr3	Hargreaves [113]	66 000
24-01-2006	FSV Mainz 05	W 3-2	H	DPqf	Pizarro 2 [81 115], Guerrero [94]	53 000
27-01-2006	Borussia Mönchengladbach	W 3-1	A	BL	Makaay 2 [13 69], Ballack [55]	54 019
4-02-2006	Bayer Leverkusen	W 1-0	H	BL	Ballack [36]	69 000
7-02-2006	Hertha BSC Berlin	D 0-0	A	BL		
12-02-2006	1.FC Nürnberg	W 2-1	H	BL	Makaay [28], Ballack [54]	69 000
18-02-2006	Hannover 96	D 1-1	A	BL	Ballack [89]	49 500
21-02-2006	Milan - ITA	D 1-1	H	CLr2	Ballack [23]	66 000
25-02-2006	Eintracht Frankfurt	W 5-2	H	BL	Guerrero 2 [21 42], Ballack 2 [33 62], Pizarro [85]	69 000
4-03-2006	Hamburger SV	L 1-2	H	BL	Scholl [83]	69 000
8-03-2006	Milan - ITA	L 1-4	A	CLr2	Ismaël [35]	78 577
11-03-2006	VfL Wolfsburg	D 0-0	A	BL		30 000
19-03-2006	Schalke 04	W 3-0	H	BL	Salihamidzic [49], Pizarro [56], Makaay [89]	69 000
25-03-2006	MSV Duisberg	W 3-1	A	BL	Salihamidzic [66], Makaay [71], Pizarro [80]	31 500
1-04-2006	1.FC Köln	D 2-2	H	BL	Sagnol [29], Makaay [39]	69 000
8-04-2006	Werder Bremen	L 0-3	A	BL		42 000
12-04-2006	FC St. Pauli	W 3-0	A	DPsf	Hargreaves [15], Pizarro 2 [84 88]	19 800
15-04-2006	Arminia Bielefeld	W 2-0	H	BL	Ballack [69], Scholl [74]	69 000
23-04-2006	FSV Mainz 05	D 2-2	A	BL	Makaay 2 [29 37p]	20 300
29-04-2006	Eintracht Frankfurt	W 1-0	N	DPf	Pizarro [59]	74 349
3-05-2006	VfB Stuttgart	W 3-1	H	BL	Santa Cruz [11], Pizarro [44], Schweinsteiger [46]	69 000
6-05-2006	1.FC Kaiserslautern	D 1-1	A	BL	Ottl [68]	50 754
13-05-2006	Borussia Dortmund	D 3-3	H	BL	Makaay [6], Schweinsteiger [48], Ballack [50]	69 000

LP = Liga-Pokal (Super Cup) • BL = Bundesliga • CL = UEFA Champions League • DP = DFB Pokal
r1 = first round • gC = Group C • r2 = second round • r3 = third round • qf = quarter-final • sf = semi-final • f = final
A = Olympiastadion, Berlin • N = Olympiastadion, Berlin

WERDER BREMEN 2005–06

Date	Opponents		Score		Comp	Scorers	Att
23-07-2005	Bayer Leverkusen	W	1-0	N	LPqf	Klasnic [19]	20 000
27-07-2005	Schalke 04	L	1-2	A	LPsf	Valdez [90]	56 781
6-08-2005	Arminia Bielefeld	W	5-2	H	BL	Klose 2 [1 82], Klasnic 2 [18 85], Baumann [36]	38 156
10-08-2005	FC Basel - SUI	L	1-2	A	CLpr3	Klose [73]	28 101
14-08-2005	FSV Mainz 05	W	2-0	H	BL	Klasnic [21], Klose [62]	20 300
21-08-2005	SG Wattenscheid 90	W	3-1	A	DPr1	Klasnic [59], Jensen [80], Hunt [82]	8 000
24-08-2005	FC Basel - SUI	W	3-0	H	CLpr3	Klasnic 2 [65 73], Borowski [68p]	30 339
27-08-2005	VfB Stuttgart	D	1-1	H	BL	Klasnic [41]	38 440
10-09-2005	1.FC Kaiserslautern	W	5-1	A	BL	Micoud [31], Klose 2 [44 78], Frings [45], Vranjes [89]	32 851
14-09-2005	Barcelona - ESP	L	0-2	H	CLgC		37 000
17-09-2005	Borussia Dortmund	W	3-2	H	BL	Klose [37], Klasnic [54], Micoud [78]	38 000
20-09-2005	Borussia Mönchengladbach	L	1-2	A	BL	Van Damme [21]	40 251
24-09-2005	Bayer Leverkusen	W	2-1	H	BL	Klose [46], Klasnic [77]	37 265
27-09-2005	Panathinaikos - GRE	L	1-2	A	CLgC	Klose [41]	31 450
1-10-2005	Hertha BSC Berlin	W	2-1	A	BL	Borowski [85], Valdez [89]	60 000
15-10-2005	1.FC Nürnberg	W	6-2	H	BL	Klose 3 [2 34 39], Klasnic 2 [66 85], Borowski [80]	39 542
18-10-2005	Udinese - ITA	D	1-1	A	CLgC	Flipe OG [64]	20 335
22-10-2005	Hannover 96	D	0-0	A	BL		48 627
25-10-2005	VfL Wolfsburg	D	2-2	H	DPr2	Klose 2 [88 105], W 5-4p	19 100
29-10-2005	Eintracht Frankfurt	W	4-1	H	BL	Frings [29], Borowski 2 [52 90], Klose [61]	41 085
2-11-2005	Udinese - ITA	W	4-3	H	CLgC	Klose [15], Baumann [24], Micoud 2 [51 67]	35 424
5-11-2005	Bayern München	L	1-3	A	BL	Klose [1]	66 000
19-11-2005	VfL Wolfsburg	W	6-1	H	BL	Baumann [6], Borowski 2 [43 52], Klose 2 [60 85], Naldo [72]	37 258
22-11-2005	Barcelona - ESP	L	1-3	A	CLgC	Borowski [22p]	67 273
26-11-2005	Schalke 04	L	1-2	A	BL	Valdez [56]	61 524
3-12-2005	MSV Duisburg	W	2-0	H	BL	Valdez [64], Borowski [73]	38 079
7-12-2005	Panathinaikos - GRE	W	5-1	H	CLgC	Micoud [2p], Valdez 2 [28 31], Klose [51], Frings [91+]	36 550
11-12-2005	1.FC Köln	W	4-1	A	BL	Naldo [34], Klose 2 [50 90], Micoud [89]	50 000
18-12-2005	Hamburger SV	D	1-1	H	BL	Micoud [45]	42 100
21-12-2005	Hannover 96	W	4-1	A	DPr3	Naldo [71], Frings [83], Balitsch OG [89], Hunt [90]	49 000
25-01-2006	FC St Pauli	L	1-3	A	DPqf	Micoud [27]	19 800
29-01-2006	Arminia Bielefeld	W	1-0	H	BL	Fahrenhorst [72]	24 196
4-02-2006	FSV Mainz 05	W	4-2	H	BL	Valdez 2 [39 69], Klasnic [45], Micoud [45]	37 717
8-02-2006	VfB Stuttgart	D	0-0	A	BL		30 000
11-02-2006	1.FC Kaiserslautern	L	0-2	H	BL		36 218
18-02-2006	Borussia Dortmund	W	1-0	A	BL	Klasnic [31]	75 200
22-02-2006	Juventus - ITA	W	3-2	H	CLr2	Schulz [39], Borowski [87], Micoud [92+]	36 500
25-02-2006	Borussia Mönchengladbach	W	2-0	H	BL	Klose [16], Klasnic [27]	39 900
4-03-2006	Bayer Leverkusen	D	1-1	A	BL	Frings [3p]	22 500
7-03-2006	Juventus - ITA	L	1-2	A	CLr2	Micoud [13]	40 226
11-03-2006	Hertha BSC Berlin	L	0-3	H	BL		37 728
18-03-2006	1.FC Nürnberg	L	1-3	A	BL	Klose [57]	40 924
25-03-2006	Hannover 96	W	5-0	H	BL	Valdez 3 [43 52 81], Micoud [45], Klose [53]	41 646
1-04-2006	Eintracht Frankfurt	W	1-0	H	BL	Klose [70p]	48 600
8-04-2006	Bayern München	W	3-0	H	BL	Schweinsteiger OG [33], Jensen.D [79], Borowski [83]	42 100
15-04-2006	VfL Wolfsburg	D	1-1	A	BL	Valdez [6]	27 996
23-04-2006	Schalke 04	D	0-0	H	BL		42 100
3-05-2006	MSV Duisburg	W	5-3	H	BL	Micoud 2 [4 16], Klose 2 [31 75], Klasnic [86]	23 104
6-05-2006	1.FC Köln	W	6-0	H	BL	Borowski 2 [11 25], Klose 2 [19 75], Klasnic 2 [51 69]	42 000
13-05-2006	Hamburger SV	W	2-1	A	BL	Klasnic [27], Klose [72]	57 000

LP = Liga-Pokal (Super Cup) • BL = Bundesliga • CL = UEFA Champions League • DP = DFB Pokal
r1 = first round • gC = Group C • r2 = second round • r3 = third round • qf = quarter-final
N = Düsseldorf

GHA – GHANA

NATIONAL TEAM RECORD
JULY 1ST 2002 TO JULY 9TH 2006

PL	W	D	L	F	A	%
45	18	12	15	63	45	53.3

FIFA/COCA-COLA WORLD RANKING

1993	1994	1995	1996	1997	1998	1999	2000	2001	2002	2003	2004	2005	High	Low
37	26	29	25	57	48	48	57	59	61	78	77	50	**15** 04/96	**89** 06/04

					2005–2006						
08/05	09/05	10/05	11/05	12/05	01/06	02/06	03/06	04/06	05/06	06/06	07/06
70	62	51	50	50	50	48	50	50	48	-	25

The Black Stars finally verified their long-standing status as one of Africa's footballing super powers, making it past the first round of the 2006 FIFA World Cup™ finals at their debut appearance. After a disappointing defeat at the hands of Italy in their opening game, Ghana were very impressive in their victories over the USA and the Czech Republic before losing against Brazil in the second round. Injuries meant that Ghana delivered a disappointing performance at the 2006 African Nations Cup finals in Egypt, where they did not get past the first round, but it was patently evident

INTERNATIONAL HONOURS
FIFA World U-17 Championship 1991 1995 Qualified for the FIFA World Cup finals™ 2006 Qualified for the FIFA Women's World Cup finals 1999 2003
CAF African Cup of Nations 1963 1965 1978 1982 CAF African Youth Championship 1993 1999
CAF African U-17 Championship 1995 1999 CAF Champions League Asante Kotoko 1970 1983 Hearts of Oak 2000

from their displays in Germany that, had they had a full squad, it would have been a different story. Players like Michael Essien, Sulley Muntari and John Mensah proved their international profile and finally achieved where the more famous names of the past, like Abedi Pele and Tony Yeboah, could not. Ghana's premier league title went to Asante Kotoko, again breaking the stranglehold that Hearts of Oak had enjoyed over the last decade. Kotoko finished seven points clear despite being pegged neck-and-neck with Hearts through most of the season.

THE FIFA BIG COUNT OF 2000

	Male	Female		Male	Female
Registered players	15 000	0	Referees	700	0
Non registered players	100 000	0	Officials	4 000	0
Youth players	10 000	0	Total involved	129 700	
Total players	125 000		Number of clubs	250	
Professional players	0	0	Number of teams	1 500	

Ghana Football Association (GFA)
General Secretariat, National Sports Council, PO Box 1272, Accra, Ghana
Tel +233 21 910170   Fax +233 21 668590
info@ghanafa.org   www.ghanafa.org
President: NYANTAKYI Kwesi   General Secretary: NSIAH Kofi
Vice-President: TBD   Treasurer: TBD   Media Officer: None
Men's Coach: DUJKOVIC Ratomir   Women's Coach: BASHIRU Hayford
GFA formed: 1957   CAF: 1958   FIFA: 1958
Yellow shirts with black trimmings, Yellow shorts, Yellow socks

RECENT INTERNATIONAL MATCHES PLAYED BY GHANA

2002	Opponents	Score		Venue	Comp	Scorers	Att	Referee
19-10	Sierra Leone	L	1-2	Freetown	Fr	Taylor [25]		Sanusie SLE
15-12	Nigeria	L	0-1	Accra	Fr			Wellington GHA
22-12	Egypt	D	0-0	Cairo	Fr			
2003								
26-01	Benin	W	3-0	Kumasi	Fr	Abbey [37], Tiero [45], Asante [87]		Amedior GHA
15-02	Benin	L	0-1	Cotonou	Fr			Lamidi BEN
27-03	Tunisia	D	2-2	Tunis	Fr	Amoah.C 2 [45 48]. L 7-8p	30 000	
30-03	Madagascar	D	3-3	Tunis	Fr	Appiah [5], Amoah.C [32], Gyan [60]. W 10-9p		
30-05	Nigeria	L	1-3	Abuja	Fr	Agyema [2]	60 000	
13-06	Kenya	L	1-3	Accra	Fr	Appiah [60]		
22-06	Uganda	D	1-1	Kumasi	CNq	Amoah.C [84]		
6-07	Rwanda	L	0-1	Kigali	CNq		40 000	
16-11	Somalia	W	5-0	Accra	WCq	Arhin Duah 2 [25 56], Boakye 2 [69 89], Gyan [82]	19 447	Bebou TOG
19-11	Somalia	W	2-0	Kumasi	WCq	Appiah [27], Adjei [90]	12 000	Chaibou NIG
2004								
28-04	Angola	D	1-1	Accra	Fr	Morgan [90]		Kotey GHA
5-06	Burkina Faso	L	0-1	Ouagadougou	WCq		25 000	Chukwujekwu NGA
14-06	Togo	D	0-0	Kumasi	Fr			
20-06	South Africa	W	3-0	Kumasi	WCq	Muntari [13], Appiah 2 [55 78]	32 000	Diatta SEN
25-06	Mozambique	W	1-0	Maputo	Fr	Gyan [72]		
3-07	Uganda	D	1-1	Kampala	WCq	Gyan [88]	20 000	El Beltagy EGY
5-09	Cape Verde Islands	W	2-0	Kumasi	WCq	Essien [24p], Veiga OG [62]	35 000	Tamuni LBY
10-10	Congo DR	D	0-0	Kumasi	WCq		30 000	Coulibaly MLI
2005								
23-03	Kenya	D	2-2	Nairobi	Fr	Gyan [23], Amoah [89]		
27-03	Congo DR	D	1-1	Kinshasa	WCq	Gyan [30]	80 000	Sowe GAM
5-06	Burkina Faso	W	2-1	Kumasi	WCq	Appiah [66p], Amoah [83]	11 920	Abd el Fatah EGY
18-06	South Africa	W	2-0	Johannesburg	WCq	Amoah [59], Essien [91+]	50 000	Guezzaz MAR
17-08	Senegal	D	0-0	London	Fr			
4-09	Uganda	W	2-0	Kumasi	WCq	Essien [10], Amoah [15]	45 000	Hicuburundi BDI
8-10	Cape Verde Islands	W	4-0	Praia	WCq	Asamoah [5], Muntari [35], Gyan [75], Attram [87]	6 500	Daami TUN
14-11	Saudi Arabia	W	3-1	Jeddah	Fr	Muntari [41], Gyan 2 [45 72]		
2006								
11-01	Togo	L	0-1	Monastir	Fr		2 500	Piccirillo FRA
15-01	Tunisia	L	0-2	Rades/Tunis	Fr		25 000	Walid Salah
23-01	Nigeria	L	0-1	Port Said	CNr1		20 000	Abd El Fatah EGY
27-01	Senegal	W	1-0	Port Said	CNr1	Amoah [13]	20 000	El Arjoun MAR
31-01	Zimbabwe	L	1-2	Ismailia	CNr1	Armando [93+]	14 000	Liuzaya CGO
1-03	Mexico	L	0-1	Frisco	Fr		19 513	Hall USA
26-05	Turkey	D	1-1	Bochum	Fr	Amoah [60]	9 738	Meier GER
29-05	Jamaica	W	4-1	Leicester	Fr	Muntari [5], OG [19], Appiah [66], Amoah [68]	11 163	Halsey ENG
4-06	Korea Republic	W	3-1	Edinburgh	Fr	Gyan [37p], Muntari [63], Essien [81]	15 000	McDonald SCO
12-06	Italy	L	0-2	Hanover	WCr1		43 000	Simon BRA
17-06	Czech Republic	W	2-0	Cologne	WCr1	Gyan [2], Muntari [82]	45 000	Elizondo ARG
22-06	USA	W	2-1	Nuremberg	WCr1	Draman [22], Appiah [47+p]	41 000	Merk GER
27-06	Brazil	L	0-3	Dortmund	WCr2		65 000	Michel SVK

Fr = Friendly match • CN = CAF African Cup of Nations • WC = FIFA World Cup™ • q = qualifier

GHANA NATIONAL TEAM RECORDS AND RECORD SEQUENCES

Records			Sequence records					
Victory	9-1	NIG 1969	Wins	8	1965-1967	Clean sheets	6	1990-1991
Defeat	2-8	BRA 1996	Defeats	6	1996	Goals scored	29	1963-1967
Player Caps	n/a		Undefeated	21	1981-1983	Without goal	5	1985
Player Goals	n/a		Without win	9	1996-1997	Goals against	15	1967-1968

GHANA COUNTRY INFORMATION

Capital	Accra	Independence	1957 from the UK	GDP per Capita	$2 200
Population	20 757 032	Status	Republic	GNP Ranking	108
Area km²	239 460	Language	English	Dialling code	+233
Population density	86 per km²	Literacy rate	66%	Internet code	.gh
% in urban areas	36%	Main religion	Christian 63%	GMT +/−	0
Towns/Cities ('000)	Accra 1 963; Kumasi 1 468; Tamale 360; Tema 351; Obuasi 144; Cape Coast 143; Obuasi 119				
Neighbours (km)	Burkina Faso 549; Togo 877; Côte d'Ivoire 668; Atlantic Ocean 539				
Main stadia	Kumasi Stadium – Kumasi 51 500; Accra Stadium – Accra 35 000; Len Clay – Obuasi 25 000				

GHANA 2005

GHANA TELECOM PREMIER LEAGUE

	Pl	W	D	L	F	A	Pts	Kotoko	Hearts	King Faisal	Arsenal	Sportive	Liberty Pros	AshantiGold	Feyenoord	RTU	Power	Bafoakwa	Hasaacas	Lions	Okwahu	Dwarfs	Hotspurs
Asante Kotoko †	30	18	9	3	37	15	63		3-1	2-0	1-0	1-2	2-1	1-0	1-0	2-1	1-1	3-1	2-0	1-0	1-0	1-0	2-0
Hearts of Oak †	30	16	8	6	47	28	56	1-1		3-2	2-1	3-1	1-0	1-0	2-1	2-1	2-2	1-0	1-1	1-0	5-0	2-3	5-1
King Faisal Babies ‡	30	15	5	10	41	32	50	0-0	2-1		1-0	1-0	1-1	2-1	0-2	3-1	3-1	2-0	1-0	5-1	1-1	2-1	3-2
Berekum Arsenal ‡	30	14	5	11	34	28	47	2-1	1-1	1-0		1-1	2-1	2-0	4-1	1-0	2-1	0-0	3-1	2-0	1-0	2-0	2-1
Real Sportive	30	13	8	9	24	25	47	0-0	1-1	2-0	1-0		1-0	1-0	2-1	0-3	1-0	1-0	1-0	1-1	0-0	1-1	2-0
Liberty Professionals	30	12	6	12	42	29	42	3-1	0-1	3-1	4-1	1-0		0-0	1-2	5-1	1-2	0-0	4-0	4-1	0-0	3-2	4-0
AshantiGold	30	12	6	12	29	24	42	0-1	0-0	1-3	1-1	1-0	1-0		1-0	0-0	2-1	2-0	2-1	5-1	1-0	1-0	5-1
Feyenoord Academy	30	11	8	11	26	29	41	0-0	0-0	1-0	2-1	0-0	0-2	1-1		1-0	1-1	0-0	1-0	1-1	1-0	2-0	1-0
Real Tamale United §	30	13	4	13	34	35	40	**0-3**	1-0	2-1	0-0	2-0	2-0	1-0	2-1		2-0	4-1	2-1	1-1	2-0	2-0	3-0
Power FC	30	10	8	12	29	31	38	1-1	2-0	1-0	0-1	0-1	3-1	0-0	0-1	0-0		2-1	2-1	1-0	0-0	2-0	1-0
Tano Bafoakwa	30	10	7	13	24	33	37	0-0	0-2	2-1	1-0	2-0	0-0	2-1	1-1	4-0	0-1		2-1	3-1	1-0	2-0	1-0
Hasaacas	30	10	6	14	30	33	36	1-2	1-1	0-0	1-0	0-0	2-0	1-0	2-0	3-1	1-1	3-0		2-0	2-0	2-0	2-1
Heart of Lions	30	10	6	14	34	42	36	0-1	0-3	1-1	3-2	0-1	1-0	0-2	1-0	1-0	0-2	2-1	5-0		2-1	4-0	1-1
Okwahu United	30	9	5	16	20	30	32	0-0	0-1	0-1	0-1	3-1	0-1	1-2	2-0	1-0	3-1	1-0	3-0	2-1		2-1	1-0
Ebusua Dwarfs	30	9	5	16	26	39	32	0-0	2-1	1-2	1-0	1-2	1-1	0-1	2-0	2-0	2-1	0-0	1-0	0-0	2-0		2-1
Hotspurs	30	9	2	19	23	47	29	0-2	1-2	0-2	2-0	2-0	0-1	1-0	3-2	1-0	1-0	1-0	0-0	0-2	1-0	2-1	

17/04/2005 - 13/11/2005 • † Qualified for the CAF Champions League • ‡ Qualified for the Confederation Cup • § Three points deducted • Match in bold awarded 3-0 • Top scorers: Prince TAGOE, Hearts, 18; Emmanuel Osei KUFFOUR, AshantiGold, 13, Eric GAWU, King Faisal, 12

RECENT LEAGUE AND CUP RECORD

Championship

Year	Champions	Pts	Runners-up	Pts	Third	Pts
1990	Hearts of Oak	78	Asante Kotoko	75		
1991	Asante Kotoko	44	Hearts of Oak	37	Great Olympics	35
1992	Asante Kotoko	40	Hearts of Oak	37	Goldfields Obuasi	33
1993	Asante Kotoko	32	Goldfields Obuasi	30	Mysterious Dwarfs	24
1994	Goldfields Obuasi	34	Asante Kotoko	27	Hearts of Oak	26
1995	Goldfields Obuasi	33	Real Tamale United	36	Asante Kotoko	33
1996	Goldfields Obuasi	51	Asante Kotoko	50	Okwahu United	46
1997	Hearts of Oak	54	Real Tamale United	51	Goldfields Obuasi	48
1998	Hearts of Oak	52	Asante Kotoko	48	Great Olympics	39
1999	Hearts of Oak	62	Cape Coast Dwarfs	53	Real Tamale United	52
2000	Hearts of Oak	57	Goldfields Obuasi	52	King Faisal Babies	46
2001	Hearts of Oak	64	Asante Kotoko	55	Goldfields Obuasi	45
2002	Hearts of Oak	78	Asante Kotoko	73	Liberty Professionals	48
2003	Asante Kotoko	75	Hearts of Oak	66	King Faisal Babies	54
2004	Hearts of Oak	1-0	Asante Kotoko			
2005	Asante Kotoko	63	Hearts of Oak	56	King Faisal Babies	50

Cup

Winners	Score	Runners-up
Asante Kotoko		Hearts of Oak
	Not played	
Voradep	2-2 3-2p	Neoplan Stars
Goldfields Obuasi	4-3	Mysterious Dwarfs
Hearts of Oak	2-1	Mysterious Dwarfs
Great Olympics		Hearts of Oak
Hearts of Oak	1-0	Ghapoha Tema
Ghapoha Tema	1-0	Okwahu United
Asante Kotoko	1-0	Real Tamale United
Hearts of Oak	3-1	Great Olympics
Hearts of Oak	2-0	Okwahu United
Asante Kotoko	1-0	King Faisal Babies
	Not played	
	Not played	
Real Tamale United	1-2 1-0	Asante Kotoko

GNB – GUINEA-BISSAU

NATIONAL TEAM RECORD
JULY 1ST 2002 TO JULY 9TH 2006

PL	W	D	L	F	A	%
4	0	2	2	4	7	25

FIFA/COCA-COLA WORLD RANKING

1993	1994	1995	1996	1997	1998	1999	2000	2001	2002	2003	2004	2005		High		Low	
131	122	118	133	148	165	173	177	174	183	186	190	186		115	07/94	191	02/05

2005–2006											
08/05	09/05	10/05	11/05	12/05	01/06	02/06	03/06	04/06	05/06	06/06	07/06
191	191	191	191	186	186	186	185	186	186	-	179

Guinea Bissau is set for another cycle of international isolation after failing to enter the qualifiers for the 2008 African Nations Cup finals. The former Portuguese colony, which has a myriad of talent at Portuguese clubs, competed in the 2006 FIFA World Cup™ qualifiers but were knocked out at the preliminary round stage by Mali. Scarce resources have been put into entering the Olympic Games qualifiers for Beijing in 2008 and a Brazilian coach, Nogueira Junior, has also been employed. In 2005 Guinea-Bissau entered the Amilcar Cabral Cup, a regional tournament for West African countries, which in 2005 was staged in neighbouring Guinea in the capital Conakry.

INTERNATIONAL HONOURS
None

Two draws in their opening round group matches meant they reached the semifinals where they lost to Senegal's under-23 side on penalties before losing to Mali in the third place play-off match. There was a second-ever league title for provincial club Os Balantas Mansoa, who had previously won the first post-independence championship in 1975. Squabbles between the federation and clubs postponed the 2006 Cup Final, eventually won by Portas Bissau who beat Benfica Bissau 2-1 after extra time, the winner coming from Iva in the 106th minute. Portas Bissau were, however, relegated from the first division.

THE FIFA BIG COUNT OF 2000

	Male	Female		Male	Female
Registered players	1 000	0	Referees	50	0
Non registered players	3 000	0	Officials	300	0
Youth players	500	0	Total involved	4 850	
Total players		4 500	Number of clubs	40	
Professional players	0	0	Number of teams	100	

Federação de Futebol da Guiné-Bissau (FFGB)
Alto Bandim (Nova Sede), Case Postale 375, Bissau 1035, Guinea-Bissau
Tel +245 201918   Fax +245 211414
federacaofutebol@hotmail.com   www.none
President: LOBATO Jose   General Secretary: CASSAMA Infali
Vice-President: GOMES VAZ Alberto   Treasurer: DAVYES Lolita Francisca Maria   Media Officer: TCHAGO Jorge
Men's Coach: NOGUEIRA JUNIOR   Women's Coach: KEITA Sidico
FFGB formed: 1974   CAF: 1986   FIFA: 1986
Red shirts, Green shorts, Red socks

RECENT INTERNATIONAL MATCHES PLAYED BY GUINEA-BISSAU

2002	Opponents	Score		Venue	Comp	Scorers	Att	Referee
No international matches played after June 2002								
2003								
10-10	Mali	L	1-2	Bissau	WCq	Dionisio Fernandes 50	22 000	Sowe GAM
14-11	Mali	L	0-2	Bamako	WCq		13 251	Seydou MTN
2004								
No International matches played in 2004								
2005								
18-11	Guinea	D	2-2	Conakry	ACr1	Manuel Fernandes 2 35p 49		
20-11	Sierra Leone	D	1-1	Conakry	ACr1	Agostino Suarez 62		
25-11	Senegal †	D	1-1	Conakry	ACsf			
27-11	Mali †	L	0-1	Conakry	AC3p			
2006								
No international matches played in 2006 before July								

AC = Amilcar Cabral Cup • WC = FIFA World Cup™
q = qualifier • r1 = first round group • sf = semi-final • 3p = third place play-off • † Not a full international

GUINEA-BISSAU NATIONAL TEAM RECORDS AND RECORD SEQUENCES

Records			Sequence records					
Victory	7-2	BEN 2001	Wins	3	1990-1991	Clean sheets	5	1987-1988
Defeat	1-6	MLI 1997	Defeats	5	1980-1981	Goals scored	6	1989-1991
Player Caps	n/a		Undefeated	11	1987-1989	Without goal	3	1985, 1997-2000
Player Goals	n/a		Without win	8	1979-1981	Goals against	13	1994-1997

RECENT LEAGUE AND CUP RECORD

	Championship						Cup		
Year	Champions	Pts	Runners-up	Pts	Third	Pts	Winners	Score	Runners-up
1997	Sporting Bissau						No tournament		
1998	Sporting Bissau						No tournament		
1999	No competition held						No tournament		
2000	Sporting Bissau	38	Benfica	36	União Bissau	36	Portas Bissau	2-1	Mavegro FC
2001	No competition held						No tournament		
2002	Sporting Bissau	39	Portas Bissau	37	União Bissau	32	Mavegro FC	3-1	Sporting Bafatá
2003	União Bissau	47	Sporting Bissau	44	Sporting Bafatá	43	Tournament not finished		
2004	Sporting Bissau	39	Benfica	28	Mavegro FC	28	Mavegro FC	1-0	Sporting Bissau
2005	Sporting Bissau	45	Atlético Bissorã	38	Mavegro FC	37	Sporting Bissau	4-2	Atlético Bissorã
2006	Os Balantas	50	Mavegro FC	47	Desportivo Mansabá	33	Portas Bissau	2-1	Benfica

GUINEA-BISSAU COUNTRY INFORMATION

Capital	Bissau	Independence	1973 from Portugal	GDP per Capita	$800
Population	1 388 363	Status	Republic	GNP Ranking	184
Area km²	36 120	Language	Portuguese	Dialling code	+245
Population density	38 per km²	Literacy rate	34%	Internet code	.gw
% in urban areas	22%	Main religion	Indigenous 50%, Muslim 45%	GMT +/-	0
Towns/Cities ('000)	Bissau 388; Bafatá 22; Gabú 14; Bissorã 12; Bolama 10; Cacheu 10; Bubaque 9				
Neighbours (km)	Senegal 338; Guinea 386; Atlantic Ocean 350				
Main stadia	24 de Setembro – Bissau 20 000; Lino Correia – Bissau 12 000				

GRE – GREECE

NATIONAL TEAM RECORD
JULY 1ST 2002 TO JULY 9TH 2006

PL	W	D	L	F	A	%
50	26	12	12	53	39	64

FIFA/COCA-COLA WORLD RANKING

1993	1994	1995	1996	1997	1998	1999	2000	2001	2002	2003	2004	2005		High		Low
34	28	34	35	42	53	34	42	57	48	30	18	16		**13** 02/05	**66**	09/98

	2005–2006										
08/05	09/05	10/05	11/05	12/05	01/06	02/06	03/06	04/06	05/06	06/06	07/06
18	20	18	17	16	16	19	21	19	20	-	32

Greece weren't the first European champions to fail to qualify for a FIFA World Cup™ but never before have the European champions failed to qualify to defend their continental title. That's the challenge facing the Greeks with Euro 2008™ looming in Austria and Switzerland; and Greece do not have a good record when it comes to qualifying for the finals. Coach Otto Rehhagel remains at the helm despite the failure to make it to the FIFA World Cup™ in Germany from what was, admittedly, perhaps the toughest of all the qualifying groups. There was also little joy for Greek clubs in European competition as both Panathinaikos and Olympiacos finished bottom of their

INTERNATIONAL HONOURS
UEFA European Championship 2004   Qualified for the FIFA World Cup™ 1994

UEFA Champions League groups. Olympiacos did have a good season at home, however, winning back-to-back doubles for the first time since the start of the National League in 1960. The aim is now to emulate the Olympiacos team of 1957-59 that won three doubles in a row. AEK and Panathinaikos may have finished just three points behind in the League, but the reality was that after winning 21 of their first 23 games, a ninth title in ten years was never really in doubt for Olympiacos. There was a scare for Greece when FIFA banned all international activity due to government interference in the running of the game, but the situation was quickly resolved.

THE FIFA BIG COUNT OF 2000

	Male	Female		Male	Female
Registered players	421 743	961	Referees	2 500	0
Non registered players	150 000	0	Officials	9 000	200
Youth players	55 311	0	Total involved	639 715	
Total players	628 015		Number of clubs	1 400	
Professional players	1 874	0	Number of teams	3 804	

Hellenic Football Federation (HFF)
137 Singrou Avenue, Nea Smirni, Athens 17121, Greece
Tel +30 210 9306000   Fax +30 210 9359666
epo@epo.gr   www.epo.gr
President: GAGATSIS Vassilis   General Secretary: ECONOMIDES Ioannis Dr
Vice-President: LYKOUREZOS Alexandros   Treasurer: GIRTZIKIS George   Media Officer: TSAPIDIS Michael
Men's Coach: REHHAGEL Otto   Women's Coach: BATSILAS Dimitrios
HFF formed: 1926   UEFA: 1954   FIFA: 1927
Blue shirts with white trimmings, Blue shorts, Blue socks or White shirts with blue trimmings, White shirts, White socks

RECENT INTERNATIONAL MATCHES PLAYED BY GREECE

2003	Opponents	Score		Venue	Comp	Scorers	Att	Referee
20-08	Sweden	W	2-1	Norrköping	Fr	Giannakopoulos [63], Kafes [65]	15 018	Hyytia FIN
6-09	Armenia	W	1-0	Yerevan	ECq	Vryzas [34]	6 500	Temmink NED
11-10	Northern Ireland	W	1-0	Athens	ECq	Tsartas [69p]	15 500	Cortez Batista POR
15-11	Portugal	D	1-1	Aveiro	Fr	Lakis [47]	30 000	Esquinas Torres ESP
2004								
18-02	Bulgaria	W	2-0	Athens	Fr	Papadopoulos [25], Vryzas [60]	6 000	Poll ENG
31-03	Switzerland	W	1-0	Irákleio	Fr	Tsartas [55]	33 000	Temmink NED
28-04	Netherlands	L	0-4	Eindhoven	Fr		25 000	Bolognino ITA
29-05	Poland	L	0-1	Szczecin	Fr		17 000	Kari FIN
3-06	Liechtenstein	W	2-0	Vaduz	Fr	Vryzas [24], Charisteas [88]	2 000	Petignat SUI
12-06	Portugal	W	2-1	Porto	ECr1	Katagounis [7], Basinas [51p]	48 761	Collina ITA
16-06	Spain	D	1-1	Porto	ECr1	Charisteas [66]	25 444	Michel SVK
20-06	Russia	L	1-2	Faro-Loule	ECr1	Vryzas [43]	24 000	Veissiere FRA
25-06	France	W	1-0	Lisbon	ECqf	Charisteas [65]	45 390	Frisk SWE
1-07	Czech Republic	W	1-0	Porto	ECsf	Dellas [105 SG]	42 449	Collina ITA
4-07	Portugal	W	1-0	Lisbon	ECf	Charisteas [57]	62 865	Merk GER
18-08	Czech Republic	D	0-0	Prague	Fr		15 050	Dougal SCO
4-09	Albania	L	1-2	Tirana	WCq	Giannakopoulos [38]	15 800	Iturralde Gonzalez ESP
8-09	Turkey	D	0-0	Piraeus	WCq		32 182	Frisk SWE
9-10	Ukraine	D	1-1	Kyiv	WCq	Tsartas [83]	56 000	Mejuto Gonzalez ESP
17-11	Kazakhstan	W	3-1	Piraeus	WCq	Charisteas 2 [24 46+], Katsouranis [85]	31 838	Kostadinov BUL
2005								
9-02	Denmark	W	2-1	Piraeus	WCq	Zagorakis [25], Basinas [32p]	32 430	Collina ITA
26-03	Georgia	W	3-1	Tbilisi	WCq	Kapsis [43], Vryzas [44], Giannakopoulos [53]	23 000	Rosetti ITA
30-03	Albania	W	2-0	Piraeus	WCq	Charisteas [33], Karagounis [84]	31 700	Layec FRA
4-06	Turkey	D	0-0	Istanbul	WCq		26 700	Merk GER
8-06	Ukraine	L	0-1	Piraeus	WCq		33 500	Temmink NED
16-06	Brazil	L	0-3	Leipzig	CCr1		42 507	Michel SVK
19-06	Japan	L	0-1	Frankfurt	CCr1		34 314	Fandel GER
22-06	Mexico	D	0-0	Frankfurt	CCr1		31 285	Amarilla PAR
17-08	Belgium	L	0-2	Brussels	Fr		20 000	Berntsen NOR
7-09	Kazakhstan	W	2-1	Almaty	WCq	Giannakopoulos [78], Lymperopoulos [94+]	18 000	Tudor ROU
8-10	Denmark	L	0-1	Copenhagen	WCq		42 099	De Bleeckere BEL
12-10	Georgia	W	1-0	Athens	WCq	Papadopoulos [17]	28 186	Trefoloni ITA
16-11	Hungary	W	2-1	Piraeus	Fr	Giannakopoulos [31], Kafes [91+]	12 500	Vink NED
2006								
21-01	Korea Republic	D	1-1	Riyadh	Fr	Zagorakis [10]		Al Shehri KSA
25-01	Saudi Arabia	D	1-1	Riyadh	Fr	Zagorakis [59p]	2 900	Mohammoud BHR
28-02	Belarus	W	1-0	Limassol	Fr	Samaras [15]	3 000	Salomir ROU
1-03	Kazakhstan	W	2-0	Nicosia	Fr	Samaras [68], Giannakopoulos [90]	2 000	Kailis CYP
25-05	Australia	L	0-1	Melbourne	Fr		95 103	Riley ENG

Fr = Friendly match • EC = UEFA EURO 2004™ • WC = FIFA World Cup™ • CC = FIFA Confederations Cup
q = qualifier • r1 = First round group • qf = quarter-final • sf = semi-final • f = final • SG = Silver goal

GREECE NATIONAL TEAM RECORDS AND RECORD SEQUENCES

Records			Sequence records					
Victory	8-0	SYR 1949	Wins	6	1994-1994	Clean sheets	4	Five times
Defeat	1-11	HUN 1938	Defeats	10	1931-1933	Goals scored	17	1934-1949
Player Caps	116	ZAGORAKIS Theodorus	Undefeated	15	2002-2004	Without goal	6	2005
Player Goals	29	ANASTOPOULOS Nikolaos	Without win	12	1954-1960	Goals against	21	1957-1964

GREECE COUNTRY INFORMATION

Capital	Athens	Independence	1829 from Ottoman Empire	GDP per Capita	$20 000
Population	10 647 529	Status	Republic	GNP Ranking	31
Area km²	131 940	Language	Greek	Dialling code	+30
Population density	80 per km²	Literacy rate	97%	Internet code	.gr
% in urban areas	65%	Main religion	Christian 98%	GMT + / –	+2
Towns/Cities ('000)	Athens 729; Thessaloníki 354; Piraeus 172; Pátra 163; Irákleio 137; Lárisa 128; Kallithea 107; Nikaia 94; Kalamaria 91; Glifada 88, Volos 84; Akharnai 82; Nea Smirni 75				
Neighbours (km)	Albania 282; FYR Macedonia 246; Bulgaria 494; Turkey 206; Mediterranean Sea 13 676				
Main stadia	Olympic – Athens 74 767; Karaiskaki – Piraeus 33 500; Toumba – Thessaloníki 28 701				

GREECE NATIONAL TEAM PLAYERS AND COACHES

Record Caps			Record Goals			Recent Coaches	
ZAGORAKIS Theodorus	1994-'06	116	ANASTOPOULOS Nikolaos	1977-'88	29	SOFIANIDIS Alekos	1988-'89
APOSTOLAKIS Efstratos	1986-'98	95	SARAVAKOS Dimitris	1982-'94	22	GEORGIADIS Antonis	1989-'91
SARAVAKOS Dimitris	1982-'94	78	PAPAIOANNOU Dimitris	1963-'78	21	PETRITSIS Stefanos	1992
MITROPOULOS Anastassios	1978-'94	76	MACHLAS Nikos	1993-'02	18	GEORGIADIS Antonis	1992
TSALOHUIDIS Panayotis	1987-'96	75	NIKOLAIDES Themistoklis	1995-'04	17	PANAGOULIAS Alketas	1992-'94
ANASTOPOULOS Nikolaos	1977-'88	73	TSALOHUIDIS Panayotis	1987-'96	16	POLYCHRONIOU Kostas	1994-'98
NIKOPOLIDIS Antonis	1999-'06	71	SIDERIS Yeorgios	1958-'69	14	IORDANESCU Anghel	1998-'99
MANOLAS Steilos	1982-'94	70	CHARISTEAS Angelos	2001-'06	14	DANIIL Vassilis	1999-'00
TSARTAS Vassilis	1993-'05	70	TSARTAS Vassilis	1993-'05	12	CHRISTIDIS Nikos	2001
						REHHAGEL Otto	2001-

CLUB DIRECTORY

Club	Town/City	Stadium	Capacity	www.	Lge	Cup
AEK	Athens	Nikos Goumas	32 000	aekfc.gr	11	13
Aris	Thessaloníki	Harilaou	18 308	arisfc.gr	3	1
Chalkidona	Piraeus	Neapolis Public	7 026	xalkhdonafc.gr	0	0
Egaleo	Athens	Egaleo	4 000		0	0
Ergotelis	Irákleio	Pankritio	33 240	ergotelis.gr	0	0
Ionikos	Piraeus	Neapolis Public	7 026	ionikos-fc.gr	0	0
Iraklis	Thessaloníki	Kaftanzoglio	28 028	iraklis-fc.gr	0	1
Kalamarias	Thessaloníki	Kalamaria	7 000		0	0
Kallithea	Athens	Kallithea	4 250	kallitheafc.gr	0	0
Kérkira	Kérkira (Corfu)	Kérkira	4 000		0	0
OFI Crete	Irákleio	Pankritio	33 240	ofi.gr	0	1
Olympiacos	Piraeus	Karaiskaki	33 500	olympiacos.org	34	22
Panathinaikos	Athens	Apostolos Nikolaidis	16 620	pao.gr	19	16
Panionios	Athens	Nea Smyrni	11 700	panionios.gr	0	2
PAOK	Thessaloníki	Toumba	28 701	paokfc.gr	2	4
Xánthi	Xánthi	Xánthi	9 500	skodaxanthifc.gr	0	0

RECENT LEAGUE AND CUP RECORD

	Championship						Cup		
Year	Champions	Pts	Runners-up	Pts	Third	Pts	Winners	Score	Runners-up
1990	Panathinaikos	53	AEK	50	PAOK	46	Olympiacos	4-2	OFI Crete
1991	Panathinaikos	54	Olympiakos	46	AEK	42	Panathinaikos	3-0 2-1	Athinaikos
1992	AEK	54	Olympiakos	51	Panathinaikos	48	Olympiacos	1-1 2-0	PAOK
1993	AEK	78	Panathinaikos	77	Olympiacos	68	Panathinaikos	1-0	Olympiacos
1994	AEK	79	Panathinaikos	72	Olympiacos	68	Panathinaikos	3-3 4-2p	AEK
1995	Panathinaikos	83	Olympiakos	67	PAOK	65	Panathinaikos	1-0	AEK
1996	Panathinaikos	83	AEK	81	Olympiacos	65	AEK	7-1	Apollon
1997	Olympiacos	84	AEK	72	OFI Crete	66	AEK	0-0 5-3p	Panathinaikos
1998	Olympiacos	88	Panathinaikos	85	AEK	74	Panionios	1-0	Panathinaikos
1999	Olympiacos	85	AEK	75	Panathinaikos	74	Olympiacos	2-0	Panathinaikos
2000	Olympiacos	92	Panathinaikos	88	AEK	66	AEK	2-0	Ionikos
2001	Olympiacos	78	Panathinaikos	66	AEK	61	PAOK	4-2	Olympiacos
2002	Olympiacos	58	AEK	58	Panathinaikos	55	AEK	2-1	Olympiacos
2003	Olympiacos	70	Panathinaikos	70	AEK	68	PAOK	1-0	Aris
2004	Panathinaikos	77	Olympiacos	75	PAOK	60	Panathinaikos	3-1	Olympiacos
2005	Olympiacos	65	Panathinaikos	64	AEK	62	Olympiacos	3-0	Aris
2006	Olympiacos	70	AEK	67	Panathinaikos	67	Olympiacos	3-0	AEK

GREECE 2005-06
HELLENIC FOOTBALL LEAGUE A DIVISION

	Pl	W	D	L	F	A	Pts	Olympiacos	AEK	Panath'kos	Iraklis	Xánthi	PAOK	Atromitos	Larisa	Kalamarias	Egaleo	Panionios	Ionikos	OFI	Levadiakos	Kallithea	Akratitos
Olympiacos †	30	23	1	6	63	23	70		3-0	3-2	2-1	2-0	1-2	3-0	4-0	2-1	5-1	5-0	0-0	4-0	1-0	2-1	2-0
AEK Athens †	30	21	4	5	42	20	67	1-3		3-0	2-0	0-0	2-1	2-1	1-0	2-1	1-1	2-0	2-1	2-0	2-0	2-0	2-0
Panathinaikos ‡	30	21	4	5	55	23	67	0-2	1-0		2-2	2-1	1-0	4-3	3-0	3-0	4-0	3-0	1-0	3-1	2-0	2-0	1-0
Iraklis Thessaloníki ‡	30	15	6	9	39	31	51	2-0	4-0	1-0		2-0	0-0	2-0	2-1	0-1	4-2	1-0	2-1	2-0	3-2	1-0	
Xánthi ‡	30	13	8	9	31	25	47	1-0	0-0	1-1	4-1		1-0	1-0	1-0	2-0	1-0	1-0	1-1	0-0	1-0	2-2	2-0
PAOK Thessaloníki ‡	30	13	7	10	44	31	46	1-2	2-1	0-1	1-0	1-0		2-2	2-2	1-2	2-0	1-0	6-1	2-0	3-1	2-1	2-0
Atromitos/Chalkidonia	30	12	6	12	36	37	42	0-1	0-0	1-0	3-2	0-1	2-1		0-0	1-1	0-0	1-3	3-2	4-0	1-0	2-1	2-0
Larisa	30	10	9	11	31	37	39	2-1	0-1	0-3	0-0	3-1	2-1	2-1		4-1	1-1	1-0	0-0	1-0	1-0	2-0	2-1
Apollon Kalamarias	30	10	8	12	32	36	38	1-2	0-1	0-1	2-0	2-1	2-2	1-2	2-2		0-0	1-0	2-1	2-1	1-1	0-0	3-0
Egaleo	30	8	9	13	23	41	33	1-3	0-2	0-2	1-1	3-2	1-0	0-1	1-0	0-0		0-3	1-1	0-0	1-0	1-0	1-0
Panionios	30	9	5	16	33	45	32	2-3	0-2	2-4	3-0	0-2	0-1	2-0	1-1	2-1	0-1		3-3	1-1	1-1	1-0	2-4
Ionikos	30	6	14	10	36	41	32	0-1	0-1	1-1	1-1	0-0	1-1	3-1	1-1	2-0	4-1	0-1		1-1	2-0	2-1	3-2
OFI Crete	30	7	10	13	23	37	31	1-0	0-1	0-2	0-1	1-1	2-1	0-0	3-2	1-2	1-0	1-1	3-0		2-0	0-0	2-2
Levadiakos	30	8	7	15	24	36	31	3-2	0-1	0-0	0-1	0-2	2-2	1-0	3-0	1-0	2-1	3-2	1-1	1-0		1-0	1-1
Kallithea	30	4	8	18	28	49	20	0-3	1-4	2-4	0-0	2-1	1-1	2-3	2-1	0-0	1-1	1-2	3-3	0-1	3-2		2-0
Akratitos	30	4	6	20	19	47	18	0-1	1-2	0-2	3-1	2-0	0-3	0-2	0-0	1-3	0-3	0-1	0-0	1-1	0-0	1-0	

27/08/2005 - 14/05/2006 • † Qualified for the UEFA Champions League • ‡ Qualified for the UEFA Cup

GREECE 2005-06 B DIVISION

	Pl	W	D	L	F	A	Pts
Ergotelis	30	16	8	6	41	23	56
Kérkira	30	17	5	8	38	26	56
Aris Thessaloníki	30	14	12	4	33	17	54
Thrasivoulos Filis	30	15	8	7	40	25	53
Veria	30	10	11	9	28	27	41
Kastoria	30	10	10	10	28	28	40
Ilysiakos	30	11	7	12	43	35	40
Kalamata	30	9	12	9	26	28	39
Ethnikos Asteras	30	8	14	8	36	40	38
Niki Volou	30	9	11	10	32	31	38
Proodeftiki	30	9	11	10	31	34	38
Chiadari	30	9	10	11	27	27	37
Olympiacos Volou	30	10	7	13	30	37	37
Panserraikos	30	10	7	13	28	37	37
Panahaiki 2005	30	9	7	14	24	29	34
Paniliakos §	30	2	4	24	16	57	9

24/09/2005 - 14/05/2006 • § one point deducted

HELLENIC CUP 2005-06

Round of 16
Olympiacos	2
Thrasivoulos Filis *	0
Panahaiki 2005	0
Xánthi *	1
Akratitos *	0 1 5p
Egaleo	0 1 4p
Apollon Kalamarias	0 1
Larisa *	0 2
Agrotikos Asteras *	2
Ergotelis	0
Panionios	1
Ethnikos Asteras *	2
Niki Volou	4
Ionikos *	1
Ethnikos Manis	1 1 3p
AEK Athens *	1 1 4p

Quarter-finals
Olympiacos *	1 1
Xánthi	1 0
Akratitos *	0 0
Larisa	1 1
Agrotikos Asteras	1 4
Ethnikos Asteras *	1 0
Niki Volou *	0 0
AEK Athens	0 2

Semi-finals
Olympiacos *	3 1
Larisa	1 0
Agrotikos Asteras	0 1
AEK Athens *	3 0

Final
Olympiacos	3
AEK Athens	0

CUP FINAL

Pankritio, Iraklion, Crete
10-05-2006, Ref: Terovitsas

Scorers - Mihalis Konstantinou [61],
Ivic OG [71], Neri Castillo [90] for Olympiacos

* Home team/home team in the first leg

GRN – GRENADA

NATIONAL TEAM RECORD
JULY 1ST 2002 TO JULY 9TH 2006

PL	W	D	L	F	A	%
25	8	3	14	54	55	38

FIFA/COCA-COLA WORLD RANKING

1993	1994	1995	1996	1997	1998	1999	2000	2001	2002	2003	2004	2005		High	Low
143	142	141	127	111	117	121	143	133	131	154	144	151		**105** 08/97	**155** 02/04

2005–2006											
08/05	09/05	10/05	11/05	12/05	01/06	02/06	03/06	04/06	05/06	06/06	07/06
149	149	149	150	151	152	152	152	154	155	-	159

2004 was a busy year for the Grenada national team with 17 international matches played - despite the huge interuptions caused by Hurricane Ivan in September that year - but since January 2005 the team hasn't played a single game. The lack of an annual Caribbean Cup has meant that the fixture list has become fragmented with matches only being played in FIFA World Cup™ qualifying years and the year before the finals of the CONCACAF Gold Cup. The women's team has been active, however, and entered the 2006 Women's Caribbean Cup, although the campaign didn't last long as they finished bottom of a first round group won by Trinidad. The under-19 team fared

INTERNATIONAL HONOURS
None

slightly better in their qualifying group for the FIFA U-19 Women's World Championship, finishing second, but an 11-0 thrashing by Trinidad showed the ground that still has to be made up by the women's game in Grenada. After the hugely disrupted League season in 2004, the Digicel Premier League returned for a full season in 2005 and despite remaining unbeaten all season, Fontenoy United could only finish as runners-up to ASOMS Paradise. It was a first championship for ASOMS (Andall School of Modern Soccer) but there was more disappointment for Fontenoy when they lost in the Cup Final to St John's Sports.

THE FIFA BIG COUNT OF 2000

	Male	Female		Male	Female
Registered players	524	0	Referees	35	0
Non registered players	1 000	125	Officials	127	5
Youth players	489	0	Total involved	2 305	
Total players		2 138	Number of clubs	30	
Professional players	0	0	Number of teams	50	

Grenada Football Association (GFA)
Deco Building, PO Box 326, St George's, Grenada
Tel +1 473 4409903   Fax +1 473 4409973
gfa@caribsurf.com   www.grenadafootball.com
President: FOLKES Ashley Ram   General Secretary: DANIEL Victor
Vice-President: CHENEY Joseph   Treasurer: DANIEL Victor   Media Officer: BASCOMBE Michael
Men's Coach: DEBELLOTTE Alister   Women's Coach: DEAN Jules
GFA formed: 1924   CONCACAF: 1969   FIFA: 1978
Green and yellow striped shirts, Red shorts, Yellow socks

RECENT INTERNATIONAL MATCHES PLAYED BY GRENADA

2003	Opponents	Score	Venue	Comp	Scorers	Att	Referee
No international matches played in 2003							
2004							
11-01	Barbados	L 0-2	Bridgetown	Fr		2 000	Small BRB
31-01	Barbados	L 0-1	St George's	Fr			
28-02	Guyana	W 5-0	St George's	WCq	Bishop [34], Phillip [39], Augustine [72], Modeste.A [81], Rennie [91]	7 000	Archundia MEX
14-03	Guyana	W 3-1	Blairmont	WCq	Charles [15], Roberts [69], Bubb [87]	1 200	Quesada Cordero CRC
8-05	St Vincent/Grenadines	D 1-1	Kingstown	Fr			
20-05	Cuba	D 2-2	Havana	Fr	Roberts [47], Bishop [75]		
2-06	St Lucia	W 2-0	St George's	Fr	Roberts [7], Bain.K [65]	2 500	
13-06	USA	L 0-3	Columbus	WCq		10 000	Navarro CAN
20-06	USA	L 2-3	St George's	WCq	Roberts [12], Charles [77]	10 000	Brizan TRI
17-10	St Lucia	L 1-3	Castries	Fr			
13-11	St Vincent/Grenadines	L 2-6	Kingstown	Fr	Rennie [42], Bishop [81]		
20-11	St Vincent/Grenadines	W 3-2	Gouyave	Fr	Modeste.A [6], Charles 2 [13 88]	3 000	Bedeau GRN
24-11	Surinam	D 2-2	Tunapuna	GCq	Charles [46], Bishop [50]	2 000	Forde BRB
26-11	Trinidad and Tobago	L 0-2	Tunapuna	GCq			Callender BRB
28-11	Puerto Rico	W 5-2	Tunapuna	GCq	OG [1], Charles [3], Rennie [58], Williams [68], Langiagne [75]		Callender BRB
12-12	St Vincent/Grenadines	L 1-3	Kingstown	GCq	Rennie [59]		Fanus LCA
19-12	St Vincent/Grenadines	L 0-1	St George's	GCq			Small BRB
2005							
23-01	Barbados	L 0-3	Bridgetown	Fr			
2006							
No international matches played in 2006 before July							

Fr = Friendly match • GC = CONCACAF Gold Cup • WC = FIFA World Cup™ • q = qualifier

GRENADA NATIONAL TEAM RECORDS AND RECORD SEQUENCES

Records			Sequence records		
Victory	14-1	AIA 1998	Wins	3	1996
Defeat	0-7	TRI 1999	Defeats	5	2002-2004
Player Caps	n/a		Undefeated	5	1997, 2004
Player Goals	n/a		Without win	10	1990-1994

			Sequence records		
			Clean sheets	2	1989, 1994
			Goals scored	15	2001-2002
			Without goal	3	1990
			Goals against	17	1996-1999

RECENT LEAGUE AND CUP RECORD

	Championship						Cup		
Year	Champions	Pts	Runners-up	Pts	Third	Pts	Winners	Score	Runners-up
1998	Fontenoy United	3-2	Saint Andrews FL						
1999	Cable Vision SAFL	30	Fontenoy United	28	GBSS	27	Queens Park Rangers		
2000	GBSS	29	Saint John's Sports	27	Fontenoy United	20	Hurricane FC	3-1	GBSS
2001	GBSS	34	Hurricane FC	22	Saint Andrews FL	22	Hurricane FC		GBSS
2002	Queens Park Rangers								
2003	Hurricane FC	45	Paradise	39	Fontenoy United	31	Hurricane FC	1-0	GBSS
2004	Abandoned due to Hurricane Ivan						Police SC	2-1	Paradise
2005	ASOMS Paradise	37	Fontenoy United	36	Hurricane	35	St John's Sports		Fontenoy United

GRENADA COUNTRY INFORMATION

Capital	Saint George's	Independence	1974 from the UK	GDP per Capita	$5 500
Population	89 357	Status	Commonwealth	GNP Ranking	174
Area km²	344	Language	English	Dialling code	+1 473
Population density	259 per km²	Literacy rate	98%	Internet code	.gd
% in urban areas	37%	Main religion	Christian	GMT +/−	-4
Towns/Cities ('000)	Saint George's 4; Gouyave 3; Grenville 2; Victoria 2				
Neighbours (km)	Atlantic Ocean and the Caribbean Sea 121				
Main stadia	National Stadium – Saint George's 9 000				

GUA – GUATEMALA

NATIONAL TEAM RECORD
JULY 1ST 2002 TO JULY 9TH 2006

PL	W	D	L	F	A	%
56	22	14	20	75	71	51.8

FIFA/COCA-COLA WORLD RANKING

1993	1994	1995	1996	1997	1998	1999	2000	2001	2002	2003	2004	2005	High	Low
120	149	145	105	83	73	73	56	67	78	77	71	56	**54** 03/03	**163** 11/95

2005–2006											
08/05	09/05	10/05	11/05	12/05	01/06	02/06	03/06	04/06	05/06	06/06	07/06
59	57	56	55	56	56	58	58	61	62	-	53

After 18 FIFA World Cup™ qualifying matches, two points was all that seperated Guatemala from a play-off place against Bahrain. In their final match they did the job that they needed to do by beating Costa Rica, but no-one could have predicted that Trinidad and Tobago would beat Mexico to pip them to the post. It was tough for a nation that had never come so close to making it to the finals. The aim for Guatemala is to match the football infrastructure in Costa Rica, a setup that has seen them make it to consecutive finals. Matching Costa Rican success in the CONCACAF Champions' Cup would be a start, but there is some catching up to do there as well. Having reached

INTERNATIONAL HONOURS
CONCACAF Championship 1967 UNCAF Championship 2001 CONCACAF Club Championship Municipal 1974, Comunicaciones 1978

the quarter-finals of the final tournament in 2004-05, Municipal lost to Costa Rica's LD Alajuelense in the Central American qualifiers in 2005-06, whilst Suchitepéquez lost heavily to Honduran champions Olimpia at the same stage. At home in the Primera División Municipal had no equals, winning both the Apertura and Clausura with some ease. After topping the League stage of both, they beat Comunicaciones 2-0 on aggregate in the Apertura final, and then Deportivo Marquense 4-1 on aggregate in the Clausura final, to win a fourth successive title. They did, however, lose to Jalapa in that most rare phenomenon in the Americas - the Cup Final.

THE FIFA BIG COUNT OF 2000

	Male	Female		Male	Female
Registered players	48 900	760	Referees	320	8
Non registered players	150 000	62 500	Officials	4 500	75
Youth players	67 500	0	Total involved	334 563	
Total players	329 660		Number of clubs	100	
Professional players	500	0	Number of teams	197	

Federación Nacional de Fútbol de Guatemala (FNFG)
2a. Calle 15-57, Zona 15, Boulevard Vista Hermosa, Guatemala City 01009, Guatemala
Tel +502 24227777   Fax +502 24227780
fedefutbol@guate.net.gt   www.fedefut.org
President: ARROYO Oscar   General Secretary: TBD
Vice-President: TBD   Treasurer: DE TORREBIARTE Adela   Media Officer: None
Men's Coach: GOMEZ Hernan   Women's Coach: GARCIA Antonio
FNFG formed: 1919   CONCACAF: 1961   FIFA: 1946
Blue shirts, White shorts, Blue socks

RECENT INTERNATIONAL MATCHES PLAYED BY GUATEMALA

2004	Opponents	Score		Venue	Comp	Scorers	Att	Referee
12-06	Surinam	D	1-1	Paramaribo	WCq	Ramirez [36]	5 500	Jimenez CRC
20-06	Surinam	W	3-1	Guatemala City	WCq	Ruiz 2 [21 85], Pezzarossi [80]	19 610	Rodriguez MEX
18-07	El Salvador	W	1-0	Los Angeles	Fr	Medina [41]		Valenzuela USA
23-07	Panama	D	1-1	Panama City	Fr	Ramirez [67]	3 000	Mejia CRC
6-08	El Salvador	W	2-0	Washington DC	Fr	Ramirez [49], Mendoza [72]	20 000	Valenzuela USA
11-08	Trinidad and Tobago	W	4-1	Guatemala City	Fr	Melgar [48], Ramirez [71], Romero [78], Estrada.W [86]	9 000	
18-08	Canada	W	2-0	Vancouver	WCq	Ruiz 2 [7 59]	6 500	Sibrian SLV
5-09	Costa Rica	W	2-1	Guatemala City	WCq	Plata 2 [58 73]	27 460	Stott USA
8-09	Honduras	D	2-2	San Pedro Sula	WCq	Ruiz [20], Pezzarossi [49]	40 000	Prendergast JAM
2-10	Jamaica	D	2-2	Fort Lauderdale	Fr	Plata [56], Davilla [59]	8 500	Vaughn USA
9-10	Costa Rica	L	0-5	San Jose	WCq		18 000	Archundia MEX
13-10	Honduras	W	1-0	Guatemala City	WCq	Ruiz [44]	26 000	Brizan TRI
10-11	Mexico	L	0-2	San Antonio (USA)	Fr			Terry USA
13-11	Bolivia	W	1-0	Washington DC	Fr	Ruiz [21]	22 000	Prus USA
17-11	Canada	L	0-1	Guatemala City	WCq		18 000	Rodriguez MEX
21-12	Venezuela	W	1-0	Caracas	Fr	Ruiz [89]	5 000	Solorzano VEN
2005								
17-01	Colombia	D	1-1	Los Angeles	Fr	Ruiz [3]	15 000	Vaughn USA
23-01	Paraguay	L	1-2	Los Angeles	Fr	Rivera [36]	20 000	Prendergast JAM
9-02	Panama	D	0-0	Panama City	WCq		10 000	Salazar USA
13-02	Haiti	W	2-1	Fort Lauderdale	Fr	Villatoro [18], Castillo [70]	10 000	Quesada CRC
19-02	Belize	W	2-0	Guatemala City	GCq	Villatoro [35], Plata [72p]	8 000	Sibrian SLV
21-02	Nicaragua	W	4-0	Guatemala City	GCq	Plata [11], Sandoval 2 [30 77], Villatoro [66]	3 000	Moreno PAN
23-02	Honduras	D	1-1	Guatemala City	GCq	Romero [22]	11 159	Archundia MEX
25-02	Costa Rica	L	0-4	Guatemala City	GCq		1 491	Quesada CRC
27-02	Panama	W	3-0	Panama City	GCq	Villatoro [7], Plata 2 [41 49]	22 506	Stott USA
26-03	Trinidad and Tobago	W	5-1	Guatemala City	WCq	Ramirez [17], Ruiz 2 [30 38], Pezzarossi 2 [78 87]	31 624	Ramdhan TRI
30-03	USA	L	0-2	Birmingham	WCq		7 000	Prus USA
20-04	Jamaica	L	0-1	Atlanta	Fr		38 000	Vazquez URU
27-04	Brazil	L	0-3	Sao Paulo	Fr		26 723	Hall USA
4-06	Mexico	L	0-2	Guatemala City	WCq		BCD	Archundia MEX
8-06	Costa Rica	L	2-3	San Jose	WCq	Villatoro [74], Rodriguez [77]	27 000	Hall USA
8-07	Jamaica	L	3-4	Carson	GCr1	Ruiz 3 [11p 48+ 87]	30 710	Ruiz COL
10-07	Mexico	L	0-4	Los Angeles	GCr1		45 311	Stott USA
13-07	South Africa	D	1-1	Houston	GCr1	Romero [37]	24 000	Sibrian SLV
17-08	Panama	W	2-1	Guatemala City	WCq	Baloy OG [70], Romero [93+]	15 000	Archundia MEX
3-09	Trinidad and Tobago	L	2-3	Port of Spain	WCq	Andrews OG [3], Romero [61]	27 000	Rodriguez MEX
7-09	USA	D	0-0	Guatemala City	WCq			Prendergast JAM
1-10	Jamaica	L	1-2	Fort Lauderdale	Fr		30 000	
8-10	Mexico	L	2-5	San Luis Potosi	WCq	Ruiz [1], Poniciano [53]	23 912	Hall USA
12-10	Costa Rica	W	3-1	Guatemala City	WCq	Poniciano [2], Garcia [16], Ruiz [30]		
2006								
19-02	USA	L	0-4	Frisco	Fr		14 453	Navarro CAN

Fr = Friendly match • GC = CONCACAF Gold Cup • WC = FIFA World Cup™ • q = qualifier • BCD = Behind closed doors

GUATEMALA NATIONAL TEAM RECORDS AND RECORD SEQUENCES

Records			Sequence records				
Victory	9-0	HON 1921	Wins	6	1967	Clean sheets	4	1984-1985
Defeat	1-9	CRC 1955	Defeats	7	2005	Goals scored	16	1957-1965
Player Caps	n/a		Undefeated	13	1996-1997	Without goal	8	1989-1991
Player Goals	n/a		Without win	14	1989-1991	Goals against	13	1953-1961

GUATEMALA COUNTRY INFORMATION

Capital	Guatemala City	Independence	1821 from Spain	GDP per Capita	$4 100
Population	14 280 596	Status	Republic	GNP Ranking	64
Area km²	108 890	Language	Spanish	Dialling code	+502
Population density	131 per km²	Literacy rate	67%	Internet code	.gt
% in urban areas	41%	Main religion	Christian	GMT + / –	-6
Towns/Cities ('000)	Guatemala City 973; Mixco 460; Villa Nueva 397; Petapa 137; Quetzaltenango 127				
Neighbours (km)	Mexico 962; Belize 266; Honduras 256; El Salvador 203; Pacific Ocean & Caribbean Sea 400				
Main stadia	Mateo Flores – Guatemala City 29 950; La Pedrera – Guatemala City 17 000				

COPA CENTENARIO 2006

Round of 16			Quarter-finals			Semi-finals			Final		
Deportivo Jalapa	0	2									
Mictlán *	0	1	Deportivo Jalapa	0	1						
Jutiapa *	0	1	Comunicaciones *	0	0						
Comunicaciones	0	4				Deportivo Jalapa	0	3			
Cobán Imperial	0	2				Deportivo Heredia *	1	1			
Sacachispas *	1	0	Cobán Imperial *	1	1						
Onassis Reforma	0	3	Deportivo Heredia	1	3						
Deportivo Heredia *	6	0							Deportivo Jalapa	1	1
Xinabajul *	1	3							Municipal *	1	0
Deportivo Marquense	0	2	Xinabajul *	2 0	4p						
Coatepeque *	2	1	Suchitepéquez	0 2	3p						
Suchitepéquez	1	5				Xinabajul *	1	1			
Antigua GFC	2	1				Municipal	1	4			
Tiquisate *	3	0	Antigua GFC *	0	1						
Universidad *	0	1	Municipal	4	3						
Municipal	2	1									

CUP FINAL

1st leg. 26-04-2006

2nd leg. 17-05-2006

* Home team in the first leg

RECENT LEAGUE AND CUP RECORD

Championship/Clausura from 2000				Apertura				Cup			
Year	Winners	Score	Runners-up	Winners	Score	Runners-up		Winners	Score	Runners-up	
1990	Municipal	1-0	Suchitepéquez					No tournament			
1991	Comunicaciones	4-2	Municipal					No tournament			
1992	Municipal	0-0 2-1	Comunicaciones					Comunicaciones	2-0	Juventud Ret'ca	
1993	Aurora	†						Aurora			
1994	Municipal	†						Suchitepéquez	2-1	Mictlán	
1995	Comunicaciones	1-0	Municipal					Municipal	3-0	Suchitepéquez	
1996	Xelajú MC	1-0 1-1	Comunicaciones					Municipal	1-1 1-0	Xelajú MC	
1997	Comunicaciones	2-0 3-1	Aurora					Amatitlan	1-1 4-3	Municipal	
1998	Comunicaciones	†						Suchitepéquez	3-1	Cobán Imperial	
1999	Comunicaciones	†						Municipal		Aurora	
2000	Municipal	0-1 2-0	Comunicaciones	Comunicaciones	1-1 2-1	Municipal		No tournament			
2001	Comunicaciones	4-0 2-3	Antigua GFC	Municipal	0-0 1-1	Comunicaciones		No tournament			
2002	Municipal	1-2 2-0	Comunicaciones	Municipal	3-0 0-3	Cobán Imperial		Deportivo Jalapa	5-2	Cobán Imperial	
2003	Comunicaciones	0-0 3-2	Cobán Imperial	Comunicaciones	2-1 1-1	Municipal		Municipal	2-1 1-0	Cobán Imperial	
2004	Cobán Imperial	3-2 2-2	Municipal	Municipal	3-2 0-0	Comunicaciones		Municipal	1-0 4-2	Deportivo Jalapa	
2005	Municipal	1-0 4-2	Suchitepéquez	Municipal	5-1 4-1	Comunicaciones		Deportivo Jalapa	3-0 0-2	Xelajú MC	
2006	Municipal	2-0 2-1	Marquense	Comunicaciones	0-0 2-0	Comunicaciones		Deportivo Jalapa	1-1 1-0	Municipal	

† Automatic champions as winners of both the regular season and the play-offs

GUATEMALA 2005-06

TORNEO APERTURA

	Pl	W	D	L	F	A	Pts	Municipal	Com'ciones	Xelajú	Marquense	Jalapa	Suchit'quez	Heredia	Antigua	Petapa	Cobán
Municipal †	18	11	5	2	35	14	38		4-0	4-0	0-2	1-0	5-1	3-1	1-1	3-0	2-1
Comunicaciones †	18	10	5	3	38	28	35	2-2		1-2	0-3	4-1	3-2	4-2	2-1	2-2	4-1
Xelajú MC †	18	10	2	6	31	22	32	0-1	1-4		2-1	8-1	2-0	0-1	1-1	3-0	3-1
Deportivo Marquense †	18	8	4	6	28	18	28	0-1	1-1	0-1		2-1	3-1	2-0	5-2	3-1	2-0
Deportivo Jalapa †	18	7	3	8	25	34	24	0-0	1-3	1-0	2-1		4-1	3-2	2-0	0-0	2-1
Suchitepéquez †	18	7	2	9	25	32	23	1-3	0-1	2-3	2-0	2-0		3-1	2-1	2-0	2-1
Deportivo Heredia	18	5	6	7	21	26	21	1-1	1-1	1-3	1-1	3-1	3-1		1-0	1-0	0-0
Antigua GFC	18	4	6	8	21	29	18	3-2	1-2	0-1	1-1	3-2	1-1	2-1		0-0	2-2
Petapa	18	1	11	6	17	28	14	1-1	2-3	1-1	2-2	1-1	0-0	1-1	2-2		3-2
Cobán Imperial	18	2	6	10	18	28	12	0-1	1-1	2-0	0-0	2-3	1-2	0-0	2-0	1-1	

30/07/2005 - 27/11/2005 • † Qualified for the play-offs • Top two receive a bye to the semi-finals

APERTURA PLAY-OFFS

Quarter-finals			Semi-finals			Final		
			Municipal ‡	0	2			
Xelajú MC	0	1	Suchitepéquez *	1	1			
Suchitepéquez *	2	0				Municipal	0	2
Deportivo Marquense‡	0	1				Comunicaciones *	0	0
Deportivo Jalapa *	1	0	Deportivo Marquense*	0	1			
			Comunicaciones	3	0			

* Home team in first leg • ‡ qualified due to better season record

GUATEMALA 2005-06

TORNEO CLAUSURA

	Pl	W	D	L	F	A	Pts	Municipal	Marquense	Suchit'quez	Xelajú	Jalapa	Cobán	Heredia	Petapa	Com'ciones	Antigua
Municipal †	18	11	6	1	41	14	39		3-0	2-0	2-0	4-0	3-1	4-0	4-2	2-2	5-1
Deportivo Marquense †	18	10	3	5	33	23	33	1-1		1-0	2-1	2-1	4-2	1-1	2-1	2-0	4-0
Suchitepéquez †	18	8	4	6	21	21	28	2-1	2-2		3-2	1-1	3-2	1-0	0-2	2-0	1-0
Xelajú MC †	18	8	3	7	24	21	27	2-2	1-2	2-1		1-1	2-1	2-1	1-0	2-2	3-0
Deportivo Jalapa †	18	7	5	6	16	21	26	0-0	1-0	2-0	1-0		1-1	2-1	2-1	1-0	1-0
Cobán Imperial †	18	6	7	5	27	24	25	0-0	1-2	1-1	1-0	3-2		1-0	2-0	4-1	1-1
Deportivo Heredia	18	6	3	9	19	24	21	1-2	2-1	0-0	5-1	2-2			1-0	2-1	3-0
Petapa	18	5	4	9	19	23	19	1-1	3-2	0-1	0-1	0-0	1-1	1-0		3-1	3-0
Comunicaciones	18	4	4	10	18	31	16	1-3	0-3	1-2	2-1	2-0	1-1	2-1	1-1		1-0
Antigua GFC	18	4	3	11	14	30	15	0-2	3-2	1-1	1-3	0-0	0-2	3-0	3-0	1-0	

21/01/2006 - 21/05/2006 • † Qualified for the play-offs • Top two receive a bye to the semi-finals • Antigua relegated due to having the worst overall season record • Cobán and Petapa entered a relegation play-off:

CLAUSURA PLAY-OFFS

Quarter-finals			Semi-finals			Final		
			Municipal	1	3			
Deportivo Jalapa *	0	0	Xelajú MC *	2	1			
Xelajú MC	1	2				Municipal	2	2
Suchitepéquez	0	4				Deportivo Marquense*	0	1
Cobán Imperial *	3	0	Suchitepéquez *	0	0			
			Deportivo Marquense	0	1			

* Home team in first leg

GUI – GUINEA

NATIONAL TEAM RECORD
JULY 1ST 2002 TO JULY 9TH 2006

PL	W	D	L	F	A	%
38	18	9	11	55	39	59.2

FIFA/COCA-COLA WORLD RANKING

1993	1994	1995	1996	1997	1998	1999	2000	2001	2002	2003	2004	2005	High	Low
63	66	63	73	65	79	91	80	108	120	101	86	79	**24** 07/06	**123** 05/03

2005–2006											
08/05	09/05	10/05	11/05	12/05	01/06	02/06	03/06	04/06	05/06	06/06	07/06
90	89	82	80	79	77	56	56	52	51	-	24

A quarter-final place at the African Nations Cup finals for Syli Nationale served notice of the potential for Guinea, who will look back on the tournament with some satisfaction. Although there was major disappointment with their elimination the hands of Senegal in the quarter-finals, Guinea impressed in the opening round group where they won all three of their matches to finish top of the standings. French coach Patrice Neveu produced admirable tactics to fit in with the physical potential of his players and it was only the third time in eight Nations Cup finals appearances that the side had made it past the first round in what was arguably their best showing since finishing as

INTERNATIONAL HONOURS
Copa Amilcar Cabral 1981 1982 1987 1988 2005   **CAF Champions League** Hafia Conakry 1972 1975 1977

runners-up in 1976. The confidence at the Nations Cup flowed from the success in the regional Amilcar Cabral Cup where Neveu had used home-based players to win the event on home soil, beating Senegal's under-23 side in the final. Both achievements made up for the disappointment of a third place finish in their FIFA World Cup™ qualifying group, behind Tunisia and Morocco. At club level there was a rare foray into the latter stage of continental competition with Fello Star Labe making the last eight of the CAF Confederation Cup. The rigours of group play, however, proved difficult for the under-resourced team, who lost all six of their matches.

THE FIFA BIG COUNT OF 2000

	Male	Female		Male	Female
Registered players	8 000	0	Referees	300	0
Non registered players	30 000	0	Officials	2 400	0
Youth players	4 000	0	Total involved	44 700	
Total players	42 000		Number of clubs	150	
Professional players	0	0	Number of teams	700	

Fédération Guinéenne de Football (FGF)
PO Box 3645, Conakry, Guinea
Tel +224 455878   Fax +224 455879
guineefoot59@yahoo.fr   www.none
President: BANGOURA Aboubacar Bruno   General Secretary: CAMARA Fode Capi
Vice-President: CONTE Sory   Treasurer: DIALLO Mamadou   Media Officer: None
Men's Coach: NEVEU Patrice   Women's Coach: CAMARA Fabert
FGF formed: 1960   CAF: 1962   FIFA: 1962
Red shirts, Yellow shorts, Green socks

RECENT INTERNATIONAL MATCHES PLAYED BY GUINEA

2002	Opponents	Score		Venue	Comp	Scorers	Att	Referee
1-09	Gambia	L	0-1	Banjul	Fr			
8-09	Liberia	W	3-0	Conakry	CNq	Camara.T [17], Fode [56], Conte [57]		Diouf SEN
12-10	Ethiopia	L	0-1	Addis Abeba	CNq			Itur KEN
2003								
12-02	Mali	L	0-1	Toulon	Fr			
30-03	Niger	W	2-0	Conakry	CNq	Mansare [40p], Sylla.A [90]		Monteiro Duatre CPV
7-06	Niger	L	0-1	Niamey	CNq			Wellington GHA
21-06	Liberia	W	2-1	Accra	CNq	Soulemane 2 [11 50]		
6-07	Ethiopia	W	3-0	Conakry	CNq	Youla 2 [32 72], Feindouno [55]		
20-08	Tunisia	D	0-0	Radès/Tunis	Fr		20 000	
12-10	Mozambique	W	1-0	Conakry	WCq	Sambegou Bangoura [70]	13 400	Ndoye SEN
16-11	Mozambique	W	4-3	Maputo	WCq	Youla [14], Sambegou Bangoura 3 [21 35 54]	50 000	Mochubela RSA
2004								
20-01	Burkina Faso	W	1-0	Saint-Maxime	Fr	Camara.T [72]		
25-01	Congo DR	W	2-1	Tunis	CNr1	Camara.T [68], Feindouno [81]	3 000	Aboubacar CIV
28-01	Rwanda	D	1-1	Bizerte	CNr1	Camara.T [48]	4 000	Sowe GAM
1-02	Tunisia	D	1-1	Radès/Tunis	CNr1	Camara.T [84]	18 000	Tessema ETH
7-02	Mali	L	1-2	Bizerte	CNqf	Feindouno [15]	1 450	El Fatah EGY
28-04	Côte d'Ivoire	L	2-4	Aix-les-Bains	Fr	Feidouno [12], Oulare [39]	2 000	
29-05	Senegal	D	1-1	Paris	Fr	Diawara [24p]	2 000	Garibian FRA
20-06	Tunisia	W	2-1	Conakry	WCq	Diawara 2 [12 46]	15 300	Codjia BEN
3-07	Malawi	D	1-1	Lilongwe	WCq	Diawara [80]	11 383	Abdulkadir TAN
5-09	Botswana	W	4-0	Conakry	WCq	Feindouno [44], Youla [54], Diawara [60], Mansare [82]	25 000	Agbenyega GHA
10-10	Morocco	D	1-1	Conakry	WCq	Mansare [50]	25 000	Monteiro Duatre CPV
17-11	Kenya	L	1-2	Nairobi	WCq	Feindouno [19p]	16 000	Abd El Fatah EGY
2005								
9-02	Mali	D	2-2	Paris	Fr	Thiam [6], Feindouno [55]		
26-03	Morocco	L	0-1	Rabat	WCq		70 000	Coulibaly MLI
5-06	Kenya	W	1-0	Conakry	WCq	Sambegou Bangoura [68]	21 000	Mbera GAB
11-06	Tunisia	L	0-2	Tunis	WCq		30 000	Lim Kee Chong MRI
16-08	Congo DR	L	1-3	Paris	Fr	Ibrahima Bangoura [70]	2 000	Piccirillo FRA
4-09	Malawi	W	3-1	Conakry	WCq	Feindouno [12], Diawara [36], Sambegou Bangoura [67]	2 518	Mana NGA
8-10	Botswana	W	2-1	Gaborone	WCq	Ousmane Bangoura 2 [73 76]	16 800	Sowe GAM
18-11	Guinea-Bissau	D	2-2	Conakry	ACr1	Soumah [7], Camara.O [75]		
22-11	Sierra Leone	W	1-0	Conakry	ACr1	Diawara [19]		
25-11	Mali	D	0-0	Conakry	ACsf	W 6-5p		
27-11	Senegal †	W	1-0	Conakry	ACf	Barujakis [5]	30 000	
2006								
7-01	Togo	W	1-0	Viry-Chatillon	Fr	Bangoura.O [65p]	2 500	Piccirillo FRA
22-01	South Africa	W	2-0	Alexandria	CNr1	Sambegou Bangoura [76], Ousmane Bangoura [87]	10 000	Benouza ALG
26-01	Zambia	W	2-1	Alexandria	CNr1	Feindouno 2 [74p 90]	24 000	Imeire NGA
30-01	Tunisia	W	3-0	Alexandria	CNr1	Ousmane Bangoura [16], Feindouno [69], Diawara [90]	18 000	Maidin SIN
3-02	Senegal	L	2-3	Alexandria	CNqf	Diawara [24], Feindouno [95+]	17 000	Codjia BEN

Fr = Friendly match • CN = CAF African Cup of Nations • AC = Amilcar Cabral Cup • WC = FIFA World Cup™ • q = qualifier • r1 = first round group • sf = semi-final • f = final • † = not a full international

GUINEA NATIONAL TEAM RECORDS AND RECORD SEQUENCES

Records			Sequence records					
Victory	14-0	MTN 1972	Wins	7	1972-1973	Clean sheets	7	1986-1987
Defeat	2-6	GHA 1975	Defeats	4	1984, 1998-1999	Goals scored	29	1973-1977
Player Caps	n/a		Undefeated	13	1980-1981	Without goal	6	1991
Player Goals	n/a		Without win	14	1983-1984	Goals against	14	1967-1969

GUINEA COUNTRY INFORMATION

Capital	Conakry	Independence	1958 from France	GDP per Capita	$2 100
Population	9 246 462	Status	Republic	GNP Ranking	129
Area km²	245 857	Language	French	Dialling code	+224
Population density	37 per km²	Literacy rate	38%	Internet code	.gn
% in urban areas	30%	Main religion	Muslim 85%	GMT + / –	0
Towns/Cities ('000)	Conakry 1 871; Nzérékoré 132; Kindia 117; Kankan 114; Labé 46; Mamou 41; Siguiri 43				
Neighbours (km)	Guinea-Bissau 386; Mali 858; Côte d'Ivoire 610; Liberia 563; Sierra Leone 652; Atlantic Ocean 320				
Main stadia	Stade 28 Septembre – Conakry 40 000				

CLUB DIRECTORY

Club	Town/City	Lge	CL
ASFAG (Association Forces Armées Guinée)	Conakry	1	0
Ashanti Golden Boys	Siguiri	0	0
ASM Sangarédi (Association Sportive Mineurs)	Boké	0	0
Athlético Coléah	Conakry	0	0
Baraka SSG	Conakry	0	0
Etoile de Guinée	Conakry	0	0
Fello Star	Labé	0	0
Friguiabé FC	Kindia	0	0
Gangan FC	Kindia	0	0
Hafia FC	Conakry	12	3
Horoya AC	Conakry	9	0
Industriel Kamsar	Kamsar	0	0
Kaloum Star	Conakry	11	0
Milo FC	Kankan	0	0
Olympique Kankande	Boké	0	0
Satellite FC	Conakry	2	0

RECENT LEAGUE AND CUP RECORD

Championship				Cup			
Year	Champions	Score	Runners-up	Winners	Score	Runners-up	
1996	Kaloum Stars	†		ASFAG Conakry			
1997	No championship played			Kaloum Stars			
1998	Kaloum Stars	†		Kaloum Stars	1-1 6-5p	Mineurs Sangaredi	
1999	No championship played			Horoya Conakry			
2000	Hafia Conakry	†		Fello Stars Labé	2-1	Horoya Conakry	
2001	Horoya Conakry	3-1	Satellite Conakry	Kaloum Stars			
2002	Satellite Conakry	3-2	Kaloum Star	Hafia Conakry	5-3	Satellite Conakry	
2003	ASFAG Conakry	†		Etoile de Guinée		Etoile de Coléah	
2004	No championship played			Fello Star Labé	2-2 5-4p	CIK Kamsar	
2005	Satellite Conakry	†	Fello Star Labé	Kaloum Stars	0-0 5-4p	Gangan Kindia	

† Championship played on a league system

GUM – GUAM

NATIONAL TEAM RECORD
JULY 1ST 2002 TO JULY 9TH 2006

PL	W	D	L	F	A	%
13	0	0	13	1	99	0

FIFA/COCA-COLA WORLD RANKING

1993	1994	1995	1996	1997	1998	1999	2000	2001	2002	2003	2004	2005	High	Low
-	-	-	188	191	198	200	199	199	200	201	2005	204	182 08/96	205 12/04

					2005–2006						
08/05	09/05	10/05	11/05	12/05	01/06	02/06	03/06	04/06	05/06	06/06	07/06
204	204	204	204	204	204	204	204	203	203	-	196

Given the heavy defeats suffered by the national team of Guam in past matches, the introduction of the AFC Challenge Cup was seen as a welcome development. Based on the premise that playing nations of a similar standard is more beneficial for the development of the game, it was hoped that the tournament would be more suited to the standards in Guam. However, at half-time in their opening match against Palestine in the Bangladesh capital Dhaka, Guam were trailing 8-0 and a repeat of the 21-0 thrashing at the hands of Korea DPR 12 months earlier looked on the cards. But after the initial shock they conceded just three more and in the next game, against hosts

Bangladesh, Guam surprised everyone by restricting them to a 3-0 victory, a scoreline that was repeated in their storm delayed match against Cambodia. It was progress of sorts but the fact remains that in 13 internationals since the start of 2003, the national team has let in 99 goals and scored just one. Unsurprisingly, they prop up the FIFA/Coca-Cola World Ranking. Local businesses have joined with the GFA to try and develop the game, donating $680,000 to upgrade the soccer facility at the Guam Sports Complex. One of those companies, Guam Shipyard, continue to be a force in the local League, their team winning both stages the 2005 Championship.

THE FIFA BIG COUNT OF 2000

	Male	Female		Male	Female
Registered players	135	137	Referees	19	2
Non registered players	400	275	Officials	75	25
Youth players	1 012	153	Total involved	2 233	
Total players	2 112		Number of clubs	9	
Professional players	0	0	Number of teams	77	

Guam Football Association (GFA)
PO Box 5093, Hagatna, Guam 96932
Tel +1 671 9225423   Fax +1 671 9225424
info@guamfootball.com   www.guamfootball.com
President: LAI Richard   General Secretary: BORDALLO Michael
Vice-President: ARTERO Pascual   Treasurer: LAI George   Media Officer: CEPEDA Joseph
Men's Coach: TSUKITATE Norio   Women's Coach: RENFRO Thomas
GFA formed: 1975   AFC: 1996   FIFA: 1996
Blue shirts, White shorts, Blue socks

RECENT INTERNATIONAL MATCHES PLAYED BY GUAM

2002	Opponents		Score	Venue	Comp	Scorers	Att	Referee
No international matches played in 2002								
2003								
24-02	Mongolia	L	0-2	Hong Kong	EACq		1 602	Huang Junjie CHN
26-02	Macao	L	0-2	Hong Kong	EACq		672	Cheung Yim Yau HKG
28-02	Chinese Taipei	L	0-7	Hong Kong	EACq		1 814	
2-03	Hong Kong	L	0-11	Hong Kong	EACq		6 862	Huang Junjie CHN
23-04	Bhutan	L	0-6	Thimphu	ACq			
25-04	Mongolia	L	0-5	Thimphu	ACq			
2004								
No international matches played in 2004								
2005								
5-03	Chinese Taipei	L	0-9	Taipei	EACq			
7-03	Hong Kong	L	0-15	Taipei	EACq			
9-03	Mongolia	L	1-4	Taipei	EACq	Pangelinan 69		
11-03	Korea DPR	L	0-21	Taipei	EACq			
2006								
1-04	Palestine	L	0-11	Dhaka	CCr1		3 000	AK Nema IRQ
3-04	Bangladesh	L	0-3	Dhaka	CCr1		18 000	U Win Cho MYA
6-04	Cambodia	L	0-3	Dhaka	CCr1		500	U Win Cho MYA

EAC = East Asian Championship • AC = AFC Asian Cup • CC = AFC Challenge Cup • q = qualifier • r1 = first round group

GUAM NATIONAL TEAM RECORDS AND RECORD SEQUENCES

Records			Sequence records					
Victory	-	Yet to win a match	Wins	0		Clean sheets	0	
Defeat	0-21	PRK 2005	Defeats	32	1975-2006	Goals scored	1	five times
Player Caps	n/a		Undefeated	0		Without goal	15	1996-2005
Player Goals	n/a		Without win	32	1975-2006	Goals against	32	1975-2006

RECENT LEAGUE AND CUP RECORD

	Overall Champions				Spring League				Fall League		
Year	Winners	Score	Runners-up		Winners	Score	Runners-up		Winners	Score	Runners-up
1998	Anderson				Anderson				Island Cargo		
1999	Silver Bullets				Carpet One				Silver Bullets		
2000	Silver Bullets	4-2	Navy		Silver Bullets				Navy	4-3	Anderson
2001					Silver Bullets	4-1	Lai National		Staywell Zoom	2-1	Guam Insurance
2002	Guam Shipyard	‡			Guam Shipyard	2-0	Guam Insurance		Guam Shipyard	4-2	IT&E Pumas
2003	Guam Shipyard	‡			Guam Shipyard	2-1	Quality Distrib's		Guam Shipyard	†	
2004	Under-18	‡			Under-18	5-0	IT&E Pumas		Under-18	4-0	Guam Shipyard
2005	Guam Shipyard	‡			Guam Shipyard	6-0	Quality Distrib's		Guam Shipyard	4-3	Crushers
2006					Guam Shipyard	6-1	Quality Distrib's				

‡ Won both stages so automatic champions • † Played on a league system • Guam Shipyard previously known as Silver Bullets

GUAM COUNTRY INFORMATION

Capital	Hagatna	Independence	Unincorporated territory of the USA	GDP per Capita	$21 000
Population	166 090	Status		GNP Ranking	n/a
Area km²	549	Language	English	Dialling code	+1 671
Population density	302 per km²	Literacy rate	99%	Internet code	.GU
% in urban areas	n/a	Main religion	Christian 99%	GMT +/−	+10
Towns/Cities ('000)	Tamuning 11; Mangilao 8; Yigo 8; Astumbo 5; Barrigada 4; Agat 4; Ordot 4				
Neighbours (km)	North Pacific Ocean 125				
Main stadia	Wettengel Rugby Field – Hagatna				

GUY – GUYANA

NATIONAL TEAM RECORD
JULY 1ST 2002 TO JULY 9TH 2006

PL	W	D	L	F	A	%
11	6	1	4	20	16	59.1

FIFA/COCA-COLA WORLD RANKING

1993	1994	1995	1996	1997	1998	1999	2000	2001	2002	2003	2004	2005	High	Low
136	154	162	153	168	161	171	183	178	169	182	182	167	**131** 07/06	**185** 02/04

2005–2006											
08/05	09/05	10/05	11/05	12/05	01/06	02/06	03/06	04/06	05/06	06/06	07/06
180	182	168	167	167	167	167	163	164	162	-	131

Just four international matches were played by Guyana in the 2005-06 season, but the matches against Dominica and then Antigua and Barbuda, brought with them a small piece of history. All four were won - the best run of consecutive victories ever achieved by the national team. The challenge is to take that form into the qualifiers for the CONCACAF Gold Cup. The Georgetown League remains the major club competition in the country and in 2005 was played on a round robin basis. It was won by Fruta Conquerors for the fourth time in five years. They finished four points ahead of Alpha United, who a month and a half later also had to settle for second place in the

INTERNATIONAL HONOURS
None

Kashif & Shanghai Cup, a tournament that brings together the top clubs from all of the regions of the country. In the final on New Year's Day 2006, Alpha United lost to Top XX from the second city of Linden. With the idea of a national championship almost dead and buried, the Cup is the nearest thing to deciding the champion team of the country. In March 2006 Alpha United did get their hands on a trophy when they beat the stylishly named Pele in the final of the Fruta Knockout Festival, another Cup competition that brings together teams from Georgetown, Linden, East Coast, East Bank, Berbice and West Demerara.

THE FIFA BIG COUNT OF 2000

	Male	Female		Male	Female
Registered players	1 500	90	Referees	4	2
Non registered players	7 000	40	Officials	480	30
Youth players	1 000	0	Total involved	10 146	
Total players	9 630		Number of clubs	30	
Professional players	0	0	Number of teams	100	

Guyana Football Federation (GFF)
Lot 17 Dadanawa Street, Section K, Campbellville, PO Box 10727, Georgetown, Guyana
Tel +592 2 278758   Fax +592 2 262641
gff@networksgy.com   www.gff.org.gy
President: KLASS Colin   General Secretary: RUTHERFORD George
Vice-President: CALLENDER Winston   Treasurer: HENRY Aubrey   Media Officer: GRANGER Frederick
Men's Coach: FRANCE Lynden   Women's Coach: FRANCE Lynden
GFF formed: 1902   CONCACAF: 1969   FIFA: 1968
Green shirts, Green shorts, Yellow socks

RECENT INTERNATIONAL MATCHES PLAYED BY GUYANA

2004	Opponents		Score	Venue	Comp	Scorers	Att	Referee
15-02	Barbados	W	2-0	Bridgetown	Fr	Hernandez 59, Richardson 86	1 200	Small BRB
28-02	Grenada	L	0-5	St George's	WCq		7 000	Archundia MEX
2-03	Trinidad and Tobago	L	0-1	Tunapuna	Fr			Randham TRI
14-03	Grenada	L	1-3	Blairmont	WCq	Harris 29	1 200	Quesada Cordero CRC
2005								
13-02	Barbados	D	3-3	Bridgetown	Fr	Richardson 21, Cadogan 36, Abrams 71	6 000	Callender BRB
30-09	Dominica	W	3-0	Linden	Fr	Abrams 10, Parks 60, Manning 81		Lancaster GUY
2-10	Dominica	W	3-0	Georgetown	Fr	McKinnon 2 19 42, Codrington 85		Kia SUR
2006								
24-02	Antigua and Barbuda	W	2-1	Linden	Fr	Abrams 3, Codrington 61		James GUY
26-02	Antigua and Barbuda	W	4-1	Linden	Fr	Pollard 34, Abrams 37, Beveney 2 40 66		Lancaster GUY

Fr = Friendly match • GC = CONCACAF Gold Cup • WC = FIFA World Cup™ • q = qualifier

GUYANA NATIONAL TEAM RECORDS AND RECORD SEQUENCES

Records			Sequence records					
Victory	14-0	AIA 1998	Wins	4	2005-2006	Clean sheets	2	1990-1991, 2005
Defeat	0-9	MEX 1987	Defeats	8	1987-1990	Goals scored	11	1984-1987
Player Caps	n/a		Undefeated	10	1984-1987	Without goal	7	1987-1990
Player Goals	n/a		Without win	10	1987-1990	Goals against	13	1992-1996

KASHIF & SHANGHAI CUP 2005-06

Quarter-finals		Semi-finals		Final	
Top XX Linden	0 5p				
Silver Shattas	0 4p	Top XX Linden	2		
Netrockers	1	Pele	1		
Pele	2			Top XX Linden	1
Conquerors	1			Alpha United	0
Victoria Kings	0	Conquerors	0		
GDF	0	Alpha United	1	1-01-2006	
Alpha United	1				

RECENT LEAGUE AND CUP RECORD

	National Championship			Georgetown League				Cup		
Year	Winners	Score	Runners-up	Winners	Score	Runners-up		Winners	Score	Runners-up
1999	Santos	0-0 4-2p	Conquerors	Conquerors				Khelwalaas	2-1	Real Victoria
2000	Not held				-			Top XX Linden	3-1	Conquerors
2001	Conquerors	†	Real Victoria	Conquerors				Top XX Linden	1-1 4-2p	Camptown
2002	Not held				-			Real Victoria	2-2 5-4p	Netrockers
2003	Not held			Conquerors	1-0	Beacon		Conquerors	1-0	Western Tigers
2004	Not held			Western Tigers	2-1	Conquerors		Camptown	1-0	Top XX Linden
2005	Not held			Conquerors	†	Alpha United		Conquerors	4-1	Dennery
2006	Not held							Top XX Linden	1-0	Alpha United

There are two main cup competitions - the Kashif & Shanghai, which is listed above, and the Mayors Cup • † Played on a league basis

GUYANA COUNTRY INFORMATION

Capital	Georgetown	Independence	1966 from the UK	GDP per Capita	$4 000
Population	705 803	Status	Republic within Commonwealth	GNP Ranking	163
Area km²	214 970	Language	English	Dialling code	+592
Population density	3 per km²	Literacy rate	98%	Internet code	.gy
% in urban areas	36%	Main religion	Christian 50%, Hindu 35%	GMT + / –	-4
Towns/Cities ('000)	Georgetown 235; Linden 44; New Amsterdam 35; Corriverton 12; Bartica 11				
Neighbours (km)	Surinam 600; Brazil 1 119; Venezuela 743; Caribbean Sea 459				
Main stadia	Georgetown Football Stadium – Georgetown 2 000				

HAI - HAITI

NATIONAL TEAM RECORD
JULY 1ST 2002 TO JULY 9TH 2006

PL	W	D	L	F	A	%
33	13	7	13	60	48	50

FIFA/COCA-COLA WORLD RANKING

1993	1994	1995	1996	1997	1998	1999	2000	2001	2002	2003	2004	2005	High	Low
145	132	153	114	125	109	99	84	82	72	96	95	98	**72** 12/02	**155** 04/96

					2005–2006						
08/05	09/05	10/05	11/05	12/05	01/06	02/06	03/06	04/06	05/06	06/06	07/06
87	91	91	91	98	100	102	103	104	106	-	123

Democratic rule may have been restored to Haiti in February 2006 but it remains one of the most impoverished states in the world with the infrastructure in a state of almost total collapse. However, apart from a break when the fighting was at its worst in 2004, the League has carried on in a remarkably organised manner. The 2005-06 season started in October with the staging of the Super Coupe d'Haiti, the first official Cup tournament played in the country since 1962. With 32 entrants it was completed before the League kicked off in November and was won by Tempête St Marc, who beat AS Mirebalais 2-1 in the final. In the Championnat d'Ouverture, Tempête's local rivals

INTERNATIONAL HONOURS
Qualified for the FIFA World Cup™ finals 1974   **CCCF Championship** 1957   **CONCACAF Champions Cup** Racing Club 1963 Violette 1984

Baltimore won a close race with Racing Gônaïves and Racing Club Haïtien to follow up their first ever title in the previous season's closing championship. They failed to make it a hat-trick of titles, however, when the Championnat de Fermeture was won by Don Bosco. With four teams in with a chance going into the final round, Don Bosco were the only winners from the quartet. They beat Victory 2-0 to win only their second title. With the men's national team inactive after February 2005, it was left to the women to fly the flag for Haiti, but after being drawn in a Caribbean Women's Cup group in Aruba they were refused visas on arrival.

THE FIFA BIG COUNT OF 2000

	Male	Female		Male	Female
Registered players	8 000	0	Referees	200	0
Non registered players	75 000	0	Officials	2 000	0
Youth players	15 000	0	Total involved	100 200	
Total players	98 000		Number of clubs	300	
Professional players	0	0	Number of teams	2 000	

Fédération Haïtienne de Football (FHF)
128 Avenue Christiophe, Case postale 2258, Port-au-Prince, Haiti
Tel +509 2440115   Fax +509 2440117
jbyves@yahoo.com
President: JEAN-BART Yves Dr   General Secretary: DESIR Lionel
Vice-President: JEAN MARIE Georges   Treasurer: BERTIN Eddy   Media Officer: CHARLES M. Louis
Men's Coach: MARCELIN Carlo   Women's Coach: LAMARRE Wilnea
FHF formed: 1904   CONCACAF: 1961   FIFA: 1933
Blue shirts, Red shorts, Blue socks

RECENT INTERNATIONAL MATCHES PLAYED BY HAITI

2002 Opponents		Score	Venue	Comp	Scorers	Att	Referee
18-11 Antigua and Barbuda	W	1-0	Port-au-Prince	GCq	Lormera [48]		Bowen CAY
22-11 Antigua and Barbuda	W	3-0	Port-au-Prince	GCq	Lormera [5], Gilles [45], Menelas [75]		Bowen CAY
2003							
23-02 Peru	L	1-5	Lima	Fr	Menelas [50]		Rivera PER
26-03 Martinique	W	2-1	Kingston	GCq	Menelas 2 [22 64]		Lee ANT
28-03 St Lucia	L	1-2	Kingston	GCq	Romulus [73]		Lee ANT
30-03 Jamaica	L	0-3	Kingston	GCq			Brizan TRI
29-07 St Kitts and Nevis	L	0-1	Basseterre	Fr			Matthew SKN
31-07 Trinidad and Tobago	W	2-0	Basseterre	Fr	Peguero [47], Chery [63]		Rawlins SKN
20-08 Venezuela	L	2-3	Maracaibo	Fr	Peguero [55], Maxo [69]	15 000	
31-08 China PR	W	4-3	Fort Lauderdale	Fr			
27-12 Bahamas	W	6-0	Miami	Fr			
2004							
31-01 Nicaragua	D	1-1	West Palm Beach	Fr			
18-02 Turks and Caicos Isl.	W	5-0	Miami	WCq	Peguero [6], Descouines 3 [43 45 50], Wadson [71]	3 000	Stott USA
21-02 Turks and Caicos Isl.	W	2-0	Hialeah	WCq	Roody [10p], Harvey OG [41]	3 000	Valenzuela USA
29-02 Nicaragua	D	1-1	Esteli	Fr			
13-03 USA	D	1-1	Miami	Fr	Boucicaut [69]	8 714	Prendergast JAM
5-05 Guatemala	L	0-1	Guatemala City	Fr		15 000	Recinos SLV
12-05 El Salvador	D	3-3	Houston	Fr	Peguero [10], Descouines [15], Lormera [82]	4 000	Terry USA
12-06 Jamaica	D	1-1	Miami	WCq	Peguero [50]	30 000	Stott USA
20-06 Jamaica	L	0-3	Kingston	WCq			Sibrian SLV
18-08 Brazil	L	0-6	Port-au-Prince	Fr		15 000	Oliveira BRA
24-11 US Virgin Islands	W	11-0	Kingston	GCq	Mesidor 3 [13 30 48], Ulcena 2 [15 78], Saint-Preux [33], Chery 2 [40 90], Lormera [57], Germain [64], Thelamour [87]	250	Piper TRI
26-11 Saint-Martin †	W	2-0	Montego Bay	GCq	Bruny [25], Thelamour [67]	500	Brizan TRI
28-11 Jamaica	L	1-3	Kingston	GCq	Ulcena [41]	4 000	Piper TRI
12-12 St Kitts and Nevis	W	1-0	Fort Lauderdale	GCq	Cadet [62]		McNab BAH
15-12 St Kitts and Nevis	W	2-0	Basseterre	GCq	Cadet [16], Dorcelus [70]		Bhimull TRI
2005							
9-01 Cuba	L	0-1	Port-au-Prince	GCq		15 000	Minyetti DOM
12-01 Costa Rica	D	3-3	San Jose	Fr	Cadet 2 [18 39], Germain [90]		Porras CRC
16-01 Cuba	D	1-1	Havana	GCq	Cadet [59]		Brizan TRI
1-02 Trinidad and Tobago	L	0-1	Port of Spain	Fr			
3-02 Trinidad and Tobago	L	1-2	Port of Spain	Fr	Romulus [47]		
6-02 Trinidad and Tobago	W	1-0	Scarborough	Fr	Germain [19p]		
13-02 Guatemala	L	1-2	Fort Lauderdale	Fr	Cadet [61]	10 000	Salazar USA
2006							

No international matches played in 2006 before July

Fr = Friendly match • GC = CONCACAF Gold Cup • WC = FIFA World Cup™ • q = qualifier • † Not a full international

HAITI NATIONAL TEAM RECORDS AND RECORD SEQUENCES

Records			Sequence records					
Victory	12-1	VIR 2001	Wins	8	1979	Clean sheets	5	1997-1998
Defeat	1-9	BRA 1959	Defeats	6	1974-75, 1984-89	Goals scored	12	1997-1999
Player Caps	n/a		Undefeated	18	1977-1980	Without goal	6	1973-1974
Player Goals	n/a		Without win	12	1973-1975	Goals against	9	1974-1975

HAITI COUNTRY INFORMATION

Capital	Port-au-Prince	Independence	1804 from France	GDP per Capita	$1 600
Population	7 656 166	Status	Republic	GNP Ranking	122
Area km²	27 750	Language	French	Dialling code	+509
Population density	275 per km²	Literacy rate	52%	Internet code	.ht
% in urban areas	32%	Main religion	Christian 96%	GMT + / –	-5
Towns/Cities ('000)	Port-au-Prince 1 234; Carrefour 439; Delmas 377; Cap-Haïtien 134; Pétionville 108				
Neighbours (km)	Dominican Republic 360; Atlantic Ocean & Caribbean Sea 1 771				
Main stadia	Stade Sylvio Cator – Port-au-Prince 10 500; Park St Victor – Cap-Haïtien 7 500				

HAITI 2005–06 DIVISION 1 OUVERTURE

	Pl	W	D	L	F	A	Pts
Baltimore St Marc	15	9	5	1	15	3	32
Racing Gônaïves	15	9	4	2	17	6	31
Racing Club Haïtien	15	6	8	1	14	7	26
Don Bosco Pétion-Ville	15	7	4	4	15	11	25
Zénith Cap Haïtien	15	6	5	4	11	8	23
Aigle Noir	15	5	4	6	17	12	19
Tempête St Marc	15	5	4	6	9	12	19
Violette AC	15	5	4	6	13	18	19
Cavaly Léogâne	15	4	6	5	11	10	18
Victory FC	15	4	5	6	13	13	17
Dynamite St Marc	15	4	5	6	13	20	17
US Frères Pétion-Ville	15	3	7	5	12	13	16
AS Capoise	15	3	7	5	11	14	16
AS Mirebalais	15	4	3	8	9	15	15
Roulado Gônaïves	15	3	5	7	14	25	14
AS Carrefour	15	3	4	8	10	17	13

4/11/2005 - 19/02/2006

HAITI 2005–06 DIVISION 1 FERMETURE

	Pl	W	D	L	F	A	Pts
Don Bosco Pétion-Ville	15	9	3	3	22	13	30
AS Mirebalais	15	8	5	2	15	5	29
Aigle Noir	15	8	3	3	23	17	27
Cavaly Léogâne	15	7	5	2	15	6	26
Victory FC	15	7	4	4	20	15	25
Tempête St Marc	15	7	3	5	14	12	24
Zénith Cap Haïtien	15	6	6	3	13	11	24
Baltimore St Marc	15	6	4	5	13	13	22
Roulado Gônaïves	15	5	5	5	12	17	20
Racing Club Haïtien	15	5	4	6	12	10	19
Violette AC	15	4	5	6	10	11	17
Racing Gônaïves	15	3	6	6	9	13	15
AS Carrefour †	15	3	4	8	7	16	13
Dynamite St Marc	15	2	5	8	3	1	11
AS Capoise	15	3	2	10	18	29	11
US Frères Pétion-Ville†	15	2	4	9	8	25	10

11/03/2006 - 28/05/2006 • † Relegated on aggregate record

SUPER COUPE D'HAITI 2005

Round of 16

Tempête St Marc	1 1 3p
Dynamite St Marc	1 1 2p
Racine de Gros Morne	
Racing Gonaïves	
Baltimore St Marc	0 3
Roulado Gônaïves	0 1
Zénith Cap Haïtien	0 2
FICA Cap Haïtien	0 2
Victory FC	0 2
Violette AC	1 0
Aigle Noir	0
Racing Club Haïtien	2
Cavaly Léogâne	1 1
AS Grand Gôave	2 0
Don Bosco	1 0
AS Mirebalais	1 1

Quarter-finals

Tempête St Marc	2
Racing Gonaïves	1
Baltimore St Marc	0 2p
FICA Cap Haïtien	0 4p
Victory FC	2
Racing Club Haïtien	0
Cavaly Léogâne	1
AS Mirebalais	2

Semi-finals

Tempête St Marc	1
FICA Cap Haïtien	0
Victory FC	0
AS Mirebalais	2

Final

Tempête St Marc	2
AS Mirebalais	1

CUP FINAL

1-11-2005

RECENT LEAGUE RECORD

Championnat Fermature

Year	Champions	Pts	Runners-up	Pts
2001				
2002	Racing Club	31	Aigle Noir	29
2003	Roulado Gônaïves	27	Victory FC	27
2004	Championship cancelled ‡			
2005	Baltimore St Marc	31	Zénith Cap Haïtien	26
2006	Don Bosco	30	AS Mirebalais	29

Championnat Ouverture

Champions	Pts	Runners-up	Pts
Roulado Gônaïves	33	Aigle Noir	26
Don Bosco †	30	Cavaly Léogane	30
Championship cancelled ‡			
AS Mirebalais	32	Racing Club	31
Baltimore St Marc	32	Racing Gônaïves	31

† Play-off: Don Bosco 2-0 1-0 Cavaly Léogâne • ‡ Don Bosco and Roulado played in a match of champions in October 2004 with Roulado winning 5-4 on penalties after a 0-0 draw

HKG – HONG KONG

NATIONAL TEAM RECORD
JULY 1ST 2002 TO JULY 9TH 2006

PL	W	D	L	F	A	%
39	13	7	19	86	70	42.3

FIFA/COCA-COLA WORLD RANKING

1993	1994	1995	1996	1997	1998	1999	2000	2001	2002	2003	2004	2005	High		Low	
112	98	111	124	129	136	122	123	137	150	142	133	117	**90**	02/96	**154**	02/03

2005–2006											
08/05	09/05	10/05	11/05	12/05	01/06	02/06	03/06	04/06	05/06	06/06	07/06
119	120	120	117	117	117	117	115	116	116	-	117

To lose a Cup Final is bad enough but spare a thought for the fans of Happy Valley whose team lost in the final of all three major Cup tournaments in Hong Kong in 2006. But that was only half of the story because Happy Valley had also lost in the final of all three tournaments in 2005. Has any team anywhere in the world ever experienced such a run of bad luck? There was redemption, however, when they reclaimed the League title from arch rivals Sun Hei in convincing fashion in a season notable for the historic first relegation of South China. Happy Valley's tale of Cup Final misery began with defeat to Kitchee in the League Cup Final in December in a seven goal thriller

INTERNATIONAL HONOURS
None

that was decided a minute before the end by Kitchee's Wilfred Bamnjo. The two then met again in March in the final of the Challenge Shield. This time the score was far more convincing for Kitchee with a 3-0 triumph, whilst the final of the HKFA Cup saw Sun Hei atone for surrendering their league title by beating Happy Valley 1-0 with a Carlo Andre Hartwig goal midway through the second half. Sun Hei also performed well in international competition, reaching the semi-final of the AFC Cup in 2005 and qualifying from the group stages in 2006. The national team's efforts to qualify for the AFC Asian Cup got off to a poor start with a home defeat to Qatar.

THE FIFA BIG COUNT OF 2000

	Male	Female		Male	Female
Registered players	3 652	119	Referees	143	1
Non registered players	20 000	220	Officials	500	60
Youth players	340	26	Total involved	25 061	
Total players	24 357		Number of clubs	116	
Professional players	220	0	Number of teams	574	

The Hong Kong Football Association Ltd (HKFA)
55 Fat Kwong Street, Homantin, Kowloon, Hong Kong
Tel +852 27129122   Fax +852 27604303
hkfa@hkfa.com
www.hkfa.com
President: FOK Timothy Tsun Ting   General Secretary: LAM Martin
Vice-President: HONG Martin   Treasurer: LI Sonny   Media Officer: TBD
Men's Coach: LAI Sun Cheung & CHUNG Tsang Wai   Women's Coach: TBD
HKFA formed: 1914   AFC: 1954   FIFA: 1954
Red shirts, Red shorts, Red socks

RECENT INTERNATIONAL MATCHES PLAYED BY HONG KONG

2003	Opponents	Score		Venue	Comp	Scorers	Att	Referee
4-08	Singapore	L	1-4	Singapore	Fr	Au Wai Lun [46]		
6-11	Uzbekistan	L	1-4	Tashkent	ACq	Law Chun Bong [45]		
8-11	Tajikistan	D	0-0	Tashkent	ACq			
10-11	Thailand	W	2-1	Tashkent	ACq	Siang Sai Ho [28], Wong Sun Liu [69]		
17-11	Thailand	L	0-4	Bangkok	ACq			
19-11	Uzbekistan	L	0-1	Bangkok	ACq			
21-11	Tajikistan	L	0-1	Bangkok	ACq			
4-12	Korea Republic	L	1-3	Tokyo	EAC	Akandu [34]	14 895	Napitupulu IDN
7-12	Japan	L	0-1	Saitama	EAC		45 145	Piromya THA
10-12	China PR	L	1-3	Yokohama	EAC	Lo Chi Kwan [75]	17 400	Piromya THA
2004								
18-02	Malaysia	W	3-1	Kuantan	WCq	Ng Wai Chiu [17], Chu Siu Kei [84], Kwok Yue Hung [93+]	12 000	Nagalingham SIN
31-03	China PR	L	0-1	Hong Kong	WCq		9 000	Rungklay THA
9-06	Kuwait	L	0-4	Kuwait City	WCq		9 000	Najm LIB
8-09	Kuwait	L	0-2	Hong Kong	WCq		1 500	Busurmankulov KGZ
13-10	Malaysia	W	2-0	Hong Kong	WCq	Chu Siu Kei [5], Wong Chun Yue [51]	2 425	Ahamd Rakhil MAS
17-11	China PR	L	0-7	Guangzhou	WCq		20 300	Lee Jong Kuk KOR
30-11	Singapore	D	0-0	Singapore	Fr	W 6-5p	3 359	
2-12	Myanmar	D	2-2	Singapore	Fr	Feng Ji Zhi, Law Chun Bong	2 000	
2005								
9-02	Brazil	L	1-7	Hong Kong	Fr	Lee Sze Ming [85]	23 425	Zhou Weixin CHN
5-03	Mongolia	W	6-0	Taipei	EACq	Chu Siu Kei [30p], Law Chun Bong [48], Wong Chun Yue [50] Lam Ka Wai [73], Chan Yiu Lun 2 [92 93]		
7-03	Guam	W	15-0	Taipei	EACq	Chan Wai Ho [1], Chan Siu Ki [7 8 18 28 30 36 42 87] Chan Yiu Lun 2 [16 31], Wong Chun Yue 3 [24 43 45] Chu Siu Kei [57], Poon Man Tik [89]		
11-03	Chinese Taipei	W	5-0	Taipei	EACq	Chan Yiu Lun 2 [7 45], Lam Ka Wai [20] Poon Yiu Cheuk [58p], Cheung Sai Ho [60]		
13-03	Korea DPR	L	0-2	Taipei	EACq			
29-05	Macao	W	8-1	Hong Kong	Fr	Chan Siu Ki 3, Lee Chi Ho, Lam Ka Wei, Leung Sze Chung, Cheng Lai Hin		
2006								
29-01	Denmark	L	0-3	Hong Kong	Fr		16 841	Iemoto JPN
1-02	Croatia	L	0-4	Hong Kong	Fr		13 971	Iemoto JPN
15-02	Singapore	D	1-1	Hong Kong	Fr	Gerard Ambassa Guy [65]	610	Ong Kim Heng MAS
18-02	India	D	2-2	Hong Kong	Fr	Gerard Ambassa Guy [3], Law Chun Bong [17]	3 672	Jae Yong Bae KOR
22-02	Qatar	L	0-3	Hong Kong	ACq		1 806	Nishimura JPN
1-03	Bangladesh	W	1-0	Dhaka	ACq	Chan Siu Ki [82]	1 000	Sarkar IND
3-06	Macao	D	0-0	Macao	Fr			

Fr = Friendly match • EAC = East Asian Championship • AC = AFC Asian Cup • WC = FIFA World Cup™ • q = qualifier • † Hong Kong League XI

HONG KONG NATIONAL TEAM RECORDS AND RECORD SEQUENCES

Records			Sequence records					
Victory	15-0	GUM 2005	Wins	7	1985	Clean sheets	4	2003
Defeat	0-7	CHN 1980 2004	Defeats	9	1977-1979	Goals scored	24	1949-1958
Player Caps	n/a		Undefeated	10	1984-1985	Without goal	7	1988-1989
Player Goals	n/a		Without win	13	1967-1968	Goals against	23	1992-1995

HONG KONG COUNTRY INFORMATION

Capital	Victoria	Independence		Special Administrative	GDP per Capita	$28 800
Population	6 855 125	Status		Region (SAR) of China	GNP Ranking	n/a
Area km²	1 092	Language		Cantonese, English	Dialling code	+852
Population density	6 277 per km²	Literacy rate		93%	Internet code	.hk
% in urban areas	100%	Main religion		Local religions	GMT + / −	+8
Towns/Cities ('000)	Hong Kong Island 1 320; Kowloon 1 990; New Territories 2 730					
Neighbours (km)	China 30; South China Sea 733					
Main stadia	Hong Kong Stadium – Hong Kong Island 40 000; Mongkok – Kowloon 8 500					

HONG KONG 2005–06

FIRST DIVISION

	Pl	W	D	L	F	A	Pts	Happy Valley	Sun Hei	Buler Rangers	Kitchee	Lanwa	Citizen	South China	HK 08
Happy Valley †	14	11	2	1	39	15	35		2-0	1-3	1-1	3-1	2-1	4-3	2-0
Sun Hei †	14	8	2	4	30	15	26	1-1		5-0	1-0	0-2	3-1	3-0	3-0
Buler Rangers	14	7	3	4	24	19	24	1-6	3-0		1-0	2-0	1-1	3-1	4-0
Kitchee	14	5	6	3	24	13	21	2-3	2-0	1-0		0-0	3-0	0-0	1-1
Lanwa	14	4	5	5	.14	20	17	1-4	1-3*	2-2	0-2		1-1	1-0	2-1
Citizen	14	3	6	5	20	25	15	1-3	2-2	0-3	4-4	1-1		1-1	3-0
South China	14	3	4	7	18	22	13	0-2	1-3	1-0	2-2	1-1	1-2		2-0
Hong Kong 08	14	0	2	12	3	43	2	0-5	0-6	0-1	0-6	0-1	0-2	0-5	

3/09/2005 - 23/04/2006 • † Qualified for the 2007 AFC Cup • Match in bold awarded 3-0

HONG KONG 2005–06 SECOND DIVISION

	Pl	W	D	L	F	A	Pts
Hong Kong FC	24	20	3	1	107	21	63
Tai Po	24	16	6	2	73	37	54
Tung Po	24	11	10	3	61	45	43
Lucky Mile	24	11	5	8	35	41	38
Fukien	24	11	1	11	41	41	34
Kwok Keung	24	10	3	10	43	51	33
Double Flower	24	8	5	11	43	50	29
Korchina	24	8	5	11	40	52	29
Eastern	24	7	6	11	43	57	27
Kwai Tsing	24	7	6	11	30	49	27
New Fair Kui Tan	24	6	4	14	39	58	22
Fire Services	24	6	4	14	29	47	22
Derico	24	3	4	17	22	57	13

CHALLENGE SHIELD 2005–06

Quarter-finals		Semi-finals		Final	
Kitchee	2				
South China	0	Kitchee	2		
Hong Kong 08	0	Lanwa	0		
Lanwa	1			Kitchee	3
Sun Hei	2			Happy Valley	0
Buler Rangers	0	Sun Hei	1 6p	19-03-2006
Citizen	0	Happy Valley	1 7p	Scorers - Gumbs 2 [45] [90],
Happy Valley	3			Jevic [86] for Kitchee

LEAGUE CUP 2005–06

Semi-finals		Finals	
Kitchee	1		
Citizen	0		
		Kitchee	4
		Happy Valley	3
Sun Hei	1 1p	10-12-2005
Happy Valley	1 3p	

FA CUP 2005–06

Quarter-finals		Semi-finals		Final	
Sun Hei	1				
Kitchee	0	Sun Hei	7		
Lanwa	1	Citizen	0		
Citizen	2			Sun Hei	1
South China	3			Happy Valley	0
Hong Kong 08	2	South China	1	Mongkok, 16-04-2006
Buler Rangers	1 3p	Happy Valley	2	Scorer - Carlo Andre Hartwig [72]
Happy Valley	1 5p			

RECENT LEAGUE AND CUP RECORD

	League				FA Cup				Challenge Shield		
Year	Champions	Score	Runners-up		Winners	Score	Runners-up		Winners	Score	Runners-up
2000	South China	2-2 4-3p	Happy Valley		Happy Valley	7-2	O & YH Union		South China	4-3	Happy Valley
2001	Happy Valley	1-0	Instant-Dict		Instant-Dict	2-1	South China		O & YH Union	1-0	Instant-Dict
2002	Sun Hei	†	Happy Valley		South China	1-0	Sun Hei		South China	3-2	Sun Hei
2003	Happy Valley	†	Sun Hei		Sun Hei	2-1	Buler Rangers		South China	2-1	Happy Valley
2004	Sun Hei	†	Kitchee		Happy Valley	3-1	Kitchee		Happy Valley	3-0	Sun Hei
2005	Sun Hei	†	Happy Valley		Sun Hei	2-1	Happy Valley		Sun Hei	4-2	Happy Valley
2006	Happy Valley	†	Sun Hei		Sun Hei	1-0	Happy Valley		Kitchee	3-0	Happy Valley

† Played on a league basis - in 2002 the Championship reverted to a single stage round robin format • ‡ Won both stages so automatic champions

HON – HONDURAS

NATIONAL TEAM RECORD
JULY 1ST 2002 TO JULY 9TH 2006

PL	W	D	L	F	A	%
46	13	17	16	62	53	46.7

FIFA/COCA-COLA WORLD RANKING

1993	1994	1995	1996	1997	1998	1999	2000	2001	2002	2003	2004	2005		High		Low	
40	53	49	45	73	91	69	46	27	40	49	59	41		20	09/01	98	11/98

	2005–2006										
08/05	09/05	10/05	11/05	12/05	01/06	02/06	03/06	04/06	05/06	06/06	07/06
39	43	40	41	41	41	42	43	41	42	-	38

There is no stopping Olimpia at the moment, as the club from the capital Tegucigalpa claimed their third consecutive championship by winning both the Torneo Apertura and Torneo Clausura. Although Victoria, from the northern coastal city of La Ceiba, finished as runners-up to Olimpia in the League stage of both the Apertura and Clausura, it was fierce rivals Marathon who contested the Apertura final against Olimpia. The team from the second city of San Pedro Sula won the home leg 2-1, but back in Tegucigalpa, Olimpia won 2-0 with goals from Luciano Emilio and then in extra time from Wilson Palacios. In the Clausura, Marathon contrived to finish joint bottom of the

INTERNATIONAL HONOURS
Qualified for the FIFA World Cup™ finals 1982 UNCAF Cup 1993 1995 CONCACAF Club Championship Olimpia 1972 1988

League stage and so missed out on the play-offs leaving Victoria to try and depose Olimpia. They drew the first leg of the final 3-3 in La Ceiba but then lost the return 1-0 before a crowd of 31,951 in Tegucigalpa, to hand Olimpia their 20th title. Earlier in the season Olimpia had lost in the final of the Torneo Interclubes de UNCAF, a tournament that also serves as a qualifying zone for the CONCACAF Champions' Cup. In the final they played LD Alajuelense and after losing the first leg in Costa Rica, Olimpia won the return to force a penalty shoot-out. That was lost, as was the tie against eventual finalists Toluca in the quarter-finals of the Champions' Cup.

THE FIFA BIG COUNT OF 2000

	Male	Female		Male	Female
Registered players	6 000	0	Referees	250	0
Non registered players	65 000	0	Officials	1 500	100
Youth players	14 000	0	Total involved	86 850	
Total players	85 000		Number of clubs	200	
Professional players	0	0	Number of teams	1 000	

Federación Nacional Autónoma de Fútbol de Honduras (FENAFUTH)
Colonia Florencia Norte, Ave. Roble, Edificio Plaza América, Ave. Roble, 1 y 2 Nivel, Tegucigalpa, Honduras
Tel +504 2311436   Fax +504 2398826
fenafuth@fenafuth.com   www.fenafuth.com
President: CALLEJAS Rafael   General Secretary: HAWIT BANEGAS Alfredo
Vice-President: ABUDOJ Jorge   Treasurer: WILLIAMS Vicente   Media Officer: BANEGAS Martin
Men's Coach: DE LA PAZ Jose   Women's Coach: GUITIERREZ ALVAREZ Cesar Efrain
FENAFUTH formed: 1951   CONCACAF: 1961   FIFA: 1951
Blue shirts, Blue shorts, Blue socks

RECENT INTERNATIONAL MATCHES PLAYED BY HONDURAS

2003	Opponents	Score		Venue	Comp	Scorers	Att	Referee
15-07	Brazil	L	1-2	Mexico City	GCr1	Leon [90p]		Navarro CAN
17-07	Mexico	D	0-0	Mexico City	GCr1		20 000	Nery SLV
11-10	Bolivia	L	0-1	Washington DC	Fr		20 000	Kennedy USA
16-11	Finland	L	1-2	Houston	Fr	Alvarez [87]	26 000	Hall USA
2004								
25-01	Norway	L	1-3	Hong Kong	Fr	Martinez.S [30]	14 603	Chan HKG
18-02	Colombia	D	1-1	Tegucigalpa	Fr	De Leon [24]	8 000	Alfaro SLV
10-03	Venezuela	L	1-2	Maracaibo	Fr	Lopez [39]	24 000	Manzur VEN
31-03	Jamaica	D	2-2	Kingston	Fr	Martinez.E [67], Núñez [78]	28 000	Brizan TRI
7-04	Panama	D	0-0	La Ceiba	Fr		10 000	Rodriguez HON
28-04	Ecuador	D	1-1	Fort Lauderdale	Fr	Pavon [31]	15 000	Saheli USA
2-06	USA	L	0-4	Foxboro	Fr		11 533	Sibrian SLV
12-06	Netherlands Antilles	W	2-1	Willemstad	WCq	Suazo 2 [9 68]	12 000	McArthur GUY
19-06	Netherlands Antilles	W	4-0	San Pedro Sula	WCq	Guevara [7], Suazo [22], Alvarez [50], Pavon [70]	30 000	Alcala MEX
28-07	Panama	D	0-0	Tegucigalpa	Fr		5 000	Zelaya HON
3-08	El Salvador	W	4-0	San Salvador	Fr	Izaguirre [4], Palacios.J 3 [5 71 75]		Aguilar SLV
18-08	Costa Rica	W	5-2	Alajuela	WCq	Suazo [22], Leon [35], Guevara 2 [77 87], Martinez.S [89]	14 000	Rodriguez MEX
4-09	Canada	D	1-1	Edmonton	WCq	Guevara [88p]	8 000	Archundia MEX
8-09	Guatemala	D	2-2	San Pedro Sula	WCq	Guevara [51], Suazo [65]	40 000	Prendergast JAM
9-10	Canada	D	1-1	San Pedro Sula	WCq	Turcios [92+]	42 000	Stott USA
13-10	Guatemala	L	0-1	Guatemala City	WCq		26 000	Brizan TRI
17-11	Costa Rica	D	0-0	San Pedro Sula	WCq		18 000	Sibrian SLV
2005								
19-02	Nicaragua	W	5-1	Guatemala City	GCq	Núñez 2 [19 84], Velásquez 3 [42 51 73]	5 306	Moreno PAN
21-02	Belize	W	4-0	Guatemala City	GCq	Velásquez [7], Núñez 2 [33 80], Palacios.W [88]	3 000	Campos NCA
23-02	Guatemala	D	1-1	Guatemala City	GCq	Velásquez [72]	3 000	Moreno PAN
25-02	Panama	W	1-0	Guatemala City	GCq	Velásquez [72]	11 159	Sibrian SLV
27-02	Costa Rica	D	1-1	Guatemala City	GCq	Núñez [58]. L 6-7p	1 491	Batres GUA
19-03	USA	L	0-1	Albuquerque	Fr		9 222	Navarro CAN
4-06	Jamaica	D	0-0	Atlanta	Fr		6 500	Valenzuela USA
2-07	Canada	W	2-1	Vancouver	Fr	Ramirez.F [52], Velásquez [56]	4 105	Valenzuela USA
6-07	Trinidad and Tobago	D	1-1	Miami	GCr1	Figueroa [43]	10 311	Navarro CAN
10-07	Colombia	W	2-1	Miami	GCr1	Velásquez 2 [79 82]	17 292	Rodriguez MEX
12-07	Panama	W	1-0	Miami	GCr1	Caballero [81]	11 000	Wyngaarde SUR
16-07	Costa Rica	W	3-2	Foxboro	GCqf	Velásquez [6], Turcios [27], Núñez [29]	22 108	Archundia MEX
21-07	USA	L	1-2	New Jersey	GCsf	Guerrero [30]	41 721	Prendergast JAM
7-09	Japan	L	4-5	Miyagi	Fr	Velásquez 3 [8 27 50], Martinez.S [45]	45 198	
2006								
25-01	Ecuador	L	0-1	Guayaquil	Fr		10 000	Ramos ECU
12-02	China PR	W	1-0	Guangzhou	Fr	Oliva [54]	20 000	Supian MAS

Fr = Friendly match • GC = CONCACAF Gold Cup • WC = FIFA World Cup™ • q = qualifier • r1 = first round group • qf = quarter-final • sf = semi-final

HONDURAS NATIONAL TEAM RECORDS AND RECORD SEQUENCES

Records			Sequence records				
Victory	10-0	NCA 1946	Wins	6	1980-81, 1985-86	Clean sheets	6	1992
Defeat	1-10	GUA 1921	Defeats	6	1963-1965	Goals scored	13	Three times
Player Caps	n/a		Undefeated	14	1991-1992	Without goal	5	1988
Player Goals	n/a		Without win	14	1987-1991	Goals against	13	1993-1995

HONDURAS COUNTRY INFORMATION

Capital	Tegucigalpa	Independence	1821 from Spain		GDP per Capita	$2 600
Population	6 823 568	Status	Republic		GNP Ranking	105
Area km²	112 090	Language	Spanish		Dialling code	+504
Population density	60 per km²	Literacy rate	76%		Internet code	.hn
% in urban areas	44%	Main religion	Christian		GMT + / –	-6
Towns/Cities ('000)		Tegucigalpa 850; San Pedro Sula 489; Choloma 139; La Ceiba 130; El Progreso 100; Choluteca 75				
Neighbours (km)		Guatemala 256; El Salvador 342; Nicaragua 922; Pacific Ocean & Caribbean Sea 820				
Main stadia		Olimpico Metropolitano – San Pedro Sula 40 000; Tiburcio Carias Andino – Tegucigalpa 35 000				

CLUB DIRECTORY

Club	Town/City	Stadium	Capacity	www.	Lge	CL
Atlético	Olancho	Estadio Ruben Guifarro	5 000		0	0
Marathón	San Pedro Sula	Olimpico Metropolitano	40 000	cdmarathon.com	5	0
Motagua	Tegucigalpa	Tiburcio Carias Andino	35 000	motagua.com	10	0
Olimpia	Tegucigalpa	Tiburcio Carias Andino	35 000	clubolimpia.com	20	2
CD Platense	Puerto Cortés	Estadio Excelsior	7 000	platensehn.com	2	0
Real España	San Pedro Sula	Estadio Francisco Morazan	18 000	realcdespana.com	8	0
Universidad	Choluteca	Estadio Fausto Flores Lagos	5 000		0	0
Municiapal Valencia	Choluteca	Estadio Fausto Flores Lagos	5 000		0	0
CD Victoria	La Ceiba	Estadio Nilmo Edwards	6 000		1	0
CD Vida	La Ceiba	Estadio Nilmo Edwards	6 000	psinet.hn/cdvida	2	0

RECENT LEAGUE RECORD

Championship/Torneo Clausura from 1998				Torneo Apertura		
Year	Champions	Score	Runners-up	Champions	Score	Runners-up
1991	Real España	0-0 2-1	Motagua			
1992	Motagua	1-0	Real España			
1993	Olimpia	‡				
1994	Real España	‡				
1995	Victoria	0-0 1-1	Olimpia			
1996	Olimpia	3-0 0-0	Real España			
1997	Olimpia	1-1 3-0	Platense	Motagua	3-0 2-1	Real España
1998	Motagua	0-0 1-0	Olimpia	Olimpia	0-0 1-0	Real España
1999	Season readjustment			Motagua	0-0 0-0 6-5p	Olimpia
2000	Motagua	1-1 1-1 3-2p	Olimpia	Olimpia	1-0 1-1	Platense
2001	Platense	1-0 1-1	Olimpia	Motagua	0-1 3-2	Marathón
2002	Marathón	4-1 0-1	Olimpia	Olimpia	1-1 2-1	Platense
2003	Marathón	1-0 3-1	Motagua	Real España	2-2 2-0	Olimpia
2004	Olimpia	1-1 1-0	Marathón	Marathón	3-2 2-1	Olimpia
2005	Olimpia	1-1 2-1	Marathón	Olimpia	1-2 2-0	Marathón
2006	Olimpia	3-3 1-0	Victoria Ceiba			

‡ Won both stages so automatic champions

HONDURAS 2005–06

TORNEO APERTURA

	Pl	W	D	L	F	A	Pts	Olimpia	Victoria	Marathón	Platense	Universidad	España	Hispano	Valencia	Vida	Motagua
Olimpia †	18	11	4	3	38	17	37		6-0	1-1	5-2	1-3	3-0	1-0	5-1	0-0	1-0
Victoria Ceiba †	18	9	3	6	30	27	30	3-1		0-1	3-0	1-0	2-0	2-2	1-0	5-4	4-1
Marathón †	18	7	8	3	30	26	29	0-2	2-3		2-2	3-1	1-1	4-4	2-0	1-1	3-2
Platense †	18	8	3	7	28	34	27	3-2	3-2	1-2		1-1	3-2	2-1	0-1	0-1	2-0
Universidad Choluteca	18	6	6	6	19	21	24	2-3	1-1	1-1	1-2		0-0	1-0	1-0	2-1	2-1
Real España	18	6	5	7	23	23	23	0-2	2-1	1-1	2-2	1-1		2-0	3-0	2-0	2-0
Hispano Comayagua	18	5	7	6	24	24	22	0-1	0-0	1-1	0-1	3-0	3-2		2-1	0-0	1-1
Municipal Valencia	18	5	5	8	15	22	20	1-1	3-0	1-2	1-2	1-0	1-0	0-0		1-1	2-2
Vida Ceiba	18	4	6	8	22	25	18	0-2	1-0	1-3	6-1	1-1	3-2	1-2	0-1		1-1
Motagua	18	3	5	10	16	26	14	1-1	0-2	3-0	2-1	0-1	0-1	1-2	0-0	1-0	

6/08/2005 - 3/12/2005 • † Qualified for the play-offs

APERTURA PLAY-OFFS

Semi-finals			Final		
Olimpia	2	0			
Platense *	0	1	Olimpia	1	2
Victoria Ceiba	0	1	Marathón *	2	0
Marathón *	3	2			

* Home team in the first leg

HONDURAS 2005–06

TORNEO CLAUSURA

	Pl	W	D	L	F	A	Pts	Olimpia	Victoria	Valencia	Motagua	Vida	España	Platense	Universidad	Marathón	Hispano
Olimpia †	18	10	7	1	27	13	37		2-2	1-0	0-1	2-2	0-0	1-0	2-2	1-0	2-0
Victoria Ceiba †	18	8	7	3	31	18	31	1-2		2-1	2-2	1-2	0-0	2-1	3-0	2-1	2-0
Municipal Valencia †	18	9	3	6	20	13	30	1-2	0-0		2-0	1-1	1-0	2-0	3-0	1-0	1-0
Motagua †	18	8	5	5	24	20	29	0-1	3-0	1-0		2-1	0-1	2-0	1-1	3-1	2-2
Vida Ceiba	18	6	9	3	21	21	27	1-1	1-5	0-0	1-2		1-1	1-1	2-1	2-1	3-2
Real España	18	5	8	5	15	17	23	0-2	1-1	2-0	1-1	0-0		0-3	0-2	3-0	2-1
Platense	18	5	7	6	19	21	22	2-2	0-2	1-0	2-1	0-0	3-3		0-1	1-0	2-1
Universidad Choluteca	18	3	8	7	15	24	17	0-3	0-0	1-2	1-1	0-1	0-0	1-1		2-2	1-2
Marathón	18	2	5	11	16	27	11	0-2	1-1	0-2	4-0	1-2	0-1	2-2	0-0		2-1
Hispano Comayagua	18	2	5	11	17	31	11	1-1	1-5	2-3	0-2	0-0	2-0	0-0	1-2	1-1	

21/01/2006 - 7/05/2006 • † Qualified for the play-offs

CLAUSURA PLAY-OFFS

Semi-finals			Final		
Olimpia ‡	1	2			
Motagua *	2	1	Olimpia	3	1
Valencia *	1	0	Victoria Ceiba *	3	0
Victoria Ceiba	1	3			

* Home team in the first leg • ‡ Qualified due to better record

AGGREGATE RELEGATION TABLE

	Pl	W	D	L	F	A	Pts
Olimpia	36	21	11	4	65	30	74
Victoria Ceiba	36	17	10	9	61	45	61
Municipal Valencia	36	14	8	14	35	35	50
Platense	36	13	10	13	47	55	49
Real España	36	11	13	12	38	40	46
Vida Ceiba	36	10	15	11	43	46	45
Motagua	36	11	10	15	40	46	43
Universidad Choluteca	36	9	14	13	34	45	41
Marathón	36	9	13	14	46	53	40
Hispano Comayagua	36	7	12	17	41	55	33

HUN – HUNGARY

NATIONAL TEAM RECORD
JULY 1ST 2002 TO JULY 9TH 2006

PL	W	D	L	F	A	%
44	17	7	20	67	55	46.6

FIFA/COCA-COLA WORLD RANKING

1993	1994	1995	1996	1997	1998	1999	2000	2001	2002	2003	2004	2005	High		Low	
50	61	62	75	77	46	45	47	66	56	72	64	74	42	08/93	87	07/96

2005–2006											
08/05	09/05	10/05	11/05	12/05	01/06	02/06	03/06	04/06	05/06	06/06	07/06
65	66	66	71	74	70	72	72	75	76	-	84

For much of the season Ujpest seemed to be heading for their first title in eight years, but a home defeat against MTK with just three rounds to go saw defending champions Drebrecen draw level. Both won in their penultimate games but another home defeat on the last day for Ujpest, this time against Fehérvár, saw Debrecen claim a second championship with a 4-1 victory over relegated Pápa. Rarely does the title leave Budapest so to have done it twice running is quite an achievement for the railway team from Hungary's second city. With so many clubs in the capital, there is huge competition for money and support whereas Debrecen and Diosgyor are the only top level clubs in

INTERNATIONAL HONOURS
Olympic Gold 1952 1964 1968

the east of the country. Budapest's woes continued just before the start of the 2006-07 season when Ferencvaros, the most famous club in the country, were relegated after being refused a license. Hungary's disappointing performance in the FIFA World Cup™ qualifiers saw coach Lothar Matthaus quit to be replaced by Peter Bozsik, the son of former national team coach Josef Bozsik, Hungary's most capped player and a member of the famous Aranycsapat of the 1950s. Having lead Zalaegerszeg to the title in 2002, Bozsik's task is to see Hungary qualify for their first finals since 1986, although their last appearance in the Euro finals goes even further back - to 1972.

THE FIFA BIG COUNT OF 2000

	Male	Female		Male	Female
Registered players	46 782	515	Referees	3 500	5
Non registered players	100 000	320	Officials	7 000	150
Youth players	73 397	288	Total involved	231 957	
Total players	221 302		Number of clubs	2 577	
Professional players	852	0	Number of teams	5 966	

Hungarian Football Federation (MLSZ)
Magyar Labdarúgó Szövetség, Koerberek-Tovaros, Kanai u. 314/24.hrsz, Budapest 1112, Hungary
Tel +36 1 5779500   Fax +36 1 5779503
mlsz@mlsz.hu   www.mlsz.hu
President: KISTELEKI Istvan   General Secretary: KMETY Ildiko
Vice-President: TBD   Treasurer: KRIZSO Ibolya   Media Officer: GANCZER Gabor
Men's Coach: BOZSIK Peter   Women's Coach: BACSO Istvan
MLSZ formed: 1901   UEFA: 1954   FIFA: 1906
Red shirts with white trimmings, White shirts, Green socks or White shirts with red trimmings, White shorts, White socks

RECENT INTERNATIONAL MATCHES PLAYED BY HUNGARY

2002	Opponents		Score	Venue	Comp	Scorers	Att	Referee
21-08	Spain	D	1-1	Budapest	Fr	Miriuta [72]	20 000	Fleischer GER
7-09	Iceland	W	2-0	Reykjavik	Fr	Löw [81], Dárdai [90]	3 190	Maisonlahti FIN
12-10	Sweden	D	1-1	Stockholm	ECq	Kenesei [5]	35 084	Stark GER
16-10	San Marino	W	3-0	Budapest	ECq	Gera 3 [49 60 87]	6 500	Orrason ISL
20-11	Moldova	D	1-1	Budapest	Fr	Dárdai [55]	6 000	Sowa AUT
2003								
12-02	Bulgaria †	L	0-1	Larnaca	Fr	Abandoned after 45' due to the weather	200	Theodotou CYP
29-03	Poland	D	0-0	Chorzow	ECq		48 000	De Santis ITA
2-04	Sweden	L	1-2	Budapest	ECq	Lisztes [65]	28 000	Cortez Batista POR
30-04	Luxembourg	W	5-1	Budapest	Fr	Gera [18], Szabics 2 [52 90], Lisztes [61], Kenesei [69]	1 205	Skomina SVN
7-06	Latvia	W	3-1	Budapest	ECq	Szabics 2 [50 58], Gera [86]	4 000	Merk GER
11-06	San Marino	W	5-0	Serravalle	ECq	Böör [5], Lisztes 2 [21 81], Kenesei [61], Szabics [77]	1 410	Clark SCO
20-08	Slovenia	L	1-2	Murska Sobota	Fr	Fehér.M [90]	5 000	Sowa AUT
10-09	Latvia	L	1-3	Riga	ECq	Lisztes [53]	7 500	Larsen DEN
11-10	Poland	L	1-2	Budapest	ECq	Szabics [49]	15 500	Mejuto Gonzalez ESP
19-11	Estonia	L	0-1	Budapest	Fr		1 000	Sedivy CZE
2004								
18-02	Armenia	W	2-0	Paphos	Fr	Szabics [63], Lisztes [75]	400	Gerasimou CYP
19-02	Latvia	W	2-1	Limassol	Fr	Tököli [82], Kenesei [85]	500	Kailis CYP
31-03	Wales	L	1-2	Budapest	Fr	Kenesei [17p]	10 000	Meyer GER
25-04	Japan	W	3-2	Zalaegerszeg	Fr	Kuttor [53], Juhasz [67], Huszti [90p]	7 000	Trivkovic CRO
28-04	Brazil	L	1-4	Budapest	Fr	Torghelle [56]	45 000	De Santis ITA
1-06	China PR	L	1-2	Beijing	Fr	Kenesei [4p]	18 000	Chiu HKG
6-06	Germany	W	2-0	Kaiserslautern	Fr	Torghelle 2 [7 31]	36 590	Bennett ENG
18-08	Scotland	W	3-0	Glasgow	Fr	Huszti 2 [45p 53], Marshall OG [73]	15 933	Duhamel FRA
4-09	Croatia	L	0-3	Zagreb	WCq		20 853	Riley ENG
8-09	Iceland	W	3-2	Budapest	WCq	Gera [62], Torghelle [75], Szabics [79]	5 461	Ovrebo NOR
9-10	Sweden	L	0-3	Stockholm	WCq		32 288	Dougal SCO
17-11	Malta	W	2-0	Ta'Qali	WCq	Gera [39], Kovacs.P [93+]	14 500	Asumaa FIN
30-11	Slovakia	L	0-1	Bangkok	Fr		750	Veerapool THA
2-12	Estonia	W	5-0	Bangkok	Fr	Rosa [12], Waltner [14], Kerekes [19], Rajczi [24], Pollak [63]	800	Tongkhan THA
2005								
2-02	Saudi Arabia	D	0-0	Istanbul	Fr		100	Dereli TUR
9-02	Wales	L	0-2	Cardiff	Fr		16 672	Richmond SCO
30-03	Bulgaria	D	1-1	Budapest	WCq	Rajczi [90]	11 586	Wegereef NED
31-05	France	L	1-2	Metz	Fr	Kerekes [78]	26 000	Allaerts BEL
4-06	Iceland	W	3-2	Reykjavik	WCq	Gera 2 [45p 56p], Huszti 73	4 613	Cardoso Batista POR
17-08	Argentina	L	1-2	Budapest	Fr	Torghelle [29]	27 000	Merk GER
3-09	Malta	W	4-0	Budapest	WCq	Torghelle 34, OG 55, Takacs 64, Rajczi 85	5 900	Godulyan UKR
7-09	Sweden	L	0-1	Budapest	WCq		20 161	Farina ITA
8-10	Bulgaria	L	0-2	Sofia	WCq		4 652	Delevic SCG
12-10	Croatia	D	0-0	Budapest	WCq		6 979	Larsen DEN
16-11	Greece	L	1-2	Piraeus	Fr	Kenesei [77]	12 500	Vink NED
14-12	Mexico	L	0-2	Phoenix	Fr		32 466	Valenzuela USA
18-12	Antigua and Barbuda	W	3-0	Fort Lauderdale	Fr	Vadocz [10], Feczesin 2 [32 80]	250	Rutty USA
2006								
24-05	New Zealand	W	2-0	Budapest	Fr	Huszti [48], Szabics [81]	5 000	Hrinak SVK
30-05	England	L	1-3	Manchester	Fr	Dardai [55]	56 323	Vink NED

Fr = Friendly match • EC = UEFA EURO 2004™ • WC = FIFA World Cup™ • q = qualifier • † Not a full international

HUNGARY NATIONAL TEAM RECORDS AND RECORD SEQUENCES

Records			Sequence records					
Victory	13-1	FRA 1927	Wins	11	1951-1952	Clean sheets	4	Five times
Defeat	0-7	ENG 1908, GER 1941	Defeats	6	1978	Goals scored	70	1949-1957
Player Caps	101	BOZSIK József	Undefeated	30	1950-1954	Without goal	1	1993
Player Goals	84	PUSKAS Ferenc	Without win	12	1994	Goals against	19	Three times

HUNGARY COUNTRY INFORMATION

Capital	Budapest	Independence	Unified in 1001	GDP per Capita	$13 900
Population	10 032 375	Status	Republic	GNP Ranking	50
Area km²	93 030	Language	Hungarian	Dialling code	+36
Population density	107 per km²	Literacy rate	99%	Internet code	.hu
% in urban areas	65%	Main religion	Christian 92%	GMT + / –	+1
Towns/Cities ('000)	Budapest 1 708; Debrecen 204; Miskolc 179; Szeged 160; Pécs 156; Györ 129; Nyiregyháza 116; Kecskemét 106; Székesfehérvár 103; Szombathely 80; Szolnok 75; Tatabánya 71; Békéscsaba 65				
Neighbours (km)	Slovakia 677; Ukraine 103; Romania 443; Serbia & Montenegro 151; Croatia 329; Slovenia 102; Austria 366				
Main stadia	Puskas Ferenc (Nep) – Budapest 68 976				

HUNGARY NATIONAL TEAM PLAYERS AND COACHES

Record Caps			Record Goals			Recent Coaches	
BOZSIK József	1947-'62	101	PUSKAS Ferenc	1945-'56	84	GLAZER Robert	1991
FAZEKAS László	1968-'83	92	KOCSIS Sándor	1948-'56	75	JENEI Imre	1992-'93
GROSICS Gyula	1947-'62	86	SCHLOSSER Imre	1906-'27	59	PUSKAS Ferenc	1993
PUSKAS Ferenc	1945-'56	85	TICHY Lajos	1955-'64	51	VEREBES József	1993-'94
GARABA Imre	1980-'91	82	SAROSI György Dr.	1931-'43	42	MESZOLY Kálmán	1994-'95
MATRAI Sándor	1956-'67	81	HIDEGKUTI Nándor	1945-'58	39	CSANK János	1996-'97
SIPOS Ferenc	1957-'66	77	BENE Ferenc	1962-'79	36	BICSKEI Bertalan	1998-'01
BALINT László	1972-'82	76	ZSENGELLER Gyula	1936-'47	32	GELLEI Imre	2001-'03
BENE Ferenc	1962-'79	76	NYILASI Tibor	1975-'85	32	MATTHAUS Lothar	2003-'05
FENYVESI Máté Dr.	1954-'66	76	ALBERT Flórián	1959-'74	31	BOZSIK Peter	2006-

CLUB DIRECTORY

Club	Town/City	Stadium	Capacity	www.	Lge	Cup
Békéscsabai EFC	Békéscsaba	Kórház Utcai	11 500	elorefc.hu	0	1
Debreceni VSC	Debrecen	Oláh Gábor Ut	7 600	dvsc.hu	2	2
Diósgyöri VTK	Miskolc	DVTK	22 000	balatonfc.hu	0	2
Fehérvár FC	Székesfehérvár	Sóstói Ut	19 000	videotonfcf.hu	0	1
Ferencvárosi TC	Budapest	Ullöi Ut	18 100	ftc.hu	28	20
Györi ETO FC	Györ	Stadion ETO	27 000	eto.hu	3	4
Honvéd FC	Budapest	Bozsik József	13 500	kispesthonved.hu	13	5
Kaposvári Rákóczi FC	Kaposvár	Vöröshadsereg Ut	14 000		0	0
MTK-Hungária FC	Budapest	Hidegkuti Nandor	12 700	mtkhungaria.hu	22	12
Nyíregyházi FC	Nyíregyháza	Sóstói Ut	16 500		0	0
Pápa TFC	Pápa	Várkerti	4 000		0	0
Pécsi MFC	Pécs	PMFC	10 000	pmfc.hu	0	1
FC Sopron	Sopron	Városi	10 000		0	1
Ujpest FC	Budapest	Szusza Ferenc	13 501	ujpestfc.hu	20	8
Vasas SC	Budapest	Illovsky Rudolf	18 000	vasassc.hu	6	4
Zalaegerszegi TE	Zalaegerszeg	ZTE	12 500	ztefc.hu	1	0

RECENT LEAGUE AND CUP RECORD

	Championship						Cup		
Year	Champions	Pts	Runners-up	Pts	Third	Pts	Winners	Score	Runners-up
1990	Ujpesti Dózsa	58	MTK-VM Budapest	58	Ferencvárosi TC	48	Pécsi MSC	2-0	Honvéd
1991	Honvéd	45	Ferencvárosi TC	40	Pécsi MSC	37	Ferencvárosi TC	1-0	Vac FC
1992	Ferencvárosi TC	46	Vac FC	45	Kispest-Honvéd	40	Ujpesti TE	1-0	Vac FC
1993	Kispest-Honvéd	43	Vac FC	42	Ferencvárosi TC	41	Ferencvárosi TC	1-1 1-1 5-3p	Haladás
1994	Vac FC	46	Kispest-Honvéd	43	Békéscsabai ESC	41	Ferencvárosi TC	3-0 2-1	Kispest-Honvéd
1995	Ferencvárosi TC	59	Ujpesti TE	52	Debreceni VSC	49	Ferencvárosi TC	2-0 3-4	Vac FC
1996	Ferencvárosi TC	66	BVSC	61	Ujpesti TE	48	Kispest-Honvéd	0-1 2-0	BVSC
1997	MTK-Hungária	85	Ujpesti TE	76	Ferencvárosi TC	74	MTK-Hungária	6-0 2-0	BVSC
1998	Ujpesti TE	73	Ferencvárosi TC	67	Vasas SC	64	MTK-Hungária	1-0	Ujpesti TE
1999	MTK-Hungária	83	Ferencvárosi TC	64	Ujpesti TE	63	Debreceni VSC	2-0	LFC Tatabánya
2000	Dunaferr FC	79	MTK-Hungária	63	Vasas SC	61	MTK-Hungária	3-1	Vasas SC
2001	Ferencvárosi TC	48	Dunaferr FC	46	Vasas SC	40	Debreceni VSC	5-2	Videoton Fehérvar
2002	Zalaegerszegi TE	71	Ferencvárosi TC	69	MTK-Hungária	59	Ujpesti TE	2-1	Haladás
2003	MTK-Hungária	66	Ferencvárosi TC	64	Debreceni VSC	53	Ferencvárosi TC	2-1	Debreceni VSC
2004	Ferencvárosi TC	57	Ujpesti TE	56	Debreceni VSC	56	Ferencvárosi TC	3-1	Honvéd FC
2005	Debreceni VSC	62	Ferencvárosi TC	56	MTK-Hungária	56	Mátav FC Sopron	5-1	Ferencvárosi TC
2006	Debreceni VSC	68	Ujpesti TE	65	Fehérvár FC	64	Fehérvár	2-2 6-5p	Vasas SC

HUNGARY 2005-06

ARANY ASZOK LIGA 1.DIVISION

	Pl	W	D	L	F	A	Pts	Debrecen	Ujpest	Fehérvár	MTK	Tatabánya	FTC	Kaposvár	Diósgyőr	Győr	Soporon	ZTE	Pécs	Honvéd	REAC	Vasas	Pápa
Debreceni VSC †	30	20	8	2	69	34	68		2-2	2-0	2-2	1-0	3-1	2-1	2-0	1-1	3-1	2-1	3-1	6-1	6-1	2-2	4-1
Ujpesti TE ‡	30	20	5	5	74	37	65	2-1		1-3	1-2	5-1	2-1	4-1	3-2	3-1	2-1	5-1	5-1	7-0	2-0	2-2	3-1
FC Fehérvár ‡	30	19	7	4	52	24	64	1-2	1-1		1-0	4-1	1-1	3-0	5-0	2-2	2-2	1-0	1-0	3-0	3-1	1-0	2-1
MTK-Hungaria	30	18	6	6	65	33	60	2-4	0-2	0-1		1-0	2-2	2-1	4-0	5-2	2-0	6-3	2-0	0-0	1-0	3-0	7-0
Tatabánya FC	30	11	8	11	46	45	41	3-3	1-1	0-1	0-1		2-3	1-0	2-1	3-3	3-2	0-1	2-0	3-1	4-0	2-2	1-1
Ferencvárosi TC	30	10	11	9	43	38	41	0-0	1-2	0-1	1-0	2-3		1-1	1-1	2-0	1-0	2-2	3-1	3-1	0-2	3-1	3-3
Kaposvári Rákóczi	30	10	7	13	35	41	37	1-2	1-2	3-0	1-3	1-1	0-0		1-3	1-0	2-0	1-1	2-2	0-0	1-0	4-1	1-0
Diósgyőri VTK	30	10	7	13	33	44	37	3-3	0-1	1-0	0-0	1-0	0-1	5-2		1-1	1-1	3-0	0-0	1-0	1-1	0-2	0-1
Győri ETO	30	9	9	12	47	50	36	1-2	2-5	2-3	1-3	0-0	1-1	4-0	1-2		2-1	2-1	1-1	1-2	2-2	2-1	4-0
FC Soporon	30	9	8	13	39	39	35	0-2	1-1	1-1	0-3	5-1	1-1	2-0	2-1	2-0		0-1	3-1	1-1	0-1	2-0	2-0
Zalaegerszegi TE	30	9	8	13	42	47	35	2-0	1-3	1-1	3-4	3-0	3-2	0-1	2-0	0-0	2-2		1-4	0-0	3-0	3-0	5-0
Pécsi MFC	30	8	9	13	37	41	33	0-2	2-0	0-2	2-2	0-1	0-0	2-1	5-0	0-1	2-1	0-0		1-0	4-0	0-0	5-0
Honvéd	30	8	8	13	33	52	33	0-1	1-0	1-1	2-2	1-3	3-1	0-2	0-1	3-2	0-3	4-0	1-1		1-3	2-2	1-0
Rákospalotai EAC	30	7	5	18	30	59	26	1-2	2-3	1-2	1-2	0-2	1-0	0-3	0-2	1-2	1-0	2-1	1-1	1-3		0-3	2-2
Vasas SC	30	5	10	15	32	47	25	0-1	2-3	0-3	2-1	1-1	0-1	0-2	2-0	1-2	1-1	0-0	3-0	1-2	2-2		1-1
Pápa TFC	30	5	7	18	30	76	22	3-3	2-1	0-2	1-3	0-5	1-5	0-0	1-3	1-4	1-2	2-1	3-1	2-2	1-3	1-0	

30/07/2005 - 3/06/2006 • † Qualified for the UEFA Champions League • ‡ Qualified for the UEFA Cup

HUNGARY 2005-06 2.DIVISION WEST

	Pl	W	D	L	F	A	Pts
Paksi SE	30	25	1	4	66	22	76
Felcsút SE	30	20	3	7	72	41	63
Gyirmót SE	30	15	12	3	53	25	57
Integrál-DAC Győr	30	15	6	9	52	38	51
Barcsi FC	30	13	3	14	42	47	42
Szombathelyi Haladás	30	12	6	12	38	37	42
Bodajk FC Siófok	30	11	7	12	39	40	40
Celldömölki VSE	30	10	8	12	31	35	38
Budakalász MSE Cora	30	9	9	12	39	43	36
Hévíz FC	30	7	14	9	32	34	35
Balatonlelle SE	30	8	9	13	30	49	33
BKV Előre	30	7	10	13	32	41	31
Dunaújvárosi Kohász	30	7	10	13	36	53	31
Mosonmagyaróvári TE	30	7	9	14	35	47	30
Kaposvölgye-Nagyberki	30	6	9	15	40	59	27
Ajka FC	30	5	10	15	27	53	25

6/08/2005 - 4/06/2006

HUNGARY 2005-06 2.DIVISION EAST

	Pl	W	D	L	F	A	Pts
Dunakanyar-Vác	28	18	7	3	61	25	61
Szolnoki MAV	28	12	13	3	45	23	49
Jászapáti VSE	28	15	3	10	54	34	48
Makó FC	28	13	8	7	44	34	47
Soroksári SC	28	13	6	9	44	34	45
Nyíregyházi Spartacus	28	12	9	7	48	30	45
Bocsi KSC	28	13	5	10	39	40	43
Kazincbarcika SC	28	12	5	11	47	42	41
Kecskeméti TE	28	9	11	8	46	49	38
Orosháza FC	28	9	9	10	51	46	36
Baktalóránrgáza VSE	28	9	8	11	41	37	35
Vecsés FC	28	8	4	16	34	54	28
Karcagi SE	28	8	4	16	36	63	28
Budafoki LC	28	6	6	16	29	51	24
Erzsébeti SMTK	28	3	2	23	19	76	11
Szentes				Withdrew			

6/08/2005 - 4/06/2006

MAGYAR KUPA 2005-06

Round of 16

Fehérvár FC *	1	2
MTK-Hungária	1	1
Rákospalotai EAC	1	3
Kaposvári Rákóczi *	1	3
Ujpesti TE *	8	1
Makó	1	0
FC Tatabánya *	0	1
Debreceni VSC	2	2
Honvéd *	2	3
BKV Előre	1	1
Zalaegerszegi TE *	1	1
FC Soporon	5	3
Pécsi MFC	2	0
Szentlőrinc *	0	1
Pápa TFC	3	1
Vasas FC *	3	2

Quarter-finals

Fehérvár FC	2	3
Kaposvári Rákóczi *	1	1
Ujpesti TE *	0	0
Debreceni VSC	1	2
Honvéd	0	1
FC Soporon *	0	0
Pécsi MFC *	0	0
Vasas FC	1	1

Semi-finals

Fehérvár FC	1	2
Debreceni VSC *	0	2
Honvéd *	1	1
Vasas FC	3	0

Final

Fehérvár FC ‡	2	6p
Vasas SC	2	5p

CUP FINAL

Üllői út, Budapest
17-05-2006, Att: 5 000, Ref: Megyebíró
Scorers - Sitku [46], Schwarz [57] for Fehérvár;
Waltner [25], Baiog [84] for Vasas

* Home team in the first leg • ‡ Qualified for the UEFA Cup

IDN – INDONESIA

INDONESIA NATIONAL TEAM RECORD
JULY 1ST 2002 TO JULY 9TH 2006

PL	W	D	L	F	A	%
36	13	10	13	70	58	50

FIFA/COCA-COLA WORLD RANKING

1993	1994	1995	1996	1997	1998	1999	2000	2001	2002	2003	2004	2005	High	Low
106	134	130	119	91	87	90	97	87	110	91	91	109	76 09/98	152 11/95

2005–2006											
08/05	09/05	10/05	11/05	12/05	01/06	02/06	03/06	04/06	05/06	06/06	07/06
97	96	98	103	109	110	110	110	110	110	-	139

As one of the four co-hosts of the 2007 AFC Asian Cup, all eyes will be on Indonesia on July 29, when Jakarta's Senayan Stadium will host the final. In the 2005-06 season, however, national team coach Peter Withe didn't have a single match in which to prepare his players for the tournament. Instead the focus was on domestic football. The Liga Indonesia reverted back to the more traditional format of an East Division and a West Division from which the top four qualified for the Big Eight play-offs and then the grand final. The winners of both divisions, Persija from the capital Jakarta and Persipura, from the city of Jayapura in the far east of the country on the border

INTERNATIONAL HONOURS
AFC Youth Championship 1961

with Papua New Guinea, made it through to the final. Before a capacity crowd of 80,000 in Jakarta, Persipura won their first professional title thanks to an extra time winner from Ian Kabes. Persija made it to the Indonesian Cup Final two months later but again they were on the losing side, this time against Arema Malang. With the scores level at 3-3 after 90 minutes, Persija went down to another extra time goal, this time from hat-trick hero Firman Utina. There was huge embarrassment for Indonesia, however, when both Persipura and Arema were thrown out of the 2006 AFC Champions League after their player registration forms were not submitted on time.

THE FIFA BIG COUNT OF 2000

	Male	Female		Male	Female
Registered players	2 525	0	Referees	669	0
Non registered players	10 000 000	0	Officials	365	0
Youth players	2 500	0	Total involved	10 006 059	
Total players	10 005 025		Number of clubs	73	
Professional players	700	0	Number of teams	73	

Football Association of Indonesia (PSSI)
Gelora Bung Karno, Pintu X-XI, Senayan, PO Box 2305, Jakarta 10023, Indonesia
Tel +62 21 5704762   Fax +62 21 5734386
pssi@pssi-football.com   www.pssi-football.com
President: HALID Nurdin   General Secretary: BESOES Nugraha
Vice-President: EFFENDI Agusman   Treasurer: YANDHU Hamka   Media Officer: HALMAHERA John
Men's Coach: WITHE Peter   Women's Coach: none
PSSI formed: 1930   AFC: 1954   FIFA: 1952
Red shirts with white trimmings, White shirts, Red socks

RECENT INTERNATIONAL MATCHES PLAYED BY INDONESIA

2002	Opponents		Score	Venue	Comp	Scorers	Att	Referee
10-11	Singapore	D	1-1	Singapore	Fr	Juraimi [38]. L 3-4p		
15-12	Myanmar	D	0-0	Jakarta	TCr1		100 000	Ebrahim BHR
17-12	Cambodia	W	4-2	Jakarta	TCr1	Arif [36], Bambang 3 [59 75 82p]	20 000	Khanthachai THA
21-12	Vietnam	D	2-2	Jakarta	TCr1	Budi [11], Arif [84]	35 000	Mohd Salleh MAS
23-12	Philippines	W	13-0	Jakarta	TCr1	Bambang 4 [2 29 34 82], Arif 4 [7 37 41 57], Budi [17], Sugiyantoro 2 [53 75], Imran [80], Licuanan OG [88]	30 000	Khanthachai THA
27-12	Malaysia	W	1-0	Jakarta	TCsf	Bambang [75]	65 000	Ebrahim BHR
29-12	Thailand	D	2-2	Jakarta	TCf	Jaris [48], Gendut [79]. L 2-4p	100 000	Mohd Salleh MAS
2003								
26-09	Malaysia	D	1-1	Kuala Lumpur	Fr	Aiboi [62]		
6-10	Bhutan	W	2-0	Jeddah	ACq	Arif 2 [19 50]		
8-10	Yemen	W	3-0	Jeddah	ACq	Uston 2 [51 90], Arif [62]		
10-10	Saudi Arabia	L	0-5	Jeddah	ACq			
13-10	Bhutan	W	2-0	Jeddah	ACq	Edwarar [19], Arif [33]		
15-10	Yemen	D	2-2	Jeddah	ACq	Edwarar [12p], Donald [38]		
17-10	Saudi Arabia	L	0-6	Jeddah	ACq			
2004								
12-02	Jordan	L	1-2	Amman	Fr	Bambang [15]		
18-02	Saudi Arabia	L	0-3	Riyadh	WCq		1 000	Al Ghafary JOR
17-03	Malaysia	D	0-0	Johor Bahru	Fr		8 000	Kim Heng MAS
31-03	Turkmenistan	L	1-3	Ashgabat	WCq	Budi [30]	5 000	Sahib Shakir IRQ
3-06	India	D	1-1	Jakarta	Fr	Ponyaro [33]		
9-06	Sri Lanka	W	1-0	Jakarta	WCq	Aiboi [30]	30 000	Nesar BAN
18-07	Qatar	W	2-1	Beijing	ACr1	Budi [26], Ponaryo [48]	5 000	Moradi IRN
21-07	China PR	L	0-5	Beijing	ACr1			Najm LIB
25-07	Bahrain	L	1-3	Jinan	ACr1	Aiboy [75]	20 000	Codjia BEN
4-09	Singapore	L	0-2	Singapore	Fr			
8-09	Sri Lanka	D	2-2	Colombo	WCq	Jaya [8], Sofyan [51]	4 000	Marshoud JOR
12-10	Saudi Arabia	L	1-3	Jakarta	WCq	Jaya [50]	30 000	Mohd Salleh MAS
17-11	Turkmenistan	W	3-1	Jakarta	WCq	Jaya 3 [20 47 59]	15 000	Shaban KUW
7-12	Laos	W	6-0	Ho Chi Minh City	TCr1	Boas [26], Jaya 2 [29 34], OG [53], Aiboy [60], Kurniawan [87]		Rungklay THA
9-12	Singapore	D	0-0	Ho Chi Minh City	TCr1		4 000	Kwong Jong Chul KOR
11-12	Vietnam	W	3-0	Hanoi	TCr1	Lessy [18], Boas [21], Jaya [45]	40 000	Ebrahim BHR
13-12	Cambodia	W	8-0	Hanoi	TCr1	Jaya 3 [9 48 57], Aiboy 2 [30 55], Kurniawan 2 [72 74], Ortisan [82]	17 000	Sun Baojie CHN
28-12	Malaysia	L	1-2	Jakarta	TCsf	Kurniawan [7]	100 000	Irmatov UZB
2005								
3-01	Malaysia	W	4-1	Kuala Lumpur	TCsf	Kurniawan [59], Yulianto [74], Jaya [77], Boas [84]	70 000	Kunsuta THA
8-01	Singapore	L	1-3	Jakarta	TCf	Mahyadi [90+3]	120 000	Kwong Jong Chul KOR
16-01	Singapore	L	1-2	Singapore	TCf	Aiboy [76]	55 000	Al Ghamdi KSA
29-03	Australia	L	0-3	Perth	Fr		14 000	Yamanishi JPN
2006								

No international matches played in 2006 before July

Fr = Friendly match • TC = ASEAN Tiger Cup • AC = AFC Asian Cup • WC = FIFA World Cup™
q = qualifier • r1 = first round group • sf = semi-final • f = final

INDONESIA NATIONAL TEAM RECORDS AND RECORD SEQUENCES

Records			Sequence records					
Victory	12-0	PHI 1972	Wins	10	1968-1969	Clean sheets	4	1987, 2004
Defeat	0-9	DEN 1974	Defeats	7	1996	Goals scored	24	1967-1969
Player Caps	n/a		Undefeated	10	Three times	Without goal	5	Three times
Player Goals	n/a		Without win	18	1985-1986	Goals against	19	1985-1986

INDONESIA COUNTRY INFORMATION

Capital	Jakarta	Independence	1945 from the Netherlands	GDP per Capita	$3 200
Population	238 452 952	Status	Republic	GNP Ranking	28
Area km²	1 919 440	Language	Bahasa Indonesia	Dialling code	+62
Population density	124 per km²	Literacy rate	87%	Internet code	.id
% in urban areas	35%	Main religion	Muslim 88%	GMT +/−	+7
Cities/Towns ('000)	Jakarta 8 987; Surabaya 3 092; Bandung 2 781; Medan 2 243; Palembang 1 507; Tangerang 1 344; Semarang 1 289; Makasar 1 268				
Neighbours (km)	Malaysia 1 782; East Timor 228; Papua New Guinea 820; Pacific Ocean & Indian Ocean 54 716				
Main stadia	Gelora Bung Karno (Senayan) – Jakarta 100 000; Gelora 10 November – Surabaya 40 000				

CLUB DIRECTORY

Club	Town/City	Stadium	Capacity	Lge	Cup
Arema	Malang	Gajayana	20 000	1	1
Delta Putra	Sidoardjo	Delta	35 000		
Persebaya	Surabaya	Gelora	30 000	2	
Persegi	Mojokerto				
Persekabpas	Pasuruan	Pogar Bangil	10 000		
Persela	Lamongan	Surajaya	12 500		
Persema	Malang	Gajayana	20 000		
Persib Maung	Bandung	Siliwangi	20 000	1	
Persiba	Balikpapan	Persiba	15 000		
Persibom	Kotamobagu	Ambang	10 000		
Persija	Jakarta	Lebak Bulus	12 000	1	
Persijap	Jepara	Kamal Djunaedi	10 000		
Persik	Kediri	Brawijaya	10 000	1	
Persikota	Tangerang	Benteng	20 000		
Persipura	Jayapura	Mandala Krida	15 000	1	
Persita	Tangerang	Benteng	20 000		
Persitara	Jakarta Utara				
Persiter	Ternate	Gelora Kieraha	15 000		
Persiwa	Wamena	Pendidkan	20 000		
Persmin	Minahasa	Maesa	15 000		
Petrokimia Putra	Gresik	Tri Dharma	25 000	1	
PKT	Bontang	Mulawarman	12 000		
PSDS	Lubuk Pakam	Baharuddin Siregar	15 000		
PSIM	Yogyakarta	Mandala Krida	25 000		
PSIS	Semarang	Jatidiri	21 000	1	
PSM	Makassar	Mattoangin	30 000	1	
PSMS	Medan	Teladan	40 000		
PSS	Sleman	Tridadi	12 000		
Semen Padang	Indarung	Haji Agus Salim	20 000		1
Sriwijaya	Palembang	Jakabaring	40 000		

COPA DJI SAM SOE 2005

Round of 16	Quarter-finals	Semi-finals	Final
Arema Malang			
PSDS	**Arema Malang** W-0		
Semen Padang	Persegi		
Persegi		**Arema Malang** 2 3	
Persebaya Surabaya		PSS Sleman 0 0	
Persipura Jayapura	Persebaya Surabaya		
Persita Tangerang	**PSS Sleman** W-0		**Arema Malang** 4
PSS Sleman			Persija 3
PSMS Medan			
Persiter	**PSMS Medan** 1 1		
Persikabo	Persik Kediri 1 0		
Persik Kediri		PSMS Medan 2 1	**CUP FINAL**
Persekaba		**Persija** 1 3	Gelora Bung Karno, Senayan, Jakarta
Persijap	Persekaba 1 0		19-11-2005, Att: 55 000, Ref: Sudrajat
Persmin	**Persija** 1 1		Scorers - Hita [20], Utina 3 [55 85 96] for Arema;
Persija			Fatecha [12], Batoum [57p], Kurniawan [89] for Persija

* Home team • ‡ Qualified for the UEFA Cup

INDONESIA 2005

LIGA INDONESIA DIVISI UTAMA WILAYA BARAT (WEST)

	Pl	W	D	L	F	A	Pts	Persija	Arema	PSIS	PSMS	Persib	Persekpas	PSS	Persita	Sriwijaya	Semen	Persikota	PSDS	Deltras	PSPS
Persija Jakarta †	26	15	4	7	42	21	49		2-2	2-1	2-1	3-0	4-2	2-0	2-0	1-0	4-0	4-0	4-0	0-1	1-0
Arema Malang †	26	13	7	6	42	20	46	1-0		1-0	3-1	1-0	2-0	4-0	1-0	1-0	1-0	5-0	5-1	4-1	3-0
PSIS Semarang †	26	10	12	4	36	21	42	1-0	1-1		1-1	3-0	3-0	4-1	1-1	3-0	1-0	3-2	1-0	2-0	3-1
PSMS Medan †	26	12	6	8	30	26	42	2-1	1-0	0-0		0-0	2-1	2-0	1-0	1-2	2-0	3-0	3-1	1-0	3-2
Persib Maung	26	10	8	8	32	26	38	1-1	2-0	0-0	1-1		1-0	0-0	2-0	1-0	3-1	3-3	4-1	3-1	0-0
Persekabpas	26	11	4	11	30	37	37	1-1	2-1	2-2	2-0	2-1		2-1	1-0	2-1	2-0	1-0	1-0	2-1	2-1
PSS Sleman	26	10	4	12	22	32	34	2-0	1-0	2-0	0-0	0-1	3-0		0-0	1-0	1-0	1-0	3-1	3-2	0-0
Persita Tangerang	26	8	8	10	31	26	32	0-1	1-1	1-0	4-0	2-0	4-0	4-1		0-0	2-0	0-1	2-2	2-2	3-2
Sriwijaya Palembang	26	9	5	12	30	34	32	1-0	2-2	1-1	1-1	1-4	2-1	1-0	0-1		3-1	0-1	2-1	3-1	4-1
Semen Padang	26	9	5	12	24	30	32	2-3	1-0	0-0	1-0	0-0	1-0	0-0		1-0		0-1	2-0	3-1	4-1
Persikota	26	7	10	9	25	35	31	0-1	0-0	1-1	1-0	0-0	2-2	0-1	1-0	1-0	1-1		3-3	3-1	1-0
PSDS Lubuk Pakam	26	8	6	12	32	45	30	1-1	1-0	1-1	1-0	1-0	2-1	4-1	2-2	2-4	2-1	1-0		0-0	3-0
Delta Putra Sidoarjo	26	7	8	11	33	43	29	1-2	2-2	2-2	1-2	1-0	1-1	1-0	1-0	2-1	1-1	2-2	3-1		2-2
PSPS Pekanbaru	26	6	7	13	29	42	25	1-0	1-1	1-1	1-2	4-2	1-0	1-0	2-2	3-0	1-2	1-1	1-0	1-2	

LIGA INDONESIA DIVISI UTAMA WILAYA TIMUR (EAST)

	Pl	W	D	L	F	A	Pts	Persipura	PSM	Persik	Persebaya	Persiba	PKT	Persema	Persela	Persmin	Persegi	Persibom	Persijap	Pelita	Petrokimia
Persipura Jayapura †	26	14	4	8	31	17	46		2-0	2-1	2-0	1-0	2-0	4-0	0-0	1-0	2-0	3-0	3-0	2-1	1-0
PSM Makassar †	26	14	3	9	42	29	45	2-1		0-0	2-0	1-0	1-0	4-0	1-1	3-0	3-0	3-1	2-0	4-2	3-2
Persik Kediri †	26	13	4	9	44	28	43	2-1	2-1		1-1	1-0	3-0	5-0	2-0	2-1	2-0	3-0	3-1	3-1	3-0
Persebaya Jayapura †	26	12	7	7	31	22	43	0-0	2-1	2-0		1-0	3-0	2-1	2-0	1-1	0-0	3-0	2-1	0-0	5-1
Persiba Balikpapan	26	13	2	11	29	26	41	2-0	4-1	2-1	3-0		2-0	1-0	1-0	2-0	4-0	1-0	1-1	2-0	1-0
PKT Bontang	26	10	6	10	29	32	36	1-0	3-2	3-0	1-0	0-0		2-2	2-1	2-0	4-1	1-1	1-1	3-1	1-2
Persema Malang	26	11	3	12	30	34	36	2-0	1-2	2-1	2-1	2-0	0-1		0-0	1-0	1-0	3-0	2-0	1-0	4-1
Persela Lamongan	26	9	8	9	27	29	35	0-1	2-1	3-2	1-2	2-0	3-1	1-0		2-1	1-1	1-0	1-1	2-1	1-0
Persmin Minahasa	26	10	4	12	24	28	34	1-1	1-0	1-0	2-0	2-1	1-0	3-1	3-0		1-0	1-2	1-0	1-2	1-1
Persegi Gianyar	26	10	4	12	27	37	34	0-1	2-1	2-3	1-0	3-1	0-0	1-0	3-2	3-1		1-0	2-1	3-0	2-1
Persibom Kotamobagu	26	10	4	12	21	30	31	0-0	1-0	2-1	1-1	3-0	1-2	1-0	1-0	0-1	2-0		1-0	2-1	1-0
Persijap Jepara	26	7	9	10	25	29	30	2-0	0-1	2-1	0-0	5-0	1-0	1-1	1-1	0-0	1-1	0-0		1-0	2-1
Pelita Krakatau Steel	26	8	5	13	28	38	29	1-0	0-0	1-1	1-2	2-0	3-0	0-3	1-1	2-0	1-0	2-1	3-1		2-2
Petrokimia Gresik	26	7	5	14	32	41	26	2-1	2-3	1-1	0-1	0-1	1-1	3-1	1-1	1-0	4-1	2-0	1-3	3-0	

5/03/2005 - 4/09/2005 • † Qualified for the play-offs • Matches in bold awarded 3-0 • Persibom deducted three points

PLAY-OFFS

West	Pl	W	D	L	F	A	Pts	PS	PM	Pe
Persija Jakarta †	3	2	1	0	5	1	7	1-0	1-1	3-0
PSIS Semarang‡	3	2	0	1	3	1	6	2-0	1-0	
PSM Makassar	3	0	2	1	3	5	2	2-2		
Persebaya	3	0	1	2	2	6	1			

East	Pl	W	D	L	F	A	Pts	PM	PK	AM
Persipura †	3	3	0	0	3	0	9	1-0	1-0	1-0
PSMS Medan ‡	3	1	1	1	2	2	4		2-1	0-0
Persik Kediri	3	1	0	2	3	3	3			2-0
Arema Malang	3	0	1	2	0	3	1			

† Qualified for the final • ‡ Qualified for the third place play-off • Third place play-off: PSIS Semarang 2-1 PSMS Medan
Final: **Persipura** 3-2 Persija. Gelora Bung Karno, Jakarta, 25-09-2005, Att: 80 000, Ref: Purwanto. Scorers - Boaz Salossa [18], Korinus Fingrew [82], Ian Kabes [101] for Persipura; Agus Indra [10], Francis Wewengkang [55] for Persija

RECENT LEAGUE RECORD

	Championship			Cup		
Year	Champions	Score	Runners-up	Champions	Score	Runners-up
1995	Persib	1-0	Petrokimia Putra	No Cup competition		
1996	Bandung Raya	2-0	PSM	No Cup competition		
1997	Persebaya	3-1	Bandung Raya	No Cup competition		
1998	Season not finished due to political unrest			No Cup competition		
1999	PSIS	1-0	Persebaya	No Cup competition		
2000	PSM	3-2	Pupuk Kaltim	No Cup competition		
2001	Persija	3-2	PSM	No Cup competition		
2002	Petrokimia Putra	2-1	Persita	No Cup competition		
2003	Persik	†	PSM	No Cup competition		
2004	Persebaya	†	PSM	No Cup competition		
2005	Persipura	3-2	Persija	Arema Malang	4-3	Persija

† Championship played on a league system

IND – INDIA

NATIONAL TEAM RECORD
JULY 1ST 2002 TO JULY 9TH 2006

PL	W	D	L	F	A	%
37	13	8	16	42	62	45.9

FIFA/COCA-COLA WORLD RANKING

1993	1994	1995	1996	1997	1998	1999	2000	2001	2002	2003	2004	2005	High	Low
100	109	121	120	112	110	106	122	121	127	127	132	127	94 02/96	143 07/04

2005–2006											
08/05	09/05	10/05	11/05	12/05	01/06	02/06	03/06	04/06	05/06	06/06	07/06
132	134	132	135	127	118	118	118	117	117	-	130

After a terrible start to the 2007 AFC Asian Cup qualifiers, which included a 6-0 mauling by Japan and a 3-0 home defeat against Yemen, the AIFF appointed Englishman Bob Houghton as only the second foreign coach of the Indian national team after Cypriot Stephen Constantine. Former coach Syed Nayeemuddin had earlier led India to victory in the South Asian Football Federation Championship in Pakistan, with a 2-0 win over Bangladesh in the final, but winning tournaments on the sub-continent should not be the only realistic aim for India and Houghton's job will be to try and make India the force in Asia that it should be. The 10th National Football League saw

INTERNATIONAL HONOURS
Asian Games 1951 1962 South Asian Federation Games 1985 1987 1995 South Asian Football Federation Cup 1995

Mumbai's Mahindra United win the title for the first time. They finished comfortably clear of the Calcutta duo of East Bengal and Mohun Bagan and in doing so completed the double, having earlier beaten Sporting Clube de Goa 2-1 in the final of the Federation Cup which had been staged in Goa. The two major local leagues in India, in Calcutta and Goa, saw title triumphs for Mohun Bagan and Dempo whilst Goa won the Santosh trophy for state selections and Army XI won the 118th Durand Cup. Remarkably Army didn't take the lead in any of their last four matches, all of which were drawn. In the final they beat Sporting Clube de Goa - on penalties.

THE FIFA BIG COUNT OF 2000

	Male	Female		Male	Female
Registered players	96 250	8 000	Referees	2 550	120
Non registered players	2 000 000	12 000	Officials	220 000	40 000
Youth players	45 000	4 000	Total involved	2 427 920	
Total players	2 165 250		Number of clubs	10 750	
Professional players	750	0	Number of teams	20 500	

All India Football Federation (AIFF)
Football House, Sector 19, Dwarka, New Dehli 110075, India
Tel +91 11 28041430   Fax +91 11 28041434
alb@sancharnet.in   www.the-aiff.com
President: DAS MUNSI Priya Ranjan   General Secretary: COLACO Alberto
Vice-President: PATEL Praful   Treasurer: SALGAOCAR Shivanand   Media Officer: None
Men's Coach: HOUGHTON Bob   Women's Coach: SINGH Moirangthem
AIFF formed: 1937   AFC: 1954   FIFA: 1948
Sky blue shirts, Navy blue shorts, Sky blue and navy blue socks

RECENT INTERNATIONAL MATCHES PLAYED BY INDIA

2002 Opponents	Score	Venue	Comp	Scorers	Att	Referee
29-08 Jamaica	L 0-3	Watford	Fr			Bennett ENG
1-09 Jamaica	D 0-0	Wolverhampton	Fr		4 030	Riley ENG
2003						
10-01 Pakistan	L 0-1	Dhaka	SAr1			Shamsuzzaman BAN
12-01 Afghanistan	W 4-0	Dhaka	SAr1	Biswas 2 30 62, D'Cunha 2 50 85		Gurung NEP
14-01 Sri Lanka	D 1-1	Dhaka	SAr1	Biswas 90		Shamsuzzaman BAN
18-01 Bangladesh	L 1-2	Dhaka	SAsf	D'Cunha 80		Kunsuta THA
20-01 Pakistan	W 2-1	Dhaka	SA3p	Vijayan 56, Yadav 100GG		Shamsuzzaman BAN
24-03 Korea DPR	L 0-2	Pyongyang	ACq			
30-03 Korea DPR	D 1-1	Margao	ACq	Vijayan 29		
16-10 Thailand	L 0-2	Bangkok	Fr			
22-10 Rwanda	W 3-1	Hyderabad	AAr1	Vijayan 13, Suresh 54, Biswas 79		
24-10 Malaysia	W 2-0	Hyderabad	AAr1	Bisht 50, Vijayan 64		
29-10 Zimbabwe	W 5-3	Hyderabad	AAsf	Vijayan 2 25 33, Bhutia 2 41 83p, Singh.R 58		
31-10 Uzbekistan	L 0-1	Hyderabad	AAf			Lu Jun CHN
2004						
18-02 Singapore	W 1-0	Margao	WCq	Singh.R 50	28 000	Yasrebi IRN
31-03 Oman	L 1-5	Kochin	WCq	Singh.R 18	48 000	Kim Heng MAS
3-06 Indonesia	D 1-1	Jakarta	Fr	Ancheri 89p		
9-06 Japan	L 0-7	Saitama	WCq		63 000	Huang Junjie CHN
22-08 Myanmar	W 2-1	Ho Chi Minh City	Fr	Prakash 2 42 83		
24-08 Vietnam	L 1-2	Ho Chi Minh City	Fr	Lawrence 87		
8-09 Japan	L 0-4	Calcutta	WCq		90 000	Hajjar SYR
13-10 Singapore	L 0-2	Singapore	WCq		3 609	Husain BHR
5-11 Kuwait	W 3-2	Kuwait City	Fr	Singh.T 48, Zirsanga 64, Yadav 75		
17-11 Oman	D 0-0	Muscat	WCq		2 000	Nurilddin Salman IRQ
2005						
12-06 Pakistan	D 1-1	Quetta	Fr	Chetri 65	20 000	Khan PAK
16-06 Pakistan	W 1-0	Peshawar	Fr	Abdul Hakim 67	15 000	Imtiaz PAK
18-06 Pakistan	L 0-3	Lahore	Fr			Asif PAK
12-08 Fiji	L 0-1	Lautoka	Fr		10 000	Fox NZL
14-08 Fiji	L 1-2	Suva	Fr	Singh.I 10	11 000	O'Leary NZL
8-12 Nepal	W 2-1	Karachi	SAr1	Mehtab Hossain 2 6 28		
10-12 Bhutan	W 3-0	Karachi	SAr1	Bhutia 45, Gawli 51, Abdul Hakim 64		
12-12 Bangladesh	D 1-1	Karachi	SAr1	Lawrence 17		
14-12 Maldives	W 1-0	Karachi	SAsf	Shivananju 38		
17-12 Bangladesh	W 2-0	Karachi	SAf	Din Wadoo 33, Bhutia 81		
2006						
18-02 Hong Kong	D 2-2	Hong Kong	Fr	Nabi 61, Bhutia 68p	3 672	Jae Yong Bae
22-02 Japan	L 0-6	Yokohama	ACq		38 025	Huang CHN
1-03 Yemen	L 0-3	New Dehli	ACq		8 000	Torky IRN
1-04 Afghanistan	W 2-0	Chittagong	CCr1	Pariyar 2 35 60	2 500	Al Ghatrifi OMA
3-04 Philippines	D 1-1	Chittagong	CCr1	Pariyar 8	2 000	Mujghef JOR
5-04 Chinese Taipei	D 0-0	Chittagong	CCr1		2 000	Gosh BAN
9-04 Nepal	L 0-3	Chittagong	CCqf		3 000	Gosh BAN

Fr = Friendly match • SA = South Asian Football Federation Cup • CC - AFC Confederation Cup • AC = AFC Asian Cup • AA = Afro-Asian Games •
WC = FIFA World Cup™
q = qualifier • r1 = first round group • qf = quarter-finalxz • sf = semi-final • f = final

INDIA NATIONAL TEAM RECORDS AND RECORD SEQUENCES

Records			Sequence records				
Victory	7-1	SRI 1963	Wins	7	1962-1964	Clean sheets	4	1966
Defeat	1-11	URS 1955	Defeats	8	1978-1980	Goals scored	21	1958-1961
Player Caps	n/a		Undefeated	7	1962-64, 1999	Without goal	6	1984-1985
Player Goals	n/a		Without win	11	1986-92, 1993	Goals against	15	1952-58, 1973-76

INDIA COUNTRY INFORMATION

Capital	New Delhi	Independence	1947 from the UK	GDP per Capita	2 900
Population	1 065 070 607	Status	Republic	GNP Ranking	12
Area km²	3 287 590	Language	Hindi, English	Dialling code	+91
Population density	324 per km²	Literacy rate	59%	Internet code	.in
% in urban areas	27%	Main religion	Hindu 71%, Muslim 12%	GMT +/−	+5.5
Towns/Cities ('000)	Mumbai 12 692; Delhi 10 928; Bangalore 4 931; Calcutta 4 631; Madras 4 328; Ahmadabad 3 719; Hyderabad 3 598; Pune 2 935; Surat 2 894; Kanpur 2 823; Jaipur 2 711				
Neighbours (km)	Bangladesh 4 053; Bhutan 605; Burma 1 463; China 3 380; Nepal 1 690; Pakistan 2 912; Indian Ocean 7 000				
Main stadia	Saltlake – Calcutta 120 000; Jawaharlal Nehru – Kochin 60 000; Jawaharlal Nehru – Margao 35 000				

INDIA 2006

10TH NATIONAL FOOTBALL LEAGUE

	Pl	W	D	L	F	A	Pts	Mahindra	East Bengal	Mohun B	Sporting	Dempo	JCT Mills	Air India	Moham'dan	Salgaocar	Fransa
Mahindra United †	17	11	3	3	27	13	36		1-0	1-2	0-1	4-3	2-1	2-0	2-0	2-2	-
East Bengal	17	9	4	4	25	16	31	0-1		3-1	4-3	5-3	1-0	0-0	1-0	1-1	2-0
Mohun Bagan	17	8	6	3	17	10	30	0-0	0-0		1-0	0-0	0-2	2-1	0-1	3-0	2-0
Sporting Clube Goa	17	6	7	4	24	16	25	0-1	3-1	0-0		2-2	1-1	3-1	3-0	1-0	3-0
Dempo Sports Club	17	6	7	4	29	22	25	0-0	1-3	1-1	0-0		3-0	0-2	3-1	2-1	0-0
JCT Mills	17	5	5	7	14	14	20	0-1	0-1	0-1	2-1	0-0		2-1	2-0	0-0	-
Air India	17	5	4	8	16	22	19	2-1	1-1	0-2	1-1	1-4	0-0		1-0	1-0	-
Mohammedan Sporting	17	5	2	10	11	25	17	0-5	0-2	0-1	1-1	0-2	2-1	1-0		1-0	0-0
Salgaocar Sports Club	17	2	6	9	15	29	12	1-2	1-0	1-1	1-1	2-5	0-3	3-1	1-1		1-1
Fransa Pax FC	9	0	4	5	2	13	4	1-2	-	-	-	-	0-0	0-3	-	-	

10/01/2006 - 21/05/2006 • † Qualified for the 2007 AFC Cup • Fransa withdrew at the halfway stage • Top scorers: Ranty SOLEYE, Dempo, 13; Baichung BHUTIA, East Bengal, 12; MacPherlin OMAGBENI, Sporting Goa, 9; Yakubu YUSIF, Mahindra Utd, 8; Chidi EDEH, Sporting Goa, 7

LEAGUE CLUB DIRECTORY

Club	Town/City	Stadium	Capacity	www.	Lge	FCup
Churchill Brothers SC	Salcete, Goa	Nehru, Margao	35 000		0	0
Dempo Sports Club	Panjim, Goa	Nehru, Margao	35 000		1	1
East Bengal Football Club	Calcutta	Saltlake	120 000	eastbengalfootballclub.com	3	4
JCT Mills	Phagwara, Punjab	Guru Govind Singh	12 000		1	0
Mahindra United	Mumbai	The Cooperage	12 000		1	2
Mohammedan Sporting	Calcutta	Mohammedan Sporting Ground	7 000		0	2
Mohun Bagan Club	Calcutta	Saltlake	120 000	mohunbaganclub.com	3	11
Salgaocar Sports Club	Vasco, Goa	Nehru, Margao	35 000		1	3
Sporting Clube de Goa	Goa	Nehru, Margao	35 000		0	0
State Bank of Travancore	Trivandrum, Kerala	Chandrashekar Nair			0	0
Tollygunge Agragami	Calcutta	Rabindra Sarobar	18 000		0	0
Vasco Sports Club	Vasco, Goa	Nehru, Margao	35 000	vascoclub.com	0	0

RECENT LEAGUE AND CUP RECORD

National Football League							Federation Cup		
Year	Champions	Pts	Runners-up	Pts	Third	Pts	Winners	Score	Runners-up
1993							Mohun Bagan	1-0	Mahindra & Mahindra
1994							Mohun Bagan	0-0 3-0p	Salgaocar
1995							JCT Mills	1-1 7-6p	East Bengal
1996							JCT Mills	1-1 5-3p	East Bengal
1996							East Bengal	2-1	Dempo
1997	JCT Mills	30	Churchill Brothers	29	East Bengal	25	Salgaocar	2-1	East Bengal
1998	Mohun Bagan	34	East Bengal	31	Salgaocar	30	Mohun Bagan	2-1	East Bengal
1999	Salgaocar	23	East Bengal	19	Churchill Brothers	15	Not played		
2000	Mohun Bagan	47	Churchill Brothers	41	Salgaocar	39	Not played		
2001	East Bengal	46	Mohun Bagan	45	Churchill Brothers	36	Mohun Bagan	2-0	Dempo
2002	Mohun Bagan	44	Churchill Brothers	42	Vasco	40	Not played		
2003	East Bengal	49	Salgaocar	44	Vasco	43	Mahindra United	1-0	Mohammedan Sporting
2004	East Bengal	49	Dempo	45	Mahindra United	41	Dempo	2-0	Mohun Bagan
2005	Dempo	47	Sporting Clube Goa	45	East Bengal	43	Mahindra United	2-1	Sporting Clube Goa
2006	Mahindra United	36	East Bengal	31	Mohun Bagan	30			

INDIA 2006
NATIONAL LEAGUE SECOND DIVISION

First Round

Group A (in Jamshedpur)	Pl	W	D	L	F	A	Pt
Churchill Brothers	5	3	1	1	14	4	10
Tata Football Academy	5	2	3	0	4	1	9
State Bank Travancore	5	2	2	1	7	8	8
Punjab Police	5	2	0	3	3	5	6
EverReady	5	1	2	2	4	6	5
Simla Youngs	5	0	2	3	3	12	2

Final Round

(In Bangalore)	Pl	W	D	L	F	A	Pt	CB	HAL	Ar	Va	SBT
Tata Football Academy	5	4	0	1	7	3	12	2-1	0-1	1-0	2-1	2-0
Churchill Brothers	5	3	1	1	6	3	10		1-0	0-0	3-1	1-0
Hindustan AL	5	3	0	2	5	4	9			2-3	1-0	1-0
Army XI	5	2	2	1	7	6	8				1-1	3-2
Vasco SC	5	0	2	3	5	9	2					2-2
State Bank Travancore	5	0	1	4	4	9	1					

Group B (in Bangalore)	Pl	W	D	L	F	A	Pt
Army XI	5	4	1	0	5	1	13
Hindustan AL	5	3	1	1	7	1	10
Vasco SC	5	3	1	1	6	2	10
Indian Bank	5	2	1	2	3	5	7
Tollygrunge Agragami	5	0	1	4	2	7	1
Assam Rifles	5	0	1	4	1	8	1

27/02/2006 - 9/05/2006 • Tata Football Academy and Churchill Brothers promoted to the National Football League

FEDERATION CUP 2005

First round		Quarter-finals		Semi-finals		Final	
Mahindra United	1						
JCT Mills	0	Mahindra United	4				
Dempo Sports Club	1	Hindustan AL SC	2				
Hindustan AL SC	2			Mahindra United	4		
East Bengal	3			Churchill Brothers	1		
Air India	1	East Bengal	0 9p				
Tollygrunge Agragami	2	Churchill Brothers	0 10p				
Churchill Brothers	4					Mahindra United ‡	2
Salgaocar Sports Club	3					Sporting Clube Goa	1
Punjab Police	1	Salgaocar Sports Club	3				
Mohun Bagan	0 5p	Vasco Sports Club	1				
Vasco Sports Club	0 6p			Salgaocar Sports Club	1 4p		
Fransa Pax FC	2			Sporting Clube Goa	1 5p		
Mohammedan Sporting	1	Fransa Pax FC	1				
State Bank Travancore	1	Sporting Clube Goa	4				
Sporting Clube Goa	2						

CUP FINAL

Nehru Stadium, Fatorda, Goa
30-10-2005, Ref: Haq

Scorers - Barreto 2 [37] [120] for Mahindra;
Omagbemi [58p] for Sporting

All matches were played in Goa • ‡ Qualified for the 2006 AFC Cup

INDIA 2005
CALCUTTA SUPER DIVISION

	Pl	W	D	L	F	A	Pts
Mohun Bagan	14	13	1	0	21	5	40
East Bengal	14	11	1	2	25	7	34
Mohammedan Sporting	14	7	2	5	21	16	23
EverReady SA	14	4	5	5	9	10	17
Eastern Railway	14	3	4	7	8	20	13
George Telegraph	14	4	0	10	8	15	12
Calcutta Port Trust	14	2	5	7	8	17	11
Tollygrunge Agragami	14	2	2	10	11	21	8

27/07/2005 - 1/10/2005

INDIA 2005
8TH GOAN PRO LEAGUE

	Pl	W	D	L	F	A	Pts
Dempo Sports Club	14	10	4	0	24	7	34
Sporting Clube Goa	14	7	3	4	20	7	24
Vasco Sports Club	14	6	6	2	18	12	24
Churchill Brothers	14	6	5	3	22	15	23
Fransa Pax FC	14	4	5	5	11	12	17
Salgaocar Sports Club	14	4	4	6	19	18	16
Raia Sporting Club	14	3	4	7	15	20	13
MPT Sports Council	14	0	1	13	7	45	1

18/09/2005 - 5/01/2006

IRL – REPUBLIC OF IRELAND

NATIONAL TEAM RECORD
JULY 1ST 2002 TO JULY 9TH 2006

PL	W	D	L	F	A	%
39	20	12	7	48	27	66.7

FIFA/COCA-COLA WORLD RANKING

1993	1994	1995	1996	1997	1998	1999	2000	2001	2002	2003	2004	2005		High		Low
10	9	28	36	47	56	35	31	17	14	14	12	24		6	08/93	57	11/98

2005–2006											
08/05	09/05	10/05	11/05	12/05	01/06	02/06	03/06	04/06	05/06	06/06	07/06
14	21	21	23	24	26	27	29	30	31	-	39

The Republic of Ireland may have finished in fourth place in their FIFA World Cup™ qualifying group, but just three points separated them from France in first place. The failure to qualify lost coach Brian Kerr his job, despite a record of 18 wins and four defeats in 33 matches. He was replaced by record cap holder Steve Staunton as the Republic look to qualify for the European Championship finals for the first time since 1988. For three years now the domestic season has run from March until November and the consensus is that by playing over the summer months, standards have risen, as have attendances, a fact reflected by stronger performances in European

INTERNATIONAL HONOURS
Qualified for the FIFA World Cup™ finals 1990 1994 2002 **UEFA U-17 Championship** 1998

competition. Shelbourne made short shrift of Glentoran in the historic meeting of the two champions from the island of Ireland in the UEFA Champions League, while in the UEFA Cup, Cork City reached the first round proper after defeating Lithuania's Ekranas and Sweden's Djurgårdens, before losing to Slavia Praha. Cork were also involved in the match of the season when on the final weekend of the League they beat Derry City 2-0 to leapfrog their rivals and win the Championship. It was not such a happy time for Shamrock Rovers, who, after financial problems and an eight points deduction, lost a relegation play-off and went down for the first time in their history.

THE FIFA BIG COUNT OF 2000

	Male	Female		Male	Female
Registered players	1 517	3 637	Referees	1 150	50
Non registered players	50 000	0	Officials	4 000	150
Youth players	132 527	1 615	Total involved	194 646	
Total players	189 296		Number of clubs	3 059	
Professional players	520	0	Number of teams	7 456	

The Football Association of Ireland (FAI)
80 Merrion Square South, Dublin 2
Tel +353 1 7037500   Fax +353 1 6610931
info@fai.ie   www.fai.ie
President: BLOOD David   General Secretary: DELANEY John
Vice-President: FLEMING Maurice   Treasurer: MURRAY Edward   Media Officer: CONROY Declan
Men's Coach: STAUNTON Steve   Women's Coach: KING Noel
FAI formed: 1921   UEFA: 1954   FIFA: 1923
Green shirts with white trimmings, White shirts, Green socks or White shirts with green trimmings, Green shorts, White socks

RECENT INTERNATIONAL MATCHES PLAYED BY THE REPUBLIC OF IRELAND

2002	Opponents		Score	Venue	Comp	Scorers	Att	Referee
21-08	Finland	W	3-0	Helsinki	Fr	Keane.Rb [12], Healy [74], Barrett [82]	12 225	Pedersen NOR
7-09	Russia	L	2-4	Moscow	ECq	Doherty [69], Morrison [76]	23 000	Colombo FRA
16-10	Switzerland	L	1-2	Dublin	ECq	Magnin OG [78]	40 000	Pedersen NOR
20-11	Greece	D	0-0	Athens	Fr		5 000	Trentalange ITA
2003								
12-02	Scotland	W	2-0	Glasgow	Fr	Kilbane [8], Morrison [16]	33 337	Braamhaar NED
29-03	Georgia	W	2-1	Tbilisi	ECq	Duff [18], Doherty [84]	15 000	Vassaras GRE
2-04	Albania	D	0-0	Tirana	ECq		20 000	Farina ITA
30-04	Norway	W	1-0	Dublin	Fr	Duff [17]	32 643	McCurry SCO
7-06	Albania	W	2-1	Dublin	ECq	Keane.Rb [6], Aliaj OG [90]	33 000	Mikulski POL
11-06	Georgia	W	2-0	Dublin	ECq	Doherty [43], Keane [58]	36 000	Iturralde Gonzalez ESP
19-08	Australia	W	2-1	Dublin	Fr	O'Shea [74], Morrison [81]	37 200	Vidlak CZE
6-09	Russia	D	1-1	Dublin	ECq	Duff [35]	36 000	Michel SVK
9-09	Turkey	D	2-2	Dublin	Fr	Connolly [35], Dunne [90]	27 000	Wegereef NED
11-10	Switzerland	L	0-2	Basel	ECq		31 006	Frisk SWE
18-11	Canada	W	3-0	Dublin	Fr	Duff [24], Keane.Rb 2 [60 84]	23 000	Whitby WAL
2004								
18-02	Brazil	D	0-0	Dublin	Fr		44 000	Frisk SWE
31-03	Czech Republic	W	2-1	Dublin	Fr	Harte [52], Keane.Rb [90]	42 000	Fisker DEN
28-04	Poland	D	0-0	Bydgoszcz	Fr		15 500	Shebek UKR
27-05	Romania	W	1-0	Dublin	Fr	Holland [85]	42 356	Jara CZE
29-05	Nigeria	L	0-3	London	Fr		7 438	D'Urso ENG
2-06	Jamaica	W	1-0	London	Fr	Barrett [26]	6 155	Styles ENG
5-06	Netherlands	W	1-0	Amsterdam	Fr	Keane.Rb [45]	42 000	Dean ENG
18-08	Bulgaria	D	1-1	Dublin	Fr	Reid [15]	31 887	Brines SCO
4-09	Cyprus	W	3-0	Dublin	WCq	Morrison [33], Reid [38], Keane.Rb [54]	36 000	Paniashvili GEO
8-09	Switzerland	D	1-1	Basel	WCq	Morrison [8]	28 000	Vassaras GRE
9-10	France	D	0-0	Paris	WCq		78 863	Dauden Ibanez ESP
13-10	Faroe Islands	W	2-0	Dublin	WCq	Keane.Rb 2 [14p 32]	36 000	Lajuks LVA
16-11	Croatia	W	1-0	Dublin	Fr	Keane.Rb [24]	33 200	Orrason ISL
2005								
9-02	Portugal	W	1-0	Dublin	Fr	O'Brien [21]	44 100	Messias ENG
26-03	Israel	D	1-1	Tel Aviv	WCq	Morrison [43]	32 150	Ivanov.V RUS
29-03	China PR	W	1-0	Dublin	Fr	Morrison [82]	35 222	Casha MLT
4-06	Israel	D	2-2	Dublin	WCq	Harte [5], Keane.Rb [11]	36 000	Vassaras GRE
8-06	Faroe Islands	W	2-0	Torshavn	WCq	Harte [51p], Kilbane [59]	5 180	Guenov BUL
17-08	Italy	L	1-2	Dublin	Fr	Reid.A [32]	44 000	Gomes Costa POR
7-09	France	L	0-1	Dublin	WCq		36 000	Fandel GER
8-10	Cyprus	W	1-0	Nicosia	WCq	Elliott [6]	13 546	Kassai HUN
12-10	Switzerland	D	0-0	Dublin	WCq		35 944	Merk GER
2006								
1-03	Sweden	W	3-0	Dublin	Fr	Duff [36], Keane.Rb [48], Miller [71]	44 109	Ledentu FRA
24-05	Chile	L	0-1	Dublin	Fr		41 200	Ingvarsson SWE

Fr = Friendly match • EC = UEFA EURO 2004™ • WC = FIFA World Cup™ • q = qualifier

REPUBLIC OF IRELAND NATIONAL TEAM RECORDS AND RECORD SEQUENCES

Records			Sequence records				
Victory	8-0	MLT 1983	Wins	8	1987-1988	Clean sheets	5	1989, 1996-1997
Defeat	0-7	BRA 1982	Defeats	5	Six times	Goals scored	17	1954-59, 2000-01
Player Caps	102	STAUNTON Stephen	Undefeated	17	1989-1990	Without goal	5	1995-1996
Player Goals	26	KEANE Robbie	Without win	20	1968-1971	Goals against	35	1966-1973

REPUBLIC OF IRELAND COUNTRY INFORMATION

Capital	Dublin	Independence	1921 from the UK	GDP per Capita	$29 600
Population	3 969 558	Status	Republic	GNP Ranking	39
Area km²	70 280	Language	English, Irish	Dialling code	+353
Population density	56 per km²	Literacy rate	98%	Internet code	.ie
% in urban areas	58%	Main religion	Roman Catholic 91%	GMT + / –	0
Towns/Cities ('000)	Dublin 1 024; Cork 189; Limerick 90; Galway 70; Waterford 48; Drogheda 33; Dundalk 33				
Neighbours (km)	UK 360; North Atlantic & Irish Sea 1 448				
Main stadia	Lansdowne Road – Dublin 47 000; Dalymount Park – Dublin 12 200				

REPUBLIC OF IRELAND NATIONAL TEAM PLAYERS AND COACHES

Record Caps			Record Goals			Recent Coaches	
STAUNTON Steve	1989-'02	102	KEANE Robbie	1998-'06	26	MEAGAN Mick	1969-'71
QUINN Niall	1986-'02	91	QUINN Niall	1986-'02	21	TUOHY Liam	1971-'73
CASCARINO Tony	1986-'00	88	STAPLETON Frank	1977-'90	20	THOMAS Sean	1973
MCGRATH Paul	1985-'97	83	ALDRIDGE John	1986-'97	19	GILES Johnny	1973-'80
BONNER Pat	1981-'96	80	CASCARINO Tony	1986-'00	19	KELLY Alan	1980
GIVEN Shay	1996-'06	76	GIVENS Don	1969-'82	19	HAND Eoin	1980-'85
HOUGHTON Ray	1986-'98	73	CANTWELL Noel	1954-'67	14	CHARLTON Jack	1986-'95
BRADY Liam	1975-'90	72	DALY Gerry	1973-'87	13	MCCARTHY Mick	1996-'02
CUNNINGHAM Kenny	1996-'05	72	DUNNE James	1930-'39	12	KERR Brian	2002-'05
			HARTE Ian	1996-'06	11	STAUNTON Steve	2006-

CLUB DIRECTORY

Club	Town/City	Stadium	Capacity	www.	Lge	Cup
Bohemians	Dublin	Dalymount Park	12 200	bohemians.ie	9	6
Bray Wanderers	Bray	Carlisle Grounds	6 500	braywanderers.ie	0	2
Cork City	Cork	Turner's Cross	11 500	corkcityfc.ie	2	1
Derry City	Londonderry	Brandywell	10 000	derrycityfc.com	2	3
Drogheda United	Drogheda	United Park	5 400	droghedaunited.ie	0	1
Finn Harps	Ballybofey	Finn Park	7 900	finnharps.com	0	1
Longford Town	Longford	Strokestown Road	10 000	longfordtownfc.com	0	2
St Patrick's Athletic	Dublin	Richmond Park	7 500	stpatsfc.com	7	2
Shamrock Rovers	Dublin	Tallaght Stadium	6 000	shamrockrovers.ie	15	24
Shelbourne	Dublin	Tolka Park	9 681	shelbournefc.ie	12	7
UCD - University College Dublin	Dublin	Belfield Park	5 250	ucd.ie/soccer	0	1
Waterford United	Waterford	RSC	8 200	waterford-united.ie	6	2

RECENT LEAGUE AND CUP RECORD

	Championship							Cup		
Year	Champions	Pts	Runners-up	Pts	Third	Pts		Winners	Score	Runners-up
1990	St Patrick's Ath	52	Derry City	49	Dundalk	42		Bray Wanderers	3-0	St Francis
1991	Dundalk	52	Cork City	50	St Patrick's Ath	44		Galway United	1-0	Shamrock Rovers
1992	Shelbourne	49	Derry City	44	Cork City	43		Bohemians	1-0	Cork City
1993	Cork City †	40	Bohemians	40	Shelbourne	40		Shelbourne	1-0	Dundalk
1994	Shamrock Rovers	66	Cork City	59	Galway United	50		Sligo Rovers	1-0	Derry City
1995	Dundalk	59	Derry City	58	Shelbourne	57		Derry City	2-1	Shelbourne
1996	St Patrick's Ath	67	Bohemians	62	Sligo Rovers	55		Shelbourne	1-1 2-1	St Patrick's Ath
1997	Derry City	67	Bohemians	57	Shelbourne	54		Shelbourne	2-0	Derry City
1998	St Patrick's Ath	68	Shelbourne	67	Cork City	53		Cork City	0-0 1-0	Shelbourne
1999	St Patrick's Ath	73	Cork City	70	Shelbourne	47		Bray Wanderers	0-0 2-2 2-1	Finn Harps
2000	Shelbourne	69	Cork City	58	Bohemians	57		Shelbourne	0-0 1-0	Bohemians
2001	Bohemians	62	Shelbourne	60	Cork City	56		Bohemians	1-0	Longford Town
2002	Shelbourne	63	Shamrock Rovers	57	St Patrick's Ath	53		Dundalk	2-1	Bohemians
2003	Bohemians	54	Shelbourne	49	Shamrock Rovers	43		Derry City	1-0	Shamrock Rovers
2003	Shelbourne	69	Bohemians	64	Cork City	53		Longford Town	2-0	St Patrick's Ath
2004	Shelbourne	68	Cork City	65	Bohemians	60		Longford Town	2-1	Waterford United
2005	Cork City	74	Derry City	72	Shelbourne	67		Drogheda United	2-0	Cork City

The Irish football calender was changed in 2003 to a spring - autumn season • † Cork City won a series of play-offs between the top three

REPUBLIC OF IRELAND 2005

PREMIER DIVISION

	Pl	W	D	L	F	A	Pts	Cork	Derry	Shelbourne	Drogheda	Longford	Bohemians	Bray	Waterford	UCD	St Pats	Shamrock	Harps
Cork City †	33	22	8	3	53	18	74		2-0 2-0	1-0	0-1 1-0	0-0	2-1	1-1 3-0	1-1	0-0 1-0	3-1 0-1	3-0	2-0
Derry City ‡	33	22	6	5	56	25	72	3-1		0-0 2-1	3-0 1-0	3-1	3-1	2-2	1-0 0-1	3-0	2-2	2-0 2-3	2-0	3-2
Shelbourne	33	20	7	6	62	25	67	0-2 0-0	1-2		3-3	1-0	2-1	4-1 5-0	1-0 5-0	1-4 2-3	1-1 1-0	1-2	3-0 1-0
Drogheda United ‡	33	12	12	9	40	33	48	0-1	0-2 1-0	0-2		1-1	2-2 3-2	3-0	1-0	1-2	1-1 1-2	1-0 0-1	0-2
Longford Town	33	12	9	12	29	32	45	0-1 0-0	0-0	0-2 0-2	1-0		1-0 1-0	2-1	1-1 2-3	0-1 0-1	1-0	2-1	1-0
Bohemians	33	13	6	14	42	47	45	0-2 1-2 0-1	2-3 2-1 0-3	3-2	2-0 1-0	1-0		2-1	1-1	1-1	1-1	1-3 0-3-1	
Bray Wanderers	33	11	6	16	40	57	39	1-2 0-1 0-3	2-2 2-2 0-2	1-1 1-2 3-1	2-1	1-0 1-0	0-1		2-1 1-0 1-0	2-3	2-1	
Waterford United	33	9	7	17	30	49	34	2-2 2-2 1-3	2-4 0-3 1-0	0-3 2-0 2-0	1-2	0-0	1-0	1-1		0-1 0-1	2-1 2-2	
UCD	33	7	12	14	28	44	33	1-5 1-0 0-2	1-1 0-2 2-2	0-0 1-1 1-3	3-2	1-0	2-3	1-0	0-0		2-2	1-1	
St Patrick's Athletic	33	7	11	15	26	36	32	0-2	1-1	0-1	0-2	0-1 1-3 0-0 0-1	2-0	1-0	3-2 0-0	1-1 3-1 2 0-0-0			
Shamrock Rovers §	33	9	8	16	33	52	27	1-3 0-2	0-2	0-2	0-2	0-2	1-0	0-2 4-2	1-2	3-2 0-1 0-1	0-2	1-0 0-0	1-4
Finn Harps	33	5	6	22	30	51	21	1-3	0-2 1-2	0-2 0-1	0-3	0-0 5-0	1-3 1-2	2-4	2-0	1-0 1-2	0-2 1-1	3-0	

16/03/2005 - 18/11/2005 • † Qualified for the UEFA Champions League • ‡ Qualified for the UEFA Cup • § Shamrock Rovers deducted eight points due to financial problems • Top scorers: Jason BYRNE, Shelbourne, 22; Mark FARREN, Derry 18; Kevin McHUGH, Finn Harps, 13; Eamon ZAYED, Bray, 12 • Relegation play-off: Shamrock Rovers 1-2 1-1 Dublin City

REPUBLIC OF IRELAND 2005
FIRST DIVISION

	Pl	W	D	L	F	A	Pts
Sligo Rovers	36	15	16	5	45	27	62
Dublin City	36	15	14	7	57	34	59
Cobh Ramblers	36	15	11	10	49	40	56
Kilkenny City	36	15	8	13	46	35	53
Galway United	36	14	11	11	46	43	53
Dundalk	36	12	13	11	44	40	49
Limerick	36	13	9	14	44	49	48
Kildare County	36	10	11	15	33	42	41
Monaghan United	36	9	9	18	36	66	36
Athlone Town	36	6	10	20	28	52	28

18/03/2005 - 19/11/2005

IRELAND LEAGUE CUP 2005

Quarter-finals

Derry City	2 5p
Drogheda Utd	2 4p
Cork City *	0
Longford Town	1
Shelbourne *	2
St Patrick's Ath	1
Waterford Utd	0
UCD *	1

Semi-finals

Derry City *	2
Longford Town	1
Shelbourne *	1
UCD	2

Final

Derry City *	2
UCD	1

Belfield Park, Dublin
20-09-2005, 2 150, Hancock
Scorers - Murphy [14], OG [45] for Derry; Byrne [40] for UCD
* Home team

FA OF IRELAND CUP 2005

Round of 16

Drogheda United	2
Dundalk *	0
Wayside Celtic	2 1
Bohemians *	2 2
UCD	1 2
Longford Town *	1 1
Cherry Orchard	0
Bray Wanderers *	1
Derry City *	3
Kildare County	1
Douglas Hall	0
Shamrock Rovers *	2
Sligo Rovers *	2
St Patrick's Athletic	1
Finn Harps	0 2
Cork City *	0 3

Quarter-finals

Drogheda United *	2
Bohemians	1
UCD	2
Bray Wanderers *	3
Derry City *	1
Shamrock Rovers	0
Sligo Rovers	1
Cork City *	3

Semi-finals

Drogheda United	2
Bray Wanderers	1
Derry City	0
Cork City	1

Final

Drogheda United ‡	2
Cork City	0

CUP FINAL

Lansdowne Road, Dublin
4-12-2005, At: 24 521, Ref: Stokes

Scorers - Gavin Whelan [52], Declan O'Brien [83] for Drogheda Utd

* Home team • ‡ Qualified for the UEFA Cup

IRN – IRAN

NATIONAL TEAM RECORD
JULY 1ST 2002 TO JULY 9TH 2006

PL	W	D	L	F	A	%
55	33	11	11	117	53	70

FIFA/COCA-COLA WORLD RANKING

1993	1994	1995	1996	1997	1998	1999	2000	2001	2002	2003	2004	2005		High		Low
59	75	108	83	46	27	49	37	29	33	28	20	19		15	07/05	122 05/96

					2005–2006						
08/05	09/05	10/05	11/05	12/05	01/06	02/06	03/06	04/06	05/06	06/06	07/06
15	18	21	19	19	19	22	19	22	23	-	47

Iran's return to the FIFA World Cup™ finals, having missed out in Korea and Japan in 2002, brought with it high expectations, especially with their strong core of Germany based players. Those expectations were not fulfiled, however, and the danger is that in the future just qualifying for the finals will be seen as the limit of their ambitions when they are potentially capable of much more. Their campaign began with a hugely disappointing defeat at the hands of Mexico in which they conceded two goals in the last 20 minutes. That meant they had to beat Portugal. Again they

INTERNATIONAL HONOURS
Qualified for the FIFA World Cup™ finals 1978 1998 2006 **AFC Asian Cup** 1968 1972 1976 **Asian Games** 1974 1990 1998 2002
AFC Asian U-19 Championship 1973 1974 1975 1976 **AFC Champions League** Esteghlal 1970 1991

more than held their own for the first hour, but this time were undone by Deco's fantastic goal and then a Ronaldo penalty and were out, finishing bottom of the group. Iran's lack of progress in the AFC Champions League also remains a source of concern. Pas lost to Al Ain in the quarter-finals of the 2005 tournament and neither Foolad nor Saba Battery made it out of the group stage in the 2006 tournament. Representing Iran in 2007 will be traditional power Esteghlal after they won the Iran Pro League in a tight finish with Pas. The Cup Final between Pirouzi and Sepahan was delayed until September after problems with the venue.

THE FIFA BIG COUNT OF 2000

	Male	Female		Male	Female
Registered players	251 620	1 470	Referees	4 965	56
Non registered players	400 000	0	Officials	48 600	1 050
Youth players	143 625	1 050	Total involved	852 436	
Total players	797 765		Number of clubs	2 535	
Professional players	20	0	Number of teams	16 829	

IR Iran Football Federation (IRIFF)
No. 2/2 Third St., Seoul Ave., 19958-73591 Tehran, Iran
Tel +98 21 88213308   Fax +98 21 8213302
info@iriff   www.iriff.ir
President: DADGAN Mohammad Dr   General Secretary: PAHLEVAN Reza
Vice-President: NOAMOOZ Naser   Treasurer: SABRIOUN Abbas   Media Officer: VAZIRI Shahram
Men's Coach: GHALENOEI Amir   Women's Coach: FATEMEH Sepanji
IRIFF formed: 1920   AFC: 1958   FIFA: 1945
White shirts with green timmings, White shorts, White socks

RECENT INTERNATIONAL MATCHES PLAYED BY IRAN

2003	Opponents	Score		Venue	Comp	Scorers	Att	Referee
5-09	Jordan	W	4-1	Tehran	ACq	Daei 2 [45 90], Vahedinikbakht [75], Mobali [82]	57 000	Ebrahim BHR
26-09	Jordan	L	2-3	Amman	ACq	Golmohammadi [6], Majidi [60]	27 000	Shaban KUW
12-10	New Zealand	W	3-0	Tehran	AO	Karimi 2 [8 20], Kaebi [65]	40 000	Kousa SYR
27-10	Korea DPR	W	3-1	Pyongyang	ACq	Karimi 2 [47 79], Navidkia [87]	30 000	
12-11	Korea DPR	W	3-0	Tehran	ACq	Daei [54p]. Abandoned 60'. Awarded 3-0 to Iran	40 000	Haj Khader SYR
19-11	Lebanon	W	3-0	Beirut	ACq	Daei [37p], Golmohammadi [61], Vahedinikbakht [80]		Al Marzouqi UAE
28-11	Lebanon	W	1-0	Tehran	ACq	Daei [22]		Rungklay THA
2-12	Kuwait	L	1-3	Kuwait City	Fr	Daei [77]	5 000	Al Qahtani QAT
2004								
18-02	Qatar	W	3-1	Tehran	WCq	Vahedi [8], Mahdavikia [44], Daei [62]	BCD	Haj Khader SYR
31-03	Laos	W	7-0	Vientiane	WCq	Daei 2 [9 17p], Enayati 2 [32 36], OG [54], Taghipour 2 [68 83]	7 000	Yang TPE
9-06	Jordan	L	0-1	Tehran	WCq		35 000	Kamikawa JPN
17-06	Lebanon	W	4-0	Tehran	WFr1	Daei 3 [15p 62 88], Nekounam [80]	20 000	Issa Hazim IRQ
21-06	Syria	W	7-1	Tehran	WFr1	Daei [29], Vahedinikbakht [30], Nosrati [45], Borhani 2 [55 85], Karimi [86], Majidi [89p]	20 000	
23-06	Iraq	W	2-1	Tehran	WFsf	Nekounam [4], Borhani [54]	15 000	Shaban KUW
25-06	Syria	W	4-1	Tehran	WFf	Karimi [34], Daei [59], Borhani [69], Nekounam [75]	20 000	Shaban KUW
20-07	Thailand	W	3-0	Chongqing	ACr1	Enayati [70], Nekounam [80], Daei [86p]	37 000	Kousa SYR
24-07	Oman	D	2-2	Chongqing	ACr1	Karimi [62], Nosrati [90]	35 000	Al Delawar BHR
28-07	Japan	D	0-0	Chongqing	ACr1		52 000	Shield AUS
31-07	Korea Republic	W	4-3	Jinan	ACqf	Karimi 3 [10 20 77], Park OG [51]	32 159	Al Fadhli KUW
3-08	China PR	D	1-1	Beijing	ACsf	Alavi [38]. L 3-4p	51 000	Najm LIB
6-08	Bahrain	W	4-2	Beijing	AC3p	Nekounam [9], Karimi [52], Daei 2 [80p 90]	23 000	Al Marzouqi UAE
8-09	Jordan	W	2-0	Amman	WCq	Vahedi [80], Daei [91+]	20 000	Lu Jun CHN
9-10	Germany	L	0-2	Tehran	Fr		110 000	Mane KUW
13-10	Qatar	W	3-2	Doha	WCq	Hashemian 2 [9 89], Borhani [78]	8 000	Kwon Jong Chul KOR
17-11	Laos	W	7-0	Tehran	WCq	Daei 4 [8 20 28 58], Nekounam 2 [63 72], Borhani [69]	30 000	Mamedov TKM
18-12	Panama	W	1-0	Tehran	Fr	Daei [38p]	8 000	Esfahanian IRN
2005								
2-02	Bosnia-Herzegovina	W	2-1	Tehran	Fr	Daei [41], Borhani [73]	15 000	
9-02	Bahrain	D	0-0	Manama	WCq		25 000	Mohd Salleh MAS
25-03	Japan	W	2-1	Tehran	WCq	Hashemian 2 [13 66]	110 000	Maidin SIN
30-03	Korea DPR	W	2-0	Pyongyang	WCq	Mahdavikia [32], Nekounam [79]	55 000	Kousa SYR
29-05	Azerbaijan	W	2-1	Tehran	Fr	Zandi [9], Nekounam [29]	30 000	Al Fadhli KUW
3-06	Korea DPR	W	1-0	Tehran	WCq	Rezaei [45]	35 000	Al Ghamdi KSA
8-06	Bahrain	W	1-0	Tehran	WCq	Nosrati [47]	80 000	Kwon Jong Chul KOR
17-08	Japan	L	1-2	Yokohama	WCq	Daei [79]	66 098	Shaban KUW
24-08	Libya	W	4-0	Tehran	Fr	Alavi [7], Nekounam 2 [41 90], Daei [56]	15 000	Delawar BHR
12-10	Korea Republic	L	0-2	Seoul	Fr		61 457	Al Ghamdi KSA
13-11	Togo	W	2-0	Tehran	Fr	Daei [11p], Hashemian [58p]		
2006								
22-02	Chinese Taipei	W	4-0	Tehran	ACq	Timotian [35], Madanchi 2 [47 60], Daei [82]	5 000	AK Nema IRQ
1-03	Costa Rica	W	3-2	Tehran	Fr	Karimi [9], Daei [16], Hashemian [34]	25 000	Marzouqi UAE
28-05	Croatia	D	2-2	Osijek	Fr	Karimi [21], Borhani [81]	19 000	Siric CRO
31-05	Bosnia-Herzegovina	W	5-2	Tehran	Fr	Madanchi [25], Rezaei [45], Hashemian [45], Enayati [88], Khatibi [90]	40 000	Mohd Salleh MAS
11-06	Mexico	L	1-3	Nuremburg	WCr1	Golmohammadi [36]	41 000	Rosetti ITA
17-06	Portugal	L	0-2	Frankfurt	WCr1		48 000	Poulat FRA
21-06	Angola	D	1-1	Leipzig	WCr1	Bakhtiarizadeh [75]	38 000	Shield AUS

Fr = Friendly match • WF = West Asian Federation Championship • AC = AFC Asian Cup • AO = AFC/OFC Challenge • WC = FIFA World Cup™
q = qualifier • r1 = first round group • qf = quarter-final • sf = semi-final • 3p = third place play-off • f = final • BCD = Behind closed doors

IRAN NATIONAL TEAM RECORDS AND RECORD SEQUENCES

Records			Sequence records					
Victory	19-0	GUM 2000	Wins	8	1974, 1996	Clean sheets	7	1977
Defeat	1-6	TUR 1950	Defeats	3	1989-1990	Goals scored	20	2000-2001
Player Caps	149	DAEI Ali	Undefeated	15	1996-1997	Without goal	4	1951-1958, 1988
Player Goals	109	DAEI Ali	Without win	10	1997	Goals against	9	1959-1963

IRAN COUNTRY INFORMATION

Capital	Tehran	Formation	1502	GDP per Capita	$7 000
Population	69 018 924	Status	Republic	GNP Ranking	35
Area km²	1 648 000	Language	Persian, Turkic	Dialling code	+98
Population density	42 per km²	Literacy rate	79%	Internet code	.ir
% in urban areas	59%	Main religion	Muslim	GMT +/−	+3.5
Towns/Cities ('000)	Tehran 7 158; Mashhad 2 307; Esfahan 1 547; Karaj 1 448; Tabriz 1 424; Shiraz 1 249; Qom 1 011; Ahvaz 854; Kermanshah 766; Orumiyeh 602; Rasht 594; Kerman 577; Zahedan 551; Hamadan 514; Arak 503; Yazd 477; Ardabil 410; Abadan 370; Zanjan 357				
Neighbours (km)	Afghanistan 936; Armenia 35; Azerbaijan 611; Iraq 1458; Pakistan 909; Turkey 499; Turkmenistan 992; Caspian Sea & Arabian Gulf 2 440				
Main stadia	Azadi – Tehran 100 000; Naghsh e Jahan – Esfahan 75 000; Yadegar e Emam – Tabriz 71 000				

NATIONAL TEAM PLAYERS AND COACHES

Record Caps			Record Goals			Recent Coaches	
DAEI Ali	1993-'06	149	DAEI Ali	1993-'06	109	IVIC Tomislav	1998
MAHDAVIKIA Mehdi	1996-'06	92	BAGHERI Karim	1993-'01	47	TALEBI Jalal	1998
KARIMI Mohammed Ali	1998-'05	92	KARIMI Mohammed Ali	1998-'06	33	POURHAYDARI Mansour	1998
ESTILI Hamid Reza	1990-'00	82	MAZLOOMI Gholamhussain	1969-'77	19	TALEBI Jalal	2000
BAGHERI Karim	1993-'01	80	PEYOUS Farshad	1984-'94	19	BRAGA Ademar Da Silva	2000
ZARINCHEH Javad	1987-'00	80	ROSTA Ali Asghar Moudir	1974-'78	18	BLAZEVIC Miroslav	2001-'02
ABEDZADEH Ahmad Reza	1987-'98	79	ROWSHAN Hassan	1974-'80	13	IVANKOVIC Branko	2002
PARVIN Ali	1970-'80	76	PARVIN Ali	1970-'80	13	SHAHROKHI Homayoun	2002
NEKOUNAM Javad	2000-'06	73				IVANKOVIC Branko	2002-'06
GOLMOHAMMADI Yaha	1996-'06	71				GHALENOEI Amir	2006-

CLUB DIRECTORY

Club	Town/City	Stadium	Capacity	Lge	Cup	CL
AbooMoslem	Mashhad	Samen	35 000	0	0	0
Bargh	Shiraz	Hafezieh	20 000	0	1	0
Esteghlal	Tehran	Azadi	110 000	5	4	2
Esteghlal	Ahvaz	Takhti	30 000	0	0	0
Fajr Sepasi	Shiraz	Hafezieh	20 000	0	1	0
Foolad	Ahvaz	Takhti	30 000	1	0	0
Malavan	Bandar Anzali	Takhti	20 000	0	3	0
Pas	Tehran	Dastgerdi	15 000	5	0	0
Pegah Gilan	Rasht	Dr Azody	20 000	0	0	0
Peykan	Tehran	Iran Khodro	10 000	0	0	0
Pirouzi (Perspolis)	Tehran	Azadi	110 000	8	3	0
Saba Battery	Tehran	Derakhshan	12 000	0	1	0
Saipa	Karaj	Enghelab	10 000	2	1	0
Sepahan	Esfehan	Naghsh e Jahan	75 000	1	1	0
Shamoushak	Noshahr	Sohada	10 000	0	0	0
Zob Ahan	Esfehan	Naghsh e Jahan	75 000	0	1	0

RECENT LEAGUE AND CUP RECORD

	Championship						Cup		
Year	Champions	Pts	Runners-up	Pts	Third	Pts	Winners	Score	Runners-up
1990	Esteghlal						Malavan	2-0	Khibar
1991	Pas						Pirouzi	2-1	Malavan
1992	Pas						No tournament held		
1993	Saipa						No tournament held		
1994	Saipa						Saipa	0-0 1-1	Jonoob
1995	Pirouzi						Bahman	0-1 2-0	TraktorSazi
1996	Pirouzi	57	Bahman	51	Esteghlal	51	Esteghlal	3-1 2-0	Bargh
1997	Pirouzi	59	Bahman	53	Sepahan	50	Bargh	1-1 3-0p	Bahman
1998	Esteghlal	58	Pas	52	Zob Ahan	45	No tournament held		
1999	Pirouzi	65	Esteghlal	53	Sepahan	53	Pirouzi	2-1	Esteghlal
2000	Pirouzi	54	Esteghlal	47	Fajr Sepasi	44	Esteghlal	3-1	Bahman
2001	Esteghlal	50	Pirouzi	46	Saipa	33	Fajr Sepasi	1-0 2-1	Zob Ahan
2002	Pirouzi	49	Esteghlal	48	Foolad	45	Esteghlal	2-1 2-2	Fajr Sepasi
2003	Sepahan	52	Pas	45	Pirouzi	44	Zob Ahan	2-2 2-2 6-5p	Fajr Sepasi
2004	Pas	53	Esteghlal	51	Foolad	47	Sepahan	3-2 2-0	Esteghlal
2005	Foolad	64	Zob Ahan	58	Esteghlal	58	Saba Battery	1-1 2-2 4-2p	AbooMoslem
2006	Esteghlal	59	Pas	58	Saipa	52			

IRAN 2005–06

IRAN PRO LEAGUE

	Pl	W	D	L	F	A	Pts	Esteghlal	Pas	Saipa	Saba	AbooMoslem	Zob Ahan	Sepahan	Foolad	Pirouzi	Fajr Sepasi	Malavan	Est AhvazA	Rah Ahan	Bargh	Sham'shak	Ghandi
Esteghlal Tehran †	30	16	11	3	44	17	59		0-0	0-0	4-1	0-0	3-0	2-1	4-1	1-0	0-0	3-3	1-0	3-0	4-1	1-1	1-0
Pas Tehran	30	16	10	4	54	29	58	1-0		1-1	0-0	2-0	3-1	4-4	7-1	2-1	4-2	3-0	1-3	2-2	0-0	1-0	1-1
Saipa Karaj	30	13	13	4	41	21	52	0-0	1-3		1-2	1-1	0-0	2-2	1-1	2-2	1-1	1-0	1-0	6-1	6-0	2-1	1-0
Saba Battery Tehran	30	13	11	6	35	31	50	1-1	2-4	1-1		1-0	1-1	3-1	1-1	2-1	0-1	3-2	0-4	1-0	1-0	2-0	1-0
AbooMoslem Mashhad	30	12	10	8	31	23	46	1-0	0-1	1-0	0-0		1-3	0-1	5-1	1-0	1-2	1-0	2-0	1-0	1-0	2-1	
Zob Ahan Esfahan	30	12	10	8	41	30	45	1-1	3-0	0-1	0-1	1-2		2-0	3-1	3-0	1-1	1-0	1-0	2-0	2-1	1-1	4-3
Sepahan Esfahan	30	12	7	11	38	32	43	1-0	1-1	0-1	0-2	1-1	2-0		2-0	2-0	3-0	0-0	2-2	1-3	1-0	4-0	1-0
Foolad Ahvaz	30	11	8	11	30	41	41	0-0	0-0	0-1	0-1	1-1	0-0	1-0		1-0	3-0	1-0	3-2	0-1	2-1	0-0	2-0
Pirouzi Tehran	30	9	11	10	39	40	38	0-0	1-0	0-0	2-2	2-2	1-1	2-3	2-3		2-4	4-1	1-0	1-1	2-1	2-1	1-0
Fajr Sepasi Shiraz	30	8	12	10	27	33	36	0-3	0-2	0-2	1-1	0-1	0-0	1-0	2-0	2-2		1-0	0-0	3-0	0-0	4-1	1-2
Malavan Anzali	30	10	6	14	29	38	36	2-3	1-1	1-4	0-0	1-0	3-1	1-0	1-0	1-3	2-0		3-2	0-1	1-0	1-0	2-0
Esteghlal Ahvaz	30	9	8	13	24	44	35	0-2	1-2	1-2	1-0	0-1	1-1	1-3	4-2	2-2	2-1	1-1		3-2	1-1	2-3	3-2
Rah Ahan Tehran	30	9	7	14	27	43	34	1-2	1-3	1-0	1-0	0-2	0-2	2-1	1-2	0-0	0-0	1-0	3-1		1-1	2-1	0-1
Bargh Shiraz	30	6	10	14	23	37	28	1-3	1-3	0-0	2-2	1-1	2-1	1-0	0-1	0-1	0-0	2-0	0-1	1-0		**3-0**	1-0
Shamoushak Noshahr	30	4	11	15	19	39	23	0-1	1-0	1-2	1-2	0-0	0-0	0-0	1-2	2-1	0-0	0-0	1-1	1-1	1-1		1-0
Shahid Ghandi Yazd	30	4	7	19	21	43	19	0-1	0-2	0-0	1-1	1-3	1-5	0-1	0-0	0-2	1-2	1-0	2-2	1-1	1-1	2-0	

1/09/2005 – 21/04/2006 • † Qualified for the AFC Champions League • Match in bold awarded 3-0 • § Zob Ahan deducted one point
Top scorers: Reza ENAYATI, Esteghlal, 21; Fereidon FAZLI, Esteghlal Ahvaz, 17; Mehdi RAJABZADEH, Zob Ahan, 14

IRAN 2005–06 AZADEGAN LEAGUE GROUP A

	Pl	W	D	L	F	A	Pts
Pegah Gilan †	22	15	3	4	42	12	48
Teraktor-Sazi Tabriz	22	14	5	3	33	16	47
Horna Tehran †	22	14	5	3	30	16	47
Oghab Tehran	22	8	8	6	28	26	32
Sanaye Arak	22	8	5	9	30	34	29
Kesht-o-Sanat Shushtar	22	7	7	8	29	32	28
Niroye Zamini Tehran	22	7	5	10	25	30	26
Shahab Zanjan	22	7	4	11	25	32	25
Nouzhen Sari	22	5	8	9	14	20	23
Dayhim Ahvaz	22	5	6	11	26	33	21
Ekbatan Tehran	22	4	9	9	20	28	21
Iran-Javan Bushehr	22	3	4	15	19	44	13

† Qualified for the play-offs
Play-off: Paykan Tehran 2-1 1-1 Pegah Gilan
Second place play-off: Homa 0-0 5-4p Teraktor
Relegation play-off: Ekbatan 0-0 3-2p Dayhim

IRAN 2005–06 AZADEGAN LEAGUE GROUP B

	Pl	W	D	L	F	A	Pts
Mes Kerman †	22	12	7	3	30	13	43
Paykan Tehran †	22	11	7	4	28	11	40
Sanat-Naft Abadan	22	11	5	6	27	14	38
Shahin Bushehr	22	11	2	9	30	28	35
Marsad Shiraz	22	10	4	8	28	25	34
Sorkh-Pushan Tehran	22	8	7	7	27	24	31
Pegah Khuzestan Shush	22	5	12	5	24	21	27
Esteghlal Kish	22	6	9	7	18	25	27
Mashin-Sazi Tabriz	22	6	7	9	21	36	25
Payam Kh. Mashhad	22	6	6	10	21	30	24
Bargh Tehran	22	5	5	11	19	25	21
Shahrdari Langerud	22	2	6	14	17	39	12

† Qualified for the play-offs
Play-off: Mes Kerman 3-1 1-1 Homa
Mas Kerman and Paykan promoted

JAAM HAZFI 2005–06

Eighth-finals

Pirouzi	3
AbooMoslem Mashhad	2
Peykan Tehran	2
Malavan Anzali	3
Esteghlal Tehran	w-o
Shahin Boshehr †	-
Zobahan Esfahan	1
Nojan Sari	2
Saba Battery	2
Sanay Arak	1
Payam Shiraz	0
Sepahan 'B'	1
Teraktorsazi Tabriz	1
Maziran Sari	0
Pas Tehran	0 3p
Sepahan	0 4p

Quarter-finals

Pirouzi	3
Malavan Anzali	1
Esteghlal Tehran †	-
Nojan Sari	w-o
Saba Battery	2
Sepahan 'B'	1
Teraktorsazi Tabriz	0
Sepahan	1

Semi-finals

Pirouzi	2 7p
Nojan Sari	2 6p
Saba Battery	1
Sepahan	3

Final

Pirouzi	
Sepahan	

CUP FINAL
Final to be played in September 2006 after the fixture was postponed from May 2006

* Home team • † Teams withdrew

IRQ – IRAQ

NATIONAL TEAM RECORD
JULY 1ST 2002 TO JULY 9TH 2006

PL	W	D	L	F	A	%
56	23	14	19	95	72	53.6

FIFA/COCA-COLA WORLD RANKING

1993	1994	1995	1996	1997	1998	1999	2000	2001	2002	2003	2004	2005	High		Low	
65	88	110	98	68	94	78	79	72	53	43	44	54	39	10/04	139	07/96

	2005–2006										
08/05	09/05	10/05	11/05	12/05	01/06	02/06	03/06	04/06	05/06	06/06	07/06
57	68	67	74	54	54	55	55	52	52	-	88

Despite the extremely serious security situation which means that no international football can be played within Iraq, the domestic League continues to function, although not without difficulty or controversy. The championship was organised along the same lines as the previous season with four preliminary groups of seven teams, each playing each other twice. The top three then qualified for the final rounds which saw Baghdad clubs Al Zawra'a and Al Quwa Al Jawiya emerge to play each other in one semi-final and Najaf and Arbil in the other. They were bad tempered encounters with the second legs of both matches abandoned. Crowd trouble put paid to the match

INTERNATIONAL HONOURS
Qualified for the FIFA World Cup™ finals 1986
Asian Games 1982 AFC Youth Championship 1975 1977 1978 1988 2000 Gulf Cup 1979 1984 1988

in Arbil on the hour whilst the Al Quwa Al Jawiya players walked off in injury time whilst losing 2-0. In the final against Najaf, Al Zawra'a needed penalties to claim their first title since 2001 after the match finished goalless. The national team rescued a poor start to their AFC Asian Cup qualifiers by beating China PR in the UAE, but whether football can continue to be played was thrown open to debate following the kidnapping of the president of the Iraqi Olympic Council and other sports officials on July 15, 2006 at a conference centre in Baghdad.

THE FIFA BIG COUNT OF 2000

	Male	Female		Male	Female
Registered players	5 815	400	Referees	504	0
Non registered players	90 000	1 000	Officials	685	415
Youth players	1 705	250	Total involved	100 774	
Total players	99 170		Number of clubs	100	
Professional players	20	0	Number of teams	152	

Iraqi Football Association (IFA)
Al Shaab Stadium, PO Box 484, Baghdad, Iraq
Tel +964 1 7743652   Fax +964 1 5372021
iraqfed@yahoo.com   www.iraqfootball.org
President: HUSSAIN Mohammed Saeed   General Secretary: AHMED A. Ibrahim
Vice-President: HUMOUD Najih   Treasurer: ABDUL KHALIQ Masounel Ahmed   Media Officer: WALID Tabra
Men's Coach: AKRAM Ahmed Salman   Women's Coach: AL MUMIN Husam Dr.
IFA formed: 1948   AFC: 1971   FIFA: 1950
White shirts, White shorts, White socks

RECENT INTERNATIONAL MATCHES PLAYED BY IRAQ

2003	Opponents		Score	Venue	Comp	Scorers	Att	Referee
12-12	Bahrain	D	2-2	Manama	Fr	Manajid Abbas [40], Hawar Tahir [76]	15 000	
15-12	Kenya	W	2-0	Manama	Fr	Hawar Taher [9], Abbas Hassan [43]		
18-12	Egypt	L	0-2	Manama	Fr			
21-12	Qatar	D	0-0	Doha	Fr			Al Qatani QAT
2004								
12-02	Japan	L	0-2	Tokyo	Fr		38 622	Kwon Jong Chul KOR
18-02	Uzbekistan	D	1-1	Tashkent	WCq	Ahmed Saleh [57]	24 000	Srinivasan IND
31-03	Palestine	D	1-1	Doha	WCq	Razak Mossa [20]	500	Al Shoufi SYR
23-05	Trinidad and Tobago	L	0-2	West Bromwich	Fr		2 000	Halsey ENG
9-06	Chinese Taipei	W	6-1	Amman	WCq	Razak Mossa 2 [2 14], Naji Fawazi [18] Manajid Abbas 2 [50 85], Jassim Fayadh [68]	2 000	Al Hail QAT
19-06	Palestine	W	2-1	Tehran	WFr1	Emad Mohammed 2 [41 83]		
21-06	Jordan	L	0-2	Tehran	WFr1			
23-06	Iran	L	1-2	Tehran	WFsf	Ahmad Abbas [30]		
25-06	Jordan	L	1-3	Tehran	WF3p	Emad Mohammed [81]		
18-07	Uzbekistan	L	0-1	Chengdu	ACr1		12 400	Kwon Jong Chul KOR
22-07	Turkmenistan	W	3-2	Chengdu	ACr1	Hawar Mohammed [12], Razzaq Farhan [81], Qusai Munir [88]		Al Fadhli KUW
26-07	Saudi Arabia	W	2-1	Chengdu	ACr1	Nashat Akram [50], Younes Khalef [86]	15 000	Kwon Jong Chul KOR
30-07	China PR	L	0-3	Beijing	ACqf			Maidin SIN
8-09	Chinese Taipei	W	4-1	Taipei	WCq	Salih Sadir 2 [4 43], Saad Attiya [75], Younes Khalef [86]	5 000	Baskar IND
7-10	Oman	L	0-1	Muscat	Fr			
13-10	Uzbekistan	L	1-2	Amman	WCq	Qusai Munir [29]	10 000	Maidin SIN
16-11	Palestine	W	4-1	Doha	WCq	Qusai Munir 2 [54 58], Emad Mohammed [65], Nashat Akram [70]	500	Al Mutlaq KSA
3-12	Yemen	W	3-1	Dubai	Fr			
10-12	Oman	L	1-3	Doha	GCr1	Razzaq Farhan [56]		
13-12	Qatar	D	3-3	Doha	GCr1	Razzaq Farhan [16], Nashat Akram [53], Haidar Hassan [90]		
16-12	UAE	D	1-1	Doha	GCr1	Qusai Munir [90p]		
2005								
26-03	Australia	L	1-2	Sydney	Fr	Mohammad Nassir [12]	30 258	O'Leary NZL
8-06	Jordan	W	1-0	Amman	Fr	Mahdi Kareem [15]		
7-08	Bahrain	D	2-2	Manama	Fr	Younis Mahmoud [52], Mohammed Nassir [75]		
13-08	Cyprus	L	1-2	Limassol	Fr	Mohammed Nassir [17]		
11-10	Qatar	D	0-0	Doha	Fr		500	
26-11	Kuwait	D	0-0	Kuwait City	Fr			
1-12	Palestine	W	4-0	Rayyan	WGr1	Razzaq Farhan [4], Hawar Mohammed Taher [56], Loay Salah [73], Ahmed Salah [86]		
5-12	Saudi Arabia	W	5-1	Rayyan	WGr1	Haidar Abdul Amir [8], Emad Mohammed [19], Nashat Akram [30], Younis Mahmoud 2 [51 78]		
8-12	Saudi Arabia	W	2-0	Doha	WGsf	Loay Saleh [33], Razzaq Farhan [85]		
10-12	Syria	D	2-2	Doha	WGf	Razzaq Farhan [45], Younis Mahmoud [78], W 4-3p		
2006								
13-02	Oman	L	0-1	Wattayah	Fr		11 000	Shaban KUW
16-02	Thailand	L	3-4	Ayutthaya	Fr	Emad Mohammed 3 [8 44 90]	25 000	Waiyabot THA
22-02	Singapore	L	0-2	Singapore	ACq		10 221	Shield AUS
1-03	China PR	W	2-1	Al Ain	ACq	Mahdi Ajeel [16], Hawar Mohammed Taher [67]	7 700	Al Saeedi UAE
15-03	Saudi Arabia	D	2-2	Jeddah	Fr	Mohammed Nassir [40], Haidar Abdul Amir [92+]		Al Hamdan KSA

Fr = Friendly • WF = West Asian Federation Championship • WG = West Asian Games • AC = AFC Asian Cup • GC = Gulf Cup • WC = FIFA World Cup™
q = qualifier • r1 = first round group • qf = quarter-final • sf = semi-final • 3p = third place play-off • f = final • GG = golden goal

IRAQ NATIONAL TEAM RECORDS AND RECORD SEQUENCES

Records			Sequence records					
Victory	10-1	BHR 1966	Wins	8	1985	Clean sheets	5	Four times
Defeat	1-7	TUR 1959	Defeats	5	1967-1969	Goals scored	21	1993-1996
Player Caps	126	HUSSAIN Saeed	Undefeated	17	1982-84, 1988-89	Without goal	3	2003-2004
Player Goals	63	HUSSAIN Saeed	Without win	9	1967-1971	Goals against	22	2004-2005

IRAQ COUNTRY INFORMATION

Capital	Baghdad	Independence	1932 from the UK	GDP per Capita	$1 500
Population	25 374 691	Status	Republic	GNP Ranking	76
Area km²	437 072	Language	Arabic, Kurdish	Dialling code	+964
Population density	58 per km²	Literacy rate	40%	Internet code	.iq
% in urban areas	75%	Main religion	Muslim	GMT + / −	+3
Towns/Cities ('000)	Baghdad 5 672; Mosul 2 066; Basra 2 016; Irbil 933; Sulimaniya 723; Kirkuk 601; Najaf 482; Karbala 434; Nasiriyah 400; Al Amarah 323; Diwaniyah 318; Al Kut 315; Al Hillah 289				
Neighbours (km)	Turkey 352; Iran 1 458; Kuwait 240; Saudi Arabia 814; Jordan 181; Syria 605; Persian Gulf 58				
Main stadia	Al Shaab − Baghdad 45 000				

CLUB DIRECTORY

Club	Town/City	Stadium	Capacity	Lge	Cup
Arbil	Arbil	Franso Hariri	40 000	0	0
Al Jaish (Army)	Baghdad			1	2
Al Mina'a	Basra	Al Mina'a Stadium	10 000	0	0
Al Najaf	Najaf	Al Najaf Stadium	12 000	0	0
Al Quwa Al Jawia (Air Force)	Baghdad	Al Quwa Al Jawia Stadium	10 000	5	7
Al Rasheed	Baghdad			3	2
Al Shurta (Police)	Baghdad	Al Kashafa Stadium	12 000	2	0
Al Talaba (Students)	Baghdad	Al Talaba Stadium	10 000	5	2
Al Zawra'a	Baghdad	Al Zawra'a Stadium	10 000	11	14

RECENT LEAGUE AND CUP RECORD

	Championship						Cup		
Year	Champions	Pts	Runners-up	Pts	Third	Pts	Winners	Score	Runners-up
1990	Al Tayaran	42	Al Rasheed	38	Al Shurta	36	Al Zawra'a	0-0 2-1	Al Shabab
1991	Al Zawra'a	46	Al Talaba	41	Al Shurta	39	Al Zawra'a	1-1 4-3p	Al Jaish
1992	Al Quwa Al Jawia	63	Al Zawra'a	61	Al Karkh	60	Al Quwa Al Jawia	2-1	Al Khutut
1993	Al Talaba	110	Al Zawra'a	103	Al Quwa Al Jawia	101	Al Zawra'a	2-1	Al Talaba
1994	Al Zawra'a	85	Al Quwa Al Jawia	77	Al Talaba	75	Al Zawra'a	2-1	Al Talaba
1995	Al Zawra'a	120	Al Quwa Al Jawia	107	Al Najaf	107	Al Zawra'a	3-0	Al Jaish
1996	Al Zawra'a	55	Al Najaf	38	Al Shurta	37	Al Zawra'a	2-1	Al Shurta
1997	Al Quwa Al Jawia	69	Al Zawra'a	67	Al Talaba	60	Al Quwa Al Jawia	1-1 8-7p	Al Shurta
1998	Al Shurta	73	Al Quwa Al Jawia	71	Al Zawra'a	70	Al Zawra'a	1-1 4-3p	Al Quwa Al Jawia
1999	Al Zawra'a	57	Al Talaba	53	Al Quwa Al Jawia	47	Al Zawra'a	1-0	Al Talaba
2000	Al Zawra'a	114	Al Quwa Al Jawia	110	Al Shurta	110	Al Zawra'a	0-0 4-3p	Al Quwa Al Jawia
2001	Al Zawra'a	70	Al Quwa Al Jawia	62	Al Shurta	60	No tournament held		
2002	Al Talaba	91	Al Quwa Al Jawia	85	Al Shurta	80	Al Talaba	1-0	Al Shurta
2003	Championship abandoned						Al Talaba	1-0	Al Shurta
2004	Championship abandoned						No tournament held		
2005	Al Quwa Al Jawia	2-0	Al Mina'a				No tournament held		
2006	Al Zawra'a	†	Al Quwa Al Jawia				No tournament held		

† Won 4-3 on penalties after a 0-0 draw

IRAQ 2005–06
FIRST ROUND GROUP 1

	Pl	W	D	L	F	A	Pts
Al Mina'a Basra †	12	8	3	1	22	9	27
Karbala †	12	8	2	2	27	15	26
Maysan Umara †	12	4	5	3	12	10	17
Nafit Al Janob Basra	12	4	2	6	11	13	14
Shatra	12	3	5	4	9	15	14
Samawa	12	1	6	5	11	13	9
Kut	12	1	3	8	8	25	6

28/10/2005 - 3/03/2006 • † Qualified for the next round

IRAQ 2005–06
FIRST ROUND GROUP 2

	Pl	W	D	L	F	A	Pts
Al Zawra'a Baghdad †	12	9	3	0	29	9	30
Samara'a †	12	5	4	3	12	15	19
Al Najaf †	12	5	3	4	19	10	18
Al Nafit Baghdad	12	4	6	2	14	15	18
Kahrabaa Baghdad	12	3	6	3	14	12	15
Al Khadimiya Baghdad	12	0	7	5	6	15	7
Amana	12	0	3	9	3	21	3

28/10/2005 - 3/03/2006 • † Qualified for the next round

IRAQ 2005–06
FIRST ROUND GROUP 3

	Pl	W	D	L	F	A	Pts
Al Shurta Baghdad †	12	9	3	0	21	4	30
Al Quwa Al Jawiya †	12	6	4	2	19	10	22
Al Jaish Baghdad †	12	5	3	4	12	10	18
Al Sina'a Baghdad	12	3	5	4	7	10	14
Diyala	12	3	4	5	5	9	13
Al Karkh Baghdad	12	3	3	6	9	14	12
Siliakh	12	0	4	8	5	21	4

28/10/2005 - 3/03/2006 • † Qualified for the next round

IRAQ 2005–06
FIRST ROUND GROUP 4

	Pl	W	D	L	F	A	Pts
Al Talaba Baghdad †	12	7	3	2	22	5	24
Duhok †	12	5	5	2	10	5	20
Arbil †	12	4	5	3	10	7	17
Sirwan Sulimaniya	12	4	5	3	11	13	17
Kirkuk	12	4	1	7	10	15	13
Ararat	12	2	5	5	6	18	11
Zakho Duhok	12	2	4	6	6	12	10

28/10/2005 - 4/03/2006 • † Qualified for the next round

CHAMPIONSHIP PLAY-OFFS

Second round

Group 1	Pl	W	D	L	F	A	Pt	Ar	Sa	AM
Arbil	4	2	1	1	7	4	7		1-0	3-0
Samara'a	4	2	0	2	4	4	6	2-1		1-0
Al Mina'a Basra	4	1	1	2	4	7	4	2-2	2-1	

Group 2	Pl	W	D	L	F	A	Pt	AZ	Du	AJ
Al Zawra'a Baghdad	4	3	1	0	8	0	10		3-0	2-0
Duhok	4	1	1	2	3	5	4	0-0		2-0
Al Jaish Baghdad	4	1	0	3	2	8	3	0-3	2-1	

Group 3	Pl	W	D	L	F	A	Pt	AN	Ka	AS
Al Najaf	4	2	1	1	5	2	7		3-1	2-0
Karbala	4	2	0	2	5	8	6	1-0		1-4
Al Shurta Baghdad	4	1	1	2	5	5	4	0-0	1-2	

Group 4	Pl	W	D	L	F	A	Pt	AQ	AT	Ma
Al Quwa Al Jawiya	4	2	1	1	7	3	7		0-1	3-0
Al Talaba Baghdad	4	2	1	1	7	6	7	1-3		4-2
Maysan Umara	4	0	2	2	4	9	2	1-1	1-1	

Semi-finals

Al Zawra'a	1 3
Al Quwa Al Jawiya	1 0

Arbil	1 1
Al Najaf	4 0

Final

Al Zawra'a	0 4p
Al Najaf	0 3p

25/03/2006 - 16/06/2006 • Matches in bold awarded 3-0 • Both semi-final second leg matches abandoned

ISL – ICELAND

NATIONAL TEAM RECORD
JULY 1ST 2002 TO JULY 9TH 2006

PL	W	D	L	F	A	%
32	8	5	19	40	60	32.8

FIFA/COCA-COLA WORLD RANKING

1993	1994	1995	1996	1997	1998	1999	2000	2001	2002	2003	2004	2005		High		Low	
47	39	50	60	72	64	43	50	52	58	58	93	94		37	09/94	107	06/07

2005–2006											
08/05	09/05	10/05	11/05	12/05	01/06	02/06	03/06	04/06	05/06	06/06	07/06
94	92	92	93	94	95	96	97	97	99	-	107

There was no stopping FH Hafnarfjördur in the 2005 Icelandic championship as the team from just outside of the capital Rejkjavik stormed to a second successive League title. FH won the first 15 of their 18 League matches to win the title by a remarkable 16 points. Having remained unbeaten in their final 16 matches of their previous season, FH's unbeaten run stretched for 31 matches over the course of 15 months before they finally lost to IA Akranes at the end of August 2005. With the destination of the title never in doubt, the relegation battle provided much of the interest. Having escaped the drop on the last day of the previous six seasons, Fram Rejkjavik's luck finally ran out.

INTERNATIONAL HONOURS
None

On the final day they lost 5-1 to FH, although it took an injury time goal from old boy Tryggvi Gudmundsson to send them down on goal difference instead of IBV. Fram then compounded their misfortune by losing in the Cup Final to Valur the following weekend. It was all change for the national team after the disappointing FIFA World Cup™ qualifying campaign, with joint coaches Asgeir Sigurvinsson and Logi Olafsson replaced by Eyjolfur Sverrisson as Iceland try to halt their decline in fortunes. Their qualifying group for UEFA Euro 2008™ has a distinctly Scandinavian feel to it, so it may offer Eidur Gudjohnsen and co the opportunity to cause a surprise or two.

THE FIFA BIG COUNT OF 2000

	Male	Female		Male	Female
Registered players	4 800	700	Referees	934	98
Non registered players	4 000	1 000	Officials	666	101
Youth players	9 000	3 500	Total involved	24 799	
Total players	23 000		Number of clubs	127	
Professional players	300	0	Number of teams	560	

Knattspyrnusamband Islands (KSI)
The Football Association of Iceland, Laugardal, Reykjavík 104, Iceland
Tel +354 5102900   Fax +354 5689793
ksi@ksi.is   www.ksi.is
President: MAGNUSSON Eggert   General Secretary: THORSTEINSSON Geir
Vice-President: JONSSON Halldor   Treasurer: STEINGRIMSSON Eggert   Media Officer: SAMARASON Omar
Men's Coach: SVERRISSON Eyjolfur   Women's Coach: SVEINSSON Jorundur Aki
KSI formed: 1947   UEFA: 1954   FIFA: 1947
Blue shirts with red and white trimmings, Blue shorts, Blue socks or White shirts with blue trimmings, Blue shirts, White socks

RECENT INTERNATIONAL MATCHES PLAYED BY ICELAND

2002	Opponents	Score		Venue	Comp	Scorers	Att	Referee
21-08	Andorra	W	3-0	Reykjavík	Fr	Gudjohnsen.E [19], Dadason 2 [26 43]	2 900	Isaksen FRO
7-09	Hungary	L	0-2	Reykjavík	Fr		3 190	Maisonlahti FIN
12-10	Scotland	L	0-2	Reykjavík	ECq		7 065	Sars FRA
16-10	Lithuania	W	3-0	Reykjavík	ECq	Helguson [49], Gudjohnsen.E 2 [61 73]	3 513	Gilewski POL
20-11	Estonia	L	0-2	Tallinn	Fr		478	Haverkort NED
2003								
29-03	Scotland	L	1-2	Glasgow	ECq	Gudjohnsen.E [48]	37 548	Temmink NED
30-04	Finland	L	0-3	Vantaa	Fr		4 005	Frojdfeldt SWE
7-06	Faroe Islands	W	2-1	Reykjavík	ECq	Sigurdsson.H [49], Gudmundsson.T [88]	6 038	Liba CZE
11-06	Lithuania	W	3-0	Kaunas	ECq	Gudjónsson.Th [59], Gudjohnsen.E [72], Hreidarsson [90]	7 500	Corpodean ROU
20-08	Faroe Islands	W	2-1	Toftir	ECq	Gudjohnsen.E [55], Marteinsson [70]	3 416	Iturralde Gonzalez ESP
6-09	Germany	D	0-0	Reykjavík	ECq		7 035	Barber ENG
11-10	Germany	L	0-3	Hamburg	ECq		50 780	Ivanov RUS
19-11	Mexico	D	0-0	San Francisco	Fr		17 000	Saheli USA
2004								
31-03	Albania	L	1-2	Tirana	Fr	Gudjónsson.Th [66]	12 000	Bertini ITA
28-04	Latvia	D	0-0	Riga	Fr		6 500	Shmolik BLR
30-05	Japan	L	2-3	Manchester	Fr	Helguson 2 [5 50]	1 500	Riley ENG
5-06	England	L	1-6	Manchester	Fr	Helguson [42]	43 500	Wegereef NED
18-08	Italy	W	2-0	Reykjavík	Fr	Gudjohnsen.E [17], Einarsson [19]	20 204	Frojdfeldt SWE
4-09	Bulgaria	L	1-3	Reykjavík	WCq	Gudjohnsen.E [51p]	5 014	Hamer LUX
8-09	Hungary	L	2-3	Budapest	WCq	Gudjohnsen.E [39], Sigurdsson.I [78]	5 461	Ovrebo NOR
9-10	Malta	D	0-0	Ta'Qali	WCq		1 130	Corpodean ROU
13-10	Sweden	L	1-4	Reykjavík	WCq	Gudjohnsen.E [66]	7 037	Busacca SUI
2005								
26-03	Croatia	L	0-4	Zagreb	WCq		17 912	Damon RSA
30-03	Italy	D	0-0	Padova	Fr		16 697	Hamer LUX
4-06	Hungary	L	2-3	Reykjavík	WCq	Gudjohnsen.E [17], Sigurdsson.K [68]	4 613	Cardoso Batista POR
8-06	Malta	W	4-1	Reykjavík	WCq	Thorvaldsson.G [27], Gudjohnsen.E [33] Gudmundsson.T [74], Gunnarsson.V [84]	4 887	Skomina SVN
17-08	South Africa	W	4-1	Reykjavík	Fr	Steinsson [25], Vidarsson [42], Helguson [67], Gunnarsson.V [73]		
3-09	Croatia	L	1-3	Reykjavík	WCq	Gudjohnsen.E [24]	5 520	Stark GER
7-09	Bulgaria	L	2-3	Sofia	WCq	Steinsson [9], Hreidarsson [16]	18 000	Demirlek TUR
7-10	Poland	L	2-3	Warsaw	Fr	Sigurdsson.K [15], Sigurdsson.H [39]	7 500	Sukhina RUS
12-10	Sweden	L	1-3	Stockholm	WCq	Arnason [11]	33 716	Ivanov.V RUS
2006								
28-02	Trinidad and Tobago	L	0-2	London	Fr		7 890	

Fr = Friendly match • EC = UEFA EURO 2004™ • WC = FIFA World Cup™ • q = qualifier

ICELAND NATIONAL TEAM RECORDS AND RECORD SEQUENCES

Records			Sequence records				
Victory	9-0	FRO 1985	Wins	4	2000	Clean sheets	3	1984
Defeat	2-14	DEN 1967	Defeats	10	1978-1980	Goals scored	7	Three times
Player Caps	101	KRISTINSSON Rúnar	Undefeated	11	1998-1999	Without goal	6	1977-1978
Player Goals	17	JONSSON Ríkhardur	Without win	17	1977-1980	Goals against	19	1978-1981

ICELAND COUNTRY INFORMATION

Capital	Reykjavík	Independence	1918 from Denmark	GDP per Capita	$30 900
Population	293 966	Status	Constitutional Republic	GNP Ranking	94
Area km²	103 000	Language	Icelandic	Dialling code	+354
Population density	3 per km²	Literacy rate	99%	Internet code	.is
% in urban areas	92%	Main religion	Christian	GMT +/-	0
Towns/Cities ('000)	Reykjavík 113; Kópavogur 26; Hafnarfjördur 22; Akureyri 16; Gardabær 9; Keflavík 7
Neighbours (km)	North Atlantic 4 988
Main stadia	Laugardalsvöllur – Reykjavík 7 176; Akranesvöllur – Akranes 4 850

NATIONAL TEAM PLAYERS AND COACHES

Record Caps			Record Goals			Recent Coaches	
KRISTINSSON Rúnar	1987-'04	101	JONSSON Ríkhardur	1947-'65	17	KJARTANSSON Gudni	1980-'81
BERGSSON Gudni	1984-'03	80	GUDJOHNSEN Eidur	1996-'06	16	ATLASON Johannes	1982-'83
KRISTINSSON Birkir	1988-'04	74	DADASON Ríkhardur	1991-'03	14	HELD Siegfried	1986-'89
GUDJOHNSEN Arnór	1979-'97	73	GUDJOHNSEN Arnór	1979-'97	14	KJARTANSSON Gudni	1989
THORDARSON Olafur	1984-'96	72	GUDJONSSON Thórdur	1993-'04	13	JOHANNSSON Bo	1990-'91
GRETARSSON Arnar	1991-'04	71	HALLGRIMSSON Matthías	1968-'78	11	ELIASSON Asgeir	1991-'95
EDVALDSSON Atli	1976-'91	70	PETURSSON Pétur	1978-'90	11	OLAFSSON Logi	1996-'97
JONSSON Sævar	1980-'92	68	SVERRISSON Eyjólfur	1990-'01	10	THORDARSON Gudjon	1997-'99
GEIRSSON Marteinn	1971-'82	67	SIGURDSSON Helgi	1993-'04	10	EDVALDSSON Atli	1999-'03
SVERRISSON Eyjólfur	1990-'01	66	GUDMUNDSSON Tryggvi	1997-'05	10	SIGURVINSSON Asgeir	2003-

CLUB DIRECTORY

Club	Town/City	Stadium	Capacity	www.	Lge	Cup
IA Akranes	Akranes	Akranesvöllur	4 850	ia.is	18	9
Fram	Reykjavík	Laugardalsvöllur	7 176	fram.is	18	7
Fylkir	Reykjavík	Fylkisvöllur	4 000	fylkir.com	0	2
Grindavík	Grindavík	Grindavíkurvöllur	2 500	umfg.is	0	0
FH Hafnarfjördur	Hafnarfjördur	Kaplakrikavöllur	4 800	fhingar.is	2	0
IBV Vestmannæyjar	Vestmannæyjar	Hásteinsvöllur	3 540	ibv.is	3	4
Keflavík	Keflavík	Keflavíkurvöllur	4 000	keflavik.is	0	3
KR Reykjavík	Reykjavík	KR-Völlur	3 000	kr.is	24	10
Thróttur	Reykjavík	Valbjarnarvöllur	2 500	throttur.is	0	0
Valur	Reykjavík	Hlidarendi	3 000	valur.is	19	9

RECENT LEAGUE AND CUP RECORD

Year	Champions	Pts	Runners-up	Pts	Third	Pts	Winners	Score	Runners-up
1990	Fram Reykjavik	38	KR Reykjavik	38	IBV Vestmannæyjar	37	Valur Reykjavik	1-1 0-0 5-4p	KR Reykjavik
1991	Víkingur Reykjavík	37	Fram Reykjavik	37	KR Reykjavik	28	Valur Reykjavik	1-1 1-0	FH Hafnarfjördur
1992	IA Akranes	40	KR Reykjavik	37	Thor Akureyri	35	Valur Reykjavik	5-2	KA Akureyri
1993	IA Akranes	49	FH Hafnarfjördur	40	Keflavík	27	IA Akranes	2-1	Keflavík
1994	IA Akranes	39	FH Hafnarfjördur	36	Keflavík	31	KR Reykjavik	2-0	Grindavík
1995	IA Akranes	49	KR Reykjavik	35	IBV Vestmannæyjar	31	KR Reykjavik	2-1	Fram Reykjavík
1996	IA Akranes	40	KR Reykjavik	37	Leiftur	29	IA Akranes	2-1	IBV Vestmannæyjar
1997	IBV Vestmannæyjar	40	IA Akranes	35	Leiftur	30	Keflavík	1-1 0-0 5-4p	IBV Vestmannæyjar
1998	IBV Vestmannæyjar	38	KR Reykjavik	33	IA Akranes	30	IBV Vestmannæyjar	2-0	Leiftur
1999	KR Reykjavík	45	IBV Vestmannæyjar	38	Leiftur	26	KR Reykjavik	3-1	IA Akranes
2000	KR Reykjavík	37	Fylkir Reykjavik	35	Grindavík	30	IA Akranes	2-1	IBV Vestmannæyjar
2001	IA Akranes	36	IBV Vestmannæyjar	36	FH Hafnarfjördur	32	Fylkir Reykjavik	2-2 5-4p	KA Akureyri
2002	KR Reykjavík	36	Fylkir Reykjavik	34	Grindavík	29	Fylkir Reykjavik	3-1	Fram Reykjavík
2003	KR Reykjavík	33	FH Hafnarfjördur	30	IA Akranes	30	IA Akranes	1-0	FH Hafnarfjördur
2004	FH Hafnarfjördur	37	IBV Vestmannæyjar	31	IA Akranes	31	Keflavík	3-0	KA Akureyri
2005	FH Hafnarfjördur	48	Valur Reykjavik	32	IA Akranes	32	Valur Reykjavik	1-0	Fram Reykjavík

ICELAND 2005

URVALSDEILD (1)

	Pl	W	D	L	F	A	Pts	FH	Valur	IA	Keflavík	Fylkir	KR	Grindavík	IBV	Fram	Þróttur
FH Hafnarfjördur †	18	16	0	2	53	11	48		2-0	2-0	2-0	1-2	2-0	8-0	3-0	3-1	3-1
Valur Reykjavík ‡	18	10	2	6	29	16	32	0-1		2-0	0-0	3-1	3-0	3-1	1-1	3-0	1-2
IA Akranes ‡	18	10	2	6	24	20	32	2-1	1-2		1-2	0-3	2-1	3-2	2-0	1-2	1-0
Keflavík	18	7	6	5	28	31	27	0-3	1-5	0-1		2-2	2-1	1-1	2-2	2-1	3-3
Fylkir Reykjavík	18	8	2	8	28	28	26	2-5	1-2	2-3	0-1		1-2	2-1	1-0	1-1	0-1
KR Reykjavík	18	8	1	9	22	24	25	0-1	2-0	0-2	1-3	1-3		3-1	1-0	1-0	3-2
Grindavík	18	5	3	10	23	41	18	1-5	0-1	1-3	2-1	3-0	0-0		2-1	3-1	1-1
IBV Vestmannæyjar	18	5	2	11	18	30	17	0-1	1-0	0-2	2-3	0-3	2-1	5-1		2-0	2-0
Fram Reykjavík	18	5	2	11	19	32	17	1-5	2-1	0-0	2-3	0-4	0-1	3-0			3-0
Þróttur Reykjavík	18	4	4	10	21	32	16	1-5	0-2	0-0	2-2	1-2	0-1	3-2	4-0	0-1	

16/05/2005 - 17/09/2005 • † Qualified for the UEFA Champions League • ‡ Qualified for the UEFA Cup
Top scorers: Tryggvi GUDMUNDSSON, FH, 16; Allan BORGVARDT, FH, 13; Hordur SVEINSSON, Keflavík, 9; Gardar GUNNLAUGSSON, Valur, 8

ICELAND 2005
1.DEILD (2)

	Pl	W	D	L	F	A	Pts
Breidablik Kópavogur	18	13	5	0	32	13	44
Vikingur Reykjavík	18	10	7	1	41	9	37
KA Akureyri	18	10	4	4	40	20	34
Fjölnir Reykjavík	18	7	1	10	29	34	22
Vikingur Olafsvík	18	6	4	8	15	30	22
Thór Akureyri	18	6	3	9	25	34	21
HK Kópavogur	18	4	8	6	18	21	20
Haukar Hafnarfjördur	18	4	5	9	23	33	17
Völsungur Husavík	18	4	4	10	17	25	16
KS Siglufjördur	18	2	7	9	14	35	13

16/05/2005 - 16/09/2005

ICELANDIC CUP 2005

Round of 16

Valur Reykjavík	5
Haukar Hafnarfjördur	1
Vikingur Reykjavík	3 5p
KR Reykjavík	3 6p
HK Kópavogur	1
Keflavík	0
Grindavík	0
Fylkir Reykjavík	1
FH Hafnarfjördur	3
KA Akureyri	1
Breidablik Kópavogur	1
IA Akranes	2
IBV Vestmannæyjar	3
Njardvík	2
Thór Akureyri	0
Fram Reykjavík	3

Quarter-finals

Valur Reykjavík	2
KR Reykjavík *	1
HK Kópavogur *	0
Fylkir Reykjavík	2
FH Hafnarfjördur *	5
IA Akranes	1
IBV Vestmannæyjar	1
Fram Reykjavík *	2

Semi-finals

Valur Reykjavík	2
Fylkir Reykjavík	0
FH Hafnarfjördur	2 6p
Fram Reykjavík	2 7p

Semis played at Laugardalsvøllur

Final

Valur Reykjavík ‡	1
Fram Reykjavík	0

CUP FINAL

Laugardalsvøllur, Reykjavík
24-09-2005, Att: 5 162, Ref: Ragnarsson

Scorer - Adalsteinsson 52 for Valur

* Home team • ‡ Qualified for the UEFA Cup

ISR – ISRAEL

NATIONAL TEAM RECORD
JULY 1ST 2002 TO JULY 9TH 2006

PL	W	D	L	F	A	%
33	14	13	6	55	37	62.1

FIFA/COCA-COLA WORLD RANKING

1993	1994	1995	1996	1997	1998	1999	2000	2001	2002	2003	2004	2005		High		Low	
57	42	42	52	61	43	26	41	49	46	51	48	44		22	06/99	71	09/93

2005–2006											
08/05	09/05	10/05	11/05	12/05	01/06	02/06	03/06	04/06	05/06	06/06	07/06
47	44	43	44	44	44	44	47	47	49	-	51

With the national team able to play all of its home matches in the 2006 FIFA World Cup™ qualifiers in Israel, it gave the team a huge boost as they finished just two points behind group winners France, and only missed out on the play-offs on goal difference to Switzerland. Despite the good campaign and with just six defeats in four years, coach Avraham Grant decided he had taken the team as far as he could and was replaced by Dror Kashtan, who just missed out on the job in 2002. The ability to watch the national team in action, however temporarily, proved to be a welcome relief for many fans given the declining interest at League matches. Part of the problem

INTERNATIONAL HONOURS
Qualified for the FIFA World Cup™ finals 1970   AFC Asian Cup 1964   AFC Champions League Hapoel Tel Aviv 1967 Maccabi Tel Aviv 1969 1971

lies with the increased politicisation of fans since the start of the second intifada in 2000, with anti Arab chants now the norm at many grounds, especially during matches played against Arab club Bnei Sakhnin. Another factor in the falling attendances may be the complete dominance of Maccabi Haifa who were once again runaway champions, becoming the first club since Hapoel Petah Tikva in the 1960s to win a hat-trick of titles. The influx of Russian oligarch money into clubs such as Hapoel Tel Aviv and Beitar Jerusalem may make the League more competitive in the long run, but the effects have yet to filter through, although Hapoel did beat Bnei Yehuda to win the Cup.

THE FIFA BIG COUNT OF 2000

	Male	Female		Male	Female
Registered players	11 212	250	Referees	1 145	0
Non registered players	70 000	0	Officials	800	150
Youth players	25 949	150	Total involved	109 656	
Total players	107 561		Number of clubs	317	
Professional players	1 620	0	Number of teams	2 127	

The Israel Football Association (IFA)
Ramat-Gan Stadium, 299 Aba Hilell Street, Ramat-Gan 52134, Israel
Tel +972 3 6171500   Fax +972 3 5702044
r.dori@israel-football.org.il   www.israel-football.org.il
President: MENAHEM Itzhak   General Secretary: ZIMMER Haim
Vice-President: LUZON Abraham   Treasurer: HALUBA Shtern   Media Officer: AIZENBERG Shaul
Men's Coach: KASHTAN Dror   Women's Coach: SCHRAIER Alon
IFA formed: 1928 & 1948   UEFA: 1992 (AFC 1956-1976)   FIFA: 1929
Blue shirts with white trimmings, White shorts, Blue socks or White shirts with blue trimmings, Blue shorts, White socks

RECENT INTERNATIONAL MATCHES PLAYED BY ISRAEL

2002	Opponents		Score	Venue	Comp	Scorers	Att	Referee
21-08	Lithuania	W	4-2	Kaunas	Fr	Afek 2 [20][64], Zandberg [47], Tal [74]	3 000	Chykun BLR
5-09	Luxembourg	W	5-0	Luxembourg	Fr	Udi 2 [1][68], Badeer [24], Keisi [79], Benayoun [85]	1 400	Allaerts BEL
12-10	Malta	W	2-0	Ta'Qali	ECq	Balili [56], Revivo [77]	5 200	Shebek UKR
20-11	FYR Macedonia	W	3-2	Skopje	Fr	Zandberg [19], Nimni [28], Biton [90]	5 000	Delevic YUG
2003								
12-02	Armenia	W	2-0	Tel Aviv	Fr	Nimni [19], Zandberg [62]	8 000	Trentlange ITA
5-03	Moldova	D	0-0	Tel Aviv	Fr		8 000	Bertini ITA
29-03	Cyprus	D	1-1	Limassol	ECq	Afek [1]	8 500	McCurry SCO
2-04	France	L	1-2	Palermo	ECq	Afek [2]	4 000	Barber ENG
30-04	Cyprus	W	2-0	Palermo	ECq	Badeer [88], Holtzman [90]	1 000	Benes CZE
7-06	Slovenia	D	0-0	Antalya	ECq		2 500	Busacca SUI
20-08	Russia	W	2-1	Moscow	Fr	Nimni [52], Balili [82]	5 000	Ishchenko UKR
6-09	Slovenia	L	1-3	Ljubljana	ECq	Revivo [69]	8 000	Fandel GER
10-09	Malta	D	2-2	Antalya	ECq	Revivo [16], Abuksis [78]	300	Blareau BEL
11-10	France	L	0-3	Paris	ECq		57 900	Bolognino ITA
2004								
18-02	Azerbaijan	W	6-0	Tel Aviv	Fr	Arbeitman 3 [9][65][69], Tal [24p], Katan 2 [45][61]	13 250	Gomes Paraty POR
30-03	Lithuania	W	2-1	Tel Aviv	Fr	Balili [34], Badeer [64]	9 872	Dougal SCO
28-04	Moldova	D	1-1	Tel Aviv	Fr	Covalenco OG [31]	4 500	Corpodean ROU
27-05	Georgia	W	1-0	Tbilisi	Fr	Badeer [33]	22 000	Oriekhov UKR
18-08	Croatia	L	0-1	Zagreb	Fr		10 000	Granat POL
4-09	France	D	0-0	Paris	WCq		43 527	Temmink NED
8-09	Cyprus	W	2-1	Tel Aviv	WCq	Benayoun [64], Badeer [75]	21 872	Shmolik BLR
9-10	Switzerland	D	2-2	Tel Aviv	WCq	Benayoun 2 [9][48]	37 976	Shield AUS
17-11	Cyprus	W	2-1	Nicosia	WCq	Keisi [17], Nimni [86]	1 624	Kaldma EST
2005								
9-02	Croatia	D	3-3	Jerusalem	Fr	Balili [38], Benayoun [74], Golan [84]	4 000	Kailis CYP
26-03	Republic of Ireland	D	1-1	Tel Aviv	WCq	Souan [90]	32 150	Ivanov.V RUS
30-03	France	D	1-1	Tel Aviv	WCq	Badeer [83]	32 150	Merk GER
4-06	Republic of Ireland	D	2-2	Dublin	WCq	Yemiel [39], Nimni [46+]	36 000	Vassaras GRE
15-08	Ukraine	D	0-0	Kyiv	Fr	W 5-3p		Mikullski POL
17-08	Poland	L	2-3	Kyiv	Fr	Badir [35], Katan [47]	2 000	Karadzic SCG
3-09	Switzerland	D	1-1	Basel	WCq	Keisi [20]	30 000	Rosetti ITA
7-09	Faroe Islands	W	2-0	Tórshavn	WCq	Nimni [54], Katan [79]	2 240	VINK NED
8-10	Faroe Islands	W	2-1	Tel Aviv	WCq	Benayoun [1], Zaudberg [91+]	31 857	Brugger AUT
2006								
1-03	Denmark	L	0-2	Tel Aviv	Fr		15 762	Sippel GER

Fr = Friendly match • EC = UEFA EURO 2004™ • WC = FIFA World Cup™ • q = qualifier

ISRAEL NATIONAL TEAM RECORDS AND RECORD SEQUENCES

Records			Sequence records					
Victory	9-0	TPE 1988	Wins	7	1973-1974	Clean sheets	4	Four times
Defeat	1-7	EGY 1934, GER 2002	Defeats	8	1950-1956	Goals scored	9	1968-69, 2000-01
Player Caps	89	BENADO Arik	Undefeated	12	1971-1973	Without goal	5	1964-1965
Player Goals	25	SPIEGLER Mordechai	Without win	22	1985-1988	Goals against	22	1934-1958

ISRAEL COUNTRY INFORMATION

Capital	Jerusalem	Formation	1948	GDP per Capita	$19 800
Population	6 199 008	Status	Republic	GNP Ranking	36
Area km²	20 770	Language	Hebrew, Arabic	Dialling code	+972
Population density	298 per km²	Literacy rate	95%	Internet code	.il
% in urban areas	91%	Main religion	Jewish 80%, Muslim 14%	GMT + / –	+2
Towns/Cities ('000)	Jerusalem 714; Tel Aviv 370; Haifa 270; Rishon LeZiyyon 222; Ashdod 202; Be'er Sheva 187				
Neighbours (km)	Lebanon 79; Syria 76; Jordan 238; West Bank 307; Egypt 266; Gaza Strip 51; Mediterranean Sea & Red Sea 273				
Main stadia	Ramat-Gan – Ramat-Gan 42 000; Teddy Maiha – Jerusalem 20 000; Bloomfield – Tel Aviv 16 500				

NATIONAL TEAM PLAYERS AND COACHES

Record Caps			Record Goals			Recent Coaches	
BENADO Arik	1995-'06	89	SPIEGLER Mordechai	1964-'77	25	SCHWEITZER David	1973-'77
HARAZI Alon	1992-'06	88	HARAZI Ronen	1992-'99	23	SHEFER Imanuel	1978-'79
SHELAH Amir	1992-'01	85	STELMACH Nahum	1956-'68	22	MANSELL Jack	1980-'81
NIMNI Avi	1992-'05	80	OHANA Eli	1984-'97	17	MIRMOVICH Yosef	1983-'86
BANIN Tal	1990-'03	78	NIMNI Avi	1992-'05	17	MIHIC Miljenko	1986-'88
BERKOVIC Eyal	1992-'04	78	MIZRAHI Alon	1992-'01	17	SHNEOR & GRUNDMAN	1988-'92
KLINGER Nir	1987-'97	77	GLAZER Yehoshua	1949-'61	16	SCHARF Shlomo	1992-'99
HAZAN Alon	1990-'00	72	FEIGENBAUM Yehoshua	1966-'77	15	MOLLER NIELSEN Richard	2000-'02
REVIVO Haim	1992-'03	67	REVIVO Haim	1992-'03	15	GRANT Avraham	2002-'06
BADIR Walid	1997-'06	62				KASHTAN Dror	2006-

CLUB DIRECTORY

Club	Town/City	Stadium	Capacity	www.	Lge	Cup
MS Ashdod	Ashdod	Ashdod Stadium	8 000		0	0
Beitar Jerusalem	Jerusalem	Teddy Maiha	20 000		4	5
Bnei Yehuda	Tel Aviv	Bloomfield	16 500	bnei-yehuda.co.il	1	2
Hapoel Beer Sheva	Beer Sheva	Vasermil	13 000		2	1
Hapoel Bnei Sakhnin	Sakhnin	Ironi Sakhnin	6 000		0	1
Hapoel Haifa	Haifa	Kiryat Eli'ezer	18 500		1	3
Hapoel Nazareth	Nazareth Illit	Ilut	9 000		0	0
Hapoel Petah Tikva	Petah Tikva	Hapoel	8 400	hapoel-pt.co.il	6	2
Hapoel Tel Aviv	Tel Aviv	Bloomfield	16 500		11	11
Maccabi Haifa	Haifa	Kiryat Eli'ezer	18 500	maccabi-haifa.nana.co.il	10	5
Maccabi Petah Tikva	Petah Tikva	Hapoel	8 400		0	2
Maccabi Tel Aviv	Tel Aviv	Bloomfield	16 500	maccabi-tlv.nana.co.il	18	22

RECENT LEAGUE AND CUP RECORD

	Championship						Cup		
Year	Champions	Pts	Runners-up	Pts	Third	Pts	Winners	Score	Runners-up
1990	Bnei Yehuda	62	Hapoel Petah Tikva	58	Maccabi Haifa	50	Hapoel Kfar Saba	1-0	Shimshon Tel Aviv
1991	Maccabi Haifa	71	Hapoel Petah Tikva	70	Beitar Tel Aviv	50	Maccabi Haifa	3-1	Hapoel Petah Tikva
1992	Maccabi Tel Aviv	75	Bnei Yehuda	62	Maccabi Haifa	48	Hapoel Petah Tikva	3-1	Maccabi Tel Aviv
1993	Beitar Jerusalem	71	Maccabi Tel Aviv	62	Bnei Yehuda	56	Maccabi Haifa	1-0	Maccabi Tel Aviv
1994	Maccabi Haifa	95	Maccabi Tel Aviv	88	Hapoel Beer Sheva	65	Maccabi Tel Aviv	2-0	Hapoel Tel Aviv
1995	Maccabi Tel Aviv	63	Maccabi Haifa	58	Hapoel Beer Sheva	50	Maccabi Haifa	2-0	Hapoel Haifa
1996	Maccabi Tel Aviv	74	Maccabi Haifa	66	Beitar Jerusalem	64	Maccabi Tel Aviv	4-1	Hapoel Ironi RL
1997	Beitar Jerusalem	69	Hapoel Petah Tikva	60	Hapoel Beer Sheva	60	Hapoel Beer Sheva	1-0	Maccabi Tel Aviv
1998	Beitar Jerusalem	69	Hapoel Tel Aviv	68	Hapoel Haifa	60	Maccabi Haifa	2-0	Hapoel Jerusalem
1999	Hapoel Haifa	71	Maccabi Tel Aviv	63	Maccabi Haifa	60	Hapoel Tel Aviv	1-1 3-1p	Beitar Jerusalem
2000	Hapoel Tel Aviv	85	Maccabi Haifa	76	Hapoel Petah Tikva	74	Hapoel Tel Aviv	2-2 4-2p	Beitar Jerusalem
2001	Maccabi Haifa	82	Hapoel Tel Aviv	75	Hapoel Haifa	71	Maccabi Tel Aviv	3-0	Maccabi Petah Tikva
2002	Maccabi Haifa	75	Hapoel Tel Aviv	67	Maccabi Tel Aviv	57	Maccabi Tel Aviv	0-0 5-4p	Maccabi Haifa
2003	Maccabi Tel Aviv	69	Maccabi Haifa	69	Hapoel Tel Aviv	67	Hapoel Ramat Gan	1-1 5-4p	Hapoel Beer Sheva
2004	Maccabi Haifa	63	Maccabi Tel Aviv	57	Maccabi Petah Tikva	56	Hapoel Bnei Sakhnin	4-1	Hapoel Haifa
2005	Maccabi Haifa	71	Maccabi Petah Tikva	60	Ashdod	50	Maccabi Tel Aviv	2-2 5-3p	Maccabi Herzliya
2006	Maccabi Haifa	75	Hapoel Tel Aviv	59	Beitar Jerusalem	58	Hapoel Tel Aviv	1-0	Bnei Yehuda

ISRAEL 2005-06
PREMIER LEAGUE

	Pl	W	D	L	F	A	Pts	Maccabi H	Hapoel TA	Beitar	Bnei Yehuda	Maccabi PT	Maccabi TA	Maccabi N	Ashdod	Hapoel PT	Hapoel KS	Hapoel UN	B. Sakhnin
Maccabi Haifa †	33	23	6	4	65	25	75		1-0 0-1	3-0	1-0 4-0	3-2 2-1	2-1	2-1 2-1	4-0		2-0	1-0 1-1	2-1 4-0	4-1
Hapoel Tel Aviv ‡	33	16	11	6	51	25	59	0-0		1-1 1-1	2-0		1-1	2-0 2-0	2-0	3-1 1-1 1-1	3-0 3-1 1-2	4-0	2-2 1-0
Beitar Jerusalem ‡	33	17	7	9	51	33	58	0-1 1-0	0-2			2-2 3-0 2-0 1-0	0-1	1-1 4-0	0-1	0-1	1-0 0-1 4-0 0-2	3-2
Bnei Yehuda Tel Aviv ‡	33	14	7	12	37	41	49	0-1	0-4 0-1	2-3		1-0	3-1 1-0	1-0	2-1 2-1 2-1 2-2 1-0 0-1	1-1	2-1 2-0
Maccabi Petah Tikva	33	12	8	13	37	38	44	1-3	2-3 2-1	1-2	0-0 1-0		3-1	2-1 2-1	2-2	2-0	0-0	2-0 1-0 2-1 1-0
Maccabi Tel Aviv	33	11	11	11	35	37	44	1-0 1-1	2-0	2-3 2-1	2-2	0-0 0-3		1-0 3-1	2-1	3-0	2-1 0-0 0-0 1-1	2-0
Maccabi Netanya	33	11	8	14	40	45	41	1-3	1-0 1-1	2-3	0-1 1-1	2-3	0-1	3-1		1-1 3-1 0-0 2-3 3-2 1-0	1-0	0-0 1-1
MS Ashdod	33	9	12	12	46	47	39	1-2 1-0	1-1	2-3 1-1	2-0	2-0 0-0 0-1 1-1	2-2		4-3	5-0	2-1 0-0	1-2
Hapoel Petah Tikva	33	9	10	14	38	50	36	3-1 0-2	0-3	0-3 1-2	2-3	2-1 1-1 2-2 1-1	1-0	0-2	3-1 1-2		2-1	0-0	0-0
Hapoel Kfar Saba	33	8	10	15	30	41	34	1-2	0-1	0-2	1-1	2-0 2-2	1-0	1-2	2-2 1-1 1-1 0-0		1-2 3-1 0-0 1-0
Hapoel Upper Nazareth	33	8	10	15	25	47	34	0-6	1-1 1-1	1-1	0-0 0-1 1-0 0-0 1-2 0-1	2-1	2-1 0-1	1-0		3-2 2-1
Hapoel Bnei Sakhnin	33	5	10	18	28	54	25	2-2 2-2	2-1	0-0 0-3	0-3	2-1	3-1 1-1	2-2	0-1 0-3 0-2 1-0	1-2	1-0	

26/08/2005 - 14/05/2006 • † Qualified for the UEFA Champions League • ‡ Qualified for the UEFA Cup • Top scorer: Shai HOLTZMAN, Ashdod, 18

ISRAEL 2005-06
LIGA LEUMIT (2)

	Pl	W	D	L	F	A	Pts
Macabi Hertzelia	33	16	9	8	42	22	57
Hakoah Ramat Gan	33	15	11	7	47	31	56
Ironi Kiriat Shmona	33	12	14	7	39	33	50
Hapeol Be'er Sheva	33	11	16	6	35	25	49
Hapoel Jerusalem	33	13	10	10	45	40	49
Hapoel Haifa	33	11	14	8	40	28	47
Hapoel Acre	33	12	10	11	32	33	46
Hapoel Ashkelon	33	10	8	15	33	40	38
Hapoel Ranana	33	8	12	13	31	36	36
Ironi Ramat Hasharon §2	33	8	13	12	30	39	35
Ironi Rishon Letzion	33	6	13	14	24	43	31
Maccabi Be'er Sheva §1	33	6	10	17	19	47	27

20/08/2004 - 27/05/2005 • § Points deducted

FA CUP 2005-06

Round of 16

Hapoel Tel Aviv	3
MS Ashdod *	0
Beitar Jerusalem *	0
Hakoah Ramat Gan	1
Hapoel Kfar Saba	1
Hapoel Marmorek *	0
Ironi Ramat Hasharon *	1
Hapoel Bnei Sakhnin	3
Maccabi Haifa	2
Hapoel Be'er Sheva *	1
Maccabi Hertzelia *	2 12p
Maccabi Petah Tikva	2 13p
Hapoel Acre	4
Maccabi Tel Aviv *	0
Maccabi Kfar Kana *	0
Bnei Yehuda Tel Aviv	1

Quarter-finals

Hapoel Tel Aviv	3
Hakoah Ramat Gan *	0
Hapoel Kfar Saba *	1
Hapoel Bnei Sakhnin	3
Maccabi Haifa *	0 4p
Maccabi Petah Tikva	0 3p
Hapoel Acre *	1
Bnei Yehuda Tel Aviv	2

Semi-finals

Hapoel Tel Aviv	2
Hapoel Bnei Sakhnin	0
Maccabi Haifa	0
Bnei Yehuda Tel Aviv	2

Final

Hapoel Tel Aviv ‡	1
Bnei Yehuda Tel Aviv	0

CUP FINAL
Ramat Gan, Tel Aviv
9-05-2006

Scorer - Ilia Yavorian [87] for Hapoel

* Home team • Semis played at Ramat Gan • ‡ Qualified for the UEFA Cup

ITA – ITALY

NATIONAL TEAM RECORD
JULY 1ST 2002 TO JULY 9TH 2006

PL	W	D	L	F	A	%
52	30	17	5	83	35	74

How to sum up a year in Italian football that had absolutely everything? On the one hand it was an Annus Mirabilis with the national team's quite unexpected and glorious triumph at the 2006 FIFA World Cup™ in Germany. On the other hand it was an Annus Horribilis of spectacular proportions with a scandal that left the nation reeling at the sheer scale of gerrymandering within the club game. The two events were not linked but there can be no doubt that for the duration of the finals in Germany the scandal bonded the players in a way that perhaps nothing else could. Italy did not look like world beaters in the group stage but their record coming into the finals was excellent having gone 18 games without defeat. Not since Vittorio Pozzo's legendary team of the 1930s had the Azzurri been on such a run. In the event Italy conceded just two goals - a deflected own goal and a penalty - and therein lay the secret of their success. Coach Marcello Lippi said after beating France in the final that there was nothing to compare with winning the World Cup and no-one in Italy would argue with him. Consolation then, for the fans of Juventus, Lazio, Fiorentina and Milan whose clubs were caught up in a scandal so serious that it challenged the integrity of Italian club

INTERNATIONAL HONOURS
FIFA World Cup™ 1934 1938 1982 2006
Olympic Gold 1936
International Cup 1930 1935   UEFA European Championship 1968   UEFA Junior Tournament 1958 1966
UEFA U-21 Championship 1992 1994 1996 2000 2004   UEFA U-19 Championship 2003   UEFA U-17 Championship 1982 1987
UEFA Champions League Milan 1963 1969 1989 1990 1994 2003, Internazionale 1964 1965, Juventus 1985 1996

football. For years there had been complaints about referees favouring the big clubs but finally there was proof that sporting fraud was indeed happening, with Juventus' general manager Luciano Moggi a central figure in the investigations. The major upshot of those investigations was that Juventus were stripped of the titles won in 2005 and 2006 and they were relegated to Serie B for the first time in their history. On appeal the other three clubs had their original punishments reduced, with Milan remarkably qualifying for the UEFA Champions League as a result. With all the changes, Inter emerged from the season as champions although their fans will derive little pleasure from the fact. Prior to the scandal it had been a memorable season on a number of fronts - Juventus won a record nine consecutive games from the start of the season; Roma then won 11 games on the trot to break the Serie A record, all without any natural strikers; while Luca Toni became the first player for over half a century to score over 30 League goals in a season. All in all a quite extraordinary year for Italian football, although it may take a long while for Serie A to regain the respect that it has so spectacularly lost.

Federazione Italiana Giuoco Calcio (FIGC)
Via Gregorio Allegri 14, Roma 00198, Italy
Tel +39 06 84911   Fax +39 06 84912526
press@figc.it   www.figc.it
President: ROSSI Guido   General Secretary: GHIRELLI Francesco Dr
Vice-President: ABETE Giancarlo Dr   Treasurer: GHIRELLI Francesco Dr   Media Officer: VALENTINI Antonello Dr
Men's Coach: DONADONI Roberto   Women's Coach: GHEDIN Pietro
FIGC formed: 1898   UEFA: 1954   FIFA: 1905
Blue shirts with white trimmings, White shorts, Blue socks or White shirts with blue trimmings, Blue shorts, White socks

RECENT INTERNATIONAL MATCHES PLAYED BY ITALY

2003	Opponents	Score		Venue	Comp	Scorers	Att	Referee
20-08	Germany	W	1-0	Stuttgart	Fr	Vieri [17]	50 128	Nielsen DEN
6-09	Wales	W	4-0	Milan	ECq	Inzaghi.F 3 [59 63 70], Del Piero [76p]	68 000	Merk GER
10-09	Serbia & Montenegro	D	1-1	Belgrade	ECq	Inzaghi.F [22]	35 000	Hamer LUX
11-10	Azerbaijan	W	4-0	Reggio Calabria	ECq	Vieri [16], Inzaghi.F 2 [24 88], Di Vaio [65]	30 000	Dougal SCO
12-11	Poland	L	1-3	Warsaw	Fr	Cassano [19]	9 000	Ovrebo NOR
16-11	Romania	W	1-0	Ancona	Fr	Di Vaio [58]	11 700	Stark GER
2004								
18-02	Czech Republic	D	2-2	Palermo	Fr	Vieri [14], Di Natale [86]	20 935	Braamhaar NED
31-03	Portugal	W	2-1	Braga	Fr	Vieri [40], Miccoli [75]	25 000	Aydin TUR
28-04	Spain	D	1-1	Genoa	Fr	Vieri [56]	30 300	Poll ENG
30-05	Tunisia	W	4-0	Tunis	Fr	Bouazizi OG [15], Cannavaro [27], Pirlo [86], Zambrotta [90]	20 000	Duhamel FRA
14-06	Denmark	D	0-0	Guimaraes	ECr1		19 595	Mejuto Gonzalez ESP
18-06	Sweden	D	1-1	Porto	ECr1	Cassano [37]	44 927	Meier SUI
22-06	Bulgaria	W	2-1	Guimaraes	ECr1	Perrotta [48], Cassano [90]	16 002	Ivanov RUS
18-08	Iceland	L	0-2	Reykjavik	Fr		20 204	Frojdfeldt SWE
4-09	Norway	W	2-1	Palermo	WCq	De Rossi [4], Toni [80]	21 463	Sars FRA
8-09	Moldova	W	1-0	Chisinau	WCq	Del Piero [32]	5 200	Benes CZE
9-10	Slovenia	L	0-1	Celje	WCq		9 262	De Bleeckere BEL
13-10	Belarus	W	4-3	Parma	WCq	Totti 2 [26p 74], De Rossi [32], Gilardino [86]	19 833	Megia Davila ESP
17-11	Finland	W	1-0	Messina	Fr	Miccoli [33]	7 043	Tudor ROU
2005								
9-02	Russia	W	2-0	Cagliari	Fr	Gilardino [56], Barone [62]	15 700	Michel SVK
26-03	Scotland	W	2-0	Milan	WCq	Pirlo 2 [35 85]	45 000	Vassaras GRE
30-03	Iceland	D	0-0	Padova	Fr		16 697	Hamer LUX
4-06	Norway	D	0-0	Oslo	WCq		24 829	Mejuto Gonzalez ESP
8-06	Serbia & Montenegro	D	1-1	Toronto	Fr	Lucarelli [83]	35 000	Depiero CAN
11-06	Ecuador	D	1-1	East Rutherford	Fr	Toni [6]	27 583	Vaughn USA
17-08	Republic of Ireland	W	2-1	Dublin	Fr	Pirlo [10], Gilardino [31]	44 000	Gomes Costa POR
3-09	Scotland	D	1-1	Glasgow	WCq	Grosso [75]	50 185	Michel SVK
7-09	Belarus	W	4-1	Minsk	WCq	Toni 3 [6 13 55], Camoranesi [45]	30 299	Temmink NED
8-10	Slovenia	W	1-0	Palermo	WCq	Zaccardo [78]	19 123	Poulat FRA
12-10	Moldova	W	2-1	Lecce	WCq	Viera [70], Gilardino [85]	28 160	Benquerenca POR
12-11	Netherlands	W	3-1	Amsterdam	Fr	Gilardino [41], Vlaar OG [45], Toni [50]	50 000	Ivanov RUS
16-11	Côte d'Ivoire	D	1-1	Geneva	Fr	Diana [86]	18 500	Bertolini SUI
2006								
1-03	Germany	W	4-1	Florence	Fr	Gilardino [4], Toni [7], De Rossi [39], Del Piero [57]	28 317	Iturralde Gonzalez ESP
31-05	Switzerland	D	1-1	Geneva	Fr	Gilardino [10]	30 000	Sippel GER
2-06	Ukraine	D	0-0	Lausanne	Fr		10 000	Nobs SUI
12-06	Ghana	W	2-0	Hannover	WCr1	Pirlo [40], Iaquinta [83]	43 000	Simon BRA
17-06	USA	D	1-1	Kaiserslautern	WCr1	Gilardino [22]	46 000	Larrionda URU
22-06	Czech Republic	W	2-0	Hamburg	WCr1	Materazzi [26], Inzaghi [87]	50 000	Archundia MEX
26-06	Australia	W	1-0	Kaiserslautern	WCr2	Totti [95+p]	46 000	Medina Cantalejo ESP
30-06	Ukraine	W	3-0	Hamburg	WCqf	Zambrotta [6], Toni 2 [59 69]	50 000	De Bleeckere BEL
4-07	Germany	W	2-0	Dortmund	WCsf	Grosso [119], Del Piero [121+]	65 000	Archundia MEX
9-07	France	D	1-1	Berlin	WCf	Materazzi [19], W 5-3p	69 000	Elizondo ARG

Fr = Friendly match • EC = UEFA EURO 2004™ • WC = FIFA World Cup™
q = qualifier • r1 = first round group • r2 = second round • qf = quarter-finals • sf = semi-finals • f = final

ITALY NATIONAL TEAM RECORDS AND RECORD SEQUENCES

Records			Sequence records			
Victory	11-3	EGY 1928	Wins	9	1938-1939	Clean sheets	12	1972-1974
Defeat	1-7	HUN 1924	Defeats	3	Three times	Goals scored	43	1931-1937
Player Caps	126	MALDINI Paolo	Undefeated	30	1935-1939	Without goal	3	Three times
Player Goals	35	RIVA Luigi	Without win	8	1958-1959	Goals against	19	1927-1930

ITALY COUNTRY INFORMATION

Capital	Rome	Formation	1870	GDP per Capita	$26,700
Population	58 057 477	Status	Republic	GNP Ranking	7
Area km²	301 230	Language	Italian	Dialling code	+39
Population density	193 per km²	Literacy rate	98.6%	Internet code	.it
% in urban areas	67%	Main religion	Christian	GMT + / −	+1
Towns/Cities ('000)	Rome 2 643; Milan 1 156; Naples 981; Turin 846; Palermo 669; Genoa 585; Bologna 367; Florence 347; Catania 307; Bari 303; Venice 259; Verona 247; Messina 237; Padova 205; Trieste 204, Brescia 193; Taranto 191; Reggio de Calabria 181; Modena 180; Prato 178; Cagliari 157; Perugia 157; Parma 173				
Neighbours (km)	Austria 430; Slovenia 232; San Marino 39; Vatican 3; France 488; Switzerland 740; Mediterranean 7 600				
Main stadia	San Siro – Milan 85 700; Olimpico – Rome 82 307; San Paolo – Naples 82 126				

NATIONAL TEAM PLAYERS AND COACHES

Record Caps			Record Goals			Recent Coaches	
MALDINI Paolo	1988-'02	126	RIVA Luigi	1965-'74	35	BERNARDINI Fulvio	1974-'75
ZOFF Dino	1968-'83	112	MEAZZA Giuseppe	1930-'39	33	BERNARDINI/BEARZOT	1975-'77
CANNAVARO Fabio	1997-'06	100	PIOLA Silvio	1935-'52	30	BEARZOT Enzo	1977-'86
FACCHETTI Giacinto	1963-'77	94	BAGGIO Roberto	1988-'04	27	VICINI Azeglio	1986-'91
TARDELLI Marco	1976-'85	81	DEL PIERO Alessandro	1995-'06	27	SACCHI Arrigo	1991-'96
BERGOMI Giuseppe	1982-'98	81	BALONCIERI Adolfo	1920-'30	25	MALDINI Cesare	1996-'98
BARESI Franco	1982-'94	81	ALTOBELLI Alessandro	1980-'88	25	ZOFF Dino	1998-'00
ALBERTINI Demetrio	1991-'02	79	GRAZIANI Francesco	1975-'83	23	TRAPATTONI Giovanni	2000-'04
DEL PIERO Alessandro	1995-'06	79	VIERI Christian	1997-'05	23	LIPPI Marcello	2004-'06
SCIREA Gaetano	1975-'86	78	MAZZOLA Sandro	1963-'74	22	DONADONI Roberto	2006-

FIFA/COCA-COLA WORLD RANKING

1993	1994	1995	1996	1997	1998	1999	2000	2001	2002	2003	2004	2005		High		Low	
2	4	3	10	9	7	14	4	6	13	10	10	12		1	11/93	16	04/98

2005–2006											
08/05	09/05	10/05	11/05	12/05	01/06	02/06	03/06	04/06	05/06	06/06	07/06
13	13	12	12	12	12	12	12	14	13	-	2

THE FIFA BIG COUNT OF 2000

	Male	Female		Male	Female
Registered players	361 239	9 221	Referees	31 170	1 240
Non registered players	2 900 000	35 000	Officials	48 184	456
Youth players	732 864	4 563	Total involved	4 123 937	
Total players	4 042 887		Number of clubs	16 123	
Professional players	3 152	0	Number of teams	63 476	

ITALY 2005–06

SERIE A

	Pl	W	D	L	F	A	Pts	Inter	Roma	Milan	Chievo	Palermo	Livorno	Empoli	Parma	Fiorentina	Ascoli	Udinese	Sampdoria	Reggina	Cagliari	Siena	Lazio	Messina	Lecce	Treviso	Juventus
Internazionale †	38	23	7	8	68	30	76	—	2-3	3-2	1-0	3-0	5-0	4-1	2-0	1-0	1-0	3-1	1-0	4-0	3-2	1-1	3-1	3-0	3-0	3-0	1-2
Roma †	38	19	12	7	70	42	69	1-1	—	1-0	4-0	1-2	3-0	1-0	4-1	1-1	2-1	0-1	0-0	3-1	4-3	2-3	1-1	2-1	3-1	1-0	1-4
Milan † §30	38	28	4	6	85	31	58	1-0	2-1	—	4-1	2-1	2-0	3-0	4-3	3-1	1-0	5-1	1-1	2-1	1-0	3-1	2-0	4-0	2-1	5-0	3-1
Chievo Verona †	38	13	15	10	54	49	54	0-1	4-4	2-1	—	0-0	2-1	2-2	1-0	0-2	1-1	2-0	1-1	4-0	2-1	4-1	2-2	2-0	3-1	0-0	1-1
Palermo ‡	38	13	13	12	50	52	52	3-2	3-3	0-2	2-2	—	0-2	2-2	4-2	1-0	1-1	2-0	0-2	1-0	2-2	1-3	3-1	1-0	3-0	1-0	1-2
Livorno ‡	38	12	13	13	37	44	49	0-0	0-0	0-3	0-0	3-1	—	2-0	2-0	2-0	2-0	0-2	0-0	1-0	0-1	2-2	2-1	2-2	2-1	1-1	1-3
Empoli	38	13	6	19	47	61	45	1-0	1-0	1-3	2-1	0-1	2-1	—	1-2	1-1	1-2	1-1	2-1	3-1	2-1	2-1	3-1	3-1	3-1	1-0	0-4
Parma ‡	38	12	9	17	46	60	45	1-0	0-3	2-3	2-1	1-1	2-1	1-0	—	2-4	0-0	1-2	1-1	4-0	1-0	1-1	1-1	1-1	2-0	1-1	0-4
Fiorentina §30	38	22	8	8	66	41	44	2-1	1-1	3-1	2-1	1-0	3-2	2-1	4-1	—	3-1	4-2	2-1	5-2	2-1	2-1	1-2	2-0	1-0	1-0	1-2
Ascoli	38	9	16	13	43	53	43	1-2	3-2	1-1	2-2	1-1	0-0	3-1	3-1	0-2	—	1-1	2-1	1-1	2-2	1-1	1-4	1-0	2-0	1-0	3-1
Udinese	38	11	10	17	40	54	43	0-1	1-4	0-4	1-1	0-0	0-2	1-0	2-0	0-0	0-1	—	2-0	1-2	2-0	1-3	2-0	4-2	1-3	1-0	2-2	0-1
Sampdoria	38	10	11	17	47	51	41	2-2	1-1	2-1	1-2	0-2	0-2	0-1	2-3	1-1	2-1	1-1	—	3-2	1-1	3-3	2-0	4-2	1-3	1-1	0-1
Reggina	38	11	8	19	39	65	41	0-4	0-3	1-4	1-3	2-2	1-1	0-2	1-1	2-0	2-0	2-1	2-1	—	3-1	1-1	1-0	3-0	2-0	1-2	0-2
Cagliari	38	8	15	15	42	55	39	2-2	0-0	0-2	2-2	1-1	1-1	4-1	3-1	0-0	2-1	2-1	2-0	2-1	—	1-0	1-1	1-0	0-0	0-1	1-1
Siena	38	9	12	17	42	60	39	0-0	0-2	0-3	0-1	1-2	0-0	1-0	2-2	1-2	3-1	1-0	0-0	0-2	2-3	—	4-2	1-2	1-0	0-3	—
Lazio §30	38	16	14	8	57	47	32	0-0	0-2	0-0	2-2	4-2	3-1	3-3	1-0	1-0	4-1	1-1	2-0	3-1	1-1	3-2	—	1-0	1-0	3-1	1-1
Messina	38	6	13	19	33	59	31	1-2	0-1	1-3	2-0	0-0	0-0	1-2	0-1	2-2	1-1	1-4	1-1	1-0	0-0	1-1	2-1	—	3-2	1-2	—
Lecce	38	7	8	23	30	57	29	0-2	2-1	0-0	2-0	0-0	1-2	1-2	1-3	0-1	2-0	3-0	3-0	3-0	0-0	0-2	1-1	0-3	—	1-1	0-3
Treviso	38	3	12	23	24	56	21	0-1	0-1	0-2	1-2	2-2	0-1	1-0	1-3	2-2	2-1	0-2	0-1	1-0	1-0	1-0	0-2	1-0	0-2	—	0-0
Juventus	38	27	10	1	71	24	91	2-0	1-1	0-0	1-0	2-1	3-0	2-1	1-1	1-1	2-1	1-0	2-0	1-0	4-0	2-0	1-1	1-0	3-1	3-1	—

27/08/2005 – 14/05/2006 • The table above represents the standings after the appeal verdicts, announced on July 25, 2006. For the original table see page 1051 • The relegation of Juventus was upheld and they will start the 2005-06 season with a 17 point penalty (reduced from 30) • Milan were originally docked 44 points for the 2005-06 season but that was reduced to 30 on appeal. They will start the 2006-07 season with a penalty of eight points (reduced from 15) • Fiorentina were docked 30 points for the 2005-06 season after their relegation to Serie B was revoked. They will start the 2006-07 season with a penalty of 19 points • Lazio were docked 30 points for the 2005-06 season after their relegation to Serie B was revoked. They will start the 2006-07 season with a penalty of 11 points√
† Qualified for the UEFA Champions League • ‡ Qualified for the UEFA Cup
Top scorers: Luca TONI, Fiorentina, 31; David TREZEGUET, Juventus, 23; David SUAZO, Cagliari, 22; Cristiano LUCARELLI, Livorno, 19; Andrij SHEVCHENKO, Milan, 19; Francesco TAVANO, Empoli, 19

ITALY 2005–06

SERIE B

	Pl	W	D	L	F	A	Pts	Atalanta	Catania	Torino	Mantova	Modena	Cesena	Arezzo	Bologna	Crotone	Brescia	Pescara	Piacenza	Bari	Triestina	Verona	Vicenza	Rimini	Albinoleffe	Avellino	Ternana	Cremonese	Catanzaro
Atalanta	42	24	9	9	61	39	81	—	1-2	2-1	2-1	0-1	2-2	2-0	1-0	1-0	2-0	1-0	3-2	1-0	3-2	1-0	3-2	0-2	0-2	0-2	0-2	0-2	0-3-1
Catania	42	22	12	8	67	42	78	4-1	—	1-1	3-0	3-2	1-0	0-0	1-3	2-2	1-3	0-3	1-0	1-1	1-0	0-2	2-0	0-2	1-2	0-3	1-2	1-3	0
Torino	42	21	13	8	51	31	76	2-2	2-1	—	2-0	2-1	1-0	1-2	0-0	0-0	1-1	1-2	1-0	0-2	1-2	1-2	0-1	0-1	0-1	0-1	1-3	0-2	0
Mantova	42	18	15	9	46	35	69	1-0	3-0	1-0	—	2-0	3-2	1-0	0-0	1-1	1-0	2-2	0-0	0-0	1-3	1-1	0-3	1-0	1-0	0-0	0-0	0
Modena	42	17	16	9	59	41	67	2-2	2-1	2-1	0-0	—	2-2	0-0	0-0	1-0	0-2	2-2	1-0	4-1	2-0	1-1	0-2	1-2	2-3	2-2	1-4-1	0
Cesena	42	18	12	12	66	54	66	0-2	1-0	1-2	2-0	2-4	—	2-1	2-0	0-0	0-1	0-2	2-2	1-0	0-2	1-1	0-2	1-2	2-3	2-3	2-2	1-4-1	0
Arezzo	42	17	15	10	45	34	66	2-0	0-0	1-2	2-1	1-1	1-0	—	1-3	2-0	0-0	1-0	0-2	2-1	3-0	1-0	1-2	0-1	2-0	3-1	1-1	1-3	0
Bologna	42	16	16	10	55	42	64	1-1	2-1	1-1	0-0	1-2	0-0	1-0	—	1-2	3-1	2-1	1-0	0-1	2-1	4-1	1-0	4-0	2-0	1-3	1-1	3-0	0
Crotone	42	18	9	15	56	48	63	1-0	3-1	1-1	1-1	1-0	2-1	0-3	0-0	—	4-2	0-0	4-0	2-1	4-2	2-0	1-0	2-0	1-3	0-3	1-3	1-2-1	0
Brescia	42	15	15	12	54	44	60	1-0	2-0	0-1	0-0	2-3	2-0	0-1	1-2	0	—	3-0	1-1	2-1	1-0	3-2	0-3	0-2	3-0	4-0	0-0	1-0	2-0
Pescara	42	14	12	16	41	50	54	2-2	0-1	0-2	1-0	1-0	0-1	3-2	2-1	3-0	2-0	3	—	1-0	1-0	5-1	1-0	3-1	1-0	1-0	2-1	0-3	1-0	1-1
Piacenza	42	13	15	14	56	52	54	3-0	1-1	0-1	3-0	0-2	2-3	2-1	3-0	3-1	0-0	—	1-3	4-0	1-0	0-1	0-0	4-0	2-1	2-1	0
Bari	42	11	18	13	43	47	51	2-1	0-2	2-2	1-2	2-2	3-1	1-0	1-1	1-0	2-2	1-1	—	1-1	1-2	1-0	3-1	2-0	2-0	1-0	1-0	0
Triestina	42	12	15	15	44	51	51	1-2	1-2	0-2	0-1	2-1	0-1	1-0	0-2	0-1	0-2	0-2	2-0	0	—	0-3	1-1	1-1	1-1	0-0	2-0	1-3	2-0
Hellas Verona	42	10	19	13	42	41	49	0-1	1-3	2-1	1-2	1-1	1-1	3-1	1-1	1-0	0-1	1-1	0-2	2-0	—	1-2	2-2	0-0	0-1	1-2	1-1	0
Vicenza	42	13	10	19	38	49	49	3-3	0-2	3-2	0-1	0-3	1-0	0-0	1-0	0-0	1-0	0-0	0-0	0-1	1-2	1-1	—	0-0	0-1	1-2-1	1-0	1-0
Rimini	42	11	15	16	42	49	48	0-0	1-2	2-1	1-3	1-1	1-2	0-1	3-1	0-0	0-0	2-0	0-2	1-2	0-0	1-0	—	1-0	3-3	2-1	2-0-4-2	0
Albinoleffe	42	10	16	16	38	52	46	2-3	2-0	0-2	1-0	0-0	3-1	0-2	2-3	2-2	2-0	2-2	0-2	2-0	1-1	0-0	1-2-2	—	2-0	1-0	0-0-0-0	0
Avellino	42	11	13	18	42	62	46	0-0	1-1	1-0	0-0	5-4	2-0	0-2	2-2	1-1	2-0	1-1	1-1	1-0	1-1	1-2	1-1	1-2-1	—	1-1	2-1	1-2-1-2-0
Ternana	42	7	18	17	36	58	39	0-0	0-0	0-0	1-1	0-1	3-0	1-0	1-1	2-2-1	1-2	2-1	1-1	1-2	2-2	3-2	1-1	1-1	1-2	2-0	2-2	—	1-1-0-2
Cremonese	42	6	12	24	36	60	30	0-1	2-4	0-1	1-2	0-1	2-3	0-1	2-2	0-1	1-2	0-1	2-1	0-1	1-1	0-0	2-2	3-2	1-0	0-1	0-2	—	2-0
Catanzaro	42	7	7	28	26	63	28	1-2	1-3	0-1	0-1	1-0	2-4	1-2	0-2	1-0	1-2	1-0	1-0	0-2	1-0	1-1	1-0	1-3	1-2	0-1	1-1	—

26/08/2005 – 28/05/2006 • Promotion play-off semi-finals: Cesena 1-1 0-1 **Torino**; Modena 0-0 1-1 **Mantova** • Play-off final: Mantova 4-2 1-3 **Torino**
Relegation play-off: Avellino 0-2 3-2 **Albinoleffe**

ITALY 2005-06 SERIE C1 GROUP A

	Pl	W	D	L	F	A	Pts
Spezia	34	17	12	5	42	22	63
Genoa ‡ §3	34	15	14	5	42	27	56
Monza ‡	34	14	14	6	35	25	56
Pavia ‡	34	15	9	10	44	29	54
Salernitana ‡	34	13	13	8	42	30	52
Cittadella	34	14	8	12	38	33	50
Teramo §3	34	14	11	9	39	35	49
Novara	34	12	12	10	40	36	48
Padova	34	11	14	9	36	32	47
Pro Patria	34	10	14	10	36	39	44
Pizzighettone	34	9	16	9	37	32	43
Giulianova	34	10	13	11	33	33	43
Ravenna	34	11	10	13	30	33	43
Pro Sesto ‡	34	11	5	18	28	48	38
Sambened‡tese§6	34	11	9	14	35	48	36
San Marino ‡	34	8	11	15	32	38	35
Lumezzane ‡	34	9	8	17	35	44	35
Fermana	34	2	7	25	18	58	13

28/08/2005 - 7/05/2006 • ‡ Entered play-offs
§ Points deducted

PLAY-OFFS SERIE C1 GROUP A

Semi-finals

Salernitana	2	1
Genoa	1	2
Pavia	1	0
Monza	1	2

Final

Monza	0	1
Genoa	2	0

SERIE C1 GROUP B

Semi-finals

Sangiovannese	0	0
Frosinone	0	0
Grosseto	1	1
Sassari Torres	0	0

Final

Grosseto	0	0
Frosinone	0	1

ITALY 2005-06 SERIE C1 GROUP B

	Pl	W	D	L	F	A	Pts
Napoli	34	19	11	4	48	20	68
Frosinone ‡	34	15	10	9	43	37	55
Sassari Torres ‡	34	12	17	5	44	32	53
Grosseto ‡	34	12	15	7	43	32	51
Sangiovannese ‡	34	12	15	7	37	34	51
Perugia	34	14	8	12	35	37	50
Lucchese	34	13	10	11	33	27	49
Martina	34	13	8	13	41	39	47
Pistoiese	34	8	18	8	28	24	42
Manfredonia	34	10	12	12	36	38	42
Lanciano	34	10	11	13	36	35	41
Gela Juve §2	34	9	16	9	31	35	41
Foggia	34	8	16	10	32	32	40
Acireale ‡	34	8	15	11	29	34	39
Pisa ‡	34	11	6	17	31	43	39
Massese ‡	34	9	11	14	21	36	38
Juve Stabia ‡	34	7	12	15	25	36	33
Chieti	34	7	7	20	24	46	28

28/08/2005 - 7/05/2006 • ‡ Entered play-offs
§ Points deducted

CLUB DIRECTORY

Club	Town/City	Stadium	Capacity	www.	Lge	Cup	CL
Ascoli	Ascoli Piceno	Cino e Lillo del Duca	28 340	ascolicalcio.net	0	0	0
Atalanta	Bergamo	Atleti Azzurri d'Italia	26 638	atalanta.it	0	1	0
Cagliari	Cagliari	Sant'Elia	39 905	cagliaricalcio.it	1	0	0
Catania	Catania	Angelo Massimino	20 800	calciocatania.it	0	0	0
Chievo	Verona	Marc'Antonio Bentegodi	42 160	chievoverona.it	0	0	0
Empoli	Empoli	Carlo Castellani	19 847	empolifc.com	0	0	0
Fiorentina	Florence	Artemio Franchi	47 232	acffiorentina.it	2	6	0
Internazionale	Milan	Giuseppe Meazza (San Siro)	85 700	inter.it	13	4	2
Lazio	Rome	Olimpico	82 307	sslazio.it	2	4	0
Livorno	Livorno	Armando Picchi	18 200	livornocalcio.it	0	0	0
Messina	Messina	San Filippo	43 000	mondomessina.it	0	0	0
Milan	Milan	Giuseppe Meazza (San Siro)	85 700	acmilan.com	17	5	6
Palermo	Palermo	Renzo Barbera	36 980	ilpalermocalcio.it	0	0	0
Parma	Parma	Ennio Tardini	28 783	fcparma.com	0	3	0
Reggina	Reggio Calabria	Oreste Granillo	27 763	regginacalcio.it	0	0	0
Roma	Rome	Olimpico	82 307	asromacalcio.it	3	7	0
Sampdoria	Genoa	Luigi Ferraris	41 917	sampdoria.it	1	4	0
Siena	Siena	Artemio Franchi	13 500	acsiena.it	0	0	0
Torino	Turin	Grande Torino	27 128		7	5	0
Udinese	Udine	Friuli	41 652	udinese.it	0	0	0

RECENT LEAGUE AND CUP RECORD

	Championship						Cup		
Year	Champions	Pts	Runners-up	Pts	Third	Pts	Winners	Score	Runners-up
1990	Napoli	51	Milan	49	Internazionale	44	Juventus	0-0 1-0	Milan
1991	Sampdoria	51	Milan	46	Internazionale	46	Roma	3-1 1-1	Sampdoria
1992	Milan	56	Juventus	48	Torino	43	Parma	0-1 2-0	Juventus
1993	Milan	50	Internazionale	46	Parma	41	Torino	3-0 2-5	Roma
1994	Milan	50	Juventus	47	Sampdoria	44	Sampdoria	0-0 6-1	Ancona
1995	Juventus	73	Lazio	63	Parma	63	Juventus	1-0 2-0	Parma
1996	Milan	73	Juventus	65	Lazio	59	Fiorentina	1-0 2-0	Atalanta
1997	Juventus	65	Parma	64	Internazionale	59	Vicenza	0-1 3-0	Napoli
1998	Juventus	74	Internazionale	69	Udinese	64	Lazio	0-1 3-1	Milan
1999	Milan	70	Lazio	69	Fiorentina	56	Parma	1-1 2-2	Fiorentina
2000	Lazio	72	Juventus	71	Milan	61	Lazio	2-1 0-0	Internazionale
2001	Roma	75	Juventus	73	Lazio	69	Fiorentina	1-0 1-1	Parma
2002	Juventus	71	Roma	70	Internazionale	69	Parma	1-2 1-0	Juventus
2003	Juventus	72	Internazionale	65	Milan	61	Milan	4-1 2-2	Roma
2004	Milan	82	Roma	71	Juventus	69	Lazio	2-0 2-2	Juventus
2005	Juventus	86	Milan	79	Internazionale	72	Internazionale	2-0 1-0	Roma
2006	Internazionale	76	Roma	69	Milan	58	Internazionale	1-1 3-1	Roma

Juventus were stripped of their titles won in 2005 and 2006

COPPA ITALIA 2005–06

Second Round			Third Round			Round of 16		
						Internazionale	1	0
Empoli	3					Parma *	0	0
Crotone *	2		Empoli *	1	6p			
Padova *	0		Parma	1	7p			
Parma	1							
Cittadella *	0	7p						
Ternana	0	6p	Cittadella *	3				
Catanzaro *	0	2p	Livorno	2				
Livorno	0	4p				Cittadella	0	0
						Lazio *	2	0

Second Round			Third Round			Round of 16		
						Sampdoria	1	2
Manfredonia *	3					Cagliari *	1	1
Albinoleffe	2		Manfredonia *	2	2p			
Grosseto *	1		Cagliari	2	4p			
Cagliari	2							
Atalanta	1							
Pisa *	0		Atalanta	4				
Avellino *	0		Siena *	0				
Siena	1					Atlalanta *	1	1
						Udinese	0	3

Second Round			Third Round			Round of 16		
						Palermo	0	5
Pavia	1	5p				Bari *	0	4
Monza *	1	4p	Pavia *	0	5p			
Ascoli	1		Bari	0	6p			
Bari *	2							
Brescia	2	7p						
Arezzo *	2	6p	Brescia *	1				
Cremonese *	0		Chievo Verona	0				
Chievo Verona	1					Brescia	1	3
						Milan *	3	4

Second Round			Third Round			Round of 16		
						Juventus	2	4
Cesena *	1					Fiorentina *	2	1
Bologna	0		Cesena *	0				
Rimini *	1		Fiorentina	1				
Fiorentina	2							
Napoli *	1							
Reggina	0		Napoli *	1				
Hellas Verona	1		Piacenza	0				
Piacenza *	2					Napoli *	0	1
						Roma	3	2

Serie A clubs playing in Europe join in at the round of 16

COPPA ITALIA 2005-06

Quarter-finals	Semi-finals	Final

Internazionale	1	1
Lazio *	1	0

Internazionale *	1	2
Udinese	0	2

Sampdoria	1	2
Udinese *	1	2

Internazionale	1	3
Roma *	1	1

Palermo	0	3
Milan *	1	0

Palermo *	2	0
Roma	1	1

Juventus *	2	1
Roma	3	0

COPPA ITALIA FINAL

First leg. Stadio Olimpico, Rome, 3-05-2006, Att: 70 000, Ref: Trefoloni

Roma	1	Mancini 55
Internazionale	1	Cruz 7

Roma - Doni - Panucci, Mexes●, Chivu (Bovo 46), Cufrè, Tommasi (Chuka 80), De Rossi, Perrotta, Kharja, Mancini (Alvarez 85), Taddei●. Tr: Spalletti

Inter - Julio Cesar - Zanetti.J, Cordoba, Samuel● (Burdisso 70), Favalli, Figo, Pizarro●, Cambiasso, Stankovic (Aparecido 73), Adriano (Martins 80●), Cruz●. Tr: Mancini

Second leg. San Siro, Milan, 11-05-2006, Att: 49 557, Att: Messina

Internazionale	3	Cambiasso 6, Cruz 45, Martins 78
Roma	1	Nonda 80

Inter - Julio Cesar - Zanetti.J, Materazzi●, Samuel, Favalli, Figo (Kily Gonzalez 81), Pizarro●, Cambiasso, Stankovic (Solari 58), Adriano (Martins 67), Cruz. Tr: Mancini

Roma - Doni - Panucci, Chivu (Kuffour 13), Bovo●, Cufrè, Kharja● (Nonda 76), Dacourt, Rossi●, Tommasi, Mancini, Chuka (Totti 54). Tr: Spalletti

* Home team in the first leg

JUVENTUS 2005-06

Date	Opponents	Score		Comp	Scorers	Att
20-08-2005	Internazionale	L 0-1	H	SC		
28-08-2005	Chievo Verona	W 1-0	H	SA	Trezeguet [36]	24 693
11-09-2005	Empoli	W 4-0	A	SA	Trezeguet 2 [10 59], Vieira [14], Camoranesi [16]	13 454
14-09-2005	Club Brugge - BEL	W 2-1	A	CLgA	Nedved [66], Trezeguet [75]	27 000
18-09-2005	Ascoli	W 2-1	H	SA	Del Piero 2 [13p 39]	27 293
21-09-2005	Udinese	W 1-0	H	SA	Vieira [37]	25 000
24-09-2005	Parma	W 2-1	A	SA	Camoranesi [44], Vieira [82]	22 050
27-09-2005	SK Rapid Wien - AUT	W 3-0	H	CLgA	Trezeguet [27], Mutu [82], Ibrahimovic [85]	11 156
2-10-2005	Internazionale	W 2-0	H	SA	Trezeguet [22], Nedved [34]	33 772
15-10-2005	Messina	W 1-0	H	SA	Del Piero [24]	30 052
18-10-2005	Bayern München - GER	L 1-2	A	CLgA	Ibrahimovic [90]	66 000
23-10-2005	Lecce	W 3-0	A	SA	Ibrahimovic [9], Mutu [79], Zalayeta [96+]	24 941
26-10-2005	Sampdoria	W 2-0	H	SA	Trezeguet [41], Mutu [57]	29 977
29-10-2005	Milan	L 1-3	A	SA	Trezeguet [76]	79 706
2-11-2005	Bayern München - GER	W 2-1	H	CLgA	Trezeguet 2 [62 85]	16 076
6-11-2005	Livorno	W 3-0	H	SA	Trezeguet [59], Ibrahimovic [60], Del Piero [93+]	28 897
19-11-2005	Roma	W 4-1	A	SA	Nedved [45], Ibrahimovic [56], Trezeguet 2 [58 61]	68 816
22-11-2005	Club Brugge - BEL	W 1-0	H	CLgA	Del Piero [80]	9 623
27-11-2005	Treviso	W 3-1	H	SA	Mutu [37], Trezeguet [42], Del Piero [83]	27 102
1-12-2005	Fiorentina	D 2-2	A	CUPr4	Pessotto [52], Mutu [69]	
4-12-2005	Fiorentina	W 2-1	A	SA	Trezeguet [8], Camoranesi [88]	43 537
7-12-2005	SK Rapid Wien - AUT	W 3-1	A	CLgA	Del Piero 2 [35 45], Ibrahimovic [42]	45 524
11-12-2005	Cagliari	W 4-0	H	SA	Nedved [9], Trezeguet 2 [17 52], Vignati OG [68]	27 587
17-12-2005	Lazio	D 1-1	A	SA	Trezeguet [26]	38 332
21-12-2005	Siena	W 2-0	H	SA	Cannavaro [13], Trezeguet [56]	25 587
7-01-2006	Palermo	W 2-1	A	SA	Mutu 2 [15 34]	33 149
10-01-2006	Fiorentina	W 4-1	H	CUPr4	Del Piero 3 [9 17 56], Mutu [21]	
15-01-2006	Reggina	W 1-0	H	SA	Del Piero [45]	30 598
18-01-2006	Chievo Verona	D 1-1	A	SA	Vieira [31]	18 673
22-01-2006	Empoli	W 2-1	H	SA	Cannavaro 2 [17 77]	26 292
26-01-2006	Roma	L 2-3	H	CUPqf	Del Piero 2 [72 94+]	
29-01-2006	Ascoli	W 3-1	A	SA	Trezeguet 3 [7 13 18]	20 510
1-02-2006	Roma	W 1-0	A	CUPqf	Mutu [48p]	
5-02-2006	Udinese	W 1-0	H	SA	Del Piero [70]	27 501
8-02-2006	Parma	D 1-1	A	SA	Ibrahimovic [45]	25 719
12-02-2006	Internazionale	W 2-1	A	SA	Ibrahimovic [63], Del Piero [85]	78 606
18-02-2006	Messina	D 2-2	A	SA	Ibrahimovic [18], Mutu [81p]	28 066
22-02-2006	Werder Bremen - GER	L 2-3	A	CLr2	Nedved [73], Trezeguet [82]	36 500
26-02-2006	Lecce	W 3-1	H	SA	Emerson [17], Kovac [44], Del Piero [91+p]	26 721
4-03-2006	Sampdoria	W 1-0	A	SA	Nedved [69]	35 369
7-03-2006	Werder Bremen - GER	W 2-1	H	CLr2	Trezeguet [65], Emerson [88]	40 226
12-03-2006	Milan	D 0-0	H	SA		45 560
18-03-2006	Livorno	W 3-1	A	SA	Trezeguet 2 [3 53], Del Piero [95+]	15 569
25-03-2006	Roma	D 1-1	H	SA	Emerson [35]	29 621
28-03-2006	Arsenal - ENG	L 0-2	A	CLqf		35 472
1-04-2006	Treviso	D 0-0	A	SA		6 586
5-04-2006	Arsenal - ENG	D 0-0	H	CLqf		46 031
9-04-2006	Fiorentina	D 1-1	H	SA	Del Piero [64]	27 656
15-04-2006	Cagliari	D 1-1	A	SA	Cannavaro [97+]	25 134
22-04-2006	Lazio	D 1-1	H	SA	Trezeguet [88]	33 898
30-04-2006	Siena	W 3-0	A	SA	Vieira [3], Trezeguet [6], Mutu [8]	16 000
7-05-2006	Palermo	W 2-1	H	SA	Nedved [31], Ibrahimovic [52]	56 488
14-05-2006	Reggina	W 2-0	A	SA	Trezeguet [20], Del Piero [94+]	8 900

SC = Supercoppa Italia • SA = Serie A • CL = UEFA Champions League • CUP = Coppa Italia
gA = group A • r2 = second round • r4 = fourth round • qf = quarter-final

MILAN 2005-06

Date	Opponents	Score		Comp	Scorers	Att
28-08-2005	Ascoli	D 1-1	A	SA	Shevchenko [66]	22 919
10-09-2005	Siena	W 3-1	H	SA	Ambrosini [15], Shevchenko [31], Kaká [82]	56 468
13-09-2005	Fenerbahçe - TUR	W 3-1	H	CLgE	Kaká 2 [18 87], Shevchenko [89]	34 619
18-09-2005	Sampdoria	L 1-2	A	SA	Gilardino [18]	30 655
21-09-2005	Lazio	W 2-0	H	SA	Shevchenko [12], Kaká [14]	57 778
25-09-2005	Treviso	W 2-0	A	SA	Shevchenko [43p], Gilardino [75]	17 389
28-09-2005	Schalke 04 - GER	D 2-2	A	CLgE	Seedorf [1], Shevchenko [59]	53 425
2-10-2005	Reggina	W 2-1	H	SA	Maldini 2 [5 20]	57 538
16-10-2005	Cagliari	W 2-0	A	SA	Gilardino [1], Shevchenko [27]	15 000
19-10-2005	PSV Eindhoven - NED	D 0-0	H	CLgE		39 298
23-10-2005	Palermo	W 2-1	H	SA	Gattuso [29], Inzaghi [79]	63 115
26-10-2005	Empoli	W 3-1	A	SA	Gilardino 2 [46 51], Vieri [56]	9 014
29-10-2005	Juventus	W 3-1	H	SA	Seedorf [14], Kaká [26], Pirlo [45]	79 706
1-11-2005	PSV Eindhoven - NED	L 0-1	A	CLgE		35 100
6-11-2005	Udinese	W 5-1	H	SA	Gilardino 2 [25 55], Seedorf [37], Pirlo [45], Kaká [79]	57 942
20-11-2005	Fiorentina	L 1-3	A	SA	Gilardino [25]	43 950
23-11-2005	Fenerbahçe - TUR	W 4-0	A	CLgE	Shevchenko 4 [16 52 70 76]	36 350
26-11-2005	Lecce	W 2-1	H	SA	Pirlo [3], Inzaghi [94+]	55 129
29-11-2005	Brescia	W 3-1	H	CUPr4	Rui Costa [26], Gilardino [40], Vieri [69]	
3-12-2005	Chievo Verona	L 1-2	A	SA	Kaladze [22]	14 733
6-12-2005	Schalke 04 - GER	W 3-2	H	CLgE	Pirlo [42], Kaká 2 [52 60]	40 200
11-12-2005	Internazionale	L 2-3	A	SA	Shevchenko [38p], Stam [85]	76 416
18-12-2005	Messina	W 4-0	H	SA	Shevchenko 2 [23p 48], Pirlo [83], Gilardino [85]	60 434
21-12-2005	Livorno	W 3-0	A	SA	Gilardino 2 [23 61], Shevchenko [72]	16 304
8-01-2006	Parma	W 4-3	H	SA	Cardone OG [27], Gilardino [29], Kaká [36], Shevchenko [81]	54 358
11-01-2006	Brescia	W 4-3	A	CUPr4	Seedorf [15], Inzaghi [31], Rui Costa 2 [48 88p]	
15-01-2006	Roma	L 0-1	A	SA		48 822
18-01-2006	Ascoli	W 1-0	H	SA	Inzaghi [5]	38 592
22-01-2006	Siena	W 3-0	A	SA	Kaká 2 [12 85], Shevchenko [70]	10 693
25-01-2006	Palermo	W 1-0	H	CUPqf	Gilardino [86]	
28-01-2006	Sampdoria	D 1-1	H	SA	Shevchenko [13p]	55 395
31-01-2006	Palermo	L 0-3	A	CUPqf		
5-02-2006	Lazio	D 0-0	A	SA		29 956
8-02-2006	Treviso	W 5-0	H	SA	Kaká [14], Shevchenko 2 [54 66], Gilardino [63], Inzaghi [74]	52 017
12-02-2006	Reggina	W 4-1	A	SA	Inzaghi 3 [14 55 96+], Gilardino [37]	12 669
18-02-2006	Cagliari	W 1-0	H	SA	Gilardino [23p]	54 599
21-02-2006	Bayern München - GER	D 1-1	H	CLr2	Shevchenko [58p]	66 000
26-02-2006	Palermo	W 2-0	A	SA	Inzaghi [73], Shevchenko [83p]	31 868
4-03-2006	Empoli	W 3-0	H	SA	Inzaghi 2 [77 86], Shevchenko [81]	54 419
8-03-2006	Bayern München - GER	W 4-1	H	CLr2	Inzaghi 2 [8 47], Shevchenko [25], Kaká [59]	78 577
12-03-2006	Juventus	D 0-0	A	SA		45 560
19-03-2006	Udinese	W 4-0	A	SA	Shevchenko 2 [42 65], Gilardino [61], Seedorf [70]	19 242
25-03-2006	Fiorentina	W 3-1	H	SA	Shevchenko [20], Kaka [48], Gattuso [60]	64 700
29-03-2006	Olympique Lyonnais - FRA	D 0-0	A	CLqf		39 500
1-04-2006	Lecce	L 0-1	A	SA		14 521
4-04-2006	Olympique Lyonnais - FRA	W 3-1	H	CLqf	Inzaghi 2 [25 88], Shevchenko [93+]	78 894
9-04-2006	Chievo Verona	W 4-1	H	SA	Nesta [29], Kaka 3 [62 70p 91+]	60 762
14-04-2006	Internazionale	W 1-0	H	SA	Kaladze [71]	74 137
18-04-2006	Barcelona - ESP	L 0-1	H	CLsf		76 883
22-04-2006	Messina	W 3-1	A	SA	Jankulovski [33], Gattuso [44], Gilardino' [92+]	26 681
26-04-2006	Barcelona - ESP	D 0-0	A	CLsf		95 661
30-04-2006	Livorno	W 2-0	H	SA	Inzaghi 2 [28 67]	62 088
7-05-2006	Parma	W 3-2	A	SA	Kaka [29p], Cafu [43], Seedorf [60]	20 631
14-05-2006	Roma	W 2-1	H	SA	Kaka [5p], Amoroso [93+p]	66 305

SA = Serie A • CL = UEFA Champions League • CUP = Coppa Italia
gE = group E • r2 = second round • r4 = fourth round • qf = quarter-final • sf = semi-final

INTERNAZIONALE 2005–06

Date	Opponents		Score		Comp	Scorers	Att
10-08-2005	Shakhtar Donetsk - UKR	W	2-0	A	CLpr3	Martins [68], Adriano [78]	25 000
24-08-2005	Shakhtar Donetsk - UKR	D	1-1	H	CLpr3	Recoba [13]	BCD
28-08-2005	Treviso	W	3-0	H	SA	Adriano 3 [32 68 79]	51 542
10-09-2005	Palermo	L	2-3	A	SA	Cruz 2 [86 94+]	31 309
13-09-2005	Artmedia Bratislava - SVK	W	1-0	A	CLgH	Cruz [17]	28 000
17-09-2005	Lecce	W	3-0	H	SA	Martins [25], Stankovic [29], Cruz [84]	48 219
21-09-2005	Chievo Verona	W	1-0	A	SA	Samuel [50]	18 000
25-09-2005	Fiorentina	W	1-0	H	SA	Martins [7]	56 207
28-09-2005	Rangers - SCO	W	1-0	H	CLgH	Pizarro [49]	BCD
2-10-2005	Juventus	L	0-2	A	SA		33 772
16-10-2005	Livorno	W	5-0	H	SA	Materazzi [11], Cruz [19], Cambiasso [49], Cordoba [51], Recoba [61]	51 413
19-10-2005	FC Porto - POR	L	0-2	A	CLgH		38 418
23-10-2005	Udinese	W	1-0	H	SA	Cruz [36]	19 134
26-10-2005	Roma	L	2-3	H	SA	Adriano 2 [67 77]	50 330
29-10-2005	Sampdoria	D	2-2	A	SA	Cambiasso [30], Cordoba [40]	27 626
1-11-2005	FC Porto - POR	W	2-1	H	CLgH	Cruz 2 [75p 82]	BCD
5-11-2005	Lazio	D	0-0	A	SA		33 367
20-11-2005	Parma	W	2-0	H	SA	Figo [70], Cambiasso [83]	47 651
23-11-2005	Artmedia Bratislava - SVK	W	4-0	H	CLgH	Figo [28], Adriano 3 [41 59 74]	BCD
27-11-2005	Messina	W	2-1	A	SA	Recoba [7], Cambiasso [61]	24 418
30-11-2005	Parma	W	1-0	A	CUPr4	Martins [74]	1 764
3-12-2005	Ascoli	W	1-0	H	SA	Adriano [24]	46 122
6-12-2005	Rangers - SCO	D	1-1	A	CLgH	Adriano [30]	50 000
11-12-2005	Milan	W	3-2	H	SA	Adriano 2 [23p 93+], Martins [63]	76 416
18-12-2005	Reggina	W	4-0	A	SA	Cordoba [2], Martins [15], Adriano [40], Pizarro [92+]	14 629
21-12-2005	Empoli	W	4-1	H	SA	Adriano [4], Cruz [50], Figo [72], Martins [90]	44 385
8-01-2006	Siena	D	0-0	A	SA		12 137
12-01-2006	Parma	D	0-0	H	CUPr4		3 294
15-01-2006	Cagliari	W	3-2	H	SA	Martins [10], Adriano 2 [14 58p]	47 354
18-01-2006	Treviso	W	1-0	A	SA	Cruz [23]	7 985
21-01-2006	Palermo	W	3-0	H	SA	Cambiasso [33], Cordoba [76], Figo [80]	48 942
24-01-2006	Lazio	D	1-1	A	CUPqf	Stankovic [26]	10 027
29-01-2006	Lecce	W	2-0	A	SA	Figo [76], Stankovic [97+]	15 832
2-02-2006	Lazio	W	1-0	H	CUPqf	Stankovic [37]	10 000
5-02-2006	Chievo Verona	W	1-0	H	SA	Cruz [7]	47 347
8-02-2006	Fiorentina	L	1-2	A	SA	Recoba [85]	41 399
12-02-2006	Juventus	L	1-2	H	SA	Samuel [77]	78 606
18-02-2006	Livorno	D	0-0	A	SA		15 017
22-02-2006	Ajax - NED	D	2-2	A	CLr2	Stankovic [49], Cruz [86]	46 663
26-02-2006	Udinese	W	3-1	H	SA	Cruz 2 [18p 49], Martins [61]	45 698
5-03-2006	Roma	D	1-1	A	SA	Materazzi [90]	56 689
11-03-2006	Sampdoria	W	1-0	H	SA	Adriano [40]	48 826
14-03-2006	Ajax - NED	W	1-0	H	CLr2	Stankovic [57]	48 489
19-03-2006	Lazio	W	3-1	H	SA	Figo [37], Recoba 2 [47 73]	48 818
22-03-2006	Udinese	W	1-0	H	CUPsf	Solari [20]	
25-03-2006	Parma	L	0-1	A	SA		16 918
29-03-2006	Villarreal - ESP	W	2-1	H	CLqf	Adriano [7], Martins [54]	49 165
1-04-2006	Messina	W	3-0	H	SA	Solari 2 [15 26], Martins [19]	45 671
4-04-2006	Villarreal - ESP	L	0-1	A	CLqf		21 700
8-04-2006	Ascoli	W	2-1	A	SA	Cruz [52p], Mihajlovic [57]	12 161
11-04-2006	Udinese	D	2-2	A	CUPsf	Solari [8], Pizarro [86]	1 681
14-04-2006	Milan	L	0-1	A	SA		74 137
22-04-2006	Reggina	W	4-0	H	SA	Cruz 2 [16p 92+], Martins [23], Cesar [28]	46 129
30-04-2006	Empoli	L	0-1	A	SA		7 068
3-05-2006	Roma	D	1-1	A	CUPf	Cruz [8]	70 030
7-05-2006	Siena	D	1-1	H	SA	Cruz [61]	47 732
11-05-2006	Roma	W	3-1	H	CUPf	Cambiasso [6], Cruz [45], Martins [78]	49 557
14-05-2006	Cagliari	D	2-2	A	SA	Cruz [11], Solari [37]	14 567

SA = Serie A • CL = UEFA Champions League • CUP = Coppa Italia • BCD = behind closed doors
pr3 = third preliminary round • gH = group H • r2 = second round • r4 = fourth round • qf = quarter-final • sf = semi-final • f = final

JAM – JAMAICA

NATIONAL TEAM RECORD
JULY 1ST 2002 TO JULY 9TH 2006

PL	W	D	L	F	A	%
57	24	18	15	86	62	57.9

FIFA/COCA-COLA WORLD RANKING

1993	1994	1995	1996	1997	1998	1999	2000	2001	2002	2003	2004	2005		High		Low
80	96	56	32	39	33	41	48	53	51	46	49	42		27	08/98	96 12/94

2005–2006											
08/05	09/05	10/05	11/05	12/05	01/06	02/06	03/06	04/06	05/06	06/06	07/06
41	41	40	43	42	42	43	45	44	46	-	78

It can't have been easy for Jamaican fans to watch the fans of fierce rivals Trinidad and Tobago having so much fun at the FIFA World Cup™ finals in Germany, but the bottom line is that twice now in the past three tournaments the Caribbean has had a representative at the finals and that represents real progress. The Jamaican national team played only five times during the season and three of those games were played in England including a first ever match against the English national team. All three matches were lost, however, and heavily, showing just how much more work needs to be done. There was success at club level when Portmore United won the Caribbean

INTERNATIONAL HONOURS
Qualified for the FIFA World Cup™ finals 1998   Caribbean Cup 1991 1998 2005

Football Union Club Championship to qualify for the final rounds of the CONCACAF Champions' Cup but they were drawn against Mexico City's America in the quarter-finals and lost 7-3 on aggregate. Having completed a domestic double in 2005, Portmore failed to defend both the League and the Cup in 2006. In the Cup Final they lost 3-2 in extra-time to Tivoli Gardens, despite being 2-0 up with just 11 minutes to play, while Waterhouse won the League title in an exciting race with Harbour View. At one point Waterhouse trailed their rivals by 13 points but by the time the two met in the last match of the season they had wrapped up the title.

THE FIFA BIG COUNT OF 2000

	Male	Female		Male	Female
Registered players	10 110	600	Referees	150	19
Non registered players	40 000	2 000	Officials	4 000	200
Youth players	10 000	800	Total involved	67 879	
Total players	63 510		Number of clubs	570	
Professional players	110	0	Number of teams	882	

Jamaica Football Federation (JFF)
20 St Lucia Crescent, Kingston 5, Jamaica
Tel +1 876 9298036   Fax +1 876 9290438
jamff@hotmail.com   www.jamaicafootballfederation.com
President: BOXHILL Crenston   General Secretary: GIBSON Burchell
Vice-President: EVANS George   Treasurer: SPEID Rudolph   Media Officer: BAILEY Earl
Men's Coach: DOWNSWELL Wendell   Women's Coach: BLAINE Vin
JFF formed: 1910   CONCACAF: 1961   FIFA: 1962
Gold shirts, Black shorts, Gold socks

RECENT INTERNATIONAL MATCHES PLAYED BY JAMAICA

2003	Opponents		Score	Venue	Comp	Scorers	Att	Referee
25-05	Nigeria	W	3-2	Kingston	Fr	Lowe 25, Johnson.J 40, Williams.A 90	25 000	Brizan TRI
6-07	Cuba	L	1-2	Kingston	Fr	Langley 86	8 500	Bowen CAY
9-07	Paraguay	W	2-0	Kingston	Fr	Byfield 11, Langley 28	10 000	Bowen CAY
13-07	Colombia	L	0-1	Miami	GCr1		15 423	Stott USA
15-07	Guatemala	W	2-0	Miami	GCr1	Lowe 30, Williams.A 72p	10 323	Pineda HON
20-07	Mexico	L	0-5	Mexico City	GCqf		10 000	Navarro CAN
7-09	Australia	L	1-2	Reading	Fr	Lisbie 22	8 050	D'Urso ENG
12-10	Brazil	L	0-1	Leicester	Fr		32 000	Styles ENG
16-11	El Salvador	W	3-0	Kingston	Fr	Fuller 6, Lisbie 72, Burton 85	15 000	Ramdhan TRI
2004								
18-02	Uruguay	W	2-0	Kingston	Fr	Lowe 9, Johnson.J 82	27 000	Gordon TRI
31-03	Honduras	D	2-2	Kingston	Fr	Lowe 8, Davis.F 53	28 000	Brizan TRI
28-04	Venezuela	W	2-1	Kingston	Fr	King 10, Williams.A 45	10 000	Ford BRB
31-05	Nigeria	L	0-2	London	Fr			Bennett ENG
2-06	Republic of Ireland	L	0-1	London	Fr		6 155	Styles ENG
12-06	Haiti	D	1-1	Miami	WCq	King 39	30 000	Stott USA
20-06	Haiti	W	3-0	Kingston	WCq	King 3 4 14 31	30 000	Sibrian SLV
18-08	USA	D	1-1	Kingston	WCq	Goodison 49	30 000	Mattus CRC
4-09	Panama	L	1-2	Kingston	WCq	Ralph 77	24 000	Batres GUA
8-09	El Salvador	W	3-0	San Salvador	WCq	King 2 3 38, Hyde 40	25 000	Alcala MEX
2-10	Guatemala	D	2-2	Fort Lauderdale	Fr	Hue 89, Jackson 90	8 500	Vaughn USA
9-10	Panama	D	1-1	Panama City	WCq	Whitmore 75	16 000	Pineda HON
13-10	El Salvador	D	0-0	Kingston	WCq		12 000	Quesada Cordero CRC
17-11	USA	D	1-1	Columbus	WCq	Williams.A 26	9 088	Navarro CAN
24-11	Saint-Martin †	W	12-0	Kingston	GCq	Dean 3 2 11 30, Hue 10, Shelton 4 17 39 45 52, Stephenson 18, Scarlett 2 20 85, West 54	2 600	Brizan TRI
26-11	US Virgin Islands	W	11-1	Kingston	GCq	Shelton 8, Dean 2 23 32, Hue 3 35 53 56, Stephenson 40 Williams.A 50, Davis.F 64, Bennett 67, Priestly 68	4 200	Piper TRI
28-11	Haiti	W	3-1	Kingston	GCq	Stephenson 20, Dean 22, Shelton 30	4 000	Piper TRI
12-12	St Lucia	D	1-1	Vieux Fort	GCq	Priestly 42		Jeanvillier MTQ
19-12	St Lucia	W	2-1	Kingston	GCq	Dean 1, Hue 67	2 500	Gutierrez CUB
2005								
20-02	Trinidad and Tobago	W	2-1	Bridgetown	GCq	Shelton 13, Williams.A 35	5 000	Callender BRB
22-02	Barbados	W	1-0	Bridgetown	GCq	Williams.A 8	2 100	Brizan TRI
24-02	Cuba	W	1-0	Bridgetown	GCq	Shelton 48	3 000	Brizan TRI
20-04	Guatemala	W	1-0	Atlanta	Fr	Shelton 14	7 000	Prus USA
4-06	Honduras	D	0-0	Atlanta	Fr		6 500	Valenzuela USA
8-07	Guatemala	W	4-3	Carson	GCr1	Shelton 3, Fuller 5, Williams.A 46+p, Hue 57	27 000	Hall USA
10-07	South Africa	D	3-3	Los Angeles	GCr1	Hue 35, Stewart 43, Bennett 80	30 710	Stott USA
13-07	Mexico	L	0-1	Houston	GCr1		45 311	Quesada CRC
16-07	USA	L	1-3	Foxboro	GCqf	Fuller 88	22 108	Batres GUA
1-10	Guatemala	W	2-1	Fort Lauderdale	Fr	Shelton 41, Crawford 70	6 000	Rutty USA
9-10	Australia	L	0-5	London	Fr		6 570	Riley ENG
2006								
11-04	USA	D	1-1	Carey	Fr	Bennett 4	8 093	Gasso MEX
29-05	Ghana	L	1-4	Leicester	Fr	Euell 58	12 000	Halsey ENG
3-06	England	L	0-6	Manchester	Fr		70 373	Plautz AUT

Fr = Friendly match • GC = CONCACAF Gold Cup • WC = FIFA World Cup™ • q = qualifier • r1 = first round group • qf = quarter-final
† Not a full international

JAMAICA NATIONAL TEAM RECORDS AND RECORD SEQUENCES

Records			Sequence records				
Victory	12-0	BVI 1994	Wins	7	2000	Clean sheets	5	Three times
Defeat	0-9	CRC 1999	Defeats	7	1967-68, 2001-02	Goals scored	19	1997
Player Caps	105	WHITMORE Theodore	Undefeated	23	1997-1998	Without goal	7	2000
Player Goals	n/a		Without win	12	1975-79, 1988-90	Goals against	23	1966-1969

JAMAICA COUNTRY INFORMATION

Capital	Kingston	Independence	1962 from the UK	GDP per Capita	$3 900
Population	2 713 130	Status	Commonweath	GNP Ranking	100
Area km²	10 991	Language	English	Dialling code	+1 876
Population density	247 per km²	Literacy rate	87%	Internet code	.jm
% in urban areas	54%	Main religion	Christian 61%	GMT + / –	-4
Towns/Cities ('000)	Kingston 584; Spanish Town 145; Portmore 102; Montego Bay 83; Mandeville 47				
Neighbours (km)	Caribbean Sea 1 022				
Main stadia	Independence Park – Kingston 35 000; Harbour View – Kingston 7 000				

JAMAICA 2005-06

NATIONAL PREMIER LEAGUE

	Pl	W	D	L	F	A	Pts	Waterhouse	Harbour V.	Tivoli G.	Portmore U.	Boys' Town	Village Utd	Arnett G.	Seba Utd	Reno	Wadadah	C. Spring	Rivoli Utd
Waterhouse	33	20	9	4	57	34	69		2-2	1-1	0-0	1-3	1-1	1-0	0-2	4-1	2-0	4-0	2-1	0-0	3-1 3-1	1-0	1-0
Harbour View	33	19	7	7	49	26	64	3-1		1-0	1-2	0-1	0-2	2-0	2-1	3-0	1-0	2-1	1-0	1-2	1-0	1-0 1-0	2-0 2-0
Tivoli Gardens	33	17	6	10	64	39	57	1-2	3-2		0-0	0-1	2-1	1-0	2-3	1-1 1-1	4-0	7-2	2-0	4-0	6-0	2-0	5-1
Portmore United	33	13	16	4	41	26	55	1-1	0-1	2-2		0-0	0-0 0-1	0-2	0-1	0-4 2-2	1-1	1-0	3-0 4-3	3-0	1-1
Boys' Town	33	12	13	8	42	31	49	2-2	0-1	0-2	2-1		2-2	1-1	2-1 1-0	1-2 2-0	2-0 2-1	1-8 3-1	0-0 0-0
Village United	33	11	15	7	41	54	48	4-1 1-1	2-1 0-1	0-3	2-3 3-1	0-0		3-0	2-2	1-0 2-4	2-2	2-1 1-1	4-0	5-3
Arnett Gardens	33	10	10	13	42	49	40	2-0 2-3	1-3	4-1	2-2	3-2 0-2	1-0 0-1		1-1	5-1 1-1	2-2	2-1 4-1	1-1	2-1
Seba United	33	10	8	15	46	51	38	0-1	0-1 1-1	3-0	0-1	1-2	4-3 2-1	0-4 0-0		1-1	0-0 1-2	2-0	1-2 1-1
Reno	33	8	10	15	30	39	34	1-2 2-3	1-2	0-1 1-2	1-1 0-0	0-0	0-0	0-1	0-3 1-3		1-0	3-1 0-0	3-0
Wadadah	33	7	11	15	39	62	32	1-3	1-5 2-2	3-1	2-1	0-1	1-0 2-0 0-3 3-3	0-1	0-0 0-2		1-1	3-1 0-0
Constant Spring	33	3	15	15	28	56	24	2-2 0-1	0-3	1-1 0-3	0-3 3-0 0-0	0-0	2-1	1-1	0-2 1-1	1-0	1-1 2-2		1-1
Rivoli United	33	2	14	17	27	58	20	1-1 1-2	1-1	1-1 1-1	3-0 2-1 1-1	1-1	2-2	0-1	1-3	0-2 1-1	2-1	0-0 2-3	

11/09/2005 - 16/04/2006 • Match in bold awarded 3-0

RED STRIPE CHAMPIONS LEAGUE KNOCK OUT CUP 2005-06

Round of 16			Quarter-finals			Semi-finals		Final	
Tivoli Gardens *	3	2							
Tafari Lions	2	0	**Tivoli Gardens** *	6	3				
Star Cosmos	2	1	Maverley	0	2				
Maverley *	3	1				**Tivoli Gardens**	3		
Rivoli United *	8	1				Arnett Gardens	2		
Bath	1	2	Rivoli United	0	2				
Clarkstown *	0	0	**Arnett Gardens** *	0	5				
Arnett Gardens	0	3				**Tivoli Gardens**	3		
Waterhouse	0	3				Portmore United	2		
Constant Spring *	0	1	**Waterhouse** *	2	2				
St George's	0	2	Reno	1	1				
Reno *	0	2				Waterhouse	1		
Harbour View	0	2				**Portmore United**	3		
Seba United *	1	0	Harbour View	1	1				
Village United *	0	0	**Portmore United** *	1	2				
Portmore United	1	4				* Home team in the first leg			

CUP FINAL

Tivoli Gardens 3
Portmore United 2

26-03-2006
Scorers - Johnson [79], Simpson [85p]
Stewart [107] for Tivoli Gardens;
Wolfe [42], Bennett [45] for Portmore

RECENT LEAGUE AND CUP RECORD

	Championship				Cup		
Year	Champions	Score	Runners-up		Winners	Score	Runners-up
1997	Seba United	2-1 2-2	Arnett Gardens		Naggo's Head	1-0	Hazard United
1998	Waterhouse	0-0 2-1	Seba United		Harbour View	1-0	Waterhouse
1999	Tivoli Gardens	3-1 0-0	Harbour View		Tivoli Gardens	2-0	Violet Kickers
2000	Harbour View	0-0 2-1	Waterhouse		Hazard United	1-0	Wadadah
2001	Arnett Gardens	2-1 2-1	Waterhouse		Harbour View	3-0	Wadadah
2002	Arnett Gardens	1-1 2-1	Hazard United		Harbour View	2-1	Rivoli United
2003	Hazard United	1-1 3-2	Arnett Gardens		Hazard United	1-0	Harbour View
2004	Tivoli Gardens	4-1 1-2	Harbour View		Waterhouse	2-1	Village United
2005	Portmore United	1-1 1-0	Tivoli Gardens		Portmore United	3-1	Harbour View
2006	Waterhouse	†	Harbour View		Tivoli Gardens	3-2	Portmore United

† Played on a League basis • Hazard United now known as Portmore United

JOR – JORDAN

NATIONAL TEAM RECORD
JULY 1ST 2002 TO JULY 9TH 2006

PL	W	D	L	F	A	%
63	26	21	16	79	55	58

FIFA/COCA-COLA WORLD RANKING

1993	1994	1995	1996	1997	1998	1999	2000	2001	2002	2003	2004	2005		High		Low	
87	113	143	146	124	126	115	105	99	77	47	40	86		37	08/04	152	07/96

2005–2006											
08/05	09/05	10/05	11/05	12/05	01/06	02/06	03/06	04/06	05/06	06/06	07/06
63	69	78	84	86	86	86	83	83	84	-	98

There was no doubt as to the team of the season in Jordan - Al Faysali - who won a first ever international trophy for the country. It came in the 2005 AFC Cup in which they beat Lebanon's Al Nejmeh in the final 4-2 on aggregate over two legs. In the first match in Amman, a Khaled Saed goal gave them a slender 1-0 lead to take to Beirut. In the second leg at the Sports City Stadium, two goals from Khaled Al Malta'ah and one from Hassouneh Qasem sealed an historic 3-2 victory. The AFC Cup is a competition which suits the Jordanians well with both Faysali and Al Wahdat qualifying from the group stages in 2006 as well. Al Faysali weren't the only club making the headlines

INTERNATIONAL HONOURS
None

in Jordan though. They may have favourites to complete a domestic double, but no-one had counted on Shabab Al Ordon, otherwise known as the Jordan Youth Club, pulling off a major surprise to win their first ever trophy. In a close race with Al Faysali, Shabab won the League on the last day of the season with a 4-1 victory over Ramtha. A week later they capped off an incredible season by beating Al Faysali 2-1 in the Cup Final to complete an unlikely double. The national team played a number of friendlies in preparation for the 2007 AFC Asian Cup qualifiers which got off to a good start with a win over Bangladesh, but that was followed by defeat against Oman.

THE FIFA BIG COUNT OF 2000

	Male	Female		Male	Female
Registered players	3 675	0	Referees	88	0
Non registered players	20 000	100	Officials	5 000	50
Youth players	782	0	Total involved	29 695	
Total players	24 557		Number of clubs	84	
Professional players	13	0	Number of teams	120	

Jordan Football Associatiom (JFA)

Al-Hussein Youth City, PO Box 962024, Amman 11196, Jordan
Tel +962 6 5657662   Fax +962 6 565 7660
jfa@nets.com.jo   www.jfa.com.jo
President: HRH Prince Ali AL-HUSSEIN   General Secretary: ZURIEKAT Fadi
Vice-President: AL-HADID Nidal   Treasurer: AL DAOUD Jamal   Media Officer: FAKHOURY Munem
Men's Coach: AL GOHARY Mahmoud   Women's Coach: MAHER Abuhantash
JFA formed: 1949   AFC: 1970   FIFA: 191958
White shirts with red trimmings, White shorts, White socks or Red shirts with with trimmings, Red shorts, Red socks

RECENT INTERNATIONAL MATCHES PLAYED BY JORDAN

2003	Opponents		Score	Venue	Comp	Scorers	Att	Referee
17-10	Lebanon	W	1-0	Amman	ACq	Aqel 85p		
12-11	Lebanon	W	2-0	Beirut	ACq	Al Sheikh 37, Al Shagran 65	15 000	
18-11	Korea DPR	W	3-0	Amman	ACq	Shelbaieh 7, Al Shboul 89, Al Zboun 90		
28-11	Korea DPR	W	3-0	Pyongyang	ACq	Awarded 3-0. Jordan refused entry into Korea DPR		
2004								
12-02	Indonesia	W	2-1	Amman	Fr	Al Sheikh 39, Mansour 45		
18-02	Laos	W	5-0	Amman	WCq	Aqel 40, Shelbaieh 45, Al Shagran 63, Ragheb 90 Shehdeh 90	5 000	Al Mozahmi OMA
21-03	Bahrain	D	0-0	Al Muharraq	Fr			
23-03	Bahrain	W	2-0	Al Muharraq	Fr	Al Zboun, Al Shboul		
31-03	Qatar	W	1-0	Amman	WCq	Mansour 70	15 000	Shaban KUW
28-04	Nigeria	L	0-2	Lagos	Fr			
30-04	Libya	L	0-1	Lagos	Fr			
19-05	Cyprus	D	0-0	Nicosia	Fr		2 500	Loizou CYP
30-05	Algeria	D	1-1	Annaba	Fr	Shelbaieh 18	20 000	Zahmoul TUN
9-06	Iran	W	1-0	Tehran	WCq	Al Shboul 83	35 000	Kamikawa JPN
17-06	Palestine	D	1-1	Tehran	WFr1	Al Shboul 3		
21-06	Iraq	W	2-0	Tehran	WFr1	Mansour 48, Shelbaieh 79		
23-06	Syria	D	1-1	Tehran	WFsf	Deeb 21. L 2-3p		
25-06	Iraq	W	3-1	Tehran	WF3p	Al Shagran 2 27 47, Abu Alieh 76		
8-07	Thailand	D	0-0	Bangkok	Fr			
19-07	Korea Rep	D	0-0	Jinan	ACr1		26 000	Maidin SIN
23-07	Kuwait	W	2-0	Jinan	ACr1	Sa'ed 90, Al Zboun 90	28 000	Lu Jun CHN
27-07	United Arab Emirates	D	0-0	Beijing	ACr1		25 000	Talaat LIB
31-07	Japan	D	1-1	Chongqing	ACqf	Shelbaieh 11. L 3-4p	52 000	Salleh MAS
18-08	Azerbaijan	D	1-1	Amman	Fr	Aqel 21	4 000	
31-08	Lebanon	D	2-2	Amman	Fr	Shelbaieh, Al Zboun		
8-09	Iran	L	0-2	Amman	WCq		20 000	Lu Jun CHN
8-10	Thailand	W	3-2	Bangkok	Fr	Al Maharmeh 2, Shehdeh		
13-10	Laos	W	3-2	Vientiane	WCq	Al Maharmeh 28, Al Shagran 2 73 76	3 000	Gosh BAN
20-10	Ecuador	W	3-0	Tripoli	Fr	Al Maltah 45, Shelbaieh 53, Suleiman 69		
22-10	Libya	L	0-1	Tripoli	Fr			Bennaceur TUN
11-11	United Arab Emirates	L	0-1	Abu Dhabi	Fr			
17-11	Qatar	L	0-2	Doha	WCq		800	Yoshida JPN
2005								
28-01	Norway	D	0-0	Amman	Fr		8 000	Al Shoufi SYR
26-03	Cyprus	L	1-2	Larnaca	Fr	Ahmet 85		
8-06	Iraq	L	0-1	Amman	Fr			
17-08	Armenia	D	0-0	Amman	Fr			
16-11	Georgia	L	2-3	Amman	Fr	Salimi 35, Saedi 59		
2006								
17-01	Côte d'Ivoire	L	0-2	Abu Dhabi	Fr			
23-01	Sweden	D	0-0	Abu Dhabi	Fr			
1-02	Thailand	D	0-0	Ayutthaya	Fr			
7-02	Kuwait	L	1-2	Kuwait City	Fr	Abdulfattah		
14-02	Kazakhstan	W	2-0	Amman	Fr	Ali 13, Aqel 53		
22-02	Pakistan	W	3-0	Amman	ACq	Aqel 30p, Shelbaieh 38, Al Shagran 41		Basma SYR
1-03	Oman	L	0-3	Wattayah	ACq		11 000	Irmatov UZB

Fr = Friendly match • WF = West Asian Federation Championship • AR = Arab Cup • AC = AFC Asian Cup • WC = FIFA World Cup™
q = qualifier • r1 = first round group • qf = quarter-final • sf = semi-final • 3p = third place play-off • f = final

JORDAN NATIONAL TEAM RECORDS AND RECORD SEQUENCES

Records			Sequence records					
Victory	6-0	TPE 2001	Wins	5	1992, 2003-2004	Clean sheets	4	1988, 2004
Defeat	0-6	SYR, ALG, CHN	Defeats	6	Three times	Goals scored	9	1992
Player Caps	n/a		Undefeated	14	2004	Without goal	7	1996-1997
Player Goals	n/a		Without win	13	1957-1966	Goals against	13	1992-1993

JORDAN COUNTRY INFORMATION

Capital	Amman	Independence	1946 from the UK	GDP per Capita	$4 300
Population	5 611 202	Status	Kingdom	GNP Ranking	90
Area km²	92 300	Language	Arabic	Dialling code	+962
Population density	61	Literacy rate	91.3%	Internet code	.jo
% in urban areas	71%	Main religion	Muslim 92%, Christian 6%	GMT + / –	+2
Towns/Cities ('000)	Amman 2 201; Irbid 1 027; Al Zarqa 915; Al Balqa 378; Al Mafraq 273; Al Karak 231				
Neighbours (km)	Syria 375; Iraq 181; Saudi Arabia 744; Israel 238; West Bank 97				
Main stadia	Al-Qwaismeh (King Abdullah International) – Amman 18 000				

JORDAN 2005–06

FIRST DIVISION

	Pl	W	D	L	F	A	Pts	Shabab AO	Faysali	Wahdat	Hussein	Ramtha	Buqa'a	Yarmouk	Shabab AH	Jazeera	Kfarsoum
Shabab Al Ordon ‡	18	13	3	2	41	19	42		1-0	2-0	0-0	4-1	2-1	1-1	3-1	1-2	4-1
Al Faysali ‡	18	12	4	2	35	13	40	0-2		1-1	2-1	2-2	1-1	1-0	3-1	5-2	2-0
Al Wahdat	18	10	5	3	35	18	35	0-1	1-1		0-1	4-1	2-1	3-0	3-3	2-1	3-0
Al Hussein	18	8	4	6	26	21	28	1-2	1-3	0-0		2-0	1-2	2-1	2-1	3-1	2-1
Al Ramtha	18	7	5	6	23	28	26	3-2	0-1	2-2	1-1		1-0	2-2	2-1	1-0	2-1
Al Buqa'a	18	6	4	8	23	23	22	2-5	0-1	1-2	1-1	0-1		3-0	2-1	1-0	3-0
Al Yarmouk	18	4	5	9	19	29	17	1-3	0-2	0-3	1-2	3-2	1-1		1-1	0-0	3-1
Shabab Al Hussein	18	4	3	11	25	37	15	2-3	0-3	0-4	**0-3**	1-2	2-0	1-0		2-3	4-0
Al Jazeera	18	3	5	10	19	33	14	3-5	0-2	1-2	3-2	0-0	1-1	**0-3**	0-1		0-0
Kfarsoum	18	2	4	12	17	42	10	0-0	0-5	2-3	2-1	2-0	1-3	1-2	3-3	2-2	

13/10/2005 – 22/05/2006 • ‡ Qualified for the 2007 AFC Cup • Matches in bold awarded 3-0

JFA CUP 2005–06

Round of 16

Shabab Al Ordon *	4
Al Jazeera	2
Al Karmel *	1
Shabab Al Hussein	3
Al Arabi	1 ?p
Al Wahdat *	1 ?p
Sahab *	0
Al Ramtha	5
Al Buqa'a *	1
Al Yarmouk	0
Mansheyat Bani Hasan	0
Al Hussein *	7
Kfarsoum *	2 ?p
Al Qawqazi	2 ?p
Al Turra *	1
Al Faysali	6

Quarter-finals

Shabab Al Ordon *	2
Shabab Al Hussein	1
Al Arabi	1
Al Ramtha *	0
Al Buqa'a	3
Al Hussein *	2
Kfarsoum *	0
Al Faysali	3

Semi-finals

Shabab Al Ordon	0 15p
Al Ramtha	0 14p
Al Buqa'a	1
Al Faysali	5

Final

Shabab Al Ordon	2
Al Faysali	1

CUP FINAL

27-05-2006

Scorers: Fadi Lafi [8], Saher Al Hejawi [75] for Shabab; Moayad Salim [90] for Faysali

* Home team • ‡ Qualified for the 2007 AFC Cup

RECENT LEAGUE AND CUP RECORD

	Championship							Cup		
Year	Champions	Pts	Runners-up	Pts	Third	Pts		Winners	Score	Runners-up
1997	Al Wihdat	41	Al Faysali	41	Al Ramtha	29		Al Wihdat	2-1	Al Ramtha
1997	Al Wihdat	47	Al Faysali	46	Al Hussein	30		No tournament due to season readjustment		
1998	Al Wihdat	34	Al Faysali	33	Al Ramtha	19		Al Faysali	2-1	Al Wihdat
1999	Al Faysali	57	Al Wihdat	49	Al Ramtha	48		Al Faysali	0-0 5-4p	Al Wihdat
2000	Al Faysali	52	Al Wihdat	44	Al Ahly	34		Al Wihdat	2-0	Al Faysali
2001	Al Faysali	48	Al Wihdat	44	Al Hussein	31		Al Faysali	2-0	Al Hussein
2002	No championship due to season readjustment							No tournament due to season readjustment		
2003	Al Wihdat	48	Al Faysali	45	Al Hussein	35		Al Faysali	2-0	Al Hussein
2004	Al Faysali	9	Al Hussein	4	Al Wihdat	4		Al Faysali	3-1	Al Hussein
2005	Al Wihdat	50	Al Hussein	36	Al Faysali	31		Al Faysali	3-0	Shabab Al Hussein
2006	Shabab Al Ordon	42	Al Faysali	40	Al Wahdat	35		Shabab Al Ordon	2-1	Al Faysali

In the 1997 play-off Al Wahdat beat Al Faisaly 4-2 on penalties following a 1-1 draw after the two clubs finished level on points

JPN – JAPAN

NATIONAL TEAM RECORD
JULY 1ST 2002 TO JULY 9TH 2006

PL	W	D	L	F	A	%
52	29	10	13	82	43	65.4

The Zico era for the Japanese national team is over and it ended in a whimper as the side barely put up a fight at the FIFA World Cup™ finals in Germany. Brazil's legendary forward can always point to the fact that he led Japan to AFC Asian Cup success in 2004, but at the finals in Germany his team didn't show the same fight and spirit that took them to the Asian title. The first game, against Australia, looked to be going Japan's way as they led 1-0 with only six minutes remaining, but they were undone by a spirited Australian fight back and lost 3-1. The defeat set the tone for the tournament and was followed by a poor scoreless draw against Croatia and a comprehensive defeat at the hands of Zico's fellow countrymen, which meant a demoralising exit in the first round. Japan have now appeared at three consecutive finals and will no doubt be amongst the Asian favourites to qualify for South Africa in 2010, but for the good of the game in the country they will have to do better than just turn up. Just before the finals, the Japanese began the defence of their Asian crown, having been forced to qualify because of the automatic qualification of the four co-hosts. In their first game they thrashed India 6-0 leaving little doubt that they will be the team to

INTERNATIONAL HONOURS
Qualified for the FIFA World Cup™ 1998 2002 2006
Qualified for the FIFA Women's World Cup 1991 1995 1999 2003
Asian Cup 1992 2000 2004
AFC U-16 Championship 1994
AFC Champions League Furukawa 1987, Jubilo Iwata 1999

beat. Success in the AFC Champions League is another thing altogether with Japanese clubs continually outshone by their Saudi and Korean Republic counterparts. Since the launch of the Champions League in its present format in 2003, not a single Japanese club has qualified from the group stage, a staggering fact given that the winners qualify for the FIFA Club World Cup in Japan. This must surely act as an incentive to improve. Despite all this, the J.League continues to flourish and provides the staple diet of most Japanese fans. In a sensational finale to the season five clubs still had a chance to clinch the title going into the last round of games. Cerezo Osaka led the table, a point ahead of cross-city rivals Gamba Osaka who in turn were a point ahead of Urawa, Kashima and JEF United. With a minute to go in the matches, all five teams were winning but then a last minute goal by FC Tokyo's Yasuyuki Konno meant Cerezo only drew their match, handing Gamba their first title on a plate. Having led the table since the start of September, only to lose top spot to Cerezo on the penultimate weekend, it was perhaps no more than Gamba deserved. The hugely popular Urawa Reds won the Emperor's Cup beating Shimizu S-Pulse in the final.

Japan Football Association (JFA)
JFA House, Football Ave., Bunkyo-ku, Tokyo 113-8311, Japan
Tel +81 3 38302004   Fax +81 3 38302005
www.jfa.or.jp/e/index.html
President: KAWABUCHI Saburo   General Secretary: HIRATA Takeo
Vice-President: OGURA Jinji   Treasurer: SAITO Koji   Media Officer: TESHIMA Hideto
Men's Coach: OSIM Ivica   Women's Coach: OHASHI Hiroshi
JFA formed: 1921   AFC: 1954   FIFA: 1929-46 & 1950
Blue shirts with white trimmings, White shorts, Blue socks

RECENT INTERNATIONAL MATCHES PLAYED BY JAPAN

2004	Opponents		Score	Venue	Comp	Scorers	Att	Referee
20-07	Oman	W	1-0	Chongqing	ACr1	Nakamura [34]	35 000	Shield AUS
24-07	Thailand	W	4-1	Chongqing	ACr1	Nakamura [21], Nakazawa 2 [56 87], Fukunishi [58]	45 000	Al Marzouqi UAE
28-07	Iran	D	0-0	Chongqing	ACr1		52 000	Shield AUS
31-07	Jordan	D	1-1	Chongqing	ACqf	Suzuki.T [14]. W 4-3p	52 000	Mohd Salleh MAS
3-08	Bahrain	W	4-3	Jinan	ACsf	Nakata.K [48], Tamada 2 [55 93], Nakazawa [90]	32 050	Maidin SIN
7-08	China PR	W	3-1	Beijing	ACf	Fukunishi [22], Nakata.K [65], Tamada [90]	62 000	Al Fadhli KUW
18-08	Argentina	L	1-2	Shizuoka	Fr	Suzuki.T [72]	45 000	Lu Jun CHN
8-09	India	W	4-0	Calcutta	WCq	Suzuki.T [45], Ono [60], Fukunishi [71], Miyamoto [87]	90 000	Hajjar SYR
13-10	Oman	W	1-0	Muscat	WCq	Suzuki.T [52]	35 000	Lu Jun CHN
17-11	Singapore	W	1-0	Saitama	WCq	Tamada [13]	58 881	Torky IRN
16-12	Germany	L	0-3	Yokohama	Fr		61 805	Shield AUS
2005								
29-01	Kazakhstan	W	4-0	Yokohama	Fr	Tamada 2 [5 60], Matsuda [11], Alex [24]	46 941	
2-02	Syria	W	3-0	Saitama	Fr	Suzuki.T [44], Miyamoto [70], Ogasawara [90]	30 000	
9-02	Korea DPR	W	2-1	Saitama	WCq	Ogasawara [4], Oguro [92+]	60 000	Al Ghamdi KSA
25-03	Iran	L	1-2	Tehran	WCq	Fukunishi [33]	110 000	Maidin SIN
30-03	Bahrain	W	1-0	Saitama	WCq	Salmeen OG [71]	67 549	Irmatov UZB
22-05	Peru	L	0-1	Niigata	KC		39 856	Michel SVK
27-05	United Arab Emirates	L	0-1	Tokyo	KC		53 123	Michel SVK
3-06	Bahrain	W	1-0	Manama	WCq	Ogasawara [34]	32 000	Mohd Salleh MAS
8-06	Korea DPR	W	2-0	Manama	WCq	Yanagisawa [67], Oguro [89]	BCD	De Bleeckere BEL
16-06	Mexico	L	1-2	Hanover	CCr1	Yanagisawa [12]	24 036	Breeze AUS
19-06	Greece	W	1-0	Frankfurt	CCr1	Oguro [76]	34 314	Fandel GER
22-06	Brazil	D	2-2	Cologne	CCr1	Nakamura [27], Oguro [88]	44 922	Daami TUN
31-07	Korea DPR	L	0-1	Daejon	EAF		23 150	Tan Hai CHN
3-08	China PR	D	2-2	Daejon	EAF	Moniwa [59], Tanaka [87]	1 827	
7-08	Korea Republic	W	1-0	Daejon	EAF	Nakazawa [86]	42 753	Tan Hai CHN
17-08	Iran	W	2-1	Yokohama	WCq	Kaji [28], Oguro [76]	66 098	Shaban KUW
7-09	Honduras	W	5-4	Miyagi	Fr	Takahara [33], Yanagisawa 2 [48 70], Nakamura [55], Ogasawara [78]	45 198	
8-10	Latvia	D	2-2	Riga	Fr	Takahara [5], Nakamura [52]	6 500	Granatas POL
12-10	Ukraine	L	0-1	Kyiv	Fr			Lajuks LVA
16-11	Angola	W	1-0	Tokyo	Fr	Matsui [90]	52 406	
2006								
10-02	USA	L	2-3	San Francisco	Fr	Maki [62], Nakazawa [90]	37 365	Elizondo ARG
18-02	Finland	W	2-0	Shizuoka	Fr	Kubo [47], Ogasawara [57]	40 702	Lee Gi Young KOR
22-02	India	W	6-0	Yokohama	ACq	Ono [32], Maki [58], Fukunishi [68], Kubo 2 [78 90], Sato [82]	38 025	Huang CHN
28-02	Bosnia-Herzegovina	D	2-2	Dortmund	Fr	Takahara [45], Nakata.H [90]	8 120	Wack GER
30-03	Ecuador	W	1-0	Oita	Fr	Sato [85]	36 507	Maidin SIN
9-05	Bulgaria	L	1-2	Osaka	Fr	Maki [76]	44 851	Megia Davila ESP
13-05	Scotland	D	0-0	Saitama	Fr		58 648	Itturalde Gonzalez ESP
30-05	Germany	D	2-2	Leverkusen	Fr	Takahara 2 [57 65]	22 500	Vassaras GRE
4-06	Malta	W	1-0	Dusseldorf	Fr	Tamada [2]	10 800	Kircher GER
12-06	Australia	L	1-3	Kaiserslautern	WCr1	Nakamura [26]	46 000	Abd El Fatah EGY
18-06	Croatia	D	0-0	Nuremberg	WCr1		41 000	De Bleeckere BEL
22-06	Brazil	L	1-4	Dortmund	WCr1	Tamada [34]	65 000	Poulat FRA

Fr = Friendly match • CC = FIFA Confederations Cup • EAF - East Asian Federation Cup • AC = AFC Asian Cup • WC = FIFA World Cup™
q = qualifier • r1 = first round group • qf = quarter-final • sf = semi-final • f = final • BCD = behind closed doors

JAPAN NATIONAL TEAM RECORDS AND RECORD SEQUENCES

Records			Sequence records		
Victory	15-0	PHI 1966	Wins	8 Four times	Clean sheets	7	2003-2004
Defeat	2-15	PHI 1917	Defeats	9 1917-1927	Goals scored	14	1966-1968
Player Caps	123	IHARA Masami	Undefeated	12 2000, 2004	Without goal	6	1988, 1989-1990
Player Goals	56	MIURA Kazuyoshi	Without win	11 1976-1977	Goals against	31	1960-1966

JAPAN COUNTRY INFORMATION

Capital	Tokyo	Formation	1600	GDP per Capita	$28 200
Population	127 333 002	Status	Constitutional Monarchy	GNP Ranking	2
Area km²	377 835	Language	Japanese	Dialling code	+81
Population density	337 per km²	Literacy rate	99%	Internet code	.jp
% in urban areas	78%	Main religion	Shinto & Buddhist 84%	GMT + / −	+9
Towns/Cities ('000)	Tokyo 8 372; Yokohama 3 603; Osaka 2 590; Nagoya 2 194; Sapporo 1 895; Kobe 1 535; Kyoto 1 458; Fukuoka 1 402; Kawasaki 1 318; Hiroshima 1 147; Saitama 1 088; Sendai 1 043; Kitakyushu 994; Chiba 926; Sakai 780; Shizuoka 700; Kunamoto 684; Sagamihara 657; Okayama 642; Hamamatsu 609; Hachioji 588; Funabashi 562				
Neighbours (km)	Pacific Ocean and the Sea of Japan 29 751				
Main stadia	Yokohama International – Yokohama 72 370; Olympic Stadium – Tokyo 57 363				

JAPAN NATIONAL TEAM PLAYERS AND COACHES

Record Caps			Record Goals			Recent Coaches	
IHARA Masami	1988-'99	123	MIURA Kazuyoshi	1990-'00	56	MORI Takaji	1981-'86
KAWAGUCHI Yoshikatsu	1997-'06	92	KAMAMOTO Kunishige	1964-'77	55	ISHII Yoshinobu	1986-'87
MIURA Kazuyoshi	1990-'00	91	TAKAGI Takuya	1992-'97	28	YOKOYAMA Kenzo	1988-'92
NAKATA Hidetoshi	1997-'06	77	HARA Hiromi	1978-'88	24	OOFT Hans	1992-'93
SANTOS Alessandro	2000-'06	75	NAKAYAMA Masashi	1990-'03	21	FALCAO Roberto	1993-'94
HASHIRATANI Tetsuji	1988-'95	71	YANAGISAWA Atsushi	1998-'06	17	KAMO Shu	1995-'97
MIYAMOTO Tsuneyasu	2000-'06	70	TAKAHARA Naohiro	2000-'06	17	OKADA Takeshi	1997-'98
NANAMI Hiroshi	1995-'01	68	NAKAMURA Shunsuke	2000-'06	16	TROUSSIER Philippe	1998-'02
MORISHIMA Hiroaki	1995-'02	65	KIMURA Kazushi	1979-'86	15	ZICO	2002-'06
INAMOTO Junichi	2000-'06	65	MIYAMOTO Teruki	1961-'71	14	OSIM Ivica	2006-

FIFA/COCA-COLA WORLD RANKING

1993	1994	1995	1996	1997	1998	1999	2000	2001	2002	2003	2004	2005		High		Low	
43	36	31	21	14	20	57	38	34	22	29	17	15		9	02/98	62	02/00

2005–2006											
08/05	09/05	10/05	11/05	12/05	01/06	02/06	03/06	04/06	05/06	06/06	07/06
17	16	16	15	15	15	18	18	17	18	-	49

THE FIFA BIG COUNT OF 2000

	Male	Female		Male	Female
Registered players	190 206	10 357	Referees	100 545	0
Non registered players	2 500 000	0	Officials	90 346	4 970
Youth players	612 152	9 673	Total involved	3 518 249	
Total players	3 322 388		Number of clubs	700	
Professional players	1 120	0	Number of teams	28 455	

JAPAN 2005

J.LEAGUE DIVISION 1

	Pl	W	D	L	F	A	Pts	Gamba	Urawa	Kashima	JEF United	Cerezo	Jubilo	Sanfrecce	Kawasaki	Marinos	Tokyo	Oita	Albirex	Omiya	Nagoya	Shimizu	Kashiwa	Verdy	Vissel
Gamba Osaka ‡	34	18	6	10	82	58	60		2-1	3-3	1-2	4-1	3-1	4-2	3-2	3-2	5-3	1-2	1-1	0-2	3-1	3-3	3-2	7-1	3-1
Urawa Reds	34	17	8	9	65	37	59	1-1		0-1	0-0	1-2	1-0	2-0	3-2	0-0	2-1	1-2	2-1	1-2	3-0	1-1	7-0	4-1	2-2
Kashima Antlers	34	16	11	7	61	39	59	2-2	2-2		2-2	0-1	2-1	1-2	2-0	0-2	1-1	1-1	7-2	2-0	1-0	2-1	4-0	2-1	4-0
JEF United	34	16	11	7	56	42	59	3-1	1-0	2-4		1-2	2-1	1-1	1-0	2-2	2-1	4-2	3-2	2-0	2-1	2-1	2-2	1-0	4-0
Cerezo Osaka	34	16	11	7	48	40	59	2-4	3-1	0-0	2-0		2-0	1-1	2-0	2-3	2-2	1-1	1-0	1-0	1-1	1-1	1-1	0-2	2-1
Jubilo Iwata	34	14	9	11	51	41	51	2-1	2-2	1-1	1-3	3-0		1-3	1-2	3-1	1-1	2-1	2-3	2-0	0-3	1-1	1-0	6-0	1-0
Sanfrecce Hiroshima	34	13	11	10	50	42	50	1-2	3-4	0-1	1-1	1-2	0-0		2-1	0-1	0-0	0-4	5-0	2-1	1-2	3-1	0-0	3-0	2-0
Kawasaki Frontale	34	15	5	14	54	47	50	2-4	3-3	2-1	1-0	3-2	0-2	1-1		2-1	1-0	0-2	1-1	3-0	2-1	0-2	0-1	3-1	1-0
Yokohama F.Marinos	34	12	12	10	41	40	48	2-2	0-1	2-1	2-1	1-1	0-1	3-1	0-2		0-0	0-3	4-1	1-2	2-1	0-1	3-1	1-0	3-1
FC Tokyo	34	11	14	9	43	40	47	2-1	0-2	0-2	2-1	2-2	1-0	2-2	1-1	4-0		0-0	4-0	3-3	1-1	1-0	0-2	0-0	1-1
Oita Trinita	34	12	7	15	44	43	43	0-2	1-0	1-1	0-1	1-2	1-2	0-1	1-0	0-2	2-1		1-3	2-1	2-0	5-0	1-1	1-2	2-1
Albirex Niigata	34	11	9	14	47	62	42	4-2	0-4	2-2	1-1	1-2	0-1	0-1	2-1	1-0	0-1	2-1		3-2	3-0	0-0	2-2	1-1	3-2
Omiya Ardija	34	12	5	17	39	50	41	1-0	1-3	0-2	0-1	1-0	0-2	0-1	1-0	3-1	1-4				3-2	3-2	1-0	2-3	1-1
Nagoya Grampus Eight	34	10	9	15	43	49	39	2-1	0-2	3-0	2-2	1-3	2-0	1-1	1-4	1-1	0-0	0-1	1-1			1-2	4-0	5-4	0-2
Shimizu S-Pulse	34	9	12	13	40	49	39	1-4	0-1	2-2	2-2	1-1	1-1	3-2	0-1	0-1	2-1	2-1	2-2				1-2	1-2	1-0
Kashiwa Reysol	34	8	11	15	39	54	35	2-1	3-0	1-3	1-2	1-0	0-4	1-1	1-1	3-2	0-1	0-1	2-1	2-1	2-2			5-1	1-0
Tokyo Verdy 1969	34	6	12	16	40	73	30	0-1	0-7	2-0	2-2	0-1	4-4	1-4	1-2	1-1	1-2	4-2	2-2	1-1	0-0	0-0	1-0		3-3
Vissel Kobe	34	4	9	21	30	67	21	1-4	0-1	0-2	1-1	3-1	0-0	2-3	1-6	0-2	1-2	2-1	1-1	0-1	1-0	1-0	0-3	0-4	

5/03/2005 - 3/12/2005 • ‡ Qualified for the AFC Champions League • Relegation play-off: Ventforet Kofu 2-1 6-2 Kashiwa Reysol

JAPAN 2005

J.LEAGUE DIVISION 2

	Pl	W	D	L	F	A	Pts	Kyoto	Avispa	Ventforet	Vegalta	Montedio	Consadole	Shonan	Sagan	Tokushima	Mito	Yokohama	Thespa
Kyoto Purple Sanga	44	30	7	7	89	40	97		3-2 0-3	2-1 2-1	0-3 1-2	1-0 1-0	0-0 4-0	2-1 4-0	0-3 0-1	1-0 2-0	1-1 3-1	1-0 2-1	3-0 6-0
Avispa Fukuoka	44	21	15	8	72	43	78	0-0 2-1		0-1 2-2	1-1 1-0	0-0 2-0	3-3 0-0	0-2 0-3	2-4 1-3	1-0 0-4	1-3 0-1	0-3 0-4	2-1 1-0
Ventforet Kofu	44	19	12	13	78	64	69	0-3 1-2	2-1 0-5		1-2 1-1	2-1 1-2	2-2 5-2	3-1 1-1	5-0 5-0	4-1 2-2	0-1 0-0	4-2 1-0	
Vegalta Sendai	44	19	11	14	66	47	68	3-1 0-1	0-2 2-2	2-1 1-1		0-1 0-0	4-0 2-2	3-2 0-0	2-1 0-0	3-2 2-1	0-3 3-0	3-0 3-4	0-4 0-1
Montedio Yamagata	44	16	16	12	54	45	64	1-3 0-3	0-1 1-3	1-1 2-0	0-0 0-2		3-0 1-0	1-0 1-1	1-3 1-0	2-2 1-3	0-1 2-3	0-1 3-0	3-0 1-1
Consadole Sapporo	44	17	12	15	57	53	63	0-1 3-3	1-1 3-3	1-2 4-0	3-2 1-0	2-3 1-0		0-0 2-0	1-0 3-0	2-0 2-0	1-1 1-0	1-2 3-2	1-2 1-1
Shonan Bellmare	44	13	15	16	46	59	54	1-2 0-0	0-2 1-0	1-1 0-1	1-1 0-1	1-1 1-2	2-0 0-0		4-3 2-0	1-0 1-2	3-0 1-0	2-1 3-2	1-2 3-2
Sagan Tosu	44	14	10	20	58	58	52	2-3 3-2	1-1 2-1	2-1 0-0	2-0 0-2	0-2 0-1	2-0 1-0	1-2 0-1		1-3 3-3	0-1 0-1	2-3 1-2	2-2 1-1
Tokushima Vortis	44	12	16	16	60	76	52	1-2 1-5	2-2 0-1	1-1 3-3	2-4 1-2	1-1 1-1	1-1 2-3	3-1 2-2	2-1		0-1 0-1	2-0 1-3	2-1 3-2
Mito Hollyhock	44	13	13	18	41	57	52	2-3 1-1	0-0 0-3	1-0 3-0	2-0 2-1	2-0 1-2	0-1 0-4	1-0 1-0	1-1 0-1	2-1 1-1		2-2 1-0	1-0 1-1
Yokohama FC	44	10	15	19	48	64	45	1-2 1-1	1-3 1-1	3-3 4-1	3-1 2-1	1-1 1-2	2-1 1-0	0-4 2-0	1-1 1-0	2-1 2-1	3-0 0-1		1-0 1-0
Thespa Kusatsu	44	5	8	31	26	82	23	0-3 0-2	1-2 0-2	1-2 0-2	0-2 0-3	0-0 1-4	2-1 1-0	0-0 0-2	1-0 2-0	1-0 1-0	1-0 1-3		

5/03/2005 - 3/12/2005

JAPAN 2005
JAPAN FOOTBALL LEAGUE (3)

	Pl	W	D	L	F	A	Pts
Ehime FC	30	21	3	6	54	26	66
YKK AP	30	20	4	6	63	28	64
Alo's Hokuriku	30	19	4	7	52	26	61
Tochigi SC	30	16	9	5	60	32	57
Honda FC	30	17	5	8	59	37	56
Sagawa Kyubin Tokyo	30	16	4	10	55	33	52
Sony Sendai	30	15	5	10	49	38	50
Gunma FC Horikoshi	30	15	3	12	53	40	48
Musashino FC	30	14	6	10	37	29	48
Sagawa Kyubin Osaka	30	13	6	11	42	36	45
Sagawa Printing	30	9	7	14	34	43	34
SC Tottori	30	9	6	15	40	58	33
Ryutsu Keizai Univ.	30	5	7	18	39	79	22
Denso	30	4	7	19	33	63	19
Honda Lock	30	3	6	21	38	79	15
Mitsubishi Mizushima	30	2	2	26	24	85	8

27/03/2005 - 4/12/2005

TOP SCORERS

ARAUJO	Gamba Osaka	33
WASHINGTON	Tokyo Verdy	22
EDMILSON	Albirex Niigata	18
SATO Hisato	Sanfrecce	18
MAGNO ALVES	Oita Trinita	18
JUNINHO	Kawasaki	16
OGURO Masashi	Gamba Osaka	16
ALEX MINEIRO	Kashima Antlers	15
CULLEN Robert	Jubilo Iwata	13

J.LEAGUE YAMAZAKI NABISCO CUP 2005

Quarter-finals			Semi-finals			Final		
JEF United *	3	2						
Jubilo Iwata	2	2	JEF United	3	2			
Shimizu S-Pulse *	0	0	Urawa Reds *	1	2			
Urawa Reds	1	1				JEF United	0	5p
Yokohama F.Marinos	1	3				Gamba Osaka	0	4p
Omiya Ardija *	0	1	Yokohama F.Marinos	0 1	1p			
Cerezo Osaka *	0	2	Gamba Osaka *	1 0	4p			
Gamba Osaka	3	2	* Home team in first leg					

National Stadium, Tokyo
5-11-2005, 45 039, Ref: Matsumura

First round played in four groups of four teams • The group winners and the two best runners-up joined Jubilo
Iwata and Yokohama Marinos in the quarter-finals

CLUB DIRECTORY

Club	Town/City	Stadium	Capacity	www.	Lge	Cup	CL
Albirex Niigata	Niigata	Big Swan	42 300	albirex.co.jp	0	0	0
Cerezo Osaka	Osaka	Nagai	50 000	cerezo.co.jp	4	3	0
Gamba Osaka	Osaka	Expo'70	23 000	gamba-osaka.net	1	1	0
JEF United	Ichihara/Chiba	Ichihara	16 933	so-net.ne.jp/jefunited	2	4	1
Jubilo Iwata	Iwata	Yamaha	16 893	jubilo-iwata.co.jp	4	2	1
Kashima Antlers	Ibaraki	Kashima	39 026	so-net.ne.jp/antlers/	4	2	0
Kashiwa Reysol	Kashiwa	Kashiwa Hitachi	15 900	reysol.co.jp	1	2	0
Kawasaki Frontale	Kawasaki	Todoroki	25 000	frontale.co.jp	0	0	0
Nagoya Grampus Eight	Toyota	Toyota	45 000	so-net.ne.jp/grampus	0	2	0
Oita Trinita	Oita	Oita	43 000	oita-trinita.co.jp	0	0	0
Omiya Ardija	Saitama	Omiya	12 500	ardija.co.jp	0	0	0
Sanfrecce Hiroshima	Hiroshima	Big Arch	50 000	sanfrecce.co.jp	5	3	0
Shimizu S-Pulse	Shizuoka	Nihondaira	20 339	s-pulse.co.jp	0	1	0
FC Tokyo	Tokyo	Komazawa Olympic	28 000	fctokyo.co.jp	0	0	0
Tokyo Verdy 1969	Tokyo	Ajinomoto	50 000	verdy.co.jp	7	5	0
Urawa Reds	Saitama	Saitama 2002	63 700	urawa-reds.co.jp	4	5	0
Vissel Kobe	Kobe	Kobe Wing	34 000	vissel-kobe.co.jp	0	0	0
Yokohama F.Marinos	Yokohama	International	72 370	so-net.ne.jp/f-marinos	5	6	0

In 1992 with the creation of the J.League clubs changed their names as follows • Yanmar Diesel → Cerezo Osaka • Matsushita → Gamba Osaka •
Furukawa Electric and JR East Furukawa merged to form JEF United • Yamaha Motors → Jubilo Iwata • Sumitomo Honda → Kashima Antlers •
Hitachi → Kashiwa Reysol • Fujitsu → Kawasaki Frontale • Toyota FC → Nagoya Grampus Eight • NIT Kanto → Oita Trinita • Mazda FC (previously
Toyo Kogyo) → Sanfrecce Hiroshima • Yomiuri Nippon → Verdy Kawasaki and then Tokyo Verdy 1969 • Mitsubishi Motors → Urawa Reds • Nissan →
Yokohama Marinos • In 1998 Yokohama Marinos merged with Yokohama Flugels (previously All Nippon Airways) to form Yokohama F.Marinos

RECENT LEAGUE AND CUP RECORD

	Championship				Emperor's Cup		
Year	Champions	Score	Runners-up		Winners	Score	Runners-up
1990	Nissan	‡	Yomiuri Nippon		Matsushita	0-0 4-3p	Nissan
1991	Yomiuri Nippon	‡	Nissan		Nissan	4-1	Yomiuri Nippon
1992	Yomiuri Nippon	‡	Nissan		Yokohama Marinos	2-1	Verdy Kawasaki
1993	Verdy Kawasaki	2-0 0-0	Kashima Antlers		Yokohama Flugels	6-2	Kashima Antlers
1994	Verdy Kawasaki	1-0 1-0	Sanfrecce Hiroshima		Bellmare Hiratsuka	2-0	Cerezo Osaka
1995	Yokohama Marinos	1-0 1-0	Verdy Kawasaki		Nagoya Grampus Eight	3-0	Sanfrecce Hiroshima
1996	Kashima Antlers	‡	Nagoya Grampus Eight		Verdy Kawasaki	3-0	Sanfrecce Hiroshima
1997	Jubilo Iwata	3-2 1-0	Kashima Antlers		Kashima Antlers	3-0	Yokohama Flugels
1998	Kashima Antlers	2-1 2-1	Jubilo Iwata		Yokohama Flugels	2-1	Shimizu S-Pulse
1999	Jubilo Iwata	2-1 1-2 4-2p	Shimizu S-Pulse		Nagoya Grampus Eight	2-0	Sanfrecce Hiroshima
2000	Kashima Antlers	0-0 3-0	Yokohama F.Marinos		Kashima Antlers	3-2	Shimizu S-Pulse
2001	Kashima Antlers	2-2 1-0	Jubilo Iwata		Shimizu S-Pulse	3-2	Cerezo Osaka
2002	Jubilo Iwata	†			Kyoto Purple Sanga	2-1	Kashima Antlers
2003	Yokohama F.Marinos	†			Jubilo Iwata	1-0	Cerezo Osaka
2004	Yokohama F.Marinos	1-0 0-1 4-2p	Urawa Reds		Tokyo Verdy 1969	2-1	Jubilo Iwata
2005	Gamba Osaka	‡	Urawa Reds		Urawa Reds	2-1	Shimizu S-Pulse

† Both stages won by the same team so no play-off was required • ‡ Played on a single stage league system with no play-off • See club directory
for pre J.League names

EMPEROR'S CUP 2005

Third Round

Montedio Yamagata *	3
MM Mizushima	0

Avispa Fukuoka *	1
Sagawa Printing	0

Vegalta Sendai *	2 8p
Sendai University	2 7p

Sagawa Kyubin Tokyo	2
Consadole Sapporo *	0

Honda Lock	1
Tochigi SC *	0

Alo's Hokuriku	2
Shonan Bellmare *	1

Kyoto Purple Sanga *	3
FC Ryukyu	0

Honda FC *	3
Fukuoka University	1

Ventforet Kofu *	1
Biwako Seikei	0

Yokohama FC *	1
Gunma FC Korikoshi	0

Sagan Tosu *	1
Tsukuba University	0

Thespa Kusatsu *	3
Ehime FC	2

Mito Hollyhock *	9
Ain Food SC	0

Tokushima Vortis *	7
Sanyo Tokushima	0

Fourth Round

Urawa Reds *	2
Montedio Yamagata	1

Avispa Fukuoka	0
FC Tokyo *	2

Yokohama F.Marinos *	4
Vegalta Sendai	0

Sagawa Kyubin Tokyo	1
Kawasaki Frontale *	5

Kashima Antlers *	7
Honda Lock	0

Tokyo Verdy 1969	2
Oita Trinita *	3

Nagoya Grampus Eight *	1
Alo's Hokuriku	0

Kyoto Purple Sanga	0
Omiya Ardija *	1

Cerezo Osaka *	1 4p
Honda FC	1 1p

Ventforet Kofu	2
JEF United *	3

Kashiwa Reysol *	2 3p
Vissel Kobe	2 1p

Yokohama FC	3 6p
Gamba Osaka *	3 7p

Jubilo Iwata *	4
Sagan Tosu	0

Thespa Kusatsu	0
Albirex Niigata *	1

Sanfrecce Hiroshima *	3
Mito Hollyhock	1

Tokushima Vortis	0
Shimizu S-Pulse *	5

Fifth Round

Urawa Reds *	2
FC Tokyo	0

Yokohama F.Marinos *	2
Kawasaki Frontale	3

Kashima Antlers *	3
Oita Trinita	0

Nagoya Grampus Eight *	1
Omiya Ardija	2

Cerezo Osaka	5
JEF United *	2

Kashiwa Reysol	3
Gamba Osaka *	5

Jubilo Iwata *	2
Albirex Niigata	1

Sanfrecce Hiroshima *	0
Shimizu S-Pulse	3

* Home team

EMPEROR'S CUP 2005

Quarter-finals   **Semi-finals**   **Final**

Urawa Reds *	2
Kawasaki Frontale	0

Urawa Reds †	4
Omiya Ardija	2

Kashima Antlers *	0
Omiya Ardija	1

Urawa Reds ‡	2
Shimizu S-Pulse	1

Cerezo Osaka	3
Gamba Osaka *	1

Cerezo Osaka	0
Shimizu S-Pulse ††	1

Jubilo Iwata *	0
Shimizu S-Pulse	1

EMPEROR'S CUP FINAL 2005

National Stadium, Tokyo, 1-01-2006, Att: 51 536, Referee: Kamikawa

Urawa Reds	2	Horinouchi 39, Maric 73
Shimizu S-Pulse	1	Ichikawa 76

Urawa - TSUZUKI Ryota - TSUBOI Keisuke, HORINOUCHI Satochi, HOSOGAI Hajime - YAMADA Nobuhisa, HASEBE Makoto, SAKAI Tomoyuki, SANTOS Alessandro, PONTE Robson - OKANO Masayuki (AKAHOSHI Takafumi 65), MARIC Tomislav. Tr: BUCHWALD Guido
Shimizu - NISHIBE Yohei - MORIOKA Ryuzo (ICHIKAWA Daisuke 65), AOYAMA Naoaki, TAKAGI Kazumichi, YAMANISHI Takahiro - CHOI Tae Uk (KITAJIMA Hideaki 80), EDAMURA Takuma (HIRAMATSU Kohei 72●84), ITO Teruyoshi, HYODO Akihiro - OKAZAKI Shinji, CHO Jae Jin. Tr: HASEGAWA Kenta

† Played at the National Stadium, Tokyo
†† Played at Ecopa Stadium, Shizuoka
‡ Qualified for the 2007 AFC Champions League

GAMBA OSAKA 2005

Date	Opponents	Score		Comp	Scorers	Att
5-03-2005	Omiya Ardija	L	0-2	H	JL		16 168
12-03-2005	Kashima Antlers	D	2-2	A	JL	Araujo[42], Fernandinho[70]	25 944
19-03-2005	Sanfrecce Hiroshima	W	4-2	H	JLCgB	Sidiclei[31], Araujo[44], Yoshihara[69], Fernandinho[80]	5 358
26-03-2005	Kawasaki Frontale	D	2-2	A	JLCgB	OG[19], Matsunami[89]	7 342
3-04-2005	Kawasaki Frontale	W	3-2	H	JL	Oguro 2[6 68], Yamaguchi[89]	9 925
9-04-2005	Urawa Reds	D	1-1	A	JL	Araujo[49]	51 249
13-04-2005	Albirex Niigata	D	1-1	H	JL	Oguro[21]	6 646
16-04-2005	Yokohama F.Marinos	D	2-2	A	JL	Saneyoshi[16], Araujo[73]	23 466
23-04-2005	FC Tokyo	W	5-3	H	JL	OG[45], Oguro 3[52 53 65], Araujo[72]	11 728
28-04-2005	JEF United Chiba	L	1-3	A	JL	Yoshihara[74]	4 885
1-05-2005	Vissel Kobe	W	3-1	H	JL	Endo[12], Oguro 2[49 74]	14 625
4-05-2005	Jubilo Iwata	L	1-2	A	JL	Araujo[30]	16 579
8-05-2005	Nagoya Grampus Eight	W	3-1	H	JL	Araujo[38], Endo[43], Maeda[76]	13 687
14-05-2005	Cerezo Osaka	W	4-2	A	JL	Oguro 2[17 89], Araujo 2[35 75]	42 053
21-05-2005	Tokyo Verdy 1969	W	5-3	H	JLCgB	Yoshihara 2[20 45], Araujo 2[31 77], Sidiclei[48]	5 472
28-05-2005	Kawasaki Frontale	W	3-2	H	JLCgB	Araujo[7], Fernandinho[41], Maeda[89]	5 391
4-06-2005	Sanfrecce Hiroshima	L	1-2	A	JLCgB	Watanabe[3]	4 455
11-06-2005	Tokyo Verdy 1969	W	2-1	A	JLCgB	Matsunami[39], Terada[68]	8 868
2-07-2005	Tokyo Verdy 1969	W	7-1	H	JL	Araujo 3[44 50 62], Oguro 2[46 79], Fernandinho[55], Miyamoto[65]	11 002
6-07-2005	Sanfrecce Hiroshima	W	2-1	A	JL	Araujo 2[47 89]	7 058
10-07-2005	Kashiwa Reysol	W	3-2	H	JL	Miyamoto[15], Fernandinho[56], Yamaguchi[82]	17 343
13-07-2005	Oita Trinita	W	2-0	A	JL	Yamaguchi[14], Endo[36]	20 743
17-07-2005	Shimizu S-Pulse	D	3-3	H	JL	Fernandinho[63], Araujo 2[88 89]	17 016
23-07-2005	Cerezo Osaka	W	4-1	H	JL	Araujo 2[43 63], Hashimoto[70], Endo[83]	22 232
6-08-2005	Cerezo Osaka	W	3-0	A	JLCqf	Sidiclei[18], Hashimoto[54], Ienaga[86]	12 863
13-08-2005	Cerezo Osaka	D	2-2	H	JLCqf	Fernandinho[17], Araujo[89]	11 155
20-08-2005	Albirex Niigata	L	2-4	A	JL	Araujo[33], Oguro[85]	41 126
24-08-2005	Jubilo Iwata	W	3-1	H	JL	Fernandinho[66], Araujo 2[73 84]	19,129
27-08-2005	Yokohama F.Marinos	W	3-2	H	JL	Watanabe 2[38 89], Oguro[72]	15 071
31-08-2005	Yokohama F.Marinos	W	1-0	H	JLCsf	Araujo[82]	7 049
3-09-2005	Tokyo Verdy 1969	W	1-0	A	JL	Araujo[77]	14 177
10-09-2005	Sanfrecce Hiroshima	W	4-2	H	JL	Araujo 3[15 51 59], Endo[26]	13 942
17-09-2005	Kashiwa Reysol	L	1-2	A	JL	Araujo[13]	11 948
24-09-2005	Kashima Antlers	D	3-3	H	JL	Araujo 2[23 89], Oguro[51]	22 884
2-10-2005	Shimizu S-Pulse	W	4-1	A	JL	OG[31], Fernandinho[41], Oguro[49], Araujo[77]	14 444
5-10-2005	Yokohama F.Marinos	L	0-1	A	JLCsf	W 4-1p	11 370
15-10-2005	Vissel Kobe	W	4-1	A	JL	Araujo 2[40 89], Endo[64], Yoshihara[68]	22 069
22-10-2005	Oita Trinita	L	1-2	H	JL	Endo[74]	18 374
30-10-2005	FC Tokyo	L	1-2	A	JL	Sidiclei[1]	34 848
5-11-2005	JEF United Chiba	D	0-0	N	JLCf	L 4-5p	45 039
9-11-2005	Yokohama FC	D	3-3	H	ECr4	Yamaguchi[55], Oguro[89], Miki[119]	2 735
12-11-2005	Urawa Reds	W	2-1	H	JL	Fernandinho[29], Araujo[83]	20 811
20-11-2005	Nagoya Grampus Eight	L	1-2	A	JL	Endo[36]	22 110
23-11-2005	Omiya Ardija	L	0-1	A	JL		10 623
26-11-2005	JEF United Chiba	L	1-2	H	JL	Endo[29]	20 833
3-12-2005	Kawasaki Frontale	W	4-2	A	JL	Araujo 2[12 89], Miyamoto[56], Endo[79]	23 113
17-12-2005	Kashiwa Reysol	W	5-3	H	ECr5	Terada[50], Oguro[75], Araujo 2[85 89], Matsunami[87]	6 618
24-12-2005	Cerezo Osaka	L	1-3	H	ECqf	Sidiclei[58]	

JL = J.League • JLC = J.League Cup • EC = Emperor's Cup
gB = Group B • r4 = fourth round • r5 = fifth round • qf = quarter-final • sf = semi-final • F = final
H = Expo '70 • **H** = Kanazawa • **A** = Nagai, Osaka • N = National Stadium, Tokyo

URAWA REDS 2005

Date	Opponents	Score		Comp	Scorers	Att
5-03-2005	Kashima Antlers	L	0-1	H	JL		52 789
12-03-2005	Kawasaki Frontale	D	3-3	A	JL	Sakai [21], Okano [80], Tanaka.MT [89]	24 332
19-03-2005	Vissel Kobe	W	2-1	A	JLCgA	Yamada [37], Emerson [42]	12 748
26-03-2005	Omiya Ardija	W	2-1	H	JLCgA	Tanaka.T [15], Emerson [23]	17 494
2-04-2005	Oita Trinita	L	0-1	A	JL		28 847
9-04-2005	Gamba Osaka	D	1-1	H	JL	Horinouchi [32]	51 249
13-04-2005	Shimizu S-Pulse	D	1-1	H	JL	Hasebe [43]	15 760
16-04-2005	FC Tokyo	W	2-0	A	JL	Emerson [48], Horinouchi [74]	40 113
23-04-2005	Cerezo Osaka	L	1-2	H	JL	Yokoyama [62]	18 850
28-04-2005	Jubilo Iwata	D	2-2	A	JL	Nagai [44], Emerson [86]	30 865
1-05-2005	Nagoya Grampus Eight	W	3-0	H	JL	Tanaka.T [35], Emerson 2 [38 64]	55 476
4-05-2005	Vissel Kobe	W	1-0	A	JL	Tanaka.T [29]	25 104
8-05-2005	JEF United Chiba	D	0-0	H	JL		50 643
15-05-2005	Yokohama F.Marinos	W	1-0	A	JL	Nagai [76]	53 097
21-05-2005	Albirex Niigata	W	2-1	H	JLCgA	Emerson [6], Suzuki [60]	30 744
28-05-2005	Vissel Kobe	W	1-0	H	JLCgA	Emerson [89]	16 735
4-06-2005	Omiya Ardija	W	3-1	A	JLCgA	Suzuki [10], Emerson [27], Tanaka.T [32]	26 397
11-06-2005	Albirex Niigata	L	0-3	A	JLCgA		39 154
3-07-2005	Albirex Niigata	W	2-1	H	JL	Yamada [58], Tanaka [64]	39 656
6-07-2005	Tokyo Verdy 1969	W	7-0	A	JL	Hasebe [8], Tanaka.MT [27], Yamada [42], Nagai [47], Tanaka.T [51], Hirakawa 2 [53 59]	22 953
9-07-2005	Omiya Ardija	L	1-2	H	JL	Tanaka.MT [44]	50 437
13-07-2005	Kashiwa Reysol	L	0-3	A	JL		23 684
18-07-2005	Sanfrecce Hiroshima	W	2-0	H	JL	Tanaka.MT [21], Tanaka.T [55]	35 658
23-07-2005	Shimizu S-Pulse	W	1-0	A	JL	Tanaka.MT [55]	21 730
6-08-2005	Shimizu S-Pulse	W	1-0	A	JLCqf	Hasebe [36]	12 572
14-08-2005	Shimizu S-Pulse	W	1-0	H	JLCqf	Hasebe [88]	31 754
20-08-2005	FC Tokyo	W	2-1	H	JL	Nagai [39], Ponte [54]	44 400
24-08-2005	Vissel Kobe	D	2-2	H	JL	Nagai [51], Ponte [89]	16 173
27-08-2005	Nagoya Grampus Eight	W	2-0	A	JL	Tanaka.MT [16], Maric [30]	18 817
31-08-2005	JEF United Chiba	L	1-3	H	JLCsf	Ponte [44]	17 265
3-09-2005	Kashima Antlers	D	2-2	A	JL	Tanaka.T [77], Ponte [86]	35 467
10-09-2005	Oita Trinita	L	1-2	H	JL	Tanaka.T [28]	35 198
18-09-2005	Sanfrecce Hiroshima	W	4-3	A	JL	Nagai [32], Ponte [44], OG [62], Nene [70]	26 083
24-09-2005	Yokohama F.Marinos	D	0-0	H	JL		49 800
2-10-2005	Cerezo Osaka	L	1-3	A	JL	Maric [74]	23 555
5-10-2005	JEF United Chiba	D	2-2	A	JLCsf	Tanaka.MT [19], Tanaka.T [27]	11 286
15-10-2005	Kashiwa Reysol	W	7-0	H	JL	Ponte [23], Tanaka.T [49], Maric 3 [54 57 63], Sakai [67], Yokoyama [89]	16 865
22-10-2005	Omiya Ardija	W	3-1	A	JL	Santos [3], Tanaka [53], Maric [69]	30 038
29-10-2005	Kashiwa Reysol	W	3-2	H	JL	Santos 2 [8 34], Tanaka.MT [76]	37 593
3-11-2005	Montedio Yamagata	W	2-1	H	ECr4	Maric 2	
12-11-2005	Gamba Osaka	L	1-2	A	JL	Santos [85]	20 811
20-11-2005	Tokyo Verdy 1969	W	4-1	H	JL	Ponte 2 [14 87], Maric [79], Tanaka.MT [89]	43 636
23-11-2005	JEF United Chiba	L	0-1	A	JL		16 261
26-11-2005	Jubilo Iwata	W	1-0	H	JL	OG [79]	54 883
3-12-2005	Albirex Niigata	W	4-0	A	JL	Horinouchi [4], Ponte [13], Maric [60], Yamada [80]	41 988
10-12-2005	FC Tokyo	W	2-0	H	ECr5	Maric, Yamada	
24-12-2005	Kawasaki Frontale	W	2-0	H	ECqf	Maric [68], Horinouchi [83]	
29-12-2005	Omiya Ardija	W	4-2	N	ECsf	Maric [23], Hasebe 2 [62 102], Yamada [95]	
1-01-2006	Shimizu S-Pulse	W	2-1	N	ECf	Horinouchi [39], Maric [73]	51 536

JL = J.League • JLC = J.League Cup • EC = Emperor's Cup
gA = Group A • r4 = fourth round • r5 = fifth round • qf = quarter-final • sf = semi-final • f = final
H = Saitama Stadium 2002, Saitama • **H** = Urawa Komaba, Saitama • **A** = Saitama Stadium 2002, Saitama• N = National Stadium, Tokyo

KAZ – KAZAKHSTAN

NATIONAL TEAM RECORD
JULY 1ST 2002 TO JULY 9TH 2006

PL	W	D	L	F	A	%
28	2	6	20	24	59	17.9

FIFA/COCA-COLA WORLD RANKING

1993	1994	1995	1996	1997	1998	1999	2000	2001	2002	2003	2004	2005	High	Low
-	153	163	156	107	102	123	120	98	117	136	147	137	**98** 12/01	**166** 05/96

2005–2006											
08/05	09/05	10/05	11/05	12/05	01/06	02/06	03/06	04/06	05/06	06/06	07/06
148	146	140	139	137	137	137	134	136	135	-	140

Kazakhstan's move to UEFA may have switched the national team's focus away from Asia to Europe but the wins over Central Asian neighbours Tajikistan and Kyrgyzstan in July 2006 provided welcome relief for the Kazakhs. It ended a run of 29 matches without a win stretching back to 2001. The true test of the progress made by the national team, however, will only come with that elusive first win over European opposition, although an earlier run of 13 successive defeats was halted with a 0-0 draw against Georgia in the 2006 FIFA World Cup™ qualifiers. The Football Union has been stringent in making sure that clubs in the country meet the UEFA Licensing

INTERNATIONAL HONOURS
None

standards and have clamped down on those who have failed to pay their players or their taxes. Kairat Almaty were the first Kazakh club to play in the UEFA Champions League and in their first game beat Slovakia's Artmedia 2-0 before losing the return 4-1, a good performance given Artmedia's later results in the competition. Aktobe Lento were surprise first time champions in the League, beating off the challenge of Tobol Kostanay thanks to a 3-0 win against Vostock on the final day of the season. Bolat Temirtau on the other hand won just one point all season! Zhenis Astana beat Kairat in the Cup Final thanks to an extra-time winner from Mendes.

THE FIFA BIG COUNT OF 2000

	Male	Female		Male	Female
Registered players	6 240	120	Referees	75	0
Non registered players	75 000	0	Officials	2 900	0
Youth players	15 040	120	Total involved	99 495	
Total players	96 520		Number of clubs	119	
Professional players	890	60	Number of teams	318	

The Football Union of Kazakhstan (FSK)
Satpayev Street 29/3, Almaty 480 072, Kazakhstan
Fax +7 3272 921885
kfo@mail.online.kz   www.fsk.kz
President: ALIYEV Rakhat   General Secretary: AKHMETOV Askar
Vice-President: PIJPERS Arno   Treasurer: TBD   Media Officer: KEPLIN Alexander
Men's Coach: TIMOFEYEV Sergei   Women's Coach: JAMANTAYEV Aitpay
FSK formed: 1914   AFC: 1994-2002, UEFA: 2002   FIFA: 1994
Blue shirts with yellow trimmings, Blue shorts, Yellow socks or Yellow shirts with blue trimmings, Yellow shorts, Blue socks

RECENT INTERNATIONAL MATCHES PLAYED BY KAZAKHSTAN

2002	Opponents	Score		Venue	Comp	Scorers	Att	Referee
7-07	Estonia	D	1-1	Almaty	Fr	Litvinenko [38]	15 000	Kapanin KAZ
2003								
12-02	Malta	D	2-2	Ta'Qali	Fr	Zhumaskaliyev [72], Tarasov [83]	200	Rogalla SUI
27-04	Faroe Islands	L	2-3	Toftir	Fr	Lunev [56], Mumanov [76]	420	Jakobsson ISL
29-04	Faroe Islands	L	1-2	Tórshavn	Fr	Lovchev [6p]	800	Bergmann ISL
6-06	Poland	L	0-3	Poznan	Fr		6 000	Fisker DEN
20-08	Portugal	L	0-1	Chaves	Fr		8 000	Rodriguez Santiago ESP
2004								
18-02	Latvia	L	1-3	Larnaca	Fr	Aksenov [23]	500	Constantinou CYP
19-02	Armenia	D	3-3	Paphos	Fr	Zhumaskaliyev 2 [53 75], Finonchenko [76]. W 3-2p	100	Loizou CYP
21-02	Cyprus	L	1-2	Larnaca	Fr	Uzdenov [68]	300	Lajaks LVA
28-04	Azerbaijan	L	2-3	Almaty	Fr	Karpovich [55], Lunev [77]	20 000	Chynybekov KGZ
8-09	Ukraine	L	1-2	Almaty	WCq	Karpovich [34]	23 000	Alves Garcia POR
9-10	Turkey	L	0-4	Istanbul	WCq		39 900	Hrinak SVK
13-10	Albania	L	0-1	Almaty	WCq		12 300	Stuchlik AUT
17-11	Greece	L	1-3	Piraeus	WCq	Baltiyev [88]	31 838	Kostadinov BUL
2005								
29-01	Japan	L	0-4	Yokohama	Fr		46 941	
26-03	Denmark	L	0-3	Copenhagen	WCq		20 980	Gilewski POL
4-06	Ukraine	L	0-2	Kyiv	WCq		45 000	Lehner AUT
8-06	Turkey	L	0-6	Almaty	WCq		20 000	Kassai HUN
17-08	Georgia	L	1-2	Almaty	WCq	Kenzhekhanov [23]	9 000	Havrilla SVK
3-09	Albania	L	1-2	Tirana	WCq	Nizovtsev [62]	3 000	Slupik POL
7-09	Greece	L	1-2	Almaty	WCq	Zhalmagambetov [53]	18 000	Tudor ROU
8-10	Georgia	D	0-0	Tbilisi	WCq		BCD	Hyytia FIN
12-10	Denmark	L	1-2	Almaty	WCq	Kuchma [86]	8 050	Trivkovic CRO
2006								
14-02	Jordan	D	0-0	Amman	Fr			
28-02	Finland	D	0-0	Larnaca	Fr	W 3-1p		
1-03	Greece	L	0-2	Nicosia	Fr		2 000	Kailis CYP
2-07	Tajikistan	W	4-1	Almaty	Fr	Zhumaskaliev [22], Familtsev [40], Kuchma [63], Tleshev [90]		
5-07	Kyrgyzstan	W	1-0	Almaty	Fr	Baltiev [20p]		

Fr = Friendly match • EC = UEFA EURO 2004™ • WC = FIFA World Cup™ • q = qualifier • BCD = behind closed doors

KAZAKHSTAN NATIONAL TEAM RECORDS AND RECORD SEQUENCES

Records			Sequence records					
Victory	7-0	PAK 1997	Wins	4	1997	Clean sheets	3	1994-1995
Defeat	1-5	JPN 1997	Defeats	13	2004-2005	Goals scored	7	2000-2001
Player Caps	34	BALTIYEV Ruslan	Undefeated	7	2001-2003	Without goal	5	1994-1995
Player Goals	12	ZUBAREV Viktor	Without win	29	2001-2006	Goals against	16	2002-

KAZAKHSTAN COUNTRY INFORMATION

Capital	Astana	Independence	1991 from USSR	GDP per Capita	$6 300
Population	15 143 704	Status	Republic	GNP Ranking	61
Area km²	2 717 300	Language	Kazakh, Russian	Dialling code	+7
Population density	5 per km²	Literacy rate	98%	Internet code	.kz
% in urban areas	60%	Main religion	Muslim 47%, Orthodox 44%	GMT +/-	+4
Towns/Cities ('000)	Almaty 1 204; Shymkent 414; Karagandy 431; Taraz 358; Astana 345; Pavlodar 329; Oskamen (Ost-Kamenogorsk) 319; Semey (Semipalatinsk) 292; Aktobe 262; Kostanay 230; Uralsk 230; Petropavl (Petropavlovsk) 200; Atyrau 146; Ekibastuz 144; Kokshetau 124;				
Neighbours (km)	Russia 6 846; China 1 533; Kyrgyzstan 1 051; Uzbekistan 2 203; Turkmenistan 379				
Main stadia	Ortalyk Tsentralnyi – Almaty 26 250; Kazhimukana Munaytpasova – Astana 12 343				

KAZAKHSTAN 2005

SUPERLEAGUE

	Pl	W	D	L	F	A	Pts	Aktobe	Tobol	Kairat	Shakhter	Irtysh	Ordabasy	Yesil	Zhenis	Okzhetpes	Atyrau	Taraz	Ekibast'ts	Alma-Ata	Vostock	Zhetysu	Bolat
Aktobe Lento †	30	22	4	4	50	27	**70**		2-1	2-1	2-1	3-1	1-0	2-0	2-1	2-1	1-0	2-0	2-0	4-3	3-0	2-1	3-1
Tobol Kostanai ‡	30	21	6	3	53	21	**69**	3-0		2-1	1-0	2-1	3-0	2-1	1-1	1-0	3-2	1-0	1-1	5-0	2-1	4-1	5-0
Kairat Almaty	30	18	8	4	56	22	**62**	2-0	0-0		2-1	1-0	3-0	3-0	1-1	1-0	3-0	4-1	2-1	1-1	3-0	1-1	5-0
Shakhter Karagandy	30	19	2	9	37	22	**59**	1-1	2-0	2-0		1-0	1-0	1-0	0-1	1-0	2-1	1-0	2-0	1-0	3-0	2-1	3-0
Irtysh Pavlodar	30	18	3	9	51	24	**57**	1-0	1-2	0-1	6-1		2-0	2-1	1-0	3-0	1-0	5-1	1-0	3-2	4-1	3-0	
Ordabasy Shymkent	30	14	7	9	30	27	**49**	0-0	1-4	0-1	2-0	1-0		2-0	0-0	2-0	2-1	1-0	2-1	1-0	3-2	2-1	1-0
Yesil-Bogatyr Petropavl	30	15	3	12	38	25	**48**	0-1	1-1	2-2	1-0	1-0	1-0		1-0	2-0	0-0	3-0	2-1	0-2	1-0	4-0	7-0
Zhenis Astana	30	11	10	9	35	23	**43**	0-2	4-0	1-2	1-0	1-1	1-1	1-0		0-1	2-0	1-1	2-0	2-0	3-0	0-0	4-0
Okzhetpes Kokshetau	30	11	4	15	26	32	**37**	0-1	1-2	0-0	0-1	0-2	1-1	1-4	0-0		3-1	1-0	3-1	1-0	3-1	4-0	
FK Atyrau	30	10	7	13	32	36	**37**	0-1	0-1	2-2	1-1	3-0	1-1	2-1	1-0	0-1		0-0	1-0	1-0	2-0	3-2	4-0
FC Taraz	30	10	6	14	32	36	**36**	3-4	0-1	0-1	1-3	1-1	0-0	1-0	1-1	1-0	6-1		1-0	2-1	0-1	3-2	3-0
Ekibastuzetc	30	8	10	12	30	32	**34**	1-2	0-0	2-2	0-1	0-0	1-0	1-0	1-1	1-0	1-1	1-0		1-1	2-0	1-1	4-1
Alma-Ata Almaty	30	9	3	18	30	43	**30**	3-1	0-2	1-0	0-2	0-1	2-3	0-1	3-2	2-0	0-1	0-1	0-0		2-0	1-2	3-2
Vostock Oskemen	30	9	1	20	24	49	**28**	0-2	0-2	0-2	1-0	0-2	1-0	1-5	0-1	2-1	1-2	1-0	0-2	1-1		4-2	3-0
Zhetysu Taldykorgan	30	4	7	19	28	60	**19**	1-1	0-0	0-3	0-1	0-2	1-1	0-2	0-1	2-0	1-1	0-2	3-4	0-2	0-2		3-2
Bolat Temirtau	30	0	1	29	15	88	**1**	1-1	0-1	2-6	0-2	0-3	1-2	0-1	1-2	0-3	0-2	0-2	1-4	1-2	0-2	1-2	

2/04/2005 - 6/11/2005 • † Qualified for the UEFA Champions League • ‡ Qualified for the UEFA Cup

FOOTBALL CUP OF KAZAKHSTAN 2005

Second round		Quarter-finals			Semi-finals			Final		
Zhenis Astana *	3									
Bolat Temirtau	0	**Zhenis Astana**	0	2						
Aktobe Lento	0	Yesil-Bogatyr *	1	0						
Yesil-Bogatyr *	1				**Zhenis Astana** *	2	2			
Vostock Oskemen *	1				FK Atyrau	2	0			
Tobol Kostanai	0	Vostock Oskemen	0	1						
Kaysar Kyzylorda *	0	**FK Atyrau** *	1	1				**Zhenis Astana** ‡		2
FK Atyrau	1							Kairat Almaty		1
FC Taraz	1									
Irtysh Pavlodar *	0	**FC Taraz** *	1	3						
Shakhter Karagandy	1	Zhetysu Taldykorgan	1	2						
Zhetysu Taldykorgan *	2				FC Taraz *	1	1			
Ordabassy Shymkent *	3				**Kairat Almaty**	2	2			
Alma-Ata Almaty	0	Ordabassy Shymkent *	0	0						
Okzhetpes Kokshetau	0	**Kairat Almaty**	2	1						
Kairat Almaty *	1									

* Home team in first leg • ‡ Qualified for the UEFA Cup

CUP FINAL

Kajimukan, Shymkent
11-11-2005, Att: 8 000, Ref: Holmatov

Scorers - Byahanski [19], Mendes [116] for Zhenis; Lutu [25] for Kairat

RECENT LEAGUE AND CUP RECORD

	Championship						Cup		
Year	Champions	Pts	Runners-up	Pts	Third	Pts	Winners	Score	Runners-up
1992	Kairat Almaty	37	Arsenal-SKIF	36	Traktor Pavlodar	36	Kairat Almaty	5-1	Fosfor Zhambul
1993	Ansat Pavlodar	34	Batyr Ekibastuz	30	Gornyak Khromtau	30	Dostyk Almaty	4-2	Taraz Zhambul
1994	Yelimay Semey	47	Ansat Pavlodar	41	Zhiger Shymkent	40	Vostock Oskemen	1-0	Aktyubinsk
1995	Yelimay Semey	67	Taraz Zhambul	62	Shakhtyor Karagandy	60	Yelimay Semipal'sk	1-0	Ordabasy Shymkent
1996	Taraz Zhambul	76	Irtysh Pavlodar	74	Yelimay Semey	74	Kairat Almaty	2-0	Vostock Oskemen
1997	Irtysh Pavlodar	56	FC Taraz	56	Kairat Almaty	53	Not played due to season readjustment		
1998	Yelimay Semey	63	Batyr Ekibastuz	59	Irtysh Pavlodar	57	Irtysh Pavlodar	2-1	Kaysar Kzyl-Orda
1999	Irtysh Pavlodar	76	Yesil Petropavlovsk	72	Kairat Almaty	64	Kaysar Kzyl-Orda	1-1 2-0p	Vostock Oskemen
2000	Zhenis Astana	74	Yesil Petropavlovsk	74	Irtysh Pavlodar	60	Kairat Almaty	5-0	Yesil Petropavlovsk
2001							Zhenis Astana	1-1 5-4p	Irtysh Pavlodar
2001	Zhenis Astana	81	FK Atyrau	70	Yesil Petropavlovsk	69	Kairat Almaty	3-1	Zhenis Astana
2002	Irtysh Pavlodar	71	FK Atyrau	63	Tobol Kostanay	52	Zhenis Astana	1-0	Irtysh Pavlodar
2003	Irtysh Pavlodar	78	Tobol Kostanay	76	Zhenis Astana	64	Kairat Almaty	3-1	Tobol Kostanai
2004	Kairat Almaty	83	Irtysh Pavlodar	79	Tobol Kostanay	77	FC Taraz	1-0	Kairat Almaty
2005	Aktobe Lento	70	Tobol Kostanay	69	Kairat Almaty	62	Zhenis Astana	2-1	Kairat Almaty

Irtysh beat Taraz 1-0 in a play-off in 1997 • Zhenis beat Petropavlovsk 2-0 in a play-off in 2000 • Two cup competitions were held in 2001

KEN – KENYA

NATIONAL TEAM RECORD
JULY 1ST 2002 TO JULY 9TH 2006

PL	W	D	L	F	A	%
57	20	21	16	76	67	53.5

FIFA/COCA-COLA WORLD RANKING

1993	1994	1995	1996	1997	1998	1999	2000	2001	2002	2003	2004	2005		High	Low
74	83	107	112	89	93	103	108	104	81	72	74	89		70 02/04	117 07/06

2005–2006											
08/05	09/05	10/05	11/05	12/05	01/06	02/06	03/06	04/06	05/06	06/06	07/06
80	87	90	92	89	90	91	94	94	95	-	117

Kenyan football's long-standing administrative malaise looks to be at an end after FIFA's intervention set up new structures for the country. The end of the impasse sets the tone for a revival in the fortunes of the country's national team, the Harambee Stars, as well as for the clubs. Plans for a professional league are in the works and the appointment of Frenchman Bernard Lama as new national coach suggests a revival of ambition. Kenya will certainly want to put the 2006 FIFA World Cup™ qualifying campaign behind them. Although they were just one place away from African Nations Cup qualification, in reality they lurched from game to game and were never in

INTERNATIONAL HONOURS

Gossage Cup 1926 1931 1941 1942 1944 1946 1953 1958 1959 1960 1961 1966 **Challenge Cup** 1967 1971 **CECAFA Cup** 1975 1981 1982 1983 2002 **CECAFA Club Championship** Luo Union 1976 1977, AFC Leopards 1979 1982 1983 1984 1997, Gor Mahia 1985, Tusker 1988 1989 2000 2001

the race. The national team lost four of their last five qualifying matches and went almost 500 minutes without a goal. A penalty shootout win for Ulinzi Stars over Tusker saw them win the League again for the third successive year but a ban from participating in continental competition for withdrawing in previous years precluded them from playing in the 2006 Champions League. Tusker, formerly know as Kenya Breweries, were also denied silverware in a controversial President's Cup Final when World Hope FC, a club jointly owned by a charity group, beat them 2-1.

THE FIFA BIG COUNT OF 2000

	Male	Female		Male	Female
Registered players	12 331	1 229	Referees	2 160	110
Non registered players	750 000	5 000	Officials	30 430	2 780
Youth players	36 864	3 686	Total involved	844 590	
Total players	909 110		Number of clubs	2 956	
Professional players	43	0	Number of teams	9 002	

Kenya Football Federation (KFF)
Nyayo Stadium, PO Box 40234, Nairobi, Kenya
Tel +254 2 602310   Fax +254 2 602294
www.none
President: SAMBU Alfred Wekesa   General Secretary: TBD
Vice-President: LAMA Bernard   Treasurer: TBD   Media Officer: None
Men's Coach: KHERI Mohammed   Women's Coach: None
KFF formed: 1960   CAF: 1968   FIFA: 1960
Red shirts with black trimmings, Red shorts, Red socks

RECENT INTERNATIONAL MATCHES PLAYED BY KENYA

2003	Opponents	Score		Venue	Comp	Scorers	Att	Referee
14-09	Rwanda	W	1-0	Kigali	Fr	Omondi [80]	10 000	
11-10	Tanzania	D	0-0	Dar es Saalam	WCq		8 864	Tessema ETH
15-11	Tanzania	W	3-0	Nairobi	WCq	Oliech 2 [9 32], Okoth Origi [30]	14 000	El Beltagy EGY
2-12	Eritrea	W	3-2	Kassala	CCr1	Omondi [27], Mathenge [91+], Mulama [93+]		
4-12	Uganda	D	1-1	Kassala	CCr1	Sunguti [93+]		
8-12	Rwanda	D	1-1	Khartoum	CCsf	Omondi [44]. L 3-4p		
10-12	Sudan	W	2-1	Khartoum	CC3p	Sunguti [24], Omondi [35]		
12-12	Egypt	L	0-1	Manama	Fr			
15-12	Iraq	L	0-2	Manama	Fr			
18-12	Bahrain	L	1-2	Manama	Fr	Omondi [65]		
21-12	United Arab Emirates	D	2-2	Abu Dhabi	Fr	Omolisi [86], Juma [90]		
2004								
16-01	Libya	L	0-2	Zawyan	Fr			
19-01	Libya	L	0-2	Tripoli	Fr			
26-01	Mali	L	1-3	Bizerte	CNr1	Mulama [58]	6 000	Tessema ETH
30-01	Senegal	L	0-3	Bizerte	CNr1		13 500	Abd El Fatah EGY
2-02	Burkina Faso	W	3-0	Bizerte	CNr1	Ake [50], Oliech [63], Baraza [83]	4 550	Sowe GAM
7-08	Uganda	D	1-1	Kampala	Fr	Obua [27p]	25 000	
18-08	Uganda	W	4-1	Nairobi	Fr	Baraza 2 [11 33], Sirengo [65], Omondi [85]	5 000	
4-09	Malawi	W	3-2	Nairobi	WCq	Barasa 2 [21 29], Oliech [25]	13 000	Mwanza ZAM
9-10	Botswana	L	1-2	Gaborone	WCq	Oliech [5]	16 500	Colembi ANG
17-11	Guinea	W	2-1	Nairobi	WCq	Oliech [10], Mukenya [61]	16 000	Abd El Fatah EGY
12-12	Sudan	D	2-2	Addis Abeba	CCr1	Simiyu [37], Baraza [73]		
14-12	Somalia	W	1-0	Addis Abeba	CCr1	Baraza [7]		
18-12	Uganda	D	1-1	Addis Abeba	CCr1	Obua [77p]		
22-12	Ethiopia	D	2-2	Addis Abeba	CCsf	Mururi [66], Baraza [85]. L 4-5p	50 000	Ssegonga UGA
25-12	Sudan	L	1-2	Addis Abeba	CC3p	Baraza [82]		
2005								
9-02	Morocco	L	1-5	Rabat	WCq	Otieno [93+]	40 000	Tamuni LBY
12-03	Rwanda	D	1-1	Nairobi	Fr	Mkenya [25]		
23-03	Ghana	D	2-2	Nairobi	Fr	Baraza [44], Sunguti [87]		
26-03	Botswana	W	1-0	Nairobi	WCq	Oliech [44]	15 000	Buenkadila COD
5-06	Guinea	L	0-1	Conakry	WCq		21 000	Mbera GAB
18-06	Morocco	D	0-0	Nairobi	WCq		50 000	Diatta SEN
17-08	Tunisia	L	0-1	Rades	WCq		60 000	Evehe CMR
3-09	Tunisia	L	0-2	Nairobi	WCq			Sowe GAM
8-10	Malawi	L	0-3	Blantyre	WCq		12 000	Codjia BEN
2006								

No international matches played in 2006 before July

Fr = Friendly match • CN = CAF African Cup of Nations • CC = CECAFA Cup • WC = FIFA World Cup™
q = qualifier • r1 = first round group • sf = semi-final • 3p = third place play-off • f = final

KENYA NATIONAL TEAM RECORDS AND RECORD SEQUENCES

Records			Sequence records					
Victory	9-0	TAN 1956	Wins	5	1993	Clean sheets	7	1983
Defeat	0-13	GHA 1965	Defeats	7	1932-1940	Goals scored	16	1931-1948
Player Caps	n/a		Undefeated	10	1997-1998	Without goal	5	1996
Player Goals	n/a		Without win	10	1984-1985	Goals against	16	1931-1948

KENYA COUNTRY INFORMATION

Capital	Nairobi	Independence	1963 from the UK	GDP per Capita	$1 000
Population	32 021 586	Status	Republic	GNP Ranking	84
Area km²	582 650	Language	Kiswahili, English	Dialling code	+254
Population density	55 per km²	Literacy rate	90%	Internet code	.ke
% in urban areas	28%	Main religion	Christian 78%, Muslim 10%	GMT +/–	+3
Towns/Cities ('000)	Nairobi 2 750; Mombasa 799; Nakuru 260; Eldoret 218; Kisumu 216; Ruiru 114; Thika 99				
Neighbours (km)	Ethiopia 861; Somalia 682; Tanzania 769; Uganda 933; Sudan 232; Indian Ocean 536				
Main stadia	Kasarani – Nairobi 60 000; Nyayo – Nairobi 20 000				

PRESIDENT'S CUP 2005

Second round		Quarter-finals		Semi-finals		Final	
World Hope	1						
Gor Mahia	0	World Hope					
Chemelil		Chemelil/Red Berets					
Red Berets				World Hope	1 0		
Mathare United	6			Mumias	1 0		
Shalimar	0	Mathare United	1				
Muruguru	0	Mumias Sugar	3				
Mumias Sugar	3					World Hope ‡	2
Coast Stars	0					Tusker	1
Nzoia Sugar †	3	Coast Stars	3				
Pipeline †	1	Securicor	0			CUP FINAL	
Securicor	0			Coast Stars	0 0		
Homegrown				Tusker	2 2		
Green Berets		Homegrown	0			12-11-2005	
Ramogi United	1	Tusker	1				
Tusker	2	† Withdrew • ‡ Qualified for the 2006 CAF Confederation Cup					

RECENT LEAGUE AND CUP RECORD

	Championship						Cup		
Year	Champions	Pts	Runners-up	Pts	Third	Pts	Winners	Score	Runners-up
1996	Kenya Breweries	71	AFC Leopards	65	Eldoret KCC	63	Mumias Sugar	1-0	Reli
1997	Utalii	66	Gor Mahia	64	Mumias Sugar	62	Eldoret KCC	4-1	AFC Leopards
1998	AFC Leopards	69	Mumias Sugar	66	Gor Mahia	60	Mathare United	2-1	Eldoret KCC
1999	Tusker						Mumias Sugar	3-2	Coast Stars
2000	Tusker	6	Oserian Fastac	4	Mumias Sugar	4	Mathare United	2-1	AFC Leopards
2001	Oserian Fastac	88	Mathare United	81	Mumias Sugar	68	AFC Leopards	2-0	Mathare United
2002	Oserian Fastac	†	Nzoia Sugar				Pipeline	1-0	Mumias Sugar
2003	Ulinzi Stars	†	Coast Stars				Chemelil	1-0	AFC Leopards
2004	Ulinzi Stars	†	Tusker				KCB	1-0	Thika United
2005	Ulinzi Stars	†	Tusker				World Hope	2-1	Tusker

† Championship play-offs • 2002: Oserian Fastac 2-2 1-0 Nzoia Sugar • 2003: Ulinzi Stars 3-3 4-2p Coast Stars • 2004: Ulinzi Stars 2-2 4-3p Tusker • 2005: Ulinzi Stars 0-0 4-2p Tusker • The original final in 2003 was won by Nzoia Sugar, who beat Tusker 2-1. It was declared void by the KFF after a number of clubs broke away. The 2003 Moi Golden Cup was also disrupted with Utalii beating Gor Mahia 2-1 in an alternative final. The dispute between the KFF, the breakaway clubs and the Kenyan Sports Ministry saw the 2004 season badly affected which lead to the intervention of FIFA and the creation of Stake-holders Transition Committee (STC). Two separate championships had been played but a play-off for all the leading clubs was organised to qualify for CAF competitions

KGZ – KYRGYZSTAN

NATIONAL TEAM RECORD
JULY 1ST 2002 TO JULY 9TH 2006

PL	W	D	L	F	A	%
18	7	2	9	18	21	44.4

FIFA/COCA-COLA WORLD RANKING

1993	1994	1995	1996	1997	1998	1999	2000	2001	2002	2003	2004	2005	High		Low	
-	166	172	168	140	151	159	174	164	171	157	150	157	121	07/06	175	11/03

2005–2006											
08/05	09/05	10/05	11/05	12/05	01/06	02/06	03/06	04/06	05/06	06/06	07/06
152	152	152	153	157	159	159	159	146	147	-	121

It was an eventful year for Kyrgyzstan with champions Dordoy-Dinamo making most of the headlines. In 2005 they qualified to take part in the inaugural AFC President's Cup, a tournament designed to give international experience to the lowest ranked clubs in the confederation. They rose to the challenge and reached the final where they played Regar TadAz from neighbours Tajikistan. They lost 3-0 but more than made amends in the 2006 edition. Once again they reached the final against Tajik opponents, but this time they won, beating Vakhsh 2-1 to land a first ever international title for Kyrgyzstan. Dordoy-Dinamo had won the double in 2005, beating SKA-Shoro in a

INTERNATIONAL HONOURS
None

championship play-off on penalties, and consigning Zhashtyk Kara-Su to a record fifth consecutive defeat in the Cup Final. Boris Podkorytov also coached the national team in the inaugural AFC Challenge Cup and although the national side couldn't quite match the achievements of Dordoy-Dinamo after being knocked out by Tajikistan in the semi-final, Podkorytov, captain Ruslan Sydykov and top scorer Roman Kornilov were all honoured with the award of the 'Pochetnaya Gramota', one of the highest civilian awards in the country. It was the first time the award had been given to footballers.

THE FIFA BIG COUNT OF 2000

	Male	Female		Male	Female
Registered players	1 392	22	Referees	101	2
Non registered players	27 060	220	Officials	1 279	19
Youth players	260	0	Total involved	30 355	
Total players	28 954		Number of clubs	20	
Professional players	0	0	Number of teams	1 109	

Football Federation of Kyrgyz Republic (FFKR)
Kurenkeeva Street 195, PO Box 1484, Bishkek 720 040, Kyrgyzstan
Tel +996 312 670573   Fax +996 312 670573
media@ffkr.kg   www.ffkr.kg
President: MURALIEV Amangeldi   General Secretary: BERDYBEKOV Klichbek
Vice-President: KUTUEV Omurbek   Treasurer: DJAMANGULOVA Raiham   Media Officer: TOKABAEV Kemel
Men's Coach: PODKORYTOV Boris   Women's Coach: UMATALIEVA Gulbara
FFKR formed: 1992   AFC: 1994   FIFA: 1994
Red shirts, Red shorts, Red socks

RECENT INTERNATIONAL MATCHES PLAYED BY KYRGYZSTAN

2002 Opponents	Score	Venue	Comp	Scorers	Att	Referee
No international matches played in 2002						
2003						
16-03 Afghanistan	L 1-2	Kathmandu	ACq	Gulov [60]		
20-03 Nepal	W 2-0	Kathmandu	ACq	Nikov 2 [27 47]		
29-11 Pakistan	W 2-0	Karachi	WCq	Boldygin [36], Chikishev [59]	10 000	Nesar BAN
3-12 Pakistan	W 4-0	Bishkek	WCq	Chikishev [18], Chertkov [28], Boldygin [67], Krasnov [9]	12 000	Mamedov TKM
2004						
18-02 Tajikistan	L 1-2	Bishkek	WCq	Berezovsky [12]	14 000	Lutfullin UZB
31-03 Syria	D 1-1	Bishkek	WCq	Ishenbaev.A [55]	17 000	Bose IND
5-06 Qatar	D 0-0	Doha	Fr			
9-06 Bahrain	L 0-5	Al Muharraq	WCq		2 800	Al Saeedi UAE
8-09 Bahrain	L 1-2	Bishkek	WCq	Kenjisariev [86]	10 000	Rungklay THA
13-10 Tajikistan	L 1-2	Dushanbe	WCq	Chikishev [84]	11 000	El Enezi KUW
10-11 Kuwait	L 0-3	Kuwait City	Fr			
17-11 Syria	W 1-0	Damascus	WCq	Amin [47]	1 000	Tongkhan THA
2005						
No international matches played in 2005						
2006						
2-04 Pakistan	L 0-1	Dhaka	CCr1		2 500	Shamsuzzaman BAN
6-04 Tajikistan	W 1-0	Dhaka	CCr1	Krasnov [22]	2 000	AK Nema IRQ
7-04 Macao	W 2-0	Dhaka	CCr1	Ablakimov [35], Ishenbaev.A [58]	1 000	Tan Hai CHN
9-04 Palestine	W 1-0	Dhaka	CCqf	Djamshidov [91]	150	U Win Cho MYA
13-04 Tajikistan	L 0-2	Dhaka	CCsf		2 000	Tan Hai CHN
5-07 Kazakhstan	L 0-1	Almaty	Fr			

Fr = Friendly match • AC = AFC Asian Cup • CC = AFC Challenge Cup • WC = FIFA World Cup™
q = qualifier • r1 = first round group • qf = quarter-final • sf = semi-final

KYRGYZSTAN NATIONAL TEAM RECORDS AND RECORD SEQUENCES

Records			Sequence records				
Victory	6-0	MDV 1997	Wins	3	2003, 2006	Clean sheets	3	2003
Defeat	0-7	IRN 1997	Defeats	8	1999-2001	Goals scored	7	2001-2004
Player Caps	30	SALO Vladimir	Undefeated	3	2003, 2006	Without goal	6	1994-1996
Player Goals	3	Four players	Without win	8	1999-2001	Goals against	8	1991-2001

KRYGYZSTAN COUNTRY INFORMATION

Capital	Bishkek	Independence	1991 from Soviet Union	GDP per Capita	$1 600
Population	5 081 429	Status	Republic	GNP Ranking	148
Area km²	198 500	Language	Kyrgyz, Russian	Dialling code	+996
Population density	25 per km²	Literacy rate	97%	Internet code	.kg
% in urban areas	39%	Main religion	Muslim 75%, Orthodox 20%	GMT +/–	+6
Towns/Cities ('000)	Bishkek 896; Os 230; Celabad 77; Karakol 70; Tokmak 63; Karabalta 63; Balikici 45				
Neighbours (km)	Kazakhstan 1 051; China 858; Tajikistan 870; Uzbekistan 1 099				
Main stadia	Spartak – Bishkek 23 000; Dynamo – Bishkek 10 000				

KYRGYZSTAN 2005

FIRST DIVISION

	Pl	W	D	L	F	A	Pts	Dordoy	SKA	Zhashtyk	Abdysh	Alay	Guardia	U-21	Al Fagir
Dordoy-Dinamo Naryn	24	19	3	2	67	12	60		0-0 1-2	3-1 4-0	2-0 3-0	6-1 4-0	4-2	2-0 2-0	3-0
SKA-Shoro Bishkek	24	19	3	2	55	12	60	0-3 0-0		4-1 4-1	0-0 7-1	3-0 4-0	1-0	1-0 3-1	3-0
Zhashtyk Kara-Su	24	12	2	10	47	39	38	0-0 0-4	0-1 0-1		4-1 4-0	0-0 5-1	4-0	5-1 3-2	2-0
Abdysh-Ata Kant	24	9	4	11	40	49	31	1-4 0-3	1-0 0-2	3-1 1-2		3-1 2-3	6-1	3-0 5-4	3-0
Alay Osh	24	7	4	13	37	56	25	1-0 2-3	0-2 2-3	2-5 2-4	1-1 1-1		6-1	1-0 5-2	3-0
Guardia Bishkek	14	5	1	8	18	37	16	1-6	0-3	2-0	2-4	3-2		0-0	3-0
Kyrgyzstan U-21	24	4	3	17	28	53	15	1-3 0-4	0-5 1-3	2-0 1-2	2-2 2-0	0-0 4-0	0-1		3-0
Al Fagir Aravan	14	1	0	13	4	38	3	0-3	0-3	0-3	0-2	0-3	1-2	3-2	

23/04/2005 - 29/10/2005 • Al Fagir withdrew after four matches • Guardia withdrew after completing the first round of matches • Zhayil Baatyr and Shumkar Kara-Su withdrew before the start • Championship play-off: Dordoy-Dinamo 1-1 4-2p SKA-Shoro (4-11-2005, Att: 5 000, Ref: Slambekov KAZ, Scorers - Sidikov [71] for Dordoy, Jumakeyev [7] for SKA) • Championship increased to 17 clubs in 2006 • Matches in bold were awarded

KYRGYZSTAN CUP 2005

Third round

Dordoy-Dinamo Naryn*	5
Guardia Bishkek	1
Alykul Osmonov Kainda	
Abdysh-Ata Kant	w-o
Happy Day Kant	0
Boo-Terek Talas *	2
Sher Bishkek *	1
SKA-Shoro Bishkek	5
Al Fagir Aravan *	1 3p
Alay Osh	1 2p
FK Batken	
Kurban-100 Kadamjay	w-o
Neftchi Kochkor-Ata	w-o
Shakhtyor Tash-Komur	
Asyl Jalal-Abad	0
Zhashtyk Kara-Su *	7

Quarter-finals

Dordoy-Dinamo Naryn	5 2
Abdysh-Ata Kant *	0 0
Happy Day Kant	0 0
SKA-Shoro Bishkek *	8 5
Al Fagir Aravan *	5 1
Kurban-100 Kadamjay	0 2
Neftchi Kochkor-Ata	
Zhashtyk Kara-Su	w-o

Semi-finals

Dordoy-Dinamo Naryn*	0 2
SKA-Shoro Bishkek	1 0
Al Fagir Aravan *	0 1
Zhashtyk Kara-Su	5 12

Final

Dordoy-Dinamo Naryn	1
Zhashtyk Kara-Su	0

CUP FINAL

Spartak Stadium, Bishkek
1-09-2005, Att: 7 200, Ref: Mashentsev

Scorer - Chikishev [77] for Dordoy-Dinamo

* Home team in first leg

RECENT LEAGUE AND CUP RECORD

	Championship						Cup		
Year	Champions	Pts	Runners-up	Pts	Third	Pts	Winners	Score	Runners-up
1992	Alga Bishkek	38	SKA Sokuluk	32	Alay Osh	27	Alga Bishkek	2-1	Alay Osh
1993	Alga-RIFF Bishkek	61	Spartak Tokmak	55	Alay Osh	53	Alga-RIFF Bishkek	4-0	Alga Bishkek
1994	Kant-Oil Kant	47	Semetey Kyzyl-Kiya	44	Ak-Maral Tokmak	43	Ak-Maral Tokmak	2-1	Alay Osh
1995	Kant-Oil Kant	31	AiK Bishkek	30	Semetey Kyzyl-Kiya	28	Semetey Kyzyl-Kiya	2-0	Dinamo Bishkek
1996	Metallurg Kadamjay	56	AiK Bishkek	56	Alay Osh	45	AiK Bishkek	2-0	Metallurg Kadamjay
1997	Dinamo Bishkek	46	Alga-PVO Bishkek	41	AiK Bishkek	40	Alga-PVO Bishkek	1-0	Alay Osh
1998	Dinamo Bishkek	36	SKA-PVO Bishkek	31	AiK Bishkek	28	SKA-PVO Bishkek	3-0	Alay Osh
1999	Dinamo Bishkek	54	SKA-PVO Bishkek	48	Polyot & Zhashtyk	47	SKA-PVO Bishkek	3-0	Semetey Kyzyl-Kiya
2000	SKA-PVO Bishkek	64	Dinamo Bishkek	52	Polyot Bishkek	48	SKA-PVO Bishkek	2-0	Alay Osh
2001	SKA-PVO Bishkek	66	Zhashtyk Kara-Su	57	Dordoy-Dinamo	53	SKA-PVO Bishkek	1-0	Zhashtyk Kara-Su
2002	SKA-PVO Bishkek	48	Zhashtyk Kara-Su	43	Dordoy-Dinamo	39	SKA-PVO Bishkek	1-0	Zhashtyk Kara-Su
2003	Zhashtyk Kara-Su	36	SKA-PVO Bishkek	31	Dordoy-Dinamo	29	SKA-PVO Bishkek	1-0	Zhashtyk Kara-Su
2004	Dordoy-Dinamo	98	SKA-Shoro Bishkek	93	Zhashtyk Kara-Su	77	Dordoy-Dinamo	1-0	Zhashtyk Kara-Su
2005	Dordoy-Dinamo	60	SKA-Shoro Bishkek	60	Zhashtyk Kara-Su	38	Dordoy-Dinamo	1-0	Zhashtyk Kara-Su

Play-off in 1996: Metallurg 1-0 AiK (now Guardia) • Play-off in 2005: Dordoy 1-1 4-2p SKA-Shoro • SKA-Shoro Bishkek previously named Alga Bishkek, Alga-PVO Bishkek then SKA-PVO Bishkek

KOR – KOREA REPUBLIC

NATIONAL TEAM RECORD
JULY 1ST 2002 TO JULY 9TH 2006

PL	W	D	L	F	A	%
68	31	18	19	107	52	58.8

Of all of the Asian qualifiers at the 2006 FIFA World Cup™ finals, Korea were once again the most impressive and although they missed out on qualifying from the group stages, they did win their first FIFA World Cup™ match on European soil. The season had started badly for the Koreans when they failed to win a game as hosts of the 2005 East Asian Football Federation Championship. That led to the replacement of coach Jo Bonfrere with his compatriot Dick Advocaat in September, nine months ahead of the finals. In Germany, after going a goal behind in their opening game against Togo, the team showed great spirit to fight back and win the game 2-1 but their best result was the heroic 1-1 draw with eventual finalists France. Again they went a goal behind but didn't panic, equalising through Manchester United's Park Ji Sung just before the end. The third match, against Switzerland, was the most disappointing and after going behind yet again, to a first half Philippe Senderos goal, a third fight back failed to produce the desired results and the Koreans were out, despite having won four points, a total that saw both Mexico and Australia qualify for the knock out rounds. A lack of European based players was cited as one reason for the failure to

INTERNATIONAL HONOURS
Qualified for the FIFA World Cup™ finals 1954 1986 1990 1994 1998 2002 2006 Qualified for the FIFA Women's World Cup finals 2003
AFC Asian Cup 1956 1960 Asian Games Football Tournament 1970 (shared) 1978 (shared) 1986 East Asian Championship 2003
AFC Youth Championship 1959 1960 1963 1978 1980 1982 1990 1996 1998 2002 2004 AFC U-17 Championship 1986 2002
AFC Champions League Daewoo Royals 1986, Ilhwa Chunma 1996, Pohang Steelers 1997 1998, Suwon Samsung Bluewings 2001 2002

go further but the Korean K-League does remain one of the strongest Leagues in Asia, attracting players from all over the world. The 2005 championship was won by Ulsan Hyundai who beat Incheon United 6-3 on aggregate to win their first title for nine years. Neither team had won either of the two stages of the championship, the first of which was won by Busan I'Park who then went went on to finish bottom of the second stage without winning a match - hardly the best preparation for the play-offs. Busan's loss of form coincided with their ignominious exit from the 2005 AFC Champions League. Having reached the semi-finals, they lost 5-0 at home to eventual winners Al Ittihad from Saudi Arabia. Not since 2002 has a Korean club won the tournament. The city of Ulsan nearly pulled off an unlikely double when K2 side Ulsan Mipo Dockyard made it to the FA Cup Final but against the backdrop of temperatures in double figures below freezing, which restricted the crowd to just over 1 000, they lost to Chonbuk Motors. In a new development, the 2006 season will see the first promotion and relegation between the K-League and K2. It also saw SK Bucheon move to the island of Jeju off the south coast of the mainland and the introduction of Gyeongnam FC as a new K-League club in the south-east of the country.

Korea Football Association (KFA)
1-131 Sinmunno, 2-ga, Jongno-Gu, Seoul 110-062, Korea Republic
Tel +82 2 7336764   Fax +82 2 7352755
fantasista@kfa.or.kr   www.kfa.or.kr
President: CHUNG Mong Joon Dr   General Secretary: KA Sam Hyun
Vice-President: KIM Ho Kon   Treasurer: CHUNG Dong Hwan   Media Officer: SONG Ki Ryong
Men's Coach: VERBEEK Pim   Women's Coach: AN Jong Goan
KFA formed: 1928   AFC: 1954   FIFA: 1948
Red shirts with blue trimmings, Blue shorts, Red socks

RECENT INTERNATIONAL MATCHES PLAYED BY KOREA REPUBLIC

2004	Opponents	Score		Venue	Comp	Scorers	Att	Referee
19-07	Jordan	D	0-0	Jinan	ACr1		26 000	Maidin SIN
23-07	United Arab Emirates	W	2-0	Jinan	ACr1	Lee Dong Gook [41], Ahn Jung Hwan [91+]	30 000	Irmatov UZB
27-07	Kuwait	W	4-0	Jinan	ACr1	Lee Dong Gook 2 [24 40], Cha Du Ri [45], Ahn Jung Hwan [75]	20 000	Maidin SIN
31-07	Iran	L	3-4	Jinan	ACqf	Seol Ki Hyun [16], Lee Dong Gook [25], Kim Nam Il [68]	20 000	Al Fadhli KUW
8-09	Vietnam	W	2-1	Ho Chi Minh City	WCq	Lee Dong Gook [63], Lee Chun Soo [76]	25 000	Yoshida JPN
13-10	Lebanon	D	1-1	Beirut	WCq	Choi Jin Cheul [8]	38 000	Irmatov UZB
17-11	Maldives	W	2-0	Seoul	WCq	Kim Do Heon [66], Lee Dong Gook [80]	64 000	Lazar SIN
19-12	Germany	W	3-1	Busan	Fr	Kim Dong Jin [16], Lee Dong Gook [71], Cho Jae Jin [87]	45 775	Mohd Salleh MAS
2005								
15-01	Colombia	L	1-2	Los Angeles	Fr	Chung Kyung Ho [2]	20 000	Fris
19-01	Paraguay	D	1-1	Los Angeles	Fr	Kim Jin Kyu [46]	9 000	Hall USA
22-01	Sweden	D	1-1	Carson	Fr	Chung Kyung Ho [70]	9 941	Stott USA
4-02	Egypt	L	0-1	Seoul	Fr		16 054	Huang Junjie CHN
9-02	Kuwait	W	2-0	Seoul	WCq	Lee Dong Gook [24], Lee Young Pyo [81]	53 287	Maidin SIN
20-03	Burkina Faso	W	1-0	Dubai	Fr	Kim Sang Sik		
25-03	Saudi Arabia	L	0-2	Dammam	WCq		25 000	Mohd Salleh MAS
30-03	Uzbekistan	W	2-1	Seoul	WCq	Lee Young Pyo [54], Lee Dong Gook [61]	62 857	Najm LIB
3-06	Uzbekistan	D	1-1	Tashkent	WCq	Park Chu Young [90]	40 000	Moradi IRN
8-06	Kuwait	W	4-0	Kuwait City	WCq	Park Chu Young [19], Lee Dong Gook [29] Chung Kyung Ho [55], Park Ji Sung [61]	15 000	Khanthama THA
31-07	China PR	D	1-1	Daejon	EAC	Kim Jin Kyu [74]	25 374	Nishimura JPN
4-08	Korea DPR	D	0-0	Jeonju	EAC		27 455	Ghahremani IRN
7-08	Japan	L	0-1	Daejon	EAC		42 753	Tan Hai CHN
14-08	Korea DPR	W	3-0	Seoul	Fr	Chung Kyung Ho [34], Kim Jin Ryong [36], Park Chu Young [68]		
17-08	Saudi Arabia	L	0-1	Seoul	WCq		61 586	Kunsuta THA
12-10	Iran	W	2-0	Seoul	Fr	Cho Won Hee [1], Kim Jin Kyu [90]	61 457	Al Ghamdi KSA
12-11	Sweden	D	2-2	Seoul	Fr	Ahn Jung Hwan [7], Kim Young Chul [51]	59 113	Wan Daxue CHN
16-11	Serbia & Montenegro	W	2-0	Seoul	Fr	Choi Jin Cheul [4], Lee Dong Gook [66]	40 127	
2006								
18-01	United Arab Emirates	L	0-1	Dubai	Fr			Al Hilali OMA
21-01	Greece	D	1-1	Riyadh	Fr	Park Chu Young [24]		Al Shehri KSA
25-01	Finland	W	1-0	Riyadh	Fr	Park Chu Young [46]	800	Al Jerman KSA
29-01	Croatia	W	2-0	Hong Kong	Fr	Kim Dong Jin [35], Lee Chin Soo [49]	16 841	Fong Yau Fat HKG
1-02	Denmark	L	1-3	Hong Kong	Fr	Cho Jae Jin [13]	13 971	Fong Yau Fat HKG
11-02	Costa Rica	L	0-1	Oakland	Fr			Vaughn USA
15-02	Mexico	W	1-0	Los Angeles	Fr	Lee Dong Gook [14]	64 128	Salazar USA
22-02	Syria	W	2-1	Aleppo	ACq	Kim D Heon [5], Lee Chin Soo [50]	35 000	Maidin SIN
1-03	Angola	W	1-0	Seoul	Fr	Park Chu Young [22]	63 255	Supian MAS
23-05	Senegal	D	1-1	Seoul	Fr	Kim Do Heon [74]	64 836	
26-05	Bosnia-Herzegovina	W	2-0	Seoul	Fr	Seol Ki Hyeon [50], Cho Jae Jin [92+]	64 835	
1-06	Norway	D	0-0	Oslo	Fr		15 487	Verbist BEL
4-06	Ghana	L	1-3	Edinburgh	Fr	Lee Eul Yong [50]	15 000	McDonald SCO
13-06	Togo	W	2-1	Frankfurt	WCr1	Lee Chun Soo [54], Ahn Jung Hwan [72]	48 000	Poll ENG
18-06	France	D	1-1	Leipzig	WCr1	Park Ji Sung [81]	43 000	Archundia MEX
23-06	Switzerland	L	0-2	Hannover	WCr1		43 000	Elizondo ARG

Fr = Friendly match • AC = AFC Asian Cup • EAC = East Asian Championship • WC = FIFA World Cup™
q = qualifier • r1 = first round group • qf = quarter-final • † Not a full international

KOREA REPUBLIC NATIONAL TEAM RECORDS AND RECORD SEQUENCES

Records			Sequence records					
Victory	16-0	NEP 2003	Wins	11	1975, 1978	Clean sheets	9	1970, 1988-1989
Defeat	0-12	SWE 1948	Defeats	3	Seven times	Goals scored	23	1975-76, 1977-78
Player Caps	135	HONG Myung Bo	Undefeated	32	1977-1978	Without goal	3	Four times
Player Goals	55	CHA Bum Kun	Without win	8	1981-1982	Goals against	11	1948-1953

KOREA REPUBLIC COUNTRY INFORMATION

Capital	Seoul	Independence	1945 from Japan	GDP per Capita	$17 800
Population	48 598 175	Status	Republic	GNP Ranking	13
Area km²	98 480	Language	Korean	Dialling code	+82
Population density	493 per km²	Literacy rate	98%	Internet code	.kr
% in urban areas	81%	Main religion	Christian 26%, Buddhist 26%	GMT +/–	+9
Towns/Cities ('000)	Seoul 10 349; Pusan 3 678; Inchon 2 580; Taegu 2 566; Taejon 1 475; Kwangju 1 416; Suwon 1 242; Koyang 1 195, Songnam 1 032; Ulsan 962; Puchon 829; Chonju 711; Ansan 650; Chongju 634; Anyang 634; Shihung 621; Changwon 526; Uijongbu 479; Chonan 365				
Neighbours (km)	North Korea 238; Sea of Japan & Yellow Sea 2 413				
Main stadia	Olympic Stadium – Seoul 69 841; Seoul Sang-am World Cup Stadium – Seoul 64 677				

CLUB DIRECTORY

Club	Town/City	Stadium	Capacity	www.	Lge	Cup	CL
Jeju United (1)	Seogwipo	World Cup Stadium	42 256	skfc.com	1	0	0
Busan I-Park (2)	Busan	Busan Asiad Main Stadium	55 982	busanipark.co.kr	4	1	0
Chonbuk Hyundai Motors	Jeonju	Jeonju World Cup Stadium	42 477	hyundai-motorsfc.com	0	3	0
Chunnam Dragons	Gwangyang	Gwangyang Football Stadium	14 284	dragons.co.kr	0	1	0
Daegu FC	Daegu	Daegu World Cup Stadium	68 014	daegufc.co.kr	0	0	0
Daejeon Citizen	Daejeon	Daejeon World Cup Stadium	42 176	fcdaejeon.com	0	1	0
Gyeongnam FC	Changwon	Changwon City Stadium	27 085	gsndfc.co.kr	0	0	0
Gwangju Sangmu Phoenix	Gwangju	Guus Hidink Stadium	42 880	gwangjusmfc.co.kr	0	0	0
Incheon United	Incheon	Incheon Munhak	51 179	incheonutd.com	0	0	0
Pohang Steelers (3)	Pohang	Steel Yard	25 000	steelers.co.kr	3	1	2
Seongnam Ilhwa Chunma (4)	Seongnam	Seongnam Stadium	27 000	seongnamilhwafc.co.kr	6	1	1
FC Seoul	Seoul	Seoul World Cup Stadium	64 677	fcseoul.com	0	0	0
Suwon Samsung Bluewings	Suwon	Suwon World Cup Stadium	44 047	fcbluewings.com	3	1	2
Ulsan Hyundai Horang-i	Ulsan	Ulsan Big Crown	43 550	horangifc.co.kr	2	0	0

Name changes (1) Yukong Elephants → Puchong Yukong → Puchong SK → Bucheon SK→ Jeju United
(2) Daewoo Royals → Pusan Daewoo Royals → Pusan Icons → Busan Icons → Busan I-Park
(3) POSCO Dolphins → POSCO Atoms → Pohang Atoms → Pohang Steelers
(4) Ilhwa Chunma → Seongnam Ilhwa Chunma
(Others) Lucky Goldstar → Anyang LG Cheetahs

FIFA/COCA-COLA WORLD RANKING

1993	1994	1995	1996	1997	1998	1999	2000	2001	2002	2003	2004	2005		High		Low	
41	35	46	44	27	17	51	40	42	20	22	22	29		17	12/98	62	02/96

2005–2006											
08/05	09/05	10/05	11/05	12/05	01/06	02/06	03/06	04/06	05/06	06/06	07/06
23	26	29	29	29	29	31	31	30	29	-	56

THE FIFA BIG COUNT OF 2000

	Male	Female		Male	Female
Registered players	2 157	180	Referees	559	6
Non registered players	500 000	4 000	Officials	968	106
Youth players	13 182	879	Total involved	522 037	
Total players	520 398		Number of clubs	54	
Professional players	417	0	Number of teams	615	

KOREA REPUBLIC 2005
K-LEAGUE FIRST STAGE

	Pl	W	D	L	F	A	Pts
Busan I'Park	12	7	4	1	17	10	25
Incheon United	12	7	3	2	20	13	24
Ulsan Hyundai Horang-i	12	7	1	4	16	13	22
Pohang Steelers	12	6	3	3	14	11	21
FC Seoul	12	5	4	3	22	19	19
Seongnam Ilhwa Chunma	12	4	4	4	18	15	16
Bucheon SK	12	4	4	4	10	10	16
Daejeon Citizen	12	2	8	2	11	11	14
Suwon Samsung Bluewings	12	3	5	4	18	19	14
Chunnam Dragons	12	3	5	4	13	14	14
Chonbuk Hyundai Motors	12	2	3	7	13	19	9
Daegu FC	12	2	3	7	14	25	9
Gwangju Sangmu Phoenix	12	1	3	8	16	23	6

15/05/2005 - 10/07/2005

KOREA REPUBLIC 2005
K-LEAGUE SECOND STAGE

	Pl	W	D	L	F	A	Pts
Seongnam Ilhwa Chunma	12	8	3	1	22	9	27
Bucheon SK	12	8	2	2	16	8	26
Daegu FC	12	6	3	3	15	11	21
Ulsan Hyundai Horang-i	12	6	3	3	15	11	21
Incheon United	12	6	3	3	16	13	21
Pohang Steelers	12	5	4	3	14	11	19
Daejeon Citizen	12	4	4	4	8	9	16
Suwon Samsung Bluewings	12	3	5	4	11	13	14
FC Seoul	12	3	4	5	15	13	13
Chunnam Dragons	12	4	1	7	10	15	13
Gwangju Sangmu Phoenix	12	3	2	7	7	15	11
Chonbuk Hyundai Motors	12	2	3	7	11	22	9
Busan I'Park	12	0	3	9	11	21	3

24/08/2005 - 9/11/2005

KOREA REPUBLIC 2005
K-LEAGUE OVERALL

	Pl	W	D	L	F	A	Pts	Incheon	Seongnam	Ulsan	Bucheon	Pohang	Seoul	Daejeon	Daegu	Suwon	Busan	Chunnam	Chonbuk	Gwangju
Incheon United ‡	24	13	6	5	36	26	45		3-2	1-0	1-0	1-0	2-2	0-1	1-1	1-1	1-1	3-1	1-2	1-2
Seongnam Ilhwa Chunma †	24	12	7	5	40	24	43	4-2		1-2	2-1	2-2	4-1	2-0	2-0	1-0	0-2	1-1	1-0	2-1
Ulsan Hyundai Horang-i ‡	24	13	4	7	31	24	43	0-1	0-0		0-1	1-3	1-0	3-1	1-1	0-1	0-0	1-0	1-0	
Bucheon SK	24	12	6	6	26	18	42	2-1	1-3	2-3		0-0	1-0	1-1	1-0	2-1	1-2	0-0	3-1	2-0
Pohang Steelers	24	11	7	6	28	22	40	0-2	2-1	2-1	0-0		2-1	1-0	1-2	2-1	1-0	1-1	2-0	1-0
FC Seoul	24	8	8	8	37	32	32	2-2	0-0	1-1	0-0	4-1		2-2	1-1	2-1	1-1	2-0	2-0	3-5
Daejeon Citizen	24	6	12	6	19	20	30	0-1	0-0	2-1	1-0	0-0	0-0		2-1	1-1	2-1	1-1	2-1	0-1
Daegu FC	24	8	6	10	29	36	30	1-1	1-0	0-2	1-2	1-1	1-2	0-0		4-3	2-2	2-0	1-4	3-2
Suwon Samsung Bluewings	24	6	10	8	29	32	28	0-2	2-2	1-2	0-0	2-0	0-3	0-0	0-0		1-1	2-1	2-2	0-2
Busan I'Park †	24	7	7	10	28	31	28	2-3	1-2	2-3	0-1	0-0	1-2	1-1	2-1	1-2		0-1	2-1	3-2
Chunnam Dragons	24	7	6	11	23	29	27	0-1	0-2	1-2	1-2	2-1	1-3	1-0	4-1	0-2	0-1		1-1	2-0
Chonbuk Hyundai Motors	24	4	6	14	24	41	18	0-1	1-5	2-3	0-2	0-2	2-1	1-1	0-2	3-4	1-1	1-0		1-1
Gwangju Sangmu Phoenix	24	4	5	15	23	38	17	2-3	1-1	1-2	0-1	0-3	0-2	2-2	0-1	0-2	1-1	0-1	0-0	

† Qualified for the play-offs as stage winners • ‡ Qualified for play-offs thanks to overall record • Matches in bold played in the first stage

K-LEAGUE PLAY-OFFS 2005

Semi-finals

Ulsan Hyundai Horang-i	2
Seongnam Ilhwa Chunma *	1

Busan I'Park *	0
Incheon United	2

Finals

Ulsan Hyundai Horang-i †	5	1
Incheon United	1	2

* At home as stage winners
† Qualified for the 2006 AFC Champions Cup

K-LEAGUE PLAY-OFF 2005 1ST LEG
Incheon Munhak, Incheon, 27-11-2005

Incheon United 1 Radoncic [89]
Ulsan Hy. Horang-i 5 Machado 2 [13 58], Lee Chun So 3 [37 45 72]

Incheon: Kim Lee Sub, Kim Hak Chul, Lim Joong Yong, Jang Kyung Jin (Kim Chi Woo 61), Seo Dong Won, Jasmin Agic, Jeon Jae Ho, Noh Jong Keun (Choi Hyo Jin 40), Bang Seung Hwan (Lee Joon Young 69), Selmir dos Santos Bezerra, Dzenan Radoncic
Ulsan: Kim Ji Hyuk, Cho Se Kwon, Yoo Kyung Ryul, Bark Byung Kyu, Kim Jung Woo, Lee Ho (Kim Young Sam 86), Hyun Young Min, Lee Jong Min, Lee Chun Soo, Choi Sung Guk (Jang Sang Won 82), Leandro Machado (Noh Jung Yoon 76)

K-LEAGUE PLAY-OFF 2005 2ND LEG
Ulsan Big Crown, Ulsan, 4-12-2005

Ulsan Hy. Horang-i 1 Lee Chun Soo [18]
Incheon United 2 Radoncic 2 [14 26]

Ulsan: Kim Ji Hyuk, Cho Se Kwon, Yoo Kyung Ryul, Park Byung Kyu, Kim Jung Woo, Lee Ho, Hyun Young Min, Lee Jong Min, Lee Chun Soo, Choi Sung Guk (Noh Jung Yoon 83), Leandro Machado (Lee Jin Ho 57) (Jang Sang Won 90)
Incheon: Sung Kyung Mo, Kim Hak Chul, Lim Joong Yong, Lee Yo Han, Kim Chi Woo, Choi Hyo Jin, Jasmin Agic, Jeon Jae Ho, Selmir dos Santos Bezerra, Dzenan Radoncic

KOREA REPUBLIC 2005
K2-LEAGUE FIRST STAGE

	Pl	W	D	L	F	A	Pts
Suwon City Office	10	7	1	2	19	10	22
Ulsan Mipo Dockyard	10	6	3	1	25	15	21
Goyang Kookmin Bank	10	6	2	2	15	6	20
Gangneung City Office	10	5	2	3	13	11	17
Gimpo Hallelujah	10	5	2	3	11	12	17
Icheon Sangmu 2	10	4	3	3	11	8	15
Incheon Korail	10	4	1	5	10	11	13
Uijeongbu Hummel Korea	10	3	3	4	10	12	12
Changwon City Office	10	2	3	5	7	13	9
Daejeon Hydro & Nuclear	10	1	2	7	7	14	5
Seosan Citizen	10	1	0	9	4	20	3

5/04/2005 - 17/06/2005
Suwon qualified to meet second stage winners for the title

KOREA REPUBLIC 2005
K2-LEAGUE SECOND STAGE

	Pl	W	D	L	F	A	Pts
Incheon Korail	10	6	3	1	14	7	21
Icheon Sangmu 2	10	5	3	2	11	6	18
Goyang Kookmin Bank	10	4	3	3	13	7	15
Gimpo Hallelujah	10	4	3	3	19	15	15
Changwon City Office	10	4	3	3	16	15	15
Suwon City Office	10	3	5	2	16	13	14
Uijeongbu Hummel Korea	10	2	7	1	7	6	13
Ulsan Mipo Dockyard	10	3	3	4	13	14	12
Gangneung City Office	10	2	3	5	7	12	9
Seosan Citizen	10	1	6	3	8	15	9
Daejeon Hydro & Nuclear	10	0	3	7	6	20	3

8/07/2005 - 29/10/2005
Championship play-off: **Incheon Korail** 2-1 2-1 Suwon City Office

KOREA REPUBLIC 2005
SAMSUNG HAUZEN CUP

	Pl	W	D	L	F	A	Pts
Suwon Samsung Bluewings	12	7	4	1	20	11	25
Ulsan Hyundai Horang-i	12	6	5	1	17	11	23
Pohang Steelers	12	4	8	0	13	9	20
Bucheon SK	12	5	3	4	14	13	18
FC Seoul	12	5	2	5	18	18	17
Incheon United	12	4	3	5	9	10	15
Daegu FC	12	4	3	5	16	18	15
Seongnam Ilhwa Chunma	12	3	5	4	9	9	14
Chunnam Dragons	12	3	5	4	11	12	14
Daejeon Citizen	12	3	4	5	9	11	13
Gwangju Sangmu Phoenix	12	3	3	6	7	13	12
Chonbuk Hyundai Motors	12	2	5	5	12	14	11
Busan I'Park	12	2	4	6	8	14	10

6/03/2005 - 8/05/2005

RECENT LEAGUE CUP RECORD

Year	Winners
1992	Ilhwa Chunma
1993	POSCO Atoms
1994	Yukong Elephants
1995	Ulsan Horang-i
1996	Puchon Yukong
1997	Pusan Daewoo Royals
1998	Pusan Daewoo Royals
	Not organised from 1999-2003
2004	Seongnam Ilhwa Chunma
2005	Suwon Samsung Bluewings

Adidas Cup 1992-97 • Hauzen Cup 2003-

RECENT LEAGUE AND CUP RECORD

	Championship						Cup		
Year	Champions	Pts	Runners-up	Pts	Third	Pts	Winners	Score	Runners-up
1990	Lucky Goldstar	39	Daewoo Royals	35	POSCO Atoms	28			
1991	Daewoo Royals	52	Ulsan Horang-i	42	POSCO Atoms	39			
1992	POSCO Atoms	35	Ilhwa Chunma	34	Ulsan Horang-i	32			
1993	Ilhwa Chunma	68	Anyang Cheetahs	59	Ulsan Horang-i	56			
1994	Ilhwa Chunma	54	Yukong Elephants	51	POSCO Atoms	50			
1995	Ilhwa Chunma	†	Pohang Atoms						
1996	Ulsan Horang-i	†	Suwon Bluewings						
1997	Pusan Royals	37	Chunnam Dragons	36	Ulsan Horang-i	30	Pohang Steelers	0-0 7-6p	Suwon Bluewings
1998	Suwon Bluewings	†					Chunnam Dragons	1-0	Ilhwa Chunma
1999	Suwon Bluewings	59	Bucheon SK	47	Chunnam Dragons	38	Anyang Cheetahs	2-1	Ulsan Horang-i
2000	Anyang Cheetahs	†	Bucheon SK				Chonbuk Hyundai	2-0	Ilhwa Chunma
2001	Ilhwa Chunma	45	Anyang Cheetahs	43	Suwon Bluewings	41	Daejeon Citizen	1-0	Pohang Steelers
2002	Ilhwa Chunma	49	Ulsan Horang-i	47	Suwon Bluewings	45	Suwon Bluewings	1-0	Pohang Steelers
2003	Ilhwa Chunma	91	Ulsan Horang-i	73	Suwon Bluewings	72	Chonbuk Hyundai	2-2 4-2p	Chunnam Dragons
2004	Suwon Bluewings	†	Pohang Steelers				Busan Icons	1-1 4-3p	Bucheon SK
2005	Ulsan Horang-i	†	Incheon United				Chonbuk Hyundai	1-0	Ulsan Dockyard

† End of season play-offs: 1995 Seognam Ilhwa Chunma 1-1 3-3 1-0 Pohang Atoms • 1996 Ulsan Hyundai Horang-i 0-1 3-1 Suwon Samsung
Bluewings • 1998 Suwon Samsung Bluewings 1-0 0-0 Ulsan Hyundai Horang-i • 2000 Anyang LG Cheetahs 4-1 1-1 (4-2p) Bucheon SK
2004 Suwon Samsung Bluewings 0-0 0-0 4-3p Pohang Steelers • 2005 Ulsan Hyundai Horang-i 5-1 1-2 Incheon United

HANA BANK FA CUP 2004

First Round

Chonbuk Hyundai Motors	2	
Korea University	0	
Gimpo Halleujah	1	
FC Seoul	2	
Seongnam Ilhwa Chunma	3	
Jungang University	2	
Suwon City	1	3p
Suwon Samsung Bluewings	1	5p
Goyang Kookmin Bank	4	
Bongshin Club	0	
Aju University	2	
Incheon United	3	
Bucheon SK	3	
Gangneung City	0	
Uijeongbu Hummel	1	
Incheon Korail	2	
Chunnam Dragons	Bye	
Hannam University	1	
Ulsan Hyundai Horang-i	3	
Daejeon Hydro & Nuclear	1	
Changwon City	0	
Hongik University	0	
Daegu FC	1	
Pohang Steelers	2	
Honam University	1	
Konkuk University	1	
Gwangju Sangmu Phoenix	6	
Daejeon Citizen	3	
Daegu University	1	
Busan I'Park	1	2p
Ulsan Mipo Dockyard	1	3p

Second Round

Chonbuk Hyundai Motors	2	
FC Seoul	1	
Seongnam Ilhwa Chunma	1	
Suwon Samsung Bluewings	3	
Goyang Kookmin Bank	2	
Incheon United	1	
Bucheon SK	2	
Incheon Korail	4	
Chunnam Dragons	2	
Ulsan Hyundai Horang-i	1	
Daejeon Hydro & Nuclear	1	
Daegu FC	4	
Pohang Steelers	0	4p
Gwangju Sangmu Phoenix	0	3p
Daejeon Citizen	1	2p
Ulsan Mipo Dockyard	1	3p

Quarter-finals

Chonbuk Hyundai Motors	3	4p
Suwon Samsung Bluewings	3	2p
Goyang Kookmin Bank	1	
Incheon Korail	2	
Chunnam Dragons	2	
Daegu FC	1	
Pohang Steelers	0	3p
Ulsan Mipo Dockyard	0	4p

Semi-finals

Chonbuk Hyundai Motors	3
Incheon Korail	1
Chunnam Dragons	1
Ulsan Mipo Dockyard	3

Final

Chonbuk Hyundai Motors †	1
Ulsan Mipo Dockyard	0

CUP FINAL

World Cup Stadium, Seoul
17-12-2005, Att: 1 000
Scorer - Milton Rodríguez 13

Cheonbuk - Lee Kwang Suk, Choi Jin Chul, Kim Hyun Soo, Jung Jong Kwan, Raphael Jose Botti Zacarias Sena, Kim Jung Kyum, Milton Rodriguez, Wang Jung Hyun, Gu Hyun Seo, Jeon Kwang Hwan, Cho Jin Soo (Yoon Jung Kwan 65) **Ulsan Mipo** - Yang Ji Won, Kim Young Ki, Kim Jong Young, Park Hee Wan (Yang Ji Hoon 83), Son Sang Ho (Woo Ju Young 56), Lee Jae Chun, Lim Joon Sik, Jeon Sang Dae (Jung Min Mu 60), Jung Jae Suk, Cho Yong Suk, Chun Jung Hee

† Qualified for the 2006 AFC Champions Cup

KSA – SAUDI ARABIA

NATIONAL TEAM RECORD
JULY 1ST 2002 TO JULY 9TH 2006

PL	W	D	L	F	A	%
68	32	18	18	112	65	60.3

Only two nations at the 2006 FIFA World Cup™ finals named squads that consisted entirely of home based players - Italy and Saudi Arabia. The results were very different. Although the Saudis avoided the embarrassments of four year's previously, they never threatened to qualify from a group that looked to offer possibilities. Coaching stability does not seem to be a trait that the Saudis set much store by and after guiding the team to the finals, coach Gabriel Calderon was sacked after Saudi lost to Iraq in the semi-finals of the West Asian Games, just six months before the finals. His replacement was Marcos Paqueta, a double winner with Al Hilal in 2005 and coach of the Brazilian FIFA World Youth Championship winning team in 2003. Had it not been for an injury time equaliser by Tunisia in the opening game of the finals in Germany, it may well have been a different story for Saudi, but the 2-2 draw handed the advantage to Spain and the Ukraine, both of whom went on to beat the Saudis. Paqueta survived in his job after the first round exit and the hope is that he can develop the game in the Kingdom and take the national team back to the level it achieved at the 1994 FIFA World Cup™. Saudi Arabia's position as one of the leading lights of Asian football isn't

INTERNATIONAL HONOURS
Qualified for the FIFA World Cup™ finals 1994 1998 2002 2006
FIFA U-17 World Championship 1989
AFC Asian Cup 1984 1988 1996   AFC Asian Youth Cup 1986 1992   AFC Asian U-17 1985 1988
AFC Champions League Al Hilal 1992 2000, Al Ittihad 2004 2005

in doubt, however. In 2004 Jeddah's Al Ittihad become only the second Saudi club to win the AFC Champions League and they retained their title in 2005, helped by the fact that they received a bye through the group stages. They beat China PR's Shandong and Korea Republic's Busan I'Park to reach the final where they faced Al Ain from the UAE. Inspired by captain Mohammed Noor, Ittihad drew away in Al Ain thanks to a late Mohamed Kallon penalty and despite the sending off of Joseph-Desire Job in the return, they won 4-2 to reclaim the trophy. Ittihad were also impressive at the 2005 FIFA Club World Championship in Tokyo, ending Egyptian Club Al Ahly's 55 match unbeaten run before narrowly losing to São Paulo in the semi-finals. Despite their dominance at the continental level, Ittihad missed out on the Saudi championship for the third year running. They lost 2-1 in the play-offs to Al Hilal who in turn lost 3-0 to Riyadh neighbours Al Shabab in the final. Shabab had topped the table in the 22 match regular season to qualify directly for the final having gone the first 14 games unbeaten. Hilal were hoping to complete a treble having earlier won the Prince Faisal Ibn Fahd Cup and the Crown Prince Cup. In the latter they beat perennial runners-up Al Ahly 1-0 with a goal from Nawaf Al Temyat.

Saudi Arabian Football Federation (SAFF)
Al Mather Quarter, Prince Faisal Bin Fahad Street, PO Box 5844, Riyadh 11432, Saudi Arabia
Tel +966 1 4822240   Fax +966 1 4821215
www.saff.com.sa
President: HRH Prince Sultan bin Fahad BIN ABDULAZIZ   General Secretary: AL-ABDULHADI Faisal
Vice-President: HRH Prince Nawaf Bin Faisal B.F. BIN ABDULAZIZ   Treasurer: AL-ATHEL Abdullah
Men's Coach: MARCOS PAQUETA   Women's Coach: None
SAFF formed: 1959   AFC: 1972   FIFA: 1959
White shirts with green trimmings, Green shorts, White socks

RECENT INTERNATIONAL MATCHES PLAYED BY SAUDI ARABIA

2004	Opponents	Score		Venue	Comp	Scorers	Att	Referee
8-09	Turkmenistan	W	1-0	Ashgabat	WCq	Al Qahtani [47]	5 000	Kwon Jong Chul KOR
6-10	Syria	D	2-2	Riyadh	Fr	Muwaled [26], Suwaid [69p]		
12-10	Indonesia	W	3-1	Jakarta	WCq	Al Meshal [9], Sulaimani [13], Al Qahtani [80]	30 000	Mohd Salleh MAS
17-11	Sri Lanka	W	3-0	Dammam	WCq	Al Harthi [6], Al Shlhoub [45p], Fallata [65]	2 000	Muflah OMA
11-12	Kuwait	L	1-2	Doha	GCr1	Al Qahtani [13]		
14-12	Yemen	W	2-0	Doha	GCr1	Al Otaibi [34], Al Saweyed [47]		
17-12	Bahrain	L	0-3	Doha	GCr1			
2005								
25-01	Tajikistan	W	3-0	Riyadh	Fr	Edris [42], Al Jamaan [60], Al Saqri [66]		
29-01	Turkmenistan	W	1-0	Riyadh	Fr	Al Shamrani [90]		
2-02	Hungary	D	0-0	Istanbul	Fr		100	Dereli TUR
29-02	Uzbekistan	D	1-1	Tashkent	WCq	Al Jaber [76]	45 000	Kamikawa JPN
14-03	Egypt	L	0-1	Dammam	Fr			
18-03	Finland	L	1-4	Dammam	Fr	Al Basha [48]		
25-03	Korea Republic	W	2-0	Dammam	WCq	Khariri [29], Al Qahtani [74]	25 000	Mohd Salleh MAS
30-03	Kuwait	D	0-0	Kuwait City	WCq		25 000	Moradi IRN
27-05	Bahrain	D	1-1	Riyadh	Fr	Khariri [35]		
3-06	Kuwait	W	3-0	Riyadh	WCq	Al Shlhoub 2 [19 50], Al Harthi [82]	72 000	Kamikawa JPN
8-06	Uzbekistan	W	3-0	Riyadh	WCq	Al Jaber 2 [8 61], Al Harthi [88]	72 000	Huang Junjie CHN
17-08	Korea Republic	W	1-0	Seoul	WCq	Al Anbar [4]	61 586	Kunsuta THA
14-11	Ghana	L	1-3	Jeddah	Fr	Al Temyat [36]		
3-12	Palestine	W	2-0	Rayyan	WGr1	Al Sawailh [18], Al Mahyani [22]		
5-12	Iraq	L	1-5	Rayyan	WGr1	Al Qadhi [53]		
8-12	Iraq	L	0-2	Rayyan	WGsf			
2006								
18-01	Sweden	D	1-1	Riyadh	Fr	Haidar [70]		
21-01	Finland	D	1-1	Riyadh	Fr	Al Shlhoub [58]	3 000	Al Anzi KUW
25-01	Greece	D	1-1	Riyadh	Fr	Khaled Aziz [89]	60 000	Jassim Mohamed BHR
27-01	Lebanon	L	1-2	Riyadh	Fr	Al Mahyani [42]		
14-02	Syria	D	1-1	Jeddah	Fr	Al Khatani [40]		
22-02	Yemen	W	4-0	Sana'a	ACq	Al Sawailh 2 [14 89], Al Shlhoub 2 [77 92+]	55 000	Al Fadhli KUW
1-03	Portugal	L	0-3	Dusseldorf	Fr		8 430	Stark GER
15-03	Iraq	D	2-2	Jeddah	Fr	Al Temyat [19], Al Jaber [59]		Al Hamdan KSA
28-03	Poland	L	1-2	Riyadh	Fr	Redha Tukar [27]	2 000	Al Mutlaq KSA
11-05	Belgium	L	1-2	Sittard	Fr	OG [35]	3 283	Bossen NED
14-05	Togo	W	1-0	Sittard	Fr	Al Hawsawi [85]	400	Braamhaar NED
26-05	Czech Republic	L	0-2	Innsbruck	Fr		4 000	
31-05	Turkey	L	0-1	Offenbach	Fr		9 000	Fleischer GER
14-06	Tunisia	D	2-2	Munich	WCr1	Al Khatani [57], Al Jaber [84]	66 000	Shield AUS
19-06	Ukraine	L	0-4	Hamburg	WCr1	.	50 000	Poll ENG
23-06	Spain	L	0-1	Kaiserslautern	WCr1		46 000	Codjia BEN

Fr = Friendly match • AR = Arab Cup • AC = AFC Asian Cup • GC = Gulf Cup • WG = West Asian Games • WC = FIFA World Cup™
q = qualifier • r1 = first round group • sf = semi-final • f = final • GG = Golden Goal

SAUDI ARABIA NATIONAL TEAM RECORDS AND RECORD SEQUENCES

Records			Sequence records					
Victory	8-0	MAC 1993	Wins	11	2001	Clean sheets	9	2001
Defeat	0-13	EGY 1961	Defeats	6	1995	Goals scored	15	2001
Player Caps	170	AL DAEYEA Mohamed	Undefeated	19	2003-2004	Without goal	5	1998
Player Goals	67	ABDULLAH Majed	Without win	10	1988	Goals against	10	1981-1982

SAUDI ARABIA COUNTRY INFORMATION

Capital	Riyadh	Formation	1932	GDP per Capita	$11 800
Population	25 795 938	Status	Monarchy	GNP Ranking	23
Area km²	1 960 582	Language	Arabic	Dialling code	+966
Population density	13 per km²	Literacy rate	78%	Internet code	.sa
% n urban areas	80%	Main religion	Muslim	GMT + / −	+3
Towns/Cities ('000)	Riyadh 3 469; Jeddah 2 545; Mecca 1 199; Medina 824; Ad Damman 568; At Taif 514; Tabuk 355; Buraydah 341; Khamis Mushayt 276; Al Hufuf 266; Al Mubarraz 258; Ha'il 236				
Neighbours (km)	Jordan 744; Iraq 814; Kuwait 222; Qatar 60; UAE 457; Oman 676; Yemen 1 458; Persian Gulf & Red Sea 2 640				
Main stadia	King Fahd International − Riyadh 70 000; Prince Abdullah Al Faisal − Jeddah 24 000				

NATIONAL COACH

	Years
AL KHARASHI Mohammad	1999
PFISTER Otto	1999
MACALA Milan	2000
AL JOHOR Nasser	2000
SANTRAC Slobodan	2001
AL JOHOR Nasser	2002
VAN DER LEM Gerard	2002-'04
AL ABODULAZIZ Nasser	2004
CALDERON Gabriel	2004-'05
MARCOS PAQUETA	2005-

CLUB DIRECTORY

Club	Town/City	Stadium	Capacity	Lge	Cup	CL
Al Ahli	Jeddah	Prince Sultan bin Fahd	15 000	2	12	0
Al Ansar	Medina	Prince Mohammed bin Abdul Aziz	10 000	0	0	0
Al Hilal	Riyadh	Prince Faisal bin Fahd	27 000	10	11	2
Al Ittifaq	Dammam	Prince Mohamed bin Fahd	35 000	2	2	0
Al Ittihad	Jeddah	Prince Abdullah Al Faisal	24 000	6	10	2
Al Nasr	Riyadh	Prince Faisal bin Fahd	27 000	6	7	0
Ohod	Medina	Prince Mohammed bin Abdul Aziz	10 000	0	0	0
Al Qadisiya	Khobar	Prince Saud bin Jalawi	10 000	0	1	0
Al Riyadh	Riyadh	Prince Faisal bin Fahd	27 000	0	1	0
Al Shabab	Riyadh	Prince Faisal bin Fahd	27 000	5	3	0
Al Ta'ee	Ha'il	Prince bin Masaad bin Jalawi	10 000	0	0	0
Al Wahda	Mecca	King Abdul Aziz	33 500	0	2	0

FIFA/COCA-COLA WORLD RANKING

1993	1994	1995	1996	1997	1998	1999	2000	2001	2002	2003	2004	2005	High		Low	
38	27	54	37	33	30	39	36	31	38	26	28	33	21	07/04	81	07/06

2005-2006											
08/05	09/05	10/05	11/05	12/05	01/06	02/06	03/06	04/06	05/06	06/06	07/06
27	28	31	32	33	33	35	34	34	34	-	81

THE FIFA BIG COUNT OF 2000

	Male	Female		Male	Female
Registered players	6 402	0	Referees	602	0
Non registered players	100 000	0	Officials	612	0
Youth players	10 316	0	Total involved	117 932	
Total players	116 718		Number of clubs	153	
Professional players	458	0	Number of teams	700	

SAUDI ARABIA 2005–06

THE CUSTODIAN OF THE TWO HOLY MOSQUES LEAGUE CUP

	Pl	W	D	L	F	A	Pts	Shabab	Hilal	Ittihad	Ahli	Ittifaq	Nasr	Hazm	Qadisiya	Wahda	Ta'ee	Abha	Ansar
Al Shabab †	22	13	6	3	47	22	45		0-1	1-1	1-2	1-0	1-2	4-2	6-1	3-0	2-0	4-0	2-1
Al Hilal †‡	22	13	5	4	41	21	44	1-1		0-1	4-1	2-0	1-1	2-2	1-0	4-0	0-2	3-2	3-1
Al Ittihad ‡	22	11	9	2	47	28	42	1-2	2-2		2-2	1-1	1-1	0-2	2-0	2-1	1-0	1-0	5-2
Al Ahli ‡	22	9	9	4	45	23	36	2-2	2-3	1-1		0-1	3-0	3-0	1-1	0-1	2-0	7-1	4-0
Al Ittifaq	22	9	6	7	31	25	33	2-2	1-1	2-2	0-0		1-0	2-2	2-1	1-2	4-0	3-2	1-0
Al Nasr	22	7	9	6	32	32	30	1-3	1-2	1-1	1-1	1-0		4-2	0-0	1-1	3-2	1-0	1-1
Al Hazm Raas	22	7	8	7	33	37	29	0-0	1-2	3-7	1-1	1-3	2-2		1-1	2-3	1-1	3-1	2-0
Al Qadisiya	22	8	5	9	23	32	29	0-3	1-0	2-4	0-3	2-1	2-1	0-1		2-1	2-2	2-0	2-0
Al Wahda	22	7	7	8	35	37	28	1-1	1-2	1-1	1-5	2-3	3-2	0-1	1-1		3-1	2-2	0-0
Al Ta'ee	22	4	6	12	24	37	18	1-2	1-0	3-4	0-0	2-1	2-4	0-1	1-2	1-1		1-2	0-0
Abha	22	3	4	15	23	57	13	0-1	0-5	1-3	2-2	1-0	2-2	1-3	1-0	1-7	1-3		2-3
Al Ansar	22	1	6	15	16	46	9	3-5	3-2	0-4	1-3	0-2	1-2	0-0	0-1	1-3	1-1	1-1	

21/09/2005 - 1/04/2006 • † Qualified for the play-off final • †‡ Qualified for the play-off semi-final • ‡ Qualified for the play-off first round

SAUDI ARABIA 2005–06 FIRST DIVISION (2)

	Pl	W	D	L	F	A	Pts
Al Khaleej Saihat	26	17	3	6	43	18	54
Al Faysali	26	13	7	6	29	18	46
Al Riyadh	26	13	6	7	37	24	45
Dhemk	26	11	8	7	32	25	41
Najran	26	10	9	7	33	29	39
Al Watani	26	10	7	9	28	26	37
Al Jabalain	26	9	8	9	23	28	35
Hajr	26	9	8	9	28	35	35
Faiha'a	26	5	15	6	28	29	30
Al Fat'h	26	8	6	12	31	35	30
Al Taawun Beraida	26	8	6	12	29	34	30
Al Sho'ala Karj	26	8	4	14	19	33	28
Ohod	26	7	5	14	27	40	26
Al Ra'ed Beraida	26	4	8	14	27	40	20

26/09/2005 - 13/04/2006

CHAMPIONSHIP PLAY-OFFS 2005–06

First round		Semi-final		Final	
		Al Hilal	2		
Al Ahli	0	Al Ittihad	1		
Al Ittihad	3			Al Shabab ‡	3
				Al Hilal	0

21-04-2006
Scorers - Zaid Al Muallad [49p], Abdu Othaif [53], Nasser Al Shamrani [83]

‡ Qualified for the 2007 AFC Champions League

CROWN PRINCE CUP 2005–06

Round of 16		Quarter-finals		Semi-finals		Final	
Al Hilal *	1						
Al Ansar	0	Al Hilal	2				
Rawdha *	0	Al Qadisiya *	0				
Al Qadisiya	8			Al Hilal *	3 2		
Al Nasr	1			Al Wahda	2 0		
Al Ittifaq *	0	Al Nasr	0				
Al Faysali	1	Al Wahda *	1				
Al Wahda	2					Al Hilal ‡	1
Al Shabab	3					Al Ahli	0
Al Hazm *	2	Al Shabab *	4				
Al Ta'ee *	3	Hamada	1				
Hamada	4			Al Shabab *	1 3		
Al Ittihad	1			Al Ahli	2 3		
Al Riyadh *	0	Al Ittihad *	1 2p			CUP FINAL	
Abha	0	Al Ahli	1 4p			King Fahd International, Riyadh, 7-04-2006	
Al Ahli *	4					Scorer - Nawaf Al Temyat [22] for Hilal	

* Home team in the first leg • ‡ Qualified for the 2007 AFC Champions League

AL ITTIHAD 2005-06

Date	Opponents	Score				Scorers
14-09-2005	Shandong Luneng - CHN	D	1-1	A	ACLqf	Mohammed Noor [48]
21-09-2005	Shandong Luneng - CHN	W	7-2	H	ACLqf	Osama Al Harbi [19], Tcheco [34], Ibrahim Sowed [56], Mohammed Kallon [6], Manaf Abushgeer 2 [77 89], Redha Tukar [81]
28-09-2005	Busan I'Park - KOR	W	5-0	A	ACLsf	Al Otaibi [55], Mohammed Kallon [62], Tcheco [65], Ali Khariri [86], Hamzah Fallatah [89]
7-10-2005	Al Wahda	D	1-1	A	LGE	Tcheco [73]
12-10-2005	Busan I'Park - KOR	W	2-0	H	ACLsf	Mohammed Kallon 2 [18 58]
26-10-2005	Al Ain - UAE	D	1-1	A	ACLf	Mohammed Kallon [85p]
5-11-2005	Al Ain - UAE	W	4-2	H	ACLf	Mohammed Kallon [2], Mohammed Noor [33], Joseph-Desire Job [57], Ahmed Dokhi Al Dosari [69]
12-11-2005	Al Hazm Raas	W	7-3	A	LGE	Joseph-Desire Job 2 [6 84], Osama Al Muwallid [32], Saeed Al Wadaani [36], Mohammed Noor [42], Hamza Falatah [45], Abdulmajid Al Tariqi [66]
26-11-2005	Al Qadisiya	W	4-2	A	LGE	Tcheco [12p], Joseph-Desire Job 2 [20 47], Manaf Aboushgeer [27]
11-12-2005	Al Ahly - EGY	W	1-0	N	CWCr1	Mohammed Noor [78]
14-12-2005	São Paulo FC - BRA	L	2-3	N	CWCsf	Mohammed Noor [33], Hamad Al Montashari [58]
18-12-2005	Deportivo Saprissa - CRC	L	2-3	N	CWC3p	Mohammed Kallon [28], Joseph-Desire Job [53p]
23-12-2005	Al Ansar	W	4-0	A	LGE	Tcheco [12], Osama Al Muwallid [33], Hamza Fallatah [61p], Ibrahim Sowed [79]
27-12-2005	Al Riyadh	W	1-0	A	CPCr1	
1-01-2006	Al Ahli	D	1-1	H	CPCqf	L 2-4p
7-01-2006	Al Ta'ee	W	1-0	H	LGE	Mohammed Kallon [55]
15-01-2006	Al Wahda	W	2-1	H	LGE	Mohammed Noor [49], Joseph-Desire Job [77]
19-01-2006	Al Nasr	D	1-1	H	LGE	Ahmed Al Ajami OG [3]
23-01-2006	Abha	W	1-0	H	LGE	Mohammed Noor [77]
27-01-2006	Al Shabab	D	1-1	A	LGE	Mohammed Kallon [74]
9-02-2006	Al Hazm Raas	L	0-2	H	LGE	
13-02-2006	Al Hilal	D	2-2	H	LGE	Mohammed Kallon [48p], Ibrahim Sowed [67]
17-02-2006	Al Ittifaq	D	2-2	A	LGE	Mohammed Kallon 2 [37 61]
20-02-2006	Al Ta'ee	W	4-3	A	LGE	Prince Tagoe 2 [19 87], Saad Al Abboud [35], Hamza Fallatah [90]
24-02-2006	Al Qadisiya	W	2-0	H	LGE	Mohammed Noor [24], Prince Tagoe [54]
28-02-2006	Al Shabab	L	1-2	H	LGE	Prince Tagoe [37]
5-03-2006	Al Ahli	D	2-2	H	LGE	Mohammed Kallon [55p], Mohammed Noor [57]
9-03-2006	Al Ittifaq	D	1-1	H	LGE	Prince Tagoe [25]
13-03-2006	Al Ansar	W	5-2	H	LGE	Mohammed Kallon 3 [9 13 45p], Prince Tagoe [35], Manaf Abushgeer [74]
17-03-2006	Al Hilal	W	1-0	A	LGE	Saad Al Harithi [83]
23-03-2006	Al Ahli	D	1-1	A	LGE	Mohammed Noor [46]
27-03-2006	Al Nasr	D	1-1	H	LGE	Hamza Fallatah [79]
1-04-2006	Abha	W	3-1	A	LGE	Saad Al Abboud [36], Mohammed Kallon 2 [67p 90]
12-04-2006	Al Ahli	W	3-0	H	LGEpo	Mohammed Kallon [34], Prince Tagoe 2 [38 56]
16-04-2006	Al Hilal	L	1-2	A	LGEpo	Mohammed Noor [110]

LGE = Custodian of the Two Holy Mosques League Cup • CPC = Crown Prince Cup • ACL = AFC Asian Champions League
r2 = second round • qf = quarter-final • sf = semi-final • f = final • po = play-off • 3p = third place play-off
N = National Stadium, Tokyo • **N** = International Stadium, Yokohama

RECENT LEAGUE AND CUP RECORD

	Championship				Cup		
Year	Champions	Score	Runners-up		Winners	Score	Runners-up
1990	Al Hilal	†	Al Ahli				
1991	Al Shabab				Al Ittihad	0-0 5-4p	Al Nasr
1992	Al Shabab	1-1 4-3p	Al Ittifaq		Al Qadisiya	0-0 4-2p	Al Shabab
1993	Al Shabab	1-0	Al Hilal		Al Shabab	1-1 5-3p	Al Ittihad
1994	Al Nasr	1-0	Al Riyadh		Al Riyadh	1-0	Al Shabab
1995	Al Nasr	3-1	Al Hilal		Al Hilal	1-0	Al Riyadh
1996	Al Hilal	2-1	Al Ahli		Al Shabab	3-0	Al Nasr
1997	Al Ittihad	2-0	Al Hilal		Al Ittihad	2-0	Al Ta'ee
1998	Al Hilal	3-2	Al Shabab		Al Ahli	3-2	Al Riyadh
1999	Al Ittihad	1-0	Al Ahli		Al Shabab	1-0	Al Hilal
2000	Al Ittihad	2-1	Al Ahli		Al Hilal	3-0	Al Shabab
2001	Al Ittihad	1-0	Al Nasr		Al Ittihad	3-0	Al Ittifaq
2002	Al Hilal	2-1	Al Ittihad		Al Ahli	2-1	Al Ittihad
2003	Al Ittihad	3-2	Al Ahli		Al Hilal	1-0	Al Ahli
2004	Al Shabab	1-0	Al Ittihad		Al Ittihad	1-0	Al Ahli
2005	Al Hilal	1-0	Al Shabab		Al Hilal	2-1	Al Qadisiya
2006	Al Shabab	3-0	Al Hilal		Al Hilal	1-0	Al Ahli

† Played on a league basis • The Crown Prince Cup took over as the main Cup competition in 1991

KUW – KUWAIT

NATIONAL TEAM RECORD
JULY 1ST 2002 TO JULY 9TH 2006

PL	W	D	L	F	A	%
67	26	20	21	95	83	55.2

FIFA/COCA-COLA WORLD RANKING

1993	1994	1995	1996	1997	1998	1999	2000	2001	2002	2003	2004	2005	High	Low
64	54	84	62	44	24	82	74	74	83	48	54	72	24 12/98	100 07/06

2005–2006											
08/05	09/05	10/05	11/05	12/05	01/06	02/06	03/06	04/06	05/06	06/06	07/06
54	61	67	68	72	73	75	72	73	74	-	100

To finish in last place in their final round Asian qualifying group for the 2006 FIFA World Cup™ was a bitter disappointment for the Kuwaitis. They didn't begin their qualifiers for the 2007 AFC Asian Cup in the best fashion either, with two draws, against Lebanon and Bahrain, although with the withdrawal of Lebanon their task of reaching the finals was made easier. The poor form of Kuwaiti clubs in the AFC Champions League continued into the 2005 tournament with both Kuwait Sports Club and Al Salmiya falling at the group stage. The 2006 tournament did bring a change in fortunes, however, with Al Qadisiya becoming the first club from the country since the

INTERNATIONAL HONOURS
Qualified for the FIFA World Cup™ finals 1982   **Asian Cup** 1980   **Gulf Cup** 1970 1972 1974 1976 1982 1986 1990 1996 1998

start of the AFC Champions League in 2003, to make it through to the quarter-finals. Qadisya were also part of an extraordinary story in the Kuwaiti championship. After remaining unbeaten for the first 24 games of the 26 match season, they still contrived to lose the title to Kuwait Sports Club. A defeat to Al Arabi in the penultimate round saw them lose the lead to their rivals. In the final round the two then met in a winner takes all clash, which Kuwait SC won 2-0 with goals from Mohamed Armoumen and Hussain Ali Baba. Qadisya gained a measure of revenge by winning the Crown Prince Cup Final between the two, but then lost in the final of the Emir Cup to Al Arabi.

THE FIFA BIG COUNT OF 2000

	Male	Female		Male	Female
Registered players	1 000	0	Referees	70	0
Non registered players	6 000	0	Officials	300	0
Youth players	1 000	0	Total involved	8 370	
Total players	8 000		Number of clubs	40	
Professional players	0	0	Number of teams	100	

Kuwait Football Association (KFA)
Udailiya, Block 4, Al-Ittihad Street, PO Box 2029, Safat 13021, Kuwait
Tel +965 2555851   Fax +965 2549955
info@kfa.org.kw   www.kfa.org.kw
President: AL-SABAH Shk. Ahmad   General Secretary: TAHER Naser Abdul-Latif
Vice-President: AL-SABAH Shk. Khaled Fahad A.   Treasurer: AL-MUTAIRY Haiyef Hussain   Media Officer: None
Men's Coach: STOICHITA Mihai   Women's Coach: None
KFA formed: 1952   AFC: 1962   FIFA: 1962
Blue shirts with white trimmings, Blue shorts, Blue socks

RECENT INTERNATIONAL MATCHES PLAYED BY KUWAIT

2004	Opponents	Score		Venue	Comp	Scorers	Att	Referee
18-02	China PR	L	0-1	Guangzhou	WCq		50 000	Roman UZB
31-03	Malaysia	W	2-0	Kuantan	WCq	Al Mutwa 75, Al Harbi 87	9 327	Matsumura JPN
1-06	Syria	L	0-1	Kuwait City	Fr			
3-06	Syria	L	1-2	Kuwait City	Fr	Mousa 50		
9-06	Hong Kong	W	4-0	Kuwait City	WCq	Seraj 12, Al Mutwa 38, Al Enezi 45, Al Dawood 75	9 000	Najm LIB
19-07	United Arab Emirates	W	3-1	Jinan	ACr1	Bashar 25, Al Mutwa 2 40 45	31 250	Al Hamdan KSA
23-07	Jordan	L	0-2	Jinan	ACr1		28 000	Lu Jun CHN
27-07	Korea Republic	L	0-4	Jinan	ACr1			Maidin SIN
26-08	Bahrain	D	0-0	Al Muharraq	Fr			
1-09	Saudi Arabia	D	1-1	Riyadh	Fr			
8-09	Hong Kong	W	2-0	Hong Kong	WCq	Al Enezi 38, Humaidan 70	1 500	Busurmankulov KGZ
29-09	Syria	D	1-1	Tripoli	Fr			
3-10	Lebanon	W	3-1	Tripoli	Fr	Bashar 42p, Al Harbi 80, Sobeih 87		
6-10	Lebanon	D	1-1	Beirut	Fr	Seraj 60		
13-10	China PR	W	1-0	Kuwait City	WCq	Jumah 47	10 000	Kunsuta THA
5-11	India	L	2-3	Kuwait City	Fr	Al Fahed 35, Bashar 54		
10-11	Kyrgyzstan	W	3-0	Kuwait City	Fr			
17-11	Malaysia	W	6-1	Kuwait City	WCq	Al Mutwa 17, Bashar 2 60 70, Saeed 2 75 85, Al Hamad 82	15 000	Lutfullin UZB
27-11	United Arab Emirates	W	1-0	Abu Dhabi	Fr	Al Harbi 50		
3-12	United Arab Emirates	D	1-1	Dubai	Fr	Al Fahad 80		
6-12	Tajikistan	W	3-0	Kuwait City	Fr	Bashar 19, Laheeb 90, Al Humaidan 90		
11-12	Saudi Arabia	W	2-1	Doha	GCr1	Al Enezi 75, Al Mutwa 86		
14-12	Bahrain	D	1-1	Doha	GCr1	Jarragh 16		
17-12	Yemen	W	3-0	Doha	GCr1	Bashar 2 18 90, Al Mutwa 82		
20-12	Qatar	L	0-2	Doha	GCsf			
23-12	Bahrain	L	1-3	Doha	GC3p	Khodeir 35		
2005								
22-01	Norway	D	1-1	Kuwait City	Fr	Bashar 27	200	Shaban KUW
26-01	Syria	W	3-2	Kuwait City	Fr	OG 8, Mussa 70, Al Humaidan 83		
2-02	Korea DPR	D	0-0	Beijing	Fr			
9-02	Korea Republic	L	0-2	Seoul	WCq		53 287	Maidin SIN
12-03	Finland	L	0-1	Kuwait City	Fr		10 000	
18-03	Armenia	W	3-1	Al Ain	Fr	Abdulreda 70, Al Mutwa 79, Al Subaih 90		
25-03	Uzbekistan	W	2-1	Kuwait City	WCq	Bashar 2 7 62	12 000	Sun Baojie CHN
30-03	Saudi Arabia	D	0-0	Kuwait City	WCq		25 000	Moradi IRN
27-05	Egypt	L	0-1	Kuwait City	Fr			
3-06	Saudi Arabia	L	0-3	Riyadh	WCq		72 000	Kamikawa JPN
8-06	Korea Republic	L	0-4	Kuwait City	WCq		15 000	Khanthama THA
29-07	United Arab Emirates	D	1-1	Geneva	Fr	Al Mutawa 43. L 6-7p		
31-07	Qatar	L	0-1	Geneva	Fr			
17-08	Uzbekistan	L	2-3	Tashkent	WCq	Al Mutwa 15, Abdulaziz 30	40 000	Mohd Salleh MAS
26-11	Iraq	D	0-0	Kuwait City	Fr			
2006								
3-02	Singapore	D	2-2	Kuwait City	Fr	Jarragh 8, Al Mutawa 30		
7-02	Jordan	W	2-1	Kuwait City	Fr	Salama 6, Ali 16		
22-02	Lebanon	D	1-1	Beirut	ACq	Al Hamad 25	8 000	Mujghef JOR
1-03	Bahrain	D	0-0	Kuwait City	ACq		16 000	Moradi IRN

Fr = Friendly match • AR = Arab Cup • AC = AFC Asian Cup 2004 • GC = Gulf Cup • WC = FIFA World Cup™
q = qualifier • r1 = first round group • sf = semi-final • 3p = third place play-off

KUWAIT NATIONAL TEAM RECORDS AND RECORD SEQUENCES

Records			Sequence records					
Victory	20-0	BHU 2000	Wins	7	1974	Clean sheets	7	1988
Defeat	0-8	EGY 1961, POR 2003	Defeats	5	1964-1965	Goals scored	17	1986-1987
Player Caps	132	ABDULAZIZ Bashar	Undefeated	21	1985-1987	Without goal	5	1988
Player Goals	74	ABDULAZIZ Bashar	Without win	12	1988	Goals against	18	1964-1971

KUWAIT COUNTRY INFORMATION

Capital	Kuwait City	Independence	1961 from the UK	GDP per Capita	$19 000
Population	2 257 549	Status	Constitutional Monarchy	GNP Ranking	54
Area km²	17 820	Language	Arabic	Dialling code	+965
Population density	126 per km²	Literacy rate	83%	Internet code	.kw
% in urban areas	97%	Main religion	Muslim 85%	GMT +/–	+3
Towns/Cities ('000)	Hitan-al-Janubiyah 203; as-Sabahiyah 187; Jalib as-Suyuh 166; as-Salimiyah 158				
Neighbours (km)	Iraq 240; Saudi Arabia 222; Persian Gulf 499				
Main stadia	Kazma Stadium – Kuwait City 20 000; National Stadium – Kuwait City 16 000				

KUWAIT 2005-06

PREMIER LEAGUE

	Pl	W	D	L	F	A	Pts	Kuwait	Qadisiya	Salmiya	Arabi	Kazma	Tadamon	Sahel	Fehayheel	Yarmouk	Nasr	Jahra	Khitan	Shabab	Solayb'hat
Al Kuwait SC †	26	21	3	2	63	10	66		2-0	2-0	0-1	2-0	4-1	1-0	2-0	3-0	3-0	0-0	6-1	2-1	5-0
Al Qadisiya	26	19	5	2	67	14	62	1-0		1-1	1-2	2-1	0-0	2-0	7-1	3-1	6-1	3-0	1-0	4-1	4-0
Salmiya	26	18	4	4	78	24	58	1-1	2-2		2-1	2-0	1-2	3-0	7-0	5-1	2-0	2-0	6-0	6-2	4-1
Al Arabi	26	17	5	4	58	15	56	1-2	0-0	5-1		1-1	1-1	2-0	1-0	4-0	2-1	3-1	1-1	1-0	2-0
Kazma	26	14	8	4	47	19	50	0-0	0-0	2-1	1-0		1-3	6-0	2-2	1-1	2-0	4-0	0-0	5-2	5-1
Al Tadamon	26	10	9	7	34	30	39	0-2	0-1	1-2	1-1	0-0		2-0	0-3	1-0	0-2	1-1	0-0	2-1	3-0
Al Sahel	26	8	7	11	23	36	31	1-3	0-3	1-4	0-4	1-1	1-1		0-0	3-1	1-0	1-0	0-1	2-0	2-0
Fehayheel	26	8	7	11	20	41	31	0-4	0-1	0-0	0-4	0-1	2-1	0-4		2-2	1-0	0-1	1-0	0-0	1-0
Al Yarmouk	26	7	8	11	32	42	29	1-3	0-1	2-3	0-2	1-2	2-2	1-1	0-0		1-0	1-0	3-0	1-0	3-3
Al Nasr	26	6	6	14	21	36	24	0-4	1-4	0-2	1-0	0-1	1-2	0-0	0-1	1-1		0-1	3-0	2-0	0-0
Jahra	26	6	6	14	21	43	24	0-2	1-2	0-2	0-3	0-6	2-2	0-0	2-1	1-2	1-1		3-1	2-0	1-2
Khitan	26	3	4	19	14	68	13	0-3	0-2	0-12	1-9	0-2	0-3	0-1	0-1	1-1	2-3	2-1		3-1	0-1
Al Shabab	26	3	3	20	25	69	12	1-3	0-12	0-5	0-3	0-1	2-3	1-1	1-2	0-3	0-0	1-2	2-1		5-2
Solaybeekhat	26	3	3	20	15	71	12	0-4	0-4	0-2	0-4	0-2	0-2	0-3	1-3	0-3	0-4	1-1	2-0	1-4	

10/11/2005 - 22/04/2006 • † Qualified for the 2007 AFC Champions League

EMIR CUP 2005-06

Quarter-finals		Semi-finals		Final	
Al Arabi	7				
Al Yarmouk	1	Al Arabi	1		
Khitan	1	Al Nasr	0	23-05-2006	
Al Nasr	2			Al Arabi †	2
Al Kuwait SC	3			Al Qadisiya	0
Al Shabab	2	Al Kuwait SC	0	Third Place Play-off	
Kazma	0	Al Qadisiya	1	Al Kuwait SC	2 3p
Al Qadisiya	4			Al Nasr	2 1p

† Qualified for the 2007 AFC Champions League

CROWN PRINCE CUP 2005-06

Semi-finals		Final	
Al Qadisiya	3		
Salmiya	2	9-05-2006	
		Al Qadisiya	2 3p
Al Tadamon	2	Al Kuwait SC	2 2p
Al Kuwait SC	5		

RECENT LEAGUE AND CUP RECORD

	Championship						Cup		
Year	Champions	Pts	Runners-up	Pts	Third	Pts	Winners	Score	Runners-up
1996	Kazma	24	Salmiya	22	Al Qadisiya	15	Al Arabi	2-1	Jahra
1997	Al Arabi						Kazma	2-0	Al Qadisiya
1998	Salmiya	64	Kazma	55	Al Qadisiya	50	Kazma	3-1	Al Arabi
1999	Al Qadisiya	1-0	Al Tadamon				Al Arabi	2-1	Al Sahel
2000	Salmiya	23	Al Qadisiya	20	Al Kuwait SC	15	Al Arabi	2-1	Al Tadamon
2001	Al Kuwait SC	28	Salmiya	24	Al Arabi	24	Salmiya	3-1	Kazma
2002	Al Arabi	26	Al Qadisiya	25	Salmiya	23	Al Kuwait SC	1-0	Jahra
2003	Al Qadisiya	28	Al Arabi	26	Kazma	24	Al Qadisiya	2-2 4-1p	Al Salimiya
2004	Al Qadisiya	2-1	Salmiya				Al Qadisiya	2-0	Al Kuwait SC
2005	Al Qadisiya	9	Al Kuwait SC	8	Al Arabi	6	Al Arabi	1-1 6-5p	Kazma
2006	Al Kuwait SC	66	Al Qadisiya	62	Salmiya	58	Al Arabi	2-2 3-2p	Al Qadisiya

LAO – LAOS

NATIONAL TEAM RECORD
JULY 1ST 2002 TO JULY 9TH 2006

PL	W	D	L	F	A	%
17	2	2	13	13	66	17.6

FIFA/COCA-COLA WORLD RANKING

1993	1994	1995	1996	1997	1998	1999	2000	2001	2002	2003	2004	2005	High	Low
146	160	152	147	143	144	156	165	162	170	167	162	170	**134** 09/98	**182** 07/06

	2005–2006									
08/05	09/05	10/05	11/05	12/05	01/06	02/06	03/06	04/06	05/06	06/06	07/06
163	164	165	165	170	170	170	171	172	172	-	182

The biggest story of the season in Laos came with the qualification of the under-17 side for the 2006 AFC U-17 Championship finals. What made the qualification all the more remarkable was that it came at the expense of Indonesia and AFC new boys Australia. In the first match of the three team group played in Vientiane, the capital of Laos, the hosts held Australia to a 0-0 draw. The Aussies then beat Indonesia 3-1, leaving Laos the task of beating Indonesia by three clear goals, which they did in style, hammering five past their ASEAN neighbours to qualify for the finals in Singapore. Their under-19 counterparts were not quite so lucky as they were knocked out of their

INTERNATIONAL HONOURS
None

qualifying group on goal difference by Vietnam. With the senior national team out of action since the end of the 2004 Tiger Cup, the youth matches were the only internatonals played during the season. There were no club internationals either with 2005 champions Vientiane FC choosing not to enter the AFC President's Cup for which they were eligible. With entry into the 2007 AFC Asian Cup now restricted, the idea was that nations such as Laos would be better served by competing in the new AFC Challenge Cup. By not taking part in the tournament, Laos have left themselves without a fixture list in-between FIFA World Cup™ qualifiers and the ASEAN Tiger Cup.

THE FIFA BIG COUNT OF 2000

	Male	Female		Male	Female
Registered players	1 100	0	Referees	50	0
Non registered players	20 000	0	Officials	300	0
Youth players	1 000	0	Total involved	22 450	
Total players	22 100		Number of clubs	50	
Professional players	0	0	Number of teams	150	

Lao Football Federation (LFF)
National Stadium, Konboulo Street, PO Box 3777, Vientiane 856-21, Laos
Tel +856 21 251593   Fax +856 21 213460
laosff@laotel.com   www.none
President: PHISSAMAY Bountiem   General Secretary: VONGSOUTHI Phouvanh
Vice-President: VONGSOUTHI Phouvanh   Treasurer: KEOMANY Khammoui   Media Officer: VILAYSAK Sisay
Men's Coach: SAVATDY Xaysana   Women's Coach: XEUNGVILAY Soulivanh
LFF formed: 1951   AFC: 1980   FIFA: 1952
Red shirts, Red shorts, Red socks

RECENT INTERNATIONAL MATCHES PLAYED BY LAOS

2002	Opponents	Score		Venue	Comp	Scorers	Att	Referee
18-12	Thailand	L	1-5	Singapore	TCr1	Phaphouvanin [66]	7 000	Rahmanvijay SIN
20-12	Singapore	L	1-2	Singapore	TCr1	Phaphouvanin [19]	10 000	Setiyono IDN
22-12	Malaysia	D	1-1	Singapore	TCr1	Phaphouvanin [29]	350	Lee Young Chun KOR
2003								
25-03	Hong Kong	L	1-5	Hong Kong	ACq	Phaphouvanin [66]		
27-03	Bangladesh	W	2-1	Hong Kong	ACq	Phonephachan [30], Phaphouvanin [38]		
29-11	Sri Lanka	D	0-0	Vientiane	WCq		4 500	Luong VIE
3-12	Sri Lanka	L	0-3	Colombo	WCq		6 000	Saleem MDV
2004								
18-02	Jordan	L	0-5	Amman	WCq		5 000	Al Mozahmi OMA
31-03	Iran	L	0-7	Vientiane	WCq		7 000	Yang Mu Sheng TPE
9-06	Qatar	L	0-5	Doha	WCq		500	Abu Armana PAL
8-09	Qatar	L	1-6	Vientiane	WCq	Chanthalome [88]	2 900	Napitupulu IDN
13-10	Jordan	L	2-3	Vientiane	WCq	Phaphouvanin [13], Thongphachan [53]	3 000	Gosh BAN
17-11	Iran	L	0-7	Tehran	WCq		30 000	Mamedov TKM
7-12	Indonesia	L	0-6	Ho Chi Minh City	TCr1			Mongkol THA
11-12	Cambodia	W	2-1	Hanoi	TCr1	Chalana 2 [63 73]	20 000	Kwong Jong Chul KOR
13-12	Singapore	L	2-6	Hanoi	TCr1	Phaphouvanin [22], Chalana [72p]	17 000	Supian MAS
15-12	Vietnam	L	0-3	Hanoi	TCr1		20 000	Mongkul THA
2005								
No international matches played in 2005								
2006								
No international matches played in 2006 before July								

TC = Tiger Cup • AC = AFC Asian Cup 2004 • WC = FIFA World Cup™ • q = qualifier • r1 = first round group

LAOS NATIONAL TEAM RECORDS AND RECORD SEQUENCES

Records			Sequence records					
Victory	4-1	PHI	Wins	3	1993-1995	Clean sheets	3	1995
Defeat	0-12	OMA 2001	Defeats	11	1970-1974	Goals scored	9	1996-1998
Player Caps	n/a		Undefeated	4	1993-1995	Without goal	8	2000-2001
Player Goals	n/a		Without win	19	1970-1993	Goals against	14	1961-1969

RECENT LEAGUE AND CUP RECORD

	Championship	Cup	
Year	Champions		Winners
2000	Vientiane Municipality		
2001			
2002	MCPTC		
2003	MCPTC		MCPTC
2004	MCPTC		Vientiane FC
2005	Vientiane FC		

LAOS COUNTRY INFORMATION

Capital	Vientiane	Independence	1953 from France	GDP per Capita	$1 700
Population	6 068 117	Status	Republic	GNP Ranking	143
Area km²	236 800	Language	Lao	Dialling code	+856
Population density	25.5 per km²	Literacy rate	66%	Internet code	.la
% in urban areas	22%	Main religion	Buddhist 60%	GMT +/−	+7
Towns/Cities ('000)	Vientiane 196; Pakxe 88; Savannakhet 66; Luang Prabang 47; Xam Nua 39; Xaignabury 31				
Neighbours (km)	China 423; Vietnam 2 130; Cambodia 541; Thailand 1 754; Burma 235				
Main stadia	National Stadium – Vientiane 18 000				

LBR – LIBERIA

NATIONAL TEAM RECORD
JULY 1ST 2002 TO JULY 9TH 2006

PL	W	D	L	F	A	%
19	4	1	14	9	38	23.7

FIFA/COCA-COLA WORLD RANKING

1993	1994	1995	1996	1997	1998	1999	2000	2001	2002	2003	2004	2005	High		Low	
123	127	87	94	94	108	105	95	73	88	110	123	135	66	07/01	143	05/06

2005–2006											
08/05	09/05	10/05	11/05	12/05	01/06	02/06	03/06	04/06	05/06	06/06	07/06
130	132	134	133	135	135	135	139	141	143	-	136

Football dominated the headlines in Liberia last year but in unusual circumstances after the former FIFA World Player of the Year George Weah made an unsuccessful bid to win the country's presidency in much anticipated elections. Weah's colourful campaign and metamorphosis from playboy soccer icon into serious politician overshadowed a disappointing run for the national side in the FIFA World Cup™ qualifiers. Liberia's Lone Star finished bottom of their qualifying group, losing all five of the qualifying matches played in 2005, finishing with just four points from 10 matches. The defeats contributed to a record sequence of eight successive losses for the side,

INTERNATIONAL HONOURS
None

stretching back to September 2004. In the six matches played in 2005, Liberia conceded 22 goals while scoring only two. The performances have come as a result of the country's football association not having the financial resources to pay for the return of the myriad Liberian footballers based around the world and a necessary reliance on less experienced home grown talent. Liberian players can be found predominantly in Asia, notably India, Indonesia and the leagues of Malaysia. Frank Jericho Nagbe has been appointed as the new national coach to replace Joseph Sayon, as Liberia seek to redress their plummeting FIFA/Coca-Cola World Ranking.

THE FIFA BIG COUNT OF 2000

	Male	Female		Male	Female
Registered players	1 360	0	Referees	42	0
Non registered players	10 000	0	Officials	400	0
Youth players	1 000	264	Total involved	13 066	
Total players	12 624		Number of clubs	80	
Professional players	25	0	Number of teams	157	

Liberia Football Association (FLFA)
Antoinette Tubman Stadium (ATS), PO Box 10-1066, Monrovia 1000, Liberia
Fax +231 227223
yansbor@yahoo.com   www.liberiansoccer.com
President: WESLEY Sombo   General Secretary: BORSAY Yanqueh
Vice-President: BESTMAN Pennoh   Treasurer: KOON Joseph S.   Media Officer: None
Men's Coach: NAGBE Frank   Women's Coach: TOGBA Lucretius
FLFA formed: 1936   CAF: 1962   FIFA: 1962
Blue shirts, White shorts, Red socks

RECENT INTERNATIONAL MATCHES PLAYED BY LIBERIA

2002	Opponents		Score	Venue	Comp	Scorers	Att	Referee
8-09	Guinea	L	0-3	Conakry	CNq		35 000	Diouf.AS SEN
13-10	Niger	W	1-0	Monrovia	CNq	Daye [80]	40 000	
2003								
30-03	Ethiopia	L	0-1	Addis Ababa	CNq		40 000	Ali Mohamed DJI
8-06	Ethiopia	W	1-0	Monrovia	CNq	Mennoh [57]	14 000	Aguidissou BEN
21-06	Guinea	L	1-2	Accra	CNq	Daye [20]		Sowe GAM
5-07	Niger	L	0-1	Niamey	CNq			
12-10	Gambia	L	0-2	Bakau	WCq		20 000	Codjia BEN
16-11	Gambia	W	3-0	Monrovia	WCq	Roberts [10], Tondo 2 [76 83]	10 000	Coulibaly MLI
2004								
6-06	Mali	W	1-0	Monrovia	WCq	Kieh [85]	30 000	Codjia BEN
20-06	Congo	L	0-3	Brazzaville	WCq		25 000	Lemghambodj MTN
4-07	Togo	D	0-0	Monrovia	WCq		30 000	Soumah GUI
4-09	Zambia	L	0-1	Lusaka	WCq		30 000	Nchengwa BOT
10-10	Senegal	L	0-3	Monrovia	WCq		26 000	Aboubacar CIV
2005								
26-03	Senegal	L	1-6	Dakar	WCq	Tondo [86]	50 000	Shelmani LBY
5-06	Mali	L	1-4	Segou	WCq	Toe [54]	11 000	Pare BFA
10-06	Sierra Leone	L	0-2	Freetown	Fr			
19-06	Congo	L	0-2	Paynesville	WCq		5 000	Sillah GAM
4-09	Togo	L	0-3	Lome	WCq		28 000	Abdel Rahman SUD
1-10	Zambia	L	0-5	Monrovia	WCq		0	Evehe CMR
2006								

No international matches played in 2006 before July

CN = CAF African Cup of Nations • WC = FIFA World Cup™ • q = qualifier

LIBERIA NATIONAL TEAM RECORDS AND RECORD SEQUENCES

Records			Sequence records					
Victory	4-0	GAM 1996, MRI 2000	Wins	4	2001	Clean sheets	4	1987-1995
Defeat	2-7	TUN 2001	Defeats	8	2004-	Goals scored	8	2001, 2001-02
Player Caps	n/a		Undefeated	11	1994-1995	Without goal	4	Six times
Player Goals	n/a		Without win	17	1971-1980	Goals against	13	1984-1986

RECENT LEAGUE AND CUP RECORD

	Championship		Cup
Year	Champions		Winners
1996	Junior Professional		Junior Professional
1997	Invincible Eleven		Invincible Eleven
1998	Invincible Eleven		Invincible Eleven
1999	LPRC Oilers		LPRC Oilers
2000	Mighty Barolle		LPRC Oilers
2001	Mighty Barolle		
2002	LPRC Oilers		Mighty Blue Angels
2003	Not finished		
2004	Mighty Barolle		LISCR FC
2005	LPRC Oilers		LPRC Oilers

LIBERIA COUNTRY INFORMATION

Capital	Monrovia	Independence	1847	GDP per Capita	$1 000
Population	3 390 635	Status	Republic	GNP Ranking	171
Area km²	111 370	Language	English	Dialling code	+231
Population density	30 per km²	Literacy rate	57%	Internet code	.lr
% in urban areas	45%	Main religion	Christian & Indigenous 40%	GMT +/-	0
Cities/Towns ('000)	Monrovia 935; Gbarnga 45; Bensonville 33; Harper 33; Buchanan 26; Zwedru 26				
Neighbours (km)	Guinea 563; Côte d'Ivoire 716; Sierra Leone 306; Atlantic Ocean 579				
Main stadia	Samuel Doe Sports Complex – Monrovia 35 000; Antoinette Tubman – Monrovia 10 000				

LBY – LIBYA

NATIONAL TEAM RECORD
JULY 1ST 2002 TO JULY 9TH 2006

PL	W	D	L	F	A	%
44	18	9	17	60	52	51.1

FIFA/COCA-COLA WORLD RANKING

1993	1994	1995	1996	1997	1998	1999	2000	2001	2002	2003	2004	2005	High		Low	
152	167	175	184	147	147	131	116	116	104	83	61	80	61	12/04	187	07/97

2005–2006											
08/05	09/05	10/05	11/05	12/05	01/06	02/06	03/06	04/06	05/06	06/06	07/06
75	80	84	83	80	80	80	84	85	86	-	79

Libya returned to the African Nations Cup finals after a 24-year hiatus and, although they were the first side eliminated, they left enough of a positive impression to suggest that their next appearance at the biennial continental championship might not be that long in coming. Coached by the bushy-moustached Croat Ilija Loncarevic, they were over-run in the opening game of the tournament by hosts Egypt but found their feet after that. In their final match, the Libyans outplayed Morocco and were unfortunate to have to settle for a goalless draw. The Nations Cup performances were a major fillip for the game, blessed with an abundance of financial backing but short on playing depth.

INTERNATIONAL HONOURS
None

Loncarevic has since been replaced by the former Egyptian international Mohsen Salah, tasked with qualifying Libya for the 2008 African Nations Cup finals. Al Ittihad edged out rivals Al Ahly of Tripoli to win the Libyan championship in a thrilling finish to the season that accentuated the bitter rivalry between the two clubs. Al Ahly gained a measure of revenge in the semi-finals of the Cup and went on to win the trophy when Ahmed Saad scored a late winner as they beat Olympic 2-1 in the final. On the administrative aside there was also a major breakthrough for the Libyan Football Federation with Jamal El Jaafri becoming the first elected leader of the organisation.

THE FIFA BIG COUNT OF 2000

	Male	Female		Male	Female
Registered players	5 000	0	Referees	300	0
Non registered players	20 000	0	Officials	1 900	0
Youth players	2 500	0	Total involved	29 700	
Total players	27 500		Number of clubs	100	
Professional players	0	0	Number of teams	500	

Libyan Football Federation (LFF)
General Sports Federations Building, Sports City, Gorji, PO Box 5137, Tripoli, Libya
Tel +218 21 4782001   Fax +218 21 4782006
libyaff@hotmail.com   www.lff.org.ly
President: EL JAAFRI Jamal Saleh   General Secretary: AL SAEDY Ahmed Abdulmagid
Vice-President: KHATABI Abdulrazag Al Tayb   Treasurer: EL MUGHRBI Abdulmula   Media Officer: BEN TAHIA Mohamad
Men's Coach: SALAH Mohsin   Women's Coach: None
LFF formed: 1962   CAF: 1965   FIFA: 1963
Green shirts with white trimmings, Green shorts, Green socks or White shirts with green trimmings, White shorts, White socks

RECENT INTERNATIONAL MATCHES PLAYED BY LIBYA

2003	Opponents		Score	Venue	Comp	Scorers	Att	Referee
11-10	São Tomé e Príncipe	W	1-0	São Tomé	WCq	Masli [85]	4 000	Yameogo BFA
16-11	São Tomé e Príncipe	W	8-0	Benghazi	WCq	Masli 3 [14 17 20], El Taib 2 [45 63], Suliman [54] Osman.A [74], El Rabty [88]	20 000	Guirat TUN
2004								
16-01	Kenya	W	2-0	Zawyan	Fr	Kara, El Kikli		
19-01	Kenya	W	2-0	Tripoli	Fr	Saad [27], Hussain [56]		
18-02	Ukraine	D	1-1	Tripoli	Fr	Kara [55]		
26-03	Qatar	W	1-0	Rome	Fr	Kara [48]		
30-04	Jordan	W	1-0	Lagos	Fr	Rewani [37]		
30-05	Burkina Faso	L	2-3	Ouagadougou	Fr	El Hamail [21], Rewani [54]		Pare BFA
6-06	Côte d'Ivoire	L	0-2	Abidjan	WCq		40 827	Colembi ANG
18-06	Cameroon	D	0-0	Misurata	WCq		7 000	Lim Kee Chong MRI
3-07	Sudan	W	1-0	Khartoum	WCq	Kara [93+]	10 000	Bennett RSA
3-09	Benin	W	4-1	Tripoli	WCq	Al Shibani [9], Kara [47], Osman.A [51], Suliman [70]	30 000	Kidane Tesfu ERI
8-10	Egypt	W	2-1	Tripoli	WCq	Kara [31], Osman.A [85]	40 000	Haimoudi ALG
20-10	Nigeria	W	2-1	Tripoli	Fr	Kara 2 [23 44]		
22-10	Jordan	W	1-0	Tripoli	Fr	Kara [59p]		
2005								
27-03	Egypt	L	1-4	Cairo	WCq	Ferjani [50]	30 000	Poulat FRA
27-05	Malawi	D	1-1	Tripoli	Fr			
3-06	Côte d'Ivoire	D	0-0	Tripoli	WCq		45 000	Lim Kee Chong MRI
19-06	Cameroon	L	0-1	Yaoundé	WCq		36 000	Coulibaly MLI
17-08	Nigeria	L	0-1	Tripoli	Fr			
24-08	Iran	L	0-4	Tehran	Fr			
2-09	Sudan	D	0-0	Tripoli	WCq			
9-10	Benin	L	0-1	Cotonou	WCq			
16-11	Congo DR	W	2-1	Paris	Fr	Shebani [25], Erwani [76]		
2-12	United Arab Emirates	D	1-1	Sharjah	Fr	Dawood [39]		
2006								
2-01	Qatar	L	0-2	Doha	Fr			
12-01	Tunisia	L	0-1	Radès/Tunis	Fr			
20-01	Egypt	L	0-3	Cairo	CNr1		65 000	Pare BFA
24-01	Côte d'Ivoire	L	1-2	Cairo	CNr1	Khamis [41]	42 000	Maidin SIN
28-01	Morocco	D	0-0	Cairo	CNr1		5 000	Daami TUN
30-05	Uruguay	L	1-2	Rades/Tunis	Fr	El Taib [61]		
2-06	Belarus	D	1-1	Rades/Tunis	Fr	Osman [90]. W 3-1p		
5-06	Ukraine	L	0-3	Gossau	Fr		2 500	Wilzhaber SUI

Fr = Friendly match • CN = CAF African Cup of Nations • WC = FIFA World Cup™ • q = qualifier • r1 = first round

LIBYA NATIONAL TEAM RECORDS AND RECORD SEQUENCES

Records			Sequence records					
Victory	21-0	OMA 1966	Wins	5	2003-04, 2004	Clean sheets	4	1996, 2003-04
Defeat	2-10	EGY 1953	Defeats	5	1953-1960	Goals scored	15	1998-1999
Player Caps	n/a		Undefeated	7	1982-1983	Without goal	6	2005
Player Goals	n/a		Without win	9	2005-2006	Goals against	16	1953-65. 1992-99

LIBYA COUNTRY INFORMATION

Capital	Tripoli	Independence	1951 from Italy	GDP per Capita	$6 400
Population	5 631 585	Status	Republic	GNP Ranking	59
Area km²	1 759 540	Language	Arabic	Dialling code	+218
Population density	3 per km²	Literacy rate	82%	Internet code	.ly
% in urban areas	86%	Main religion	Muslim	GMT +/−	+1
Towns/Cities ('000)	Tripoli 1 150; Benghazi 650; Misurata 386; Al Aziziyah 287; Tarhunah 210; Al-Hums 201; Az-Zawiyah 186; Zuwarah 180; Ajdabiya 134; Surt 128; Sabha 126; Tubruq 121				
Neighbours (km)	Egypt 1 115 km; Sudan 383; Chad 1 055; Niger 354; Algeria 982; Tunisia 459; Mediterranean 1 770				
Main stadia	11 June Stadium – Tripoli 80 000; 28 March Stadium – Benghazi 60 000				

LIBYA 2005-06

SUPER DIVISION

	Pl	W	D	L	F	A	BP	Pts	Ittihad	Ahly T	Akhdar	Tahaddi	Olympique	Ahly B
Al Ittihad Tripoli †	10	8	2	0	21	4	1	27		0-0	3-0	3-1	1-0	4-0
Al Ahly Tripoli	10	7	3	0	15	4	3	27	1-1		3-1	4-0	1-0	2-1
Al Akhdar Darnah §1	10	3	1	6	6	12	1	10	0-2	0-1		0-1	1-0	2-1
Al Tahaddi Benghazi	10	3	1	6	8	18	0	10	1-3	1-2	0-2		1-0	0-3
Olympique Az-Zwiyah	10	1	4	5	3	6	3	10	1-2	0-0	0-0	0-0		2-0
Al Ahly Benghazi	10	2	1	7	7	16	0	7	0-2	0-1	1-0	1-3	0-0	

7/04/2006 – 12/05/2006 • † Qualified for the CAF Champions League • BP = Bonus points from the first round groups • Match in bold awarded 2-0 • §1 = One point deducted

LIBYA 2005-06 RELEGATION GROUP A

	Pl	W	D	L	F	A	BP	Pts
Rafik Sorman	10	5	2	3	13	12	3	20
Al Soukour	10	6	1	3	9	7	0	19
Al Hilal Benghazi	10	5	3	2	16	7	0	18
Al Wahda	10	5	3	2	15	10	0	18
Al Mustaqbal Tripoli	10	3	2	5	12	11	0	11
Al Magd	10	0	1	9	7	25	1	2

7/4/2006 - 14/05/2006 • BP = Bonus points from the first round groups

LIBYA 2005-06 RELEGATION GROUP B

	Pl	W	D	L	F	A	BP	Pts
Al Charara	10	5	3	2	15	11	1	19
Al Shat Tripoli	10	5	2	3	15	12	0	17
Al Madina Tripoli	10	4	3	3	12	8	0	15
Al Uruba	10	2	5	3	10	9	3	14
Al Swihli Misurata	10	3	5	2	12	12	0	14
Al Harati	10	1	2	7	4	16	0	5

7/4/2006 - 13/05/2006 • BP = Bonus points from the first round groups

AL FATIH CUP 2005-06

Round of 16		Quarter-finals		Semi-finals		Final	
Al Ahly Tripoli *	2						
Al Tahaddi Benghazi	1	Al Ahly Tripoli	2 3				
Al Najma	1	Rafik Sorman *	0 1				
Rafik Sorman *	3			Al Ahly Tripoli	2 0		
Al Nasr Tripoli	0 4p			Al Ittihad Tripoli *	1 0		
Al Swihli Misurata *	0 3p	Al Nasr Tripoli	0 0				
Al Mustaqbal Tripoli *	0	Al Ittihad Tripoli *	1 1				
Al Ittihad Tripoli	2					Al Ahly Tripoli ‡	2
Al Charara *	3					Olympique Az-Zwiyah	1
Al Ahly Benghazi	1	Al Charara *	2 1				
Al Uruba	2	Al Madina Tripoli	2 0				
Al Madina Tripoli *	3			Al Charara *	1 0		
Al Shat Tripoli *	5			Olympique Az-Zwiyah	1 1		
Al Wifak Sabrata	1	Al Shat Tripoli *	0 1				
Al Akhdar Darnah *	0 2p	Olympique Az-Zwiyah	1 1				
Olympique Az-Zwiyah	0 4p						

CUP FINAL

26-05-2006

Scorers - Mohammed Al Shoshan [30], Ahmad Saad [81] for Ahly; Akram Al Hamale [15] for Olympique

* Home team in the first leg • ‡ Qualified for the CAF Confederation Cup

RECENT LEAGUE AND CUP RECORD

	Championship						Cup		
Year	Champions	Pts	Runners-up	Pts	Third	Pts	Winners	Score	Runners-up
1997	Al Tahaddi Benghazi	54	Al Ahly Tripoli	53	Al Ittihad Tripoli	51	Al Nasr Benghazi	1-1 4-3p	Al Yarmouk
1998	Al Mahalah Tripoli						Al Shaat Tripoli	1-1 4-2p	Al Hilal Benghazi
1999	Al Mahalah Tripoli	30	Al Shat Tripoli	23	Al Hilal Benghazi	21	Al Ittihad Ytripoli	2-0	Al Tahaddi Benghazi
2000	Al Ahly Tripoli	1-0	Al Hilal Benghazi				Al Ahly Tripoli	2-0	Al Shawehly Misurata
2001	Al Medina Tripoli	1-1	Al Tahaddi Benghazi						
2002	Al Ittihad Tripoli	67	Al Nasr Benghazi	67	Al Hilal Benghazi	52			
2003	Al Ittihad Tripoli	65	Al Nasr Benghazi	52	Al Hilal Benghazi	43			
2004	Olympique Az-Zwiyah	57	Al Ittihad Tripoli	52	Al Ahly Tripoli	51	Al Ittihad Tripoli	0-0 8-7p	Al Hilal
2005	Al Ittihad Tripoli	51	Al Uruba	43	Olympique Az-Zwiyah	42	Al Ittihad Tripoli	3-0	Al Akhdar
2006	Al Ittihad Tripoli	27	Al Ahly Tripoli	27	Al Akhdar Darnah	10	Al Ahly Tripoli	2-1	Olympique Az-Zwiyah

Al Medina won the 2001 Championship on penalties after a 1-1 draw

LCA – ST LUCIA

NATIONAL TEAM RECORD
JULY 1ST 2002 TO JULY 9TH 2006

PL	W	D	L	F	A	%
22	9	3	10	45	39	47.7

FIFA/COCA-COLA WORLD RANKING

1993	1994	1995	1996	1997	1998	1999	2000	2001	2002	2003	2004	2005		High		Low
139	157	114	134	142	139	152	135	130	112	130	114	128		**108** 04/03		**157** 12/94

2005–2006											
08/05	09/05	10/05	11/05	12/05	01/06	02/06	03/06	04/06	05/06	06/06	07/06
118	117	117	125	128	128	128	129	130	131	-	115

The story of the season in St Lucia was the historic run by Northern United in the CFU Caribbean Cup. The 2005 champions made it to the semi-finals before losing to Robinhood of Surinam, but no club from the country had ever progressed that far before. It made up for a poor 2006 season in which none of the clubs from Castries or Vieux Fort, the two traditional football centres on the island, fared well. Instead it was clubs from the three towns of Anse La Raye, Canaries and Soufrière, located on the Caribbean Sea coast, who provided all four finalists for the two tournaments played. The 27 team St Lucia Premier League was divided into two first round groups

INTERNATIONAL HONOURS
None

with the top four of each qualifying for the knock out stages. Former champions VSADC from Castries made it through to the semi-finals but lost 2-1 to Anse La Raye who qualified to meet Canaries, winners over Big Players in the other semi-final. At the Mindoo Philip Ground in Castries, Canaries claimed their first title thanks to a 3-2 penalty shoot-out victory after the match had finished 2-2. The previous week Canaries had lost a penalty shoot-out by the same score after a 1-1 draw, in the final of the Kentucky Fried Chicken/CLICO FA Cup, against Elite Challengers. It was a first Cup triumph for Soufrière based side.

THE FIFA BIG COUNT OF 2000

	Male	Female		Male	Female
Registered players	2 025	100	Referees	37	4
Non registered players	1 500	0	Officials	300	15
Youth players	500	0	Total involved	4 481	
Total players	4 125		Number of clubs	39	
Professional players	25	0	Number of teams	119	

St Lucia Football Association (SLFA)
La Clery, PO Box 255, Castries, St Lucia
Tel +1 758 4530687   Fax +1 758 4560510
gs_slfa@hotmail.com   www.none
President: LARCHER Oswald W.   General Secretary: JOSEPH Germaine
Vice-President: SEALEY John   Treasurer: JOSEPH Germaine   Media Officer: HALL Gilroy
Men's Coach: MILLAR Carson   Women's Coach: ANDERSON Trevor
SLFA formed: 1979   CONCACAF: 1988   FIFA: 1988
Colours: White with yellow/blue/black stripe, White with yellow/blue/black stripe, White/blue/yellow

RECENT INTERNATIONAL MATCHES PLAYED BY ST LUCIA

2002	Opponents	Score	Venue	Comp	Scorers	Att	Referee
9-10	Martinique †	L 0-4	Riviere-Pilote	Fr			
6-11	Martinique †	L 0-2	Vieux Fort	Fr			
13-11	St Kitts and Nevis	L 1-2	Port of Spain	GCq	Lastic 78		Forde BRB
17-11	Trinidad and Tobago	W 1-0	Port of Spain	GCq	McVane 54		Forde BRB
2003							
26-03	Jamaica	L 0-5	Kingston	GCq		22 000	Brizan TRI
28-03	Haiti	W 2-1	Kingston	GCq	Emmanuel 45, Flavius 90	14 500	Lee ATG
30-03	Martinique	L 4-5	Kingston	GCq	Elva 21, Mark 38, Jean 52, Joseph.V 56	7 200	Lee ATG
2004							
1-02	Guadeloupe †	L 0-2		Fr			
8-02	St Vincent/Grenadines	L 1-2	Castries	Fr			
22-02	British Virgin Islands	W 1-0	Tortola	WCq	Elva 55	800	Stewart JAM
21-03	St Vincent/Grenadines	D 1-1	Kingstown	Fr	Elva 15		
28-03	British Virgin Islands	W 9-0	Vieux Fort	WCq	Emmanuel 2 13p 66, Joseph.E 26, Jean 2 28 52 Skeete 2 49 55, Elva 69, Baptiste 90	665	Corrivault CAN
2-06	Grenada	L 0-2	St George's	Fr		2 500	
13-06	Panama	L 0-4	Panama City	WCq		15 000	Phillip GRN
20-06	Panama	L 0-3	Vieux Fort	WCq		400	Gurley VIN
17-10	Grenada	W 3-1	Castries	Fr	Gilbert 3		
2-11	St Kitts and Nevis	D 1-1	Basseterre	GCq	Gilbert 67		Bedeau GRN
4-11	Montserrat	W 3-0	Basseterre	GCq	St Lucia awarded match 3-0		
6-11	Antigua and Barbuda	W 2-1	Basseterre	GCq	Elva 22, Gilbert 27		Bedeau GRN
12-12	Jamaica	D 1-1	Vieux Fort	GCq	Joseph.E 23		Jeanvillier MTQ
19-12	Jamaica	L 1-2	Kingston	GCq	Elva 23	2 500	Gutierrez CUB
2005							

No international matches played in 2005

2006

No international matches played in 2006 before July

Fr = Friendly match • GC = CONCACAF Gold Cup • WC = FIFA World Cup™ • q = qualifier • † Not a full international

NATIONAL TEAM RECORDS AND RECORD SEQUENCES

Records			Sequence records					
Victory	14-1	VIR 2001	Wins	5	2000	Clean sheets	5	1990-1991
Defeat	0-5	TRI 1995, JAM 2003	Defeats	5	1996	Goals scored	14	1999-2000
Player Caps	n/a		Undefeated	7	1982-1983	Without goal	3	2004
Player Goals	n/a		Without win	6	1996-1997	Goals against	12	2001-02

RECENT LEAGUE AND CUP RECORD

Championship		Cup
Year	Champions	Winners
2000	Roots Alley Ballers	Rovers United
2001	VSADC	VSADC
2002	VSADC	VSADC
2003	season readjustment	18 Plus
2004	Roots Alley Ballers	Northern United
2005	Northern United	No tournament played
2006	Canaries	Elite Challengers

ST LUCIA COUNTRY INFORMATION

Capital	Castries	Independence	1979 from the UK	GDP per Capita	$5 400
Population	164 213	Status	Parliamentary democracy	GNP Ranking	165
Area km²	616	Language	English	Dialling code	+1758
Population density	266 per km²	Literacy rate	67%	Internet code	.lc
% in urban areas	48%	Main religion	Christian	GMT +/−	-4
Towns/Cities ('000)	Castries 13; Vieux Fort 4; Micoud 3; Dennery 3; Soufrière 3; Gros Islet 2				
Neighbours (km)	Atlantic Ocean & Carribbean Sea 158				
Main stadia	Bones Park – Castries 20 000; National Stadium – Vieux Fort				

LES – LESOTHO

NATIONAL TEAM RECORD
JULY 1ST 2002 TO JULY 9TH 2006

PL	W	D	L	F	A	%
30	6	10	14	29	44	36.7

FIFA/COCA-COLA WORLD RANKING

1993	1994	1995	1996	1997	1998	1999	2000	2001	2002	2003	2004	2005	High	Low
138	135	149	162	149	140	154	136	126	132	120	144	145	120 12/03	165 04/97

2005–2006											
08/05	09/05	10/05	11/05	12/05	01/06	02/06	03/06	04/06	05/06	06/06	07/06
146	147	147	146	145	146	146	146	147	141	-	133

Tragedy befell football in Lesotho in 2005 with the death in a car crash of the charismatic president of the country's football association, Thabo Makakole. A past candidate for a place on the Confederation of African Football's executive committee, his passing cast a shadow over the game in the country, which was again restricted to regional competition. With Lesotho not making it to the group phase of the 2006 FIFA World Cup™ qualifiers, focus was again firmly placed on achieving a result in the COSAFA Castle Cup. The Basotho capital Maseru hosted the first of the 2006 mini-tournaments but 'Likuena' (the Crocodiles) looked short of practice as they edged past

INTERNATIONAL HONOURS
None

Mozambique on penalties, only to be solidly beaten by Germany-bound Angola. It was a baptism of fire for Motheo Mohapi, the new national coach, who only five years earlier had been a regular member of the national side's midfield. He replaced the German Johnny Hey, in charge for only two matches before returning to Europe. Likhopo won the Premier League in Lesotho for a second successive season as they continued to buy up all the top talent in the country. Their CAF Champions League campaign, however, lasted just two matches, beaten on aggregate by South Africa's Mamelodi Sundowns in the first round of the competition.

THE FIFA BIG COUNT OF 2000

	Male	Female		Male	Female
Registered players	27 400	0	Referees	70	0
Non registered players	5 000	0	Officials	2 000	0
Youth players	2 000	10 000	Total involved	43 770	
Total players	41 700		Number of clubs	100	
Professional players	0	0	Number of teams	910	

Lesotho Football Association (LEFA)
Old Polo Ground, PO Box 1879, Maseru-100, Lesotho
Tel +266 22311879   Fax +266 22310586
lefa@leo.co.ls   www.lefa.org.ls
President: PHAFANE Salemane   General Secretary: MOKALANYANE Boniface
Vice-President: MOSOTHOANE Pitso   Treasurer: TBD   Media Officer: MONNE
Men's Coach: MOHAPI Motheo   Women's Coach: MASIMONA Lethoia
LEFA formed: 1932   CAF: 1964   FIFA: 1964
Blue shirts, Green shorts, White socks

RECENT INTERNATIONAL MATCHES PLAYED BY LESOTHO

2003	Opponents	Score		Venue	Comp	Scorers	Att	Referee
9-03	Botswana	W	1-0	Gaborone	Fr	Mpakanyane [13]		
16-03	Congo DR	D	2-2	Maseru	Fr	Phiri [60], Maseela [89]		
19-03	Swaziland	L	0-1	Mbabane	Fr		400	
22-03	Mozambique	D	0-0	Maputo	CCr1	L 4-5p		Lwanja MWI
16-05	Botswana	L	1-2	Maseru	Fr	Ramafole [17]		
21-05	Malawi	D	0-0	Maseru	Fr			
25-05	Swaziland	W	2-1	Maseru	Fr	Potse 2 [87 89]		
14-06	Senegal	L	0-3	Dakar	CNq			
6-07	Gambia	W	1-0	Maseru	CNq	OG [89]		
4-10	Swaziland	W	5-2	Maseru	Fr	OG 13, Mpakanyane 2 [49 53], Mosothoane [55], Ramafole [89]		
8-10	South Africa	L	0-3	Maseru	Fr			
11-10	Botswana	L	1-4	Gaborone	WCq	Ramafole [64]	10 000	Manuel Joao ANG
16-11	Botswana	D	0-0	Maseru	WCq		9 000	Shikapande ZIM
2004								
29-02	Botswana	D	0-0	Maseru	CCr1	L 10-11p	10 000	Mufeti NAM
15-12	Botswana	D	1-1	Maseru	Fr			
2005								
19-03	Namibia	L	1-2	Maseru	Fr			
1-06	Swaziland	L	3-4	Somhlolo	Fr			
11-06	Malawi	L	1-2	Lusaka	CCr1	Potse [46]		Mpanisi ZAM
26-06	Mozambique	L	0-1	Maputo	Fr			
2006								
14-04	Swaziland	W	5-0	Maseru	Fr	Ramafole [27], Mothoane [38], Shale 2 [64 74], Muso [85]		
16-04	Swaziland	D	2-2	Maseru	Fr	Seema [83], Shale [88]		
29-04	Mozambique	D	0-0	Maseru	CCr1	W 5-4p		Jovinala MWI
30-04	Angola	L	1-3	Maseru	CCr1	Moletsane [89]		Mlangeni SWZ
10-05	South Africa	D	0-0	Maseru	Fr			

Fr = Friendly match • CN = CAF African Cup of Nations • CC = COSAFA Castle Cup • WC = FIFA World Cup™ • q = qualifier • r1 = first round group

LESOTHO NATIONAL TEAM RECORDS AND RECORD SEQUENCES

Records			Sequence records				
Victory	4-0	BOT 1992	Wins	3	1979	Clean sheets	3	1992
Defeat	0-7	COD 1993	Defeats	6	1995-1997	Goals scored	6	1992
Player Caps	n/a		Undefeated	7	1992	Without goal	3	Three times
Player Goals	n/a		Without win	11	1981-1992	Goals against	12	2000-2001

RECENT LEAGUE AND CUP RECORD

Championship		Cup	
Year	Champions		Winners
2000	Lesotho Prisons Service		RLDF Maseru
2001	RLDF Maseru		
2002	Lesotho Prisons Service		
2003	Matlama FC Maseru		
2004	RLDF Maseru		
2005	Likhopo Maseru		
2006	Likhopo Maseru		

LESOTHO COUNTRY INFORMATION

Capital	Maseru	Independence	1966 from the UK	GDP per Capita	3 000
Population	1 865 040	Status	Constutional Monarchy	GNP Ranking	153
Area km²	30 355	Language	Sesotho, English	Dialling code	+266
Population density	61 per km²	Literacy rate	84%	Internet code	.ls
% in urban areas	23%	Main religion	Christian 80%	GMT +/−	+2
Towns/Cities ('000)	Maseru 194; Hlotse 46; Mafeteng 40; Maputsoa 31; Teyateyaneng 25; Mohale's Hoek 22				
Neighbours (km)	South Africa 909				
Main stadia	National Stadium − Maseru 20 000				

LIB – LEBANON

NATIONAL TEAM RECORD
JULY 1ST 2002 TO JULY 9TH 2006

PL	W	D	L	F	A	%
. 35	8	9	18	36	60	35.7

FIFA/COCA-COLA WORLD RANKING

1993	1994	1995	1996	1997	1998	1999	2000	2001	2002	2003	2004	2005	High	Low
108	129	134	97	90	85	111	110	93	119	115	105	125	**85** 12/98	**145** 11/95

2005–2006											
08/05	09/05	10/05	11/05	12/05	01/06	02/06	03/06	04/06	05/06	06/06	07/06
113	118	122	120	125	126	121	120	121	122	-	112

In July 2006 Lebanon was supposed to have hosted the West Asian Championship but the tournament became the first sporting casualty of the cross border hostilities with Israel. It was soon followed by the decision to withdraw the national team from the 2007 AFC Asian Cup and the hope is that football does not return to the dark days of the 1970s and 1980s when it almost ceased to be played in the country. The irony is that in the wake of hosting the 2000 AFC Asian Cup, the game in Lebanon was flourishing. In 2005 Al Nejmeh had made history by reaching the AFC Cup Final, the first Lebanese team to get that far in a continental competition. A narrow 1-0 defeat in the 1st

INTERNATIONAL HONOURS
None

leg in Amman against Jordan's Al Faysali brought hope for the home leg, but Nejmeh had to be content with the runners-up spot after losing the return 3-2. In the 2005-06 championship, Nejmeh, along with Beirut rivals Al Ansar, dominated the League. The two met on the final weekend of the season with Ansar holding a three point advantage. When Ali Nasereddine put Nejmeh 2-0 up at half time, the title looked to be theirs but second half goals from Hawar Al Mullah Mohamed and Fadi Ghosin won the title for Ansar. A week later they completed the ninth double in their history when they beat Al Hikma 3-1 in the Cup Final.

THE FIFA BIG COUNT OF 2000

	Male	Female		Male	Female
Registered players	21 912	0	Referees	155	0
Non registered players	300 000	0	Officials	2 680	0
Youth players	5 000	0	Total involved	329 747	
Total players	326 912		Number of clubs	174	
Professional players	62	0	Number of teams	2 070	

Lebanese Football Association (FLFA)
Verdun Street - Bristol, Radwan Center, PO Box 4732, Beirut, Lebanon
Tel +961 1 745745   Fax +961 1 349529
libanfa@cyberia.net.lb   www.lebanesefa.com
President: HAYDAR Hachem   General Secretary: ALAMEH Rahif
Vice-President: KAMAR EDDINE Ahmad   Treasurer: AL RABA'A Mahmoud   Media Officer: None
Men's Coach: TBD   Women's Coach: None
FLFA formed: 1933   AFC: 1964   FIFA: 1935
Red shirts, White shorts, Red socks

RECENT INTERNATIONAL MATCHES PLAYED BY LEBANON

2002	Opponents	Score		Venue	Comp	Scorers	Att	Referee
1-09	Jordan	L	0-1	Damascus	WAr1			
3-09	Iran	L	0-2	Damascus	WAr1		2 000	Haj Khader SYR
19-12	Saudi Arabia	L	0-1	Kuwait City	ARr1		700	El Beltagy EGY
21-12	Syria	L	1-4	Kuwait City	ARr1	Kassas [54]	1 000	Guezzaz MAR
24-12	Yemen	W	4-2	Kuwait City	ARr1	Antar.R 3 [11 51 60], Hojeij [62]	1 000	Hamza KUW
26-12	Bahrain	D	0-0	Kuwait City	ARr1		1 000	Guirat TUN
2003								
15-08	Syria	D	0-0	Damascus	Fr	Abandoned at half-time		
22-08	Syria	W	1-0	Beirut	Fr	Ali Atwi [57]		
4-09	Korea DPR	W	1-0	Pyongyang	ACq	Farah [56]		
19-09	Bahrain	L	3-4	Manama	Fr	Kassas [53], Mohammed [69], Al Jamal [86]		
17-10	Jordan	L	0-1	Amman	ACq			
3-11	Korea DPR	D	1-1	Beirut	ACq	Hamieh [58]	25 000	
12-11	Jordan	L	0-2	Beirut	ACq		15 000	
19-11	Iran	L	0-3	Beirut	ACq			Al Marzouqi UAE
28-11	Iran	L	0-1	Tehran	ACq			Rungklay THA
16-12	Kuwait	L	0-2	Larnaca	Fr			
18-12	Kuwait	D	0-0	Larnaca	Fr			
2004								
8-02	Bahrain	W	2-1	Beirut	Fr	Chahoud [90], Al Jamal [90]		
18-02	Korea Republic	L	0-2	Suwon	WCq		22 000	Al Dosari KSA
23-03	Syria	L	0-1	Jounieh	Fr			
31-03	Vietnam	W	2-0	Nam Dinh	WCq	Antar.R [83], Hamieh [88]	25 000	Irmatov UZB
26-05	Bahrain	D	2-2	Beirut	Fr	Ali Atwi [70], Balout [81]		
9-06	Maldives	W	3-0	Beirut	WCq	Zein [21], Antar.R [87], Nasseredine [93+]	18 000	Nurilddin Salman IRQ
17-06	Iran	L	0-4	Tehran	WAr1			
19-06	Syria	L	1-3	Tehran	WAr1	Zein [65]		
3-07	China PR	L	0-6	Chongqing	Fr			
31-08	Jordan	D	2-2	Amman	Fr			
8-09	Maldives	W	5-2	Male	WCq	Nasseredine 2 [4 58], Antar.F [44], Chahoud [63], Antar.R [75]	12 000	Al Ajmi OMA
3-10	Kuwait	L	1-3	Tripoli	Fr	Chahoud [64]		
6-10	Kuwait	D	1-1	Beirut	Fr	Chahoud [45]		
13-10	Korea Republic	D	1-1	Beirut	WCq	Nasseredine [27]	38 000	Irmatov UZB
17-11	Vietnam	D	0-0	Beirut	WCq		1 000	Ebrahim BHR
1-12	Qatar	L	1-4	Doha	Fr	Nasseredine		
2005								
2-02	Bahrain	L	1-2	Doha	Fr	Ali Atwi		
2006								
27-01	Saudi Arabia	W	2-1	Riyadh	Fr	Ghaddar [14], Nasseredine [70]		
22-02	Kuwait	D	1-1	Beirut	ACq	Nasseredine [67]	8 000	Mujghef JOR

Fr = Friendly match • WA = West Asian Federation Cup • AR = Arab Cup • AC = AFC Asian Cup • WC = FIFA World Cup™
q = qualifier • r1 = first round group

LEBANON NATIONAL TEAM RECORDS AND RECORD SEQUENCES

Records			Sequence records					
Victory	11-1	PHI 1967	Wins	6	1995-1996	Clean sheets	4	1997
Defeat	0-8	IRQ 1959	Defeats	5	1979-1985	Goals scored	10	1993-1996
Player Caps	n/a		Undefeated	9	1993-96, 1996-97	Without goal	11	1974-1988
Player Goals	n/a		Without win	11	1998	Goals against	11	1997-1998

LEBANON COUNTRY INFORMATION

Capital	Beirut	Independence	1944 from France	GDP per Capita	$4 800
Population	3 777 218	Status	Republic	GNP Ranking	70
Area km²	10 400	Language	Arabic	Dialling code	+961
Population density	363 per km²	Literacy rate	87%	Internet code	.lb
% in urban areas	87%	Main religion	Muslim 60%, Christian 39%	GMT + / –	+2
Towns/Cities ('000)	Beirut 1 252; Tripoli 229; Sidon 163; Sour 135; Nabatiye 98; Jounieh 96; Zahlah 78				
Neighbours (km)	Syria 375; Israel 79; Mediterranean Sea 225				
Main stadia	Camille Chamoun – Beirut 57 000; International Olympic – Tripoli 22 400				

LEBANON 2005–06

PREMIER LEAGUE

	Pl	W	D	L	F	A	Pts	Ansar	Nijmeh	Safa	Mabarra	Ahed	S. Zghorta	Tadamon	Tripoli	Rayyan	Racing
Al Ansar †	18	15	2	1	50	14	47		2-2	3-2	3-2	2-0	3-0	2-1	1-0	2-1	5-1
Al Nijmeh	18	14	2	2	46	14	44	1-0		0-0	3-1	3-2	2-0	2-0	0-1	2-0	6-1
Safa	18	9	5	4	21	21	32	0-5	0-4		2-1	1-0	0-2	1-1	0-0	1-0	5-2
Al Mabarra	18	9	2	7	34	21	29	0-3	2-3	0-1		1-1	3-1	2-0	0-0	5-0	2-0
Al Ahed	18	8	3	7	37	19	27	1-2	2-1	0-1	1-2		2-2	1-0	5-1	0-1	3-0
Salam Zghorta	18	5	5	8	17	30	20	1-4	0-1	1-1	0-1	0-8		1-0	1-0	1-0	2-2
Al Tadamon Tyre	18	3	6	9	13	26	15	1-1	1-5	1-3	2-1	1-3	1-0		1-1	0-0	2-1
Tripoli SC	18	2	8	8	8	21	14	0-2	1-4	0-0	0-2	1-1	2-2	0-0		0-1	0-0
Al Rayyan	18	4	2	12	10	30	14	1-4	0-2	0-1	1-2	0-3	0-3	2-1	0-1		2-1
Racing Beirut	18	1	3	12	12	52	8	0-6	1-5	1-2	0-7	0-4	0-0	0-0	1-0	1-1	

12/11/2005 – 13/05/2006 • † Qualified for AFC Cup

FA CUP 2005–06

Round of 16		Quarter-finals		Semi-finals		Final	
Al Ansar *	3						
Al Ahly Sidon	1	Al Ansar	2 3				
Tripoli SC	0	Al Nijmeh *	0 4				
Al Nijmeh *	1			Al Ansar *	1 2		
Racing Beirut *	3			Al Ahed	0 1		
Nijmeh Maaraka	1	Racing Beirut	1 0				
Homenetmen	1	Al Ahed *	2 1				
Al Ahed *	3					Al Ansar	3
Al Mabarra *	3					Al Hikma	1
Al Rayyan	1	Al Mabarra	0 0 5p				
Mahabbah Tripoli	1 2p	Salam Zghorta *	0 0 4p				
Salam Zghorta *	1 3p			Al Mabarra	1 1	**CUP FINAL**	
Shabab Sahel	2			Al Hikma *	0 2	Beirut, 21-05-2006	
Al Tadamon Tyre *	1	Shabab Sahel	0 0			Scorers - Fabio 2, Hoiwar Mulla for Ansar;	
Safa *	1	Al Hikma *	1 1			Yousuf Al Gohery for Hikma	
Al Hikma	2			* Home team/Home team in the first leg			

RECENT LEAGUE AND CUP RECORD

	Championship						Cup		
Year	Champions	Pts	Runners-up	Pts	Third	Pts	Winners	Score	Runners-up
1997	Al Ansar	65	Al Nijmeh	58	Homenetmen	49	Al Nijmeh	2-0	Al Ansar
1998	Al Ansar	63	Al Nijmeh	53	Al Tadamon	43	Al Nijmeh	2-1	Homenmen
1999	Al Ansar	48	Safa	38	Al Tadamon	36	Al Ansar	2-1	Homenmen
2000	Al Njmeh	47	Al Ansar	44	Al Akha 'a-Ahly	33	Shabab Al Sahel	1-1 5-4p	Safa
2001	Championship cancelled due to match fixing scandal						Al Tadamon	2-1	Al Ansar
2002	Al Nijmeh	61	La Sagesse	60	Al Tadamon	59	Al Ansar	2-0	Al Ahed
2003	Olympic Beirut	54	Al Nijmeh	53	Al Ahed	50	Olympic Beirut	3-2	Al Nijmeh
2004	Al Ansar	54	Al Ahed	47	Olympic Beirut	35	Al Ahed	2-1	Al Nijmeh
2005	Al Nijmeh	44	Al Ansar	44	Al Ahed	36	Al Ahed	2-1	Olympic Beirut
2006	Al Ansar	47	Al Nijmeh	44	Safa	32	Al Ansar	3-1	Al Hikma

LIE – LIECHTENSTEIN

NATIONAL TEAM RECORD
JULY 1ST 2002 TO JULY 9TH 2006

PL	W	D	L	F	A	%
30	3	4	23	21	63	16.7

FIFA/COCA-COLA WORLD RANKING

1993	1994	1995	1996	1997	1998	1999	2000	2001	2002	2003	2004	2005	High	Low
160	156	157	154	158	159	125	147	150	147	148	142	122	122 12/05	165 09/98

2005–2006											
08/05	09/05	10/05	11/05	12/05	01/06	02/06	03/06	04/06	05/06	06/06	07/06
139	123	126	124	122	123	124	124	124	123	-	124

The qualifiers for the 2006 FIFA World Cup™ proved that you dismiss Liechtenstein at your peril. The national team may not win many games but they are now capable of causing an upset or two and very rarely get beaten by more than a couple of goals in a game. Group winners Portugal and runners-up Slovakia both left Vaduz having dropped points at the excellent Rheinpark Stadion, while fellow minnows Luxembourg were comprehensively beaten twice as the tiny principality collected eight points from their 12 matches, an unimaginable figure before the qualifiers started. The task for Martin Andermatt's men is to see if they can maintain their current standing in a strong

INTERNATIONAL HONOURS
None

UEFA Euro 2008™ qualifying group and perhaps even improve upon their highest-ever position of 122 in the revised FIFA/Coca-Cola World Ranking. Domestically FC Vaduz continued to make the headlines, winning a ninth successive Cup Final with a 4-2 victory over FC Balzers, and they even won a UEFA Cup tie against Moldova's Dacia, although they lost in the next round to Besiktas. Vaduz had a disappointing season in the Swiss Second Division, however, especially having just missed out on promotion to the Super League the season before, but their ninth consecutive triumph in the Liechtenstein Cup is a world record that is growing by the year.

THE FIFA BIG COUNT OF 2000

	Male	Female		Male	Female
Registered players	708	22	Referees	30	0
Non registered players	300	40	Officials	200	0
Youth players	745	50	Total involved	2 095	
Total players	1 865		Number of clubs	7	
Professional players	8	0	Number of teams	100	

Liechtensteiner Fussballverband (LFV)
Landstrasse 149, 9494 Schaan, Postfach 165, 9490 Vaduz, Liechtenstein
Tel +423 2374747   Fax +423 2374748
info@lfv.li   www.lfv.li
President: WALSER Reinhard   General Secretary: OSPELT Roland
Vice-President: HILTI Fredi   Treasurer: GERNER Urs   Media Officer: FROMMELT Judith
Men's Coach: ANDERMATT Martin   Women's Coach: None
LFV formed: 1934   UEFA: 1992   FIFA: 1974
Blue shirts with white trimmings, Red shorts, Blue socks or Red shirts with white trimmings, Blue shorts, Red Socks

RECENT INTERNATIONAL MATCHES PLAYED BY LIECHTENSTEIN

2003	Opponents	Score	Venue	Comp	Scorers	Att	Referee
29-03	England	L 0-2	Vaduz	ECq		3 548	Kasnaferis GRE
2-04	Slovakia	L 0-4	Trnava	ECq			Ceferin SVN
30-04	Saudi Arabia	W 1-0	Vaduz	Fr	Burgmeier.F [22]	1 200	Rogalla SUI
7-06	Macedonia FYR	L 1-3	Skopje	ECq	Beck.R [18]	6 000	Jara CZE
20-08	San Marino	D 2-2	Vaduz	Fr	Frick.M [16], Burgmeier.F [23]	850	Wildhaber SUI
6-09	Turkey	L 0-3	Vaduz	ECq		3 548	Van Egmond NED
10-09	England	L 0-2	Manchester	ECq		64 931	Fisker DEN
11-10	Slovakia	L 0-2	Vaduz	ECq		800	Hyytia FIN
2004							
28-04	San Marino	L 0-1	Serravalle	Fr		700	Sammut MLT
3-06	Greece	L 0-2	Vaduz	Fr		2 000	Petignat SUI
6-06	Switzerland	L 0-1	Zürich	Fr		10 200	Drabek AUT
18-08	Estonia	L 1-2	Vaduz	WCq	D'Elia [49]	912	Bozinovski MKD
3-09	Netherlands	L 0-3	Utrecht	Fr		15 000	Brines SCO
8-09	Slovakia	L 0-7	Bratislava	WCq		5 620	Delevic SCG
9-10	Portugal	D 2-2	Vaduz	WCq	Burgmeier.F [48], Beck.T [76]	3 548	Panic BIH
13-10	Luxembourg	W 4-0	Luxembourg	WCq	Stocklasa.Mt [41], Burgmeier.F 2 [44] [85], Frick.M [57p]	3 748	Jara CZE
17-11	Latvia	L 1-3	Vaduz	WCq	Frick.M [32]	1 460	Szabo HUN
2005							
26-03	Russia	L 1-2	Vaduz	WCq	Beck.T [40]	2 400	Bernsten NOR
4-06	Estonia	L 0-2	Tallinn	WCq		3 000	Whitby WAL
8-06	Latvia	L 0-1	Riga	WCq		8 000	Eriksson SWE
17-08	Slovakia	D 0-0	Vaduz	WCq		1 150	Layec FRA
3-09	Russia	L 0-2	Moscow	WCq		18 123	Hyytia FIN
7-09	Luxembourg	W 3-0	Vaduz	WCq	Frick [38], Fischer [77], Beck [92+]	2 300	Skomina SVN
8-10	Portugal	L 1-2	Aveiro	WCq	Fischer [32]	29 000	Gilewski POL
12-11	FYR Macedonia	L 1-2	Vaduz	Fr	D'Elia [35]	1 350	Nobs SUI
2006							
2-06	Togo	L 0-1	Vaduz	Fr		2 700	Schorgenhofer AUT
7-06	Australia	L 1-3	Ulm	Fr	OG [8]	5 872	Stark GER

Fr = Friendly match • EC = UEFA EURO 2004™ • WC = FIFA World Cup™ • q = qualifier

NATIONAL TEAM PLAYERS AND COACHES

Record Caps			Record Goals			Recent Coaches	
HASLER Daniel	1993-'06	66	FRICK Mario	1990-'06	8	RIEDL Alfred	1997
FRICK Mario	1990-'06	62	BURGMEIER Franz	1999-'06	5	BURZLE Erich	1998
TELSER Martin	1996-'06	61	STOCKLASA Martin	1996-'06	5	LOOSE Ralf	1998-'03
STOCKLASA Martin	1996-'06	58	BECK Thomas	1993-'06	3	HORMANN Walter	2003-'04
BECK Thomas	1993-'06	48				ANDERMATT Martin	2004-

LIECHTENSTEIN NATIONAL TEAM RECORDS AND RECORD SEQUENCES

Records			Sequence records				
Victory	4-0	LUX 2004	Wins	3	1981-1982	Clean sheets	2	1981-82, 1999
Defeat	1-11	MKD 1996	Defeats	17	1995-1998	Goals scored	4	2004-2005
Player Caps	66	HASLER Daniel	Undefeated	3	1981-1982	Without goal	11	1994-96, 2000-02
Player Goals	8	FRICK Mario	Without win	29	1984-1998	Goals against	22	1995-1999

LIECHTENSTEIN COUNTRY INFORMATION

Capital	Vaduz	Formation	1719	GDP per Capita	$25 000
Population	33 436	Status	Constitutional Monarchy	GNP Ranking	144
Area km²	160	Language	German	Dialling code	+423
Population density	208 per km²	Literacy rate	100%	Internet code	.li
% in urban areas	21%	Main religion	Christian 83%	GMT + / –	+1
Towns/Cities ('000)	Schaan 6; Vaduz 5; Triesen 5; Balzers 4; Eschen 4; Mauren 3; Triesenberg 2				
Neighbours (km)	Austria 34; Switzerland 41				
Main stadia	Rheinpark Stadion – Vaduz 8 000				

LTU – LITHUANIA

NATIONAL TEAM RECORD
JULY 1ST 2002 TO JULY 9TH 2006

PL	W	D	L	F	A	%
34	10	5	19	36	49	36.8

FIFA/COCA-COLA WORLD RANKING

1993	1994	1995	1996	1997	1998	1999	2000	2001	2002	2003	2004	2005	High		Low	
85	59	43	48	45	54	50	85	97	100	101	100	100	42	08/97	118	09/04

2005–2006											
08/05	09/05	10/05	11/05	12/05	01/06	02/06	03/06	04/06	05/06	06/06	07/06
92	95	97	98	100	102	100	96	99	93	-	69

At times during the season there seemed to be more stories with Lithuanian interest emanating from Edinburgh than from Vilnius. Tycoon Roman Romanov's roller coaster reign at Heart of Midlothian saw the Edinburgh club win the Scottish FA Cup and finish second in the League, with four Lithuanian players and, by the end of the campaign, a Lithuanian coach in Valdas Ivanauskas. At home, the 2005 season was dominated by Ekranas and FBK Kaunas who once again were in a different class to the other teams in the League. FBK, another club in the Romanov stable, were looking for a seventh consecutive championship but Ekranas, coached by Virjinijus Liubsys, who

INTERNATIONAL HONOURS
None

had led them to their previous title success in 1993, won the League with three rounds to spare thanks to a 3-1 victory against Atlantas. Four days earlier FBK had beaten Vetra Vilnius 3-1 in the Cup Final to retain the trophy. One of the traditional giants of the Lithuanian game, Zalgiris Vilnius, had a terrible season and they have now won just one championship in 14 seasons, prompting the inevitable talk of a take-over by Romanov. After a bright start to their 2006 FIFA World Cup™ qualifying campaign, the Lithuanian national team finished it on a low, winning just two matches - both against San Marino.

THE FIFA BIG COUNT OF 2000

	Male	Female		Male	Female
Registered players	17 069	100	Referees	125	5
Non registered players	35 000	500	Officials	1 200	100
Youth players	12 179	450	Total involved	66 728	
Total players	65 298		Number of clubs	60	
Professional players	224	0	Number of teams	1 135	

Lithuanian Football Federation (LFF)
Seimyniskiu 15, 2005 Vilnius, Lithuania
Tel +370 52638741   Fax +370 52638740
info@futbolas.lt   www.futbolas.lt
President: VARANAVICIUS Liutauras   General Secretary: KVEDARAS Julius
Vice-President: BABRAVICIUS Gintautas   Treasurer: ZYGELIENR Dalia   Media Officer: ZIZAITE Vaiva
Men's Coach: LIUBINSKAS Algimantas   Women's Coach: VIKTORAVICIUS Rimas
LFF formed: 1922   UEFA: 1992   FIFA: 1923-1943 & 1992
Yellow shirts with green trimmings, Green shorts, Yellow socks or Green shirts with yellow trimming, Green shorts, Green socks

RECENT INTERNATIONAL MATCHES PLAYED BY LITHUANIA

2002	Opponents		Score	Venue	Comp	Scorers	Att	Referee
21-08	Israel	L	2-4	Kaunas	Fr	Fomenka [10], Poskus [32]	3 000	Chykun BLR
7-09	Germany	L	0-2	Kaunas	ECq		8 500	Poll ENG
12-10	Faroe Islands	W	2-0	Kaunas	ECq	Razanauskas [23p], Poskus [37]	2 500	Delevic YUG
16-10	Iceland	L	0-3	Reykjavík	ECq		3 513	Gilewski POL
2003								
12-02	Latvia	L	1-2	Antalya	Fr	OG [34]	700	
29-03	Germany	D	1-1	Nuremberg	ECq	Razanauskas [73]	40 754	Esquinas Torres ESP
2-04	Scotland	W	1-0	Kaunas	ECq	Razanauskas [75p]	8 000	Stuchlik AUT
30-04	Romania	L	0-1	Kaunas	Fr		5 000	Sipailo LVA
11-06	Iceland	L	0-3	Kaunas	ECq		7 500	Corpodean ROU
3-07	Estonia	W	5-1	Valga	BC	Morinas [39], Cesnauskis.D [45], Velicka [72] Bezykornovas [84], Cesnauskas.E [90]	800	Ingvarsson SWE
4-07	Latvia	L	1-2	Valga	BC	Tamosauskas [73]	500	Frojdfeldt SWE
20-08	Bulgaria	L	0-3	Sofia	Fr		2 000	Bolognino ITA
10-09	Faroe Islands	W	3-1	Toftir	ECq	Morinas 2 [23 57], Vencevicius [88]	2 175	Trivcovic CRO
11-10	Scotland	L	0-1	Glasgow	ECq		50 343	Colombo FRA
14-12	Poland	L	1-3	Ta'Qali	Fr	Butrimavicius [5]	100	Attard MLT
2004								
30-03	Israel	L	1-2	Tel Aviv	Fr	OG [43]	9 782	Dougal SCO
28-04	Belarus	L	0-1	Minsk	Fr		8 000	Ivanov RUS
5-06	Portugal	L	1-4	Alcochete	Fr	Vencevicius [74p]	25 000	Wilmes LUX
18-08	Russia	L	3-4	Moscow	Fr	Danilevicius [40], Poskus [83], Barasa [89]	3 500	Mikulski POL
4-09	Belgium	D	1-1	Charleroi	WCq	Jankauskas [73]	19 218	Loizou CYP
8-09	San Marino	W	4-0	Kaunas	WCq	Jankauskas 2 [18 50], Danilevicius [65], Gedgaudas [92+]	4 000	Jareci ALB
13-10	Spain	D	0-0	Vilnius	WCq		9 114	Poulat FRA
17-11	San Marino	W	1-0	Serravalle	WCq	Cesnauskis.D [41]	1 457	Nalbandyan ARM
2005								
9-02	Georgia	L	0-1	Tbilisi	Fr		1 000	Gadiyev AZE
30-03	Bosnia-Herzegovina	D	1-1	Sarajevo	WCq	Stankevicius [60]	6 000	Baskakov RUS
21-05	Latvia	W	2-0	Kaunas	BC	Morinas 2 [25 81]		
4-06	Spain	L	0-1	Valencia	WCq		25 000	Farina ITA
17-08	Belarus	W	1-0	Vilnius	Fr	Cesnauskis.D [45]	2 500	Sipailo LVA
3-09	Serbia & Montenegro	L	0-2	Belgrade	WCq		20 203	Nielsen DEN
7-09	Bosnia-Herzegovina	L	0-1	Vilnius	WCq		4 000	Kassai HUN
8-10	Serbia & Montenegro	L	0-2	Vilnius	WCq		1 500	Wegereef NED
12-10	Belgium	D	1-1	Vilnius	WCq	OG [82]	1 500	Riley ENG
2006								
1-03	Albania	W	2-1	Tirana	Fr	Savenas [34], Danilevicius [41]		Pieri ITA
2-05	Poland	W	1-0	Belchatow	Fr	Gedgaudas [14]	3 200	Bozinovski MKD

Fr = Friendly match • EC = UEFA EURO 2004™ • BC = Baltic Cup • WC = FIFA World Cup™ • q = qualifier

LITHUANIA NATIONAL TEAM RECORDS AND RECORD SEQUENCES

Records			Sequence records				
Victory	7-0	EST 1995	Wins	3	1992	Clean sheets	3	2004
Defeat	0-10	EGY 1924	Defeats	10	1936-1938	Goals scored	15	1934-1937
Player Caps	65	SKARBALIUS Aurelijus	Undefeated	5	1935, 1992	Without goal	4	1993, 1997
Player Goals	12	LINGIS Antanas	Without win	13	1936-1939	Goals against	18	1923-1936

LITHUANIA COUNTRY INFORMATION

Capital	Vilnius	Independence	1991 from the USSR	GDP per Capita	$11 400
Population	3 607 899	Status	Republic	GNP Ranking	82
Area km²	65 200	Language	Lithuanian, Russian	Dialling code	+370
Population density	55 per km²	Literacy rate	99%	Internet code	lt
% in urban areas	72%	Main religion	Christian	GMT +/-	+2
Towns/Cities ('000)	Vilnius 542; Kaunas 374; Klaipeda 192; Siauliai 130; Panevezys 117; Alytus 70				
Neighbours (km)	Latvia 453; Belarus 502; Poland 91; Russia 227; Baltic Sea 99				
Main stadia	Zalgirio – Vilnius 15 030; Aukstaitijos – Panevezys 10 000; Darius Girenas – Kaunas 8 476				

NATIONAL TEAM PLAYERS AND COACHES

Record Caps			Record Goals			Recent Coaches	
SKARBALIUS Aurelijus	1991-'05	65	LINGIS Antanas	1928-'38	12	LATOZA Kestutis	1998-'99
STAUCE Gintaras	1992-'04	61	BALTUSNIKAS Virginijus	1990-'98	9	TAUTKUS Robertas	1999-'00
TERESKINAS Andrius	1991-'00	56	CITAVICIUS Jaroslavas	1926-'33	8	STANKUS Stasys	2000
SKERLA Andrius	1996-'06	46	IVANAUSKAS Valdas	1992-'00	8	KVEDARAS Julius	2000
JANKAUSKAS Edgaras	1995-'05	45	JANKAUSKAS Edgaras	1995-'05	8	ZELKEVICIUS Benjaminas	2000-'03
ZIUKAS Tomas	1994-'98	45				LIUBINSKAS Algimantas	2003-

CLUB DIRECTORY

Club	Town/City	Stadium	Capacity	www.	Lge	Cup
Atlantas	Klaipeda	Centrinis	5 000	atlantas.lt	0	2
Ekranas	Panevezys	Aukstaitijos	10 000	fk-ekranas.lt	1	2
FBK Kaunas	Kaunas	Darius Girenas	8 476	fbk.rodiklis.lt	6	3
Nevezis	Kedainiai	Kedainlu	3 000		0	0
KFK Siauliai	Siauliai	Savlvaldybes	2 430		0	0
FK Silute	Silute	Centrinis	5 000		0	0
Suduva	Marijampole	Suduvos	4 000	fksuduva.lt	0	0
Vetra	Vilnius			fkvetra.lt	0	0
FK Vilnius	Vilnius	Zalgirio	15 030	zalgiris-vilnius.lnx.lt	0	0
Zalgiris	Vilnius	Zalgirio	15 030		3	5

RECENT LEAGUE AND CUP RECORD

	Championship						Cup		
Year	Champions	Pts	Runners-up	Pts	Third	Pts	Winners	Score	Runners-up
1990	Sirijus Klaipeda	†	Zalgiris Vilnius				Sirijus Klaipeda	0-0 4-3p	Zalgiris Vilnius
1991	Zalgiris Vilnius	3-1	Neris Vilnius				Zalgiris Vilnius	1-0	Tauras Siauliai
1992	Zalgiris Vilnius	39	Panerys Vilnius	38	Sirijus Klaipeda	33	Makabi Vilnius	1-0	Zalgiris Vilnius
1993	Ekranas Panevezys	46	Zalgiris Vilnius	43	Panerys Vilnius	36	Zalgiris Vilnius	1-0	Sirijus Klaipeda
1994	ROMAR Mazeikiai	38	Zalgiris Vilnius	37	Ekranas Panevezys	31	Zalgiris Vilnius	4-2	Ekranas Panevezys
1995	Inkaras Kaunas ‡	36	Zalgiris Vilnius	36	ROMAR Mazeikiai	34	Inkaras Kaunas	2-1	Zalgiris Vilnius
1996	Inkaras Kaunas	56	Kareda Siauliai	52	Zalgiris Vilnius	50	Kareda Siauliai	1-0	Inkaras Kaunas
1997	Kareda Siauliai	64	Zalgiris Vilnius	56	Inkaras Kaunas	53	Zalgiris Vilnius	1-0	Inkaras Kaunas
1998	Kareda Siauliai	79	Zalgiris Vilnius	77	Ekranas Panevezys	68	Ekranas Panevezys	1-0	FBK Kaunas
1999	Kareda Siauliai	59	Kareda Siauliai	58	FBK Kaunas	57	Kareda Siauliai	3-0	FBK Kaunas
1999	FBK Kaunas	41	Zalgiris Vilnius	36	Atlantas Klaipeda	33			
2000	FBK Kaunas	86	Zalgiris Vilnius	83	Atlantas Klaipeda	67	Ekranas Panevezys	1-0	Zalgiris Vilnius
2001	FBK Kaunas	85	Atlantas Klaipeda	69	Zalgiris Vilnius	69	Atlantas Klaipeda	1-0	Zalgiris Vilnius
2002	FBK Kaunas	78	Atlantas Klaipeda	67	Ekranas Panevezys	55	FBK Kaunas	3-1	Süduva Marijampole
2003							Atlantas Klaipeda	1-1 3-1p	Vetra Rudiskes
2003	FBK Kaunas	68	Ekranas Panevezys	62	Vetra	47	Zalgiris Vilnius	3-1	Ekranas Panevezys
2004	FBK Kaunas	65	Ekranas Panevezys	62	Atlantas Klaipeda	50	FBK Kaunas	0-0 2-1p	Atlantas Klaipeda
2005	Ekranas Panevezys	92	FBK Kaunas	82	Süduva Marijampole	59	FBK Kaunas	2-0	Vetra Vilnius

Two leagues were played in 1999 and an extra cup competition held in 2003 due to a change in the season calendar • † Sirijus won 4-3 on penalties after a 0-0 draw • ‡ Inkaras beat Zalgiris 2-0 in a play-off

LITHUANIA 2005

A LYGA

	Pl	W	D	L	F	A	Pts	Ekranas	Kaunas	Suduva	Vetra	Vilnius	Silute	Atlantas	Zalgiris	Siauliai	Nevezis
Ekranas Panevezys †	36	29	5	2	87	23	92		1-0 0-0	2-0 4-1	8-0 1-0	5-1 2-0	2-1 3-0	0-0 1-2	2-0 4-0	1-0 1-5	1-0 4-1
FBK Kaunas ‡	36	26	4	6	89	25	82	1-2 2-3		3-0 3-1	0-2 3-0	0-0 1-0	4-1 5-0	2-1 2-0	4-0 3-2	5-1 0-0	5-0 3-0
Suduva Marijampole ‡	36	16	11	9	67	43	59	2-2 1-2	0-1 3-4		2-2 1-1	2-2 1-1	4-1 2-1	1-0 2-1	1-1 2-0	1-0 0-0	5-0 5-1
Vetra Vilnius	36	17	6	13	45	45	57	0-2 1-1	0-1 0-3	1-0 0-2		2-1 2-0	1-0 3-1	0-2 3-2	2-0 2-1	2-1 2-0	1-0 2-1
FK Vilnius	36	11	14	11	36	29	47	0-1 0-1	1-0 0-0	0-0 1-1	0-0 1-1		0-1 5-1	1-0 4-1	2-0 0-1	0-0 1-1	1-1 3-0
FK Silute	36	12	8	16	44	61	44	1-5 0-2	0-4 1-4	1-1 0-0	2-0 3-1	1-1 1-1		3-0 1-0	1-0 0-1	4-1 2-1	3-2 3-0
Atlantas Klaipeda	36	11	8	17	40	52	41	0-1 1-3	1-3 0-5	1-0 1-3	1-0 1-3	0-1 1-0	0-0 2-2		2-2 1-1	3-1 2-0	5-1 2-2
Zalgiris Vilnius	36	11	8	17	40	52	41	0-4 0-2	0-2 2-3	2-4 0-1	1-0 1-1	1-0 0-0	2-0 0-0	1-2 0-1		0-0 1-1	4-0 5-2
KFK Siauliai	36	8	9	19	40	61	33	2-2 1-3	1-0 2-3	1-3 1-4	1-2 1-0	0-1 0-2	2-1 1-4	2-0 1-1	2-3 0-4		4-0 2-2
Nevezis Kedainiai	36	0	5	31	18	115	5	0-4 0-5	0-8 0-2	1-5 1-6	0-6 0-2	0-2 0-3	0-0 1-3	0-0 0-3	0-2 1-2	0-2 1-2	

12/04/2005 - 12/11/2005 • † Qualified for the UEFA Champions League • ‡ Qualified for the UEFA Cup • Top scorers: Mantas SAVENAS, Ekranas, 27; Tomas RADZINEVICIUS, Suduva, 25; Povilas LUKSYS, Ekranas, 19; Ricardas BENIUSIS, FBK Kaunas, 16; Andrius VELICKA, FBK Kaunas, 15

LITHUANIA 2005
LFF 1 LYGA (2)

	Pl	W	D	L	F	A	Pts
Alytis Alytus	34	25	6	3	92	21	81
Kauno Jegeriai	34	23	6	5	83	18	75
Vetra-2 Vilnius	34	21	8	5	70	20	71
Polonija Vilnius	34	21	5	8	85	33	66
Gelezinis Vilkas Vilnius	34	18	7	9	66	41	61
KFK Siauliai-2	34	17	7	10	54	45	58
LKKA Teledema Kaunas	34	17	6	11	67	46	57
Suduva-2 Marijampole	34	16	7	11	57	38	55
Lietava Jonava	34	17	4	13	63	48	55
Kruoja Pakruojis	34	16	5	13	64	50	53
Atletas Kaunas	34	13	5	16	49	45	44
Babrungas Plunge	34	12	6	16	48	54	42
Kursiai Neringa	34	9	7	18	42	58	34
Vilkmerge Ukmerge	34	8	8	18	34	60	32
FK Vilnius-2	34	8	4	22	32	61	28
Utenis Utena	34	9	1	24	40	115	28
Tauras Erra Taurage	34	7	6	21	45	83	27
Rodovitas Klaipeda	34	0	0	34	19	174	0

9/04/2005 - 29/10/2005

LFF TAURE 2005-06

First round

First round			Quarter-finals			Semi-finals			Final		
FBK Kaunas *	4	8									
Vetra-2 Vilnius	0	0	FBK Kaunas *	1	1						
FK Vilnius	1	0	KFK Siauliai	0	1						
KFK Siauliai *	1	1				FBK Kaunas *	0	1			
FK Silute *	5	2				Ekranas Panevezys	0	0			
Babrungas Plunge	1	0	FK Silute *	1	0						
Lietava Jonava	0	0	Ekranas Panevezys	1	2						
Ekranas Panevezys *	3	5							FBK Kaunas ‡		2
Atlantas Klaipeda *	6	0							Vetra Vilnius		0
Nevezis Kedainiai	1	0	Atlantas Klaipeda	0	1						
Polonija Vilnius	0		Zalgiris Vilnius *	0	0						
Zalgiris Vilnius *	4					Atlantas Klaipeda	1	0			
Suduva Marijampole *	12	4				Vetra Vilnius *	1	1			
Rodovitas Klaipeda	0	0	Suduva Marijampole	0	2						
Kauno Jegeriai	0	1	Vetra Vilnius *	1	1						
Vetra Vilnius *	4	0									

* Home team in the first leg • ‡ Qualified for the UEFA Cup

CUP FINAL
Vetra Stadium, Vilnius
22-10-2005, Ref: Zuta
Scorers - Ricardas Beniusis [102],
Eimantas Poderis [118] for FBK

LUX – LUXEMBOURG

NATIONAL TEAM RECORD
JULY 1ST 2002 TO JULY 9TH 2006

PL	W	D	L	F	A	%
34	0	2	32	10	109	2.9

FIFA/COCA-COLA WORLD RANKING

1993	1994	1995	1996	1997	1998	1999	2000	2001	2002	2003	2004	2005	High	Low
111	128	100	123	138	143	124	139	142	148	153	155	150	93 04/96	194 07/06

2005–2006											
08/05	09/05	10/05	11/05	12/05	01/06	02/06	03/06	04/06	05/06	06/06	07/06
155	155	152	152	150	151	151	151	152	152	-	194

F'91 Dudelange made history in July 2005 by becoming the first team from Luxembourg in 42 years to win through a European Cup tie. Their unfortunate opponents were Bosnian side Zrinjski who won the first leg in Luxembourg 1-0. They seemed to be on course for qualification until injury-time in the return in Mostar when Thomas Gruszczynski scored for Dudelange to force extra time. Incredibly Dudelange scored three more to secure a famous victory, and a second preliminary round tie against Rapid Vienna, which unsurprisingly was lost. Dudelange continued their domination of the domestic scene by achieving their first League and Cup double. They finished comfortably ahead of Jeunesse

INTERNATIONAL HONOURS
None

d'Esch in the League and then consigned Jeunesse to another runners-up spot by beating them 3-2 in the Cup Final. How the national team could do with some of the Dudelange spirit. With just two draws in the 34 games played between the 2002 and 2006 FIFA World Cups, no other nation in the world can match such a poor record - at least with that many games played. Luxembourg already hold the world record for the number of consecutive matches without a win but they are now within touching distance of beating that record. The 3-0 defeat at home to Ukraine in June 2006 was their 76th match without winning, just four short of the total they set between 1980 and 1995.

THE FIFA BIG COUNT OF 2000

	Male	Female		Male	Female
Registered players	17 148	403	Referees	225	6
Non registered players	4 000	0	Officials	1 000	50
Youth players	9 434	0	Total involved	32 266	
Total players	30 985		Number of clubs	120	
Professional players	150	0	Number of teams	490	

Fédération Luxembourgeoise de Football (FLF)

PO Box 5, Monderange 3901, Luxembourg
Tel +352 4886651   Fax +352 48866582
flf@football.lu   www.football.lu
President: PHILIPP Paul   General Secretary: WOLFF Joel
Vice-President: SCHAACK Charles   Treasurer: DECKER Erny   Media Officer: DIEDERICH Marc
Men's Coach: HELLERS Guy   Women's Coach: JEAN Romain
FLF formed: 1908   UEFA: 1954   FIFA: 1910
Red shirts with white trimmings, Red shorts, Red socks or White shirts with blue trimmings, White shorts, White socks

RECENT INTERNATIONAL MATCHES PLAYED BY LUXEMBOURG

2002 Opponents	Score	Venue	Comp	Scorers	Att	Referee
21-08 Morocco	L 0-2	Luxembourg	Fr		1 650	
5-09 Israel	L 0-5	Luxembourg	Fr		1 400	Allaerts BEL
12-10 Denmark	L 0-2	Copenhagen	ECq		40 259	Bede HUN
16-10 Romania	L 0-7	Luxembourg	ECq		2 000	Lajuks LVA
20-11 Cape Verde Islands	D 0-0	Hesperange	Fr			
2003						
29-03 Bosnia-Herzegovina	L 0-2	Zenica	ECq		10 000	Hyytia FIN
2-04 Norway	L 0-2	Luxembourg	ECq		3 000	Dobrinov BUL
30-04 Hungary	L 1-5	Budapest	Fr	Strasser [25]	1 205	Skomina SVN
11-06 Denmark	L 0-2	Luxembourg	ECq		6 869	Baskakov RUS
19-08 Malta	D 1-1	Luxembourg	Fr	Strasser [53p]		Lehner AUT
6-09 Romania	L 0-4	Ploiesti	ECq		4 500	Yefet ISR
10-09 Bosnia-Herzegovina	L 0-1	Luxembourg	ECq		3 500	Kapitanis CYP
11-10 Norway	L 0-1	Oslo	ECq		22 255	Szabo HUN
20-11 Moldova	L 1-2	Hesperange	Fr	Schauls [77]	623	
2004						
31-03 Bosnia-Herzegovina	L 1-2	Luxembourg	Fr	Huss [87]	2 000	Rogalla SUI
28-04 Austria	L 1-4	Innsbruck	Fr	Huss [63]	9 400	Skomina SVN
29-05 Portugal	L 0-3	Agueda	Fr		9 000	Styles ENG
18-08 Slovakia	L 1-3	Bratislava	WCq	Strasser [2]	5 016	Kassai HUN
4-09 Estonia	L 0-4	Tallinn	WCq		3 000	Kelly IRL
8-09 Latvia	L 3-4	Luxembourg	WCq	Braun [11], Leweck [55], Cardoni [62]	2 125	Kasnaferis GRE
9-10 Russia	L 0-4	Luxembourg	WCq		3 670	Braamhaar NED
13-10 Liechtenstein	L 0-4	Luxembourg	WCq		3 478	Jara CZE
17-11 Portugal	L 0-5	Luxembourg	WCq		8 045	Godulyan UKR
2005						
30-03 Latvia	L 0-4	Riga	WCq		8 203	Kovacic CRO
8-06 Slovakia	L 0-4	Luxembourg	WCq		2 108	Styles ENG
3-09 Portugal	L 0-6	Faro-Loule	WCq		25 300	Van Egmond NEd
7-09 Liechtenstein	L 0-3	Vaduz	WCq		2 300	Skomina SVN
8-10 Russia	L 1-5	Moscow	WCq	Reiter [51]	20 000	Tudor ROU
12-10 Estonia	L 0-2	Luxembourg	WCq		2 010	Dereli TUR
16-11 Canada	L 0-1	Hesperange	Fr			Gomes Costa POR
2006						
1-03 Belgium	L 0-2	Luxembourg	Fr	Abandoned after 65 minutes due to snow		Einwaller AUT
27-05 Germany	L 0-7	Freiburg	Fr		23 000	Rogalla SUI
3-06 Portugal	L 0-3	Metz	Fr		19 157	Duhamel FRA
8-06 Ukraine	L 0-3	Luxembourg	Fr			Vervecken BEL

Fr = Friendly match • EC = UEFA EURO 2004™ • WC = FIFA World Cup™ • q = qualifier

LUXEMBOURG NATIONAL TEAM RECORDS AND RECORD SEQUENCES

Records			Sequence records					
Victory	6-0	AFG 1948	Wins	3	1939-1943	Clean sheets	3	1995
Defeat	0-9	GER 1936, ENG 1960 1982	Defeats	32	1980-1985	Goals scored	7	1948-1951
Player Caps	87	WEIS Carlo	Undefeated	4	1963	Without goal	9	1980-81, 1984-85
Player Goals	16	MART Léon	Without win	80	1980-1995	Goals against	31	1987-1995

LUXEMBOURG COUNTRY INFORMATION

Capital	Luxembourg	Independence	1839 from the Netherlands	GDP per Capita	$55 100
Population	462 690	Status	Constitutional Monarchy	GDP Ranking	
Area km²	2 586	Language	Luxembourgish, German, French	Dialling code	+352
Population density	179 per km²	Literacy rate	100%	Internet code	.lu
% in urban areas	89%	Main religion	Christian	GMT + / −	+1
Towns/Cities ('000)	Luxembourg 76; Esch-sur-Alzette 28; Dudelange 18; Schifflange 8; Battembourg 7				
Neighbours (km)	Germany 138; France 73; Belgium 148;				
Main stadia	Stade Josy Barthel – Luxembourg 8 250; Stade de la Frontière – Esch-sur-Alzette 5 400				

NATIONAL TEAM PLAYERS AND COACHES

Record Caps			Record Goals			Recent Coaches	
WEIS Carlo	1978-'98	87	MART Léon	1939-'45	16		
KONTER François	1955-'69	77	KEMP Gustave	1938-'45	15		
LANGERS Roby	1980-'98	73	LIBAR Camille	1938-'47	14	PHILIPP Paul	1985-'01
STRASSER Jeff	1993-'06	70	KETTEL Nicolas	1946-'59	13	SIMONSEN Allan	2001-'04
CARDONI Manuel	1993-'04	69	MULLER François	1949-'54	12	HELLERS Guy	2004-

The above caps and goals are inclusive of many games not considered as full internationals by their opponents

CLUB DIRECTORY

Club	Town/City	Stadium	Capacity	www.	Lge	Cup
Avenir Beggen	Walferdange	Henri Dunant	5 500	wichtelweb.net	6	7
F91 Dudelange	Dudelange	Jos Nosbaum	5 000	f91.lu	5	2
Etzella Ettelbruck	Ettelbruck	Deich	4 500	fc-etzella.lu	0	1
CS Grevenmacher	Luxembourg	Op Flohr	4 500	csg.lu	1	3
Käerjéng 97	Bascharage	Bechel	3 000	un-kaerjeng.lu	0	0
Jeunesse d'Esch	Esch-sur-Alzette	Stade de la Frontière	7 500	jeunesse-esch.lu	27	12
CS Pétange	Pétange	Municipal	3 000		0	1
Racing Union Luxembourg	Luxembourg	Achille Hammerel	6 000	racing-fc.lu	0	0
US Rumelange	Rumelange	Municipal	4 000	usrumelange.lu	0	2
Swift Hesperange	Grevenmacher	Alfonse Theis	5 000		0	1
Victoria Rosport	Rosport	Um Camping	2 500	fcvictoriarosport.lu	0	0
Wiltz 71	Wiltz	Gétzt	3 000	fcwiltz.lu	0	0

RECENT LEAGUE AND CUP RECORD

	Championship							Cup		
Year	Champions	Pts	Runners-up	Pts	Third	Pts		Winners	Score	Runners-up
1990	Union Luxembourg	29.5	Avenir Beggen	27.5	Jeunesse Esch	26.5		Swift Hesperange	3-3 7-1	AS Differdange
1991	Union Luxembourg	28	Jeunesse Esch	25	AC Spora	22.5		Union Luxembourg	3-0	Jeunesse Esch
1992	Union Luxembourg	26	Avenir Beggen	26	Jeunesse Esch	23		Avenir Beggen	1-0	CS Petange
1993	Union Luxembourg	28.5	Union Luxembourg	27.5	Jeunesse Esch	23		Avenir Beggen	5-2	F'91 Dudelange
1994	Avenir Beggen	28.5	CS Grevenmacher	24	Union Luxembourg	23		Avenir Beggen	3-1	F'91 Dudelange
1995	Jeunesse d'Esch	35	CS Grevenmacher	35	Avenir Beggen	30		CS Grevenmacher	1-1 3-2	Jeunesse d'Esch
1996	Jeunesse d'Esch	48	CS Grevenmacher	47	Union Luxembourg	42		Union Luxembourg	3-1	Jeunesse d'Esch
1997	Jeunesse d'Esch	56	CS Grevenmacher	50	Union Luxembourg	38		Jeunesse d'Esch	2-0	Union Luxembourg
1998	Jeunesse d'Esch	54	Union Luxembourg	53	CS Grevenmacher	43		CS Grevenmacher	2-0	Avenir Beggen
1999	Jeunesse d'Esch	51	F'91 Dudelange	47	Avenir Beggen	45		Jeunesse d'Esch	3-0	FC Mondercange
2000	F'91 Dudelange	57	CS Grevenmacher	46	Jeunesse d'Esch	46		Jeunesse d'Esch	4-1	FC Mondercange
2001	F'91 Dudelange	63	CS Grevenmacher	59	CS Hobscheid	46		Etzella Ettelbruck	5-3	FC Wiltz
2002	F'91 Dudelange	62	CS Grevenmacher	58	Union Luxembourg	47		Avenir Beggen	1-0	F'91 Dudelange
2003	CS Grevenmacher	59	F'91 Dudelange	52	Jeunesse d'Esch	48		CS Grevenmacher	1-0	Etzella Ettelbruck
2004	Jeunesse d'Esch	68	F'91 Dudelange	59	Etzella Ettelbruck	48		F'91 Dudelange	3-1	Etzella Ettelbruck
2005	F'91 Dudelange	70	Etzella Ettelbruck	64	Jeunesse d'Esch	45		CS Petange	5-0	Cebra
2006	F'91 Dudelange	64	Jeunesse d'Esch	53	Etzella Ettelbruck	49		F'91 Dudelange	3-2	Jeunesse d'Esch

LUXEMBOURG 2005-06

DIVISION NATIONALE

	Pl	W	D	L	F	A	Pts	Dudelange	Jeunesse	Etzella	Grev'cher	Wiltz	Kaerjeng	Racing	Petange	Swift	Victoria	Rumelange	Avenir
F'91 Dudelange	22	16	3	3	63	15	51		2-0	3-1	1-2	2-0	4-0	5-0	5-1	3-1	3-0	6-1	4-1
Jeunesse d'Esch	22	14	2	6	49	19	44	0-3		3-0	4-2	1-1	2-0	4-0	0-1	1-1	2-0	5-0	8-0
Etzella Ettelbruck	22	13	1	8	48	36	40	1-0	2-1		2-1	1-2	1-3	1-3	5-0	2-1	4-2	4-1	5-0
CS Grevenmacher	22	12	2	8	51	27	38	1-1	0-2	4-1		3-1	2-1	0-2	2-1	3-0	0-1	4-0	2-0
FC Wiltz 71	22	9	7	6	36	27	34	1-1	1-3	4-3	0-0		3-1	1-2	1-0	0-0	3-0	1-0	4-0
UN Kaerjeng	22	10	4	8	36	33	34	0-4	1-4	2-2	5-1	2-0		2-1	3-1	1-1	1-0	1-0	3-0
Racing Union	22	10	4	8	31	30	34	1-0	0-1	1-0	0-2	2-2	1-0		1-3	3-0	5-0	0-2	0-0
CS Petange	22	10	2	10	29	33	32	0-1	1-2	1-3	1-0	1-1	2-1	1-2		1-0	2-0	4-2	2-0
Swift Hesperange	22	6	8	8	31	37	26	1-6	2-1	2-3	3-1	2-0	0-0	3-2	1-1		2-2	1-0	1-1
Victoria Rosport	22	6	5	11	24	42	23	2-4	1-0	1-2	1-4	2-2	1-1	1-3	1-0	4-3		1-0	1-1
US Rumelange	22	3	3	16	20	58	12	0-4	1-4	0-2	0-6	1-3	3-5	1-1	1-3	1-1	0-0		4-1
Avenir Beggen	22	0	5	17	10	71	5	1-1	0-1	1-3	0-11	0-5	0-3	1-1	1-2	1-5	1-1	1-2	

6/08/2005 - 2/04/2006 • † Qualified for championship play-off • ‡ To relegation Group A • ‡‡ To relegation Group B

CHAMPIONSHIP PLAY-OFF

	Pl	W	D	L	F	A	Pts	FD	JE	EE	Gr
F'91 Dudelange †	28	20	4	4	83	22	64		9-0	3-2	0-0
Jeunesse d'Esch ‡	28	17	2	9	58	36	53	1-4		3-1	1-0
Etzella Ettelbruck ‡	28	16	1	11	59	47	49	0-3	2-0		2-0
CS Grevenmacher	28	13	3	12	58	39	42	4-1	1-4	2-4	

8/04/2006 - 14/05/2006 • † Qualified for the UEFA Champions League • ‡ Qualified for the UEFA Cup

RELEGATION PLAY-OFF

Group A	Pl	W	D	L	F	A	Pts	Wi	RU	SH	Ru
FC Wiltz 71	28	13	8	7	49	36	47		1-1	2-0	3-1
Racing Union	28	12	5	11	40	39	41	2-3		3-0	3-1
Swift Hesperange	28	9	9	10	41	44	36	5-1	2-0		2-0
US Rumelange ‡	28	4	4	20	25	70	16	0-3	2-0	1-1	

Group B	Pl	W	D	L	F	A	Pts	Pe	Ka	VR	AB
CS Petange	28	12	4	12	39	40	40		3-0	1-1	2-0
UN Kaerjeng	28	10	7	11	44	46	37	3-3		3-3	0-1
Victoria Rosport	28	8	8	12	34	50	32	2-1	0-0		0-2
Avenir Beggen ‡	28	4	5	19	18	79	17	1-0	3-2	1-4	

8/04/2006 - 14/05/2006 • ‡ To relegation play-off

LUXEMBOURG 2005-06 PROMOTION HONNEUR (2)

	Pl	W	D	L	F	A	Pts
FC Differdange 03	26	17	5	4	52	21	56
Progres Niedercorn	26	16	7	3	58	23	55
FC Mondercange ‡	26	16	5	5	73	22	53
FC Mamer 32 ‡	26	16	2	8	49	41	50
FC Cessange 01	26	12	7	7	39	29	43
FC Rapid Hamm	26	13	3	10	54	39	42
Mertert-Wasserbillig	26	11	6	9	55	37	39
FC 72 Erpeldange	26	11	4	11	46	45	37
Sporting Mertzig	26	8	6	12	42	62	30
Koeppchen Wormeldange	26	9	3	14	44	66	30
Jeunesse Canach	26	8	2	15	35	60	26
CS Obercorn	26	6	4	16	28	54	22
Minerva Lintgen	26	4	5	17	34	65	17
AS Colmar-Berg	26	3	5	17	28	72	14

8/09/2005 - 26/05/2006 • ‡ qualified for play-offs
Play-offs: FC Mondercange 3-2 Avenir Beggen
FC Mamer 0-0 4-3p US Rumelange

COUPE DE LUXEMBOURG 2005–06

Round of 16

F'91 Dudelange	10
Mertert-Wasserbillig *	0
FC Mondercange	1
Progres Niedercorn *	3
CS Petange	2 7p
Schieren *	2 6p
FC Differdange 03 *	2
Racing Union	4
Victoria Rosport	2
Hostert *	0
CS Grevenmacher	0
Etzella Ettelbruck *	3
Swift Hesperange	2
FC Wiltz 71 *	1
Colmarberg *	0
Jeunesse d'Esch	2

Quarter-finals

F'91 Dudelange *	4 6p
Progres Niedercorn	4 5p
CS Petange *	1 4p
Racing Union	1 5p
Victoria Rosport *	2
Etzella Ettelbruck	1
Swift Hesperange	0
Jeunesse d'Esch *	2

Semi-finals

F'91 Dudelange	3
Racing Union	1
Victoria Rosport	0
Jeunesse d'Esch	1

Final

F'91 Dudelange	3
Jeunesse d'Esch ‡	2

* Home team • ‡ Qualified for the UEFA Cup

CUP FINAL

Josy Barthel, Luxembourg, 20-05-2006
Scorers - Gruczynski 2 [66] [68],
Hug [71] for Dudelange;
Stakloso [10], Pouget [29] for Jeunesse

LVA – LATVIA

NATIONAL TEAM RECORD
JULY 1ST 2002 TO JULY 9TH 2006

PL	W	D	L	F	A	%
51	15	15	21	59	77	44.1

FIFA/COCA-COLA WORLD RANKING

1993	1994	1995	1996	1997	1998	1999	2000	2001	2002	2003	2004	2005		High	Low
86	69	60	82	75	77	62	92	106	79	51	65	69		51 12/03	107 03/02

2005–2006											
08/05	09/05	10/05	11/05	12/05	01/06	02/06	03/06	04/06	05/06	06/06	07/06
64	63	64	70	69	66	67	68	69	70	-	82

It took a long time in coming - 15 years to be precise - but a team other than Skonto Riga has finally won the Latvian championship. After finishing either second or third for the past seven seasons, Metalurgs of Leipaja finally put an end to Skonto's world record run of 14 consecutive titles. If there is consolation to be had for Skonto, it's that their record is likely to remain unchallenged for many years to come given that Rosenborg's record run in Norway also ended in 2005 at 13 successive titles. Not only did Metalurgs win the title but they did so with relative ease, finishing 13 points ahead of Skonto and losing just once all season - to Ventspils. Having lost the title to Skonto

INTERNATIONAL HONOURS
Baltic Cup 1928 1932 1933 1936 1937 1993 1995 2001 2003

in 2004 after conceding a last minute penalty in the match between the two on the final day of the season, success was sweet for the Metalurg fans. They did, however, lose the Cup Final to Ventspils who completed a hat-trick of wins. With the game goalless after 90 minutes, Metalurgs took the lead in extra time but goals from Vits Rimkus and Igors Slesarcuks consigned the champions to a fourth defeat in a final of a tournament they have yet to win. In light of their qualification for the European Championship finals in Portugal in 2004, the national team had a disappointing end to their 2006 FIFA World Cup™ qualifying campaign, finishing below neighbours Estonia.

THE FIFA BIG COUNT OF 2000

	Male	Female		Male	Female
Registered players	1 420	10	Referees	215	0
Non registered players	14 000	0	Officials	400	30
Youth players	5 640	235	Total involved	21 950	
Total players	21 305		Number of clubs	51	
Professional players	210	0	Number of teams	256	

Latvian Football Federation (LFF)
Latvijas Futbola Federacija, Augsiela 1, Riga LV1009, Latvia
Tel +371 7292988   Fax +371 7317606
futbols@lff.lv   www.lff.lv
President: INDRIKSONS Guntis   General Secretary: MEZECKIS Janis
Vice-President: GORKSS Juris   Treasurer: BAHAREVA Nina   Media Officer: HARTMANIS Martins
Men's Coach: ANDREJEVS Jurjis   Women's Coach: BANDOLIS Agris
LFF formed: 1921   UEFA: 1992   FIFA: 1923-43, 1992
Carmine red shirts with white trimmings, Carmine red shorts, Carmine red socks or White shirts, White shorts, White socks

RECENT INTERNATIONAL MATCHES PLAYED BY LATVIA

2003	Opponents	Score		Venue	Comp	Scorers	Att	Referee
20-08	Uzbekistan	L	0-3	Riga	Fr		4 000	Shandor UKR
6-09	Poland	L	0-2	Riga	ECq		9 000	Vassaras GRE
10-09	Hungary	W	3-1	Riga	ECq	Verpakovskis 2 [38 51], Bleidelis [42]	7 500	Larsen DEN
11-10	Sweden	W	1-0	Stockholm	ECq	Verpakovskis [23]	32 095	De Santis ITA
15-11	Turkey	W	1-0	Riga	ECpo	Verpakovskis [29]	8 000	Veissiere FRA
19-11	Turkey	D	2-2	Istanbul	ECpo	Laizans [66], Verpakovskis [77]	25 000	Frisk SWE
20-12	Kuwait	L	0-2	Larnaca	Fr			Kapitanis CYP
2004								
18-02	Kazakhstan	W	3-1	Larnaca	Fr	Pahars [40], Laizans 2 [45 56]	500	Constantinou CYP
19-02	Hungary	L	1-2	Limassol	Fr	Stepanovs [64]	100	Kailis CYP
21-02	Belarus	L	1-4	Limassol	Fr	Zemlinskis [37p]	100	Theodotou CYP
31-03	Slovenia	W	1-0	Celje	Fr	Verpakovskis [36]	1 500	Stredak SVK
28-04	Iceland	D	0-0	Riga	Fr		6 500	Shmolik BLR
6-06	Azerbaijan	D	2-2	Riga	Fr	Verpakovskis [53], Zemlinskis [82p]	8 000	Maisonlahti FIN
15-06	Czech Republic	L	1-2	Aveiro	ECr1	Verpakovskis [45]	21 744	Veissiere FRA
19-06	Germany	D	0-0	Porto	ECr1		22 344	Riley ENG
23-06	Netherlands	L	0-3	Braga	ECr1		27 904	Milton Nielsen DEN
18-08	Wales	L	0-2	Riga	Fr		6 500	Ivanov RUS
4-09	Portugal	L	0-2	Riga	WCq		9 500	Poll ENG
8-09	Luxembourg	W	4-3	Luxembourg	WCq	Verpakovskis [4], Zemlinskis [40p], OG [65], Prohorenkovs [67]	2 125	Kasnaferis GRE
9-10	Slovakia	L	1-4	Bratislava	WCq	Verpakovskis [3]	13 025	Farina ITA
13-10	Estonia	D	2-2	Riga	WCq	Astafjevs [65], Laizans [82]	8 500	Meyer GER
17-11	Liechtenstein	W	3-1	Vaduz	WCq	Verpakovskis [7], Zemlinskis [57], Prohorenkovs [89]	1 460	Szabo HUN
1-12	Oman	L	2-3	Manama	Fr	Rimkus [66], Rubins [68]		
3-12	Bahrain	D	2-2	Manama	Fr	Kolesnicenko [22p], Zakresevskis [35], L 2-4p	2 000	Al Hilali OMA
2005								
8-02	Finland	L	1-2	Nicosia	Fr	Zemlinskis [62p]	102	Kailis CYP
9-02	Austria	D	1-1	Limassol	Fr	Visnakovs [70], W 5-3p	50	Theodotou CYP
30-03	Luxembourg	W	4-0	Riga	WCq	Bleidelis [32], Laizans [38p], Verpakovskis 2 [73 90]	8 203	Kovacic CRO
21-05	Lithuania	L	0-2	Kaunas	BC			
4-06	Russia	L	0-3	St Pertersburg	WCq		21 575	Poulat FRA
8-06	Liechtenstein	W	1-0	Riga	WCq	Bleidelis [17]	8 000	Eriksson SWE
17-08	Russia	D	1-1	Riga	WCq	Astafjevs [6]	10 000	Poll ENG
3-09	Estonia	L	1-2	Tallinn	WCq	Laizans [90]	8 970	Undiano Mallenco ESP
7-09	Slovakia	D	1-1	Riga	WCq	Laizans [74]	8 800	Plautz AUT
8-10	Japan	D	2-2	Riga	Fr	Rimkus [67], Rubins [89]	6 500	Granatas POL
12-10	Portugal	L	0-3	Porto	WCq		35 000	Frojdfeldt SWE
12-11	Belarus	L	1-3	Minsk	Fr	Visnakovs [24]	8 300	Egorov RUS
24-12	Thailand	D	1-1	Phang Nga	Fr	Solonicins [19]		
26-12	Korea DPR	D	1-1	Phuket	Fr	Karlsons [65]		
30-12	Korea DPR	W	2-1	Phuket	Fr	Karlsons [38], Prohorenkovs [40]		
2006								
28-05	USA	L	0-1	Hartford	Fr		24 636	Dipiero CAN

Fr = Friendly match • EC = UEFA EURO 2004™ • BC = Baltic Cup • WC = FIFA World Cup™ • q = qualifier • po = play-off • r1 = first round group

LATVIA NATIONAL TEAM RECORDS AND RECORD SEQUENCES

Records				Sequence records			
Victory	8-1	EST 1942	Wins	4	1936	Clean sheets	2	
Defeat	0-12	SWE 1927	Defeats	5	1999-2000	Goals scored	10	Three times
Player Caps	125	ASTAFJEVS Vitalijs	Undefeated	6	1937, 1938	Without goal	5	1998-1999
Player Goals	24	PETERSONS Eriks	Without win	10	1995-1997	Goals against	21	1933-1937

LATVIA COUNTRY INFORMATION

Capital	Riga	Independence	1991 from the Soviet Union	GDP per Capita	$10 200
Population	2 306 306	Status	Republic	GNP Ranking	98
Area km²	64 589	Language	Latvian, Russian	Dialling code	+371
Population density	35 per km²	Literacy rate	99%	Internet code	.lv
% in urban areas	73%	Main religion	Christian	GMT + / –	+2
Towns/Cities ('000)	Riga 742; Daugavpils 111; Liepāja 82; Jelgava 62; Jurmala 54; Ventspils 42				
Neighbours (km)	Estonia 339; Russia 217; Belarus 141; Lithuania 453; Baltic Sea 531				
Main stadia	Stadions Skonto – Riga 9 300				

NATIONAL TEAM PLAYERS AND COACHES

Record Caps			Record Goals			Recent Coaches	
ASTAFJEVS Vitalijs	1992-'06	125	PETERSONS Eriks	1929-'39	24	GILIS Janis	1992-'97
ZEMLINSKIS Mihails	1992-'05	104	VERPAKOVSKIS Maris	1999-'06	19	DZODZUASHVILI Revaz	1997-'99
BLEIDELIS Imants	1995-'05	94	PAHARS Marians	1996-'04	15	JOHNSON Gary	1999-'01
STEPANOVS Igors	1995-'05	86	SEIBELIS Albert	1925-'39	14	STARKOVS Alexandrs	2001-'04
STOLCERS Andrejs	1994-'05	81	VESTERMANS Ilja	1935-'38	13	ANDREJEVS Jurijs	2004-
LAIZANS Juris	1998-'06	74	ZEMLINSKIS Mihails	1992-'05	12		
BLAGONADEZDINS Olegs	1992-'04	70	ASTAFJEVS Vitalijs	1992-'06	12		
IVANOVS Valerijs	1992-'01	69	LAIZANS Juris	1998-'06	11		
KOLINKO Alexander	1997-'06	66					

CLUB DIRECTORY

Club	Town/City	Stadium	Capacity	www.	Lge	Cup
FC Dinaburg	Daugavpils	Celtnieka Stadions	4 070	dinaburg.com	0	0
FK Jurmala	Jurmala			fcjurmala.lv	0	0
FHK Leipajas Metalurgs	Liepaja	Daugavas Stadions	5 000	sport.metalurgs.lv	1	0
Olimps	Riga	Stadions Skonto	9 300		0	0
FK Riga	Riga	Latvijas Universitates	5 000		0	1
Skonto FC	Riga	Stadions Skonto	9 300	skontofc.lv	14	7
Venta	Kuldiga				0	0
FK Ventspils	Ventspils	Olimpiska Centra	3 200	fkventspils.lv	0	3

RECENT LEAGUE AND CUP RECORD

	Championship							Cup		
Year	Champions	Pts	Runners-up	Pts	Third	Pts		Winners	Score	Runners-up
1991	Skonto Riga	32	Pardaugava Riga	26	Olimpija Liepaja	25		Celtnieks	0-0 3-1p	Skonto Riga
1992	Skonto Riga	38	RAF Jelgava	38	VEF Riga	33		Skonto Riga	1-0	Daugava Kompar
1993	Skonto Riga	34	Olimpija Riga	26	RAF Jelgava	26		RAF Jelgava	1-0	Pardaugava Riga
1994	Skonto Riga	42	RAF Jelgava	33	DAG Riga	29		Olimpija Riga	2-0	DAG Riga
1995	Skonto Riga	78	Vilan-D Daugavpils	51	RAF Jelgava	48		Skonto Riga	3-0	DAG Liepaja
1996	Skonto Riga	73	Daugava Riga	61	Dinaburg Daugavpils	47		RAF Jelgava	2-1	Skonto Riga
1997	Skonto Riga	64	Daugava Riga	43	Dinaburg Daugavpils	42		Skonto Riga	2-1	Dinaburg Daugavpils
1998	Skonto Riga	67	Liepajas Metalurgs	57	FK Ventspils	54		Skonto Riga	1-0	Liepajas Metalurgs
1999	Skonto Riga	69	Liepajas Metalurgs	60	FK Ventspils	56		FK Riga	1-1 6-5p	Skonto Riga
2000	Skonto Riga	75	FK Ventspils	65	Liepajas Metalurgs	55		Skonto Riga	4-1	Liepajas Metalurgs
2001	Skonto Riga	68	FK Ventspils	67	Liepajas Metalurgs	64		Skonto Riga	2-0	Dinaburg Daugavpils
2002	Skonto Riga	73	FK Ventspils	71	Liepajas Metalurgs	51		Skonto Riga	3-0	Liepajas Metalurgs
2003	Skonto Riga	73	Liepajas Metalurgs	68	FK Ventspils	61		FK Ventspils	4-0	Skonto Riga
2004	Skonto Riga	69	Liepajas Metalurgs	66	FK Ventspils	55		FK Ventspils	2-1	Skonto Riga
2005	Liepajas Metalurgs	71	Skonto Riga	58	FK Ventspils	55		FK Ventspils	2-1	Liepajas Metalurgs

Play-off in 1992: Skonto 3-2 RAF

LATVIA 2005

VIRSLIGA

	Pl	W	D	L	F	A	Pts	Metalurgs	Skonto	Ventspils	Dinaburg	Riga	Jurmala	Olimps	Venta
Liepajas Metalurgs †	28	22	5	1	85	19	71		4-2 1-1	2-0 2-1	4-2 5-0	5-1 6-0	3-1 1-0	3-0 5-0	5-1 9-0
Skonto Riga ‡	28	17	7	4	59	25	58	1-1 1-1		1-0 1-1	3-0 1-1	0-2 4-0	3-1 2-1	0-2 3-0	3-0 3-0
FK Ventspils ‡	28	16	7	5	56	30	55	3-0 1-5	1-3 2-2		1-1 3-1	0-0 1-1	1-0 2-1	3-2 6-1	5-1 2-0
Dinaburg Daugavpils	28	9	8	11	37	43	35	1-2 2-2	1-2 1-3	0-1 3-3		0-0 2-2	1-0 1-0	3-0 1-1	1-0 3-0
FK Riga	28	9	7	12	32	46	34	0-1 0-3	0-4 1-1	0-2 1-3	3-0 1-2		3-2 1-1	1-0 1-1	0-2 4-2
FK Jurmala	28	9	5	14	37	38	32	0-1 0-1	3-2 0-3	2-2 0-1	1-2 1-0	3-0 1-0		1-0 4-3	0-0 4-0
Olimps Riga	28	5	4	19	24	68	19	0-6 0-4	1-5 0-1	0-3 0-1	2-1 1-1	0-2 0-3	0-3 1-1		2-1 5-2
Venta Kuldiga	28	2	3	23	18	79	9	0-0 1-3	0-3 0-1	0-1 0-6	1-3 0-3	0-1 0-4	2-2 2-4	3-0 0-2	

4/04/2004 - 11/11/2004 • † Qualified for the UEFA Champions League • ‡ Qualified for the UEFA Cup
Relegation/promotion play-off: Olimps Riga 0-2 Ditton Daugavpils

LATVIA 2005
PIRMALIGA (2)

	Pl	W	D	L	F	A	Pts
Skonto-2 Riga	26	20	5	1	81	18	65
FK Ventspils-2	26	15	7	4	98	25	52
Dizvanagi Rezekne	26	15	3	8	68	43	48
Liepajas Metalurgs-2	26	14	5	7	57	23	47
Ditton Daugavpils	26	14	5	7	59	28	47
FK Valmiera	26	9	8	9	37	39	35
JFC Skonto Riga	26	8	11	7	44	31	35
FK Riga-2	26	10	5	11	33	41	35
FK Jurmala-2/Flaminko	26	9	7	10	48	48	34
Zibens/Zemes. Ilukste	26	7	8	11	45	56	29
FK Jelgava	26	8	2	16	43	59	26
Auda Riga	26	8	2	16	27	46	26
Alberts Riga	26	5	3	18	39	111	18
Ogres Sporta	26	3	3	20	30	141	12

1/05/2004 - 6/11/2004 • Skonto, Ventspils and Liepajas were ineligible for promotion due to their links with teams in the Virsliga • Dinaburg-2 & Venta-2 withdrew

LATVIJAS KAUSS 2005

Fourth Round		Quarter-finals		Semi-finals		Final	
FK Ventspils	0 3p						
Dizvanagi Rezekne *	0 1p	FK Ventspils	2				
FK Valmiera *	1	FK Jurmala *	0				
FK Jurmala	5			FK Ventspils	1		
FK Riga	2			Skonto Riga	0		
Alberts Riga *	0	FK Riga *	1				
FK Jelgava *	0	Skonto Riga	2				
Skonto Riga	5					FK Ventspils ‡	2
Olimps Riga	2					Liepajas Metalurgs	1
JFC Skonto Riga *	0	Olimps Riga *	2				
Ditton Daugavpils *	0	Venta Kuldiga	0				
Venta Kuldiga	4			Olimps Riga	0		
Dinaburg Daugavpils	8			Liepajas Metalurgs	1		
FK Plavinas *	0	Dinaburg Daugavpils	1				
Auda Riga *	0	Liepajas Metalurgs *	2				
Liepajas Metalurgs	7						

* Home teams • ‡ Qualified for the UEFA Cup

CUP FINAL

Skonto, Riga
25-09-2005, Att: 4 000, Ref: Lajuks
Scorers - Rimkus [99], Slesarcuks [111] for
Ventspils; Miceika [94] for Metalurgs

MAC – MACAU

NATIONAL TEAM RECORD
JULY 1ST 2002 TO JULY 9TH 2006

PL	W	D	L	F	A	%
13	2	2	9	9	32	23.1

FIFA/COCA-COLA WORLD RANKING

1993	1994	1995	1996	1997	1998	1999	2000	2001	2002	2003	2004	2005	High	Low
166	175	180	172	157	174	176	180	180	188	184	188	192	**156** 09/97	**192** 12/05

2005–2006											
08/05	09/05	10/05	11/05	12/05	01/06	02/06	03/06	04/06	05/06	06/06	07/06
190	190	190	190	192	192	192	192	192	192	-	183

After a run of six defeats, including a humiliating 8-1 thrashing at the hands of Hong Kong, the Macau Football Association decided drastic action was needed to restore some pride to the national team and to avoid further embarrassment at the 2006 AFC Challenge Cup in Bangladesh. They appealed to the Japan Football Association for help, who responded by sending Masanaga Kageyama on a year's contract to coach the national team. The effects were immediate. Although Macau lost the opening fixture of the AFC Challenge Cup to eventual winners Tajikistan, they did manage an encouraging draw with Pakistan in the second match. More impressively they held

INTERNATIONAL HONOURS
None

Hong Kong to a goalless draw in the annual encounter between the two, a marked improvement on the previous year. There was not such good progress at youth level, however. In November the under-17 team played their Asian Youth Championship qualifiers in Korea Republic and suffered a nasty shock when they lost 14-0 to the hosts and then 26-0 to Japan. At club level the Campeonato Primeiro Divisao was won by Polícia de Segurança Pública in a short 14 game season, but despite the introduction of the AFC President's Cup for the champions of small nations like Macau, Police didn't enter the tournament.

THE FIFA BIG COUNT OF 2000

	Male	Female		Male	Female
Registered players	3 710	0	Referees	60	0
Non registered players	2 000	10	Officials	600	4
Youth players	622	0	Total involved	7 006	
Total players		6 342	Number of clubs	174	
Professional players	0	0	Number of teams	276	

Macau Football Association (AFM)
Avenida Dr. Sun Yat Sen, Edificio Wa Fung Kok, 15 Andar, Bloco A, Taipa, Macau
Tel +853 830287   Fax +853 830409
futebol@macau.ctm.net   www.macaufa.com
President: CHEUNG Vitor Lup Kwan   General Secretary: REGO Alexander
Vice-President: CHONG Coc Veng   Treasurer: CHIO Kam Vai   Media Officer: None
Men's Coach: KAGEYAMA Masanaga   Women's Coach: None
AFM formed: 1939   AFC: 1976   FIFA: 1976
Green shirts, Green shorts, Green socks

RECENT INTERNATIONAL MATCHES PLAYED BY MACAO

2002	Opponents	Score		Venue	Comp	Scorers	Att	Referee
No international matches played in 2002								
2003								
22-02	Mongolia	W	2-0	Hong Kong	EAq	Che Chi Man 34p, Chan Man Hei 82	6 055	Matsumura JPN
24-02	Hong Kong	L	0-3	Hong Kong	EAq		1 602	Park Sang Gu KOR
26-02	Guam	W	2-0	Hong Kong	EAq	De Sousa 2 37 77	672	Cheung Yim Yau HKG
2-03	Chinese Taipei	L	1-2	Hong Kong	EAq	Hoi Man Io 35	6 862	
21-03	Pakistan	L	0-3	Singapore	ACq			
23-03	Singapore	L	0-2	Singapore	ACq			
23-11	Chinese Taipei	L	0-3	Taipei	WCq		2 000	Napitupulu IDN
29-11	Chinese Taipei	L	1-3	Macau	WCq	Lei Fu Weng 87	250	Zhou Weixin CHN
2004								
No international matches played in 2004								
2005								
21-05	Hong Kong	L	1-8	Hong Kong	Fr	Chung Koon Kan 86		
2006								
2-04	Tajikistan	L	0-4	Dhaka	CCr1		2 000	Mombini IRN
6-04	Pakistan	D	2-2	Dhaka	CCr1	Chan Kin Seng 2 16 52	1 000	Shamsuzzaman BAN
7-04	Kyrgyzstan	L	0-2	Dhaka	CCr1		1 000	Tan Hai CHN
3-06	Hong Kong	D	0-0	Macau	Fr			

Fr = Friendly match • EA = East Asian Championship • AC = AFC Asian Cup • CC = AFC Challenge Cup • WC = FIFA World Cup™
q = qualifier • r1 = first round group

MACAO NATIONAL TEAM RECORDS AND RECORD SEQUENCES

Records			Sequence records					
Victory	5-1	PHI	Wins	2	1997-1990	Clean sheets	1	Six times
Defeat	0-10	JPN 1997 (Twice)	Defeats	9	2000-2001	Goals scored	5	1975-1978
Player Caps	n/a		Undefeated	2	Three times	Without goal	5	1985-1987
Player Goals	n/a		Without win	10	2003-2006	Goals against	15	1992-1997

MACAO 2005
CAMPEONATO 1° DIVISAO

	Pl	W	D	L	F	A	Pts
Polícia	14	10	2	2	41	12	**32**
Lam Pak	14	9	2	3	37	13	**29**
Monte Carlo	14	6	5	3	32	24	**23**
Va Luen	14	6	4	4	23	21	**22**
Alfândega	14	6	3	5	24	23	**21**
Heng Tai	14	4	2	8	29	40	**14**
Kuan Tai	14	1	5	8	17	43	**8**
Kei Lun	14	2	1	11	13	40	**7**

4/01/2005 - 22/04/2005

RECENT LEAGUE RECORD

Year	Champions
1996	GD Artilheiros
1997	GD Lam Park
1998	GD Lam Park
1999	GD Lam Park
2000	Polícia de Segurança Pública
2001	GD Lam Park
2002	Monte Carlo
2003	Monte Carlo
2004	Monte Carlo
2005	Polícia de Segurança Pública

MACAO COUNTRY INFORMATION

Capital	Macao	Status	Special administrative region of China	GDP per Capita	$19 400
Population	445 286			GNP Ranking	n/a
Area km²	25.4 per km²	Language	Portuguese, Cantonese	Dialling code	+853
Population density	17 530	Literacy rate	94%	Internet code	.mo
% in urban areas	100%	Main religion	Buddhist 50%, Christian 15%	GMT + / –	+8
Towns/Cities ('000)	Macao 445				
Neighbours (km)	China 0.34; South China Sea 41				
Main stadia	Campo Desportivo – Macao 15 000				

MAD – MADAGASCAR

NATIONAL TEAM RECORD
JULY 1ST 2002 TO JULY 9TH 2006

PL	W	D	L	F	A	%
21	4	4	13	15	39	28.6

FIFA/COCA-COLA WORLD RANKING

1993	1994	1995	1996	1997	1998	1999	2000	2001	2002	2003	2004	2005		High		Low	
89	111	132	140	163	150	134	114	122	101	118	147	149		81	08/93	169	05/98

2005–2006											
08/05	09/05	10/05	11/05	12/05	01/06	02/06	03/06	04/06	05/06	06/06	07/06
150	150	150	149	149	150	150	150	151	151	-	156

The only major change for Malagasy football over the last 12 months was a new nickname for the national side. Results remained disappointing for the side now known as "Berea" after an animal indigenous to the large tropical island. Previously the national side had been known as the Scorpions, although the sting had gone out of the tail in recent years. Madagascar played just two internationals in 2005, and only two more in 2006, both of which were lost, to Botswana and Swaziland in the COSAFA Castle Cup. There was, however, a first taste of international success in Durban, South Africa in December when the country's under-20 side beat Lesotho 1-0 to win the

INTERNATIONAL HONOURS
Indian Ocean Games 1990 1993

COSAFA U-20 Championship. It was a first-ever junior success for Madagascar, whose only previous football titles had come in the Indian Ocean Islands Games. Players like Paulin Voavy and Pamphile Rabefitia are earmarked to play a major part for the Malagasy in the 2008 African Nations Cup qualifiers. At club level, USCAFOOT left a trail of destruction in their wake in the CAF Champions League, reaching the third round before being solidly beaten by Asante Kotoko of Ghana in May 2006. But they did manage a win on the away goals rule over the highly rated Mamelodi Sundowns of South Africa, a source of much satisfaction for Madagascar.

THE FIFA BIG COUNT OF 2000

	Male	Female		Male	Female
Registered players	15 000	800	Referees	316	18
Non registered players	40 000	300	Officials	525	20
Youth players	400	0	Total involved	57 106	
Total players	56 500		Number of clubs	200	
Professional players	0	0	Number of teams	800	

Fédération Malagasy de Football (FMF)
26 rue de Russie, Isoraka, PO Box 4409, Tananarive 101, Madagascar
Tel +261 20 2268374   Fax +261 20 2268373
fmf@blueline.mg   www.none
President: AHMAD   General Secretary: RABIBISOA Anselme
Vice-President: RAZAFINDKIAKA Sylvain   Treasurer: ZAFINANDRO René   Media Officer: RANJALAHY Sylvain
Men's Coach: RANDRIAMBOLOLONA Jeremia   Women's Coach: ANDRIANTANASASOA Herihaja
FMF formed: 1961   CAF: 19   FIFA: 1962
Red shirts with green trimmings, White shorts, Green socks

RECENT INTERNATIONAL MATCHES PLAYED BY MADAGASCAR

2002	Opponents	Score	Venue	Comp	Scorers	Att	Referee
21-07	South Africa	D 0-0	Port Elizabeth	CCqf	L 1-4p	8 000	Colembi ANG
8-09	Egypt	W 1-0	Antananarivo	CNq	Menakely [73]		Nkole ZAM
12-10	Mauritius	W 1-0	Port Louis	CNq	Menakely [18]	1 819	Maillet SEY
2003							
22-02	Mauritius	W 2-1	Antananarivo	CCr1	Menakely [16p], Radonamahafalison [33]	25 000	Motau RSA
27-03	Cameroon	L 0-2	Tunis	Fr		14 000	Zahmoul TUN
29-03	South Africa	L 0-2	Johannesburg	Fr		5 000	Shikapande ZAM
30-03	Ghana	D 3-3	Tunis	Fr	OG [47], Rasonaivo [82], Randriandelison [88]. L 9-10p		
24-04	Algeria	L 1-4	Amiens	Fr	Menakely [78p]	1 295	Garibian FRA
27-04	Mali	L 0-5	Paris	Fr			
20-06	Egypt	L 0-6	Port Said	CNq			
6-07	Mauritius	L 0-2	Antananarivo	CNq			
13-07	Swaziland	L 0-2	Mbabane	CCqf		8 000	Mpofu BOT
28-08	Seychelles	D 1-1	Curepipe	IOG	Menakely [32]	1 000	Lim Kee Chong MRI
30-08	Mauritius	L 1-3	Curepipe	IOG	Ralaitafika [54]	4 500	Ramsamy REU
11-10	Benin	D 1-1	Antananarivo	WCq	Edmond [28]	5 131	Maillet SEY
16-11	Benin	L 2-3	Cotonou	WCq	Radonamahafalison [15], Rakotondramanana [23]	20 000	Imiere NGA
2004							
18-04	Mozambique	L 0-2	Maputo	CCr1		28 000	Damon RSA
2005							
26-02	Mauritius	L 0-2	Curepipe	CCq			Fakude SWZ
23-10	Mauritius	W 2-0	Antananarivo	Fr	Randriamalala [16p], Andriatsima [80]		
2006							
20-05	Botswana	L 0-2	Gaborone	CCr1			Colembi ANG
21-05	Swaziland	L 0-2	Gaborone	CCr1			Malepa BOT

Fr = Friendly match • CN = CAF African Cup of Nations • CC = COSAFA Cup • IOG = Indian Ocean Games • WC = FIFA World Cup™
q = qualifier • r1 = first round group • qf = quarter-final • 3p = third place play-off

MADAGASCAR NATIONAL TEAM RECORDS AND RECORD SEQUENCES

Records			Sequence records				
Victory	8-1	CGO 1960	Wins	8	1957-1963	Clean sheets	4	1990, 1992-93
Defeat	0-7	MRI 1952	Defeats	8	2001	Goals scored	14	1957-1965
Player Caps	n/a		Undefeated	10	1979-1980	Without goal	6	2001
Player Goals	n/a		Without win	14	2003-2005	Goals against	17	1971-1980

MADAGASCAR COUNTRY INFORMATION

Capital	Antananarivo	Independence	1960 from France	GDP per Capita	$800
Population	17 501 871	Status	Republic	GNP Ranking	119
Area km²	587 040	Language	French, Malagasy	Dialling code	+261
Population density	29 per km²	Literacy rate	68%	Internet code	.mg
% in urban areas	27%	Main religion	Indigenous 52%, Christian 41%	GMT +/−	+3
Towns/Cities ('000)	Antananarivo 1 391; Toamasina 206; Antsirabé 183; Fianarantsoa 167; Mahajanga 155; Toliary 115; Antsiranana 82; Antanifotsy 70; Ambovombe 66; Amparafaravola 51				
Neighbours (km)	Indian Ocean 4 828				
Main stadia	Mahamasina – Antananarivo 22 000				

MADAGASCAR 2005 NATIONAL CHAMPIONSHIP

Group A	Pl	W	D	L	F	A	Pts
USA Foot †	5	4	1	0	14	2	13
Adema Antananarivo †	5	3	2	0	13	2	11
RFM Mahasolo †	5	2	1	2	9	7	7
St Paul Marovoay	5	2	1	2	15	15	7
ASUT Toliara	5	1	0	4	6	21	3
Herita Antsohihy	5	0	1	4	6	16	1

Group B	Pl	W	D	L	F	A	Pts
USJF/Ravinala †	5	4	0	0	9	1	12
Eco Redipharm †	5	1	2	1	3	1	5
Jirama Fianarantsoa †	5	1	1	2	2	5	4
EFFI PMU Itasy	5	0	3	1	2	4	3
Ascum Mahajanga	5	0	2	2	2	7	2
TAM Morondava				Withdrew			

Second Stage	Pl	W	D	L	F	A	Pts
USJF/Ravinala ‡	5	5	0	0	13	5	15
USCAFOOT ‡	5	4	0	1	11	3	12
Adema Antananarivo ‡	5	2	1	2	5	7	7
Eco Redipharm ‡	5	1	2	2	5	8	5
Jirama Fianarantsoa	5	1	1	3	9	12	4
RFM Mahasolo	5	0	0	5	7	15	0

10/09/2005 - 18/09/2005 • † Qualified for the second stage
• ‡ Qualified for the play-offs

MADAGASCAR 2005 CHAMPIONSHIP PLAY-OFFS

Semi-finals		Finals	
USCAFOOT	3		20-11-2005
Adema Antanarivo	1		Mahamasina, Antananarivo
		USCAFOOT †	0
		USJF/Ravinala	0

Eco Redipharm	0
USJF/Ravinala ‡	1

‡ Match abandoned when Eco Redipharm walked off
† Qualified for the CAF Champions League

COUPE DE MADAGASCAR 2005

Round of 16		Quarter-finals		Semi-finals		Final	
USCAFOOT	1						
COSFA	0	USCAFOOT	1				
Air Force Betsiboka	0	Jirama Toamasina	0				
Jirama Toamasina	1			USCAFOOT	3		
Fanilon Soavimasoandro	w-o			Adema Antanarivo	1		
Fortior Toamasina		Fanilon Soavimasoandro	2 1p				
Ajesaia	0	Adema Antanarivo	2 4p			USCAFOOT	2
Adema Antanarivo	1					USJF/Ravinala ‡	1
Stade Olympique	1 3p						
Ihorombe	1 1p	Stade Olympique	2				
Amboasary Atsimo	0	EEF Afoma Ambositra	0				
EEF Afoma Ambositra	1			Stade Olympique	0	CUP FINAL	
RTS Soavinandriana	1			USJF/Ravinala	2		
Jirama Antsirabe	0	RTS Soavinandriana	0			9-10-2005	
USERJ	0	USJF/Ravinala	4			Mahamasina, Antananarivo	
USJF/Ravinala	1			‡ Qualified for the CAF Confederation Cup			

RECENT LEAGUE AND CUP RECORD

	Championship		Cup		
Year	Champions	Winners	Score	Runners-up
1998	DSA Antananarivo	FC Djivan Farafangana	2-0	Fortior Club Mahajanga
1999	Fortior Toamasina	FC Djivan Farafangana	3-0	Akon'Ambatomena
2000	Fortior Toamasina	FC Djivan Farafangana	1-0	FC Jirama Antsirabe
2001	Stade Olympique Antananarivo (SOE)	US Transfoot Toamasina	1-0	Fortior Toamasina
2002	Adema Antananarivo	Fortior Toamasina	3-0	US Transfoot Toamasina
2003	Eco Redipharm Tamatave	Léopards Transfoot	1-0	SOE Antananarivo
2004	USJF/Ravinala	USJF/Ravinala	2-1	USCAFOOT Antananarivo
2005	USCAFOOT Antananarivo	USCAFOOT Antananarivo	2-1	USJF/Ravinala

MAR – MOROCCO

NATIONAL TEAM RECORD
JULY 1ST 2002 TO JULY 9TH 2006

PL	W	D	L	F	A	%
53	26	15	12	75	34	63.2

FIFA/COCA-COLA WORLD RANKING

1993	1994	1995	1996	1997	1998	1999	2000	2001	2002	2003	2004	2005		High		Low	
30	33	38	27	15	13	24	28	36	35	38	33	36		**10**	04/98	**41**	08/02

2005–2006											
08/05	09/05	10/05	11/05	12/05	01/06	02/06	03/06	04/06	05/06	06/06	07/06
34	36	35	35	36	35	36	37	36	36	-	40

Missing out on the 2006 FIFA World Cup™ finals was a bitter pill for Morocco to swallow. A controversial 2-2 draw against Tunisia in the final match saw them miss out by only the slimmest of margins, having remained unbeaten during the qualifying campaign. That left Moroccan football to suffer the consequences, notably the enforced departure of coach Badou Zaki. Attempts to replace him with the fabled French coach Philippe Troussier collapsed just six weeks into his tenure, when Troussier's demands on the hiring of supporting staff fell outside of the Moroccan football federation's budget. That left Mohamed Fakhir with just two weeks to prepare his side for the African

INTERNATIONAL HONOURS
Qualified for the FIFA World Cup™ finals 1970 1986 1994 1998 CAF African Cup of Nations 1976
African Youth Championship 1997 CAF Champions League FAR Rabat 1985, Raja Casablanca 1989 1997 1999, Wydad Casablanca 1992

Nations Cup finals in Egypt. His decision to make several controversial changes to the squad hampered the country's chances and as a result, Morocco failed to make it past the first round. Fakhir was handed the job just a month after he led the army club FAR Rabat to victory in the CAF Confederation Cup Final over Dolphin FC of Nigeria. FAR Rabat, Moroccan champions in 2005, were unable to successfully defend their title as Wydad Casablanca, coached by the Portuguese José Romão, clinched the championship for the first time in 13 years.

THE FIFA BIG COUNT OF 2000

	Male	Female		Male	Female
Registered players	30 639	913	Referees	1 556	0
Non registered players	120 000	0	Officials	6 000	0
Youth players	100 119	1 737	Total involved	260 964	
Total players	253 408		Number of clubs	400	
Professional players	100	0	Number of teams	3 374	

Fédération Royale Marocaine de Football (FRMF)
51 Bis Avenue Ibn Sina, Agdal, Case Postale 51, Rabat 10 000, Morocco
Tel +212 37 672706   Fax +212 37 671070
contact@fedefoot.ma   www.frmf.ma
President: BENSLIMANE Housni   General Secretary: BENCHEIKH Larci
Vice-President: AOUZAL Mohamed   Treasurer: EL AOUFIR Larbi   Media Officer: MOUFID Mohamed
Men's Coach: FAKHIR Mohammed   Women's Coach: ALAOUI Slimani
FRMF formed: 1955   CAF: 1966   FIFA: 1960
Green shirts with red trimmings, Green shorts, Green socks or Red shirts with green trimmings, Red shorts, Red socks

RECENT INTERNATIONAL MATCHES PLAYED BY MOROCCO

2002	Opponents	Score		Venue	Comp	Scorers	Att	Referee
10-09	Trinidad and Tobago	W	2-0	Marrakech	Fr	Chamakh 2 [38 49]		Yaacoubi TUN
11-10	Tunisia	D	0-0	Tunis	Fr		13 000	Layec FRA
15-11	Burkina Faso	W	1-0	Meknés	Fr	Ouaddou [24]	25 000	Boukhtir TUN
18-11	Mali	L	0-1	Casablanca	Fr		6 000	Shelmani LBY
19-11	Mali	L	0-1	Meknés	Fr			
2004								
27-01	Nigeria	W	1-0	Monastir	CNr1	Youssef Hadji [77]	15 000	Ndoye SEN
31-01	Benin	W	4-0	Sfax	CNr1	Chamakh [15], Mokhtari [73], Ouaddou [75], El Karkouri [80]	20 000	Maillet SEY
4-02	South Africa	D	1-1	Sousse	CNr1	Safri [38p]	6 000	Guirat TUN
8-02	Algeria	W	3-1	Sfax	CNqf	Chamakh [90], Youssef Hadji [113], Zairi [120]	22 000	Shelmani LBY
11-02	Mali	W	4-0	Sousse	CNsf	Mokhtari 2 [14 58], Youssef Hadji [80], Baha [90]	15 000	Sharaf CIV
14-02	Tunisia	L	1-2	Tunis	CNf	Mokhtari [38]	60 000	Ndoye SEN
18-02	Switzerland	W	2-1	Rabat	Fr	Adjou [78], Iajour [82]	1 700	Berber ALG
31-03	Angola	W	3-1	Casablanca	Fr	Baha 2 [67 74], Zairi [77]	7 000	Risha EGY
28-04	Argentina	L	0-1	Casablanca	Fr		65 000	Ndoye SEN
28-05	Mali	D	0-0	Bamako	Fr		35 000	Sidibe MLI
5-06	Malawi	D	1-1	Blantyre	WCq	Safri [25]	30 040	Mususa ZIM
3-07	Botswana	W	1-0	Gaborone	WCq	Mokhtari [30]	22 000	Dlamini SWZ
4-09	Tunisia	D	1-1	Rabat	WCq	El Karkouri [74]	45 000	Auda EGY
10-10	Guinea	D	1-1	Conakry	WCq	Chamakh [5]	25 000	Monteiro Duarte CPV
17-11	Burkina Faso	W	4-0	Rabat	Fr	Oulmers [52], Boukhari [68], Sarssar [78], Abdessadki [82]	5 000	Keita MLI
2005								
9-02	Kenya	W	5-1	Rabat	WCq	Zairi 3 [12 39 90], Diane [46], Youssef Hadji [81]	40 000	Tamuni LBY
26-03	Guinea	W	1-0	Rabat	WCq	Youssef Hadji [62]	70 000	Coulibaly MLI
4-06	Malawi	W	4-1	Rabat	WCq	Chamakh [16], Youssef Hadji 2 [21 75], Kharja [72]	48 000	Buenkadila COD
18-06	Kenya	D	0-0	Nairobi	WCq		50 000	Diatta SEN
17-08	Togo	L	0-1	Rouen	Fr			
3-09	Botswana	W	1-0	Rabat	WCq	El Karkouri [56]	25 000	Benouza ALG
8-10	Tunisia	D	2-2	Tunis/Rades	WCq	Chamakh [3], El Karkouri [42]	60 000	Abd El Fatah EGY
15-11	Cameroon	D	0-0	Clairfontaine	Fr			
2006								
9-01	Congo DR	W	3-0	Rabat	Fr	Chamakh [32], Aboucherouane [52], Armoumen [67]		
14-01	Zimbabwe	W	1-0	Marrakech	Fr	Armoumen [89]		
17-01	Angola	D	2-2	Marrakech	Fr	Chamakh [6], Youssef Hadji [8]		
21-01	Côte d'Ivoire	L	0-1	Cairo	CNr1		8 000	Damon RSA
24-01	Egypt	D	0-0	Cairo	CNr1		75 000	Codjia BEN
23-01	Libya	D	0-0	Cairo	CNr1		5 000	Daami TUN
23-05	USA	W	1-0	Nashville	Fr	Madihi [90]	26 141	Navarro CAN
28-05	Mali	L	0-1	Paris	Fr			Garibian FRA
4-06	Colombia	L	0-2	Barcelona	Fr		11 000	Segura Garcia ESP

Fr = Friendly match • AR = Arab Cup • CN = CAF African Cup of Nations • WC = FIFA World Cup™
q = qualifier • r1 = first round group • qf = quarter-final • sf = semi-final • 3p = third place play-off • f = final

MOROCCO NATIONAL TEAM RECORDS AND RECORD SEQUENCES

Records			Sequence records					
Victory	7-0	TOG 1979	Wins	8	1997	Clean sheets	9	1997
Defeat	0-6	HUN 1964	Defeats	4	1994	Goals scored	12	1975-1976
Player Caps	115	NAYBET Noureddine	Undefeated	15	1983-84, 1996-97	Without goal	6	1983
Player Goals	n/a		Without win	7	1988	Goals against	9	1959-1961

MOROCCO COUNTRY INFORMATION

Capital	Rabat	Independence	1956 from France	GDP per Capita	$4 000
Population	32 209 101	Status	Constitutional Monarchy	GNP Ranking	57
Area km²	446 550	Language	Arabic, French, Berber	Dialling code	+212
Population density	72 per km²	Literacy rate	51%	Internet code	.ma
% in urban areas	48%	Main religion	Muslim 99%	GMT + / –	0
Towns/Cities ('000)	Casablanca 3 609; Rabat 1 894; Fès 1 160; Marrakech 942; Tanger 825; Agadir 656; Meknès 583; Salé 521; Oujda 433; Kénitra 420; Tetouan 365; Safi 278; Mohammedia 155;				
Neighbours (km)	Spain (Ceuta & Melilla) 15; Algeria 1 559; Western Sahara 443; North Atlantic & Mediterranean Sea 1 835				
Main stadia	Stade Mohammed V – Casablanca 67 000; Stade Moulay Abdallah – Rabat 52 000				

CLUB DIRECTORY

Club	AKA	Town/City	Stadium	Capacity	www.	Lge	Cup	CL
AS Salé	ASS	Salé	Narche Verte	4 000		0	0	0
SC Chabab	SCCM	Mohammedia	El Bachir	5 000	chabab.org	1	1	0
COD Meknès	CODM	Meknès	Stade d'Honneur	20 000	codm-meknes.com	1	1	0
Forces Armées Royales	FAR	Rabat	Moulay Abdallah	52 000	supporters-asfar.com	11	8	1
Hassania US	HUSA	Agadir	Al Inbiaâte	15 000		2	0	0
Ittihad Zemmouri	IZK	Khemisset	Stade du 20 Août	6 000		0	0	0
Ittihad Riadi	IRT	Tanger	Stade de Marchan	14 000		0	0	0
Jeunesse Al Massira	JSM	Laâyoune	Cheikh Laaghdef	40 000		0	0	0
Kawkab AC	KACM	Marrakech	El Harti	25 000		2	6	0
Maghreb AS	MAS	Fès	Complexe Sportif	45 000	massawi.com	4	2	0
Mouloudia Club	MCO	Oujda	Stade d'Honneur	35 000		1	4	0
Olympique Club	OCK	Khouribga	Stade Municipal	5 000	ock.ma	0	0	0
Olympique Club	OCS	Safi			ocs.ma	0	0	0
Raja CA	RCA	Casablanca	Stade Mohammed V	67 000	rajacasablanca.com	8	5	3
Union Touarga	UST	Rabat				0	0	0
Wydad AC	WAC	Casablanca	Stade Mohammed V	67 000	wydad.com	11	9	1

RECENT LEAGUE AND CUP RECORD

	Championship						Cup		
Year	Champions	Pts	Runners-up	Pts	Third	Pts	Winners	Score	Runners-up
1990	Wydad Casablanca	72	Ittihad Riadi Tanger	66	Kawkab Marrakech	65	Olympic Casablanca	0-0 4-2p	FAR Rabat
1991	Wydad Casablanca	72	FAR Rabat	68	Ittihad Riadi Tanger	63	Kawkab Marrakech	1-0	KAC Kénitra
1992	Kawkab Marrakech	74	Raja Casablanca	66	Wydad Casablanca	64	Olympic Casablanca	1-0	Raja Casablanca
1993	Wydad Casablanca	72	Raja Casablanca	64	Renaissance Settat	64	Kawkab Marrakech	1-0	Maghreb Fès
1994	Olympic Casablanca	76	Wydad Casablanca	66	FAR Rabat	64	Wydad Casablanca	1-0	Olympic Khouribga
1995	COD Meknès	66	Olympic Casablanca	65	Kawkab Marrakech	65	FUS Rabat	2-0	Olympic Khouribga
1996	Raja Casablanca	57	Olympic Khouribga	48	Wydad Casablanca	47	Raja Casablanca	1-0	FAR Rabat
1997	Raja Casablanca	55	Wydad Casablanca	53	Renaissance Settat	53	Wydad Casablanca	1-0	Kawkab Marrakech
1998	Raja Casablanca	67	Kawkab Marrakech	53	Wydad Casablanca	51	Wydad Casablanca	2-1	FAR Rabat
1999	Raja Casablanca	62	Kawkab Marrakech	58	Olympic Khouribga	54	FAR Rabat	1-0	Chabab Mohammedia
2000	Raja Casablanca	59	Wydad Casablanca	54	Maghreb Fès	53	Majd Casablanca	1-1 8-7p	Renaissance Settat
2001	Raja Casablanca	64	FUS Rabat	55	Maghreb Fès	48	Wydad Casablanca	1-0	Maghreb Fès
2002	Hassania Agadir	65	Wydad Casablanca	62	Raja Casablanca	55	Raja Casablanca	2-0	Maghreb Fès
2003	Hassania Agadir	54	Raja Casablanca	52	Wydad Casablanca	52	FAR Rabat	1-0	Wydad Casablanca
2004	Raja Casablanca	56	FAR Rabat	56	AS Salé	51	FAR Rabat	0-0 3-0p	Wydad Casablanca
2005	FAR Rabat	62	Raja Casablanca	60	Wydad Casablanca	50	Raja Casablanca	0-0 5-4p	Olympic Khouribga
2006	Wydad Casablanca	61	FAR Rabat	58	Olympic Khouribga	53			

MOROCCO 2005-06
CHAMPIONNAT DU GNFE1

	Pl	W	D	L	F	A	Pts	WAC	FAR	OCK	RCA	HUSA	CODM	DHJ	IZK	ASS	OCS	MCO	MAT	JSM	IRT	SCCM	UTS
Wydad Casablanca †	30	17	10	3	33	16	61		1-0	2-1	1-2	1-1	1-1	0-0	0-0	1-0	1-0	2-1	2-0	1-0	2-0	1-0	3-0
FAR Rabat	30	16	10	4	41	14	58	0-0		1-1	2-0	2-0	3-1	2-0	1-1	3-1	0-0	3-1	1-1	3-1	2-1	5-0	1-0
Olympique Khouribga	30	15	8	7	44	23	53	2-0	2-1		1-2	0-1	2-0	1-0	4-0	4-0	0-3	1-0	0-0	2-1	2-0	3-1	3-0
Raja Casablanca	30	13	12	5	34	24	51	1-1	0-1	0-0		1-1	0-0	3-2	1-1	2-0	2-1	1-1	0-0	3-2	0-0	1-0	0-0
HUS Agadir	30	14	7	9	31	24	49	2-1	1-0	1-0	1-3		3-0	1-0	1-0	1-0	2-1	2-0	1-0	0-1	2-2	0-1	3-0
COD Meknès	30	10	11	9	23	25	41	0-1	0-1	1-1	1-0	2-1		1-1	1-0	0-0	1-0	2-1	2-1	1-1	0-0	0-0	0-0
DH Jadida	30	8	16	6	29	26	40	1-2	1-0	2-2	1-1	1-0	1-1		1-0	1-1	1-0	1-0	0-0	0-0	4-2	0-1	1-1
IZ Khemisset	30	8	12	10	20	26	36	1-1	1-1	1-2	1-0	1-1	1-0	1-1		2-1	1-0	0-1	0-0	0-0	0-1	0-0	1-0
AS Salé	30	8	11	11	18	26	35	0-1	0-0	0-0	0-2	2-1	2-1	1-1	0-1		1-0	0-0	3-0	0-0	2-1	2-1	1-0
Olympique Safi	30	9	7	14	26	27	34	1-1	0-0	2-0	3-2	0-1	0-1	2-2	1-0	0-1		0-0	1-0	1-1	2-1	3-1	0-1
Mouloudia Oujda	30	8	10	12	27	30	34	0-1	0-0	1-2	1-1	3-1	0-1	0-0	2-0	1-0	0-0		2-2	3-2	1-1	1-0	3-1
MA Tétouan	30	7	12	11	19	27	33	1-2	0-1	2-1	2-3	0-1	1-0	1-1	1-1	0-0	1-0	1-0		0-0	0-0	0-0	0-1
JS Massira	30	5	17	8	23	26	32	0-0	0-0	0-3	0-0	1-0	1-1	1-1	3-1	0-0	0-1	2-2	2-0		1-1	3-1	0-0
IR Tanger	30	6	11	13	22	29	29	1-1	0-1	0-0	0-1	0-0	1-0	0-0	0-1	2-0	3-1	0-1	0-1	1-0		1-2	2-0
Chabab Mohammedia	30	6	9	15	15	35	27	0-1	0-4	0-0	0-1	0-0	1-2	0-1	1-1	0-0	1-3	1-0	1-2	0-0	1-0		0-0
US Touarga §2	30	4	9	17	12	39	19	0-1	0-2	1-4	0-1	1-0	0-2	1-3	**0-2**	0-0	1-0	2-1	1-2	0-0	1-1	0-1	

16/08/2003 - 15/05/2004 • † Qualified for the CAF Champions League • Match in bold awarded 2-0 • §2 = two points deducted

MOROCCO 2005-06
CHAMPIONNAT DU GNFE2

	Pl	W	D	L	F	A	Pts
Maghreb Fès	30	16	12	2	33	14	60
Kawkab Marrakech	30	16	10	4	32	18	58
CAY Berrechid	30	13	8	9	32	28	47
Racing Casablanca	30	11	12	7	26	23	45
RS Berkane	30	13	5	12	32	36	44
US Mohamedia	30	9	13	8	25	23	40
US Sidi Kacem	30	10	10	10	21	22	40
Kénitra AC	30	8	15	7	27	20	39
Rachad Bernoussi	30	9	10	11	28	31	37
Hilal Nador	30	8	11	11	20	26	35
Stade Marocain	30	8	11	11	20	23	35
WW Sidi Othmane	30	7	11	12	27	35	32
FUS Rabat	30	5	17	8	14	18	32
RS Settat	30	8	9	13	26	31	31
NR Marrakech	30	7	9	14	24	27	30
Fath Riadi Nador	30	5	11	14	17	29	26

3/09/2005 - 27/05/2006

COUPE DU TRONE 2005-06

Round of 16		Quarter-finals		Semi-finals		Final
HUS Agadir	1					
Wydad Casablanca	0	HUS Agadir	w-o			
NR Marrakech	0	Raja Casablanca				
Raja Casablanca	1			HUS Agadir	1	
AS Salé	2			COD Meknès	0	
FAR Rabat	0	AS Salé	0			
MA Tétouan	0	COD Meknès	1			
COD Meknès	1					HUS Agadir
IR Tanger	2					Olympique Khouribga
Etoile Tanger	1	IR Tanger	1 4p			
Kénitra AC	1 8p	IZ Khemisset	1 2p			CUP FINAL
IZ Khemisset	1 9p			IR Tanger	0	
Rachad Bernoussi	0 4p			Olympique Khouribga	4	
US Mohamedia	0 2p	Rachad Bernoussi	0			The 2006 Coupe du Trône final was delayed until the start of the new season
Jeunesse Ben Guérir	0 3p	Olympique Khouribga	2			
Olympique Khouribga	0 4p				* Home team	

MAS – MALAYSIA

NATIONAL TEAM RECORD
JULY 1ST 2002 TO JULY 9TH 2006

PL	W	D	L	F	A	%
40	12	7	21	52	64	38.7

FIFA/COCA-COLA WORLD RANKING

1993	1994	1995	1996	1997	1998	1999	2000	2001	2002	2003	2004	2005	High	Low
79	89	106	96	87	113	117	107	111	128	116	120	123	75 08/93	128 12/02

2005–2006											
08/05	09/05	10/05	11/05	12/05	01/06	02/06	03/06	04/06	05/06	06/06	07/06
111	116	115	116	123	124	125	126	127	127	-	146

The shift in the dates of Malaysia's Super League saw the completion of three championships in just over two years with Perlis winning the 2005 championship ahead of defending champions Pahang. The story of the season though, was the unlikely treble won by Selangor. They beat Negeri Sembilan in the final of the Premier League, Malaysia's second division in July 2005, then went on to win the FA Cup in September by beating Perak 4-2 before a capacity crowd in the Shah Alam Stadium. Remarkably, they then went on to beat champions Perlis in the final of the Malaysia Cup, regarded by many as the highlight of the domestic season. In the clash between the Super League

INTERNATIONAL HONOURS
Southeast Asian Games 1961 1977 1979 1989

and Premier League champions, Selangor's Bambang Pamungas became only the fourth player to score a hat-trick in the final as his team won 3-0. The 2006 season promised much for Selangor and a promoted side did go on to win the Super League, but it wasn't Selangor. Instead Negeri Sembilan won a first ever title, finishing comfortably clear of Melaka Telecom. The Malaysian National team had a relatively quiet year with just two matches, against New Zealand and Singapore. To help preparations for the 2007 AFC Asian Cup, which they will co-host, there will be a welcome return for the Merdeka Cup, one of the oldest national team competitions in Asia.

THE FIFA BIG COUNT OF 2000

	Male	Female		Male	Female
Registered players	2 400	250	Referees	3 500	0
Non registered players	300 000	800	Officials	16 000	100
Youth players	800	100	Total involved	323 950	
Total players	304 350		Number of clubs	600	
Professional players	800	0	Number of teams	2 800	

Football Association of Malaysia (FAM)
3rd Floor Wisma FAM, Jalan SS5A/9, Kelana Jaya, Selangor Darul Ehsan 47301, Malaysia
Tel +60 3 78733100   Fax +60 3 78757984
gensec@fam.org.my   www.fam.org.my
President: HRH Sultan AHMAD SHAH   General Secretary: AKBAR KHAN Dato' Dell
Vice-President: RITHAUDDEEN Tengka   Treasurer: KEAP TAI Cheong   Media Officer: KHAWARI Ahmad
Men's Coach: BICSKEI Bertalan   Women's Coach: ZHANG Hong
FAM formed: 1933   AFC: 1954   FIFA: 1956
Yellow shirts with black trimmings, Yellow shorts, Yellow socks

RECENT INTERNATIONAL MATCHES PLAYED BY MALAYSIA

2002	Opponents	Score		Venue	Comp	Scorers	Att	Referee
16-07	Singapore	L	1-2	Kuantan	Fr	Bin Jamlus [35]	25 000	
11-12	Cambodia	W	5-0	Kuala Lumpur	Fr	Marjan 2, Omar, Mahayuddin, Rakhli		
18-12	Singapore	W	4-0	Singapore	TCr1	Rakhli [30], Mahayuddin 2 [49 65], Yusoff [69]	40 000	Lee Young Chun KOR
20-12	Thailand	W	3-1	Singapore	TCr1	Rakhli [43], Tengku [66], Mahayudin [86]	7 000	Luong The Tai VIE
22-12	Laos	D	1-1	Singapore	TCr1	Jamil [28]	350	Lee Young Chun KOR
27-12	Indonesia	L	0-1	Jakarta	TCsf		65 000	Ebrahim BHR
29-12	Vietnam	L	1-2	Jakarta	TC3p	Mahayuddin [56]	25 000	Midi Nitrorejo IDN
2003								
26-09	Indonesia	D	1-1	Kuala Lumpur	Fr	Saari [90]		
8-10	Myanmar	W	4-0	Kuala Lumpur	ACq	Tengku 2 [34 79], Gilbert [67p], OG [85]	4 500	Yang CHN
10-10	Iraq	D	0-0	Kuala Lumpur	ACq		5 000	Kunthama THA
12-10	Bahrain	D	2-2	Kuala Lumpur	ACq	Shukor [80], Yosri [90]	15 000	Matsumura JPN
20-10	Iraq	L	1-5	Manama	ACq	Omar [53]	500	Al Saeedi UAE
22-10	Bahrain	L	1-3	Manama	ACq	Mahayuddin [32]	18 000	Najm LIB
24-10	Myanmar	L	1-2	Isa Town	ACq	Omar [86]	200	Al Harrassi OMA
24-10	India	L	0-2	Hyderabad	AAG			
26-10	Rwanda	L	1-2	Hyderabad	AAG	Amri [28]		
2004								
7-02	Japan	L	0-4	Ibaraki	Fr		29 530	Moradi IRN
18-02	Hong Kong	L	1-3	Kuantan	WCq	Talib [39p]	12 000	Nagalimgam SIN
17-03	Indonesia	D	0-0	Johor Bahru	Fr		8 000	Kim Heng MAS
31-03	Kuwait	L	0-2	Kuantan	WCq		9 327	Matsumura JPN
9-06	China PR	L	0-4	Tianjin	WCq		35 000	Park Sang Gu KOR
12-07	Singapore	W	2-0	Kuala Lumpur	Fr			
19-08	Thailand	W	2-1	Bangkok	Fr	Kit Hong [8], Vellu [57]		
8-09	China PR	L	0-1	Penang	WCq		14 000	Karim BHR
13-10	Hong Kong	L	0-2	Hong Kong	WCq		2 425	Ghandour LIB
1-11	Singapore	W	2-1	Singapore	Fr	Bin Jamlus [68], Amri [90]	3 293	Luong The Tai VIE
17-11	Kuwait	L	1-6	Kuwait City	WCq	Mohd [19]	15 000	Lutfullin UZB
8-12	East Timor †	W	5-0	Kuala Lumpur	TCr1	Kit Kong [27], Amri 2 [47 83], Saari [67], Adan [85]	6 000	Lazar SIN
10-12	Philippines	W	4-1	Kuala Lumpur	TCr1	Kit Kong [17], Bin Jamlus 2 [67 77p], Hussein [74]		Napitupulu IDN
12-12	Myanmar	L	0-1	Kuala Lumpur	TCr1		10 000	Hsu Chao Lo TPE
14-12	Thailand	W	2-1	Kuala Lumpur	TCr1	Bin Jamlus 2 [63 65]	10 000	Moradi IRN
28-12	Indonesia	W	2-1	Jakarta	TCsf	Kit Kong 2 [28 47]	100 000	Irmatov UZB
2005								
3-01	Indonesia	L	1-4	Kuala Lumpur	TCsf	Bin Jamlus [26]	70 000	Kunsuta THA
15-01	Myanmar	W	2-1	Singapore	TC3p	Bin Jamlus [15], Nor [56]	2 000	Vo Minh Tri VIE
4-06	Singapore	L	0-2	Singapore	Fr		18 000	Kunsuta THA
8-06	Singapore	L	1-2	Penang	Fr	Ayob [25]	10 000	Napitupulu IDN
2006								
19-02	New Zealand	L	0-1	Christchurch	Fr		10 100	O'Leary NZL
23-02	New Zealand	L	1-2	Albany	Fr	Safee Sali [24]	8 702	Fox NZL
31-05	Singapore	D	0-0	Singapore	Fr	L 4-5p	18 604	Li Yuhong CHN
3-06	Singapore	D	0-0	Paroi	Fr	L 7-8p		

Fr = Friendly match • TC = ASEAN Tiger Cup • AC = AFC Asian Cup • AAG = Afro-Asian Games • WC = FIFA World Cup™
q = qualifier • r1 = first round group • sf = semi-final • 3p = third place play-off • † not a full international

MALAYSIA NATIONAL TEAM RECORDS AND RECORD SEQUENCES

Records			Sequence records					
Victory	15-1	PHI 1962	Wins	6	1975, 1989	Clean sheets	5	1979
Defeat	2-8	NZL 1967	Defeats	7	1980-81, 2003-04	Goals scored	14	1999-2000
Player Caps	n/a		Undefeated	10	1961-1962, 1971	Without goal	5	1997-1998
Player Goals	n/a		Without win	12	2003-2004	Goals against	15	1970-1971

MALAYSIA COUNTRY INFORMATION

Capital	Kuala Lumpur	Independence	1963 from the UK	GDP per Capita	$9 000
Population	23 522 482	Status	Constitutional Monarchy	GNP Ranking	42
Area km²	329 750	Language	Malay, English, Chinese	Dialling code	+60
Population density	71 per km²	Literacy rate	88%	Internet code	.my
% in urban areas	54%	Main religion	Muslim 45%, Buddhist 15%	GMT + / –	+8
Towns/Cities ('000)	Kuala Lumpur 1 453; Klang 879; Subang Jaya 833; Johor Bahru 802; Ipoh 673; Ampang Jaya 644; Kuching 570; Petaling Jaya 520; Shah Alam 481; Kota Kinabalu 457; Sandakan 392; Kuantan 366				
Neighbours (km)	Brunei 381; Indonesia 1 782; Thailand 506; South China Sea 4 675				
Main stadia	Bukit Jalil – Kuala Lumpur 100 200; Shah Alam – Shah Alam 69 372; Darul Makmur – Kuantan 40 000				

MALAYSIA 2005

SUPER LEAGUE

	Pl	W	D	L	F	A	Pts	Perlis	Pahang	Perak	Melaka Telecom	Selangor MPPJ	Penang	Selangor Pub. Bank	Sabah
Perlis †	21	14	3	4	43	19	45		5-1 2-1	2-2	1-2 4-0	2-0 4-0	2-0 1-0	0-1	5-0
Pahang	21	10	5	6	37	29	35	0-1		4-1 1-0	3-0	3-2	4-1 2-1	1-2 0-0	3-3 3-2
Perak	21	9	3	9	33	25	30	1-2 3-1	0-0		0-0 3-1	2-1	0-1	1-0	2-0 3-0
Melaka Telecom	21	7	7	7	23	28	28	0-0	1-1 3-2	3-0		0-1 3-1	0-1	1-2 0-0	3-3
Selangor MPPJ	21	8	3	10	29	38	27	2-3	1-2 1-1	3-1 1-5	0-0		2-1	2-4 2-1	2-1
Penang	21	8	1	12	27	31	25	1-2	3-2	2-1 0-3	0-1 0-1	2-3 1-3		3-1 1-0	3-0
Selangor Public Bank	21	7	4	10	22	30	25	0-2 3-3	0-1	2-1 0-4	1-2	1-0	1-1		1-3 1-0
Sabah	21	6	4	11	25	39	22	2-0 0-1	0-2	1-0	1-1 4-1	1-1 0-1	0-4 2-1	2-1	

29/01/2005 - 9/05/2005 • † Qualified for the AFC Cup

MALAYSIA 2005 PREMIER LEAGUE (2) GROUP A

	Pl	W	D	L	F	A	Pts
Selangor	21	16	3	2	61	25	51
Kedah	21	13	7	1	44	11	46
Selangor MK Land	21	14	4	3	61	29	46
Kuala Lumpur	21	8	7	6	34	30	31
Brunei	21	6	3	12	29	43	21
Penang NTFA	21	4	5	12	27	51	17
Kelantan TNB	21	4	2	15	28	62	14
Melaka	21	3	1	17	17	50	10

6/02/2005 - 10/07/2005

CHAMPIONSHIP PREMIER LEAGUE
Selangor　　　4
Negeri Sembilan　2

MALAYSIA 2005 PREMIER LEAGUE (2) GROUP B

	Pl	W	D	L	F	A	Pts
Negeri Sembilan	21	16	1	4	45	19	49
Terengganu	21	13	4	4	34	18	43
Selangor PKNS	21	13	2	6	46	25	41
Johor FC	21	10	6	5	27	16	36
Perak Jenderata	21	7	5	9	20	32	26
Johor	21	6	2	13	18	29	20
Sarawak	21	3	5	13	23	38	14
Police	21	2	3	16	15	51	9

6/02/2005 - 10/07/2005

FA CUP 2005

Second Round		Quarter-finals		Semi-finals		Final	
Selangor	3 2						
Selangor MK Land *	1 1	Selangor	1 5				
Perlis *	4 2 2p	Kelantan *	1 4				
Kelantan	1 5 4p			Selangor	2 3		
Selangor PKNS *	1 1 8p			Selangor Public Bank*	2 1		
Kedah	1 1 7p	Selangor PKNS	3 1				
KL Maju Holdings *	1 0	Selangor Public Bank*	3 3				
Selangor Public Bank	5 5					Selangor †	4
Kuala Lumpur	2 3					Perak	2
Kelantan TNB *	2 2	Kuala Lumpur	1 1 4p				
Johor *	0 0	Terengganu *	1 1 1p				
Terengganu	1 0			Kuala Lumpur	0 3		
Sabah	3 3			Perak *	2 2		
Shahzan Muda *	2 0	Sabah *	0 0				
Penang	0 1	Perak	5 2				
Perak *	6 2						

* Home team in the first leg • † Qualified for the AFC Cup

CUP FINAL

Shah Alam Stadium, 24-09-2005
Att: 80 000, Ref: Ibrahim Muhamad
Scorers - Bambang Pamungkas 2 [8] [87],
Elie Aiboy [43], Brian Fuentes [68] for Selangor;
Abdoulaye Traore [24], Mohd Noor Ismail [89]
for Perak

MALAYSIA CUP 2005

Quarter-finals			Semi-finals			Final	
Selangor	2	1					
Penang	1	1	Selangor	3	1		
Kedah	2 1	2p	Terengganu	1	1		
Terengganu	0 3	4p				Selangor	3
Perak	1	1				Perlis	0
Melaka Telekom	0	1	Perak	1	0		
Pahang	1	1	Perlis	2	1		
Perlis	3	0					

Bukit Jalil, 1-10-2005, Att 90 000

MALAYSIA CUP

Year	Winners	Score	Runners-up
1996	Selangor	1-1 5-3p	Sabah
1997	Selangor	1-0	Pahang
1998	Perak	1-1 5-3p	Terengganu
1999	Brunei	2-1	Sarawak
2000	Perak	2-0	Negeri Sembilan
2001	Terengganu	2-1	Perak
2002	Selangor	1-0	Sabah
2003	Selangor MPPJ	3-0	Sabah
2004	Perlis	1-0	Kedah
2005	Selangor	3-0	Perlis

MALAYSIA 2005-06

SUPER LEAGUE

	Pl	W	D	L	F	A	Pts	Negeri Sembilan	Melaka Telecom	Perak	Perlis	Selangor MPPJ	Pulau Pinang	Pahang	Selangor
Negeri Sembilan Naza†	21	12	4	5	26	14	40		1-0	5-1	2-1 1-0	0-1	2-0 2-0	1-0 1-1	2-1
Melaka Telekom	21	9	6	6	29	27	33	0-1 0-0		0-2	0-0	1-0 0-3	3-2 5-2	1-1	1-2 2-2
Perak	21	9	3	9	32	29	30	2-1 0-2	0-1 0-1		4-0 0-2	1-2	2-3	2-0	2-0 0-0
Perlis	21	8	6	7	26	25	30	0-0	1-1 2-4	2-2		1-0	1-0 1-0	1-1 1-0	6-1 3-2
Selangor MPPJ	21	9	2	10	28	27	29	3-0 1-2	1-3	2-1	3-1 1-2		2-1	0-2 3-0	3-2
Pulau Pinang E&O	21	8	4	9	30	31	28	1-0	1-1	3-1 1-3	1-0	0-0 3-0		1-1	3-1 4-3
Pahang	21	7	6	8	21	24	27	1-0	1-2 0-1	0-2 3-1	1-1	2-0	1-1 2-1		1-3 1-0
Selangor	21	5	3	13	31	46	18	0-2 1-1	5-2	1-4 1-1	1-0	1-2 3-2	0-2	1-2	

3/12/2005 - 23/05/2006 • † Qualified for the AFC Cup

MALAYSIA 2005-06 PREMIER LEAGUE (2) GROUP A

	Pl	W	D	L	F	A	Pts
Kedah	21	13	3	5	39	22	42
Terengganu	21	12	5	4	47	21	41
Brunei DPMM FC	21	9	6	6	40	33	33
Sarawak	21	8	6	7	40	39	30
Johor	21	7	5	9	23	26	26
Kelantan	21	7	5	9	29	35	26
Perak UPB	21	5	4	12	28	43	19
Pulau Pinang NTFA	21	3	6	12	15	42	15

4/12/2005 - 22/05/2006

CHAMPIONSHIP PREMIER LEAGUE

Melaka	0
Kedah	1

MALAYSIA 2005-06 PREMIER LEAGUE (2) GROUP B

	Pl	W	D	L	F	A	Pts
Melaka	21	13	4	4	48	24	43
Selangor PKNS	21	11	6	4	39	25	39
Johor FC	21	9	8	4	38	27	35
Sabah	21	7	7	7	32	31	28
Kuala Lumpur	21	8	3	10	28	31	27
PDRM	21	7	3	11	30	44	24
Pahang Shahzan	21	5	7	9	30	41	22
Kelantan TNB	21	3	4	14	16	38	13

4/12/2005 - 22/05/2006

Promotion play-offs: Selangor PKNS 0-3 2-3 **Sarawak**; Johor FC 2-3 2-4 **Selangor**; Sabah 0-1 0-1 **Terengganu**; **Brunei DPMM FC** 0-0 2-1 Pahang; Sawawak, Terengganu and DPMM promoted, Selangor remain in the Super League • Play-offs second round: Pahang 3-2 1-1 Sabah; Selangor PKNS 1-4 1-1 **Johor FC**; Johor FC promoted whilst Pahang remain in the Super League

RECENT LEAGUE AND CUP RECORD

	Championship						FA Cup		
Year	Champions	Pts	Runners-up	Pts	Third	Pts	Winners	Score	Runners-up
1995	Pahang	65	Selangor	54	Sarawak	54	Sabah	3-1	Pahang
1996	Sabah	58	Kedah	57	Negri Sembilan	57	Kedah	1-0	Sarawak
1997	Sarawak	54	Kedah	50	Sabah	49	Selangor	1-0	Penang
1998	Penang	41	Pahang	40	Brunei	35	Johor	1-0	Sabah
1999	Pahang	34	Penang	31	Negri Sembilan	29	Kuala Lumpur	0-0 5-3p	Terengganu
2000	Selangor	45	Penang	43	Perak	41	Terengganu	1-1 4-3p	Penang
2001	Penang	50	Terengganu	41	Kelantan	38	Selangor	1-0	Sarawak
2002	Perak	60	Selangor	56	Sabah	47	Penang	1-0	Perak
2003	Perak	47	Kedah	45	Perlis	45	Negeri Sembilan	2-1	Perlis
2004	Pahang	47	Selangor Public Bank	38	Perlis	36	Perak	3-0	Terengganu
2005	Perlis	45	Pahang	35	Perak	30	Selangor	4-2	Perak
2006	Negeri Sembilan	40	Melaka Telekom	33	Perak	30			

MDA – MOLDOVA

NATIONAL TEAM RECORD
JULY 1ST 2002 TO JULY 9TH 2006

PL	W	D	L	F	A	%
34	8	9	17	26	47	36.8

FIFA/COCA-COLA WORLD RANKING

1993	1994	1995	1996	1997	1998	1999	2000	2001	2002	2003	2004	2005	High	Low
-	118	109	117	131	116	93	94	103	111	106	114	107	**89** 02/00	**149** 07/94

2005–2006											
08/05	09/05	10/05	11/05	12/05	01/06	02/06	03/06	04/06	05/06	06/06	07/06
113	107	108	108	107	107	107	107	104	104	-	77

Such is the domination of Sheriff Tiraspol in Moldovan club football that they must be starting to think about the possibilities of beating Skonto Riga's world record of 14 consecutive titles. They are not halfway there yet but the ease with which they won their sixth successive title must be a source of worry to the other teams in the league. The club's Georgian captain Vazha Takhnishvili has been an integral part of all six championship winning teams whilst Alexey Kuchuk, son of coach Leonid Kuchuk, finished the season as top scorer. Sheriff lost just once all season, to neighbours Tiligul-Tiras, after having gone the first 18 games unbeaten. Unsurprisingly, they also

INTERNATIONAL HONOURS
None

won the Cup, beating Nistru Otaci 2-0 in the final. Nistru's defender Alexandru Stadiiciuc had a nightmare start to the game when he scored an own goal after just 60 seconds. Sheriff were formed in 1997 and the Cup was a tenth trophy in their short history. The national team on the other hand had a FIFA World Cup™ campaign to forget after finishing bottom of a group won by world champions-to-be Italy. Their one win came in September against Belarus. There were two further victories in the Malta Tournament in February and although Moldova were represented by the under-21 team, the matches have been classed as full internationals by FIFA.

THE FIFA BIG COUNT OF 2000

	Male	Female		Male	Female
Registered players	793	85	Referees	316	18
Non registered players	63 000	2 500	Officials	252	20
Youth players	2 300	165	Total involved	57 106	
Total players	68 843		Number of clubs	200	
Professional players	0	0	Number of teams	800	

Football Association of Moldova (FMF)
Federatia Moldoveneasca de Fotbal, Str. Tricolorului nr. 39, Chisinau MD-2012, Moldova
Tel +373 22 210413   Fax +373 22 210432
fmf@mfotbal.mldnet.com   www.fmf.md
President: CEBANU Pavel   General Secretary: CEBOTARI Nicolai
Vice-President: ANGHEL Mihai   Treasurer: SOROCEAN Victor   Media Officer: VATAMANU Vasile
Men's Coach: TESLEV Anatolii   Women's Coach: PUSICOV Evgheni
FMF formed: 1990   UEFA: 1992   FIFA: 1994
Red shirts, Blue shirts, Red socks or Blue shirts, Red shorts, Blue socks

GAMES PLAYED BY MOLDOVA IN THE 2006 FIFA WORLD CUP™ CYCLE

2002	Opponents	Score		Venue	Comp	Scorers	Att	Referee
21-08	Estonia	L	0-1	Tallinn	Fr		1 500	Kaldma EST
7-09	Austria	L	0-2	Vienna	ECq		18 300	Dougal SCO
12-10	Czech Republic	L	0-2	Chisinau	ECq		4 000	Irvine NIR
20-11	Hungary	D	1-1	Budapest	Fr	Patula 16	6 000	Sowa AUT
2003								
12-02	Georgia	D	2-2	Tbilisi	Fr	Golban 75, Dadu 84p	7 000	Hovanisyan ARM
5-03	Israel	D	0-0	Tel Aviv	Fr		8 000	Bertini ITA
29-03	Belarus	L	1-2	Minsk	ECq	Cebotari 14	7 500	Verbist BEL
2-04	Netherlands	L	1-2	Tiraspol	ECq	Boret 16	12 000	Sars FRA
7-06	Austria	W	1-0	Tiraspol	ECq	Frunza 60	10 000	Paraty Silva POR
11-06	Czech Republic	L	0-5	Olomouc	ECq		12 907	Jakobsson ISL
20-08	Turkey	L	0-2	Ankara	Fr		15 300	Plautz AUT
10-09	Belarus	W	2-1	Tiraspol	ECq	Dadu 23, Covaliciuc 88	7 000	Delevic SCG
11-10	Netherlands	L	0-5	Eindhoven	ECq		30 995	Siric CRO
20-11	Luxembourg	W	2-1	Hesperange	Fr	Golban 19, Dadu 90	623	Duhamel FRA
2004								
14-02	Malta	D	0-0	Ta'Qali	Fr		600	Vialichka BLR
16-02	Belarus	L	0-1	Ta'Qali	Fr		40	Attard MLT
18-02	Estonia	L	0-1	Ta'Qali	Fr		100	Sammut MLT
31-03	Azerbaijan	W	2-1	Chisinau	Fr	Dadu 2 42p 84	5 500	Godulyan UKR
28-04	Israel	D	1-1	Tel Aviv	Fr	Rogaciov 71	4 500	Corpodean ROU
18-08	Georgia	W	1-0	Tiraspol	Fr	Miterev 68	8 000	Godulyan UKR
4-09	Slovenia	L	0-3	Celje	WCq		3 620	Hyytia FIN
8-09	Italy	L	0-1	Chisinau	WCq		5 200	Benes CZE
9-10	Belarus	L	0-4	Minsk	WCq		21 000	Dereli TUR
13-10	Scotland	D	1-1	Chisinau	WCq	Dadu 28	7 000	Jakobsson ISL
2005								
9-02	Azerbaijan	D	0-0	Baku	Fr		1 500	
30-03	Norway	D	0-0	Chisinau	WCq		5 000	Meyer GER
4-06	Scotland	L	0-2	Glasgow	WCq		45 317	Braamhaar NED
3-09	Belarus	W	2-0	Chisinau	WCq	Rogaciov 2 17 49	5 000	Duhamel FRA
7-09	Slovenia	L	1-2	Chisinau	WCq	Rogaciov 31	7 200	Baskakov RUS
8-10	Norway	L	0-1	Oslo	WCq		23 409	Bennett RSA
12-10	Italy	L	1-2	Lecce	WCq	Gatcan 76	28 160	Benquerenca POR
2006								
25-02	Malta	W	2-0	Ta'Qali	Fr	Namasco 46, Bugaiov 73	1 125	Silagava GEO
27-02	Georgia	W	5-1	Ta'Qali	Fr	Zislis 2 5 13, Alexeev 48, Namasco 55p, Golovatenco 72	330	Casha MLT
18-05	Azerbaijan	D	0-0	Chisinau	Fr			

Fr = Friendly match • EC = UEFA EURO 2004™ • WC = FIFA World Cup™ • q = qualifier

MOLDOVA NATIONAL TEAM RECORDS AND RECORD SEQUENCES

Records			Sequence records					
Victory	2-0	Four times	Wins	3	1994	Clean sheets	2	2000, 2005
Defeat	0-6	SWE 2001	Defeats	9	1996-1998	Goals scored	7	1998-1999
Player Caps	64	CLESCENKO Serghei	Undefeated	3	Six times	Without goal	7	1997-98, 2000-01
Player Goals	10	CLESCENKO Serghei	Without win	10	1996-98, 2002-03	Goals against	25	1994-1998

MOLDOVA COUNTRY INFORMATION

Capital	Chisinau	Independence	1991 from the USSR	GDP per Capita	$1 800
Population	4 446 455	Status	Republic	GNP Ranking	146
Area km²	33 843	Language	Moldovan, Russian	Dialling code	+373
Population density	131 per km²	Literacy rate	99%	Internet code	.md
% in urban areas	52%	Main religion	Christian	GMT + / –	+2
Towns/Cities ('000)	Chisinau 713; Tiraspol 196; Balti 150; Tighina 128; Rabnita 61; Orhei 49; Cahul 44				
Neighbours (km)	Ukraine 939; Romania 450				
Main stadia	Complex Sheriff – Tiraspol 14 000; Stadionul Republica – Chisinau 8 084				

NATIONAL TEAM PLAYERS AND COACHES

Record Caps				Record Goals				Recent Coaches	
CLESCENKO Serghei	1991-'06	64		CLESCENKO Serghei	1991-'06	10		CARAS Ion	1993-'97
REBEJA Radu	1991-'06	57		MITEREV Iurie	1995-'05	8		DANILIANT Ivan	1998-'99
TESTIMITANU Ion	1991-'06	50		ROGACIOV Serghei	1996-'06	7		MATIURA Alexandr	1999-'01
CATINSUS Valeriu	1999-'06	49		DADU Serghei	2002-'06	6		SPIRIDON Alexandr	2001-'02
GAIDAMASCIUC Vladimir	1992-'01	45		TESTIMITANU Ion	1995-'06	6		PASULKO Victor	2002-'05
STROENCO Serghei	1992-'01	45						TESLEV Anatolii	2006-

CLUB DIRECTORY

Club	Town/City	Stadium	Capacity	www.	Lge	Cup
FC Dacia	Chisinau	Baza CSF Zimbru		fcdacia.com	0	0
FC Nistru	Otaci	Calarasauca			0	1
FC Sheriff	Tiraspol	Complex Sheriff	14 000	fc.sheriff.md	6	4
CS Steaua	Chisinau	Speia			0	0
CS Tiligul-Tiras	Tiraspol	Orasenesc			0	3
FC Tiraspol	Tiraspol	Complex Sheriff	14 000		0	0
FC Unisport-Auto	Chisinau	Dinamo			0	0
CSF Zimbru	Chisinau	Baza CSF Zimbru		zimbru.md	8	4

RECENT LEAGUE AND CUP RECORD

	Championship							Cup		
Year	Champions	Pts	Runners-up	Pts	Third	Pts		Winners	Score	Runners-up
1992	Zimbru Chisinau	35	Tiligul Tiraspol	35	Bugeac Comrat	33		Bugeac Comrat	5-0	Tiligul Tiraspol
1993	Zimbru Chisinau	50	Tiligul Tiraspol	47	Moldova Boroseni	41		Tiligul Tiraspol	1-0	Dinamo Chisinau
1994	Zimbru Chisinau	52	Tiligul Tiraspol	49	Codru Calarasi	40		Tiligul Tiraspol	1-0	Nistru Otaci
1995	Zimbru Chisinau	67	Tiligul Tiraspol	66	Olimpia Balti	57		Tiligul Tiraspol	1-0	Zimbru Chisinau
1996	Zimbru Chisinau	81	Tiligul Tiraspol	74	Constructorul	74		Constructorul	2-1	Tiligul Tiraspol
1997	Constructorul	81	Zimbru Chisinau	70	Tiligul Tiraspol	68		Zimbru Chisinau	0-0 7-6p	Nistru Otaci
1998	Zimbru Chisinau	69	Tiligul Tiraspol	59	Constructorul	54		Zimbru Chisinau	1-0	Constructorul
1999	Zimbru Chisinau	61	Constructorul	51	Tiligul Tiraspol	39		Sheriff Tiraspol	2-1	Constructorul
2000	Zimbru Chisinau	82	Sheriff Tiraspol	81	Constructorul	65		Constructorul	1-0	Zimbru Chisinau
2001	Sheriff Tiraspol	67	Zimbru Chisinau	66	Tiligul Tiraspol	41		Sheriff Tiraspol	0-0 5-4p	Nistru Otaci
2002	Sheriff Tiraspol	67	Nistru Otaci	52	Zimbru Chisinau	46		Sheriff Tiraspol	3-2	Nistru Otaci
2003	Sheriff Tiraspol	60	Zimbru Chisinau	50	Nistru Otaci	42		Zimbru Chisinau	0-0 4-2p	Nistru Otaci
2004	Sheriff Tiraspol	65	Nistru Otaci	57	Zimbru Chisinau	49		Zimbru Chisinau	2-1	Sheriff Tiraspol
2005	Sheriff Tiraspol	70	Nistru Otaci	54	Dacia Chisinau	45		Nistru Otaci	1-0	Dacia Chisinau
2006	Sheriff Tiraspol	71	Zimbru Chisinau	53	FC Tiraspol	37		Sheriff Tiraspol	2-0	Nistru Otaci

MOLDOVA 2005-06

DIVIZIA NATIONALA

	Pl	W	D	L	F	A	Pts	Sheriff	Zimbru	Tiraspol	Tiligul-Tiras	Nistru	Dacia	P'tehnica	Dinamo
Sheriff Tiraspol †	28	22	5	1	57	11	71		3-0 0-0	1-0 2-1	2-0 2-1	2-0 4-1	5-1 3-0	4-0 1-0	3-1 4-0
Zimbru Chisinau ‡	28	15	8	5	47	20	53	0-1 2-3		2-1 1-0	2-0 1-0	1-1 2-0	0-1 2-1	5-2 1-1	5-1 7-0
FC Tiraspol	28	8	13	7	24	21	37	0-2 0-0	0-1 0-0		0-0 2-1	0-0 1-0	2-2 2-2	1-0 1-1	1-0 0-0
Tiligul-Tiras Tiraspol	28	7	13	8	22	23	34	1-1 2-1	1-1 0-0	1-1 0-0		1-0 0-0	0-0 3-1	3-0 0-1	0-0 1-1
Nistru Otaci ‡	28	6	13	9	24	27	31	0-0 0-0	2-1 1-1	0-1 1-1	0-1 0-0		1-2 3-0	1-1 2-1	1-0 3-1
Dacia Chisinau	28	7	9	12	28	39	30	0-1 0-1	0-2 1-1	1-2 1-2	1-1 2-0	0-0 1-1		0-2 1-0	2-1 5-2
Politehnica Chisinau	28	5	10	13	18	37	25	0-1 0-2	0-4 0-1	1-0 0-0	2-1 0-1	1-3 1-1	1-1 0-0		2-2 1-0
Dinamo Bender	28	2	9	17	17	59	15	0-1 1-7	0-3 0-1	0-4 1-1	2-2 0-1	2-1 1-1	0-2 1-0	0-0 0-0	

13/08/2005 - 12/06/2005 • † Qualified for the UEFA Champions League • ‡ Qualified for the UEFA Cup • No relegation • Top scorers: Alexei KUCIUK, Sheriff, 13; Sergiu CHIRILOV, Zimbru, 11; Razvan COCIS, Sheriff, 10

MOLDOVA 2005-06
DIVIZIA A (2)

	Pl	W	D	L	F	A	Pts
Zimbru-2 Chisinau	28	23	4	1	79	13	73
Sheriff-2 Tiraspol	28	20	5	3	71	28	65
Olimpia Balti	28	18	5	5	66	23	59
Iskra-Stali Ribnita	28	17	7	4	54	31	58
FC Floreni	28	13	9	6	45	31	48
FC Rapid	28	12	10	6	42	23	46
CSCA-Agro	28	12	7	9	46	31	43
Intersport-Aroma	28	10	9	9	26	25	39
USC Gagauziya	28	10	7	11	46	28	37
Energetic	28	8	6	14	27	42	30
Tiligul-Tiras-2	28	8	5	15	31	40	29
Moldova 03	28	6	6	16	27	66	24
Goliador-SS-11	28	3	7	18	19	62	16
FC Glodeni	28	2	2	24	12	89	8
Avenarex	28	1	5	22	14	73	8
FC Otaci				Withdrew after 15 rounds			

6/08/2005 - 27/05/2006 • Top two ineligible for promotion

CUPA MOLDOVEI 2005-06

Round of sixteen

Sheriff Tiraspol

Intersport-Aroma

FC Tiraspol

Zimbru Chisinau

Dacia Chisinau

Tiligul-Tiras Tiraspol

Politehnica Chisinau

Nistru Otaci

Quarter-finals

| Sheriff Tiraspol | 4 | 3 |
| Intersport-Aroma | 0 | 0 |

| FC Tiraspol | 0 | 0 |
| Zimbru Chisinau | 2 | 1 |

| Dacia Chisinau | 0 | 1 |
| Tiligul-Tiras Tiraspol | 0 | 0 |

| Politehnica Chisinau | 0 | 3 |
| Nistru Otaci | 4 | 0 |

Semi-finals

| Sheriff Tiraspol | 2 | 2 |
| Zimbru Chisinau | 1 | 2 |

| Dacia Chisinau | 0 | 0 |
| Nistru Otaci | 0 | 1 |

Final

| Sheriff Tiraspol | 2 |
| Nistru Otaci ‡ | 0 |

CUP FINAL

Republica, Chisinau
10-05-2006, Ref: Cepoi

Scorers - Stadiiciuc OG [1], Omotoiossi [60] for Sheriff

* Home team in the first leg • ‡ Qualified for the UEFA Cup

MDV – MALDIVES

NATIONAL TEAM RECORD
JULY 1ST 2002 TO JULY 9TH 2006

PL	W	D	L	F	A	%
25	8	5	12	44	37	42

FIFA/COCA-COLA WORLD RANKING

1993	1994	1995	1996	1997	1998	1999	2000	2001	2002	2003	2004	2005	High	Low
148	162	169	176	160	166	143	154	147	152	141	139	133	**136** 11/04	**183** 09/97

2005–2006											
08/05	09/05	10/05	11/05	12/05	01/06	02/06	03/06	04/06	05/06	06/06	07/06
142	142	146	147	133	133	133	136	137	137	-	126

That the Maldives is considered to be a 'developing' and not an 'emerging' nation by the Asian Football Confederation is a tribute to the enormous progress made by the national team and the club sides in the country over the past decade. Just four internationals were played in 2005, at the South Asian Football Federation Cup in Karachi. The Maldives got off to a dream start scoring nine against Afghanistan, a record score for the tournament. They then beat Sri Lanka and drew with hosts Pakistan to top their first round group before losing to India in a close fought match in the semi-finals. The 2005 edition of the AFC Cup saw the story of the season when 2004 champions

INTERNATIONAL HONOURS
None

New Radiant qualified from their first round group. They then beat Jordan's Al Hussein in the quarter-finals and held eventual winners Al Faysali to a 1-1 draw in the first leg of the semi-finals, before losing the return in Amman 4-1. Never before had a team from the Maldives progressed so far in an Asian club competition, although they did fail to make it past the group stage in the 2006 tournament. New Radiant lost in two finals at home in the 2005-06 season - against Victory in both the National Championship final in October and the Cup Winners Cup, but they did beat Valencia to win the 19th edition of the FA Cup.

THE FIFA BIG COUNT OF 2000

	Male	Female		Male	Female
Registered players	3 305	0	Referees	130	0
Non registered players	13 600	1 200	Officials	20	0
Youth players	1 556	55	Total involved	19 866	
Total players	19 716		Number of clubs	127	
Professional players	105	0	Number of teams	367	

Football Association of Maldives (FAM)
Ujaalaa Hin'gun, Maafannu, Male 20388, Maldives
Tel +960 317006   Fax +960 317005
famaldvs@dhivehinet.net.mv   www.famaldives.gov.mv
President: SHAKOOR Abdul   General Secretary: ISMAIL Ibrahim
Vice-President: TBD   Treasurer: RASHEED Hussain   Media Officer: TBD
Men's Coach: IODAN Ivanov   Women's Coach: ATHIF Mohamed
FAM formed: 1982   AFC: 1986   FIFA: 1986
Red shirts, Green shorts, White socks

RECENT INTERNATIONAL MATCHES PLAYED BY THE MALDIVES

2002	Opponents	Score	Venue	Comp	Scorers	Att	Referee
No international matches played in 2002 after June							
2003							
11-01	Bhutan	W 6-0	Dhaka	SAFr1	Nizam [2], Luthfy [11], Shiham 3 [24 25 67], Umar [80]		Vidanagamage SRI
13-01	Bangladesh	L 0-1	Dhaka	SAFr1		20 000	Vidanagamage SRI
15-01	Nepal	W 3-2	Dhaka	SAFr1	Nizam [63], Luthfy [75], Umar [85]	15 000	Kunsuta THA
18-01	Pakistan	W 1-0	Dhaka	SAFsf	Fazeel [12]		Gurung NEP
20-01	Bangladesh	D 1-1	Dhaka	SAFf	Umar [58]. L 3-5p	46 000	Vidanagamage SRI
4-03	Singapore	L 1-4	Singapore	Fr	Umar [44]		Abdul Bashir SIN
21-03	Brunei Darussalam	D 1-1	Malé	ACq	Umar [42]		
25-03	Myanmar	L 0-2	Malé	ACq			
29-11	Mongolia	W 1-0	Ulaan-Baatar	WCq	Nizam [24]	2 000	Yang Zhiqiang CHN
3-12	Mongolia	W 12-0	Malé	WCq	Ashfaq 4 [4 61 63 68], Nizam [42], Fazeel 2 [46+ 49+], Ghani [65], Thariq [74], OG [75], Nazeeh [80]	9 000	Arambekade SRI
2004							
18-02	Vietnam	L 0-4	Hanoi	WCq		25 000	Fong KKG
31-03	Korea Republic	D 0-0	Malé	WCq		12 000	Vidanagamage SRI
31-05	Oman	L 0-3	Muscat	Fr			
3-06	Oman	L 1-4	Muscat	Fr			
9-06	Lebanon	L 0-3	Beirut	WCq		18 000	Nurilddin Salman IRQ
31-08	Oman	L 0-1	Malé	Fr			
3-09	Oman	L 1-2	Malé	Fr			
8-09	Lebanon	L 2-5	Malé	WCq	Fazeel [79], Umar [88]	12 000	Al Ajmi OMA
13-10	Vietnam	W 3-0	Malé	WCq	Thariq [29], Ashfaq 2 [68 85]	10 000	Haq IND
17-11	Korea Republic	L 0-2	Seoul	WCq		64 000	Lazar SIN
18-12	Sri Lanka	D 0-0	Malé	Fr			
2005							
7-12	Afghanistan	W 9-1	Karachi	SAFr1	Umar [11], Fazeel 3 [27 45 69], Ashfaq 2 [32 88], Thariq 3 [45 46 86], Maqsood [39]		
9-12	Sri Lanka	W 2-0	Karachi	SAFr1	Ashfaq [15], Umar [82p]		
11-12	Pakistan	D 0-0	Karachi	SAFr1			
14-12	India	L 0-1	Karachi	SAFsf			
2006							
No international matches played in 2006 before July							

Fr = Friendly match • SAF = South Asian Football Federation Cup • AC = AFC Asian Cup • WC = FIFA World Cup™
q = qualifier • r1 = first round group • sf = semi-final • f = final

MALDIVES NATIONAL TEAM RECORDS AND RECORD SEQUENCES

Records			Sequence records				
Victory	6-0	CAM 2001	Wins	3	1999	Clean sheets	2	1993, 1999, 2003
Defeat	0-17	IRN 1997	Defeats	12	1996-1997	Goals scored	7	1999
Player Caps	n/a		Undefeated	4	2000	Without goal	6	1997
Player Goals	n/a		Without win	23	1985-1997	Goals against	14	1996-1997

MALDIVES COUNTRY INFORMATION

Capital	Malé	Independence	1965 from the UK	GDP per Capita	$3 900
Population	339 330	Status	Republic	GNP Ranking	168
Area km²	300	Language	Maldivian Dhiveti	Dialling code	+960
Population density	1 131 per km²	Literacy rate	97%	Internet code	.mv
% in urban areas	27%	Main religion	Muslim	GMT +/−	+5
Towns/Cities ('000)	Malé 85; Hithadoo 9; Fuvammulah 8; Kulhudhuffushi 8; Thinadhoo 5; Naifaru 4				
Neighbours (km)	Indian Ocean 644				
Main stadia	Galolhu National Stadium – Male				

MALDIVES 2005

MALE LEAGUE

	Pl	W	D	L	F	A	Pts	Valencia	Victory	Radiant	Hurriyya	IFC	Eagles	Vyansa	GZJ
Valencia	7	5	2	0	20	9	17		2-1	1-1	3-1	6-2	5-3	0-0	3-1
Victory	7	5	1	1	24	5	16			1-0	0-0	5-1	5-1	3-1	9-0
New Radiant	7	5	1	1	20	10	16				5-2	3-1	3-2	3-1	5-2
Hurriyya	7	3	1	3	14	11	10					0-1	4-0	5-1	2-1
Island FC	7	3	1	3	11	18	10						2-1	3-2	1-1
Eagles	7	1	1	5	13	23	4							5-3	1-1
Vyansa	7	1	1	5	10	20	4								2-1
Guraidhoo ZJ	7	0	2	5	7	23	2								

28/05/2005 - 30/06/2005 • Top six qualify for the Dhivehi League

MALDIVES 2005

DHIVEHI LEAGUE

	Pl	W	D	L	F	A	Pts	Hurriyya	Radiant	Valencia	Victory	IFC	Hiriyaa	FEJ	Eagles
Hurriyya †	12	7	4	1	35	10	25		2-0	0-0	2-2	1-2	5-0	3-0	1-0
New Radiant	12	7	3	2	28	10	24	2-2		2-2	2-1	0-1	4-0	9-0	2-0
Valencia	12	6	5	1	35	15	23	1-1	1-1		2-1	1-1	5-1	6-1	2-1
Victory	12	7	1	4	44	16	22	2-3	1-2	4-2		4-1	6-1	4-1	4-0
Island FC	12	4	3	5	19	36	15	1-12	0-1	1-10	0-3		4-1	5-0	3-3
Hiriyaa	12	1	2	9	10	49	5	0-3	0-3	1-3	0-12	0-0		4-4	2-0
Foakaidhoo EJ	7	1	1	5	7	31	4								1-0
Eagles	7	0	1	6	4	15	1								

19/07/2004 - 26/09/2004 • Top four qualify for the National Championship play-offs • † Qualified for the AFC Cup

NATIONAL CHAMPIONSHIP 2005

Preliminary round		Semi-finals		Final	
		Victory	2		
Victory	5	Hurriyya	1		
Valencia	1			Victory	1
		Major semi-final		New Radiant	0
		Hurriyya	1	**31-10-2005**	
		New Radiant	6	Scorer - Ismail Mohamed [37] for Victory	

CUP WINNERS CUP 2006

	Pl	W	D	L	F	A	Pts
New Radiant	4	4	0	0	11	4	12
Victory	4	2	1	1	10	5	7
Valencia	4	1	1	2	10	8	4
Hurriyya	4	0	2	2	4	9	2
Vyansa	4	0	2	2	3	12	2

Final: Victory 3-3 2-1p New Radiant • 30-03-2006; Scorers: Henrikson, Nafiu, Assad for Victory; Fazeel, Ashfaaq 2 for New Radiant

FA CUP 2006

Quarter-finals		Semi-finals		Final	
New Radiant	2				
Guraidhoo ZJ	1	New Radiant	3		
Hurriyya	1	Victory	1		
Victory	2			New Radiant †	2
Eagles	2			Valencia	0
Island FC	1	Eagles	1	**16-04-2006**	
Maziya	1	Valencia	3	Scorers - Nita [63], Umar [85]	
Valencia	2	† Qualified for the AFC Cup			

RECENT LEAGUE AND CUP RECORD

	National Championship				FA Cup				Cup Winners Cup		
Year	Winners	Score	Runners-up		Winners	Score	Runners-up		Winners	Score	Runners-up
1997	New Radiant	2-1	Hurriyya		New Radiant	2-0	Valencia		Valencia		
1998	Valencia	1-1 2-0	Victory		New Radiant	1-0	Hurriyya		Valencia	2-0	New Radiant
1999	Valencia	2-1	Hurriyya		Valencia	2-2 2-1	New Radiant		New Radiant	3-1	Victory
2000	Victory				Victory	3-0	Hurriyya		New Radiant		
2001	Victory	2-1	Valencia		New Radiant	1-1 2-0	Valencia		Victory	1-1 5-4p	Valencia
2002	Victory	4-2	Valencia		IFC	2-0	New Radiant		Victory	4-3	Valencia
2003	Victory	2-1	Valencia		IFC	1-0	Valencia		New Radiant	1-1 3-1p	Valencia
2004	New Radiant	1-1 6-5p	Valencia		Valencia	2-0	Victory		Valencia	1-0	IFC
2005	Victory	1-0	New Radiant		New Radiant	2-0	Valencia		Valencia	2-1	Victory
2006					New Radiant	2-0	Valencia		Victory	3-3 2-1p	New Radiant

MEX – MEXICO

NATIONAL TEAM RECORD
JULY 1ST 2002 TO JULY 9TH 2006

PL	W	D	L	F	A	%
71	38	16	17	131	59	64.8

It was an historic year for Mexico with the under-17 team winning a first world championship for the country but it ended in disappointment when, after promising so much, the senior national team crashed out of the 2006 FIFA World Cup™ finals in Germany in the second round, having only just made it through the group stage. There are, however, encouraging signs that Mexico are beginning to feel more comfortable at the top table of world football. The accusation levelled in the past has been that Mexico is only represented at the world level because the country has a relatively easy passage through the CONCACAF qualifiers, and there may be an element of truth in that, but the performance at the FIFA U-17 World Championship in Peru made critics stand up and take notice. In the final they were more than a match for their Brazilian counterparts and in Carlos Vela had one of the potential future stars of world football, while the half volley scored by Omar Esparza that put Mexico 2-0 ahead would have graced the final of any competition. Success in Peru had some commentators saying that the senior team could seriously challenge for the FIFA World Cup™ in Germany. Just before the tournament captain Rafael Marquez had played an

INTERNATIONAL HONOURS

Qualified for the FIFA World Cup™ finals 1930 1950 1954 1958 1962 1966 1970 (hosts) 1978 1986 (hosts) 1994 1998 2002 2006

FIFA Confederations Cup 1999   **Qualified for the FIFA Women's World Cup finals** 1999

North American Championship 1947 1949   **CONCACAF Championship** 1965 1971   **CONCACAF Gold Cup** 1993 1996 1998 2003

CONCACAF U-20 1962 1970 1973 1976 1978 1980 1984 1990 1992   **CONCACAF U-17** 1985 1987 1991 1996

CONCACAF Club Championship Guadalajara 1962 Toluca 1968 2003 Cruz Azul 1969 1970 1971 1996 1997 America 1977 1990 1992 2006 UAG Tecos 1978 UNAM Pumas 1980 1982 1989 Atlante 1983 Puebla 1991 Necaxa 1999 Pachuca 2002

instrumental role in helping Barcelona win the UEFA Champions League, becoming the first Mexican to win the European Cup, but he could take Mexico no further than the second round in Germany. The team struggled in the first round group. Late goals from Omar Bravo and Zinha gave the team a 3-1 win in the opening match against Iran, but that was followed by a 0-0 draw against Angola and a 2-1 defeat at the hands of Portugal, although four points proved to be enough to take Mexico through to the next round. Perhaps their best performance was against Argentina in a pulsating match in Leipzig which was only lost thanks to a wonder goal by Maxi Rodriguez. After the finals Marquez suggested that more players should get experience in Europe, despite the fact that the Mexican League is perhaps the strongest in the Americas. In the 2005-06 season, the Apertura Championship was won by Toluca and the Clausura by Mexico's oldest club Pachuca while there was international success for Club América. They won the CONCACAF Champions' Cup to qualify for the 2006 FIFA Club World Cup after beating Toluca in an all-Mexican final.

Federación Mexicana de Fútbol Asociación, A.C. (FMF)

Colima No. 373, Colonia Roma, Mexico D.F. 06700, Mexico

Tel +52 55 52410166   Fax +52 55 52410191

ddemaria@femexfut.org.mx   www.femexfut.org.mx

President: DE LA TORRE Jose Alberto   General Secretary: DE MARIA Decio

Vice-President: TBD   Treasurer: TBD   Media Officer: KOCHEN Juan Jose

Men's Coach: TBD   Women's Coach: CUELLAR Leonardo

FMF formed: 1927   CONCACAF: 1961   FIFA: 1929

Green shirts with white trimmings, White shorts, Red socks or White shirts with green trimmings, Green shorts, White socks

RECENT INTERNATIONAL MATCHES PLAYED BY MEXICO

2004	Opponents		Score	Venue	Comp	Scorers	Att	Referee
10-10	St Vincent/Grenadines	W	1-0	Kingstown	WCq	Borgetti [25]	2 500	Alfaro SLV
13-10	Trinidad and Tobago	W	3-0	Puebla	WCq	Naelson [19], Lozano 2 [55 84]	37 000	Sibrian SLV
27-10	Ecuador	W	2-1	New Jersey	Fr	Fonseca 2 [42 47]		Prus USA
10-11	Guatemala	W	2-0	San Antonio, USA	Fr	Osorno [67], Medina.A [69]	21 921	Terry USA
13-11	St Kitts and Nevis	W	5-0	Miami	WCq	Altamirano [31], Fonseca 2 [40 57], Santana 2 [49 91]	18 312	Moreno PAN
17-11	St Kitts and Nevis	W	8-0	Monterrey	WCq	Altamirano [10p], Perez.L 3 [21 49 78], Fonseca 2 [44 56] Osorno [52], Santana [67]	12 000	Stott USA
2005								
26-01	Sweden	D	0-0	San Diego	Fr		35 521	Hall USA
9-02	Costa Rica	W	2-1	San Jose	WCq	Lozano 2 [8 10]	22 000	Batres GUA
23-02	Colombia	D	1-1	Culiacan	Fr	Fonseca [5]	10 000	Gasso MEX
9-03	Argentina	D	1-1	Los Angeles	Fr	OG [23]	51 345	Hall USA
27-03	USA	W	2-1	Mexico City	WCq	Borgetti [30], Naelson [32]	84 000	Sibrian SLV
30-03	Panama	D	1-1	Panama City	WCq	Morales [26]	13 000	Pineda HON
27-04	Poland	D	1-1	Chicago	Fr	Morales [52]	54 427	Kennedy USA
4-06	Guatemala	W	2-0	Guatemala City	WCq	Zinha [41], Cabrera OG [45]	26 723	Hall USA
8-06	Trinidad and Tobago	W	2-0	Monterrey	WCq	Borgetti [63], Perez.L [88]	32 833	Stott USA
16-06	Japan	W	2-1	Hanover	CCr1	Zinha [39], Fonseca [64]	24 036	Breeze AUS
19-06	Brazil	W	1-0	Hanover	CCr1	Borgetti [59]	43 677	Rosetti ITA
22-06	Greece	D	0-0	Frankfurt	CCr1		31 285	Amarilla PAR
26-06	Argentina	D	1-1	Hanover	CCsf	Salcido [104]	40 718	Rosetti ITA
29-06	Germany	L	3-4	Leipzig	CCsf	Fonseca [40], Borgetti 2 [58 85]	43 335	Breeze AUS
8-07	South Africa	L	1-2	Carson	GCr1	Rodriguez.F [83]	27 000	Quesada CRC
10-07	Guatemala	W	4-0	Los Angeles	GCr1	Borgetti 2 [5 14], Galindo [54], Bravo [65]	30 710	Ruiz COL
13-07	Jamaica	W	1-0	Houston	GCr1	Medina [19]	45 311	Quesada CRC
17-07	Colombia	L	1-2	Houston	GCqf	Pineda [65]	60 050	Sibrian SLV
17-08	Costa Rica	W	2-0	Mexico City	WCq	Borgetti [63], Fonseca [86]	27 000	Pineda HON
3-09	USA	L	0-2	Columbus	WCq		24 685	Batres GUA
7-09	Panama	W	5-0	Mexico City	WCq	Perez.L [31], Marquez [54], Borgetti [59], Fonseca [75], Pardo [76]	40 000	Hall USA
8-10	Guatemala	W	5-2	San Luis Potosi	WCq	Franco [19], Fonseca 4 [48 51 62 66]	30 000	Prendergast JAM
12-10	Trinidad and Tobago	L	1-2	Port of Spain	WCq	Lozano [38]	23 000	Pineda HON
26-10	Uruguay	W	3-1	Guadalajara	Fr	Salcido [16], Martinez [47p], Perez.L [53]	45 000	Guajardo MEX
16-11	Bulgaria	L	0-3	Phoenix	Fr		35 526	Hall USA
14-12	Hungary	W	2-0	Phoenix	Fr		32 466	Valenzuela USA
2006								
25-01	Norway	W	2-1	San Francisco	Fr	Fonseca [36], Perez.L [87]	44 729	Vaughn USA
15-02	Korea Republic	L	0-1	Los Angeles	Fr		64 128	Salazar USA
1-03	Ghana	W	1-0	Frisco	Fr	Franco [75]	19 513	Hall USA
29-03	Paraguay	W	2-1	Chicago	Fr	Bravo 2 [30p 81]	46 510	Kennedy USA
5-05	Venezuela	W	1-0	Pasadena	Fr	Bravo [57p]	58 147	Vaughn USA
12-05	Congo DR	W	2-1	Mexico City	Fr	Fonseca 2 [3 41]	75 000	Flores MEX
27-05	France	L	0-1	Paris	Fr		80 000	Daami TUN
1-06	Netherlands	L	1-2	Eindhoven	Fr	Borgetti [19]	35 000	Frojdfeldt SWE
11-06	Iran	W	3-1	Nuremberg	WCr1	Bravo 2 [28 76], Zinha [79]	41 000	Rosetti ITA
16-06	Angola	D	0-0	Hanover	WCr1		43 000	Maidin SIN
21-06	Portugal	L	1-2	Gelsenkirchen	WCr1	Fonseca [29]	52 000	Michel SVK
24-06	Argentina	L	1-2	Leipzig	WCr2	Marquez [6]	43 000	Busacca SUI

Fr = Friendly match • GC = CONCACAF Gold Cup • CA = Copa America • CC = FIFA Confederations Cup • WC = FIFA World Cup™
q = qualifier • r1 = first round group • r2 = second round • qf = quarter-final • sf = semi-final • f = final

MEXICO NATIONAL TEAM RECORDS AND RECORD SEQUENCES

Records			Sequence records					
Victory	11-0	VIN 1992	Wins	8	1947-49, 2004	Clean sheets	6	1965-1966
Defeat	0-8	ENG 1961	Defeats	7	1950-1952	Goals scored	22	1930-1950
Player Caps	178	SUAREZ Claudio	Undefeated	21	2004-2005	Without goal	5	1975-1976
Player Goals	38	BORGETTI Jared	Without win	11	1971	Goals against	12	1957-1960

MEXICO COUNTRY INFORMATION

Capital	Mexico City	Independence	1836 from Spain	GDP per Capita	$9 000
Population	104 959 594	Status	Federal Republic	GNP Ranking	10
Area km²	1 972 550	Language	Spanish	Dialling code	+52
Population density	53 per km²	Literacy rate	92%	Internet code	.mx
% in urban areas	75%	Main religion	Christian	GMT +/–	-6
Towns/Cities ('000)	Mexico City 8 657; Guadalajara 1 640; Juárez 1 403; Puebla 1 392; Tijuana 1 376; Nezahualcóyotl 1 232; Monterrey 1 122; Léon 1 114; Zapopan 987; Naucalpan 846; Guadalupe 724; Mérida 717; Tlalnepantla 715; Chihuahua 708; Aguascalientes 658; Acapulco 652; Querétaro 611				
Neighbours (km)	Belize 250; Guatemala 962; USA 3 141; Pacific & Gulf of Mexico 9 330				
Main stadia	Azteca – Mexico City 101 000; Jalisco – Guadalajara 63 163; Universitario – Monterrey 45 000				

NATIONAL TEAM PLAYERS AND COACHES

Record Caps			Record Goals			Recent Coaches	
SUAREZ Claudio	1992-'06	178	BORGETTI Jared	1997-'06	38	VELARDE Mario	1987-'89
CAMPOS Jorge	1991-'03	130	HERMOSILLO Carlos	1984-'97	35	GUERRA Alberto	1990
PARDO Pavel	1996-'06	129	HERNANDEZ Luis	1995-'02	35	LAPUENTE Manuel	1991
RAMIREZ Ramón	1991-'00	121	BORJA Enrique	1966-'75	31	MENOTTI Luis Cesar	1992
GARCIA ASPE Alberto	1988-'02	109	ALVES 'Zague' Luis Roberto	1988-'02	30	BARON Miguel	1993-'95
HERMOSILLO Carlos	1984-'97	90	BLANCO Cuauhtémoc	1995-'06	30	MILUTINOVIC Bora	1995-'97
HERNANDEZ Luis	1995-'02	85	FLORES Luis	1983-'93	29	LAPUENTE Manuel	1997-'00
ALVES Zague Luis Roberto	1988-'02	84	GARCIA Postigo Luis	1991-'99	29	MEZA Enrique	2000-'01
CARMONA Salvador	1996-'05	84	SANCHEZ Hugo	1977-'98	29	AGUIRRE Javier	2001-'02
BLANCO Cuauhtmémoc	1995-'06	84	GALINDO Benjamin	1983-'97	28	LA VOLPE Ricardo	2002-'06

FIFA/COCA-COLA WORLD RANKING

1993	1994	1995	1996	1997	1998	1999	2000	2001	2002	2003	2004	2005	High		Low	
16	15	12	11	5	10	10	12	9	8	7	7	5	4	02/98	19	11/94

2005–2006											
08/05	09/05	10/05	11/05	12/05	01/06	02/06	03/06	04/06	05/06	06/06	07/06
5	5	6	7	5	7	6	7	6	4	-	18

THE FIFA BIG COUNT OF 2000

	Male	Female		Male	Female
Registered players	208 481	1 518	Referees	3 832	95
Non registered players	5 000 000	2 000 000	Officials	20 000	600
Youth players	215 696	6 030	Total involved	7 456 252	
Total players	7 431 725		Number of clubs	1 493	
Professional players	15 000	0	Number of teams	20 009	

CLUB DIRECTORY

Club	Town/City	Stadium	Capacity	www.	Lge	Cup	CL
América	Mexico City	Azteca	101 000	esmas.com/clubamerica	14	6	4
Atlante	Mexico City	Azteca	101 000	club-atlante.com	4	3	1
Atlas	Guadalajara	Jalisco	65 000	atlas.com.mx	1	4	0
Cruz Azul	Mexico City	Azul	35 161	cruz-azul.com.mx	8	2	5
Guadalajara	Guadalajara	Jalisco	65 000	chivasdecorazon.com.mx	10	2	1
Jaguares (Chiapas)	Tuxtla Gutierrez	Victor Manuel Reyna	25 000		0	0	0
Monarcas Morelia	Morelia	Jose Morelos y Pavon	41 552		1	0	0
Monterrey	Monterrey	Tecnologico	32 662		2	1	0
Necaxa	Aguascalientes	Victoria	20 000		7	7	1
Pachuca	Pachuca	Hidalgo	25 000	tuzos.com.mx	7	2	1
Querétaro	Querétaro	La Corregidora	50 000		0	0	0
San Luis	San Luis Potosi	Alfonso Lastras	24 000		0	0	0
Santos Laguna	Torreón	Corona	20 010		2	0	0
Tigres UANL	Monterrey	Universitario	43 000	tigres.com.mx	2	2	0
Toluca	Toluca	Nemesio Diez	27 000	deportivotolucafc.com	8	2	2
UAG Tecos	Guadalajara	3 de Marzo	22 988		1	1	1
UNAM Pumas	Mexico City	Olimpico	72 988	pumasunam.com.mx	5	1	3
Veracruz	Veracruz	Luis Pirata Fuente	35 000		2	1	0

RECENT LEAGUE RECORD

	Championship Play-off/Clausura				Apertura		
Year	Champions	Score	Runners-up		Winners	Score	Runners-up
1990	Puebla	2-1 4-3	Universidad Guadalajara				
1991	UNAM Pumas	1-0 2-3	América				
1992	León	2-0 0-0	Puebla				
1993	Atlante	1-0 3-0	Monterrey				
1994	UAG Tecos	2-0 0-1	Santos Laguna				
1995	Necaxa	2-0 1-1	Cruz Azul				
1996	Necaxa	1-1 0-0	Atlético Celaya		Santos Laguna	0-1 4-2	Necaxa
1997	Guadalajara	1-1 6-1	Neza		Cruz Azul	1-0 1-1	Leon
1998	Toluca	1-2 5-2	Necaxa		Necaxa	0-0 2-0	Guadalajara
1999	Toluca	3-3 2-2 5-4p	Atlas		Pachuca	2-2 1-0	Cruz Azul
2000	Toluca	2-0 5-1	Santos Laguna		Monarcas Morelia	3-1 0-2 5-4p	Toluca
2001	Santos Laguna	1-2 3-1	Pachuca		Pachuca	2-0 1-1	Tigres UANL
2002	América	0-2 3-0	Necaxa		Toluca	0-1 4-1	Monarcas Morelia
2003	Monterrey	3-1 0-0	Monarcas Morelia		Pachuca	3-1 0-1	Tigres UANL
2004	UNAM Pumas	1-1 0-0 5-4p	Guadalajara		UNAM Pumas	2-1 1-0	Monterrey
2005	América	1-1 6-3	UAG Tecos		Toluca	3-3 3-0	Monterrey
2006	Pachuca	0-0 1-0	San Luis				

MEXICO 2005–06

PRIMERA DIVISION NACIONAL (APERTURA)

Group 1

Team	Pl	W	D	L	F	A	Pts	Amé	Nec	Tec	Mor	SLu	Atl	Tol	Pac	San	Dor	Pum	Ver	Mon	CrA	Tig	Ats	Jag	Gua
América †	17	12	2	3	34	22	38		4-1			3-1	4-3			2-1	2-1		1-2		1-0	3-1			0-0
Necaxa †	17	9	4	4	35	31	31						2-1	0-0	2-1	4-3		2-0			3-1	3-2	3-5		
UAG Tecos †	17	7	3	7	27	28	24	1-2	3-2			2-1			1-2	3-2	3-1	2-2	2-1					1-1	
Monarcas Morelia	17	6	2	9	27	29	20	1-2	3-4						3-1		1-0	2-2	2-1	2-2			0-2	1-0	
San Luis	17	4	4	9	18	25	16						2-1	2-1		2-2		4-1		1-0	1-2			1-1	1-2
Atlante	17	4	3	10	29	37	15	2-1	0-1	4-3					0-0				4-5	0-2		2-0		1-1	

Group 2

Team	Pl	W	D	L	F	A	Pts	Amé	Nec	Tec	Mor	SLu	Atl	Tol	Pac	San	Dor	Pum	Ver	Mon	CrA	Tig	Ats	Jag	Gua
Toluca †	17	9	3	5	27	21	30	0-1				2-1	1-0		1-1	2-2					2-1		2-1	0-1	3-0
Pachuca †	17	7	7	3	26	18	28	0-0			1-0	1-3	0-0	3-2		2-1					0-0			5-1	0-0
Santos Laguna	17	5	5	7	31	31	20							3-1	4-1		0-0		1-2		3-2	1-4	2-2		3-0
Dorados	17	5	3	9	20	31	18	1-1	0-2	2-1					3-1			0-3			1-0	1-3		2-1	
UNAM Pumas	17	4	4	9	17	34	16	1-2							0-0	2-3	0-3		1-3	2-0	0-5	1-0			1-0
Veracruz	17	3	6	8	24	34	15		2-3						2-3	1-3	2-2	1-1			0-1	0-5	2-1		

Group 3

Team	Pl	W	D	L	F	A	Pts	Amé	Nec	Tec	Mor	SLu	Atl	Tol	Pac	San	Dor	Pum	Ver	Mon	CrA	Tig	Ats	Jag	Gua
Monterrey †	17	10	5	2	32	20	35	4-1	1-1						2-1	1-2	2-2	1-1	1-1			2-1	1-0		
Cruz Azul †	17	9	3	5	34	20	30			5-1	2-1	3-0	5-3			2-2			1-2					3-1	0-0
Tigres †	17	6	4	7	30	25	22						1-0			1-3	2-2	3-1	3-1		1-2		1-2		1-1
Atlas	17	6	3	8	22	24	21	1-3				2-1				1-0	1-0	3-2			1-2	0-1		0-0	2-2
Jaguares	17	5	8	4	30	27	20	4-3	1-1	3-3	1-0							5-1			5-1	2-2	1-2		1-1
Guadalajara	17	4	7	6	16	22	19	1-2	1-0	1-2					3-2					1-0	1-1	2-3		1-1	

30/07/2005 - 26/11/2005 • † Qualified for the play-offs • §3 = Three points deducted • Top scorers (incl play-offs): Sebastian ABREU, Dorados, 11; Walter GAITAN, Tigres, 11; Kléber PEREIRA, América, 11; Vicente Matias VUOSO, Santos, 11

MEXICO 2005–06

PRIMERA DIVISION NACIONAL (CLAUSURA)

Group 1

Team	Pl	W	D	L	F	A	Pts	Atl	SLu	Mor	Tec	Amé	Nec	Pac	Tol	Dor	Pum	Ver	San	Jag	CrA	Gua	Tig	Ats	Mon
Atlante †	17	8	3	6	19	15	27		1-1		1-0			1-2	0-0	0-0	1-0			1-2	2-0				0-1
San Luis †	17	7	4	6	23	19	25					2-0	3-0	2-3	1-3		3-0		1-1	2-1				0-0	2-1
Monarcas Morelia †	17	5	7	5	19	20	22	0-2	1-0			3-1				1-1		3-3			1-3	0-1	2-0		
UAG Tecos	17	6	4	7	18	29	22	0-2	2-1			0-5			1-1			0-1	2-1	2-2				2-1	1-1
América	17	6	3	8	20	23	21							3-0	2-1	2-3	1-0	1-3		1-3				2-1	1-1
Necaxa	17	5	3	9	19	28	18	1-2						0-0	0-1	1-0	5-1	0-1	1-0		1-2				1-4

Group 2

Team	Pl	W	D	L	F	A	Pts	Atl	SLu	Mor	Tec	Amé	Nec	Pac	Tol	Dor	Pum	Ver	San	Jag	CrA	Gua	Tig	Ats	Mon
Pachuca †	17	9	4	4	33	19	31					4-1			1-0	1-1	0-0	0-1					0-0	3-0	3-0
Toluca †	17	7	3	7	22	19	24					2-3	3-1			3-1		2-1	2-1	1-2		1-1			0-1
Dorados	17	4	10	3	24	24	22	1-0				2-0					1-3	1-1	0-0			2-2	1-1	1-1	3-1
UNAM Pumas	17	5	7	5	15	16	22	1-0	0-1					0-0				2-0	1-0	2-1	1-1		0-0		
Veracruz	17	5	5	7	16	19	20	1-0	3-0	1-1	1-2	0-1							1-1		2-3		1-1		1-0
Santos Laguna	17	3	9	5	20	25	18	3-4							0-0	1-1	2-2	1-1		1-1	0-2		2-1		1-1

Group 3

Team	Pl	W	D	L	F	A	Pts	Atl	SLu	Mor	Tec	Amé	Nec	Pac	Tol	Dor	Pum	Ver	San	Jag	CrA	Gua	Tig	Ats	Mon
Jaguares †	17	9	3	5	28	18	30	1-0	1-1					3-0	2-0	2-4						1-0	3-1	2-2	
Cruz Azul †	17	9	3	5	29	20	30					1-3	3-1	3-2	2-1				3-1	3-0		4-1		1-1	1-1
Guadalajara †	17	6	5	6	19	26	23	1-3				1-0		3-2	0-2				2-2	1-1			1-0	1-0	0-3
Tigres	17	4	9	4	15	15	21	0-2				2-3	0-0	1-1	1-2				1-1	1-0	1-0				2-1
Atlas	17	5	5	7	23	23	20	1-1						2-3		0-1			0-0	2-0	3-3		0-2		1-0
Monterrey	17	5	3	9	17	21	18	3-0	0-1	1-0	2-3			2-1								0-3	0-1	1-2	

20/01/2006 - 30/04/2006 • † Qualified for the play-offs • Top scorers (incl play-offs): Salvador CABANAS, Jaguares, 11; Sebastian ABREU, Dorados, 11; Emmanuel VILLA, Atlas, 10; Ariel GONZALEZ, San Luis, 10; César DELGADO, Cruz Azul, 9; Patricio GALAZ, Atlante, 9

APERTURA PLAY-OFFS

Quarter-finals		Semi-finals		Final	
Toluca *	1 0				
Cruz Azul	0 0	Toluca	0 2		
Necaxa	0 0	Pachuca *	0 1		
Pachuca *	2 2			Toluca *	3 3
Tigres *	1 4			Monterrey	3 0
América	3 1	Tigres *	1 1		
UAG Tecos *	0 0	Monterrey	0 2		
Monterrey	3 4	* Home team in the first leg			

APERTURA FINAL

First leg. Nemesio Diez, Toluca, 15-12-2006

Toluca	3	Sánchez 32, Abundis 45, Díaz 87
Monterrey	3	Pérez 3, Casartelli 8, Paulo Cesar OG 61

Second leg. Tecnologico, Monterrey, 18-12-2005

Monterrey	0	
Toluca	3	Sánchez 2 50 91+, Díaz 93+

CLAUSURA PLAY-OFFS

Quarter-finals		Semi-finals		Final	
Pachuca	1 3				
Morelia *	2 1	Pachuca	2 2		
Jaguares	3 2	Guadalajara*	1 3		
Guadalajara *	2 4			Pachuca	0 1
Toluca *	2 1			San Luis *	0 0
Cruz Azul	1 1	Toluca *	1 1		
Atlante	0 0	San Luis	2 2		
San Luis *	1 0	* Home team in the first leg			

CLAUSURA FINAL

First leg. 18-05-2006

San Luis	0	
Pachuca	0	

Second leg. Hidalgo, Pachuca, 21-05-2006

Pachuca	1	Richard Nuñez 79p
San Luis	0	

MEXICO 2005–06
PRIMERA A (2) APERTURA

Group 1	Pl	W	D	L	F	A	Pts
Correcaminos †	19	12	4	3	38	20	40
Puebla †	19	10	3	6	29	22	33
Indios Ciudad Juárez †	19	10	2	7	29	26	32
Tigres Los Mochis	19	8	3	8	32	29	27
Tampico Madero	19	7	5	7	21	27	26
Group 2							
Durango †	19	6	8	5	25	25	26
León †	19	6	7	6	30	28	25
Tabasco Villahermosa	19	7	4	8	21	32	25
Petroleros Salamanca	19	6	5	8	21	28	23
Lobos BUAP	19	5	4	10	24	37	19
Group 3							
Cruz Azul Oaxaca †	19	10	3	6	34	24	33
Querétaro †	19	10	3	6	23	17	33
Coyotes Sonora †	19	10	2	7	35	25	32
Coatzacoalcos	19	6	4	9	26	29	22
Atlético Mexiquense	19	4	7	8	22	24	19
Group 4							
Chivas Coras †	19	9	3	7	27	25	30
Tijuana †	19	5	8	6	26	26	23
Rayados Monterrey	19	5	4	10	32	35	19
Iraputo	19	3	9	7	30	37	18
Aguilas Riviera Maya	19	4	6	9	15	24	18

7/08/2005 - 19/11/2005 • † Qualified for the play-offs •
Repechaje: León 1-0 3-3 Indios; Tijuana 1-4 2-4 Coyotes

MEXICO 2005–06
PRIMERA A (2) CLAUSURA

Group 1	Pl	W	D	L	F	A	Pts
Correcaminos †	19	10	5	4	31	23	35
Indios Ciudad Juárez †	19	8	6	5	29	17	30
Tampico Madero †	19	9	2	8	28	20	29
Tigres Los Mochis	19	4	7	8	19	27	19
Puebla	19	3	5	11	16	32	14
Group 2							
León †	19	8	6	5	32	24	30
Petroleros Salamanca †	19	8	6	5	22	18	30
Lobos BUAP	19	8	3	8	28	30	27
Durango	19	6	8	5	22	22	26
Tabasco Villahermosa	19	8	2	9	22	23	26
Group 3							
Querétaro †	19	9	7	3	26	18	34
Cruz Azul Oaxaca †	19	8	7	4	27	21	31
Atlético Mexiquense	19	8	3	8	27	27	27
Coatzacoalcos	19	6	4	9	22	28	22
Coyotes Sonora	19	4	7	8	24	27	19
Group 4							
Chivas Coras †	19	9	5	5	19	14	32
Rayados Monterrey †	19	8	5	6	29	22	29
Zacatepec	19	6	6	7	23	23	24
Iraputo	19	4	6	9	17	28	18
Tijuana	19	4	4	11	13	32	16

15/01/2006 - 5/05/2006 • † Qualified for the play-offs •
Repechaje: Rayados 1-0 1-0 Tampico Madero

APERTURA PLAY-OFFS

Quarter-finals		Semi-finals		Final	
Puebla	1 2				
Chivas Tepic	2 1	Puebla	1 1		
Querétaro	1 2	Coyotes	2 0		
Coyotes	2 2			Puebla	1 1
León	2 2			Cruz Azul	1 0
Correcaminos	0 1	León	1 1		
Durango	2 2	Cruz Azul	1 2		
Cruz Azul	2 2				

CLAUSURA PLAY-OFFS

Quarter-finals		Semi-finals		Final	
Querétaro	1 2				
Petroleros	1 1	Querétaro	1 3		
León	2 1	Cruz Azul	2 0		
Cruz Azul	2 1			Querétaro	1 2
Correcaminos	2 2			Indios	2 1
Rayados	0 0	Correcaminos	1 1		
Chivas	0 1	Indios	1 2		
Indios	0 3				

CHAMPIONSHIP PLAY-OFF

Puebla   2-1 1-2 4-5p   **Querétaro**
Querétaro replace Dorados in the Primera Division

MGL – MONGOLIA

NATIONAL TEAM RECORD
JULY 1ST 2002 TO JULY 9TH 2006

PL	W	D	L	F	A	%
12	3	2	7	11	42	33.3

FIFA/COCA-COLA WORLD RANKING

1993	1994	1995	1996	1997	1998	1999	2000	2001	2002	2003	2004	2005	High	Low
-	-	-	-	-	196	198	196	187	193	179	185	179	**179** 12/03	**200** 02/00

2005–2006											
08/05	09/05	10/05	11/05	12/05	01/06	02/06	03/06	04/06	05/06	06/06	07/06
180	180	181	179	179	179	179	179	179	179	-	-

Mongolia's absence from the 2006 AFC Challenge Cup meant that there were no international matches played during the season by the national team. With entry to the AFC Asian Cup being denied to the so called 'emerging' nations of Asia, Mongolia's fixture list is in danger of consisting largely of games in the qualifying tournament of the East Asian Football Federation Championship. With the distances involved and the difficulty of travel, friendly matches have never been an option for the national team. The two youth teams did see some action in their respective qualifying groups for the AFC Youth Championship and the AFC U-17 Championship. The under-17 team

INTERNATIONAL HONOURS
None

played in a qualifying group in neighbouring China PR where they lost 11-0 to the hosts but only narrowly lost to a late goal against Chinese Taipei. The under-20 team played their qualifying games in Korea Republic where they lost 13-0 to the hosts and then to another very late winner against Hong Kong in a 3-4 defeat. Encouraging signs perhaps, but until the senior team enters mainstream competition it may count for little in the long run. There are also opportunities for club teams to take part in the AFC President's Cup, reserved for the champions of the emerging nations, but 2005 champions Khoromkhon didn't enter the tournament.

THE FIFA BIG COUNT OF 2000

	Male	Female		Male	Female
Registered players	650	0	Referees	10	0
Non registered players	10 000	0	Officials	70	0
Youth players	700	30	Total involved	11 460	
Total players	11 380		Number of clubs	27	
Professional players	150	0	Number of teams	74	

Mongolia Football Federation (MFF)
PO Box 259, Ulaan-Baatar 210646, Mongolia
Tel +976 11 312145   Fax +976 11 312145
ubmaya@yahoo.com   www.none
President: AMARJARGAL Renchinnyam   General Secretary: GANBOLD Buyannemekh
Vice-President: TBD   Treasurer: OYUNTSETSEG Davaa   Media Officer: BAYARTSOGT Ganjuur
Men's Coach: OTGONBAYAR Ishdorj   Women's Coach: TBD
MFF formed: 1959   AFC: 1998   FIFA: 1998
White shirts, Red shorts, White socks

RECENT INTERNATIONAL MATCHES PLAYED BY MONGOLIA

2002	Opponents	Score		Venue	Comp	Scorers	Att	Referee
	No international matches played in 2002							
2003								
22-02	Macao	L	0-2	Hong Kong	EAq		6 055	Chan Siu Kee HKG
24-02	Guam	W	2-0	Hong Kong	EAq	Tugsbayar [52], Lumbengarav [59]	1 602	Huang Junjie CHN
26-02	Chinese Taipei	L	0-4	Hong Kong	EAq		672	Chan Siu Kee HKG
28-02	Hong Kong	L	0-10	Hong Kong	EAq		1 814	
25-04	Guam	W	5-0	Thimphu	ACq	Batyalat [20], Tugsbayar 3 [26 56 90], Lunmbengaran [61]		
27-04	Bhutan	D	0-0	Thimphu	ACq			
29-11	Maldives	L	0-1	Ulaan-Baatar	WCq		2 000	Yang Zhiqiang CHN
3-12	Maldives	L	0-12	Malé	WCq		9 000	Arambekade SRI
2004								
	No international matches played in 2004							
2005								
5-03	Hong Kong	L	0-6	Taipei	EAq			
7-03	Korea DPR	L	0-6	Taipei	EAq			
9-03	Guam	W	4-1	Taipei	EAq	Tugsbayar 2 [31 34], Bayarzorig [46], Buman-Uchral [81]		
13-03	Chinese Taipei	D	0-0	Taipei	EAq			
2006								
	No international matches played in 2006 before July							

EA = EAFF East Asian Championship • AC = AFC Asian Cup • WC = FIFA World Cup™ • q = qualifier

MONGOLIA NATIONAL TEAM RECORDS AND RECORD SEQUENCES

Records			Sequence records					
Victory	5-0	GUM 2003	Wins	1		Clean sheets	2	2003
Defeat	0-15	UZB 1998	Defeats	11	1998-2001	Goals scored	1	
Player Caps	n/a		Undefeated	2	2003, 2005	Without goal	5	2001, 2003-2005
Player Goals	n/a		Without win	13	1998-2003	Goals against	13	1998-2003

RECENT LEAGUE RECORD

	Championship		
Year	**Champions**	**Score**	**Runners-up**
1997	Delger	2-1	Erchim
1998	Erchim		Delger
1999	ITI Bank Bars		Erchim
2000	Erchim		Sonor
2001	Khangarid		Mon Uran
2002	Erchim		Khangarid
2003	Khangarid	2-1	Mon Uran
2004	Khangarid	1-0	Khoromkon
2005	Khoromkhon	1-0	Khangarid

MONGOLIA COUNTRY INFORMATION

Capital	Ulaan-Baatar	Independence	1921 from China	GDP per Capita	$1 800
Population	2 751 314	Status	Republic	GNP Ranking	156
Area km²	1 564 116	Language	Khalkha Mongol	Dialling code	+976
Population density	2 per km²	Literacy rate	97%	Internet code	.mn
% in urban areas	61%	Main religion	Buddhist 50%, None 40%	GMT +/–	+8
Towns/Cities ('000)	Ulaan-Baatar 844; Ërdènèt 76; Darhan 72; Cojbalsan 44; Ölgij 30; Sahnsand 28; Ulaangorn 28				
Neighbours (km)	China 4 677; Russia 3 543				
Main stadia	National Sports Stadium – Ulaan-Baatar 20 000				

MKD – FYR MACEDONIA

NATIONAL TEAM RECORD

JULY 1ST 2002 TO JULY 9TH 2006

PL	W	D	L	F	A	%
37	11	9	17	42	55	41.9

FIFA/COCA-COLA WORLD RANKING

1993	1994	1995	1996	1997	1998	1999	2000	2001	2002	2003	2004	2005	High	Low
-	90	94	86	92	59	68	76	89	85	92	92	87	**58** 01/99	**147** 05/94

2005–2006											
08/05	09/05	10/05	11/05	12/05	01/06	02/06	03/06	04/06	05/06	06/06	07/06
92	96	93	90	87	87	88	91	91	91	-	70

Following an awful campaign in the 2006 FIFA World Cup™ qualifiers which saw the national team only just avoid the wooden spoon in a group containing Armenia and Andorra, the football federation appointed the Slovenian Srecko Katanec as coach. The benefits were felt almost immediately with impressive wins over Ecuador and Turkey in friendlies before the finals in Germany. The wooden spoon was avoided thanks to two wins over Armenia which spared the blushes of finishing below minnows Andorra, a team they meet again in the UEFA Euro 2008™ qualifiers. Twice Katanec engineered Slovenia's path to the finals of major tournaments - in 2000

INTERNATIONAL HONOURS

None

in Belgium and the Netherlands and in 2002 in Korea/Japan, although a repeat of that is unlikely given the presence of England, Russia, Croatia and Israel in the group. In the Macedonian championship there was a second title in a row for Skopje club Rabotniki, coached by Gjorgi Jovanovski. Having won a hat-trick of titles with Sloga Jugomagnat, it was title number five for the former national team coach. Rabotniki's biggest challenge came from promoted club Makedonija Skopje who finished second, above traditional top dogs in the city, Vardar. Makedonija also won an exciting Cup Final against Shkendija to win their first trophy.

THE FIFA BIG COUNT OF 2000

	Male	Female		Male	Female
Registered players	11 223	0	Referees	820	0
Non registered players	17 000	0	Officials	1 000	0
Youth players	11 500	0	Total involved	41 543	
Total players	39 723		Number of clubs	594	
Professional players	223	0	Number of teams	919	

Football Federation of Macedonia (FFM)

8-ma Udarna brigada 31-a, Skopje 1000, FYR Macedonia

Tel +389 23 222603   Fax +389 23 165448

fsm@fsm.org.mk   www.ffm.com.mk

President: HADZI-RISTESKI Haralampie   General Secretary: MITROVSKI Lazar

Vice-President: BEDZETI Redzep   Treasurer: MITROVSKI Lazar   Media Officer: NIKOLOVSKI Zoran

Men's Coach: KATANEC Srecko   Women's Coach: DIMOVSKI Dobre

FFM formed: 1908   UEFA: 1994   FIFA: 1994

Red shirts with white trimmings, Red shorts, Red socks or White shirts with red trimmings, White shorts, White socks

RECENT INTERNATIONAL MATCHES PLAYED BY FYR MACEDONIA

2002	Opponents		Score	Venue	Comp	Scorers	Att	Referee
21-08	Malta	W	5-0	Skopje	Fr	Stojkov [37], Sakiri 2 [40 60], Hristov [54], Pandev [86]	4 000	Supraha CRO
8-09	Liechtenstein	D	1-1	Vaduz	ECq	Hristov [7]	2 300	Godulyan UKR
12-10	Turkey	L	1-2	Skopje	ECq	Grozdanovski [2]	15 000	Fisker DEN
16-10	England	D	2-2	Southampton	ECq	Sakiri [10], Trajanov [24]	32 095	Dauden Ibanez ESP
20-11	Israel	L	2-3	Skopje	Fr	Vasoski [63], Sedloski [89]	5 000	Delevic SCG
2003								
9-02	Croatia	D	2-2	Sibenik	Fr	Sedloski [10p], Toleski [60]	4 000	Zrnic BIH
14-02	Poland	L	0-3	Split	Fr		500	Trivkovic POL
29-03	Slovakia	L	0-2	Skopje	ECq		11 000	Duhamel FRA
2-04	Portugal	L	0-1	Lausanne	Fr		14 258	Nobs SUI
7-06	Liechtenstein	W	3-1	Skopje	ECq	Sedloski [39p], Krstev [51], Stojkov [82]	6 000	Jara CZE
11-06	Turkey	L	2-3	Istanbul	ECq	Grozdanovski [24], Sakiri [28]	23 000	Rosetti ITA
20-08	Albania	W	3-1	Prilep	Fr	Naumoski [9], Pandev [36], Dimitrovski [77]	3 000	Mihajlevic SCG
6-09	England	L	1-2	Skopje	ECq	Hristov [28]	20 500	De Bleeckere BEL
10-09	Slovakia	D	1-1	Zilina	ECq	Dimitrovski [62]	2 286	Sundell SWE
11-10	Ukraine	D	0-0	Kyiv	Fr		13 000	Orlic MDA
2004								
27-01	China PR	D	0-0	Shanghai	Fr		25 000	Lee Yu CHN
29-01	China PR	L	0-1	Shanghai	Fr		17 500	Zhig Yang CHN
18-02	Bosnia-Herzegovina	W	1-0	Skopje	Fr	Pandev [20]	8 000	Vrajkov BUL
31-03	Ukraine	W	1-0	Skopje	Fr	Stavrevski [26]	16 000	Karagic SCG
28-04	Croatia	L	0-1	Skopje	Fr		15 000	Arzuman TUR
11-06	Estonia	W	4-2	Tallinn	Fr	Sedloski [11], Popov [15], Pandev [31], Grozdanovski [65]	1 500	Fröjfeldt SWE
18-08	Armenia	W	3-0	Skopje	WCq	Pandev [5], Sakiri [37], Sumolikoski [90]	4 375	Guenov BUL
4-09	Romania	L	1-2	Craiova	WCq	Vasoski [70]	14 500	Plautz AUT
9-10	Netherlands	D	2-2	Skopje	WCq	Pandev [45], Stojkov [71]	15 000	Frojdfeldt SWE
13-10	Andorra	L	0-1	Andorra La Vella	WCq		350	Podeschi SMR
17-11	Czech Republic	L	0-2	Skopje	WCq		7 000	Meier SUI
2005								
9-02	Andorra	D	0-0	Skopje	WCq		5 000	Verbist BEL
30-03	Romania	L	1-2	Skopje	WCq	Maznov [31]	15 000	Ovrebo NOR
4-06	Armenia	W	2-1	Yerevan	WCq	Pandev 2 [29p 47]	2 870	Mikulski POL
8-06	Czech Republic	L	1-6	Teplice	WCq	Pandev [13]	14 150	Dauden Ibanez ESP
17-08	Finland	L	0-3	Skopje	WCq		6 800	Messias ENG
7-09	Finland	L	1-5	Tampere	WCq	Maznov [48]	6 467	Jakobsson ISL
12-10	Netherlands	D	0-0	Amsterdam	WCq		50 000	Farina ITA
12-11	Liechtenstein	W	2-1	Vaduz	Fr	Ilijoski [82], Nuhiji [90]	1 350	Nobs SUI
2006								
1-03	Bulgaria	L	0-1	Skopje	Fr		8 000	
28-05	Ecuador	W	2-1	Madrid	Fr	Maznov [28], Mitreski [73p]	4 000	
4-06	Turkey	W	1-0	Krefeld	Fr	Maznov [82]	7 000	

Fr = Friendly match • EC = UEFA EURO 2004™ • WC = FIFA World Cup™ • q = qualifier

FYR MACEDONIA NATIONAL TEAM RECORDS AND RECORD SEQUENCES

Records			Sequence records				
Victory	11-1	LIE 1996	Wins	4	1993-1994	Clean sheets	2	
Defeat	1-6	CZE 2005	Defeats	3	Five times	Goals scored	8	2002-2003
Player Caps	70	SHAKIRI Artim	Undefeated	8	1998	Without goal	4	2001-2002
Player Goals	16	HRISTOV Giorgji	Without win	19	2000-2002	Goals against	13	2001-2002

FYR MACEDONIA COUNTRY INFORMATION

Capital	Skopje	Independence	1991 from Yugoslavia	GDP per Capita	$6 700
Population	2 071 210	Status	Republic	GNP Ranking	126
Area km²	25 333	Language	Macedonian, Albanian	Dialling code	+389
Population density	82 per km²	Literacy rate	n/a	Internet code	.mk
% in urban areas	60%	Main religion	Christian 70%, Muslim 29%	GMT + / –	+1
Towns/Cities ('000)	Skopje 475; Kumanovo 108; Bittola 86; Prilep 74; Tetovo 73; Veles 58; Ohrid 55; Gostivar 51				
Neighbours (km)	Serbia and Montenegro 221; Bulgaria 148; Greece 246; Albania 151				
Main stadia	City Stadium – Skopje 22 000; City Stadium – Tetovo 20 500				

NATIONAL TEAM PLAYERS AND COACHES

Record Caps			Record Goals			Recent Coaches	
SHAKIRI Artim	1996-'06	70	HRISTOV Giorgji	1995-'05	16	KANATLAROVSKI Dragan	1999-'01
SEDLOSKI Goce	1996-'06	68	SHAKIRI Artim	1996-'06	15	JOVANOVSKI Gjore	2001-'02
HRISTOV Giorgji	1995-'05	48	PANDEV Goran	2002-'06	9	ILIEVSKI Nikola	2002-'04
MILOSHEVSKI Petar	1998-'06	45	CIRIC Sasa	1995-'04	8	KANATLAROVSKI Dragan	2004-'05
MICEVSKI Toni	1993-'02	43	BOSKOVSKI Zoran	1993-'96	5	SANTRAC Slobodan	2005
NIKOLOVSKI Igor Sasha	1995-'02	43	STOJKOVSKI Mitko	1994-'02	5	KATANEC Srecko	2006-

CLUB DIRECTORY

Club	Town/City	Stadium	Capacity	www.	Lge	Cup
Baskimi	Kumanovo	Gradski Arena	7 000		0	1
Belasica Geras Cunev	Strumica	Mladost	6 370	belasica.com.mk	0	0
Bregalnica	Stip	City Stadium	10 000		0	0
Cementarnica	Skopje	Cementarnica	2 000		0	1
Makedonija Gorce Petrov	Skopje	Gorce Petrov	3 000		0	1
Napredok	Kicevo	City Stadium	5 000		0	0
Pobeda	Prilep	Goce Delcev	15 000		1	1
Rabotnicki Kometal	Skopje	City Stadium	22 000		2	0
Shkendija	Tetovo	City Stadium	20 500		0	0
Sileks	Kratovo	Sileks	3 000		3	2
Sloga Jugomagnat	Skopje	Cair	4 500	sloga-jugomagnat.com.mk	3	3
Vardar	Skopje	City Stadium	22 000	fkvardar.com.mk	5	4

RECENT LEAGUE AND CUP RECORD

	Championship						Cup		
Year	Champions	Pts	Runners-up	Pts	Third	Pts	Winners	Score	Runners-up
1993	Vardar Skopje	61	Sileks Kratovo	40	Balkan Skopje	40	Vardar Skopje	1-0	Pelister Bitola
1994	Vardar Skopje	51	Sileks Kratovo	44	Balkan Stokokomerc	37	Sileks Kratovo	1-1 4-2p	Pelister Bitola
1995	Vardar Skopje	76	Sileks Kratovo	60	Sloga Jugomagnat	58	Vardar Skopje	2-1	Sileks Kratovo
1996	Sileks Kratovo	70	Sloga Jugomagnat	58	Vardar Skopje	57	Sloga Jugomagnat	0-0 5-3p	Vardar Skopje
1997	Sileks Kratovo	62	Pobeda Prilep	54	Sloga Jugomagnat	42	Sileks Kratovo	4-2	Sloga Jugomagnat
1998	Sileks Kratovo	48	Sloga Jugomagnat	43	Makedonija Skopje	42	Vardar Skopje	2-0	Sloga Jugomagnat
1999	Sloga Jugomagnat	60	Sileks Kratovo	57	Pobeda Prilep	53	Vardar Skopje	2-0	Sloga Jugomagnat
2000	Sloga Jugomagnat	61	Pobeda Prilep	52	Rabotnicki Skopje	50	Sloga Jugomagnat	6-0	Pobeda Prilep
2001	Sloga Jugomagnat	63	Vardar Skopje	63	Pobeda Prilep	56	Pelister Bitola	2-1	Sloga Jugomagnat
2002	Vardar Skopje	37	Belasica Strumica	36	Cementarnica	27	Pobeda Prilep	3-1	Cementarnica
2003	Vardar Skopje	72	Belasica Strumica	69	Pobeda Prilep	65	Cementarnica	4-4 3-2p	Sloga Jugomagnat
2004	Pobeda Prilep	71	Sileks Kratovo	66	Vardar Skopje	60	Sloga Jugomagnat	1-0	Napredok Kicevo
2005	Rabotnicki Skopje	78	Vardar Skopje	72	Pobeda Prilep	55	Baskimi Kumanovo	2-1	Madzari Skopje
2006	Rabotnicki Skopje	72	Makedonija Skopje	69	Vardar Skopje	64	Makedonije Skopje	3-2	Shkendija Tetovo

FYR MACEDONIA 2005–06

PRVA LIGA

	Pl	W	D	L	F	A	Pts	Rabotnicki	Makedonija	Vardar	Pobeda	Shkendija	Baskimi	Renova	Vlazrimi	Sileks	Bregalnica	Cement'ica	Belasica
Rabotnicki Skopje †	33	21	9	3	64	26	72		1-0	1-0 1-3 1-1	3-0	2-0 0-0 1-0	3-1 2-1 4-0	3-1 1-0		7-2		3-1	3-0
Makedonija Skopje ‡	33	21	6	6	55	23	69	0-3 0-0		1-0	1-0 3-0	1-0	3-0 2-0 3-0 0-0	0-3 0-6	2-3 1-1 1-1	1-0		4-0	1-0
Vardar Skopje ‡	33	19	7	7	42	19	64	0-2	1-0 0-0		1-1	1-0 2-2	3-1	1-1	2-0 3-0	2-0	1-0 1-0	1-1 2-0	2-1 3-0
Pobeda Prilep	33	16	6	11	58	46	54	3-3	1-1	0-1 2-0		1-0 3-0	3-1	2-1	1-0 1-2	2-1	1-0 1-2	3-0 3-0	1-0 3-0 2-1
Shkendija Tetovo	33	15	4	14	48	47	49	2-1 2-1 2-1	0-1	2-1	4-5		0-1 1-0	2-1 1-1	2-2 1-5	1-4 1-2	2-1	1-4	1-0 2-0
Baskimi Kumanovo	33	13	6	14	50	49	45	1-1	5-0	0-1 1-1 2-1 2-0	4-2			3-2	0-1 2-1	1-1	2-2 2-3 3-2	2-1 1-0 6-0	
Renova Cepciste	33	13	5	15	45	49	44	1-1	2-0	0-1 1-0 2-0 3-0	0-2	1-0 4-3			4-3	1-1	2-1 2-1 2-1 2-1	2-3	
Vlazrimi Kicevo	33	13	4	16	44	57	43	0-1	0-1	1-0	2-4	1-0	2-2 4-3 2-1			0-1 3-2 2-1 1-0 4-0 0-0 3-1 3-0			
Sileks Kratovo	33	10	11	12	54	58	41	2-4	0-2	0-2 0-0 2-2 4-2	1-1	4-1 3-0 1-2 1-0	1-1				4-3 3-3	3-2	1-0
Bregalnica Stip	33	10	6	17	44	55	36	1-2 0-0 4-1	1-2	0-3	2-0	2-0 0-0	0-1	2-1	1-1	1-2		1-0 0-0 3-1	6-1
Cementarnica Skopje	33	8	8	17	38	51	32	2-2 0-0 2-0 2-0	0-1	2-2	1-2 3-1	1-0	2-0	3-1 2-0 3-2	1-2				3-0 1-1
Belasica Strumica	33	2	2	29	22	84	8	1-2 0-3 0-2 1-4	0-2		2-5 1-2 0-3	0-2	2-0 0-2	0-1 1-1 4-6	0-1	0-2			

7/08/2005 – 21/05/2006 • † Qualified for the UEFA Champions League • ‡ Qualified for the UEFA Cup

Relegation play-offs: Karaorman 3-3 3-4p Bregalnica; Madzari 0-1 Sileks • Top scorers: Stevica RISTIC, Sileks, 27; Filip IVANOVSKI, Makedonija, 22

FYR MACEDONIA 2005–06
VTORA LIGA (2)

	Pl	W	D	L	F	A	Pts
Pelister Bitola	30	19	4	7	52	22	61
Napredok Kicevo	30	15	7	8	44	39	52
Karaorman Struga	30	15	5	10	47	38	50
Madzari Skopje	30	11	8	11	33	30	41
Sloga Jugomagnat	30	11	7	12	35	39	40
Skopje	30	11	7	12	30	36	40
Turnovo	30	11	6	13	39	36	39
Metalurg Skopje	30	10	7	13	29	36	37
Lozar Demir Kapija	30	10	7	13	34	45	37
Teteks Tetovo	30	11	2	17	36	45	35
Novatsi	30	9	4	17	29	42	31
Mladnost							Expelled after 15 rounds

6/08/2005 – 20/05/2006

CUP OF MACEDONIA 2005–06

Round of sixteen
Makedonija Skopje *	2 2
Napredok Kicevo	0 2
Karaorman	2 0
Cementarnica Skopje *	3 1
Teteks Tetovo *	3 1
Lokomotiva	1 2
Belasica Strumica *	1 0
Sileks Kratovo	2 3
Bregalnica Stip *	2 2
Baskimi Kumanovo	1 2
Kozuv	0 0
Vardar Skopje *	3 2
Pobeda Prilep *	3 2
Vlazrimi Kicevo	0 2
Renova Cepchiste	0 1
Shkendija Tetovo *	4 1

Quarter-finals
Makedonija Skopje *	1 1
Cementarnica Skopje	0 0
Teteks Tetovo	0 2
Sileks Kratovo *	3 3
Bregalnica Stip	3 0
Vardar Skopje *	1 0
Pobeda Prilep	0 2
Shkendija Tetovo *	2 2

Semi-finals
Makedonija Skopje *	1 2
Sileks Kratovo	1 1
Bregalnica Stip	
Shkendija Tetovo *	

Final
Makedonija Skopje ‡	3
Shkendija Tetovo	2

CUP FINAL
City Stadium, Skopje
24-05-2006
Scorers – Artim Polozani 60, Nuri Mustafi 75, Filip Ivanovski 93+ for Makedonija; Vasko Stefanov OG 68, Marjan Belcev 84 for Shkendija

* Home team in the first leg • ‡ Qualified for the UEFA Cup

MLI – MALI

NATIONAL TEAM RECORD
JULY 1ST 2002 TO JULY 9TH 2006

PL	W	D	L	F	A	%
37	21	6	10	55	31	64.9

FIFA/COCA-COLA WORLD RANKING

1993	1994	1995	1996	1997	1998	1999	2000	2001	2002	2003	2004	2005	2006	High	Low
70	52	52	67	80	70	72	98	112	73	54	51	63		43 09/04	117 10/01

2005–2006											
08/05	09/05	10/05	11/05	12/05	01/06	02/06	03/06	04/06	05/06	06/06	07/06
60	55	58	59	63	62	64	64	65	66	-	63

In spite of a fine reservoir of playing talent, Mali's national team suffered a surprising relapse in their results less than two years after finishing third at the 2004 African Nations Cup finals in Tunisia. Expected to be among the contenders for a place at the 2006 FIFA World Cup™ finals in Germany, the 'Aigles' crashed spectacularly in their qualifying group and even suffered a ban on their home stadium in Bamako due to the rioting that followed their home defeat against Togo. Such was the bewilderment at the sudden slump that Mali went through four coaches in the qualifying campaign; first Henri Stambouli, then another Frenchman in Alain Mozan before

INTERNATIONAL HONOURS
None

turning to former international goalkeeper Abdoulaye Keita and finally Pierre Lechantre, who was already on a hiding to nothing when he took the job. Their final tally was just two wins out of 10 matches and a paltry eight points. Now the coaching mantle has been turned over to Jean-Francois Jodar, who comes for his first African adventure following a stint in the Middle East. Stade Malien, coached by Ghana's former African Footballer of the Year, Abdul Razak, were runaway winners of the championship but they were embarrassingly eliminated in the second round of the 2006 CAF Champions League by Renacimiento of Equatorial Guinea.

THE FIFA BIG COUNT OF 2000

	Male	Female		Male	Female
Registered players	3 900	0	Referees	462	8
Non registered players	1 000 000	1 500	Officials	4 336	462
Youth players	6 980	510	Total involved	1 018 158	
Total players	1 012 890		Number of clubs	407	
Professional players	0	0	Number of teams	103 400	

Fédération Malienne de Football (FMF)
Avenue du Mali, Hamdallaye ACI 2000, PO Box 1020, Bamako 12582, Mali
Tel +223 2238844   Fax +223 2224254
malifoot@afribone.net.ml   www.none
President: KEITA Salif   General Secretary: TRAORE Jacouba
Vice-President: KEITA Karounga   Treasurer: TRAORE Brehima   Media Officer: KOUYATE Mamadou
Men's Coach: JODAR Jean-Francois   Women's Coach: LAICO Moustapha
FMF formed: 1960   CAF: 1963   FIFA: 1962
Green shirts, Yellow shorts, Red socks

RECENT INTERNATIONAL MATCHES PLAYED BY MALI

2002	Opponents		Score	Venue	Comp	Scorers	Att	Referee
8-09	Zimbabwe	L	0-1	Harare	CNq		50 000	Mochubela RSA
2-10	Mauritania	W	2-1	Bamako	Fr			
5-10	Mauritania	W	2-0	Bamoko	Fr			
13-10	Seychelles	W	3-0	Bamako	CNq	Keita.S [31], Sidibe.M [77], Coulibaly.Dr [85]	50 000	Sorie SLE
20-11	Morocco	W	3-1	Rabat	Fr	Sidibe.D [56], Coulibaly.Dr 2 [80 90]	15 000	Tahiri MAR
2003								
12-02	Guinea	W	1-0	Toulon	Fr	Doukantie [20]		
30-03	Eritrea	W	2-0	Asmara	CNq	Thiam [54], Coulibaly.Dr [90]		Abdulkadir TAN
27-04	Madagascar	W	2-0	Paris	Fr	Toure.B [25], Bagayoko [73]		
7-06	Eritrea	W	1-0	Bamako	CNq	Coulibaly.S [20]		Aboubacar CIV
22-06	Zimbabwe	D	0-0	Bamako	CNq			
5-07	Seychelles	W	2-0	Victoria	CNq	Traore.S [60], Bagayoko [90]	5 000	Lim Kee Chong MRI
10-10	Guinea-Bissau	W	2-1	Bissau	WCq	Keita.S [8], Coulibaly.S [69]	22 000	Sowe GAM
14-11	Guinea-Bissau	W	2-0	Bamako	WCq	Coulibaly.S [15], Sidibe.D [84p]	13 251	Seydou MTN
19-11	Morocco	W	1-0	Meknes	Fr	Coulibaly.Dv [35]	6 000	Shelmani LBY
2004								
15-01	Algeria	W	2-0	Algiers	Fr	Traore.D [4], Toure.B [57]	7 000	Zehmoun TUN
26-01	Kenya	W	3-1	Bizerte	CNr1	Sissoko [27], Kanoute 2 [63 82]	6 000	Tessema ETH
30-01	Burkina Faso	W	3-1	Tunis	CNr1	Kanoute [33], Diarra.M [37], Coulibaly.S [78]	1 500	Shelmani LBY
2-02	Senegal	D	1-1	Tunis	CNr1	Traore.D [33]	7 550	Evehe CAM
7-02	Guinea	W	2-1	Bizerte	CNqf	Kanoute [45], Diarra.M [90]	1 450	Abd El Fatah EGY
11-02	Morocco	L	0-4	Sousse	CNsf		15 000	Aboubacar CIV
13-02	Nigeria	L	1-2	Monastir	CN3p	Abouta [70]	2 500	Sowe GAM
28-04	Tunisia	L	0-1	Sfax	Fr		8 000	Shelmani LBY
28-05	Morocco	D	0-0	Bamako	Fr		35 000	
6-06	Liberia	L	0-1	Monrovia	WCq		30 000	Codjia BEN
19-06	Zambia	D	1-1	Bamako	WCq	Kanoute [80]	19 000	Sowe GAM
4-07	Congo	L	0-1	Brazzaville	WCq		20 000	Evehe CMR
18-08	Congo DR	W	3-0	Paris	Fr	Keita.S 2 [2 21], Kanoute [81]		Bruno FRA
5-09	Senegal	D	2-2	Bamako	WCq	Diallo.M [4], Kanoute [54]	45 000	Guezzaz MAR
10-10	Togo	L	0-1	Lome	WCq		45 000	Njike CMR
2005								
9-02	Guinea	D	2-2	Paris	Fr	Traore.D [8], Diao [51]	2 000	
27-03	Togo	L	1-2	Bamako	WCq	Coulibaly.S [12]	45 000	Agbenyega GHA
5-06	Liberia	W	4-1	Liberia	WCq	Coulibaly.D 2 [7p 34], Diamoutene [48p], Diarra.M [75]	11 000	Pare BFA
12-06	Algeria	W	3-0	Arles	Fr	Coulibaly.D [33], Dissa 2 [58 79]	2 000	Derrien FRA
17-06	Zambia	L	1-2	Chililabombwe	WCq	Coulibaly.S [73]	29 000	Colembi ANG
3-09	Congo	W	2-0	Bamako	WCq	Demba [48], Sissoko [51]	10 000	Mbera GAB
8-10	Senegal	L	0-3	Dakar	WCq		30 000	Maillet SEY
2006								
28-05	Morocco	W	1-0	Paris	Fr	Kanoute [70]		Garibian FRA

Fr = Friendly match • CN = CAF African Cup of Nations • WC = FIFA World Cup™
q = qualifier • r1 = first round group • qf = quarter-final • sf = semi-final • 3p = third place play-off

MALI NATIONAL TEAM RECORDS AND RECORD SEQUENCES

Records				Sequence records				
Victory	6-0	MTN 1975		Wins	8	2002-2003	Clean sheets	6	2003
Defeat	1-8	KUW 1997		Defeats	5	1997	Goals scored	11	1971-1972
Player Caps	n/a			Undefeated	18	2002-2004	Without goal	4	Three times
Player Goals	n/a			Without win	8	1989-90, 1995-96	Goals against	12	1987-1988

MALI COUNTRY INFORMATION

Capital	Bamako	Independence	1960 from France	GDP per Capita	$900
Population	11 956 788	Status	Republic	GNP Ranking	134
Area km²	1 240 000	Language	French, Bambara	Dialling code	+223
Population density	10 per km²	Literacy rate	46%	Internet code	.ml
% in urban areas	27%	Main religion	Muslim 90%	GMT + / –	0
Towns/Cities ('000)	Bamako 1 297; Sikasso 144; Mopti 109; Koutiala 100; Kayes 97; Ségou 95; Nioro 72				
Neighbours (km)	Algeria 1 376; Niger 821; Burkina Faso 1 000; Cote d'Ivoire 532; Guinea 858; Senegal 419; Mauritania 2 237				
Main stadia	Stade 26 Mars – Bamako 50 000; Stade Omnisports – Sikasso 20 000				

MALI 2005

PREMIERE DIVISION

	Pl	W	D	L	F	A	Pts	Stade	Cercle	Real	Djoliba	CSK	ASB	Nianan	Comune II	USFAS	Tata	Sigui	Biton	Débo	Mandé
Stade Malien †	26	20	4	2	45	13	64		0-1	0-0	1-1	1-0	0-0	3-0	5-2	3-1	3-0	1-0	3-1	3-0	3-0
Cercle Olympique	26	16	7	3	42	13	55	0-1		5-1	1-2	0-0	4-0	1-0	2-1	1-0	1-3	3-1	5-0	4-0	3-2
Réal Bamako	26	13	8	5	41	19	47	1-2	0-0		1-1	1-0	1-1	3-0	0-0	5-0	1-1	4-1	1-1	1-1	1-0
Djoliba	26	12	8	6	37	22	44	2-1	0-0	0-1		0-1	0-2	0-2	3-0	2-0	1-0	2-0	4-0	0-1	1-1
Centre Salif Keita	26	11	6	9	26	20	39	0-2	0-1	1-0	0-1		1-0	1-2	4-0	0-1	2-2	2-0	2-0	1-0	0-0
AS Bamako	26	10	8	8	32	23	38	0-1	0-1	2-0	3-2	3-0		0-1	4-1	4-0	0-0	1-0	4-0	2-1	0-0
Nianan Koulikoro	26	10	6	10	27	28	36	1-2	0-4	0-1	1-1	0-2	2-0		0-2	0-0	0-0	0-1	6-0	0-2	2-0
Comune II Bamako	26	8	7	11	20	36	31	1-3	0-0	0-2	1-1	1-1	1-0	0-1		1-4	1-0	0-0	1-0	0-2	0-0
USFAS Bamako	26	8	5	13	30	44	29	1-2	1-1	0-5	1-2	3-2	3-1	1-1	0-4		1-2	2-0	2-1	3-0	1-1
Tata National Sikasso	26	5	10	11	22	33	25	0-0	0-0	2-4	1-1	0-2	1-2	1-3	0-0	2-0		2-0	0-0	2-1	0-1
Sigui Kayes	26	5	9	12	15	36	24	0-2	1-0	0-2	1-4	0-0	2-2	1-1	1-1	2-1	1-0		0-1	2-1	0-0
Biton Ségou	26	6	6	14	19	43	24	1-2	0-1	0-0	0-2	1-2	0-0	1-1	3-1	2-4	2-1	0-0		2-1	1-0
Débo Club Mopti	26	6	5	15	24	33	23	0-1	0-1	1-2	1-1	1-2	1-1	1-2	0-0	0-0	1-1	1-1	2-1		3-0
Mandé Bamako	26	3	9	14	13	30	18	0-2	0-1	0-3	1-3	0-0	0-0	0-1	0-1	1-0	5-0	1-1	0-2	0-1	

7/01/2005 - 18/09/2005 • † Qualified for the CAF Champions League • ‡ Qualified for the CAF Confederation Cup • Matches in bold were awarded by the Federation • Top scorer: Jacques Koffi N'GUESSAN, Real Bamako, 18

COUPE DU MALI 2005

Round of 16		Quarter-finals		Semi-finals		Final	
AS Bamako	3						
Mamahira Kati	0	AS Bamako †	2				
Al Farouk Timbuktu	0	Nianan Koulikoro	0				
Nianan Koulikoro	1			AS Bamako	2		
Tata Sikasso	1			Stade Malien	1		
Mali Sadio Kayes	0	Tata Sikasso	1				
Renaissance Ségou	1	Stade Malien	2				
Stade Malien	11					AS Bamako ‡	1 5p
Sigui Kayes	1 5p					Djoliba	1 4p
Maliano-Belge Mopti	1 4p	Sigui Kayes	1				
Sonni Gao	1	USFAS Bamako	0				
USFAS Bamako	4			Sigui Kayes	0		CUP FINAL
Débo Club Mopti	1 5p			Djoliba	2		
Bakaridian Baraouéli	1 4p	Débo Club Mopti	0				Stade Bambeba Traoré, Sikasso
Tadona Sikasso	0	Djoliba	2	‡ Qualified for the CAF Confed Cup			22-09-2005, Ref: Koman Coulibaly
Djoliba	1			† Match abandoned at half-time and awarded 2-0 to AS Bamoko			Scorers: Boubacar Coulibaly 73p for ASB; Oumar Koné 76 for Djoliba

RECENT LEAGUE AND CUP RECORD

	Championship						Cup		
Year	Champions	Pts	Runners-up	Pts	Third	Pts	Winners	Score	Runners-up
2000	Stade Malien	52	Djoliba	47	Centre Salif Keita	40	Cercle Olympique	1-0	Stade Malien
2001	Stade Malien	66	Djoliba	54	Cercle Olympique	45	Stade Malien	5-0	Mamahira Kati
2002	Stade Malien	68	Djoliba	61	Centre Salif Keita	54	Cercle Olympique	2-1	Stade Malien
2003	Stade Malien	62	Djoliba	60	Cercle Olympique	53	Djoliba	2-1	Tata National
2004	Djoliba	63	Stade Malien	58	Centre Salif Keita	58	Djoliba	2-0	Nianan
2005	Stade Malien	64	Cercle Olympique	55	Réal Bamako	47	AS Bamako	1-1 5-4p	Djoliba

MLT – MALTA

NATIONAL TEAM RECORD
JULY 1ST 2002 TO JULY 9TH 2006

PL	W	D	L	F	A	%
33	1	8	24	21	95	15.1

FIFA/COCA-COLA WORLD RANKING

1993	1994	1995	1996	1997	1998	1999	2000	2001	2002	2003	2004	2005	High		Low	
83	78	90	122	133	130	116	119	131	122	129	134	118	66	09/94	137	03/05

2005–2006											
08/05	09/05	10/05	11/05	12/05	01/06	02/06	03/06	04/06	05/06	06/06	07/06
138	127	125	123	118	119	19	122	123	125	-	122

Despite encouraging draws at home to Iceland, Croatia and Bulgaria, the Maltese national team, as expected, finished bottom of their FIFA World Cup™ qualifying group and have now won just one international since the finals in Korea/Japan in 2002. The fact that they won four and drew two games in the seven months before those finals, only highlights a drop in form that is reminiscent of the bad old days of the 1980s and mid 1990s. It's now nearly ten years since Malta have won away from home and since that win away to Hungary in August 1997, they have just three draws to their name from their travels. Their new Czech coach Dusan Fitzel certainly has his work cut

INTERNATIONAL HONOURS
None

out to improve results. The Premier League in Malta was won by Birkirkara for only the second time in their history. Having finished runners-up to Sliema Wanderers for the past three seasons they turned the tables on their rivals and the margin of victory would have been greater had they not lost to Sliema on the final day of the season. The FA Trophy final saw Nigerian striker Haruna Doda score just before half-time against Floriana to give Hibernians their third straight 1-0 victory in the 2005-06 competition and a seventh title overall. The win also denied Floriana the chance to equal Sliema Wanderers' record haul of 19 Cups.

THE FIFA BIG COUNT OF 2000

	Male	Female		Male	Female
Registered players	6 350	200	Referees	101	5
Non registered players	3 000	0	Officials	2 000	50
Youth players	4 000	75	Total involved	15 781	
Total players	13 625		Number of clubs	56	
Professional players	350	0	Number of teams	198	

Malta Football Association (MFA)
280 St Paul Street, Valletta VLT 07, Malta
Tel +356 21 232581   Fax +356 21 245136
info@mfa.com.mt   www.mfa.com.mt
President: MIFSUD Joseph Dr   General Secretary: GAUCHI Joseph
Vice-President: BARTOLO Carmelo   Treasurer: MANFRE Alex   Media Officer: VELLA Alex
Men's Coach: FITZEL Dusan   Women's Coach: BRINCAT Pierre
MFA formed: 1900   UEFA: 1960   FIFA: 1959
Red shirts with white trimmings, White shorts, Red socks or White shirts with red trimmings, Red shorts, White socks

RECENT INTERNATIONAL MATCHES PLAYED BY MALTA

2002	Opponents	Score		Venue	Comp	Scorers	Att	Referee
21-08	FYR Macedonia	L	0-5	Skopje	Fr		4 000	Supraha CRO
7-09	Slovenia	L	0-3	Ljubljana	ECq		7 000	Borovilos GRE
12-10	Israel	L	0-2	Ta'Qali	ECq		5 200	Shebek UKR
16-10	France	L	0-4	Ta'Qali	ECq		10 000	Tudor ROU
20-11	Cyprus	L	1-2	Nicosia	ECq	Mifsud.Mc 90	5 000	Guenov BUL
2003								
12-02	Kazakhstan	D	2-2	Ta'Qali	Fr	Bogdanovic 15, Nwoko 61	200	Rogalla SUI
29-03	France	L	0-6	Lens	ECq		40 775	Bozinovski MKD
30-04	Slovenia	L	1-3	Ta'Qali	ECq	Mifsud.Mc 90	5 000	Hanacsek HUN
7-06	Cyprus	L	1-2	Ta'Qali	ECq	Dimech 72	3 000	Brugger AUT
19-08	Luxembourg	D	1-1	Luxembourg	Fr	Giglio 55	2 000	Lehner AUT
10-09	Israel	D	2-2	Antalya	ECq	Mifsud.Mc 51p, Carabott 52	300	Blareau BEL
11-12	Poland	L	0-4	Larnaca	Fr		300	Kasnaferis GRE
2004								
14-02	Moldova	D	0-0	Ta'Qali	Fr		600	Vialichka BLR
16-02	Estonia	W	5-2	Ta'Qali	Fr	Barbara 2 12 60, Said 28, Turner 57, Zahra 87		Orlic MDA
18-02	Belarus	L	0-4	Ta'Qali	Fr			Kaldma EST
31-03	Finland	L	1-2	Ta'Qali	Fr	Mifsud.Mc 90		Trefoloni ITA
27-05	Germany	L	0-7	Freiburg	Fr		22 000	Stredak SVK
18-08	Faroe Islands	L	2-3	Toftir	Fr	Giglio 50, Mifsud.Mc 65	1 932	Laursen DEN
4-09	Sweden	L	0-7	Ta'Qali	WCq		4 200	Jakov ISR
9-10	Iceland	D	0-0	Ta'Qali	WCq		1 130	Corpodean ROU
13-10	Bulgaria	L	1-4	Sofia	WCq	Mifsud.Mc 11	16 800	Richards WAL
17-11	Hungary	L	0-2	Ta'Qali	WCq		14 500	Asumaa FIN
2005								
9-02	Norway	L	0-3	Ta'Qali	Fr		1 000	Malcolm NIR
30-03	Croatia	L	0-3	Zagreb	WCq		15 510	Kapitanis CYP
4-06	Sweden	L	0-6	Gothenburg	WCq		35 593	Ivanov.N RUS
8-06	Iceland	L	1-4	Reykjavík	WCq	Said 58	4 887	Skomina SVN
17-08	Northern Ireland	D	1-1	Ta'Qali	Fr	Woods 35	1 850	Riley ENG
3-09	Hungary	L	0-4	Budapest	WCq		5 900	Godulyan UKR
7-09	Croatia	D	1-1	Ta'Qali	WCq	Wellman 74	916	Briakos GRE
12-10	Bulgaria	D	1-1	Ta'Qali	WCq	Zahra 79	2 844	Godulyan UKR
2006								
25-02	Moldova	L	0-2	Ta'Qali	Fr		1 125	Silagava GEO
1-03	Georgia	L	0-2	Ta'Qali	Fr		1 100	Banari MDA
4-06	Japan	L	0-1	Dusseldorf	Fr		10 800	Kircher GER

Fr = Friendly match • EC = UEFA EURO 2004™ • WC = FIFA World Cup™ • q = qualifier

MALTA NATIONAL TEAM RECORDS AND RECORD SEQUENCES

Records			Sequence records					
Victory	5-0	AZE 1994	Wins	3	1981, 1999-2000	Clean sheets	4	1999-2000
Defeat	1-12	ESP 1983	Defeats	16	1982-1985	Goals scored	7	1991-1992
Player Caps	121	CARABOTT David	Undefeated	6	2001-2002	Without goal	8	2000-2001
Player Goals	23	BUSUTTIL Carmel	Without win	34	1994-1998	Goals against	29	1996-19999

MALTA COUNTRY INFORMATION

Capital	Valletta	Independence	1964 from the UK	GDP per Capita	$17 700
Population	396 851	Status	Republic	GNP Ranking	124
Area km²	316	Language	Maltese, English	Dialling code	+356
Population density	1 255 per km²	Literacy rate	92%	Internet code	.mt
% in urban areas	89%	Main religion	Christian	GMT + / −	+1
Towns/Cities ('000)	Birkirkara 22; Qormi 18; Mosta 18; Sliema 11; Hamrun 11; Naxxar 10; Gzira 7; Valletta 7				
Neighbours (km)	Mediterranean Sea 196				
Main stadia	Ta'Qali Stadium – Ta'Qali 17 797				

NATIONAL TEAM PLAYERS AND COACHES

Record Caps			Record Goals			Recent Coaches	
CARABOTT David	1987-'05	121	BUSUTTIL Carmel	1982-'01	23	HEESE Horst	1988-'91
BUSUTTIL Carmel	1982-'01	111	CARABOTT David	1987-'05	12	PSAYLA Pippo	1991-'93
BRINCAT Joe	1988-'04	102	MIFSUD Michael	2000-'06	11	GEDIN Pietro	1993-'95
BUTTIGIEG John	1984-'00	95	SUDA Hubert	1988-'03	8	GATT Robert	1996
VELLA Silvio	1988-'00	90	AGIUS Gilbert	1993-'06	6	KOSANOVIC Milorad	1996-'97
AGIUS Gilbert	1993-'06	89	BRINCAT Joe	1988-'04	6	ILIC Josef	1997-'01
DEGIORGIO Michael	1981-'92	74	LAFERLA Kristian	1986-'98	6	HELD Siggi	2001-'03
SUDA Hubert	1988-'03	70	XUEREB Raymond	1971-'85	6	HEESE Horst	2003-'05
CHETCUTI Jeffrey	1994-'05	69				FITZEL Dusan	2006-

CLUB DIRECTORY

Club	Town/City	Stadium	Capacity	www.	Lge	Cup
Birkirkara	Birkirkara	Ta'Qali	17 797	birkirkarafc.com	2	3
Floriana	Floriana	Ta'Qali	17 797	florianafc.com	25	18
Hibernians	Paola	Hibernians Ground	8 000	hibernians.com	9	7
Lija	Lija	Ta'Qali	17 797		0	0
Marsaxlokk	Marsaxlokk	Ta'Qali	17 797	marsaxlokkfc.com	0	0
Msida St Joseph	Msida	Ta'Qali	17 797	msidastjoseph.com	0	0
Pietà Hotspurs	Pietà	Ta'Qali	17 797	pietahotspurs.com	0	0
Sliema Wanderers	Sliema	Ta'Qali	17 797	eswfc.com	26	19
Saint Patrick	Zabbar	Ta'Qali	17 797		0	0
Valletta	Valletta	Ta'Qali	17 797	vallettafcofficial.net	18	11

RECENT LEAGUE AND CUP RECORD

	Championship						Cup		
Year	Champions	Pts	Runners-up	Pts	Third	Pts	Winners	Score	Runners-up
1990	Valletta	28	Sliema Wanderers	24	Hamrun Spartans	23	Sliema Wanderers	1-0	Birkirkara
1991	Hamrun Spartans	24	Valletta	19	Floriana	18	Valletta	2-1	Sliema Wanderers
1992	Valletta	33	Floriana	24	Hamrun Spartans	23	Hamrun Spartans	3-3 2-1	Valletta
1993	Floriana	29	Hamrun Spartans	24	Valletta	24	Floriana	5-0	Sliema Wanderers
1994	Hibernians	31	Floriana	28	Valletta	27	Floriana	2-1	Valletta
1995	Hibernians	43	Sliema Wanderers	39	Valletta	37	Valletta	1-0	Hamrun Spartans
1996	Sliema Wanderers	46	Valletta	42	Floriana	37	Valletta	0-0 1-0	Sliema Wanderers
1997	Valletta	67	Birkirkara	60	Floriana	53	Valletta	2-0	Hibernians
1998	Valletta	65	Birkirkara	63	Sliema Wanderers	56	Hibernians	2-1	Valletta
1999	Valletta	70	Birkirkara	68	Sliema Wanderers	47	Valletta	1-0	Birkirkara
2000	Birkirkara	46	Sliema Wanderers	39	Valletta	36	Sliema Wanderers	4-1	Birkirkara
2001	Valletta	46	Sliema Wanderers	40	Birkirkara	36	Valletta	3-0	Birkirkara
2002	Hibernians	43	Sliema Wanderers	36	Birkirkara	31	Birkirkara	1-0	Sliema Wanderers
2003	Sliema Wanderers	42	Birkirkara	37	Valletta	35	Birkirkara	1-0	Sliema Wanderers
2004	Sliema Wanderers	43	Birkirkara	39	Hibernians	35	Sliema Wanderers	2-0	Marsaxlokk
2005	Sliema Wanderers	40	Birkirkara	38	Hibernians	35	Birkirkara	2-1	Msida St Joseph
2006	Birkirkara	42	Sliema Wanderers	37	Marsaxlokk	36	Hibernians	1-0	Floriana

MALTA 2005–06

PREMIER LEAGUE

	Pl	W	D	L	F	A	Pts	Birkirkara	Sliema	Marsaxlokk	Hibernians	Valletta	Msida	Floriana	Spurs	Mosta	Spartans
Birkirkara † (21)	28	19	5	4	68	27	42		2-1 1-1	1-1 1-0	2-0 1-0	4-2 3-0	4-1 5-0	1-1	4-1	6-0	2-1
Sliema Wanderers ‡ (20)	28	17	5	6	58	27	37	2-1 2-1		0-0 0-1	0-2 3-4	3-0 2-1	2-1 4-1	1-0	0-1	2-0	4-1
Marsaxlokk (17)	28	16	5	7	52	36	36	2-0 1-1	1-2 2-1		1-4 1-0	2-3 3-4	1-0 1-0	1-1	1-3	5-1	4-3
Hibernians ‡ (19)	28	14	4	10	49	37	28	5-2 1-3	0-3 0-3	0-1 3-1		1-2 1-3	2-0 0-0	1-1	2-1	3-2	1-0
Valletta (12)	28	10	5	13	37	49	24	0-2 0-0	1-3 1-2	0-4 0-2	2-0 2-2		1-3 2-2	1-1	1-0	1-0	1-2
Msida St Joseph (11)	28	6	7	15	40	59	15	2-5 1-4	1-4 3-3	1-1 3-4	2-4 1-1	0-1 1-2		4-2	4-2	4-1	2-1
Floriana (10)	24	6	9	9	36	37	18	0-1	0-0	1-2	0-3	2-1	0-0		0-2 1-1	4-4 0-1	1-3 3-0
Pietà Spurs (8)	24	6	6	12	31	47	17	0-2	0-3	1-4	0-4	0-0	0-0	1-3 2-1		3-3 2-2	2-3 1-1
Mosta (4)	24	5	5	14	34	65	16	2-3	0-6	1-3	0-3	0-3	2-1	0-3 3-3	3-1 3-1		0-3 0-0
Hamrun Spartans (10)	24	6	3	15	35	56	12	0-6	1-1	1-2	0-2	4-2	0-2	2-4 2-4	2-4 0-2	2-1 3-5	

5/08/2005 – 14/05/2006 • † Qualified for the UEFA Champions League • ‡ Qualified for the UEFA Cup • Points taken forward for the final round in brackets

MALTA 2005–06
FIRST DIVISION

	Pl	W	D	L	F	A	Pts
St George's	18	10	5	3	27	14	35
Marsa	18	9	6	3	33	20	33
Mqabba	18	9	4	5	28	18	31
Tarxien Rainbows	18	8	5	5	25	18	29
Senglea Athletic	18	8	3	7	21	23	27
St Patrick	18	7	5	6	29	22	26
San Gwann	18	7	2	9	23	25	23
Naxxar Lions	18	6	2	10	32	38	20
Lija Athletic	18	5	3	10	20	33	18
St Andrews	18	1	5	12	13	40	8

10/09/2005 – 14/05/2006

FA TROPHY 2005–06

Round of 16		Quarter-finals		Semi-finals		Final	
Hibernians	Bye						
		Hibernians	1				
St Patrick	2	Hamrun Spartans	0				
Hamrun Spartans	3			Hibernians	1		
Valletta	Bye			Birkirkara	0		
		Valletta	0				
		Birkirkara	2				
Birkirkara	Bye					Hibernians ‡	1
Sliema Wanderers	Bye					Floriana	0
		Sliema Wanderers	2				
Marsa	0	Marsaxlokk	0				
Marsaxlokk	2			Sliema Wanderers	0		
Msida St Joseph	2			Floriana	2		
San Gwann	1	Msida St Joseph	0				
Senglea Athletic	0	Floriana	2				
Floriana	4						

‡ Qualified for the UEFA Cup

CUP FINAL

National Stadium, Ta'Qali
26-05-2006, Ref: Sammut
Scorer – Haruna Doda [44] for Hibernians

MOZ – MOZAMBIQUE

NATIONAL TEAM RECORD
JULY 1ST 2002 TO JULY 9TH 2006

PL	W	D	L	F	A	%
26	8	8	10	23	28	46.2

FIFA/COCA-COLA WORLD RANKING

1993	1994	1995	1996	1997	1998	1999	2000	2001	2002	2003	2004	2005	High		Low	
104	94	76	85	67	80	101	112	128	125	127	126	130	66	11/97	134	07/05

2005–2006											
08/05	09/05	10/05	11/05	12/05	01/06	02/06	03/06	04/06	05/06	06/06	07/06
130	130	130	130	130	130	130	132	133	127	-	126

As one of the cradles of African football's glorious past, and as the birthplace of legends like Eusebio, Mario Coluna and Matateu, Mozambique has been unable to live up to the legacy set by some of the continent's first genuine superstars. Coluna, in his role as President of the Federação Moçambicana de Futebol, has made great strides in developing the infrastructure of football, seeking to take advantage of the economic boom in a country fast recovering from the ravages of civil war. There was bitter disappointment then, when in early 2006, Mozambique did not make the cut for the final four candidates to host the 2010 African Nations Cup finals, despite being regarded as one

INTERNATIONAL HONOURS
None

of the favourites to win the vote. The national team failed for a second successive year to make it out of the group phase of the regional COSAFA Castle Cup, beaten by Zimbabwe in 2005 and by Lesotho in 2006, albeit on penalties. But the side have not had a chance to use foreign-based players like Armando Sa, Dario Monteiro and Paito in recent years because of their failure to get through to the group phase of the 2006 FIFA World Cup™ qualifiers. Ferroviario Beira struck a blow for the provincial clubs with Cup success in November, beating Costa do Sol in a dramatic final, while national coach Artur Semedo steered Ferroviario Maputo to success in the League.

THE FIFA BIG COUNT OF 2000

	Male	Female		Male	Female
Registered players	5 259	100	Referees	415	0
Non registered players	50 000	0	Officials	4 597	25
Youth players	5 725	0	Total involved	66 121	
Total players	61 084		Number of clubs	150	
Professional players	168	0	Number of teams	208	

Federação Moçambicana de Futebol (FMF)
Av. Samora Machel, Número 11-2 Andar, Maputo 1467, Mozambique
Tel +258 1 300366   Fax +258 1 300367
fmfbol@tvcabo.co.mz   www.none
President: COLUNA Mario   General Secretary: MONTEIRO Manuel
Vice-President: GAFUR Amir Abdul   Treasurer: NHANCOLO Luis   Media Officer: MONTEIRO Manuel
Men's Coach: SEMEDO Artur   Women's Coach: MACUACUA Chadreque
FMF formed: 1976   CAF: 1978   FIFA: 1980
Red shirts with black trimmings, Black shorts, Red socks

RECENT INTERNATIONAL MATCHES PLAYED BY MOZAMBIQUE

2002	Opponents	Score		Venue	Comp	Scorers	Att	Referee
6-07	Zambia	L	0-3	Lusaka	CCqf			Ndoro ZIM
9-09	Central African Rep.	D	1-1	Bangui	CNq	Fumo 60		Ndong EQG
13-10	Congo	L	0-3	Maputo	CNq			Lwanja MWI
2003								
22-03	Lesotho	D	0-0	Maputo	CCrl	W 5-4p		Lwanja MWI
30-03	Burkina Faso	W	1-0	Maputo	CNq	Monteiro Dario 89		Nunkoo MRI
7-06	Burkina Faso	L	0-4	Ouagadougou	CNq		25 000	Ould Mohamed MTN
22-06	Central African Rep.	W	1-0	Maputo	CNq	Jossias 73p	15 000	
6-07	Congo	D	0-0	Brazzaville	CNq			
27-07	Zambia	L	2-4	Lusaka	CCqf	To 44, Tico-Tico 60	10 000	Katjimune NAM
12-10	Guinea	L	0-1	Conakry	WCq		13 400	Ndoye SEN
9-11	Swaziland	W	2-0	Maputo	Fr			
16-11	Guinea	L	3-4	Maputo	WCq	Monteiro Dario 3 75 80 89	50 000	Mochubela RSA
2004								
11-04	Swaziland	W	2-0	Maputo	Fr	Nando 42, Amilcar 72		
18-04	Madagascar	W	2-0	Maputo	CCrl	Tico-Tico 64, Fala-Fala 89	28 000	Damon RSA
26-05	Botswana	D	0-0	Maputo	Fr		2 000	
31-05	Swaziland	D	1-1	Maputo	Fr	Nelinho 43	5 000	
13-06	Malawi	W	2-0	Maputo	CCqf	Mabedi OG 42, To 62	30 000	Kaoma ZAM
25-06	Ghana	L	0-1	Maputo	Fr			
19-09	Angola	L	0-1	Maputo	CCsf		50 000	Jovinala MWI
2005								
16-04	Zimbabwe	L	0-3	Windhoek	CCrl			Mufeti NAM
26-06	Lesotho	W	1-0	Maputo	Fr			
28-08	Zimbabwe	D	0-0	Mutare	Fr			
2006								
29-04	Lesotho	D	0-0	Maseru	CCrl	L 4-5p		Jovinala MWI
30-04	Mauritius	D	0-0	Maseru	CCrl			Moeketsi LES
24-06	Swaziland	W	4-0	Maputo	Fr	Macamo 12, Butoana 22, Manoso 60, Massima 79		
25-06	Malawi	L	1-2	Maputo	Fr	Lomba Da Costa		

Fr = Friendly match • CN = CAF African Cup of Nations • CC = COSAFA Cup • WC = FIFA World Cup™ • q = qualifier

MOZAMBIQUE NATIONAL TEAM RECORDS AND RECORD SEQUENCES

Records			Sequence records				
Victory	6-1	LES 1980	Wins	5	1989-1990	Clean sheets	4	Four times
Defeat	0-6	ZIM 1979, ZIM 1980	Defeats	7	1998	Goals scored	15	1980-1982
Player Caps	n/a		Undefeated	7	1995	Without goal	3	1986, 1989, 1991
Player Goals	n/a		Without win	18	1985-1989	Goals against	17	1985-1989

MOZAMBIQUE COUNTRY INFORMATION

Capital	Maputo	Independence	1975 from Portugal	GDP per Capita	$1 200
Population	18 811 731	Status	Republic	GNP Ranking	123
Area km²	801 590	Language	Portuguese, Makhuwa, Tsonga	Dialling code	+258
Population density	23 per km²	Literacy rate	47%	Internet code	.mz
% in urban areas	34%	Main religion	Indigenous 50%, Christian 30%	GMT +/−	+2
Towns/Cities ('000)	Maputo 1 191; Matola 544; Beira 531; Nampula 388; Chomoio 257; Nacala 225; Quelimane 188				
Neighbours (km)	South Africa 491; Swaziland 105; Zimbabwe 1 231; Zambia 419; Malawi 1 569; Tanzania 756; Indian Ocean 2 470				
Main stadia	Estádio da Machava – Maputo 6 000; Estádio do Ferroviário – Beira 7 000				

MOZAMBIQUE 2005

CAMPEONATO NACIONAL DA 1ª DIVISAO

	Pl	W	D	L	F	A	Pts	Ferro M.	Costa	GD Maputo	Maxaquene	Têxtil	Academ'ca	Ferro B.	Chingale	Ferro Nam.	Lichinga	Matchedje	Ferro Nac.
Ferroviário Maputo †	22	13	7	2	34	7	46		1-0	3-0	0-0	1-0	1-0	3-1	4-0	2-0	6-0	3-0	4-1
Costa do Sol	22	12	5	5	24	10	41	0-0		0-0	0-0	2-1	1-2	1-1	4-0	1-0	1-0	1-0	1-0
Desportivo Maputo	22	12	5	5	30	16	41	0-1	1-1		1-0	4-1	4-0	1-0	2-1	3-0	2-1	0-1	2-1
Maxaquene	22	10	8	4	15	11	38	0-1	1-0	1-0		1-0	1-1	1-0	0-2	0-0	1-0	1-0	1-0
Têxtil Púnguè	22	7	8	7	23	21	29	1-1	0-1	1-0	1-1		2-1	1-0	1-1	0-0	0-0	3-0	4-1
Académica Maputo	22	7	6	9	18	25	27	0-0	1-4	0-1	0-0	2-0		0-1	2-1	1-0	2-2	0-0	3-1
Ferroviário Beira	22	6	8	8	18	17	26	1-1	1-0	0-1	1-2	0-1	1-2		2-2	0-0	2-0	0-0	1-0
Chingale Tete	22	6	8	8	18	24	26	1-0	0-1	1-1	2-0	3-3	0-0	0-0		0-0	0-2	2-0	0-0
Ferroviário Nampula	22	5	10	7	10	13	25	1-0	1-0	1-1	0-1	1-1	0-1	0-0	1-0		2-0	0-0	2-0
Lichinga	22	5	9	8	13	22	24	1-1	0-2	0-0	0-1	1-0	1-0	1-1	1-0	0-0		2-0	1-1
Matchedje	22	3	6	13	12	28	15	0-1	0-1	1-4	1-0	0-2	0-1	1-4	0-1	1-0	0-0		6-0
Ferroviário Nacala	22	2	8	12	13	34	14	0-0	0-2	1-2	1-1	0-0	3-1	1-0	0-1	1-1	0-0	1-1	

2/04/2005 - 30/10/2005 • † Qualified for the CAF Champions League

TACA NACIONAL 2005

Round of 16

Ferroviário Beira	4
Benfica Macúti	3
Quelimane	0
Chingale Tete	4
Sporting Nampula	2
Desportiva Pembe	1
Vilanculos	0
Maxaquene	1
Matchedje	1 3p
Incomatí Xinavane	1 1p
Matchedje Chimoio	1
Desportivo Chimoio	3
Ferroviário Maputo	4
Teka Mahala Gaza	0
Académica Maputo	0
Costa do Sol	2

Quarter-finals

Ferroviário Beira	1
Chingale Tete	0
Sporting Nampula	0
Maxaquene	4
Matchedje	1
Desportivo Chimoio	0
Ferroviário Maputo	1 2p
Costa do Sol	1 4p

Semi-finals

Ferroviário Beira	2
Maxaquene	1
Matchedje	0
Costa do Sol	4

Final

Ferroviário Beira ‡	1
Costa do Sol	0

‡ Qualified for the CAF Confederation Cup

CUP FINAL

Machava, Maputo
20-11-2005, Att: 20 000

Scorer - Leonel [93] for Beira

CLUB DIRECTORY

Club	City/Town	Stadium	Capacity	Lge	Cup
Costa do Sol	Maputo	Costa do Sol	10 000	8	9
Desportivo	Maputo	Desportivo	4 000	5	1
Ferroviário	Beira	Ferroviário	7 000	0	2
Ferroviário	Maputo	Machava	60 000	7	4
Ferroviário	Nampula	Nampula	4 000	1	1
Lichinga	Lichinga	Lichinga	3 000	0	0
Matchedje	Maputo	Costa do Sol	10 000	2	1
Maxaquene	Maputo	Maxaquene	15 000	4	6
Têxtil Púnguè	Beira	Chiveve	5 000	1	0

RECENT LEAGUE AND CUP RECORD

	Championship							Cup		
Year	Champions	Pts	Runners-up	Pts	Third	Pts		Winners	Score	Runners-up
1999	Ferroviário Maputo	23	Costa do Sol	23	Chingale Tete	14		Costa do Sol	5-0	Sporting Nampula
2000	Costa do Sol	51	Ferroviário Maputo	47	Matchadje	38		Costa do Sol	1-0	Matchadje
2001	Costa do Sol	45	Ferroviário Maputo	38	Maxaquene	33		Maxaquene	3-1	Textáfrica Chimoio
2002	Ferroviário Maputo	50	Maxaquene	46	Costa do Sol	43		Costa do Sol	2-0	Académica Maputo
2003	Maxaquene	47	Costa do Sol	43	Desportivo Maputo	40		Ferroviário Nampula	1-1 5-4p	Ferroviário Maputo
2004	Ferroviário Nampula	44	Desportivo Maputo	42	Ferroviário Maputo	35		Ferroviário Maputo	5-1	Textáfrica Chimoio
2005	Ferroviário Maputo	46	Costa do Sol	41	Desportivo Maputo	41		Ferroviário Beira	1-0	Costa do Sol

MRI – MAURITIUS

NATIONAL TEAM RECORD
JULY 1ST 2002 TO JULY 9TH 2006

PL	W	D	L	F	A	%
22	8	3	11	21	32	43.2

FIFA/COCA-COLA WORLD RANKING

1993	1994	1995	1996	1997	1998	1999	2000	2001	2002	2003	2004	2005		High		Low
133	146	154	150	151	148	118	118	124	126	123	140	143		116	08/00	158 05/96

2005–2006											
08/05	09/05	10/05	11/05	12/05	01/06	02/06	03/06	04/06	05/06	06/06	07/06
144	145	145	144	143	144	144	144	145	146	-	135

For all their honest endeavour and intentions, Mauritius still battle to make much progress with their national side, eliminated early yet again in the regional COSAFA Castle Cup. The side suffered a 5-1 thrashing at the hands of Germany-bound Angola in April in the 2006 tournament and it has been more than a year since their last win in an international. An ageing team is the cause of concern for Mauritius as they look ahead to a tough qualifying group for the 2008 African Nations Cup finals containing FIFA World Cup™ finalists Tunisia. There has been a dearth of young talent coming through, despite widespread development of the football infrastructure on the

INTERNATIONAL HONOURS
None

island. After four successive titles, AS Port Louis 2000 were deposed as champions at the end of the 2005/06 season by Pamplemousse SC, who easily won the Super League play-offs, 10 points clear of the defending champions who finished fifth. ASPL 2000 were also hammered by Orlando Pirates of South Africa in the second round of the African Champions League, losing both home and away in the tie. Curepipe Starlight were MFA Cup winners but only after a marathon penalty shootout over Savanne SC following a goalless draw. It ended 9-8 to Starlight at the newly-revamped George V stadium.

THE FIFA BIG COUNT OF 2000

	Male	Female		Male	Female
Registered players	11 250	522	Referees	88	2
Non registered players	6 000	200	Officials	4 000	0
Youth players	4 170	0	Total involved	26 232	
Total players	22 142		Number of clubs	62	
Professional players	0	0	Number of teams	637	

Mauritius Football Association (MFA)
Football House, Trianon, Mauritius
Tel +230 4652200   Fax +230 4547909
mfaho@intnet.mu   www.none
President: PERSUNNOO Dinnanathlall   General Secretary: VUDDAMALAY Ananda
Vice-President: CHITBAHAL Bhai Mustapha   Treasurer: BOWUD A.H. Nazir   Media Officer: NG PING MAN Laval
Men's Coach: DORASAMI Rajen and L'AIGUILLE France   Women's Coach: ROSE Eddy
MFA formed: 1952   CAF: 1962   FIFA: 1962
Red shirts, Red shorts, Red socks

RECENT INTERNATIONAL MATCHES PLAYED BY MAURITIUS

2002 Opponents		Score	Venue	Comp	Scorers	Att	Referee
1-08 Swaziland	W	1-0	Mbabane	Fr	Zuel [2]		
3-08 Swaziland	D	0-0	Big Bend	Fr			Sitriongomyane SWZ
26-09 Seychelles	W	1-0	Port Louis	Fr	Laboiteuse [70]	166	Roopnah MRI
12-10 Madagascar	L	0-1	Port Louis	CNq		1 819	Maillet SEY
2003							
22-02 Madagascar	L	1-2	Antananarivo	CCr1	Appou [50]	25 000	Motau RSA
29-03 Egypt	L	0-1	Port Louis	CNq		800	
8-06 Egypt	L	0-7	Cairo	CNq		40 000	Abdalla LBY
6-07 Madagascar	W	2-0	Antananarivo	CNq	Perle [13], Appou [30p]		
30-08 Madagascar	W	3-1	Curepipe	IOr1	Appou 2 [11p 56], Perle [15]	4 500	Ramsamy REU
2-09 Seychelles	D	0-0	Curepipe	IOr1			
4-09 Comoros †	W	5-0	Curepipe	IOsf	Perle 2 [8 87], Appou 2 [42p 70], Cundasamy [49]	4 500	Labrosse SEY
6-09 Reunion	W	2-1	Curepipe	IOf	Cundasamy [41], Ithier [83]	10 000	Labrosse SEY
11-10 Uganda	L	0-3	Kampala	WCq		6 800	Tangawarima ZIM
16-11 Uganda	W	3-1	Curepipe	WCq	Naboth [37], Mourgine [70], Louis [82]	2 465	Maillet SEY
2004							
10-01 South Africa	W	2-0	Curepipe	CCr1	Lekgetho OG [53], Perle [81]	5 230	Raolimanana MAD
31-07 Zambia	L	1-3	Lusaka	CCqf	Appou [70]		Manuel ZIM
2005							
26-02 Madagascar	W	2-0	Curepipe	CCr1	Appou [44], Louis [48]		Fakude SWZ
27-02 South Africa	L	0-1	Curepipe	CCr1			Mnkantjo ZIM
23-10 Madagascar	L	0-2	Antananarivo	Fr			
2006							
29-04 Angola	L	1-5	Maseru	CCr1	Louis [2]		Moeketsi LES
30-04 Mozambique	D	0-0	Maseru	CCr1	L 4-5p		Jovinala MWI
26-06 Tanzania	L	1-2	Victoria	Fr	Godon [17]		
28-06 Seychelles	L	1-2	Victoria	Fr	Mourgine [90]		

Fr = Friendly match • CN = CAF African Cup of Nations • CC = COSAFA Cup • IO = Indian Ocean Games • WC = FIFA World Cup™
q = qualifier • r1 = first round group • qf = quarter-final • sf = semi-final • f = final • † not a full international

MAURITIUS NATIONAL TEAM RECORDS AND RECORD SEQUENCES

Records			Sequence records				
Victory	15-0	REU 1950	Wins	17	1947-1955	Clean sheets	4	1957-1958
Defeat	0-7	EGY 2003	Defeats	6	1974-1975	Goals scored	25	1947-1958
Player Caps	n/a		Undefeated	17	1947-1955	Without goal	6	1994-1995
Player Goals	n/a		Without win	9	Three times	Goals against	10	1999-2000

MAURITIUS COUNTRY INFORMATION

Capital	Port Louis	Independence	1968 from the UK	GDP per Capita	$11 400
Population	1 220 481	Status	Republic	GNP Ranking	116
Area km²	2 040	Language	French, English	Dialling code	+230
Population density	598 per km²	Literacy rate	85%	Internet code	.mu
% in urban areas	41%	Main religion	Hindu 52%, Christian 28%	GMT +/–	+4
Towns/Cities ('000)	Port Louis 155; Beau Bassin-Rose Hill 110; Vascoas-Pheinix 107; Curepipe 84; Quatre Bras 80				
Neighbours (km)	Indian Ocean 2 740				
Main stadia	George V Stadium – Curepipe 10 000; Auguste Vollaire – Port Louis				

MAURITIUS 2005–06

PREMIER LEAGUE FIRST STAGE

	Pl	W	D	L	F	A	Pts	Savanne	ASPL 2000	Pampl'ses	BB/RH	PAS Mates	ASVP	Faucon	Starlight	Olympique	Grand Port	Petite RN	Arsenal
Savanne SC †	11	8	3	0	19	2	27		0-0	1-1	5-0	0-0			1-0			2-0	
AS Port-Louis 2000 †	11	8	2	1	24	9	26						1-0	0-1	3-1	4-1		3-1	
Pamplemousses SC †	11	5	4	2	22	10	19	2-2							1-3	4-0	2-0		3-1
Beau-Bassin Rose Hill †	11	5	2	4	9	12	17			0-2		2-1	0-0	1-0		1-0		1-0	
Pointe-aux-Sables †	11	3	7	1	9	2	16			0-0			0-0	1-0		2-0		1-1	5-0
AS Vacoas-Phoenix †	11	4	4	3	12	8	16	0-1		0-0					3-3	0-1	4-1		1-0
Faucon Flacq SC †	11	4	3	4	19	16	15	0-1				1-1			2-0	3-0			3-3
Curepipe Starlight SC†	11	4	3	4	13	13	15			1-2			0-0	1-1			3-1	2-1	
Olympique Moka ‡	11	4	1	6	15	18	13	0-1					1-0		1-4		2-2		4-1
Grand Port United ‡	11	2	2	7	10	24	8	0-2	1-5	0-3	1-0	0-0		0-1					
Petite Rivière Noire ‡	11	2	1	8	10	26	7				1-5			0-2	0-2	0-5	2-1		4-2
Arsenal Wanderers	11	0	2	9	13	35	2	1-5	1-2			1-3			1-1		2-4		

9/10/2005 - 4/12/2005 • † Qualified for the Super League play-offs • ‡ Entered the promotion/relegation group

MAURITIUS 2005–06

PREMIER LEAGUE SUPER LEAGUE PLAY-OFFS

	Pl	W	D	L	F	A	Pts	Pampl'ses	ASVP	Starlight	Savanne	ASPL 2000	PAS Mates	BB/RH	Faucon
Pamplemouses SC †	14	8	4	2	27	16	28		0-0	0-2	2-2	3-2	3-0	2-1	3-0
AS Vacoas-Phoenix	14	5	8	1	13	9	23	2-2		2-1	1-1	0-1	1-0	2-1	0-0
Curepipe Starlight SC	14	5	5	4	19	17	20	1-3	2-2		2-1	3-1	0-1	1-1	2-1
Savanne SC	14	5	5	4	22	20	20	4-3	1-1	2-1			0-3	2-2	2-4
AS Port-Louis 2000	14	5	3	6	15	20	18	1-2	0-0	2-2	0-2		3-1	1-1	2-1
Pointe-aux-Sables	14	4	4	5	11	11	16	0-2	0-0	0-0	1-1			0-1	0-1
Beau-Bassin/Rose Hill	14	4	2	7	16	17	14	0-1	0-2	0-1	0-3	2-1			2-0
Faucon Flacq	14	2	3	9	10	23	9	1-1		1-1	0-1	1-2	0-2	0-5	

9/03/2006 - 28/05/2006 • † Qualified for the CAF Champions League
Play-off: Faucon Flacq 2-2 2-0 Sodnac Quatre-Bornes

MAURITIUS 2005–06 PROMOTION/RELEGATION

	Pl	W	D	L	F	A	Pts
Petite Rivière Noire	5	4	0	1	17	9	12
Grand Port United	5	3	1	1	10	5	10
Olympique Moka	5	3	1	1	10	5	10
Sodnac Quatre-Bornes	5	1	2	2	6	7	5
AS Quatre-Bornes	5	1	1	3	5	12	4
Savanne St Aubin	5	0	1	4	6	16	1

4/02/2006 - 8/04/2006

MFA CUP 2005–06

Quarter-finals		Semi-finals		Final	
C'pipe Starlight	0				
AS Quatre-Bornes	6	C'pipe Starlight	5		
KS Briquetterie	1	Vacoas-Phoenix	2		
Vacoas-Phoenix	8			C'pipe Starlight ‡	0 9p
ASPL 2000	3			Savanne SC	0 8p
PAS Mates	0	ASPL 2000	1		
Petite RN	0	**Savanne SC**	2	Curepipe, 4-06-2006	
Savanne SC	1	‡ Qualified for Confed Cup			

RECENT LEAGUE AND CUP RECORD

	Championship						Cup		
Year	Champions	Pts	Runners-up	Pts	Third	Pts	Winners	Score	Runners-up
1996	Sunrise Flacq						Sunrise Flacq	2-1	Scouts Club
1997	Sunrise Flacq						Fire Brigade BB/RH	3-1	Sunrise Flacq
1998	Scouts Club	28	Fire Brigade BB/RH	21	Sunrise Flacq	20	Fire Brigade BB/RH	3-0	Scouts Club
1999	Fire Brigade BB/RH	39	Scouts Club	38	Sunrise Flacq	35			
2000									
2001	Olympique Moka	57	AS Port Louis 2000	44	US Beau-Basin/RH		US Beau-Basin/RH	2-1	Olympique Moka
2002	AS Port Louis 2000	58	US Beau-Basin/RH	52	Faucon Flacq	40	AS Port Louis 2000	3-0	Olympique Moka
2003	AS Port Louis 2000	26	Faucon Flacq SC	21	US Beau-Basin/RH	21	Savanne SC	1-1 4-2p	AS Port Louis 2000
2004	AS Port Louis 2000	56	Pamplemousses SC	43	Savanne SC	37	Savanne SC	3-2	Faucon Flacq SC
2005	AS Port Louis 2000	31	Savanne SC	26	US Beau-Basin/RH	23	AS Port Louis 2000	2-0	PAS Mates
2006	Pamplemousses SC	28	AS Vacoas-Phoenix	23	Curepipe Starlight	20	Curepipe Starlight	0-0 9-8p	Svanne SC

In 2000 there was a major re-organisation of football in Mauritius after major incidents on the pitch that year • Sunrise Flacq became Olympique de Moka; Fire Brigade merged with Real Pamplemousses to form Pamplemousses SC; Mahebourg United became Grand Port United

MSR - MONTSERRAT

NATIONAL TEAM RECORD
JULY 1ST 2002 TO JULY 9TH 2006

PL	W	D	L	F	A	%
5	0	0	5	5	34	0

FIFA/COCA-COLA WORLD RANKING

1993	1994	1995	1996	1997	1998	1999	2000	2001	2002	2003	2004	2005	High		Low	
-	-	-	-	-	-	201	202	203	203	204	202	202	196	07/06	205	10/04

2005–2006											
08/05	09/05	10/05	11/05	12/05	01/06	02/06	03/06	04/06	05/06	06/06	07/06
202	202	202	202	202	202	202	202	202	202	-	196

In the wake of the devastation caused by the eruption of Mount Soufriere in 1995, the population of Montserrat fell from 10,000 regular inhabitants to just under 5,000. Even with a population of 10,000 the country would have been the smallest nation affiliated to FIFA, so to lose half of that number has made the running of football a challenging task at the best of times. That the football association managed to field a team in the 2006 FIFA World Cup™ qualifiers, and in the 2005 CONCACAF Gold Cup qualifiers, was a miracle in itself. Since then, however, they have had to admit defeat. They simply couldn't find enough players to enter either the FIFA Women's World

INTERNATIONAL HONOURS
None

Cup or the FIFA Women's U-19 World Championship. Most of those who moved abroad have ended up in London, and the FA has issued a plea to the football players amongst them to contact them with a view to playing for the country. In the future it may well be easier for matches and training camps to be organised in England. The lack of available players has also had an effect on the Montserrat League. The Royal Montserrat Police Force found themselves without any opponents for the 2005 season and so the League had to be cancelled, a situation the FA are trying to rectify for the 2006 season by creating two new teams.

THE FIFA BIG COUNT OF 2000

	Male	Female		Male	Female
Registered players	100	0	Referees	5	0
Non registered players	100	0	Officials	20	0
Youth players	100	0	Total involved	325	
Total players	300		Number of clubs	4	
Professional players	0	0	Number of teams	7	

Montserrat Football Association Inc. (MFA)
PO Box 505, Woodlands, Montserrat
Tel +1 664 4918744   Fax +1 664 4918801
monfa@candw.ms   www.montserrat-football.com
President: CASSELL Vincent   General Secretary: MILNE Carole
Vice-President: POLLIDORE Clement   Treasurer: TBD   Media Officer: None
Men's Coach: COOPER Scott   Women's Coach: READ Darren & LABORDE Ottley
MFA formed: 1994   CONCACAF: 1996   FIFA: 1996
Green shirts with black and white stripes, Green shorts, Green socks

RECENT INTERNATIONAL MATCHES PLAYED BY MONTSERRAT

2002	Opponents	Score	Venue	Comp	Scorers	Att	Referee
No international matches played in 2002 after June							
2003							
No international matches played in 2003							
2004							
29-02	Bermuda	L 0-13	Hamilton	WCq		3 000	Kennedy USA
21-03	Bermuda	L 0-7	Plymouth	WCq		250	Charles DMA
31-10	St Kitts and Nevis	L 1-6	Basseterre	GCq	Adams [81]		Bedeau GRN
2-11	Antigua and Barbuda	L 4-5	Basseterre	GCq	Bramble [36], Fox [41], Mendes [50], Farrel [61]		Phillip GRN
4-11	St Lucia	L 0-3	Basseterre	GCq	St Lucia awarded the match 3-0		
2005							
No international matches played in 2005							
2006							
No international matches played in 2006 before July							

Fr = Friendly match • GC = CONCACAF Gold Cup • WC = FIFA World Cup™ • q = qualifier

MONTSERRAT NATIONAL TEAM RECORDS AND RECORD SEQUENCES

Records			Sequence records					
Victory	3-2	AIA 1995	Wins	2	1995	Clean sheets	1	1995
Defeat	0-13	BER 2004	Defeats	16	1995-2004	Goals scored	3	1996-99, 2000-01
Player Caps	n/a		Undefeated	2	1995	Without goal	4	2004-2004
Player Goals	n/a		Without win	16	1995-2004	Goals against		

RECENT LEAGUE RECORD

Championship	
Year	Champions
1996	Royal Montserrat Police Force
1997	Abandoned
1998	Not held
1999	Not Held
2000	Royal Montserrat Police Force
2001	Royal Montserrat Police Force
2002	Not held due to season readjustment
2003	Royal Montserrat Police Force
2004	Ideal SC
2005	Not held

MONTSERRAT COUNTRY INFORMATION

Capital	Plymouth	Status	UK Dependent Territory	GDP per Capita	$3 400
Population	9 245			GNP Ranking	n/a
Area km²	102	Language	English	Dialling code	+1 664
Population density	91 per km²	Literacy rate	97%	Internet code	.ms
% in urban areas	n/a	Main religion	Christian	GMT + / −	-4
Towns/Cities	Cork Hill 732; Salem 680; Saints Johns 627; Bransby Point 550; Davy Hill 366; Geralds 314				
Neighbours (km)	Caribbean Sea 40				
Main stadia	Blakes Estate Football Ground – Plymouth				

MTN – MAURITANIA

MAURITANIA NATIONAL TEAM RECORD
JULY 1ST 2002 TO JULY 9TH 2006

PL	W	D	L	F	A	%
11	1	2	8	4	22	18.2

FIFA/COCA-COLA WORLD RANKING

1993	1994	1995	1996	1997	1998	1999	2000	2001	2002	2003	2004	2005	High	Low
144	137	85	113	135	142	160	161	177	180	165	175	178	**85** 12/95	**182** 05/03

				2005–2006							
08/05	09/05	10/05	11/05	12/05	01/06	02/06	03/06	04/06	05/06	06/06	07/06
176	176	178	178	178	178	178	178	178	178	-	166

Mauritania remained occasional participants in a myriad of continental competitions but with little success to show for their endeavour. The Saharan country, with a standing in the lower echelons of the FIFA/Coca-Coca World Ranking, has sent clubs to both African and Arab competitions but they have made little headway in either. At national team level, Mauritania will return to the field after an absence of almost three years, in the qualifiers for the 2008 African Nations Cup in Ghana, where they were drawn in a group with holders Egypt, Burundi and Botswana. With a record of just one win in the past ten years, it is unlikely that they will test Egypt

INTERNATIONAL HONOURS
None

but the hope is that the team can start to gain experience and build for the future. Their absence from the 2005 Amilcar Cabral Cup in nearby Guinea, however, did little to suggest that the national team is a sporting priority. The 2006 league title was taken by ASC Mauritel, who just edged Entente Sebka in the four-team play-off for the title. It was their first championship since 2000. Mauritel are ineligible to play in the 2007 CAF Champions League and participation from Mauritanian clubs has been haphazard in recent years. ASC Ksar did play in the Arab Champions League, but were beaten 7-0 on aggregate by Al Hilal of Sudan in September 2005.

THE FIFA BIG COUNT OF 2000

	Male	Female		Male	Female
Registered players	2 933	0	Referees	90	5
Non registered players	6 000	0	Officials	200	0
Youth players	1 288	0	Total involved	10 516	
Total players	10 221		Number of clubs	52	
Professional players	10	0	Number of teams	160	

Fédération de Foot-Ball de la République Islamique de Mauritanie (FFM)
Case postale 566, Nouakchott, Mauritania
Tel +222 5 241860   Fax +222 5 241861
ffrim@mauritel.mr   www.none
President: ABBAS Moulay Mohamed   General Secretary: BOUGHOURBAL Abdel Aziz
Vice-President: OULD KLEIB Abdallahi   Treasurer: OULD LIMAM AHMED Sidi Mohamed   Media Officer: None
Men's Coach: TBD   Women's Coach: FALL Rey
FFM formed: 1961   CAF: 1968   FIFA: 1964
Green shirts with yellow trimmings, Yellow shorts, Green socks

RECENT INTERNATIONAL MATCHES PLAYED BY MAURITANIA

2002	Opponents	Score		Venue	Comp	Scorers	Att	Referee
6-09	Cape Verde Islands	L	0-2	Nouakchott	CNq			Sillah GAM
2-10	Mali	L	1-2	Bamako	Fr	Ibrahim Ould Malha 70		
5-10	Mali	L	0-2	Bamako	Fr			
13-10	Togo	L	0-1	Lome	CNq			Kaba LBR
2003								
29-03	Kenya	L	0-4	Nairobi	CNq		30 000	Berhane ERI
31-05	Gambia	L	1-4	Banjul	Fr	Mouhamed Khouma		
6-06	Kenya	D	0-0	Nouakchott	CNq		6 000	Keita GUI
21-06	Cape Verde Islands	L	0-3	Praia	CNq			
5-07	Togo	D	0-0	Nouakchott	CNq		2 000	Djingarey NIG
12-10	Zimbabwe	L	0-3	Harare	WCq		55 000	Damon RSA
14-11	Zimbabwe	W	2-1	Nouakchott	WCq	Langlet 3, Sidibe.A 10	3 000	Keita GUI
2004								
No international matches played in 2004								
2005								
No international matches played in 2005								
2006								
No international matches played in 2006 before July								

Fr = Friendly match • CN = CAF African Cup of Nations • WC = FIFA World Cup™ • q = qualifier

MAURITANIA NATIONAL TEAM RECORDS AND RECORD SEQUENCES

Records			Sequence records					
Victory	3-0	LBR 1984	Wins	2	1983, 1995	Clean sheets	4	1994-95, 1995-96
Defeat	0-14	GUI 1972	Defeats	11	1976-1979	Goals scored	9	1979-1980
Player Caps	n/a		Undefeated	7	1994-95, 1995-96	Without goal	5	1983-1984
Player Goals	n/a		Without win	34	1995-2003	Goals against	25	1963-1979

RECENT LEAGUE AND CUP RECORD

	Championship		Cup		
Year	Champions	Winners	Score	Runners-up	
1995	ASC Sonalec	Air Mauritanie			
1996	No Tournament held	ASC Imarguens			
1997	No tournament held	ASC Sonalec	2-0	AS Garde Nationale	
1998	AS Garde Nationale	ASC Sonalec	3-2	SDPA Trarza	
1999	SDPA Rosso	ASC Police	2-1	AS Garde Nationale	
2000	ASC Mauritel	Air Mauritanie	4-0	ASC Gendrim	
2001	FC Nouadhibou	AS Garde Nationale			
2002	FC Nouadhibou	No tournament held			
2003	NASR Sebkha	ASC Entente Sebkha	1-0	ACS Ksar	
2004	ACS Ksar	FC Nouadhibou	1-0	ACS Ksar	
2005	NASR Sebkha	Entente Sebkha	2-1	ASC Socogim	
2006	ASC Mauritel	NASR Sebkha	1-0	FC Trarza Rosso	

MAURITANIA COUNTRY INFORMATION

Capital	Nouakchott	Independence	1960 from France	GDP per Capita	$1 800
Population	2 998 563	Status	Republic	GNP Ranking	154
Area km²	1 030 700	Language	Arabic, French, Pulaar	Dialling code	+222
Population density	3 per km²	Literacy rate	47%	Internet code	.mr
% in urban areas	54%	Main religion	Muslim	GMT +/−	0
Towns/Cities ('000)	Nouakchott 709; Nouadhibou 80; Kifah 68; Kayhaydi 51; Zuwarat 44; an-Na'mah 36				
Neighbours (km)	Western Sahara 1 561; Algeria 463; Mali 2 237; Senegal 813; North Atlantic 754				
Main stadia	Stade National – Nouakchott 40 000				

MWI – MALAWI

NATIONAL TEAM RECORD
JULY 1ST 2002 TO JULY 9TH 2006

PL	W	D	L	F	A	%
42	10	14	18	46	69	40.5

FIFA/COCA-COLA WORLD RANKING

1993	1994	1995	1996	1997	1998	1999	2000	2001	2002	2003	2004	2005		High	Low
67	82	89	88	97	89	114	113	120	95	105	109	106		**67** 12/93	**124** 06/01

2005–2006											
08/05	09/05	10/05	11/05	12/05	01/06	02/06	03/06	04/06	05/06	06/06	07/06
108	108	105	104	106	106	106	106	107	107	-	80

Malawi continued to set an ambitious agenda but their youthful national team flattered to deceive over the last 12 months. The central African country, known as the 'warm heart of Africa', finished last in their FIFA World Cup™ qualifying group, winning their only match in the final group encounter at home to Kenya. That 3-0 win was one of two matches under English caretaker coach Michael Hennigan, who had been recommended by the Football Association in London to go out on a short term contract to help Malawi's cause. Former international Yasin Osman stepped aside after an embarrassing home defeat by Botswana in the FIFA World Cup™ qualifier, returning to his

INTERNATIONAL HONOURS
None

post as the Secretary General of the Football Association of Malawi. The helm of the organisation was taken over by the youthful marketing executive Walter Nyamilandu, a rare example of the accession to power in an African association of a former international footballer. Immediately he sought to rid the Super League of the continual crowd violence, which has become a blight on the game in Malawi, by imposing tougher sanctions on the clubs. Big Bullets, who lost the sponsorship and patronage of the country's former president Bakili Maluzi, won a seventh successive League title while ADMARC Tigers needed a penalty shoot-out to take Cup success.

THE FIFA BIG COUNT OF 2000

	Male	Female		Male	Female
Registered players	2 704	63	Referees	10	0
Non registered players	27 000	0	Officials	1 680	0
Youth players	2 000	63	Total involved	33 520	
Total players	31 830		Number of clubs	66	
Professional players	4	0	Number of teams	105	

Football Association of Malawi (FAM)
Mpira House, Old Chileka Road, PO Box 865, Blantyre, Malawi
Tel +265 1 623197   Fax +265 1 623204
gensec@fam.mw   www.fam.mw
President: NYAMILANDU MANDA Walter   General Secretary: OSMAN Yasin
Vice-President: ANDERSON Zimba   Treasurer: TBD   Media Officer: TAKOMANA Harold
Men's Coach: ZIESE Burkhard   Women's Coach: MBOLEMBOLE Stuart
FAM formed: 1966   CAF: 1968   FIFA: 1967
Red shirts, White shorts, Red socks

RECENT INTERNATIONAL MATCHES PLAYED BY MALAWI

2002	Opponents	Score		Venue	Comp	Scorers	Att	Referee
7-07	Zimbabwe	W	3-2	Blantyre	Fr	Kanyenda [13p], Maduka [37], Nundwe [51]	35 000	Kafatiya MWI
8-07	Zimbabwe	D	2-2	Lilongwe	Fr	Kondowe [28], Nkhwazi [87]	20 000	
10-08	Zambia	W	1-0	Blantyre	CCsf	Kanyenda [66p]	60 000	Phomane LES
21-09	South Africa	L	1-3	Blantyre	CCf	Mabedi [44p]	60 000	Shikapande ZAM
28-09	South Africa	L	0-1	Durban	CCf		20 000	Mususa ZIM
12-10	Angola	W	1-0	Lilongwe	CNq	Mwafulirwa [87]	40 000	Tangawarima ZIM
2003								
22-02	Congo DR	D	1-1	Blantyre	Fr			
23-02	Congo DR	L	2-3	Lilongwe	Fr			
16-03	Zimbabwe	D	0-0	Harare	Fr		10 000	Bwanya ZIM
29-03	Nigeria	L	0-1	Blantyre	CNq		60 000	Nkole ZAM
17-05	Zambia	L	0-1	Blantyre	Fr			Lwanja MWI
21-05	Lesotho	D	0-0	Maseru	Fr			
25-05	Botswana	D	1-1	Gaborone	CCqf	Chavula [86]. W 3-1p	25 000	Infante MOZ
7-06	Nigeria	L	1-4	Lagos	CNq	Kanyenda [7]		Ndoye SEN
6-07	Angola	L	1-5	Luanda	CNq	Mgangira [78]	10 000	
16-08	Zambia	D	1-1	Blantyre	CCsf	Mwafulirwa [35]		Mnkantjo ZIM
27-09	Zimbabwe	L	1-2	Blantyre	CCf	Mwafulirwa [83]	60 000	Bennett RSA
5-10	Zimbabwe	L	0-2	Harare	CCf		25 000	Nkole ZAM
12-10	Ethiopia	W	3-1	Addis Abeba	WCq	Kanyenda 2 [39 55], Mgangira [88]	20 000	Abd El Fatah EGY
15-11	Ethiopia	D	0-0	Lilongwe	WCq		20 000	Abdel Rahman SUD
2004								
22-05	Zambia	W	2-0	Kitwe	Fr	Mwakasungula [15], Munthali [70]	20 000	Nkole ZAM
5-06	Morocco	D	1-1	Blantyre	WCq	Munthali [35]	30 040	Mususa ZIM
13-06	Mozambique	L	0-2	Maputo	CCqf		30 000	Kaoma ZAM
19-06	Botswana	L	0-2	Gaborone	WCq		15 000	Awuye UGA
3-07	Guinea	D	1-1	Lilongwe	WCq	Mpinganjira [71]	11 383	Abdulkadir TAN
6-07	Swaziland	L	1-2	Blantyre	Fr			
8-07	Swaziland	D	1-1	Lilongwe	Fr			
4-09	Kenya	L	2-3	Nairobi	WCq	Munthali [41], Mabedi [90p]	13 000	Mwanza ZAM
9-10	Tunisia	D	2-2	Blantyre	WCq	Mwafulirwa [19], Chipatala [37]	20 000	Awuye UGA
2005								
27-02	Zimbabwe	W	2-1	Blantyre	Fr	Tambala [45], Phiri.V [51]		
26-03	Tunisia	L	0-7	Tunis	WCq		30 000	Abdel Rahman SUD
27-05	Libya	D	1-1	Tripoli	Fr			
4-06	Morocco	L	1-4	Rabat	WCq	Chipatala [10]	48 000	Buenkadila COD
11-06	Lesotho	W	2-1	Lusaka	CCr1	Chitsulo [54], Zakazaka [73]		Mpanisi ZAM
12-06	Zambia	L	1-2	Lusaka	CCr1	Maduka [55]		Nhlapo RSA
18-06	Botswana	L	1-3	Blantyre	WCq	Mwafulirwa [48]	20 000	Gabonamong BOT
4-09	Guinea	L	1-3	Conakry	WCq	Mkandwire [36]	2 518	Mana NGA
8-10	Kenya	W	3-0	Blantyre	WCq	Zakazaka [6], Mkandawire 2 [49 61]	12 000	Codjia BEN
2006								
24-06	Zimbabwe	D	1-1	Maputo	Fr	Chipatala [6]. W 2-1p		
25-06	Mozambique	W	2-1	Maputo	Fr	Wadabwa [29], Kamwendo		
6-07	Botswana	W	2-1	Lilongwe	Fr	Zakazaka [57], Wadabwa [49]		
8-07	Botswana	D	0-0	Blantyre	Fr	L 2-3p		

Fr = Friendly match • CN = CAF African Cup of Nations • CC = COSAFA Cup • WC = FIFA World Cup™
q = qualifier • r1 = first round group • qf = quarter-final • sf = semi-final • f = final

MALAWI NATIONAL TEAM RECORDS AND RECORD SEQUENCES

Records			Sequence records					
Victory	8-1	BOT 1968	Wins	8	1984	Clean sheets	5	1989
Defeat	0-7	ZAM 1969, TUN 2005	Defeats	9	1962-1968	Goals scored	13	1986-1987
Player Caps	n/a		Undefeated	15	1989-1990	Without goal	5	Three times
Player Goals	n/a		Without win	14	1998-2000	Goals against	18	1971-1975

MALAWI COUNTRY INFORMATION

Capital	Lilongwe	Independence	1964 from the UK	GDP per Capita	$600
Population	11 906 855	Status	Republic	GNP Ranking	
Area km²	118 480	Language	English, Chichewa	Dialling code	+265
Population density	100 per km²	Literacy rate	62%	Internet code	.mw
% in urban areas	14%	Main religion	Christian 75%, Muslim 20%	GMT + / –	+2
Towns/Cities ('000)	Lilongwe 647; Blantyre 585; Mzuzu 128; Zomba 81; Kasungu 42; Mangochi 40; Karonga 34				
Neighbours (km)	Mozambique 1 569; Zambia 837; Tanzania 475				
Main stadia	Chichiri – Blantyre 60 000; Chivo – Lilongwe 40 000				

MALAWI 2005 SUPER LEAGUE

	Pl	W	D	L	F	A	Pts
Big Bullets	26	16	7	3	44	13	55
MTL Wanderers	26	16	6	4	48	18	54
Silver Strikers	26	15	8	3	52	23	53
CIVO United	26	15	7	4	39	16	52
ADMARC Tigers	26	10	8	8	37	28	38
Blue Eagles	26	9	10	7	25	21	37
Super ESCOM	26	9	8	9	33	31	35
Dwangwa United	25	8	7	10	31	38	31
Red Lions	26	8	7	11	24	31	31
Cobbe Barracks	26	8	3	15	28	51	27
Sammy's United	26	5	9	12	26	43	24
Moyale Barracks	26	5	7	14	28	47	22
KRADD Eagles	26	4	6	16	19	46	18
MAFCO	25	2	7	16	23	51	13

19/02/2005 - 18/12/2005

FAM CUP 2005

Quarter-finals			Semi-finals			Final		
ADMARC Tigers	2	2						
Silver Strikers	2	0	ADMARC Tigers	1	3p			
Blue Eagles	1		Big Bullets	1	1p			
Big Bullets	2					ADMARC Tigers	1	5p
CIVO United †	3					MTL Wanderers	1	4p
Dwangwa Utd	2		CIVO United	0		12-11-2005		
Red Lions	0		MTL Wanderers	1		Scorers - Chisomo Ngowe for ADMARC;		
MTL Wanderers	1		† Dwangwa walked off			Joel Chipofya for MTL		

RECENT LEAGUE AND CUP RECORD

	Championship							Cup		
Year	Champions	Pts	Runners-up	Pts	Third	Pts		Winners	Score	Runners-up
1996	Telecom Wanderers									
1997	Telecom Wanderers									
1998	Telecom Wanderers									
1999	Bata Bullets	62	Telecom Wanderers	60	Red Lions	44		Bata Bullets	3-0	MDC United
2000	Bata Bullets	44	MDC United	41	Silver Strikers	40		Telecom Wanderers	2-1	Bata Bullets
2001	Total Big Bullets	69	MTL Wanderers	66	MDC United	44		Moyale Barracks	1-0	Super ESCOM
2002	Total Big Bullets	62	Silver Strikers	50	MDC United	45		Total Big Bullets	1-0	MTL Wanderers
2003	Bakili Bullets	70	MTL Wanderers	69	MDC United	60		Final between Wanderers and Bullets abandoned		
2004	Bakili Bullets		MTL Wanderers		Silver Strikers			No competition		
2005	Big Bullets	55	MTL Wanderers	54	Silver Strikers	53		ADMARC Tigers	1-1 5-4p	MTL Wanderers

Bakili Bullets previously known as Bata Bullets and Total Big Bullets • MTL Wanderers previously known as Limbe Leaf Wanderers and Telecom Wanderers

MYA - MYANMAR

NATIONAL TEAM RECORD
JULY 1ST 2002 TO JULY 9TH 2006

PL	W	D	L	F	A	%
24	8	3	13	39	47	39.6

FIFA/COCA-COLA WORLD RANKING

1993	1994	1995	1996	1997	1998	1999	2000	2001	2002	2003	2004	2005		High		Low
110	124	115	104	114	115	126	124	151	162	140	144	147		**97** 04/96	**163**	07/06

2005–2006										
08/05	09/05	10/05	11/05	12/05	01/06	02/06	03/06	04/06	05/06	06/06	07/06
144	141	141	142	147	148	148	148	149	149	163	

Finance and Revenue landed yet another championship trophy to add to their growing collection when they won the 2005-06 Premier League, and they won it in some style. In a short 15 game tournament, they and the Ministry of Commerce, the Ministry of Energy and the Ministry of Transport were a cut above the rest. Despite winning their first 12 matches in the 16 team league, Finance and Revenue were doggedly pursued by Commerce who went unbeaten in their first 12 games. Both lost just once, Commerce against Construction and Finance, and Revenue on the last weekend - against Commerce. Aside from the Premier League there are a number of other

INTERNATIONAL HONOURS

Asian Games 1966 1970   **SEA Games** 1965 1967 1969 1971   **AFC Youth Championship** 1961 1963 1964 1966 1968 1969 1970

competitions played through the year the most notable of which is the State and Division League for regional combinations. The 2006 title was won by Ayeyarwady Division who beat Shan South State 5-3 on penalties after the final ended in a 1-1 draw. The Premier League also operates a pre-season and a post-season tournament with the former won by Kanbawza, who beat Finance and Revenue 2-0 in the final, and the latter by the Ministry of Energy, 2-1 victors over YC Development Committee. On the international scene the national team have not played since the 2004 Tiger Cup, whilst the women's team qualified for the AFC Women's Championship.

THE FIFA BIG COUNT OF 2000

	Male	Female		Male	Female
Registered players	79 500	2 000	Referees	188	18
Non registered players	180 000	3 500	Officials	2 500	100
Youth players	10 000	1 200	Total involved	279 006	
Total players	276 200		Number of clubs	573	
Professional players	0	0	Number of teams	3 620	

Myanmar Football Federation (MFF)
National Football Training Centre, Thuwunna Thingankyun, Township, Yangon, Myanmar
Tel +951 577366   Fax +951 570000
mff@myanmar.com.mm   www.myanmarfootball.org
President: ZAW Zaw   General Secretary: AUNG Tin
Vice-President: NAING Zaw Win   Treasurer: ZAW Than   Media Officer: OO Tin Tun
Men's Coach: KOLEV Ivan   Women's Coach: AYE Maung
MFF formed: 1947   AFC: 1954   FIFA: 1957
Red shirts, White shorts, Red socks

RECENT INTERNATIONAL MATCHES PLAYED BY MYANMAR

2003	Opponents		Score	Venue	Comp	Scorers	Att	Referee
23-03	Brunei Darussalam	W	5-0	Malé	ACq	Win Htike [10], Aung Kyaw Moe [14], Yan Paing 2 [45 66] Lwin Oo [75]		
25-03	Maldives	W	2-0	Malé	ACq	Win Htike [52], Zaw Zaw [65]		
8-10	Malaysia	L	0-4	Kuala Lumpur	ACq		4 500	Yang Zhiqiang CHN
10-10	Bahrain	L	1-3	Kuala Lumpur	ACq	Soe Myat Min [77]	500	Naglingham SIN
12-10	Iraq	L	0-3	Kuala Lumpur	ACq		500	Yang Zhiqiang CHN
20-10	Bahrain	L	0-4	Manama	ACq		15 000	Al Harrassi OMA
22-10	Iraq	L	1-3	Manama	ACq	Zaw Zaw [45]	300	Yasrebi IRN
24-10	Malaysia	W	2-1	Isa Town	ACq	Soe Myat Min [25], Fadzli OG [43]	200	Al Harrassi OMA
2004								
17-03	China PR	L	0-2	Guangzhou	Fr			
20-08	Vietnam	L	0-5	Ho Chi Minh	Fr			
22-08	India	L	1-2	Ho Chi Minh	Fr	Win Nawng [81]		
27-11	Singapore	L	0-1	Singapore	Fr			
2-12	Hong Kong	D	2-2	Singapore	Fr	Yan Paing 2 [28 84]		
8-12	Philippines	W	1-0	Kuala Lumpur	TCr1	San Day Thien [92+]	1 000	Vo Minh Tri VIE
10-12	Thailand	D	1-1	Kuala Lumpur	TCr1	Zaw Lynn Tun [89]		Moradi IRN
12-12	Malaysia	W	1-0	Kuala Lumpur	TCr1	Soe Myat Min [20]	10 000	Hsu Chao Lo TPE
16-12	East Timor †	W	3-1	Kuala Lumpur	TCr1	Soe Myat Min [4], San Day Thien [43], Myo Hlaing Win [51]	1 000	Hsu Chao Lo TPE
29-12	Singapore	L	3-4	Kuala Lumpur	TCsf	Soe Myat Min 2 [34 90], Min Thu [36]	12 000	Rungklay THA
2005								
2-01	Singapore	L	2-4	Singapore	TCsf	Soe Myat Min [15], Aung Kyaw Moe [50]	30 000	Kamikawa JPN
15-01	Malaysia	L	1-2	Singapore	TC3p	Soe Myat Min [52]	2 000	Vo Minh Tri VIE
2006								

No international matches played in 2006 before July

Fr = Friendly match • TC = Tiger Cup • AC = AFC Asian Cup
q = qualifier • r1 = 1st round • sf = semi-final • 3p = 3rd place play-off • † Not a full international

MYANMAR NATIONAL TEAM RECORDS AND RECORD SEQUENCES

Records			Sequence records					
Victory	9-0	SIN 1969	Wins	8	1971-1972	Clean sheets	7	1966-1967
Defeat	1-9	MAS 1977	Defeats	7	1957-1961	Goals scored	14	1964-1966
Player Caps	n/a		Undefeated	14	1970-1971	Without goal	4	1987-1991
Player Goals	n/a		Without win	9	1987-1993	Goals against	11	2003-2004

MYANMAR RECENT LEAGUE RECORD

Championship		Interstate Championship		
Year	Champions	Winners	Score	Runners-up
2002	Finance & Revenue Yangon	Mandalay		Sagaing
2003	Finance & Revenue Yangon	Shan State	2-0	Kayin State
2004	Finance & Revenue Yangon			
2005	Finance & Revenue Yangon			
2006	Finance & Revenue Yangon	Ayeyrwady	1-1 5-3p	Shan State

MYANMAR COUNTRY INFORMATION

Capital	Yangon (Rangoon)	Independence	1948 from the UK	GDP per Capita	$1 800
Population	42 720 196	Status	Republic	GNP Ranking	52
Area km²	678 500	Language	Burmese	Dialling code	+95
Population density	63 per km²	Literacy rate	85%	Internet code	.mm
% in urban areas	29%	Main religion	Buddhist 90%	GMT +/–	+6.5
Towns/Cities ('000)	Yangon 4 477; Mandalay 1 208; Mawlamyine 439; Bago 244; Pathein 237; Monywa 182				
Neighbours (km)	China 2 185; Laos 235; Thailand 1 800; Bangladesh 193; India 1 463; Indian Ocean 1 930				
Main stadia	Bogyoke Aung San – Yangon 40 000; Thuwanna YTC – Yangon 30 000				

NAM – NAMIBIA

NATIONAL TEAM RECORD
JULY 1ST 2002 TO JULY 9TH 2006

PL	W	D	L	F	A	%
13	2	3	8	8	19	26.9

FIFA/COCA-COLA WORLD RANKING

1993	1994	1995	1996	1997	1998	1999	2000	2001	2002	2003	2004	2005	High	Low
156	123	116	103	86	69	80	87	101	123	144	158	161	**68** 11/98	**161** 07/94

2005–2006											
08/05	09/05	10/05	11/05	12/05	01/06	02/06	03/06	04/06	05/06	06/06	07/06
159	159	160	160	161	161	161	161	163	164	-	167

Namibia continued to plummet down the FIFA/Coca-Cola World Ranking, moving down almost 100 places from the high of 68 they reached when they participated at the 1998 African Nations Cup finals. The Brave Warriors, eliminated in the preliminary round of the qualifiers for the 2006 FIFA World Cup™ finals in November 2003, suffered from a lack of competition and without a coach for almost a year were left kicking their heels in self-imposed isolation. In May 2006 they moved to restart their national side with the appointment of Ben Bamfuchile as their new national coach. The former Zambian international has signed four year contract and been handed the exacting

INTERNATIONAL HONOURS
None

task of reviving football in the arid southern African nation. Namibia continue to produce talent but the best players are quickly whisked out of the country with the likes of Collin Benjamin (Hamburg) and Razundura Tjikuzu (Duisburg) competing in the Bundesliga. Domestic potential was displayed at the start of 2006 when champions Civics caused a major upset by beating the Angolan champions Sagrada Esperance in the first round of the CAF Champions League, winning the first leg 4-0 in Windhoek. Civics, who are based in the capital, have emerged as the dominant force in Namibian football with a runway annexation of the championship.

THE FIFA BIG COUNT OF 2000

	Male	Female		Male	Female
Registered players	4 000	0	Referees	100	0
Non registered players	8 000	0	Officials	600	0
Youth players	2 000	0	Total involved	14 700	
Total players		14 000	Number of clubs	50	
Professional players	0	0	Number of teams	200	

Namibia Football Association (NFA)
Richard Kamumuka Street, Soccer House, Katutura, PO Box 1345, Windhoek 9000, Namibia
Tel +264 61 265691   Fax +264 61 265693
nfass@iafrica.com.na   www.none
President: DAMASEB Petrus   General Secretary: GAWESEB Alpheus
Vice-President: MUINJO John   Treasurer: RIJATUA Tjeripo   Media Officer: BEU Kauta
Men's Coach: BAMFUCHILE Ben   Women's Coach: FREYER Gabriel
NFA formed: 1990   CAF: 1990   FIFA: 1992
Red shirts, Red shorts, Red socks

RECENT INTERNATIONAL MATCHES PLAYED BY NAMIBIA

2002	Opponents	Score		Venue	Comp	Scorers	Att	Referee
7-09	Algeria	L	0-1	Windhoek	CNq		13 000	Tangawarima ZIM
2003								
16-03	Botswana	L	0-1	Windhoek	CCr1			Kakudze SWA
30-03	Chad	L	0-2	N'Djamena	CNq			Dimanche CTA
7-06	Chad	W	2-1	Windhoek	CNq	Diergaardt 24, Hummel 76p	5 000	Bernardo Colembi ANG
20-06	Algeria	L	0-1	Blida	CNq		30 000	Auda EGY
7-09	Angola	L	0-2	Luanda	Fr		5 000	Antonio De Sousa ANG
20-09	Angola	L	1-3	Windhoek	Fr	Hindjou 4		
12-10	Rwanda	L	0-3	Kigali	WCq		22 000	Abdulkadir TAN
15-11	Rwanda	D	1-1	Windhoek	WCq	Shipanga 39	9 000	Mbera GAB
2004								
28-04	Botswana	D	0-0	Windhoek	Fr		1 500	
9-05	Angola	L	1-2	Luanda	CCr1	Petrus 70	4 000	Ngcamphalala SWA
2005								
19-03	Lesotho	W	2-1	Maseru	Fr	Guriras, Malgas		
16-04	Botswana	D	1-1	Windhoek	CCr1	Botes 35. L 4-5p		Sentso LES
2006								

No international matches played in 2006 before July

Fr = Friendly match • CN = CAF African Cup of Nations • CC = COSAFA Cup • WC = FIFA World Cup™ • q = qualifier • r1 = first round group

NAMIBIA NATIONAL TEAM RECORDS AND RECORD SEQUENCES

Records			Sequence records					
Victory	8-2	BEN 2000	Wins	3	1997	Clean sheets	3	1995-1996, 1996
Defeat	2-8	EGY 2001	Defeats	7	2001-03	Goals scored	15	1997-1998
Player Caps	n/a		Undefeated	8	1995-1996	Without goal	5	1992-1993, 2001
Player Goals	n/a		Without win	8	1998	Goals against	25	1997-1998

CLUB DIRECTORY

Club	Town/City	Lge	Cup
Benfica	Tsumeb	1	0
Black Africans	Windhoek	5	3
Blue Waters	Walvis Bay	4	1
Chief Santos	Tsumeb	2	4
Civics	Windhoek	2	1
Eleven Arrows	Walvis Bay	1	0
Orlando Pirates	Walvis Bay	1	1
Ramblers	Windhoek	1	1
Tigers	Windhoek	0	2

NAMIBIA COUNTRY INFORMATION

Capital	Windhoek	Independence	1990 from South Africa	GDP per Capita	$7 200
Population	1 954 033	Status	Republic	GNP Ranking	125
Area km²	825 415	Language	English, Afrikaans, Oshivambo	Dialling code	+264
Population density	2 per km²	Literacy rate	84%	Internet code	.na
% in urban areas	37%	Main religion	Christian 80%	GMT +/–	+2
Towns/Cities ('000)	Windhoek 268; Rundu 58; Walvis Bay 52; Oshakati 34; Swakopmund 25; Katima Mulilo 25				
Neighbours (km)	Angola 1 376; Zambia 233; Botswana 1 360; South Africa 967; South Atlantic 1 572				
Main stadia	Independence Stadium – Windhoek 25 000				

NAMIBIA 2005-06 PREMIER LEAGUE

	Pl	W	D	L	F	A	Pts
Civics †	22	16	5	1	55	19	53
Ramblers	22	14	2	6	51	30	44
Blue Waters	22	11	7	4	36	20	40
Orlando Pirates	22	8	7	7	35	29	31
Black Africa	22	8	6	8	33	29	30
Eleven Arrows	22	9	2	11	44	45	29
United Africa Tigers	22	8	4	10	39	35	28
Oshakati City	22	7	7	8	32	40	28
African Stars	22	5	11	6	25	27	26
SK Windhoek	22	6	5	11	26	44	23
Chief Santos	22	4	6	12	31	42	18
Touch and Go	22	4	2	16	27	74	14

12/11/2005 - 27/05/2006 • † Qualified for the CAF Champions League

MTL NFA CUP 2005-06

Round of 16		Quarter-finals		Semi-finals †		Final	
Orlando Pirates	5						
Deportivo Aaves	2	Orlando Pirates	1 5p				
Golden Bees	0	Civics	1 4p				
Civics	3			Orlando Pirates	1 4p		
Chief Santos	6			Ramblers	1 2p		
United Stars	1	Chief Santos	1				
African Stars	1	Ramblers	2			Orlando Pirates	1
Ramblers	2					SK Windhoek	0
Oshakati City	5						
Touch and Go	4	Oshakati City	2				
Black Africa	0 4p	Blue Waters	0				
Blue Waters	0 5p			Oshakati City	0 1p		
Eleven Arrows	6			SK Windhoek	0 3p		
Arsenal	0	Eleven Arrows	0				
United Africa Tigers	0 3p	SK Windhoek	1				
SK Windhoek	0 4p						

† Semi-finals played in Walvis Bay
‡ Qualified for the CAF Confederation Cup

CUP FINAL
Windhoek
4-06-2006
Scorer - Etienne Beukes [106] for Pirates

RECENT LEAGUE AND CUP RECORD

	Championship						Cup		
Year	Champions	Pts	Runners-up	Pts	Third	Pts	Winners	Score	Runners-up
1998	Black Africans	46	Civics	39	Chief Santos	37	Chief Santos	1-0	Tigers
1999	Black Africans	56	Life Fighters	43	Blue Waters	40	Chief Santos	1-0	Tigers
2000	Blue Waters	54	Black Africans	45	Nashua Young Ones	40	Chief Santos	4-2	Life Fighters
2001	No Championship due to season readjustment						Not held due to season readjustment		
2002	Liverpool	57	Blue Waters	56	Chief Santos	56	Orlando Pirates	2-1	Tigers
2003	Chief Santos						Civics	4-2	Tigers
2004	Blue Waters	72	Civics	69	Orlando Pirates	62	Black Africans	2-0	Life Fighters
2005	Civics	71	Blue Waters	69	Ramblers	61	Ramblers	2-2 5-4p	Black Africa
2006	Civics	53	Ramblers	44	Blue Waters	40	Orlando Pirates	1-0	SK Windhoek

NCA – NICARAGUA

NATIONAL TEAM RECORD
JULY 1ST 2002 TO JULY 9TH 2006

PL	W	D	L	F	A	%
18	5	3	10	15	38	36.1

FIFA/COCA-COLA WORLD RANKING

1993	1994	1995	1996	1997	1998	1999	2000	2001	2002	2003	2004	2005	High	Low
155	168	174	179	182	188	193	191	188	186	173	158	152	150 08/93	193 05/01

2005–2006											
08/05	09/05	10/05	11/05	12/05	01/06	02/06	03/06	04/06	05/06	06/06	07/06
156	156	156	154	152	153	153	153	156	157	-	161

The Nicaraguan women's team was the only senior national team that saw action in the past year when they entered the FIFA Women's World Cup for the first time. They were drawn in a qualifying group played in Mexico and after a 9-0 defeat at the hands of their hosts they did beat El Salvador 2-1 to salvage some pride. The only men's international action during the season saw 2005 champions Diriangén enter the CONCACAF Champions' Cup. Against Suchitepéquez in the first round of the Central American qualifiers, they did the hard work by drawing 2-2 in Guatemala, but then lost the return in Diriamba. Championship runners-up Parmalat had also qualified but ceased

INTERNATIONAL HONOURS
None

to exist thanks to the bankruptcy of their parent company, the Italian food giant Parmalat. Diriangén were once again the team to beat in the Primera Division. After experimenting with two champions a year between 2003 and 2005 there is now a play-off between the winners of the Apertura and the Clausura. After winning the former, Diriangén came within a whisker of winning both but lost in the Clausura final against Real Estelí. That meant two more games between the two and this time Diriangén made no mistake, although an Real Estelí injury time winner in the second leg meant the championship was won on goal difference.

THE FIFA BIG COUNT OF 2000

	Male	Female		Male	Female
Registered players	10 000	600	Referees	1 197	15
Non registered players	50 000	1 000	Officials	1 500	100
Youth players	25 480	1 400	Total involved	91 292	
Total players	88 480		Number of clubs	200	
Professional players	0	0	Number of teams	1 879	

Federación Nicaragüense de Fútbol (FENIFUT)
Hospital Bautista 1, Cuadra abajo, 1 cuadra al Sur y 1/2 cuadra abajo, Managua 976, Nicaragua
Tel +505 2227035   Fax +505 2227885
fenifut@tmx.com.ni   www.fenifut.org.ni
President: ROCHA LOPEZ Julio   General Secretary: LOPEZ SANDERS Rolando
Vice-President: QUINTANILLA Manuel   Treasurer: TBD   Media Officer: ROSALES Marlon
Men's Coach: CRUZ Mauricio   Women's Coach: URROZ Edward
FENIFUT formed: 1931   CONCACAF: 1968   FIFA: 1950
Blue shirts, White shorts, Blue socks

RECENT INTERNATIONAL MATCHES PLAYED BY NICARAGUA

2002	Opponents		Score	Venue	Comp	Scorers	Att	Referee
17-11	Cayman Islands	W	1-0	Grand Cayman	Fr			
2003								
11-02	Honduras	L	0-2	Panama City	GCq			Aguilar SLV
13-02	El Salvador	L	0-3	Panama City	GCq			Moreno PAN
15-02	Costa Rica	L	0-1	Colon	GCq			Aguilar SLV
18-02	Guatemala	L	0-5	Panama City	GCq		5 000	Moreno PAN
21-02	Panama	W	1-0	Panama City	GCq	Palacios [83]		Aguilar SLV
2004								
31-01	Haiti	D	1-1	West Palm Beach	Fr	Palacios [41]	53	
29-02	Haiti	D	1-1	Esteli	Fr	Calero [58]		
31-03	Bermuda	L	0-3	Hamilton	Fr			Crockwell BER
2-04	Bermuda	L	1-2	Hamilton	Fr	Palacios [72p]		Raynor BER
30-04	Bermuda	W	2-0	Diriamba	Fr	Solorzano [4], Palacios [30]	800	
2-05	Bermuda	W	2-0	Esteli	Fr	Rocha [8], Palacios [46]	4 000	Reyes NCA
4-06	Costa Rica	L	1-5	San Carlos	Fr	Lopez.F [1]	BCD	
13-06	St Vincent/Grenadines	D	2-2	Diriamba	WCq	Palacios [37], Calero [79]	7 500	Delgado CUB
20-06	St Vincent/Grenadines	L	1-4	Kingstown	WCq	Palacios [60]	5 000	Brohim DMA
2005								
19-02	Honduras	L	1-5	Guatemala City	GCq	Bustos [54]	5 306	Moreno PAN
21-02	Guatemala	L	0-4	Guatemala City	GCq		8 000	Sibrian SLV
23-02	Belize	W	1-0	Guatemala City	GCq	Vilchez [85]	3 000	Quesada CRC
2006								

No international matches played in 2006 before July

Fr = Friendly match • GC = CONCACAF Gold Cup • WC = FIFA World Cup™ • q = qualifier • BCD = behind closed doors

NICARAGUA NATIONAL TEAM RECORDS AND RECORD SEQUENCES

Records			Sequence records					
Victory	3-1	PAN 1967	Wins	2	2004	Clean sheets	2	2004
Defeat	1-11	ANT 1950	Defeats	25	1986-2001	Goals scored	7	2004-2005
Player Caps	n/a		Undefeated	3	2003-2004	Without goal	8	1999-2001
Player Goals	n/a		Without win	33	1975-2001	Goals against	55	1966-2002

NICARAGUA COUNTRY INFORMATION

Capital	Managua	Independence	1838 from Spain	GDP per Capita	$2 300
Population	5 359 759	Status	Republic	GNP Ranking	140
Area km²	129 494	Language	Spanish	Dialling code	+505
Population density	41 per km²	Literacy rate	67%	Internet code	.ni
% in urban areas	63%	Main religion	Christian 85%	GMT + / –	-6
Towns/Cities ('000)	Managua 1 140; Léon 150; Chinandega 128; Masaya 123; Granada 92; Estelí 92; Tipitapa 89				
Neighbours (km)	Costa Rica 309; Honduras 922; Caribbean Sea & Pacific Ocean 910				
Main stadia	Estadio Dennis Martinez – Managua 30 000; Cacique Diriangen – Diriamba				

NICARAGUA 2005-06

PRIMERA DIVISION TORNEO APERTURA

	Pl	W	D	L	F	A	Pts	Real Estelí	Diriangén	D Masatepe	Scorpión	Walter Fer.	América	Dep. Jalapa	Real Madriz	Bluefields	At. Estelí
Real Estelí †	18	14	3	1	39	5	45		2-1	1-0	3-0	0-0	1-0	3-0	4-1	5-0	4-0
Diriangén †	18	12	3	3	40	15	39	0-0		1-0	3-1	4-1	3-0	2-2	1-0	8-1	0-0
Deportivo Masatepe †	18	10	3	5	28	16	33	0-3	2-1		2-2	2-0	1-1	2-1	0-0	5-0	2-0
Scorpión †	18	9	4	5	31	24	31	1-3	3-0	1-0		1-1	0-2	4-1	1-0	3-0	2-2
Dep. Walter Ferreti	18	8	3	7	24	31	27	0-2	0-4	2-1	2-3		1-0	4-0	2-2	3-2	2-1
América	18	6	5	7	23	20	23	0-1	1-2	1-2	2-3	5-1		1-0	1-0	0-0	3-1
Deportivo Jalapa	18	6	3	9	25	29	21	1-0	1-3	0-1	0-0	0-1	2-2		2-0	**3-0**	2-0
Real Madriz	18	3	6	9	20	25	15	1-1	0-2	0-2	1-2	2-0	0-0	1-3		0-0	5-0
Deportivo Bluefields	18	2	5	11	18	51	11	0-3	1-2	2-5	0-3	0-1	1-1	5-4	2-2		2-2
Atlético Estelí	18	1	3	14	14	46	6	0-3	0-3	0-1	2-1	2-3	1-3	0-3	2-5	1-2	

23/07/2005 - 20/11/2005 • † Qualified for the Apertura play-offs • Match in bold was awarded 3-0

NICARAGUA 2005-06

PRIMERA DIVISION TORNEO CLAUSURA

	Pl	W	D	L	F	A	Pts	Diriangén	Scorpión	Real Estelí	Bluefields	D Masatepe	América	Walter Fer.	Dep. Jalapa	At. Estelí	Real Madriz
Diriangén †	9	6	1	2	21	12	19		2-1				2-1	3-1		5-1	1-0
Scorpión †	9	5	3	1	24	15	18	4-2					5-1	2-2		4-0	3-2
Real Estelí †	9	4	4	1	12	7	16		1-1			0-0		2-1	2-1	3-0	
Deportivo Bluefields †	9	3	5	1	18	16	14	3-3	2-2					2-1	2-2	**3-0**	
Deportivo Masatepe †	9	3	4	2	24	18	13			1-1	4-4			5-2	3-0	5-0	
América †	9	3	3	3	16	15	12			1-2	1-2	3-3			2-1		
Dep. Walter Ferreti	9	2	2	5	10	14	8	1-0	1-2				1-1				0-0
Deportivo Jalapa	9	2	2	5	11	17	8	0-3	4-1				1-3				1-0
Atlético Estelí	9	2	1	6	6	25	7			0-3				1-0	1-1		3-1
Real Madriz	9	1	3	5	8	11	6			0-0	3-0	1-1	1-2				

8/01/2006 - 5/03/2006 • † Qualified for the Clausura Hexagonal • Match in bold was awarded 3-0

APERTURA PLAY-OFFS

Semi-finals			Finals		
Diriangén	0	1			
Dep Masatepe	0	0	Diriangén	0 1 4p	
Scorpión	0	2	Real Estelí	0 1 3p	
Real Estelí	2	1	11/12/2005 & 18/12/2005		

CLAUSURA PLAY-OFFS

Semi-finals			Finals		
Real Estelí	4	1			
América	2	0	Real Estelí	2 3	
Dep Masatepe	0	2	Diriangén	1 2	
Diriangén	2	1	7/05/2006 & 14/05/2006		

CHAMPIONSHIP FINAL

First leg, Estelí, 21-05-2006
Real Estelí 1 López 62
Diriangen 2 Sánchez 16, Mendieta 72
Second leg, Diriamba, 28-05-2006
Diriangén 0
Real Estelí 1 Calero 93+
Diriangén are 2006 champions on away goals

CLAUSURA HEXAGONAL

	Pl	W	D	L	F	A	Pts	RE	Di	DM	Am	Sc	DB
Real Estelí †	5	4	1	0	11	2	13		0-0	2-0			4-1
Diriangén †	5	2	3	0	8	4	9				2-1	1-1	3-0
Deportivo Masatepe †	5	2	1	2	13	9	7	2-2				2-3	6-1
América †	5	2	1	2	7	9	7	0-3				1-1	
Scorpión	5	1	2	2	6	8	5	1-2		1-3			2-1
Deportivo Bluefields	5	0	0	5	4	17	0				1-2		

12/03/2006 - 12/04/2006 • † Qualified for the Clausura play-offs

RECENT LEAGUE RECORD

Championship/Clausura 2004-2005				Apertura		
Year	Champions	Score	Runners-up	Winners	Score	Runners-up
1999	Real Estelí	0-0 3-1p	Diriangén			
2000	Diriangén	1-0	Deportivo Walter Ferreti			
2001	Deportivo Walter Ferreti	0-0 0-0 5-3p	Diriangén			
2002	Deportivo Jalapa	1-1 4-0	Deportivo Walter Ferreti			
2003	Real Estelí	0-1 3-0	Diriangén			
2004	Real Estelí	1-0 0-0	Diriangén			
2005	Diriangén	1-0 0-1 3-2p	Parmalat	Real Estelí	0-0 1-0	Diriangén
2006	Diriangén	2-1 0-1	Real Estelí	Diriangén	0-0 1-0	Real Estelí

NCL – NEW CALEDONIA

NEW CALEDONIA NATIONAL TEAM RECORD
JULY 1ST 2002 TO JULY 9TH 2006

PL	W	D	L	F	A	%
12	5	2	5	28	19	50

FIFA/COCA-COLA WORLD RANKING

1993	1994	1995	1996	1997	1998	1999	2000	2001	2002	2003	2004	2005	High	Low
-	-	-	-	-	-	-	-	-	-	-	186	187	**185** 07/05	**185** 06/05

					2005–2006						
08/05	09/05	10/05	11/05	12/05	01/06	02/06	03/06	04/06	05/06	06/06	07/06
185	185	186	185	187	187	187	187	188	188	-	171

New Caledonia are no longer FIFA's newest member following the admission of Timor-Leste and Comoros at the 2005 FIFA Congress in Marrakech and already the country is beginning to make its mark in the Oceania Football Confederation. 2005 champions AS Magenta Nouméa entered the OFC Club Championship for the second year running and although they couldn't match the extraordinary results of the previous year when they were just one game away from qualifying for the FIFA Club World Championship in Tokyo, they were involved in a close first round group and were just one point behind Fiji's Nokia Eagles who qualified for the semi-finals. Magenta also

INTERNATIONAL HONOURS
None

qualified for the annual Coupe des Clubs Champions d'Outre Mer in 2005 although they didn't win either of the two matches played at the finals in France. Magenta's supremacy at home was challenged in the 2005-06 season by AS Mont-Doré. Having become used to finishing runners up to Magenta in recent seasons, Mont-Doré finally won the division d'honneur for the first time after finishing seven points clear of JS Baco, another team very familiar with the runners-up spot. The Cup Final also saw Mont-Doré face Baco, but despite scoring an injury time equaliser, Baco lost in extra-time to a Wakanumune goal and had to settle for yet another runners-up spot.

THE FIFA BIG COUNT OF 2000

	Male	Female		Male	Female
Registered players	n/a	n/a	Referees	n/a	n/a
Non registered players	n/a	n/a	Officials	n/a	n/a
Youth players	n/a	n/a	Total involved	n/a	
Total players	n/a		Number of clubs	n/a	
Professional players	n/a	n/a	Number of teams	n/a	

Fédération Calédonienne de Football (FCF)

7 bis, rue Suffren Quartien latin, BP 560, 99845 Nouméa CEDEX 99845, New Caledonia

Tel +687 272383   Fax +687 263249

fedcalfoot@canl.nc   www.none

President: FOURNIER Claude   General Secretary: VIRCONDELET Laurent

Vice-President: TOGNA Daniel   Treasurer: SALVATORE Jean-Paul   Media Officer: none

Men's Coach: MARTINENGO Serge   Women's Coach: none

FCF formed: 1928   OFC: 19   FIFA: 2004

Grey shirts, Red shorts, Grey socks

RECENT INTERNATIONAL MATCHES PLAYED BY NEW CALEDONIA

2002	Opponents	Score		Venue	Comp	Scorers	Att	Referee
6-07	Fiji	L	1-2	Auckland	OCr1	Sinedo [79]	1 000	Rugg NZL
8-07	Australia	L	0-11	Auckland	OCr1		200	Rugg NZL
10-07	Vanuatu	L	0-1	Auckland	OCr1		500	Ariiotima TAH
2003								
30-06	Papua New Guinea	W	2-0	Suva	SPr1	Djamali [69], Hmae [81]		Shah FIJ
1-07	Micronesia †	W	18-0	Suva	SPr1	Hmae 4 [3 41 49 53], Poatinda 6 [8 9 29 33 66 76] Wajoka 3 [15 62 85], Elmour [16], Joseph [71], Jacques [78] Theodore [80], Jacky [84]	3 000	Moli SOL
3-07	Tonga	W	4-0	Suva	SPr1	Djamali [10], Dokunengo [30], Cawa [54], Kabeu [74]	700	Shah FIJ
5-07	Tahiti	W	4-0	Nadi	SPr1	Lameu 2 [10 41], Djamali [31], Poatinda [88]	3 000	Shah FIJ
9-07	Vanuatu	D	1-1	Lautoka	SPsf	Kabeu [44], W 4-3p	7 000	Shah FIJ
11-07	Fiji	L	0-2	Suva	SPf		10 000	Attison VAN
2004								
12-05	Tahiti	D	0-0	Honiara	WCq		14 000	Rakaroi FIJ
15-05	Solomon Islands	L	0-2	Honiara	WCq		20 000	Attison VAN
17-05	Cook Islands	W	8-0	Honiara	WCq	Wajoka [3], Hmae 6 [20 35 40 42 52 85], Djamali [25]	400	Singh FIJ
19-05	Tonga	W	8-0	Honiara	WCq	Hmae 2 [4 45], Poatinda 3 [26 42 79], Wajoka 2 [54 58] Kaume [72]	14 000	Fred VAN
2005								
No international matches played in 2005								
2006								
No international matches played in 2006 before July								

Fr = Friendly match • OC = OFC Oceania Nations Cup • SP = South Pacific Games • WC = FIFA World Cup™
q = qualifier • r1 = first round group • sf = semi-final • f = final • † Not a full international

NEW CALEDONIA NATIONAL TEAM RECORDS AND RECORD SEQUENCES

Records			Sequence records				
Victory	18-0	GUM 1991	Wins	6	1964-1966	Clean sheets	4	1987
Defeat	0-8	AUS 1980	Defeats	6	1995-1998	Goals scored	31	1951-1966
Player Caps	n/a		Undefeated	9	1969	Without goal	3	1988
Player Goals	n/a		Without win	6	1995-1998	Goals against	15	1969-1973

RECENT LEAGUE AND CUP RECORD

	Division d'Honneur				National Championship			Cup		
Year	Champions	Pts	Runners-up	Pts	Champions	Score	Runners-up	Winners	Score	Runners-up
1997					JS Baco	2-1	CA Saint-Louis	CA Saint-Louis	1-1 4-3p	FC Gaïcha
1998					AS Poum	4-2	JS Traput Lifou	JS Traput Lifou	1-1 4-3p	CS Nékoué
1999					FC Gaïcha	2-2 4-3p	AS Auteuil	JS Traput Lifou	1-0	AS Auteuil
2000					JS Baco	1-0	JS Traput Lifou	AS Magenta	1-1 4-1p	JS Traput Lifou
2001					JS Baco	1-0	AS Mont-Doré	AS Magenta	4-3	AS Mont-Doré
2002	JS Baco	49	AS Magenta	42	AS Mont-Doré	2-2 4-3p	JS Baco	AS Magenta	5-2	JS Ouvéa
2003	AS Magenta	62	JS Baco	54	AS Magenta	5-3	JS Baco	AS Magenta	1-0	JS Baco
2004	AS Magenta	73	AS Mont-Doré	59	AS Magenta	3-1	AS Mont-Doré	AS Magenta	2-1	AS Mont-Doré
2005	AS Magenta	73	JS Baco	61	AS Magenta	3-2	AS Mont-Doré	AS Magenta	2-1	JS Baco
2006	AS Mont-Doré	49	JS Baco	42				AS Mont Dore	2-1	JS Baco

NEW CALEDONIA COUNTRY INFORMATION

Capital	Nouméa	Status	French overseas territory	GDP per Capita	$15 000
Population	213 679			GNP Ranking	n/a
Area km²	19 060	Language	French	Dialling code	+687
Population density	11 per km²	Literacy rate	91%	Internet code	.nc
% in urban areas	n/a	Main religion	Christian 60%	GMT +/-	+11
Towns/Cities ('000)	Nouméa 93; Mont-Doré 26; Dumbéa 21; Wé 11; Paita 10; Tadine 8; Poindimié 5; Houailu 5				
Neighbours (km)	South Pacific Ocean 2 254				
Main stadia	Nouméa-Daly Magenta – Nouméa				

NED – NETHERLANDS

NATIONAL TEAM RECORD
JULY 1ST 2002 TO JULY 9TH 2006

PL	W	D	L	F	A	%
51	30	13	8	91	32	71.6

The defeat by Portugal in the second round of the 2006 FIFA World Cup™ is something most Dutch fans will want to forget. The bad tempered affair was spoilt by four dismissals, flagrant diving and all manner of other misdeeds which left both sides discredited and the Dutch out of a tournament in which they had promised so much more. Over the two years from taking over in 2004, coach Marco Van Basten had discarded a number of the established old guard and developed a young team around a number of emerging talents such as Arjen Robben and Robin Van Persie. There was experience in the team, with Giovanni Van Bronckhorst, Phillip Cocu and Edwin Van der Sar, but the consensus after the defeat by Portugal was that this was a tournament too soon for the Dutch and that Euro finals in Austria and Switzerland represented a better opportunity for Van Basten's side. One positive from the defeat by Portugal was Van der Sar becoming the most capped Dutch player of all time, overtaking the 112 caps of Frank de Boer. In the League, PSV Eindhoven reinforced their position as the leading Dutch club of the past decade by winning their sixth championship in ten seasons and they barely broke out in a sweat to do it. Despite the loss of key

INTERNATIONAL HONOURS
Qualified for the FIFA World Cup™ finals 1934 1938 1974 1978 1990 1994 1998 2006
UEFA European Championship 1988   **UEFA European U-21 Championship** 2006
UEFA Champions League Feyenoord 1970 Ajax 1971 1972 1973 1995 PSV Eindhoven 1988

players such as Mark Van Bommel and Park Ji Sung at the start of the season, only Feyenoord and Groningen managed to beat PSV and after the defeat to Feyenoord in early December, PSV finished the season with a run of 15 wins and four draws in their remaining 19 matches. For coach Guus Hiddink, it was his last season in charge before taking over the challenging role of Russian national team coach but he didn't end his reign with a second successive double. In the Cup Final in Rotterdam, Ajax spoilt those dreams, in no small part due to Klaas-Jan Huntelaar whose extraordinary goalscoring feats after signing for Ajax in the mid season transfer window was one of the stories of the season. In the Cup Final against PSV he gave Ajax the lead just after half time. A Michael Lamey equaliser just five minutes later looked to have sent the match into extra time, but Huntelaar scored the winner three minutes into added time. It was his 24th goal in just 26 appearances for the club, helping to turn around a potentially disastrous season. Ajax still only finished fourth, signalling the end for coach Danny Blind who was replaced by Henk Ten Cate, but thanks to a bizarre post season play-off system, they managed to qualify for the UEFA Champions League, much to the dismay of second placed AZ Alkmaar, who had to settle for the UEFA Cup.

Koninklijke Nederlandse Voetbalbond (KNVB)
Woudenbergseweg 56-58, PO Box 515, Am Zeist 3700, Netherlands
Tel +31 343 499201   Fax +31 343 499189
concern@knvb.nl   www.knvb.nl
President: SPRENGERS Mathieu Dr   General Secretary: BEEN Harry
Vice-President: LESTERHUIS Hans   Treasurer: HOOGENDOORN Jan Willem   Media Officer: DE LEEDE Rob
Men's Coach: VAN BASTEN Marco   Women's Coach: PAUW Vera
KNVB formed: 1889   UEFA: 1954   FIFA: 1904
Orange shirts with white trimmings, White shorts, Orange socks or White shirts with orange trimmings, Orange shorts, White socks

RECENT INTERNATIONAL MATCHES PLAYED BY THE NETHERLANDS

2003	Opponents		Score	Venue	Comp	Scorers	Att	Referee
20-08	Belgium	D	1-1	Brussels	Fr	Makaay [55]	38 000	Fandel GER
6-09	Austria	W	3-1	Rotterdam	ECq	Van der Vaart [30], Lkuivert [60], Cocu [54]	47 000	Poulat FRA
10-09	Czech Republic	L	1-3	Prague	ECq	Van der Vaart [62]	18 356	Cortez Batista POR
11-10	Moldova	W	5-0	Eindhoven	ECq	Kluivert [43], Sneijder [51], Van Hooijdonk [74p] Van der Vaart [80], Robben [89]	30 995	Siric CRO
15-11	Scotland	L	0-1	Glasgow	ECpo		50 670	Hauge NOR
19-11	Scotland	W	6-0	Amsterdam	ECpo	Sneijder [14], Ooijer [32], Van Nistelrooij 3 [37 51 67] De Boer.F [65]	51 000	Michel SVK
2004								
18-02	United States	W	1-0	Amsterdam	Fr	Robben [56]	29 700	Ovrebo NOR
31-03	France	D	0-0	Rotterdam	Fr		50 000	Stark GER
28-04	Greece	W	4-0	Eindhoven	Fr	Makaay [50], Zenden [58], Heitinga [61], Van Hooijdonk [89]	25 000	Bolognino ITA
29-05	Belgium	L	0-1	Eindhoven	Fr		32 500	Colombo FRA
1-06	Faroe Islands	W	3-0	Lausanne	Fr	Van der Vaart [29], Makaay [51], Overmars [58]	3 200	Leuba SUI
5-06	Republic of Ireland	L	0-1	Amsterdam	Fr		42 000	Dean ENG
15-06	Germany	D	1-1	Porto	ECr1	Van Nistelrooij [81]	52 000	Frisk SWE
19-06	Czech Republic	L	2-3	Aveiro	ECr1	Bouma [4], Van Nistelrooij [19]	29 935	Mejuto Gonzalez ESP
23-06	Latvia	W	3-0	Braga	ECr1	Van Nistelrooij 2 [27p 35], Makaay [84]	27 904	Milton Nielsen DEN
26-06	Sweden	D	0-0	Faro-Loule	ECqf	W 5-4p	27 286	Michel SVK
30-06	Portugal	L	1-2	Lisbon	ECsf	Jorge Andrade OG [63]	46 679	Frisk SWE
18-08	Sweden	D	2-2	Stockholm	Fr	Sneijder [17], Van Bommel [43]	20 377	Styles ENG
3-09	Liechtenstein	W	3-0	Utrecht	Fr	Van Bommel [23], Ooijer [56], Landzaat [78]	15 000	Brines SCO
8-09	Czech Republic	W	2-0	Amsterdam	WCq	Van Hooijdonk 2 [34 84]	48 488	Merk GER
9-10	FYR Macedonia	D	2-2	Skopje	WCq	Bouma [42], Kuyt [65]	15 000	Frojdfeldt SWE
13-10	Finland	W	3-1	Amsterdam	WCq	Sneijder [39], Van Nistelrooij 2 [41 63]	50 000	Bennett ENG
17-11	Andorra	W	3-0	Barcelona	WCq	Cocu [21], Robben [31], Sneijder [78]	2 000	Yefet ISR
2005								
9-02	England	D	0-0	Birmingham	Fr		40 705	Frojdfeldt SWE
26-03	Romania	W	2-0	Bucharest	WCq	Cocu [1], Babel [84]	19 000	Medina Cantalejo ESP
30-03	Armenia	W	2-0	Eindhoven	WCq	Castelen [3], Van Nistelrooij [33]	35 000	Trefoloni ITA
4-06	Romania	W	2-0	Rotterdam	WCq	Robben [26], Kuyt [47]	47 000	De Santis ITA
8-06	Finland	W	4-0	Helsinki	WCq	Van Nistelrooij [36], Kuyt [76], Coco [85], Van Persie [87]	37 786	Hamer LUX
17-08	Germany	D	2-2	Rotterdam	Fr	Robben 2 [3 46]	45 500	Hauge NOR
3-09	Armenia	W	1-0	Yerevan	WCq	Van Nistelrooij [64]	1 747	Dougal SCO
7-09	Andorra	W	4-0	Eindhoven	WCq	Van der Vaart [23], Cocu [27], Van Nistelrooij 2 [43 89]	34 000	Hanacsek HUN
8-10	Czech Republic	W	2-0	Prague	WCq	Van der Vaart [31], Opdam [38]	17 478	Sars FRA
12-10	FYR Macedonia	D	0-0	Amsterdam	WCq		50 000	Farina ITA
12-11	Italy	L	1-3	Amsterdam	Fr	Babel [38]	50 000	Ivanov RUS
2006								
1-03	Ecuador	W	1-0	Amsterdam	Fr	Kuijt [48]	35 000	Benquerenca POR
27-05	Cameroon	W	1-0	Rotterdam	Fr	Van Nistelrooij [23]	46 228	Plautz AUT
1-06	Mexico	W	2-1	Eindhoven	Fr	Heitinga [53], Babel [57]	35 000	Frojdfeldt SWE
4-06	Australia	D	1-1	Rotterdam	Fr	Van Nistelrooij [9]	49 000	Dean ENG
11-06	Serbia & Montenegro	W	1-0	Leipzig	WCr1	Robben [18]	37 216	Merk GER
16-06	Côte d'Ivoire	W	2-1	Stuttgart	WCr1	Van Persie [23], Van Nistelrooij [27]	52 000	Ruiz COL
21-06	Argentina	D	0-0	Frankfurt	WCr1		48 000	Medina Cantalejo ESP
25-06	Portugal	L	0-1	Nuremberg	WCr2		41 000	Ivanov.V RUS

Fr = Friendly match • EC = UEFA EURO 2004™ • WC = FIFA World Cup™ • q = qualifier • r1 = first round group • qf = quarter-final

NETHERLANDS NATIONAL TEAM RECORDS AND RECORD SEQUENCES

Records			Sequence records					
Victory	9-0	FIN 1912, NOR 1972	Wins	7	1971-72, 2002-03	Clean sheets	6	1987, 2004-05
Defeat	2-12	ENG 1907	Defeats	8	1949-1950	Goals scored	23	1912-1920
Player Caps	113	VAN DER SAR Edwin	Undefeated	17	2001-2003	Without goal	3	1949-50, 1968
Player Goals	40	KLUIVERT Patrick	Without win	12	1951-1953	Goals against	24	1938-1948

NETHERLANDS COUNTRY INFORMATION

Capital	The Hague	Formation	1579	GDP per Capita	$28 600
Population	16 318 199	Status	Constitutional Monarchy	GNP Ranking	14
Area km²	41 526	Language	Dutch	Dialling code	+31
Population density	393 per km²	Literacy rate	99%	Internet code	.nl
% in urban areas	89%	Main religion	Christinan 52%	GMT + / –	+1
Towns/Cities ('000)	Amsterdam 745; Rotterdam 603; The Hague 476; Utrecht 267; Eindhoven 210; Tilburg 206; Almere 186; Groningen 179; Breda 168; Nijmegen 158; Apeldoorn 157; Enschede 154; Haarlem 147; Arnhem 144; Zaanstad 141; Amersfoort 139; 's-Hertogenbosch 135				
Neighbours (km)	Germany 577; Belgium 450; North Sea 451				
Main stadia	Amsterdam ArenA – Amsterdam 51 859; Stadion Feijenoord (De Kuip) – Rotterdam 51 180; Philips Stadion – Eindhoven 36 500; Gelredome – Arnhem 29 000				

NATIONAL TEAM PLAYERS AND COACHES

Record Caps			Record Goals			Recent Coaches	
VAN DER SAR Edwin	1995-'06	113	KLUIVERT Patrick	1994-'04	40	LIBREGTS Thijs	1988-'89
DE BOER Frank	1990-'04	112	BERGKAMP Dennis	1990-'00	37	DE RUITER Nol	1990
COCU Philip	1996-'06	101	WILKES Faas	1946-'61	35	BEENHAKKER Leo	1990
OVERMARS Marc	1993-'04	86	LENSTRA Abe	1940-'59	33	MICHELS Rinus	1990-'92
WINTER Aron	1987-'00	84	CRUIJFF Johan	1966-'77	33	ADVOCAAT Dick	1992-'94
KROL Ruud	1969-'83	83	BAKHUYS Bep	1928-'37	28	HIDDINK Guus	1994-'98
BERGKAMP Dennis	1990-'00	79	VAN NISTELROOIJ Ruud	1998-'06	28	RIJKAARD Frank	1998-'00
KLUIVERT Patrick	1994-'04	79	SMIT Kick	1934-'46	26	VAN GAAL Louis	2000-'01
KOEMAN Ronald	1983-'94	78	VAN BASTEN Marco	1983-'92	24	ADVOCAAT Dick	2002-'04
SEEDORF Clarence	1994-'04	77	VENTE Leen	1933-'40	19	VAN BASTEN Marco	2004-

THE FIFA BIG COUNT OF 2000

	Male	Female		Male	Female
Registered players	527 900	35 000	Referees	76 000	10 000
Non registered players	250 000	0	Officials	5 400	400
Youth players	418 000	30 000	Total involved	1 352 700	
Total players	1 260 900		Number of clubs	4 050	
Professional players	900	0	Number of teams	58 868	

FIFA/COCA-COLA WORLD RANKING

1993	1994	1995	1996	1997	1998	1999	2000	2001	2002	2003	2004	2005	High		Low	
7	6	6	9	22	11	19	8	8	6	4	6	3	2	11/93	25	05/98

2005–2006											
08/05	09/05	10/05	11/05	12/05	01/06	02/06	03/06	04/06	05/06	06/06	07/06
3	2	2	3	3	3	3	3	3	3	-	6

CLUB DIRECTORY

Club	Town/City	Stadium	Capacity	www.	Lge	Cup	CL
ADO Den Haag	The Hague	Zuiderpark	11 000	adodenhaag.nl	2	1	0
Ajax	Amsterdam	Amsterdam ArenA	51 859	ajax.nl	29	16	4
AZ Alkmaar	Alkmaar	Alkmaarderhout	8 372	az.nl	1	3	0
Excelsior	Rotterdam	Woudestein	3 527	sc-excelsior.nl	0	0	0
Feyenoord	Rotterdam	Feijenoord Stadion (De Kuip)	51 180	feyenoord.nl	14	10	1
FC Groningen	Groningen	Oosterpark	13 000	fcgroningen.nl	0	0	0
SC Heerenveen	Heerenveen	Abe Lenstra	17 653	sc-heerenveen.nl	0	0	0
Heracles	Almelo	Polman	8 500		2	0	0
NAC Breda	Breda	MyCom Stadion	17 064	nac.nl	1	1	0
NEC Nijmegan	Nijmegan	De Goffert	12 500	nec-nijmegan.nl	0	0	0
PSV Eindhoven	Eindhoven	Philips Stadion	36 500	psv.nl	19	8	1
RKC Waalwijk	Waalwijk	Mandemakers	7 500	rkcwaalwijk.nl	0	0	0
Roda JC	Kerkrade	Parkstad Limburg	19 200	rodajc.nl	0	2	0
Sparta	Rotterdam	Sparta Stadion (Het Kassel)	11 500	sparta-rotterdam.nl	6	3	0
FC Twente	Enschede	Arke Stadion	13 500	fctwente.nl	0	2	0
FC Utrecht	Utrecht	Nieuw Galgenwaard	18 500	fc-utrecht.nl	0	3	0
Vitesse	Arnhem	Gelredome	29 000	vitesse.com	0	0	0
Willem II	Tilburg	Willem II	14 700	willem-ii.nl	3	2	0

RECENT LEAGUE AND CUP RECORD

	Championship						Cup		
Year	Champions	Pts	Runners-up	Pts	Third	Pts	Winners	Score	Runners-up
1990	Ajax	49	PSV Eindhoven	48	Twente Enschede	42	PSV Eindhoven	1-0	Vitesse Arnhem
1991	PSV Eindhoven	53	Ajax	53	FC Groningen	46	Feyenoord	1-0	BVV Den Bosch
1992	PSV Eindhoven	58	Ajax	55	Feyenoord	49	Feyenoord	3-0	Roda JC Kerkrade
1993	Feyenoord	53	PSV Eindhoven	51	Ajax	49	Ajax	6-2	SC Heerenveen
1994	Ajax	54	Feyenoord	51	PSV Eindhoven	44	Feyenoord	2-1	NEC Nijmegan
1995	Ajax	61	Roda JC Kerkrade	54	PSV Eindhoven	47	Feyenoord	2-1	FC Volendam
1996	Ajax	83	PSV Eindhoven	77	Feyenoord	63	PSV Eindhoven	5-2	Sparta Rotterdam
1997	PSV Eindhoven	77	Feyenoord	73	Twente Enschede	65	Roda JC Kerkrade	4-2	SC Heerenveen
1998	Ajax	89	PSV Eindhoven	72	Vitesse Arnhem	70	SC Heerenveen	3-1	Twente Enschede
1999	Feyenoord	80	Willem II Tilburg	65	PSV Eindhoven	61	Ajax	2-0	Fortuna Sittard
2000	PSV Eindhoven	84	SC Heerenveen	68	Feyenoord	64	Roda JC Kerkrade	2-0	NEC Nijmegan
2001	PSV Eindhoven	83	Feyenoord	66	Ajax	61	Twente Enschede	0-0 4-3p	PSV Eindhoven
2002	Ajax	73	PSV Eindhoven	68	Feyenoord	64	Ajax	3-2	FC Utrecht
2003	PSV Eindhoven	84	Ajax	83	Feyenoord	80	FC Utrecht	4-1	Feyenoord
2004	Ajax	80	PSV Eindhoven	74	Feyenoord	68	FC Utrecht	1-0	Twente Enschede
2005	PSV Eindhoven	87	Ajax	77	AZ Alkmaar	64	PSV Eindhoven	4-0	Willem II Tilburg
2006	PSV Eindhoven	84	AZ Alkmaar	74	Feyenoord	71	Ajax	2-1	PSV Eindhoven

NETHERLANDS 2005–06

EREDIVISIE

	Pl	W	D	L	F	A	Pts	PSV	AZ	Feyenoord	Ajax	Groningen	Utrecht	Heerenveen	Roda JC	FC Twente	NEC	Vitesse	RKC	Heracles	Sparta	ADO	NAC	Willem II	RBC
PSV Eindhoven †	34	26	6	2	71	23	84		3-0	1-1	1-0	1-1	1-0	4-1	3-2	1-1	1-0	2-1	2-0	1-0	3-0	3-0	3-0	4-1	2-0
AZ Alkmaar ‡	34	23	5	6	78	32	74	1-2		1-0	4-2	1-1	2-3	2-1	2-0	0-0	3-2	1-1	3-0	2-2	3-0	3-1	3-2	5-1	7-0
Feyenoord ‡	34	21	8	5	79	34	71	1-0	2-0		3-2	4-1	3-0	5-1	0-0	4-2	3-0	0-0	1-1	7-1	4-0	0-2	2-0	6-1	2-0
Ajax †	34	18	6	10	66	41	60	0-0	1-0	1-2		3-2	1-4	0-0	4-1	2-1	4-1	2-1	4-1	0-0	6-0	2-2	1-1	1-0	6-0
FC Groningen ‡	34	16	8	10	46	43	56	0-0	0-0	1-1	3-2		2-1	2-0	1-0	1-0	3-0	2-0	0-0	0-1	3-1	3-2	2-0	1-0	1-0
FC Utrecht	34	16	7	11	48	44	55	1-2	1-2	3-1	1-0	0-2		2-0	2-1	1-3	1-1	1-0	3-1	1-0	1-1	1-1	2-2	1-4	4-1
SC Heerenveen ‡	34	14	8	12	63	58	50	2-3	2-4	1-1	4-2	4-0	1-1		5-4	3-1	2-1	4-1	2-1	1-2	0-0	3-0	2-1	3-3	2-0
Roda JC Kerkrade	34	15	5	14	57	54	50	0-3	1-4	2-3	2-1	1-3	2-1	2-1		2-0	0-1	3-2	1-0	2-1	1-1	3-1	3-3	0-2	5-1
FC Twente Enschede	34	13	8	13	44	36	47	0-1	1-3	1-3	2-3	1-1	3-0	1-2	1-0		0-1	0-1	2-0	1-0	2-0	1-0	3-1	0-1	4-1
NEC Nijmegen	34	13	8	13	43	43	47	0-2	0-2	1-2	1-0	2-2	0-0	4-1	0-3	0-3		1-0	1-3	2-0	0-0	5-0	1-1	2-0	3-1
Vitesse Arnhem	34	13	5	16	52	54	44	1-3	0-5	0-1	0-2	2-0	1-0	2-2	1-3	1-2	1-1		4-2	5-1	3-1	3-1	2-1	2-1	5-1
RKC Waalwijk	34	11	6	17	48	58	39	4-4	0-1	2-1	2-4	2-1	2-3	2-2	2-0	0-0	1-3	0-1		0-2	3-2	3-0	4-1	1-0	1-1
Heracles Almelo	34	11	6	17	35	58	39	1-1	0-2	0-4	1-3	2-1	1-1	1-1	0-1	0-4	0-2	3-1	0-2		1-0	1-3	4-2	1-0	3-0
Sparta Rotterdam	34	10	7	17	34	50	37	0-1	0-1	1-3	1-2	1-0	0-1	1-2	2-3	1-0	1-3	1-0	3-2	2-0		2-3	1-0	3-2	5-0
ADO Den Haag	34	10	5	19	36	62	35	0-2	0-2	2-1	1-2	2-1	2-3	1-0	1-1	0-0	0-1	2-0	2-1	1-2	0-2		0-3	1-1	3-0
NAC Breda	34	8	9	17	45	66	33	2-6	2-1	3-3	0-2	2-2	0-1	0-3	0-4	1-1	2-1	2-2	1-2	2-1	0-0	4-1		1-0	2-1
Willem II Tilburg	34	7	7	20	45	66	28	0-3	1-3	1-3	0-2	5-0	0-1	4-3	2-2	1-1	2-2	3-4	1-2	0-0	1-0	0-2	1-0		3-1
RBC Roosendaal	34	1	6	27	22	90	9	1-2	0-5	2-2	0-2	1-2	1-2	0-2	0-2	1-1	2-0	0-3	1-1	1-2	1-1	1-2	1-2	1-1	

12/08/2005 - 16/04/2006 • † Qualified for the UEFA Champions League • ‡ Qualified for the UEFA Cup
Champions League play-offs: Groningen 3-1 1-2 AZ; Ajax 3-0 4-2 Feyenoord; Ajax 2-0 1-2 Groningen; Ajax qualify for the UEFA Champions League whilst Groningen, Feyenoord and AZ qualify for the UEFA Cup • UEFA Cup play-offs: FC Twente 2-0 3-1 FC Utrecht; Roda JC 0-0 0-0 Heerenveen; FC Twente 0-1 0-5 Heerenveen; Heerenveen qualified for the UEFA Cup • Top scorers: Klaas Jan Huntelaar, Heerenveen/Ajax, 33; Shota Arveladze, AZ Alkmaar, 22; Dirk Kuijt, Feyenoord, 22; Jefferson Farfan, PSV, 21; Salomon Kalou, Feyenoord, 15; Arouna Koné, Roda JC/PSV, 13

NETHERLANDS 2005–06

EERSTE DIVISIE

	Pl	W	D	L	F	A	Pts	Excelsior	VVV	Volendam	Helmond	Graafschap	Emmen	Den Bosch	Haarlem	Dordrecht	AGOVV	TOP Oss	Zwolle	MVV	Veendam	Cambuur-L	Stormvogels	Eindhoven	Go Ahead	Omniworld	Fortuna
Excelsior	38	22	9	7	68	25	75		3-1	3-1	3-0	4-1	3-0	0-1	1-2	0-1	2-1	2-2	2-1	1-0	3-0	4-0	4-0	1-0	2-1	2-1	3-0
VVV Venlo †	38	20	8	10	53	34	68	1-0		3-2	2-1	3-0	2-0	1-0	4-1	2-2	3-0	2-0	1-0	1-3	1-1	1-1	1-0	0-1	3-0	0-1	1-1
FC Volendam †	38	19	9	10	59	43	66	0-0	0-0		3-0	1-0	5-2	4-2	5-0	1-1	3-1	1-2	1-1	0-0	1-1	2-0	0-0	1-0	1-2	2-0	2-0
Helmond Sport †	38	19	7	12	62	55	64	3-3	1-1	4-2		1-2	2-1	4-2	1-0	1-0	1-2	4-1	2-1	2-0	0-2	1-2	2-0	3-1	3-1	3-1	3-0
De Graafschap †	38	17	11	10	63	51	62	1-1	0-2	3-1	2-2		0-1	1-0	0-0	1-3	0-0	4-2	4-2	3-3	0-0	2-1	2-2	2-0	1-1	2-0	2-1
FC Emmen	38	18	6	14	68	56	60	0-2	1-2	4-1	1-1	2-2		3-1	0-2	2-5	3-0	1-0	2-0	4-2	2-2	2-1	3-0	0-2	1-2	2-5	7-0
FC Den Bosch	38	16	11	11	62	51	59	0-1	1-1	1-0	1-0	2-0	2-2		2-0	2-5	1-4	0-2	1-3	3-1	2-0	1-1	5-3	0-0	1-1	4-1	
Haarlem †	38	17	8	13	57	51	59	0-0	2-0	4-0	0-1	1-0	0-2	1-1		2-3	1-0	1-2	0-0	4-1	0-0	2-2	0-4	5-0	3-2	1-1	
FC Dordrecht	38	15	11	12	61	45	56	1-0	5-0	0-1	0-2	2-2	1-2	2-2	0-1		1-2	2-1	1-2	1-0	0-0	1-5	0-1	1-1	5-2	3-0	
AGOVV Apeldoorn †	38	17	5	16	64	62	56	0-1	1-0	1-2	2-1	2-2	3-3	0-0	2-1		2-2	1-4	2-1	1-3	1-2	0-1	4-2	1-5	2-3	3-0	
TOP Oss †	38	15	10	13	51	53	55	0-1	1-0	1-2	2-1	1-0	3-3	3-1	1-2	0-1		2-1	3-1	0-2	1-0	1-2	1-1	1-1	1-3	3-1	
FC Zwolle †	38	15	9	14	57	52	54	0-5	1-1	1-1	3-0	2-3	1-0	0-0	1-0	0-1	1-3	2-3		4-1	2-1	1-0	2-2	2-1	4-0	2-1	
MVV Maastricht	38	13	12	13	58	61	51	0-0	2-0	0-2	1-0	1-0	4-1	1-1	4-1	2-1	2-2	0-0	2-2		2-1	3-4	2-0	1-0	2-2	7-1	3-1
BV Veendam	38	14	9	15	54	60	51	2-1	0-1	2-3	1-3	0-1	1-3	0-3	1-1	1-3	2-1	0-0	0-0	2-3		4-1	0-2	3-1	2-0	2-2	
Cambuur-Leeuwarden	38	12	14	12	48	50	47	0-1	1-1	2-1	0-0	1-1	1-1	1-0	4-0	0-0	2-3	1-1	0-0	3-0	4-1		1-1	1-0	2-1	1-0	2-2
Storm. Telstar Velsen	38	9	13	16	37	53	40	0-1	0-1	0-2	2-1	1-3	2-0	1-4	1-1	3-1	1-1	1-3	1-1	1-0	1-1	1-3		0-1	1-0	2-2	1-1
FC Eindhoven	38	11	6	21	53	65	39	0-6	1-3	1-2	0-0	2-3	1-2	2-4	1-3	0-0	1-2	5-0	1-0	0-3	3-1	3-1	2-0		2-1	2-0	1-1
Go Ahead Eagles	38	8	11	19	45	70	35	1-0	1-0	1-2	1-3	1-2	1-4	0-1	3-0	2-1	1-0	1-1	1-1	1-1	4-0	2-2	2-1	1-2		1-4	1-1
Omniworld Almere	38	7	8	23	50	87	29	1-1	0-5	1-1	0-1	3-3	3-4	1-2	2-4	1-3	0-4	0-1	1-3	1-2	2-0	3-1	3-2	2-2			1-1
Fortuna Sittard	38	2	11	25	35	85	17	1-1	0-2	0-1	2-3	1-2	0-2	1-2	0-3	0-3	2-3	2-1	0-1	1-3	1-3	0-0	1-2	3-2	2-3		

12/08/2005 - 7/04/2006 • † Qualified for the play-offs • §3 = three points deducted
Promotion play-offs: Zwolle 1-1 3-1 Haarlem; Top Oss 3-0 2-0 AGOVV; Helmond Sport 0-1 3-2 1-2 Volendam; Zwolle 2-4 2-6 Willem II; De Graafschap 1-1 4-2 VVV Venlo; TOP Oss 0-0 2-2 1-3 NAC Breda; Volendam 1-2 0-0 NAC Breda; De Graafschap 0-1 1-2 Willem II; NAC and Willem II remain in the Eredivisie • Top scorer: Berry POWEL, Den Bosch, 19

GATORADE CUP 2005-06

Third Round		Fourth Round		Quarter-finals		Semi-finals		Final	
BV Emmen	0	**Ajax**	6						
FC Eindhoven *	2	FC Eindhoven *	1	**Ajax**	3				
VVV Venlo	2	VVV Venlo	0	SC Heerenveen *	0				
FC Utrecht *	1	**SC Heerenveen** *	2			**Ajax** *	4		
						Roda JC Kerkrade	1		
Helmond Sport *	1	**Helmond Sport** *	2						
De Treffers/Kegro	0	Jong Ajax	1	**Helmond Sport** *	0				
AGOVV Apeldoorn	0			**Roda JC Kerkrade**	2				
Jong Ajax *	1	Feyenoord	0					**Ajax**	2
		Roda JC Kerkrade *	1					PSV Eindhoven	1
Go Ahead Eagles *	0								
Roda JC Kerkrade	1								
		AZ Alkmaar *	2	**AZ Alkmaar** *	4				
NAC Breda	2 4p	NEC Nijmegan	0	MVV	0				
NEC Nijmegan *	2 5p					**AZ Alkmaar**			
		Willem II	1			**PSV Eindhoven** *			
AFC *	0	**MVV** *	3						
MVV	2								
FC Groningen *	3	**FC Groningen** *	3	**FC Groningen** *	2				
ADO Den Haag	0	FC Volendam	0	**PSV Eindhoven**	3				
FC Dordrecht *	0								
FC Volendam	4	FC Twente	0						
FC Twente	2	**PSV Eindhoven** *	3						
RKC Waalwijk *	1								

* Home team ● Clubs playing in Europe join in the fourth round

AMSTEL CUP FINAL

De Kuip, Rotterdam
7-05-2006, At: 30 776, Ref. Vink
Scorers - Huntelaar 2 48 92+ for PSV, Lamey 53 for Ajax

Ajax - Stekelenburg - Boakye, Heitinga, Vermaelen ●,
Emanuelson, Galasek ●●● 64, Sneijder ●, Charisteas
(Maduro 65), Huntelaar ●, Rosenberg (Babel 46).
Boukhari. Tr: Blind

PSV - Gomes - Ooijer, Addo, Bali ●, Lamey ●●● 71, Afellay
(Kone,A 59) Cocu, Simons, Beasley, Hesselink, Farfan.
Tr: Hiddink

PSV EINDHOVEN 2005–06

Date	Opponents	Score		Comp	Scorers	Att
5-08-2005	Ajax	L 1-2	A	SC	Bouma [51]	32 000
13-08-2005	Heracles Almelo	D 1-1	A	ED	Cocu [84]	8 100
21-08-2005	Vitesse Arnhem	W 2-1	H	ED	Farfan [32], Cocu [45]	32 600
28-08-2005	Roda JC Kerkrade	W 3-0	A	ED	Farfan [38], Beasley [68], Cocu [86]	14 000
10-09-2005	FC Utrecht	W 1-0	H	ED	Kone [49]	32 000
13-09-2005	FC Schalke 04 - GER	W 1-0	H	CLgE	Vennegoor of Hesselink [33]	30 000
18-09-2005	FC Groningen	L 0-1	A	ED		12 500
24-09-2005	RBC Roosendaal	W 2-0	H	ED	Simons [7], Farfan [47]	32 200
28-09-2005	Fenerbahçe - TUR	L 0-3	A	CLgE		37 079
2-10-2005	SC Heerenveen	W 3-2	A	ED	Kone 3 [36 56 69]	21 000
15-10-2005	AZ Alkmaar	W 3-0	H	ED	Cocu 2 [43 82], Vennegoor of Hesselink [86]	33 700
19-10-2005	Milan - ITA	D 0-0	A	CLgE		39 298
23-10-2005	Ajax	W 1-0	H	ED	Simons [10p]	34 700
29-10-2005	FC Twente Enschede	W 1-0	H	ED	Afellay [70]	13 100
1-11-2005	Milan - ITA	W 1-0	H	CLgE		35 100
5-11-2005	Sparta Rotterdam	W 3-0	H	ED	Farfan 2 [34 74], Beasley [35]	33 300
19-11-2005	RKC Waalwijk	D 4-4	A	ED	Farfan 3 [14 44 51], Robert [90]	7 400
23-11-2005	FC Schalke 04 - GER	L 0-3	A	CLgE		53 994
27-11-2005	ADO Den Haag	W 3-0	H	ED	Vennegoor of Hesselink 2 [60 73], Kone [86]	33 000
3-12-2005	NAC Breda	W 3-0	H	ED	Vennegoor of Hesselink [53], Farfan [78], Kone [88]	33 000
6-12-2005	Fenerbahçe - TUR	W 2-0	H	CLgE	Cocu [14], Farfan [85]	35 000
11-12-2005	Feyenoord	L 0-1	A	ED		45 000
17-12-2005	Willem II Tilburg	W 4-1	H	ED	Vennegoor of Hesselink 2 [19 42], Farfan [63], Varyrynen [90]	33 100
20-12-2005	FC Twente Enschede	W 3-0	H	GCr4	Farfan [45], Vennegoor of Hesselink 2 [58 90]	
26-12-2005	NEC Nijmegan	W 2-0	A	ED	Kone [6], Beasley [90]	11 750
29-12-2005	FC Twente Enschede	D 1-1	H	ED	Cocu [70]	33 200
15-01-2006	Sparta Rotterdam	W 1-0	A	ED	Gudelj OG [75]	9 100
20-01-2006	RKC Waalwijk	W 2-0	H	ED	Farfan [4], Beasley [76]	32 500
29-01-2006	ADO Den Haag	W 2-0	A	ED	Farfan [55], Cocu [78]	6 341
1-02-2006	FC Groningen	W 3-2	A	GCqf	Cocu 2 [5 27], Farfan [25]	
4-02-2006	Roda JC Kerkrade	W 3-2	H	ED	Vennegoor of Hesselink 2 [7p 53], Aissati [65]	32 000
8-02-2006	FC Utrecht	W 2-1	H	ED	Farfan 2 [22 78]	19 615
11-02-2006	Heracles Almelo	W 1-0	H	ED	Farfan [72]	32 900
17-02-2006	Vitesse Arnhem	W 3-1	A	ED	Farfan 2 [45 90], Lamey [85]	19 845
21-02-2006	Olympique Lyonnais - FRA	L 0-1	H	CLr2		35 000
26-02-2006	AZ Alkmaar	W 2-1	A	ED	Vennegoor of Hesselink [3], Kone [6]	8 571
4-03-2006	SC Heerenveen	W 4-1	H	ED	Kone 2 [37 83], Cocu [41], Alex [75]	33 400
8-03-2006	Olympique Lyonnais - FRA	L 0-4	A	CLr2		37 901
11-03-2006	Ajax	D 0-0	A	ED		48 741
18-03-2006	NEC Nijmegan	W 1-0	H	ED	Farfan [77]	33 000
22-03-2006	AZ Alkmaar	W 2-0	H	GCsf	Simons [103], Farfan [119]	
25-03-2006	Willem II Tilburg	W 3-0	A	ED	Aissati [5], Addo [45], Kone [46]	14 100
1-04-2006	RBC Roosendaal	W 2-1	A	ED	Afellay [60], Alex [66]	5 000
9-04-2006	FC Groningen	D 1-1	H	ED	Farfan [47]	33 500
12-04-2006	Feyenoord	D 1-1	H	ED	Cocu [70]	34 300
16-04-2006	NAC Breda	W 6-2	A	ED	Vennegoor of Hesselink 2 [4 48], Farfan 2 [21 49], Vayrynen [62], Cocu [90]	14 950
7-05-2006	Ajax	L 1-2	N	GCf	Lamey [53]	30 776

SC = Johan Cruijff Super Cup • ED = Eredivisie • GC = Gatorade Cup • CL = UEFA Champions League
pr3 = third preliminary round • gE = Group E • r2 = second round • r4 = fourth round • qf = quarter-final • sf = semi-final • f = final
N = De Kuip, Rotterdam

AJAX 2005-06

Date	Opponents	Score		Comp	Scorers	Att
5-08-2005	PSV Eindhoven	W 2-1	H	SC	Boukhari [72], Babel [78]	32 000
10-08-2005	Brøndby IF - DEN	D 2-2	A	CLpr3		24 917
20-08-2005	RBC Roosendaal	W 2-0	A	ED	Pienaar [59], Rosenberg [85]	5 000
24-08-2005	Brøndby IF - DEN	W 3-1	H	CLpr3		39 750
28-08-2005	Feyenoord	L 1-2	H	ED	Charisteas [79]	49 567
10-09-2005	Willem II Tilburg	W 2-0	A	ED	Galásek [35], Charisteas [86]	12 800
14-09-2005	Sparta Praha - CZE	D 1-1	A	CLgB	Sneijder [91+]	15 386
18-09-2005	AZ Alkmaar	L 2-4	A	ED	Sneijder 2 [10 45]	8 600
21-09-2005	ADO Den Haag	D 2-2	H	ED	Maduro [20], Sneijder [28]	42 854
24-09-2005	Roda JC Kerkrade	W 4-1	H	ED	Charisteas 2 [28 40], Pienaar [70], Galasek [86p]	48 586
27-09-2005	Arsenal - ENG	L 1-2	H	CLgB	Rosenberg [71]	43 250
2-10-2005	Sparta Rotterdam	W 2-1	A	ED	De Jong 2 [63 77]	11 000
15-10-2005	Heracles Almelo	D 0-0	H	ED		49 650
18-10-2005	FC Thun - SUI	W 2-0	H	CLgB	Anastasiou 2 [36 55]	44 772
23-10-2005	PSV Eindhoven	L 0-1	A	ED		34 700
28-10-2005	SC Heerenveen	D 0-0	H	ED		47 500
2-11-2005	FC Thun - SUI	W 4-2	A	CLgB	Sneijder [10], Anastasiou [63], De Jong [91+], Boukhari [93+]	30 919
6-11-2005	NEC Nijmegen	L 0-1	A	ED		12 500
19-11-2005	FC Twente Enschede	W 2-0	H	ED	Majstorovic OG [70], Rosenberg [90]	45 120
22-11-2005	Sparta Praha - CZE	W 2-1	H	CLgB	De Jong 2 [68 89]	46 158
27-11-2005	FC Utrecht	L 0-1	A	ED		22 137
4-12-2005	RKC Waalwijk	W 4-1	H	ED	Maduro [45], Sneijder [48], Rosenberg [84], Babel [86]	47 812
7-12-2005	Arsenal - ENG	D 0-0	A	CLgB		35 376
11-12-2005	Vitesse Arnhem	W 2-0	H	ED	Galásek [17p], Charisteas [75]	24 400
18-12-2005	NAC Breda	W 2-0	A	ED	Rosenberg [39], Sneijder [80]	15 933
22-12-2005	FC Eindhoven	W 6-1	A	GCr4	Charisteas [4], Sneijder 2 [14 62], Demouge OG [16], Boukhari [19], Vermaelen [81]	4 500
27-12-2005	FC Groningen	W 3-2	H	ED	Rosenberg [7], Charisteas 2 [18 67]	48 547
30-12-2005	SC Heerenveen	L 2-4	A	ED	Vermaelen [79], Galásek [90p]	21 200
15-01-2006	NEC Nijmegen	D 1-1	H	ED	Rosenberg [12]	48 000
22-01-2006	FC Twente Enschede	W 3-2	A	ED	Rosenberg [51], Maduro [89], Emanuelson [90]	13 250
29-01-2006	FC Utrecht	L 1-4	H	ED	Rosenberg [46]	45 000
2-02-2006	SC Heerenveen	W 3-0	A	GCqf	Rosales [9], Huntelaar [89], Emanuelson [92+]	20 500
5-02-2006	Feyenoord	L 2-3	A	ED	Rosenberg [23], Huntelaar [90]	45 000
8-02-2006	Willem II Tilburg	W 1-0	H	ED	Rosenberg [55]	37 000
12-02-2006	ADO Den Haag	W 2-1	A	ED	Grygera [30], Huntelaar [55]	6 500
19-02-2006	RBC Roosendaal	W 6-0	H	ED	Huntelaar 4 [4 71 78 83], Rosenberg 2 [28 86]	46 383
22-02-2006	Internazionale - ITA	D 2-2	H	CLr2	Huntelaar [16], Rosales [20]	46 663
26-02-2006	Heracles Almelo	W 3-1	A	ED	Huntelaar [45], Timisela [82], Babel [90]	8 500
5-03-2006	Sparta Rotterdam	W 6-0	H	ED	Boukhari 2 [5 14], Huntelaar 3 [40 56 62], Vermaelen [53]	47 476
11-03-2006	PSV Eindhoven	D 0-0	H	ED		48 741
14-03-2006	Internazionale - ITA	L 0-1	A	CLr2		48 489
19-03-2006	FC Groningen	L 2-3	A	ED	Huntelaar [17], Vermaelen [68]	20 000
22-03-2006	Roda JC Kerkrade	W 4-1	H	GCsf	Huntelaar 2 [93 109], Babel 2 [95 106]	26 449
26-03-2006	NAC Breda	D 1-1	H	ED	Huntelaar [2]	47 700
2-04-2006	Roda JC Kerkrade	L 1-2	A	ED	Huntelaar [18]	16 200
9-04-2006	AZ Alkmaar	W 1-0	H	ED	Boukhari [33]	50 150
12-04-2006	Vitesse Arnhem	W 2-1	H	ED	Huntelaar [89], Charisteas [90]	46 686
16-04-2006	RKC Waalwijk	W 4-2	A	ED	Heitinga [25], Huntelaar 2 [44p 87], Boukhari [50]	7 400
20-04-2006	Feyenoord	W 3-0	H	EDpo	Rosales [27], Heitinga [79], Huntelaar [80]	34 364
23-04-2006	Feyenoord	W 4-2	A	EDpo	Rosales [34], Huntelaar [40], Boukhari [51], Mitea [81]	35 000
26-04-2006	FC Groningen	W 2-0	H	EDpo	Rosenberg [9], Charisteas [69]	38 060
3-05-2006	FC Groningen	L 1-2	A	EDpo	Sneijder [88]	19 610
7-05-2006	PSV Eindhoven	W 2-1	N	GCf	Huntelaar 2 [48 90]	30 776

SC = Johan Cruijff Super Cup • ED = Eredivisie • GC = Gatorade Cup • CL = UEFA Champions League
pr3 = third preliminary round • gE = Group E • r2 = second round • r4 = fourth round • qf = quarter-final • sf = semi-final • f = final
po = play-off for European places • N = De Kuip, Rotterdam

NEP – NEPAL

NATIONAL TEAM RECORD
JULY 1ST 2002 TO JULY 9TH 2006

PL	W	D	L	F	A	%
19	5	2	12	20	56	31.6

FIFA/COCA-COLA WORLD RANKING

1993	1994	1995	1996	1997	1998	1999	2000	2001	2002	2003	2004	2005	High		Low	
124	138	147	151	155	176	157	166	156	165	165	177	175	**124**	12/93	**181**	11/05

2005–2006										
08/05	09/05	10/05	11/05	12/05	01/06	02/06	03/06	04/06	05/06	06/06	07/06
178	179	180	181	175	175	175	175	169	169	-	164

For so long a backwater in football terms, Nepal is currently reaping the benefits of the AFC Vision Asia programme which has streamed entry into tournaments according to the standards in the member countries and in which Nepal is classified as an 'emerging' nation. In May 2005, Three Star Club took part in the inaugural AFC President's Cup and reached the semi-finals, before losing to Tajikistan's Regar TadAz, who went on to win the tournament. In April 2006 the national team took part in the inaugural AFC Challenge Cup and after qualifying from their first round group sensationally beat India to reach the semi-finals. They then drew with Sri Lanka and were

INTERNATIONAL HONOURS
South Asian Games 1984 1993

only denied a place in the final on penalties. Two semi-final appearances in 12 months was uncharted territory for Nepalese football and the ramifications can only be positive. In-between, the national team also took part in the South Asian Football Federation Championship in Bangladesh but defeats by both India and Bangladesh saw them exit after the first round. The prospect of international competition has also helped the domestic championship, which in the 2005-06 season was won by Manang Marsyangdi Club, although they weren't quite so successful as Three Star had been in the 2005 AFC President's Cup, losing in the first round of the 2006 tournament.

THE FIFA BIG COUNT OF 2000

	Male	Female		Male	Female
Registered players	2 500	0	Referees	200	0
Non registered players	100 000	0	Officials	800	0
Youth players	2 500	0	Total involved	106 000	
Total players	105 000		Number of clubs	100	
Professional players	0	0	Number of teams	400	

All-Nepal Football Association (ANFA)
ANFA House, Ward No.4, Bishalnagar, PO Box 12582, Kathmandu, Nepal
Tel +977 1 5539059   Fax +977 1 4424314
ganesht@ntc.net.np   www.none
President: THAPA Ganesh   General Secretary: SHRESTHA Narendra
Vice-President: BISTA Mahesh   Treasurer: SHAH Birat Jun   Media Officer: None
Men's Coach: THAPA Shyam   Women's Coach: KISHOR K.C.
ANFA formed: 1951   AFC: 1971   FIFA: 1970
Red shirts, Red shorts, Red socks

RECENT INTERNATIONAL MATCHES PLAYED BY NEPAL

2003	Opponents	Score		Venue	Comp	Scorers	Att	Referee
18-03	Afghanistan	W	4-0	Kathmandu	ACq	Rayamajhi 2 [35][88], Khadka [39], Lama [90]		Haq IND
20-03	Kyrgyzstan	L	0-2	Kathmandu	ACq			
25-09	Oman	L	0-7	Incheon	ACq			
27-09	Vietnam	L	0-5	Incheon	ACq			
29-09	Korea Republic	L	0-16	Incheon	ACq			
19-10	Oman	L	0-6	Muscat	ACq			Al Ghafary JOR
21-10	Vietnam	L	0-2	Muscat	ACq			
24-10	Korea Republic	L	0-7	Muscat	ACq			
2004								
No international matches played in 2004								
2005								
8-12	India	L	1-2	Karachi	SAFr1	Basanta Thapa [35]		
10-12	Bangladesh	L	0-2	Karachi	SAFr1			
12-12	Bhutan	W	3-1	Karachi	SAFr1	Surendra Tamang [10], Basanta Thapa [16], Bijay Gurung [29]		
2006								
2-04	Bhutan	W	2-0	Chittagong	CCr1	Pradeep Maharjan 2 [52][68]	3 500	Gosh BAN
4-04	Brunei Darussalam	L	1-2	Chittagong	CCr1	Tashi Tsering [60]	2 500	Al Ghatrifi OMA
6-04	Sri Lanka	D	1-1	Chittagong	CCr1	Pradeep Maharjan [75p]	2 500	Lee Gi Young KOR
9-04	India	W	3-0	Chittagong	CCqf	Pradeep Maharjan 2 [16][26], Basanta Thapa [28]	3 000	Gosh BAN
12-04	Sri Lanka	D	1-1	Chittagong	CCsf	Basanta Thapa [82], L 3-5p	2 500	Lee Gi Young KOR

Fr = Friendly match • SAF = South Asian Football Federation Cup • CC = AFC Challenge Cup • AC = AFC Asian Cup
q = qualifier • r1 = first round group • qf = quarter-final • sf = semi-final

NEPAL NATIONAL TEAM RECORDS AND RECORD SEQUENCES

Records			Sequence records				
Victory	7-0	BHU 1999	Wins	3	1982	Clean sheets	2	Four times
Defeat	0-16	KOR 2003	Defeats	10	1997-1998	Goals scored	6	2005-2006
Player Caps	n/a		Undefeated	3	1982, 1993, 2006	Without goal	13	1987-1989
Player Goals	n/a		Without win	20	1987-93, 1995-98	Goals against	21	1996-1999

RECENT LEAGUE AND CUP RECORD

Championship		Cup	
Year	Champions		Winners
1995	New Road Team		
1996	No Tournament		
1997	Three Star Club		Tribhuvan Army Club
1998	Three Star Club		Mahendra Police
1999	No tournament		Mahendra Police
2000	Manang Marsyangdi		
2001	No tournament		
2002	No tournament		Mahendra Police
2003	Manang Marsyangdi		Manang Marsyangdi
2004	Three Star Club		Mahendra Police
2005	Season readjustment		
2006	Manang Marsyangdi		

The Cup from 1997 to 1999 refers to the National League Cup, in 2002 to the Tribhuvan Challenge Shield and for 2003 and 2004 to the Khukuri Gold Cup

NEPAL 2005-06
ANFA A DIVISION

	Pl	W	D	L	F	A	Pts
Manang Marsyangdi	28	21	5	2	84	20	68
Three Star Club	28	19	6	3	65	18	63
Tribhuvan Army Club	28	19	4	5	67	30	61
Mahendra Police Club	28	17	9	2	52	18	60
Gyanendra APT Team	28	13	7	8	53	31	46
New Road Team	28	12	8	8	51	33	44
Ranipokhari Corner	28	10	7	11	52	61	37
Sankata Boys Sp. Club	28	10	4	14	46	56	34
Brigade Boys Club	28	10	2	16	51	68	32
Boys Union Club	28	7	7	14	37	67	28
Jawalakhel Youth Club	28	6	9	13	39	50	27
Friends Club	28	6	8	14	27	46	26
Machhindra FC	28	7	5	16	33	59	26
Mahabir Club	28	6	4	18	28	74	22
Boudha FC	28	2	5	21	26	80	11

26/08/2005 - 21/02/2006

NEPAL COUNTRY INFORMATION

Capital	Kathmandu	Formation	1769	GDP per Capita	$1 400
Population	27 070 666	Status	Constitutional Monarchy	GNP Ranking	107
Area km²	140 800	Language	Nepali	Dialling code	+977
Population density	19 per km²	Literacy rate	45%	Internet code	.np
% in urban areas	14%	Main religion	Hindu 86%, Buddhism 8%	GMT +/-	5.75
Towns/Cities ('000)	Kathmandu 790; Pokhara 186; Laltipur 183; Biratnagar 183; Birganj 133; Bharatpur 107				
Neighbours (km)	China 1 236; India 1 690				
Main stadia	Dasarath Rangasala – Kathmandu 25 000				

NGA – NIGERIA

NATIONAL TEAM RECORD
JULY 1ST 2002 TO JULY 9TH 2006

PL	W	D	L	F	A	%
44	24	11	9	69	40	67

Failure to qualify for the 2006 FIFA World Cup™ finals stung the sensibilities of Nigerian football but a measure of pride was restored at the African Nations Cup tournament in Egypt at the beginning of the year. Although the Super Eagles did not win the continental championship, finishing third yet again, they were among the best sides on display and unveiled several new stars in a youthful line-up that holds out much potential for the immediate future. Nigeria finished second to Angola in their 2006 FIFA World Cup™ qualifying group, tied on the same number of points and with a better goal difference, but failing to qualify for the tournament in Germany because of a poor head-to-head record against the Angolans. The setback in their campaign came when a typically languid attitude to a home tie against the Angolans back-fired horribly. A far from full strength team were held to 1-1 draw in Kano, handing the initiative to their opponents who went on to take a surprise first place. Nigeria were left to lick their wounds at the Nations Cup finals where new coach Augustine Eguavoen showed much faith in the youthful talent of Obafemi Martins, Victor Obinna and John Obi Mikel. They took up the mantle as long-time captain Austin

INTERNATIONAL HONOURS
Qualified for the FIFA World Cup™ finals 1994 1998 2002   Qualified for the FIFA Women's World Cup finals 1991 1995 1999 2003
Olympic Games Gold 1996   FIFA U-17 World Championship 1985 1993
CAF African Cup of Nations 1980 1994   African Women's Championship 1991 1995 1998 2000 2002 2004
African Youth Championship 1983 1985 1987 1989 2005   African U-17 Championship 2001   African Women's U-19 Championship 2002 2004
CAF Champions League Enyimba 2003 2004

Okocha battled with injury, only to return in the latter stages of the tournament to mark his final international appearances. Nigeria romped through their opening round group, beat Tunisia on penalties in the quarter-finals before losing to Cote d'Ivoire in the semi-finals. The Super Eagles then won the third place play-off match against Senegal. At the same time as the national side were suffering a shock FIFA World Cup™ exit, Enyimba lost their two-year hold on the CAF Champions League title with elimination at the group phase of the competition. Dolphin FC became Nigeria's first representatives in the final of the CAF Condeferation Cup, but despite winning the first leg at home in Port Harcourt, they lost the return 3-0 in Rabat to Morocco's Royal Armed Forces, to lose the tie 3-1 on aggregate. Enyimba may well have seen their continental crown slip away but they still remain the dominant force at home. In the League they won all of their 18 home matches conceding just four goals, form that helped them to a fourth title in five years. They also won the Coca-Cola FA Cup for the first time when they beat Lobi Stars on penalties in the final in Port Harcourt to claim the three million Naira first prize along with a newly minted trophy.

Nigeria Football Association (NFA)
Plot 2033, Olusegun Obasanjo Way, Zone 7, Wuse Abuja, PO Box 5101 Garki, Abuja, Nigeria
Tel +234 9 5237326   Fax +234 9 5237327
info@nigeriafa.com   www.nigeriafa.com
President: GALADIMA Ibrahim   General Secretary: TBD
Vice-President: AGWU Felix Anyansi   Treasurer: TBD   Media Officer: SAMUEL Kaalu
Men's Coach: EGUAVOEN Augustine   Women's Coach: IZILEIN Godwin
NFA formed: 1945   CAF: 1959   FIFA: 1959
Green shirts with white trimmings, Green shorts, Green socks

RECENT INTERNATIONAL MATCHES PLAYED BY NIGERIA

2003	Opponents		Score	Venue	Comp	Scorers	Att	Referee
16-02	Gambia	W	1-0	Banjul	Fr	Ugochukwu [10]	30 000	
29-03	Malawi	W	1-0	Blantyre	CNq	Utaka [10]	60 000	Nkole ZAM
25-05	Jamaica	L	2-3	Kingston	Fr	Ugochukwu [65], Kanu [80]	25 000	Brizan TRI
30-05	Ghana	W	3-1	Abuja	Fr	Aiyegbeni 2 [49p 71], Enakhire [82]	8 000	
7-06	Malawi	W	4-1	Lagos	CNq	Aiyegbeni 2 [10 17], Kanu 2 [22 35]	40 000	Ndoye SEN
11-06	Brazil	L	0-3	Abuja	Fr		30 000	Quartey GHA
21-06	Angola	D	2-2	Benin City	CNq	Uche [56], Odemwigie [62p]	15 000	
26-07	Venezuela	W	1-0	Watford	Fr	Okocha [8]	1 000	
20-08	Japan	L	0-3	Tokyo	Fr		54 860	Kim Tae Young KOR
2004								
27-01	Morocco	L	0-1	Monastir	CNr1		15 000	Ndoye SEN
31-01	South Africa	W	4-0	Monastir	CNr1	Yobo [4], Okocha [64p], Odemwingie 2 [81 83]	15 000	Bujsaim UAE
4-02	Benin	W	2-1	Sfax	CNr1	Lawal [35], Utaka [76]	15 000	Abd el Fatah EGY
8-02	Cameroon	W	2-1	Monastir	CNqf	Okocha [45], Utaka [73]	14 750	Guezzaz MAR
11-02	Tunisia	D	1-1	Tunis	CNsf	Okocha [67p], L 3-5p	56 000	Coffi BEN
13-02	Mali	W	2-1	Monastir	CN3p	Okocha [16], Odemwingie [47]	2 500	Sowe GAM
28-04	Jordan	W	2-0	Lagos	Fr	Akueme [16], Nworgu [82]	40 000	
29-05	Republic of Ireland	W	3-0	London	Fr	Ogbeche 2 [36 69], Martins [49]	7 438	D'Urso ENG
31-05	Jamaica	W	2-0	London	Fr	Utaka [17], Ogbeche [55]	15 000	Bennett ENG
5-06	Rwanda	W	2-0	Abuja	WCq	Martins 2 [55 88]	35 000	Pare BFA
20-06	Angola	L	0-1	Luanda	WCq		40 000	Nkole ZAM
3-07	Algeria	W	1-0	Abuja	WCq	Yobo [84]	35 000	Hisseine CHA
5-09	Zimbabwe	W	3-0	Harare	WCq	Aghahowa [3], Enakahire [28], Aiyegbeni [48p]	60 000	Mandzioukouta CGO
9-10	Gabon	D	1-1	Libreville	WCq	Aiyegbeni [50]	26 000	Yameogo BFA
20-10	Libya	L	1-2	Tripoli	Fr	Ezeji [17]	50 000	Guirat TUN
22-10	Ecuador	D	2-2	Tripoli	Fr	Ademola, Ezeji [78], L 3-4p	50 000	
17-11	South Africa	L	1-2	Johannesburg	Fr	Makinwa [62]	39 817	Marange ZIM
2005								
26-03	Gabon	W	2-0	Port Harcourt	WCq	Aghahowa [79], Kanu [81]	16 489	Hicuburundi BDI
5-06	Rwanda	D	1-1	Kigali	WCq	Martins [78]	30 000	Kidane ERI
18-06	Angola	D	1-1	Kano	WCq	Okocha [5]	17 000	Abd el Fatah EGY
17-08	Libya	W	1-0	Tripoli	Fr	Martins [20]		
4-09	Algeria	W	5-2	Oran	WCq	Martins 3 [20p 88 90], Utaka [42], Obodo [81]	11 000	Shelmani LBY
8-10	Zimbabwe	W	5-1	Abuja	WCq	Martins 2 [35 75p], Ayila [62], Kanu [80p], Odemwingie [89]	45 000	Pare BFA
16-11	Romania	L	0-3	Bucharest	Fr		500	Banari MDA
2006								
23-01	Ghana	W	1-0	Port Said	CNr1	Taiwo [86]	20 000	Abd El Fatah EGY
27-01	Zimbabwe	W	2-0	Port Said	CNr1	Obodo [57], Mikel [61]	10 000	Coulibaly MLI
31-01	Senegal	W	2-1	Port Said	CNr1	Martins 2 [79 88]	5 000	Damon RSA
4-02	Tunisia	D	1-1	Port Said	CNqf	Nsofor [6], W 6-5p	15 000	Maillet SEY
7-02	Côte d'Ivoire	L	0-1	Alexandria	CNsf		20 000	Damon RSA
9-02	Senegal	W	1-0	Cairo	CN3p	Lawal [79]	11 354	Coulibaly MLI

Fr = Friendly match • CN = CAF African Cup of Nations • WC = FIFA World Cup™
q = qualifier • r1 = first round group • qf = quarter-final • sf = semi-final • 3p = third place play-off

NIGERIA NATIONAL TEAM RECORDS AND RECORD SEQUENCES

Records			Sequence records		
Victory	8-1	UGA 1991	Wins	5	Four times	Clean sheets	6	1992-1993
Defeat	0-7	GHA 1955	Defeats	5	1963-1964	Goals scored	26	1972-1976
Player Caps	86	LAWAL Muda	Undefeated	12	1993-94, 1999-00	Without goal	4	Three times
Player Goals	37	YEKINI Rashidi	Without win	9	1985-1987	Goals against	11	1965-1967

NIGERIA COUNTRY INFORMATION

Capital	Abuja	Independence	1960 from the UK	GDP per Capita	$900
Population	137 253 133	Status	Republic	GNP Ranking	
Area km²	923 768	Language	English, Hausa, Yoruba, Igbo	Dialling code	+234
Population density	148 per km²	Literacy rate	68%	Internet code	.ng
% in urban areas	39%	Main religion	Muslim 50%, Christian 40%	GMT + / –	+1
Cities/Towns ('000)	Lagos 8 789; Kano 3 626; Ibadan 3 565; Kaduna 1 582; Port Harcourt 1 148; Benin 1 125; Maiduguri 1 112; Zaria 975; Aba 897; Ogbomosho 861; Jos 816; Ilorin 814; Oyo 736; Enugu 653; Abeokuta 593; Sokoto 563; Onitsha 561; Warri 536; Oshogbo 499; Okene 479				
Neighbours (km)	Chad 87; Cameroon 1 690; Benin 773; Niger 1 497; Atlantic Ocean (Gulf of Guinea) 853				
Main stadia	Abuja Stadium – Abuja 60 000; Surulere – Lagos 45 000; Liberty Stadium – Ibadan 35 000				

NATIONAL TEAM PLAYERS AND COACHES

Record Caps			Record Goals			Recent Coaches	
LAWAL Muda	1975-'85	86	YEKINI Rashidi	1984-'98	37	AMODU Shuaibu	1996-'97
RUFAI Peter	1981-'98	61	ODEGBAMI Segun	1976-'81	23	SINCLAIR Monday	1997
ATUEGBU Aloy	1974-'81	60	OYAREKHUA Sunday	1969-'76	16	TROUSSIER Philippe	1997-'98
NWOSU Henry	1980-'91	59	SIASIA Samson	1987-'98	16	MILUTINOVIC Bora	1988
YEKINI Rashidi	1984-'98	58	USIYEN Thompson	1976-'81	15	LIBREGTS Thijs	1988-'89
KESHI Stephen	1981-'94	57	AGHAHOWA Julius	2000-'06	13	BONFRERE Jo	1999-'01
CHUKWU Christian	1974-'81	54	AMOKACHI Daniel	1990-'99	12	AMODU Shuaibu	2001-'02
ADESINA Ademola	1982-'90	52	EKPE Asuquo	1956-'65	12	ONIGBINDE Adegboye	2002
OKALA Emma	1972-'80	51	OLAYOMBO Kenneth	1966-'76	12	CHUKWU Christian	2002-'05
GEORGE Finidi, SIASIA Samson		50	LAWAL Muda	1975-'85	11	EGUAVOEN Augustine	2005-

FIFA/COCA-COLA WORLD RANKING

1993	1994	1995	1996	1997	1998	1999	2000	2001	2002	2003	2004	2005		High		Low	
18	12	27	63	71	65	76	52	40	29	35	21	24		5	04/94	82	11/99

2005–2006											
08/05	09/05	10/05	11/05	12/05	01/06	02/06	03/06	04/06	05/06	06/06	07/06
30	29	23	25	24	24	12	12	12	11	-	11

THE FIFA BIG COUNT OF 2000

	Male	Female		Male	Female
Registered players	35 000	660	Referees	737	151
Non registered players	500 000	17 000	Officials	10 353	714
Youth players	25 000	0	Total involved	589 615	
Total players	577 660		Number of clubs	365	
Professional players	1 400	0	Number of teams	1 320	

NIGERIA 2005

PREMIER LEAGUE

	Pl	W	D	L	F	A	Pts	Enyimba	Rangers	Nationale	Gombe	Sh. Stars	Dolphin	Berger	Sharks	Lobi	Kwara Utd	Pillars	Insurance	Nasarawa	Tornadoes	El Kanemi	Wikki	NPA	Gabros	Zamfara	Gateway
Enyimba †	38	21	9	8	63	22	72		1-0	3-0	3-0	3-1	2-1	4-1	2-0	3-0	2-0	3-0	2-0	4-1	4-0	2-0	3-0	4-0	**0-3**	3-0	2-0
Enugu Rangers †	38	20	7	11	33	22	67	1-1		1-0	0-0	2-0	1-0	1-0	1-0	2-0	2-0	1-0	1-0	1-0	0-1	1-0	1-0	1-0	2-0	3-1	1-0
Iwuanyanwu Nationale‡	38	20	5	13	35	30	65	0-0	1-0		1-0	2-0	1-0	1-0	1-0	1-0	2-1	2-0	2-0	3-0	2-1	2-0	2-0	2-1	0-1	1-0	1-1
Gombe United	38	19	7	12	37	28	64	**0-3**	0-0	1-0		1-0	1-0	0-0	1-0	1-2	1-1	1-0	2-0	2-0	1-2	1-1	1-0	1-0	1-0	1-0	2-0
Shooting Stars	38	17	7	14	40	35	58	0-0	1-0	1-0	1-0		3-0	1-2	0-1	2-1	1-0	1-2	1-1	1-0	3-1	1-0	3-0	1-0	2-1	4-0	2-1
Dolphin	38	18	4	16	37	34	58	2-0	1-0	1-1	1-1	1-0		2-0	2-1	1-0	1-0	2-0	2-0	2-1	2-1	2-0	0-0	2-1	2-1	1-0	2-0
Julius Berger	38	17	4	17	33	38	55	0-0	3-0	2-0	1-0	2-1	1-0		0-1	1-0	1-0	1-0	2-1	0-1	1-0	1-0	1-0	1-0	1-0	3-0	0-0
Sharks	38	16	6	16	42	37	54	3-1	1-0	1-0	0-3	1-1	0-2	2-1		1-0	0-0	2-2	1-0	4-0	1-0	3-1	2-0	2-1	2-1	4-0	3-0
Lobi Stars ‡	38	15	8	15	41	38	53	1-0	0-0	2-0	3-1	2-2	2-1	1-0	1-1		1-0	3-0	1-0	1-1	1-0	3-0	1-0	1-0	2-0	2-0	3-0
Kwara United	38	15	8	15	32	32	53	1-0	2-0	3-0	0-0	0-0	1-0	2-1	1-0	2-1		1-0	**3-0**	2-1	1-1	2-0	1-0	3-1	1-0	3-0	1-0
Kano Pillars	38	15	5	17	37	40	53	1-0	1-0	0-1	1-1	1-0	2-1	2-1	2-1	1-0	2-1		4-1	3-1	2-0	1-0	1-0	4-1	2-0	1-1	1-0
Bendel Insurance	38	16	3	19	44	49	51	0-3	2-2	1-2	3-0	1-0	4-0	3-1	1-0	3-0	2-0	3-0		1-0	1-0	1-0	2-1	2-1	2-1	2-1	**0-3**
Nasarawa United	38	16	3	19	39	50	51	0-1	0-2	2-1	2-1	3-0	1-0	3-1	2-0	1-0	2-1	3-1		2-0	2-1	3-1	2-0	2-1	3-0	2-1	3-0	3-2	2-0
Niger Tornadoes	38	14	8	16	38	35	50	1-1	0-1	3-0	0-1	1-1	1-0	1-1	3-0	2-0	1-0	1-0	2-1	0-0		2-0	3-0	2-1	3-0	3-2	2-0
El Kanemi Warriors	38	15	5	18	39	39	50	1-0	1-0	0-1	1-0	1-0	3-0	1-0	3-0	1-1	1-0	6-2	2-0	1-0		4-1	1-0	0-1	2-2	5-0
Wikki Tourists	38	14	8	16	28	33	50	0-0	0-0	1-0	2-1	2-1	2-0	0-0	1-0	3-0	1-0	1-0	2-1	0-0	0-0		0-0	2-0	2-1	2-0
Ports Authority	38	13	8	17	40	47	47	1-1	0-1	2-1	1-0	1-0	2-1	2-1	3-0	3-1	2-1	0-0	1-1	2-1	1-2	1-0	1-0		2-1	2-1	1-0
Gabros International	38	13	7	18	36	49	46	2-1	1-2	1-0	2-1	0-0	1-2	1-0	2-2	2-0	2-2	2-0	2-2	2-0	2-1	2-1	1-1	1-1		1-0	1-0
Zamfara United	38	12	8	18	34	47	44	0-0	1-0	0-1	1-0	2-0	1-0	0-1	1-1	1-0	0-0	2-1	1-1	0-0	2-1	0-1	0-1	3-1	2-2		2-0
Gateway	38	8	10	20	27	50	34	1-1	4-2	0-1	2-2	0-1	0-0	0-1	0-4	0-0	1-1	0-2	2-0	2-0	1-1	1-1	2-1	2-1		

12/02/2005 - 18/12/2005 • † Qualified for the CAF Champions League • ‡ Qualified for the CAF Confederation Cup • Matches in bold awarded 3-0

CLUB DIRECTORY

Club	Town/City	Stadium	Capacity	Lge	Cup	CL
Bendel Insurance	Benin City	Samuel Ogbemudia	20 000	2	3	0
Dolphin (Prev Eagle Cement)	Port Harcourt	Liberation Stadium	25 000	2	2	0
El Kanemi Warriors	Maiduguri	El Kamemi Stadium	10 000	0	2	0
Enugu Rangers	Enugu	Nnamdi Azikiwe	25 000	5	5	0
Enyimba	Aba	Enyimba Sports Stadium	10 000	4	1	2
Gabros International	Nnewi	Nnewi Township Stadium	5 000	0	0	0
Gombe United	Gombe	Abubakar Umar Memorial	10 000	0	0	0
Heartland (Prev Iwuanyanwu Nationale)	Owerri	Dan Anyiam	10 000	5	1	0
Julius Berger	Lagos	Kashimawo Abiola	15 000	2	2	0
Kano Pillars	Kano	Sani Abacha	25 000	0	1	0
Kwara United	Ilorin	Kwara State Stadium	10 000	0	0	0
Lobi Stars	Makurdi	Aper Aku	15 000	1	0	0
Mighty Jets	Jos	Rwang Pam	15 000	1	0	0
Niger Tornados	Minna	Minna Township Stadium	5 000	0	1	0
Nigerian Ports Authority	Warri	Warri Township Stadium	20 000	0	2	0
Plateau United	Jos	Rwang Pam	15 000	0	1	0
Shooting Stars	Ibadan	Lekan Salami	18 000	5	8	0
Wikki Tourists	Bauchi	Abubakar Balewa	25 000	0	1	0

RECENT LEAGUE AND CUP RECORD

Championship

Year	Champions	Pts	Runners-up	Pts	Third	Pts
1990	Iwuanyanwu Nat.					
1991	Julius Berger	58	Shooting Stars	57	Plateau United	54
1992	Stationery Stores	63	Shooting Stars	62	Iwuanyanwu Nat.	57
1993	Iwuanyanwu Nat.	57	Bendel Insurance	56	Concord	54
1994	BCC Lions	63	Shooting Stars	59	Enyimba	59
1995	Shooting Stars					
1996	Udoji United	58	Jasper United	58	Sharks	58
1997	Eagle Cement	59	Jasper United	58	Shooting Stars	51
1998	Shooting Stars	57	Kwara United	53	Enugu Rangers	53
1999	Lobi Stars	5	Iwuanyanwu Nat.	5	Plateau United	4
2000	Julius Berger	7	Katsina United	6	Lobi Stars	3
2001	Enyimba	9	Ports Authority	4	Gombe United	3
2002	Enyimba	61	Enugu Rangers	57	Kano Pillars	56
2003	Enyimba	63	Julius Berger	58	Enugu Rangers	58
2004	Dolphin	62	Enyimba	60	Bendel Insurance	56
2005	Enyimba	72	Enugu Rangers	67	Iwuanyanwu Nat.	65

Cup

Winners	Score	Runners-up
Stationery Stores	0-0 5-4p	Enugu Rangers
El Kanemi Warriors	3-2	Kano Pillars
El Kanemi Warriors	1-0	Stationery Stores
BCC Lions	1-0	Plateau United
BCC Lions	1-0	Julius Berger
Shooting Stars	2-0	Katsina United
Julius Berger	1-0	Katsina United
BCC Lions	1-0	Katsina United
Wikki Tourists	0-0 3-2	Plateau United
Plateau United	1-0	Iwuanyanwu Nat.
Niger Tornados	1-0	Enugu Rangers
Dolphin	2-0	El Kanemi Warriors
Julius Berger	3-0	Yobe Stars
Lobi Stars	2-0	Sharks
Dolphin	1-0	Enugu Rangers
Enyimba	1-1 6-5p	Lobi Stars

COCA-COLA FA CUP 2005

Third Round		Fourth Round		Quarter-finals		Semi-finals		Final	
Enyimba		**Enyimba**	2 1	**Enyimba**	2 1	**Enyimba**	1	**Enyimba**	1 6p
Yerima		Paulson	0 3	Gombe United	0 3	Sharks	0	Lobi Stars ‡	1 5p
Julius Berger	0								
Paulson	1								
SEC Abuja	1	SEC Abuja	0 1 5p						
Shooting Stars	0	**Gombe United**	1 0 6p						
Sunshine	1								
Gombe United	1								
Dolphin	0 5p	**Dolphin**	3 1	Dolphin					
Yobe Stars	0 3p	Keffi United	0 1	**Sharks**					
Kano Pilars	1								
Keffi United	2								
El Kamemi Warriors	5	**El Kamemi Warriors**	1 0						
Moulam	0	**Sharks**	0 3						
Bendel Insurance	1								
Sharks	1								
Iwuanyanwu Nationale	2	**Iwuanyanwu Nationale**	2 3	**Iwuanyanwu Nationale**		**Iwuanyanwu Nationale**			
Ranchers Bees	0	Gateway	2 0	Bayelsa		**Lobi Stars**			
Ports Authority	0								
Gateway	1								
Kwara United	2	**Kwara United**	0 1 4p						
Zamfara	1	**Bayelsa**	1 0 5p						
Gabros International									
Bayelsa									
Nasarawa United	1	**Nasarawa United**	1 2	Nasarawa United					
Niger Tornadoes	0	Enugu Rangers	1 1	**Lobi Stars**					
Gashaka	1								
Enugu Rangers	4								
Arugo Owerri	2	Arugo Owerri	1 0						
Wikki Tourists	1	**Lobi Stars**	1 3						
OUK	0								
Lobi Stars	1								

CUP FINAL

Liberation Stadium, Port Harcourt, 19-11-2005

Scorers - Atonda Sakibu 93 for Enyimba;
Stephen Saviour 92 for Lobi Stars

‡ Qualified for the CAF Confederation Cup

NIG – NIGER

NATIONAL TEAM RECORD
JULY 1ST 2002 TO JULY 9TH 2006

PL	W	D	L	F	A	%
10	3	1	6	7	20	35

FIFA/COCA-COLA WORLD RANKING

1993	1994	1995	1996	1997	1998	1999	2000	2001	2002	2003	2004	2005	High	Low
81	70	93	129	150	154	164	182	191	184	164	173	177	**68** 11/94	**196** 08/02

2005–2006											
08/05	09/05	10/05	11/05	12/05	01/06	02/06	03/06	04/06	05/06	06/06	07/06
175	175	176	176	177	177	177	177	177	177	-	169

After three years of inactivity on the international front, the chance to watch matches in the qualifiers for the 2008 African Nations Cup was a welcome prospect for fans in the country. The national team from this arid Saharan country has not played since a 0-6 defeat by Algeria at the start of the qualifiers for the 2006 FIFA World Cup™ finals but the draw for the Nations Cup was not particularly kind. They were paired with Nigeria, Uganda and Lesotho, all three of whom were positioned substantially higher in the FIFA/Coca-Cola World Ranking of July 2006, just before the qualifiers got under way. In a surprise move, the federation appointed Togo's Tchanille Bana to

INTERNATIONAL HONOURS
None

lead the national side in a rare approach to a foreign coach, Bana having previously taken Togo to the finals of the Nations Cup. He had also previously worked at club level with Sahel SC and JS Tenere in Niger. Domestic competition was plagued with disputes over results and refereeing which, coupled with numerous protests, left the championship in a state of chaos. L'Association Sportive des Forces Nationales d'Intervention et de Sécurité (AS/FNIS) were Niger's entrants in the 2006 CAF Champions League but they were bundled out in the first round by CS Sfaxien of Tunisia in a one-sided tie. Sahel SC were also first round losers in the CAF Confederation Cup.

THE FIFA BIG COUNT OF 2000

	Male	Female		Male	*Female
Registered players	6 377	0	Referees	50	1
Non registered players	30 000	0	Officials	609	25
Youth players	1 054	0	Total involved	38 116	
Total players	37 431		Number of clubs	127	
Professional players	20	0	Number of teams	922	

Fédération Nigerienne de Football (FENIFOOT)
Avenue Francois Mitterand, Case postale 10299, Niamey, Niger, Niger
Tel +227 20725127   Fax +227 20725127
fenifoot@intnet.ne   www.none
President: DIALLO Amadou   General Secretary: ABDOU Sani
Vice-President: DIAMBEIDOU Oumarou   Treasurer: HASSANE DIABRI Ounteini   Media Officer: None
Men's Coach: BANA Tchanille   Women's Coach: ACOSTA Frederic
FENIFOOT formed: 1967   CAF: 1967   FIFA: 1967
Orange shirts, White shorts, Green socks

RECENT INTERNATIONAL MATCHES PLAYED BY NIGER

2002 Opponents	Score		Venue	Comp	Scorers	Att	Referee
7-09 Ethiopia	W	3-1	Niamey	CNq	Tankary 2 [55 61], Abdoulaye [80]	35 000	Pare BFA
3-10 Morocco	L	1-6	Rabat	Fr	Hamidou	4 300	Rouaissi MAR
13-10 Liberia	L	0-1	Monrovia	CNq		40 000	
2003							
7-03 Benin	D	1-1	Cotonou	Fr	L 1-3p		
30-03 Guinea	L	0-2	Conakry	CNq		25 000	Monteiro Duarte CPV
7-06 Guinea	W	1-0	Niamey	CNq	Tankary [69]	50 000	Wellington GHA
22-06 Ethiopia	L	0-2	Addis Abeba	CNq		25 000	
5-07 Liberia	W	1-0	Niamey	CNq	Alhassan [90p]		
11-10 Algeria	L	0-1	Niamey	WCq		20 126	Coulibaly MLI
14-11 Algeria	L	0-6	Algiers	WCq		50 000	El Arjoun MAR
2004							
No international matches played in 2004							
2005							
No international matches played in 2005							
2006							
No international matches played in 2006 before July							

Fr = Friendly match • CN = CAF African Cup of Nations • WC = FIFA World Cup™ • q = qualifier

NIGER NATIONAL TEAM RECORDS AND RECORD SEQUENCES

Records			Sequence records					
Victory	7-1	MTN 1990	Wins	2	1981	Clean sheets	2	1983
Defeat	1-9	GHA 1969	Defeats	9	1969-1972	Goals scored	5	1994-1995
Player Caps	n/a		Undefeated	4	Three times	Without goal	5	1987-1988
Player Goals	n/a		Without win	23	1963-1976	Goals against	25	1963-1980

RECENT LEAGUE AND CUP RECORD

	Championship		Cup		
Year	Champions	Winners	Score	Runners-up
1998	Olympic FC Niamey	JS Ténéré Niamey	4-0	Liberté FC Niamey
1999	Olympic FC Niamey	JS Ténéré Niamey	2-0	Sahel SC Niamey
2000	JS Ténéré Niamey	JS Ténéré Niamey	3-1	Olympic FC Niamey
2001	JS Ténéré Niamey	Akokana Agadez	1-1 5-4p	Jangorzo Maradi
2002	No competition held	Tournament not held		
2003	Sahel SC Niamey	Olympic FC Niamey	4-1	Alkali Nassara Zinder
2004	Sahel SC Niamey	Sahel SC Niamey	2-1	Akokana Agadez
2005				

NIGER COUNTRY INFORMATION

Capital	Niamey	Independence	1960 from France	GDP per Capita	$800
Population	11 360 538	Status	Republic	GNP Ranking	138
Area km²	1 267 000	Language	French, Hausa, Djerma	Dialling code	+227
Population density	9 per km²	Literacy rate	17%	Internet code	.ne
% in urban areas	17%	Main religion	Muslim 80%	GMT +/-	+1
Towns/Cities ('000)	Niamey 774; Zinder 191; Maradi 163; Agadez 88; Arlit 83; Tahoua 80; Dosso 49				
Neighbours (km)	Chad 1 175; Nigeria 1 497; Benin 266; Burkina Faso 628; Mali 821; Algeria 956; Libya 354				
Main stadia	General Seyni Kountche – Niamey 30 000; Municipal – Zinder 10 000; Municipal – Maradi 10 000				

NIR – NORTHERN IRELAND

NATIONAL TEAM RECORD
JULY 1ST 2002 TO JULY 9TH 2006

PL	W	D	L	F	A	%
35	6	12	17	23	45	34.3

FIFA/COCA-COLA WORLD RANKING

1993	1994	1995	1996	1997	1998	1999	2000	2001	2002	2003	2004	2005	High	Low
39	45	45	64	93	86	84	93	88	103	122	107	103	33 05/94	124 03/04

2005–2006											
08/05	09/05	10/05	11/05	12/05	01/06	02/06	03/06	04/06	05/06	06/06	07/06
116	101	104	101	103	103	102	98	96	96	-	75

With just six wins to celebrate in-between FIFA World Cups, it's not been easy being a Northern Ireland fan - with one notable exception. The wins over St Kitts, Trinidad, Azerbaijan and the two wins over Estonia may have all been met with muted celebrations, but not the historic win over England, which was celebrated long into the Belfast night. Not since 1972 had Northern Ireland beaten the English and it was only their seventh win in 98 meetings between the two. It was also the first time they had beaten England in Belfast since 1932. David Healy's second half winner is sure to be remembered for many years to come and there can be no doubt that under coach Lawrie

INTERNATIONAL HONOURS
Qualified for the FIFA World Cup™ finals 1958 1982 1986   **British International Championship** 1903 1914 1956 1958 1959 1964 1980 1984

Sanchez, Northern Ireland have managed to restore some sense of pride and purpose in the national team. Domestically, Glentoran will be glad to see the back of the season in which they were consigned to second place in all three major competitions and in all of them by arch rivals Linfield. In the League Linfield went the opening 25 matches unbeaten before losing to Distillery in April, the only defeat they suffered in the League all season as they marched on to a 46th title, just five shy of the world record held by Rangers. In the League Cup Final in December they beat Glentoran 3-0 and they followed that up with 2-1 victory in the Irish Cup Final in May to secure the treble.

THE FIFA BIG COUNT OF 2000

	Male	Female		Male	Female
Registered players	20 370	1 000	Referees	425	2
Non registered players	17 000	0	Officials	3 000	50
Youth players	15 000	2 000	Total involved	58 847	
Total players	55 370		Number of clubs	1 278	
Professional players	370	0	Number of teams	2 128	

Irish Football Association (IFA)
20 Windsor Avenue, Belfast, BT9 6EG, United Kingdom
Tel +44 28 90669458   Fax +44 28 90667620
enquiries@irishfa.com   www.irishfa.com
President: BOYCE Jim   General Secretary: WELLS Howard J C
Vice-President: KENNEDY Raymond   Treasurer: MARTIN David   Media Officer: HARRISON Sueann
Men's Coach: SANCHEZ Lawrie   Women's Coach: WYLIE Alfie
IFA formed: 1880   UEFA: 1954   FIFA: 1911-20, 1924-28, 1946
Green shirts with blue trimmings, White shorts, Green socks or White shirts with green trimmings, Green shorts, White socks

RECENT INTERNATIONAL MATCHES PLAYED BY NORTHERN IRELAND

2002	Opponents	Score		Venue	Comp	Scorers	Att	Referee
21-08	Cyprus	D	0-0	Belfast	Fr		6 922	Jones WAL
12-10	Spain	L	0-3	Albacete	ECq		16 000	Michel SVK
16-10	Ukraine	D	0-0	Belfast	ECq		9 288	Bolognino ITA
2003								
12-02	Finland	L	0-1	Belfast	Fr		6 137	McDonald SCO
29-03	Armenia	L	0-1	Yerevan	ECq		10 321	Beck LIE
2-04	Greece	L	0-2	Belfast	ECq		7 196	Gilewski POL
3-06	Italy	L	0-2	Campobasso	Fr		18 270	Cortez Batista POR
11-06	Spain	D	0-0	Belfast	ECq		11 365	Larsen DEN
6-09	Ukraine	D	0-0	Donetsk	ECq		24 000	Stark GER
10-09	Armenia	L	0-1	Belfast	ECq		8 616	Stredak SVK
11-10	Greece	L	0-1	Athens	ECq		15 500	Cortez Batista POR
2004								
18-02	Norway	L	1-4	Belfast	Fr	Healy [56]	11 288	Thomson SCO
31-03	Estonia	W	1-0	Tallinn	Fr	Healy [45]	2 900	Petteri FIN
28-04	Serbia & Montenegro	D	1-1	Belfast	Fr	Quinn [18]	9 690	Richards WAL
30-05	Barbados	D	1-1	Bridgetown	Fr	Healy [71]	8 000	Brizan TRI
2-06	St Kitts and Nevis	W	2-0	Basseterre	Fr	Healy [78], Jones [82]	5 000	Matthew SKN
6-06	Trinidad and Tobago	W	3-0	Port of Spain	Fr	Healy 2 [4 65], Elliott [41]	5 500	Callender BRB
18-08	Switzerland	D	0-0	Zurich	Fr		4 000	Vollquartz DEN
4-09	Poland	L	0-3	Belfast	WCq		12 487	Wegereef NED
8-09	Wales	D	2-2	Cardiff	WCq	Whitley [10], Healy [21]	63 500	Messina ITA
9-10	Azerbaijan	D	0-0	Baku	WCq		6 460	Hanacsek HUN
13-10	Austria	D	3-3	Belfast	WCq	Healy [36], Murdock [58], Elliott [93+]	11 810	Shield AUS
2005								
9-02	Canada	L	0-1	Belfast	Fr		11 156	Attard MLT
26-03	England	L	0-4	Manchester	WCq		62 239	Stark GER
30-03	Poland	L	0-1	Warsaw	WCq		13 515	Frojdfeldt SWE
4-06	Germany	L	1-4	Belfast	Fr	Healy [15p]	14 000	Richmond SCO
17-08	Malta	D	1-1	Ta'Qali	Fr	Healy [9]	1 850	Riley ENG
3-09	Azerbaijan	W	2-0	Belfast	WCq	Elliott [60], Feeney [84]	12 000	Stanisic SCG
7-09	England	W	1-0	Belfast	WCq	Healy [73]	14 069	Busacca SUI
8-10	Wales	L	2-3	Belfast	WCq	Duff [47], Davis [50]	13 451	Bossen NED
12-10	Austria	L	0-2	Vienna	WCq		12 500	Briakos GRE
15-11	Portugal	D	1-1	Belfast	Fr	Feeney [53]	20 000	Webb ENG
2006								
1-03	Estonia	W	1-0	Belfast	Fr	Sproule [2]	13 600	Vink NED
21-05	Uruguay	L	0-1	New Jersey	Fr		4 152	
26-05	Romania	L	0-2	Chicago	Fr		15 000	Kennedy USA

Fr = Friendly match • EC = UEFA EURO 2004™ • WC = FIFA World Cup™ • q = qualifier

NORTHERN IRELAND NATIONAL TEAM RECORDS AND RECORD SEQUENCES

Records			Sequence records					
Victory	7-0	WAL 1930	Wins	3	1968, 1984	Clean sheets	6	1985-1986
Defeat	0-13	ENG 1882	Defeats	11	1884-87, 1959-61	Goals scored	13	1933-1938
Player Caps	119	JENNING Pat	Undefeated	9	1979-80, 1985-86	Without goal	13	2002-2003
Player Goals	19	HEALY David	Without win	21	1947-1953	Goals against	46	1882-1897

NORTHERN IRELAND COUNTRY INFORMATION

Capital	Belfast	Status	Part of the UK	GDP per Capita	$27 700
Population	1 716 942			GNP Ranking	4
Area km²	14 120	Language	English	Dialling code	+44
Population density	121 per km²	Literacy rate	99%	Internet code	.uk
% in urban areas	89%	Main religion	Christian	GMT + / –	0
Towns/Cities ('000)	Belfast 585; Londonderry 86; Bangor 62; Newtonabbey 59; Craigavon 57; Lisburn 45				
Neighbours (km)	Ireland Republic 360; Irish Sea & North Atlantic				
Main stadia	Windsor Park – Belfast 20 332; The Oval – Belfast 15 000				

NATIONAL TEAM PLAYERS AND COACHES

Record Caps			Record Goals			Recent Coaches	
JENNINGS Pat	1964-'86	119	HEALY David	2000-'06	19	PEACOCK Bertie	1962-'67
DONHAGY Mal	1980-'94	91	CLARKE Colin	1986-'93	13	BINGHAM Billy	1967-'71
MCILROY Sammy	1972-'87	88	GILLESPIE William	1913-'31	12	NEILL Terry	1971-'75
NICHOLL Jimmy	1976-'86	73	BAMBRICK Joe	1929-'38	12	CLEMENTS Dave	1975-'76
HUGHES Michael	1992-'04	71	ARMSTRONG Gerry	1977-'86	12	BLANCHFLOWER Danny	1976-'79
GILLESPIE Keith	1995-'05	68	QUINN Jimmy	1985-'96	12	BINGHAM Billy	1980-'93
MCCREERY David	1976-'90	67	DOWIE Iain	1990-'00	12	HAMILTON Bryan	1994-'98
WORTHINGTON Nigel	1984-'97	66	STANFIELD Oli	1887-'97	11	MCMENEMY Lawrie	1998-'99
O'NEILL Martin	1972-'85	64				MCILROY Sammy	2000-'03
ARMSTRONG Gerry	1977-'86	63				SANCHEZ Lawrie	2004-

CLUB DIRECTORY

Club	Town/City	Stadium	Capacity	www.	Lge	Cup
Ards	Newtownards	Taylor's Avenue	6 000		1	4
Ballymena United	Ballymena	The Showgrounds	8 000	ballymenaunited.com	0	6
Cliftonville	Belfast	Solitude	6 000	cliftonvillefc.net	3	8
Coleraine	Coleraine	The Showgrounds	6 500	colerainefc.com	1	5
Crusaders	Belfast	Seaview	6 500		4	2
Dungannon Swifts	Dungannon	Stangmore Park	3 000	dungannonswifts.co.uk	0	0
Glentoran	Belfast	The Oval	15 000	glentoran.net	22	20
Institute	Drumahoe	YMCA Grounds	2 000		0	0
Larne	Larne	Inver Park	6 000	wwwlarnefc.net	0	0
Limavady United	Limavady	The Showgrounds	1 500		0	0
Linfield	Belfast	Windsor Park	20 332	linfieldfc.com	46	37
Lisburn Distillery	Lisburn	New Grosvenor	8 000	lisburn-distillery.net	6	12
Loughgall	Loughgall	Lakeview Park	3 000	loughgallfc.org	0	0
Newry City	Newry	The Showgrounds	6 500		0	0
Omagh	Omagh	St Julians Road	4 500		0	0
Portadown	Portadown	Shamrock Park	8 000	portadownfc.co.uk	4	3

RECENT LEAGUE AND CUP RECORD

	Championship						Cup		
Year	Champions	Pts	Runners-up	Pts	Third	Pts	Winners	Score	Runners-up
1990	Portadown	55	Glenavon	54	Glentoran	44	Glentoran	3-0	Portadown
1991	Portadown	71	Bangor City	61	Glentoran	60	Portadown	2-1	Glenavon
1992	Glentoran	77	Portadown	65	Linfield	60	Glenavon	2-1	Linfield
1993	Linfield	66	Crusaders	66	Bangor	64	Bangor	1-0	Ards
1994	Linfield	70	Portadown	68	Glenavon	68	Linfield	2-0	Bangor
1995	Crusaders	67	Glenavon	60	Portadown	50	Linfield	3-1	Carrick Rangers
1996	Portadown	56	Crusaders	52	Glentoran	46	Glentoran	1-0	Glenavon
1997	Crusaders	46	Coleraine	43	Glentoran	41	Glenavon	1-0	Cliftonville
1998	Cliftonville	68	Linfield	64	Portadown	60	Glentoran	1-0	Glenavon
1999	Glentoran	78	Linfield	70	Crusaders	62	Portadown	w/o	Cliftonville
2000	Linfield	79	Coleraine	61	Glenavon	61	Glentoran	1-0	Portadown
2001	Linfield	75	Glenavon	62	Glentoran	57	Glentoran	1-0	Linfield
2002	Portadown	75	Glentoran	74	Linfield	62	Linfield	2-1	Portadown
2003	Glentoran	90	Portadown	80	Coleraine	73	Coleraine	1-0	Glentoran
2004	Linfield	73	Portadown	70	Lisburn Distillery	55	Glentoran	1-0	Coleraine
2005	Glentoran	74	Linfield	72	Portadown	58	Portadown	5-1	Larne
2006	Linfield	75	Glentoran	63	Portadown	54	Linfield	2-1	Glentoran

NORTHERN IRELAND 2005-06

PREMIER LEAGUE

	Pl	W	D	L	F	A	Pts	Linfield	Glentoran	Portadown	Swifts	Cliftonville	Newry City	Ballymena	Distillery	Coleraine	Limavady	Loughgall	Larne	Glenavon	Armagh	Institute	Ards
Linfield †	30	23	6	1	88	23	75		0-0	4-0	1-1	1-0	3-1	3-2	1-3	7-2	2-0	2-0	8-1	2-1	5-0	2-0	2-0
Glentoran ‡	30	19	6	5	60	28	63	1-4		5-1	3-1	0-0	3-2	1-2	0-0	3-0	0-1	1-0	5-1	1-0	2-0	3-1	2-1
Portadown ‡	30	16	6	8	56	36	54	0-0	0-0		2-3	3-1	5-1	6-1	1-2	2-0	5-1	2-1	2-2	4-0	1-2	0-1	3-2
Dungannon Swifts	30	13	10	7	61	41	50	2-3	2-1	0-1		1-0	1-1	2-2	2-2	6-1	3-2	3-0	3-0	6-0	2-1	2-1	4-2
Cliftonville	30	13	8	9	45	35	47	1-1	1-1	0-2	0-3		0-0	2-2	2-1	0-1	0-1	1-0	2-2	2-1	8-1	2-0	0-1
Newry City	30	12	9	9	45	35	45	1-1	1-3	0-2	2-1	3-1		2-0	0-3	2-0	1-0	0-0	0-0	1-2	1-2	5-0	2-1
Ballymena United	30	13	6	11	42	48	45	0-2	0-4	2-3	4-3	0-2	0-0		1-0	1-0	1-3	3-2	1-0	2-3	3-0	1-0	1-1
Lisburn Distillery	30	12	8	10	44	38	44	0-6	1-4	1-0	0-0	0-0	0-0	2-1		1-2	1-2	2-3	3-1	1-2	3-1	4-1	1-0
Coleraine	30	11	4	15	40	57	37	0-1	0-0	1-1	2-0	0-2	1-3	0-1	1-0		0-2	1-3	2-1	0-0	4-0	2-5	2-4
Limavady United	30	9	9	12	42	49	36	2-2	0-2	0-2	1-1	1-2	1-4	2-2	1-1	3-3		0-1	1-0	1-1	3-0	3-3	1-0
Loughgall	30	9	7	14	33	38	34	1-2	2-3	0-0	0-1	2-3	0-3	1-0	0-0	2-3	2-1		1-1	1-1	2-1	2-0	2-3
Larne	30	7	9	14	42	63	30	2-4	1-3	2-1	1-0	2-4	1-1	1-2	3-1	1-4	2-3	0-0		2-2	2-3	1-1	3-1
Glenavon	30	7	9	14	35	59	30	0-5	0-3	0-1	2-2	2-2	1-4	2-2	2-2	1-2	2-1	0-4	2-3		1-3	0-0	1-0
Armagh City	30	9	3	18	38	69	30	0-1	5-2	2-2	0-0	1-3	2-1	0-1	1-6	3-0	3-3	0-1	1-2	0-4			3-0
Institute	30	6	8	16	37	58	26	2-9	1-3	1-2	3-3	2-3	2-3	0-0	0-1	0-2	0-1	1-1	0-1	1-1	1-2		2-1
Ards	30	6	2	22	31	62	20	0-4	0-1	1-2	3-3	0-1	1-3	1-3	0-1	2-5	2-1	1-0	1-3	1-0	0-2	1-4	

17/09/2005 - 29/04/2006 • † Qualified for the UEFA Champions League • ‡ Qualified for the UEFA Cup • Match in bold awarded 1-0
Play-off: **Donegal Celtic** 3-1 0-0 Institute

NORTHERN IRELAND 2005-06
FIRST DIVISION (2)

	Pl	W	D	L	F	A	Pts
Crusaders	22	20	1	1	51	13	61
Donegal Celtic	22	13	5	4	41	25	44
Dundela	22	10	5	7	32	28	35
Bangor	22	10	3	9	42	32	33
Banbridge Town	22	8	6	8	29	29	30
Tobermore United	22	8	5	9	33	37	29
Carrick Rangers	22	8	4	10	25	29	28
Coagh United	22	8	3	11	25	26	27
HW Welders	22	7	4	11	21	31	25
Moyola Park	22	7	3	12	32	50	24
Ballyclare Comrades	22	6	5	11	32	37	23
Ballymoney United	22	3	4	15	18	44	13

24/09/2005 - 13/05/2006

LEAGUE CUP 2005-06

Quarter-finals		Semi-finals		Final	
Linfield *	4				
Dung'on Swifts	0	Linfield †	5		
Limavady Utd	0	Lisburn Distillery	0		
Lisburn Distillery *	6			Linfield	3
Portadown *	4			Glentoran	0
Armagh City	2	Portadown	1	Windsor Park, 10-12-2005
Newry City	1	Glentoran ‡	2	Scorer - Ferguson 3 [3] [49] [75]
Glentoran *	2			

* Home team • † At Seaview • ‡ At Windsor Park

IRISH CUP 2005-06

Round of 16		Quarter-finals		Semi-finals		Final	
Linfield *	1 3						
Loughgall	1 1	Linfield *	3				
Coleraine	0	Glenavon	0				
Glenavon *	3			Linfield †	3		
Lisburn Distillery *	0 2			Bangor	1		
Ballymena United	0 1	Lisburn Distillery *	0				
Limvady United *	1	Bangor	1			Linfield	2
Bangor	3					Glentoran ‡	1
Larne *	3						
Carrick Rangers	0	Larne *	2				
Portstewart	0	Newington YC	1			CUP FINAL	
Newington YC	1			Larne	0	Windsor Park, Belfast	
Portadown	1 3			Glentoran ††	2	6-05-2006	
Dungannon Swifts *	1 1	Portadown	0			Scorers - Peter Thompson 2 [45] [65] for	
Ballyclare Comrades	0	Glentoran *	2			Linfield; Michael Halliday [44] for Glentoran	
Glentoran *	1						

* Home team • ‡ Qualified for the UEFA Cup • † At Seaview • †† At Windsor Park

NOR – NORWAY

NATIONAL TEAM RECORD
JULY 1ST 2002 TO JULY 9TH 2006

PL	W	D	L	F	A	%
53	23	14	16	66	52	56.6

FIFA/COCA-COLA WORLD RANKING

1993	1994	1995	1996	1997	1998	1999	2000	2001	2002	2003	2004	2005		High		Low	
4	8	10	14	13	14	7	14	26	26	42	35	38		2	10/93	52	07/06

2005–2006											
08/05	09/05	10/05	11/05	12/05	01/06	02/06	03/06	04/06	05/06	06/06	07/06
36	37	37	38	38	37	39	39	40	40	-	52

The story of the season in the Norwegian championship was the fall from power of Trondheim's Rosenborg BK, who, after 13 years at the top, were knocked off their pedestal by Oslo club Vålerenga IF. Rosenborg had survived a number of last day scares during those 13 triumphs, notably in 2004 when they denied Vålerenga the title on goal difference, but they were not involved in the 2005 finale as once again the League went down to the wire. Newly promoted Start Kristiansand went into the final day a point ahead of Vålerenga with a home game against relegation threatened Fredrikstad, a match Start lost 3-1. That meant Vålerenga's draw against Odd Grenland

INTERNATIONAL HONOURS
Qualified for the FIFA World Cup™ finals 1938 1994 1998
FIFA Women's World Cup 1995   Women's Olympic Gold 2000   European Women's Championship 1987 1993

was enough to give them the title for the first time since 1984. In the Cup Final Arild Sundgot scored a last minute penalty for Lillestrøm to send the match into extra time, but goals from Daniel Berg and John Andreas Husøy won the trophy for Molde, who then won their relegation play-off against Moss. Following their Euro 2004 play-off defeat by Spain, Norway had enjoyed a successful two years but key defeats in their FIFA World Cup™ qualifying group meant another play-off, this time against the Czech Republic. Both matches were lost 1-0.

THE FIFA BIG COUNT OF 2000

	Male	Female		Male	Female
Registered players	90 292	21 319	Referees	4 000	1 000
Non registered players	60 000	25 000	Officials	4 000	1 000
Youth players	162 846	53 367	Total involved	422 824	
Total players	412 824		Number of clubs	1 820	
Professional players	800	30	Number of teams	15 431	

Norges Fotballforbund (NFF)
Ullevaal Stadion, Sognsveien 75J, Serviceboks 1 Ullevaal Stadion, Oslo 0840, Norway
Tel +47 21029300   Fax +47 21029301
nff@fotball.no   www.fotball.no
President: KAAFJORD Sondre   General Secretary: ESPELUND Karen
Vice-President: HAMMERSLAND Mette   Treasurer: RIBERG Rune   Media Officer: SOLHEIM Roger
Men's Coach: HAREIDE Age   Women's Coach: BERNTSEN Bjarne
NFF formed: 1902   UEFA: 1954   FIFA: 1908
Red shirts with white and blue trimmings, White shorts, Blue socks or White shirts with blue trimmings, White shorts, White socks

RECENT INTERNATIONAL MATCHES PLAYED BY NORWAY

2003	Opponents	Score		Venue	Comp	Scorers	Att	Referee
20-08	Scotland	D	0-0	Oslo	Fr		12 858	Vuorela FIN
6-09	Bosnia-Herzegovina	L	0-1	Zenica	ECq		18 000	Bre FRA
10-09	Portugal	L	0-1	Oslo	Fr		11 014	Bennett ENG
11-10	Luxembourg	W	1-0	Oslo	ECq	Flo.TA [18]	22 255	Szabo HUN
15-11	Spain	L	1-2	Valencia	ECpo	Iversen [14]	53 000	Poll ENG
19-11	Spain	L	0-3	Oslo	ECpo		25 106	Collina ITA
2004								
22-01	Sweden	W	3-0	Hong Kong	Fr	Johnsen.F [44], Flo.H 2 [54 63]	10 000	Fong HKG
25-01	Honduras	W	3-1	Hong Kong	Fr	Brattbakk [27], Johnsen.F [39], Hoseth [86]	14 603	Chan HKG
28-01	Singapore	W	5-2	Singapore	Fr	Stadheim [18], Aas [42], Flo.H 2 [59 70], Brattbakk [67]	5 000	Supian MAS
18-02	Northern Ireland	W	4-1	Belfast	Fr	Gamst Pedersen 3 [17 35], Iversen [43], OG [57]	11 288	Thomson SCO
31-03	Serbia & Montenegro	W	1-0	Belgrade	Fr	Andresen [76p]	8 000	Panic BIH
28-04	Russia	W	3-2	Oslo	Fr	Andresen [25], Rushfeldt [43], Solli [62]	11 435	Wegereef NED
27-05	Wales	D	0-0	Oslo	Fr		14 137	Hansson SWE
18-08	Belgium	D	2-2	Oslo	Fr	Johnsen.F [32], Riseth [59]	16 669	Slupik POL
4-09	Italy	L	1-2	Palermo	WCq	Carew [1]	21 463	Sars FRA
8-09	Belarus	D	1-1	Oslo	WCq	Riseth [39]	25 272	Costa POR
9-10	Scotland	W	1-0	Glasgow	WCq	Iversen [54p]	51 000	Allaerts BEL
13-10	Slovenia	W	3-0	Oslo	WCq	Carew [7], Pedersen.M [60], Odegaard [89]	24 907	Ivanov RUS
16-11	Australia	D	2-2	London	Fr	Iversen [42], Gamst Pedersen [72]	7 364	Styles ENG
2005								
22-01	Kuwait	D	1-1	Kuwait City	Fr	Kvisvik [49]	200	Shaban KUW
25-01	Bahrain	W	1-0	Manama	Fr	Kvisvik [49]	4 000	Al Bannai UAE
28-01	Jordan	D	0-0	Amman	Fr		8 000	Al Shoufi SYR
9-02	Malta	W	3-0	Ta'Qali	Fr	Rushfeldt 2 [71 80], Riise [82]	1 000	Malcolm NIR
30-03	Moldova	D	0-0	Chisinau	WCq		5 000	Meyer GER
20-04	Estonia	W	2-1	Tallinn	Fr	Johnsen.F [24], Braaten [54]	2 500	Vink NED
24-05	Costa Rica	W	1-0	Oslo	Fr	Johnsen.F [77]	21 251	Van Egmond NED
4-06	Italy	D	0-0	Oslo	WCq		24 829	Mejuto Gonzalez ESP
8-06	Sweden	W	3-2	Stockholm	Fr	Riise [60], Helstad [64], Iversen [65]	15 345	Jara CZE
17-08	Switzerland	L	0-2	Oslo	Fr		19 623	Vollquartz DEN
3-09	Slovenia	W	3-2	Celje	WCq	Carew [3], Lundekvam [23], Pedersen [92+]	10 055	Medina Cantalejo ESP
7-09	Scotland	L	1-2	Oslo	WCq	Arst [89]	24 904	Hamer LUX
8-10	Moldova	W	1-0	Oslo	WCq	Rushfeldt [50]	23 409	Bennett RSA
12-10	Belarus	W	1-0	Minsk	WCq	Helstad [70]	13 222	Plautz AUT
12-11	Czech Republic	L	0-1	Oslo	WCpo		24 264	Busacca SUI
16-11	Czech Republic	L	0-1	Prague	WCpo		17 464	Poll ENG
2006								
25-01	Mexico	L	1-2	San Francisco	Fr	Vaagen Moen [9]	44 729	Vaughn USA
29-01	USA	L	0-5	Carson	Fr		16 366	Acosta COL
1-03	Senegal	L	1-2	Dakar	Fr	Hagen [41]	45 000	Pare BFA
24-05	Paraguay	D	2-2	Oslo	Fr	Johnsen.F 2 [22 61]	10 227	Olsiak SVK
1-06	Korea Republic	D	0-0	Oslo	Fr		15 487	Verbist BEL

Fr = Friendly match • EC = UEFA EURO 2004™ • WC = FIFA World Cup™ • q = qualifier • po = qualifying play-off

NORWAY NATIONAL TEAM RECORDS AND RECORD SEQUENCES

Records			Sequence records				
Victory	12-0	FIN 1946	Wins	9	1999	Clean sheets	6	Three times
Defeat	0-12	DEN 1917	Defeats	9	1908-1913	Goals scored	21	1929-1933
Player Caps	104	SVENSSEN Thorbjørn	Undefeated	17	1997-98	Without goal	7	1975-1976
Player Goals	33	JUVE Jørgen	Without win	27	1908-18	Goals against	20	1908-1916

NORWAY COUNTRY INFORMATION

Capital	Oslo	Independence	1905 from Sweden	GDP per Capita	$37 800
Population	4 574 560	Status	Constitutional Monarchy	GNP Ranking	27
Area km²	324 220	Language	Norwegian	Dialling code	+47
Population density	14 per km²	Literacy rate	100%	Internet code	.no
% in urban areas	73%	Main religion	Christian	GMT + / –	+1
Towns/Cities ('000)	Oslo 808; Bergen 214; Stavanger 173; Trondheim 145; Fredrikstad-Sarpsborg 97; Kristiansand 67; Tromsø 53; Bodø 34; Larvik 23; Halden 22; Harstad 19; Lillehammer 19				
Neighbours (km)	Russia 196; Finland 736; Sweden 1 619; North Sea & North Atlantic 21 925				
Main stadia	Ullevaal Stadion – Oslo 25 572; Lerkendal – Trondheim 21 166				

NATIONAL TEAM PLAYERS AND COACHES

Record Caps			Record Goals			Recent Coaches	
SVENSSEN Thorbjørn	1947-'62	104	JUVE Jørgen	1928-'37	33	JOHANNESSEN Oivind	1970-'71
BERG Henning	1992-'04	100	GUNDERSEN Einar	1917-'28	26	CURTIS George	1972-'74
THORSTVEDT Erik	1982-'96	97	HENNUM Harald	1949-'60	25	ANDREASSEN Kjell	1974-'77
LEONHARDSEN Oyvind	1990-'03	86	FLO Tore André	1995-'04	23	EGGEN Nils Arne	
REKDAL Kjetil	1987-'00	83	THORESEN Gunnar	1946-'59	22	FOSSEN Tor Røste	1978-'87
MYKLAND Erik	1990-'00	78	SOLSKJAER Ole Gunnar	1995-'04	21	GRIP Tord	1987-'88
GRONDALEN Svein	1973-'84	77	FJORTOFT Jan Age	1986-'96	20	STADHEIM Ingvar	1988-'90
FLO Tore André	1995-'04	76	IVERSEN Odd	1967-'79	19	OLSEN Egil	1990-'98
BJORNEBYE Stig Inge	1989-'00	75	LEONHARDSEN Oyvind	1990-'03	19	SEMB Nils Johan	1998-'03
FJORTOFT Jan Age	1986-'96	71	NILSEN Olav	1962-'71	18	HAREIDE Age	2003-

CLUB DIRECTORY

Club	Town/City	Stadium	Capacity	www.	Lge	Cup
Aalesunds FK	Aalesund	Kråmyra	9 600	aafk.no	0	0
FK Bodø/Glimt	Bodø	Aspmyra	6 100	glimt.no	0	2
SK Brann	Bergen	Brann Stadion	17 600	brann.no	2	6
Fredrikstad FK	Fredrikstad	Fredrikstad Stadion	10 000	fredrikstadfk.no	9	10
Hamarkameratene	Hamar	Briskeby	8 000	hamkam.no	0	0
Lillestrøm SK	Lillestrøm	Aråsen	12 250	lsk.no	5	4
SFK Lyn	Oslo	Ullevaal	25 572	lyn.no	2	8
Molde FK	Molde	Molde Stadion	11 167	moldefk.no	0	2
Odd Grenland	Skien	Odd Stadion	9 008	oddgrenland.no	0	12
Rosenborg BK	Trondheim	Lerkendal	21 166	rosenborg.no	19	9
IK Start	Kristiansand	Kristiansand Stadion	12 000	ikstart.no	2	0
Tromsø IL	Tromsø	Alfheim	9 362	til.no	0	2
Vålerenga IF	Oslo	Ullevaal	25 572	vif.no	5	3
Viking FK	Stavanger	Viking Stadion	15 300	viking-fk.no	8	5

RECENT LEAGUE AND CUP RECORD

Championship						Cup		
Year	Champions	Pts	Runners-up	Pts	Third	Pts	Winners	Score	Runners-up
1990	Rosenborg BK	44	Tromsø IL	42	Molde FK	40	Rosenborg BK	5-1	Fyllingen
1991	Viking SK	41	Rosenborg BK	36	IK Start	34	Strømsgodset	3-2	Rosenborg BK
1992	Rosenborg BK	46	Kongsvinger	40	IK Start	39	Rosenborg BK	3-2	Lillestrøm
1993	Rosenborg BK	47	FK Bodø/Glimt	45	Lillestrøm	42	FK Bodø/Glimt	2-0	Strømsgodset
1994	Rosenborg BK	49	Lillestrøm	41	Viking SK	39	Molde FK	3-2	Lyn Oslo
1995	Rosenborg BK	62	Molde FK	47	FK Bodø/Glimt	43	Rosenborg BK	1-1 3-1	SK Brann
1996	Rosenborg BK	59	Lillestrøm	46	Viking SK	43	Tromsø IL	2-1	FK Bodø/Glimt
1997	Rosenborg BK	61	SK Brann	50	Strømsgodset	46	Vålerenga IF	4-2	Strømsgodset
1998	Rosenborg BK	63	Molde FK	54	Stabæk	53	Stabæk	3-1	Rosenborg BK
1999	Rosenborg BK	56	Molde FK	50	SK Brann	49	Rosenborg BK	2-0	SK Brann
2000	Rosenborg BK	54	SK Brann	47	Viking SK	45	Odd Grenland	2-1	Viking SK
2001	Rosenborg BK	57	Lillestrøm	56	Viking SK	49	Viking SK	3-0	Bryne FK
2002	Rosenborg BK	56	Molde FK	50	Lyn Oslo	47	Vålerenga	1-0	Odd Grenland
2003	Rosenborg BK	61	FK Bodø/Glimt	47	Stabæk	42	Rosenborg BK	3-1	FK Bodø/Glimt
2004	Rosenborg BK	48	Vålerenga IF	48	SK Brann	40	SK Brann	4-1	Lyn Oslo
2005	Vålerenga IF	46	IK Start	45	Lyn Oslo	44	Molde FK	4-2	Lillestrøm

NORWAY 2005

TIPPELIGAEN

	Pl	W	D	L	F	A	Pts	Vålerenga	Start	Lyn	Lillestrøm	Viking	Brann	Rosenborg	Tromsø	Odd	Ham-Kam	Fredrikstad	Molde	Aalesunds	Bodø/Glimt
Vålerenga IF †	26	13	7	6	40	27	46		1-1	0-1	0-0	1-2	2-1	0-2	1-1	3-0	2-1	0-0	3-1	3-1	3-1
IK Start ‡	26	13	6	7	47	35	45	3-0		1-1	3-1	5-2	3-2	5-2	1-1	4-0	2-1	1-3	1-0	4-5	2-0
FC Lyn Oslo ‡	26	12	8	6	37	21	44	1-1	1-1		1-0	2-1	1-0	3-2	0-1	1-2	1-0	1-1	6-1	0-0	6-0
Lillestrøm SK	26	12	6	8	37	31	42	2-1	2-0	1-0		2-0	1-0	1-1	1-2	2-3	1-0	3-0	2-2	3-0	2-0
Viking FK	26	12	5	9	37	32	41	0-0	1-1	0-0	3-1		0-0	3-2	3-2	1-0	1-3	2-1	2-3	3-0	2-1
SK Brann ‡	26	10	7	9	43	32	37	1-2	1-0	3-0	6-2	2-1		4-1	0-0	2-2	2-0	4-0	2-0	0-0	2-3
Rosenborg BK	26	10	4	12	50	42	34	2-3	3-0	0-1	1-2	0-2	4-1		1-1	6-0	4-0	0-1	1-1	2-2	2-0
Tromsø IL	26	8	10	8	31	30	34	0-1	3-1	0-0	1-1	1-0	1-1	1-2		0-1	1-0	2-0	2-1	1-1	2-2
Odd Grenland	26	9	6	11	28	51	33	2-2	2-0	0-2	0-2	1-0	0-0	0-5	1-1		2-2	2-1	2-1	2-1	2-1
Hamarkameratene	26	8	7	11	31	37	31	3-1	0-2	1-0	2-3	0-0	1-1	0-3	3-2	2-1		1-1	4-1	2-1	2-0
Fredrikstad FK	26	8	7	11	35	44	31	0-4	1-2	2-1	1-1	2-1	2-3	5-1	4-2	1-1	1-1		1-1	1-4	3-2
Molde FK ‡	26	8	6	12	40	46	30	1-3	0-1	1-3	2-0	1-2	3-1	4-1	2-1	4-0	1-1	2-1		2-2	1-1
Aalesunds FK	26	6	9	11	30	42	27	0-2	1-2	1-1	1-0	2-1	2-1	0-1	2-1	0-1	2-1	1-1	1-0		1-1
Bodø/Glimt	26	6	6	14	29	45	24	0-1	1-1	3-1	1-1	0-3	2-1	0-1	2-1	5-1	2-0	1-2	2-0	0-0	

10/04/2005 - 29/10/2005 • † Qualified for the UEFA Champions League • ‡ Qualified for the UEFA Cup • Play-off: Moss 2-3 0-2 **Molde FK**
Top scorers: Ole Martin ARST, Tromsø, 16; Egil OSTENSTAD, Viking, 14; Thorstein HELSTAD, Rosenborg, 13; Arild SUNDGOT, Lillestrøm, 11

NORWAY 2005
ADECCOLIGAEN (2)

	Pl	W	D	L	F	A	Pts
Stabæk	30	20	7	3	63	23	67
Sandefjord	30	19	5	6	58	37	62
Moss FK	30	17	7	6	54	30	58
Hønefoss BK	30	17	5	8	52	41	56
Bryne	30	14	8	8	55	33	50
Pors Grenland	30	13	11	6	47	45	50
Sogndal	30	11	8	11	47	51	41
Strømsgodset	30	11	7	12	46	45	40
IL Hødd	30	10	7	13	53	54	37
Kongsvinger	30	11	4	15	41	48	37
Follo	30	8	10	12	40	47	34
Løv-Ham	30	9	4	17	31	47	31
Mandalskameratene	30	7	8	15	41	54	29
Skeid	30	8	5	17	39	58	29
FK Tønsberg	30	6	7	17	36	56	25
Alta	30	5	5	20	28	62	20

10/04/2005 - 30/10/2005

NM-CUP 2005

Round of 16		Quarter-finals		Semi-finals		Final	
Molde FK	2						
Bodø/Glimt *	1	Molde FK *	2				
Alta	0	Odd Grenland	1				
Odd Grenland *	6			Molde FK *	1		
Hamarkameratene *	2			Hønefoss BK	0		
Bryne FK	0	Hamarkameratene	0				
Rosenborg BK *	1	Hønefoss BK *	4				
Hønefoss BK	2					Molde FK ‡	4
Vålerenga IF	3					Lillestrøm	2
IK Start *	2	Vålerenga IF *	2				
Aalesunds FK	2	SK Brann	1				
SK Brann *	3			Vålerenga IF	0		
Stabæk *	4			Lillestrøm *	2		
Fredrikstad FK	2	Stabæk	1				
Viking FK *	0	Lillestrøm *	3				
Lillestrøm	2						

CUP FINAL
Ullevaal, Oslo
6-11-2005, Att: 25 182, Ref: Sandmoen

Scorers - Friend [25], Konate [65], Hestad [94],
Husøy [108] for Molde;
Mouelhi [46], Sundgot [90p] for Lillestrøm

* Home team • ‡ Qualified for the UEFA Cup

NZL – NEW ZEALAND

NATIONAL TEAM RECORD
JULY 1ST 2002 TO JULY 9TH 2006

PL	W	D	L	F	A	%
27	11	2	14	53	44	44.4

FIFA/COCA-COLA WORLD RANKING

1993	1994	1995	1996	1997	1998	1999	2000	2001	2002	2003	2004	2005	High	Low
77	99	102	132	120	103	100	91	84	49	88	95	120	**47** 08/02	**136** 11/96

2005–2006											
08/05	09/05	10/05	11/05	12/05	01/06	02/06	03/06	04/06	05/06	06/06	07/06
109	111	116	118	120	121	122	115	120	118	-	117

These are exciting times for football in New Zealand as the game there emerges from the shadow cast over it for years by Australia. Rather than following their neighbours into the Asian Football Confederation, the Kiwis seem determined to forge a place for themselves in the international game by exploiting all of the opportunities available to them through the OFC. The first of those came in May 2006 when Auckland City won the Oceania Club Championship which was staged in their home town. In the 2005 tournament they had been knocked out in the first round group but they had no such trouble this time around against opposition from Papua New Guinea, the Solomon

INTERNATIONAL HONOURS
Oceania Nations Cup 1973 1998 2002   Oceania Women's Championship 1983 1991
Oceania Youth Championship 1980 1992 Oceania U-17 Championship 1997

Islands and Tahiti to qualify for the semi-finals. There they met Nokia Eagles from Fiji whom they beat 9-1. They then beat Tahiti's Piraé 3-1 in the final, thanks to a hat-trick by South African Keryn Jordan, to qualify for the FIFA Club World Cup in Japan. The hope is that with such a prize on offer on a regular basis, the championship in New Zealand will be seen as an attractive prospect for players. In 2006 it was won for the second time by Auckland City after they won both the regular season and the Grand Final, although it took penalties in the latter to beat Canterbury.

THE FIFA BIG COUNT OF 2000

	Male	Female		Male	Female
Registered players	17 525	6 700	Referees	400	7
Non registered players	35 000	2 000	Officials	9 240	6 160
Youth players	60 725	14 098	Total involved	151 855	
Total players	136 048		Number of clubs	311	
Professional players	25	0	Number of teams	7 088	

New Zealand Soccer Inc (NZS)
Albany, PO Box 301 043, Auckland, New Zealand
Tel +64 9 4140175   Fax +64 9 4140176
tracy@soccernz.co.nz   www.nzsoccer.com
President: MORRIS John   General Secretary: SEATTER Graham
Vice-President: TBD   Treasurer: ELDERKIN Peter   Media Officer: GRAY Kent
Men's Coach: HERBERT Ricki   Women's Coach: JONES Allan
NZS formed: 1891   OFC: 1966   FIFA: 1948
White shirts with black trimmings, White shorts, White socks

RECENT INTERNATIONAL MATCHES PLAYED BY NEW ZEALAND

2002	Opponents	Score		Venue	Comp	Scorers	Att	Referee
5-07	Tahiti	W	4-0	Auckland	OCr1	Nelsen [30], Vicelich [49], Urlovic [80], Campbell [88]	1 000	Atisson VAN
7-07	Papua New Guinea	W	9-1	Auckland	OCr1	Killen 4 [9 10 28 51], Campbell 2 [27 85], Nelson [54] Burton [87], De Gregorio [90]	2 200	Rakaroi FIJ
9-07	Solomon Islands	W	6-1	Auckland	OCr1	Vicelich 2 [28 45], Urlovic [42], Campbell 2 [50 75], Burton [88]	300	Atisson VAN
12-07	Vanuatu	W	3-0	Auckland	OCsf	Burton 2 [13 65], Killen [23]	1 000	Breeze AUS
14-07	Australia	W	1-0	Auckland	OCf	Nelsen [78]	4 000	Ariiotima TAH
12-10	Estonia	L	2-3	Tallinn	Fr	Hickey [41], Lines [45]	800	Pedersen NOR
16-10	Poland	L	0-2	Ostrowiec	Fr		8 000	Layec FRA
2003								
27-05	Scotland	D	1-1	Edinburgh	Fr	Nelsen [47]	10 016	Ingvarsson SWE
8-06	USA	L	1-2	Richmond	Fr	Coveny [23]	9 116	Liu CAN
18-06	Japan	L	0-3	Paris	CCr1		36 038	Codjia BEN
20-06	Colombia	L	1-3	Lyon	CCr1	De Gregorio [27]	22 811	Batres GUA
22-06	France	L	0-5	Paris	CCr1		36 842	Moradi IRN
12-10	Iran	L	0-3	Tehran	AO		40 000	Kousa SYR
2004								
29-05	Australia	L	0-1	Adelaide	WCq		12 100	Larsen DEN
31-05	Solomon Islands	W	3-0	Adelaide	WCq	Fisher [36], Oughton [81], Lines [90]	217	Iturralde Gonzalez ESP
2-06	Vanuatu	L	2-4	Adelaide	WCq	Coveny 2 [61 75]	356	Farina ITA
4-06	Tahiti	W	10-0	Adelaide	WCq	Coveny 3 [6 38 46+], Fisher 3 [16 22 63], Jones [72] Oughton [74], Nelsen 2 [82 87]	200	Shield AUS
6-06	Fiji	W	2-0	Adelaide	WCq	Bunce [8], Coveny [56]	300	Larsen DEN
2005								
9-06	Australia	L	0-1	London	Fr		9 023	Dean ENG
2006								
19-02	Malaysia	W	1-0	Christchurch	Fr	Old [87]	10 100	O'Leary NZL
23-02	Malaysia	W	2-1	Albany	Fr	Banks [18], Barron [88]	8 702	Fox NZL
25-04	Chile	L	1-4	Rancagua	Fr	Smeltz [14]	8 000	Osorio CHI
27-04	Chile	L	0-1	La Calera	Fr			Acosta CHI
24-05	Hungary	L	0-2	Budapest	Fr		5 000	Hrinak SVK
27-05	Georgia	W	3-1	Altenkirchen	Fr	Coveny 2 [35 53], Killen [37]	1 000	
31-05	Estonia	D	1-1	Tallinn	Fr	Hay [27]	3 000	Rasmussen DEN
4-06	Brazil	L	0-4	Geneva	Fr		32 000	Laperriere SUI

Fr = Friendly match • OC = OFC Oceania Nations Cup • CC = FIFA Confederations Cup • AO = Asia/Oceania Challenge • WC = FIFA World Cup™ •
q = qualifier • r1 = first round group

NATIONAL TEAM PLAYERS AND COACHES

Record Caps			Record Goals			Recent Coaches	
SUMNER Steve	1976-'86	105	COVENY Vaughan	1992-'06	28	JONES Allan	1983-'84
TURNER Brian	1967-'82	102	NEWALL Jock	1951-'52	28	FALLON Kevin	1985-'88
COLE Duncan	1978-'83	92	SUMNER Steve	1976-'86	27	ADSHEAD John	1989
ELRICK Adrian	1975-'84	91	NELSON Keith	1977-'83	26	MARSHALL Ian	1989-'94
MCGARRY Michael	1986-'97	87	TURNER Brian	1967-'82	25	CLARK Bobby	1994-'95
EVANS Ceri	1980-'93	85	MCGARRY Michael	1986-'97	22	PRITCHETT Keith	1996-'97
SIBLEY Tony	1972-'81	85	COXON ROY	1951-'52	20	MCGRATH Joe	1997-'98
ZORICICH Chris	1988-'03	77	TURNER Grant	1980-'86	19	DUGDALE Ken	1998-'02
JACKSON Chris	1990-'03	72	THOMAS Earle	1967-'78	18	WAITT Mick	2002-'04
Caps/goals include unofficial matches			WALKER Colin	1984-'88	18	HERBERT Ricki	2004-

NEW ZEALAND NATIONAL TEAM RECORDS AND RECORD SEQUENCES

Records			Sequence records				
Victory	13-0	FIJ 1981	Wins	9	1951-1954	Clean sheets	10	1981
Defeat	0-10	AUS 1936	Defeats	16	1927-1951	Goals scored	22	1951-1967
Player Caps	105	SUMNER Steve	Undefeated	11	1981	Without goal	5	1997-1998
Player Goals	28	COVENY/NEWALL	Without win	16	1927-1951	Goals against	19	1927-1951

NEW ZEALAND COUNTRY INFORMATION

Capital	Wellington	Independence	1907 from the UK	GDP per Capita	$21 600
Population	3 993 817	Status	Commonnwealth	GNP Ranking	48
Area km²	268 680	Language	English, Maori	Dialling code	+64
Population density	15 per km²	Literacy rate	99%	Internet code	.nz
% in urban areas	86%	Main religion	Christian	GMT +/–	+12
Towns/Cities ('000)	Aukland 417; Manukau 383; Christchurch 364; North Shore 207; Wellington 179; Waitakere 166; Hamilton 152; Dunedin 114; Tauranga 110; Lower Hutt 101; Palmerston North 75; Hastings 61				
Neighbours (km)	South Pacific Ocean 15 134				
Main stadia	Ericsson Stadium – Auckland 50 000; North Harbour Stadium – Albany, Auckland 25 000				

NEW ZEALAND 2005–06

NEW ZEALAND FOOTBALL CHAMPIONSHIP

	Pl	W	D	L	F	A	Pts	Auckland	Manawatu	Canterbury	Wellington	Otago	Waitakere	Waikato	Hawkes Bay
Auckland City †	21	16	0	5	63	28	48		4-1 2-1	2-3 4-3	5-3	4-1 0-1	5-1	4-0	3-0 6-0
YoungHeart Manawatu†	21	14	4	3	50	29	46	1-2		1-0 1-0	2-1	0-0 3-2	2-1 2-1	2-1	5-2 8-1
Canterbury United	21	13	2	6	36	22	41	2-1	0-1		4-0 2-3	2-1	2-1 1-1	2-1 2-1	2-1
Team Wellington	21	8	4	9	43	53	28	4-6 0-4	2-2 1-3	2-0		1-1	3-3	4-2 2-2	2-1 4-2
Otago United	21	7	6	8	27	25	27	2-3	0-0	1-1 0-2	2-1 1-2		1-0 0-1	0-0	3-3
Waitakere United	21	6	4	11	38	41	22	1-2 1-2	3-3	1-2	3-2 1-4	2-1		7-1 1-2	3-2
Waikato	21	6	4	11	31	44	22	2-1 1-0	1-3 3-4	0-1	6-0	0-4 0-2	2-2		1-0
Hawkes Bay United	21	1	2	18	17	63	5	0-3	1-4	0-2 0-3	1-2	0-3 0-1	0-3 1-0	1-1 2-4	

15/10/2004 - 12/03/2005 • Top five qualified for the play-offs: Play-offs: First round: Manawatu 0-0 4-5p Canterbury; Wellington 2-2 4-1p Otago;
Second round: Auckland 3-0 Canterbury; Manawatu 2-3 Wellington; Third round: Canterbury 3-2 Wellington
Grand Final: **Auckland City** 3-3 4-3p Canterbury • † Qualified for the 2006 OFC Champions Cup • Napier City renamed Hawkes Bay United

CHATHAM CUP 2005

Round of sixteen		Quarter-finals		Semi-finals		Final	
Central United *	4						
Hamilton Wanderers	2	**Central United**	2				
North Shore United *	2	East Coast Bays *	1				
East Coast Bays	3			**Central United**	3		
Papakura *	2			Halswell United *	1		
Bay Olympic	1	Papakura	1				
Roslyn Wakari *	3	**Halswell United** *	2				
Halswell United	4					**Central United**	2
Wellington Olympic *	5					Palmerston N. Marist	1
Mosgiel	2	**Wellington Olympic**	4				
Tauranga City United *	1 4p	Eastern Suburbs *	1				
Eastern Suburbs	1 5p			Wellington Olympic *	1	CUP FINAL	
Lower Hutt City	5			**Palmerston N. Marist**	2	North Harbour Stadium, Albany	
Gisborne City *	1	Lower Hutt City	1			5-09-2005, Ref: Fox	
Naenae	0	**Palmerston N. Marist** *	2			Scorers Urlovic 21, Sykes 80 for Central;	
Palmerston N. Marist *	2				* Home team	Hill 84 for Palmerston North	

RECENT LEAGUE AND CUP RECORD

	Championship					Chatham Cup		
Year	Champions	Score	Runners-up		Winners	Score	Runners-up	
1997	Waitakere City	3-1	Napier City Rovers		Central United	3-2	Napier City Rovers	
1998	Napier City Rovers	5-2	Central United		Central United	5-0	Dunedin Technical	
1999	Central United	3-1	Dunedin Technical		Dunedin Technical	4-0	Waitakere City	
2000	Napier City Rovers	0-0 4-2p	University Mt Wellington		Napier City Rovers	4-1	Central United	
2001	Central United	3-2	Miramar Rangers		University Mt Wellington	3-3 5-4p	Central United	
2002	Miramar Rangers	3-1	Napier City Rovers		Napier City Rovers	2-0	Tauranga City United	
2003	Miramar Rangers	3-2	East Auckland		University Mt Wellington	3-1	Melville United	
2004	No tournament held				Miramar Rangers	1-0	Waitakere City	
2005	Auckland City	3-2	Waitakere United		Central United	2-1	Palmerston North Marist	
2006	Auckland City	3-3 4-3	Canterbury United					

OMA – OMAN

NATIONAL TEAM RECORD
JULY 1ST 2002 TO JULY 9TH 2006

PL	W	D	L	F	A	%
48	29	8	11	94	41	68.7

FIFA/COCA-COLA WORLD RANKING

1993	1994	1995	1996	1997	1998	1999	2000	2001	2002	2003	2004	2005	High	Low
97	71	98	91	81	58	92	106	91	96	62	56	91	**50** 08/04	**117** 07/03

					2005–2006						
08/05	09/05	10/05	11/05	12/05	01/06	02/06	03/06	04/06	05/06	06/06	07/06
68	78	80	79	91	92	89	81	82	82	-	86

The 2006 Premier League season saw a three-horse-race between Muscat, Al Nahda and Al Tali'aa, and it went down to the wire. Going into the final day, all three were level on points with Tali'aa and Nahda playing each other. Too many draws had meant that despite losing just once all season, Tali'aa had not been able to pull away from their challengers and once again a draw was to cost them dear after a Salem Shamsi's equaliser for Nahda on 79 minutes. Meanwhile, Muscat beat Dhofar 4-3 with Mohamed Toqi scoring the all important championship winner just before half time. Earlier in the season none of the trio had made it past the quarter-finals of the Sultan Qaboos

INTERNATIONAL HONOURS
AFC U-17 Championship 1996 2000

Cup which was won by Al Nasr Salalah who beat Seeb 3-1 in the final. The win meant that Al Nasr qualified for the 2006 AFC Cup after Omani clubs were allowed back into the competition and they were the first club to qualify from the group stage and reach the quarter-finals. There was a return to the national team coaching job for Milan Macala who replaced Croat Srecko Juricic who was sacked after Oman's disappointing defeat by the UAE in the first game of their 2007 AFC Asian Cup qualifying group. Before Macala's appointment, local coach Hamed Al Azzani had steered the team to a 3-0 win over Jordan in Oman's second group match.

THE FIFA BIG COUNT OF 2000

	Male	Female		Male	Female
Registered players	1 765	0	Referees	120	0
Non registered players	10 000	0	Officials	600	0
Youth players	5 110	0	Total involved	17 595	
Total players	16 875		Number of clubs	51	
Professional players	0	0	Number of teams	153	

Oman Football Association (OFA)
Al Farahidy Street, PO Box 3462, Ruwi 112, Oman
Tel +968 24 787636   Fax +968 24 787632
omanfa@omantel.net.om   www.none
President: AL KHALILI Shk. Khalil   General Secretary: AL RAISI Fahad
Vice-President: AL FARSI Abdullah   Treasurer: AL LAWATI Jamil Ali Sultan   Media Officer: AL RAWAHI Aiman
Men's Coach: MACALA Milan   Women's Coach: None
OFA formed: 1978   AFC: 1979   FIFA: 1980
White shirts, White shorts, White socks

GAMES PLAYED BY OMAN IN THE 2006 FIFA WORLD CUP™ CYCLE

2003	Opponents		Score	Venue	Comp	Scorers	Att	Referee
18-12	Azerbaijan	W	1-0	Muscat	Fr	Saleh [84]		
20-12	Estonia	W	3-1	Muscat	Fr	Saleh 2 [6 71], Al Dhabat [80]	1 000	Al Harrassi OMA
26-12	Kuwait	D	0-0	Kuwait City	GC			Al Saeedi UAE
28-12	Yemen	D	1-1	Kuwait City	GC	Bashir [65]		Sadeq KUW
31-12	United Arab Emirates	W	2-0	Kuwait City	GC	Ahmed Mubarak [32], Saleh [51]		Al Qahtani QAT
2004								
3-01	Bahrain	L	0-1	Kuwait City	GC			
6-01	Saudi Arabia	L	1-2	Kuwait City	GC	Amad Ali [62]		
11-01	Qatar	W	2-0	Kuwait City	GC	Bashir [45p], Al Maimani [77]		
14-02	Korea Republic	L	0-5	Ulsan	Fr		26 514	Yoshida JPN
18-02	Japan	L	0-1	Saitama	WCq		60 270	Abdul Hamid MAS
31-03	India	W	5-1	Kochin	WCq	Amad Ali [12], Ahmed Mubarak 2 [26 49], Al Hinai 2 [60 88]	48 000	Kim Heng MAS
31-05	Maldives	W	3-0	Muscat	Fr			
3-06	Maldives	W	4-1	Muscat	Fr			
9-06	Singapore	W	7-0	Muscat	WCq	Al Maimani 4 [9 44 64 86], Khalifa Ayil 2 [25 53], Hahdid [39]	2 000	Ebrahim BHR
20-07	Japan	L	0-1	Chongqing	ACr1		35 000	Shield AUS
24-07	Iran	D	2-2	Chongqing	ACr1	Amad Ali 2 [32 41]	35 000	Al Delawar BHR
28-07	Thailand	W	2-0	Chengdu	ACr1	OG [11], Amad Ali [49]	13 000	Lu Jun CHN
31-08	Maldives	W	1-0	Malé	Fr			
3-09	Maldives	W	2-1	Malé	Fr			
8-09	Singapore	W	2-0	Singapore	WCq	Yousef Shaaban [3], Amad Ali [82]	4 000	Arambekade SRI
7-10	Iraq	W	1-0	Muscat	Fr			
13-10	Japan	L	0-1	Muscat	WCq		35 000	Lu Jun CHN
17-11	India	D	0-0	Muscat	WCq		2 000	Nurilddin Salman IRQ
1-12	Latvia	W	3-2	Manama	Fr	Ahmed Mubarak [39], Khalifa Ayil [62], Kamouna [90]		
3-12	Finland	D	0-0	Manama	Fr	W 4-3p		
10-12	Iraq	W	3-1	Doha	GCr1	Amad Ali 2 [29 46], Khalifa Ayil [53]		
13-12	United Arab Emirates	W	2-1	Doha	GCr1	Mudhafir [74], Al Maimani [85]		
16-12	Qatar	L	1-2	Doha	GCr1	Kamouna [26]		
20-12	Bahrain	W	3-2	Doha	GCsf	Amad Ali 2 [44 83], Al Maimani [50]		
24-12	Qatar	D	2-2	Doha	GCf	Al Maimani [26]. L 4-5p		
2005								
11-10	United Arab Emirates	D	2-2	Al Ain	Fr	Saleh 2 [60 85]		
25-10	Syria	D	0-0	Muscat	Fr			
3-12	Syria	L	1-3	Al Gharrafa	WGr1	Al Maghni [35]		
2006								
6-02	Singapore	W	1-0	Doha	Fr	Salah [90]		
13-02	Iraq	W	1-0	Wattayah	Fr	Khalifa Ayel [77]	11 000	Shaban KUW
22-02	United Arab Emirates	L	0-1	Dubai	ACq		15 000	Al Ghamdi KSA
1-03	Jordan	W	3-0	Wattayah	ACq	Saleh [7], Sulaiman [18], Al Maghni [54]	11 000	Irmatov UZB

Fr = Friendly match • GC = Gulf Cup • WG = West Asian Games • AC = AFC Asian Cup • WC = FIFA World Cup™
q = qualifier • r1 = first round group • sf = semi-final • f = final

OMAN NATIONAL TEAM RECORDS AND RECORD SEQUENCES

Records			Sequence records					
Victory	12-0	LAO 2001	Wins	7	2003	Clean sheets	5	2001
Defeat	0-21	LBY 1966	Defeats	17	1976-1984	Goals scored	11	1994, 2001
Player Caps	n/a		Undefeated	10	2003	Without goal	8	1965-1976
Player Goals	n/a		Without win	29	1965-1984	Goals against	28	1965-1984

OMAN COUNTRY INFORMATION

Capital	Muscat	Independence	1650 Portuguese Expulsion	GDP per Capita	$13 100
Population	2 903 165	Status	Monarchy	GNP Ranking	75
Area km²	212 460	Language	Arabic	Dialling code	+968
Population density	13 per km²	Literacy rate	75%	Internet code	.om
% in urban areas	13%	Main religion	Muslim	GMT +/−	+4
Towns/Cities ('000)	Muscat 871; Salalah 178; Suhar 138; 'Ibri 88; Nizwa 86; as-Suwayq 86; Sur 77, Saham 76				
Neighbours (km)	Saudi Arabia 676; UAE 410; Yemen 288; Arabian Sea & Persian Gulf 2 092				
Main stadia	Sultan Qaboos – Muscat 39 000, Nizwa Complex – Nizwa 11 000				

OMAN 2005-06

PREMIER LEAGUE

	Pl	W	D	L	F	A	Pts	Muscat	Nahda	Tali'aa	Nasr	Sur	Urooba	Seeb	Bahla	Dhofar	Majees	Suwaiq	Oman
Muscat ‡	22	13	6	3	33	15	45		2-2	0-1	2-0	1-0	1-0	1-2	3-1	4-3	1-0	1-0	1-0
Al Nahda	22	12	7	3	39	18	43	1-1		2-2	1-0	1-0	2-3	2-0	2-0	3-1	4-0	1-0	4-0
Al Tali'aa	22	11	10	1	35	22	43	0-0	1-1		4-3	3-3	2-1	2-1	0-0	1-0	4-1	0-0	1-0
Al Nasr Salalah	22	11	2	9	32	27	35	1-2	1-0	2-2		3-1	0-0	2-0	0-1	0-1	2-1	2-1	3-1
Sur	22	9	6	7	26	25	33	0-4	3-1	0-0	2-1		1-0	3-1	0-0	1-0	0-2	0-0	0-0
Al Urooba Sur	22	9	5	8	26	25	32	2-1	0-1	1-1	1-3	0-2		0-0	3-1	2-1	2-1	3-2	2-0
Seeb	22	7	6	9	21	24	27	0-0	1-1	3-1	2-0	0-2	2-1		0-0	1-3	0-0	0-2	0-0
Bahla	22	6	7	9	27	37	25	1-3	1-4	1-1	1-0	1-3	0-3	2-1		1-2	5-2	3-3	4-2
Dhofar Salalah	22	6	5	11	22	26	23	0-0	0-1	1-2	0-1	2-0	0-0	1-0	1-1		0-1	1-1	0-1
Majees	22	6	4	12	22	37	22	0-3	0-0	0-1	2-3	2-1	0-0	0-1	1-3	2-1		2-2	2-1
Suwaiq	22	4	9	9	27	29	21	0-1	1-1	0-1	0-1	2-3	3-0	1-4	3-0	2-2	2-1		2-2
Oman	22	1	7	14	17	42	10	1-1	1-4	2-5	2-4	1-1	1-2	0-2	0-0	1-2	1-2	0-0	

9/11/2005 - 19/05/2006 • ‡ Qualified for the AFC Cup

SULTAN QABOOS CUP 2005-06

Round of 16		Quarter-finals		Semi-finals		Final	
Al Nasr Salalah	7						
Fanja	1	Al Nasr Salalah	2				
Oman	0	Bahla	0				
Bahla	2			Al Nasr Salalah	2 4		
Sohar	2			Al Urooba Sur	1 3		
Masna'aa	0	Sohar	0				
Al Nahda	2	Al Urooba Sur	4				
Al Urooba Sur	3					Al Nasr Salalah ‡	3
Sur	1					Seeb	1
Dhofar Salalah	0	Sur	3				
Salam	0	Al Tali'aa	2				
Al Tali'aa	1			Sur	1 0 4p		
Saham	1			Seeb	1 0 5p	CUP FINAL	
Muscat	0	Saham	1				
Medhaibi	0	Seeb	3		14-11-2005		
Seeb	1			‡ Qualified for the AFC Cup			

Scorers - Mohamed Mubarak 2, Hassan Zohr for Nasr; Donald for Seeb

RECENT LEAGUE AND CUP RECORD

	Championship						Cup		
Year	Champions	Pts	Runners-up	Pts	Third	Pts	Winners	Score	Runners-up
2000	Al Urooba	42	Al Nasr	36	Seeb	31	Al Nasr	2-1	Al Urooba
2001	Dhofar	41	Al Urooba	36	Seeb	36	Al Urooba	1-0	Al Nasr
2002	Al Urooba	38	Sur	37	Seeb	30	Al Nasr	2-1	Dhofar
2003	Rowi	65	Dhofar	63	Al Nasr	55	Rowi	2-0	Seeb
2004	Al Nasr	46	Muscat	45	Al Urooba	41	Dhofar	1-0	Muscat
2005	Dhofar	46	Al Urooba	44	Muscat	40	Al Nasr	3-1	Seeb
2006	Muscat	45	Al Nahda	43	Al Tali'aa	43			

Muscat were formed by the merger of Rowi and Bustan

PAK – PAKISTAN

NATIONAL TEAM RECORD
JULY 1ST 2002 TO JULY 9TH 2006

PL	W	D	L	F	A	%
24	8	4	12	18	31	41.7

FIFA/COCA-COLA WORLD RANKING

1993	1994	1995	1996	1997	1998	1999	2000	2001	2002	2003	2004	2005	High		Low	
142	158	160	173	153	168	179	190	181	178	168	177	158	141	02/94	192	05/01

2005–2006											
08/05	09/05	10/05	11/05	12/05	01/06	02/06	03/06	04/06	05/06	06/06	07/06
169	169	170	168	158	158	157	155	153	153	-	153

It was a busy, if not necessarily successful year for the Pakistan national team with entry into three tournaments, one of which Pakistan hosted. In December Karachi welcomed eight nations from the Indian subcontinent and beyond for the sixth edition of the South Asian Football Federation Championship, a tournament Pakistan has yet to win. That unwanted record was maintained thanks to a defeat in the semi-final against Bangladesh although goalkeeper Jaffar Khan went more than five hours without conceding a goal. When he did, it took a penalty from Bangladeshi striker Mohammad Sujan to beat him. Later in the month Bangladesh then beat Pakistan again, over two

INTERNATIONAL HONOURS
South Asian Federation Games 1989 1991 2004

legs in a pre-qualifying round of the 2007 AFC Asian Cup. Following the withdrawal of Sri Lanka, Pakistan were given a fortunate reprieve and took the vacant spot in group C. Their first two matches in the group ended in defeat and were followed by a rather ignominious first round exit in their third tournament of the year, the AFC Challenge Cup, courtesy of Tajikistan and Kyrgyzstan. There is clearly also a lot of work to be done at club level with WAPDA, the 2004 Pakistani champions, being knocked out after the first round of the 2005 AFC President's Cup, and 2005 champions Pakistan Army suffering a similar fate in the 2006 edition.

THE FIFA BIG COUNT OF 2000

	Male	Female		Male	Female
Registered players	37 000	0	Referees	340	0
Non registered players	800 000	0	Officials	6 750	0
Youth players	20 000	0	Total involved	864 090	
Total players	857 000		Number of clubs	2 500	
Professional players	0	0	Number of teams	2 570	

Pakistan Football Federation (PFF)
Opposite Punjab Football Stadium, Ferozepur Road, Lahore, Pakistan
Tel +92 42 9230821   Fax +92 42 9230823
mail@pff.com.pk   www.pff.com.pk
President: SALEH HAYAT Makhdoom Syed   General Secretary: ARSHAD KHAN LODHI Muhammad
Vice-President: LIAQAT ALI Agha Syed   Treasurer: HAYAT Ali Khan   Media Officer: ALI WAHIDI Syed Akber
Men's Coach: LUFTI Tariq   Women's Coach: None
PFF formed: 1948   AFC: 1954   FIFA: 1948
Green shirts, Green shorts, Green socks

RECENT INTERNATIONAL MATCHES PLAYED BY PAKISTAN

2002	Opponents	Score		Venue	Comp	Scorers	Att	Referee
No international matches played in 2002 after June								
2003								
10-01	India	W	1-0	Dhaka	SAFr1	Sarfraz Rasool 50		Hossain BAN
12-01	Sri Lanka	W	2-1	Dhaka	SAFr1	Zahid Niaz 50, Sarfraz Rasool 86		Ghosh BAN
14-01	Afghanistan	W	1-0	Dhaka	SAFr1	Sarfraz Rasool 9		Ghosh BAN
18-01	Maldives	L	0-1	Dhaka	SAFsf			Gurung NEP
20-01	India	L	1-2	Dhaka	SAF3p	Sarfraz Rasool 66		Hassan BAN
21-03	Macao	W	3-0	Singapore	ACq	Qadeer Ahmed 2 27 65, Sarfraz Rasool 51		
25-03	Singapore	L	0-3	Singapore	ACq			
29-11	Kyrgyzstan	L	0-2	Karachi	WCq		10 000	Nesar BAN
3-12	Kyrgyzstan	L	0-4	Bishkek	WCq		12 000	Mamedov TKM
2004								
No international matches played in 2004								
2005								
12-06	India	D	1-1	Quetta	Fr	Essa 81	20 000	Khan PAK
16-06	India	L	0-1	Peshawar	Fr		15 000	Imtiaz PAK
18-06	India	W	3-0	Lahore	Fr	Essa 2, Tanveer Ahmed 45+, Arif Mehmood 46		Asif PAK
7-12	Sri Lanka	W	1-0	Karachi	SAFr1	Imran Hussain 38		
9-12	Afghanistan	W	1-0	Karachi	SAFr1	Muhammad Essa 55		
11-12	Maldives	D	0-0	Karachi	SAFr1			
14-12	Bangladesh	L	0-1	Karachi	SAFsf			
22-12	Bangladesh	D	0-0	Dhaka	ACq			
26-12	Bangladesh	L	0-1	Karachi	ACq			
2006								
18-02	Palestine	L	0-3	Manama	Fr			
22-02	Jordan	L	0-3	Amman	ACq			Basma SYR
1-03	United Arab Emirates	L	1-4	Karachi	ACq	Muhammad Essa 60	10 000	Tongkhan THA
2-04	Kyrgyzstan	W	1-0	Dhaka	CCr1	Muhammad Essa 59	2 500	Shamsuzzaman BAN
4-04	Tajikistan	L	0-2	Dhaka	CCr1		5 000	Tan Hai CHN
6-04	Macau	D	2-2	Dhaka	CCr1	Adeel 12, Muhammad Essa 43	1 000	Shamsuzzaman BAN

Fr = Friendly match • SA = South Asian Federation Cup • AC = AFC Asian Cup • CC = AFC Challenge Cup • WC = FIFA World Cup™
q = qualifier • r1 = first round group • sf = semi-final • f = final

PAKISTAN NATIONAL TEAM RECORDS AND RECORD SEQUENCES

Records			Sequence records					
Victory	7-0	THA 1960	Wins	3	2003	Clean sheets	5	1952-1953
Defeat	1-9	IRN 1969	Defeats	14	1992-1993	Goals scored	13	1953-1959
Player Caps	n/a		Undefeated	5	1952-1953	Without goal	6	Three times
Player Goals	n/a		Without win	19	1992-1993	Goals against	21	1965-1981

PAKISTAN COUNTRY INFORMATION

Capital	Islamabad	Independence	1947 from the UK	GDP per Capita	$2 100
Population	159 196 336	Status	Republic	GNP Ranking	44
Area km²	803 940	Language	Punjabi 48%, English	Dialling code	+92
Population density	198 per km²	Literacy rate	45%	Internet code	.pk
% in urban areas	35%	Main religion	Muslim	GMT +/−	+5
Towns/Cities ('000)	Karachi 11 627; Lahore 6 312; Faisalabad 2 507; Rawalpindi 1 743; Multan 1 437; Hyderabad 1 386; Gujranwala 1 384; Peshawar 1 219; Islamabad 756; Quetta 733; Bahawalpur 552				
Neighbours (km)	China 523; India 2 912; Iran 909; Afghanistan 2 430; Arabian Sea 1 046				
Main stadia	Jinnah Sport Stadium – Islamabad 48 200; National Stadium – Karachi 34 228				

PAKISTAN 2005

NATIONAL FOOTBALL LEAGUE A DIVISION

	Pl	W	D	L	F	A	Pts	Army	WAPDA	KRL	PTCL	NBP	Afghan	HBL	KPT	Navy	Panther	Wohaib	PWD
Pakistan Army †	22	16	3	3	52	9	51		3-1	3-0	2-0	1-1	4-0	5-0	4-0	2-1	2-0	10-0	2-0
WAPDA	22	13	6	3	43	15	45	1-0		3-0	0-1	1-0	4-2	3-0	2-1	2-0	4-1	2-1	2-0
Khan Research Labs	22	12	5	5	41	24	41	0-2	0-0		5-2	3-1	3-0	2-1	1-3	3-0	4-0	2-0	5-0
Pakistan Telecoms CL	22	11	3	8	36	26	36	1-3	2-1	2-2		1-0	6-2	1-2	3-0	1-0	3-1	3-0	3-0
National Bank of Pak.	22	9	8	5	31	19	35	0-0	0-0	2-1	1-1		0-1	1-0	3-2	0-0	2-0	1-0	2-1
Afghan Club	22	10	4	7	25	27	34	1-0	1-1	1-2	1-0	1-0		3-1	2-1	0-1		2-1	3-0
Habib Bank Ltd	22	7	5	10	24	36	26	1-3	2-2	1-1	1-3	1-5	1-1		2-1	1-0	1-2	2-0	0-0
Karachi Port Trust	22	6	6	10	27	35	24	1-0	0-0	0-2	1-0	1-1	0-0	2-2		1-3	6-4	0-1	3-1
Pakistan Navy	22	5	6	11	17	26	21	1-2	0-0	1-1	1-0	0-5	0-1	0-1	1-1		1-1	1-1	3-0
Panther Club	22	6	2	13	20	44	20	0-2	0-4	0-1	1-0	2-2	0-3	1-0	1-0	2-1		1-0	1-3
Wohaib Club	22	5	5	12	16	41	20	0-0	0-8	1-1	1-1	1-1	2-0	0-1	1-2	1-0	3-1		1-0
Public Works Dept	22	3	3	16	14	44	12	0-2	1-2	1-2	1-2	1-3	0-0	0-3	1-1	0-2	2-1	2-1	

31/07/2005 - 23/10/2005 • † Qualified for the 2006 AFC Presidents Cup • Top scorers: Imran HUSSEIN, Army, 21; Qadeer AHMED, KRL, 16

17TH NATIONAL FOOTBALL CHALLENGE CUP 2005

Second Round Groups   **Semi-finals**   **Final**

Group A †	Pl	W	D	L	F	A	Pts	WP	KE	PN	PP	PC
Khan Research	5	5	0	0	11	4	15	1-0	1-0	1-0	4-1	4-3
WAPDA	5	4	0	1	14	3	12		3-0	3-0	4-0	4-2
Karachi Electric	5	3	0	2	7	5	9			3-0	3-1	1-0
Pakistan Navy	5	2	0	3	3	7	6				1-0	2-0
Pakistan Police	5	1	0	4	3	12	3					1-0
Panther Club	5	0	0	5	5	12	0					

Semi-finals:
Pakistan Telecoms   3
Khan Research Labs   1

Group B ‡	Pl	W	D	L	F	A	Pts	PT	NB	KP	SG	HE
Pakistan Army	5	5	0	0	8	0	15	2-0	1-0	2-0	2-0	1-0
Pakistan Telecoms	5	4	0	1	16	6	12		3-2	3-0	1-0	9-2
National Bank of P.	5	2	1	2	18	5	7			0-0	8-1	8-0
Karachi Port Trust	5	2	1	2	11	7	7				5-2	6-0
Sindh Govt Press	5	1	0	4	9	16	3					6-0
Higher Ed. Comm.	5	0	0	5	2	30	0					

Semi-finals:
Pakistan Army   0
WAPDA   1

† Played in Faisalabad • ‡ Played in Rawalpindi

Final

Pakistan Telecoms   2
WAPDA   1

CUP FINAL
Army Sports Complex, Rawalpindi Cantt
5-08-2005, Ref: Imtiaz
Scorers - Adeel Ahmed [11],
Muhammad Ejaz 'Ghoza' [68] for PTCL;
Syed Raza [66] for WAPDA

RECENT LEAGUE AND CUP RECORD

	Championship				Cup		
Year	Champions	Score	Runners-up		Winners	Score	Runners-up
1990	Punjub Red		Pakistan Int. Airlines		Karachi Port Trust		HBFC
1991	WAPDA		Habib Bank		Marker Club		Karachi Port Trust
1992	Pakistan Int. Airlines	†	Pakistan Army		Crescent Textile Mills		Marker Club
1993	Pakistan Army	†	WAPDA		National Bank		Pakistan Steel
1994	Crescent Textile Mills	1-0	WAPDA		Frontier Constabulary		Pakistan Air Force
1995	Pakistan Army	1-0	Allied Bank		No tournament held		
1996	No tournament held				Allied Bank	3-1	Pakistan Army
1997	Allied Bank	0-0 3-0p	Pakistan Int. Airlines		No tournament held		
1998	Pakistan Int. Airlines	1-1 3-1p	Allied Bank		Allied Bank	1-0	Karachi Port Trust
1999	Allied Bank	0-0 4-3p	Pakistan Navy		Allied Bank	1-1 5-4p	Khan Research Labs
2000	Allied Bank	1-0	Habib Bank		Pakistan Army	1-0	Allied Bank
2001	WAPDA	1-1 4-3p	Khan Research Labs		Pakistan Army		Khan Research Labs
2002	No tournament held				Allied Bank	1-1 4-2p	WAPDA
2003	WAPDA	0-0 4-2p	Pakistan Army		Pakistan Telecoms	1-1 ‡	Karachi Port Trust
2004	WAPDA	†	Pakistan Army		No tournament held		
2005	Pakistan Army	†	WAPDA		Pakistan Telecoms	2-1	WAPDA

† Played on a league basis • ‡ Won on the toss of a coin • The PFF does not recognise the National Championships in 1992, 1993 and 1994 as official tournaments

PAN – PANAMA

NATIONAL TEAM RECORD
JULY 1ST 2002 TO JULY 9TH 2006

PL	W	D	L	F	A	%
50	12	14	24	45	72	38

FIFA/COCA-COLA WORLD RANKING

1993	1994	1995	1996	1997	1998	1999	2000	2001	2002	2003	2004	2005	High	Low
132	140	126	101	119	131	138	121	109	129	125	100	78	**97** 03/05	**150** 10/95

2005–2006											
08/05	09/05	10/05	11/05	12/05	01/06	02/06	03/06	04/06	05/06	06/06	07/06
77	76	78	78	78	78	79	81	81	81	-	59

With the heroics of their CONCACAF Gold Cup campaign behind them, a campaign which saw the national team lose in the final on penalties, it was back down to earth with a bump for Panama. Having made it to the final round of the FIFA World Cup™ qualifiers before the Gold Cup, they proceeded to lose their remaining five games and finished bottom of the group. A year that had promised and delivered so much ended on a low given that four of the six team group made it to the finals in Germany. 2006 saw the women pick up the baton from the men with qualification for the Women's Gold Cup after knocking out Guatemala and Costa Rica in a group staged in Panama.

INTERNATIONAL HONOURS
None

Although the Panamanian national teams have made giant strides in recent years, the same can't be said for the clubs and once again there was disappointment in the CONCACAF Champions' Cup with both San Francisco and Arabe Unido failing to get past the first round of the Torneo Interclubes de UNCAF, the Central American qualifying section. Like most other countries in the Americas, Panama has an Apertura and a Clausura but, unusually for the region, the winners of both play-off for the title at the end of the year. The 2005 final saw Plaza Amador beat San Francisco 2-0 to win the title for the second time in four seasons.

THE FIFA BIG COUNT OF 2000

	Male	Female		Male	Female
Registered players	25 300	3 250	Referees	263	20
Non registered players	25 000	6 000	Officials	1 500	0
Youth players	20 080	1 075	Total involved	82 488	
Total players	80 705		Number of clubs	100	
Professional players	300	250	Number of teams	860	

Federación Panameña de Fútbol (FEPAFUT)
Estadio Rommel Fernández, Puerta 24, Ave. Jose Aeustin Araneo, Apartado postal 8-391 Zona 8, Panama
Tel +507 2333896   Fax +507 2330582
fepafut@sinfo.net   www.fepafut.com
President: ALVARADO Ariel   General Secretary: ALVAREZ Ruben
Vice-President: ARCE Fernando   Treasurer: SARMIENTO Raul   Media Officer: BOLVARAN Arturo
Men's Coach: TBD   Women's Coach: DEVEAUX Noel
FEPAFUT formed: 1937   CONCACAF: 1961   FIFA: 1938
Red shirts, Red shorts, Red socks

RECENT INTERNATIONAL MATCHES PLAYED BY PANAMA

2004 Opponents		Score	Venue	Comp	Scorers	Att	Referee
28-01 El Salvador	D	1-1	San Salvador	Fr	Garces [10]		
16-03 Cuba	D	1-1	Havana	Fr	Phillips [7]		Rojas Corbeas CUB
18-03 Cuba	L	0-3	Havana	Fr			Yero Rodriguez CUB
7-04 Honduras	D	0-0	La Ceiba	Fr		10 000	Rodriguez HON
28-04 Bermuda	W	4-1	Panama City	Fr	Phillips 2 [25 90], Dely Valdes.JC [66], Tejada [68]		
1-05 Guatemala	W	2-1	Guatemala City	Fr	Julio Dely Valdes 2 [35 64p]	11 615	Argueta SLV
13-06 St Lucia	W	4-0	Panama City	WCq	Julio Dely Valdes [5], Tejada [18], Phillips [39], Brown [75]		Phillip GRN
20-06 St Lucia	W	3-0	Vieux Fort	WCq	Tejada [14], Julio Dely Valdes [88], Blanco [89]	400	Gurley VIN
23-07 Guatemala	D	1-1	Panama City	Fr	Dely Valdes.J [72]	3 000	Mejia CRC
28-07 Honduras	D	0-0	Tegucigalpa	Fr		6 000	Zelaya HON
18-08 El Salvador	L	1-2	San Salvador	WCq	Julio Dely Valdes [36]	11 400	Navarro CAN
4-09 Jamaica	W	2-1	Kingston	WCq	Brown [2], Julio Dely Valdes [90]	24 000	Batres GUA
8-09 USA	D	1-1	Panama City	WCq	Brown [69]	15 000	Rodriguez MEX
9-10 Jamaica	D	1-1	Panama City	WCq	Brown [24]	16 000	Pineda HON
13-10 USA	L	0-6	Washington DC	WCq		22 000	Ramdhan TRI
17-11 El Salvador	W	3-0	Panama City	WCq	Brown [4], Baloy [7], Garces [21]	9 502	Archundia MEX
18-12 Iran	L	0-1	Tehran	Fr			Esfahanian IRN
2005							
26-01 Ecuador	L	0-2	Ambato	Fr		5 000	Vasco ECU
29-01 Ecuador	L	0-2	Babahoyo	Fr			
9-02 Guatemala	D	0-0	Panama City	WCq		20 000	Prendergast JAM
19-02 El Salvador	W	1-0	Guatemala City	GCq	Solis [77]	10 000	Archundia MEX
23-02 Costa Rica	L	0-1	Guatemala City	GCq		3 000	Archundia MEX
25-02 Honduras	L	0-1	Guatemala City	GCq		11 159	Sibrian SLV
27-02 Guatemala	L	0-3	Guatemala City	GCq		1 491	Quesada CRC
26-03 Costa Rica	L	1-2	San Jose	WCq	Brown [58p]	8 000	Rodriguez MEX
30-03 Mexico	D	1-1	Panama City	WCq	Tejada [75]	13 000	Pineda HON
25-05 Venezuela	D	1-1	Caracas	Fr	Brown [34]	15 000	Brand VEN
4-06 Trinidad and Tobago	L	0-2	Port of Spain	WCq		18 000	Prendergast JAM
8-06 USA	L	0-3	Panama City	WCq		15 000	Navarro CAN
6-07 Colombia	W	1-0	Miami	GCr1	Tejada [70]	10 311	Batres GUA
10-07 Trinidad and Tobago	D	2-2	Miami	GCr1	Tejada 2 [24 90]	17 292	Wyngaarde SUR
12-07 Honduras	L	0-1	Miami	GCr1		11 000	Wyngaarde SUR
17-07 South Africa	D	1-1	Houston	GCqf	Jorge Dely Valdes [48] W 5-3p	60 050	Prendergast JAM
21-07 Colombia	W	3-2	New Jersey	GCsf	Phillips 2 [11 72], Jorge Dely Valdes 26	41 721	Sibrian SLV
24-07 USA	D	0-0	New Jersey	GCf	L 1-3p	31 018	Batres GUA
17-08 Guatemala	L	1-2	Guatemala City	WCq	Jorge Dely Valdes [19]	24 000	Sibrian SLV
3-09 Costa Rica	L	1-3	Panama City	WCq	Tejada [90]	21 000	Stott USA
7-09 Mexico	L	0-5	Mexico City	WCq		40 000	Hall USA
8-10 Trinidad and Tobago	L	0-1	Panama City	WCq		1 000	Navarro CAN
12-10 USA	L	0-2	Boston	WCq		2 500	Alcala MEX
27-10 Bahrain	L	0-5	Manama	Fr			
2006							

No international matches played in 2006 before July

Fr = Friendly match • GC = CONCACAF Gold Cup • WC = FIFA World Cup™
q = qualifier • r1 = first round group • qf = quarter-final • sf = semi-final • f = final

PANAMA NATIONAL TEAM RECORDS AND RECORD SEQUENCES

Records			Sequence records				
Victory	12-0	PUR 1946	Wins	4	2001, 2003	Clean sheets	3	2000
Defeat	0-11	CRC 1938	Defeats	9	1976-1977	Goals scored	11	1946-50, 1974-75
Player Caps	n/a		Undefeated	7	2001, 2003	Without goal	6	1984-1985
Player Goals	n/a		Without win	13	1950-1963	Goals against	17	1975-1979

PANAMA COUNTRY INFORMATION

Capital	Panamá	Independence	1903	GDP per Capita	$6 300
Population	3 000 463	Status	Republic	GNP Ranking	87
Area km²	78 200	Language	Spanish	Dialling code	+507
Population density	38 per km²	Literacy rate	92%	Internet code	.pa
% in urban areas	53%	Main religion	Christian	GMT + / –	-5
Towns/Cities ('000)	Panamá 408; San Miguelito 321; Tocumen 88; David 82; Arraiján 77; Colón 76; Las Cumbres 69				
Neighbours (km)	Colombia 225; Costa Rica 330; Caribbean and North Pacific 2 490				
Main stadia	Rommel Fernandez – Panamá 25 000; Armando Dely Valdez – Colón 3 000				

PANAMA 2005

ANAPROF PRIMERA PROFESIONAL APERTURA

	Pl	W	D	L	F	A	Pts	Tauro	San Fran	Arab Un.	Plaza	Chorrillo	Alianza	Chiriquí	Sporting	Veragüense	Colón
Tauro †	18	11	5	2	22	7	38		1-3	3-1	0-0	0-0	1-0	3-0	0-1	0-0	3-0
San Francisco †	18	11	4	3	38	15	37	0-1		0-2	1-0	5-1	2-0	1-1	3-1	7-1	5-1
Arabe Unido †	18	11	4	3	31	11	37	1-1	0-2		4-0	1-0	0-0	1-1	5-1	3-0	3-0
Plaza Amador †	18	8	6	4	28	19	30	0-1	1-1	1-1		0-0	3-1	5-1	2-1	2-1	2-1
El Chorrillo	18	7	6	5	26	18	27	1-1	0-0	0-2	1-3		0-1	2-1	2-0	2-1	6-0
Alianza	18	5	6	7	16	20	21	0-2	2-3	1-0	2-2	1-1		0-1	1-1	3-0	2-1
Atlético Chiriquí	18	5	6	7	15	24	21	0-1	0-0	1-3	1-0	0-3	1-1		0-0	1-1	2-1
Sporting '89	18	4	5	9	13	21	17	0-1	0-1	0-1	0-2	1-1	2-0	0-1		0-0	2-0
Atlético Veragüense	18	3	4	11	9	30	13	0-2	1-0	0-1	1-1	0-2	0-1	1-0	0-2		1-2
Colón River	18	1	2	15	14	47	5	0-1	2-4	0-2	2-4	1-4	0-0	1-3	1-1	1-2	

11/02/2005 - 7/05/2005 • † Qualified for the Apertura play-offs • Match in bold awarded • Play-offs: Semi-finals - **Plaza Amador** 1-0 0-0 Tauro; **Arabe Unido** 2-1 2-1 San Francisco; Final - **Plaza Amador** 3-1 Arabe Unido. Plaza Amador won the Apertura

PANAMA 2005

ANAPROF PRIMERA PROFESIONAL CLAUSURA

	Pl	W	D	L	F	A	Pts	Veragüense	San Fran	Tauro	Alianza	Arabe Un.	Chiriquí	Chorrillo	Sporting	Plaza	Colón
Atlético Veragüense †	16	9	6	1	29	15	33		3-1	3-4	1-0	1-1	2-1	1-0	5-2	2-1	-
San Francisco †	16	9	4	3	34	21	31	1-1		2-4	3-3	0-1	1-0	2-0	4-3	2-2	1-2	-
Tauro †	16	8	5	3	35	22	29	1-1	1-1		2-3	6-1	3-1	0-2	1-1	3-1	-
Alianza †	16	6	4	6	25	26	22	0-2	1-3	0-2		1-1	5-4	2-2	1-0	2-2	-
Arabe Unido	16	4	7	5	18	20	19	1-1	1-2	1-0	2-1		0-1	0-0	1-1	3-0	-
Atlético Chiriquí	16	4	5	7	20	25	17	1-2	1-5	1-1	2-3	1-0		0-0	3-0	1-1	-
El Chorrillo	16	4	5	7	19	24	17	0-2	0-3	1-3	2-0	3-3	0-2		0-0	2-1	-
Sporting '89	16	3	6	7	17	26	15	0-3	2-4	0-2	2-0	0-0	0-0	1-3		4-0	-
Plaza Amador	16	2	4	10	17	35	10	1-1	0-1	2-3	1-5	1-3	1-1	2-1	1-2		-
Colón River				Colón withdrew				-	-	-	-	-	-	-	-	-	-

15/07/2005 - 26/10/2005 • † Qualified for the Clausura play-offs • Play-offs: Semi-finals - San Francisco 3-1 1-0 Tauro; Alianza 1-1 1-2 Atlético Veragüense; Final - **San Francisco** 2-0 Atlético Veragüense. San Francisco won the Clausura
Overall championship final: **PLAZA AMADOR** 2-0 San Francisco (Rommel Fernandez, Panama City, 20-11-2005, Ref: Vidal. Scorers: Angel Lombardo 47, Jose Justavino 90 for Plaza)

CLUB DIRECTORY

Club	Town/City	Lge	CL
Alianza		0	0
Deportivo Arabe Unido	Colón	3	0
Atlético Chiriquí	San Cristobal	0	0
Atlético Veraguense	Veraguas	0	0
Colón River	Colón	0	0
El Chorrillo	Balboa	0	0
Plaza Amador	Panama City	5	0
Sporting 89	San Miguelito	0	0
San Francisco	La Chorrera	2	0
Tauro	Panama City	6	0

RECENT LEAGUE RECORD

	Championship		
Year	Winners	Score	Runners-up
1997	Tauro	1-0	Euro Kickers
1998	Tauro	1-0	Deportivo Arabe Unido
1999	Deportivo Arabe Unido	3-0	Tauro
2000	Tauro	2-0	Plaza Amador
2001	Panama Viejo	4-3	Tauro
2001	Deportivo Arabe Unido	†	
2002	Plaza Amador	2-0	Deportivo Arabe Unido
2003	Tauro	†	
2004	Deportivo Arabe Unido	†	
2005	Plaza Amador	2-0	San Francisco

† Won both Apertura and Clausura so automatic champions

PAR – PARAGUAY

NATIONAL TEAM RECORD
JULY 1ST 2002 TO JULY 9TH 2006

PL	W	D	L	F	A	%
48	19	16	13	54	49	56.2

FIFA/COCA-COLA WORLD RANKING

1993	1994	1995	1996	1997	1998	1999	2000	2001	2002	2003	2004	2005		High		Low	
61	87	64	38	29	25	17	10	13	18	22	30	30		8	03/01	103	05/95

2005–2006											
08/05	09/05	10/05	11/05	12/05	01/06	02/06	03/06	04/06	05/06	06/06	07/06
35	34	33	30	30	30	33	33	33	33	-	19

A third consecutive qualification for the FIFA World Cup™ finals was greeted with genuine optimism in Paraguay that the national team could match the exploits of the team in France in 1998 and in Korea in 2002 by qualifying for the second round once again. That was always going to be tough after the draw paired Paraguay with England and Sweden and so it proved to be despite the useful blend of youth and experience brought together by veteran Uruguayan coach Anibal Ruiz. In-between conceding a third minute goal to England and a last minute goal to Sweden, Paraguay

INTERNATIONAL HONOURS
Qualified for the FIFA World Cup™ finals 1930 1950 1958 1986 1998 2002 2006 Copa America 1953 1979
South America U-23 1992 Juventud de America 1971 South America U-16 2004 Copa Libertadores Olimpia 1979 1990 2002

played well but both matches were lost and they were out after the second round of games. One of the notable features of recent seasons in Paraguayan club football has been the decline of traditional giants Olimpia and in 2005 their main rivals Cerro Porteño had little trouble in securing both the Apertura and Clausura and hence the overall title. But the performance of the year was surely that of Libertad who not only won the Apertura in 2006 but also their first round group in the 2006 Copa Libertadores. They then went on to beat Mexico's Tigres and Argentina's River Plate to reach the semi-finals for only the second time, where they lost to Brazil's Internacional.

THE FIFA BIG COUNT OF 2000

	Male	Female		Male	Female
Registered players	200 000	0	Referees	400	0
Non registered players	500 000	0	Officials	2 000	150
Youth players	20 000	251	Total involved	722 801	
Total players	720 251		Number of clubs	1 100	
Professional players	180	0	Number of teams	2 000	

Asociación Paraguaya de Fútbol (APF)
Estadio de los Defensores del Chaco, Calle Mayor Martinez 1393, Asuncion, Paraguay
Tel +595 21 480120   Fax +595 21 480124
apf@telesurf.com.py   www.apf.org.py
President: HARRISON Oscar   General Secretary: FILARTIGA Arturo
Vice-President: NAPOUT Juan Angel   Treasurer: ZACARIAS Emilio Dr   Media Officer: BATTILANA Guillermo Eloy
Men's Coach: RUIZ Anibal   Women's Coach: VON LUCKEN Esteban
APF formed: 1906   CONMEBOL: 1921   FIFA: 1925
Red and white striped shirts, Blue shorts, Blue socks

RECENT INTERNATIONAL MATCHES PLAYED BY PARAGUAY

2002	Opponents	Score		Venue	Comp	Scorers	Att	Referee
2-07	El Salvador	W	1-0	San Francisco	Fr	Samudio [3]		Valenzuela USA
6-07	USA	L	0-2	Columbus	Fr			Navarro CAN
9-07	Jamaica	L	0-2	Kingston	Fr			Bowen CAY
20-08	Panama	W	2-1	Panama City	Fr	Campos [6], Gamarra [17]		Porras CRC
6-09	Peru	L	1-4	Lima	WCq	Gamarra [24]	42 557	Baldassi ARG
10-09	Uruguay	W	4-1	Asuncion	WCq	Cardozo 3 [26 58 72], Paredes [53]	15 000	Ruiz COL
15-11	Ecuador	W	2-1	Asuncion	WCq	Santa Cruz [29], Cardozo [75]	12 000	Arandia BOL
18-11	Chile	W	1-0	Santiago	WCq	Paredes [30]	61 923	Mendez URU
2004								
31-03	Brazil	D	0-0	Asuncion	WCq		40 000	Ruiz COL
28-04	Korea Republic	D	0-0	Incheon	Fr		26 237	Kamikawa JPN
1-06	Bolivia	L	1-2	La Paz	WCq	Cardozo [33]	23 013	Rezende BRA
6-06	Argentina	D	0-0	Buenos Aires	WCq		37 000	Simon BRA
8-07	Costa Rica	W	1-0	Arequipa	CAr1	Dos Santos [85p]	30 000	Ruiz COL
11-07	Chile	D	1-1	Arequipa	CAr1	Cristaldo [79]	15 000	Mendez URU
14-07	Brazil	W	2-1	Arequipa	CAr1	González.J [29], Bareiro [71]	8 000	Hidalgo PER
18-07	Uruguay	L	1-3	Tacna	CAqf	Gamarra [16]	20 000	Baldassi ARG
5-09	Venezuela	W	1-0	Asuncion	WCq	Gamarra [52]	30 000	Mendez URU
9-10	Colombia	D	1-1	Barranquilla	WCq	Gavilan [77]	25 000	Elizondo ARG
13-10	Peru	D	1-1	Asuncion	WCq	Paredes [13]	30 000	Ruiz COL
17-11	Uruguay	L	0-1	Montevideo	WCq		35 000	Simon BRA
2005								
19-01	Korea Republic	D	1-1	Los Angeles	Fr	Cardozo [45p]	10 000	Hall USA
23-01	Guatemala	W	2-1	Los Angeles	Fr	Cuevas [14], Dos Santos [74]		
27-03	Ecuador	L	2-5	Quito	WCq	Cardozo [10p], Cabanas [14]	32 449	Mendez URU
30-03	Chile	W	2-1	Asuncion	WCq	Morinigo [37], Cardozo [59]	10 000	Elizondo ARG
5-06	Brazil	L	1-4	Porto Alegre	WCq	Santa Cruz [72]	45 000	Vazquez URU
7-06	Bolivia	W	4-1	Asuncion	WCq	Gamarra [17], Santa Cruz [46+], Caceres [54], Nunez [68]	5 534	Brand VEN
17-08	El Salvador	W	3-0	Ciudad del Este	Fr	Barreto [22], Valdez [45], Dos Santos [75]	12 000	
3-09	Argentina	W	1-0	Asuncion	WCq	Santa Cruz [14]	32 000	Simon BRA
8-10	Venezuela	W	1-0	Maracaibo	WCq	Valdez [64]	13 272	Elizondo ARG
12-10	Colombia	L	0-1	Asuncion	WCq		12 374	Rezende BRA
11-11	Togo	W	4-2	Tehran	Fr	Lopez.D 2 [13 51], Bonet [56], Dos Santos [67]		
2006								
1-03	Wales	D	0-0	Cardiff	Fr		12 324	McDonald SCO
29-03	Mexico	L	1-2	Chicago	Fr	Cuevas [2]	46 510	Kennedy USA
24-05	Norway	D	2-2	Oslo	Fr	Gamarra [48], Valdez [54]	10 227	Olsiak SVK
27-05	Denmark	D	1-1	Aarhus	Fr	Cardozo [20]	20 047	Bennett ENG
31-05	Georgia	W	1-0	Dornbirn	Fr	Valdez [40]	2 000	Gangle AUT
10-06	England	L	0-1	Frankfurt	WCr1		48 000	Rodriguez MEX
15-06	Sweden	L	0-1	Berlin	WCr1		72 000	Michel SVK
20-06	Trinidad and Tobago	W	2-0	Kaiserslautern	WCr1	OG [25], Cuevas [86]	46 000	Rosetti ITA

Fr = Friendly match • CA = Copa America • WC = FIFA World Cup™ • q = qualifier • r1 = 1st round • qf = quarter-final

PARAGUAY NATIONAL TEAM RECORDS AND RECORD SEQUENCES

Records			Sequence records					
Victory	7-0	BOL 1949	Wins	8	1947-1949	Clean sheets	5	1947-49, 1988
Defeat	0-8	ARG 1926	Defeats	8	1959-1961	Goals scored	15	1958-1960
Player Caps	109	GAMARRA Carlos	Undefeated	14	1985-1986	Without goal	4	1981-83, 1993
Player Goals	25	CARDOZA Jose	Without win	20	1959-1962	Goals against	20	1931-1942

PARAGUAY COUNTRY INFORMATION

Capital	Asunción	Independence	1811	GDP per Capita	$4 700
Population	6 191 368	Status	Republic	GNP Ranking	99
Area km²	406 750	Language	Spanish, Guarani	Dialling code	+595
Population density	15 per km²	Literacy rate	94%	Internet code	.py
% in urban areas	53%	Main religion	Christian	GMT + / –	-4
Towns/Cities ('000)	Asunción 508; Ciudad del Este 260; San Lorenzo 228; Luque 210; Capiatá 199; Lambaré 126				
Neighbours (km)	Brazil 1 290; Argentina 1 880; Bolivia 750				
Main stadia	Defensores del Chaco – Asuncion 40 000; Feliciano Cáceres – Luque 24 000				

NATIONAL TEAM PLAYERS AND COACHES

Record Caps			Record Goals			Recent Coaches	
GAMARRA Carlos Alberto	1993-'06	109	CARDOZO Jose	1991-'06	25	MANERA Lujan	
ACUNA Roberto	1993-'06	96	ARRUA Saturnino	1969-'80	13	KIESE Carlos	
AYALA Celso	1993-'05	85	ROMERO Julio Cesar	1979-'86	13	MARKARIAN Sergio	1991-'93
CARDOZO Jose	1991-'06	82	SANTA CRUZ Roque	1999-'06	13	VALDIR PAREIR	1993-'95
FERNANDEZ Roberto	1976-'89	78	RIVAS Gerardo	1921-'26	12	KUBALA Ladislao	1995-'96
TORALES Juan	1979-'89	77	GAMARRA Carlos Alberto	1993-'06	12	CARPEGGIANI Paulo Cesar	1996-'98
CANIZA Denis	1996-'06	77	BENITEZ Miguel Angel	1996-'99	11	ALMEYDA Hugo Ever	1998-'99
CHILAVERT Jose-Luis	1989-'03	74	GONZALEZ Aurelio	1924-'37	10	MARKARIAN Sergio	1999-'01
STRUWAY Estanislao	1991-'02	74	PAREDES Carlos Alberto	1998-'06	10	MALDINI Cesare	2001-'02
PAREDES Carlos Alberto	1998-'06	71	VILLALBA Juan	1945-'47	10	RUIZ Anibal	2002-

CLUB DIRECTORY

Club	Town/City	Stadium	Capacity	www.	Lge	CL
3 de Febrero	Ciudad del Este	Ciudad del Este	25 000		0	0
12 de Octubre	Itaugua	Juan Pettengil	8 000		0	0
Cerro Porteño	Asuncion	General Pablo Rojas	25 000	clubcerro.com	27	0
General Caballero	Zeballos Cue				0	0
Guaraní	Asuncion	Rogelio Livieres	10 000		9	0
Libertad	Asuncion	Alfredo Stroessner	16 000		10	0
Nacional	Asuncion	Arsenio Erico	4 500		6	0
Olimpia	Asuncion	Manuel Ferreira	20 000	clubolimpia.com.py	38	3
Sportivo Luqueño	Luque	Feliciano Cáceres	24 000		2	0
Tacuary	Tacuary	Toribio Vargas	4 000		0	0

RECENT LEAGUE RECORD

	Championship		
Year	Winners	Score	Runners-up
1990	Cerro Porteño	2-0 2-1	Libertad
1991	Sol de América	1-1 2-1	Cerro Porteño
1992	Cerro Porteño	2-2 0-0 5-0	Libertad
1993	Olimpia	‡	Cerro Porteño
1994	Cerro Porteño	1-1 0-0 4-3p	Olimpia
1995	Olimpia	2-1 0-1 8-7p	Cerro Porteño
1996	Cerro Porteño	1-2 5-1	Guaraní
1997	Olimpia	1-0 1-1	Cerro Porteño
1998	Olimpia	2-2 3-1	Cerro Porteño
1999	Olimpia	1-0 3-2	Cerro Porteño
2000	Olimpia	†	
2001	Cerro Porteño	†	Sportivo Luqueño
2002	Libertad	2-1 4-1	12 de Octubre
2003	Libertad	†	Guaraní
2004	Cerro Porteño	†	
2005	Cerro Porteño	†	Libertad

† Won both Apertura and Clausura so automatic champions

PARAGUAY 2005

DIVISION PROFESIONAL APERTURA

	Pl	W	D	L	F	A	Pts	Cerro	Guaraní	Nacional	3 Febrero	12 Octubre	Tacuary	Libertad	Luqueño	Caballero	Olimpia
Cerro Porteño	18	10	6	2	30	15	36		0-0	1-0	1-3	3-0	1-1	2-1	2-1	1-0	5-0
Guaraní	18	9	4	5	21	18	31	1-3		0-0	1-0	2-1	1-3	1-0	1-0	1-0	1-0
Nacional	18	9	3	6	25	22	30	0-2	1-0		2-4	2-1	3-1	0-3	2-1	4-3	1-0
3 de Febrero	18	7	7	4	24	17	28	0-1	3-1	2-2		1-1	1-1	2-1	2-1	1-0	0-0
12 de Octubre	18	6	8	4	22	22	26	1-1	2-1	0-3	0-0		1-1	2-1	4-2	2-0	1-1
Tacuary	18	4	11	3	24	19	23	2-2	1-1	2-3	1-0	0-1		0-0	1-1	2-2	3-1
Libertad	18	4	7	7	21	23	19	1-2	2-2	0-2	3-3	1-1	0-4		0-0	3-1	3-0
Sportivo Luqueño	18	3	8	7	20	22	17	1-1	1-2	0-0	2-1	1-1	0-0	1-1		5-1	1-2
General Caballero	18	2	7	9	16	28	13	2-1	1-2	1-0	0-0	1-1	1-1	0-1	1-1		1-1
Olimpia	18	2	7	9	10	27	13	1-1	0-3	1-0	0-2	1-2	0-0	1-1	0-1	1-1	

11/02/2005 - 25/06/2005 • Cerro won the Apertura and qualified to meet the Clausura champions for the 2005 title
† Qualified for the Copa Sudamericana 2005

PARAGUAY 2005

DIVISION PROFESIONAL CLAUSURA

	Pl	W	D	L	F	A	Pts	Cerro	Libertad	Olimpia	3 Febrero	Nacional	Luqueño	Tacuary	Guaraní	12 Octubre	Caballero
Cerro Porteño †	18	11	3	4	34	20	36		0-1	3-1	1-1	0-1	3-0	2-0	1-0	1-1	2-0
Libertad †	18	9	5	4	30	23	32	2-3		1-1	3-2	0-0	5-2	3-1	4-1	4-1	2-1
Olimpia	18	9	4	5	29	20	31	4-1	1-0		0-2	1-1	1-1	3-0	0-2	3-1	1-0
3 de Febrero	18	8	4	6	31	25	28	1-2	4-0	3-2		3-2	1-1	1-0	0-1	0-0	3-1
Nacional †	18	7	6	5	24	20	27	0-1	1-1	1-3	3-0		2-1	0-0	1-2	3-2	1-0
Sportivo Luqueño	18	6	5	7	27	26	25	2-4	1-1	0-0	1-1			4-1	3-2	2-1	2-0
Tacuary	18	6	6	6	26	31	24	2-5	0-0	3-2	6-3	0-0	2-1		1-0	1-1	1-0
Guaraní	18	6	2	10	18	25	20	2-1	0-1	0-1	0-1	3-2	0-3	3-3		0-0	0-2
12 de Octubre	18	2	8	8	18	33	14	1-1	2-1	0-2	0-5	2-4	1-1	1-1	0-2		2-0
General Caballero	18	3	1	14	15	29	10	1-3	2-1	1-3	2-0	0-1	0-1	2-4	1-0	2-2	

5/08/2005 - 12/12/2005 • Cerro won the Clausura and having won the Apertura were automatically the overall champions for 2005 • Match in bold later awarded as a win for Libertad • Play-off for second place: Guaraní 2-1 1-4 Libertad • † Qualified for the Copa Libertadores 2006 • General Caballero relegated • 2 de Mayo and Fernando de la Mora promoted with the league extended to 11 teams

PARAGUAY 2006

DIVISION PROFESIONAL APERTURA

	Pl	W	D	L	F	A	Pts	Libertad	Cerro	Tacuary	Luqueño	12 Octubre	Olimpia	2 Mayo	Nacional	Guaraní	3 Febrero	Mora
Libertad	20	13	3	4	42	20	42		1-2	2-1	1-1	5-1	3-1	0-1	3-1	3-2	1-0	5-1
Cerro Porteño	20	12	4	4	36	22	40	0-2		1-3	2-0	3-0	1-0	1-1	4-3	1-1	4-1	2-1
Tacuary	20	10	4	6	34	33	34	2-1	1-0		2-2	0-0	2-3	3-1	1-0	2-1	3-2	1-0
Sportivo Luqueño	20	9	6	5	39	29	33	1-3	2-2	1-1		5-0	2-1	6-1	2-1	2-1	2-0	2-3
12 de Octubre	20	8	4	8	25	31	28	1-0	2-1	2-1	1-1		1-0	2-0	4-2	1-1	1-1	4-2
Olimpia	20	8	3	9	34	30	27	1-2	0-1	6-1	1-2	1-0		2-0	3-1	3-2	2-3	2-2
2 de Mayo	20	6	7	7	29	33	25	0-0	2-3	3-3	2-2	3-0			0-0	3-0	1-0	0-0
Nacional	20	6	6	8	42	36	24	2-2	1-1	2-0	5-1	1-0	1-1	5-6		2-2	5-2	3-0
Guaraní	20	6	3	11	34	43	21	2-4	1-4	3-2	1-0	4-3	1-1	2-1	1-5		1-1	5-1
3 de Febrero	20	5	4	11	29	41	19	0-3	1-2	3-4	2-0	2-0	1-3	2-2	1-0	2-2		3-4
Fernando de la Mora	20	3	3	14	21	47	12	0-2	0-1	0-1	0-4	0-2	0-2	2-1	2-2	1-2	1-2	

27/01/2006 - 3/06/2006 • Libertad won the Apertura and qualified to meet the Clausura champions for the 2006 title
‡ Qualified for the Copa Sudamericana 2006 • Top scorers: Hernan LOPEZ, Olimpia, 19; Oscar CARDOZO, Nacional, 15

PER – PERU

NATIONAL TEAM RECORD
JULY 1ST 2002 TO JULY 9TH 2006

PL	W	D	L	F	A	%
40	12	13	15	54	54	46.2

FIFA/COCA-COLA WORLD RANKING

1993	1994	1995	1996	1997	1998	1999	2000	2001	2002	2003	2004	2005		High		Low
73	72	69	54	38	72	42	45	43	82	74	66	66		**34** 09/97	**86**	02/03

2005–2006											
08/05	09/05	10/05	11/05	12/05	01/06	02/06	03/06	04/06	05/06	06/06	07/06
75	70	63	65	66	66	67	66	67	66	-	42

Peru hadn't hosted a major international tournament for years when, just like the proverbial bus, along came two in quick succession. After hosting the Copa América in 2004 it was the turn of the FIFA U-17 World Championship in September 2005, making only its second appearance on South American soil. Once again the Peruvian supporters made the tournament a success although there wasn't much for the home fans to cheer about as Peru finished bottom of their first round group. In the 2006 FIFA World Cup™ qualifiers the senior team brought their poor campaign to an end with a 4-1 win over Bolivia, which at least meant that they avoided the wooden spoon. Having

INTERNATIONAL HONOURS
Qualified for the FIFA World Cup™ finals 1930 1970 1978 1982   Copa America 1939 1975

finished ninth in the 2002 qualifiers as well, this seems to be Peru's station in South America at present. Peruvian clubs are not faring much better internationally either with the 2005 Apertura winners, Ciencieno, and the 2005 Clausura winners, Sporting Cristal, both failing to make it past the group stage of the 2006 Copa Libertadores. In December the two had met in the championship final played in Arequipa where a Carlos Zegarra goal just before half time won a 15th title for Sporting Cristal. It was the second time Ciencieno had lost in the final and not since Unión Huaral in 1989 has anyone other than Alianza, Universitario or Sporting Cristal won the title.

THE FIFA BIG COUNT OF 2000

	Male	Female		Male	Female
Registered players	262 500	800	Referees	1 940	40
Non registered players	750 000	30 000	Officials	1 300	300
Youth players	150 800	1 000	Total involved	1 198 680	
Total players	1 195 100		Number of clubs	2 500	
Professional players	2 500	0	Number of teams	11 000	

Federación Peruana de Fútbol (FPF)
Av. Aviación 2085, San Luis, Lima 30, Peru
Tel +51 1 2258236   Fax +51 1 2258240
fepefutbol@fpf.org.pe   www.fpf.com.pe
President: BURGA Manuel Dr   General Secretary: QUINTANA Javier
Vice-President: PASTOR Julio   Treasurer: ALEMAN Lander   Media Officer: DEL AGUILA Wilmer
Men's Coach: NAVARRO Franco   Women's Coach: None
FPF formed: 1922   CONMEBOL: 1926   FIFA: 1926
White shirts with a red sash, White shorts, White socks

RECENT INTERNATIONAL MATCHES PLAYED BY PERU

2002	Opponents	Score		Venue	Comp	Scorers	Att	Referee
No international matches played in 2002								
2003								
23-02	Haiti	W	5-1	Lima	Fr	Soto.Js 2 [13p 83], Serrano [19], Soto.Jg [26], Farfan [84]		Rivera PER
30-03	Chile	L	0-2	Santiago	Fr		39 662	Amarilla PAR
2-04	Chile	W	3-0	Lima	Fr	Quinteros [17], Pizarro 2 [48 49]	25 000	Ruiz COL
30-04	Paraguay	L	0-1	Lima	Fr			Lopez COL
11-06	Ecuador	D	2-2	New Jersey	Fr	Silva [42], Mendoza [52]		Terry USA
26-06	Venezuela	W	1-0	Miami	Fr	Carmona [74]		Kennedy USA
2-07	Guatemala	W	2-1	San Francisco	Fr	Silva [15], Orejuela [35]		Hall USA
24-07	Uruguay	L	3-4	Lima	Fr	Farfan 2 [27 56], Marengo [46]		Garay PER
30-07	Uruguay	L	0-1	Montevideo	Fr			Mendez URU
20-08	Mexico	W	3-1	New Jersey	Fr	Pizarro [1], Zegarra [31], Solano [33]		Hall USA
27-08	Guatemala	D	0-0	Lima	Fr			Lecca PER
6-09	Paraguay	W	4-1	Lima	WCq	Solano [34], Mendoza [42], Soto.Jg [83], Farfan [90]	42 557	Baldassi ARG
9-09	Chile	L	1-2	Santiago	WCq	Mendoza [57]	54 303	Gimenez ARG
16-11	Brazil	D	1-1	Lima	WCq	Solano [50]	70 000	Ruiz COL
19-11	Ecuador	D	0-0	Quito	WCq		34 361	Gonzalez Chaves PAR
2004								
18-02	Spain	L	1-2	Barcelona	Fr	Solano [21]	23 580	Layec FRA
31-03	Colombia	L	0-2	Lima	WCq		29 325	Rezende BRA
28-04	Chile	D	1-1	Antofagasta	Fr	Zúñiga [91+]	23 000	Amarilla PAR
1-06	Uruguay	W	3-1	Montevideo	WCq	Solano [13], Pizarro [18], Farfan [61]	30 000	Selman CHI
6-06	Venezuela	D	0-0	Lima	WCq		40 000	Larrionda URU
30-06	Argentina	L	1-2	East Rutherford	Fr	Solano [36p]	41 013	Stott USA
6-07	Bolivia	D	2-2	Lima	CAr1	Pizarro [68p], Palacios [86]	45 000	Baldassi ARG
9-07	Venezuela	W	3-1	Lima	CAr1	Farfan [34], Solano [62], Acasiete [72]	43 000	Selman CHI
12-07	Colombia	D	2-2	Trujillo	CAr1	Solano [58], Maestri [60]	25 000	Rodriguez Moreno MEX
17-07	Argentina	L	0-1	Chiclayo	CAqf		25 000	Amarilla PAR
4-09	Argentina	L	1-3	Lima	WCq	Soto.Jg [62]	28 000	Simon BRA
9-10	Bolivia	L	0-1	La Paz	WCq		23 729	Reinoso ECU
13-10	Paraguay	D	1-1	Asuncion	WCq	Solano [74]	30 000	Ruiz COL
17-11	Chile	W	2-1	Lima	WCq	Farfan [56], Guerrero [85]	39 752	Baldassi ARG
2005								
27-03	Brazil	L	0-1	Goiania	WCq		49 163	Amarilla PAR
30-03	Ecuador	D	2-2	Lima	WCq	Guerrero [1], Farfan [58]	40 000	Chandia CHI
22-05	Japan	W	1-0	Niigata	Fr	Vassallo [94+]	39 856	Michel SVK
24-05	United Arab Emirates	D	0-0	Toyota	Fr		6 536	Nishimura JPN
4-06	Colombia	L	0-5	Barranquilla	WCq		15 000	Torres PAR
7-06	Uruguay	D	0-0	Lima	WCq		31 515	Baldassi ARG
17-08	Chile	W	3-1	Tacna	Fr	Vilchez [28], Guerrero [59], Villalta [64]		Ortube BOL
3-09	Venezuela	L	1-4	Maracaibo	WCq	Farfan [63]	6 000	Rezende BRA
9-10	Argentina	L	0-2	Buenos Aires	WCq		36 977	Torres PAR
12-10	Bolivia	W	4-1	Tacna	WCq	Vassallo [11], Acasiete [38], Farfan 2 [45 82]	14 774	Sequeira ARG
2006								
10-05	Trinidad and Tobago	D	1-1	Port of Spain	Fr	Vasallo [31]	20 000	Prendergast JAM

Fr = Friendly match • CA = Copa América • WC = FIFA World Cup™ • q = qualifier • r1 = first round group • qf = quarter-final

PERU NATIONAL TEAM RECORDS AND RECORD SEQUENCES

Records			Sequence records		
Victory	9-1	ECU 1938	Wins	9	1937-1939
			Clean sheets	4	1996
Defeat	0-7	BRA 1997	Defeats	9	1965-1968
			Goals scored	12	1937-1941
Player Caps	113	PALACIOS Roberto	Undefeated	12	1937-1941
			Without goal	3	Eight times
Player Goals	26	CUBILLAS Teófilo	Without win	15	1965-1969
			Goals against	16	1959-1965

PERU COUNTRY INFORMATION

Capital	Lima	Independence	1821 from Spain	GDP per Capita	$5 100
Population	27 544 305	Status	Constitutional Republic	GNP Ranking	46
Area km²	1 285 220	Language	Spanish, Quechua	Dialling code	+51
Population density	21 per km²	Literacy rate	90%	Internet code	.pe
% in urban areas	72%	Main religion	Christian	GMT + / –	-5
Towns/Cities ('000)	Lima 7 646; Arequipa 844; Trujillo 750; Chiclayo 582; Iquitos 439; Huancayo 380; Piura 326; Chimbote 320; Cusco 313, Pucallpa 311; Tacna 280; Juliaca 247; Ica 247; Sullana 162				
Neighbours (km)	Ecuador 1 420; Colombia 1 496; Brazil 1 560; Bolivia 900; Chile 160; South Pacific 2 414				
Main stadia	Estadio Nacional – Santiago 45 574; Monumental 'U' – Santiago 80 093				

NATIONAL TEAM PLAYERS AND COACHES

Record Caps				Record Goals				Recent Coaches	
PALACIOS Roberto	1992-'05	117		CUBILLAS Teófilo	1968-'82	26			
CHUMPITAZ Héctor	1965-'81	105		FERNANDEZ Teodoro	1935-'47	24			
SOTO Jorge	1992-'05	101		SOLANO Nolberto	1994-'05	20			
DIAZ Rubén Toribio	1972-'85	89		PALACIOS Roberto	1992-'05	19			
JAYO Juan José	1994-'05	89		SOTIL Hugo	1970-'79	18			
REYNOSO Juan	1986-'00	84		RAMIREZ Oswaldo	1969-'82	17		OBLITAS Juan Carlos	1996-'99
OLIVARES Percy	1987-'01	83		NAVARRO Franco	1980-'89	16		MATURANA Francisco	1999-'00
VELASQUEZ José	1972-'85	82		LEON Pedro Pablo	1963-'73	15		URIBE Julio César	2000-'03
CUBILLAS Teófilo	1968-'82	81		GOMEZ SANCHEZ Oscar	1953-'59	14		AUTUORI Paulo	2003-'05
SOLANO Nolberto	1994-'05	77		ALCALDE Jorge	1935-'39	13		TERNERO Freddy	2005-'06
								NAVARRO Franco	2006-

CLUB DIRECTORY

Club	Town/City	Stadium	Capacity	www.	Lge
Alianza Atlético	Sullana	Campeones del '36	10 000		0
Alianza Lima	Lima	Alejandro Villanueva	35 000	alianzalima.net	19
Coronel Bolognesi	Tacna	Modelo	19 850		0
Cienciano	Cusco	Inca Garcilaso de la Vega	42 056	cienciano.com	0
FBC Melgar	Arequipa	Mariano Melgar	20 000	fbcmelgar.com	1
Sport Boys	Callao	Miguel Grau	15 000	clubsportboys.com.pe	6
Sporting Cristal	Lima	San Martin de Porres	18 000		15
Unión Huaral	Huaral	Julio Lores Colan	10 000		2
Atlético Universidad	Arequipa	Monumental UNSA	40 217		0
Universidad César Vallejo	Trujillo	Mansiche	25 036		0
Universitario	Lima	Teodoro Fernández	80 093	universitario.com.pe	24

RECENT LEAGUE RECORD

	Championship							Championship Play-off		
Year	Champions	Pts	Runners-up	Pts	Third	Pts		Winners	Score	Runners-up
1990								Universitario	4-2	Sport Boys
1991								Sporting Cristal	†	
1992	Universitario	43	Sporting Cristal	40	FBC Melgar	37				
1993	Universitario	45	Alianza Lima	41	Sport Boys	41				
1994	Sporting Cristal	53	Universitario	42	Alianza Lima	40				
1995	Sporting Cristal	96	Alianza Lima	84	Universitario	84				
1996	Sporting Cristal	69	Alianza Lima	60	Universitario	58				
1997										
1998								Alianza Lima	†	
1999								Universitario	2-1 1-2 4-2p	Sporting Cristal
2000								Universitario	3-0 0-1	Alianza Lima
2001								Universitario	†	
2002								Alianza Lima	3-2 0-1 4-2p	Cienciano
2003								Sporting Cristal	‡	
2004								Alianza Lima	2-1	Sporting Cristal
2005								Alianza Lima	0-0 5-4p	Sporting Cristal
								Sporting Cristal	1-0	Cienciano

† Won both Apertura and Clausura so automatic champions. ‡ Apertura champions Universitario forfeited their place in the play-off by failing to finish in the top 4 of the Clausura

PERU 2005

PRIMERA DIVISION APERTURA

	PI	W	D	L	F	A	Pts	Cienciano	Univer'tario	Alianza	Cristal	Bolognesi	Ancash	San Martín	Sport Boys	Melgar	At. Univ	C. Vallejo	Unión	Alianza At.
Cienciano	24	16	3	5	37	21	51		2-0	3-1	2-0	2-1	1-0	1-0	3-0	1-0	4-3	3-0	1-0	4-1
Universitario	24	13	9	2	40	20	48	1-0		2-2	1-0	1-1	2-1	2-1	4-1	4-0	3-2	1-0	1-2	5-2
Alianza Lima	24	9	11	4	43	25	38	6-2	0-0		2-0	0-0	4-0	1-1	2-1	0-1	1-1	3-1	0-0	5-0
Sporting Cristal	24	9	9	6	34	28	36	1-2	2-2	1-1		1-2	2-0	1-1	4-1	3-3	2-0	1-1	3-2	1-1
Coronel Bolognesi	24	8	11	5	25	20	35	0-0	0-0	2-2	0-0		2-1	2-0	1-1	3-1	2-1	1-1	0-2	0-0
Sport Ancash	24	10	4	10	28	33	34	2-1	0-0	4-1	0-1	2-1		2-1	1-0	3-2	2-1	1-0	2-1	3-2
Univ. San Martín	24	8	7	9	28	26	31	2-0	1-3	1-1	1-2	1-1	1-0		3-2	2-1	5-0	2-0	0-1	0-0
Sport Boys	24	8	7	9	31	34	31	1-0	1-1	1-0	1-1	0-2	4-0	1-1		2-1	1-0	2-1	2-1	2-2
FBC Melgar	24	7	6	11	32	42	27	0-1	0-2	2-6	1-1	2-0	3-2	3-0	2-1		1-1	3-2	2-2	2-3
Atlético Universidad	24	5	8	11	26	40	23	1-1	1-1	0-1	1-2	1-0	1-0	1-0	2-2	0-0		2-2	0-0	1-0
Univ. César Vallejo	24	4	10	10	27	36	22	0-1	0-2	1-1	1-0	0-2	1-1	0-0	1-1	2-0	3-2		3-0	3-3
Unión Huaral	24	4	9	11	24	32	21	0-1	1-1	1-1	1-2	1-1	1-0	1-2	1-0	0-1	2-3	2-2		2-3
Alianza Atlético	24	3	10	11	29	47	19	1-1	0-1	0-2	1-3	0-1	1-1	0-2	0-3	1-1	5-1	2-2	1-1	

5/03/2005 - 31/07/2005 • Cienciano qualified to meet the winners of the Clausura in the 2005 Championship decider

PERU 2005

PRIMERA DIVISION CLAUSURA

	PI	W	D	L	F	A	Pts	Cristal	San Martín	Bolognesi	Univer'tario	Cienciano	Ancash	Melgar	At. Univ	Alianza At.	Sport Boys	Alianza	C. Vallejo	Unión
Sporting Cristal †	24	15	7	2	37	13	52		2-2	2-0	2-1	1-0	3-1	4-0	2-0	5-1	0-0	0-0	1-1	2-0
Univ. San Martín	24	14	6	4	40	20	48	1-0		0-2	1-0	2-0	4-0	7-1	2-1	1-0	1-0	0-3	0-0	1-1
Coronel Bolognesi ‡	24	14	2	8	38	32	44	1-2	1-2		0-2	2-1	1-3	3-0	1-2	2-0	2-2	3-2	2-1	2-2
Universitario †	24	11	7	6	31	20	40	0-1	1-1	1-2		4-0	1-0	1-1	1-0	1-0	2-0	2-1	2-2	3-0
Cienciano †	24	9	6	9	33	30	33	3-0	2-2	0-1	1-1		1-2	4-0	3-1	3-1	5-1	2-1	3-2	2-1
Sport Ancash	24	9	5	10	27	32	32	0-0	0-1	3-1	1-2	0-1		2-2	3-2	1-0	2-0	1-0	1-0	2-0
FBC Melgar	24	9	5	10	26	37	32	0-2	0-2	0-1	1-1	3-0	0-0		1-0	2-0	1-0	2-0	2-1	3-1
Atlético Universidad	24	9	4	11	35	39	31	1-2	3-1	2-3	3-1	0-0	2-0	0-3		2-1	2-0	1-0	3-3	2-0
Alianza Atlético	24	9	3	12	29	39	30	0-0	1-4	1-2	0-1	1-0	2-2	1-0	3-1		4-3	2-1	4-2	1-0
Sport Boys	24	7	7	10	23	30	28	0-1	0-2	1-0	0-0	1-1	2-0	4-1	2-2	0-0		1-0	3-2	1-0
Alianza Lima	24	7	5	12	26	23	26	0-0	0-0	1-2	0-0	2-0	3-0	1-0	3-3	4-1	2-0		0-1	0-1
Univ. César Vallejo	24	5	7	12	31	39	22	1-4	2-1	1-2	1-0	1-1	2-2	1-2	3-0	2-3	0-0	1-0		0-1
Unión Huaral	24	4	4	16	16	38	16	0-1	0-2	1-2	2-3	0-0	2-1	1-1	1-2	0-2	0-2	0-2	2-1	

6/08/2005 - 18/12/2005 • Sporting Cristal qualified to meet the winners of the Apertura in the 2005 championship decider
2005 Championship play-off: Sporting Cristal 1-0 Cienciano (Arequipa, 21-12-2005; Scorer - Carlos Zegarra 44)
Univ. César Vallejo and Atlético Universidad relegated • † Qualified for the 2006 Copa Libertadores • ‡ Qualified for the 2006 Copa Sudamericana

PERU 2006

PRIMERA DIVISION APERTURA

	PI	W	D	L	F	A	Pts	Alianza	Cristal	Bolognesi	Cienciano	San Martín	Universitario	Alianza At.	Ancash	Unión	José Gálvez	Melgar	Sport Boys
Alianza Lima	22	13	7	2	33	13	46		1-0	2-1	1-0	2-0	1-1	2-0	2-0	2-0	2-0	4-1	1-0
Sporting Cristal	22	13	6	3	37	17	45	2-0		3-1	1-1	1-0	3-1	3-0	2-0	1-1	2-1	3-0	2-0
Coronel Bolognesi	22	9	7	6	32	24	34	1-2	0-1		4-2	2-2	1-0	2-0	1-1	1-0	1-0	3-0	3-0
Cienciano	22	9	6	7	26	17	33	0-0	2-0	3-1		1-2	0-1	3-0	1-0	0-0	3-0	1-1	3-0
Univ. San Martín	22	9	6	7	30	30	33	1-1	2-2	2-1	0-0		1-0	0-1	3-3	1-0	0-3	1-0	2-1
Universitario	22	8	7	7	30	22	31	1-1	3-3	1-1	1-0	2-3		1-1	2-0	5-0	1-0	1-2	3-0
Alianza Atlético	22	8	5	9	26	35	29	0-3	1-4	1-3	3-1	2-1	0-0		2-2	3-2	0-0	3-1	2-0
Sport Ancash	22	6	7	9	24	31	25	1-1	1-0	1-2	0-1	1-0	2-1	0-2		0-0	3-1	0-0	3-2
Unión Huaral	22	6	6	10	20	30	24	0-1	0-1	2-2	1-0	3-2	1-0	0-1	2-1		0-0	1-1	0-3
José Gálvez	22	6	4	12	20	30	22	0-2	1-2	1-0	1-2	2-4	1-1	2-2	3-0	0-3		2-0	1-0
FBC Melgar	22	5	7	10	20	32	22	2-1	0-0	0-0	0-0	1-2	0-2	3-1	2-4	3-1	2-0		1-2
Sport Boys	22	3	6	13	17	34	15	1-1	1-1	0-0	0-2	1-1	1-2	2-1	1-1	2-3	0-1	0-0	

3/02/2006 - 25/06/2006 • Alianza qualified to meet the winners of the Clausura in the 2006 Championship decider

PHI – PHILIPPINES

NATIONAL TEAM RECORD
JULY 1ST 2002 TO JULY 9TH 2006

PL	W	D	L	F	A	%
12	0	2	10	7	42	8.3

FIFA/COCA-COLA WORLD RANKING

1993	1994	1995	1996	1997	1998	1999	2000	2001	2002	2003	2004	2005	High		Low	
163	171	166	166	175	175	181	179	175	181	189	188	191	162	08/93	193	11/04

2005–2006											
08/05	09/05	10/05	11/05	12/05	01/06	02/06	03/06	04/06	05/06	06/06	07/06
187	187	187	187	191	191	191	191	191	191	-	192

With a history of poor results at international level, the Philippines national team is often a reluctant participant in tournaments, with the fixture list based around the biennial Tiger Cup. Given that the team didn't even enter the 2006 FIFA World Cup™ the introduction of the AFC Challenge Cup has given the national team a second outlet and the tournament seems well suited to their standard. Although they didn't win a match in Bangladesh all three games were close. After an opening defeat by Chinese Taipei, India were held to a 1-1 draw in one of the most impressive performances by the Philippines in a number of years. The final match against Afghanistan also finished 1-1 and although

INTERNATIONAL HONOURS
Far-Eastern Games 1913

they didn't progress to the knock out round it was a performance that will give encouragement. In November and December Manila had hosted the South East Asian Games during which the under-23 team managed to beat Cambodia - for the first time ever in the tournament. In domestic football the National Men's Open Championship was held in February 2006 with the football associations of eight regions taking part. In the final the Negros Occidental FA (NOFA) beat the National Capital Region FA (NCRFA) 2-1 in Iloilo. The three year old Ang Liga was won for the first time by Saint Benilde who deposed two-time champions San Beda College on penalties in the final.

THE FIFA BIG COUNT OF 2000

	Male	Female		Male	Female
Registered players	4 000	2 500	Referees	178	0
Non registered players	400 000	1 000	Officials	150	80
Youth players	12 000	4 000	Total involved	423 908	
Total players	423 500		Number of clubs	500	
Professional players	0	0	Number of teams	1 320	

Philippine Football Federation (PFF)
Room 405, Building B, Philsports Complex, Meralco Avenue, Pasig City, Metro Manila 1604, Philippines
Tel +63 2 6871594   Fax +63 2 6871598
domeka13@hotmail.com   www.philfootball.info
President: ROMUALDEZ Juan Miguel   General Secretary: GARAMENDI Domeka B.
Vice-President: ARANETA Pablito   Treasurer: MORAN Daniel   Media Officer: FORMOSO M. Eduardo
Men's Coach: CASLIB Jose Ariston   Women's Coach: MARO Marlon
PFF formed: 1907   AFC: 1954   FIFA: 1930
Blue shirts, Blue shorts, Blue socks or Red shirts, Red shorts, Red socks

RECENT INTERNATIONAL MATCHES PLAYED BY THE PHILIPPINES

2002 Opponents	Score	Venue	Comp	Scorers	Att	Referee
11-12 Singapore	L 0-2	Singapore	Fr			Nagalingham SIN
17-12 Myanmar	L 1-6	Jakarta	TCr1	Gonzales [81]		Mohd Salleh MAS
19-12 Vietnam	L 1-4	Jakarta	TCr1	Canedo [71]		Nagalingham SIN
21-12 Cambodia	L 0-1	Jakarta	TCr1			Napitupulu IDN
23-12 Indonesia	L 1-13	Jakarta	TCr1	Go [78]		Khanthachai THA
2003						
No international matches played in 2003						
2004						
8-12 Myanmar	L 0-1	Kuala Lumpur	TCr1		1 000	Napitupulu IDN
10-12 Malaysia	L 1-4	Kuala Lumpur	TCr1	Gould [93+]		Napitupulu IDN
14-12 East Timor †	W 2-1	Kuala Lumpur	TCr1	Caligdong 2 [89] [92+]	100	Napitupulu IDN
16-12 Thailand	L 1-3	Kuala Lumpur	TCr1	Caligdong [27]	300	Lazar SIN
2005						
No international matches played in 2005 before August						
2006						
26-03 Thailand	L 0-5	Chonburi	Fr			
1-04 Chinese Taipei	L 0-1	Chittagong	CCr1		4 000	Lee Gi Young KOR
3-04 India	D 1-1	Chittagong	CCr1	Valeroso [19]	2 000	Mujghef JOR
5-04 Afghanistan	D 1-1	Chittagong	CCr1	Valeroso [59]	3 000	Mujghef JOR

Fr = Friendly match • TC = ASEAN Tiger Cup • CC = AFC Challenge Cup • r1 = 1st round • † Not a full international

PHILIPPINES NATIONAL TEAM RECORDS AND RECORD SEQUENCES

Records			Sequence records					
Victory	15-2	JPN 1917	Wins	2	1972	Clean sheets	2	1972
Defeat	0-15	JPN 1967	Defeats	23	1958-1971	Goals scored	6	1923-1930
Player Caps	n/a		Undefeated	3	1972, 1991	Without goal	14	1980-1983
Player Goals	n/a		Without win	38	1977-1990	Goals against	33	1972-1982

RECENT LEAGUE AND CUP RECORD

National Men's Open Championship				ANG Liga		
Year	Champions	Pts	Runners-up	Winners	Score	Runners-up
2003	National Capital Region	4-1	Laguna	San Beda College	1-0	University of Santo Tomas
2004	National Capital Region	0-0 4-3p	Negros Occidental	San Beda College	2-1	University of Santo Tomas
2005	Negros Occidental	2-1	National Capital Region	Saint Benilde	0-0 7-6p	San Beda College

PHILIPPINES COUNTRY INFORMATION

Capital	Manila	Independence	1946 from the USA	GDP per Capita	$4 600
Population	86 241 697	Status	Republic	GNP Ranking	41
Area km²	300 000	Language	Filipino, English	Dialling code	+63
Population density	274 per km²	Literacy rate	92%	Internet code	.ph
% in urban areas	54%	Main religion	Christian	GMT +/−	+8
Towns/Cities ('000)	Manila 10 443; Davao 1 212; Cebu 758; Antipolo 549; Zamboanga 460; Bacolod 454; Cagayan 445; Dasmariñas 441; Dadiangas 432; Iloilo 387; San Jose del Monte 357				
Neighbours (km)	Philippine Sea & South China Sea 36 289				
Main stadia	José Rizal Memorial Stadium – Manilla 30 000; Pana-ad Stadium – Bacolod 15 000				

PLE – PALESTINE

NATIONAL TEAM RECORD
JULY 1ST 2002 TO JULY 9TH 2006

PL	W	D	L	F	A	%
34	7	9	18	48	56	33.8

FIFA/COCA-COLA WORLD RANKING

1993	1994	1995	1996	1997	1998	1999	2000	2001	2002	2003	2004	2005	High	Low
-	-	-	-	-	184	170	171	145	151	139	126	137	**125** 11/04	**191** 08/99

	2005–2006										
08/05	09/05	10/05	11/05	12/05	01/06	02/06	03/06	04/06	05/06	06/06	07/06
133	136	136	137	137	137	138	121	115	115	-	120

That Palestine plays any football at all is an achievement in itself but there may be a long wait before the national team can play a home match, especially after the Palestine Stadium in Gaza was damaged by an Israeli missile attack which left a big hole in the middle of the pitch. Unsurprisingly the AFC rejected a request to use the stadium for international matches although FIFA has promised to build an international standard stadium when circumstances permit. Instead the team leads a nomadic existence entering what tournaments it can. In the 2005-06 season that meant the West Asian Games in Doha, followed by the opening two games in the qualifiers for the 2007 AFC

INTERNATIONAL HONOURS
None

Asian Cup, and ending with an appearance at the AFC Challenge Cup in Bangladesh, a tournament in which they were ranked second. That was certainly evident against minnows Guam who were thrashed 11-0, a record score for the Palestinians, with striker Fahed Attal scoring six of them. After qualifying easily for the quarter-finals it was to great surprise that Palestine were knocked out at that stage by Krygyzstan. There is little domestic football played in any of the Palestinian territories at present, with the situation made even more difficult by the political turmoil that has accompanied the change of government following the Palestinian elections.

THE FIFA BIG COUNT OF 2000

	Male	Female		Male	Female
Registered players	5 000	0	Referees	285	0
Non registered players	20 000	130	Officials	980	8
Youth players	12 000	60	Total involved	38 463	
Total players	37 190		Number of clubs	377	
Professional players	0	0	Number of teams	1 215	

Palestine Football Association (PFA)
Al Yarmuk, Gaza
Tel +970 8 2834339   Fax +970 8 2825208
info@palfa.com   www.palfa.com
President: AFIFI Ahmed   General Secretary: MEKKY Bader Yassin
Vice-President: ALBEDD Georg   Treasurer: ZAQOUI Jamal   Media Officer: HASAN Khwalda
Men's Coach: NASSER Asmi   Women's Coach: SHAHWAN Necola & HANIA Bish
PFA formed: 1928, 1962   AFC: 1998   FIFA: 1998
White shirts, Black shorts, White socks

RECENT INTERNATIONAL MATCHES PLAYED BY PALESTINE

2002	Opponents		Score	Venue	Comp	Scorers	Att	Referee
24-09	Qatar	D	1-1	Doha	ACq	Aziz 90		
27-09	Qatar	L	1-2	Doha	ACq	Florentio 77		
5-10	Kuwait	L	1-2	Kuwait City	ACq	Abdullah 62		
8-10	Kuwait	L	0-4	Kuwait City	ACq			
19-10	Singapore	L	0-2	Singapore	ACq		2 787	Sarkar IND
22-10	Singapore	D	0-0	Singapore	ACq		3 076	Vidanagamage SRI
2004								
18-02	Chinese Taipei	W	8-0	Doha	WCq	Alkord 10, Habaib 2 20 32, Atura 43, Beshe 2 52 86 Amar 76, Keshkesh 82	1 000	Al Yarimi YEM
26-03	Syria	D	1-1	Damascus	Fr			
31-03	Iraq	D	1-1	Doha	WCq	Beshe 72	500	Al Shoufi SYR
9-06	Uzbekistan	L	0-3	Tashkent	WCq		35 000	Moradi IRN
17-06	Jordan	D	1-1	Tehran	WAr1	Alkord 12		
19-06	Iraq	L	1-2	Tehran	WAr1	Alkord 40		
2-09	Bahrain	L	0-1	Al Muharraq	Fr			
8-09	Uzbekistan	L	0-3	Rayyan	WCq		400	Maidin SIN
14-10	Chinese Taipei	W	1-0	Taipei	WCq	Amar 94+	500	Rasheed MDV
16-11	Iraq	L	1-4	Doha	WCq	Zaatara 71	500	Al Mutlaq KSA
2005								
1-12	Iraq	L	0-4	Al Rayyan	WGr1			
3-12	Saudi Arabia	L	0-2	Al Rayyan	WGr1			
2006								
7-02	Syria	L	0-3	Damascus	Fr			
16-02	Bahrain	W	2-0	Al Muharraq	Fr	Allam 26, Attal 88		
18-02	Pakistan	W	3-0	Manama	Fr	Attal 2 55 75, Salem 85		
22-02	China PR	L	0-2	Guangzhou	ACq		16 500	Kwon Jong Chul KOR
1-03	Singapore	W	1-0	Amman	ACq	Attal 75	1 000	Al Hilali OMA
1-04	Guam	W	11-0	Dhaka	CCr1	Keshkesh 6, Attal 6 14 20 25 32 45 86, Atura 22, Al Amour 39, Al Kord 2 59 67	3 000	AK Nema IRQ
3-04	Cambodia	W	4-0	Dhaka	CCr1	Keshkesh 10, Al Sweirki 2 12 75, Attal 30	2 500	AK Nema IRQ
5-04	Bangladesh	D	1-1	Dhaka	CCr1	Attal 30	22 000	Mombini IRN
9-04	Kyrgyzstan	L	0-1	Dhaka	CCqf		150	U Win Cho MYA

Fr = Friendly match • AC = AFC Asian Cup • AR = Arab Cup • WA = West Asian Championship • WC = FIFA World Cup™
q = qualifier • r1 = 1st round

PALESTINE NATIONAL TEAM RECORDS AND RECORD SEQUENCES

Records			Sequence records				
Victory	11-0	GUM 2006	Wins	3	2006	Clean sheets	3	1976-1992, 2006
Defeat	1-8	EGY 1953	Defeats	4	2001-02, 2003	Goals scored	8	1953-1965
Player Caps	n/a		Undefeated	4	1999, 2006	Without goal	3	2003
Player Goals	n/a		Without win	14	2001-2003	Goals against	13	2001-2003

The organisation of a Palestinian championship and cup tournament is sporadic and often haphazrad due to the political and geographical difficulties. Champions in the past have included Rafah Services club in 1996, Shabab Al Amari in 1997, Khadamat Rafah in 1998 and Al Aqsa in 2002

PALESTINE COUNTRY INFORMATION

Capital	Ramallah	Independence	1993	GDP per Capita	$600
Population	3 636 195	Status	Republic	GNP Ranking	n/a
Area km²	6 220	Language	Arabic	Dialling code	+972
Population density	584 per km²	Literacy rate	n/a	Internet code	.il
% in urban areas	n/a	Main religion	Muslim	GMT +/−	+2
Towns/Cities	Ramallah; Nablus; Jericho; Hebron; Gaza; Bethlehem				
Neighbours (km)	For the West Bank and Gaza: Israel 358; Jordan 97; Egypt 11; Mediterranean Sea 40				
Main stadia	None				

PNG – PAPUA NEW GUINEA

NATIONAL TEAM RECORD
JULY 1ST 2002 TO JULY 9TH 2006

PL	W	D	L	F	A	%
11	2	3	6	24	30	31.8

FIFA/COCA-COLA WORLD RANKING

1993	1994	1995	1996	1997	1998	1999	2000	2001	2002	2003	2004	2005		High		Low
-	-	-	169	167	172	183	192	196	167	172	161	166		**160** 06/04		**197** 02/02

2005–2006											
08/05	09/05	10/05	11/05	12/05	01/06	02/06	03/06	04/06	05/06	06/06	07/06
165	165	164	164	166	166	166	168	168	168	-	174

For the second year running the only international football involving Papua New Guinea came in the OFC Club Championship where, once again, national champions Sobou FC represented the country. Just as in 2005 when they finished bottom of their first round group without a point, they found the going tough in Auckland, losing 7-0 to hosts Auckland City, 7-0 to Tahiti's Piraé and 7-1 to Marist from the Solomon Islands. Clearly there is some catching-up to do although the sport is becoming increasingly popular and there are well established tournaments throughout the country. The three biggest have traditionally been the tournaments in Port Moresby, Lae and Lahi, with the

INTERNATIONAL HONOURS
South Pacific Mini Games 1989

latter producing the most successful teams in the National Championship. This brings together representatives from eight of the local leagues at the end of each year and in 2005 Sobou won their fifth consecutive title when they beat Cosmos from Port Moresby 4-2 in the final, in a tournament held in Madang. September 2006 sees the launch of a new semi-pro National Soccer League in an attempt to raise standards in local football. The League will run in parallel with the current competitions with the champions meeting the winners of the amateur National Championship for the right to take part in future OFC Club Championships.

THE FIFA BIG COUNT OF 2000

	Male	Female		Male	Female
Registered players	7 000	0	Referees	500	0
Non registered players	23 000	0	Officials	1 800	0
Youth players	8 000	0	Total involved	40 300	
Total players	38 000		Number of clubs	400	
Professional players	0	0	Number of teams	2 500	

Papua New Guinea Football Association (PNGFA)
Lae 411, PO Box 957, Morobe Province, Papua New Guinea
Tel +675 4751359   Fax +675 4751399
pngsoka@datec.net.pg   www.pngfootball.com.pg
President: CHUNG David   General Secretary: DIMIRIT Mileng
Vice-President: DANIELS Seth   Treasurer: TBD   Media Officer: None
Men's Coach: TBD   Women's Coach: TBD
PNGFA formed: 1962   OFC: 1966   FIFA: 1963
Red shirts with yellow trimmings, Black shorts, Yellow socks or Yellow shirts with red trimmings, Red shorts, Yellow socks

RECENT INTERNATIONAL MATCHES PLAYED BY PAPUA NEW GUINEA

2002	Opponents	Score		Venue	Comp	Scorers	Att	Referee
5-07	Solomon Islands	D	0-0	Auckland	OCr1		1 000	Breeze AUS
7-07	New Zealand	L	1-9	Auckland	OCr1	Aisa [35p]	1 000	Rakaroi FIJ
9-07	Tahiti	L	1-3	Auckland	OCr1	Davani [43]	800	Rakaroi FIJ
2003								
14-06	Solomon Islands	L	3-5	Port Moresby	Fr			
30-06	New Caledonia	L	0-2	Suva	SPr1			Shah FIJ
1-07	Tonga	D	2-2	Suva	SPr1	Sow [41], Habuka [76]	3 000	Singh FIJ
3-07	Tahiti	L	0-3	Suva	SPr1		1 000	Attison VAN
2004								
10-05	Vanuatu	D	1-1	Apia	WCq	Wasi [73]	500	Breeze AUS
12-05	Fiji	L	2-4	Apia	WCq	Davani [12], Komboi [44]	400	Diomis AUS
17-05	American Samoa	W	10-0	Apia	WCq	Davani 4 [23 24 40 79], Lepani 3 [26 28 64], Wasi [34] Komboi [37], Lohai [71]	150	Afu SOL
19-05	Samoa	W	4-1	Apia	WCq	Davani [16], Lepani 2 [37 55], Komeng [68]	300	Diomis AUS
2005								
No international matches played in 2005								
2006								
No international matches played in 2006 before July								

Fr = Friendly match • OC = OFC Nations Cup • SP = South Pacific Games • WC = FIFA World Cup™ • q = qualifier • r1 = first round group

PAPUA NEW GUINEA NATIONAL TEAM RECORDS AND RECORD SEQUENCES

Records			Sequence records					
Victory	10-0	ASA 2004	Wins	4	2002	Clean sheets	2	2002
Defeat	2-11	AUS 1980	Defeats	6	1998-2000	Goals scored	7	2000-2002
Player Caps	n/a		Undefeated	5	1993-97, 2002	Without goal	4	1990-1993
Player Goals	n/a		Without win	10	1985-1986	Goals against	12	1980-1993

RECENT LEAGUE AND CUP RECORD

	National Championship			Port Moresby			Lae			Lahi		
Year	Winners	Score	Finalist	Winners	Score	Finalist	Winners	Score	Finalist	Winners	Score	Finalist
1997	ICF Univ'sity	2-0	Babaka							Guria		Sobou
1998	ICF Univ'sity	1-0	Blue Kumuls	ICF Univ'sity	2-1	Rapatona	Mopi	3-2	Bulolo Utd	Sobou	4-2	Guria
1999	Guria	2-1	Rapatona	Defence	1-1 4-2p	PS United	Bara	1-0	Buresong	Sobou	1-1 5-4p	Guria
2000	Unitech	3-2	Guria	PS United	1-0	Rapatona	Poro SC	1-1 4-3p	Blue Kumuls	Sobou	1-0	Unitech
2001	Sobou	3-1	ICF Univ'sity	ICF Univ'sity	1-0	PS United	Blue Kumuls	2-1	Goro	Unitech	2-0	Sobou
2002	Sobou	1-0	PS United	ICF Univ'sity	3-1	Rapatona	Tarangau	2-0	Poro SC	Sobou	w/o	Unitech
2003	Sobou	1-0	Unitech	Cosmos	2-1	ICF Univ'sity	Blue Kumuls		HC West	Unitech	2-0	Sobou
2004	Sobou	2-0	HC Water	Rapatona	1-0	PS Rutz	HC West	2-1	Tarangau	Sobou	3-0	Bismarck
2005	Sobou	4-2	Cosmos	PS Rutz	2-0	ICF Univ'sity	Blue Kumuls	2-1	HC West	Unitech	4-2	Sobou

The National Championship is held over the course of a week with representatives from the regional leagues. The most successful of the regional leagues in the National Championship are Port Moresby, Lae and Lahi. Others include Alotau, East Sepik, Enga, Goroka, Kerema, Kompian, Kokopo, Madang, Manus, Mount Hagen, New Ireland, Popondetta, Sogeri, Tari, Wabag, Wau and Wewak

PAPUA NEW GUINEA COUNTRY INFORMATION

Capital	Port Moresby	Independence	1975 from Australia	GDP per Capita	$2 200
Population	5 420 280	Status	Constitutional Monarchy	GNP Ranking	131
Area km²	462 840	Language	Melanesian Pidgin, English	Dialling code	+675
Population density	12 per km²	Literacy rate	64%	Internet code	.pg
% in urban areas	16%	Main religion	Christian	GMT +/−	+10
Towns/Cities ('000)	Port Moresby 283; Lae 76; Arawa 40; Mount Hagen 33; Popondetta 28; Madang 27; Kokopo 26				
Neighbours (km)	Indonesia 820; South Pacific Ocean & Coral Sea 5 152				
Main stadia	Hubert Murray – Port Moresby 10 000				

POL – POLAND

NATIONAL TEAM RECORD
JULY 1ST 2002 TO JULY 9TH 2006

PL	W	D	L	F	A	%
56	33	7	16	104	58	65.2

FIFA/COCA-COLA WORLD RANKING

1993	1994	1995	1996	1997	1998	1999	2000	2001	2002	2003	2004	2005	High		Low	
28	29	33	53	48	31	32	43	33	34	25	25	22	**20**	08/93	**61**	03/98

2005–2006											
08/05	09/05	10/05	11/05	12/05	01/06	02/06	03/06	04/06	05/06	06/06	07/06
22	17	23	23	22	22	26	26	28	29	-	30

After such a good qualifying campaign, Poland's performance at the 2006 FIFA World Cup™ finals was a huge disappointment for the huge number of fans who made the short trip across the border to watch the games, especially the calamitous defeat by Ecuador in the first match. After that there was no way back for the Poles with an injury time defeat at the hands of Germany in the second match making the victory over Costa Rica in the final match meaningless. The irony was that Germany reached the semi-finals of the tournament thanks to the goals of Miroslav Klose and Lukas Podolski, both born in Poland of Polish parents. After the tournament Dutchman Leo

INTERNATIONAL HONOURS
Qualified for the FIFA World Cup Finals 1938 1974 1978 1982 1986 2002 2006

Beenhaaker was appointed as national team coach to help Poland qualify for the European Championship, the finals of which they have yet to qualify for. In the Polish League Wisla Krakow's three year reign as champions was brought to an end by Legia Warsaw after an unusually turbulent season behind the scenes at Wisla. The White Star, as they are known, are the richest club in Poland thanks to the backing of millionaire Boguslaw Cupial, but the failure once again to qualify for the UEFA Champions League group stage hit hard. With restrictions on foreigners in the League relaxed, Pogon Szczecin came up with a novel idea - they signed 20 Brazilians.

THE FIFA BIG COUNT OF 2000

	Male	Female		Male	Female
Registered players	382 703	540	Referees	8 570	22
Non registered players	380 000	6 300	Officials	15 000	400
Youth players	217 068	950	Total involved	1 011 553	
Total players	987 561		Number of clubs	7 763	
Professional players	1 150	65	Number of teams	27 107	

Polish Football Association (PZPN)
Polski Zwiazek Pilki Noznej, Miodowa 1, Warsaw 00-080, Poland
Tel +48 22 5512315   Fax +48 22 5512240
pzpn@pzpn.pl   www.pzpn.pl
President: LISTKIEWICZ Michal   General Secretary: KRECINA Zdzislaw
Vice-President: KOLATOR Eugeniusz   Treasurer: SPECZIK Stanislaw   Media Officer: KOCIEBA Michal
Men's Coach: BEENHAKKER Leo   Women's Coach: STEPCZAK Jan
PZPN formed: 1919   UEFA: 1954   FIFA: 1923
White shirts with red trimmings, Red shorts, White socks or Red shirts with white trimmings, Red shorts, Red socks

RECENT INTERNATIONAL MATCHES PLAYED BY POLAND

2003	Opponents	Score	Venue	Comp	Scorers	Att	Referee
20-08	Estonia	W 2-1	Tallinn	Fr	Sobolewski [52], Wichniarek [90]	4 500	Johannesson SWE
6-09	Latvia	W 2-0	Riga	ECq	Szymkowiak [36], Klos [38]	9 000	Vassaras GRE
10-09	Sweden	L 0-2	Chorzow	ECq		20 000	Riley ENG
11-10	Hungary	W 2-1	Budapest	ECq	Niedzielan 2 [10 62]	15 500	Mejuto Gonzalez ESP
12-11	Italy	W 3-1	Warsaw	Fr	Bak [6], Klos [18], Krzynowek [85]	9 000	Ovrebo NOR
16-11	Serbia & Montenegro	W 4-3	Plock	Fr	Niedzielan [27], Rasiak [30], Kosowski [73], Zurawski [82]	9 000	Weiner GER
11-12	Malta	W 4-0	Ta'Qali	Fr	Bieniuk [54], Mila [57], Sikora [83], Burkhardt [88]	300	Kasnaferis GRE
14-12	Lithuania	W 3-1	Ta'Qali	Fr	Rasiak [8], Mila [11], Jelen [50]	100	Attard MLT
2004							
18-02	Slovenia	W 2-0	Cadiz	Fr	Mila [24], Niedzielan [65]	100	Barea Lopez ESP
21-02	Faroe Islands	W 6-0	San Fernando	Fr	Kryszalowicz 4 [9 39 41 42], Klos [60], Kukielka [86]	100	Cascales ESP
31-03	USA	L 0-1	Plock	Fr		10 500	Skjerven NOR
28-04	Republic of Ireland	D 0-0	Bydgoszcz	Fr		15 500	Shebek UKR
29-05	Greece	W 1-0	Szczecin	Fr	Kapsis OG [17]	17 000	Kari FIN
5-06	Sweden	L 1-3	Stockholm	Fr	Gorawski [89]	28 281	Kelly IRL
11-07	USA	D 1-1	Chicago	Fr	Wlodarczyk [76]	39 529	Petrescu CAN
18-08	Denmark	L 1-5	Poznan	Fr	Zurawski [76]	4 500	Bebek CRO
4-09	Northern Ireland	W 3-0	Belfast	WCq	Zurawski [4], Wlodarczyk [36], Krzynowek [56]	12 487	Wegereef NED
8-09	England	L 1-2	Chorzow	WCq	Zurawski [47]	30 000	Farina ITA
9-10	Austria	W 3-1	Vienna	WCq	Kaluzny [10], Krzynowek [78], Frankowski [90]	46 100	Cardoso Batista POR
13-10	Wales	W 3-2	Cardiff	WCq	Frankowski [72], Zurawski [81], Krzynowek [85]	56 685	Sars FRA
17-11	France	D 0-0	Paris	Fr		50 480	Benquerenca POR
2005							
9-02	Belarus	L 1-3	Warsaw	Fr	Zurawski [51]	6 000	Zuta LTU
26-03	Azerbaijan	W 8-0	Warsaw	WCq	Frankowski 3 [12 63 66], Hajiyev OG [16], Kosowski [40], Krzynowek [72], Saganowski 2 [84 90]	9 000	Vollquartz DEN
30-03	Northern Ireland	W 1-0	Warsaw	WCq	Zurawski [87]	13 515	Frojdfeldt SWE
27-04	Mexico	D 1-1	Chicago	Fr	Brozek [71]	54 427	Kennedy USA
29-05	Albania	W 1-0	Szczecin	Fr	Zurawski [1]	14 000	Weiner GER
4-06	Azerbaijan	W 3-0	Baku	WCq	Frankowski [28], Klos [57], Zurawski [81]	10 458	Undiano Mallenco ESP
15-08	Serbia & Montenegro	W 3-2	Kyiv	Fr	Frankowski 2 [30 42p], Rasiak [37]	2 000	Orekhov UKR
17-08	Israel	W 3-2	Kyiv	Fr	Szymkowiak [19], Rasiak 2 [77 89]	2 000	Karadzic SCG
3-09	Austria	W 3-2	Chorzow	WCq	Smolarek [13], Kosowski [22], Zurawski [67]	40 000	De Santis ITA
7-09	Wales	W 1-0	Warsaw	WCq	Zurawski [52]	13 500	Larsen DEN
7-10	Iceland	W 3-2	Warsaw	Fr	Krzynowek [25], Baszczynski [56], Smolarek [63]	7 500	Sukhina RUS
12-10	England	L 1-2	Manchester	WCq	Frankowski [45]	65 467	Nielsen DEN
13-11	Ecuador	W 3-0	Barcelona	Fr	Klos [2] Smolarek [58], Mila [90]	6 000	Moreno Delgado ESP
16-11	Estonia	W 3-1	Ostrowiec	Fr	Lewandowski [8], Mila [57], Piechna [87]	8 500	Hyytia FIN
2006							
1-03	USA	L 0-1	Kaiserslautern	Fr		13 395	Kinhofer GER
28-03	Saudi Arabia	W 2-1	Riyadh	Fr	Sosin 2 [7 63]	2 000	Al Mutlaq KSA
2-05	Lithuania	L 0-1	Belchatow	Fr		5 000	Bozinovski MKD
14-05	Faroe Islands	W 4-0	Wronki	Fr	Mila [15], Rasiak 2 [48 84], Saganowski [73]	4 000	Prus USA
30-05	Colombia	L 1-2	Chorzow	Fr	Jelen [91+]	40 000	Szabo HUN
3-06	Croatia	W 1-0	Wolfsburg	Fr	Smolarek [54]	10 000	Meyer GER
9-06	Ecuador	L 0-2	Gelsenkirchen	WCr1		52 000	Kamikawa JPN
14-06	Germany	L 0-1	Dortmund	WCr1		65 000	Medina Cantalejo ESP
20-06	Costa Rica	W 2-1	Hanover	WCr1	Bosacki 2 [33 66]	43 000	Maidin SIN

Fr = Friendly match • EC = UEFA EURO 2004™ • WC = FIFA World Cup™ • q = qualifier • r1 = first round group

POLAND NATIONAL TEAM RECORDS AND RECORD SEQUENCES

Records				Sequence records			
Victory	9-0	NOR 1963		Wins	7	Four times	
Defeat	0-8	DEN 1948		Defeats	6	1933-1934	
Player Caps	100	LATO Grzegorz		Undefeated	13	2000-2001	
Player Goals	48	LUBANSKI Wlodzimeirz		Without win	13	1995-1996	
				Clean sheets	4	1978, 1979, 2003	
				Goals scored	28	1978-1980	
				Without goal	6	1999-2000	
				Goals against	17	1957-1960	

POLAND COUNTRY INFORMATION

Capital	Warsaw	Independence	1918	GDP per Capita	$11 100
Population	38 626 349	Status	Republic	GNP Ranking	26
Area km²	312 685	Language	Polish	Dialling code	+48
Population density	123 per km²	Literacy rate	99%	Internet code	.pl
% in urban areas	65%	Main religion	Christian	GMT +/–	+1
Towns/Cities ('000)	Warsaw 1 651; Lódz 768; Kraków 755; Wroclaw 634; Poznan 570; Gdánsk 461; Szczecin 413; Bydgoszcz 366; Lublin 360; Katowice 317; Bialystok 291; Gdynia 253; Czestochowa 248				
Neighbours (km)	Russia 206; Lithuania 91; Belarus 407; Ukraine 526; Slovakia 444; Czech Republic 658; Germany 456; Baltic Sea 491				
Main stadia	Slaski – Chorzow 43 000; Florian Kryger – Szczecin 17 783; Wojska Polskiego – Warsaw 15 278				

NATIONAL TEAM PLAYERS AND COACHES

Record Caps			Record Goals			Recent Coaches	
LATO Grzegorz	1971-'84	100	LUBANSKI Wlodzimierz	1963-'80	48	STREJLAU Andrzej	1989-'93
DEYNA Kazimierz	1968-'78	97	LATO Grzegorz	1971-'82	45	CMIKIEWICZ Leslaw	1993
ZMUDA Wladyslaw	1973-'86	91	DEYNA Kazimierz	1968-'78	41	APOSTEL Henryk	1994-'95
SZYMANOWSKI Antoni	1970-'80	82	POL Ernest	1956-'65	39	STACHURSKI Wladyslaw	1996
BONIEK Zbigniew	1976-'88	80	CIESLIK Gerard	1947-'58	27	PIECHNICZEK Antoni	1996-'97
BAK Jacek	1993-'06	75	SZARMACH Andrzej	1973-'82	25	WOJCIK Janusz	1997-'99
LUBANSKI Wlodzimierz	1963-'80	75	BONIEK Zbigniew	1976-'88	24	ENGEL Jerzy	2000-'02
WALDOCH Tomasz	1991-'02	74	WILIMOWSKI Ernest	1934-'39	21	BONIEK Zbigniew	2002
SWIERCZEWSKI Piotr	1992-'03	70	DZIEKANOWSKI Dariusz	1981-'90	20	JANAS Pawel	2002-'06
KLOS Tomasz	1998-'05	69	KOSECKI Roman	1988-'95	19	BEENHAAKER Leo	2006-

CLUB DIRECTORY

Club	Town/City	Stadium	Capacity	www.	Lge	Cup
Arka	Gdynia	Arka	12 000	arka.gdynia.pl	0	1
Cracovia	Kraków	Jana Pawla II	10 000	cracovia.pl	5	0
Górnik Zabrze	Zabrze	Górnika	18 000	gornikzabrze.pl	14	6
Groclin Grodzisk	Grodzisk	Groclin	7 000	dyskobolia.com.pl	0	1
GKS Belchayow	Belchatow	GKS	7 000	gksbelchatow.pl	0	0
GKS Górnik Leczna	Leczna	Górnik	7 000	gornik.leczna.com	0	0
Korona Kielce	Kielce	Korona	7 000	korona-lielce.pl	0	0
Legia Warszawa	Warsaw	Wojska Polskiego	15 278	legia.pl	8	12
MKS Odra Wodzislaw	Wodzislaw	Odry	6 607	odra.wodzislaw.pl	0	0
Wisla Plock	Plock	Gorskiego	12 500	wisla.plock.pl	0	1
Pogon Szczecin	Szczecin	Florian Kryger	17 783	pogonszczecin.pl	0	0
Lech Poznan	Poznan	Lecha	27 500	lech.poznan.pl	5	4
Wisla Kraków	Kraków	Wisly	10 410	wislaw.krakow.pl	10	4
Zaglebie Lubin	Lubin	Zaglebia	32 420	zaglebie-lubin.pl	1	0

RECENT LEAGUE AND CUP RECORD

Championship							Cup		
Year	Champions	Pts	Runners-up	Pts	Third	Pts	Winners	Score	Runners-up
1990	Lech Poznan	42	Zaglebie Lubin	40	GKS Katowice	40	Legia Warszawa	2-0	GKS Katowice
1991	Zaglebie Lubin	44	Górnik Zabrze	40	Wisla Kraków	40	GKS Katowice	1-0	Legia Warszawa
1992	Lech Poznan	49	GKS Katowice	44	Widzew Lódz	43	Miedz Legnica	1-1 4-3p	Górnik Zabrze
1993	Legia Warszawa †	47	LKS Lódz †	47	Lech Poznan †	47	GKS Katowice	1-1 5-4p	Ruch II Chorzów
1994	Legia Warszawa	48	GKS Katowice	47	Górnik Zabrze	46	Legia Warszawa	2-0	LKS Lódz
1995	Legia Warszawa	51	Widzew Lódz	45	GKS Katowice	42	Legia Warszawa	2-0	GKS Katowice
1996	Widzew Lódz	88	Legia Warszawa	85	Hutnik Kraków	52	Ruch Chorzów	1-0	GKS Belchatów
1997	Widzew Lódz	81	Legia Warszawa	77	Odra Wodzislaw	55	Legia Warszawa	2-0	GKS Katowice
1998	LKS Lódz	66	Polonia Warszawa	63	Wisla Kraków	61	Amica Wronki	5-3	Aluminium Konin
1999	Wisla Kraków	73	Widzew Lódz	56	Legia Warszawa	56	Amica Wronki	1-0	GKS Belchatów
2000	Polonia Warszawa	65	Wisla Kraków	56	Ruch Chorzów	55	Amica Wronki	2-2 3-0	Wisla Kraków
2001	Wisla Kraków	62	Pogon Szczecin	53	Legia Warszawa	50	Polonia Warszawa	2-1 2-2	Górnik Zabrze
2002	Legia Warszawa	42	Wisla Kraków	41	Amica Wronki	36	Wisla Kraków	4-2 4-0	Amica Wronki
2003	Wisla Kraków	68	Groclin Grodzisk	62	GKS Katowice	61	Wisla Kraków	0-1 3-0	Wisla Plock
2004	Wisla Kraków	65	Legia Warszawa	60	Amica Wronki	48	Lech Poznan	2-0 0-1	Legia Warszawa
2005	Wisla Kraków	62	Groclin Grodzisk	51	Legia Warszawa	47	Groclin Grodzisk	2-0 0-1	Zaglebie Lubin
2006	Legia Warszawa	66	Wisla Krakow	64	Zaglebie Lubin	49	Wisla Plock	3-2 3-1	Zaglebie Lubin

† Lech Poznan proclaimed champions following match fixing involving Legia and LKS

POLAND 2005-06

LIGA POLSKA
ORANGE EKSTRAKLASA

	Pl	W	D	L	F	A	Pts	Legia	Wisla	Zaglebie	Amica	Korona	Lech	Odra	Groclin	Cracovia	GKS	Pogon	Wisla	G. Leczna	G. Zabrze	Arka	Polonia
Legia Warszawa †	30	20	6	4	47	17	66		1-2	1-0	1-0	1-0	3-1	2-1	0-2	5-0	1-0	2-0	3-0	0-2	3-2	2-0	1-0
Wisla Krakow ‡	30	19	7	4	50	20	64	0-0		2-0	0-0	2-2	5-1	1-0	2-1	3-0	3-0	2-1	4-0	1-0	2-0	3-1	2-0
Zaglebie Lubin	30	14	7	9	45	32	49	0-1	2-1		2-0	3-3	4-5	2-0	2-0	3-1	2-1	1-1	2-0	2-0	3-0	4-0	1-0
Amica Wronki	30	14	7	9	50	28	49	0-2	0-1	3-1		0-3	1-4	4-0	2-0	1-1	3-1	4-1	2-0	6-0	3-1	1-1	3-0
Korona Kielce	30	12	11	7	46	33	47	2-2	1-0	1-1	2-1		1-1	0-1	3-0	0-0	0-0	0-1	2-3	1-1	4-1	1-0	3-2
Lech Poznan	30	11	9	10	45	45	42	1-0	2-1	0-1	1-1	0-0		1-2	4-1	1-0	1-1	1-1		1-0	3-2	1-1	1-2
Odra Wodzislaw Slaski	30	10	10	10	23	27	40	1-2	1-1	0-0	0-4	1-1	2-1		1-0	1-0	0-2	1-0	1-0	0-0	1-0	1-2	0-1
Groclin Dy. Grodzisk	30	10	7	13	37	45	37	0-4	2-4	1-0	2-2	0-3	3-1	0-0		4-1	3-1	1-3	3-0	1-1	0-1	2-1	1-2
Cracovia	30	10	7	13	32	44	37	1-1	1-1	0-0	1-0	2-3	3-2	1-0	1-3		2-1	1-0	3-1	0-1	1-2	2-1	3-0
GKS Belchatow	30	9	10	11	30	32	37	0-3	0-0	3-0	1-2	1-2	1-1	0-3	2-2	2-0		2-0	3-0	1-1	0-0	1-1	2-0
Pogon Szczecin	30	9	10	11	29	34	37	2-2	1-2	1-0	0-3	4-2	0-0	1-0	1-3	1-2	0-0		2-0	2-1	1-1	0-0	2-0
Wisla Plock ‡	30	10	4	16	30	45	34	0-1	1-2	3-2	0-1	1-0	5-1	0-0	2-0	1-0	0-1	0-0		2-1	1-0	1-1	4-0
Górnik Leczna	30	7	12	11	23	31	33	0-0	1-1	1-3	1-0	3-0	0-0	0-0	0-0	1-1	0-1	0-2	0-1		1-0	1-1	0-1
Górnik Zabrze	30	8	5	17	29	46	29	0-1	0-1	2-2	0-2	0-3	0-3	1-1	0-0	3-0	0-1	2-1	4-0	2-0		2-0	2-1
Arka Gdynia	30	4	15	11	21	33	27	0-0	1-0	0-1	1-1	0-2	0-2	1-1	0-0	1-1	2-0	0-0	1-1	1-1	3-0		0-1
Polonia Warszawa	30	6	7	17	20	45	25	0-2	0-1	1-1	0-0	1-1	2-1	0-3	1-2	1-3	0-0	1-1	0-1	0-3	4-1	0-0	

24/07/2005 - 13/05/2006 • † Qualified for the UEFA Champions League • ‡ Qualified for the UEFA Cup • Relegation play-off: Jagiellonia 0-2 1-2 Arka

POLAND 2005-06
II LIGA

	Pl	W	D	L	F	A	Pts
Widzew Lodz	34	18	8	8	53	28	62
LKS Lodz	34	15	13	6	42	21	58
Jagiellonia Bialystok	34	15	11	8	48	30	56
Slask Wroclaw	34	16	8	10	38	35	56
Zaglebie Sosnowiec	34	15	9	10	48	34	54
Zawisza Bydgoszcz	34	13	14	7	38	26	53
Ruch Chorzów	34	14	9	11	50	36	51
Piast Gliwice §10	34	15	13	6	44	33	48
Ostrowiec Swietokrzyski	34	12	10	12	37	41	46
Lechia Gdansk	34	11	12	11	33	39	45
Górnik Polkowice	34	12	9	13	36	37	45
Heko Czermno	34	10	13	11	40	42	43
Podbeskidzie	34	9	14	11	37	38	41
Radomiak Radom	34	8	11	15	39	46	35
Polonia Bytom	34	9	8	17	32	51	35
Swit Nowy Dwór	34	7	9	18	27	54	30
Szczakowianka	34	7	8	19	28	63	29
Drweca Nowe Miasto	34	5	11	18	31	47	26

29/07/2005 - 10/06/2006 • §10 = ten points deducted

PUCHAR POLSKI 2005-06

Round of sixteen		Quarter-finals		Semi-finals		Final	
Wisla Plock *	3 0						
Podbeskidzie	0 0	Wisla Plock *	1 1				
Pogon Szczecin	0 2	Kujawiak Wloclawek	0 1				
Kujawiak Wloclawek *	1 1			Wisla Plock *	0 1		
Odra Wodzislaw Slaski	0 3			Lech Poznan	0 0		
Amica Wronki *	0 2	Odra Wodzislaw Slaski	0 0				
Radomiak Radom	0 0	Lech Poznan *	1 0				
Lech Poznan *	2 2					Wisla Plock ‡	3 3
Korona Kielce						Zaglebie Lubin *	2 1
Groclin Grodzisk *		Korona Kielce	0 3				
Hetman Zamosc *	0 0	Legia Warszawa *	2 0				
Legia Warszawa	4 6			Korona Kielce	0 0		
Polonia Warszawa	3 2			Zaglebie Lubin *	2 0		
Jagiellonia Bialystok *	1 3	Polonia Warszawa	1 0				
Wisla Krakow	1 0	Zaglebie Lubin *	0 3				
Zaglebie Lubin *	1 1						

* Home team in the first leg • ‡ Qualified for the UEFA Cup

CUP FINAL

1st leg. 26-04-2006
Scorers - Jackiewicz [63], Arboleda [77] for Lubin; Jelen 2 [1 56], Belada [89] for Plock
2nd leg. 3-05-2006
Magdon [68], Gevorgyan [73], Truszczynski [86] for Plock; Piszczek [82]

POR – PORTUGAL

NATIONAL TEAM RECORD
JULY 1ST 2002 TO JULY 9TH 2006

PL	W	D	L	F	A	%
54	33	13	8	111	40	73.1

The Portuguese national team has never known two years quite like it; a European Championship final appearance, a place in the FIFA World Cup™ semi-finals, a record breaking unbeaten run of 19 games, but perhaps most importantly they have given the fans a chance to revel in what coach Luiz Felipe Scolari called the 'warrior spirit' he has instilled in his players. After losing to the Republic of Ireland in a friendly in February 2005, Portugal went on a run of 15 victories and three draws in the following 18 games, although it has to be said that none of the victories were against top ranked nations. That test didn't come until the last group game at the finals in Germany against Mexico. Having beaten Angola and Iran, Portugal made it three wins out of three to top the group and qualify for the knock out stage for the first time since 1966. The second round encounter with the Netherlands should have been one of the games of the tournament and although Portugal's 1-0 win was certainly memorable, that was more because of the four dismissals rather than for the football. Portuguese goalkeeper Ricardo was the hero of the penalty shoot-out victory over England in the quarter-final, just as he had been in the Euro 2004 quarter-final between the two.

INTERNATIONAL HONOURS
Qualified for FIFA World Cup™ finals 1966 1986 2002 2006
FIFA World Youth Championship 1989 1991
UEFA Youth Tournament 1961   **UEFA U-18 Championship** 1994 1999   **UEFA U-17 Championship** 1989 1995 1996 2000 2003
Intercontinental Cup FC Porto 1987 2004   **UEFA Champions League** Benfica 1961 1962, FC Porto 1987 2004

However, Scolari's Portugal express had begun to show signs of running out of steam in the England match and against France in the semi-final that was certainly the case. A Zinedine Zidane penalty settled the game in France's favour and Portugal had lost a FIFA World Cup™ semi-final for the second time. The encouraging news amid the disappointment at missing out on the final was that Scolari, despite offers from elsewhere - notably from England - had decided to stay on as coach which should see Portugal as one of the favourites for the UEFA Euro 2008™ finals. The domestic season was dominated by the battle of the Dutch coaches with Co Adriaanse's FC Porto beating Ronald Koeman's Benfica to the post in both the Super League and the Taça Portugal. Having suffered a post-Mourinho, post-Champions League hangover in the 2004-05 season, it was back to business as usual for Porto who won their 11th championship since 1990. There was also a Cup triumph to celebrate as they more than made up for the previous trophyless season. Benfica did have the better season in Europe, however, knocking out Manchester United in the last match of the group stage, comfortably beating defending champions Liverpool in the second round and then only narrowly losing to eventual winners Barcelona in the quarter-finals.

Federaçao Portuguesa de Futebol (FPF)
Rua Alexandre Herculano, no.58, Apartado 24013, Lisbon 1250-012, Portugal
Tel +351 21 3252700   Fax +351 21 3252780
secretario_geral@fpf.pt   www.fpf.pt
President: MADAIL Gilberto, Dr   General Secretary: BROU Angelo
Vice-President: BROU Angelo   Treasurer: PACHECO LAMAS Carlos   Media Officers: COSTA Onofre & HENRIQUE Bruno
Men's Coach: SCOLARI Luiz Felipe   Women's Coach: AUGUSTO Jose
FPF formed: 1914   UEFA: 1954   FIFA: 1923
Red shirts with green trimmings, Green shorts, Red socks or White shirts with blue trimmings, Blue shorts, White socks

RECENT INTERNATIONAL MATCHES PLAYED BY PORTUGAL

2003	Opponents	Score		Venue	Comp	Scorers	Att	Referee
11-10	Albania	W	5-3	Lisbon	Fr	Figo [6], Simão [48], Rui Costa [55], Pauleta [57], Miguel [64]	5 000	Garibian FRA
15-11	Greece	D	1-1	Aveiro	Fr	Pauleta [60]	30 000	Esquinas Torres ESP
19-11	Kuwait	W	8-0	Leiria	Fr	Pauleta 4 [10 20 45 52], Figo [33], Nuno Gomes 3 [69 75 87]	22 000	Ingvarsson SWE
2004								
18-02	England	D	1-1	Faro/Loule	Fr	Pauleta [68]	27 000	Kassai HUN
31-03	Italy	L	1-2	Braga	Fr	Nuno Valente [5]	25 000	Aydin TUR
28-04	Sweden	D	2-2	Coimbra	Fr	Pauleta [33], Nuno Gomes [90]	15 000	Ceferin SVN
29-05	Luxembourg	W	3-0	Agueda	Fr	Figo [13], Nuno Gomes [28], Rui Costa [36]	9 000	Styles ENG
5-06	Lithuania	W	4-1	Alcochete	Fr	Couto [3], Pauleta [13], Nuno Gomes [81], Postiga [90]	25 000	Wilmes LUX
12-06	Greece	L	1-2	Porto	ECr1	Ronaldo [90]	48 761	Collina ITA
16-06	Russia	W	2-0	Lisbon	ECr1	Maniche [7], Rui Costa [89]	55 000	Hauge NOR
20-06	Spain	W	1-0	Lisbon	ECr1	Nuno Gomes [57]	52 000	Frisk SWE
24-06	England	D	2-2	Lisbon	ECqf	Postiga [83], Rui Costa [110]. W 6-5p	65 000	Meier SUI
30-06	Netherlands	W	2-1	Lisbon	ECsf	Ronaldo [26], Maniche [58]	46 679	Frisk SWE
4-07	Greece	L	0-1	Lisbon	ECf		62 865	Merk GER
4-09	Latvia	W	2-0	Riga	WCq	Ronaldo [57], Pauleta [58]	9 500	Poll ENG
8-09	Estonia	W	4-0	Leiria	WCq	Ronaldo [75], Postiga 2 [83 91+], Pauleta [86]	27 214	Demirlek TUR
9-10	Liechtenstein	D	2-2	Vaduz	WCq	Pauleta [23], Hasler OG [39]	3 548	Panic BIH
13-10	Russia	W	7-1	Lisbon	WCq	Pauleta [26], Ronaldo 2 [39 69], Deco [45], Simão [82] Petit 2 [89 92+]	27 258	Vassaras GRE
17-11	Luxembourg	W	5-0	Luxembourg	WCq	Federspiel OG [11], Ronaldo [28], Maniche [52] Pauleta 2 [67 82]	8 045	Godulyan UKR
2005								
9-02	Republic of Ireland	L	0-1	Dublin	Fr		44 100	Messias ENG
26-03	Canada	W	4-1	Barcelos	Fr	Manuel Fernandes [2], Pauleta [11], Postiga [81] Nuno Gomes [90]	13 000	Ishchenko UKR
30-03	Slovakia	D	1-1	Bratislava	WCq	Postiga [62]	21 000	Sars FRA
4-06	Slovakia	W	2-0	Lisbon	WCq	Fernando Meira [21], Ronaldo [42]	64 000	Collina ITA
8-06	Estonia	W	1-0	Tallinn	WCq	Ronaldo [32]	10 280	Riley ENG
17-08	Egypt	W	2-0	Ponta Delgada	Fr	Fernando Meira [50], Postiga [69]	20 000	Granat POL
3-09	Luxembourg	W	6-0	Faro-Loule	WCq	Jorge [24], Carvalho [30], Pauleta 2 [38 57], Simão 2 [80 85]	25 300	Van Egmond NED
7-09	Russia	D	0-0	Moscow	WCq		28 800	Merk GER
8-10	Liechtenstein	W	2-1	Aveiro	WCq	Pauleta [48], Nuno Gomes [85]	29 000	Gilewski POL
12-10	Latvia	W	3-0	Porto	WCq	Pauleta 2 [20 22], Hugo Viana [86]	35 000	Frojdfeldt SWE
12-11	Croatia	W	2-0	Coimbra	Fr	Petit [32], Pauleta [65]	15 000	Nielsen DEN
15-11	Northern Ireland	D	1-1	Belfast	Fr	OG [40]	20 000	Webb ENG
2006								
1-03	Saudi Arabia	W	3-0	Dusseldorf	Fr	Ronaldo 2 [30 85], Maniche [45]	7 500	Stark GER
27-05	Cape Verde Islands	W	4-1	Evora	Fr	Pauleta 3 [1 38 83], Petit [60]	10 000	Van Egmond NED
3-06	Luxembourg	W	3-0	Metz	Fr	Simão 2 [47 72p], Figo [85]	19 157	Duhamel FRA
11-06	Angola	W	1-0	Cologne	WCr1	Pauleta [4]	45 000	Larrionda URU
17-06	Iran	W	2-0	Frankfurt	WCr1	Deco [63], Ronaldo [80p]	48 000	Poulat FRA
21-06	Mexico	W	2-1	Gelsenkirchen	WCr1	Maniche [6], Simão [24p]	52 000	Michel SVK
25-06	Netherlands	W	1-0	Nuremberg	WCr2	Maniche [23]	41 000	Ivanov.V RUS
1-07	England	D	0-0	Gelsenkirchen	WCqf	W 3-1p	52 000	Elizondo ARG
5-07	France	L	0-1	Munich	WCsf		66 000	Larrionda URU
8-07	Germany	L	1-3	Stuttgart	WC3p	Nuno Gomes [88]	52 000	Kamikawa JPN

Fr = Friendly match • EC = UEFA EURO 2004™ • WC = FIFA World Cup™
q = qualifier • r1 = first round group • qf = quarter-final • sf = semi-final • 3p = third place play-off • f = final

PORTUGAL NATIONAL TEAM RECORDS AND RECORD SEQUENCES

Records			Sequence records				
Victory	8-0	LIE, LIE, KUW	Wins	9	1966	Clean sheets	8	1998-1999
Defeat	0-10	ENG 1947	Defeats	7	1957-59, 1961-62	Goals scored	16	1966-1967
Player Caps	127	FIGO Luis	Undefeated	19	2005-2006	Without goal	4	1996-1997
Player Goals	47	PAULETA	Without win	13	1949-1953	Goals against	17	1949-1953

PORTUGAL COUNTRY INFORMATION

Capital	Lisbon	Independence	1640	GDP per Capita	$18 000
Population	10 524 145	Status	Republic	GNP Ranking	34
Area km²	92 391	Language	Portuguese	Dialling code	+351
Population density	114 per km²	Literacy rate	93%	Internet code	.pt
% in urban areas	36%	Main religion	Christian	GMT + / –	0
Towns/Cities ('000)	Lisbon 2 561; Porto 1 218; Braga 121; Coimbra 106; Funchal 98; Aveiro 54; Evora 45; Leiria 45; Faro 41; Sesimbra 41; Guimarães 40; Portimão 38; Castelo Branco 33				
Neighbours (km)	Spain 1 214; North Atlantic 1 793				
Main stadia	Estadio da Luz – Lisbon 65 647; Estadio do Dragão – Porto 50 948; Estadio José Alvalade – Lisbon 46 955; Estadio Algarve – Faro-Loulé 30 305; Dr. Magalhães Pessoa – Leiria 29 869				

NATIONAL TEAM PLAYERS AND COACHES

Record Caps			Record Goals			Recent Coaches	
FIGO Luis	1991-'06	127	PAULETA	1997-'06	47	RUI SEABRA	1986-'87
FERNANDO COUTO	1990-'04	110	EUSEBIO	1961-'73	41	JUCA	1987-'89
RUI COSTA	1993-'04	94	FIGO Luis	1991-'06	32	JORGE Artur	1989
PAULETA	1997-'06	88	RUI COSTA	1993-'04	26	QUEIROZ Carlos	1990-'93
JOAO V. PINTO	1991-'02	81	NUNO GOMES	1996-'05	24	VINGADA Eduardo	1994
VITOR BAIA	1990-'02	80	JOAO V. PINTO	1991-'02	23	OLIVEIRA Antonio	1994-'96
JOAO D. PINTO	1983-'96	70	NENE	1971-'84	22	JORGE Artur	1996-'97
NENE	1971-'84	66	JORDAO	1972-'89	15	HUMBERTO COELHO	1998-'00
EUSEBIO	1961-'73	64	PEYROTEO Fernando	1938-'49	14	OLIVEIRA Antonio	2000-'02
HUMBERTO COELHO	1968-'83	64	TORRES José	1963-'73	14	SCOLARI Luiz Felipe	2002-

CLUB DIRECTORY

Club	Town/City	Stadium	Capacity	www.	Lge	Cup	CL
Académica de Coimbra	Coimbra	Cidade de Coimbra	30 154	academica-oaf.pt	0	1	0
Desportivo Aves	Vila das Aves	Estádio do CD Aves	8 560	cdaves.pt	0	0	0
SC Beira-Mar	Aveiro	Municipal de Aveiro	31 498	beiramar.pt	0	1	0
SL Benfica	Lisbon	Estádio da Luz	65 647	slbenfica.pt	31	24	2
Boavista FC	Porto	Estádio do Bessa	28 263	boavistafc.pt	1	5	0
SC Braga	Braga	Municipal de Braga	30 359	scbraga.pt	0	1	0
CF Estrella Amadora	Amadora	José Gomes	25 000	brigadatricolor.pt	0	1	0
Gil Vicente FC	Barcelos	Municipal de Barcelos	12 540	gilvicente.bcl.pt	0	0	0
CS Marítimo	Funchal	Estádio dos Barreiros	14 000	csmaritimo-madeira.pt	0	0	0
CD Nacional	Funchal	Estádio dos Barreiros	14 000	nacional-da-madeira.com	0	0	0
Naval 1° Maio	Figueira da Foz	Municipal	10 000	figueira.net/naval	0	0	0
FC Paços Ferreira	Paços de Ferreira	Mata Real	15 000	fcpf.com.pt	0	0	0
FC Porto	Porto	Estádio do Dragão	50 948	fcporto.fc	21	13	2
Sporting CP	Lisbon	José Alvalade	46 955	sporting.pt	18	13	0
Vitória FC	Setúbal	Estádio do Bonfim	25 000	vitoriafutebolclub.pt	0	3	0
União Leiria	Leiria	Magalhães Pessoa	29 869	udl.leirianet.pt	0	0	0

RECENT LEAGUE AND CUP RECORD

	Championship								Cup		
Year	Champions	Pts	Runners-up	Pts	Third	Pts			Winners	Score	Runners-up
1990	FC Porto	59	Benfica	55	Sporting CP	46			Estrela Amadora	1-1 2-0	SC Farense
1991	Benfica	69	FC Porto	67	Sporting CP	56			FC Porto	3-1	SC Beira-Mar
1992	FC Porto	56	Benfica	46	Sporting CP	44			Boavista	2-1	FC Porto
1993	FC Porto	54	Benfica	52	Sporting CP	45			Benfica	5-2	Boavista FC
1994	Benfica	54	FC Porto	52	Sporting CP	51			FC Porto	0-0 2-1	Sporting CP
1995	FC Porto	62	Sporting CP	53	Benfica	49			Sporting CP	2-0	Marítimo
1996	FC Porto	84	Benfica	73	Sporting CP	67			Benfica	3-1	Sporting CP
1997	FC Porto	85	Sporting CP	72	Benfica	58			Boavista	3-2	Benfica
1998	FC Porto	77	Benfica	68	Vitória Guimarães	59			FC Porto	3-1	SC Braga
1999	FC Porto	79	Boavista	71	Benfica	65			Beira-Mar	1-0	Campomaiorense
2000	Sporting CP	77	FC Porto	73	Benfica	69			FC Porto	1-1 2-0	Sporting CP
2001	Boavista	77	FC Porto	76	Sporting CP	62			FC Porto	2-0	Marítimo
2002	Sporting CP	75	Boavista	70	FC Porto	68			Sporting CP	1-0	Leixões
2003	FC Porto	86	Benfica	75	Sporting CP	59			FC Porto	1-0	União Leiria
2004	FC Porto	82	Benfica	74	Sporting CP	73			Benfica	2-1	FC Porto
2005	Benfica	65	FC Porto	62	Sporting CP	61			Vitória Setúbal	2-1	Benfica
2006	FC Porto	79	Sporting CP	72	Benfica	67			FC Porto	1-0	Vitória Setúbal

PORTUGAL 2005-06

SUPERLIGA

	Pl	W	D	L	F	A	Pts	Porto	Sporting	Benfica	Braga	Nacional	Boavista	Un. Leiria	Setúbal	E. Amadora	Marítimo	P. Ferreira	Gil Vicente	Naval	Académica	Belenenses	Rio Ave	Guimarães	Penafiel
FC Porto †	34	24	7	3	54	16	79		1-1	0-2	1-1	3-0	1-0	1-0	0-0	1-0	1-0	3-0	3-0	1-0	5-1	2-0	3-0	3-1	3-1
Sporting CP †	34	22	6	6	50	24	72	0-1		2-1	1-0	1-0	1-0	2-1	1-0	0-1	1-1	3-0	2-0	0-0	0-1	2-1	3-0	2-0	2-0
SL Benfica †	34	20	7	7	51	29	67	1-0	1-3		1-0	1-0	1-0	4-0	1-0	1-0	2-0	2-2	1-2	2-3	1-1	1-0	2-0	2-0	4-0
Sporting Braga ‡	34	17	7	10	38	22	58	1-0	1-3	3-2		0-0	3-2	3-2	1-0	1-0	1-0	0-1	1-1	2-0	2-3	1-1	1-0	2-0	5-0
CD Nacional Funchal ‡	34	14	10	10	40	32	52	0-1	2-1	1-1	1-0		1-0	1-4	2-2	1-2	2-1	2-2	2-0	2-0	2-2	4-0	1-1	1-1	2-0
Boavista	34	12	14	8	37	29	50	1-1	2-2	0-2	0-0	0-3		2-0	0-0	2-1	1-1	4-1	1-0	3-0	2-1	0-2	2-1	1-1	2-1
União Leiria	34	13	8	13	44	42	47	1-3	0-1	3-1	0-1	0-0	0-0		0-2	1-1	0-0	3-0	3-0	2-1	0-2	2-2	5-2	1-0	1-1
Vitória FC Setúbal ‡	34	14	4	16	28	33	46	0-2	1-2	0-1	1-0	1-1	0-2	2-0		1-0	0-1	0-1	1-0	4-1	0-1	1-0	1-0	0-1	2-0
Estrela Amadora	34	12	9	13	31	33	45	2-1	0-0	1-2	0-0	0-2	1-1	1-2	1-0		2-2	0-0	1-0	2-1	3-2	1-2	0-0	0-1	1-0
CS Marítimo Funchal	34	10	14	10	38	37	44	2-2	1-2	0-1	1-0	2-0	1-1	3-0	1-0	1-0		1-1	1-1	2-1	2-2	1-0	0-0	0-1	2-2
Paços Ferreira	34	11	9	14	38	49	42	0-1	3-0	3-1	1-0	0-1	0-1	1-2	2-1	1-2	1-2		1-0	3-1	2-1	1-1	2-1	1-1	2-2
Gil Vicente	34	11	7	16	37	42	40	0-1	2-2	1-3	2-1	0-1	0-1	1-2	5-0	1-1	1-0	2-0		2-0	4-3	1-0	1-0	1-1	2-2
Naval 1º de Maio	34	11	6	17	35	48	39	2-3	0-2	1-1	0-1	3-1	2-2	0-2	0-3	2-0	2-0	1-0	1-4		0-1	2-1	1-0	0-0	4-0
Académica Coimbra	34	10	9	15	37	48	39	0-1	0-3	0-0	0-3	0-0	0-2	1-3	0-1	1-0	2-2	3-0	2-0	2-2		0-1	2-2	3-1	5-0
Os Belenenses	34	11	6	17	40	42	39	1-3	0-1	1-2	0-1	0-1	1-3	3-1	0-2	0-1	2-0	0-2	2-3	0-0	1-2		3-1	5-0	1-0
Rio Ave	34	8	10	16	34	53	34	0-0	1-3	0-1	1-2	0-2	1-1	1-2	1-0	2-1	2-2	2-2	1-0	0-1	1-4	2-1		3-1	2-0
Vitória SC Guimarães	34	8	10	16	28	41	34	0-2	0-1	2-0	0-2	0-0	1-1	0-3	4-0	0-1	1-0	0-2	2-0	0-2	1-1	2-2	1-1		3-1
Penafiel	34	2	9	23	21	61	15	0-1	0-1	1-3	0-0	1-2	0-0	1-1	0-1	0-1	3-2	2-1	0-1	1-0	0-3	0-2	0-1	0-3	

19/08/2005 - 7/05/2006 • † Qualified for the UEFA Champions League • ‡ Qualified for the UEFA Cup • Top scorers: MEYONG, Belenenses, 17; JOAO TOMAS, Braga, 15; LIEDSON, Sporting, 15; NUNO GOMES, Benfica, 15; ANDRE PINTO, Nacional, 14; JOEANO, Académica, 13

PORTUGAL 2005-06

LIGA DE HONRA (2)

	Pl	W	D	L	F	A	Pts	Beira-Mar	Aves	Leixões	Varzim	Olhanense	Santa Clara	Gondomar	Chaves	Estoril	Feirense	Vizela	Portimonense	Moreirense	Sp. Covilhã	Barreirense	Marco	Ovarense	Maia
SC Beira-Mar	34	18	14	2	45	18	68		2-1	0-0	1-0	1-0	2-1	2-1	0-0	3-1	1-0	3-0	0-0	2-0	2-0	0-0	3-2	2-0	4-0
Desportivo Aves	34	18	10	5	47	30	64	1-1		1-0	1-0	1-0	1-1	2-0	1-1	2-1	2-1	3-2	0-0	4-2	2-1	1-1	2-0	1-1	1-0
Leixões	34	17	11	6	47	19	62	0-0	2-1		1-2	2-1	2-1	1-1	1-1	4-1	0-0	1-3	3-1	1-0	1-2	3-0	3-1	3-1	0-0
Varzim SC	34	13	13	8	47	39	52	0-2	2-1	2-1		0-0	1-0	0-3	0-0	1-0	3-3	3-1	1-0	1-2	3-0	3-1	3-1	0-0	
Olhanense	34	13	13	8	41	28	52	0-0	0-1	1-0	1-1		2-0	1-2	0-0	0-0	2-2	1-0	1-1	3-0	5-2	1-1	2-1	4-0	3-3
CD Santa Clara	34	13	12	9	45	32	51	0-0	1-0	2-3	2-0	0-0		3-1	2-0	0-2	2-0	2-0	0-0	3-0	4-1	3-1	1-0	2-1	2-0
Gondomar	34	14	9	11	56	41	51	2-2	1-0	0-0	1-1	1-2	2-2		1-2	2-0	0-0	5-5	2-0	0-1	1-1	1-0	0-2	2-1	1-0
GD Chaves	34	13	11	10	40	36	50	0-2	0-1	1-2	2-0	0-0	0-0	1-1		1-3	4-1	0-2	1-0	0-0	3-1	1-0	2-1	2-0	
GD Estoril-Praia	34	11	12	11	44	43	45	1-1	1-1	0-3	1-3	0-1	0-0	1-0	3-4		5-2	1-0	4-1	2-1	1-1	2-1	2-0	3-2	3-2
Feirense	34	12	8	14	44	44	44	1-2	2-1	1-1	2-2	2-0	2-1	2-0	0-0	1-1		2-2	0-2	3-0	1-0	1-1	4-3	0-2	
Vizela	34	11	11	12	42	48	44	1-2	2-1	0-0	2-2	1-0	1-2	1-2	2-2	1-0	1-0		0-0	2-1	2-1	2-0	4-3	0-2	
Portimonense	34	10	13	11	36	36	43	1-1	2-2	0-0	2-2	0-1	3-1	1-3	1-0	2-1	0-2	2-0		0-1	0-0	2-0	3-0	1-1	2-0
Moreirense	34	11	9	13	36	37	42	2-2	0-1	1-1	2-2	2-0	2-1	2-0	0-0	1-1	1-0	0-2	0-2		3-0	1-0	1-1	3-0	0-1
Sporting Covilhã	34	10	12	12	37	42	42	1-0	1-2	1-2	3-7	1-2	0-0	1-2	0-0	5-5	2-0	0-1	2-1	2-1		2-2	1-0	2-0	1-1
Barreirense	34	8	11	15	31	41	35	0-0	2-1	0-2	1-1	2-0	1-0	1-4	1-1	0-0	1-1	3-0	0-0	1-0			2-3	4-0	1-1
Marco	34	7	8	19	32	63	29	1-0	0-2	0-5	2-2	0-0	1-1	1-2	2-4	1-1	1-1	0-0	0-1	1-0	1-2			0-2	3-2
Ovarense	34	6	7	21	36	72	25	2-1	1-3	0-1	2-4	0-3	1-1	0-4	2-3	0-0	2-0	1-2	1-3	1-1	1-2	1-0	1-3		4-4
FC Maia	34	6	6	22	30	67	24	0-1	0-0	0-2	1-2	1-3	2-1	2-4	3-2	0-0	0-2	1-2	0-3	0-4	1-2	1-0	0-2	0-2	

21/08/2005 - 7/05/2006

TAÇA DE PORTUGAL 2005-06

Fifth Round		Round of sixteen		Quarter-finals		Semi-finals		Final	
FC Porto	2	FC Porto	Bye	FC Porto	2	FC Porto	1 5p	FC Porto	1
Naval 1° de Maio *	1			CS Marítimo Funchal *	1	Sporting CP	1 4p	Vitória FC Setúbal ‡	0
Vila Meã	2	Vila Meã	0						
Sporting Covilhã *	1	CS Marítimo Funchal *	3						
Portomosense *	0								
CS Marítimo Funchal	2								
Académica Coimbra	0 3p	Académica Coimbra	2	Académica Coimbra *	0				
Louletano *	0 2p	Desportivo Aves *	1	Sporting CP	2				
Sporting Braga	1 2p								
Desportivo Aves *	1 4p								
Parades *	3	Parades	1						
Lagoa	1	Sporting CP *	2						
Vizela	1								
Sporting CP *	2								
Vitória SC Guimarães *	4	Vitória SC Guimarães *	2	Vitória SC Guimarães	1	Vitória SC Guimarães	1 2p		
GD Estoril-Praia	0	UD Oliveirense	0	SL Benfica *	0	Vitória FC Setúbal	1 3p		
Aljustrelense *	1								
UD Oliveirense	0								
CD Nacional Funchal *	2	CD Nacional Funchal	0 3p						
Fátima	0	SL Benfica *	0 5p						
Tourizense *	0								
SL Benfica	2								
Boavista *	3	Boavista	1	Boavista	1				
Abrantes	0	Estrela Amadora *	0	Vitória FC Setúbal *	2				
Souropires *	1								
Estrela Amadora	3								
Lixa *	1	Lixa *	0						
Ribeirão	0	Vitória FC Setúbal	2						
Pinhalnovense *	0 4p								
Vitória FC Setúbal	0 5p								

CUP FINAL

Estádio Nacional, Lisbon
14-05-2006, Ref: Duarte Gomes

Scorer - Adriano 31 for Porto

Porto - Helton - Bosingwa, Pepe, Pedro Emanuel, Lucho González, Paulo Assunção, Anderson (Cech 75), Ricardo Quaresma (Jorginho 67), Adriano, McCarthy (Ibson 85). Alan. Tr: Co Adriaanse

Setúbal - Rubinho - Janício, Veríssimo, Auri, Adalto (Sougou 57), Binho (Fonseca 81), Sandro, Ricardo Chaves (Pedro Oliveira 67), Bruno Ribeiro, Silvestre Varela, Carlitos. Tr: Hélio Sousa

* Home team • ‡ Qualified for the UEFA Cup

FC PORTO 2005-06

Date	Opponents	Score		Comp	Scorers
21-08-2005	Estrela Amadora	W 1-0	H	SL	Ricardo Costa [60]
26-08-2005	Naval 1° do Maio	W 3-2	A	SL	César Peixoto 2 [45 52], Hugo Almeida [82]
10-09-2005	Rio Ave	W 3-0	H	SL	Quaresma [88], Alan [94+], Hugo Almeida [96+]
13-09-2005	Rangers - SCO	L 2-3	A	CLgH	Pepe 2 [47 71]
18-09-2005	Sporting Braga	D 0-0	A	SL	
24-09-2005	Os Belenenses	W 2-0	H	SL	McCarthy [17], Jorginho [57]
28-09-2005	Artmedia Bratislava - SVK	L 2-3	H	CLgH	Lucho González [32], Diego [39]
2-10-2005	CS Marítimo Funchal	D 2-2	A	SL	Lisandro Lopez [75], César Peixoto [78]
15-10-2005	SL Benfica	L 0-2	H	SL	
19-10-2005	Internazionale - ITA	W 2-0	H	CLgH	Materazzi OG [22], McCarthy [35]
23-10-2005	CD National Funchal	W 1-0	A	SL	Hugo Almeida [48]
26-10-2005	Marco	W 1-0	H	TPr4	Ivanildo [28]
29-10-2005	Vitória FC Setúbal	D 0-0	H	SL	
1-11-2005	Internazionale - ITA	L 1-2	A	CLgH	Hugo Almeida [16]
6-11-2005	Paços Ferreira	W 1-0	A	SL	Quaresma [11]
19-11-2005	Académica Coimbra	W 5-1	H	SL	Lucho González 2 [10 96+], Lisandro Lopez 2 [19 79], César Peixoto [73]
23-11-2005	Rangers - SCO	D 1-1	H	CLgH	Lisandro Lopez [60]
28-11-2005	Gil Vicente	W 1-0	A	SL	Lucho González [1]
2-12-2005	Sporting CP	D 1-1	H	SL	Jorginho [67]
6-12-2005	Artmedia Bratislava - SVK	D 0-0	A	CLgH	
11-12-2005	União Leiria	W 3-1	A	SL	Laranjeiro OG [40], Lisandro Lopez [42], Diego [93+]
17-12-2005	Penafiel	W 3-1	H	SL	Lucho González 2 [39 44], Lisandro Lopez [57]
22-12-2005	Vitória SC Guimarães	W 2-0	A	SL	Quaresma [21], Jorginho [60]
8-01-2006	Boavista	W 1-0	H	SL	Quaresma [22]
11-01-2006	Naval 1° do Maio	W 2-1	A	TPr5	Diego [26], Lucho González [79p]
15-01-2006	Estrela Amadora	L 1-2	A	SL	Lucho González [62]
21-01-2006	Naval 1° do Maio	W 1-0	H	SL	Fernando OG [30]
29-01-2006	Rio Ave	D 0-0	A	SL	
6-02-2006	Sporting Braga	D 1-1	H	SL	Lucho González [57]
11-02-2006	Os Belenenses	W 2-0	A	SL	Adriano 2 [43 54]
19-02-2006	CS Marítimo Funchal	W 1-0	H	SL	Raul Meireles [21]
26-02-2006	SL Benfica	L 0-1	A	SL	
5-03-2006	CD National Funchal	W 3-0	H	SL	McCarthy [16], Pepe [44], Lucho González [52]
10-03-2006	Vitória FC Setúbal	W 2-0	H	SL	Adriano [41], Raul Meireles [51]
15-03-2006	CS Marítimo Funchal	W 2-1	A	TPqf	McCarthy 2 [22 96]
18-03-2006	Paços Ferreira	W 3-0	H	SL	McCarthy [31], Adriano [47], Lisandro Lopez [74]
22-03-2006	Sporting CP	D 1-1	H	TPsf	McCarthy [114]. W 5-4p
26-03-2006	Académica Coimbra	W 1-0	A	SL	Hugo Almeida [72]
2-04-2006	Gil Vicente	W 3-0	H	SL	Marek Cech [49], Quaresma [83], Ibson [91+]
8-04-2006	Sporting CP	W 1-0	A	SL	Jorginho [85]
14-04-2006	União Leiria	W 1-0	H	SL	Adriano [44]
22-04-2006	Penafiel	W 1-0	A	SL	Adriano [48]
30-04-2006	Vitória SC Guimarães	W 3-1	H	SL	Lucho González 2 [60 89], Adriano [95]
6-05-2006	Boavista	D 1-1	A	SL	Lisandro Lopez [21]
14-05-2006	Vitória FC Setúbal	W 1-0	N	TPf	Adriano [31]

SL = SuperLiga • TP = Taça de Portugal • CL = UEFA Champions League
gH = group H • r4 = fourth round • r5 = fifth round • qf = quarter-final • sf = semi-final • f = final • N = Estadio Nacional, Lisbon

FIFA/COCA-COLA WORLD RANKING

1993	1994	1995	1996	1997	1998	1999	2000	2001	2002	2003	2004	2005	High		Low	
20	20	16	13	30	36	15	6	4	11	17	9	10	4	03/01	43	08/98

2005–2006											
08/05	09/05	10/05	11/05	12/05	01/06	02/06	03/06	04/06	05/06	06/06	07/06
9	9	9	10	10	10	10	10	8	7	-	8

THE FIFA BIG COUNT OF 2000

	Male	Female		Male	Female
Registered players	40 169	2 593	Referees	3 967	27
Non registered players	170 000	3 600	Officials	8 000	200
Youth players	47 198	722	Total involved	303 476	
Total players	291 282		Number of clubs	2 530	
Professional players	2 244	0	Number of teams	10 382	

PRK – KOREA DPR

NATIONAL TEAM RECORD
JULY 1ST 2002 TO JULY 9TH 2006

PL	W	D	L	F	A	%
36	11	10	15	62	48	44.4

FIFA/COCA-COLA WORLD RANKING

1993	1994	1995	1996	1997	1998	1999	2000	2001	2002	2003	2004	2005	High	Low
62	84	117	144	166	158	172	142	136	124	117	95	82	**57** 11/93	**181** 11/98

2005–2006											
08/05	09/05	10/05	11/05	12/05	01/06	02/06	03/06	04/06	05/06	06/06	07/06
89	85	86	85	82	82	82	87	88	88	-	91

It was a busy year for the various national teams of the Democratic People's Republic of Korea with the senior men's team starting the season with an appearance in the East Asian Football Federation Championship across the border in the south. They started with a great win over Japan which was followed by a draw with Korea Republic and then a defeat by China PR to finish third in the four team tournament. A final FIFA World Cup™ qualifying game against Bahrain was won but by then there was no chance to make it to the finals in Germany. The under-17 team was the next in action at the FIFA U-17 World Championship in Peru where a great win over the Côte

INTERNATIONAL HONOURS
Qualified for the FIFA World Cup™ finals 1966   Qualified for the FIFA Women's World Cup finals 1999 2003
Asian Games 1978   Asian Women's Championship 2001 2003   Women's Asian Games 2002

d'Ivoire and a draw against Italy saw them qualify for the last eight. Against Brazil, another great effort saw them equalise late on to take the game to extra time before losing 3-1. The senior team was back in action in December at the 36th King's Cup in Thailand where they impressed by reaching the final although they lost 2-1 to Latvia. Then it was the turn of the women as the under-19 team qualified for the FIFA U-20 Women's World Championship in Russia and the senior team made sure of their berth in the FIFA women's World Cup in China PR in 2007.

THE FIFA BIG COUNT OF 2000

	Male	Female		Male	Female
Registered players	5 000	0	Referees	300	0
Non registered players	100 000	0	Officials	1 000	0
Youth players	5 000	0	Total involved	111 300	
Total players	110 000		Number of clubs	150	
Professional players	0	0	Number of teams	800	

DPR Korea Football Association (PRK)
Kumsongdong, Kwangbok Street, Mangyongdae Dist., PO Box 56, Pyongyang, Korea DPR
Tel +850 2 182228164   Fax +850 2 3814403
noc-kp@co.chesin.com   www.none
President: RIM Kyong Man   General Secretary: KIM Jong Su
Vice-President: MUN Jang Hong   Treasurer: JANG Su Myong   Media Officer: None
Men's Coach: HAN Hyong Yi   Women's Coach: KIM Kwang Min
PRK formed: 1945   AFC: 1974   FIFA: 1958
White shirts, White shorts, White socks

RECENT INTERNATIONAL MATCHES PLAYED BY KOREA DPR

2003	Opponents	Score		Venue	Comp	Scorers	Att	Referee
24-03	India	W	2-0	Pyongyang	ACq	So Hyok Chol 2 [22 80]		
30-03	India	D	1-1	Margao	ACq	Choe Hyun U [85]		
4-09	Lebanon	L	0-1	Pyongyang	ACq			
27-10	Iran	L	1-3	Pyongyang	ACq	Myong Song Chol [65]	30 000	
3-11	Lebanon	D	1-1	Beirut	ACq	Kim Yong Chol [61]		
12-11	Iran	L	0-3	Tehran	ACq			
18-11	Jordan	L	0-3	Amman	ACq			
28-11	Jordan	L	0-3	Pyongyang	ACq	Match awarded 3-0 to Jordan		
2004								
18-02	Yemen	D	1-1	Sana'a	WCq	Hong Yong Jo [85]	15 000	Husain BHR
31-03	United Arab Emirates	D	0-0	Pyongyang	WCq		20 000	Zhou Weixin CHN
9-06	Thailand	W	4-1	Bangkok	WCq	Kim Yong Su 2 [42 71], Sin Yong Nam [52], Hong Yong Jo [67]	30 000	Tseytlin UZB
8-09	Thailand	W	4-1	Pyongyang	WCq	An Yonh Hak 2 [49 73], Hong Yong Jo [55], Ri Hyok Chol [60]	20 000	Moradi IRN
13-10	Yemen	W	2-1	Pyongyang	WCq	Ri Han Ja [1], Hong Yong Jo [64]	15 000	Vo Minh Tri VIE
17-11	United Arab Emirates	L	0-1	Dubai	WCq		2 000	Abdul Hamid MAS
2005								
2-02	Kuwait	D	0-0	Beijing	Fr			
9-02	Japan	L	1-2	Saitama	WCq	Nam Song Chol [61]	60 000	Al Ghamdi KSA
7-03	Mongolia	W	6-0	Taipei	EAq	Kim Kwang Hyok 3 [18 39 66], Ri Hyok Chol 2 [22 30] Hong Yong Jo [64]		
9-03	Chinese Taipei	W	2-0	Taipei	EAq	Choe Chol Man 2 [13 14]		
11-03	Guam	W	21-0	Taipei	EAq	Hong Yong Jo 2 [6 17], Choe Chol Man 3 [10 37 54] Kim Kwang Hyok 7 [21 43 61 63 71 76 77], Park Nam Chol [83] Kim Yong Jun 3 [29 39 49], Kang Jin Hyok 5 [31 44 65 84 91+]		
13-03	Hong Kong	W	2-0	Taipei	EAq	Kang Jin Hyok [43], Ri Myong Sam [64]		
25-03	Bahrain	L	1-2	Pyongyang	WCq	Pak Song Gwan [63]	50 000	Rungklay THA
30-03	Iran	L	0-2	Pyongyang	WCq		55 000	Kousa SYR
3-06	Iran	L	0-1	Tehran	WCq		35 000	Al Ghamdi KSA
8-06	Japan	L	0-2	Bangkok	WCq		BCD	De Bleeckere BEL
31-07	Japan	W	1-0	Daejon	EA	Kim Yong Jun [25]	23 150	Tan Hai CHN
4-08	Korea Republic	D	0-0	Jeonju	EA		27 455	Ghahremani IRN
7-08	China PR	L	0-2	Daegu	EA			
14-08	Korea Republic	L	0-3	Seoul	Fr			
17-08	Bahrain	W	3-2	Manama	WCq	Choe Chol Man [28], Kim Chol Ho [43], An Chol Hyok [89]	3 000	Maidin SIN
26-12	Latvia	D	1-1	Phuket	Fr	An Chol Hyok [26]		
28-12	Thailand	W	2-0	Phuket	Fr	Kim Chol Ho [7], Hong Yong Jo [9]		
30-12	Latvia	L	1-2	Phuket	Fr	Hong Yong Jo [47]		
2006								

Ni international matches played in 2006 before July

Fr = Friendly match • AC = AFC Asian Cup 2004 • EA = East Asian Championship • WC = FIFA World Cup™ • q = qualifier

KOREA DPR NATIONAL TEAM RECORDS AND RECORD SEQUENCES

Records			Sequence records					
Victory	21-0	GUM 2005	Wins	8	1993	Clean sheets	4	Four times
Defeat	1-6	BUL 1974	Defeats	5	1993	Goals scored	18	1992-1993
Player Caps	n/a		Undefeated	13	1978-1980	Without goal	4	1989-1990
Player Goals	n/a		Without win	15	1993-2000	Goals against	12	1993-2000

KOREA DPR COUNTRY INFORMATION

Capital	Pyongyang	Independence	1945 from Japan	GDP per Capita	$1 400
Population	22 912 177	Status	Communist Republic	GNP Ranking	68
Area km²	120 540	Language	Korean	Dialling code	+850
Population density	190 per km²	Literacy rate	99%	Internet code	.kp
% in urban areas	61%	Main religion	None	GMT +/−	+9
Towns/Cities ('000)	Pyongyang 2 787; Hamhung 840; Chongjin 689, Nampo 670; Sinuiju 385; Wonsan 355; Phyongsong 323; Sariwon 300; Haeju 271; Kanggye 264; Kimchaek 237; Hyesan 210				
Neighbours (km)	Korea Republic 238; China 1 416; Russia 19; Sea of Japan & Yellow Sea 2 495				
Main stadia	Kim Il-Sung Stadium – Pyongyang 70 000; Yanggakdo – Pyongyang 30 000				

PUR – PUERTO RICO

NATIONAL TEAM RECORD
JULY 1ST 2002 TO JULY 9TH 2006

PL	W	D	L	F	A	%
5	0	1	4	3	17	10

FIFA/COCA-COLA WORLD RANKING

1993	1994	1995	1996	1997	1998	1999	2000	2001	2002	2003	2004	2005		High		Low
105	112	128	149	169	182	186	195	195	198	200	194	195		97	03/94	202 11/04

2005–2006											
08/05	09/05	10/05	11/05	12/05	01/06	02/06	03/06	04/06	05/06	06/06	07/06
194	194	194	193	195	195	195	195	196	196	-	190

One would be hard pushed to find a nation affiliated to FIFA in which football plays such a low profile. For the second year running there was no international action on any front with the women's under-19 and women's senior team failing to enter the Caribbean qualifiers for either of the FIFA world tournaments. Coming on the heels of the men's team not entering the 2006 FIFA World Cup™ there is a danger that Puerto Rico will lose the right to vote at upcoming FIFA Congresses. There is a healthy club scene in Puerto Rico although the emphasis is largely focused on the club as a social centre, and as an outlet for junior teams. Fraigicomar, the Puerto Rican

INTERNATIONAL HONOURS
None

champions in 2005, are a good example. They run teams from the age of six upwards and one look at their website leaves little doubt that the priority remains very much on the kids. The Liga Mayor is the senior men's competition in the country and after a first round group, from which all six teams rather bizarrely qualified for the play-offs, Real Quintana beat Fraigicomar 2-1 in the final to win the title. All six teams then joined with teams from the Liga Premier to take part in the end of year National Championship. In the final at the Estadio Juan Ramón Loubriel in Bayamón, Fraigicomar beat Huracanes 1-0.

THE FIFA BIG COUNT OF 2000

	Male	Female		Male	Female
Registered players	8 000	0	Referees	300	0
Non registered players	36 000	0	Officials	2 000	1 000
Youth players	10 000	0	Total involved	56 400	
Total players	54 000		Number of clubs	200	
Professional players	0	0	Number of teams	800	

Federación Puertorriquena de Fútbol (FPF)
392 Juan B. Rodriguez, Parque Central Hato Rey, PR 00918, San Juan 00918, Puerto Rico
Tel +1 787 7652895   Fax +1 787 7672288
jserralta@yahoo.com   www.fedefutbolpr.com
President: SERRALTA Joe   General Secretary: RODRIGUEZ Esteban
Vice-President: JIMENEZ Mickey   Treasurer: VILLEGAS Miguel   Media Officer: None
Men's Coach: VILLAREJO Luis   Women's Coach: ROSA Jorge Oscar
FPF formed: 1940   CONCACAF: 1962   FIFA: 1960
White shirts with red stripes and blue sleeves, White shorts, White socks

RECENT INTERNATIONAL MATCHES PLAYED BY PUERTO RICO

2002	Opponents	Score		Venue	Comp	Scorers	Att	Referee
7-07	Guadeloupe	L	0-4	Baie-Mahault	GCq			Ibrahim DMA
21-07	Guadeloupe	L	0-2	San Juan	GCq			Richard DMA
2003								
No international matches played in 2003								
2004								
24-11	Trinidad and Tobago	L	0-5	Tunapuna	GCq		2 000	Callender BRB
26-11	Surinam	D	1-1	Marabella	GCq	Ortiz 80		Forde BRB
28-11	Grenada	L	2-5	Malabar	GCq	Garcia 85, Nieves 86		Callender BRB
2005								
No international matches played in 2005								
2006								
No international matches played in 2006 before July								

GC = CONCACAF Gold Cup • q = qualifier

PUERTO RICO NATIONAL TEAM RECORDS AND RECORD SEQUENCES

Records			Sequence records					
Victory	4-0	CAY 1993	Wins	4	1993	Clean sheets	4	1993
Defeat	0-9	CUB 1995	Defeats	15	1949-1965	Goals scored	6	1988-1992
Player Caps	n/a		Undefeated	4	1993	Without goal	6	1982-1988
Player Goals	n/a		Without win	37	1940-1970	Goals against	26	1949-1970

PUERTO RICO 2005 LIGA MAYOR

	Pl	W	D	L	F	A	Pts
Fraigcomar †	10	7	3	0	25	7	24
Real Quintana †	10	6	4	0	34	7	22
Huracanes Caguas ‡	10	4	4	2	11	13	16
Atléticos Añasco ‡	10	4	0	6	21	24	12
Vaqueros Bayamón ‡	10	2	2	6	20	37	8
Tornados Humacao ‡	10	0	1	9	12	35	1

7/08/2004 - 24/10/2005 • † Qualified for the semi-finals
‡ Qualified for the quarter-finals

LIGA MAYOR PLAY-OFFS

Quarter-finals	Semi-finals	Final	
	Real Quintana		
Tornados	Huracanes		
Huracanes		Real Quintana	2
Atlético Añasco		Fraigcomar	1
Vaqueros	Atlético Añasco		
	Fraigcomar		

RECENT LEAGUE RECORD

	Championship	Liga Mayor		
Year	Champions	Winners	Score	Runners-up
1997	Académicos Quintana	Leones Maunabo		Islanders San Juan
1998	Académicos Quintana	Islanders San Juan	3-0	Brujos Guayama
1999	CF Nacional Carolina	Islanders San Juan		Cardenales
2000	Académicos Quintana	Vaqueros Bayamón	1-0	Gigantes Carolina
2001	Académicos Quintana	Islanders San Juan	4-3	Brujos Guayama
2002	Académicos Quintana	Vaqueros Bayamón	3-0	Islanders San Juan
2003	Not held	Sporting Carolina	2-1	Vaqueros Bayamón
2004	Not held	Sporting San Lorenzo	1-0	Huracanes Caguas
2005	Fraigcomar	Real Quintana	2-1	Fraigcomar

PUERTO RICO COUNTRY INFORMATION

Capital	San Juan	Status	Commonwealth associated with the US	GDP per Capita	$16 800
Population	3 897 960			GNP Ranking	n/a
Area km²	9 104	Language	Spanish, English	Dialling code	+1 787
Population density	428 per km²	Literacy rate	94%	Internet code	.pr
% in urban areas	71%	Main religion	Christian	GMT +/-	-5
Towns/Cities ('000)	San Juan 418; Bayamón 203; Carolina 170; Ponce 152; Caguas 86; Guaynabo 81; Mayagüez 76				
Neighbours (km)	Caribbean Sea & North Atlantic 501				
Main stadia	Estadio Sixto Escobar – San Juan 18 000; Country Club – San Juan 2 500				

QAT – QATAR

NATIONAL TEAM RECORD
JULY 1ST 2002 TO JULY 9TH 2006

PL	W	D	L	F	A	%
49	20	14	15	76	58	55.1

FIFA/COCA-COLA WORLD RANKING

1993	1994	1995	1996	1997	1998	1999	2000	2001	2002	2003	2004	2005		High	Low
54	60	83	69	70	60	107	102	80	62	65	66	95		**51** 08/93	**107** 12/99

					2005–2006						
08/05	09/05	10/05	11/05	12/05	01/06	02/06	03/06	04/06	05/06	06/06	07/06
68	75	77	81	95	89	90	77	76	78	-	76

The highlight of the season for the Qatari national team was a first visit by Argentina to the country in a match staged to raise funds for the victims of the Asian tsunami disaster. Qatar held their own for more than an hour before conceding three goals in three minutes to lose the game 3-0. The 2007 AFC Asian Cup qualifying campaign got off to a solid start with wins over Hong Kong and Uzbekistan as Qatar set out out to qualify for their third successive appearance in the finals. In preparation for the 2006 Asian Games to be held in Doha, there was a trial run with the West Asian Games in December in 2005 with Doha hosting all of the football tournament, although Qatar did

INTERNATIONAL HONOURS
Gulf Cup 1992 2004

not enter its full national team, unlike some of the other competing nations. Domestically, the Q-League continues to attract players from the world over and it was won in 2006 by Al Sadd. In the final round the top two teams faced each other with Al Arabi needing to win to force a play-off but Ecuador's Carlos Tenorio scored twice for Sadd in a 2-1 win to give them their 11th championship. Al Rayyan were the other trophy winners, beating Al Gharrafa on penalties after a 1-1 draw in the Amir Cup Final, but there was huge disappointment in the 2006 AFC Champions League after neither Gharrafa nor Al Sadd managed to make it through the group stage.

THE FIFA BIG COUNT OF 2000

	Male	Female		Male	Female
Registered players	1 943	0	Referees	85	0
Non registered players	2 370	0	Officials	1 040	0
Youth players	1 598	0	Total involved	7 036	
Total players	5 911		Number of clubs	16	
Professional players	4	0	Number of teams	45	

Qatar Football Association (QFA)
7th Floor, QNOC Building, Cornich, PO Box 5333, Doha, Qatar
Tel +974 4944411   Fax +974 4944414
football@qatarolympics.org   www.qatar-football.com
President: AL-THANI Shk. Hamad Bin Khalifa   General Secretary: AL-MOHANNADI Saud
Vice-President: TBD   Treasurer: AL-OBAIDLY Abdulaziz Hassan   Media Officer: AL-KAWARI Khalid
Men's Coach: MUSOVIC Dzemaludin   Women's Coach: None
QFA formed: 1960   AFC: 1972   FIFA: 1970
White shirts, White shorts, White socks

RECENT INTERNATIONAL MATCHES PLAYED BY QATAR

2003	Opponents	Score		Venue	Comp	Scorers	Att	Referee
4-09	Algeria	L	0-1	Paris	Fr		400	
14-09	Kuwait	L	1-2	Kuwait City	ACq	Ghanim Al Shemmari [27]	20 000	
20-09	Kuwait	D	2-2	Doha	ACq	Sayed Al Bashir 2 [20 82]		Al Hamdan KSA
24-09	Palestine	D	1-1	Doha	ACq	Meshal Abdullah [47]		Abdul Kadir Nema IRQ
27-09	Palestine	W	2-1	Doha	ACq	Muhyeddin [68], Hamza [90]		Mujghef JOR
19-11	Singapore	W	2-0	Doha	ACq	Ali Bechir [11], Mubarak Mustafa [29]		
29-11	Singapore	W	2-0	Singapore	ACq	Abdullah Kouni [42], Ali Bechir [55]		Hanlumyaung THA
21-12	Iraq	D	0-0	Doha	Fr			Al Qatani QAT
27-12	Bahrain	D	0-0	Kuwait City	GC			Kassai HUN
29-12	Saudi Arabia	D	0-0	Kuwait City	GC			Meier SUI
2004								
3-01	United Arab Emirates	D	0-0	Kuwait City	GC			
5-01	Yemen	W	3-0	Kuwait City	GC	Mubarak Mustafa [22], Meshal Abdulla [39], Salmeen [58]		
8-01	Kuwait	W	2-1	Kuwait City	GC	Salmeen [41], Mubarak Mustafa [58]		
11-01	Oman	L	0-2	Kuwait City	GC			
13-02	Bahrain	W	2-0	Doha	Fr			
18-02	Iran	L	1-3	Tehran	WCq	Waleed Rasoul [70]		Haj Khader SYR
26-03	Libya	L	0-1	Rome	Fr			
31-03	Jordan	L	0-1	Amman	WCq		15 000	Shaban KUW
31-05	Turkmenistan	W	5-0	Doha	Fr	Mijbel [2], Ali Bechir 3 [15 60 88], Moussa [44]		
5-06	Kyrgyzstan	D	0-0	Doha	Fr			
9-06	Laos	W	5-0	Doha	WCq	Fazli 2 [17 37], Waleed Jassim 2 [69 86], Ali Bechir [89]	500	Abu Armana PAL
18-07	Indonesia	L	1-2	Beijing	ACr1	Magid [83]	5 000	Moradi IRN
21-07	Bahrain	D	1-1	Beijing	ACr1	Wesam Rizak [58p]		Toru JPN
25-07	China PR	L	0-1	Beijing	ACr1		60 000	Moradi IRN
8-09	Laos	W	6-1	Vientiane	WCq	Abdulmajid [36], Nasser Mubarak [42], Ali Bechir [50], Waleed Rasoul [70], Meshal Abdulla [86], Saad Al Shammari [89]	2 900	Napitupulu IDN
8-10	Syria	L	1-2	Doha	Fr			
13-10	Iran	L	2-3	Doha	WCq	Bilal Rajab [18], Golmohammadi OG [75]	8 000	Kwon Jong Chul KOR
17-11	Jordan	W	2-0	Doha	WCq	Salem Al Hamad [60], Nayef Al Khater [75]	800	Yoshida JPN
1-12	Lebanon	W	4-1	Doha	Fr			
5-12	Yemen	W	3-0	Doha	Fr			
10-12	United Arab Emirates	D	2-2	Doha	GCr1	Waleed Jassim [90], Wisam Rizq [93+]		
13-12	Iraq	D	3-3	Doha	GCr1	Bilal Mohammed [38], Waleed Jassim 2 [43p 57]		
16-12	Oman	W	2-1	Doha	GCr1	Sattam Al Shamari [10], Ali Bechir [27]		
20-12	Kuwait	W	2-0	Doha	GCsf	Ali Bechir [39], Nasir Kamil [90p]		
24-12	Oman	D	1-1	Doha	GCf	Wissam Rizq [4]. W 5-4p		
2005								
29-07	Egypt	L	0-5	Geneva	Fr			
31-07	Kuwait	W	1-0	Geneva	Fr	Waleed Jassim [37]		
11-10	Iraq	D	0-0	Doha	Fr			
16-11	Argentina	L	0-3	Doha	Fr			Al Fadhli KUW
2006								
2-01	Libya	W	2-0	Doha	Fr	Adel Lamy 2 [55 61]		
14-02	Tajikistan	W	2-0	Doha	Fr	Sayd Bechir, Waleed Jassim		
22-02	Hong Kong	W	3-0	Hong Kong	ACq	Abdulrahman [11], Sayd Bechir [44], Magid Hassan [95+]	1 806	Nishimura JPN
1-03	Uzbekistan	W	2-1	Doha	ACq	Adel Lamy [45], Ali Naser [49]	7 000	Sun Baoje CHN

Fr = Friendly match • AC = AFC Asian Cup • GC = Gulf Cup • WC = FIFA World Cup™ • q = qualifier • r1 = first round group • sf = semi-final • f = final

QATAR NATIONAL TEAM RECORDS AND RECORD SEQUENCES

Records			Sequence records					
Victory	8-0	AFG 1984, LIB 1985	Wins	5	1988, 1996, 2001	Clean sheets	7	2003-2004
Defeat	0-9	KUW 1973	Defeats	8	1972-1974	Goals scored	12	1996
Player Caps	n/a		Undefeated	11	2001, 2003-04	Without goal	4	1998, 2003-04
Player Goals	n/a		Without win	11	1970-1974	Goals against	15	1994-1996

QATAR COUNTRY INFORMATION

Capital	Doha	Independence	1971 from the UK	GDP per Capita	$21 500
Population	840 290	Status	Monarchy	GNP Ranking	92
Area km²	11 437	Language	Arabic	Dialling code	+974
Population density	73 per km²	Literacy rate	82%	Internet code	.qa
% in urban areas	91%	Main religion	Muslim	GMT + / −	+3
Towns/Cities ('000)	Doha 344; Al Rayyan 272; Umm Salal 29; Al Wakra 26; Khor 19				
Neighbours (km)	Saudi Arabia 60; Persain Gulf 563				
Main stadia	Khalifa International – Doha 45 000				

QATAR 2005-06

Q-LEAGUE

	Pl	W	D	L	F	A	Pts	Sadd	Qatar	Arabi	Rayyan	Ahli	Gharrafa	Khor	Wakra	Shamal	Siliya
Al Sadd †	27	16	4	7	48	32	52		1-0 2-2	1-2	2-1	3-4 3-0	2-1 1-2	2-2	0-1 1-0	0-2 2-1	3-0 3-0
Qatar SC	27	14	7	6	49	34	49	0-1		1-1	0-1 3-1	2-0	1-1 1-0	1-0 2-0	5-3	5-3	4-1
Al Arabi	27	13	7	7	41	36	46	3-1 1-2	2-4 3-1		0-0	3-2 1-4	3-4 1-0	2-1	1-0	1-1 2-1	1-2 1-1
Al Rayyan	27	12	5	10	30	28	41	0-1 2-0	1-2	2-3 0-1		0-2 2-0	2-2 0-0	3-2	1-2 0-0	0-1	1-0 0-2
Al Ahli	27	11	6	10	44	40	39	1-1	0-2 1-1	0-1	0-1		1-1 2-1	2-4	2-3	6-2 2-1	1-1 2-1
Al Gharrafa	27	8	10	9	29	30	34	0-0	0-2	0-1	1-0	1-3		1-1	0-2	3-1 1-2	2-0 1-1
Khor	27	9	6	12	44	49	33	1-3 2-3	0-0	2-1 2-0	1-1 1-2	2-2 0-4	0-1 1-1		1-2 3-2	6-4	1-0
Al Wakra	27	8	8	11	29	32	32	1-3	1-2 0-1	0-0 3-3	0-1	1-0 0-0	0-0 0-1	1-0		2-1 2-0	1-0 1-0
Shamal	27	6	5	16	41	56	23	1-2	2-2 3-1	0-2	1-2 0-1	3-1	1-1	6-2 1-5	1-1		0-1 1-1
Al Siliya	27	5	8	14	29	47	23	2-5	2-2 2-3	1-1	2-3	0-1	1-3	0-1 2-3	2-2	2-1	

*16/09/2005 - 3/04/2006 • † Qualified for AFC Champions League

AMIR CUP 2005-06

Round of sixteen		Quarter-finals		Semi-finals		Final		
Al Rayyan	Bye							
		Al Rayyan	3					
Al Siliya	0	Al Ahli	2					
Al Ahli	1			Al Rayyan	1			
Al Arabi	Bye			Al Wakra				
		Al Arabi	1					
Al Maitheer	0	Al Wakra	2			Al Rayyan †	1	5p
Al Wakra	1					Al Gharrafa	1	3p
Qatar SC	Bye							
		Qatar SC	2					
Al Khritiyat	1	Khor	0					
Khor	5			Qatar SC	1			
Al Sadd	Bye			Al Gharrafa	4			
		Al Sadd	1					
Shamal	2	Al Gharrafa	2					
Al Gharrafa	3							

CUP FINAL

13-05-2006

Scorers - Bouchaib Al Mubaraki [15] for Rayyan; Sergio Ricardo [59] for Gharrafa

† Qualified for AFC Champions League

RECENT LEAGUE AND CUP RECORD

	Championship							Amir Cup		
Year	Champions	Pts	Runners-up	Pts	Third	Pts		Winners	Score	Runners-up
1997	Al Arabi	34	Al Rayyan	32	Al Ittihad	29		Al Ittihad	1-1 3-2p	Al Rayyan
1998	Al Ittihad	32	Al Rayyan	29	Al Sadd	26		Al Ittihad	4-3	Al Ahli
1999	Al Wakra	39	Al Ittihad	34	Al Sadd	33		Al Rayyan	2-1	Al Ittihad
2000	Al Sadd	38	Al Rayyan	34	Al Arabi	26		Al Sadd	2-0	Al Rayyan
2001	Al Wakra	32	Al Arabi	29	Al Taawun	28		Qatar SC	3-2	Al Sadd
2002	Al Ittihad	41	Qatar SC	29	Al Rayyan	25		Al Ittihad	3-1	Al Sadd
2003	Qatar SC	34	Al Sadd	31	Khor	31		Al Sadd	2-1	Al Ahli
2004	Al Sadd	42	Qatar SC	34	Al Arabi	31		Al Rayyan	3-2	Qatar SC
2005	Al Gharrafa	66	Al Rayyan	52	Khor	48		Al Sadd	0-0 5-4p	Al Wakra
2006	Al Sadd	52	Qatar SC	49	Al Arabi	46		Al Rayyan	1-1 5-3p	Al Gharrafa

Name changes: Al Ittihad → Al Gharrafa; Al Taawun → Khor

ROU – ROMANIA

NATIONAL TEAM RECORD
JULY 1ST 2002 TO JULY 9TH 2006

PL	W	D	L	F	A	%
40	23	6	11	70	33	65

FIFA/COCA-COLA WORLD RANKING

1993	1994	1995	1996	1997	1998	1999	2000	2001	2002	2003	2004	2005		High	Low
13	11	11	16	7	12	8	13	15	24	27	29	27		**3** 09/97	**35** 08/04

					2005–2006						
08/05	09/05	10/05	11/05	12/05	01/06	02/06	03/06	04/06	05/06	06/06	07/06
31	32	28	27	27	27	30	26	25	25	-	26

Romania may not have qualified for the 2006 FIFA World Cup™ finals in Germany but coach Victor Piturca is building a team that is gaining in strength all the time. Had they been grouped with anyone other than the Netherlands and the Czech Republic, they may well have made it to Germany. They finished off their campaign with three straight wins making eight in total out of 12 games played and hopes are now high that they can make an impact at UEFA Euro 2008™. They will certainly start as favourites along with the Netherlands to reach the finals from their qualifying group. Although they have some players based in the big European leagues most are based at home

INTERNATIONAL HONOURS
Balkan Cup 1931 1933 1936 1980   **UEFA Junior Tournament** 1962   **UEFA Champions League** Steaua Bucuresti 1986

where club football has become more competitive. For the first time in nearly twenty years, Romanian clubs found themselves at the centre of attention in Europe when Steaua and Rapid were drawn together in the quarter-finals of the UEFA Cup. Steaua won that grudge match and only a miracle recovery by Middlesbrough denied them a place in the final. Steaua and Rapid were also involved in a close race for the title that went down to the final day and which was won by Steaua. With Rapid needing to win away at Jiul Petrosani, they had five players sent off and so forfeited the match 3-0. The previous month, however, they had beaten National 1-0 in the Cup Final.

THE FIFA BIG COUNT OF 2000

	Male	Female		Male	Female
Registered players	52 650	176	Referees	6 085	17
Non registered players	500 000	4 000	Officials	13 252	35
Youth players	54 890	1 500	Total involved	632 605	
Total players	613 216		Number of clubs	2 276	
Professional players	3 920	0	Number of teams	3 852	

Romanian Football Federation (FRF)

Federatia Romana de Fotbal, House of Football, Str. Serg. Serbanica Vasile 12, Bucharest 022186, Romania
Tel +40 21 3250678   Fax +40 21 3250679
frf@frf.ro   www.frf.ro
President: SANDU Mircea   General Secretary: KASSAI Adalbert
Vice-President: DRAGOMIR Dumitru   Treasurer: FILIMON Vasile   Media Officer: ZAHARIA Paul Daniel
Men's Coach: PITURCA Victor   Women's Coach: STAICU Gheorghe
FRF formed: 1909   UEFA: 1954   FIFA: 1923
Yellow shirts with red trimmings, Yellow shorts, Yellow socks or White shirts with red trimmings, White shorts, White socks

RECENT INTERNATIONAL MATCHES PLAYED BY ROMANIA

2002	Opponents	Score		Venue	Comp	Scorers	Att	Referee
21-08	Greece	L	0-1	Constanta	Fr		15 000	Toat TUR
7-09	Bosnia-Herzegovina	W	3-0	Sarajevo	ECq	Chivu [8], Munteanu.D [8], Ganea [27]	4 000	Cortez Batista POR
12-10	Norway	L	0-1	Bucharest	ECq		25 000	Ivanov RUS
16-10	Luxembourg	W	7-0	Luxembourg	ECq	Moldovan 2 [2 5], Radoi [24], Contra 3 [45 47 86], Ghioane [80]	2 000	Lajuks LVA
20-11	Croatia	L	0-1	Timisoara	Fr		40 000	Megyebiro HUN
2003								
12-02	Slovakia	W	2-1	Larnaca	Fr	Munteanu.D [39], Ganea [41]	150	Papaioannou GRE
29-03	Denmark	L	2-5	Bucharest	ECq	Mutu [5], Munteanu.D [47]	55 000	Mejuto Gonzalez ESP
30-04	Lithuania	W	1-0	Kaunas	Fr	Bratu [63]	5 000	Sipailo LVA
7-06	Bosnia-Herzegovina	W	2-0	Craiova	ECq	Mutu [46], Ganea [88]	36 000	Bossen NED
11-06	Norway	D	1-1	Oslo	ECq	Ganea [64]	24 890	Michel SVK
20-08	Ukraine	W	2-0	Donetsk	Fr	Mutu 2 [29p 57]	28 000	Yegorov RUS
6-09	Luxembourg	W	4-0	Ploiesti	ECq	Mutu [39], Pancu [42], Ganea [44], Bratu [77]	4 500	Yefet ISR
10-09	Denmark	D	2-2	Copenhagen	ECq	Mutu [61], Pancu [72]	42 049	Meier SUI
11-10	Japan	D	1-1	Bucharest	Fr	Mutu [17]	10 000	Carmona Mendez ESP
16-11	Italy	L	0-1	Ancona	Fr		11 700	Stark GER
2004								
18-02	Georgia	W	3-0	Larnaca	Fr	Mutu 2 [30 70], Cernat [87]	300	Lajuks LVA
31-03	Scotland	W	2-1	Glasgow	Fr	Chivu [37], Pancu [51]	20 433	Hyytia FIN
28-04	Germany	W	5-1	Bucharest	Fr	Plesan [21], Rat [23], Danciulescu 2 [35 43], Caramarin [85]	21 000	Rosetti ITA
27-05	Republic of Ireland	L	0-1	Dublin	Fr		42 356	Jara CZE
18-08	Finland	W	2-1	Bucharest	WCq	Mutu [50], Petre [90]	17 500	Gilewski POL
4-09	FYR Macedonia	W	2-1	Craiova	WCq	Pancu [15], Mutu [88]	14 500	Plautz AUT
8-09	Andorra	W	5-1	Andorra la Vella	WCq	Cernat 2 [1 17], Pancu 2 [5 83], Niculae [70]	1 100	Kircher GER
9-10	Czech Republic	L	0-1	Prague	WCq		16 028	Rosetti ITA
17-11	Armenia	D	1-1	Yerevan	WCq	Ciprian [29]	1 403	De Bleeckere BEL
2005								
9-02	Slovakia	D	2-2	Larnaca	Fr	Niculae [35], Ilie [87]	500	Kapitanis CYP
26-03	Netherlands	L	0-2	Bucharest	WCq		19 000	Medina Cantalejo ESP
30-03	FYR Macedonia	W	2-1	Skopje	WCq	Mitea 2 [18 58]	15 000	Ovrebo NOR
24-05	Moldova	W	2-0	Bacau	Fr	Niculescu [8], Dica [55]	6 000	Salomir ROU
4-06	Netherlands	L	0-2	Rotterdam	WCq		47 000	De Santis ITA
8-06	Armenia	W	3-0	Constanta	WCq	Petre [29], Bucur 2 [40 78]	5 146	Briakos GRE
17-08	Andorra	W	2-0	Constanta	WCq	Mutu 2 [29 41]	8 200	Jakov ISR
3-09	Czech Republic	W	2-0	Constanta	WCq	Mutu 2 [28 56]	7 000	Hauge NOR
8-10	Finland	W	1-0	Helsinki	WCq	Mutu [41p]	11 500	Guenov BUL
12-11	Côte d'Ivoire	L	1-2	Le Mans	Fr	Iencsi [52]	5 377	Fautrel FRA
16-11	Nigeria	W	3-0	Bucharest	Fr	Niculae [15], Petre [48], Rosu [90]	500	Banari MDA
2006								
28-02	Armenia	W	2-0	Nicosia	Fr	Maftei [72], Cocis [86]	1 000	Tsacheilidis GRE
1-03	Slovenia	W	2-0	Larnaca	Fr	Mazilu [22], OG [53]	300	Vialichka BLR
23-05	Uruguay	L	0-2	Los Angeles	Fr		10 000	Stott USA
26-05	Northern Ireland	W	2-0	Chicago	Fr	Buga [7], Niculae [11]	15 000	Kennedy USA
27-05	Colombia	D	0-0	Chicago	Fr		15 000	Hall USA

Fr = Friendly match • EC = UEFA EURO 2004™ • WC = FIFA World Cup™ • q = qualifier

ROMANIA NATIONAL TEAM RECORDS AND RECORD SEQUENCES

Records			Sequence records					
Victory	9-0	FIN 1973	Wins	8	1996-1997	Clean sheets	5	1996-97, 1999
Defeat	0-9	HUN 1948	Defeats	4	1924-25, 1979	Goals scored	16	1971-1972
Player Caps	130	MUNTEANU Dorinel	Undefeated	17	1989-1990	Without goal	4	1947-1948
Player Goals	35	HAGI Gheorghe	Without win	20	1968-1971	Goals against	21	1933-1937

ROMANIA COUNTRY INFORMATION

Capital	Bucharest	Independence	1878 from Ottoman Empire	GDP per Capita	$7 000
Population	22 355 551	Status	Republic	GNP Ranking	53
Area km²	237 500	Language	Romanian, Hungarian	Dialling code	+40
Population density	94 per km²	Literacy rate	98%	Internet code	.ro
% in urban areas	55%	Main religion	Christian	GMT + / –	+2
Towns/Cities ('000)	Bucharest 1 877; Iasi 318; Cluj-Napoca 316; Timisoara 315; Craiova 304; Constanta 303; Galati 294; Brasov 276; Ploiesti 228; Braila 213; Oradea 203; Bacau 171; Arad 169; Pitesti 167				
Neighbours (km)	Ukraine 531; Moldova 450; Bulgaria 608; Serbia 476; Hungary 443; Black Sea 225				
Main stadia	Stadionul Lia Manoliu – Bucharest 60 120; Stadionul Giulesti – Bucharest 19 100				

NATIONAL TEAM PLAYERS AND COACHES

Record Caps			Record Goals			Recent Coaches	
MUNTEANU Dorinel	1991-'06	130	HAGI Gheorghe	1983-'00	35	CONSTANTIN Gheorghe	1990-'91
HAGI Gheorghe	1983-'00	125	BODOLA Iuliu	1931-'39	30	RADULESCU Mircea	1991-'92
POPESCU Gheorghe	1988-'03	115	MOLDOVAN Dinu	1993-'05	25	DINU Cornel	1992-'93
BOLONI Ladislau	1975-'88	104	BOLONI Ladislau	1975-'88	24	IORDANESCU Anghel	1993-'98
PETRESCU Dan	1989-'00	95	CAMATARU Rodion	1978-'90	22	PITURCA Victor	1998-'99
STELEA Bogdan	1988-'05	91	IORDANESCU Anghel	1971-'81	22	IENEI Emeric	2000
KLEIN Michael	1981-'91	90	GEORGESCU Dudu	1973-'84	21	BOLONI Ladislau	2000-'01
LACATUS Marius	1984-'98	84	RADUCIOIU Florin	1992-'00	21	HAGI Gheorghe	2001
REDNIC Mircea	1981-'91	83	DOBAY Stefan	1930-'39	20	IORDANESCU Anghel	2002-'04
LUNG Silviu	1979-'93	77	DUMITRESCU Ilie	1989-'98	20	PITURCA Victor	2004-

CLUB DIRECTORY

Club	Town/City	Stadium	Capacity	www.	Lge	Cup	CL
Apulum Alba Iulia	Iulia	Cetate	18 000		0	0	0
Arges Pitesti	Pitesti	Nicolae Dobrin	15 170		2	0	0
FCM Bacau	Bacau	Dumitru Sechelariu	17 500	fcmbacau.ro	0	0	0
FC Brasov	Brasov	Tineretului	12 670	fcbrasov.ro	0	0	0
CFR Cluj	Cluj	Gruia	6 000		0	0	0
Universitatea Craiova	Craiova	Ion Oblemenco	27 915	fcuniversitatea.ro	4	6	0
Dinamo Bucuresti	Bucuresti	Dinamo	15 138	fcdinamo.ro	17	12	0
Farul Constanta	Constanta	Gheorghe Hagi	15 520	fcfarul.ro	0	0	0
Gloria Bistrita	Bistrita	Gloria	15 000	cfgloria.ro	0	1	0
Politehnica Iasi	Iasi	Emil Alexandrescu	12 500	politehnicaiasi.ro	0	0	0
National Bucuresti	Bucuresti	Cotroceni	14 542	nationalfc.ro	0	1	0
Otelul Galati	Galati	Otelul	13 932		0	0	0
Politehnica AEK Timisoara	Timisoara	Dan Paltinisanu	40 000		0	2	0
Rapid Bucuresti	Bucuresti	Giulesti	19 100	fcrapid.ro	3	12	0
Sportul Studentesc	Bucuresti	Aurica Radulescu	15 000	fcsportulstudentesc.ro	0	0	0
Steaua Bucuresti	Bucuresti	Ghencea	27 063	steaua.ro	23	21	1

RECENT LEAGUE AND CUP RECORD

	Championship						Cup		
Year	Champions	Pts	Runners-up	Pts	Third	Pts	Winners	Score	Runners-up
1990	Dinamo Bucuresti	57	Steaua Bucuresti	56	Universit. Craiova	44	Dinamo Bucuresti	6-4	Steaua Bucuresti
1991	Universit. Craiova	50	Steaua Bucuresti	50	Dinamo Bucuresti	43	Universit. Craiova	2-1	FC Bacau
1992	Dinamo Bucuresti	55	Steaua Bucuresti	48	Electroput. Craiova	39	Steaua Bucuresti	1-1 4-3p	Politehn. Timisoara
1993	Steaua Bucuresti	48	Dinamo Bucuresti	47	Universit. Craiova	37	Universit. Craiova	2-0	Dacia Unirea Braila
1994	Steaua Bucuresti	53	Universit. Craiova	40	Dinamo Bucuresti	39	Gloria Bistrita	1-0	Universit. Craiova
1995	Steaua Bucuresti	77	Universit. Craiova	68	Dinamo Bucuresti	65	Petrolul Ploiesti	1-1 5-3p	Rapid Bucuresti
1996	Steaua Bucuresti	71	National Bucuresti	60	Rapid Bucuresti	59	Steaua Bucuresti	3-1	Gloria Bistrita
1997	Steaua Bucuresti	73	National Bucuresti	68	Dinamo Bucuresti	59	Steaua Bucuresti	4-2	National Bucuresti
1998	Steaua Bucuresti	80	Rapid Bucuresti	78	Arges Pitesti	65	Rapid Bucuresti	1-0	Universit. Craiova
1999	Rapid Bucuresti	89	Dinamo Bucuresti	82	Steaua Bucuresti	66	Steaua Bucuresti	2-2 4-2p	Rapid Bucuresti
2000	Dinamo Bucuresti	84	Rapid Bucuresti	72	Ceahlaul P. Neamt	57	Dinamo Bucuresti	2-0	Universit. Craiova
2001	Steaua Bucuresti	60	Dinamo Bucuresti	51	FC Brasov	50	Dinamo Bucuresti	4-2	Rocar Bucuresti
2002	Dinamo Bucuresti	60	National Bucuresti	58	Rapid Bucuresti	50	Rapid Bucuresti	2-1	Dinamo Bucuresti
2003	Rapid Bucuresti	63	Steaua Bucuresti	56	Gloria Bistrita	45	Dinamo Bucuresti	1-0	National Bucuresti
2004	Dinamo Bucuresti	70	Steaua Bucuresti	64	Rapid Bucuresti	55	Dinamo Bucuresti	2-0	Otelul Galati
2005	Steaua Bucuresti	63	Dinamo Bucuresti	62	Rapid Bucuresti	57	Dinamo Bucuresti	1-0	Farul Constanta
2006	Steaua Bucuresti	64	Rapid Bucuresti	59	Dinamo Bucuresti	56	Rapid Bucuresti	1-0	National Bucuresti

ROMANIA 2005-06

DIVIZIA A

	Pl	W	D	L	F	A	Pts	Steaua	Rapid	Dinamo	Sportul	Ecomax	National	Farul	Politehnica	Otelul	Gloria	Poli	Arges	Jiul	Vaslui	Pandurii	Bacau
Steaua Bucuresti †	30	19	7	4	49	16	64		0-2	2-2	4-1	2-0	4-0	3-0	2-1	4-0	0-1	1-0	0-0	1-0	2-2	1-0	1-0
Rapid Bucuresti ‡	30	17	8	5	47	23	59	0-0		3-0	3-0	1-0	1-0	0-0	0-0	4-0	1-0	1-0	1-1	3-0	1-1	3-0	2-1
Dinamo Bucuresti ‡	30	17	5	8	56	32	56	1-1	5-2		4-5	5-0	2-1	0-1	1-0	0-3	3-1	1-1	1-2	1-1	1-2	3-0	6-0
Sportul Studentesc	30	17	5	8	54	35	56	1-2	1-0	0-2		1-1	0-1	3-1	3-1	2-1	2-1	1-0	4-0	3-0	4-0	2-1	
Ecomax Cluj	30	14	8	8	36	27	50	1-0	1-3	1-0	0-0		0-0	3-0	2-0	0-1	0-0	0-0	2-2	0-0	1-0	1-2	4-0
National Bucuresti	30	13	7	10	32	37	46	0-0	1-0	2-0	2-1	0-4		1-0	1-0	3-2	2-0	1-1	0-1	1-1	0-1	3-2	1-0
Farul Constanta	30	14	3	13	39	38	45	1-4	1-2	0-1	2-2	1-2	4-0		4-2	0-1	3-0	1-0	2-0	1-0	2-1	1-0	2-0
Politehnica Timisoara	30	10	10	10	34	31	40	0-0	1-3	0-0	0-0	2-2	2-1	3-2		0-2	4-0	3-0	0-0	1-0	2-0	1-0	2-0
Otelul Galati	30	10	9	11	35	37	39	0-3	3-3	1-4	2-3	0-1	2-0	0-1	0-2		1-0	0-0	0-0	1-1	1-1	1-1	0-0
Gloria Bistrita	30	11	6	13	27	34	39	1-0	2-1	1-2	2-0	1-2	0-2	1-0	1-1	0-0		1-0	1-0	0-0	1-1	4-0	2-1
Politehnica Unirea Iasi	30	11	6	13	28	31	39	0-1	1-4	0-2	1-0	1-0	2-3	3-1	0-1	0-1	1-1		3-2	2-0	1-0	1-0	4-0
Arges Pitesti	30	8	8	14	27	37	32	0-1	1-1	0-1	2-2	0-1	2-3	1-2	1-1	0-5	2-0	3-0		2-1	1-0	0-1	0-0
Jiul Petrosani	30	7	9	14	28	39	30	1-2	3-0	1-3	1-3	5-1	2-0	3-1	1-1	0-3	0-2	0-2	0-1		0-0	1-1	2-0
SC Vaslui	30	6	11	13	23	37	29	0-4	0-1	1-2	0-3	0-3	0-0	0-2	1-1	0-0	2-0	1-1	3-0	1-2		2-1	1-1
Pandurii Targu Jiu	30	6	7	17	22	44	25	1-2	0-0	0-2	0-1	0-1	1-1	1-2	3-2	2-2	2-1	0-1	1-0	1-0	0-0		2-1
FCM Bacau	30	3	5	22	16	55	14	0-2	0-1	0-1	1-2	0-2	2-2	1-1	1-0	0-4	1-2	0-1	3-2	1-2	0-2	1-0	

5/08/2005 - 7/06/2006 • † Qualified for the UEFA Champions League • ‡ Qualified for the UEFA Cup • Promotion play-offs: Forex 2-0 Bihor; Urziceni 4-2 Bihor; Bihor 0-1 Urziceni • Unirea Valahorum promoted

ROMANIA 2005-06 DIVIZIA B SERIA 1

	Pl	W	D	L	F	A	Pts
Ceahlaul Piatra Neamt	30	20	6	4	59	20	66
Forex Brasov	30	18	5	7	55	31	59
FC Brasov	30	17	8	5	57	22	58
FC Botosani	30	15	4	11	32	29	49
Cetatea Suceava	30	14	4	12	43	34	46
Dacia Unirea Braila	30	12	9	9	31	28	45
Precizia Sacele	30	12	9	9	26	24	45
Dunarea Galati	30	12	7	11	29	26	43
Gloria Buzau	30	12	7	11	37	29	43
Altay Constanta	30	12	6	12	33	37	42
Callatis Mangalia	30	11	6	13	34	39	39
FCM Targoviste	30	10	8	12	29	30	38
Petrolul Moinesti	30	8	8	14	33	44	32
Laminorul Roman	30	7	7	16	30	47	28
Portul Constanta	30	7	6	17	35	60	27
Midia Navodari	30	1	4	25	6	69	7

20/08/2005 - 3/06/2006

See page 1052 for Divizia B Seria 3 table

ROMANIA 2005-06 DIVIZIA B SERIA 2

	Pl	W	D	L	F	A	Pts
Universitatea Craiova	30	20	4	6	41	14	64
Unirea Val. Urziceni	30	18	5	7	55	24	59
Petrolul Ploesti	30	17	5	8	47	29	56
CS Otopeni	30	15	9	6	37	18	54
Dunarea Giurgiu	30	16	3	11	35	33	51
Ramnicu Valcea	30	11	12	7	37	27	45
Poiana Campina	30	12	9	9	34	28	45
Dacia Mioveni	30	12	8	10	36	30	44
FC Caracal	30	13	4	13	35	38	43
Astra Ploiesti	30	12	4	14	45	48	40
Minerul Motru	30	9	10	11	32	34	37
Inter-Gaz Bucuresti	30	9	9	12	30	40	36
Electromag. Bucuresti	30	10	2	18	27	56	32
Juventus Colentina	30	7	4	19	29	49	25
Dinamo II Bucuresti	30	4	8	18	25	43	20
FC Sibiu	30	3	8	19	12	46	17

20/08/2005 - 3/06/2006

CUPA ROMANIEI 2005-06

Round of 16		Quarter-finals		Semi-finals		Final	
Rapid Bucuresti	3						
Cetatea Suceava	2	Rapid Bucuresti	1				
SC Vaslui	1	Politehnica Un. Iasi	0				
Politehnica Un. Iasi	2			Rapid Bucuresti	4 3		
Politehnica Timisoara	3			Petrolul Ploesti	1 3		
FCM Targoviste	1	Politehnica Timisoara	2				
Dinamo Bucuresti	1	Petrolul Ploesti	3				
Petrolul Ploesti	2					Rapid Bucuresti ‡	1
Farul Constanta	4					National Bucuresti	0
Rapid-2 Bucuresti	3	Farul Constanta	1				
FCM Bacau	0	Jiul Petrosani	0				
Jiul Petrosani	2			Farul Constanta	1 1		
Otelul Galati	2			National Bucuresti	0 4		
Pandurii Targu Jiu	0	Otelul Galati	0 3p				
Universitatea Craiova	0 3p	National Bucuresti	0 4p				
National Bucuresti	0 4p						

CUP FINAL

National, Bucharest
17-05-2006, Att: 12 000, Ref: Corpodean

Scorer: Daniel Niculae[91] for Rapid

* Home team in the first leg • ‡ Qualified for the UEFA Cup

RSA – SOUTH AFRICA

NATIONAL TEAM RECORD
JULY 1ST 2002 TO JULY 9TH 2006

PL	W	D	L	F	A	%
56	23	15	18	70	66	54.5

FIFA/COCA-COLA WORLD RANKING

1993	1994	1995	1996	1997	1998	1999	2000	2001	2002	2003	2004	2005	High		Low	
95	56	40	19	31	26	30	20	35	30	36	38	49	**16**	08/96	**109**	08/93

2005–2006											
08/05	09/05	10/05	11/05	12/05	01/06	02/06	03/06	04/06	05/06	06/06	07/06
38	42	46	48	49	49	50	52	51	53	-	72

As future hosts of the FIFA World Cup™ finals, South Africa has been awash in a growing football fever that has, at times, threatened to swamp the country like a tidal wave. Yet this enthusiasm has contrasted starkly with performances on the pitch. South Africa's national side 'Bafana Bafana' have gone through their worst slump over the last 12 months with three wins in 18 games and a disastrous showing in both the 2006 FIFA World Cup™ qualifiers and the African Nations Cup finals. In June 2005, South Africa were top of their qualifying group and needed four points from their last three matches to book a third successive trip to the finals. Yet out of a total

INTERNATIONAL HONOURS
CAF African Cup of Nations 1996 **CAF Champions League** Orlando Pirates 1995

of nine points they managed just one and allowed Ghana to storm past them and grab the place in Germany. Coach Stuart Baxter was replaced by the veteran Romanian-born Ted Dumitru, who brazenly changed the squad and its style of play and then saw South Africa lose all three matches at the African Nations Cup finals. They became the first side in 20 years to depart the tournament with no points and no goals. Domestic success went to Mamelodi Sundowns who won the League ahead of Orlando Pirates while Kaiser Chiefs also beat Pirates into second place in the first Cup Final meeting between the two since 1988.

THE FIFA BIG COUNT OF 2000

	Male	Female		Male	Female
Registered players	40 000	4 000	Referees	700	0
Non registered players	400 000	8 000	Officials	10 000	0
Youth players	60 000	2 000	Total involved	524 700	
Total players	514 000		Number of clubs	300	
Professional players	250	0	Number of teams	2 000	

South African Football Association (SAFA)
First National Bank Stadium, PO Box 910, Johannesburg 2000, South Africa
Tel +27 11 4943522   Fax +27 11 4943013
raymond.hack@safa.net   www.safa.net
President: OLIPHANT Molefi   General Secretary: HACK Raymond
Vice-President: KHOZA Irvin   Treasurer: HULYO Gronie   Media Officer: MARAWA Gugu
Men's Coach: TBD   Women's Coach: MAKALAKALANE Augustine
SAFA formed: 1991   CAF: 1992   FIFA: 1992
White shirts with yellow stripes, White shorts, White socks

RECENT INTERNATIONAL MATCHES PLAYED BY SOUTH AFRICA

2003	Opponents	Score		Venue	Comp	Scorers	Att	Referee
22-06	Côte d'Ivoire	W	2-1	Johannesburg	CNq	Bartlett [21], Nomvete [65]	35 000	Maillet SEY
6-07	Burundi	W	2-0	Bujumbura	CNq	Mokoena [1], Fredricks [30]	8 000	Teshome ETH
19-07	Zimbabwe	L	0-1	East London	CC		7 000	Raolimanana MAD
8-10	Lesotho	W	3-0	Maseru	Fr	Moshoeu [23], Seema OG [66], Raselemane [72]	20 000	
11-10	Costa Rica	W	2-1	Johannesburg	Fr	Nomvete [75], Mayo [87]		Bwanya ZIM
15-11	Egypt	L	1-2	Cairo	Fr	McCarthy [50]	10 000	Mohammed LBY
19-11	Tunisia	L	0-2	Tunis	Fr		12 000	Chaibu NGA
2004								
10-01	Mauritius	L	0-2	Curepipe	CC		5 230	Raolimanana MAD
18-01	Senegal	L	1-2	Dakar	Fr	Nomvete [15]	50 000	El Achiri MAR
27-01	Benin	W	2-0	Sfax	CNr1	Nomvete 2 [58 76]	12 000	Coulibaly MLI
31-01	Nigeria	L	0-4	Monastir	CNr1		15 000	Bujsaim UAE
4-02	Morocco	D	1-1	Sousse	CNr1	Mayo [29]	6 000	Guirat TUN
30-03	Australia	L	0-1	London	Fr		16 108	Halsey ENG
5-06	Cape Verde Islands	W	2-1	Bloemfontein	WCq	Mabizela 2 [40 68]	30 000	Tessema ETH
20-06	Ghana	L	0-3	Kumasi	WCq		32 000	Diatta SEN
3-07	Burkina Faso	W	2-0	Johannesburg	WCq	Pienaar [14], Bartlett [42]	25 000	Ramanampamonjy MAD
18-08	Tunisia	W	2-0	Tunis	Fr	McCarthy [2], Arsendse [82]	4 000	Zekrini ALG
5-09	Congo DR	L	0-1	Kinshasa	WCq		85 000	Hicuburundi BDI
10-10	Uganda	W	1-0	Kampala	WCq	McCarthy [68p]	50 000	Gasingwa RWA
17-11	Nigeria	W	2-1	Johannesburg	Fr	Bartlett [2], Vilakazi [60]	39 817	Marang ZIM
2005								
9-02	Australia	D	1-1	Durban	Fr	McCarthy [12]		Lim Kee Chong MRI
26-02	Seychelles	W	3-0	Curepipe	CCr1	Mphela 2 [12 16], Chabangu [44]	3 000	Roheemun MRI
27-02	Mauritius	W	1-0	Curepipe	CCr1	Mphela [36]	3 500	Mnkantjo ZIM
26-03	Uganda	W	2-1	Johannesburg	WCq	Fortune [21p], Pienaar [71]	20 000	Chukwujekwu NGA
4-06	Cape Verde Islands	W	2-1	Praia	WCq	McCarthy [10], Buckley [12]	6 000	Benouza ALG
18-06	Ghana	L	0-2	Johannesburg	WCq		50 000	Guezzaz MAR
8-07	Mexico	W	2-1	Carson	GCr1	Evans [28], Van Heerden [41]	27 000	Sibrian SLV
10-07	Jamaica	D	3-3	Los Angeles	GCr1	Raselemane [35], Ndela [41], Nomvete [56]	30 710	Stott USA
13-07	Guatemala	D	1-1	Houston	GCr1	Nkosi [45]	45 311	Sott USA
17-07	Panama	D	1-1	Houston	GCqf	Ndela [68]	60 050	Prendergast JAM
13-08	Zambia	D	2-2	Mmabatho	CCsf	Ndela [63], Raselemane [68]. L 8-9p		Raolimanana MAD
17-08	Iceland	L	1-4	Rejklavik	Fr	Buckley [28]		
3-09	Burkina Faso	L	1-3	Ouagadougou	WCq	Zuma [75]	25 000	Codjia BEN
7-09	Germany	L	2-4	Bremen	Fr	Bartlett [28p], McCarthy [51]	28 100	Gilewski POL
8-10	Congo DR	D	2-2	Durban	WCq	Zuma 2 [5 52]	35 000	Mbera GAB
12-11	Senegal	L	2-3	Port Elizabeth	Fr	Zuma [9], Nomvete [68]		Ndoye SEN
2006								
14-01	Egypt	W	2-1	Cairo	Fr	OG [13], McCarthy [44]		
22-01	Guinea	L	0-2	Alexandria	CNr1		10 000	Benouza ALG
26-01	Tunisia	L	0-2	Alexandria	CNr1		10 000	Evehe CMR
30-01	Zambia	L	0-1	Alexandria	CNr1		4 000	Abd El Fatah EGY
10-05	Lesotho	D	0-0	Maseru	Fr		15 000	
20-05	Swaziland	W	1-0	Gaborone	CCr1	Mhlongo [13]		Malepa BOT
21-05	Botswana	D	0-0	Gaborone	CCr1	L 5-6p		Infante MOZ

Fr = Friendly match • CN = CAF African Cup of Nations • CC = COSAFA Cup • GC = CONCACAF Gold Cup • WC = FIFA World Cup™
q = qualifier • r1 = first round group • qf = quarter-final • sf = semi-final • f = final

SOUTH AFRICA NATIONAL TEAM RECORDS AND RECORD SEQUENCES

Records			Sequence records					
Victory	8-0	AUS 1955	Wins	7	1947-50, 1954-92	Clean sheets	7	1997-1997, 2002
Defeat	1-5	AUS 1947	Defeats	3	Five times	Goals scored	12	1947-1950
Player Caps	74	BARTLETT Shaun	Undefeated	15	1994-1996	Without goal	4	2006
Player Goals	29	BARTLETT Shaun	Without win	9	1997-1998, 2005	Goals against	17	2005-2006

SOUTH AFRICA COUNTRY INFORMATION

Capital	Pretoria	Independence	1934	GDP per Capita	$10 700
Population	42 718 530	Status	Republic	GNP Ranking	30
Area km²	1 219 912	Language	Afrikaans, English, Zulu	Dialling code	+27
Population density	35 per km²	Literacy rate	86%	Internet code	.za
% in urban areas	51%	Main religion	Christian	GMT +/−	+2
Towns/Cities ('000)	Johannesburg 5 226; Cape Town 4 302; Durban 3 120; Pretoria 1 884; Port Elizabeth 1 224; Pietermarizburg 750; Vereeniging 730; Bloemfontein 463; Welkom 432; East London 421				
Neighbours (km)	Mozambique 491; Swaziland 430; Lesotho 909; Botswana 1 840; Namibia 967; Zimbabwe 225; South Atlantic & Indian Ocean 2 798				
Main stadia	FNB – Johannesburg 90 000; ABSA – Durban 55 000; Newlands – Cape Town 50 900				

NATIONAL TEAM PLAYERS AND COACHES

Record Caps			Record Goals			Recent Coaches	
BARTLETT Shaun	1995-'05	74	BARTLETT Shaun	1995-'05	29	TROUSSIER Philippe	1998
MOSHOEU John	1993-'04	73	MCCARTHY Benedict	1997-'05	27	MOLOTO Trott	1998-'00
RADEBE Lucas	1992-'03	70	MASINGA Phil	1992-'01	18	QUEIROZ Carlos	2000-'02
ARENDSE Andre	1994-'04	67	NOMVETE Siyabonga	1999-'05	13	SONO Jomo	2002
MKHALELE Helman	1994-'01	66	KHUMALO Theophilus	1992-'01	9	MASHABA Ephraim	2002-'03
FISH Mark	1993-'04	62	BUCKLEY Delron	1998-'05	9	KUBHEKA Kenneth	2003
MCCARTHY Benedict	1997-'05	62	MKHALELE Helman	1994-'01	8	MASHABA Ephraim	2003
BUCKLEY Delron	1998-'05	60	MOSHOEU John	1993-'04	8	PHUMO April	2004
MASINGA Phil	1992-'01	58	WILLIAMS Mark	1992-'97	8	BAXTER Stuart	2004-'05
NOMVETE Siyabonga	1999-'05	57				DUMITRU Ted	2005-'06

CLUB DIRECTORY

Club	Town/City	Stadium	Capacity	www.	Lge	Cup	CL
Ajax	Capetown	Newlands	50 900	ajaxct.com	0	0	0
Black Leopards	Johannesburg	Thohoyandou		blackleopardsfc.com	0	0	0
Bloemfontein Celtic	Bloemfontein	Seisa Ramabodu	20 000	bloemfonteincelticfc.co.za	0	1	0
Bush Bucks	East London	Absa		bushbucks.co.za	1	0	0
Dynamos	Pietersburg	Giyani	35 000		0	0	0
Golden Arrows	Durban	King Zwelithini	25 000		0	0	0
Jomo Cosmos	Johannesburg	Makhulong		jomocosmos.co.za	1	1	0
Kaizer Chiefs	Johannesburg	FNB	90 000	kaizerchiefs.co.za	5	4	0
Manning Rangers	Durban	Chatsworth	35 000		2	0	0
Moroka Swallows	Johannesburg	Rand	30 000	morokaswallows.co.za	0	3	0
Orlando Pirates	Johannesburg	JHB		orlandopiratesfc.com	3	2	1
Santos	Cape Town	Athlone	25 000		1	2	0
Silver Stars	Johannesburg	Peter Mokaba			0	0	0
SuperSport United	Pretoria	Securicor Loftus	52 000	sufc.co.za	0	2	0
Sundowns	Pretoria	Securicor Loftus	52 000	sundownsfc.com	6	2	0
Wits University	Johannesburg	BidVest		witsfc.co.za	0	0	0

RECENT LEAGUE AND CUP RECORD

	Championship						Cup		
Year	Champions	Pts	Runners-up	Pts	Third	Pts	Winners	Score	Runners-up
1990	Mamelodi Sundowns	55	Kaizer Chiefs	55	Orlando Pirates	48	Jomo Cosmos	1-0	Amazulu
1991	Kaizer Chiefs	57	Mamelodi Sundowns	53	Fairway Stars	46	Moroka Swallows	3-1 2-0	Jomo Cosmos
1992	Kaizer Chiefs	60	Hellenic	57	Wits University	51	Kaizer Chiefs	1-1 1-0	Jomo Cosmos
1993	Mamelodi Sundowns	55	Moroka Swallows	52	Amazulu	48	Witbank Aces	1-0	Kaizer Chiefs
1994	Orlando Pirates	50	Cape Town Spurs	49	Umtata Bucks	41	Vaal Professionals	1-0	Qwa Qwa Stars
1995	Cape Town Spurs	71	Mamelodi Sundowns	66	Orlando Pirates	60	Cape Town Spurs	3-2	Pretoria City
1996	Not played due to season adjustment						Orlando Pirates	1-0	Jomo Cosmos
1997	Manning Rangers	74	Kaizer Chiefs	66	Orlando Pirates	64	No tournament played		
1998	Mamelodi Sundowns	68	Kaizer Chiefs	63	Orlando Pirates	57	Mamelodi Sundowns	1-1 1-1 6-5p	Orlando Pirates
1999	Mamelodi Sundowns	75	Kaizer Chiefs	75	Orlando Pirates	60	SuperSport United	2-1	Kaizer Chiefs
2000	Mamelodi Sundowns	75	Orlando Pirates	64	Kaizer Chiefs	60	Kaizer Chiefs	1-0	Mamelodi Sundowns
2001	Orlando Pirates	61	Kaizer Chiefs	60	Mamelodi Sundowns	59	Santos Cape Town	1-0	Mamelodi Sundowns
2002	Santos Cape Town	64	SuperSport United	59	Orlando Pirates	57	No tournament played		
2003	Orlando Pirates	61	SuperSport United	55	Wits University	54	Santos Cape Town	2-0	Ajax Cape Town
2004	Kaizer Chiefs	63	Ajax Cape Town	57	SuperSport United	53	Moroka Swallows	3-1	Manning Rangers
2005	Kaizer Chiefs	62	Orlando Pirates	60	Mamelodi Sundowns	56	SuperSport United	1-0	Wits University
2006	Mamelodi Sundowns	57	Orlando Pirates	54	Kaizer Chiefs	50	Kaizer Chiefs	0-0 5-3p	Orlando Pirates

SOUTH AFRICA 2005-06

PREMIER SOCCER LEAGUE

	Pl	W	D	L	F	A	Pts	Sundowns	Pirates	Chiefs	Swallows	Stars	Arrows	SuperSport	Santos	Cosmos	Celtic	Ajax	Leopards	Dynamos	Classic	Bush Bucks	Free State
Mamelodi Sundowns †	30	16	9	5	45	19	57		0-0	3-1	1-2	1-0	1-1	2-2	1-1	0-2	1-0	1-1	5-1	1-0	3-1	5-1	0-0
Orlando Pirates †	30	14	12	4	39	24	54	1-1		0-1	1-0	1-1	1-0	1-1	2-0	1-0	3-0	2-1	1-0	2-0	0-0	3-1	1-1
Kaizer Chiefs	30	12	14	4	39	26	50	1-0	2-0		1-1	2-4	2-1	0-1	0-0	0-0	2-0	0-0	0-0	2-1	0-0	0-0	5-2
Moroka Swallows	30	12	10	8	39	33	46	1-2	3-1	1-1		2-2	0-0	3-0	2-3	2-1	1-0	1-5	2-1	1-0	1-1	1-1	1-0
Silver Stars	30	11	9	10	34	32	42	0-1	2-2	1-2	1-0		3-1	0-4	0-1	1-1	2-1	0-2	1-0	1-1	0-1	0-1	1-1
Golden Arrows	30	9	13	8	32	28	40	0-2	2-1	1-3	2-1	1-0		2-3	2-2	1-0	0-0	2-0	0-0	3-0	2-0	3-0	1-1
SuperSport United	30	10	10	10	43	41	40	0-1	1-3	1-1	1-0	1-1	1-0		2-2	0-3	1-1	2-1	0-2	2-1	1-1	6-0	2-0
Cape Town Santos	30	7	17	6	35	32	38	0-0	3-3	1-3	1-0	1-1	1-1	2-2		2-0	1-2	0-1	0-0	3-1	2-0	1-1	2-0
Jomo Cosmos	30	10	8	12	31	32	38	0-1	0-0	1-1	0-2	2-1	1-1	1-0	1-1		2-1	4-2	2-3	1-2	1-0	1-2	2-1
Bloemfontein Celtic	30	9	10	11	35	37	37	2-1	0-2	1-1	0-1	1-1	0-0	1-1	3-3	1-0		2-0	1-2	1-1	4-1	4-1	2-2
Ajax Cape Town	30	8	11	11	40	42	35	0-2	0-0	2-2	2-1	1-1	1-1	4-1	0-0	2-1	1-1		1-0	0-1	3-1	1-2	1-1
Black Leopards	30	9	7	14	31	39	34	1-0	0-1	2-2	1-1	0-2	1-0	0-2	1-0	2-0	3-1	3-3		0-1	2-1	1-1	2-3
Dynamos	30	7	10	13	24	38	31	0-4	1-1	0-2	2-1	0-1	0-0	2-0	0-0	0-0	0-2	2-1	3-2		1-1	2-3	0-0
Tembisa Classic	30	7	9	14	23	37	30	0-3	1-2	1-0	0-0	0-1	1-2	0-2	2-1	1-2	0-1	2-0	2-0	1-0		2-1	1-1
Umtata Bush Bucks	30	6	12	12	25	48	30	0-2	1-1	0-1	1-1	1-4	0-0	1-3	0-0	0-0	0-1	2-2	1-0	0-1	1-1		0-0
Free State Stars	30	4	17	9	34	41	29	0-0	1-2	1-1	2-4	0-1	2-2	2-2	0-0	1-2	3-1	3-1	2-1	1-1	0-0	1-2	

3/08/2005 - 13/05/2006 • † Qualified for the CAF Champions League • Play-offs: Bucks 0-2 1-2 Vasco; Benoni 3-1 1-0 Pillars; Benoni 0-0 1-0 Vasco (Bucks relegated, Benoni promoted) • Top scorers: Mame NIANG, Swallows, 14; Alton MEIRING, Arrows, 13

SOUTH AFRICA 2005-06
MVELA GOLDEN LEAGUE (2)

	Pl	W	D	L	F	A	Pts
Wits University	30	23	2	5	55	26	71
City Pillars	30	17	8	5	57	36	59
Vasco da Gama	30	16	8	6	59	38	56
Benoni Premier United	30	14	10	6	41	30	52
PJ Stars Kings	30	13	8	9	49	40	47
Mabopane Y. Masters	30	11	8	11	43	48	41
Nathi Lions	30	11	6	13	39	39	39
Zulu Royals	30	9	11	10	32	31	38
Winners Park	30	9	10	11	37	37	37
Durban Stars	30	10	5	15	39	48	35
Pretoria University	30	7	14	9	38	48	35
Manning Rangers	30	7	10	13	33	44	31
Witbank Spurs	30	8	5	17	40	51	29
Maritzburg United	30	6	11	13	23	38	29
FC Fortune	30	5	13	12	34	51	28
Bloemfontein Tigers	30	5	9	16	29	43	24

12/08/2005 - 7/05/2006

ABSA CUP 2005-06

Second Round		Quarter-finals		Semi-finals		Final	
Kaizer Chiefs	5						
City Pillars	4	Kaizer Chiefs	1				
Witbank Spurs	0	Black Leopards	0				
Black Leopards	2			Kaizer Chiefs	0 2p		
Bloemfontein Tigers	3			Mamelodi Sundowns	0 1p		
Blackburn Rovers	0	Bloemfontein Tigers	0				
Mabopane Y. Masters	0	Mamelodi Sundowns	4				
Mamelodi Sundowns	1					Kaizer Chiefs	0 5p
Tembisa Classic	1 4p					Orlando Pirates	0 3p
Ajax Cape Town	1 3p	Tembisa Classic	2				
Moroka Swallows	1	Cape Town Santos	1				
Cape Town Santos	2			Tembisa Classic	1	CUP FINAL	
Hanover Park	2			Orlando Pirates	2		
Nathi Lions	1	Hanover Park				ABSA Stadium, Durban	
PJ Stars	0	Orlando Pirates				20-05-2006	
Orlando Pirates	2						

MAMELODI SUNDOWNS 2005-06

Date	Opponents	Score		Comp	Scorers
30-07-2005	Black Leopards	W 1-0	N	TCsf	Ntwagae [77]
30-07-2005	Bloemfontein Celtic	D 1-1		TCf	Moriri [61], W 7-6p
3-08-2005	Silver Stars	W 1-0	A	PSL	Moriri [87]
10-08-2005	Ajax Cape Town	W 2-0	A	PSL	Torrealba [16], Moriri [45]
14-08-2005	Ajax Cape Town	W 2-0	H	SEqf	Mendu [34], Sandile Ndlovu [50]
23-08-2005	Golden Arrows	D 1-1	H	PSL	Sandile Ndlovu [79]
28-08-2005	SuperSport United	L 0-1	H	SEsf	
10-09-2005	Jomo Cosmos	W 1-0	A	PSL	Sandile Ndlovu [45]
14-09-2005	Black Leopards	L 0-1	A	PSL	
21-09-2005	Bloemfontein Celtic	W 1-0	H	PSL	Moriri [65]
24-09-2005	Cape Town Santos	D 0-0	A	PSL	
28-09-2005	Dynamos	W 1-0	H	PSL	Sandile Ndlovu [62]
1-10-2005	Golden Arrows	W 4-0	H	LCr1	Chabangu 2 [52 64], Peter Ndlovu [85], Sapula [88]
12-10-2005	Moroka Swallows	L 1-2	H	PSL	Moriri [73p]
16-10-2005	Tembisa Classic	W 3-0	A	PSL	Moriri [40], Nyandoro [42], Dladla [65]
25-10-2005	Umtata Bush Bucks	W 5-1	H	PSL	Dladla [42], Torrealba [44], Mazibuko [80], Moriri [85], Ngwenya [88]
30-10-2005	Free State Stars	D 0-0	A	PSL	
2-11-2005	Ajax Cape Town	D 1-1	A	LCqf	Torrealba [56], L 4-5p
16-11-2005	SuperSport United	D 2-2	H	PSL	Moriri [13], Moriri [34]
26-11-2005	Orlando Pirates	D 1-1	A	PSL	Sapula [43]
4-12-2005	Golden Arrows	W 2-0	A	PSL	Torrealba [15], Masehe [33]
7-12-2005	Ajax Cape Town	D 1-1	H	PSL	Sandile Ndlovu [93+]
11-12-2005	Free State Stars	D 0-0	H	PSL	
17-12-2005	Black Leopards	W 5-1	H	PSL	Moriri 2 [19 78], Ndlovu [31], Torrealba [83], Ngwenya [85]
21-12-2005	Dynamos	W 4-0	A	PSL	Torrealba [5], Peter Ndlovu [31p], Moriri [63p], Sandile Ndlovu [70]
15-02-2006	Kaizer Chiefs	L 0-1	A	PSL	
19-02-2006	Likhopo - LES	W 1-0	A	CLpr	Sandile Ndlovu
22-02-2006	Kaizer Chiefs	W 3-1	H	PSL	Dladla 2 [35 46], Moriri [83]
26-02-2006	Bloemfontein Celtic	L 1-2	A	PSL	Sandile Ndlovu [6]
2-03-2006	Cape Town Santos	D 1-1	H	PSL	Dladla [37]
5-03-2006	Likhopo - LES	W 3-0	H	CLpr	Ngwenya 2 [40 57], Torrealba [52]
11-03-2006	Golden Arrows	W 1-0	A	CUPr1	Ngwenya [89]
15-03-2006	Moroka Swallows	W 2-1	A	PSL	Ngwenya [30], Saula [76]
19-03-2006	USCAFOOT - MAD	D 1-1	A	CLr1	Ngwenya [48]
26-03-2006	Mabopane Young Masters	W 1-0	H	CUPr2	Ngwenya [30]
29-03-2006	Umtata Bush Bucks	W 2-0	A	PSL	Ngwenya 2 [23 71]
2-04-2006	USCAFOOT - MAD	D 2-2	H	CLr1	Moriri [35], Sandile Ndlovu [89]
5-04-2006	Jomo Cosmos	L 0-2	H	PSL	
8-04-2006	Silver Stars	W 1-0	A	PSL	Kannemeyer [86]
16-04-2006	Bloemfontein Young Tigers	W 4-0	A	CUPqf	Torrealba 2 [2 46], Chabangu [63], Sheppard [69]
19-04-2006	SuperSport United	W 1-0	A	PSL	Nyandoro [87]
26-04-2006	Temisa Classic	W 3-1	H	PSL	Sandile Ndlovu [61], Nyandoro [65], Torrealba [77]
29-04-2006	Kaizer Chiefs	D 0-0	H	CUPsf	L 1-2p
13-05-2006	Orlando Pirates	D 0-0	H	PSL	

TC = Telekom Charity Cup • PSL = Premier Soccer League • SE = SAA Supa8 Cup • LC = Coca-Cola League Cup • CL = CAF Champions League •
CUP = ABSA Cup • pr = preliminary round • r1 = first round • r2 = second round • qf = quarter-final • sf = semi-final • f = final
N = FNB Stadium • H = Loftus Stadium • H = HM Pitje Stadium • H = Super Stadium • H - Odi Stadium

SAA SUPA 8 CUP 2005

First Round		Semi-finals		Final	
B'fontein Celtic	2				
Kaizer Chiefs	1	B'fontein Celtic	1 5p		
Silver Stars	0	Orlando Pirates	1 3p		
Orlando Pirates	3			B'fontein Celtic	1
Sundowns	2			SuperSport Utd	0
Ajax Cape Town	0	Sundowns	0	Olen Park, Potchefstroom
Moroka Swallows		SuperSport Utd	1	17-09-2005
SuperSport Utd				Scorer - Rotson Kilambe [64] for Celtic

KAIZER CHIEFS 2005–06

Date	Opponents		Score		Comp	Scorers
30-07-2005	Bloemfontein Celtic	L	1-2	N	TCsf	Chalwe [14]
6-08-2005	Umtata Bush Bucks	W	1-0	A	PSL	Chalwe [73]
9-08-2005	Free State Stars	D	1-1	A	PSL	Moshoeu [67]
20-08-2005	Bloemfontein Celtic	L	1-2	H	SEqf	Agyemang [1]
25-08-2005	Ajax Cape Town	D	0-0	H	PSL	
11-09-2005	Dynamos	W	2-0	A	PSL	Zwane 2 [39 90]
14-09-2005	Golden Arrows	W	3-1	A	PSL	Djiehou [25], McCarthy [29], Moshoeu [84]
21-09-2005	Jomo Cosmos	D	1-1	A	PSL	Djiehou [1]
25-09-2005	Bloemfontein Celtic	D	1-1	A	PSL	Argeymang [84]
28-09-2005	Black Leopards	D	0-0	H	PSL	
12-10-2005	Cape Town Santos	D	0-0	H	PSL	
16-10-2005	Moroka Swallows	D	1-1	A	PSL	Schalkwyk [26]
22-10-2005	Tembisa Classic	W	2-1	H	LCr1	Moshoeu [37], McCarthy [55]
26-10-2005	Tembisa Classic	D	0-0	H	PSL	
29-10-2005	Orlando Pirates	W	2-0	H	PSL	Obua [3], Schalkwyk [85]
5-11-2005	Jomo Cosmos	L	0-2	H	LCqf	
16-11-2005	Silver Stars	L	2-4	H	PSL	Agyemang [7], Chalwe [57]
27-11-2005	SuperSport United	D	1-1	A	PSL	Agyemang [63]
4-12-2005	Ajax Cape Town	D	2-2	A	PSL	Nzama [38], Mototo [76]
7-12-2005	Free State Stars	W	5-2	H	PSL	Radebe 2 [17 20], Agyemang [26], Kaizer Motaung Jnr [15], Zwane [79]
10-12-2005	Orlando Pirates	W	1-0	A	PSL	Obua [25]
17-12-2005	Golden Arrows	W	2-1	H	PSL	Chalwe [36], Kaizer Motaung Jnr [75]
22-12-2005	Black Leopards	D	2-2	A	PSL	Mathebula [27], Radebe [64]
15-02-2006	Mamelodi Sundowns	W	1-0	H	PSL	Obua [24p]
18-02-2006	Dynamos	W	2-1	H	PSL	McCarthy [12], Mototo [68]
22-02-2006	Mamelodi Sundowns	L	1-3	A	PSL	Obua [31]
25-02-2006	Jomo Cosmos	D	0-0	H	PSL	
4-03-2006	Bloemfontein Celtic	W	2-0	H	PSL	Obua [62], Schalkwyk [73]
11-03-2006	SuperSport United	W	3-1	H	CUPr1	Agyemang 2 [57 76], Mathebula [65]
15-03-2006	Cape Town Santos	W	3-1	A	PSL	Schalkwyk 2 [25 82], Mayo [45]
18-03-2006	Moroka Swallows	D	1-1	H	PSL	Schalkwyk [55]
25-03-2006	City Pillars	W	5-4	H	CUPr2	Kaizer Motaung Jnr [11], Moshoeu [18], Agyemang 2 [91+ 100], Nzama [120]
2-04-2006	Tembisa Classic	L	0-1	A	PSL	
8-04-2006	Umtata Bush Bucks	D	0-0	H	PSL	
15-04-2006	Black Leopards	W	1-0	H	CUPqf	Obua [48]
23-04-2006	Silver Stars	W	2-1	A	PSL	Mayo [16], Tau [47]
29-04-2006	Mamelodi Sundowns	D	0-0	A	CUPsf	W 2-1p
13-05-2006	SuperSport United	L	0-1	H	PSL	
20-05-2006	Orlando Pirates	D	0-0	N	CUPf	

TC = Telekom Charity Cup • PSL = Premier Soccer League • SE = SAA Supa 8 Cup • LC = Coca-Cola League Cup • CUP = ABSA Cup
r1 = first round • r2 = second round • qf = quarter-final • sf = semi-final • f = final
H = FNB Stadium • H = Olympia Stadium • N = FNB Stadium • N = ABSA Stadium, Durban

COCA-COLA LEAGUE CUP 2005

First Round		Quarter-finals		Semi-finals		Final
Jomo Cosmos	1 3p					
Silver Stars	1 1p	Jomo Cosmos	2			
Tembisa Classic	1	Kaizer Chiefs	0			
Kaizer Chiefs	2			Jomo Cosmos	1	
Bloemfontein Celtic	2			Orlando Pirates	0	
Dynamos	1	Bloemfontein Celtic	0 2p			
Black Leopards	2 3p	Orlando Pirates	0 4p			
Orando Pirates	2 4p					Jomo Cosmos	1 4p
Ajax Cape Town	1					SuperSport United	1 1p
Umtata Bush Bucks	0	Ajax Cape Town	1 5p			
Golden Arrows	0	Mamelodi Sundowns	1 4p			
Mamelodi Sundowns	4			Ajax Cape Town	0	CUP FINAL
Cape Town Santos	0 2p			SuperSport United	3	
Moroka Swallows	0 1p	Cape Town Santos	0			3-12-2005
Free State Stars	1	SuperSport United	1			Scorers – Teboho Mokoena [108] for Cosmos;
SuperSport United	2					Mandla Zwane [109] for SuperSport

RUS – RUSSIA

NATIONAL TEAM RECORD
JULY 1ST 2002 TO JULY 9TH 2006

PL	W	D	L	F	A	%
36	13	13	10	57	45	54.2

FIFA/COCA-COLA WORLD RANKING

1993	1994	1995	1996	1997	1998	1999	2000	2001	2002	2003	2004	2005		High		Low	
14	13	5	7	12	40	18	21	21	23	24	32	34		3	04/96	40	12/98

2005–2006										
08/05	09/05	10/05	11/05	12/05	01/06	02/06	03/06	04/06	05/06	06/06	07/06
29	30	30	34	34	34	34	35	37	37	-	34

After missing out on qualifying for the 2006 FIFA World Cup™ finals in Germany, the appointment of Guus Hiddink as national team coach signalled the intent of the Russian Football Union to make the country a major force in international football. Hiddink certainly has the credentials and the material to work with given Russia's increasing profile, especially at club level where the League gets more cosmopolitan by the year. Russia's best known football oligarch may be spending his money in west London but there seems to be plenty of cash around at home to tempt players and coaches from abroad. Joining Hiddink in Russia after the finals in Germany was Dick Advocaat,

INTERNATIONAL HONOURS
Qualified for the FIFA World Cup™ finals 1994 2002 UEFA European Championship 1960 UEFA U-17 Championship 2006 UEFA Women's U-19 2005

appointed coach of Zenit St Petersburg in an attempt by Russia's second city to break the stranglehold of the capital on the League and Cup. Of the 28 trophies at stake in both competitions since the break up of the Soviet Union, 25 have been won by clubs from Moscow and 2005 was no different. CSKA Moscow began an extraordinary run by winning the UEFA Cup in May 2005, the Russian Cup 11 days later, the League title in November and then a second consecutive Russian Cup in May 2006, to complete the most remarkable 12 months in the history of the club. It's something, however, that may not be repeated given Sibneft's decision to withdraw their sponsorship.

THE FIFA BIG COUNT OF 2000

	Male	Female		Male	Female
Registered players	603 920	2 290	Referees	44 000	36
Non registered players	2 955 000	8 000	Officials	17 000	1 000
Youth players	192 000	1 300	Total involved	3 824 546	
Total players	3 762 510		Number of clubs	17 816	
Professional players	3 920	190	Number of teams	155 980	

Football Union of Russia (RFU)
8 Luzhnetskaya Naberezhnaja, Moscow 119 992, Russia
Tel +7 495 6372056   Fax +7 501 4867997
rfs@roc.ru   www.rfs.ru
President: MUTKO Vitaliy   General Secretary: BREZGIN Boris
Vice-President: SIMONIAN Nikita   Treasurer: GROUZDEV Victor   Media Officer: CHERNOV Alexander
Men's Coach: HIDDINK Guus   Women's Coach: BYSTRITSKIY Yury
RFU formed: 1912   UEFA: 1992   FIFA: 1992
White shirts with blue trimmings, White shorts, White socks or Blue shirts with white trimmings, Blue shorts, Blue socks

RECENT INTERNATIONAL MATCHES PLAYED BY RUSSIA

2002	Opponents		Score	Venue	Comp	Scorers	Att	Referee
21-08	Sweden	D	1-1	Moscow	Fr	Kerzhakov [55]	23 000	Poulat FRA
7-09	Republic of Ireland	W	4-2	Moscow	ECq	Karyaka [20], Beschastnykh [24], Kerzhakov [71], OG [88]	23 000	Colombo FRA
16-10	Albania	W	4-1	Volgograd	ECq	Kerzhakov [3], Semak 2 [42 55], Onopko [52]	18 000	Sundell SWE
2003								
12-02	Cyprus	W	1-0	Limassol	Fr	Khokhlov [43]	300	Efthimiadis GRE
29-03	Albania	L	1-3	Shkoder	ECq	Karyaka [77]	16 000	Allaerts BEL
30-04	Georgia	L	0-1	Tbilisi	ECq		11 000	Wack GER
7-06	Switzerland	D	2-2	Basel	ECq	Ignashevich 2 [24 67p]	30 500	Dauden Ibanez ESP
20-08	Israel	L	1-2	Moscow	Fr	Semak [86]	5 000	Ishchenko UKR
6-09	Republic of Ireland	D	1-1	Dublin	ECq	Ignashevich [42]	36 000	Michel SVK
10-09	Switzerland	W	4-1	Moscow	ECq	Bulykin 3 [20 33 59], Mostovoi [72]	29 000	Collina ITA
11-10	Georgia	W	3-1	Moscow	ECq	Bulykin [29], Titov [45], Sychev [73]	30 000	Plautz AUT
15-11	Wales	D	0-0	Moscow	ECpo		29 000	Cortez Batista POR
19-11	Wales	L	0-1	Cardiff	ECpo		73 062	Mejuto Gonzalez ESP
2004								
31-03	Bulgaria	D	2-2	Sofia	Fr	Sychev 2 [9 31]	14 938	Alves Garcia POR
28-04	Norway	L	2-3	Oslo	Fr	Radimov [85], Kirichenko [90]	11 435	Wegereef NED
25-05	Austria	D	0-0	Graz	Fr		9 600	Vuorela FIN
12-06	Spain	L	0-1	Faro-Loule	ECr1		28 182	Meier SUI
16-06	Portugal	L	0-2	Lisbon	ECr1		59 273	Hauge NOR
20-06	Greece	W	2-1	Faro-Loule	ECr1	Kirichenko [2], Bulykin [17]	24 347	Veissiere FRA
18-08	Lithuania	W	4-3	Moscow	Fr	Khokhlov [22], Karyaka [53], Bulykin [66], Sychev [88]	3 500	Mikulski POL
4-09	Slovakia	D	1-1	Moscow	WCq	Bulykin [14]	11 500	Mejuto Gonzalez ESP
9-10	Luxembourg	W	4-0	Luxembourg	WCq	Sychev 3 [56 69 86], Arshavin [62]	3 670	Braamhaar NED
13-10	Portugal	L	1-7	Lisbon	WCq	Arshavin [79]	27 258	Vassaras GRE
17-11	Estonia	W	4-0	Krasnodar	WCq	Karyaka [23], Izmailov [25], Sychev [32], Loskov [67p]	29 000	Busacca SUI
2005								
9-02	Italy	L	0-2	Cagliari	Fr		15 700	Michel SVK
26-03	Liechtenstein	W	2-1	Vaduz	WCq	Kerzhakov [23], Karyaka [37]	2 400	Berntsen NOR
30-03	Estonia	D	1-1	Tallinn	WCq	Arshavin [18]	8 850	Paparesta ITA
4-06	Latvia	W	2-0	Sankt Peterburg	WCq	Arshavin [56], Loskov [78p]	21 575	Poulat FRA
8-06	Germany	D	2-2	Mönchengladbach	Fr	Anyukov [26], Arshavin [91+]	46 228	Plautz AUT
17-08	Latvia	D	1-1	Riga	WCq	Arshavin [24]	10 000	Poll ENG
3-09	Liechtenstein	W	2-0	Moscow	WCq	Kerzhakov 2 [27 66]	18 123	Hyytia FIN
7-09	Portugal	D	0-0	Moscow	WCq		28 800	Merk GER
8-10	Luxembourg	W	5-1	Moscow	WCq	Izmailov [6], Kerzhakov [17], Pavluchenko [69], Kirichenko 2 [74 93+]	20 000	Tudor ROU
12-10	Slovakia	D	0-0	Bratislava	WCq		22 317	Rosetti ITA
2006								
1-03	Brazil	L	0-1	Moscow	Fr		19 000	Busacca SUI
27-05	Spain	D	0-0	Albacete	Fr		20 000	Ferreira POR

Fr = Friendly match • EC = UEFA EURO 2004™ • WC = FIFA World Cup™ • q = qualifier • po = play-off • r1 = first round group

RUSSIA NATIONAL TEAM RECORDS AND RECORD SEQUENCES

Records			Sequence records				
Victory	7-0	SMR 1995	Wins	12	1995-1996	Clean sheets	4	1992-93, 2000
Defeat	0-16	GER 1912	Defeats	6	1998	Goals scored	23	1998-2001
Player Caps	109	ONOPKO Victor	Undefeated	17	1995-1996	Without goal	3	Three times
Player Goals	26	BESCHASTNYKH Vladimir	Without win	8	1912-1914, 1998	Goals against	8	Three times

RUSSIA COUNTRY INFORMATION

Capital	Moscow	Independence	1991 from Soviet Union	GDP per Capita	$8 900
Population	143 782 238	Status	Republic	GNP Ranking	19
Area km²	17 075 200	Language	Russian	Dialling code	+7
Population density	8 per km²	Literacy rate	99%	Internet code	.ru
% in urban areas	76%	Main religion	Christian	GMT + / –	+2-12

Towns/Cities ('000)	Moscow 10 381; Sankt Peterburg 4 039; Novosibirsk 1 419; Yekaterinburg 1 287; Nizhny Novgorod 1 284; Samara 1 134; Omsk 1 129; Kazan 1 104; Rostov-na-Donu 1 074; Chelyabinsk 1 062; Ufa 1 033; Volgograd 1 010; Perm 982; Krasnoyarsk 907; Saratov 863
Neighbours (km)	Korea DPR 19; China 3 645; Mongolia 3 485; Kazakhstan 6 846; Azerbaijan 284; Georgia 723; Ukraine 1 576; Belarus 959; Poland 206; Lithuania 227; Latvia 217; Estonia 294; Finland 1 340; Norway 196; Arctic Ocean & Pacific Ocean 37 653
Main stadia	Luzhniki – Moscow 84 745; Kirov – Sankt Peterburg; Metallurg – Samara 35 330; Tsentralnyi – Volgograd 32 120; Lokomotiv – Moscow 30 979; Kuban – Krasnodar 28 800

CLUB DIRECTORY

Club	Town/City	Stadium	Capacity	www.	Lge	Cup
Amkar Perm	Perm	Zvezda	20 000	amkar.ru	0 - 0	0 - 0
CSKA Moskva	Moskva	Eduard Streltsov	14 274	cska-football.ru	2 - 7	3 - 5
Dinamo Moskva	Moskva	Dinamo	36 540	fcdynamo.ru	0 - 11	1 - 6
Lokomotiv Moskva	Moskva	Lokomotiv	30 979	fclm.ru	2 - 0	4 - 2
Luch Vladivostock	Vladivostock	Dinamo	10 500	luch-vlad.ru	0 - 0	0 - 0
FC Moskva	Moskva	Eduard Streltsov	14 274	fcmoscow.ru	0 - 0	0 - 0
FC Rostov	Rostov-na-Donu	Olimp 21-Vek	15 600	fc-rostov.ru	0 - 0	0 - 0
Rubin Kazan	Kazan	Tsentralnyi	25 000	rubin-kazan.ru	0 - 0	0 - 0
Krylya Sovetov Samara	Samara	Metallurg	35 330	kc-kampara.ru	0 - 0	0 - 0
Saturn Moskovskaya Oblast	Ramenskoe	Saturn	16 726	Saturn-fc.ru	0 - 0	0 - 0
Shinnik Yaroslavl	Yaroslavl	Shinnik	22 984	shinnik.yar.ru	0 - 0	0 - 0
Spartak Moskva	Moskva	Luzhniki	84 745	rus.spartak.com	9 - 12	3 - 10
Spartak Nalchik	Nalchik	Spartak	18 000	spartak-nalchik.ru	0 - 0	0 - 0
Tom Tomsk	Tomsk	Trud	15 500	football.tomsk.ru	0 - 0	0 - 0
Torpedo Moskva	Moskva	Luzhniki	84 745	torpedo.ru	0 - 3	1 - 6
Zenit Sankt Peterburg	Sankt Peterburg	Petrovski	21 838	fc-zenit.ru	0 - 1	1 - 1

In the championships and cups column, the first of the two figures indicates titles won in Russia, the second titles won in the Soviet era

RECENT LEAGUE AND CUP RECORD

	Championship						Cup		
Year	Champions	Pts	Runners-up	Pts	Third	Pts	Winners	Score	Runners-up
1992	Spartak Moskva	24	Spartak Vladikavkaz	17	Dinamo Moskva	16			
1993	Spartak Moskva	53	Rotor Volgograd	42	Dinamo Moskva	42	Torpedo Moskva	1-1 5-3p	CSKA Moskva
1994	Spartak Moskva	39	Dinamo Moskva	39	Lokomotiv Moskva	36	Spartak Moskva	2-2 4-2p	CSKA Moskva
1995	Spartak Vladikavkaz	71	Lokomotiv Moskva	65	Spartak Moskva	63	Dinamo Moskva	0-0 8-7p	Rotor Volograd
1996	Spartak Moskva	72	Alania Vladikavkaz	72	Rotor Volgograd	70	Lokomotiv Moskva	3-2	Spartak Moskva
1997	Spartak Moskva	73	Rotor Volgograd	68	Dinamo Moskva	68	Lokomotiv Moskva	2-0	Dinamo Moskva
1998	Spartak Moskva	59	CSKA Moskva	56	Lokomotiv Moskva	55	Spartak Moskva	1-0	Lokomotiv Moskva
1999	Spartak Moskva	72	Lokomotiv Moskva	65	CSKA Moskva	55	Zenit St-Peterburg	3-1	Dynamo Moskva
2000	Spartak Moskva	70	Lokomotiv Moskva	62	Torpedo Moskva	55	Lokomotiv Moskva	3-2	CSKA Moskva
2001	Spartak Moskva	60	Lokomotiv Moskva	56	Zenit St-Peterburg	56	Lokomotiv Moskva	2-1	Anzhi Makhachkala
2002	Lokomotiv Moskva	66	CSKA Moskva	66	Spartak Moskva	55	CSKA Moskva	2-0	Zenit St-Peterburg
2003	CSKA Moskva	59	Zenit St-Peterburg	56	Rubin Kazan	53	Spartak Moskva	1-0	FK Rostov
2004	Lokomotiv Moskva	61	CSKA Moskva	60	Krylya S. Samara	56	Terek Groznyi	1-0	Krylya S. Samara
2005	CSKA Moskva	62	Spartak Moskva	56	Lokomotiv Moskva	56	CSKA Moskva	1-0	FK Khimki
2006							CSKA Moskva	3-0	Spartak Moskva

RUSSIA 2005

PREMIER LEAGUE

	Pl	W	D	L	F	A	Pts	CSKA	Spartak	Lokomotiv	Rubin	FK Moskva	Zenit	Torpedo	Dinamo	Shinnik	Tomsk	Saturn	Amkar	Rostov	Krylya	Alania	Terek
CSKA Moskva †	30	18	8	4	48	20	62		1-0	0-0	2-1	1-1	1-1	2-0	2-0	2-0	2-0	1-0	3-1	2-1	5-0	4-3	3-0
Spartak Moskva †	30	16	8	6	47	26	56	1-3		1-2	3-0	0-2	1-1	1-0	5-1	1-1	2-1	1-0	1-1	2-0	1-0	5-1	3-0
Lokomotiv Moskva ‡	30	14	14	2	41	18	56	3-2	1-1		1-0	0-0	0-0	0-3	4-1	0-0	2-0	1-1	1-1	4-0	1-0	3-0	4-0
Rubin Kazan ‡	30	14	9	7	45	31	51	1-0	0-0	3-1		1-1	1-0	5-1	2-1	2-0	0-0	0-0	2-0	1-1	2-1	4-2	1-1
FK Moskva	30	14	8	8	36	26	50	0-0	3-1	0-1	0-1		2-0	1-1	2-1	3-2	4-1	0-1	1-0	1-0	0-1	1-0	2-1
Zenit Sankt-Peterburg	30	13	10	7	45	26	49	1-0	1-1	1-1	0-1	2-2		1-1	4-1	0-0	1-0	1-0	5-1	4-2	4-1	3-1	5-1
Torpedo Moskva	30	12	9	9	37	33	45	0-2	1-3	0-1	1-1	2-0	0-4		2-1	0-0	3-0	2-0	2-1	3-1	0-0	3-0	2-1
Dinamo Moskva	30	12	2	16	36	46	38	1-2	0-1	0-0	3-1	0-2	1-2	2-1		1-0	0-0	1-0	1-2	2-1	3-1	1-0	0-1
Shinnik Yaroslavl	30	9	11	10	26	31	38	1-1	1-3	0-2	3-2	0-1	1-0	1-3	2-1		0-0	1-0	1-1	2-1	3-1	1-0	2-1
Tom Tomsk	30	9	10	11	28	33	37	0-0	0-1	0-0	1-2	3-2	2-0	1-1	3-2	0-0		0-3	3-0	1-2	4-2	0-0	2-0
Saturn Ramenskoe	30	8	9	13	23	25	33	0-1	1-1	0-0	0-0	1-2	0-0	1-0	0-1	1-0	0-2		2-0	2-0	1-1	3-1	3-2
Amkar Perm	30	7	12	11	25	36	33	0-1	0-0	3-4	1-0	0-0	1-0	0-0	4-1	0-0	0-0	3-2		1-0	1-1	0-0	0-0
FK Rostov	30	8	7	15	26	41	31	0-2	0-1	1-1	0-1	1-0	0-1	1-1	0-3	2-2	2-0	0-0	2-0		2-1	1-0	1-0
Krylya Sovetov Samara	30	7	8	15	29	44	29	2-2	1-3	0-0	2-2	4-1	3-0	0-1	0-1	1-0	1-1	1-0	1-1	2-1		2-0	0-1
Alania Vladikavkaz	30	5	8	17	27	53	23	1-1	2-1	0-0	4-3	0-2	0-3	2-2	2-4	1-1	1-2	1-1	0-1	0-0	2-0		1-0
Terek Groznyi	30	5	5	20	20	50	14	1-0	1-2	0-3	1-5	0-0	0-0	0-1	0-1	0-1	0-1	1-0	2-2	2-3	2-0	1-2	

12/03/2005 - 12/11/2005 • † Qualified for the UEFA Champions League • ‡ Qualified for the UEFA Cup
Top scorers: Dmitriy KIRICHENKO, FK Moskva, 14; DERLEI, Dinamo, 13; Igor SHEMSHOV, Torpedo, 12; Roman PAVLYUCHENKO, Spartak, 11

RUSSIA 2005
FIRST DIVISION (2)

	Pl	W	D	L	F	A	Pts
Luch Vladivostock	42	27	11	4	81	32	92
Spartak Nalchik	42	25	11	6	67	36	86
KamAz Chelny	42	26	6	10	80	32	84
FK Khimki	42	23	13	6	75	36	82
Kuban Krasnodar	42	23	12	7	55	25	81
Dinamo Makhachkala	42	23	7	12	64	41	76
Ural Yekaterinburg	42	21	10	11	51	34	73
FK Oryol	42	17	12	13	55	48	63
Spartak Chelyabinsk	42	16	13	13	60	53	61
Chkalovets Novosibirsk	42	15	11	16	51	53	56
Anzhi Makhachkala	42	14	13	15	47	48	55
SKA Khabarovsk	42	15	9	18	40	43	54
Dinamo Bryansk	42	13	13	16	44	49	52
Volga Astrakhan	42	14	9	19	50	56	51
Lokomotiv Chita	42	14	8	20	57	67	50
Avangard Kursk	42	11	15	16	36	45	48
Fakel Voronezh	42	13	7	22	39	60	46
Metallurg Novokuznetsk	42	10	15	17	48	61	45
Amur Blagoveshchensk	42	10	7	25	44	70	37
Metallurg Lipetsk	42	7	5	30	40	78	26
PetroTrust St Peterburg	42	7	5	30	37	107	26
Sokol Saratov §6	42	7	10	25	37	84	25

27/03/2005 - 6/11/2005 • Top scorer: Yevgeniy Alkhimov, Lokomotiv, 24 • §6 = six points deducted

NATIONAL TEAM PLAYERS AND COACHES

Record Caps				Record Goals				Recent Coaches	
ONOPKO Viktor	1992-'04	109		BESCHASTNYKH Vladimir	1992-'03	26		SADYRIN Pavel	1992-'94
KARPIN Valeri	1992-'03	72		KARPIN Valeri	1992-'03	17		ROMANTSEV Oleg	1994-'96
BESCHASTNYKH Vladimir	1992-'03	71		KOLYVANOV Igor	1992-'98	12		IGNATIEV Boris	1996-'98
ALENICHEV Dmitri	1996-'05	55		KIRYAKOV Sergei	1992-'98	10		BYSHOVETS Anatoliy	1998
NIKIFOROV Yuri	1993-'02	55		MOSTOVOI Alexsandr	1992-'04	10		ROMANTSEV Oleg	1998-'02
SMERTIN Aleksei	1998-'06	54		SYCHEV Dmitri	2002-'06	10		GAZZAEV Valeriy	2002-'03
KHOKHLOV Dmitri	1996-'05	53		RADCHENKO Dimitri	1992-'97	9		YARTSEV Georgy	2003-'05
KOVTUN Yuri	1994-'03	50		SIMUTENKOV Igor	1994-'98	9		SYOMIN Yuri	2005
MOSTOVOI Alexsandr	1992-'04	50		KERZHAKOV Alexandr	2002-'06	8		HIDDINK Guus	2006-
KHLESTOV Dmitri	1992-'02	49							

RUSSIAN CUP 2005-06

Fifth Round

CSKA Moskva *	2	1
Torpedo Vladimir	1	1
Tom Tomsk *	3	0
Spartak Kostroma	2	2
Shinnik Yaroslavl	0	4
Metalurg Lipetsk *	1	0
Vityaz Podolsk	0	1
Rubin Kazan *	1	2
Torpedo Moskva	2	2
Volgar Astrakhan *	0	0
Dinamo Makhachkala *	1	2
FK Moskva	4	2
Terek Groznyi *	5	1
Spartak Nalchik	0	1
Kuban Krasnodar *	1	0
Zenit Sank-Peterburg	1	0
Saturn Ramenskoe *	1	2
Ural Yekaterinburg	1	1
Lada Togliatti *	1	0
Amkar Perm	0	2
Krylya Sovetov Samara *	4	0
Saturn Yegoryevsk	1	1
Dinamo Bryansk *	0	0
Dinamo Moskva	0	4
Lokomotiv Moskva *	2	1
Metalurg Novokuznetsk	0	1
Alania Vladikavkaz *	2 0	4p
Lokomotiv Chita	0 2	5p
Luch Vladivostock *	2	1
FK Rostov	1	1
Okean Nakhodka	0	1
Spartak Moskva *	6	2

Sixth Round

CSKA Moskva *	5	3
Spartak Kostroma	0	0
Shinnik Yaroslavl	1	0
Rubin Kazan *	0	2
Torpedo Moskva *	1	3
FK Moskva	2	1
Terek Groznyi	0	1
Zenit Sank-Peterburg *	2	0
Saturn Ramenskoe	1	0
Amkar Perm *	0	0
Krylya Sovetov Samara *	2 0	1p
Dinamo Moskva	0 2	3p
Lokomotiv Moskva	Bye	
Lokomotiv Chita †		
Luch Vladivostock	0	0
Spartak Moskva * ††	1	1

Quarter-finals

CSKA Moskva	1	4
Rubin Kazan *	1	1
Torpedo Moskva	0	2
Zenit Sank-Peterburg *	2	3
Saturn Ramenskoe *	3	1
Dinamo Moskva	0	3
Lokomotiv Moskva	2	1
Spartak Moskva *	2	2

Semi-finals

CSKA Moskva *	1	3
Zenit Sank-Peterburg	0	0
Saturn Ramenskoe	1	1
Spartak Moskva *	1	3

Final

CSKA Moskva	3
Spartak Moskva	0

CUP FINAL

Luzhniki, Moscow
20-05-2006, Att. 67 000, Ref. Ivanov.V

Scorers - J6 Alves2 43 93+, Vágner Love 90 for CSKA

CSKA - Akinfeev - Berezutskiy,V. Ignashevich, Berezutskiy,A, Semberas, Dudu, Aldonin*, Zhirkov* (Tatarchuk 89), Carvalho (Taranov 33), J6 Alves, Vágner Love* (Grigoryev 92+)

Spartak - Kowalewski* - Tamas, Jiancsi, Stranzl*, Bystrov,V, Mozart•88, Covalciuc (Pavlenko 79), Rodriguez* (Owusu-Abeye 55), Titov, Cavenaghi (Bazhenov 46), Pavlyuchenko*

* Home team in the first leg • † Expelled from the tournament • †† Both legs in Moscow

CSKA MOSKVA 2005

Date	Opponents	Score				Scorers	Crowd
17-02-2005	Benfica - POR	W	2-0	H	UCr3	Berezutskiy.V [12], Vágner Love [60]	28 000
24-02-2005	Benfica - POR	D	1-1	A	UCr3	Ignashevich [49]	25 000
1-03-2005	FK Moskva	W	3-1	A	CUPr6	Samodin [45], Daniel Carvalho [62], Gusev [91+]	1 200
5-03-2005	FK Moskva	W	3-1	H	Cupr6	Olic [11], Laizans [35], Daniel Carvalho [63]	1 500
10-03-2005	Partizan Beograd - SCG	D	1-1	A	UCr4	Aldonin [17]	18 000
13-03-2005	Terek Groznyi	W	3-0	H	PL	Olic [19], Daniel Carvalho [61], Rahmic [82]	9 000
17-03-2005	Partizan Beograd - SCG	W	2-0	H	UCr4	Daniel Carvalho [69], Vágner Love [85p]	28 500
20-03-2005	Tom Tomsk	D	0-0	A	PL		14 000
3-04-2005	Lokomotiv Moskva	D	0-0	H	PL		30 000
7-04-2005	AJ Auxerre - FRA	W	4-0	H	UCqf	Odiah [21], Ignashevich [63p], Vágner Love [71], Gusev [77]	26 000
10-04-2005	Krylya Sovetov Samara	W	5-0	H	PL	Krasic [31], Olic 2 [42p 79], Kouba OG [58], Laizans [85]	15 000
14-04-2005	AJ Auxerre - FRA	L	0-2	A	UCqf		13 000
17-04-2005	Zenit Sankt-Peterburg	L	0-1	A	PL		21 400
20-04-2005	Saturn Ramenskoe	W	2-1	H	CUPqf	Laizans [88], Aldonin [93+]	4 000
28-04-2005	Parma - ITA	D	0-0	A	UCsf		7 298
5-05-2005	Parma - ITA	W	3-0	H	UCsf	Daniel Carvalho 2 [11 54], Berezutskiy.V [61]	30 000
10-05-2005	Saturn Ramenskoe	D	0-0	A	CUPqf		13 000
13-05-2005	Zenit Sankt-Peterburg	L	0-1	A	CUPsf		15 000
18-05-2005	Sporting CP - POR	W	3-1	A	UCf	Berezutskiy.A [57], Zhirkov [66], Vágner Love [75]	48 000
22-05-2005	Spartak Moskva	W	3-1	A	PL	Aldonin [51], Berezutskiy.V [28]	66 500
25-05-2005	Zenit Sankt-Peterburg	W	2-0	H	CUPsf	Aldonin [11], Daniel Carvalho [33]	17 000
29-05-2005	FK Khimki	W	1-0	N	CUPf	Zhirkov [68]	25 000
12-06-2005	Rubin Kazan	L	0-1	A	PL		18 200
15-06-2005	Saturn Ramenskoe	W	1-0	H	PL	Gusev [6]	5 500
19-06-2005	Amkar Perm	W	3-1	H	PL	Krasic [7], Vágner Love 2 [74 91+]	7 800
22-06-2005	Shinnik Yaroslavl	D	1-1	A	PL	Zhirkov [63]	18 000
25-06-2005	FK Rostov	W	2-0	A	PL	Olic 2 [52p 61p]	14 000
2-07-2005	Dinamo Moskva	W	2-0	H	PL	Dudu Cearense [15], Olic [17p]	11 000
6-07-2005	Torpedo Vladimir	W	2-1	H	CUPr5	Gusev [41], Samodin [51]	4 500
9-07-2005	Alania Vladikavkaz	D	1-1	A	PL	Vágner Love [56]	25 000
13-07-2005	Torpedo Vladimir	D	1-1	A	CUPr5	Krasic [65]	18 000
17-07-2005	Terek Groznyi	L	0-1	A	PL		8 000
20-07-2005	Torpedo Moskva	W	2-0	H	PL	Berezutskiy.V [20], Odiah [82]	7 000
24-07-2005	Tom Tomsk	W	2-0	H	PL	Ignashevich [20], Vágner Love [32]	7 000
30-07-2005	Lokomotiv Moskva	L	2-3	A	PL	Berezutskiy.A [17], Olic [58]	28 555
3-08-2005	FK Moskva	D	1-1	H	PL	Olic [92+]	7 500
6-08-2005	Krylya Sovetov Samara	D	2-2	A	PL	Ignashevich [4], Gusev [43]	16 000
10-08-2005	Torpedo Moskva	W	2-0	A	PL	Gusev [13], Olic [55]	8 500
21-08-2005	Zenit Sankt-Peterburg	D	1-1	H	PL	Ignashevich [61p]	28 000
10-09-2005	Shinnik Yaroslavl	W	2-0	H	PL	Gusev [2], Dudu Cearense [94+]	6 300
15-09-2005	FC Midtjylland - DEN	W	3-1	H	UCr1	Gusev [21], Daniel Carvalho 2 [76 79]	BCD
18-09-2005	Saturn Ramenskoe	W	1-0	A	PL	Dudu Cearense [8]	16 500
24-09-2005	Spartak Moskva	W	1-0	H	PL	Daniel Carvalho [6]	35 000
29-09-2005	FC Midtjylland - DEN	W	3-1	A	UCr1	Daniel Carvalho 2 [61 77], Samodin [76]	7 022
2-10-2005	FK Moskva	D	0-0	A	PL		9 200
16-10-2005	Rubin Kazan	W	2-1	H	PL	Odiah [11], Ignashevich [51]	6 500
20-10-2005	Olympique Marseille - FRA	L	1-2	H	UCgF	Vágner Love [80]	
23-10-2005	Amkar Perm	W	1-0	A	PL	Daniel Carvalho [43]	19 100
30-10-2005	FK Rostov	W	2-1	H	PL	Zhirkov [20], Vágner Love [25]	7 500
3-11-2005	SC Heerenveen - NED	D	0-0	A	UCgF		
6-11-2005	Dinamo Moskva	W	2-1	A	PL	Berezutskiy.A [55], Daniel Carvalho [73]	27 000
19-11-2005	Alania Vladikavkaz	W	4-3	H	PL	Ignashevich [24], Salugin [36], Vágner Love 2 [66 77]	10 000
24-11-2005	Levski Sofia	W	2-1	H	UCgF	Vágner Love 2 [49 73]	
1-12-2005	Dinamo Bucureşti - ROM	L	0-1	A	UCgF		

SC = Super Cup • CUP = Russian Cup • PL = Premier League • CL = UEFA Champions League
pr2 = second preliminary round • pr3 = third preliminary round • r6 = sixth round • qf = quarter-final • gH = group H
H = Kubán, Krasnodar • *H* = Lokomotiv • H = Dinamo • **H** = Luzhniki

RWA – RWANDA

NATIONAL TEAM RECORD
JULY 1ST 2002 TO JULY 9TH 2006

PL	W	D	L	F	A	%
49	16	12	21	54	68	44.9

FIFA/COCA-COLA WORLD RANKING

1993	1994	1995	1996	1997	1998	1999	2000	2001	2002	2003	2004	2005	High		Low	
-	-	168	159	172	107	146	128	144	130	109	99	89	89	12/05	178	07/99

2005–2006											
08/05	09/05	10/05	11/05	12/05	01/06	02/06	03/06	04/06	05/06	06/06	07/06
104	106	105	106	89	90	91	92	93	94	-	103

Rwanda have long shrugged off their tag as one of African football's minnows but their bid to win a second CECAFA Cup title fell short in December. The 'Amavubi' (wasps) again hosted the annual regional tournament, for which the country's president Paul Kagame is an enthusiastic financial backer, but lost 1-0 to defending champions Ethiopia in the final. Rwanda also turned in a disappointing performance in the FIFA World Cup™ qualifiers, leading to the dismissal of their youthful Swedish coach Roger Palmgren, who has stayed on in the East African country to run a youth development scheme. Palmgren had sought to build on the achievements of Ratomir

INTERNATIONAL HONOURS
CECAFA Cup 1999

Dujkovic, the Serbian who was later to take charge of Ghana in the 2006 FIFA World Cup™ finals in Germany. Dujkovic qualified Rwanda for a first-ever African Nations Cup finals appearance in Tunisia, but just one point taken out of a possible 15 points in their last five qualifiers for the 2006 finals in Egypt, saw them miss out on a second appearance. For the 2008 Nations Cup qualifiers, Rwanda have appointed the German coach Michael Nees. Army club APR FC were the League and Cup double winners in domestic competition, comfortably ahead of arch rivals Rayon Sport in the League standings and 1-0 winners over ATRACO in the Cup Final.

THE FIFA BIG COUNT OF 2000

	Male	Female		Male	Female
Registered players	4 000	0	Referees	200	0
Non registered players	25 000	0	Officials	1 400	0
Youth players	2 000	0	Total involved	32 600	
Total players	31 000		Number of clubs	100	
Professional players	0	0	Number of teams	500	

Fédération Rwandaise de Football Amateur (FERWAFA)
Case Postale 2000, Kigali, Rwanda
Tel +250 518525   Fax +250 518523
ferwafa@yahoo.fr   www.none
President: KAZURA Jean-Bosco   General Secretary: KALISA Jules Cesar
Vice-President: NGOGA Martin Charles   Treasurer: ITANGISHAKA Bernard   Media Officer: None
Men's Coach: NEES Michael   Women's Coach: None
FERWAFA formed: 1972   CAF: 1976   FIFA: 1978
Green shirts with red and yellow trimmings, Green shorts, Red socks

RECENT INTERNATIONAL MATCHES PLAYED BY RWANDA

2003	Opponents		Score	Venue	Comp	Scorers	Att	Referee
29-03	Uganda	D	0-0	Kigali	CNq			Bakhit SUD
7-06	Uganda	W	1-0	Kampala	CNq	Gatete [39]	50 000	Gizate ETH
6-07	Ghana	W	1-0	Kigali	CNq	Gatete [49]	40 000	
14-09	Kenya	L	0-1	Kigali	Fr		10 000	
12-10	Namibia	W	3-0	Kigali	WCq	Elias [43], Karekezi [52], Lomani [58]	22 000	Abdulkadir TAN
22-10	India	L	1-3	Hyderabad	AA	Balinda [61]		
26-10	Malaysia	W	2-1	Hyderabad	AA	Iraguha 2 [81 87]		
29-10	Uzbekistan	L	1-2	Hyderabad	AA	Mulisa [73]		
31-10	Zimbabwe	D	2-2	Hyderabad	AA	Milly [37], Iraguha [75]. L 3-5p		
15-11	Namibia	D	1-1	Windhoek	WCq	Lomani [37]	9 000	Mbera GAB
2-12	Zanzibar †	D	2-2	Khartoum	CCrl	Kerekezi 2 [40p 56]		Segonga UGA
4-12	Sudan	L	0-3	Khartoum	CCrl			
8-12	Kenya	D	1-1	Khartoum	CCsf	Lomani [30]. W 4-3p		
10-02	Uganda	L	0-2	Khartoum	CCf			Itur KEN
2004								
8-01	Egypt	L	1-5	Port Said	Fr	Said [87]	10 000	
24-01	Tunisia	L	1-2	Tunis	CNrl	Elias [31]	60 000	Evehe CMR
28-01	Guinea	D	1-1	Bizerte	CNrl	Kamanazi [90]	4 000	Sowe GAM
1-02	Congo DR	W	1-0	Bizerte	CNrl	Said [74]	700	N'Doye SEN
28-05	Uganda	D	1-1	Kigali	Fr	Kamanazi [5]		
5-06	Nigeria	L	0-2	Abuja	WCq		35 000	Pare BFA
19-06	Gabon	W	3-1	Kigali	WCq	Said 2 [4 64], Mulisa [27]	16 325	Abdulkadir TAN
3-07	Zimbabwe	L	0-2	Kigali	WCq			Chilinda MWI
14-08	Uganda	W	2-1	Kampala	Fr	Mulisa, Karekezi		
28-08	Zambia	L	1-2	Kitwe	Fr	Gaseruka [71]	15 000	Mwanza ZAM
5-09	Angola	L	0-1	Luanda	WCq		30 000	Damon RSA
9-10	Algeria	D	1-1	Kigali	WCq	Said [9]	20 000	Abdel Rahman SUD
11-12	Zanzibar †	W	4-2	Addis Abeba	CCrl	Lomani 3 [8 28 48], Karekezi [24]	20 000	
13-12	Burundi	L	1-3	Addis Abeba	CCrl	Gatete [59]		
15-12	Ethiopia	D	0-0	Addis Abeba	CCrl		20 000	
19-12	Tanzania	W	5-1	Addis Abeba	CCrl	Lomani 3, Karekezi, Sibomana		
2005								
12-03	Kenya	D	1-1	Niarobi	Fr	Bolla [10]		
27-03	Algeria	L	0-1	Oran	WCq		20 000	Abd El Fatah EGY
5-06	Nigeria	D	1-1	Kigali	WCq	Gatete [53]	30 000	Kidane ERI
18-06	Gabon	L	0-3	Libreville	WCq		10 000	El Arjoun MAR
4-09	Zimbabwe	L	1-3	Harare	WCq	OG [30]	55 000	Ssegona UGA
8-10	Angola	L	0-1	Kigali	WCq		25 000	Guezzaz MAR
26-11	Zanzibar †	L	0-1	Kigali	CCrl			
30-11	Eritrea	W	2-1	Kigali	CCrl	Gatete, Lomani 2		
4-12	Burundi	W	2-0	Kigali	CCrl			
6-12	Tanzania	W	3-1	Kigali	CCrl	Lomani 2, Gatete		
8-12	Uganda	W	1-0	Kigali	CCsf	Karekezi [115]		
10-12	Ethiopia	L	0-1	Kigali	CCf			
2006								

No international matches in 2006 before July

Fr = Friendly match • CN = CAF African Cup of Nations • CC = CECAFA Cup • AA = Afro-Asian Games • WC = FIFA World Cup™
q = qualifier • r1 = first round group • sf = semi-final • f = final • † Not a full international

RWANDA NATIONAL TEAM RECORDS AND RECORD SEQUENCES

Records			Sequence records				
Victory	4-1	DJI 1999	Wins	4	2005	Clean sheets	4	1999
Defeat	1-6	COD 1976	Defeats	5	1976-77, 1983-86	Goals scored	14	2000-2001
Player Caps	n/a		Undefeated	10	1998-2000	Without goal	3	1983-1986
Player Goals	n/a		Without win	16	1983-1996	Goals against	11	2003-2004

RWANDA COUNTRY INFORMATION

Capital	Kigali	Independence	1962 from Belgium	GDP per Capita	$1 300
Population	7 954 013	Status	Repulblic	GNP Ranking	139
Area km²	26 338	Language	Kinyarwanda, English, French	Dialling code	+250
Population density	301 per km²	Literacy rate	70%	Internet code	.rw
% in urban areas	6%	Main religion	Christian	GMT +/–	+2
Towns/Cities ('000)	Kigali 745; Butare 89; Gitarama 87; Ruhengeri 86; Gisenyi 83; Byumba 70; Cyangugu 63				
Neighbours (km)	Tanzania 217; Burundi 290; Congo DR 217; Uganda 169				
Main stadia	Stade Amahoro – Kigali 15 000				

RWANDA 2005–06 CHAMPIONNAT NATIONAL

	Pl	W	D	L	F	A	Pts
APR FC Kigali	26	21	1	4	63	14	64
Rayon Sport Kigali	26	18	4	4	52	23	58
Police Kibungo	26	16	4	6	39	21	52
Kiyovu Sport Kigali	26	15	5	6	35	19	50
Mukura Victory Butare	26	15	3	8	32	24	48
Kigali FC	26	12	8	6	39	23	44
Zèbres Byumba	26	9	5	12	24	38	32
Jeunesse Kigali	26	8	6	12	23	33	30
KIST Kigali	26	8	3	15	24	36	27
Etincelles Gisenyi	26	6	8	12	22	33	26
Marines Gisenyi	26	5	9	12	22	39	24
Renaissance Kigali	26	4	9	13	15	30	21
Flash Gitarama	26	4	5	17	21	45	17
Mukungwa Ruhengeri	26	3	6	17	18	40	15

15/01/2005 - 30/10/2006

COUPE AMAHORO 2006

Quarter-final groups	Semi-finals		Final	
Group winners				
APR FC	APR FC	3		
Group winners	KIST	1		
KIST			APR FC	1
Group winners			ATRACO	0
La Jeunesse	LA Jeunesse	2		
Group winners	ATRACO	3	Stade Amahoro, Kigali, 4-07-2006	
ATRACO			Scorer - Abbas Rassou 54 for APR	

RECENT LEAGUE AND CUP RECORD

	Championship		Cup		
Year	Champions	Winners	Score	Runners-up	
1995	APR FC Kigali	Rayon Sports Butare			
1996	APR FC Kigali				
1997	Rayon Sports Butare	Rwanda FC			
1998	Rayon Sports Butare	Rayon Sports Butare	w-o	Kiyovu Sports	
1999	APR FC Kigali				
2000	APR FC Kigali				
2001	APR FC Kigali	Citadins	0-0 6-5p	APR FC	
2002	Rayon Sports Butare	APR FC Kigali	2-1	Rayon Sports Butare	
2003	APR FC Kigali				
2004	Rayon Sports Butare				
2005	APR FC Kigali	Rayon Sports Butare	3-0	Mukura Victory	
2006	APR FC Kigali	APR FC Kigali	1-0	ATRACO	

SAM – SAMOA

NATIONAL TEAM RECORD
JULY 1ST 2002 TO JULY 9TH 2006

PL	W	D	L	F	A	%
5	1	1	3	5	11	30

FIFA/COCA-COLA WORLD RANKING

1993	1994	1995	1996	1997	1998	1999	2000	2001	2002	2003	2004	2005	High	Low
-	-	-	177	183	164	180	173	172	163	176	179	182	**166** 03/02	**188** 07/06

2005–2006											
08/05	09/05	10/05	11/05	12/05	01/06	02/06	03/06	04/06	05/06	06/06	07/06
178	178	179	180	182	182	182	183	183	183	-	188

With the national team out of action since Samoa hosted a preliminary round group in the 2006 FIFA World Cup™ qualifiers in 2004, the women's under-19 team has been the only representative side to take the field since then. In the OFC qualifiers for the FIFA U-20 Women's World Championship, they performed heroics by reaching the semi-finals after topping their first round group with wins over Fiji, New Caledonia and Papua New Guinea. In the semi-final they met Tonga and were 2-1 up midway through the second half before conceding a second penalty and then a third goal to lose 3-2. It was a spirited performance which bodes well for the senior women's

INTERNATIONAL HONOURS
None

team in the 2007 OFC qualifying tournament for the FIFA Women's World Cup. The OFC Club Championship provided international action for the men and for the second year running Tunaimato Breeze qualified to take part. In the 2005 edition they had been beaten by Papua New Guinea's Sobou 7-0 on aggregate in a preliminary qualifying round and in 2006 they took part in another qualifying tournament, this time played as a four team group in Fiji. They got off to a great start by beating Nikao Sokattack of the Cook Islands but then lost to hosts Nokia Eagles and could only draw with Tonga's Lotoha'apai and ended up finishing second to miss out on the finals.

THE FIFA BIG COUNT OF 2000

	Male	Female		Male	Female
Registered players	1 000	0	Referees	50	0
Non registered players	1 000	0	Officials	250	0
Youth players	1 000		Total involved	3 300	
Total players	3 000		Number of clubs	50	
Professional players	0	0	Number of teams	200	

Samoa Football Soccer Federation (SFSF)
Tuanaimato, PO Box 6172, Apia, Samoa
Tel +685 7783210   Fax +685 22855
www.soccersamoa.ws
President: ROEBECK Tautulu   General Secretary: SOLIA Tilomai
Vice-President: PAPALII Seiuli Poasa   Treasurer: LINO Maiava Visesio   Media Officer: SOLIA Tilomai
Men's Coach: BRAND David   Women's Coach: Brand David
SFSF formed: 1968   OFC: 1984   FIFA: 1986
Blue shirts, Blue shorts, Red socks

RECENT INTERNATIONAL MATCHES PLAYED BY SAMOA

2002	Opponents	Score	Venue	Comp	Scorers	Att	Referee
No international matches played in 2002 after June							
2003							
No international matches played in 2003							
2004							
5-05	Cook Islands	D 0-0	Auckland	Fr			
10-05	American Samoa	W 4-0	Apia	WCq	Bryce 12, Fasavalu 2 30 53, Michael 66	500	Afu SOL
15-05	Vanuatu	L 0-3	Apia	WCq		650	Breeze AUS
17-05	Fiji	L 0-4	Apia	WCq		450	Diomis AUS
19-05	Papua New Guinea	L 1-4	Apia	WCq	Michael 69	300	Diomis AUS
2005							
No international matches played in 2005							
2006							
No international matches played in 2006 before July							

Fr = Friendly match • WC = FIFA World Cup™ • q = qualifier

SAMOA NATIONAL TEAM RECORDS AND RECORD SEQUENCES

Records			Sequence records				
Victory	5-0	ASA 2002	Wins	3	1998-2000	Clean sheets	2	2002, 2004
Defeat	0-13	TAH 1981	Defeats	8	1979-1981	Goals scored	8	1998-2000
Player Caps	n/a		Undefeated	3	1998-2000	Without goal	4	1983-1988
Player Goals	n/a		Without win	8	1979-1981	Goals against	22	1979-1998

RECENT LEAGUE AND CUP RECORD

	Championship		Cup		
Year	Champions	Winners	Score	Runners-up
1997	Kiwi	Kiwi		Vaivase-tai
1998	Vaivase-tai	Togafuafua		
1999	Moata'a	Moaula		Moata'a
2000	Titavi	Gold Star	4-1	Faatoia
2001	Gold Star	Strickland Brothers	3-3 5-4p	Moata'a
2002	Strickland Brothers	Vaivase-tai		Hosanna
2003	Strickland Brothers	Strickland Brothers	5-2	Moata'a
2004	Strickland Brothers	Tunaimato Breeze	3-2	Central United
2005	Tunaimato Breeze			

SAMOA COUNTRY INFORMATION

Capital	Apia	Independence	1962 from New Zealand	GDP per Capita	$5 600
Population	177 714	Status	Constitutional Monarchy	GNP Ranking	178
Area km²	2 944	Language	Samoan, English	Dialling code	+685
Population density	60 per km²	Literacy rate	99%	Internet code	.ws
% in urban areas	21%	Main religion	Christian	GMT +/−	-11
Towns/Cities ('000)	Apia 40; Vaitele 5; Faleasiu3; Vailele 3; Leauvaa 3; Faleula 2; Siusega 2; Malie 2; Fasitoouta 2				
Neighbours (km)	South Pacific Ocean 403				
Main stadia	Toleafoa J.S. Blatter Complex – Apia				

SCG – SERBIA AND MONTENEGRO

NATIONAL TEAM RECORD
JULY 1ST 2002 TO JULY 9TH 2006

PL	W	D	L	F	A	%
41	13	12	16	48	52	46.3

FIFA/COCA-COLA WORLD RANKING

1993	1994	1995	1996	1997	1998	1999	2000	2001	2002	2003	2004	2005		High		Low	
-	-	-	-	-	-	-	-	-	19	41	46	47		19	12/02	55	10/04

	2005–2006										
08/05	09/05	10/05	11/05	12/05	01/06	02/06	03/06	04/06	05/06	06/06	07/06
49	48	42	47	47	47	47	46	46	44	-	36

And then there was one... The declaration of independence made on June 4, 2006 by the parliament in Montenegro formally brought to a close the union of southern Slavs that had come into existence after the first world war. With it went 90 years of an often glorious history in football, a history that had thrown up numerous teams to be admired. The final hurrah came at the 2006 FIFA World Cup™ in Germany although the performance will go down as one of the least glorious in the annals of the game within the region. Yet it had promised so much, as the Serbia and Montenegro national team had won their qualifying group ahead of Spain and in the process had

INTERNATIONAL HONOURS
Qualified for the FIFA World Cup™ finals 2006   UEFA Champions League Crvena Zvezda 1991

conceded just one goal. With defence such a key part of coach Ilija Petkovic's strategy it was to general amazement that they let in six against Argentina in the finals in perhaps the most lopsided game of the tournament. The task is now to disentangle the football structures in both Serbia and Montenegro although it is the Montenegrins who will have to apply to join FIFA. The Serbs will also keep the history of Yugoslavia rather than having to start their records from scratch. Having won the double in the last season of the old order, Red Star will be hoping to do the same when a truly Serbian League kicks off for the first time.

THE FIFA BIG COUNT OF 2000

	Male	Female		Male	Female
Registered players	250 800	450	Referees	8 000	30
Non registered players	120 000	2 000	Officials	375 000	150
Youth players	100 100	120	Total involved	856 650	
Total players	473 470		Number of clubs	2 821	
Professional players	800	0	Number of teams	7 527	

Football Association of Serbia (FSS)
Fudbalski savez Srbije, Terazije 35, PO Box 263, Belgrade 11000, Serbia
Tel +381 11 3234253   Fax +381 11 3233433
fsj@beotel.yu   www.fsj.co.yu
President: KARADZIC Tomislav   General Secretary: DAMJANOVIC Zoran
Vice-President: SAVICEVIC Dejan   Treasurer: BRDARIC   Media Officer: POPOVIC Miodrag
Men's Coach: CLEMENTE Javier   Women's Coach: KRSTIC Perica
FSSCG formed: 1919   UEFA: 1954   FIFA: 1919
Blue shirts with white trimmings, White shorts, Red socks or White shirts with blue trimmings, White shorts, White socks

RECENT INTERNATIONAL MATCHES PLAYED BY SERBIA AND MONTENEGRO

2002	Opponents	Score		Venue	Comp	Scorers	Att	Referee
21-08	Bosnia-Herzegovina	W	2-0	Sarajevo	Fr	Krstajic [34], Kovacevic.D [41]	9 000	Siric CRO
6-09	Czech Republic	L	0-5	Prague	Fr		5 435	Baskakov RUS
12-10	Italy	D	1-1	Naples	ECq	Mijatovic [27]	50 000	Mejuto Gonzalez ESP
16-10	Finland	W	2-0	Belgrade	ECq	Kovacevic.D [56], Mihajlovic [84p]	30 000	Wegereef NED
20-11	France	L	0-3	Paris	Fr		60 000	Iturralde Gonzalez ESP
2003								
12-02	Azerbaijan	D	2-2	Podgorica	ECq	Mijatovic [34p], Lazetic [52]	8 000	Granat POL
27-03	Bulgaria	L	1-2	Krusevac	Fr	Kovacevic.D [29]	10 000	Lazarevski MKD
30-04	Germany	L	0-1	Bremen	Fr		22 000	De Bleeckere BEL
3-06	England	L	1-2	Leicester	Fr	Jestrovic [45]	30 900	Allaerts BEL
7-06	Finland	L	0-3	Helsinki	ECq		17 343	Colombo FRA
11-06	Azerbaijan	L	1-2	Baku	ECq	Boskovic [27]	5 000	Fisker DEN
20-08	Wales	W	1-0	Belgrade	ECq	Mladenovic [73]	25 000	Frisk SWE
10-09	Italy	D	1-1	Belgrade	ECq	Ilic [82]	35 000	Hamer LUX
11-10	Wales	W	3-2	Cardiff	ECq	Vukic [4], Milosevic [82], Ljuboja [87]	72 514	Stuchlik AUT
16-11	Poland	L	3-4	Plock	Fr	Boskovic [70], Vukic [79], Iliev [89]	9 000	Weiner GER
2004								
31-03	Norway	L	0-1	Belgrade	Fr		8 000	Panic BIH
28-04	Northern Ireland	D	1-1	Belfast	Fr	Paunovic [7]	9 690	Richards WAL
11-07	Slovakia	W	2-0	Fukuoka	Fr	Milosevic [6], Jestrovic [90]	6 100	Yoshida JPN
13-07	Japan	L	0-1	Yokohama	Fr		57 616	Lennie AUS
18-08	Slovenia	D	1-1	Ljubljana	Fr	Jestrovic [49]	7 000	Ovrebo NOR
4-09	San Marino	W	3-0	Serravalle	WCq	Vukic [4], Jestrovic 2 [15 83]	1 137	Kholmatov KAZ
9-10	Bosnia-Herzegovina	D	0-0	Sarajevo	WCq		22 440	Veissiere FRA
13-10	San Marino	W	5-0	Belgrade	WCq	Milosevic [35], Stankovic 2 [45 50], Koroman [53], Vukic [69]	4 000	Isaksen FRO
17-11	Belgium	W	2-0	Brussels	WCq	Vukic [7], Kezman [60]	28 350	Frojdfeldt SWE
2005								
9-02	Bulgaria	D	0-0	Sofia	Fr		3 000	Guenov BUL
30-03	Spain	D	0-0	Belgrade	WCq		48 910	Busacca SUI
4-06	Belgium	D	0-0	Belgrade	WCq		16 662	Ivanov.V RUS
8-06	Italy	D	1-1	Toronto	Fr	Zigic [25]	35 000	Depiero CAN
15-08	Poland	L	2-3	Kyiv	Fr	Zigic [32], Vidic [59]	2 000	Orekhov UKR
17-08	Ukraine	L	1-2	Kyiv	Fr	Kezman [90]		
3-09	Lithuania	W	2-0	Belgrade	WCq	Kezman [18], Ilic [74]	20 203	Nielsen DEN
7-09	Spain	D	1-1	Madrid	WCq	Kezman [68]	51 491	Poll ENG
8-10	Lithuania	W	2-0	Vilnius	WCq	Kezman [44], Vukic [85]	1 500	Wegereef NED
12-10	Bosnia-Herzegovina	W	1-0	Belgrade	WCq	Kezman [7]	46 305	Vassaras GRE
13-11	China PR	W	2-0	Nanjing	Fr	Djordjevic [50], Zigic [64]	30 000	
16-11	Korea Republic	L	0-2	Seoul	Fr		40 127	
2006								
1-03	Tunisia	W	1-0	Rades/Tunis	Fr	Kezman [11]	6 000	Haimoudi ALG
27-05	Uruguay	D	1-1	Belgrade	Fr	Stankovic [17]	30 000	Kos SVN
11-06	Netherlands	L	0-1	Leipzig	WCr1		37 216	Merk GER
16-06	Argentina	L	0-6	Gelsenkirchen	WCr1		52 000	Rosetti ITA
21-06	Côte d'Ivoire	L	2-3	Munich	WCr1	Zigic [10], Ilic [20]	66 000	Rodriguez MEX

Fr = Friendly match • EC = UEFA EURO 2004™ • WC = FIFA World Cup™ • q = qualifier

SERBIA AND MONTENEGRO NATIONAL TEAM RECORDS AND RECORD SEQUENCES

Records			Sequence records					
Victory	10-0	VEN 1972	Wins	10	1978-1980	Clean sheets	7	2004-2005
Defeat	0-7	CZE, URU, CZE	Defeats	6	1931-1932	Goals scored	36	1959-1962
Player Caps	101	MILOSEVIC Savo	Undefeated	16	1996-1998	Without goal	4	1971-72, 1977-78
Player Goals	38	BOBEK Stjepan	Without win	7	2002-2003	Goals against	19	1920-1927

SERBIA AND MONTENEGRO COUNTRY INFORMATION

Capital	Belgrade	Independence	1992 (break up of Yugoslavia)	GDP per Capita	$2 200
Population	10 825 900	Status	Republic	GNP Ranking	86
Area km²	102 350	Language	Serbian, Albanian	Dialling code	+381
Population density	105 per km²	Literacy rate	93%	Internet code	.yu
% in urban areas	57%	Main religion	Christian 70%, Muslim 19%	GMT + / –	+1
Towns/Cities ('000)	Belgrade 1 115; Pristina 254; Novi Sad 194; Nis 173; Prizren 159; Podgorica 157				
Neighbours (km)	Romania 476; Bulgaria 318; FYR Macedonia 221; Albania 287; Bosnia and Herzegovina 527; Croatia 266; Hungary 151				
Main stadia	Maracana – Belgrade 51 328; Partizana – Belgrade 30 887				

NATIONAL TEAM PLAYERS AND COACHES

Record Caps			Record Goals			Recent Coaches	
MILOSEVIC Savo	1994–'06	101	BOBEK Stjepan	1946–'56	38	SANTRAC Slobodan	1994–'98
DZAJIC Dragan	1964–'79	85	GALIC Milan	1959–'65	37	ZIVADINOVIC Milan	1998–'99
STOJKOVIC Dragan	1983–'01	84	MARJANOVIC Blagoje	1926–'38	36	BOSKOV Vujadin	1999–'00
MIJATOVIC Predrag	1990–'03	73	MILOSEVIC Savo	1994–'06	35	PETKOVIC Ilija	2000–'01
VUJOVIC Zlatko	1979–'90	70	MITIC Rajko	1946–'57	32	DJORIC Milovan	2001
ZEBEC Branko	1951–'61	65	BAJEVIC Dusan	1970–'79	29	3 man commision	2001
JOKANOVIC Slavisa	1991–'02	64	VESELINOVIC Todor	1953–'61	28	SAVICEVIC Dejan	2001–'03
BOBEK Stjepan	1946–'56	63	MIJATOVIC Predrag	1990–'03	27	PETKOVIC Ilija	2003–'06
MIHAJLOVIC Sinisa	1991–'03	63	KOSTIC Borivoje	1956–'63	26	CLEMENTE Javier	2006–
			VUJOVIC Zlatko	1979–'90	25		

CLUB DIRECTORY

Club	Town/City	Stadium	Capacity	www.	Lge	Cup	CL
FK Buducnost	Banatski Dvor	Mirko Vucurevic	2 400		0	0	0
FK Buducnost	Podgorica (Montenegro)	Gradski Pod Goricom	15 300	fkbuducnost.co.yu	0	0	0
Crvena Zvezda (Red Star)	Beograd	Crvena Zvezda	51 328	fc-redstar.net	24	21	1
FK Hajduk Kula	Kula	Hajduk	11 000	fchajduk.com	0	0	0
FK Habitfarm Javor	Ivanjica	Gradski	5 000		0	0	0
FK Jedinstvo	Bijelo Polje (Montenegro)	Gradski	7 500		0	0	0
FK Obilic	Beograd	Milos Obilic	4 508	fcobilic.co.yu	1	0	0
OFK Beograd	Beograd	Omladinski	13 912	ofkbeograd.com	0	4	0
FK Partizan	Beograd	Partizana	30 887	partizan.co.yu	19	9	0
Rad	Beograd	Na Banjici	6 000		0	0	0
FK Radnicki Novi Beograd	Beograd	Cika Daca	22 058		0	0	0
FK Smederevo	Smederevo	Kraj Stare Zelezare	16 565	fcsartid.co.yu	0	1	0
FK Vojvodina	Novi Sad	Gradski	15 745	fcvojvodina.co.yu	2	0	0
FK Zeleznik	Zeleznik	Zeleznik	8 350	fczeleznik.co.yu	0	0	0
FK Zemun	Zemun	Gradski	10 000	fkzemun.co.yu	0	0	0
FK Zeta	Golubovci (Montenegro)	Tresnjica	5 000		0	0	0

RECENT LEAGUE AND CUP RECORD

	Championship						Cup		
Year	Champions	Pts	Runners-up	Pts	Third	Pts	Winners	Score	Runners-up
1990	Crvena Zvezda	51	Dinamo Zagreb	42	Hajduk Split	38	Crvena Zvezda	1-0	Hajduk Split
1991	Crvena Zvezda	54	Dinamo Zagreb	46	Partizan Beograd	41	Hajduk Split	1-0	Crvena Zvezda
1992	Crvena Zvezda	50	Partizan Beograd	46	Vojvodina Novi Sad	42	Partizan Beograd	1-0 2-2	Crvena Zvezda
1993	Partizan Beograd	65	Crvena Zvezda	51	Vojvodina Novi Sad	46	Crvena Zvezda	0-1 1-0 5-4p	Partizan Beograd
1994	Partizan Beograd	42	Crvena Zvezda	37	Vojvodina Novi Sad	31	Partizan Beograd	3-2 6-1	Spartak Subotica
1995	Crvena Zvezda	42	Partizan Beograd	38	Vojvodina Novi Sad	37	Crvena Zvezda	4-0 0-0	FK Obilic
1996	Partizan Beograd	60	Crvena Zvezda	48	Vojvodina Novi Sad	43	Crvena Zvezda	3-0 3-1	Partizan Beograd
1997	Partizan Beograd	84	Crvena Zvezda	78	Vojvodina Novi Sad	53	Crvena Zvezda	0-0 1-0	Vojvodina Novi Sad
1998	FK Obilic	86	Crvena Zvezda	84	Partizan Beograd	70	Partizan Beograd	0-0 2-0	FK Obilic
1999	Partizan Beograd	66	FK Obilic	64	Crvena Zvezda	51	Crvena Zvezda	4-2	Partizan Beograd
2000	Crvena Zvezda	105	Partizan Beograd	101	FK Obilic	89	Crvena Zvezda	4-0	Napredak Krusevac
2001	Crvena Zvezda	88	Partizan Beograd	86	FK Obilic	63	Partizan Beograd	1-0	Crvena Zvezda
2002	Partizan Beograd	81	Crvena Zvezda	66	Sartid Smederevo	58	Crvena Zvezda	1-0	Sartid Smederevo
2003	Partizan Beograd	89	Crvena Zvezda	70	OFK Beograd	63	Sartid Smederevo	1-0	Crvena Zvezda
2004	Crvena Zvezda	74	Partizan Beograd	63	FK Zeleznik	58	Crvena Zvezda	1-0	Buducnost Dvor
2005	Partizan Beograd	80	Crvena Zvezda	74	Zeta Golubovci	59	Zeleznik Beograd	1-0	Crvena Zvezda
2006	Crvena Zvezda	78	Partizan Beograd	71	Vozdovac Beograd	51	Crvena Zvezda	4-2	OFK Beograd

Croatian and Slovenian clubs withdrew from the league after the 1991 season • Bosnian and Macedonian clubs followed after the 1992 season

SERBIA AND MONTENEGRO 2005-06

PRVA SAVEZNA LIGA

	Pl	W	D	L	F	A	Pts	Red Star	Partizan	Vozdovac	Hajduk	Zeta	OFK	Borac	Buducnost	Vojvodina	Zemun	Smederevo	Habitfarm	Rad	Buducnost	Obilic	Jedinstvo
Crvena Zvezda †	30	25	3	2	73	23	78		2-0	3-1	4-1	3-2	2-0	1-0	5-1	3-1	2-1	2-0	2-0	1-0	4-0	4-2	4-0
Partizan Beograd ‡	30	22	5	3	53	17	71	0-0		2-3	0-0	1-0	0-1	1-0	2-0	3-0	0-0	2-1	6-0	2-0	3-0	4-2	2-0
Vozdovac Beograd	30	15	6	9	52	38	51	0-2	1-3		2-1	1-0	0-1	4-0	1-1	2-0	1-2	3-0	2-1	2-1	4-1	3-0	3-1
Hajduk Kula ‡	30	13	11	6	41	26	50	2-2	0-0	2-0		3-1	3-0	2-2	1-0	0-0	6-1	1-0	3-0	1-0	1-0	1-0	2-0
Zeta Golubovci	30	14	5	11	42	36	47	2-2	1-3	1-0	5-3		0-0	3-1	1-0	2-1	1-0	0-0	1-0	1-0	3-0	4-1	3-0
OFK Beograd ‡	30	13	5	12	35	29	44	0-1	0-1	2-2	2-1	0-1		1-1	0-1	1-0	2-0	3-0	3-2	1-0	3-0	3-1	4-0
Borac Cacak	30	12	8	10	32	27	44	2-1	0-2	0-1	1-0	0-1	1-1		0-1	1-0	2-0	4-0	0-0	2-1	2-0	1-3	2-0
Buducnost Dvor	30	13	5	12	34	31	44	0-3	1-1	0-0	2-0	3-1	1-0	0-1		1-0	3-0	2-0	1-1	0-1	2-1	3-0	5-1
Vojvodina Novi Sad	30	11	10	9	28	27	43	1-0	2-3	2-2	0-0	3-1	1-0	0-1	1-0		2-1	1-0	1-1	2-0	0-0	1-0	2-0
FK Zemun	30	11	8	11	34	39	41	0-2	0-2	2-2	2-2	2-1	3-1	1-1	2-0	1-1		0-0	1-0	0-0	3-1	2-0	2-1
FC Smederevo	30	11	6	13	30	37	39	1-3	0-1	1-2	1-1	4-1	2-1	0-0	1-1	1-0	3-2		1-0	0-1	1-1	3-1	1-0
Habitfarm Ivanjica	30	8	8	14	22	35	32	1-2	0-1	0-1	0-0	1-0	1-0	0-2	4-2	2-2	2-0	1-0		1-0	0-0	0-0	1-0
Rad Beograd	30	9	4	17	27	35	31	2-4	1-2	3-1	0-0	3-0	1-2	0-3	0-1	1-1	0-1	0-2	1-0		2-1	1-1	2-0
Buducnost Podgorica §3	30	6	10	14	24	43	25	1-2	0-1	2-0	0-0	1-1	2-2	1-1	0-2	0-0	1-1	1-2	3-1	2-1		2-1	2-0
Obilic Beograd	30	3	6	21	23	53	15	2-3	0-2	2-5	0-1	0-0	0-1	0-0	1-0	0-0	0-1	0-2	0-2	0-0	0-1		5-0
Jedinstvo Bijelo Polje	30	3	2	25	18	72	11	0-4	2-3	2-2	1-3	0-4	0-1	2-1	2-0	1-1	0-2	2-3	0-2	1-4	0-1	2-1	

7/08/2004 – 28/05/2005 • † Qualified for the UEFA Champions League • ‡ Qualified for the UEFA Cup • §3 = Three points deducted

II LIGA GRUPA SRBIJA (2)

	Pl	W	D	L	F	A	Pts
Bezanija Novi Beograd	38	25	7	6	70	25	82
Mladost Apatin	38	23	9	6	56	18	78
Pivara Celarevo	38	22	9	7	63	29	75
Cukaricki Stankom	38	22	8	8	59	29	74
Srem Sremska	38	17	9	12	47	41	60
Napredak Krusevac	38	17	7	14	49	43	58
Macva Sabac	38	14	13	11	54	55	55
Radnicki Nis	38	13	13	12	44	42	52
BASK Beograd	38	13	12	13	43	41	51
Sevojno	38	14	9	15	37	40	51
Spartak Subotica	38	14	8	16	47	54	50
Mladenovac	38	12	11	15	36	46	47
Vlasina Vlasotince	38	13	7	18	50	52	46
Radnicki Pirot	38	10	14	14	37	47	44
Novi Pazar	38	11	11	16	34	53	44
Jedinstvo Ub	38	11	7	20	47	58	40
PSK Pancevo	38	11	7	20	37	54	40
Radnicki Kragujevac	38	10	9	19	36	59	39
Novi Sad	38	9	8	21	31	53	35
OFK Nis	38	7	6	25	26	64	27

13/08/2005 – 8/06/2006

II LIGA GRUPA CRNA GORA (2)

	Pl	W	D	L	F	A	Pts
Rudar Pljevlja	36	22	6	8	58	34	72
Sutjeska Niksic	36	15	11	10	40	28	56
Kom Podgorica	36	14	10	12	37	32	52
Grbalj Radanovici	36	14	9	13	34	34	51
Mogren Budva	36	12	12	12	36	32	48
Petrovac	36	11	14	11	33	34	47
Decic Tuzi	36	11	14	11	32	34	47
Zora Spuz	36	11	14	11	34	35	47
Mornar Bar §1	36	9	7	20	23	46	33
Bokelj Kotor	36	7	11	18	30	48	32

12/08/2005 – 26/05/2006 • §1 = One point deducted
Montenegro (Crna Gora) will have an independent league
from 2006 with Zeta Golubovci, Buducnost Podgorica and
Jedinstvo Bijelo Polje joining from the Prva Savezna Liga

KUP SCG 2005-06

Round of 16		Quarter-finals		Semi-finals		Final	
Crvena Zvezda	2						
Mladost Podgorica	1	Crvena Zvezda	2				
Crvena Stijena	0	Smederevo	0				
Smederevo	4			Crvena Zvezda	5		
Timok Zajecar	1 5p			Radnicki Nis	0		
Partizan Beograd	1 4p	Timok Zajecar	0				
FK Zemun	0 1p	Radnicki Nis	2				
Radnicki Nis	0 3p					Crvena Zvezda	4
Kolubara Lazarevac	1					OFK Beograd ‡	2
Radnicki Sombor	0	Kolubara Lazarevac	0 5p				
Rad Beograd	0	Vlasina Vlasotince	0 4p				
Vlasina Vlasotince	2			Kolubara Lazarevac	1		
Hajduk Kula	2			OFK Beograd	4		
Sutjeska Niksic	0	Hajduk Kula	0				
Obilic Beograd	1	OFK Beograd	1				
OFK Beograd	2			‡ Qualified for the UEFA Cup			

CUP FINAL

Partizan, Belgrade
10-05-2006, Att: 10 757, Ref: Vukadinovic
Scorers – Zigic 2 [66] [101], Purovic [73],
Basta [117] for Red Star,
Rakic [10], Bisevac OG [59] for OFK

SCO – SCOTLAND

NATIONAL TEAM RECORD
JULY 1ST 2002 TO JULY 9TH 2006

PL	W	D	L	F	A	%
40	12	12	16	43	53	45

FIFA/COCA-COLA WORLD RANKING

1993	1994	1995	1996	1997	1998	1999	2000	2001	2002	2003	2004	2005		High		Low	
24	32	26	29	37	38	20	25	50	59	54	86	60		20	10/99	88	03/05

2005–2006											
08/05	09/05	10/05	11/05	12/05	01/06	02/06	03/06	04/06	05/06	06/06	07/06
86	74	62	61	60	60	61	62	62	59	-	41

There have been challenges to the Old Firm of Celtic and Rangers in the past, most notably in the early 1980s by Aberdeen, and the major talking point of the season was if Edinburgh club Hearts could be the latest to break the stranglehold of the Glasgow giants. Under wealthy Lithuanian Vladimir Romanov, Hearts set out their stall from the start winning their first eight League games only for coach George Burley to walk out over disagreements with the Lithuanian's unorthodox approach to running the club. The changes at Hearts allowed Celtic, under new coach Gordon Strachan to eventually build up a healthy lead at the top of the table, but Hearts never relinquished

INTERNATIONAL HONOURS
British International Championship 41 times from 1884 to 1977 **UEFA Champions League** Celtic 1967

second place. Hearts also brought to an end one of the all-time great Scottish FA Cup stories when they beat Gretna in the final. Gretna, a non League club just four years previously but transformed by philanthropist Brooks Mileson, were the first team from the third tier of League football to make it to the final, which they only lost on penalties. In Europe there was disaster for Celtic but joy for Rangers as they made it past the group stage of the UEFA Champions League for the first time. Their striker Kris Boyd had a remarkable season. Signed in the January transfer window from Kilmarnock, he finished as top scorer for both clubs - the first time that has ever happened.

THE FIFA BIG COUNT OF 2000

	Male	Female		Male	Female
Registered players	30 000	0	Referees	2 097	33
Non registered players	50 000	7 500	Officials	8 000	150
Youth players	95 000	2 000	Total involved	194 780	
Total players	184 500		Number of clubs	5 879	
Professional players	2 785	0	Number of teams	8 969	

The Scottish Football Association (SFA)
Hampden Park, Glasgow G42 9AY, United Kingdom
Tel +44 141 6166000   Fax +44 141 6166001
info@scottishfa.co.uk   www.scottishfa.co.uk
President: McBETH John   General Secretary: TAYLOR David
Vice-President: PEAT George   Treasurer: TBD   Media Officer: MITCHELL Andrew
Men's Coach: SMITH Walter   Women's Coach: SIGNEUL Anna
SFA formed: 1873   UEFA: 1954   FIFA: 1910-20, 1924-28, 1946
Dark blue shirts with white trimmings, White shorts, Dark blue socks or yellow shirts with black trimmings, Back shorts, yellow socks

RECENT INTERNATIONAL MATCHES PLAYED BY SCOTLAND

2002	Opponents	Score		Venue	Comp	Scorers	Att	Referee
21-08	Denmark	L	0-1	Glasgow	Fr		28 766	Irvine NIR
7-09	Faroe Islands	D	2-2	Toftir	ECq	Lambert [62], Ferguson [83]	4 000	Granat POL
12-10	Iceland	W	2-0	Reykjavik	ECq	Dailly [6], Naysmith [63]	7 065	Sars FRA
15-10	Canada	W	3-1	Edinburgh	Fr	Crawford 2 [11 73], Thompson [50]	16 207	Huyghe BEL
20-11	Portugal	L	0-2	Braga	Fr		8 000	Anghelinei ROM
2003								
12-02	Republic of Ireland	L	0-2	Glasgow	Fr		33 337	Braamhaar NED
29-03	Iceland	W	2-1	Glasgow	ECq	Miller.K [12], Wilkie [70]	37 548	Temmink NED
2-04	Lithuania	L	0-1	Kaunas	ECq		8 000	Stuchlik AUT
30-04	Austria	L	0-2	Glasgow	Fr		12 189	Vollquartz DEN
27-05	New Zealand	D	1-1	Edinburgh	Fr	Crawford [10]	10 016	Ingvarsson SWE
7-06	Germany	D	1-1	Glasgow	ECq	Miller.K [69]	48 037	Messina ITA
20-08	Norway	D	0-0	Oslo	Fr		12 858	Vuorela FIN
6-09	Faroe Islands	W	3-1	Glasgow	ECq	McCann [7], Dickov [45], McFadden [74]	40 901	Ceferin SVN
10-09	Germany	L	1-2	Dortmund	ECq	McCann [60]	67 000	Frisk SWE
11-10	Lithuania	W	1-0	Glasgow	ECq	Fletcher [70]	50 343	Colombo FRA
15-11	Netherlands	W	1-0	Glasgow	ECpo	McFadden [22]	50 670	Hauge NOR
19-11	Netherlands	L	0-6	Amsterdam	ECpo		51 000	Michel SVK
2004								
18-02	Wales	L	0-4	Cardiff	Fr		47 124	Ross NIR
31-03	Romania	L	1-2	Glasgow	Fr	McFadden [57]	20 433	Hyytia FIN
28-04	Denmark	L	0-1	Copenhagen	Fr		22 485	Ingvarsson SWE
27-05	Estonia	W	1-0	Tallinn	Fr	McFadden [76]	4 000	Poulsen DEN
30-05	Trinidad and Tobago	W	4-1	Edinburgh	Fr	Fletcher [6], Holt [14], Caldwell.G [23], Quashie [34]	16 187	Vink NED
18-08	Hungary	L	0-3	Glasgow	Fr		15 933	Duhamel FRA
3-09	Spain	D	1-1	Valencia	Fr	McFadden [17]. Abandoned 59'	11 000	Bre FRA
8-09	Slovenia	D	0-0	Glasgow	WCq		38 279	Larsen DEN
9-10	Norway	L	0-1	Glasgow	WCq		51 000	Allaerts BEL
13-10	Moldova	D	1-1	Chisinau	WCq	Thompson [31]	7 000	Jakobsson ISL
17-11	Sweden	L	1-4	Edinburgh	Fr	McFadden [78p]	15 071	Jara CZE
2005								
26-03	Italy	L	0-2	Milan	WCq		45 000	Vassaras GRE
4-06	Moldova	W	2-0	Glasgow	WCq	Dailly [52], McFadden [88]	45 317	Braamhaar NED
8-06	Belarus	D	0-0	Minsk	WCq		28 287	Benquerencia POR
17-08	Austria	D	2-2	Graz	Fr	Miller.K [3], O'Connor [39]	13 800	Dereli TUR
3-09	Italy	D	1-1	Glasgow	WCq	Miller.K [13]	50 185	Michel SVK
7-09	Norway	W	2-1	Oslo	WCq	Miller.K 2 [20 30]	24 904	Hamer LUX
8-10	Belarus	L	0-1	Glasgow	WCq		51 105	Szabo HUN
12-10	Slovenia	W	3-0	Celje	WCq	Fletcher [4], McFadden [47], Hartley [84]	9 100	Temmink NED
12-11	USA	D	1-1	Glasgow	Fr	Webster [37]	26 708	Undiano Mallenco ESP
2006								
1-03	Switzerland	L	1-3	Glasgow	Fr	Miller.K [55]	20 952	Coue FRA
11-05	Bulgaria	W	5-1	Kobe	Fr	Boyd 2 [13 43], McFadden [69], Burke 2 [76 88]	5 780	Kamikawa JPN
13-05	Japan	D	0-0	Saitama	Fr		56 648	Iturralde Gonzalez ESP

Fr = Friendly match • EC = UEFA EURO 2004™ • WC = FIFA World Cup™ • q = qualifier

SCOTLAND NATIONAL TEAM RECORDS AND RECORD SEQUENCES

Records			Sequence records			
Victory	11-0	NIR 1901	Wins	13	Clean sheets	7	1925-27,1996-97
Defeat	0-7	URU 1954	Defeats	5	2002	Goals scored	32	1873-1988
Player Caps	102	DALGLISH Kenny	Undefeated	22	1879-1887	Without goal	4	1971
Player Goals	30	LAW Denis/DALGLISH	Without win	9	1997-1998	Goals against	14	1957-1958

SCOTLAND COUNTRY INFORMATION

Capital	Edinburgh	Status	Part of the UK	GDP per Capita	$27 300
Population	5 057 400			GNP Ranking	4
Area km²	77 000	Language	English	Dialling code	+44
Population density	66 per km²	Literacy rate	99%	Internet code	.uk
% in urban areas	89%	Main religion	Christian	GMT + / –	0
Towns/Cities ('000)	Glasgow 610; Edinburgh 435; Aberdeen 183; Dundee 151; Paisley 73; East Kilbride 74				
Neighbours (km)	England 164				
Main stadia	Hampden Park – Glasgow 50 670; Parkhead – Glasgow 60 506; Ibrox – Glasgow 50 420				

NATIONAL TEAM PLAYERS AND COACHES

Record Caps			Record Goals			Recent Coaches	
DALGLISH Kenny	1972-'87	102	DALGLISH Kenny	1972-'87	30	BROWN Bobby	1967-'71
LEIGHTON Jim	1983-'99	91	LAW Denis	1959-'74	30	DOCHERTY Tommy	1971-'72
MCLEISH Alex	1980-'93	77	GALLACHER Hugh	1924-'35	23	ORMOND Willie	1972-'77
MCSTAY Paul	1984-'97	76	REILLY Lawrie	1949-'57	22	MACLEOD Ally	1977-'78
BOYD Tom	1991-'01	72	MCCOIST Ally	1986-'98	19	STEIN Jock	1978-'85
MILLER Willie	1975-'90	65	HAMILTON Robert	1899-'11	14	FERGUSON Alex	1985-'86
MCGRAIN Danny	1973-'82	62	JOHNSTON Mo	1984-'92	14	ROXBURGH Andy	1986-'93
GOUGH Richard	1983-'93	61	MCCOLL Robert	1896-'08	13	BROWN Craig	1993-'02
MCCOIST Ally	1986-'98	61	SMITH John	1877-'84	13	VOGTS Bertie	2002-'04
DAILLY Christian	1997-'06	61	WILSON Andrew Nesbit	1920-'23	13	SMITH Walter	2004-

CLUB DIRECTORY

Club	Town/City	Stadium	Capacity	www.	Lge	Cup	CL
Aberdeen	Aberdeen	Pittodrie	21 487	afc.co.uk	4	7	0
Celtic	Glasgow	Celtic Park	60 554	celticfc.net	39	33	1
Dundee United	Dundee	Tannadice Park	14 223	dundeeunitedfc.co.uk	1	1	0
Dunfermline Athletic	Dunfermline	East End Park	12 500	dafc.co.uk	0	2	0
Falkirk	Falkirk	Falkirk Stadium	6 123	falkirkfc.co.uk	0	2	0
Heart of Midlothian	Edinburgh	Tynecastle	17 412	heartsfc.co.uk	4	6	0
Hibernian	Edinburgh	Easter Road	17 400	hibernianfc.co.uk	4	2	0
Inverness Caledion Thistle	Inverness	Caledonian Stadium	7 400	hmssneck.com/official	0	0	0
Kilmarnock	Kilmarnock	Rugby Park	18 128	kilmarnockfc.co.uk	1	3	0
Motherwell	Motherwell	Fir Park	13 742	motherwellfc.co.uk	1	2	0
Rangers	Glasgow	Ibrox	50 444	rangers.co.uk	51	31	0
St Mirren	Paisley, Glasgow	St Mirren Park	10 866	saintmirren.net	0	3	0

RECENT LEAGUE AND CUP RECORD

Championship						Cup		
Year	Champions	Pts	Runners-up	Pts	Third	Pts	Winners	Score	Runners-up
1990	Rangers	51	Aberdeen	44	Heart of Midlothian	44	Aberdeen	0-0 9-8p	Celtic
1991	Rangers	55	Aberdeen	53	Celtic	41	Motherwell	4-3	Dundee United
1992	Rangers	72	Heart of Midlothian	63	Celtic	62	Rangers	2-1	Airdrieonians
1993	Rangers	73	Aberdeen	64	Celtic	60	Rangers	2-1	Aberdeen
1994	Rangers	58	Aberdeen	55	Motherwell	54	Dundee United	1-0	Rangers
1995	Rangers	69	Motherwell	54	Hibernian	53	Celtic	1-0	Airdrieonians
1996	Rangers	87	Celtic	83	Aberdeen	55	Rangers	5-1	Heart of Midlothian
1997	Rangers	80	Celtic	75	Dundee United	60	Kilmarnock	1-0	Falkirk
1998	Celtic	74	Rangers	72	Heart of Midlothian	67	Heart of Midlothian	2-1	Rangers
1999	Rangers	77	Celtic	71	St. Johnstone	57	Rangers	1-0	Celtic
2000	Rangers	90	Celtic	69	Heart of Midlothian	54	Rangers	4-0	Aberdeen
2001	Celtic	97	Rangers	82	Hibernian	66	Celtic	3-0	Hibernian
2002	Celtic	103	Rangers	85	Livingston	58	Rangers	3-2	Celtic
2003	Rangers	97	Celtic	97	Heart of Midlothian	63	Rangers	1-0	Dundee
2004	Celtic	98	Rangers	81	Heart of Midlothian	68	Celtic	3-1	Dunfermline Ath.
2005	Rangers	93	Celtic	92	Hibernian	61	Celtic	1-0	Dundee United
2006	Celtic	85	Heart of Midlothian	65	Rangers	62	Heart of Midlothian	1-1 4-2p	Gretna

SCOTLAND 2005-06

BANK OF SCOTLAND PREMIER LEAGUE

	Pl	W	D	L	F	A	Pts	Celtic	Hearts	Rangers	Hibs	Kilmarnock	Aberdeen	Inverness	Motherwell	Dundee U	Falkirk	Dunf'mline	Livingstone
Celtic †	38	28	7	3	93	37	91		1-1 1-0	3-0 0-0	3-2 1-1	4-2 2-0	2-0 3-0	2-1 2-1	5-0	2-0-3 3-3	1-2-1	0-1	2-1
Heart of Midlothian †	38	22	8	8	71	31	73	2-3 3-0		1-0 1-1	4-0 4-1	1-0 2-0	2-0 1-2	0-0	2-1 3-0	3-0	5-0 2-0 4-0	2-1
Rangers ‡	38	21	10	7	67	37	73	3-1 0-1 1-0 2-0			0-3 2-0 3-0 4-0 0-0 1-1	1-1	2-0 1-0	3-0	2-2	5-1 1-0 3-0 4-1
Hibernian	38	17	5	16	61	56	56	0-1 1-2 2-0 2-1 2-1 1-1-2		2-1	1-2 0-4 1-2 0-2	2-1	2-1 3-1	2-3	1-1 3-1 3-0 7-0
Kilmarnock	38	15	10	13	63	64	55	0-1 1-4 2-4 1-0 2-3 1-3 2-3 1		4-2 0-0	2-2	4-1 2-0	2-1	1-1 2-1 3-2 1-0 3-0 3-1
Aberdeen	38	13	15	10	46	40	54	1-3 2-2 1-1 0-1 3-2 2-0 0-1 1-0 1-2 2-2		0-0	2-2 2-2	2-0	3-0 1-0	0-0	0-0 3-0
Inverness CT	38	15	13	10	51	38	58	1-1 0-1 0-0 1-2 3 2-0 2-2 3-3 1-1 0-1		1-2 0-1 1-1 1-0 0-3 2-0 2-1 1-1 3-0 1-0
Motherwell	38	13	10	15	55	61	49	4-4 1-3 1-1 0-1 1-3 2-2 2-2 3-1 0-2 0-1		4-5 2-0 5-0 3-1 1-0 1-1 1-0 2-1
Dundee United	38	7	12	19	41	66	33	2-4 0-3 1-0 0-1-4 1-0 0-0 2-2-1 1-1 1-1 2-4 1-1 1-1		2-1 0-2 2-1 0-1 2-0 3-1
Falkirk	38	8	9	21	35	64	33	0-3 2-2 1-2 1-1-2 0-2 0-0-1 1-2 1-2 0-2 1-4 0-1 1-1 1-3 1-0		1-2 0-0 1-1 1-0
Dunfermline Athletic	38	8	9	21	33	68	33	0-4 1-8 1-4 3-3 1-2 0-1 0-2 1-0 0-1-2 2-0 3-3 2-2 1-1 1-0 1-1		0-1 3-2
Livingstone	38	4	6	28	25	79	18	0-5 0-2 1-4 2-3 2-2 1-2 0-3 0-0 1-1 2-1 1-2 0-1 1-0 3-1 0-2 0-1 1-0 1-0	

16/08/2005 - 22/05/2006 • † Qualified for the UEFA Champions League • ‡ Qualified for the UEFA Cup • Matches in bold are away not home matches
Top scorers: Kris BOYD, Kilmarnock/Rangers, 32; John HARTSON, Celtic, 18; Craig DARGO, Inverness CT, 17

FIRST DIVISION (2)

	Pl	W	D	L	F	A	Pts
St Mirren	36	23	7	6	52	28	76
St Johnstone	36	18	12	6	59	34	66
Hamilton Acad'ical	36	15	14	7	53	39	59
Ross County	36	14	14	8	47	40	56
Clyde	36	15	10	11	54	42	55
Airdrie United	36	11	12	13	57	43	45
Dundee	36	9	16	11	43	50	43
Queen of the South	36	7	12	17	31	54	33
Stranraer †	36	5	14	17	33	53	29
Brechin City	36	2	11	23	28	74	17

6/08/2005 - 29/04/2006 • † Play-off

PLAY-OFFS

DIV 1 & 2

Semi-finals

Stranraer	1	2
Partick Thistle	3	1
Morton	0	0
Peterhead	0	1

Final

Partick Thistle	1	2	4p
Peterhead	2	1	2p

SECOND DIVISION (3)

	Pl	W	D	L	F	A	Pts
Gretna	36	28	4	4	97	30	88
Morton †	36	21	7	8	58	33	70
Peterhead †	36	17	6	13	53	47	57
Partick Thistle †	36	16	9	11	57	56	57
Stirling Albion	36	15	6	15	54	63	51
Ayr United	36	10	12	14	56	61	42
Raith Rovers	36	11	9	16	44	54	42
Forfar Athletic	36	12	4	20	44	55	40
Alloa Athletic †	36	8	8	20	36	77	32
Dumbarton	36	7	5	24	40	63	26

6/08/2005 - 29/04/2006 • † Play-off

THIRD DIVISION (4)

	Pl	W	D	L	F	A	Pts
Cowdenbeath	36	24	4	8	81	34	76
Berwick Rangers †	36	23	7	6	54	27	76
Stenhousemuir †	36	23	4	9	78	38	73
Arbroath †	36	16	7	13	57	47	55
Elgin City	36	15	7	14	55	58	52
Queen's Park	36	13	12	11	47	42	51
East Fife	36	13	4	19	48	64	43
Albion Rovers	36	7	8	21	39	60	29
Montrose	36	6	10	20	31	59	28
East Stirling	36	6	5	25	28	89	23

6/08/2005 - 29/04/2006

DIV 2 & 3

Semi-finals

Arbroath	1	0
Alloa Athletic	1	1
Stenhousemuir	0	0
Berwick Rangers	1	0

Final

Alloa Athletic	4	1
Berwick Rangers	0	2

RECENT LEAGUE CUP RECORD

Year	Winners	Score	Runners-up
1997	Rangers	4-3	Heart of Mid'thian
1998	Celtic	3-0	Dundee United
1999	Rangers	2-1	St Johnstone
2000	Celtic	2-0	Aberdeen
2001	Celtic	3-0	Kilmarnock
2002	Rangers	4-0	Ayr United
2003	Rangers	2-1	Celtic
2004	Livingston	2-0	Hibernian
2005	Rangers	5-1	Motherwell
2006	Celtic	3-0	Dunfermline Ath.

CIS INSURANCE SCOTTISH LEAGUE CUP 2005-06

Third Round

Celtic *	2
Falkirk	1
Clyde	2
Rangers *	5
Aberdeen	2
Stranraer *	0
St Mirren *	0
Motherwell	2
Livingston *	1
Heart of Midlothian	0
Dundee United	0
Inverness CT *	2
Hibernian	2
Ayr United *	1
Kilmarnock *	3
Dunfermline Athletic	4

Quarter-finals

Celtic *	2
Rangers	0
Aberdeen	0
Motherwell *	1
Livingston *	2
Inverness CT	1
Hibernian	0
Dunfermline Athletic *	3

Semi-finals

Celtic ‡	2
Motherwell	1
Livingston	0
Dunfermline Athletic †	1

Final

Celtic	3
Dunfermline Athletic	0

LEAGUE CUP FINAL

Hampden Park, Glasgow
19-03-2005, Att: 50 090, Ref: Dougal
Scorers - Zurawski[43], Maloney[76], Dublin[90] for Celtic

* Home team • † Easter Road, Edinburgh • ‡ Hampden Park, Glasgow

TENNENTS SCOTTISH FA CUP 2005-06

Third Round		Fourth Round		Quarter-finals		Semi-finals		Final	
Heart of Midlothian *	2								
Kilmarnock	1	Heart of Midlothian *	3						
Dundee United *	2	Aberdeen	0						
Aberdeen	3			Heart of Midlothian *	2				
Inverness Caledonian T. *	1 2			Partick Thistle	1				
Ayr United	1 0	Inverness Caledonian T. *	2 1 2p						
Stirling Albion *	0	Partick Thistle	2 1 4p						
Partick Thistle	1					Heart of Midlothian	4		
Falkirk *	2					Hibernian	0		
Brechin City	1	Falkirk *	1 1						
Forfar Athletic	0	Ross County	1 0						
Ross County *	5			Falkirk *	1				
Rangers *	5			Hibernian	5				
Peterhead	0	Rangers *	0						
Arbroath	0	Hibernian	3						
Hibernian *	6							Heart of Midlothian	1 4p
Dundee *	2							Gretna ‡	1 2p
Stranraer	0	Dundee *	1 2						
Dunfermline Athletic *	3	Airdrie United *	1 0						
Airdrie United	4			Dundee	0 3				
Alloa Athletic *	1 1			Hamilton Academical *	0 2				
Livingston	1 1	Alloa Athletic	0 0						
Queen of the South *	1 0	Hamilton Academical *	0 3						
Hamilton Academical	1 1					Dundee	0		
St Mirren *	3					Gretna	3		
Motherwell	0	St Mirren	0 3						
Queen's Park	2	Spartans *	0 0						
Spartans *	3			St Mirren	0				
Clyde *	2			Gretna *	1				
Celtic	1	Clyde *	0 0						
St Johnstone	0	Gretna	0 4						
Gretna *	1								

* Home team ● Both semi-finals played at Hampden Park ● ‡ Qualified for the UEFA Cup

SCOTTISH CUP FINAL

Hampden Park, Glasgow
13-05-2006, Att: 51 232. Ref: McDonald

Scorers – Skacel 39 for Hearts; McGuffie 76 for Gretna

Hearts - Gordon, Neilson, Pressley, Tall, Fyssas●, Cesnauskis (Mikoliunas 86), Aguiar (Brellier 72), Hartley●●120, Skacel●, Bednar (Pospisil 70), Jankauskas

Gretna - Main, Birch●, Townsley, Innes, Nicholls (Graham 55), McGuffie, Tosh●, O'Neil, Skelton, Grady, Deuchar (McQuilken 103)

Penalties: Pressley ✓, Grady ✓, Neilson ✓, Birch ✓, Skacel ✓, Townsley ✗, Pospisil ✓, Skelton ✗

CELTIC 2005-06

Date	Opponents	Score		Comp	Scorers	Att
27-07-2005	Artmedia Bratislava - SVK	L	0-5	A	CLpr2	17 632
30-07-2005	Motherwell	D	4-4	A	SPL	Hartson 3 [14 32 44p], Beattie [91+]	9 903
2-08-2005	Artmedia Bratislava - SVK	W	4-0	H	CLpr2	Thompson [21p], Hartson [44], McManus [54], Beattie [82]	50 063
6-08-2005	Dundee United	W	2-0	H	SPL	Hartson [37], Beattie [88]	56 532
13-08-2005	Falkirk	W	3-1	H	SPL	Hartson [49], Thompson 2 [75 91+]	57 782
20-08-2005	Rangers	L	1-3	A	SPL	Maloney [86p]	49 699
28-08-2005	Dunfermline Athletic	W	4-0	A	SPL	Zurawski 2 [5 74], Hartson [10], Nakamura [58]	9 244
10-09-2005	Aberdeen	W	2-0	H	SPL	Zurawski [13], Petrov [61]	59 607
18-09-2005	Hibernian	W	1-0	A	SPL	Petrov [5]	15 649
21-09-2005	Falkirk	W	2-1	H	LCr3	Zurawski [62], Hartson [94]	19 422
24-09-2005	Inverness Caledonian Thistle	W	2-1	H	SPL	Beattie 2 [57 67]	57 247
1-10-2005	Livingston	W	5-0	A	SPL	McManus [36], Maloney [45], Zurawski [51], Sutton [62], Beattie [72]	9 115
15-10-2005	Heart of Midlothian	D	1-1	H	SPL	Beattie [13]	60 100
23-10-2005	Kilmarnock	W	1-0	A	SPL	Petrov [24]	10 544
26-10-2005	Motherwell	W	5-0	H	SPL	Petrov 3 [14 23 79], Maloney [17], Nakamura [67]	57 388
30-10-2005	Dundee United	W	4-2	A	SPL	Hartson [17], Sutton [28], Archibald OG [32], Pearson [88]	11 942
6-11-2005	Falkirk	W	3-0	A	SPL	Maloney [41], McGeady [42], Hartson [69]	6 459
9-11-2005	Rangers	W	2-0	H	LCqf	Maloney [26], Balde [82]	57 813
19-11-2005	Rangers	W	3-0	H	SPL	Hartson [12], Balde [56], McGeady [61]	58 997
26-11-2005	Dunfermline Athletic	L	0-1	H	SPL		58 203
4-12-2005	Aberdeen	W	3-1	A	SPL	McGeady [56], Petrov [58], Telfer [64]	17 031
10-12-2005	Hibernian	W	3-2	H	SPL	Hartson 2 [40 65], Maloney [57]	59 895
18-12-2005	Inverness Caledonian Thistle	D	1-1	H	SPL	Hartson [21]	7 382
26-12-2005	Livingston	W	2-1	H	SPL	Maloney [39p], Nakamura [87]	57 000
1-01-2006	Heart of Midlothian	W	3-2	A	SPL	Pearson [55], McManus 2 [87 91+]	17 378
8-01-2006	Clyde	L	1-2	A	SCr3	Zurawski [84]	8 000
14-01-2006	Kilmarnock	W	4-2	H	SPL	Nakamura [3], Maloney [16p], McManus [53], Zurawski [67]	59 995
22-01-2006	Motherwell	W	3-1	A	SPL	Zurawski [17], McGeady [71], Hartson [85]	11 503
28-01-2006	Dundee United	D	3-3	H	SPL	Hartson [9], Zurawski [49], Petrov [67]	59 875
1-02-2006	Motherwell	W	2-1	N	LCsf	Zurawski [28], Maloney [89]	22 595
8-02-2006	Falkirk	W	2-1	H	SPL	Keane [34], McManus [44]	56 672
12-02-2006	Rangers	W	1-0	A	SPL	Zurawski [12]	49 788
19-02-2006	Dunfermline Athletic	W	8-1	A	SPL	Petrov [3], Hartson [24], Zurawski 4 [32 40 56 88], Maloney [74], Lennon [82]	9 015
4-03-2006	Aberdeen	W	3-0	H	SPL	Petrov [66], Maloney [75], Zurawski [89]	60 018
12-03-2006	Hibernian	W	2-1	A	SPL	Maloney [36p], McManus [60]	16 985
19-03-2006	Dunfermline Athletic	W	3-0	N	LCf	Zurawski [43], Maloney [76], Dublin [90]	50 090
22-03-2006	Inverness Caledonian Thistle	W	2-1	H	SPL	McManus [35], Maloney [79]	57 451
26-03-2006	Livingston	W	2-0	A	SPL	Zurawski [47], Maloney [52p]	7 486
5-04-2006	Heart of Midlothian	W	1-0	H	SPL	Hartson [4]	59 699
9-04-2006	Kilmarnock	W	4-1	A	SPL	Nakamura 2 [8 82], Hartson [64], Dublin [84]	10 978
16-04-2006	Hibernian	D	1-1	H	SPL	Zurawski [76]	60 047
23-04-2006	Rangers	D	0-0	H	SPL		59 684
30-04-2006	Heart of Midlothian	L	0-3	A	SPL		16 795
3-05-2006	Kilmarnock	W	2-0	H	SPL	Zurawski [55], Varga [63]	48 649
7-05-2006	Aberdeen	D	2-2	A	SPL	Hartson [5], Maloney [6]	14 597

SPL = Scottish Premier League • CL = UEFA Champions League • LC = League Cup • SC = Scottish FA Cup
pr2 = second preliminary round • r3 = third round • qf = quarter-final • sf = semi-final • f = final • N = Hampden Park, Glasgow

HEART OF MIDLOTHIAN 2005-06

Date	Opponents	Score			Comp	Scorers	Att
30-07-2005	Kilmarnock	W	4-2	A	SPL	Skacel [12], Bednar [46], Mikoliunas [61], Hartley [89p]	7 487
7-08-2005	Hibernian	W	4-0	H	SPL	Skacel [13], Hartley [58p], Simmons [71], Mikoliunas [83]	16 459
14-08-2005	Dundee United	W	3-0	A	SPL	Pressley [6], Bednar [12], Scakel [90]	11 654
20-08-2005	Aberdeen	W	2-0	H	SPL	Skacel [20], Pospisal [85]	16 139
23-08-2005	Queen's Park	W	2-0	A	LCr2	Jankauskas 2 [15 44]	2 429
27-08-2005	Motherwell	W	2-1	H	SPL	Skacel [41], Jankauskas [70]	16 213
11-09-2005	Livingston	W	4-1	A	SPL	Skacel [11], Webster [27], Hartley 2 [34 63p]	8 405
17-09-2005	Inverness Caledonian Thistle	W	1-0	A	SPL	Skacel [28]	6 704
21-09-2005	Livingston	L	0-1	H	LCr3		3 805
24-09-2005	Rangers	W	1-0	H	SPL	Bednar [14]	17 379
2-10-2005	Falkirk	D	2-2	A	SPL	Pressley 2 [72 91+]	6 342
15-10-2005	Celtic	D	1-1	A	SPL	Skacel [16]	60 100
22-10-2005	Dunfermline Athletic	W	2-0	H	SPL	Skacel [21], Pospisil [23]	16 500
26-10-2005	Kilmarnock	W	1-0	H	SPL	Jankauskas [35]	16 536
29-10-2005	Hibernian	L	0-2	H	SPL		17 180
5-11-2005	Dundee United	W	3-0	H	SPL	Hartley [4], Skacel [26], Pospisil [57]	16 617
20-11-2005	Aberdeen	D	1-1	A	SPL	Skacel [64]	14 901
26-11-2005	Motherwell	D	1-1	A	SPL	Hartley [91+p]	8 131
3-12-2005	Livingston	W	2-1	H	SPL	Skacel 2 [8 15]	16 583
10-12-2005	Inverness Caledonian Thistle	D	0-0	H	SPL		16 373
17-12-2005	Rangers	L	0-1	A	SPL		49 723
26-12-2005	Falkirk	W	5-0	H	SPL	Hartley [20], Skacel [25], Elliot 2 [41 91+], Pospisil [73]	16 538
1-01-2006	Celtic	L	2-3	H	SPL	Jankauskas [6], Pressley [8]	17 378
7-01-2006	Kilmarnock	W	2-1	H	SCr3	Pressley [24], McAllister [75]	12 831
14-01-2006	Dunfermline Athletic	W	4-1	A	SPL	Pressley [28], Pospisil 2 [54 67], Skacel [81]	8 277
21-01-2006	Kilmarnock	L	0-1	A	SPL		8 811
28-01-2006	Hibernian	W	4-1	H	SPL	Hartley 2 [27 44p], Skacel [41], Elliot [50]	17 371
4-02-2006	Aberdeen	W	3-0	H	SCr4	Pospisil [21], Elliot [34], Pressley [45]	17 353
7-02-2006	Dundee United	D	1-1	A	SPL	Hartley [83p]	10 584
11-02-2006	Aberdeen	L	1-2	H	SPL	Elliot [9]	16 895
18-02-2006	Motherwell	W	3-0	H	SPL	Jankauskas 2 [4 14], Elliot [78]	16 976
25-02-2006	Partick Thistle	W	2-1	H	SCqf	Jankauskas [6], Cesnauskas [63]	16 365
5-03-2006	Livingston	W	3-2	A	SPL	Aguiar [17], Jankauskas [72], Bednar [87]	5 058
11-03-2006	Inverness Caledonian Thistle	D	0-0	A	SPL		5 027
19-03-2006	Rangers	D	1-1	H	SPL	Jankauskas [9]	17 040
25-03-2006	Falkirk	W	2-1	A	SPL	Hartley [22], Jankauskas [81]	5 966
2-04-2006	Hibernian	W	4-0	N	SCsf	Hartley 3 [28 59 88p], Jankauskas [81]	43 180
5-04-2006	Celtic	L	0-1	A	SPL		59 699
8-04-2006	Dunfermline Athletic	W	4-0	H	SPL	Pospisil [7], Bednar [14], Mikoliunas [25], Makela [82]	16 973
15-04-2006	Kilmarnock	W	2-0	H	SPL	Hartley [70], Berra [87]	16 497
22-04-2006	Hibernian	L	1-2	A	SPL	Bednar [49]	16 654
30-04-2006	Celtic	W	3-0	H	SPL	McManus OG [7], Hartley [9], Bednar [63]	16 795
3-05-2006	Aberdeen	W	1-0	H	SPL	Hartley [54p]	17 327
7-05-2006	Rangers	L	0-1	A	SPL		49 792
13-05-2006	Gretna	D	1-1	N	SCf	Skacel [39], W 4-1p	51 232

SPL = Scottish Premier League • LC = League Cup • SC = Scottish FA Cup
r2 = second round • r3 = third round • r4 = fourth round • qf = quarter-final • sf = semi-final • f = final • N = Hampden Park, Glasgow

RANGERS 2005–06

Date	Opponents	Score	Comp	Scorers	Att
31-07-2005	Livingston	W 3-0	H	SPL	Prso [23], Pierre-Fanfan [53], Løvenkrands [92+]	49 613
6-08-2005	Inverness Caledonian Thistle	W 1-0	A	SPL	Ferguson [69]	7 512
9-08-2005	Anorthosis Famagusta - CYP	W 2-1	A	CLpr3	Novo [64], Ricksen [71]	16 990
14-08-2005	Aberdeen	L 2-3	A	SPL	Prso [39], Løvenkrands [49]	18 182
20-08-2005	Celtic	W 3-1	H	SPL	Prso [34], Buffel [51], Novo [88p]	49 699
24-08-2005	Anorthosis Famagusta -CYP	W 2-0	H	CLpr3	Buffel [38], Prso [57]	48 500
27-08-2005	Hibernian	L 0-3	H	SPL		49 754
10-09-2005	Falkirk	D 1-1	A	SPL	Novo [39p]	6 500
13-09-2005	FC Porto - POR	W 3-2	H	CLgH	Løvenkrands [35], Prso [59], Kyrgiakos [85]	48 599
17-09-2005	Kilmarnock	W 3-0	H	SPL	Prso [9p], Ferguson [67], Greer OG [82]	49 076
20-09-2005	Clyde	W 5-2	H	LCr3	Buffel 2 [5 74], Nieto 2 [98 113], Andrews [111]	30 104
24-09-2005	Heart of Midlothian	L 0-1	A	SPL		17 379
28-09-2005	Internazionale - ITA	L 0-1	A	CLgH		BCD
1-10-2005	Dunfermline Athletic	W 5-1	H	SPL	Buffel [15], Prso [38], Nieto [71], Løvenkrands [75], McCormack [86]	48 374
16-10-2005	Dundee United	D 0-0	A	SPL		11 696
19-10-2005	Artmedia Bratislava - SVK	D 0-0	H	CLgH		49 013
22-10-2005	Motherwell	W 2-0	H	SPL	Burke [1], Lovenkrands [72]	49 215
26-10-2005	Livingston	D 2-2	A	SPL	Ferguson [15], Burke [54]	9 481
29-10-2005	Inverness Caledonian Thistle	D 1-1	H	SPL	Thompson [54]	47 867
1-11-2005	Artmedia Bratislava - SVK	D 2-2	A	CLgH	Prso [3], Thompson [44]	19 492
5-11-2005	Aberdeen	D 0-0	H	SPL		49 717
9-11-2005	Celtic	L 0-2	A	LCqf		57 183
19-11-2005	Celtic	L 0-3	A	SPL		58 997
23-11-2005	FC Porto - POR	D 1-1	A	CLgH	McCormack [83]	39 439
27-11-2005	Hibernian	L 1-2	A	SPL	Ferguson [59]	16 958
3-12-2005	Falkirk	D 2-2	H	SPL	Ireland OG [31], Løvenkrands [56p]	48 042
6-12-2005	Internazionale - ITA	D 1-1	H	CLgH	Løvenkrands [38]	49 170
11-12-2005	Kilmarnock	W 3-2	A	SPL	Løvenkrands 3 [16 42 72]	12 426
17-12-2005	Heart of Midlothian	W 1-0	H	SPL	Løvenkrands [35]	49 723
26-12-2005	Dunfermline Athletic	D 3-3	A	SPL	Løvenkrands 2 [22 65p], Burke [67]	9 481
31-12-2005	Dundee United	W 3-0	H	SPL	Buffel [68], Thompson [83], Løvenkrands [86]	49 141
7-01-2006	Peterhead	W 5-0	H	SCr3	Kyrgiakos [35], Boyd 3 [50p 54 71], McCormack [75]	39 870
15-01-2006	Motherwell	W 1-0	H	SPL	Løvenkrands [55]	10 689
21-01-2006	Livingston	W 4-1	H	SPL	Boyd 2 [8 56], Prso 2 [89 91+]	49 211
29-01-2006	Inverness Caledonian Thistle	W 3-2	A	SPL	Boyd 2 [6 58p], Andrews [27]	7 380
4-02-2006	Hibernian	L 0-3	H	SCr4		40 722
8-02-2006	Aberdeen	L 0-2	A	SPL		17 087
12-02-2006	Celtic	L 0-1	H	SPL		49 788
18-02-2006	Hibernian	W 2-0	H	SPL	Boyd [40], Ferguson [74]	49 720
22-02-2006	Villarreal - ESP	D 2-2	H	CLr2	Løvenkrands [22], Peña OG [82]	49 372
4-03-2006	Falkirk	W 2-1	A	SPL	Boyd [57], Twaddle OG [70]	6 343
7-03-2006	Villarreal - ESP	D 1-1	A	CLr2	Løvenkrands [12]	19 828
11-03-2006	Kilmarnock	W 4-0	H	SPL	Boyd [13], Rodriguez [71], Prso [85p], Løvenkrands [87]	49 442
19-03-2006	Heart of Midlothian	D 1-1	A	SPL	Buffel [65]	17 040
25-03-2006	Dunfermline Athletic	W 1-0	H	SPL	Kyrgiakos [70]	49 017
2-04-2006	Dundee United	W 4-1	A	SPL	Prso [30], Boyd 3 [31 54 83]	11 213
8-04-2006	Motherwell	W 1-0	H	SPL	Boyd [27]	49 481
15-04-2006	Aberdeen	D 1-1	H	SPL	Boyd [51]	48 987
23-04-2006	Celtic	D 0-0	A	SPL		59 684
29-04-2006	Kilmarnock	W 3-1	H	SPL	Andrews 2 [51 79], Boyd [64]	11 583
2-05-2006	Hibernian	W 2-1	A	SPL	Boyd 2 [36 74]	14 773
7-05-2006	Heart of Midlothian	W 2-0	H	SPL	Boyd 2 [36 74]	49 792

SPL = Scottish Premier League • CL = UEFA Champions League • UC = UEFA Cup • LC = League Cup • SC = Scottish FA Cup
pr3 = third preliminary round • r1 = first round • gF = Group F • r3 = third round • qf = quarter-final • sf = semi-final • f = final

SEN – SENEGAL

NATIONAL TEAM RECORD
JULY 1ST 2002 TO JULY 9TH 2006

PL	W	D	L	F	A	%
43	20	12	11	61	37	60.5

FIFA/COCA-COLA WORLD RANKING

1993	1994	1995	1996	1997	1998	1999	2000	2001	2002	2003	2004	2005	High	Low
56	50	47	58	85	95	79	88	65	27	33	31	30	**26** 06/04	**95** 12/98

2005–2006											
08/05	09/05	10/05	11/05	12/05	01/06	02/06	03/06	04/06	05/06	06/06	07/06
40	35	34	30	30	30	29	28	29	28	-	35

Senegal achieved the extraordinary feat of finishing fourth at the 2006 African Nations Cup finals despite winning only two matches. Three points was surprisingly enough to allow them to progress from their first round group and they took full advantage by beating Guinea 3-2 in the quarter-finals. After that came defeat by Egypt, albeit controversially, in the semi-final, and Nigeria in the bronze medal play-off match. The mediocrity of the achievement was little consolation for a country which followed up its record-equalling quarter-final place at the 2002 FIFA World Cup™ finals with failure to qualify for the 2006 tournament in Germany. After the departure of charismatic

INTERNATIONAL HONOURS
Copa Amilcar Cabral 1979 1980 1983 1984 1985 1986 1991 2001

coach Bruno Metsu, Senegal rarely sparkled and a 2-2 home draw with Togo in June 2005 signalled the end of their FIFA World Cup™hopes as well as the career of Metsu's successor, Guy Stephan. He was ultimately replaced by the much-travelled Pole, Henryk Kasperczak. Senegal divided their domestic championship into two groups and changed the timing of the season, abandoning the calendar year format favoured in Africa. AS Douanes finished ahead of perennial rivals Diaraf Dakar in both their group and then the four-team play-off group, ensuring a first championship in nine years, as well as the double, having earlier won the Cup Final 1-0 against DUC Dakar.

THE FIFA BIG COUNT OF 2000

	Male	Female		Male	Female
Registered players	6 593	0	Referees	3 230	0
Non registered players	40 000	0	Officials	2 700	0
Youth players	146 689	0	Total involved	199 212	
Total players	193 282		Number of clubs	82	
Professional players	50	0	Number of teams	12 200	

Fédération Sénégalaise de Football (FSF)
VDN-Ouest-Foire en face du CICES, Case Postale 13021, Dakar, Senegal
Tel +221 8692828   Fax +221 8200592
fsf@senegalfoot.sn   www.senegalfoot.sn
President: NDOYE Mbaye   General Secretary: CISSE Victor
Vice-President: NDIAYE Momar   Treasurer: DIAGNE Blaise   Media Officer: SECK Mbacke
Men's Coach: KASPERCZAK Henryk   Women's Coach: DIABY Bassouare
FSF formed: 1960   CAF: 1963   FIFA: 1962
White shirts with yellow trimmings, White shorts, White socks or Green shirts with yellow trimmings, Green shorts, Green socks

RECENT INTERNATIONAL MATCHES PLAYED BY SENEGAL

2002	Opponents	Score		Venue	Comp	Scorers	Att	Referee
8-09	Lesotho	W	1-0	Maseru	CNq	Camara.H [44]	60 000	Mangaliso SWZ
12-10	Nigeria	D	2-2	Dakar	Fr	Camara.S [84], Sarr [90]	50 000	Diatta SEN
19-11	South Africa	D	1-1	Johannesburg	Fr	Niang [68], W 4-1p	40 000	Tangawarima ZIM
2003								
12-02	Morocco	L	0-1	Paris	Fr		8 000	Piccirillo FRA
30-03	Gambia	D	0-0	Banjul	CNq		30 000	Djingarey NIG
30-04	Tunisia	L	0-1	Tunis	Fr			
31-05	Cape Verde Islands	W	2-1	Dakar	Fr	Camara.S [50], Diao [62]	20 000	Santos GNB
7-06	Gambia	W	3-1	Dakar	CNq	Diatta [5], Camara.H [36], Diouf [73]		Guirat TUN
14-06	Lesotho	W	3-0	Dakar	CNq	Diouf [26p], Camara 2 [66 71]		
10-09	Japan	W	1-0	Niigata	Fr	Diop.PB [6]	40 000	Moradi IRN
10-10	Egypt	L	0-1	Cairo	Fr		20 000	
15-11	Côte d'Ivoire	W	1-0	Dakar	Fr	Diouf [89]	50 000	Daami TUN
2004								
18-01	South Africa	W	2-1	Dakar	Fr	Diop.PM [29], Mabizela OG [83]	50 000	El Achiri MAR
26-01	Burkina Faso	D	0-0	Tunis	CNr1		2 000	Guezzaz MAR
30-01	Kenya	W	3-0	Bizerte	CNr1	Niang 2 [4 31], Diop.PB [19]	13 500	Abd El Fatah EGY
2-02	Mali	D	1-1	Tunis	CNr1	Beye [45]	7 550	Evehe CMR
7-02	Tunisia	L	0-1	Tunis	CNqf		57 000	Bujsaim UAE
29-05	Guinea	D	1-1	Paris	Fr	Guaye [82]	2 000	Garibian FRA
5-06	Congo	W	2-0	Dakar	WCq	Diatta [59], Ndiaya [77]	18 000	Benouza ALG
13-06	Cape Verde Islands	W	3-1	Praia	Fr	Gueye [65], Kamara.D 2 [71 74]	10 000	
20-06	Togo	L	1-3	Lome	WCq	Diop.PB [81]	25 000	El Arjoun MAR
3-07	Zambia	W	1-0	Dakar	WCq	Gueye [21]	50 000	Monteiro Duarte CPV
18-08	Côte d'Ivoire	L	1-2	Avignon	Fr	Camara [12]	5 000	
5-09	Mali	D	2-2	Bamako	WCq	Camara.H [45], Dia [84]	45 000	Guezzaz MAR
10-10	Liberia	W	3-0	Monrovia	WCq	Diop.PB [41], Camara.H 2 [50 73]	26 000	Aboubacar CIV
17-11	Algeria	W	2-1	Toulon	Fr	Niang [35], Gueye [41]	4 000	Bata FRA
2005								
9-02	Cameroon	L	0-1	Creteil	Fr			
26-03	Liberia	W	6-1	Dakar	WCq	Fadiga [19], Diouf 2 [45p 84], Faye [56], Camara.H [72], Ndiaye [75]	50 000	Shelmani LBY
5-06	Congo	D	0-0	Brazzaville	WCq		40 000	Damon RSA
18-06	Togo	D	2-2	Dakar	WCq	Niang [15], Camara.H [30]	50 000	Guirat TUN
17-08	Ghana	D	0-0	London	Fr			
3-09	Zambia	W	1-0	Chililabombwe	WCq	Diouf [57]	20 000	Abd El Fatah EGY
8-10	Mali	W	3-0	Dakar	WCq	Camara.H 2 [18 65], Diouf [23]	30 000	Maillet SEY
12-11	South Africa	W	3-2	Port Elizabeth	Fr	Camara.S [3], Kamara [22], Momar N'Diaye [85]		N'Doye SEN
2006								
14-01	Congo DR	D	0-0	Dakar	Fr			
23-01	Zimbabwe	W	2-0	Port Said	CNr1	Camara.C [60], Issa Ba [80]	15 000	Abdel Rahman SUD
27-01	Ghana	L	0-1	Port Said	CNr1		20 000	El Arjoun MAR
31-01	Nigeria	L	1-2	Port Said	CNr1	Camara.S [59]	5 000	Damon RSA
3-02	Guinea	W	3-2	Alexandria	CNqf	Diop.PB [62], Niang [84], Camara.H [93+]	17 000	Codjia BEN
7-02	Egypt	L	1-2	Cairo	CNsf	Kamara [54]	74 000	Evehe CMR
9-02	Nigeria	L	0-1	Cairo	CN3p		11 354	Coulibaly MLI
1-03	Norway	W	2-1	Dakar	Fr	Moussa N'Diaye [20], Gueye [36]	45 000	Pare BFA
23-05	Korea Republic	D	1-1	Seoul	Fr	Moussa N'Diaye [80]	64 836	

Fr = Friendly match • CN = CAF African Cup of Nations • WC = FIFA World Cup™ • q = qualifier • r1 = first round group • qf = quarter-final

SENEGAL NATIONAL TEAM RECORDS AND RECORD SEQUENCES

Records			Sequence records			
Victory	6-0	MTN 1984	Wins	11	1985-1986	Clean sheets	6	1999-2000
Defeat	0-4	Seven times	Defeats	4	1969-1970	Goals scored	14	1999
Player Caps	n/a		Undefeated	12	1987-1989	Without goal	7	1987
Player Goals	n/a		Without win	12	2000-2001	Goals against	22	1965-1970

SENEGAL COUNTRY INFORMATION

Capital	Dakar	Independence	1960 from France	GDP per Capita	$1 600
Population	10 852 147	Status	Republic	GNP Ranking	115
Area km²	196 190	Language	French, Wolof, Pulaar	Dialling code	+221
Population density	55 per km²	Literacy rate	40%	Internet code	.sn
% in urban areas	42%	Main religion	Muslim	GMT + / −	+0
Towns/Cities ('000)	Dakar 2 406; Thiès 257; Mbour 183; Kaolack 177; Saint Louis 162; Ziguinchor 161; Diourbel 101; Louga 80; Tambacounda 75; Kolda 60; Mbacké 55; Tivaouane 51; Richard-Toll 45				
Neighbours (km)	Mauritania 813; Mali 419; Guinea 330; Guinea-Bissau 338; Gambia 740; Atlantic Ocean 531				
Main stadia	Stade Léopold Senghor (Stade de l'Amitié) – Dakar 60 000				

SENEGAL 2005

CHAMPIONNAT NATIONAL 1ERE DIVISION

	Pl	W	D	L	F	A	Pts	Port Auto.	Diaraf	CSS	Sonacos	Casa	HLM	US Gorée	DUC	Jeanne d'Arc	GFC	Douanes	USO	Ndiambour	Rail	Saloum	Stade	Renaissance	ETICS
Port Autonome Dakar †	34	19	10	5	46	24	67		1-2	1-1	3-0	1-0	1-0	0-1	2-0	3-3	4-1	0-2	1-0	**2-0**	1-0	1-1	0-0	1-0	3-1
ASC Diaraf †	34	13	15	6	26	12	54	0-1		0-1	0-0	0-0	1-0	0-0	0-0	0-0	2-0	1-0	0-1	0-1	5-0	2-0	1-0	1-1	**2-0**
CSS Richard-Toll ‡	34	12	13	9	35	24	49	2-1	0-0		0-0	2-1	2-0	2-0	0-0	0-0	1-1	0-0	3-0	1-2	3-0	1-0	1-2	0-1	1-1
Sonacos Djourbel	34	12	13	9	23	22	49	2-0	0-0	0-3		0-0	0-0	0-0	1-0	1-1	0-1	1-0	2-0	1-0	1-0	0-0	1-2	1-0	3-1
Casa Sport Ziguinchor	34	12	11	11	25	27	47	0-2	0-1	1-0	0-2		0-0	2-1	0-3	2-1	0-0	0-0	3-0	3-2	2-0	1-0	0-0	4-0	1-0
ASC HLM Dakar	34	10	16	8	26	21	46	1-2	1-1	2-1	0-2	1-1		0-2	1-1	0-0	2-0	0-0	1-0	1-0	3-0	0-0	0-1	1-1	1-0
US Gorée	34	11	13	10	30	27	46	0-1	0-0	1-1	2-0	1-1	0-2		0-2	0-1	0-2	2-1	1-0	1-1	0-1	1-1	0-1	1-1	2-0
DUC Dakar	34	10	15	9	34	27	45	1-1	1-0	0-1	0-0	1-0	0-0	1-2		2-1	1-1	1-2	0-1	1-0	1-1	0-0	1-2	1-2	3-0
Jeanne d'Arc	34	10	16	8	35	30	44	1-1	2-2	3-0	0-1	1-1	0-0	2-2	0-0		0-1	**0-2**	2-0	1-0	0-0	1-0	2-1	1-2	2-1
Guédiawaye FC Dakar	34	9	17	8	20	24	44	0-1	0-0	0-0	0-0	1-0	0-0	1-1	0-0	1-2		0-2	0-0	0-0	0-0	2-0	1-2	0-0	1-1
AS Douanes Dakar	34	9	16	9	29	21	43	1-2	0-1	2-0	0-0	0-1	1-1	0-1	2-2	0-0	0-1		0-0	0-0	0-0	0-0	3-0	1-0	4-2
US Ouakam	34	10	11	13	30	37	41	0-2	0-1	1-0	1-1	3-1	0-0	1-0	0-0	4-1	1-1	1-1		1-1	1-4	0-0	3-0	3-3	1-0
ASEC Ndiambour	34	9	14	11	23	30	41	1-1	0-0	0-0	0-2	0-1	1-2	1-1	1-1	0-2	0-0	0-0	1-3		2-1	1-2	1-1	2-1	1-1
US Rail Thiès	34	10	11	13	31	41	41	1-1	1-0	1-1	1-1	2-0	1-0	0-0	2-2	1-1	1-1	2-2	0-1	0-1		1-0	1-1	2-1	1-2
ASC Saloum Kaolack	34	9	12	13	26	30	39	2-2	0-1	2-1	2-0	0-0	1-0	1-0	1-0	2-1	0-1	0-3	3-1	2-0	1-0		0-2	2-0	3-1
Stade Mbour	34	7	17	10	25	31	38	0-0	0-1	0-1	0-0	0-0	1-1	0-1	1-1	1-0	2-1	1-1	0-0	1-2	0-0	0-0		1-1	2-2
Renaissance Yoff	34	8	13	13	29	37	37	0-2	0-0	0-1	2-0	0-0	0-3	1-0	1-2	0-0	1-0	0-0	1-0	3-0	1-2	2-2	0-0		3-1
ETICS Mboro	34	6	7	21	26	56	25	0-1	1-0	1-5	0-1	2-0	0-0	0-2	0-3	0-2	0-1	1-0	1-0	0-0	2-2	0-1	2-2	2-1	

8/01/2005 - 1/10/2005 • † Qualified for the CAF Champions League • ‡ Qualified for the CAF Confederation Cup • Matches in bold awarded

RECENT LEAGUE AND CUP RECORD

	Championship					
Year	Champions	Pts	Runners-up	Pts	Third	Pts
1991	Port Autonome	40	ASC Ndiambour	38	SIDEC Dakar	37
1992	ASC Ndiambour	41	Jeanne d'Arc	39	Port Autonome	37
1993	AS Douanes	54	ASC Diaraf	52	Jeanne d'Arc	46
1994	ASC Ndiambour	†	US Rail Thiès			
1995	ASC Diaraf	2-1	ESO			
1996	Sonacos	‡	Linguère			
1997	AS Douanes	46	Jeanne d'Arc	45	Linguère	43
1998	ASC Ndiambour	47	ASC Diaraf	46	AS Douanes	39
1999	Jeanne d'Arc	53	ASC Ndiambour	46	CSS Richard-Toll	43
2000	ASC Diaraf	37	Port Autoname	36	ASC Ndiambour	35
2001	Jeanne d'Arc	47	ASC Ndiambour	45	US Gorée	44
2002	Jeanne d'Arc	52	Sonacos	42	ASC Ndiambour	39
2003	ASC Diaraf	51	ASC Diaraf	47	AS Douanes	43
2004	ASC Diaraf	72	AS Douanes	69	ASC Ndiambour	65
2005	Port Autonome	67	ASC Diaraf	54	CSS Richard-Toll	49
2006	AS Douanes	14	ASC Diaraf	7	US Gorée	6

	Cup	
Winners	Score	Runners-up
ASC Diaraf	2-1	Jeanne d'Arc
US Gorée	2-1	ASC Diaraf
ASC Diaraf	2-0	Linguère
ASC Diaraf	1-0	CSS
ASC Diaraf	2-0	AS Douanes
US Gorée	1-0	ASC Ndiambour
AS Douanes	3-1	Linguère
ASC Yeggo	1-0	US Gorée
ASC Ndiambour	1-1 3-0p	Sonacos
Port Autonome	4-0	AS Saloum
Sonacos	1-0	US Gorée
AS Douanes	1-1 4-1p	Sonacos
AS Douanes	1-0	ASC Thiès
AS Douanes	2-1	ASC Diaraf
AS Douanes	1-0	DUC Dakar

† Ndiambour won 4-3 on penalties after a 0-0 draw • ‡ Sonacos 3-0 0-1 Linguère

SENEGAL 2005–06

CHAMPIONNAT NATIONAL 1ERE DIVISION POULE A

	Pl	W	D	L	F	A	Pts	Douanes	Diaraf	GFC	Stade	Sonacos	Yakaar	CSS	DUC	Ndiambour
AS Douanes Dakar †	16	7	7	2	16	8	28		1-1	2-1	0-1	0-0	1-2	2-1	0-0	3-0
ASC Diaraf Dakar †	16	5	9	2	13	10	24	1-1		0-0	2-1	1-2	0-0	0-0	2-1	1-0
Guédiawaye FC Dakar	16	4	8	4	10	11	20	0-2	0-0		0-1	0-0	0-0	0-0	0-0	1-0
Stade Mbour	16	4	8	4	9	10	20	0-1	1-1	1-3		0-0	0-0	0-0	0-0	1-0
Sonacos Djoubel	16	3	10	3	7	10	19	0-0	0-0	0-1	0-0		0-0	1-1	2-1	0-0
ASC Yakaar Rufisque	16	3	9	4	10	9	18	0-1	0-0	1-2	1-0	3-0		0-0	1-2	0-0
CSS Richard-Toll	16	3	8	5	11	13	17	0-1	2-1	1-1	2-3	0-1	2-1		1-0	0-1
DUC Dakar	16	2	10	4	11	12	16	1-1	0-1	1-1	0-0	3-1	1-1	1-1		0-0
ASEC Ndiambour	16	2	9	5	4	8	15	0-0	1-2	2-0	0-0	0-0	0-0	0-0	0-0	

4/01/2006 - 7/06/2006 • † Qualified for the play-offs

SENEGAL 2005–06

CHAMPIONNAT NATIONAL 1ERE DIVISION POULE B

	Pl	W	D	L	F	A	Pts	HLM	Gorée	Port Auto	Jeanne d'Arc	Xam-Xam	Casa Sport	Saloum	USO	Rail
ASC HLM Dakar †	16	9	5	2	20	10	32		1-1	3-0	0-1	1-0	1-0	2-1	0-0	3-1
US Gorée †	16	6	9	1	21	12	27	2-2		0-0	2-2	0-0	4-1	2-1	3-1	2-1
Port Autonome Dakar	16	6	8	2	15	10	26	1-1	0-0		0-0	0-0	2-1	1-1	1-0	2-2
Jeanne d'Arc	16	7	5	4	14	13	26	1-0	0-1	0-0		0-2	2-0	1-1	1-1	2-0
ASC Xam-Xam Dakar	16	5	5	6	12	10	20	0-1	1-1	0-3	0-1		0-0	0-0	3-0	1-0
Casa Sport Ziguinchor	16	5	4	7	13	15	19	0-0	0-0	0-1	4-0	2-1		0-1	0-0	2-1
ASC Saloum Kaolack	16	4	5	7	10	15	17	1-2	1-0	0-2	0-1	1-0	1-2		1-0	0-0
US Ouakam	16	4	4	8	10	16	16	1-2	1-1	1-0	2-0	0-2	0-1	2-0		0-1
US Rail Thiès	16	2	3	11	8	22	9	0-1	0-2	1-2	0-2	0-2	1-0	0-0	0-1	

4/01/2006 - 8/06/2006 • † Qualified for the play-offs

SENEGAL 2005–06

CHAMPIONNAT NATIONAL 1ERE DIVISION PLAY-OFFS

	Pl	W	D	L	F	A	Pts	Douanes	Diaraf	Goreé	HLM
AS Douanes Dakar †	6	4	2	0	12	4	14		1-0	2-0	3-2
ASC Diaraf Dakar †	6	1	4	1	8	8	7	2-2		2-2	2-1
US Goree	6	1	3	2	6	11	6	0-4	2-2		0-0
ASC HLM Dakar	6	0	3	3	4	7	3	0-0	0-0	1-2	

21/06/2006 - 8/07/2006 • † Qualified for the CAF Champions League

COUPE NATIONALE 2005

Eighth-finals		Quarter-finals		Semi-finals		Final	
AS Douanes	1						
Stade Thiaroye	0	AS Douanes	0 4p				
St Louis Foot Center	0	US Gorée	0 3p				
US Gorée	3			AS Douanes	1		
ETICS Mboro	1			Casa Sport	0		
Port Autonome	0	ETICS Mboro	0				
US Ouakam	0	Casa Sport	1			AS Douanes ‡	1
Casa Sport	1					DUC Dakar	0
Sonacos	2						
Ndiambour Louga	0	Sonacos					
Diamono Diourbel	0	Jeunesse Fass		Sonacos	0		
Jeunesse Fass	2			DUC Dakar	2		
ASC Diaraf	4						
CNEPS Thiès	0	ASC Diaraf	0 3p				
Xam-Xam Yarakh	1	DUC Dakar	0 4p				
DUC Dakar	2						

‡ Qualified for the CAF Confederation Cup

CUP FINAL
Stade de l'Amitie, Dakar
16-10-2005, Ref: Seck
Scorer - Maguette Mbengue Dème 90 for Douanes

SEY – SEYCHELLES

NATIONAL TEAM RECORD
JULY 1ST 2002 TO JULY 9TH 2006

PL	W	D	L	F	A	%
15	4	3	8	10	23	36.7

FIFA/COCA-COLA WORLD RANKING

1993	1994	1995	1996	1997	1998	1999	2000	2001	2002	2003	2004	2005		High		Low
157	175	176	175	181	181	192	188	192	185	163	173	176		141 07/06		195 07/02

2005–2006											
08/05	09/05	10/05	11/05	12/05	01/06	02/06	03/06	04/06	05/06	06/06	07/06
174	173	174	174	176	176	176	176	176	176	-	141

An ambitious federation with a vision for the future is beginning to see some of the fruits of its labour, but Africa's smallest country is always going to be hampered by its lack of population. With only around 80,000 citizens, playing resources on the islands are limited although there is no end of opportunity. Driven by the Seychelles Football Federation president Suketu Patel, a member of the executive committee of the CAF and several FIFA standing committees, the Seychelles boast an energetic administration, a specialist referees development officer and a picturesque home for their football, complete with artificial pitches just metres away from the tropical beaches that have

INTERNATIONAL HONOURS
None

made the country such a picture of paradise. The Seychelles played their only international football of the past 12 months during the FIFA World Cup finals in Germany. The independence anniversary tournament in Victoria provided the newly-named 'Pirates', a nickname chosen in a public competition, with unprecedented back-to-back wins over traditional rivals Mauritius and Tanzania. It ensured a highest-ever ranking of 141 for the Seychelles in the FIFA/Coca-Cola World Ranking. In domestic competition, La Passe won their third title in the last four years while the Seychelles Marketing Board took a first ever trophy with Cup success.

THE FIFA BIG COUNT OF 2000

	Male	Female		Male	Female
Registered players	1 328	140	Referees	39	5
Non registered players	400	0	Officials	295	0
Youth players	1 028	0	Total involved	3 235	
Total players	2 896		Number of clubs	55	
Professional players	0	0	Number of teams	55	

Seychelles Football Federation (SFF)
People's Stadium, PO Box 843, Victoria, Mahe, Seychelles
Tel +248 324632   Fax +248 225468
sff@seychelles.net   www.sff.sc
President: PATEL Suketu   General Secretary: TBD
Vice-President: ADAM Nicholas   Treasurer: MATHIOT Justin   Media Officer: none
Men's Coach: SHUNGU Rahoul   Women's Coach: none
SFF formed: 1979   CAF: 1986   FIFA: 1986
Red shirts, Red shorts, Red socks

RECENT INTERNATIONAL MATCHES PLAYED BY THE SEYCHELLES

2002	Opponents	Score		Venue	Comp	Scorers	Att	Referee
8-09	Eritrea	W	1-0	Victoria	CNq	Victor [50]	3 000	Ravelontsalama MAD
26-09	Mauritius	L	0-1	Port Louis	Fr		166	Roopnah MRI
13-10	Mali	L	0-3	Bamako	CNq		50 000	Sorie SLE
2003								
30-03	Zimbabwe	L	1-3	Harare	CNq	Zialor [90]	60 000	Bernardo Colembi ANG
7-06	Zimbabwe	W	2-1	Victoria	CNq	Balde [73p], Zialor [87]	12 000	Mangaliso SWZ
21-06	Eritrea	L	0-1	Asmara	CNq			
5-07	Mali	L	0-2	Victoria	CNq		5 000	Lim Kee Chong MRI
28-08	Madagascar	D	1-1	Curepipe	IOr1	Balde [87]	1 000	Lim Kee Chong MRI
2-09	Mauritius	D	0-0	Curepipe	IOr1			
4-09	Reunion	L	0-1	Curepipe	IOr1		1 000	
11-10	Zambia	L	0-4	Victoria	WCq		2 700	Lim Kee Chong MRI
15-11	Zambia	D	1-1	Lusaka	WCq	Suzette [69]	30 000	Abdulkadir TAN
2004								
No international matches played in 2004								
2005								
26-02	South Africa	L	0-3	Curepipe	CCr1			Roheemun MRI
2006								
28-06	Mauritius	W	2-1	Victoria	Fr	Brutus [47], Ladouche		
30-06	Tanzania	W	2-1	Victoria	Fr	Rose [23], Zialor [81]		

Fr = Friendly match • CN = CAN African Cup of Nations • IO = Indian Ocean Games • CC = COSAFA Castle Cup • WC = FIFA World Cup™
q = qualifier • r1 = first round group

SEYCHELLES NATIONAL TEAM RECORDS AND RECORD SEQUENCES

Records			Sequence records					
Victory	9-0	MDV 1979	Wins	2	2006	Clean sheets	1	
Defeat	0-6	MAD 1990	Defeats	11	1992-1996	Goals scored	4	1979-1983
Player Caps	n/a		Undefeated	2	Four times	Without goal	3	Three times
Player Goals	n/a		Without win	14	1992-1998	Goals against	17	1990-1998

SEYCHELLES 2004 FIRST DIVISION

	Pl	W	D	L	F	A	Pts
La Passe	18	13	5	0	47	14	44
St Louis Victoria	18	12	5	1	31	11	41
Anse Réunion	18	9	4	5	28	21	31
St Michael United	18	8	5	5	23	15	29
Red Star	18	7	3	8	17	19	24
Seychelles MB	18	7	2	9	23	19	23
Sunshine Victoria	18	7	1	10	25	29	22
Light Stars	18	6	3	9	25	24	22
Survivors	18	3	3	12	18	37	12
Baie St Anne 96ers	18	2	1	15	10	58	7

2/06/2005 - 30/10/2005

RECENT LEAGUE AND CUP RECORD

	Championship		Cup		
Year	Champions	Winners	Score	Runners-up	
1996	St Michel United	St Louis			
1997	St Michel United	St Michel			
1998	Red Star	St Michel United	4-0	Ascot	
1999	St Michel United	Red Star	2-1	Sunshine	
2000	St Michel United	Sunshine	1-1 4-2p	Red Star	
2001	Red Star	St Michel United	2-1	Sunshine	
2002	La Passe	Anse Reunion	2-1	Red Star	
2003	St Michel United	St Louis	2-1	Light Stars	
2004	La Passe	Red Star	1-0	Anse Réunion	
2005	La Passe	Seychelles MB	1-0	Anse Réunion	

SEYCHELLES COUNTRY INFORMATION

Capital	Victoria	Independence	1976 from the UK	GDP per Capita	$7 800
Population	80 832	Status	Republic	GNP Ranking	169
Area km²	455	Language	English, French, Creole	Dialling code	+248
Population density	177 per km²	Literacy rate	58%	Internet code	.sc
% in urban areas	54%	Main religion	Christian	GMT +/−	+4
Towns/Cities	Victoria 26 361				
Neighbours (km)	Indian Ocean 491				
Main stadia	Stade Linité – Victoria 12 000				

SIN – SINGAPORE

NATIONAL TEAM RECORD
JULY 1ST 2002 TO JULY 9TH 2006

PL	W	D	L	F	A	%
49	21	10	18	70	66	53.1

FIFA/COCA-COLA WORLD RANKING

1993	1994	1995	1996	1997	1998	1999	2000	2001	2002	2003	2004	2005	High	Low
75	95	104	92	103	81	104	101	115	118	106	112	92	73 08/93	121 09/04

2005–2006											
08/05	09/05	10/05	11/05	12/05	01/06	02/06	03/06	04/06	05/06	06/06	07/06
99	99	95	95	92	92	93	92	92	92	-	111

With the finals of the 2007 AFC Asian Cup being played right on their doorstep, Singapore are determined not to miss out on what would virtually be a home tournament for them. They started off their qualifiers in style by beating Iraq 2-0 at home but then lost to Palestine in Amman. With China PR the other team in the group, making the finals won't be easy. In the friendly match against Cambodia in October 2005 Singapore completed a run of nine successive wins and 13 matches unbeaten to establish a record that may take some time to eclipse. The run was ended in January with a 1-2 defeat at the hands of Denmark. Club football continues to thrive in the coun-

INTERNATIONAL HONOURS
Tiger Cup 1998 2002

try with Tampines Rovers successfully defending their S.League title to claim an AFC Cup spot for 2006. The other went to Cup winners Home United, AFC Cup semi-finalists in 2004. In the Cup Final they beat Woodlands Wellington 3-2 in an exciting game to win the trophy for the fourth time in six seasons, with the winner coming from Indra Sahdan Daud three minutes into injury time. In the 2005 AFC Cup both Tampines Rovers and Home United had qualified from their first round groups but then fell at the quarter-final stage; Tampines to eventual winners Al Faysali from Jordan and Home United to eventual runners-up Al Nejmeh from Lebanon.

THE FIFA BIG COUNT OF 2000

	Male	Female		Male	Female
Registered players	1 280	0	Referees	125	0
Non registered players	50 000	300	Officials	120	20
Youth players	5 700	0	Total involved	57 545	
Total players	57 280		Number of clubs	136	
Professional players	200	0	Number of teams	563	

Football Association of Singapore (FAS)
100 Tyrwhitt Road, Singapore 207542
Tel +65 63483477   Fax +65 63921194
johnkoh@fas.org.sg   www.fas.org.sg
President: HO Peng Kee   General Secretary: KOH John
Vice-President: ZAINUDIN Nordin   Treasurer: CHAN Ket Teck   Media Officer: HO Stanley
Men's Coach: AVRAMOVIC Radojko   Women's Coach: NOOR Abdullah B.
FAS formed: 1892   AFC: 1954   FIFA: 1952
Red shirts with white trimmings, Red shorts, Red socks

RECENT INTERNATIONAL MATCHES PLAYED BY SINGAPORE

2003	Opponents		Score	Venue	Comp	Scorers	Att	Referee
4-03	Maldives	W	4-1	Singapore	Fr	Baksin [8], Indra Sahdan Daud [17], Fadhil [22], Juraimi [67]		Bashir MAS
23-03	Macao	W	2-0	Singapore	ACq	Baksin [18], Indra Sahdan Daud [59]		
25-03	Pakistan	W	3-0	Singapore	ACq	Indra Sahdan Daud 2 [4 33p], Noh Alam Shah [66]		
4-08	Hong Kong	W	4-1	Singapore	Fr	Bennett [7], Juaimi [16], Indra Sahdan Daud 2 [67 77]		
4-09	Kuwait	L	1-3	Singapore	ACq	Goncalves [50]		Sun Baojie CHN
16-09	Oman	L	1-3	Singapore	Fr	Indra Sahdan Daud [66]		Abdul Hamid MAS
27-09	Kuwait	L	0-4	Kuwait City	ACq			
19-10	Palestine	W	2-0	Singapore	ACq	Juraimi [18], Noh Alam Shah [89]		Sarkar IND
22-10	Palestine	D	0-0	Singapore	ACq			Vidanagamage SRI
19-11	Qatar	L	0-2	Doha	ACq			
29-11	Qatar	L	0-2	Singapore	ACq			Hamlumyaung THA
2004								
28-01	Norway	L	2-5	Singapore	Fr	Bennett [45], Ishak [51]	5 000	Supian MAS
18-02	India	L	0-1	Margoa	WCq		28 000	Yasrebi IRN
31-03	Japan	L	1-2	Singapore	WCq	Indra Sahdan Daud [62]	6 000	Bae Jae Yong KOR
9-06	Oman	L	0-7	Muscat	WCq		2 000	Ebrahim BHR
12-07	Malaysia	L	0-2	Kuala Lumpur	Fr		2 000	
4-09	Indonesia	W	2-0	Singapore	Fr		3 030	Vo Minh Tri VIE
8-09	Oman	L	0-2	Singapore	WCq		4 000	Arambekade SRI
8-10	United Arab Emirates	L	1-2	Singapore	Fr	Masturi [60]	2 809	Ong MAS
13-10	India	W	2-0	Singapore	WCq	Indra Sahdan Daud [73], Kairul Amri Mohd [76]	3 609	Husain BHR
1-11	Malaysia	L	1-2	Singapore	Fr	Dickson [21]	3 293	Luong VIE
17-11	Japan	L	0-1	Saitama	WCq		58 881	Torky IRN
27-11	Myanmar	W	1-0	Singapore	Fr	Noh Alam Shah [78]	4 881	Hadi IDN
30-11	Hong Kong	D	0-0	Singapore	Fr	L 5-6p	3 359	Phaengsupha THA
7-12	Vietnam	D	1-1	Ho Chi Minh City	TCr1	Indra Sahdan Daud [70]	20 000	Sun Baojie CHN
9-12	Indonesia	D	0-0	Ho Chi Minh City	TCr1		4 000	Kwon Jong Chul KOR
13-12	Laos	W	6-2	Hanoi	TCr1	Jailani [7], Indra Sahdan Daud 2 [19 74], OG [41], Casmir 2 [45 90p]	17 000	Supian MAS
15-12	Cambodia	W	3-0	Hanoi	TCr1	Dickson [21], Khaizan [27], Khairul Amri [54]	2 000	Ebrahim BHR
29-12	Myanmar	W	4-3	Kuala Lumpur	TCsf	Bennet [21], Casmir [39], Noh Alam Shah [64], Ishak [82]	12 000	Rungklay THA
2005								
2-01	Myanmar	W	4-2	Singapore	TCsf	Noh Alam Shah 3 [74 94 95], Casmir [110]	30 000	Kamikawa JPN
8-01	Indonesia	W	3-1	Jakarta	TCf	Bennett [5], Khairul Amri [39], Casmir [69]	120000	Kwon Jong Chul KOR
16-01	Indonesia	W	2-1	Singapore	TCf	Indra Sahdan Daud [5], Casmir [40p]	55 000	Al Ghamdi KSA
4-06	Malaysia	W	2-0	Singapore	Fr	Noh Alam Shah 2 [32 93+]	18 000	Kunsuta THA
8-06	Malaysia	W	2-1	Pinang	Fr	Noh Alam Shah [19], Bennett [66]	10 000	Napitupulu IDN
11-10	Cambodia	W	2-0	Phnom Penh	Fr	Shahril Ishak 2 [44 88]		
2006								
26-01	Denmark	L	1-2	Singapore	Fr	Indra Sahdan Daud [89]	10 392	Srinivasan IND
3-02	Kuwait	D	2-2	Kuwait City	Fr	Khairul Amri [73], Indra Sahdan Daud [90]		
6-02	Oman	L	0-1	Doha	Fr			
15-02	Hong Kong	D	1-1	Hong Kong	Fr	Noh Alam Shah [66p]	610	Heng MAS
22-02	Iraq	W	2-0	Singapore	ACq	Khairul Amri [24], Noh Alam Shah [83]	10 221	Shield AUS
1-03	Palestine	L	0-1	Amman	ACq		1 000	Al Hilali OMA
31-05	Malaysia	D	0-0	Singapore	Fr	W 5-4p	18 604	Li Yuhong CHN
3-06	Malaysia	D	0-0	Paroi	Fr	W 8-7p		

Fr = Friendly match • AC = AFC Asian Cup • TC = ASEAN Tiger Cup • WC = FIFA World Cup™
q = qualifier • r1 = first round group • sf = semi-final • f = final

SINGAPORE NATIONAL TEAM RECORDS AND RECORD SEQUENCES

Records			Sequence records				
Victory	8-1	IDN 1986	Wins	9	2004-2005	Clean sheets	4	1985
Defeat	0-9	MYA 1969	Defeats	9	1977	Goals scored	14	1993-1995
Player Caps	105	ISKANDAR Aide	Undefeated	13	2004-2005	Without goal	5	1976-1977
Player Goals	n/a		Without win	19	1966-1968	Goals against	36	1966-1970

SINGAPORE COUNTRY INFORMATION

Capital	Singapore City	Independence	1965 from Malaysia	GDP per Capita	$23 700
Population	4 353 893	Status	Republic	GNP Ranking	38
Area km²	693	Language	Chinese, English, Malay	Dialling code	+65
Population density	6 282 per km²	Literacy rate	92%	Internet code	.sg
% in urban areas	100%	Main religion	Buddhist 54%, Muslim 15%	GMT + / –	+8
Towns/Cities ('000)	Singapore City 3 547				
Neighbours (km)	Strait of Singapore & Johore Strait 193				
Main stadia	Jalan Besar – Singapore 6 000; National Stadium – Singapore 55 000				

SINGAPORE 2005

S.LEAGUE

	Pl	W	D	L	F	A	Pts	Tampines	SAF	Woodlands	Home Utd	Albirex	Young Lions	Balestier	Geylang	Sinchi	Paya Lebar
Tampines Rovers †	27	18	3	6	77	35	57		3-2 3-5	2-2	2-1 3-5	2-2 2-4	1-0	3-0	7-0	4-1	2-0 5-0
Sing. Armed Forces	27	15	7	5	54	41	52	3-2		5-1 2-4	1-0	1-0	1-1 3-0	1-1 3-2	1-0 3-3	0-1	3-2
Woodlands Wellington	27	15	5	7	57	44	50	0-3 1-2	2-0		0-0	2-1 2-1	2-2	3-3 4-1	1-4 2-0	3-1	4-1 4-0
Home United	27	14	4	9	62	44	46	0-2	0-1 5-1	4-0 4-2		0-3	3-0	3-2	4-4 3-1	2-1 1-0	4-0 3-2
Albirex Niigata	27	12	8	7	50	33	44	0-0	2-3 2-2	0-0	4-0 3-2		1-3 4-2	0-1 0-0	4-1	0-0 2-0	2-0
Young Lions	27	12	6	9	44	37	42	1-3 3-1	2-2	2-3 3-1	2-2 2-3	0-0		3-1	0-1	1-0	2-0 3-1
Balestier Khalsa	27	10	6	11	45	52	36	2-0 1-4	1-1	1-3	3-2 0-5	1-3	0-1 0-2		2-2 4-3	1-2	3-1
Geylang United	27	7	5	15	38	57	26	0-3 0-2	0-1	0-2	0-3	1-1 2-3	1-0 0-2	0-1		3-1 2-1	4-0
Sinchi	27	7	3	17	27	56	24	0-4 0-5	0-2 2-2	2-4 0-3	2-0	2-1	1-3 0-2	2-3 0-3	2-2		2-1
Paya Lebar Punggol	27	1	1	25	23	78	4	0-5	0-1 2-4	0-2	2-3	1-2 1-3	2-2	1-4 0-3	3-2 1-2	2-3 0-1	

1/03/2005 - 28/10/2005 • † Qualified for the AFC Cup

SINGAPORE CUP 2005

First round

Home United	Bye
DPMM Brunei	0
Sinchi *	2
Young Lions *	1
Geylang United	0
Tampines Rovers	Bye
Sing. Armed Forces	1
Balestier Khalso *	0
Paya Lebar Punggol *	1
Indonesia U-23	2
Albirex Niigata *	1
Thai Provincial EA	0
Tampines Rovers	0
Woodlands Wellington*	2

Quarter-finals

Home United	3 1
Sinchi *	1 0
Young Lions	1 2
Tampines Rovers *	3 2
Sing. Armed Forces *	3 6
Indonesia U-23	0 1
Albirex Niigata	3 2
Woodlands Wellington*	5 1

Semi-finals

Home United *	2 2
Tampines Rovers	3 0
Sing. Armed Forces	2 0
Woodlands Wellington*	2 1

Final

Home United †	3
Woodlands Wellington	2

* Home Team in the first leg • † Qualified for the AFC Cup

CUP FINAL

National Stadium, Kallang
6-11-2005, Att: 12 000, Ref: Abdul Malik
Scorers - Indra Sahdan Daud 2 60 93+, Fadzuhasny Juraimi 63 for Hime Utd; Lucian Dronca 7, Azmi Mahamud 78 for Woodlands

RECENT LEAGUE AND CUP RECORD

	Championship					
Year	Champions	Pts	Runners-up	Pts	Third	Pts
1997	Sing. Armed Forces	37	Tanjong Pagar Utd	34	Woodlands Well'ton	33
1998	Sing. Armed Forces	46	Tanjong Pagar Utd	46	Geylang United	38
1999	Home United	51	Sing. Armed Forces	49	Tanjong Pagar Utd	41
2000	Sing. Armed Forces	52	Tanjong Pagar Utd	43	Geylang United	41
2001	Geylang United	76	Sing. Armed Forces	74	Home United	72
2002	Sing. Armed Forces	84	Home United	64	Geylang United	59
2003	Home United	85	Geylang United	71	Sing. Armed Forces	69
2004	Tampines Rovers	63	Home United	53	Young Lions	47
2005	Tampines Rovers	57	Sing. Armed Forces	52	Woodlands Well'ton	50

Cup		
Winners	Score	Runners-up
Sing. Armed Forces	4-2	Woodlands Well'ton
Tanjong Pagar Utd	2-0	Sing. Armed Forces
Sing. Armed Forces	3-1	Jurong
Home United	1-0	Sing. Armed Forces
Home United	8-0	Geylang United
Tampines Rovers	1-0	Jurong
Home United	2-1	Geylang United
Tampines Rovers	4-1	Home United
Home United	3-2	Woodlands Well'ton

SKN – ST KITTS AND NEVIS

NATIONAL TEAM RECORD
JULY 1ST 2002 TO JULY 9TH 2006

PL	W	D	L	F	A	%
28	13	2	13	49	49	50

FIFA/COCA-COLA WORLD RANKING

1993	1994	1995	1996	1997	1998	1999	2000	2001	2002	2003	2004	2005		High	Low
166	175	150	121	127	132	137	146	129	109	134	118	129		**108** 07/04	**176** 11/94

2005–2006											
08/05	09/05	10/05	11/05	12/05	01/06	02/06	03/06	04/06	05/06	06/06	07/06
122	124	124	128	129	129	129	131	132	133	-	136

Football in St Kitts and Nevis continues to grow despite the country having one of the smaller populations in the Caribbean. Teams were entered into both the FIFA Women's World Cup and the FIFA U-20 Women's World Championship although unsurprisingly neither made it past the first round of the Caribbean qualifiers. The senior team fared slightly better in their group in Jamaica starting off with a 3-2 win over Antigua and Barbuda. That was followed by a 3-2 reverse at the hands of St Lucia before a heavy 11-0 defeat by hosts Jamaica. St Kitts hosted a four team group in the U-20 event but that couldn't stop three straight defeats without a single goal being scored.

INTERNATIONAL HONOURS
None

In the men's game there was no entry into the CONCACAF Champions' Cup despite the fact that the league in the country is well organised and structured. There was some controversy when after the first round group stage, the Super Four play-offs suddenly turned into the Super Five play-offs, bringing the championship to a standstill. Garden Hotspurs had complained that their elimination on goal difference was unfair due to an awarded match and they were backed up by the National Olympic Committee. It had no bearing on the outcome of the championship as Village Superstars retained their title after beating St Paul's United 6-1 on aggregate in the final.

THE FIFA BIG COUNT OF 2000

	Male	Female		Male	Female
Registered players	825	0	Referees	0	0
Non registered players	500	0	Officials	100	
Youth players	500	75	Total involved	2 000	
Total players	1 900		Number of clubs	31	
Professional players	0	0	Number of teams	32	

St Kitts and Nevis Football Association (SKNFA)
Warner Park, PO Box 465, Basseterre, St Kitts and Nevis
Tel +1 869 4668502   Fax +1 869 4659033
info@sknfa.com   www.sknfa.com
President: JENKINS Peter   General Secretary: AMORY Spencer Leonard
Vice-President: FRASER Sylvester   Treasurer: AMORY Spencer Leonard   Media Officer: None
Men's Coach: TAYLOR Leonard & BROWNE Elvis   Women's Coach: none
SKNFA formed: 1932   CONCACAF: 1992   FIFA: 1992
Green shirts, Red shorts, Yellow socks

RECENT INTERNATIONAL MATCHES PLAYED BY ST KITTS AND NEVIS

2002	Opponents	Score		Venue	Comp	Scorers	Att	Referee
25-07	Chinese Taipei	W	3-0	Basseterre	Fr			
27-07	Barbados	W	3-0	Basseterre	Fr	Issac, Francis, Gumbs		
28-07	Trinidad and Tobago	W	2-1	Basseterre	Fr	Sargeant [49], Issac [75]	800	
29-10	Antigua and Barbuda	D	1-1	Basseterre	Fr			
13-11	St Lucia	W	2-1	Port of Spain	GCq	Isaac 2 [38 56]		Forde BRB
15-11	Trinidad and Tobago	L	0-2	Port of Spain	GCq		3 500	Faneijte ANT
2003								
29-07	Haiti	W	1-0	Basseterre	Fr	Isaac [3]		Matthew SKN
2-08	Trinidad and Tobago	L	1-2	Basseterre	Fr	Francis [50]		
2004								
1-02	Antigua and Barbuda	L	0-1	St John's	Fr			
18-02	US Virgin Islands	W	4-0	St Thomas	WCq	Huggins [26], Lake 2 [50 64], Isaac [62]	225	Brizan TRI
20-03	British Virgin Islands	W	4-0	Basseterre	Fr			
21-03	Antigua and Barbuda	L	2-3	Basseterre	Fr			
31-03	US Virgin Islands	W	7-0	Basseterre	WCq	Lake 5 [8 38 46 56 77], Isaac 2 [80 90]	800	Recinos SLV
23-05	St Vincent/Grenadines	W	3-2	Basseterre	Fr	Lake [9], Hodge [25], Willock [63]		Matthew SKN
2-06	Northern Ireland	L	0-2	Basseterre	Fr		5 000	Matthew SKN
13-06	Barbados	W	2-0	Bridgetown	WCq	Gumbs [78], Newton [88]	3 700	Alfaro SLV
19-06	Barbados	W	3-2	Basseterre	WCq	Gomez [16], Willock 2 [22 29]	3 500	Pineda HON
4-09	Trinidad and Tobago	L	1-2	Basseterre	WCq	Isaac [40]	2 800	Castillo GUA
10-09	St Vincent/Grenadines	L	0-1	Kingstown	WCq		4 000	Delgado CUB
10-10	Trinidad and Tobago	L	1-5	Marabella	WCq	Gumbs [43p]	7 000	Valenzuela USA
13-10	St Vincent/Grenadines	L	0-3	Basseterre	WCq		500	Whittaker CAY
31-10	Montserrat	W	6-1	Basseterre	GCq	Francis 3 [9 45 86], Connonier [36], Isaac [57], Hodge [83]		Bedeau GRN
2-11	St Lucia	D	1-1	Basseterre	GCq	Francis [14]		Bedeau GRN
4-11	Antigua and Barbuda	W	2-0	Basseterre	GCq	Sargeant [34], Isaac [45]		Phillip GRN
13-11	Mexico	L	0-5	Miami	WCq		18 312	Moreno PAN
17-11	Mexico	L	0-8	Monterrey	WCq		12 000	Stott USA
12-12	Haiti	L	0-1	Fort Lauderdale	GCq		2 500	McNab BAH
15-12	Haiti	L	0-2	Basseterre	GCq		1 000	Bhimull TRI
2005								
No international matches played in 2005								
2006								
No international matches played in 2006 before July								

Fr = Friendly match • GC = CONCACAF Gold Cup • WC = FIFA World Cup™ • q = qualifier

ST KITTS AND NEVIS NATIONAL TEAM RECORDS AND RECORD SEQUENCES

Records			Sequence records					
Victory	9-1	MSR 1994	Wins	4	1996, 2002	Clean sheets	3	1991-1992
Defeat	0-8	MEX 2004	Defeats	4	2004 (Twice)	Goals scored	10	1998-99, 2001
Player Caps	n/a		Undefeated	10	2001-2002	Without goal	4	2004
Player Goals	n/a		Without win	5	1996	Goals against	14	1998-2000

ST KITTS AND NEVIS COUNTRY INFORMATION

Capital	Basseterre	Independence	1983 from the UK	GDP per Capita	$8 800
Population	38 836	Status	Constitutional Monarchy	GNP Ranking	177
Area km²	261	Language	English	Dialling code	+1869
Population density	148 per km²	Literacy rate	97%	Internet code	.kn
% in urban areas	42%	Main religion	Christian	GMT +/−	-4
Towns/Cities	Basseterre 12 920; Charlestown 1 538; Saint Paul's 1 483; Sadlers 986; Middle Island 887				
Neighbours (km)	Caribbean Sea 135				
Main stadia	Warner Park – Basseterre 6 000				

ST KITTS 2005-06 PREMIER DIVISION

	Pl	W	D	L	F	A	Pts
Newtown United †	18	13	4	1	44	11	43
Village Superstars †	18	11	1	6	39	20	34
St Paul's United †	18	9	2	7	21	19	29
Conaree United	18	8	4	6	23	15	28
Garden Hotspurs †	18	9	1	8	24	17	28
St Peter's	18	4	1	13	11	46	13
Cayon Rockets	18	2	1	15	12	46	7

21/11/2004 - 5/03/2005 • † Qualified for play-offs

ST KITTS 2005-06 PREMIER DIVISION SUPER FOUR

	Pl	W	D	L	F	A	Pts
Village Superstars †	3	3	0	0	7	3	9
St Paul's United †	3	1	1	1	2	2	4
Garden Hotspurs	3	1	0	2	7	8	3
Newtown United	3	0	1	2	4	7	1

12/03/2005 - 23/03/2005 • † Qualified for the final

ST KITTS AND NEVIS 2005-06 PREMIER DIVISION FINAL

Champions	Score	Runners-up
Village Superstars	3-1 3-0	St Paul's United

RECENT LEAGUE AND CUP RECORD

	Championship				Cup		
Year	Champions	Score	Runners-up		Winners	Score	Runners-up
1997	Newtown United						
1998	Newtown United						
1999	St Paul's United	3-0 0-1 4-2	Garden Hotspurs				
2000	No tournament due to season adjustment						
2001	Garden Hotspurs	3-0 0-0 3-4p 1-0	Village Superstars				
2002	Cayon Rockets	0-0 3-2p 3-0	Garden Hotspurs		Cayon Rockets		
2003	Village Superstars	0-1 2-1 0-0 5-4p	Newtown United		Village Superstars	1-0	Newtown United
2004	Newtown United	0-1 1-0 2-0	Village Superstars		Village Superstars	3-1	Cayon Rockets
2005	Village Superstars	1-0 2-1	St Peter's				
2006	Village Superstars	3-1 3-0	St Paul's United				

SLE – SIERRA LEONE

NATIONAL TEAM RECORD
JULY 1ST 2002 TO JULY 9TH 2006

PL	W	D	L	F	A	%
13	5	3	5	12	10	50

FIFA/COCA-COLA WORLD RANKING

1993	1994	1995	1996	1997	1998	1999	2000	2001	2002	2003	2004	2005		High	Low
76	76	58	84	84	111	120	129	138	133	146	160	163		51 01/96	165 05/06

	2005–2006										
	08/05	09/05	10/05	11/05	12/05	01/06	02/06	03/06	04/06	05/06	06/06	07/06
	162	162	162	162	163	163	163	163	165	165	-	155

Sierra Leone's slow development after years of absence from real international competition, and a dearth of domestic league competition, began with participation in the regional Amilcar Cabral Cup at the end of 2005. Without any of their overseas-based players, the national team played against Guinea and Guinea Bissau in their first competitive internationals since elimination at the hands of Congo at the start of the 2006 FIFA World Cup™ qualifiers in November 2003, but they didn't make it past the first round in Conakry. At club level, East End Lions represented the country in the 2006 CAF Champions League but the gulf between them and the established clubs in the

INTERNATIONAL HONOURS
Copa Amilcar Cabral 1993 1995

West African region was cruelly exposed when they lost both home and away to ASEC Abidjan from Cote d'Ivoire in the first round. In 2007 it will be the turn of new champions FC Kallon, the side that is bankrolled by Sierra Leone's most high profile export - Mohamed Kallon. In 2005 he helped Saudi club Al Ittihad to win the Asian Champions League title while on loan from Monaco. It was the first time a player from Sierra Leone had won continental honours. FC Kallon have only been in existence for the last five years and Kallon is building a modern training facility for the team on the outskirts of the capital Freetown.

THE FIFA BIG COUNT OF 2000

	Male	Female		Male	Female
Registered players	600	240	Referees	246	17
Non registered players	15 000	150	Officials	2 120	80
Youth players	5 640	0	Total involved	24 093	
Total players	21 630		Number of clubs	24	
Professional players	0	0	Number of teams	196	

Sierra Leone Football Association (SLFA)
21 Battery Street, Kingtom, PO Box 672, Freetown, Sierra Leone
Tel +232 22 240071   Fax +232 22 241339
Starssierra@yahoo.com   www.slfa.tk
President: KHADI Nahim   General Secretary: BAH Alimu
Vice-President: BANGURA Bassie   Treasurer: TBD   Media Officer: none
Men's Coach: SHERINGTON J.J.   Women's Coach: MOSES
SLFA formed: 1967   CAF: 1967   FIFA: 1967
Green shirts, Green shorts, Green socks

RECENT INTERNATIONAL MATCHES PLAYED BY SIERRA LEONE

2002	Opponents	Score		Venue	Comp	Scorers	Att	Referee
25-08	Gambia	L	0-1	Banjul	Fr			
8-09	Equatorial Guinea	W	3-1	Malabo	CNq	Bah 38, Sesay 46, Mansaray 68		Neto STP
12-10	Gabon	W	2-0	Freetown	CNq	Kpaka 45, Bah 52		Ekoue TOG
19-10	Ghana	W	2-1	Freetown	Fr	Massaquoi 24, Kemokai Kallon 36		Sanusie SLE
2003								
29-03	Morocco	D	0-0	Freetown	CNq			Kabu LBR
8-06	Morocco	L	0-1	Casablanca	CNq			Abd El Fatah EGY
22-06	Equatorial Guinea	W	2-0	Freetown	CNq	Mohanned Kallon 71, Kabbah 90		
6-07	Gabon	L	0-2	Libreville	CNq			
12-10	Congo	L	0-1	Brazzaville	WCq		4 800	Mana NGA
16-11	Congo	D	1-1	Freetown	WCq	Koroma 58	20 000	Monteiro Lopes CPV
2004								
No international matches played in 2004								
2005								
12-06	Gambia	W	1-0	Freetown	Fr	Kpaka 56		
20-11	Guinea-Bissau	D	1-1	Conakry	ACr1	Moustapha Bangoura 49		
22-11	Guinea	L	0-1	Conakry	ACr1			
2006								
No international matches played in 2006 before July								

Fr = Friendly match • CN = CAF African Cup of Nations • AC = Amilcar Cabral Cup • WC = FIFA World Cup™ • q = qualifier

SIERRA LEONE NATIONAL TEAM RECORDS AND RECORD SEQUENCES

Records			Sequence records					
Victory	5-1	NIG 1976, NIG 1995	Wins	4	1986	Clean sheets	5	1984, 1991-92
Defeat	0-5	MWI 1978, GHA 2000	Defeats	6	1982-83, 1996	Goals scored	11	1985-1987
Player Caps	n/a		Undefeated	14	1991-1993	Without goal	6	1982-83, 1996
Player Goals	n/a		Without win	9	1971-1973	Goals against	19	1976-1983

RECENT LEAGUE AND CUP RECORD

	Championship	Cup	
Year	Champions		Winners
1995	Mighty Blackpool		
1996	Mighty Blackpool		
1997	East End Lions		
1998	Mighty Blackpool		
1999	East End Lions		
2000	Mighty Blackpool		Mighty Blackpool
2001	Mighty Blackpool		Old Edwardians
2002	No tournament		No tournament
2003	No tournament		
2004	No tournament		
2005	East End Lions		
2006	FC Kallon		

SIERRA LEONE COUNTRY INFORMATION

Capital	Freetown	Independence	1961 from UK	GDP per Capita	$500
Population	5 883 889	Status	Republic	GNP Ranking	160
Area km²	71 740	Language	English, Mende, Krio	Dialling code	+232
Population density	82 per km²	Literacy rate	31%	Internet code	.sl
% in urban areas	36%	Main religion	Muslim 60%	GMT +/−	0
Towns/Cities ('000)	Freetown 1 190; Koidu 111; Bo 80; Kenema 70; Makeni 54; Lunsar 21; Waterloo 21				
Neighbours (km)	Guinea 652; Liberia 306; North Atlantic Ocean 402				
Main stadia	National Stadium – Freetown 36 000				

SLV – EL SALVADOR

NATIONAL TEAM RECORD
JULY 1ST 2002 TO JULY 9TH 2006

PL	W	D	L	F	A	%
34	7	7	20	24	57	30.9

FIFA/COCA-COLA WORLD RANKING

1993	1994	1995	1996	1997	1998	1999	2000	2001	2002	2003	2004	2005		High		Low	
66	80	82	65	64	92	96	83	86	94	95	106	124		60	10/93	147	07/06

2005–2006										
08/05	09/05	10/05	11/05	12/05	01/06	02/06	03/06	04/06	05/06	06/06	07/06
115	118	120	120	124	125	126	127	128	129	-	147

In July 2006 El Salvador plummeted to their lowest ever position in the FIFA Coca-Cola World Ranking. At 147 they are on a par with the likes of Antigua, Chinese Taipei and the Seychelles, and that's not something to be expected from a former FIFA World Cup™ finalist. Indeed they are the lowest ranked of any nation that has in the past qualified for the finals and of their Central American rivals they are above only Nicaragua and Belize. Their ranking is not helped by the fact that the national team tends to go into hibernation in-between tournaments and since February 2005 El Salvador have played just one match, a 3-0 defeat by Paraguay. At home in the League,

INTERNATIONAL HONOURS
Central American Championship 1943   Central American and Caribbean Games 1954 2002
CONCACAF Champions Cup Alianza 1967 Aguila 1976 Deportivo FAS 1979

the Torneo Apertura threw up a totally unexpected final with both Vista Hermosa and Isidro-Metapán appearing for the first time in the showcase game. A 2-0 win gave Vista Hermosa a first championship but they didn't manage to defend the title in the Clausura, the final of which saw a more familiar line-up in which Aguila beat Deportivo FAS 4-2. In the 2005-06 CONCACAF Champions' Cup, Costa Rican opposition put paid to the hopes of both Luis Angel Firpo and Deportivo FAS early on in the Central American qualifiers.

THE FIFA BIG COUNT OF 2000

	Male	Female		Male	Female
Registered players	24 497	310	Referees	258	0
Non registered players	250 000	0	Officials	610	0
Youth players	5 546	0	Total involved	281 221	
Total players	280 353		Number of clubs	200	
Professional players	216	0	Number of teams	15 630	

Federacion Salvadorena de Futbol (FESFUT)
Avenida José Matias Delgado, Frente al Centro Español, Colonia Escalón, Zona 10, San Salvador CA 1029, El Salvador
Tel +503 22096200   Fax +503 22637528
rcalvo@fesfut.org.sv   www.fesfut.org.sv
President: CALVO Rodrigo   General Secretary: BERNAL Marvin
Vice-President: TORRES Jose Humberto   Treasurer: DIAZ Mario   Media Officer: LOPEZ Eduardo Alegria
Men's Coach: CONTRERAS Armando   Women's Coach: HERRERA Jose
FESFUT formed: 1935   CONCACAF: 1961   FIFA: 1938
Blue shirts with white trimmings, Blue shorts, Blue socks

RECENT INTERNATIONAL MATCHES PLAYED BY EL SALVADOR

2002	Opponents	Score		Venue	Comp	Scorers	Att	Referee
17-11	USA	L	0-2	Washington DC	Fr		13 590	Prendergast JAM
2003								
17-01	Guatemala	D	0-0	Santa Ana, USA	Fr		6 000	Gack USA
19-01	Guatemala	D	0-0	Los Angeles	Fr		6 000	Jackson USA
9-02	Panama	W	2-1	Panama City	GCq	Galdamez [70], Corrales [77]	7 000	Pineda HON
11-02	Costa Rica	L	0-1	Panama City	GCq		500	Batres GUA
13-02	Nicaragua	W	3-0	Panama City	GCq	Corrales [5], Velasquez [27], Mejia [89]		Moreno PAN
15-02	Honduras	W	1-0	Colon	GCq	Murgas [81]	600	Batres GUA
20-02	Guatemala	L	0-2	Panama City	GCq		500	Ramos MEX
29-06	Honduras	D	1-1	San Pedro Sula	Fr	Mejia [80]	5 000	Porras CRC
2-07	Paraguay	L	0-1	San Francisco	Fr			Valenzuela USA
6-07	Mexico	W	2-1	Carson	Fr	Mejia [30], Corrales [60]	19 271	Hall USA
8-07	Guatemala	L	1-2	Houston	Fr	Murgas [68]	21 047	Hall USA
12-07	USA	L	0-2	Boston	GCr1		33 652	Ramos MEX
16-07	Martinique	W	1-0	Boston	GCr1	Gonzalez.M [76]	10 361	Batres GUA
19-07	Costa Rica	L	2-5	Boston	GCqf	Murgas [34p], Pacheco [53]	15 627	Ramos MEX
16-11	Jamaica	L	0-3	Kingston	Fr		12 000	Ramdhan TRI
2004								
28-01	Panama	D	1-1	San Salvador	Fr	Velasquez [36]		
31-03	Guatemala	L	0-3	San Salvador	Fr		5 047	Aguilar Chicas SLV
28-04	Colombia	L	0-2	Washington DC	Fr		23 000	Vaughn USA
12-05	Haiti	D	3-3	Houston	Fr	Gochez [29], Murgas [43p], Martinez.J [72]	4 000	Terry USA
13-06	Bermuda	W	2-1	San Salvador	WCq	Martinez.J [14], Velasquez [54]	12 000	Campos NCA
20-06	Bermuda	D	2-2	Hamilton	WCq	Pacheco 2 [20 41p]	4 000	Whittaker CAY
18-07	Guatemala	L	0-1	Los Angeles	Fr			Valenzuela USA
3-08	Honduras	L	0-4	San Salvador	Fr			Aguilar Chicas SLV
6-08	Guatemala	L	0-2	Washington DC	Fr		20 000	Valenzuela USA
18-08	Panama	W	2-1	San Salvador	WCq	Velasquez [7], Rodriguez.J [45]	11 400	Navarro CAN
4-09	USA	L	0-2	Boston	WCq		25 266	Brizan TRI
8-09	Jamaica	L	0-3	San Salvador	WCq		25 000	Alcala MEX
9-10	USA	L	0-2	San Salvador	WCq		20 000	Batres GUA
13-10	Jamaica	D	0-0	Kingston	WCq		12 000	Quesada Cordero CRC
17-11	Panama	L	0-3	Panama City	WCq		9 502	Archundia MEX
2005								
19-02	Panama	L	0-1	Guatemala City	GCq		10 000	Archundia MEX
21-02	Costa Rica	L	1-2	Guatemala City	GCq	Alas [40]	3 000	Batres GUA
17-08	Paraguay	L	0-3	Ciudad del Este	Fr		12 000	
2006								

No international matches played in 2006 before July

Fr = Friendly match • GC = CONCACAF Gold Cup • WC = FIFA World Cup™ • q = qualifier

EL SALVADOR NATIONAL TEAM RECORDS AND RECORD SEQUENCES

Records			Sequence records					
Victory	9-0	NCA 1929	Wins	5	1967-1968	Clean sheets	5	1981-1982
Defeat	0-8	MEX 1988	Defeats	7	1989	Goals scored	11	1999-2000
Player Caps	n/a		Undefeated	10	1981-1982	Without goal	6	1971-72, 2004-05
Player Goals	39	DIAZ ARCE Raul	Without win	10	1989	Goals against	18	1930-1941

EL SALVADOR COUNTRY INFORMATION

Capital	San Salvador	Independence	1841 from Spain	GDP per Capita	$4 800
Population	6 587 541	Status	Republic	GNP Ranking	80
Area km²	21 040	Language	Spanish	Dialling code	+503
Population density	313 per km²	Literacy rate	80%	Internet code	.sv
% in urban areas	45%	Main religion	Christian	GMT + / –	-6
Towns/Cities ('000)	San Salvador 526; Soyapango 329; Santa Ana 176; San Miguel 161; Mejicanos 160				
Neighbours (km)	Guatemala 203; Honduras 342; North Pacific Ocean 307				
Main stadia	Estadio Cuscatlán – San Salvador 39 000				

EL SALVADOR 2005–06

PRIMERA DIVISION PROFESIONAL TORNEO APERTURA

	Pl	W	D	L	F	A	Pts	Metapán	V. Hermosa	LA Firpo	Once Mun.	S. Salvador	Aguila	FAS	Alianza	Chalat'ango	Balboa
Isidro-Metapán †	18	10	6	2	25	13	36		2-1	2-1	1-0	2-0	1-0	1-0	4-1	0-0	3-1
Vista Hermosa †	18	10	1	7	28	26	31	1-2		1-0	2-1	5-1	2-1	2-0	1-3	3-1	3-2
Luis Angel Firpo †	18	7	6	5	27	17	27	1-1	3-0		1-1	1-2	1-0	2-1	3-0	4-1	2-2
Once Municipal †	18	7	5	6	25	20	26	2-1	4-0	1-0		0-0	2-2	4-1	2-1	0-1	2-1
San Salvador	18	6	6	6	22	26	24	1-1	1-2	0-3	4-1		1-1	0-3	2-1	3-1	1-0
Aguila	18	5	8	5	23	17	23	1-1	1-0	0-0	2-0	1-1		1-1	3-1	6-1	1-1
Deportivo FAS	18	5	7	6	21	21	22	0-0	1-2	1-1	0-0	0-0	0-1		1-1	3-0	2-1
Alianza	18	5	5	8	20	27	20	1-0	1-1	1-1	2-1	1-1	2-1	0-1		1-2	1-2
Chalatenango	18	5	5	8	15	29	20	0-1	1-0	1-2	0-0	0-2	1-0	2-2	0-0		2-1
Atlético Balboa	18	3	5	10	26	36	14	2-2	1-2	2-1	1-4	3-2	1-1	3-4	1-2	1-1	

13/08/2005 - 27/11/2005 • † Qualified for the play-offs • Top scorers: Alex ERAZO, Aguila, 7, Cristian GIL, V. Hermosa, 7; Franklin WEBSTER, LA Firpo, 7
Play-off semi-finals: LA Firpo 1-0 1-2 2-4p **Vista Hermosa**; Once Municipal 1-2 0-0 **Isidro-Metapán** • Final: Isidro-Metapán 0-2 **Vista Hermosa** •
Vista Hermosa won the Apertura

EL SALVADOR 2005–06

PRIMERA DIVISION PROFESIONAL TORNEO CLAUSURA

	Pl	W	D	L	F	A	Pts	Aguila	FAS	V. Hermosa	Metapán	Alianza	Balboa	S. Salvador	Chalat'ango	Once Mun.	LA Firpo
Aguila †	18	9	5	4	24	19	32		2-0	1-0	1-0	0-2	2-1	1-4	2-0	3-0	0-0
Deportivo FAS †	18	6	8	4	26	17	26	2-2		2-0	0-1	3-1	0-0	2-1	4-0	3-0	2-0
Vista Hermosa †	18	8	2	8	27	22	26	2-3	2-2		3-1	1-0	2-0	1-2	1-2	3-0	2-0
Isidro-Metapán †	18	7	5	6	21	22	26	2-0	1-1	2-1		1-0	2-1	1-1	3-3	4-1	0-0
Alianza	18	7	4	7	29	26	25	1-1	2-1	2-3	1-1		2-1	1-1	3-0	3-0	1-2
Atlético Balboa	18	6	5	7	26	23	23	2-1	1-1	2-0	4-0	2-2		1-0	1-1	3-2	2-0
San Salvador	18	6	5	7	28	32	23	2-3	1-1	2-4	1-0	3-4	2-1		2-2	1-1	3-1
Chalatenango	18	5	7	6	19	26	22	0-0	1-1	1-0	0-1	1-2	2-1	1-2		1-0	2-1
Once Municipal	18	5	6	7	24	30	21	1-1	2-1	0-0	1-0	2-0	3-3	6-0	1-1		3-2
Luis Angel Firpo	18	5	5	8	18	23	20	1-1	1-1	0-0	2-0	3-1	3-2	3-0	1-0	1-1	

29/01/2006 - 5/06/2006 • † Qualified for the play-offs • Match in bold awarded • Top scorers:
Play-off semi-finals: Isidro-Metapán 3-1 0-4 **Aguila**; Vista Hermosa 0-0 0-1 **Deportivo FAS** • Final: **Aguila** 4-2 Deportivo FAS • Aguila won the
Clausura • Relegation play-off: **Chalatenango** 5-0 1-2 Municipal Limeño • Atlético Balboa relegated, Nacional promoted

RECENT LEAGUE AND CUP RECORD

	Championship/Clausura from 2000				Apertura		
Year	Champions	Score	Runners-up		Winners	Score	Runners-up
1997	Alianza	0-0 3-2	Luis Angel Firpo				
1998	Luis Angel Firpo	2-0	Deportivo FAS				
1999	Luis Angel Firpo	1-1 5-4p	Deportivo FAS		Aguila	1-0	Municipal Limeño
2000	Luis Angel Firpo	1-1 10-9p	AD El Tránsito		Aguila	3-2	Municipal Limeño
2001	Aguila	1-1 2-1	Deportivo FAS		Alianza	2-1	Luis Angel Firpo
2002	Deportivo FAS	4-0	Alianza		Deportivo FAS	3-1	San Salvador
2003	San Salvador	3-1	Luis Angel Firpo		Deportivo FAS	2-2 5-3p	Aguila
2004	Alianza	1-1 3-2p	Deportivo FAS		Deportivo FAS	0-0 4-3p	Atlético Balboa
2005	Deportivo FAS	3-1	Luis Angel Firpo		Vista Hermosa	2-0	Isidro-Metapán
2006	Aguila	4-2	Deportivo FAS				

SMR – SAN MARINO

NATIONAL TEAM RECORD
JULY 1ST 2002 TO JULY 9TH 2006

PL	W	D	L	F	A	%
20	1	1	18	5	72	7.5

FIFA/COCA-COLA WORLD RANKING

1993	1994	1995	1996	1997	1998	1999	2000	2001	2002	2003	2004	2005	High	Low
121	131	951	165	173	179	150	168	158	160	162	164	155	**118** 09/03	**191** 07/06

2005–2006										
08/05	09/05	10/05	11/05	12/05	01/06	02/06	03/06	04/06	05/06	06/06	07/06
161	161	157	157	155	156	156	158	160	161	-	191

Within the space of three years San Marino have plummeted down the FIFA/Coca-Cola World Ranking and are now perilously close to the bottom. They are not, however, the worst ranked nation in Europe anymore with that honour going to Luxembourg, who were three places below them in July 2006 when the new ranking system was introduced. In the 2006 FIFA World Cup™ qualifiers, San Marino lost every match they played, scoring just twice and letting in 40 goals in the ten games played. The San Marino championship saw a new name on the trophy when Murata beat Pennarossa 1-0 in the final thanks to an Alex Gasperoni goal. They had won their first round

INTERNATIONAL HONOURS
None

group to qualify for a rather bizarre play-off system that requires some explanation. In the first round the second and third placed teams from each group play each other. The second round sees the first placed teams from the groups face the winners of the first round ties. In the third round the losers in the first and second round play each other whilst the fourth round sees the winners from the second round play each other for a place in the final. The losers of that game then play the winners of the other fourth round match, between the two third round winners, in the semi-final. All clear now? In the rather more straightforward Coppa Titano, Libertas beat Tre Penne 4-1 in the final.

THE FIFA BIG COUNT OF 2000

	Male	Female		Male	Female
Registered players	800	0	Referees	30	0
Non registered players	300	0	Officials	200	10
Youth players	600	0	Total involved	1 940	
Total players		1 700	Number of clubs	32	
Professional players	0	0	Number of teams	60	

Federazione Sammarinese Giuoco Calcio (FSGC)
Viale Campo dei Giudei 14, Rep. San Marino 47890
Tel +378 054 9990515   Fax +378 054 9992348
fsgc@omniway.sm   www.fsgc.sm
President: CRESCENTINI Giorgio   General Secretary: CASADEI Luciano
Vice-President: CECCOLI Pier Luigi   Treasurer: GUIDI Joseph   Media Officer: ELISA Felici
Men's Coach: MAZZA Gianpaolo   Women's Coach: none
FSGC formed: 1931   UEFA: 1988   FIFA: 1988
Light blue shirts with white trimmings, Light blue shorts, Light blue socks or White shirts, White shorts, White socks

RECENT INTERNATIONAL MATCHES PLAYED BY SAN MARINO

2002 Opponents		Score	Venue	Comp	Scorers	Att	Referee
7-09 Poland	L	0-2	Serravalle	ECq		2 000	McKeon IRE
16-10 Hungary	L	0-3	Budapest	ECq		6 500	Orrason ISL
20-11 Latvia	L	0-1	Serravalle	ECq		600	Khudiev AZE
2003							
2-04 Poland	L	0-5	Ostrowiec	ECq		8 500	Loizou CYP
30-04 Latvia	L	0-3	Riga	ECq		7 500	Byrne IRE
7-06 Sweden	L	0-6	Serravalle	ECq		2 184	Delevic SCG
11-06 Hungary	L	0-5	Serravalle	ECq		1 410	Clark SCO
20-08 Liechtenstein	D	2-2	Vaduz	Fr	Gasperoni 39, Ciacci 45	850	Wildhaber SUI
6-09 Sweden	L	0-5	Gothenburg	ECq		31 098	Messner AUT
2004							
28-04 Liechtenstein	W	1-0	Serravalle	Fr	Selva 5	700	Sammut MLT
4-09 Serbia & Montenegro	L	0-3	Serravalle	WCq		1 137	Kholmatov KAZ
8-09 Lithuania	L	0-4	Kaunas	WCq		4 000	Jareci ALB
13-10 Serbia & Montenegro	L	0-5	Belgrade	WCq		4 000	Isaksen FRO
17-11 Lithuania	L	0-1	Serravalle	WCq		1 457	Nalbandyan ARM
2005							
9-02 Spain	L	0-5	Almeria	WCq		12 580	Clark SCO
30-03 Belgium	L	1-2	Serravalle	WCq	Selva 41	871	Kasnaferis GRE
4-06 Bosnia-Herzegovina	L	1-3	Serravalle	WCq	Selva 39	750	Demirlek TUR
7-09 Belgium	L	0-8	Antwerp	WCq		8 207	Stokes IRL
8-10 Bosnia-Herzegovina	L	0-3	Zenica	WCq		8 500	Hamer LUX
12-10 Spain	L	0-6	Serravalle	WCq		3 426	Meyer GER
2006							

No international matches played in 2006 before July

Fr = Friendly match • EC = UEFA EURO 2004™ • WC = FIFA World Cup™ • q = qualifier

SAN MARINO NATIONAL TEAM RECORDS AND RECORD SEQUENCES

Records			Sequence records		
Victory	1-0	LIE 2004	Wins	1	2004	Clean sheets	1	1993, 2004
Defeat	0-10	NOR	Defeats	36	1993-2001	Goals scored	2	2005
Player Caps	48	GENNARI Mirco	Undefeated	1	Four times	Without goal	10	1995-1998
Player Goals	6	SELVA Andy	Without win	64	1990-2004	Goals against	50	1993-2004

NATIONAL TEAM PLAYERS AND COACHES

Record Caps			Record Goals			Recent Coaches	
GENNARI Mirco	1992-'03	48	SELVA Andy	1998-'05	6	LEONI Giorgio	1990-'95
MATTEONI Ivan	1990-'03	44				BONINI Massimo	1996-'98
GOBBI Luca	1990-'02	41				MAZZA Gianpaolo	1998-
GASPERONI Federico	1996-'05	41					
GUERRA William	1987-'99	40					
MONTAGNA Paolo	1995-'05	40					

SAN MARINO COUNTRY INFORMATION

Capital	San Marino	Formation	301	GDP per Capita	$34 600
Population	28 503	Status	Republic	GNP Ranking	185
Area km²	61	Language	Italian	Dialling code	+378
Population density	467 per km²	Literacy rate	96%	Internet code	.sm
% in urban areas	94%	Main religion	Christian	GMT +/-	+1
Towns/Cities	Serravalle 9 258; Borgo Maggiore 6 627; San Marino 4 598; Domagnano 2 724; Fiorentino 2 082				
Neighbours (km)	Italy 39				
Main stadia	Stadio Olimpico – Serravalle 2 210				

SAN MARINO 2005-06 CAMPIONATO DILETTANTI GIRONE A

	Pl	W	D	L	F	A	Pts
Tre Fiori †	21	14	5	2	37	12	47
Domagnano †	21	12	6	3	52	23	42
Tre Penne †	21	11	6	4	27	15	39
Folgore/Falciano	21	9	4	8	22	25	31
La Fiorita	21	7	7	7	31	35	28
Faetano	21	6	3	12	32	40	21
Cosmos	21	5	5	11	13	22	20
San Giovanni	21	1	2	18	13	60	5

23/09/2005 - 10/04/2006 • † Qualified for the play-offs

SAN MARINO 2005-06 CAMPIONATO DILETTANTI GIRONE B

	Pl	W	D	L	F	A	Pts
Murata †	20	15	4	1	49	20	49
Pennarossa †	20	12	6	2	38	19	42
Libertas †	20	10	3	7	42	22	33
Virtus	20	7	4	9	23	33	25
Juvenes/Dogana	20	3	8	9	27	44	17
Cailungo	20	4	4	12	11	25	16
Fiorentino	20	3	3	14	30	52	12

23/09/2005 - 10/04/2006 • † Qualified for the play-offs

CAMPIONATO DILETTANTI PLAY-OFFS

First round: Domagnano 1-4 **Libertas**; Pennarossa 1-1 2-3p **Tre Penne**
Second round: **Tre Fiori** 1-0 Tre Penne; **Murata** 3-1 Libertas
Third round: **Tre Penne** 1-1 5-3p Domagnano; Libertas 0-2 **Pennarossa**
Fourth round: Tre Fiori 0-1 **Murata**; Tre Penne 2-3 **Pennarossa**
Semi-final: Tre Fiori 1-2 **Pennarossa**

FINAL

Champions	Score	Runners-up
Murata	1-0	Pennarossa

CLUB DIRECTORY

Club	Lge	Cup
Cailungo	0	1
Cosmos	1	3
Dogana	0	0
Domagnano	4	3
Faetano	3	1
Folgore	3	2
Fiorentino (ex Montevito)	1	0
La Fiorita	2	2
Libertas	1	4
Murata	1	0
Pennarossa	1	2
San Giovanni	0	0
Tre Fiori	4	2
Tre Penne	0	0
Virtus	0	1

COPPA TITANO 2005-06

Quarter-finals		Semi-finals		Final	
Libertas	2				
Tre Fiori	1	**Libertas**	4		
Cailungo	0	Pennarossa	3		
Pennarossa	2			**Libertas**	4
Juvenes/Dogana	2			Tre Penne	1
Murata	0	Juvenes/Dogana	1	Serravalle, 23-06-2006	
Domagnano	2	**Tre Penne**	3	Scorers - Vannucci 2 35 76p,	
Tre Penne	3			Toccaceli 87, Ghiotti 92+ for	
				Libertas; Cibelli 50 for TP	

RECENT LEAGUE AND CUP RECORD

	Championship				Cup		
Year	Champions	Score	Runners-up		Winners	Score	Runners-up
1990	La Fiorita	1-0	Cosmos		Domagnano	2-0	Juvenes
1991	Faetano	1-0	Tre Fiori		Libertas	2-0	Faetano
1992	Montevito	4-2	Libertas		Domagnano	1-1 4-2p	Tre Fiori
1993	Tre Fiori	2-0	Domagnano		Faetano	1-0	Libertas
1994	Tre Fiori	2-0	La Fiorita		Faetano	3-1	Folgore
1995	Tre Fiori	1-0	La Fiorita		Cosmos	0-0 3-1p	Faetano
1996	Libertas	4-1	Cosmos		Domagnano	2-0	Cosmos
1997	Folgore Falciano	2-1	La Fiorita		Murata	2-0	Virtus
1998	Folgore Falciano	2-1	Tre Fiori		Faetano	4-1	Cosmos
1999	Faetano	1-0	Folgore Falciano		Cosmos	5-1	Domagnano
2000	Folgore Falciano	3-1	Domagnano		Tre Penne	3-1	Folgore
2001	Cosmos	3-1	Folgore Falciano		Domagnano	1-0	Tre Fiori
2002	Domagnano	1-0	Cailungo		Domagnano	6-1	Cailungo
2003	Domagnano	2-1	Pennarossa		Domagnano	1-0	Pennarossa
2004	Pennarossa	2-2 4-2p	Domanano		Pennarossa	3-0	Domagnano
2005	Domagnano	2-1	Murata		Pennarossa	4-1	Tre Penne
2006	Murata	1-0	Pennarossa		Libertas	4-1	Tre Penne

SOL – SOLOMON ISLANDS

NATIONAL TEAM RECORD
JULY 1ST 2002 TO JULY 9TH 2006

PL	W	D	L	F	A	%
21	9	4	8	40	45	52.4

FIFA/COCA-COLA WORLD RANKING

1993	1994	1995	1996	1997	1998	1999	2000	2001	2002	2003	2004	2005		High	Low
149	163	170	171	130	128	144	130	134	142	156	130	140		**124** 10/98	**177** 08/96

					2005–2006						
08/05	09/05	10/05	11/05	12/05	01/06	02/06	03/06	04/06	05/06	06/06	07/06
136	138	138	138	140	140	140	140	143	144	-	151

With Australia gone from the OFC, the challenge for the bigger countries in Oceania, like the Solomon Islands, is to try to match New Zealand at both national team and club level. If they can do that there is the possibility of qualifying for FIFA events such as the men's and women's age-restricted tournaments, the FIFA Confederations Cup and the FIFA Club World Cup. The Solomon Islands are positioned to do that. After all, they knocked New Zealand out of the 2006 FIFA World Cup™ qualifiers to set up a play-off with Australia in September 2005. Rarely does a team of European based stars visit Honiara, but a big crowd at the Lawson Tama Stadium got to see a full

INTERNATIONAL HONOURS
Melanesian Cup 1994

strength Aussie side beat the Solomons 2-1, the first leg having been lost 7-0 in Sydney. The OFC Club championship offers great possibilities but the club set-up in the Solomons has yet to match that in Tahiti for instance. In the first round group stage of the 2006 finals in Auckland, Tahiti's AS Piraé beat Marist FC of Honiara 10-1 in the opening game and although Marist restricted Auckland to a 3-1 victory in the second match, the difference in class was marked. Marist had qualified for the event having won the National Club Championship in February 2006, but all that consisted of was five games in a first round group, a semi-final and a final - a total of seven games in ten days.

THE FIFA BIG COUNT OF 2000

	Male	Female		Male	Female
Registered players	1 000	0	Referees	100	0
Non registered players	2 000	0	Officials	300	0
Youth players	1 000	0	Total involved	4 400	
Total players	4 000		Number of clubs	100	
Professional players	0	0	Number of teams	200	

Solomon Islands Football Federation (SIFF)

Lawson Tama, PO Box 854, Honiara, Solomon Islands
Tel +677 26496   Fax +677 26497
administration@siff.com.sb   www.siff.com.sb
President: ALUFURAI Martin   General Secretary: NGAVA Edward
Vice-President: BELAMA Peter   Treasurer: MAAHANUA Aloysio   Media Officer: PITUVAKA Francis
Men's Coach: ANDRIOLI Ayrton   Women's Coach: MASUAKU Rex
SIFF formed: 1978   OFC: 1988   FIFA: 1988
Green shirts, Blue shorts, White socks

RECENT INTERNATIONAL MATCHES PLAYED BY THE SOLOMOM ISLANDS

2002	Opponents	Score		Venue	Comp	Scorers	Att	Referee
5-07	Papua New Guinea	D	0-0	Auckland	OCq		1 000	Breeze AUS
7-07	Tahiti	L	2-3	Auckland	OCq	Daudau [8], Menapi [25]	1 000	Breeze AUS
9-07	New Zealand	L	1-6	Auckland	OCq	Faarodo [73]	300	Atisson VAN
2003								
14-06	Papua New Guinea	W	5-3	Port Moresby	Fr	Samani [12], Menapi 2 [?? ??p], Mehau [??], Suri [??p]		
1-07	Vanuatu	D	2-2	Suva	SPr1	Menapi 2 [49 57]		Shah FIJ
3-07	Kiribati †	W	7-0	Suva	SPr1	Waita [8], Menapi 5 [43 48 52 55 74], Mehau [78]	700	Ariiotima TAH
5-07	Tuvalu †	W	4-0	Nausori	SPr1	Maniadalo [16], Menapi 2 [27 87], Suri [80]	2 500	Bayung PNG
7-07	Fiji	L	1-2	Lautoka	SPr1	Menapi [68]	6 000	Ariiotima TAH
2004								
3-04	Vanuatu	W	2-1	Port Vila	Fr	Menapi 2 [52 71]	4 000	Lencie VAN
6-04	Vanuatu	W	2-1	Port Vila	Fr	Suri [34], Menapi [??]		
10-05	Tonga	W	6-0	Honiara	WCq	Faarodo 3 [12 30 77], Maemae 2 [62 76], Samani [79]	12 385	Attison VAN
12-05	Cook Islands	W	5-0	Honiara	WCq	Waita [21], Omokirio [27], Samani [45], Maemae [70], Leo [81]	14 000	Fred VAN
15-05	New Caledonia	W	2-0	Honiara	WCq	Omokirio [10], Suri [42]	20 000	Attison VAN
19-05	Tahiti	D	1-1	Honiara	WCq	Suri [80]	18 000	Rakaroi FIJ
29-05	Vanuatu	W	1-0	Adelaide	WCq	Suri [51p]	200	Shield AUS
31-05	New Zealand	L	0-3	Adelaide	WCq		217	Iturralde Gonzalez ESP
2-06	Tahiti	W	4-0	Adelaide	WCq	Faarodo [9], Menapi 2 [14 80], Suri [42]	50	Rakaroi FIJ
4-06	Fiji	W	2-1	Adelaide	WCq	Kakai [16], Houkarawa [82]	1 500	Attison VAN
6-06	Australia	D	2-2	Adelaide	WCq	Menapi 2 [43 75]	1 500	Iturralde Gonzalez ESP
9-10	Australia	L	1-5	Honiara	OCf	Suri [60]	21 000	O'Leary NZL
12-10	Australia	L	0-6	Sydney	OCf		19 208	Rakaroi FIJ
2005								
3-09	Australia	L	0-7	Sydney	WCq		16 000	Mohd Salleh MAS
6-09	Australia	L	1-2	Honiara	WCq	Faarodo [49]	16 000	Maidin SIN
2006								

No international matches played in 2006 before July

Fr = Friendly match • OC = OFC Oceania Nations Cup • SP = South Pacific Games • WC = FIFA World Cup™
q = qualifier • r1 = first round group • f = final • † Not a full international

SOLOMON ISLANDS NATIONAL TEAM RECORDS AND RECORD SEQUENCES

Records			Sequence records					
Victory	16-0	COK 1995	Wins	5	1994, 2004	Clean sheets	3	Three times
Defeat	0-8	NCL 1966	Defeats	5	1992-1993	Goals scored	14	2002-2004
Player Caps	n/a		Undefeated	7	2004	Without goal	4	1989-1990
Player Goals	n/a		Without win	9	1963-1975	Goals against	21	1997-2001

RECENT LEAGUE AND CUP RECORD

	National Club Championship		S.League	S.League Cup		Cup	Honiara League
Year	Winners	Finalist				Winners	Champions
2003	Koloale	4-0 Auki Kingz	Not played	Not played		Not played	Koloale
2004	Central Reales	w-o Makuru	JP Su'uria	Wan Toks		Not played	Makuru
2005	Not played		JP Su'uria	JP Su'uria		Honiara Warriors	Not played
2006	Marist	1-0 Koloale					

In the S.League Makuru are known as JP Su'uria, Marist as Systek Kingz and Uncles as Wan Toks

SOLOMON ISLANDS COUNTRY INFORMATION

Capital	Honiara	Independence	1978 from the UK	GDP per Capita	$1 700
Population	523 617	Status	Constitutional Monarchy	GNP Ranking	180
Area km²	28 450	Language	Melanesian, English	Dialling code	+677
Population density	18 per km²	Literacy rate	n/a	Internet code	.sb
% in urban areas	17%	Main religion	Christian	GMT +/–	+11
Towns/Cities ('000)	Honiara 56; Gizo 6; Auki 4; Buala 2; Tulagi 1; Kirakira 1				
Neighbours (km)	South Pacific Ocean 5 313				
Main stadia	Lawson Tama Stadium – Honiara 10 000				

SOM – SOMALIA

NATIONAL TEAM RECORD
JULY 1ST 2002 TO JULY 9TH 2006

PL	W	D	L	F	A	%
12	2	0	10	5	33	16.7

FIFA/COCA-COLA WORLD RANKING

1993	1994	1995	1996	1997	1998	1999	2000	2001	2002	2003	2004	2005	High		Low	
-	159	165	178	187	190	197	194	197	190	191	193	184	158	04/95	199	04/00

2005–2006										
08/05	09/05	10/05	11/05	12/05	01/06	02/06	03/06	04/06	05/06	06/06	07/06
188	188	188	188	184	184	184	184	185	185	-	179

Remarkably, given the total absence of order, government or civil society in Somalia, the country still manages to field a national football team almost every year and has even entered the past two FIFA World Cup™ tournaments. However, because of the ravaged infrastructure, and the absence of security and organisation in Mogadishu and elsewhere, the country has not hosted an international match for 20 years, the last game in Mogadishu being a Nations Cup qualifier against Uganda in October 1986. In November 2005, a 2-1 win over Djibouti marked only their second win in international football since 1994 and got them off to a bright start at the annual CECAFA

INTERNATIONAL HONOURS
None

Cup, in Kigali, Rwanda. But the lack of international exposure caught up with Somalia's footballers after that, heavily beaten by Sudan, Uganda and eventual winners Ethiopia in their next three opening round group matches. Somali club Elman, champions since the turn of the century, entered both the 2005 and 2006 editions of the CECAFA Club Championship but not the CAF Champions League. Somali junior sides are also set to play in the preliminaries of the African U-20 and U-17 championships, but again they have to play both legs of their preliminary round ties away from home.

THE FIFA BIG COUNT OF 2000

	Male	Female		Male	Female
Registered players	1 560	120	Referees	1 000	0
Non registered players	25 000	590	Officials	3 120	30
Youth players	2 080	160	Total involved	33 660	
Total players	29 510		Number of clubs	32	
Professional players	0	0	Number of teams	112	

Somali Football Federation (SFF)
DHL Mogadishu, Mogadishu BN 03040, Somalia
Tel +252 1 216363   Fax +252 1 600000
sofofed@hotmail.com   www.none
President: ALI Mohiadin Hassan   General Secretary: ARAB Abdiqani Said
Vice-President: MOHAMUD Nor   Treasurer: HUSSEIN DUNTE Abdiraham   Media Officer: None
Men's Coach: TBD   Women's Coach: None
SFF formed: 1951   CAF: 1968   FIFA: 1960
Sky blue shirts, Sky blue shorts, White socks

RECENT INTERNATIONAL MATCHES PLAYED BY SOMALIA

2002	Opponents	Score		Venue	Comp	Scorers	Att	Referee
1-12	Uganda	L	0-2	Arusha	CCr1			Juma Ali TAN
3-12	Rwanda	L	0-1	Arusha	CCr1			
5-12	Zanzibar †	L	0-1	Arusha	CCr1			
7-12	Ethiopia	W	1-0	Arusha	CCr1			
2003								
16-11	Ghana	L	0-5	Accra	WCq		19 447	Bebou TOG
19-11	Ghana	L	0-2	Kumasi	WCq		12 000	Chaibou NIG
2004								
12-12	Uganda	L	0-2	Addis Abeba	CCr1			
14-12	Kenya	L	0-1	Addis Abeba	CCr1			
18-12	Sudan	L	0-4	Addis Abeba	CCr1			
2005								
27-11	Djibouti	W	2-1	Kigali	CCr1	Abdul Hakim, Mahmoud Sharki		
29-11	Sudan	L	1-4	Kigali	CCr1	Mohamed Sheikh		
1-12	Uganda	L	0-7	Kigali	CCr1			
5-12	Ethiopia	L	1-4	Kigali	CCr1			
2006								

No international matches played in 2006 before July

Fr = Friendly match • CC = CECAFA Cup • WC = FIFA World Cup™ • q = qualifier • r1 = first round group • † Not a full international

SOMALIA NATIONAL TEAM RECORDS AND RECORD SEQUENCES

Records			Sequence records					
Victory	5-2	MTN 1985	Wins	1		Clean sheets	1	
Defeat	2-9	CMR 1960	Defeats	7	1995-2000	Goals scored	4	Six times
Player Caps	n/a		Undefeated	4	1978-1980	Without goal	8	2000-2002
Player Goals	n/a		Without win	17	1995-2002	Goals against	10	1994-2000

RECENT LEAGUE RECORD

Championship	
Year	**Champions**
1995	Alba
1996	No tournament
1997	No tournament
1998	Ports Authority
1999	No tournament
2000	Elman
2001	Elman
2002	Elman
2003	Elman
2004	Elman
2005	Elman

SOMALIA COUNTRY INFORMATION

Capital	Mogadishu	Independence	1960	GDP per Capita	$500
Population	8 304 601	Status	Republic	GNP Ranking	151
Area km²	637 657	Language	Somali	Dialling code	+252
Population density	13 per km²	Literacy rate	37%	Internet code	.so
% in urban areas	26%	Main religion	Muslim	GMT +/−	+3
Towns/Cities ('000)	Mogadishu 2 590; Hargeysa 478; Marka 320; Berbera 242; Kismayo 234; Jamame 185				
Neighbours (km)	Kenya 682; Ethiopia 1 600; Djibouti 58; Gulf of Aden & Indian Ocean 3 025				
Main stadia	Mogadishu Stadium - Mogadishu 35 000				

SRI – SRI LANKA

NATIONAL TEAM RECORD
JULY 1ST 2002 TO JULY 9TH 2006

PL	W	D	L	F	A	%
32	7	9	16	28	56	35.9

FIFA/COCA-COLA WORLD RANKING

1993	1994	1995	1996	1997	1998	1999	2000	2001	2002	2003	2004	2005	High	Low
126	139	135	126	136	134	153	149	143	139	135	140	144	**122** 08/98	**164** 06/00

2005–2006											
08/05	09/05	10/05	11/05	12/05	01/06	02/06	03/06	04/06	05/06	06/06	07/06
140	142	144	144	144	145	145	145	135	136	-	138

Sri Lanka has been one of the major beneficiaries of the AFC's decision to stream Asian nations according to the standard of football in the country. Whereas in the past it was a rare event for any Sri Lankan team to register an international victory, both the national team and the club sides are now able to push for international honours. In the inaugural AFC Challenge Cup, a tournament designed for the 16 lowest ranked nations in Asia, the Sri Lankan national team won their first round group, beat Chinese Taipei in the quarter-finals and Nepal on penalties in the semi-final, to qualify for the final. No one had expected the team to get that far and in the final against Tajikistan

INTERNATIONAL HONOURS
None

they were comprehensively outplayed in a 4-0 defeat. The experience, however, was an overwhelmingly positive one for football in Sri Lanka and built upon the success of 2004 club champions Blue Star at the inaugural AFC President's Cup played in May 2005. They lost in the semi-finals to Kyrgyz side Dordoi-Dynamo, but only after a penalty shoot-out. Ratnams did not fare so well in the second edition the following year, but the tournament gives an added edge to club football in the country. In 2005 Negombo Youth won a remodelled championship that involved two first round groups and play-offs, whilst Ratnams won the Cup beating Negombo Youth in the final.

THE FIFA BIG COUNT OF 2000

	Male	Female		Male	Female
Registered players	20 560	200	Referees	258	0
Non registered players	70 000	0	Officials	5 000	150
Youth players	22 000	0	Total involved	118 168	
Total players	112 760		Number of clubs	1 110	
Professional players	0	0	Number of teams	1 366	

Football Federation of Sri Lanka (FFSL)
100/9 Independence Avenue, Colombo 07, Sri Lanka
Tel +94 11 2686120   Fax +94 11 2682471
ffsl@srilankafootball.com   www.srilankafootball.com
President: PANDITHARATHNE Thilina   General Secretary: SALLY B.H.H.
Vice-President: GAMINI Randeni   Treasurer: RANJITH Rodrigo   Media Officer: PERERA Rukmal
Men's Coach: SAMPATH PERERA Kolonnage   Women's Coach: DE SILVA Clement
FFSL formed: 1939   AFC: 1958   FIFA: 1950
White shirts, White shorts, White socks

RECENT INTERNATIONAL MATCHES PLAYED BY SRI LANKA

2002	Opponents	Score		DhakaVCCfenue	Comp	Scorers	Att	Referee
27-11	Vietnam	L	1-2	Colombo	Fr	Channa Edribandanage [78]		Deshapriya SRI
29-11	Vietnam	D	1-1	Colombo	Fr	Nazar [90]		Pingamage SRI
1-12	Vietnam	D	2-2	Colombo	Fr	Steinwall [??], Maduranga [??]		
2003								
10-01	Afghanistan	W	1-0	Dhaka	SAFr1	Steinwall [43]		Gurung NEP
12-01	Pakistan	L	1-2	Dhaka	SAFr1	Siyaguna [90]		Gosh BAN
14-01	India	D	1-1	Dhaka	SAFr1	Abeysekera [90]		Shamsuzzaman BAN
21-03	East Timor	W	3-2	Colombo	ACq	Kasun Weerarathna 2 [36 89], Channa Edribandanage [44]		
25-03	Chinese Taipei	W	2-1	Colombo	ACq	Kumara [13], Channa Edribandanage [79]		
15-10	Syria	L	0-5	Damascus	ACq			
18-10	Syria	L	0-8	Damascus	ACq			
9-11	Turkmenistan	L	0-1	Balkanabat	ACq			
12-11	Turkmenistan	L	0-3	Ashgabat	ACq			
18-11	United Arab Emirates	L	1-3	Dubai	ACq	Channa Edribandanage [31]		
22-11	United Arab Emirates	L	0-3	Dubai	ACq			
29-11	Laos	D	0-0	Vientiane	WCq		4 500	Luong The Tai VIE
3-12	Laos	W	3-0	Colombo	WCq	Channa Edribandanage [35], Kasun Weerarathna [59], Hameed [93+]	6 000	Saleem MDV
2004								
18-02	Turkmenistan	L	0-2	Ashgabat	WCq		11 000	Al Bannai UAE
31-03	Saudi Arabia	L	0-1	Colombo	WCq		6 000	Chynybekov KGZ
9-06	Indonesia	L	0-1	Jakarta	WCq		30 000	Nesar BAN
8-09	Indonesia	D	2-2	Colombo	WCq	Steinwall [81], Karunaratne [82]	4 000	Marshoud JOR
9-10	Turkmenistan	D	2-2	Colombo	WCq	Perera [47], Mudiyanselage [57]	4 000	Al Bannai UAE
17-11	Saudi Arabia	L	0-3	Dammam	WCq		2 000	Muflah OMA
18-12	Maldives	D	0-0	Male	Fr			
2005								
7-12	Pakistan	L	0-1	Karachi	SAFr1			
9-12	Maldives	L	0-2	Karachi	SAFr1			
11-12	Afghanistan	L	1-2	Karachi	SAFr1	Karunaratne [85]		
2006								
2-04	Brunei Darusalaam	W	1-0	Chittagong	CCr1	Kasun Weerarathna [74]	2 000	Saidov UZB
4-04	Bhutan	W	1-0	Chittagong	CCr1	Karu [45]		Saidov UZB
6-04	Nepal	D	1-1	Chittagong	CCr1	Izzadeen [19]	2 500	Lee Gi Young KOR
8-04	Chinese Taipei	W	3-0	Chittagong	CCqf	Izzadeen [44], Sanjaya [70], Ratnayaka [90]	2 500	Al Ghatrifi OMA
12-04	Nepal	D	1-1	Chittagong	CCsf	Kasun Weerarathna [65], W 5-3p	2 500	Lee Gi Young KOR
16-04	Tajikistan	L	0-4	Dhaka	CCf		2 000	Mombini IRN

Fr = Friendly match • SAF = South Asian Federation Cup • AC = AFC Asian Cup • CC = AFC Challenge Cup • WC = FIFA World Cup™
q = qualifier • r1 = first round group • qf = quarter-final • sf = semi-final • f = final

SRI LANKA NATIONAL TEAM RECORDS AND RECORD SEQUENCES

Records			Sequence records				
Victory	4-0	SIN, NEP, PAK	Wins	3	1996-97, 2002	Clean sheets	2	Five times
Defeat	0-8	IDN 1972, SYR 2003	Defeats	12	1972-79, 1979-84	Goals scored	12	2002-2003
Player Caps	n/a		Undefeated	7	2001-2002	Without goal	10	1991-1993
Player Goals	n/a		Without win	15	1954-72, 1984-93	Goals against	35	1952-1979

SRI LANKA COUNTRY INFORMATION

Capital	Colombo	Independence	1948 from UK	GDP per Capita	$3 700
Population	19 905 165	Status	Republic	GNP Ranking	73
Area km²	65 610	Language	Sinhala, Tamil, English	Dialling code	+94
Population density	303 per km²	Literacy rate	92.3%	Internet code	.lk
% in urban areas	22%	Main religion	Buddhist, Hindu	GMT +/–	+5.5
Towns/Cities ('000)	Colombo 648; Dehiwala-Mount Lavinia 215; Jaffna 169; Negombo 137; Chavakachcheri 121; Kotte 118; Kandy 111; Trincomalee 108; Kalmunai 100; Galle 93; Point Pedro 89				
Neighbours (km)	Indian Ocean 1 340				
Main stadia	Sugathadasa Stadium – Colombo 25 000				

SRI LANKA 2005–06 GROUP A

	Pl	W	D	L	F	A	Pts
Negombo Youth †	18	14	2	2	44	14	44
Ratnams †	18	11	4	3	36	16	37
Blue Star †	18	9	3	6	27	33	30
Police	18	7	5	6	27	20	26
Air Force	18	7	4	7	15	21	25
Army	18	6	5	7	25	31	23
Saunders	18	4	7	7	18	24	19
Jupiters	18	4	6	8	18	24	18
Renown	18	4	6	8	25	25	18
Java Lane	18	1	4	13	21	48	7

4/08/2005 - 7/01/2006 • † Qualified for play-offs

SRI LANKA 2005–06 GROUP B

	Pl	W	D	L	F	A	Pts
Navy †	14	9	4	1	22	8	31
York Kandy	14	6	5	3	16	11	23
Red Sun	14	5	5	4	11	9	20
Matara	14	6	2	6	17	19	20
New Young	14	4	5	5	16	17	17
Old Bens	14	3	6	5	9	15	15
Super Beach	14	3	5	6	10	13	14
Victory	14	3	2	9	9	18	11

9/09/2005 - 7/01/2006 • † Qualified for play-offs
Play-off semi-finals: Negombo youth beat Navy; Blue Star beat Ratnams • Championship final: **Negombo Youth** 3-2 Blue Star (12-02-2006. Scorers - Nalin Nandakumara [10], Thushara Gunaratne [22], Nimal Anthony [64] for Negombo; Mohamed Farsan 2 [40] [72] for Blue Star)

HOLCIM FA CUP 2005–06

Round of 16		Quarter-finals		Semi-finals		Final	
Ratnams	w-o						
Java Lane		Ratnams	5				
New Young	6	Police	2				
Police	7			Ratnams	3		
Air Force	7			Saunders	0		
Jupiters	6	Air Force					
Matara	1	Saunders					
Saunders	2					Ratnams	2 5p
Navy	8					Negombo Youth	2 3p
Renown	7	Navy	8				
Army	7	Kandy York	0				
Kandy York	8			Navy	4		
Blue Star	4			Negombo Youth	5		
Old Bens	1	Blue Star	0				
Red Sun	0	Negombo Youth	2				
Negombo Youth	5						

Round of sixteen scores include penalties where relevant

CUP FINAL
Sugathadasa, Colombo
24-06-2006

Scorers - Kasun Jayasuriya [75], Naufer [84] for Ratnams; Karunaratne [35], Nimal Fernando [70] for Negombo

RECENT LEAGUE AND CUP RECORD

	Championship		Cup	
Year	Champions	Winners	Score	Runners-up
1996	Saunders	Old Benedictans		Renown
1997	Saunders	Saunders	1-0	Police
1998	Ratnams			
1999	Saunders	Saunders	3-2	Renown
2000	Ratnams	Ratnams	2-1	Saunders
2001	Saunders	Saunders	4-0	Negombo Youth
2002	Saunders			
2003	Negombo Youth	Renown	1-0	Air Force
2004	Blue Stars	Ratnams	2-2 4-2p	Renown
2005	Saunders	Ratnams	3-1	Saunders
2006	Negombo Youth	Ratnams	2-2 5-3p	Negombo Youth

CLUB DIRECTORY

Club	Town/City	Lge	Cup
Blue Stars	Kalutara	1	0
Jupiters	Colombo	0	0
Negombo Youth	Negombo	2	0
Old Bens	Colombo	1	1
Pettah United	Colombo	1	0
Ratnams	Colombo	2	4
Renown	Colombo	3	5
Saunders	Colombo	12	6
York	Kandy	0	1

STP – SAO TOME E PRINCIPE

NATIONAL TEAM RECORD
JULY 1ST 2002 TO JULY 9TH 2006

PL	W	D	L	F	A	%
3	0	0	3	1	12	0

FIFA/COCA-COLA WORLD RANKING

1993	1994	1995	1996	1997	1998	1999	2000	2001	2002	2003	2004	2005	High	Low
-	-	-	-	-	194	187	181	186	191	192	195	197	179 08/00	198 05/06

	2005–2006										
08/05	09/05	10/05	11/05	12/05	01/06	02/06	03/06	04/06	05/06	06/06	07/06
195	196	196	196	197	197	197	197	198	198	-	196

The development of football in one of Africa's smallest countries remained stagnant as a lack of finances and bitter in-fighting plagued the sport in the tiny island state. Sao Tome e Principe announced they were to skip the qualifiers for the African Nations Cup again, failing to enter the 2008 competition because it would cost an estimated US$750 000 for their national side to participate, a sum beyond their resources according to federation president Manuel Dende. The domestic competition was brought to a premature halt in December for a second successive season when the last round of the championship was annulled by the country's sports ministry. It was the final straw

INTERNATIONAL HONOURS
None

in a long dispute between the FSF and half of the 10 clubs in the first division. The dispute had begun six months earlier as the clubs demanded promised pay outs for achievements in the previous season, and it escalated into a judicial battle over compulsory medical tests for top flight footballers. The five clubs – Vitoria Riboque, Cruz Vermelha, Allianca Nacional, Andorinha and Caixao Grande – were all relegated but later reinstated into an expanded 14-team first division after the intervention of sports minister Jorge Lopes. The dispute was settled in time to get the new season off to a promising start in May 2006, after two years of bitter wrangling.

THE FIFA BIG COUNT OF 2000

	Male	Female		Male	Female
Registered players	500	0	Referees	20	0
Non registered players	500	0	Officials	100	0
Youth players	150	0	Total involved	1 270	
Total players	1 150		Number of clubs	10	
Professional players	0	0	Number of teams	20	

Federação Santomense de Futebol (FSF)
Rua Ex-João de Deus No QXXIII - 426/26, Casa postale 440, São Tomé, São Tomé e Príncipe
Tel +239 90 3672   Fax +239 2 21333
futebol@cstome.net   www.fsf.st
President: DENDE Manuel   General Secretary: BARROS Ricardino
Vice-President: DA GRACA ANDRADE Celestino   Treasurer: DA GRACA ANDRADE Celestino   Media Officer: none
Men's Coach: TBD   Women's Coach: TBD
FSF formed: 1975   CAF: 1986   FIFA: 1986
Green shirts, Yellow shorts, Green socks

RECENT INTERNATIONAL MATCHES PLAYED BY SAO TOME E PRINCIPE

2002	Opponents	Score		Venue	Comp	Scorers	Att	Referee
No international matches played in 2002 after June								
2003								
11-10	Libya	L	0-1	São Tomé	WCq		4 000	Yameogo JPN
12-11	Equatorial Guinea	L	1-3	Malabo	Fr			
16-11	Libya	L	0-8	Benghazi	WCq		20 000	Guirat TUN
2004								
No international matches played in 2004								
2005								
No international matches played in 2005								
2006								
No international matches played in 2006 before July								

Fr = Friendly match • WC = FIFA World Cup™ • q = qualifier

SAO TOME E PRINCIPE NATIONAL TEAM RECORDS AND RECORD SEQUENCES

Records			Sequence records					
Victory	2-0	EQG 1999, SLE 2000	Wins	2	1999-2000	Clean sheets	2	1999-2000
Defeat	0-11	CGO 1976	Defeats	6	1998-1999	Goals scored	2	1999-2000, 2000
Player Caps	n/a		Undefeated	2	1999-2000	Without goal	3	1999
Player Goals	n/a		Without win	11	1976-1999	Goals against	11	1976-1999

RECENT LEAGUE AND CUP RECORD

	League	Cup			São Tomé	Príncipe
Year	Champions	Winners	Score	Finalist	Champions	Champions
1995	Inter Bom-Bom	Caixão Grande			Inter Bom-Bom	
1996	Caixão Grande	Aliança Nacional				
1997	No Tournament	No Tournament				
1998	Os Operários	Sporting Praia Cruz				
1999	Sporting Praia Cruz	Vitória Riboque	3-2	Os Operários	Sporting Praia Cruz	Os Operários
2000	Inter Bom-Bom	Sporting Praia Cruz	3-1	Caixão Grande	Inter Bom-Bom	GD Sundy
2001	Bairros Unidos	GD Sundy	4-3	Vitória Riboque	Bairros Unidos	GD Sundy
2002	No tournament	No Tournament				
2003	Inter Bom Bom	Os Operários	1-0	UDESCAI	Inter Bom-Bom	1º de Maio
2004	Os Operários	No Tournament			UDESCAI	Os Operários
2005	No Tournament	No Tournament			No Tournament	No Tournament

SAO TOME E PRINCIPE COUNTRY INFORMATION

Capital	Sao Tomé	Independence	1975 from Portugal	GDP per Capita	$1 200
Population	181 565	Status	Republic	GNP Ranking	190
Area km²	1 001	Language	Portuguese	Dialling code	+239
Population density	185 per km²	Literacy rate	79%	Internet code	.st
% in urban areas	46%	Main religion	Christian	GMT +/–	0
Towns/Cities ('000)	Sao Tomé 62; Santo Amaro 8; Neves 7; Santana 7; Trinidade 7; São José dos Agnolares 2				
Neighbours (km)	Atlantic Ocean/Gulf of Guinea 209				
Main stadia	Estadio Nacional 12 de Julho – São Tomé 6 500				

SUD – SUDAN

NATIONAL TEAM RECORD
JULY 1ST 2002 TO JULY 9TH 2006

PL	W	D	L	F	A	%
56	19	14	23	72	78	46.4

FIFA/COCA-COLA WORLD RANKING

1993	1994	1995	1996	1997	1998	1999	2000	2001	2002	2003	2004	2005		High	Low
119	116	86	74	108	114	132	132	118	106	103	114	92		**74** 12/96	**137** 04/00

2005–2006											
08/05	09/05	10/05	11/05	12/05	01/06	02/06	03/06	04/06	05/06	06/06	07/06
102	93	94	93	92	92	93	95	95	97	-	113

As one of the founder members of the Confederation of African Football, Sudan enjoy an exalted place in the annals of the continent's football. They are also past hosts and winners of the African Nations Cup title, but it has now been decades since the Arabic-speaking country made any impact on the African football scene, consigned to a role in the supporting cast. Their absence from the Nations Cup stretched even further when they finished fifth in their FIFA World Cup™ qualifying group, which also served as a preliminary group for the 2006 African Nations Cup finals in Egypt, their immediate northern neighbours. Sudan were also unable to reach the last four at the CECAFA

INTERNATIONAL HONOURS
CAF African Cup of Nations 1970   CECAFA Cup 1980

Cup in Kigali, Rwanda in December 2005, but there was a brief foray back to past heady heights as Al Hilal reached the semi-final of the Arab Champions League, only to suffer a heavy aggregate defeat at the hands of eventual winners Raja Casablanca. Al Hilal also lost to Orlando Pirates in the third round of the Champions League, the second successive year that Sudanese representatives had made it to the cusp of qualification for the group phase but failed. At home Al Hilal and great rivals Al Merreikh predictably dominated the 2005 season. Hilal were unbeaten all season in League and Cup although they did lose on penalties to Merreikh in the Cup Final.

THE FIFA BIG COUNT OF 2000

	Male	Female		Male	Female
Registered players	18 000	0	Referees	1 000	0
Non registered players	80 000	0	Officials	7 000	0
Youth players	10 000	0	Total involved	116 000	
Total players	108 000		Number of clubs	400	
Professional players	0	0	Number of teams	2 500	

Sudan Football Association (SFA)
Bladia Street, Khartoum, Sudan
Tel +249 183 773495   Fax +249 183 776633
www.sudanfootball.com
President: SHADDAD Kamal, Dr   General Secretary: ABDELMAGEED Eldin
Vice-President: EL MAZZAL Ahmed Elhag   Treasurer: EL KHATEM Mustasim Gaffar Dr   Media Officer: none
Men's Coach: AHMED Mohamed   Women's Coach: None
SFA formed: 1936   CAF: 1957   FIFA: 1948
Red shirts, White shorts, Black socks

RECENT INTERNATIONAL MATCHES PLAYED BY SUDAN

2003	Opponents	Score		Venue	Comp	Scorers	Att	Referee
5-03	Congo DR	L	1-3	Khartoum	Fr			
29-03	Benin	W	3-0	Khartoum	CNq	Tambal 2 [34 71], Motaz [68]	20 000	Buenkadila COD
21-05	Uganda	D	0-0	Kampala	Fr			
24-05	Kenya	D	1-1	Khartoum	Fr			
8-06	Benin	L	0-3	Cotonou	CNq			Coulibaly MLI
21-06	Zambia	D	1-1	Lusaka	CNq	Galag [23]		Maxim KEN
17-09	Yemen	L	2-3	Sana'a	Fr	Ammar Ibrahim [64], Amir Damir [83]		
19-09	Yemen	W	2-1	Sana'a	Fr			
12-10	Eritrea	W	3-0	Khartoum	WCq	Tambal [68], El Rasheed [72], Ahmed Mugahid [89p]	18 000	Tamuni LBY
16-11	Eritrea	D	0-0	Asmara	WCq		12 000	Abdulle Ahmed SOM
30-11	Zanzibar †	W	4-0	Khartoum	CCrl	El Rasheed 2 [10 45], Aldoud [50], Saleh Mohammed [90p]		
4-12	Rwanda	W	3-0	Khartoum	CCrl	El Rasheed [11], Gibril [60], Onsa [87]		
8-12	Uganda	D	0-0	Khartoum	CCsf	L 3-4p		
10-12	Kenya	L	1-2	Khartoum	CC3p	Almazir Muhamoud [30p]		
2004								
19-04	Syria	L	1-2	Khartoum	Fr	Kabir [65]		
21-04	Syria	D	0-0	Khartoum	Fr			
22-05	Uganda	W	2-1	Khartoum	Fr	Muhamed Mohamed, Ali Musa		
25-05	Zambia	L	0-2	Khartoum	Fr			
6-06	Egypt	L	0-3	Khartoum	WCq		10 000	Kidane Tesfu ERI
20-06	Benin	D	1-1	Cotonou	WCq	Abd laziz [47+]	20 000	Guezzaz MAR
3-07	Libya	L	0-1	Khartoum	WCq		10 000	Bennett RSA
5-09	Côte d'Ivoire	L	0-5	Abidjan	WCq		20 000	Mana NGA
9-10	Cameroon	D	1-1	Omdurman	WCq	Agab Sido [17]	30 000	Buenkadila COD
12-12	Kenya	D	2-2	Addis Abeba	CCrl	Mustafa Ali [45p], Kamal [79]		
14-12	Uganda	W	2-1	Addis Abeba	CCrl	Kamal [3], El Rasheed [75]		
18-12	Somalia	W	4-0	Addis Abeba	CCrl	Mustafa Haitham [46], Hameedama [63], Tambal [69], Omar Mohamed [90]		
22-12	Burundi	L	1-2	Addis Abeba	CCsf	Mustafa Haitham [54p]		
25-12	Kenya	W	2-1	Addis Abeba	CC3p	Kamal 2 [30 60]	30 000	
2005								
12-03	Ethiopia	W	3-1	Khartoum	Fr			
27-03	Cameroon	L	1-2	Yaoundé	WCq	Tambal [41]	30 000	Diatta SEN
22-05	Chad	W	4-1	Khartoum	Fr			
27-05	Chad	D	1-1	Khartoum	Fr			
5-06	Egypt	L	1-6	Cairo	WCq	Tambal [83]	20 000	Mususa ZIM
17-08	Benin	W	1-0	Omdurman	WCq	Tambal [20]	12 000	Maillet SEY
2-09	Libya	D	0-0	Tripoli	WCq		20 000	Pare BFA
8-10	Côte d'Ivoire	L	1-3	Omdurman	WCq	Tambal [89]	20 000	Damon RSA
24-11	Ethiopia	L	1-5	Khartoum	Fr			
29-11	Somalia	W	4-1	Kigali	CCrl	Eldod Badreldin 2, Agab Sido, Tambal		
1-12	Ethiopia	L	1-3	Kigali	CCrl	Galag		
3-12	Uganda	L	0-3	Kigali	CCrl			
5-12	Djibouti	W	4-0	Kigali	CCrl	Tambal, Agab Sido, Alaa, Eldin		
2006								
4-06	Algeria	L	0-1	Algiers	Fr			

Fr = Friendly match • CN = CAF African Cup of Nations • CC = CECAFA Cup • AR = Arab Cup • WC = FIFA World Cup™
q = qualifier • rl = first round group • sf = semi-final • 3p = third place play-off • † Not an official international

SUDAN NATIONAL TEAM RECORDS AND RECORD SEQUENCES

Records			Sequence records					
Victory	15-0	OMA 1965	Wins	5	1965	Clean sheets	5	2003
Defeat	0-8	KOR 1979	Defeats	5	2000-2001	Goals scored	12	1996-1998
Player Caps	n/a		Undefeated	9	1968-1969	Without goal	4	2000-2001
Player Goals	n/a		Without win	9	1980-1982	Goals against	15	1996-1998

SUDAN COUNTRY INFORMATION

Capital	Khartoum	Independence	1956 from Egypt and UK	GDP per Capita	$1 900
Population	39 148 162	Status	Republic	GNP Ranking	83
Area km²	2 505 810	Language	Arabic, English, Nubian	Dialling code	+249
Population density	15 per km²	Literacy rate	61%	Internet code	.sd
% in urban areas	25%	Main religion	Muslim	GMT + / –	+2
Towns/Cities ('000)	Omdurman 2 810; Khartoum 1 974; Khartoum North 1 530; Niyala 499; Port Sudan 459; Kassala 401; El Obeid 393; Kusti 345; Wad Madani 332; Gadaref 322, El Fasher 252				
Neighbours (km)	Eritrea 605; Ethiopia 1 606; Kenya 232; Uganda 435; Congo DR 628; Central African Republic 1 165; Chad 1 360; Libya 383; Egypt 1 273; Red Sea 853				
Main stadia	National Stadium – Khartoum 20 000; El Merriekh – Omdurman 30 000				

SUDAN 2005

PREMIER LEAGUE

	Pl	W	D	L	F	A	Pts	Hilal	Merreikh	Hilal PS	Jazeerat	Khartoum	Merghani	Amal	Mawrada	Ittihad	Hay Al Arab	Shambat	Taka
Al Hilal Omdurman †	22	18	4	0	58	10	58		3-0	1-0	1-0	2-0	2-0	6-1	5-1	3-1	7-1	3-0	4-1
Al Merreikh Omdurman‡	22	18	2	2	61	8	56	0-0		1-0	4-0	2-0	6-0	3-1	5-0	3-0	5-0	3-0	2-0
Al Hilal Port Sudan	22	10	5	7	21	16	35	1-2	1-0		1-0	1-1	0-0	1-1	0-0	3-0	2-0	1-0	2-1
Jazeerat Al-Feel	22	7	6	9	27	29	27	0-0	0-4	1-1		1-3	0-1	2-2	2-2	2-2	0-1	6-1	2-1
Khartoum-3	22	7	6	9	22	30	27	1-5	1-3	2-0	2-1		0-2	2-2	0-1	2-1	0-1	2-0	2-1
Al Merghani Kassala	22	8	3	11	20	32	27	1-2	0-3	1-0	0-2	0-2		1-1	3-0	1-0	1-0	4-2	1-1
Al Amal Atbara	22	5	11	6	22	29	26	0-0	1-2	2-1	1-1	0-0	2-1		1-1	0-1	1-0	1-0	0-0
Al Mawrada Omdurman	22	5	10	7	19	29	25	0-2	0-1	0-1	0-2	1-1	3-0	3-1		1-1	2-1	1-0	1-1
Al Ittihad Wad Medani	22	5	7	10	18	28	22	0-2	0-0	2-0	0-1	1-0	1-2	2-3	1-1		2-1	1-2	1-0
Hay Al Arab Pt. Sudan	22	5	6	11	14	32	21	0-0	1-3	0-1	1-0	0-0	2-1	1-1	1-1	0-0		0-1	1-3
Al Shambat Khartoum	22	6	3	13	16	37	21	1-5	0-5	1-2	0-1	4-0	1-0	1-0	0-0	0-0	1-1		1-0
Al Taka Kassala	22	3	7	12	16	34	16	1-3	0-6	0-2	1-3	1-1	2-0	0-0	0-0	1-1	0-1	1-0	

16/02/2005 - 23/10/2005 • † Qualified for the CAF Champions League • ‡ Qualified for the CAF Confederations Cup • Al Ahli Atbara and Al Nil Wad Medani promoted • Relegation play-off: Hay Al Arab 0-0 3-1p Al Shambat
Top scorers: Haitham TAMBAL, Hilal Omdurman, 19; Faisal AL AJAB, Merreikh Omdurman, 19

SUDAN CUP 2005

Quarter-finals			Semi-finals		Final		
Al Merreikh	1	5					
Al Hilal Kadougli	0	0	Al Merreikh	3			
Jazeerat Al Feel	1	0	Al Mawrada	0			
Al Mawrada	2	0			Al Merreikh	0	4p
Al Hilal Port Sudan	0	1			Al Hilal	0	2p
Dakka Barbar	0	0	Al Hilal Port Sudan	0	1		
Al Merreikh Nyala	0	0	Al Hilal	0	4	14-12-2005	
Al Hilal	1	6					

RECENT LEAGUE AND CUP RECORD

	Championship		Cup		
Year	Champions		Winners	Score	Runners-up
1998	Al Hilal		Al Mawrada		
1999	Al Hilal		Al Mawrada		
2000	Al Merreikh		Al Hilal	3-0	Al Ahly
2001	Al Merreikh		Al Merreikh	1-0	Al Mawrada
2002	Al Merreikh				
2003	Al Hilal				
2004	Al Hilal		Al Hilal	0-0 3-2p	Al Merreikh
2005	Al Hilal		Al Merreikh	0-0 4-2p	Al Hilal

SUI – SWITZERLAND

NATIONAL TEAM RECORD
JULY 1ST 2002 TO JULY 9TH 2006

PL	W	D	L	F	A	%
43	19	15	9	68	46	61.6

FIFA/COCA-COLA WORLD RANKING

1993	1994	1995	1996	1997	1998	1999	2000	2001	2002	2003	2004	2005		High		Low	
12	7	18	47	62	83	47	58	63	44	44	51	35		3	08/93	83	12/98

2005–2006											
08/05	09/05	10/05	11/05	12/05	01/06	02/06	03/06	04/06	05/06	06/06	07/06
42	38	38	36	35	36	37	35	35	35	-	13

When Switzerland was awarded the co-hosting of UEFA Euro 2008™, few thought that the national team would be able to make much of an impact in the tournament. How wrong they may be. The long-term planning at youth level is beginning to reap dividends at senior level and in 23 games following their appearance at Euro 2004 in Portugal, Switzerland lost just once - in the intimidating atmosphere of Istanbul in the 2006 FIFA World Cup™ play-off. Despite losing that game, the Swiss still qualified for the finals in Germany where they made it through the group stage for only the third time. That their second round match against Ukraine was a huge disappointment is beyond

INTERNATIONAL HONOURS
Qualified for the FIFA World Cup™ finals 1934 1938 1950 1954 1962 1966 1994 2006

doubt, especially their inability to score in the penalty shoot-out, but the experience will have served the team well. At the heart of the Swiss renaissance is club football which has gone through a hugely positive transformation, and the last game of the 2006 season saw the top two face each other in a thrilling finale. Three minutes into injury time with the score 1-1, FC Basel were on course for a hat-trick of titles but then Iulian Filipescu scored to win the match, and a first title in 25 years, for FC Zurich on goal difference. Remarkably, it was Basel's first home defeat in 60 matches. Second division FC Sion also caused a sensation by beating BSC Young Boys to win the Cup.

THE FIFA BIG COUNT OF 2000

	Male	Female		Male	Female
Registered players	89 980	4 000	Referees	4 540	60
Non registered players	200 000	25 000	Officials	250 000	200
Youth players	115 800	3 000	Total involved	692 580	
Total players	437 780		Number of clubs	1 453	
Professional players	300	0	Number of teams	11 800	

Schweizerischer Fussball-Verband (SFV/ASF)
Worbstrasse 48, Postfach, Bern 15 3000, Switzerland
Tel +41 31 9508111   Fax +41 31 9508181
sfv.asf@football.ch   www.football.ch
President: ZLOCZOWER Ralph   General Secretary: GILLIERON Peter
Vice-President: CORNELLA Guido   Treasurer: POMA Giuseppe   Media Officer: BENOIT Pierre
Men's Coach: KUHN Koebi   Women's Coach: VON SIEBENTHAL Beatrice
SFV/ASF formed: 1895   UEFA: 1954   FIFA: 1904
Red shirts with white trimmings, White shorts, Red socks or White shirts with red trimmings, Red shorts, White socks

RECENT INTERNATIONAL MATCHES PLAYED BY SWITZERLAND

2002	Opponents	Score	Venue	Comp	Scorers	Att	Referee
21-08	Austria	W 3-2	Basel	Fr	Yakin.H [19], Frei [41], Yakin.M [76]	23 500	Rosetti ITA
8-09	Georgia	W 4-1	Basel	ECq	Frei [37], Yakin.H [62], Muller.P [74], Chapuisat [81]	20 500	Hrinak SVK
12-10	Albania	D 1-1	Tirana	ECq	Yakin.M [37]	15 000	Erdemir TUR
16-10	Republic of Ireland	W 2-1	Dublin	ECq	Yakin.H [45], Celestini [87]	40 000	Pedersen NOR
2003							
12-02	Slovenia	W 5-1	Nova Gorica	Fr	Yakin.H [3], Haas [29], Frei 2 [36 78], Cabanas [49]	3 500	Abraham HUN
2-04	Georgia	D 0-0	Tbilisi	ECq		10 000	Trivkovic CRO
30-04	Italy	L 1-2	Geneva	Fr	Frei [6]	30 000	Ledentu FRA
7-06	Russia	D 2-2	Basel	ECq	Frei 2 [14 16]	30 500	Dauden Ibanez ESP
11-06	Albania	W 3-2	Geneva	ECq	Haas [11], Frei [32], Cabanas [72]	26 000	Bennett ENG
20-08	France	L 0-2	Geneva	Fr		30 000	Allaerts BEL
10-09	Russia	L 1-4	Moscow	ECq	Karyaka OG [12]	29 000	Collina ITA
11-10	Republic of Ireland	W 2-0	Basel	ECq	Yakin.H [6], Frei [60]	31 006	Frisk SWE
2004							
18-02	Morocco	L 1-2	Rabat	Fr	Frei [90]	3 000	Berber ALG
31-03	Greece	L 0-1	Heraklion	Fr		33 000	Temmink NED
28-04	Slovenia	W 2-1	Geneva	Fr	Celestini [66], Yakin.H [85]	7 500	Bossen NED
2-06	Germany	L 0-2	Basel	Fr		30 000	Messina ITA
6-06	Liechtenstein	W 1-0	Zurich	Fr	Gygax [90]	10 200	Drabek AUT
13-06	Croatia	D 0-0	Leiria	ECr1		24 090	Cortez Batista POR
17-06	England	L 0-3	Coimbra	ECr1		28 214	Ivanov.V RUS
21-06	France	L 1-3	Coimbra	ECr1	Vonlanthen [26]	28 111	Michel SVK
18-08	Northern Ireland	D 0-0	Zurich	Fr		4 000	Vollquartz DEN
4-09	Faroe Islands	W 6-0	Basel	WCq	Vonlanthen 3 [10 14 57], Rey 3 [29 44 55]	11 880	Tudor ROM
8-09	Republic of Ireland	D 1-1	Basel	WCq	Yakin.H [17]	28 000	Vassaras GRE
9-10	Israel	D 2-2	Tel Aviv	WCq	Frei [26], Vonlanthen [34]	37 976	Shield AUS
2005							
9-02	United Arab Emirates	W 2-1	Dubai	Fr	Gygax [9], Muller.P [79]	1 000	El Hilali OMA
26-03	France	D 0-0	Paris	WCq		79 373	De Santis ITA
30-03	Cyprus	W 1-0	Zurich	WCq	Frei [87]	16 066	Dougal SCO
4-06	Faroe Islands	W 3-1	Toftir	WCq	Wicky [25], Frei 2 [72 84]	2 047	Gumienny BEL
17-08	Norway	W 2-0	Oslo	Fr	Frei [50], OG [59]	19 623	Vollquartz DEN
3-09	Israel	D 1-1	Basel	WCq	Frei [6]	30 000	Rosetti ITA
7-09	Cyprus	W 3-1	Nicosia	WCq	Frei [15], Senderos [71], Gygax [84]	2 561	Ivanov.N RUS
8-10	France	D 1-1	Berne	WCq	Magnin [80]	31 400	Hauge NOR
12-10	Republic of Ireland	D 0-0	Dublin	WCq		35 944	Merk GER
12-11	Turkey	W 2-0	Berne	WCpo	Senderos [41], Behrami [86]	31 130	Michel SVK
16-11	Turkey	L 2-4	Istanbul	WCpo	Frei [2p], Streller [84]	42 000	De Bleeckere BEL
2006							
1-03	Scotland	W 3-1	Glasgow	Fr	Barnetta [21], Gygax [41], Cabanas [69]	20 952	Coue FRA
27-05	Côte d'Ivoire	D 1-1	Basel	Fr	Barnetta [32]	20 000	Vuorela FIN
31-05	Italy	D 1-1	Geneva	Fr	Gygax [32]	30 000	Sippel GER
3-06	China PR	W 4-1	Zurich	Fr	Frei 2 [40 49p], Streller 2 [47 73]	16 000	Stokes IRL
13-06	France	D 0-0	Stuttgart	WCr1		52 000	Ivanov.V RUS
19-06	Togo	W 2-0	Dortmund	WCr1	Frei [16], Barnetta [88]	65 000	Amarilla PAR
23-06	Korea Republic	W 2-0	Hanover	WCr1	Snderos [23], Frei [77]	43 000	Elizondo ARG
26-06	Ukraine	D 0-0	Cologne	WCr2	L 0-3p	45 000	Archundia MEX

Fr = Friendly match • EC = UEFA EURO 2004™ • WC = FIFA World Cup™ • q = qualifier • po = play-off

SWITZERLAND NATIONAL TEAM RECORDS AND RECORD SEQUENCES

Records			Sequence records				
Victory	9-0	LTU 1924	Wins	5	1960-1961	Clean sheets	4	1973
Defeat	0-9	ENG 1909, HUN 1911	Defeats	11	1928-1930	Goals scored	22	1921-1924
Player Caps	117	HERMANN Heinz	Undefeated	14	2004-2005	Without goal	5	1985
Player Goals	34	ABEGGLEN/TURKYILMAZ	Without win	16	1928-1930	Goals against	45	1926-1932

SWITZERLAND COUNTRY INFORMATION

Capital	Bern	Formation	1291	GDP per Capita	$32 700
Population	7 450 867	Status	Federal Republic	GNP Ranking	17
Area km²	41 290	Language	German 64%, French 19%, Italian 7%	Dialling code	.ch
Population density	180 per km²	Literacy rate	99%	Internet code	+41
% in urban areas	61%	Main religion	Christian	GMT + / –	+1
Towns/Cities ('000)	Zürich 346; Geneva 181; Basel 164; Bern 123; Lausanne 118; Winterthur 91; St Gallen 72; Luzern 57; Biel 49; Thun 41; La Chaux-de-Fonds 36; Köniz 35; Schaffhausen 34, Neuchâtel 31				
Neighbours (km)	Austria 164; Liechtenstein 41; Italy 740; France 573; Germany 334				
Main stadia	St Jakob Park – Basel 42 500; Stade de Genève – Geneva 30 000; Letzigrund – Zürich 30 000				

NATIONAL TEAM PLAYERS AND COACHES

Record Caps			Record Goals			Recent Coaches	
HERMANN Heinz	1978-'91	117	ABEGGLEN Max 'Xam'	1922-'37	34	JEANDUPEUX Daniel	1986-'89
GEIGER Alain	1980-'96	112	TURKYILMAZ Kubilay	1988-'01	34	WOLFISBERG Paul	1989
CHAPUISAT Stéphane	1989-'04	103	ABEGGLEN Trello	1927-'43	29	STIELIKE Ueli	1989-'91
VOGEL Johan	1995-'06	89	FATTON Jacky	1946-'55	29	HODGSON Roy	1992-95
MINELLI Severino	1930-'43	80	FREI Alexander	2001-'06	27	JORGE Artur	1996
SFORZA Ciriaco	1991-'01	79	KNUP Adrian	1989-'96	26	FRINGER Rolf	1996-'97
EGLI André	1979-'94	79	HUGI Josef	1951-'61	23	GRESS Gilbert	1998-'99
HENCHOZ Stéphane	1993-'05	72	ANTENEN Charly	1948-'62	22	ZAUGG Hanspeter	2000
BICKEL Alfred	1936-'54	71	AMADO Lauro	1935-'48	21	TROSSERO Enzo	2000-'01
WICKY Raphael	1996-'06	71	CHAPUISAT Stéphane	1989-'04	21	KUHN Koebi	2001-

CLUB DIRECTORY

Club	Town/City	Stadium	Capacity	www.	Lge	Cup
FC Aarau	Aarau	Brügglifeld Stadion	13 500	fcaarau.ch	3	1
FC Basel	Basel	St Jakob Park	31 539	fcb.ch	11	7
Grasshopper-Club	Zürich	Hardturm Stadion	17 666	gcz.ch	26	18
FC Luzern	Luzern	Allmend	18 400	fcl.ch	1	2
FC Schaffhausen	Schaffhausen	Breite Stadion	6 000	fcschaffhausen.ch	0	0
FC St. Gallen	St. Gallen	Espenmoos Stadion	11 300	fcsg.ch	2	1
FC Sion	Sion	Tourbillon	13 000	fc-sion.ch	2	10
FC Thun	Thun	Lachen Stadion	7 250	fcthun.ch	0	0
BSC Young Boys	Berne	Neufeld Stadion	12 000	bscyb.ch	11	6
FC Zürich	Zürich	Letzigrund Stadion	19 400	fcz.ch	10	7

RECENT LEAGUE AND CUP RECORD

	Championship						Cup		
Year	Champions	Pts	Runners-up	Pts	Third	Pts	Winners	Score	Runners-up
1990	Grasshopper-Club	31	Lausanne-Sports	31	Neuchâtel Xamax	30	Grasshopper-Club	2-1	Neuchâtel Xamax
1991	Grasshopper-Club	33	FC Sion	29	Neuchâtel Xamax	29	FC Sion	3-2	BSC Young Boys
1992	FC Sion	33	Neuchâtel Xamax	31	Grasshopper-Club	30	FC Luzern	3-1	FC Lugano
1993	FC Aarau	34	BSC Young Boys	28	FC Lugano	27	FC Lugano	4-1	Grasshopper-Club
1994	Servette FC	34	Grasshopper-Club	33	FC Sion	31	Grasshopper-Club	4-0	FC Schaffhausen
1995	Grasshopper-Club	37	FC Lugano	30	Neuchâtel Xamax	28	FC Sion	4-2	Grasshopper-Club
1996	Grasshopper-Club	52	FC Sion	47	Neuchâtel Xamax	43	FC Sion	3-2	Servette FC
1997	FC Sion	49	Neuchâtel Xamax	46	Grasshopper-Club	45	FC Sion	3-3 5-4p	FC Luzern
1998	Grasshopper-Club	57	Servette FC	41	Lausanne-Sports	40	Lausanne-Sports	2-2 4-3p	FC St. Gallen
1999	Servette FC	46	Grasshopper-Club	46	Lausanne-Sports	45	Lausanne-Sports	2-0	Grasshopper-Club
2000	FC St. Gallen	54	Lausanne-Sports	44	FC Basel	40	FC Zürich	2-2 3-0p	Lausanne-Sports
2001	Grasshopper-Club	46	FC Lugano	41	FC St. Gallen	40	Servette FC	3-0	Yverdon-Sports
2002	FC Basel	55	Grasshopper-Club	45	FC Lugano	42	FC Basel	2-1	Grasshopper-Club
2003	Grasshopper-Club	57	FC Basel	56	Neuchâtel Xamax	35	FC Basel	6-0	Neuchâtel Xamax
2004	FC Basel	85	BSC Young Boys	72	Servette FC	52	FC Wil	3-2	Grasshopper-Club
2005	FC Basel	70	FC Thun	60	Grasshopper-Club	50	FC Zürich	3-1	FC Luzern
2006	FC Zürich	78	FC Basel	78	BSC Young Boys		FC Sion	1-1 5-3p	BSC Young Boys

SWITZERLAND 2005-06

AXPO SUPER LEAGUE

	Pl	W	D	L	F	A	Pts	Zürich	Basel	Young Boys	Grasshoppers	Thun	St Gallen	Aarau	Sch'hausen	Xamax	Yverdon
FC Zürich †	36	23	9	4	86	36	78	—	2-4 1-1	1-1 3-3	4-2 2-0	2-2 1-0	3-0 1-0	3-0 6-0	5-0 0-0	3-2 4-1	1-1 4-1
FC Basel ‡	36	23	9	4	87	42	78	2-1 1-2	—	1-1 2-0	1-0 2-1	5-1 2-0	1-0 3-1	7-2 1-1	1-0 1-1	3-0 2-1	3-1 2-1
BSC Young Boys ‡	36	17	11	8	60	46	62	3-1 0-1	1-6 4-2	—	0-3 1-1	0-0 2-1	1-0 2-0	0-0 2-1	3-1 1-2	3-2 3-1	2-2 2-1
Grasshopper-Club	36	14	13	9	44	33	55	1-0 0-0	2-2 1-1	1-1 1-0	—	2-0 3-1	3-1 2-1	1-1 0-0	1-1 0-1	0-1 3-0	2-2 3-2
FC Thun	36	14	7	15	50	53	49	1-6 1-3	3-0 1-1	1-1 1-1	2-1 0-1	—	5-1 3-1	2-0 1-1	0-3 2-1	2-3 3-0	3-0 1-0
FC St Gallen	36	11	7	18	51	56	40	1-3 2-3	3-3 2-2	0-1 1-3	1-1 0-2	5-1 1-0	—	2-1 1-1	0-0 3-0	7-1 1-0	2-1 2-0
FC Aarau	36	8	11	17	29	63	35	1-1 1-1	0-2 1-5	1-0 1-5	0-1 1-0	2-1 0-1	1-4 1-0	—	0-2 1-1	2-0 3-1	1-1 1-0
FC Schaffhausen	36	7	12	17	32	55	33	0-2 1-4	1-2 0-4	3-2 1-1	0-2 1-3	1-1 1-3	0-1 0-0	1-1 0-0	—	1-1 0-0	1-2 1-1
Neuchâtel Xamax	36	9	6	21	41	70	33	3-5 0-1	3-2 1-2	1-3 1-3	0-0 1-0	0-2 0-0	0-1 2-2	2-0 2-0	1-0 2-0	—	4-0 2-0
Yverdon-Sports	36	9	5	22	38	64	32	0-2 0-3	1-2 1-3	0-3 1-1	2-0 0-1	2-0 0-1	1-0 2-1	4-1 3-1	0-1 0-4	4-1 2-1	—

13/07/2005 - 14/05/2006 • † Qualified for the UEFA Champions League • ‡ Qualified for the UEFA Cup • Top scorers: Alhassan KEITA, Zürich, 20; DANIEL, BSC Young Boys, 18; Matias DELGADO, Basel, 18 • Relegation play-off: FC Sion 0-0 3-0 Neuchâtel Xamax • FC Sion promoted

SWITZERLAND 2005-06

CHALLENGE LEAGUE (2)

	Pl	W	D	L	F	A	Pts	Luzern	Sion	Lausanne	Chiasso	CDF	Wohlen	Wil	Vaduz	Bellinzona	Lugano	Baulmes	Concordia	Kriens	Winterthur	Y. Fellows	Locarno	Baden	Meyrin
FC Luzern	34	24	7	3	69	33	79	—	2-1	1-1	2-1	5-1	0-1	2-1	2-1	1-0	3-2	1-0	5-1	2-2	2-0	3-3	1-0	3-0	3-0
FC Sion	34	22	6	6	61	24	72	1-0	—	1-2	1-1	1-1	2-0	2-0	4-1	4-1	3-0	0-1	1-0	2-0	2-0	4-0	2-1	1-0	1-0
Lausanne-Sport	34	20	8	6	64	42	68	4-1	2-2	—	1-0	4-3	1-0	3-3	3-1	3-0	1-0	3-0	3-0	2-0	5-4	1-3	2-1	3-1	1-1
FC Chiasso	34	17	8	9	51	31	59	1-1	1-0	2-0	—	3-0	5-0	0-3	4-0	0-0	0-2	1-0	1-0	0-2	1-1	1-2	1-0	3-0	2-0
La Chaux-de-Fonds	34	15	13	6	60	44	58	0-0	1-0	1-0	3-1	—	2-2	5-3	0-0	2-4	4-1	1-1	1-1	1-1	1-1	2-1	1-2	2-0	
FC Wohlen	34	15	7	12	50	40	52	1-2	3-0	0-1	0-0	1-0	—	1-2	3-1	5-1	3-1	1-1	1-0	0-4	0-0	5-0	1-1	3-0	
FC Wil 1900	34	14	9	11	61	55	51	1-2	2-2	3-1	2-5	1-4	2-0	—	2-0	0-1	2-2	1-1	5-1	2-0	4-3	0-0	4-2	2-0	2-2
FC Vaduz	34	13	7	14	57	54	46	3-3	0-0	2-1	1-3	0-3	1-1	0-1	—	2-4	1-4	0-0	4-1	1-1	4-3	3-1	3-1	3-0	4-0
AC Bellinzona	34	12	10	12	43	45	46	0-2	1-2	2-2	0-0	0-2	2-0	0-0	2-0	—	2-0	1-0	2-2	3-0	0-0	2-2	2-0	2-0	
AC Lugano	34	10	11	13	41	52	41	2-2	0-3	1-1	3-1	0-0	0-0	0-3	0-4	2-0	—	1-1	3-0	1-1	2-1	3-2	0-0	1-1	4-1
FC Baulmes	34	9	13	12	36	45	40	0-1	0-1	1-2	2-3	2-2	1-0	2-0	0-3	2-0	2-1	—	0-1	2-2	1-3	1-1	2-1	1-0	1-1
Concordia Basel	34	10	9	15	44	57	39	0-1	0-1	1-3	0-0	2-2	1-0	2-0	0-3	2-0	2-1		—	2-2	2-1	1-1	4-3	1-1	1-0
SC Kriens	34	9	12	13	42	56	39	0-1	0-5	4-2	0-2	0-2	0-2	2-0	3-2	2-3	1-2	1-0	4-1	—	1-0	0-0	0-2	2-2	1-1
FC Winterthur	34	10	7	17	62	53	37	0-1	4-4	1-2	2-1	2-3	2-3	2-3	1-2	4-0	4-0	1-1	1-0	6-0	—	0-1	1-1	3-1	4-0
Young Fellows Juventus	34	8	14	12	39	53	35	1-5	0-2	0-1	1-3	2-2	0-1	4-2	1-0	0-4	0-0	1-1	0-0	2-3	0-4	—	1-1	3-0	0-0
FC Locarno	34	7	7	20	35	60	28	1-4	0-2	1-2	0-1	0-1	1-4	3-1	1-0	1-1	0-1	1-0	0-2	2-0	3-3	2-1	—	2-1	1-0
FC Baden 1897	34	6	9	19	30	59	27	1-2	0-1	1-2	1-2	0-3	1-2	2-2	1-0	1-1	1-1	2-4	1-0	0-0	0-1	3-1	1-0	—	3-2
FC Meyrin	34	1	11	22	26	68	14	2-3	0-3	0-0	0-1	2-3	2-0	0-0	2-3	0-2	1-2	0-2	2-0	0-1	1-4	2-3	1-1		—

15/07/2005 - 14/05/2006 • Young Fellows deducted three points

SWISSCOM CUP 2005-06

Round of 16
- FC Sion * — 1
- AC Bellinzona — 0
- FC Küssnacht * — 1
- FC Locarno — 2
- Servette Geneva * — 1 5p
- FC Thun — 1 4p
- FC Luzern — 0
- FC Winterthur * — 2
- FC Zürich — 4
- FC Basel * — 3
- FC Schaffhausen * — 0 4p
- FC Aarau — 0 5p
- AC Lugano * — 2
- FC Wil 1900 — 1
- SC Kriens * — 1
- BSC Young Boys — 2

Quarter-finals
- FC Sion — 1
- FC Locarno * — 0
- Servette Geneva * — 1
- FC Winterthur — 3
- FC Zürich — 1 3p
- FC Aarau * — 1 2p
- AC Lugano * — 1
- BSC Young Boys — 2

Semi-finals
- FC Sion — 1
- FC Winterthur * — 0
- FC Zürich * — 1
- BSC Young Boys — 4

Final
- FC Sion ‡ — 1 5p
- BSC Young Boys — 1 3p

SWISS CUP FINAL

Stade de Suisse, Berne
17-04-2006, Att: 30 569, Ref: Rutz

Scorers - Goran Obradovic [55] for Sion; Carlos Varela [16] for Young Boys

* Home team • ‡ Qualified for the UEFA Cup

SUR – SURINAM

NATIONAL TEAM RECORD
JULY 1ST 2002 TO JULY 9TH 2006

PL	W	D	L	F	A	%
11	4	4	3	24	13	54.5

FIFA/COCA-COLA WORLD RANKING

1993	1994	1995	1996	1997	1998	1999	2000	2001	2002	2003	2004	2005		High		Low
117	104	124	131	145	160	162	164	141	141	158	149	152		92	07/94	168 04/01

					2005–2006						
08/05	09/05	10/05	11/05	12/05	01/06	02/06	03/06	04/06	05/06	06/06	07/06
151	151	151	151	152	153	153	153	157	158	-	150

To pick an all-time XI of players who could have appeared for Surinam is an easy task. The coach would be Frank Rijkaard of European Champions Barcelona. The captain would be Ruud Gullit, the midfield would be marshalled by Aron Winter and Edgar Davids... the list goes on. But they all chose not to play for Surinam, if indeed they even thought about it in the first place. Therein lies Surinam's problem because if a player from Surinam, or of Surinamese origin, shows any promise he will almost certainly be picked up by a Dutch system noted for its scouting and youth development. This isn't to say that Surinam is devoid of football. Quite the opposite, but imagine the possibilities.

INTERNATIONAL HONOURS
CONCACAF Champions Cup Transvaal 1973 1981

2005 champions Robinhood showed that they can be a force in the Caribbean when they entered the CONCACAF Champions' Cup and almost made it to the quarter-finals after reaching the final of the CFU Caribbean championship. Both matches in the final against Jamaica's Portmore United were played at home, and had they held on to their two goal advantage in the first match, they may well have been crowned Caribbean champions, but they conceded a goal late in the game and then lost the second leg 4-0. Robinhood did win the SVB Cup in 2006 but were runners-up to Walking Bout Co in the championship.

THE FIFA BIG COUNT OF 2000

	Male	Female		Male	Female
Registered players	4 659	750	Referees	125	20
Non registered players	12 500	200	Officials	250	50
Youth players	1 463	0	Total involved	20 017	
Total players	19 572		Number of clubs	30	
Professional players	0	0	Number of teams	257	

Surinaamse Voetbal Bond (SVB)
Letitia Vriesdelaan 7, PO Box 1223, Paramaribo, Surinam
Tel +597 473112   Fax +597 479718
svb@sr.net   www.svb.sr
President: GISKUS Louis   General Secretary: FELTER Harold
Vice-President: KOORNDIJK Ronald   Treasurer: GOBARDHAN Waldo   Media Officer: POCORNI Dennis
Men's Coach: KOSWAL Leo   Women's Coach: FELTER Harold
SVB formed: 1920   CONCACAF: 1964   FIFA: 1929
White shirts, Green shorts, Green socks

RECENT INTERNATIONAL MATCHES PLAYED BY SURINAM

2002	Opponents	Score		Venue	Comp	Scorers	Att	Referee
28-07	Aruba	W	2-0	Oranjestad	GCq	Kejansi [55], Sandvliet [62]		Faneijte ATG
11-08	Aruba	W	6-0	Paramaribo	GCq	Zinhagel 2 [28 47], Kejansi 3 [35 57 84], Kinsaini [63]	2 500	Mercera ATG
2003								
No international matches played in 2003								
2004								
10-01	Netherlands Antilles	D	1-1	Paramaribo	Fr	Sandvliet [53]		Jol NED
17-01	Netherlands Antilles	L	0-2	Willemstad	Fr			
28-02	Aruba	W	2-1	Oranjestad	WCq	Felter [54p], Zinhagel [63]	2 108	Moreno PAN
27-03	Aruba	W	8-1	Paramaribo	WCq	Kinsaini 2 [6 49], Loswijk [14], Felter 3 [18 65 66], Sandvliet [42], Zinhagel [90]	4 000	Prendergast JAM
12-06	Guatemala	D	1-1	Paramaribo	WCq	Purperhart [14]	5 500	Jimenez CRC
20-06	Guatemala	L	1-3	Guatemala City	WCq	Brandon [82]	19 610	Rodriguez MEX
24-11	Grenada	D	2-2	Tunapuna	GCq	Modeste OG [27], Sandvliet [59]	2 000	Forde BRB
26-11	Puerto Rico	D	1-1	Marabella	GCq	Sandvliet [45]		Forde BRB
28-11	Trinidad and Tobago	L	0-1	Malabar	GCq			Forde BRB
2005								
No international matches played in 2005								
2006								
No international matches played in 2006 before July								

Fr = Friendly match • GC = CONCACAF Gold Cup • WC = FIFA World Cup™ • q = qualifier

SURINAM NATIONAL TEAM RECORDS AND RECORD SEQUENCES

Records			Sequence records					
Victory	8-1	ARU 2004	Wins	4	1992	Clean sheets	4	1980
Defeat	1-8	MEX 1977	Defeats	5	1997	Goals scored	9	1990-1992
Player Caps	n/a		Undefeated	9	1990-1992	Without goal	2	Six times
Player Goals	n/a		Without win	6	Four times	Goals against	22	1994-1999

SURINAM 2005-06 HOOFDKLASSE

	Pl	W	D	L	F	A	Pts
Walking Bout Co	26	17	6	3	75	33	57
Robinhood	26	16	8	2	78	35	56
Inter Moengotapoe	26	13	9	4	45	31	48
FCS Nacional	26	14	5	7	66	36	47
Royal '95	26	13	5	8	61	36	44
Super Red Eagles	26	11	4	11	41	47	37
Cosmos	26	11	3	12	47	51	36
Leo Victor	26	8	10	8	51	46	34
Transvaal	26	10	4	12	39	35	34
Voorwaarts	26	9	4	13	36	42	31
Boskamp	26	5	7	14	28	62	22
Randjiet Boys	26	5	5	16	28	62	20
Takdier Boys	26	4	8	14	31	67	20
Boma Star	26	5	4	17	30	73	19

7/10/2005 - 28/05/2006

SVB CUP 2005-06

Quarter-finals		Semi-finals		Final	
Robinhood	2 3p				
Transvaal	2 1p	Robinhood	4		
Boma Star	0	Kamal Dewaker	0		10-06-2006
Kamal Dewaker	2			Robinhood	1 7p
Leo Victor	3			Inter Mo'tapoe	1 6p
Voorwaarts	2	Leo Victor	2		
Eendracht	0	Inter Mo'tapoe	6		
Inter Mo'tapoe	3				

RECENT LEAGUE RECORD

Year	Champions	Pts	Runners-up	Pts	Third	Pts
2000	Transvaal	57	SNL	54	Royal '95	49
2001	No Competition					
2002	Voorwaarts	67	SNL	63	Royal '95	52
2003	FCS National	52	Robinhood	50	House of Billiards	43
2004	Walking Bout Co	55	Inter Moengotapoe	47	Transvaal	46
2005	Robinhood	62	Royal '95	54	Walking Bout Co	53
2006	Walking Bout Co	57	Robinhood	56	Inter Moengotapoe	48

SURINAM COUNTRY INFORMATION

Capital	Paramaribo	Independence	1975 from the Netherlands	GDP per Capita	$4 000
Population	436 935	Status	Republic	GNP Ranking	158
Area km²	163 270	Language	Dutch, English, Surinamese	Dialling code	+597
Population density	2.6 per km²	Literacy rate	93%	Internet code	.sr
% in urban areas	50%	Main religion	Christian, Hindu, Muslim,	GMT +/–	-3
Cities/Towns ('000)	Paramaribo 220; Lelydorp 17; Nieuw Nickerie 13; Moengo 7; Meerzorg 6; Nieuw Amsterdam 5				
Neighbours (km)	French Guiana 510; Brazil 597; Guyana 600; North Atlantic Ocean 386				
Main stadia	André Kamperveen Stadion – Paramaribo 18 000				

SVK – SLOVAKIA

NATIONAL TEAM RECORD
JULY 1ST 2002 TO JULY 9TH 2006

PL	W	D	L	F	A	%
41	14	16	11	59	46	53.7

FIFA/COCA-COLA WORLD RANKING

1993	1994	1995	1996	1997	1998	1999	2000	2001	2002	2003	2004	2005	High		Low	
150	43	35	30	34	32	21	24	47	55	50	53	45	**17**	05/97	**150**	12/93

2005–2006											
08/05	09/05	10/05	11/05	12/05	01/06	02/06	03/06	04/06	05/06	06/06	07/06
45	45	45	45	45	44	45	41	43	41	-	44

Slovakia surpassed all expectations in the 2006 FIFA World Cup™ qualifiers by finishing second in their group - ahead of Russia - to qualify for a play-off against Spain. There they met their match with a 5-1 defeat in Madrid but once again the national team is beginning to show its undoubted potential. That defeat and the 2-1 reverse against Portugal in the group were the only two defeats in the past two seasons and if coach Dusan Galis can help turn some of the large number of drawn matches into victories, Slovakia may not be waiting too long before they appear in the finals of a major tournament. The national team will also soon be able to play in a new national stadium

INTERNATIONAL HONOURS
None

which will be built to replace the old Tehelné Pole. The success in Europe of the previously unknown Artmedia Bratislava was also a shot in the arm for football in the country. Their 5-0 victory at home over Celtic and the 3-2 away victory over FC Porto - both former European champions - were of particular note as they came within a whisker of qualifying for the knockout stage at the first attempt. The distractions of their European adventure and the loss of key players in the winter transfer window, however, gave MFK Ruzomberok the opportunity to celebrate their centenary in style by winning the League and Cup, neither of which had they won before.

THE FIFA BIG COUNT OF 2000

	Male	Female		Male	Female
Registered players	115 680	578	Referees	92	15
Non registered players	75 000	1 500	Officials	696	100
Youth players	127 175	397	Total involved	321 233	
Total players	320 330		Number of clubs	2 427	
Professional players	1 918	0	Number of teams	7 298	

Slovak Football Association (SFZ)
Slovensky futbalovy zväz, Junácka 6, 832 80, Bratislava, Slovakia
Tel +421 2 49249151   Fax +421 2 49249595
international@futbalsfz.sk   www.futbalsfz.sk
President: LAURINEC Frantisek   General Secretary: TITTEL Dusan
Vice-President: OBLOZINSKY Juraj   Treasurer: KOVAC Peter   Media Officer: LAMACOVA-DUCKA Karolina
Men's Coach: GALIS Dusan   Women's Coach: URVAY Frantisek
SFZ formed: 1993   UEFA: 1994   FIFA: 1907/1994
Blue shirts with white trimmings, Blue shorts, Blue socks or White shirts with blue trimmings, White shorts, White socks

RECENT INTERNATIONAL MATCHES PLAYED BY SLOVAKIA

2002	Opponents	Score		Venue	Comp	Scorers	Att	Referee
21-08	Czech Republic	L	1-4	Olomouc	Fr	Nemeth.S [16]	11 986	Douros GRE
7-09	Turkey	L	0-3	Istanbul	ECq		19 750	Lopez Nieto ESP
12-10	England	L	1-2	Bratislava	ECq	Nemeth.S [24]	30 000	Messina ITA
20-11	Ukraine	D	1-1	Bratislava	Fr	Karhan [61p]	2 859	Marczyk POL
2003								
12-02	Romania	L	1-2	Larnaca	Fr	Vittek [6]	150	Papaioannou GRE
13-02	Cyprus	W	3-1	Larnaca	Fr	Reiter [1], Vittek 2 [62 82]	250	Kapitanis CYP
29-03	FYR Macedonia	W	2-0	Skopje	ECq	Petras [28], Reiter [90]	11 000	Duhamel FRA
2-04	Liechtenstein	W	4-0	Trnava	ECq	Reiter [19], Nemeth.S 2 [51 64], Janocko [90]	BCD	Ceferin SVN
30-04	Greece	D	2-2	Puchov	Fr	Nemeth.S 2 [13 87]	2 863	Messner AUT
7-06	Turkey	L	0-1	Bratislava	ECq		15 000	Hauge NOR
11-06	England	L	1-2	Middlesbrough	ECq	Janocko [31]	35 000	Stark GER
20-08	Colombia	D	0-0	New Jersey	Fr		16 000	Stott USA
10-09	FYR Macedonia	D	1-1	Zilina	ECq	Nemeth.S [25]	2 286	Sundell SWE
11-10	Liechtenstein	W	2-0	Vaduz	ECq	Vittek 2 [40 56]	800	Hyytia FIN
10-12	Kuwait	W	2-0	Larnaca	Fr	Breska [53], Dovicovic [71]		
2004								
31-03	Austria	D	1-1	Bratislava	Fr	Mintal [72]	4 500	Vidlak CZE
28-04	Ukraine	D	1-1	Kyiv	Fr	Varga [65]	18 000	Ryszka POL
29-05	Croatia	L	0-1	Rijeka	Fr		10 000	Kassai HUN
9-07	Japan	L	1-3	Hiroshima	Fr	Babnic [65]	34 458	Breeze AUS
11-07	Serbia & Montenegro	L	0-2	Fukuoka	Fr		6 100	Yoshida JPN
18-08	Luxembourg	W	3-1	Bratislava	WCq	Vittek [26], Gresko [48], Demo [89]	5 016	Kassai HUN
4-09	Russia	D	1-1	Moscow	WCq	Vittek [87]	11 500	Mejuto Gonzalez ESP
8-09	Liechtenstein	W	7-0	Bratislava	WCq	Vittek 3 [15 59 81], Karhan [42], Nemeth.S [84], Mintal [85], Zabavnik [92+]	5 620	Delevic SCG
9-10	Latvia	W	4-1	Bratislava	WCq	Nemeth.S [36], Reiter [50], Karhan 2 [55 87]	13 025	Farina ITA
17-11	Slovenia	D	0-0	Trnava	Fr		5 482	Skjerven NOR
30-11	Hungary	W	1-0	Bangkok	Fr	Porazik [47]	750	Veerapool THA
2-12	Thailand	D	1-1	Bangkok	Fr	Durica [65p], W 5-4p	5 000	Chappanimutu MAS
2005								
9-02	Romania	D	2-2	Larnaca	Fr	Vittek [12], Karhan [44]	500	Kapitanis CYP
26-03	Estonia	W	2-1	Tallinn	WCq	Mintal [58], Reiter [65]	3 051	Frojdfeldt SWE
30-03	Portugal	D	1-1	Bratislava	WCq	Karhan [8]	21 000	Sars FRA
4-06	Portugal	L	0-2	Lisbon	WCq		64 000	Collina ITA
8-06	Luxembourg	W	4-0	Luxembourg	WCq	Nemeth [5], Mintal [15], Kisel [54], Reiter [60]	2 108	Styles ENG
17-08	Liechtenstein	D	0-0	Vaduz	WCq		1 150	Layec FRA
3-09	Germany	W	2-0	Bratislava	Fr	Karhan 2 [20p 38]	9 276	Braamahr NED
7-09	Latvia	D	1-1	Riga	WCq	Vittek [35]	8 800	Plautz AUT
8-10	Estonia	W	1-0	Bratislava	WCq	Hlinka [72]	12 800	Allaerts BEL
12-10	Russia	D	0-0	Bratislava	WCq		22 317	Rosetti ITA
12-11	Spain	L	1-5	Madrid	WCpo	Nemeth [49]	47 210	De Santis ITA
16-11	Spain	D	1-1	Bratislava	WCpo	Holosko [50]	23 587	Merk GER
2006								
1-03	France	W	2-1	Paris	Fr	Nemeth.S [62], Valachovic [82]	55 000	Thomson SCO
20-05	Belgium	D	1-1	Trnava	Fr	Holosko [64]	4 174	Kassai HUN

Fr = Friendly match • EC = UEFA EURO 2004™ • WC = FIFA World Cup™ • q = qualifier • po = play-off • BCD = Behind closed doors

SLOVAKIA NATIONAL TEAM RECORDS AND RECORD SEQUENCES

Records			Sequence records				
Victory	7-0	LIE 2004	Wins	3	Five times	Clean sheets	4	2000
Defeat	1-6	CRO 1942	Defeats	5	2001	Goals scored	8	1996-1997
Player Caps	78	KARHAN Miroslav	Undefeated	12	2000-2001	Without goal	4	2001
Player Goals	22	NEMETH Slizard	Without win	6	Four times	Goals against	11	2002-2003

SLOVAKIA COUNTRY INFORMATION

Capital	Bratislava	Independence	1993 from Czechoslovakia	GDP per Capita	$13 300
Population	5 423 567	Status	Republic	GNP Ranking	60
Area km^2	48 845	Language	Slovak, Hungarian	Dialling code	+421
Population density	111 per km^2	Literacy rate	n/a	Internet code	.sk
% in urban areas	59%	Main religion	Christian	GMT + / –	+1
Cities/Towns ('000)	Bratislava 423; Kosice 236; Presov 94; Nitra 86; Zilna 86; Banska Bystrica 82; Trnava 69				
Neighbours (km)	Ukraine 97; Hungary 677; Austria 91; Czech Republic 215; Poland 444				
Main stadia	Tehelné Pole – Bratislava 30 087; Anton Malatinsky – Trnava 18 448				

NATIONAL TEAM PLAYERS AND COACHES

Record Caps			Record Goals			Recent Coaches	
KARHAN Miroslav	1995-'06	78	NEMETH Szilard	1996-'06	22	VENGLOS Jozef Dr	1993-'95
NEMETH Szilard	1996-'06	57	VITTEK Robert	2001-'06	13	JANKECH Jozef	1995-'98
VARGA Stanislav	1997-'05	53	DUBOVSKY Peter	1994-'00	12	GALIS Dusan	1998
TOMASCHEK Robert	1994-'01	52	JANCULA Tibor	1995-'01	9	RADOLSKY Dusan	1998-'99
DZURIK Peter	1997-'03	45	REITER Lubomir	2001-'05	9	ADEMEC Jozef	1999-'01
KONIG Miroslav	1997-'04	45	KARHAN Miroslav	1995-'06	9	JURKEMIK Ladislav	2001-'03
TITTEL Dusan	1994-'98	44	TIMKO Jaroslav	1994-'97	7	GALIS Dusan	2003-
BALIS Igor	1995-'01	40	TITTEL Dusan	1994-'98	7		
JANOCKO Vladimir	1999-'05	40					

CLUB DIRECTORY

Club	Town/City	Stadium	Capacity	www.	Lge	Cup
Artmedia Petrzalka	Bratislava	Petrzalka Stadion	8 000	fcartmedia.sk	1	1
Dukla Banská Bystrica	Banská Bystrica	DAC Stadion	16 490	fkdukla.sk	0	1
Inter Bratislava	Bratislava	Pasienky Stadion	13 295	askinter.sk	2	3
Matador Púchov	Púchov	Matador	5 964	fkmatadorpuchov.sk	0	1
FC Rimavská Sobota	Rimavská Sobota	Rimavská Sobota	8 000		0	0
MFK Ruzomberok	Ruzomberok	MFK Stadion	5 030	futbalruza.sk	1	1
FK AS Trencín	Trencin	Mestsky Stadion	15 712	astn.sk	0	0
Spartak Trnava	Trnava	Anton Malatinsky	18 448	spartak.sk	0	1
MSK Zilina	Zilina	Pod Dubnon	6 233	mskzilina.sk	3	0
ZTS Dubnica	Dubnica Nad	Mestsky Stadion	8 000	fkdubnica.sk	0	0

RECENT LEAGUE AND CUP RECORD

	Championship						Cup		
Year	Champions	Pts	Runners-up	Pts	Third	Pts	Winners	Score	Runners-up
1994	Slovan Bratislava	50	Inter Bratislava	40	Dunajska Streda	36	Slovan Bratislava	2-1	Tatran Presov
1995	Slovan Bratislava	72	1.FC Kosice	52	Inter Bratislava	50	Inter Bratislava	1-1 3-1p	Dunajska Streda
1996	Slovan Bratislava	75	1.FC Kosice	65	Spartak Trnava	63	Chemlon Humenné	2-1	Spartak Trnava
1997	1.FC Kosice	70	Spartak Trnava	69	Slovan Bratislava	50	Slovan Bratislava	1-0	Tatran Presov
1998	1.FC Kosice	68	Spartak Trnava	66	Inter Bratislava	60	Spartak Trnava	2-0	1.FC Kosice
1999	Slovan Bratislava	70	Inter Bratislava	68	Spartak Trnava	64	Slovan Bratislava	3-0	Dukla B. Bystrica
2000	Inter Bratislava	70	1.FC Kosice	61	Slovan Bratislava	57	Inter Bratislava	1-1 4-2p	1.FC Kosice
2001	Inter Bratislava	80	Slovan Bratislava	71	SCP Ruzomberok	55	Inter Bratislava	1-0	SCP Ruzomberok
2002	MSK Zilina	69	Matador Púchov	62	Inter Bratislava	56	Koba Senec	1-1 4-2p	Matador Púchov
2003	MSK Zilina	70	Artmedia Bratislava	67	Slovan Bratislava	63	Matador Púchov	2-1	Slovan Bratislava
2004	MSK Zilina	64	Dukla B. Bystrica	64	SCP Ruzomberok	55	Artmedia Bratislava	2-0	Trans Licartovce
2005	Artmedia Bratislava	72	MSK Zilina	65	Dukla B. Bystrica	52	Dukla B. Bystrica	2-1	Artmedia Bratislava
2006	MFK Ruzomberok	80	Artmedia Bratislava	74	Spartak Trnava	68	MFK Ruzomberok	0-0 4-3p	Spartak Trnava

Slovak clubs took part in the Czechoslovak League until the end of the 1992-1993 season

SLOVAKIA 2005-06

CORGON LIGA

	Pl	W	D	L	F	A	Pts	Ruz'berok	Artmedia	Trnava	Zilina	Nitra	Dukla	Trencin	Dubnica	Inter	Púchov
MFK Ruzomberok †	36	26	2	8	65	28	80		1-0 3-0	4-1 2-1	2-0 2-1	2-0 2-0	2-0 1-0	1-0 3-0	1-0 3-1	1-2 3-1	3-1 3-1
Artmedia Bratislava ‡	36	23	5	8	58	33	74	2-1 2-0		0-2 2-1	1-1 1-2	1-1 2-0	2-0 1-0	3-0 3-1	2-2 3-2	7-1 1-0	2-0 1-0
Spartak Trnava ‡	36	21	5	10	57	31	68	2-0 2-1	1-3 1-0		4-1 2-1	2-0 0-1	1-0 1-1	1-0 3-0	2-1 4-1	3-0 0-0	4-0 1-0
MSK Zilina	36	18	6	12	69	44	60	0-1 1-2	1-2 0-1	1-0 2-1		2-5 2-1	2-0 2-0	1-2 5-0	3-0 0-0	5-2 1-1	1-2 3-1
FC Nitra	36	12	9	15	42	48	45	2-2 2-3	1-0 0-2	3-1 1-1	0-2 2-2		0-3 2-1	3-1 3-1	0-0 2-2	2-0 1-0	3-1 1-1
Dukla Banská Bystrica	36	12	6	18	37	42	42	0-2 0-5	3-0 0-0	0-1 1-2	0-4 2-2	2-0 2-0		2-0 0-1	4-1 2-3	1-0 2-1	3-1 2-0
AS Trencin	36	11	9	16	31	49	42	1-0 1-0	1-1 3-1	0-0 1-0	0-1 2-1	2-1 1-1	2-1 0-0		2-0 1-2	2-0 1-2	1-1 1-3
Dubnica nad Váhom	36	10	10	16	41	55	39	3-0 1-1	0-2 0-1	0-3 0-2	2-4 1-4	0-1 2-1	1-0 0-0	1-1 1-1		1-1 2-1	1-1 1-1 0-1
Inter Bratislava	36	7	9	20	27	62	30	0-3 0-1	1-2 1-2	1-0 2-2	0-4 1-1	1-2 2-0	1-1 0-0	0-0 0-0	0-3 0-2		1-1 2-1
Matador Púchov	36	7	5	24	29	64	26	0-2 0-2	1-2 1-3	1-3 0-2	1-5 0-1	0-0 1-0	0-1 0-2	2-1 2-1	0-2 1-3	3-0 0-1	

16/07/2005 - 31/05/2006 • † Qualified for the UEFA Champions League • ‡ Qualified for the UEFA Cup

SLOVAKIA 2005-06
II LIGA (2)

	Pl	W	D	L	F	A	Pts
MFK Kosice	30	23	4	3	67	12	73
Slovan Bratislava	30	19	6	5	47	25	63
FC Senec	30	19	3	8	65	35	60
Tatran Presov	30	15	7	8	37	22	52
LAFC Lucenec	30	15	7	8	40	34	52
Rimavská Sobota	30	17	5	8	49	23	50
Zemplin Michalovce	30	14	6	10	38	30	48
Vion Zlaté Moravce	30	14	6	10	33	25	48
Slovan Duslo Sala	30	13	6	11	42	29	45
Sport Podbrezová	30	12	8	10	39	30	44
HFC Humenné	30	10	7	13	35	45	37
DAC Dunajská Streda	30	7	6	17	27	51	27
Odeva Lipany	30	6	4	20	27	61	22
Spartak Trnava B	30	4	5	21	17	56	17
Druzstevnik Bác	30	3	7	20	17	63	16
FC Nitra B	30	4	3	23	25	64	15

22/07/2005 - 28/05/2006

SLOVENSKY POHAR 2005-06

Second Round		Quarter-finals		Semi-finals		Final	
MFK Ruzomberok *	1						
Matador Púchov	0	MFK Ruzomberok	3 0				
Dukla Banská Bystrica	0	AS Trencin *	0 0				
AS Trencin *	3			MFK Ruzomberok *	2 0 6p		
FC Senec	2			Artmedia Bratislava	0 2 5p		
Sport Podbrezova *	1	FC Senec	0 1				
Inter Bratislava *	0	Artmedia Bratislava *	1 1				
Artmedia Bratislava	2					MFK Ruzomberok	0 4p
FC Nitra *	1 5p					Spartak Trnava ‡	0 3p
MSK Zilina	1 3p	FC Nitra	2 2				
Odeva Lipany	0	Slovan Duslo Sala *	2 1				
Slovan Duslo Sala *	3			FC Nitra *	1 1		
Eldus Mocenok *	3			Spartak Trnava	3 1		
Rimavská Sobota	0	Eldus Mocenok *	0 0				
MFK Kosice	0	Spartak Trnava	4 1				
Spartak Trnava *	1						

CUP FINAL
Bratislava, 8-05-2006

* Home team/home team in the first leg • ‡ Qualified for the UEFA Cup

SVN – SLOVENIA

NATIONAL TEAM RECORD
JULY 1ST 2002 TO JULY 9TH 2006

PL	W	D	L	F	A	%
35	11	9	15	36	49	4.3

FIFA/COCA-COLA WORLD RANKING

1993	1994	1995	1996	1997	1998	1999	2000	2001	2002	2003	2004	2005		High	Low
134	81	71	77	95	88	40	35	25	36	31	42	68		25 12/01	134 02/94

					2005–2006						
08/05	09/05	10/05	11/05	12/05	01/06	02/06	03/06	04/06	05/06	06/06	07/06
48	52	61	63	68	69	70	69	71	71	-	61

By qualifying for the finals of Euro 2000 and the 2002 FIFA World Cup™ the Slovenian national team has been saddled with expectations that can perhaps only rarely be matched. In the 2006 FIFA World Cup™ qualifiers, two defeats at the hands of Norway put to an end any hopes of reaching a fourth consecutive play-off, and they even ended up finishing behind Scotland in the final standings. There is huge satisfaction, however, in the knowledge they were the only team to beat Italy on their journey to becoming world champions. Indeed that 1-0 victory in Celje was the last time the Italians lost a match. In the Slovenian League, Gorica won the title by beating bottom club Rudar

INTERNATIONAL HONOURS
Qualified for the FIFA World Cup™ finals 2002

4-0 on the last day of the season to deny Domzale a first-ever title. That made it three in a row for Pavel Pinni's men as they seek to match the seven in a row won by Maribor between 1997 and 2003. Olimpija from the capital Ljubljana are the only other club to have won the title in the 15 seasons since independence. There was a new name on the Cup, however, with Koper beating the holders Publikum Celje on penalties after the match had ended 1-1. Koper's goal and winning penalty was scored by captain Mladen Rudonja, who also happens to be the president of the club, bringing a whole new meaning to the concept of presidential interference in team matters.

THE FIFA BIG COUNT OF 2000

	Male	Female		Male	Female
Registered players	15 072	90	Referees	912	2
Non registered players	50 000	200	Officials	4 500	40
Youth players	10 063	55	Total involved	80 934	
Total players	75 480		Number of clubs	243	
Professional players	354	0	Number of teams	1 510	

Football Association of Slovenia (NZS)

Nogometna Zveza Slovenije, Cerinova 4, PO Box 3986, Ljubljana 1001, Slovenia

Tel +386 1 5300400   Fax +386 1 5300410

nzs@nzs.si   www.nzs.si

President: ZAVRL Rudi   General Secretary: JOST Dane

Vice-President: FRANTAR Anton   Treasurer: JOST Dane   Media Officer: STANIC Uros

Men's Coach: OBLAK Branko   Women's Coach: CIRKVENCIC Zoran

NZS formed: 1920   UEFA: 1992   FIFA: 1992

White shirts with green trimmings, White shorts, White socks or Green shirts with white trimmings, Green shorts, Green socks

RECENT INTERNATIONAL MATCHES PLAYED BY SLOVENIA

2002	Opponents	Score		Venue	Comp	Scorers	Att	Referee
21-08	Italy	W	1-0	Trieste	Fr	Cimirotic [32]	11 080	Brugger AUT
7-09	Malta	W	3-0	Ljubljana	ECq	OG [37], Siljak [59], Cimirotic [90]	7 000	Borovilos GRE
12-10	France	L	0-5	Paris	ECq		77 619	Milton Nielsen DEN
2003								
12-02	Switzerland	L	1-5	Nova Gorica	Fr	Rakovic [79]	3 500	Abraham HUN
2-04	Cyprus	W	4-1	Ljubljana	ECq	Siljak 2 [5 14], Zahovic [39p], Ceh.N [43]	5 000	Gomes Costa POR
30-04	Malta	W	3-1	Ta'Qali	ECq	Zahovic [15], Siljak 2 [37 57]	5 000	Hanacsek HUN
7-06	Israel	D	0-0	Antalya	ECq		2 500	Busacca SUI
20-08	Hungary	W	2-1	Murska Sobota	Fr	Sukalo [3], Cimirotic [75]	5 000	Sowa AUT
6-09	Israel	W	3-1	Ljubljana	ECq	Siljak [35], Knavs [37], Ceh.N [78]	8 000	Fandel GER
10-09	France	L	0-2	Ljubljana	ECq		8 000	Messina ITA
11-10	Cyprus	D	2-2	Limassol	ECq	Siljak 2 [12 42]	2 346	Ovrebo NOR
15-11	Croatia	D	1-1	Zagreb	ECpo	Siljak [22]	35 000	Merk GER
19-11	Croatia	L	0-1	Ljubljana	ECpo		9 000	Meier SUI
2004								
18-02	Poland	L	0-2	Cadiz	Fr		100	Barea Lopez ESP
31-03	Latvia	L	0-1	Celje	Fr		1 500	Stredak SVK
28-04	Switzerland	L	1-2	Geneva	Fr	Zahovic [45]	7 500	Bossen NED
18-08	Serbia & Montenegro	D	1-1	Ljubljana	Fr	Ceh.N [83]	8 000	Ovrebo NOR
4-09	Moldova	W	3-0	Celje	WCq	Acimovic 3 [5 27 48]	3 620	Hyytia FIN
8-09	Scotland	D	0-0	Glasgow	WCq		38 279	Larsen DEN
9-10	Italy	W	1-0	Celje	WCq	Cesar [82]	9 262	De Bleeckere BEL
13-10	Norway	L	0-3	Oslo	WCq		24 907	Ivanov.V RUS
17-11	Slovakia	D	0-0	Trnava	Fr		5 482	Skjerven NOR
2005								
9-02	Czech Republic	L	0-3	Celje	Fr		4 000	Strahonja CRO
26-03	Germany	L	0-1	Celje	Fr		9 000	Poll ENG
30-03	Belarus	D	1-1	Celje	WCq	Rodic [44]	6 450	Al Ghamdi KSA
4-06	Belarus	D	1-1	Minsk	WCq	Ceh.N [17]	29 042	Hansson SWE
17-08	Wales	D	0-0	Swansea	Fr		10 016	Stokes IRL
3-09	Norway	L	2-3	Celje	WCq	Cimirotic [4], Zlogar [83]	10 055	Medina Cantalejo ESP
7-09	Moldova	W	2-1	Chisinau	WCq	Lavric [47], Marvic [58]	7 200	Baskakov RUS
8-10	Italy	L	0-1	Palermo	WCq		19 123	Poulat FRA
12-10	Scotland	L	0-3	Celje	WCq		9 100	Temmink NED
2006								
28-02	Cyprus	W	1-0	Larnaca	Fr	Ljubijankic [84]		
1-03	Romania	L	0-2	Larnaca	Fr		300	Vialichka BLR
31-05	Trinidad and Tobago	W	3-1	Celje	Fr	Novakovic 3 [4 16 77]	2 500	Tanovic SCG
4-06	Côte d'Ivoire	L	0-3	Evry-Bondoufle	Fr		8 000	

Fr = Friendly match • EC = UEFA EURO 2004™ • WC = FIFA World Cup™ • q = qualifier • po = play-off

SLOVENIA NATIONAL TEAM RECORDS AND RECORD SEQUENCES

Records			Sequence records				
Victory	7-0	OMA 1999	Wins	4	1998	Clean sheets	4	2002
Defeat	0-5	FRA 1999, FRA 2002	Defeats	4	1997, 1998	Goals scored	9	2001-2002
Player Caps	80	ZAHOVIC Zlatko	Undefeated	8	2001	Without goal	4	2004-2005
Player Goals	35	ZAHOVIC Zlatko	Without win	8	2003-04, 2004-05	Goals against	13	1997-1998

SLOVENIA COUNTRY INFORMATION

Capital	Ljubljana	Independence	1991 from Yugoslavia	GDP per Capita	$19 000
Population	2 011 473	Status	Republic	GNP Ranking	65
Area km²	20 273	Language	Slovenian, Serbo-Croat	Dialling code	+386
Population density	99 per km²	Literacy rate	99%	Internet code	.si
% in urban areas	64%	Main religion	Christian	GMT + / –	+1
Towns/Cities ('000)	Ljubljana 255; Maribor 89; Celje 37; Kranj 35; Velenje 26; Koper 23; Ptuj 18; Trbovlje 16				
Neighbours (km)	Hungary 102; Croatia 670; Italy 232; Austria 330; Adriatic Sea 46				
Main stadia	Ljudski Vrt – Maribor 10 210; Sportni Park – Celje 8 600; Bezigrad – Ljubljana 8 211				

NATIONAL TEAM PLAYERS AND COACHES

Record Caps			Record Goals			Recent Coaches	
ZAHOVIC Zlatko	1992-'04	80	ZAHOVIC Zlatko	1992-'04	35	PRASNIKAR Bojan	1992-'93
CEH Ales	1992-'02	74	UDOVIC Saso	1993-'00	16	VERDENIK Zdenko	1993-'97
NOVAK Dzoni	1992-'02	71	SILJAK Ermin	1994-'05	14	PRASNIKAR Bojan	1997-'98
ACIMOVIC Milenko	1998-'06	69	ACIMOVIC Milenko	1998-'06	13	KATANEC Srecko	1998-'02
GALIC Marinko	1994-'02	66	GLIHA Primoz	1993-'98	10	PRASNIKAR Bojan	2002-'04
RUDONJA Mladen	1994-'03	65	OSTERC Milan	1997-'02	8	OBLAK Branco	2004-
KARIC Amir	1996-'04	64	CEH Nastja	2001-'06	6		
PAVLIN Miran	1994-'04	63	PAVLIN Miran	1994-'04	5		
KNAVS Aleksander	1998-'05	63	CIMIROTIC Sebastjan	1998-'05	5		
SIMEUNOVIC Marko	1992-'04	57					

CLUB DIRECTORY

Club	Town/City	Stadium	Capacity	www.	Lge	Cup
NK Bela Krajina	Crnomelj	Bela Krajina Stadion	1 500		0	0
NK Domzale	Domzale	Sportni Park	3 212	nogometniklub-domzale.si	0	0
NK Drava	Ptuj	Mestni Stadion	1 950	nkptuj-klub.si	0	0
NK Gorica	Nova Gorica	Sportni Park	4 200	nd-gorica.com	4	2
FC Koper	Koper	SRC Bonifika Stadion	3 557	nkkoper.net	0	1
NK Ljubljana	Ljubljana	ZSD Ljubljana Stadion	5 000		0	0
NK Maribor	Maribor	Ljudski vrt Stadion	10 210	nkmaribor.com	7	5
NK Mura	Murska Sobota	Fazanerija Stadion	5 400	snkmura.com	0	1
NK Olimpija Ljubljana	Ljubljana	Bezigrad Stadion	8 211	nkolimpija.com	4	4
NK Primorje	Ajdovscina	Primorje Stadion	3 000	nkprimorje.com	0	0
NK Publikum	Celje	Sportni Park	8 600	publikum.com	0	1
NK Zagorje	Zagorje Obsavi	Zagorje Stadion	2 000		0	0

RECENT LEAGUE AND CUP RECORD

	Championship						Cup		
Year	Champions	Pts	Runners-up	Pts	Third	Pts	Winners	Score	Runners-up
1992	Olimpija Ljubljana	66	NK Maribor	59	Izola Belvedur	56	NK Maribor	0-0 4-3p	Olimpija Ljubljana
1993	Olimpija Ljubljana	52	NK Maribor	48	Mura Murska Sobota	46	Olimpija Ljubljana	2-1	Publikum Celje
1994	Olimpija Ljubljana	51	Mura Murska Sobota	45	NK Maribor	42	NK Maribor	0-1 3-1	Mura Murska Sobota
1995	Olimpija Ljubljana	44	NK Maribor	42	ND Gorica	41	Mura Murska Sobota	1-1 1-0	Publikum Celje
1996	ND Gorica	67	Olimpija Ljubljana	64	Mura Murska Sobota	58	Olimpija Ljubljana	1-0 1-1	Primorje Ajdovscina
1997	NK Maribor	71	Primorje Ajdovscina	66	ND Gorica	65	NK Maribor	0-0 3-0	Primorje Ajdovscina
1998	NK Maribor	67	Mura Murska Sobota	67	ND Gorica	65	Rudar Velenje	1-2 3-0	Primorje Ajdovscina
1999	NK Maribor	66	ND Gorica	62	Rudar Velenje	56	NK Maribor	3-2 2-0	Olimpija Ljubljana
2000	NK Maribor	81	ND Gorica	62	Rudar Velenje	58	Olimpija Ljubljana	1-2 2-0	Korotan Prevalje
2001	NK Maribor	62	Olimpija Ljubljana	60	Primorje Ajdovscina	56	ND Gorica	0-1 4-2	Olimpija Ljubljana
2002	NK Maribor	66	Primorje Ajdovscina	60	FC Koper	56	ND Gorica	4-0 2-1	Aluminij Kidricevo
2003	NK Maribor	62	Publikum Celje	55	Olimpija Ljubljana	54	Olimpija Ljubljana	1-1 2-2	Publikum Celje
2004	ND Gorica	56	Olimpija Ljubljana	55	NK Maribor	54	NK Maribor	4-0 3-4	Koroska Dravograd
2005	ND Gorica	65	Domzale	52	Publikum Celje	52	Publikum Celje	1-0	ND Gorica
2006	ND Gorica	73	Domzale	71	NK Koper	57	NK Koper	1-1 5-3p	Publikum Celje

Slovenian clubs played in the Yugoslav League until the end of the 1990-1991 season

SLOVENIA 2005–06

SIMOBIL LIGA

	Pl	W	D	L	F	A	Pts	Gorica	Domzale	Koper	Maribor	Drava	Publikum	Nafta	Primorje	Bela Krajina	Rudar
ND Gorica †	36	21	10	5	75	30	73		1-1 2-0	3-0 0-0	4-1 2-1	2-0 4-0	2-1 2-0	2-0 1-1	2-0 2-0	4-0 5-0	0-0 4-0
Domzale ‡	36	20	11	5	69	28	71	1-1 1-1		4-1 2-0	2-1 2-0	1-0 0-2	5-0 2-1	2-0 3-1	3-0 2-0	4-0 2-1	4-1 3-0
NK Koper ‡	36	16	9	11	49	39	57	2-0 1-1	2-2 2-0		2-3 2-0	0-1 1-1	2-0 2-2	0-2 2-0	1-1 1-0	2-1 2-0	2-1 3-0
NK Maribor	36	16	6	14	51	42	54	2-1 4-1	0-0 1-3	1-2 0-1		2-1 2-1	0-2 1-2	1-0 5-1	2-0 2-0	1-1 0-0	1-1 1-0
Drava Ptuj	36	15	9	12	50	46	54	3-2 0-1	1-1 1-1	1-0 1-1	0-3 3-2		1-0 4-1	3-2 2-0	4-1 0-0	3-0 0-1	1-0 2-1
Publikum Celje	36	15	4	17	48	59	49	2-1 0-4	3-2 0-3	3-3 0-2	0-0 1-0	2-0 3-1		1-3 2-1	2-0 0-1	0-3 2-0	2-1 4-2
Nafta Lendava	36	13	7	16	42	52	46	2-4 1-4	0-1 0-0	1-0 0-1	0-4 1-0	1-0 0-0	2-1 0-0		1-0 2-0	1-1 3-3	5-0 2-1
Primorje Ajdovscina	36	11	10	15	43	50	43	2-2 1-3	2-2 0-0	2-0 1-0	2-1 0-3	6-2 2-2	1-0 2-4	2-0 0-0		2-1 2-2	6-1 1-1
Bela Krajina Crnomelj	36	7	13	16	35	61	34	1-1 1-1	1-1 0-1	1-3 0-3	2-2 0-1	1-1 1-5	1-0 3-1	1-4 3-0	1-0 0-1		1-0 1-1
Rudar Velenje	36	2	9	25	28	83	15	1-2 0-3	0-8 2-0	2-1 2-2	0-1 2-3	0-0 1-3	0-1 2-4	1-3 1-2	0-4 1-1	0-0 2-2	

22/07/2005 - 3/06/2006 • † Qualified for the UEFA Champions League • ‡ Qualified for the UEFA Cup • Play-off: Dravinja 2-2 0-0 Bela Krajina
Top scorers: Miran BURGIC, Gorica, 24; Valter BIRSA, Gorica, 18; Oskar DROBNE, Koper, 18; Viktor TRENEVSKI, Drava, 16

SLOVENIA 2005–06 2.SNL (2)

	Pl	W	D	L	F	A	Pts
Factor Ljubljana	27	15	5	7	37	27	50
Dravinja Duol Konjice	27	14	7	6	46	24	49
Supernova Triglav	27	13	9	5	36	18	48
Aluminij Kidricevo	27	12	7	8	37	24	43
Krsko	27	10	10	7	34	36	40
Tinex Sencur	27	8	9	10	34	43	33
Livar Ivancna Gorica	27	7	6	14	31	38	27
Zagorje	27	5	11	11	22	34	26
Svoboda Ljubljana	27	7	4	16	26	33	25
Koroska Dravograd §3	27	6	8	13	26	52	23

12/08/2005 - 3/06/2006 • §3 = three points deducted

POKAL HERVIS 2005–06

Round of 16		Quarter-finals		Semi-finals		Final	
NK Koper	2 4p						
Bela Krajina Crnomelj *	2 2p	NK Koper *	2				
Zagorje *	0	Domzale	1				
Domzale	3			NK Koper	2 0		
Rudar Velenje *	1 5p			NK Gorica *	0 1		
Drava Ptuj	1 4p	Rudar Velenje *	0				
Primorje Ajdovscina	0	NK Gorica	1				
NK Gorica *	2					NK Koper ‡	1 5p
NK Maribor	8					Publikum Celje	1 3p
Tehnotim Pesnica *	1	NK Maribor *	1				
Aluminij Kidricevo	0	Avtoplus Korte	0				
Avtoplus Korte *	1			NK Maribor			
Livar Ivancna Gorica *	1			Publikum Celje *			
Nafta Lendava	0	Livar Ivancna Gorica	1				
Brda	0	Publikum Celje *	5				
Publikum Celje *	2			* Home team/home team in the first leg • ‡ Qualified for the UEFA Cup			

CUP FINAL

Petrol Arena, Celje
24-05-2006, Att: 4 000, Ref: Ceferin

Scorers - Dejan Rusic 75 for Koper; Mladen Rudonja 5 for Publikum

SWE – SWEDEN

NATIONAL TEAM RECORD
JULY 1ST 2002 TO JULY 9TH 2006

PL	W	D	L	F	A	%
56	23	20	13	106	56	58.9

FIFA/COCA-COLA WORLD RANKING

1993	1994	1995	1996	1997	1998	1999	2000	2001	2002	2003	2004	2005	High		Low	
9	3	13	17	18	18	16	23	16	25	19	13	14	2	11/94	31	08/98

2005–2006											
08/05	09/05	10/05	11/05	12/05	01/06	02/06	03/06	04/06	05/06	06/06	07/06
15	10	13	14	14	14	15	16	16	16	-	22

Going into the 2006 FIFA World Cup™ finals in Germany there was little optimism amongst Swedish fans after six friendlies in the build up to the tournament had failed to produce a single win. A 0-0 draw against tiny Trinidad and Tobago in the first match of the finals confirmed those feelings and had it not been for a last minute Freddie Ljungberg winner against Paraguay, Sweden might have been on the first plane home. That was followed, however, by a spirited performance against England and another last minute goal, this time by Henrik Larsson, to maintain their record of not having lost to the English since 1968. Two early German goals and the dismissal of Teddy

INTERNATIONAL HONOURS
Olympic Games Gold 1948　**Qualified for the FIFA World Cup™ finals** 1934 1938 1950 1959 (Hosts) 1970 1974 1978 1990 1994 2002 2006
Women's European Championship 1984　**Qualified for the FIFA Women's World Cup** 1991 1995 1999 2003

Lucic in the second round, however, brought to an end the Swedish campaign. 2005 proved to be a great year for Stockholm club Djurgården, who, for the second time in four seasons won the League and Cup double. Such has been their domination since 2002 that they have won three of the four League titles and three of the four Cups contested since then. The 2006 season saw the return of Henrik Larsson to Swedish club football after an absence of thirteen years. He had been an instrumental figure in Barcelona's victory over Arsenal in the final of the Champions League.

THE FIFA BIG COUNT OF 2000

	Male	Female		Male	Female
Registered players	123 612	25 535	Referees	15 300	1 200
Non registered players	300 000	75 000	Officials	10 000	200
Youth players	37 397	14 864	Total involved	603 108	
Total players	576 408		Number of clubs	3 228	
Professional players	1 500	0	Number of teams	25 000	

Svenska Fotbollförbundet (SVFF)
PO Box 1216, Solna 17 123, Sweden
Tel +46 8 7350900　　　Fax +46 8 7350901
svff@svenskfotboll.se　　　www.svenskfotboll.se
President: LAGRELL Lars-Ake　　　General Secretary: HELLSTROMER Sune
Vice-President: MADSEN Bengt　　　Treasurer: SAHLSTROEM Kjell　　　Media Officer: NYSTEDT Jonas
Men's Coach: LAGERBACK Lars　　　Women's Coach: DOMANSKI LYFORS Marika
SVFF formed: 1904　　　UEFA: 1954　　　FIFA: 1954
Yellow shirts with blue trimmings, Blue shorts, Yellow socks or Blue shirts with yellow trimmings, Blue shorts, Blue socks

RECENT INTERNATIONAL MATCHES PLAYED BY SWEDEN

2003 Opponents	Score	Venue	Comp	Scorers	Att	Referee
20-08 Greece	L 1-2	Norrköping	Fr	Svensson.A [16]	15 018	Hyytia FIN
6-09 San Marino	W 5-0	Gothenburg	ECq	Jonson.M [33], Jakobsson [49], Ibrahimovic 2 [56 83p], Kallstrom [68p]	31 098	Messner AUT
10-09 Poland	W 2-0	Chorzow	ECq	Nilsson [2], Mellberg [36]	20 000	Riley ENG
11-10 Latvia	L 0-1	Stockholm	ECq		32 095	De Santis ITA
18-11 Egypt	L 0-1	Cairo	Fr		15 000	Abdallah LBY
2004						
22-01 Norway	L 0-3	Hong Kong	Fr		10 000	Fong HKG
18-02 Albania	L 1-2	Tirana	Fr	Selakovic [50]	15 000	Paparesta ITA
31-03 England	W 1-0	Gothenburg	Fr	Ibrahimovic [54]	40 464	Ovrebo NOR
28-04 Portugal	D 2-2	Coimbra	Fr	Kallstrom [17], OG [86]	15 000	Ceferin SVN
28-05 Finland	W 3-1	Tammerfors	Fr	Anders Andersson [30], Allback 2 [45 82]	16 500	Undiano Mallenco ESP
5-06 Poland	W 3-1	Stockholm	Fr	Larsson [42], Jakobsson [54], Allback [72]	28 281	Kelly IRL
14-06 Bulgaria	W 5-0	Lisbon	ECr1	Ljungberg [32], Larsson 2 [57 58], Ibrahimovic [78p], Allback [90]	31 652	Riley ENG
18-06 Italy	D 1-1	Porto	ECr1	Ibrahimovic [85]	44 927	Meier SUI
22-06 Denmark	D 2-2	Porto	ECr1	Larsson [47p], Jonson.M [89]	26 115	Merk GER
26-06 Netherlands	D 0-0	Faro-Loule	ECqf		27 286	Michel SVK
18-08 Netherlands	D 2-2	Stockholm	Fr	Jonson.M [4], Ibrahimovic [69]	20 377	Styles ENG
4-09 Malta	W 7-0	Ta'Qali	WCq	Ibrahimovic 4 [4 11 14 71], Ljungberg 2 [46 74], Larsson [76]	4 200	Jakov ISR
8-09 Croatia	L 0-1	Gothenburg	WCq		40 023	Dauden Ibanez ESP
9-10 Hungary	W 3-0	Stockholm	WCq	Ljungberg [26], Larsson [50], Svensson.A [67]	32 288	Dougal SCO
13-10 Iceland	W 4-1	Reykjavik	WCq	Larsson 2 [24 39], Allback [27], Wilhelmsson [45]	7 037	Busacca SUI
17-11 Scotland	W 4-1	Edinburgh	Fr	Allback 2 [27 49], Elmander [72], Berglund [73]	15 071	Jara CZE
2005						
22-01 Korea Republic	D 1-1	Carson	Fr	Rosenberg [86]	9 941	Stott USA
26-01 Mexico	D 0-0	San Diego	Fr		35 521	Hall USA
9-02 France	D 1-1	Paris	Fr	Ljungberg [11]	59 923	Rodriguez Santiago ESP
26-03 Bulgaria	W 3-0	Sofia	WCq	Ljungberg 2 [17 92+p], Edman [74]	42 530	Fandel GER
4-06 Malta	W 6-0	Gothenburg	WCq	Jonson [6], Svensson.A [18], Wilhelmsson [29], Ibrahimovic [40], Ljungberg [57], Elmander [81]	35 593	Ivanov.N RUS
8-06 Norway	L 2-3	Stockholm	Fr	Kallstrom [16], Elmander [68]	15 345	Jara CZE
17-08 Czech Republic	W 2-1	Gothenburg	Fr	Larsson [19], Rosenberg [26]	23 117	Bennett ENG
3-09 Bulgaria	W 3-0	Stockholm	WCq	Ljungberg [60], Mellberg [75], Ibrahimovic [90]	35 000	De Bleeckere BEL
7-09 Hungary	W 1-0	Budapest	WCq	Ibrahimovic [91+]	20 161	Farina ITA
8-10 Croatia	L 0-1	Zagreb	WCq		34 015	De Santis ITA
12-10 Iceland	W 3-1	Stockholm	WCq	Ibrahimovic [29], Larsson [42], Kallstrom [91+]	33 176	Ivanov.V RUS
12-11 Korea Republic	D 2-2	Seoul	Fr	Elmander [9], Rosenberg [57]	59 113	Wan Daxue CHN
2006						
18-01 Saudi Arabia	D 1-1	Riyadh	Fr	Svensson.A [32]		Al Amri KSA
23-01 Jordan	D 0-0	Abu Dhabi	Fr		1 000	Almulla UAE
1-03 Republic of Ireland	L 0-3	Dublin	Fr		44 109	Ledentu FRA
25-05 Finland	D 0-0	Gothenburg	Fr		25 754	Gilewski POL
2-06 Chile	D 1-1	Stockholm	Fr	Larsson [32]	34 735	Stark GER
10-06 Trinidad and Tobago	D 0-0	Dortmund	WCr1		62 959	Maidin SIN
15-06 Paraguay	W 1-0	Berlin	WCr1	Ljungberg [89]	72 000	Michel SVK
20-06 England	D 2-2	Cologne	WCr1	Allback [51], Larsson [90]	45 000	Busacca SUI
24-06 Germany	L 0-2	Munich	WCr2		66 000	Simon BRA

Fr = Friendly match • EC = UEFA EURO 2004™ • WC = FIFA World Cup™
q = qualifier • r1 = first round group • r2 = second round • qf = quarter-final

SWEDEN NATIONAL TEAM RECORDS AND RECORD SEQUENCES

Records			Sequence records					
Victory	12-0	LVA 1927, KOR 1948	Wins	11	2001	Clean sheets	9	2001
Defeat	1-12	ENG 1908	Defeats	6	1908-1909	Goals scored	28	1958-1962
Player Caps	143	RAVELLI Thomas	Undefeated	23	2000-2002	Without goal	4	1998
Player Goals	49	RYDELL Sven	Without win	15	1920-1921	Goals against	17	1925-1927

SWEDEN COUNTRY INFORMATION

Capital	Stockholm	Independence	1523		GDP per Capita	$26 800
Population	8 986 400	Status	Constitutional monarchy		GNP Ranking	21
Area km²	449 964	Language	Swedish		Dialling code	+46
Population density	20 per km²	Literacy rate	99%		Internet code	.se
% in urban areas	83%	Main religion	Lutheran		GMT + / –	+1
Towns/Cities ('000)	Stockolm 1 253; Göteborg 515; Malmö 261; Uppsala 127; Västeras 107; Örebro 98; Linköping 96; Helsingborg 91; Jönköping 83; Norrköping 82; Lund 76; Umeå 74; Gävle 63; Borås 63;					
Neighbours (km)	Finland 614; Norway 1 619; Baltic Sea & Gulf of Bothnia 3 218					
Main stadia	Råsunda – Solna, Stockholm 37 000; Nya Ullevi – Göteborg 43 200					

NATIONAL TEAM PLAYERS AND COACHES

Record Caps			Record Goals			Recent Coaches	
RAVELLI Thomas	1981-'97	143	RYDELL Sven	1923-'32	49	NYMAN Lennart	1962-'65
NILSSON Roland	1986-'00	116	NORDAHL Gunnar	1942-'48	43	BERGMARK Orvar	1966-'70
NORDQVIST Björn	1963-'78	115	LARSSON Henrik	1993-'06	36	ERICSON Georg	1971-'79
ANDERSSON Patrick	1991-'02	96	GREN Gunnar	1940-'58	32	ARNESSON Lars	1980-'85
BERGMARK Orvar	1951-'65	94	ANDERSSON Kennet	1990-'00	31	NORDIN Olle	1986-'90
LARSSON Henrik	1993-'06	93	DAHLIN Martin	1991-'00	29	ANDERSSON Nils	1990
ALEXANDERSSON Niclas	1993-'06	91	SIMONSSON Agne	1957-'67	27	SVENSSON Tommy	1991-'97
LUCIC Teddy	1995-'06	85	BROLIN Tomas	1990-'95	26	SVENSSON/SODERBERG Tommy	1997
ANDERSSON Kennet	1990-'00	83	ALLBACK Marcus	1999-'06	24	SODERBERG/LAGERBACK	1998-'04
HELLSTROM Ronnie	1968-'80	77	KAUFELDT Per	1922-'29	23	LAGERBACK Lars	2004-

CLUB DIRECTORY

Club	Town/City	Stadium	Capacity	www.	Lge	Cup
AIK Solna	Stockholm			aik.se	10	7
Djurgårdens IF	Stockholm	Stockholms Stadion	14 500	dif.se	11	4
IF Elfsborg	Borås	Borås Arena	14 500	elfsborg.se	4	2
GAIS Göteborg	Gothenburg			gais.se	6	1
Gefle IF	Gävle	Strömvallen	6 200	geflefotboll.com	0	0
BK Häcken	Gothenburg	Rambergsvallen	8 480	hacken.o.se	0	0
Halmstads BK	Halmstad	Orjans Vall	15 500	halmstadsbk.se	4	1
Hammarby	Stockholm	Söderstadion	16 000	hammarbyfotboll.se	1	0
Helsingborgs IF	Helsingborg	Olympia Stadion	16 673	hif.se	6	2
IFK Göteborg	Gothenburg	Gamla Ullevi	15 845	ifkgoteborg.se	17	4
Kalmar FF	Kalmar	Fredriksskans	8 500	kalmarff.se	0	2
Malmö FF	Malmö	Malmö Stadion	26 500	mff.se	15	14
Orgryte IS	Gothenburg	Gamla Ullevi	15 845	ois.o.se	14	1
Osters IF	Växjö			osterfotboll.com	4	1

RECENT LEAGUE AND CUP RECORD

	Championship						Cup		
Year	Champions	Pts	Runners-up	Pts	Third	Pts	Winners	Score	Runners-up
1991	IFK Göteborg	36	IFK Norrköping	31	Orebro SK	28	IFK Göteborg	3-2	AIK Stockholm
1992	AIK Stockholm	34	IFK Norrköping	32	Osters IF	30	No tournament due to a season readjustment		
1993	IFK Göteborg	59	IFK Norrköping	54	AIK Stockholm	46	Degerfors IF	3-0	Landskrona BoIS
1994	IFK Göteborg	54	Orebro SK	52	Malmö FF	49	IFK Norrköping	4-3	Helsingborgs IF
1995	IFK Göteborg	46	Helsingborgs IF	42	Halmstads BK	41	Halmstads BK	3-1	AIK Stockholm
1996	IFK Göteborg	56	Malmö FF	46	Helsingborgs IF	44	AIK Stockholm	1-0	Malmö FF
1997	Halmstads BK	52	IFK Göteborg	49	Malmö FF	46	AIK Stockholm	2-1	IF Elfsborg
1998	AIK Stockholm	46	Helsingborgs IF	44	Hammarby IF	42	Helsingborgs IF	1-1 1-1 3-0p	Orgryte IS
1999	Helsingborgs IF	54	AIK Stockholm	53	Halmstads BK	48	AIK Stockholm	1-0 0-0	IFK Göteborg
2000	Halmstads BK	52	Helsingborgs IF	46	AIK Stockholm	45	Orgryte IS	2-0 0-1	IFK Göteborg
2001	Hammarby IF	48	Djurgårdens IF	47	AIK Stockholm	45	IF Elfsborg	1-1 9-8p	AIK Stockholm
2002	Djurgårdens IF	52	Malmö FF	46	Orgryte IS	44	Djurgårdens IF	1-0	AIK Stockholm
2003	Djurgårdens IF	58	Hammarby IF	51	Malmö FF	48	IF Elfsborg	2-0	Assyriska
2004	Malmö FF	52	Halmstads BK	50	IFK Göteborg	47	Djurgårdens IF	3-1	IFK Göteborg
2005	Djurgårdens IF	53	IFK Göteborg	49	Kalmar FF	43	Djurgårdens IF	2-0	Atvidabergs FF

SWEDEN 2005

ALLSVENSKAN	Pl	W	D	L	F	A	Pts	Djurgårdens	Göteborg	Kalmar	Hammarby	Malmö	Hels'borgs	Elfsborg	Häcken	Orgryte	Halmstads	Gefle	Landskrona	Sundsvall	Assyriska
Djurgårdens IF †	26	16	5	5	60	26	53		0-0	2-2	2-0	5-2	8-1	2-1	2-2	6-1	3-1	0-1	4-0	3-1	
IFK Göteborg ‡	26	14	7	5	38	22	49	1-3		0-0	1-0	2-1	0-0	1-1	1-0	3-0	4-0	0-1	4-2	2-0	0-3
Kalmar FF	26	11	10	5	36	21	43	0-2	0-0		3-0	0-2	2-0	1-1	2-0	2-1	2-0	1-0	2-2	0-0	1-0
Hammarby IF	26	12	7	7	43	30	43	2-1	3-2	0-0		1-1	6-2	0-0	3-1	0-0	2-1	0-1	4-0	0-0	3-0
Malmö FF	26	12	5	9	38	27	41	1-3	1-2	1-0	0-1		2-0	1-1	2-1	1-0	2-1	3-0	5-0	6-2	2-2
Helsingborgs IF	26	12	3	11	32	38	39	2-0	0-2	2-2	2-1	0-1		3-0	0-1	1-0	2-0	2-1	1-0	2-1	2-0
Elfsborg IF	26	10	7	9	35	43	37	1-2	0-2	1-0	4-1	3-1	2-0		2-0	1-0	1-1	1-0	1-2	2-1	1-3
BK Häcken	26	11	3	12	29	29	36	1-0	3-1	1-1	1-3	1-0	3-0	2-2		1-2	0-1	2-1	3-0	1-0	0-2
Orgryte IS	26	10	5	11	37	38	35	0-0	1-2	3-3	3-2	1-1	1-2	4-2	0-4		2-1	2-0	2-1	4-1	2-0
Halmstads BK	26	9	5	12	38	38	32	3-1	0-2	0-1	1-2	0-0	2-0	1-1	1-0	4-2		1-4	5-1	6-0	5-0
Gefle IF ‡	26	9	4	13	27	33	31	1-3	0-2	1-2	1-1	2-1	1-2	1-2	0-0	0-2	2-0		0-0	2-1	1-0
Landskrona BoIS	26	8	6	12	26	44	30	0-2	1-1	1-1	0-3	0-1	4-3	4-1	0-1	1-0	0-0	0-1		1-0	2-1
GIF Sundsvall	26	6	7	13	31	46	25	1-1	0-0	0-2	2-1	2-0	1-1	3-1	3-0	3-2	1-3	2-2	2-2		5-0
Assyriska FF	26	4	2	20	17	52	14	0-2	2-3	0-7	1-2	0-2	0-1	1-2	0-1	0-1	0-0	0-3	0-1	1-0	

9/04/2005 - 23/10/2005 • † Qualified for the UEFA Champions League • ‡ Qualified for the UEFA Cup • Relegation play-off: GAIS 2-1 0-0 Landskrona
Top scorers: Gunnar THORVALDSSON, Halmstads, 16; AFONSO ALVES, Malmö, 14; Hasse BERGGREN, Elfsborg, 13; AILTON Almeida, Orgryte, 13

SWEDEN 2005 — SUPERETTAN (2)

	Pl	W	D	L	F	A	Pts
AIK Stockholm	30	19	7	4	56	27	64
Osters IF	30	17	4	9	48	36	55
GAIS Göteborg	30	14	10	6	52	35	52
Ljungskile SK	30	13	11	6	41	29	50
Orebro SK	30	12	9	9	40	32	45
IF Brommapojkarna	30	13	5	12	48	42	44
IFK Norrköping	30	12	8	10	44	40	44
Falkenbergs FF	30	11	8	11	38	43	41
Väsby United	30	11	6	13	32	40	39
Atvidabergs FF	30	9	11	10	36	32	38
Trelleborgs FF	30	9	9	12	34	34	36
Mjällby AIF	30	9	8	13	44	49	35
Degerfors IF	30	9	7	14	31	36	34
Bodens BK	30	9	5	16	28	48	32
Västerås SK	30	7	6	17	35	62	27
Västra Frölunda IF	30	7	4	19	32	54	25

16/04/2005 - 22/10/2005

SVENSKA CUPEN 2005

Fourth round
- Djurgårdens IF — 5
- Enskede IK * — 1
- Kalmar FF — 1 4p
- IFK Olme * — 1 5p
- BK Häcken * — 0 4p
- Malmö FF — 0 3p
- IFK Göteborg * — 1
- IF Elfsborg — 2
- IFK Norrköping * — 2
- GIF Sundsvall — 0
- Orgryte IS * — 1 2p
- Assyriska FF — 1 4p
- GAIS Göteborg * — 2
- Halmstads BK — 1
- Trelleborgs FF — 0
- Atvidabergs FF * — 1

Quarter-finals
- Djurgårdens IF — 6
- IFK Olme * — 0
- BK Häcken — 3
- IF Elfsborg * — 4
- IFK Norrköping — 2 11p
- Assyriska FF * — 2 10p
- GAIS Göteborg — 1 4p
- Atvidabergs FF * — 1 5p

Semi-finals
- Djurgårdens IF — 2
- IF Elfsborg — 1
- IFK Norrköping — 0
- Atvidabergs FF — 1

Final
- Djurgårdens IF — 2
- Atvidabergs FF ‡ — 0

CUP FINAL
Råsunda, Solna, Stockholm
29-10-2005, Att: 11 613, Ref: Hansson
Scorers - Toni Kuivasto [36], Tobias Hysén [89] for Djurgården

* Home team • ‡ Qualified for the UEFA Cup

SWZ – SWAZILAND

NATIONAL TEAM RECORD
JULY 1ST 2002 TO JULY 9TH 2006

PL	W	D	L	F	A	%
32	7	8	17	29	65	34.4

FIFA/COCA-COLA WORLD RANKING

1993	1994	1995	1996	1997	1998	1999	2000	2001	2002	2003	2004	2005		High		Low	
99	125	148	160	165	149	127	137	132	116	114	126	134		92	10/93	174	10/97

2005–2006											
08/05	09/05	10/05	11/05	12/05	01/06	02/06	03/06	04/06	05/06	06/06	07/06
129	132	133	131	134	134	134	137	139	138	-	153

Swaziland continued to struggle with the effects of limited international competition, occasionally showing glimpses of potential but then slumping back into character. The national side, Sihlangu, have dropped almost 30 places on the FIFA/Coca-Cola World Ranking over the last 12 months, their competitive outlook restricted to the regional COSAFA Castle Cup due to the failure to make it to the group phase of the 2006 FIFA World Cup™ qualifiers. However, in beating Madagascar in the COSAFA Castle Cup in Gaborone in May 2006 there was evidence of potential for the 2008 African Nations Cup qualifiers. Youthful Belgian coach Jan van Winkel looked to be a positive

INTERNATIONAL HONOURS
None

force for the national side but unfortunately for the Swazis, after just two months he was on his way, after being offered a role on the coaching staff at Club Brugge. The continuing export of top talent to the professional league in neighbouring South Africa also holds out much promise and the first-ever Swazi to play in Europe, winger Denis Masina, was a regular at his Belgian club KV Mechelen. Royal Leopards emerged as League winners in May 2006, the first time they had won the championship and also the first success for a parastatal team, in this case the Police side. They were led to the title by Musa Zwane, who also serves as the assistant national coach.

THE FIFA BIG COUNT OF 2000

	Male	Female		Male	Female
Registered players	3 000	0	Referees	100	0
Non registered players	3 500	0	Officials	700	0
Youth players	1 500	0	Total involved	8 800	
Total players	8 000		Number of clubs	50	
Professional players	0	0	Number of teams	200	

National Football Association of Swaziland (NFAS)
Sigwaca House, Plot 582, Sheffield Road, PO Box 641, Mbabane H100, Swaziland
Tel +268 4046852   Fax +268 4046206
nfas@swazi.net   www.nfas.org.sz
President: MTHETHWA Adam   General Secretary: MNGOMEZULU Frederick
Vice-President: SHONGWE Timothy   Treasurer: MNGOMEZULU Frederick   Media Officer: None
Men's Coach: TBD   Women's Coach: THWALA Christian
NFAS formed: 1968   CAF: 1976   FIFA: 1978
Blue shirts, Gold shorts, Red socks

RECENT INTERNATIONAL MATCHES PLAYED BY SWAZILAND

2002	Opponents	Score	Venue	Comp	Scorers	Att	Referee
1-08	Mauritius	L 0-1	Mbabane	Fr			
3-08	Mauritius	D 0-0	Big Bend	Fr			Sitriongomyane SWZ
24-08	South Africa	L 1-4	Polokwane	CCsf	Sibusiso Dlamini [58]	30 000	Katjimune NAM
7-09	Botswana	D 0-0	Gaborone	CNq			Moeketsi LES
6-10	Lesotho	D 0-0	Big Bend	Fr		4 000	
13-10	Libya	W 2-1	Mbabane	CNq	Gamedze [81], Nhleko [83]		Bernardo Colembi ANG
2003							
19-03	Lesotho	W 1-0	Mbabane	Fr	Mfanizle Dlamini [51]	400	
30-03	Congo DR	D 1-1	Mbabane	CNq	Mfanizle Dlamini [9]		Katjimune NAM
25-05	Lesotho	L 1-2	Maseru	Fr	Mkhwanazi [35]	5 000	
8-06	Congo DR	L 0-2	Kinshasa	CNq		60 000	Benjamin MRI
22-06	Botswana	W 3-2	Mbabane	CNq	Siza Dlamini 2 [7 25], Sibusiso Dlamini [18]	35 000	
5-07	Libya	L 2-6	Tripoli	CNq	Bongali Dlamini 2		
13-07	Madagascar	W 2-0	Mbabane	CCqf	Siza Dlamini [30], Mfanizle Dlamini [51]	8 000	Mpofu BOT
31-08	Zimbabwe	L 0-2	Harare	CCsf		25 000	Antonio De Souza ANG
6-09	Botswana	L 0-3	Mbabane	Fr			
4-10	Lesotho	L 2-5	Maseru	Fr			
12-10	Cape Verde Islands	D 1-1	Mbabane	WCq	Siza Dlamini [64]	5 000	Teshome ERI
9-11	Mozambique	L 0-2	Maputo	Fr			
16-11	Cape Verde Islands	L 0-3	Praia	WCq		6 000	Aboubacar CIV
2004							
11-04	Mozambique	L 0-2	Maputo	Fr			
31-05	Mozambique	D 1-1	Maputo	Fr	Maziya [83p]	5 000	
27-06	Zimbabwe	L 0-5	Mbabane	CCqf			Infante MOZ
6-07	Malawi	W 2-1	Blantyre	Fr			
8-07	Malawi	D 1-1	Lilongwe	Fr			
2005							
1-06	Lesotho	W 4-3	Somhlolo	Fr			
11-06	Zambia	L 0-3	Lusaka	CCrl			Chidoda BOT
2006							
14-04	Lesotho	L 0-5	Maseru	Fr			
16-04	Lesotho	D 2-2	Maseru	Fr	Nkosingiphile Dlamini [5], Matsebula [15]		
20-05	South Africa	L 0-1	Gaborone	CCrl			Malepa BOT
21-05	Madagascar	W 2-0	Gaborone	CCrl	Msibi [54], Mamba [82]		Malepa BOT
24-06	Mozambique	L 0-4	Maputo	Fr			
25-06	Zimbabwe	L 1-2	Maputo	Fr			

Fr = Friendly match • CN = CAF African Cup of Nations • CC = COSAFA Castle Cup • WC = FIFA World Cup™
q = qualifier • rl = first round group • qf = quarter-final • sf = semi-final

SWAZILAND NATIONAL TEAM RECORDS AND RECORD SEQUENCES

Records			Sequence records					
Victory	4-1	LES 1999	Wins	3	1999, 2001-2002	Clean sheets	2	1968, 2001, 2002
Defeat	1-9	ZAM 1978	Defeats	8	1969-1989	Goals scored	8	1998-1999
Player Caps	n/a		Undefeated	9	2001-2002	Without goal	6	1993-1997
Player Goals	n/a		Without win	18	1969-1990	Goals against	15	1981-1990

SWAZILAND COUNTRY INFORMATION

Capital	Mbabane	Independence	1968 from the UK	GDP per Capita	$4 900
Population	1 169 241	Status	Monarchy	GNP Ranking	147
Area km²	17 363	Language	English, siSwati	Dialling code	+46
Population density	67 per km²	Literacy rate	81%	Internet code	.sz
% in urban areas	31%	Main religion	Christian 60%	GMT +/−	+1
Towns/Cities ('000)	Manzini 110; Mbabane 76; Big Bend 10; Malkerns 9; Nhlangano 9; Mhlume 8; Hluti 6				
Neighbours (km)	Mozambique 105; South Africa 430				
Main stadia	Somholo National Stadium – Mbabane 30 000				

SWAZILAND 2005-06

MTN PREMIER LEAGUE

	Pl	W	D	L	F	A	Pts	Leopards	Buffaloes	Highlanders	Swallows	Mambas	Rovers	Sundowns	XI Men	Chiefs	Wanderers	Pirates	RSSC Utd
Royal Leopards †	22	13	4	5	39	19	43		1-1	0-0	0-4	2-0	3-2	2-1	3-1	0-1	1-1	2-0	4-0
Young Buffaloes	22	11	7	4	37	20	40	1-0		2-0	2-0	0-0	1-3	3-0	4-1	2-1	2-2	4-0	2-1
Mbabane Highlanders	22	10	7	5	32	19	37	0-1	1-1		3-2	0-1	1-2	2-1	4-1	2-0	3-0	2-2	1-0
Mbabane Swallows	22	11	4	7	35	24	37	1-2	0-2	1-1		1-1	4-1	2-1	0-1	5-1	2-0	0-0	1-0
Green Mamba	22	8	9	5	27	18	33	1-0	3-0	0-0	2-3		0-0	0-2	0-0	1-0	1-0	6-1	3-0
Mhlambanyatsi Rovers	22	7	9	6	29	28	30	1-5	0-0	2-2	1-2	2-2		1-1	3-1	0-0	2-1	1-1	2-0
Manzini Sundowns	22	7	6	9	27	26	27	1-2	2-3	0-0	3-0	0-0	1-0		0-1	1-1	2-1	1-1	1-1
Eleven Men in Flight	22	7	4	11	23	34	25	1-1	1-0	0-2	0-1	2-2	0-0	1-2		5-0	0-3	3-4	1-0
Malanti Chiefs	22	7	4	11	19	30	25	1-2	**0-0**	0-2	2-1	2-1	0-1	3-2	2-0		1-2	2-0	0-1
Manzini Wanderers	22	6	6	10	23	30	24	1-0	1-5	0-2	1-1	1-2	1-1	0-1	0-1	1-0		1-1	3-0
Moneni Pirates	22	4	9	9	21	42	21	0-3	2-1	1-4	0-2	0-0	1-4	2-1	2-0	1-1	1-1		0-0
RSSC United	22	5	3	14	14	36	18	0-5	1-1	**2-0**	2-0	2-1	1-0	0-3	1-2	0-1	1-2	3-1	

30/09/2005 - 4/06/2006 • † Qualified for the CAF Champions League • Match in bold awarded
Top scorers: Mzwandile MAMBA, Leopards, 11; Mduduzi MDLULI, Highlanders, 11; Jabulani DLAMINI, Buffaloes, 10

SWAZI BANK CUP 2005-06

Round of 16		Quarter-finals		Semi-finals		Final	
Mbabane Swallows	3						
Illovo FC	2	**Mbabane Swallows**	3				
Midas City	0 1p	Hub Sundowns	1				
Hub Sundowns	0 3p			**Mbabane Swallows**	4		
Moneni City Stars	2 5p			Royal Leopards	3		
Mhlambanyatsi Rovers	2 3p	Moneni City Stars	2 0p				
RSSC United	0 1p	**Royal Leopards**	2 3p			**Mbabane Swallows**	1
Royal Leopards	0 3p					Malanti Chiefs	0
Manzini Sundowns	1						
Manzini Wanderers	0	**Manzini Sundowns**	1 3p				
Moneni Pirates	0	Young Buffaloes	1 0p				
Young Buffaloes	1			Manzini Sundowns	0		
Umbelebele Cosmos	1			**Malanti Chiefs**	1		
Mbabane Highlanders	0	Umbelebele Cosmos	1				
Eleven Men in Flight	1	**Malanti Chiefs**	2				
Malanti Chiefs	3						

CUP FINAL

Mbabane Swallows 1 | **Malanti Chiefs 0**

Somhlolo, Mbabane
2-04-2006, Att: 8 000, Ref: Nhleko

Scorer - Menzi Gamedze [100] for Swallows

RECENT LEAGUE AND CUP RECORD

	Championship							Cup		
Year	Champions	Pts	Runners-up	Pts	Third	Pts		Winners	Score	Runners-up
1996	XI Men in Flight	69	Denver Sundowns	66	C&M Eagles	56				
1997	Mbabane High'ders	54	XI Men in Flight	52	Mbabane Swallows	52		Mbabane High'ders		
1998	No championship due to season readjustment									
1999	Manzini Wanderers	48	Mbabane High'ders	45	Mbabane Swallows	44		Mbabane High'ders		
2000	Mbabane High'ders	52	Green Mamba	45	Mbabane Swallows	37		Mhlume United		
2001	Mbabane High'ders	48	Manzini Wanderers	42	Mbabane Swallows	40		XI Men in Flight	1- 4-3p	Mbabane Swallows
2002	Manzini Wanderers	46	Mhlam'yatsi Rovers	43	Mbabane Swallows	43				
2003	Manzini Wanderers	45	Mhlam'yatsi Rovers	42	Mbabane Swallows	38				
2004	Mhlam'yatsi Rovers	50	Mbabane High'ders	45	Green Mamba	37		Green Mamba	5-1	Denver Sundowns
2005	Mbabane Swallows	43	Green Mamba	43	Royal Leopards	39		Hub Sundowns	2-0	Malanti Chiefs
2006	Royal Leopards	43	Young Buffaloes	40	Mbabane High'ders			Mbabane Swallows	1-0	Malanti Chiefs

SYR – SYRIA

NATIONAL TEAM RECORD
JULY 1ST 2002 TO JULY 9TH 2006

PL	W	D	L	F	A	%
56	19	15	22	89	86	47.3

FIFA/COCA-COLA WORLD RANKING

1993	1994	1995	1996	1997	1998	1999	2000	2001	2002	2003	2004	2005	High		Low	
82	105	136	115	98	84	109	100	90	91	85	85	98	**78**	08/03	**145**	05/96

					2005–2006						
08/05	09/05	10/05	11/05	12/05	01/06	02/06	03/06	04/06	05/06	06/06	07/06
96	102	107	107	98	100	95	89	90	90	-	110

After the successes of 2004 when both Al Jaish and Al Wahda reached the final of the inaugural AFC Cup, the Asian Football Confederation decided that Syria was no longer a 'developing' football nation but deserved to be considered as 'mature'. A compliment indeed, but Jaish and Wahda found the going a lot tougher having been promoted to the 2005 AFC Champions League. Both finished bottom of their groups with Wahda failing to get a single point. The 2006 AFC Champions League had two different Syrian entrants with champions Al Ittihad and League runners-up Al Karama, and it was Karama who caused a sensation by winning their group and qualifying for the quarter-finals.

INTERNATIONAL HONOURS
Asian Youth Championship 1994

At the same time they also won the 2006 League title in Syria but were denied the chance to win the Cup when they were thrown out of the competition. Crowd trouble had disrupted their semi-final first leg match against Teshrin after the referee turned down a Karama penalty appeal near the end. Al Ittihad then beat Teshrin 3-0 in the final to win the tournament. The national team's attempt to qualify for the AFC Asian Cup for the first time since 1996 got off to a shaky start with a defeat by Korea Republic in a difficult group also containing Iran, while earlier the Syrians had lost to Iraq on penalties in the final of the football tournament of the West Asian Games.

THE FIFA BIG COUNT OF 2000

	Male	Female		Male	Female
Registered players	4 263	0	Referees	600	0
Non registered players	194 750	0	Officials	3 240	0
Youth players	27 007		Total involved	229 860	
Total players		226 020	Number of clubs	157	
Professional players	20	0	Number of teams	694	

Syrian Arab Federation for Football (FASF)
Maysaloon Street, PO Box 22296, Damascus, Syria
Tel +963 11 3335866   Fax +963 11 3331511
toufiksarhan@hotmail.com   www.syrian-soccer.com
President: AHMAD Jappan Dr   General Secretary: SARHAN Toufik
Vice-President: FARES Taj Addin   Treasurer: SELOU Aref   Media Officer: none
Men's Coach: RADINOVICH Milosaf   Women's Coach: None
FASF formed: 1936   AFC: 1970   FIFA: 1937
Red shirts, Red shorts, Red socks

RECENT INTERNATIONAL MATCHES PLAYED BY SYRIA

2004	Opponents	Score		Venue	Comp	Scorers	Att	Referee
18-02	Bahrain	L	1-2	Al Muharraq	WCq	Shekh Eleshra 80	5 000	Khanthama THA
23-03	Lebanon	W	1-0	Jounieh	Fr			
26-03	Palestine	D	1-1	Damascus	Fr			
31-03	Kyrgyzstan	D	1-1	Bishkek	WCq	Meaataz Kailouni 86	17 000	Bose IND
19-04	Sudan	W	2-1	Khartoum	Fr			
21-04	Sudan	D	0-0	Khartoum	Fr			
1-06	Kuwait	W	1-0	Kuwait City	Fr			
3-06	Kuwait	W	2-1	Kuwait City	Fr	Raja Rafe 22, Maher Al Sayed 55p		
10-06	Tajikistan	W	2-1	Homs	WCq	Yahia Al Mhd. 76, Raja Rafe 80	18 000	Al Fadhli KUW
19-06	Lebanon	W	3-1	Tehran	WAr1	Maen Al Rashed 7, Shekh Eleshra 27, Raja Rafe 45		
21-06	Iran	L	1-7	Tehran	WAr1	Maher Al Sayed 82		
23-06	Jordan	D	1-1	Tehran	WAsf	Raja Rafe 55, W 3-2p		
25-06	Iran	L	1-4	Tehran	WAf	Raja Rafe 3		
26-08	Yemen	W	2-1	Sana'a	Fr			
28-08	Yemen	L	1-2	Sana'a	Fr			
8-09	Tajikistan	W	1-0	Dushanbe	WCq	Raja Rafe 35	18 000	Mohd Salleh MAS
29-09	Kuwait	D	1-1	Tripoli (LIB)	Fr			
6-10	Saudi Arabia	D	2-2	Riyadh	Fr	Raja Rafe 7, Rafat 90p		
8-10	Qatar	W	2-1	Doha	Fr			
13-10	Bahrain	D	2-2	Damascus	WCq	Shekh Eleshra 12, Jehad Al Houssain 18	35 000	Moradi IRN
17-11	Kyrgyzstan	L	0-1	Damascus	WCq		1 000	Tongkhan THA
2005								
26-01	Kuwait	L	2-3	Kuwait City	Fr	Amneh 39, Raja Rafe 74		
2-02	Japan	L	0-3	Saitama	Fr			
25-10	Oman	D	0-0	Muscat	Fr			
16-11	United Arab Emirates	L	0-3	Damascus	Fr			
3-12	Oman	W	3-1	Al Gharrafa	WGr1	Yhya Al Rachedd 41, Rafat 68, Alaya 81		
10-12	Iraq	D	2-2	Doha	WGf	Amena 19, Jehad Al Houssain 91+, L 3-4p		
2006								
30-01	Bahrain	D	1-1	Manama	Fr	Zyad Chabbo 6		
7-02	Palestine	W	3-0	Damascus	Fr			
14-02	Saudi Arabia	D	1-1	Jeddah	Fr	OG 45		
22-02	Korea Republic	L	1-2	Aleppo	ACq	Firas Al Khatib 49	35 000	Maidin SIN
1-03	Chinese Taipei	W	4-0	Taipei	ACq	Zyad Chabbo 2 29 58, Jehad Al Houssain 45, Firas Al Khatib 64	700	O Il Son PRK
2-05	United Arab Emirates	L	1-2	Dubai	Fr	Zyad Chabbo		

Fr = Friendly match • WA = West Asian Championship • WAG = West Asian Games • AR = Arab Championship • AC = AFC Asian Cup • WC = FIFA World Cup™ • q = qualifier • r1 = first round group • sf = semi-final • 3p = third place play-off • f = final

SYRIA NATIONAL TEAM RECORDS AND RECORD SEQUENCES

Records			Sequence records					
Victory	13-0	OMA 1965	Wins	4	1998, 2001, 2004	Clean sheets	5	1985
Defeat	0-8	GRE 1949, EGY 1951	Defeats	9	1977-1978	Goals scored	14	2004
Player Caps	n/a		Undefeated	10	1987-1988	Without goal	4	Three times
Player Goals	n/a		Without win	13	1981-1983	Goals against	15	1981-1983

SYRIA COUNTRY INFORMATION

Capital	Damascus	Independence	1946 from France	GDP per Capita	$3 300
Population	18 016 874	Status	Republic	GNP Ranking	72
Area km²	185 180	Language	Arabic, Kurdish, Armenian	Dialling code	+963
Population density	97 per km²	Literacy rate	76%	Internet code	.sy
% in urban areas	52%	Main religion	Muslim	GMT +/–	+2
Towns/Cities ('000)	Aleppo 2 139; Damascus 1 576; Homs 736; Latakia 431; Hama 348; ar-Raqqah 261				
Neighbours (km)	Iraq 605; Jordan 375; Israel 76; Lebanon 375; Turkey 822; Mediterranean Sea 193				
Main stadia	Abbasiyyin – Damascus 45 000				

SYRIA 2005-06

FIRST DIVISION

	Pl	W	D	L	F	A	Pts	Karama	Jaish	Wahda	Ittihad	Jabala	Majd	Hottin	Teshrin	Taliya	Foutoua	Qardaha	Horriya	Nwa'ir	Jihad
Al Karama Homs †	26	17	5	4	60	19	56		3-0	1-1	3-1	1-0	2-0	4-0	0-0	2-1	6-1	2-0	3-1	6-0	4-1
Al Jaish Damascus	26	15	8	3	48	21	53	1-1		0-1	1-1	3-0	1-1	3-3	3-2	1-1	2-0	0-0	5-0	4-1	3-0
Al Wahda Damascus	26	14	9	3	30	12	51	1-2	1-2		1-1	1-0	3-0	2-0	2-0	0-0	1-0	1-0	0-0	2-1	1-0
Al Ittihad Aleppo	26	10	10	6	33	20	40	1-0	1-1	0-0		0-0	3-0	2-0	5-0	2-1	3-0	0-0	2-2	0-1	2-0
Jabala	26	10	6	10	36	30	36	2-3	1-1	1-2	0-0		4-0	1-0	1-3	2-0	1-0	2-3	1-1	1-0	3-1
Al Majd Damascus	26	9	9	8	34	33	36	1-0	1-0	1-1	1-0	0-0		1-2	0-2	0-1	1-1	4-2	8-2	2-2	4-0
Hottin Latakia	26	9	8	9	43	38	35	1-1	0-3	0-0	2-0	3-1	2-2		2-3	1-2	2-1	3-2	4-0	1-0	9-1
Teshrin Latakia	26	9	7	10	36	34	34	2-2	0-1	0-1	2-1	1-1	1-1	2-0		1-1	1-2	0-1	1-2	5-0	3-1
Al Taliya Hama	26	8	10	8	29	32	34	1-4	1-2	0-0	1-0	2-0	2-1	1-1	2-2		1-1	3-1	1-1	0-0	2-1
Al Foutoua Deir ez-Zor	26	9	6	11	33	37	33	1-0	1-4	1-2	1-1	1-0	0-1	2-2	2-3	2-1		4-0	3-0	1-1	2-0
Qardaha	26	9	5	12	32	38	32	0-3	0-2	2-0	1-2	0-1	1-1	1-1	1-0	4-1	3-1		1-1	0-2	4-0
Al Horriya Aleppo	26	7	9	10	25	45	30	2-1	0-1	0-0	1-3	1-2	0-0	1-1	1-0	2-1	0-2	1-2		2-1	2-1
Al Nwa'ir	26	6	6	14	27	49	24	0-3	1-2	0-3	1-1	2-6	1-2	2-1	0-1	0-1	1-1	2-1	1-1		2-1
Al Jihad Qameshli	26	0	2	24	12	70	2	0-3	0-2	0-3	0-1	1-5	0-1	0-2	1-1	1-1	0-2	1-2	0-1	1-5	

7/10/2005 - 21/05/2006 • † Qualified for the 2007 AFC Champions League

FASF CUP 2005-06

Round of 16			Quarter-finals			Semi-finals			Final	
Al Ittihad *	1	1								
Al Wahda	0	1	Al Ittihad	2	1					
Hottin *	1	1								
Al Taliya	2	1	Al Taliya *	1	0	Al Ittihad	0 1 4p			
Jabala *	0	4				Al Jaish *	1 0 3p			
Qardaha	1	1	Jabala	1	0					
Al Naw'ir	1	1								
Al Jaish *	1	3	Al Jaish *	2	2				Al Ittihad †	3
Al Karama	4	0							Teshrin Latakia	0
Al Jalaa *	0	0	Al Karama *	4	2					
Efrin	3	0								
Al Majd *	2	3	Al Majd	1	1	Al Karama * ‡	0	0	CUP FINAL	
Al Horriya	1 0 5p					Teshrin Latakia	0	3	29-06-2006	
Al Jihad *	0 1 4p		Al Horriya	1	2				Scorers - Abdufattah Al Ahga [1],	
Musfat Banyas *	0	4							Bakry Tarab 2 [20] [39] for Ittihad	
Teshrin Latakia	0	5	Teshrin Latakia *	2	3					

* Home team in the first leg • ‡ Karama expelled • † Qualified for the AFC Cup

RECENT LEAGUE AND CUP RECORD

	Championship						Cup		
Year	Champions	Pts	Runners-up	Pts	Third	Pts	Winners	Score	Runners-up
1990	Al Foutoua	43	Al Karama	43	Al Wathba	34	Al Foutoua	1-0	Al Karama
1991	Al Foutoua	44	Jabala	37	Al Shourta	34	Al Foutoua	1-0	Yaqaza
1992	Al Horriya	42	Jabala	41	Al Ittihad	38	Al Horriya	1-0	Hottin
1993	Al Ittihad						Al Wahda	4-0	Hottin
1994	Al Horriya						Al Ittihad		
1995	Al Ittihad						Al Karama	3-0	Hottin
1996	Al Karama	62	Hottin	51	Teshrine	45	Al Karama	3-0	Jabala
1997	Teshrine	60	Al Jaish	57	Al Karama	49	Al Jaish	2-0	Jabala
1998	Al Jaish	62	Al Karama	48	Hottine	46	Al Jaish	5-2	Al Karama
1999	Al Jaish	58	Al Karama	55	Al Wahda	44	Jabala	2-2 3-0p	Jabala
2000	Jabala	51	Hottin	50	Teshrine	50	Al Jaish	4-1	Jabala
2001	Al Jaish	60	Al Karama	51	Al Ittihad	49	Hottin	1-0	Al Jaish
2002	Al Jaish	37	Al Ittihad	35	Al Wahda	29	Al Jaish	3-0	Jabala
2003	Al Jaish	57	Al Ittihad	54	Qardah	47	Al Wahda	5-2	Al Ittihad
2004	Al Wahda	60	Al Karama	58	Teshrine	54	Al Jaish	0-0 4-2p	Teshrine
2005	Al Ittihad	53	Al Karama	50	Al Wahda	44	Al Ittihad	3-1	Al Majd
2006	Al Karama	56	Al Jaish	53	Al Wahda	51	Al Ittihad	3-0	Teshrin

TAH – TAHITI

NATIONAL TEAM RECORD
JULY 1ST 2002 TO JULY 9TH 2006

PL	W	D	L	F	A	%
19	8	3	8	23	41	50

FIFA/COCA-COLA WORLD RANKING

1993	1994	1995	1996	1997	1998	1999	2000	2001	2002	2003	2004	2005		High	Low
141	148	156	158	161	123	139	131	127	115	33	124	141		**111** 08/02	**172** 09/98

	2005–2006										
08/05	09/05	10/05	11/05	12/05	01/06	02/06	03/06	04/06	05/06	06/06	07/06
135	137	138	140	141	141	141	142	144	145	-	164

Of the Oceania Football Confederation member nations, Tahiti ranks well behind Papua New Guinea, New Zealand, Fiji and the Solomon Islands in terms of population. When it comes to club football, however, the country is more than a match for its rivals. In the 2005 OFC Club Championship AS Piraé reached the semi-finals but in 2006 they went one better by reaching the final. In the first round group they beat Marist from the Solomon Islands 10-1 and then Sobou from Papua New Guinea 7-0 before narrowly losing to hosts Auckland City 1-0. In the semi-finals Piraé faced New Zealand side YoungHeart Manawatu and, thanks to goals from Jose Hmae and Naea

INTERNATIONAL HONOURS
South Pacific Games & Mini Games 1966 1975 1979 1981 1983 1985 1993 1995

Bennett early in the first half, they beat them 2-1 to reach the final. That meant another game against Auckland City which this time they lost 3-1. Gone was the opportunity to take part in the FIFA Club World Cup, but Tahitian sides have proved they can win games against the Kiwis so participation in the future is not out of the question. The League in Tahiti runs from September to June and is divided into two stages. Piraé won the first stage to qualify for the second which involved the top five clubs. They won that by four points from Tefana to win the championship for the third time in six seasons. Tefana won the Cup by beating Temarii 2-0 in the final.

THE FIFA BIG COUNT OF 2000

	Male	Female		Male	Female
Registered players	5 582	152	Referees	55	3
Non registered players	4 050	135	Officials	55	4
Youth players	3 660	86	Total involved	13 782	
Total players	13 665		Number of clubs	184	
Professional players	0	0	Number of teams	589	

Fédération Tahitienne de Football (FTF)
Rue Coppenrath, Stade de Fautaua, Case postale 50858, Pirae 98716, Tahiti, French Polynesia
Tel +689 540954   Fax +689 419629
contact@ftf.pf   www.ftf.pf
President: HAERERAAROA Eugene   General Secretary: DAVIO Vairani
Vice-President: ARIIOTIMA Henri Thierry   Treasurer: MARTIN Jean-François   Media Officer: LATEYRON Chrystele
Men's Coach: KAUTAI Gerard   Women's Coach: KAUTAI Gerard
FTF formed: 1989   OFC: 1990   FIFA: 1990
Red shirts, White shorts, Red socks

RECENT INTERNATIONAL MATCHES PLAYED BY TAHITI

2002	Opponents		Score	Venue	Comp	Scorers	Att	Referee
5-07	New Zealand	L	0-4	Auckland	OCr1		1 000	Attison VAN
7-07	Solomon Islands	W	3-2	Auckland	OCr1	Booene 42, Tagawa 57, Fatupua-Lecaill 90	1 000	Breeze AUS
9-07	Papua New Guinea	W	3-1	Auckland	OCr1	Garcia 29, Tagawa 2 49 64	800	Rakaroi FIJ
12-07	Australia	L	1-2	Auckland	OCsf	Zaveroni 38	400	Rugg NZL
14-07	Vanuatu	W	1-0	Auckland	OC3p	Auraa 65	1 000	Rakaroi FIJ
2003								
30-06	Micronesia †	W	17-0	Suva	SPr1	Tagawa 4 8 10 19 33, OG 17, Guyon 3 32 41 56 Bennett 4 48 70 76 86, Tchen 69, Papaaura 71 Senechal 72, Lecaill 78, Terevaura 81		Rakaroi FIJ
3-07	Papua New Guinea	W	3-0	Suva	SPr1	Bennett 2 13 69, Tagawa 62	1 000	Attison VAN
5-07	New Caledonia	L	0-4	Nadi	SPr1		3 000	Shah FIJ
7-07	Tonga	W	4-0	Lautoka	SPr1	Tagawa 2 2 27, Bennett 2 81 83	3 000	Shah FIJ
9-07	Fiji	L	1-2	Lautoka	SPsf	Papura 4	8 000	Attison VAN
11-07	Vanuatu	L	0-1	Suva	SP3p		6 000	Rakaroi FIJ
2004								
10-05	Cook Islands	W	2-0	Honiara	WCq	Temataua 2, Moretta 80	12 000	Singh FIJ
12-05	New Caledonia	D	0-0	Honiara	WCq		14 000	Rakaroi FIJ
17-05	Tonga	W	2-0	Honiara	WCq	Wajoka 1, Temataua 78	400	Sosongan PNG
19-05	Solomon Islands	D	1-1	Honiara	WCq	Simon 30	18 000	Rakaroi FIJ
29-05	Fiji	D	0-0	Adelaide	WCq		3 000	Farina ITA
31-05	Australia	L	0-9	Adelaide	WCq		1 200	Attison VAN
2-06	Solomon Islands	L	0-4	Adelaide	WCq		50	Rakaroi FIJ
4-06	New Zealand	L	0-10	Adelaide	WCq		200	Shield AUS
6-06	Vanuatu	W	2-1	Adelaide	WCq	Temataua 40, Wajoka 89	300	Rakaroi FIJ
2005								
No international matches played in 2005								
2006								
No international matches played in 2006 before July								

Fr = Friendly match • OC = OFC Oceania Cup • SP = South Pacific Games • WC = FIFA World Cup™
q = qualifier • r1 = first roundgroup • sf = semi-final • 3p = third place play-off • † Not a full international

TAHITI NATIONAL TEAM RECORDS AND RECORD SEQUENCES

Records			Sequence records					
Victory	30-0	COK 1971	Wins	10	1978-1980	Clean sheets	5	1995
Defeat	0-10	NZL 2004	Defeats	5	1996-1997	Goals scored	17	1981-1983
Player Caps	n/a		Undefeated	17	1981-1983	Without goal	4	2004
Player Goals	n/a		Without win	17	1959-1963	Goals against	20	1953-1963

RECENT LEAGUE AND CUP RECORD

Championship		Cup		
Year	Champions	Winners	Score	Runners-up
2001	AS Pirae	AS Dragon Papeete	2-1	AS Vénus Mahina
2002	AS Vénus Mahina	AS Pirae	1-0	AS Vénus Mahina
2003	AS Pirae	AS Manu-Ura Paea	0-0 4-3p	AS Pirae
2004	AS Manu-Ura Paea	AS Tefana	1-1 5-4p	AS Pirae
2005	AS Tefana	AS Manu-Ura Paea	0-0 10-9p	AS Pirae
2006	AS Pirae	AS Tefana	2-0	AS Temarii

TAHITI COUNTRY INFORMATION

Capital	Papeete	Status	French Overseas Possession, part of French Polynesia	GDP per Capita	$17 920
Population	266 339			GNP Ranking	n/a
Area km²	4 167	Language	French, Tahitian	Dialling code	+689
Population density	62 per km²	Literacy rate	98%	Internet code	.pf
% in urban areas	n/a	Main religion	Christian	GMT + / -	-10
Towns/Cities ('000)	Faaa 29; Papeete 26; Punaauia 25; Pirae 14; Mahina 14; Paea 13; Papara 10; Arue 9				
Neighbours (km)	South Pacific Ocean 2 525				
Main stadia	Stade de Fautaua – Pirae; Stade Pater – Papeete 15 000				

TAN – TANZANIA

NATIONAL TEAM RECORD
JULY 1ST 2002 TO JULY 9TH 2006

PL	W	D	L	F	A	%
28	6	5	17	22	47	30.4

FIFA/COCA-COLA WORLD RANKING

1993	1994	1995	1996	1997	1998	1999	2000	2001	2002	2003	2004	2005	High		Low	
98	74	70	89	96	118	128	140	149	153	159	172	165	65	02/95	175	11/05

2005–2006											
08/05	09/05	10/05	11/05	12/05	01/06	02/06	03/06	04/06	05/06	06/06	07/06
173	174	175	175	165	165	165	167	167	167	-	143

The election of Jakaya Kikwete as President of Tanzania in October 2005 has had positive implications for football in the East African country with the prospect of increased support for the game. The recruitment of a Brazilian coach for the Taifa Stars was arranged with the direct interest of the President and Tanzania can now take part in the 2008 African Nations Cup qualifiers with new-found optimism as they try to reach the finals in Ghana. Only once before, in 1980, has the national team made it to the finals. Improving football in Tanzania, beset by allegations of corruption by previous administrations of the Football Association of Tanzania, was one of the campaign

INTERNATIONAL HONOURS
CECAFA Cup 1974 1994

promises of President Kikwete. Brazilian Marciano Maximo has been hired to try and turn a corner for the country and in June 2006 the national team played a rare set of friendly matches when they travelled to the Seychelles for games against their hosts as well as Mauritius. Prior to that the only exposure for the side over the last 36 months has been in the CECAFA Cup, where Tanzania is split in its representation. The mainland sends one team and Zanzibar another. There was a close contest in the 2005 Mainland League with Young Africans, otherwise known as YANGA, deposing reigning champions Simba in a tight race that also included Moro United.

THE FIFA BIG COUNT OF 2000

	Male	Female		Male	Female
Registered players	12 000	0	Referees	400	0
Non registered players	100 000	0	Officials	3 500	0
Youth players	12 000	0	Total involved	127 900	
Total players	124 000		Number of clubs	400	
Professional players	0	0	Number of teams	2 000	

The Football Association of Tanzania (FAT)
Karume Memorial Stadium, Uhuru/Shaurimoyo Street, PO Box 1574, Dar-es-Salaam, Tanzania
Tel +255 74 4264181   Fax +255 22 2861815
www.none
President: TENGA Leodgar   General Secretary: TBD
Vice-President: MAGORI Crescentius   Treasurer: TBD   Media Officer: None
Men's Coach: MSOLLA Mshind   Women's Coach: BAKARI Mohamed
FAT formed: 1930   CAF: 1960   FIFA: 1964
Green shirts, Black shorts, Green socks

RECENT INTERNATIONAL MATCHES PLAYED BY TANZANIA

2003	Opponents	Score		Venue	Comp	Scorers	Att	Referee
11-10	Kenya	D	0-0	Dar-es-Salaam	WCq		8 864	Tessema ETH
11-11	Uganda	L	1-2	Kampala	Fr	Abu Masula		
15-11	Kenya	L	0-3	Nairobi	WCq		14 000	El Beltagy EGY
2004								
13-12	Zanzibar †	L	2-4	Addis Abeba	CCr1	Maxime [23], Machupa [32]		
15-12	Burundi	L	0-2	Addis Abeba	CCr1			
17-12	Ethiopia	L	0-2	Addis Abeba	CCr1			
19-12	Rwanda	L	1-5	Addis Abeba	CCr1			
2005								
28-11	Burundi	W	2-1	Kigali	CCr1			
2-12	Zanzibar †	D	1-1	Kigali	CCr1			
4-12	Eritrea	W	1-0	Kigali	CCr1	Nurdin Bakari [38]		
6-12	Rwanda	L	1-3	Kigali	CCr1	Sammy Kessy		
2006								
26-06	Mauritius	W	2-1	Victoria	Fr	Abdi Kassim 2 [2p 19]		
30-06	Seychelles	L	1-2	Victoria	Fr	Salum Ussi [15]		

Fr = Friendly match • CN = CAF African Cup of Nations • CC = CECAFA Cup • WC = FIFA World Cup™
q = qualifier • r1 = first round group • sf = semi-final • f = final • † Not a full international

TANZANIA NATIONAL TEAM RECORDS AND RECORD SEQUENCES

Records			Sequence records					
Victory	7-0	SOM 1995	Wins	5	1994	Clean sheets	5	1994
Defeat	0-9	KEN 1956	Defeats	6	Four times	Goals scored	11	1993-1994
Player Caps	n/a		Undefeated	9	1973-1975	Without goal	4	Four times
Player Goals	n/a		Without win	28	1984-1990	Goals against	12	2001-2002

TANZANIA 2005 MAINLAND LEAGUE

	Pl	W	D	L	F	A	Pts
Young Africans	28	18	7	3	43	16	61
Moro United	28	17	7	4	38	15	58
Simba SC	28	16	8	4	36	20	56
Kagera Sugar	28	13	7	8	33	21	46
Ashanti United	28	11	12	5	31	22	45
JKT Ruvu Stars	28	12	7	9	39	29	43
Mtibwa Sugar	28	11	6	11	41	30	39
Police Dodoma	28	8	10	10	24	30	34
Transit Camp	28	7	9	12	22	37	30
Arusha FC	28	6	11	11	28	35	29
Prisons Mbeya	28	6	11	11	25	32	29
Bandari	28	8	5	15	25	39	29
Twiga Sports	28	5	10	13	20	32	25
Kahama United	28	3	12	13	20	38	21
Maji Maji Songea	28	5	6	17	16	43	21
Mji Mpwapwa				Withdrew			

26/03/2005 - 23/10/2005

RECENT LEAGUE AND CUP RECORD

	Tanzanian Mainland	Cup
Year	Champions	Winners
1990	Simba SC Dar es Salaam	Small Simba
1991	Young Africans Dar es Salaam	Railways Morogoro
1992	Young Africans Dar es Salaam	Pamba FC Mwamba
1993	Young Africans Dar es Salaam	Malindi
1994	Simba SC Dar es Salaam	Young Africans Dar es Salaam
1995	Simba SC Dar es Salaam	Simba SC Dar es Salaam
1996	Young Africans Dar es Salaam	Sigara
1997	Young Africans Dar es Salaam	Tanzania Stars
1998	Young Africans Dar es Salaam	Tanzania Stars
1999	Mtibwa Sugar	Young Africans Dar es Salaam
2000	Mtibwa Sugar	Simba SC Dar es Salaam
2001	Simba SC Dar es Salaam	Polisi Zanzibar
2002	Young Africans Dar es Salaam	Ruvu Stars
2003	Simba SC Dar es Salaam	
2004	Simba SC Dar es Salaam	
2005	Young Africans Dar es Salaam	

TANZANIA COUNTRY INFORMATION

Capital	Dodoma	Independence	1964 from the UK	GDP per Capita	$600
Population	36 588 225	Status	Republic	GDP Ranking	88
Area km²	945 087	Language	Swahili, English	Dialling code	+255
Population density	38 per km²	Literacy rate	78%	Internet code	.tz
% in urban areas	24%	Main religion	Muslim 35%, Christian 30%	GMT +/−	+3
Towns/Cities ('000)	Dar es Salaam 2 698; Mwanza 436; Zanzibar 403; Arusha 341; Mbeya 291; Morogoro 250; Tanga 224; Dodoma 180; Kigoma 164; Moshi 156; Tabora 145; Songea 126, Musoma 121				
Neighbours (km)	Mozambique 756; Malawi 475; Zambia 338; Congo DR 459; Burundi 451; Rwanda 217; Uganda 396; Kenya 769; Indian Ocean 1 424				
Main stadia	National Stadium – Dar-es-Salaam 15 000; CCM Kirumba – Mwanza 30 000				

TCA – TURKS AND CAICOS ISLANDS

NATIONAL TEAM RECORD
JULY 1ST 2002 TO JULY 9TH 2006

PL	W	D	L	F	A	%
2	0	0	2	0	7	0

FIFA/COCA-COLA WORLD RANKING

1993	1994	1995	1996	1997	1998	1999	2000	2001	2002	2003	2004	2005	High		Low	
-	-	-	-	-	-	196	200	200	202	203	203	203	192	05/99	204	05/06

2005–2006											
08/05	09/05	10/05	11/05	12/05	01/06	02/06	03/06	04/06	05/06	06/06	07/06
203	203	203	203	203	203	203	203	203	204	-	196

As far as goals to games ratios go, forget Luca Toni's exploits in Serie A for Fiorentina. Kirkland Harris of Cost Right scored 21 goals in just nine Leagues matches in the 2005-06 Turks and Caicos League Championship and he wasn't the only one firing them in. Sadrac Mondestine scored 16 in nine games for Beaches FC, Noel Frankley hit the back of the net 15 times for Provopool and Dady Aristide 13 times for Caribbean All Stars - all scoring at more than a goal a game! The champions were Beaches FC, an apt name for a club in one of the world's top tourist destinations. It was their second title in five years and prevented KPMG United winning a hat-trick. Beaches then did the

INTERNATIONAL HONOURS
None

double when they beat Provopool 2-1 after extra-time in the MFL Cup Final. History was made when the senior women's team entered the 2007 FIFA Women's World Cup, the first time they had taken part in the tournament. Playing in the 2006 Women's Caribbean Cup, which acted as a qualifying zone, Turks and Caicos received a bye to the group stage after the Bahamas withdrew from their preliminary round tie, and although they didn't win a point in the group, there were no big defeats as they lost to Bermuda, the US Virgin Islands and the hosts, in a tournament played in the Dominican Republic.

THE FIFA BIG COUNT OF 2000

	Male	Female		Male	Female
Registered players	120	30	Referees	15	0
Non registered players	200	200	Officials	30	20
Youth players	400	0	Total involved	1 015	
Total players	950		Number of clubs	6	
Professional players	0	0	Number of teams	6	

Turks and Caicos Islands Football Association (TCIFA)
Tropicana Plaza, Leeward Highway, PO Box 626, Providenciales, Turks and Caicos Islands
Tel +1 649 9415532　　Fax +1 649 9415554
tcifa@tciway.tc　　www.football.tc
President: BRYAN Christopher　　General Secretary: BIEN-AIME Sonia
Vice-President: SLATTERY James　　Treasurer: DOUGLAS Jenny　　Media Officer: None
Men's Coach: COOK Charles　　Women's Coach: COOK Charles
TCIFA formed: 1996　　CONCACAF: 1998　　FIFA: 1998
White shirts, White shorts, White socks

RECENT INTERNATIONAL MATCHES PLAYED BY TURKS AND CAICOS

2002	Opponents	Score	Venue	Comp	Scorers	Att	Referee
No international matches played in 2002							
2003							
No international matches played in 2003							
2004							
18-02	Haiti	L 0-5	Miami †	WCq		3 000	Stott USA
21-02	Haiti	L 0-2	Hialeah †	WCq		3 000	Valenzuela USA
2005							
No international matches played in 2005							
2006							
No international matches played in 2006 before July							

WC = FIFA World Cup™ • q = qualifier • † Both matches played in the USA

TURKS AND CAICOS ISLANDS NATIONAL TEAM RECORDS AND RECORD SEQUENCES

Records			Sequence records					
Victory	-		Wins	0		Clean sheets	0	
Defeat	0-8	SKN 2000	Defeats	6	2000-2004	Goals scored	1	1999, 2000
Player Caps	n/a		Undefeated	1	1999	Without goal	3	2000
Player Goals	n/a		Without win	8	1999-2004	Goals against	8	1999-2004

TURKS AND CAICOS ISLANDS 2005-06 MFL LEAGUE

	Pl	W	D	L	F	A	Pts
Beaches	9	6	1	2	39	15	19
Cost Right	9	5	3	1	28	18	18
Caribbean All Stars	10	5	2	3	31	21	17
KPMG United	10	4	2	4	25	18	14
Povopool	9	3	1	5	16	33	10
SWA Sharks	9	0	1	8	12	46	1

1/10/2005 - 18/05/2006

RECENT LEAGUE AND CUP RECORD

	Championship						Cup		
Year	Champions	Pts	Runners-up	Pts	Third	Pts	Winners	Score	Runners-up
1999	Tropic All Stars	15	Fleches Rapides	13	Provo	7	No tournament		
2000	Masters	16	Beaches	10	Sans Complex	4	Masters	2-0	Beaches
2001	Sharks	1-0	Projetech				No tournament		
2002	Beaches †	2-2	Barefoot				No tournament		
2003	Caribbean All Stars	28	Master Hammer	25	KPMG United	13	Caribbean All Stars	2-1	Master Hammer
2004	KPMG United	27	Caribbean All Stars	22	Police	14	Police	4-3	KPMG United
2005	KPMG United	30	Caribbean All Stars	25	Cost Right	14			
2006	Beaches	19	Cost Right	18	Caribbean All Stars	17	Beaches	2-1	Provopool

† Final abandoned at 2-2. Beaches declared champions

TURKS AND CAICOS ISLANDS COUNTRY INFORMATION

Capital	Cockburn Town	Status	Overseas territory of the UK	GDP per Capita	$9 600
Population	19 956			GNP Ranking	n/a
Area km²	430	Language	English	Dialling code	+1649
Population density	46 per km²	Literacy rate	98%	Internet code	.tc
% in urban areas	n/a	Main religion	Christian	GMT +/−	-4
Towns/Cities	Cockburn Town 5 525; Cockburn Harbour 1 744				
Neighbours (km)	North Atlantic Ocean 389				
Main stadia	National Development Facility – Providenciales 1 500				

TGA – TONGA

NATIONAL TEAM RECORD
JULY 1ST 2002 TO JULY 9TH 2006

PL	W	D	L	F	A	%
7	1	1	5	4	27	21.4

FIFA/COCA-COLA WORLD RANKING

1993	1994	1995	1996	1997	1998	1999	2000	2001	2002	2003	2004	2005	High		Low	
-	-	-	164	174	163	178	185	173	175	180	183	185		163	10/98	189 07/06

2005–2006										
08/05	09/05	10/05	11/05	12/05	01/06	02/06	03/06	04/06	05/06	06/06 07/06
184	184	184	184	185	185	185	185	186	187	- 189

As the third smallest member of the OFC in terms of population, Tonga will find it difficult to challenge the bigger nations in the confederation but the women's under-19 team showed great spirit in the qualifying tournament for the FIFA U-20 Women's World Championship and were just 90 minutes away from making the finals in Russia. Their progress at a tournament held in Samoa showed the benefits of careful planning and preparation, in no small measure due a successfully implemented GOAL programme. The under-19s beat the Solomon Islands and Vanuatu in the first round to qualify for the semi-finals, where they beat the hosts 3-2. That meant a final against New

INTERNATIONAL HONOURS
None

Zealand, a game they lost 6-0, but just reaching the final was probably the outstanding achievement in the history of the game in Tonga. At club level, the 2005 champions Lotoha'apai from the capital Nuku'alofa, were forced to pre-qualify for the 2006 OFC Club Championship and never really came close to qualifying for the finals in New Zealand. At a tournament played in Fiji, a 5-1 defeat at the hands of local club Nokia Eagles put paid to any hope of winning the group. It was the fourth time Lotoha'apai had qualified to take part in the OFC Club Championship and a victory over Nikao Sokattak in the second match was their first ever in the competition.

THE FIFA BIG COUNT OF 2000

	Male	Female		Male	Female
Registered players	1 824	272	Referees	78	24
Non registered players	500	100	Officials	87	36
Youth players	864	288	Total involved	4 073	
Total players	3 848		Number of clubs	91	
Professional players	0	0	Number of teams	203	

Tonga Football Association (FTF)
Loto Tonga Soko Center, Off Taufa'Ahau Road - 'Atele, PO Box 852, Nuku'alofa, Tonga
Tel +676 30233   Fax +676 30240
tfa@kalianet.to   www.tongafootball.com
President: VEEHALA Hon   General Secretary: FUSIMALOHI Ahongalu
Vice-President: FUSITUA Hon   Treasurer: AHO Lui   Media Officer: None
Men's Coach: JANKOVIC Milan   Women's Coach: None
FTF formed: 1965   OFC: 1994   FIFA: 1994
Red shirts, White shorts, Red socks

RECENT INTERNATIONAL MATCHES PLAYED BY TONGA

2002	Opponents	Score	Venue	Comp	Scorers	Att	Referee
No international matches played in 2002 after June							
2003							
1-07	Papua New Guinea	D 2-2	Suva	SPr1		3 000	Singh FIJ
3-07	New Caledonia	L 0-4	Suva	SPr1		700	Shah FIJ
5-07	Micronesia †	W 7-0	Nausori	SPr1	Fonua [5], Tevi [15], Uhatahi 2 [22 36], Feao 2 [34 55], Uele [72]	1 000	Moli SOL
7-07	Tahiti	L 0-4	Lautoka	SPr1		3 000	Shah FIJ
2004							
10-05	Solomon Islands	L 0-6	Honiara	WCq		12 385	Attison VAN
15-05	Cook Islands	W 2-1	Honiara	WCq	Uhatahi [46], Vaitaki [61]	15 000	Sosongan PNG
17-05	Tahiti	L 0-2	Honiara	WCq		400	Sosongan PNG
19-05	New Caledonia	L 0-8	Honiara	WCq		14 000	Fred VAN
2005							
No international matches played in 2005							
2006							
No international matches played in 2006 before July							

Fr = Friendly match • SP = South Pacific Games • WC = FIFA World Cup™ • q = qualifier • r1 = first round group • † Not a full international

TONGA NATIONAL TEAM RECORDS AND RECORD SEQUENCES

Records			Sequence records				
Victory	5-0	ASA 2001	Wins	3	1994-1996	Clean sheets	2	1996
Defeat	0-22	AUS 2001	Defeats	4	1998-2000	Goals scored	4	1994-96, 2000-01
Player Caps	n/a		Undefeated	4	1994-1996	Without goal	4	1993-1994
Player Goals	n/a		Without win	6	1983-1994	Goals against	12	2001-2004

TONGA CHAMPIONS

Year	Champions
1998	SC Lotoha'apai Nuku'alofa
1999	SC Lotoha'apai Nuku'alofa
2000	SC Lotoha'apai Nuku'alofa
2001	SC Lotoha'apai Nuku'alofa
2002	SC Lotoha'apai Nuku'alofa
2003	SC Lotoha'apai Nuku'alofa
2004	SC Lotoha'apai Nuku'alofa
2005	SC Lotoha'apai Nuku'alofa

TONGA COUNTRY INFORMATION

Capital	Nuku'alofa	Independence	1970 from the UK	GDP per Capita	$2 200
Population	110 237	Status	Constitutional Monarchy	GNP Ranking	186
Area km²	748	Language	Tongan, English	Dialling code	+676
Population density	147 per km²	Literacy rate	98%	Internet code	.to
% in urban areas	41%	Main religion	Christian	GMT +/-	+13
Towns/Cities ('000)	Nuku'alofa 23; Mu'a 5; Neiafu 4; Haveloloto 3; Vaini 3; Tofoa-Koloua 2; Pangai 2				
Neighbours (km)	South Pacific Ocean 419				
Main stadia	Mangweni Stadium – Nuku'alofa 3 000				

THA – THAILAND

NATIONAL TEAM RECORD
JULY 1ST 2002 TO JULY 9TH 2006

PL	W	D	L	F	A	%
42	14	11	17	67	67	47.6

FIFA/COCA-COLA WORLD RANKING

1993	1994	1995	1996	1997	1998	1999	2000	2001	2002	2003	2004	2005	High		Low	
69	85	77	57	54	45	60	61	61	66	60	79	111	**43**	09/98	**113**	07/06

2005–2006											
08/05	09/05	10/05	11/05	12/05	01/06	02/06	03/06	04/06	05/06	06/06	07/06
95	94	101	105	111	109	109	108	108	108	-	113

May 2006 saw the opening of the National Football Center in Thailand and at the ceremony the talk was of pushing to qualify for the 2010 FIFA World Cup™ finals in South Africa. But as one local commentator cautiously pointed out, it might be wise to learn to walk before attempting to run. Making an impact at the 2007 AFC Asian Cup, which the Thais are co-hosting, will be a big test for Chanwit Polchiwin's side which has no real history to build upon in the tournament. Progress has not been helped by the PR gaffe of the year which saw Thai clubs Tobacco and Provincial Electrical Authority bear the full brunt of the AFC's wrath by being thrown out of the

INTERNATIONAL HONOURS
SEA Games 1965 1975 1981 1983 1985 1993 1995 1997 1999 2001 2003 **Tiger Cup** 1996 2000 2002
AFC Champions League Thai Farmers Bank 1994 1995

AFC Champions League for failing to register their squads on time. From 2007 only one Thai club will qualify for the Champions League with the other going into the AFC Cup. The club scene was not helped either by the setting up of a rival League to the FAT Premier League. The Pro League is more national in its composition and has the backing of the Ministry of Tourism and Sports but it has caused a schism which cannot be good for the future of the game in the country. The Premier League, which finished two months ahead of its rival, was won by Bangkok University.

THE FIFA BIG COUNT OF 2000

	Male	Female		Male	Female
Registered players	9 680	100	Referees	1 000	3
Non registered players	300 000	10 000	Officials	5 000	3
Youth players	15 000	0	Total involved	340 786	
Total players	334 780		Number of clubs	132	
Professional players	480	0	Number of teams	1 624	

The Football Association of Thailand (FAT)

National Stadium, Gate 3, Rama 1 Road, Patumwan, Bangkok 10330, Thailand
Tel +66 2 2164691   Fax +66 2 2154494
www.none
President: GETKAEW Vijit Dr   General Secretary: MAKUDI Worawi
Vice-President: WATTANAWONGKEEREE Pisarn   Treasurer: MULULIM Samart   Media Officer: None
Men's Coach: PHOLCHIVIN Chanwit   Women's Coach: PONGPANICH Prapol
FAT formed: 1916   AFC: 1957   FIFA: 1925
Red shirts, Red shorts, Red socks

RECENT INTERNATIONAL MATCHES PLAYED BY THAILAND

2003	Opponents	Score		Venue	Comp	Scorers	Att	Referee
16-02	Korea DPR	D	2-2	Thailand	Fr	Chaikamdee [27], Thonglao [55]		
18-02	Qatar	D	1-1	Bangkok	Fr	Chaiman [55p]		Lee Gi Young KOR
20-02	Sweden	L	1-4	Bangkok	Fr	Vachiraban [80]		Lee Gi Young KOR
22-02	Qatar	W	3-1	Bangkok	Fr	Noyvach 2 [24 33], Cheoychiew [76]		
16-10	India	W	2-0	Bangkok	Fr	Phorueundee [64], Chaikamdee [78]		
6-11	Takijistan	L	0-1	Tashkent	ACq			
8-11	Uzbekistan	L	0-3	Tashkent	ACq			
10-11	Hong Kong	L	1-2	Tashkent	ACq	Thonglao [64]		
17-11	Hong Kong	W	4-0	Bangkok	ACq	Noyvech [24], Thonglao [35], Chaikamdee 2 [79 88p]		
19-11	Tajikistan	W	1-0	Bangkok	ACq	Chaiman [83p]		
21-11	Uzbekistan	W	4-1	Bangkok	ACq	Noyvech [38], Surasiang [56], Tongmaen [78], Chaikamdee [81]		
2004								
18-02	United Arab Emirates	L	0-1	Al Ain	WCq		4 000	Sun Baojie CHN
31-03	Yemen	W	3-0	Sana'a	WCq	Chaikamdee [69], Surasiang [71], Senamuang [88]	25 000	Mansour LIB
9-06	Korea DPR	L	1-4	Bangkok	WCq	Senamuang [51]	30 000	Tseytlin UZB
5-07	Bahrain	L	0-2	Bangkok	Fr			
8-07	Jordan	D	0-0	Bangkok	Fr			
10-07	Trinidad and Tobago	W	3-2	Bangkok	Fr	Vachiraban [47], Suksomkit [53], Pichitpong [87]		
20-07	Iran	L	0-3	Chongqing	ACr1		37 000	Kousa SYR
24-07	Japan	L	1-4	Chongqing	ACr1	Suksomkit [11]	45 000	Al Marzouqi UAE
28-07	Oman	L	0-2	Chengdu	ACr1		13 000	Lu Jun CHN
19-08	Malaysia	L	1-2	Bangkok	Fr	Chaiman [90]		
8-09	Korea DPR	L	1-4	Pyongyang	WCq	Suksomkit [72]	20 000	Moradi IRN
8-10	Jordan	L	2-3	Bangkok	Fr			
13-10	United Arab Emirates	W	3-0	Bangkok	WCq	Jakapong [10], Nanok [30], Chaiman [67]	15 000	Nishimura JPN
17-11	Yemen	D	1-1	Bangkok	WCq	Siriwong [95+]	15 000	Baskar IND
30-11	Estonia	D	0-0	Bangkok	Fr	W 4-3p	35 000	Mat Amin MAS
2-12	Slovakia	D	1-1	Bangkok	Fr	Joemdee [15p]. L 4-5p	5 000	Chappanimutu MAS
10-12	Myanmar	D	1-1	Kuala Lumpur	TCr1	Chaiman [14]		Moradi IRN
12-12	East Timor †	W	8-0	Kuala Lumpur	TCr1	Yodyingyong [17], Domthaisong [41], Jitkuntod [53], Chaiman [59], Chaikamdee 3 [63 65 67], Konjan [84]		Vo Minh Try VIE
14-12	Malaysia	L	1-2	Kuala Lumpur	TCr1	Chaikamdee [45]	10 000	Moradi IRN
16-12	Philippines	W	3-1	Kuala Lumpur	TCr1	Poolsap [42], Sainui [56], Domthaisong [89]	300	Vo Minh Try VIE
21-12	Germany	L	1-5	Bangkok	Fr	Chaikamdee [57]	15 000	Maidin SIN
2005								
24-12	Latvia	D	1-1	Phang Nga	Fr	Teeratep [56]		
28-12	Korea DPR	L	0-2	Phuket	Fr			
2006								
1-02	Jordan	D	0-0	Ayutthaya	Fr			
16-02	Iraq	W	4-3	Ayutthaya	Fr	Prat 2 OG [10], Nirut [12], Apichate [55]		
26-03	Philippines	W	5-0	Chonburi	Fr	Bunkham [13], Teeratep 2 [20 44], Jaiharn [58], Phona [90]		

Fr = Friendly match • TC = ASEAN Tiger Cup • AC = AFC Asian Cup • WC = FIFA World Cup™
q = qualifier • r1 = 1st round • sf = semi-final • f = final • † Not a full international

THAILAND NATIONAL TEAM RECORDS AND RECORD SEQUENCES

Records			Sequence records					
Victory	10-0	BRU 1970	Wins	8	1993	Clean sheets	4	Five times
Defeat	0-8	CZE 1968	Defeats	11	1959-1961	Goals scored	19	1960-1963
Player Caps	117	KIATISUK SENAMUANG	Undefeated	11	1995-1996	Without goal	9	1990-1991
Player Goals	64	KIATISUK SENAMUANG	Without win	23	1959-1963	Goals against	31	1959-1965

THAILAND COUNTRY INFORMATION

Capital	Bangkok	Foundation	1238	GDP per Capita	$7 400
Population	64 865 523	Status	Constitutional Monarchy	GNP Ranking	32
Area km²	514 000	Language	Thai	Dialling code	+66
Population density	126 per km²	Literacy rate	92%	Internet code	.th
% in urban areas	20%	Main religion	Buddhist	GMT + / –	+7
Towns/Cities ('000)	Bangkok 5 104; Samut Prakan 388; Nonthaburi 375; Udon Thani 247; Chon Buri 219; Nakhon Ratchasima 208; Chiang Mai 201; Hat Yai 191; Pak Kret 183; Si Racha 179				
Neighbours (km)	Laos 1 754; Cambodia 803; Malaysia 506; Myanmar 1 800; Gulf of Thailand 3 219				
Main stadia	Rajamangala – Bangkok 65 000; Suphachalasai – Bangkok 30 000				

THAILAND 2006

FAT PREMIER LEAGUE

	Pl	W	D	L	F	A	Pts	Bangkok Un	Osotspa	BEC Tero	Tobacco	BBL	Army	Port	Chonburi	KTB	PEA	Thai-Honda	Suphanburi
Bangkok University †	22	11	6	5	25	17	39		1-1	0-0	1-0	1-2	1-0	3-1	1-1	1-1	0-0	1-0	2-1
Osotspa ‡	22	10	8	4	35	20	38	1-2		2-2	3-2	2-0	6-1	1-1	3-3	4-1	3-0	1-1	1-0
BEC Tero Sasana	22	9	9	4	32	14	36	2-1	1-0		1-1	1-0	8-1	1-1	0-1	0-1	2-0	0-0	5-0
Thailand Tobacco	22	9	8	5	30	24	35	1-0	0-0	1-0		1-2	1-1	2-1	2-2	1-0	1-1	0-2	0-1
Bangkok Bank	22	10	4	8	26	28	34	2-1	0-1	0-2	1-2		3-4	1-0	3-2	0-0	2-1	1-1	1-0
Royal Thai Army	22	7	9	6	31	38	30	0-1	1-0	1-1	2-2	1-0		3-0	1-1	1-1	3-2	2-3	1-0
Port Authority	22	7	7	8	21	28	28	0-1	0-0	1-1	0-3	1-1	2-1		0-0	0-0	1-0	2-1	3-2
Chonburi	22	5	12	5	29	28	27	0-2	1-1	0-0	2-3	3-0	2-2	1-3		2-2	1-0	1-1	0-1
Krung Thai Bank	22	5	10	7	22	26	25	1-2	0-1	0-2	2-2	1-1	2-2	3-0	0-2		1-2	1-0	1-0
Provincial Electrical	22	6	4	12	23	32	22	0-1	1-2	2-0	1-3	1-2	1-2	1-2	2-2	1-1		2-1	1-0
Thai-Honda	22	4	9	9	23	26	21	1-1	2-1	0-0	1-2	0-0	1-2	1-1	1-2	0-1			1-1
Suphanburi	22	4	4	14	18	34	16	2-1	0-1	1-1	1-2	1-2	1-1	1-0	0-1	1-1	2-3	2-5	

28/01/2006 - 2/07/2006 • † Qualified for the 2007 AFC Champions League • ‡ Qualified for the 2007 AFC Cup

RECENT LEAGUE RECORD

	Championship					
Year	Champions	Pts	Runners-up	Pts	Third	Pts
1997	Royal Thai Air Force	42	Sinthana	42	Bangkok Bank	38
1998	Sinthana	42	Royal Thai Air Force	40	BEC Tero Sasana	38
1999	Royal Thai Air Force	39	Port Authority	39	BEC Tero Sasana	39
2000	BEC Tero Sasana	49	Royal Thai Air Force	41	Thai Farmers Bank	37
2002	BEC Tero Sasana	50	Osotapa	44	Bangkok Bank	35
2003	Krung Thai Bank	36	BEC Tero Sasana	35	Port Authority	33
2004	Krung Thai Bank	38	BEC Tero Sasana	34	Osotapa	33
2005	Thailand Tobacco	34	Electical Authority	32	Osotapa	32
2006	Bangkok University	39	Osotspa	38	BEC Tero Sasana	36

TJK – TAJIKISTAN

NATIONAL TEAM RECORD
JULY 1ST 2002 TO JULY 9TH 2006

PL	W	D	L	F	A	%
25	12	3	10	35	28	54

FIFA/COCA-COLA WORLD RANKING

1993	1994	1995	1996	1997	1998	1999	2000	2001	2002	2003	2004	2005	High	Low
-	155	164	163	118	120	119	134	154	168	137	136	141	114 07/97	180 10/03

	2005–2006										
08/05	09/05	10/05	11/05	12/05	01/06	02/06	03/06	04/06	05/06	06/06	07/06
141	140	143	141	141	141	141	141	125	121	-	116

Tajikistan has never known success like it. It all started with the 2005 AFC President's Cup, a tournament designed to give international experience to the clubs of the so-called 'emerging' nations of Asia. Champions Regar TadAz represented Tajikistan and they went on to win it, beating Dordoi-Dynamo of neighbours Kyrgyzstan 3-0 in the final in Kathmandu. 12 months later it was the turn of Vakhsh to enter and they too reached the final. Despite having beaten Dordoi-Dynamo in the group stage, they lost 2-1 in the final, thanks to an extra time winner from Ildar Amirov. Disappointment for Vakhsh but it did beg the question as to how much longer Tajikistan should be

INTERNATIONAL HONOURS
None

considered an 'emerging' nation, especially after the performance the previous month in the AFC Challenge Cup, a tournament created for the national teams of the emerging nations. Despite a group stage defeat by Kyrgyzstan, the Tajiks had little trouble brushing aside hosts Bangladesh in the quarter-finals, Kyrgyzstan in the semi-finals and Sri Lanka in the final, to become the first nation to have their name inscribed on the trophy. Domestically, Vakhsh were a penalty shoot-out away from winning the double but after losing the Cup final to Regar, they did end their rivals four-season reign as champions, to win the title for only the second time.

THE FIFA BIG COUNT OF 2000

	Male	Female		Male	Female
Registered players	750	0	Referees	45	0
Non registered players	30 000	0	Officials	240	0
Youth players	1 600	0	Total involved	32 635	
Total players	32 350		Number of clubs	125	
Professional players	0	0	Number of teams	200	

Tajikistan Football Federation (TFF)
14/ Ainy Street, Dushanbe 734 025, Tajikistan
Tel +992 372 212447   Fax +992 372 510157
tff@tajikfootball.org   www.none
President: KOSIMOV Sukhrob   General Secretary: DAVLATOV Sherali
Vice-President: TURSUNOV Valery   Treasurer: KHOLOV Sherali   Media Officer: BURIEV Aloviddin
Men's Coach: NAZAROV Sharif   Women's Coach: SATTOROV Shavkat
TFF formed: 1936   AFC: 1994   FIFA: 1994
White shirts, White shorts, White socks

RECENT INTERNATIONAL MATCHES PLAYED BY TAJIKISTAN

2002	Opponents	Score		Venue	Comp	Scorers	Att	Referee
No international matches played in 2002								
2003								
6-11	Thailand	W	1-0	Tashkent	ACq	Fuzailov [79]		
8-11	Hong Kong	D	0-0	Tashkent	ACq			
10-11	Uzbekistan	D	0-0	Tashkent	ACq			
17-11	Uzbekistan	L	1-4	Bangkok	ACq	Burkhanov [65]		
19-11	Thailand	L	0-1	Bangkok	ACq			
21-11	Hong Kong	W	1-0	Bangkok	ACq	Muhidinov [68]		
26-11	Bangladesh	W	2-0	Dhaka	WCq	Hamidov [11], Hakimov [51]	6 000	Khanthachai THA
30-11	Bangladesh	W	2-0	Dushanbe	WCq	Kholomatov [15], Rabiev [83]	12 000	Pereira IND
2004								
18-02	Kyrgyzstan	W	2-1	Bishkek	WCq	Burkhanon 2 [31 53]	14 000	Lutfullin UZB
31-03	Bahrain	D	0-0	Dushanbe	WCq		17 000	Maidin SIN
10-06	Syria	L	1-2	Homs	WCq	Kholomatov [35]	18 000	Al Fadhli KUW
8-09	Syria	L	0-1	Dushanbe	WCq		18 000	Mohd Salleh MAS
13-10	Kyrgyzstan	W	2-1	Dushanbe	WCq	Rabiev [19], Hakimov [37]	11 000	Naser Al Enezi KUW
17-11	Bahrain	L	0-4	Manama	WCq		15 000	Sun Baojie CHN
6-12	Kuwait	L	0-3	Kuwait City	Fr			
2005								
25-01	Saudi Arabia	L	0-3	Riyadh	Fr			
9-11	Afghanistan	W	4-0	Dushanbe	Fr	Hakimov 2 [28 31], Makhmudov [45], Ashurmamadov [67]		
2006								
14-02	Qatar	L	0-2	Doha	Fr			
2-04	Macau	W	4-0	Dhaka	CCr1	Makhmudov [9], Rabiev [13], Rabimov [56], Khojaev [77]	2 000	Mombini IRN
4-04	Pakistan	W	2-0	Dhaka	CCr1	Hakimov [14], Irgashev [20]	5 000	Tan Hai CHN
6-04	Kyrgyzstan	L	0-1	Dhaka	CCr1		2 000	AK Nema IRQ
10-04	Bangladesh	W	6-1	Dhaka	CCqf	Rabimov [2], Makhmudov [20], Muhidinov [31], Hakimov [51], Rabiev [65], Nematov [81]	15 000	AK Nema IRQ
13-04	Kyrgyzstan	W	2-0	Dhaka	CCsf	Rabiev 2 [51 92+]	2 000	Tan Hai CHN
16-04	Sri Lanka	W	4-0	Dhaka	CCf	Muhidinov 3 [1 61 71], Makhmudov [45]	2 000	Mombini IRN
2-07	Kazakhstan	L	1-4	Almaty	Fr	Saidov [75]		

Fr = Friendly match • AC = AFC Asian Cup • ACC = AFC Challenge Cup • WC = FIFA World Cup™ • q = qualifier

TAJIKISTAN NATIONAL TEAM RECORDS AND RECORD SEQUENCES

Records					Sequence records		
Victory	16-0	GUM 2000	Wins	4	2003-2004	Clean sheets	3	1997, 2003, 2003
Defeat	0-5	UZB 1996, IRN 1998	Defeats	3	Three times	Goals scored	5	1997-98, 1998-99
Player Caps	n/a		Undefeated	5	2003-2004	Without goal	3	1993-94, 2004-05
Player Goals	n/a		Without win	5	1998-1999	Goals against	7	1998-1999

TAJIKISTAN COUNTRY INFORMATION

Capital	Dushanbe	Independence	1991 from the USSR	GDP per Capita	$1 000
Population	7 011 556	Status	Republic	GNP Ranking	152
Area km²	143 100	Language	Tajik, Russian	Dialling code	+992
Population density	49 per km²	Literacy rate	99%	Internet code	.tj
% in urban areas	32%	Main religion	Muslim	GMT +/ –	+5
Towns/Cities ('000)	Dushanbe 543; Khujand 144; Kulob 78; Qurgonteppa 60; Uroteppa 52; Konibodom 50				
Neighbours (km)	China 414; Afghanistan 1 206; Uzbekistan 1 161 Kyrgyzstan 870;				
Main stadia	National Stadium – Dushanbe 20 000				

TAJIKISTAN 2005

PREMIER DIVISION

	Pl	W	D	L	F	A	Pts	Vakhsh	Regar	Parvoz	CSKA	Khujand	HIMA	SKA Pamir	Ravshan	Saroy	Danghara
Vakhsh Qurgonteppa †	18	15	2	1	41	12	47		2-1	1-1	1-0	2-0	4-1	3-0	0-0	5-0	2-0
Regar-TadAZ	18	13	3	2	46	9	42	1-0		2-0	1-0	2-1	3-1	7-0	2-0	3-0	9-0
Parvoz B. Gafurov	18	10	4	4	38	20	34	0-2	1-4		2-0	3-1	4-1	2-0	2-1	6-1	3-0
CSKA Dushanbe	18	9	1	8	31	23	28	1-3	0-0	1-0		1-3	2-1	2-0	2-1	4-1	**7-1**
FK Khujand	18	8	3	7	28	19	27	2-3	1-0	1-1	1-2		2-0	1-0	1-1	3-0	**3-0**
HIMA Dushanbe	18	6	5	7	29	29	23	3-4	1-1	0-0	2-1	0-0		3-2	1-0	7-2	1-1
SKA Pamir Dushanbe	18	5	4	9	30	36	19	0-1	2-4	0-0	3-5	1-0	0-0		4-4	6-0	3-1
Ravshan Kulob	18	4	5	9	21	29	17	1-3	0-0	3-4	1-0	0-2	2-1	0-3		3-1	3-1
Saroy Kamar	18	3	2	13	18	55	11	0-2	0-3	2-4	2-1	2-1	0-2	2-2	1-1		4-1
FK Danghara	18	2	1	15	11	61	7	1-3	0-3	0-5	0-2	1-5	1-4	1-4	1-0	1-0	

28/03/2005 - 5/11/2005 • † Qualified for the AFC President's Cup • Match in bold awarded • Top scorers: Ahtam HAMROKULOV, Vakhsh, 12; Nazir RIZOMOV, Vakhsh, 12; Suhrob HAMIDOV, Regar TadAZ, 11

TAJIKISTAN CUP 2005

First round

Regar-TadAZ	Bye	
Saroy Kamar	1	2
SKA Farhor *	1	2
SKA Pamir	Bye	
FK Khujand	Bye	
CSKA Dushanbe	Bye	
Parvoz B. Gafurov	Bye	
HIMA Dushanbe	0	2
Ravshan Kulob *	1	0
Vahdat	0	0
Vakhsh Qurgonteppa *	5	2

Quarter-finals

Regar-TadAZ *	11	5
SKA Farhor	0	2
SKA Pamir *	0	0
FK Khujand	0	3
CSKA Dushanbe *	0	2
Parvoz B. Gafurov	0	1
HIMA Dushanbe	1	0
Vakhsh Qurgonteppa *	2	1

Semi-finals

Regar-TadAZ	1	1
FK Khujand	0	0
CSKA Dushanbe	1	2
Vakhsh Qurgonteppa	1	1

Final

Regar-TadAZ	1	3p
Vakhsh Qurgonteppa	1	1p

CUP FINAL

National Stadium, Dushanbe
5-10-2005, Att: 10 000, Ref: Jurayev

Scorers - Hamidov 87 for Regar; Habibulloyev 24p for Vakhsh

* Home team in the first leg

RECENT LEAGUE AND CUP RECORD

Year	Championship Champions	Pts	Runners-up	Pts	Third	Pts	Cup Winners	Score	Runners-up
1992	Pamir Dushanbe	33	Regar TadAZ	26	Vakhsh Qur'teppa	24	Pamir Dushanbe	1-0	Regar TadAZ
1993	Sitora Dushanbe	55	Pamir Dushanbe	52	P'takor Proletarsk	42	Sitora Dushanbe	0-0 5-3p	Ravshan Kulyab
1994	Sitora Dushanbe	47	Pamir Dushanbe	45	P'takor Proletarsk	43	Ravshan Kulyab	2-1	Shodmon Ghissar
1995	Pamir Dushanbe	67	Istravshan	57	Sitora Dushanbe	52	Pakhtakor Dzh'lovsk	0-0 3-2p	Regar TadAZ
1996	Dinamo Dushanbe	73	Sitora Dushanbe	71	Khojent	64		Not played	
1997	Vakhsh Qurgonteppa	59	Ranjbar Vosse	55	Khujand	52	Vakhsh Qurgonteppa	4-0	Khujand
1998	Varzob Dushanbe	56	Khujand	44	Saddam Sarband	42	Khujand	2-1	Ranjbar Vose
1999	Varzob Dushanbe	57	Khuja Gazimalik	49	Ravshan Kulyab	46	Varzob Dushanbe	4-2p	Regar TadAZ
2000	Varzob Dushanbe	87	Regar TadAZ	77	Khujand	68		Not played	
2001	Regar TadAZ	50	Panjsher Kolk'bad	38	Pamir Dushanbe	32	Regar TadAZ	4-2	Varzob Dushanbe
2002	Regar TadAZ	58	Khujand	53	Farrukh Ghissar	44	Khujand	3-0	Vakhsh Qurgonteppa
2003	Regar TadAZ	81	Khujand	72	Aviator	71	Vakhsh Qurgonteppa		
2004	Regar TadAZ	86	Vakhsh Qurgonteppa	85	Aviator	71	Aviator B. Gafurov	5-0	Uroteppa
2005	Vakhsh Qurgonteppa	47	Regar Tursunzoda	42	Parvoz B. Gafurov	34	Regar TadAZ	1-1 4-2p	Vakhsh Qurgonteppa

Tajik clubs took part in the Soviet league until the end of the 1991 season

TKM – TURKMENISTAN

NATIONAL TEAM RECORD
JULY 1ST 2002 TO JULY 9TH 2006

PL	W	D	L	F	A	%
22	9	4	9	37	31	50

FIFA/COCA-COLA WORLD RANKING

1993	1994	1995	1996	1997	1998	1999	2000	2001	2002	2003	2004	2005		High		Low
-	108	133	141	134	122	129	125	114	134	99	98	116		**86**	04/04	**150** 04/97

	2005–2006											
08/05	09/05	10/05	11/05	12/05	01/06	02/06	03/06	04/06	05/06	06/06	07/06	
107	109	111	112	116	116	116	118	119	120	-	148	

With just two senior international matches played in 2005 the focus in Turkmenistan was very much on club football, which was probably not such a bad thing either given terrible run endured by the national team since April 2004. The decision not to enter the the 2007 AFC Asian Cup, however, has left the national team in a position where they may not play any competitive matches until the qualifiers for the 2010 FIFA World Cup™, a period of nearly four years. That's hardly ideal given the excellent campaign which led to qualification for the 2004 AFC Asian Cup finals in China PR. After years as the top teams in the country, both Nisa Ashgabat and Kopetdag Ashgabat

INTERNATIONAL HONOURS
None

have seen their dominance eroded in the past three years and, in a sign of the times, the championship was won by MTTU in only their second season in the top flight. MTTU, the team of the International Turkmen-Turkish University, finished 10 points ahead of Gazcy with 2004 double winners Nebitchi Balkanabat in third place. There were first time winners of the Turkmenistan Cup as well, with Merv, from the industrial city of Mary in the Karakum desert, beating Kopetdag 3-1 on penalties in the final played on Independence Day. Both MTTU and Merv qualified for the 2006 AFC Cup but both finished bottom of their first round group and failed to make the quarter-finals.

THE FIFA BIG COUNT OF 2000

	Male	Female		Male	Female
Registered players	868	0	Referees	50	0
Non registered players	15 000	0	Officials	112	0
Youth players	300	0	Total involved	16 330	
Total players	16 168		Number of clubs	12	
Professional players	264	0	Number of teams	95	

Football Association of Turkmenistan (FFT)
15 A. Niyazova Street, Stadium Kopetdag, Ashgabat 744 001, Turkmenistan
Tel +993 12 362392   Fax +993 12 3632355
footballtkm@mail.ru   www.none
President: YUSUPOV Aman   General Secretary: SATYLOV Meret
Vice-President: SAPAEV Allabergen   Treasurer: LEONOVA Natalya   Media Officer: IVANNIKOV Evgeniy
Men's Coach: KURBANMAMEDOV Rakhim   Women's Coach: None
FFT formed: 1992   AFC: 1994   FIFA: 1994
Green shirts, White shorts, Green socks

RECENT INTERNATIONAL MATCHES PLAYED BY TURKMENISTAN

2002 Opponents	Score	Venue	Comp	Scorers	Att	Referee
No international matches played in 2002						
2003						
19-10 United Arab Emirates	W 1-0	Ashgabat	ACq	Bayramov.V [43]		
30-10 United Arab Emirates	D 1-1	Sharjah	ACq	Bayramov.V [40]		
9-11 Sri Lanka	W 1-0	Balkanabat	ACq	Agabaev [9]		
12-11 Sri Lanka	W 3-0	Ashgabat	ACq	Agayev 2 [25 70], Bayramov.V [45]		
19-11 Afghanistan	W 11-0	Ashgabat	WCq	Ovekov 2 [6 35], Kuliev 3 [8 22 81], Bayramov.N [27] Berdyev [42], Agabaev 3 [49 65 67], Urazov [90]	12 000	Busurmankulov KGZ
23-11 Afghanistan	W 2-0	Kabul	WCq	Kuliev 2 [85 91+]	6 000	Khan PAK
28-11 Syria	D 1-1	Damascus	ACq	Urazov [16]		Sadeq KUW
3-12 Syria	W 3-0	Ashgabat	ACq	Not played. Turkmenistan awarded match 3-0		
2004						
18-02 Sri Lanka	W 2-0	Ashgabat	WCq	Ovekov [40], Bayramov.N [56]	11 000	Al Bannai UAE
17-03 Yemen	W 2-1	Sana'a	Fr			
31-03 Indonesia	W 3-1	Ashgabat	WCq	Bayramov.V 2 [10 74], Kuliev [35]	5 000	Sahib Shakir IRQ
28-04 Armenia	L 0-1	Yerevan	Fr		7 500	
31-05 Qatar	L 0-5	Doha	Fr			
9-06 Saudi Arabia	L 0-3	Riyadh	WCq		1 000	Khanthama THA
18-07 Saudi Arabia	D 2-2	Chengdu	ACr1	Bayramov.N [7], Kuliev [90]	12 400	Al Qahtani KSA
22-07 Iraq	L 2-3	Chengdu	ACr1	Bayramov.V [15], Kuliev [85]	22 000	Al Fadhli KUW
26-07 Uzbekistan	L 0-1	Chongqing	ACr1		34 000	Kousa SYR
8-09 Saudi Arabia	L 0-1	Ashgabat	WCq		5 000	Kwon Jong Chul KOR
9-10 Sri Lanka	D 2-2	Colombo	WCq	Bayramov.D [20], Nazarov [70]	4 000	Al Bannai UAE
17-11 Indonesia	L 1-3	Jakarta	WCq	Durdiyev [25]	15 000	Shaban KUW
2005						
29-01 Saudi Arabia	L 0-1	Riyadh	Fr			
3-08 Bahrain	L 0-5	Manama	Fr			
2006						
No international matches played in 2006 before July						

Fr = Friendly match • AC = AFC Asian Cup • WC = FIFA World Cup™ • q = qualifier

TURKMENISTAN NATIONAL TEAM RECORDS AND RECORD SEQUENCES

Records			Sequence records				
Victory	11-0	AFG 2003	Wins	4	2003, 2003-2004	Clean sheets	4	2003
Defeat	1-6	KUW 2000	Defeats	3	Four times	Goals scored	14	2001-2004
Player Caps	n/a		Undefeated	13	2001-2004	Without goal	3	2004
Player Goals	n/a		Without win	11	2004-2005	Goals against	13	2004-2005

TURKMENISTAN COUNTRY INFORMATION

Capital	Ashgabat	Independence	1991 from the USSR	GDP per Capita	$5 800
Population	4 863 169	Status	Republic	GNP Ranking	113
Area km²	488 100	Language	Turkmen, Russian, Uzbek	Dialling code	+993
Population density	10 per km²	Literacy rate	98%	Internet code	.tm
% in urban areas	45%	Main religion	Muslim	GMT +/–	+5
Cities/Towns ('000)	Ashgabat 979; Turkmenabat 234; Dasoguz 199; Mary 114; Balkanabat 87; Bayramali 75				
Neighbours (km)	Uzbekistan 1 621; Afghanistan 744; Iran 992; Kazakhstan 379; Caspian Sea 1 768				
Main stadia	Olympic Stadium – Ashgabat 30 000; Köpetdag – Ashgabat 26 000				

TURKMENISTAN 2005

FIRST DIVISION

	Pl	W	D	L	F	A	Pts	HTTU	Gazcy	Nebitchi	Nisa	Merv	Sagadam	Turan	Kopetdag	Ahal
MTTU Ashgabat ‡	32	22	6	4	77	20	72		1-0 2-0	1-0 5-0	1-0 3-1	2-0 5-0	8-0 2-0	1-0 4-0	5-0 6-3	2-0 7-0
Gazcy Gaz-Acak	32	18	8	6	54	18	62	2-1 0-0		1-0 1-0	1-1 3-0	0-0 3-0	4-0 3-1	4-0 4-1	3-0 3-0	3-0 3-0
Nebitchi Balkanabat	32	17	7	8	48	29	58	3-2 4-0	1-0 2-1		1-1 5-0	2-2 2-0	0-0 2-0	3-1 2-1	2-0 1-1	3-2 2-1
Nisa Ashgabat	32	10	11	11	31	38	41	0-1 1-4	0-0 1-1	2-0 1-1		0-1 1-0	2-1 0-0	2-0 0-1	3-1 1-2	5-5 1-0
Merv Mary	32	10	9	13	28	38	39	0-0 2-1	1-1 0-1	1-0 0-1	2-0 0-0		1-0 3-2	2-1 0-0	1-2 3-0	0-0 2-0
Sagadam Turkmenbasy	32	10	6	16	33	49	36	0-1 0-0	1-0 0-1	0-2 2-0	0-1 2-1	2-0 2-0		2-1 0-2	0-0 2-1	0-0 6-3
Turan Dasoguz	32	9	8	15	33	50	35	0-3 1-1	1-1 0-2	1-0 1-1	0-0 1-1	1-1 3-2	3-1 0-3		3-2 1-1	3-1 3-0
Kopetdag Ashgabat	32	7	9	16	29	56	30	0-0 2-2	0-4 0-1	0-0 1-3	0-1 0-1	1-0 1-1	2-2 0-1	2-0 1-0		2-1 3-1
Ahal Annau	32	6	6	20	37	72	24	0-2 1-4	3-2 1-1	0-2 0-3	1-0 1-2	3-0 1-3	3-1 3-2	3-0 0-3	3-0 1-1	

2/04/2005 - 26/11/2005 • ‡ Qualified for the 2006 AFC Cup • Match in bold awarded
Top scorers: Berdimyrat SAMYRADOV, HTTU, 30; Hamza ALLOMOV, Turan, 20; Mammedaly GARADANOV, HTTU, 18

TURKMENISTAN CUP 2005

Preliminary Round			Quarter-finals			Semi-finals			Final		
Merv Mary	Bye										
			Merv Mary								
Turan Dasoguz *	0	0	Gazcy Gaz-Acak								
Gazcy Gaz-Acak	1	2									
						Merv Mary	2	2			
Nisa Ashgabat	Bye					Sagadam Turk'basy *	0	0			
			Nisa Ashgabat		0	0					
			Sagadam Turk'basy *		1	3					
Sagadam Turk'basy	Bye										
MTTU Ashgabat	Bye								Merv Mary ‡	1	3p
			MTTU Ashgabat *		5	0			Kopetdag Ashgabat	1	1p
			Nebitchi Balkanabat		1	3					
Nebitchi Balkanabat	Bye										
Ahal Annau	Bye					MTTU Ashgabat *	4	1			
			Ahal Annau *		2	0	Kopetdag Ashgabat	3	2		
			Kopetdag Ashgabat		3	1					
Kopetdag Ashgabat	Bye										

* Home team in the first leg • ‡ Qualified for the 2006 AFC Cup

CUP FINAL

28-10-2005

Scorers - Anton Kuçerenkov [27] for Merv;
Ata Babayev OG [5]

RECENT LEAGUE AND CUP RECORD

	Championship								Cup		
Year	Champions	Pts	Runners-up	Pts	Third	Pts		Winners	Score	Runners-up	
1992	Kopetdag Ashgabat	54	Nebitchi Balkanabat	47	Akhal Akdashayak	46					
1993	Kopetdag Ashgabat	14	Byuzmeyin	11	Nebitchi Balkanabat	9		Kopetdag Ashgabat	4-0	Merv Mary	
1994	Kopetdag Ashgabat	31	Nisa Ashgabat	24	Merv Mary	20		Kopetdag Ashgabat	2-0	Turan Dasoguz	
1995	Kopetdag Ashgabat	84	Nisa Ashgabat	79	Nebitchi Balkanabat	61		Turan Dasoguz	4-3	Kopetdag Ashgabat	
1996	Kopetdag Ashgabat	83	Kopetdag Ashgabat	74	Exkavatorshchik	60		No tournament due to season re-adjustment			
1997	No tournament due to season re-adjustment							Kopetdag Ashgabat	2-0	Nisa Ashgabat	
1998	Kopetdag Ashgabat		Nisa Ashgabat					Nisa Ashgabat	3-0	Nebitchi Balkanabat	
1999	Nisa Ashgabat	78	Kopetdag Ashgabat	67	Dagdan Ashgabat	60		Kopetdag Ashgabat	3-1	Nebitchi Balkanabat	
2000	Kopetdag Ashgabat	56	Nebitchi Balkanabat	41	Nisa Ashgabat	37		Kopetdag Ashgabat	5-0	Nisa Ashgabat	
2001	Nisa Ashgabat	77	Kopetdag Ashgabat	68	Nebitchi Balkanabat	60		Kopetdag Ashgabat	2-0	Nebitchi Balkanabat	
2002	Sagadam Turk'basy	67	Nisa Ashgabat	63	Garagam Turk'abat	59		Garagam Turk'abat	0-0 4-2p	Sagadam Turk'basy	
2003	Nisa Ashgabat	92	Nebitchi Balkanabat	79	Sagadam Turk'basy	76		Nebitchi Balkanabat	2-1	Nisa Ashgabat	
2004	Nebitchi Balkanabat	84	Nisa Ashgabat	78	Merv Mary	67		Nebitchi Balkanabat	1-0	Asudalyk Ashgabat	
2005	MTTU Ashgabat	72	Gazcy Gazojak	62	Nebitchi Balkanabat	58		Merv Mary	1-1 3-1p	Kopetdag Ashgabat	

Turkmen clubs took part in the Soviet league until the end of the 1991 season

TLS – TIMOR-LESTE

NATIONAL TEAM RECORD
JULY 1ST 2002 TO JULY 9TH 2006

PL	W	D	L	F	A	%
0	0	0	0	0	0	0

FIFA/COCA-COLA WORLD RANKING

1993	1994	1995	1996	1997	1998	1999	2000	2001	2002	2003	2004	2005	High	Low
-	-	-	-	-	-	-	-	-	-	-	-	-	-	-

2005–2006											
08/05	09/05	10/05	11/05	12/05	01/06	02/06	03/06	04/06	05/06	06/06	07/06
-	-	-	-	-	-	-	-	-	-	-	-

After three years of affiliation to the Asian Football Confederation, Timor-Leste (or East Timor in its anglicised version) became the 207th member of FIFA at the Marrakech Congress in September 2005. For 24 years after the Portuguese left in 1975, Timor-Leste was part of Indonesia and it is estimated that up to 100,000 people may have been killed in the struggle for independence. After a referendum in 1999 showed overwhelming support for a break from Indonesia, it wasn't until May 2002 that independence finally came. Four years on, the country has yet to fully recover from the fighting that wrecked the infrastructure during this period and once again the country has

INTERNATIONAL HONOURS
None

suffered instability. The move to join FIFA was certainly symbolic but a year on from admission to the world body, the national team has yet to play an official international. Matches were played in the 2004 AFC Asian Cup qualifiers and in the 2004 ASEAN Tiger Cup but as these came before affiliation to FIFA, they are not part of the official record. Football is the number one sport in the country and there are over 2000 clubs but the need for a stadium to host international matches is the most pressing concern. It may be a while, however, before the people of Timor-Leste can watch the national team play in the capital Dili for the first time.

THE FIFA BIG COUNT OF 2000

	Male	Female		Male	Female
Registered players	n/a	n/a	Referees	n/a	n/a
Non registered players	n/a	n/a	Officials	n/a	n/a
Youth players	n/a	n/a	Total involved	n/a	
Total players		n/a	Number of clubs	n/a	
Professional players	n/a	n/a	Number of teams	n/a	

Federaçao Futebol Timor-Leste (FFTL)
Rua 12 de Novembro Sta. Cruz, Dili, Timor-Leste
Tel +670 3322231   Fax +670 3317430
federacao_futebol@yahoo.com   www.none
President: LAY Francisco Kalbuadi   General Secretary: SAMENTO Amandio
Vice-President: CABRAL FERNANDES Filomeno Pedro   Treasurer: FEREIRA Jesuina M.   Media Officer: TIMOTIO Antonio
Men's Coach: PAULO Joao   Women's Coach: DE ARAUJO Marcos
FFTL formed: 2002   AFC: 2002   FIFA: 2005
Red shirts, Black shorts, Red socks

RECENT INTERNATIONAL MATCHES PLAYED BY TIMOR-LESTE

2002	Opponents	Score	Venue	Comp	Scorers	Att	Referee
No international matches played before 2003							
2003							
21-03	Sri Lanka	L 2-3	Colombo	ACq			
23-03	Chinese Taipei	L 0-3	Colombo	ACq			
2004							
8-12	Malaysia	L 0-5	Kuala Lumpur	TCr1			
12-12	Thailand	L 0-8	Kuala Lumpur	TCr1			
14-12	Philippines	L 1-2	Kuala Lumpur	TCr1	Anai 59		
16-12	Myanmar	L 1-3	Kuala Lumpur	TCr1	Diamantino 15p		
2005							
No international matches played in 2005							
2006							
No international matches played in 2006 before July							

AC = AFC Asian Cup • TC = ASEAN Tiger Cup • q = qualifier • r1 = first round group • Matches played before September 2005 are not full internationals

TIMOR-LESTE NATIONAL TEAM RECORDS AND RECORD SEQUENCES

Records			Sequence records				
Victory	-	Never won a match	Wins	0		Clean sheets	0	
Defeat	0-8	THA 2004	Defeats	6	2003-	Goals scored	2	2004
Player Caps	n/a		Undefeated	0		Without goal	3	2003-2004
Player Goals	n/a		Without win	6	2003-	Goals against	6	2003-

TIMOR-LESTE COUNTRY INFORMATION

Capital	Dili	Independence	2002 from Indonesia	GDP per Capita	$400
Population	1 040 880	Status	Republic	GNP Ranking	143
Area km²	15 077	Language	Tetum, Portuguese	Dialling code	+670
Population density	69 per km²	Literacy rate	58%	Internet code	.tp
% in urban areas	8%	Main religion	Christian 93%	GMT + / –	+8
Towns/Cities ('000)	Dili 159; Dare 18; Los Palos 17; Baucau 14; Ermera 12; Maliana 12				
Neighbours (km)	Indonesia 228; Timor Sea, Savu Sea and Banda Sea 706				
Main stadia	Estadio Nacional, Dili 5 000				

TOG – TOGO

NATIONAL TEAM RECORD
JULY 1ST 2002 TO JULY 9TH 2006

PL	W	D	L	F	A	%
37	16	5	16	42	46	50

FIFA/COCA-COLA WORLD RANKING

1993	1994	1995	1996	1997	1998	1999	2000	2001	2002	2003	2004	2005	High	Low
113	86	92	87	78	68	87	81	71	86	94	89	56	**48** 07/06	**123** 06/94

2005–2006										
08/05	09/05	10/05	11/05	12/05	01/06	02/06	03/06	04/06	05/06	06/06	07/06
66	54	49	56	56	56	59	58	59	61	-	48

Togo reached the heady heights of a place at the FIFA World Cup™ finals, but the fairy tale qualification was tarnished in the end by several months of folly that preceded and then overshadowed their participation in Germany. Led by the goals of lanky striker Emmanuel Adebayor, who signed for Arsenal at the start of 2006, Togo caused a major upset by pipping Senegal to top place in the qualifying group. 'Les Eperviers' had only a modest record in FIFA World Cup preliminaries before, but inspired by the former Nigerian captain Stephen Keshi they created a tight-knit squad and drew inspiration from dollops of team spirit to qualify in dramatic fashion. It was mostly

INTERNATIONAL HONOURS
Qualified for the FIFA World Cup™ finals 2006

downhill, thereafter, as Keshi clashed with Adebayor at the start of January's African Nations Cup finals, leading to acrimony within the squad that played a direct role in a mediocre performance that saw them lose all three of their opening round group games. Keshi was fired after the tournament and replaced by the German Otto Pfister who had just one match before having to name his final 23 man squad for the FIFA World Cup™ finals. He then had to watch as the players and officials became embroiled in an embarrassing row over payment and match bonuses. On the pitch the West Africans again lost all three games in their group.

THE FIFA BIG COUNT OF 2000

	Male	Female		Male	Female
Registered players	1 535	162	Referees	585	40
Non registered players	14 000	235	Officials	2 410	190
Youth players	4 015	85	Total involved	23 257	
Total players	20 032		Number of clubs	565	
Professional players	35	0	Number of teams	565	

Fédération Togolaise de Football (FTF)
Case postale 5, Lome, Togo
Tel +228 2212698   Fax +228 2221413
eperviers@ftf.tg   www.ftf.tg
President: GNASSINGBE Balakiyem Rock   General Secretary: ASSOGBAVI Komlan
Vice-President: DOGBATSE Winny   Treasurer: ADJETE Tino   Media Officer: ATTOLOU Messan
Men's Coach: PFISTER Otto   Women's Coach: ZOUNGBEDE Paul
FTF formed: 1960   CAF: 1963   FIFA: 1962
Yellow shirts with green trimmings, Green shorts, White socks or Green shirts with white trimmings, Green shorts, White socks

RECENT INTERNATIONAL MATCHES PLAYED BY TOGO

2002	Opponents		Score	Venue	Comp	Scorers	Att	Referee
1-09	Libya	L	0-4	Lomé	Fr			
2-09	Libya	L	0-4	Misurata	Fr			
7-09	Kenya	L	0-3	Nairobi	CNq		20 000	Abdulkadir TAN
13-10	Mauritania	W	1-0	Lomé	CNq	Adebayor [23]		Kaba LBR
2003								
29-03	Cape Verde Islands	L	1-2	Praia	CNq	Wondu [37]		Nandigna GNB
8-06	Cape Verde Islands	W	5-2	Lomé	CNq	Sania [2], Touré.S 2 [23 32], De Souza [72], Adebayor [78]		Pare BFA
22-06	Kenya	W	2-0	Lomé	CNq	Faria 2 [21 56p]		Rembangouet GAB
5-07	Mauritania	D	0-0	Nouakchott	CNq		2 000	Djingarey NIG
11-10	Equatorial Guinea	L	0-1	Bata	WCq		25 000	Evehe CMR
16-11	Equatorial Guinea	W	2-0	Lomé	WCq	Adebayor [43], Salifou [53]	12 000	Mandzioukouta CGO
2004								
20-05	Benin	W	1-0	Cotonou	Fr	Kadafi [53]		
23-05	Benin	D	1-1	Lomé	Fr	Salou [50p]		
5-06	Zambia	L	0-1	Lusaka	WCq		40 000	Damon RSA
14-06	Ghana	D	0-0	Kumasi	Fr			
20-06	Senegal	W	3-1	Lomé	WCq	Adebayor [30], Senaya 2 [76 85]	25 000	El Arjoun MAR
4-07	Liberia	D	0-0	Monrovia	WCq		30 000	Soumah GUI
5-09	Congo	W	2-0	Lomé	WCq	Adebayor 2 [37 80]	20 000	Mbera GAB
10-10	Mali	W	1-0	Lomé	WCq	Adebayor [23]	45 000	Njike CMR
2005								
27-03	Mali	W	2-1	Bamako	WCq	Salifou [78], Mamam [91+]	45 000	Agbenyega GHA
29-05	Burkina Faso	W	1-0	Lomé	Fr			
5-06	Zambia	W	4-1	Lomé	WCq	Adebayor 2 [12 88], Toure.S [44], Kader Coubadja [65]	15 000	Guezzaz MAR
18-06	Senegal	D	2-2	Dakar	WCq	Olufade [11], Adebayor [71]	50 000	Guirat TUN
17-08	Morocco	W	1-0	Rouen	Fr	Dogbe [20]		
4-09	Liberia	W	3-0	Lomé	WCq	Adebayor 2 [52 93+], Mamam [69]	28 000	Abdel Rahman SUD
8-10	Congo	W	3-2	Brazzaville	WCq	Adebayor [40], Kader Coubadja 2 [60 70]	20 000	Shelmani LBY
11-11	Paraguay	L	2-4	Tehran	Fr	Mamam [33], Soulieman [34]		
13-11	Iran	L	0-2	Tehran	Fr			
2006								
7-01	Guinea	L	0-1	Viry-Chatillon	Fr			
11-01	Ghana	W	1-0	Monastir	Fr	Olufade [77]	2 500	Piccirillo FRA
21-01	Congo DR	L	0-2	Cairo	CNr1		6 000	Daami TUN
25-01	Cameroon	L	0-2	Cairo	CNr1		3 000	Sowe GAM
29-01	Angola	L	2-3	Cairo	CNr1	Kader Coubadja [24], Maman [67]	4 000	El Arjoun MAR
14-05	Saudi Arabia	L	0-1	Sittard	Fr		400	Braamhaar NED
2-06	Liechtenstein	W	1-0	Vaduz	Fr	Kader Coubadja [52]	2 700	Schorgenhofer AUT
13-06	Korea Republic	L	1-2	Frankfurt	WCr1	Kader Coubadja [31]	48 000	Poll ENG
19-06	Switzerland	L	0-2	Dortmund	WCr1		65 000	Amarilla PAR
23-06	France	L	0-2	Cologne	WCr1		45 000	Larrionda URU

Fr = Friendly match • CN = CAF African Cup of Nations • WC = FIFA World Cup™ • q = qualifier

TOGO NATIONAL TEAM RECORDS AND RECORD SEQUENCES

Records			Sequence records					
Victory	4-0	Six times	Wins	5	2004-2005	Clean sheets	3	Six times
Defeat	0-7	MAR 1979, TUN 2000	Defeats	5	1977-79, 1999-00	Goals scored	12	1956-1957
Player Caps	n/a		Undefeated	12	2004-2005	Without goal	5	2002
Player Goals	n/a		Without win	14	1992-94, 1999-00	Goals against	9	1983-1984

TOGO COUNTRY INFORMATION

Capital	Lomé	Independence	1960 from France	GDP per Capita	$1 500
Population	5 556 812	Status	Republic	GNP Ranking	149
Area km²	56 785	Language	French	Dialling code	+228
Population density	97 per km²	Literacy rate	60%	Internet code	.tg
% in urban areas	31%	Main religion	Indigenous 51% Christian 29%	GMT + / –	0
Towns/Cities ('000)	Lomé 726; Kpalimé 110; Sokodé 108; Kara 94; Atakpamé 92; Bassar 55; Tsévié 55; Aného 47				
Neighbours (km)	Benin 644; Ghana 877; Burkina Faso 126; Atlantic Ocean/Bight of Benin 56				
Main stadia	Stade General Eyadema (Kegue) – Lomé 20 000				

TOGO 2005–06 CHAMPIONNAT NATIONAL

	Pl	W	D	L	F	A	Pts
Maranatha FC Fiokpo	28						61
AS Douanes Lomé	28						50
Etoile Filante Lomé	28						47
Dynamic Togolais (DyTo)	28						41
ASKO Kara	28						40
AS Togo-Port Lomé	28						40
AC Merlan Lomé	28						40
Togo Télécom Lomé	28						36
Semassi Sokodé	28						32
Doumbé FC	28						32
Gomico Kpalimé	28						30
Omnisports Agaza Lomé	28						28
Tchaoudjo AC Sokodé	28						27
Kotoko Lavié	28						23
Abou Ossé Anié	28						13
Kakadlé Défalé				Withdrew			

24/09/2005 - 29/04/2006

COUPE DU TOGO 2005–06

Quarter-finals		Semi-finals		Final	
AS Togo-Port *	4				
AS Dankpen	0	AS Togo-Port	0 1		
Unisport Sokodé	0 3p	DyTo * †	0 1		
DyTo	0 5p			AS Togo-Port	1 5p
Doumbé *	3 4p			ASKO Kara	1 4p
Etoile Filante	3 2p	Doumbé	1 0		
US Koroki	2 3p	ASKO Kara *	3 2		
ASKO Kara *	2 4p				

Municipal, Lomé, 7-05-2006
Scorers - Alassane [44] for Port; Farouk [86] for ASKO Kara

* Home team in first leg • † DyTo disqualified

RECENT LEAGUE AND CUP RECORD

	Championship						Cup		
Year	Champions	Pts	Runners-up	Pts	Third	Pts	Winners	Score	Runners-up
1995	Semassi Sokodé	38	Etoile Filante Lomé	32	ASKO Kara Lomé	30	ASKO Kara Lomé	1-0	Semassi Sokodé
1996	ASKO Kara Lomé						Doumbé	2-1	Etoile Filante Lomé
1997	Dynamic Togolais	43	Etoile Filante Lomé	40	Agaza Lomé	37	No tournament		
1998	No tournament						No tournament		
1999	Semassi Sokodé						Agaza Lomé	1-0	Entente 2 Lomé
2000	Season unfinished						No tournament		
2001	Dynamic Togolais	17	Maranatha Fiokpo	16	ASKO Kara Lomé	14	Dynamic Togolais	3-0	Sara Sport Bafilo
2002	AS Douanes	63	Maranatha Fiokpo	63	Dynamic Togolais	51	Dynamic Togolais	2-0	Doumbé
2003	No tournament due to season readjustment						Maranatha Fiokpo		
2004	Dynamic Togolais	59	Maranatha Fiokpo	54	Kakadle Defale	51	AS Douanes	2-1	Foadam Dapaong
2005	AS Douanes	31	Dynamic Togolais	26	Togo Télécom	20	Dynamic Togolais	1-0	Agaza Lomé
2006	Maranatha Fiokpo	61	AS Douanes	50	Etoile Filante	47	AS Togo-Port	1-1 5-4p	ASKO Kara

TPE – CHINESE TAIPEI

NATIONAL TEAM RECORD
JULY 1ST 2002 TO JULY 9TH 2006

PL	W	D	L	F	A	%
26	9	2	15	41	60	38.5

FIFA/COCA-COLA WORLD RANKING

1993	1994	1995	1996	1997	1998	1999	2000	2001	2002	2003	2004	2005		High	Low
161	170	178	174	154	169	174	162	170	166	150	155	156		**149** 04/97	**180** 07/96

2005–2006											
08/05	09/05	10/05	11/05	12/05	01/06	02/06	03/06	04/06	05/06	06/06	07/06
153	153	155	156	156	156	157	157	155	156	-	149

Chinese Taipei was one of five countries to get entry into both the 2007 AFC Asian Cup qualifiers and the inaugural AFC Challenge Cup but there can be little doubt where the national team felt more comfortable. 4-0 defeats by Iran and Syria left Chinese Taipei rooted to the bottom of an AFC Asian Cup qualifying group also containing Korea Republic and that is almost certainly where they will remain. In the 2006 AFC Challenge Cup in Bangladesh on the other hand, a 1-0 win over the Philippines and draws with both Afghanistan and India, saw the team qualify for the quarter-finals. They lost that 3-0 to Sri Lanka but in the future the AFC Challenge Cup offers the country the best

INTERNATIONAL HONOURS
Asian Games 1954 1958

route to success, especially with the winners guaranteed a place in the finals of the AFC Asian Cup. In domestic football, the 11 year reign of Taiwan Power Company as champions of the Taiwan Men's League finally came to an end when they were deposed by Tatung in 2005. Taiwan Power Company had taken part in the inaugural AFC President's Cup but didn't make it past the group stage, but in the 2006 tournament in Malaysia, Tatung did. They beat both Pakistan Army and Bhutan's Transport United to finish runners-up in the group behind Khemara of Cambodia. Inexperience told in the semi-final against Tajikistan's Vakhsh and they lost 3-1.

THE FIFA BIG COUNT OF 2000

	Male	Female		Male	Female
Registered players	500	250	Referees	110	10
Non registered players	80 000	600	Officials	480	155
Youth players	1 520	420	Total involved	84 045	
Total players	83 290		Number of clubs	50	
Professional players	0	0	Number of teams	127	

Chinese Taipei Football Association (CTFA)
2F No. Yu Men St., 104 Taipei, Taiwan 104
Tel +886 2 25961184   Fax +886 2 25951594
ctfa7155@ms59.hinet.net   www.ctfa.com.tw
President: CHIOU I-Jen   General Secretary: DER Chia Lin
Vice-President: SHI Hwei-Yow   Treasurer: LIN Shiu Yi   Media Officer: BEARE Alexander James
Men's Coach: TOSHIAKI Imai   Women's Coach: CHOU Tai Ying
CTFA formed: 1924   AFC: 1954-75, 1990   FIFA: 1954
Blue shirts, Blue shorts, White socks

RECENT INTERNATIONAL MATCHES PLAYED BY CHINESE TAIPEI

2003	Opponents	Score		Venue	Comp	Scorers	Att	Referee
23-11	Macao	W	3-0	Taipei	WCq	Chuang Yao Tsung [23], Chen Jui Te [52], Chang Wu Yeh [57]	2 000	Napitupulu IDN
29-11	Macao	W	3-1	Macao	WCq	Chen Jui Te 2 [14 69], Chiang Shih Lu [66]	250	Zhou Weixin CHN
2004								
18-02	Palestine	L	0-8	Doha	WCq		1 000	Al Yarimi YEM
31-03	Uzbekistan	L	0-1	Taipei	WCq		2 500	Midi Nitrorejo IDN
9-06	Iraq	L	1-6	Amman	WCq	Huang Wei Yi [57]	2 000	Al Hail QAT
8-09	Iraq	L	1-4	Taipei	WCq	Huang Wei Yi [82]	5 000	Baskar IND
14-10	Palestine	L	0-1	Taipei	WCq		500	Rasheed MDV
17-11	Uzbekistan	L	1-6	Tashkent	WCq	Huang Wei Yi [64]	20 000	Basma SYR
2005								
5-03	Guam	W	9-0	Taipei	EAq	Tu Ming Feng [8], Kuo Yin Hung 3 [10 20 69], Chiang Shih Lu 2 [56 70], He Ming Chan 3 [66 83 93+]		
9-03	Korea DPR	L	0-2	Taipei	EAq			
11-03	Hong Kong	L	0-5	Taipei	EAq			
13-03	Mongolia	D	0-0	Taipei	EAq			
2006								
22-02	Iran	L	0-4	Tehran	ACq		5 000	AK Nema IRQ
1-03	Syria	L	0-4	Taipei	ACq		700	O Il Son PRK
1-04	Philippines	W	1-0	Chittagong	CCr1	Chuang Wei Lun [20]	4 000	Lee Gi Young KOR
3-04	Afghanistan	D	2-2	Chittagong	CCr1	Chuang Wei Lun [48], Liang Chien Wei [73]	2 500	Lee Gi Young KOR
5-04	India	D	0-0	Chittagong	CCr1		2 000	Gosh BAN
8-04	Sri Lanka	L	0-3	Chittagong	CCqf		2 500	Al Ghatrifi OMA

Fr = Friendly match • EA = East Easian Championship • AC = AFC Asian Cup • CC = AFC Challenge Cup • WC = FIFA World Cup™ • q = qualifier

CHINESE TAIPEI NATIONAL TEAM RECORDS AND RECORD SEQUENCES

Records			Sequence records				
Victory	9-0	PHI 1967, GUM 2005	Wins	8	1958-1960	Clean sheets	3	1981
Defeat	1-10	IDN 1968	Defeats	9	1988-92, 1992-96	Goals scored	15	1966-1967
Player Caps	n/a		Undefeated	11	1957-1960	Without goal	12	2000-2002
Player Goals	n/a		Without win	19	1988-1996	Goals against	15	1867-1968

CHINESE TAIPEI 2005 FIRST DIVISION

	Pl	W	D	L	F	A	Pts
Tatung	14	13	1	0	45	6	40
Taiwan Power Co.	14	10	0	4	51	16	30
Army	14	8	1	5	27	27	25
Ming Chuan University	14	6	5	3	32	16	23
Taiwan College of P.E.	14	7	1	6	27	23	22
Taipei P.E. College	14	4	1	9	16	30	13
San Chung	14	2	0	12	13	62	6
Ilan Youth	14	1	1	12	14	45	4

19/03/2005 - 6/11/2005

RECENT LEAGUE RECORD

Year	Champions
1993	Flying Camel (Fei To)
1994	Taiwan Power Company Taipei
1995	Taiwan Power Company Taipei
1996	Taiwan Power Company Taipei
1997	Taiwan Power Company Taipei
1998	Taiwan Power Company Taipei
1999	Taiwan Power Company Taipei
2000	Not played
2001	Taiwan Power Company Taipei
2002	Taiwan Power Company Taipei
2003	Taiwan Power Company Taipei
2004	Taiwan Power Company Taipei
2005	Tatung

CHINESE TAIPEI COUNTRY INFORMATION

Capital	Taipei	Independence	1949	GDP per Capita	$23 400
Population	22 749 838	Status	Republic	GNP Ranking	16
Area km²	35 980	Language	Mandarin, Min	Dialling code	+886
Population density	632 per km²	Literacy rate	96%	Internet code	.tw
% in urban areas	69%	Main religion	Buddhist, Confucian, Taoist	GMT +/–	+8
Towns/Cities ('000)	Taipei 2 514; Kaoshiung 1 512; Taichung 1 083; Tainan 734; Panchiao 491; Hsinchu 413				
Neighbours (km)	Taiwan Strait, East China Sea, Philippine Sea & South China Sea 1 566				
Main stadia	Chung Shan Soccer Stadium – Taipei 25 000				

TRI – TRINIDAD AND TOBAGO

NATIONAL TEAM RECORD
JULY 1ST 2002 TO JULY 9TH 2006

PL	W	D	L	F	A	%
79	33	12	34	102	102	49.4

FIFA/COCA-COLA WORLD RANKING

1993	1994	1995	1996	1997	1998	1999	2000	2001	2002	2003	2004	2005		High		Low
88	91	57	41	56	51	44	29	32	47	70	63	50		**25** 06/01		**95** 04/94

2005–2006											
08/05	09/05	10/05	11/05	12/05	01/06	02/06	03/06	04/06	05/06	06/06	07/06
53	56	53	51	50	50	51	49	47	47	-	64

Football fans in Trinidad and Tobago will be hoping that the national team's appearance in the 2006 FIFA World Cup™ finals in Germany won't be a once in a lifetime experience, but as the smallest nation ever to qualify for the finals, that may well be the case. Fans of the Soca Warriors, with their elaborate Indian headdresses, certainly added to the occasion whilst the draw with Sweden in their opening game was the highlight of an odyssey that had begun two years previously in Santo Domingo. The hiring of coach Leo Beenhaaker was the turning point, culminating in the historic 2-1 win over Mexico, which meant Trinidad qualified for a play-off against Bahrain. Having drawn

INTERNATIONAL HONOURS
Qualified for the FIFA World Cup™ finals 2006 **Caribbean Cup** 1981 1989 1992 1994 1995 1996 1997 1999 2001 **Champions Cup** Defence Force 1978 1985

1-1 at home, they looked to have blown their chances but the giant Dennis Lawrence scored with a header just after half time to take Trinidad to the finals. In Germany it looked as if they might follow up their heroics against Sweden with a draw against England but they were denied by two late goals, having had an earlier chance cleared off the line by John Terry. Going into the third match Trinidad still had a chance to qualify for the second round but lost 2-0 to Paraguay. Despite the disappointment felt by captain Dwight Yorke and his players, just qualifying for the finals had sealed their place in the history books, having taken part in one of the great World Cup adventures.

THE FIFA BIG COUNT OF 2000

	Male	Female		Male	Female
Registered players	2 362	230	Referees	380	16
Non registered players	13 000	1 500	Officials	570	75
Youth players	10 100	500	Total involved	28 733	
Total players	27 692		Number of clubs	135	
Professional players	200	0	Number of teams	963	

Trinidad and Tobago Football Federation (TTFF)
24-26 Dundonald Street, PO Box 400, Port of Spain, Trinidad and Tobago
Tel +1 868 6237312   Fax +1 868 6238109
admin@tttff.com   www.tnt.fifa.com
President: CAMPS Oliver   General Secretary: GRODEN Richard
Vice-President: TIM KEE Raymond   Treasurer: RUDOLPH Thomas   Media Officer: FUENTES Shaun
Men's Coach: RIJSBERGEN Wim   Women's Coach: SHABAZZ Jamaal
TTFF formed: 1908   CONCACAF: 1964   FIFA: 1963
Red shirts with white trimmings, Red shorts, Red socks or White shirts with red trimmings, White shorts, White socks

RECENT INTERNATIONAL MATCHES PLAYED BY TRINIDAD AND TOBAGO

2004	Opponents	Score		Venue	Comp	Scorers	Att	Referee
24-11	Puerto Rico	W	5-0	Tunapuna	GCq	Glenn 3 [13 43 48], King 81p, Smith.C [89]	2 000	Callender BRB
26-11	Grenada	W	2-0	Marabella	GCq	Pierre.N [22p], Gray [50]		Callender BRB
28-11	Surinam	W	1-0	Malabar	GCq	Glenn [65]		Forde BRB
12-12	British Virgin Islands	W	4-0	Tortola	GCq	Pierre.N 2 [7 65], Jemmott [75], Spann [90]	1 600	Arthur LCA
19-12	British Virgin Islands	W	2-0	Tunapuna	GCq	Pierre.N [21], Eve [61]		Lancaster GUY
2005								
9-01	St Vincent/Grenadines	W	3-1	Marabella	GCq	Glasgow [51], Fitzpatrick 2 [54 62]	1 688	Chance ANT
12-01	Antigua and Barbuda	L	1-2	St John's	Fr	Pierre.N [55]	2 000	
16-01	St Vincent/Grenadines	L	0-1	Kingstown	GCq		1 450	Pine JAM
21-01	Azerbaijan	W	1-0	Port of Spain	Fr	Sealy [41]	500	
23-01	Azerbaijan	W	2-0	Marabella	Fr	Pierre.N [21], Smith.C [67]	1 000	Gordon TRI
1-02	Haiti	W	1-0	Port of Spain	Fr	Pierre.A 59	1 500	
3-02	Haiti	W	2-1	Port of Spain	Fr	John [21], Glenn [43]		
6-02	Haiti	L	0-1	Scarborough	Fr			
9-02	USA	L	1-2	Port of Spain	WCq	Eve [87]	11 000	Archundia MEX
20-02	Jamaica	L	1-2	Bridgetown	GCq	Pierre.N [37]	5 000	Callender BRB
22-02	Cuba	L	1-2	Bridgetown	GCq	Glen 13	2 100	Lancaster GUY
24-02	Barbados	W	3-2	Bridgetown	GCq	Smith.C 11, Glenn 30, Eve 84	3 000	Prendergast JAM
26-03	Guatemala	L	1-5	Guatemala City	WCq	Edwards 32	22 506	Stott USA
30-03	Costa Rica	D	0-0	Port of Spain	WCq		8 000	Navarro CAN
25-05	Bermuda	W	4-0	Port of Spain	Fr	OG 34, Jones.K 46, Lawrence 51, John 65	400	
27-05	Bermuda	W	1-0	Marabella	Fr	John 17		
4-06	Panama	W	2-0	Port of Spain	WCq	John 34, Lawrence 71		Prendergast JAM
8-06	Mexico	L	0-2	Monterrey	WCq			
6-07	Honduras	D	1-1	Miami	GCr1	Birchall 28	10 311	Navarro CAN
10-07	Panama	D	2-2	Miami	GCr1	Andrews 17, Glen 91+	17 292	Wyngaarde SUR
12-07	Colombia	L	0-2	Miami	GCr1		11 000	Rodriguez MEX
17-08	USA	L	0-1	Hartford	WCq		25 500	Rodriguez MEX
3-09	Guatemala	W	3-2	Port of Spain	WCq	Latapy [48], John 2 [85 86]	15 000	Archundia MEX
7-09	Costa Rica	L	0-2	San Jose	WCq		17 000	Batres GUA
8-10	Panama	W	1-0	Panama City	WCq	John [61]	1 000	Navarro CAN
12-10	Mexico	W	2-1	Port of Spain	WCq	John 2 [43 69]	23 000	Pineda HON
12-11	Bahrain	D	1-1	Port of Spain	WCpo	Birchall [76]	24 991	Shield AUS
16-11	Bahrain	W	1-0	Manama	WCpo	Lawrence [49]	35 000	Ruiz COL
2006								
28-02	Iceland	W	2-0	London	Fr	Yorke 2 [9 52p]	7 890	
10-05	Peru	D	1-1	Port of Spain	Fr	Jones [74]	20 000	Prendergast JAM
27-05	Wales	L	1-2	Graz	Fr	John [32]	8 000	Messner AUT
31-05	Slovenia	L	1-3	Celje	Fr	Birchall [26]	2 500	Tanovic SCG
3-06	Czech Republic	L	0-3	Prague	Fr		15 910	Johannesson SWE
10-06	Sweden	D	0-0	Dortmund	WCr1		62 959	Maidin SIN
15-06	England	L	0-2	Nuremberg	WCr1		41 000	Kamikawa JPN
20-06	Paraguay	L	0-2	Kaiserslautern	WCr1		46 000	Rosetti ITA

Fr = Friendly match • GC = CONCACAF Gold Cup • WC = FIFA World Cup™ • q = qualifier • po = play-off • r1 = first round group

TRINIDAD AND TOBAGO NATIONAL TEAM RECORDS AND RECORD SEQUENCES

Records			Sequence records					
Victory	11-0	ARU 1989	Wins	8	1996, 1999	Clean sheets	5	2000, 2004
Defeat	0-7	MEX 2000	Defeats	6	1955-1957	Goals scored	19	1998-1999
Player Caps	118	EVE Angus	Undefeated	9	1996, 1999	Without goal	4	1990, 2006
Player Goals	64	JOHN Stern	Without win	13	1983-1985	Goals against	15	1976-1979

TRINIDAD AND TOBAGO COUNTRY INFORMATION

Capital	Port of Spain	Independence	1962 from the UK	GDP per Capita	$9 500
Population	1 096 585	Status	Republic	GNP Ranking	96
Area km²	5 128	Language	English, Hindi	Dialling code	+1 868
Population density	213 per km²	Literacy rate	98%	Internet code	.tt
% in urban areas	72%	Main religion	Christian 43%, Hindu 23%	GMT + / −	+4
Towns/Cities ('000)	Chaguanas 72; San Juan 56; San Fernando 56; Port of Spain 49; Arima 35; Marabella 26				
Neighbours (km)	Caribbean Sea & Atlantic Ocean 362				
Main stadia	Hasely Crawford Stadium – Port of Spain 27 000; Manny Ramjohn Stadium – Marabella 10 000; Marvin Lee Stadium – Tunapuna 8 000; Dr João Havelange Centre of Excellence – Macoya				

TRINIDAD AND TOBAGO 2005

PROFESSIONAL LEAGUE

	Pl	W	D	L	F	A	Pts	Williams	Jabloteh	Caledonia	Defence	NE Stars	Petrotrin	Tobago
Williams Connection	23	17	3	3	69	20	54		2-1 1-1	3-0 5-0	5-2 2-2	4-0 3-2	4-1 2-2	7-0 4-0
San Juan Jabloteh	23	11	6	6	47	21	39	1-0 1-0		0-0 2-0	7-0 1-2	1-2 1-1	4-1 4-0	7-0
Caledonia AIA/Fire	23	10	4	4	26	32	34	0-3 1-4	0-1 2-1		1-4 1-0	1-0 1-0	2-0 2-2	4-1 2-2
Defence Force	23	8	7	7	36	38	31	0-4 1-3	1-1 1-1	2-0 0-0		0-0 1-4	3-0 1-2	4-0
North-East Stars	23	8	6	6	33	32	30	1-2 1-2	2-1 3-0	0-2 1-0	1-1 0-1		2-1 0-1	4-3 5-2
United Petrotrin	23	6	6	6	26	46	24	0-3 3-1	0-3 1-1	0-3 0-2	2-3 1-0	0-0 1-1		3-2
Tobago United	18	0	4	4	21	69	4	0-5	0-4 2-3	1-2	2-2 0-5	3-3	2-2 1-3	

9/04/2005 - 10/12/2005 • Top scorers: Gefferson GOULART, Williams, 13; Earl JEAN, Williams, 11 • League expanded to 10 teams for 2006

TRINIDAD AND TOBAGO 2005 SPORTWORLD NATIONAL SUPER LEAGUE (2)

	Pl	W	D	L	F	A	Pts
Joe Public	22	19	2	1	78	16	59
Crab Connection	22	16	4	2	51	28	52
WASA	22	13	3	6	42	32	42
Superstar Rangers	22	12	5	5	55	33	41
Police	22	11	5	6	41	32	38
Couva Players United	22	8	6	8	44	47	30
Angostura 1976 Phoenix	22	9	3	10	38	48	30
PLIPDECO Caroni	22	6	8	8	35	40	26
Stokely Vale	22	6	1	15	46	56	19
M & M Harvard	22	4	5	13	28	43	17
Maraval Youth Academy	22	2	6	14	25	62	12
Media 21	22	1	2	19	22	68	5

15/06/2005 - 4/12/2005

FA TROPHY 2005

Quarter-finals		Semi-finals		Final	
SJ Jabloteh	3				
Pele Pele	1	SJ Jabloteh	2		
Couva Players	1	NE Stars	0		
NE Stars	2			SJ Jabloteh	2
Defence F. Res	2 3p			Defence Force	1
Maraval YA	2 1p	Defence F. Res	0	30-11-2005	
Williams Con.	2 12p	Defence Force	2	Scorers - Baptiste ¹⁶, Marcano ⁷² for Jabloteh; Lewis ⁴ for Defence Force	
Defence Force	1 3p				

FIRST CITIZENS BANK CUP 2005

Quarter-finals		Semi-finals		Final	
Williams Con.	bye				
		Williams Con.	4		
NE Stars	1	Defence Force	0		
Defence Force	2			Williams Con.	3
United Petrotrin	4			SJ Jabloteh	1
Caledonia AIA	2	United Petrotrin	0	Manny Ramjohn, Marabella 30-09-2005	
Tobago United	1	SJ Jabloteh	2		
SJ Jabloteh	5				

RECENT LEAGUE AND CUP RECORD

	Championship						Cup		
Year	Champions	Pts	Runners-up	Pts	Third	Pts	Winners	Score	Runners-up
1997	Defence Force	53	Joe Public	52	Caledonia AIA	44	United Petrotrin		Superstar Rangers
1998	Joe Public	51	Caledonia AIA	45	Queen's Park	44	San Juan Jabloteh	3-2	Defence Force
1999	Defence Force	64	Joe Public	55	Williams Connection	55	Williams Connection		Joe Public
2000	Williams Connection	52	Defence Force	51	San Juan Jabloteh	47	Williams Connection	1-1 5-4p	Joe Public
2001	Williams Connection	37	Joe Public	35	Defence Force	24	Joe Public	1-0	Carib
2002	San Juan Jabloteh	65	Williams Connection	62	Joe Public	48	Williams Connection	5-1	Arima Fire
2003	San Juan Jabloteh	92	Williams Connection	80	North East Stars	64	North East Stars	2-2 4-1p	Williams Connection
2004	North East Strikers	57	Williams Connection	51	San Juan Jabloteh	51		Not played	
2005	Williams Connection	54	San Juan Jabloteh	39	Caledonia AIA/Fire	34	San Juan Jabloteh	2-1	Defence Force

The semi-pro league was introduced in 1996, followed by a professional league in 1999

TUN – TUNISIA

NATIONAL TEAM RECORD
JULY 1ST 2002 TO JULY 9TH 2006

PL	W	D	L	F	A	%
52	26	15	11	79	50	64.4

FIFA/COCA-COLA WORLD RANKING

1993	1994	1995	1996	1997	1998	1999	2000	2001	2002	2003	2004	2005	High		Low	
32	30	22	23	23	21	31	26	28	41	45	35	28	19	02/98	46	11/03

					2005–2006						
08/05	09/05	10/05	11/05	12/05	01/06	02/06	03/06	04/06	05/06	06/06	07/06
31	23	27	28	28	28	23	24	21	21	-	31

Tunisia presented the sole picture of consistency from Africa at the 2006 FIFA World Cup™ finals, participating for a third successive time while all the other African representatives were newcomers. It's a measure of the professionalism, capabilities and fluid organisation of Tunisian football that a nation with a population of around ten million can prove such a consistent force. The 'Carthage Eagles', however, did not take advantage of a solid opportunity to break new ground for themselves by qualifying for the second round at the tournament in Germany, drawing with Saudi Arabia and then losing to both Spain and the Ukraine in first round action. Defeat on post-match

INTERNATIONAL HONOURS
Qualified for the FIFA World Cup™ finals 1978 1998 2002 2006 CAF African Cup of Nations 2004
CAF Champions League Club Africain 1991, Esperance 1994

penalties also denied them a successful defence of their African Nations Cup title earlier in the year in Egypt, as they succumbed to Nigeria after extra time in the quarter-finals. At club level Etoile du Sahel reached a second successive CAF Champions League final but were convincingly beaten by Egypt's Al Ahly over the two legs. It added to a nightmare of bridesmaid's performances by Etoile, who finished second for the seventh successive time in the Tunisian league, throwing away a strong position to allow Esperance to replace CS Sfaxien as champions.

THE FIFA BIG COUNT OF 2000

	Male	Female		Male	Female
Registered players	26 271	0	Referees	910	10
Non registered players	45 000	0	Officials	5 920	0
Youth players	6 262	0	Total involved	84 373	
Total players		77 533	Number of clubs	552	
Professional players	311	0	Number of teams	1 309	

Fédération Tunisienne de Football (FTF)
Stade annexe d'El Menzah, Cité Olympique, Tunis 1003, Tunisia
Tel +216 71 793760   Fax +216 71 783843
directeur@ftf.org.tn   www.ftf.org.tn
President: BEN AMMAR Hamouda   General Secretary: DARRAGI Amor
Vice-President: BACCAR Mohieddine   Treasurer: HAMMAMI Mahmoud   Media Officer: None
Men's Coach: LEMERRE Roger   Women's Coach: None
FTF formed: 1956   CAF: 1960   FIFA: 1960
Red shirts with white trimmings, White shorts, Red socks or White shirts with red trimmings, White shorts, White socks

RECENT INTERNATIONAL MATCHES PLAYED BY TUNISIA

2003	Opponents	Score		Venue	Comp	Scorers	Att	Referee
11-10	Morocco	D	0-0	Tunis	Fr		13 000	Layec FRA
19-11	South Africa	W	2-0	Tunis	Fr	Braham [43], Ayari [88]	12 000	Diabate SEN
2004								
14-01	Benin	W	2-0	Djerba	Fr	Jaziri [31], Hagui [43]	6 000	
17-01	Benin	W	2-1	Tunis	Fr	Santos [9], Saidi [90]	25 000	
24-01	Rwanda	W	2-1	Radès/Tunis	CNr1	Jaziri [26], Santos [56]	60 000	Evehe CMR
28-01	Congo DR	W	3-0	Radès/Tunis	CNr1	Santos 2 [55 87], Braham [65]	20 000	Damon RSA
1-02	Guinea	D	1-1	Radès/Tunis	CNr1	Ben Achour [58]	18 000	Tessema ETH
7-02	Senegal	W	1-0	Radès/Tunis	CNqf	Mnari [65]	57 000	Ali Bujsaim UAE
11-02	Nigeria	D	1-1	Radès/Tunis	CNsf	Badra [82p], W 5-3p	56 000	Codjia BEN
14-02	Morocco	W	2-1	Radès/Tunis	CNf	Santos [5], Jaziri [52]	60 000	Ndoye SEN
31-03	Côte d'Ivoire	L	0-2	Tunis	Fr		10 000	Haimoudi ALG
28-04	Mali	W	1-0	Sfax	Fr	Jedidi [56]	8 000	Shelmani LBY
30-05	Italy	L	0-4	Radès/Tunis	Fr		30 000	Duhamel FRA
5-06	Botswana	W	4-1	Radès/Tunis	WCq	Ribabro [9], Hagui 2 [35 79], Zitouni [74]	2 844	Abdel Rahman SUD
20-06	Guinea	L	1-2	Conakry	WCq	Braham [67]	15 300	Codjia BEN
18-08	South Africa	L	0-2	Tunis	Fr		4 000	Zekrini ALG
4-09	Morocco	D	1-1	Rabat	WCq	Santos [11]	45 000	Auda EGY
9-10	Malawi	D	2-2	Blantyre	WCq	Jaziri [82], Ghodhbane [89]	20 000	Awuye UGA
2005								
26-03	Malawi	W	7-0	Radès/Tunis	WCq	Guemamdia [3], Santos 4 [12 52 75 77], Clayton [60p], Ghodhbane [80]	30 000	Abdel Rahman SUD
27-05	Angola	W	4-1	Tunis	Fr	Zitouni 2 [20 70], Mehedhebi 2 [51 89]	4 000	
4-06	Botswana	W	3-1	Gaborone	WCq	Nafti [20], Santos [44], Wissem [76]	20 000	Mana NGA
11-06	Guinea	W	2-0	Tunis	WCq	Clayton [36p], Chadli [78]	30 000	Lim Kee Chong MRI
15-06	Argentina	L	1-2	Cologne	CCr1	Guemamdia [72p]	28 033	Rosetti ITA
18-06	Germany	L	0-3	Cologne	CCr1		44 377	Prendergast JAM
21-06	Australia	W	2-0	Leipzig	CCr1	Santos 2 [26 70]	23 952	Chandia CHI
17-08	Kenya	W	1-0	Radès/Tunis	WCq	Guemamdia [2]	60 000	Evehe CMR
3-09	Kenya	W	2-0	Nairobi	WCq	Guemamdia [2], Jomaa [85]		Sowe GAM
8-10	Morocco	D	2-2	Radès/Tunis	WCq	Clayton [18], Chadli [69]	60 000	Abd El Fatah EGY
11-11	Congo DR	D	2-2	Paris	Fr	Ben Saada [19], Santos [65]		Garibian FRA
16-11	Egypt	W	2-1	Cairo	Fr	Guemamdia 2 [55 57]		
2006								
12-01	Libya	W	1-0	Radès/Tunis	Fr	Ltifi [73]		
15-01	Ghana	W	2-0	Radès/Tunis	Fr	Melliti [60], Ghodhbane [75p]	25 000	Wahid Salah
22-01	Zambia	W	4-1	Alexandria	CNr1	Santos 3 [35 82 90], Bouazizi [51]	16 000	Maillet SEY
26-01	South Africa	W	2-0	Alexandria	CNr1	Santos [32]	10 000	Evehe CMR
30-01	Guinea	L	0-3	Alexandria	CNr1		18 000	Maidin SIN
4-02	Nigeria	D	1-1	Port Said	CNqf	Hagui [49]	15 000	Maillet SEY
1-03	Serbia & Montenegro	L	0-1	Radès/Tunis	Fr		6 000	Haimoudi ALG
30-05	Belarus	W	3-0	Radès/Tunis	Fr	Namouchi [34p], Santos [46], Jomaa [90]	20 000	
2-06	Uruguay	D	0-0	Radès/Tunis	Fr	L 1-3p		
14-06	Saudi Arabia	D	2-2	Munich	WCr1	Jaziri [23], Jaidi [92+]	66 000	Shield AUS
19-06	Spain	L	1-3	Stuttgart	WCr1	Mnari [8]	52 000	Simon BRA
23-06	Ukraine	L	0-1	Berlin	WCr1		72 000	Amarilla PAR

Fr = Friendly match • CN = CAF African Cup of Nations • CC = FIFA Confederations Cup • WC = FIFA World Cup™
q = qualifier • r1 = first round group • qf = quarter-final • sf = semi-final • f = final

TUNISIA NATIONAL TEAM RECORDS AND RECORD SEQUENCES

Records			Sequence records					
Victory	7-0	TOG 2000, MWI 2005	Wins	7	1963	Clean sheets	6	1965
Defeat	1-10	HUN	Defeats	5	1988	Goals scored	14	1961-1963
Player Caps	n/a		Undefeated	11	1975-1977	Without goal	7	2002
Player Goals	n/a		Without win	14	2002	Goals against	13	1960-1962

TUNISIA COUNTRY INFORMATION

Capital	Tunis	Independence	1956 from France	GDP per Capita	$6 900
Population	9 974 722	Status	Republic	GNP Ranking	62
Area km²	163 610	Language	Arabic, French	Dialling code	+216
Population density	61 per km²	Literacy rate	74%	Internet code	.tn
% in urban areas	57%	Main religion	Muslim	GMT + / −	+1
Towns/Cities ('000)	Tunis 1 160; Sfax 276; Sousse 163; Kairouan 119; Bizerte 115; Gabès 111; Kasserine 82; Gafsa 81; Jarjis 79; Ben Arous 78; Masakin 64; Medenine 64; Monastir 64; Djerba 62				
Neighbours (km)	Algeria 965; Libya 459; Mediterranean Sea 1 148				
Main stadia	Stade 7 Novembre – Rades (Tunis) 60 000; El Menzah – Tunis 45 000; Stade Olympique – Sousse 28 000; Stade Taïeb-Mhiri – Sfax 22 000; Moustapha Ben Jenat – Monastir 20 000				

CLUB DIRECTORY

Club	AKA	Town/City	Stadium	Capacity	www.	Lge	Cup	CL
Avenir Sportif de la Marsa	ASM	Marsa, Tunis	Stade Chtioui	6 000		0	5	0
Club Africain	CA	Tunis	El Menzah	45 000	club-africain.com	9	11	1
Club Athletic Bizertin	CAB	Bizerte	Stade Municipal	20 000	cabizertin.com	1	2	0
Club Sportif de Hammam Lif	CSHL	Hammam Lif	Stade Boui Kournine	8 000		1	2	0
Club Sportif Sfaxien	CSS	Sfax	Stade Taïeb-Mhiri	22 000	css.org.tn	7	3	0
El Gawafel Sportives de Gafsa	EGSG	Gafsa				0	0	0
EO Goulette et Kram	EOKG	Kram				0	0	0
Etoile Sportive Beni Khalled	ESBK	Beni Khalled	Stade Habib Tajouri	5 000		0	0	0
Etoile Sportive du Sahel	ESS	Sousse	Stade Olympique	28 000	etoile-du-sahel.com	7	7	0
Espérance Sportive de Tunis	EST	Tunis	El Menzah	45 000	est.org.tn	20	10	1
Espérance Sportive de Zarzis	ESZ	Zarzis	Stade Jlidi	7 000		0	1	0
Olympique de Béjà	OB	Béjà	Stade Municipal	8 000		0	1	0
Stade Tunisien	ST	Tunis	Stade Zouiten	18 000	stadetunisien.com	4	6	0
Union Sportive Monastir	USMO	Monastir	Moustapha Benn Jenat	20 000	usmonastir.com	0	0	0

RECENT LEAGUE AND CUP RECORD

	Championship						Cup		
Year	Champions	Pts	Runners-up	Pts	Third	Pts	Winners	Score	Runners-up
1990	Club Africain	83	Espérance Tunis	83	Stade Tunisien	82	AS Marsa	3-2	Stade Tunisien
1991	Espérance Tunis	82	Club Africain	75	Etoile du Sahel	65	Espérance Tunis	2-1	Etoile du Sahel
1992	Club Africain	84	CA Bizertin	83	Espérance Tunis	67	Club Africain	2-1	Stade Tunisien
1993	Espérance Tunis	43	JS Kairouan	32	CA Bizertin	27	Olympique Béja	0-0 3-1p	AS Marsa
1994	Espérance Tunis	43	Club Africain	33	Etoile du Sahel	32	AS Marsa	1-0	Etoile du Sahel
1995	CS Sfaxien	38	Espérance Tunis	37	Etoile du Sahel	37	CS Sfaxien	2-1	Olympique Béja
1996	Club Africain	63	Etoile du Sahel	58	Espérance Tunis	52	Etoile du Sahel	2-1	JS Kairouan
1997	Etoile du Sahel	64	Espérance Tunis	61	CS Sfaxien	45	Espérance Tunis	1-0	CS Sfaxien
1998	Espérance Tunis	69	Club Africain	59	Etoile du Sahel	48	Club Africain	1-1 4-2p	Olympique Béja
1999	Espérance Tunis	38	CA Bizertin	25	CS Sfaxien	24	Espérance Tunis	2-1	Club Africain
2000	Espérance Tunis	60	Etoile du Sahel	53	CS Sfaxien	35	Club Africain	0-0 4-2p	CS Sfaxien
2001	Espérance Tunis	57	Etoile du Sahel	38	Club Africain	36	CS Hammam-Lif	1-0	Etoile du Sahel
2002	Espérance Tunis	46	Etoile du Sahel	39	Club Africain	35	Tournament not finished		
2003	Espérance Tunis	57	Etoile du Sahel	38	Club Africain	35	Stade Tunisien	1-0	Club Africain
2004	Espérance Tunis	53	Etoile du Sahel	44	Club Africain	42	CS Sfaxien	2-0	Espérance Tunis
2005	CS Sfaxien	58	Etoile du Sahel	58	Club Africain	56	ES Zarzis	2-0	Espérance Tunis
2006	Espérance Tunis	56	Etoile du Sahel	55	Club Africain	47	Espérance Tunis	2-2 5-4p	Club Africain

TUNISIA 2005-06

LIGUE NATIONALE A

	Pl	W	D	L	F	A	Pts	Espérance	Etoile	Club Africain	Sfaxien	Monastir	Zarzis	Stade	Gafsa	Marsa	Hammam-L	Bizertin	Kram	Jendouba	Kairouan
Espérance Tunis †	26	17	5	4	42	21	56		1-2	2-0	3-1	2-1	1-1	0-0	3-2	2-0	4-1	0-0	3-0	1-0	4-2
Etoile du Sahel †	26	16	7	3	30	11	55	2-1		1-0	2-0	2-1	2-0	1-0	2-0	2-1	2-0	1-0	1-1	1-1	3-1
Club Africain ‡	26	12	9	3	37	19	47	1-2	1-0		2-0	3-0	1-0	1-1	0-0	1-0	5-1	4-0	1-1	1-1	1-0
CS Sfaxien ‡	26	12	9	5	35	16	45	1-2	1-0	0-0		1-0	4-1	0-1	5-1	2-0	5-0	0-0	0-0	1-0	2-0
US Monastir	26	11	8	7	22	20	41	2-1	1-0	0-0	0-0		0-0	1-0	2-0	2-0	2-1	0-0	0-0	1-0	1-0
ES Zarzis	26	7	9	10	20	26	30	0-0	0-0	1-2	2-2	0-1		1-1	0-1	2-0	1-0	1-0	2-0	1-0	0-1
Stade Tunisien	26	7	8	11	24	25	29	0-1	1-3	1-1	0-1	2-0	4-1		2-0	1-1	1-1	0-0	1-2	0-1	1-0
EGS Gafsa	26	6	11	9	28	36	29	1-1	1-0	0-0	1-1	1-1		2-3		2-1	2-1	2-2	2-0	2-0	2-2
AS Marsa	26	6	10	10	19	30	28	1-2	0-0	1-1	0-0	1-0	0-1	1-0	0-0		1-1	1-1	1-1	2-1	1-0
CS Hammam-Lif	26	7	7	12	28	41	28	1-2	0-1	3-3	0-1	0-1	1-0	3-2	2-1	0-0		2-0	3-1	1-0	1-1
CA Bizertin	26	4	13	9	15	23	25	0-2	0-1	1-2	0-1	2-0	1-1	1-0	0-0	3-1	0-0		2-1	0-0	1-1
EOG Kram	26	5	10	11	16	30	25	0-1	0-0	0-2	0-5	1-1	0-1	0-1	1-0	1-2	1-0	0-0		1-1	2-0
Jendouba Sport	26	5	9	12	16	22	24	2-0	0-0	1-1	1-1	0-0	0-0	1-2	2-0	1-2	1-2	1-0	0-0		0-1
JS Kairouan	26	5	7	14	24	36	22	0-1	0-1	2-3	0-1	3-2	1-1	1-0	1-1	3-0	3-3	1-1	0-2	0-1	

31/07/2005 - 16/04/2006 • † Qualified for the CAF Champions League • ‡ Qualified for the CAF Confederation Cup

TUNISIA 2005-06
LIGUE NATIONAL B (2)

	Pl	W	D	L	F	A	Pts
Olympique Béjà	26	16	2	8	38	27	50
ES Hammam-Sousse	26	13	6	7	35	24	45
AS Kasserine	26	10	9	7	28	22	39
El Makarem Mahdia	26	10	8	8	24	18	38
CS Korba	26	9	10	7	35	34	37
Stade Gabésien	26	9	9	8	33	23	36
AS Ariana	26	7	12	7	20	19	33
ES Béni Khalled	26	9	6	11	24	27	33
AS Gabès	26	7	12	7	20	23	33
CO Médenine	26	9	5	12	27	34	32
Stir Zarzouna Bizerte	26	8	8	10	29	34	32
AS Djerba	26	7	11	8	25	28	32
Stade Sfaxien	26	7	6	13	27	38	27
Mégrine Sports	26	4	10	12	17	31	22

28/08/2005 - 15/04/2006

COUPE NATIONALE 2005-06

Fourth Round

Esperánce Tunis *	4
Olympique Kef	2
ES Zarzis	1 3p
CA Bizertin *	1 4p
Stade Tunisien	3
US Siliana *	1
JS Kaairouan	3 3p
CS Hilal Msaken *	3 4p
EGS Gafsa *	0 4p
Stade Gabésien	0 3p
LPS Tozeur	0
AS Mohammedia *	1
CS Hammam-Lif *	2
Etoile du Sahel	1
CO Kerkennah *	0
Club Africain	1

Quarter-finals

Esperánce Tunis	2
CA Bizertin *	0
Stade Tunisien	1 3p
CS Hilal Msaken *	1 4p
EGS Gafsa	6
AS Mohammadia *	1
CS Hammam-Lif *	0 2p
Club Africain	0 4p

Semi-finals

Esperánce Tunis *	3
CS Hilal Msaken	0
EGS Gafsa *	0
Club Africain	1

Final

Esperánce Tunis	2 5p
Club Africain ‡	2 4p

* Home team • ‡ Qualified for the CAF Confederation Cup

CUP FINAL

Stade 7 Novembre, Radès
12-05-2006, Att: 50 000, Ref: Ragalla SUI
Scorers - Michael Eneramo [8], Kamel Zaiem [46] for Esperánce; Borhan Ghannem [24], Omer Bargougui [72] for Club Africain

TUR – TURKEY

NATIONAL TEAM RECORD
JULY 1ST 2002 TO JULY 9TH 2006

PL	W	D	L	F	A	%
52	25	16	11	89	59	63.5

FIFA/COCA-COLA WORLD RANKING

1993	1994	1995	1996	1997	1998	1999	2000	2001	2002	2003	2004	2005	High		Low	
52	48	30	31	43	57	29	30	23	9	8	14	11	5	06/04	67	10/93

2005–2006											
08/05	09/05	10/05	11/05	12/05	01/06	02/06	03/06	04/06	05/06	06/06	07/06
12	12	11	11	11	11	11	11	13	14	-	27

It was a miserable year for Turkish football with the national team failing to qualify for their second major championship in a row, whilst Trabzonspor's defeat at the hands of Anorthosis Famagusta from Cyprus in the UEFA Champions League was particularly humiliating given that Anorthosis have been homeless since the invasion of northern Cyprus by Turkish troops in 1974. It was the FIFA World Cup™ exit, however, that made the most headlines, with the Turks accused of poor sportsmanship and intimidation towards Switzerland in the second leg of their play-off in Istanbul, right from the moment their guests arrived at the airport. It ended with a melee after the

INTERNATIONAL HONOURS
Qualified for the FIFA World Cup™ finals 2002 **UEFA European U-17 Championship** 1994 2005

final whistle and so appalled were FIFA that there was even talk of expelling Turkey from the 2010 FIFA World Cup™. In the event they escaped with a three match ban on supporters attending home matches and suspensions for those involved in the fight. Domestically, the Championship provided one of the most exciting finishes ever. Both Galatasaray and Fenerbahçe were tied on 80 points going into their final fixtures, but Fenerbahçe's galaxy of stars failed to beat Denizlispor as Galatasaray beat Kayserispor. There was also disappointment for Fenerbahçe in the Cup as they failed to end a 23-year drought in the competition with defeat in the final by Besiktas.

THE FIFA BIG COUNT OF 2000

	Male	Female		Male	Female
Registered players	575 327	327	Referees	4 567	141
Non registered players	750 000	50	Officials	200 000	200
Youth players	350 076	85	Total involved	1 880 773	
Total players	1 675 865		Number of clubs	5 240	
Professional players	5 577	0	Number of teams	14 405	

Türkiye Futbol Federasyonu (TFF)
Konaklar Mah. Ihlamurlu Sok. 9, 4. Levent, Istanbul, Turkey
Tel +90 212 2827020   Fax +90 212 2827016
tff@tff.org.tr   www.tff.org
President: ULUSOY Haluk   General Secretary: ARIBOGAN Lütfi
Vice-President: KAPULLUOGLU Kemal   Treasurer: BATMAZ Erdal   Media Officer: UGUR Ilker
Men's Coach: TERIM Fatih   Women's Coach: KIZILET Ali
TFF formed: 1923   UEFA: 1962   FIFA: 1923
White shirts with red trimmings, White shorts, White socks or Red shirts with white trimmings, Red shorts, Red socks

RECENT INTERNATIONAL MATCHES PLAYED BY TURKEY

2003	Opponents	Score		Venue	Comp	Scorers	Att	Referee
19-06	USA	W	2-1	St Etienne	CCr1	Okan Yilmaz 39p, Tuncay Sanli 70	16 944	Larrionda URU
21-06	Cameroon	L	0-1	Paris	CCr1		43 743	Amarilla PAR
23-06	Brazil	D	2-2	St Etienne	CCr1	Karadeniz 53, Okan Yilmaz 81	29 170	Merk GER
26-06	France	L	2-3	Paris	CCsf	Karadeniz 42, Tuncay Sanli 48	41 195	Larrionda URU
28-06	Colombia	W	2-1	St Etienne	CC3p	Tuncay Sanli 2, Okan Yilmaz 86	18 237	Shield AUS
20-08	Moldova	W	2-0	Ankara	Fr	Nihat Kahveci 30, Okan Yilmaz 55	15 300	Plautz AUT
6-09	Liechtenstein	W	3-0	Vaduz	ECq	Tumer Metin 14, Okan Buruk 41, Hakan Sukur 50	3 548	Van Egmond NED
9-09	Republic of Ireland	D	2-2	Dublin	Fr	Hakan Sukur 52, Okan Yilmaz 86	27 000	Wegereef NED
11-10	England	D	0-0	Istanbul	ECq		42 000	Collina ITA
15-11	Latvia	L	0-1	Riga	ECpo		8 000	Veissiere FRA
19-11	Latvia	D	2-2	Istanbul	ECpo	Ilhan Mansiz 21, Hakan Sukur 64	25 000	Frisk SWE
2004								
18-02	Denmark	L	0-1	Adana	Fr		15 000	Wack GER
31-03	Croatia	D	2-2	Zagreb	Fr	Zafer Biryol 73, Cagdas Atan 78	12 000	Lopes Ferreira POR
28-04	Belgium	W	3-2	Brussels	Fr	Basturk 43, Tolga Seyhan 68, Karadeniz 89	25 000	Van Egmond NED
21-05	Australia	W	3-1	Sydney	Fr	Umit Ozat 42, Hakan Sukur 2 69 76	28 326	Kamikawa JPN
24-05	Australia	W	1-0	Melbourne	Fr	Nihat Kahveci 45	28 953	Rugg NZL
2-06	Korea Republic	W	1-0	Seoul	Fr	Hakan Sukur 22	51 185	Maidin SIN
5-06	Korea Republic	L	1-2	Daegu	Fr	Hakan Sukur 44	45 284	Yoshida JPN
18-08	Belarus	W	2-1	Denizli	Fr	Hakan Sukur 14	18 000	Mrkovic BIH
4-09	Georgia	D	1-1	Trabzon	WCq	Fatih Tekke 49, Malkhaz Asatiani 85	10 169	Medina Cantalejpo ESP
8-09	Greece	D	0-0	Piraeus	WCq		32 182	Frisk SWE
9-10	Kazakhstan	W	4-0	Istanbul	WCq	Karadeniz 17, Nihat Kahveci 50, Fatih Tekke 2 90 93+	39 900	Hrinak SVK
13-10	Denmark	D	1-1	Copenhagen	WCq	Nihat Kahveci 70	41 331	De Santis ITA
17-11	Ukraine	L	0-3	Istanbul	WCq		40 468	Cardoso Batista POR
2005								
26-03	Albania	W	2-0	Istanbul	WCq	Necati Ates 3p, Basturk 5	32 000	Plautz AUT
30-03	Georgia	W	5-2	Tbilisi	WCq	Tolga Seyhan 12, Fatih Tekke 2 20 35, Koray Avci 72, Tuncay Sanli 89	10 000	Hauge NOR
4-06	Greece	D	0-0	Istanbul	WCq		26 700	Merk GER
8-06	Kazakhstan	W	6-0	Almaty	WCq	Fatih Tekke 2 13 85, Ibrahim Toraman 15, Tuncay Sanli 2 41 90, Halil Altintop 88	20 000	Kassai HUN
17-08	Bulgaria	L	1-3	Sofia	Fr	Fatih Tekke 21	25 000	Zografos GRE
3-09	Denmark	D	2-2	Istanbul	WCq	Okan Buruk 47, Tumer Metin 81	29 721	Mejuto Gonzalez ESP
7-09	Ukraine	W	1-0	Kyiv	WCq	Tumer Metin 55	67 000	Sars FRA
8-10	Germany	W	2-1	Istanbul	Fr	Halil Altintop 25, Nuri 89	25 000	Messina ITA
12-10	Albania	W	1-0	Tirana	WCq	Tumer Metin 58	8 000	Dauden Ibanez ESP
12-11	Switzerland	L	0-2	Berne	WCpo		31 130	Michel SVK
16-11	Switzerland	W	4-2	Istanbul	WCpo	Tuncay Sanli 3 22 36 89, Necati Ates 52p	42 000	De Bleeckere BEL
2006								
1-03	Czech Republic	D	2-2	Izmir	Fr	Umit Karan 2 89 90	58 000	Meyer GER
12-04	Azerbaijan	D	1-1	Baku	Fr	Hasan Kabze 78		Paniashvili GEO
24-05	Belgium	D	3-3	Genk	Fr	Necati Ates 2, Hasan Kabze 27, Tuncay Sanli 75	15 000	Stuchlik AUT
26-05	Ghana	D	1-1	Bochum	Fr	Nihat Kahveci 17	9 738	Meier GER
31-05	Saudi Arabia	W	1-0	Offenbach	Fr	Necati Ates 59	9 000	Fleischer GER
2-06	Angola	W	3-2	Arnhem	Fr	Necati Ates 53, Nihat Kahveci 71, Halil Altintop 85	1 200	Wegereef NED
4-06	FYR Macedonia	L	0-1	Krefeld	Fr		7 000	

Fr = Friendly match • EC = UEFA EURO 2004™ • CC = FIFA Confederation Cup • WC = FIFA World Cup™
q = qualifier • po = play-off • r1 = first round group • sf = semi-final • 3p = third place play-off

TURKEY NATIONAL TEAM RECORDS AND RECORD SEQUENCES

Records			Sequence records			
Victory	7-0	SYR, KOR, SMR	Wins	5	1995, 2002	Clean sheets	4	1958-1959
Defeat	0-8	POL, ENG, ENG	Defeats	8	1980-1982	Goals scored	15	1925-1931
Player Caps	108	RUSTU Reçber	Undefeated	15	1998-1999	Without goal	8	1980-1982
Player Goals	46	HAKAN Sükür	Without win	17	1989-1992	Goals against	19	1923-1931

TURKEY COUNTRY INFORMATION

Capital	Ankara	Independence	1923 out of Ottoman Empire	GDP per Capita	$6 700
Population	68 893 918	Status	Republic	GNP Ranking	24
Area km²	780 580	Language	Turkish	Dialling code	+90
Population density	88 per km²	Literacy rate	86%	Internet code	.tr
% in urban areas	69%	Main religion	Muslim 99%	GMT + / –	+2
Towns/Cities ('000)	Istanbul 9 797; Ankara 3 519; Izmir 2 501; Bursa 1 413; Adana 1 249; Gaziantep 1 066; Konya 876; Antalya 758; Diyarbakir 645; Mersin 612; Kayseri 593; Eskisehir 515; Urfa 449				
Neighbours (km)	Georgia 252; Armenia 268; Azerbaijan 9; Iran 499; Iraq 352; Syria 822; Greece 206; Bulgaria 240; Mediterranean Sea & Black Sea 7 200				
Main stadia	Olimpiyat – Istanbul 81 653; Atatürk – Izmir 63 000; Sükrü Saracoglu – Istanbul 46 231				

NATIONAL TEAM PLAYERS AND COACHES

Record Caps			Record Goals			Recent Coaches	
RUSTU Reçber	1994–'06	108	HAKAN Sükür	1992–'05	46	TERPAN Tinaz	1988-'89
BULENT Korkmaz	1990-'05	102	LEFTER Kücükandonyadis	1948-'61	20	TERIM Fatih	1990
HAKAN Sükür	1992-'05	102	OKTAY Metin	1956-'65	19	PIONTEK Sepp	1990-'93
TUGAY Kerimoglu	1990-'03	92	TURAN Cemil	1969-'79	19	TERIM Fatih	1993-'96
ALPAY Ozalan	1995-'05	90	ZEKI-RIZA Sporel	1923-'32	15	DENIZLI Mustafa	1996-'00
OGUN Temizkanoglu	1990-'02	76	ARIF Erdem	1994-'03	11	GUNES Senol	2000-'04
ABDULLAH Ercan	1990-'03	71	ERTUGRUL Saglam	1993-'97	11	YANAL Ersun	2004-'05
OGUZ Cetin	1988-'98	70	NIHAT Kahveci	2000-'06	11	TERIM Fatih	2005-

CLUB DIRECTORY

Club	Town/City	Stadium	Phone	www.	Lge	Cup
Akçaabat Sebatspor	Trabzon	Fatih Stadi	6 200	akcaabatsebatspor.org.tr	0	0
MKE Ankaragücü	Ankara	19 Mayis Stadi	21 250	ankaragucu.org.tr	0	2
BB Ankaraspor	Ankara	19 Mayis Stadi	21 250	ankaraspor.net	0	0
Besiktas JK	Istanbul	Inönü Stadi	32 750	bjk.com.tr	10	6
Denizlispor	Denizli	Atatürk Stadi	15 000	denizlispor.cc	0	0
Diyarbakirspor	Diyarbakir	Atatürk Stadi	16 000	diyarbakirspor.com	0	0
Fenerbahçe SK	Istanbul	Sükrü Saracoglu	46 231	fenerbahce.org	16	4
Galatasaray SK	Istanbul	Ali Sami Yen	18 000	galatasaray.org	16	14
Gaziantepspor	Gaziantep	Kamil Ocak Stadi	19 000	gaziantepspor.org.tr	0	0
Gençlerbirligi SK	Ankara	19 Mayis Stadi	21 250	genclerbirligi.org.tr	0	2
Istanbulspor AS	Istanbul	Zeytinburnu	17 500	istanbulspor.com.tr	0	0
Kayserispor	Kayseri	Atatürk Stadi	21 300	kayserispor.org.tr	0	0
Konyaspor	Konya	Atatürk Stadi	19 440	konyaspor.org.tr	0	0
Malatyaspor	Malatya	Inönü Stadi	15 000	malatyaspor.org.tr	0	0
Caykur Rizespor	Rize	Atatürk Stadi	10 800		0	1
Sakaryaspor	Sakarya	Atatürk Stadi	14 500	sakaryasporluyuz.com	0	1
Samsunspor	Samsun	19 Mayis Stadi	13 500	samsunspor.org.tr	0	0
Trabzonspor	Trabzon	Hüseyin Avni Aker	21 700	trabzonspor.org.tr	6	7

RECENT LEAGUE AND CUP RECORD

	Championship						Cup		
Year	Champions	Pts	Runners-up	Pts	Third	Pts	Winners	Score	Runners-up
1990	Besiktas	75	Fenerbahçe	70	Trabzonspor	68	Besiktas	2-0	Trabzonspor
1991	Besiktas	69	Galatasaray	64	Trabzonspor	51	Galatasaray	3-1	Ankaragücü
1992	Besiktas	76	Fenerbahçe	71	Galatasaray	60	Trabzonspor	0-3 5-1	Bursaspor
1993	Galatasaray	66	Besiktas	66	Trabzonspor	60	Galatasaray	1-0 2-2	Besiktas
1994	Galatasaray	70	Fenerbahçe	69	Trabzonspor	59	Besiktas	3-2 0-0	Galatasaray
1995	Galatasaray	79	Trabzonspor	76	Galatasaray	69	Trabzonspor	3-2 1-0	Galatasaray
1996	Fenerbahçe	84	Trabzonspor	82	Besiktas	69	Galatasaray	1-0 1-1	Fenerbahçe
1997	Galatasaray	82	Besiktas	74	Fenerbahçe	73	Kocaelispor	1-0 1-1	Trabzonspor
1998	Galatasaray	75	Fenerbahçe	71	Trabzonspor	66	Besiktas	1-1 1-1 4-2p	Galatasaray
1999	Galatasaray	78	Besiktas	77	Fenerbahçe	72	Galatasaray	0-0 2-0	Besiktas
2000	Galatasaray	79	Besiktas	75	Gaziantepspor	62	Galatasaray	5-3	Antalyaspor
2001	Fenerbahçe	76	Galatasaray	73	Gaziantepspor	68	Gençlerbirligi	2-2 4-1p	Fenerbahçe
2002	Galatasaray	78	Fenerbahçe	75	Besiktas	62	Kocaelispor	4-0	Besiktas
2003	Besiktas	85	Galatasaray	75	Gençlerbirligi	66	Trabzonspor	3-1	Gençlerbirligi
2004	Fenerbahçe	76	Trabzonspor	72	Besiktas	62	Trabzonspor	4-0	Gençlerbirligi
2005	Fenerbahçe	80	Trabzonspor	77	Galatasaray	76	Galatasaray	5-1	Fenerbahçe
2006	Galatasaray	83	Fenerbahçe	81	Besiktas	54	Besiktas	3-2	Fenerbahçe

TURKEY 2005–06

SUPER LIG

	Pl	W	D	L	F	A	Pts	Gala	F'bahçe	Besiktas	Trabzon	Kayseri	G'birligi	Konya	Sivas	Caykur	K. Erciyes	Gaz'tep	Vestel	MKE	Ankara	Denizli	Malatya	Samsun	Diy'bakir
Galatasaray †	34	26	5	3	82	34	83	—	0-1	3-2	4-1	3-0	3-0	2-1	2-0	4-2	4-2	6-0	4-2	2-0	4-0	1-1	5-2	3-2	2-0
Fenerbahçe †	34	25	6	3	90	34	81	4-0	—	2-2	2-2	3-0	3-0	5-0	3-0	1-1	4-2	1-0	2-1	2-1	2-1	6-2	2-0	5-2	2-2
Besiktas ‡	34	15	9	10	52	39	54	1-2	1-2	—	0-1	0-0	2-1	0-1	0-1	0-1	2-2	0-1	3-1	4-2	3-0	2-0	2-2	3-2	1-1
Trabzonspor ‡	34	15	7	12	51	42	52	1-1	2-3	1-2	—	2-1	1-1	1-2	0-0	3-1	0-0	2-0	0-2	3-1	2-3	3-0	1-0	2-1	3-0
Kayserispor	34	15	6	13	59	42	51	1-3	1-0	0-1	4-2	—	2-0	1-0	2-2	3-1	1-2	0-1	7-2	1-2	2-1	2-2	2-0	6-3	3-0
Gençlerbirligi	34	14	9	11	47	39	51	2-1	0-0	0-2	1-0	3-2	—	1-1	0-1	1-3	3-0	3-1	2-1	1-1	2-1	3-3	2-0	0-1	4-0
Konyaspor	34	12	10	12	39	43	46	0-1	2-4	0-1	0-0	1-0	0-3	—	2-1	3-1	2-0	3-2	1-1	2-0	0-0	0-0	0-2	4-2	5-1
Sivasspor	34	10	13	11	34	44	43	0-0	2-3	1-3	2-1	0-5	2-1	1-1	—	1-2	3-0	0-0	1-0	3-1	2-2	1-0	1-1	0-3	4-1
Caykur Rizespor	34	10	11	13	35	44	41	0-3	1-2	1-0	1-6	0-0	1-1	1-1	1-0	—	2-2	0-0	4-1	1-0	1-1	1-2	1-0	1-2	2-0
Kayseri Erciyesspor	34	9	13	12	36	47	40	1-2	0-3	1-1	1-0	0-0	2-0	0-0	0-0	0-2	—	1-0	2-1	1-2	0-1	2-0	1-1	2-2	0-2
Gaziantepspor	34	10	10	14	34	50	40	2-2	0-2	2-2	0-2	1-4	1-1	2-0	0-0	1-1	1-2	—	1-1	1-1	3-3	1-0	1-0	0-1	2-0
Vestel Manisaspor	34	11	7	16	52	61	40	1-4	5-3	0-1	1-2	1-0	0-3	0-0	3-1	1-1	0-2	1-2	—	2-2	1-0	4-2	4-3	3-0	0-3
MKE Ankaraguçu	34	10	9	15	43	48	39	0-1	1-4	2-3	1-2	2-0	1-1	3-0	0-0	1-0	1-2	2-1	0-2	—	3-2	1-1	0-1	1-1	5-1
Ankaraspor	34	9	12	13	44	51	39	1-2	2-1	2-0	0-2	1-3	0-0	0-0	1-0	1-1	1-2	2-1	0-2		—	1-3	1-2	3-3	3-3
Denizlispor	34	9	10	15	41	50	37	1-2	1-1	1-1	0-1	1-3	0-2	5-2	4-0	2-0	1-1	1-2	1-1	0-0	1-1	—	1-0	1-2	1-0
Malatyaspor	34	9	9	16	34	50	36	1-1	0-3	1-1	1-1	2-1	1-3	1-0	0-0	1-0	2-2	2-0	0-5	0-0	0-2	0-1	—	3-0	1-2
Samsunspor	34	9	9	16	45	62	36	1-2	0-5	1-3	3-1	0-0	2-0	1-1	1-2	0-0	1-1	2-3	1-1	2-1	0-1	1-2	1-2	—	1-0
Diyarbakirspor	34	8	5	21	31	69	29	1-3	0-4	1-3	3-0	0-2	0-2	0-3	1-1	1-0	2-1	1-2	0-2	0-3	1-2	1-0	3-2	0-0	—

16/08/2004 – 15/05/2005 • † Qualified for the UEFA Champions League • ‡ Qualified for the UEFA Cup • Match in bold was awarded

TURKEY 2005–06
2. LIG A

	Pl	W	D	L	F	A	Pts
Bursaspor	34	21	8	5	56	26	71
Antalyaspor	34	20	7	7	68	34	67
Altay Izmir †	34	18	10	6	54	39	64
Sakaryaspor †	34	17	9	8	54	36	60
Istanbulspor †	34	16	6	12	58	35	54
Orduspor †	34	14	12	8	53	42	54
Istanbul BB	34	13	13	8	43	31	52
Türk Telecom Ankara	34	11	12	11	40	40	45
Kocaelispor	34	11	12	11	41	41	45
Elazigspor	34	11	12	11	40	45	45
Mardinspor	34	11	10	13	38	41	43
Gaziantep BB	34	12	5	17	47	52	41
Karsiyaka Izmir	34	11	10	13	47	49	41
Usakspor	34	11	7	16	40	54	40
Akçaabat Sebatspor	34	7	13	14	37	54	34
Idman Yurdu Mersin	34	6	11	17	30	54	29
Yozgatspor	34	6	10	18	32	55	28
Dardanel Canakkale	34	5	4	25	23	73	19

27/08/2005 – 14/05/2006 • † Qualified for the play-offs

Play-off semi-finals: Altay Izmir 1-0 Orduspor; Sakaryaspor 2-2 5-3p Istanbulspor
Play-off final: Altay Izmir 1-4 Sakaryaspor

TURKIYE KUPASI 2005–06

Third round groups	Quarter-finals		Semi-finals		Final	
(Five teams in each group)						
Group A Pts	Besiktas *	2 0				
Galatasaray 10	Kayserispor	0 1				
Malatyaspor 10			Besiktas	3 2		
			Gaziantepspor *	1 0		
Group B Pts	Malatyaspor *	1 0				
Gaziantepspor 10	Gaziantepspor	0 2				
Fenerbahçe 7					Besiktas ‡	3
					Fenerbahçe	2
Group C Pts	Denizlispor *	1 1				
Kayserispor 9	Samsunspor	0 1				
Denizlispor 0			Denizlispor *	0 0		
			Fenerbahçe	4 3		
Group D Pts	Galatasaray	1 3				
Samsunspor 9	Fenerbahçe *	2 2				
Besiktas 7						

* Home team in the first leg • ‡ Qualified for the UEFA Cup

CUP FINAL

Atatürk Staium, Izmir
3-05-2006

Scorers – Tümer Metin 2 [25][113],
Gökhan Gülec [29] for Besiktas;
Alex [55], Mehmet Yozgatli [79] for Fenerbahçe

UAE – UNITED ARAB EMIRATES

NATIONAL TEAM RECORD
JULY 1ST 2002 TO JULY 9TH 2006

PL	W	D	L	F	A	%
52	17	18	17	71	71	50

FIFA/COCA-COLA WORLD RANKING

1993	1994	1995	1996	1997	1998	1999	2000	2001	2002	2003	2004	2005	High	Low
51	46	75	60	50	42	54	64	60	89	75	82	85	**42** 11/98	**111** 10/03

2005–2006											
08/05	09/05	10/05	11/05	12/05	01/06	02/06	03/06	04/06	05/06	06/06	07/06
85	88	89	88	85	85	84	80	78	71	-	90

Dubai's Al Ahli won their first league title for over a quarter of a century when they beat cross-town rivals Al Wahda 4-1 in a play-off after the two had finished equal on points. There was huge controversy surrounding the run in, however, when two former Wahda players were caught in a police sting trying to bribe five Sharjah players before the final fixture between Wahda and Sharjah. In the event Wahda came back from 3-1 down at half-time to win the match 6-3 and secure the play-off against Al Ahli. Al Jazeera were also in contention going into the final round but finished two points adrift despite a 3-1 win over Al Shabab. Al Ain joined Al Ahli in the 2007 AFC

INTERNATIONAL HONOURS
None

Champions League when they beat Sharjah 2-1 in the final of the President's Cup to ensure their participation in the Champions League for a fifth straight season. The win also secured Al Ain a Cup double as they had already beaten Al Wahda 2-1 in the lesser Vice President's Cup. On the international front, early elimination from the 2006 FIFA World Cup™ meant a season of friendly matches, the most notable being against world champions Brazil. The 8-0 thrashing gave an indication as to the UAE's level on the world stage but there is still plenty to play for in Asia and the 2007 AFC Asian Cup qualifiers got off to a solid start with victories over Oman and Pakistan.

THE FIFA BIG COUNT OF 2000

	Male	Female		Male	Female
Registered players	727	0	Referees	150	0
Non registered players	10 000	0	Officials	300	0
Youth players	2 047	0	Total involved	13 224	
Total players	12 774		Number of clubs	10	
Professional players	0	0	Number of teams	29	

United Arab Emirates Football Association (UAEFA)
PO Box 916, Abu Dhabi, United Arab Emirates
Tel +971 2 4445600   Fax +971 2 4448558
uaefa@uae-football.org.ae   www.uaefootball.org
President: AL SERKAL Yousuf   General Secretary: BIN DAKHAN Mohammed
Vice-President: AL ROAMITHI Mohamed   Treasurer: AL KHOURI Younes Haji   Media Officer: None
Men's Coach: RABIE Jumaa   Women's Coach: None
UAEFA formed: 1971   AFC: 1974   FIFA: 1972
White shirts with red trimmings, White shorts, White socks

RECENT INTERNATIONAL MATCHES PLAYED BY THE UNITED ARAB EMIRATES

2003	Opponents	Score		Venue	Comp	Scorers	Att	Referee
14-12	Azerbaijan	D	3-3	Dubai	Fr	Nawaf Mubarak [5], Moh'd Sirour [54], Moh'd Omar [72p]		Mohamed UAE
21-12	Kenya	D	2-2	Abu Dhabi	Fr	Mohamed Omar 2 [41p 45]		
26-12	Saudi Arabia	L	0-2	Kuwait City	GC			Ebrahim BHR
29-12	Kuwait	W	2-0	Kuwait City	GC	Rashed Al Kalbani [70], Mohamed Sirour [77]		Kassai HUN
31-12	Oman	L	0-2	Kuwait City	GC			Al Qahtani QAT
2004								
3-01	Qatar	D	0-0	Kuwait City	GC			
7-01	Bahrain	L	1-3	Kuwait City	GC	Faysal Khalil 7		
11-01	Yemen	W	3-0	Kuwait City	GC	Moh'd Omar [6], Moussa Hatab [21], Moh'd Sirour [89]		
18-02	Thailand	W	1-0	Al Ain	WCq	Mohamed Rashid [22]	4 000	Sun Baojie CHN
31-03	Korea DPR	D	0-0	Pyongyang	WCq		20 000	Zhou Weixin CHN
31-05	Bahrain	L	2-3	Dubai	Fr			
9-06	Yemen	W	3-0	Al Ain	WCq	Rashid Abdulrahman [24], Mohamed Omar 2 [28 73]	5 000	Sapaev TKM
10-07	China PR	D	2-2	Hohhot	Fr	Khamis [48], Ismail Matar [60]		
19-07	Kuwait	L	1-3	Jinan	ACr1	Mohamed Rashid [47]	31 250	Al Hamdan KSA
23-07	Korea Republic	L	0-2	Jinan	ACr1		30 000	Irmatov UZB
27-07	Jordan	D	0-0	Beijing	ACr1		25 000	Najm LIB
8-09	Yemen	L	1-3	Sana'a	WCq	Mohamed Omar [26]	17 000	Al Ghamdi KSA
8-10	Singapore	W	2-1	Singapore	Fr	Fahed Masoud [25], Khamis [26]		
13-10	Thailand	L	0-3	Bangkok	WCq		15 000	Nishimura JPN
11-11	Jordan	W	4-0	Abu Dhabi	Fr			
17-11	Korea DPR	W	1-0	Dubai	WCq	Saleh Obeid [58]	2 000	Abdul Hamid MAS
22-11	Belarus	L	2-3	Dubai	Fr	Saleh Obeid [21], Fahed Masoud [75]	600	Kaliq BHR
27-11	Kuwait	L	0-1	Abu Dhabi	Fr			
3-12	Kuwait	D	1-1	Dubai	Fr	Basheer Saeed [26]		
10-12	Qatar	D	2-2	Doha	GCr1	Subait Khatir [41p], Ismail Matar [83]		
13-12	Oman	L	1-2	Doha	GCr1	Fahed Masoud [46+]		
16-12	Iraq	D	1-1	Doha	GCr1	Faisal Khalil [68]		
2005								
9-02	Switzerland	L	1-2	Dubai	Fr	Ismail Matar [21]	1 000	Al Hilali OMA
24-05	Peru	D	0-0	Tokyo	Fr		6 536	
27-05	Japan	W	1-0	Tokyo	Fr	Haidar Ali [68]		Lubos SVK
29-07	Kuwait	D	1-1	Geneva	Fr	Salam Saad [10], W 7-6p		
31-07	Egypt	D	0-0	Geneva	Fr	L 4-5p		
23-09	Benin	D	0-0	Dubai	Fr			
11-10	Oman	D	2-2	Al Ain	Fr	Ismail Matar 2 [19 85]		
12-11	Brazil	L	0-8	Abu Dhabi	Fr		50 000	Abd El Fatah EGY
16-11	Syria	W	3-0	Damascus	Fr	Saeed Alkas [23], Ismail Matar [34], Faisal Khalil [88]		
2-12	Libya	D	1-1	Sharjah	Fr	Abdul Rahman Juma [60]		
2006								
18-01	Korea Republic	W	1-0	Dubai	Fr	Faisal Khalil [22]		Al Hilali OMA
22-02	Oman	W	1-0	Dubai	ACq	Ismail Matar [15]	15 000	Al Ghamdi KSA
1-03	Pakistan	W	4-1	Karachi	ACq	Subait Al Mekhaini [68], Ismail Matar [78], Salam Saad [81], Saeed Alkas [88]	10 000	Tongkhan THA
2-05	Syria	W	2-1	Dubai	Fr	Nawaf Mubarak [40], Faisal Khalil [90]		

Fr = Friendly match • AC = AFC Asian Cup • GC = Gulf Cup • WC = FIFA World Cup™
q = qualifier • r1 = first round group

UNITED ARAB EMIRATES NATIONAL TEAM RECORDS AND RECORD SEQUENCES

Records			Sequence records					
Victory	12-0	BRU 2001	Wins	5	1993, 1998	Clean sheets	4	1985, 1993, 1996
Defeat	0-8	BRA 2005	Defeats	9	1990-1992	Goals scored	18	1999-2000
Player Caps	164	AL TALYANI Adnan	Undefeated	16	1996-1997	Without goal	4	1974-1976, 1980
Player Goals	53	AL TALYANI Adnan	Without win	14	1974-1979	Goals against	14	2002-2003

UNITED ARAB EMIRATES COUNTRY INFORMATION

Capital	Abu Dhabi	Independence	1971 from the UK	GDP per Capita	$23 200
Population	2 523 915	Status	Federation	GNP Ranking	49
Area km²	82 880	Language	Arabic	Dialling code	+971
Population density	30 per km²	Literacy rate	77%	Internet code	.ae
% in urban areas	84%	Main religion	Muslim	GMT + / –	+4
Towns/Cities ('000)	Dubai 1 137; Abu Dhabi 603; Sharjah 543; al-Ayn 408; Ras al-Haymah 115; al-Fujayrah 62
Neighbours (km)	Oman 410; Saudi Arabia 457; Persian Gulf & Gulf of Oman 1 318
Main stadia	Zayed – Abu Dhabi 49 500; Al Ahli Club – Dubai 12 000; Al Ain Club – Al Ain 12 000

CLUB DIRECTORY

Club	Towns/City	Stadium	Capacity	Lge	Cup	CL
Al Ahli	Dubai	Al Maktoum	12 000	4	6	0
Al Ain	Al Ain	Tahnoon Bin Mohammed	10 000	9	4	1
Dhafra	Dhafra			0	0	0
Dubai	Dubai			0	0	0
Emirates	Ras Al Khaima			0	0	0
Al Ittihad	Kalba			0	0	0
Al Jazeera	Abu Dhabi	Mohammed Bin Zayed	15 000	0	0	0
Al Khaleej	Khor Fakkan			0	0	0
Al Nasr	Dubai	Al Maktoum	12 000	3	3	0
Al Sha'ab	Sharjah	Sharjah Stadium	12 000	0	1	0
Al Shabab	Dubai	Al Maktoum	12 000	2	4	0
Sharjah	Sharjah	Sharjah Stadium	12 000	4	8	0
Al Wahda	Dubai	Al Nuhayyan	12 000	3	1	0
Al Wasl	Dubai	Al Maktoum	12 000	6	1	0

RECENT LEAGUE AND CUP RECORD

	Championship						Cup		
Year	Champions	Pts	Runners-up	Pts	Third	Pts	Winners	Score	Runners-up
1990	Al Shabab	40	Al Wasl	40	Sharjah	39	Al Shabab		
1991	Tournament not finished						Sharjah		
1992	Al Wasl	46	Sharjah	45	Bani Yas	44	Bani Yas	2-1	Al Nasr
1993	Al Ain	35	Al Wasl	27	Sharjah	26	Al Sha'ab		
1994	Sharjah	29	Al Ain	29	Al Nasr	23	Al Shabab	1-0	Al Ain
1995	Al Shabab	29	Al Ain	23	Al Wasl	18	Sharjah	0-0 5-4p	Al Ain
1996	Sharjah	39	Al Wasl	35	Al Ain	25	Al Ahli	4-1	Al Wahda
1997	Al Wasl	19	Al Nasr	16	Al Wahda	16	Al Shabab	1-1 5-4p	Al Nasr
1998	Al Ain	32	Sharjah	30	Al Wasl	23	Sharjah	3-2	Al Wasl
1999	Al Wahda	65	Al Ain	57	Al Nasr	56	Al Ain	1-0	Al Shabab
2000	Al Ain	47	Al Nasr	46	Al Wahda	45	Al Wahda	1-1 8-7p	Al Wasl
2001	Al Wahda	50	Al Ahly	42	Al Jazeera	38	Al Ain	3-2	Al Sha'ab
2002	Al Ain	47	Al Jazeera	38	Al Sha'ab	37	Al Ahli	3-1	Al Jazeera
2003	Al Ain	48	Al Wahda	43	Al Ahli	34	Sharjah	1-1 6-5p	Al Wahda
2004	Al Ain	15	Al Ahli	13	Al Shabab	7	Al Ahli	2-1	Al Sha'ab
2005	Al Wahda	62	Al Ain	57	Al Jazeera	53	Al Ain	3-1	Al Wahda
2006	Al Ahli	47	Al Wahda	47	Al Jazeera	45	Al Ain	2-1	Sharjah

1990 title play-off: Al Shabab 2-1 Al Wasl • 1994 title play-off: Sharjah 1-0 Al Ain • 2006 title play-off: Al Ahli 4-1 Al Wahda

UNITED ARAB EMIRATES 2005-06

PREMIER LEAGUE

	Pl	W	D	L	F	A	Pts	Ahli	Wahda	Jazeera	Ain	Nasr	Shabab	Sharjah	Wasl	Sha'ab	Emirates	Bani Yas	Dibba
Al Ahli †	22	15	2	5	64	30	47		3-4	2-1	1-0	2-1	2-1	0-0	1-0	2-1	2-2	7-1	4-1
Al Wahda	22	14	5	3	44	24	47	2-0		1-2	4-1	1-3	1-2	2-1	2-1	2-0	5-1	4-2	6-0
Al Jazeera	22	14	3	5	43	35	45	1-1	1-5		2-1	2-1	1-2	3-2	2-0	2-2	2-1	2-0	2-0
Al Ain	22	13	2	7	42	23	41	1-2	1-0	4-0		1-0	1-2	1-0	2-1	2-1	5-0	6-2	0-0
Al Nasr	22	11	2	9	50	35	35	3-0	2-2	1-3	0-1		4-2	2-2	0-2	3-2	3-0	3-0	4-2
Al Shabab	22	10	4	8	40	39	34	1-2	2-2	1-3	2-1	4-3		0-0	2-1	0-2	0-0	0-3	3-1
Sharjah	22	8	6	8	52	41	30	1-3	3-6	6-1	2-1	4-3	2-4		1-1	1-2	6-0	2-1	7-1
Al Wasl	22	9	2	11	33	32	29	0-3	3-1	0-2	2-3	3-1	2-4	2-3		2-0	2-1	1-0	3-0
Al Sha'ab	22	6	7	9	30	39	25	0-1	0-5	3-3	0-0	0-4	2-1	5-4	0-0		2-0	1-1	1-2
Emirates	22	4	6	12	21	48	18	0-0	1-4	1-3	0-1	0-3	1-0	1-1	1-0	3-3		3-1	3-1
Bani Yas	22	3	4	15	24	56	13	1-4	0-2	0-2	2-5	1-3	2-4	1-1	1-4	0-0	2-0		2-2
Dibba Al Hisn	22	1	5	16	24	65	8	2-2	1-3	1-3	0-4	1-3	3-3	1-3	2-3	1-3	2-2	0-1	

31/08/2005 - 21/05/2006 • † Qualified for the AFC Champions League • ‡ Championship play-off: Al Ahli 4-1 Al Wahda (Tahnoon Bin Mohammed, Al Ain, 26-05-2006, Scorers: Salem Khamis 19p, Farhad Majidi, Faisal Khalil 75, OG for Ahli; Darko Metrovic 71 for Wahda)

UNITED ARAB EMIRATES 2005-06
SECOND DIVISION GROUP A

	Pl	W	D	L	F	A	Pts
Al Ittihad †	14	9	2	3	34	18	29
Al Arabi †	14	9	1	4	25	21	28
Dubai †	14	8	2	4	23	20	26
Hamra Island	14	6	5	3	22	18	23
Ramms	14	5	3	6	25	25	18
Ras Al Khaima	14	5	2	7	30	28	17
Al Urooba	14	3	1	10	16	26	10
Masafi	14	2	2	10	17	36	8

16/09/2004 - 30/03/2005 • † Qualified for play-offs

UNITED ARAB EMIRATES 2005-06
SECOND DIVISION GROUP B

	Pl	W	D	L	F	A	Pts
Ajman †	14	11	0	3	44	18	33
Ahli Fujeira †	14	8	2	4	29	15	26
Al Khaleej †	14	7	4	3	29	14	25
Hatta	14	7	3	4	31	24	24
Dhafra	14	6	2	6	30	21	20
Dibba Fujeira	14	5	1	8	21	38	16
Himriya	14	4	2	8	16	33	14
Thaid	14	0	2	12	10	47	2

16/09/2004 - 30/03/2005 • † Qualified for play-offs

UNITED ARAB EMIRATES 2005-06
SECOND DIVISION FINAL ROUND

	Pl	W	D	L	F	A	Pts
Ahli Fujeira	10	5	4	1	17	11	19
Dubai	10	5	3	2	17	9	18
Al Ittihad	10	5	3	2	23	17	18
Al Kahaleej	10	5	1	4	22	18	16
Ajman	10	2	2	6	11	16	8
Al Arabi	10	0	3	7	7	26	3

16/09/2004 - 30/03/2005 • Play-off: Dubai 2-2 3-1p Ittihad

PRESIDENT'S CUP 2005-06

Round of 16			Quarter-finals groups		Semi-finals		Final	
Al Ain *	3							
Al Himriya	0		Group A	Pts				
Bani Yas	1	4p	Al Wahda	5				
Al Shabab *	1	5p	Al Nasr	5	Al Ain	3		
Al Jazeera *	4		Al Shabab	5	Al Nasr	2		
Dibba Al Hisn	1		Al Jazeera	0				
Ras Al Khaima	0							
Al Nasr *	4						Al Ain †	2
Al Wahda *	5						Sharjah	1
Ajman	0		Group B	Pts				
Hatta *	1	2p	Al Ain	7				
Dubai	1	4p	Sharjah	6	Al Wahda	3 2p		
Al Wasl	3		Dubai	4	Sharjah	3 4p		
Al Ahli *	2		Al Wasl	0				
Al Sha'ab *	0							
Sharjah	1							

* Home team • † Qualified for the AFC Champions League

CUP FINAL
Zayed Sports City, Abu Dhabi
3-04-2006

Scorers - Nenad Jestrovic 60, Ali Al Wehaibi 80 for Al Ain; Javad Nekounam 63 for Sharjah

UGA – UGANDA

NATIONAL TEAM RECORD
JULY 1ST 2002 TO JULY 9TH 2006

PL	W	D	L	F	A	%
58	19	18	21	69	64	48.3

FIFA/COCA-COLA WORLD RANKING

1993	1994	1995	1996	1997	1998	1999	2000	2001	2002	2003	2004	2005	High		Low	
94	93	74	81	109	105	108	103	119	102	103	109	101	66	04/95	121	07/02

2005–2006											
08/05	09/05	10/05	11/05	12/05	01/06	02/06	03/06	04/06	05/06	06/06	07/06
110	110	110	109	101	96	97	98	97	97	-	99

The Cranes were no more than a supporting act in the 2006 FIFA World Cup™ qualifiers but will have drawn heart from the competitive nature with which they tackled the campaign. There was disappointment, however, at the end of 2005 in the CECAFA Cup where Uganda, traditionally a dominant force, left empty-handed from tournament in Kigali after a defeat by hosts Rwanda in the semi-final. Egyptian-born coach Mahmoud Abbas departed after the FIFA World Cup™ qualifiers and following a few false starts the Hungarian Laszlo Csaba was drafted in as his replacement. In the League, SC Villa were denied an eighth successive league title when they lost on penalties to

INTERNATIONAL HONOURS
CECAFA Cup 1973 1976 1977 1989 1990 1992 1996 2000 2003

Police in the Super League play-off. The competition had been divided into three sections with an American-style play-off for the top eight teams, which culminated in victory for the policemen in the deciding game. Uganda Revenue Authority won the Kakungulu Cup to qualify for the 2006 edition of the CAF Confederation Cup. The taxmen achieved a 2-1 win over Kampala CC in last October's final. Ugandan clubs have been in great form in the annual CECAFA Club Championship, winning two of the last three tournaments. In May 2006 Police beat Tanzania's Moro United 2-1 in the final, SC Villa having won it the year before.

THE FIFA BIG COUNT OF 2000

	Male	Female		Male	Female
Registered players	17 000	0	Referees	600	0
Non registered players	60 000	0	Officials	5 000	0
Youth players	10 000	0	Total involved	92 600	
Total players	87 000		Number of clubs	400	
Professional players	0	0	Number of teams	2 000	

Federation of Uganda Football Associations (FUFA)
FUFA House, Plot No. 879, Kyadondo Block 8, Mengo Wakaliga Road, PO Box 22518, Kampala, Uganda
Tel +256 41 272702   Fax +256 41 272702
fufaf@yahoo.com   www.fufa.co.ug
President: MULINDWA Lawrence   General Secretary: TBD
Vice-President: BARIGYE Richard   Treasurer: TBD   Media Officer: MULINDWA Rogers
Men's Coach: CSABA Laszlo   Women's Coach: None
FUFA formed: 1924   CAF: 1959   FIFA: 1959
Yellow shirts, Yellow shorts, Yellow socks

RECENT INTERNATIONAL MATCHES PLAYED BY UGANDA

2003	Opponents	Score		Venue	Comp	Scorers	Att	Referee
29-03	Rwanda	D	0-0	Kigali	CNq			Bakhit SUD
21-05	Sudan	D	0-0	Kigali	Fr			
29-05	Tanzania	W	3-1	Kampala	Fr	Kasongo 2 [39 88], Ssozi [44p]		
31-05	Tanzania	W	1-0	Kampala	Fr			
7-06	Rwanda	L	0-1	Kampala	CNq		50 000	Gizate ETH
22-06	Ghana	D	1-1	Kumasi	CNq	Bajaba [16]		
11-10	Mauritius	W	3-0	Kampala	WCq	Bajope [52], Mubiru [68], Obua [92+]	6 800	Tangwarima ZIM
11-11	Tanzania	W	2-1	Kampala	Fr	Ssali, Lubega		Kalyango UGA
16-11	Mauritius	L	1-3	Curepipe	WCq	Obua [113]	2 465	Maillet SEY
30-11	Eritrea	W	2-1	Kassala	CCr1	Kabagambe [43], Kabeta [60]		
4-12	Kenya	D	1-1	Kassala	CCr1	Obua [47]		
8-12	Sudan	D	0-0	Khartoum	CCsf	W 4-3p		
10-12	Rwanda	W	2-0	Khartoum	CCf	Lubega [48], Obua [54]		Itur KEN
2004								
22-05	Sudan	L	1-2	Khartoum	Fr	Ojara		
28-05	Rwanda	D	1-1	Kigali	Fr	Tabala [71]		
6-06	Congo DR	W	1-0	Kampala	WCq	Sekajja [75]	45 000	Maillet SEY
19-06	Cape Verde Islands	L	0-1	Praia	WCq		5 000	Coulibaly MLI
3-07	Ghana	D	1-1	Kampala	WCq	Obua [46+]	20 000	El Beltagy EGY
7-08	Kenya	D	1-1	Kampala	Fr	Obua [27p]	25 000	
14-08	Rwanda	L	1-2	Kampala	Fr	Sebalata		
18-08	Kenya	L	1-4	Nairobi	Fr	Tabula [55]	5 000	
22-08	Zimbabwe	L	0-2	Harare	Fr		3 000	
4-09	Burkina Faso	L	0-2	Ouagadougou	WCq		30 000	Ould Lemghambodj MTN
10-10	South Africa	L	0-1	Kampala	WCq		50 000	Gasingwa RWA
12-12	Somalia	W	2-0	Addis Abeba	CCr1	Kalungi 2 [30 42]		
14-12	Sudan	L	1-2	Addis Abeba	CCr1	Mwesigwa [83]		
18-12	Kenya	D	1-1	Addis Abeba	CCr1	Obua [77p]		
2005								
8-01	Egypt	L	0-3	Cairo	Fr			
26-03	South Africa	L	1-2	Johennesburg	WCq	Obua [63p]	20 000	Chukwujekwu NGA
5-06	Congo DR	L	0-4	Kinshasa	WCq		80 000	Daami TUN
18-06	Cape Verde Islands	W	1-0	Kampala	WCq	Serunkuma [36]	5 000	Kidane ERI
4-09	Ghana	L	0-2	Kumasi	WCq		45 000	Hicuburundi BDI
8-10	Burkina Faso	D	2-2	Kampala	WCq	Masaba [30], Serunkuma [71]	1 433	Benouza ALG
27-11	Ethiopia	D	0-0	Kigali	CCr1			
30-11	Djibouti	W	6-1	Kigali	CCr1	Masaba [12p], Nsereko 2 [27 29], Serunkuma [47], Mawejje [85], Muganga [89]		
1-12	Somalia	W	7-0	Kigali	CCr1	Massa 2 [15 24], Nsereko 18, Mubiru 2 [64 73], Vincent [78], Ryekwassa [88]		
3-12	Sudan	W	3-0	Kigali	CCr1	Massa [4], Serunkuma [35], Mubiru [92+]		
8-12	Rwanda	L	0-1	Kigali	CCsf			
10-12	Zanzibar †	D	0-0	Kigali	CC3p	L 4-5p		
27-12	Egypt	L	0-2	Cairo	Fr			
29-12	Ecuador	W	2-1	Cairo	Fr	Massa [47], Mwanga [54]		
2006								

No international matches played in 2006 before July

Fr = Friendly match • CN = CAF African Cup of Nations • CC = CECAFA Cup • WC = FIFA World Cup™
q = qualifier • r1 = first round group • sf = semifinal • 3p = third place play-off • f = final • † Not a full international

UGANDA NATIONAL TEAM RECORDS AND RECORD SEQUENCES

Records			Sequence records					
Victory	13-1	KEN 1932	Wins	7	1932-1940	Clean sheets	5	1996-1998
Defeat	0-6	TUN 1999	Defeats	5	1978-1979, 2004	Goals scored	19	1931-1952
Player Caps	n/a		Undefeated	15	1996-1998	Without goal	4	1995, 1999
Player Goals	n/a		Without win	11	1995-1996	Goals against	15	1999-2000

UGANDA COUNTRY INFORMATION

Capital	Kampala	Independence	1962 from the UK	GDP per Capita	$1 400
Population	26 404 543	Status	Republic	GNP Ranking	106
Area km²	236 040	Language	English, Ganda	Dialling code	+3
Population density	111 per km²	Literacy rate	69%	Internet code	.ug
% in urban areas	13%	Main religion	Christian 66%, Muslim 16%	GMT +/−	+3
Towns/Cities ('000)	Kampala 1 353; Gulu 146; Lira 119; Jinja 93; Mbarara 79; Mbale 76; Mukono 67; Kasese 67				
Neighbours (km)	Kenya 933; Tanzania 396; Rwanda 169; Congo DR 765; Sudan 435;				
Main stadia	National Stadium – Kampala 40 000				

UGANDA 2005 SUPER LEAGUE GROUP A

	Pl	W	D	L	F	A	Pts
SC Villa Kampala †	8	6	2	0	11	1	20
Masaka Local Council†	8	3	3	2	9	9	12
URA Kampala †	8	2	5	1	8	4	11
Lugazi United	8	1	2	5	8	15	5
Mbarara United	8	1	2	5	6	13	5

11/06/2005 - 23/07/2005 • † Qualified for play-offs

UGANDA 2005 SUPER LEAGUE GROUP B

	Pl	W	D	L	F	A	Pts
Express RE Kampala †	8	5	2	1	10	4	17
SC Simba †	8	5	1	2	15	6	16
Kampala United	8	3	1	4	7	12	10
Kinyara Sugar	8	2	2	4	4	7	8
Kakira Sugar	8	1	2	5	6	13	5

11/06/2005 - 20/07/2005 • † Qualified for play-offs

UGANDA 2005 SUPER LEAGUE GROUP C

	Pl	W	D	L	F	A	Pts
Police Jinja †	8	5	3	0	12	2	18
Victor †	8	4	3	1	11	7	15
Kampala City Council†	8	4	2	2	18	9	14
Mityana UTODA	8	1	1	6	12	14	4
Gulu United	8	1	1	6	4	25	4

10/06/2005 - 20/07/2005 • † Qualified for play-offs

SUPER LEAGUE PLAY-OFFS

Quarter-finals		Semi-finals		Final	
Police Jinja *	4 0				
Masaka LC	2 0	Police Jinja	1 2	* Home team in the 1st leg	
URA Kampala	1 3	Express RE *	1 1		
Express RE *	1 3			Police Jinja †	0 3p
Kampala CC *	3 2			SC Villa	0 1p
SC Simba	2 0	Kampala CC *	0 1	Namboole, 23-09-2005	
Victor	0 0	SC Villa	2 2		
SC Villa *	1 1	† Qualified for the CAF Champions League			

SDCA CUP 2005

Quarter-finals		Semi-finals		Final	
SC Villa	3				
Mityana UTODA	1	SC Villa	1		
Kinyara Sugar	0	Kampala CC	0		
Kampala CC	w-o			SC Villa	1
URA Kampala	1			Masaka LC	0
Police Jinja	0	URA Kampala	1 2p	25-02-2005	
Kakira Sugar		Masaka LC	1 3p		
Masaka LC					

KAKUNGULU CUP 2005

Quarter-finals		Semi-finals		Final	
URA Kampala	3				
Wolves Young	0	URA Kampala	0 4		
Corporate XI		Kinyara Sugar	1 2		
Kinyara Sugar				URA Kampala ‡	2
SC Villa	1 1			Kampala CC	1
Masaka LC	0 0	SC Villa	2 1	Nakivubo, 21-10-2005	
Jogoos Young	1 1	Kampala CC	3 1		
Kampala CC	2 2	‡ Qualified for the CAF Confederation Cup			

RECENT LEAGUE AND CUP RECORD

	Championship						Cup		
Year	Champions	Pts	Runners-up	Pts	Third	Pts	Winners	Score	Runners-up
1995	Express	74	Umeme Jinja	61	SC Villa	52	Express	2-0	Posta
1996	Express	75	Kampala CC	65	SC Villa	65	Umeme Jinja	1-0	Nile FC
1997	Kampala CC	76	Umeme Jinja	73	Express	72	Express	4-1	Umeme Jinja
1998	SC Villa	45	Express	44	SC Simba	39	SC Villa	2-0	SC Simba
1999	SC Villa	94	Express	92	SC Simba	76	Mbale Heroes	0-0 3-0p	Lyantonde
2000	SC Villa	75	Kampala CC	70	Express	65	SC Villa	1-0	Military Police
2001	SC Villa	70	Kampala CC	65	Mbale Heroes	48	Express	3-1	SC Villa
2002	SC Villa	79	Express	63	Kampala CC	61	SC Villa	2-1	Express
2003	SC Villa	72	Express	72	Kampala CC	53	Express	3-1	Police
2004	SC Villa	67	Express	57	URA Kampala	57	Kampala CC	1-1 3-2	Express
2005	Police Jinja	†	SC Villa				URA Kampala	2-1	Kampala CC

† Police won 3-1 on penalties after a 0-0 draw

UKR – UKRAINE

NATIONAL TEAM RECORD
JULY 1ST 2002 TO JULY 9TH 2006

PL	W	D	L	F	A	%
45	17	17	11	51	37	56.7

FIFA/COCA-COLA WORLD RANKING

1993	1994	1995	1996	1997	1998	1999	2000	2001	2002	2003	2004	2005	High		Low	
90	77	71	59	49	47	27	34	45	45	60	57	40	22	04/99	132	09/93

2005–2006											
08/05	09/05	10/05	11/05	12/05	01/06	02/06	03/06	04/06	05/06	06/06	07/06
36	39	39	40	40	40	41	42	41	45	-	15

An appearance in the quarter-finals of the 2006 FIFA World Cup™ in Germany exceeded all expectations and cemented Ukraine's position at the top table of European and world football. The national team's form at the finals may have been hit and miss but the performance gives the country a platform and a reputation on which to build. They showed character to recover from their 4-0 mauling at the hands of Spain in the opening match, qualifying for the knockout stage after comfortable wins over Saudi Arabia and Tunisia. They also held their nerve to win the penalty shoot-out against the Swiss after a poor second round game and although they lost 3-0 to the

INTERNATIONAL HONOURS
Qualified for the FIFA World Cup™ finals 2006

Italians in the quarter-finals, the score was not a fair reflection. With three goals in the tournament, Andriy Shevchenko cemented his reputation but Ukraine's rise in fortunes has its roots in the club game at home, where most of the squad are based. The League is one of the most competitive and well financed in Europe, attracting players from around the world and whereas in years past Dynamo Kyiv reigned almost unopposed, they now have powerful challengers in Shakhtar Donetsk from the mining region of the country. After both finished the season level on points, Shakhtar won the play-off 2-1 with an extra time winner from their Nigerian striker Julius Aghahowa.

THE FIFA BIG COUNT OF 2000

	Male	Female		Male	Female
Registered players	27 059	1 100	Referees	12 000	7
Non registered players	600 000	5 000	Officials	15 200	33
Youth players	120 000	100	Total involved	780 499	
Total players	753 259		Number of clubs	1 088	
Professional players	2 010	300	Number of teams	8 487	

Football Federation of Ukraine (FFU)
Laboratorna Str. 1, PO Box 293, Kyiv 03150, Ukraine
Tel +380 44 2528498   Fax +380 44 2528513
ffu@ffu.org.ua   www.ffu.org.ua
President: SURKIS Grigoriy   General Secretary: BANDURKO Oleksandr
Vice-President: BANDURKO Oleksandr   Treasurer: MISCHENKO Lyudmyla   Media Officer: NYKONENKO Valeriy
Men's Coach: BLOKHIN Oleg   Women's Coach: KULAYER Volodymyr
FFU formed: 1991   UEFA: 1992   FIFA: 1992
Yellow shirts with blue trimmings, Yellow shorts, Yellow socks or Blue shirts with yellow trimming, Blue shorts, Blue socks

RECENT INTERNATIONAL MATCHES PLAYED BY UKRAINE

2002	Opponents		Score	Venue	Comp	Scorers	Att	Referee
7-09	Armenia	D	2-2	Yerevan	ECq	Serebrennikov [2], Zubov [33]	9 000	Vuorela FIN
12-10	Greece	W	2-0	Kyiv	ECq	Vorobei [51], Voronin [90]	50 000	Temmink NED
16-10	Northern Ireland	D	0-0	Belfast	ECq		9 288	Bolognino ITA
20-11	Slovakia	D	1-1	Bratislava	Fr	Melaschenko [84]	2 859	Marczyk POL
2003								
12-02	Turkey	D	0-0	Izmir	Fr		40 000	Attard MLT
29-03	Spain	D	2-2	Kyiv	ECq	Voronin [11], Horshkov [90]	82 000	Riley ENG
2-04	Latvia	W	1-0	Kyiv	Fr	Kalinichenko [83p]	3 700	Michel SVK
30-04	Denmark	L	0-1	Copenhagen	Fr		15 599	Mikulski POL
7-06	Armenia	W	4-3	Lviv	ECq	Horshkov [28], Shevchenko 2 [66p 73], Fedorov [90]	35 000	Albrecht GER
11-06	Greece	L	0-1	Athens	ECq		15 000	De Bleckere BEL
20-08	Romania	L	0-2	Donetsk	Fr		28 000	Egorov RUS
6-09	Northern Ireland	D	0-0	Donetsk	ECq		24 000	Stark GER
19-09	Spain	L	1-2	Elche	ECq	Shevchenko [84]	38 000	Hauge NOR
11-10	FYR Macedonia	D	0-0	Kyiv	Fr		13 000	Orlic MDA
2004								
18-02	Libya	D	1-1	Tripoli	Fr	Pukanych [14]	40 000	El Arjoun MAR
31-03	FYR Macedonia	L	0-1	Skopje	Fr		16 000	Karagic SCG
28-04	Slovakia	D	1-1	Kyiv	Fr	Venhlynskyi [13]	18 000	Ryszka POL
6-06	France	L	0-1	Paris	Fr		66 646	Ceferin SVN
18-08	England	L	0-3	Newcastle	Fr		35 387	McCurry SCO
4-09	Denmark	D	1-1	Copenhagen	WCq	Husin [56]	36 335	Meier SUI
8-09	Kazakhstan	W	2-1	Almaty	WCq	Byelik [14], Rotan [90]	23 000	Oliveira POR
9-10	Greece	D	1-1	Kyiv	WCq	Shevchenko [48]	56 000	Mejuto Gonzalez ESP
13-10	Georgia	W	2-0	Lviv	WCq	Byelik [12], Shevchenko [79]	28 000	Stark GER
17-11	Turkey	W	3-0	Istanbul	WCq	Husyev [8], Shevchenko 2 [17 88]	40 468	Cardoso Batista POR
2005								
9-02	Albania	W	2-0	Tirana	WCq	Rusol [40], Gusin [59]	12 000	Bennett ENG
30-03	Denmark	W	1-0	Kyiv	WCq	Voronin [68]	60 000	Michel SVK
4-06	Kazakhstan	W	2-0	Kyiv	WCq	Shevchenko [18], Avdeyev OG [83]	45 000	Lehner AUT
8-06	Greece	W	1-0	Piraeus	WCq	Gusin [82]	33 500	Temmink NED
15-08	Israel	D	0-0	Kyiv	Fr	L 3-5p		Mikulski POL
17-08	Serbia & Montenegro	W	2-1	Kyiv	Fr	Rebrov [61], Nazarenko [72]		
3-09	Georgia	D	1-1	Tbilisi	WCq	Rotan [43]	BCD	Ovrebo NOR
7-09	Turkey	L	0-1	Kyiv	WCq		67 000	Sars FRA
8-10	Albania	D	2-2	Dnipropetrovsk	WCq	Shevchenko [45], Rotan [86]	24 000	Verbist BEL
12-10	Japan	W	1-0	Kyiv	Fr	Husin [89p]		Lajuks LVA
2006								
28-02	Azerbaijan	D	0-0	Baku	Fr			Sipailo LVA
28-05	Costa Rica	W	4-0	Kyiv	Fr	Nazarenko [27], Vorobei [33], Kalinichenko [38], Bielik [56]	25 000	Ivanov.N RUS
2-06	Italy	D	0-0	Lausanne	Fr		10 000	Nobs SUI
5-06	Libya	W	3-0	Gossau	Fr	Yezerskyi [49], Bielik [87], Vorobei [89]	2 500	Wilzhaber SUI
8-06	Luxembourg	W	3-0	Luxembourg	Fr	Voronin [55], Shevchenko [83], Kalinichenko [84]		Vervecken BEL
14-06	Spain	L	0-4	Leipzig	WCr1		43 000	Busacca SUI
19-06	Saudi Arabia	W	4-0	Hamburg	WCr1	Rusol [4], Rebrov [36], Shevchenko [46], Kalinichenko [84]	50 000	Poll ENG
23-06	Tunisia	W	1-0	Berlin	WCr1	Shevchenko [70p]	72 000	Amarilla PAR
26-06	Switzerland	D	0-0	Cologne	WCr2		45 000	Archundia MEX
30-06	Italy	L	0-3	Hamburg	WCqf		50 000	De Bleeckere BEL

Fr = Friendly match • EC = UEFA EURO 2004™ • WC = FIFA World Cup™ • q = qualifier • BCD = Behind closed doors

UKRAINE NATIONAL TEAM RECORDS AND RECORD SEQUENCES

Records			Sequence records				
Victory	4-0	GEO 1998, AND 1999	Wins	6	2004-2005	Clean sheets	7	2004-2005
Defeat	0-4	CRO 1995	Defeats	2	Six times	Goals scored	10	1995-1996
Player Caps	74	REBROV Serhiy	Undefeated	13	1998-1999	Without goal	3	2003
Player Goals	31	SHEVCHENKO Andriy	Without win	11	2003-2004	Goals against	8	2004

UKRAINE COUNTRY INFORMATION

Capital	Kiev	Independence	1991 from the USSR	GDP per Capita	$5 400
Population	47 732 079	Status	Republic	GNP Ranking	56
Area km²	603 700	Language	Ukrainian, Russian	Dialling code	+380
Population density	79 per km²	Literacy rate	99%	Internet code	.ua
% in urban areas	70%	Main religion	Christian	GMT + / –	+2
Towns/Cities ('000)	Kyiv 2 514; Kharkiv 1 430; Dnipropetrovsk 1 032; Odessa 1 001; Donetsk 987; Zaporizhzhya 796; Lviv 686; Kryvyi Rih 652; Mykolayiv 510; Mariupol 481; Luhansk 451; Makiyivka 376; Vinnytsya 352; Simferopol 342; Sevastopol 332; Kherson 320; Poltava 317; Chernihiv 307; Cherkasy 297				
Neighbours (km)	Russia 1 576; Romania 531; Moldova 939; Hungary 103; Slovakia 97; Poland 526; Belarus 891; Black Sea & Caspian Sea 2 782				
Main stadia	NSK Olimpiyskiy – Kyiv 83 160; Shakhtor – Donetsk 31 547; Ukrajina – Lviv 28 058				

NATIONAL TEAM PLAYERS AND COACHES

Record Caps			Record Goals			Recent Coaches	
REBROV Serhiy	1993-'06	74	SHEVCHENKO Andriy	1995-'06	31	PAVLOV Nikolay	1992
SHOVKOVSKYI Oleksandr	1994-'06	73	REBROV Serhiy	1993-'06	15	BAZYLEVYCH Oleg	1993-'94
SHEVCHENKO Andriy	1995-'06	69	GUSIN Andriy	1993-'06	9	SZABO Jozsef	1994
GUSIN Andriy	1993-'06	69	GUSEINOV Timerlan	1993-'97	8	KONKOV Anatoliy	1995
VASHCHUK Vladyslav	1996-'06	61	VOROBEY Andriy	1994-'06	7	SZABO Jozsef	1996-'99
TYMOSCHUK Anatoliy	2000-'06	59	LEONENKO Viktor	1992-'97	6	LOBANOVSKYI Valeriy	2000-'01
HOLOVKO Olexandr	1995-'04	58	MAXIMOV Yuriy	1992-'02	5	BURYAK Leonid	2001-'03
VOROBEY Andriy	1994-'06	56	POPOV Serhiy	1993-'03	5	BLOKHIN Oleg	2003-

CLUB DIRECTORY

Club	Town/City	Stadium	Capacity	www.	Lge	Cup
FC Arsenal	Kyiv	CSK ZSU	12 000		0	0
FC Borysfen Boryspil	Kyiv	Stadion Kolos	7 500	fcborisfen.kiev.ua	0	0
FC Chernomorets	Odesa	Tsentralnyi	30 767	chernomorets.odessa.ua	0	2
FC Dnipro	Dnipropetrovsk	Stadion Meteor	26 345	fcdnipro.dp.ua	0 - 2	0 - 1
FC Dynamo Kyiv	Kyiv	Valeriy Lobanovskyi	16 888	fcdynamo.kiev.ua	11 - 13	8 - 9
FC Illychivets	Mariupil	Stadion Illchivets	13 000	fcilyich.com.ua	0	0
FC Kryvbas	Kryvyi Rih	Stadion Metalurh	29 782	fckrivbass.dp.ua	0	0
FC Metallist	Kharkiv	Stadion Metallist	28 000	metallist.kharkov.ua	0	0 - 1
FC Metalurh	Donetsk	RSK Olimpiyskiy	24 510	metalurg.donetsk.ua	0	0
FC Metalurh	Zaporizhya	Stadion Metalurh	24 000	fcmetalurg.com.ua	0	0
FC Obolon	Kyiv	Stadion Obolon	6 000	fc.obolon.ua	0	0
FC Shakhtar Donetsk	Donetsk	Stadion Shakhtor	31 547	shakhtar.com	3	5 - 4
FC Tavriya	Simferopol	Stadion Tavriya	20 013	fctavriya.crimea.ua	1	0
FC Volyn	Lutsk	Stadion Avanhard	11 574	fcvolyn.com	0	0
FC Vorskla	Poltava	Stadion Vorskla	24 810	vorskla.com.au	0	0
FC Zakarpattya	Uzhgorod	Stadion Avanhard	12 000		0	0

Where clubs have won trophies in both the Soviet era and post independence, the figure for the Soviet era is given second

RECENT LEAGUE AND CUP RECORD

Championship							Cup		
Year	Champions	Pts	Runners-up	Pts	Third	Pts	Winners	Score	Runners-up
1992	Tavriya Simferopol	1-0	Dynamo Kyiv				Ch'morets Odesa	1-0	Metallist Kharkiv
1993	Dynamo Kyiv	44	Dn. Dnipropetrovsk	44	Ch'morets Odesa	38	Dynamo Kyiv	2-1	Karpaty L'viv
1994	Dynamo Kyiv	56	Shakhtar Donetsk	49	Ch'morets Odesa	48	Ch'morets Odesa	0-0 5-3p	Tavriya Simferopol
1995	Dynamo Kyiv	83	Ch'morets Odesa	73	Dn. Dnipropetrovsk	65	Shakhtar Donetsk	1-1 7-6p	Dn. Dnipropetrovsk
1996	Dynamo Kyiv	79	Ch'morets Odesa	73	Dn. Dnipropetrovsk	63	Dynamo Kyiv	2-0	Nyva Vinnitsa
1997	Dynamo Kyiv	73	Shakhtar Donetsk	62	Vorskla Poltava	58	Shakhtar Donetsk	1-0	Dn. Dnipropetrovsk
1998	Dynamo Kyiv	72	Shakhtar Donetsk	67	Karpaty L'viv	57	Dynamo Kyiv	2-1	CSCA Kyiv
1999	Dynamo Kyiv	74	Shakhtar Donetsk	65	Kryvbas Kryvyi Rih	59	Dynamo Kyiv	3-0	Karpaty L'viv
2000	Dynamo Kyiv	84	Shakhtar Donetsk	66	Kryvbas Kryvyi Rih	60	Dynamo Kyiv	1-0	Kryvbas Kryvyi Rih
2001	Dynamo Kyiv	64	Shakhtar Donetsk	63	Dn. Dnipropetrovsk	55	Shakhtar Donetsk	2-1	CSCA Kyiv
2002	Shakhtar Donetsk	66	Dynamo Kyiv	65	Metalurh Donetsk	42	Shakhtar Donetsk	3-2	Dynamo Kyiv
2003	Dynamo Kyiv	73	Shakhtar Donetsk	70	Metalurh Donetsk	60	Dynamo Kyiv	2-1	Shakhtar Donetsk
2004	Dynamo Kyiv	73	Shakhtar Donetsk	70	Dn. Dnipropetrovsk	57	Shakhtar Donetsk	2-0	Dn. Dnipropetrovsk
2005	Shakhtar Donetsk	80	Dynamo Kyiv	73	Metalurh Donetsk	49	Dynamo Kyiv	1-0	Shakhtar Donetsk
2006	Shakhtar Donetsk	75	Dynamo Kyiv	75	Ch'morets Odesa	45	Dynamo Kyiv	1-0	Metalurh Zapor'hja

Ukrainian clubs played in the Soviet league until the end of the 1991 season

UKRAINE 2005-06

PREMIER LEAGUE

	Pl	W	D	L	F	A	Pts	Shakhtar	Dynamo	Ch'morets	Illychivets	Metalist	Dnipro	Tavriya	Metalurh Z	Metalurh D	Vorskla	Stal	Arsenal	Kharkiv	Kryvbas	Volyn	Z'Pattya
Shakhtar Donetsk †	30	23	6	1	64	14	75		0-1	2-0	6-0	2-0	2-0	1-1	3-1	2-0	0-0	1-1	1-0	3-0	1-0	2-0	3-0
Dynamo Kyiv †	30	23	6	1	68	20	75	2-2		4-1	1-1	2-2	0-2	2-0	1-1	3-1	0-0	4-0	3-1	1-0	3-1	7-1	4-1
Chernomorets Odesa ‡	30	13	6	11	36	31	45	0-1	0-1		1-2	5-2	0-0	1-2	0-0	1-0	1-2	2-2	1-1	1-0	2-1	2-0	2-0
Illychivets Mariupil	30	12	7	11	30	34	43	1-2	1-2	0-1		0-2	0-0	0-1	1-0	1-0	3-2	3-0	3-5	2-1	1-0	1-1	2-0
Metalist Kharkiv	30	12	7	11	35	42	43	1-5	1-2	1-1	1-1		0-6	2-0	3-1	2-0	0-1	1-0	1-2	1-0	1-0	1-0	4-1
Dnipro Dnipropetrovsk	30	11	10	9	33	23	43	2-2	0-3	1-2	0-1	0-0		1-3	3-0	1-0	0-0	0-1	1-0	2-0	1-0	0-0	4-0
Tavriya Simferopol	30	11	6	13	29	31	39	0-3	0-0	1-1	0-1	0-1	0-1		1-0	3-0	2-3	5-2	0-1	2-1	1-0	1-2	1-0
Metalurh Zaporizhya ‡	30	11	6	13	32	40	39	0-3	1-2	1-0	2-1	0-0	0-2	1-0		3-1	0-2	2-1	2-2	3-6	2-1	1-0	3-0
Metalurh Donetsk	30	10	9	11	35	35	39	1-3	0-3	3-2	0-0	3-1	1-1	0-0	0-0		2-0	5-0	2-2	1-1	3-2	4-0	1-0
Vorskla Poltava	30	9	10	11	28	34	37	0-2	0-4	1-2	1-0	0-1	1-1	2-3	3-1	1-1		1-0	2-0	0-0	0-0	2-0	0-0
Stal Alchevsk	30	9	9	12	26	39	36	1-3	1-2	0-1	1-0	1-1	0-0	1-0	1-1	1-1	2-0		1-0	0-0	0-1	2-2	1-0
Arsenal Kyiv	30	9	8	13	31	39	35	0-0	0-2	0-1	0-2	1-1	1-0	1-0	1-2	0-2	2-0	1-1		0-0	1-1	2-1	2-1
FC Kharkiv	30	9	6	15	29	36	33	2-3	0-3	0-1	3-0	1-0	0-1	0-0	1-0	1-0	2-0	0-1	3-1		1-1	3-2	1-0
Kryvbas Kryvyi Rih	30	9	6	15	27	35	33	0-2	0-1	1-0	0-1	2-1	2-2	2-0	1-0	0-1	2-2	2-1	1-2	3-1		2-1	1-0
Volyn Lutsk	30	9	6	15	31	45	33	0-1	1-3	0-3	0-0	3-0	2-1	0-0	0-1	1-2	2-1	0-1	2-1	2-0	3-0		3-1
Zakarpattya Uzhgorod	30	3	6	21	17	53	15	0-3	1-2	2-1	1-1	2-3	1-2	0-1	0-2	0-0	1-1	0-2	2-1	2-1	0-0	1-1	

12/07/2005 - 10/05/2006 • † Qualified for the UEFA Champions League • ‡ Qualified for the UEFA Cup

UKRAINE 2005-06
FIRST DIVISION (2)

	Pl	W	D	L	F	A	Pts
Zorja Luhansk	34	27	6	1	73	14	87
Karpaty Lviv §3	34	26	5	3	53	14	80
Obolon Kyiv	34	22	6	6	51	19	72
Naftovyk-Ukrnafta	34	17	7	10	50	35	58
Dynamo 2 Kyiv	34	15	7	12	51	36	52
Hazovyk-Skala Stryj	34	14	10	10	35	33	52
Podillja Khmelnytskyj	34	14	7	13	39	37	49
Stal Dniprodzerzhinsk	34	13	9	12	34	29	48
Krymteplystja Molodizhne	34	12	11	11	35	34	47
Spartak Ivano-Frank'sk	34	10	15	9	33	31	45
Shakhter 2 Donetsk	34	12	8	14	37	42	44
Helios Kharkiv	34	12	8	14	26	35	44
Dynamo Simferopol	34	10	8	16	40	51	38
Enerhetyk Burshtyn	34	8	12	14	31	44	36
CSCA Kyiv	34	8	8	18	25	52	32
Borysfen Boryspil	34	3	14	17	23	46	23
Spartak Sumy	34	5	5	24	28	68	20
FC Bershad §9	34	3	4	27	14	60	4

30/07/2005 - 23/06/2006 • § = points deducted

Championship play-off: Shakhter Donetsk 2-1 Dynamo Kyiv (Stadion Metalurh, Kryvyj Rih, Att: 29 734. Scorers: Marica [60], Aghahowa [100] for Shakhter; Rodolfo [80] for Dynamo) • Top scorers: BRANDAO, Shakhter, 15; Emmanuel OKODUWA, Arsenal, 15; Olexandr KOSYRIN, Chernomorets/Metalurh Donetsk, 13; Serhiy REBROV, Dynamo, 13; Vasyl SACHKO, Volyn, 13

FFU CUP 2005-06

Third Round		Quarter-finals		Semi-finals		Final	
Dynamo Kyiv *	1						
Metalist Kharkiv	0	Dynamo Kyiv *	2				
Stal Alchevsk *	1	Metalurh Donetsk	0				
Metalurh Donetsk	2			Dynamo Kyiv	2 1		
Vorskla Poltava *	1			Karpaty Lviv *	0 0		
Dnipro Dnipropetrovsk	0	Vorskla Poltava	0				
Shakhtar Donetsk	0	Karpaty Lviv *	1			Dynamo Kyiv	1
Karpaty Lviv *	1					Metalurh Zaporizhya ‡	0
Illychivets Mariupil	1						
Hazovyk-Skala Stryj *	0	Illychivets Mariupil *	2				
Stal Dniprodzerzhinsk*	0	Arsenal Kyiv	0				
Arsenal Kyiv	2			Illychivets Mariupil	1 1		
Kryvbas Kryvyj Rih *	2			Metalurh Zaporizhya *	2 1		
Tavriya Simferopol	0	Kryvbas Kryvyj Rih	0				
Veres Rivne *	2	Metalurh Zaporizhya *	3				
Metalurh Zaporizhya	4						

* Home team/home team in the 1st leg • ‡ Qualified for the UEFA Cup

CUP FINAL

Kyiv
2-05-2006, Att: 25 000

Scorer: Kleber [48] for Dynamo

URU – URUGUAY

NATIONAL TEAM RECORD
JULY 1ST 2002 TO JULY 9TH 2006

PL	W	D	L	F	A	%
46	18	15	13	63	62	55.4

Uruguay were the only former FIFA World Cup™ winners not present at the finals in Germany. Having finished in fifth place in the South American qualifiers the national team faced Australia once again in a play-off and with both nations winning their home legs 1-0 it meant a penalty shoot-out to decide who would travel to Germany - the first time penalties had been used to directly qualify any nation for the finals. Under intense pressure both Dario Rodrigues and Marcelo Zalayeta missed their kicks and when John Aloisi scored, Uruguay missed out. Coach Jorge Fossati quit in the aftermath and was eventually succeeded by the veteran Oscar Tabarez, who had led Uruguay to the FIFA World Cup finals™ back in 1990. He is fortunate that it is possible for half of the South American nations to qualify for the finals so getting to South Africa in 2010 remains a realistic hope but all is not well in Uruguay. In the words of former national team captain Paolo Monetro, Uruguay has "a thousand teams - all of them broke - who play on five pitches, all of which are a disaster, and eight people turn up to watch." In a bid to get in line with much of the rest of the world, the Uruguayan season was switched from the calendar year to the timing used by

INTERNATIONAL HONOURS
FIFA World Cup™ 1930 1950   **Olympic Gold** 1924 1928
Qualified for the FIFA World Cup™ finals 1930 (hosts) 1950 1954 1962 1966 1970 1986 1990 2002
Copa América 1916 1917 1920 1923 1924 1926 1935 1942 1956 1959 1967 1983 1987 1995
Panamerican Games 1983 **Juventud de América** 1954 1958 1964 1975 1977 1979 1981
Copa Toyota Libertadores Peñarol 1960 1961 1966 1982 1987 Nacional 1971 1980 1988

most European countries with the finish midway through the year. That meant a short interim championship in the first half of 1995, a tournament that ended in controversy after Defensor and Nacional both finished the campaign on equal points. Nacional had won their final game against Rocha thanks to a penalty seven minutes into injury-time. Defensor cried foul and refused to take part in the play-off and so the title was awarded to Nacional. Rocha were surprise winners of the following season's Apertura but only because Nacional had three points deducted following crowd trouble dating back to 2004. Worse was to follow in the Clausura, however, when a gang of Peñarol fans stabbed to death a Cerro fan after a fixture between the two on March 11, 2006. The League was suspended for three weeks as football faced its most grave crisis in years. Peñarol's 12 point deduction meant that they finished bottom of the Clausura, a totally new experience for one of the 'big two' of Uruguayan football. Nacional were crowned champions after beating Rocha in a play-off to win their sixth title in nine years, having won just one in the previous 14 years. Uruguayan hopes now rest with them to win a first Copa Libertadores for the country since 1988.

Asociación Uruguaya de Fútbol (AUF)
Guayabo 1531, Montevideo 11200, Uruguay
Tel +59 82 4004814   Fax +59 82 4090550
auf@auf.org.uy   www.auf.org.uy
President: FIGUEREDO Eugenio   General Secretary: ALMADA Jorge Dr
Vice-President: DAMIANI Juan Pedro   Treasurer: PASTORINI Daniel Dr   Media Officer: GONZALEZ Heber
Men's Coach: FOSSATI Jorge   Women's Coach: DUARTE Juan
AUF formed: 1900   CONMEBOL: 1916   FIFA: 1923
Sky blue with white trimmings, Black shorts, Black socks

RECENT INTERNATIONAL MATCHES PLAYED BY URUGUAY

2003	Opponents	Score		Venue	Comp	Scorers	Att	Referee
28-03	Japan	D	2-2	Tokyo	Fr	Forlan [21], Lembo [25]	54 039	Kim Tae Young KOR
8-06	Korea Republic	W	2-0	Seoul	Fr	Hiornos [12], Abreu [53]		Yoshida JPN
16-07	Argentina	D	2-2	La Plata	Fr	Chevanton [7], Milito OG [37]	35 000	Gonzalez PAR
24-07	Peru	W	4-3	Lima	Fr	Liguera 2 [10 72], Sosa [49], Vigneri [79]		Garay Evia PER
30-07	Peru	W	1-0	Montevideo	Fr	Liguera [54]	9 000	Mendez URU
20-08	Argentina	L	2-3	Florence	Fr	Forlan [2], Abreu [57]	3 000	De Santis ITA
7-09	Bolivia	W	5-0	Montevideo	WCq	Forlan [17], Chevanton 2 [40 61], Abeijon [83], Bueno [88]	39 253	Ricaldi
10-09	Paraguay	L	1-4	Asuncion	WCq	Chevanton [24]	15 000	Ruiz COL
15-10	Mexico	W	2-0	Chicago	Fr	Perrone 2 [27 63]		Kennedy USA
15-11	Chile	W	2-1	Montevideo	WCq	Chevanton [31], Romero [49]	60 000	Martin ARG
19-11	Brazil	D	3-3	Curitiba	WCq	Forlan 2 [57 76], Gilberto Silva OG [78]	28 000	Elizondo ARG
2004								
18-02	Jamaica	L	0-2	Kingston	Fr		27 000	Gordon TRI
31-03	Venezuela	L	0-3	Montevideo	WCq		40 094	Ortube BOL
1-06	Peru	L	1-3	Montevideo	WCq	Forlan [72]	30 000	Selman CHI
6-06	Colombia	L	0-5	Barranquilla	WCq		7 000	Amarilla PAR
7-07	Mexico	D	2-2	Chiclayo	CAr1	Bueno [42], Montero [87]	25 000	Hidalgo PER
10-07	Ecuador	W	2-1	Chiclayo	CAr1	Forlan [61], Bueno [79]	25 000	Brand VEN
13-07	Argentina	L	2-4	Piura	CAr1	Estoyanoff [7], Sanchez.V [39]	24 000	Selman CHI
18-07	Paraguay	W	3-1	Tacna	CAqf	Bueno [40p], Silva 2 [65 88]	20 000	Baldassi ARG
21-07	Brazil	D	1-1	Lima	CAsf	Sosa [22], L 3-5p	10 000	Rodriguez Moreno MEX
24-07	Colombia	W	2-1	Cusco	CA3p	Estoyanoff [4], Sanchez.V [88]	35 000	Ortube BOL
5-09	Ecuador	W	1-0	Montevideo	WCq	Bueno [57]	28 000	Hidalgo PER
9-10	Argentina	L	2-4	Buenos Aires	WCq	Rodriguez.C [63], Chevanton [86]	50 000	Souza BRA
12-10	Bolivia	D	0-0	La Paz	WCq		24 349	Rezende BRA
17-11	Paraguay	W	1-0	Montevideo	WCq	Montero [78]	35 000	Simon BRA
2005								
26-03	Chile	D	1-1	Santiago	WCq	Regueiro [4]	55 000	Ruiz COL
30-03	Brazil	D	1-1	Montevideo	WCq	Forlan [48]	60 000	Baldassi ARG
4-06	Venezuela	D	1-1	Maracaibo	WCq	Forlan [2]	12 504	Brazenas ARG
7-06	Peru	D	0-0	Lima	WCq		31 515	Baldassi ARG
17-08	Spain	L	0-2	Gijon	Fr		25 885	Benquerenca POR
4-09	Colombia	W	3-2	Montevideo	WCq	Zalayeta 3 [42 51 86]	60 000	Elizondo ARG
8-10	Ecuador	D	0-0	Quito	WCq		37 270	Rezende BRA
12-10	Argentina	W	1-0	Montevideo	WCq	Recoba [46]	55 000	Souza BRA
26-10	Mexico	L	1-3	Guadalajara	Fr	Abreu [17]	45 000	Guajardo MEX
12-11	Australia	W	1-0	Montevideo	WCpo	Rodriguez.D [37]	55 000	Larsen DEN
16-11	Australia	L	0-1	Sydney	WCpo		82 698	Medina Cantalejo ESP
2006								
1-03	England	L	1-2	Liverpool	Fr	Pouso [26]	40 013	Farina ITA
21-05	Northern Ireland	W	1-0	New Jersey	Fr	Estoyanoff [33]	4 152	
23-05	Romania	W	2-0	Los Angeles	Fr	Vargas 2 [46 59]	10 000	Stott USA
27-05	Serbia & Montenegro	D	1-1	Belgrade	Fr	Godin [82]	30 000	Kos SVN
30-05	Libya	W	2-1	Radès/Tunis	Fr	Vigneri [15], Abreu [34]		
4-06	Tunisia	D	0-0	Radès/Tunis	Fr	W 3-1p		

Fr = Friendly match • CA = Copa América • WC = FIFA World Cup™
q = qualifier • po = play-off • r1 = first round group • qf = quarter-final • sf = semi-final • 3p = third place play-off

URUGUAY NATIONAL TEAM RECORDS AND RECORD SEQUENCES

Records			Sequence records					
Victory	9-0	BOL 1927	Wins	7	1941-42, 1980-81	Clean sheets	6	1969-1970
Defeat	0-6	ARG 1902	Defeats	5	1916	Goals scored	20	1953-1956
Player Caps	78	RODRIGUEZ Rodolfo	Undefeated	14	1967-1968	Without goal	4	1925, 1968. 1976
Player Goals	31	SCARONE Héctor	Without win	9	1986	Goals against	18	1961-1963

URUGUAY COUNTRY INFORMATION

Capital	Montevideo	Independence	1828 from Spain		GDP per Capita	$12 800
Population	3 339 237	Status	Republic		GNP Ranking	66
Area km²	176 220	Language	Spanish		Dialling code	+598
Population density	19 per km²	Literacy rate	98%		Internet code	uy
% in urban areas	90%	Main religion	Christian		GMT + / –	-3
Towns/Cities ('000)	Montevideo 1 305; Ciudad de la Costa 112; Salto 104; Paysandú 78; Las Piedras 73; Rivera 68					
Neighbours (km)	Argentina 579; Brazil 985; South Atlantic Ocean 660					
Main stadia	Estadio Centenario – Montevideo 73 609					

NATIONAL TEAM PLAYERS AND COACHES

Record Caps			Record Goals			Recent Coaches	
RODRIGUEZ Rodolfo	1976-'86	78	SCARONE Héctor	1917-'30	31	FLEITAS Roberto	1994
FRANCESCOLI Enzo	1982-'97	72	ROMANO Angel	1911-'27	28	NUNEZ Hector	1994-'96
ROMANO Angel	1911-'27	68	MIGUEZ Omar	1950-'58	27	AHUNTCHAIN Juan	1996-'97
AGUILERA Carlos	1982-'97	65	PETRONE Pedro	1923-'30	24	MASPOLI Roque	1997
RECOBA Alvaro	1995-'05	64	AGUILERA Carlos	1982-'97	23	PUA Victor	1997-'99
BARRIOS Jorge	1980-'92	61	MORENA Fernando	1971-'83	22	PASSARELLA Daniel	1999-'00
MONTERO Paolo	1991-'05	61	PIENDIBENE José	1909-'22	21	PUA Victor	2001-'03
GUTIERREZ Nelson	1983-'90	56	CASTRO Héctor	1924-'35	20	CARRASCO Juan	2003-'04
HERRERA José	1988-'97	56	VARELA Severino	1935-'42	19	FOSSATI Jorge	2004-'05
GARCIA Pablo	1997-'06	55	SCARONE Carlos	1909-'22	18	TABAREZ Oscar	2006-

CLUB DIRECTORY

Club	Town/City	Stadium	Capacity	www.	Lge	CL
Club Bella Vista	Montevideo	Jose Nasazzi	15 000		1	0
CS Cerrito	Montevideo	Estadio Charrua	12 000		0	0
CA Cerro	Montevideo	Luis Troccoli	25 000		0	0
CA Plaza	Colonia	Supicci	12 000		0	0
Danubio FC	Montevideo	Jardines del Hipodromo	16 000	danubio.org.uy	2	0
Defensor Sporting Club	Montevideo	Luis Franzini	18 000		3	0
CA Fénix	Montevideo	Parque Capurro	10 000		0	0
Liverpool FC	Montevideo	Estadio Belvedere	9 500		0	0
Club Nacional de Fútbol	Montevideo	Estadio Centenario	73 609	nacional.com.uy	41	3
Paysandú FC	Paysandú	Parque Artigas	25 000		0	0
CA Peñarol	Montevideo	Estadio Centenario	73 609	penarol.org	47	5
Rampla Juniors FC	Montevideo	Estadio Olimpico	9 500	rampla.com	1	0
River Plate	Montevideo	Federico Saroldi	12 000		4	0
Rocha FC	Rocha	Mario Sobrero	8 000		0	0
Tacuarembó FC	Tacuarembó	Raul Goyenola	12 000		0	0
Montevideo Wanderers	Montevideo	Alfredo Victor Viera	12 500	mwfc.com.uy	0	0

FIFA/COCA-COLA WORLD RANKING

1993	1994	1995	1996	1997	1998	1999	2000	2001	2002	2003	2004	2005		High		Low	
17	37	32	43	40	76	46	32	22	28	21	16	18		14	05/94	76	12/98

2005–2006											
08/05	09/05	10/05	11/05	12/05	01/06	02/06	03/06	04/06	05/06	06/06	07/06
25	25	17	18	18	18	21	23	22	22	-	14

THE FIFA BIG COUNT OF 2000

	Male	Female		Male	Female
Registered players	107 873	600	Referees	400	0
Non registered players	85 000	1 000	Officials	2 000	100
Youth players	7 212	100	Total involved	204 285	
Total players	201 785		Number of clubs	1 100	
Professional players	1 000	0	Number of teams	2 000	

URUGUAY 2005

PRIMERA DIVISION PROFESSIONAL — TORNEO ESPECIAL

	PI	W	D	L	F	A	Pts	Nacional	Defensor	Peñarol	Danubio	Rocha	Liverpool	Rentistas	Miramar	Wanderers	River Plate	Cerrito	Tacuarembó	Fénix	Paysandú	Rampla Jun	Plaza	Cerro	Colonia
Nacional	17	12	5	0	39	16	41					3-2	1-1				2-0	2-2		4-0	1-0	3-1		1-0	3-2
Defensor Sporting	17	12	5	0	33	13	41	1-1					1-0				2-2	4-2		1-0	4-1	3-1		2-2	2-0
Peñarol	17	10	5	2	28	19	35	2-2	1-1		2-1			2-2	1-3	2-1		2-2				1-0			
Danubio	17	8	4	5	23	16	28	1-1	0-2				1-0	1-1		5-2		0-1						2-0	2-0
Rocha	17	6	7	4	27	21	25		2-3	0-1				1-1				2-1	0-0	1-1	1-0			6-1	1-1
Liverpool	17	7	4	6	26	25	25	1-3		1-2				2-0	1-5		3-3	0-1						1-0	3-0
Rentistas	17	6	6	5	30	25	24	1-5	0-0	1-2						2-2	5-1	3-3	2-0	1-1					4-0
Miramar Misiones	17	7	2	8	33	29	23	1-3	1-2							1-2	1-2	1-2	1-1		4-1	3-1			1-2
Montevideo Wanderers	17	6	5	6	30	33	23	1-2									2-0	2-2	2-4	2-1	2-0			3-1	0-0
River Plate	17	6	4	7	34	32	22			0-1	0-2	0-1						4-2	2-1	5-1	3-4	2-2		3-1	
Cerrito	17	5	6	6	21	19	21												0-1	3-0	0-0	2-0	2-1	4-2	2-2
Tacuarembó	17	5	6	6	17	18	21	0-1		2-2			1-2							3-1	1-1	0-1		2-1	0-0
Fénix	17	5	4	8	19	26	19			0-1	0-1		2-0		2-0						2-0	4-4		1-2	1-2
Paysandú	17	3	5	9	23	34	14			1-2	1-3		3-3	1-3					3-1			2-2		0-1	2-2
Rampla Juniors	17	3	5	9	19	31	14					2-2		1-1		1-4			1-2				0-0	1-0	0-0 2-1
Plaza Colonia	17	3	5	9	8	27	14	1-4	0-3		0-2						1-0				0-3	0-0		0-0	2-0
Cerro	17	3	4	10	20	30	13		0-2					0-1	0-1	0-3	1-2			2-1	2-3			2-0	4-2
Colonia Juan Lacaze	17	3	4	10	15	31	13		0-3			1-1	1-2		1-2	2-0	1-1					1-1	1-3		

3/03/2005 - 3/07/2005 • There was supposed to be a play-off between Nacional and Defensor for the title but Defensor withdrew in protest. In their final game of the season against Rocha, Nacional had been awarded a penalty seven minutes into injury time to win the game and draw level with Defensor • Match in bold awarded • Top scorers: Pablo GRANOCHE, Miramar, 16; ZINHO, Rentistas, 14; Sergio BLANCO, Wanderers, 12; Osvaldo CANOBBIO, River, 11

URUGUAY 2005-06

PRIMERA DIVISION PROFESSIONAL — TABLA ANUAL

	PI	W	D	L	F	A	Pts	Nacional	Defensor	Danubio	C. Español	Rampla Jun	Rentistas	Cerrito	Liverpool	Rocha	River Plate	Bella Vista	Cerro	Colonia	Wanderers	Tacuarembó	Peñarol	Miramar	Plaza	Fénix	Paysandú
Nacional §3 †	33	21	9	3	63	28	69		2-2	1-2	1-1	2-1	1-0	1-0	0-4	0-0	2-1	0-2	5-1	2-0	2-2	1-0	4-1				5-0
Defensor Sporting ‡	33	15	12	6	55	36	57	1-3		4-0		4-2	2-2	4-1	1-2	0-2	1-0	1-1	4-3	2-0	0-0	1-0	1-1	1-0		1-2	2-0
Danubio ‡	33	17	6	10	67	49	57	3-4	0-1		0-2	3-1	0-1	2-0	5-2	1-2	2-1	2-1	2-3	3-0	3-1	4-2	0-1	3-1			3-3
Central Español ‡	16	8	3	5	19	16	55	1-1		0-2		2-1	2-0		0-2		2-1	2-0		1-0	0-3	2					
Rampla Juniors ‡	33	14	7	12	59	54	49	3-0	1-2	2-0	3-1		2-0	2-2	2-2	1-0	1-4		0-5	3-5	1-0	4-1	1-0	1-1		5-1	
Rentistas ‡	33	14	6	13	49	44	48	1-3	0-1	1-1	5-2			1-3	2-1	1-0	1-2	4-2	1-3	0-1	2-2	1-3	3-0	4-1		3-2	
Cerrito	33	11	15	7	37	34	48	1-1	2-1	1-1	1-1	0-3	2-1		1-1	1-0	0-0	1-2	1-1	1-1	1-1	1-1	1-0	1-0			0-1
Liverpool	33	12	11	10	46	45	47	0-4	2-5	1-2	4-0	2-2	1-2	0		1-0	2-1	3-1	1-2	3-3	0-0	1-2	2-1			3-1	
Rocha	33	13	6	14	55	54	45	2-4	2-2	4-2		2-1	1-2	2-0	2-1		2-1		4-1	5-3	3-1	1-1	0-1	2-2	3-0	3-1	
River Plate	33	12	8	13	43	42	44	0-2	2-2	0-3		2-2	2-0	0-1	1-2	2-1		2-1	1-1	0-0	1-0	0-1	0-3	1-2		4-2	
Bella Vista	16	3	7		18	19	39	1-2		1-0	1-2		1-1		1-1	1-0			0-1	1-0	1-1						
Cerro §6	33	11	10	12	46	41	37	1-2	1-1	1-1	0-2	2-1	2-2	1-1	0-0	3-0	1-1			5-1	2-4	1-0	0-0	0-1	2-0		
Colonia Juan Lacaze	33	9	10	14	35	49	37	0-0	0-0	0-2	0-1	0-2	0-3	0-2	0-0	2-0	0-2		0-1		1-1	0-0	1-0	3-2	0-0		
Montevideo Wanderers	33	8	12	13	45	51	36	0-1	0-1	1-2		1-3	2-1	3-2	1-1	1-0	1-2		2-0	1-2		3-1	1-1	1-1		3-2	
Tacuarembó	33	8	11	14	25	40	35		1-1	1-0	1-1	2-1	2-0	0-3	1-0	0-0		1-4	1-1				1-0	1-0			
Peñarol §12	33	11	11	11	42	51	32	0-0	1-2	1-2	7	1-0	1-1	0-0	1-3	4-4	2-4	1-0	4-1	1-5	0-0	2-1			3-2		
Miramar Misiones	33	6	14	13	35	48	32	1-1	1-4	3-3	0-3	0-0	0-1	0-1	3-3	1-1	0-2	1-0	2-2	3-2	1-1	2-1			0-0		
Plaza Colonia	17	5	6	6	15	23	21	1-1	0-0		1-0		0-0		1-0	3-0	0-0									2-2	
Fénix	17	3	4	7	18	31	13	1-2		0-2		1-3		0-1	0-1		1-1	2-2	2-2		2-0	2-0					
Paysandú	17	1	5	11	18	39	8	0-2	0-1		2-3	2-3		1-1	1-5	2-0		1-3			2-2						

20/08/2005 - 19/06/2006 • † Qualified for the Copa Libertadores 2007 • ‡ Qualified for the Copa Artigas • Apertura matches are in the shaded boxes • Match in bold was awarded 2-0 • The points for Central Español and Bella Vista are rounded up to reflect a full season
Top scorers: José Pedro CARDOSO, Rocha, 17; Ignacio GONZALEZ, Danubio 13

URUGUAY 2005-06
TORNEO APERTURA

	Pl	W	D	L	F	A	Pts
Rocha	17	10	3	4	37	25	33
Nacional §3	17	9	7	1	32	16	31
Danubio	17	8	3	6	36	25	27
Rampla Juniors	17	8	2	7	35	25	26
Colonia Juan Lacaze	17	6	8	3	23	19	26
Cerrito	17	6	7	4	20	18	25
Peñarol	17	6	7	4	22	26	25
River Plate	17	6	6	5	24	22	24
Rentistas	17	7	3	7	21	22	24
Liverpool	17	5	7	5	19	18	22
Defensor Sporting	17	5	7	5	21	21	22
Cerro	17	5	7	5	23	25	22
Plaza Colonia	17	5	6	6	15	23	21
Montevideo Wanderers	17	4	8	5	27	32	20
Miramar Misiones	17	3	9	5	18	18	18
Tacuarembó	17	4	5	8	13	21	17
Fénix	17	3	4	10	22	31	13
Paysandú	17	1	5	11	18	39	8

20/08/2005 - 17/12/2005 • Relegation based on results over the whole of 2005 • Relegation play-off: Plaza 2-2 0-1 Cerro §3 = three points deducted

URUGUAY 2005-06
TORNEO CLAUSURA

	Pl	W	D	L	F	A	Pts
Nacional	16	12	2	2	31	12	38
Defensor Sporting	16	10	5	1	34	15	35
Danubio	16	9	3	4	31	24	30
Central Español	16	8	3	5	19	16	27
Liverpool	16	7	4	5	27	27	25
Rentistas	16	7	3	6	28	22	24
Cerrito	16	5	8	3	17	16	23
Rampla Juniors	16	6	5	5	24	29	23
River Plate	16	6	2	8	19	20	20
Bella Vista	16	5	4	7	18	19	19
Tacuarembó	16	4	6	6	12	19	18
Montevideo Wanderers	16	4	4	8	18	19	16
Cerro §6	16	6	3	7	23	16	15
Miramar Misiones	16	3	5	8	17	30	14
Rocha	16	3	3	10	18	29	12
Colonia Juan Lacaze	16	3	2	11	12	30	11
Peñarol §12	16	5	4	7	20	25	7

18/02/2006 - 19/06/2006 • Relegation based on results over the whole of the 2005 and 2005-06 seasons • § = points deducted

CHAMPIONSHIP PLAY-OFFS

Semi-finals

Rocha	1	0
Nacional	4	2

Finals

Nacional †	

The winners of the Apertura and Clausura met to determine who would play the team with the best overall record in the final. As Nacional had the best overall record they only had to win the semi-final

† Qualified for the 2007 Copa Libertadores

CHAMPIONSHIP FINAL 2006

Estadio Parque Central, Montevideo, 25-06-2006, Ref: Silvera

Nacional	2	Luis Suarez [62], Sebastian Vasquez [77]
Rocha	0	

Nacional - Jorge BAVA - Mauricio VICTORINO, Diego JAUME, Ignacio PALLAS, Daniel LEITES, Sebastian VAZQUEZ, Marco VANZINI (Agustin VIANA 79), Jorge BRITEZ, Javier DELGADO, Luis SUAREZ, Gonzalo CASTRO (Jose Luis GARCES 79). Tr: Martin LASARTE

Rocha - Alvaro GARCIA - Cristiano ARAUJO, Pablo SEIJAS (Marcelo SEGALES 71), Diego BONELLI, Diego CIZ (Ruben PREDAJA 67), Alvaro BECERRA, Martin GONZALEZ, Leonardo MALDONADO, Luis MAGUREGUY (Mauro ALDAVE 67), Heber CARO, José CARDOZO. Tr: Hector MENDEZ

URUGUAY 2006
COPA ARTIGAS

	Pl	W	D	L	F	A	Pts	Da	Na	CE	Re	RJ
Defensor Sporting †	5	3	2	0	9	3	11	1-1	1-1	2-0	3-1	2-0
Danubio †	5	3	1	1	16	7	10		1-3	5-0	4-2	5-1
Nacional ‡	5	2	2	1	8	6	8			1-1	0-3	3-0
Central Español ‡	5	2	1	2	5	9	7				2-1	2-0
Rentistas	5	1	1	3	9	11	4					2-2
Rampla Juniors	5	0	1	4	3	14	1					

28/06/2006 - 13/07/2006 • † Qualified for the 2007 Copa Libertadores • ‡ Qualified for the 2006 Copa Sudamericana

URUGUAY LEAGUE RECORD

Year	Winners	Score	Runners-up
1995	Peñarol	1-0 1-2 3-1	Nacional
1996	Peñarol	1-0 1-1	Nacional
1997	Peñarol	1-0 3-0	Defensor Sporting
1998	Nacional	†	
1999	Peñarol	1-1 1-1 2-1	Nacional
2000	Nacional	1-0 1-1	Peñarol
2001	Nacional	2-2 2-1	Danubio
2002	Nacional	2-1 2-1	Danubio
2003	Peñarol	1-0	Nacional
2004	Danubio	1-0	Nacional
2005	Nacional	w-o	Defensor Sporting
2006	Nacional	4-1 2-0	Rocha

† Automatic champions as winners of both the Apertura and Clausura

USA - UNITED STATES OF AMERICA

NATIONAL TEAM RECORD
JULY 1ST 2002 TO JULY 9TH 2006

PL	W	D	L	F	A	%
65	38	15	12	111	45	70

Just before the 2006 FIFA World Cup™ finals kicked off in Germany, the USA national team was ranked as the fourth best in the world, but there were few who believed that Bruce Arena's team had what it took to reach a semi-final that their ranking suggested they should. In the event they didn't get past the first round and after their 3-0 opening game reverse against the Czech Republic, it looked as if their ranking would be made to look ridiculous. Against Italy in the next match, however, the USA showed a determination and a fighting spirit that did the team proud in very difficult circumstances. The 1-1 draw was only one of two games that the world champions didn't win, whilst the American goal was the only one Italy conceded from open play in the whole tournament. A victory against Ghana in their final game would have still seen the USA through but a debatable penalty just before half time gave the Ghanaians a 2-1 advantage they held on to. There was disappointment and criticism at home of the team but if you bear in mind that Italy went on to win the title, the Czech Republic were ranked number two in the world and that Ghana are almost certainly the best team in Africa at the moment, then the performance doesn't look too bad.

INTERNATIONAL HONOURS

FIFA Women's World Cup 1991 1999   **Women's Olympic Gold** 1996 2004   **FIFA U-19 Women's World Championship** 2002
Qualified for the FIFA World Cup™ 1930 1934 1950 1990 1994 1998 2002 2006
CONCACAF Gold Cup 1991 2002 2005   **CONCACAF Women's Gold Cup** 1991 1993 1994 2000 2002
Panamerican Games 1991   **CONCACAF U-17** 1983 1992
CONCACAF Champions Cup DC United 1998 Los Angeles Galaxy 2000

Remarkably, Major League Soccer carried on during the finals despite the fact that 11 of the squad played for teams in the League. World Cup or no World Cup the show must go on. The 2005 season was dominated by Los Angeles Galaxy who became the third club after DC United in 1996 and Chicago Fire in 1998 to do the double of MLS Cup and the US Open Cup. The season opened with two new franchises - Real Salt Lake and Chivas USA, the latter an offshoot of Chivas Guadalajara of Mexico. Neither fared well and it was San Jose who finished the regular season with the best record. In MLS, however, that counts for little and they were knocked out in the first round of the play-offs by Galaxy, who then beat Colorado Rapids to qualify for the Championship game. There they met New England who had won the Eastern Conference in the regular season and the conference final. MLS Cup 2005 was won by a solitary extra time goal from Guatemalan Guillermo 'Pando' Ramirez who had endured a nightmare season for the club before then. A source of concern was the abject performance by both Galaxy and DC United in the CONCACAF Champions' Cup, both of whom were knocked out by Costa Rican clubs.

US Soccer Federation (USSF)
US Soccer House, 1801 S. Prairie Avenue, Chicago IL 60616, USA
Tel +1 312 8081300   Fax +1 312 8081301
communications@ussoccer.org   www.ussoccer.com
President: GULATI Sunil   General Secretary: FLYNN Dan
Vice-President: EDWARDS Mike   Treasurer: GOAZIOU Bill   Media Officer: MOORHOUSE Jim
Men's Coach: TBD   Women's Coach: RYAN Greg
USSF formed: 1913   CONCACAF: 1961   FIFA: 1914
White shirts with a red and blue panel on the left, Blue shorts, White socks

RECENT INTERNATIONAL MATCHES PLAYED BY THE USA

2004	Opponents	Score		Venue	Comp	Scorers	Att	Referee
13-06	Grenada	W	3-0	Columbus	WCq	Beasley 2 [45 71], Vanney [90]	9 137	Navarro CAN
20-06	Grenada	W	3-2	St George's	WCq	Donovan [6], Wolff [19], Beasley [76]	15 267	Brizan TRI
11-07	Poland	D	1-1	Chicago	Fr	Bocanegra	39 529	
18-08	Jamaica	D	1-1	Kingston	WCq	Ching [88]	27 000	Mattus CRC
4-09	El Salvador	W	2-0	Boston	WCq	Ching [5], Donovan [68]	25 266	Brizan TRI
8-09	Panama	D	1-1	Panama City	WCq	Jones.C [91+]	14 500	Rodriguez MEX
9-10	El Salvador	W	2-0	San Salvador	WCq	McBride [29], Johnson [75]	20 000	Batres GUA
13-10	Panama	W	6-0	Washington	WCq	Donovan 2 [21 56], Johnson 3 [69 84 86], Torres OG [89]	19 793	Ramdhan TRI
17-11	Jamaica	D	1-1	Columbus	WCq	Johnson [15]	9 088	Navarro CAN
2005								
9-02	Trinidad and Tobago	W	2-1	Port of Spain	WCq	Johnson [23], Lewis [53]	11 000	Archundia MEX
9-03	Colombia	W	3-0	Fullerton	Fr	Noonan [25], Marshall [33], Mathis [66]	7 086	Rodriguez MEX
19-03	Honduras	W	1-0	Albuquerque	Fr	Johnson [45]	9 222	Navorro CAN
27-03	Mexico	L	1-2	Mexico City	WCq	Lewis [58]	84 000	Sibrian SLV
30-03	Guatemala	W	2-0	Birmingham	WCq	Johnson [11], Ralston [69]	31 624	Ramdhan TRI
28-05	England	L	1-2	Chicago	Fr	Dempsey [79]	47 637	Archundia MEX
4-06	Costa Rica	W	3-0	Salt Lake City	WCq	Donovan 2 [10 62], McBride [87]	40 576	Batres GUA
8-06	Panama	W	3-0	Panama City	WCq	Bocanegra [6], Donovan [19], McBride [39]	15 000	Navarro CAN
7-07	Cuba	W	4-1	Seattle	GCr1	Dempsey [44], Donovan 2 [87 92+], Beasley [89]	15 831	Pineda HON
9-07	Canada	W	2-0	Seattle	GCr1	Hutchinson OG [48], Donovan [90]	15 109	Brizan TRI
12-07	Costa Rica	D	0-0	Boston	GCr1		15 211	Archundia MEX
16-07	Jamaica	W	3-1	Boston	GCqf	Wolff [6], Beasley 2 [42 83]	22 108	Batres GUA
21-07	Honduras	W	2-1	New Jersey	GCsf	O'Brien [86], Onyewu [92+]	41 721	Prendergast JAM
24-07	Panama	D	0-0	New Jersey	GCf		31 018	Batres GUA
17-08	Trinidad & Tobago	W	1-0	Hartford	WCq	McBride [2]	25 500	Rodriguez MEX
3-09	Mexico	W	2-0	Columbus	WCq	Ralston [53], Beasley [57]	24 685	Batres GUA
7-09	Guatemala	D	0-0	Guatemala City	WCq		27 000	Rodriguez MEX
8-10	Costa Rica	L	0-3	San Jose	WCq		18 000	Archundia MEX
12-10	Panama	W	2-0	Boston	WCq	Martino [51], Twellman [57]	2 500	Alcala MEX
12-11	Scotland	D	1-1	Glasgow	Fr	Wolff [9p]	26 708	Undiano Mallenco ESP
2006								
22-01	Canada	D	0-0	San Diego	Fr		6 077	Archundia MEX
29-01	Norway	W	5-0	Carson	Fr	Twellman 3 [5 18 76], Pope [67], Klein [87]	16 366	Ruiz COL
10-02	Japan	W	3-2	San Francisco	Fr	Pope [24], Dempsey [39], Twellman [50]	37 365	Elizondo ARG
19-02	Guatemala	W	4-0	Frisco	Fr	Olsen [38], Ching [45], Johnsen [47], Klein [71]	14 453	Navarro CAN
1-03	Poland	W	1-0	Kaiserslautern	Fr	Dempsey [48]	13 395	Kinhofer GER
22-03	Germany	L	1-4	Dortmund	Fr	Cherundolo [85]	64 500	Frojdfeldt SWE
11-04	Jamaica	D	1-1	Cary	Fr	Olsen [25]	8 093	Gasso MEX
23-05	Morocco	L	0-1	Nashville	Fr		26 141	Navarro CAN
26-05	Venezuela	W	2-0	Cleveland	Fr	Ching [36], Dempsey [69]	29 745	Morales MEX
28-05	Latvia	W	1-0	Hartford	Fr	McBride [43]	24 636	Dipiero CAN
12-06	Czech Republic	L	0-3	Gelsenkirchen	WCr1		52 000	Amarilla PAR
17-06	Italy	D	1-1	Kaiserslautern	WCr1	OG [27]	46 000	Larrionda URU
22-06	Ghana	L	1-2	Nuremberg	WCr1	Dempsey [43]	41 000	Merk GER

Fr = Friendly match • CC = FIFA Confederations Cup • GC = CONCACAF Gold Cup • WC = FIFA World Cup™
q = qualifier • r1 = first round group • qf = quarter-final • sf = semi-final • 3p = third place play-off • f = final

USA NATIONAL TEAM RECORDS AND RECORD SEQUENCES

Records			Sequence records		
Victory	8-1	CAY 1993	Wins	6	1997-1998
Defeat	0-11	NOR 1948	Defeats	13	1973-1975
Player Caps	164	JONES Cobi	Undefeated	16	2004-2005
Player Goals	34	WYNALDA Eric	Without win	16	1973-1976
			Clean sheets	5	2003
			Goals scored	23	2004-2005
			Without goal	5	1990-1991
			Goals against	14	1973-1976

USA COUNTRY INFORMATION

Capital	Washington DC	Independence	1776 from Great Britain	GDP per Capita	$37 800
Population	293 027 571	Status	Republic	GNP Ranking	1
Area km²	9 631 418	Language	English, Spanish	Dialling code	+1
Population density	30 per km²	Literacy rate	97%	Internet code	.us
% in urban areas	76%	Main religion	Christian	GMT + / –	-6 to -11
Towns/Cities ('000)	New York 22 313; Los Angeles 17 542; Chicago 9 418; Washington-Baltimore 8 036; San Francisco 7 533; Philadelphia 6 254; Boston 5 908; Dallas 5 896; Detroit 5 885; Houston 5 194; Atlanta 4 716; San Diego 4 688; Miami 4 286; Phoenix 3 792; Seattle 3 769; Minneapolis 3 162; Cleveland 2 956; Denver 2 685; Saint Louis 2 629; Tampa 2 584; Portland 2 467; Pittsburgh 2 332; Cincinnati 2 038; Sacramento 1 980; Las Vegas 1 952				
Neighbours (km)	Canada 8 893; Mexico 3 141; North Atlantic, North Pacific & Gulf of Mexico 19 924				
Main stadia	Rose Bowl – Pasadena 92 542; Gillette Stadium – Foxboro/Boston 68 756; RFK Memorial – Washington 56 454; Home Depot Centre – Carson 27 000; Crew Stadium – Columbus 22 555				

CLUB DIRECTORY

Club	Town/City	Stadium	Capacity	www.	Lge	Cup	CL
Chicago Fire	Chicago	Soldier Field	20 000	chicagofire.mlsnet.com	1	3	0
Chivas USA	Carson/Los Angeles	Home Depot Centre	27 000	chivas.usa.mlsnet.com	0	0	0
Colorado Rapids	Denver	Invesco Field	76 125	coloradorapids.com	0	0	0
Columbus Crew	Columbus	Crew Stadium	22 555	thecrew.com	0	1	0
FC Dallas	Dallas	Pizza Hut Park	21 193	fcdallas.mlsnet.com	0	1	0
DC United	Washington	RFK Memorial	56 454	dcunited.mlsnet.com	4	1	1
Houston Dynamo	Houston	Robertson Stadium	33 000	houstondynamo.com	0	0	0
Kansas City Wizards	Kansas City	Arrowhead	79 451	kc.wizards.mlsnet.com	1	1	0
Los Angeles Galaxy	Carson/Los Angeles	Home Depot Centre	27 000	la.galaxy.mlsnet.com	2	2	1
MetroStars	New York/New Jersey	Giants Stadium	80 242	metrostars.mlsnet.com	0	0	0
New England Revolution	Foxboro/Boston	Gillette Stadium	68 756	revolutionsoccer.net	0	0	0
Real Salt Lake	Salt Lake	Rice-Eccles	46 500	real.saltlake.mslnet.com	0	0	0

NATIONAL TEAM PLAYERS AND COACHES

Record Caps			Record Goals			Recent Coaches	
JONES Cobi	1992-'04	164	WYNALDA Eric	1990-'00	34	CHYZOWYCH Walter	1976-'80
AGOOS Jeff	1988-'03	134	MCBRIDE Brian	1993-'06	30	GANSLER Bob	1982
BALBOA Marcelo	1988-'00	128	DONOVAN Landon	2000-'06	25	PANAGOULIAS Alkis	1983-'85
REYNA Claudio	1994-'06	112	MOORE Joe-Max	1992-'02	24	OSIANDER Lothar	1986-'88
CALIGIURI Paul	1984-'98	110	MURRAY Bruce	1985-'93	21	GANSLER Bob	1989-'91
WYNALDA Eric	1990-'00	106	STEWART Earnie	1990-'04	17	KOWALSKI John	1991
STEWART Earnie	1990-'04	101	JONES Cobi	1992-'04	15	MILUTINOVIC Bora	1991-'95
MOORE Joe-Max	1992-'02	100	BALBOA Marcelo	1988-'00	13	SAMPSON Steve	1996-'98
MEOLA Tony	1988-'06	100	PEREZ Hugo	1984-'94	13	ARENA Bruce	1998-'06

FIFA/COCA-COLA WORLD RANKING

1993	1994	1995	1996	1997	1998	1999	2000	2001	2002	2003	2004	2005		High		Low	
22	23	19	18	26	23	22	16	24	10	11	11	8		4	04/06	35	10/97

2005–2006											
08/05	09/05	10/05	11/05	12/05	01/06	02/06	03/06	04/06	05/06	06/06	07/06
6	7	7	8	8	7	6	5	4	5	-	16

USA THE FIFA BIG COUNT OF 2000

	Male	Female		Male	Female
Registered players	159 928	102 049	Referees	87 150	17 850
Non registered players	8 400 000	5 600 000	Officials	487 500	262 500
Youth players	2 178 000	1 452 000	Total involved	18 746 977	
Total players	17 891 977		Number of clubs	1 690	
Professional players	6 928	49	Number of teams	10 945	

USA 2005

MAJOR LEAGUE SOCCER — REGULAR SEASON

Eastern Conference	Pl	W	D	L	F	A	Pts	NE Revs	DC United	Chicago Fire	MetroStars	Wizards	Crew	Earthquakes	Dallas	Rapids	LA Galaxy	Salt Lake	Chivas
New England Revs †	32	17	8	7	55	37	59	—	1-0 2-1	2-0 1-0	4-2 1-0	1-1 2-3	0-3 3-1	0-2	3-2	0-0	1-1	4-1	1-0
DC United †	32	16	6	10	58	37	54	3-4 2-0	—	1-1 4-3	3-0 1-2	3-2 0-1	3-1 2-2	3-0	0-2	2-0	2-3	5-1	3-0
Chicago Fire †	32	15	4	13	49	50	49	0-3 1-0	4-3 2-3	—	0-3 2-2	1-1 2-3	1-1 1-2	2-1	2-0	2-1	2-1	3-1	5-2
NY/NJ MetroStars †	32	12	11	9	53	49	47	2-2 5-4	0-0 1-4	0-1 2-1	—	2-2 2-2	3-2 2-1	0-1	3-2	1-1	2-1	0-0	3-3
Kansas City Wizards	32	11	12	9	52	44	45	0-2 2-0	0-1 1-3	0-0 1-1	0-0 1-0	—	1-1 0-1	1-0	3-3	3-2	2-2	3-2	3-0
Columbus Crew	32	11	5	16	34	45	38	1-3 1-1	1-0 0-1	0-2 1-2	0-3 1-0	0-4 2-0	—	1-2	1-0	1-0	3-0	2-0	0-1

Western Conference	Pl	W	D	L	F	A	Pts	NE Revs	DC United	Chicago Fire	MetroStars	Wizards	Crew	Earthquakes	Dallas	Rapids	LA Galaxy	Salt Lake	Chivas
San Jose Earthquakes †	32	18	10	4	53	31	64	2-2	0-0	2-0	2-1	3-2	2-1	—	0-0 1-1	1-0 1-1	3-0 2-1	3-0 2-2	3-3 3-0
FC Dallas †	32	13	9	10	52	44	48	1-2	1-2	2-1	2-2	2-2	2-1	2-2 0-2	—	2-1 1-0	0-1 0-4	1-3 0-2	1-2 0-2 2-2
Colorado Rapids †	32	13	6	13	40	37	45	2-0	1-0	4-1	1-1	2-1	2-0	0-1 1-2	0-0 1-3	—	1-0 2-0	0-1 3-0	2-1 1-1
Los Angeles Galaxy †	32	13	6	13	44	45	45	1-1	0-1	1-2	2-2	2-2	0-0	2-1 1-3	2-0 2-1	3-2 4-1	—	3-1 1-0	3-1 2-0
Real Salt Lake	32	5	5	22	30	65	20	0-1	1-3	0-3	2-2	2-4	1-2	2-2 0-1	0-2 3-0	1-0 0-1	2-1 1-1	—	2-0 2-1
Chivas USA	32	4	6	22	31	67	18	1-0	0-2	0-1	0-2	1-1	0-3	1-1 2-1	2-5 1-3	1-3 0-2	0-1 1-0	5-1	—

2/04/2005 - 16/10/2005 • † Qualified for the play-offs • Top scorers: Taylor TWELLMAN, NE Revs, 17; Jaime MORENO, DC United, 16

MLS PLAY-OFFS 2005

Conference semi-finals

Los Angeles Galaxy *	3	1
San Jose Earthquakes	1	1
FC Dallas	0	2 4p
Colorado Rapids *	0	2 5p
Chicago Fire *	0	4
DC United	0	0
NY/NJ MetroStars *	1	1
New England Revolution	0	3

Conference finals

Los Angeles Galaxy	2
Colorado Rapids	0
Chicago Fire	0
New England Revolution	1

MLS Cup

Los Angeles Galaxy	1
New England Revolution	0

* Home team/home team in the first leg

MLS CUP 2005

Home Depot Centre, Carson, 13-11-2005, Att: 21 193 Referee: Stott

Los Angeles Galaxy 1 Ramirez [107]
New England Revolution 0

Galaxy - Kevin HARTMAN - Todd DUNIVANT, Chris ALBRIGHT, Peter VAGENAS, Landon DONOVAN, Ned GRABAVOY (Guillermo RAMIREZ 66), Cobi JONES (Ednaldo DA CONCEICAO 109), Tyrone MARSHALL, Ugo IHEMELU, Herculez GOMEZ (Alan GORDON 119), Paulo NAGAMURA. Tr: Steve SAMPSON
Revolution - Matt REIS - Clint DEMPSEY, Daniel HERNANDEZ (Andy DORMAN 91+), Jay HEAPS, Joe FRANCHINO, Pat NOONAN (Jose CANCELA 64), Steve RALSTON, James RILEY (Ryan LATHAM 107), Taylor TWELLMAN, Shairie JOSEPH. Tr: Steve NICHOL

USA 2005 — USL FIRST DIVISION (2)

	Pl	W	D	L	F	A	Pts
Montreal Impact	28	18	7	3	37	15	61
Rochester Raging Rhinos	28	15	6	7	45	27	51
Vancouver Whitecaps	28	12	9	7	37	21	45
Seattle Sounders	28	11	11	6	33	25	44
Portland Timbers	28	10	9	9	40	42	39
Richmond Kickers	28	10	9	9	28	30	39
Puerto Rico Islanders	28	10	8	10	46	43	38
Atlanta Silverbacks	28	10	3	15	40	52	33
Charleston Battery	28	9	5	14	27	36	32
Minnesota Thunder	28	7	10	11	37	42	31
Virginia Beach Mariners	28	7	7	14	26	39	28
Toronto Lynx	28	3	8	17	26	50	17

The top six qualified for the play-offs

USL FIRST DIVISION PLAY-OFFS

Quarter-finals: Richmond Kickers 0-0 0-0 5-4p Vancouver Whitecaps; Seattle Sounders 1-0 2-0 Portland Timbers;
Semi-finals: Richmond Kickers 3-1 1-1 Rochester Raging Rhinos; Seattle Sounders 2-2 2-1 Montreal Impact;
Final: Seattle Sounders 1-1 4-3p Richmond Kickers

RECENT LEAGUE AND CUP RECORD

	Championship			Cup		
Year	Champions	Score	Runners-up	Winners	Score	Runners-up
1996	DC United	3-2	Los Angeles Galaxy	DC United	3-0	Rochester Rhinos
1997	DC United	2-1	Colorado Rapids	Dallas Burn	0-0 5-3p	DC United
1998	Chicago Fire	2-0	DC United	Chicago Fire	2-1	Columbus Crew
1999	DC United	2-0	Los Angeles Galaxy	Rochester Rhinos	2-0	Colorado Rapids
2000	Kansas City Wizards	1-0	Chicago Fire	Chicago Fire	2-1	Miami Fusion
2001	San Jose Earthquakes	2-1	Los Angeles Galaxy	Los Angeles Galaxy	2-1	New England Revolution
2002	Los Angeles Galaxy	1-0	New England Revolution	Columbus Crew	1-0	Los Angeles Galaxy
2003	San Jose Earthquakes	4-2	Chicago Fire	Chicago Fire	1-0	MetroStars
2004	DC United	3-2	Kansas City Wizards	Kansas City Wizards	1-0	Chicago Fire
2005	Los Angeles Galaxy	1-0	New England Revolution	Los Angeles Galaxy	1-0	FC Dallas

LAMAR HUNT US OPEN CUP 2005

Third Round	Fourth Round	Quarter-finals	Semi-finals	Final

Third Round		Fourth Round		Quarter-finals		Semi-finals		Final	
Charlotte Eagles *	2	Los Angeles Galaxy	5						
Chivas USA	3	Chivas USA *	2	Los Angeles Galaxy	2				
Portland Timbers *	2	Portland Timbers *	0	San Jose Earthquakes *	1	Los Angeles Galaxy		Los Angeles Galaxy *	1
Seattle Sounders	0	San Joe Earthquakes	2			Minnesota Thunder		FC Dallas	0
Atlanta Silverbacks *	1	Kansas City Wizards *	6						
Des Moines Menace	5	Des Moines Menace	1	Kansas City Wizards *	1				
Real Salt Lake	4	Colorado Rapids	1	Minnesota Thunder	3				
Minnesota Thunder *	6	Minnesota Thunder *	4						
Chicago Fire	3	Chicago Fire	3	Chicago Fire	1 5p				
Western Mass Pioneers *	1	New England Revolution*	2	Rochester Raging Rhinos*	1 4p	Chicago Fire	0		
Virginia Beach Mariners	1	NY/NJ MetroStars	1			FC Dallas *	1		
Rochester Raging Rhinos*	2	Rochester Raging Rhinos*	3						
Ocean City Barons	4	DC United	3	DC United	1 1p				
Richmond Kickers *	8	Richmond Kickers *	1	FC Dallas	1 4p				
Wilmington Hammerheads	1	Columbus Crew *	1						
FC Dallas *	3	FC Dallas	3						

* Home team

CUP FINAL

Home Depot Centre, Carson, Los Angeles
28-09-2005, Att: 10 000, Ref: Prus

Scorer – Herculez Gomez 25 for LA Galaxy

Galaxy: HARTMAN Kevin – ALBRIGHT Chris, IHEMELU Ugo,
MARSHAL Tyrone, DUNIVANT Todd, JONES Cobi, SARAGOSA
Marcelo, VAGENAS Peter, DONOVAN Landon, NGWENYA
Joseph (GORDON Alan 95+), GOMEZ Herculez (UMANA
Michael 91+). Tr: SAMPSON Steve

FC Dallas: GARLICK Scott – RHINE Bobby (JOLLEY Steve
86), GOODSON Clarence, VANNEY Greg, WAGENFUHR
David, ALVAREZ Arturo (THOMPSON Abe 69), O'BRIEN
Ronnie (PAREJA Oscar 53), TALLEY Carey (PITCHKOLAN
Aaron 54), WILSON Mark, NUÑEZ Ramon, MINA Roberto.
Tr: CLARKE Colin

UZB – UZBEKISTAN

NATIONAL TEAM RECORD
JULY 1ST 2002 TO JULY 9TH 2006

PL	W	D	L	F	A	%
36	18	10	8	62	38	63.9

FIFA/COCA-COLA WORLD RANKING

1993	1994	1995	1996	1997	1998	1999	2000	2001	2002	2003	2004	2005	High		Low	
-	78	97	109	79	66	55	71	62	98	81	47	59	46	03/05	119	11/96

2005–2006											
08/05	09/05	10/05	11/05	12/05	01/06	02/06	03/06	04/06	05/06	06/06	07/06
62	57	57	58	59	59	61	61	59	60	-	50

Uzbekistan were involved in a bizarre incident during their FIFA World Cup™ play-off against Bahrain and it cost them a chance of playing in the finals in Germany. With Uzbekistan leading 1-0, the Japanese referee disallowed an Uzbek penalty for encroachment but instead of ordering a retake, he gave a free kick to Bahrain. Uzbekistan lodged a protest, which they came to regret, as FIFA ordered a replay on the grounds of a technical error. The replay was drawn 1-1 and Bahrain's away goal was the difference between the two teams after the 0-0 draw in Manama. The Uzbeks felt that they had been punished twice; for not having the penalty retaken, and for having the original

INTERNATIONAL HONOURS
Asian Games 1994

win taken away. In club football, Pakhtakor continued their dominance over the rest of the teams with a fourth consecutive double of League and Cup and they will be out to beat the world record of seven held by Georgia's Dinamo Tbilisi. Their 1-0 Cup Final win over Neftchi Fergana was their fifth in a row. In the AFC Champions League, however, Pakhtakor have struggled to match the standard of the top Arab clubs with whom they are grouped every year. In the 2005 tournament they finished second behind Saudi's Al Ahli whilst in 2006 they just missed out on the quarter-finals after failing to beat Kuwait's Al Qadiyisa at home in the crucial deciding match.

THE FIFA BIG COUNT OF 2000

	Male	Female		Male	Female
Registered players	4 000	0	Referees	200	0
Non registered players	130 000	0	Officials	1 300	0
Youth players	4 000	0	Total involved	139 500	
Total players	138 000		Number of clubs	150	
Professional players	0	0	Number of teams	600	

Uzbekistan Football Federation (UFF)
O'zbekiston Futbol Federatsiyasi, Massiv Almazar, Furkat Street 15/1, Tashkent 700 003, Uzbekistan
Tel +998 71 1441684   Fax +998 71 1441683
info@uzfootball.com   www.uzfootball.com
President: USMANOV Mirabror   General Secretary: RAKHMATULLAEV Sardor
Vice-President: RAKHIMOV Bakhtier   Treasurer: ISKHAKOVA Zemfira   Media Officer: RIZAEV Sanjar
Men's Coach: NEPOMNIACHI Valeri   Women's Coach: YUMANGULOV Abdurahman
UFF formed: 1946   AFC: 1994   FIFA: 1994
White shirts with blue trimmings, White shorts, White socks or Blue shirts with white trimmings, Blue shorts, Blue socks

RECENT INTERNATIONAL MATCHES PLAYED BY UZBEKISTAN

2002 Opponents	Score		Venue	Comp	Scorers	Att	Referee
21-08 Azerbaijan	L	0-2	Baku	Fr		7 000	Abdullayev AZE
2003							
2-04 Belarus	D	2-2	Minsk	Fr	Khvostunov [66]p, Geynrikh [69]	4 000	Lajuks LVA
30-04 Belarus	L	1-2	Tashkent	Fr	Shishelov [43]	4 000	Kolpakov KGZ
20-08 Latvia	W	3-0	Riga	Fr	Akopyants [41], Soliev [80], Geynrikh [86]	4 000	Shandor UKR
11-10 United Arab Emirates	D	2-2	Dubai	Fr	Karpenko [40], Djeparov [86]		
25-10 Burkina Faso	W	1-0	Hyderabad	AAr1	Krusheinitskiy [66]		
27-10 Zimbabwe	D	1-1	Hyderabad	AAr1	Suyunov [50]		
29-10 Rwanda	W	2-1	Hyderabad	AAsf	Saidov [63], Boyev [102]		
31-10 India	W	1-0	Hyderabad	AAf	Inomov [90]		Lu Jun CHN
6-11 Hong Kong	W	4-1	Tashkent	ACq	Akopyants [1], Shishelov 2 [17 65], Soliev [28]		
8-11 Thailand	W	3-0	Tashkent	ACq	Shatskikh [23], Shishelov 2 [27 70]		
10-11 Tajikistan	D	0-0	Tashkent	ACq			
17-11 Tajikistan	W	4-1	Bangkok	ACq	Shishelov 2 [8 36], Kapadze [50], Koshekev [61]		
19-11 Hong Kong	W	1-0	Bangkok	ACq	Shirshov [32]		
21-11 Thailand	L	1-4	Bangkok	ACq	Koshekev [88]		
2004							
18-02 Iraq	D	1-1	Tashkent	WCq	Soliev [78]	24 000	Srinivasan IND
31-03 Chinese Taipei	W	1-0	Taipei	WCq	Koshekev [59]	2 500	Midi Nitrorejo IDN
28-05 Azerbaijan	L	1-3	Baku	Fr	Tadjiyev [45]	12 000	
9-06 Palestine	W	3-0	Tashkent	WCq	Soliev [93+]	45 000	Kamikawa JPN
18-07 Iraq	W	1-0	Chengdu	ACr1	Kasimov [22]	12 400	Kwon Jong Chul KOR
22-07 Saudi Arabia	W	1-0	Chengdu	ACr1	Geynrikh [11]	22 000	Codjia BEN
26-07 Turkmenistan	W	1-0	Chongqing	ACr1	Kasimov [57]	34 000	Kousa SYR
30-07 Bahrain	D	2-2	Chengdu	ACqf	Geynrikh [60], Shishelov [86]. L 3-4p	18 000	Salmeen BHR
8-09 Palestine	W	3-0	Rayyan	WCq	Kasimov [9], Djeparov [32], Bikmoev [78]	400	Maidin SIN
13-10 Iraq	W	2-1	Amman	WCq	Shatskikh [10], Geynrikh [22]	10 000	Maidin SIN
17-11 Chinese Taipei	W	6-1	Tashkent	WCq	Geynrikh [5], Kasimov 3 [12 45 85], Shatskikh [18], Koshekev [34]	20 000	Basma SYR
2005							
9-02 Saudi Arabia	D	1-1	Tashkent	WCq	Soliev [93+]	45 000	Kamikawa JPN
25-03 Kuwait	L	1-2	Kuwait City	WCq	Geynrikh [77]	12 000	Sun Baojie CHN
30-03 Korea Republic	L	1-2	Seoul	WCq	Geynrikh [78]	62 857	Najm LIB
3-06 Korea Republic	D	1-1	Tashkent	WCq	Shatskikh [63]	40 000	Moradi IRN
8-06 Saudi Arabia	L	0-3	Riyadh	WCq		72 000	Huang Junjie CHN
17-08 Kuwait	W	3-2	Tashkent	WCq	Djeparov [41p], Shatskikh [51], Soliev [76]	40 000	Mohd Saleh MAS
3-09 Bahrain †	W	1-0	Tashkent	WCpo	Kasimov [12]		
8-10 Bahrain	D	1-1	Tashkent	WCpo	Shatskikh [19]	55 000	Busacca SUI
12-10 Bahrain	D	0-0	Manama	WCpo		25 000	Poll ENG
2006							
22-02 Bangladesh	W	5-0	Tashkent	ACq	Geynrikh 2 [10 52], Djeparov [24], Shatskikh 2 [34 84]	12 000	Ebrahim BHR
1-03 Qatar	L	1-2	Doha	ACq	OG [20]	7 000	Sun Baoje CHN

Fr = Friendly match • AA - Afo-Asian Games • AC = AFC Asian Cup • WC = FIFA World Cup™
q = qualifier • po = play-off • r1 = first round group • qf = quarter-final • sf = semi-final • f = final • † Matched annulled due to referee error

UZBEKISTAN NATIONAL TEAM RECORDS AND RECORD SEQUENCES

Records			Sequence records				
Victory	15-0	MGL 1998	Wins	8	1994	Clean sheets	4	2004
Defeat	1-8	JPN 2000	Defeats	4	2000-2001	Goals scored	18	2003-2005
Player Caps	65	KASIMOV Mirdjalal	Undefeated	11	1994, 2001	Without goal	3	2000-2001
Player Goals	29	KASIMOV Mirdjalal	Without win	6	1997	Goals against	9	2004-2005

UZBEKISTAN COUNTRY INFORMATION

Capital	Tashkent	Independence	1991 from the USSR	GDP per Capita	$1 700
Population	26 410 416	Status	Republic	GNP Ranking	78
Area km²	447 400	Language	Uzbek, Russian	Dialling code	+7
Population density	59 per km²	Literacy rate	99%	Internet code	.uz
% in urban areas	41%	Main religion	Muslim	GMT + / −	+5
Cities/Towns ('000)	Tashkent 1 978; Namangan 432; Samarkand 319; Andijon 318; Bukhara 247; Nukus 230; Karshi 222; Kukon 187; Chirchik 167; Fergana 164; Cizak 152; Urganch 150; Termiz 140				
Neighbours (km)	Kyrgyzstan 1 099; Tajikistan 1 161; Afghanistan 137; Turkmenistan 1 621; Kazakhstan 2 203				
Main stadia	Pakhtakor – Tashkent 54 000; Markaziy – Bukhara 40 000				

NATIONAL TEAM PLAYERS AND COACHES

Record Caps			Record Goals			Recent Coaches	
KASIMOV Mirdjalal	1992-'05	65	KASIMOV Mirdjalal	1992-'05	29		
SHIRSHOV Nikolai	1996-'05	63	SHKVRIN Igor	1992-'00	20		
FEDOROV Andrei	1994-'06	62	IRISMETOV Zhafar	1997-'01	18		
DAVLETOV Fevzi	1994-'05	51	SHATSKIKH Maksim	1999-'06	17		
KHVOSTUNOV Alexandr	1997-'04	47	SHIRSHOV Nikolai	1996-'05	13	KHAYDAROV Ravshan	2002-'05
ASHURMATOV Bahtiyor	1997-'05	42	MAKSUDOV Shukhrat	1992-'97	11	GEODE Heinz-Jurgen	2005
ALIKULOV Asror	1999-'06	41	ABDURAIMOV Azamat	1992-'97	10	KHAYDAROV Ravshan	2005
AKOPYANTS Andrey	1998-'05	40	GEYNRIKH Alexander	2002-'06	10	HOUGHTON Bob	2005
BUGALO Pavel	1995-'00	35	LEBEDEV Sergei	1994-'01	10	NEPOMNIACHI Valeri	2006-

CLUB DIRECTORY

Club	Town/City	Lge	Cup
FK Andijon	Andijon	0	0
FK Bukhara (FK Buxoro)	Bukhara (Buxoro)	0	0
Lokomotiv	Tashkent (Toshkent)	0	0
Mash'al	Muborak	0	0
Metallurg	Bekobod	0	0
Nasaf	Karshi (Qarshi)	0	0
Navbahor	Namangan	1	3
Neftchi	Fergana (Farg'ona)	5	2
Pakhtakor (Paxtakor)	Tashkent (Toshkent)	6	7
Kizilgum (Qizilqum)	Zarafshon	0	0
Samarqand-Dinamo	Samarkand (Samarqand)	0	0
Sho'rtan	Guzor	0	0
Sogdiana (So'g'diyona)	Jizak (Jizzox)	0	0
Topolon (To'Palang)	Sariasia (Sariosiyo)	0	0
Traktor	Tashkent (Toshkent)	0	0
Xorazm	Urganch	0	0

RECENT LEAGUE AND CUP RECORD

	Championship						Cup		
Year	Champions	Pts	Runners-up	Pts	Third	Pts	Winners	Score	Runners-up
1992	Pakhtakor Tashkent	51	Neftchi Fergana	51	Sogdiana Jizak	48	Navbahor Nam'gan	0-0 6-5p	Temirulchi Kukon
1993	Neftchi Fergana	52	Pakhtakor Tashkent	47	Navbahor Nam'gan	43	Pakhtakor Tashkent	3-0	Navbahor Nam'gan
1994	Neftchi Fergana	51	Nurafshon Bukhara	44	Navbahor Nam'gan	40	Neftchi Fergana	2-0	FK Yangier
1995	Neftchi Fergana	76	MHSK Tashkent	74	Navbahor Nam'gan	72	Navbahor Nam'gan	1-0	MHSK Tashkent
1996	Navbahor Nam'gan	74	Neftchi Fergana	72	MHSK Tashkent	62	Neftchi Fergana	0-0 5-4p	Pkhtakor Tashkent
1997	MHSK Tashkent	90	Neftchi Fergana	81	Navbahor Nam'gan	68	Pakhtakor Tashkent	3-2	Neftchi Fergana
1998	Pakhtakor Tashkent	76	Neftchi Fergana	70	Navbahor Nam'gan	59	Navbahor Nam'gan	2-0	Neftchi Fergana
1999	Dustlik Tashkent	64	Neftchi Fergana	63	Navbahor Nam'gan	61	No tournament		
2000	Dustlik Tashkent	94	Neftchi Fergana	90	Nasaf Karshi	85	Dustlik Tashkent	4-1	Samarkand Dinamo
2001	Neftchi Fergana	84	Pakhtakor Tashkent	72	Nasaf Karshi	71	Pakhtakor Tashkent	2-1	Neftchi Fergana
2002	Pakhtakor Tashkent	74	Neftchi Fergana	69	Kizilgum Zarafshon	59	Pakhtakor Tashkent	6-3	Neftchi Fergana
2003	Pakhtakor Tashkent	77	Neftchi Fergana	71	Navbahor Nam'gan	63	Pakhtakor Tashkent	3-1	Nasaf Karshi
2004	Pakhtakor Tashkent	69	Neftchi Fergana	65	Navbahor Nam'gan	57	Pakhtakor Tashkent	3-2	Traktor Tashkent
2005	Pakhtakor Tashkent	65	Mashal Muborak	59	Nasaf Karshi	51	Pakhtakor Tashkent	1-0	Neftchi Fergana

Uzbek clubs played in the Soviet league until the end of the 1991 season • Pakhtakor and Neftchi shared the title in 1992

UZBEKISTAN 2005

O'ZBEKISTON CHEMPIONATI OLIY LIGA

	Pl	W	D	L	F	A	Pts	Pakhtakor	Mashal	Nasaf	Traktor	Neftchi	Navbahor	Kizilgum	Dinamo	Topolon	Lokomtiv	Metallurg	Bukhara	Shurton	Sogdiana
Pakhtakor Tashkent †	26	21	2	3	78	15	65		1-2	2-0	5-2	2-0	2-0	2-0	2-0	4-0	5-1	5-2	3-0	4-0	5-0
Mashal Muborak †	26	19	2	5	54	24	59	0-0		0-2	2-1	2-0	2-1	2-1	3-1	3-1	3-1	3-1	4-0	3-0	5-1
Nasaf Karshi	26	16	3	7	50	31	51	3-2	1-0		2-2	2-1	2-0	4-0	3-0	3-1	2-1	4-0	2-1	1-2	2-1
Traktor Taskent	26	13	2	11	48	43	41	1-4	3-5	4-2		2-1	2-0	2-1	4-2	0-3	1-2	1-2	2-0	3-1	5-1
Neftchi Fergana	26	13	1	12	40	28	40	1-0	1-3	2-1	2-1		3-0	1-0	1-0	4-0	4-0	1-0	4-2	5-0	2-0
Navbahor Namangan	26	12	3	11	31	31	39	0-3	0-0	2-1	3-0	1-0		2-1	2-1	1-0	3-0	1-0	2-0	3-2	4-0
Kizilgum Zarafshon	26	11	4	11	33	32	37	0-1	0-1	3-1	2-1	1-0	1-0		3-1	5-0	1-1	2-1	2-2	1-0	0-0
Samarkand Dinamo	26	11	3	12	28	32	36	0-0	0-2	0-0	0-1	2-1	1-0	3-0		4-2	1-0	2-1	2-0	1-0	3-2
Topolon Sariosia	26	11	2	13	33	45	35	0-3	2-1	2-0	1-2	1-0	1-1	1-0	2-1		1-2	4-2	3-1	0-0	4-2
Lokomotiv Taskent	26	9	3	14	39	46	30	1-6	2-0	1-2	1-1	2-1	1-1	1-3	0-1	0-1		2-0	4-2	1-2	5-0
Metallurg Bekobod	26	9	2	15	32	47	29	1-3	0-2	2-3	1-2	1-3	1-0	3-1	1-1	2-1	1-0		2-0	2-1	2-1
FK Bukhara	26	9	2	15	37	59	29	0-8	4-0	2-2	0-3	2-1	2-3	2-3	1-0	2-1	4-3	3-1		2-1	1-0
Shurton Guzor ‡	26	6	1	19	23	56	19	0-3	0-5	0-4	0-2	3-1	3-1	0-2	0-1	1-2	0-3	1-3	3-1		2-0
Sogdiana Jizak ‡	26	5	4	17	16	53	19	1-3	0-1	0-1	1-0	0-0	1-0	0-0	1-0	1-0	1-4	0-0	0-3	2-1	

19/03/2005 - 7/11/2005 • † Qualified for the 2006 AFC Champions League • ‡ To relegation/promotion play-off • Top scorers: Anvar SOLIEV, Pakhtakor, 29; Zafar KHOLMURADOV, Nasaf, 24; Shurat MIRKHOLDIRSHOYEV, Mashal, 20

UZBEKISTAN 2005 BIRINCHI LIGA (2)

	Pl	W	D	L	F	A	Pts
FK Andijon	34	27	3	4	85	20	84
Xorazm-2003 Urganch	34	27	2	5	93	32	83
Osiyo Tashkent ‡	34	20	7	7	68	32	67
FK Vobkent ‡	34	21	4	9	75	44	67
Kimyogar Chirchik	34	21	1	12	72	46	64
Sementchi Kuvasoy	34	20	1	13	79	44	61
Gallakor Gallaorol	34	17	4	13	64	58	55
Surhom Termiz	34	17	2	15	47	57	53
FK Shahrixon	34	16	3	15	59	55	51
OTMK Olmalik	34	13	10	11	43	50	49
FK Hazorasp	34	12	5	17	53	57	41
Zarafshon Navai	34	11	7	16	43	59	40
FK Qo'qon 1912	34	10	7	17	48	69	37
Lochin Shorchi	34	10	7	17	40	63	37
Sidaryo Guliston	34	10	4	20	50	56	34
Shakhontohur Tashkent	34	7	4	23	45	89	25
Nasaf 2 Karshi	34	8	0	26	33	95	24
AOZSK Andijon	34	2	3	29	17	88	9

12/04/2005 - 6/11/2005 • ‡ Qualified for play-offs

PROMOTION/RELEGATION

	Pl	W	D	L	F	A	Pts
Shurton Guzor	3	3	0	0	14	3	9
Sogdiana Jizak	3	2	0	1	7	5	6
FK Vobkent	3	1	0	2	5	9	3
Osiyo Tashkent	3	0	0	3	1	10	0

13/11/2005 - 17/11/2005

UZBEKISTAN CUP 2005

Second Round			Quarter-finals			Semi-finals			Final	
Pakhtakor Tashkent	Bye									
			Pakhtakor Tashkent	4	0					
Kizilgum Zarafshon	1	3	Nasaf Karshi *	1	0					
Nasaf Karshi *	3	2				Pakhtakor Tashkent	4	3		
Lokomotiv Tashkent *	3	1				Navbahor Namangan *	4	1		
Surhom Termiz	0	2	Lokomotiv Tashkent	0	0					
Sogdiana Jizak *	2	1	Navbahor Namangan *	3	1				Pakhtakor Tashkent	1
Navbahor Namangan	1	3							Neftchi Fergana	0
FK Bukhara	3	2								
Shurton Guzor *	1	0	FK Bukhara *	5	0					
Samarkand-Dinamo *	2	1	Traktor Tashkent	0	1					
Traktor Taskent	1	3				FK Bukhara *	1	0		
Mashal Muborak *	4	0				Neftchi Fergana	0	3		
FK Andijon	0	0	Mashal Muborak *	1	0					
Osiyo Tashkent *	0	0	Neftchi Fergana	5	3					
Neftchi Fergana	2	4								

* Home team/home team in the first leg

CUP FINAL

Pakhtakor Stadium, Taskent
26-11-2005, Att: 5 000, Ref: Karimov

Scorer - Soliev 24 for Pakhtakor

VAN – VANUATU

NATIONAL TEAM RECORD
JULY 1ST 2002 TO JULY 9TH 2006

PL	W	D	L	F	A	%
20	7	4	9	29	24	45

FIFA/COCA-COLA WORLD RANKING

1993	1994	1995	1996	1997	1998	1999	2000	2001	2002	2003	2004	2005		High		Low	
164	172	179	180	186	177	184	167	168	156	160	143	146		**139**	08/04	**188**	04/00

2005–2006										
08/05	09/05	10/05	11/05	12/05	01/06	02/06	03/06	04/06	05/06	06/06	07/06
147	148	148	148	146	147	147	146	147	148	-	161

The 1300 kilometre archipelago of Vanuatu has 82 islands which makes the task of running football by the Vanuatu Football Federation a difficult one. In 2005 changes were made to the VFF constitution which saw the recognition of six provincial associations with the organisation of the two main Leagues in the country passing from the VFF to these associations - the Port Vila League to the Shefa FA and the Luganville League to the Sanma FA. The changes were not universally welcomed and there was talk of break away Leagues and rival associations, particularly in Port Vila. Amidst all this Tafea FC chalked up their 12th consecutive title in the Port Vila League and are now just

INTERNATIONAL HONOURS
Melanesian Cup 1990

two away from equalling Skonto's world record of 14. There is some debate, though, as to whether the winners of a regional League not under the control of the VFF can be considered as national champions. By winning the Port Vila League Tafea did, however, earn the right to take part in the 2006 OFC Club Championship, qualifying directly for the finals in New Zealand. Having reached the semi-finals in 2005, hopes were high of a repeat performance and they came within a minute of achieving that, but a last minute goal by Benjamin Totori of New Zealand's YoungHeart Manawatu saw them edged out on goal difference by Fiji's Nokia Eagles in a very tight group.

THE FIFA BIG COUNT OF 2000

	Male	Female		Male	Female
Registered players	1 000	0	Referees	100	0
Non registered players	1 000	0	Officials	200	0
Youth players	1 000	0	Total involved	3 300	
Total players	3 000		Number of clubs	100	
Professional players	0	0	Number of teams	200	

Vanuatu Football Federation (VFF)

PO Box 266, Port Vila, Vanuatu
Tel +678 25236   Fax +678 25236
jimmy_nipo@yahoo.com   www.sportingpulse.com.au
President: TRONQUET Jacques   General Secretary: NIPO Jimmy
Vice-President: MALTOCK Lambert   Treasurer: WARSAL Leon Katty   Media Officer: None
Men's Coach: BUZZETTI Juan   Women's Coach: BUZZETTI Juan
VFF formed: 1934   OFC: 1988   FIFA: 1988
Gold shirts, Black shorts, Gold socks

RECENT INTERNATIONAL MATCHES PLAYED BY VANUATU

2002	Opponents	Score	Venue	Comp	Scorers	Att	Referee
6-07	Australia	L 0-2	Auckland	OCr1		1 000	Ariiotima TAH
8-07	Fiji	W 1-0	Auckland	OCr1	Marango [6]	800	Sosongan PNG
10-07	New Caledonia	W 1-0	Auckland	OCr1	Iwai [76]	500	Ariiotima TAH
12-07	New Zealand	L 0-3	Auckland	OCsf		1 000	Breeze AUS
14-07	Tahiti	L 0-1	Auckland	OC3p		1 000	Rakaroi FIJ
2003							
30-06	Fiji	D 0-0	Suva	SPr1			Ariiotima TAH
1-07	Solomon Islands	D 2-2	Suva	SPr1	Mermer [22], Qorig [47]		Shah FIJ
3-07	Tuvalu †	W 1-0	Suva	SPr1	Tabe [86]	700	Bayung PNG
7-07	Kiribati †	W 18-0	Lautoka	SPr1	Mermer 4 [4 15 51 53], Chillia 4 [10 22 29 30], Iwai 5 [27 40 41 63 64], Tabe [35], Vava [47], Thomsen [54], Demas [62], Pita [83]	2 000	Bayung PNG
9-07	New Caledonia	D 1-1	Lautoka	SPsf	Laki [54]. L 3-4p	7 000	Shah FIJ
11-07	Tahiti	W 1-0	Suva	SP3p	Mermer [57]	6 000	Rakaroi FIJ
2004							
3-04	Solomon Islands	L 1-2	Port-Vila	Fr	Chillia [41]	4 000	Fred VAN
6-04	Solomon Islands	L 1-2	Port-Vila	Fr			
10-05	Papua New Guinea	D 1-1	Apia	WCq	Lauru [92+]	500	Breeze AUS
12-05	American Samoa	W 9-1	Apia	WCq	Qorig 2 [30 47+], Mermer 3 [37 56 91+], Poida [55], Chilea [65], Maleb 2 [80 92+]	400	Fox NZL
15-05	Samoa	W 3-0	Apia	WCq	Mermer [13], Chillia 55, Maleb 57	650	Breeze AUS
19-05	Fiji	W 3-0	Apia	WCq	Thomsen [46+], Lauru 2 [63 65]	200	Breeze AUS
29-05	Solomon Islands	L 0-1	Adelaide	WCq		200	Shield AUS
31-05	Fiji	L 0-1	Adelaide	WCq		500	Ariiotima TAH
2-06	New Zealand	W 4-2	Adelaide	WCq	Chillia [37], Bibi [64], Maleb [72], Qoriz [88]	356	Farina ITA
4-06	Australia	L 0-3	Adelaide	WCq		4 000	Ariiotima TAH
6-06	Tahiti	L 1-2	Adelaide	WCq	Iwai [23]	300	Rakaroi FIJ
2005							
No international matches played in 2005							
2006							
No international matches played in 2006 before July							

Fr = Friendly match • OC = OFC Oceania Cup • SP = South Pacific Games • WC = FIFA World Cup™
q = qualifier • r1 = first round group • sf = semi-final • 3p = third place play-off • † Not a full international

VANUATU NATIONAL TEAM RECORDS AND RECORD SEQUENCES

Records			Sequence records				
Victory	13-1	SAM 1981	Wins	3	2004	Clean sheets	2	Five times
Defeat	0-9	NZL 1951	Defeats	6	Three times	Goals scored	13	1996-2000
Player Caps	n/a		Undefeated	6	2003	Without goal	3	1992, 2003-2004
Player Goals	n/a		Without win	9	1979-1981	Goals against	23	1951-1979

RECENT LEAGUE RECORD

Year	Port Vila Football League
2002	Tafea FC
2003	Tafea FC
2004	Tafea FC
2005	Tafea FC

VANUATU COUNTRY INFORMATION

Capital	Port-Vila	Independence	1980 from UK and France	GDP per Capita	$2 900
Population	202 609	Status	Republic	GNP Ranking	183
Area km²	12 200	Language	English, French, Bislama	Dialling code	+678
Population density	16 per km²	Literacy rate	53%	Internet code	.vu
% in urban areas	19%	Main religion	Christian	GMT + / –	+11
Towns/Cities ('000)	Port-Vila 35; Luganville 13; Norsup 3; Port Olry 2; Isangel ; Sola 1				
Neighbours (km)	South Pacific Ocean 2 528				
Main stadia	Korman Stadium – Port-Vila				

VEN – VENEZUELA

NATIONAL TEAM RECORD
JULY 1ST 2002 TO JULY 9TH 2006

PL	W	D	L	F	A	%
43	14	8	21	51	58	41.9

FIFA/COCA-COLA WORLD RANKING

1993	1994	1995	1996	1997	1998	1999	2000	2001	2002	2003	2004	2005		High		Low	
93	110	127	111	115	129	110	111	81	69	57	62	67		48	04/04	129	12/98

2005–2006											
08/05	09/05	10/05	11/05	12/05	01/06	02/06	03/06	04/06	05/06	06/06	07/06
67	57	71	67	67	68	69	70	71	71	-	68

The hosting of the 2007 Copa América promises to be a seminal event in the history of football in Venezuela, a nation that has always been just a little bit suspicious of the game. Whether lack of success is the cause of the disinterest or as a result of it is open to debate, but huge steps have been taken in the past few years and a successful Copa América would seal that progress. In the 2006 FIFA World Cup™ qualifiers the national team under Richard Paez finished eighth in the ten team South American group, the second tournament in a row that the wooden spoon has been avoided. The task now is to win a Copa América game for the first time since 1967 and there won't be a

INTERNATIONAL HONOURS
None

better opportunity than when hosting the tournament. The upswing in fortunes for the national team has been accompanied by an improvement at club level with Venezuelan clubs no longer an easy target in the Copa Libertadores. In the 2006 tournament Unión Atlético Maracaibo came close to qualifying from their group but lost on the final day to Internacional to miss out by a point. Earlier in the season, they had won the Apertura title but couldn't win the Clausura as well to claim the overall title as they had done the previous season. Instead they had to play-off against Caracas, the Clausura winners, and after drawing the first leg in Maracaibo lost the return in Caracas 3-0.

THE FIFA BIG COUNT OF 2000

	Male	Female		Male	Female
Registered players	7 592	1 289	Referees	512	68
Non registered players	500 000	10 000	Officials	8 000	300
Youth players	22 563	2 115	Total involved	552 439	
Total players	543 559		Number of clubs	400	
Professional players	372	0	Number of teams	1 557	

Federación Venezolana de Fútbol (FVF)
Avda. Santos Erminy Ira, Calle las Delicias Torre Mega II, P.H. Quitar P.H., Caracas 1050, Venezuela
Tel +58 212 7624472   Fax +58 212 7620596
sec_presidencia_fvf@cantv.net   www.fvf.org.ve
President: ESQUIVEL Rafael   General Secretary: GARCIA-REGALADO Jesus
Vice-President: CABEZAS Temistocles   Treasurer: SANGLADE Luis Ignacio   Media Officer: GOUSSOT Zaiddy
Men's Coach: HERNANDEZ Ramon & PAEZ Richard   Women's Coach: ALONSO Lino
FVF formed: 1926   CONMEBOL: 1965   FIFA: 1952
Burgundy shirts with white trimmings, White shorts, White socks

RECENT INTERNATIONAL MATCHES PLAYED BY VENEZUELA

2002	Opponents	Score		Venue	Comp	Scorers	Att	Referee
21-08	Bolivia	W	2-0	Caracas	Fr	Noriega [17], González.H [20]	25 000	Ibarra VEN
20-10	Ecuador	W	2-0	Caracas	Fr	Rey [30], Moreno [79]	24 000	Brand VEN
20-11	Uruguay	W	1-0	Caracas	Fr	Páez [49]	26 000	Solorzano VEN
2003								
29-03	USA	L	0-2	Seattle	Fr		17 819	Seifert CAN
2-04	Jamaica	W	2-0	Caracas	Fr	Urdaneta [11p], Páez [38]	25 000	Díaz ECU
30-04	Trinidad and Tobago	W	3-0	San Cristobal	Fr	Arango 2 [30 38], Noriega [75]	25 000	Rivero VEN
7-06	Honduras	W	2-1	Miami	Fr	Urdaneta [14], Arango [36]	15 000	Terry USA
26-06	Peru	L	0-1	Miami	Fr			Kennedy USA
3-07	Trinidad and Tobago	D	2-2	Port of Spain	Fr	Casseres 2 [1 49]	7 500	Piper TRI
26-07	Nigeria	L	0-1	Watford	Fr		1 000	
20-08	Haiti	W	3-2	Maracaibo	Fr	Vielma [78], González.H [83], Rivero [87]	15 000	Manzur VEN
6-09	Ecuador	L	0-2	Quito	WCq		14 997	Selman CHI
9-09	Argentina	L	0-3	Caracas	WCq		24 783	Vazquez URU
15-11	Colombia	W	1-0	Barranquilla	WCq	Arango [9]	20 000	Chandia CHI
18-11	Bolivia	W	2-1	Maracaibo	WCq	Rey [90], Arango [92+]	30 000	Reinoso ECU
2004								
18-02	Australia	D	1-1	Caracas	Fr	Arango [91+]	16 000	Ruiz COL
10-03	Honduras	W	2-1	Maracaibo	Fr	Vera [35p], Noriega [53]	24 000	Manzur VEN
31-03	Uruguay	W	3-0	Montevideo	WCq	Urdaneta [19], González.H [67], Arango [77]	40 094	Ortube BOL
28-04	Jamaica	L	1-2	Kingston	Fr	Arango [27]	10 000	Ford BRB
1-06	Chile	L	0-1	San Cristobal	WCq		23 040	Torres PAR
6-06	Peru	D	0-0	Lima	WCq		40 000	Larrionda URU
6-07	Colombia	L	0-1	Lima	CАr1		45 000	Rezende BRA
9-07	Peru	L	1-3	Lima	CАr1	Margiotta [74]	43 000	Selman CHI
12-07	Bolivia	D	1-1	Trujillo	CАr1	Moran [27]	25 000	Mattus CRC
18-08	Spain	L	2-3	Las Palmas	Fr	Rojas.J [46+], Castellín [92+]	32 000	Rodomonti ITA
5-09	Paraguay	L	0-1	Asuncion	WCq		30 000	Mendez URU
9-10	Brazil	L	2-5	Maracaibo	WCq	Moran 2 [79 90]	26 133	Chandia CHI
14-10	Ecuador	W	3-1	San Cristobal	WCq	Urdaneta [20p], Moran 2 [72 80]	13 800	Lecca PER
17-11	Argentina	L	2-3	Buenos Aires	WCq	Moran [31], Vielma [72]	30 000	Hidalgo PER
21-12	Guatemala	L	0-1	Caracas	Fr		6 000	Solorzano VEN
2005								
9-02	Estonia	W	3-0	Maracaibo	Fr	Paez [20], Margiotta [33], Maldonado [83]	12 000	Vazquez ECU
26-03	Colombia	D	0-0	Maracaibo	WCq		18 000	Simon BRA
29-03	Bolivia	L	1-3	La Paz	WCq	Maldonado [71]	7 908	Lecca PER
25-05	Panama	D	1-1	Caracas	Fr	Maldonado [4]	15 000	Brand VEN
4-06	Uruguay	D	1-1	Maracaibo	WCq	Maldonado [74]	12 504	Brazenas ARG
8-06	Chile	L	1-2	Santiago	WCq	Moran [82]	35 506	Torres PAR
17-08	Ecuador	L	1-3	Loja	Fr	Torrealba [70]	10 000	Vasco ECU
3-09	Peru	W	4-1	Maracaibo	WCq	Maldonado [17], Arango [68], Torrealba 2 [73 79]	6 000	Rezende BRA
8-10	Paraguay	L	0-1	Maracaibo	WCq		13 272	Elizondo ARG
12-10	Brazil	L	0-3	Belem	WCq		47 000	Baldassi ARG
2006								
1-03	Colombia	D	1-1	Maracaibo	Fr	Gomez [48]	15 000	Carpio ECU
5-05	Mexico	L	0-1	Pasadena	Fr		57 000	Vaughn USA
26-05	USA	L	0-2	Cleveland	Fr		29 745	Morales MEX

Fr = Friendly match • CA = Copa América • WC = FIFA World Cup™ • q = qualifier • r1 = first round group

VENEZUELA NATIONAL TEAM RECORDS AND RECORD SEQUENCES

Records				Sequence records			
Victory	6-0	PUR 1946	Wins	4	2001	Clean sheets	4	2002
Defeat	0-11	ARG 1975	Defeats	9	1989-1991	Goals scored	8	1946-1956
Player Caps	77	URDANETA Gabriel	Undefeated	6	1946-1956	Without goal	5	1990-1991
Player Goals	15	MORAN Ruberth	Without win	26	1989-1993	Goals against	21	1993-96, 1999-01

VENEZUELA COUNTRY INFORMATION

Capital	Caracas	Independence	1821 from Spain	GDP per Capita	$4 800
Population	25 017 387	Status	Republic	GNP Ranking	33
Area km²	912 050	Language	Spanish	Dialling code	+58
Population density	27 per km²	Literacy rate	93%	Internet code	.ve
% in urban areas	93%	Main religion	Christian	GMT + / –	-4
Towns/Cities ('000)	Maracaibo 1 948; Caracas 1 815; Valencia 1 385; Barquisimeto 809; Ciudad Guayana 746; Barcelona 424; Maturin 410; Maracay 395; Petare 365; Turmero 344; Ciudad Bolivar 291				
Neighbours (km)	Guyana 743; Brazil 2 200; Colombia 2 050; Atlantic Ocean & Caribbean Sea 2 800				
Main stadia	Pachenricho Romero – Maracaibo 35 000; Pueblo Nuevo – San Cristobal 27 500; Olimpico – Caracas 25 000				

NATIONAL TEAM PLAYERS AND COACHES

Record Caps			Record Goals			Recent Coaches	
URDANETA Gabriel	1996-'05	77	MORAN Ruberth	1996-'05	15		
REY José Manuel	1997-'05	71	ARANGO Juan	1999-'06	11		
JIMENEZ Leopoldo	1999-'05	64	URDANETA Gabriel	1996-'05	9	SANTANA Rafael	1987
MORAN Ruberth	1996-'05	62	GARCIA Juan	1993-'04	7	MORENO Carlos	1989
VALLENILLA Luis	1996-'05	61	DOLGETTA José Luis	1993-'97	6	PIGNANELLI Victor	1990-'91
ROJAS Jorge	1996-'06	57	REY José Manuel	1997-'05	6	DUJKOVIC Ratomir	1992-'94
ARANGO Juan	1999-'06	54	CASTELLIN Rafael	1996-'05	5	SANTANA Rafael	1994-'96
DUDAMEL Rafael	1993-'05	54	FEBLES Pedro	1979-'89	5	BORRERO Eduardo	1997
MEA VITALI Miguel	1999-'06	50	NORIEGA Daniel	1996-'05	5	PASTORIZA Omar	1998-'00
PAEZ Ricardo	2000-'06	49	PAEZ Ricardo	2000-'06	5	PAEZ Richard	2000-

CLUB DIRECTORY

Club	Town/City	Stadium	Capacity	Lge
Carabobo FC	Valencia	Missael Delgado	15 000	0
Caracas FC	Caracas	Estadio Olimpico	25 000	8
Deportivo Táchira	San Cristobal	Pueblo Nuevo	30 000	4
Estudiantes FC	Merida	Guillermo Soto Rosas	15 000	2
Deportivo ItalChacao	Caracas	Brigido Iriarte	15 000	5
Deportivo ItalMaracaibo	Maracaibo	Pachenricho Romero	35 000	0
AC Mineros de Guayana	Puerto Ordaz	Polideportivo Cachamay	15 000	1
Monagas SC	Maturin	Polideportivo Maturin	4 000	0
Trujillanos FC	Valera	Luis Loreto Lira	15 000	0
Unión Atlético Maracaibo	Maracaibo	Pachenricho Romero	35 000	1

RECENT LEAGUE RECORD

	Championship						Championship Play-off		
Year	Champions	Pts	Runners-up	Pts	Third	Pts	Winners	Score	Runners-up
1990	CS Maritimo	43	Unión At. Táchira	43	Minervén	42			
1991	Univ. de Los Andes	39	CS Maritimo	37	Atlético Zamora	36			
1992	Caracas FC	43	Minervén	42	CS Maritimo	39			
1993	CS Maritimo	41	Minervén	41	Caracas FC	40	CS Maritimo	0-1 1-0 7-6p	Minervén
1994	Caracas FC	43	Trujillanos	40	Minervén	39			
1995	Caracas FC	17	Minervén	16	Trullianos	14			
1996	Minervén	22	Mineros de Guayana	20	Caracas FC	19			
1997	Caracas FC						Caracas	3-1 5-0	Atlético Zulia
1998	Atlético Zulia						Atlético Zulia	1-0 4-0	Estudiantes
1999	ItalChacao						ItalChacao	5-1 2-1	Unión At. Táchira
2000	Deportivo Táchira	15	ItalChacao	7	Estudiantes	6			
2001	Caracas FC	35	Trujillanos	33	ItalChacao	32			
2002	Nacional Táchira						Nacional Táchira	3-3 0-0 5-3p	Estudiantes
2003	Caracas FC						Caracas FC	1-1 3-0	Unión At. Maracaibo
2004	Caracas FC	†							
2005	Unión At. Maracaibo	†							
2006	Caracas FC						Caracas FC	1-1 3-0	Unión At. Maracaibo

† Automatic champions as winners of both the Apertura and Clausura

VENEZUELA 2005-06

PRIMERA DIVISION TORNEO APERTURA 2005

	Pl	W	D	L	F	A	Pts	Unión	Táchira	Mineros	Carabobo	Caracas	ItalMara'bo	Aragua	Trujillanos	Estudiantes	Monagas
Unión At. Maracaibo ‡	18	12	5	1	28	11	41		3-2	2-1	1-1	2-1	3-1	3-0	4-1	1-1	2-1
Deportivo Táchira	18	9	4	5	32	23	31	0-1		1-1	2-2	1-0	2-1	4-0	2-1	3-2	1-1
Mineros de Guyana	18	7	6	5	24	19	27	0-1	2-1		2-2	1-0	3-2	0-2	3-0	1-2	1-0
Carabobo FC	18	7	6	5	28	24	27	0-2	1-2	1-1		1-3	0-1	3-0	2-1	2-2	1-0
Caracas FC	18	7	3	8	28	25	24	2-0	1-3	1-1	1-3		1-1	4-1	1-0	2-1	1-1
Dep. ItalMaracaibo	18	6	6	6	23	22	24	0-1	2-3	1-1	2-2	1-0		1-1	0-0	2-0	2-3
Aragua FC	18	6	4	8	16	27	22	0-0	0-3	1-2	3-2	1-0	0-1		0-0	3-1	2-1
Trujillanos FC	18	4	6	8	14	24	18	1-1	1-1	1-0	0-1	1-4	0-1	2-1		2-1	1-1
Estudiantes FC	18	3	6	9	21	30	15	0-1	1-0	1-1	1-2	3-2	1-3	0-0	1-1		2-2
Monagas SC	18	3	6	9	19	28	15	0-0	3-1	0-3	0-2	3-4	1-1	0-1	0-2	2-1	

10/08/2005 - 19/12/2005 • ‡ Qualified for the overall championship final • Top scorer: Juan GARCIA, Dep. Tachira, 15

VENEZUELA 2005-06

PRIMERA DIVISION TORNEO CLAUSURA 2006

	Pl	W	D	L	F	A	Pts	Caracas	Táchira	Carabobo	Mineros	Monagas	Aragua	Unión	ItalMara'bo	Estudiantes	Trujillanos
Caracas FC ‡	18	10	6	2	29	14	36		0-0	4-0	2-2	2-0	4-2	2-1	2-1	1-0	2-1
Deportivo Táchira	18	8	7	3	25	21	31	2-1		1-1	1-0	2-2	3-1	1-0	1-0	1-0	3-0
Carabobo FC	18	7	6	5	26	22	27	2-1	6-2		0-0	1-1	2-0	0-2	4-1	3-2	1-1
Mineros de Guyana	18	7	6	5	21	22	27	0-0	1-1	1-0		3-2	1-0	1-1	2-1	4-3	2-1
Monagas SC	18	5	10	3	21	15	25	0-0	3-1	1-0	2-0		0-0	0-0	0-0	3-0	3-0
Aragua FC	18	7	4	7	21	21	25	0-2	0-0	1-0	3-0	0-0		2-1	3-1	1-0	0-0
Unión At. Maracaibo	18	3	11	4	21	20	20	1-1	1-1	1-1	2-1	1-1	1-2		2-2	1-1	1-1
Dep. ItalMaracaibo	18	1	7	10	18	32	19	0-0	1-2	1-2	0-2	2-2	1-3	1-1		4-2	1-1
Estudiantes	18	5	3	10	27	33	18	2-3	2-1	1-2	2-0	1-1	3-2	1-1	2-0		3-0
Trujillanos FC	18	3	8	7	18	27	17	0-2	2-2	1-1	1-1	2-0	1-0	0-2	2-2	4-1	

8/01/2006 - 14/05/2006 • ‡ Qualified for the overall championship final • Top scorers: Daniel ARISMENDI, Carabobo, 9; Jesus GOMEZ, Estudiantes, 9; Championship Final: Unión At. Maracaibo 1-1 0-3 **Caracas FC** • Caracas are Venezuelan champions in 2006

PRIMERA DIVISION AGGREGATE

	Pl	W	D	L	F	A	Pts
Deportivo Táchira †	36	17	11	8	57	44	62
Unión At. Maracaibo †	36	15	16	5	49	31	61
Caracas FC †	36	17	9	10	57	39	60
Carabobo FC ‡	36	14	12	10	54	46	54
Mineros de Guyana ‡	36	14	12	10	45	41	54
Aragua FC	36	13	8	15	37	48	47
Monagas SC	36	8	16	12	40	43	40
Trujillanos	36	7	14	15	32	51	35
Dep. ItalMaracaibo	36	7	13	16	41	54	34
Estudiantes	36	8	9	19	48	63	33

† Qualified for Copa Libertadores 2007 • ‡ Qualified for Copa Sudamericana • Top scorer: Juan GARCIA, Táchira, 21

VENEZUELA 2005-06 ASCENSO APERTURA (2) GRUPO CENTRO-OCCIDENTE

	Pl	W	D	L	F	A	Pts
UPEL Nacional †	14	7	5	2	18	8	26
Deportivo Maracaibo	14	7	4	3	20	15	25
UCLA FC	14	5	5	4	13	13	20
Zamora FC	14	6	2	6	19	22	20
Portuguesa FC	14	5	4	5	17	17	19
Llaneros de Guanare	14	4	6	4	17	13	18
Sport Zulia	14	5	3	6	16	15	18
Unión At. El Vigía	14	2	1	11	11	28	7

21/08/2005 - 1/12/2005 • † Qualified for Apertura final

VENEZUELA 2005-06 ASCENSO APERTURA (2) GRUPO CENTRO-ORIENTE

	Pl	W	D	L	F	A	Pts
Deportivo Galicia †	14	8	4	2	27	10	28
Deportivo ItalChacao	14	9	1	4	32	16	28
Deportivo Anzoátegui	14	8	2	4	16	15	26
Unión Lara	14	6	7	1	33	17	25
Caracas FC 'B'	14	5	2	7	21	22	17
Hermandad Gallega	14	3	5	6	21	26	14
Nueva Cádiz	14	2	4	8	11	25	10
Escuela San Tomé	14	2	1	11	10	40	7

20/08/2005 - 1/12/2005 • † Qualified for Apertura final
Apertura final: Dep Galicia 2-3 2-3 **UPEL Nacional**

VENEZUELA 2005-06 ASCENSO CLAUSURA (2)

	Pl	W	D	L	F	A	Pts
Portuguesa FC	18	11	5	2	34	14	38
Zamora FC	18	11	5	2	31	15	38
Unión Lara	18	11	4	3	36	21	37
Deportivo Anzoátegui	18	9	3	6	31	25	30
UPEL Nacional	18	6	5	7	19	19	23
Caracas FC 'B'	18	6	4	8	20	24	22
UCLA FC	18	6	3	9	23	30	21
Deportivo Italchacao	18	5	5	8	19	19	20
Deportivo Maracaibo	18	3	3	12	20	41	12
Deportivo Galicia	18	3	1	14	14	39	10

15/01/2006 - 20/05/2006

VGB – BRITISH VIRGIN ISLANDS

NATIONAL TEAM RECORD
JULY 1ST 2002 TO JULY 9TH 2006

PL	W	D	L	F	A	%
15	4	1	10	15	38	30

FIFA/COCA-COLA WORLD RANKING

1993	1994	1995	1996	1997	1998	1999	2000	2001	2002	2003	2004	2005		High		Low
-	-	-	-	180	187	161	172	163	161	175	165	171		**160**	03/00	**187** 02/99

					2005–2006						
08/05	09/05	10/05	11/05	12/05	01/06	02/06	03/06	04/06	05/06	06/06	07/06
164	163	163	163	171	171	171	172	173	173	-	168

The women's national team of the British Virgin Islands entered the FIFA Women's World Cup for the first time and were drawn to play the US Virgin Islands in a preliminary round of the 2006 Caribbean Cup, which served as part of the qualifying tournament. A 3-1 defeat in the home leg in Road Town put paid to any hopes of progress, but a week later they made what must be the shortest away trip in international football, across The Narrows to Charlotte Amalie less than 20 miles away. The stress of the journey can't be blamed for their 5-0 defeat but it was a very useful experience for the team. Seven months earlier the women's under-19 team had taken part in the

INTERNATIONAL HONOURS
None

qualifiers for the FIFA Women's U-20 World Championship, but came away from their qualifying group in the Dominican Republic considerably worse off for the experience. Their opening match against Haiti had to be abandoned after 39 minutes with the score at 11-0 because the BVI had been reduced to just six players. Against the hosts they then lost 25-0 - a record score for a women's game in a FIFA match - before rounding off the tournament with a resounding 12-0 defeat at the hands of the US Virgin Islands. In domestic football, Hairoun beat Rangers 3-2 in a play-off to end Rangers' eight year reign as champions of Virgin Gorda.

THE FIFA BIG COUNT OF 2000

	Male	Female		Male	Female
Registered players	208	28	Referees	11	1
Non registered players	100	15	Officials	4	0
Youth players	214	93	Total involved	674	
Total players	658		Number of clubs	10	
Professional players	0	0	Number of teams	21	

British Virgin Islands Football Association (BVIFA)
Botanic Station Road, Road Town, PO Box 4269, Tortola, British Virgin Islands
Tel +1 284 4945655   Fax +1 284 4948968
bvifa@surfbvi.com   www.bvifa.com
President: GRANT Kenrick   General Secretary: DASENT Llewellyn
Vice-President: LIBURD Aubrey   Treasurer: DASENT Llewellyn   Media Officer: FAYE Anatole
Men's Coach: DAVIES Ben   Women's Coach: PETERSON Azille
BVIFA formed: 1974   CONCACAF: 1996   FIFA: 1996
Gold shirts, Green shorts, Green socks

RECENT INTERNATIONAL MATCHES PLAYED BY THE BRITISH VIRGIN ISLANDS

2002	Opponents	Score		Venue	Comp	Scorers	Att	Referee
6-07	Anguilla	W	2-1	Tortola	Fr	Baptiste [42], Huggins [44]		
14-07	St Lucia	L	1-3	Tortola	GCq	Huggins [53]		
28-07	St Lucia	L	1-8	Castries	GCq	Azile [36]		
2003								
No international matches played in 2003								
2004								
28-01	Dominica	L	0-1	Tortola	Fr			Matthew SKN
30-01	US Virgin Islands	W	5-0	Tortola	Fr	OG [18], Williams [24], Morris 2 [26 56], Ferron [88]		
1-02	Dominica	L	1-2	Tortola	Fr	Morris [28]		Charles DMA
22-02	St Lucia	L	0-1	Tortola	WCq		800	Stewart JAM
20-03	St Kitts and Nevis	L	0-4	Basseterre	Fr			
28-03	St Lucia	L	0-9	Vieux Fort	WCq		665	Corrivault CAN
25-09	US Urgin Islands	W	2-1	Tortola	Fr	Heileger [48], Etienne [55]		
24-11	St Vincent/Grenadines	D	1-1	Kingstown	GCq	Haynes [53]	300	Prendergast JAM
26-11	Cayman Islands	L	0-1	Kingstown	GCq			
28-11	Bermuda	W	2-0	Kingstown	GCq	James 2 [12 24]	400	Matthews SKN
12-12	Trinidad and Tobago	L	0-4	Tortola	GCq		16 000	Arthur LCA
19-12	Tinidad and Tobago	L	0-2	Tunapuna	GCq			Lancaster GUY
2005								
No international matches played in 2005								
2006								
No international matches played in 2006 before July								

Fr = Friendly match • GC = CONCACAF Gold Cup • WC = FIFA World Cup™ • q = qualifier

BRITISH VIRGIN ISLANDS NATIONAL TEAM RECORDS AND RECORD SEQUENCES

Records			Sequence records					
Victory	5-0	PUR, AIA, VIR	Wins	2	1999	Clean sheets	2	1999, 2001
Defeat	0-12	JAM 1994	Defeats	8	1997-1998	Goals scored	6	1999-2000
Player Caps	n/a		Undefeated	6	2000-2001	Without goal	3	Five times
Player Goals	n/a		Without win	10	1991-1997	Goals against	18	1992-1999

RECENT LEAGUE RECORD

	Tortola	Virgin Gorda
Year	Champions	Champions
1996	Black Lions	Spice United
1997	No tournament	Beverly Hills
1998	BDO Binder Stingers	United Kickers
1999	Veterans	
2000	HBA Panthers	Rangers
2001	HBA Panthers	Rangers
2001	Future Stars United	Rangers
2002	HBA Panthers	No tournament
2003		Rangers
2004	Valencia	Rangers
2005		Hairoun

BRITISH VIRGIN ISLANDS COUNTRY INFORMATION

Capital	Road Town	Status	Overseas territory of the UK	GDP per Capita	$16 000
Population	22 187			GNP Ranking	n/a
Area km²	153	Language	English	Dialling code	+1284
Population density	145 per km²	Literacy rate	97%	Internet code	.vg
% in urban areas	NA	Main religion	Christian	GMT +/−	-4
Towns/Cities	Road Town 8 449; Spanish Town 355				
Neighbours (km)	Caribbean Sea & Atlantic Ocean 80				
Main stadia	Shirley Recreational Field – Road Town, Tortola 2 000				

VIE – VIETNAM

NATIONAL TEAM RECORD
JULY 1ST 2002 TO JULY 9TH 2006

PL	W	D	L	F	A	%
29	13	5	11	60	51	53.4

FIFA/COCA-COLA WORLD RANKING

1993	1994	1995	1996	1997	1998	1999	2000	2001	2002	2003	2004	2005		High		Low	
135	151	122	99	104	98	102	99	105	108	98	103	120		84	09/98	156	11/95

2005–2006											
08/05	09/05	10/05	11/05	12/05	01/06	02/06	03/06	04/06	05/06	06/06	07/06
106	112	113	114	120	121	122	124	125	126	-	141

For the co-hosts of the 2007 AFC Asian Cup not to play any internationals in the 18 months following the 2004 Tiger Cup, would seem to be a foolhardy thing to do. But that is exactly what Vietnam have done, preferring instead to concentrate their efforts in a series of mini-tournaments in the region before the finals in July 2007. It will be the first time since 1960 that Vietnam will have appeared in the finals and although they will have a passionate home support behind them in the modern My Dinh National Stadium in Hanoi, that may not be enough to get them past the first stage. Vietnam's international sporting prestige suffered a blow in 2006 with the decision by the

INTERNATIONAL HONOURS
South East Asian Games 1959

AFC to take away one of the two Champions League places allocated to the country. Only the champions will now qualify with the other team playing in the AFC Cup instead. Vietnam's record in the Champions League hasn't been good with both Gach Dong Tam and Da Nang failing to pick up a single point in the 2006 tournament. At home, 2005 was a good year for Dong Tam. Having won a first ever Championship, they followed that up with a comprehensive 5-0 win in the Cup Final against Hai Phong to win the trophy for the first time as well. The finish of the 2006 season was delayed due to the FIFA World Cup™ finals in Germany.

THE FIFA BIG COUNT OF 2000

	Male	Female		Male	Female
Registered players	1 652	176	Referees	180	20
Non registered players	985 000	50 000	Officials	18 000	2 000
Youth players	1 948	0	Total involved	1 058 976	
Total players	1 038 776		Number of clubs	200	
Professional players	0	0	Number of teams	18 300	

Vietnam Football Federation (VFF)
Liên Doàn Bong Dá Viêt Nam, 18 Ly van Phuc, Dong Da District, Hanoi 844, Vietnam
Tel +84 4 8452480   Fax +84 4 8233119
vff@hn.vnn.vn   www.vff.org.vn
President: NGUYEN Trong Hy   General Secretary: TRAN Quoc Tuan
Vice-President: LE The Tho   Treasurer: LE Hung Dung   Media Officer: NGUYEN Trung Lan
Men's Coach: RIEDL Alfred   Women's Coach: MAI Chung Duc
VFF formed: 1962   AFC: 1954   FIFA: 1964
Red shirts, Red shorts, Red socks

RECENT INTERNATIONAL MATCHES PLAYED BY VIETNAM

2002	Opponents	Score		Venue	Comp	Scorers	Att	Referee
27-11	Sri Lanka	W	2-1	Colombo	Fr	Nguyen Minh Phoung [32], Nhuyen Duc Thang [62]		Arambakade SRI
29-11	Sri Lanka	D	1-1	Colombo	Fr	Trinh Xuan Thanh [49]		Pingamage SRI
1-12	Sri Lanka	D	2-2	Colombo	Fr	Le Huynh Duc		
8-12	Thailand	L	1-2	Bangkok	Fr	Huynh Hong Son [13]		
15-12	Cambodia	W	9-2	Jakarta	TCr1	Huynh Hong Son [10], Tran Truong Giang 2 [14 41], Nguyen Quoc Trung [24], Le Huynh Duc 2 [58 73], Nguyen Minh Phuong [70], Trinh Xuan Thanh [83], Pham Van Quyen [89]	5 000	Nagalingam SIN
19-12	Philippines	W	4-1	Jakarta	TCr1	Huynh Hong Son 2 [55 69], Le Huynh Duc 2 [68p 72]	2 000	Nagalingam SIN
21-12	Indonesia	D	2-2	Jakarta	TCr1	Phan Van Tai Em [53], Le Huynh Duc [57]	35 000	Mohd Salleh MAS
23-12	Myanmar	W	4-2	Jakarta	TCr1	Trinh Xuan Thanh [37], Dang Phuong Nam 2 [49 67], Le Huynh Duc [72]	2 000	Nagalingam SIN
27-12	Thailand	L	0-4	Jakarta	TCsf		10 000	Nagalingam SIN
29-12	Malaysia	W	2-1	Jakarta	TC3p	Tran Truong Giang [45], Nguyen Minh Phuong [59]	25 000	Midi Nitrorejo IDN
2003								
12-02	Albania	L	0-5	Bastia Umbra	Fr			Nicoletti ITA
25-09	Korea Republic	L	0-5	Incheon	ACq			
27-09	Nepal	W	5-0	Incheon	ACq	Pham Van Quyen 3 [14 22 36], Nguyen Huu Thang [23], Phan Thanh Binh [90]		
29-09	Oman	L	0-6	Incheon	ACq			
19-10	Korea Republic	W	1-0	Muscat	ACq	Pham Van Quyen [73]		
21-10	Nepal	W	2-0	Muscat	ACq	Nguyen Minh Phuong [49], Phan Thanh Binh [51]		
24-10	Oman	L	0-2	Muscat	ACq			
2004								
18-02	Maldives	W	4-0	Hanoi	WCq	Phan Van Tai Em 2 [9 60], Nguyen Minh Hai [13], Pham Van Quyen [80p]	25 000	Fong HKG
31-03	Lebanon	L	0-2	Nam Dinh	WCq		25 000	Irmatov UZB
9-06	Korea Republic	L	0-2	Daejeon	WCq		40 019	Al Mehannah KSA
20-08	Myanmar	W	5-0	Ho Chi Minh City	Fr	Le Cong Vinh 2, Thach Boa Khanh, Nguyen Minh Phuong, Pham Van Quyen		
24-08	India	W	2-1	Ho Chi Minh City	Fr	Le Cong Vinh [21], Thach Boa Khanh [57]		
8-09	Korea Republic	L	1-2	Ho Chi Minh City	WCq	Phan Van Tai Em [49]	25 000	Yoshida JPN
13-10	Maldives	L	0-3	Male	WCq		10 000	Haq IND
17-11	Lebanon	D	0-0	Beirut	WCq		1 000	Ebrahim BHR
7-12	Singapore	D	1-1	Ho Chi Minh City	TCr1	Thach Boa Khanh [51]	20 000	Sun Baojie CHN
9-12	Cambodia	W	9-1	Ho Chi Minh City	TCr1	Thach Boa Khanh 2 [8 23], Le Cong Vinh 3 [58 87 89], OG [63], Dang Van Thanh 2 [71 83], Nguyen Huu Thang [83]	8 000	Supian MAS
11-12	Indonesia	L	0-3	Hanoi	TCr1		40 000	Sun Baojie CHN
15-12	Laos	W	3-0	Hanoi	TCr1	Le Cong Vinh [9], Nguyen Minh Phuong [41], Thach Bao Khanh [74]	20 000	Rungklay THA

2005

No international matches played in 2005

2006

No international matches played in 2006 before July

Fr = Friendly match • TC = ASEAN Tiger Cup • AC = AFC Asian Cup • WC = FIFA World Cup™
q = qualifier • r1 = first round group • sf = semi-final • 3p = third place play-off

VIETNAM NATIONAL TEAM RECORDS AND RECORD SEQUENCES

Records			Sequence records					
Victory	11-0	GUM 2000	Wins	6	1966	Clean sheets	6	1999
Defeat	1-9	IDN 1971	Defeats	10	1997	Goals scored	23	1949-1958
Player Caps	n/a		Undefeated	8	1954-1956	Without goal	4	1997
Player Goals	n/a		Without win	12	1974-1993	Goals against	22	1956-1959

VIETNAM COUNTRY INFORMATION

Capital	Hanoi	Independence	1954 from France	GDP per Capita	$2 500
Population	82 689 518	Status	Republic	GNP Ranking	58
Area km²	329 560	Language	Vietnamese	Dialling code	+84
Population density	251 per km²	Literacy rate	90%	Internet code	.vn
% in urban areas	21%	Main religion	Buddhist, Hoa Hao, Cao Dai	GMT + / −	+7
Towns/Cities ('000)	Ho Chi Minh City 3 467; Hanoi 1 431; Hai Phong 602; Da Nang 472; Bien Hoa 407; Hue 287
Neighbours (km)	Cambodia 1 228; China 1 281; Laos 2 130; South China Sea & Gulf of Tonkin 3 444
Main stadia	My Dinh – Hanoi 40 000; San Chi Lang – Da Nang 28 000; Thong Nhat – Ho Chi Minh City 25 000

VIETNAM CUP 2005

Round of 16			Quarter-finals			Semi-finals			Final		
Gach Dong Tam	0	6p									
Ton Hoa Sen Can Tho*	0	5p	Gach Dong Tam *	3	3p						
Ngan Hang Dong *	2		Binh Dinh	3	1p						
Binh Dinh	3					Gach Dong Tam	4				
Hoa Phat	2					Khatoco Khanh Hoa *	0				
LG HN ACB *	0		Hoa Phat	0							
The Cong *	0		Khatoco Khanh Hoa *	4							
Khatoco Khanh Hoa	1								Gach Dong Tam	5	
Hoang Anh Gia Lai *	3								Hai Phong	0	
Da My Nghe	0		Hoang Anh Gia Lai	2							
Buu Dien	0		Binh Duong *	1							
Binh Duong *	2					Hoang Anh Gia Lai *	0	1p			
Song Lam Nghe An	1					Hai Phong	0	3p			
Thanh Hoa *	0		Song Lam Nghe An	0							
Song Da Nam Dinh	0		Hai Phong *	1							
Hai Phong *	1										

CUP FINAL

20-08-2005, Long An

Scorers - Tai Em 2 [12][91]+, Carlos 2 [33][42], Fungai Tostao Kwashi [85]

* Home team

RECENT LEAGUE AND CUP RECORD

	Championship						Cup		
Year	Champions	Pts	Runners-up	Pts	Third	Pts	Winners	Score	Runners-up
2000	Song Lam Nghe An	43	Cong An HCMC	42	Cong An Hanoi	37	Cang Saigon	2-1	Cong An HCMC
2001	Song Lam Nghe An	36	Nam Dinh	34	The Cong	29	Cong An HCMC	2-1	Cong An Hanoi
2002	Cang Saigon	32	Song Lam Nghe An	28	Ngan Hang Dong	26	Song Lam Nghe An	1-0	Thua Thien
2003	Hoang Anh Gia Lai	43	Gach Dong Tam	40	Nam Dinh	36	Binh Dinh	2-1	Ngan Hang Dong
2004	Hoang Anh Gia Lai	46	Nam Dinh	44	Gach Dong Tam	38	Binh Dinh	2-0	The Cong
2005	Gach Dong Tam	42	Da Nang	38	Binh Duong	38	Gach Dong Tam	5-0	Hai Phong

Cong An = Police • The Cong = Army • Cang Saigon = Saigon Port • HCMC = Ho Chi Minh City

VIN – ST VINCENT AND THE GRENADINES

NATIONAL TEAM RECORD
JULY 1ST 2002 TO JULY 9TH 2006

PL	W	D	L	F	A	%
22	9	5	8	40	37	52.3

FIFA/COCA-COLA WORLD RANKING

1993	1994	1995	1996	1997	1998	1999	2000	2001	2002	2003	2004	2005		High		Low
129	144	95	93	122	138	141	127	125	144	169	137	130		**80** 08/96		**170** 02/04

	2005–2006										
08/05	09/05	10/05	11/05	12/05	01/06	02/06	03/06	04/06	05/06	06/06	07/06
128	128	127	126	130	131	131	133	133	133	-	129

The international season in St Vincent and the Grenadines didn't get off to the best of starts when in August the women's under-19 team travelled to St Lucia for a FIFA Women's U-20 World Championship qualifying group. A 4-1 defeat at the hands of the hosts was followed by an embarrassing 18-0 reversal at the hands of Trinidad and Tobago and a 10-0 defeat by Grenada. Thankfully that form wasn't carried over into the 2006 Caribbean Cup in which the senior women's team took part in May 2006. Making their debut in what was a qualifying group for the FIFA Women's World Cup, the team acquitted themselves well by beating Dominica 2-0 and Grenada 5-0.

INTERNATIONAL HONOURS
None

As was to be expected they lost to Trinidad to miss out on the final round of the Caribbean Cup but the goals count of eight scored and only four conceded was very encouraging. In the men's game there was no international activity but big efforts have been made to improve the club structure with the launch in 2004 of the National Club Championship, won by Samba in its first season. In 2005, nine teams entered the Premier League which was won by Newmill Hope International. They went through the 16 match season unbeaten, finishing eight points ahead of SVM System Three with defending champions Samba back in fourth place.

THE FIFA BIG COUNT OF 2000

	Male	Female		Male	Female
Registered players	1 000	106	Referees	4	0
Non registered players	1 100	170	Officials	410	15
Youth players	3 000	40	Total involved	5 845	
Total players	5 416		Number of clubs	272	
Professional players	5	0	Number of teams	272	

Saint Vincent and the Grenadines Football Federation (SVGFF)
Murray's Road, PO Box 1278, Saint George, St Vincent and the Grenadines
Tel +1 784 4561092   Fax +1 784 4572193
svgfootball@vincysurf.com   www.svgvincyheat.com
President: LEACOCK St Clair   General Secretary: BENNETT Earl
Vice-President: ROBINSON Clyde   Treasurer: HUGGINS Trevor   Media Officer: WILLIAMS Asberth
Men's Coach: VRANES Zoran   Women's Coach: McCARTHY Seamus
SVGFF formed: 1979   CONCACAF: 1988   FIFA: 1988
Green shirts, Blue shorts, Green socks

RECENT INTERNATIONAL MATCHES PLAYED BY ST VINCENT AND THE GRENADINES

2004	Opponents		Score	Venue	Comp	Scorers	Att	Referee
8-02	St Lucia	W	2-1	Castries	Fr			
21-03	St Lucia	D	1-1	Kingstown	Fr	Charles [39]		
8-05	Grenada	D	1-1	Kingstown	Fr	Guy [6]		
23-05	St Kitts and Nevis	L	2-3	Basseterre	Fr	Haynes [10], Samuel [32]		Matthew SKN
13-06	Nicaragua	D	2-2	Diriamba	WCq	Haynes [9], Samuel [43]	7 500	Delgado CUB
20-06	Nicaragua	W	4-1	Kingstown	WCq	Samuel 2 [14 79], James [15], Alonso OG [86]	5 000	Brohim DMA
18-08	Trinidad and Tobago	L	0-2	Kingstown	WCq		5 000	Vaughn USA
10-09	St Kitts and Nevis	W	1-0	Kingstown	WCq	Jack [23]	4 000	Delgado CUB
6-10	Mexico	L	0-7	Pachuca	WCq		21 000	Liu CAN
10-10	Mexico	L	0-1	Kingstown	WCq		2 500	Alfaro SLV
13-10	St Kitts and Nevis	W	3-0	Basseterre	WCq	Velox 2 [19 85], Samuel [65]	500	Whittaker CAY
13-11	Grenada	W	6-2	Kingstown	Fr	James 2 [12 27], John [19], Joseph [71], Gonsalves [74], Velox [88]		Moss VIN
17-11	Trinidad and Tobago	L	1-2	Port of Spain	WCq	Haynes [49]	10 000	Batres GUA
20-11	Grenada	L	2-3	Gouyave	Fr	Gonsalves [18], Haynes [58]	3 000	Bedeau CAN
24-11	British Virgin Islands	D	1-1	Kingstown	GCq	Forde [69]	300	Prendergast JAM
26-11	Bermuda	D	3-3	Kingstown	GCq	Pierre [7], Haynes [52], Samuel [54]		
28-11	Cayman Islands	W	4-0	Kingstown	GCq	Samuel [20], Forde [43p], Haynes [51], Gonsalves [80]	850	Prendergast JAM
12-12	Grenada	W	3-1	Kingstown	GCq	Samuel [10], Guy [23], Velox [64]		Fanus LCA
19-12	Grenada	W	1-0	St George's	GCq	Francis [6]	1 000	Small BRB
2005								
9-01	Trinidad and Tobago	L	1-3	Port of Spain	GCq	Haynes [25]	1 688	Chance ATG
16-01	Trinidad and Tobago	W	1-0	Kingstown	GCq	Forde [66p]	1 450	Pine JAM
30-01	Barbados	L	1-3	Bridgetown	Fr	Guy [14]		
2006								
No international matches played in 2006 before July								

Fr = Friendly match • GC = CONCACAF Gold Cup • WC = FIFA World Cup™ • q = qualifier

ST VINCENT AND THE GRENADINES NATIONAL TEAM RECORDS AND RECORD SEQUENCES

Records			Sequence records					
Victory	9-0	MSR 1995, VIR 2000	Wins	5	1999-2000	Clean sheets	4	1995
Defeat	0-11	MEX 1992	Defeats	7	1992-1993, 2000	Goals scored	21	1996-2000
Player Caps	n/a		Undefeated	8	1995	Without goal	7	1992-1993
Player Goals	n/a		Without win	10	1996	Goals against	12	1996-1998

ST VINCENT AND THE GRENADINES 2005-06 PREMIER LEAGUE

	Pl	W	D	L	F	A	Pts
Hope International	16	12	4	0	36	7	40
SVM System Three	16	10	2	4	27	17	32
Prospect United	16	8	5	3	28	17	29
Samba	16	7	4	5	22	13	25
Stingers	16	6	6	4	19	18	24
Under-20	16	6	5	5	29	15	23
Buccament Warriors	16	1	6	9	15	29	9
Hot Spurs	16	1	5	10	17	38	8
Rose Place	16	0	5	11	11	49	5

ST VINCENT AND THE GRENADINES COUNTRY INFORMATION

Capital	Kingstown	Independence	1979 from the UK	GDP per Capita	$2 900
Population	117 193	Status	Parliamentary Democracy	GNP Ranking	176
Area km²	389	Language	English	Dialling code	+1809
Population density	301 per km²	Literacy rate	96%	Internet code	.vc
% in urban areas	46%	Main religion	Christian	GMT +/−	-4
Towns/Cities ('000)	Kingstown 17; Barroualie 2; Georgetown 2; Layou 2; Byera 1; Biabou 1				
Neighbours (km)	Caribbean Sea & Atlantic Ocean 84				
Main stadia	Arnos Vale Playing Ground – Kingstown 18 000				

VIR – US VIRGIN ISLANDS

NATIONAL TEAM RECORD
JULY 1ST 2002 TO JULY 9TH 2006

PL	W	D	L	F	A	%
9	0	0	9	4	56	0

FIFA/COCA-COLA WORLD RANKING

1993	1994	1995	1996	1997	1998	1999	2000	2001	2002	2003	2004	2005	High		Low	
-	-	-	-	-	-	194	198	198	197	199	196	196	190	04/99	200	09/04

2005–2006											
08/05	09/05	10/05	11/05	12/05	01/06	02/06	03/06	04/06	05/06	06/06	07/06
195	195	195	195	196	196	196	196	197	197	-	196

It proved to be a busy year for the women's teams of the US Virgin Islands with both the senior team and the under-19 team making their competitive international debuts. In the FIFA Women's World Cup, the senior team beat their close neighbours the British Virgin Islands 8-1 on aggregate in a preliminary round tie to qualify for the first group stage of the 2006 Caribbean Cup. In a tournament in the Dominican Republic, they more than held their own against their more powerful hosts despite losing 3-1 and were 1-0 up against Bermuda before conceding four in the last half an hour. They did register a win in the final game, beating the Turks and Caicos Islands 2-0 to finish

INTERNATIONAL HONOURS
None

third in the group. The qualifiers for the FIFA Women's U-20 World Championship had also seen the under-19s travel to the Dominican Republic, although their hosts were slightly less charitable in the opening match, winning 8-0. There then followed a 14-0 drubbing at the hands of Haiti before a morale boosting 12-0 win over the British Virgin Islands. Overall it was an encouraging season showing that progress is being made on the international front. In men's club football, the final of the 5th USVI Championship between the top two teams of both the St Croix Soccer League and the St Thomas Soccer League saw New Vibes beat Positive Vibes 4-2 after extra-time.

THE FIFA BIG COUNT OF 2000

	Male	Female		Male	Female
Registered players	200	85	Referees	1	0
Non registered players	800	50	Officials	13	4
Youth players	600	275	Total involved	2 028	
Total players	2 010		Number of clubs	9	
Professional players	0	60	Number of teams	22	

U.S.V.I. Soccer Federation Inc. (USVISA)
AQ Building Contant, Suite 205, PO Box 306627, St Thomas VI 0080-6627, US Virgin Islands
Tel +1 340 7142828   Fax +1 340 7142830
usvisoccer@vipowernet.net   www.none
President: MARTIN Derrick   General Secretary: MONTICEUX Glen
Vice-President: FAHIE Collister   Treasurer: TBD   Media Officer: none
Men's Coach: WILLIAMS Clifton   Women's Coach: WOREDE Yohannes
USVISA formed: 1992   CONCACAF: 1998   FIFA: 1998
Royal blue shirts, Royal blue shorts, Royal blue socks

RECENT INTERNATIONAL MATCHES PLAYED BY THE US VIRGIN ISLANDS

2002	Opponents	Score		Venue	Comp	Scorers	Att	Referee
16-08	Dominican Republic	L	1-6	Santo Domingo	GCq	Sheppard [44]		Forde BRB
18-08	Dominican Republic	L	1-5	Santo Domingo	GCq	Sheppard [69]		Jean Lesly HAI
2003								
No international matches played in 2003								
2004								
30-01	British Virgin Islands	L	0-5	Road Town	Fr			
31-01	Dominica	L	0-5	St Thomas	Fr			Matthew SKN
18-02	St Kitts and Nevis	L	0-4	St Thomas	WCq		225	Brizan TRI
31-03	St Kitts and Nevis	L	0-7	Basseterre	WCq		800	Recinos SLV
25-09	British Virgin Islands	L	1-2	Road Town	Fr	Challenger [65]		
24-11	Haiti	L	0-11	Kingston	GCq		250	Piper TRI
26-11	Jamaica	L	1-11	Kingston	GCq	Lauro [72]	4 200	Piper TRI
28-11	St Martin †	D	0-0	Kingston	GCq		200	Brizan TRI
2005								
No international matches played in 2005								
2006								
No international matches played in 2006 before July								

Fr = Friendly match • GC = CONCACAF Gold Cup • WC = FIFA World Cup™ • q = qualifier • † Not a full international

US VIRGIN ISLANDS NATIONAL TEAM RECORDS AND RECORD SEQUENCES

Records			Sequence records					
Victory	1-0	BVI 1998	Wins	1	1998	Clean sheets	1	1998, 1999
Defeat	1-14	LCA 2001	Defeats	17	2000-2004	Goals scored	3	2001-2002
Player Caps	n/a		Undefeated	3	1998-1999	Without goal	4	1999-2000, 2004
Player Goals	n/a		Without win	19	1999-2004	Goals against	17	2000-2004

RECENT LEAGUE RECORD

	Overall Championship			St Thomas/St John	St Croix
Year	Champions	Score	Runners-up	Champions	Champions
1998				MI Roc Masters	Helenites
1999				MI Roc Masters	Unique FC
2000	United We Stand Upsetters	5-1	Helenites	United We Stand Upsetters	Helenites
2001		Not played			Not played
2002	Hatian Stars	1-0	United We Stand Upsetters	Waitikubuli United	Helenites
2003		Not played		Waitikubuli United	Helenites
2004		Not played			Helenites
2005	Positive Vibes	2-0	Helenites	Positive Vibes	Helenites
2006	New Vibes	4-2	Positive Vibes	Positive Vibes	Helenites

US VIRGIN ISLANDS COUNTRY INFORMATION

Capital	Charlottte Amalie	Status	US Unincorpoated Territory	GDP per Capita	$17 500
Population	108 775			GNP Ranking	n/a
Area km²	352	Language	English, Spanish, Creole	Dialling code	+1340
Population density	309 per km²	Literacy rate	n/a	Internet code	.vi
% in urban areas	n/a	Main religion	Christian	GMT +/–	-4
Towns/Cities ('000)	Charlotte Amalie 10; Anna's Retreat 8; Charlotte Amalie West 5; Frederiksted Southeast 3				
Neighbours (km)	Caribbean Sea & Atlantic Ocean 188				
Main stadia	Lionel Roberts – Charlotte Amalie, St Thomas 9 000				

WAL – WALES

NATIONAL TEAM RECORD
JULY 1ST 2002 TO JULY 9TH 2006

PL	W	D	L	F	A	%
33	12	9	12	39	34	50

FIFA/COCA-COLA WORLD RANKING

1993	1994	1995	1996	1997	1998	1999	2000	2001	2002	2003	2004	2005	High		Low	
29	41	61	80	102	97	98	109	100	52	66	68	71	27	08/93	113	09/00

2005–2006											
08/05	09/05	10/05	11/05	12/05	01/06	02/06	03/06	04/06	05/06	06/06	07/06
83	82	73	72	71	72	74	76	74	74	-	58

An outstanding season for TNS Llansantffraid started with a dream tie against European champions Liverpool in the first preliminary round of the UEFA Champions League, and although both ties were lost, the mood of celebration carried right through the season for the club. Not until the beginning of April were TNS beaten, having remained undefeated for their first 29 matches. A defeat by Carmarthen Town was just one of two in the League all season, the other coming in the very last game, against Aberystwyth, a match that had previously been abandoned because of snow with TNS leading 2-1. A defeat by Llanelli in the Cup put paid to their hopes of a successive

double. Instead, Rhyl beat Bangor to win the Cup for the second time in three years. The long era of Barry Town's dominance is well and truly over with both TNS and Rhyl now setting the standard in the Welsh League. The national team had an upbeat end to their FIFA World Cup™ qualifying campaign with victories over Northern Ireland and Azerbaijan but they still only finished one place off the bottom of their group. The draw for their UEFA Euro 2008™ qualifying group was not particularly kind with John Toshack and his squad facing difficult trips to Germany, the Czech Republic, Slovakia and the Republic of Ireland.

THE FIFA BIG COUNT OF 2000

	Male	Female		Male	Female
Registered players	38 946	400	Referees	1 062	12
Non registered players	30 000	0	Officials	10 500	125
Youth players	28 700	600	Total involved	110 345	
Total players	98 646		Number of clubs	1 830	
Professional players	320	0	Number of teams	4 615	

The Football Association of Wales, Ltd (FAW)
11/12 Neptune Court, Vanguard Way, Cardiff, CF24 5PJ, United Kingdom
Tel +44 29 20435830   Fax +44 29 20496953
info@faw.co.uk   www.faw.org.uk
President: EVANS Tegwyn MBE   General Secretary: COLLINS David
Vice-President: REES Peter   Treasurer: WILLIAMS Idwal   Media Officer: COLLINS David
Men's Coach: TOSHACK John MBE   Women's Coach: BEATTIE Andy
FAW formed: 1876   UEFA: 1954   FIFA: 1910-20, 1924-28, 1946
Red shirts, Red shorts, Red socks or White shirts, White shorts, White socks

RECENT INTERNATIONAL MATCHES PLAYED BY WALES

2002	Opponents	Score		Venue	Comp	Scorers	Att	Referee
21-08	Croatia	D	1-1	Varazdin	Fr	Davies.S [11]	6 000	Frohlich GER
7-09	Finland	W	2-0	Helsinki	ECq	Hartson [30], Davies.S [72]	35 833	Plautz AUT
6-10	Italy	W	2-1	Cardiff	ECq	Davies.S [11], Bellamy [70]	70 000	Vessiere FRA
20-11	Azerbaijan	W	2-0	Baku	ECq	Speed [10], Hartson [70]	8 000	Huyghe BEL
2003								
12-02	Bosnia-Herzegovina	D	2-2	Cardiff	Fr	Earnshaw [8], Hartson [74]	25 000	Malcolm NIR
29-03	Azerbaijan	W	4-0	Cardiff	ECq	Bellamy [1], Speed [40], Hartson [44], Giggs [52]	72 500	Leuba SUI
26-05	USA	L	0-2	San Jose	Fr		12 282	Archundia MEX
20-08	Serbia & Montenegro	L	0-1	Belgrade	ECq		25 000	Frisk SWE
6-09	Italy	L	0-4	Milan	ECq		68 000	Merk GER
10-09	Finland	D	1-1	Cardiff	ECq	Davies.S [3]	72 500	Dauden Ibanez ESP
11-10	Serbia & Montenegro	L	2-3	Cardiff	ECq	Hartson [24p], Earnshaw [90]	72 514	Stuchlik AUT
15-11	Russia	D	0-0	Moscow	ECpo		29 000	Cortez Batista POR
19-11	Russia	L	0-1	Cardiff	ECpo		73 062	Mejuto Gonzalez ESP
2004								
18-02	Scotland	W	4-0	Cardiff	Fr	Earnshaw 3 [1 35 58], Taylor [78]	47 124	Ross NIR
31-03	Hungary	W	2-1	Budapest	Fr	Koumas [20], Earnshaw [81]	10 000	Meyer GER
27-05	Norway	D	0-0	Oslo	Fr		14 137	Hansson SWE
30-05	Canada	W	1-0	Wrexham	Fr	Parry [21]	10 805	McKeon IRL
18-08	Latvia	W	2-0	Riga	Fr	Hartson [80], Bellamy [89]	10 000	Ivanov RUS
4-09	Azerbaijan	D	1-1	Baku	WCq	Speed [47]	8 000	Trivkovic CRO
8-09	Northern Ireland	D	2-2	Cardiff	WCq	Hartson [32], Earnshaw [74]	63 500	Messina ITA
9-10	England	L	0-2	Manchester	WCq		65 224	Hauge NOR
13-10	Poland	L	2-3	Cardiff	WCq	Earnshaw [56], Hartson [90]	56 685	Sars FRA
2005								
9-02	Hungary	W	2-0	Cardiff	Fr	Bellamy 2 [63 80]	16 672	Richmond SCO
26-03	Austria	L	0-2	Cardiff	WCq		47 760	Allaerts BEL
30-03	Austria	L	0-1	Vienna	WCq		29 500	Mejuto Gonzalez ESP
17-08	Slovenia	D	0-0	Swansea	Fr		10 016	Stokes IRL
3-09	England	L	0-1	Cardiff	WCq		70 715	Ivanov.V RUS
7-09	Poland	L	0-1	Warsaw	WCq		13 500	Larsen DEN
8-10	Northern Ireland	W	3-2	Belfast	WCq	Davies [27], Robinson [37], Giggs [81]	13 451	Bossen NED
12-10	Azerbaijan	W	2-0	Cardiff	WCq	Giggs 2 [3 51]	32 628	Hansson SWE
16-11	Cyprus	L	0-1	Limassol	Fr		1 000	Jakov ISR
2006								
1-03	Paraguay	D	0-0	Cardiff	Fr		12 324	McDonald SCO
27-05	Trinidad and Tobago	W	2-1	Graz	Fr	Earnshaw 2 [38 87]	8 000	Messner AUT

Fr = Friendly match • EC = UEFA EURO 2004™ • WC = FIFA World Cup™ • q = qualifier

WALES NATIONAL TEAM RECORDS AND RECORD SEQUENCES

Records			Sequence records					
Victory	11-0	NIR 1888	Wins	6	1980-1981	Clean sheets	4	1981, 1991
Defeat	0-9	SCO 1878	Defeats	8	1897-1900	Goals scored	16	1950-1954
Player Caps	92	SOUTHALL Neville	Undefeated	8	1980-1981	Without goal	6	1971-72, 1973-74
Player Goals	28	RUSH Ian	Without win	12	1896-00, 1999-01	Goals against	28	1891-1900

WALES COUNTRY INFORMATION

Capital	Cardiff	Status	Part of the UK	GDP per Capita	$22 160
Population	2 935 283			GNP Ranking	4
Area km²	20 798	Language	English, Welsh	Dialling code	+44
Population density	141 per km²	Literacy rate	99%	Internet code	.uk
% in urban areas	89%	Main religion	Christian	GMT +/−	0
Towns/Cities ('000)	Cardiff 305; Swansea 223; Newport 137; Wrexham 128; Rhondda 59; Merthyr Tydfil 55; Barry 51; Cwmbran 48; Llanelli 47; Neath 46; Bridgend 41; Pontypool 35; Port Talbot 35				
Neighbours (km)	England 468				
Main stadia	Millennium Stadium – Cardiff 74 500; Racecourse Ground – Wrexham 15 891				

NATIONAL TEAM PLAYERS AND COACHES

Record Caps			Record Goals			Recent Coaches	
SOUTHALL Neville	1982-'98	92	RUSH Ian	1980-'96	28	BOWEN Dave	1964-'74
SPEED Gary	1990-'04	85	ALLCHURCH Ivor	1951-'66	23	SMITH Mike	1974-'79
SAUNDERS Dean	1986-'01	75	FORD Trevor	1947-'57	23	ENGLAND Mike	1980-'88
NICHOLAS Peter	1979-'92	73	SAUNDERS Dean	1986-'01	22	WILLIAMS David	1988
RUSH Ian	1980-'96	73	HUGHES Mark	1984-'99	16	YORATH Terry	1988-'93
HUGHES Mark	1984-'99	72	JONES Cliff	1954-'70	16	TOSHACK John	1994
JONES Joey	1976-'86	72	CHARLES John	1950-'65	15	SMITH Mike	1994-'95
ALLCHURCH Ivor	1951-'66	68	HARTSON John	1997-'05	14	GOULD Bobby	1995-'99
FLYNN Bryan	1975-'84	66	TOSHACK John	1969-'80	13	HUGHES Mark	1999-'04
MELVILLE Andrew	1989-'04	65	LEWIS Billy	1885-'98	12	TOSHACK John	2004-

CLUB DIRECTORY

Club	Town/City	Stadium	Capacity	www.	Lge	Cup
Aberystwyth Town	Aberystwyth	Park Avenue	2 300	atfcnews.co.uk	0	1
Afan Lido	Port Talbot	Sports Ground	4 200	afanlidofc.co.uk	0	0
Airbus UK	Broughton				0	0
Bangor City	Bangor	Farrar Road	2 000	bangorcityfc.com	2	5
Caernarfon Town	Caernarfon	The Oval	2 000	caernarfontown.net	0	0
Caersws	Caersws	Recreation Ground	2 500	caerswsfc.com	0	0
Carmarthen Town	Carmarthen	Richmond Park	2 300	carmarthentownafc.net	0	0
Cefn Druids	Wrexham	Plaskynaston Lane	2 500	cefndruids.co.uk	0	0
Connah's Quay Nomads	Connah's Quay	Deeside Stadium	4 000	nomadsfc.co.uk	0	0
Cwmbran Town	Cwmbran	Cwmbran Stadium	7 877	cwmbrantownafc.org.uk	1	0
Haverfordwest County	Haverfordwest	Bridge Meadow	2 500	haverfordwestcounty.com	0	0
Llanelli	Llanelli	Stebonheath Park	3 700	llanelli-afc.co.uk	0	0
TNS Llansantffraid	Llansantffraid	Treflan	2 000	tnsfc.co.uk	3	2
Newtown	Newtown	Latham Park	5 000	newtonafc.co.uk	0	1
Porthmadog	Porthmadog	Y Traeth	4 000	geocities.com/port_fc	0	0
Port Talbot Town	Port Talbot	Victoria Road	2 000	porttalbotafc.co.uk	0	0
Rhyl	Rhyl	Belle View	3 000	rhylfc.com	1	4
Welshpool Town	Welshpool	Maes-y-Dre	3 000		0	0

RECENT LEAGUE AND CUP RECORD

	Championship						Cup		
Year	Champions	Pts	Runners-up	Pts	Third	Pts	Winners	Score	Runners-up
1993	Cwmbran Town	87	Inter Cardiff	83	Aberystwyth Town	78	Cardiff City	5-0	Rhyl
1994	Bangor City	83	Inter Cardiff	81	Ton Petre	71	Barry Town	2-1	Cardiff City
1995	Bangor City	88	Afan Lido	79	Ton Petre	77	Wrexham	2-1	Cardiff City
1996	Barry Town	97	Newtown	80	Conwy United	76	TNS Llansantffraid	3-3 3-2p	Barry Town
1997	Barry Town	105	Inter Cardiff	84	Ebbw Vale	78	Barry Town	2-1	Cwmbran Town
1998	Barry Town	104	Newtown	78	Ebbw Vale	77	Bangor City	1-1 4-2p	Nomads
1999	Barry Town	76	Inter Cardiff	63	Cwmbran Town	57	Inter Cardiff	1-1 4-2p	Carmarthen Town
2000	TNS Llansantffraid	76	Barry Town	74	Cwmbran Town	69	Bangor City	1-0	Cwmbran Town
2001	Barry Town	77	Cwmbran Town	74	Carmarthen Town	58	Barry Town	2-0	TNS Llansantffraid
2002	Barry Town	77	TNS Llansantffraid	70	Bangor City	69	Barry Town	4-1	Bangor City
2003	Barry Town	83	TNS Llansantffraid	80	Bangor City	71	Barry Town	2-2 4-3	Cwmbran Town
2004	Rhyl	77	TNS Llansantffraid	76	Haverfordwest Cty	62	Rhyl	1-0	TNS Llansantffraid
2005	TNS Llansantffraid	78	Rhyl	74	Bangor City	67	TNS Llansantffraid	1-0	Carmarthen Town
2006	TNS Llansantffraid	86	Llanelli	68	Rhyl	64	Rhyl	2-0	Bangor City

Welsh clubs playing in the English league system have been ineligible to take part in the Welsh Cup since 1995

WALES 2005–06

LEAGUE OF WALES

Team	Pl	W	D	L	F	A	Pts	TNS	Llanelli	Rhyl	Carmarthen	Port Talbot	Welshpool	Aberystwyth	Haver'west	Bangor	Caersws	Porthmadog	Connah's Q	Caernarfon	Cefn Druids	Airbus	Newtown	Cwmbran	Quins
TNS Llansantffraid †	34	27	5	2	87	17	86		0-0	1-0	4-1	1-0	1-1	5-0	2-0	2-0	2-0	7-0	2-0	2-1	4-1	3-0	3-1	1-0	7-0
Llanelli ‡	34	21	5	8	64	28	68	0-2		1-1	0-2	3-1	0-0	2-1	0-1	5-0	5-0	2-2	2-0	3-1	1-0	3-0	2-2	0-1	1-0
Rhyl ‡	34	18	10	6	65	30	64	0-0	0-1		1-0	3-0	3-0	4-1	1-1	4-1	0-0	3-0	2-1	2-1	1-1	1-1	3-1	1-2	5-2
Carmarthen Town	34	17	6	11	62	42	57	2-1	0-1	1-1		1-1	2-0	1-0	2-3	0-2	1-3	3-1	1-1	1-1	3-0	2-1	6-0	1-1	8-0
Port Talbot Town	34	15	11	8	47	30	56	1-1	0-1	1-0	3-0		1-1	0-3	0-0	1-1	0-2	0-0	2-1	0-0	1-1	1-0	4-0	3-2	2-1
Welshpool Town	34	15	9	10	59	48	54	1-2	3-2	3-1	3-0	2-1		1-4	1-1	2-0	2-2	1-0	4-1	0-0	3-2	3-3	1-2	5-1	2-1
Aberystwyth Town	34	14	10	10	59	48	52	2-0	4-1	1-2	1-1	0-3	6-2		1-1	1-0	0-0	4-1	1-2	1-1	2-1	2-2	3-1	3-1	0-0
Haverfordwest County	34	12	14	8	49	36	50	0-1	0-2	2-2	1-2	1-3	2-1	1-1		1-1	0-0	1-1	2-0	2-2	0-0	1-1	1-1	3-0	7-0
Bangor City §5	34	14	3	17	51	54	45	2-3	1-3	0-3	1-2	3-2	2-4	3-1	0-1		1-2	1-2	0-2	1-0	2-1	1-0	3-1	0-3	5-1
Caersws	34	11	12	11	44	56	45	0-2	1-4	1-1	1-2	1-1	0-2	1-1	1-0	0-6		2-1	1-0	3-4	1-0	3-1	2-1	1-2	2-2
Porthmadog	34	12	8	14	57	59	44	2-2	1-2	2-1	3-0	1-1	2-0	0-2	1-4	1-2	3-3		2-2	2-3	5-0	3-1	1-1	5-1	4-0
Connah's Quay Nomads	34	10	8	16	36	46	38	0-2	1-0	0-1	0-1	0-1	2-0	1-0	1-1	0-1	1-3	0-2		2-1	1-0	3-0	0-2	2-2	1-0
Caernarfon Town	34	9	10	15	47	55	37	1-3	0-3	0-2	0-2	0-1	1-1	4-2	0-2	1-1	6-0	1-2	4-2		1-1	0-1	4-0	3-2	2-1
NEWI Cefn Druids	34	7	11	16	42	58	32	0-6	2-5	1-1	2-0	0-0	1-0	2-2	0-1	2-2	2-0	1-1	2-2	3-2		0-0	3-0	0-0	7-0
Airbus UK	34	8	8	18	35	60	32	0-5	1-0	1-2	1-3	0-1	0-2	0-1	1-2	2-1	1-1	0-1	2-2	1-2	3-2		0-2	1-3	3-0
Newtown §5	34	10	6	18	42	61	31	0-3	0-3	1-4	2-1	0-1	1-1	1-3	2-3	0-1	0-2	3-1	1-1	1-2	2-3	0-3		4-1	5-0
Cwmbran Town §13	34	8	8	18	42	73	19	1-4	0-1	1-7	3-2	2-5	1-2	1-3	3-2	1-2	2-2	3-1	2-1	0-1	1-2	1-1	0-1		1-1
Cardiff Grange Quins §1	34	4	4	26	23	110	15	0-3	0-5	0-2	0-6	0-5	0-5	2-5	1-0	2-3	0-5	0-2	1-4	4-1	3-1	0-1	0-1	1-1	

27/08/2005 - 30/04/2006 • † Qualified for the UEFA Champions League • ‡ Qualified for the UEFA Cup • § = points deducted

FAW PREMIER CUP 2005–06

Quarter-finals		Semi-finals		Final	
Swansea City	1				
Rhyl *	0	Swansea City	3		
Cardiff City	1	Carmarthen Town *	2		
Carmarthen Town *	2			Swansea City	2
TNS Llansantffraid	5			Wrexham *	1
Newtown *	2	TNS Llansantffraid	3 4p		
Newport County *	0	Wrexham *	3 5p		
Wrexham	2				

Racecourse Ground, Wrexham, 29-03-2006
Scorers – Williams OG 36, Rory Fallon 42 for Swansea; Simon Spender 71 for Wrexham

* Home team

WELSH CUP 2005–06

Eighth-finals		Quarter-finals		Semi-finals		Final	
Rhyl	5						
NEWI Cefn Druids *	3	Rhyl *	5				
Pontypridd Town *	0	Goytre United	2				
Goytre United	5			Rhyl †	2 5p		
Llangefni Town	3			Port Talbot Town	2 4p		
Caersws *	1	Llangefni Town	0				
Cwmbran Town *	1	Port Talbot Town *	2				
Port Talbot Town	3					Rhyl ‡	2
Llanelli *	1					Bangor City	0
TNS Llansantffraid	0	Llanelli *	3				
Bala Town	0	Caernarfon Town	0				
Caernarfon Town *	4			Llanelli	0		
Carmarthen Town	2			Bangor City †	1		
Prestatyn Town *	1	Carmarthen Town	0				
Newtown	1	Bangor City *	1				
Bangor City *	2						

CUP FINAL

Racecourse Ground, Wrexham
7-05-2006

* Home team • † Played in Aberystwyth • ‡ Qualified for the UEFA Cup

YEM – YEMEN

NATIONAL TEAM RECORD
JULY 1ST 2002 TO JULY 9TH 2006

PL	W	D	L	F	A	%
36	6	7	23	45	92	26.4

FIFA/COCA-COLA WORLD RANKING

1993	1994	1995	1996	1997	1998	1999	2000	2001	2002	2003	2004	2005	High	Low
91	103	123	139	128	146	158	160	135	145	132	124	139	**90** 08/93	**163** 07/00

2005–2006											
08/05	09/05	10/05	11/05	12/05	01/06	02/06	03/06	04/06	05/06	06/06	07/06
124	131	131	134	139	139	139	130	131	132	-	125

The 2005 season saw Aden's Al Tilal win the title for the first time since 1990 although the run in to the Championship was disrupted by the civil unrest and riots in the country, a situation which caused the cancellation altogether of the second division. With the football association plagued by political interference from the Yemeni Ministry of Youth and Sport, FIFA stepped in and suspended the YFF from any international activity between August and November 2005. The threat was only lifted when fresh elections were held in March 2006. The chaos left Yemen without any international club football for the second season running although the hope is that clubs will return for the 2007

INTERNATIONAL HONOURS
None

AFC Cup. The lifting of the suspension came just in time for the national team to take part in the qualifiers for the 2007 AFC Asian Cup. Grouped with both Saudi Arabia and Japan, two nations who between them have won all of the past six tournaments, progress is unlikely but there was an encouraging 3-0 win over India in New Dehli to celebrate. The 2006 Championship kicked off in January and was won by Al Saqr of Taizz, who became only the second club from outside of San'a and Aden to win the League. They followed in the footsteps of Al Sha'ab from Ibb, who won the League in 2003 and 2004.

THE FIFA BIG COUNT OF 2000

	Male	Female		Male	Female
Registered players	2 000	0	Referees	100	0
Non registered players	60 000	0	Officials	400	0
Youth players	2 000	0	Total involved	64 500	
Total players	64 000		Number of clubs	100	
Professional players	0	0	Number of teams	200	

Yemen Football Association (YFF)
Quarter of Sport Al Jeraf, (Stadium Ali Mushen), PO Box 908, Sanaa-Yemen, Al Thawra City, Yemen
Tel +967 1 310923   Fax +967 1 310921
S.G@yemenfootball.org   www.yemenfootball.org
President: AL-EISSI Ahmed Saleh   General Secretary: SHAIBANI Hammed
Vice-President: AL AWAEJ Najeeb   Treasurer: AL NADRY Khaled   Media Officer: None
Men's Coach: AL RAEA Ahmad S.   Women's Coach: None
YFF formed: 1962   AFC: 1972   FIFA: 1980
Green shirts, Green shorts, Green socks

RECENT INTERNATIONAL MATCHES PLAYED BY YEMEN

2002	Opponents	Score		Venue	Comp	Scorers	Att	Referee
17-12	Syria	L	0-4	Kuwait City	ARr1		300	Al Saeedi UAE
21-12	Bahrain	L	1-3	Kuwait City	ARr1	Al Slimi [89]	1 000	Al Baltaji EGY
24-12	Lebanon	L	2-4	Kuwait City	ARr1	Al Qadimi [24], Ali Abboud [70]	1 000	Hamza KUW
26-12	Saudi Arabia	D	2-2	Kuwait City	ARr1			
2003								
17-09	Sudan	W	3-2	Sana'a	Fr	Al Minj [17], Ali Mubarak [54], Al Shihri [76]		
19-09	Sudan	L	1-2	Sana'a	Fr			
27-09	Syria	L	2-8	Jeddah	Fr			
6-10	Saudi Arabia	L	0-7	Jeddah	ACq			
8-10	Indonesia	L	0-3	Jeddah	ACq			
10-10	Bhutan	W	8-0	Jeddah	ACq	Al Qassayi 3 [20 25 82], Al Habishi [36], Al Shiri [60], Al Salmi 2 [67 88], Al Hijam [74]		
13-10	Saudi Arabia	L	1-3	Jeddah	ACq	Al Qassayi [12]		
15-10	Indonesia	D	2-2	Jeddah	ACq	Al Salmi [31p], Al Omqi [59]		
17-10	Bhutan	W	4-0	Jeddah	ACq	Al Hijam 2 [3 20], Al Omqi [33], Al Salmi [81]		
28-12	Oman	D	1-1	Kuwait City	GC	Fawzi Bashir [65]		Abdul Sadeq KUW
30-12	Bahrain	L	1-5	Kuwait City	GC	Al Salmi [14p]		Al Hamdan KSA
2004								
1-01	Kuwait	L	0-4	Kuwait City	GC			
5-01	Qatar	L	0-3	Kuwait City	GC			
8-01	Saudi Arabia	L	0-2	Kuwait City	GC			
11-01	United Arab Emirates	L	0-3	Kuwait City	GC			
18-02	Korea DPR	D	1-1	Sana'a	WCq	Al Selwi [73]	15 000	Husain BHR
17-03	Turkmenistan	L	1-2	Sana'a	Fr	Saleh Al Shekri [40p]		
31-03	Thailand	L	0-3	Sana'a	WCq		25 000	Mansour LIB
9-06	United Arab Emirates	L	0-3	Al Ain	WCq		5 000	Sapaev TKM
26-08	Syria	L	1-2	Sana'a	Fr			
28-08	Syria	W	2-1	Sana'a	Fr			
8-09	United Arab Emirates	W	3-1	Sana'a	WCq	Al Nono 2 [22 77], Abduljabar [49]	17 000	Al Ghamdi KSA
13-10	Korea DPR	L	1-2	Pyongyang	WCq	Jaber [76]	15 000	Vo Minh Tri VIE
1-11	Zambia	D	2-2	Dubai	Fr	Al Nono [83], Al Qaar [90]		
17-11	Thailand	D	1-1	Bangkok	WCq	Al Shehri [69]	15 000	Baskar IND
3-12	Iraq	L	1-3	Dubai	Fr	Nashwan Abdulaziz [28]		
5-12	Qatar	L	0-3	Doha	Fr			
11-12	Bahrain	D	1-1	Doha	GCr1	Nasser Ghazi [47]		
14-12	Saudi Arabia	L	0-2	Doha	GCr1			
17-12	Kuwait	L	0-3	Doha	GCr1			
2005								
No international matches played in 2005								
2006								
22-02	Saudi Arabia	L	0-4	Sana'a	ACq		55 000	Al Fadhli KUW
1-03	India	W	3-0	New Delhi	ACq	Salem Abdullah [6], Fekri Al Hubaishi [43], Ali A Nono [56p]	8 000	Torky IRN

Fr = Friendly match • GC = Gulf Cup • AC = AFC Asian Cup • AR = Arab Cup • WC = FIFA World Cup™ • q = qualifier • r1 = first round group

YEMEN NATIONAL TEAM RECORDS AND RECORD SEQUENCES

Records			Sequence records					
Victory	11-2	BHU 2000	Wins	2	1989-1990, 2004	Clean sheets	4	1989-1990
Defeat	1-15	ALG 1973	Defeats	10	1965-1975	Goals scored	7	2001
Player Caps	n/a		Undefeated	5	2001	Without goal	5	1994-1996
Player Goals	n/a		Without win	12	1981-1989	Goals against	17	1976-1990

YEMEN COUNTRY INFORMATION

Capital	Sana'a	Unification	1990	GDP per Capita	$800
Population	20 024 867	Status	Republic	GNP Ranking	93
Area km²	527 970	Language	Arabic	Dialling code	+967
Population density	38 per km²	Literacy rate	50%	Internet code	.ye
% in urban areas	34%	Main religion	Muslim	GMT + / −	+3
Towns/Cities ('000)	Sana'a 1 937; Hudayda 617; Taizz 615; Aden 550; Mukalla 258; Ibb 234; Damar 158;				
Neighbours (km)	Oman 288; Saudi Arabia 1 458; Red Sea & Arabian Sea 1 906				
Main stadia	Ali Moshen – Sana'a 25 000				

YEMEN 2005

PREMIER LEAGUE

	Pl	W	D	L	F	A	Pts	Tilal	Saqr	Ahly	Sha'ab Ibb	Hilal	Sha'ab H	Shabab J	Shula	May 22	Yarmuk	Wahda	Ittihad	Shabab B	Sha'ab S
Al Tilal Aden	26	16	6	4	47	25	54		4-3	1-0	2-1	3-0	4-1	0-0	1-0	5-3	1-0	3-0	3-0	0-0	1-3
Al Saqr Taizz	26	13	8	5	41	23	47	2-2		0-1	0-0	1-1	3-3	0-1	0-0	3-0	1-1	1-0	5-0	2-0	2-0
Al Ahly Sana'a	26	12	9	5	42	25	45	0-1	1-2		0-0	1-1	1-0	3-1	2-2	2-0	4-1	3-4	2-1	2-1	1-1
Al Sha'ab Ibb	26	12	8	6	40	25	44	1-0	3-0	0-0		2-2	2-1	1-0	0-3	2-1	2-1	2-1	0-0	3-1	1-0
Al Hilal Hudayda	26	10	9	7	44	33	39	1-4	1-3	1-1	2-1		1-0	5-1	1-1	3-1	5-0	1-1	4-0	4-0	1-1
Al Sha'ab Had. Mukalla	26	10	6	10	40	33	36	0-0	2-1	1-1	2-2	2-1		1-2	3-0	1-0	0-1	3-1	3-1	4-1	4-1
Shabab Al Jeel Hudayda	26	9	6	11	34	41	33	2-3	0-1	1-2	3-2	1-3	0-0		1-1	4-1	0-2	2-1	2-0	3-0	0-0
Shula Aden	26	7	11	8	32	33	32	1-1	0-1	1-3	1-0	0-0	3-0	1-2		1-2	2-1	2-0	3-0	2-2	2-1
May 22 Sana'a	26	9	5	12	35	44	32	2-1	0-2	0-2	1-0	1-2	2-0	2-2	2-2		1-0	1-4	5-1	0-2	0-0
Yarmuk Al Rawda Sana'a	26	9	4	13	31	40	31	1-2	1-3	1-1	1-4	1-0	1-0	5-2	2-1	3-3		0-2	1-0	4-1	1-0
Al Wahda Sana'a	26	8	7	11	37	44	31	1-0	0-2	0-3	0-4	3-3	2-3	1-1	2-2	1-1	2-1		3-0	4-0	1-1
Ittihad Ibb	26	7	7	12	24	44	28	2-3	0-0	1-1	2-2	2-1	2-1	4-1	1-1	1-2	2-1	0-0		1-0	1-0
Shabab Al Baydaa	26	7	5	14	26	41	26	0-1	1-2	3-2	1-1	2-0	0-0	0-1	5-0	0-2	1-0	4-0	0-0		1-0
Al Sha'ab Sana'a	26	3	9	14	17	39	18	1-1	1-1	0-3	0-4	0-1	1-5	2-1	0-0	0-2	0-0	1-3	0-2	3-0	

3/02/2005 - 12/08/2005 • † Qualified for the AFC Cup • Matches in bold were awarded

PRESIDENTS CUP 2005

Quarter-finals

Hilal Al Sahely	2
Saioon	1
Al Sha'ab Ibb	0
Al Sha'ab Mukalla	1
Al Sabeen	1
Salam Sada	0
Al Saqr	1 3p
Al Rasheed Taizz	1 4p

Semi-finals

Hilal Al Sahely	1 2
Al Sha'ab Mukalla	1 0
Al Sabeen	2 1 2p
Al Rasheed Taizz	1 2 4p

Final

Hilal Al Sahely	3
Al Rasheed Taizz	1

3-10-2005
Scorers - Muhamad Rajah [70], Issam Abdul Ghani [85], Yasser Bassehy [93+] for Hilal; Isfahan Jueesa [3] for Rasheed

RECENT LEAGUE AND CUP RECORD

	Championship							Cup		
Year	Champions	Pts	Runners-up	Pts	Third	Pts		Winners	Score	Runners-up
1997	Al Wahda Sana'a	42	Al Tilal Aden	39	Al Ahly Hudayda	37		Al Ahly Hudayda	1-0	Al Sha'ab Mukalla
1998	Al Wahda Sana'a	48	Al Ahly Sana'a	47	Al Shoala Aden	44		Al Ittihad Ibb	1-0	Al Shoala Aden
1999	Al Ahly Sana'a							No tournament		
2000	Al Ahly Sana'a	†	Al Tali'aa Taizz					Al Sha'ab Mukalla	0-0 5-4p	Al Shoala Aden
2001	Al Ahly Sana'a							Al Ahly Sana'a	2-1	Al Tilal Aden
2002	Al Wahda Sana'a	63	Al Ahly Sana'a	50	Al Hilal Hudayda	39		Al Sha'ab Ibb	4-0	Al Tadamun
2003	Al Sha'ab Ibb	46	Al Tilal Aden	43	Al Hilal Hudayda	36		Al Sha'ab Ibb	2-1	Al Sha'ab Mukalla
2004	Al Sha'ab Ibb	46	Al Ahly Sana'a	44	Al Tilal Aden	39		Al Ahly Sana'a	2-0	Al Sha'ab Ibb
2005	Al Tilal Aden	54	Al Saqr Taizz	47	Al Ahli Sana'a	45		Hilal Al Sahely	3-1	Al Rasheed Taizz

† 1999 championship final: Al Ahly 1-2 5-1 Al Tali'aa

ZAM – ZAMBIA

NATIONAL TEAM RECORD
JULY 1ST 2002 TO JULY 9TH 2006

PL	W	D	L	F	A	%
52	21	20	11	70	47	59.6

FIFA/COCA-COLA WORLD RANKING

1993	1994	1995	1996	1997	1998	1999	2000	2001	2002	2003	2004	2005	High		Low	
27	21	25	20	21	29	36	49	64	67	68	70	58	15	02/96	80	05/04

2005–2006											
08/05	09/05	10/05	11/05	12/05	01/06	02/06	03/06	04/06	05/06	06/06	07/06
56	64	58	57	58	58	57	57	56	57	-	62

Zambia consolidated their position amongst the consistent competitors in African football but without ever threatening to realise their undoubted potential. Qualification for the African Nations Cup finals in Egypt came as expected with third place in their FIFA World Cup™ qualifying group. At one stage the Zambians had been well positioned for a serious bid at a first-ever place at the FIFA World Cup™ finals but hat dream died with a 0-1 home defeat by Senegal in Chililabombwe in September 2005. At the Nations Cup finals, an early lead in their first game against Tunisia turned into a 4-1 defeat and in their second group match they lost to a last-minute goal by Guinea.

INTERNATIONAL HONOURS
CECAFA Cup 1984   COSAFA Castle Cup 1997 1998

A consolation win over regional rivals South Africa did little to temper a sudden outburst of public anger against coach Kalusha Bwalya, up to that point the long-time darling of Zambian football. He resigned soon after to be replaced by Patrick Phiri. In the League, the bank-sponsored ZANACO, coached by former national team captain Fighton Simukonda, regained their title but in the CAF Champions League they were again eliminated early, keeping up Zambia's record of never having qualified for the group phase of the competition. Army side Green Buffaloes won their first major trophy in 25 years when they beat Red Arrows in the Mosi Cup Final.

THE FIFA BIG COUNT OF 2000

	Male	Female		Male	Female
Registered players	7 409	720	Referees	497	9
Non registered players	728 100	3 450	Officials	3 800	79
Youth players	3 173	450	Total involved	747 687	
Total players	743 302		Number of clubs	428	
Professional players	49	0	Number of teams	24 350	

Football Association of Zambia (FAZ)
Football House, Alick Nkhata Road, Long Acres, PO Box 34751, 34751 Lusaka, Zambia
Tel +260 1 250940   Fax +260 1 250946
faz@zamnet.zm   www.faz.co.zm
President: MULONGA Teddy   General Secretary: MUSONDA John Brig Gen
Vice-President: BWALYA Kalusha   Treasurer: MWEEMBA Rix   Media Officer: MWANSA Mbulakulima
Men's Coach: PHIRI Patrick   Women's Coach: BANDA E.
FAZ formed: 1929   CAF: 1964   FIFA: 1964
Copper shirts, Black shorts, Copper socks

RECENT INTERNATIONAL MATCHES PLAYED BY ZAMBIA

2003	Opponents	Score		Venue	Comp	Scorers	Att	Referee
29-03	Tanzania	W	1-0	Dar es Salaam	CNq	Lungu [25]	23 000	Haislemelk ETH
17-05	Malawi	W	1-0	Blantyre	Fr	Mumbi [88]		Lwanja MWI
7-06	Tanzania	W	2-0	Lusaka	CNq	Milanzi 2 [44 71]	30 000	Chilinda MWI
21-06	Sudan	D	1-1	Lusaka	CNq	Chalwe [72]		Maxim KEN
6-07	Benin	L	0-3	Cotonou	CNq		40 000	Monteiro Duarte CPV
27-07	Mozambique	W	4-2	Lusaka	CCqf	Mwandilla 2 [51 80], Milanzi [84], Msesuma [89]	10 000	Katjimune NAM
16-08	Malawi	D	1-1	Blantyre	CCsf	Chalwe [89]. L 2-4p	55 000	Mnkantjo ZIM
11-10	Seychelles	W	4-0	Victoria	WCq	Kampamba [8], Fichite [44], Milanzi [52], Numba [75]	2 700	Lim Kee Chong MRI
15-11	Seychelles	D	1-1	Lusaka	WCq	Milanzi [7]	30 000	Abdulkadir TAN
2004								
1-05	Zimbabwe	D	1-1	Lusaka	Fr	Chansa [79]		
16-05	Zimbabwe	D	0-0	Harare	Fr			
22-05	Malawi	L	0-2	Kitwe	Fr		20 000	Nkole ZAM
25-05	Sudan	W	2-0	Khartoum	Fr	Numba [9], Chalwe [39]		
5-06	Togo	W	1-0	Lusaka	WCq	Mulenga [11]	40 000	Damon RSA
19-06	Mali	D	1-1	Bamako	WCq	Milanzi [25]	19 000	Sowe GAM
3-07	Senegal	L	0-1	Dakar	WCq		50 000	Monteiro Duarte CPV
31-07	Mauritius	W	3-1	Lusaka	CCqf	Mulenga [11], Numba [55], Bwalya.K [58]		Manuel ZIM
28-08	Rwanda	W	2-1	Kitwe	Fr	Kaposa [8], Mwamdila [38]	15 000	Mwanza ZAM
4-09	Liberia	W	1-0	Lusaka	WCq	Bwalya.K [91+]	30 000	Nchengwa BOT
30-09	Botswana	L	0-1	Gaborone	Fr			Chidoda BOT
10-10	Congo	W	3-2	Brazzaville	WCq	Mbesuma 3 [2 37 65]	20 000	Yacoubi TUN
24-10	Zimbabwe	D	0-0	Harare	CCsf	W 5-4p	25 000	Simisse MRI
1-11	Yemen	D	2-2	Dubai	Fr	Mwale [32], Nsofwa [58]		
20-11	Angola	D	0-0	Lusaka	CCf	L 4-5p		Lwanja MWI
2005								
26-02	Botswana	D	0-0	Gaborone	Fr			
26-03	Congo	W	2-0	Chililabombwe	WCq	Tana [1], Mbesuma [44]	20 000	Maillet SEY
5-06	Togo	L	1-4	Lome	WCq	Kampamba [15]	15 000	Guezzaz MAR
11-06	Swaziland	W	3-0	Lusaka	CCr1	Mbesuma 2 [44 46], Kalaba [56]		Chidoda BOT
12-06	Malawi	W	2-1	Lusaka	CCr1	Mbesuma 2 [79 85]		Nhlapo RSA
18-06	Mali	W	2-1	Chililabombwe	WCq	Chalwe [26], Mbesuma [85]	29 000	Colembi ANG
13-08	South Africa	D	2-2	Mmabatho	CCsf	Chamanga [18], Chris Katongo [24]. W 9-8p		Raolimanana MAD
14-08	Zimbabwe	L	0-1	Mmabatho	CCf			Massango MOZ
3-09	Senegal	L	0-1	Chililabombwe	WCq		20 000	Abd El Fatah EGY
25-09	Congo DR	D	2-2	Chililabombwe	Fr	Mweetwa [41], Luipa [57]		
27-09	Congo DR	D	0-0	Lubumbashi	Fr			
1-10	Liberia	W	5-0	Monrovia	WCq	Lwipa 2 [50 82], Mweetwa 2 [51 63], Numba [61]	BCD	Evehe CMR
11-12	Congo DR	D	1-1	Lubumbashi	Fr	Numba [15]		
14-12	Congo DR	W	4-1	Chingola	Fr	Milanzi 2 [2 62], Dube Phiri [10], Kasonde [13]		
31-12	Zimbabwe	D	1-1	Harare	Fr	Dube Phiri [84]		
2006								
22-01	Tunisia	L	1-4	Alexandria	CNr1	Chamanga [9]	16 000	Maillet SEY
26-01	Guinea	L	1-2	Alexandria	CNr1	Tana [34]	24 000	Imeire NGA
30-01	South Africa	W	1-0	Alexandria	CNr1	Chris Katongo [75]	4 000	Abd El Fatah EGY
14-05	Botswana	D	0-0	Gaborone	Fr	L 4-5p		

Fr = Friendly match • CC = COSAFA Castle Cup • CN = CAF African Cup of Nations • WC = FIFA World Cup™
q = qualifier • BCD = Behind closed doors

ZAMBIA NATIONAL TEAM RECORDS AND RECORD SEQUENCES

Records			Sequence records				
Victory	9-0	KEN 1978	Wins	8	1964-1966	Clean sheets	7	1997-1998, 2000
Defeat	1-10	COD 1969	Defeats	4	Four times	Goals scored	19	1966-1971
Player Caps	n/a		Undefeated	11	Three times	Without goal	4	2001
Player Goals	n/a		Without win	11	1999-2000	Goals against	10	1966-1968

ZAMBIA COUNTRY INFORMATION

Capital	Lusaka	Independence	1964 from the UK	GDP per Capita	$800
Population	10 462 436	Status	Republic	GNP Ranking	128
Area km²	752 614	Language	English, Bemba, Kaonda	Dialling code	+260
Population density	14 per km²	Literacy rate	80%	Internet code	.zm
% in urban areas	43%	Main religion	Christian 63%	GMT + / –	+2
Towns/Cities ('000)	Lusaka 1 267; Kitwe 400; Ndola 394; Kabwe 189; Chingola 148; Mufulira 120; Luanshya 113				
Neighbours (km)	Tanzania 338; Malawi 837; Mozambique 419; Zimbabwe 797; Namibia 233; Angola 1 110; Congo DR 1 930				
Main stadia	Independence Stadium – Lusaka 30 000; Dola Hill – Ndola 23 000; Nchanga – Chingola 20 000				

CLUB DIRECTORY

Club	Town/City	Lge	Cup
Chambishi	Chambishi	0	0
Forest Rangers	Ndola	0	0
Green Buffaloes	Lusaka	6	1
Kabwe Warriors	Kabwe	5	5
Kitwe United	Kitwe	0	0
Konkola Blades	Chililabombwe	0	3
Lusaka Celtic	Lusaka	0	1
Lusaka Dynamos	Lusaka	0	0
Mufulira Wanderers	Mufulira	9	9
Nakambala Leopards	Mazabuka	0	0
National Assembly	Lusaka	0	0
Nchanga Rangers	Chingola	2	1
Nkana (ex Nkana Red Devils)	Kitwe	11	6
Nkwazi	Lusaka	0	0
Power Dynamos	Kitwe	5	6
Red Arrows	Lusaka	1	0
Zanaco	Lusaka	3	1
ZESCO United	Ndola	0	0

BP TOP-8 CUP 2005

First Round		Semi-finals		Final	
Kabwe Warriors	1 4p				
ZESCO United	1 2p	Kabwe Warriors	4		
Power Dynamos	1	Kitwe United	3		
Kitwe United	2			Kabwe Warriors	2
Red Arrows	2			Green Buffaloes	1
Nat. Assembly	0	Red Arrows	1 4p	Woodlands, Lusaka, 12-11-2005	
Zanaco	2	Green Buffaloes	1 5p	Scorers - Silioni Jere [35], Joseph Bwalya [43] for Rangers, Jimmy	
Green Buffaloes	3			Mumba [89] for Buffaloes	

RECENT LEAGUE AND CUP RECORD

	Championship						Cup		
Year	Champions	Pts	Runners-up	Pts	Third	Pts	Winners	Score	Runners-up
1990	Nkana						Power Dynamos		
1991	Power Dynamos	61	Nkana	58	Mufulira Wanderers	50	Nkana		
1992	Nkana						Nkana		
1993	Nkana	60	Power Dynamos	60	Roan United	54	Nkana		
1994	Power Dynamos	53	Zamsure	51	Mufulira Wanderers	50	Roan United		
1995	Mufulira Wanderers	60	Power Dynamos	54	Zamsure	50	Mufulira Wanderers	1-0	Rumlex
1996	Mufulira Wanderers						Roan United	1-0	Nchanga Rangers
1997	Power Dynamos	66	Nkana	64	Nchanga Rangers	56	Power Dynamos	1-0	City of Lusaka
1998	Nchanga Rangers	56	Kabwe Warriors	49	Nkana	48	Konkola Blades	2-1	Zanaco
1999	Nkana	57	Zamsure	55	Nchanga Rangers	54	Zamsure		Power Dynamos
2000	Power Dynamos	56	Nkana	52	Zanaco	50	Nkana	0-0 7-6p	Green Buffaloes
2001	Nkana	60	Zanaco	57	Kabwe Warriors	55	Power Dynamos	1-0	Kabwe Warriors
2002	Zanaco	61	Power Dynamos	60	Green Buffaloes	60	Zanaco	2-2 3-2p	Power Dynamos
2003	Zanaco	69	Green Buffaloes	59	Kabwe Warriors	57	Power Dynamos	1-0	Kabwe Warriors
2004	Red Arrows	62	Green Buffaloes	55	Zanaco	53	Lusaka Celtic	2-1	Kabwe Warriors
2005	Zanaco	65	Zesco United	54	Power Dynamos	52	Green Buffaloes	2-1	Red Arrows

The main Cup tournament was known as the Castle Cup from 1962-74, the Independence Cup from 1975-92 and then as the Mosi Cup from 1993

ZAMBIA 2005

PREMIER LEAGUE

	Pl	W	D	L	F	A	Pts	Zanaco	ZESCO	Dynamos	Nchanga	Chambishi	Red Arrows	Buffaloes	Kitwe Utd	N Assembly	Nkwazi	Kabwe	Lusaka Dy	Afrisports	Mufulira	Y. Arrows	Chilanga
Zanaco †	30	18	11	1	48	14	65		2-0	2-0	0-0	2-1	2-0	1-0	4-0	1-0	2-0	1-1	2-0	3-0	3-1	5-2	1-1
ZESCO United ‡	30	15	9	6	30	16	54	1-0		0-0	2-0	0-0	2-1	2-0	2-1	0-1	2-0	0-1	0-0	1-0	0-0	0-0	1-0
Power Dynamos	30	13	13	4	31	19	52	2-2	2-0		0-2	1-0	1-1	1-1	3-0	0-1	0-0	3-1	0-0	1-1	2-1	1-0	1-0
Nchanga Rangers	30	11	13	6	37	29	46	0-0	0-0	1-1		1-0	0-1	2-0	0-1	1-1	1-1	1-2	1-0	1-0	3-2	1-1	4-1
Chambishi	30	13	7	10	29	21	46	0-0	1-0	0-2	1-2		1-1	1-0	1-1	4-1	0-1	0-0	1-2	1-0	3-0	0-1	1-0
Red Arrows	30	13	6	11	42	31	45	0-3	1-2	2-1	3-0	1-1		1-1	0-1	1-2	3-1	2-0	1-1	1-0	5-1	0-2	4-0
Green Buffaloes	30	12	8	10	34	26	44	0-1	2-2	0-0	0-1	0-2	1-0		1-0	2-0	0-1	1-0	2-2	2-0	2-0	2-1	4-1
Kitwe United	30	11	10	9	25	26	43	0-0	0-1	0-1	1-0	1-1	0-1	1-1		2-0	0-0	1-0	2-0	3-2	1-0	0-0	1-0
National Assembly	30	10	8	11	31	33	38	0-0	0-1	1-2	2-2	2-0	0-1	1-1	0-1		1-0	2-2	0-1	1-0	1-1	2-1	
Nkwazi	30	9	11	10	27	29	38	1-3	0-1	0-0	1-1	1-0	2-1	1-0	2-2	3-0		1-1	0-2	1-2	0-0	1-0	2-0
Kabwe Warriors	30	8	13	9	32	34	37	0-0	1-1	1-1	2-2	0-1	2-0	2-2	2-1	0-1	1-3		2-1	0-3	3-0	2-2	2-1
Lusaka Dynamos	30	9	9	12	28	29	36	0-1	0-0	0-0	0-1	3-0	0-2	0-0	1-1	1-2	1-1	1-0		0-1	5-1	0-1	2-0
Afrisports Kitwe	30	8	10	12	31	35	34	2-2	0-2	1-1	2-2	0-2	1-0	1-0	1-0	1-1	1-1	2-2	0-1		3-0	2-0	3-0
Mufulira Wanderers	30	7	8	15	32	52	29	1-1	1-0	1-2	3-3	0-3	1-2	1-3	0-1	2-2	1-0	0-0	4-1	3-0		1-0	2-2
Young Arrows	30	6	8	16	21	41	26	1-3	1-5	0-1	1-1	0-1	0-3	1-2	0-2	1-0	1-1	0-2	2-1	0-0	1-2		1-0
Chilanga Heroes	30	1	6	22	12	55	9	0-1	0-1	0-1	0-3	0-1	1-3	0-4	0-0	0-5	2-1	0-0	1-2	2-2	0-2	0-0	

12/03/2005 - 6/11/2005 • † Qualified for the CAF Champions League • ‡ Qualified for the CAF Confederation Cup • Top scorers: Dube PHIRI, Young Arrows/Red Arrows, 28; Ignatius LWIPA, Afrisports, 16, Cosmas BANDA, Zanaco, 15; Joseph BWALYA, Kabwe, 15; Maybin MWABA, Nchanga 14

COCA-COLA CUP 2005

Quarter-finals		Semi-finals		Final	
Forest Rangers	2				
ZESCO United	1	Forest Rangers	1 4p		
Young Zanaco	1	Zanaco	1 3p		
Zanaco	4			Forest Rangers	1
Power Dynamos	2			Red Arrows	0
Nchanga Rang.	1	Power Dynamos	0	Arthur Davies Stadium, Kitwe	
Green Buffaloes	0	Red Arrows	3	24-09-2005	
Red Arrows	1			Scorer - Frazer Mweza 55 for Rangers	

MOSI CUP 2005

Round of 16		Quarter-finals		Semi-finals		Final	
Green Buffaloes *	4						
Mufulira Wanderers	1	Green Buffaloes	1				
Lime Hotspurs	1	Lusaka City Council *	0				
Lusaka City Council *	2			Green Buffaloes	2		
Power Dynamos	4			Livingstone Pirates	1		
Nkana FC *	0	Power Dynamos *	1				
ZESCO United	0	Livingstone Pirates	2			Green Buffaloes	2
Livingstone Pirates *	1					Red Arrows	1
Kabwe Warriors	2						
Chilanga Heroes *	0	Kabwe Warriors	1				
Lusaka Dynamos	2 8p	National Assembly *	0	Kabwe Warriors	1		
National Assembly *	2 9p			Red Arrows	3		
Nchanga Rangers *	2						
Chambishi	1	Nchanga Rangers	1				
Zamcoal Diggers	0	Red Arrows *	2				
Red Arrows *	4					* Home team	

CUP FINAL

Woodlands Stadium, Lusaka
17-12-2005

Scorers - Sebastian Mwansa 50, Geoffrey Nsama 88 for Green Buffaloes; Dube Phiri 26 for Red Arrows

ZIM – ZIMBABWE

NATIONAL TEAM RECORD
JULY 1ST 2002 TO JULY 9TH 2006

PL	W	D	L	F	A	%
58	27	16	15	83	60	60.3

FIFA/COCA-COLA WORLD RANKING

1993	1994	1995	1996	1997	1998	1999	2000	2001	2002	2003	2004	2005	High		Low	
46	51	59	71	74	74	67	68	68	57	53	60	53	**40**	04/95	**92**	03/98

2005–2006											
08/05	09/05	10/05	11/05	12/05	01/06	02/06	03/06	04/06	05/06	06/06	07/06
51	49	52	54	53	53	52	53	55	55	-	66

Zimbabwe has battled with economic and political problems in recent times, problems that have had a real effect on football in the country. Remarkably, however, the past two years have arguably been the most successful in the history of the national team. Victory in the 2005 COSAFA Castle Cup was an unexpected boon for coach Charles Mhlauri, forced to play the tournament without the bulk of his first choice players because they were not released by their clubs. Zimbabwe first overcame Angola 2-1 and then beat Zambia for the first time ever in a competitive international to win the title. Less than two months later Zimbabwe suffered an embarrassing 5-1 defeat by Nigeria

INTERNATIONAL HONOURS
CECAFA Cup 1985 COSAFA Castle Cup 2000 2003

in the FIFA World Cup™ qualifiers but still managed to qualify for the 2006 African Nations Cup finals, for the second tournament in a row. The Warriors were eliminated after successive defeats by Senegal and Nigeria but ended with a surprise 2-1 win over Ghana. Mhlauri also experienced success at club level at the helm of CAPS United. They won the championship easily even though they ended just two points ahead of Masvingo United, winners of two of the three Cup competitions played during the season. CAPS were disqualified from the CAF Champions League in March 2006 for using a falsely registered player.

THE FIFA BIG COUNT OF 2000

	Male	Female		Male	Female
Registered players	25 548	490	Referees	703	11
Non registered players	42 000	600	Officials	2 015	51
Youth players	5 374	0	Total involved	76 792	
Total players	74 012		Number of clubs	27	
Professional players	68	0	Number of teams	1 134	

Zimbabwe Football Association (ZIFA)
53 Livingstone Avenue, Causeway, PO Box CY 114, Harare, Zimbabwe
Tel +263 4 721026   Fax +263 4 731265
zifa@africaonline.co.zw   www.zimbabwesoccer.com
President: NYATHANGA Wellington   General Secretary: MASHINGAIDZE Jonathan
Vice-President: MADZORERA Tendai   Treasurer: TBD   Media Officer: None
Men's Coach: MHLAURI Charles   Women's Coach: BOWERS Vernon
ZIFA formed: 1965   CAF: 1965   FIFA: 1965
Green shirts, Yellow shorts, Green socks

RECENT INTERNATIONAL MATCHES PLAYED BY ZIMBABWE

2003	Opponents	Score		Venue	Comp	Scorers	Att	Referee
12-10	Mauritania	W	3-0	Harare	WCq	Ndlovu.A [23], Tembo [47], Ndlovu.P [57]	55 000	Damon RSA
23-10	Burkina Faso	W	4-1	Hyderabad	AAr1	Nyoni 2 [3 74], Mbano 2 [26 82]		
27-10	Uzbekistan	D	1-1	Hyderabad	AAr1	Tsipa [12]		
29-10	India	L	3-5	Hyderabad	AAsf	Mbano [4], Mashiri [81], Chipunza [87]		Mohd Salleh MAS
31-10	Rwanda	D	2-2	Hyderabad	AA3p	Nyoni [65], Mbano [90]. W 5-3p		
14-11	Mauritania	L	1-2	Nouakchott	WCq	Mbwando [81]	3 000	Keita GUI
13-12	Botswana	W	2-0	Selibe-Phikwe	Fr	Chandida [30], Sandaka [80]	7 000	
2004								
25-01	Egypt	L	1-2	Sfax	CNr1	Ndlovu.P [46]	22 000	Pare BFA
29-01	Cameroon	L	3-5	Sfax	CNr1	Ndlovu.P 2 [8 47p], Nyandoro [89]	15 000	Aboubacar CIV
3-02	Algeria	W	2-1	Sousse	CNr1	Luphahala 2 [65 71]	10 000	Maillet SEY
1-05	Zambia	D	1-1	Lusaka	Fr	Ndlovu.B [89]		
16-05	Zambia	D	0-0	Harare	Fr			
24-05	Egypt	L	0-2	Cairo	Fr		10 000	
5-06	Gabon	D	1-1	Libreville	WCq	Kaondera [82]	25 000	Quartey GHA
20-06	Algeria	D	1-1	Harare	WCq	Raho OG [60]	65 000	Ntambidila COD
27-06	Swaziland	W	5-0	Mbabane	CCqf	Kasinuayo [7], Ndlovu.P 3 [41 58 81], OG [54]. Abandoned 83'		Infante MOZ
3-07	Rwanda	W	2-0	Kigali	WCq	Ndlovu.P [41], Nengomasha [79]		Chilinda MWI
18-08	Botswana	W	2-0	Bulawayo	Fr	Ncube [67], Sibanda [87]	5 000	
22-08	Uganda	W	2-0	Harare	Fr	Moyo [28], Ncube [81]	3 000	
5-09	Nigeria	L	0-3	Harare	WCq		60 000	Mandzioukouta COD
10-10	Angola	L	0-1	Luanda	WCq		17 000	Lwanja MWI
24-10	Zambia	D	0-0	Harare	CCsf	L 4-5p	25 000	Simisse MRI
2005								
27-02	Malawi	L	1-2	Blantyre	Fr	Tsipa [54]		
16-03	Botswana	D	1-1	Harare	Fr	Chimedza [53]	3 000	
27-03	Angola	W	2-0	Harare	WCq	Kawondera [60], Mwaruwari [69]		Codjia BEN
16-04	Mozambique	W	3-0	Windhoek	CCr1	Chimedza 2 [66p 78], Sandaka [82]		Mufeti NAM
17-04	Botswana	W	2-0	Windhoek	CCr1	Badza [21], Sandaka [58]		Braga Mavunza ANG
5-06	Gabon	W	1-0	Harare	WCq	Ndlovu.P [52]	55 000	Ssegonga UGA
19-06	Algeria	D	2-2	Oran	WCq	Kawondera [33], Ndlovu.P [87]	15 000	Pare BFA
13-08	Angola	W	2-1	Mmabatho	CCsf	Chandida [59], Sandaka [76]		Kapanga MWI
14-08	Zambia	W	1-0	Mmabatho	CCf	Chandida [84]		Massango MOZ
28-08	Mozambique	D	0-0	Mutare	Fr			
4-09	Rwanda	W	3-1	Harare	WCq	Kawondera [4], Mwaruwari [43], Rambanapasi [78]	55 000	Ssegona UGA
8-10	Nigeria	L	1-5	Abuja	WCq	Mwaruwari [70]	45 000	Pare BFA
31-12	Zambia	D	1-1	Harare	Fr	Mbwando [63]		
2006								
5-01	Egypt	L	0-2	Alexandria	Fr			
14-01	Morocco	L	0-1	Marrakech	Fr			
23-01	Senegal	L	0-2	Port Said	CNr1		15 000	Abdel Rahman SUD
27-01	Nigeria	L	0-2	Port Said	CNr1		10 000	Coulibaly MLI
31-01	Ghana	W	2-1	Ismailia	CNr1	Chimedza [60], Mwaruwari [68]	14 000	Louzaya CGO
24-06	Malawi	D	1-1	Maputo	Fr	Gwekwerere [28p]. L 1-2p		
25-06	Swaziland	W	2-1	Maputo	Fr	Gwekwerere [14], Matema [73]		

Fr = Friendly match • CN = CAF African Cup of Nations • CC = COSAFA Castle Cup • AA = Afro-Asian Games • WC = FIFA World Cup™
q = qualifier • r1 = first round group • qf = quarter-final • sf = semi-final • 3p = third place play-off • f = final

ZIMBABWE NATIONAL TEAM RECORDS AND RECORD SEQUENCES

Records			Sequence records					
Victory	7-0	BOT 1990	Wins	6	2003	Clean sheets	5	2002-2003
Defeat	0-5	CIV 1989, COD 1995	Defeats	5	1997-1998	Goals scored	12	2003-2004
Player Caps	n/a		Undefeated	13	1981-1982	Without goal	4	1988
Player Goals	n/a		Without win	9	1995-96, 1997-98	Goals against	11	1995-1996

ZIMBABWE COUNTRY INFORMATION

Capital	Harare	Independence	1980	GDP per Capita	$1 900
Population	12 671 860	Status	Republic	GNP Ranking	104
Area km²	390 580	Language	English, Shona, Sindebele	Dialling code	+263
Population density	32 per km²	Literacy rate	90%	Internet code	.zw
% in urban areas	32%	Main religion	Christian	GMT + / –	+2
Towns/Cities ('000)	Harare 2 213; Bulawayo 897; Chitungwiza 456; Mutare 253; Gweru 201; Kwekwe 116; Kadoma 100				
Neighbours (km)	Mozambique 1 231; South Africa 225; Botswana 813; Zambia 797				
Main stadia	National Sports Stadium – Harare 60 000; Barbourfields – Bulawayo 25 000; Rufaro - Harare 20 000; Lancashire Steel - Kwekwe 10 000				

CLUB DIRECTORY

Club	Town/City	Lge	Cup
Black Rhinos	Harare	2	1
Buymore	Chitungwiza	0	0
CAPS United	Harare	4	8
Chapungu United	Gweru	0	1
Dynamos	Harare	17	8
Highlanders	Bulawayo	6	2
Hwange (ex Wankie)	Hwange	0	3
Lancashire Steel	Kwekwe	0	0
Masvingo United	Masvingo	0	2
Monomatapa United	Harare	0	0
Motor Action	Mutare	0	0
Mwana Africa	Bindura	0	0
Railstars	Bulawayo	0	0
Shabanie Mine	Shabanie Mine	0	0
Shooting Stars	Harare	0	0
Zimbabwe Saints	Bulawayo	2	3

OK WOZA BHORA CUP 2005

First Round		Semi-finals		Final	
Masvingo Utd	2				
Railstars	0	**Masvingo Utd**	1		
Sundowns	1	Motor Action	0		
Motor Action	2			**Masvingo Utd**	1 5p
CAPS United	1			Highlanders	1 4p
Lancashire Steel	0	CAPS United	0	Bulawayo, 2-10-2005	
Monomatapa	1	**Highlanders**	1	Scorers - Wonder Sithole 82 for	
Highlanders	2			Masvingo; Ralph Matema 68 for Highlanders	

RECENT LEAGUE AND CUP RECORD

	Championship						Cup		
Year	Champions	Pts	Runners-up	Pts	Third	Pts	Winners	Score	Runners-up
1990	Highlanders	38	CAPS United	30	Dynamos	30	Highlanders		
1991	Dynamos		Black Rhinos				Wankie	3-1	Cranbonne Bullets
1992	Black Aces	38	CAPS United	32	Black Mambas	27	CAPS United		
1993	Highlanders	40	CAPS United	35	Chapungu	35	Tanganda		
1994	Dynamos	62	Highlanders	51	Mhangura	50	Blackpool		
1995	Dynamos	58	Blackpool	58	Black Aces	53	Chapungu United		
1996	Dynamos	71	Dynamos	68	Blackpool	54	Dynamos		
1997	Dynamos	68	CAPS United	57	Black Aces	50	CAPS United	3-2	Dynamos
1998	No championship due to calender reorganisation						CAPS United		
1999	Highlanders	72	Dynamos	71	Zimbabwe Saints	54	Amazulu		
2000	Highlanders	78	AmaZulu	76	Dynamos	66	No tournament		
2001	Highlanders	62	AmaZulu	59	Shabanie Mine	51	Highlanders	4-1	Shabanie Mine
2002	Highlanders	72	Black Rhinos	52	AmaZulu	50	Masvingo United	2-2 4-3p	Railstars
2003	AmaZulu	51	Highlanders	50	Dynamos	48	Dynamos	2-0	Highlanders
2004	CAPS United	79	Highlanders	64	Shabanie Mine	51	CAPS United	1-0	Wankie
2005	CAPS United	58	Masvingo United	56	Highlanders	51	Masvingo United	1-1 3-1p	Highlanders

The main Cup tournament was known as the Castle Cup from 1962-97 and then as the ZIFA Unity Cup from 2001

ZIMBABWE 2004

NATIONAL PREMIER SOCCER LEAGUE

	Pl	W	D	L	F	A	Pts	CAPS Utd	Masvingo	Highlanders	Motor	Buymore	Lancashire	Railstars	Shabanie	Dynamos	Hwange	Mono'tapa	Rhinos	Chapungu	Sundowns	AmaZulu	Wild Cats
CAPS United †	30	17	7	6	37	21	58		2-0	0-0	0-0	0-0	3-0	1-0	2-0	2-1	0-1	2-1	0-3	3-2	1-0	1-0	1-2
Masvingo United	30	17	5	8	44	30	56	0-1		3-2	2-1	0-0	1-0	4-1	3-1	1-2	3-1	1-2	3-2	1-2	3-1	1-0	1-0
Highlanders	30	13	12	5	30	20	51	2-1	0-0		2-1	2-0	0-1	1-0	2-1	1-1	1-1	1-0	1-0	1-0	0-0	1-0	0-0
Motor Action	30	13	7	10	46	31	46	2-0	0-1	0-0		2-1	3-2	1-1	0-1	1-4	1-0	1-0	3-1	4-0	5-2	2-0	0-1
Buymore Chitungwiza	30	13	5	12	40	31	44	0-2	1-0	1-0	2-0		3-2	2-3	1-1	0-1	1-4	1-0	1-2	1-1	3-0	3-1	4-0
Lancashire Steel	30	13	5	12	39	35	44	1-1	0-0	3-1	2-1	2-0		2-0	1-2	1-0	0-1	1-1	4-0	1-0	1-1	3-1	2-1
Railstars	30	13	2	15	39	43	41	2-4	0-1	2-1	2-1	1-0	1-3		3-2	0-1	0-1	1-0	4-2	1-0	0-1	4-0	1-0
Shabanie Mine	30	12	5	13	37	41	41	0-1	1-2	2-2	0-1	1-1	1-3	1-0		3-1	2-1	1-0	1-0	3-2	4-2	2-0	2-1
Dynamos	30	11	7	12	38	38	40	1-2	3-1	0-0	0-5	1-1	1-1	5-0	1-0		1-1	0-1	3-2	2-1	0-2	0-0	2-1
Hwange	30	10	10	10	29	30	40	0-0	1-2	0-0	1-1	3-1	1-0	1-0	0-0	1-1		0-1	3-2	1-2	1-1	1-2	0-0
Monomatapa United	30	11	7	12	27	29	40	0-0	1-1	0-2	0-0	1-0	1-0	3-2	2-1	3-0	0-1		2-3	0-2	0-0	3-2	0-1
Black Rhinos	30	11	6	13	43	43	39	0-4	1-0	0-1	1-1	1-2	1-0	1-1	2-3	1-3	2-1	1-1		1-2	3-0	2-0	5-1
Chapungu United	30	12	3	15	35	43	39	0-0	2-3	0-0	3-1	1-2	2-1	0-2	1-1	3-1	1-2	0-1	0-2		1-0	1-3	5-1
Njube Sundowns	30	10	6	14	29	40	36	2-0	1-2	0-1	0-5	1-0	2-1	2-0	2-0	2-1	1-1	2-0	1-3	1-2		2-0	1-0
AmaZulu	30	11	1	18	41	54	34	1-2	0-3	2-4	0-1	1-0	6-1	1-4	4-1	3-2	3-1	1-1	2-3	2-0	2-0		1-0
Eiffel Wildcats	30	5	8	17	16	41	23	0-1	1-1	1-1	2-2	0-3	0-2	1-0	0-0	0-2	0-2	1-1	2-1	0-1	1-1	0-1	

12/03/2005 - 11/12/2005 • † Qualified for the CAF Champions League • Edmore MUFEMA, Motor Action, 17; Philip MARUFU, Chapungu, 16

INDEPENDENCE CUP 2005

Quarter-finals		Semi-finals		Final	
Motor Action	2				
Dynamos	1	Motor Action	1 5p		
Black Rhinos	3 2p	CAPS United	1 4p		
CAPS United	3 3p			Motor Action	2
Shabanie Mine	1			Highlanders	0
AmaZulu	0	Shabanie Mine	1		
Hwange	1 3p	Highanders	2		
Highlanders	1 4p				

Bulawayo, 18-04-2005
Scorers - Clyde Musiya [6], Salim Milanzi [84] for Motor Action

---

ZIFA UNITY CUP 2005

Round of 16		Quarter-finals		Semi-finals		Final	
Masvingo United	2						
Black Rhinos	1	Masvingo United	5				
Mwana Africa	1	CAPS United	1				
CAPS United	3			Masvingo United	0 5p		
Buymore	2			Motor Action	0 3p		
Monomatapa United	0	Buymore	0				
Eiffel Wildcats	0	Motor Action	2				
Motor Action	4					Masvingo United	1 3p
AmaZulu	2					Highlanders	1 1p
Shabanie Mine	0	AmaZulu	1 4p				
Njube Sundowns		Lancashire Steel	1 5p				
Lancashire Steel				AmaZulu	0		
Chapungu United	2			Highlanders	3		
Railstars	0	Chapungu United	1				
Hwange	0 1p	Highlanders	2				
Highlanders	0 3p						

CUP FINAL

22-12-2005

Scorers - Wonder Sithole [4] for Masvinga; Obadiah Tarumbwa [11] for Highlanders

PART THREE

THE
CONFEDERATIONS

AFC

ASIAN FOOTBALL CONFEDERATION

After the giant step forward made by Asian teams at the 2002 FIFA World Cup™, it was back down to earth with a bump at the 2006 finals in Germany with Iran, Japan, Korea Republic and Saudi Arabia all returning home after the first round. Of the AFC teams, Australia - who only joined on January 1st - achieved the most, coming agonisingly close to a quarter-final spot before being knocked-out by the Italians courtesy of a highly contentious penalty. Despite it being a World Cup year, there was plenty of action involving teams that hadn't qualified for Germany 2006. In December, India won the sixth South Asian Football Federation Cup, played in Pakistan, beating Bangladesh 2-0 in the final, while April saw Bangladesh host the inaugural AFC Challenge Cup. Designed to give the lesser nations meaningful experience of international competition and the chance of getting their hands on some silverware, it was a resounding success with the AFC once again providing a blueprint that other confederations would do well to consider. Two ex-Soviet

THE FIFA BIG COUNT OF 2000 FOR THE AFC

	Male	Female		Male	Female
Registered players	963 054	26 771	Referees	127 289	294
Non registered players	31 932 830	125 355	Officials	506 876	81 735
Youth players	1 278 492	25 867	Total involved	99 836 726	6 180 338
Children & Occasional	65 020 000	5 920 000	in football	106 008 563	
Professionals	8 185	316	Number of clubs	29 095	
Total players	105 300 870		Number of teams	134 876	

republics made it through to the semi-finals with Tajikistan beating Kyrgyzstan to set up a final against Sri Lanka. They won that 4-0 to write their names into the record books. The Tajiks were also leading lights in a new club competition for the smaller nations of Asia - the AFC President's Cup. Regar TadAZ won the 2005 tournament beating Kyrgyzstan's Dordoi-Dinamo 3-0 in the final, although there was revenge for Dordoi-Dinamo when they beat Vahsh 2-1 in another Kyrgyzstan-Tajikistan final in 2006. The second edition of the AFC Cup for middle ranking nations was won by Jordan's Al Faysali who beat Lebanon's Al Nejmeh in the final, while the blue ribbon event of the Asian club calendar, the AFC Champions League, was won for the second year running by Saudi's Al Ittihad. They beat UAE's Al Ain in only the second all-Arab final, and the first since 1989. That meant a place in the FIFA Club World Championship 2005 in Japan, where they beat African champions, Al Ahly, in the first round before losing to São Paulo in the semis.

Asian Football Confederation (AFC)

AFC House, Jalan 1/155B, Bukit Jalil, 57000 Kuala Lumpur, Malaysia
Tel +60 3 89943388   Fax +60 3 89946168
media@the-afc.com   www.the-afc.com
President: BIN HAMMAM Mohamed QAT   General Secretary: VELAPPAN Peter Dato' MAS
AFC Formed: 1954

AFC EXECUTIVE COMMITTEE

President: BIN HAMMAM Mohamed QAT   Vice-President: ZHANG Jilong CHN   Vice-President: FERNANDO V. Manilal SRI
Vice-President: TENGKU Abdullah Ibni Ahmad Shah   Hon Treasurer: BOUZO Farouk, Gen SYR   FIFA Vice-President: CHUNG Mong Joon, Dr KOR
FIFA Executive Member: MAKUDI Worawi   FIFA Executive Member: OGURA Junji

MEMBERS OF THE EXECUTIVE COMMITTEE

DAS MUNSHI Priya Ranjan IND   NOOMOOZ Naser Gen IRN   HUSSAIN Mohammed Saeed IRQ
TAHIR Dali IDN   THAPA Ganesh NEP   AL KHALILI Khalil Ahmed Hilal, Sheikh OMA
ROMUALDEZ Juan Miguel PHI   RAHIMOV Bahtier UZB   AL DABAL Abdullah Khaled KSA
General Secretary: VELAPPAN Peter Dato' MAS   Legal Advisor: GANESAN N. SIN

MAP OF AFC MEMBER NATIONS

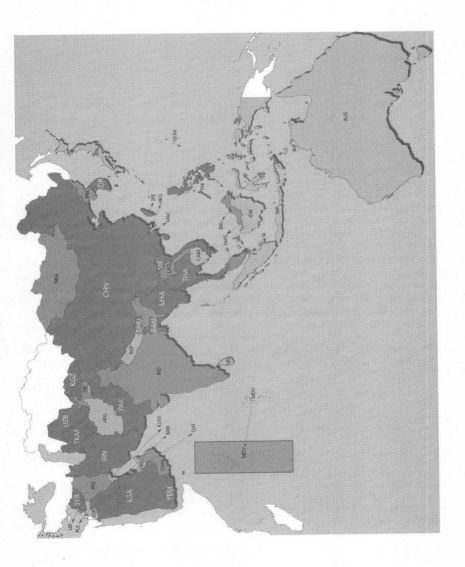

ASIAN TOURNAMENTS

AFC ASIAN CUP

Year	Host Country	Winners	Score	Runners-up	Venue
1956	Hong Kong	Korea Republic	2-1	Israel	Government Stadium, Hong Kong
1960	Korea Republic	Korea Republic	3-0	Israel	Hyochang Park, Seoul
1964	Israel	Israel	2-0	India	Bloomfield, Jaffa
1968	Iran	Iran	3-1	Burma	Amjadieh, Tehran
1972	Thailand	Iran	2-1	Korea Republic	Suphachalasai, Bangkok
1976	Iran	Iran	1-0	Kuwait	Azadi, Tehran
1980	Kuwait	Kuwait	3-0	Korea Republic	Kuwait City
1984	Singapore	Saudi Arabia	2-0	China PR	National Stadium, Singapore
1988	Qatar	Saudi Arabia	0-0 4-3p	Korea Republic	Khalifa, Doha
1992	Japan	Japan	1-0	Saudi Arabia	Main Stadium, Hiroshima
1996	UAE	Saudi Arabia	0-0 4-2p	United Arab Emirates	Zayed, Abu Dhabi
2000	Lebanon	Japan	1-0	Saudi Arabia	Camille Chamoun, Beirut
2004	China PR	Japan	3-1	China PR	Workers' Stadium, Beijing

From 1956 to 1968 the tournament was played as a league. The result listed is that between the winners and runners-up

The four major powers in Asia – Iran, Japan, Korea Republic and Saudia Arabia – have shared all bar two of the titles in Asia's premier competition for national teams, although of the six editions played since 1984, Japan and Saudi have been crowned Asian champions three times each. The most surprising aspect has been the failure of Korea Republic, despite qualifying for every FIFA World Cup™ since 1986, to add another title to the two won in 1956 and 1960. From the late 1960s to the late 1970s Iran were the undisputed kings of the continent winning every game they played and a hat-trick of titles. Kuwait became the first Arab nation to win the tournament, in 1980, but since then it has been all Japan and Saudi Arabia. The lack of any real success on the part of China PR is another surprising feature and in 2004 they became only the second nation to lose a final on home soil, eight years after the United Arab Emirates had done so. Traditionally held every four years, the next tournament, to be co-hosted by Indonesia, Malaysia, Thailand and Vietnam, will be held after a break of three years to avoid clashing with other continental championships.

AFC WOMEN'S CHAMPIONSHIP

Year	Host Country	Winners	Score	Runners-up	Venue
1975	Hong Kong	New Zealand	3-1	Thailand	Hong Kong
1977	Chinese Tapei	Chinese Taipei	3-1	Thailand	Taipei
1979	India	Chinese Taipei	2-0	India	Calicut
1981	Hong Kong	Chinese Taipei	5-0	Thailand	Hong Kong
1983	Thailand	Thailand	3-0	India	Bangkok
1986	Hong Kong	China PR	2-0	Japan	Hong Kong
1989	Hong Kong	China PR	1-0	Chinese Taipei	Hong Kong
1991	Japan	China PR	5-0	Japan	Fukuoka
1993	Malaysia	China PR	3-0	Korea DPR	Sarawak
1995	Malaysia	China PR	2-0	Japan	Sabah
1997	China PR	China PR	2-0	Korea DPR	Guangdong
1999	Philippines	China PR	3-0	Chinese Taipei	Bacalod
2001	Chinese Taipei	Korea DPR	2-0	Japan	Taipei
2003	Thailand	Korea DPR	2-1	China PR	Bangkok
2006	Australia	China PR	2-2 4-2p	Australia	Adelaide

The AFC Women's Championship is the longest running of all the continental championships for women though not surprisingly it has been dominated by East Asia with the countries of the Middle East yet to enter a single tournament. China PR has emerged as the most successful nation with seven consecutive titles though they were recently knocked off their perch by the North Koreans, winners of two of the past three events. Japan have made it to four finals but have yet to win.

FOOTBALL TOURNAMENT OF THE ASIAN GAMES

Year	Host Country	Winners	Score	Runners-up	Venue
1951	India	India	1-0	Iran	New Delhi
1954	Philippines	Chinese Taipei	5-2	Korea Republic	Manilla
1958	Japan	Chinese Taipei	3-2	Korea Republic	Tokyo
1962	Indonesia	India	2-1	Korea Republic	Djakarta
1966	Thailand	Burma	1-0	Iran	Bangkok
1970	Thailand	Burma	0-0 †	Korea Republic	Bangkok
1974	Iran	Iran	1-0	Israel	Tehran
1978	Thailand	Korea Republic	0-0 †	Korea DPR	Bangkok
1982	India	Iraq	1-0	Kuwait	New Dehli
1986	Korea Republic	Korea Republic	2-0	Saudi Arabia	Seoul
1990	China PR	Iran	0-0 4-1p	Korea DPR	Beijing
1994	Japan	Uzbekistan	4-2	China PR	Hiroshima
1998	Thailand	Iran	2-0	Kuwait	Bangkok
2002	Korea Republic	Iran	2-1	Japan	Busan

† Gold medal shared in 1970 and 1978

For many years the Football Tournament of the Asian Games rivalled the Asian Cup in importance meaning the continent had a major championship every other year. The range of winners has been more diverse than in the Asian Cup with Japan and Saudi Arabia yet to win gold. The Asian Games operate as a regional version of the Olympics so in the amateur days this was not an issue given the lack of professional players on the continent. In 2002, as with the Olympics, the football tournament was turned into a U-23 tournament with three older players allowed.

WOMEN'S FOOTBALL TOURNAMENT OF THE ASIAN GAMES

Year	Host Country	Winners	Score	Runners-up	Venue
1990	China PR	China PR	5-0	Japan	Beijing
1994	Japan	China PR	2-0	Japan	Hiroshima
1998	Thailand	China PR	1-0	Korea DPR	Bangkok
2002	Korea Republic	Korea DPR	0-0	China PR	Busan

In 1990 and 1994 the tournament was played as a league. The result listed is that between the winners and runners-up

Given the strength of women's football in East Asia and in particular in China PR, it was a natural progression to introduce the sport to the Games when Beijing was host in 1990. The Chinese won that year and have remained dominant although they have faced a strong challenge at the past two Games from the North Koreans, which has also been the case at the AFC Women's Championship. The 2006 Asian Games will represent a major breakthrough for the women's game when Qatar are the hosts. It will only be the second time that a West Asian country has hosted the Games and the first since Iran in 1974, and it means that for the first time a major women's football tournament will be held in an Arab country.

AFC CHALLENGE CUP

Year	Host Country	Winners	Score	Runners-up	Venue
2006	Bangladesh	Tajikistan	4-0	Sri Lanka	Bangabandhu, Dhaka

The AFC Challenge Cup for national teams was launched in 2006 for the lower ranked nations on the continent in order to give these nations the realistic prospect of winning competitive honours.

AFC UNDER 17 CHAMPIONSHIP WINNERS

Year	Host Country	Winners	Runners-up	Year	Host Country	Winners	Runners-up
1984	Qatar	Saudi Arabia	Qatar	1996	Thailand	Oman	Thailand
1986	Qatar	Korea Republic	Qatar	1998	Qatar	Thailand	Qatar
1988	Thailand	Saudi Arabia	Bahrain	2000	Vietnam SR	Oman	Iran
1990	UAE	Qatar	UAE	2002	UAE	Korea Republic	Yemen
1992	Saudi Arabia	China PR	Qatar	2004	Japan	China PR	Korea DPR
1994	Qatar	Japan	Qatar				

AFC YOUTH CHAMPIONSHIP WINNERS

Year	Host Country	Winners	Runners-up
1959	Malaysia	Korea Republic	Malaysia
1960	Malaysia	Korea Republic	Malaysia
1961	Thailand	Burma & Indonesia	
1962	Thailand	Thailand	Korea Republic
1963	Malaysia	Burma & Korea Republic	
1964	Vietnam	Burma & Israel	
1965	Japan	Israel	Burma
1966	Philippines	Burma & Israel	
1967	Thailand	Israel	Indonesia
1968	Korea Republic	Burma	Malaysia
1969	Thailand	Burma & Thailand	
1970	Philippines	Burma	Indonesia
1971	Japan	Israel	Korea Republic
1972	Thailand	Israel	Korea Republic
1973	Iran	Iran	Japan
1974	Thailand	India & Iran	
1975	Kuwait	Iran & Iraq	

AFC YOUTH CHAMPIONSHIP WINNERS

Year	Host Country	Winners	Runners-up
1976	Thailand	Iran & Korea DPR	
1977	Iran	Iraq	Iran
1978	Bangladesh	Iraq & Korea Republic	
1980	Thailand	Korea Republic	Qatar
1982	Thailand	Korea Republic	China PR
1984	UAE	China PR	Saudi Arabia
1986	Saudi Arabia	Saudi Arabia	Bahrain
1988	Qatar	Iraq	Syria
1990	Indonesia	Korea Republic	Korea DPR
1992	UAE	Saudi Arabia	Korea Republic
1994	Indonesia	Syria	Japan
1996	Korea Republic	Korea Republic	China PR
1998	Thailand	Korea Republic	Japan
2000	Iran	Iraq	Japan
2002	Qatar	Korea Republic	Japan
2004	Malaysia	Korea Republic	China PR

Asia has a long history of youth tournaments dating back to the 1950s when the Youth Championship was held annually although it was largely confined to the countries of East and South-East Asia. Burma (now Myanmar) had the best record before the 1970s with seven titles but since then they have won none as the countries of the Middle East joined the AFC and began flexing their muscles. Since the 1980s the Championship has been held every two years to tie in with the FIFA World Youth Championship for which it serves as a qualifying tournament. The South Koreans remain the most successful nation in the history of the AFC Youth Championship with 11 titles. The AFC U-17 Championship was introduced in 1984 to coincide with the launch of the FIFA U-17 World Championship. No country has won that title more than twice although Saudi Arabia did follow up their 1988 Championship victory by winning the world title a year later.

ASIAN CHAMPIONS CUP AND AFC CHAMPIONS LEAGUE FINALS

Year	Winners	Country	Score	Country	Runners-up
1967	Hapoel Tel Aviv	ISR	2-1	MAS	Selangor
1968	Maccabi Tel Aviv	ISR	1-0	KOR	Yangzee
1970	Taj Club	IRN	2-1	ISR	Hapoel Tel Aviv
1971	Maccabi Tel Aviv	ISR	W-O	IRQ	Police Club
1986	Daewoo Royals	KOR	3-1	KSA	Al Ahly
1987	Furukawa	JPN	4-3	KSA	Al Hilal
1988	Yomiuri	JPN	W-O	KSA	Al Hilal
1989	Al Saad	QAT	2-3 1-0	IRQ	Al Rasheed
1990	Liaoning	CHN	2-1 1-1	JPN	Nissan
1991	Esteghlal SC	IRN	2-1	CHN	Liaoning
1992	Al Hilal	KSA	1-1 4-3p	IRN	Esteghlal SC
1993	Pas	IRN	1-0	KSA	Al Shabab
1994	Thai Farmers Bank	THA	2-1	OMA	Omani Club
1995	Thai Farmers Bank	THA	1-0	QAT	Al Arabi
1996	Ilhwa Chunma	KOR	1-0	KSA	Al Nasr
1997	Pohang Steelers	KOR	2-1	KOR	Ilhwa Chunma
1998	Pohang Steelers	KOR	0-0 6-5p	CHN	Dalian
1999	Jubilo Iwata	JPN	2-1	IRN	Esteghlal SC
2000	Al Hilal	KSA	3-2	JPN	Jubilo Iwata
2001	Suwon Samsung Bluewings	KOR	1-0	JPN	Jubilo Iwata
2002	Suwon Samsung Bluewings	KOR	0-0 4-2p	KOR	Anyang LG Cheetahs
2003	Al Ain	UAE	2-0 0-1	THA	BEC Tero Sasana
2004	Al Ittihad	KSA	1-3 5-0	KOR	Seongnam Ilhwa Chunma
2005	Al Ittihad	KSA	1-1 4-2	UAE	Al Ain

ASIAN CUP WINNERS' CUP FINALS

Year	Winners	Country	Score	Country	Runners-up
1991	Pirouzi	IRN	0-0 1-0	BHR	Al Muharraq
1992	Nissan	JPN	1-1 5-0	KSA	Al Nasr
1993	Nissan	JPN	1-1 1-0	IRN	Pirouzi
1994	Al-Qadisiyah	KSA	4-2 2-0	HKG	South China
1995	Yokohama Flugels	JPN	2-1	UAE	Al Shaab
1996	Bellmare Hiratsuka	JPN	2-1	IRQ	Al Talaba
1997	Al Hilal	KSA	3-1	JPN	Nagoya Grampus Eight
1998	Al Nasr	KSA	1-0	KOR	Suwon Samsung Bluewings
1999	Al Ittihad	KSA	3-2	KOR	Chunnam Dragons
2000	Shimizu S-Pulse	JPN	1-0	IRQ	Al Zawra
2001	Al Shabab	KSA	4-2	CHN	Dalian Shide
2002	Al Hilal	KSA	2-1	KOR	Chonbuk Hyundai Motors

Discontinued after 2002 following the creation of the AFC Champions League

ASIAN SUPER CUP

Year	Winners	Country	Score	Country	Runners-up
1995	Yokohama Flugels	JPN	1-1 3-2	THA	Thai Farmers Bank
1996	Ilhwa Chunma	KOR	5-3 1-0	JPN	Bellmare Hiratsuka
1997	Al Hilal	KSA	1-0 1-1	KOR	Pohang Steelers
1998	Al Nasr	KSA	1-1 0-0	KOR	Pohang Steelers
1999	Jubilo Iwata	JPN	1-0 1-2	KSA	Al Ittihad
2000	Al Hilal	KSA	2-1 1-1	JPN	Shimizu S-Pulse
2001	Suwon Samsung Bluewings	KOR	2-2 2-1	KSA	Al Shabab
2002	Suwon Samsung Bluewings	KOR	1-0 0-1 4-2p	KSA	Al Hilal

Discontinued after 2002 following the creation of the AFC Champions League

AFC CUP

Year	Winners	Country	Score	Country	Runners-up
2004	Al Jaish	SYR	3-2 0-1	SYR	Al Wahda
2005	Al Faysali	JOR	1-0 3-2	LIB	Al Nejmeh

AFC PRESIDENT'S CUP

Year	Winners	Country	Score	Country	Runners-up
2005	Regar TadAZ	TJK	3-0	KGZ	Dordoy-Dinamo
2006	Dordoy-Dinamo	KGZ	2-1	TJK	Vakhsh

It is in club football where Asia has seriously lagged behind the rest of the world and nowhere has this been more evident than in the Asian Champion Teams' Cup, or the AFC Champions League as the competition is now known. After an initial burst of enthusiasm in the 1960s, mainly thanks to Israeli and Iranian clubs, it went into a prolonged hibernation to finally re-emerge in 1986. Support for the new tournament was still patchy and the logistics remained cumbersome thanks to the large distances clubs were forced to travel to play games. As part of his bold Vision Asia development strategy, AFC President Mohamed bin Hammam placed the development of club football at the heart of this strategy, hence the launch of the AFC Champions League in 2002. A key element was the streaming of the nations in the Confederation so that the AFC Champions League is now open to only the top 14 ranked 'mature' countries. A second tier of 14 'developing' countries entered the new AFC Cup while the President's Cup for the lowest ranked 'emerging' nations was launched in the 2005 season. It is a policy aimed at increasing the competitive nature of the club game in these countries by holding out the real prospect of honours for nations unlikely ever to win the Champions League. Historically Saudi and Korean clubs have been the most successful in the Champions Cup and AFC Champions League with nine titles between them whilst Iran, Japan and China PR have underachieved given the strength of their domestic leagues. Seven clubs have been Asian Champions twice - Maccabi Tel Aviv, Esteghlal (once as Taj), Al Hilal, Thai Farmers Bank, Pohang Steelers, Suwon Bluewings and Al Ittihad - although no club has managed to win it more.

WEST ASIAN FOOTBALL FEDERATION CHAMPIONSHIP

Year	Host Country	Winners	Score	Runners-up	Venue
2000	Jordan	Iran	1-0	Syria	Malek Abdullah, Amman
2002	Syria	Iraq	3-2	Jordan	Al Abbassiyyine, Damascus
2004	Iran	Iran	4-1	Syria	Tehran

GULF CUP

Year	Host Country	Winners	Runners-up
1970	Bahrain	Kuwait	Bahrain
1972	Saudi Arabia	Kuwait	Saudi Arabia
1974	Kuwait	Kuwait	Saudi Arabia
1976	Qatar	Kuwait	Iraq
1979	Iraq	Iraq	Kuwait
1982	UAE	Kuwait	Bahrain
1984	Oman	Iraq	Qatar
1986	Bahrain	Kuwait	UAE
1988	Saudi Arabia	Iraq	UAE

GULF CUP

Year	Host Country	Winners	Runners-up
1990	Kuwait	Kuwait	Qatar
1992	Qatar	Qatar	Bahrain
1994	UAE	Saudi Arabia	UAE
1996	Oman	Kuwait	Qatar
1998	Bahrain	Kuwait	Saudi Arabia
2002	Saudi Arabia	Saudi Arabia	Qatar
2004	Kuwait	Saudi Arabia	Bahrain
2005	Qatar	Qatar	Oman

FOOTBALL TOURNAMENT OF THE SOUTH ASIAN GAMES

Year	Host Country	Winners	Score	Runners-up	Venue
1984	Nepal	Nepal	4-2	Bangladesh	Dasharath Rangashala, Kathmandu
1985	Bangladesh	India	1-1 4-1p	Bangladesh	Dhaka
1987	India	India	1-0	Nepal	Salt Lake, Calcutta
1989	Pakistan	Pakistan	1-0	Bangladesh	Islamabad
1991	Sri Lanka	Pakistan	2-0	Maldives	Colombo
1993	Bangladesh	Nepal	2-2 4-3p	India	Dhaka
1995	India	India	1-0	Bangladesh	Madras
1999	Nepal	Bangladesh	1-0	Nepal	Dasharath Rangashala, Kathmandu
2004	Pakistan	Pakistan	1-0	India	Jinnah Stadium, Islamabad

SOUTH ASIAN FOOTBALL FEDERATION CUP

Year	Host Country	Winners	Score	Runners-up	Venue
1993	Pakistan	India	2-0	Sri Lanka	Lahore
1995	Sri Lanka	Sri Lanka	1-0	India	Colombo
1997	Nepal	India	5-1	Maldives	Dasharath Rangashala, Kathmandu
1999	Goa	India	2-0	Bangladesh	Margao
2003	Bangladesh	Bangladesh	1-1 5-3p	Maldives	Bangabandu, Dhaka
2005	Pakistan	India	2-0	Bangladesh	Karachi

ASEAN TIGER CUP

Year	Host Country	Winners	Score	Runners-up	Venue
1996		Thailand	1-0	Malaysia	
1998	Vietnam	Singapore	1-0	Vietnam	Hanoi Stadium, Hanoi
2000	Thailand	Thailand	4-1	Indonesia	Bangkok
2002	Indonesia/Sin'pore	Thailand	2-2 4-2p	Indonesia	Gelora Senayan, Jakarta
2004	Malaysia/Vietnam	Singapore	3-1 2-1	Indonesia	Jakarta, Singapore

EAST ASIAN CHAMPIONSHIP

Year	Host Country	Winners	Score	Runners-up	Venue
2003	Japan	Korea Republic	0-0	Japan	International, Yokohama
2005	Korea Republic	China PR	2-2	Japan	World Cup Stadium, Daejeon

The 2003 tournament was played as a league. The result listed is that between the winners and runners-up

Regional tournaments in Asia are particularly strong dating back to 1911, when the Far East Olympics were first held, and they play a hugely important role given the vast size of the continent. The Middle East has the West Asian Football Federation Championship and the Gulf Cup; Central Asia has the South Asian Games and the South Asian Football Federation Cup; and the nations of Eastern Asia take part in either the ASEAN Tiger Cup or the East Asian Championship.

AFC ASIAN CUP 2007

QUALIFYING GROUPS

Group A		Pts	Group B		Pts	Group C		Pts	Group D		Pts
Japan	JPN	3	Iran	IRN	3	UAE	UAE	6	Australia	AUS	3
Saudi Arabia	KSA	3	Syria	SYR	3	Oman	OMA	3	Kuwait	KUW	1
Yemen	YEM	3	Korea Republic	KOR	3	Jordan	JOR	3	Bahrain	BHR	1
India	IND	0	Chinese Taipei	TPE	0	Pakistan	PAK	0	Lebanon withdrew		

Group E		Pts	Group F		Pts
China PR	CHN	3	Qatar	QAT	6
Singapore	SIN	3	Uzbekistan	UZB	3
Iraq	IRQ	3	Hong Kong	HKG	3
Palestine	PLE	3	Bangladesh	BAN	0

Tables as of August 15, 2006 • Indonesia, Malaysia, Thailand and Vietnam qualified automatically as hosts • The final tournament will be held in all four countries from July 7 to July 29, 2007, with the final in Jakarta • The top two in each qualifying group qualify for the finals • Bangladesh and Pakistan met in a preliminary round but both teams made it to the group stage after the withdrawl of Sri Lanka

GROUP A

Ali Moshen Stadium, Sana'a
22-02-2006, 16:00, 55 000, Al Fadhli KUW

YEM	0	4		KSA

Ahmed Al Sawailh 2 [14 89]
Mohammed Al Shlhoub 2 [77 92+]

YEMEN				SAUDI ARABIA	
1 ABDULWALI Muaad				AL DEAYEA Mohammad	1
2 SALEM Mohammed	86			FALLATAH Redha	3
4 AFARA Khaled			23	AL MONTASHARI Hamad	4
5 AL BAADANI Yaser				AL GHANNAM Abdullatif	8
6 SAEED ABDULLAH Salem				AL SHALHOUB Mohammed	10
10 AL NONO Ali				KHATHRAN Abdul Aziz	12
14 AL OMQY Ali				AL BAHRI Ahmed	15
15 AL WORAFI Akram				AL THAKER Khaled	16
18 Al Aroomi Fadhl	80	59		AL TEMYAT Nawaf	18
19 Awn Esam	60	71		AL QAHTANI Yasser	20
40 Al Hubaishi Fekri				AL SUWAILH Ahmed	31
Tr: SAADANE Rabeh				Tr: PAQUETA Marcos	
9 YAHYA Radwan	60	59		HAIDAR Mohammed	7
13 Al Wadi	86	23		AL HARBI Osama	13
24 EISSA Nashwan	80	71		AL KWYKBI Alaa	32

Nissan Stadium, Yokohama
22-02-2006, 19:20, 38 025, Huang CHN

JPN	6	0		IND

Ono [32], Maki [58], Fukunishi [68],
Kubo 2 [78 90], Sato [82]

JAPAN				INDIA	
23 KAWAGUCHI Yoshikatsu				NANDY Sandip	1
5 MIYAMOTO Tsuneyasu	72			SHIVANANJU Manju	3
8 OGASAWARA Mitsuo				WADOO Mehrajuddin	4
9 KUBO Tatsuhiko		77		HUSSAIN Mehtab	7
14 SANTOS Alessandro				NABI Syed Rahim	10
15 FUKUNISHI Takashi				GAWLI Mahesh	14
18 ONO Shinji	72			BHUTIA Bhaichung	15
21 KAJI Akira				SINGH Irungbam	17
22 NAKAZAWA Yuji				NAIR Ajayan	18
35 HASEBE Makoto				MARIA Sanjeev	23
36 MAKI Seiichiro	76	82		PRADEEP NP	41
Tr: ZICO				Tr: NAEEMUDDIN Syed	
4 ENDO Yasuhito	72			SINGH Manjit	9
24 MONIWA Teruyuki	72			SINGH Lukram James	16
37 SATO Hisato	76				

Dr. Ambedkar Stadium, New Dehli
1-03-2006, 14:30, 8 000, Torky IRN

IND	0	3		YEM

Salem Abdullah [6], Fekri Al
Hubaishi [43], Ali Al Nono [56p]

INDIA				YEMEN	
1 NANDY Sandjip				ABDULWALI Muaad	1
4 WADOO Mehrajuddin	61			SALEM Mohammed	2
7 HUSSAIN Mehtab	74			SAEED ABDULLAH Salem	6
10 NABI Syed Rahim				AL-NONO Ali	10
15 BHUTIA Bhaichung				AL-WADI Ahmed	13
16 SINGH Lukram James		70		AL-OMQY Ali	14
17 SINGH Irungbam				AL-WORAFI akram	15
23 MARIA Sanjeev				MUNASSAR Mohanad	16
41 PRADEEP NP		83		AL AROOMI Fadhl	18
42 MANDAL Deepak				AWN Esam	19
44 FERNANDIS Micky		85		AL-HUBAISHI Fekri	40
Tr: NAEEMUDDIN Syed				Tr: AL MAJHALI Abdulmannan	
9 SINGH Manjit	42	85		AHMED Fathi	7
19 HAKKIM Abdul	61	70		AL-TAHOOS Mohammed	8
25 SINGH Dharamjit	74	83		EISSA Nashwan	24

GROUP B

Al Hamdania Stadium, Aleppo		
22-02-2006, 14:00, 35 000, Maidin SIN		

SYR 1 2 KOR

Firas Al Khatib [49] — Kim Do Heon [5], Lee Chun Soo [50]

SYRIA				KOREA REPUBLIC	
1	AL AZHAR Mhd.Redwan			LEE Woon Jae	1
2	MOHAMMAD Rafat			KIM Dong Jin	3
4	ISTANBALI Mohammad			CHOI Jin Cheul	4
6	ALHOUSSAIN Jehad			KIM Jin Kyu	6
8	ALAMENA Mahmoud	76	85	KIM Do Heon	8
10	AL KHATIB Firas		95	LEE Chun Soo	14
15	AL KHOUJAH Anas	95	54	CHUNG Kyung Ho	16
17	DAKKA Abd			LEE Ho	17
19	AL RACHED Mhd.Yhya			KIM Nam Il	19
20	CHAABO Zyad			LEE Dong Gook	20
23	ESMAEEL Feras	25		CHO Won Hee	23
	Tr: RADENOVIC Miloslav			Tr: ADVOCAAT Dick	
5	BARAKAT Adeb	95	54	PARK Chu Young	10
18	ALHOUSSAIN Abd	76	85	KIM Sang Sik	13
30	DYAB Ali	25	95	BAEK Ji Hoon	21

Azadi, Tehran		
22-02-2006, 15:30, 5 000, Abdul Kadir Nema IRQ		

IRN 4 0 TPE

Timotian [35], Madanchi 2 [47 60], Daei [82]

IRAN				CHINESE TAIPEI	
30	TALEBLOO Vahid			LU Kun-Chi	1
4	GOLMOHAMMADI Yahya			KAO Hao-Chieh	2
6	NEKONAM Javad			TSAI Sheng-An	3
10	DAEI Ali			KUO Chun-Yi	4
13	KAEBI Hossein			CHENG Yung-Jen	5
15	ALAVI Sayyed	46		FENG Pao-Hsiang	6
18	JABARI Kordgeshlaghi		69	CHANG Fu Hsiang	14
20	NOSRATI Mohammad			LEE Meng-Chian	18
24	TIMOTIAN Andranik	75	82	CHUANG Wei-Lun	19
27	ZARE Sattar			LIANG Chien-Wei	23
40	PAKIKHTIBI Rasoul	65	46	CHEN Po-Liang	30
	Tr: IVANKOVIC Branko			Tr: IMAI Toshiaki	
23	KAZEMIAN Javad	75	82	HUANG Cheng-Tsung	7
29	AKBARPOUR Sivavash	65	69	TAI Hung-Hsu	8
36	MADANCHI Mehrzad	46	46	CHEN Yi-Wei	15

Chungsan Stadium, Taipei		
1-03-2006, 18:00, 700, O Il Son PRK		

TPE 0 4 SYR

Zyad Chabbo 2 [29 58], Jehad Al Houssain [45], Firas Al Khatib [64]

CHINESE TAIPEI				SYRIA	
1	LU Kun-Chi		76	AL AZHAR Mhd.Redwan	1
2	KAO Hao-Chieh			MOHAMMAD Rafat	2
3	TSAI Sheng-An		73	HOMSI Majd	3
4	KUO Chun-Yi			ISTANBALI Mohammad	4
5	CHENG Yung-Jen		71	ALHOUSSAIN Jehad	6
6	FENG Pao-Hsing			ALAMENA Mahmoud	8
8	TAI Hung-Hsu			AL KHATIB Firas	10
14	CHANG Fu Hsiang	76		AL KHOUJA Anas	15
19	CHUANG Wei-Lun			DAKKA Abd	17
23	LIANG Chien-Wei			AL RACHED Mhd.Yhya	19
24	LIN Che-Min			CHAABO Zyad	20
	Tr: IMAI Toshiaki			Tr: RADENOVIC Miloslav	
7	HUANG Cheng-Tsung	76	71	KAILOUNI Meaataz	7
			73	SHAHROUR Salah	12
			76	AL HAFEZ Adnan	22

GROUP C

International Stadium, Amman		
22-02-2006, 18:00, Basma SYR		

JOR 3 0 PAK

Hatem Aqel [30p], Mahmoud Shelbaieh [38], Badran Al Shagran [41]

JORDAN				PAKISTAN	
12	ELAMAIREH Lo'ai			KHAN Jaffer	1
3	ALMALTA'AH Khaled			AKRAM Naveed	2
4	ABU ALIEH Qusai			ISHAQ Samar	5
5	KHAMEES Mohammad			GONDAL Usman	6
7	KHALIL Amer	58		HUSSAIN Imran	9
8	SH.QASEM Hassouneh			ESSA Muhammad	10
9	SHELBAIEH Mahmoud			AZIZ Abdul	11
13	JABER Rafat	78	44	IMRAN Mohammad	14
16	SULEIMAN Faisal		46	WASEEM Mohammad	16
17	AQEL Hatem			MUNIR Khalid	19
20	AL SHAGRAN Badran	70		HASSAN Misbahul	23
	Tr: AL GOHARY Mahmoud			Tr: SHAREEDA Salman	
11	AL ZBOUN Anas	78	67	SHAH Farooq	8
18	MAHMOUD Hasan	58	46	AHMED Jamil	17
21	IBRAHIM Ahmad	70	44 67	ALI Abid	24

Al Nasr Stadium, Dubai		
22-02-2006, 19:00, 15 000, Al Ghamdi KSA		

UAE 1 0 OMA

Ismail Matar [15]

UAE				OMAN	
17	AL BADRANI Waleed			AL HABS Ali	26
2	AL JENAIBI Abdulraheem		94	AL NOOBI Mohamed	2
3	SALEH Mohammed			AL WAHAIBI Juma	3
4	ALJESMI Omran		63	MOHAMED Hashim	9
5	ALHAWASIN Ali	89	75	BAIT DOORBEEN Fawzi	10
7	AHMED Mohammed	66	79	AL MAHAURI Ahmed	12
8	MOHAMED Haidar	63		AL AJMI Ismail	15
10	ALJUNAIBI Ismaeil Matar			AL GHEILANI Hassan	17
11	AL JUNAIBI Faisal			AL HOSNI Amad	20
21	MAJEED Humaid		67	AL MUKHAINI Ahmed	21
23	AL BALOOSHI Mohamed			AL NAUFALI Khalifa	25
	Tr: BATHENAY Dominique			Tr: JURCIC Srecko	
12	AL SAEDI Helal	89	67	AL TOUQI Sultan	7
18	AL WEHAIBI Ali	63	75	AL MAIMANI Badar	8
24	AL MEKHAINI	66	63	AL MAGHIN Hassan	27

Police Stadium, Wattayyah
1-03-2006, 19:00, 11 000, Irmatov UZB

OMA   **3**   **0**   **JOR**

Hashem Saleh [7], Ismael Sulaiman [18],
Hassan Zaher Al Maghni [54]

OMAN			JORDAN	
26 AL HABSI Ali			ELAMAIREH Lo'ai	12
3 AL WAHAIBI Juma			ALMALTA'AH Khaled	3
4 SUWAILIM Said			ABU ALIEH Qusai	4
8 AL MAIMANI Badar	68		BANI YASEEN Bashar	6
9 MOHAMED Hashim Saleh	81		KHALIL Amer	7
10 BAIT DOORBEEN Fawzi			SH.QASEM Hassouneh	8
15 AL AJMI Ishmail Sulaiman	56		SHELBAIEH Mahmoud	9
17 AL GHEILANI Hassan	56		JABER Rafat	13
20 AL HOSNI Amad	22		SULEIMAN Faisal	16
21 AL MUKHAINI Ahmed			AQEL Hatem	17
25 AL NAUFALI Khalifa			MAHMOUD Hasan	18
Tr: JURCIC Srecko			Tr: AL GOHARY Mahmoud	
6 AL MUKHAINI Mohamed	85	56	AL ZBOUN Anas	11
7 AL TOUQI Sultan	68	81	AL SHAGRAN Badran	20
27 AL MAGHNI Hassan	85	22	56	IBRAHIM Amad	21

People's Stadium, Karachi
1-03-2006, 21:00, 10 000, Tongkhan THA

PAK   **1**   **4**   **UAE**

Muhammad Essa [60]   Subait Al Mekhaini [68], Ismaeil Matar [78]
Salam Saad [81], Saeed Alkas [88]

PAKISTAN			UAE	
1 KHAN Jaffar			AL BADRANI Waleed	17
2 AKRAM Naveed			AL JENAIBI Abdulraheem	2
8 SHAH Farooq	61		SALEH Mohammed	3
9 HUSSAIN Imran			ALJESMI Omran	4
10 ESSA Muhammad		66	AHMED Mohammed	7
11 AZIZ Abdul			ALJUNAIBI Ismaeil Matar	10
13 KHAN Safiullah	32	87	AL JUNAIBI Faisal	11
14 IMRAN Mohammad		65	AL SAEDI Helal	12
19 MUNIR Khalid	78		AL WEHAIBI Ali	18
22 HAMZA Javeed			MAJEED Humaid	21
23 HASSAN Misbahul			AL BALOOSHI Mohamed	25
Tr: SHAREEDA Salman			Tr: BATHENAY Dominique	
5 ISHAQ Samar	32	87	ALKAS Saeed	19
20 RIAZ Faheem	61	66	ALABADLA Salem Saad	23
21 ISMAIL Muhammad	78	65	AL MEKHAINI Subait	24

GROUP D

National Stadium, Manama
22-02-2006, 18:35, 2 500, Mohd Salleh MAS

BHR   **1**   **3**   **AUS**

Hussain Ali Abdulla [35]   Thompson [53], Skoko [79], Elrich [87p]

BAHRAIN			AUSTRALIA	
1 AL THANI Ali Hasan			COVIC Ante	12
2 HASAN Mohamed			SKOKO Josip	8
3 MARZOOQ Abdulla	86	46	THWAITE Michael	16
7 AL WADAEI Sayed			WILKSHIRE Luke	20
8 AL DOSERI Rashed	77		ELRICH Ahmad	21
9 ABDULLA Husain			THOMPSON Archie	22
10 SALMEEN Mohamed			BEAUCHAMP Michael	26
14 ALI Salman			CECCOLI Alvin	27
16 MOHAMED HUSAIN Sayed	83		MCDONALD Scott	31
18 HABIB Husain	62		NORTH Jade	35
29 HUBAIL Mohamed			MCKAIN Jonathan	36
Tr: PERUZOVIC Luka			Tr: ARNOLD Graham	
27 MUSAIFER Ali Aamer	77	46	HOLMAN Brett	25
30 HUBAIL Aala	62	83	CARNEY David	30

Municipal Stadium, Beirut
22-02-2006, 19:00, 8 000, Mujghef JOR

LIB   **1**   **1**   **KUW**

Ali Nasseredine [67]   Fahad Al Hamad [25]

LEBANON			KUWAIT	
1 EL SAMAD Ziyad			AL KHALDI Nawaf	22
3 MOHAMAD Youssef			JARRAGH Mohammad	3
6 ANTAR Faissal			AL HAJERI Naser	4
7 BAALBAKI Nabil			AL-SHAMARI Nohayr	5
9 KASSAS Mohammad			ZADAH Khaled	7
11 GHADDAR Mohamad	83	91	AL MUTAIRI Khalaf	10
12 EL CHOUM Ahmad			AL EIDAN Ahmad	12
13 MTEIREK Ali			AL MUTWA Badar	17
16 AL JAMAL Nasrat	52		AL ATAIQI Jarah	18
21 HAMIEH Khaled			AL HAMAD Fahad	20
27 EL ATAT Ali	65		SHAHEEN Fahad	30
Tr: RUSTOM Emile			Tr: STOICHITA Mihai	
15 MAATOUK Hassan	83	91	AL HUMAIDAN Nawaf	25
23 ATWI Abbas Ali	65			
30 NASSEREDINE Ali	52			

Kuwait SC Stadium, Kuwait City
1-03-2006, 18:15, 16 000, Moradi IRN

KUW   **0**   **0**   **BHR**

KUWAIT			BAHRAIN	
22 AL KHALDI Nawaf			AL THANI Ali Hassan	1
3 JARRAGH Mohammad			HASAN Mohamed	2
4 AL HAJERI Naser		73	AL WADAEI Sayed	7
5 AL-SHAMARI Nohayr			AL DOSERI Rashed	8
10 AL MUTAIRI Khalaf	87		ABDULLA Husain	9
12 AL EIDAN Ahmad			SALMEEN Mohamed	10
17 AL MUTWA Bader			ALI Salman	14
18 AL ATAIQI Jarah			MOHAMED HUSAIN Sayed	16
20 AL HAMAD Fahad	80		AL ANEZI Hamad	24
30 SHAHEEN Fahad			HUBAIL Mohamed	29
41 AL NAMASH Ali	90	65	HUBAIL Aala	30
Tr: STOICHITA Mihai			Tr: AL THAWADI Riyadh	
7 ZADAH Khaled	90	73	HABIB Husain	18
25 AL HUMAIDAN Nawaf	80	65	MOHAMED RASHED Ahmed	20
26 FAIROOZ Mousaed	87			

GROUP E

National Stadium, Singapore
22-02-2006, 19:30, 10 221, Shield AUS

SIN 2 0 IRQ

Khairul Amri [24], Noh Alam Shah [83]

SINGAPORE				IRAQ	
18	LIONEL Lewis			ABBAS Noor	22
2	SHI Jiayi			MOHAMMED Yasser	4
5	SAHAK Aide Iskandar			ALI Nashat	5
6	KAIZAN Baihakki	81	79	RIDHA Emad	7
8	NOH Alam Shah			M.KHALEF Younes	10
10	DAUD Indra Sahdan			TAHER Hawar	11
14	SHUNMUGHAM Subramani			HASSAN Haiedar	12
15	MUSTAFIC Fahrudin			REHEMA Ali	15
16	BENNETT Daniel		69	AJEEL Mahdi	18
19	MOHAMMAD Khairul Amri	71	46	TAHIR Haitham	19
23	ABDUL HALIM Isa	62		ABOUDY Qusay	24
	Tr: AVRAMOVIC Radojko			Tr: SALMAN Akram	
11	SHAHUL HAMEED Fazrul	71	69	AL SADWN Salih	6
20	Rahman Mohamed Noh	62	46	MOSSA Razak	9
21	Emuejeraye Precious	81	79	HASSAN Haidar A.	14

Tianhe Sports Centre, Guangzhou
22-02-2006, 19:30, 16 500, Kwon Jong Chul KOR

CHN 2 0 PLE

Du Wei [23], Li Weifeng [62]

CHINA PR				PALESTINE	
1	LI Lei Lei			SALEH Ramzi	21
2	DU Wei			ATURA Francisco	2
5	LI Wei Feng			JENDEYA Saeb	5
8	LI Tie			ZAATARA Imad	9
11	TAO Wei	68		ABULATIFA Fady	11
13	CAO Cheng			ABUSIDU Majed	15
16	JI Mingyi		82	AMER Taysir	17
24	ZHAO Xuri			AL AMOUR Ismail	18
28	DONG Fangzho	90		ABDALLAH Pablo	24
32	HAO Junmin			ADAUY Roberto	25
33	LI Yi	81	36	KHALIL Omar	34
	Tr: Zhu Guanghu			Tr: VICZKO Tamas	
10	CHEN Tao	68	82	ATTAL Fahed	16
17	ZOU Jie	90	36	ALKORD Ziyad	29
35	GAO Lin	81			

Khalifa Bin Zayed Stadium, Al Ain
1-03-2006, 16:00, 7 700, Al Saeedi UAE

IRQ 2 1 CHN

Mahdi Ajeel [16]
Hawar Mohammed Taher [67]
Tao Wei [54]

IRAQ				CHINA PR	
22	ABBAS Noor			LI Lei Lei	1
3	GATEE Bassim			DU Wei	2
4	MOHAMMED Yasser			ZHANG Yaokun	4
10	M.KHALEF Younes			LI Wei Feng	5
11	TAHER Hawar		46	LI Tie	8
14	HASSAN Haidar A.			TAO Wei	11
15	REHEMA Ali			ZHAO Junzhe	15
18	AJEEL Mahdi	87		JI Mingyi	16
19	TAHIR Haitham		54	SHI Jun	19
24	ABOUDY Qusay			ZHAO Xuri	24
27	HAJI Jasim		74	DONG Fangzhuo	28
	Tr: SALMAN Akram			Tr: Zhu Guanghu	
32	ISMAIL Khalid	87	46	SHAO Jiayi	6
			54	CHEN Tao	10
			74	ZOU Jie	17

International Stadium, Amman
1-03-2006, 16:00, 1 000, Al Hilali OMA

PLE 1 0 SIN

Fahed Attal [75]

PALESTINE				SINGAPORE	
21	SALEH Ramzi			LIONEL Lewis	18
2	ATURA Francisco			SHI Jiayi	2
5	JENDEYA Saeb			SAHAK Aide Iskandar	5
8	AL SWEIRKI Ibrahim		61	NOH Alam Shah	8
9	ZAATARA Imad	64		DAUD Indra Sahdan	10
11	ABULATIFA Fady			SHUNMUGHAM Subramani	14
12	SALEM Fady			MUSTAFIC Fahrudin	15
15	ABUSIDU Majed			BENNETT Daniel	16
17	AMER Taysir	90		MOHAMMAD Khairul Amri	19
24	ABDALLAH Pablo	64		EMUEJERAYE Precious	21
25	ADAUY Roberto		46	ABDUL HALIM Isa	23
	Tr: VICZKO Tamas			Tr: AVRAMOVIC Radojko	
3	ESHBAIR Hamada	90	61	SHAHUL HAMEED Fazrul	11
10	AL WAARA Khaldun	64	46	RAHMAN Mohamed Noh	20
16	ATTAL Fahed	64	79		

GROUP F

Pakhtakor Stadium, Tashkent
22-02-2006, 16:00, 12 000, Ebrahim BHR

UZB 5 0 BAN

Geynrikh 2 [10] [52], Djeparov [24],
Shatskikh 2 [34] [84]

UZBEKISTAN				BANGLADESH	
1	SAFONOV Evgene		15	HOQUE Md.Aminul	1
3	FYODOROV Andrey			HOSSAIN Firoj	2
5	ALIQULOV Asror			BARMAN Rajani	4
8	DJEPAROV Server	72		MAMUN Md.	6
9	SOLIEV Anvarjon	32	80	MUNNA Motiur	7
10	KARPENKO Victor			ARMAN Md.	8
13	BIKMOEV Marat	54	54	AHMED Md.	10
15	GEYNRIKH Alexander			KHAN Arif	13
16	SHATSKIKH Maksim			AZIZ Arman	15
18	KAPADZE Timur			SUJAN Md.	19
25	DENISOV Vitaliy	76		AMELI Md.	21
	Tr: NEPOMNIATCHI Valeriy			Tr: BABLOO Hasanuzzaman	
6	KOSHELEV Leonid	54	54	KANCHAN Md.	11
17	NIKOLAEV Alexey	32	80	UZZAL Mehedi	17
33	RADKEVICH Vladimir	76	15	BHATTACHARJEE Biplob	20

Hong Kong Stadium, Hong Kong
22-02-2006, 20:00, 1 806, Nishimura JPN

HKG 0 3 QAT

Hussain Yaser Abdulrahman [11]
Sayd Bechir [44] Magid Hassan [95+]

HONG KONG				QATAR	
19	FAN Chun Yip			AHMED Mohamed	1
3	MAN Pei Tak			AL BERIK Abdulla	4
6	NG Wai Chiu			NASSER Ali	7
9	CHAN Siu Ki	70		ALSHAMMRI Saad	8
10	CHAN Yiu Lun			BECHIR Sayd	9
18	LEE Wai Man			ABDULRAHMAN Hussain	10
20	POON Yiu Cheuk		90	MOHD Adel	16
21	CHAN Ho Man	46		ABDULMAJID Wesam	17
23	AMBASSA Guy Gerard		85	JASSIM ABDULLA Waleed	18
25	SZETO Man Chun			KONI Abdulla	21
28	SHAM Kwok Fai		66	RAJAB Bilal	30
	Tr: Lai Sun Cheung			Tr: MUSOVIC Dzemaludin	
7	CHU Siu Kei	70	85	SIDDIQ Majadi	5
8	CHEUNG Sai Ho	46	90	HASSAN Magid	12
			66	AL GHANIM Ibrahim	14

Bangabandhu, Dhaka 1-03-2006, 16:00, 1 000, Sarkar IND			
BAN	**0**	**1**	**HKG**
			Chan Siu Ki [82]

BANGLADESH			HONG KONG
20 BHATTACHARJEE Biplob			FAN Chun Yip 19
2 HOSSAIN Firoj			NG Wai Chiu 4
4 BARMAN Rajani			CHEUNG Sai Ho 8
6 AL-MAMUN Md.			CHAN Yiu Lun 10
7 MUNNA Motiur	71	55	LO Chi Kwan 14
8 ARMAN Md.	80	67	LEE Wai Man 18
9 FARHAD Ariful			POON Yiu Cheuk 20
10 AHMAD Md.		60	CHAN Ho Man 21
13 JOY Arif			AMBASSA GUY Gerard 23
15 AZIZ Arman	85		SZETO Man Chun 25
19 SUJAN Md.			SHAM Kwok Fai 28
Tr: BABLOO Hasanuzzaman			Tr: Lai Sun Cheung
11 KANCHAN Md.	85	67	MAN Pei Tak 3
17 UZZAL Mehedi	80	60	CHAN Siu Ki 9
18 RAHMAN Asadur	71	55	LAW Chun Bong 11

Al Sadd Stadium, Doha 1-03-2006, 20:00, 7 000, Sun Baoje CHN			
QAT	**2**	**1**	**UZB**
Adel Mohd Lamy [45], Ali Naser [49]			Bilal OG [20]

QATAR			UZBEKISTAN
1 AHMED Mohamed			SAFONOV Evgene 1
4 AL BERIK Abdulla			FYODOROV Andrey 3
5 SIDDIQ Majadi			ALIQULOV Asror 5
7 NASSER Ali		77	KOSHELEV Leonid 6
8 ALSHAMMRI Saad		50	KARPENKO Victor 10
10 ABDULRAHMAN Hussain	81		KIRYAN Vladislav 14
12 HASSAN Magid	88	62	GEYNRIKH Alexander 15
16 MOHD Adel	93		SHATSKIKH Maksim 16
17 ABDULMAJID Wesam			NIKOLAEV Alexey 17
21 KONI Abdulla			KAPADZE Timur 18
30 RAJAB Bilal			INNOMOV Islom 24
Tr: MUSOVIC Dzemaludin			Tr: NEPOMNIATCHI Valeriy
2 ADAM Maaz	93	77	BAYRAMOV Renat 7
18 ABDULLA Meshaal	81	50	SOLIEV Anvarjon 9
19 FARTOOS Ali	88	62	KHOLMURODOV Zafar 29

AFC CHALLENGE CUP BANGLADESH 2006

AFC CHALLENGE CUP BANGLADESH 2006

First round groups		Quarter-final groups		Semi-finals		Final	
	Pts						
India	5						
Chinese Taipei	5	Tajikistan	6				
Philippines	2	Bangladesh	1				
Afghanistan	2						
				Tajikistan	2		
	Pts			Kyrgyzstan	0		
Sri Lanka	7						
Nepal	4	Palestine	0				
Brunei Darussalam	4	Kyrgyzstan	1				
Bhutan	1						
						Tajikistan	4
	Pts					Sri Lanka	0
Palestine	7						
Bangladesh	7	Nepal	3				
Cambodia	3	India	0				
Guam	0						
				Nepal	1 3p		
	Pts			Sri Lanka	1 5p		
Tajikistan	6						
Kyrgyzstan	6	Chinese Taipei	0				
Pakistan	4	Sri Lanka	3				
Macau	1						

GROUP A	PL	W	D	L	F	A	GD	PTS	IND	TPE	PHI	AFG
1 India	3	1	2	0	3	1	+2	5		0-0	1-1	2-0
2 Chinese Taipei	3	1	2	0	3	2	+1	5			1-0	2-2
3 Philippines	3	0	2	1	2	3	-1	2				1-1
4 Afghanistan	3	0	2	1	3	5	-2	2				

Ma Aziz, Chittagong
1-04-2006, 15:30, 2 500, Al Ghatrifi OMA

IND   2   0   AFG

Vimal Pariyar 2 [35] [60]

INDIA			AFGHANISTAN	
21 PAUL Shilton			AMIRI Shamsuddin	1
2 SINGH Parwinder			AMIRI Islamuddin	2
4 NADUPARAMPIL Pradeep			SAADAT Bashir Ahmad	3
5 MASIH Rakesh			HUSSAINI Qudratullah	4
9 SINGH Bungo Thokchom	70		GULLESTANI Abdul	5
13 XAVIER Vijay Kumar	60	81	MAHMOUDI Raza	6
16 LEPCHA Ong Tshering			MAQSOOD Sayed	7
18 ANTO Rino			ABBASI Ahmad Wahid	8
24 PARIYAR Vimal	92	78	QADAMI Hafizullah	9
25 LARAMLUAHA			AFSHAR Mohammad	10
30 HAMAR Lalmalsawma			AHMADI Ali	11
Tr: AKHMEDOV Islam			Tr: STAERK Klaus	
15 PAITE Khanthang	60	81	YARZADA Ali Ahmad	14
26 VASHUM Reisangmi	70	78	BAYAT Mustafa	16
29 ELANGBAM Hirohito	92			

Ma Aziz, Chittagong
3-04-2006, 15:30, 2 000, Mujghef JOR

PHI   1   1   IND

Valeroso [19]
Vimal Pariyar [8]

PHILIPPINES			INDIA	
22 SACAPANO Eduard			PAUL Shilton	21
2 ITALIA Bervic			SINGH Parwinder	2
5 ORCULLO Gerald		82	NADUPARAMPIL Pradeep	4
6 GONZALES Andres			MASIH Rakesh	5
8 VILLON Mark Peterson			SINGH Bungo Thokchom	9
10 PEREZ Rolly	67	79	PAITE Khanthang	15
12 DELA CRUZ Wilson			LEPCHA Ong Tshering	16
16 GUNN Leigh James	84		ANTO Rino	18
18 BORROMEO Alexander			PARIYAR Vimal	24
23 JIAO Jeremias			HMAR Zadinmawia	27
29 VALEROSO Mark Alvin	74	77	HAMAR Lalmalsawma	30
Tr: CASLIB Jose Ariston			Tr: AKHMEDOV Islam	
11 LIMAN Jeffrey	67	82	DEEP Warum	3
20 ARANETA Ian	74	77	PACHUAU Lalawmpuia	14
26 ALLADO Marjo	84	79	VASHUM Reisangmi	26

Ma Aziz, Chittagong
5-04-2006, 15:30, 2 000, Gosh BAN

IND   0   0   TPE

INDIA			CHINESE TAIPEI	
21 PAUL Shilton			HSU Jen-Feng	12
2 SINGH Parwinder			KAO Hao-Chieh	2
4 NADUPARAMPIL Pradeep	71		CHENG Yung-Jen	5
5 MASIH Rakesh			FENG Pao-Hsing	6
9 SINGH Bungo Thokchom	80	89	TAI Hung-Hsu	8
15 PAITE Khanthang	47		HUANG Shih-Chan	10
16 LEPCHA Ong Tshering			CHANG Fu-Hsiang	14
18 ANTO Rino			KUO Chan-Yu	16
24 PARIYAR Vimal	91		LEE Meng-Chian	18
27 HMAR Zadinmawia			CHUANG Wei-Lun	19
30 HAMAR Lalmalsawma	71		TSENG Tail-Lin	22
Tr: AKHMEDOV Islam			Tr: IMAI Toshiaki	
13 XAVIER Vijay Kumar	91	89	HUANG Cheng-Tsung	7
25 LALRAMLUAHA	80			
26 VASHUM Reisangmi	47			

Ma Aziz, Chittagong
1-04-2006, 18:00, 4 000, Lee Gi Young KOR

TPE   1   0   PHI

Chuang Wei Lun [20]

CHINESE TAIPEI			PHILIPPINES	
12 HSU Jen-Feng			SACAPANO Eduard	22
2 KAO Hao-Chieh			ITALIA Bervic	2
3 TSAI Sheng-An			ORCULLO Gerald	5
4 KUO Chun-Yi	46		GONZALES Andres	6
5 CHENG Yung-Jen			VILLON Mark Peterson	8
11 LIN Po-Yuan	65	82	LIMAN Jeffrey	11
14 CHANG Fu-Hsiang			DELA CRUZ Wilson	12
18 LEE Meng-Chian			BORROMEO Alexander	18
19 CHUANG Wei-Lun			ARANETA Ian	20
22 TSENG Tail-Lin	46*	55	JIAO Jeremias	23
23 LIANG Chien-Wei		39	SUBERE Winnie	24
Tr: IMAI Toshiaki			Tr: CASLIB Jose Ariston	
7 HUANG Cheng-Tsung	46*	55	CALIGDONG Emelio	13
8 TAI Hung-Hsu	65	82	BRILLANTES Luisito	17
10 HUANG Shih-Chan	46	39	VALEROSO Mark Alvin	29

Ma Aziz, Chittagong
3-04-2006, 18:00, 2 500, Lee Gi Young KOR

AFG   2   2   TPE

Hafizullah Qadami 2 [20] [23]
Chuang Wei Lun [48]
Liang Chien Wei [73]

AFGHANISTAN			CHINESE TAIPEI	
1 AMIRI Shamsuddin			HSU Jen-Feng	12
3 SAADAT Bashir Ahmad			KAO Hao-Chieh	2
4 HUSSAINI Qudratullah			TSAI Sheng-An	3
5 GULLESTANI Abdul			KUO Chun-Yi	4
6 MAHMOUDI Raza			CHENG Yung-Jen	5
7 MAQSOOD Sayed			FENG Pao-Hsing	6
8 ABBASI Ahmad Wahid	89	64	TAI Hung-Hsu	8
9 QADAMI Hafizullah	91	88	CHANG Fu-Hsiang	14
10 AFSHAR Mohammad	86		LEE Meng-Chian	18
11 AHMADI Ali			CHUANG Wei-Lun	19
21 AZIZI Manochahr			LIANG Chien-Wei	23
Tr: STAERK Klaus			Tr: IMAI Toshiaki	
15 AKHWAN Souraj	86	88	LIN Che-Min	24
16 BAYAT Mustafa	91	64	CHEN Po-Liang	30
17 KOHISTANI Mohammad	89			

Ma Aziz, Chittagong
5-04-2006, 18:00, 3 000, Mujghef JOR

PHI   1   1   AFG

Valeroso [59]
Sayed Maqsood [28]

PHILIPPINES			AFGHANISTAN	
22 SACAPANO Eduard			AMIRI Shamsuddin	1
2 ITALIA Bervic		76	SAADAT Bashir Ahmad	3
5 ORCULLO Gerald			GULLESTANI Abdul	5
6 GONZALES Andres			MAHMOUDI Raza	6
8 VILLON Mark Peterson	89	90	MAQSOOD Sayed	7
10 PEREZ Rolly			ABBASI Ahmad Wahid	8
12 DELA CRUZ Wilson		75	QADAMI Hafizullah	9
16 GUNN Leigh James	87		AFSHAR Mohammad	10
18 BORROMEO Alexander			AHMADI Ali	11
23 JIAO Jeremias			YARZADA Ali Ahmad	14
29 VALEROSO Mark Alvin	73		AZIZI Manochahr	21
Tr: CASLIB Jose Ariston			Tr: STAERK Klaus	
17 BRILLANTES Luisito	87	76	AMIRI Islamuddin	2
20 ARANETA Ian	73	75	BAYAT Mustafa	16
26 ALLADO Marjo	89	90	ATIQULLAH	5

GROUP B	PL	W	D	L	F	A	GD	PTS	SRI	NEP	BRU	BHU
1 Sri Lanka	3	2	1	0	3	1	+2	7		1-1	1-0	1-0
2 Nepal	3	1	1	1	4	3	+1	4			1-2	2-0
3 Brunei Darussalam	3	1	1	1	2	2	=	4				0-0
4 Bhutan	3	0	1	2	0	3	-3	1				

Ma Aziz, Chittagong
2-04-2006, 15:30, 2 000, Saidov UZB

SRI 1 0 BRU

Kasun [74]

SRI LANKA		BRUNEI DARUSSALAM	
1 THILAKARATNE Sugath		MD.NOOR Azman Ilham 25	
2 HETTIHARACHCHIGE Dumidu	88	BUJANG Mardi 2	
3 KAMALDEEN Fuard		PG DAMIT Pg Sallehuddin 3	
4 WELL DON Rohan		WAHIT Md.Safari 5	
6 NAUFER Izzadeen	71	AMBON Christopher 7	
7 SIYAGUNA Chathura		BUJANG Hardi 8	
8 BIYAGAMA Rajitha		WAHIT Riwandi 9	
10 EDIRIBANDANAGE Channa		ABDUL LAMIT Hardyman 10	
18 AMARASINHA Sanjaya		PG RAMLEE Kamarul 17	
19 DEHIWALAGE Nimal	58 67	TUAH Ratano 19	
23 STEINWALL Duddley		MUHAMAD SALEH Azwan 20	
Tr: SAMPATH PERERA Kolonnage		Tr: HJ MUSTAFA Mohd Ali	
9 GALBODAPAYAGALAGE Karu 71	88	LUPAT Yunus 15	
11 WEERARATHNA Kasun	58 67	MD.SALLEH Adie Arsham 21	

Ma Aziz, Chittagong
2-04-2006, 18:00, 3 500, Gosh BAN

NEP 2 0 BHU

Pradeep Maharjan 2 [52 68]

NEPAL		BHUTAN	
1 MALLA Bikash		SINGYE Jigme 1	
5 KC Anjan		KHANDU Sangay 2	
6 GURUNG Lok Bandhu		TSHERING Tandin 3	
7 TAMANG Surendra	68	PEMA 4	
8 KHADAGI Rajesh	46 60	TSHERING Passang 5	
13 GOUCHAN Vishad		DORJI Kinley 7	
14 TSERING Tashi		WANGCHUK 8	
17 MAHARJAN Pradeep	71	DORJI Wangay 10	
19 THAPA Sagar		DORJI Ugyen 15	
22 THAPA Basanta Kumar	74	DENDUP Nawang 16	
23 GURUNG Bijay		GURUNG Karun 18	
Tr: THAPA Shyam		Tr: BASNET Kharga	
10 BUDHATHOKI Ramesh	68 60	PRADHAN Bikash 9	
11 KHADKA Hari	74 71	GYELTSHEN 12	
12 TAMANG Raju	46		

Ma Aziz, Chittagong
4-04-2006, 15:30, Saidov UZB

BHU 0 1 SRI

Karu [45]

BHUTAN		SRI LANKA	
1 SINGYE Jigme		THILAKARATNE Sugath 1	
2 KHANDU Sangay		HETTIHARACHCHIGE Dumidu 2	
3 TSHERING Tandin		KAMALDEEN Fuard 3	
4 PEMA		WELL DON Rohan 4	
5 TSHERING Passang	19	SIYAGUNA Chathura 7	
7 DORJI Kinley		GALBODAPAYAGALAGE Karu 9	71
8 WANGCHUK	90	EDIRIBANDANAGE Channa 10	
10 DORJI Wangay		WEERARATHNA Kasun 11	
15 DORJI Ugyen		ABDUL AZEEZ Fazlur 14	
16 DENDUP Nawang		AMARASINHA Sanjaya 18	54
18 GURUNG Karun	89	STEINWALL Duddley 23	
Tr: BASNET Kharga		Tr: SAMPATH PERERA Kolonnage	
9 PRADHAN Bikash	89 71	ELPITIYA Nuwanth 12	
12 GYELTSHEN	19 54	RATHNAYAKA Ratnayaka 15	
13 TENZIN Sonam	90		

Ma Aziz, Chittagong
4-04-2006, 18:00, 2 500, Al Ghatrifi OMA

BRU 2 1 NEP

Safari [47], Sallehuddin [70]   Tashi Tsering [60]

BRUNEI DARUSSALAM		NEPAL	
25 MD.NOOR Azman Ilham		MALLA Bikash 1	
2 BUJANG Mardi	67	K.C.,Anjan 5	
3 PG DAMIT Pg Sallehuddin		GURUNG Lok Bandhu 6	
5 WAHIT Md.Safari		TAMANG Surendra 7	
7 AMBON Christopher		TAMANG Raju 12	
9 WAHIT Riwandi	78	GOUCHAN Vishad 13	
10 ABDUL LAMIT Hardyman		TSERING Tashi 14	
12 HANAFIAH Helman	46	MAHARJAN Pradeep 17	
17 PG RAMLEE Kamarul	84	THAPA Sagar 19	
20 MUHAMAD SALEH Azwan		THAPA Basanta Kumar 22	
21 MD.SALLEH Adie Arsham	90 67	GURUNG Bijay 23	
Tr: HJ MUSTAFA Mohd Ali		Tr: THAPA Shyam	
6 AHAR Philip	90 46	SUBEDI Suman 3	
8 BUJANG Hardi	67 67	RAI Ju Manu 9	
19 TUAH Ratano	84 78	BUDHATHOKI Ramesh 10	

Ma Aziz, Chittagong
6-04-2006, 15:30, 2 500, Lee Gi Young KOR

SRI 1 1 NEP

Izzadeen [19]   Pradeep Maharjan [75p]

SRI LANKA		NEPAL	
1 THILAKARATNE Sugath		THAPA Ritesh 20	
2 HETTIHARACHCHIGE Dumidu	32	SUBEDI Suman 3	
3 KAMALDEEN Fuard		K.C. Anjan 5	
4 WELL DON Rohan		GURUNG Lok Bandhu 6	
6 NAUFER Izzadeen	70	TAMANG Raju 12	
7 SIYAGUNA Chathura	91	GOUCHAN Vishad 13	
8 BIYAGAMA Rajitha	61	TSERING Tashi 14	
10 EDIRIBANDANAGE Channa	70	MAHARJAN Pradeep 17	
11 WEERARATHNA Kasun		THAPA Sagar 19	
15 RATHNAYAKA Ratnayaka	83	THAPA Basanta Kumar 22	
18 AMARASINHA Sanjaya		GURING Bijay 23	
Tr: SAMPATH PERERA Kolonnage		Tr: THAPA Shyam	
9 GALBODAPAYAGALAGE Karu 70	32	TAMANG Surendra 7	
17 WELLALA Gunaratne	61 91	KHADAGI Rajesh 8	
23 STEINWALL Duddley	83 91	BISHWAS Ram Kumar 26	

Ma Aziz, Chittagong
6-04-2006, 18:00, 2 000, Al Ghatrifi OMA

BHU 0 0 BRU

BHUTAN		BRUNEI DARUSSALAM	
1 SINGYE Jigme		MD.NOOR Azman Ilham 25	
2 KHANDU Sangay		BUJANG Mardi 2	
3 TSHERING Tandin		PG DAMIT Pg Sallehuddin 3	
4 PEMA		AMBON Christopher 7	
7 DORJI Kinley		BUJANG Hardi 8	
8 WANGCHUK	45	WAHIT Riwandi 9	
10 DORJI Wangay		ABDUL LAMIT Hardyman 10	75
12 GYELTSHEN		HANAFIAH Helman 12	59
15 DORJI Ugyen		PG RAMLEE Kamarul 17	
16 DENDUP Nawang		MUHAMAD SALEH Azwan 20	
18 GURUNG Karun		MD.SALLEH Adie Arsham 21	
Tr: BASNET Kharga		Tr: HJ MUSTAFA Mohd Ali	
9 PRADHAN Bikash	45 75	LUPAT Yunus 15	
	59	TUAH Ratano 19	

GROUP C		PL	W	D	L	F	A	GD	PTS		PLE	BAN	CAM	GUM
1	Palestine	3	2	1	0	16	1	+15	7			1-1	4-0	11-0
2	Bangladesh	3	2	1	0	6	2	+4	7		1-1		2-1	3-0
3	Cambodia	3	1	0	2	4	6	-2	3		4-0	2-1		3-0
4	Guam	3	0	0	3	0	17	-17	0		11-0	3-0	3-0	

Bangabandhu, Dhaka
1-04-2006, 15:30, 3 000, Abdul Kadir Nema IRQ

PLE   1   0   GUM

Ahmed Keshkesh [6], Fahed Attal 6 [14 20 25 32 45 86]
Francisco Atura [22], Ismail Al Amour [39], Zyad Al Kord 2 [59 67]

PALESTINE			GUAM	
22	DWAIMA Iyad		MALUWELMENG Brett	1
2	ATURA Francisco	58	BUSH James	2
3	ESHBAIR Hamada		LANDSTROM Weneisom	3
5	JENDEYA Saeb	78	HAMMOND Sho	7
8	AL SWEIRIKI Ibrahim	72	JAMISON Alan	8
12	SALEM Fady		ESPINOSA Randy	9
14	OMAR Mohanad		GADIA Dominic Tacadina	12
16	ATTAL Fahed		SCHALLHORN Uri	14
18	AL AMOUR Ismail	59	TORRES Pele	15
19	ABUSELEISEL Ammar	56	UNPINGCO Carlo	18
20	KESHKESH Ahmed	43	MERFALEN Elias	19
	Tr: SABAAH Mohammed		Tr: TSUKITATE Norio	
24	ABDALLAH Pablo	72 56	MANTANONA Ricfrancis	6
28	ABUKESHEK Mohammed	59 43	SANTOS Christopher	16
29	ALKORD Ziyad	58 78	WADE Craig	29

Bangabandhu, Dhaka
3-04-2006, 15:30, 2 500, Abdul Kadir Nema IRQ

CAM   0   4   PLE

Ahmed Keshkesh [10], Ibrahim Al
Sweirki 2 [12 75], Fahed Attal [30]

CAMBODIA			PALESTINE	
25	OUK Mic		DWAIMA Iyad	22
2	KEO Kosal	46*	ATURA Francisco	2
3	LAR Pichseyla		ESHBAIR Hamada	3
4	KOUCH Sokumpheak		JENDEYA Saeb	5
5	SAM Minar	46	AL SWEIRIKI Ibrahim	8
8	POK Chan Than	79	SALEM Fady	12
9	SENG Narath	72	OMAR Mohanad	14
11	CHAN Rithy		ATTAL Fahed	16
14	SREY Veasna	62	AL AMOUR Ismail	18
17	HOUT Sokunthea		ABUSELEISEL Ammar	19
22	TIENG Tiny	38	KESHKESH Ahmed	20
	Tr: JO Yong Choi		Tr: SABAAH Mohammed	
13	SOK Buntheang	79 38	ABUKESHEK Mohammed	7
16	THUL Sothearith	46* 72	BESHE Roberto	28
20	CHEA Veasna	46 62	ALKORD Ziyad	29

Bangabandhu, Dhaka
5-04-2006, 15:30, 22 000, Mombini IRN

PLE   1   1   BAN

Fahed Attal [30]

Mahadi Tapu [55]

PALESTINE			BANGLADESH	
21	SALEH Ramzi		HOQUE Md. Aminul	1
2	ATURA Francisco		AHMED Abu	3
3	ESHBAIR Hamada		ISLAM Kazi	5
5	JENDEYA Saeb		KANCHAN Md.Rokon	11
10	AL WAARA Khaldun	55	AZIZ Arman	15
16	ATTAL Fahed		RAHMAN Asadur	18
18	AL AMOUR Ismail	56	SAZIB Md	25
19	ABUSELEISEL Ammar	75	TAPU Mahadi	26
24	ABDALLAH Pablo	72	PARVEZ Zahed	27
28	BESHE Roberto	29 68	RINTU Shahriar	29
29	ALKORD Ziyad		FAISAL Md.Waly	30
	Tr: SABAAH Mohammed		Tr: CRUCIANI Diego	
8	AL SWEIRIKI Ibrahim	55 56	HOSSAIN Md	16
12	SALEM Fady	29 68	UZZAL Mehedi	17
14	OMAR Mohanad	72 75	HASAN AMELI Md	21

Bangabandhu, Dhaka
1-04-2006, 18:00, 35 000, Tan Hai CHN

BAN   2   1   CAM

Alfaz Ahmad [31], Hasan Ameli [64]

Chan Rithy [68]

BANGLADESH			CAMBODIA	
1	HOQUE Md. Aminul		OUK Mic	25
4	BARMAN Rajani		KEO Kosal	2
5	ISLAM Kazi		LAR Pichseyla	3
10	AHMAD Md	89	KOUCH Sokumpheak	4
12	HOSSEN Md.Monwar	54	SAM Minar	5
13	JOY Arif		POK Chan Than	8
14	PARVEZ Mostofo	79	SENG Narath	9
16	HOSSAIN Md		OM Thavrak	10
17	UZZAL Mehedi	76	CHAN Rithy	11
21	HASAN AMELI Md	71	SOK Buntheang	13
25	SAZIB Md		TIENG Tiny	22
	Tr: CRUCIANI Diego		Tr: JO Yong Choi	
11	KANCHAN Md.Rokon	76 71	SREY Veasna	14
15	AZIZ Arman	89 79	HOUT Sokunthea	17
27	PARVEZ Zahed	54		

Bangabandhu, Dhaka
3-04-2006, 18:00, 18 000, U Win Cho MYA

GUM   0   3   BAN

Hasam Ameli [49]
Abul Hossein 2 [83 85]

GUAM			BANGLADESH	
1	MALUWELMENG Brett		HOQUE Md. Aminul	1
2	BUSH James		BARMAN Rajani	4
3	LANDSTROM Weneisom		ISLAM Kazi	5
7	HAMMOND Sho	86 56	AHMAD Md	10
9	ESPINOSA Randy	78	HOSSEN Md.Monwar	12
12	GADIA Dominic Tacadina	82	JOY Arif	13
14	SCHALLHORN Uri		PARVEZ Mostofo	14
15	TORRES Pele		HOSSAIN Md	16
18	UNPINGCO Carlo		UZZAL Mehedi	17
19	MERFALEN Elias	54 88	HASAN AMELI Md	21
23	CUNLIFFE Jason		SAZIB Md	25
	Tr: TSUKITATE Norio		Tr: CRUCIANI Diego	
8	JAMISON Alan	78 82	AZIZ Arman	15
16	SANTOS Christopher	54 88	TAPU Mahadi	26
29	WADE Craig	86 56	RINTU Shahriar	29

Army Stadium, Dhaka
6-04-2006, 14:00, 500, U Win Cho MYA

CAM   3   0   GUM

Sok Buntheang [37], Keo Kosal [40],
Kouch Sokumpheak [63]

CAMBODIA			GUAM	
25	OUK Mic		MALUWELMENG Brett	1
2	KEO Kosal		BUSH James	2
3	LAR Pichseyla		LANDSTROM Weneisom	3
4	KOUCH Sokumpheak	85	JAMISON Alan	8
8	POK Chan Than	73	ESPINOSA Randy	9
9	SENG Narath	89	GADIA Dominic Tacadina	12
10	OM Thavrak		SCHALLHORN Uri	14
13	SOK Buntheang	68	TORRES Pele	15
14	SREY Veasna		UNPINGCO Carlo	18
16	THUL Sothearith	54	MERFALEN Elias	19
22	TIENG Tiny	46	CUNLIFFE Jason	23
	Tr: JO Yong Choi		Tr: TSUKITATE Norio	
7	TY Bun Vi Chet	68 85	MANTANONA Ricfrancis	6
17	HOUT Sokunthea	89 46	HAMMOND Sho	7
20	CHEA Veasna	73 54	LAANAN Joseph	20

GROUP D	PL	W	D	L	F	A	GD	PTS	TJK	KGZ	PAK	MAC
1 Tajikistan	3	2	0	1	6	1	+5	6		0-1	2-0	4-0
2 Kyrgyzstan	3	2	0	1	3	1	+2	6	0-1		2-0	
3 Pakistan	3	1	1	1	3	4	-1	4				2-2
4 Macau	3	0	1	2	2	8	-6	1				

Bangabandhu, Dhaka
2-04-2006, 15:30, 2 000, Mombini IRN

TJK   4   0   MAC

Makhmudov [9], Rabiev [13],
Rabimov [56], Khojaev [77]

TAJIKISTAN			MACAU	
1 KHABIBULLOEV Aslidin			CHU Hon Ming Wialliam	1
4 KHUJJAMOV Subkhon			KU Weng Nin	3
5 NEGMATOV Alexei			LAO Pak Kin	6
6 NOSIROV Naim			CHEANG Cheng Paulo	8
7 RABIMOV Ibrauim		80	DE SOUSA Geofredo	10
9 MAKHMUDOV Khurshed	71	52	CHEANG Chon Man	11
15 HAKIMOV Numondzhon		80	MOK Kin Fong	15
17 OEV Dzhamolidin			LEI Fu Weng	16
18 MUHIDINOV Dzhomikhon	67		CHAN Man Hei	23
19 IRGASHEV Odil			LAM Ka Pou	24
20 RABIEV Yusuf	77		UN Tak Lan	26
Tr: NAZAROV Sharif			Tr: KAGEYAMA Masanaga	
10 DZHABAROV Shukhrat	71	52	LEONG Lap San	12
21 KHOJAEV Rustam	67	80	CHAN Kin Seng	19
22 SADYKOV Makhmadhi	77	80	KONG Cheng Hou	21

Bangabandhu, Dhaka
4-04-2006, 15:30, 5 000, Tan Hai CHN

PAK   0   2   TJK

Hakimov [14], Irgashev [20]

PAKISTAN			TAJIKISTAN	
1 KHAN Jaffar			KHABIBULLOEV Aslidin	1
2 AKRAM Naveed			KHUJJAMOV Subkhon	4
4 SHAHID Muhammad			NEGMATOV Alexei	5
5 ISHAQ Samar			NOSIROV Naim	6
7 HAMEED Zahid	25		RABIMOV Ibrauim	7
10 ESSA Muhammad			MAKHMUDOV Khurshed	9
11 AZIZ Abdul			HAKIMOV Numondzhon	15
14 IMRAN Mohammad			OEV Dzhamolidin	17
22 HAMZA Javeed	59	63	MUHIDINOV Dzhomikhon	18
26 AYUB Muhammad Asif	85	73	IRGASHEV Odil	19
30 ADEEL		83	RABIEV Yusuf	20
Tr: SHAREEDA Salman			Tr: NAZAROV Sharif	
8 SHAH Farooq	25	83	NEMATOV Shujoat	11
12 KHAN Naveed	85	73	KHOJAEV Rustam	21
20 RIAZ Faheem	59	63	SADYKOV Makhmadhi	27

Bangabandhu, Dhaka
6-04-2006, 16:00, 1 000, Shamsuzzaman BAN

PAK   2   2   MAC

Adeel [12], Muhammad Essa [43]   Chan Kin Seng 2 [16 52]

PAKISTAN			MACAU	
1 KHAN Jaffar			CHU Hon Ming Wialliam	1
2 AKRAM Naveed			KU Weng Nin	3
4 SHAHID Muhammad			LAO Pak Kin	6
5 ISHAQ Samar			CHEANG Cheng Paulo	8
8 SHAH Farooq		17	DE SOUSA Geofredo	10
10 ESSA Muhammad		78	LEONG Lap San	12
11 AZIZ Abdul		70	MOK Kin Fong	15
14 IMRAN Mohammad			CHAN Kin Seng	19
22 HAMZA Javeed			CHAN Man Hei	23
24 ALI Abbas	32		LAM Ka Pou	24
30 ADEEL			UN Tak Lan	26
Tr: SHAREEDA Salman			Tr: KAGEYAMA Masanaga	
26 AYUB Muhammad Asif	32	70	CHEANG Chon Man	11
		78	LEI Fu Weng	16
		17	KONG Cheng Hou	21

Bangabandhu, Dhaka
2-04-2006, 18:00, 2 500, Shamsuzzaman BAN

KGZ   0   1   PAK

Muhammad Essa [59]

KYRGYZSTAN			PAKISTAN	
1 VOLKOV Vladislav			KHAN Jaffar	1
3 SAMSALIEV Talant	91		AKRAM Naveed	2
4 SYDYKOV Ruslan			SHAHID Muhammad	4
5 KNIAZEV Sergey			ISHAQ Samar	5
7 ISHENBAEV Azamat		86	HAMEED Zahid	7
9 HARCHENKO Vadim	80		ESSA Muhammad	10
10 DJAMSHIDOV Ruslan			AZIZ Abdul	11
11 KORNILOV Roman	76		IMRAN Mohammad	14
12 BOKOEV Aibek		76	HAMZA Javeed	22
13 KUDRENKO Igor			AYUB Muhammad Asif	26
17 ASKAROV Davron			ADEEL	29
Tr: PODKORYTOV Boris			Tr: SHAREEDA Salman	
2 AMIN Viacheslav	91	76	HUSSAIN Imran	9
15 VEREVKIN Vladimir	76	86	RIAZ Faheem	20
18 KRASNOV Andrey	80			

Bangabandhu, Dhaka
6-04-2006, 14:00, 2 000, Abdul Kadir Nema IRQ

TJK   0   1   KGZ

Krasnov [22]

TAJIKISTAN			KYRGYZSTAN	
1 KHABIBULLOEV Aslidin			VOLKOV Vladislav	1
2 CHORIEV Farrukh		46	AMIN Viacheslav	2
3 NURIDINOV Iskandar			SAMSALIEV Talant	3
5 NEGMATOV Alexei			SYDYKOV Ruslan	4
7 RABIMOV Ibraguim			KNIAZEV Sergey	5
10 DZHABAROV Shukhrat	78		HARCHENKO Vadim	9
18 MUHIDINOV Dzhomikhon	24		DJAMSHIDOV Ruslan	10
21 KHOJAEV Rustam			KUDRENKO Igor	13
22 SADYKOV Makhmadhli	46		AMIROV Ildar	14
25 TABAROV Rustam		60	VEREVKIN Vladimir	15
27 SAIDOV Kamil		82	KRASNOV Andrey	18
Tr: NAZAROV Sharif			Tr: PODKORYTOV Boris	
9 MAKHMUDOV Khurshed	78	60	ISHENBAEV Azamat	7
11 NEMATOV Shujoat	24	46	VALIEV Timur	8
19 IRGASHEV Odil	46	82	ASKAROV Davron	17

Bangabandhu, Dhaka
7-04-2006, 14:00, 1 000, Tan Hai CHN

MAC   0   2   KGZ

Ablakimov [35], Ishenbaev [58]

MACAU			KYRGYZSTAN	
1 CHU Hon Ming William			VOLKOV Vladislav	1
3 KU Weng Nin			SAMSALIEV Talant	3
8 CHEANG Cheng Paulo			SYDYKOV Ruslan	4
10 DE SOUSA Geofredo	66		KNIAZEV Sergey	5
11 CHEANG Chon Man	45		HARCHENKO Vadim	9
12 LEONG Lap San		68	DJAMSHIDOV Ruslan	10
15 MOK Kin Fong	66		BOKOEV Aibek	12
19 CHAN Kin Seng			KUDRENKO Igor	13
21 KONG Cheng Hou		54	AMIROV Ildar	14
23 CHAN Man Hei		46	KRASNOV Andrey	18
26 UN Tak Lan			ABLAKIMOV Roman	19
Tr: KAGEYAMA Masanaga			Tr: PODKORYTOV Boris	
14 HUNG Luis	66	68	ASKAROV Sardorbek	6
16 LEI Fu Weng	45	46	ISHENBAEV Azamat	7
28 HO Man Hou	66	54	ASKAROV Davron	17

QUARTER-FINALS

Ma Aziz, Chittagong
8-04-2006, 15:30, 2 500, Al Ghatrifi OMA

SRI	3 0	TPE

Izzadeen [44], Sanjaya [70], Ratnayaka [90]

SRI LANKA		CHINESE TAIPEI	
1 THILAKARATNE Sugath		LU Kun-Chi 1	
2 HETTIHARACHCHIGE Dumidu		KAO Hao-Chieh 2	
3 KAMALDEEN Fuard		KUO Chun-Yi 4	
4 WELL DON Rohan		FENG Pao-Hsing 6	
6 NAUFER Izzadeen		TAI Hung-Hsu 8	
7 SIYAGUNA Chathura	46	HUANG Tzu-Jung 9	
8 BIYAGAMA Rajitha	77	HUANG Shih-Chan 10	
10 EDIRIBANDANAGE Channa		CHANG Fu-Hsiang 14	
11 WEERARATHNA Kasun	46	KUO Chan-Yu 16	
18 AMARASINHA Sanjaya	92	LIANG Chien-Wei 23	
23 STEINWALL Duddley		LIN Che-Min 24	
Tr: SAMPATH PERERA Kolonnage		Tr: IMAI Toshiaki	
15 RATHNAYAKA Ratnayaka	77	HUANG Cheng-Tsung 7	46
17 WELLALA Gunaratne	92	TSENG Tai-Lin 22	80
		CHEN Po-Liang 30	46 80

Bangabandhu, Dhaka
9-04-2006, 15:30, 150, U Win Cho MYA

PLE	0 1	KGZ

Djamshidov [91]

PALESTINE		KYRGYZSTAN	
21 SALEH Ramzi		VOLKOV Vladislav 1	
2 ATURA Francisco		SAMSALIEV Talant 3	64
3 ESHBAIR Hamada		SYDYKOV Ruslan 4	
5 JENDEYA Saeb		KNIAZEV Sergey 5	
8 AL SWEIRKI Ibrahim		VALIEV Timur 8	67
12 SALEM Fady	38	HARCHENKO Vadim 9	
14 OMAR Mohanad	77	BOKOEV Aibek 12	
16 ATTAL Fahed		KUDRENKO Igor 13	
19 ABUSELEISEL Ammar		ASKAROV Davron 17	
28 BESHE Roberto		KRASNOV Andrey 18	
29 ALKORD Ziyad		ABLAKIMOV Roman 19	46
Tr: SABAAH Mohammed		Tr: PODKORYTOV Boris	
10 AL WAARA Khaldun	77	AMIN Viacheslav 2	64
24 ABDALLAH Pablo	38	ISHENBAEV Azamat 7	46
		DJAMSHIDOV Ruslan 10	67

Ma Aziz, Chittagong
9-04-2006, 15:30, 3 000, Gosh BAN

IND	0 3	NEP

Pradeep Maharjan 2 [16 26]
Basanta Thapa [28]

INDIA		NEPAL	
20 BHATTACHARJA Arindam		MALLA Bikash 1	
2 SINGH Parwinder		K.C. Anjan 5	
4 NADUPARAMPIL Pradeep		GURUNG Lok Bandhu 6	
5 MASIH Rakesh	79	TAMANG Surendra 7	
9 SINGH Bungo Thokchom		TAMANG Raju 12	
13 XAVIER Vijay Kumar	89 72	GOUCHAN Vishad 13	
16 LEPCHA Ong Tshering		TSERING Tashi 14	
18 ANTO Rino	86	MAHARJAN Pradeep 17	
24 PARIYAR Vimal		THAPA Sagar 19	
25 LALRAMLUAHA	63 86	THAPA Basanta Kumar 22	
27 HMAR Zaidinmawia		GURUNG Bijay 23	
Tr: AKHMEDOV Islam		Tr: THAPA Shyam	
3 DEEP Warun	86 86	SUBEDI Suman 3	
14 PACHAUA Lalawmpuia	63 72	NEUPAME Nabin 4	
26 VASHUM Reisangmi	89 79	RAI Ju Manu 9	

Bangabandhu, Dhaka
10-04-2006, 15:30, 15 000, Abdul Kadir Nema IRQ

TJK	6 1	BAN

Rabimov [2], Makhmudov [20], Muhidinov [31], Hakimov [51], Rabiev [65], Nematov [81]
Alfaz Ahmad [17]

TAJIKISTAN		BANGLADESH	
1 KHABIBULLOEV Aslidin		HOQUE Md. Aminul 1	
4 KHUJJAMOV Subkhon		BARMAN Rajani 4	
5 NEGMATOV Alexei	74	ISLAM Kazi 5	
6 NOSIROV Naim		AHMAD Md 10	62
7 RABIMOV Ibrauim		KANCHAN Md. Rokon 11	52
9 MAKHMUDOV Khurshed		HOSSEN Md. Monwar 12	46
15 HAKIMOV Numondzhon		AZIZ Arman 15	
17 OEV Dzhamolidin		HOSSAIN Md 16	
18 MUHIDINOV Dzhomikhon	67	UZZAL Mehedi 17	
19 IRGASHEV Odil	72	SAZIB Md 25	
20 RABIEV Yusuf		FASIAL Md 30	
Tr: NAZAROV Sharif		Tr: CRUCIANI Diego	
11 NEMATOV Shujoat	67 62	HASAN AMELI Md 21	64
21 KHOJAEV Rustam	72 52	TAPU Mahadi 26	
25 TABAROV Rustam	74 46	PARVEZ Zahed 27	

SEMI-FINALS

Ma Aziz, Chittagong
12-04-2006, 15:30, 2 500, Lee Gi Young KOR

SRI	1 1	NEP

Kasun [65]
Sri Lanka won 5-3 on penalties
Basanta Thapa [82]

SRI LANKA		NEPAL	
1 THILAKARATNE Sugath		MALLA Bikash 1	
2 HETTIHARACHCHIGE Dumidu		K.C. Anjan 5	
3 KAMALDEEN Fuard		GURUNG Lok Bandhu 6	
4 WELL DON Rohan	115	TAMANG Surendra 7	
6 NAUFER Izzadeen	82	TAMANG Raju 12	
7 SIYAGUNA Chathura		GOUCHAN Vishad 13	
8 BIYAGAMA Rajitha	61	TSERING Tashi 14	
10 EDIRIBANDANAGE Channa		MAHARJAN Pradeep 17	
11 WEERARATHNA Kasun	86	THAPA Sagar 19	
18 AMARASINHA Sanjaya		THAPA Basanta Kumar 22	
23 STEINWALL Duddley		GURUNG Bijay 23	
Tr: SAMPATH PERERA Kolonnage		Tr: THAPA Shyam	
15 RATHNAYAKA Ratnayaka	86 115	NEUPANE Nabin 4	
17 WELLALA Gunaratne	61 107	KHADAGI Rajesh 8	
	82 107	BISHWAS Ram Kumar 26	

Bangabandhu, Dhaka
13-04-2006, 15:30, 2 000, Tan Hai CHN

KGZ	0 2	TJK

Rabiev 2 [51 92+]

KYRGYZSTAN		TAJIKISTAN	
1 VOLKOV Vladislav		KHABIBULLOEV Aslidin 1	
2 AMIN Viacheslav		KHUJJAMOV Subkhon 4	
3 SAMSALIEV Talant		NEGMATOV Alexei 5	
4 SYDYKOV Ruslan		NOSIROV Naim 6	
5 KNIAZEV Sergey		RABIMOV Ibrauim 7	90
7 ISHENBAEV Azamat		MAKHMUDOV Khurshed 9	
9 HARCHENKO Vadim		HAKIMOV Numondzhon 15	
10 DJAMSHIDOV Ruslan	55	OEV Dzhamolidin 17	
11 KORNILOV Roman	74 76	MUHIDINOV Dzhomikhon 18	
12 BOKOEV Aibek	55 79	IRGASHEV Odil 19	
13 KUDRENKO Igor		RABIEV Yusuf 20	
Tr: PODKORYTOV Boris		Tr: NAZAROV Sharif	
6 ASKAROV Sardorbek	55 76	NEMATOV Shujoat 11	
15 VEREVKIN Vladimir	74 79	KHOJAEV Rustam 21	
17 ASKAROV Davron	55 90	TABAROV Rustam 25	

AFC Challenge Cup Final   **Bangabandhu, Dhaka**   **16-04-2006**

Kick-off: 15:30   Attendance: 2 000

SRI LANKA   0   4   TAJIKISTAN

Dzhomikhon Muhidinov 3 [1] [61] [71], Khurshed Makhmudov [45]

		SRI LANKA	
1	GK	THILAKARATNE Sugath	
2	DF	HETTIHARACHCHIGE Dumidu	
3	DF	KAMALDEEN Fuard	
4	DF	WELL DON Rohan	
6	DF	NAUFER Izzadeen	
18	DF	AMARASINHA Sanjaya	65
23	DF	STEINWALL Duddley	
7	MF	SIYAGUNA Chathura	
8	MF	BIYAGAMA Rajitha	86
10	FW	EDIRIBANDANAGE Channa	78
11	FW	WEERARATHNA Kasun	
		Tr: SAMPATH PERERA Kolonnage	

		Substitutes	
9	FW	GALBODAPAYAGALAGE Karu	78
12	FW	ELPITIYA Nuwanth	
14	MF	ABDUL AZIZ Fazlur	
15	MF	RATHNAYAKA Ratnayaka	
16	DF	KALUTHANTHRIGE Nisal	65
17	MF	WELLALA Gunaratne	86
22	GK	ASANKA Viraj	
25	GK	HERATH MUDIYANSELAGE Kumara	
19	FW	DEHIWALAGE Nimal	

MATCH OFFICIALS

REFEREE

MOMBINI Hedayat IRN

ASSISTANTS

PALVANOV Rashid TKM

TUMIN Mohd Kamil MAS

4TH OFFICIAL

TAN Hai CHN

	TAJIKISTAN		
69	KHABIBULLOEV Aslidin	GK	1
	KHUJAMOV Subkhon	DF	4
	NEGMATOV Alexei	DF	5
	NOSIROV Naim	DF	6
	OEV Dzhamolidin	DF	17
	RABIMOV Ibraguim	MF	7
75	MAKHMUDOV Khurshed	MF	9
77	IRGASHEV Odil	MF	19
	RABIEV Yusus	MF	20
	HAKIMOV Numondzhon	FW	15
	MUHIDINOV Dzhomikhon	FW	18
	Tr: NAZAROV Sharif		

	Substitutes		
	CHORIEV Farrukh	MF	2
	NURIDINOV Iskandar	DF	3
75	DZHABAROV Shukhrat	FW	10
	NEMATOV Shujoat	FW	11
69	MUKANIN Alexandr	GK	16
	KHOJAEV Rustam	MF	21
	SADYKOV Makhmadhli	MF	22
	TABAROV Rustam	DF	25
77	SAIDOV Kamil	FW	27

We lacked finishing. But I am happy that with nine new and young players in the side, that we came this far. It's been a long time since we played in the final of a major tournament and the runners-up trophy will make people back home happy.

Kolonnage Sampath Perera

We came here to win the trophy and we are the champions. Certainly, this victory is going to develop the game in our country. We have also proved that we are capable of playing at a higher level. I congratulate my players for keeping the tempo from the start and winning it.

Sharif Nazarov

AFC CHAMPIONS LEAGUE 2005

AFC CHAMPIONS LEAGUE 2005

| Group Stage | Quarter-finals | Semi-finals | Final |

Group Stage

Group A

		Pts
Pas	IRN	16
Al Salmiya	KUW	9
Al Rayyan	QAT	7
Al Shorta	IRQ	2

Group B

		Pts
Al Ain	UAE	13
Sepahan	IRN	11
Al Shabab	KSA	10
Al Wahda	SYR	0

Group C

		Pts
Al Sadd	QAT	12
Neftchi	UZB	9
Kuwait SC	KUW	7
Al Ahli	UAE	7

Group D

		Pts
Al Ahli	KSA	15
Pakhtakor	UZB	9
Al Zawra'a	IRQ	7
Al Jaish	SYR	4

Group E

		Pts
Shenzhen	CHN	13
Suwon Bluewings	KOR	13
Jubilo Iwata	JPN	9
Hoang Anh	VIE	0

Group F

		Pts
Shandong	CHN	18
Yokohama Marinos	JPN	12
PSM Makassar	IDN	4
BEC Tero	THA	1

Group G

		Pts
Busan I'Park	KOR	18
Krung Thai	THA	9
Persebaya	IDN	4
Binh Dinh	VIE	4

Quarter-finals

Al Ittihad	1	7
Shandong *	1	2

Al Sadd	0	1
Busan I'Park *	3	2

Shenzhen	1	3
Al Ahli *	2	1

Pas	1	3
Al Ain *	1	3

Semi-finals

Al Ittihad	5	2
Busan I'Park *	0	0

Shenzhen	0	0
Al Ain *	6	0

Final

Al Ittihad	1	4
Al Ain *	1	2

† Al Ittihad (KSA) given a bye to the quarter-finals as holders • * Home team in the first leg

GROUP A

Dastgerdi, Tehran, 9-03-2005, 16:00, 8 000, Irmatov UZB

Pas	2	Nekounam 2 [27 91+p]
Al Rayyan	1	De Boer.F [64]

Kuwait Stadium, Kuwait City, 9-03-2005, 18:00, 300, Al Ghamdi KSA

Al Salmiya	3	Dago 2 [2p 51], Ali Asel [62]
Al Shorta	1	Qusei [80]

Ahmed Bin Ali, Doha, 16-03-2005, 18:25, 5 000, Mujghef JOR

Al Rayyan	2	Kameel [30], De Boer.F [67]
Al Salmiya	1	Salman [62]

International, Zerqa City, 15-03-2005, 15:00, 100, Mansour LIB

Al Shorta	1	Iead Misheihd [30]
Pas	1	Traore [62]

Ahmed Bin Ali, Doha, 6-04-2005, 18:35, 2 000, Karim BHR

Al Rayyan	2	Benarbia [66], Anderson [76]
Al Shorta	0	

Dastgerdi, Tehran, 6-04-2005, 17:00. 6 000, Mujghef JOR

Pas	5	Traore [51], Bayati Niya 3 [65 84 86], Nekounam [79]
Al Salmia	1	Al Buraiki [38]

International, Amman, 19-04-2005, 15:00, 150, Haj Khader SYR

Al Shorta	0	
Al Rayyan	0	

Friendship & Peace, Kazma, 20-04-2005, 18:30, 1 000, Haq IND

Al Salmia	0	
Pas	1	Nekounam [90p]

Ahmed Bin Ali, Doha, 11-05-2005, 18:50, 2 000, Al Hamdan KSA

Al Rayyan	1	Jassim [38]
Pas	2	Borhani [71], Abolghasempour [80]

International, Amman, 10-05-2005, 15:00, 100, Al Hafi JOR

Al Shorta	0	
Al Salmia	1	Al Ammar [29]

Dastgerdi, Tehran, 25-05-2005, 18:00, 3 000, Mamedov TKM

Pas	1	Pashaei [86]
Al Shorta	0	

Friendship & Peace, Kazma, 25-05-2005, 18:50, 200, Najm LIB

Al Salmia	2	Khalaf [28], Uzoma-[42]
Al Rayyan	0	

Group A	Pl	W	D	L	F	A	Pts
Pas	6	5	1	0	12	4	16
Al Salmiya	6	3	0	3	8	9	9
Al Rayyan	6	2	1	3	6	7	7
Al Shorta	6	0	2	4	2	8	2

GROUP B

Tahnon Bin Mohammed, Al Ain, 9-03-2005, 19:00, 10 000, Ebrahim BHR

Al Ain	3	Shehab Ahmed [42], Edilson 2 [54 82]
Al Wahda	0	

King Fahad International, Riyadh, 9-03-2005, 20:30, 2 000, Al Fadki KUW

Al Shabab	1	Attram [26]
Sepahan	1	Karimi [84]

Abbassiyn, Damascus, 16-03-2005, 15:00, 10 000, AK Nema IRQ

Al Wahda	1	Traore [91+]
Al Shabab	2	Attram [56], Manga [60]

Naghsh-E-Jahan, Esfahan, 16-03-2005, 15:00, 35 000, Kousa SYR

Sepahan	1	Bezik [36]
Al Ain	1	Ahmed Mubarak [49]

Abbassiyn, Damascus, 6-04-2005, 17:00, 8 000, Al Fadhli KUW

Al Wahda	1	Al Shareef [67]
Sepahan	3	Khatibi 3 [6 65 94+]

Tahnon Bin Mohammed, Al Ain, 6-04-2005, 19:30, 8 000, Al Hail QAT

Al Ain	3	Edilson 2 [29 31], Subait Khater [47]
Al Shabab	0	

Naghsh-E-Jahan, Esfahan, 20-04-2005, 17:00, 12 000, Chynybekov KGZ

Sepahan	2	Khatibi [21p], Bezik [33]
Al Wahda	0	

King Fahad International, Riyadh, 20-04-2005, 20:45, 5 000, Shaban KUW

Al Shabab	1	Attram [77]
Al Ain	0	

Naghsh-E-Jahan, Esfahan, 11-05-2005, 17:30, 26 000, Saidov UZB

Sepahan	1	Hadi Aghily [37]
Al Shabab	0	

Abbassiyn, Damascus, 11-05-2005, 18:00, Salman IRQ

Al Wahda	2	Maher Al Sayed 2 [58 65]
Al Ain	3	Sanogo [80], Khamis [83], Subait Khater [95+]

Tahnon Bin Mohammed, Al Ain, 25-05-2005, 20:00, 9 000, Ebrahim BHR

Al Ain	3	Subait Khater [11], Sanogo 2 [31 70]
Sepahan	2	Karimi [69], Bengar [82]

King Fahad International, Riyadh, 25-05-2005, 21:00, 500, Mujghef JOR

Al Shabab	3	Nashat Akram [6], Abdulaziz bin Saran 2 [35p 78]
Al Wahda	1	Jaafar [72]

Group B	Pl	W	D	L	F	A	Pts
Al Ain	6	4	1	1	13	6	13
Sepahan	6	3	2	1	10	6	11
Al Shabab	6	3	1	2	7	7	10
Al Wahda	6	0	0	6	5	16	0

GROUP C

GAR Sports Complex, Tashkent, 9-03-2005, 15:00, 2 000, Haq IND

Neftchi Fergana	1	Holmatov [52]
Kuwait SC	0	

Al Sadd SC, Doha, 9-03-2005, 18:30, 3 000, Mujghef JOR

Al Sadd	2	Hussain Yasser 2 [14 50]
Al Ahli	0	

Rashid, Dubai, 16-03-2005, 16:30, 4 000, Al Mutlaq KSA

Al Ahli	3	Ali Karimi [47], Faisal Khalil 2 [55 92+]
Neftchi Fergana	0	

Kuwait SC, Kuwait City, 16-03-2005, 20:00, 4 000, Moradi IRN

Kuwait SC	0	
Al Sadd	1	Hossein Kaebi [39p]

Fergana Stadium, Fergana, 6-04-2005, 17:00, 14 500, Ebrahim BHR

Neftchi Fergana	2	Berdiyev [73], Otakuziev [84]
Al Sadd	0	

Kuwait SC, Kuwait City, 6-04-2005, 20:00, 1 500, Abbas SYR

Kuwait SC	1	Faraj Laheeb [50]
Al Ahli	0	

Al Sadd SC, Doha, 20-04-2005, 18:45, 3 000, Mansour LIB

Al Sadd	3	Chippo [30], Hossein Kaebi [50], Jafal Al Kuwari [60]
Neftchi Fergana	2	Alijonov [20], Holmatov [46]

Rashid, Dubai, 20-04-2005, 18:30, 5 000, Salman IRQ

Al Ahli	3	Faisal Khalil [14], Ali Karimi [53], Salem Khamis [59]
Kuwait SC	3	Bashar Abdullah 2 [16 73], Al Ataiqi [44]

Rashid, Dubai, 11-05-2005, 19:45, 3 000, Al Delawar BHR

Al Ahli	2	Ali Karimi [71p], Mashmoom Mahboob [93+]
Al Sadd	1	Adil Aziz OG [3]

Kuwait SC, Kuwait City, 11-05-2005, 20:30, 2 500, Abbas SYR

Kuwait SC	1	Adel Al Anezi [80p]
Neftchi Fergana	0	

GAR Sports Complex, Tashkent, 25-05-2005, Mombini IRN

Neftchi Fergana	3	Match awarded 3-0 to Neftchi after Al
Al Ahli	0	Ahli failed to fulfill the fixture

Al Sadd SC, Doha, 25-05-2005, 19:15, 5 000, Al Mutlaq KSA
| Al Sadd | 1 | Carlos Tenorio [44] |
| Kuwait SC | 0 | |

Group C	Pl	W	D	L	F	A	Pts
Al Sadd	6	4	0	2	8	6	12
Neftchi	6	3	0	3	8	7	9
Kuwait SC	6	2	1	3	5	6	7
Al Ahli	6	2	1	3	8	10	7

GROUP D

Tripoli Municipal, Tripoli, 8-03-2005, 14:30, 500, Mansour LIB
| Al Zawra'a | 1 | Abduljabar [26p] |
| Al Ahli | 2 | Al Jassam [7], Abuyabis [31] |

Al Abbassiyn, Damascus, 9-03-2005, 15:00, 5 000, Al Saeedi UAE
| Al Jaish | 0 | |
| Pakhtakor T'kent | 2 | Djeparov [22], Ilhomjon [45] |

Pakhtakor, Tashkent, 16-03-2005, 16:30, 12 000, Al Hail QAT
| Pakhtakor T'kent | 1 | Djeparov [54p] |
| Al Zawra'a | 2 | Ala'a Sattar [8], Fawzi Abdulsada [89] |

Prince Faisal, Jeddah, 16-03-2005, 20:30, 8 000, Shaban KUW
| Al Ahli | 3 | Rogerio [5], Abuyabis [39], Flavio [76] |
| Al Jaish | 1 | Zeno [70] |

Tripoli Municipal, Tripoli, 5-04-2005, 14:30, 500, Ghahremani IRN
| Al Zawra'a | 1 | Abdulsada [57p] |
| Al Jaish | 5 | Zeno 3 [19 30 48], Chaabo [61], Yosef Hasan [92+] |

Prince Faisal, Jeddah, 6-04-2005, 20:40, 12 000, Najm LIB
| Al Ahli | 3 | Alessandro [58], Al Hawsawi [83], Sulaimani [87] |
| Pakhtakor T'kent | 0 | |

Al Abbassiyn, Damascus, 20-04-2005, 17:00, 5 000, Al Delawar BHR
| Al Jaish | 0 | |
| Al Zawra'a | 0 | |

Pakhtakor, Tashkent, 20-04-2005, 17:00, 8 000, Mujghef JOR
| Pakhtakor T'kent | 2 | Koshelov [22], Soliev [60] |
| Al Ahli | 1 | Rogerio [36] |

Pakhtakor, Tashkent, 11-05-2005, 17:00, 8 000, Haq IND
| Pakhtakor T'kent | 4 | Abdullayev [48], Koshelov [52], Djeparov [70] Soliev [80] |
| Al Jaish | 1 | Al Hariri [68] |

Prince Faisal, Jeddah, 11-05-2005, 20:50, 4 000, Najm LIB
| Al Ahli | 5 | Flavio [11], Al Zahrani [28], Rogerio [32], Alessandro 2 [71 92] |
| Al Zawra'a | 1 | Abdulzahra [45] |

Tripoli Municipal, Tripoli, 24-05-2005, 14:30, 100, Al Saeedi UAE
| Al Zawra'a | 1 | Ali Jawad [60] |
| Pakhtakor T'kent | 0 | |

Al Abbassiyn, Damascus, 25-05-2005, 18:00, 1 000, Al Hail QAT
| Al Jaish | 0 | |
| Al Ahli | 4 | Al Hawsawi [26], Alessandro 2 [37 49], Al Shari [75] |

Group D	Pl	W	D	L	F	A	Pts
Al Ahli	6	5	0	1	18	5	15
Pakhtakor	6	3	0	3	9	8	9
Al Zawra'a	6	2	1	3	6	13	7
Al Jaish	6	1	1	4	7	14	4

GROUP E

Shenzhen Stadium, Shenzhen, 9-03-2005, 15:30, 6 000, Rungklay THA
| Shenzhen | 1 | Li Yi [56] |
| Jubilo Iwata | 0 | |

Gia Lai, Pleiku City, 9-03-2005, 16:00, 8 000, Abdul Hamid MAS
| Hoang Anh GL | 1 | Chalermsan [72] |
| Suwon Bluewings | 5 | Nadson [9], Neretjlak [16], Park KH [50], An HY 2 [52 64] |

World Cup Stadium, Suwon, 16-03-2005, 19:00, 10 263, Maidin SIN
| Suwon Bluewings | 0 | |
| Shenzhen | 0 | |

Yamaha, Shizuoka, 16-03-2005, 19:00, 8 171, Mohd Salleh MAS
| Jubilo Iwata | 6 | Nishi [23], Choi YS 2 [29 58], Gral 2 [67 90], Cullen [76] |
| Hoang Anh GL | 0 | |

Shenzhen Stadium, Shenzhen, 6-04-2005, 15:30, 2 600, Napitupulu IDN
| Shenzhen | 5 | Oyawole [34], Li Yi 2 [39 50], Wang Xinxin [52] Zhang Yonghai [82] |
| Hoang Anh GL | 0 | |

Yamaha, Shizuoka, 6-04-2005, 19:00, 8 529, Nagalingham SIN
| Jubilo Iwata | 0 | |
| Suwon Bluewings | 1 | Nadson [30] |

Gia Lai, Pleiku City, 20-04-2005, 16:00, 8 000, Khanthama THA
| Hoang Anh GL | 0 | |
| Shenzhen | 2 | Oyawole [77], Li Jianhua [80] |

World Cup Stadium, Suwon, 20-04-2005, 19:00, 21 032, Mohd Salleh MAS
| Suwon Bluewings | 2 | Kim NI [62], Sandro [85] |
| Jubilo Iwata | 1 | Fujita [4] |

World Cup Stadium, Suwon, 11-05-2005, 19:00, 5 013, Napitupulu IDN
| Suwon Bluewings | 6 | Kim Dong Hun [1], Lee BK 2 [11 15], Cho WH 34 Cardoso [49], Kim Do Heon [75] |
| Hoang Anh GL | 0 | |

Yamaha, Shizuoka, 11-05-2005, 19:00, 5 344, Mohd Salleh MAS
| Jubilo Iwata | 3 | Funatani [56], Ohta 2 [80 85] |
| Shenzhen | 0 | |

Gia Lai, Pleiku City, 25-05-2005, 16:00, 6 000, Arambakade SRI
| Hoang Anh GL | 0 | |
| Jubilo Iwata | 1 | Kawaguchi [16] |

Shenzhen Stadium, Shenzhen, 25-05-2005, 19:30, 19 000, Kunsuta THA
| Shenzhen | 1 | Xin Feng [29] |
| Suwon Bluewings | 0 | |

Group E	Pl	W	D	L	F	A	Pts
Shenzhen	6	4	1	1	9	3	13
Suwon Bluewings	6	4	1	1	14	3	13
Jubilo Iwata	6	3	0	3	11	4	9
Hoang Anh GL	6	0	0	6	1	25	0

GROUP F

Rajamangala, Bangkok, 9-03-2005, 16:00, 700, Nagalingham SIN
| BRC Tero | 0 | |
| PSM Makassar | 1 | Moreno [78] |

Mitsuzawa, Yokohama, 9-03-2005, 19:00, 9 000, Kwon Jong Chul KOR
| Yokohama Marinos | 0 | |
| Shandong | 1 | Gao Yao [67] |

Shandong SC, Jinan, 16-03-2005, 14:30, 30 000, Lee Gi Young KOR
| Shandong | 1 | Li Jinyu [29] |
| BEC Tero | 0 | |

Matoangin, Makassar, 16-03-2005, 19:30, 15 000, Arambakade SRI
| PSM Makassar | 0 | |
| Yokohama Marinos | 2 | Oshima [30], Yamazaki [63] |

Tupatemee, Bangkok, 6-04-2005, 16:00, 2 000, Lee Gi Young KOR
| BEC Tero | 1 | Kongpraphun [66] |
| Yokohama Marinos | 2 | Ahn Jung Hwan 2 [25 41] |

Matoangin, Makassar, 6-04-2005, 19:30, 10 000, Abdul Hamid MAS
| PSM Makassar | 0 | |
| Shandong | 1 | Han Peng [83] |

Mitsuzawa, Yokohama, 20-04-2005, 19:00, 6 062, Maidin SIN
| Yokohama Marinos | 2 | Sakata [45], Ahn Jung Hwan [57] |
| BEC Tero | 0 | |

Shandong SC, Jinan, 20-04-2005, 19:30, 20 000, Kwon Jong Chul KOR
| Shandong | 6 | Zheng Zhi 3 [4 6 52p], Han Peng [32], Lihui [35], Haibin [87] |
| PSM Makassar | 1 | Moreno [72] |

Shandong SC, Jinan, 11-05-2005, 19:30, 30 000, Lee Gi Young KOR
Shandong 2 Zheng Zhi 2 [39] [94+]
Yokohama Marinos 1 Nasu [7]
Matoangin, Makassar, 11-05-2005, 19:30, 3 000, Nagalingham SIN
PSM Makassar 2 Fagundez [46], Bachri [78]
BEC Tero 2 Thonglao 2 [45] [86]
Tupatemee, Bangkok, 25-05-2005, 16:00, 1 000, Mohd Salleh MAS
BEC Tero 0
Shandong 4 Danciulescu 2 [3] [64], Liu Zhao [23], Lu Zheng [92+]
Mitsuzawa, Yokohama, 25-05-2005, 19:00, 6 379, Kwon Jong Chul KOR
Yokohama Marinos 3 Dutra [75], Ueno [79], Oku [82]
PSM Makassar 0

Group F	Pl	W	D	L	F	A	Pts
Shandong	6	6	0	0	15	2	18
Yokohama F.Marinos	6	4	0	2	10	4	12
PSM Makassar	6	1	1	4	4	14	4
BEC Tero	6	0	1	5	3	12	1

GROUP G

Asiad Main Stadium, Busan, 9-03-2005, 19:00, 10 512, Kamikawa JPN
Busan I'Park 8 Luciano 2 [23] [49], Felix 2 [35] [62], Bae Hyo Sung [43] Popo [52], Kim Yoo Jin [69], Do Xuan Hung OG [83]
Binh Dinh 0
Gelora, Surabaya, 9-03-2005, 15:30, 30 000, Matsumura JPN
Persebaya 1 Kaewkhew OG [86]
Krung Thai Bank 2 Promkeaw 2 [21] [51]
Rangsit, Bangkok, 16-03-2005, 16:00, 500, Yoshida JPN
Krung Thai Bank 0
Busan I'Park 2 Lee Jung Hyo 2 [37] [67]

Quy Nhon, Binh Dinh, 16-03-2005, 15:30, 4 000, Gosh BAN
Binh Dinh 0
Persebaya 0
Asiad Main Stadium, Busan, 6-04-2005, 19:00, 675, Zhou Weixin CHN
Busan I'Park 4 Lee Jung Hyo [52], Popo [65], Do Hwa Sung 2 [69] [75]
Persebaya 0
Quy Nhon, Binh Dinh, 6-04-2005, 15:30, Gosh BAN
Binh Dinh 1 Srimaka [44p]
Krung Thai Bank 2 Jittrong [38], Kunlawong [80]
Gelora 10th November, Surabaya, 20-04-2005, 15:30, 11 000, Nishimura JPN
Persebaya 0
Busan I'Park 3 Lee Jung Hyo [9], Do Hwa Sung [38], Popo [87]
Tupatemee, Bangkok, 20-04-2005, 16:00, 500, Sun Baojie CHN
Krung Thai Bank 0
Binh Dinh 1 Srimaka [19p]
Quy Nhon, Binh Dinh, 11-05-2005, 15:30, 3 000, Huang Junjie CHN
Binh Dinh 0
Busan I'Park 4 Do Hwa Sung [9], Luciano 2 [15 45], Nzeina [82]
Tupatemee, Bangkok, 11-05-2005, 16:00, 500, Nishimura JPN
Krung Thai Bank 1 Kaewkheaw [20]
Persebaya 0
Gelora 10th November, Surabaya, 25-05-2005, 15:30, 1500, Maidin SIN
Persebaya 1 Fernando [15]
Binh Dinh 0
Busan Asiad Main Stadium, Busan, 25-05-2005, 611, Gosh BAN
Busan I'Park 4 Nzeina 2 [14 66], Kim Tae Min [19], Hae Jae Woong [51]
Krung Thai Bank 0

Group G	Pl	W	D	L	F	A	Pts
Busan I'Park	6	6	0	0	25	0	18
Krung Thai	6	3	0	3	5	9	9
Persebaya	6	1	1	4	2	10	4
Binh Dinh	6	1	1	4	2	15	4

QUARTER-FINALS

1st leg. Shandong Sports Centre, Shandong
14-09-2005, 20:05, 35 000, Nishimura JPN
Shandong 1
Li Xiaopeng [53]
Yang Cheng - Wang Chao (Xuan Weiwei 76), Shu Chang, Predrag Pazin, Jiao Zhe, Li Xiaopeng, Zheng Zhi•, Gao Yao, Zhou Haibin (Song Lihui 80), Han Peng, Ionel Danciulescu (Cui Peng 61)
Al Ittihad 1
Noor [48]
Mabrouk Zaid - Ahmed Dokhi, Redha Tukar, Al Harbi•, Adnan Ibrahim•, Ali Khariri•, Mohammed Noor•, Mohamed Kallon, Manaf Abushgeer (Ibrahim Sowed 76), Job, Tcheco• (Khamis Owairan 87)

2nd leg. Prince Faisal, Jeddah
21-09-2005, 20:15, 12 000, Gharemani IRN
Al Ittihad 7
Al Harbi [19], Tcheco [34], Sowed [56], Kallon [66] Abushgeer 2 [77 89], Tukar [81]
Mabrouk Zaid - Ahmed Dokhi, Redha Tukar, Al Harbi, Adnan Ibrahim, Ali Khariri, Mohammed Noor•, Ibrahim Sowed, Mohamed Kallon• (Manaf Abushgeer 76), Job, Tcheco
Shandong 2
Li Xiaopeng [16], Cui Peng [61]
Yang Cheng - Wang Chao, Shu Chang, Predrag Pazin•90, Jiao Zhe, Song Lihui (Lu Zheng 54), Li Xiaopeng, Zheng Zhi•90, Gao Yao• (Cui Peng• 58), Zhou Haibin, Han Peng

1st leg. Busan Asiad Main Stadium, Busan
14-09-2005, 19:05, 2 000, Junjie CHN
Busan I'Park 3
Da Silva 2 [20 88], Yoon Hee Jun [91+]
Kim Yong Dae - Park Joon Hong, Bae Hyo Sung, Yoon Hee Jun, Lee Jang Kwan, Lim Kwan Sik, Kim Jae Young, Laktionov, Popo, Luciano, Da Silva
Al Sadd 0
Basel Samith - Jafal Al Kuwari, Essa Al Kuwari•, Al Bareek•, Abdullah Koni•, Ali Nasser Saleh•81, Wesam Rizik, Mased Al Hamad, Clayton, Tenorio (Bilal Abu Hamdeh 87), Mohamed Gholam (Magid Hassan 71)

2nd leg. Al Sadd SC, Doha
21-09-2005, 16:45, 3 000, Najm LIB
Al Sadd 1
Tenorio [92+]
Mohamed Saqr - Jafal Al Kuwari, Al Bareek, Abdullah Koni, Al Dahri (Khalid Al Hajari 90), Mased Al Hamad, Magid Hassan, Clayton (Emerson 46), Tenorio, Mohamed Gholam Bilal Abu Hamdeh• 67)
Busan I'Park 2
Lim Kwan Sik [21], Han Jae Woong [79]
Kim Yong Dae - Park Joon Hong•, Bae Hyo Sung, Yoon Hee Jun•, Lee Jang Kwan, Lim Kwan Sik•, Kim Jae Young• (Do Hwa Sung 69), Laktionov (Lee Jung Hyo 46), Popo (Han Jae Woong 64), Luciano, Da Silva•

1st leg. Prince Faisal, Jeddah
14-09-2005, 20:20, 16 000, Kunsuta THA
Al Ahli 1
Rogerio [62], Yang Chen OG [88]
Al Naje - Al Qadi, Youssef Rabeh, Al Mowallad (Al Hawasawi 55), Waleed Gahdali (Rogerio 46), Hussain Sulaimani, Al Shehri, Al Mohammedi (Al Kaebari 70), Al Abdulla, Al Gizani, Al Meshal
Shenzhen 1
Al Qad OG [76]
Li Leilei - Li Weifeng•, Zhang Yonghai, Zhou Ting••86, Li Ming, Yuan Lin, Marek Zajac, Li Jianhua (Huang Yunfeng 90), Wang Hongwei, Yang Chen, Li Yi

2nd leg. Shenzhen Stadium, Shenzhen
21-09-2005, 19:35, 23 000
Shenzhen 3
Zajac [6], Li Yi 2 [15 98]
Li Leilei - Li Weifeng••120, Zhang Yonghai (Li Ming• 89), Yuan Lin, Marek Zajac, Wang Xinxin, Li Jianhua, Wang Hongwei (Huang Yunfeng 77), Lu Bofei (Li Fei 71), Yang Chen, Li Yi•
Al Ahli 1
Sulaimani [20]
Al Bsisi - Al Qadi, Youssef Rabeh, Al Mowallad (Al Hawasawi 61), Waleed Gahdali, Hussain Sulaimani•, Al Shehri, Al Mohammedi (Rogerio 79), Al Abdulla, Al Gizani (Al Kaebari 71), Al Meshal

1st leg. Tahnon Bin Mohammed, Al Ain
14-09-2005, 19:15, 7 000, Irmatov UZB

Al Ain	1
	Nosrati OG [43]

Mutaz Abdulla - Juma Khater, Ali Msarri, Abdulla Ali (Rami Yaslam 68), Humaid Fakher• (Nasser Khamis 83), Blanco, Shehab Ahmed, Subait Khater•, Onyekachi, Tejada

Pas	1
	Borhani [24]

Roudbarian•60 - Shakouri, Nosrati, Assad, Nekounam, Pashaei, Shirzadeh, Moniei• (Nakisa 62), Traore (Jamshidi 84), Borhani• (Razagharid 82), Koushki

2nd leg. Dastgerdi, Tehran
21-09-2005, 18:05, 8 000, Maidin SIN

Pas	3
	Borhani 2 [34 47], Traore [75]

Nakisa - Shakouri, Nosrati, Ahmed Assad (Khoraj 79), Nekounam, Pashaei, Moniei (Shirzadeh 79), Traore, Borhani (Bayatiniya 77), Jamshidi, Koushki•

Al Ain	3
	Tejada [61p], Helal Saeed 2 [83 84]

Mutaz Abdulla - Juma Khater, Ali Msarri•, Humaid Fakher, Blanco, Helal Saeed, Gharib Harib (Ali Ahmed 58), Shehab Ahmed, Subait Khater (Nasser Khamis• 81), Onyekachi, Tejada

SEMI-FINALS

1st leg. Gudeok Stadium, Busan
28-09-2005, 20:05, 22 450, Maidin SIN

Busan I'Park	0

Kim Yong Dae, Park Joon Hong, Bae Hyo Sung, Yoon Hee Jun, Lee Jang Kwan, Lim Kwan Sik•, Kim Jae Young (Do Hwa Sung 80), Lee Jung Hyo (Laktionov 63), Popo, Luciano, Park Seong Bae (Han Jae Woong 63)

Al Ittihad	5
	Al Otaibi [55], Kallon [62], Tcheco [65]
	Ali Khariri [86], Hamzah Idris [89]

Mabrouk Zaid•, Ahmed Dokhi, Redha Tukar•, Al Harbi•, Adnan Ibrahim, Al Khariri, Ibrahim Sowed, Mohamed Kallon (Khamis Owairan 82), Manaf Abushgeer, Tcheco, Al Otaibi (Hamzah Idris 78)

2nd leg. Prince Faisal, Jeddah
12-10-2005, 22:15, 10 000, Mohd Salleh MAS

Al Ittihad	2
	Kallon 2 [18 58]

Mabrouk Zaid, Ahmed Dokhi, Al Harbi, Adnan Ibrahim, Al Montashari, Al Khariri, Mohammed Noor (Mohammed Haidar 79), Ibrahim Sowed, Mohamed Kallon (Job 69), Manaf Abushgeer, Tcheco (Khamis Owairan 71)

Busan I'Park	0

Kim Yong Dae, Shin Young Rok, Bae Hyo Sung, Kim Yoo Jin, Lee Jang Kwan•, Lim Kwan Sik, Kim Jae Young• (Shin Soo Jin 79), Laktionov• (Lee Jung Hyo 62), Do Hwa Sung, Popo, Da Silva

1st leg. Tahnon Bin Mohammed, Al Ain
28-09-2005, 19:05, 12 000, Kunsuta THA

Al Ain	6
	Subait Khater 2 [4 81], Onyekachi 3 [10 22 77]
	Shehab Ahmed [28]

Mutaz Abdulla - Juma Khater, Ali Msarri, Abdulla Ali, Humaid Fakher (Rami Yaslam 66), Blanco, Helal Saeed, Shehab Ahmed, Subait Khater• (Nassib Ishaq 87), Onyekachi, Tejada

Shenzhen	0

Li Leilei - Zhang Yonghai (Li Ming 46), Zhou Ting•, Yuan Lin, Xin Feng, Marek Zajac, Wang Xinxin (Lu Bofei 46), Li Jianhua, Wang Hongwei, Yang Chen•, Li Yi

2nd leg. Shenzhen Stadium, Shenzhen
12-10-2005, 19:35, 6 500, Kamikawa JPN

Shenzhen	0

Zhou Jia - Zhang Yonghai•, Yuan Lin, Marek Zajac, Huang Yunfeng, Li Fei (Xin Feng 90), Li Jianhua, Wang Hongwei (Zhou Ting• 27), Lu Bofei, Yang Chen, Li Yi

Al Ain	0

Mutaz Abdulla - Juma Khater, Ali Msarri (Musallem Fayez 76), Ali Ahmed, Abdulla Ali•, Fahad Ali, Blanco (Gharib Harib 61), Helal Saeed, Shehab Ahmed, Onyekachi, Tejada• (Rami Yaslam 71)

AFC CHAMPIONS LEAGUE FINAL FIRST LEG
Tahnon Bin Mohammed, Al Ain, 15 000
26-10-2005, 22:05, Kwong Jong Chul KOR, Lui CHN, Kim Dae Young KOR

AL AIN	1		1	AL ITTIHAD

Msarri [50]   Kallon [85p]

Al Ain			Al Ittihad	
1	ABDULLA Mutaz		ZAID Mabrouk	1
3	KHATER Juma		DOKHI Ahmed	2
6	MSARRI Ali		AL HARBI Osama	13
7	AHMED Ali		IBRAHIM Adnan	20
16	ALI Abdulla		AL MONTASHARI Hamad	21
19	ALI Fahd		KHARIRI Saud Ali	14
8	BLANCO Alberto	64	SOWED Ibrahim	27
20	SAEED Helal	46	KALLON Mohamed	3
24	KHATER Subait	76	ABUSHGEER Manaf	8
10	ONYEKACHI Nwoha	69	67	JOB Joseph-Desire	10
14	TEJADA Luis		TCHECO	11
	Tr: MACALA Milan		Tr: IORDANESCU Anghel	
	Substitutes		Substitutes	
21	HARIB Gharib	46	76	HAIDAR Mohammed	7
23	AHMED Shehab	69	67	IDRIS Hamzah	9
			64	NOOR Mohammed	18

AFC CHAMPIONS LEAGUE FINAL SECOND LEG
Prince Abdullah Al Faisal, Jeddah 25 000
5-11-2005, 19:45, Maidin SIN, Allberdiyev TKM, Prempanich THA

AL ITTIHAD	4		2	AL AIN

Kallon [2], Noor [33], Job [57], Dokhi [69]   Shehab Ahmed [55p], Tejada [90]

Al Ittihad				Al Ain	
1	ZAID Mabrouk			ABDULLA Mutaz	1
2	DOKHI Ahmed			KHATER Juma	3
13	AL HARBI Osama			MSARRI Ali	6
20	IBRAHIM Adnan			AHMED Ali	7
21	AL MONTASHARI Hamad	71		ALI Abdulla	16
14	KHARIRI Saud Ali	80		ALI Fahd	19
18	NOOR Mohammed	62		FAKHER Humaid	25
3	KALLON Mohamed	90		BLANCO Alberto	8
8	ABUSHGEER Manaf	87		AHMED Shehab	23
10	JOB Joseph-Desire	77		KHATER Subait	24
11	TCHECO	78		ONYEKACHI Nwoha	10
	Tr: IORDANESCU Anghel			Tr: MACALA Milan	
	Substitutes			Substitutes	
6	OWAIRAN Khamis	78	62	YASLAM Rami	13
7	HAIDAR Mohammed	87	80	HARIB Gharib	21
9	IDRIS Hamzah	90	71	TEJADA Luis	14

AFC CUP 2005

AFC CUP 2005			
Group Stage	**Quarter-finals**	**Semi-finals**	**Final**

Group A		Pts
Al Faysali	JOR	14
Nebitchi Balkanabat	TKM	8
East Bengal	IND	7
Muktijoddha	BAN	4

Al Faysali *	1 1
Tampines Rovers	0 0

Group B		Pts
Al Hussein	JOR	9
Al Ahed	LIB	9
Dempo	IND	0

Al Faysali	1 4
New Radiant *	1 1

Al Hussein	0 0
New Radiant *	1 0

Group C		Pts
Al Nejmeh	LIB	12
Nisa Ashgabat	TKM	2
Brothers Union	BAN	2

Al Faysali *	1 3
Al Nejmeh	0 2

Group D		Pts
Sun Hei	HKG	12
Tampines Rovers	SIN	11
Valencia	MDV	5
Perak	MAS	4

Sun Hei	0 3
Al Ahed *	1 1

Sun Hei	0 2
Al Nejmeh *	3 3

Group E		Pts
Home United	SIN	13
New Radiant	MDV	10
Pahang	MAS	9
Happy Valley	HKG	1

Home United *	0 2
Al Nejmeh	3 2

* Home team in the first leg

GROUP A

Ammam International, Amman, 9-03-2005, 1 000, Abbas SYR

Al Faysali	1	Mansour [6]
Nebitchi	1	Arazov [56]

Salt Lake, Kolkota, 9-03-2005, 30 000, Chynybekov KGZ

East Bengal	0	
Muktijoddah	0	

Nebitchi Stadium, Balkanabat, 16-03-2005, 7 000, Saidov UZB

Nebitchi	3	Alikperov [1], Meredov [60], Arazov [83]
East Bengal	2	Secco [52], Bhutia [92+]

Bangabandhu National, Dhaka, 16-03-2005, 3 000, Napitupulu IDN

Muktijoddah	0	
Al Faysali	3	Mansour [35], Al Maharmeh [62], Al Tall [85]

Olympic Stadium, Balkanabat, 6-04-2005, 200, Saidov UZB

Nebitchi	0	
Muktijoddah	1	Mohd Aminul Hoque [93+]

Ammam International, Amman, 6-04-2005, 1 000, Al Hamdan KSA

Al Faysali	5	Mansour 2 [13 43 73], Halasa 2 [50 69]
East Bengal	0	

Salt Lake, Kolkota, 20-04-2005, 10 000, Irmatov UZB

East Bengal	0	
Al Faysali	1	Aqel [31p]

Bangabandhu National, Dhaka, 20-04-2005, 2 000, Mombini IRN

Muktijoddah	1	Annamyradov OG [72]
Nebitchi	2	Alikperov 2 [4 39p]

Olympic Stadium, Balkanabat, 11-05-2005, 300, Moradi IRN

Nebitchi	3	Karadanov 2 [28 45], Hojageldiyev [29]
Al Faysali	3	Al Maharmeh 2 [12 27], Aqel [88p]

Bangabandhu National, Dhaka, 11-05-2005, 5 000, Chynybekov KGZ

Muktijoddah	0	
East Bengal	1	Bijen Singh [75]

Salt Lake, Kolkota, 25-05-2005, 800, Irmatov UZB

East Bengal	3	Jeremiah 3 [28 57 63]
Nebitchi	2	Bazarov [53], Arazov [88]

Ammam International, Amman, 25-05-2005, 2 000, Nema IRQ

Al Faysali	2	Mansour 2 [12 24]
Muktijoddah	1	Hery [48]

Group A	Pl	W	D	L	F	A	Pts
Al Faysali	6	4	2	0	15	5	14
Nebitchi Balkanabat	6	2	2	2	11	11	8
East Bengal	6	2	1	3	6	11	7
Muktijoddha	6	1	1	4	3	8	4

GROUP B

Beirut Municipal Stadium, Beirut, 9-03-2005, 2 000, Salman IRQ

Al Ahed	1	Shahgeldyan [55]
Dempo SC	0	

Al Hassan International, Irbid City, 16-03-2005, 7 000, Al Delawar BHR

Al Hussein	4	Al Riahna 2 [28 38], Al Sheyab [52], Athamnah [83]
Al Ahed	0	

Jawaharial Nehru, Goa, 6-04-2005, 8 000, Busurmankulov KGZ

Dempo	0	
Al Hussein	3	Al Zboun [32], Hatamleh [75], Ehmoud [91+]

Al Hassan International, Irbid City, 20-04-2005, 10, Al Marzouqi UAE

Al Hussein	2	Al Riahna [52], Al Zboun [80]
Dempo	0	

Jawaharial Nehru, Goa, 11-05-2005, 3 000, Gosh BAN

Dempo	0	
Al Ahed	1	Maatouk [72]

Beirut Municipal Stadium, Beirut, 25-05-2005, 100, Al Fadhli KUW

Al Ahed	4	Maatouk 2 [28 30], Ayoub 2 [54 76]
Al Hussein	2	Al Zboun [23], Al Sheyab [83]

Group B	Pl	W	D	L	F	A	Pts
Al Hussein	4	3	0	1	11	4	9
Al Ahed	4	3	0	1	6	6	9
Dempo SC	4	0	0	4	0	7	0

GROUP C

Bangabandhu National, Dhaka, 9-03-2005, 3 000, Mombini IRN

Brothers Union	1	Khokon [86]
Nisa Ashgabat	1	Urazov [17]

Sports City, Beirut, 16-03-2005, 3 000, Al Marzouqi UAE

Al Nejmeh	4	Hjeij [1], Kassas 2 [3 13], Atwi [86]
Brothers Union	1	Rana [24]

Olympic Stadium, Ashgabat, 6-04-2005, 500, Haq IND

Nisa Ashgabat	0	
Al Nejmeh	1	Kassas [86]

Sports City, Beirut, 20-04-2005, 3 000, Al Mutlaq KSA

Al Nejmeh	1	Atwi [76]
Nisa Ashgabat	0	

Olympic Stadium, Ashgabat, 11-05-2005, 1 000, Al Marzouqi UAE

Nisa Ashgabat	0	
Brothers Union	0	

Bangabandhu National, Dhaka, 25-05-2005, 1 000, Haq IND

Brothers Union	0	
Al Nejmeh	2	Ghaddar 2 [44 82]

Group C	Pl	W	D	L	F	A	Pts
Al Nejmeh	4	4	0	0	8	1	12
Nisa Ashgabat	4	0	2	2	1	3	2
Brothers Union	4	0	2	2	2	7	2

GROUP D

Mongkok, Hong Kong, 9-03-2005, 1 100, Napitupulu IDN

Sun Hei	6	Hartwig [16], Lau Chi Keung [59], Akosah 2 [59 73] Poon Man Tik [91+], Chu Siu Kei [93+]
Valencia	1	Kvasz [80]

Perak Stadium, Ipoh, 9-03-2005, 2 000, Sun Baojie CHN

Perak	2	Keita Mandjou [38], Syamsul Mohd Saad [72]
Tampines Rovers	1	Hucika [22]

National Stadium, Male, 16-03-2005, 3 896, Haq IND

Valencia	1	Ali Ashfaq [39]
Perak	1	Mohd Nor Ismail [41]

Tampines Stadium, Singapore, 16-03-2005, 2 626, Kamikawa JPN

Tampines Rovers	1	Aliff Shafaein [50]
Sun Hei	1	Hartwig [19]

Tampines Stadium, Singapore, 6-04-2005, 2 000, Yoshida JPN

Tampines Rovers	1	Grabovac [12]
Valencia	0	

Perak Stadium, Ipoh, 6-04-2005, 2 000, Kamikawa JPN

Perak	0	
Sun Hei	1	Akosah [71]

National Stadium, Male, 20-04-2005, 3 000, Mamedov TKM

Valencia	0	
Tampines Rovers	4	Luthfy OG [48], Grabovac [61] Noh Alam Shah [68], Aliff Shafaein [77]

Mongkok, Hong Kong, 6-04-2005, 1 109, Napitupulu IDN

Sun Hei	2	Akosah 2 [31 87]
Perak	1	Chan Wing Hoong [37]

National Stadium, Male, 11-05-2005, 2 489, Gedara SRI

Valencia	1	Kvasz [61]
Sun Hei	1	Chu Siu Kei [95+]

Tampines Stadium, Singapore, 11-05-2005, 1 500, Khanthama THA
Tampines Rovers 4 Noh Alam Shah 2 [5][82], Grabovac [32], Hucika [41]
Perak 2 Traore [29], Mandjou [56]
Mongkok, Hong Kong, 25-05-2005, 1 500, Yoshida JPN
Sun Hei 1 Hartwig [90]
Tampines Rovers 1 Noh Alam Shah [26]
Perak Stadium, Ipoh, 25-05-2005, 800, Midi Nitrorejo IDN
Perak 1 Syamsul Mohd Saad [37p]
Valencia 2 Mukhthar Nasser [45], Ali Umar [84]

Group D	Pl	W	D	L	F	A	Pts
Sun Hei	6	3	3	0	12	5	12
Tampines Rovers	6	3	2	1	12	6	11
Valencia	6	1	2	3	5	14	5
Perak	6	1	1	4	7	11	4

GROUP E

National Stadium, Male, 9-03-2005, 5 000, Mamedov TKM
New Radiant 2 Simeonov [44], Fazeel [83]
Happy Valley 0
Bishan, Singapore, 9-03-2005, 1 963, Khanthama THA
Home United 2 De Oliveira [23], Fahmie Abdullah [77]
Pahang 1 Tchoutang [3p]
Mongkok, Hong Kong, 16-03-2005, 1 000, Rungklay THA
Happy Valley 0
Home United 1 De Oliveira [74]
Darul Makmur, Kuantan, 16-03-2005, 4 000, Huang Junjie CHN
Pahang 1 Hairuddin Omar [89]
New Radiant 0

National Stadium, Male, 6-04-2005, 5 000, Gedara SRI
New Radiant 1 Kasirye [40]
Home United 0
Mongkok, Hong Kong, 6-04-2005, 420, Rungklay THA
Happy Valley 1 Kwok Yue Hung [45]
Pahang 1 Mahayuddin [62]
Bishan, Singapore, 20-04-2005, 1 488, Huang Junjie CHN
Home United 2 Goncalves [8], De Oliveira [64]
New Radiant 0
Darul Makmur, Kuantan, 20-04-2005, 10 000, Gosh BAN
Pahang 3 Mohd Zulkifli Yusuf [25], Tchoutang [30]
Mahayuddin [53]
Happy Valley 1 Alcantara [21]
Mongkok, Hong Kong, 11-05-2005, 147, Zhou Weixin CHN
Happy Valley 0
New Radiant 2 Simeonov [20], Fazeel [50]
Darul Makmur, Kuantan, 11-05-2005, 3 000, Yoshida JPN
Pahang 3 Talib [18], Mahayuddin [30], Tchoutang [91+]
Home United 3 Iskandar [23], Goncalves [28], De Oliveira [53]
National Stadium, Male, 25-05-2005, 5 127, Sun Baojie CHN
New Radiant 1 Abdulla Mohamed [85]
Pahang 1 Mahayuddin [78]
Bishan, Singapore, 25-05-2005, 1 552, Busurmankulov KGZ
Home United 5 Sahdan Daud [21], Juraimi 3 [30][70][78], Kumar [49]
Happy Valley 0

Group E	Pl	W	D	L	F	A	Pts
Home United	6	4	1	1	13	5	13
New Radiant	6	3	1	2	6	4	10
Pahang	6	2	3	1	10	8	9
Happy Valley	6	0	1	5	2	14	1

QUARTER-FINALS

1st leg. Amman International, Amman	2nd leg. Tampines Stadium, Singapore	1st leg. National Stadium, Male
14-09-2005, 19:00, 7 000, Kousa SYR	21-09-2005, 19:30, 3 105, Haq IND	14-09-2005, 16:00, 7 200, Nagalingam SIN
Al Faysali 1	**Tampines Rovers** 0	**New Radiant** 1
Al Maharmeh [64]		Thariq [85]
Elamaireh - Khamees, Krsteski (Al Maharmeh 30), Aqel, Shawish, Sh. Qasem●, Nemer, Abu Alieh, Odtallah (Al Otabe● 63), Mansour, Al Tall (Al Tawaiha 73)	Hafez Mawasi - Muratovic, Nazri Nasir, Zul Zainal●, Tan Kim Leng (Jauharmi 60), Chaiyaphuak, Mustafic●37, Aliff Safiee (Ibrahim Md Noh 44), Mohamed Rafi Ali (Tan Teng Chuan 78), Noh Alam Shah, Grabovac	Sooriyaarachche - Simeonov, Jameel, Nasir (Nimal 62), Ahmed Saeed, Sifan● (Janah 80), Sabah Ibrahim●, Fazeel●, Naaz●, Ahmed Mohamed● (Niyaaz 84), Thariq
Tampines Rovers 0	**Al Faysali** 1	**Al Hussein** 0
	Al Tall [31]	
Hafez Mawasi - Muratovic, Nazri Nasir●, Zul Zainal, Tan Kim Leng (Satria Mad 71), Azhar Md Salleh, Chaiyaphuak●, Mustafic, Aliff Safiee (Azlan Alipah 52), Noh Alam Shah (Jauharmi 81), Grabovac	Elamaireh - Khamees, Krsteski, Al Shboul (Al Malta'ah 83), Aqel●, Shawish, Sh. Qasem●, Nemer, Abu Alieh (Mansour 68), Al Maharmeh (Shamoun 43), Al Tall	Abdallah Yousef - Obeidat, Al Jomah●, Hnoun, Bani-Hani●, Ababneh●, Al Sheyab (Al Khateeb 86), Muhsen, Hatamleh (Bani Yaseen 82), Al Zboun, Al Riahna (Athamnah 61)

2nd leg. Al Hassan International, Irbed	1st leg. Beirut Municipal, Beirut	2nd leg. Hong Kong Stadium, Hong Kong
21-09-2005, 20:00, 5 000, Al Marzouqi UAE	14-09-2005, 20:00, 1 000, Al Delawar BHR	21-09-2005, 20:00, 1 700, Khanthama THA
Al Hussein 0	**Al Ahed** 1	**Sun Hei** 3
	Haidar [39]	Akosah [42], Lee Kin Wo [52], Sanvel Keung [90]
Abdallah Yousef - Al Jomah, Hnoun, Al Khateeb●, Bani-Hani (Al Bals 59), Ababneh (Al Riahna 59), Al Sheyab, Muhsen, Hatamleh, Athamnah (Bani Yaseen 66), Al Zboun	Hachem - Bangura, Marmar, Mezher, Baydoun, Haidar, Nassrallah (Kobeissi 85), Bah, El Ali (Ayoub 70), Abou Atiq (Trad 78), Maatouk	Chan Ka Ki - Chung Kin Hei, Hartwig, Lee Wai Lun, Kai Cheuk, Cordeiro, Lau Chi Keung, Chu Siu Kei (Chan Ho Man 62), Chan Yiu Lun (Lee Kin Wo 46), Lo Chi Kwan● (Leung Chi Wing 75), Akosah
New Radiant 0	**Sun Hei** 0	**Al Ahed** 1
		Abou Atiq [45]
Sooriyaarachche● - Nimal●, Simeonov, Jameel, Nasir, Sifan, Sabah Ibrahim, Fazeel●, Naaz● (Janah 84), Ahmed Mohamed (Ahmed Saeed 62) (Azim Hussein 93+), Thariq●●●51	Chan Ka Ki - Chung Kin Hei, Hartwig, Lee Wai Lun, Cordeiro, Lau Chi Keung●, Chu Siu Kei, Lee Kin Wo (Chan Yiu Lun 64), Akosah●, Wong Chun Yue (Lo Chi Kwan 72), Chan Ho Man (Poon Man Tik 58)	Hachem● - Bangura (Kobeissi 62) (Ayoub 90), Marmar●, Mezher●, Baydoun, Haidar, Nassrallah, Bah, El Ali (Trad 48), Abou Atiq, Maatouk

1st leg. Bishan Stadium, Singapore
14-09-2005, 19:30, 1 536, Gedara SRI
Home United   **0**
Lionel - Aide Sahak●●●51, Shunmugham, Srikerd, Aidil Sahak●, De Oliveira, Imran Sahib (Kamal Haja 58), Baksin, Indra Sahdan Daud, Goncalves, Suksomkit
Al Nejmeh   **3**
Ali Mohamad 24, Hjeij 53, Ali Atwi 73
El Fattal - Dokmak, Zaher, Ali Mohamad, Khaled Hamieh, El Najjarine, Yehia Hachem, Abbas Atwi, Moussa Hjeij (Ghaddar 66), Kabbout (Ahmad Moghrabi 57), Ali Nassereddine (Hayssam Atwi 81)

2nd leg. Sports City, Beirut
21-09-2005, 19:30, 4 000, Al Mutlaq KSA
Al Nejmeh   **3**
Nassereddine 35, Ghaddar 59, Ali Mohamad 72
El Fattal - Dokmak, Zaher, Ali Mohamad●, Khaled Hamieh, El Najjarine, Yehia Hachem●, Abbas Atwi, Moussa Hjeij (Moghrabi 78), Kabbout (Ghaddar 27), Ali Nassereddine (Halawi● 63)
Home United   **2**
Sahdan Daud 18, Kamal Haja 49
Lionel - Mohamed Salleh, Shunmugham, Srikerd, Aidil Sahak (Mohammad Abdullah 40) (Abdul Samat 43), De Oliveira, Kamal Haja● (Juraimi 74), Baksin, Indra Sahdan Daud●, Goncalves, Suksomkit

SEMI-FINALS

1st Leg. National Stadium, Male
28-09-2005, 16:00, 10 000, Al Saeedi UAE
New Radiant   **1**
Niyaz 52
Sooriyaarachche - Nimal, Simeonov●●●93+, Jameel, Ahmed Janah● (Mohamed Hussein● 50), Nasir, Ahmed Saeed, Sifan, Sabah Ibrahim, Ahmed Mohamed (Azim Hussein 15), Niyaaz (Abdulla Mohamed 74)
Al Faysali   **1**
Al Shboul 20
Elamaireh - Khamees, Krsteski●, Al Malta'ah (Al Maharmeh 45), Al Shboul, Aqel, Shawish, Nemer, Abu Alieh●, Shamoun● (Mansour 72), Al Tall

2nd Leg. Amman International, Amman
12-10-2005, 20:30, 18 000, Al Fadhli KUW
Al Faysali   **4**
Mansour 2 8 42, Al Tall, Al Shboul
Elamaireh (Abu Hamid 75) - Khamees (Al Mutasim 75), Krsteski, Al Malta'ah, Al Shboul, Aqel, Shawish, Sh. Qasem●, Abu Alieh, Mansour, Al Tall (Halasa 77)
New Radiant   **1**
Thariq
Sooriyaarachche - Nimal, Jameel, Nasir, Ahmed Saeed, Sifan, Sabah Ibrahim (Mohamed Hussain 87), Fazeel (Janah 86), Naaz, Thariq, Niyaaz (Azim Hussein 73)

2nd Leg. Sports City, Beirut
28-09-2005, 19:30, 6 000, Ebrahim BHR
Al Nejmeh   **3**
Ghaddar 2 25 57, Nassereddine 69
El Fattal - Dokmak, Zaher, Ali Mohamad, Khaled Hamieh, El Najjarine, Yehia Hachem, Abbas Atwi (Hayssam Atwi 95+), Moussa Hjeij (Duah 79), Ghaddar●, (Ahmad Moghrabi 88), Ali Nassereddine
Sun Hei   **0**
Chan Ka Ki - Chung Kin Hei (Leung Chi Wing 61), Hartwig●, Lee Wai Lun●, Lai Kai Cheuk, Lau Chi Keung, Chu Siu Kei (Chan Ho Man 71), Lee Kin Wo (Chan Yiu Lun 67), Lo Chi Kwan, Poon Man Tik, Akosah

1st Leg. Hong Kong Stadium, Hong Kong
12-10-2005, 20:00, 4 652, Al Hamdan KSA
Sun Hei   **2**
Lai Kai Chuk 8, Akosah 24
Chan Ka Ki - Hartwig●, Lee Wai Lun, Lai Kai Cheuk, Leung Chi Wing, Lau Chi Keung●, Chu Siu Kei (Lo Chi Kwan 46), Chan Yiu Lun, Lee Kin Wo (Chan Ho Man 68), Poon Man Tik (Chung Kin Hei 87), Akosah
Al Nejmeh   **3**
Nassereddine 25, Hamieh 45, Ghaddar 89
El Fattal● - Dokmak●, Zaher, Ali Mohamad, Khaled Hamieh●, El Najjarine, Yehia Hachem, Abbas Atwi (Hayssam Atwi 83), Moussa Hjeij (Ghaddar 70), Ahmad Moghrabi (Duah● 29), Ali Nassereddine

AFC CUP FINAL FIRST LEG
Amman International, Amman
19-10-2005, 21:00, 10 000, Moradi IRN, Al Kadri SYR, Al Khalifi QAT

AL FAYSALI	1	0	AL NEJMEH

Khaled Saed 36

Al Faysali			Al Nejmeh
22 ELAMAIREH Lo'ai			EL FATTAL Wahid 22
7 KHAMEES Mohammad			DOKMAK Hussein 3
10 KRSTESKI Darko			ZAHER Hussein 6
12 AL MALTA'AH Khaled			MOHAMAD Ali 7
14 AL SHBOUL Haitham			HAMIEH Khaled 21
17 AQEL Hatem			EL NAJJARINE Bilal 24
20 SHAWISH Mohammad		46	HACHEM Yehia 8
6 SH. QASEM Hassouneh			ATWI Abbas 10
13 ABU ALIEH Qusai			DUAH Emmanuel 15
19 MANSOUR Moayad 60		90	HJEIJ Moussa 20
27 AL TALL Siraj 53		70	NASSEREDDINE Ali 30
Tr: SMILANEC Branko			Tr: MEZIANE Omar
Substitutes			Substitutes
8 NEMER Khaled 60		46	GHADDAR Mohamad 11
11 AL MAHARMEH Abdelhadi 53		70	ATWI Hayssam 19
		90	MOGHRABI Ahmad 25

AFC CUP FINAL SECOND LEG
Sport City, Beirut
26-10-2005, 21:00, 15 000, Al Ghamdi KSA, Ghuloum UAE, Al Traifi KSA

AL NEJMEH	2	3	AL FAYSALI

Moussa Hjeij 2 35 73   Al Malta'ah 2 20 59, Qasem 88

Al Nejmeh			Al Faysali
22 EL FATTAL Wahid			ELAMAIREH Lo'ai 22
3 DOKMAK Hussein	24		KHAMEES Mohammad 7
6 ZAHER Hussein			KRSTESKI Darko 10
7 MOHAMAD Ali			AL MALTA'AH Khaled 12
21 HAMIEH Khaled	24		AL SHBOUL Haitham 14
24 EL NAJJARINE Bilal			AQEL Hatem 17
10 ATWI Abbas			SHAWISH Mohammad 20
15 DUAH Emmanuel			SH. QASEM Hassouneh 6
20 HJEIJ Moussa			ABU ALIEH Qusai 13
11 GHADDAR Mohamad			AL MAHARMEH Abdelhadi 11
30 NASSEREDDINE Ali			MANSOUR Moayad 19
Tr: MEZIANE Omar			Tr: SMILANEC Branko
Substitutes			Substitutes

AFC PRESIDENT'S CUP 2005

AFC PRESIDENT'S CUP NEPAL 2005

Group Stage			Semi-finals		Final

Group A		Pts
Regar TadAZ	TJK	7
Three Star Club	NEP	5
Taiwan Power Co	TPE	4
Transport United	BHU	0

Semi-finals	
Regar TadAZ	6
Blue Star SC	0

Final	
Regar TadAZ	3
Dordoy-Dinamo	0

Group B		Pts
Dordoy-Dinamo	KGZ	6
Blue Star SC	SRI	6
WAPDA	PAK	3
Hello United	CAM	3

Semi-finals		
Three Star Club	0	3p
Dordoy-Dinamo	0	4p

GROUP A

Halchowk, Kathmandu, 4-05-2005, 16:00, 2 000, Vidanagamage SRI

Regar TadAZ	6	Makhmudov 2 [18 89], Muhidinov 3 [35 37 56], Tabarov [86p]
Transport United	1	Dendup [68]

Dasrath, Kathmandu, 4-05-2005, 17:00, 15 000, Kunsuta THA

Three Star Club	1	Maharjan [38]
Taiwan Power Co	1	Chen Chi Feng [36]

Halchowk, Kathmandu, 6-05-2005, 16:00, 2 000, Midi Nitrorejo IDN

Regar TadAZ	3	Irgashev [7], Muhidinov [18], Tabarov [40]
Taiwan Power Co	0	

Dasrath, Kathmandu, 6-05-2005, 16:00, 8 000, Busurmankulov KGZ

Three Star Club	2	Gouchan.V [10], Maharjan [43]
Transport United	1	Chopel [37]

Halchowk, Kathmandu, 8-05-2005, 16:00, 600, Busurmankulov KGZ

Taiwan Power Co	1	Chiang Shih Lu [40]
Transport United	0	

Dasrath, Kathmandu, 8-05-2005, 16:00, 12 000, Vidanagamage SRI

Three Star Club	0	
Regar TadAZ	0	

Group A	Pl	W	D	L	F	A	Pts
Regar TadAZ	3	2	1	0	9	1	7
Three Star Club	3	1	2	0	3	2	5
Taiwan Power Company	3	1	1	1	10	2	4
Transport United	3	0	0	3	2	9	0

GROUP B

Halchowk, Kathmandu, 5-05-2005, 16:00, 1 000, Shamsuzzaman BAN

Dordoy-Dinamo	6	Kasymov 2 [24 43], Krasnov 2 [25 39], Chikishev [28], Berezovsky [71]
Hello United	1	Ieng Saknida [40]

Dasrath, Kathmandu, 5-05-2005, 16:00, 400, Nguyen VIE

Blue Star SC	1	Steinwall [26]
WAPDA	0	

Halchowk, Kathmandu, 7-05-2005, 16:00, 1 000, Kunsuta THA

Hello United	2	Hok Sochetra 2 [48 92+]
WAPDA	1	Arif Mehmood [16]

Dasrath, Kathmandu, 7-05-2005, 16:00, 2 000, Shamsuzzaman BAN

Dordoy-Dinamo	8	Kasymov [1], Krohmal [11], Krasnov [15], Berezovsky [16], Jumagulov [42], Chertkov [64], Ishenbaev 2 [76 81]
Blue Star SC	1	Steinwall [19]

Halchowk, Kathmandu, 9-05-2005, 16:00, 500, Pereira IND

WAPDA	1	Mehmood Arif [81]
Dordoy-Dinamo	0	

Dasrath, Kathmandu, 9-05-2005, 16:00, 800, Midi Nitrorejo IDN

Blue Star SC	3	Steinwall 2 [32p 72], Fawzan [90]
Hello United	2	Hang Sokunthea [60], Hok Sochetra [79p]

Group A	Pl	W	D	L	F	A	Pts
Dordoy-Dinamo	3	2	0	1	14	3	6
Blue Star SC	3	2	0	1	5	10	6
WAPDA	3	1	0	2	2	3	3
Hello United	3	1	0	2	5	10	3

SEMI-FINALS AND FINAL

Semi-final. Dashrath, Kathmandu
12-05-2005, 16:00, 10 000, Pereira IND

Regar TadAZ	6

Khamidov 2 [13 43], Makhmudov [41] Umarbaev [70], Rustamov [74], Nematov [91+]
Khodjimurodov - Tabarov (c), Turdiev, Rustamov - Rakhimov (Umarbaev 57), Makhmudov, Tuhtaev, Dzhabarov, Irgashev - Khamidov (Nematov 46), Muhidinov (Kholbekov 76). Tr: Habibuloev

Blue Star SC	0

Thilakaratne - Steinwall, Ramees, Murshid*, Hamza (c) - Imran (Farzeen 46), Najeem (Chathura 74), Rawme - Irshan, Nafais, Farsin (Asmeer 31). Tr: Ratnayaka Mudiyanselage

Semi-final. Dashrath, Kathmandu
12-05-2005, 19:00, 22 000, Shamsuzzaman BAN

Three Star Club	0	3p

Singh.UM - Shrestha.S, Singh.J, Gurung.LB, Anjan.KC - Khadagi.R, Gurung.B, Gouchan.V (Khadka.N 119), Rajbhandari.P, Maharjan.P - Shahukhala (Tamang.SB 100). Tr: Dhruba Bahadur

Dordoy-Dinamo	0	4p

Djalilov - Samsaliev, Sydykov* (c), Kononov, Kasymov - Krohmal (Kniazev 118), Chertkov, Pilipas - Berezovsky, Krasnov (Jumagulov 65), Chikishev (Ishenbaev 77). Tr: Tiagusov

Final. Dashrath, Kathmandu
14-05-2005, 19:00, 8 000, Kunsuta THA

Regar TadAZ	3

Rakhimov [7], Irgashev [70p], Makhmudov [72]
Khodjimurodov - Tabarov (c), Turdiev, Rustamov - Rakhimov, Makhmudov, Tuhtaev (Choriev 89), Dzhabarov (Umarbaev 64), Irgashev - Khamidov, Muhidinov (Nematov 58). Tr: Habibuloev

Dordoy-Dinamo	0

Djalilov - Samsaliev, Sydykov (c)*, Kononov, Kasymov* - Krohmal (Ishenbaev 62), Chertkov, Pilipas - Berezovsky, Krasnov (Kniazev 77), Chikishev (Jumagulov 46). Tr: Tiagusov

AFC CHAMPIONS LEAGUE 2006

AFC CHAMPIONS LEAGUE 2006

Group Stage			Quarter-finals	Semi-finals	Final

Group A		Pts
Al Qadisiya	KUW	11
Pakhtakor Tashkent	UZB	10
Al Ittihad	SYR	8
Foolad	IRN	4

Group B		Pts		
Al Ain	UAE	13		
Al Hilal	KSA	10	Al Ittihad *
Mash'al	UZB	8	Al Karama
Al Mina'a	IRQ	2	

Group C		Pts
Al Karama	SYR	12
Saba Battery	IRN	10
Al Wahda	UAE	7
Al Gharafa	QAT	6

Al Qadisiya *
Al Ain

Group D		Pts
Al Shabab	KSA	13
Al Sadd	QAT	13
Al Quwa Al Jawiya	IRQ	6
Al Arabi	KUW	3

Group E		Pts	
Jeonbuk Motors	KOR	13	Shanhai Shenhua *
Dalian	CHN	12	Jeonbuk Motors
Gamba Osaka	JPN	10	
Da Nang	VIE	0	

Group F		Pts
Ulsan Hyundai	KOR	6
Tokyo Verdy	JPN	0

Ulsan Horang-i *
Al Shabab

Group G		Pts
Shanghai Shenhua	CHN	6
Dong Tam	VIE	0

† Al Ittihad (KSA) given a bye to the quarter-finals as holders • * Home team in the first leg
Remaining ties: Quarter-finals 13/09/2006 & 20/09/2006; Semi-finals 27/09/2006 & 18/10/2006; Final 1/11/2006 & 8/11/2006

GROUP A

		Pl	W	D	L	F	A	Pts	KUW	UZB	SYR	IRN
Al Qadisiya	KUW	6	3	2	1	9	11	11		2-1	1-0	2-0
Pakhtakor Tashkent	UZB	6	3	1	2	11	7	10	2-2		2-0	2-0
Al Ittihad	SYR	6	2	2	2	6	7	8	2-2	2-1		0-0
Foolad	IRN	6	1	1	4	8	9	4	6-0	1-3	1-2	

GROUP A MATCHDAY 1
Pakhtakor, Tashkent
8-03-2006, 16:30, 11 000, Sarkar IND

Pakhtakor Tashkent   2
Inomov [18], Kletsov [85]

Nesterov - Aliqulov, Klestkov* - Kiryan, Innomov*, Ponomarev (Rahimov 66), Kapadze, Bayramov - Djeparov, Soliev (Iheruome 90), Z.Tadjiyev (Abdulaev 66)

Al Ittihad   0

M.Karkar - M.Al Rashad, M.Homsi, K.Aryan (S.Shahrour 67), M.I.Aziza, M.Sayed (D.Hemidi 77), W.Aian (M.Boudaka 46), H.A.Hassan* - M.Al Amena, M.Yahia Al Rached - A.Aga

---

GROUP A MATCHDAY 1
Dastgerdi, Tehran
8-03-2006, 15:00, 2 000, Ebrahim BHR

Foolad   6
Rameshgar [11], Soleimani [27], Badavi [33], Khaziravi [54], Ahmadi [59], Montazeri [72]

Mirzapour - Pejman, Jalal, Kabi, Badavi - Sarlak, Nori, Mojahed* (Shaveroy 76), Ahmadi* (L.Hamidi 69) - Rameshgar* (Hojat 66), Soleimani

Al Qadisiya   0

N.Al Khaledi - A.Al Namash, A.Al Shamali, N.Al Shammari, M.Abdul Rahman* (H.Saadoun 65) - B.Keita, N.Al Mutairi (T.Seydou 46), A.Al Dawood*, Lucio (A.Abdullah 46) - B.Al Mutwa, S.Khalaf

---

GROUP A MATCHDAY 2
Friendship & Peace, Kuwait City
22-03-2006, 20:00, 5 000, Tongkhan THA

Al Qadisiya   2
Al Otaibi [89], Al Mutwa [91+]

N.Al Khaledi - A.Al Namash, A.Al Shamali, N.Al Shammari, M.Jamal - B.Keita, A.Al Dawood (T.Seydou 63), Lucio - B.Al Mutwa, S.Khalaf (N.Al Mutairi 82), A.Abdullah (M.Rashed 82)

Pakhtakor Tashkent   1
Soliev [44]

Nesterov - Aliqulov*, Klestkov, Suyunov (Ponomarev 52) - Rahimov (Z.Tadjiyev 76), Kiryan, Innomov, Kapadze, Bayramov* - Djeparov, Soliev*

GROUP A MATCHDAY 2
Al Hamadania, Aleppo
22-03-2005, 14:00, 4 500, Al Hamdan KSA

Al Ittihad   0

M.Karkar* - M.Homsi, D.Hemidi, M.I.Aziza, M.Sayed (A.Habal 64), W.Aian (Z.Al Kaddour 90), M.Boudaka, Y.Shikhaleshreh - M.Al Amena (R.Al Abrach 83), M.Yahia Al Rached - A.Aga

Foolad   0

Mirzapour - Pejman, Kabi, Badavi, Alavi - Omid, Sarlak, Mojahed (Adel 68), Ahmadi (L.Hamidi 74) - Soleimani, Emad (Rameshgar* 40)

GROUP A MATCHDAY 3
Pakhtakor, Tashkent
12-04-2006, 17:00, 10 000, Al Saeedi UAE

Pakhtakor Tashkent   2
Tadjiev [13], Djeperov [37]

Nesterov - Aliqulov, Klestkov, Suyunov (Ponomarev 52) - Abdullaev (K.Tadjiev 87), Kiryan, Innomov*, Kapadze*, Ponomarev (Rahimov 77) - Djeparov, Z.Tadjiyev (Iheruome 92+)

Foolad   0

Emad - Pejman, Jalal, Kabi, Badavi* - Omid* (Zandipour 81), Adel, Alavi (M.Hamidi 68), Soleimani (L.Hamidi 57), Nori, Mojahed**53

GROUP A MATCHDAY 3
Al Hamadania, Aleppo
12-04-2006, 19:00, 7 000, Mansour LIB

Al Ittihad   0
Homsi [23], Aga [84]

Y.Jarkas - M.Homsi, D.Hemidi*, M.I.Aziza, M.Sayed*, B.Tarrab, Y.Shikhaleshreh - M.Al Amena*, M.Yahia Al Rached (M.Al Beef 81) - M.Al Damen (W.Aian* 61), A.Aga* (K.Aryan 85)

Al Qadisiya   2
Al Mutwa [20p], Tarab OG [90]

N.Al Khaledi - A.Al Namash*, A.Al Shamali, M.Abdul Rahman, M.Jamal - B.Keita*, A.Al Dawood (N.Al Mutairi 85), Lucio (T.Seydou 76) - B.Al Mutwa, S.Khalaf, A.Abdullah (M.Rashed 85)

GROUP A MATCHDAY 4
Dastgerdi, Tehran
26-04-2006, 17:00, 1 500, Mujghef JOR

Foolad   1
Soleimani [34]

Mirzapour - Pejman, Jalal, Kabi, Badavi, Alavi (L.Hamidi 62) - Adel (Omid 69), Nori, Mojahed - Soleimani (Rameshgar 90), Emad*

Pakhtakor Tashkent   3
Bayramov [46], Kiryan [48], Tadjiev [57]

Nesterov (Juraev 25) - Aliqulov, Klestkov, Suyunov* - Kiryan, Innomov*, Kapadze, Bayramov* - Djeparov*, Soliev (Ponomarev 75), Z.Tadjiyev (K.Tadjiev 87)

GROUP A MATCHDAY 4
Friendship & Peace, Kuwait City
26-04-2006, 19:00, 3 500, Al Hilali OMA

Al Qadisiya   1
Al Mutwa [84]

N.Al Khaledi - A.Al Namash, A.Al Shamali, N.Al Shammari, M.Abdul Rahman* - B.Keita (T.Seydou 63), N.Al Mutairi (SH.Saleh 72), M.Fahad, Lucio (A.Al Dawood 85) - B.Al Mutwa, S.Khalaf*

Al Ittihad   0

M.Karkar - M.Al Rashad (M.Al Beef 87), M.Homsi, D.Hemidi*, M.I.Aziza*, M.Sayed, W.Aian - M.Al Amena* (Y.Shikhaleshreh 77), M.Yahia Al Rached* - M.Al Damen (M.Boudaka* 55), A.Aga

---

GROUP A MATCHDAY 5
Friendship & Peace, Kuwait City
3-05-2006, 19:05, 19 000, Al Ghamdi KSA

Al Qadisiya   2
Al Mutwa 2 [5] [93+]

N.Al Khaledi - A.Al Namash, A.Al Shamali, H.Saadoun, N.Al Shammari - B.Keita*, M.Fahad*, Lucio (A.Al Dawood 69) - B.Al Mutwa, S.Khalaf (M.Rashed* 75), A.Abdullah* (SH.Salej 89)

Foolad   0

Hori - Pejman, Jalal (Alavi* 72), Badavi - Omid, Adel (Nori 16), Sarlak (L.Hamidi 67), Mojahed, Ahmadi* - Soleimani*, Rameshgar

---

GROUP A MATCHDAY 5
Al Hamadania, Aleppo
3-05-2006, 20:00, 3 000, Nema IRQ

Al Ittihad   2
Al Rashad [17], Al Damen [45]

M.Karkar - M.Al Rashad (M.Al Beef 87), M.Homsi*, M.I.Aziza, M.Sayed, W.Aian, B.Tarrab - M.Yahia Al Rached*, A.Habal* (Y.Shikhaleshreh 78) - M.Al Damen (M.Boudaka 46), A.Aga (K.Aryan 90+3)

Pakhtakor Tashkent   1
Ponomarev [20]

Juraev - Aliqulov, Klestkov*, K.Tadjiev* (Abdulaev 46), Suyunov - Kiryan, Ponomarev, Kapadze - Djeparov, Soliev, Z.Tadjiyev

---

GROUP A MATCHDAY 6
Pakhtakor, Tashkent
17-05-2006, 18:00, 15 000, Shamsuzzaman

Pakhtakor Tashkent   2
Bayramov [12], Soliev [90]

Juraev* - Aliqulov*, Klestkov, Suyunov - Kiryan, Innomov (Iheruome* 46), Ponomarev (Abdulaev 70), Kapadze, Bayramov - Djeparov*, Z.Tadjiyev (Soliev 64)

Al Qadisiya   2
Hussain Ali [7], Salama [58]

N.Al Khaledi - A.Al Namash (M.Nida* 75), F.Hussain* (H.Saadoun 81), N.Al Shammari, B.Keita* - N.Al Mutairi, M.Fahad*, A.Al Dawood - B.Al Mutwa, S.Khalaf (SH.Salej 80*), A.Abdullah

---

GROUP A MATCHDAY 6
Dastgerdi, Tehran
17-05-2006, 17:00, 500, Nurilddin IRQ

Foolad   1
Kolahkaj [77]

Hori - M.Sharifi, Pejman, Jalal, Badavi - Omid*, Adel*, Sarlak, Nori (Zandipour 46), Mojahed (Soleimani 46) - Hojat (A.Amiri 76)

Al Ittihad   2
Al Damen [21], Aga [74]

M.Karkar - D.Hemidi, M.I.Aziza, M.Sayed (M.Al Beef 87), W.Aian, M.Boudaka - M.Al Rashad 83), Y.Shikhaleshreh - M.Al Amena, A.Habal - M.Al Damen (K.Aryan 70), A.Aga

GROUP B

		Pl	W	D	L	F	A	Pts	UAE	KSA	UZB	IRQ
Al Ain	UAE	6	3	2	1	9	11	11		2-0	2-1	2-1
Al Hilal	KSA	6	3	1	2	11	7	10	2-1		5-0	3-1
Mash'al	UZB	6	2	2	2	6	7	8	1-1	2-1		2-2
Al Mina'a	IRQ	6	1	1	4	8	9	4	1-2	1-1	0-1	

GROUP B MATCHDAY 1
Tahnon Bin Mohammed, Al Ain
8-03-2006, 19:30, 12 000, Moradi IRN
Al Ain   **2**
Faisal Ali [42], Clesly [49]
Waleed - Saleh●, Fahad, Humaid, A.Juma - Diaky, Helal, Subait - Jestrovic (Shehab 22), Fasial (Gharib 63), Clesly

Al Hilal   **0**
Al Deayea - Al Dossary, Tavares, Al Mousa● - Al Thaker● (Suwaileh● 32), Camaho, Al Shalhoub (Al Ghannam 46), Al Ghamdi, Al Gahtani●, Al Bargan - Al Jaber (Al Suwailh 46)

GROUP B MATCHDAY 1
Sabah Al Salem, Kuwait City
8-03-2006, 16:00, 200, Al Yarimi YEM
Al Mina'a   **0**

S.Sadam - A.Sajjad, A.Emad, A.Baha●, A.Ala'a, S.Nawaf - F.Ghazi (I.Husam 56), F.Naif (H.Bashar 87), J.Satar, F.Nawaf - H.Ehsan

Mashal Muborak   **1**
Zafar Kholmurodov [31]
Y.Tsoy - K.Kenjayev, D.Vaniev, A.Gafurov, Hayrulla Karimov, Hamza Karimov, B.Karaev - R.Kadirov● - Z.Kholmurodov (J.Hasanov 74), SH.Mirhoidirshaev (V.Klishin● 66), B.Vahobov (R.Gofurov 90)

GROUP B MATCHDAY 2
Nasaf Stadium, Karshi
22-03-2006, 15:00, 10 000, Najm LIB
Mashal Muborak   **1**
Shuhratbek Mirholdirshaev [94+]
Y.Tsoy - K.Kenjayev, D.Vaniev, A.Gafurov (R.Gafurov 59), Hayrulla Karimov●, Hamza Karimov●, B.Karaev (J.Hasanov 46) - R.Kadirov● (A.Ostap 67) - SH.Mirhoidirshaev, V.Klishin, B.Vahobov

Al Ain   **1**
Ibrahim Diaky [15]
Waleed - A.Wahaibi, Saleh, Fahad (K.Juma 85), Humaid, A.Juma● - Diaky, Helal●, Shehab (Gharib 72), Subait - Fasial (Jestrovic 69)

GROUP B MATCHDAY 2
King Fahd International, Riyadh
22-03-2006, 20:30, 23 000, Al Fadhli KUW
Al Hilal   **3**
Tavares [31], Al Anbar [60], Al Qahtani [91+]
Al Deayea - Tavares, Al Mefarej, Khathranm - Al Ghannam, Camaho, Al Temyat, Al Ghamdi (Al Mousa 73), Al Bargan - Al Jaber (Al Qahtani 70), Al Anbar (Al Dosari 80)

Al Mina'a   **1**
Muneer Hamoud [45]
S.Sadam - A.Sajjad, A.Emad, J.Ali, A.Ala'a, S.Nawaf●, H.Muneer - F.Ghazi (F.Naif 88), J.Satar, F.Nawaf - H.Ehsan

GROUP B MATCHDAY 3
Tahnon Bin Mohammed, Al Ain
12-04-2006, 19:30, 10 000, Basma SYR
Al Ain   **2**
Nenad Jestrovic 2 [14 37p]
Waleed - A.Wahaibi, Saleh, K.Juma, Humaid (Fasial 87), A.Juma - Diaky (Gharib 90+3), Helal, Shehab, Subait - Jestrovic●

Al Mina'a   **1**
Satar Jabbar [15]
S.Sadam - A.Sajjad●, A.Emad, J.Ali●, Ala, S.Nawaf, H.Muneer (F.Ghazi 56) - F.Naif (H.Ehsan 78), J.Satar, F.Nawaf● - T.Nasir

GROUP B MATCHDAY 3
King Fahd International, Riyadh
12-04-2006, 20:45, 20 000, Maidin SIN
Al Hilal   **5**
Al Mouri [30], Oliveira [34], Al Suwailh 2 [63 85]
Camacho [79]
Al Shammari - Al Dossary, Tavares, Al Mousa (Al Bashir 83) - Al Thaker, Camaho, Al Shalhoub, Oliveira● (Al Abdulsalam 85), Al Bargan● - Al Jaber (Al Suwailh 60), Al Mouri●

Mashal Muborak   **0**
Y.Tsoy - K.Kenjayev, D.Vaniev (J.Hasanov 65), A.Gafurov (R.Gafurov 55), Hayrulla Karimov●72, Hamza Karimov, B.Karaev - A.Ostap● - SH.Mirhoidirshaev, V.Klishin, B.Vahobov (V.Djalilov 68)

GROUP B MATCHDAY 4
Friendship & Peace, Kuwait City
26-04-2006, 21:15, 1 000, Moradi IRN
Al Mina'a   **1**
Nawaf Falah [7]
S.Sadam Al Abody Sajjad, A.Emad, J.Ali, Ala●, S.Nawaf● (Abbas Sajjad 70), H.Muneer - F.Naif, J.Satar (T.Nasir 45), F.Nawaf S.Usama (H.Bashar 76)

Al Ain   **2**
Clesly [64p], Ibrahim Diaky [66]
Waleed - A.Wahaibi, Saleh (Abdullah 89), K.Juma, Humaid, A.Juma - Diaky, Helal, Shehab (Clesly 54), Subait - Fasial (Sultan 88)

GROUP B MATCHDAY 4
Nasaf Stadium, Karshi
26-04-2006, 16:00, 5 500, Ebrahim BHR
Mashal Muborak   **2**
Botir Karaev [50], Zafar Kholmurodov [82]
P.Butenko - K.Kenjayev●90, D.Vaniev●, A.Gafurov, Hamza Karimov, B.Karaev - R.Kadirov (Z.Kholmurodov● 57), J.Hasanov, R.Gofurov (V.Klishin 85), A.Ostap● (J.Jiyamuradov 46●84) - SH.Mirhoidirshaev●

Al Hilal   **1**
Abdullah Al Dosari [92+p]
Al Shammari - Abulaziz● (Badr Al Dosari 58), Tavares, Al Mousa, Al Mefarej - Oliveira (Al Kharashi 53), Al Bargan, Al Abdulsalam●, - Abdullah Al Dosari, Al Suwailh, Al Mouri (Al Mobarak 65)

GROUP B MATCHDAY 5
King Fahd International, Riyadh
3-05-2006, 20:45, 15 000, Marshoud JOR
Al Hilal   **2**
Camacho [33], Al Shalhoub [86p]
Al Deayea - Tavares, Al Mousa●, Al Mefarej - Camacho (Al Mobarak 64), Al Shalhoub, Al Ghamdi, Al Gahtini (Al Doassary 90), Al Bargan, Al Abdulsalam, - Al Jaber

Al Ain   **1**
Nenad Jestrovic [49]
Waleed - A.Wahaibi, Saleh, K.Juma● (Fasial 88), Humaid (Fahad 83), A.Juma● - Diaky, Helal, Subait - Jestrovic, Clesley

GROUP B MATCHDAY 5
Nasaf Stadium, Karshi
3-05-2006, 18:00, 3 000, Arambakade SRI
Mashal Muborak   **2**
Hasanov [30], Mirholdirshaev [72]
P.Butenko - D.Vaniev, D.Djalilov (B.Vahobov 46), A.Gafurov, Hayrulla Karimov, Hamza Karimov, B.Karaev (V.Klishan 76) - R.Kadirov (Z.Kholmurodov 41), J.Hasanov, R.Gofurov - SH.Mirhoidirshaev

Al Mina'a   **2**
Abbas Sajjad [12], Mokhlas Abdulsattar [60]
S.Sadam● - Al Abody Sajjad, A.Emad, J.Ali, Ala, Abbas Sajjad, H.Muneer - F.Naif, F.Nawaf (M.Hussain● 79) - A.Mokhlas● (H.Ehsan 70), S.Usama (H.Bashar 76)

GROUP B MATCHDAY 6
Tahnon Bin Mohammed, Al Ain
17-05-2006, 19:45, 7 000, Kwon Jong Chul KOR
Al Ain   **2**
Nenad Jestrovic 2 [35 45]
Waleed - Mahboub, Saleh, K.Juma, Humaid - Diaky (Shehab 89), Gharib, Subait - Jestrovic, Fasial (Helal 77)

Mashal Muborak   **1**
Zafar Kholmurodov [23]
P.Butenko - D.Vaniev, D.Djalilov, A.Gafurov, Hayrulla Karimov●, Hamza Karimov - R.Kadirov (L.Turaev 83), J.Hasanov - Z.Kholmurodov, A.Ibragimov (SH.Mirhoidirshaev● 78), V.Klishin (Vahobov 57)

GROUP B MATCHDAY 6
Sabah Al Salem, Kuwait City
17-05-2006, 18:45, 2 000, Kousa SYR
Al Mina'a   **1**
Nawaf Falah [34]
S.Sadam● - Al Abody Sajjad, A.Emad, Ala, S.Nawaf (H.Bashar 73), H.Muneer - F.Naif, M.Hussain (I.Husam 83), F.Nawaf● - A.Mokhlas (F.Ghazi 77), S.Usama

Al Hilal   **1**
Giovanni Oliveira [48]
Al Otaibi - Al Dossary, Tavares●, Al Mefarej (Al Kharashi 85), Badr Al Dossari (Al Jaber 40) - Camaho, Al Shalhoub, Oliveira, Al Bargan, Al Abdulsalam - Abdullah Al Dossari (Al Mobarak 63)

GROUP C

		Pl	W	D	L	F	A	Pts	SYR	IRN	UAE	QAT
Al Karama	SYR	6	4	0	2	10	11	12		1-0	2-1	3-1
Saba Battery	IRN	6	3	1	2	13	8	10	1-2		2-2	4-1
Al Wahda	UAE	6	2	1	3	14	15	7	4-2	2-4		2-0
Al Gharafa	QAT	6	2	0	4	11	14	6	4-0	0-2	5-3	

GROUP C MATCHDAY 1
Al Gharafa, Doha
8-03-2006, 18:30, 1 500, Al Hamdan KSA

Al Gharafa 0

A.Al Kabbi - H.Shami, Mugib●, B.Mohmed - Lawrence●, El Assas●●60, S.Al Shammeri●, Soud Sabah (M.Al Haj 46) - Sergio●83, Jamal Johar●, Aala Hubail

Saba Battery 2
Ali Daei 2 ⁴⁸ ⁵³

A.Tolja - Bakhtiari, Golmohammadi, Navazi, Asadi● - Akbari (Mohammadi 79), Mahdizadeh, Beigi - A.Daei, Zolrahmi● (Ghasemian 64), Alen● (Zarei 85)

GROUP C MATCHDAY 1
Khaled Ibn Al Waleed, Homs
8-03-2006, 19:00, 25 000, Mujghef JOR

Al Karama 2
Al Hamwi ⁴⁵, Ahmad Turkmani ⁸⁷

M.Balhous● - H.Abbas, J.Kassab, A.Kojah● - S.Atassi (N.Sibaee 85), J.Hussen, A.Rifaee, M.Hamwi● (B.Abduldaym● 91), E.Mundo, A.Jineyat - A.Turkmani● (F.Oudeh 95)

Al Wahda 1
Ismail Matar ¹³

A.Baset● - S.Abdulla (S.Al Menhali 89), B.Bajic, A.Omar, S.Zayed● - A.Tawfeeq (A.Al Noubi 80), M.Fahed, A.Al Jenaibi - I.Matar, N.Mauro●, S.Mitrovic

---

GROUP C MATCHDAY 2
Al Nahyan, Abu Dhabi
22-03-2006, 19:20, 9 000, Ebrahim BHR

Al Wahda 2
Ismail Matar ²⁷, Mauro ⁴⁵

A.Baset - B.Bajic, A.Omar, S.Zayed (J.Ali 78), S.Basheer - A.Salam●, A.Al Noubi●, A.Al Jenaibi - I.Matar (A.Haidar 46+), S.Al Menhali (A.Hasan 92+), N.Mauro

Al Gharafa 0

A.Al Kabbi - H.Shami, Mugib, B.Mohmed●, Mustafa - Lawrence, S.Al Shammeri, M.Al Haj, Ali Fatah● (A.Al Mazroei 83) - Jamal Johar (M.Al Allaq 17), Aala Hubail●

GROUP C MATCHDAY 2
Saba Battery, Tehran
22-03-2006, 16:00, 5 000, Salman IRQ

Saba Battery 1
Ali Daei ¹⁷

A.Tolja - Bakhtiari, Golmohammadi, Navazi, Asadi - Akbari, Mahdizadeh (M.Hoseiny 81), Beigi - A.Daei, Zolrahmi (Mohammadi 75), Alen● (Ghasemian 61)

Al Karama 2
Al Hussen ⁶⁴, Mohanad Ibrahem ⁸⁹

A.Hafz - N.Sibaee (B.Abduldaym 84), H.Abbas, J.Kassab, A.Kojah - J.Hussen (F.Oudeh 89), A.Rifaee, M.Hamwi, E.Mundo, A.Jineyat - A.Turkmani● (M.Ibrahem 77)

GROUP C MATCHDAY 3
Al Gharafa, Doha
12-04-2006, 18:30, 1 000, Salman IRQ

Al Gharafa 4
Ala'a Hubail 2 ⁶⁰ᵖ ⁷¹, Ismail Ali ⁸¹, Lawrence ⁸⁹

A.Al Kabbi - H.Shami (Ali Fatah 90+1), Mugib, Shaheen Ali (Ishmaiel Ali 70), B.Mohmed●, Mustafa - Lawrence, S.Al Shammeri, M.Al Haj - Aala Hubail● (A.Al Mazroei 90+1)

Al Karama 0

A.Hafz - H.Abbas, J.Kassab, B.Abduldaym (F.Oudeh 89), A.Kojah (H.Masree 81) - J.Hussen, A.Rifaee, M.Hamwi, E.Mundo (M.Abdulkader 73), A.Jineyat - M.Ibrahem●

GROUP C MATCHDAY 3
Saba Battery, Tehran
12-04-2006, 16:00, 6 500, Irmatov UZB

Saba Battery 2
Ghasemian ²⁴, Akbari ²⁷

A.Tolja - Bakhtiari, Golmohammadi, Navazi, Asadi - Akbari, Ghasemian (Mahdizadeh 66), Beigi, Bayat (Zarei● 71) - A.Daei, Alen

Al Wahda 2
Mauro ⁶⁰, Slavisa Mitrovic ⁶¹

A.Baset - B.Bajic, A.Omar, S.Basheer - A.Salam, M.Fahed, A.Haidar, A.Al Jenaibi● - I.Matar (A.Al Noubi 93), N.Mauro, S.Mitrovic

---

GROUP C MATCHDAY 4
Khaled Ibn Al Waleed, Homs
26-04-2006, 20:00, 35 000, Shaban KUW

Al Karama 3
Ahmad Turkmani 2 ⁶⁷ ⁷⁴, Rifaee ⁸³ᵖ

M.Balhous - H.Abbas, J.Kassab●, A.Kojah● - S.Atassi (B.Abduldaym 83), J.Hussen, A.Rifaee●, M.Hamwi● (F.Oudeh 88), E.Mundo, A.Jineyat - A.Turkmani● (M.Ibrahem 93)

Al Gharafa 1
Otman El Assas ⁶⁵

A.Al Kabbi - H.Shami, Mugib●, Shaheen Ali (Ali Fatah 82), Mustafa● - Lawrence, El Assas, S.Al Shammeri, M.Al Haj● (A.Al Mazroei 87) - Ismaiel Ali●, Sergio

---

GROUP C MATCHDAY 4
Al Nahyan, Abu Dhabi
26-04-2006, 19:40, 8 000, Abdul Bashir SIN

Al Wahda 2
Golmohammadi OG ⁴⁰, Fahed Masoud ⁸⁶

A.Baset - B.Bajic (A.Al Noubi 79), A.Omar, S.Basheer - A.Salam●, M.Fahed, A.Haidar, A.Al Jenaibi - I.Matar●, N.Mauro (A.Tawfeeq 90), S.Mitrovic (S.Al Menhali 65)

Saba Battery 4
Alen ²⁹, Beigi 2 ³³ ⁵², Bakhtiari ⁴⁸

A.Tolja - Bakhtiari, Golmohammadi, Navazi (Mahdizadeh 79), Asadi● - Akbari●, Yousefi● (Bayat 83), Zarei●, Beigi - A.Daei, Alen (Daghigi 69)

GROUP C MATCHDAY 5
Saba Battery, Tehran
3-05-2006, 16:00, 5 000, Ebrahim BHR

Saba Battery 4
Alen ⁷², Ali Daei 2 ⁷⁷ ⁸², Golmohammadi ⁹²⁺

A.Tolja - Bakhtiari, Navazi - Akbari (K.Mahmoudi 90), Yousefi (Daghigi 80), Mahdizadeh, Beigi, Bayat - A.Daei, Alen (Soltani 84)

Al Gharafa 1
Al Mazroai ⁵⁵

M.Al Gamdi● - H.Shami (M.Al Mazroai● 46), Shaheen Ali, N.Al Enzi, B.Mohmed (Mustafa 61) - S.Al Shammeri, M.Al Haj●, Ali Fatah - Ismaiel Ali, A.Al Mazroei (F.Al Naemi 76), F.Al Shammeri

---

GROUP C MATCHDAY 5
Al Nahyan, Abu Dhabi
3-05-2006, 19:40, 7 000, Najm LIB

Al Wahda 4
Hasan ¹⁹, Tawfeeq ²¹, M.Ali ⁶⁴, Al Menhali ⁸⁴

A.Baset - S.Abdulla (Y.Mater 77), J.Ali, B.Bajic●, M.Ali, S.Zayed, A.Talal● - A.Tawfeeq, A.Al Noubi (A.Al Hajeri 86), A.Hasan - S.Al Menhali●

Al Karama 2
Rifaee ³²ᵖ, Jineyat ⁴⁰

M.Balhous - N.Sibaee (B.Abduldaym 67), H.Abbas, J.Kassab - J.Hussen, A.Rifaee, E.Mundo (M.Ead● 67), F.Oudeh, A.Jineyat - A.Turkmani (M.Ibrahem 75)

GROUP C MATCHDAY 6
Al Gharafa, Doha
17-05-2006, 18:30, 200, Al Ghamdi KSA

Al Gharafa 5
Ala'a Hubail 3 ²³ ⁶⁶ ⁷³, Al Shammari ²⁹, Ricardo ⁷²ᵖ

Abdulaziz - H.Shami (A.Al Hajeri 45), Mugib, Shaheen Ali●, B.Mohmed, Mustafa● - Lawrence●, S.Al Shammeri - Ismaiel Ali, F.Al Shammeri (Sergio 52), Aala Hubail (A.Al Mazroai 88)

Al Wahda 3
Hasan ¹⁵, Al Menhali 2 ⁶⁰ ⁸⁹

A.Baset - J.Ali●, B.Bajic, M.Ali, S.Zayed, A.Talal (A.Eisa 80) - A.Tawfeeq, A.Al Noubi (A.Al Hajeri 45), M.Othman, A.Hasan - S.Al Menhali (A.Al Menhali 58)

GROUP C MATCHDAY 6
Khaled Ibn Al Waleed, Homs
17-05-2006, 20:00, 35 000, Al Hilali OMA

Al Karama 1
Rifaee ³¹

M.Balhous - N.Sibaee, H.Abbas, J.Kassab, A.Kojah - J.Hussen, A.Rifaee, M.Hamwi (M.Ibrahem 83), E.Mundo, Jineyat - A.Turkmani (A.Akari 8) (B.Abduldaym 92+)

Saba Battery 0

Karamollahi - Bakhtiari, Golmohammadi, Asadi - Akbari (Mahdizadeh 90 +2), Yousefi (Navazi 81), Zarei●, Beigi●, Bayat● (Margousi 80) - A.Daei, Alen

GROUP D

		Pl	W	D	L	F	A	Pts	KSA	QAT	IRQ	KUW
Al Shabab	KSA	6	4	1	1	9	6	13		0-0	2-1	2-0
Al Sadd	QAT	6	4	1	1	13	5	13	2-3		3-0	4-1
Al Quwa Al Jawiya	IRQ	6	2	0	4	5	9	6	0-2	0-2		3-0
Al Arabi	KUW	6	1	0	5	5	12	3	3-0	1-2	0-1	

GROUP D MATCHDAY 1
Sabah Al Salem, Kuwait City
8-03-2006, 18:30, 3 000, Torky IRN

Al Arabi   **0**

Yousef - M Essa, Aziz, A.Alanezi (Aldhuwaihi 67), F.Dabes• - Jarragh•, Alshuwaye, Malek, Talal• - Khaled (Almutawa 87), Alkhatib

Al Quwa Al Jawiya   **1**
Safwan [76]

K.Oasam - A.Mukhalad, M.Fareed, H.Ali, R.Hader•, KH.Muaad, SH.Radhi - A.Safwan (A.Ahmed 83), A.Hussein• - S.Louai (D.Waleed 86), M.Ali• (S.Hussein 90+3)

GROUP D MATCHDAY 1
King Fahd International, Riyadh
8-03-2006, 20:30, 5 000, Al Saeedi UAE

Al Shabab   **0**

Khojah - Abdulmohsen, Sadeeq, Al Bahari (Hassan 46), Abdoh (Bashar 69), Zaid• - Ahmed•, Al Muwaine, Nashat - Attram, Fisal (Nassir 75)

Al Sadd   **0**

Mohamed - Jafal, Al Berik•, Kone• - Ali (Al Dahri 78), Rizik, Al Hamad, Magid• (Mohammed 86), Rabia - Tenorio, Felipe (Hussain• 66)

GROUP D MATCHDAY 2
Al Sadd Sports Club, Doha
22-03-2006, 18:30, 3 000, Al Ghatrifi OMA

Al Sadd   **4**
Al Khalfan [32], Tenorio [51p], Jafal [61], Yusef [73]

Mohamed - Al Kuwari, Bilal• (Jafal 55), Kone - Rizik•, Al Hamad, Al Khalfan, Rabia (Al Berik 70) - Tenorio (Yusef 63), Felipe, Afef

Al Arabi   **1**
Alkhatib [48]

Yousef (Ghanem 65) - M.Essa, Musaed, A.Alanezi• - Jarragh, Alshuwaye, Malek•, Talal - Khaled, Alkhatib, K.Kalaf

GROUP D MATCHDAY 2
Municipal, Tripoli
22-03-2006, 14:30, 500, Marshoud JOR

Al Quwa Al Jawiya   **0**

K.Oasam• - A.Mukhalad, M.Fareed, H.Ali•, R.Hader, KH.Muaad (A.Ahmed 51), SH.Radhi (M.Muhand 78) - A.Safwan (KH.Ghanm 71), A.Hussein - S.Louai, M.Ali

Al Shabab   **2**
Attram 2 [36p 45]

Khojah - Abdulmohsen, Sadeeq•, Al Bahari, Abdoh (Bashar 68), Zaid - Ahmed, Al Muwaine, Nashat (Naji 81) - Attram, Fisal (Abdullah 87)

GROUP D MATCHDAY 3
Sabah Al Salem, Kuwait City
12-04-2006, 18:45, 3 000, Ebrahim BHR

Al Arabi   **3**
Alkhatib 2 [21 87], Jarragh [68]

Yousef - M Essa (A.Muosa 83), Aziz (Fahad 71), Musaed, F.Dabes - Jarragh, Malek, Talal - Khaled, Alkhatib, Raja• (K.Kalaf• 35)

Al Shabab   **0**

Khojah - Abdulmohsen, Sadeeq, Hassan• (Al Bahari 62), Zaid - Ahmed, Al Muwaine, Nashat (Al Halail 84) - Naji (Nassir 46), Attram, Fisal

GROUP D MATCHDAY 3
Municipal, Tripoli
12-04-2006, 16:30, 300, Marshoud JOR

Al Quwa Al Jawiya   **0**

H.Ali - A.Mukhalad, H.Ali, KH.Muaad•, SH.Radhi - D.Waleed, KH.Ali, A.Alaa (A.Safwan 67), A.Hussein - S.Louai, M.Ali

Al Sadd   **2**
Tenorio [58], Magid [87]

Mohamed - Al Berik, Kone - Ali• (Al Kuwari 83), Rizik, Al Hamad, Rabia - Tenorio, Felipe, Afef (Magid 75), Yusef (Hussain 46)

GROUP D MATCHDAY 4
King Fahd International, Riyadh
26-04-2006, 20:45, 1 500, Kousa SYR

Al Shabab   **2**
Nassir [11], Attram [13]

Khojah - Abdulmohsen (Sadeeq 46), Hamdan, Abdoh•, Zaid (Al Astaa 74), Sanad - Ahmed, Al Muwaine (Mansour• 57), Nashat - Attram, Nassir

Al Arabi   **0**

Yousef - M Essa, Aziz, Musaed, F.Dabes (A.Alanezi 66) - Alshuwaye (Ashknany 77), Malek, Talal• - Khaled, Alkhatib, Saud• (Almutawa 51)

GROUP D MATCHDAY 4
Al Sadd Sports Club, Doha
26-04-2006, 18:45, 2 500, Mansour LIB

Al Sadd   **3**
Jafal [23], Felipe [83], Magid [90]

Mohamed - Jafal, Al Berik, Kone - Rizik, Hussain, Al Khalfan (Ali 64), Rabia - Tenorio (Magid 88), Felipe, Afef (Al Hamad 75)

Al Quwa Al Jawiya   **0**

H.Ali - H.Ali, R.Hader (A.Mukhalad 78), KH.Muaad, SH.Radhi - KH.Ali, M.Muhand, K.Homoodi, A.Alaa (D.Waleed 46), A.Safwana (A.Hussein 65) - S.Louai•

GROUP D MATCHDAY 5
Municipal, Tripoli
3-05-2006, 16:30, 1 000, Saidov UZB

Al Quwa Al Jawiya   **3**
Safwan 2 [31 45], Homoodi [74]

K.Oasam - A.Mukhalad (KH.Muaad 32), R.Hader, SH.Radhi (S.Hussain 89) - D.Waleed•, KH.Ali, K.Homoodi, A.Safwana, A.Hussein - M.Ali, KH.Ghanm (M.Fareed 73)

Al Arabi   **0**

Yousef - Aziz, A.Alanezi, F.Dabes - Ashknany (Aldhuwaihi 64), Khaled (Alqhareeb 46), Malek•, Fahad, A.Muosa - K.Kalaf, Almutawa (Alkhatib 46)

GROUP D MATCHDAY 5
Al Sadd Sports Club, Doha
3-05-2006, 19:00, 3 000, Maidin SIN

Al Sadd   **2**
Tenorio 2 [83 90]

Mohamed - Jafal, Al Berik, Kone• - Ali• (Felipe 46), Rizik•, Hussain•, Magid (Al Khalfan 67), Talal (Afef 59), Rabia - Tenorio

Al Shabab   **3**
Nashat [22], Nassir [39], Attram [56]

Khojah• - Sadeeq, Hamdan, Hassan, Abdoh• (Mansour 58), Zaid• - Ahmed, Al Muwaine, Nashat• - Attram (Al Obili 85), Nassir (Fisal 69)

GROUP D MATCHDAY 6
Sabah Al Salem, Kuwait City
17-05-2006, 21:15, 250, Al Saeedi UAE

Al Arabi   **1**
Alqhareeb [34]

Yousef - Aziz, Musaed, A.Alanezi, F.Dabes••71, Alqhareeb (Fahad 68) - Ashknany•, A.Mousa (K.Kalaf 80), Talal - Alkhatib, Raja (Almutwa 66)

Al Sadd   **2**
Felipe [63], Yusef [79]

Mohamed - Jafal, Al Kuwari• (Yusef 66), Al Berik - Al Hamad, Magid, Al Khalfan (Jadoua 89), Talal• - Felipe•, Afef (Al Dahri 82)

GROUP D MATCHDAY 6
King Fahd International, Riyadh
17-05-2006, 21:15

Al Shabab   **2**
Nassir [41], Nashat [69]

Khojah - Al Astaa, Sadeeq (Naji 65), Hamdan, Hassan - Mansour, Ahmed, Al Muwaine, Nashat• - Attram (Al Bahari 72), Nassir (Sanad 89)

Al Quwa Al Jawiya   **1**
Khodair [35]

K.Oasam - M.Fareed•, H.Ali, KH.Muaad (A.Alaa 85), SH.Radhi (R.Hader 59) - D.Waleed•, KH.Ali, K.Homoodi (S.Hussain 74) - S.Louai, M.Ali, KH.Ghanm

GROUP E

		Pl	W	D	L	F	A	Pts	KOR	CHN	JPN	VIE
Jeonbuk Hyundai Motors	KOR	6	4	1	1	11	5	13		3-1	3-2	3-0
Dalian Shide	CHN	6	4	0	2	7	6	12	1-0		2-0	1-0
Gamba Osaka	JPN	6	3	1	2	26	7	10	1-1	3-0		15-0
Da Nang	VIE	6	0	0	6	1	27	0	0-1	0-2	1-5	

GROUP E MATCHDAY 1
Chi Lang, Da Nang
8-03-2006, 16:00, 10 000, Lee Gi Young KOR

Da Nang 0

Vo Van Hahn - Ma Tri, Nguyen Huu Hung● (Pham Minh Duc 54), Le Quang Cuong, Nguyen Manh Dung, Nguyen Binh Minh● - Le Hong Minh, Truong Quang Tuan (Giang Thanh Thong 61) - Phan Thanh Phuc●, Tran Van Hung (Le Huynh Duc 52), Nuro

Dalian Shide 2
Zuo Jie [39], Ji Ming Yi [48]

Chen Dong - Zhai Yan Peng, Zhang Yaokun, Wang Sheng, Ji Ming Yi, Liu Yu● - Yankovic, Hu Zhao Jun (Zhao Xuri 70), Zhang Yalin (Quan Lei 46) - Pantelic (Yang Song 74), Zou Jie

GROUP E MATCHDAY 1
Jeonju World Cup Stadium, Jeonju
8-03-2006, 19:00, 2 700, Shield AUS

Jeonbuk Hyundai Motors 3
Milton [30p], Kim Hyeung Bum 2 [71 85]

Lee Kwang Suk - Choi Chul Soon●, Choi Jin Cheul, Kim Young Sun, Kim Hyun Su (Kim Hyeung Bum 62) - Chung Jung Kwan (Jang Ji Hyun 21), Botti (Lee Hyun Seung 79), Yeom Kihun, Kim Jung Kyum - Milton, Zecarlo

Gamba Osaka 2
Endo [16], Magno Alves [59]

Fujigaya - Sidiclei, Yamaguchi, Kaji (Miyamoto 63) - Endo, Fernandinho (Maeda 63), Futagawa (Bando 87), Ienaga, Myojin●, Hashimoto - Magno Alves

GROUP E MATCHDAY 2
Jin Zhou, Dalian
22-03-2006, 14:30, 12 000, Irmatov UZB

Dalian Shide 1
Zou Jie [41]

Chen Dong - Zhai Yan Peng, Zhang Yaokun, Wang Sheng, Ji Ming Yi●, Liu Yu - Zhao Xuri (Liu Cheng 83), Yankovic●, Hu Zhao Jun - Pantelic● (Quan Lei 79), Zou Jie

Jeonbuk Hyundai Motors 0

Lee Kwang Suk - Jung Inwhan (Kim Hyeung Bum 52), Choi Jin Cheul●, Kim Hyun Su, Kim Ihno - Botti, Yeom Kihun, Kim Jung Kyum, Choo Woon Ki - Cho Jin Soo, Zecarlo (Milton 64)

GROUP E MATCHDAY 2
Expo '70, Osaka
22-03-2006, 19:00, 3 832, Abdul Bashir SIN

Gamba Osaka 15
Endo [7p], Fernandinho 4 [19 20 36 77], Bando [24]
Alves 4 [41 48 68 85], Maeda 2 [76 79], Miyamoto [81]
Hashimoto [84], Ienaga [90]

Fujigaya - Sidiclei (Futagawa 46), Miyamoto, Yamaguchi, Kaji - Endo, Fernandinho, Ienaga, Myojin (Hashimoto 46) - Magno Alves, Bando (Maeda 65)

Da Nang 0

Vo Van Hahn - Ma Tri, Nguyen Huu Hung (Le Huynh Duc 46), Pham Hung Dung, Nguyen Manh Dung, Nguyen Binh Minh (Le Quang Cuong 79) - Giang Thanh Thong, Le Hong Minh - Truong Quang Tuan - Tran Van Hung, Nuro (Pham Minh Duc 46)

GROUP E MATCHDAY 3
Jeonju World Cup Stadium, Jeonju
12-04-2006, 19:00, 750, Tongkhan THA

Jeonbuk Hyundai Motors 3
Milton [24], Kim Hyeung Bum [41], Botti [82]

Kwoun Sun Tae - Choi Chul Soon, Choi Jin Cheul (Chung Jung Kwan 46), Kim Hyun Su, Wang Jung Hyun - Yeom Kihun, Kim Jung Kyum, Kim Hyeung Bum, Jang Ji Hyun (Botti 46) - Milton (Lee Hyun Seung 61) Zecarlo

Da Nang 0

Vo Van Hahn - Ma Tri, Pham Hung Dung, Le Quang Cuong (Tran Van Hung 22), Nguyen Manh Dung, Nguyen Binh Minh, Hoang Hai Thuong● - Giang Thanh Thong (Pham Minh Duc 46), Le Hong Minh● - Phan Thanh Phuc (Truong Quang Tuan 83), Le Huynh Duc

GROUP E MATCHDAY 3
Expo '70, Osaka
12-04-2006, 19:00, 5 555, Shield AUS

Gamba Osaka 3
Endo [48p], Magno Alves 2 [56 71]

Fujigaya - Sidiclei (Aoki 81), Miyamoto, Yamaguchi, Kaji - Endo, Fernandinho (Bando 73), Ienaga, Maeda (Futagawa 46), Hashimoto - Magno Alves

Dalian Shide 0

Chen Dong - Zhang Yaokun, Wang Sheng●, Ji Ming Yi, Liu Yu - Zhao Xuri●, Yankovic (T.Zhu 68), Hu Zhao Jun, Zhao Ming Jian● (Quan Lei 63) - Pantelic (Yan Song 61), Zou Jie

GROUP E MATCHDAY 4
Chi Lang, Da Nang
26-04-2006, 16:00, 4 000, Sarkar IND

Da Nang 0

Tran Duc Cuong - Ma Tri● (Rogerio 68), Pham Hung Dung, Nguyen Manh Dung, Pham Minh Duc, Nguyen Binh Minh, Hoang Hai Thuong - Giang Thanh Thong (Le Hyun Duc 46), Le Hong Minh - Phan Thanh Phuc (Truong Quang Tuan 46), Tran Van Hung

Jeonbuk Hyundai Motors 1
Ze Carlo [21]

Lee Kwang Suk - Choi Chul Soon●, Kim Inho, Wang Jung Hyun - Botti, Choo Woon Ki, Kim Kyung Ryang, Lee Hyun Seung, Kim Young Sin (Chun Jae Woon 53) - Zecarlo●, Jung Soo Jong (Kim Jong Chun 52)

GROUP E MATCHDAY 4
Jin Zhou, Dalian
26-04-2006, 19:00, 20 000, Mohd Salleh MAS

Dalian Shide 2
Hu Zhaojun [19], Zhang Yaokun [48]

Chen Dong - Zhang Yaokun, Wang Sheng, Ji Ming Yi, Liu Yu - Zhao Xuri, Yankovic (Zhang Peng 83), Yan Song (Liu Cheng 86), Quan Lei, Hu Zhao Jun - Zou Jie

Gamba Osaka 0

Fujigaya - Sidiclei, Miyamoto, Yamaguchi, Kaji - Endo, Fernandinho (Nakayama 66), Ienaga●, Maeda (Bando 59), Hashimoto - Magno Alves

GROUP E MATCHDAY 5
Expo '70, Osaka
3-05-2006, 14:00, 12 470, Breeze AUS

Gamba Osaka 1
Yamaguchi [73]

Fujigaya - Sidiclei, Miyamoto (Bando 83), Yamaguchi, Kaji - Endo, Fernandinho (Nakayama 46), Ienaga, Maeda (Futagawa 35), Hashimoto - Magno Alves

Jeonbuk Hyundai Motors 1
Cho Jin Soo [45]

Kwoun Sun Tae - Choi Jin Cheul, Kim Hyun Su, Kim Inho●, Wang Jung Hyun - Chung Jung Kwan, Botti, Jeon Kwang Hwan (Kim Young Sun 83), Kim Jung Kyum - Cho Jin Soo (Yeom Kihun 59), Zecarlo● (Milton 64)

GROUP E MATCHDAY 5
Jin Zhou, Dalian
3-05-2006, 19:00, 10, 0 ‖ Son PRK

Dalian Shide 1
Liu Cheng [3]

Chen Dong - Tang Tian, Liu Cheng, Zhai Yan Peng, Ji Ming Yi - Yankovic, Quan Lei, Hu Zhao Jun (Yan Song 70), Zhou Ming Jian - Zou Jie (Wang Shouting 57), Zhang Peng

Da Nang 0

Tran Duc Cuong - Nguyen Huu Hung, Pham Hung Dung, Nguyen Manh Dung, Pham Minh Duc (Giang Thanh Thong 82), Nguyen Binh Minh, Hoang Hai Thuong - Rogerio● (Ma Tri 87), Le Hong Minh●, Truong Quang Tuuan - Le Hyun Duc (Phan Thanh Phuc 72)

GROUP E MATCHDAY 6
Chi Lang, Da Nang
17-05-2006, 16:00, 5 000, Abdul Bashir SIN

Da Nang 1
Rogerio [72p]

Tran Duc Cuong - Ma Tri, Nguyen Huu Hung●, Pham Hung Dung●90, Nguyen Manh Dung, Pham Minh Duc, Nguyen Binh Minh (Hoang Hai Thuong 78) - Rogerio, Truong Quang Tuuan● - Phan Thanh Phuc (Giang Thanh Thong 66), Le Hyun Duc●

Gamba Osaka 5
Fernandinho 2 [21 45], Magno Alves [35]
Futagawa [52], Yamaguchi [75]

Fujigaya (Matsuyo 64) - Sidiclei, Yamaguchi, Aoki - Fernandinho, Futagawa (Miki 79), Ienaga, Myojin, Hashimoto - Magno Alves (Nakayama 64), Bando

GROUP E MATCHDAY 6
Jeonju World Cup Stadium, Jeonju
17-05-2006, 19:00, 5 400, Mohd Salleh MAS

Jeonbuk Hyundai Motors 3
Kim Hyeung Bum 2 [67 88], Wang Jung Hyun [81]

Kwoun Sun Tae - Kim Young Sun, Kim Hyun Su, Kim Inho, Wang Jung Hyun - Chung Jung Kwan (Choi Chul Soon 46), Botti (Milton● 61), Yeom Kihun (Lee Hyun Seung 54), Jeon Kwang Hwan, Kim Hyeung Bum - Cho Jin Soo

Dalian Shide 1
Zou Jie [58]

Chen Dong - Zhai Yan Peng (Liu Cheng 50), Zhang Yaokun, Wang Sheng, Ji Ming Yi - Zhao Xuri, Yankovic (Yan Song 76), Quan Lei, Hu Zhao Jun - Pantelic, Zou Jie● (Zhang Peng 64)

GROUP F

		Pl	W	D	L	F	A	Pts	KOR	JPN
Ulsan Hyundai Horang-i	KOR	2	2	0	0	3	0	6		1-0
Tokyo Verdy 1969	JPN	2	0	0	2	0	3	0	0-2	

GROUP F MATCHDAY 1
National Stadium, Tokyo
8-03-2006, 19:00, 4 436, Mohd Salleh MAS

Tokyo Verdy 1969   0

Mizuhara - Hagimura•, Togawa, Yanagisawa (Lio 74) - Sugawara, Anailson, Ono, Kanazawa• (Nagai 82), Hiroyama (Fujita 74) - Basilio•, Saito

Ulsan Hyundai Horang-i   2
Choi Sung Kuk [57], Machado [71]

Kim Jee Hyuk - Vinicius (Lee Sang Ho 85), Park Byung Gyu, Cho Se Kwon (Jang Sang Won 70), You Kyoung Youl, Park Dong Hyuk, Byun Sung Hwan - Park Kyu Seon•, Lee Chun Soo (Leandro 79) - Machado, Choi Sung Kuk

GROUP F MATCHDAY 2
Ulsan Munsu, Ulsan
22-03-2006, 19:30, 3 150, Sun Baejie CHN

Ulsan Hyundai Horang-i   1
Lee Chun Soo [43]

Kim Jee Hyuk - Vinicius, Park Byung Gyu, You Kyoung Youl•69, Park Dong Hyuk (Seo Deok Kyu 64), Jang Sang Won - Lee Ho, Lee Sang Ho, Kim Young Sam - Lee Chun Soo (Choi Kwang Hee 90), Machado• (Byun Sung Hwan• 75)

Tokyo Verdy 1969   0

Takagi - Hagimura, Togawa•, Dedimar (Hiroyama 67), Aoba• (Fujita 51) - Ohashi, Anailson, Ono, Kanazawa - Lio (Saito 67), Hiramoto

GROUP G

		Pl	W	D	L	F	A	Pts	CHN	VIE
Shanghai Shenhua	CHN	2	2	0	0	7	7	6		3-1
Dong Tam	VIE	2	0	0	2	3	3	0	2-4	

GROUP G MATCHDAY 1
Yuan Shen, Shanghai
8-03-2006, 19:35, 7 000, Kim Dong Jin KOR

Shanghai Shenhua   3
Wang Ke [8], Xie Hui 2 [11] [51]

Yu Weiliang - Li Yinan•, Du Wei, Cheng Liang (Zheng Kewei 84), Li Weifeng•••65 - Xiao Zhanbo, Jovanovic, Wang Ke (Sun Xiang 71), Yu Tao, Sun Ji - Xie Hui (Gao Lin 67)

Dong Tam   1
Antonio Rodrigues [66p]

Santos - Nguyen Van Hung, Bruno•, Luu Minh Tri, Vo Phi Thuong - Nguyen Minh Phuong•, Phan Thanh Giang, Truong Van Tam (Nguyen Tuan Phong 58), Nguyen Hoang Thuong• - Antonio Rodrigues, Nguyen Ngoc Thanh• (Nguyen Viet Thang 46)

GROUP G MATCHDAY 2
Long An, Long An
3-05-2006, 16:00, 5 000, Abdul Bashir SIN

Dong Tam   2
Antonio Rodrigues [29], Fabio [61]

Santos - Nguyen Van Hung, Bruno - Nguyen Minh Phuong, Phan Van Tai Em, Nguyen Tuan Phong (Vo Cong Thanh• 68), Phan Thanh Giang, Nguyen Thanh Truc (Luu Minh Tri 77), Nguyen Hoang Thuong• - Nguyen Viet Thang, Antonio Rodrigues

Shanghai Shenhua   4
Goa Lin 3 [42] [90] [93+], Yu Tao [65]

Yu Weiliang - Du Wei•, Ng Waichiu, Li Chengming•, Chen Lei - Xiao Zhanbo (Zheng Kewei 46), Yu Tao, Shen Longyuan (Sun Ji 61), Wang Hongliang• - Xie Hui•, Mao Jian Qing (Gao Lin 42)

AL AIN

Goalkeepers		
1	Mutaz Abdulla	UAE
12	Waleed Salem	UAE
22	Zakareya Ahmed	UAE
30	Abdulla Sultan	UAE
Defenders		
2	Mahboub Juma	UAE
3	Juma Khater	UAE
4	Musallem Fayez	UAE
6	Ali Msarri	UAE
7	Ali Ahmed	UAE
16	Abdulla Ali	UAE
17	Saleh Obaid	UAE
19	Fahad Ali	UAE
25	Humaid Fakher	UAE
26	Abdulla Mousa	UAE
28	Fawzi Fayez	UAE
29	Juma Abdulla	UAE
Midfielders		
5	Sultan Rashed	UAE
10	Ibrahim Diaky	CIV
13	Rami Yaslam	UAE
18	Ahmed Khalfan	UAE
20	Helal Saeed	UAE
21	Gharib Harib	UAE
23	Shehab Ahmed	UAE
24	Subait Khater	UAE
Forwards		
8	Nenad Jestrovic	SCG
9	Faisal Ali	UAE
11	Kelly	BRA
14	Nassib Ishaq	UAE
15	Nasser Khamis	UAE
27	Salem Abdulla	UAE

AL ARABI

Goalkeepers		
1	Yousef Al Thuwaini	KUW
22	Falah Dabsha	KUW
26	Muhamaad Ghanem	KUW
Defenders		
2	Muhammad Issa	KUW
3	Abdulaziz Fadhel	KUW
5	Musaed Abdullah	KUW
6	Abdullah Layesh	KUW
12	Ahmad Saiedi	KUW
23	Abdullah Boloshi	KUW
27	Fahad Dabes	KUW
30	Hussain Al Qhareeb	KUW
Midfielders		
4	Mohammad Jarragh	KUW
8	Homoud Majed	KUW
11	Mohammad Ashkanani	KUW
13	Khaled Nassar	KUW
15	Nawaf Al Shuwaye	KUW
16	Mubarak Kamshad	KUW
18	Jasem Al Owisi	KUW
19	Malek Al Qallaf	KUW
20	Fahad Al Farhan	KUW
21	Ahmad Mousa	KUW
25	Talal Khalfan	OMA
28	Meshal Al Thuwaini	KUW
Forwards		
7	Khaled Abdulkuddous	KUW
9	Ahmad Al Dhuwaihi	KUW
10	Firas Al Khatib	SYR
14	Saud Sweid	KUW
17	Khaled Khalaf	KUW
24	Raja Rafe	SYR
29	Abdullah Al Mutawa	KUW

CHONBUK

Goalkeepers		
1	Lee Kwang Suk	KOR
21	Kwoun Sun Tae	KOR
23	Lee Kwang Hyeon	KOR
27	Sung Kyung Il	KOR
Defenders		
2	Choi Chul Soon	KOR
3	Jung In Whan	KOR
4	Choi Jin Cheul	KOR
5	Kim Young Sun	KOR
6	Kim Hyun Su	KOR
16	Chun Jae Woon	KOR
20	Kim In Ho	KOR
28	Wang Jung Hyun	KOR
29	Kim Jong Chun	KOR
Midfielders		
7	Kim Jae Young	KOR
8	Chung Jung Kwan	KOR
10	Botti	BRA
11	Yeom Ki Hun	KOR
12	Jeon Kwang Hwan	KOR
17	Choo Woon Ki	KOR
19	Kim Kyung Ryang	KOR
22	Kim Hyeung Bum	KOR
24	Lee Hyun Seung	KOR
26	Jang Ji Hyun	KOR
30	Kim Young Sin	KOR
Forwards		
9	Milton Rodriguez	COL
14	Cho Jin Soo	KOR
15	Ze Carlo	BRA
18	Park Jung Hwan	KOR
25	Jung Soo Jong	KOR

DALIAN

Goalkeepers		
1	Chen Dong	CHN
22	Yu Ziqian	CHN
23	Sun Shoubo	CHN
Defenders		
2	Tang Tian	CHN
3	Liu Cheng	CHN
4	Zhai Yanpeng	CHN
5	Feng Xiaoting	CHN
6	Zhang Yaokun	CHN
12	Wang Sheng	CHN
16	Ji Mingyi	CHN
20	Liu Yu	CHN
21	Tan Wangsong	CHN
24	Zhang Hongyang	CHN
28	Yan Shipeng	CHN
29	Lu Qiang	CHN
Midfielders		
7	Zhao Xuri	CHN
9	Zoran Jankovic	BUL
11	Yan Song	CHN
13	Quan Lei	CHN
14	Hu Zhaojun	CHN
15	Zhao Mingjian	CHN
25	Wang Shouting	CHN
26	Zhang Yalin	CHN
27	Didier Njewel	CMR
Forwards		
8	Zhu Ting	CHN
10	Miodrag Pantelic	SCG
17	Zou Jie	CHN
18	Zhang Peng	CHN
19	Ma Shuai	CHN
30	Guo Feng	CHN

DA NANG

Goalkeepers		
1	Vo Van Hanh	VIE
25	Tran Duc Cuong	VIE
26	Nguyen Thanh Binh	VIE
Defenders		
2	Ma Tri	VIE
3	Thai Quang Vu	VIE
4	Nguyen Huu Hung	VIE
5	Pham Hung Dung	VIE
12	Le Quang Cuong	VIE
15	Nguyen Manh Dung	VIE
16	Rogerio	BRA
19	Pham Minh Duc	VIE
21	Nguyen Binh Minh	VIE
22	Hoang Hai Thuong	VIE
Midfielders		
11	Giang Thanh Thong	VIE
17	Le Hong Minh	VIE
18	Truong Quang Tuan	VIE
Forwards		
7	Phan Thanh Phuc	VIE
9	Tran Van Hung	VIE
10	Le Huynh Duc	VIE
23	Nuro Amiro Tualibudine	MOZ

DONG TAM

Goalkeepers		
1	Santos	BRA
25	Nguyen Tien Phong	VIE
26	Nguyen Huynh Q Cuong	VIE
27	Nguyen Thanh Tuan	VIE
Defenders		
2	Tran Nguyen Nhan	VIE
3	Phan Van Giau	VIE
4	Nguyen Van Hung	VIE
5	Bruno	BRA
6	Le Luu Quang	VIE
12	Luu Minh Tri	VIE
23	Vo Phi Thuong	VIE
Midfielders		
7	Nguyen Minh Phuong	VIE
10	Phan Van Tai Em	VIE
15	Nguyen Tuan Phong	VIE
16	Phan Thanh Giang	VIE
17	Truong Van Tam	VIE
19	Nguyen Thanh Truc	VIE
20	Nguyen Hoang Thuong	VIE
21	Doan Bach Bao Hung	VIE
22	Nguyen Xuan Hoang	VIE
Forwards		
8	Nguyen Viet Thang	VIE
9	Antonio	BRA
11	Huynh Ngoc Quang	VIE
14	Nguyen Ngoc Thanh	VIE
24	Vo Cong Thanh	VIE

FOOLAD

Goalkeepers		
1	Ebrahim Mirzapour	IRN
22	Hassan Hori	IRN
25	Davood Jolaei	IRN
30	Farshad Bakhtiarizadeh	IRN
Defenders		
2	Maki Sharifi	IRN
3	Pejman Montazeri	IRN
4	Farhad Alkhamis	IRN
5	Jalal Kameli Mofrad	IRN
6	Saman Mousavi	IRN
13	Hossein Kaebi	IRN
14	Ali Badavi	IRN
15	Sayyed Mohammad Alavi	IRN
Midfielders		
7	Omid Sharifinasab	IRN
8	Adel Kolahkaj	IRN
11	Siamak Sarlak	IRN
12	Abdolkareim Shaverdy	IRN
16	Mohsen Hamidi	IRN
18	Milad Nori	IRN
19	Mojahed Khaziravi	IRN
20	Nader Ahmadi	IRN
23	Eman Mobali	IRN
26	Milad Zanidpour	IRN
Forwards		
9	Asghar Rameshgar	IRN
10	Lafteh Hamidi	IRN
17	Meysam Soleimani	IRN
21	Emad Mohammed	IRQ
24	Daniel Okechukwu	NGA
27	Hojat Chaharmahali	IRN
28	Karim Hezbaeepour	IRN
29	Ali Amiri	IRN

GAMBA OSAKA

Goalkeepers		
1	Naoki Matsuyo	JPN
12	Atsushi Kimura	JPN
22	Yosuke Fujigaya	JPN
23	Suguru Hino	JPN
Defenders		
2	Sidiclei	BRA
3	Toru Irie	JPN
4	Noritada Saneyoshi	JPN
5	Tsuneyasu Miyamoto	JPN
6	Satoshi Yamaguchi	JPN
13	Kazuki Teshima	JPN
15	Ryota Aoki	JPN
21	Akira Kaji	JPN
25	Daiki Niwa	JPN
Midfielders		
7	Yasuhito Endo	JPN
8	Fernandinho	BRA
10	Takahiro Futagawa	JPN
14	Akihiro Ienaga	JPN
16	Masafumi Maeda	JPN
17	Tomokazu Myojin	JPN
20	Shinichi Terada	JPN
24	Toshihiro Matsushita	JPN
26	Michihiro Yasuda	JPN
27	Hideo Hashimoto	JPN
29	Yasunobu Matsuoka	JPN
30	Shigeru Yokotani	JPN
Forwards		
9	Magno Alves	BRA
11	Ryuji Bando	JPN
18	Ryota Miki	JPN
19	Satoshi Nakayama	JPN
28	Hideya Okamoto	JPN

AL GHARAFA

Goalkeepers		
1	Amer Al Kaabi	QAT
21	Mohammed Al Gamdi	QAT
22	Abdulaziz Ali	QAT
	Defenders	
6	Hamad Shami	QAT
19	Mugib Hamid	QAT
23	Shaheen Ali	QAT
24	Naief Al Enzi	QAT
26	Bilal Mohammed	QAT
28	Mustafa Abdulla	QAT
	Midfielders	
2	Abdulaziz Al Shammari	QAT
4	Lawrence Quaye	QAT
5	Othman El Assas	MAR
8	Saad Al Shammari	QAT
12	Fahid Al Shammari	QAT
15	Mohammed Al Haj	QAT
16	Ali Fath	QAT
20	Soud Sabah	QAT
	Forwards	
3	Ismaiel Ali	QAT
7	Abdulla Al Mazroui	QAT
9	Marzouq Al Qutaiti	QAT
11	Sergio Ricardo	BRA
13	Mousa Al Allaq	QAT
14	Fahad Al Naemi	QAT
17	Mohamed Al Mazroui	QAT
27	Jamal Johar	QAT
29	Fahad Al Shammari	QAT
30	A'ala Hubail	BHR

AL HILAL

Goalkeepers		
1	Mohammed Al Daeyea	KSA
22	Fahad Al Shammari	KSA
29	Bandar Almass	KSA
30	Hasan Al Otaibi	KSA
	Defenders	
2	Turki Suwaileh	KSA
3	Abdulaziz Hulayyil	KSA
4	Ahmad Khaleel	KSA
14	Marcelo Tavares	BRA
16	Kamil Al Mousa	KSA
17	Fahad Al Mefareg	KSA
19	Abdulaziz Kahthran	KSA
24	Meshari Al Bashir	KSA
	Midfielders	
5	Abdullatif Al Ghannam	KSA
6	Khaled Aziz	KSA
8	Camacho	BRA
10	Mohammad Al Shlhoub	KSA
11	Nawaf Al Temyat	KSA
13	Omar Al-Ghamdi	KSA
15	Giovanni	BRA
21	Sultan Al Bargan	KSA
23	Badr Al Dosari	KSA
25	Abdulaziz Al Abdulsalam	KSA
28	Fahad Ghazi	KSA
	Forwards	
7	Abdullah Al Dosary	KSA
9	Sami Al Jaber	KSA
12	Bader Al Kharashi	KSA
18	Ahmed Al Suwaileh	KSA
20	Yasser Al Qahtani	KSA
26	Mohammed Al Anbar	KSA
27	Meshal Al Mouri	KSA

AL ITTIHAD (SYR)

Goalkeepers		
1	Mahmoud Karkar	SYR
30	Yasser Jarkas	SYR
	Defenders	
2	Maan Al Rashad	SYR
3	Majd Homsi	SYR
4	Omar Hemidi	SYR
6	Mohammed Ibrahim	SYR
7	Aobada Sayed	SYR
12	Zakaria Al Kaddour	SYR
14	Wael Aian	SYR
15	Mohamed Boudaka	SYR
16	Bakri Tarrab	SYR
20	Salah Shahrour	SYR
21	Yousef Shikhaleshreh	SYR
24	Haidar Abdulrazzaq	IRQ
	Midfielders	
5	Khaled Aryan	SYR
17	Mahmoud Al Amena	SYR
19	Yahia Al Rached	SYR
23	Ayman Habal	SYR
	Forwards	
8	Mohamed Al Damen	SYR
10	Abdul Aga	SYR
11	Radwan Al Abrach	SYR
13	Mahmoud Al Beef	SYR
18	Anas Sari	SYR
25	Ahmad Saleh	IRQ

AL KARAMA

Goalkeepers		
1	Mosab Balhous	SYR
22	Adnan Al Hafez	SYR
30	Fahd Saleh	SYR
	Defenders	
2	Naser Al Sebai	SYR
4	Hassan Abbas	SYR
5	Jehad Kassab	SYR
13	Belal Abduldaim	SYR
14	Anas Al Khouja	SYR
16	Tarek Al Hourani	SYR
26	Abdulhadi Khalaf	SYR
	Midfielders	
3	Saffir Atasi	SYR
6	Jehad Al Hussien	SYR
7	Abdul Kader Refai	SYR
9	Mohamad Al Hamwi	SYR
10	Iyad Mando	SYR
11	Fahd Aodi	SYR
15	Mohamad Eid	SYR
18	Mahmoud Al Mallul	SYR
20	Hassan Masri	SYR
21	Aatef Jenyat	SYR
24	Mohamad Abdulkader	SYR
	Forwards	
8	Mohanad Ibrahim	SYR
12	Ahmad Turkmani	SYR
19	Abdalrahman Akkari	SYR

MASHAL

Goalkeepers		
1	Yuriy Tsoy	UZB
12	Pavel Butenko	RUS
26	Botir Nasirov	UZB
27	Pavel Sinelnikov	UZB
	Defenders	
2	Komoliddin Kenjayev	UZB
3	Dilyaver Vaniev	UZB
5	Vitaliy Djalilov	UZB
6	Anvar Gafurov	UZB
7	Hayrulla Karimov	UZB
14	Hamza Karimov	UZB
15	Gabit Sapargaliev	UZB
16	Artyom Filiposyan	UZB
17	Botir Karaev	UZB
28	Jahongir Jiyamuradov	UZB
	Midfielders	
4	Mirdjalal Kasimov	UZB
8	Rustam Kadirov	UZB
10	Rustam Kurbanbayev	UZB
13	Lutfulla Turaev	UZB
19	Jasur Hasanov	UZB
22	Rashidjon Gofurov	UZB
25	Anatolie Ostap	MDA
29	Jonibek Hamdamov	UZB
30	Valeriy Dotsenko	UKR
	Forwards	
9	Zafar Kholmurodov	UZB
11	Shuhratbek Mirholdirshaev	UZB
18	Aziz Ibragimov	UZB
20	Viktor Klishin	UZB
21	Bakhriddin Vahobov	UZB
23	Josur Boboev	UZB
24	Botir Qodirqulov	UZB

AL MINA'A

Goalkeepers		
1	Sadam Salman	IRQ
12	Medhat Abdulhussain	IRQ
20	Esmail Hashem	IRQ
	Defenders	
2	Sajjad Abdulkadim	IRQ
3	Jehad Madloul	IRQ
4	Emad Ouda	IRQ
5	Baha Abdullatif	IRQ
6	Ali Jassim	IRQ
13	Ala'a Abdulhussain	IRQ
14	Nawaf Sallal	IRQ
26	Muneer Hamoud	IRQ
28	Haider Naeem	IRQ
	Midfielders	
7	Ghazi Fahad	IRQ
11	Naif Falah	IRQ
15	Satar Jabbar	IRQ
16	Bashar Hadi	IRQ
18	Hussain Abdulmohsin	IRQ
21	Sajjad Abdulkazem	IRQ
25	Nawaf Falah	IRQ
	Forwards	
8	Mokhlas Abdulsattar	IRQ
9	Nasir Talaa	IRQ
10	Ehsan Hadi	IRQ
22	Husam Ibrahim	IRQ
30	Usama Shayyal	IRQ

PAKHTAKOR

Goalkeepers		
1	Eldor Tadjibaev	UZB
12	Ignatiy Nesterov	UZB
30	Temur Juraev	UZB
	Defenders	
2	Rahmatullo Berdimurodov	UZB
3	Gochguly Gochguliyev	TKM
5	Asror Aliqulov	UZB
13	Aleksander Kletskov	UZB
21	Komoloddin Tadjiev	UZB
24	Anzur Ismailov	UZB
27	Ilhomjon Suyunov	UZB
	Midfielders	
4	Anvar Berdiev	UZB
6	Ibrohimjon Rahimov	UZB
8	Server Djeperov	UZB
11	Sadriddin Abdullaev	UZB
14	Vladislav Kiryan	UZB
15	Islom Inomov	UZB
16	Shuhrat Yuldashev	UZB
17	Vyacheslav Ponomarev	UZB
18	Timur Kapadze	UZB
20	Ildar Magdeev	UZB
22	Renat Bayramov	UZB
23	Andrey Vlasichev	UZB
25	Odil Ahmedov	UZB
26	Sirojiddin Sayfiev	UZB
28	Aleksey Klikunov	UZB
	Forwards	
7	Uche Iheruome	NGA
9	Anvarjon Soliev	UZB
10	Zaynitdin Tadjiev	UZB
19	Akmal Suyarov	UZB
29	Farhod Tadjiev	UZB

AL QADISIYA

Goalkeepers		
1	Bader Al Jumah	KUW
21	Nayef Al Zoufairi	KUW
22	Nawaf Al Khaldi	KUW
	Defenders	
2	Ali Al Namash	KUW
3	Saqer Khodair	KUW
4	Hussain Ali	KUW
5	Nawaf Auda	KUW
6	Fayez Bander	KUW
11	Ali Al Shamali	KUW
13	Mesaed Neda	KUW
23	Saadoun Al Shammari	KUW
25	Nohayer Al Shammari	KUW
26	Tareq Al Khulaifi	KUW
28	Abdulrahman Al Zahamil	KUW
30	Jamal Mubarak	KUW
	Midfielders	
8	Saleh Al Hendi	KUW
12	Brahima Keita	CIV
14	Naser Al Adwani	KUW
18	Fawaz Buhamad	KUW
19	Nawaf Al Mutairi	KUW
20	Abdulrahman Mussa	KUW
24	Mohammad Fahad	KUW
27	Khaled Al Namash	KUW
29	Lucio	BRA
	Forwards	
7	Khalaf Salama	KUW
10	Mohammad Al Otaibi	KUW
15	Seydou Traore	BFA
16	Ahmad Kamshad	KUW
17	Bader Al Mutwa	KUW

AL QUWA AJ			SABA BATTERY			AL SADD			AL SHABAB		
Goalkeepers			Goalkeepers			Goalkeepers			Goalkeepers		
1	Wissam Kassid	IRQ	1	Almir Tolja	BIH	1	Jabor Salem	QAT	1	Rashed Al Mugren	KSA
21	Ali Jalel	IRQ	21	Ali Mardan Rashidi	IRN	19	Talal Salem	QAT	22	Saeid Al Harbi	KSA
22	Allaa Qatea	IRQ	30	Asghar Karamollahi	IRN	22	Basel Samith	QAT	23	Waleed Ali	KSA
	Defenders			Defenders		30	Mohamed Saqr	QAT	30	Mohammad Khojah	KSA
2	Jassim Ghulam	IRQ	2	Mojtaba Hosseiny	IRN		Defenders			Defenders	
3	Mukhalad Ali	IRQ	3	Amir Reza Alvandipour	IRN	2	Jafal Al Kuwari	QAT	2	Abdullah Al Astaa	KSA
4	Fareed Majeed	IRQ	4	Sohrab Bakhtiarizadeh	IRN	3	Essa Al Kuwari	QAT	3	Abdulmohsen Al Dosari	KSA
5	Ali Hossein Rehema	IRQ	5	Kazem Mahmoudi	IRN	4	Abdullah Al Bareek	QAT	4	Saleh Sadeeq	KSA
6	Haidar Raheem	IRQ	6	Yahya Golmohammadi	IRN	17	Bilal Abu Hamdeh	QAT	5	Mohammed bin Hamdan	KSA
12	Ibrahim Ahmed	IRQ	7	Mohammad Navazi	IRN	20	Abdulla Al Asseiri	QAT	6	Ahmed Al Bahari	KSA
13	Muayad Khaled	IRQ	25	Morteza Asadi	IRN	21	Abdullah Koni	QAT	13	Hassan Maaz	KSA
14	Aqeel Kassem	IRQ		Midfielders		28	Emad Al Dahri	QAT	14	Abdullah Shuhail	KSA
27	Radhi Shnaishil	IRQ	8	Mohsen Soltani	IRN		Midfielders		15	Abdoh Autef	KSA
	Midfielders		9	Yadollah Akbari	IRN	5	Ezzat Jadoua	QAT	17	Zaid Al Mowalad	KSA
8	Hussain Saddam	IRQ	12	Hossain Yousefi	IRN	6	Ali Nasser Saleh	QAT	20	Faisal Al Obili	KSA
9	Waleed Dahd	IRQ	14	Mohammad Shahriari	IRN	7	Wesam Rizik	QAT	24	Sanad Shrahilee	KSA
11	Ali Khodair	IRQ	19	Ali Ghasemian	IRN	8	Mased Al Hamad	QAT	29	Hosein Fllath	KSA
15	Muhand Ali	IRQ	20	Mostafa Mahdizadeh	IRN	9	Hussain Yasser	QAT		Midfielders	
16	Homoodi Kathem	IRQ	23	Amir H Feshangchi	IRN	12	Magid Mohammed	QAT	7	Mansour Al Dosari	KSA
17	Alaa Abdulwahed	IRQ	24	Masoud Zarei	IRN	14	Khalfan Ibrahim	QAT	8	Abdullah Al Dosari	KSA
18	Mohamed Abdulhassan	IRQ	26	Saeid Bagi	IRN	15	Talal Al Bloushi	QAT	11	Ahmed Ateef	KSA
19	Ahmed Iyad	IRQ	27	Amir Khanmohammadi	IRN	18	Hamood Abdulla	QAT	16	Bashar Al Ashur	KSA
23	Safwan Abdulghani	IRQ		Forwards		23	Tahir Zakariya	QAT	19	Yousef Al Muwaine	KSA
25	Hussein Ali Hussein	IRQ	10	Ali Daei	IRN	25	Ahmad Mohd Musa	QAT	25	Nashat Akram	IRQ
28	Rafid Mohammed	IRQ	11	Babak Zolrahmi	IRN	27	Mohamed Rabia	OMA	26	Mohammed Al Halail	KSA
	Forwards		15	Alen Avdic	BIH		Forwards			Forwards	
7	Louai Salah	IRQ	16	Robert Margousi	IRN	11	Carlos Tenorio	ECU	9	Osei Kuffour	GHA
10	Ali Mansour	IRQ	18	Ali Asghar Mohammadi	IRN	13	Felipe	BRA	10	Naji Majrashi	KSA
20	Ghanim Khodair	IRQ	28	Mohsen Bayat	IRN	16	Mohamed Gholam	QAT	12	Fahad Fallata	KSA
26	Moustfa Kareem	IRQ	29	Saeed Daghighi	IRN	24	Ali Afef	QAT	18	Godwin Attram	GHA
						26	Yusuf Ahmed	QAT	21	Abdulaziz bin Saran	KSA
						29	Khalid Al Hajari	QAT	27	Fisal bin Sultan	KSA
									28	Nassir Al Shamrani	KSA

SHANGHAI			TOKYO VERDY			ULSAN HORANG-I			AL WAHDA		
Goalkeepers			Goalkeepers			Goalkeepers			Goalkeepers		
1	Yu Weiliang	CHN	1	Hiroki Mizuhara	JPN	1	Seo Dong Myung	KOR	1	Husain Ali	UAE
12	Zhou Yajun	CHN	12	Satoshi Tokizawa	JPN	21	Bae Kwan Young	KOR	18	Ramadan Malallah	UAE
21	Qiu Shenjiong	CHN	21	Yoshinari Takagi	JPN	25	Kim Jee Hyuk	KOR	22	Abdulbaset Al Hammadi	UAE
22	Liu Yunfei	CHN	26	Takaya Kurokawa	JPN	27	Hwang Sun Il	KOR	30	Abdulla Fayrouz	UAE
	Defenders			Defenders			Defenders			Defenders	
2	Yao Lijun	CHN	2	Shigenori Hagimura	JPN	2	Vinicius	BRA	3	Abdulla Salem	UAE
3	Gu Cao	CHN	3	Taisei Fujita	JPN	3	Park Byung Gyu	KOR	4	Ali Jumaa	UAE
4	Li Yinan	CHN	4	Kenta Togawa	JPN	4	Cho Se Kwon	KOR	6	Branimir Bajic	BIH
5	Du Wei	CHN	5	Dedimar	BRA	5	You Kyoung Youl	KOR	7	Mohamed Ali	UAE
6	Ng Wai Chiu	HKG	13	Masayuki Yanagisawa	JPN	6	Park Dong Hyuk	KOR	8	Omar Ali	UAE
13	Cheng Liang	CHN	19	Kenichi Uemura	JPN	13	Lee Hyun Min	KOR	12	Salem Zayed	UAE
14	Sun Xiang	CHN	24			14	Jang Sang Won	KOR	13	Talal Abdulla	UAE
23	Li Weifeng	CHN	27	Yukihiro Aoba	JPN	22	Seo Deok Kyu	KOR	15	Fahed Masoud	UAE
28	Dong Yang	CHN	28	Takumi Hayama	JPN	23	Byun Sung Hwan	KOR	19	Faisal Ali	UAE
30	Xue Zhiqiang	CHN	29	Naoki Mihara	JPN	29	Jang Jae Wan	KOR	21	Basheer Saeed	UAE
	Midfielders			Midfielders			Midfielders		28	Eisa Ahmed	UAE
7	Xiao Zhanbo	CHN	6	Tomo Sugawara	JPN	7	Park Kyu Seon	KOR		Midfielders	
11	Ivan Jovanovic	SCG	7	Masahiro Ohashi	JPN	8	Lee Ho	KOR	2	Tawfeeq Abdul Razzaq	UAE
15	Wang Ke	CHN	8	Hideki Nagai	JPN	9	Noh Jung Yoon	KOR	5	Abdul Salam Jumaa	UAE
16	Yu Tao	CHN	10	Anailson	BRA	11	Kwon Seok Keun	KOR	9	Abdulla Belal	UAE
17	Sun Ji	CHN	11	Harutaka Ono	JPN	12	Jun Hyun Joon	KOR	14	Yaser Matar	UAE
18	Zheng Kewei	CHN	14	Masatomo Kuba	JPN	16	Lee Sang Ho	KOR	16	Mohamed Othman	UAE
19	Li Chengming	CHN	15	Shin Kanazawa	JPN	17	Lee Jong Min	KOR	23	Haidar Alo Ali	UAE
20	Chen Lei	CHN	17	Takuya Sato	JPN	19	Choi Kwang Hee	KOR	24	Abdulraheem Jumaa	UAE
24	Shen Longyuan	CHN	20	Nozomi Hiroyama	JPN	24	Park Won Hong	KOR	25	Mahmoud Khamis	UAE
25	Xu Wen	CHN	22	Tetsuhiro Kina	JPN	26	Kim Young Sam	KOR	29	Hasan Ameen	UAE
26	Wang Hongliang	CHN	23	Kento Tsurumaki	JPN	28	Kim Min Oh	KOR		Forwards	
	Forwards			Forwards			Forwards		10	Ismail Matar	UAE
8	Xie Hui	CHN	9	Basilio	BRA	10	Lee Chun Soo	KOR	11	Saleh Al Menhali	UAE
10	Zhang Yuning	CHN	16	Kazunori Iio	JPN	15	Machado	BRA	17	Maurito	ANG
27	Mao Jianqin	CHN	18	Ryosuke Kijima	JPN	18	Choi Sung Kuk	KOR	20	Ahmed Al Hajeri	UAE
29	Gao Lin	CHN	25	Kazuki Hiramoto	JPN	20	Leandro	BRA	26	Belal Jumaa	UAE
			30	Masaki Saito	JPN	30	Yang Dong Hyen	KOR	27	Slavisa Mitrovic	BIH

AFC CUP 2006

AFC CUP 2006

Group Stage			Quarter-finals	Semi-finals	Final

Group A		Pts	Quarter-finals
Al Muharraq	BHR	11	Tampines Rovers *
Al Ahed	LIB	10	Wihdat
Mahindra United	IND	9	
Brothers Union	BAN	2	

Group B		Pts
Al Nasr	OMA	12
Dempo SC	IND	4
Merv Mary	TKM	1

Al Faysali *
Sun Hei

Group C		Pts
Al Wihdat	JOR	6
Mohemmedan SC	BAN	0

Group D		Pts
Al Faysali	JOR	7
Al Nejmeh	LIB	7
MTTU	TKM	2

Selangor *
Al Nejmeh

Group E		Pts
Sun Hei	HKG	13
Perlis	MAS	11
Home United	SIN	6
New Radiant	MDV	4

Group F		Pts
Tampines Rovers	SIN	15
Selangor	MAS	15
Happy Valley	HKG	4
Hurriyya	MDV	1

Al Nasr *
Al Muharraq

Remaining ties: Quarter-finals 12-09-2006 & 19-09-2006; Semi-finals 26-09-2006 & 17-10-2006; Final 26-10-2006 & 2-11-2006
* Home team in the first leg

GROUP A

National Stadium, Manama, 7-03-2006, 18:15, 1 000, AK Nema IRQ

| Al Muharraq | 2 | Leandson [47], Bashar Bani Yaseen [54] |
| Brothers Union | 0 | |

Sport City, Beirut, 7-03-2006, 19:30, 1 000, Al Ghatrifi OMA

| Al Ahed | 2 | Abu Bakarr Bah [8], Ahmad Trad [28] |
| Mahindra United | 2 | Steven Dias [33], David Adjei [38] |

Bangabandhu, Dhaka, 21-03-2006, 16:00, 1 000, Shrestha NEP

| Brothers Union | 2 | Abul Hossain [52], Hasan Ameli [68] |
| Mahindra United | 2 | Yusif Yakubu [67], Jose Barreto Ramires [70] |

Municipal, Beirut, 21-03-2006, 19:30, 300, Kousa SYR

| Al Ahed | 0 | |
| Al Muharraq | 2 | Al Sharqawi [45], Ebrahim Almuqla [90] |

National Stadium, Manama, 11-04-2006, 18:30, 500, Al Yarimi YEM

| Al Muharraq | 1 | Leandson [62] |
| Mahindra United | 1 | Sushanth [66] |

Bangabandhu, Dhaka, 18-04-2006, 16:00, 500, Arambakade SRI

| Brothers Union | 1 | Mahadi Tapu [39] |
| Al Ahed | 3 | Bassem Marmar [4], El Ali [49], Abbas Kenaan [75] |

PJN, Fatorda, Goa, 25-04-2006, 16:15, 2 000, Tongkhan THA

| Mahindra United | 0 | |
| Al Muharraq | 1 | Abdulla Al Dakeel [9] |

Municipal, Beirut, 25-04-2006, 20:30, 300, Al Ghamdi KSA

| Al Ahed | 6 | Osama Haidar 2 [13 21 36], Issam Ayoub [23], Ali Yaakoub [73], Hassan Maatouk [78] |
| Brothers Union | 2 | Hasan Ameli [70], Mahadi Tapu [87] |

Bangabandhu, Dhaka, 2-05-2006, 16:00, 300, Basma SYR

| Brothers Union | 0 | |
| Al Muharraq | 0 | |

PJN, Fatorda, Goa, 2-05-2006, 16:15, 700, Mohd Salleh MAS

| Mahindra United | 2 | Surajit Bose [78], David Adjei [80] |
| Al Ahed | 1 | Mahmoud El Ali [51] |

National Stadium, Manama, 16-05-2006, 18:45, 400, Mombini IRN

| Al Muharraq | 2 | Abdulla Al Dakeel 2 [45 93+] |
| Al Ahed | 4 | Hassan Nassrallah [18], Issam Ayoub [59], Hassan Matouk 2 [76 86] |

PJN, Fatorda, Goa, 16-05-2006, 19:00, 200, Al Yarmi YEM

| Mahindra United | 1 | Shanmugam Venkatesh [90] |
| Brothers Union | 0 | |

Group A	Pl	W	D	L	F	A	Pts
Al Muharraq	6	3	2	1	8	5	11
Al Ahed	6	3	1	2	16	11	10
Mahindra United	6	2	3	1	8	7	9
Brothers Union	6	0	2	4	5	14	2

GROUP B

Salalah SC, Salalah, 7-03-2006, 19:15, 500, Shaban KUW

| Al Nasr Salalah | 3 | Mohammed Matoona 2 [61 80], Al Hinai [86] |
| Dempo | 1 | Ranti Soleye [75p] |

Olympic Stadium, Ashgabat, 21-03-2006, 14:00, 150, Torky IRN

| Merv Mary | 2 | Oleg Yuzbashyan 2 [80 91+] |
| Dempo SC | 2 | Ranti Soleye [12], Joaquim Abranches [86] |

Salalah SC, Salalah, 11-04-2006, 19:15, 300, Al Ghamdi KSA

| Al Nasr Salalah | 4 | Mubarak Al Hinai 2 [11 49], Hisham Al Kahali [39], Hamdi Hoobees Al Shar [59] |
| Merv Mary | 1 | Kurbanmuhammedov [64] |

Olympic Stadium, Ashgabat, 25-04-2006, 14:00, 200, Mombini IRN

| Merv Mary | 0 | |
| Al Nasr Salalah | 2 | Mubarak Al Hinai [11], Haitham Tabook [38] |

PJN, Fatorda, Goa, 2-05-2006, 19:00, 1 000, U Win Cho MYA

| Dempo SC | 0 | |
| Al Nasr Salalah | 1 | Ashoor Bait Shamiah [55] |

PJN, Fatorda, Goa, 16-05-2006, 16:15, 200, Saidov UZB

| Dempo SC | 6 | Johnny Cruz [20], Samir Naik [24], Clifford Miranda 2 [42 78], Beto Mendes Silva 2 [68 86] |
| Merv Mary | 1 | Kurbanmuhammedov [90] |

Group B	Pl	W	D	L	F	A	Pts
Al Nasr Salaleh	4	4	0	0	10	2	12
Dempo SC	4	1	1	2	9	7	4
Merv Mary	4	0	1	3	4	14	1

GROUP C

Amman Stadium, 18-04-2006, 17:00, 5 000, Shaban KUW

| Al Wihdat | 7 | Mahmoud Shelbaieh 3 [8 54 56], Rafat Ali Jaber 2 [47 72], Hasan Abdel Fattah 2 [55 70] |
| Mohammedan SC | 0 | |

Bangabandhu, Dhaka, 25-04-2006, 2 000, Saidov UZB

| Mohammedan SC | 1 | Paul Nwachukwu [85p] |
| Al Wihdat | 2 | Mahmoud Shelbaieh 2 [61 64] |

Group C	Pl	W	D	L	F	A	Pts
Al Wihdat	2	2	0	0	9	1	6
Mohammedan SC	2	0	0	2	1	9	0

GROUP D

Municipal, Saida, 7-03-2006, 19:00, 350, Ebrahim BHR

| Al Nejmeh | 6 | Ali Nasereddine 3 [25 55 57], Faissal Antar [28], Moussa Hjeij [34], Mohamed Ghaddar [74] |
| MTTU | 2 | Dovlet Bayramov [76], Mamedaly Karadanov [79] |

Amman International, 21-03-2006, 17:00, 7 000, Al Yarimi YEM

| Al Faysali | 2 | Khaled Almalta'ah [13], Patrick Agbo [45] |
| Al Nejmeh | 0 | |

Olympic Stadium, Ashgabat, 11-04-2006, 18:00, 1 000, Sarkar IND

| MTTU | 1 | Yazguly Hojageldiyev [33] |
| Al Faysali | 1 | Haitham Al Shboul [30] |

King Abdullah, Amman, 25-04-2006, 17:00, 700, Basma SYR

| Al Faysali | 4 | Abdelhadi Al Maharmeh 2 [15 17], Hassouneh Qasem [81], Khaled Al Maltaa'h [95+] |
| MTTU | 3 | Berdy Shamuradov 2 [44 65], Hangeldiyev [57] |

Olympic Stadium, Ashgabat, 2-05-2006, 1 900, Al Saeei UAE

| MTTU | 2 | Berdy Shamuradov [4], Maksim Belyh [58] |
| Al Nejmeh | 2 | Mohamad Ghaddar 2 [75 91+] |

Sport City, Beirut, 16-05-2006, 19:00, 1 000, Al Fadhli KUW

| Al Nejmeh | 2 | Emmanuel Duah [22], Ali Nasereddine [65] |
| Al Faysali | 1 | Khaled Almalta'ah [56] |

Group D	Pl	W	D	L	F	A	Pts
Al Faysali	4	2	1	1	8	6	7
Al Nejmeh	4	2	1	1	10	7	7
MTTU	4	0	2	2	8	13	2

GROUP E

National Stadium, Male, 7-03-2006, 16:00, 12 000, Tongkhan THA
New Radiant 0
Sun Hei 2 Julius Akosah 2 [19] [28]

Bishan, Singapore, 7-03-2006, 19:30, 1 624, Gosh BAN
Home United 2 Egmar 2 [7] [62]
Perlis 3 Phillimon Chipeta 3 [52] [57] [89]

Mongkok, Hong Kong, 21-03-2006, 20:00, 2000, Kim Dong Jin KOR
Sun Hei 0
Home United 1 Indra Sahdan Daud [70]

Utama, Kangar, 21-03-2006, 20:45, 3 500, Tan Hai CHN
Perlis 6 Manzoor [45], Phillimon Chipeta 3 [49] [72] [77], Zacharia Simukonda 2 [55] [66]
New Radiant 0

Mongkok, Hong Kong, 11-04-2006, 20:00, 493, Moradi IRN
Sun Hei 0
Perlis 0

National Stadium, Male, 11-04-2006, 16:00, 8 000, Shrestha NEP
New Radiant 5 Ali Umar [10], Ali Ashfaq [67], Ahmed Thariq 2 [70] [92+], Cristian Nitta [94+p]
Home United 3 Rosman [4], Indra Sahdan Daud [79], Egmar [83]

Bishan, Singapore, 25-04-2006, 19:30, 1 212, O Il Son PRK
Home United 2 Indra Sahdan Daud [21], Egmar [60]
New Radiant 0

Utama, Kangar, 25-04-2006, 20:45, 6 000, Shrestha NEP
Perlis 1 Zacharia Simukonda [69]
Sun Hei 2 Fladimir Freitas [13], Chu Siu Kei [16]

Mongkok, Hong Kong, 2-05-2006, 15:30, 100, Lee Gi Young KOR
Sun Hei 5 Lai Kai Cheuk [4], Fladimir Freitas [31], Julius Akosah 3 [49] [63] [64]
New Radiant 2 Cristian Nitta 2 [3] [56]

Utama, Kangar, 2-05-2006, 20:45, 4 000, Tongkhan THA
Perlis 1 Phillimon Chipeta [73]
Home United 0

National Stadium, Male, 16-05-2006, 16:00, 1 000, Arambakade SRI
New Radiant 0
Perlis 0

Bishan, Singapore, 16-05-2006, 19:00, 1 287, Ebrahim BHR
Home United 0
Sun Hei 2 Fladimir Freitas [22p], Julius Akosah [57]

Group E	Pl	W	D	L	F	A	Pts
Sun Hei	6	4	1	1	11	4	13
Perlis	6	3	2	1	11	4	11
Home United	6	2	0	4	8	11	6
New Radiant	6	1	1	4	7	18	4

GROUP F

Shah Alam, Bukit Jalil, 7-03-2006, 20:45, 3 000, Tan Hai CHN
Selangor 1 Brian Fuentes [11]
Tampines Rovers 0

Mongkok, Hong Kong, 7-03-2006, 20:00, 500, Arambakade SRI
Happy Valley 3 Sham Kwok Keung [32], Gerard Ambassa [37], Lee Sze Ming [76]
Hurriya 0

Tampines, Singapore, 21-03-2006, 19:30, 3 021, Williams AUS
Tampines Rovers 3 Aliff Safiee [45], Noh Alam Shah 2 [48] [70]
Happy Valley 1 Fabio [30]

National Stadium, Male, 21-03-2006, 16:00, 5 000, Sarkar IND
Hurriya 1 Masey Abdul Ghafoor [90]
Selangor 3 Brian Fuentes [29p], Elie Aiboy [63], Bambang Pamungkas [66]

Tampines, Singapore, 11-04-2006, 19:30, 2 500, Nishimura JPN
Tampines Rovers 3 Mirko Grabovac [44], Aliff Safiee [49], Peres [89]
Hurriya 1 Sinaz Hilmy [90]

Shah Alam, Bukit Jalil, 11-04-2006, 20:45, 1 000, Kwon Jong Chul KOR
Selangor 4 Shukor Adnan [42], Surendran Davaghan [52], Brian Fuentes 2 [64] [72]
Happy Valley 3 Evanor [14], Fabio [71p], Lee Wai Man [74]

Mongkok, Hong Kong, 25-04-2006, 20:00, 407, U Win Cho MYA
Happy Valley 2 Evanor [19], Gerard Ambassa [74]
Selangor 3 Razman Roslan [29], Brian Fuentes [71], Sanba Kalasigaram [88]

National Stadium, Male, 25-04-2006, 16:00, 1 000, Gosh BAN
Hurriya 0
Tampines Rovers 4 Rafi Ali 2 [15] [24], Aliff Safiee [51] Noh Alam Shah [81]

Tampines, Singapore, 2-05-2006, 19:30, 3 868, Nishimura JPN
Tampines Rovers 3 Peres 2 [32] [51], Mirko Grabovac [60]
Selangor 2 Bambang Pamungkas 2 [56] [82]

National Stadium, Male, 2-05-2006, 16:00, 400, Sarkar IND
Hurriya 1 Shinaz Hilmy [36]
Happy Valley 1 Li Chun Yip Ricky [21]

KLFA, Cheras, 16-05-2006, 20:45, 3 000, U Win Cho MYA
Selangor 1 Ahmed Samau OG [27]
Hurriya 0

Mongkok, Hong Kong, 16-05-2006, 20:45, 66, Matsumra JPN
Happy Valley 0
Tampines Rovers 4 Noh Alam Shah 3 [57] [76] [81], Ibrahim Md. Noh [85]

Group F	Pl	W	D	L	F	A	Pts
Tampines Rovers	6	5	0	1	17	5	15
Selangor	6	5	0	1	14	9	15
Happy Valley	6	1	1	4	10	15	4
Hurriyya	6	0	1	5	3	15	1

AFC PRESIDENT'S CUP 2006

AFC PRESIDENT'S CUP MALAYSIA 2006

Group Stage			Semi-finals	Final

Group A		Pts
Khemara	CAM	7
Tatung	TPE	6
Transport United	BHU	3
Pakistan Army	PAK	1

Semi-finals	
Dordoy-Dinamo	3
Khemara	0

Final	
Dordoy-Dinamo	2
Vakhsh	1

Group B		Pts
Vakhsh	TJK	6
Dordoy-Dinamo	KGZ	6
Manang MC	NEP	3
Ratnam SC	SRI	3

Semi-finals	
Tatung	1
Vakhsh	3

GROUP A

Sarawak Stadium, Kuching, 10-05-2006, 17:30, 100, Gosh BAN		
Tatung	4	Maulay OG [11], Wu Chun I [25], Hsu Che Hao [49], Chuang Yao Tsung [91+]
Pakistan Army	1	Jaffar Hussain [29]

Sarawak Stadium, Kuching, 10-05-2006, 20:00, 100, Sarkar IND		
Khemara	2	Srey Veasna [45], Kim Song U [90]
Transport United	1	Wangchuk Ugyen [66]

Sarawak Stadium, Kuching, 12-05-2006, 18:30, 100, Sarkar IND		
Transport United	1	Wangay Dorji [90]
Pakistan Army	0	

Sarawak Stadium, Kuching, 13-05-2006, 10:00, 50, Ebrahim BHR		
Khemara	5	Kim Song U [56], Choe Ung Chon 3 [59 72 77], Kosal Keo [92+]
Tatung	1	Hsu Che Hao [12]

Sarawak Stadium, Kuching, 14-05-2006, 16:00, 50, Sarkar IND		
Khemara	1	Chacha Shahbbir [36]
Pakistan Army	1	Kompheak Kouch [48]

Sarawak Stadium, Kuching, 14-05-2006, 18:30, 50, Ebrahim BHR		
Tatung	5	Lin Kuei Pin [53], Chuang Yao Tsung 3 [71 72 75],
Transport United	0	Hsu Che Hao [89]

Group A	Pl	W	D	L	F	A	Pts
Khemara	3	2	1	0	8	3	**7**
Tatung	3	2	0	1	10	6	**6**
Transport United	3	1	0	2	2	7	**3**
Pakistan Army	3	0	1	2	2	6	**1**

GROUP B

Sarawak Stadium, Kuching, 11-05-2006, 17:30, 100, Tongkhan THA		
Ratnam SC	2	Kasun [66], Rawmy [89]
Manang MC	0	

Sarawak Stadium, Kuching, 11-05-2006, 20:00, 100, Sun Baoije CHN		
Vakhsh	3	Khamrakulov [24], Karabaev [62], Nazarov [81]
Dordoy-Dinamo	0	

Sarawak Stadium, Kuching, 13-05-2006, 16:00, 100, Sun Baojie CHN		
Dordoy-Dinamo	3	Kornilov [21], Krasnov [66], Ishenbaev [89]
Ratnam SC	0	

Sarawak Stadium, Kuching, 13-05-2006, 18:30, 100, Tongkhan THA		
Manang MC	3	Anil Gurung [20], Basanta Thakali [60], Khum Gurung [90]
Vakhsh	1	Rizomov [80]

Sarawak Stadium, Kuching, 15-05-2006, 16:30, 100, Tongkhan THA		
Dordoy-Dinamo	2	Kornilov 2 [23 69]
Manang MC	0	

Negeri Stadium, Kuching, 15-05-2006, 16:30, 50, Gosh BAN		
Vakhsh	2	Rizomov [47], Izzadeen OG [75]
Ratnam SC	1	Channa Ediribandanage [81]

Group B	Pl	W	D	L	F	A	Pts
Vakhsh	3	2	0	1	6	4	**6**
Dordoy-Dinamo	3	2	0	1	5	3	**6**
Manang Marshyangdi Club	3	1	0	2	3	5	**3**
Ratnam Sports Club	3	1	0	2	3	5	**3**

SEMI-FINALS AND FINAL

Semi-final. Sarawak Stadium, Kuching 17-05-2006, 20:00, 200, Gosh BAN

Dordoy-Dinamo	3

Roman Kornilov 2 [33 76], Azamat Ishenbaev [41]
Volkov - Samsaliev, Sydykov∗, Kniazev - Bokoev, Ishenbaev, Kasymov (Ahatov 46), Harchenko - Kornilov, Krasnov (Verevkin 53), Chikishev (Jumagulov 80). Tr: Podkorytov

Khemara	0

Ouk Mic - Lar Seyla, Thul Thearith (Sam Minar∗ 79), Om Thavrak, Chan Rithy (Srey Veasna 77), Tieng Tiny - Pok Chanthan, Kim Song U, Sok Buntheang (Keo Kosal 78) - Kouch Kompheak, Choe Ung Chon. Tr: Jo Yong Chol

Semi-final. Sarawak Stadium, Kuching 18-05-2006, 20:00, 100, Sarkar IND

Vakhsh	3

Khamrakulov [43], Savankulov [81], Ortikov [83]
Khabibulloev - Savankulov∗, Negmatov∗ (Zoirov 87), Nazarov, Zakhurbekov - Nuridinov, Sabourov, Ortikov - Rizomov (Karabaev 84), Faizullaev (Samiev 61), Khamrakulov. Tr: Turaqulov

Tatung	1
	Chuang Yao Tsung [57]

Wang Shyh Kuen - Kao Hao Chieh, Tsai Hui Kai∗, Chen Jeng I, Yu Chih Hung (Hsu Chia Cheng 68), Chen Chung Tzu, Wu Chun I, Lin Kuei Pin, Hou Sheng Chung (Hsu Che Hao 78) - Huang Wei Yi (Chang Chih Chung 88), Chuang Yao Tsung. Tr: Chiang Mu Tsai

Final. Sarawak Stadium, Kuching 21-05-2006, 20:00, 500, Sun Baojie CHN

Dordoy-Dinamo	2
	Ildar Amirov 2 [37 105]

Volkov - Ahatov, Samsaliev, Sydykov, Kniazev - Bokoev, Ishenbaev (Kydyraliev 120), Harchenko - Kornilov, Amirov (Verevkin 111), Krasnov (Jumagulov 72). Tr: Podkorytov

Vakhsh	1
	Sohib Savankulov [53]

Khabibulloev - Savankulov, Negmatov, Nazarov, Zakhurbekov - Nuridinov, Sabourov, Ortikov - Rizomov, Faizullaev (Samiev 80), Khamrakulov. Tr: Turaqulov

REGIONAL TOURNAMENTS IN ASIA IN 2005

SOUTH EAST ASIAN GAMES MANILA 2005

First Round Group Stage

	Pl	W	D	L	F	A	Pts	MAS	PHI	CAM
Thailand	3	3	0	0	4	1	9	2-1	1-0	1-0
Malaysia	3	2	0	1	10	4	6		4-2	5-0
Philippines	3	1	0	2	6	7	3			4-2
Cambodia	3	0	0	3	2	10	0			

	Pl	W	D	L	F	A	Pts	IDN	SIN	LAO	MYA
Vietnam	4	3	0	1	11	4	9	0-1	2-1	8-2	1-0
Indonesia	4	2	2	0	5	0	8		0-0	4-0	0-0
Singapore	4	2	1	1	3	2	7			1-0	1-0
Laos	4	1	0	3	5	15	3				3-2
Myanmar	4	0	1	3	2	5	1				

Held in Manila, Philippines from 20-11-2005 to 4-12-2005

Semi-finals

Thailand	3
Indonesia	1
Malaysia	1
Vietnam	2

Final

Thailand	3
Vietnam	0

Third place play-off

Malaysia	1
Indonesia	0

EAST ASIAN CHAMPIONSHIP KOREA REPUBLIC 2005

Preliminary Group Stage

	Pl	W	D	L	F	A	Pts	HKG	TPE	MGL	GUM
Korea DPR	4	4	0	0	31	0	12	2-0	2-0	6-0	21-0
Hong Kong	4	3	0	1	27	2	9		5-0	6-0	16-0
Chinese Taipei	4	1	1	2	9	7	4			0-0	9-0
Mongolia	4	1	1	2	4	12	4				4-0
Guam	4	0	0	4	0	50	0				

Final Group Stage

	Pl	W	D	L	F	A	Pts	JPN	PRK	KOR
China PR	3	1	2	0	5	3	5	2-2	2-0	1-1
Japan	3	1	1	1	3	3	4		0-1	1-0
Korea DPR	3	1	1	1	1	2	4			0-0
Korea Republic	3	0	2	1	1	2	2			

Korea DPR qualified to join China PR, Japan and Korea Republic in the final tournament • Preliminary group stage held in Taipei from 5-03-2005 to 13-03-2005 • Final group stage held in Korea Republic from 31-07-2005 to 7-08-2005

WEST ASIAN GAMES DOHA 2005

First Round Group Stage

	Pl	W	D	L	F	A	Pts	QAT	KUW
Iran	2	2	0	0	8	1	6	4-1	4-0
Qatar	2	1	0	1	3	5	3		2-1
Kuwait	2	0	0	2	1	6	0		

	Pl	W	D	L	F	A	Pts	KSA	PAL
Iraq	2	2	0	0	9	1	6	5-1	4-0
Saudi Arabia	2	1	0	1	3	5	3		2-0
Palestine	2	0	0	2	0	6	0		

	Pl	W	D	L	F	A	Pts	BHR	OMA
Syria	2	1	1	0	5	3	4	2-2	3-1
Bahrain	2	0	2	0	4	4	2		2-2
Oman	2	0	1	1	3	5	1		

Held in Qatar from 1-12-2005 to 10-12-2005

Semi-finals

Iraq	2
Saudi Arabia	0
Iran	0 1p
Syria	0 4p

Final

Iraq	2 4p
Syria	2 3p

Third place play-off

Iran	2
Saudi Arabia	1

SOUTH ASIAN FOOTBALL FEDERATION CHAMPIONSHIP PAKISTAN 2005

First Round Group Stage

	Pl	W	D	L	F	A	Pts	PAK	AFG	SRI
Maldives	3	2	1	0	11	1	7	0-0	9-1	2-0
Pakistan	3	2	1	0	2	0	7		1-0	1-0
Afghanistan	3	1	0	2	3	11	3			2-1
Sri Lanka	3	0	0	3	1	5	0			

	Pl	W	D	L	F	A	Pts	IND	NEP	BHU
Bangladesh	3	2	1	0	6	1	7	1-1	2-0	3-0
India	3	2	1	0	6	2	7		2-1	3-0
Nepal	3	1	0	2	4	5	3			3-1
Bhutan	3	0	0	3	1	9	0			

Held in Karachi, Pakistan from 7-12-2005 to 17-12-2005

Semi-finals

India	1
Maldives	0
Pakistan	0
Bangladesh	1

Final

India	2
Bangladesh	0

CAF

CONFEDERATION AFRICAINE DE FOOTBALL

The predicted African disaster at the 2006 FIFA World Cup™ finals never materialised and, had Ghana believed that they could actually beat Brazil, the world champions were there for the taking. Instead, Ghana had to settle for a second-round finish, the only Africans to make it past the first round, but by no means the only ones to impress. The absence of Cameroon, Nigeria, Senegal and Morocco had prompted many critics to fear the worst, with four African debutants at the finals. But even tiny Togo, despite the threat of player strikes and wrangles over coaches, gave all of their opponents a tough fight. Especially unlucky were Côte d'Ivoire, who found themselves in a treacherous group but still managed to play some of the best football of the tournament. They were also the only one of the five qualifiers not to have a miserable time at the Africa Cup of Nations finals in Egypt in February. Angola, Togo and Ghana all fell there at the first hurdle, while defending champions, Tunisia, lost to Nigeria on penalties in the quarter-finals. Côte d'Ivoire's quarter-final

THE FIFA BIG COUNT OF 2000 FOR CAF

	Male	Female		Male	Female
Registered players	610 997	13 724	Referees	26 798	499
Non registered players	5 607 300	111 329	Officials	189 443	5 392
Youth players	621 238	19 932	Total involved	21 332 631	1 451 476
Children & Occasional	14 300 000	1 300 000	in football	22 806 652	
Professionals	3 653	600	Number of clubs	13 302	
Total players	22 584 520		Number of teams	195 886	

victory over Cameroon was an epic with all 22 players scoring from the spot in the shoot-out before the African Footballer of the Year, Samuel Eto'o, missed second time around. In the final the Ivorians met hosts Egypt. Once again penalties were needed, but this time Côte d'Ivoire weren't so clinical, handing Egypt a record fifth title. There were regional titles in 2005 for Zimbabwe, Ethiopia and Guinea and, at club level, for SC Villa of Uganda and then in 2006 for Police FC of Uganda in the CECAFA Club Championship. At continental level, the CAF Confederation Cup was won by Morocco's FAR Rabat while the CAF African Champions League was won for the fourth time by Al Ahly. In the final they beat Tunisia's Etoile du Sahel 3-0 on aggregate to crown a glorious year. Their run of 55 matches without defeat was finally ended in the FIFA Club World Championship 2005 in Japan by Al Ittihad of Saudi Arabia. It proved to be a disappointing tournament for Al Ahly, who also lost to Sydney FC in the match for fifth place.

Confédération Africaine de Football (CAF)

PO Box 23, 3 Abdel Khalek Sarwat Street, El Hay El Motamayez, 6th October City, Egypt

Tel +20 2 8371000   Fax +20 2 8370006

info@cafonline.com   www.cafonline.com

President: HAYATOU Issa CMR   General Secretary: FAHMY Mustapha EGY

CAF Formed: 1957

CAF EXECUTIVE COMMITTEE

President: HAYATOU Issa CMR   1st Vice-President: MEMENE Seyi TOG   2nd Vice-President: OLIPHANT Molefi RSA

ORDINARY MEMBERS OF THE EXECUTIVE COMMITTEE

PATEL Suketu SEY	ADAMU Amos Dr. NGA	RAOURAOUA Mohamed ALG
DIAKITE Amadou MLI	REDA Hani Abu EGY	DJIBRINE Adoum CHA
BARANSANANIYE Moses BDI	KAMACH Thierry CTA	CAMARA Almamy Kabele GUI
MUSABYIMANA Celestin RWA	General Secretary: FAHMY Mustapha EGY	Co-opted: ALOULOU Slim
	FIFA Exco: CHIBOUB Slim TUN	

MAP OF CAF MEMBER NATIONS

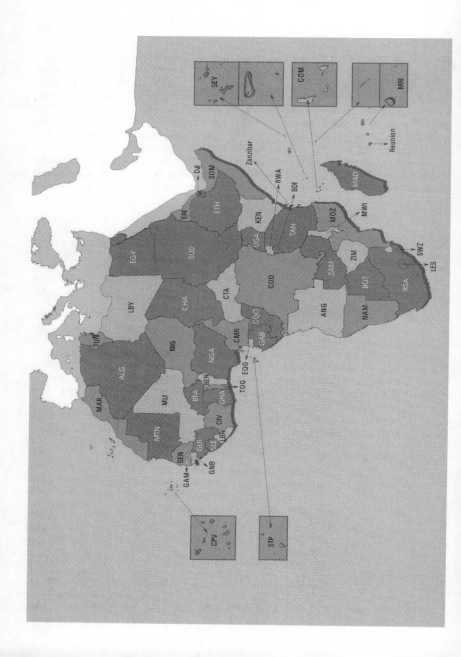

AFRICAN TOURNAMENTS

CAF AFRICA CUP OF NATIONS

Year	Host Country	Winners	Score	Runners-up	Venue
1957	Sudan	Egypt	4-0	Ethiopia	Khartoum Stadium, Khartoum
1959	Egypt	Egypt	2-1	Sudan	Al Ahly Stadium, Cairo
1962	Ethiopia	Ethiopia	2-0	Egypt	Haile Selassie, Addis Abeba
1963	Ghana	Ghana	3-0	Sudan	Accra Stadium, Accra
1965	Tunisia	Ghana	3-2	Tunisia	Zouiten, Tunis
1968	Ethiopia	Congo Kinshasa	1-0	Ghana	Haile Selassie, Addis Abeba
1970	Sudan	Sudan	1-0	Ghana	Municipal, Khartoum
1972	Cameroon	Congo	3-2	Mali	Omnisports, Yaoundé
1974	Egypt	Zaire	2-2 2-0	Zambia	International, Cairo
1976	Ethiopia	Morocco	1-1	Guinea	Addis Abeba Stadium
1978	Ghana	Ghana	2-0	Uganda	Accra Stadium, Accra
1980	Nigeria	Nigeria	3-0	Algeria	Surulere, Lagos
1982	Libya	Ghana	1-1 7-6p	Libya	11th June Stadium, Tripoli
1984	Côte d'Ivoire	Cameroon	3-1	Nigeria	Houphouët Boigny, Abidjan
1986	Egypt	Egypt	0-0 5-4p	Cameroon	International, Cairo
1988	Morocco	Cameroon	1-0	Nigeria	Mohamed V, Casablanca
1990	Algeria	Algeria	1-0	Nigeria	Stade Olympique, Algiers
1992	Senegal	Côte d'Ivoire	0-0 11-10p	Ghana	Stade de l'Amite, Dakar
1994	Tunisia	Nigeria	2-1	Zambia	El Menzah, Tunis
1996	South Africa	South Africa	2-0	Tunisia	Soccer City, Johannesburg
1998	Burkina Faso	Egypt	2-0	South Africa	Stade du 4 Août, Ouagadougou
2000	Ghana/Nigeria	Cameroon	2-2 4-3p	Nigeria	Surulere, Lagos
2002	Mali	Cameroon	0-0 3-2p	Senegal	Stade du 26 Mars, Bamako
2004	Tunisia	Tunisia	2-1	Morocco	Rades, Tunis
2006	Egypt	Egypt	0-0 4-2p	Côte d'Ivoire	International, Cairo

Thirteen different countries have triumphed at the 25 CAF Africa Cup of Nations tournaments and this lack of domination by one country and the fact that it is played every two years means the competition gives a very good indication of the footballing prowess on the continent. The great teams from the past have all managed to inscribe their name on the trophy - the Egyptian team of the late 1950s; Ghana at the time of independence in the 1960s; Zaire in the early 1970s; Cameroon in the 1980s; and the Nigerians of the mid-1990s. Fifteen nations have hosted the tournament which has grown from a three team round robin in the early years into a 16 team spectacular. For the 2006 edition the FIFA World Cup™ qualifiers doubled up as Nations Cup qualifiers to ease the fixture load and this remains the plan for those editions played in future FIFA World Cup™ years. In 2006 Egypt hosted the tournament for the fourth time and won a record fifth title, moving one ahead of Ghana who will hope to draw level again when they host the tournament in 2008. Remarkably the other previous joint record holders, Cameroon, have won all their four titles away from home.

CAF AFRICAN WOMEN'S CHAMPIONSHIP

Year	Host Country	Winners	Score	Runners-up	Venue
1991		Nigeria	2-0 4-0	Cameroon	
1995		Nigeria	4-1 7-1	South Africa	
1998	Nigeria	Nigeria	2-0	Ghana	Abeokuta
2000	South Africa	Nigeria	2-0	South Africa	Johannesburg
2002	Nigeria	Nigeria	2-0	Ghana	Lagos
2004	South Africa	Nigeria	5-0	Cameroon	Johannesburg

With relatively little empowerment of women on the continent the game is not particulary widespread but the chance of a place in the FIFA Women's World Cup provided the spur for CAF to introduce a women's Championship. To date Nigeria has won all six tournaments with Cameroon, South Africa and Ghana each losing in the final twice.

AFRICAN YOUTH CHAMPIONSHIP

Year	Host Country	Winners	Score	Runners-up	Venue
1979		Algeria	2-1 2-3	Guinea	Algiers, Conakry
1981		Egypt	1-1 2-0	Cameroon	Douala, Cairo
1983		Nigeria	2-2 2-1	Côte d'Ivoire	Abidjan, Lagos
1985		Nigeria	1-1 2-1	Tunisia	Tunis, Lagos
1987		Nigeria	2-1 3-0	Togo	Lomé, Lagos
1989		Nigeria	2-1 2-0	Mali	Bamako, Lagos
1991	Egypt	Egypt	2-1	Côte d'Ivoire	Cairo
1993	Mauritius	Ghana	2-0	Cameroon	Bellevue
1995	Nigeria	Cameroon	4-0	Burundi	Lagos
1997	Morocco	Morocco	1-0	South Africa	Meknès
1999	Ghana	Ghana	1-0	Nigeria	Accra
2001	Ethiopia	Angola	2-0	Ghana	Addis Abeba
2003	Burkina Faso	Egypt	4-3	Côte d'Ivoire	Ouagadougou
2005	Benin	Nigeria	2-0	Egypt	Cotonou

AFRICAN U–17 CHAMPIONSHIP

Year	Host Country	Winners	Score	Runners-up	Venue
1995	Mali	Ghana	3-1	Nigeria	Bamako
1997	Botswana	Egypt	1-0	Mali	Gaborone
1999	Guinea	Ghana	3-1	Burkina Faso	Conakry
2001	Seychelles	Nigeria	3-0	Burkina Faso	Victoria
2003	Swaziland	Cameroon	1-0	Sierra Leone	Mbabane
2005	Gambia	Gambia	1-0	Ghana	Bakau

AFRICAN WOMEN'S U–19 CHAMPIONSHIP

Year	Host Country	Winners	Score	Runners-up	Venue
2002		Nigeria	6-0 3-2	South Africa	
2004		Nigeria	1-0 0-0	South Africa	

Africa's youth tournaments came from the need to play qualifiers for the FIFA age-restricted competitions. Until the 1990s they were played on a home and away basis but since 1991 in the Youth Championship and 1995 in the U-17s, there has been a final tournament in a designated country. This has given those countries unlikely to host the CAF Africa Cup of Nations a chance to organise a major football tournament.

FOOTBALL TOURNAMENT OF THE AFRICAN GAMES

Year	Host Country	Winners	Score	Runners-up	Venue
1965	Congo	Congo	0-0 †	Mali	Brazzaville
1973	Nigeria	Nigeria	2-0	Guinea	Lagos
1978	Algeria	Algeria	1-0	Nigeria	Algiers
1987	Kenya	Egypt	1-0	Kenya	Nairobi
1991	Egypt	Cameroon	1-0	Tunisia	Cairo
1995	Zimbabwe	Egypt	3-1	Zimbabwe	Harare
1999	South Africa	Cameroon	0-0 4-3p	Zambia	Johannesburg
2003	Nigeria	Cameroon	2-0	Nigeria	Abuja

† Decided on number of corner-kicks awarded. Congo won 7-2

WOMEN'S FOOTBALL TOURNAMENT OF THE AFRICAN GAMES

Year	Host Country	Winners	Score	Runners-up	Venue
2003	Nigeria	Nigeria	1-0	South Africa	Abuja

At one time the football tournament of the African Games carried enormous prestige but it is only since 1987 that it has been played on a regular basis. Cameroon and Egypt have dominated since then although it is now staged as an age-restricted tournament as at the Olympics. The 1965 final at the Brazzaville Games threw up an interesting historical curiosity. After the hosts Congo and Mali could only draw 0-0, the game was decided not on penalties but by the number of corner kicks won which many believe is a much fairer system.

CAF CHAMPIONS LEAGUE

Year	Winners	Country	Score	Country	Runners-up
1965	Oryx Douala	CMR	2-1	MLI	Stade Malien
1966	Stade Abidjan	CIV	1-3 4-1	MLI	AS Real Bamako
1967	Tout Puissant Englebert	ZAI	1-1 2-2	GHA	Asante Kotoko
1968	Tout Puissant Englebert	ZAI	5-0 1-4	TOG	Etoile Filante
1969	Al Ismaili	EGY	2-2 3-1	ZAI	Tout Puissant Englebert
1970	Asante Kotoko	GHA	1-1 2-1	ZAI	Tout Puissant Englebert
1971	Canon Yaoundé	CMR	0-3 2-0 1-0	GHA	Asante Kotoko
1972	Hafia FC Conakry	GUI	4-2 3-2	UGA	Simba FC
1973	AS Vita Kinshasa	ZAI	2-4 3-0	GHA	Asante Kotoko
1974	CARA Brazzaville	CGO	4-2 2-1	EGY	Mehalla Al Kubra
1975	Hafia FC Conakry	GUI	1-0 2-1	NGA	Enugu Rangers
1976	Mouloudia d'Algiers	ALG	3-0 0-3 4-1p	GUI	Hafia FC Conakry
1977	Hafia FC Conakry	GUI	1-0 3-2	GHA	Hearts of Oak
1978	Canon Yaoundé	CMR	0-0 2-0	GUI	Hafia FC Conakry
1979	Union Douala	CMR	0-1 1-0 5-3p	GHA	Hearts of Oak
1980	Canon Yaoundé	CMR	2-2 3-0	ZAI	AS Bilima
1981	JE Tizi-Ouzou	ALG	4-0 1-0	ZAI	AS Vita Kinshasa
1982	Al Ahly Cairo	EGY	3-0 1-1	GHA	Asante Kotoko
1983	Asante Kotoko	GHA	0-0 1-0	EGY	Al Ahly Cairo
1984	Zamalek	EGY	2-0 1-0	NGA	Shooting Stars
1985	FAR Rabat	MAR	5-2 1-1	ZAI	AS Bilima
1986	Zamalek	EGY	2-0 0-2 4-2p	CIV	Africa Sports
1987	Al Ahly Cairo	EGY	0-0 2-0	SUD	Al Hilal
1988	Entente Setif	ALG	0-1 4-0	NGA	Iwuanyanwu Owerri
1989	Raja Casablanca	MAR	1-0 0-1 4-2p	ALG	Mouloudia d'Oran
1990	JS Kabylie	ALG	1-0 0-1 5-3p	ZAM	Nkana Red Devils
1991	Club Africain	TUN	5-1 1-1	UGA	Nakivubo Villa
1992	Wydad Casablanca	MAR	2-0 0-0	SUD	Al Hilal
1993	Zamalek	EGY	0-0 0-0 7-6p	GHA	Asante Kotoko
1994	Espérance Tunis	TUN	0-0 3-1	EGY	Zamalek
1995	Orlando Pirates	RSA	2-2 1-0	CIV	ASEC Mimosas
1996	Zamalek	EGY	1-2 2-1 4-2p	NGA	Shooting Stars
1997	Raja Casablanca	MAR	0-1 1-0 5-4p	GHA	Obuasi Goldfields
1998	ASEC Mimosas	CIV	0-0 4-1	ZIM	Dynamos
1999	Raja Casablanca	MAR	0-0 0-0 4-3p	TUN	Espérance Tunis
2000	Hearts of Oak	GHA	2-1 3-1	TUN	Espérance Tunis
2001	Al Ahly Cairo	EGY	1-1 3-0	RSA	Pretoria Sundowns
2002	Zamalek	EGY	0-0 1-0	MAR	Raja Casablanca
2003	Enyimba	NGA	2-0 0-1	EGY	Al Ismaili
2004	Enyimba	NGA	1-2 2-1 5-3p	TUN	Etoile du Sahel
2005	Al Ahly Cairo	EGY	0-0 3-0	TUN	Etoile du Sahel

Previously known the African Cup of Champion Clubs, the CAF Champions League is unpredictable and never short of controversy, but it remains hugely entertaining despite the growing number of African players who will never compete in it thanks to moves to Europe at increasingly young ages. The heart of the rivalry in the tournament lies between the Arab North African countries and the sub-Saharan countries. Until the 1980s the latter held the upper hand but for 17 years between 1981 and 1997 only Ghana's Asante Kotoko and Orlando Pirates from South Africa managed to prise the Cup from the north. Since 1995 the honours have been split evenly, although club football in North Africa is run along more professional lines and suffers less from an exodus of leading players. It has proved difficult for any club, however, to maintain a consistant presence in the tournament with the possible exception of the two Egyptian giants Al Ahly and record title holders Zamalek. In 2004 Enyimba became only the second club to retain the title and the first since 1968. They were also the 19th different club from 13 different countries to have won the title. No other continent has such a range of winners.

CAF CUP WINNERS' CUP

Year	Winners	Country	Score	Country	Runners-up
1975	Tonnerre Yaoundé	CMR	1-0 4-1	CIV	Stella Abidjan
1976	Shooting Stars	NGA	4-1 0-1	CMR	Tonnerre Yaoundé
1977	Enugu Rangers	NGA	4-1 1-1	CMR	Canon Yaoundé
1978	Horoya AC Conakry	GUI	3-1 2-1	ALG	MA Hussein-Dey
1979	Canon Yaoundé	CMR	2-0 6-0	KEN	Gor Mahia
1980	TP Mazembe	ZAI	3-1 1-0	CIV	Africa Sports
1981	Union Douala	CMR	2-1 0-0	NGA	Stationery Stores
1982	Al Mokaoulum	EGY	2-0 2-0	ZAM	Power Dynamos
1983	Al Mokaoulum	EGY	1-0 0-0	TOG	Agaza Lomé
1984	Al Ahly Cairo	EGY	1-0 0-1 4-2p	CMR	Canon Yaoundé
1985	Al Ahly Cairo	EGY	2-0 0-1	NGA	Leventis United
1986	Al Ahly Cairo	EGY	3-0 0-2	GAB	AS Sogara
1987	Gor Mahia	KEN	2-2 1-1	TUN	Espérance Tunis
1988	CA Bizerte	TUN	0-0 1-0	NGA	Ranchers Bees
1989	Al Merreikh	SUD	1-0 0-0	NGA	Bendel United
1990	BCC Lions	NGA	3-0 1-1	TUN	Club Africain
1991	Power Dynamos	ZAM	2-3 3-1	NGA	BCC Lions
1992	Africa Sports	CIV	1-1 4-0	BDI	Vital'O
1993	Al Ahly Cairo	EGY	1-1 1-0	CIV	Africa Sports
1994	DC Motema Pembe	ZAI	2-2 3-0	KEN	Kenya Breweries
1995	JS Kabylie	ALG	1-1 2-1	NGA	Julius Berger
1996	Al Mokaoulum	EGY	0-0 4-0	ZAI	Sodigraf
1997	Etoile du Sahel	TUN	2-0 0-1	MAR	FAR Rabat
1998	Espérance Tunis	TUN	3-1 1-1	ANG	Primeiro Agosto
1999	Africa Sports	CIV	1-0 1-1	TUN	Club Africain
2000	Zamalek	EGY	4-1 0-2	CMR	Canon Yaoundé
2001	Kaiser Chiefs	RSA	1-1 1-0	ANG	Inter Luanda
2002	Wydad Casablanca	MAR	1-0 1-2	GHA	Asante Kotoko
2003	Etoile du Sahel	TUN	0-2 3-0	NGA	Julius Berger

Discontinued after the 2003 tournament and replaced by the CAF Confederation Cup

CAF CUP

Year	Winners	Country	Score	Country	Runners-up
1992	Shooting Stars	NGA	0-0 3-0	UGA	Nakivubo Villa
1993	Stella Abidjan	CIV	0-0 2-0	TAN	SC Simba
1994	Bendel Insurance	NGA	0-1 3-0	ANG	Primeiro de Maio
1995	Etoile du Sahel	TUN	0-0 2-0	GUI	Kaloum Star
1996	Kawkab Marrakech	MAR	1-3 2-0	TUN	Etoile du Sahel
1997	Esperance Tunis	TUN	0-1 2-0	ANG	Petro Atlético
1998	CS Sfaxien	TUN	1-0 3-0	SEN	ASC Jeanne d'Arc
1999	Etoile du Sahel	TUN	1-0 1-2	MAR	Wydad Casablanca
2000	JS Kabylie	ALG	1-1 0-0	EGY	Al Ismaili
2001	JS Kabylie	ALG	1-2 1-0	TUN	Etoile du Sahel
2002	JS Kabylie	ALG	4-0 0-1	CMR	Tonnerre Youndé
2003	Raja Casablanca	MAR	2-0 0-0	CMR	Cotonsport Garoua

Discontinued after the 2003 tournament and replaced by the CAF Confederation Cup

CAF CONFEDERATION CUP

Year	Winners	Country	Score	Country	Runners-up
2004	Hearts of Oak	GHA	1-1 1-1 8-7p	GHA	Asante Kotoko
2005	FAR Rabat	MAR	0-1 3-0	NGA	Dolphin Port Harcourt

With the decision to allow more than one team from each country into the CAF Champions League, CAF decided in 2003 to discarded the Cup Winners' Cup and the CAF Cup in favour of a 'best of the rest' tournament - the CAF Confederation Cup. Teams knocked out in early rounds of the Champions League enter the Confederation Cup at the intermediate stage after which there is a group stage with the winners of each group contesting the final.

COSAFA CUP

Year	Host Country	Winners	Score	Runners-up	Venue
1997	Home and away	Zambia	1-1	Namibia	Windhoek
1998	Home and away	Zambia	1-0	Zimbabwe	Harare
1999	Home and away	Angola	1-0 1-1	Namibia	Luanda & Windhoek
2000	Home and away	Zimbabwe	3-0 3-0	Lesotho	Maseru & Bulawayo
2001	Home and away	Angola	0-0 1-0	Zimbabwe	Luanda & Harare
2002	Home and away	South Africa	3-1 1-0	Malawi	Blantyre & Durban
2003	Home and away	Zimbabwe	2-1 2-0	Malawi	Blantyre & Harare
2004	Home and away	Angola	0-0 5-4p	Zambia	Lusaka
2005	Home and away	Zimbabwe	1-0	Zambia	Mafikeng

The 1997 and 1998 tournaments were played as a league. The result listed is that between the winners and runners-up

COPA AMILCAR CABRAL

Year	Host Country	Winners	Score	Runners-up	Venue
1979	Guinea-Bissau	Senegal	1-0	Mali	Bissau
1980	Gambia	Senegal	1-0	Gambia	Banjul
1981	Mali	Guinea	0-0 6-5p	Mali	Bamako
1982	Cape Verde	Guinea	3-0	Senegal	Praia
1983	Mauritania	Senegal	3-0	Guinea-Bissau	Nouakchott
1984	Sierra Leone	Senegal	0-0 5-3p	Sierra Leone	Freetown
1985	Gambia	Senegal	1-0	Gambia	Banjul
1986	Senegal	Senegal	3-1	Sierra Leone	Dakar
1987	Guinea	Guinea	1-0	Mali	Conakry
1988	Guinea-Bissau	Guinea	3-2	Mali	Bissau
1989	Mali	Mali	3-0	Guinea	Bamako
1991	Senegal	Senegal	1-0	Cape Verde Islands	Dakar
1993	Sierra Leone	Sierra Leone	2-0	Senegal	Freetown
1995	Mauritania	Sierra Leone	0-0 4-2p	Mauritania	Nouakchott
1997	Gambia	Mali	1-0	Senegal	Banjul
2000	Cape Verde	Cape Verde Islands	1-0	Senegal	Praia
2001	Mali	Senegal	3-1	Gambia	Bamako
2005	Guinea	Guinea	1-0	Senegal	Conakry

COUPE CEMAC

Year	Host Country	Winners	Score	Runners-up	Venue
2003	Congo	Cameroon	3-2	Central African Rep.	Brazzaville
2005	Gabon	Cameroon	1-0	Chad	Libreville

There is a long and rich history of regional tournaments in Africa dating back to 1926 when William Gossage sponsored an annual competition between Kenya and Uganda. From 1945 it was extended to include Tanganyika and then Zanzibar from 1949 and was a popular feature of the football calendar. With independence the name of the competition was changed to the Challenge Cup in 1967. With the creation in 1973 of CECAFA – the Confederation of East and Central African Football Associations – the tournament was renamed as the CECAFA Cup and expanded to include Zambia and Somalia; Malawi joined in 1975, Sudan in 1980, Zimbabwe in 1982, Ethiopia in 1983, Seychelles in 1992, Eritrea and Djibouti in 1994, Rwanda in 1995 and finally Burundi in 1998. The Southern African contingent left to join COSAFA in the aftermath of South Africa's return to international football with the first COSAFA Castle Cup held in 1997 and contested since by Angola, Botswana, Lesotho, Madagascar, Malawi, Mauritius, Mozambique, Namibia, Seychelles, South Africa, Swaziland, Zambia and Zimbabwe. The situation in West Africa has been much more fragmented although the Copa Amilcar Cabral has stood the test of time unlike many other tournaments in the region. The Coupe CEMAC is the latest addition to the list of tournaments. Introduced in 2003 entries come from the member states of the Communauté Economique et Monétaire de l'Afrique Central.

CECAFA CUP

Year	Host Country	Winners	Score	Runners-up
1973	Uganda	Uganda	2-1	Tanzania
1974	Tanzania	Tanzania	1-1 5-3p	Uganda
1975	Zambia	Kenya	0-0 5-4p	Malawi
1976	Zanzibar	Uganda	2-0	Zambia
1977	Somalia	Uganda	0-0 5-3p	Zambia
1978	Malawi	Malawi	3-2	Zambia
1979	Kenya	Malawi	3-2	Kenya
1980	Sudan	Sudan	1-0	Tanzania
1981	Tanzania	Kenya	1-0	Tanzania
1982	Uganda	Kenya	1-1 5-3p	Uganda
1983	Kenya	Kenya	1-0	Zimbabwe
1984	Uganda	Zambia	0-0 3-0p	Malawi
1985	Zimbabwe	Zimbabwe	2-0	Kenya
1986	Sudan	Not held		
1987	Ethiopia	Ethiopia	1-1 5-4p	Zimbabwe
1988	Malawi	Malawi	3-1	Zambia
1989	Kenya	Uganda	3-3 2-1	Malawi
1990	Zanzibar	Uganda	2-0	Sudan
1991	Uganda	Zambia	2-0	Kenya
1992	Tanzania	Uganda	1-0	Tanzania
1993	Uganda	Not held		
1994	Kenya	Tanzania	2-2 4-3p	Uganda
1995	Uganda	Zanzibar	1-0	Uganda
1996	Sudan	Uganda	1-0	Sudan
1997		Not held		
1998	Rwanda	Not held		
1999	Rwanda	Rwanda B	3-1	Kenya
2000	Uganda	Uganda	2-0	Uganda B
2001	Rwanda	Ethiopia	2-1	Kenya
2002	Tanzania	Kenya	3-2	Tanzania
2003	Sudan	Uganda	2-0	Rwanda
2004	Ethiopia	Ethiopia	3-0	Burundi
2005	Rwanda	Ethiopia	1-0	Rwanda

CECAFA CLUB CHAMPIONSHIP

Year	Winners	Country	Score	Country	Runners-up
1974	Simba SC	TAN	1-0 †	KEN	Abaluhya FC
1975	Young Africans	TAN	2-0	TAN	Simba SC
1976	Luo Union	KEN	2-1	TAN	Young Africans
1977	Luo Union	KEN	2-1	SOM	Horsed
1978	Kamapala City Council	UGA	0-0 3-2p	TAN	Simba SC
1979	Abaluhya FC	KEN	1-0	UGA	Kampala City Council
1980	Gor Mahia	KEN	3-2	KEN	Abaluhya FC
1981	Gor Mahia	KEN	1-0	TAN	Simba SC
1982	AFC Leopards	KEN	1-0	ZIM	Rio Tinto
1983	AFC Leopards	KEN	2-1	MWI	Admarc Tigers
1984	AFC Leopards	KEN	2-1	KEN	Gor Mahia
1985	Gor Mahia	KEN	2-0	KEN	AFC Leopards
1986	El Merreikh	SUD	2-2 4-2p	TAN	Young Africans
1987	Nakivubo Villa	UGA	1-0	SUD	El Merreikh
1988	Kenya Breweries	KEN	2-0	SUD	El Merreikh
1989	Kenya Breweries	KEN	3-0	TAN	Coastal Union
1990	Not held				
1991	Simba SC	TAN	3-0	UGA	Nikivubo Villa
1992	Simba SC	TAN	1-1 5-4p	TAN	Young Africans
1993	Young Africans	TAN	2-1	UGA	Nakivubo Villa

CECAFA CLUB CHAMPIONSHIP (CONT'D)

Year	Winners	Country	Score	Country	Runners-up
1994	El Merreikh	SUD	2-1	UGA	Express FC
1995	Simba SC	TAN	1-1 5-3p	UGA	Express FC
1996	Simba SC	TAN	1-0	RWA	APR FC
1997	AFC Leopards	KEN	1-0	KEN	Kenya Breweries
1998	Rayyon Sport	RWA	2-1	ZAN	Mlandege
1999	Young Africans	TAN	1-1 4-1p	UGA	SC Villa
2000	Tusker FC	KEN	3-1	RWA	APR FC
2001	Tusker FC	KEN	0-0 3-0p	KEN	Oserian
2002	Simba SC	TAN	1-0	BDI	Prince Louis
2003	SC Villa	UGA	1-0	TAN	Simba SC
2004	APR FC	RWA	3-1	KEN	Ulinzi Stars
2005	SC Villa	UGA	3-0	RWA	APR FC
2006	Police FC	UGA	2-1	TAN	Moro United

PAST AFRICAN PLAYER OF THE YEAR AWARDS

PLAYER OF THE YEAR 1970

KEITA Salif	Saint-Étienne	MLI	54
POKOU Laurent	ASEC Abidjan	CIV	28
ABOUGREISHA Ali	Ismaili	EGY	28
KALALA Pierre	TP Englebert	ZAI	19
LALMAS Hacène	CR Belcourt	ALG	15
SORY Petit	Hafia	GUI	9
ALLAL Ben Kassou	FAR Rabat	MAR	5
MENSAH Robert	Asante Kotoko	GHA	5
KOFI Osei	Asante Kotoko	GHA	5
Four players with four votes			

PLAYER OF THE YEAR 1971

SUNDAY Ibrahim	Asante Kotoko	GHA	29
MENSAH Robert	Asante Kotoko	GHA	15
OBENGUE Lea	Canon	CMR	13
POKOU Laurent	ASEC Abidjan	CIV	8
ATTOUGA Sadok	Club Africain	TUN	8
KIBONGE Mafu	Victoria Club	ZAI	6
M'PELE Francois	Ajaccio	CGO	6
KOUM Emmanuel	Monaco	CMR	6
LALMAS Hacène	CR Belcourt	ALG	6
KALLET BIALY Ernest	Africa Sports	CIV	6

PLAYER OF THE YEAR 1972

SOULEYMANE Cherif	Hafia	GUI	21
BWANGA Tshimen	TP Mazembe	ZAI	16
SORY Petit	Hafia	GUI	14
HANY Moustafa	Al Ahly	EGY	12
FARRAS Ahmed	Mohammedia	MAR	11
HADEFI Miloud	MO Oran	ALG	11
MALIK Jabir	Asante Kotoko	GHA	10
ABOUGREISHA Ali	Ismaili	EGY	8
MINGA Jean-Noel	CARA	CGO	8
N'TUMBA Kalala	Vita	ZAI	8

PLAYER OF THE YEAR 1973

BWANGA Tshimen	TP Mazembe	ZAI	49
KAZADI Mwamba	TP Mazembe	ZAI	44
POKOU Laurent	ASEC Abidjan	CIV	41
KAKOKO Etepe	Imana	ZAI	29
FARRAS Ahmed	Mohammedia	MAR	18
SAM Yaw	Asante Kotoko	GHA	16
KEMBO Kembo Uba	Vita	ZAI	15
SOULEYMANE Cherif	Hafia	GUI	9
Three players with eight votes			

PLAYER OF THE YEAR 1974

MOUKILA Paul	CARA	CGO	57
LOBILO Boba	Vita	ZAI	32
SHEHATA Hassan	Zamalek	EGY	28
CHAMA Dickson	Gr'n Buffaloes	ZAM	16
FARRAS Ahmed	Mohammedia	MAR	14
N'DAYE Mulamba	Vita	ZAI	10
KAKOKO Etepe	Imana	ZAI	8
Five players with six votes			

PLAYER OF THE YEAR 1975

FARRAS Ahmed	Mohammedia	MAR	28
N'JO LEA Mamadou	Hafia	GUI	24
MILLA Roger	Canon	CMR	24
DHIAB Tarak	Esperance	TUN	16
SAGNA Christophe	Jeanne d'Arc	SEN	15
SORY Petit	Hafia	GUI	10
LARBI Ahardane	Wydad	MAR	9
GAAFAR Farouk	Zamalek	EGY	7
ATTOUGA Sadok	Club Africain	TUN	7
Three players with five votes			

PLAYER OF THE YEAR 1976

MILLA Roger	Tonnerre	CMR	33
CAMARA Papa	Hafia	GUI	32
BENCHEIKH Ali	MC Alger	ALG	27
SYLLA Bengally	Hafia	GUI	26
FARRAS Ahmed	Mohammedia	MAR	12
BETROUNI Rachid	MC Alger	ALG	12
LARBI Ahardane	Wydad	MAR	11
ATTOUGA Sadok	Club Africain	TUN	11
DHIAB Tarak	Esperance	TUN	10
SORY Petit	Hafia	GUI	10

PLAYER OF THE YEAR 1977

DHIAB Tarak	Espérance	TUN	45
CAMARA Papa	Hafia	GUI	33
ODEGBAMI Segun	Shooting Stars	NGA	29
POLO Mohamed	Olympics	GHA	15
BWALYA Thomas	Mufulira	ZAM	6
BENCHEIKH Ali	MC Alger	ALG	5
ATTOUGA Sadok	Club Africain	TUN	4
GAAFAR Farouk	Zamalek	EGY	3
BAHAMBOULA Jonas	Diable Noir	CGO	3
SOULEYMANE Cherif	Hafia	GUI	3

PLAYER OF THE YEAR 1978

ABDUL RAZAK Karim	Asante Kotoko	GHA	58
BENCHEIKH Ali	MP Algiers	ALG	33
N'KONO Thomas	Canon	CMR	29
CHUKWU Christian	Enugu Rangers	NGA	25
SYLLA Bengally	Hafia	GUI	20
DHIAB Tarak	Al Ahly Jeddah	TUN	18
LAHZANI Temime	Espérance	TUN	12
MANGA-ONGUENE J	Canon	CMR	10
OMONDI Philip	Kampala CC	UGA	9
Four players with four votes			

PLAYER OF THE YEAR 1979

N'KONO Thomas	Canon	CMR	55
ARMAH Adolf	Hearts of Oak	GHA	23
BANGOURA Kerfalla	Horoya	GUI	15
CAMPAORE Abdoulaye	Bobo Dioulasso	BFA	13
OLUOCH Nahashion	Gor Mahia	KEN	9
KIYIKA Tokodia	Imana	ZAI	8
AGBONIFO Felix	Shooting Stars	NGA	7
MIEZAN Pascal	ASEC Abidjan	CIV	6
LAWAL Muda	Shooting Stars	NGA	5
Four players with four votes			

PLAYER OF THE YEAR 1980

MANGA-ONGUENE J	Canon	CMR	64
ODEGBAMI Segun	Shooting Stars	NGA	41
ABEGA Théophile	Canon	CMR	18
BELLOUMI Lakhdar	GCR Mascara	ALG	13
MAYELE Ayel	AS Bilima	ZAI	12
N'KONO Thomas	Canon	CMR	12
KOUICI Mustapha	CR Belcourt	MAR	11
MASSENGO Elunga	TP Mazembe	ZAI	7
BENSAOULA Tadj	MC Oran	ALG	6
KAZADI Mwamba	TP Mazembe	ZAI	6

PLAYER OF THE YEAR 1981

BELLOUMI Lakhdar	GCR Mascara	ALG	78
N'KONO Thomas	Canon	CMR	54
FERGANI Ali	JE Tizi-Ouzou	ALG	26
EKOULE Eugène	Union Douala	CMR	18
ABEGA Théophile	Canon	CMR	16
BOUDERBALA Aziz	Wydad	MAR	16
ODEGBAMI Segun	Shooting Stars	NGA	8
KEITA Cheik	Kaloum Stars	GUI	6
KOUADIO Koffi	ASEC Abidjan	CIV	4
ZAKI Badou	Wydad	MAR	4

PLAYER OF THE YEAR 1982

N'KONO Thomas	Español	CMR	83
ASSAD Salah	Mulhouse	ALG	54
BELLOUMI Lakhdar	GCR Mascara	ALG	36
EL KHATIB Mahmoud	Al Ahly Cairo	EGY	28
ABEGA Théophile	Canon	CMR	23
KAUMBA Peter	Power Dynamos	ZAM	23
ASASE Albert	Asante Kotoko	GHA	22
AFRIYIE Opoku	Asante Kotoko	GHA	13
MADJER Rabah	Hussein Dey	ALG	9
MERZEKANE Chaabane	Hussein Dey	ALG	8

PLAYER OF THE YEAR 1983

EL KHATIB Mahmoud	Al Ahly Cairo	EGY	98
N'TI Opoku	Asante Kotoko	GHA	89
MOUTAIROU Rafiou	Agaza Lomé	TOG	19
ABEGA Théophile	Canon	CMR	18
BELL Joseph Antoine	Al Mokaouloum	CMR	18
ABDUL RAZAK Karim	Al Mokaouloum	GHA	18
SECK Cheikh	Diaraf Dakar	SEN	11
NASSER Mohamed Ali	Al Ahly Cairo	EGY	7
HADDAOUI Mustapha	Rajan	MAR	7
MADJER Rabah	Racing Paris	ALG	7

PLAYER OF THE YEAR 1984

ABEGA Théophile	Toulouse	CMR	124
YOUSSEF Ibrahim	Zamalek	EGY	65
BELL Joseph Antoine	Al Mokaouloum	CMR	65
NWOSU Henry	Nigerian Bank	NGA	47
ABOU ZEID Taher	Al Ahly Cairo	EGY	28
FOFANA Youssouf	Cannes	CIV	28
EL KHATIB Mahmoud	Al Ahly Cairo	EGY	28
KESHI Stephen	Nigerian Bank	NGA	16
BELLOUMI Lakhdar	GCR Mascara	ALG	12
MSIYA Clifton	Berrick Power	MWI	12

PLAYER OF THE YEAR 1985

TIMOUMI Mohamed	FAR Rabat	MAR	113
MADJER Rabah	Porto	ALG	45
MENAD Djamel	JE Tizi-Ouzou	ALG	39
YOUSSEF Ibrahim	Zamalek	EGY	39
ZAKI Badou	Wydad	MAR	33
FOFANA Youssouf	Monaco	CIV	31
BELLOUMI Lakhdar	GCR Mascara	ALG	20
PELE Abedi	Dragons	GHA	19
BOCANDE Jules	Metz	SEN	17
Two players with 16 votes			

PLAYER OF THE YEAR 1986

ZAKI Badou	Real Mallorca	MAR	125
BOUDERBALA Aziz	Sion	MAR	88
MILLA Roger	Montpellier	CMR	80
ABOU ZEID Taher	Al Ahly	EGY	47
TIMOUMI Mohamed	Real Murcia	MAR	35
BOCANDE Jules	PSG	SEN	13
DOLMY Abdelmajid	Raja	MAR	13
PELE Abedi	Niort	GHA	13
CHABALA Efford	Nkana	ZAM	11
DRID Nacer	MP Oran	ALG	11

PLAYER OF THE YEAR 1987

MADJER Rabah	Porto	ALG	130
FOFANA Youssouf	Monaco	CIV	63
OMAM BIYIK François	Laval	CMR	52
ABDELGHANI Magdi	Al Ahly Cairo	EGY	37
ABOU ZEID Taher	Al Ahly Cairo	EGY	25
MALUNGA Kennedy	Club Brugge	MWI	24
DAWO Peter	Gor Mahia	KEN	21
PELE Abedi	Marseille	GHA	17
AYOYI Ambrose	AFC Leopards	KEN	15
MILLA Roger	Montpellier	CMR	14

PLAYER OF THE YEAR 1988

BWALYA Kalusha	Cercle Brugge	ZAM	111
MILLA Roger	Montpellier	CMR	68
FOFANA Youssouf	Monaco	CIV	40
WEAH George	Monaco	LBR	32
BOUDERBALA Aziz	Racing Paris	MAR	27
RUFAI Peter	Lokeren	NGA	27
KESHI Stephen	Anderlecht	NGA	14
KUNDE Emmanuel	Reims	CMR	14
KINGAMBO Jacques	St Truidense	ZAI	13
BELL Joseph Antoine	Toulon	CMR	12

PLAYER OF THE YEAR 1989

WEAH George	Monaco	LBR	133
BELL Joseph Antoine	Bordeaux	CMR	105
BWALYA Kalusha	PSV	ZAM	49
PELE Abedi	Lille OSC	GHA	40
OMAM BIYIK François	Laval	CMR	31
ABDELGHANI Magdi	Beira Mar	EGY	30
SHOUBEIR Ahmed	Al Ahly Cairo	EGY	28
TATAW Stephen	Tonnerre	CMR	19
KESHI Stephen	Anderlecht	NGA	18
HASSAN Hossam	Al Ahly Cairo	EGY	17

PLAYER OF THE YEAR 1990

MILLA Roger	No Club	CMR	209
EL OUAZANI Cherif	Aydinspor	ALG	64
MADJER Rabah	Porto	ALG	60
OMAM BIYIK François	Stade Rennais	CMR	60
SHOUBEIR Ahmed	Al Ahly Cairo	EGY	49
RAMZY Hany	Neuchâtel	EGY	41
MAKANAKY Cyrille	Málaga	CMR	34
WEAH George	Monaco	LBR	26
PELE Abedi	Marseille	GHA	23
HASSAN Hossam	PAOK	EGY	22

PLAYER OF THE YEAR 1991

PELE Abedi	Marseile	GHA	159
WEAH George	Monaco	LBR	106
OMAM BIYIK François	Cannes	CMR	52
BWALYA Kalusha	PSV	ZAM	30
LAMPETY Nii	Anderlecht	GHA	29
YEBOAH Anthony	Ein. Frankfurt	GHA	20
MENDY Roger	Monaco	SEN	18
TRAORE Abdoulaye	ASEC Abidjan	CIV	16
FOFANA Youssouf	Monaco	CIV	14
BOUDERBALA Aziz	Lyon	EGY	13

PLAYER OF THE YEAR 1992

PELE Abedi	Marseille	GHA	198
WEAH George	PSG	LBR	161
YEBOAH Anthony	Ein. Frankfurt	GHA	64
TRAORE Abdoulaye	ASEC Abidjan	CIV	36
GOUAMENE Alain	Raja	CIV	33
N'DORAM Japhet	Nantes	CIV	28
NDLOVU Peter	Coventry City	ZIM	24
YEKINI Rashidi	Vitoria Setubal	NGA	20
BWALYA Kalusha	PSV	ZAM	15
DAOUDI Rachid	Wydad	MAR	14

PLAYER OF THE YEAR 1993

PELE Abedi	Lyonnais	GHA	119
YEBOAH Anthony	Ein. Frankfurt	GHA	117
YEKINI Rashidi	Vitoria Setubal	NGA	104
IKPEBA Victor	Monaco	NGA	57
WEAH George	PSG	LBR	56
BWALYA Kalusha	PSV	ZAM	48
OMAM BIYIK François	RC Lens	CMR	28
DAOUDI Rachid	Wydad	MAR	20
NDLOVU Peter	Coventry City	ZAM	19
TRAORE Abdoulaye	ASEC Abidjan	CIV	16

PLAYER OF THE YEAR 1994

WEAH George	PSG	LBR	148
AMUNIKE Emmanuel	Sporting CP	NGA	133
AMOKACHI Daniel	Everton	NGA	99
YEKINI Rashidi	Olympiakos	NGA	87
BWALYA Kalusha	América	ZAM	37
YEBOAH Anthony	Ein. Frankfurt	GHA	32
GEORGE Finidi	Ajax	NGA	31
TIEHI Joël	Le Havre	CIV	22
N'DORAM Japhet	Nantes	CHA	18
OKOCHA Jay-Jay	Ein. Frankfurt	NGA	18

CAF PLAYER OF THE YEAR 1992

PELE Abedi	Marseille	GHA
GOUAMENE Alain	Raja	CIV
YEKINI Rashidi	Vitoria Setubal	NGA
WEAH George	PSG	LBR
DAOUDI Rachid	Wydad	MAR
MAGUY Serge Alain	Africa Sports	CIV
YEBOAH Anthony	Ein. Frankfurt	GHA
RAMZY Hany	Neuchatel	EGY
NDAW Moussa	Wydad	SEN
AMOKACHI Daniel	Club Brugge	NGA

CAF PLAYER OF THE YEAR 1993

YEKINI Rashidi	Vitoria Setubal	NGA
PELE Abedi	Marseille	GHA
WEAH George	PSG	LBR
YEBOAH Anthony	Ein. Frankfurt	GHA
OMAM BIYIK François	RC Lens	CMR
NAYBET Nouredine	Nantes	MAR
IKPEBA Victor	Monaco	NGA
BELL Joseph Antoine	Saint-Etienne	CMR
Three players in 9th place		

CAF PLAYER OF THE YEAR 1994

AMUNIKE Emmanuel	Sporting CP	NGA
WEAH George	PSG	LBR
YEKINI Rashidi	Olympiakos	NGA
GEORGE Finidi	Ajax	NGA
AMOKACHI Daniel	Everton	NGA
N'DORAM Japhet	Nantes	CHA
TIEHI Joel	Le Havre	CIV
OKOCHA Jay-Jay	Ein. Frankfurt	NGA
MAGUY Serge Alain	Africa Sports	CIV
OLISEH Sunday	FC Liège	NGA

CAF PLAYER OF THE YEAR 1995

WEAH George	Milan	LBR
N'DORAM Japhet	Nantes	CHA
GEORGE Finidi	Ajax	NGA
YEBOAH Anthony	Leeds	GHA
KANU Nwankwo	Ajax	NGA
AMUNIKE Emmanuel	Sporting CP	NGA
AMOKACHI Daniel	Everton	NGA
TIEHI Joel	Martigues	CIV
ONDO Valery	Mbilinga	GAB
Two players in 10th place		

CAF PLAYER OF THE YEAR 1996

KANU Nwankwo	Internazionale	NGA
WEAH George	Milan	LBR
AMOKACHI Daniel	Besiktas	NGA
FISH Mark	Lazio	RSA
GEORGE Finidi	Betis	NGA
N'DORAM Japhet	Nantes	CHA
BWALYA Kalusha	América	ZAM
AMUNIKE Emmanuel	Sporting CP	NGA
OLISEH Sunday	1.FC Köln	NGA
YEBOAH Anthony	Leeds United	GHA

CAF PLAYER OF THE YEAR 1997

IKPEBA Victor	Monaco	NGA	56
N'DORAM Japhet	Monaco	CHA	40
WEST Taribo	Internazionale	NGA	35
OLISEH Sunday	Ajax	NGA	24
SONGO'O Jacques	Deportivo LC	CMR	17
WEAH George	Milan	LBR	15
SELLIMI Adel	Nantes	TUN	12
GEORGE Finidi	Betis	NGA	9
PAULAO	Coimbra	ANG	7
M'BOMA Patrick	Gamba Osaka	CMR	6

CAF PLAYER OF THE YEAR 1998

HADJI Mustapha	Deportivo LC	MAR	76
OKOCHA Jay-Jay	PSG	NGA	74
OLISEH Sunday	Ajax	NGA	58
HASSAN Hossam	Al Ahly Cairo	EGY	34
MCCARTHY Benni	Ajax	RSA	24
GUEL Tchiressoua	ASEC Abidjan	CIV	16
AKONNOR Charles	Fortuna Köln	GHA	12
FOE Marc-Vivien	RC Lens	CMR	10
GEORGE Finidi	Betis	NGA	8
SONG Rigobert	Salernitana	CMR	6

CAF PLAYER OF THE YEAR 1999

KANU Nwankwo	Arsenal	NGA	46
KUFFOUR Samuel	Bayern	GHA	44
BAKAYOKO Ibrahima	Marseille	CIV	42
WEAH George	Milan	LBR	40
OKOCHA Jay-Jay	PSG	NGA	30
DINDANE Aruna	ASEC Abidjan	CIV	28
IKPEBA Victor	Dortmund	NGA	26
BENARBIA Ali	PSG	ALG	24
HADJI Mustapha	Coventry City	MAR	24
BADRA Khaled	Espérance	TUN	22

CAF PLAYER OF THE YEAR 2000

M'BOMA Patrick	Parma	CMR	123
LAUREN Etame-Mayer	Arsenal	CMR	36
ETO'O Samuel	Real Mallorca	CMR	29
GEREMI Njitap	Real Madrid	CMR	27
KANU Nwankwo	Arsenal	NGA	21
NAYBET Nouredine	Deportivo LC	MAR	20
HASSAN Hossam	Zamalek	EGY	17
NONDA Shabani	Monaco	COD	11
BARTLETT Shaun	Charlton	RSA	10
RAMY Hani	Werder	EGY	10

CAF PLAYER OF THE YEAR 2001

DIOUF El-Hadji	RC Lens	SEN	93
KUFFOUR Samuel	Bayern	GHA	66
ETO'O Samuel	Real Mallorca	CMR	34
KALLON Mohamed	Internazionale	SLE	28
NAYBET Nouredine	Deportivo LC	MAR	24
FADIGA Khalilou	Auxerre	SEN	22
BAGAYOKO Mamadou	Strasbourg	MLI	16
M'BOMA Patrick	Sunderland	CMR	15
RAMY Hani	Werder	EGY	12
Two players with 10 votes		

CAF PLAYER OF THE YEAR 2002

DIOUF El-Hadji	Liverpool	SEN	93
DIOP Papa Bouba	RC Lens	SEN	46
HOSSAM Ahmed	Celta Vigo	EGY	42
FADIGA Khalilou	Auxerre	SEN	41
LAUREN Etame-Mayer	Arsenal	CMR	35
CAMARA Henri	Sedan	SEN	20
AGHAHOWA Julius	Shakhtar	NGA	19
TRABELSI Hatem	Ajax	TUN	19
DIAO Salif	Liverpool	SEN	17
KEITA Seydou	RC Lens	MLI	16

CAF PLAYER OF THE YEAR 2003

ETO'O Samuel	Mallorca	CMR

CAF PLAYER OF THE YEAR 2004

ETO'O Samuel	Barcelona	CMR	116
DROGBA Didier	Chelsea	CIV	90
OKOCHA Jay-Jay	Bolton	NGA	68
MCCARTHY Benni	Porto	RSA	31
ADEBAYOR Emmanuel	Monaco	TOG	21

CAF PLAYER OF THE YEAR 2005

ETO'O Samuel	Barcelona	CMR	108
DROGBA Didier	Chelsea	CIV	106
ESSIEN Michael	Chelsea	GHA	50

CAF AFRICA CUP OF NATIONS EGYPT 2006

CAF AFRICA CUP OF NATIONS EGYPT 2006

First round groups	Pts	Quarter-finals		Semi-finals		Final		
Egypt	7							
Côte d'Ivoire	6	Egypt	4					
Morocco	2	Congo DR	1					
Libya	1							
				Egypt	2			
	Pts			Senegal	1			
Cameroon	9							
Congo DR	4	Guinea	2					
Angola	4	Senegal	3					
Togo	0							
						Egypt	0	4p
	Pts					Côte d'Ivoire	0	2p
Guinea	9							
Tunisia	6	Nigeria	1	6p				
Zambia	3	Tunisia	1	5p				
South Africa	0							
				Nigeria	0			
	Pts			Côte d'Ivoire	1			
Nigera	9							
Senegal	3	Cameroon	1	11p		3rd Place Play-off		
Ghana	3	Côte d'Ivoire	1	12p		Nigeria	1	
Zimbabwe	3					Senegal	0	

GROUP A	PL	W	D	L	F	A	GD	PTS		CIV	MAR	LBY
1 Egypt	3	2	1	0	6	1	+5	7		3-1	0-0	3-0
2 Côte d'Ivoire	3	2	0	1	4	4	=	6			1-0	2-1
3 Morocco	3	0	2	1	0	1	-1	2				0-0
4 Libya	3	0	1	2	1	5	-4	1				

International Stadium, Cairo
20-01-2006, 19:00, 65 000, Pare BFA

EGY 3 0 LBY

Mido [17], Aboutrika [22],
Ahmed Hassan [78]

EGYPT				LIBYA	
1 EL HADARY Essam		74		DE AGUSTINI Luis	12
3 ABDELWAHAB Mohamed	88			SHIBANI Younes	5
20 GOMAA Wael				RAMLI Marei	6
5 EL SAQQA Abdel Zaher				MAKLOUF Mahmoud	17
17 HASSAN Ahmed (C)				DAOUD Omar	4
4 SAID Ibrahim				HAMADI Osama	18
22 ABOUTRIKA Mohamed	79			SLIL Abdulnaser	23
11 SHAWKY Mohamed †		76		MUNTASIR Jihad	7
12 BARAKAT Mohamed		63		SAAD Ahmed	10
19 ZAKI Amr	81			TARHUNI Nader	16
15 EL SAYED Abdel Wahed				REWANI Salem	20
Tr: SHEHATA Hassan				Tr: LONCAREVIC Ilija	
6 MOSTAFA Hassan	79	63		TAYEB Tarek	14
10 MOTEAB Emad	81	76		GHZALLA Muftah	21
13 EL SAYED Tarek	88				

International Stadium, Cairo
21-01-2006, 14:00, 8 000, Damon RSA

MAR 0 1 CIV

Drogba [38]

MOROCCO				COTE D'IVOIRE	
1 El JARMOUNI Tarek				† TIZIE Jean-Jacques	1
2 REGRAGUI Walid				EBOUE Emmanuel	21
5 EL KARKOURI Talal				KOUASSI Blaise Kossi	6
6 NAYBET Noureddine (C)				TOURE Kolo	4
15 SAFRI Youssef				BOKA Arthur	3
11 YAACOUBI Mohammed	85			TOURE Yaya	19
21 EL KADDOURI Badr				ZOKORA Didier	5
13 KHARJA Houssine	83			AKALE Kanga	2
18 CHIPPO Youssef				FAE Emerse	7
17 CHAMAKH Marouane		65		(C) DROGBA Didier	11
20 HADJI Youssef		77		KALOU Bonaventure	8
Tr: FAKHIR Mohamed				Tr: MICHEL Henri	
9 BOUSSABON Ali	83	65		KONE Arouna	9
19 ABOUCHEROUANE Hicham	85	77		KONE Bakary	14

International Stadium, Cairo
24-01-2006, 17:15, 42 000, Maidin SIN

LBY 1 2 CIV

Khamis [41]

Drogba [10], Yaya Toure [74]

LIBYA				COTE D'IVOIRE	
21 GHZALLA Muftah				TIZIE Jean-Jacques	1
2 OSMAN Walid		70		YAPI YAPO Gilles	10
3 SHUSHAN Naji				MEITE Abdoulaye	12
5 SHIBANI Younes				BOKA Arthur	3
6 RAMLI Marei	86			ZORO Marc	13
16 TARHUNI Nader				TOURE Kolo	4
18 HAMADI Osama		88		TOURE Yaya	19
19 KHAMIS Abdesalam				ZOKORA Didier	5
7 MUNTASIR Jihad	72			AKALE Kanga	2
14 TAYEB Tarek (C) †	78	82		KONE Arouna	9
15 KARA Nader				(C) DROGBA Didier	11
Tr: LONCAREVIC Ilija				Tr: MICHEL Henri	
8 HUSSIEN Khaled	86	88		FAE Emerse	7
10 SAAD Ahmed	78	70		KALOU Bonaventure	8
20 REWANI Salem	72	82		KONE Bakary	14

International Stadium, Cairo
24-01-2006, 20:00, 75 000, Codjia BEN

EGY 0 0 MAR

EGYPT				MOROCCO	
1 EL HADARY Essam †				El JARMOUNI Tarek	1
3 ABDELWAHAB Mohamed				EL KARKOURI Talal	5
5 EL SAQQA Abdel Zaher				(C) NAYBET Noureddine	6
20 GOMAA Wael				EL ARMINE Erbate	16
17 HASSAN Ahmed (C)	65	76		REGRAGUI Walid	2
4 SAID Ibrahim				EL KADDOURI Badr	21
7 FATHI Ahmed	50			YAACOUBI Mohammed	11
11 SHAWKY Mohamed				KHARJA Houssine	13
12 BARAKAT Mohamed				SAFRI Youssef	15
15 HOSSAM Ahmed Mido	79	84		CHAMAKH Marouane	17
19 ZAKI Amr		71		HADJI Youssef	20
Tr: SHEHATA Hassan				Tr: FAKHIR Mohamed	
6 MOSTAFA Hassan	50	71		BOUSSABON Ali	9
10 MOTEAB Emad	79	76		CHIPPO Youssef	18
22 ABOUTRIKA Mohamed	65	84		ABOUCHEROUANE Hicham	19

Military Stadium, Cairo
28-01-2006, 19:00, Maillet SEY, 74 000

EGY 3 1 CIV

Moteab 2 [8 70], Aboutrika [61]

Arouna Kone [43]

EGYPT				COTE D'IVOIRE	
1 EL HADARY Essam		59		TIZIE Jean-Jacques	1
3 ABDELWAHAB Mohamed	63			DOMORAUD Cyrille	17
20 GOMAA Wael				KOUASSI Blaise Kossi	6
5 EL SAQQA Abdel Zaher		69		DEMEL Guy	20
12 BARAKAT Mohamed				EBOUE Emmanuel	21
17 HASSAN Ahmed (C)				TIENE Siaka	18
4 SAID Ibrahim		83		TOURE Yaya	19
22 ABOUTRIKA Mohamed †	76			FAE Emerse	7
11 SHAWKY Mohamed				N'DRI Christian Koffi	22
15 HOSSAM Ahmed Mido	23			KALOU Bonaventure	8
10 MOTEAB Emad				KONE Arouna	9
Tr: SHEHATA Hassan				Tr: MICHEL Henri	
6 MOSTAFA Hassan	63	83		AKALE Kanga	2
9 HASSAN Hosam	23	69		KONE Bakary	14
13 EL SAYED Tarek	63	59		BOUBACAR Barry	23

International Stadium, Cairo
28-01-2006, 19:00, 5 000, Daami TUN

LBY 0 0 MAR

LIBYA				MOROCCO	
12 DE AGUSTINI Luis				El JARMOUNI Tarek	1
2 OSMAN Walid				REGRAGUI Walid	2
3 SHUSHAN Naji				EL KARKOURI Talal	5
4 DAOUD Omar				(C) NAYBET Noureddine	6
6 RAMLI Marei		86		SAFRI Youssef	15
14 TAYEB Tarek (C)				EL KADDOURI Badr	21
16 TARHUNI Nader †		73		YAACOUBI Mohammed	11
18 HAMADI Osama				KHARJA Houssine	13
19 KHAMIS Abdesalam				CHAMAKH Marouane	17
10 SAAD Ahmed		58		ABOUCHEROUANE Hicham	19
15 KARA Nader				HADJI Youssef	20
Tr: LONCAREVIC Ilija				Tr: FAKHIR Mohamed	
		58		BOUSSABON Ali	9
		73		MADIHI Mohamed	10
		86		EL ARMINE Erbate	16

GROUP B

		PL	W	D	L	F	A	GD	PTS	COD	ANG	TOG
1	Cameroon	3	3	0	0	7	1	+6	9	2-0	3-1	2-0
2	Congo DR	3	1	1	1	2	2	=	4		0-0	2-0
3	Angola	3	1	1	1	4	5	-1	4			3-2
4	Togo	3	0	0	3	2	7	-5	0			

Military Stadium, Cairo
21-01-2006, 17:15, 8 000, Guezzaz MAR

CMR 3 – 1 ANG

Eto'o 3 [21 39 78] — Flavio [31p]

#	CAMEROON			ANGOLA	#
16	SOULEYMANOU Hamidou			JOAO RICARDO	1
3	ATOUBA Timothee			JACINTO	2
5	KALLA Raymond			JAMBA	3
8	Njitap GEREMI			LEBO-LEBO	4
4	SONG Rigobert (C)		72	MARCO ABREU	23
11	MAKOUN Jean			FIGUEIREDO	7
7	NGOM KOME Daniel	83		ANDRE	8
14	SAIDOU Alioum			MENDONCA	14
18	DOUALA Roudolphe		65	EDSON	13
9	ETO'O Samuel †	89		AKWA (C)	10
15	WEBO Pierre Achille	75	60	FLAVIO	16
	Tr: JORGE Artur			Tr: GONCALVES Luis Oliveira	
10	EMANA Achille	89	60	MANTORRAS	9
20	OLEMBE Salomon	83	65	ZE KALANGA	17
21	BOYA Pierre	75	72	DELGADO	21

Military Stadium, Cairo
21-01-2006, 20:00, 6 000, Daami TUN

TOG 0 – 2 COD

Mputu [42], Lua Lua [61]

#	TOGO			CONGO DR	#
16	AGASSA Kossi			KALEMBA Pascal	1
21	ATTE-OUDEYI Zanzan			KINKELA Christian	7
15	ROMAO Alaixys	53		ILUNGA Herita	15
10	MAMAN Cherif Toure	85		BOKESE Gladys	18
3	ABALO Jean-Paul (C)			KABUNDI Felicien	20
18	SENAYA Junior Yao		62	MPUTU Tresor	8
6	AZIAWONOU Yao			TSHIOLOLA Tshinyama	4
14	OLUFADE Adekanmi	59	84	† MATUMONA Zola	10
12	AKOTO Eric			MBAYO Marcel	11
17	COUBADJA Kader		86	MBALA Biscotte	5
13	MATHIAS Emmanuel			LUALUA Lomana (C)	9
	Tr: KESHI Stephen			Tr: LE ROY Claude	
4	ADEBAYOR Emmanuel	59	62	MATINGOU Franck	12
7	SALIFOU Moustapha	53	84	ILONGO Ngasanya	14
9	DOGBE Mikael	85	86	MUSASA Kabamba	21

Military Stadium, Cairo
25-01-2006, 17:15, 2 000, Diatta SEN

ANG 0 – 0 COD

#	ANGOLA			CONGO DR	#
1	JOAO RICARDO			KALEMBA Pascal	1
3	JAMBA			BOKESE Gladys	18
5	KALI			KINKELA Christian	7
20	LOCO			KABUNDI Felicien	20
21	DELGADO			ILUNGA Herita	15
7	FIGUEIREDO	75	69	MPUTU Tresor	8
8	ANDRE		92	MATUMONA Zola	10
14	MENDONCA	47	81	MBAYO Marcel	11
13	EDSON			MBALA Biscotte	5
16	FLAVIO	58		TSHIOLOLA Tshinyama	4
10	AKWA			LUALUA Lomana	9
	Tr: GONCALVES Luis Oliveira			Tr: LE ROY Claude	
6	MILOY	75	92	MILAMBO Mutamba	6
11	JONHSON	47	69	MATINGOU Franck	12
15	MAURITO	58	81	MUSASA Kabamba	21

Military Stadium, Cairo
25-01-2006, 20:00, 3 000, Sowe GAM

CMR 2 – 0 TOG

Eto'o [68], Meyong Ze [86]

#	CAMEROON			TOGO	#
16	SOULEYMANOU Hamidou			AGASSA Kossi	16
3	ATOUBA Timothee			MATHIAS Emmanuel	13
4	SONG Rigobert		84	AZIAWONOU Yao	6
5	KALLA Raymond	56	81	SENAYA Junior Yao	18
8	Njitap GEREMI			ADEBAYOR Emmanuel	4
11	MAKOUN Jean			ASSEMOASSA Ludovic	20
14	SAIDOU Alioum			TCHANGAI Massamasso	5
18	DOUALA Roudolphe	76		KASSIM Gouyazou	23
7	NGOM KOME Daniel			ABALO Jean-Paul Yaovi	3
15	WEBO Pierre Achille	69		SALIFOU Moustapha	7
9	ETO'O Samuel		74	MAMAN Cherif Toure	10
	Tr: JORGE Artur			Tr: KESHI Stephen	
20	OLEMBE Salomon	76	84	OLUFADE Adekanmi	14
22	MEYONG ZE Albert	69	81	ROMAO Alaixys	15
23	BIKEY Andre	56	74	COUBADJA Kader	17

International Stadium, Cairo
29-01-2006, 19:00, 4 000, El Arjoun MAR

ANG 3 – 2 TOG

Flavio 2 [9 39], Maurito [86] — Cougbadja [24], Cherif Toure Maman [67]

#	ANGOLA			TOGO	#
1	JOAO RICARDO			TCHAGNIROU Ourou	1
3	JAMBA		61	ROMAO Alaixys	15
5	KALI			COUBADJA Kader	17
20	LOCO	72		ABALO Jean-Paul Yaovi	3
21	DELGADO		85	SENAYA Junior Yao	18
7	FIGUEIREDO			TCHANGAI Massamasso	5
8	ANDRE			ASSEMOASSA Ludovic	20
13	EDSON	55	78	SALIFOU Moustapha	7
15	MAURITO		30	KASSIM Gouyazou	23
16	FLAVIO			MAMAM Gafarou	8
10	AKWA	61		MAMAN Cherif Toure	10
	Tr: GONCALVES Luis Oliveira			Tr: KESHI Stephen	
9	MANTORRAS	61	61	AZIAWONOU Yao	6
17	ZE KALANGA	55	78	SHERIF Cougbadja	11
18	LOVE	72	85	OLUFADE Adekanmi	14

Military Stadium, Cairo
29-01-2006, 19:00, 5 000, Coulibaly MLI

CMR 2 – 0 COD

Geremi [31], Eto'o [33]

#	CAMEROON			CONGO DR	#
1	KAMENI Idris Carlos			KALEMBA Pascal	1
2	ATEBA Jean Hugues			ILUNGA Herita	15
4	SONG Rigobert		72	BOKESE Gladys	18
6	ANGBWA Benoit			KINKELA Christian	7
23	BIKEY Andre			KABUNDI Felicien	20
8	Njitap GEREMI		46	MBAYO Marcel	11
14	SAIDOU Alioum			TSHIOLOLA Tshinyama	4
20	OLEMBE Salomon	90	79	MBALA Biscotte	5
21	BOYA Pierre	64		MATUMONA Zola	10
22	MEYONG ZE Albert	46	46	LELO Mbele	17
9	ETO'O Samuel			LUALUA Lomana	9
	Tr: JORGE Artur			Tr: LE ROY Claude	
10	EMANA Achille	64	79	MUBIALA Cyrille	2
13	FEUTCHINE Guy	90	46	MILAMBO Mutamba	6
15	WEBO Pierre Achille	46	46	MUSASA Kabamba	21

GROUP C	PL	W	D	L	F	A	GD	PTS
1 Guinea	3	3	0	0	7	1	+6	9
2 Tunisia	3	2	0	1	6	4	+2	6
3 Zambia	3	1	0	2	3	6	-3	3
4 South Africa	3	0	0	3	0	5	-5	0

	TUN	ZAM	RSA
TUN		3-0	2-1	2-0
ZAM		4-1		2-0
RSA				1-0

Harras El Hedoud, Alexandria
22-01-2006, 17:15, 16 000, Maillet SEY

TUN 4 1 ZAM

Santos 3 [35 82 90], Bouazizi [51]

Chamanga [9]

TUNISIA			ZAMBIA	
1 BOUMNIJEL Ali			KOLOLA George	16
13 BOUAZIZI Riadh			HACHILENSA Clive	19
3 HAGUI Karim			MUSONDA Joseph	4
14 CHEDLI Adel			SINYANGWE Mark	6
4 MELLITI Sofiane	79		NKETANI Kennedy	3
15 JAIDI Radhi		62	CHANSA Isaac	8
5 JAZIRI Ziad	72		KATONGO Chris	11
10 GHODHBANE Kaies		62	NUMBA Mumamba	14
11 DOS SANTOS Francileudo			CHAMANGA James	22
20 CLAYTON Jose	67	88	NJOVU Lameck	23
6 TRABELSI Hatem			MBESUMA Collins	9
Tr: LEMERRE Roger			Tr: BWALYA Kalusha	
8 NAMOUCHI Hamed	79	62	SINKALA Andrew	17
12 MNARI Jouhar	72	62	KATONGO Felix	20
19 AYARI Anis	67	88	CHAMANGA James	22

Harras El Hedoud, Alexandria
26-01-2006, 17:15, 24 000, Imeire NGA

ZAM 1 2 GUI

Tana [34]

Feindouno 2 [74p 90]

ZAMBIA			GUINEA	
16 KOLOLA George			DIARSO Naby	1
3 NKETANI Kennedy			CAMARA Ibrahima	3
4 MUSONDA Joseph			SYLLA Mohamed	18
6 SINYANGWE Mark			BALDE Bobo	5
18 MWANZA Billy			JABI Daouda	21
20 KATONGO Felix	77	90	THIAM Pablo	6
17 SINKALA Andrew			MANSARE Fode	7
11 KATONGO Chris		75	BANGOURA Sambegou	9
22 CHAMANGA James			FEINDOUNO Pascal	2
23 NJOVU Lameck		55	BANGOURA Ibrahima	11
9 MBESUMA Collins			KALABANE Oumar	15
Tr: BWALYA Kalusha			Tr: NEVEU Patrice	
8 CHANSA Isaac	77	90	SYLLA Kanfory	8
		75	DIAWARA Kaba	19
		55	YATTARA Ibrahima	20

Harras El Hedoud, Alexandria
30-01-2006, 19:00, 18 000, Maidin SIN

TUN 0 3 GUI

Ousame Bangoura [16]
Feindouno [69], Diawara [90]

TUNISIA			GUINEA	
22 KASRAOUI Hamdi			DIARSO Naby	1
4 MELLITI Sofiane		57	KALABANE Oumar	15
21 HAJ MASSAOUD Amir			KABA Mamadi	4
8 NAMOUCHI Hamed	79		DIALLO Mamadou Alimou	17
23 LTIFI Amine	55		SYLLA Kanfory	8
9 GMAMDIA Haukel			DIAWARA Kaba	19
10 GHODHBANE Kaies			BANGOURA Ismael	10
12 MNARI Jouhar		56	YATTARA Ibrahima	20
13 JAIDI Radhi	59		CISSE Morlaye	12
2 MERDASSI Issam	83		SOUARE Ibrahima	14
20 CLAYTON Jose		79	BANGOURA Ousmane	13
Tr: LEMERRE Roger			Tr: NEVEU Patrice	
3 HAGUI Karim	59	56	FEINDOUNO Pascal	2
14 CHEDLI Adel	79	57	CAMARA Ibrahima	3
17 JEMAA Issam	55	79	CAMARA Sekouba	23

Harras El Hedoud, Alexandria
22-01-2006, 20:00, 10 000, Benouza ALG

RSA 0 2 GUI

Sambegou Bangoura [76]
Ousmane Bangoura [87]

SOUTH AFRICA			GUINEA	
1 MARLIN Calvin			DIARSO Naby	1
2 TAU Jimmy			FEINDOUNO Pascal	2
3 TSHABALALA Daniel			KALABANE Oumar	15
4 KATZA Ricardo			CAMARA Ibrahima	3
5 MABIZELA Mbulelo		69	DIAWARA Kaba	19
13 BANGOURA Ousmane			BALDE Bobo	5
10 BANGOURA Ismael			JABI Daouda	21
14 SOUARE Ibrahima	57		THIAM Pablo	6
23 CAMARA Sekouba	65	84	MANSARE Fode	7
17 DIALLO Mamadou Alimou			SYLLA Kanfory	8
15 KALABANE Oumar		72	BANGOURA Ismael	10
Tr: DUMITRU Ted			Tr: NEVEU Patrice	
7 MANSARE Fode	57	69	BANGOURA Sambegou	9
20 YATTARA Ibrahima	65	72	BANGOURA Ibrahima	11
		84	BANGOURA Ousmane	13

Harras El Hedoud, Alexandria
26-01-2006, 20:00, 10 000, Evehe CMR

TUN 2 0 RSA

Santos [32], Benachour [57]

TUNISIA			SOUTH AFRICA	
1 BOUMNIJEL Ali			MARLIN Calvin	1
14 CHEDLI Adel			TSHABALALA Daniel	3
3 HAGUI Karim			ISSA Pierre	13
15 JAIDI Radhi		66	KATZA Ricardo	4
7 BEN SAADA Chaouki			MABIZELA Mbulelo	5
19 AYARI Anis		84	MERE Vuyo	21
8 NAMOUCHI Hamed			VAN HEERDEN Elrio	11
11 DOS SANTOS Francileudo	83		VILAKAZI Benedict	10
12 MNARI Jouhar			NOMVETE Siyabonga	14
6 TRABELSI Hatem			McCARTHY Benni	17
18 BENACHOUR Slim	77	74	ZUMA Sibusiso	15
Tr: LEMERRE Roger			Tr: DUMITRU Ted	
9 GMAMDIA Haukel	77	66	GAXA Siboniso	6
17 JEMAA Issam	83	84	MPHELA Katlego	18
		74	NKOSI Siyabonga	20

Alexandria Stadium, Alexandria
30-01-2006, 19:00, 4 000, Abd El Fatah EGY

ZAM 1 0 RSA

Chris Katongo [75]

ZAMBIA			SOUTH AFRICA	
1 MWEENE Kennedy			MARLIN Calvin	1
19 HACHILENSA Clive			TAU Jimmy	2
4 MUSONDA Joseph		63	TSHABALALA Daniel	3
3 NKETANI Kennedy			MASILELA Tshepo	19
6 SINYANGWE Mark			MABIZELA Mbulelo	5
20 KATONGO Felix	64		ISSA Pierre	13
17 SINKALA Andrew		80	NKOSI Siyabonga	20
11 KATONGO Chris			TSHABALALA Siphiwe	7
22 CHAMANGA James			GUMBI Mlungisi	8
9 MBESUMA Collins		68	NOMVETE Siyabonga	14
23 NJOVU Lameck	69		MPHELA Katlego	18
Tr: BWALYA Kalusha			Tr: DUMITRU Ted	
2 PHIRI Dube	64	63	VAN HEERDEN Elrio	11
10 BAKALA Ian	69	68	MAKHANYA Joseph	12
		80	MOKOENA Lebohang	23

GROUP D		PL	W	D	L	F	A	GD	PTS		SEN	GHA	ZIM
1	Nigeria	3	3	0	0	5	1	+4	9		2-1	1-0	2-0
2	Senegal	3	1	0	2	3	3	=	3			0-1	2-0
3	Ghana	3	1	0	2	2	3	-1	3				1-2
4	Zimbabwe	3	1	0	2	2	5	-3	3				

Port Said Stadium, Port Said
23-01-2006, 17:15, 20 000, Abd El Fatah EGY

NGA   1   0   GHA

Taiwo 86

NIGERIA		
1	ENYEAMA Vincent	
2	YOBO Joseph	
3	TAIWO Ismaila	89
5	ODIAH Chidi	
6	ENAKARHIRE Joseph	
16	ORUMA Wilson	73
18	OBODO Christian	87
13	AYILA Yusuf	
17	AGHAHOWA Julius	80
20	ODEMWINGIE Peter	82
9	ODEMWINGIE Peter	
	Tr: EGUAVOEN Augustine	
4	KANU Nwankwo	80 73
14	NSOFOR Obinna	81 89
21	NWANERI Obinna	87

GHANA		
ADJEI Sammy	1	
DRAMANI Haminu	23	
PAPPOE Emmanuel	6	
MENSAH John	5	
AHMED Issah	21	
YAKUBU Abubakari	18	
PAINTSIL John	15	
KUFFOUR Samuel Osei	4	
KINGSTON Laryea	7	
APPIAH Stephen	10	
AMOAH Matthew	14	
Tr: DUJKOVIC Ratomir		
SARPEI Hans	8	
FRIMPONG Joetex	13	

Port Said Stadium, Port Said
27-01-2006, 17:15, 20 000, El Arjoun MAR

GHA   1   0   SEN

Amoah 13

GHANA		
1	ADJEI Sammy	
23	DRAMANI Haminu	
15	PAINTSIL John	62
5	MENSAH John	
18	YAKUBU Abubakari	
6	PAPPOE Emmanuel	46
21	AHMED Issah	67
7	KINGSTON Laryea	62
10	APPIAH Stephen	90
13	FRIMPONG Joetex	83
14	AMOAH Matthew	87 66
	Tr: DUJKOVIC Ratomir	
9	TAGOE Prince	87 66
17	EDUSEI Daniel	90 67
19	MOHAMMED Hamza	83 46

SENEGAL		
SYLVA Tony	1	
COLY Ferdinand	17	
BEYE Habib	21	
DIATTA Lamine	13	
DIAWARA Souleymane	5	
DIAGNE-FAYE Abdoulaye	20	
BA Issa	10	
FAYE Amdy	12	
BARRY Rahmane	6	
CAMARA Henri	7	
DIOUF El Hadji	11	
Tr: SARR Abdoulaye		
NIANG Mamadou	8	
KAMARA Diomansy	15	
DIOP Pape Bouba	19	

Port Said Stadium, Port Said
31-01-2006, 19:00, 5 000, Damon RSA

NGA   2   1   SEN

Martins 2 79 88   Souleymane Camara 59

NIGERIA		
1	ENYEAMA Vincent	
2	YOBO Joseph	
3	TAIWO Ismaila	
5	ODIAH Chidi	
6	ENAKARHIRE Joseph	68
8	MIKEL John Obi	
13	AYILA Yusuf	78
18	OBODO Christian	57
9	MARTINS Obafemi	44
19	MAKINWA Stephen	52
7	UTAKA John	77
	Tr: EGUAVOEN Augustine	
4	KANU Nwankwo	52 68
11	LAWAL Garba	57 44
14	NSOFOR Obinna	77 78

SENEGAL		
SYLVA Tony	1	
DIATTA Lamine	13	
DAF Omar	2	
DIAWARA Souleymane	5	
COLY Ferdinand	17	
FAYE Amdy	12	
KAMARA Diomansy	15	
DIOP Pape Bouba	19	
BARRY Rahmane	6	
CAMARA Henri	7	
DIOUF El Hadji	11	
Tr: SARR Abdoulaye		
DIAKHATE Pape Malickou	4	
CAMARA Souleymane	9	
DIAGNE-FAYE Abdoulaye	20	

Port Said Stadium, Port Said
23-01-2006, 20:00, 15 000, Abdel Rahman SUD

ZIM   0   2   SEN

Henri Camara 60, Issa Ba 80

ZIMBABWE		
23	MUZADZI Gift	
6	MAKONESE Zvenyika	
21	MATOLA James	
13	CHIMEDZA Cephas	
14	MBWANDO George	
3	NYANDORO Esrom	
19	KASINAUYO Edzai	85
20	DINHA Edelbert	61 62
9	MWARUWARI Benjani	
10	KAWONDERA Shingi	
12	NDLOVU Peter	67 79
	Tr: MHLAURI Charles	
11	LUPHAHLA Joel	67 62
8	NENGOMASHA Tinashe	61 79
18	BADZA Brian	85

SENEGAL		
SYLVA Tony	1	
COLY Ferdinand	17	
BEYE Habib	21	
DIATTA Lamine	13	
DIAWARA Souleymane	5	
DIAGNE-FAYE Abdoulaye	20	
FAYE Amdy	12	
KAMARA Diomansy	15	
BARRY Rahmane	6	
CAMARA Henri	7	
DIOUF El Hadji	11	
Tr: SARR Abdoulaye		
NIANG Mamadou	8	
BA Issa	10	

Port Said Stadium, Port Said
27-01-2006, 20:00, 10 000, Coulibaly MLI

NGA   2   0   ZIM

Obodo 57, Mikel 61

NIGERIA		
1	ENYEAMA Vincent	
2	YOBO Joseph	
3	TAIWO Ismaila	
5	ODIAH Chidi	
6	ENAKARHIRE Joseph	
13	AYILA Yusuf	70
16	ORUMA Wilson	53
18	OBODO Christian	85 88
17	AGHAHOWA Julius	53
7	UTAKA John	
9	MARTINS Obafemi	80
	Tr: EGUAVOEN Augustine	
4	KANU Nwankwo	53 70
8	MIKEL John Obi	53 80
11	LAWAL Garba	85 88

ZIMBABWE		
MUZADZI Gift	23	
YOHANE Charles	11	
CHIMEDZA Cephas	13	
MATOLA James	21	
MAKONESE Zvenyika	6	
DINHA Edelbert	20	
NENGOMASHA Tinashe	8	
LUPHAHLA Joel	7	
NYANDORO Esrom	3	
MWARUWARI Benjani	9	
KAWONDERA Shingi	10	
Tr: MHLAURI Charles		
NDLOVU Bekithemba	4	
NDLOVU Peter	12	
MUSHANGAZHIKE Gilbert	17	

Ismailia Stadium, Ismailia
31-01-2006, 19:00, 14 000, Louzaya CGO

GHA   1   2   ZIM

Armando 93+   Chimedza 60, Mwaruwari 68

GHANA		
1	ADJEI Sammy	
23	DRAMANI Haminu	65
15	PAINTSIL John	
17	EDUSEI Daniel	
5	MENSAH John	
18	YAKUBU Abubakari	55
6	PAPPOE Emmanuel	
21	AHMED Issah	
10	APPIAH Stephen	
9	TAGOE Prince	46 53
13	FRIMPONG Joetex	
	Tr: DUJKOVIC Ratomir	
12	ATTRAM Godwin	65 86
19	MOHAMMED Hamza	55 53
20	ARMANDO Baba	46

ZIMBABWE		
KAPINI Tapuwa	16	
MAKONESE Zvenyika	6	
CHIMEDZA Cephas	13	
MATOLA James	21	
NENGOMASHA Tinashe	8	
DINHA Edelbert	20	
NYANDORO Esrom	3	
LUPHAHLA Joel	7	
MWARUWARI Benjani	9	
NDLOVU Peter	12	
MUSHANGAZHIKE Gilbert	17	
Tr: MHLAURI Charles		
KAWONDERA Shingi	10	
KASINAUYO Edzai	19	

QUARTER-FINALS

International Stadium, Cairo
3-02-2006, 19:00, 74 000, Sowe GAM

EGY 4   1 COD

Ahmed Hassan 2 32 89, Hossam Hassan 41, Moteab 58   Ibrahim Said OG 45

EGYPT			CONGO DR		
1 EL HADARY Essam			KALEMBA Pascal 1		
13 EL SAYED Tarek	78		NSUMBU Dituabanza 3		
5 EL SAQQA Abdel Zaher			ILUNGA Herita 15		
20 GOMAA Wael		46	KINKELA Christian 7		
4 SAID Ibrahim		46	MUBIALA Cyrille 2		
17 HASSAN Ahmed			MBAYO Marcel 11		
11 SHAWKY Mohamed			TSHIOLOLA Tshinyama 4		
12 BARAKAT Mohamed		52	MUSASA Kabamba 21		52
19 ZAKI Amr	73		MBALA Biscotte 5		
9 HASSAN Hosam	67		MATUMONA Zola 10		
10 MOTEAB Emad		58	LUALUA Lomana 9		
Tr: SHEHATA Hassan			Tr: LE ROY Claude		
3 ABDELWAHAB Mohamed	78	46	LUBANZADIO Nono 13		46
6 MOSTAFA Hassan	67	52	MUSASA Kabamba 21		52
14 ALI Abdel Halim	73				

Harras El Hedoud, Alexandria
3-02-2006, 15:00, 17 000, Codjia BEN

GUI 2   3 SEN

Diawara 24, Feindouno 95+   Pape Bouba Diop 62, Niang 84, Henri Camara 93+

GUINEA			SENEGAL		
1 DIARSO Naby			SYLVA Tony 1		
2 FEINDOUNO Pascal			DIAWARA Souleymane 5		
15 KALABANE Oumar		40	COLY Ferdinand 17		40
11 BANGOURA Ibrahima			DIATTA Lamine 13		
19 DIAWARA Kaba	68		DAF Omar 2		
5 BALDE Bobo			KAMARA Diomansy 15		
21 JABI Daouda			DIOP Pape Bouba 19		
6 THIAM Pablo	54		FAYE Amdy 12		
7 MANSARE Fode			CAMARA Henri 7		
8 SYLLA Kanfory		57	CAMARA Souleymane 9		57
13 BANGOURA Ousmane	81	88	MENDY Frederic 14		88
Tr: NEVEU Patrice			Tr: SARR Abdoulaye		
9 BANGOURA Sambegou	68	40	DIAKHATE Pape Malickou 4		40
10 BANGOURA Ismael	81	57	NIANG Mamadou 8		57
14 SOUARE Ibrahima	54	88	BA Issa 10		88

Military Stadium, Cairo
4-02-2006, 19:00, 4 000, Sowe GAM

CMR 1   1 CIV

Meyong Ze 96   Bakary Kone 91
CIV won 12-11 on pens

CAMEROON			COTE D'IVOIRE		
16 SOULEYMANOU Hamidou			TIZIE Jean-Jacques 1		
3 ATOUBA Timothee			KOUASSI Blaise Kossi 6		
4 SONG Rigobert			BOKA Arthur 3		
23 BIKEY Andre			TOURE Kolo 4		
8 Njitap GEREMI		115	EBOUE Emmanuel 21		
11 MAKOUN Jean			FAE Emerse 7		
14 SAIDOU Alioum		97	AKALE Kanga 2		
20 OLEMBE Salomon	80	88	TOURE Yaya 19		
7 NGOM KOME Daniel			ZOKORA Didier 5		
9 ETO'O Samuel			KONE Arouna 9		
15 WEBO Pierre Achille		34	DROGBA Didier 11		
Tr: JORGE Artur			Tr: MICHEL Henri		
18 DOUALA Roudolphe	80	115	ZORO Marc 13		115
22 MEYONG ZE Albert	34 88	97	KONE Bakary 14		88
			N'DRI Christian Koffi 22		97

Port Said Stadium, Port Said
4-02-2006, 15:00, 15 000, Maillet SEY

NGA 1   1 TUN

Nsofor 6   Hagui 49
NGA won 6-5 on pens

NIGERIA			TUNISIA		
1 ENYEAMA Vincent			BOUMNIJEL Ali 1		
2 YOBO Joseph		48	TRABELSI Hatem 6		
3 TAIWO Ismaila			CLAYTON Jose 20		
5 ODIAH Chidi		97	BOUAZIZI Riadh 13		
6 ENAKARHIRE Joseph			HAGUI Karim 3		
8 MIKEL John Obi			CHEDLI Adel 14		
13 AYILA Yusuf		68	MELLITI Sofiane 4		
7 UTAKA John	59		JAIDI Radhi 15		
9 MARTINS Obafemi			JAZIRI Ziad 5		
14 NSOFOR Obinna			NAMOUCHI Hamed 8		
19 MAKINWA Stephen	90		DOS SANTOS Francilieudo 11		80
Tr: EGUAVOEN Augustine			Tr: LEMERRE Roger		
4 KANU Nwankwo	59	80	GMAMDIA Haukel 9		80
11 LAWAL Garba	90	68	BENACHOUR Slim 18		
21 NWANERI Obinna	97	48	HAJ MASSAOUD Amir 21		48

SEMI-FINALS

International Stadium, Cairo
7-02-2006, 19:00, 74 000, Evehe CMR

EGY 2   1 SEN

Ahmed Hassan 36p, Zaki 80   Kamara 54

EGYPT			SENEGAL		
1 EL HADARY Essam			SYLVA Tony 1		
3 ABDELWAHAB Mohamed			DIATTA Lamine 13		
5 EL SAQQA Abdel Zaher			DAF Omar 2		
20 GOMAA Wael			DIAKHATE Pape Malickou 4		
12 BARAKAT Mohamed			DIAWARA Souleymane 5		
17 HASSAN Ahmed			FAYE Amdy 12		
4 SAID Ibrahim			KAMARA Diomansy 15		
22 ABOUTRIKA Mohamed			DIOP Pape Bouba 19		
11 SHAWKY Mohamed			NIANG Mamadou 8		
15 HOSSAM Ahmed Mido	79		MENDY Frederic 14		
10 MOTEAB Emad	90		CAMARA Henri 7		
Tr: SHEHATA Hassan			Tr: SARR Abdoulaye		
9 HASSAN Hosam	90	86	CAMARA Souleymane 9		86
19 ZAKI Amr	79	89	BA Issa 10		89
			DIOUF El Hadji 11		66

Harras El Hedoud, Alexandria
7-02-2006, 15:00, 20 000, Damon RSA

CIV 1   0 NGA

Drogba 47

COTE D'IVOIRE			NIGERIA		
1 TIZIE Jean-Jacques			ENYEAMA Vincent 1		
10 YAPI YAPO Gilles	58		YOBO Joseph 2		
12 MEITE Abdoulaye			TAIWO Ismaila 3		
3 BOKA Arthur			ODIAH Chidi 5		
4 TOURE Kolo			ENAKARHIRE Joseph 6		
21 EBOUE Emmanuel	67	54	MIKEL John Obi 8		54
19 TOURE Yaya			KAITA Sani 22		
5 ZOKORA Didier			MARTINS Obafemi 9		
22 N'DRI Christian Koffi			NSOFOR Obinna 14		
8 KALOU Bonaventure	77	63	ODEMWINGIE Peter 20		63
11 DROGBA Didier	74		KANU Nwankwo 4		74
Tr: MICHEL Henri			Tr: EGUAVOEN Augustine		
7 FAE Emerse	56	54	OKOCHA Jay-Jay 10		54
9 KONE Arouna	77	74	AGHAHOWA Julius 17		74
13 ZORO Marc	67	63	MAKINWA Stephen 19		63

Third place play-off. Military Stadium, Cairo
9-02-2006, 18:00, 11 354, Coulibaly MLI

NGA   1   0   SEN

Lawal [79]

NIGERIA				SENEGAL	
1	ENYEAMA Vincent			DIOUF Mamadou	16
2	YOBO Joseph			NDAW Guirane	3
3	TAIWO Ismaila			DRAME Boukary	18
5	ODIAH Chidi			DIAKHATE Pape Malickou	4
21	NWANERI Obinna			DAF Omar	2
10	OKOCHA Jay-Jay	67		DIAGNE-FAYE Abdoulaye	20
18	OKOCHA Jay-Jay		62	DJIBA Dino	23
11	LAWAL Garba			BA Issa	10
14	NSOFOR Obinna	78		KAMARA Diomansy	15
7	UTAKA John		70	BARRY Rahmane	6
9	MARTINS Obafemi		78	CAMARA Souleymane	9
	Tr: EGUAVOEN Augustine			Tr: SARR Abdoulaye	
4	KANU Nwankwo	78	70	CAMARA Henri	7
16	ORUMA Wilson	67	78	NIANG Mamadou	8
			62	DIOP Pape Bouba	19

PENALTY SHOOT-OUT

Cameroon First		Côte d'Ivoire Second	
ETO'O Samuel	✔	DROGBA Didier	✔
Njitap GEREMI	✔	TOURE Kolo	✔
ATOUBA Timothee	✔	KONE Bakary	✔
NGOM KOME Daniel	✔	FAE Emerse	✔
ZE MEYONG Albert	✔	KONE Arouna	✔
MAKOUN Jean	✔	KOUASSI Blaise	✔
SONG Rigobert	✔	N'DRI Christian	✔
SAIDOU Alioum	✔	BOKA Arthur	✔
DOUALA Rudolphe	✔	ZOKORA Didier	✔
BIKEY Stephane	✔	ZORO Marco	✔
HAMIDOU Souleymane	✔	TIZIE Jean-Jacques	✔
ETO'O Samuel	✘	DROGBA Didier	✔
Cote d'Ivoire qualified for the semis 12-11 on penalties			

PENALTY SHOOT-OUT

Nigeria First		Tunisia Second	
YOBO Joseph	✘	NAMOUCHI Hamed	✔
TAIWO Taye	✔	GUEMAMDIA Haikel	✔
AYILA Yusuf	✘	CHEDLI Adel	✘
NSOFOR Obinna	✔	BENACHOUR Slim	✘
MARTINS Obafemi	✔	CLAYTON	✔
MIKEL Jon Obi	✔	BOUMNIJEL Ali	✔
ENYEAMA Vincent	✔	YAHIA Alaeddine	✔
KANU Nwankwo	✔	BOUAZIZI Riadh	✘
Nigeria qualify for the semis 6-5 on penalties			

Final. International Stadium, Cairo
10-02-2006, 18:00, 74 000, Mourad Daami TUN

EGYPT   0   0   COTE D'IVOIRE
4 ^P_S_O 2

		EGYPT			
1	GK	EL HADARY Essam			
3	DF	ABDELWAHAB Mohamed			
20	DF	GOMAA Wael	21		
5	DF	EL SAQQA Abdel Zaher			
11	MF	SHAWKY Mohamed			
12	MF	BARAKAT Mohamed			
17	MF	HASSAN Ahmed		61	
4	DF	SAID Ibrahim	113	91	
22	MF	ABOUTRIKA Mohamed			
19	FW	ZAKI Amr			
10	FW	MOTEAB Emad	81		
		Tr: SHE HATA Hassan			
6	MF	MOSTAFA Hassan	81	61	
7	MF	FATHI Ahmed	21	91	
14	FW	ALI Abdel Halim	113		

	COTE D'IVOIRE		
TIZIE Jean-Jacques	GK	1	
KOUASSI Blaise Kossi	DF	6	
BOKA Arthur	DF	3	
TOURE Kolo	DF	4	
EBOUE Emmanuel	DF	21	
FAE Emerse	MF	7	
AKALE Kanga	MF	2	
TOURE Yaya	MF	19	
ZOKORA Didier	MF	5	
KONE Arouna	FW	9	
DROGBA Didier	FW	11	
Tr: MICHEL Henri			
KALOU Bonaventure	FW	8	
KONE Bakary	FW	14	

PENALTY SHOOT-OUT

Egypt First		Côte d'Ivoire Second	
HASSAN Ahmed	✔	DROGBA Didier	✘
ABDELWAHAB Moh.	✔	TOURE Kolo	✔
ALI Abdelhalim	✘	KONE Bakary	✘
ZAKI Amr	✔	EBOUE Emmanuel	✔
ABOUTRIKA Moh.	✔		
Egypt win the Cup of Nations 4-2 on penalties			

REGIONAL TOURNAMENTS IN AFRICA IN 2005

COSAFA CASTLE CUP 2005

First Round		First Round finals		Semi-finals		Final	
Zimbabwe	3						
Mozambique	0	Zimbabwe	2				
Namibia	1 1p	Botswana	0				
Botswana	1 2p			Zimbabwe	2		
Mauritius	2			Angola	1		
Madagascar	0	Mauritius	0			Zimbabwe	1
Seychelles	0	South Africa	1			Zambia	0
South Africa	3			South Africa	2 8p		
Malawi	2			Zambia	2 9p		
Lesotho	1	Malawi	1				
Swaziland	0	Zambia	2				
Zambia	3						

* Home team • The holders Angola received a bye to the semi-finals • Semi-finals and final played in South Africa from 13-08-2005 to 14-08-2005

CECAFA CUP RWANDA 2005

First Round Group Stage

Group A	Pl	W	D	L	F	A	Pts	RWA	TAN	BDI	ERI
Zanzibar	4	3	1	0	7	2	10	1-0	1-1	2-1	3-0
Rwanda	4	3	0	1	8	4	9		3-1	2-0	3-2
Tanzania	4	2	1	1	5	5	7			2-1	1-0
Burundi	4	0	1	3	2	6	1				0-0
Eritrea	4	0	1	3	2	7	1				

Group B	Pl	W	D	L	F	A	Pts	ETH	SUD	SOM	DJI
Uganda	4	3	1	0	16	1	10	0-0	3-0	7-0	6-1
Ethiopia	4	3	1	0	12	2	10		3-1	3-1	6-0
Sudan	4	2	0	2	7	12	6			4-1	4-0
Somalia	4	1	0	3	6	10	3				2-1
Djibouti	4	0	0	4	2	18	0				

Played in Rwanda from 26-11-2005 to 10-12-2005

Semi-finals

Ethiopia	4
Zanzibar	0
Uganda	0
Rwanda	1

Final

Ethiopia	1
Rwanda	0

Third place play-off

Zanzibar	0 5p
Uganda	0 4p

COPA AMILCAR CABRAL GUINEA 2005

First Round Group Stage

Group A	Pl	W	D	L	F	A	Pts	GNB	SLE
Guinea	2	1	1	0	3	2	4	2-2	1-0
Guinea-Bissau	2	0	2	0	3	3	2		1-1
Sierra Leone	2	0	1	1	1	2	1		

Group B	Pl	W	D	L	F	A	Pts	MLI	GAM
Senegal	2	1	1	0	2	1	4	1-1	1-0
Mali	2	1	1	0	2	1	4		1-0
Gambia	2	0	0	2	0	2	0		

Played in Guinea from 18-11-2005 to 27-11-2005

Semi-finals

Guinea	0 6p
Mali	0 5p
Guinea-Bissau	1 0p
Senegal	1 3p

Final

Guinea	1
Senegal	0

Third place play-off

Mali	1
Guinea-Bissau	0

CAF CHAMPIONS LEAGUE 2005

First Round

Team	Code	Leg 1	Leg 2
SC Villa *	UGA	1	2
Adulis Club	ERI	0	0
Renaissance	CHA	0	3
Olympique Az Zwiyah *	LBY	2	2
Diables Noirs	CGO	0	0 2p
Red Arrows *	ZAM	0	0 3p
CAPS United *	ZIM	4	4
Lesotho Defence Force	LES	1	3
Ferroviario Nampula	MOZ	1	1
Simba SC *	TAN	2	1
Mhlambanyatsi Rovers	SWZ	0	1
Ajax Cape Town *	RSA	1	1
ASFA Yennega	BFA	0	2 5p
TP Mazembe Englebert *	COD	2	0 4p
Fello Stars Labé	GUI	1	1
Diaraf Dakar *	SEN	2	0
Blue Waters	NAM	0	2
Atlético Aviação *	ANG	3	1
KMKM Zanzibar	ZAN	1	0
Tusker *	KEN	4	3
DC Motema Pembe *	COD	3	0
Rayon Sport	RWA	0	2
Donjo	BEN	0	0
Racing Bafoussam *	CIV	1	2
Renacimiento	EQG	0	1
Dolphin *	NGA	3	0
Mangasport	GAB	0	1
Sagrada Esperança *	ANG	0	2
Al Hilal *	SUD	2	1
Awassa City	ETH	1	1
La Passe *	SEY	2	1
USJA/Ravinala	MAD	2	4
Kaizer Chiefs *	RSA	2	1
AS Port Louis 2000	MRI	0	2
ASC Ksar	MTN		
FAR Rabat *	MAR	4	0
Asante Kotoko	GHA	w-o	
Wallidan ‡	GAM		
AS Douanes	SEN	1	1
Djoliba *	MLI	1	0

Second Round

Team	Code	Leg 1	Leg 2
Al Ahly	EGY	0	6
SC Villa *	UGA	0	0
Olympique Az Zwiyah *	LBY	0	0
USM Alger	ALG	2	5
Red Arrows	ZAM	1	2
CAPS United *	ZIM	1	1
Simba SC *	TAN	1	0
Enyimba	NGA	1	4
Ajax Cape Town	RSA	0	1 5p
ASFA-Yennega *	BFA	1	0 3p
JS Kabylie	ALG	0	0
Fello Stars Labé *	GUI	1	0
Atlético Aviação *	ANG	2	0
Cotonsport Garoua	CMR	0	1
Tusker *	KEN	0	1
Zamalek	EGY	1	3
Raja Casablanca	MAR	1	2
DC Motema Pembe *	COD	1	0
Racing Bafoussam *	CMR	1	1
Africa Sports	CIV	0	3
Dolphin *	NGA	4	1
Hearts of Oak	GHA	0	2
Sagrada Esperança *	ANG	2	0
ASEC Mimosas	CIV	2	1
Espérance Tunis	TUN	0	5
Al Hilal *	SUD	2	1
USJA/Ravinala *	MAD	0	1
Kaizer Chiefs	RSA	1	4
FAR Rabat	MAR	0	2
Asante Kotoko *	GHA	1	0
AS Douanes *	SEN	0	1
Etoile du Sahel	TUN	0	3

Third Round

Team	Leg 1	Leg 2
Al Ahly	1	2
USM Alger *	0	2
Red Arrows	0	1
Enyimba *	3	6
Ajax Cape Town *	2	0 3p
Fello Stars Labé	0	2 2p
Atlético Aviação *	1	0
Zamalek	1	2
Raja Casablanca	1	1
Africa Sports *	1	0
Dolphin *	2	0 3p
ASEC Mimosas	0	2 5p
Espérance Tunis *	4	1
Kaizer Chiefs	0	2
FAR Rabat *	1	0
Etoile du Sahel	0	2

* Home team in the first leg • Losing teams in the second round enter the CAF Confederation Cup • ‡ Wallidan withdrew • w-o = walk-over

CAF CHAMPIONS LEAGUE 2005

CAF CHAMPIONS LEAGUE 2005

Champions League Stage   **Semi-finals**   **Final**

Group A		Pts	EGY	MAR	NGA	RSA
Al Ahly	EGY	14		1-0	2-1	2-0
Raja Casablanca	MAR	8	1-1		1-0	1-1
Enyimba	NGA	7	0-1	2-0		2-0
Ajax Cape Town	RSA	3	0-0	0-3	1-1	

Al Ahly	2	2
Zamalek *	1	0

Al Ahly	0	3
Etoile du Sahel *	0	0

Raja Casablanca *	0	0
Etoile du Sahel	1	1

Group B		Pts	TUN	EGY	CIV	TUN
Etoile du Sahel	TUN	10		2-1	2-1	1-1
Zamalek	EGY	9	1-1		2-1	1-1
ASEC Mimosas	CIV	6	1-1	1-1		1-0
Espérance Tunis	TUN	4	1-1	1-2	0-0	

FIRST ROUND

30-01-2005
SC Villa 1 Ssentongo 4
Adulis Club 0

13-02-2005
Adulis Club 0
SC Villa 2 Ssentongo 23,

28-01-2005
Olympique 2 Kames 68, Daood 80
Renaissance 0

20-02-2005
Renaissance 3 Misdongarde 70, Asde 84, Ahmat 88
Olympique 2 Kara 35p, Al Sweae 68

30-01-2005
Red Arrows 0
Diables Noirs 0

13-02-2005
Diables Noirs 0
Red Arrows 0 — Red Arrows W 3-2p

30-01-2005
CAPS United 4 Tsipa 2 16 19, Badza 44, Chimedza 48
Lesotho DF 1 Ranchobe 76

13-02-2005
Lesotho DF 3 Ranchobe 5, Ntakha 61, Majara 80
CAPS United 4 Chimedza 13, Tsipa 48, ?, Badza 81

30-01-2005
Simba SC 2 Costa 73p, Sued 78
Ferroviário 1 Carlos 1

13-02-2005
Ferroviário 1 Domingos 22
Simba SC 1 Abdalla 31

30-01-2005
Ajax Cape Town 1 Tshabalala 35
Mhlambanyatsi 0

13-02-2005
Mhlambanyatsi 1 Mathonsi 85p
Ajax Cape Town 1 Kitambala 34

30-01-2005
TP Mazembe 2 Mukadi 51, Dieu 89
ASFA-Yennega 0

12-02-2005
ASFA-Yennega 2 Makela OG 37, Kombeogo 46p
TP Mazembe 0 — ASFA-Yennega W 5-4p

29-01-2005
ASC Diaraf 2 Bâ Camara OG 10, Niang 58
Fello Stars Labé 1 Camara.l 35

13-02-2005
Fello Stars Labé 1 Camara.l 82
ASC Diaraf 0

30-01-2005
Atlético Aviacão 3 Milex 34, Cabungula 2 57p 62
Blue Waters 0

12-02-2005
Blue Waters 2 Shipanga 2
Atlético Aviacão 1 Lofo

29-01-2005
Tusker 4 Gitau 6, Odhiambo 2 29 46, Mariga 84
KMKM Zanzibar 1 Semsue 16

12-02-2005
KMKM Zanzibar 0
Tusker 3 Gitau 10, Malanda 2 18 27

30-01-2005
Motema Pembe 3 Ngidi 61, Luyeye 2 88 90
Rayon Sport 0

13-02-2005
Rayon Sport 2 Papy 46, Sibomana 63
Motema Pembe 0

Douala, 30-01-2005
Racing Bafous'm 1 Youmsi 40
Donjo 0

13-02-2005
Donjo 0
Racing Bafous'm 1 Vascomo 2 21 81

30-01-2005
Dolphin 3 Ojobo 12, Ezeji 43, Osunwa 90
Renacimiento 0

13-02-2005
Renacimiento 1 Doe 87
Dolphin 0

Luanda, 29-01-2005
Sagrada Esp'nça 0
Mangasport 0

13-02-2005
Mangasport 1 Batti 63
Sagrada Esp'nça 2 Dos Santos 6, Da Silva 8

29-01-2005
Al Hilal 2 Godwin 38, Tahir 47
Awassa City 1 Ashamo 75

13-02-2005
Awassa City 1 Demeke
Al Hilal 1 Hishad 69

29-01-2005
La Passe 2 Ladouce 55, Rajaonarivelo OG 80
USJF/Ravinala 2 Rabefitia 2 14 49

13-02-2005
USJA Ravinala 4 Ralaitafika 35, Randriamihaja 14, Rabefitia 2 64p 84
La Passe 1 Saindina 71

29-01-2005
Kaizer Chiefs 2 Chalwe 7, Mbesuma 59p
Port Louis 2000 0

13-02-2005
Port Louis 2000 2 Mounthaly 2 26 49
Kaizer Chiefs 1 Zwane 32

29-01-2005
FAR Rabat 4 Ouchella 2 12 32, Armoumen 57, Afoui 86
ASC Ksar 0

11-02-2005
ASC Ksar 1 Diallo 93+
FAR Rabat 0

Kumasi, 30-01-2005
Asante Kotoko - Wallidan withdrew
Wallidan -

30-01-2005
Djoliba AC 1 Abouta 29p
AS Douanes 1 Fall 34

12-02-2005
AS Douanes 1 Samb 87
Djoliba AC 0

SECOND ROUND

4-03-2005
SC Villa 0
Al Ahly Cairo 0

19-03-2005
Al Ahly Cairo 6 Imed 23, Baraket 2 56 90, Tarika 2 65 87, Nahas 85
SC Villa 0

Tripoli, 6-03-2005
Olympique 0
USM Alger 2 Ammour 2 53 59

Algiers, 18-03-2005
USM Alger 5 Doucoure 2 5 37, Belkheir 2 83 90, Enerami 68
Olympique 0

		6-03-2005
CAPS United	1	Tsipa [28]
Red Arrows	1	Gondwe [53]
		19-03-2005
Red Arrows	2	Banda [41], Katuka [77]
CAPS United	1	Chimedza [45]
		Mwanza, 6-03-2005
Simba SC	1	Nduka [66]
Enyimba	1	Olumo [42]
		20-03-2005
Enyimba	4	Olomu [1], Frimpong [11], Mohamed [84], Adegoke [88]
Simba SC	0	
		6-03-2005
ASFA Yennega	1	Issouf [87]
Ajax Cape Town	0	
		20-03-2005
Ajax Cape Town	1	Shabalala [48]
ASFA Yennega	0	Ajax W 5-3p
		6-03-2005
Fello Stars Labé	1	Tsipa [25]
JS Kabylie	0	
		18-03-2005
JS Kabylie	0	
Fello Stars Labé	0	
		6-03-2005
Atlético Aviacão	2	Arsenio [10], Lofo [85]
Cotonsport	0	
		20-03-2005
Cotonsport	1	Belinga
Atlético Aviacão	0	
		5-03-2005
Tusker	0	
Zamalek	1	Halim Ali [73]
		20-03-2005
Zamalek	3	Tarek [10], Sameh [25], Abdelhalim [60]
Tusker	1	Mariga [90]
		6-03-2005
Motema Pembe	1	Baribu [15p]
Raja Casablanca	1	Rachid [80]
		19-03-2005
Raja Casablanca	2	Sherouane [2], Mohsen [88]
Motema Pembe	0	
		5-03-2005
Racing Bafous'm	1	Anior [54]
Africa Sports	0	
		19-03-2005
Africa Sports	3	Kassiaty [45], Shaibu [47], Brou [74]
Racing Bafous'm	1	Mbianda [45]
		6-03-2005
Dolphin	4	Osunwa [18], Idahor [55], Ojobo [62], Bello [79]
Hearts of Oak	0	
		20-03-2005
Hearts of Oak	2	Tagoe 2 [75 79]
Dolphin	1	Osunwa [83]
		Luanda, 5-03-2005
Sagrada Esp'nça	2	Chinho 2 [43 80p]
ASEC Mimosas	2	Mamadou [59], Kane [90]
		Abidjan, 20-03-2005
ASEC Mimosas	1	Foneye [14]
Sagrada Esp'nça	0	
		6-03-2005
Al Hilal	2	Hytham.T [47], Hytham.K [61]
Esperánce Tunis	0	
		Tunis, 19-03-2005
Esperánce Tunis	5	Kamel [68], Moyin 2 [75 88], Master [77], Amine [89]
Al Hilal	1	Hytham.T
		6-03-2005
USJF/Ravinala	0	
Kaizer Chiefs	1	Mbesuma [75]

		19-03-2005
Kaizer Chiefs	4	Mbesuma 2 [6 22], Mbambo [26], Zwane [69]
USJF/Ravinala	1	Ralaitafika [44]
		6-03-2005
Asante Kotoko	1	Chipsah [77]
FAR Rabat	0	
		19-03-2005
FAR Rabat	2	Ajeddou
Asante Kotoko	0	
		5-03-2005
AS Douanes	0	
Etoile du Dahel	0	
		19-03-2005
Etoile du Sahel	3	Chikaoui [45], Mhadbi [50], Jedidi [87]
AS Douanes	1	Bdiane [90]

THIRD ROUND

		Algiers, 8-04-2005
USM Alger	0	
Al Ahly Cairo	1	Barakat [6]
		Cairo, 22-04-2005
Al Ahly Cairo	2	El Nahas [45], Moteab [55]
USM Alger	2	Achiou [42], Hamdoud [94+p]
		10-04-2005
Enyimba	3	Frimpong 2 [17p 90], Sakibu [82]
Red Arrows	0	
		23-04-2005
Red Arrows	1	Mwamba [4]
Enyimba	6	Frimpong [18], Olomo [30], Ogunbiyi [59] David 2 [63 65], Obeoah [77]
		10-04-2005
Ajax Cape Town	2	August 2 [41 73]
Fello Stars Labé	0	
		24-05-2005
Fello Stars Labé	2	Camara.I [48], Camara.A [88]
Ajax Cape Town	0	Ajax W 3-2p
		9-04-2005
Atlético Aviacão	1	Lofo [34]
Zamalek	1	Hamza [12]
		24-04-2005
Zamalek	2	Wael [23p], Halim Ali [60]
Atlético Aviacão	0	
		10-04-2003
Africa Sports	1	Djedjed [26]
Raja Casablanca	1	Iajour [75]
		23-04-2003
Raja Casablanca	1	Redouane [90]
Africa Sports	0	
		10-04-2004
Dolphin	2	Idahor 2 [18 87]
ASEC Mimosas	0	
		24-04-2005
ASEC Mimosas	2	Foneye [9], Koivogui [66]
Dolphin	0	ASEC W 5-3p
		9-04-2005
Esperánce Tunis	4	Zaiem 2 [12p 15p], Dos Santos [20], Mnari [83]
Kaizer Chiefs	0	
		23-04-2005
Kaizer Chiefs	2	Moshoeu [63], Mbambo [90]
Esperánce Tunis	1	Dos Santos [76]
		10-04-2005
FAR Rabat	1	Armoumen [57p]
Etoile du Sahel	0	
		23-04-2005
Etoile du Sahel	2	Beya [18p], Traore.K [50]
FAR Rabat	0	

GROUP A

		Pl	W	D	L	F	A	Pts	EGY	MAR	NGA	RSA
Al Ahly Cairo	EGY	6	4	2	0	7	2	14		1-0	2-1	2-0
Raja Casablanca	MAR	6	2	2	2	6	5	8	1-1		1-0	1-1
Enyimba	NGA	6	2	1	3	6	5	7	0-1	2-0		2-0
Ajax Cape Town	RSA	6	0	3	3	2	9	3	0-0	0-3	1-1	

GROUP A MATCHDAY 1
Arab Contractors, Cairo
26-06-2005, 20:30, Benouza ALG

Al Ahly 1

Shawky [54]

Al Hadari - El Shater●38, Ahmed El Sayed, Al Nahhas, Shady Mohamed, Gilberto (Aboumosalem● 75), Barakat, Shawky, Hassan Mostafa, Aboutrika (Wael Riad 83'), Bilal● (Moteab 61). Tr: Manuel Jose

Raja Casablanca 0

El Had - El Haimeur (Soulaimani 75), Erbate, Loue, Jrindou, Misbah●38, Masloub●, Daoudi● (Sakim 87), Alloudi, Zemmama, Aboucherouane. Tr: Moldovan

GROUP A MATCHDAY 1
Athlone Stadium, Cape Town
26-06-2005, 15:15, Hicuburundi BDI

Ajax Cape Town 1

Ogar OG [17]

Josephs, Isaacs, Mouyouma, Mubiala, Mofokeng (Paulse 46), Shumana, Evans, Dlangudlangu (Scott 70), Carelse (Shabalala 29'), Motlhajwa, Mugeyi. Tr: Igesund

Enyimba 1

Frimpong [9]

Aiyenugba, Aliyu, Adegoke, Ogar, Yusuf Mohamed, Raji, Sakibu (Obediah 68), Johnson, Olomu, Ogunbiyi, Frimpong● (Fasindo 76). Tr: Emordi

GROUP A MATCHDAY 2
Mohamed V, Casablanca
9-07-2005, 20:30, Ndoye SEN

Raja Casablanca 1

Zemmama [51]

El Had - El Haimeur (Fatah 46), Erbate, Loue, Bouarib, Soulaimani (Suleiman 67), Sami, Daoudi, Alloudi, Zemmama●, Aboucherouane●89. Tr: Moldovan

Ajax Cape Town 1

Shumana [85]

Josephs - Isaacs, Mouyouma●, Mubiala●77, Mofokeng● (Shumana 65), Evans, Mulekelayi, Shabalala, Cale, Motlhajwa (Paulse 47), Mugeyi (Scott 68). Tr: Igesund

GROUP A MATCHDAY 2
Aba Stadium, Aba
10-07-2005, 16:00Lim Kee Chong MRI

Enyimba 0

Aiyenugba - Aliyu, Adegoke, Ogar, Uche, Yusuf Mohamed, Sakibu (Obediah 74), Johnson (Njoku 69), Olomu, Ogunbiyi, Frimpong (Fasindo 62). Tr: Emordi

Al Ahly Cairo 1

Moteab [12]

Al Hadari - Ahmed El Sayed, Mensah (Ahmed Hassan● 16) (Shady Mohamed 89), Al Nahhas, Wael Gomaa, Barakat, Gilberto, Hassan Mostafa, Shawky●, Aboutrika, Moteab (Osama Hosni 80). Tr: Manuel Jose

GROUP A MATCHDAY 3
Sekka Hadid, Cairo
22-07-2005, 20:30, Evehe CMR

Al Ahly Cairo 2

El Sayed [8], Moteab [89]

Al Hadari - El Shater (Shady Mohamed 85), Wael Gomaa, Al Nahhas, Ahmed El Sayed, Hossam Ashour, Barakat, Gilberto, Hassan Mostafa●, Shawky, Aboutrika (Flavio 85), Moteab. Tr: Manuel Jose

Ajax Cape Town 0

Josephs● - Isaacs●, Mouyouma, Evans, Mofokeng, Shumana (Dlangudlangu● 77), Mulekelayi, Shabalala (Scott 46), Cale, Motlhajwa (Paulse 46), Mugeyi. Tr: Igesund

GROUP A MATCHDAY 3
Mohamed V, Casablanca
23-07-2005, 20:30, Sowe GAM

Raja Casablanca 1

Jrindou [78]

Chadli●, Erbate, Loue (Abdelouahed, 68), Daoudi●68, Jrindou, Masloub (Alloudi 83), Soulaimani, Sakim, Zemmama, Harouach (Fofana 63), Iajour. Tr: Moldovan

Enyimba 0

Aiyenugba, Aliyu, Adegoke●, Uche, Yusuf Mohamed, Ogar, David, Johnson, Olomu● (Mba 89), Ogunbiyi (Tyavkase, 79), Frimpong (Sakibu 58). Tr: Emordi

GROUP A MATCHDAY 4
Athlone Stadium, Cape Town
7-08-2005, 15:15, Colembi ANG

Ajax Cape Town 0

Josephs - Mouyouma, Evans, Mofokeng, Mulekelayi (Paulse 34), Shabalala●, Cale, Motlhajwa (Dlangudlangu 70), Mugeyi●, Shumana (Poggenpoel 85), Fanteni. Tr: Igesund

Al Ahly Cairo 0

Al Hadari - El Shater, Wael Gomaa, Al Nahas, Ahmed El Sayed, Gilberto, Hassan Mostafa, Shawky●, Flavio (Barakat 70), Aboutrika (Osama Hosni 83), Moteab● (Wael Riad 89). Tr: Manuel Jose

GROUP A MATCHDAY 4
Aba Stadium, Aba
7-08-2005, 16:15, Shelmani LBY

Enyimba 2

Frimpong 2 [30] [49]

Aiyegnuba - Adegoke, Raji, Ogar, Yusuf Mohamed, Aliyu, Johnson, Lawal (Okoli 69), Ogunbiyi (Mbah 87), Tyavkase, Frimpong● (Sakibu 63). Tr: Emordi

Raja Casablanca 0

El Had - El Haimeur, Abdelouahed●, Erbate●, Loue●, Jrindou, Soulaimani, Sakim (Harouach 65), Alloudi, Zemmama, Iajour (Masloub 46). Tr: Moldovan

GROUP A MATCHDAY 5
Mohamed V, Casablanca
20-08-2005, 20:30, Daami TUN

Raja Casablanca 1

Alloudi [65]

Chadli - El Haimeur, Abdelouahed, Loue, Jrindou, Soulaimani (Fofana 53), Masloub, Misbah●, Alloudi●, Zemmama (Daoudi 83), Iajour (Maiga 72). Tr: Moldovan

Al Ahly Cairo 1

Moteab [89]

Al Hadari - El Shater (Aboutrika 73), Wael Gomaa●, Al Nahhas, Ahmed El Sayed, Gilberto (Wael Riad 85), Barakat●, Shady Mohamed, Hossam Ashour (Shawky● 44), Flavio●, Moteab. Tr: Manuel Jose

GROUP A MATCHDAY 5
Aba Stadium, Aba
21-08-2005, 16:00, Kidane ERI

Enyimba 2

David [61], Tyavkase [85]

Aiyegnuba - Yusuf Mohamed, Adegoke (Emigo, 75), Aliyu, Raji, Ogar, David, Fasindo (Sakibu 69), Johnson, Ogunbiyi, Tyavkase. Tr: Emordi

Ajax Cape Town 0

Petim - Isaacs, Mubiala, Mouyouma●, Evans●, Mofokeng, Mulekelayi (Shumana 84), Cale, Mugeyi (Scott 70), Paulse (Shabalala● 58), Fanteni. Tr: Igesund

GROUP A MATCHDAY 6
Athlone Stadium, Cape Town
11-09-2005, 19:00, Lim Kee Chong MRI

Ajax Cape Town 0

Josephs - Mofokeng, Mubiala, Poggenpoel, Mulekelayi, Shumana, Cale●, Scott, Dlangudlangu, Motlhajwa, Fanteni (Paulse 54). Tr: Igesund

Raja Casablanca 3

Fofana [5], Alloudi [41], Iajour [59]

Chadli - El Haimeur, Abdelouahed, Loue, Soulaimani●, Misbah, Alloudi● (Fatah 82), Zemmama (Remch 88), Daoudi, Fofana (Harouach 68), Iajour. Tr: Moldovan

GROUP A MATCHDAY 6
Sekka Hadid, Cairo
11-09-2005, 20:00, Coulibaly MLI

Al Ahly Cairo 2

Osama Hosni 2 [39] [81]

Al Hadari - El Shater, Rami Adel, Ahmed El Sayed, Al Nahhas, Ahmed Hassan, Shady Mohamed, Gilberto (Abdelwahab 68), Hossam Ashour (Wael Gomaa 76), Osama Hosni, Flavio (Wael Riad 85). Tr: Manuel Jose

Enyimba 1

Sakibu [27]

Aiyegnuba - Yusuf Mohamed, Adegoke, Ogar, Aliyu (Sakibu 12), Raji (Njoku 80), Uche●, Ogunbiyi, Olomu, Tyavkase (Chukwu 89), Frimpong. Tr: Emordi

GROUP B

	Pl	W	D	L	F	A	Pts			
Etoile du Sahel	TUN	6	2	4	0	7	5	10	2-1	2-1	1-1
Zamalek	EGY	6	2	3	1	8	7	9	1-1		2-1	1-1
ASEC Mimosas	CIV	6	1	3	2	5	6	6	1-1	1-1		1-0
Espérance Tunis	TUN	6	0	4	2	3	5	4	1-1	1-2	0-0

GROUP B MATCHDAY 1
Felix Houphouet-Boigny, Abidjan
26-06-2005, 15:15, Mbera GAB

ASEC Mimosas 1

Koivogui [79]

Dimy - Ndri, Dacosta, Doumbia●, Bakary Soro, Kouamé, Ya Konan, Emmanuel Kone, Kane (Taina Soro 68), Die (Koivogui● 48), Beko Fofana (Seydou Kone 50). Tr: Liewig

Zamalek 1

Tarek El Sayed [30]

El Sayed - Mahmoud●, Abdelhadi, Wael El Quabbani, Seddek, Tarek El Sayed (Abdelwahed 66), Aboul Ela, Tarek Said, Gamal Hamza, Abdelhalim Ali (Hazem Emam 80), Youssef Sameh (El Moataz● 72). Tr: Bucker

GROUP B MATCHDAY 2
International, Cairo
10-07-2005, 20:30, Damon RSA

Zamalek 1

Wael El Quabbani [92+]

El Sayed - Abdelhadi, Seddek●, Wael El Quabbani, Tarek El Sayed, Ibrahim Said, Tarek Said●, Aboul Ela, Hazem Emam (Gamal Hamza 62), Abdelhalim Ali (Abdelwahed 89), Hossam Ossama (Abdellatif 82). Tr: Buckner

Etoile du Sahel 0

Bokri [88]

Ejide - Sellami, Ghezal●, Ben Frej● (Ettraoui● 58), Bokri●, Zouaghi●, Miladi, Hammi●, Melliti (Ben Nasr 89), Jedidi, Traore (Gilson 79). Tr: Chetali

GROUP B MATCHDAY 4
Stade Olympique, Sousse
6-08-2005, 19:00, Ssegonga UGA

Etoile du Sahel 2

Jedidi [7], Melliti [52]

Ejide - Ben Mohamed, Ali Arouri, Ghezal, Sellami, Ahmed Hammi, Zouaghi, Bokri (Gilson 46), Melliti, Jedidi (Ettraoui 75), Opara (Chikhaoui 62). Tr: Bazdarevic

ASEC Mimosas 1

Ya Konan [25]

Dimy - Ndri, Dacosta, Doumbia●44, Bakary Soro●, Kocou (Taina Soro 68), Kouamé, Emmanuel Koné, Diomandé (Adenon 46), Ya Konan (Dié 80), Koivogui. Tr: Liewig

GROUP B MATCHDAY 5
Sekka Hadid, Cairo
21-08-2005, 20:30, Maillet SEY

Zamalek 2

Gamal Hamza [2], Wael El Quabbani [80p]

El Sayed - Abdelhadi, Wael El Quabbani, El Moataz●, El Bakry, Tarek El Sayed, Ibrahim Said, Hazem Emam (Quaye 53), Gamal Hamza (Sameh Youssef 75), Aboul Ela (Hossama Ossama 46), Abdelhalim Ali●. Tr: Gaafar

ASEC Mimosas 1

Fofana [72]

Dimy - N'Dri, Dacosta, Bakary Soro, Kocou (Tayoro 46), Adenon, Kouamé, Emmanuel Koné, Ya Konan (Diomandé 50), Beko Fofana (Dié 80), Koivogui. Tr: Liewig

GROUP B MATCHDAY 1
Stade Olympique, Sousse
2-07-2005, 19:00, Pare BFA

Etoile du Sahel 0

Ejide - Nasri (Ben Frej 10), Miladi, Sellami, Ghezal, Zouaghi, Bokri, Melliti (Ben Nasr 88), Gilson (Ettraoui 46), Taylor●75, Jedidi. Tr: Chetali

Esperánce Tunis 1

Tizie - Yaken●, El Bekri, Nwaneri, Clayton (Udeh● 38) (Hamdi Harbaoui 87), Azaiez●, Sghaier, Zaiem, Melki, Dos Santos●80, Kasdaoui● (Ongfiang 63). Tr: Mahjoubi

GROUP B MATCHDAY 3
Felix Houphouet-Boigny, Abidjan
24-07-2005, 15:15, Musasa ZIM

ASEC Mimosas 1

Koivogui [7]

Dimy - Ndri, Dacosta, Adenon, Bakary Soro, Kocou, Kouame, Ya Konan● (Seydou Kone 88), Emmanuel Kone, Diomande (Taina Soro 61), Koivogui (Die 79). Tr: Liewig

Etoile du Sahel 1

Ben Nasr [86p]

Ejide - Ghezal, Miladi, Ben Frej●, Melliti●, Bokri (Ben Nasr 63), Sellemi, Hammi, Taylor (Chikaoui 73), Opara, Jedidi (Trabelsi 79). Tr: Mlik

GROUP B MATCHDAY 4
7 Novembre, Rades, Tunis
7-08-2004, 20:00, Agbenyenga GHA

Esperánce Tunis 1

Ongfiang [53]

Tizie - Chaabani, Mathias, Nwaneri, Yaken (Ltaief 76), Clayton, Belhadj, Zaïem●, Ongfiang, Dos Santos (Udeh 63), Zitouni. Tr: Mahjoub

Zamalek 2

Hazem Emam [67], Quaye [72]

El Sayed - Abdelhadi, Mahmoud●, Wael El Quabbani, El Moataz, Tarek El Sayed (Hazem Emam 67'), Ibrahim Said, Abdelwahed●, Tarek Said, Quaye● (Aboul Ela● 80'), Abdelhalim Ali. Tr: Buckner

GROUP B MATCHDAY 6
Stade Olympique, Sousse
10-09-2005, 18:00, Benouza ALG

Etoile du Sahel 2

Opara [50], Bokri [53]

Ejide - Zouaghi, Ali Arouri, Ghezal●, Sellami, Ettraoui, Bargui, Bokri, Ben Nasr (Jebnoun 66), Gilson (Melliti 85), Emeka Opara (Sabeur Trabelsi● 74). Tr: Bazdarevic

Zamalek 1

Tarek El Sayed [64]

El Sayed - Adel Fathi●, El Bakry●, Wael El Quabbani, Abdelhadi, Tarek El Sayed, Hazem Emam, Ibrahim Said (Gamal Hamza 73), Aboul Ela, Abdelhalim Ali, Quaye● (Sameh Youssef 51). Tr: Gaafar

GROUP B MATCHDAY 2
7 Novembre, Rades, Tunis
9-07-2005, 20:00, Avdelrahman SUD

Esperánce Tunis 0

Tizié - Mathias, Clayton, Nwaneri, Azaïez, Sghaïer (El Bekri 82), Udeh (Ben Yahia 87), Melki, Ongfiang, Zitouni, Harbaoui (Ltaief 67). Tr: Mahjoubi

ASEC Mimosas 0

Dimy - Doumbia●, Kouamé, Kocou, Dacosta, Ndri, Emmanuel Koné (Taina Soro 79), Ya Konan (Beko Fofana 83), Bakary Soro, Koivogui (Die 72), Diomande. Tr: Liewig

GROUP B MATCHDAY 3
Arab Contractors, Cairo
24-07-2005, 20:30, Codjia BEN

Zamalek 1

Abdelwahed [36]

El Sayed - Abdelhadi, El Moataz, Wael El Quabbani, Tarek El Sayed● (Gamal Hamza 80), Ibrahim Said●, Tarek Said, Abdelwahed, Hazem Emam (Aboul Ela 38), Abdelhalim Ali, Edson (Quaye 65). Tr: Buckner

Esperánce Tunis 1

Chaabani [44]

Tizie● - Mathias, Nwaneri, Chaabani, El Bekri● (Udeh 60), Yaken●, Clayton (Kasdaoui 46), Belhadj, Melki●, Ongfiang● (Jabeur 81), Zitouni. Tr: Mahjoub

GROUP B MATCHDAY 5
7 Novembre, Rades, Tunis
20-08-2005, 20:00, Shelmani LBY

Esperánce Tunis 1

Ltaief [31]

Tizié - Yaken●, El Bekri, Nwaneri, Chaabani, Belhadj●, Ben Yahia (Kasdaoui 76'), Melki, Ongfiang, Dos Santos (Zitouni 46'), Ltaief● (Bhaïri 82'). Tr: Ben Yahia ·

Etoile du Sahel 1

Melliti [6]

Ejide - Ben Frej●, Ali Arouri, Sellami, Ghezal, Zouaghi●, Hammi●, Melliti, Bokri (Ettraoui 69'), Gilson, Opara● (Chikhaoui 60'). Tr: Bazdarevic

GROUP B MATCHDAY 6
Felix Houphouet-Boigny, Abidjan
10-09-2005, 16:00, Buenkadila COD

ASEC Abidjan 1

Diaby [89]

Dimy - Tayoro, N'Dri, Dacosta, Adenon, Kouamé, Emmanuel Koné●, Ya Konan (Diaby 83), Diomandé, Modibo Kane (Faye 79), Koffi Konan (Dié 60). Tr: Liewig

Esperánce Tunis 0

Kasraoui - Mathias, Nwaneri, Chaabani●, Guizani●, Azaiez●, Bhaïri, Sghaier, Ouji, Dos Santos, Kasdaoui. Tr: Belhassan Meriah

SEMI-FINALS

1st Leg. Military Stadium, Cairo
25-09-2005. Codjia BEN

Zamalek   **1**

Hazem Emam [74]

Abou Moncef - Abdelhadi, El Quabbani, El Bakry•, El Moataz•, Adel Fathi (Sameh Youssef 70), Tarek El Sayed, Ibrahim Said (Hazem Emam 51), Aboul Ela, Abdelhalim Ali (Gamal Hamza 63), Abdellatif. Tr: Gaafar

Al Ahly Cairo   **2**

Moteab [27], Barakat [44]

Al Hadari – El Shater (Shady Mohamed 60), Ahmed El Sayed, Wael Gomaa, Al Nahhas, Barakat, Hossam Ashour (Abdelwahab 89), Gilberto, Hassan Mostafa, Motaeb, Aboutrika• (Flavio 74). Tr: Manuel Jose

2nd Leg. Military Stadium, Cairo
15-10-2005. Shelmani LBY

Al Ahly Cairo   **2**

Barakat 2 [62] [73]

Al Hadari - El Shater•, Ahmed El Sayed•, Wael Gomaa, Al Nahhas, Shawky, Barakat, Gilberto, Hassan Mostafa (Hossam Ashour 46), Motaeb (Osama Hosni 88), Aboutrika (Abdelhafiz 82). Tr: Manuel Jose

Zamalek   **0**

Abou Moncef - El Moataz, El Quabbani, Sameh Youssef, Tarek El Sayed, Ibrahim Said, Abdelwahed, Abouela, Awule Quaye• (Hazem Emam 68'), Abdelhalim Ali, Gamal Hamza (Abdellatif 61'). Tr: Gaafar

1st Leg. Mohamed V, Casablanca
24-09-2005, Maillet SEY

Raja Casablanca   **0**

Chadli - El Haimeur, Abdelouahed, Edgard Loue, Masloub, Misbah, Soulaimani (Maiga 63), Harouach• (Zemmama 66), Daoudi, Fofana (Sami 83), lajour. Tr: Moldovan

Etoile du Sahel   **1**

Opara [59]

Ejide - Ben Frej, Ali Arouri, Sellami, Zouaghi, Bargui, Ettraoui, Zouaghi, Bokri, Opara• (Trabelsi 78), Gilson (Melliti• 71). Tr: Bazdarevic

2nd Leg. Stade Olympique, Sousse
15-10-2005, Bennett RSA

Etoile du Sahel   **1**

Zouaghi.K [64]

Ejide - Ghezal, Ali Arouri, Sellami, Zouaghi, Hammi, Ettraoui, Zouaghi, Bokri (Bargui 64), Chikaoui (Ben Nasr• 71), Gilson (Trabelsi 89). Tr: Bazdarevic

Raja Casablanca   **0**

Chadli - El Haimeur, Abdelouahed•67, Loue, Sami (lajour 63), Masloub, Alloudi, Maiga, Daoudi•, Fofana (Soulaimani 57), Zemmama (Remch 69). Tr: Moldovan

---

CAF CHAMPIONS LEAGUE FINAL 1ST LEG
Stade Olympique, Sousse
29-10-2005, 20 000, El Arjoun MAR

ETOILE DU SAHEL 0   0   AL AHLY CAIRO

	Etoile			Al Ahly	
16	Austin EJIDE			Essam AL HADARI	1
15	Lotfi SELLAMI			Islam EL SHATER	2
13	Sabeur BEN FREJ			GILBERTO Amaral	12
2	Seif GHEZAL			Emad AL NAHHAS	16
14	Kais ZOUAGHI			Wael GOMAA	10
6	Ahmed HAMDI			Ahmed EL SAYED	5
4	Chaker ZOUAGHI			Mohamed SHAWKY	17
3	Marouene BOKRI	81		Hassan MOSTAFA	14
8	Mohamed JEDIDI		92	Mohamed ABOUTRIKA	22
27	Manuel GILSON			Emad MOTEAB	13
28	Emeka OPARA	62		Mohamed BARAKAT	8
	Tr: BAZDAREVIC Mehmed			Tr: MANUEL JOSE	
	Substitutes			Substitutes	
18	Mejdi ETTRAOUI	81	92	Osama HOSNI	18
17	Yassine CHIKAOUI	62			
11	Saber TRABELSI	85			

CAF CHAMPIONS LEAGUE FINAL 2ND LEG
Military Stadium, Cairo
12-11-2005, 35 000, Pare BFA

AL AHLY CAIRO   3   0   ETOILE DU SAHEL

Abou Tarika [20], Hosni [51]
Barakat [90]

	Al Ahly			Etoile	
1	Essam AL HADARI			Austin EJIDE	16
12	GILBERTO Amaral	32		Lotfi SELLAMI	15
16	Emad AL NAHHAS			Sabeur BEN FREJ	13
26	Wael GOMAA			Seif GHEZAL	2
5	Ahmed EL SAYED			Kais ZOUAGHI	14
17	Mohamed SHAWKY			Ahmed HAMDI	6
14	Hassan MOSTAFA			Chaker ZOUAGHI	4
22	Mohamed ABOUTRIKA		67	Marouene BOKRI	3
13	Emad MOTEAB		79	Mohamed JEDIDI	8
8	Mohamed BARAKAT			Manuel GILSON	27
18	Osama HOSNI		53	Emeka OPARA	28
	Tr: MANUEL JOSE			Tr: BAZDAREVIC Mehmed	
	Substitutes			Substitutes	
3	Mohamed ABDELWAHAB	32	53	Yassine CHIKAOUI	17
2	Islam EL SHATER	66	67	Bassem BEN NASR	10
			79	Saber TRABELSI	11

AJAX CAPE TOWN

Goalkeepers

1	Andre PETIM	RSA
16	Moeneeb JOSEPHS	RSA

Defenders

4	Dominic ISAACS	RSA
22	Shane POGGENPOEL	RSA
23	Cyrille MUBAILA	COD
24	Thierry MOUYOUMA	GAB
25	Brett EVANS	RSA
28	George MOFOKENG	RSA

Midfielders

5	Franklyn CALE	RSA
6	Mfundo SHUMANA	RSA
11	Kanku MULEKELAYI	COD
12	Granwald SCOTT	RSA
21	Seuntjie MOTLHAJWA	RSA
30	Lunga DLANGUDLANGU	RSA

Forwards

7	Nhlanhla SHABALALA	RSA
9	Nathan PAULSE	RSA
10	Brent CARELSE	RSA
19	Wilfred MUGEYI	ZIM
29	Thembinkosi FANTENI	RSA

AL AHLY

Goalkeepers

1	Essam AL HADARI	EGY

Defenders

2	Islam EL SHATER	EGY
3	Mohamed ABDELWAHAB	EGY
5	Ahmed EL SAYED	EGY
15	Ahmed ABOUMOSALEM	EGY
19	Akwety MENSAH	GHA
26	Wael GOMAA	EGY
30	Rami ADEL	EGY

Midfielders

6	El Sayed ABDELHAFIZ	EGY
7	Shady MOHAMED	EGY
8	Mohamed BARAKAT	EGY
10	Wael RIAD	EGY
14	Hassan MOSTAFA	EGY
16	Emad AL NAHHAS	EGY
17	Mohamed SHAWKY	EGY
18	Osama HOSNI	EGY
24	Ahmed HASSAN	EGY
25	Hissam ASHOUR	EGY

Forwards

11	Ahmed BILAL	EGY
12	GILBERTO Amaral	ANG
13	Emad MOTEAB	EGY
22	Mohamed ABOUTRIKA	EGY
23	FLAVIO Amado	ANG

ASEC MIMOSAS

Goalkeepers

16	Stephane DIMY	CIV

Defenders

4	Adou Peter TAYORO	CIV
5	Bakary SORO	CIV
11	Alli NDRI	CIV
12	Goore DACOSTA	CIV
13	Arthur KOCOU	CIV
15	Mamadou DOUMBIA	CIV
27	Abdou ADENON	CIV

Midfielders

8	Didier YA KONAN	CIV
10	Emmanuel KONE	CIV
14	Desire KOUAME	CIV
18	Me A. DIOMANDE	CIV
22	Abdrahmane DIABY	CIV
24	Modibo KANE	CIV

Forwards

2	Alhassane KOIVOGUI	CIV
6	Beko FOFANA	CIV
9	Seydou KONE	CIV
17	Fonéyé Vincent DIE	CIV
20	Brahima FAYE	SEN
28	Taina Adama SORO	CIV
29	Romeo Koffi KONAN	CIV

ENYIMBA

Goalkeepers

1	Dele AIYENUGBA	NGA

Defenders

4	Musa ALIYU	NGA
6	Nojim RAJI	NGA
7	Mohammed LAWAL	NGA
8	Yusuf MOHAMMED	NGA
14	Mutiu ADEGOKE	NGA
25	Chidozie JOHNSON	NGA
27	Odey OGAR	NGA
28	Ekene EMIGO	NGA
29	Sheriff UCHE	NGA

Midfielders

3	Kevin NJOKU	NGA
10	Sunday MBA	NGA
11	Atanda SAKIBU	NGA
15	Ifeanyi OBEDIAH	NGA
16	Solomon DAVID	NGA
23	Daniel NJOKU	NGA
26	Prince Wilson OLOMU	NGA

Forwards

12	Joetex FRIMPONG	GHA
13	Mouri OGUNBIYI	BEN
17	Chimaobi CHUKWU	NGA
20	Too Chukwu OKOLI	NGA
21	Eric FASINDO	NGA
30	David TYAVKASE	NGA

ESPERANCE

Goalkeepers

16	Jean-Jacques TIZIE	CIV
22	Hamdi KASRAOUI	TUN

Defenders

2	Emmanuel MATHIAS	TOG
3	Obinna NWANERI	NGA
5	Moyin CHAABANI	TUN
6	Larbi JABEUR	TUN
13	Wissem EL BEKRI	TUN
14	Walid YAKEN	TUN
17	Walid AZAIEZ	TUN
19	Wajih SGHAIER	TUN
20	Mohamed GUIZANI	TUN
30	Jose CLAYTON	TUN

Midfielders

4	Damian UDEH	NGA
8	Mohamed BELHADJ	TUN
10	Ziad BHAIRI	TUN
11	Mourad MELKI	TUN

Forwards

7	Ahmed BEN YAHIA	TUN
9	Ali ZITOUNI	TUN
12	Abdelkrim OUJI	TUN
15	Marcos DOS SANTOS	BRA
18	Hamdi HARBAOUI	TUN
21	Salama KASDAOUI	TUN
23	Kamel Zaiem	TUN
24	Amine LTAIEF	TUN
25	Frank-Olivier ONGFIANG	CMR

ETOILE DU SAHEL

Goalkeepers

16	Austin EJIDE	NGA

Defenders

2	Seif GHEZAL	TUN
4	Chaker ZOUAGHI	TUN
13	Sabeur BEN FREJ	TUN
14	Kais ZOUAGHI	TUN
15	Lotfi SELLAMI	TUN
23	Mohamed Ali AROURI	TUN
26	Anis NASRI	TUN
29	Mejdi BEN MOHAMED	TUN

Midfielders

3	Marouene BOKRI	TUN
6	Ahmed HAMDI	TUN
10	Bassem BEN NASR	TUN
12	Hakim BARGUI	TUN
17	Yassine CHIKAOUI	TUN
18	Mejdi ETTRAOUI	TUN
19	Mohamed JABNOUN	TUN
20	Charles TAYLOR	GHA
21	Khaled MELLITI	TUN

Forwards

5	Mohamed MILADI	TUN
8	Mohamed JEDIDI	TUN
11	Saber TRABELSI	TUN
27	Manuel GILSON	CPV
28	Emeka OPARA	NGA
30	Kandia TRAORE	GHA

RAJA

Goalkeepers

1	Mustapha CHADLI	MAR
22	Yassine EL HAD	MAR

Defenders

3	Redouane EL HAIMEUR	MAR
4	Abdel ABDESSAMAD	MAR
8	Abdellatif JRINDOU	MAR
13	Khalid BOUARBI	MAR
16	El Armine ERBATE	MAR
23	Reda SAKIM	MAR
24	Tajeddine SAMI	MAR
26	Said FATAH	MAR
27	Edgard LOUE	CIV
28	Yassine REMCH	MAR

Midfielders

5	Modibo MAIGA	MLI
6	Nourdine HAROUACH	MAR
7	Soufiane ALLOUDI	MAR
11	Nabil MASLOUB	MAR
17	Rachid SOULAIMANI	MAR
19	Hicham MISBAH	MAR
20	Hassan DAOUDI	MAR
25	Marouane ZEMMAMA	MAR
30	Musa Suleiman	NGA

Forwards

9	Mouhssine IAJOUR	MAR
10	Abdoulkarim FOFANA	GUI
29	Hicham ABOUCHEROUANE	MAR

ZAMALEK

Goalkeepers

16	Abdelwahed EL SAYED	EGY
25	Mohamed ABOU MONCEF	EGY

Defenders

1	Medhat ABDELHADI	EGY
3	Mohamed SEDDEK	EGY
5	Mahmoud MAHMOUD	EGY
6	Adel FATHI	EGY
12	Mohamed ABDELWAHED	EGY
13	Tarek EL SAYED	EGY
15	Wael EL QUABBANI	EGY
21	Ahmed EL BAKRI	EGY

Midfielders

4	Ibrahim SAID	EGY
11	Mohamed ABOULELA	EGY
14	Hazem EMAM	EGY
18	Gamal HAMZA	EGY
19	Tarek SAID	EGY
27	El Moatez MOHAMED	EGY

Forwards

9	Sameh YOUSSEF	EGY
10	Walid Salah ABDELLATIF	EGY
24	Abdelhalim ALI	EGY
28	Hossam OSSAMA	EGY
29	Awule QUAYE	GHA
30	Edson SOUSA	CPV

CAF CONFEDERATION CUP 2005

First Round

CD Ela Nguema *	EQG	0	1
Muni Sport	CGO	0	1
CO Bouaflé	CIV	0	0
CS Cilu Lukala *	COD	5	3
AS Douanes Lomé	TOG	3	0
Mogas 90 *	BEN	1	1
DUC Dakar *	SEN	1 0 1p	
COD Meknès	MAR	0 1 3p	
ASAC Concorde	MTN	w-o	
Heart of Lions ‡ *	GHA		
AS Nianan Koulikoro *	MLI	1	0
Olympique Khouribga	MAR	1	1
CI Kamsar	GUI	w-o	
Armed Forces ‡ *	GAM		
Ferroviário Maputo *	MOZ	w-o	
Wankie ‡	ZIM		
Kipanga *	ZAN	1	0
Kampara City Council	UGA	1	1
APR FC	RWA	0	3
Green Buffaloes *	ZAM	1	1
ASF Bobo-Dioulasso *	BFA	3	0
Al Ittihad Tripoli	LBY	0	4
FC 105 Libreville	GAB	1	2
Gazelle *	CHA	3	0
Banks SC *	ETH	w-o	
Chemelil Sugar ‡	KEN		
Prisons SC	TAN	1	1
USCA Foot *	MAD	4	0
Botswana Defence Force *	BOT	3	1
Sonangol	ANG	1	1
Savanne SC *	MRI	2	0
Red Star	SEY	0	4

Second Round

Enugu Rangers	NGA	1	3
CD Ela Nguema *	EQG	0	1
CS Cilu Lukala *	COD	2	0
Union Douala	CMR	1	1
Stella Abidjan	CIV	0	3
AS Douanes Lomé *	TOG	1	0
COD Meknès *	MAR	0	0
AS Marsa	TUN	1	2
Bamboutos Mbouda	CMR	0	2
ASAC Concorde *	MTN	0	0
Olympique Khouribga *	MAR	2	0
MC Oran	ALG	0	4
Bendel Insurance	NGA	1	3
CI Kamsar *	GUI	1	1
ASC Ndiambour	SEN	0	1
King Faisal Babes *	GHA	3	1
Al Ismaily	EGY	1	2
Ferroviário Maputo	MOZ	0	0
Kampala City Council *	UGA	0	0
APR FC	RWA	0	1
Al Ittihad Tripoli *	LBY	3	2
JS Kairouan	TUN	0	3
Inter Clube	ANG	1	1
FC 105 Libreville *	GAB	3	3
Al Mokawloon	EGY	0	3
Banks SC *	ETH	0	1
USCA Foot *	MAD	3	0
Al Merreikh	SUD	1	3
FC St-Eloi Lipopo	COD	0	2
Botswana Defence Force *	BOT	1	0
Red Star *	SEY	1	0
SuperSport United	RSA	4	9

Third Round

Enugu Rangers *	3	0
Union Doala	1	1
Stella Abidjan *	1	0
AS Marsa	0	2
Bamboutos Mbouda	1	1
MC Oran *	2	0
Bendel Insurance *	0	0
King Faisal Babes	0	1
Al Ismaily	w-o	
APR FC † *		
Al Ittihad Tripoli *	3	0
FC 105 Libreville	1	2
Al Mokawloon	1	3
Al Merreikh *	3	0
FC St-Eloi Lupopo *	2 0 2p	
SuperSport United	0 2 3p	

* Home team in the first leg • ‡ Team withdrew • † APR expelled • w-o = walk over

CAF CONFEDERATION CUP 2005

CAF CONFEDERATION CUP 2005

Intermediate Round　　　**Group Stage**　　　　　　**Final**

| FAR Rabat * † | MAR | 1 1 |
| Enugu Rangers | NGA | 0 2 |

| USM Alger * † | ALG | 1 1 4p |
| AS Marsa | TUN | 1 1 5p |

Group A	Pts	MAR	GHA	TUN	GUI
FAR Rabat	16		2-1	1-0	1-0
King Faisal Babes	12	1-2		1-0	2-0
AS Marsa	7	0-0	1-2		3-1
Fello Star Labé	0	0-1	0-1	1-2	

| Fello Star Labé * † | GUI | 1 3 |
| Bamboutos Mbouda | CMR | 0 0 |

| Red Arrows * † | ZAM | 1 2 |
| King Faisal Babes | GHA | 1 3 |

| FAR Rabat | | 0 3 |
| Dolphin * | | 1 0 |

| Al Ismaily | EGY | w-0 |
| Kaizer Ciefs ‡ * † | RSA | |

| Atlético Aviação * † | ANG | 1 1 |
| FC 105 Libreville | GAB | 1 2 |

Group B	Pts	NGA	EGY	EGY	GAB
Dolphin	14		0-0	2-1	3-0
Al Ismaily	11	1-1		0-1	6-0
Al Mokawloon	6	0-1	2-3		2-1
FC 105 Libreville	3	2-3	0-1	1-0	

| Al Mokawloon | EGY | 0 3 |
| Africa Sports * † | CIV | 0 0 |

| SuperSport United | RSA | 1 2 |
| Dolphin * † | NGA | 4 2 |

† Champions League second round losers that entered at the Intermediate round

FIRST ROUND

	30-01-2005	
CD Ela Nguema	0	
Muni Sport	0	

	13-02-2005	
Muni Sport	1	Moloyai [47]
CD Ela Nguema	1	Ibrahim [37]

	Kinshasa, 28-01-2005	
CS Cilu Lukala	5	Somwe [25], Ngokene [41], Ilonga [51], Mfunsu 2 [62 90p]
CO Bouaflé	0	

	12-02-2005	
CO Bouaflé	0	
CS Cilu Lukala	3	Ngokene [22], Basisila 2 [44 87]

	30-01-2005	
Mogas 90	1	Bouraima [64]
Douanes Lomé	3	Ekeka [18], Ddey [38], Kayode [90]

	13-02-2005	
Douanes Lomé	0	
Mogas 90	1	Erice [88]

	30-01-2005	
DUC Dakar	1	Diallo [72]
COD Meknès	0	

	12-02-2005	
COD Meknès	1	Klippa
DUC Dakar	0	

	30-01-2005	
Heart of Lions	-	Heart of Lions withdrew
ASAC Concorde	-	

	29-01-2005	
Nianan Koulikoro	1	Traore.M [40]
Oly. Khouribga	1	Abdel [82p]

	12-02-2005	
Oly. Khouribga	1	Souari [61]
Nianan Koulikoro	0	

	30-01-2005	
KI Kamsar	-	Armed Forces Banjul withdrew
Armed Forces	-	

Ferroviário Maputo	-	Wankie withdrew
Wankie	-	

	29-01-2005	
Kipanga	1	Simon [78]
Kampala CC	1	Sserunkuma [75]

	12-02-2005	
Kampala CC	1	Sserunkuma [80]
Kipanga	0	

	29-01-2005	
Green Buffaloes	1	Mwandila [44]
APR FC	0	

	12-02-2005	
APR FC	3	Munyambegu [16], Lomani 2 [57 59]
Green Buffaloes	1	Sinyengwe [71]

	29-01-2005	
ASFB	3	Diallo [13], Tapsoba [26], Banse [86]
Al Ittihad Tripoli	0	

	18-02-2005	
Al Ittihad Tripoli	4	Rewani 2 [5 45p], Mhemed [30], Wuyden [68]
ASFB	0	

	30-01-2005	
Gazelle	3	Mahamat [35], Dossingar [44], Gaius [60]
FC 105 Libreville	1	Bimiti [55]

	12-02-2005	
FC 105 Libreville	2	Bouity [34], Ngouami [90]
Gazelle	0	

	30-01-2005	
Banks	-	Chemelil Sugar withdrew
Chemelil Sugar	-	

	30-01-2005	
USCA Foot	4	Rakodondravelo 2 [17 49], Rakotoarivelo [27], Imma [71]
Prisons	1	Ntupa [60]

	Morogoro, 12-02-2005	
Prisons	1	Shamte [70]
USCA Foot	0	

	29-01-2005	
Botswana DF	3	Gabolwelwe [4], Modirelabangwe [43], Gabaitsane [64]
Sonangol	1	Evaristo [85]

	12-02-2005	
Sonangol	1	Arsenio [58p]
Botswana DF	1	Kadissa [44]

	30-01-2005	
Savanne SC	2	Pitchia [57], Hollingsworth [65]
Red Star	0	

	12-02-2005	
Red Star	4	Brutus [31], Morel [33], Rose [73], Volcere [76]
Savanne SC	0	

SECOND ROUND

	6-03-2005	
CD Ela Nguema	0	
Enugu Rangers	1	Okeke [72]

	20-03-2005	
Enugu Rangers	3	Ozokwo [56], Edward [64], Nnaemeka [85]
CD Ela Nguema	1	Silvestre [51]

	Kinshasa, 4-03-2005	
CS Cilu Lukala	2	Basisila [51p], Tshabola [78]
Union Douala	1	Belinga [11]

	20-03-2005	
Union Douala	1	Belinga [33]
CS Cilu Lukala	0	

	6-03-2005	
Douanes Lomé	1	Kodjo [68]
Stella Adjamé	0	

	18-03-2005	
Stella Adjamé	3	Paul [5], Samba [23], Toualy [59]
Douanes Lomé	0	

	5-03-2005	
COD Meknès	0	
AS Marsa	1	Hirech [85]

	19-03-2005	
AS Marsa	2	Zoubeir [34], Hirech [46]
COD Meknès	0	

	4-03-2005	
ASAC Concorde	0	
Bamboutos	0	

	19-03-2005	
Bamboutos	2	Ambadiang [7], Essosso [34]
ASAC Concorde	0	

	5-03-2005	
Oly. Khouribga	2	Souari [4], Fella [27]
MC Oran	0	

	19-03-2005	
MC Oran	4	Daoud [15], Zerouki [28], Chaib [50], Benzerga [72]
Oly. Khouribga	0	

	5-03-2005	
CI Kamsar	1	Bangoura [45]
Bendel Insurance	1	Austin [32]

20-03-2005		
Bendel Insurance	3	Okoye [37], Okoh [53], Imadu [60]
CI Kamsar	1	Keita [89]
5-03-2005		
King Faisal	3	Al Hassan [8], Gawu 2 [59 85]
ASC Ndiambour	0	
19-03-2005		
ASC Ndiambour	1	Diop [89p]
King Faisal	1	Al Hassan [7]
6-03-2005		
Ferroviário Maputo	0	
Al Ismaily	1	Abu Greisha [20]
18-03-2005		
Al Ismaily	2	Abu Greisha [10], Fatahi [41]
Ferroviário Maputo	0	
5-03-2005		
Kampala CC	0	
APR FC	0	
19-03-2005		
APR FC	1	Kayimba [77]
Kampala CC	0	
4-03-2005		
Al Ittihad Tripoli	3	Marouani 2 [9 71p], Rhouma [85]
JS Kairouan	0	
18-03-2005		
JS Kairouan	3	Seifallah [65], Zouheir [81], Ismael [85]
Al Ittihad Tripoli	2	El Beid 2 [45 56]
5-03-2005		
FC 105 Libreville	3	Mbaya [26], Bouity [52], Kethevoama [85]
Inter Clube	1	Nsele [40]
18-03-2005		
Inter Clube	1	Marcos [42]
FC 105 Libreville	3	Tamboulas [55], Kethevoama [57], Edou [84]
6-03-2005		
Banks	0	
Al Mokawloon	0	
20-03-2005		
Al Mokawloon	3	El Sherbeny [33], Zeid [51], Abdel Ghani [54p]
Banks	1	Ekka [25]
5-03-2005		
USCA Foot	3	Rakotondrabe [35], Andriamasy [76], Andriantsima [87]
Al Merreikh	1	Badr [33]
19-03-2005		
Al Merreikh	3	Cheikh 2 [22 43p], Lomami [86p]
USCA Foot	0	
5-03-2005		
Botswana DF	1	Mabogo [15]
FC Saint-Eloi	0	
20-03-2005		
FC Saint-Eloi	2	Witakenge [18], Twite [89]
Botswana DF	0	
5-03-2005		
Red Star	1	Brutus [6]
SuperSport Utd	4	Studzinski 2 [28 53], Tsabedze 2 [29 67]
19-03-2005		
SuperSport Utd	9	Mokoro 3 [5 35 76], Klate 2 [24 82], Mathopa 2 [29 33], Relemane 2 [37 64]
Red Star	0	

THIRD ROUND

10-04-2005		
Enugu Rangers	3	Odita [19p], Nnam [55], Okeke [61]
Union Douala	1	Zolang [38]

10-04-2005		
Enugu Rangers	3	Odita [19p], Nnam [55], Okeke [61]
Union Douala	1	Zolang [38]
24-04-2005		
Union Douala	1	Nouazi [80]
Enugu Rangers	0	
9-04-2005		
Stella Adjamé	1	Samba [60]
AS Marsa	0	
23-04-2005		
AS Marsa	2	Mouihbi [7], Kaddeche [45]
Stella Adjamé	0	
10-04-2005		
MC Oran	2	Benzerga [23], Daoud [45]
Bamboutos	1	Lele [83]
23-04-2005		
Bamboutos	1	Emmanuel [81p]
MC Oran	0	
10-04-2005		
Bendel Insurance	0	
King Faisal	0	
24-04-2005		
King Faisal	1	Opoku [44]
Bendel Insurance	0	
10-04-2005		
APR FC	-	Tie awarded to Ismaily
Al Ismaily	-	
8-04-2005		
Al Ittihad Tripoli	3	Al Masli 2 [52 89], Al Tarhouni [90]
FC 105 Libreville	1	Foxi [80]
23-04-2005		
FC 105 Libreville	2	Tchingoma [14], Bouity [21]
Al Ittihad Tripoli	0	
9-04-2005		
Al Merreikh	3	Al Agab 2 [28 87], Al Saoudi [57]
Al Mokawloon	1	Abdel Ghani [43]
23-04-2005		
Al Mokawloon	3	Abdel Ghani 2 [49 68], El Sherbeny [86]
Al Merreikh	0	
11-04-2005		
FC Saint-Eloi	2	Milambo [57], Kabange [83]
SuperSport Utd	0	
23-04-2005		
SuperSport Utd	2	Raselmane [3], Klate [79]
FC Saint-Eloi	0	SuperSport W 3-2p

INTERMEDIATE ROUND

7-05-2005			
FAR Rabat	1	Armoumen [45]	
Enugu Rangers	0		
23-05-2005			
Enugu Rangers	2	Odita [43], Ledor [79]	
FAR Rabat	1	Ouadouch [18]	
6-05-2005			
USM Alger	1	Achiou [90]	
AS Marsa	1	El Hirech [39]	
21-05-2005			
AS Marsa	1	El Hirech [39]	
USM Alger	1	Doucoure [45]	Marsa W 5-4p
8-05-2005			
Fellow Stars Labé	1	Mantigui [50]	
Bamboutos	0		

	22-05-2005
Bamboutos	0
Fellow Stars Labé	3 Camara.A 2 [37] [90], Camara.I [63]

	7-05-2005
Red Arrows	1 Banda [16]
King Faisal	1 Gawu [49]

	22-05-2005
King Faisal	3 Antwi 2 [32] [54p], Gawu [86]
Red Arrows	2 Hangunyu [11], Gondwe [49]

	8-05-2005
Kaizer Chiefs	- Kaizer Chiefs withdrew
Al Ismaily	-

	8-05-2005
Atlético Aviação	1 Silva [90]
FC 105 Libreville	1 Otomo [11]

	21-05-2005
FC 105 Libreville	2 Bouity [20], Otomo [89]
Atlético Aviação	1 Pereira [6]

	8-05-2005
Africa Sports	0
Al Mokawloon	0

	21-05-2005
Al Mokawloon	3 Abdel Ghani [20p], Fahim [68], Muharam [80]
Africa Sports	0

	8-05-2005
Dolphin	4 Osunwa 3 [17] [29] [64], Idahor [58]
SuperSport Utd	1 Nnodim OG [90]

	21-05-2005
SuperSport Utd	2 Raselmane 2 [23] [48]
Dolphin	2 Ojobo [7], Osunwa [41]

GROUP A

	23-07-2005
AS Marsa	0
FAR Rabat	0

	24-07-2005
Fello Stars Labé	0
King Faisal	1 Gawu [58]

	6-08-2005
King Faisal	1 Yahuza [71p]
AS Marsa	0

	7-08-2005
FAR Rabat	1 Kedioui [90]
Fello Stars Labé	0

	20-08-2005
Fello Stars Labé	1 Yady [88]
AS Marsa	2 El Hirech 2 [5] [57]

	21-08-2005
King Faisal	1 Abubakar [79]
FAR Rabat	2 El Fadli [48], Kaddioui [60]

	10-09-2005
AS Marsa	3 Azak [25], Al Hirech [51], Al Mouihbi [69]
Fello Stars Labé	1 Camara.C [71]

	10-09-2005
FAR Rabat	2 Bouaouda [23], Kaddioui [89]
King Faisal	1 Abubakar [49]

Rabat, 24-09-2005, 20:00, Mana NGA	
FAR Rabat	1 Ajeddou [72]
AS Marsa	0

25-09-2005, 15:00, Ssegonga UGA	
King Faisal	2 Gawu [25], Abubakar [88]
Fello Stars Labé	0

Marsa, 15-10-2005, 17:00, Evehe CMR	
AS Marsa	1 Ben Chaeouaa [90]
King Faisal	2 Habib [72], Gawu [79]

Conakry, 15-10-2005, 15:00, Shelmani LBY	
Fello Stars Labé	0
FAR Rabat	1 Ajraoui [48]

Group A	Pl	W	D	L	F	A	Pts
FAR Rabat	6	5	1	0	7	2	16
King Faisal Babes	6	4	0	2	9	5	12
AS Marsa	6	2	1	3	6	6	7
Fello Star Labé	6	0	0	6	2	11	3

GROUP B

	23-07-2005
FC 105 Libreville	0
Al Ismaily	1 Gamal [49]

	24-07-2005
Dolphin	2 Chinwo [6], Osunwa [90]
Al Mokawloon	1 Zaki [62]

Mehalla, 5-08-2005	
Al Ismaily	1 Fathi [24]
Dolphin	1 Idahor [12]

	7-08-2005
Al Mokawloon	2 Zaki [78p], Mesailhi [90]
FC 105 Libreville	1 Tamboulas [48]

	19-08-2005
Al Mokawloon	2 Abdelhakim [35], Zain [48]
Al Ismaily	3 Abougreisha [4]

	21-08-2005
Dolphin	3 Osunwa 2 [20] [90], Ndala [25]
FC 105 Libreville	0

	9-09-2005
Al Ismaily	0
Al Mokawloon	1 Zain [26]

	11-09-2005
FC 105 Libreville	2 Dosso OG [06], Otomo [90]
Dolphin	3 Idahor [29], Eguakun 2 [61] [80]

Cairo, 24-09-2005, 19:00, Lim Kee Chong MRI	
Al Mokawloon	0
Dolphin	1 Idahor [44]

25-09-2005, 20:00, Daami TUN	
Al Ismaily	6 Akruye [12], Moawad [13], Gamal.O [48], Celino [70], Gamal.Y [80], Fathi [92+]
FC 105 Libreville	0

Libreville, 15-10-2005, 16:00, Buenkadila COD	
FC 105 Libreville	1 Tchingoma [56]
Al Mokawloon	0

Port Harcourt, 16-10-2005, 16:00, Benouza ALG	
Dolphin	0
Al Ismaily	0

Group B	Pl	W	D	L	F	A	Pts
Dolphin	6	4	2	0	10	4	14
Al Ismaily	6	3	2	1	11	4	11
Al Mokawloon	6	2	0	4	6	8	6
FC 105 Libreville	6	1	0	5	4	15	3

CAF CONFEDERATION CUP FINAL 1ST LEG
Liberation Stadium, Port Harcourt
6-11-2005, 12 000, Sillah GAM

DOLPHIN FC	1	0	FAR RABAT

Bello [85]

Dolphin		FAR Rabat	
EJIOGU Chijioke		TARIK Jermouni	
MICHAEL Olajide		EL FADLI Mohamed	
EYIMOFE Joseph		EL HOUSAINE Ouchia	
EGUAKUN Efosa		JAAFARI	
OSUNWA Kelechi	58	SERRAJ Adil	
IDAHOR Endurance		HAFID Abdessadek	
EMMAH Godwin		BOUBOU Noureddine	
BABAYARO Victor		EL MAAROFI Khalid	
NNODIM Obina		NAOUM Yassine	82
DOSSO David	80	AJEDDOU Ahmed	79
NDALA Ibrahim	51	AJRAOUI Ahmed	60
Tr: ABDULLAHI Musa		Tr: FAKHAR Muhammed	
Substitutes		Substitutes	
AKHIOBARE Jacob	51	OUADOUCH Jawad	60
BELLO Bola	58	BENKASSOU Mounir	79
WOBO Uwazuoke	80	BOUAOUDA Jaouad	82

CAF CONFEDERATION CUP FINAL 2ND LEG
Moulay Abdallah, Rabat
19-11-2005, 40 000, Guirat TUN

FAR RABAT	3	0	DOLPHIN FC

Serraj 2 [10] [45], Ajraoui [63]

FAR Rabat		Dolphin	
TARIK Jermouni		EJIOGU Chijioke	
EL FADLI Mohamed		EMMAH Godwin	
JAAFARI		CHINWO Kennedy	
SERRAJ Adil		EYIMOFE Joseph	
BOUAOUDA Jaouad		DOSSO David	
ABDESSADEQ		NNODIM Obina	
BOUBOU Noureddine		EGUAKUN Efosa	
NAOUM Yassine		BABAYARO Victor	
KADDIOUI Idrissi	90	IDAHOR Endurance	
AJEDDOU Ahmed	84	OSUNWA Kelechi	80
AJRAOUI Ahmed	83	WOBO Uwazuoke	53
Tr: FAKHAR Muhammed		Tr: ABDULLAHI Musa	
Substitutes		Substitutes	
BENKASSOU Mounir	83	BELLO Bola	53
EL MAAROFI Khalid	84	AKHIOBARE Jacob	80
OUCHLA	90		

REGIONAL TOURNAMENTS IN AFRICA IN 2006

COUPE DE LA CEMAC EQUATORIAL GUINEA 2006

First Round Group Stage

Group A	Pl	W	D	L	F	A	Pts	CHA	CGO
Equatorial Guinea	2	1	1	0	2	0	4	1-1	2-1
Chad	2	0	2	0	1	1	2		0-0
Congo	2	0	1	1	1	2	1		

Group B	Pl	W	D	L	F	A	Pts	GAB	CTA
Cameroon	2	1	1	0	2	0	4	0-0	2-0
Gabon	2	0	2	0	2	2	2		2-2
Central African Rep	2	0	1	1	2	4	1		

Played in Equatorial Guinea from 4-03-2006 to 14-03-2006 ● Cameroon did not send their full senior team

Semi-finals

Equatorial Guinea	0 4p
Gabon	0 2p

Chad	1 0p
Cameroon	1 3p

Final

Equatorial Guinea	1
Cameroon	0

Third place play-off

Gabon	2 7p
Chad	2 6p

REGIONAL CLUB TOURNAMENTS IN AFRICA

CECAFA KAGAME INTER-CLUB CUP TANZANIA 2005

First round groups

Group A		Pl	W	D	L	F	A	Pts	RWA	TAN	BDI	SOM
SC Villa	UGA	4	3	1	0	8	0	10	0-0	1-0	2-0	5-0
Rayon Sport	RWA	4	2	1	1	7	2	7		1-2	5-0	1-0
Simba SC	TAN	4	2	1	1	4	2	7			0-0	2-0
Atletico Olympique	BDI	4	1	1	2	3	9	4				3-2
Elman	SOM	4	0	0	4	2	11	0				

Group B		Pl	W	D	L	F	A	Pts	TAN	ETH	KEN	ZAN
APR FC	RWA	4	4	0	0	10	1	12	2-0	2-1	2-0	4-0
Mtibwa Sugar	TAN	4	2	1	1	6	5	7		1-1	3-2	2-0
Awassa Kenema	ETH	4	1	2	1	4	4	5			1-1	1-0
Ulinzi Stars	KEN	4	1	1	2	4	6	4				1-0
KMKM	ZAN	4	0	0	4	0	8	0				

Semi-finals

SC Villa	1
Mtibwa Sugar	0

Rayon Sport	1	3p
APR FC	1	4p

Final

SC Villa	3
APR FC	0

Third place play-off

Rayon Sport	0	4p
Mtibwa Sugar	0	2p

The tournament took place in Tanzania from 23-04-2005 to 8-05-2005 and was played in Mwanza and Arusha

CECAFA KAGAME INTER-CLUB CUP TANZANIA 2006

First round groups

Group A		Pl	W	D	L	F	A	Pts	ETH	KEN	BDI	ZAN
Young Africans	TAN	4	3	1	0	6	2	10	0-0	3-1	2-1	1-0
Saint George	ETH	4	3	1	0	5	1	10		3-1	1-0	1-0
Ulinzi Stars	KEN	4	2	0	2	5	7	6			1-0	2-1
Inter Stars	BDI	4	1	0	3	3	4	3				2-0
Polisi	ZAN	4	0	0	4	1	6	0				

Group B		Pl	W	D	L	F	A	Pts	TAN	UGA	SUD	DJI
APR FC	RWA	4	4	0	0	8	1	12	1-0	1-0	2-1	4-0
Simba SC	TAN	4	3	0	1	10	2	9		2-1	3-0	5-0
Police FC	UGA	4	2	0	2	8	7	6			3-1	4-3
Al Hilal	SUD	4	1	0	3	8	8	3				6-0
SID	DJI	4	0	0	4	3	19	0				

Group C		Pl	W	D	L	F	A	Pts	TAN	SOM	ERI
SC Villa	UGA	3	2	1	0	4	2	7	1-0	1-1	2-1
Moro United	TAN	3	2	0	1	8	3	6		5-0	3-2
Elman	SOM	3	1	1	1	4	8	4			3-2
Al Tahir	ERI	3	0	0	3	5	8	0			

Quarter-finals

Police FC	1
Young Africans	0

SC Villa	1	1p
Ulinzi Stars	1	3p

APR FC	0	4p
Saint George	0	2p

Simba SC	1
Moro United	2

Semi-finals

Police FC	
Ulinzi Stars	

APR FC	0
Moro United	2

Final

Police FC	2
Moro United	1

Third place play-off

APR FC	4
Ulinzi Stars	0

The tournament took place in Tanzania from 12-05-2006 to 28-05-2006

CONCACAF

CONFEDERATION OF NORTH, CENTRAL AMERICAN AND
CARIBBEAN ASSOCIATION FOOTBALL

Trinidad and Tobago's victory over Bahrain in their intercontinental FIFA World Cup™ play-off meant that CONCACAF had a record four entrants in the finals, but the success four years' previously in Japan and Korea was not built upon, with Trinidad, Costa Rica and the USA all going out in the first round. Only seeded Mexico made it through to the knock-out stage, but despite giving Argentina their toughest game of the tournament, the second round was as far as they went. Mexico had arrived in Germany on the back of an historic triumph in the 2005 FIFA U-17 World Championship in Peru. Their 3-0 win over Brazil in the final gave Mexico and the CONCACAF region a first world title at any level. That there is potential in the region is beyond doubt as both Costa Rica and the USA topped their first round groups in Peru, and a Mexican, Rafael Marquez, helped Barcelona to a UEFA Champions League title. But it may take more to help further raise the profile of football in the region. The 2005 CONCACAF club champions, Deportivo Saprissa

THE FIFA BIG COUNT OF 2000 FOR CONCACAF

	Male	Female		Male	Female
Registered players	625 537	147 782	Referees	102 257	24 083
Not registered players	15 656 500	7 877 050	Officials	635 916	314 045
Youth players	3 064 691	1 698 518	Total involved	28 809 582	10 851 837
Children & Occasional	8 700 000	790 000	in football	39 636 379	
Professionals	24 681	359	Number of clubs	12 852	
Total players	38 560 078		Number of teams	115 830	

of Costa Rica, represented the confederation at the FIFA Club World Championship in Japan, winning their first round match against Sydney FC. They lost in the semi-final to Liverpool but did win the third place play-off against Al Ittihad. With the prospect of a place at the FIFA Club World Cup (as the tournament will now be known), the big Mexican clubs put in a concerted effort in the 2006 CONCACAF Champions' Cup. The two regional qualifying stages were won by Jamaica's Portmore United and Liga Deportiva Alajuelense of Costa Rica. In the final knock-out rounds, the Costa Ricans provided two of the semi-finalists but it was Mexico's América and Toluca that contested the final. After a scoreless first match in Toluca, América won the return in the Azteca to claim a record-equalling fifth title. The coming year will see three major tournaments in the region, with both the finals of the men's and the women's CONCACAF Gold Cup and Canada hosting the FIFA U-20 World Cup in July 2007.

Confederation of North, Central American and Caribbean Association Football (CONCACAF)
725, Fifth Avenue, Trump Tower, 17th Floor, New York, NY 1022, USA
Tel +1 212 3080 044   Fax +1 212 3081 851
mail@concacaf.net   www.concacaf.com
President: WARNER Jack A. TRI   General Secretary: BLAZER Chuck USA
CONCACAF Formed: 1961

CONCACAF EXECUTIVE COMMITTEE
President: WARNER Jack A. TRI
Vice-President: AUSTIN Lisle BRB   Vice-President: SALGUERO Rafael GUA   Vice-President: ROTHENBURG Alan USA
ORDINARY MEMBERS OF THE EXECUTIVE COMMITTEE
BURRELL Horace Capt. JAM   BANEGAS Alfredo HON   CANEDO WHITE Guillermo MEX
FIFA Exco: SASSO SASSO Isaac CRC   FIFA Exco: BLAZER Chuck USA

MAP OF CONCACAF MEMBER NATIONS

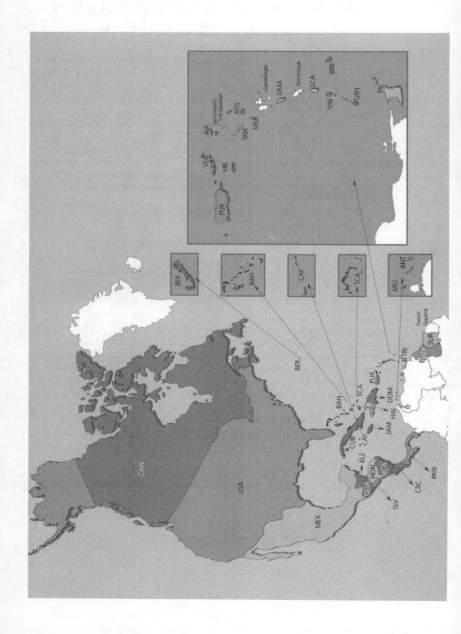

CENTRAL AMERICAN, NORTH AMERICAN AND CARIBBEAN TOURNAMENTS

CCCF CHAMPIONSHIP WINNERS

Year	Host Country	Winners	Runners-up
1941	Costa Rica	Costa Rica	El Salvador
1943	El Salvador	El Salvador	Guatemala
1946	Costa Rica	Costa Rica	Guatemala
1948	Costa Rica	Costa Rica	Guatemala
1951	Panama	Panama	Costa Rica
1953	Costa Rica	Costa Rica	Honduras
1955	Costa Rica	Costa Rica	Neth. Antilles
1957	Haiti	Haiti	Curacao
1960	Costa Rica	Costa Rica	Neth. Antilles
1961	Costa Rica	Costa Rica	El Salvador

CONCACAF CHAMPIONSHIP WINNERS

Year	Host Country	Winners	Runners-up
1963	El Salvador	Costa Rica	El Salvador
1965	Guatemala	Mexico	Guatemala
1967	Honduras	Guatemala	Mexico
1969	Costa Rica	Costa Rica	Guatemala
1971	Trinidad	Mexico	Haiti
1973	Haiti	Haiti	Trinidad
1977	Mexico	Mexico	Haiti
1981	Honduras	Honduras	El Salvador
1985	Home & Away	Canada	Honduras
1989	Home & Away	Costa Rica	USA

CONCACAF GOLD CUP

Year	Host Country	Winners	Score	Runners-up	Venue
1991	USA	USA	0-0 4-3p	Honduras	Coliseum, Los Angeles
1993	Mexico/USA	Mexico	4-0	USA	Azteca, Mexico City
1995	USA	Mexico	2-0	Brazil	Coliseum, Los Angeles
1998	USA	Mexico	1-0	USA	Coliseum, Los Angeles
2000	USA	Canada	2-0	Colombia	Coliseum, Los Angeles
2002	USA	USA	2-0	Costa Rica	Rose Bowl, Pasadena
2003	Mexico/USA	Mexico	1-0	Brazil	Azteca, Mexico City
2005	USA	USA	0-0 3-1	Panama	Giants Stadium, New Jersey

Not until the introduction of the CONCACAF Gold Cup in 1991 did the region have a proper continental championship. Prior to the creation of CONCACAF in 1961 there had been a tournament based largely around Central America with occasional Caribbean entrants, which had been dominated by Costa Rica. In 1963 CONCACAF introduced a championship staged every other year until 1971 but they singularly failed in their attempts to make the Americans and especially the Mexicans take it seriously. From 1991 either Mexico or the USA have hosted every tournament and provided the winners with the exception of Canada in 2000.

CONCACAF WOMEN'S GOLD CUP

Year	Host Country	Winners	Score	Runners-up	Venue
1991	Haiti	United States	5-0	Canada	Port au Prince
1993	USA	United States	1-0	Canada	Long Island
1994	Canada	United States	6-0	Canada	Montreal
1998	Canada	Canada	1-0	Mexico	Toronto
2000	USA	United States	1-0	Brazil	Foxboro, Boston
2002	USA/Canada	United States	2-1	Canada	Rose Bowl, Pasadena

CONCACAF WOMEN'S U–19 GOLD CUP

Year	Host Country	Winners	Score	Runners-up	Venue
2004	Canada	Canada	2-1	USA	Frank Clair, Ottawa

If there is one area in which CONCACAF can claim to be world beaters it is in women's football with both the USA and Canada ranked amongst the highest levels of the game. The Women's Gold Cup coincided with the launch of the men's competition and since then the USA have won five of the six tournaments played, beating Canada in the final of four of them. Canada won on home soil in 1998, beating the USA in an historic semi-final before defeating Mexico in the final, the only other team from the CONCACAF area to reach the final. It is hard to imagine any nation seriously threatening the North American dominance in either this or the U-19 event.

CONCACAF YOUTH CHAMPIONS

Year	Host Country	Winners	Runners-up
1954	Costa Rica	Costa Rica	Panama
1956	El Salvador	El Salvador	Neth. Antilles
1958	Guatemala	Guatemala	Honduras
1960	Honduras	Costa Rica	Honduras
1962	Panama	Mexico	Guatemala
1964	Guatemala	El Salvador	
1970	Cuba	Mexico	Cuba
1973	Mexico	Mexico	Guatemala
1974	Canada	Mexico	Cuba
1976	Puerto Rico	Mexico	Honduras

CONCACAF YOUTH CHAMPIONS

Year	Host Country	Winners	Runners-up
1978	Honduras	Mexico	Canada
1980	USA	Mexico	USA
1982	Guatemala	Honduras	USA
1984	Trinidad	Mexico	Canada
1986	Trinidad	Canada	USA
1988	Guatemala	Costa Rica	Mexico
1990	Guatemala	Mexico	Trinidad
1992	Canada	Mexico	USA
1994	Honduras	Honduras	Costa Rica
1996	Mexico	Canada	Mexico

CONCACAF UNDER 17 CHAMPIONS

Year	Host Country	Winners	Runners-up
1983	Trinidad	USA	Trinidad
1985	Mexico	Mexico	Costa Rica
1987	Honduras	Mexico	USA
1988	Trinidad	Cuba	USA

CONCACAF UNDER 17 CHAMPIONS

Year	Host Country	Winners	Runners-up
1991	Trinidad	Mexico	USA
1992	Cuba	USA	Mexico
1994	El Salvador	Costa Rica	USA
1996	Trinidad	Mexico	USA

Youth tournaments have a long, if patchy, history in the CONCACAF region. At both U-19 and U-17 levels they have served as qualifiers for the FIFA events but since 1996 once the qualifying nations have been identified the principle of determining the champions at each level has been abandoned.

CARIBBEAN CUP

Year	Host Country	Winners	Score	Runners-up	Venue
1989	Barbados	Trinidad & Tobago	2-1	Grenada	Bridgetown
1990	Trinidad	Not completed			
1991	Jamaica	Jamaica	2-0	Trinidad & Tobago	Kingston
1992	Trinidad	Trinidad & Tobago	3-1	Jamaica	Port of Spain
1993	Jamaica	Martinique	0-0 6-5p	Jamaica	Kingston
1994	Trinidad	Trinidad & Tobago	7-2	Martinique	Port of Spain
1995	Cayman/Jamaica	Trinidad & Tobago	5-0	St Vincent	George Town
1996	Trinidad	Trinidad & Tobago	2-0	Cuba	Port of Spain
1997	Antigua/St Kitts	Trinidad & Tobago	4-0	St Kitts	St John's
1998	Jamaica/Trinidad	Jamaica	2-1	Trinidad & Tobago	Port of Spain
1999	Trinidad	Trinidad & Tobago	2-1	Cuba	Port of Spain
2001	Trinidad	Trinidad & Tobago	3-0	Haiti	Port of Spain
2005	Barbados	Jamaica	1-0 †	Cuba	Waterford

† Final tournament played as a league. The match listed is that between the top two.

UNCAF CUP

Year	Host Country	Winners	Score	Runners-up	Venue
1991	Costa Rica	Costa Rica	2-0	Honduras	San José
1993	Honduras	Honduras	2-0	Costa Rica	Tegucigalpa
1995	El Salvador	Honduras	3-0	Guatemala	San Salvador
1997	Guatemala	Costa Rica	1-1	Guatemala	Mateo Flores, Guatemala City
1999	Costa Rica	Costa Rica	1-0	Guatemala	San José
2001	Honduras	Guatemala	2-0	Costa Rica	Tegucigalpa
2003	Panama	Costa Rica	1-1	Guatemala	Rommel Fernández, Panama City
2005	Guatemala	Costa Rica	1-1 7-6p	Honduras	Mateo Flores, Guatemala City

All Final tournaments played as a league except for 1995 and 2005. The matches listed are those between the top two

The UNCAF Cup, played between the nations of Central America, is a prestigious event that doubles up as a qualifying competition for the Gold Cup, as does the Caribbean Cup. Trinidad and Tobago along with Jamaica have dominated the latter tournament with Martinique in 1993 the only country to break the duopoly whilst Costa Rica have won five of the eight UNCAF championships.

CONCACAF CHAMPIONS' CUP

Year	Winners	Country	Score	Country	Runners-up
1962	Guadalajara CD	MEX	1-0 5-0	GUA	Comunicaciones
1963	Racing Club Haïtienne	HAI	W-O	MEX	Guadalajara CD
1964	Not completed				
1965	Not completed				
1966	-				
1967	Alianza	SLV	1-2 3-0́ 5-3	ANT	Jong Colombia
1968	Toluca	MEX	W-O †		
1969	Cruz Azul	MEX	0-0 1-0	GUA	Comunicaciones
1970	Cruz Azul	MEX	W-O †		
1971	Cruz Azul	MEX	5-1	CRC	LD Alajuelense
1972	Olimpia	HON	0-0 2-0	SUR	Robinhood
1973	Transvaal	SUR	W-O †		
1974	Municipal	GUA	2-1 2-1	SUR	Transvaal
1975	Atletico Español	MEX	3-0 2-1	SUR	Transvaal
1976	Aguila	SLV	6-1 2-1	SUR	Robinhood
1977	América	MEX	1-0 0-0	SUR	Robinhood
1978	Universidad Guadalajara	MEX	W-O †		
1979	Deportivo FAS	SLV	1-0 8-0	ANT	Jong Colombia
1980	UNAM Pumas	MEX	2-0	HON	Universidad de Honduras
1981	Transvaal	SUR	1-0 1-1	SLV	Atlético Marte
1982	UNAM Pumas	MEX	2-2 3-0	SUR	Robinhood
1983	Atlante	MEX	1-1 5-0	SUR	Robinhood
1984	Violette	HAI	W-O †		
1985	Defence Force	TRI	2-0 0-1	HON	Olimpia
1986	LD Alajuelense	CRC	4-1 1-1	SUR	Transvaal
1987	América	MEX	2-0 1-1	TRI	Defence Force
1988	Olimpia	HON	2-0 2-0	TRI	Defence Force
1989	UNAM Pumas	MEX	1-1 3-1	CUB	Piñar del Rio
1990	América	MEX	2-2 6-0	CUB	Piñar del Rio
1991	Puebla	MEX	3-1 1-1	TRI	Police FC
1992	América	MEX	1-0	CRC	LD Alajuelense
1993	Deportivo Saprissa	CRC	2-2 ‡	MEX	Leon
1994	CS Cartagines	CRC	3-2	MEX	Atlante
1995	Deportivo Saprissa	CRC	1-0 ‡	GUA	Municipal
1996	Cruz Azul	MEX	1-1 ‡	MEX	Necaxa
1997	Cruz Azul	MEX	5-3	USA	Los Angeles Galaxy
1998	DC United	USA	1-0	MEX	Toluca
1999	Necaxa	MEX	2-1	CRC	LD Alajuelense
2000	LA Galaxy	USA	3-2	HON	Olimpia
2001	Not completed				
2002	Pachuca	MEX	1-0	MEX	Morelia
2003	Toluca	MEX	3-3 2-1	MEX	Morelia
2004	LD Alajuelense	CRC	1-1 4-0	CRC	Deportivo Saprissa
2005	Deportivo Saprissa	CRC	2-0 1-2	MEX	UNAM Pumas
2006	América	MEX	0-0 2-1	MEX	Toluca

† 1968 Toluca were champions after Aurora GUA and Transvaal SUR were disqualified • 1970 Cruz Azul were champions after Deportivo Saprissa CRC and Transvaal SUR withdrew • 1978 Universidad Guadalajara are listed as the winners by default though Comunicaciones GUA and Defence Force TRI are also considered joint winners by CONCACAF • 1984 Violette were champions after Guadalajara and New York Freedoms withdrew
‡ 1993, 1995 & 1996 finals played as a league • The match listed is that between the top two

The entry of MLS clubs in the late 1990's and, more significantly, the prospect of a place at the FIFA Club World Cup has given the CONCACAF Champions' Cup a significant boost. Mexican clubs remain the mainstay of the tournament winning the title on 22 occasions but Costa Rican clubs have provided an unexpected challenge in recent years. They, along with Mexico and the USA, are the only countries to have provided the winners since 1989. Cruz Azul and América remain the most successful teams with five titles. Robinhood have lost all five finals they have played in.

CONCACAF CHAMPIONS' CUP 2005–06

CONCACAF CHAMPIONS' CUP 2005-06 REGIONAL ROUNDS

First Round	Quarter-Finals	Semi-finals	Finals

TORNEO INTERCLUBES DE UNCAF

First Round

LD Alajuelense	CRC	4	6
Placencia Pirates *	BLZ	1	0

Arabe Unido *	PAN	0	1
Municipal	GUA	0	4

Luis Angel Firpo *	SLV	4	2
Comunicaciones	GUA	2	2

San Francisco *	PAN	0	1
Pérez Zeledón	CRC	0	3

Deportivo Saprissa	CRC	0	2
Deportivo FAS *	SLV	0	0

Parmalat	NCA		
Marathón	HON	w-o	

Suchitepéquez *	GUA	2	2
Diriangén	NCA	2	0

Eagles FC	BLZ	0	0
Olímpia *	HON	3	1

Quarter-Finals

LD Alajuelense *	CRC	5	0
Municipal	GUA	2	1

Luis Angel Firpo	SLV	0	2
Pérez Zeledón *	CRC	4	2

Deportivo Saprissa*	CRC	4 0 4p
Marathón	HON	0 4 3p

Suchitepéquez *	GUA	1	0
Olímpia	HON	4	4

Semi-finals

LD Alajuelense	0	3
Pérez Zeledón *	1	0

Deportivo Saprissa *	1	1
Olímpia	3	1

Finals

LD Alajuelense	1 0 4p
Olímpia *	0 1 2p

Third place play-off

Deportivo Saprissa*	2 0 5p
Pérez Zeledón	0 2 3p

Alajuelense, Olimpia and Saprissa qualify for the final rounds

CFU CARIBBEAN CHAMPIONSHIP

First Round

G. Bazaar Dublanc	DMA	1	0
Hoppers †	ATG	2	4

Sagicor South East	DMA	0	1
Bassa †	ATG	6	2

Positive Vibes	VIR	2	0
Northern United *	LCA	0	5

Victory Boys	ANT	0	3
Royal 95 *	SUR	0	1

Britannia ‡	ARU	1	0
Robinhood	SUR	2	2

Quarter-Finals

Portmore United	JAM	3	7
Hoppers †	ATG	0	0

Bassa *	ATG	1	2
Centro Barber	ANT	1	6

Northern United	LCA	1	1
Victory Boys *	ANT	1	0

North East Stars	TRI		
Robinhood	SUR	w-o	

Semi-finals

Portmore United	3	0
Centro Barber †	1	1

Northern United	1	2
Robinhood *	3	4

Finals

Portmore United	1	4
Robinhood †	2	0

Portmore United qualify for the final rounds

* Home team in the first leg • † Home team in both legs • ‡ Both legs played in Trinidad

CONCACAF CHAMPIONS' CUP 2005-06

Quarter-Finals   **Semi-finals**   **Final**

América	MEX	2	5
Portmore United *	JAM	1	2

América		2	0
LD Alajuelense *		1	0

New England Revolution *	USA	0	0
LD Alajuelense	CRC	0	1

América		0	2
Toluca *		0	1

Deportivo Saprissa	CRC	0	3
Los Angeles Galaxy *	USA	0	2

Deportivo Saprissa		0	3
Toluca *		2	2

Olímpia *	HON	0	1
Toluca	MEX	2	2

* Home team in the first leg
American and Mexican teams qualified directly for the final rounds

FIRST ROUND
UNCAF

1st leg. Michael Ashcroft, Mango Creek, 28-07-2005. Rodriguez PAN

Placencia Pirates	1	Palacio [31]
LD Alajuelense	4	López [11], Díaz [35], Hernández [83p], Ruiz [90]

2nd leg. Alejandro Morera Soto, Alajuela, 2-08-2005, Garcia PAN

LD Alajuelense	6	OG [52], Ledezma 2 [61] [90p], Jiménez [69] Rodríguez.M [77], Scott [86]
Placencia Pirates	0	

1st leg. Armando Dely Valdez, Cólon, 28-07-2005, Mejia CRC

Arabe Unido	0	
Municipal	0	

2nd leg. Mateo Flores, Guatemala City, 4-08-2005

Municipal	4	Figueroa [21], Plata 2 [29] [45], García [37]
Arabe Unido	1	Avila [34]

1st leg. Sergio Torres, Usulután, 28-07-2005, Bardales HON

Luis Angel Firpo	4	Martínez.A [30], Martínez.M 2 [35] [90], Castro [74]
Comunicaciones	2	Pavón [33], Fonseca [46]

2nd leg. Cementos Progreso, Guatemala City, 2-08-2005, Quesada CRC

Comunicaciones	2	Pavón [20], Fonseca [56]
Luis Angel Firpo	2	Martínez.JM [53], Martínez.J [81]

1st leg. Muquita Sanchez, La Chorrera, 27-07-2005, Rodas GUA

San Francisco	0	
Pérez Zeledón	0	

2nd leg. Municipal, San Isidro, 4-08-2005

Pérez Zeledón	3	Lara [45p], González.B [58] [93+]
San Francisco	1	Tello [56]

1st leg. Oscar Quiteño, Santa Ana, 26-07-2005, Castillo GUA

Deportivo FAS	0	
Dep. Saprissa	2	Saborio [49], Solis [74]

2nd leg. Ricardo Saprissa, San José, 3-08-2005, Mejia GUA

Dep. Saprissa	0	
Deportivo FAS	0	

1st leg. 26-07-2005

Marathón	w-o	
Parmalat		

1st leg. Carlos Salazar Hijo, Mazatenango, 27-07-2005, Carranza HON

Suchitepéquez	2	Trujillo [20p], Loaiza [46]
Diriangén	2	Palacios 2 [69] [87]

2nd leg. Cacique Diriangén, Diriamba, 3-08-2005, Alfaro SLV

Diriangén	0	
Suchitepéquez	2	Villatoro 2 [13] [56]

1st leg. Tiburcio Carias Andino, Tegucigalpa, 27-07-2005, Campos NCA

Olímpia	3	Tosello [12], Ferreira [60], Velasquez [75]
Eagles FC	0	

2nd leg. People's Stadium, Belize City, 4-08-2005

Eagles FC	0	
Olímpia	1	Figueroa

FIRST ROUND
CFU

1st leg. Gray's Farm, 22-09-2005

G. Bazaar Dublanc	1	Casimir [86]
Hoppers	2	Thomas [5], Peters [76]

2nd leg. Gray's Farm, 24-09-2005

Hoppers	4	Roberts [15], Frederick 2 [19] [72], Thomas [59]
G. Bazaar Dublanc	0	

1st leg. All Saint's, 23-09-2005

Sagicor South East	0	
Bassa	6	Burton 2 [6] [29], Anthony [41], Thomas 2 [45] [63] Romeo [89]

2nd leg. All Saint's, 25-09-2005

Bassa	2	Jeffers [19], Williams [42]
Sagicor South East	1	Cliffy [52]

1st leg. Gros Islet, 12-09-2005

Northern United	0	
Positive Vibes	2	Guy [61], Teshiera [80]

2nd leg. St Croix, 1-10-2005

Positive Vibes	0	
Northern United	5	Lastic [4], McDonald [18], Pamphile [24] McPhee 2 [55] [62]

1st leg. Andre Kamperveen, Paramaribo, 12-09-2005, Callender GUY

Royal '95	0	
Victory Boys	0	

2nd leg. Bandariba, 24-09-2005

Victory Boys	3	Moscoso, Germain [38], Ashar [67]
Royal '95	1	Emanuelson [75]

1st leg. Marvin Lee, Macoya, 27-09-2005, Ramdhen TRI

Britannia	1	De Lange [37]
Robinhood	2	Massie [45], Kinsaini [71]

2nd leg. Marvin Lee, Macoya, 29-09-2005

Robinhood	2	Brown [29], Massie [32]
Britannia	0	

QUARTER-FINALS
UNCAF

1st leg. Alejandro Morera Soto, Alajuela, 22-09-2005

LD Alajuelense	5	Arias [1], Díaz [12], Gabas [60], Ledezma [69] Myrie [72]
Municipal	2	Plata [46], Medina [63]

2nd leg. Mateo Flores, Guatemala City, 28-09-2005

Municipal	1	Ponciano [2]
LD Alajuelense	0	

1st leg. Municipal, San Isidro, 21-09-2005

Pérez Zeledón	4	Lara [37], Steer [51], Gabriels [65], González.B [90]
Luis Angel Firpo	0	

2nd leg. Serio Torres, Usulután, 27-09-2005

Luis Angel Firpo	2	Martínez.J [22], Merino [42]
Pérez Zeledón	2	Lara [48], Gabriels [81]

1st leg. Ricardo Saprissa, San José, 20-09-2005

Dep. Saprissa	4	Núñez [6], Gómez.R 2 [45] [86], Azofeifa [83]
Marathón	0	

2nd leg. Olímpico, San Pedro Sula, 28-09-2005

Marathón	4	Cacho 3 [9] [12] [26], Pacheco [60]
Dep. Saprissa	0	Saprissa won 4-3p

1st leg. Carlos Salazar Hijo, Mazatenango, 21-09-2005

Suchitepéquez	1	Trujillo [78p]
Olímpia	4	Palacios [15], Turcios [26], Ferreira [46], Cárcamo [88]

2nd leg. Tiburcio Carias Andino, Tegucigalpa, 29-09-2005

Olímpia	4	Emilio 2 [42] [49], Velásquez [86], Morales [90o]
Suchitepéquez	0	

QUARTER-FINALS
CFU

1st leg. Recreational Ground, St John's, 14-10-2005, Small BRB

Hoppers	0	
Portmore United	3	Morrison.J [39], Daley [51], Deer [69]

2nd leg. Recreational Ground, St John's, 16-10-2005, Small BRB

Portmore United	7	Wolfe [25], Daley 2 [30] [74], Watson [47], Reid [65], Morrison.G [68], Swaby [82]
Hoppers	0	

1st leg. Recreational Ground, St John's, 12-10-2005, Giles LCA

Bassa	1	Burton [77]
Centro Barber	1	Palomina [86]

2nd leg. Ergilio Hato, Willemstad, 26-10-2005, Piper TRI

Centro Barber	6	Meulens [11], Martis [29], Bernardus 2 [31] [46], Cassiani 2 [70] [75]
Bassa	2	Thomas [2], Christian [59]

1st leg. Ergilio Hato, Willemstad, 21-10-2005, Brizan TRI

Victory Boys	1	Privania [19]
Northern United	1	McPhee [59]

2nd leg. Mindoo Phillip Park, Castries, 29-10-2005, Willet ATG

Northern United	1	Lastic [82]
Victory Boys	0	

Robinhood	w-o
North East Stars	

SEMI-FINALS
UNCAF

1st leg. Municipal, San Isidro, 19-10-2005, Rodas GUA

Pérez Zeledón	1	Steer [27]
LD Alajuelense	0	

2nd leg. Alejandro Morera Soto, Alajuela, 25-10-2005

LD Alajuelense	3	Diaz [9], Lopez.W [66], Hernandez.C [77]
Pérez Zeledón	0	

1st leg. Ricardo Saprissa, San José, 18-10-2005. Aguilar SLV

Dep. Saprissa	1	Alemán [75]
Olímpia	3	Ferreira [27], Figueroa [38], Emilio [87p]

2nd leg. Tiburcio Carias Andino, Tegucigalpa, 27-10-2005, Moreno PAN

Olímpia	1	Ferreira [60]
Dep. Saprissa	1	Gómez.R [5]

SEMI-FINALS
CFU

1st leg. Ergilio Hato, Willemstad, 30-11-2005, Wijngaarde SUR

Centro Barber	1	Molina [39]
Portmore United	3	Modeste [4], Morrissey 2 [28] [90]

2nd leg. Ergilio Hato, Willemstad, 3-12-2005, Wijngaarde SUR

Portmore United	0	
Centro Barber	1	OG [85]

1st leg. Andre Kamperveen, Paramaribo, 9-11-2005

Robinhood	3	
Northern United	1	

2nd leg. Mindoo Phillip Park, Castries, 23-11-2005, Piper TRI

Northern United	2	Evans [12], McPhee [79]
Robinhood	4	Maasie 2 [14] [27], Zebeda [63], Huur [83]

THIRD PLACE
UNCAF

1st leg. Ricardo Saprissa, San José, 22-11-2005, Pineda HON

Dep. Saprissa	2	Gonzalez.R [16], Saborio [83]
Pérez Zeledón	0	

2nd leg. Municipal, San Isidro, 29-11-2005, Aguilar SLV

Pérez Zeledón	2	Lara [32], Quesada [55]
Dep. Saprissa	0	Saprissa won 5-3p

FINAL
UNCAF

1st leg. Tiburcio Carias Andino, Tegucigalpa, 23-11-2005, Sibrian SLV

Olímpia	0	
LD Alajuelense	1	Gaba [16]

2nd leg. Alejandro Morera Soto, Alajuela, 30-11-2005, Batres GUA

LD Alajuelense	0	
Olímpia	1	Emilio [35]	Alajuelense won 4-2p

FINAL
CFU

1st leg. Andre Kamperveen, Paramaribo, 9-12-2005, Brizan TRI

Robinhood	2	Browne [49], Maasie [72]
Portmore United	1	Modeste [86]

2nd leg. Andre Kamperveen, Paramaribo, 11-12-2005, Brizan TRI

Portmore United	4	Daley [15], Morrison.C [50], Wolfe [58], Morrisey [77]
Robinhood	0	

QUARTER-FINALS

1st leg. Minute Maid Stadium, Houston
22-02-2006, 8 500, Kennedy USA

Portmore United	1
	Wolfe.K [51]

Barrett - Modeste, Stewart•, Sawyers, Mitchell, Morrison• (Wolfe.W 66), Daley (Wolfe.R 77), Austin•, Wolfe.K, Lowe, Deerr (Morrissey 79). Tr: Young

América	2
	Padilla [61p], Zepeda [73]

Navarrete - Rodríguez.I, Cervantes• (Rojas.R• 36), Castro•, Infante, Arguello (Soares 17), Villa•, Torres, Jiménez.C, Boas (Zepeda 57), Padilla. Tr: Aguado

2nd leg. Alejandro Soto, Alajuela
8-03-2006, Prendergast JAM

LD Alajuelense	1
	Hernández.C [90]

Alfaro - Marín, Montero, Fonseca (Jiménez.E 61), López.W (Scott• 61), Ruiz.B, Wallace, Hernández.C, Martínez.E (Gabas 71), Castro, Rodríguez.M. Tr: Villalobos

New England Revolution	0

Reis - Dempsey, Hernandez.D, Heaps, Franchino, Ralston (Cancela 61), Riley, Lochhead, Twellman, Joseph.S•, Dorman. Tr: Nicol

2nd leg. Azteca, Mexico City
8-03-2006, Sibrian SLV

América	5
Padilla 3 [4] [56] [90], Fernández [57], Cervantes [80]	

Navarrete - Rodríguez.I, Castro, Rojas.O (Mendoza 71), Cervantes, Soares, Padilla, Villa, Jiménez.C, Torres (Silva 74), Zepeda (Fernández.S 49). Tr: Lapuente

Portmore United	2
	Bennett [24], Morrison [82]

Barrett• - Modeste, Stewart, Mitchell•, Sawyers, Powell, Morrison, Daley, Wolfe.K (Wolfe.W• 26), Bennett (Bootha 65), Deerr (Swaby 76). Tr: Young

1st leg. Home Depot Center, Carson
23-03-2006, 8 103, Rodriguez MEX

Los Angeles Galaxy	0

Hartman - Roberts, Ihemelu•, Marshall, Sturgis, Jones, Saragoza (Gordon 75), Vagenas, Gómez.H, González.G (Gardner 46), Donovan. Tr: Sampson

Deportivo Saprissa	0

Porras - Bennett, Fonseca•, Badilla, Drummond.J, Stewart•, López.J, Brenes (Centeno• 81), Solís (Phillip 74), Avila (Bolaños 72), Drummond.G. Tr: Medford

1st leg. National SC, Hamilton, Bermuda
22-02-2006, 1 500, Liu CAN

New England Revolution	0

Reis - Dempsey, Hernández•, Heaps, Franchino, Noonan (Latham 83), Riley, Lochhead, Twellman•, Joseph.S, Joseph.A, Dorman (Cancela 75). Tr: Nicol

LD Alajuelense	0

Alfaro - Wallace, Marín, Rodríguez.M, Castro, Oviedo•, Montero, Hernández.C, Fonseca.R (Myrie 75), Ruiz.B• (Scott 86), López.W (Martínez.E 60). Tr: Villalobos

2nd leg. Ricardo Saprissa, San José
8-03-2006, Archundia MEX

Deportivo Saprissa	3
	Centeno [46], Solís [56], Parks [95]

Porras - Badilla, Bennett, Cordero (Drummond.J 81), Parks, Nuñez (Solís 46), Azofeifa, Centeno•, Balaños, Gómez.R, Saborio (López.J 107). Tr: Medford

Los Angeles Galaxy	2
	Grarner [20], Donovan [40]

Hartman - Albright, Marshall•, Ihemelu, Sturgis (Gordon 103), Vagenas, Saragoza• (Dunseth 66), Jones (Da Conceicao 81), Grarner, Gómez.H, Donovan. Tr: Sampson

1st leg. Olímpico, San Pedro Sula
22-02-2006, 14 306, Hall USA

Olímpia	0

Escobar - Avila, Figueroa.M, Palacios, Avila
(Barahona 76), García.O•, Thomas, Palacios, Tilguath
(Turcios 46), Cáracomo (Tosello 69), Emilio.
Tr: Espinoza

Toluca	2
	Díaz.R 24, Cruzalta 90

Lozano - Espinoza•, Almazán, Dueñas•, Cruzalta•,
Castillejos, Rosada, García.E•, Díaz.R (De la Torre.D 72)
(Esparza 88), Lozano• (Valadez 60), Abundis•.
Tr: Gallego

2nd leg. Nemesio Diez, Toluca
8-03-2006, Stott USA

Toluca	2
	Rosada 47, Silva 53

Lozano - Rosada, Díaz.R (Valadez 71), Espinosa,
Castillejos• (Cruzalta 61), Ponce, Viades, Lozano
(Silva 46), Abundis•, Garcia.E, Gamboa. Tr: Gallego

Olímpia	1
	Cárcamo 21

James - Barahona, Thomas, Morales, Figueroa.M,
Garcia.O• (Tilguath 80), Bonilla•, Palacios, Turcios
(López.W 85), Martínez.J (Valet 59), Cáracomo.
Tr: Espinoza

SEMI-FINALS

1st leg. Alejandro Soto, Alajuela
23-03-2006, 18 000, Hall USA

LD Alajuelense	1
	Scott 67

Alfaro - Marín, Rodríguez.M, Castro, Wallace,
Oviedo•, Martínez.M (Myrie 71), Hernández.C, Ruiz,
Díaz (Fonseca.R 60), Jiménez.E (Scott.E 60).
Tr: Villalobos

América	2
	Soares 65, Boas 76

Navarrete - Rodríguez.I, Rojas.O, Fernández.S
(Blanco 46), Castro, Villa, Cervantes, Soares, Torres•
(López.C 46), Giménez.C, Padilla (Boas 63).
Tr: Lapuente

2nd leg. Azteca, Mexico City
29-03-2006, Navarro CAN

América	0

Ochoa - Rodríguez.I, Rojas.O, Rojas.R, López.C, Villa,
Pardo, Soares, Torres•, Giménez.C (Zepeda 79), Boas.
Tr: Lapuente

LD Alajuelense	0

Alfaro - Marín, Wallace (Izaguirre 81), Montero•,
Chinchilla, Castro, Rodríguez, Hernández, Ruiz
(Jiménez.E 75), Scott (Fonseca.R 67), Díaz.
Tr: Villalobos

1st leg. Nemesio Diez, Toluca
22-03-2006, Vaughn USA

Toluca	2
	Silva 2 22 62

Cristante - Da Silva, Rosada, De la Torre.M, Dueñas,
Alzamán, Cruzalta, López.I, Díaz (De la Torre.D 76),
Silva (Toledo 81), Sánchez.V (Castillejos 85).
Tr: Gallego

Deportivo Saprissa	0

Porras - Parks, Cordero, Drummond.J•, Badilla,
Azofeifa, Muñoz (Philip 76), Bolaños, Brenes
(Avila• 63), Solís (Drummond.G• 63), Gómez.
Tr: Medford

2nd leg. Ricardo Saprissa, San José
29-03-2006, Prendergast JAM

Deportivo Saprissa	3
	Azofeifa 46, Saborío 58, Drummond 90

Porras - Cordero, Drummond.J, Parks, López.J•
(Drummond.G 77), Azofeifa•, Bolaños•, Centeno,
Brenes (Alemán• 69), Solís (Saborío 56), Gómez.R.
Tr: Medford

Toluca	2
	Valaez 60, Sánchez.V 87

Cristante• - Da Silva•, Rosada•, De la Torre.M,
Dueñas, Alzamán, Cruzalta, Toledo•, Díaz (Valaez 59)
(Espinosa 87), Silva (Ponce 77), Sánchez.V.
Tr: Gallego

CONCACAF CHAMPIONS CUP FINAL 1ST LEG
Nemesio Diez, Toluca
12-04-2006, 20 000, Pineda HON

TOLUCA	0	0		AMERICA

CD Toluca			Club América
CRISTANTE Rolando			NAVARRETE Armando
CRUZALTA Jose Manuel			ROJAS Oscar Adrian
ALMAZAN Miguel Angel			DAVINO Duilio
DA Silva Paulo César			ROJAS Ricardo
DUENAS Edgar			RODRIGUEZ Ismael
DE LA TORRE Manuel			MENDOZA Alvin
ROSADA Javier Ariel		66	GIMENEZ Christian
PONCE Sergio Amaury			VILLA German
DIAZ Rodrigo Ezequiel	60		SOARES Irenio José
SANCHEZ Vicente Martín			BOAS Kleber
SILVA Carlos Esquivel	70		BLANCO Cuauhtemoc
Tr: GALLEGO Americo			Tr: LAPUENTE Manuel
Substitutes			Substitutes
ABUNDIS José Manuel	60	66	LOPEZ Claudio
DE LA TORRE Diego	70		

CONCACAF CHAMPIONS CUP FINAL 2ND LEG
Azteca, Mexico City
19-04-2006, 35 920, Hall USA

AMERICA	2	1		TOLUCA

Boas 105, Davino 115

Da Silva 93

Club América				CD Toluca
NAVARRETE Armando				CRISTANTE Rolando
RODRIGUEZ Ismael	22	109		DA Silva Paulo César
ROJAS Oscar Adrian				ROSADA Javier Ariel
DAVINO Duilio				DE LA TORRE Manuel
LOPEZ Claudio		81		DIAZ Rodrigo Ezequiel
BLANCO Cuauhtemoc		89		SANCHEZ Vicente Martín
SOARES Irenio José		91		ALMAZAN Miguel Angel
ROJAS Ricardo				TOLEDO Josúe
PADILLA Aaron		46		PONCE Sergio Amaury
VILLA German				CRUZALTA Jose Manuel
TORRES Francisco Javier		59		VALADEZ Ismael
Tr: LAPUENTE Manuel				Tr: GALLEGO Americo
Substitutes				Substitutes
GIMENEZ Christian	22	109	81	CASTILLEJOS Iván
ARGUELLO Alejandro	91		89	ABUNDIS José Manuel
BOAS Kleber			46	59	SILVA Carlos Esquivel

CONMEBOL

CONFEDERACION SUDAMERICANA DE FUTBOL

Not since 1958 had the possibility of a South American nation winning the FIFA World Cup™ in Europe looked such a strong possibility. With the majority of Brazil's and Argentina's players based in Europe, Germany was almost a home-from-home for the two South American giants. Even Ecuador, never previously very good away from the altitude of home, joined in the fun by knocking out Poland and qualifying for the second round. Only an exquisite David Beckham free-kick and the width of the English goalpost stopped them progressing to the quarter-finals to join Brazil and Argentina. Many predicted a Brazil-Argentina final, but no-one had accounted for the resurgent French, who for the third time shattered Brazilian dreams; or for the deadly accuracy of the Germans, who knock out Argentina in a penalty shoot-out. South America will now have to wait until at least 2018 for another shot a winning a second title on European soil. One world championship that did make its way to South America in the 2005-06 season was the FIFA Club

THE FIFA BIG COUNT OF 2000 FOR CONMEBOL

	Male	Female		Male	Female
Registered players	1 619 285	13 019	Referees	17 265	203
Not registered players	11 345 000	97 300	Officials	114 835	3 070
Youth players	2 122 337	9 666	Total involved	21 533 624	693 436
Children & Occasional	6 280 000	570 000	in football	22 191 980	
Professionals	34 902	178	Number of clubs	23 334	
Total players	22 056 607		Number of teams	95 241	

World Championship, won by São Paulo FC. In the final against European champions Liverpool, an heroic goalkeeping display by Rogerio Ceni and a solitary goal from Mineiro saw the Brazilians win the trophy. In the first of the South American club competitions, the 2005 Copa Sudamericana, Boca Juniors became the first club to retain the trophy in the short four-year history of the tournament. Their opponents in the final, UNAM Pumas, almost became the first Mexican club to win a South American trophy, but they lost the penalty shoot-out in Buenos Aires. The 2006 Copa Libertadores was interrupted after the first leg of the quarter-finals by the FIFA World Cup™ and there was bad news for Argentina when it resumed with all three Argentine clubs failing to make it to the semi-finals. Instead Brazil's good run in the tournament continued with both Internacional and São Paulo FC meeting in the second successive all-Brazilian final, a tie won by Internacional who were crowned South American champions for the first time in their history.

Confederación Sudamericana de Fútbol (CONMEBOL)
Autopista Aeropuerto Internacional y Leonismo Luqueño, Luque, Gran Asuncion, Paraguay
Tel +595 21 645781   Fax +595 21 645791
conmebol@conmebol.com.py   www.conmebol.com
President: LEOZ Nicolás, Dr PAR   General Secretary: DELUCA Eduardo ARG
CONMEBOL Formed: 1916

CONMEBOL EXECUTIVE COMMITTEE
President: LEOZ Nicolás, Dr PAR

Vice-President: FIGUEREDO Eugenio URU   General Secretary: DELUCA Eduardo ARG   Treasurer: OSUNA Romer BOL

DIRECTORS OF THE EXECUTIVE COMMITTEE

ESQUIVEL Rafael VEN   DELFINO Nicolás PER   HARRISON Oscar PAR
CHEDID Nabí Abí BRA   ACOSTA ESPINOSA Francisco ECU   FINA Alvaro COL
ABDALAH José CHI

MAP OF CONMEBOL MEMBER NATIONS

SOUTH AMERICAN TOURNAMENTS

COPA AMERICA

Year	Host Country	Winners	Score	Runners-up	Venue
1910	Argentina ††	Argentina	4-1	Uruguay	‡ Racing Club, Buenos Aires
1916	Argentina †	Uruguay	0-0	Argentina	‡ Racing Club, Buenos Aires
1917	Uruguay	Uruguay	1-0	Argentina	‡ Parque Pereira, Montevideo
1919	Brazil	Brazil	1-0	Uruguay	§ Laranjeiras, Rio de Janeiro
1920	Chile	Uruguay	1-1	Argentina	* Sporting Club, Vina del Mar
1921	Argentina	Argentina	1-0	Brazil	* Sportivo Barracas, Buenos Aires
1922	Brazil	Brazil	3-0	Paraguay	§ Laranjeiras, Rio de Janeiro
1923	Uruguay	Uruguay	2-0	Argentina	‡ Parque Central, Montevideo
1924	Uruguay	Uruguay	0-0	Argentina	‡ Parque Central, Montevideo
1925	Argentina	Argentina	2-2	Brazil	‡ Bombonera, Buenos Aires
1926	Chile	Uruguay	2-0	Argentina	* Sport de Nunoa, Santiago
1927	Peru	Argentina	3-2	Uruguay	* Estadio Nacional, Lima
1929	Argentina	Argentina	4-1	Paraguay	* San Lorenzo, Buenos Aires
1935	Peru †	Uruguay	3-0	Argentina	‡ Estadio Nacional, Lima
1937	Argentina	Argentina	2-0	Brazil	‡ San Lorenzo, Buenos Aires
1939	Peru	Peru	2-1	Uruguay	‡ Estadio Nacional, Lima
1941	Chile †	Argentina	1-0	Uruguay	* Estadio Nacional, Santiago
1942	Uruguay	Uruguay	1-0	Argentina	‡ Centenario, Montevideo
1945	Chile †	Argentina	3-1	Brazil	* Estadio Nacional, Santiago
1946	Argentina †	Argentina	2-0	Brazil	‡ Monumental, Buenos Aires
1947	Ecuador	Argentina	6-0	Paraguay	* Estadio Capwell, Guayaquil
1949	Brazil	Brazil	7-0	Paraguay	§ Sao Januario, Rio de Janeiro
1953	Lima	Paraguay	3-2	Brazil	§ Estadio Nacional, Lima
1955	Chile	Argentina	1-0	Chile	‡ Estadio Nacional, Santiago
1956	Uruguay †	Uruguay	1-0	Argentina	‡ Centenario, Montevideo
1957	Peru	Argentina	3-0	Brazil	‡ Estadio Nacional, Lima
1959	Argentina	Argentina	1-1	Brazil	‡ Monumental, Buenos Aires
1959	Ecuador †	Uruguay	5-0	Argentina	* Modelo, Guayaquil
1963	Bolivia	Bolivia	5-4	Brazil	‡ Felix Capriles, Cochabamba
1967	Uruguay	Uruguay	1-0	Argentina	‡ Centenario, Montevideo
1975		Peru	0-1 2-0 1-0	Colombia	Bogota, Lima, Caracas
1979		Paraguay	3-0 0-1 0-0	Chile	Asuncion, Santiago, Buenos Aires
1983		Uruguay	2-0 1-1	Brazil	Montevideo & Salvador
1987	Argentina	Uruguay	1-0	Chile	Monumental, Buenos Aires
1989	Brazil	Brazil	1-0	Uruguay	‡ Maracana, Rio de Janeiro
1991	Chile	Argentina	3-2	Brazil	* Estadio Nacional, Santiago
1993	Ecuador	Argentina	2-1	Mexico	Monumental, Guayaquil
1995	Uruguay	Uruguay	1-1 5-3p	Brazil	Centenario, Montevideo
1997	Bolivia	Brazil	3-1	Bolivia	Hernando Siles, La Paz
1999	Paraguay	Brazil	3-0	Uruguay	Defensores del Chaco, Asuncion
2001	Colombia	Colombia	1-0	Mexico	El Campin, Bogota
2004	Peru	Brazil	2-2 4-2p	Argentina	Estadio Nacional, Lima
2007	Venezuela				

† Extraordinario tournaments are recognised as official tournaments though the teams did not compete for the Copa America • †† Unofficial tournament that is not part of the official records • ‡ Tournament played on a league system. The final game was between the top two teams
** Tournament played on a league system. The game listed between the top two teams was not the final match in the tournament • § Tournament played on a league system. The game listed was a play-off after the top two teams finished level on points.

Following the demise of the British International Championship, the Copa América is now the longest-running international competition in the world, dating back to 1916 though some historians like to point to a tournament played in 1910 that was referred to at the time as the "South American Championship". Argentina and Uruguay have always been the most enthusiastic proponents of the Copa América and each has been champions 14 times lending credence to the belief among many

South Americans that the real home of football on the continent lies around the River Plate estuary and the cities of Montevideo and Buenos Aires and not further north in Brazil. In the first 33 editions spanning 73 years the Brazilians won the title just three times and never outside of Rio de Janeiro. Aside from these three, Peru in 1939 and 1975, and Paraguay in 1953 and 1979, have been champions twice while Bolivia in 1963 and Colombia in 2001 have both won the title once. Only Venezuela, Ecuador and Chile have failed to win it with Venezuela yet to win a single match since beating Bolivia the first time they took part in 1967. Historically the tournament has usually been played on a league system although since the 1970s a group stage followed by knock-out rounds has been the preferred format. Another innovation has been the invitation extended to Mexico to take part since 1993, along with another guest, most commonly Costa Rica or the USA. Now held every two years the Copa América has finally caught the imagination of the Brazilians and in recent years they have been the most successful nation winning three of the past four editions and their 1997 triumph in Bolivia was their first away from home. The past three FIFA World Cup™ qualifying campaigns in South America, in which each of the ten nations plays each other home and away, has to a certain extent cast a shadow over the Copa América. It is difficult to argue against the fact that the top team, at the end of what amounts to a three-year campaign, should be regarded as the best team on the continent rather than the Copa America champions. However, the Copa América remains an important landmark in the fixture list and it rarely fails to entertain.

SOUTH AMERICAN WOMEN'S CHAMPIONSHIP

Year	Host Country	Winners	Score	Runners-up	Venue
1991	Brazil	Brazil	6-1	Chile	‡ Maringá
1995	Brazil	Brazil	2-0	Argentina	Uberlândia
1998	Argentina	Brazil	7-1	Argentina	Mar del Plata
2003	Peru	Brazil	3-2	Argentina	** Lima

‡ Tournament played on a league system. The final game was between the top two teams • ** Tournament played on a league system. The game listed between the top two teams was not the final match in the tournament.

SOUTH AMERICAN WOMEN'S U-20 CHAMPIONSHIP

Year	Host Country	Winners	Score	Runners-up	Venue
2004		Brazil	5-2	Paraguay	
2006	Chile	Brazil	1-0	Argentina	Sausalito, Viña del Mar

‡ Tournament played on a league system. The final game was between the top two teams

The South American Women's Championship was introduced in 1991 as a qualifying tournament for the FIFA Women's World Cup and has been played as such ever since. Brazil have dominated since the start, a pattern that has continued in the under 20 competition which was introduced in 2004 to tie in with the FIFA U-20 Women's Word Championship.

SOUTH AMERICA PRE-OLIMPICO

Year	Host Country	Winners	Runners-up
1960	Peru	Argentina	Peru
1964	Peru	Argentina	Brazil
1968	Colombia	Brazil	Colombia
1971	Colombia	Brazil	Colombia
1976	Brazil	Brazil	Uruguay
1980	Colombia	Argentina	Colombia
1984	Ecuador	Brazil	Chile
1987	Bolivia	Brazil	Argentina
1992	Paraguay	Paraguay	Colombia
1996	Argentina	Brazil	Argentina
2000	Brazil	Brazil	Chile
2004	Chile	Argentina	Paraguay

Open to non-professionals only prior to 1984 • The 1987 tournament was open to any player who had not played in a FIFA World Cup™ match • Since 1992 it has been an U-23 tournament

SUDAMERICANA SUB-17

Year	Host Country	Winners	Runners-up
1985	Argentina	Argentina	Brazil
1986	Peru	Bolivia	Brazil
1988	Ecuador	Brazil	Argentina
1991	Paraguay	Brazil	Uruguay
1993	Colombia	Colombia	Chile
1995	Peru	Brazil	Argentina
1997	Paraguay	Brazil	Argentina
1999	Uruguay	Brazil	Paraguay
2002	Peru	Brazil	Argentina
2003	Bolivia	Argentina	Brazil
2005	Venezuela	Brazil	Uruguay

From 1985-1988 the championship was a U-16 tournament but since 1991 it has operated as an U-17 championship

SUDAMERICANA SUB-20

Year	Host Country	Winners	Runners-up
1954	Venezuela	Uruguay	Brazil
1958	Chile	Uruguay	Argentina
1964	Colombia	Uruguay	Paraguay
1967	Paraguay	Argentina	Paraguay
1971	Paraguay	Paraguay	Uruguay
1974	Chile	Brazil	Uruguay
1975	Peru	Uruguay	Chile
1977	Venezuela	Uruguay	Brazil
1979	Uruguay	Uruguay	Argentina
1981	Ecuador	Uruguay	Brazil
1983	Bolivia	Brazil	Uruguay

SUDAMERICANA SUB-20

Year	Host Country	Winners	Runners-up
1985	Paraguay	Brazil	Paraguay
1987	Colombia	Colombia	Brazil
1988	Argentina	Brazil	Colombia
1991	Venezuela	Brazil	Argentina
1992	Colombia	Brazil	Uruguay
1995	Bolivia	Brazil	Argentina
1997	Chile	Argentina	Brazil
1999	Argentina	Argentina	Uruguay
2001	Ecuador	Brazil	Argentina
2003	Uruguay	Argentina	Brazil
2005	Colombia	Colombia	Brazil

SUPERCOPA JOAO HAVELANGE

Year	Winners	Country	Score	Country	Runners-up
1988	Racing Club	ARG	2-1 1-1	BRA	Cruzeiro
1989	Boca Juniors	ARG	0-0 0-0 5-3p	ARG	Independiente
1990	Olimpia	PAR	3-0 3-3	URU	Nacional Montevideo
1991	Cruzeiro	BRA	0-2 3-0	ARG	River Plate
1992	Cruzeiro	BRA	4-0 0-1	ARG	Racing Club
1993	São Paulo FC	BRA	2-2 2-2 5-3p	BRA	Flamengo
1994	Independiente	ARG	1-1 1-0	ARG	Boca Juniors
1995	Independiente	ARG	2-0 0-1	BRA	Flamengo
1996	Velez Sarsfield	ARG	1-0 2-0	BRA	Cruzeiro
1997	River Plate	ARG	0-0 2-1	BRA	São Paulo FC

Discontinued in 1997 and replaced by the Copa Mercosur and Copa Merconorte

COPA MERCOSUR

Year	Winners	Country	Score	Country	Runners-up
1998	Palmeiras	BRA	1-2 3-1 1-0	BRA	Cruzeiro
1999	Flamengo	BRA	4-3	BRA	Palmeiras
2000	Vasco da Gama	BRA	2-0 0-1 4-3	BRA	Palmeiras
2001	San Lorenzo	ARG	0-0 1-1 4-3p	BRA	Flamengo

COPA MERCONORTE

Year	Winners	Country	Score	Country	Runners-up
1998	Atlético Nacional Medellin	COL	3-1 1-0	COL	Deportivo Cali
1999	América Cali	COL	1-2 1-0	COL	Independiente Santa Fé
2000	Atlético Nacional Medellin	COL	0-0 2-1	COL	Millonarios
2001	Millonarios	COL	1-1 1-1 3-1p	ECU	Emelec

Both the Copa Mercosur and Copa Merconorte were discontinued in 2001 and were replaced by the Copa Sudamericana

COPA CONMEBOL

Year	Winners	Country	Score	Country	Runners-up
1992	Atlético Mineiro	BRA	2-0 0-1	PAR	Olimpia
1993	Botafogo	BRA	1-1 2-2 3-1p	URU	Peñarol
1994	São Paulo FC	BRA	6-1 0-3	URU	Peñarol
1995	Rosario Central	ARG	0-4 4-0 4-3p	BRA	Atlético Mineiro
1996	Lanús	ARG	2-0 0-1	COL	Independiente Santa Fé
1997	Atlético Mineiro	BRA	4-1 1-1	ARG	Lanús
1998	Santos	BRA	1-0 0-0	ARG	Rosario Central
1999	Talleres Cordoba	ARG	2-4 3-0	BRA	CSA

COPA SUDAMERICANA

Year	Winners	Country	Score	Country	Runners-up
2002	San Lorenzo	ARG	4-0 0-0	COL	Atlético Nacional Medellin
2003	Cienciano	PER	3-3 1-0	ARG	River Plate
2004	Boca Juniors	ARG	0-1 2-0	BOL	Bolivar
2005	Boca Juniors	ARG	1-1 1-1 4-3p	MEX	Pumas UNAM

COPA LIBERTADORES DE AMERICA

Year	Winners	Country	Score	Country	Runners-up
1960	Peñarol	URU	1-0 1-1	PAR	Olimpia
1961	Peñarol	URU	1-0 1-1	BRA	Palmeiras
1962	Santos	BRA	2-1 2-3 3-0	URU	Peñarol
1963	Santos	BRA	3-2 2-1	ARG	Boca Juniors
1964	Independiente	ARG	0-0 1-0	URU	Nacional Montevideo
1965	Independiente	ARG	1-0 1-3 4-1	URU	Peñarol
1966	Peñarol	URU	2-0 2-3 4-2	ARG	River Plate
1967	Racing Club	ARG	0-0 0-0 2-1	URU	Nacional Montevideo
1968	Estudiantes LP	ARG	2-1 1-3 2-0	BRA	Palmeiras
1969	Estudiantes LP	ARG	1-0 2-0	URU	Nacional Montevideo
1970	Estudiantes LP	ARG	1-0 0-0	URU	Peñarol
1971	Nacional Montevideo	URU	0-1 1-0 2-0	ARG	Estudiantes LP
1972	Independiente	ARG	0-0 2-1	PER	Universitario
1973	Independiente	ARG	1-1 0-0 2-1	CHI	Colo Colo
1974	Independiente	ARG	1-2 2-0 1-0	BRA	São Paulo FC
1975	Independiente	ARG	0-1 3-1 2-0	CHI	Union Española
1976	Cruzeiro	BRA	4-1 1-2 3-2	ARG	River Plate
1977	Boca Juniors	ARG	1-0 0-1 0-0 5-4p	BRA	Cruzeiro
1978	Boca Juniors	ARG	0-0 4-0	COL	Deportivo Cali
1979	Olimpia	PAR	2-0 0-0	ARG	Boca Juniors
1980	Nacional Montevideo	URU	0-0 1-0	BRA	Internacional PA
1981	Flamengo	BRA	2-1 0-1 2-0	CHI	Cobreloa
1982	Peñarol	URU	0-0 1-0	CHI	Cobreloa
1983	Grêmio	BRA	1-1 2-1	URU	Peñarol
1984	Independiente	ARG	1-0 0-0	BRA	Grêmio
1985	Argentinos Juniors	ARG	1-0 0-1 1-1 5-4p	COL	América Cali
1986	River Plate	ARG	2-1 1-0	COL	América Cali
1987	Peñarol	URU	0-2 2-1 1-0	COL	América Cali
1988	Nacional Montevideo	URU	0-1 3-0	ARG	Newell's Old Boys
1989	Atlético Nacional Medellín	COL	0-2 2-0 5-4p	PAR	Olimpia
1990	Olimpia	PAR	2-0 1-1	ECU	Barcelona
1991	Colo Colo	CHI	0-0 3-0	PAR	Olimpia
1992	São Paulo FC	BRA	1-0 0-1 3-2p	ARG	Newell's Old Boys
1993	São Paulo FC	BRA	5-1 0-2	CHI	Universidad Catolica
1994	Velez Sarsfield	ARG	1-0 0-1 5-3p	BRA	São Paulo FC
1995	Grêmio	BRA	3-1 1-1	COL	Atlético Nacional Medellin
1996	River Plate	ARG	0-1 2-0	COL	América Cali
1997	Cruzeiro	BRA	0-0 1-0	PER	Sporting Cristal
1998	Vasco da Gama	BRA	2-0 2-1	ECU	Barcelona
1999	Palmeiras	BRA	0-1 2-1 4-3p	COL	Deportivo Cali
2000	Boca Juniors	ARG	2-2 0-0 4-2p	BRA	Palmeiras
2001	Boca Juniors	ARG	1-0 0-1 3-1p	MEX	Cruz Azul
2002	Olimpia	PAR	0-1 2-1 4-2p	BRA	São Caetano
2003	Boca Juniors	ARG	2-0 3-1	BRA	Santos
2004	Once Caldas	COL	0-0 1-1 2-0p	ARG	Boca Juniors
2005	São Paulo FC	BRA	1-1 4-0	BRA	Atlético Paranaense
2006	Internacional	BRA	2-1 2-2	BRA	São Paulo FC

There are currently two club tournaments held in South America with the Copa Libertadores held in the first half of the year and the Copa Sudamericana towards the end. The Copa Libertadores is the senior of the two and has been held annually since 1960. The Copa Sudamericana is the latest in a long line of secondary tournaments following on from the Supercopa João Havelange, the Copa Mercosur and the Copa Merconorte. In the 1990s there was even a third tournament, the Copa CONMEBOL, but that lasted just eight years.

PAST SOUTH AMERICAN PLAYER OF THE YEAR AWARDS

Historically there have been two different awards for South American Footballer of the Year. From 1971 until 1992 *El Mundo* newspaper in Caracas awarded the accolade which was open to South Americans playing anywhere in the world. Since 1986 *El Pais* of Montevideo has given the award to the best South American playing within the Americas.

PLAYER OF THE YEAR 1971

TOSTAO	Cruzeiro	BRA	24
PASTORIZA Omar	Independiente	ARG	21
ARTIME Luis	Nacional	ARG	19
CUBILLAS Teófilo	Alianza	PER	17
GERSON	São Paulo FC	BRA	16
PELE	Santos	BRA	15
MAZURKIEWICZ Lad.	Atlético MG	URU	13
JAIRZINHO	Botafogo	BRA	11
RIVELINO Roberto	Corinthians	BRA	10
CHUMPITAZ Hector	Universitario	PAR	9

PLAYER OF THE YEAR 1972

CUBILLAS Teófilo	Alianza	PER	41
PELE	Santos	BRA	32
JAIRZINHO	Botafogo	BRA	28
TOSTAO	Vasco	BRA	16
ADEMIR da Guia	Palmeiras	BRA	15
M. CASTILLO Julio	Peñarol	URU	15
ALONSO Norberto	River Plate	ARG	11
FIGUEROA Elias	Internacional	CHI	11
FISCHER Rodolfo	Botafogo	ARG	9
REINOSO Carlos	América, Mex	CHI	6

PLAYER OF THE YEAR 1973

PELE	Santos	BRA	54
BRINDISI Miguel	Huracán	ARG	43
RIVELINO Roberto	Corinthians	BRA	33
MORENA Fernando	Peñarol	URU	19
CASZELY Carlos	Colo Colo	CHI	17
FIGUEROA Elias	Internacional	CHI	10
JAIRZINHO	Botafogo	BRA	6
SOTIL Hugo	CF Barcelona	PER	6
AYALA Ruben	Atlético Madrid	ARG	6
Two players with five votes			

PLAYER OF THE YEAR 1974

FIGUEROA Elias	Internacional	CHI	39
MARINHO Francisco	Botafogo	BRA	24
BABINGTON Carlos	Wattenschied	ARG	22
PEREIRA Luis	Palmeiras	BRA	20
PELE	Santos	BRA	15
MORENA Fernando	Peñarol	URU	14
BOCHINI Ricardo	Independiente	ARG	14
HOUSEMAN Rene	Huracán	ARG	11
CASZELY Carlos	Levante	CHI	8
RIVELINO	Fluminense	BRA	7

PLAYER OF THE YEAR 1975

FIGUEROA Elias	Internacional	CHI	50
ALONSO Norberto	River Plate	ARG	24
MORENA Fernando	Peñarol	URU	23
NELINHO	Cruzeiro	BRA	20
PEREIRA Luis	Atlético Madrid	BRA	16
SOTIL Hugo	CF Barcelona	PER	12
SCOTTA Horacio	San Lorenzo	ARG	11
CUBILLAS Teófilo	FC Porto	PER	10
BOCHINI Ricardo	Independiente	ARG	10
LEIVINHA	Atlético Madrid	BRA	7

PLAYER OF THE YEAR 1976

FIGUEROA Elias	Palestino	CHI	51
ZICO	Flamengo	BRA	34
RIVELINO Roberto	Fluminense	BRA	31
GATTI Hugo	Boca Juniors	ARG	29
PEREIRA Luis	Atlético Madrid	BRA	19
MORENA Fernando	Peñarol	URU	12
PASSARELLA Daniel	River Plate	ARG	10
PAULO CESAR	Fluminense	BRA	10
ALONSO Norberto	River Plate	ARG	10
LEIVINHA	Atlético Madrid	BRA	9

PLAYER OF THE YEAR 1977

ZICO	Flamengo	BRA
RIVELINO Roberto	Fluminense	BRA
FIGUEROA Elias	Palestino	CHI
PELE	NY Cosmos	BRA
FILLOL Ubaldo	River Plate	ARG
BOCHINI Ricardo	Independiente	ARG
CUBILLAS Teófilo	Alianza	PER
GATTI Hugo	Boca Juniors	ARG
BERTONI Daniel	Independiente	ARG
HOUSEMAN Rene	Huracán	ARG

PLAYER OF THE YEAR 1978

KEMPES Mario	Valencia	ARG	78
FILLOL Ubaldo	River Plate	ARG	59
DIRCEU Guimaraes	América, Mex	BRA	48
PASSARELLA Daniel	River Plate	ARG	29
CUBILLAS Teófilo	Alianza	PER	19
FIGUEROA Elias	Palestino	CHI	7
BOCHINI Ricardo	Independiente	ARG	6
CUETO César	Alianza	PER	5
RIVELINO Roberto	Fluminense	BRA	4
ARDILES Osvaldo	Tottenham	ARG	3

PLAYER OF THE YEAR 1979

MARADONA Diego	Argentinos J	ARG	80
ROMERO Julio Cesar	Sp. Luqueño	PAR	40
FALCAO Roberto	Internacional	BRA	29
FILLOL Ubaldo	River Plate	ARG	26
ZICO	Flamengo	BRA	15
MORENA Fernando	Rayo Vallecano	URU	13
CASZELY Carlos	Colo Colo	CHI	11
PASSARELLA Daniel	River Plate	ARG	9
KEMPES Mario	Valencia	ARG	9
DIAZ Ramón	River Plate	ARG	7

PLAYER OF THE YEAR 1980

MARADONA Diego	Argentinos J	ARG
ZICO	Flamengo	BRA
VICTORINO Waldemar	Nacional	URU
FILLOL Ubaldo	River Plate	ARG
PAZ Ruben	Peñarol	URU
PASSARELLA Daniel	River Plate	ARG
TONINHO CEREZO	Atlético MG	BRA
SOCRATES	Corinthians	BRA
RODRIGUES Rodolfo	Nacional	URU
ROMERO Julio Cesar	NY Cosmos	PAR

PLAYER OF THE YEAR 1981

ZICO	Flamengo	BRA
MARADONA Diego	Boca Juniors	ARG
JUNIOR	Flamengo	BRA
URIBE Julio	Sporting Cristal	PER
YANEZ Patricio	San Luis	CHI
PASSARELLA Daniel	River Plate	ARG
FALCAO Roberto	Roma	BRA
SOCRATES	Corinthians	BRA
FIGUEROA Elias	Ft Lauderdale	CHI
PAZ Ruben	Peñarol	URU

PLAYER OF THE YEAR 1982

ZICO	Flamengo	BRA
FALCAO Roberto	Roma	BRA
MARADONA Diego	Barcelona	ARG
MORENA Fernando	Peñarol	URU
JUNIOR	Flamengo	BRA
SOCRATES	Corinthians	BRA
PASSARELLA Daniel	Fiorentina	ARG
SANCHEZ Hugo	Atlético Madrid	MEX

PLAYER OF THE YEAR 1983

SOCRATES	Corinthians	BRA	59
FILLOL Ubaldo	Argentinos J	ARG	30
EDER	Atlético MG	BRA	29
MORENA Fernando	Peñarol	URU	25
DIOGO Victor	Peñarol	URU	17
GARECA Ricardo	Boca Juniors	ARG	15
RODRIGUEZ Rodolfo	Santos	URU	13
AGUILERA Ramon	Nacional	URU	10
JUNIOR	Flamengo	BRA	9
PAZ Ruben	Peñarol	URU	8

PLAYER OF THE YEAR 1984

FRANCESCOLI Enzo	River Plate	URU	43
FILLOL Ubaldo	Flamengo	ARG	36
BOCHINI Ricardo	Independiente	ARG	25
RODRIGUEZ Rodolfo	Santos	URU	20
GARECA Ricardo	Boca Juniors	ARG	17
DE LEON Hugo	Grêmio	URU	17
BURRUCHAGA Jorge	Independiente	ARG	13
MARCICO Alberto	FC Oeste	ARG	11
DIOGO Victor	Palmeiras	URU	8
MORENA Fernando	Peñarol	URU	7

PLAYER OF THE YEAR 1985

ROMERO Julio Cesar	Fluminense	PAR
FRANCESCOLI Enzo	River Plate	URU
BORGHI Claudio	Argentinos J	ARG
CABANAS Roberto	América Cali	PAR
CASAGRANDE Walter	Corinthians	BRA
FERNANDEZ Roberto	América Cali	PAR
ZICO	Flamengo	BRA
BATISTA Daniel	Argentinos J	ARG
RENATO GAUCHO	Grêmio	BRA
RODRIGUEZ Rodolfo	Santos	URU

PLAYER OF THE YEAR 1986

MARADONA Diego	Napoli	ARG
CARECA	São Paulo FC	BRA
SANCHEZ Hugo	Real Madrid	MEX
BURRUCHAGA Jorge	FC Nantes	ARG
ROMERO Julio Cesar	Fluminense	PAR
VALDANO Jorge	Real Madrid	ARG
FRANCESCOLI Enzo	Racing Paris	URU
JOSIMAR	Botafogo	BRA
RUGGERI Oscar	River Plate	ARG
NEGRETE Manuel	Sporting CL	MEX

PLAYER OF THE YEAR 1987

VALDERRAMA Carlos	Deportivo Cali	COL
CABANAS Roberto	América Cali	PAR
ALZAMENDI Antonio	River Plate	URU
AGUIRRE Diego	Peñarol	URU
ROJAS Roberto	Colo Colo	CHI
MARANGONI Claudio	Independiente	ARG
PERDOMO Jose	Peñarol	URU
LETELIER Juan Carlos	Cobreloa	CHI
REDIN Bernardo	Deportivo Cali	COL
RODRIGUEZ Rodolfo	Santos	URU

PLAYER OF THE YEAR 1988

PAZ Ruben	Racing Club	URU
DE LEON Hugo	Nacional	URU
GEOVANI SILVA	Vasco	BRA
TAFFAREL Claudio	Internacional	BRA
FABBRI Nestor	Racing Club	ARG
REDIN Bernardo	Deportivo Cali	COL
BATISTA Daniel	River Plate	ARG
URIBE Julio	Sporting Cristal	PER
POLILLA	River Plate	BRA

PLAYER OF THE YEAR 1989

MARADONA Diego	Napoli	ARG
SOSA Ruben	Lazio	URU
BEBETO	Vasco	BRA
ROMARIO	PSV	BRA
CARECA	Napoli	BRA
HIGUITA Rene	At. Nacional	COL
BATISTA Daniel	River Plate	ARG
ALEMAO	Napoli	BRA
DUNGA Carlos	Fiorentina	BRA
REDIN Bernardo	Deportivo Cali	COL

PLAYER OF THE YEAR 1990

MARADONA Diego	Napoli	ARG
CANIGGIA Claudio	Atalanta	ARG
HIGUITA Rene	At. Nacional	COL
CARECA	Napoli	BRA
ALEMAO	Napoli	BRA
GOYCOECHEA Sergio	Racing Club	ARG
SANCHEZ Hugo	Real Madrid	MEX
CONEJO Luis	Albacete	CRC
VALDERRAMA Carlos	Montpellier	COL

PLAYER OF THE YEAR 1991

BATISTUTA Gabriel	Fiorentina	ARG
CANIGGIA Claudio	Atalanta	ARG
ZAMORANO Ivan	Sevilla	CHI
ROCHA Ricardo	Real Madrid	BRA
RUGGERI Oscar	Vélez	ARG
RODRIGUEZ Leonardo	Toulon	ARG
LATORRE Diego	Boca Juniors	ARG
VALDERRAMA Carlos	Real Valladolid	COL

PLAYER OF THE YEAR 1992

MARADONA Diego	Sevilla	ARG	32
BEBETO	Deportivo LC	BRA	31
RAI	São Paulo FC	BRA	25
BATISTUTA Gabriel	Fiorentina	ARG	24
CANIGGIA Claudio	Roma	ARG	21
FONSECA Daniel	Napoli	URU	18
ROMARIO	PSV	BRA	17
CABANAS Roberto	Boca Juniors	PAR	14
ZAMORANO Ivan	Real Madrid	CHI	13
MULLER	São Paolo FC	BRA	10

PLAYER OF THE YEAR 1986

ALZAMENDI Antonio	River Plate	URU
CARECA	São Paulo FC	BRA
ROMERO Julio Cesar	Fluminense	PAR

PLAYER OF THE YEAR 1987

VALDERRAMA Carlos	Deportivo Cali	COL	56
TRASANTE Obdulio	Peñarol	URU	27
PERDOMO José	Peñarol	URU	25
DOMINGUEZ Alfonso	Peñarol	URU	23
ALZAMENDI Antonio	River Plate	URU	23
JOSIMAR	Flamengo	BRA	18
GUTIERREZ Nelson	River Plate	URU	17
AGUIRRE Diego	Peñarol	URU	15
PAZ Ruben	Racing Club	URU	10
2 players with 9 votes			

PLAYER OF THE YEAR 1988

PAZ Ruben	Racing Club	URU
DE LEON Hugo	Nacional	URU
SALDANHA José	Nacional	URU

PLAYER OF THE YEAR 1989

BEBETO	Vasco	BRA	74
MAZINHO	Vasco	BRA	42
HIGUITA Rene	At. Nacional	COL	34
OSTOLAZA Santiago	Nacional	URU	32
BATISTA Sergio	River Plate	ARG	30
DE LEON Hugo	Nacional	URU	29
AGUINAGA Alex	Necaxa	ECU	28
SIMON Juan	Boca Juniors	ARG	23
DOMINGUEZ Alfonso	Peñarol	URU	22
MORENO Carlos	Independiente	ARG	21

PLAYER OF THE YEAR 1990

AMARILLA Raúl	Olimpia	PAR	57
DA SILVA Ruben	River Plate	URU	32
ALVAREZ Leonel	At. Nacional	COL	25
HIGUITA René	At. Nacional	COL	25
BASUALDO Fabian	River Plate	ARG	23

PLAYER OF THE YEAR 1991

Player	Club	Country	Votes
RUGGERI Oscar		ARG	44
DIAZ Ramón		ARG	28
TOLEDO Patricio		CHI	23
ASTRADA Leonardo		ARG	21
BORRELLI Juan José		ARG	18
TILICO Mario		BRA	18
MENDOZA Gabriel		CHI	15
BASUALDO Fabian		ARG	13
DEL SOLAR José		PER	13
Three players with 12 votes			

PLAYER OF THE YEAR 1992

Player	Club	Country	Votes
RAI	São Paulo FC	BRA	55
GOYCOECHEA Sergio	Olimpia	ARG	24
ACOSTA Alberto	Newell's OB	ARG	20
GAMBOA Fernando	San Lorenzo	ARG	20
CAFU	São Paulo FC	BRA	18
RENATO Gaúcho	Cruzeiro	BRA	17
JUNIOR	Flamengo	BRA	14
BOIADEIRO	Boca Juniors	BRA	13
MARCICO Alberto	Cruzeiro	ARG	13
ISLAS Luis	Independiente	ARG	10

PLAYER OF THE YEAR 1993

Player	Club	Country	Votes
VALDERRAMA Carlos	Atlético Junior	COL	46
ETCHEVERRY Marco	Colo Colo	BOL	30
CAFU	São Paulo FC	BRA	28
RINCON Freddy	Palmeiras	COL	28
ALVAREZ Leonel	América Cali	COL	18
MULLER	São Paulo FC	BRA	18
GOYCOECHEA Sergio	Olimpia	ARG	12
PEREA Luis Carlos	Ind. Medellin	COL	11
KANAPKIS Fernando	Mandiyu	URU	11
MARADONA Diego	Newell's OB	ARG	11

PLAYER OF THE YEAR 1994

Player	Club	Country	Votes
CAFU	São Paulo FC	BRA	36
CHILAVERT Jose Luis	Vélez	PAR	35
LOPEZ Gustavo	Independiente	ARG	22
RAMBERT Sebastian	Independiente	ARG	21

PLAYER OF THE YEAR 1995

Player	Club	Country	Votes
FRANCESCOLI Enzo	River Plate	URU	34
MARADONA Diego	Boca Juniors	ARG	28
EDMUNDO	Flamengo	BRA	24
ROMARIO	Flamengo	BRA	23
CHILAVERT Jose Luis	Vélez	PARA	21

PLAYER OF THE YEAR 1996

Player	Club	Country	Votes
CHILAVERT Jose Luis	Vélez	PAR	80
FRANCESCOLI Enzo	River Plate	URU	69
ORTEGA Ariel	River Plate	ARG	41
VALDERRAMA Carlos	Tampa Bay	COL	41
ARCE Francisco	Grêmio	PAR	27
GAMARRA Carlos	Cerro Porteño	PAR	26
SALAS Marcelo	River Plate	CHI	23
ACUNA Roberto	Independiente	PAR	18
SORIN Juan Pablo	River Plate	ARG	18
AYALA Celso	River Plate	PAR	17

PLAYER OF THE YEAR 1997

Player	Club	Country	Votes
SALAS Marcelo	River Plate	CHI	87
SOLANO Nolberto	Boca Juniors	PER	39
CHILAVERT Jose Luis	Vélez	PAR	37
AYALA Celso	River Plate	PAR	36
GALLARDO Marcelo	River Plate	ARG	35
FRANCESCOLI Enzo	River Plate	URU	28
DENILSON	São Paulo FC	BRA	27
BERMUDEZ Jorge	Boca Juniors	COL	26
ASTRADA Leonardo	River Plate	ARG	23
EDMUNDO	Vasco	BRA	23

PLAYER OF THE YEAR 1998

Player	Club	Country	Votes
PALERMO Martin	Boca Juniors	ARG	73
GAMARRA Carlos	Corinthians	PAR	70
CHILAVERT Jose Luis	Vélez	PAR	63
ARCE Francisco	Palmeiras	PAR	44
SERNA Mauricio	Boca Juniors	COL	41
FELIPE	Vasco	BRA	27
GALLARDO Marcelo	River Plate	ARG	27
MARCELINO	Corinthians	BRA	24
BERMUDEZ Jorge	Boca Juniors	COL	22
CAGNA Diego	Boca Juniors	ARG	21

PLAYER OF THE YEAR 1999

Player	Club	Country	Votes
SAVIOLA Javier	River Plate	ARG	55
ARCE Francisco	Palmeiras	PAR	45
RIQUELME Juan	Boca Juniors	ARG	42
CHILAVERT Jose Luis	Vélez	PAR	36
Cordoba Ivan	San Lorenzo	COL	33
ALEX	Palmeiras	BRA	28
AIMAR Pablo	River Plate	ARG	27
VAMPETA	Corinthians	BRA	23
Three players with 22 votes			

PLAYER OF THE YEAR 2000

Player	Club	Country	Votes
ROMARIO	Vasco	BRA	67
RIQUELME Juan	Boca Juniors	ARG	64
CORDOBA Oscar	Boca Juniors	COL	53
PALERMO Martin	Boca Juniors	ARG	53
AIMAR Pablo	River Plate	ARG	38
SERNA Mauricio	Boca Juniors	COL	38
SORIN Juan Pablo	Cruzeiro	ARG	37
ARCE Francisco	Palmeiras	PAR	36
BERMUDEZ Jorge	Boca Juniors	COL	36
GAMARRA Carlos	Flamengo	PAR	32

PLAYER OF THE YEAR 2001

Player	Club	Country	Votes
RIQUELME Juan	Boca Juniors	ARG	88
CORDOBA Oscar	Boca Juniors	COL	59
ROMARIO	Vasco	BRA	41
ARCE Francisco	Palmeiras	PAR	39
SORIN Juan Pablo	Cruzeiro	ARG	37
YEPES Mario	River Plate	COL	36
ORTEGA Ariel	River Plate	ARG	31
LEMBO Alejandro	Nacional	URU	29
SERNA Mauricio	Boca Juniors	COL	27
Two players with 20 votes			

PLAYER OF THE YEAR 2002

Player	Club	Country	Votes
CARDOZO José	Toluca	PAR	39
ORTEMAN Sergio	Olimpia	URU	32
LEMBO Alejandro	Nacional	URU	30
D'ALESSANDRO Andrés	River Plate	ARG	29
KAKA	São Paulo FC	BRA	27
MILITO Gabriel	Independiente	ARG	25
ARCE Francisco	Palmeiras	PAR	24
SAJA Sebastian	San Lorenzo	ARG	23
DELGADO Marcelo	Boca Juniors	ARG	18
ROBINHO	Santos	BRA	16

PLAYER OF THE YEAR 2003

Player	Club	Country	Votes
TEVEZ Carlos	Boca Juniors	ARG	73
CARDOZO José	Toluca	PAR	39
DIEGO	Santos	BRA	33
BATTAGLIA Sebastián	Boca Juniors	ARG	26
RODRIGUEZ Clemente	Boca Juniors	ARG	18
SCHIAVI Rolando	Boca Juniors	ARG	17
ALEX	Cruzeiro	BRA	16
ROBINHO	Santos	BRA	14
ABBONDANZIERI Rob.	Boca Juniors	ARG	14
SOSA Marcelo	Danubio	URU	13

PLAYER OF THE YEAR 2004

Player	Club	Country	Votes
TEVEZ Carlos	Boca Juniors	ARG	76
MASCHERANO Javier	River Plate	ARG	56
GONZALEZ Luis	River Plate	ARG	37
ROBINHO	Santos	BRA	37
HENAO Juan Carlos	Once Caldas	COL	32
CARDOZO José	Toluca	PAR	26
LEO	Santos	BRA	24
ELANO	Santos	BRA	23
LUGANO Diego	São Paulo FC	URU	22
SCHIAVI Rolando	Boca Juniors	ARG	22

PLAYER OF THE YEAR 2005

Player	Club	Country	Votes
TEVEZ Carlos	Corinthians	ARG	77
LUGANO Diego	São Paulo FC	URU	54
CICINHO	São Paulo FC	BRA	37
ROGERIO Ceni	São Paulo FC	BRA	31
PALACIO Rodrigo	Boca Juniors	ARG	36
GAGO Fernando	Boca Juniors	ARG	25
GUSTAVO NERY	Corinthians	BRA	25
GAMARRA Carlos	Palmeiras	PAR	22
BILOS Daniel	Boca Juniors	ARG	21
MASCHERANO Javier	Corinthians	ARG	21

COPA TOYOTA LIBERTADORES 2006

COPA TOYOTA LIBERTADORES 2006

Preliminary Round

| Chivas Guadalajara | MEX | 3 | 5 |
| Colo Colo * | CHI | 1 | 3 |

| Independiente Santa Fe | COL | 2 | 0 |
| Defensor Sporting * | URU | 2 | 0 |

| Goiás EC | BRA | 1 | 3 |
| Deportivo Cuenca * | ECU | 1 | 0 |

| Universitario | PER | 2 | 0 |
| Nacional Asunción * | PAR | 2 | 0 |

| Palmeiras * | BRA | 2 | 4 |
| Deportivo Táchira | VEN | 0 | 2 |

| River Plate * | ARG | 6 | 2 |
| Oriente Petrolero | BOL | 0 | 0 |

* Home team in the first leg

Group Stage

Grupo 1

		Pts	BRA	MEX	VEN	PER
São Paulo FC	BRA	12		1-2	2-0	4-1
Chivas Guadalajara	MEX	12	2-1		1-1	0-0
Caracas FC	VEN	5	1-2	0-0		4-0
Cienciano	PER	4	0-2	0-1	2-1	

Grupo 2

		Pts	COL	ARG	PER	BOL
Independiente Santa Fe	COL	10		3-1	2-1	2-2
Estudiantes LP	ARG	10	1-0		4-3	2-1
Sporting Cristal	PER	7	1-2	2-2		2-1
Bolívar	BOL	7	1-0	1-0	1-2	

Grupo 3

		Pts	BRA	ARG	CHI	BOL
Goiás EC	BRA	11		3-0	0-0	2-0
Newell's Old Boys	ARG	8	0-0		2-0	2-0
Unión Española	CHI	8	0-2	1-1		1-0
The Strongest	BOL	6	1-0	3-2	0-1	

Grupo 4

		Pts	BRA	MEX	CHI	COL
Corinthians	BRA	13		1-0	2-2	3-0
Tigres UNAL	MEX	10	2-0		1-0	5-4
Universidad Católica	CHI	10	2-3	3-2		2-1
Deportivo Cali	COL	1	0-1	2-2	2-3	

Grupo 5

		Pts	ARG	ECU	URU	PER
Vélez Sarsfield	ARG	16		2-2	3-0	4-3
LDU Quito	ECU	10	1-3		5-0	4-0
Rocha	URU	5	0-5	3-2		0-0
Universitario	PER	2	0-1	1-2	1-1	

Grupo 6

		Pts	BRA	URU	VEN	MEX
Internacional	BRA	14		3-0	4-0	3-2
Nacional Montevideo	URU	9	0-0		0-0	2-0
Union At. Maracaibo	VEN	8	1-1	2-3		3-0
Pumas UNAM	MEX	1	1-2	1-1	0-1	

Grupo 7

		Pts	COL	BRA	PAR	ARG
Atlético Nacional	COL	10		1-2	2-2	1-0
Palmeiras	BRA	9	3-2		2-3	0-0
Cerro Porteño	PAR	8	1-5	0-0		1-3
Rosario Central	ARG	5	1-2	2-2	0-2	

Grupo 8

		Pts	PAR	ARG	ECU	BRA
Libertad	PAR	11		2-0	4-1	1-0
River Plate	ARG	9	1-0		4-3	4-1
El Nacional	ECU	6	1-1	2-0		1-1
Paulista	BRA	6	0-0	2-1	0-0	

COPA TOYOTA LIBERTADORES 2006

2nd Round			Quarter-finals			Semi-finals			Final		
Internacional	2	0									
Nacional *	1	0									
			Internacional	1	2						
			LDU Quito *	2	0						
Atlético Nacional *	0	0									
LDU Quito	4	1									
						Internacional	0	2			
						Libertad *	0	0			
River Plate *	3	3									
Corinthians	2	1									
			River Plate *	2	1						
			Libertad	2	3						
Tigres UANL *	0 0 3p										
Libertad	0 0 5p										
									Internacional	2	2
									São Paulo FC *	1	2
Chivas Guadalajara*	3	1									
Indep. Santa Fe	0	3									
			Chivas Guadalajara*	0	2						
			Vélez Sarsfield	0	1						
Newell's Old Boys *	2	2									
Vélez Sarsfield	4	2									
						Chivas Guadalajara*	0	0			
						São Paulo FC	1	3			
Estudiantes LP *	2	1									
Goiás EC	0	3									
			Estudiantes LP *	1 0 3p							
			São Paulo FC	0 1 4p							
Palmeiras *	1	1									
São Paulo FC	1	2									

* Home team in the first leg

PRELIMINARY ROUND

1st Leg. Monumental, Santiago
24-01-2006, Silvera URU

Colo Colo   **1**
Fernández.M [49]

Bravo.C - Villarroel Meneses 71), Henríquez, Riffo*, González.A*, Sanhueza, Jerez, Fernández.M, Valdivia, Suazo (Leal* 84), Mancilla (Fierro 58). Tr: Borghi

Chivas Guadalajara   **3**
Bravo.O 2 [35] [52], Morales [46p]

Sánchez.O* - Rodríguez.F, Reynoso, Salcido, Martínez.D* (Barrera 55), Sol, Pineda*, Morales, Santana (Vela 83), Bravo.O* (Borboa 75), Medina. Tr: Westerhoff.H

2nd Leg. Jalisco, Guadalajara
31-01-2006, Brand VEN

Chivas Guadalajara   **5**
Medina 2 [24] [78], Santana [34], Rodríguez [36], Bautista [81]

Sánchez.O - Rodríguez.F, Reynoso (García 64), Salcido, Martínez.D (Barrera 72), Sol, Pineda***71, Morales, Santana (Bautista* 54), Bravo.O, Medina. Tr: Westerhoff.H

Colo Colo   **3**
Suazo 3 [39] [67] [76]

Bravo.C - González.A, Ayala*, Henríquez, Mena (Aceval 68), Sanhueza, Jerez, Fernández.M (Meneses* 86), Valdivia*, Suazo, Mancilla (Fierro 45). Tr: Borghi

---

1st Leg. Parque Central, Montevideo
27-01-2006, Lopes BRA

Defensor Sporting   **2**
Olivera [86], Itthurralde [90]

Castillo - Itthurralde, Semperena, Martínez.W, Pereira, González.A, Díaz, Fajardo (Difiori 45), Olivera, Vila (Navarro 68), Peinado (Cuello 45). Tr: Da Silva

Independiente Santa Fé   **2**
Olveira [35], Preciado [81]

Martínez.L - Pachón*, Nájera, Olveira, Delgado, Gómez.G*, Ramírez.J*, Ortiz, Gamarra (Montoya 65), Preciado (Suárez.J 87), Armani (Yanes 77). Tr: González.G

2nd Leg. El Campín, Bogotá
2-02-2006, Reinoso ECU

Independiente Santa Fé   **0**

Martínez.L - Pachón*, Nájera, Olveira, Delgado, Gómez.G*, Ramírez.J (Suárez.J 11), Ortiz, Gamarra (Yanes* 61), Preciado*, Armani (Montoya 65). Tr: González.G

Defensor Sporting   **0**

Castillo* - Itthurralde*67, Esmerode*, Lamas, González.A, Díaz.C (Difiori 66), Pereira* (De Souza* 86), Ferreira, Cuello*, Olivera (Peinado 61), Fajardo*. Tr: Da Silva

---

1st Leg. Alejandro Serrano Aguilar, Cuenca
26-01-2006, Rivera PER

Deportivo Cuenca   **1**
Matamoros [57]

Klimowicz - Gámez, Fleitas, Parra, Bohorquez, Mina* (Alvarado 83), Gutiérrez.C*, Matamoros*, Guerra, Quiñónez, Calderón (España 34). Tr: Barragán

Goiás EC   **1**
Rogério Corrêa [14]

Harlei - Leonardo*, Cléber*, Jadilson, Rogério Corrêa, Fabiano, Júlio Santos*, Cléber Gaúcho (Vitor 87), Jefferson Feijão (Romerito 71), Nonato (Welliton 78), Danilo Portugal*. Tr: Geninho

---

2nd Leg. Serra Dourada, Goiania
1-02-2006, Vázquez URU

Goiás EC   **3**
Jadilson [29], Romerito 2 [75] [81p]

Harlei - Leonardo*, Cléber (Vitor 84), Jadilson, Rogério Corrêa, Fabiano*, Júlio Santos*, Juliano* (Jardel 89), Romerito, Nonato (Welliton 69), Danilo Portugal. Tr: Geninho

Deportivo Cuenca   **0**

Klimowicz - Gámez*, Fleitas, Parra***78, Bohorquez, Mina, Gutiérrez.C, Matamoros (Hurtado* 79), Alvarado (España 45), Guerra, Quiñónez (Romero 82). Tr: Barragán

---

1st Leg. Defensores del Chaco, Asunción
24-01-2006, Pezzotta ARG

Nacional   **2**
Centurión OG [62], Moisela OG [66]

Cárdenas* - Irrazabal, Martínez.A (Escobar.P 87), Meza, Ramos, Martins*, Barreto*, Arriola, Monges* (Cantero 77), González.C (Bogado.C 61), Cardozo

Universitario   **2**
Moisela [64], Sangoy [93+]

Flores - Herrera*, Guadalupe*, Centurión, Moisela*, Pereda (Maldonaldo 75), Bernales, Hernández, Alonso (Mendoza 75), Alva, Rosell (Sangoy 46). Tr: Sánchez.J

2nd Leg. Monumental, Lima
31-01-2006, López COL

Universitario   **0**

Flores - Guadelupe, Centurión, Moisela, Herrera***38, Pereda (Ruiz 53), Bernales (Mendoza 46), Alonso*, Hernández, Alva*, Sangoy (Rosell* 73). Tr: Sánchez.J

Nacional   **0**

Cárdenas*92+ - Irrazabal, Martínez.A, Escobar.P, Barreto, Martins, Monges (Bogado.C 53), Ramos* (Bogado.A 73), González.C*, Cardozo, Arriola* (Escobar.F 77)

1st Leg. Palestra Itália, São Paulo
25-01-2006, Grance PAR

Palmeiras   **2**
Marcinho [19], Gamarra [49]

Marcos - Paulo Baier, Daniel, Gamarra, Lúcio, Marcinho Guerreiro*, Edmundo (Reinaldo* 45), Correa (Gioino 45), Ricardinho (Cristian 67), Marcinho, Washington. Tr: Leão

Deportivo Táchira   **0**

Morales* - Boada, Perozo, Lancken (Valbuena* 35) (Hernández.E 62), Cuevas, Villafráz, Ospina, González.J (Campos 87), Chacón*, Rondón, García.J. Tr: Plasencia

---

2nd Leg. Olímpico, San Cristóbal
1-02-2006, Ruiz COL

Deportivo Táchira   **2**
García.J [69], González.J [73]

Morales - Chacón, Boada, Perozo*, Cuevas* (Hernández.E 74), Villafráz (Márquez* 64), Ospina, Fernández.M, González.J, García.J, Rondón. Tr: Plasencia

Palmeiras   **4**
Washington 2 [13] [45], Edmundo [60], Marcinho [73]

Marcos - Paulo Baier* (Alceu 60), Daniel*, Gamarra, Lúcio, Marcinho Guerreiro, Edmundo, Correa, Ricardinho (Cristian 70), Marcinho (Leonardo Silva 77), Washington*. Tr: Leão

---

2nd Leg. Ramón Aguilera, Santa Cruz
2-02-2006, Fagundes BRA

Oriente Petrolero   **0**

Galarza - Hoyos, Espínola, Vaca, Gutiérrez* (Méndez.L* 46), Campos (Durán 78), Uriona*, Maurício, Arce, Astudillo (Pérez.U 82), Palavicini. Tr: Antelo

River Plate   **2**
Toja [15], Vaca OG [23]

Carrizo - Alvarez, Talamonti, Gerlo, Domínguez**52, Barrado, San Martín*, Toja, Gallardo (Pusineri* 64), Figueroa (Aban 83), Oberman (Mareque 56). Tr: Passarella

---

1st Leg. Monumental, Buenos Aires
26-01-2006, Selman CHI

River Plate   **6**
Santana [20], Montenegro [37], Gallardo [39p] [57p], Farías [34], San Martín [46]

Carrizo - Ferrari, Cáceres, Gerlo, Mareque, Santana, Ahumada, Patiño, Gallardo, Montenegro, Farías. Tr: Passarella

Oriente Petrolero   **0**

Galarza - Hoyos, Vaca*, Espínola, Gutiérrez*, Pizarro*, Durán, Melgar, Agoglia*, Pérez.U, Arce. Tr: Amodeo

GRUPO 1

		Pl	W	D	L	F	A	Pts	BRA	MEX	VEN	PER
São Paulo FC	BRA	6	4	0	2	12	6	12		1-2	2-0	4-1
Chivas Guadalajara	MEX	6	3	3	0	6	3	12	2-1		1-1	0-0
Caracas FC	VEN	6	1	2	3	7	7	5	1-2	0-0		4-0
Cienciano	PER	6	1	1	4	3	12	4	0-2	0-1	2-1	

GROUP 1 MATCHDAY 1
Inca Garcilaso de la Vega, Cusco
8-02-2006, 21:30, Carpio ECU

Cienciano	0

Ibáñez - Portilla, Butrón, Villalta, Huertas, De la Haza, Ferrari, García.J (Ramírez.L 74), Salas (Torres 74), Mostto, Silva• (Ross 66). Tr: Valencia

Chivas Guadalajara	1
	Morales [91+]

Sánchez.O - Rodríguez.F, Reynoso, Salcido•, Martínez.D, Sol, Morales.R•, Santana•, Bautista (Borboa 82), Medina (Vela 80), Bravo. Tr: Westerhoff

---

GROUP 1 MATCHDAY 1
Brígido Iriarte, Caracas
1-03-2006, 21:00, 2 450, Duarte COL

Caracas FC	1
	Rey [72p]

Toyo - Olivares (Casanova 65), Vizcarrondo, Rey•, Rouga, Vera•, Jiménez.E, Rojas.J (Depablos 72), González.C, Guerra, Carpintero (Serna 69). Tr: Sanvicente

São Paulo FC	2
	Danilo [35], Aloísio [62]

Bosco• - André Dias•, Edcarlos, Júnior, Mineiro, Josué, Danilo (Ramalho 91), Alex Dias (Thiago 57), Aloísio, Souza, Alex. Tr: Ramalho

---

GROUP 1 MATCHDAY 2
Jalisco, Guadalajara
7-03-2006, 20:15, 13 072, Rivera PER

Chivas Guadalajara	1
	Santana [57]

Sánchez.O - Rodríguez.F, Reynoso, Salcido, Martínez.D, Sol•, Pineda• (Medina• 46), Morales.R, Bautista (Borboa• 46), Santana (García.J 66), Bravo. Tr: Westerhoff

Caracas FC	1
	Carpintero [75]

Toyo - Olivares (Casanova 73), Vizcarrondo, Rey, Rouga, Vera, Jiménez.E (Serna 61), Rojas.J, González.C• (Depablos 75), Guerra•, Carpintero. Tr: Sanvicente

---

GROUP 1 MATCHDAY 2
Morumbí, São Paulo
8-03-2006, 21:45, Vázquez URU

São Paulo FC	4
	Fabão [2], Alex Dias [20], Thiago [66], Souza [77]

Rogério Ceni - Fabão• (Edcarlos 34), Lugano, André Dias, Souza•, Mineiro, Josué•, Danilo, Júnior (Richarylson 68), Alex Dias (Thiago 64), Aloísio. Tr: Ramalho

Cienciano	1
	Silva [30]

Ibáñez - Huertas (Butrón• 45), Lugo, Villalta, Guizasola, Ferrari, Bazalar, De la Haza• (Mostto 62), García.J, Salas (Torres 74), Silva. Tr: Valencia

---

GROUP 1 MATCHDAY 3
Inca Garcilaso de la Vega, Cusco
14-03-2006, 21:30, Gamboa BOL

Cienciano	2
	García [11], Silva [74]

Ibáñez - Huertas, Lugo•, Villalta, Portilla, Ferrari•, Bazalar (Ramírez.L 72), De la Haza (Mostto 46), García.J, Salas (Torres 59), Silva. Tr: Valencia

Caracas FC	1
	Serna [53]

Toyo - Olivares• (Serna• 46), Vizcarrondo, Rey•, Rouga, Vera•, Jiménez.E (Varga 82), Rojas.J, González.C (Casanova• 71), Guerra•, Carpintero. Tr: Sanvicente

---

GROUP 1 MATCHDAY 3
Jalisco, Guadalajara
21-03-2006, 20:30, 21 512, Selman CHI

Chivas Guadalajara	2
	Bautista [39], Bravo [68]

Sánchez.O - Rodríguez.F, Reynoso, Salcido, Martínez.D, Sol (Barrera• 22), Bautista (García.J 82), Santana (Medina 63), Bravo•. Tr: De La Torre

São Paulo FC	1
	Danilo [25]

Rogério Ceni - Fabão (Leandro 80), Lugano, André Dias, Souza, Mineiro, Josué, Danilo, Richarylson, Thiago, Aloísio• (Alex Dias 82). Tr: Ramalho

---

GROUP 1 MATCHDAY 4
Brígido Iriarte, Caracas
28-03-2006, 19:00, Duque COL

Caracas FC	4
	Serna [44], Rey [57], Rojas 2 [59 75]

Toyo - Olivares, Vizcarrondo, Rey, Rouga•, Vera•, Jiménez.E, Rojas.J (Pérez.G 85), González.C (Guerra 77), Serna (Depablos 86), Carpintero•. Tr: Sanvicente

Cienciano	0

Ibáñez• - Huertas, Lugo, Villalta•, Portilla•90, Ferrari, Bazalar (Fernández.C• 46), De la Haza, García.J, Mostto, Silva. Tr: Valencia

---

GROUP 1 MATCHDAY 4
Morumbí, São Paulo
5-04-2006, 21:45, 44 648, Giménez ARG

São Paulo FC	1
	Aloísio [30]

Rogério Ceni - Fabão, Edcarlos (Lima 82), Lugano (Richarylson 60), Júnior, Mineiro•, Josué, Leandro, Danilo, Thiago, Aloísio. Tr: Ramalho

Chivas Guadalajara	2
	Santana [44], Martínez [80]

Sánchez.O• - Rodríguez.F•, Reynoso, Salcido•, Martínez.D, Araujo, Pineda•, Morales.R (Medina 69), Bautista (García.J 81), Santana (Barrera 67), Bravo•••72. Tr: De La Torre

---

GROUP 1 MATCHDAY 5
Brígido Iriarte, Caracas
12-04-2006, 18:30, Haro ECU

Caracas FC	0

Toyo - Olivares (Casanova 76), Vizcarrondo, Rey, Rouga, Vera•, Jiménez.E (Guerra 67), Rojas.J, González.C, Serna•, Carpintero (Espinoza 83). Tr: Sanvicente

Chivas Guadalajara	0

Talavera• - Armas, García.J, Reynoso, Barrera (Magallón 71), Martínez.D, Araujo, Vela (Solís 79), Santana, Borboa (Medina 49), Bautista. Tr: De La Torre

---

GROUP 1 MATCHDAY 5
Inca Garcilaso de la Vega, Cusco
12-04-2006, 19:45, Torres PAR

Cienciano	0

Ibáñez - Araujo (Salas 46), Lugo, Villalta, Ferrari•••72, Bazalar, De la Haza, Fernández.C, Torres• (Silva 29), Ross, Mostto (Ccahuantico 74). Tr: Uribe

São Paulo FC	2
	Aloísio [21], Mineiro [42]

Rogério Ceni - Fabão•, André Dias•, Lugano•, Júnior (Richarylson 60), Mineiro, Josué• (Ramalho 77), Souza, Danilo, Thiago, Aloísio (Alex Dias 83). Tr: Ramalho

---

GROUP 1 MATCHDAY 6
Jalisco, Guadalajara
20-04-2006, 20:00, Ortubé BOL

Chivas Guadalajara	0

Talavera - Reynoso, García, Armas, Martínez, Sol (Magallón 67), Araujo, Vela (Solís• 72), Medina, Bautista, Borboa (Santana• 54). Tr: De la Torre

Cienciano	0

Ibáñez - Huertas, Lugo, Villalta, Portilla, Ccahuantico, Ramírez.L (Torres 67), Salas, García.J•, Silva (Mostto 60), Rodríguez.R (Ross 60). Tr: Uribe

---

GROUP 1 MATCHDAY 6
Morumbí, São Paulo
20-04-2006, 22:00

São Paulo FC	2
	Danilo [57], Rogério Ceni [92+p]

Rogério Ceni - André Dias, Fabão (Alex Dias 55), Lugano•, Júnior, Mineiro, Josué, Danilo, Aloísio (Leandro 83), Thiago (Rodrigo Fabri 92+), Souza. Tr: Ramalho

Caracas FC	2

Toyo - Godoy, Bustamente•••50, Vizcarrondo•, Pérez.E, Vera, Depablos, Pérez.G, Casanova (Rouga 54), Vargas (Serna 67), Guerra (Rojas.J 63). Tr: Sanvicente

GRUPO 2

		Pl	W	D	L	F	A	Pts	COL	ARG	PER	BOL
Independiente Santa Fe	COL	6	3	1	2	9	7	10		3-1	2-1	2-2
Estudiantes La Plata	ARG	6	3	1	2	10	10	10	1-0		4-3	2-1
Sporting Cristal	PER	6	2	1	3	11	12	7	1-2	2-2		2-1
Bolívar	BOL	6	2	1	3	7	8	7	1-0	1-0	1-2	

GROUP 2 MATCHDAY 1
Hernando Siles, La Paz
7-02-2006, 19:45, Torres PAR

Bolívar 1
Gutiérrez 83

Zayas - Mores, Sánchez.O, De Souza, Torrico (Balderas 71), Pachi, Angulo, Reyes, Gutiérrez.L, Mercado (Ribeiro 45), Menacho•. Tr: Aragonés

Estudiantes LP 0

Herrera• - Alvarez, Ortiz, Alayes, Núñez•, Gelabert• (Cardozo 78), Huerta, Braña•, Cominges•, Sosa (Carrusca 61), Calderón (Lugüercio 61). Tr: Burruchaga

GROUP 2 MATCHDAY 2
Centenario, Quilmes, Buenos Aires
21-02-2006, 21:15, 16 146, Silvera URU

Estudiantes LP 4
Calderón 2 55p 65, Pavone 79, Lugüercio 90

Herrera - Cáceres, Alayes•, Núñez•, Araujo• (Sosa 46), Carrusca (Lugüercio 66), Cardozo, Esmerado, Galván• (Cominges 46), Calderón, Pavone. Tr: Burruchaga

Sporting Cristal 3
Soto 2 17p 37, Prado 32

Delgado• - Prado•, Araujo, Rodríguez.A, Vílchez, Marczuk, Torres•, Zegarra•, Quinteros• (Casas 90), Soto (Soria 70), Leal (Vassallo 82). Tr: Del Solar

GROUP 2 MATCHDAY 4
Hernando Siles, La Paz
15-03-2006, 20:45, Haro ECU

Bolívar 1
Menacho 58

Zayas - Mores, Sánchez.O, De Souza, Ribeiro, Pachi, Angulo, Reyes, Vaca Diez (Cuéllar 46), Gutiérrez.L•, Menacho (Mercado 74). Tr: Aragonés

Sporting Cristal 2
Leal 20, Quinteros 89

Delgado• - Prado, Vílchez•, Araujo, Rodríguez.A, Marczuk (Chiroque 46) (Colán 68), Torres, Zegarra, Quinteros•, Soto (Casas 84), Leal•. Tr: Del Solar

GROUP 2 MATCHDAY 5
Nacional, Lima
4-04-2006, 21:30, Larrionda URU

Sporting Cristal 2
Soto 20p, Chiroque 75

Delgado - Prado, Vílchez, Araujo, Rodríguez.A•, Torres, Zegarra (Vassallo 57), Quinteros, Soto, Lobatón (Chiroque 67), Leal• (Marczuk 81). Tr: Del Solar

Estudiantes LP 2
Pavone 34, Calderón 88

Herrera - Cáceres•, Alayes, Angeleri (Galván 81), Núñez•, Gelabert (Sosa 82), Cardozo (Lugüercio• 81), Braña, Huerta•, Calderón, Pavone. Tr: Burruchaga

GROUP 2 MATCHDAY 1
Nacional, Lima
9-02-2006, 21:30, Brand VEN

Sporting Cristal 1
Soto 38

Delgado - Prado, Araujo•, Rodríguez.A, Marczuk, Torres (Soria 74), Zegarra, Quinteros, Soto (Lobatón 70), Vassallo, Leal. Tr: Del Solar

Independiente Santa Fe 2
Yanes 62, Montoya 89

Martínez.L - Pachón•, Olveira•, Nájera, Delgado, Gómez.G, Ortiz, Montoya, Gamarra (Suárez.J 41••69), Armani (Yanes 46), Preciado (Cano 76). Tr: González.G

GROUP 2 MATCHDAY 3
Nacional, Lima
8-03-2006, 15:15, Gaciba BRA

Sporting Cristal 2
Vassallo 52, Torres 82

Delgado - Prado, Araujo, Rodríguez.A, Marczuk, Torres•, Zegarra• (Soria 45), Quinteros, Soto (Casas 85), Leal (Lobatón 70), Vassallo. Tr: Del Solar

Bolívar 1
Pachi 79

Zayas - Mores, Sánchez.O (Guatía 72), De Souza, Ribeiro, Almaraz (Camacho 25), Pachi, Justiniano (Cuéllar 69), Reyes, Gutiérrez.L, Menacho. Tr: Aragonés

GROUP 2 MATCHDAY 4
Centenario, Quilmes, Buenos Aires
21-03-2006, 19:00

Estudiantes LP 1
Lugüercio 87

Herrera - Cáceres, Alayes, Angeleri, Basanta (Núñez 65), Sosa (Lugüercio 65), Cardozo (Galván 79), Huerta, Cominges•, Calderón, Pavone. Tr: Burruchaga

Independiente Santa Fe 0

Martínez.L• - Pachón• (Gómez.M 89), Tierradentro (Olveira 56), Fawcett, Nájera, Suárez.J, Gómez.G, Ramírez.J, Largacha• (Hidalgo 65), Montoya, Yanes. Tr: Gareca

GROUP 2 MATCHDAY 6
El Campín, Bogotá
13-04-2006, 17:45, Reinoso ECU

Independiente Santa Fe 2
Suárez 7, Yanes 40

Martínez.L - Tierradentro, Fawcett, Nájera, Suárez.J, Delgado, Gómez.G (Díaz 88), Ramírez.J, Yanes (Largacha 73), Preciado, Montoya (Pachón 80). Tr: Gareca

Sporting Cristal 1
Bonnet 90

Delgado - Prado, Vílchez, Araujo, Rodríguez.A, Torres, Zegarra, Quinteros, Soto (Bonnet 71), Colán (Vassallo 19), Leal. Tr: Del Solar

GROUP 2 MATCHDAY 2
El Campín, Bogotá
15-02-2006, 21:15, Garay PER

Independiente Santa Fe 2
Preciado 53p, Montoya 54

Martínez.L - Pachón, Olveira, Nájera, Delgado•••90, Cano• (Hidalgo 46), Gómez.G, Ortiz•, Montoya, Yanes, Preciado. Tr: González.G

Bolívar 2
Gutiérrz 44, Menacho 47

Zayas - Mores•, Sánchez.O, De Souza, Torrico, Almaraz (Ribeiro 87), Pachi (Vaca Diez 79), Angulo•••88, Reyes, Gutiérrez.L, Menacho• (Cuéllar 84). Tr: Aragonés

GROUP 2 MATCHDAY 3
El Campín, Bogotá
9-03-2006, 18:30, Simon BRA

Independiente Santa Fe 3
Montoya 33, Gómez 66, Yanes 89

Martínez.L - Tierradentro, Fawcett, Nájera, Suárez.J•, Gómez.G, Ramírez.J, Largacha (Hidalgo• 68), Montoya (Díaz 89), Yanes•, Gómez.M (Marín 82). Tr: Gareca

Estudiantes LP 1
Pavone 23

Herrera - Cáceres•, Alayes, Alvarez• (Cominges 74), Núñez, Esmerado•, Carrusca (Sosa 82), Cardozo, Gelabert (Galván 78), Calderón, Pavone. Tr: Burruchaga

GROUP 2 MATCHDAY 5
Hernando Siles, La Paz
28-03-2006, 21:15, 6 993, Souza BRA

Bolívar 1

Zayas• - Mores• (Cuéllar 46), Sánchez.O, De Souza, Ribeiro, Pachi, Angulo•, Reyes, Vaca Diez, Gutiérrez.L, Menacho (Torrico 46) (Camacho 79). Tr: Aragonés

Independiente Santa Fe 0

Martínez.L - Pachón•, Olveira, Fawcett, Nájera, Suárez.J (Díaz 85), Gómez.G•, Gómez.M, Ramírez.J, Largacha (Yanes 65), Hidalgo (Montoya 58). Tr: Gareca

GROUP 2 MATCHDAY 6
Centenario, Quilmes, Buenos Aires
13-04-2006, 19:45, Simon BRA

Estudiantes LP 2
Pavone 2 38 91+

Herrera - Cáceres, Alayes•, Angeleri•, Núñez (Lugüercio 72), Gelabert, Sosa (Galván 68), Braña (Carrusca 63), Huerta, Calderón, Pavone•. Tr: Burruchaga

Bolívar 1
Cuéllar 25

Zayas - Mores, Sánchez.O•, De Souza, Torrico•, Camacho (Ribeiro 90), Angulo•, Reyes•, Cuéllar, Gutiérrez.L (Mercado 65), Menacho (Pachi 68). Tr: Aragonés

GRUPO 3

		Pl	W	D	L	F	A	Pts	BRA	ARG	CHI	BOL
Goiás EC	BRA	6	3	2	1	7	1	11		3-0	0-0	2-0
Newell's Old Boys	ARG	6	2	2	2	7	7	8	0-0		2-0	2-0
Unión Española	CHI	6	2	2	2	3	5	8	0-2	1-1		1-0
The Strongest	BOL	6	2	0	4	4	8	6	1-0	3-2	0-1	

GROUP 3 MATCHDAY 1
Hernando Siles, La Paz
9-02-2006, 18:00, Selman CHI

The Strongest 3
Britos [34], Baldivieso [60], Suárez.R [82]

Caballero - Paz.J, Mena, Rivero, Gutiérrez.R (Jáuregui 84), Britos•, Arévalo•, Coelho, Baldivieso, Paz.L (Fernández.S 87), Cabrera (Suárez.R 58). Tr: Barrientos

Newell's Old Boys 2
Colace [43], Steinert [82]

Villar - Ré•, Spolli•, Rivera, Cejas (Rodas 72), Zapata, Colace, Penta (Lucero 78), Aguirre, Steinert, Borghello (Cereseto 56). Tr: Pumpido

GROUP 3 MATCHDAY 1
Santa Laura, Santiago
14-02-2006, 19:00, Torres PAR

Unión Española 0

Gaona - Miranda, Toro, Acuña.C•, Norambuena, Rojas.F (Vidangossy 73), Reyes.J•, Pereira•, Sierra (Jara.L 46), Tapia.H (Ferrero 57), Neira. Tr: Carvallo

Goiás EC 2
Danilo Portugal [20], Fabiano [85]

Harlei - Vitor, Rogério Corrêa• (Aldo 82), Leonardo, Fabiano (Rafael Dias 90), Júlio Santos•, Jadilson, Danilo Portugal, Juliano• (Nonato• 46), Romerito, Welliton. Tr: Geninho

GROUP 3 MATCHDAY 2
Coloso, Rosario
21-02-2006, 19:00, 21 015, Souza BRA

Newell's Old Boys 2
Scocco 2 [49] [65]

Villar - Ré, Spolli, Gavilán, Husain (Cejas 44), Colace•, Penta (Steinert 46), Aguirre, Belluschi, Ortega.A•, Scocco (Roadas 84). Tr: Pumpido

Unión Española 0

Gaona - Miranda, Toro, Acuña.C (Sierra 60), Vergara•, Rojas.F•, Reyes.J•, Pereira, Jara.L (Ferrero 79), Tapia.H (Vidangossy 79), Neira. Tr: Carvallo

GROUP 3 MATCHDAY 2
Serra Dourada, Goiania
22-02-2006, 19:30, Amarilla PAR

Goiás EC 2
Nonato [16], Romerito [33]

Harlei - Vitor, Rogério Corrêa•, Leonardo•, Fabiano (Cléber Gaúcho 89), Júlio Santos•, Jadilson, Danilo Portugal, Nonato•, Romerito, Welliton. Tr: Geninho

The Strongest 0

Caballero - Paz.J, Mena, Rivero• (Jáuregui 46), Gutiérrez.R•, Zenteno, Arévalo•, Coelho (Fernández.S 71), Baldivieso, Paz.L, Suárez.R (Cabrera 46). Tr: Barrientos

GROUP 3 MATCHDAY 3
Santa Clara, Santiago
28-02-2006, 21:15, Haro ECU

Unión Española 1
Pereira [65]

Bravo - Miranda, Vergara•, Toro, Rojas.F, Reyes.J, Pereira•, Sierra, Jara.L (Arenas 87), Montecinos (Vidangossy 79), Neira. Tr: Carvallo

The Strongest 0

Caballero - Mena•85, Paz.J•, Jáuregui, Gutiérrez.R, Arévalo, Britos• (Suárez.R 75), Coelho, Cabrera (Fernández.S 65), Baldivieso•, Paz.L. Tr: Barrientos

GROUP 3 MATCHDAY 3
Serra Dourada, Goiania
15-03-2006, 19:30, Silvera URU

Goiás EC 3
Welliton 2 [18] [19], Romerito [80p]

Harlei - Rogério Corrêa, Leonardo, Fabiano• (Vampeta 97+), Júlio Santos•, Cléber, Jadilson, Danilo Portugal, Romerito, Souza• (Nonato 74), Welliton (Cléber Gaúcho 95+). Tr: Geninho

Newell's Old Boys 0

Villar - Ré•, Spolli•, Gavilán, Husain• (Colace 45), Aguirre•••78, Belluschi (Peralta 83), Zapata, Lucero (Cejas 45), Ortega.A, Scocco. Tr: Pumpido

GROUP 3 MATCHDAY 4
Coloso, Rosario
22-03-2006, 19:30, Vázquez URU

Newell's Old Boys 2

Villar - Ré, Spolli, Gavilán (Peralta 67), Rivera•, Cejas, Husain (Colace• 67), Belluschi•, Zapata•, Ortega.A (Cereseto 75), Scocco•93+. Tr: Pumpido

Goiás EC 0

Harlei - Rogério Corrêa, Leonardo, Fabiano•, Júlio Santos•, Cléber, Jadilson•, Danilo Portugal•91, Vampeta (Nonato 70), Souza (Aldo 92+•93+), Welliton• (Cléber Gaúcho 70). Tr: Geninho

GROUP 3 MATCHDAY 4
Hernando Siles, La Paz
29-03-2006, 21:00, 6 618, Gaciba BRA

The Strongest 0

Caballero - Paz.J, Jáuregui, Gutiérrez.R (Flores.Z 60), Sánchez.J, Arévalo•, Britos (Cardozo 64), Cristaldo, Cabrera, Baldivieso (Coelho 73), Paz.L. Tr: Luna

Unión Española 1
Tapia [90]

Gaona - Norambuena, Reyes.P, Vergara, Riquelme, Reyes.J•, Pereira (Jara.L 55), Toro, Sierra (Villagra 55), Tapia.H (Ferrero 57), Neira (Vidangossy 64). Tr: Carvallo

GROUP 3 MATCHDAY 5
Hernando Siles, La Paz
5-04-2006, 18:30, 6 533, Rivera PER

The Strongest 1
Gutiérrez.R [72]

Caballero - Coelho, Jáuregui, Mena, Rocabado (Gutiérrez.R 58), Arévalo, Cardozo, Cristaldo•, Flores.Z (Britos 79), Cabrera (Fernández.S 70), Paz.L•. Tr: Luna

Goiás EC 0

Harlei - Vitor, Rogério Corrêa, Leonardo•••82, Fabiano (Rafael Dias• 66), Júlio Santos•, Jadilson•, Cléber Gaúcho•, Nonato•, Vampeta, Welliton. Tr: Geninho

GROUP 3 MATCHDAY 5
Santa Laura, Santiago
11-04-2006, 20:15, 6 980, Amarilla PAR

Unión Española 1
Sierra [25]

Gaona• - Miranda•, Reyes.P, Vergara, Rojas.F, Reyes.J• (Villagra 76), Pereira (Toro 53), Jara.L (Vidangossy 65), Sierra, Tapia.H, Neira. Tr: Carvallo

Newell's Old Boys 1
Steinert [86]

Villar - Ré, Spolli•••28, Gavilán, Formica•, Husain•, Belluschi•, Zapata• (Rodas 77), Peralta, Cejas, Cereseto (Steinert 58). Tr: Pumpido

GROUP 3 MATCHDAY 6
Coloso, Rosario
19-04-2006, 19:30, Torres PAR

Newell's Old Boys 2
Zapata [8], Steinert [52]

Villar - Ré, Gavilán, Aguirre, Husain, Belluschi, Zapata (Colace• 77), Peralta (Lucero 77), Cejas• (Rodas• 64), Ortega.A, Steinert. Tr: Pumpido

The Strongest 0

Caballero - Coelho, Jáuregui, Mena, Rocabado, Gutiérrez.R (Zenteno 24), Arévalo•, Cristaldo•, Flores.Z (Cardozo 71), Cabrera (Cuellar 74), Paz.L. Tr: Luna

GROUP 3 MATCHDAY 6
Serra Dourada, Goiania
19-04-2006, 19:30, Viera URU

Goiás EC 0

Harlei - Leyrielton, Rogério Corrêa, Fabiano•, Júlio Santos, Jadilson, Cléber Gaúcho (Vampeta 80), Danilo Portugal, Romerito (Juliano 46), Souza (Nonato 66), Welliton. Tr: Geninho

Unión Española 0

Gaona - Miranda, Reyes.P, Vergara, Norambuena, Acuña Jara.L 72), Torro, Villagra, Sierra•, Tapia.H (Montecinos 82), Neira. Tr: Carvallo

GRUPO 4

		Pl	W	D	L	F	A	Pts	BRA	MEX	CHI	COL
Corinthians	BRA	6	4	1	1	10	6	13		1-0	2-2	3-0
Tigres UANL	MEX	6	3	1	2	12	10	10	2-0		1-0	5-4
Universidad Católica	CHI	6	3	1	2	12	11	10	2-3	3-2		2-1
Deportivo Cali	COL	6	0	1	5	9	16	1	0-1	2-2	2-3	

GROUP 4 MATCHDAY 1
San Carlos de Apoquindo, Santiago
8-02-2006, 21:15, Oliveira BRA

Universidad Católica 3
Fuenzalida [5], Quinteros 2 [7 68]

Buljubasich - Rubilar, Zenteno, Imboden•, Fuenzalida (Ponce 80), Ormeño, Pérez.E•, Arrué• (Osorio 80), Conca, Rubio (Núñez.L 81), Quinteros.J. Tr: Pellicer

Tigres UANL 2
González.S [1], De Nigris [74]

Rodríguez.R - García.L (Peralta 46), Martínez.E, Santos, Montano, Escudero (Saavedra 46), Veiga, Palacios (Mendoza 75), Morales•, González.S, De Nigris. Tr: España

GROUP 4 MATCHDAY 1
Pascual Guerrero, Cali
15-02-2006, 19:00, Elizondo ARG

Deportivo Cali 0

Ramírez.J - Hurtado•, Rivas•63, Caballero, Benítez, Patiño•, Díaz.O, Domínguez, Ciciliano (Moringo 78), Escobar.H (Carrillo• 61), Pérez.B (Mera 78). Tr: Sarmiento

Corinthians 1
Ricardinho [79]

Marcelo - Dyego Coelho• (Eduardo Ratinho 91+), Betão, Wescley, Gustavo Nery, Marcelo Mattos•, Bruno Octávio, Carlos Alberto• (Rafael Moura• 70), Ricardinho, Tévez, Nilmar (Roger 81). Tr: Lopes

GROUP 4 MATCHDAY 2
Universitario, Monterrey
21-02-2006, 20:30, Gaciba BRA

Tigres UANL 5
De Nigris [20], Santos [39], Morales [49], Gaitán 2 [56 80]

Rodríguez.R - Saavedra, Martínez.E, Santos•, Briseño, Montano, Morales, Veiga• (Palacios 85), Gaitán (Peralta 85), González.S, De Nigris. Tr: Ferretti

Deportivo Cali 4
Domínguez 2 [12 90p], Carrillo 2 [16 41]

Ramírez.J - Hurtado, Caballero, Mera•, Benítez, Patiño (Tapia.A 77), Díaz.O, Domínguez, Ciciliano (Escobar.H 60), Carrillo (López.J• 46), Pérez.B. Tr: Sarmiento

GROUP 4 MATCHDAY 2
Pacaembú, São Paulo
22-02-2006, 21:45, Baldassi ARG

Corinthians 2
Roger [21], Nilmar [61]

Marcelo - Dyego Coelho, Betão•, Wescley, Gustavo Nery•, Marcelo Mattos, Rosnei (Carlos Alberto 59), Ricardinho, Roger• (Rafael Moura 78), Tévez•, Nilmar. Tr: Lopes

Universidad Católica 2
Quinteros 2 [52 63]

Buljubasich - Rubilar, Zenteno (Muñoz 16), Imboden•, Fuenzalida (Osorio 80), Ormeño•, Pérez.E•, Arrué•••87, Conca, Quinteros.J•, Quinteros.L (Núñez.L 72). Tr: Pellicer

GROUP 4 MATCHDAY 3
Universitario, Monterrey
9-03-2006, 20:00, 27 500, Chandia CHI

Tigres UANL 2
Martínez.E [53], Peralta [88]

Hernández.E - Saavedra (García.L 60), Martínez.E, Santos•, Briseño, Montano (Peralta 61), Morales• (Palacios• 82), Veiga, Gaitán, González.S, De Nigris. Tr: Ferretti

Corinthians 1
Herrera - Betão, Marcus Vinícius•, Mascherano, Gustavo Nery, Wendel (Rosnei 59), Marcelo Mattos•51, Ricardinho, Roger (Carlos Alberto 46), Tévez• (Renato 76), Nilmar. Tr: Lopes

GROUP 4 MATCHDAY 3
San Carlos de Apoquindo, Santiago
21-03-2006, 20:15, 11 875, Rivera PER

Universidad Católica 2
Ormeño 2 [25 43]

Buljubasich - Muñoz, Zenteno•, Rubilar, Fuenzalida (Rosende 75), Osorio, Ormeño, Ponce (Núñez.N• 46), Conca, Rubio (Núñez.L 67), Quinteros.J. Tr: Pellicer

Deportivo Cali 1
Valdés [34]

González.D - Hurtado•, Caballero, Mera, Benítez•, Patiño, Valdés, Herrera (Escobar.H 80), Domínguez (Ciciliano 82), Carrillo (Díaz.O 46), Pérez.B. Tr: Sarmiento

GROUP 4 MATCHDAY 4
Pacaembú, São Paulo
22-03-2006, 21:45, Torres PAR

Corinthians 1
Tévez [27]

Marcelo - Dyego Coelho (Eduardo Ratinho 77), Betão, Marcus Vinícius, Gustavo Nery• (Rubens Júnior 84), Rosnei, Mascherano, Xavier•, Ricardinho, Roger• (Renato 66), Tévez. Tr: Lopes

Tigres UANL 0

Hernández.E - Saavedra, García.L (Escudero 58), Martínez.E, Montano, Ramírez.L, Veiga, Palacios (Cerda 58), Mendoza•, Ramírez.C, Silvera•. Tr: Ferretti

GROUP 4 MATCHDAY 4
Pascual Guerrero, Cali
30-03-2006, 21:30, Haro ECU

Deportivo Cali 2
Herrera [14], Pérez.B [81]

González.D - Hurtado•, Caballero, Mera, García.J, Díaz.O•, Valdés (Moríngo 60), Herrera•, Domínguez (Ciciliano 46), Carrillo (Escobar.H 46), Pérez.B•. Tr: Sarmiento

Universidad Católica 3
Quinteros.J [30], Ponce [50], Conca [92+]

Buljubasich - Rubilar•, Zenteno, Imboden, Fuenzalida• (Osorio 58), Ormeño, Arrué (Núñez.N• 76), Ponce, Conca, Rubio• (Núñez.L 79), Quinteros.J•. Tr: Pellicer

GROUP 4 MATCHDAY 5
San Carlos de Apoquindo, Santiago
6-04-2006, 21:30, 17 578, Silvera URU

Universidad Católica 2
Arrué 2 [2 38]

Buljubasich - Rubilar, Zenteno•, Imboden•, Fuenzalida (Osorio 58), Ormeño•, Arrué• (Núñez.N 76), Ponce, Conca, Rubio (Núñez.L• 79), Quinteros.J•. Tr: Pellicer

Corinthians 3
Tévez 23, Nilmar 2 [37 60]

Herrera• - Betão•, Dyego Coelho, Mascherano, Gustavo Nery•73, Wendel•57, Marcelo Mattos, Ricardinho• (Xavier 78), Carlos Alberto (Renato 88), Tévez, Nilmar (Rubens Júnior 75). Tr: Braga

GROUP 4 MATCHDAY 5
Pascual Guerrero, Cali
11-04-2006, 21:30, Paniagua BOL

Deportivo Cali 2
Moríngo [41], Pérez.B [52]

González.D - Herrera, Caballero, Rivas•, Benítez, Patiño, Valdés (De la Cruz 82), Moríngo (Olave 76), Domínguez, Escobar.H (Carrillo 53), Pérez.B. Tr: Sarmiento

Tigres UANL 2
González.S 2 [16 48]

Hernández.E - Saavedra (Ramírez.L 85), Balderos, Santos, Briseño, Veiga, Gaitán, Morales•, Montano (Escudero 46), Peralta, González.S• (De Nigris 87). Tr: Ferretti

GROUP 4 MATCHDAY 6
Universitario, Monterrey
19-04-2006, 19:45, Giménez ARG

Tigres UANL 1
Ramírez.C [91]

Hernández.E - Saavedra, Martínez.E, Santos•, Briseño•••83, Morales (Mendoza.J 67), Montano, Peralta (Veiga• 62), Gaitán, González.S, De Nigris (Ramírez.C 79). Tr: Ferretti

Universidad Católica 0

Buljubasich - Rubilar (Muñoz 61), Zenteno, Imboden, Fuenzalida, Ormeño•, Ponce (Pérez.E 61), Osorio•, Conca, Rubio (Quinteros.L 76), Quinteros.J. Tr: Pellicer

GROUP 4 MATCHDAY 6
Pacaembú, São Paulo
19-04-2006, 21:45, 33 918, Garay PER

Corinthians 2
Marcus Vinícius [6], Tévez [28], Nilmar [81]

Herrera - Dyego Coelho, Betão, Mascherano, Marcelo Mattos• (Xavier 62), Marcus Vinicius, Rubens Júnior, Carlos Alberto, Ricardinho (Roger• 72), Tévez (Renato 82), Nilmar. Tr: Braga

Deportivo Cali 0

González.D - Herrera•, Olave, Caballero•43, Rivas•, Benítez, Patiño, Valdés•, De la Cruz• (Escobar.H 80), Moríngo (Tapia.A 89), Pérez.B (Trujillo 86). Tr: Sarmiento

GRUPO 5

		Pl	W	D	L	F	A	Pts	ARG	ECU	URU	PER
Vélez Sarsfield	ARG	6	5	1	0	18	6	16		2-2	3-0	4-3
Liga Deportiva Universitaria	ECU	6	3	1	2	16	9	10	1-3		5-0	4-0
Rocha	URU	6	1	2	3	4	16	5	0-5	3-2		0-0
Universitario	PER	6	0	2	4	5	12	2	0-1	1-2	1-1	

GROUP 5 MATCHDAY 1
Domingo Miguel, Maldonado
7-02-2006, 19:30, Osses CHI

Rocha   **0**

García.A - González.N (Becerra* 78), Sosa, Bonelli, Ciz, Esquivel (Rodríguez.R 60), González.H, Maguregui, Segales*, Caro (Maldonado 83), Cardoso. Tr: González.L

Universitario   **0**

Flores* - Mendoza.J*, Guadalupe*, Centurión, Moisela, Hernández.LA, Bernales (Ruiz.M 88), Pereda, Alonso (Hernández.L 90), Alva, Sangoy (Rosell 79). Tr: Sánchez.J

GROUP 5 MATCHDAY 1
La Casa Blanca, Quito
7-02-2006, 21:00, Ruiz COL

LDU Quito   **1**
     Urrutia [55]

Mora - Reasco, Espínola, Espinoza, Obregón*, Ambrosi, Urrutia (Cevallos 67), Méndez.E*, Palacios, Delgado, Murillo (Candelario 75). Tr: Oblitas

Vélez Sarsfield   **3**
     Somoza [36], Gracián [65], Zárate.R [84]

Sessa* - Cubero*, Pellerano, Bustamente, Bustos, Somoza, Broggi, Gracián (Sena 75), Castromán (Enría 80), Zárate.R* (Zárate.M 89). Tr: Russo

---

GROUP 5 MATCHDAY 2
José Amalfitani, Buenos Aires
14-02-2006, 21:15, Ortubé BOL

Vélez Sarsfield   **3**
     Centurion [34], Gracián [75], Castromán [83]

Sessa - Cubero, Pellerano, Pellegrino, Broggi, Bustos, Somoza*, Centurion (Sena 79), Gracián (Ocampo 83), Castromán* (Enría 86), Zárate.R. Tr: Russo

Rocha   **0**

García.A - González.N*, Sosa (Maldonado 77), Bonelli, Ciz, Becerra (Delgado* 68), González.H, Maguregui, Segales, Caro (Araujo 68), Cardoso*. Tr: González.L

GROUP 5 MATCHDAY 2
Monumental, Lima
16-02-2006, 21:30, Pozo CHI

Universitario   **1**
     Sangoy [23]

Flores - Mendoza.J (Herrera 72), Guadalupe, Centurión, Moisela*, Hernández.LA (Magallanes 81), Pereda, Alonso, Maldonado* (Mendoza.M 62), Alva*, Sangoy*. Tr: Sánchez.J

LDU Quito   **2**
     Delgado 2 [12 51]

Mora - Reasco, Espínola, Espinoza, Obregón*, Ambrosi, Urrutia, Obregón, Méndez.E*, Palacios, Delgado (Cevallos 92+), Murillo (Vela 73). Tr: Oblitas

---

GROUP 5 MATCHDAY 3
Monumental, Lima
7-03-2006, 19:00, S 204, Souza BRA

Universitario   **0**

Carvallo - Mendoza.J (Pereda 76), Guadalupe, Centurión*, Moisela (Mendoza.M 82), Hernández.LD, Ruiz, Alonso, Cevasco, Alva, Maceratesi (Sangoy 65). Tr: Sánchez.J

Vélez Sarsfield   **1**
     Gracián [71]

Peratta* - Cubero*, Pellerano, Pellegrino (Uglessich* 69), Broggi, Bustos, Somoza, Centurion (Bustamente 41), Gracián, Castromán* (Sena 90), Zárate.R. Tr: Russo

---

GROUP 5 MATCHDAY 3
Domingo Miguel, Maldonado
7-03-2006, 19:45, 1 850, Grance PAR

Rocha   **3**
     Cardoso 2 [7 81], Segales [28]

Lemos - González.N, Sosa, Bonelli*, Ciz*, Becerra* (Maldonado 60), González.H, Esquivel* (Seijas 90), Segales, Caro, Cardoso (Larrosa 82). Tr: González.L

LDU Quito   **2**
     Delgado [16], Urrutia [82]

Mora - Reasco, Espínola, Espinoza, Obregón, Ambrosi, Urrutia*, Obregón (Iza 77), Méndez.E (Cevallos 65), Palacios (Candelario 89), Delgado, Murillo*. Tr: Oblitas

---

GROUP 5 MATCHDAY 4
José Amalfitani, Buenos Aires
14-03-2006, 19:00, Grance PAR

Vélez Sarsfield   **4**
     Bustamente [5], Escudero 2 [42 87], Zárate.M [45]

Peratta - Ladino, Pellerano, Alcaráz, Bustamente (Soto 85), Sena, Somoza, Escudero* (Broggi 88), Ocampo*43, Castromán* (Zárate.R 82), Zárate.M*. Tr: Russo

Universitario   **3**
     Maceratesi [1], Sangoy [7], Centurion [23]

Carvallo - Centurión*, Moisela*, Hernández.LD*, Lozada*, Ruiz, Alonso (Rosell 77), Cevasco (Herrera 46), Alva*, Maceratesi (Mendoza.M 79), Sangoy. Tr: Sánchez.J

GROUP 5 MATCHDAY 4
La Casa Blanca, Quito
16-03-2006, 21:30, Brand VEN

LDU Quito   **5**
     Murillo [13], Urrutia 2 [25 61], Méndez [64]
     Candelario [65]

Mora - Reasco, Espínola, Espinoza*, Ambrosi, Urrutia*, Vera, Méndez.E (Candelario 79), Palacios (Cevallos 86), Delgado, Murillo (Iza 66). Tr: Oblitas

Rocha   **0**

Lemos - González.N*, Sosa, Bonelli (Seijas 60), Ciz (Noguez 24), González.H*, Esquivel, Toscanini* (Araujo 50), Segales, Caro*, Cardoso. Tr: González.L

GROUP 5 MATCHDAY 5
La Casa Blanca, Quito
6-04-2006, 16:00, Duarte COL

LDU Quito   **4**
     Delgado [28], Vera [40], Méndez [51], Guerrón [81]

Mora - Reasco, Espínola*, Espinoza*67, Ambrosi, Urrutia, Vera*, Méndez.E (Candelario 75), Palacios (Campos 69), Delgado, Murillo (Guerrón.JD 62). Tr: Oblitas

Universitario   **0**

Flores - Mendoza.J, Moisela, Hernández.LD, Ruiz*, Pereda (Bernales 75), Alonso (Maldonado 39), Cevasco, Alva*67, Magallanes*, Sangoy*. Tr: Núnes

---

GROUP 5 MATCHDAY 5
Domingo Miguel, Maldonado
11-04-2006, 19:00, Selman CHI

Rocha   **0**

Lemos - González.N*, Sosa, Bonelli*, Ciz (Noguez 70), González.H, Becerra, Maguregui* (Maldonado 49), Segales, Caro, Cardoso (Rodríguez.R 35). Tr: González.L

Vélez Sarsfield   **5**
     Ereros 3 [1 33 71], Zárate.M [9], Bustamente [56]

Sessa - Cubero, Pellerano (Ladino 69), Alcaráz, Bustamente, Sena*, Bustos (Pellegrino 57), Broggi, Centurion (Batalla 66), Ereros*, Zárate.M. Tr: Russo

---

GROUP 5 MATCHDAY 6
Monumental, Lima
18-04-2006, 17:30, Duque COL

Universitario   **5**
     Magallanes [63]

Carvallo - Guadalupe, Centurión, Lozada (Hernández.LD 70), Rivas, Herrera, Bernales, Maldonaldo, Alonso (Magallanes 53), Mendoza.M, Rosell (Sangoy 46). Tr: Núnes

Rocha   **1**
     Cardoso [76]

Magarzo - Sosa, Bonelli, Araujo*, Noguez*, Esquivel, Becerra, Rodríguez.R (Maguregui 65), Caro (Larrosa 81), Toscanini (González.H 65), Cardoso. Tr: González.L

GROUP 5 MATCHDAY 6
José Amalfitani, Buenos Aires
18-04-2006, 19:30, Amarilla PAR

Vélez Sarsfield   **2**
     Ereros [55], Centurion [59p]

Peratta* - Ladino, Pellegrino, Alcaráz, Soto, Sena, Cubero*, Centurion (Escudero 85), Ocampo (Batalla 82), Ereros, Zárate.M. Tr: Russo

LDU Quito   **2**
     Urrutia [30], Palacios [57]

Mora - Reasco*, Espínola, Espinoza, Méndez.JK, Urrutia, Vera*, Méndez.E, Palacios (Guerrón.JD 90), Larrea* (Murillo 46), Delgado. Tr: Oblitas

GRUPO 6

		Pl	W	D	L	F	A	Pts	BRA	URU	VEN	MEX
Internacional	BRA	6	4	2	0	13	4	14		3-0	4-0	3-2
Nacional Montevideo	URU	6	2	3	1	6	6	9	0-0		0-0	2-0
UA Maracaibo	VEN	6	2	2	2	7	8	8	1-1	2-3		3-0
Pumas UNAM	MEX	6	0	1	5	4	12	1	1-2	1-1	0-1	

GROUP 6 MATCHDAY 1
Parque Central, Montevideo
8-02-2006, 20:00, Baldassi ARG

Nacional Montevideo 2
Castro 2 [16] [62p]

Bava - Jaume, Victorino, Paniagua●, Franco (Mansilla 86), Vanzini, Viana, Vázquez, Albín (Britez 81), Márquez, Castro (Garcés 66). Tr: Lasarte

Pumas UNAM 0

Patiño - Verón●●72, Palacios (Leandro Augusto● 62), Salinas, Castro, Moreno, Victorino, Torres● (Iñiguez 45), Pinheiro, Botero (Roma 45), Marioni. Tr: España

GROUP 6 MATCHDAY 1
Pachencho, Maracaibo
16-02-2006, 18:000, Ramos ECU

UA Maracaibo 1
Maldonado [88]

Angelucci - Martínez (Yori 55), Bovaglio, Fuenmayor, Fernández●, González.A, Beraza, García● (Figueroa 75), González.H, Maldonado, Cásseres (Guerra 85). Tr: Maldonado

Internacional 1
Ceará [48]

Clemer - Ceará, Bolívar, Fabiano Eller, Rubens Cardoso●, Edinho, Fabinho●, Tinga (Jorge Wagner 78), Iarley (Perdigão 83), Michel (Adriano 69), Fernandão. Tr: Braga

GROUP 6 MATCHDAY 2
Olímpico Universitario, Mexico City
22-02-2006, 21:00, Lopes BRA

Pumas UNAM 0

Bernal - Moreno, Beltrán, Salinas, López, Galindo, Leandro Augusto, Victorino (Toledo 45), Torres (Roma 45), Iñiguez (Palacios 70), Marioni. Tr: España

UA Maracaibo 1
Castellín [39]

Angelucci - Rodríguez (Yori 73), Bovaglio, Fuenmayor, Fernández, González.A●, Beraza, González.H, Figueroa●, Castellín (Maldonado 71), Cásseres (García 63). Tr: Maldonado

GROUP 6 MATCHDAY 2
Beira-Rio, Porto Alegre
23-02-2006, 19:45, 31 170, Elizondo ARG

Internacional 3
Michel [20], Fernandão [22], Rubens Cardoso [89]

Clemer - Ceará, Bolívar, Fabiano Eller, Rubens Cardoso, Fabinho, Perdigão, Tinga (Adriano● 82), Iarley (Jorge Wagner 84), Michel (Mossoró 70), Fernandão●. Tr: Braga

Nacional Montevideo 0

Bava - Jaume●62, Victorino●, Paniagua, Leites, Vanzini●, Britez, Martínez (Mansilla● 72), Albín (Franco 57), Garcés, Castro. Tr: Lasarte

GROUP 6 MATCHDAY 3
Olímpico Universitario, Mexico City
8-03-2006, 21:00, Selman CHI

Pumas UNAM 1
López [43]

Bernal - Moreno●, Beltrán●, Castro, López●, Galindo, Leandro Augusto (Palacios 72), Victorino●, Torres● (Morales 45), Roma (Botero 77), Marioni. Tr: España

Internacional 2
Rentería [63], Fernandão [80]

Clemer - Ceará, Bolívar, Fabiano Eller, Rubens Cardoso (Jorge Wagner 75), Edinho (Mossoró 62), Fabinho●, Tinga, Iarley, Michel● (Rentería 62), Fernandão. Tr: Braga

GROUP 6 MATCHDAY 3
Parque Central, Montevideo
9-03-2006, 19:15, 11 009, Torres PAR

Nacional Montevideo 0

Bava - Pallas (Leites 57), Victorino, Paniagua, Franco (Juárez 78), Vanzini●, Viana●, Martínez, Albín, Garcés (Márquez 62), Castro. Tr: Lasarte

UA Maracaibo 0

Angelucci - Rodríguez●●●90, González.J●, Bovaglio, Fernández●, González.A●, Beraza, González.H, Figueroa (García 80), Castellín (Maldonado 58), Cásseres. Tr: Maldonado

GROUP 6 MATCHDAY 4
Pachencho, Maracaibo
16-03-2006, 18:00, Baldassi ARG

UA Maracaibo 2
Cásseres [2], Maldonado [91+]

Angelucci - Martínez●, González.J, Bovaglio, Fernández (Suanno 81), González.A, Beraza, González.H, Figueroa (Maldonado 64), Castellín (Guerra 72), Cásseres●. Tr: Maldonado

Nacional Montevideo 3
Vázquez [57], Castro [67], Albín [87]

Bava - Jaume, Victorino, Paniagua (Márquez 38), Leites, Vanzini (Britez 84), Viana, Vázquez, Martínez (Albín● 46), Garcés●36, Castro. Tr: Lasarte

GROUP 6 MATCHDAY 4
Beira-Rio, Porto Alegre
22-03-2006, 21:45, 37 593, Pezzotta ARG

Internacional 3
Michel [37], Fernandão [52], Adriano [76]

Clemer - Ceará, Bolívar, Fabiano Eller, Rubens Cardoso●, Fabinho●, Perdigão● (Mossoró 46), Tinga, Iarley (Rentería 46), Michel (Adriano 67), Fernandão●. Tr: Braga

Pumas UNAM 2
Galindo [4], Botero [35]

Bernal - Moreno, Salinas, Castro●85, Morales (Velarde 82), Galindo●, Espinosa, Palacios●, Roma (Hernández 69), Botero (Rosas 72), Marioni. Tr: España

GROUP 6 MATCHDAY 5
Pachencho, Maracaibo
30-03-2006, 18:00, 28 515, Duarte COL

UA Maracaibo 3
Cásseres [50], Maldonado [77], Castellín [90]

Angelucci - Yori●, Fuenmayor, Martínez, Bovaglio●, Fernández●, González.A, Beraza, Figueroa (Suanno 90), Maldonado (Castellín 78), Cásseres (González.H 81). Tr: Maldonado

Pumas UNAM 0

Bernal - Beltrán, Verón, Morales (Pinheiro 68), Galindo●, Victorino, Palacios●, López (Marioni 65), Roma, Hernández, Botero (Leandro Augusto 46). Tr: España

GROUP 6 MATCHDAY 5
Parque Central, Montevideo
4-04-2006, 19:00, 7 525, Amarilla PAR

Nacional Montevideo 0

Bava - Jaume, Victorino●, Leites, Vanzini, Viana, Vázquez, Márquez● (Martínez● 75), Castro, Juárez● (Suárez 65), Delgado● (Albín 56). Tr: Lasarte

Internacional 0

Clemer - Ceará, Bolívar, Fabiano Eller●, Rubens Cardoso, Fabinho●, Tinga●, Iarley (Rafael Sóbis 75), Rentería (Jorge Wagner 75), Michel (Mossoró 46), Adriano●. Tr: Braga

GROUP 6 MATCHDAY 6
Olímpico Universitario, Mexico City
18-04-2006, 20:00, Elizondo ARG

Pumas UNAM 1
Leites OG [66]

Bernal - Beltrán●, Verón●●●54, Victorino (Toledo 60), Palacios, López● (Velarde (Morales● 60), Castro, Leandro Augusto, Iñiguez (Hernández 80), Marioni. Tr: España

Nacional Montevideo 1
Martínez [79]

Bava - Jaume●, Victorino, Leites, Vanzini, Viana●, Vázquez, Delgado (Martínez 74), Albín (Britez 45), Márquez, Castro (Mansilla 88). Tr: Lasarte

GROUP 6 MATCHDAY 6
Beira-Rio, Porto Alegre
18-04-2006, 22:00, 17 001, Chandía CHI

Internacional 4
Adriano [35], Bolívar [77], Michel [82], Rentería [85]

Clemer - Eldel Granja, Bolívar, Fabiano Eller, Tinga (Iarley 37), Perdigão, Fernandão, Rafael Sóbis (Rentería 76), Edinho, Jorge Wagner, Adriano● (Michel 78). Tr: Braga

UA Maracaibo 0

Angelucci - Yori, Fuenmayor, Martínez●, Bovaglio, Fernández●, González.A●●●90, Beraza, Figueroa (González.H 61), Castellín (Maldonado 57), Cásseres (García 80). Tr: Maldonado

GRUPO 7

		Pl	W	D	L	F	A	Pts	COL	BRA	PAR	ARG
Atlético Nacional Medellín	COL	6	3	1	2	13	9	10		1-2	2-2	1-0
Palmeiras	BRA	6	2	3	1	9	8	9	3-2		2-3	0-0
Cerro Porteño	PAR	6	2	2	2	9	12	8	1-5	0-0		1-3
Rosario Central	ARG	6	1	2	3	6	8	5	1-2	2-2	0-2	

GROUP 7 MATCHDAY 1
Atanasio Girardot, Medellín
9-02-2006, 19:15, Souza BRA

Atlético Nacional	1
	Díaz [14]

Saldarriaga - Mendoza, Vera, Marín (Bedoya 82), Díaz (Mosquera 21), Chará, Amaya•, Casañas•, Morales, Aristizábal, Rambal (Hurtado• 54). Tr: Escobar.S

Rosario Central	0

Ojeda - Loeschbor, Moreira, Villagra, Calgaro (Di María 70), Raldes, Díaz••••84, Coudet•, Castillo, Vitti (Rubén 60), Eluchans (Encina 61). Tr: Zof

GROUP 7 MATCHDAY 1
La Olla, Asunción
15-02-2006, 18:45, Vázquez URU

Cerro Porteño	0

Barreto - Pérez.F, Benítez.P, González.E•, Grana•, Avalos (Da Silva 65), Cristaldo•, Fretes, Achucarro, Genes (Giménez 46), Devaca. Tr: Costas

Palmeiras	1

Sérgio - Paulo Baier, Daniel (Leonardo Silva 14), Gamarra, Marcinho Guerreiro•, Lúcio•, Edmundo, Correa•, Enílton (Washington 67), Marcinho•, Valdomiro (Ricardinho• 46). Tr: Emerson Leão

GROUP 7 MATCHDAY 2
Gigante, Rosario
23-02-2006, 22:00, 19 503, Fagundes BRA

Rosario Central	0

Alvarez - Fassi, Rivarola, Grabowski, Borzani, Raldes, Alemanno (Zelaya 65), Coudet, Rubén, Vitti (Vecchio 56), Moreira (Calgaro 46). Tr: Zof

Cerro Porteño	2
	Avalos [46], Borzani OG [56]

Barreto - Pérez.F, Benítez.P, González.E•, Grana•, Avalos (Da Silva 65), Cristaldo•, Fretes, Achucarro, Genes (Giménez 46), Devaca. Tr: Costas

GROUP 7 MATCHDAY 2
Parque Antarctica, São Paulo
2-03-2006, 21:15, Larrionda URU

Palmeiras	3
	Marcinho [18], Edmundo [35p], Douglas [71]

Sérgio - Paulo Baier, Leonardo Silva•, Douglas (Valdomiro 75), Marcinho Guerreiro, Márcio Careca, Edmundo•, Correa, Enílton (Washington 32), Marcinho, Ricardinho (Alceu 85). Tr: Emerson Leão

Atlético Nacional	2
	Marcelo Ramos [31], Aristizábal [73]

Saldarriaga - Mendoza•, Passo•••89, Marín, Díaz•, Chará, Amaya, Ramírez (Hurtado 80), Casañas (Marrugo 80), Marcelo Ramos, Aristizábal. Tr: Escobar.S

GROUP 7 MATCHDAY 3
La Olla, Asunción
14-03-2006, 20:15, Giménez ARG

Cerro Porteño	1
	Fretes [39]

Navarro - Benítez.P, González.E (Escobar 58), Grana•, Avalos, Cristaldo (Giménez 31) (Cardozo 72), Fretes•, Achucarro•, Devaca•, Báez•75, Salcedo. Tr: Costas

Atlético Nacional	5
	Marín 2 [18 74], Galván [26], Aristizábal 2 [27 45]

Castillo - Soto, Díaz, Vera, Marín, Bedoya•64, Chará, Amaya, Ramírez•56, Galván (Mosquera 71), Aristizábal• (Marcelo Ramos 62). Tr: Navarrete

GROUP 7 MATCHDAY 3
Parque Antarctica, São Paulo
15-03-2006, 21:45, Torres PAR

Palmeiras	0

Sérgio - Paulo Baier (Ricardinho 46), Daniel, Douglas (Alceu• 46), Gamarra, Marcinho Guerreiro•, Lúcio, Edmundo•, Correa, Marcinho, Enílton (Washington 55). Tr: Emerson Leão

Rosario Central	0

Castellano• - Moreira•, Raldes•, Fassi•, Villagra, Encina• (Coudet 75), Ledesma• (Grabowski 79), Borzani•, Rubén•, Vitti (Zelaya 69), Eluchans. Tr: Astrada

GROUP 7 MATCHDAY 4
Gigante, Rosario
23-03-2006, 21:15, Silvera URU

Rosario Central	2
	Rubén [6], Ledesma [89]

Castellano - Fassi, Rivarola•, Villagra (Moreira 63), Borzani•, Raldes, Ledesma, Coudet (Di María 75), Rubén•, Vitti, Eluchans (Encina 67). Tr: Astrada

Palmeiras	2
	Washington 2 [18 88]

Sérgio - Paulo Baier• (Alceu• 76), Daniel•, Gamarra, Marcinho Guerreiro, Lúcio, Edmundo• (Enílton 64), Marcinho•, Correa, Washington, Leonardo Silva•. Tr: Emerson Leão

GROUP 7 MATCHDAY 4
Atanasio Girardot, Medellín
23-03-2006, 21:30, Reinoso ECU

Atlético Nacional	2
	Marcelo Ramos [75], Marín [90]

Castillo - Soto (Rambal 66), Passo, Vera (Mosquera• 37), Mendoza, Marrugo, Marín, Chará, Hurtado (Marcelo Ramos 56), Galván, Aristizábal•. Tr: Navarrete

Cerro Porteño	2
	Salcedo [29], Avalos [78]

Barreto - Pérez.F•, Benítez.P, González.E•, Grana, Avalos (Ovelar 83), Cristaldo, Fretes• (Irala 68), Achucarro (Giménez 64), Devaca•, Salcedo. Tr: Costas

GROUP 7 MATCHDAY 5
Atanasio Girardot, Medellín
4-04-2006, 19:15, Chandia CHI

Atlético Nacional	1
	Díaz [93+]

Castillo - Soto (Rambal 85), Díaz, Bedoya, Mendoza, Amaya, Marrugo (Chará 51), Marín (Marcelo Ramos 75), Ramírez, Galván, Aristizábal•. Tr: Navarrete

Palmeiras	2
	Correa [13], Leonardo Silva [24]

Sérgio - Paulo Baier, Amaral, Daniel•, Gamarra, Marcinho Guerreiro, Lúcio, Marcinho (Enílton 86), Correa•, Washington, Leonardo Silva•. Tr: Emerson Leão

GROUP 7 MATCHDAY 5
Defensores del Chaco, Asunción
6-04-2006, 19:15, Selman CHI

Cerro Porteño	1
	Salcedo [49]

Barreto - Pérez.F, Benítez.P (Achucarro 68), González.E•, Grana, Avalos, Giménez•, Fretes (Escobar 36), Devaca, Báez, Salcedo. Tr: Costas

Rosario Central	3
	Rubén 2 [43 72], Encina [75]

Alvarez - Loeschbor, Raldes, Moreira, Villagra, Encina (Borzani 75), Ledesma•, Vecchio (Díaz 60), Rubén•, Vitti•, Eluchans (Di María 69). Tr: Astrada

GROUP 7 MATCHDAY 6
Gigante, Rosario
13-04-2006, 22:00, 23 289, Larrionda URU

Rosario Central	1
	Villagra [75]

Alvarez - Fassi, Rivarola (Villagra• 44), Raldes•77, Moreira, Borzani, Encina, Coudet (Vecchio 54), Rubén, Vitti, Eluchans (Di María 46). Tr: Astrada

Atlético Nacional	2
	Aristizábal [31], Marín [45]

Saldarriaga - Soto•, Díaz, Bedoya, Mendoza, Chará•, Amaya, Marín, Ramírez (Hurtado 87), Galván (Marrugo 87), Aristizábal•77. Tr: Navarrete

GROUP 7 MATCHDAY 6
Parque Antarctica, São Paulo
13-04-2006, 22:00, Ortubé BOL

Palmeiras	2
	Marcinho 2 [70 89]

Sérgio - Paulo Baier•, Douglas•45, Daniel• (Leonardo Silva 37), Marcinho Guerreiro, Lúcio, Marcinho, Correa•, Edmundo (Alceu 46), Washington, Ricardinho (Enílton 60). Tr: Emerson Leão

Cerro Porteño	3
	Salcedo [55], Avalos 2 [61 83]

Barreto - Cardozo, Pérez.F•, González.E• (Ramírez 73), Grana, Avalos (Cabrera 89), Giménez (Achucarro 55), Cristaldo, Devaca, Báez•45, Salcedo•. Tr: Costas

GRUPO 8

		Pl	W	D	L	F	A	Pts	PAR	ARG	ECU	BRA
Libertad	PAR	6	3	2	1	8	4	11		2-0	4-1	1-0
River Plate	ARG	6	3	0	3	11	10	9	2-0		4-3	4-1
El Nacional	ECU	6	1	3	2	8	10	6	1-1	2-0		1-1
Paulista	BRA	6	1	3	2	4	7	6	0-0	2-1	0-0	

GROUP 8 MATCHDAY 1
Olímpico Atahualpa, Quito
14-02-2006, 21:30, Duarte COL

El Nacional 1
Borja [68]

Ibarra - Castro, De Jesús.O, Guagua, Quiroz, Ordóñez (Benítez 46), Borja, Lara, Castillo, Ayoví (Figueroa 46), De Jesús.E. Tr: Almeida

Paulista 1
Abraão [81]

Rafael - Bosco, Dema, Rever (Nivaldo 69), Gleydson, Amaral•, Wilson (Fabio Vidal 46), Jean Carlos (Abraão 66), Muñoz, Lucas, Beto. Tr: Mancini

GROUP 8 MATCHDAY 1
Defensores del Chaco, Asunción
16-02-2006, 21:15, Larrionda URU

Libertad 2
Barone [60], Gamarra [88]

Bobadilla - Balbuena, Sarabia, Barone, Hidalgo, Villarreal (Robles 82), Riveros, Guiñazú, Bonet, Romero (Garnier 75), López (Gamarra 87). Tr: Martino

River Plate 0

Lux - Ferrari•, Cáceres, Talamonti, Alvarez, Pusineri (Patiño 59), Ahumada•, Toja•••76, Gallardo (Aban 61), Montenegro, Farías (Figueroa 77). Tr: Passarella

GROUP 8 MATCHDAY 2
Jayme Pinheiro, Jundiaí
2-03-2006, 19:00, Selman CHI

Paulista 0

Rafael - Bosco•, Dema, Rever•, Fabio Vidal, Gleydson (Jean Carlos 45), Amaral, Sammir, Wilson (Beto 69), Wesley (Abraão 67), Muñoz. Tr: Mancini

Libertad 0

Bobadilla• - Damiani, Balbuena, Sarabia, Martínez.R, Cáceres•, Villarreal, Guiñazú, Bonet (Robles 80), Romero (Garnier 77), López. Tr: Martino

GROUP 8 MATCHDAY 2
Monumental, Buenos Aires
8-03-2006, 19:30, 15 957, Ruiz COL

River Plate 4
Farías [4], Santana [68], Montenegro [79], Gallardo [82]

Lux - Ferrari•, Cáceres, Talamonti (Tula 45), Mareque•, Alvarez, Santana, Ahumada, Gallardo•, Montenegro (Zapata 82), Aban (Oberman 54•••89), Farías. Tr: Passarella

El Nacional 3
Lara [30], Borja 2 [38 50]

Ibarra - Castro•, Calle, De Jesús.O, Guagua•, Cagua• (Ayoví 83), Quiroz, Borja, Lara (Benítez 81), Castillo, Hidalgo•. Tr: Almeida

GROUP 8 MATCHDAY 3
Monumental, Buenos Aires
16-03-2006, 21:15, Chandia CHI

River Plate 4
Santana [10], Montenegro 2 [13 51], Aban [82]

Lux - Ferrari, Cáceres, Tula, Domínguez, Santana, Ahumada (Mareque 87), Zapata (Lima 66), Patiño (Pusineri 46), Montenegro, Aban. Tr: Passarella

Paulista 1
Muñoz [28p]

Rafael - Bosco (Beto 78), Dema•, Rever, Fabio Vidal, Gleydson (Lucas 60), Amaral, Wilson, Abraão•, Muñoz, Jailson (Wesley 66). Tr: Mancini

GROUP 8 MATCHDAY 3
Defensores del Chaco, Asunción
23-03-2006, 18:00, Baldassi ARG

Libertad 4
Martínez.R [5], Riveros [60], Villarreal [69], López [71]

Bobadilla - Damiani• (Balbuena 63), Sarabia, Hidalgo, Martínez.R, Riveros, Villarreal, Guiñazú•, Romero (Garnier 65), López (Gamarra 74), Bonet. Tr: Martino

El Nacional 1
Borja [19]

Ibarra - Castro•, De Jesús.O, Guagua•, Cagua, Quiroz, Borja, Lara (Chalá 64•82), Castillo•, Benítez (Ayoví 73), Hidalgo• (Vera 45). Tr: Almeida

GROUP 8 MATCHDAY 4
Olímpico Atahualpa, Quito
30-03-2006, 19:15, Chandia CHI

El Nacional 1
Borja [11]

Sánchez.R - Castro•, Guagua, Quiroz, Ordóñez (Ayoví 64), Borja, Lara•, Castillo, Benítez, Caicedo (De Jesús.O 46), Quiñónez (De Jesús.E 46). Tr: Almeida

Libertad 1
Martínez [86]

Bobadilla - Balbuena, Sarabia, Hidalgo (Robles 68), Martínez.R, Riveros•, Villarreal (Gamarra 74), Guiñazú, Romero (Martínez.O 54), López, Bonet. Tr: Martino

GROUP 8 MATCHDAY 4
Jayme Pinheiro, Jundiaí
5-04-2006, 19:30, Torres PAR

Paulista 2
Amaral [6], Jailson [17]

Rafael• - Lucas, Dema, Rever•, Beto, Gleydson•, Amaral, Wilson, Muñoz (Bosco 76), Douglas, Jailson (Jean Carlos 72). Tr: Mancini

River Plate 1
Patiño [18]

Lux - Alvarez•, Cáceres, Tula•, Mareque, Pusineri (Zapata 62), Ahumada•, San Martin, Patiño• (Montenegro 73), Oberman, Aban (Farías 62). Tr: Passarella

GROUP 8 MATCHDAY 5
Defensores del Chaco, Asunción
12-04-2006, 18:30, 1 033, Ruiz COL

Libertad 1
Hidalgo [19]

Bobadilla• - Balbuena•, Sarabia, Hidalgo, Martínez.R, Riveros, Villarreal, Guiñazú, Romero (Garnier 60), López (Gamarra 85), Bonet (Robles 91). Tr: Martino

Paulista 0

Rafael - Lucas, Dema•, Rever, Beto (Fabio Vidal 69), Gleydson, Amaral, Wilson, Muñoz (Luiz Henrique 73), Douglas• (Jean Carlos 55), Jailson. Tr: Mancini

GROUP 8 MATCHDAY 5
Olímpico Atahualpa, Quito
12-04-2006, 19:45, Chandia CHI

El Nacional 2
Gerlo OG [11], Quiroz [38p]

Ibarra - Castro, De Jesús.O•, Guagua, Quiroz, Borja, Lara• (Benítez 65), Castillo•, Caicedo, Chalá (Hidalgo 82), Ayoví (Cotera 90). Tr: Almeida

River Plate 0

Lux - Alvarez•, Talamonti, Gerlo, Tula, San Martin, Patiño, Lima, Toja (Santana 63), Oberman, Aban. Tr: Passarella

GROUP 8 MATCHDAY 6
Monumental, Buenos Aires
20-04-2006, 19:45, Simon BRA

River Plate 1
Zapata [68]

Lux - Ferrari•, Cáceres, Gerlo, Mareque, Santana (Oberman 59), Ahumada, Zapata, Patiño (Gallardo 59), Montenegro (Pusineri 87), Farías. Tr: Passarella

Libertad 0

Bobadilla - Balbuena, Sarabia, Damiani, Hidalgo, Riveros, Villarreal, Guiñazú• (Martínez.O 58), Garnier (Robles 75), Gamarra (Romero 70), Bonet. Tr: Martino

GROUP 8 MATCHDAY 6
Jayme Pinheiro, Jundiaí
20-04-2006, 19:45, Selman CHI

Paulista 0

Rafael• - Lucas, Dema, Rever, Beto• (Abraão 74), Gleydson, Amaral, Wilson•, Muñoz (Jean Carlos 60), Fabio Vidal, Jailson (Nivaldo 80). Tr: Mancini

El Nacional 0

Ibarra - Castro, De Jesús.O, Hidalgo• (Figueroa 75), Guagua•, Quiroz, Borja, Lara (Cotera 83), Benítez, Castillo•, Caicedo. Tr: Almeida

ROUND OF SIXTEEN

1st Leg. Parque Central, Montevideo
27-04-2006, 19:00, 10 221, Ruiz COL

Nacional   **1**

Vanzini [29]

Bava* – Jaume*, Victorino, Pallas*, Vanzini, Viana (Martínez.J 62), Vázquez (Suárez.L 72), Brítez, Albín*, Márquez (Juárez 62), Castro. Tr: Lasarte

Internacional   **2**

Jorge Wagner [45], Rentería [64]

Clemer* – Bolívar, Edinho, Fabiano Eller, Eldel Granja, Fabinho, Alex* (Ediglê 80*82), Jorge Wagner, Adriano (Michel 65), Fernandão, Rafael Sóbis (Rentería 45**75). Tr: Braga

2nd Leg. Atanasio Girardot, Medellín
2-05-2006, 18:15, Fagundes BRA

Atlético Nacional   **0**

Ospina - Díaz.C, Mendoza*, Passo* (Echeverry 53), Soto*, Amaya*86, Casañas (Chará 53), Marín***88, Hurtado (Rambal 71), Aristizábal*, Galván. Tr: Navarrete

LDU Quito   **1**

Méndez [40]

Mora - Reasco, Espínola*, Espinoza, Ambrosi, Vera, Obregón*86, Urrutia, Méndez.E (Candelario 79), Palacios (Murillo 71), Delgado (Graziani 84). Tr: Oblitas

1st Leg. Universitario, Monterrey
27-04-2006, 21:30, Larrionda URU

Tigres UANL   **0**

Hernández.E - Saavedra, Martínez.E, Santos, Balderas, Escudero, Montano, Peralta (Gaitán 45), Morales (Palacios* 21), Moreno, López.A (González.S 58). Tr: Ferreti

Libertad   **0**

Bobadilla - Balbuena, Sarabia, Martínez.R*, Hidalgo*, Riveros, Villarreal, Guiñazú* (Robles 83), Lopez.H (Garnier 88), Gamarra (Romero 59), Bonet. Tr: Martino

2nd Leg. El Campín, Bogotá
2-05-2006, 20:45, Selman CHI

Independiente Santa Fe   **3**

Preciado [36], Largacha [50], Montoya [87p]

Martínez.L - Suárez.J, Nájera, Tierradentro, Delgado, Ortiz (Hidalgo 69), Gómez.G, Ramírez.J (Largacha 46), Montoya, Fawcett (Gómez.M 22), Preciado. Tr: Gareca

Chivas Guadalajara   **1**

Reynoso [9]

Sánchez.O - Reynoso, García.J, Armas, Barrera, Martínez.D*, Magallón, Esparza*, Rodríguez (Sol 61), Santana (Vela* 46), Bautista (Borboa 81). Tr: De la Torre

1st Leg. Centenario, Quilmes
25-04-2006, 20:15, 18 776, Chandia CHI

Estudiantes LP   **2**

Galván [80], Calderón [91+p]

Herrera - Angeleri, Alayes, Cáceres, Núñez (Lugüerico 71), Gelabert* (Galván* 75), Braña (Carrusca* 64), Huerta, Sosa, Pavone, Calderón*. Tr: Burruchaga

Goiás EC   **0**

Harlei - Leonardo***89, Júlio Santos*, Rogério Corrêa, Jadílson (Aldo* 89), Fabiano, Cléber, Danilo Portugal*, Vampeta (Cléber Gaúcho 75), Souza*70, Roni (Nonato 77). Tr: Geninho

2nd Leg. Beira-Rio, Porto Alegre
3-05-2006, 21:45, 26 225, Torres PAR

Internacional   **0**

Clemer – Eldel Granja, Bolívar*, Fabiano Eller*, Fabinho, Fernandão, Edinho, Mossoró (Iarley 59), Jorge Wagner, Alex (Perdigão 83), Adriano (Michel 83). Tr: Braga

Nacional   **0**

Bava – Jaume, Victorino, Vázquez, Vanzini, Suárez.L* (Martínez.J 73), Albín, Pallas*, Brítez* (Márquez 79), Castro, Viana*. Tr: Lasarte

2nd Leg. Monumental, Buenos Aires
26-04-2006, 21:45, 38 910, Amarilla PAR

River Plate   **3**

Farías [25], Ferrari [30], Santana [80]

Lux - Gerlo, Cáceres, Talamonti***85, Ferrari*, Santana, Ahumada*, Domínguez*, Gallardo (Patiño 83), Aban (Higuain 77), Farías* (Tula 86). Tr: Passarella

Corinthians   **3**

Tévez [15], Xavier [90]

Silvio Luiz – Dyego Coelho (Roger 88), Betão*, Marcus Vinícius*, Rubens Júnior, Mascherano***66, Marcelo Mattos, Carlos Alberto, Ricardinho (Eduardo Ratinho 86), Tévez, Nilmar (Xavier 68). Tr: Braga

2nd Leg. Defensores del Chaco, Asunción
4-05-2006, 18:15, Elizondo ARG

Libertad   **0 5p**

Bobadilla - Bonet, Sarabia*, Hidalgo, Martínez.R (Damiani 31), Balbuena, Riveros*, Guiñazú* (Martínez.O 74), Villarreal (Robles 65), Gamarra, López.H. Tr: Martino

Tigres UANL   **0 3p**

Hernández.E - Saavedra, Santos, Martínez.E, Balderas, Briseño, Peralta, Veiga (Palacios 81), Montano, Gaitán (González.S 90), Moreno. Tr: Ferreti

2nd Leg. Coloso de Parque, Rosario
27-04-2006, 21:15, 20 640, Elizondo ARG

Newell's Old Boys   **2**

Spolli [32], Scocco [53]

Villar - Gavilán (Cejas 45), Aguirre*, Spolli*, Ré, Belluschi, Husain*, Zapata (Steinert 75), Peralta*, Ortega.A, Scocco*. Tr: Pumpido

Vélez Sarsfield   **4**

Zárate [16], Somoza 2 [51p 66p], Ereros [52]

Sessa - Cubero, Pellegrino, Pellerano, Bustamante*, Bustos*, Somoza, Broggi* (Sena 65), Gracián* (Ocampo 90), Ereros (Fernandes 76), Zárate.M***56. Tr: Russo

1st Leg. La Casa Blanca, Quito
25-04-2006, 20:30, 11 303, Rivera PER

LDU Quito   **4**

Murillo 2 [10 13], Vera [63], Candelario [75]

Mora - Reasco, Espínola, Espinoza, Ambrosi, Vera, Urrutia*, Méndez.E (Guerrón 90), Murillo (Candelario 74), Palacios (Obregón 85), Delgado. Tr: Oblitas

Atlético Nacional   **0**

Saldarriaga - Soto, Díaz.C, Mendoza, Bedoya*, Chará, Amaya, Marín*, Ramírez.A (Marrugo* 10), Marcelo Ramos (Echeverry 50), Galván (Hurtado 78). Tr: Navarrete

1st Leg. Pacaembú, São Paulo
4-05-2006, 21:45, 32 089, Chandia CHI

Corinthians   **1**

Nilmar [39]

Silvio Luiz – Betão, Marcello Mattos, Nilmar, Tévez, Ricardinho, Dyego Coelho (Eduardo Ratinho 78), Carlos Alberto (Rafael Moura 76), Xavier (Roger 65), Marcus Vinícius*, Rubens Júnior. Tr: Braga

River Plate   **1**

Dyego Coelho OG [56], Higuain 2 [71 81]

Lux - Gerlo, Cáceres, Tula, Ferrari, Santana*, Ahumada, Domínguez, Gallardo*, Aban* (Higuain 65), Farías*. Tr: Passarella

1st Leg. Jalisco, Guadalajara
26-04-2006, 21:50, Viera URU

Chivas Guadalajara   **3**

Esparza [45], Borboa [51], Medina [80]

Talavera - Reynoso*, García.J*, Armas (Medina 36), Martínez.D*, Santana, Rodríguez (Sol 73), Bautista, Borboa (Parra 80), Esparza*, Araujo. Tr: De la Torre

Independiente Santa Fe   **0**

Martínez.L - Suárez.J, Tierradentro, Nájera, Fawcett (Delgado 60), Gómez.G (Ortiz 73), Pachón, Ramírez.J, Montoya*, Yanes***58, Preciado (Largacha 65). Tr: Gareca

1st Leg. José Amalfitani, Buenos Aires
3-05-2006, 19:15, 14 270, Giménez ARG

Vélez Sarsfield   **2**

Somoza [76p], Ocampo [92+]

Sessa - Cubero, Pellegrino, Pellerano, Bustamante, Bustos, Somoza, Broggi (Sena 78), Gracián (Ocampo 86), Ereros (Fernandes 70), Castromán*. Tr: Russo

Newell's Old Boys   **2**

Scocco [53], Colace [84]

Villar - Spolli*, Torren*, Ré, Husain***63, Belluschi*, Zapata (Colace 55), Peralta*, Ortega.A* (Rodas 78), Steinert, Scocco. Tr: Pumpido

2nd Leg. Serra Dourada, Goiania
4-05-2006, 19:15, 17 895, Ruiz COL

Goiás EC   **4**

Vítor [51], Nonato [65], Juliano [91]

Harlei - Vítor (Juliano* 75), Rogerio Corrêa*, Fabiano, Júlio Santos*, Jadílson, Danilo Portugal* (Leyrielton 80), Nonato, Roni, Romerito, Welliton. Tr: Geninho

Estudiantes LP   **1**

Calderón [76]

Herrera - Angeleri*, Alayes, Cáceres, Núñez, Braña*, Huerta*, Gelabert* (Cardozo* 73), Sosa (Carrusca 80), Calderón* (Galván 88), Pavone. Tr: Burruchaga

1st Leg. Parque Antarctica, São Paulo
26-04-2006, 19:15, Simon BRA

Palmeiras	1
	Edmundo [36p]

Sérgio - Wendel, Daniel● (Thiago Gomes 26), Gamarra, Márcio Careca (Reinaldo 81), Marcinho Guerreiro, Paulo Baier, Marcinho●, Correa●, Edmundo●, Washington (Juninho Paulista 62). Tr: Vilar

São Paulo FC	1
	Aloisio [23]

Rogério Ceni - André Dias, Fabão●, Lugano, Júnior, Mineiro●, Josué, Danilo●, Aloisio●, Thiago (Leandro 77), Souza. Tr: Ramalho

2nd Leg. Morumbi, São Paulo
3-05-2006, 21:45, 55 080, Souza BRA

São Paulo FC	2
	Aloisio [13], Rogério Ceni [86p]

Rogério Ceni● - André Dias●, Fabão, Lugano●, Júnior (Edcarlos 89), Mineiro, Josué, Leandro●68, Danilo●, Aloisio● (Thiago 76), Souza. Tr: Ramalho

Palmeiras	1
	Washington [58]

Sérgio - Paulo Baier●●92+, Thiago Gomes●●93+, Gamarra, Marcinho Guerreiro●●93+, Lúcio, Edmundo, Correa, Washington●, Marcinho (Cristian 18, Leandro Silva 88), Wendel (Ricardinho 76). Tr: Vilar

QUARTER-FINALS

1st Leg. La Casa Blanca, Quito
10-05-2006, 17:30, 16 016, Elizondo ARG

LDU Quito	2
	Delgado [58], Graziani [84]

Mora – Reasco, Espínola, Espinoza, Ambrosi, Vera, Urrutia (Candelario 81), Méndez, Palacios (Graziani 65), Murillo (Guerrón 72), Delgado. Tr: Oblitas

Internacional	1
	Jorge Wagner [25]

Marcelo – Eldel Granja●, Bolívar, Fabiano Eller, Fabinho, Perdigão● (Ceará 61), Fernandão (Rentería 68), Edinho●, Michel●, Jorge Wagner●, Alex (Rubens Cardoso 74). Tr: Braga

2nd Leg. Beira-Rio, Porto Alegre
19-07-2006, 19:15, 34 664, Larrionda URU

Internacional	2
	Rafael Sóbis [52], Rentería [87]

Clemer – Eldel Granja, Bolívar, Fabiano Eller●, Fabinho, Tinga (Adriano 57), Fernandão, Rafael Sóbis (Rentería 83), Edinho, Jorge Wagner, Alex (Perdigão 89). Tr: Braga

LDU Quito	0

Mora – Reasco, Espínola, Espinoza, Ambrosi, Obregón (Murillo 64), Vera● (Candelario● 83), Urrutia, Méndez (Graziani 86), Palacios, Delgado. Tr: Oblitas

1st Leg. Monumental, Buenos Aires
11-05-2006, 21:15, Simon BRA

River Plate	2
	Montenegro [76], Farías [81]

Lux – Gerlo, Cáceres (Montenegro 74), Talamonti, Ferrari, Santana (Pusineri 45●●●87), Ahumada●, Domínguez (Zapata 62), Gallardo, Higuain, Farías. Tr: Passarella

Libertad	2
	Bonet 2 [38 77]

Bobadilla – Damiani, Sarabia, Balbuena, Hidalgo, Bonet, Villarreal, Riveros●, Guiñazú (Robles● 80), Gamarra (Romero 38) (Garnier 90), López.H. Tr: Martino

2nd Leg. Defensores del Chaco, Asunción
18-07-2006, 20:15, Selman CHI

Libertad	3
	López [16], Aquino [40], Riveros [47]

Bobadilla – Bonet, Sarabia, Balbuena, Hidalgo, Riveros●, Villarreal, Guiñazú, Aquino (Robles 79), López.H, Gamarra (Romero 67). Tr: Martino

River Plate	1
	Farías [76]

Lux – Tuzzio, Cáceres, Gerlo, Ferrari, Ahumada, Zapata, Domínguez (Fernández.A 46), Gallardo●62, Aban (Farías 46), Higuain. Tr: Passarella

1st Leg. Jalisco, Guadalajara
9-05-2006, 21:15, 15 504, Chandia CHI

Chivas Guadalajara	0

Michel – Armas, García.J●, Reynoso, Martínez.D (Medina 60), Barrera, Rodríguez.J, Solis, Magallón, Bautista, Santana (Borboa 67). Tr: De la Torre

Vélez Sarsfield	0

Sessa – Cubero●, Pellegrino, Pellerano, Bustamante (Sena● 62), Bustos, Somoza, Broggi, Gracián, Zárate.M●, Ereros (Fernandes 75). Tr: Russo

2nd Leg. José Amalfitani, Buenos Aires
20-07-2006, 21:45, Torres PAR

Vélez Sarsfield	1
	Batalla [82]

Sessa – Cubero, Pellegrino, Bustamante, Bustos, Somoza●, Ocampo (Batalla 56), Pellerano●, Escudero, Zárate.M, Ereros (Fernandes 56). Tr: Russo

Chivas Guadalajara	2
	Morales [27p], Bautista [73]

Sánchez.O – Rodríguez.F, Reynoso, Magallón, Martínez.D●, Morales, Pineda● (Solís 60), Bravo (Esparaza 68), Bautista●, Araujo, Rodríguez.J● (Santana 64). Tr: De la Torre

1st Leg. Centenario, Quilmes
10-05-2006, 21:45, 21 677, Selman CHI

Estudiantes LP	1
	Alayes [86]

Herrera – Alvarez, Alayes, Cáceres, Núñez (Carrusca 65), Braña●, Huerta (Lugüercio 65), Gelabert (Galván 77), Sosa, Pavone●4, Calderón. Tr: Burruchaga

São Paulo FC	0

Rogério Ceni● – André Dias●4, Fabão, Lugano●●●73, Júnior, Mineiro, Josué●, Alex Dias (Lenílson 55) (Edcarlos 75), Danilo, Aloisio●, Souza. Tr: Ramalho

2nd Leg. Morumbi, São Paulo
19-07-2006, 21:45, 66 056, Chandia CHI

São Paulo FC	1 4p
	Edcarlos [44p]

Rogério Ceni – Alex, Fabão, Edcarlos, Souza, Josué, Mineiro, Júnior●, Danilo, Ricardo Oliveira, Leandro (Thiago 72). Tr: Ramalho

Estudiantes LP	0 3p

Herrera – Angeleri●, Alayes, Ortiz, Alvarez●, Galván (Cominges● 67), Braña, Huerta (Cardozo 89), Sosa (Carrusca 79), Lugüercio, Calderón●3●. Tr: Simeone

SEMI-FINALS

1st Leg. Defensores del Chaco, Asunción
27-07-2006, 20:45, Baldassi ARG

Libertad	0

González.H - Bonet, Sarabia, Balbuena•, Hidalgo, Riveros, Villarreal, Aquino (Samudio 74), Guiñazú•, López.H, Gamarra (Romero 54) (Cáceres 87). Tr: Martino

Internacional	0

Clemer - Indio, Bolívar, Fabiano Eller•, Jorge Wagner, Fabinho, Edinho (Wellington Monteiro 77), Ceará, Alex (Iarley 68), Rafael Sóbis (Rentería• 86), Fernandão. Tr: Braga

---

2nd Leg. Beira-Rio, Porto Alegre
3-08-2006, 21:45, 44 064, Ruiz COL

Internacional	2
	Alex 62, Fernandão 68

Clemer - Indio, Bolívar•, Fabiano Eller, Fabinho (Rentería 61), Fernandão•, Rafael Sóbis•, Indio (Wellington Monteiro 73), Ceará, Edinho•, Jorge Wagner, Alex (Perdigão 90). Tr: Braga

Libertad	0

González.H - Bonet, Balbuena, Hidalgo (Romero 70), Sarabia•, Cáceres, Riveros•, Villarreal (Aquino 85), Guiñazú, López.H•, Gamarra (Samudio 73). Tr: Martino

---

1st Leg. Jalisco, Guadalajara
26-07-2006, 20:00, 47 440, Larrionda URU

Chivas Guadalajara	0

Sánchez.O - Rodríguez.F•, Reynoso, Magallón, Araujo, Esparza, Rodríguez.J (Santana 63), Pineda (Avila 70), Morales (Medina 87), Bravo, Bautista. Tr: De la Torre

São Paulo FC	1
	Rogério Ceni 84p

Rogério Ceni - Fabão, Edcarlos, Lugano•, Júnior, Mineiro, Josué, Leandro• (Lenílson 74), Danilo (Richaryson 86), Ricardo Oliveira• (Aloisio 61), Souza. Tr: Ramalho

---

2nd Leg. Morumbí, São Paulo
2-08-2006, 21:45, 66 750, Giménez ARG

São Paulo FC	3
	Leandro 32, Mineiro 39, Ricardo Oliveira 47

Rogério Ceni - Fabão, Edcarlos, Lugano, Júnior (Richaryson 75), Mineiro, Josué, Leandro, Danilo (Lenílson 57), Ricardo Oliveira• (Aloisio 80), Souza•. Tr: Ramalho

Chivas Guadalajara	0

Sánchez.O - Rodríguez.F, Reynoso•73, Magallón•, Martínez.D, Araujo•, Rodríguez.J•, Morales (Medina 46), Bravo•, Santana• (Patlán 78), Bautista•. Tr: De la Torre

---

COPA LIBERTADORES FINAL 1ST LEG
Morumbí, São Paulo
9-08-2006, 21:45, 71 456, Larrionda URU

SAO PAULO FC 1   2 INTERNACIONAL

Edcarlos 75   Rafael Sóbis 2 53 61

SAO PAULO FC			INTERNACIONAL	
1	ROGERIO CENI		CLEMER	1
3	FABAO		BOLIVAR	3
4	EDCARLOS	76	FABIANO ELLER	4
5	LUGANO Diego	38	FABINHO	5
6	JUNIOR		TINGA	7
7	MINEIRO		FERNANDAO	9
8	JOSUE	9 78	RAFAEL SOBIS	11
9	LEANDRO	86 56	CEARA	14
10	DANILO	63	EDINHO	15
12	RICARDO OLIVEIRA		JORGE WAGNER	23
21	SOUZA	74	ALEX	24
	Tr: RAMALHO Muricy		Tr: BRAGA Abel	
	Substitutes		Substitutes	
14	ALOISIO	76 74	INDIO	13
20	RICHARLYSON	86 78	MICHEL	18
23	LENILSON	63 56	WELLINGTON MONTEIRO	21

COPA LIBERTADORES FINAL 2ND LEG
Beira-Rio, Porto Alegre
16-08-2006, 22:00, 55 000, Elizondo ARG

INTERNACIONAL 2   2   SAO PAULO FC

Fernandão 29, Tinga 66   Fabão 50, Lenílson 85

INTERNACIONAL			SAO PAULO FC	
1	CLEMER		ROGERIO CENI	1
3	BOLIVAR		FABAO	3
4	FABIANO ELLER	70	EDCARLOS	4
7	TINGA	66	LUGANO Diego	5
9	FERNANDAO		JUNIOR	6
11	RAFAEL SOBIS	82	MINEIRO	7
13	INDIO		LEANDRO	9
14	CEARA	58	DANILO	10
15	EDINHO		ALOISIO	14
23	JORGE WAGNER	58	RICHARLYSON	20
24	ALEX	78	SOUZA	21
	Tr: BRAGA Abel		Tr: RAMALHO Muricy	
	Substitutes		Substitutes	
16	EDIGLE	82 70	ALEX DIAS	11
18	MICHEL	78 58	THIAGO	19
		58	LENILSON	23

AT. NACIONAL

Goalkeepers
1 SALDARRIAGA Andrés David
12 CASTILLO Breiner Clemente
25 OSPINA David

Defenders
2 MENDOZA Humberto Antonio
3 VERA Luciano
5 PASSO Oscar Enrique
6 SOTO Hugo Emilio
15 DÍAZ Carlos Alberto

Midfielders
4 MARÍN Vladimir
8 MORALES Hugo Alberto
10 HURTADO Héctor Hugo
13 AMAYA José Antonio
16 CHARÁ Luis Felipe
17 MARRUGO Cristian Camilo
18 ZÚÑIGA Juan Camilo
20 BEDOYA Gerardo Albero
21 MOSQUERA Juan Carlos
22 PULGARÍN Juan Fernando
23 RAMÍREZ Aldo Leao
24 CASAÑAS Andrés Felipe

Forwards
7 MARCELO RAMOS
9 ARISTIZÁBAL Victor Hugo
11 RAMBAL Jairo Oliver
14 VALENCIA Carmelo Enrique
19 GALVÁN Sergio Alejandro

BOLIVAR

Goalkeepers
1 ZAYAS Joel Fernando
12 TORO Ellioth
25 LANZ Pablo Javier

Defenders
2 DE SOUZA André Felipe
3 SANDY Marco Antonio
5 MORES Aldo Andrés
6 SANCHEZ Oscar Carmelo
13 GUATÍA Ovidio
14 ALVARENGA Carlos Edgar
19 TORRICO Luis Aníbal

Midfielders
4 CAMACHO Carlos
7 RIBEIRO Luis Gatty
8 REYES Leonel
9 GUTIÉRREZ Límberg
11 PACHI Daner Jesús
15 BALDERAS Ricardo
16 ALMARAZ José Luis
17 VACA DIEZ Getulio
20 JUSTINIANO Raúl
21 ANGULO Carmelo

Forwards
18 CUÉLLAR Miguel Ángel
22 MENACHO Martín
23 CHIORAZZO Horacio
24 MERCADO Miguel

CARACAS

Goalkeepers
1 TOYO Javier Eduardo
12 GUZMAN Euro Iván
22 DI MAIO Manuel Antonio

Defenders
2 VIZCARRONDO Oswaldo
3 REY José Manuel
4 GODOY Daniel José
15 PEREZ Edder Alfonso
16 BUSTAMENTE Jaime Andrés
19 ROMERO Giovanny Michael
21 ROUGA Enrique Andrés
24 GONZALEZ Raúl

Midfielders
5 PEREZ Giovanny Leonardo
6 OLIVARES Weymar Franck
8 VERA Luis Enrique
10 ROJAS Jorge Alberto
11 GONZALEZ César Eduardo
17 JIMENEZ Edgar Hernán
18 GUERRA Alejandro Abraham
20 VARGAS Ronald Alejandro
23 DEPABLOS Pedro Javier

Forwards
7 CARPINTERO Wilson Alberto
9 SERNA Jorge Horacio
13 ESPINOZA Ever
14 CASANOVA Jorge Francisco
25 ROMERO Miguel Angel

CERRO PORTENO

Goalkeepers
1 BARRETO Diego Daniel
12 NAVARRO Hilario Bernardo
25 ORTIZ Paolo Roberto

Defenders
2 CARDOZO Juan Antonio
3 PÉREZ Fidel Amado
4 CABRERA Nelson David
5 BENÍTEZ Lidio
6 BENÍTEZ Pedro Juan
11 CRISTALDO Ernesto Rubén
13 BAZÁN Wilfrido Guzmán
22 DEVACA José Ricardo
23 BÁEZ Carlos

Midfielders
7 GONZÁLEZ Edgar Daniel
8 GRANA Mario Darío
14 RAMÍREZ Esteban Javier
15 FRETES Wálter Milcíades
16 IRALA Pedro Ríchar
18 ESCOBAR Pablo Daniel
21 GENES Carlos Daniel
24 SALCEDO José Domingo

Forwards
9 ÁVALOS Erwin Lorenzo
10 GIMÉNEZ Pablo Junior
17 ACHUCARRO Jorge Daniel
19 OVELAR Roberto
20 DA SILVA Alejandro Damián

CHIVAS

Goalkeepers
1 SÁNCHEZ Oswaldo
12 TALAVERA Alfredo
22 MICHEL Luis Ernesto

Defenders
2 MARTÍNEZ Diego Alfonso
3 RODRÍGUEZ Francisco Javier
4 REYNOSO Héctor
5 SALCIDO Carlos Arnoldo
6 RAMÍREZ Christian
7 PINEDA Gonzalo
8 GARCÍA Jhonny
17 BARRERA Jorge Armando
24 ARAUJO Patricio Gabriel

Midfielders
11 MORALES Ramón
15 SOL Manuel Bernardo
18 ARMAS Christian Michel
19 MAGALLÓN José Jonny
20 PÉREZ Max Ricardo
25 SOLÍS Edgar Iván

Forwards
9 BRAVO Omar
10 MEDINA Alberto
13 PARRA Marco Antonio
14 VELA Manuel Alejandro
16 BORBOA Edwin Alejandro
21 SANTANA Sergio Alejandro
23 BAUTISTA Adolfo

CIENCIANO

Goalkeepers
1 IBÁÑEZ Oscar
12 CISNEROS Jesús
21 ALVA Víctor

Defenders
2 VILLALTA Miguel Ángel
3 BUTRÓN Jahir
4 ARAUJO Jorge
5 LUGO Carlos
13 PORTILLA Giuliano
15 HUERTAS Miguel
19 GUIZASOLA Guillermo

Midfielders
6 CCAHUANTICO César
8 BAZALAR Juan Carlos
10 GARCÍA Julio
14 FERNÁNDEZ Carlos
16 MASÍAS Fernando
18 TORRES Miguel
20 RAMÍREZ Luis
22 FERRARI Jean
23 SALAS Hilden
25 DE LA HAZA Paolo

Forwards
7 MOSTTO Miguel
9 SILVA Roberto
11 RODRÍGUEZ Ramón
18 LAGORIO Federico
24 ROSS Douglas Junior

CORINTHIANS

Goalkeepers
1 MARCELO
12 HERRERA Johnny Cristian
22 JÚLIO CÉSAR

Defenders
2 BETÃO
6 DOMÍNGUEZ Sebastián Enrique
13 MARINHO
16 WESCLEY
24 MARCUS VINÍCIUS

Midfielders
3 MASCHERANO Javier Alejandro
4 GUSTAVO NERY
5 MARCELO MATTOS
7 ROGER
8 ROSINEI
11 RICARDINHO
14 DYEGO COELHO
15 WENDEL
17 RENATO
19 CARLOS ALBERTO
20 XAVIER
21 BRUNO OCTÁVIO
23 EDUARDO RATINHO
25 RUBENS JÚNIOR

Forwards
9 NILMAR
10 TÉVEZ Carlos Alberto
18 RAFAEL MOURA

DEPORTIVO CALI

Goalkeepers
1 RAMÍREZ Juan Pablo
12 GONZÁLEZ David
21 MENESES John Visman

Defenders
2 CABALLERO Darío Raúl
3 RIVAS Nelson Enríquez
4 OLAVE Jámison
5 MERA José Hermes
14 VALDÉS Diego Fernando
16 GARCÍA Juan Geovanni
17 BENÍTEZ Jair
22 HURTADO Freddy Andrés

Midfielders
6 DÍAZ Oscar
8 HERRERA Jarol
10 CICILIANO Ricardo Manuel
13 PATIÑO Hernando
15 TAPIA Anthony David
18 ARCE Luis Felipe
19 LÓPEZ Jorge Enríque
20 MORÍNIGO Gustavo Eliseo
23 DOMÍNGUEZ Álvaro José
25 DE LA CRUZ Rolan

Forwards
7 PÉREZ Blas Antonio Miguel
9 TRUJILLO Iván Rodrigo
11 CARRILLO Armando José
24 ESCOBAR Habynson

ESTUDIANTES LP

Goalkeepers
1 HERRERA Martín Horacio
12 TABORDA César Omar
25 ALBIL Damián Gonzálo

Defenders
2 ÁLVAREZ Pablo Sebastián
3 ARAUJO Carlos Luciano
4 CÁCERES Juan Daniel
6 ALAYES Agustín
13 BASANTA José María
14 ANGELERI Marcos Alberto
19 ORTIZ Fernando
24 NÚÑEZ Jorge Martín

Midfielders
5 GELABERT Marcos Agustín
7 SOSA José Ernesto
8 ESMERADO Gastón Rubén
10 CARRUSCA Marcelo Adrián
11 COMINGES Juan Elías
15 HUERTA Juan Augusto
18 CARDOZO Horacio Ramón
20 GALVÁN Diego Alberto
22 BRAÑA Rodrigo

Forwards
9 CALDERÓN José Luis
16 PAVONE Hugo Mariano
17 LUGÜERCIO Pablo Ariel
21 SENGER Dante Adrián
23 GUERRERO Francisco Gabriel

GOIAS EC

Goalkeepers
1 HARLEI
12 RODRIGO CALAÇA
22 PEDRO HENRIQUE

Defenders
3 ROGÉRIO CORRÊA
4 LEONARDO
5 FABIANO
14 RAFAEL DIAS
15 JÚLIO SANTOS
23 ALDO

Midfielders
2 CLÉBER
6 JADILSON
7 DANILO PORTUGAL
8 CLÉBER GAÚCHO
13 VITOR
16 VAMPETA
17 LEYRIELTON
18 LUCIANO ALMEIDA
19 JULIANO
21 JORGE MUTT
24 FÁBIO BAHIA

Forwards
9 NONATO
10 JEFFERSON FEIJÃO
11 DALMO
16 JARDEL
20 ROMERITO
24 SOUZA
25 WELLITON

INDEP. SANTA FE

Goalkeepers
1 MARTÍNEZ Luis Enrique
12 CARABALÍ Eulín Fabián
25 GARCÍA Luis Alejandro

Defenders
2 PACHÓN Pablo César
3 OLVEIRA Nelson Artigas
6 GARRIDO Iván Alonso
15 NÁJERA Álvaro Francisco
18 TIERRADENTRO Jhonn Fredy

Midfielders
4 DÍAZ Fabián Camilo
5 GÓMEZ Gabriel Enrique
7 ORTIZ Carlos Alberto
8 SUÁREZ Jairo Andrés
9 GAMARRA Luis Daniel
10 MONTOYA David Fernando
13 FAWCETT César Antonio
16 CANO John Alexander
17 RAMÍREZ Juan Carlos
19 DELGADO Edgar Francisco
20 MARÍN Raúl Esneider

Forwards
11 GÓMEZ Mario Efraín
14 YANES Luis Alfredo
21 HIDALGO Carlos Daniel
22 ARMANI Diego Leandro
23 PRECIADO Leider Calimento
24 LARGACHA José

INTERNACIONAL

Goalkeepers
1 CLEMER
12 MARCELO
22 RENÁN

Defenders
2 ELDEL GRANJA
3 BOLÍVAR
4 FABIANO ELLER
13 ÍNDIO
16 EDIGLÊ

Midfielders
5 FABINHO
6 RUBENS CARDOSO
7 TINGA
8 PERDIGÃO
14 CEARÁ
15 EDINHO
17 MOSSORÓ
18 MICHEL
23 JORGE WAGNER
24 ÁLVARO
25 ADRIANO

Forwards
9 FERNANDÃO
10 IARLEY
11 RAFAEL SÓBIS
19 RENTERÍA Wason Libardo
20 LÉO
21 GUSTAVO

LIBERTAD

Goalkeepers
1 BOBADILLA Aldo Antonio
12 GONZÁLEZ Horacio Javier
25 ACOSTA Roberto Carlos

Defenders
2 BARONE Deivis
3 BALBUENA Edgar Gabriel
4 VERA Arnaldo Andrés
13 BOGADO Rolando Marciano
15 MARTÍNEZ Ricardo Julián
22 MARTÍNEZ Gonzalo

Midfielders
5 HIDALGO Emilio Martín
6 RIVEROS Cristian Miguel
7 ROBLES Edgar Arnulfo
8 VILLARREAL Javier Alejandro
10 MARTÍNEZ Osvaldo David
11 BONET Carlos
14 SARABIA Pedro Alcides
16 LUZARDI Hugo Américo
17 GUIÑAZÚ Pablo Horacio
18 CÁCERES Víctor Javier
20 DAMIANI Raúl Hernán
21 GARNIER Pablo Sebastián

Forwards
9 LÓPEZ Hernán Rodrigo
19 ROMERO Nelson David
23 ORTELLADO Júlio César
24 GAMARRA Roberto Carlos

LDU QUITO

Goalkeepers
1 PRETI Luis Humberto
12 MORA Cristian Rafael
22 BORJA Jaime Sandro

Defenders
2 CAMPOS Jairo Rolando
3 JÁCOME Rolando Santiago
6 GUERRÓN Juan Kely
17 ESPINOZA Giovanny Patricio
21 BALSECA Cristian Paul
23 ESPÍNOLA Carlos Alberto

Midfielders
4 AMBROSI Paul Vicente
5 OBREGÓN Alfonso Andrés
8 URRUTIA Patricio Javier
10 PALACIOS Roberto Carlos
13 REASCO Neicer
14 IZA Wálter Ramiro
15 CANDELARIO Moisés Antonio
16 LARREA Pedro Sebastián
20 VERA Enrique Daniel
24 VILLALBA Jonathan Mauricio

Forwards
7 MÉNDEZ Édison Vicente
9 DELGADO Agustín Javier
11 MURILLO Elkin Antonio
18 CEVALLOS Diego Marcelo
19 GUERRÓN Joffre David
25 PUTAN Ángel Enrique

UA MARACAIBO

Goalkeepers
1 ANGELUCCI Gilberto
12 HERNÁNDEZ Tulio
22 ANGULO Alexis

Defenders
2 RODRÍGUEZ Renier
3 GONZÁLEZ José
4 DÍAZ Dickson
13 FUENMAYOR Juan
21 YORI Rubén
24 BOVAGLIO Lucas
25 MARTÍNEZ Elvis

Midfielders
5 GARCÍA Gamadiel
6 FERNÁNDEZ Pedro
7 GONZÁLEZ Héctor
10 BERAZA Guillermo
14 LUZARDO Gregory
16 SUANNO Vicente
18 FIGUEROA Darío
20 GONZÁLEZ Andree

Forwards
8 MALDONADO Giancarlo
9 GUERRA Dioni
11 CASTELLÍN Rafael
17 GUTIÉRREZ José Félix
19 RENTERÍA Emilio
23 CÁSSERES Cristian

NACIONAL M'DEO

Goalkeepers
1 BAVA Jorge
12 ÁLVAREZ Lucero
25 VIERA Alexis

Defenders
2 JAUME Diego
4 LEITES Daniel
5 VICTORINO Mauricio
7 CABALLERO Pablo
16 PANIAGUA Ignacio
17 PALLAS Ignacio
21 MANSILLA Marcelo

Midfielders
3 FRANCO Maureen
6 VÁZQUEZ Sebastián
8 VANZINI Marco
10 ALBÍN Juan
13 MARTÍNEZ Jorge Andrés
18 BRÍTEZ Jorge
20 DELGADO Javier
23 COELHO Wálter Fabián
24 VIANA Agustín

Forwards
9 SUÁREZ Luis
11 MÁRQUEZ Andrés
14 GARCÉS José Luis
15 MORALES Gerardo
19 CASTRO Gonzalo
22 JUÁREZ Carlos

EL NACIONAL

Goalkeepers
1 COROZO Rixon Javier
12 IBARRA Oswaldo Johvani
22 SÁNCHEZ Robinson Geovanny

Defenders
2 CASTRO Carlos Ernesto
3 CALLE Renán
6 GUAGUA Jorge Daniel
14 CAICEDO Pavel Cipriano
16 CASTILLO Segundo Alejandro
21 CAGUA Jhon Patricio

Midfielders
4 DE JESÚS Omar Andrés
5 HIDALGO Carlos Ramón
7 QUIROZ Mario David
10 LARA Christian Rolando
15 SÁNCHEZ Wellington Eduardo
19 QUIÑÓNEZ Pedro Ángel
20 AYOVÍ Wálter Orlando
23 DE JESÚS Erik Rolando

Forwards
8 ORDÓÑEZ Ebelio Agustín
9 BORJA Félix Alexander
11 BENÍTEZ Christian Rogelio
13 FERNÁNDEZ Ángel Oswaldo
17 FIGUEROA Gustavo Omar
18 VERA Danny Alejandro
24 COTERA Manuel Antonio
25 CHALÁ Cléver Manuel

NEWELL'S OB

Goalkeepers
1 VILLAR Justo Wilmar
12 GUZMÁN Nahuel Ignacio
22 GUTIÉRREZ Marcos Juan

Defenders
2 SPOLLI Nicolás Federico
3 SERI Martín
6 RIVERA Germán Ricardo
13 TORREN Miguel Ángel
16 RÉ Germán David
23 AGUIRRE Gastón Damián

Midfielders
4 HUSAIN Claudio Daniel
5 COLACE Hugo Roberto
8 PERALTA Adrián Maximiliano
10 PENTA Marcelo Alejandro
11 LUCERO Oscar Adrián
15 ZAPATA Ariel Hernán
20 GAVILÁN Diego Antonio
24 RODAS Gustavo Ariel
25 BELLUSCHI Fernando Daniel

Forwards
7 ORTEGA Arnaldo riel
9 CERESETO Lucio Darío
17 BORGHELLO Iván Emiliano
18 CEJAS Mauro Emiliano
19 STEINERT Héctor Damián
21 SCOCCO Ignacio Martín

PALMEIRAS

Goalkeepers
1 MARCOS
12 SÉRGIO
24 DIEGO

Defenders
3 DANIEL
4 GAMARRA Carlos Alberto
13 LEONARDO SILVA
14 VALDOMIRO
15 DOUGLAS

Midfielders
2 AMARAL
5 MARCINHO GUERREIRO
6 LÚCIO
8 PAULO BAIER
10 JUNINHO PAULISTA
11 MARCINHO
16 CORREA
17 MÁRCIO CARECA
18 REINALDO
20 ALCEU
21 RICARDINHO
22 CRISTIAN

Forwards
7 EDMUNDO
9 ENÍLTON
19 GIOINO Sergio Alejandro
23 WASHINGTON
25 CLÁUDIO

PAULISTA

Goalkeepers
1 RAFAEL
12 VICTOR
24 ROBSON

Defenders
2 BOSCO
3 DEMA
4 REVER
6 FABIO VIDAL
13 LUCAS
14 NIVALDO
15 THIAGO GAMA

Midfielders
5 GLEYDSON
7 AMARAL
8 WILSON
10 JEAN CARLOS
16 DOUGLAS
17 SAMMIR
20 BETO
22 FERNANDO
23 LUIZ HENRIQUE
25 GRINGO

Forwards
9 ABRAÃO
11 MUÑOZ León Darío
18 WESLEY
19 JAILSON
21 PEDRO HENRIQUE

PUMAS UNAM

Goalkeepers
1 PALACIOS Miguel Alejandro
12 BERNAL Sergio Arturo
13 PATIÑO Víctor Odin

Defenders
2 SALINAS Raúl Alberto
3 BELTRÁN Joaquín
4 VERÓN Darío Anastacio
5 CASTRO Israel
6 MORENO Héctor Alfredo
14 MORALES Fernando
18 VELARDE Efraín
23 PALACIOS Marco Antonio

Midfielders
7 LEANDRO AUGUSTO
8 PINHEIRO
10 VICTORINO Cesareo
11 LÓPEZ José Luis
16 GALINDO Gerardo Gabriel
17 TOLEDO José David
24 TORRES Franz Eric
25 ESPINOSA Fernando

Forwards
9 MARIONI Bruno
15 BOTERO Joaquín
19 ROSAS Luis Ricardo
20 IÑIGUEZ Ismael
21 HERNÁNDEZ Gerardo
22 ROMA

RIVER PLATE

Goalkeepers
1 LUX Germán Darío
12 CARRIZO Juan Pablo
25 OLAVE Juan Carlos

Defenders
2 CÁCERES Julio César
6 TULA Cristian
16 GERLO Danilo Telmo
22 TALAMONTI Leonardo José

Midfielders
3 DOMÍNGUEZ Federico Hernán
4 FERRARI Paulo
5 AHUMADA Diego Adrián
8 MONTENEGRO Daniel Gastón
10 GALLARDO Marcelo David
13 LIMA René Martín
14 TOJA Juan Carlos
15 SAN MARTÍN Andrés
18 SANTANA Jonathan
20 PUSINERI Lucas Andrés
21 ZAPATA Víctor Eduardo
23 MAREQUE Lucas Armando
24 ÁLVAREZ Cristian Andrés
26 PATINO Jairo Leonardo

Forwards
7 ABAN Gonzalo Daniel
9 FIGUEROA Luciano
11 FARÍAS Ernesto Antonio
19 OBERMAN Gustavo Andrés

ROCHA

Goalkeepers
1 GARCÍA Álvaro Marcelo
12 LEMOS Oscar Andrés
22 MAGARZO Damián

Defenders
2 SOSA Diego Roberto
3 SEIJAS ablo Martín
4 SARLI Pablo
6 CIZ Diego
16 NOGUEZ Darwin
23 BONELLI Diego

Midfielders
8 ESQUIVEL Pablo abriel
8 MALDONADO Leonardo
11 LARROSA Martín
15 ARAUJO Cristiano
18 MAGUREGUI Luis Alejandro
20 GONZÁLEZ Nelson Matías
21 NOVICK Marcel
25 BECERRA Álvaro

Forwards
7 GONZÁLEZ Herley Martín
9 SEGALES Marcelo
10 CARO Héber Alfonso
13 PALAVECCINO Nahuel
14 DELGADO Andrés
17 RODRÍGUEZ Ruben
19 CARDOSO José Pedro
24 TOSCANINI Luis Jesús

ROSARIO CENT.

Goalkeepers
1 OJEDA juan Marcelo
12 ÁLVAREZ Cristián Dario
25 CASTELLANO Hernán Dario

Defenders
2 LOESCHBOR Gabriel Alejandro
3 ARANA Ronald
6 RALDES Ronald
13 RIVAROLA Germán Ezequiel
16 FASSI Ramiro Fernando
20 GRABOWSKI Juan Fernando
24 MOREIRA Ricardo Ariel

Midfielders
4 VILLAGRA Cristian Carlos
5 BORZANI Leonardo Luis
8 COUDET Eduardo Germán
14 DI MARÍA Ángel Fabián
15 ENCINA Hernán Fabián
17 VECCHIO Emilio Gabriel
19 DÍAZ Andrés Alejandro
21 CALGARO Daniel Agustín
22 LEDESMA Damián David
23 ELUCHANS Juan Eduardo

Forwards
7 ALEMANNO Germán Ariel
9 RUBÉN Marco Gastón
10 VITTI Pablo Ernesto
11 ZELAYA Emilio José
18 CASTILLO José Alfredo

SAO PAULO

Goalkeepers
- 1 CENI Rogério
- 22 BOSCO
- 24 BRUNO

Defenders
- 2 ANDRE DIAS
- 3 FABAO
- 4 EDCARLOS
- 5 LUGANO Diego Alfredo
- 23 FLAVIO
- 25 ALEX

Midfielders
- 6 JUNIOR
- 7 MINEIRO
- 8 JOSUE
- 10 DANILO
- 13 RAMALHO
- 15 DENILSON
- 16 FABIO SANTOS
- 18 RODRIGO FABRI
- 20 RICHARYLSON
- 21 SOUZA

Forwards
- 9 LEANDRO
- 11 ALEX DIAS
- 12 ROGER
- 14 ALOISIO
- 17 LIMA
- 19 THIAGO

SPORT. CRISTAL

Goalkeepers
- 1 DELGADO Erick Guillermo
- 12 VEGA Jhonny Martín
- 25 CASTELL Josué

Defenders
- 2 RODRÍGUEZ Alberto Junior
- 3 SALAZAR Javier Bohuslav
- 13 VÁSQUEZ Jersson
- 14 ARAUJO Norberto Carlos
- 15 COLÁN Henry Juan
- 17 VÍLCHEZ Walter Ricardo
- 22 PRADO Amilton Jair

Midfielders
- 1 QUINTEROS Henry Edson
- 4 SOTO Jorge Antonio
- 5 MARCZUK Carlos Alberto
- 6 TORRES Rainer
- 8 SORIA David
- 16 LOBATÓN Carlos Augusto
- 20 ZEGARRA Carlos Alberto
- 21 ISMODES Damián
- 23 CASAS César Carlos

Forwards
- 7 BONNET Luis Alberto
- 9 LEAL Sergio William
- 10 CHIROQUE William Medardo
- 18 ZÚÑIGA Herlyn Israel
- 19 VASSALLO Gustavo Enrique
- 24 WATARI Takashi

THE STRONGEST

Goalkeepers
- 1 CABALLERO Ever Alexis
- 12 SAHONERO Mauricio José
- 21 ISSA Diego Gabriel

Defenders
- 2 GUTIÉRREZ Ronald
- 4 SÁNCHEZ Juan Carlos
- 5 BONO Diego Alfredo
- 6 ARÉVALO Wilder
- 13 MENA Alejandro Damián
- 15 PAZ Juan Carlos
- 16 ROCABADO Pedro Adrián
- 23 FLORES Zackary
- 25 JÁUREGUI Sergio Antonio

Midfielders
- 3 RIVERO Rosauro
- 7 CRISTALDO Luis Héctor
- 8 COELHO Sandro
- 10 BALDIVIESO Julio César
- 14 BRITOS Gustavo Daniel
- 20 ZENTENO Edson Marcelo
- 22 CARDOZO Jaime

Forwards
- 9 CABRERA Diego Aroldo
- 11 FERNÁNDEZ Sergio Enrique
- 17 SUÁREZ Roger
- 18 PAZ Líder
- 19 CUELLAR Adrián
- 24 ROBLES Jaime

TIGRES UNAL

Goalkeepers
- 1 HERNÁNDEZ Edgar Adolfo
- 12 URBINA Jesús Yair
- 25 RODRÍGUEZ Rogelio

Defenders
- 2 MARTÍNEZ Emilio Damián
- 3 BALDERAS Sindey
- 4 VEIGA Argemiro
- 6 BRISEÑO Gabriel Omar
- 9 GONZÁLEZ Sebastián
- 13 GARCÍA Luis Ángel
- 18 CHÁVEZ Jesús Roberto
- 20 RUVALCABA Nicolás René
- 21 ESCUDERO Enrique
- 24 RAMÍREZ Luis Rolando

Midfielders
- 5 SANTOS Julio César
- 10 PERALTA Sixto Raimundo
- 16 MORALES Carlos Adrián
- 17 PALACIOS Jesús Alejandro
- 19 MONTANO Juan Nazario
- 23 SAAVEDRA Javier

Forwards
- 7 GAITÁN Wálter Nicolás
- 8 RAMÍREZ Carlos Alberto
- 11 DE NIGRIS Jesús Aldo
- 14 MENDOZA José Luis
- 15 CERDA Emmanuel
- 22 SILVERA Néstor Andrés

UNION ESPANOLA

Goalkeepers
- 1 BRAVO Jaime
- 12 NAVARETTE Mauricio
- 25 GAONA Julio

Defenders
- 2 VERGARA Adán
- 3 REYES Pedro
- 4 ROJAS Francisco
- 18 TORO Juan Pablo
- 19 RIQULME Omar
- 20 MIRANDA Sebastián
- 22 VILCHEZ Gabriel
- 24 NORUMBUENA Alexis

Midfielders
- 5 PEREIRA Emerson
- 6 REYES Joel
- 10 SIERRA José
- 11 JARA Luis
- 14 LATORRE Claudio
- 16 ACUNA Clarence
- 17 ARENAS Raúl
- 21 VILLAGRA Gonzalo

Forwards
- 7 VIDANGOSSY Mathias
- 8 PARRA Ignacio
- 9 FERRO Francis
- 13 NIERA Manuel Alejandro
- 15 MONTECINOS Cristián
- 23 TAPIA Héctor

UN. CATOLICA

Goalkeepers
- 1 BULJUBASICH José María
- 12 WIRTH Rainer Klaus
- 25 GARCÉS Paulo

Defenders
- 2 RUBILAR Jaime
- 3 MUÑOZ Claudio
- 4 ZENTENO Mauricio
- 5 PÉREZ Eros
- 6 ROSENDE Diego
- 8 VÁSQUEZ Iván
- 13 IMBODEN Facundo Jorge
- 14 GONZÁLEZ Marcos Andrés
- 15 ACEVEDO Albert
- 16 GAETE Alejandro

Midfielders
- 7 ARRUÉ Francisco
- 10 CONCA Darío Leonardo
- 19 FUENZALIDA José Pedro
- 21 PONCE Miguel
- 22 ISLA Mauricio
- 23 OSORIO Alejandro
- 24 ORMEÑO Jorge

Forwards
- 9 QUINTEROS Jorge Roberto
- 16 NÚÑEZ Luis
- 17 QUINTEROS Luis Ignacio
- 18 RUBIO Eduardo
- 20 NÚÑEZ Nicolás

UNIVERSITARIO

Goalkeepers
- 1 FERNÁNDEZ Raúl
- 12 CARVALLO José Aurelio
- 21 FLORES Juan Ángel

Defenders
- 2 CENTURIÓN Germán
- 3 NEYRA Donny Renzo
- 4 LOZADA Percy
- 6 MENDOZA José Adolfo
- 13 MOISELA José Alberto
- 16 GUADALUPE Luis Alberto
- 17 HERRERA Jhoel Alexander
- 19 HERNÁNDEZ Luis Daniel
- 24 RIVAS Willy

Midfielders
- 5 HERNÁNDEZ Luis Alberto
- 8 PEREDA José Antonio
- 10 MALDONALDO Paolo Freddy
- 14 RUIZ Marco Antonio
- 15 CEVASCO Miguel Ángel
- 18 ALONSO Arnaldo
- 20 BERNALES Gregorio Abel
- 23 MAGALLANES Alex Segundo

Forwards
- 7 ALVA Piero Fernando
- 9 SANGOY Gastón Maximiliano
- 11 MACERATESI Rafael Nazareno
- 22 MENDOZA Mauricio
- 25 ROSELL Víctor Alonso

VELEZ

Goalkeepers
- 1 SESSA Gastón Alejandro
- 12 PERATTA Sebastián Darío
- 25 ESCOBAR Fernando Oscar

Defenders
- 2 UGLESSICH Mariano Esteban
- 3 BROGGI Ariel Esteban
- 4 LADINO Santiago Andrés
- 6 BUSTAMANTE Marcelo Hernán
- 13 SOTO Carlos Andrés
- 15 PELLERANO Hernán Darío
- 16 PELLEGRINO Maximiliano
- 21 ALCARÁZ Walter Oscar

Midfielders
- 5 CUBERO Fabián Alberto
- 10 GRACIÁN Leandro
- 14 BUSTOS Andrés Maximiliano
- 18 SOMOZA Leandro Ariel
- 19 BATALLA Pablo Martín
- 20 CENTURION Emanuel Andrés
- 22 SENA Sergio Román
- 23 ESCUDERO Damian Ariel
- 24 OCAMPO Ramón Dario

Forwards
- 7 ENRÍA Claudio Marcelo
- 8 CASTROMÁN Lucas Martín
- 9 ZÁRATE Mauro Matías
- 11 ZÁRATE Rolando David
- 17 EREROS Sebastián Adolfo

COPA NISSAN SUDAMERICANA 2005

Preliminary Round

Danubio	URU	3	1
Defensor Sporting *	URU	2	3
Cerro Porteño	PAR	2 1	4p
Guaraní *	PAR	1 2	3p
Universitario *	PER	1 1	1p
Alianza Atlético	PER	1 1	4p
Universidad Católica	CHI	2	0
Universidad de Chile *	CHI	1	1
Deportivo Cali *	COL	2 0	6p
At Nacional Medellin	COL	0 2	7p
Trujillanos *	VEN	3	2
Mineros	VEN	1	1
Bolivar	BOL	1	1
The Strongest *	BOL	2	2
LDU Quito	ECU	3	2
El Nacional *	ECU	4	1

First Round

Boca Juniors	ARG	Bye	
Defensor Sporting	URU	0	1
Cerro Porteño *	PAR	2	1
Rosario Central	ARG	0	1
Newell's Old Boys *	ARG	0	0
São Paulo FC	BRA	1	1
Internacional *	BRA	2	1
Fluminense *	BRA	2 1	4p
Santos	BRA	1 2	2p
Estudiantes LP	ARG	0	2
Banfield *	ARG	2	1
DC United	USA	Bye	
Alianza Atlético	PER	0	2
Universidad Católica *	CHI	5	0
Vélez Sarsfield	ARG	Bye	
Juventude *	BRA	1	1
Cruzeiro	BRA	3	0
At Nacional Medellin	COL	5	2
Trujillanos *	VEN	1	0
CF América	MEX	Bye	
Corinthians	BRA	2	1
Goiás *	BRA	0	1
River Plate	ARG	Bye	
The Strongest *	BOL	2	3
LDU Quito	ECU	1	0
Pumas UNAM	MEX	Bye	

Round of 16

Boca Juniors	2	5
Cerro Porteño *	2	1
Rosario Central *	0	1
Internacional	1	1
Fluminense *	3	0
Banfield	1	0
DC United *	1	2
Universidad Católica	1	3
Vélez Sarsfield *	2	1
Cruzeiro	0	2
Atlético Nacional Medellin	3	1
CF América *	3	4
Corinthians *	0	1
River Plate	0	1
The Strongest	1	2
Pumas UNAM *	3	1

* Home team in the first leg

COPA NISSAN SUDAMERICANA 2005

COPA NISSAN SUDAMERICANA 2005

Quarter-finals		Semi-finals		Final	
Boca Juniors	0 4				
Internacional *	1 1				
		Boca Juniors *	2 1		
		Universidad Católica	2 0		
Fluminense *	2 0				
Universidad Católica	1 2				
				Boca Juniors	1 1 4p
				Pumas UNAM *	1 1 3p
Vélez Sarsfield	2 2				
CF América *	0 0				
		Vélez Sarsfield *	0 0		
		Pumas UNAM	0 4		
Corinthians *	2 0				
Pumas UNAM	1 3				

PRELIMINARY ROUND

1st leg. Luis Franzini, Montevideo, 16-08-2005, Cabrera URU

Defensor Sporting	2	Taborda 2 [3] [81]
Danubio	3	González.IM [10], Salgueiro [64], Lima [86]

2nd leg. Parque Central, Montevideo, 23-08-2005, Viera URU

Danubio	1	Salgueiro [7]
Defensor Sporting	3	Semperena [29], Pereira [63], Taborda [64]

1st leg. Manuel Ferreira, Asunción, 9-08-2005, Torres PAR

Guaraní	1	Garay [93+]
Cerro Porteño	2	Achucarro 2 [11] [16]

2nd leg. La Olla, Asuncion, 23-08-2005, Amarilla PAR

Cerro Porteño	1	Dos Santos [75p]	
Guaraní	2	Chávez [23], Irala [43p]	Cerro won 4-3p

1st leg. Monumental, Lima, 10-08-2005, Carrillo PER

Universitario	1	Tonelotto [76]
Alianza Atlético	1	Ramírez [74]

2nd leg. Campeones del '36, Sullana, 24-08-2005, Morales PER

Alianza Atlético	1	Ferreira [24]	
Universitario	1	Tonelotto [56]	Alianza won 4-1p

1st leg. Nacional, Santiago, 11-08-2005, Ponce CHI

Univ. de Chile	1	Olivera [2]
Univ. Católica	2	Quinteros.JR [42], Rubio [82p]

2nd leg. Nacional, Santiago, 25-08-2005, Osses CHI

Univ. Católica	0	
Univ. de Chile	1	Droguett [51]

1st leg. Pascual Guerrero, Cali, 16-08-2005, Paneso COL

Deportivo Cali	2	Ciciliano [26p], Rivas [64]
At. Nacional	0	

2nd leg. Atanasio Girardot, Medellín, 23-08-2005, Hoyos COL

At. Nacional	2	Echeverry [11], Morales [24]	
Deportivo Cali	0		Atlético Nacional won 7-6p

1st leg. Farid Richard, Barquisimento, 18-08-2005, Soto VEN

Trujillanos	3	Zapata 2 [52] [68], Cordero [82]
Mineros	1	Noriega [70]

2nd leg. Cachamay, Puerto Ordaz, 24-08-2005, Manzur VEN

Mineros	1	Noriega [43p]
Trujillanos	2	Zapata [10], Santo [78]

1st leg. Hernando Siles, La Paz, 11-08-2005, Paniagua BOL

The Strongest	2	Gutiérrez [58], Escobar [80]
Bolívar	1	Fischer [20]

2nd leg. Hernando Siles, La Paz, 25-08-2005, Ortubé BOL

Bolívar	1	Andaveris [25]
The Strongest	2	Ricaldi [52], Paz [76]

1st leg. Olímpico Atahualpa, 9-08-2005, Hara Inca ECU

El Nacional	3	Quiroz [36], Chalá [59], García [78]
LDU Quito	4	Garcés [20], Salas [40], Reasco [72], Aguinaga [85]

2nd leg. Casa Blanca, Quito, 25-08-2005, Alarcón ECU

LDU Quito	1	Palacios [83]
El Nacional	2	Lara [12], Quiroz [57p]

FIRST ROUND

1st leg. Antonio Sarubbi, Ciudad del Este, 30-08-2005, Pozo CHI

Cerro Porteño	2	Salcedo [42], Da Silva [50]
Defensor Sporting	0	

2nd leg. Parque Central, Montevideo, 6-09-2005, Lopes BRA

Defensor Sporting	1	Martínez [77p]
Cerro Porteño	1	Dos Santos [29]

1st leg. Coloso, Rosario, 18-08-2005, Pompei ARG

Newell's Old Boys	0
Rosario Central	0

2nd leg. Gigante, Rosario, 29-08-2005, Elizondo ARG

Rosario Central	1	Rivarola [45]
Newell's Old Boys	0	

1st leg. Beira-Rio, Porto Alegre, 17-08-2005, Rezende BRA

Internacional	2	Elder Granja [35], Gustavo [58]
São Paulo FC	1	Mineiro [39]

2nd leg. Morumbí, São Paulo, 1-09-2005, Lopes BRA

São Paulo FC	1	Souza [41]
Internacional	1	Fernandão [68p]

1st Leg. São Januario, Rio de Janeiro, 17-08-2005, Gaciba BRA

Fluminense	2	Tuta [43], Gabriel [64]
Santos	1	Elton [55]

2nd leg. Vila Belmiro, Santos, 31-08-2005, Simon BRA

Santos	2	Edmilson [82], Geilson [89]	
Fluminense	1	Tuta [45]	Fluminense won 4-2p

1st leg. Florencio Sola, Buenos Aires, 16-08-2005, Furchi ARG

Banfield	2	Galván [15], Civelli [24]
Estudiantes LP	0	

2nd leg. Luis Jorge Hirsch, La Plata, 25-08-2005, Pompei ARG

Estudiantes LP	2	Pavone [13], Carrusca [23p]
Banfield	1	Galarza [56]

1st leg. San Carlos, Santiago, 30-08-2005, Martín ARG

Univ. Católica	5	Rubio 2 [17] [25], Conca [67], Núñez 2 [79] [84]
Alianza Atlético	0	

2nd leg. Miguel Grau, Piura, 7-09-2005, López COL

Alianza Atlético	2	Ferreira [2], Miranda [57]
Univ. Católica	0	

1st leg. Alfredo Jaconi, Caxias do Sul, 17-08-2005, Carvalho BRA

Juventude	1	Tucho [21]
Cruzeiro	3	Diego 2 [9] [37], Martinez [32]

2nd leg. Mineirão, Belo Horizonte, 1-09-2005, Fagundes BRA

Cruzeiro	0	
Juventude	1	Ederson [2]

1st leg. José Pachencho Romero, Maracaibo, 30-08-2005, Reinoso ECU

Trujillanos	1	Brignani [51]
At. Nacional	5	Morales [4], Marcelo Ramos [36], Marrugo [44], Aristizábal [62], Ramírez [87]

2nd leg. Atanasio Girardot, Medellín, 8-09-2005, Ortubé BOL

At. Nacional	2	Marcelo Ramos [35], Marrugo [48]
Trujillanos	0	

1st leg. Serra Dourada, Goiás, 17-08-2005, Souza Mendonça BRA

Goiás	0	
Corinthians	2	Dinelson [18], Fabricio [35]

2nd leg. Pacaembú, São Paulo, 31-08-2005, Pena BRA

Corinthians	1	Ronny [25]
Goiás	1	Paulo Baier [87p]

1st leg. Hernando Siles, La Paz, 30-08-2005, Grance PAR

The Strongest	2	Escobar [54], Coelho [67]
LDU Quito	1	Reasco [37]

2nd leg. Casa Blanca, Quito, 8-09-2005, Rivera PER

LDU Quito	0	
The Strongest	3	Coelho [22], Escobar [52], Cristaldo [68]

Boca Juniors, DC United, Vélez Sarsfield, América, River Plate and Pumas UNAM all received byes

ROUND OF 16

1st leg. Defensores del Chaco, Asuncion, 21-09-2005, Rezende BRA

Cerro Porteño	2	Fretes [20], Benítez [31]
Boca Juniors	2	Cardozo [2], Palacio [12]

2nd leg. Ernesto Martearena, Salta, 29-09-2005, Simon BRA

Boca Juniors	5	Krupoviesa [9], Palermo [66], B Schelotto [75], Cardozo [87], Insúa [89]
Cerro Porteño	1	Avalos [69]

1st leg. Gigante de Arroyito, Rosario, 15-09-2005, Selman CHI

| Rosario Central | 0 | |
| Internacional | 1 | Rafael Sobis [69] |

2nd leg. Beira-Rio, Porto Alegre, 29-09-2005, Vázquez URU

| Internacional | 1 | Jorge Wagner [54p] |
| Rosario Central | 1 | Rivarola [58] |

1st Leg. São Januario, Rio de Janeiro, 14-09-2005, Ortubé BOL

| Fluminense | 3 | Leandro [14], Tuta 2 [70 86] |
| Banfield | 1 | Datolo [13] |

2nd leg. Florencio Sola, Buenos Aires, 28-09-2005, Amarilla PAR

| Banfield | 0 | |
| Fluminense | 0 | |

1st leg. RFK, Washington, 13-09-2005, Torres PAR

| DC United | 1 | Walker [80] |
| Univ. Católica | 1 | Quinteros.JR [48] |

2nd leg. San Carlos, Santiago, 22-09-2005, Duque COL

| Univ. Católica | 3 | Quinteros.JR 2 [39 85], Conca [77] |
| DC United | 2 | Gómez [14], Buljubasich OG [26] |

1st Leg. José Amalfitani, Buenos Aires, 14-09-2005, Silvera URU

| Vélez Sarsfield | 2 | Castroman 2 [26 34] |
| Cruzeiro | 0 | |

2nd leg. Minerão, Belo Horizonte, 28-09-2005, Torres PAR

| Cruzeiro | 2 | Diego 2 [15 74] |
| Vélez Sarsfield | 1 | Castroman [40] |

1st leg. Coliseum, Los Angeles, 21-09-2005, Brand VEN

| CF América | 3 | López [25], Kléber Boas [65], Giménez [85] |
| At. Nacional | 3 | Bedoya [1], Aristizábal [40], Hurtado [91+] |

2nd leg. Atanasio Girardot, Medellín, 5-10-2005, Baldassi ARG

| At. Nacional | 1 | Marcelo Ramos [22] |
| CF América | 4 | Padilla [59], Kléber Boas 3 [70 77 83] |

1st leg. Morumbí, São Paulo, 14-09-2005, Vázquez URU

| Corinthians | 0 | |
| River Plate | 0 | |

2nd leg. Monumental, Buenos Aires, 28-09-2005, Chandía CHI

| River Plate | 1 | Santana [15] |
| Corinthians | 1 | Marinho [91+] |

1st Leg. Olimpico Universitario, Mexico City, 20-09-2005, Giménez ARG

| Pumas UNAM | 3 | Marioni [5], De Nigris [42], Cardetti [89] |
| The Strongest | 1 | Escobar [83] |

2nd leg. Hernando Siles, La Paz, 5-10-2005, Silvera URU

| The Strongest | 2 | Paz 2 [34 46] |
| Pumas UNAM | 1 | Da Silva [40] |

QUARTER-FINALS

1st Leg. Beira-Rio, Porto Alegre
19-10-2005, 19:30, Torres PAR

| Internacional | 1 |
| | Fernandão [93+] |

Clemer - Edinho•, Ediglê, Vinicius, Ceará, Jorge Wagner, Perdigão•, Ricardinho (Gustavo 77), Tinga, Rafael Sobis, Fernandão. Tr: Muricy Ramalho

| Boca Juniors | 0 |

Abbondanzieri•(after final whistle) - Calvo, Schiavi, Díaz•, Krupoviesa, Cagna, Gago, Cardozo (Marino 45), Insúa (Silvestre 90), Palermo, Palacio (Delgado 76). Tr: Alfio Basile

2nd Leg. Bombonera, Buenos Aires
10-11-2005, 21:00, Amarilla PAR

| Boca Juniors | 4 |

Medrán - Schiavi•, Krupoviesa, Calvo•, Gago, Díaz, Palacio, Cagna (Cardoso 70), Palermo, Insúa (Barros Schelotto• 70), Bilos (Vargas• 79). Tr: Alfio Basile

| Internacional | 1 |

Clemer - Elder Granaja, Ediglê (Gustavo 80), Vinicius•, Jorge Wagner (Wellington 86), Gavilán, Edinho, Tinga, Ricardinho (Alex 86), Rafael Sobis, Fernandão. Tr: Muricy Ramalho

1st Leg. São Januario, Rio de Janeiro
18-10-2005, 21:15, Baldassi ARG

| Fluminense | 2 |
| | Juan [23], Petkovic [36] |

Kleber - Schneider (Preto Casagrande 50), Gabriel Santos•, Igor, Juan, Milton Do'o, Arouca• (Romeu 74), Gabriel, Petkovic, Rodrigo Tiuí (Juninho 75), Tuta•. Tr: Abel Braga

| Universidad Católica | 1 |
| | Ponce [89] |

Buljubasich - Rubilar, Zenteno•, Imboden, Núñez (Fuenzalida 66), Ormeño, Arrué (Vásquez 67), Ponce, Conca, Rubio, Quinteros.JR (Quinteros.I 76). Tr: Jorge Pellicer

2nd Leg. San Carlos, Santiago
9-11-2005, 21:00, Giménez ARG

| Universidad Católica | 2 |
| | Quinteros.JR [41], Arrué [65] |

Buljubasich - Rubilar, Zenteno, Imboden, Fuenzalida (Osorio 64), Ormeño, Pérez, Arrué (Vásquez• 80), Conca, Rubio, Quinteros.JR. Tr: Jorge Pellicer

| Fluminense | 0 |

Kleber - Igor•, Gabriel Santos, Gabriel•, Milton Do'o• (Maicon 87), Juan, Leandro•, Petkovic (Rodrigo Tiuí 62), Lino, Tuta, Preto Casagrande (Schneider 73). Tr: Abel Braga

1st Leg. Azul, Mexico City
26-10-2005, 19:30, Chandía CHI

| CF América | 0 |

Ochoa - Castro, Rojas.OA, Davino (Mendoza 73), López (Navia 56), Blanco•, Irenio Soares (Villa 72), Pardo•, Rojas.RF, Giménez, Kléber Boas. Tr: Mario Carrillo

| Vélez Sarsfield | 2 |
| | Pellegrino [6], Gracián [55] |

Sessa - Cubero, Uglessich, Pellegrino, Bustamente, Sena, Somoza•, Centurión (Bustos 52), Gracián•, Valdemarin (Ereros 30) (Ladino 89), Zárate.M. Tr: Miguel Angel Russo

2nd Leg. José Amalfitani, Buenos Aires
2-11-2005, 21:30, Simon BRA

| Vélez Sarsfield | 2 |
| | Bustamante [65], Somoza [77p] |

Sessa• - Cubero, Pellegrino, Pellerano, Bustamente, Sena, Somoza, Centurión (Bustos 76), Gracián (Broggi 79), Enría (Ereros 81), Zárate.M. Tr: Miguel Angel Russo

| CF América | 0 |

Ochoa - Castro, Rodríguez, Rojas.RF• (Giménez 60), Rojas.OA, Davino, Pardo, Villa•, Blanco, Kléber Boas (Padilla 72), López. Tr: Mário Carrillo

1st Leg. Pacaembú, São Paulo
19-10-2005, 21:50, Ruiz COL

| Corinthians | 2 |
| | Hugo [34], Bobô [70] |

Fábio Costa - Eduardo Ratinho•, Marinho, Wescley, Hugo (Dyego Coelho 76), Marcelo Mattos, Fabricio•, Rosinei (Tévez 46), Roger, Carlos Alberto, Bobô (Dinelson 72). Tr: Antonio Lopes

| Pumas UNAM | 1 |
| | De Nigris [90+2] |

Bernal - López.I (López.JL 89), Beltrán•, Verón, Pineda, Castro (Espinosa 91), Galindo, Augusto, Da Silva, De Nigris•, Botero• (Iñíguez 74). Tr: Hugo Sánchez

2nd Leg. Olímpico Universitario, Mexico City
9-11-2005, 18:00, Elizondo ARG

| Pumas UNAM | 3 |
| | Marioni 2 [68 92+], Augusto [87] |

Bernal - Castro, Beltrán, Verón•, Pineda, Palacios•, Galindo (Marioni 65), Augusto•, Iñíguez (López.JL 74), Da Silva•, De Nigris Botero 78). Tr: Hugo Sánchez

| Corinthians | 0 |

Fábio Costa - Betão, Bruno Octávio, Dyego Coelho (Eduardo Ratinho• 58), Wescley, Ronny (Hugo 45), Wendel•, Fabricio•, Carlos Alberto (Dinelson 72), Bobô, Jô. Tr: Antonio Lopes

SEMI-FINALS

1st Leg. Bombonera, Buenos Aires
23-11-2005, 19:45, Ruiz COL

Boca Juniors	2
	Insúa [70], Palermo [83]

Abbondanzieri - Silvestre, Morel, Ibarra, Gago, Díaz, Barros Schelotto, Ledesma (Battaglia 68), Palermo, Cardozo (Insúa 45), Bilos (Palacio 68). Tr: Alfio Basile

Universidad Católica	2
	Imboden [74], Quinteros.JR [78]

Buljubasich - Rubilar, Zenteno, Imboden, Fuenzalida (Núñez 72), Ormeño•, Arrué (Vásquez 64), Pérez, Conca•, Rubio (Quinteros.I 88), Quinteros.JR. Tr: Jorge Pellicer

2nd Leg. San Carlos, Santiago
1-12-2005, 21:15, Simon BRA

Universidad Católica	0

Buljubasich - Rubilar (Muñoz 89), Zenteno•, Imboden, Fuenzalida (Núñez 70), Ormeño•, Pérez (Quinteros.I 78), Arrué, Conca, Rubio, Quinteros.JR. Tr: Jorge Pellicer

Boca Juniors	1
	Schiavi [59]

Abbondanzieri - Ibarra, Schiavi•, Díaz•, Krupoviesa•, Gago, Battaglia (Ledesma 72), Insúa (Silvestre 88), Bilos, Palacio (Barros Schelotto 84), Palermo•. Tr: Alfio Basile

1st Leg. José Amalfitani, Buenos Aires
23-11-2005, 22:10, Fagundes BRA

Vélez Sarsfield	0

Sessa - Cubero, Pellegrino, Pellerano (Uglessich 21), Bustamente•, Sena, Somoza, Centurión (Ocampo 51), Gracián, Enría (Zárate.M 79), Zárate.R. Tr: Miguel Angel Russo

Pumas UNAM	0

Bernal• - Pineda, Verón, Beltrán, Castro, Augusto, Palacios, Galindo, Da Silva• (Iñiguez 67), De Nigris, Marioni•. Tr: Miguel España

2nd Leg. Olimpico Universitario, Mexico City
30-11-2005, 19:15, Larrionda URU

Pumas UNAM	4
	Palacios [17], Marioni 3 [50 77 87]

Bernal - Beltrán, Verón, Castro• (Botero 83), Pineda•, Augusto (López.JL 76), Galindo, Palacios, De Nigris (Iñiguez 45), Marioni, Da Silva. Tr: Miguel España

Vélez Sarsfield	0

Sessa - Cubero•38, Uglessich•, Alcaraz, Bustamente•, Bustos, Somoza•, Sena, Gracián, Enría (Valdemarín 56), Zárate.R (Zárate.M 56). Tr: Miguel Angel Rosso

COPA SUDAMERICANA FINAL 1ST LEG
Olimpico Universitario, Mexico City
6-12-2005, 19:15, Larrionda URU

PUMAS UNAM 1 1 BOCA JUNIORS

Botero [53]   Palacio [30]

	PUMAS UNAM			BOCA JUNIORS	
12	BERNAM Sergio			ABBONDANZIERI Roberto	1
3	BELTRAN Joaquín			SCHIAVI Rolando	2
4	VERON Darío			KRUPOVIESA Juan	3
5	CASTRO Israel			IBARRA Hugo	4
6	PINEDA Gonzalo			DIAZ Daniel	6
23	PALACIOS Marco Antonio			GAGO Fernando	5
16	GALINDO Gerardo			LEDESMA Pablo	21
7	AUGUSTO Leandro		75	BILOS Daniel	23
8	DE NIGRIS Antonio	45	86	INSUA Federico	10
9	MARIONI Bruno		85	PALERMO Martín	9
10	DA SILVA Ailton	45		PALACIO Rodrigo	14
	Tr: ESPANA Miguel			Tr: BASILE Alfio	
	Substitutes			Substitutes	
15	BOTERO Joaquín	45	85	DELGADO Marcelo	16
20	INIGUEZ Ismael	45	75	CARDOZO Neri	19
			86	SILVESTRE Matías	22

COPA SUDAMERICANA FINAL 2ND LEG
La Bombonera, Buenos Aires
18-12-2005, 21:45, Amarilla PAR

BOCA JUNIORS 1 1 PUMAS UNAM

Palermo [31]   Marioni [54p]

	BOCA JUNIORS			PUMAS UNAM	
1	ABBONDANZIERI Roberto			BERNAM Sergio	12
4	IBARRA Hugo			PALACIOS Marco Antonio	23
2	SCHIAVI Rolando			BELTRAN Joaquín	3
6	DIAZ Daniel			VERON Darío	4
3	KRUPOVIESA Juan			CASTRO Israel	5
8	BATTAGLIA Sebastián			GALINDO Gerardo	16
5	GAGO Fernando	70		PINEDA Gonzalo	6
23	BILOS Daniel	84	78	BOTERO Joaquín	15
10	INSUA Federico			AUGUSTO Leandro	7
14	PALACIO Rodrigo	86	46	DA SILVA Ailton	10
9	PALERMO Martín			MARIONI Bruno	9
	Tr: BASILE Alfio			Tr: ESPANA Miguel	
	Substitutes			Substitutes	
7	B SCHELOTTO Guillermo	84	46	INIGUEZ Ismael	20
16	DELGADO Marcelo	86	78	CARDETTI Martín	22
21	LEDESMA Pablo	70			

PENALTY SHOOT-OUT

Pumas first		Boca second	
Leandro Augusto	✗	Barros Schelotto	✗
Pineda	✔	Insúa	✔
Beltrán	✗	Palermo	✔
Cardetti	✔	Schiavi	✔
Marioni	✔	Delgado	✔
Galindo	✗	Abbondanieri	✔

Boca Juniors win the Copa Sudamericana 4-3 on penalties

OFC

OCEANIA FOOTBALL CONFEDERATION

After 24 years out in the cold, Oceania finally had a qualification for the FIFA World Cup™ to celebrate when Australia at last made it past the intercontinental play-off against the fifth placed nation in the South American qualifiers. Having fallen at the last hurdle against Argentina, Iran and Uruguay in the previous three tournaments, the Australians overcame the Uruguayans on penalties to qualify for Germany amid scenes of huge celebration across the country. It was ironic, however, that when they played in Germany they were no longer members of the OFC, following their move to the Asian Football Confederation at the beginning of the year. Australia's absence from the OFC seriously threatens the integrity of the organisation. The major OFC power is now New Zealand, a former World Cup winning nation at rugby, a sport that dominates in a number of the small island states spread around the Pacific Ocean which make up the rest of the OFC. There is a case to be made for the standard of football in the region as a whole benefiting by a mass

THE FIFA BIG COUNT OF 2000 FOR OFC

	Male	Female		Male	Female
Registered players	106 469	13 677	Referees	4 483	104
Not registered players	322 100	10 285	Officials	18 602	6 650
Youth players	153 149	20 482	Total involved	1 205 028	101 198
Children & Occasional	600 000	50 000	in football	1 306 001	
Professionals	225	0	Number of clubs	2 801	
Total players	1 276 162		Number of teams	24 968	

defection to the AFC. The other side of the coin, though, is that the direct qualification of an OFC member to all of FIFA's competitions apart from the FIFA World Cup™ gives OFC countries direct experience of football at the top level - something that undeniably helped Australia. Whatever the arguments, there is little doubt that New Zealand stands to benefit most. With a place at the FIFA Club World Cup for the winners of the OFC Club Championship, there is a real incentive for the OFC members to develop club football. New Zealand's Auckland City started out as favourites for the 2006 tournament, held at Auckland's North Harbour Stadium, although Tahiti's AS Piraé had knocked out Auckland City at the group stage of the 2005 tournament and were paired with them again. This time they both qualified and then made it to the final, where a Keryn Jordan hat-trick secured a berth in Japan for the Kiwis in a 3-1 victory over the South Sea Islanders - the first time a club from outside of Australia had won the tournament.

Oceania Football Confederation (OFC)
Ericsson Stadium, 12 Maurice Road, Penrose, PO Box 62 586, Auckland 6, New Zealand
Tel +64 9 5258161　　　Fax +64 9 5258164
info@ofcfoot.org.nz　　　www.oceaniafootball.com
President: TEMARII Reynald TAH
General Secretary: NICHOLAS Tai COK
Vice-President: LULU Johnny VAN　　　Treasurer: HARMON Lee COK
OFC Formed: 1966

OFC EXECUTIVE COMMITTEE
President: TEMARII Reynald TAH

Senior Vice-President: LULU Johnny VAN	1st Vice-President: BURGESS Mark NZL	2nd Vice-President: WICKHAM Adrian SOL
3rd Vice-President: OTT Richard ASA	Treasurer: HARMON Lee COK	CHUNG David PNG
FOURNIER Claude NCL	HARERAAROA Eugene TAH	General Secretary NICHOLAS Tai COK
	FIFA Exco: FUSIMALOHI 'Ahongalu TGA	

MAP OF OFC MEMBER NATIONS

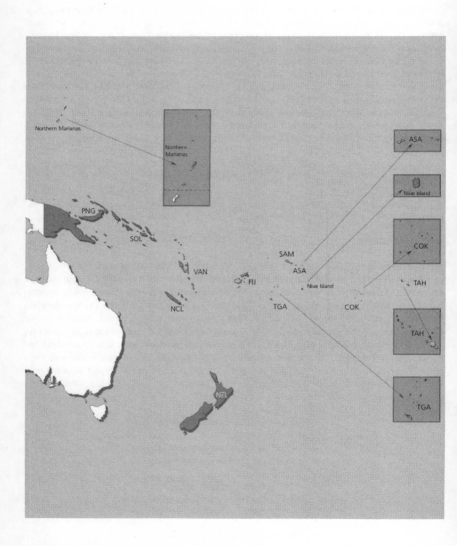

OCEANIA TOURNAMENTS

OCEANIA NATIONS CUP

Year	Host Country	Winners	Score	Runners-up	Venue
1973	New Zealand	New Zealand	2-0	Tahiti	Auckland
1980	New Caledonia	Australia	4-2	Tahiti	Nouméa
1996	Home & away	Australia	6-0 5-0	Tahiti	Papeete & Canberra
1998	Australia	New Zealand	1-0	Australia	Brisbane
2000	Tahiti	Australia	2-0	New Zealand	Stade de Pater, Papeete
2002	New Zealand	New Zealand	1-0	Australia	Ericsson Stadium, Auckland
2004	Home & away	Australia	5-1 6-0	Solomon Islands	Honaria & Sydney

Only since the advent of the FIFA Confederations Cup has the Oceania Nations Cup become a permanent fixture in the calender and unsurprisingly it has only ever been won by Australia or New Zealand. Following the departure of Australia from the OFC on January 1, 2006, New Zealand may think that they will have it all their way, although the Solomon Islands, finalists in the latest tournament in 2004 might think otherwise. Indeed, all of the smaller members of the OFC will be buoyed by the fact that at least one of them will be guaranteed a place in future finals.

OCEANIA WOMEN'S CHAMPIONSHIP

Year	Host Country	Winners	Score	Runners-up	Venue
1983	New Caledonia	New Zealand	3-2	Australia	Nouméa
1986	New Zealand	Chinese Taipei	4-1	Australia	Christchurch
1989	Australia	Chinese Taipei	1-0	New Zealand	Brisbane
1991	Australia	New Zealand	1-0 0-1 †	Australia	Sydney
1995	Papua New Guinea	Australia	1-2 1-0 †	New Zealand	Port Moresby
1998	New Zealand	Australia	3-1	New Zealand	Mount Smart, Auckland
2003	Australia	Australia	2-0 †	New Zealand	Belconnen, Canberra

† The 1991, 1995 and 2003 tournaments were played as leagues • The results shown are those between the top two teams

OCEANIA WOMEN'S U-19 CHAMPIONSHIP

Year	Host Country	Winners	Score	Runners-up	Venue
2002	Tonga	Australia	6-0	New Zealand	Nuku'alofa
2004	Papua New Guinea	Australia	14-1	Papua New Guinea	Lloyd Robson Oval, Port Moresby

Australia have developed into the most consistent power in women's football in the OFC so their departure will be a loss to the confederation with only New Zealand having a team of any great strength.

OCEANIA YOUTH CHAMPIONSHIP

Year	Host Country	Winners	Score	Runners-up	Venue
1974	Tahiti	Tahiti	2-0	New Zealand	Papeete
1978	New Zealand	Australia	5-1 †	Fiji	Auckland
1980	Fiji	New Zealand	2-0	Australia	Suva
1982	Papua New Guinea	Australia	4-3	New Zealand	Port Moresby
1985	Australia	Australia	3-2 †	Israel	Sydney
1987	New Zealand	Australia	1-1 †	Israel	Auckland
1988	Fiji	Australia	1-0	New Zealand	Suva
1990	Fiji	Australia	6-0 †	New Zealand	Suva
1992	Tahiti	New Zealand	1-0 †	Tahiti	Papeete
1994	Fiji	Australia	1-0	New Zealand	Suva
1996	Tahiti	Australia	2-1	New Zealand	Papeete
1998	Samoa	Australia	2-0	Fiji	Apia
2001	New Cal/Cook Is	Australia	1-2 3-1	New Zealand	Auckland & Coffs Harbour
2003	Vanuatu/Fiji	Australia	11-0 4-0	Fiji	Melbourne & Ba
2005	Solomon Islands	Australia	3-0	Solomon Islands	Honiara

† The 1978, 1985, 1987, 1990 and 1992 tournaments were played as leagues • The results shown are those between the top two teams

OCEANIA U-17 CHAMPIONSHIP

Year	Host Country	Winners	Score	Runners-up	Venue
1983	New Zealand	Australia	2-1	New Zealand	Mount Smart, Auckland
1986	Chinese Taipei	Australia	0-1	New Zealand	CKF Stadium, Kaohsiung
1989	Australia	Australia	5-1	New Zealand	
1991	New Zealand	Australia	1-1 1-0	New Zealand	Napier
1993	New Zealand	Australia	3-0	Soloman Islands	
1995	Vanuatu	Australia	1-0	New Zealand	
1997	New Zealand	New Zealand	1-0	Australia	
1999	Fiji	Australia	5-0	Fiji	Churchill Park, Lautoka
2001	Samoa/Cook Isl	Australia	3-0 6-0	New Zealand	Canberra & Auckland
2003	Home & away	Australia	3-1 4-0	New Caledonia	Nouméa
2005	New Caledonia	Australia	1-0	Vanuatu	Nouméa

From 1983 to 1991 the tournaments were played as leagues. The results shown are those between the top two teams

With a guaranteed place for Oceania at the FIFA World Youth Championship and the FIFA U-17 World Championship, Australia has long been a regular qualifier at these events which has helped enormously at encouraging young talent in the country. The challenge will now be for the other countries to develop their youth systems to take advantage of Australia's absence.

SOUTH PACIFIC GAMES WINNERS

Year	Host Country	Winners	Runners-up
1963	Fiji	New Caledonia	Fiji
1966	New Caledonia	Tahiti	New Caledonia
1969	Papua New Guinea	New Caledonia	Tahiti
1971	Tahiti	New Caledonia	Tahiti
1975	Guam	Tahiti	New Caledonia
1979	Fiji	Tahiti	Fiji
1983	Western Samoa	Tahiti	Fiji
1987	New Caledonia	New Caledonia	Tahiti
1991	Papua New Guinea	Fiji	Solomon Isl
1995	Tahiti	Tahiti	Solomon Isl
1999	Guam	Not played	
2003	Fiji	Fiji	New Caledonia

MELANESIAN CUP WINNERS

Year	Host Country	Winners	Runners-up
1988	Solomon Islands	Fiji	Solomon Isl
1989	Fiji	Fiji	New Caledonia
1990	Vanuatu	Vanuatu	New Caledonia
1992	Vanuatu	Fiji	New Caledonia
1994	Solomon Islands	Solomon Isl	Fiji
1996	Papua New Guinea	Papua NG	Solomon Isl
1998	Vanuatu	Fiji	Vanuatu
2000	Fiji	Fiji	Solomon Isl

SOUTH PACIFIC MINI GAMES WINNERS

Year	Host Country	Winners	Runners-up
1981	Solomon Islands	Tahiti	New Caledonia
1985	Cook Islands	Tahiti	
1989	Tonga	Papua NG	
1993	Vanuatu	Tahiti	Fiji

POLYNESIAN CUP WINNERS

Year	Host Country	Winners	Runners-up
1994	Samoa	Tahiti	Tonga
1996	Tonga	Tonga	Samoa
1998	Cook Islands	Tahiti	Cook Islands
2000	Tahiti	Tahiti	Cook Islands

For the Pacific islands, these smaller tournaments have been the lifeblood of football, representing until now the only real prospect of success and as a result they are very popular with the fans. Tahiti and Fiji have been the most consistent performers.

OFC CLUB CHAMPIONSHIP

Year	Winners	Country	Score	Country	Runners-up
1987	Adelaide City	AUS	1-1 4-1p	NZL	Mount Wellington
1999	South Melbourne	AUS	5-1	FIJ	Nadi
2001	Wollongong City Wolves	AUS	1-0	VAN	Tafea FC
2005	Sydney FC	AUS	2-0	NCL	AS Magenta
2006	Auckland City	NZL	3-1	TAH	AS Piraé

The OFC Club Championship is now an established part of the football calender, held annually to qualify a club for the FIFA Club World Cup in Japan. Tournaments have, with one exception, been organised to co-incide with a FIFA tournament and all were won by Australian clubs before their departure to the AFC.

OFC CLUB CHAMPIONSHIP NEW ZEALAND 2006

PRELIMINARY ROUND

Govind Park, Ba, Fiji, 6-02-2006, Varman FIJ

Nikao Sokattak 1 Tisam [15]
Tuanaimato Breeze 2 Faaiuaso 2 [72] [77]

Govind Park, Ba, Fiji, 6-02-2006, Averii TAH

Lotoha'apai FC 1 Vaihu [31]
Nokia Eagles Utd 5 Tamanisu [17], Nawatu [41], Duguca [59], Sabutu 2 [81] [88]

Govind Park, Ba, Fiji, 8-02-2006, Rakoroi FIJ

Lotoha'apai FC 3 Moala [54], Makasini [61], Uhatahi [67]
Nikao Sokattak 1 Willis [10]

Govind Park, Ba, Fiji, 8-02-2006, Wohler TAH

Nokia Eagles Utd 2 Tamanisau [55], Bolaitoga [77]
Tuanaimato Breeze 1 Faaiuaso [27]

Govind Park, Ba, Fiji, 10-02-2006, Varman FIJ

Tuanaimato Breeze 1 Esau [32]
Lotoha'apai FC 1 Uhatahi [85]

Govind Park, Ba, Fiji, 10-02-2006, Averii TAH

Nokia Eagles Utd 0
Nikao Sokattak 0

Preliminary round		Pl	W	D	L	F	A	Pts
Nokia Eagles United	FIJ	3	2	1	0	7	2	**7**
Tuanaimato Breeze	SAM	3	1	1	1	4	4	4
Lotoha 'apai SC	TGA	3	1	1	1	5	7	4
Nikao Sokattak	COK	3	0	1	2	2	5	1

GROUP A

North Harbour, Auckland, 10-05-2006, O'Leary NZL

Marist FC 1 Iniga [90+]
AS Piraé 10 Hmae 3 [21p] [51] [90], Naea Bennett 3 [31] [47] [65], Faauiaso [44], OG [66], Williams 2 [68] [81]

North Harbour, Auckland, 10-05-2006, Fred VAN

Auckland City 7 Jordan [10], Young [37], Mulrooney [53], Bryan Little [63], Graham Little 2 [67] [75], Hayne [89]
Sobou FC 0

North Harbour, Auckland, 13-05-2006, Averii TAH

Auckland City 3 Urlovic [14], Young [31], Graham Little [84p]
Marist FC 1 Misiga [68]

North Harbour, Auckland, 14-05-2006, Fred VAN

AS Piraé 7 Williams 3 [16] [54] [79], Luenu 2 [27] [64],
Sobou FC 0 Faauiaso 2 [77] [90]

North Harbour, Auckland, 16-05-2006, O'Leary NZL

Sobou FC 1 Wate [45] Wagiro [74], Misiga [82]
Marist FC 7 Samani 3 [31] [37] [43], Iniga [45], Wayne [54],

North Harbour, Auckland, 16-05-2006, Williams AUS

AS Piraé 0
Auckland City 1 Graham Little [85]

Group B		Pl	W	D	L	F	A	Pts
Auckland City	NZL	3	3	0	0	11	1	**9**
AS Piraé	TAH	3	2	0	1	17	2	6
Marist FC Honiara	SOL	3	1	0	2	9	14	3
Sobou Lahi	PNG	3	0	0	3	1	21	0

GROUP B

North Harbour, Auckland, 11-05-2006, O'Leary NZL

AS Magenta 0
Tafea FC 1 Vava [90]

North Harbour, Auckland, 11-05-2006, Averii TAH

Nokia Eagles Utd 2 Turuva [18p], Namaqa [75]
YoungHeart 2 Menapi [38], Totori [58]

North Harbour, Auckland, 13-05-2006, Williams AUS

AS Magenta 0
YoungHeart 3 Menapi [22], Boyens [87], Totori [88]

North Harbour, Auckland, 14-05-2006, Williams AUS

Tafea FC 0
Nokia Eagles 4 Namaqa [57], Vakatalasau [79], Hassan 2 [83] [90]

Bill McKinlay Park, Auckland, 16-05-2006, Averii TAH

Tafea FC 3 Nake 2 [23] [49], Mermer [47]
YoungHeart 3 Menapi [56], Robinson [72], Totori [89]

Bill McKinlay Park, Auckland, 16-05-2006, Fred VAN

Nokia Eagles 0
AS Magenta 1 Kaqea [83]

Group B		Pl	W	D	L	F	A	Pts
YoungHeart Manawatu	NZL	3	1	2	0	8	5	**5**
Nokia Eagles	FIJ	3	1	1	1	6	3	4
Tafea FC Port Vila	VAN	3	1	1	1	4	7	4
AS Magenta Nouméa	NCL	3	1	0	2	1	4	3

SEMI-FINALS AND FINAL

Semi-final. North Harbour, Auckland
19-05-2006, Williams AUS

Auckland City 9
Sykes [37], Seaman [52], Jordan [55], Young 2 [61] [62]
Hayne [68], Bunce [84], Graham Little 2 [89] [90]

Nicholson - Bunce, Seaman● (Cunneen 72), Perry,
Pritchett, Bryan Little (Hyde 65), Young, Sykes, Jordan
(Graham Little 67), Hayne, Van Steeden

Nokia Eagles 1
Sykes [17]
Tamanisau - Vula●64, Waqa (Dunadamu 47)
(Hassan 68), Turuva, Namaqa●, Vakatalesau, Qoro,
Tiwa, Bolaitoga, Gordon (Mudalier 70), Toma

Semi-final. North Harbour, Auckland
19-05-2006, Fred VAN

YoungHeart Manawatu 1
Totori [61]

Englefield - Cheriton (Banks 52), Menapi, Cowan,
Sandbrook, Totori, Boyens●, Robinson, Maemae●,
Adams●, Singh

AS Piraé 2
Hmae [1], Naea Bennett [8]

Torohia - Faaiuaso (Luenu 70) (Papani 79), Ly Waut,
Steven Bennett (Poroiae 26), Simon, Hmae, Li Fung
Kuee, Charriere●, Sin joux, Naea Bennett●, Zaveroni

Final. North Harbour, Auckland
21-05-2006, Williams AUS

Auckland City 3
Jordan 3 [21] [41] [64p]

Nicholson - Bunce, Seaman●, Perry●, Pritchett,
Young●, Sykes, Jordan (Coombes 80), Graham Little,
Cunneen●, Van Steeden●

AS Piraé 1
Faaiuaso [84]

Torohia● - Faaiuaso, Ly Waut, Steven Bennett (Heirani
Bennett 46), Simon, Hmae, Li Fung Kuee, Williams,
Pirowae, Charriere, Zaveroni●

UEFA

UNION DES ASSOCIATIONS EUROPEENNES DE FOOTBALL

It was a triumphant year for European football in the end, with Italy winning the FIFA World Cup™ and all four semi-finalists coming from the continent. The superb show put on by Germany showed the depth of passion there is for football in Europe and it made for a spectacular tournament. Add into the mix the superb performances of Barcelona in winning the UEFA Champions League and it is hard not to come to the conclusion that European football is riding the crest of a wave. Across the continent, many of the best players in the world play good football before big crowds in modern stadiums - and are handsomely rewarded for the pleasure. The stars of football have joined the stars of music and film as the icons of the day. Yet there are areas for concern. There were claims of match-fixing in some of the smaller leagues on the continent while in the major leagues there has been growing supporter disaffection at the widening gap between the rich and the poor. Chelsea, Lyon, Bayern Munich, Barcelona and Juventus were just so far

THE FIFA BIG COUNT OF 2000 FOR UEFA

	Male	Female		Male	Female
Registered players	8 562 596	276 323	Referees	399 919	16 650
Not registered players	17 351 201	967 291	Officials	1 752 808	17 936
Youth players	8 553 560	429 883	Total involved	51 773 742	3 078 790
Children & Occasional	15 100 000	1 370 000	in football	54 798 167	
Professionals	53 658	707	Number of clubs	223 676	
Total players	52 610 854		Number of teams	981 345	

ahead of their rivals that their respective leagues were less of a competition and more of a procession. The performance of the year was without question Barcelona in the UEFA Champions League. The bookmakers favourites from the outset they more than lived up to the billing. The Catalans won nine and drew four of the 13 games they played beating opposition from Germany, Italy, Greece, England and Portugal on their way to the title. The much criticised UEFA Cup also provided fans with some spectacular football, especially those in Middlesbrough who twice saw their team haul back three-goal deficits - against FC Basel and Steaua - to qualify for the final. There their luck ran out, however, against Sevilla as Spain made a clean sweep of the European trophies. The Spanish under-19 team also added to the Spanish fiesta when they won the UEFA European U-19 Championship in Poland, while there were continental titles for the Dutch under-21 team, the Russian under-17 team and the German women's under-19 team.

Union des associations européennes de football (UEFA)

Route de Genève 46, 1260 Nyon, Switzerland

Tel +41 22 9944444   Fax +41 22 9944488

info@uefa.com   www.uefa.com

President: JOHANSSON Lennart SWE   Chief Executive: OLSSON Lars-Christer SWE

UEFA Formed: 1954

UEFA EXECUTIVE COMMITTEE

President: JOHANSSON Lennart SWE   1st Vice-President: ERZIK Senes TUR   2nd Vice-President: OMDAL Per Ravn NOR

3rd Vice-President: VILLAR LLONA Angel Maria ESP   4th Vice-President: THOMPSON Geoffrey ENG   Treasurer: SPRENGERS Mathieu, Dr

ORDINARY MEMBERS OF THE EXECUTIVE COMMITTEE

CARRARO Franco ITA   KOLOSKOV Viacheslav, Dr RUS   LEFKARITIS Marios CYP

MAGNUSSON Eggert ISL   MAYER-VORFELDER Gerhard GER   MIFSUD Joseph, Dr MLT

PLATINI Michel FRA   SPIESS Giangiorgio SUI   Chief Executive: OLSSON Lars-Christer SWE

Co-opted: SURKIS Grigory UKR   Co-opted: MADAIL Gilberto, Dr POR

FIFA Exco member: D'HOOGHE Michel, Dr BEL   FIFA vice-president: WILL David SCO

MAP OF UEFA MEMBER NATIONS

EUROPEAN TOURNAMENTS

UEFA EUROPEAN CHAMPIONSHIP

Year	Host Country	Winners	Score	Runners-up	Venue
1960	France	Soviet Union	2-1	Yugoslavia	Parc des Princes, Paris
1964	Spain	Spain	2-1	Soviet Union	Bernabeu, Madrid
1968	Italy	Italy	1-1 2-0	Yugoslavia	Stadio Olimpico, Roma
1972	Belgium	Germany FR	3-0	Soviet Union	Heysel, Brussels
1976	Yugoslavia	Czechoslovakia	2-2 5-4p	Germany FR	Crvena Zvezda, Belgrade
1980	Italy	Germany FR	2-1	Belgium	Stadio Olimpico, Rome
1984	France	France	2-0	Spain	Parc des Princes, Paris
1988	Germany FR	Netherlands	2-0	Soviet Union	Olympiastadion, Munich
1992	Sweden	Denmark	2-0	Germany	Nya Ullevi, Gothenburg
1996	England	Germany	2-1	Czech Republic	Wembley, London
2000	Belgium/Netherlands	France	2-1	Italy	Feijenoord Stadion, Rotterdam
2004	Portugal	Greece	1-0	Portugal	Stadio da Luz, Lisbon

The UEFA European Championship is the second youngest of the Confederation championships after the Oceania Nations Cup. At first there was a patchy response to the tournament and it was not until the third edition that the Germans, the most succesful nation to date with three titles, bothered to enter. The French are the only other team to have been European Champions more than once and the wide range of winners has been a prominent feature and one of the major reasons for the continued success of the tournament. Only England of the traditional powers has failed to win the title but it has been the triumphs of the smaller nations such as Czechoslovakia, Netherlands, Denmark and most recently Greece that have caught the imagination. Only since 1980 has the UEFA European Championship had a final tournament along the lines of the current system. From 1980 to 1992 the finals had eight teams which was expanded to 16 in 1996 in no small part because UEFA's membership had grown from 32, which it had been for much of the post-war period, to beyond 50 as the political boundaries of Europe were redrawn. Eleven nations have hosted the finals but home advantage has never been a serious factor. On seven occasions the hosts have been beaten in the semi-finals, and in only three of the 12 tournaments have they actually won the title – and not since 1984 – while in 2004 Portugal became the first host nation to lose the final itself. Belgium and the Netherlands co-hosted Euro 2000™ and this system is likely to prove popular in the future with Austria and Switzerland scheduled to do the same in 2008.

UEFA EUROPEAN WOMEN'S CHAMPIONSHIP

Year	Host Country	Winners	Score	Runners-up	Venue
1984		Sweden	1-0 0-1 4-3p	England	Gothenburg & Luton
1987	Norway	Norway	2-1	Sweden	Oslo
1989	Germany FR	Germany FR	4-1	Norway	Osnabrück
1991	Denmark	Germany	3-1	Norway	Aalborg
1993	Italy	Norway	1-0	Italy	Cesena
1995	Germany	Germany	3-2	Sweden	Kaiserslautern
1997	Norway/Sweden	Germany	2-0	Italy	Oslo
2001	Germany	Germany	1-0	Sweden	Donaustadion, Ulm
2005	England	Germany	3-1	Norway	Ewood Park, Blackburn

The UEFA Women's Championship is now a flourishing event in its own right drawing good crowds into the stadiums and earning widespread coverage in the media. An unofficial European Championship was played in Italy in 1979 but since then there have been nine official tournaments, six of which have been won by Germany. The Scandinavian countries remain strong and provided the two other winners in Norway and Sweden. The eight-team final tournament was introduced for 1997 in Norway and Sweden. Although early editions often doubled up as FIFA Women's World Cup qualifiers, these are now held separately.

UEFA EUROPEAN UNDER–21 CHAMPIONSHIP

Year	Host Country	Winners	Score	Runners-up	Venue
1978		Yugoslavia	1-0 4-1	German DR	Halle & Mostar
1980		Soviet Union	0-0 1-0	German DR	Rostock & Moscow
1982		England	3-1 2-3	Germany FR	Sheffield & Bremen
1984		England	1-0 2-0	Spain	Seville & Sheffield
1986		Spain	1-2 2-1 3-0p	Italy	Rome & Valladolid
1988		France	0-0 3-0	Greece	Athens & Besançon
1990		Soviet Union	4-2 3-1	Yugoslavia	Sarajevo & Simferopol
1992		Italy	2-0 0-1	Sweden	Ferrara & Växjö
1994	France	Italy	1-0	Portugal	Montpellier
1996	Spain	Italy	1-1 4-2p	Spain	Barcelona
1998	Romania	Spain	1-0	Greece	Bucharest
2000	Slovakia	Italy	2-1	Czech Republic	Bratislava
2002	Switzerland	Czech Republic	0-0 3-1p	France	St Jakob Park, Basel
2004	Germany	Italy	3-0	Serbia & Montenegro	Ruhrstadion, Bochum
2006	Portugal	Netherlands	3-0	Ukraine	Bessa, Oporto

Since 1992 the tournament has doubled as a qualifying tournament for the Olympic Games in the respective years

UEFA EUROPEAN UNDER–19 CHAMPIONSHIP

Year	Host Country	Winners	Score	Runners-up	Venue
1981	West Germany	Germany FR	1-0	Poland	Düsseldorf
1982	Finland	Scotland	3-1	Czechoslovakia	Helsinki
1983	England	France	1-0	Czechoslovakia	White Hart Lane, London
1984	Soviet Union	Hungary	0-0 3-2p	Soviet Union	Zentralny, Moscow
1986	Yugoslavia	German DR	3-1	Italy	Subotica
1988	Czechoslovakia	Soviet Union	3-1	Portugal	Frydek-Mistek
1990	Hungary	Soviet Union	0-0 4-2p	Portugal	Bekescsaba
1992	Germany	Turkey	2-1	Portugal	Bayreuth
1993	England	England	1-0	Turkey	City Ground, Nottingham
1994	Spain	Portugal	1-1 4-1p	Germany	Merida
1995	Greece	Spain	4-1	Italy	Katerini
1996	France/Luxemb	France	1-0	Spain	Besançon
1997	Iceland	France	1-0	Portugal	Reykjavík
1998	Cyprus	Republic of Ireland	1-1 4-3p	Germany	Larnaca
1999	Sweden	Portugal	1-0	Italy	Norrköping
2000	Germany	France	1-0	Ukraine	Nürnberg
2001	Finland	Poland	3-1	Czech Republic	Helsinki
2002	Norway	Spain	1-0	Germany	Ullevaal, Oslo
2003	Liechtenstein	Italy	2-0	Portugal	Rheinpark Stadion, Vaduz
2004	Switzerland	Spain	1-0	Turkey	Colovray, Nyon
2005	Nth. Ireland	France	3-1	England	Windsor Park, Belfast
2006	Poland	Spain	2-1	Scotland	Miejski, Poznan

Played as an U-18 tournament from 1981 to 2001

UEFA EUROPEAN WOMEN'S UNDER–19 CHAMPIONSHIP

Year	Host Country	Winners	Score	Runners-up	Venue
1998		Denmark	2-0 2-3	France	Aabenraa & Niederbronn-les-Bains
1999	Sweden	Sweden	1-0	Germany	Bromölla
2000	France	Germany	4-2	Spain	La Libération, Boulogne
2001	Norway	Germany	3-2	Norway	Aråsen, Lillestrom
2002	Sweden	Germany	3-1	France	Olympia, Helsingborg
2003	Germany	France	2-0	Norway	Alfred Kunze Sportpark, Leipzig
2004	Finland	Spain	2-1	Germany	Pohjola Stadion, Vantaa
2005	Hungary	Russia	2-2 6-5p	France	ZTE, Zalaegerszeg
2006	Switzerland	Germany	3-0	France	Neufeld, Berne

The first three tournaments were played as U-18 championships

UEFA EUROPEAN UNDER-17 CHAMPIONSHIP

Year	Host Country	Winners	Score	Runners-up	Venue
1982	Italy	Italy	1-0	Germany FR	Falconara
1984	Germany FR	Germany FR	2-0	Soviet Union	Ulm
1985	Hungary	Soviet Union	4-0	Greece	Budapest
1986	Greece	Spain	2-1	Italy	Athens
1987	France	Italy	1-0	Soviet Union	Paris
1988	Spain	Spain	0-0 4-2p	Portugal	Teresa Rivero, Madrid
1989	Denmark	Portugal	4-1	German DR	Vejle
1990	East Germany	Czechoslovakia	3-2	Yugoslavia	Erfurt
1991	Swtzerland	Spain	2-0	Germany	Wankdorf, Berne
1992	Cyprus	Germany	2-1	Spain	Ammokostos, Larnaca
1993	Turkey	Poland	1-0	Italy	Inönü, Istanbul
1994	Rep. Ireland	Turkey	1-0	Denmark	Tolka Park, Dublin
1995	Belgium	Portugal	2-0	Spain	Brussels
1996	Austria	Portugal	1-0	France	Wien
1997	Germany	Spain	0-0 5-4p	Austria	Celle
1998	Scotland	Republic of Ireland	2-1	Italy	McDiarmid Park, Perth
1999	Czech Republic	Spain	4-1	Poland	Olomouc
2000	Israel	Portugal	2-1	Czech Republic	Ramat Gan, Tel Aviv
2001	England	Spain	1-0	France	Stadium of Light, Sunderland
2002	Denmark	Switzerland	0-0 4-2p	France	Farum Park, Farum
2003	Portugal	Portugal	2-1	Spain	Fontelo Municipal, Viseu
2004	France	France	2-1	Spain	Gaston Petit, Chateauroux
2005	Italy	Turkey	2-0	Netherlands	E. Mannucci, Pontedera
2006	Luxembourg	Russia	2-2 5-3p	Czech Republic	Josy Barthel, Luxembourg

Played as an U-16 tournament prior to 2002

Europe has a long history of youth football dating back to the launch of the International Youth Tournament by the English FA in 1948. UEFA took over the running of that event in 1956 and it remained largely unaltered until 1980 when it was replaced by two new tournaments, for players under 16 and players under 18. These have since changed to Under-17 and Under-19 Championships to tie in with the systems used by FIFA for their World Championships at these levels. In 1998 UEFA launched their Under-19 Championship for women which, like the men's events, doubles up when required as a qualifying tournament for the FIFA World Championships. UEFA has one other age-restricted event, the UEFA European Under-21 Championship which mirrors the qualifying groups of the senior men's team, with games often played the previous day. Tournaments are played over two years and since 1992 every second edition has doubled up as a qualifing tournament for the Olympic Games. Unlike South America, youth football has been viewed with varying degrees of scepticism in Europe and this has showed in results on the world stage.

UEFA WOMEN'S CUP

Year	Winners	Country	Score	Country	Runners-up
2002	1.FFC Frankfurt	GER	2-0	SWE	Umeå IK
2003	Umeå IK	SWE	4-1 3-0	DEN	Fortuna Hjørring
2004	Umeå IK	SWE	3-0 5-0	GER	1.FFC Frankfurt
2005	1.FFC Turbine Potsdam	GER	2-0 3-1	SWE	Djurgården/Alvsjö
2006	1.FFC Frankfurt	GER	4-0 3-2	GER	1.FFC Turbine Potsdam

Of all of the recent additions to the UEFA calendar the UEFA Women's Cup is potentially the most interesting. Whereas women's football in the USA has had its foundations in the college system, in Europe the link with men's clubs has been stronger and could develop further if the UEFA Women's Cup fulfils its potential and prompts clubs to become more serious about funding their female sections. For the 2005 tournament 42 of UEFA's 52 members entered teams, up from 22 in the first tournament in 2001, although it is the German and Scandinavian teams that have so far been the most successful.

UEFA CHAMPIONS LEAGUE

Year	Winners	Country	Score	Country	Runners-up
1956	Real Madrid	ESP	4-3	FRA	Stade de Reims
1957	Real Madrid	ESP	2-0	ITA	Fiorentina
1958	Real Madrid	ESP	3-2	ITA	Milan
1959	Real Madrid	ESP	2-0	FRA	Stade de Reims
1960	Real Madrid	ESP	7-3	FRG	Eintracht Frankfurt
1961	Benfica	POR	3-2	ESP	Barcelona
1962	Benfica	POR	5-3	ESP	Real Madrid
1963	Milan	ITA	2-1	POR	Benfica
1964	Internazionale	ITA	3-1	ESP	Real Madrid
1965	Internazionale	ITA	1-0	POR	Benfica
1966	Real Madrid	ESP	2-1	YUG	Partizan Beograd
1967	Celtic	SCO	2-1	ITA	Internazionale
1968	Manchester United	ENG	4-1	POR	Benfica
1969	Milan	ITA	4-1	NED	Ajax
1970	Feyenoord	NED	2-1	SCO	Celtic
1971	Ajax	NED	2-0	GRE	Panathinaikos
1972	Ajax	NED	2-0	ITA	Internazionale
1973	Ajax	NED	1-0	ITA	Juventus
1974	Bayern München	FRG	1-1 4-0	ESP	Atlético Madrid
1975	Bayern München	FRG	2-0	ENG	Leeds United
1976	Bayern München	FRG	1-0	FRA	AS Saint-Étienne
1977	Liverpool	ENG	3-1	FRG	Borussia Mönchengladbach
1978	Liverpool	ENG	1-0	BEL	Club Brugge
1979	Nottingham Forest	ENG	1-0	SWE	Malmö FF
1980	Nottingham Forest	ENG	1-0	FRG	Hamburger SV
1981	Liverpool	ENG	1-0	ESP	Real Madrid
1982	Aston Villa	ENG	1-0	FRG	Bayern München
1983	Hamburger SV	FRG	1-0	ITA	Juventus
1984	Liverpool	ENG	1-1 4-2p	ITA	Roma
1985	Juventus	ITA	1-0	ENG	Liverpool
1986	Steaua Bucuresti	ROU	0-0 2-0p	ESP	Barcelona
1987	FC Porto	POR	2-1	FRG	Bayern München
1988	PSV Eindhoven	NED	0-0 6-5p	POR	Benfica
1989	Milan	ITA	4-0	ROU	Steaua Bucuresti
1990	Milan	ITA	1-0	POR	Benfica
1991	Crvena Zvezda Beograd	YUG	0-0 5-3p	FRA	Olympique Marseille
1992	Barcelona	ESP	1-0	ITA	Sampdoria
1993	Olympique Marseille	FRA	1-0	ITA	Milan
1994	Milan	ITA	4-0	ESP	Barcelona
1995	Ajax	NED	1-0	ITA	Milan
1996	Juventus	ITA	1-1 4-2p	NED	Ajax
1997	Borussia Dortmund	GER	3-1	ITA	Juventus
1998	Real Madrid	ESP	1-0	ITA	Juventus
1999	Manchester United	ENG	2-1	GER	Bayern München
2000	Real Madrid	ESP	3-0	ESP	Valencia
2001	Bayern München	GER	1-1 5-4p	ESP	Valencia
2002	Real Madrid	ESP	2-1	GER	Bayer Leverkusen
2003	Milan	ITA	0-0 3-2p	ITA	Juventus
2004	FC Porto	POR	3-0	FRA	Monaco
2005	Liverpool	ENG	3-3 3-2p	ITA	Milan
2006	Barcelona	ESP	2-1	ENG	Arsenal

Europe's top club competition needs little introduction although how it is referred to may need a little explanation. Launched in 1955 as the European Champion Clubs' Cup it was often known simply as the European Cup. In 1992 it was rebranded as the UEFA Champions League, although technically speaking many of the teams taking part are not the champions of their respective leagues and half of the competition is actually run on a knock-out basis and not a league system. There are few higher honours for a footballer than lifting the European Champions Clubs' Cup, as the trophy itself is still known, and the final in May remains one of the major highlights of the year. Before 1955 clubs from different countries only met in friendly matches with two major exceptions. The annual Mitropa Cup, which started in 1927, brought together the top teams from Italy, Czechoslovakia, Hungary, Austria, Switzerland and Yugoslavia and was at its most powerful before the Second World War; and the Latin Cup, played in the post-war period between the champions of Spain, Portugal, France and Italy. Ironically the 1955 Latin Cup final was contested by Real Madrid and Stade de Reims, the two teams which a year later made it to the final of the first European Cup. The southern European nations benefited from the competitive edge that the Latin Cup had given them and it wasn't until Celtic's victory in 1967 that a club from outside of Spain, Italy or Portugal won the Cup. Most notable was Real Madrid's achievement in winning the first five tournaments and with nine triumphs they remain the most successful team. Milan are second with six although their titles have been more widespread over time than Real's showing slightly more consistency than their rivals. 1967 marked a complete shift in the balance of power with clubs from northern Europe completely dominating the competition for most of the next two decades. English clubs won six titles in a row between 1977 and 1982 while Bayern München and Ajax each won a hat-trick of titles. Heysel in 1985 marked the next watershed. That one of the worst disasters in European football should come in the European Cup final was difficult to take but it meant that UEFA could ban English clubs and the fans that had followed them abroad. It also meant the balance of power shifted south once again coinciding with the rise of the great Milan team of the late 1980s and early 1990s, a team that, in the eyes of many, rivals the Real Madrid of the 1950s as the greatest in the history of the competition. The 1991-92 season saw the first shake up in the European Cup with two groups of four replacing the quarter-finals, the winners of which qualified for the final, while the following year it was rebranded the UEFA Champions League. Since then the format has been tinkered with on a number of occasions with four first round groups introduced for the 1994-95 season, six first round groups for the 1997-98 season and finally eight first round groups and four second round groups for the 1999-2000 season. Most dramatically of all perhaps was the decision taken for the 1997-98 season which allowed more than the champions from each country to take part. For the top countries that now means entry for the top four teams, a situation which has led to some criticism, but it does satisfy the needs of the clubs whilst balancing the integrity of the national leagues. It has often been said that a European League is inevitable one day, but in many respects it is already with us in the form of the UEFA Champions League and much to UEFA's credit it has come without the clubs breaking away to form an independent body. Since the formation of the UEFA Champions League there has been a remarkble leveling of standards with no one team able to dominate the competition. Only a revived Real Madrid have come close but the past 16 tournaments have been won by 12 different clubs from eight countries. Spain head the rankings with 11 titles followed by England and Italy with 10 each.

FAIRS CUP

Year	Winners	Country	Score	Country	Runners-up
1958	Barcelona	ESP	2-2 6-0	ENG	London Select XI
1960	Barcelona	ESP	0-0 4-1	ENG	Birmingham City
1961	Roma	ITA	2-2 2-0	ENG	Birmingham City
1962	Valencia	ESP	6-2 1-1	ESP	Barcelona
1963	Valencia	ESP	2-1 2-0	YUG	Dinamo Zagreb
1964	Real Zaragoza	ESP	2-1	ESP	Valencia
1965	Ferencváros	HUN	1-0	ITA	Juventus
1966	Barcelona	ESP	0-1 4-2	ESP	Real Zaragoza
1967	Dinamo Zagreb	YUG	2-0 0-0	ENG	Leeds United
1968	Leeds United	ENG	1-0 0-0	HUN	Ferencváros
1969	Newcastle United	ENG	3-0 3-2	HUN	Ujpesti Dózsa
1970	Arsenal	ENG	1-3 3-0	BEL	RSC Anderlecht
1971	Leeds United	ENG	2-2 1-1	ITA	Juventus

UEFA CUP

Year	Winners	Country	Score	Country	Runners-up
1972	Tottenham Hotspur	ENG	2-1 1-1	ENG	Wolverhampton Wanderers
1973	Liverpool	ENG	3-0 0-2	FRG	Borussia Mönchengladbach
1974	Feyenoord	NED	2-2 2-0	ENG	Tottenham Hotspur
1975	Borussia Mönchengladbach	FRG	0-0 5-1	NED	FC Twente Enschede
1976	Liverpool	ENG	3-2 1-1	BEL	Club Brugge
1977	Juventus	ITA	1-0 1-2	ESP	Athletic Bilbao
1978	PSV Eindhoven	NED	0-0 3-0	FRA	SEC Bastia
1979	Borussia Mönchengladbach	FRG	1-1 1-0	YUG	Crvena Zvezda Beograd
1980	Eintracht Frankfurt	FRG	2-3 1-0	FRG	Borussia Mönchengladbach
1981	Ipswich Town	ENG	3-0 2-4	NED	AZ 67 Alkmaar
1982	IFK Göteborg	SWE	1-0 3-0	FRG	Hamburger SV
1983	RSC Anderlecht	BEL	1-0 1-1	POR	Benfica
1984	Tottenham Hotspur	ENG	1-1 1-1 4-3p	BEL	RSC Anderlecht
1985	Real Madrid	ESP	3-0 0-1	HUN	Videoton SC
1986	Real Madrid	ESP	5-1 0-2	FRG	1.FC Köln
1987	IFK Göteborg	SWE	1-0 1-1	SCO	Dundee United
1988	Bayer Leverkusen	FRG	0-3 3-0 3-2p	ESP	Español
1989	Napoli	ITA	2-1 3-3	FRG	VfB Stuttgart
1990	Juventus	ITA	3-1 0-0	ITA	Fiorentina
1991	Internazionale	ITA	2-0 0-1	ITA	Roma
1992	Ajax	NED	2-2 0-0	ITA	Torino
1993	Juventus	ITA	3-1 3-0	GER	Borussia Dortmund
1994	Internazionale	ITA	1-0 1-0	AUT	Austria Salzburg
1995	Parma	ITA	1-0 1-1	ITA	Juventus
1996	Bayern München	GER	2-0 3-1	FRA	Bordeaux
1997	Schalke 04	GER	1-0 0-1 4-1p	ITA	Internazionale
1998	Internazionale	ITA	3-0	ITA	Lazio
1999	Parma	ITA	3-0	FRA	Olympique Marseille
2000	Galatasaray	TUR	0-0 4-1p	ENG	Arsenal
2001	Liverpool	ENG	5-4	ESP	CD Alavés
2002	Feyenoord	NED	3-2	GER	Borussia Dortmund
2003	FC Porto	POR	3-2	SCO	Glasgow Celtic
2004	Valencia	ESP	2-0	FRA	Olympique Marseille
2005	CSKA Moskva	RUS	3-1	POR	Sporting CP
2006	Sevilla	ESP	4-0	ENG	Middlesbrough

There was a time when winning the UEFA Cup was seen as a more challenging task than winning the European Champions Clubs' Cup. With up to three or four clubs from the top nations taking part, compared to just one in the European Cup, the depth and quality of opposition was stronger, Unless clubs successfully defended their national title, the teams in the European Cup were not necessarily the form teams. More often than not these teams were playing in the UEFA Cup. Rather bizarrely the tournament was at first restricted to teams from cities that had staged a major international trade fair. Renamed in 1971 the UEFA Cup enjoyed its golden era over the next three decades. Juventus, Inter, Liverpool and Barcelona are the most successful clubs in its history with three titles, while Italy, England and Spain share 10 titles apiece. Despite this fine and glorious history, the UEFA Cup now finds itself in a crisis which UEFA has tried to address by rebranding it and introducing a group stage to try and appeal to the fans. The problem, however, dates back to the decision in 1997 to allow more than one club per country into the UEFA Champions League. Qualifying for the UEFA Cup and not the UEFA Champions League is now seen by the top clubs as a major disaster, hardly good for the credibility of the tournament. Furthermore, the problem is exacerbated by the clubs finishing third in the Champions League groups then playing in the UEFA Cup and more often than not going on to win it. This decline in prestige has had one good side effect; perhaps because the pressure is not so intense or the fear of failure so great, every final in recent years has been an entertaining and classic extravaganza.

PAST UEFA AWARDS

MOST VALUABLE PLAYER

1998	RONALDO	BRA	Internazionale
1999	BECKHAM David	ENG	Manchester United
2000	REDONDO Fernando	ARG	Real Madrid
2001	EFFENBERG Stefan	GER	Bayern München
2002	ZIDANE Zinedine	FRA	Real Madrid
2003	BUFFON Gianluigi	ITA	Juventus
2004	DECO	POR	FC Porto
2005	GERRARD Steven	ENG	Liverpool

BEST GOALKEEPER

1998	SCHMEICHEL Peter	DEN	Manchester United
1999	KAHN Oliver	GER	Bayern München
2000	KAHN Oliver	GER	Bayern München
2001	KAHN Oliver	GER	Bayern München
2002	KAHN Oliver	GER	Bayern München
2003	BUFFON Gianluigi	ITA	Juventus
2004	BAIA Vitor	POR	FC Porto
2005	CECH Petr	CZE	Chelsea

BEST DEFENDER

1998	HIERRO Fernando	ESP	Real Madrid
1999	STAM Jaap	NED	Manchester United
2000	STAM Jaap	NED	Manchester United
2001	AYALA Fabian	ARG	Valencia
2002	ROBERTO CARLOS	BRA	Real Madrid
2003	ROBERTO CARLOS	BRA	Real Madrid
2004	CARVALHO Ricardo	POR	FC Porto
2005	TERRY John	ENG	Chelsea

BEST MIDFIELDER

1998	ZIDANE Zinedine	FRA	Juventus
1999	BECKHAM David	ENG	Manchester United
2000	MENDIETA Gaizka	ESP	Valencia
2001	MENDIETA Gaizka	ESP	Lazio
2002	BALLACK Michael	GER	Bayern München
2003	NEDVED Pavel	CZE	Juventus
2004	DECO	POR	FC Porto
2005	KAKA	BRA	Milan

BEST FORWARD

1998	RONALDO	BRA	Internazionale
1999	SHEVCHENKO Andriy	UKR	Milan
2000	RAUL	ESP	Real Madrid
2001	RAUL	ESP	Real Madrid
2002	VAN NISTELROOIJ Ruud	NED	Manchester United
2003	RAUL	ESP	Real Madrid
2004	MORIENTES Fernando	ESP	Monaco
2005	RONALDINHO	BRA	Barcelona

COACH OF THE YEAR

1998	LIPPI Marcelo	ITA	Juventus
1999	FERGUSON Alex	SCO	Manchester United
2000	CUPER Hector	ARG	Valencia
2001	HITZFELD Ottmar	GER	Bayern München
2002	DEL BOSQUE Vicente	ESP	Real Madrid
2003	ANCELOTTI Carlo, ITA, Milan & MOURINHO Jose, POR, FC Porto		
2004	MOURINHO Jose, POR, FC Porto & BENITEZ Raffa, ESP, Valencia		
2005	BENITEZ Raffa, ESP, Valencia & GAZZAEV Valeri, RUS, CSKA		

PAST EUROPEAN PLAYER OF THE YEAR AWARDS

The Ballon d'Or is awarded by *France Football* magazine and since 1995 has been open to non Europeans playing with European clubs

BALLON D'OR 1956

MATTHEWS Stanley	Blackpool	ENG	47
DI STEFANO Alfredo	Real Madrid	ESP	44
KOPA Raymond	Reims	FRA	33
PUSKAS Ferenc	Honved	HUN	32
YACHIN Lev	Dyn. Moskva	URS	19
BOZSIK Jozsef	Honved	HUN	15
OCWIRK Ernst	Sampdoria	AUT	9
KOCSIS Sandor	Honved	HUN	6
Three players with four votes			

BALLON D'OR 1957

DI STEFANO Alfredo	Real Madrid	ESP	72
WRIGHT Billy	Wolves	ENG	19
KOPA Raymond	Real Madrid	FRA	16
EDWARDS Duncan	Man United	ENG	16
KUBALA Lazslo	Barcelona	ESP	15
CHARLES John	Juventus	WAL	14
STRELITSOV Edward	Torp. Moskva	URS	12
TAYLOR Tommy	Man Utd	ENG	10
BOZSIK Jozsef	Honved	HUN	9
NETTO Igor	Dyn. Moskva	URS	9

BALLON D'OR 1958

KOPA Raymond	Real Madrid	FRA	71
RAHN Helmut	RW Essen	FRG	40
FONTAINE Just	Reims	FRA	23
HAMRIN Kurt	Fiorentina	SWE	15
CHARLES John	Juventus	WAL	15
WRIGHT Billy	Wolves	ENG	9
HAYNES Johnny	Fulham	ENG	7
GREGG Harry	Man United	NIR	6
SZYMANIAK Horst	Wuppertaler SV	FRG	6
LIEDHOLM Nils	Milan	SWE	6

BALLON D'OR 1959

DI STEFANO Alfredo	Real Madrid	ESP	80
KOPA Raymond	Reims	FRA	42
CHARLES John	Juventus	WAL	24
SUAREZ Luis	Barcelona	ESP	22
SIMONSSON Agne	Örgryte IS	SWE	20
TICHY Lajos	Honved	HUN	18
PUSKAS Ferenc	Real Madrid	HUN	16
GENTO Francisco	Real Madrid	ESP	12
RAHN Helmut	1.FC Köln	FRG	11
SZYMANIAK Horst	Karlsruher SC	FRG	8

BALLON D'OR 1960

SUAREZ Luis	Barcelona	ESP	54
PUSKAS Ferenc	Real Madrid	HUN	37
SEELER Uwe	Hamburger SV	FRG	33
DI STEFANO Alfredo	Real Madrid	ESP	32
YACHIN Lev	Dyn. Moskva	URS	28
KOPA Raymond	Reims	FRA	14
CHARLES John	Juventus	WAL	11
CHARLTON Bobby	Man United	ENG	11
SIVORI Omar	Juventus	ITA	9
SZYMANIAK Horst	Karlsruher SC	FRG	9

BALLON D'OR 1961

SIVORI Omar	Juventus	ITA	46
SUAREZ Luis	Internazionale	ESP	40
HAYNES Johnny	Fulham	ENG	22
YACHIN Lev	Dyn. Moskva	URS	21
PUSKAS Ferenc	Real Madrid	ESP	16
DI STEFANO Alfredo	Real Madrid	ESP	13
SEELER Uwe	Hamburger SV	FRG	13
CHARLES John	Juventus	WAL	10
GENTO Francisco	Real Madrid	ESP	8
Seven players with five votes			

BALLON D'OR 1962

MASOPUST Josef	Dukla Praha	CZE	65
EUSEBIO	Benfica	POR	53
SCHNELLINGER K-H	1.FC Köln	FRG	33
SEKULARAC Dragoslav	Crvena Zvezda	YUG	26
JURION Joseph	Anderlecht	BEL	15
RIVERA Gianni	Milan	ITA	14
GREAVES Jimmy	Tottenham	ENG	11
GALIC Milan	Partizan	YUG	10
CHARLES John	Roma	WAL	9
GOROCS Janos	Ujpesti Dózsa	HUN	6

BALLON D'OR 1963

YACHIN Lev	Dyn. Moskva	URS	73
RIVERA Gianni	Milan	ITA	56
GREAVES Jimmy	Tottenham	ENG	51
LAW Denis	Man United	SCO	45
EUSEBIO	Benfica	POR	19
SCHNELLINGER K-H	Mantova	FRG	16
SEELER Uwe	Hamburger SV	FRG	9
SUAREZ Luis	Internazionale	ESP	5
TRAPATTONI Giovanni	Milan	ITA	5
CHARLTON Bobby	Man United	ENG	5

BALLON D'OR 1964

LAW Denis	Man United	SCO	61
SUAREZ Luis	Internazionale	ESP	43
AMANCIO	Real Madrid	ESP	38
EUSEBIO	Benfica	POR	31
VAN HIMST Paul	Anderlecht	BEL	28
GREAVES Jimmy	Tottenham	ENG	19
CORSO Mario	Internazionale	ITA	17
YACHIN Lev	Dyn. Moskva	URS	15
RIVERA Gianni	Milan	ITA	14
VORONIN Valerie	Torp. Moskva	URS	13

BALLON D'OR 1965

EUSEBIO	Benfica	POR	67
FACCHETTI Giacinto	Internazionale	ITA	59
SUAREZ Luis	Internazionale	ITA	45
VAN HIMST Paul	Anderlecht	BEL	25
CHARLTON Bobby	Man United	ENG	19
ALBERT Florian	Ferencváros	HUN	14
RIVERA Gianni	Milan	ITA	10
ASPARUCHOV Georgi	Levski Sofia	BUL	9
MAZZOLA Sandro	Internazionale	ITA	9
VORONIN Valerie	Torp. Moskva	URS	9

BALLON D'OR 1966

CHARLTON Bobby	Man United	ENG	81
EUSEBIO	Benfica	POR	80
BECKENBAUER Franz	Bayern	FRG	59
MOORE Bobby	West Ham Utd	ENG	31
ALBERT Florian	Ferencváros	HUN	23
BENE Ferenc	Ujpesti Dózsa	HUN	8
YACHIN Lev	Dyn. Moskva	URS	6
BALL Alan	Everton	ENG	6
FARKAS János	Vasas	HUN	6
TORRES José	Benfica	POR	5

BALLON D'OR 1967

ALBERT Florian	Ferencváros	HUN	68
CHARLTON Bobby	Man United	ENG	40
JOHNSTONE Jimmy	Celtic	SCO	39
BECKENBAUER Franz	Bayern	FRG	37
EUSEBIO	Benfica	POR	26
GEMMEL Tommy	Celtic	SCO	21
MULLER Gerd	Bayern	FRG	19
BEST George	Man United	NIR	18
CHISLENKO Igor	Torp. Moskva	URS	9
Three players with eight votes			

BALLON D'OR 1968

BEST George	Man United	NIR	61
CHARLTON Bobby	Man United	ENG	53
DZAJIC Dragan	Crvena Zvezda	YUG	46
BECKENBAUER Franz	Bayern	FRG	36
FACCHETTI Giacinto	Internazionale	ITA	30
RIVA Gigi	Cagliari	ITA	22
AMANCIO	Real Madrid	ESP	21
EUSEBIO	Benfica	POR	15
RIVERA Gianni	Milan	ITA	13
Two players with eight votes			

BALLON D'OR 1969

RIVERA Gianni	Milan	ITA	83
RIVA Gigi	Cagliari	ITA	79
MULLER Gerd	Bayern	FRG	38
CRUYFF Johan	Ajax	NED	30
KINDVALL Ove	Feyenoord	SWE	30
BEST George	Man United	ENG	21
BECKENBAUER Franz	Bayern	FRG	18
PRATI Pierino	Milan	ITA	17
JEKOV Peter	CSKA Sofia	BUL	14
CHARLTON Jackie	Leeds United	ENG	10

BALLON D'OR 1970

MULLER Gerd	Bayern	FRG	77
MOORE Bobby	West Ham Utd	ENG	69
RIVA Gigi	Cagliari	ITA	65
BECKENBAUER Franz	Bayern	FRG	32
Wolfgang Overath	1.FC Köln	FRG	29
DZAJIC Dragan	Crvena Zvezda	YUG	24
CRUYFF Johan	Ajax	NED	13
BANKS Gordon	Stoke City	ENG	8
MAZZOLA Sandro	Internazionale	ITA	8
Four players with seven votes			

BALLON D'OR 1971

CRUYFF Johan	Ajax	NED	116
MAZZOLA Sandro	Internazionale	ITA	57
BEST George	Man United	NIR	56
NETZER Gunter	Gladbach	FRG	30
BECKENBAUER Franz	Bayern	FRG	27
MULLER Gerd	Bayern	FRG	18
SKOBLAR Josip	Marseille	YUG	18
CHIVERS Martin	Tottenham	ENG	13
KEIZER Piet	Ajax	NED	9
Two players with seven votes			

BALLON D'OR 1972

BECKENBAUER Franz	Bayern	FRG	81
MULLER Gerd	Bayern	FRG	79
NETZER Gunter	Gladbach	FRG	79
CRUYFF Johan	Ajax	NED	73
KEIZER Piet	Ajax	NED	13
DEYNA Kazimierz	Legia	POL	6
BANKS Gordon	Stoke City	ENG	4
HULSHOFF Barry	Ajax	NED	4
LUBANSKI Wlodzimierz	Gornik Zabrze	POL	4
MOORE Bobby	West Ham Utd	ENG	4

BALLON D'OR 1973

CRUYFF Johan	Barcelona	NED	96
ZOFF Dino	Juventus	ITA	47
MULLER Gerd	Bayern	FRG	44
BECKENBAUER Franz	Bayern	FRG	30
BREMNER Billy	Leeds United	SCO	22
DEYNA Kazimierz	Legia	POL	16
EUSEBIO	Benfica	POR	14
RIVERA Gianni	Milan	ITA	12
EDSTROM Ralf	Eindhoven	SWE	11
HOENESS Uli	Bayern	FRG	11

BALLON D'OR 1974

CRUYFF Johan	Barcelona	NED	116
BECKENBAUER Franz	Bayern	FRG	105
DEYNA Kazimierz	Legia	POL	35
BREITNER Paul	Real Madrid	FRG	32
NEESKENS Johan	Barcelona	NED	21
LATO Grzegorz	Stal Mielec	POL	16
MULLER Gerd	Bayern	FRG	14
GADOCHA Robert	Legia	POL	11
BREMNER Billy	Leeds United	SCO	9
Three players with four votes			

BALLON D'OR 1975

BLOKHIN Oleg	Dynamo Kiev	URS	122
BECKENBAUER Franz	Bayern	FRG	42
CRUYFF Johan	Barcelona	NED	27
VOGTS Berti	Gladbach	FRG	25
MAIER Sepp	Bayern	FRG	20
GEELS Ruud	Ajax	NED	18
HEYNCKES Jupp	Gladbach	FRG	17
BREITNER Paul	Real Madrid	FRG	14
TODD Colin	Derby County	ENG	12
GEORGESCU Dudu	Din. Bucuresti	ROM	11

BALLON D'OR 1976

BECKENBAUER Franz	Bayern	FRG	91
RENSENBRINK Rob	Anderlecht	NED	75
VIKTOR Ivo	Dukla Praha	CZE	52
KEEGAN Kevin	Liverpool	ENG	32
PLATINI Michel	AS Nancy	FRA	19
ONDRUS Anton	Slovan	CZE	16
CRUYFF Johan	Barcelona	NED	12
CURKOVIC Ivan	Saint-Etienne	YUG	12
Three players with nine votes			

BALLON D'OR 1977

SIMONSEN Allan	Gladbach	DEN	74
KEEGAN Kevin	Liverpool	ENG	71
PLATINI Michel	AS Nancy	FRA	70
BETTEGA Roberto	Juventus	ITA	39
CRUYFF Johan	Barcelona	NED	23
FISCHER Klaus	Schalke 04	FRG	21
NYILASI Tibor	Ferencváros	HUN	13
RENSENBRINK Rob	Anderlecht	NED	13
GEORGESCU Dudu	Din. Bucuresti	ROU	6
3 players with 5 votes			

BALLON D'OR 1978

KEEGAN Kevin	Hamburger SV	ENG	87
KRANKL Hans	Rapid Wien	AUT	81
RENSENBRINK Rob	Anderlecht	NED	50
BETTEGA Roberto	Juventus	ITA	28
ROSSI Paolo	Vicenza	ITA	23
HELLSTROM Ronnie	Kaiserslautern	SWE	20
KROL Ruud	Ajax	NED	20
DALGLISH Kenny	Liverpool	SCO	10
SIMONSEN Allan	Gladbach	DEN	10
SHILTON Peter	Nottm Forest	ENG	9

BALLON D'OR 1979

KEEGAN Kevin	Hamburger SV	ENG	118
RUMMENIGGE K-H	Bayern	FRG	52
KROL Ruud	Ajax	NED	41
KALTZ Manni	Hamburger SV	FRG	27
PLATINI Michel	Saint-Etienne	FRA	23
ROSSI Paolo	Perugia	ITA	16
BRADY Liam	Arsenal	IRL	13
FRANCIS Trevor	Nottm Forest	ENG	13
BONIEK Zbigniew	Wisla Krakow	POL	9
NEHODA Zdenek	Dukla Praha	CZE	9

BALLON D'OR 1980

RUMMENIGGE K-H	Bayern	FRG	122
SCHUSTER Bernd	Barcelona	FRG	34
PLATINI Michel	Saint-Etienne	FRA	33
VAN MOER Wilfred	SK Beveren	BEL	27
CEULEMANS Jan	Club Brugge	BEL	20
HRUBESCH Horst	Hamburger SV	FRG	18
PROHASKA Herbert	Internazionale	AUT	16
MULLER Hansi	VfB Stuttgart	FRG	11
BRADY Liam	Juventus	IRL	11
KALTZ Manni	Hamburger SV	FRG	10

BALLON D'OR 1981

RUMMENIGGE K-H	Bayern	FRG	106
BREITNER Paul	Bayern	FRG	64
SCHUSTER Bernd	Barcelona	FRG	39
PLATINI Michel	Saint-Etienne	FRA	36
BLOKHIN Oleg	Dynamo Kyiv	URS	14
ZOFF Dino	Juventus	ITA	13
SHENGELIA Ramas	Dynamo Tbilisi	URS	10
CHIVADZE Alexander	Dynamo Tbilisi	URS	9
BRADY Liam	Juventus	IRL	7
WARK John	Ipswich Town	SCO	7

BALLON D'OR 1982

ROSSI Paolo	Juventus	ITA	115
GIRESSE Alain	Bordeaux	FRA	64
BONIEK Zbigniew	Juventus	POL	53
RUMMENIGGE K-H	Bayern	FRG	51
CONTI Bruno	Roma	ITA	48
DASAYEV Rinat	Spartak Moskva	URS	17
LITTBARSKI Pierre	1.FC Köln	FRG	10
ZOFF Dino	Juventus	ITA	9
PLATINI Michel	Juventus	FRA	5
SCHUSTER Bernd	Barcelona	FRG	4

BALLON D'OR 1983

PLATINI Michel	Juventus	FRA	110
DALGLISH Kenny	Liverpool	SCO	26
SIMONSEN Allan	Vejle BK	DEN	25
STRACHAN Gordon	Aberdeen	SCO	24
MAGATH Felix	Hamburger SV	FRG	20
DASAYEV Rinat	Spartak Moskva	URS	15
PFAFF Jean-Marie	Bayern	BEL	15
OLSEN Jesper	Ajax	DEN	14
RUMMENIGGE K-H	Bayern	FRG	14
ROBSON Bryan	Man United	ENG	13

BALLON D'OR 1984

PLATINI Michel	Juventus	FRA	128
TIGANA Jean	Bordeaux	FRA	57
ELKJAER Preben	Hellas Verona	DEN	48
RUSH Ian	Liverpool	WAL	44
CHALANA	Bordeaux	POR	18
SOUNESS Graeme	Sampdoria	SCO	16
SCHUMACHER Harald	1.FC Köln	FRG	12
RUMMENIGGE K-H	Internazionale	FRG	10
GIRESSE Alain	Bordeaux	FRA	9
ROBSON Bryan	Man United	ENG	7

BALLON D'OR 1985

PLATINI Michel	Juventus	FRA	127
ELKJAER Preben	Hellas Verona	DEN	71
SCHUSTER Bernd	Barcelona	FRG	46
LAUDRUP Michael	Juventus	DEN	14
RUMMENIGGE K-H	Internazionale	FRG	13
BONIEK Zbigniew	Roma	POL	12
PROTASOV Oleg	Dnepr	URS	10
BRIEGEL Hans-Peter	Hellas Verona	FRG	9
DASAYEV Rinat	Spartak Moskva	URS	8
ROBSON Bryan	Man United	ENG	8

BALLON D'OR 1986

BELANOV Igor	Dynamo Kyiv	URS	84
LINEKER Gary	Barcelona	ENG	62
BUTRAGUENO Emilio	Real Madrid	ESP	59
AMOROS Manuel	Monaco	FRA	22
ELKJAER Preben	Hellas Verona	DEN	22
RUSH Ian	Liverpool	WAL	20
ZAVAROV Alexander	Dynamo Kyiv	URS	20
VAN BASTEN Marco	Ajax	NED	10
DUCADAM Helmut	Steaua	ROU	10
ALTOBELLI Alessandro	Internazionale	ITA	9

BALLON D'OR 1987

GULLIT Ruud	Milan	NED	106
FUTRE Paolo	Atlético Madrid	POR	91
BUTRAGUENO Emilio	Real Madrid	ESP	61
MICHEL Gonzales	Real Madrid	ESP	29
LINEKER Gary	Barcelona	ENG	13
BARNES John	Liverpool	ENG	10
VAN BASTEN Marco	Milan	NED	10
VIALLI Gianluca	Sampdoria	ITA	9
ROBSON Bryan	Man United	ENG	7
ALLOFS Klaus	Marseille	FRG	6

BALLON D'OR 1988

VAN BASTEN Marco	Milan	NED	129
GULLIT Ruud	Milan	NED	88
RIJKAARD Frank	Milan	NED	45
MIKHAILICHENKO Alex	Dynamo Kyiv	URS	41
KOEMAN Ronald	PSV	NED	39
MATTHAUS Lothar	Bayern	FRG	10
VIALLI Gianluca	Sampdoria	ITA	7
BARESI Franco	Milan	ITA	5
KLINSMANN Jürgen	VfB Stuttgart	FRG	5
ZAVAROV Alexander	Juventus	URS	5

BALLON D'OR 1989

VAN BASTEN Marco	Milan	NED	119
BARESI Franco	Milan	ITA	80
RIJKAARD Frank	Milan	NED	43
MATTHAUS Lothar	Internazionale	FRG	24
SHILTON Peter	Derby County	ENG	22
STOJKOVIC Dragan	Crvena Zvezda	YUG	19
GULLIT Ruud	Milan	NED	16
HAGI Georgi	Steaua	ROU	11
KLINSMANN Jürgen	Internazionale	FRG	11
Two players with 10 votes			

BALLON D'OR 1990

MATTHAUS Lothar	Internazionale	FRG	137
SCHILLACI Salvadore	Juventus	ITA	84
BREHME Andreas	Internazionale	FRG	68
GASCOIGNE Paul	Tottenham	ENG	43
BARESI Franco	Milan	ITA	37
KLINSMANN Jürgen	Internazionale	FRG	12
SCIFO Enzo	AJ Auxerre	BEL	12
BAGGIO Roberto	Juventus	ITA	8
RIJKAARD Frank	Milan	NED	7
BUCHWALD Guido	VfB Stuttgart	FRG	6

BALLON D'OR 1991

PAPIN Jean-Pierre	Marseille	FRA	141
PANCEV Darko	Crvena Zvezda	YUG	42
SAVICEVIC Dejan	Crvena Zvezda	YUG	42
MATTHAUS Lothar	Internazionale	FRG	42
PROSINECKI Robert	Real Madrid	YUG	34
LINEKER Gary	Tottenham	ENG	33
VIALLI Gianluca	Sampdoria	ITA	18
BELODEDIC Miodrag	Crvena Zvezda	YUG	15
HUGHES Mark	Man United	WAL	12
WADDLE Chris	Marseille	ENG	11

BALLON D'OR 1992

VAN BASTEN Marco	Milan	NED	98
STOICHKOV Hristo	Barcelona	BUL	80
BERGKAMP Dennis	Ajax	NED	53
HASSLER Thomas	Roma	GER	42
SCHMEICHEL Peter	Man United	DEN	41
LAUDRUP Brian	Fiorentina	DEN	32
LAUDRUP Michael	Barcelona	DEN	22
KOEMAN Ronald	Barcelona	NED	14
CHAPUISAT Stéphane	Dortmund	SUI	10
Two players with eight votes			

BALLON D'OR 1993

BAGGIO Roberto	Juventus	ITA	142
BERGKAMP Dennis	Internazionale	NED	83
CANTONA Eric	Man United	FRA	34
BOKSIC Alen	Lazio	CRO	29
LAUDRUP Michael	Barcelona	DEN	27
BARESI Franco	Milan	ITA	24
MALDINI Paolo	Milan	ITA	19
KOSTADINOV Emil	FC Porto	BUL	11
CHAPUISAT Stéphane	Dortmund	SUI	9
GIGGS Ryan	Man United	WAL	9

BALLON D'OR 1994

STOICHKOV Hristo	Barcelona	BUL	210
BAGGIO Roberto	Juventus	ITA	136
MALDINI Paolo	Milan	ITA	109
BROLIN Tomas	Parma	SWE	68
HAGI Georghe	Barcelona	ROU	68
KLINSMANN Jürgen	Tottenham	GER	43
RAVELLI Thomas	IFK Göteborg	SWE	21
LITMANEN Jari	Ajax	FIN	12
DESAILLY Marcel	Milan	FRA	8
SAVICEVIC Dejan	Milan	YUG	8

BALLON D'OR 1995

WEAH George	Milan	LBR	144
KLINSMANN Jürgen	Bayern	GER	108
LITMANEN Jari	Ajax	FIN	67
DEL PIERO Alex	Juventus	ITA	57
KLUIVERT Patrick	Ajax	NED	47
ZOLA Gianfranco	Parma	ITA	41
MALDINI Paolo	Milan	ITA	36
OVERMARS Marc	Ajax	NED	33
SAMMER Matthias	Dortmund	GER	18
LAUDRUP Michael	Real Madrid	DEN	17

BALLON D'OR 1996

SAMMER Matthias	Dortmund	GER	144
RONALDO	Barcelona	BRA	141
SHEARER Alan	Newcastle Utd	ENG	109
DEL PIERO Alex	Juventus	ITA	65
KLINSMANN Jürgen	Bayern	GER	60
SUKER Davor	Real Madrid	CRO	38
CANTONA Eric	Man United	FRA	24
DESAILLY Marcel	Milan	FRA	22
DJORKAEFF Youri	Internazionale	FRA	20
WEAH George	Milan	LBR	17

BALLON D'OR 1997

RONALDO	Internazionale	BRA	222
MIJATOVIC Predrag	Real Madrid	YUG	72
ZIDANE Zinedine	Juventus	FRA	63
BERGKAMP Dennis	Arsenal	NED	53
ROBERTO CARLOS	Real Madrid	BRA	47
MOLLER Andreas	Dortmund	GER	40
RAUL	Real Madrid	ESP	35
SCHMEICHEL Peter	Man United	DEN	19
KOHLER Jürgen	Dortmund	GER	17
Two players with 16 votes			

BALLON D'OR 1998

ZIDANE Zinedine	Juventus	FRA	244
SUKER Davor	Real Madrid	CRO	68
RONALDO	Internazionale	BRA	66
OWEN Michael	Liverpool	ENG	51
RIVALDO	Barcelona	BRA	45
BATISTUTA Gabriel	Fiorentina	ARG	43
THURAM Lilian	Parma	FRA	36
BERGKAMP Dennis	Arsenal	NED	28
DAVIDS Edgar	Juventus	NED	28
DESAILLY Marcel	Chelsea	FRA	19

BALLON D'OR 1999

RIVALDO	Barcelona	BRA	219
BECKHAM David	Man United	ENG	154
SHEVCHENKO Andriy	Milan	UKR	64
BATISTUTA Gabriel	Fiorentina	ARG	48
FIGO Luis	Barcelona	POR	38
KEANE Roy	Man United	IRL	36
VIERI Christian	Internazionale	ITA	33
VERON Juan Seb.	Lazio	ARG	30
RAUL	Real Madrid	ESP	27
MATTHAUS Lothar	Bayern	GER	16

BALLON D'OR 2000

FIGO Luis	Real Madrid	POR	197
ZIDANE Zinedine	Juventus	FRA	181
SHEVCHENKO Andriy	Milan	UKR	85
HENRY Thierry	Arsenal	FRA	57
NESTA Alessandro	Lazio	ITA	39
RIVALDO	Barcelona	BRA	39
BATISTUTA Gabriel	Roma	ARG	26
MENDIETA Gaizka	Valencia	ESP	22
RAUL	Real Madrid	ESP	18
Two players with 10 votes			

BALLON D'OR 2001

OWEN Michael	Liverpool	ENG	176
RAUL	Real Madrid	ESP	140
KAHN Oliver	Bayern	GER	114
BECKHAM David	Man United	ENG	102
TOTTI Francesco	Roma	ITA	57
FIGO Luis	Real Madrid	POR	56
RIVALDO	Barcelona	BRA	20
SHEVCHENKO Andriy	Milan	UKR	18
HENRY Thierry	Arsenal	FRA	14
ZIDANE Zinedine	Real Madrid	FRA	14

BALLON D'OR 2002

RONALDO	Real Madrid	BRA	171
ROBERTO CARLOS	Real Madrid	BRA	145
KAHN Oliver	Bayern	GER	114
ZIDANE Zinedine	Real Madrid	FRA	78
BALLACK Michael	Bayern	GER	67
HENRY Thierry	Arsenal	FRA	54
RAUL	Real Madrid	ESP	38
RIVALDO	Milan	BRA	29
BASTURK Yildiray	Leverkusen	TUR	13
DEL PIERO Alex	Juventus	ITA	12

BALLON D'OR 2003

NEDVED Pavel	Juventus	CZE	190
HENRY Thierry	Arsenal	FRA	128
MALDINI Paolo	Milan	ITA	123
SHEVCHENKO Andriy	Milan	UKR	67
ZIDANE Zinedine	Real Madrid	FRA	64
VAN NISTELROOY Ruud	Man United	NED	61
RAUL	Real Madrid	ESP	32
ROBERTO CARLOS	Real Madrid	BRA	27
BUFFON Gianluigi	Juventus	ITA	19
BECKHAM David	Real Madrid	ENG	17

BALLON D'OR 2004

SHEVCHENKO Andriy	Milan	UKR	175
DECO	Barcelona	POR	139
RONALDINHO	Barcelona	BRA	133
HENRY Thierry	Arsenal	FRA	80
ZAGORAKIS Theodoros	Bologna	GRE	44
ADRIANO	Internazionale	BRA	23
NEDVED Pavel	Juventus	CZE	23
ROONEY Wayne	Man United	ENG	22
RICARDO CARVALHO	Chelsea	POR	18
VAN NISTELROOY Ruud	Man United	NED	18

BALLON D'OR 2005

RONALDINHO	Barcelona	BRA	225
LAMPARD Frank	Chelsea	ENG	148
GERRARD Steven	Liverpool	ENG	142
HENRY Thierry	Arsenal	FRA	41
SHEVCHENKO Andriy	Milan	UKR	33
MALDINI Paolo	Milan	ITA	23
ADRIANO	Internazionale	BRA	22
IBRAHIMOVIC Zlatan	Juventus	SWE	21
KAKA	Milan	BRA	19
Two players with 18 votes			

UEFA CHAMPIONS LEAGUE 2005-06

First Qualifying Round

Haka Valkeakoski *	FIN	1	2
Pyunik Yerevan	ARM	0	2
F'91 Dudelange *	LUX	0	4
Zrinjski Mostar *	BIH	1	0
Rabotnicki Skopje*	MKD	6	0
Skonto Riga	LVA	0	1
Levadia Tallinn *	EST	1	0
Dinamo Tbilisi	GEO	0	2
Glentoran *	NIR	1	1
Shelbourne	IRL	2	4
ND Gorica *	SVN	2	0
SK Tirana		0	3
HB Tórshavn *	FRO	2	0
FBK Kaunas	LTU	4	4
Liverpool *	ENG	3	3
TNS Llansantffraid	WAL	0	0
Neftchi Baku *	AZE	2	2
FH Hafnarfjördur	ISL	0	1
Dinamo Minsk *	BLR	1	0
Anorthosis F'gusta	CYP	1	1
Kairat Almaty *	KAZ	2	1
Artmedia	SVK	0	4
Sliema Wanderers *	MLT	1	0
Sheriff Tiraspol	MDA	4	2

Second Qualifying Round

Vålerenga IF *	NOR	1	4
Haka Valkeakoski *	FIN	0	1
F'91 Dudelange *	LUX	1	2
Rapid Wien	AUT	6	3
Rabotnicki Skopje *	MKD	1	0
Lokomotiv Moskva	RUS	1	2
Dinamo Tbilisi *	GEO	0	1
Brøndby IF	DEN	2	3
Malmö FF *	SWE	3	2
Maccabi Haifa	ISR	2	2
Dynamo Kyiv *	UKR	2	0
FC Thun	SUI	2	1
Debreceni VSC *	HUN	3	5
Hajduk Split	CRO	0	0
Shelbourne *	IRL	0	1
Steaua Bucuresti	ROU	0	4
SK Tirana *	ALB	0	0
CSKA Sofia	BUL	2	2
FBK Kaunas *	LTU	1	0
Liverpool	ENG	3	2
RSC Anderlecht *	BEL	5	0
Neftchi Baku	AZE	0	1
Anorthosis F'gusta*	CYP	3	0
Trabzonspor	TUR	1	1
Artmedia *	SVK	5	0
Celtic	SCO	0	4
Partizan Beograd *	SCG	1	1
Sheriff Tiraspol	MDA	0	0

Third Qualifying Round

Vålerenga IF *	NOR	1	0 3p
Club Brugge	BEL	0	1 4p
Rapid Wien *	AUT	1	1
Lokomotiv Moskva	RUS	1	0
Brøndby IF *	DEN	2	1
Ajax	NED	2	3
Malmö FF *	SWE	0	0
FC Thun	SUI	1	3
FC Basel *	SUI	2	0
Werder Bremen	GER	1	3
Sporting CP *	POR	0	2
Udinese	ITA	1	3
Wisla Kraków *	POL	3	1
Panathinaikos	GRE	1	4
Everton *	ENG	1	1
Villarreal	ESP	2	2
Manchester Utd *	ENG	3	3
Debreceni VSC	HUN	0	0
Steaua Bucuresti *	ROU	1	2
Rosenborg BK	NOR	1	3
CSKA Sofia *	BUL	1	1
Liverpool	ENG	3	0
Real Betis *	ESP	1	2
AS Monaco	FRA	0	2
RSC Anderlecht *	BEL	2	2
Slavia Praha	CZE	1	0
Shakhtar Donetsk *	UKR	0	1
Internazionale	ITA	2	1
Anorthosis F'gusta*	CYP	1	0
Rangers	SCO	2	2
Artmedia *	SVK	0	0 4p
Partizan Beograd	SCG	0	0 3p

Group Stage

Group A		Pts
Juventus	ITA	15
Bayern München	GER	13
Club Brugge	BEL	7
Rapid Wien	AUT	0

Group B		Pts
Arsenal	ENG	16
Ajax	NED	11
Thun	SUI	4
Sparta Praha	CZE	2

Group C		Pts
Barcelona	ESP	16
Werder Bremen	GER	7
Udinese	ITA	7
Panathinaikos	GRE	4

Group D		Pts
Villarreal	ESP	10
Benfica	POR	8
Lille OSC	FRA	6
Manchester United	ENG	6

Group E		Pts
Milan	ITA	11
PSV Eindhoven	NED	10
Schalke 04	GER	8
Fenerbahçe	TUR	4

Group F		Pts
Olymp. Lyonnais	FRA	16
Real Madrid	ESP	10
Rosenborg BK	NOR	4
Olympiacos	GRE	4

Group G		Pts
Liverpool	ENG	12
Chelsea	ENG	11
Real Betis	ESP	7
RSC Anderlecht	BEL	3

Group H		Pts
Internazionale	ITA	13
Rangers	SCO	7
Artmedia	SVK	6
FC Porto	POR	5

* Home team in the first leg • Teams placed third in the group stage qualify for the UEFA Cup as do the third qualifying round losers

UEFA CHAMPIONS LEAGUE 2005–06

UEFA CHAMPIONS LEAGUE 2005-06

Round of Sixteen			Quarter-finals			Semi-finals			Final	
Barcelona	2	1								
Chelsea *	1	1								
			Barcelona	0	2					
			Benfica *	0	0					
Liverpool	0	0								
Benfica *	1	2								
						Barcelona	1	0		
						Milan *	0	0		
Olympique Lyonnais	1	4								
PSV Eindhoven *	0	0								
			Olympique Lyonnais*	0	1					
			Milan	0	3					
Bayern München *	1	1								
Milan	1	4								
									Barcelona	2
									Arsenal	1
Villarreal	2	1								
Rangers *	2	1								
			Villarreal	1	1					
			Internazionale *	2	0					
Ajax *	2	0								
Internazionale	2	1								
						Villarreal	0	0		
						Arsenal *	1	0		
Juventus	2	2								
Werder Bremen *	3	1								
			Juventus	0	0					
			Arsenal *	2	0					
Real Madrid *	0	0								
Arsenal	0	1								

* Home team in first leg

FIRST QUALIFYING ROUND

1st Leg. Tehtaan Kenttä, Valkeakoski
13-07-2005, 1 325, Berezka UKR

Haka Valkeakoski	1
	Pasoja 26

Vilmunen; Kangaskorpi, Karjalainen, Pasoja, Innanen (Eerola 79), Kauppila*, Manninen, Nenonen (Okkonen 52), Popovich, Salli, Lehtinen (Fowler 63). Tr: Huttunen

Pyunik Yerevan	0

Bete; Tigranyan (Aleksanyan 88), Tadevosyan*, Hovsepyan, Mkrtchyan, Voskanyan, Diawara (Pachajyan 71), Arzumanyan, Nazaryan, Davityan, Lombe (Sahakyan 84). Tr: Wisman

---

2nd Leg. Republican, Yerevan
20-07-2005, 3 395, Corpodean ROU

Pyunik Yerevan	2
	Pachajyan 3, Diawara 30

Gasparyan; Tigranyan, Tadevosyan*, Hovsepyan, Mkrtchyan, Voskanyan (Aleksanyan 75), Diawara, Arzumanyan, Pachajyan, Nazaryan, Davityan (Petrosyan 75). Tr: Wisman

Haka Valkeakoski	2
	Mattila 38, Fowler 63

Vilmunen; Kangaskorpi, Karjalainen (Fowler 46), Okkonen, Pasoja, Eerola, Innanen*, Kauppila, Manninen (Juuti 84), Salli, Mattila (Rosenberg 69). Tr: Huttunen

---

1st Leg. Jos Nosbaum, Dudelange
13-07-2005, 1 308, Attard MLT

F'91 Dudelange	0

Joubert; Borbiconi, Mouny, Baudry, Mazurier (Bellini 61), Di Gregorio (El Aouad 68), Martine, Crapa, Kabongo, Remy (Saboga 78), Gruszczynski. Tr: Le Flochmoan

Zrinjski Mostar	1
	Maric.B 15

Mitrovic; Vidic, Dzidic, Papic, Zurzinov*, Mulina, Smajic*, Maric.B (Zizovic 62), Avdic (Vasilj 46), Karadza, Djuric (Semren 80). Tr: Dzidic

---

2nd Leg. Gradski, Mostar
20-07-2005, 3 600, Gvardis RUS

Zrinjski Mostar	0

Mitrovic; Vidic*, Dzidic, Papic*, Zurzinov*, Mulina*, Smajic, Maric.B (Avdic 54), Zizovic (Semren* 77), Karadza*, Djuric (Landeka 54). Tr: Dzidic

F'91 Dudelange	4
Gruszczynski 2 93 105, Di Gregorio 96, Hug 112	

Joubert; Borbiconi*, Mouny, Baudry, Martine, Crapa* (Di Gregorio 77), El Aouad (Gruszczynski 49), Kabongo, Remy, Hug*, Cleiton (Bellini* 57). Tr: Le Flochmoan

---

1st Leg. Gradski, Skopje
12-07-2005, 3 000, Paixão POR

Rabotnicki Skopje	6
Kralevski 30, Ignatov 56p, Nuhiji 2 65 84	
Trajcev 69, Maznov 76	

Madzovski; Stojanov, Karcev, Kralevski*, Jovanoski, Trajcev, Stojanov, Ignatov (Mihajlovic 89), Nuhiji, Maznov (Ilijoski 84), Pejcic (Toleski 82). Tr: Jovanovski

Skonto Riga	0

Piedels; Zakresevskis, Isakovs, Zemlinskis (Adjam 74), Nguimbat*, Korgalidze (Pereplyotkin 61), Visnakovs (Kalnins 56), Blanks, Menteshashvili, Eliava, Chaladze. Tr: Andrejevs

---

2nd Leg. Skonto, Riga
20-07-2005, 1 945, Jakov ISR

Skonto Riga	1
	Pereplyotkin 90

Piedels; Zakresevskis, Isakovs, Nguimbat* (Zemlinskis 75), Ussanov*, Eliava, Visnakovs, Menteshashvili*, Semjonovs (Kalnins 81), Pereplyotkin, Miholaps (Blanks 73). Tr: Andrejevs

Rabotnicki Skopje	0

Madzovski; Karcev (Ilievski 75), Kralevski, Jovanoski, Stojanov.I, Mihajlovic*, Jankep, Stojanov.P* (Trajcev 73), Ignatov (Pejcic 61), Toleski, Ilijoski. Tr: Jovanovski

---

1st Leg. Kadriorg, Tallinn
12-07-2005, 1 600, Courtney NIR

Levadia Tallinn	1
	Nahk 45p

Kotenko; Kalimullin*, Cepauskas, Sisov, Hohlov-Simson, Nahk, Vassiljev, Dovydenas, Dmitrijev*, Teniste (Kazimir 46), Leitan (Purke* 60). Tr: Rüütli

Dinamo Tbilisi	0

Sturua; Aladashvili*, Orbeldaze*, Gigauri, Kandelaki, Odikadze, Nozadze, Babunashvili, Navalovsky, Megreladze (Bobokhidze 63), Melkadze. Tr: Tskhadadze

---

2nd Leg. Boris Paichadze, Tbilisi
19-07-2005, 5 000, Supraha CRO

Dinamo Tbilisi	2
	Melkadze 48, Orbeldaze 50

Sturua; Aladashvili, Kemoklidze*, Orbeldaze, Kandelaki, Odikadze**76, Nozadze, Babunashvili (Makharadze 73), Chelidze (Gigauri 66), Bobokhidze (Akobia 80), Melkadze. Tr: Tskhadadze

Levadia Tallinn	0

Kotenko; Kalimullin, Cepauskas, Sisov, Hohlov-Simson, Vassiljev*, Nahk, Dmitrijev (Sadrin 60), Kazimir, Dovydenas (Purke 64), Zelinskih* (Leitan 46). Tr: Rüütli

---

1st Leg. The Oval, Belfast
13-07-2005, 2 810, Kasnaferis GRE

Glentoran	1
	Ward 77

Morris; Nixon, Holmes, Walker, Leeman*, Keegan, Ward, Tolan (Halliday 68), Parkhouse* (Morgan 68), McCallion*, Lockhart. Tr: Coyle

Shelbourne	2
	Byrne.J 2 55 65p

Delaney; Heary, Crawley (Moore* 45), Hawkins, Rogers, Hoolahan*, Cahill, Byrne.S*, Byrne.J (Crawford 79), Crowe (Fitzpatrick 76), Baker. Tr: Fenlon

---

2nd Leg. Tolka Park, Dublin
20-07-2005, 6 400, Sippel GER

Shelbourne	4
Heary 13, Byrne.J 2 32p 71, Crowe 58	

Delaney; Heary, Crawley, Rogers, Hawkins*, Cahill*, Byrne.S, Baker, Hoolahan (Crawford* 73), Crowe (Fitzpatrick 83), Byrne.J (O'Neill 83). Tr: Fenlon

Glentoran	1
	McCann 21

Morris; Nixon*, Holmes, Walker, Leeman**31, Ward (Parkhouse 65), McCann (Keegan 46) (Melaugh 88), McCallion, Morgan, Halliday, Lockhart. Tr: Coyle

---

1st Leg. Sportni Park, Nova Gorica
13-07-2005, 1 432, Nalbandyan ARM

ND Gorica	2
	Kovacevic.M 66, Birsa 82

Pirih; Suler, Handanagic, Srebrnic, Krsic, Zivec, Kovacevic.N, Ranic (Demirovic 80), Burgic (Birsa 65), Kovacevic.M, Pus. Tr: Pinni

SK Tirana	2

Hidi; Sina, Dabulla, Pisha*, Bulku, Rraklli, Mukaj*, Salihi, Hajdari, Ahmataj, Bakalli. Tr: Starova

---

2nd Leg. Qemal Stafa, Tirana
20-07-2005, 5 000, Coue FRA

SK Tirana	3
	Rraklli 38, Dabulla 42, Salihi 47

Hidi; Sina, Dabulla, Pisha, Bulku, Rraklli (Merkoci 78), Mukaj, Salihi, Hajdari, Ahmataj* (Tafaj 85), Patushi (Bakalli 75). Tr: Starova

ND Gorica	0

Pirih; Suler, Handanagic, Srebrnic, Pus*, Krsic (Sabec 77), Kovacevic.N*, Zivec (Demirovic 62), Ranic*, Kovacevic.M*, Birsa (Burgic 55). Tr: Pinni

---

1st Leg. Tórsvøllur, Torshavn
13-07-2005, 400, Sandmoen NOR

HB Torshavn	2
	Lag 2 29 62

Johannesen; Joensen.Jo, Nielsen.M, Joensen.Ja, Lag* (Mortensen 74 *92+), Nolsøe.Ru*, Borg*, Jespersen (Mortansson 46), Larsen, Nielsen.K, Danielsen* (Akselsen 61). Tr: Fernandez

FBK Kaunas	4
Velicka 2 2 25, Klimek 35, Zelmikas 63	

Kurskis; Zelmikas*, Kancelskis, Manchkhava*, Barevicius, Klimek (Rimkevicius 74), Velicka, Baguzis (Kunevicius 74), Poderis*, Kvaratskhelia* (Papeckys 46), Tamosauskas. Tr: Piskarev

---

2nd Leg. Vetra, Vilnius
19-07-2005, 2 180, Georgiev BUL

FBK Kaunas	4
Velicka 44, Rimkevicius 2 63 82, Zelmikas 90	

Kurskis*; Zelmikas, Kancelskis, Manchkhava, Barevicius (Maciulis 66), Klimek* (Rimkevicius 46), Papeckys, Velicka, Baguzis, Poderis (Pacevicius 72), Tamosauskas*. Tr: Piskarev

HB Torshavn	0

Johannesen*; Joensen.Jo, Nielsen.M (Danielsen 59), Joensen.Ja, Lag (Mortansson 59), Nolsøe.Ru*, Borg, Larsen (Akselsen 59), Nielsen.K*, Nolsøe.Ra, Jacobsen. Tr: Eystberg

---

1st Leg. Anfield, Liverpool
13-07-2005, 44 760, Van Der Velde BEL

Liverpool	3
	Gerrard 3 8 21 89

Reina; Finnan, Hyypiä, Riise, Gerrard, Le Tallec, Alonso, Morientes, Carragher, Warnock (Zenden 64), Potter (Cissé 76). Tr: Benítez

TNS Llansantffraid	0

Doherty; Taylor, King, Baker*, Evans, Holmes (Lawless 72), Ruscoe, Wilde (Beck 59), Wood, Ward (Leah 82), Jackson. Tr: McKenna

2nd Leg. Racecourse Ground, Wrexham
19-07-2005, 8 009, Bertolini SUI

TNS Llansantffraid   **0**

Doherty; Taylor, King, Baker, Evans (Jackson 78), Holmes, Ruscoe, Beck (Ward 68), Toner, Hogan, Wood (Williams 58). Tr: McKenna

Liverpool   **3**
Cissé 26, Gerrard 2 82 83

Reina; Finnan, Hyypiä, Riise, Cissé, Le Tallec (García 58), Alonso (Gerrard 68), Hamann, Carragher (Whitbread 53), Zenden, Potter. Tr: Benítez

1st Leg. Tofikh Bakhramov, Baku
12-07-2005, 8 000, Bebek CRO

Neftchi Baku   **2**
Mammadov 20, Mishura 92+

Hasanzade; Abramidze, Sadygov, Abbasov, Chertoganov, Boret, Mammadov (Mishura 59), Nabiyev, Adamia, Tagizade•, Cordas (Musayev 82). Tr: Miravadov

FH Hafnarfjördur   **0**

Lárusson; Helgason, Vidarsson, Nielsen•, Bjarnason, Ásgeirsson (Gardarsson 92+), Borgvardt, Bett, Gudmundsson, Gudjónsson (Snorrason 46), Sævarsson•. Tr: Jóhannesson

2nd Leg. Kaplakrikavöllur, Hafnarfjördur
20-05-2005, 1 873, Kaldma EST

FH Hafnarfjördur   **1**
Borgvardt 60

Lárusson; Helgason, Nielsen, Bjarnason (Albertsson 80), Ásgeirsson, Bett (Björnsson 70), Gudmundsson•, Stefánsson (Snorrason 57), Sævarsson, Borgvardt, Vidarsson•. Tr: Jóhannesson

Neftchi Baku   **2**
Mishura 51, Nabiyev 75

Hasanzade; Abramidze•, Sadygov, Abbasov, Chertoganov•43, Boret•, Adamia, Nabiyev (Rahmanov 85), Tagizade•, Mammadov (Gafitullin 90), Mishura (Musayev 71). Tr: Miravadov

1st Leg. Dinamo, Minsk
12-07-2005, 3 803, Skomina SVN

Dinamo Minsk   **1**
Lentsevich 58

Lesko; Tigorev, Lentsevich, Chalei, Volodenkov•, Razin (Kovel 26), Pavlyukovich, Zoubek (Kachuro 58), Edu, Kislyak (Rozhkov 86), Kozyr. Tr: Ryabokon

Anorthosis Famagusta   **1**
Frousos 44

Georgallides; Xenidis, Nikolaou (Konstantinou 85), Katsavakis, Poursaitidis, Ketsbaia•, Haber, Louka•, Tsitaishvili, Kinkladze (Maragos 76), Frousos (Tsolakides 46). Tr: Ketsbaia

2nd Leg. GSP, Nicosia
20-07-2005, 6 687, Brines SCO

Anorthosis Famagusta   **1**
Samaras 71

Georgallides; Katsavakis, Nikolaou (Konstantinou 88), Haber, Poursaitidis (Tsolakides 64), Tsitaishvili, Kinkladze (Kampantais 46), Louka•, Maragos, Ketsbaia, Samaras. Tr: Ketsbaia

Dinamo Minsk   **0**

Lesko; Tigorev, Lentsevich, Chalei, Volodenkov, Kovel, Pavlyukovich, Zoubek (Kachuro 64), Edu• (Rozhkov 77), Kislyak•, Kozyr. Tr: Ryabokon

1st Leg. Tsentralny, Almaty
12-07-2005, 7 000, Rogalla SUI

Kairat Almaty   **2**
Fomenko 39, Artemov 70

Naboychenko; Artemov•, Sosnovschi•, Smakov, Irismetov, Lovtchev•, Likhobabenko, Aksenov (Assanbayev 37), Diku (Bogomolov• 52), Fomenko•, Karpenko (Irismetov 46). Tr: Petrushin

Artmedia Bratislava   **0**

Cobej; Debnár• (Kotula 80), Stano, Durica, Mikulic, Obzera•, Tchul (Hellebrand 72), Gajdos, Borbély, Burák, Kozák (Vascák 62). Tr: Weiss

2nd Leg. National, Senec
20-07-2005, 3 204, Shmolik BLR

Artmedia Bratislava   **4**
Borbély 21, Tchul 52, Kozák 94p, Stano 121+

Cobej; Kotula, Debnár, Durica, Hellebrand (Mikulic 72), Vascák (Gajdos 76), Fodrek, Obzera, Tchul (Stano 83), Borbély•, Kozák. Tr: Weiss

Kairat Almaty   **1**
Bogomolov 91

Naboychenko; Artemov•, Sosnovschi•, Smakov, Abdulin, Lovtchev, Likhobabenko, Aksenov (Karpenko 60), Diku (Bogomolov 58), Fomenko, Assanbayev (Tlekhougov 86). Tr: Petrushin

1st Leg. Ta'Qali, Ta'Qali
12-05-2005, 443, Ross NIR

Sliema Wanderers   **1**
Bogdanovic 72

Akanji; Brincat (Muscat 63), Di Lello, Said, Turner (Farrugia 84), Bogdanovic•, Doncic•, Chetcuti, Woods• (Mifsud 84), Anonam, Giglio•. Tr: Aquilina

Sheriff Tiraspol   **4**
Epureanu 2 21 62, Kuchuk 25, Florescu 51

Hutan; Tassembedo, Testemitanu (Dinu 58), Tarkhnishvili, Florescu, Kuchuk, Derme, Ionescu (Goginashvili• 57), Epureanu (Gnanou 63), Cocis, Lacusta. Tr: Kouchouk

2nd Leg. Sheriff, Tiraspol
20-07-2005, 8 800, Culcu TUR

Sheriff Tiraspol   **2**
Derme 78, Cocis 83

Pasenco; Tassembedo (Goginashvili 73), Gumenuk, Testemitanu, Tarkhnishvili, Florescu (Dinu 67), Derme, Ionescu• (Kuchuk 59), Epureanu, Cocis, Lacusta. Tr: Kouchouk

Sliema Wanderers   **0**

Akanji; Brincat, Di Lello•, Said, Turner, Bogdanovic, Doncic, Chetcuti, Woods (Mifsud 75), Anonam (Muscat 86), Giglio (Lombardi 86). Tr: Aquilina

SECOND QUALIFYING ROUND

1st Leg. Ullevål, Oslo
26-07-2005, 6 297, Kelly IRL

Vålerenga   **1**
Dos Santos 50p

Arason; Brocken•, Holm, Muri, Dos Santos, Holm•, Hoseth (Gashi 56), Ishizaki (Berre 46), Mabizela (Grindheim 46), Flo.TA, Waehler. Tr: Rekdal

Haka Valkeakoski   **0**

Vilmunen; Kangaskorpi, Okkonen, Pasoja, Innanen (Rosenberg 90), Kauppila•, Manninen (Eerola 82), Popovich, Salli•, Mattila (Lehtinen 51), Fowler. Tr: Huttunen

2nd Leg. Tehtaan Kenttä, Valkeakoski
3-08-2005, 2 051, Webb ENG

Haka Valkeakoski   **1**
Lehtinen 9

Vilmunen; Kangaskorpi, Okkonen• (Rosenberg 75), Pasoja, Eerola, Innanen, Manninen (Nenonen 58), Popovich, Salli, Lehtinen (Mattila 68), Fowler. Tr: Huttunen

Vålerenga   **4**
Wæhler 26, Flo.TA 2 28 74, Iversen 59

Arason; Brocken, Holm, Dos Santos•, Holm (Ishizaki 70), Gashi•, Iversen (Hulsker 62), Grindheim (Mabizela 68), Johnsen, Flo.TA, Waehler. Tr: Rekdal

1st Leg. Jos Nosbaum, Dudelange
27-07-2005, 18:00, 1 562, Thomson SCO

F'91 Dudelange   **1**
Martine 8

Joubert; Borbiconi, Mouny, Baudry, Di Gregorio• (Gruszczynski• 58), Martine (El Aouad 79), Crapa (Bellini 72), Kabongo, Remy, Hug, Cleiton. Tr: Le Flochmoan

SK Rapid Wien   **6**
Lawaree 2 2 65, Akagündüz 2 3 15
Hofmann 5, Kienast 84

Payer; Adamski, Korsós, Hlinka, Ivanschitz, Lawaree, Akagündüz (Kienast 72), Hofmann (Dollinger 46), Bejbl, Dober• (Martínez 38), Vláhovic. Tr: Hickersberger

2nd Leg. Gerhard Hanappi, Vienna
3-08-2005, 20:15, 8 623, Briakos GRE

SK Rapid Wien   **3**
Lawaree 2 47 81, Dollinger 86

Hedl; Adamski•, Korsós, Hlinka, Lawaree, Garics, Martínez (Kavlak 70), Dollinger, Kienast (Kincl 63), Prenner, Tosun (Valachovic 63). Tr: Hickersberger

F'91 Dudelange   **2**
Tosun OG 7, Gruszczynski 37

Joubert; Borbiconi, Mouny, Baudry, Bellini (Martine 75), Crapa, El Aouad, Kabongo• (Franceschi 66), Remy•, Gruszczynski (Di Gregorio• 54), Zeghdane. Tr: Le Flochmoan

1st Leg. Gardski, Skopje
27-07-2005, 20:00, 7 000, McDonald SCO

FK Rabotnicki   **1**
Nuhiji 12

Madzovski; Igorce Stojanov, Karcev•, Kralevski, Jovanoski, Trajcev, Pance Stojanov (Mihajlovic 72), Ignatov (Jankep 92+), Nuhiji, Maznov (Ilijoski 75), Pejcic. Tr: Jovanovski

Lokomotiv Moskva   **1**
Sychev 91+

Ovchinnikov; Lima, Evseev, Sennikov, Khokhlov (Samedov 62), Asatiani, Gurenko, Bilyaletdinov, Kanyenda• (Lebedenko 75), Sychev, Poliakov. Tr: Eshtrekov

2nd Leg. Lokomotiv, Moscow
3-08-2005, 20:00, 19 648, Vollquartz DEN

Lokomotiv Moskva   **2**
Sychev 75, Asatiani 85

Ovchinnikov; Bikey, Lima• (Sennikov 82), Sychev, Pachinine, Evseev, Khokhlov, Asatiani, Samedov (Maminov 73), Gurenko, Bilyaletdinov Lebedenko 89). Tr: Eshtrekov

FK Rabotnicki   **0**

Madzovski; Igorce Stojanov (Ilija Stojanov• 14), Karcev•, Kralevski, Jovanoski•, Trajcev, Pance Stojanov, Ignatov (Jankep 55), Nuhiji (Ilijoski 77), Maznov, Pejcic. Tr: Jovanovski

1st Leg. Boris Paichadze, Tbilisi
26-07-2005, 8 000, Szabo HUN

Dinamo Tbilisi	0

Sturua; Aladashvili, Gigauri, Orbeldaze, Amisulashvili●●40, Kandelaki, Nozadze (Grigalashvili● 81), Babunashvili, Makharadze, Bobokhidze (Akobia● 46), Melkadze (Iashvili 63). Tr: Tskhadadze

Brøndby	2
	Skoubo 59, Elmander 83

Ankergren; Nielsen, Johansen.D, Lantz (Absalonsen 55), Daugaard, Retov, Skoubo (Kamper● 70), Elmander, Sennels, Agger, Jørgensen (Lorentzen 78). Tr: Laudrup.M

2nd Leg. Brøndby, Copenhagen
3-08-2005, 13 165, Weiner GER

Brøndby	3
	Lorentzen 2 9 42, Kamper 86

Ankergren; Nielsen, Johansen.D (Schmidt 75), Lantz, Lorentzen, Daugaard, Skoubo, Elmander (Kamper 57), Sennels, Agger, Jørgensen (Absalonsen 65). Tr: Laudrup.M

Dinamo Tbilisi	1
	Iashvili 65

Sturua; Aladashvili, Gigauri (Kemoklidze 46), Orbeldaze, Kandelaki (Akobia 73), Nozadze, Odikadze, Babunashvili, Makharadze, Melkadze, Megreladze (Iashvili 46). Tr: Tskhadadze

---

1st Leg. Malmö Stadion, Malmö
27-07-2005, 20:00, 10 960, Rodriguez ESP

Malmö FF	3

Osmanovski 33, Andersson.D 48p, Mattisson 68

Asper; Anders Andersson (Abelsson 89), Persson●, Mattison, Elanga, Alves, Osmanovski●, Høiland, Patrik Andersson, Bech (Olsson 86), Daniel Andersson. Tr: Prahl

Maccabi Haifa	2
	Harazi 2, Colautti 44

Davidovitch; Harazi, Benado, Keise, Boccoli, Colautti●, Tal●, Saban (Olarra 75), Xavir, Zandberg (Biruk 88), Katan (Arbaitman 86). Tr: Levy

---

2nd Leg. Bloomfield, Tel Aviv
3-08-2005, 19:00, 14 450, Tudor ROU

Maccabi Haifa	1
	Colautti 10, Arbeitman 60

Davidovitch; Harazi, Benado, Keise, Boccoli, Colautti, Tal, Xavir, Zandberg (Biruk 77), Olarra, Katan (Arbeitman 56●●70). Tr: Levy

Malmö FF	2
	Alves 21, Abelsson 89

Asper; Anders Andersson (Litmanen 61), Persson● (Abelsson 85), Olsson, Elanga, Alves, Osmanovski (Barlay 88), Høiland, Patrik Andersson, Bech, Daniel Andersson●. Tr: Prahl

---

1st Leg. Valery Lobanovskiy, Kyiv
26-07-2005, 30 000, Delevic SCG

Dynamo Kyiv	2
	Gusev 20, Shatskikh 40

Shovkovskiy; Rodolfo, Rebrov, Leko (Aliyev 69), Belkevich (Rincón 58), Rotan, Shatskikh (Verpakovskis● 58), Gusev, Nesmachniy, Gavrancic, Yussuf. Tr: Buriak

FC Thun	2
	Lustrinelli 38, Aegerter 66

Jakupovic; Vieira (Bernardi 29), Milicevic, Pimenta (Rodrigues 90), Gerber (Gonçalves 40), Deumi●, Aegerter●, Lustrinelli, Ferreira, Pallas, Hodzic. Tr: Schönenberger

---

2nd Leg. Wankdorf, Berne
3-08-2005, 20:15, 25 728, Oliveira POR

FC Thun	1
	Bernardi 92+

Jakupovic; Gonçalves●, Milicevic, Pimenta (Bernardi 86), Gerber, Deumi, Aegerter●, Lustrinelli (Rodrigues 92+), Ferreira (Vieira 75), Pallas, Hodzic. Tr: Schönenberger

Dynamo Kyiv	0

Shovkovskiy; Rodolfo, Cernat, Rotan (Belkevich 68), Shatskikh (Kleber 61), Gavrancic, Gusev, Nesmachniy, Yussuf, Da Costa●91+), Cesnauskis● (Rincón 56). Tr: Buriak

---

1st Leg. Oláh Gábor, Debrecen
27-07-2005, 20:45, 7 065, Kircher GER

Debreceni VSC	3
	Bogdanovic 2 26 40, Kerekes 58

Csernyanszki; Maté, Szatmári●, Dombi, Sandor, Bogdanovic (Brnovic 79), Kerekes (Bernáth 72), Habi (Kiss 64), Nikolov, Halmosi, Eger. Tr: Supka

Hajduk Split	0

Kale; Dolonga, Blatnjak, Kranjcar, Bartulovic●, Damjanovic, Pralija, Zilic, Granic, Grgurovic (Makarin 80), Busic. Tr: Blazevic

---

2nd Leg. Poljud, Split
3-08-2005, 20:15, 15 300, Havrilla SVK

Hajduk Split	0

Kale; Dolonga●, Blatnjak (Munhoz 46), Kranjcar, Bartulovic, Damjanovic, Zilic, Granic, Biscevic● (Makarin 85), Grgurovic●, Busic. Tr: Blazevic

Debreceni VSC	5
	Halmosi 2 1 27, Kerekes 22, Sidibe 76, Kiss 90

Csernyanszki; Maté, Szatmári, Vukmir, Dombi, Sandor, Bogdanovic (Kiss 56), Kerekes (Sidibe 57), Nikolov●, Halmosi (Böör 76), Eger. Tr: Supka

---

1st Leg. Tolka Park, Dublin
27-07-2005, 19:30, 8 500, Lajuks LVA

Shelbourne	0

Delaney; Heary, Rogers, Crawley●, Hawkins●, Baker, Cahill, Stuart Byrne (Crawford 36), Moore, Jason Byrne (Fleming 78), Crowe (Harris 75). Tr: Fenlon

Steaua Bucuresti	0

Khomutovski; Radoi, Dica● (Oprita 89), Bostina, Nesu, Nicolita● (Dinita 82), Iacob (Cristea 81), Ogararu, Paraschiv●, Ghionea, Lovin●. Tr: Protassov

---

2nd Leg. Ghencea, Bucharest
3-08-2005, 20:30, 8 781, Colombo FRA

Steaua Bucuresti	4

Nicolita 18, Iacob 27, Dinita 61, Oprita 94+p

Khomutovski; Radoi, Dica●5, Bostina (Oprita 75), Nesu, Nicolita (Paraschiv 89), Baciu, Iacob (Dinita 46●●●89), Ogararu, Ghionea, Lovin. Tr: Protassov

Shelbourne	1
	Byrne.J 38

Delaney; Heary, Rogers●5, Crawley (Fleming 77), Harris, Cahill, Stuart Byrne, Moore● (Hoolahan 65), Baker (Ndo● 80), Jason Byrne, Crowe. Tr: Fenlon

---

1st Leg. Qemal Stafa, Tirana
27-07-2005, 20:30, 6 000, Jakobsson ISL

KF Tirana	0

Hidi; Sina (Fagu 90), Dabulla●, Pisha, Bulku, Rraklli (Merkoci 46), Mukaj, Salihi●, Hajdari (Behari● 70), Ahmataj, Patushi●. Tr: Starova

CSKA Sofia	2
	Gueye 89, Gargorov 92+

Hmaruc; Zábavník, Iliev.V●, Gueye, Tiago Silva (Matic 93+), Hdiouad, Yanev, Gargorov, Todorov, Sakaliev (Dah Zadi 61), Matko (Petar Dimitrov 70). Tr: Jesic

---

2nd Leg. Balgarska Armia, Sofia
3-08-2005, 20:45, 3 100, Ingvarsson SWE

CSKA Sofia	2
	Zadi 2, Todorov 90

Hmaruc; Zábavník, Iliev.V● (Matic 57), Gueye, Tiago Silva, Hdiouad, Yanev, Gargorov (Yurukov 77), Todorov●, Sakaliev (Petar Dimitrov 57), Dah Zadi. Tr: Jesic

KF Tirana	0

Hidi; Dabulla, Pisha, Behari, Bulku●, Rraklli●, Salihi● (Fagu 82), Sina●, Ahmataj (Tafaj 63), Patushi, Merkoci (Bakalli● 58). Tr: Starova

---

1st Leg. S. Darius & S. Girenas, Kaunas
26-07-2005, 6 747, Fisker DEN

FBK Kaunas	1
	Barevicius 21

Kurskis; Zelmikas, Pacevicius (Petrenko● 45), Kancelskis, Manchkhava, Barevicius (Papeckys 72), Rimkevicius, Klimek, Baguzis, Poderis, Tamosauskas (Maciulis 88). Tr: Piskarev

Liverpool	3
	Cissé 27, Carragher 30, Gerrard 55p

Reina; Hyypiä, Riise, Gerrard (Sissoko 60), Cissé, Alonso, Crouch (Morientes 75), Josemi, Carragher, Potter (García 63), Zenden●. Tr: Benítez

---

2nd Leg. Anfield, Liverpool
2-08-2005, 43 000, Paparesta ITA

Liverpool	2
	Gerrard 77, Cissé 86

Carson; Finnan, Hyypiä, García, Crouch (Potter 55), Hamann (Gerrard 75), Morientes (Cissé 46), Sissoko, Warnock, Zenden, Whitbread. Tr: Benítez

FBK Kaunas	0

Kilijonas; Zelmikas, Kancelskis, Manchkhava, Rimkevicius, Baguzis, Poderis (Maciulis 88), Kvaratskhelia, Kunevicius, Petrenko (Klimek 46), Pehlic (Barevicius 66). Tr: Piskarev

---

1st Leg. Vanden Stock, Brussels
26-07-2005, 20:30, 21 055, Ceferin SVN

RSC Anderlecht	5

Tihinen 21, Jestrovic 24, Mpenza.M 32

Goor 35, Vanderhaeghe 77

Zitka; Deschacht, Vanderhaeghe, Jestrovic (Serhat Akin 74), Mbo Mpenza (Zewlakow 65), Goor, Wilhelmsson, Zetterberg (Baseggio 81), Kompany, Tihinen, Vanden Borre. Tr: Vercauteren

Neftchi Baku	0

Hasanzade (Micovic 46); Abramidze, Rashad F. Sadygov, Abbasov, Boret, Adamia, Nabiyev, Mammadov, Mishura (Subasic 74), Gafitullin (Getman 10), Cordas. Tr: Miravadov

1st Leg. Tofikh Bakhramov, Baku
3-08-2005, 20:00, 8 000, Kassai HUN

Neftchi Baku	1
	Boret 5p

Micovic; Getman●, Abramidze, Boret, Rashad F.
Sadygov, Abbasov, Nabiyev (Cordas 90), Mammadov,
Subasic (Mishura 76), Tagizade, Rashad A. Sadygov
(Musayev 69). Tr: Miravadov

RSC Anderlecht	0

Zitka; Deschacht, Vanderhaeghe, Zewlakow, Mbo
Mpenza (Jestrovic 70), Goor (Serhat Akin 62), Hasi,
Wilhelmsson, Kompany● (De Man 83), Tihinen,
Vanden Borre. Tr: Vercauteren

1st Leg. GSP, Nicosia
26-07-2005, 14 700, Skjerven NOR

Anorthosis Famagusta	3

Nikolaou 25, Frousos 83, Tsitaishvili 90
Georgallides; Kampantais● (Frousos 77), Poursaitidis,
Maragos●, Ketsbaia (Kinkladze 54), Nikolaou,
Tsitaishvili, Xenidis, Samaras (Haxhi● 20),
Katsavakis, Haber●. Tr: Ketsbaia & Mechael

Trabzonspor	1
	Fatih Tekke 75

Jefferson; Emrah Eren, Erdinç Yavuz, Fabiano (Tayfun Cora
81), Celaleddin Koçak (Eul Yong Lee 88), Hüseyin Çimsir,
Volkan Bekiroglu, Szymkowiak, Yattara●●45, Gökdeniz
Karadeniz, Mehmet Yilmaz (Fatih Tekke 65). Tr: Senol Günes

2nd Leg. Hüseyin Avni Aker, Trabzon
3-08-2005, 18 500, Lehner AUT.

Trabzonspor	1
	Fatih Tekke 40

Jefferson; Emrah Eren●, Erdinç Yavuz (Özgür Bayer 69),
Fabiano, Celaleddin Koçak, Hüseyin Çimsir, Adem Kocak
(Mehmet Yilmaz 46), Szymkowiak, Volkan Bekiroglu (Eul Yong
Lee 59), Gökdeniz Karadeniz, Fatih Tekke. Tr: Senol Günes

Anorthosis Famagusta	0

Georgallides●; Ketsbaia (Konstantinou 66), Haber●,
Frousos● (Xenidis 75), Katsavakis●●73, Nikolaou,
Tsitaishvili, Haxhi, Louka, Poursaitidis, Maragos
(Kinkladze 57). Tr: Ketsbaia

1st Leg. Tehelné Pole, Bratislava
27-07-2005, 17 632, Dereli TUR

Artmedia Bratislava	5

Halenár 3 43 76 89, Vascak 57, Mikulic 78
Cobej; Debnár, Durica, Kotula, Vascak (Mikulic 63),
Obzera (Burák 80), Tschul (Stano 85), Halenár,
Borbély, Fodrek, Kozák. Tr: Weiss

Celtic	0

Marshall; Telfer, Camara, Varga, Balde●, Petrov●,
Lennon, Sutton (McGeady 17), Thompson
(Aliadière 65), Zurawski (Maloney 60), Hartson.
Tr: Strachan

2nd Leg. Parkhead, Glasgow
2-08-2005, 19:45, 50 063, Undiano ESP

Celtic	4

Thompson 21p, Hartson 44, McManus 54
Beattie 82
Boruc; Telfer, Camara, Balde●, McManus, Petrov,
Wallace (Maloney 54), Lennon, Thompson●
(Aliadière 63), Zurawski (Beattie 63), Hartson.
Tr: Strachan

Artmedia Bratislava	0

Cobej; Debnár●, Durica, Vascak (Mikulic 74), Obzera,
Tschul, Halenár (Bukvic 88), Borbély, Fodrek, Burák
(Stano 68), Kozák. Tr: Weiss

1st Leg. Partizan, Belgrade
27-07-2005, 19:30, 13 116, Slupik POL

Partizan Beograd	1
	Odita 63

Kralj; Vukevic, Mirkovic, Bajic, Brnovic●, Radonjic
(Boya 46), Lomic, Odita (Grubejsic 82), Radovic,
Rnic●, Nadj (Vukajilovic 73). Tr: Vermezovic

Sheriff Tiraspol	0

Hutan; Tassembedo, Gumenuk● (Bychkov 84),
Tarkhnishvili, Florescu, Kuchuk (Dinu 55), Derme,
Ionescu (Goginashvili 58), Epureanu, Cocis, Lacusta.
Tr: Kouchouk

2nd Leg. Sheriff, Tiraspol
3-08-2005, 20:30, 11 000, Garibian FRA

Sheriff Tiraspol	0

Hutan; Tassembedo, Gumenuk●, Testemitanu,
Tarkhnishvili, Florescu● (Kuchuk 84), Derme, Ionescu
(Goginashvili 73), Epureanu, Cocis, Lacusta.
Tr: Kouchouk

Partizan Beograd	1
	Odita 74

Kralj; Vukcevic, Mirkovic (Cirkovic 89), Bajic●,
Brnovic, Boya, Lomic, Odita, Radovic (Babovic 82),
Djordjevic, Nadj (Marinkovic 92+). Tr: Vermezovic

THIRD QUALIFYING ROUND

1st Leg. Ullevål, Oslo
9-08-2005, 21:00, 13 778, Hrinak SVK

Vålerenga IF	1
	Iversen 57

Arason; Skiri, Brocken, Holm●, Dos Santos, Gashi,
Iversen●, Grindheim●, Johnsen, Flo.TA (Hoseth 74),
Waehler. Tr: Rekdal

Club Brugge	0

Butina; De Cock, Vermant, Valgaeren, Klukowski,
Clement, Verheyen●, Englebert, Balaban (Blondel 82),
Leko, Maertens● (Ishiaku 77). Tr: Ceulemans

2nd Leg. Jan Breydel, Brugge
24-08-2005, 20:30, 20 144, Plautz AUT

Club Brugge	1 4p
	Balaban 79

Butina; Vermant (1✓), Valgaeren, Klukowski (2✓),
Clement, Verheyen● (Blondel● 110) (3✓), Englebert,
Balaban (5✓), Leko (Van Tornhout 78), Maertens,
Vanaudenaerde (Dufer 69) (4✗). Tr: Ceulemans

Vålerenga IF	0 3p

Arason; Skiri (3✓), Muri, Dos Santos (5✗), Holm
(Hulsker 78) (2✗), Gashi● (4✓), Berre (Mathisen 62)
(Brocken 86), Iversen● (1✓), Grindheim, Johnsen,
Waehler●84. Tr: Rekdal

1st Leg. Gerhard Hanappi, Vienna
10-08-2005, 20:45, 18 000, Cardoso POR

SK Rapid Wien	1
	Valachovic 75p

Payer; Adamski (Dollinger 77), Korsós (Dober 86),
Hlinka●, Ivanschitz, Akagündüz, Hofmann, Martínez,
Bejbl, Kincl, Vláhovic. Tr: Hickersberger

Lokomotiv Moskva	1
	Samedov 9

Ovchinnikov●; Bikey●●●73, Lima●, Maminov,
Sennikov●, Khokhlov (Evseev 92+), Asatiani,
Lebedenko (Ruopolo 79), Samedov (Pashinin 76),
Gurenko, Bilyaletdinov. Tr: Eshtrekov

2nd Leg. Lokomotiv, Moscow
23-08-2005, 19:00, 28 000, Mejuto ESP

Lokomotiv Moskva	0

Ovchinnikov; Maminov●, Pashinin, Evseev, Sennikov,
Khokhlov, Asatiani, Lebedenko, Samedov (Izmailov
57), Gurenko (Ruopolo 85), Bilyaletdinov. Tr:
Eshtrekov

SK Rapid Wien	1
	Valachovic 84

Payer; Adamski, Korsós (Martínez 74), Hlinka,
Ivanschitz, Akagündüz (Lawaree 54), Hofmann, Bejbl●,
Dober, Kincl, Vláhovic. Tr: Hickersberger

1st Leg. Brøndby Stadion, Brøndby
10-08-2005, 19:00, 24 917, De Santis ITA

Brøndby IF	2

Skoubo 33, Escudé OG 93+
Ankergren; Rytter, Nielsen, Lantz● (Absalonsen 81),
Lorentzen (Daugaard 67), Retov, Skoubo●, Elmander,
Sennels, Agger, Jørgensen (Kamper 39). Tr: Laudrup.M

Ajax	2

Rosenberg 31, Babel 73
Vonk; Trabelsi, Grygera●, Escudé, Maduro, Pienaar,
Babel, De Jong●, Emanuelson, Rosenberg (Christeas
88), Boukhari (Sneijder 76). Tr: Blind

2nd Leg. Amsterdam ArenA, Amsterdam
24-08-2005, 20:30, 39 750, Merk GER

Ajax	3

Babel 50, Sneijder 2 80 89
Vonk; Trabelsi, Grygera, Escudé, Maduro●, Pienaar
(Galásek 82), Babel, De Jong, Emanuelson,
Rosenberg● (Heitinga 90), Boukhari (Sneijder 62).
Tr: Blind

Brøndby IF	1
	Elmander 44

Ankergren; Rytter, Nielsen●, Lantz (Daugaard 81),
Lorentzen (Kamper 57), Retov, Skoubo, Elmander,
Sennels, Agger●, Jørgensen (Absalonsen 47).
Tr: Laudrup.M

1st Leg. Malmö Stadion, Malmö
10-08-2005, 18:45, 12 237, Dauden ESP

Malmö FF — **0**

Asper; Anders Andersson, Abelsson, Elanga, Alves, Osmanovski, Høiland●, Patrik Andersson (Holgersson 87), Litmanen (Lawan 85), Pode, Daniel Andersson. Tr: Prahl

FC Thun — **1**

Adriano [33]

Jakupovic; Gonçalves, Milicevic●, Bernardi, Pimenta, Gerber (Rodrigues 85), Deumi (Vieira 15), Lustrinelli, Ferreira (Eren Sen 78), Pallas, Hodzic. Tr: Schönenberger

---

2nd Leg. Wankdorf, Berne
23-08-2005, 20:15, 31 243, Farina ITA

FC Thun — **3**

Bernardi [25], Lustrinelli 2 [40] [65]

Jakupovic; Gonçalves, Milicevic, Bernardi●, Pimenta (Rodrigues 79), Gerber (Vieira 69), Aegerter, Lustrinelli (Eren Sen 84), Ferreira, Pallas, Hodzic. Tr: Schönenberger

Malmö FF — **0**

Asper; Abelsson, Olsson (Litmanen 64), Mattisson, Elanga, Alves, Osmanovski (Anders Andersson 62), Høiland, Bech, Pode (Barlay 79), Daniel Andersson●. Tr: Prahl

---

1st Leg. St Jakob-Park, Basel
10-08-2005, 20:45, 28 101, Allaerts BEL

FC Basel — **2**

Degen.D [28], Rossi [52]

Zuberbühler; Quennoz●, Sterjovski (Kulaksizoglu 71), Petric, Chipperfield (Rossi 46), Malick Ba, Kléber, Delgado (Ergic 65), Degen, Smiljanic, Zanni. Tr: Gross

Werder Bremen — **1**

Klose [73]

Reinke; Pasanen, Naldo, Umit Davala● (Owomoyela 65), Vranjes, Micoud, Klose, Klasnic, Frings, Van Damme● (Schulz 46), Borowski. Tr: Schaaf

---

2nd Leg. Weserstadion, Bremen
24-08-2005, 20:45, 30 339, Nielsen DEN

Werder Bremen — **3**

Klasnic 2 [65] [73], Borowski [68p]

Reinke; Pasanen, Naldo, Baumann (Jensen 46), Micoud, Klose●79, Owomoyela, Klasnic (Valdez 73), Frings, Borowski, Schulz. Tr: Schaaf

FC Basel — **1**

Zuberbühler; Quennoz (Sterjovski 69), Chipperfield, Malick Ba●, Kléber, Delgado, Degen●, Eduardo●, Smiljanic, Zanni, Rossi (Ergic 82). Tr: Gross

---

1st Leg. José Alvalade, Lisbon
10-08-2005, 21:15, 35 000, Vassaras GRE

Sporting CL — **0**

Ricardo; Anderson Polga, Sá Pinto●, Rodrigo Tello, Miguel Garcia● (Rogério 57), Roudolphe Douala, Beto, Deivid (Silva 79), Custódio (Nani 70), João Moutinho, Edson●. Tr: José Peseiro

Udinese — **1**

Iaquinta [27p]

De Sanctis; Bertotto, Obodo●, Zenoni●, Iaquinta●, Di Natale● (Rossini 82), Natali●, Muntari (Mauri 72), Felipe, Barreto (Vidigal 41), Candela. Tr: Cosmi

---

1st Leg. Friuli, Udine
23-08-2005, 20:45, 23 526, Hauge NOR

Udinese — **3**

Iaquinta [23p], Natali [35], Barreto [91+]

De Sanctis; Bertotto●, Obodo, Zenoni, Vidigal, Iaquinta, Di Natale (Barreto 81), Natali, Muntari (Mauri 70), Felipe●, Candela●. Tr: Cosmi

Sporting CL — **2**

Douala [39], Pinilla [92+]

Ricardo; Rogério (Pinilla 81), Anderson Polga, Luís Loureiro, Sá Pinto (Deivid 46), Rodrigo Tello (Edson 46), Roudolphe Douala, Beto, Fábio Rochemback, João Moutinho, Liedson. Tr: José Peseiro

---

1st Leg. Wisly, Krakow
9-08-2005, 20:45, 7 227, Larsen DEN

Wisla Kraków — **3**

Brozek [13], Uche [52], Frankowski [70]

Majdan; Błaszczykowski● (Stolarczyk 76), Głowacki, Klos, Dudka, Uche, Sobolewski● (Jean Paulista 68), Cantoro, Zienczuk, Brozek (Penksa 65), Frankowski. Tr: Engel

Panathinaikos — **1**

Olisadebe [4]

Galinovic; Kotsios, Morris, Flavio Conceição●, Gekas, Olisadebe●, Papadopoulos (Charalambides 81), Wooter (Theodoridis 75), Seric, Vintra●, Biscan (Tziolis 63). Tr: Malesani

---

2nd Leg. Spyros Louis, Athens
23-08-2005, 21:45, 43 741, Riley ENG

Panathinaikos — **3**

Morris [62], Olisadebe [65], Papadopoulos [86], Kotsios [115]

Galinovic●; Kotsios●, Morris, Flavio Conceição●, Gekas, Olisadebe● (Andric 69), Wooter (Papadopoulos● 60), Seric●, Charalambides, Vintra, Biscan (Leontiou 74). Tr: Malesani

Wisla Kraków — **1**

Sobolewski [78]

Majdan●; Klos, Baszczynski, Dudka, Głowacki, Sobolewski●●89, Cantoro, Uche (Kuzba 74), Zienczuk (Jean Paulista 60), Brozek (Penska 62), Frankowski●. Tr: Engel

---

1st Leg. Goodison Park, Liverpool
9-08-2005, 20:05, 37 685, Ovrebo NOR

Everton — **1**

Beattie [42]

Martyn; Yobo, Weir, Arteta, Beattie (Marcus Bent 63), Davies, Kilbane (Ferguson 63), Cahill, Phil Neville, Hibbert●, Pistone (McFadden 80). Tr: Moyes

Villarreal — **2**

Figueroa [27], Josico [46]

Barbosa; Gonzalo Rodríguez●, Arruabarrena, Forlán● (Guayre 85), Josico, Riquelme●, Figueroa● (Tacchinardi 65), Sorín (Peña 89), Quique Alvarez, Venta, Senna. Tr: Pellegrini

---

2nd Leg. El Madrigal, Villarreal
24-08-2005, 22:00, 17 586, Collina ITA

Villarreal — **2**

Sorín [20], Forlán [92+]

Barbosa; Gonzalo Rodríguez, Arruabarrena, Forlán, Josico, Riquelme, Figueroa (Tacchinardi 82), Sorín, Quique Alvarez, Venta (Kromkamp 15), Senna. Tr: Pellegrini

Everton — **1**

Arteta [69]

Martyn; Yobo, Weir, Arteta, Marcus Bent, Ferguson, Davies (McFadden 79), Kilbane● (Osman● 57), Cahill, Phil Neville, Hibbert●. Tr: Moyes

---

1st Leg. Old Trafford, Manchester
9-08-2006, 20:05, 51 701, Medina ESP

Manchester United — **3**

Rooney [7], Van Nistelrooij [49], Ronaldo [36]

Van der Sar; Gary Neville, Ferdinand, Silvestre, O'Shea, Fletcher, Scholes, Keane● (Smith 67), Ronaldo (Park Ji Sung 67), Van Nistelrooij (Rossi 81), Rooney. Tr: Ferguson

Debreceni VSC — **0**

Csernyanszki; Maté●, Szatmári, Vukmir●, Dombi (Böör 85), Sandor, Bogdanovic, Kerekes (Sidibe 52), Nikolov●, Halmosi, Eger. Tr: Supka

---

2nd Leg. Nepstadion, Budapest
24-08-2005, 20:30, 27 000, Busacca SUI

Debreceni VSC — **0**

Csernyanszki; Maté●, Vukmir, Dombi (Szatmári 56), Sandor, Bogdanovic (Brnovic 46), Kerekes, Halmosi, Kiss, Eger, Böör (Madar 77). Tr: Supka

Manchester United — **3**

Heinze 2 [20] [61], Richardson [65]

Van der Sar; Gary Neville (Richardson 16), Heinze, Ferdinand, Brown, Smith●, Scholes (Bardsley 46), Fletcher (Miller 61), Ronaldo, Van Nistelrooij, Giggs. Tr: Ferguson

---

1st Leg. Ghencea, Bucharest
10-08-2005, 21:00, 11 514, Braamhaar NED

Steaua Bucureşti — **1**

Iacob [30]

Khomutovski; Radoi, Bostina●, Nesu, Nicolita, Iacob, Ogararu●, Cristea, Paraschiv, Ghionea, Lovin. Tr: Protassov

Rosenborg BK — **1**

Helstad [85]

Espen Johnsen; Basma, Strand (Winsnes 79), Berg, Frode Johnsen, Riseth, Solli, Lago, Helstad (Ødegaard 87), Braaten (Storflor 63), Dorsin. Tr: Hansen & Høgmo

---

2nd Leg. Lerkendal, Trondheim
23-08-2005, 20:45, 13 051, Sars FRA

Rosenborg BK — **3**

Solli [38], Ødegaard [57], Radoi OG [60]

Espen Johnsen; Wisnes, Basma, Strand, Berg, Frode Johnsen, Riseth, Lago (Ødegaard● 46), Storflor (Braaten 46), Helstad (Solli 15), Dorsin. Tr: Hansen & Høgmo

Steaua Bucureşti — **2**

Radoi [74], Iacob [76]

Khomutovski; Radoi, Bostina, Nesu (Oprita 35), Nicolita, Marin (Dinita 85), Iacob●, Ogararu, Paraschiv, Ghionea, Lovin●. Tr: Protassov

---

1st Leg. Vassil Levski, Sofia
10-08-2005, 21:45, 16 553, Wegereef NED

CSKA Sofia — **1**

Dimitrov.V [45]

Hmaruc; Zábavník, Tiago Silva, Gueye, Matic, Hdiouad●, Yanev (Petar Dimitrov 35), Gargorov, Velizar Dimitrov (Sakaliev 58), Dah Zadi (Yordanov 79), Todorov. Tr: Jesic

Liverpool — **3**

Cissé [25], Morientes 2 [31] [58]

Reina; Finnan, Hyypiä, Riise, Gerrard (Sissoko 70), Cissé, Luis Garcia●, Xabi Alonso (Hamann 65), Morientes (Barragán 78), Carragher, Warnock●. Tr: Benítez

1st Leg. Anfield, Liverpool
23-08-2005, 20:05, 42 175, Stark GER

Liverpool 0

Carson; Finnan, Hyypiä, Riise, Cissé (Sinama-Pongolle 82), Hamann, Josemi, Morientes, Sissoko, Warnock (Zenden 64), Potter (Luis García 46). Tr: Benítez

CSKA Sofia 1

Iliev.V [16]

Maksic; Velizar Dimitrov, Zábavník, Dah Zadi (Petar Dimitrov 84), Valentin Iliev, Hdiouad, Yurukov (Sakaliev 71), Gargorov, Tiago Silva, Gueye, Todorov. Tr: Jesic

1st Leg. Ruíz de Lopera, Seville
9-08-2005, 22:00, 19 122, Poll ENG

Real Betis 1

Edu [93+]

Doblas; Luis Fernández•, Juanito Gutiérrez, Rivas, Dani Martín (Xisco Muñoz 65), Fernando Fernández (Denílson 57), Joaquín Sánchez, Rivera•, Marcos Assunção (Arzu García 77), Edu, Melli. Tr: Serra Ferrer

AS Monaco 0

Roma; Evra•, Modesto•, Bernardi, Chevantón (Maoulida 69), Sorlin• (Gigliotti 82), Maicon, Zikos, Squillaci, Meriem, Adebayor. Tr: Deschamps

2nd Leg. Stade Louis II, Monaco
23-08-2005, 20:45, 13 011, Michel SVK

AS Monaco 2

Gerard [33], Maoulida [63]

Warmuz; Evra, Modesto, Bernardi•, Gerard López, Sorlin (Gigliotti 83), Maicon, Kapo, Squillaci•, Meriem (Maoulida 62), Adebayor. Tr: Deschamps

Real Betis 2

Oliveira 2 [17] [77]

Doblas•; Luis Fernández, Juanito Gutiérrez, Rivas, Ricardo Oliveira, Joaquín Sánchez• (Varela• 57), Rivera• (Lozano 77), Marcos Assunção, Xisco Muñoz• (Nano 59), Edu, Melli. Tr: Serra Ferrer

1st Leg. Vanden Stock, Brussels
10-08-2005, 20:30, 17 866, Baskakov RUS

RSC Anderlecht 2

Goor [7], Mpenza.M [38]

Zitka; Deschacht, Vanderhaeghe, Jestrovic (Wilhelmsson 62), Mbo Mpenza, Goor, Zetterberg (Baseggio 81), Serhat Akin, Kompany, Tihinen, Vanden Borre. Tr: Vercauteren

Slavia Praha 1

Jarolim [21]

Kozácik; Latka, Vlcek• (Pesir 84), Holenák, Gedeon, Jarolím•, Zboncák•, Piták• (Zábojnik 92+), Hrdlicka (Svento 46), Kovác•, Suchy. Tr: Jarolim

2nd Leg. Evzena Rosického, Prague
24-08-2005, 20:05, 17 216, Poulat FRA

Slavia Praha 0

Kozácik; Svec (Fort 46), Holenák•, Zboncák, Piták, Suchy, Gedeon• (Zábojnik 65), Lukás Jarolím, Latka, Hrdlicka (Svento 61), Vlcek•. Tr: Karel Jarolim

RSC Anderlecht 2

Serhat [72], Mpenza.M [85]

Zitka; Deschacht, Vanderhaeghe•, Mbo Mpenza, Goor•, Wilhelmsson (Zetterberg 86), Serhat Akin (Delorge 85), Kompany, Tihinen, De Man, Vanden Borre (Zewlakow 90). Tr: Vercauteren

1st Leg. Regional, Donetsk
10-08-2005, 21:00, 25 000, Hamer LUX

Shakhter Donetsk 0

Lastuvka; Srna, Rat, Tymoschuk, Matuzalem•, Brandão•, Bielik (Marica 71), Hübschman, Duljaj• (Fernandinho 69), Elano (Jadson Rodriguez 57), Barcauan. Tr: Lucescu

Internazionale 2

Martins [68], Adriano [78]

Júlio César; Córdoba•, Javier Zanetti, Stankovic, Adriano•, Verón (Pizarro 76), Solari (Zé Maria 64), Favalli, Cambiasso•, Materazzi, Martins. Tr: Mancini

2nd Leg. San Siro, Milan
24-08-2005, 21:00, BCD, Fandel GER

Internazionale 1

Recoba [13]

Júlio César; Córdoba, Javier Zanetti, Stankovic (Pizarro• 46), Adriano (Julio Cruz 81), Verón• (Zé Maria 73), Solari•, Cambiasso, Recoba, Materazzi•, Womé. Tr: Mancini

Shakhter Donetsk 1

Elano [24]

Lastuvka; Matuzalem, Lewandowski, Srna, Rat, Tymoschuk, Brandão, Hübschman, Duljaj (Fernandinho 86), Elano (Jadson Rodriguez 64), Marica (Bielik 71). Tr: Lucescu

1st Leg. GSP, Nicosia
9-08-2005, 21:00, 16 990, De Bleeckere BEL

Anorthosis Famagusta 1

Frousos [72]

Georgallides; Poursaitidis (Tsolakides 74), Haxhi•, Louka, Xenidis•, Maragos (Konstantinou 83), Frousos, Kinkladze, Ketsbaia, Tsitaishvili (Kampantais 70), Nikolaou. Tr: Ketsbaia

Rangers 2

Novo [64], Ricksen [71]

Waterreus; Pierre-Fanfan, Andrews•, Rodriguez, Ball•, Ricksen•, Ferguson, Murray, Buffel (Løvenkrands 58), Novo (Burke 82), Prso (Thompson 74). Tr: McLeish

2nd Leg. Ibrox, Glasgow
24-08-2005, 19:45, 48 500, Ivanov.V RUS

Rangers 2

Buffel [38], Prso [57]

Waterreus; Pierre-Fanfan•, Rodriguez, Ball, Ricksen, Ferguson, Murray (Rae 85), Buffel (McCormack• 74), Novo, Prso (Thompson 66), Løvenkrands. Tr: McLeish

Anorthosis Famagusta 0

Georgallides; Poursaitidis•, Katsavakis, Louka, Xenidis, Haber, Maragos (Konstantinou 51), Nikolaou, Ketsbaia (Samaras 64), Tsitaishvili (Tsolakides 72), Frousos. Tr: Ketsbaia

1st Leg. Tehelné Pole, Bratislava
10-08-2005, 20:00, 16 127, Frojdfeldt SWE

Artmedia Bratislava 0

Cobej; Stano, Durica, Kotula, Vascak (Gomes 89), Tchul, Halenár, Borbély, Fodrek, Petrás (Obzera 59), Kozák. Tr: Weiss

Partizan Beograd 0

Kralj; Vukcevic, Mirkovic, Bajic (Emeghara• 46), Brnovic, Boya•, Lomic•, Djordjevic, Odita, Tomic, Nadj•. Tr: Vermezovic

2nd Leg. Partizan, Belgrade
23-08-2005, 20:00, 26 345, Bennett ENG

Partizan Beograd 0 3p

Kralj; Vukcevic (4✓), Mirkovic• (2✗), Brnovic (6✗), Boya (5✗), Lomic• (Bajic 106) (3✓), Djordjevic, Emeghara, Odita (Radovic 68), Tomic (Grubejsic 76), Nadj (1✓). Tr: Vermezovic

Artmedia Bratislava 0 4p

Cobej; Debnár (5✓), Durica (6✓), Vascak (Gomes 95) (4✗), Tchul (Stano 55), Halenár (3✓), Borbély•, Fodrek (1✓), Petrás, Burák (Mikulic 110), Kozák• (2✗). Tr: Weiss

GROUP A

		Pl	W	D	L	F	A	Pts	ITA	GER	BEL	AUT
Juventus	ITA	6	5	0	1	12	5	15		2-1	1-0	3-0
Bayern München	GER	6	4	1	1	10	4	13	2-1		1-0	4-0
Club Brugge	BEL	6	2	1	3	6	7	7	1-2	1-1		3-2
Rapid Wien	AUT	6	0	0	6	3	15	0	1-3	0-1	0-1	

GROUP A MATCHDAY 1
Ernst Happel, Vienna
14-09-2005, 20:45, 47 540, Sars FRA

SK Rapid Wien 0

FC Bayern München 1
Guerrero 60

Payer - Dober*, Valachovic (≠81), Bejbl*, Adamski - Hofman, Korsos (Martinez 64), Hlinka, Ivanschitz (Dollinger 84) - Kincl, Lawaree (Akagunduz 74). Tr: Hickersberger

Kahn - Sagnol*, Lucio, Ismael, Lizarazu (Demichelis 52) - Schweinsteiger (Deisler 83), Hargreaves*, Scholl, Ze Roberto - Pizarro (Guerro* 52), Makaay. Tr: Magath

---

GROUP A MATCHDAY 1
Jan Breydel, Brugge
14-09-2005, 20:45, 27 000, Medina ESP

Club Brugge 1
Yulu-Matondo 85

Juventus 2
Nedved 66, Trezeguet 75

Stijnen - Spilar*, Maertens, Valgaeren (Victor 74) - De Cock, Vermant (Leko 84), Englebert, Vanaudenaerde - Yulu-Matondo, Portillo (Blondel 52), Balaban. Tr: Ceulemans

Abbiati - Blasi, Kovac*, Cannavaro, Zambrotta - Camoranesi (Giannichedda 88), Emerson, Vieira*••89, Nedved* - Trezeguet (Zalayeta 88), Ibrahimovic. Tr: Capello

---

GROUP A MATCHDAY 2
Delle Alpi, Turin
27-09-2005, 20:45, 11 156, Hansson SWE

Juventus 3
Trezeguet 27, Mutu 82, Ibrahimovic 85

SK Rapid Wien 0

Abbiati - Pessotto, Thuram, Cannavaro, Zambrotta - Camoranesi (Mutu 65),Giannichedda (Blasi 83), Emerson, Nedved - Trezeguet (Del Piero 59), Ibrahimovic. Tr: Capello

Payer - Dober (Martinez 76), Valachovic*, Bejbl, Adamski - Hofman, Korsos, Hlinka, Ivanschitz - Kincl, Akagunduz (Lawaree 53). Tr: Hickersberger

---

GROUP A MATCHDAY 2
Allianz-Arena, Munich
27-09-2005, 20:45, 66 000, Ovrebo NOR

FC Bayern München 1
Demichelis 32

Club Brugge 0

Kahn - Sagnol*, Lucio, Ismael, Lizarazu (Scholl 52) - Schweinsteiger, Demichelis, Ballack* (Jeremies 83), Ze Roberto - Makaay, Guerro (Santa Cruz 72). Tr: Magath

Butina - De Cock, Maertens, Vandelannoite* - Duffer, Englebert (Roelandts 85), Vermant*, Blondel - Verheyen (Yulu-Matondo 75), Balaban, Leko (Portillo 68). Tr: Ceulemans

---

GROUP A MATCHDAY 3
Allianz-Arena, Munich
18-10-2005, 20:45, 66 000, Vassaras GRE

FC Bayern München 2
Deisler 32, Demichelis 39

Juventus 1
Ibrahimovic 90

Kahn - Sagnol, Lucio, Ismael, Lizarazu (Schweinsteiger 30) - Deisler, Demichelis, Ballack, Ze Roberto - Makaay, Santa Cruz (Scholl 88). Tr: Magath

Abbiati - Blasi (Chiellini 46), Thuram*, Cannavaro, Zambrotta - Camoranesi (Del Piero 46), Emerson, Giannichedda*, Nedved - Ibrahimovic, Trezeguet (Mutu 66). Tr: Capello

---

GROUP A MATCHDAY 3
Ernst Happel, Vienna
18-10-2005, 20:45, 43 200, Dougal SCO

SK Rapid Wien 0

Club Brugge 1
Balaban 75

Payer - Dober* (Martin Hiden 54), Valachovic, Bejbl (Martinez 73), Adamski - Hofman, Korsos, Hlinka, Ivanschitz - Kincl, Lawaree (Akagunduz 73). Tr: Hickersberger

Butina - Vanaudenaerde, Spilar, Maertens (Englebert 70), Blondel - Vermant, Clement, Leko - Dufer (Roelandts 90), Portillo (Verheyen 70), Balaban. Tr: Ceulemans

---

GROUP A MATCHDAY 4
Delle Alpi, Turin
2-11-2005, 20:45, 16 076, Michel SVK

Juventus 2
Trezeguet 2 62 85

FC Bayern München 1
Deisler 66

Abbiati - Thuram, Kovac* (Camoranesi* 58) (Mutu 76), Cannavaro, Chiellini - Emerson, Vieira*, Del Piero (Nedved 46), Zambrotta - Trezeguet, Ibrahimovic*••90. Tr: Capello

Kahn - Sagnol, Lucio, Ismael, Schweinsteiger*, Deisler, Demichelis (Scholl 87), Ballack, Ze Roberto*, Makaay (Guerro 88) Pizarro. Tr: Magath

---

GROUP A MATCHDAY 4
Jan Breydel, Brugge
2-11-2005, 20:45, 27 541, Yefet ISR

Club Brugge 3
Portillo 9, Balaban 25, Verheyen 63

SK Rapid Wien 2
Kincl 1, Hofman 81

Butina - Vanaudenaerde, Maertens, Spilar, Blondel* - Vermant*, Clement, Leko (Roelandts 86) - Verheyen, Portillo (Simoes de Oliveira* 90), Balaban (Englebert 83). Tr: Ceulemans

Payer - Dober* (Garics 83), Martin Hiden, Bejbl, Adamski - Hofman, Korsos, Hlinka, Dollinger (Martinez 70) - Kincl*, Lawaree (Akagunduz 70). Tr: Hickersberger

---

GROUP A MATCHDAY 5
Allianz-Arena, Munich
22-11-2005, 20:45, 66 000, Dauden ESP

FC Bayern München 4
Deisler 21, Karimi 54, Makaay 2 72 77

SK Rapid Wien 0

Kahn - Sagnol*, Lucio, Ismael*, Lizarazu (Lahm 63) - Deisler, Demichelis, Karimi (Guerro 82), Ze Roberto (Scweinsteiger 46) - Makaay, Pizarro. Tr: Magath

Payer - Korsos, Martin Hiden, Bejbl*, Katzer - Hofman, Valachovic (Martinez 68), Hlinka (Garics 80), Ivanschitz (Dollinger 84) - Akagunduz, Kincl*. Tr: Hickersberger

---

GROUP A MATCHDAY 5
Delle Alpi, Turin
22-11-2005, 20:45, 9 623, Styles ENG

Juventus 1
Del Piero 80

Club Brugge 0

Abbiati - Zambrotta*, Thuram, Cannavaro, Chiellini - Camoranesi (Mutu 81), Emerson, Vieira, Nedved - Trezeguet (Zalayeta 84), Del Piero. Tr: Capello

Butina - Maertens, Spilar, Clement* (Englebert 50) - Vanaudenaerde, Verheyen, Vermant, Leko, Gvozdenovic (Lange 84) - Dufer (Serebrennikov 81), Portillo. Tr: Ceulemans

---

GROUP A MATCHDAY 6
Ernst Happel, Vienna
7-12-2005, 20:45, 45 524, Jara CZE

SK Rapid Wien 1
Kincl 52

Juventus 3
Del Piero 2 35 45, Ibrahimovic 42

Payer - Dober, Martin Hiden, Valachovic, Katzer - Korsos (Martinez 81), Hlinka, Hofman, Ivanschitz - Kincl, Akagunduz (Kienast 86). Tr: Hickersberger

Abbiati - Balzaretti, Kovac, Thuram*, Chiellini - Camoaranesi* (Giannichedda 78), Blasi, Vieira, Mutu (Pessotto 61) - Del Piero, Ibrahimovic (Zalayeta 46). Tr: Capello

---

GROUP A MATCHDAY 6
Jan Breydel, Brugge
7-12-2005, 27 860, Duhamel FRA

Club Brugge 1
Portillo 32

FC Bayern München 1
Pizarro 21

Butina - Clement, Maertens, Spilar - Vandelannoite, Vermant, Englebert (Vanaudenaerde 90), Roelandts - Yulu-Matondo (Dufer 88), Lange (Gvozdenovic 77), Portillo. Tr: Ceulemans

Kahn - Lahm, Demichelis, Ismael, Lizarazu - Deisler, Hargreaves (Schweinsteiger 67), Ballack, Karimi (Ze Roberto 46) - Makaay (Guerro 46), Pizarro*. Tr: Magath

GROUP B

		Pl	W	D	L	F	A	Pts	ENG	NED	SUI	CZE
Arsenal	ENG	6	5	1	0	10	2	16		0-0	2-1	3-0
Ajax	NED	6	3	2	1	10	6	11	1-2		2-0	2-1
FC Thun	SUI	6	1	1	4	4	9	4	0-1	2-4		1-0
Sparta Praha	CZE	6	0	2	4	2	9	2	0-2	1-1	0-0	

GROUP B MATCHDAY 1
Highbury, London
14-09-2005, 19:45, 34 498, Gilewski POL

Arsenal 2

Gilberto 51, Bergkamp 92+

Almunia - Lauren, Toure•, Campbell, Cole - Ljungberg (Hleb 81), Fabregas (Bergkamp 72), Gilberto Silva, Pires - Van Persie•45, Reyes (Owusu-Abeyie 81). Tr: Wenger

FC Thun 0

Ferreira 53

Jakupovic - Orman, Hodzic•, Milicevic, Goncalves• - Gerber (Leandro 72), Bernardi, Aegerter, Ferreira•, Adriano Pimenta (Gelson 57) - Lustrinelli (Faye 88). Tr: Schonenberger

---

GROUP B MATCHDAY 1
Sparta Stadium, Prague
14-09-2005, 20:45, 15 386, Larsen DEN

Sparta Praha 1

Matusovic 66

Blazek - Kadlec, Lukas, Petras, Pospech - Kisel, Poborsky, Polacek (Dosek 79), Sivok, Zelenka - Slepicka (Matusovic 49). Tr: Hrebik

Ajax 1

Sneijder 91+

Vonk - Trablesi, Grygera, Maduro, Emanuelson - Galasek• (Heitinga 90), Sneijder, Lindenbergh - Pienaar (Rosales 81), Rosenberg (Haristeas 76), Babel. Tr: Blind

---

GROUP B MATCHDAY 2
Wankdorf, Berne
27-09-2005, 20:45, 30 783, Layec FRA

FC Thun 1

Hodzic 89

Jakupovic - Orman (Gerber 46), Milicevic, Deumi•, Goncalves - Hodzic•, Aegerter, Leandro, Adriano Pimenta (Gelson 83), Ferreira - Lustrinelli (Sen 79). Tr: Schonenberger

Sparta Praha 0

Blazek - Pospech, Petras, Petrous•, Kadlec• - Kisel, Sivok, Hasek, Zelenka (Dosek 79), Polacek - Slepicka (Herzan 60). Tr: Hrebik

---

GROUP B MATCHDAY 2
Amsterdam ArenA, Amsterdam
27-09-2005, 20:45, 43 250, Medina ESP

Ajax 1

Rosenberg 71

Vonk• - De Jong, Grygera•, Vermaelen, Emanuelson (Juanfran 85) - Galasek• - Pienaar•, Lindenbergh - Babel, Haristeas (Rosenberg 57), Boukhari (Manucharyan 70). Tr: Blind

Arsenal 2

Ljungberg 2, Pires 69p

Almunia• - Lauren, Toure•, Campbell, Cole - Hleb (Cygan 90), Fabregas, Flamini, Pires (Clichy 88) - Ljungberg, Reyes (Owusu-Abeyie 81). Tr: Wenger

---

GROUP B MATCHDAY 3
Amsterdam ArenA, Amsterdam
18-10-2005, 20:45, 44 772, Rosetti ITA

Ajax 2

Anastasiou 2 36 55

Stekelenburg - Trablesi, Grygera, Maduro, Emanuelson - De Jong, Galasek, Pienaar (Boukhari 84) - Rosales (Heitinga 90), Anastasiou (Babel 82), Sneijder. Tr: Blind

FC Thun 0

Jakupovic - Orman, Deumi, Milicevic, Goncalves - Leandro, Aegerter, Ferreira, Adriano Pimenta (Sen 74) - Gelson (Duruz 85), Lustrinelli (Omar 85). Tr: Schonenberger

---

GROUP B MATCHDAY 3
Sparta Stadium, Prague
18-10-2005, 20:45, 12 528, Stark GER

Sparta Praha 0

Blazek - Pergl (Matusovic 70), Petrous, Lukas•, Kadlec - Petras, Pospech, Polacek - Zelenka, Kisel, Slepicka (Dosek 77). Tr: Griga

Arsenal 2

Henry 2 21 74

Lehman - Lauren, Toure, Cygan, Clichy• - Fabregas (Owusu-Abeyie 81), Flamini, Gilberto Silva, Pires - Van Persie• (Eboue 72), Reyes (Henry 15). Tr: Wenger

---

GROUP B MATCHDAY 4
Wankdorf, Berne
2-11-2005, 20:45, 30 919, Hrinak SVK

FC Thun 2

Lustrinelli 56, Adriano 74

Jakupovic - Goncalves•, Milicevic• (Adriano Pimenta 42), Deumi, Orman (Gerber 67) - Leandro (Sen 81), Bernardi, Hodzic, Aegerter, Ferreira• - Lustrinelli. Tr: Schonenberger

Ajax 4

Sneijder27, Anastasiou63, De Jong91+, Boukhari93+

Stekelenburg - Heitinga, Grygera, Maduro, Emanuelson - Pienaar, De Jong, Galasek•, Sneijder (Boukhari 88), Babel - Anastasiou•. Tr: Blind

---

GROUP B MATCHDAY 4
Highbury, London
2-11-2005, 19:45, 35 155, Sars FRA

Arsenal 3

Henry 23, Van Persie 2 82 86

Almunia - Lauren, Toure, Campbell, Clichy - Pires (Fabregas 73), Gilberto Silva, Flamini, Reyes (Eboue 82) - Bergkamp, Henry (Van Persie 67). Tr: Wenger

Sparta Praha 0

Blazek - Pergl, Petrous, Lukas, Kadlec - Pospech, Petras• (Jeslinek 79), Hasek, Polacek (Slepicka 58), Zelenka - Matusovic. Tr: Griga

---

GROUP B MATCHDAY 5
Amsterdam ArenA, Amsterdam
22-11-2005, 20:45, 46 158, Ivanov.V RUS

Ajax 2

De Jong 2 68 89

Stekelenburg - Trablesi, Grygera, Vermaelen, Emanuelson - Maduro, Sneijder, Lindenbergh (De Jong 53) - Pienaar, Anastasiou (Rosenberg 62), Boukhari. Tr: Blind

Sparta Praha 1

Petras 90

Blazek - Petras, Lukas, Petrous, Kadlec - Herzan (Simak 85), Hasek - Pospech, Zelenka (Slepicka 69), Polacek - Dosek. Tr: Griga

---

GROUP B MATCHDAY 5
Wankdorf, Berne
22-11-2005, 20:45, 31 330, Cardoso POR

FC Thun 0

Jakupovic - Orman, Hodzic, Deumi•35, Goncalves (Bernardi 90) - Ferreira•, Milicevic, Aegerter, Leandro• - Adriano Pimenta, Lustrinelli• (Sen 84). Tr: Schonenberger

Arsenal 1

Pires 88p

Almunia - Eboue, Senderos, Campbell, Cygan• (Lauren• 67) - Ljungberg, Song (Fabregas 56), Flamini, Reyes• - Van Persie, Henry (Pires 70). Tr: Wenger

---

GROUP B MATCHDAY 6
Sparta Stadium, Prague
7-12-2005, 20:45, 9 233, Riley ENG

Sparta Praha 0

Blazek - Pospech, Petras•78, Petrous, Kadlec - Simak (Jeslinek 60), Zelenka, Hasek (Herzan 82), Polacek - Dosek•, Slepicka (Matusovic 66). Tr: Griga

FC Thun 0

Jakupovic - Orman, Hodzic, Goncalves•85, Duruz• - Adriano Spadoto (Sen 57), Aegerter, Bernardi (Savic• 70), Leandro - Adriano Pimenta, Lustrinelli (Gelson 83). Tr: Schonenberger

---

GROUP B MATCHDAY 6
Highbury, London
7-12-2005, 20:45, 35 376, Iturralde ESP

Arsenal 0

Almunia - Eboue, Toure, Senderos, Lauren (Gilberto 73) - Hleb• (Fabregas 62), Larsson, Flamini•, Reyes (Van Persie 65) - Owusu-Abeyie, Henry (≠45). Tr: Wenger

Ajax 0

Stekelenburg - Heitinga•, Grygera (Trablesi 15), Vermaelen, Juanfran - Maduro (De Jong 29), Sneijder, Galasek - Pienaar, Rosenberg, Boukhari (Babel 80). Tr: Blind

GROUP C

		Pl	W	D	L	F	A	Pts	ESP	GER	ITA	GRE
Barcelona	ESP	6	5	1	0	16	2	16		3-1	4-1	5-0
Werder Bremen	GER	6	2	1	3	12	12	7	0-2		4-3	5-1
Udinese	ITA	6	2	1	3	10	12	7	0-2	1-1		3-0
Panathinaikos	GRE	6	1	1	4	4	16	4	0-0	2-1	1-2	

GROUP C MATCHDAY 1
Friuli, Udine
14-09-2005, 20:45, 21 398, Benquerenca POR
Udinese 3
Iaquinta 3 [28 73 76]
De Sanctis - Juarez (Sensini 86), Natali, Felipe - Zenoni, Vidigal, Obodo (Pinzi 68), Sulley Muntari, Candela - Iaquinta, Di Natale (Di Michele 79).
Tr: Cosmi
Panathinaikos 0

Galinovic - Goumas, Morris, Kotsios - Nilsson, Biscan, Gonzalez, Seric - Charalambides (Gekas 70), Wooter (Leontiou 79), Torghelle. Tr: Malesani

GROUP C MATCHDAY 1
Weserstadion, Bremen
14-09-2005, 20:45, 37 000, Hauge NOR
Werder Bremen 0

Reinke - Owomoyela, Pasanen, Naldo, Schulz - Frings, Bauman (Jensen 63), Micoud, Borowski - Haedo Valdez (Hunt 83), Klasnic. Tr: Schaaf
Barcelona 2
Deco [13], Ronaldinho [76p]
Valdes - Belletti (Edmilson 46), Puyol, Oleguer●, Van Bronckhorst - Xavi (Van Bommel 79), Marquez●, Deco● - Guily (Messi 66), Eto'o, Ronaldinho.
Tr: Rijkaard

GROUP C MATCHDAY 2
Camp Nou, Barcelona
27-09-2005, 20:45, 74 730, Bennett ENG
Barcelona 4
Ronaldinho 3 [13 32 90p], Deco [41]
Valdes - Belletti, Puyol●, Oleguer, Van Bronckhorst - Van Bommel● (Iniesta 62) - Xavi, Deco - Messi (Ezquerro 70), Eto'o (Larsson 81), Ronaldinho.
Tr: Rijkaard
Udinese 1
Felipe [24]
De Sanctis - Bertotto, Natali (Juarez 34), Felipe - Zenoni, Vidigal●●●49, Obodo, Sulley Muntari (Di Michele● 79), Candela - Barreto, Di Natale (Mauri 52). Tr: Cosmi

GROUP C MATCHDAY 2
Spyros Louis, Athens
27-09-2005, 21:45, 31 450, Poulat FRA
Panathinaikos 2
González [5p], Mantzios [8]
Galinovic - Vintra, Morris, Goumas (Kotsios 43), Darlas - Nilsson, Flavio Conceicao●, Gonzalez, Seric● - Torghelle (Tziolis● 58), Mantzios (Gekas 72).
Tr: Malesani
Werder Bremen 1
Klose [41]
Reinke - Owomoyela, Andreasen●, Naldo, Schulz (Haedo Valdez 75) - Frings●, Bauman (Hunt 63), Micoud, Borowski - Klose, Klasnic●●●86. Tr: Schaaf

GROUP C MATCHDAY 3
Spyros Louis, Athens
18-10-2005, 21:45, 56 804, De Bleeckere BEL
Panathinaikos 0

Galinovic - Vintra, Biscan, Morris, Darlas - Nilsson, Flavio Conceicao, Gonzalez (Papadopolous 76), Seric● (Wooter 88) - Mantzios, Torghelle● (Leontiou 58). Tr: Malesani
Barcelona 0

Valdes - Belletti, Puyol, Marquez, Van Bronckhorst - Xavi● (Iniesta 75) - Van Bommel● (Motta 56), Deco - Larsson (Messi 67), Eto'o, Ronaldihno. Tr: Rijkaard

GROUP C MATCHDAY 3
Friuli, Udine
18-10-2005, 20:45, 20 335, Temmink NED
Udinese 1
Di Natale [86]
De Sanctis - Bertotto, Sensini, Felipe - Zenoni (Mauri 76), Pinzi● (Di Natale 76), Obodo, Sulley Muntari, Candela - Di Michele (Barreto 58), Iaquinta●. Tr: Cosmi
Werder Bremen 1
Felipe OG [64]
Reinke - Owomoyela, Andreasen, Naldo, Schulz - Frings, Bauman, Micoud●, Borowski - Haedo Valdez● (Hunt 84), Klose. Tr: Schaaf

GROUP C MATCHDAY 4
Camp Nou, Barcelona
2-11-2005, 20:45, 64 321, Temmink NED
Barcelona 3
Van Bommel [1], Eto'o 3 [14 40 65], Messi [34]
Valdes - Oleguer, Puyol, Edmilson, Van Bronckhorst - Xavi (Ezquerro 70) - Van Bommel (Gabri 61), Iniesta (Motta 50) - Messi, Eto'o, Ronaldinho. Tr: Rijkaard
Panathinaikos 0

Galinovic - Vintra, Biscan (Kostios 46), Morris●, Darlas (Tziolis 61) - Flavio Conceicao, Leontiou - Nilsson, Seric (Wooter 79) - Gonzalez, Papadopolous. Tr: Malesani

GROUP C MATCHDAY 4
Weserstadion, Bremen
2-11-2005, 20:45, 35 424, Baskakov RUS
Werder Bremen 4
Klose [15], Baumann [24], Micoud 2 [51 67]
Reinke - Owomoyela (Fahrenhorst 68), Andreasen, Naldo, Schulz - Bauman (Vranjes 86), Frings●, Borowski, Micoud - Klose, Haedo Valdez (Hunt● 80). Tr: Schaaf
Udinese 3
Di Natale 2 [54 57], Schulz OG [60]
De Sanctis - Bertotto, Sensini, Felipe - Zenoni● (Mauri 50), Pinzi●●●71, Obodo, Sulley Muntari (Di Natale 30), Candela - Iaquinta, Di Michele (Motta● 73). Tr: Cosmi

GROUP C MATCHDAY 5
Spyros Louis, Athens
22-11-2005, 21:45, 30 147, Poll ENG
Panathinaikos 1
Charalambides [45]
Galinovic - Morris, Kostios, Goumas, Darlas● - Charalambides, Flavio Conceicao, Gonzalez, Leontiou (Torghelle 83) - Mantzios, Papadopolous (Andric 64). Tr: Malesani
Udinese 2
Iaquinta [81], Candela [83]
De Sanctis - Bertotto●, Sensini●, Felipe - Zenoni●, Obodo, Sulley Muntari (Mauri 75), Candela - Di Natale (Baretto 62), Di Michele (Rossini 80), Iaquinta●. Tr: Cosmi

GROUP C MATCHDAY 5
Camp Nou, Barcelona
22-11-2005, 20:45, 67 273, Larsen DEN
Barcelona 3
Gabri [14], Ronaldinho [26], Larsson [71]
Valdes - Oleguer, Puyol, Marquez● (Belletti 74), Van Bronckhorst - Gabri (Iniesta 77), Motta, Deco - Guily (Ezquerro 65), Larsson, Ronaldihno. Tr: Rijkaard
Werder Bremen 1
Borowski [22p]
Reinke - Owomoyela, Fahrenhorst●, Naldo, Schulz - Bauman, Frings, Borowski, Micoud - Haedo Valdez, Klose (Hunt 59). Tr: Schaaf

GROUP C MATCHDAY 6
Friuli, Udine
7-12-2005, 20:45, 33 570, Braamhaar NED
Udinese 0

De Sanctis - Bertotto, Sensini, Juarez - Zenoni (Tissone 38), Vidigal●, Obodo●, Sulley Muntari (Mauri 64), Candela - Di Natale, Iaquinta (Di Michele 75). Tr: Cosmi
Barcelona 2
Ezquerro [85], Iniesta [90]
Jorquera - Belletti, Puyol, Oleguer, Van Bronckhorst - Gabri (Iniesta 75), Edmilson, Deco - Guily, Larsson, Ezquerro. Tr: Rijkaard

GROUP C MATCHDAY 6
Weserstadion, Bremen
7-12-2005, 20:45, 36 550, Frojdfeldt SWE
Werder Bremen 5
Micoud 2 [2p], Valdez 2 [28 31], Klose [51], Frings [91+]
Reinke - Owomoyela, Fahrenhorst, Andreasen, Schulz (Pasanen 50) - Vranjes●, Bauman (D Jensen 75), Micoud, Frings - Klose, Haedo Valdez (Hunt 79). Tr: Schaaf
Panathinaikos 1
Morris [53]
Galinovic● - Vintra●, Biscan, Morris, Darlas (Wooter 72) - Nilsson (Kostios 79), Flavio Conceicao, Tziolis, Papadopolous - Gonzalez●, Torghelle● (Mantzios). Tr: Malesani

GROUP D

		Pl	W	D	L	F	A	Pts	ESP	POR	FRA	ENG
Villarreal	ESP	6	2	4	0	3	1	10		1-1	1-0	0-0
Benfica	POR	6	2	2	2	5	5	8	0-1		1-0	2-1
Lille OSC	FRA	6	1	3	2	1	2	6	0-0	0-0		1-0
Manchester United	ENG	6	1	3	2	3	4	6	0-0	2-1	0-0	

GROUP D MATCHDAY 1
Estádio da Luz, Lisbon
14-09-2005, 19:45, 32 176, Temmink NED

Benfica 1
Miccoli $^{92+}$

Moreira - Nelson, Luisao, Ricardo Rocha● (Anderson 46), Leo - Giovanni (Mantorras 80), Petit (Karagounis 67), Manuel Fernandes, Simao - Miccoli, Nuno Gomes. Tr: Koeman

Lille OSC 0

Sylva - Chalme, Plestan●, Schmitz, Tafforeau - Cabaye●, Makoun, Gygax● (Debuchy 46), Bodmer, Dernis (Lichtsteiner 84) - Moussilou (Odemwingie 71). Tr: Puel

GROUP D MATCHDAY 1
El Madrigal, Villarreal
14-09-2005, 20:45, 19 550, Nielsen DEN

Villarreal 0

Viera - Kromkamp, Rodriguez●, Quique Alvarez, Arruabarrena - Hector Font● (Roger 70), Josico (Tacchinardi 46), Marcos Senna, Sorin - Guayre (Figueroa 66), Forlan. Tr: Pellegrini

Manchester United 0

Van der Sar - O'Shea, Ferdinand, Silvestre, Heinze (Richardson 46) - Christiano Ronaldo (Giggs 80), Fletcher, Scholes, Smith● - Rooney●●64, Van Nistelrooy (Park 80). Tr: Ferguson

GROUP D MATCHDAY 2
Old Trafford, Manchester
27-09-2005, 19:45

Manchester United 2
Giggs ^{39}, Van Nistelrooij ^{85}

Van der Sar - Bardsley, Ferdinand, O'Shea, Richardson - Christiano Ronaldo, Fletcher, Smith●, Scholes, Giggs - Van Nistelrooy. Tr: Ferguson

Benfica 1
Simão ^{59}

Moreira - Nelson, Luisao●, Ricardo Rocha, Leo - Beto (Mantorras 86), Petit, Manuel Fernandes (Giovanni 86), Simao - Miccoli (Joao Pereira 80), Nuno Gomes●. Tr: Koeman

GROUP D MATCHDAY 2
Stade de France, Paris
27-09-2005, 20:45, 35 153, Frojdfeldt SWE

Lille OSC 0

Sylva - Lichtsteiner, Plestan, Rafael Schmitz●, Tafforeau - Debuchy, Makoun, Bodmer (Dumont 46), Acimovic (Dernis 84) - Odemwingie, Moussilou (Fauvergue 73). Tr: Puel

Villarreal 0

Viera - Kromkamp, Pena, Quique Alvarez (Rodriguez 46), Arruabarrena● - Riquelme, Tacchinardi●, Josico, Sorin (Marcos Senna 46) - Forlan (Guayre 84), Figueroa. Tr: Pellegrini

GROUP D MATCHDAY 3
Old Trafford, Manchester
18-10-2005, 19:45, 60 626, Farina ITA

Manchester United 0

Van der Sar - Bardsley, Ferdinand●, Silvestre, O'Shea● - Christiano Ronaldo, Fletcher, Scholes●●63, Smith, Giggs (Park 84) - Van Nistelrooy. Tr: Ferguson

Lille OSC 0

Sylva - Vitakic●, Tavlaridis, Rafael Schmitz●, Tafforeau● - Debuchy (Keita 84), Makoun, Bodmer, Chalme - Acimovic (Dernis 60), Odemwingie (Moussilou 73). Tr: Puel

GROUP D MATCHDAY 3
El Madrigal, Villarreal
18-10-2005, 20:45, 15 072, Meyer GER

Villarreal 1
Riquelme ^{72p}

Viera - Kromkamp, Cesar Arzo, Gonzalo, Arruabarrena (Josico 46) - Santi Carzola, Tacchinardi (Roger 84), Riquelme, Sorin - Jose Mari (Figueroa 79), Forlan. Tr: Pellegrini

Benfica 1
Manuel Fernandes ^{77}

Quim (Rui Nereu 28) - Nelson, Luisao, Anderson, Ricardo Rocha - Karagounis (Karyaka 65), Petit, Manuel Fernandes - Giovanni (Beto 89), Nuno Gomes, Simao. Tr: Koeman

GROUP D MATCHDAY 4
Estádio da Luz, Lisbon
2-11-2005, 19:45, 48 014, De Bleeckere BEL

Benfica 0

Rui Nereu - Nelson, Luisao, Anderson (Nuno Assis 83), Leo - Giovanni (Mantorras 70), Manuel Fernandes, Petit, Karagounis (Joao Pereira 70), Simao - Nuno Gomes●. Tr: Koeman

Villarreal 1
Senna ^{81}

Barbosa - Javi Venta●, Rodriguez●, Quique Alvarez, Arruabarrena - Josico, Marcos Senna (Pena 90), Riquelme, Sorin● - Jose Mari (Guayre 70), Forlan (Figueroa 50). Tr: Pellegrini

GROUP D MATCHDAY 4
Stade de France, Paris
2-11-2005, 20:45, 66 470, Merk GER

Lille OSC 1
Acimovic ^{38}

Sylva - Chalme, Tavlaridis●, Rafael Schmitz, Tafforeau● - Debuchy, Bodmer, Makoun●, Dernis (Gygax 79) - Acimovic (Cabaye 76), Moussilou (Odemwingie 84). Tr: Puel

Manchester United 0

Van der Sar - O'Shea, Ferdinand, Brown, Silvestre● - Christiano Ronaldo (Rossi 89), Fletcher, Smith, Richardson (Park 65) - Rooney●, Van Nistelrooy. Tr: Ferguson

GROUP D MATCHDAY 5
Old Trafford, Manchester
22-11-2005, 19:45, 67 471, De Santis ITA

Manchester United 0

Van der Sar - Brown (Neville 73), Ferdinand, Silvestre●, O'Shea - Fletcher (Park 53), Smith (Saha 82), Scholes●, Christiano Ronaldo - Rooney, Van Nistelrooy●. Tr: Ferguson

Villarreal 0

Barbosa - Javi Venta, Rodriguez, Pena, Arruabarrena - Roger (Hector Font 66), Tacchinardi● (Josico● 79), Marcos Senna●, Sorin - Figueroa (Xisco 86), Jose Mari. Tr: Pellegrini

GROUP D MATCHDAY 5
Stade de France, Paris
22-11-2005, 20:45, 76 187, Busacca SUI

Lille OSC 0

Sylva - Lichtsteiner, Tavlaridis●, Rafael Schmitz●, Tafforeau - Chalme (Mirallas 69), Bodmer, Makoun●, Dernis - Acimovic (Fauvergue 87), Moussilou (Abouchrouane 75). Tr: Puel

Benfica 0

Quim - Alcides, Luisao, Anderson, Ricardo Rocha - Nelson, Beto, Petit, Leo - Nuno Gomes, Miccoli (Mantorras 44). Tr: Koeman

GROUP D MATCHDAY 6
Estádio da Luz, Lisbon
7-12-2005, 19:45, 62 174, Vassaras GRE

Benfica 2
Geovanni ^{16}, Beto ^{34}

Quim - Alcides, Luisao, Anderson, Leo (Ricardo Rocha 89) - Nuno Assis (Joao Pereira 73), Petit●, Beto● - Nelson, Nuno Gomes, Giovanni● (Mantorras 81). Tr: Koeman

Manchester United 1
Scholes ^{6}

Van der Sar - Neville●, Ferdinand●, Silvestre, O'Shea (Richardson 85) - Christiano Ronaldo, Fletcher● (Park 67), Smith, Scholes, Giggs (Saha 60) - Rooney, Van Nistelrooy. Tr: Ferguson

GROUP D MATCHDAY 6
El Madrigal, Villarreal
7-12-2005, 20:45, 15 751, Ivanov.V RUS

Villarreal 1
Guayre ^{67}

Viera - Kromkamp, Rodriguez, Pena, Arruabarrena - Marcos Senna, Josico●, Sorin (Hector Font 36), Riquelme - Jose Mari (Guayre 59), Forlan (Roger 83). Tr: Pellegrini

Lille OSC 0

Sylva - Chalme, Tavlaridis, Vitakic, Tafforeau - Lichtsteiner (Moussilou 70), Dumont, Bodmer, Makoun, Dernis (Acimovic 60) - Odemwingie (Mirallas 75). Tr: Puel

GROUP E

		Pl	W	D	L	F	A	Pts	ITA	NED	GER	TUR
Milan	ITA	6	3	2	1	12	6	11		0-0	3-2	3-1
PSV Eindhoven	NED	6	3	1	2	4	6	10	1-0		1-0	2-0
Schalke 04	GER	6	2	2	2	12	9	8	2-2	3-0		2-0
Fenerbahçe	TUR	6	1	1	4	7	14	4	0-4	3-0	3-3	

GROUP E MATCHDAY 1
San Siro, Milan
13-09-2005, 20:45, 34 619, Riley ENG

Milan	3
	Kaká 2 [18] [87], Shevchenko [89]

Dida - Cafu, Nesta, Maldini, Kaladze - Gattuso (Vogel 71), Pirlo (Serginho 71), Kaka, Ambrosini - Shevchenko, Vieri (Gilardino 78). Tr: Ancelotti

Fenerbahçe	1
	Alex [63p]

Volkan● - Serkan, Onder, Fabio Luciano, Umit - Marco Aurelio, Selcuk, Alex, Appiah (Kemal 53) (Nobre 90) - Anelka, Tuncay. Tr: Daum

---

GROUP E MATCHDAY 1
Philips Stadion, Eindhoven
13-09-2005, 20:45, 30 000, Baskakov RUS

PSV Eindhoven	1
	Hesselink [33]

Gomes - Lucius, Ooijer, Addo, Reiziger - Cocu (Lamey 82), Simons●, Afellay● - Farfan, Vennegoor of Hesselink (Robert 87), Beasley. Tr: Hiddink

Schalke 04	0

Rost - Rafinha●, Bordon, Krstajic, Altintop (Bajramovic 87) - Ernst (Varela 79), Poulsen, Lincoln, Kobiashvilli● - Kuranyi, Sand (Larsen 72). Tr: Rangnick

---

GROUP E MATCHDAY 2
Arena AufSchalke, Gelsenkirchen
28-09-2005, 20:45, 53 425, Larsen DEN

Schalke 04	2
	Larsen [3], Altintop [70]

Rost - Rafinha, Bordon, Rodriguez, Krstajic - Ernst (Altintop 68), Poulsen● (Bajramovic 85), Lincoln, Kobiashvilli - Kuranyi (Sand 74), Larsen. Tr: Rangnick

Milan	2
	Seedorf [1], Shevchenko [59]

Dida - Cafu (Stam 76), Nesta, Maldini, Kaladze - Gattuso, Pirlo, Kaka● (Rui Costa 74), Seedorf - Gilardino (Vieri 70), Shevchenko. Tr: Ancelotti

---

GROUP E MATCHDAY 2
Sükrü Saraçoglu, Istanbul
28-09-2005, 21:45, 37 079, Mejuto ESP

Fenerbahçe	3
	Alex 2 [40p] [68], Appiah [92+]

Volkan - Serkan, Onder, Fabio Luciano, Umit - Marco Aurelio●, Appiah, Selcuk, Nobre (Mehmet 90), Alex (Kemal 90), Anelka. Tr: Daum

PSV Eindhoven	0

Gomes - Ooijer●, Alex, Addo, Lucius (Ferreyra 54) - Cocu, Simons, Afellay - Farfan, Vennegoor of Hesselink●●●45, Beasley. Tr: Hiddink

---

GROUP E MATCHDAY 3
San Siro, Milan
19-10-2005, 20:45, 39 298, Plautz AUT

Milan	0

Dida - Cafu, Stam, Maldini, Kaladze - Gattuso, Pirlo, Kaka, Seedorf (Serginho 75) - Shevchenko (Inzaghi● 49), Vieri. Tr: Ancelotti

PSV Eindhoven	0

Gomes - Reiziger●, Alex, Ooijer, Lamey - Afellay, Simons, Cocu - Beasley, Robert (Aissati 63), Farfan. Tr: Hiddink

---

GROUP E MATCHDAY 3
Sükrü Saraçoglu, Istanbul
19-10-2005, 21:45, 38 118, Hamer LUX

Fenerbahçe	3
	Fábio [14], Márcio [73], Appiah [79]

Volkan - Serkan, Onder, Fabio Luciano●, Umit - Selcuk, Marco Aurelio● (Tuncay 67), Appiah - Alex●●●87, Nobre, Anelka. Tr: Daum

Schalke 04	3
	Lincoln 2 [59] [62], Kuranyi [77]

Rost - Rafinha●, Bordon, Rodriguez●, Krstajic - Altintop, Poulsen, Lincoln, Kobiashvilli● - Sand (Kuranyi 46), Larsen. Tr: Rangnick

---

GROUP E MATCHDAY 4
Arena AufSchalke, Gelsenkirchen
1-11-2005, 20:45, 53 993, Medina ESP

Schalke 04	2
	Kuranyi [32], Sand [91+]

Rost - Rafinha●, Bordon, Rodriguez, Krstajic - Altintop (Sand 64), Ernst (Varela 82), Lincoln, Poulsen, Kobiashvilli - Kuranyi (Bajramovic 90). Tr: Rangnick

Fenerbahçe	0

Volkan - Serkan, Fabio Luciano●40, Onder, Umit● - Appiah, Selcuk, Nobre (Mehmet 46), Marco Aurelio●●●55 - Tuncay●, Anelka. Tr: Daum

---

GROUP E MATCHDAY 4
Philips Stadion, Eindhoven
1-11-2005, 20:45, 35 100, Poll ENG

PSV Eindhoven	1
	Farfán [12]

Gomes - Ooijer, Alex, Lamey - Afellay (Reiziger 58), Simons, Aissati, Cocu - Beasley, Vennegoor of Hesselink, Farfan (Addo 85). Tr: Hiddink

Milan	0

Dida - Stam●●●84, Nesta, Maldini, Kaladze (Serginho 46) - Seedorf, Pirlo, Kaka, Gattuso● (Jankulovski 46) - Vieri, Gilardino (Shevchenko 74). Tr: Ancelotti

---

GROUP E MATCHDAY 5
Arena AufSchalke, Gelsenkirchen
23-11-2005, 20:45, 53 994, Michel SVK

Schalke 04	3
	Kobiashvili 3 [18p] [72] [79p]

Rost - Altintop●, Bordon●, Rodriguez, Krstajic - Poulsen, Lincoln, Ernst - Varela (Asamoah 73), Kuranyi (Sand 85), Kobiashvilli (Bajramovic 89). Tr: Rangnick

PSV Eindhoven	0

Gomes - Reiziger (Sibon 78), Ooijer, Alex, Lamey - Afellay, Cocu, Simons (Lucius 46) - Farfan, Robert, Aissati (Vennegoor of Hesselink 46). Tr: Hiddink

---

GROUP E MATCHDAY 5
Sükrü Saraçoglu, Istanbul
23-11-2005, 21:45, 36 350, Hauge NOR

Fenerbahçe	0

Volkan - Serkan, Servet, Onder, Deniz● - Selcuk (Kemal 28), Umit, Appiah - Mehmet (Nobre 46), Anelka, Tuncay. Tr: Daum

Milan	4
	Shevchenko 4 [16] [52] [70] [76]

Dida - Simic, Nesta, Maldini●, Serginho - Gattuso (Vogel 80), Pirlo, Kaka (Rui Costa 19), Seedorf - Gilardino (Vieri 75), Shevchenko. Tr: Ancelotti

---

GROUP E MATCHDAY 6
San Siro, Milan
6-12-2005, 20:45, 40 200, Mejuto ESP

Milan	3
	Pirlo [42], Kaká 2 [52] [60]

Dida - Stam, Nesta, Maldini (Simic 31) (Kaladze 79), Serginho - Gattuso●, Pirlo●, Kaka, Seedorf - Inzaghi (Gilardino 85), Shevchenko. Tr: Ancelotti

Schalke 04	2
	Poulsen [44], Lincoln [66]

Rost - Rafinha, Bordon, Rodriguez●, Krstajic● (Larsen 84) - Poulsen, Ernst● (Asamoah● 46) - Lincoln, Altintop, Kobiashvilli● - Kuranyi (Sand 84). Tr: Rangnick

---

GROUP E MATCHDAY 6
Philips Stadion, Eindhoven
6-12-2005, 20:45, 35 000, Poulat FRA

PSV Eindhoven	2
	Cocu [14], Farfán [85]

Gomes - Lucius, Ooijer, Alex, Lamey - Simons, Afellay (Assiati 25), Cocu● - Farfan, Vennegoor of Hesselink, Robert● (Reiziger 67). Tr: Hiddink

Fenerbahçe	0

Volkan - Serkan●, Onder, Fabio Luciano, Umit - Appiah, Alex, Marco Aurelio, Tuncay - Nobre (Semih● 79), Anelka. Tr: Daum

GROUP F

		Pl	W	D	L	F	A	Pts	FRA	ESP	NOR	GRE
Olympique Lyonnais	FRA	6	5	1	0	13	4	16		3-0	2-1	2-1
Real Madrid	ESP	6	3	1	2	10	8	10	1-1		4-1	2-1
Rosenborg BK	NOR	6	1	1	4	6	11	4	0-1	0-2		1-1
Olympiacos	GRE	6	1	1	4	7	13	4	1-4	2-1	1-3	

GROUP F MATCHDAY 1
Stade Gerland, Lyon
13-09-2005, 20:45, 40 309, De Santis ITA

Olympique Lyonnais　　　　3
Carew [21], Juninho [26], Wiltord [31]

Coupet - Reveillere, Cris, Cacapa, Berthod● - Tiago (Pedretti 86), Diarra●, Juninho(≠42) - Wiltord (Govou 80), Carew (Fred 72), Malouda. Tr: Houllier

Real Madrid　　　　0

Casillas - Michel Salgado●, Ivan Helguera, Sergio Ramos, Roberto Carlos - Beckham●, Pablo Garcia●, Julio Baptista, Gravesen (Guti 61) - Robinho, Raul. Tr: Luxemburgo

GROUP F MATCHDAY 1
Karaiskaki, Piraeus
13-09-2005, 21:45, 33 448, Farina ITA

Olympiacos　　　　1
Lago OG [19]

Nikopolidis - Mavrogenidis, Anatolakis, Kostoulas, Georgatos - Rivaldo (Dani 87), Toure (Kafes 89), Stoltidis - Babangida (Okkas 80), Costantinou, Djordjevic. Tr: Sollied

Rosenborg BK　　　　3
Skjelbred [42], Mavrogenidis OG [48], Storflor [94+]

E Johnsen● - Strand, Kvarme, Lago, Dorsin - Skjelbred (Riseth 85), Berg, Winsnes (Braaten 66) - Solli, Helstad (F Johnsen 80), Storflor. Tr: Høgmo

GROUP F MATCHDAY 2
Lerkendal, Trondheim
28-09-2005, 20:45, 20 620, Baskakov RUS

Rosenborg BK　　　　0

E Johnsen - Strand (Basma 66), Kvarme, Riseth, Dorsin - Skjelbred, Berg●, Solli - Braaten, Helstad (F Johnsen 68), Storflor (Odegaard● 59). Tr: Høgmo

Olympique Lyonnais　　　　1
Cris [45]

Coupet - Reveillere, Cris, Cacapa, Berthod - Govu (Wiltord 89), Tiago, Diarra, Juninho, Malouda - Carew (Fred 90). Tr: Houllier

GROUP F MATCHDAY 2
Bernabéu, Madrid
28-09-2005, 20:45, 64 327, Merk GER

Real Madrid　　　　2
Raúl [9], Soldado [86]

Casillas - Michel Salgado (Diogo 80), Ivan Helguera, Sergio Ramos●91+, Roberto Carlos - Beckham, Pablo Garcia● (Gravesen 85), Julio Baptista (Soldado 79), Guti● - Robinho, Raul. Tr: Luxemburgo

Olympiacos　　　　1
Kafes [48]

Nikopolidis - Mavrogenidis (Kapsis 40), Anatolakis, Kostoulas, Georgatos - Kafes●, Toure, Stoltidis● (Babangida 90) - Rivaldo●, Costantinou (Okkas● 85) Djordjevic. Tr: Sollied

GROUP F MATCHDAY 3
Bernabéu, Madrid
19-10-2005, 20:45, 64 870, Bennett ENG

Real Madrid　　　　4
Woodgate [48], Raúl [52], Helguera [68], Beckham [82]

Casillas - Diogo, Woodgate (Mejia 85), Ivan Helguera, Roberto Carlos - Beckham, Pablo Garcia●, Robinho, Zidane (Gravesen 70) - Raul, Julio Baptista (Guti 46). Tr: Luxemburgo

Rosenborg BK　　　　1
Strand [40]

E Johnsen - Basma, Kvarme, Riseth, Dorsin - Braaten, Strand (Tettey 46), Skjelbred (Wisnes 75), Solli, Storflor - Helstad (F Johnsen 63). Tr: Høgmo

GROUP F MATCHDAY 3
Stade Gerland, Lyon
19-10-2005, 20:45, 38 093, Poll ENG

Olympique Lyonnais　　　　2
Juninho [4], Govou [89]

Coupet - Reveillere, Cris, Cacapa, Abidal - Tiago, Diarra, Juninho - Govu (Clement 90), Fred (Carew 70), Malouda (Wiltord 75). Tr: Houllier

Olympiacos　　　　1
Kafes [84]

Nikopolidis - Pantos, Kapsis, Anatolakis (Babangida 90), Kostoulas, Erol - Toure, Stoltidis (Costantinou 86) - Kafes, Okkas, Djordjevic. Tr: Sollied

GROUP F MATCHDAY 4
Lerkendal, Trondheim
1-11-2005, 20:45, 21 270, Stark GER

Rosenborg BK　　　　0

E Johnsen - Basma, Kvarme, Riseth, Dorsin (Stensaas 73) - Strand (Odegaard 82), Skjelbred, Solli - Braaten, F Johnsen, Storflor (Helstad 65). Tr: Høgmo

Real Madrid　　　　2
Dorsin OG [26], Guti [41]

Casillas - Michel Salgado (Mejia 46), Pavon, Woodgate, Roberto Carlos● - Beckham (De la Red 90), Diogo●, Sergio Ramos, Guti● (Raul Bravo● 83) - Robinho, Raul. Tr: Luxemburgo

GROUP F MATCHDAY 4
Karaiskaki, Piraeus
1-11-2005, 21:45, 30 848, Frojdfeldt SWE

Olympiacos　　　　1
Babangida [3]

Giannou - Pantos, Kostoulas● (Erol 66), Anatolakis●, Georgatos - Kafes, Toure, Rivaldo - Babangida, Okkas (D'Acol 81), Djordjevic (Stoltidis 66). Tr: Sollied

Olympique Lyonnais　　　　4
Juninho [41], Carew 2 [44 57], Diarra [55]

Coupet● - Reveillere, Cris, Cacapa, Abidal - Govu, Tiago● (Clement 75), Diarra, Juninho (Pedretti 78), Malouda (Wiltord 68) - Carew●. Tr: Houllier

GROUP F MATCHDAY 5
Bernabéu, Madrid
23-11-2005, 20:45, 67 304, De Bleeckere BEL

Real Madrid　　　　1
Guti [41]

Casillas - Diogo, Pavon, Ivan Helguera, Roberto Carlos - Pablo Garcia, Sergio Ramos - Beckham● (Michel Salgado 78), Zidane (Julio Baptista 75), Guti● - Robinho. Tr: Luxemburgo

Olympique Lyonnais　　　　1
Carew [72]

Coupet - Reveillere●, Cris●, Cacapa●, Monsoreau (Fred 69) - Tiago●, Diarra, Juninho● (Clement 90) - Govou (Wiltord 69), Carew, Malouda. Tr: Houllier

GROUP F MATCHDAY 5
Lerkendal, Trondheim
23-11-2005, 20:45, 21 270, Allaerts BEL

Rosenborg BK　　　　1
Helstad [88]

E Johnsen - Basma, Riseth, Kvarme, Dorsin - Strand (Helstad 27), Solli, Skjelbred (Winsnes 10) - Braaten (Odegaard 63), F Johnsen, Storflor. Tr: Høgmo

Olympiacos　　　　1
Rivaldo [25]

Nikopolidis - Pantos●●●85, Anatolakis, Schurrer, Erol - Kafes, Toure, Stoltidis●, Babangida (Okkas 71) - Rivaldo (Maric 86), Dani●. Tr: Sollied

GROUP F MATCHDAY 6
Stade Gerland, Lyon
6-12-2005, 20:45, 40 425, Dauden ESP

Olympique Lyonnais　　　　2
Benzema [33], Fred [93+]

Vercoutre - Reveillere (Clerc 83), Cris, Diata, Monsoreau - Pedretti●, Benzema (Beynie 90), Clement - Wiltord, Carew (Fred 55), Ben Arfa. Tr: Houllier

Rosenborg BK　　　　1
Braaten [68]

E Johnsen - Basma, Kvarme, Lago●, Dorsin - Wisnes, Riseth● (Tettey 81), F Johnsen - Braaten, Helstad (Odegaard 57), Storflor (Eguren● 83). Tr: Høgmo

GROUP F MATCHDAY 6
Karaiskaki, Piraeus
6-12-2005, 21:45, 30 496, Nielsen DEN

Olympiacos　　　　2
Bulut [50], Rivaldo [87]

Nikopolidis - Mavrogenidis, Kapsis, (Kostoulas 65), Schurrer, Erol - Toure●, Stoltidis, Rivaldo - Kafes (Babangida 80), Dani (Okkas 58), Djordjevic. Tr: Sollied

Real Madrid　　　　1
Sergio Ramos [7]

Diego Lopez - Diogo●, Pavon, Sergio Ramos, Raul Bravo - Balboa (Adrian Martin 58), De la Red● (Javi Garcia 81), Gravesen, Robinho (Jurado 80) - Julio Baptista●, Soldado. Tr: Caro

GROUP G

		Pl	W	D	L	F	A	Pts	ENG	ENG	ESP	BEL
Liverpool	ENG	6	3	3	0	6	1	12		0-0	0-0	3-0
Chelsea	ENG	6	3	2	1	7	1	11	0-0		4-0	1-0
Real Betis	ESP	6	2	1	3	3	7	7	1-2	1-0		0-1
RSC Anderlecht	BEL	6	1	0	5	1	8	3	0-1	0-2	0-1	

GROUP G MATCHDAY 1
Stamford Bridge, London
13-09-2005, 19:45, 29 575, Stark GER

Chelsea 1
Lampard [19]
Cech - Paulo Ferreira, Terry, Ricardo Carvalho, Gallas - Makelele - Duff (J Cole 76), Essien (Huth 90), Lampard, Robben (Wright-Phillips○ 67) - Drogba. Tr: Mourinho

RSC Anderlecht 0
Zitka - Zewlakow (Jestrovic 81), Juhsaz, Tihinen, Deschacht - Vanden Borre, Vanderhaege○ (Delorge 90), De Man, Goor - Mpenza, Serhat○ (Wilhelmsson 69). Tr: Vercauteren

GROUP G MATCHDAY 1
Ruíz de Lopera, Seville
13-09-2005, 20:45, 34 862, Plautz AUT

Real Betis 1
Arzu [51]
Doblas - Melli, Juanito (Xisco 46), Rivas, Oscar Lopez - Arzu (Capi 72), Fernando (Dani 36), Marcos Assuncao - Joaquin, Ricardo Oliveira, Varela. Tr: Serra Ferrer

Liverpool 2
Sinama-Pongolle [2], Luis Garcia [14]
Reina○ - Josemi, Carragher○, Hyypia, Traore - Luis Garcia, Sissoko, Xabi Alonso, Zenden (Riise 65) - Sinama-Pongolle (Gerrard 73), Crouch (Cisse 58). Tr: Benitez

GROUP G MATCHDAY 2
Anfield, Liverpool
28-09-2005, 19:45, 42 743, De Santis ITA

Liverpool 0
Reina - Finnan, Carragher, Hyypia, Traore - Luis Garcia, Hamann, Gerrard, Xabi Alonso○ - Crouch, Cisse (Sinama-Pongolle 77). Tr: Benitez

Chelsea 0
Cech - Paulo Ferreira, Ricardo Carvalho, Terry○, Gallas - Makelele○ - Duff (Crespo 74), Essien, Lampard○, Robben○ (Wright-Phillips 64) - Drogba (Huth 90). Tr: Mourinho

GROUP G MATCHDAY 2
Vanden Stock, Brussels
28-09-2005, 20:45, 21 078, Rosetti ITA

RSC Anderlecht 0
Proto - Vanden Borre, De Man, Tihinen (Serhat 80), Deschacht - Vanderhaege (Baseggio 85) - Wilhelmsson, Zetterberg, Goor - Mpenza, Jestrovic. Tr: Vercauteren

Real Betis 1
Oliveira [69]
Doblas - Melli, Juanito○, Rivas○ (Nano 72), Oscar Lopez○ - Varela○, Rivera, Miguel Angel, Xisco (Fernando 76) - Joaquin (Marcos Assuncao 90), Ricardo Oliveira. Tr: Serra Ferrer

GROUP G MATCHDAY 3
Stamford Bridge, London
19-10-2005, 19:45, 36 457, Hauge NOR

Chelsea 4
Drogba [24], Carvalho [44], Cole J [59], Crespo [64]
Cudicini - Gallas○, Ricardo Carvalho, Terry, Del Horno - Makelele (Diarra 75) - Wright-Phillips○ (Gudjohnsen 66), Essien, Lampard, J Cole - Drogba (Crespo 46). Tr: Mourinho

Real Betis 0
Doblas - Oscar Lopez (Xisco○ 46), Juanito, Rivas○, Melli - Varela○, Rivera○, Miguel Angel (Marcos Assuncao 55), Edu - Joaquin○, Ricardo Oliveira. Tr: Serra Ferrer

GROUP G MATCHDAY 3
Vanden Stock, Brussels
19-10-2005, 20:45, 21 824, Busacca SUI

RSC Anderlecht 0
Proto - Vanden Borre, Tihinen (Traore 50), De Man, Deschacht (Serhat 75) - Wilhelmsson, Vanderhaege (Baseggio 61), Zetterberg, Goor - Jestrovic, Mpenza. Tr: Vercauteren

Liverpool 1
Cissé [20]
Reina○ - Josemi, Carragher, Hyypia, Traore - Luis Garcia, Xabi Alonso○, Hamann, Riise (Warnock 88) - Sissoko (Zenden 82), Cisse (Kewell 75). Tr: Benitez

GROUP G MATCHDAY 4
Anfield, Liverpool
1-11-2005, 19:45, 42 607, Nielsen DEN

Liverpool 3
Morientes [34], Luis Garcia [61], Cissé [89]
Reina - Finnan, Carragher, Hyypia, Riise - Gerrard (Kewell 78), Xabi Alonso, Sissoko○, Luis Garcia - Crouch (Cisse 71), Morientes (Zenden 52). Tr: Benitez

RSC Anderlecht 0
Proto - Zewlakow, Juhsaz, Tihinen - Wilhelmsson, Vanderhaege (Pujol 69), De Man, Goor - Zetterberg, Serhat (Jestrovic 69○75), Mpenza (Baseggio 81). Tr: Vercauteren

GROUP G MATCHDAY 4
Ruíz de Lopera, Seville
1-11-2005, 20:45, 34 131, Hamer LUX

Real Betis 1
Dani [28]
Contreras○ - Varela○, Juanito, Nano (Castellini 20), Melli○ - Joaquin, Rivera, Arzu, Edu - Capi○ (Fernando 84), Ricardo Oliveira (Dani○ 25). Tr: Serra Ferrer

Chelsea 0
Cech - Paulo Ferreira, Ricardo Carvalho, Terry, Gallas - Essien, Makelele, Lampard - J Cole○ (Wright-Phillips○ 46), Gudjohnsen (Drogba○ 46), Robben○ (Duff○ 65). Tr: Mourinho

GROUP G MATCHDAY 5
Anfield, Liverpool
23-11-2005, 19:45, 42 077, Poulat FRA

Liverpool 0
Reina - Finnan, Carragher, Hyypia, Riise - Gerrard (Potter 89), Hamann○, Sissoko, Zenden - Crouch (Kewell 84), Morientes (Cisse 67). Tr: Benitez

Real Betis 0
Doblas - Melli, Juanito, Rivas, Oscar Lopez○ - Joaquin, Marco Assuncao (Capi 70), Rivera, Arzu, Xisco - Fernando (Israel 78). Tr: Serra Ferrer

GROUP G MATCHDAY 5
Vanden Stock, Brussels
23-11-2005, 20:45, 21 845, Farina ITA

RSC Anderlecht 0
Proto – Zewlakow, Kompany, Tihinen, Deschacht - Vanden Borre, Vanderhaege (Lachtchouk 46), Goor - Wilhelmsson, Mpenza (Zetterberg 60), Serhat (Efret 75). Tr: Vercauteren

Chelsea 2
Crespo [8], Carvalho [15]
Cech - Galls, Ricardo Carvalho, Terry○, Del Horno○ - J Cole (Diarra 63), Lampard, Essien, Duff - Gudjohnsen (Geremi 78), Crespo (C Cole 86). Tr: Mourinho

GROUP G MATCHDAY 6
Stamford Bridge, London
6-12-2005, 19:45, 41 598, Fandel GER

Chelsea 0
Cech - Paulo Ferreira (Del Horno 46), Ricardo Carvalho○, Terry, Gallas - Essien - Robben (C Cole 73), Gudjohnsen, Lampard○, Duff (Wright-Phillips 73) - Drogba. Tr: Mourinho

Liverpool 0
Reina - Finnan, Carragher, Hyypia, Traore○ - Luis Garcia (Sinama-Pongolle 80), Hamann, Gerrard, Sissoko, Riise (Kewell 60) - Crouch (Morientes 69). Tr: Benitez

GROUP G MATCHDAY 6
Ruíz de Lopera, Seville
6-12-2005, 20:45, 24 277, Ceferin SVN

Real Betis 0
Doblas - Oscar Lopez, Lembo, Rivas, Castellini - Israel (Joaguin 46), Rivera, Juande (Marco Assuncao 70), Juanlu (Xisco 46) - Capi, Fernando○. Tr: Serra Ferrer

RSC Anderlecht 1
Kompany [44]
Zitka - Juhasz○, Kompany, Tiote (Zetterberg 83), Deschacht - Lovre○ (Tihinen 69), Delorge, Goor - Baseggio (Zewlakow 69), Pujol, Iachtchouk○. Tr: Vercauteren

GROUP H

		Pl	W	D	L	F	A	Pts	ITA	SCO	SVK	POR
Internazionale	ITA	6	4	1	1	9	4	13		1-0	4-0	2-1
Rangers	SCO	6	1	4	1	7	7	7	1-1		0-0	3-2
Artmedia Bratislava	SVK	6	1	3	2	5	9	6	0-1	2-2		0-0
FC Porto	POR	6	1	2	3	8	9	5	2-0	1-1	2-3	

GROUP H MATCHDAY 1
Ibrox, Glasgow
13-09-2005, 19:45, 48 599, Wegereef NED

Rangers 3

Løvenkrands 35, Prso 59, Kyrgiakos 85

Waterreus - Ricksen, Rodriguez, Kyrgiakos, Bernard - Namouchi (Novo 72), Murray, Ferguson, Lovenkrands (Buffel 56) - Prso•, Jeffers (Thompson 84). Tr: McLeish

FC Porto 2

Pepe 2 47 71

Victor Baia - Pepe, Pedro Emanuel (Sonkaya 41), Ricardo Costa, Cesar Peixoto - Lucho Gonzalez•, Diego (Ricardo Quaresma 65), Ibson - Alan (Hugo Almeida• 65), Sokota, Jorginho. Tr: Adriaanse

GROUP H MATCHDAY 1
Tehelné Pole, Bratislava
13-09-2005, 20:45, 28 000, Poulat FRA

Artmedia Bratislava 0

Cobej - Petras, Bednar, Durica, Urbanek (Konecny 73) - Vascak, Kozak, Stano• (Gomes 62), Fodrek - Hartig (Mikulic 71), Halenar. Tr: Weiss

Internazionale 1

Cruz 17

Julio Cesar - Cordoba, Materazzi, Samuel, Wome - Figo (Matins 80), Veron•••56, C Zanetti•, Stankovic - Cruz (Pizarro 65), Adriano. Tr: Mancini

GROUP H MATCHDAY 2
O Dragão, Oporto
28-09-2005, 19:45, 38 708, Busacca SUI

FC Porto 2

Lucho González 32, Diego 39

Victor Baia - Bosingwa•, Ricardo Costa (Alan 76), Bruno Alves, Cesar Peixoto - Ibson, Diego (Hugo Almeida 76), Lucho Gonzalez - Ricardo Quaresma•, McCarthy, Jorginho. Tr: Adriaanse

Artmedia Bratislava 3

Petrás 45, Kozák 54, Borbély 74

Cobej - Burnak (Halenar• 46), Borbely, Durica, Urbanek - Vascak, Debnar, Kozak, Fodrek• - Petras• (Stano• 79), Hartig (Obzera• 84). Tr: Weiss

GROUP H MATCHDAY 2
San Siro, Milan
28-09-2005, 20:45, BCD, Vassaras GRE

Internazionale 1

Pizarro 49

Julio Cesar - Cordoba•, Materazzi, Samuel, Wome - Figo• (Ze Maria 75), Pizarro, Cambiasso, Solari (Killy Gonzalez 84) - Martins (Recoba 60), Cruz. Tr: Mancini

Rangers 0

Waterreus• - Ricksen, Rodriguez, Kyrgiakos, Bernard - Namouchi (Thompson 89), Murray (Nieto 84), Ferguson, Lovenkrands - Buffel (Jeffers 77), Prso. Tr: McLeish

GROUP H MATCHDAY 3
O Dragão, Oporto
19-10-2005, 19:45, 38 418, Ivanov.R RUS

FC Porto 2

Materazzi OG 22, McCarthy 35

Victor Baia - Bosingwa, Pedro Emanuel, Pepe•, Cech - Lucho Gonzalez, Jorginho (Ibson 90), Pablo Assuncao - Ricardo Quaresma (Ivanildo 82), McCarthy (Alan 60), Hugo Almeida. Tr: Adriaanse

Internazionale 2

Julio Cesar - Cordoba•, Materazzi, Samuel, Favalli• - Figo (Ze Maria 82), Pizarro (Recoba 53), Veron, Cambiasso, Solari (Adriano 67) - Cruz•. Tr: Mancini

GROUP H MATCHDAY 3
Ibrox, Glasgow
19-10-2005, 19:45, 49 013

Rangers 0

Waterreus - Ricksen, Rodriguez, Kyrgiakos (Andrews 59), Bernard• - Namouchi (Burke• 75), Ferguson, Hemdani, Lovenkrands - Nieto (Thompson 38), Prsov•. Tr: McLeish

Artmedia Bratislava 0

Cobej - Petras, Debnar, Durica, Urbanek - Vascak (Obzera• 69), Kozak, Borbely•, Fodrek - Helenar (Tchur 73), Hartig (Stano 83). Tr: Weiss

GROUP H MATCHDAY 4
San Siro, Milan
1-11-2005, 20:45, BCD, Mejuto ESP

Internazionale 2

Cruz 2 75p 82

Julio Cesar - Burdisso, Materazzi, Samuel (Mihajlovic 66), Favalli - Figo, Pizarro, Veron, Wome (Cambiasso 54) - Adriano (Cruz 61), Martins. Tr: Mancini

FC Porto 1

Almeida 16

Victor Baia - Bosingwa•, Pedro Emanuel, Pepe, Cech - Ricardo Quaresma, Lucho Gonzalez, Pablo Assuncao (Bruno Alves 62), Jorginho, Alan (Raul Meireles 46) - Hugo Almeida (McCarthy 76). Tr: Adriaanse

GROUP H MATCHDAY 4
Tehelné Pole, Bratislava
1-11-2005, 20:45, 19 492, Meyer GER

Artmedia Bratislava 2

Borbély 8, Kozák 59

Cobej - Petras, Debnar, Durica, Urbanek - Vascak (Tchur 83), Kozak, Borbely, Fodrek• - Obzera (Stano 87), Hartig (Halenar 73). Tr: Weiss

Rangers 2

Prso 3, Thompson 44

Waterreus - Hutton, Rodriguez, Kyrgiakos•, Bernard (Murray 90) - Ricksen, Ferguson•, Hemdani, Lovenkrands - Thompson (Jeffers 70), Prso. Tr: McLeish

GROUP H MATCHDAY 5
O Dragão, Oporto
23-11-2005, 19:45, 39 439, Fandel GER

FC Porto 1

Lisandro López 60

Victor Baia - Bosingwa, Pedro Emanuel (Hugo Almeida 46), Pepe, Cesar Peixoto - Lucho Gonzalez, Pablo Assuncao, Diego (Bruno Alves 63) - Jorginho, Lopez, Ricardo Quaresma•. Tr: Adriaanse

Rangers 1

McCormack 83

Waterreus - Ricksen, Andrews, Kyrgiakos, Murray• - Hemdani• - Namouchi, A Rae (Thompson 64), Ferguson•, Lovenkrands (Burke 77) - Jeffers (McCormack 75). Tr: McLeish

GROUP H MATCHDAY 5
San Siro, Milan
23-11-2005, 20:45, BCD, Riley ENG

Internazionale 4

Figo 28, Adriano 3 41 59 74

Julio Cesar - J Zanetti, Cordoba (C Zanetti 67) Samuel, Wome - Figo (Burdisso 46), Cambiasso, Veron (Stankovic 60), Solari - Recoba, Adriano. Tr: Mancini

Artmedia Bratislava 0

Cobej - Petras•, Debnar, Durica, Urbanek (Stano 79) - Vascak (Mikulic 68), Kozak (Tchur 68), Borbely, Fodrek, Obzera - Halenar. Tr: Weiss

GROUP H MATCHDAY 6
Ibrox, Glasgow
6-12-2005, 19:45, 49 170, Plautz AUT

Rangers 1

Løvenkrands 38

Waterreus - Ricksen, Andrews•, Kyrgiakos•, Murray - Namouchi, Ferguson, Malcolm, Burke - Buffel, Lovenkrands. Tr: McLeish

Internazionale 1

Adriano 30

Toldo - Andreolli (J Zanetti 68), Mihajlovic, Materazzi (Momente• 40), Burdisso - Solari, C Zanetti•••87, Pizzaro•, Wome - Martins, Adriano. Tr: Mancini

GROUP H MATCHDAY 6
Tehelné Pole, Bratislava
6-12-2005, 20:45, 9 542, Merk GER

Artmedia Bratislava 0

Cobej - Petras, Debnar•, Durica, Urbanek• - Stano - Obzera, (Halenar 88), Kozak, Borbely, Fodrek - Hartig (Vascak 61). Tr: Weiss

FC Porto 0

Victor Baia - Ricardo Costa, Pepe, Pedro Emanuel• (Bosingwa• 59), Cesar Peixoto• - Lucho Gonzalez, Pablo Assuncao, Diego• (Hugo Almeida 46) - Ricardo Quaresma (Jorginho 72), McCarthy, Lopez. Tr: Adriaanse

ROUND OF SIXTEEN

1st Leg. Stamford Bridge, London
22-02-2006, 19:45, 39 521, Hauge NOR

Chelsea　　　　　　　　　　　**1**
　　　　　　　　Thiago Motta OG [59]

Cech - Ferreira, Carvalho, Terry, Del Horno•37 - Cole.J (Geremi 40), Gudjohnsen, Makelele, Lampard, Robben (Wright-Phillips 78) - Crespo (Drogba 46). Tr: Mourinho

Barcelona　　　　　　　　　　**2**
　　　　　　　　　　Terry OG [72], Eto'o [80]

Valdés - Oleguer•, Puyol•, Márquez, Van Bronckhorst (Sylvinho 69) - Deco (Iniesta 85), Edmilson, Thiago Motta (Larsson 66) - Messi, Eto'o, Ronaldinho. Tr: Rijkaard

---

2nd Leg. Camp Nou, Barcelona
7-03-2006, 20:45, 98 436, Merk GER

Barcelona　　　　　　　　　　**1**
　　　　　　　　　　　　Ronaldinho [78]

Valdés - Oleguer, Puyol•, Márquez, Van Bronckhorst - Deco, Edmilson, Thiago Motta• - Messi (Larsson 25), Eto'o, Ronaldinho. Tr: Rijkaard

Chelsea　　　　　　　　　　　**1**
　　　　　　　　　　　Lampard [92+p]

Cech - Ferreira, Carvalho, Terry, Gallas - Cole.J• (Huth 83), Makelele, Robben, Lampard, Duff (Gudjohnsen 58) - Drogba (Crespo 58). Tr: Mourinho

---

1st Leg. Estádio da Luz, Lisbon
21-02-2006, 19:45, 63 702, Plautz AUT

Benfica　　　　　　　　　　　**1**
　　　　　　　　　　　　Luisão [84]

Moretto - Alcides, Luisão, Anderson, Léo (Ricardo Rocha 87) - Petit, Beto• (Karagounis 58), Manuel Fernandes - Robert (Nélson 77), Nuno Gomes, Simão. Tr: Koeman

Liverpool　　　　　　　　　　**0**

Reina - Finnan, Carragher, Hyypiä, Riise - Luis García•, Sissoko (Hamann• 35), Xabi Alonso, Kewell - Morientes (Gerrard 78), Fowler (Cissé 66). Tr: Benítez

---

2nd Leg. Anfield, Liverpool
8-03-2006, 19:45, 42 744, De Santis ITA

Liverpool　　　　　　　　　　**0**

Reina - Finnan, Carragher, Traoré, Warnock (Hamann 70) - Luis García, Gerrard•, Xabi Alonso•, Kewell (Cissé 63) - Morientes (Fowler 70), Crouch•. Tr: Benítez

Benfica　　　　　　　　　　　**2**
　　　　　　　　　Simão [36], Miccoli [89]

Moretto - Alcides, Luisão, Anderson, Léo - Robert• (Ricardo Rocha 70), Beto, Manuel Fernandes• - Geovanni (Karagounis 60), Nuno Gomes• (Miccoli 77), Simão. Tr: Koeman

---

1st Leg. Philips Stadion, Eindhoven
21-02-2006, 20:45, 35 000, Vassaras GRE

PSV Eindhoven　　　　　　　　**0**

Gomes - Reiziger, Ooijer, Alex, Lamey - Simons, Afellay (Koné 73), Cocu - Farfán, Hesselink, Culina (Alssati 54). Tr: Hiddink

Olympique Lyonnais　　　　　　**1**
　　　　　　　　　　　　Juninho [65]

Coupet - Clerc, Cris (Wiltord• 46), Müller, Abidal - Tiago, Diarra•, Juninho• - Govou••81, Carew (Fred 63), Malouda. Tr: Houllier

---

2nd Leg. Stade Gerland, Lyon
8-03-2006, 20:45, 37 901, Riley ENG

Olympique Lyonnais　　　　　　**4**
　　　Tiago 2 [26 45], Wiltord [71], Fred [90]

Coupet - Clerc, Cris, Müller, Abidal - Tiago (Clément 80), Diarra, Juninho• (Pedretti 76) - Wiltord, Carew (Fred 65), Malouda. Tr: Houllier

PSV Eindhoven　　　　　　　　**0**

Gomes - Lucius, Addo, Alex (Alssati 76), Reiziger - Simons, Afellay•, Cocu••••43 - Culina (Väyrynen 57), Koné, Farfán (Beasey 57). Tr: Hiddink

---

1st Leg. Allianz-Arena, Munich
21-02-2006, 20:45, 66 000, De Bleeckere BEL

Bayern München　　　　　　　**1**
　　　　　　　　　　　　Ballack [23]

Rensing - Sagnol, Lucio, Ismaël, Lahm - Salihamidzic (Karimi 58), Demichelis, Ballack, Zé Roberto (Scholl 77) - Pizarro, Makaay (Guerrero 80). Tr: Magath

Milan　　　　　　　　　　　　**1**
　　　　　　　　　　Shevchenko [58p]

Dida (Kalac 69) - Stam, Nesta, Kaladze, Serginho - Gattuso• (Vogel 85), Pirlo, Kaká, Seedorf• (Jankulovski 90) - Shevchenko, Gilardino. Tr: Ancelotti

---

2nd Leg. San Siro, Milan
8-03-2006, 20:45, 78 577, Ivanov.V RUS

Milan　　　　　　　　　　　　**4**
　　Inzaghi 2 [8 47], Shevchenko [25], Kaká [59]

Dida - Stam, Nesta•, Kaladze, Serginho - Vogel•, Pirlo, Kaká (Rui Costa 86), Seedorf - Shevchenko (≠23) (Ambrosini 76), Inzaghi (Gilardino 72). Tr: Ancelotti

Bayern München　　　　　　　**1**
　　　　　　　　　　　　Ismaël [35]

Kahn - Sagnol•, Lucio, Ismaël, Lizarazu (Zé Roberto 52) - Deisler (Scholl 63), Demichelis•, Ballack, Schweinsteiger - Pizarro, Makaay (Guerrero• 46). Tr: Magath

---

1st Leg. Ibrox, Glasgow
22-02-2006, 19:45, 49 372, Poulat FRA

Rangers　　　　　　　　　　　**1**
　　　　　　Løvenkrands [22], Peña OG [82]

Waterreus - Hutton, Kyrgiakos, Rodriguez, Smith.S - Burke, Hemdani, Ferguson, Namouchi (Buffel 69) - Løvenkrands (Novo 75), Prso (Boyd 89). Tr: McLeish

Villarreal　　　　　　　　　　**2**
　　　　　　　　Riquelme [8p], Forlán [35]

Viera - Javi Venta, Peña, Gonzalo, Arruabarrena (Sorín 61) - Senna, Josico, Riquelme (Arzo 90), Tacchinardi - José María (Roger García 84), Forlán. Tr: Pellegrini

---

2nd Leg. El Madrigal, Villarreal
7-03-2006, 20:45, 19 828, Hamer LUX

Villarreal　　　　　　　　　　**1**
　　　　　　　　　　Arruabarrena [49]

Viera• - Javi Venta (Font 46), Peña, Gonzalo, Arruabarrena• - Senna, Tacchinardi•, Riquelme (Calleja 86), Josico• - José María (Franco• 46), Forlán. Tr: Pellegrini

Rangers　　　　　　　　　　　**1**
　　　　　　　　　　Løvenkrands [12]

Waterreus - Hutton•, Rodriguez, Kyrgiakos, Murray• - Burke (Novo 87), Ferguson, Hemdani, Namouchi - Buffel• (Boyd 64), Løvenkrands. Tr: McLeish

---

1st Leg. Amsterdam ArenA, Amsterdam
22-02-2006, 20:45, 46 663, Stark GER

Ajax　　　　　　　　　　　　**2**
　　　　　　　　Huntelaar [16], Rosales [20]

Stekelenburg - Trabelsi, Heitinga, Vermaelen, Emanuelson - Maduro, Lindenbergh, Boukhari - Rosales (Babel 89), Huntelaar, Rosenberg•. Tr: Blind

Internazionale　　　　　　　　**2**
　　　　　　　　Stankovic [49], Cruz [86]

Toldo - Javier Zanetti, Córdoba•, Samuel, Burdisso - Figo, Cambiasso, Stankovic, César (Pizarro• 46) - Cruz•, Adriano (Martins 65). Tr: Mancini

---

2nd Leg. San Siro, Milan
14-03-2006, 20:45, 48 489, Frojdfeldt SWE

Internazionale　　　　　　　　**1**
　　　　　　　　　　　Stankovic [57]

Toldo - Javier Zanetti, Materazzi, Samuel, Womé - Figo, Verón (Cristiano Zanetti 74), Cambiasso, Stankovic - Adriano, Martins (Recoba 84). Tr: Mancini

Ajax　　　　　　　　　　　　**0**

Stekelenburg - Trabelsi, Maduro, Vermaelen• - Juanfran - Pienaar, Lindenbergh, Boukhari - Rosales (Babel 72), Huntelaar, Rosenberg (Charisteas 74). Tr: Blind

---

1st Leg. Weserstadion, Bremen
22-02-2006, 20:45, 36 500, Mejuto ESP

Werder Bremen　　　　　　　　**3**
　　　　　Schulz [39], Borowski [87], Micoud [92+]

Wiese - Owomoyela, Fahrenhorst, Naldo, Schulz• - Frings, Baumann, Micoud, Borowski - Klose (Valdez 68), Klasnic. Tr: Schaaf

Juventus　　　　　　　　　　　**2**
　　　　　　　　Nedved [73], Trezeguet [82]

Buffon - Blasi, Thuram, Cannavaro, Balzaretti• - Camoranesi (Zalayeta 74), Emerson, Vieira•, Nedved• - Trezeguet•, Ibrahimovic (Del Piero 59). Tr: Capello

---

2nd Leg. Delle Alpi
7-03-2006, 20:45, 40 226, Poll ENG

Juventus　　　　　　　　　　　**2**
　　　　　　　　Trezeguet [65], Emerson [88]

Buffon - Zebina, Thuram, Cannavaro, Zambrotta (Balzaretti 70) - Camoranesi (Mutu 57), Emerson, Vieira, Nedved• - Trezeguet, Ibrahimovic (Del Piero• 57). Tr: Capello

Werder Bremen　　　　　　　　**1**
　　　　　　　　　　　Micoud [13]

Wiese - Owomoyela, Fahrenhorst, Naldo, Schulz - Frings, Baumann• (Pasanen 73), Micoud•, Borowski - Klose, Klasnic (Valdez 81). Tr: Schaaf

---

1st Leg. Bernabéu, Madrid
21-02-2006, 20:45, 74 000, Farina ITA

Real Madrid　　　　　　　　　**1**

Casillas• - Cicinho•, Sergio Ramos, Woodgate (Mejia 9), Roberto Carlos - Beckham, Guti, Graveson (Baptista 76), Zidane, Robinho (Raúl 63) - Ronaldo. Tr: López Caro

Arsenal　　　　　　　　　　　**1**
　　　　　　　　　　　　Henry [47]

Lehmann - Eboué, Touré, Senderos, Flamini - Ljungberg, Hleb (Pirès 76), Gilberto, Fabregas• (Song 95+), Reyes• (Diaby 80) - Henry. Tr: Wenger

2nd Leg. Highbury, London
8-03-2006, 19:45, 35 487, Michel SVK

Arsenal 0

Lehmann - Eboué, Touré, Senderos, Flamini - Hleb
(Bergkamp 87), Fabregas, Ljungberg, Gilberto, Reyes
(Pirès 68) - Henry•. Tr: Wenger

Real Madrid 0

Casillas - Michel Salgado (Robinho 84), Sergio
Ramos, Raúl Bravo•, Roberto Carlos• - Beckham,
Graveson• (Baptista 68), Guti•, Zidane - Ronaldo,
Raúl (Cassano 73). Tr: López Caro

QUARTER-FINALS AND SEMI-FINALS

Quarter-final 1st Leg. Estádio da Luz, Lisbon
28-03-2006, 19:45, 65 000, Bennett ENG

Benfica 0

Moretto - Ricardo Rocha, Luisão, Anderson, Léo -
Beto, Petit, Manuel Fernandes - Simão, Geovanni
(Karagounis 68), Robert (Miccoli• 46). Tr: Koeman

Barcelona 0

Valdes - Belletti•, Oleguer, Thiago Motta,
Van Bronckhorst - Deco• (Gabri 76), Van Bommel,
Iniesta• - Larsson (Giuly 76), Eto'o, Ronaldinho.
Tr: Rijkaard

Quarter-final 2nd Leg. Camp Nou, Barcelona
5-04-2006, 20:45, 89 475, Michel SVK

Barcelona 2
Ronaldinho [19], Eto'o [89]

Valdes - Belletti, Puyol, Oleguer, Van Bronckhorst -
Van Bommel (Edmilson 85), Iniesta, Deco• - Larsson
(Giuly 86), Eto'o•, Ronaldinho (≠5). Tr: Rijkaard

Benfica 0

Moretto - Ricardo Rocha, Luisão•, Anderson•, Léo -
Beto (Robert 72), Petit, Manuel Fernandes• (Marcel
82) - Geovanni (Karagounis 55), Miccoli, Simão. Tr:
Koeman

Quarter-final 1st Leg. Stade Gerland, Lyon
29-03-2006, 20:45, 39 500, Plautz AUT

Olympique Lyonnais 0

Coupet - Clerc, Cris, Caçapa, Abidal - Tiago•, Diarra,
Pedretti (Clément 68) - Wiltord, Carew (Fred 63),
Malouda. Tr: Houllier

Milan 0

Dida - Costacurta• (Maldini 62), Nesta, Kaladze,
Serginho - Gattuso, Pirlo (Vogel 85), Kaká, Seedorf -
Gilardino (Inzaghi 62), Shevchenko. Tr: Ancelotti

Quarter-final 2nd Leg. San Siro, Milan
4-04-2006, 20:45, 78 894, Hauge NOR

Milan 3
Inzaghi 2 [25 88], Shevchenko [93+]

Dida - Stam (Costacurta 24), Nesta, Kaladze,
Serginho• - Gattuso• (Maldini• 78), Pirlo
(Ambrosini 71), Kaká, Seedorf - Inzaghi•,
Shevchenko. Tr: Ancelotti

Olympique Lyonnais 1
Diarra [31]

Coupet - Clerc, Cris, Caçapa, Abidal - Juninho,
Diarra, Malouda - Wiltord, Fred (Carew 71), Govou
(Réveillère 83). Tr: Houllier

Quarter-final 1st Leg. San Siro, Milan
29-03-2006, 20:45, 49 165, Sars FRA

Internazionale 2
Adriano [7], Martins [54]

Toldo - Javier Zanetti, Córdoba, Samuel•, Womé -
Stankovic (Kily González 82), Verón•, Cambiasso,
César (Materazzi 69) - Recoba• (Martins 28),
Adriano. Tr: Mancini

Villarreal 1
Forlán [1]

Viera - Javi Venta, Gonzalo, Peña, Sorín• - Riquelme,
Arzo (Quique Alvarez 60), Senna•, Calleja
(Cazorla 87) - José María (Franco 76), Forlán.
Tr: Pellegrini

Quarter-final 2nd Leg. El Madrigal, Villarreal
4-04-2006, 20:45, 21 700, Vassaras GRE

Villarreal 1
Arruabarrena [58]

Viera• - Javi Venta, Quique Alvarez, Peña,
Arruabarrena - Senna, Tacchinardi•, Riquelme, Sorín
(Josico 78) - Forlán (Calleja 90), José María
(Franco 78). Tr: Pellegrini

Internazionale 0

Toldo - Córdoba, Materazzi, Samuel, Javier Zanetti -
Figo• (Mihajlovic 75), Cambiasso, Verón (Cruz 85),
Stankovic - Recoba (Martins• 56), Adriano.
Tr: Mancini

Quarter-final 1st Leg. Highbury, London
28-03-2006, 20:45, 35 472, Frojdfeldt SWE

Arsenal 2
Fabregas [40], Henry [69]

Lehmann - Eboué, Touré, Senderos, Flamini - Pirès,
Fabregas, Hleb, Gilberto, Reyes (Van Persie 82) -
Henry. Tr: Wenger

Juventus 0

Buffon - Zebina••• 89, Thuram, Cannavaro,
Zambrotta - Camoranesi••• 87, Emerson, Vieira•,
Mutu (Chiellini 72) - Ibrahimovic, Trezeguet•
(Zalayeta 79). Tr: Capello

Quarter-final 2nd Leg. Delle Alpi, Turin
5-04-2006, 20:45, 46 031, Fandel GER

Juventus 0

Buffon - Zambrotta, Kovac, Cannavaro, Chiellini•
(Balzaretti 66) - Mutu (Zalayeta 61), Emerson,
Giannichedda, Nedved••• 77 - Trezeguet,
Ibrahimovic. Tr: Capello

Arsenal 0

Lehmann - Eboué, Touré, Senderos, Flamini• - Hleb
(Diaby 87), Ljungberg, Gilberto, Fabregas, Reyes•
(Pirès 63) - Henry. Tr: Wenger

Semi-final 1st Leg. San Siro, Milan
18-04-2006, 20:45, 76 883, Sars FRA

Milan 0

Dida - Stam (Cafu 77), Kaladze, Nesta•, Serginho -
Gattuso (Ambrosini 74), Pirlo (Maldini 67), Kaká,
Seedorf - Shevchenko, Gilardino. Tr: Ancelotti

Barcelona 1
Giuly [57]

Valdes - Oleguer• (Thiago Motta 75), Puyol•,
Márquez, Van Bronckhorst - Van Bommel, Edmilson,
Iniesta - Giuly (Belletti 70), Eto'o, Ronaldinho (Maxi
López 89). Tr: Rijkaard

Semi-final 2nd Leg. Camp Nou, Barcelona
26-04-2006, 20:45, 95 661, Merk GER

Barcelona 0

Valdes - Belletti, Márquez, Puyol, Van Bronckhorst -
Iniesta, Edmilson•, Deco - Giuly (Larsson 69), Eto'o
(Van Bommel 89), Ronaldinho. Tr: Rijkaard

Milan 0

Dida - Stam, Costacurta• (Cafu 64), Kaladze,
Serginho - Gattuso (Rui Costa 68), Pirlo, Kaká,
Seedorf - Shevchenko, Inzaghi (Gilardino 79).
Tr: Ancelotti

Semi-final 1st Leg. Highbury, London
19-04-2006, 20:45, 35 438, Plautz AUT

Arsenal 1
Touré [41]

Lehmann - Eboué, Touré, Senderos, Flamini - Hleb
(Bergkamp 80), Gilberto, Ljungberg (Van Persie 81),
Fabregas, Pirès - Henry. Tr: Wenger

Villarreal 0

Barbosa - Javi Venta, Quique Alvarez•, Arzo•,
Arruabarrena - Senna, Riquelme•, Tacchinardi•,
Sorín (Josico 73) - José María (Franco• 55), Forlán
(Calleja 94+). Tr: Pellegrini

Semi-final 2nd Leg. El Madrigal, Villarreal
25-04-2006, 20:45, 23 000, Ivanov.V RUS

Villarreal 0

Barbosa - Javi Venta, Peña, Quique Alvarez,
Arruabarrena (Roger García 82) - Riquelme (≠90),
Josico (José María 63), Senna, Sorín - Forlán, Franco.
Tr: Pellegrini

Arsenal 0

Lehmann - Eboué, Touré, Campbell, Flamini (Clichy 9)
- Hleb, Fabregas, Gilberto, Ljungberg, Reyes
(Pirès 69) - Henry. Tr: Wenger

Final   **Stade de France, Paris**   **17-05-2005**

Kick-off: 19:20   Attendance: 79 500

BARCELONA   2   1   ARSENAL

Samuel Eto'o [76], Juliano Belletti [81]   Sol Campbell [37]

		BARCELONA			MATCH STATS						ARSENAL		
1	GK	Victor VALDES						**18**		Jens LEHMANN	GK	**1**
4	DF	Rafael MARQUEZ		18	Shots	8			Ashley COLE	DF	3
5	DF	Carles PUYOL		9	Shots on Goal	5	18		Robert PIRES	MF	7
8	FW	Ludovic GIULY		20	Fouls Committed	16			Fredrik LJUNGBERG	MF	8
9	FW	Samuel ETO'O		3	Corner Kicks	4	85		Aleksandr HLEB	MF	13
10	MF	RONALDINHO		1	Offside	1			Thierry HENRY	FW	**14**
12	DF	Giovanni VAN BRONCKHORST		64	Possession %	36	74		Cesc FABREGAS	MF	15
15	DF	EDMILSON	46						GILBERTO	MF	19
17	MF	Mark VAN BOMMEL	61		MATCH OFFICIALS				Sol CAMPBELL	DF	23
20	MF	DECO			REFEREE				Emmanuel EBOUE	DF	**27**
23	DF	OLEGUER Presas	71		Terje HAUGE NOR				Kolo Abib TOURE	DF	28
		Tr: RIJKAARD Frank			ASSISTANTS				Tr: WENGER Arsene		
		Substitutes			Arild SUNDET NOR				Substitutes		
25	GK	Albert JORQUERA			Steinar HOLVIK NOR		18		Manuel ALMUNIA	GK	24
2	DF	Juliano BELLETTI	71		4TH OFFICIAL		85		José Antonio REYES	FW	9
3	MF	Thiago MOTTA			Tom Henning ØVREBØ NOR				Dennis BERGKAMP	FW	10
6	MF	XAVI Hernandez							Robin VAN PERSIE	FW	11
7	FW	Henrik LARSSON	61				74		Mathieu FLAMINI	MF	16
16	DF	SYLVINHO							Philippe SENDEROS	DF	20
24	MF	Andrés INIESTA	46						Gael CLICHY	DF	22

We never thought the game was lost. After having seen what Liverpool did last year we told ourselves not to throw in the towel. We covered ourselves in the spirit of Liverpool.
Samuel Eto'o

The equaliser was very important and broke something mentally for Arsenal. After that we were in control.
Frank Rijkaard

The way we lost is very difficult to take because we played fantastically, like we have the whole European season. But in the final, people only remember the team that has won.
Arsene Wenger

We can be proud, we can be more than proud, but I'm sorry, some of the refereeing today was horrendous.
Thierry Henry

MATCH HIGHLIGHTS

3' Victor Valdes saves well to deny Thierry Henry. **4'** Valdes saves once again from Henry from the ensuing corner. **8'** Ludovic Giuly shoots from an acute angle straight at Jens Lehmann. **18'** Lehmann brings down Samuel Eto'o on the edge of the box and although Ludovic Giuly scores a free kick is given and Lehmann becomes the first player to be sent off in a European Cup final. **37'** Sol Campbell heads home a Henry free kick after Emmanuel Eboue wins a dubious free kick. **45+2'** Manuel Almunia turns an Eto'o shot onto the post. **63'** Aleksandr Hleb shoots just wide. **67'** Valdes makes a fine save to deny Ljungberg. **70'** Henry breaks clear but his shot has no power and Valdes saves. **76'** Eto scores after a brilliant pass from Henrik Larsson. **81'** Larsson is once again provider as he sets up Belletti whose shot is deflected in off Almunia's leg.

MATCH REPORT

The eagerly anticipated spectacle failed to materialise in a match shaped by the early sending-off of Arsenal goalkeeper Jens Lehmann. From then on Barcelona dominated the play but conceded just before half-time. Barcelona pressed forward for the rest of the game and although they looked vulnerable to the Arsenal counter, their pressure paid off with two late goals against a rapidly tiring opposition that conceded for the first time in 10 games. For Barcelona it was a second European Cup triumph but for Arsenal the disappointment at failing to win their first was tangible.

AJAX

	Goalkeepers	
1	Maarten Stekelenburg	NED
12	Hans Vonk	RSA
26	Bogdan Lobont	ROU
30	Kenneth Vermeer	NED
35	Henrik Moisander	FIN
	Defenders	
2	Hatem Trabelsi	TUN
3	Zdenek Grygera	CZE
4	Johnny Heitinga	NED
5	Julien Escudé	FRA
15	Thomas Vermaelen	BEL
19	Urby Emanuelson	NED
31	Emanuel Boakye	GHA
33	Robbert Schilder	NED
	Midfielders	
	Didi Longuet	NED
6	Tomás Galásek	CZE
8	Hedwiges Maduro	NED
10	Steven Pienaar	RSA
16	Nigel de Jong	NED
18	Wesley Sneijder	NED
21	Olaf Lindenbergh	NED
22	Juanfran	ESP
37	Per Weihrauch	DEN
	Forwards	
7	Mauro Rosales	ARG
9	Angelos Charisteas	GRE
11	Ryan Babel	NED
17	Yannis Anastasiou	GRE
24	Markus Rosenberg	SWE
27	Edgar Manucharyan	ARM
28	Nourdin Boukhari	NED
32	Vurnon Anita	NED
36	Javier Martina	NED

ANDERLECHT

	Goalkeepers	
1	Daniel Zitka	CZE
13	Silvio Proto	BEL
25	Jan Van Steenberghe	BEL
	Defenders	
4	Yves Vanderhaeghe	BEL
5	Roland Juhász	HUN
6	Michal Zewlakow	POL
19	Laurent Delorge	BEL
27	Vincent Kompany	BEL
30	Hannu Tihinen	FIN
34	Lamine Traoré	BFA
37	Anthony Vanden Borre	BEL
	Midfielders	
3	Olivier Deschacht	BEL
7	Goran Lovre	SCG
10	Walter Baseggio	BEL
14	Bart Goor	BEL
15	Besnik Hasi	ALB
17	Christian Wilhelmsson	SWE
20	Fabrice Ehret	FRA
21	Pär Zetterberg	SWE
28	Anatoli Gerk	RUS
31	Mark De Man	BEL
41	Cheik Ismael Tiote	CIV
99	Marius Mitu	ROU
	Forwards	
8	Nenad Jestrovic	SCG
9	Mbo Mpenza	BEL
11	Grégory Pujol	FRA
22	Oleg Iachtchouk	UKR
24	Serhat Akin	TUR
36	Jonathan Legear	BEL
42	Regis Lacroix	BEL

ARSENAL

	Goalkeepers	
1	Jens Lehmann	GER
21	Mart Poom	EST
24	Manuel Almunia	ESP
42	Vito Mannone	ITA
	Defenders	
3	Ashley Cole	ENG
12	Lauren	CMR
18	Pascal Cygan	FRA
20	Philippe Senderos	SUI
22	Gaël Clichy	FRA
23	Sol Campbell	ENG
27	Emmanuel Eboué	CIV
28	Kolo Abib Touré	CIV
37	Ryan Garry	ENG
	Midfielders	
7	Robert Pirès	FRA
8	Fredrik Ljungberg	SWE
13	Aleksandr Hleb	BLR
15	Cesc Fabregas	ESP
16	Mathieu Flamini	FRA
17	Alexandre Song	CMR
19	Gilberto	BRA
29	Sebastian Larsson	SWE
35	Patrick Cregg	IRL
36	Johan Djourou	SUI
43	Ryan Smith	ENG
	Forwards	
9	José Antonio Reyes	ESP
10	Dennis Bergkamp	NED
11	Robin van Persie	NED
14	Thierry Henry	FRA
26	Quincy Owusu-Abeyie	NED
33	Nicklas Bendtner	DEN
41	Arturo Lupoli	ITA

ARTMEDIA

	Goalkeepers	
1	Juraj Cobej	SVK
18	Lubos Kamenár	SVK
30	Stefan Kollár	SVK
	Defenders	
2	Ondrej Debnár	SVK
4	Ján Durica	SVK
5	Ales Hellebrand	CZE
17	Balázs Borbély	SVK
23	Roman Konecny	SVK
24	Peter Burák	SVK
	Midfielders	
3	Pavol Stano	SVK
13	Daniel Tchul	CZE
15	Vratislav Gajdos	SVK
16	Lukás Hartig	CZE
20	Branislav Fodrek	SVK
21	Peter Petrás	SVK
22	Ales Urbánek	CZE
25	Ján Kozák	SVK
	Forwards	
8	Blazej Vascák	SVK
9	Fabio Luis Gomes	BRA
10	Martin Mikulic	SVK
12	Branislav Obzera	SVK
14	Juraj Halenár	SVK
19	Milorad Bukvic	SCG

BARCELONA

	Goalkeepers	
1	Víctor Valdés	ESP
25	Albert Jorquera	ESP
28	Rubén Martínez	ESP
	Defenders	
2	Juliano Belletti	BRA
4	Rafael Márquez	MEX
5	Carles Puyol	ESP
12	Giovanni v.Bronckhorst	NED
15	Edmílson	BRA
16	Sylvinho	BRA
23	Oleguer Presas	ESP
26	Rodri	ESP
29	Carlos Peña	ESP
32	Damiá Abella	ESP
	Midfielders	
3	Thiago Motta	BRA
6	Xavi Hernández	ESP
10	Ronaldinho	BRA
17	Mark van Bommel	NED
18	Gabri García	ESP
20	Deco	POR
24	Andrés Iniesta	ESP
27	Pitu	ESP
30	Lionel Messi	ARG
31	Joan Verdú	ESP
	Forwards	
7	Henrik Larsson	SWE
8	Ludovic Giuly	FRA
9	Samuel Eto'o	CMR
11	Maxi López	ARG
14	Santiago Ezquerro	ESP

BAYERN

	Goalkeepers	
1	Oliver Kahn	GER
22	Michael Rensing	GER
29	Bernd Dreher	GER
36	Jan Schlösser	GER
	Defenders	
2	Willy Sagnol	FRA
3	Lucio	BRA
6	Martin Demichelis	ARG
18	Andreas Görlitz	GER
21	Philipp Lahm	GER
25	Valérien Ismaël	FRA
69	Bixente Lizarazu	FRA
	Midfielders	
7	Mehmet Scholl	GER
8	Ali Karimi	IRN
11	Zé Roberto	BRA
13	Michael Ballack	GER
16	Jens Jeremies	GER
20	Hasan Salihamidzic	BIH
23	Owen Hargreaves	ENG
26	Sebastian Deisler	GER
31	Bastian Schweinsteiger	GER
39	Andreas Ottl	GER
40	Markus Steinhöfer	GER
	Forwards	
10	Roy Makaay	NED
14	Claudio Pizarro	PER
24	Roque Santa Cruz	PAR
33	José Paolo Guerrero	PER

BENFICA

	Goalkeepers	
1	José Moreira	POR
12	Quim	POR
24	Bruno Costa	POR
43	Rui Nereu	POR
	Defenders	
3	Anderson	BRA
4	Luisão	BRA
5	Léo	BRA
13	Alcides	BRA
18	Manuel Dos Santos	FRA
22	Nélson	CPV
25	Tiago Gomes	POR
27	João Pereira	POR
33	Ricardo Rocha	POR
	Midfielders	
6	Petit	POR
7	Carlitos	POR
8	Bruno Aguiar	POR
10	Georgios Karagounis	GRE
14	Manuel Fernandes	POR
15	Nuno Assis	POR
16	Beto	BRA
17	Andrei Kariaka	RUS
26	Fernando Alexandre	POR
28	Hélio Roque	POR
39	João Coimbra	POR
	Forwards	
9	Mantorras	ANG
11	Geovanni	BRA
20	Simão	POR
21	Nuno Gomes	POR
30	Fabrizio Miccoli	ITA
35	João Vilela	POR
46	Vasco Firmino	POR

BETIS

	Goalkeepers	
1	Pedro Contreras	ESP
13	Antonio Doblas	ESP
	Defenders	
2	Luis Fernández	ESP
3	Alejandro Lembo	URU
4	Juanito Gutiérrez	ESP
5	David Rivas	ESP
16	Nano	ESP
22	Paolo Castellini	ITA
27	Melli	ESP
	Midfielders	
7	Fernando Varela	ESP
8	Arzu García	ESP
9	Fernando Fernández	ESP
10	Juan José Cañas	ESP
14	Capi	ESP
15	Miguel Ángel Lozano	ESP
18	Alberto Rivera	ESP
19	Óscar López	ESP
20	Marcos Assunção	BRA
24	Edu	BRA
25	Juanlu	ESP
	Forwards	
6	Dani Martín	ESP
12	Ricardo Oliveira	BRA
17	Joaquín Sánchez	ESP
21	Xisco Muñoz	ESP
26	Israel Bascón	ESP

CHELSEA

Goalkeepers

1	Petr Cech	CZE
23	Carlo Cudicini	ITA
40	Lenny Pidgeley	ENG
41	Yves Ma-Kalambay	BEL

Defenders

2	Glen Johnson	ENG
3	Asier Del Horno	ESP
6	Ricardo Carvalho	POR
13	William Gallas	FRA
18	Wayne Bridge	ENG
20	Paulo Ferreira	POR
26	John Terry	ENG
29	Robert Huth	GER
32	Steven Watt	SCO

Midfielders

4	Claude Makelele	FRA
5	Michael Essien	GHA
8	Frank Lampard	ENG
10	Joe Cole	ENG
11	Damien Duff	IRL
14	Geremi	CMR
16	Arjen Robben	NED
19	Lassana Diarra	FRA
24	Shaun Wright-Phillips	ENG
42	Anthony Grant	ENG
44	Michael Mancienne	ENG

Forwards

9	Hernán Crespo	ARG
12	Carlton Cole	ENG
15	Didier Drogba	CIV
22	Eidur Gudjohnsen	ISL

CLUB BRUGGE

Goalkeepers

1	Tomislav Butina	CRO
13	Glenn Verbauwhede	BEL
23	Stijn Stijnen	BEL

Defenders

2	Olivier De Cock	BEL
4	Joos Valgaeren	BEL
5	Michael Klukowski	CAN
6	Philippe Clement	BEL
15	Marek Spilár	SVK
17	Ivan Gvozdenovic	SCG
26	Birger Maertens	BEL
32	Günther Vanaudenaerde	BEL
33	Jason Vandelannoite	BEL

Midfielders

3	Sven Vermant	BEL
8	Gaëtan Englebert	BEL
11	Jonathan Blondel	BEL
14	Grégory Dufer	BEL
16	Serhiy Serebrennikov	UKR
18	Ivan Leko	CRO
27	Vincent Provoost	BEL
28	Bart Vlaeminck	BEL
31	Kévin Roelandts	BEL

Forwards

7	Gert Verheyen	BEL
9	Manasseh Ishiaku	NGA
10	Bosko Balaban	CRO
19	Rune Lange	NOR
21	Sebastian Hermans	BEL
22	Javier Portillo	ESP
29	Dieter Van Tornhout	BEL
30	Victor Simões	BRA
34	Jeanvion Yulu-Matondo	BEL

FENERBAHÇE

Goalkeepers

1	Volkan Demirel	TUR
22	Serdar Kulbilge	TUR
34	Rüstü Reçber	TUR

Defenders

2	Fábio Luciano	BRA
3	Servet Çetin	TUR
5	Ümit Özat	TUR
6	Mahmut Erdogdu	TUR
17	Can Arat	TUR
19	Önder Turaci	TUR
24	Deniz Baris	TUR

Midfielders

4	Stephen Appiah	GHA
7	Mehmet Yozgatli	TUR
15	Marco Aurélio	BRA
18	Gürhan Gürsoy	TUR
20	Alex	BRA
21	Selçuk Sahin	TUR
27	Kemal Aslan	TUR
30	Serkan Balci	TUR

Forwards

8	Zafer Biryol	TUR
10	Tuncay Sanli	TUR
11	Márcio Nobre	BRA
16	Kerim Zengin	TUR
23	Semih Sentürk	TUR
29	Olcan Adin	TUR
39	Nicolas Anelka	FRA

INTERNAZIONALE

Goalkeepers

1	Francesco Toldo	ITA
12	Júlio César	BRA
22	Paolo Orlandoni	ITA

Defenders

2	Iván Córdoba	COL
3	Nicolás Burdisso	ARG
4	Javier Zanetti	ARG
11	Sinisa Mihajlovic	SCG
13	Zé Maria	BRA
16	Giuseppe Favalli	ITA
23	Marco Materazzi	ITA
25	Walter Samuel	ARG
33	Pierre Womé	CMR

Midfielders

5	Dejan Stankovic	SCG
6	Cristiano Zanetti	ITA
7	Luís Figo	POR
8	David Pizarro	CHI
14	Juan Sebastián Verón	ARG
18	Kily González	ARG
19	Esteban Cambiasso	ARG
21	Santiago Solari	ARG
40	Abdoulaye Diarra	CIV
41	Jacopo Ravasi	ITA
55	Daniel Maa Boumsong	CMR

Forwards

9	Julio Cruz	ARG
10	Adriano	BRA
20	Alvaro Recoba	URU
30	Obafemi Martins	NGA
42	Domenico Germinale	ITA
43	Basty O. Kyeremateng	GHA
44	Matteo Momente	ITA

JUVENTUS

Goalkeepers

1	Gianluigi Buffon	ITA
12	Antonio Chimenti	ITA
32	Christian Abbiati	ITA
43	Claudio Scarzanella	ITA

Defenders

3	Giorgio Chiellini	ITA
6	Robert Kovac	CRO
7	Gianluca Pessotto	ITA
14	Federico Balzaretti	ITA
15	Domenico Criscito	ITA
21	Lilian Thuram	FRA
26	Gladstone D. Valentina	ITA
27	Jonathan Zebina	FRA
28	Fabio Cannavaro	ITA

Midfielders

4	Patrick Vieira	FRA
8	Emerson	BRA
11	Pavel Nedved	CZE
16	Mauro Camoranesi	ITA
19	Gianluca Zambrotta	ITA
20	Manuele Blasi	ITA
23	Giuliano Giannichedda	ITA
24	Ruben Olivera	URU

Forwards

9	Zlatan Ibrahimovic	SWE
10	Alessandro Del Piero	ITA
17	David Trezeguet	FRA
18	Adrian Mutu	ROU
25	Marcelo Zalayeta	URU

LILLE

Goalkeepers

1	Tony Sylva	SEN
16	Grégory Malicki	FRA
30	Laurent Pichon	FRA

Defenders

3	Alexis Zywiecki	FRA
4	Efstathios Tavlaridis	GRE
5	Rafael Schmitz	BRA
6	Dante Bonfim	BRA
19	Peter Franquart	FRA
20	Grégory Tafforeau	FRA
22	Milivoje Vitakic	SCG
25	Nicolas Plestan	FRA
26	Stephan Lichtsteiner	SUI
28	Dieudonné Owona	FRA

Midfielders

2	Mathieu Debuchy	FRA
7	Yohan Cabaye	FRA
8	Geoffrey Dernis	FRA
10	Daniel Gygax	SUI
11	Hicham Aboucherouane	MOR
12	Mathieu Bodmer	FRA
15	Milenko Acimovic	SVN
17	Jean Makoun	CMR
18	Kévin Barralon	FRA
21	Matthieu Chalmé	FRA
24	Samuel Robail	FRA
29	Stéphane Dumont	FRA

Forwards

9	Matt Moussilou	FRA
11	Nicolas Fauvergue	FRA
14	Peter Odemwingie	NGA
23	Kader Keita	CIV
27	Kevin Mirallas	BEL
34	Larsen Touré	FRA

LIVERPOOL

Goalkeepers

1	Jerzy Dudek	POL
20	Scott Carson	ENG
25	José Manuel Reina	ESP

Defenders

3	Steve Finnan	IRL
4	Sami Hyypiä	FIN
6	John Arne Riise	NOR
17	Josemi	ESP
21	Djimi Traoré	FRA
23	Jamie Carragher	ENG
28	Stephen Warnock	ENG
31	David Raven	ENG
36	Antonio Barragán	ESP
37	Zak Whitbread	ENG

Midfielders

7	Harry Kewell	AUS
8	Steven Gerrard	ENG
10	Luis García	ESP
14	Xabi Alonso	ESP
16	Dietmar Hamann	GER
22	Mohamed Sissoko	FRA
30	Boudewijn Zenden	NED
32	Besian Idrizaj	AUT
34	Darren Potter	IRL
35	Daniel Guthrie	ENG
38	David Mannix	ENG

Forwards

9	Djibril Cissé	FRA
15	Peter Crouch	ENG
19	Fernando Morientes	ESP
24	Florent Sinama-Pongolle	FRA
33	Neil Mellor	ENG

LYON

Goalkeepers

1	Grégory Coupet	FRA
25	Joan Hartock	FRA
30	Rémy Vercoutre	FRA

Defenders

3	Cris	BRA
5	Claudio Caçapa	BRA
12	Anthony Réveillère	FRA
15	Lamine Diatta	SEN
20	Eric Abidal	FRA
23	Jérémy Berthod	FRA
24	Sylvain Monsoreau	FRA
27	Johann Truchet	FRA
31	François Clerc	FRA
36	Alexis Genet	FRA
37	Sandy Paillot	FRA

Midfielders

6	Jérémy Clément	FRA
7	Mahamadou Diarra	MLI
8	Juninho Pernambucano	BRA
10	Florent Malouda	FRA
21	Tiago	POR
26	Benoît Pedretti	FRA
32	Romain Beynie	FRA
39	Aurelien Brugniaud	FRA
40	Anthony Mounier	FRA

Forwards

9	John Carew	NOR
11	Fred	BRA
13	Pierre-Alain Frau	FRA
14	Sidney Govou	FRA
18	Hatem Ben Arfa	FRA
19	Karim Benzema	FRA
22	Sylvain Wiltord	FRA
34	Julien Viale	FRA

MAN UTD

Goalkeepers
1	Tim Howard	USA
19	Edwin van der Sar	NED
30	Luke Steele	ENG

Defenders
2	Gary Neville	ENG
4	Gabriel Heinze	ARG
5	Rio Ferdinand	ENG
6	Wes Brown	ENG
22	John O'Shea	IRL
26	Phil Bardsley	ENG
27	Mikaël Silvestre	FRA
28	Gerard Piqué	ESP
44	Adam Eckersley	ENG
47	Jonny Evans	NIR

Midfielders
13	Ji-Sung Park	KOR
16	Roy Keane	IRL
17	Liam Miller	IRL
18	Paul Scholes	ENG
23	Kieran Richardson	ENG
24	Darren Fletcher	SCO
25	Quinton Fortune	RSA
45	David Fox	ENG
46	Lee Martin	ENG

Forwards
7	Cristiano Ronaldo	POR
8	Wayne Rooney	ENG
9	Louis Saha	FRA
10	Ruud van Nistelrooij	NED
11	Ryan Giggs	WAL
14	Alan Smith	ENG
20	Ole Gunnar Solskjær	NOR
40	Sylvan Ebanks-Blake	ENG
42	Giuseppe Rossi	ITA

MILAN

Goalkeepers
1	Dida	BRA
12	Valerio Fiori	ITA
16	Zeljko Kalac	AUS
40	Eros Favaretto	ITA

Defenders
2	Cafu	BRA
3	Paolo Maldini	ITA
4	Kakha Kaladze	GEO
5	Alessandro Costacurta	ITA
13	Alessandro Nesta	ITA
17	Dario Simic	CRO
31	Jaap Stam	NED
42	Davide Astori	ITA
46	Lino Marzoratti	ITA

Midfielders
8	Gennaro Gattuso	ITA
10	Rui Costa	POR
14	Johann Vogel	SUI
18	Marek Jankulovski	CZE
20	Clarence Seedorf	NED
21	Andrea Pirlo	ITA
22	Kaká	BRA
23	Massimo Ambrosini	ITA
27	Serginho	BRA

Forwards
7	Andriy Shevchenko	UKR
9	Filippo Inzaghi	ITA
11	Alberto Gilardino	ITA
32	Christian Vieri	ITA
41	Matteo Ardemagni	ITA

OLYMPIACOS

Goalkeepers
29	Theodoros Dougeroglou	GRE
33	Erwin Lemmens	BEL
34	Kleopas Giannou	GRE
71	Antonios Nikopolidis	GRE

Defenders
5	Michalis Kapsis	GRE
12	Gabriel Schürrer	ESP
14	Dimitrios Mavrogenidis	GRE
19	Athanasios Kostoulas	GRE
22	Erol Bulut	TUR
25	Spyridon Vallas	GRE
26	Christos Lisgaras	GRE
30	Anastasios Pantos	GRE
32	Georgios Anatolakis	GRE

Midfielders
1	Pantelis Kafes	GRE
6	Ieroklis Stoltidis	GRE
7	Nery Alberto Castillo	URU
8	Milos Maric	SCG
10	Rivaldo	BRA
11	Predrag Djordjevic	SCG
15	Yaya Touré	CIV
17	Ioannis Taralidis	GRE
21	Grigorios Georgatos	GRE
27	Zhora Hovhannisyan	ARM

Forwards
9	Ioannis Okkas	CYP
18	D'Acol	BRA
20	Dani García	ESP
23	Michalis Konstantinou	CYP
40	Haruna Babangida	NGA

PANATHINAIKOS

Goalkeepers
1	Mario Galinovic	CRO
12	Pierre Ebede	CMR
17	Michael Shimitras	CYP
33	Markos Vellidis	GRE

Defenders
4	Ilias Kotsios	GRE
5	Nasief Morris	RSA
8	Ioannis Goumas	GRE
19	Anthony Seric	CRO
24	Loukas Vintra	GRE
31	Filippos Darlas	GRE
32	Theodoros Tripotseris	GRE
35	Stefanos Siontis	GRE
37	Ioannis Stathis	GRE

Midfielders
6	Flavio Conceição	BRA
10	Ezequiel González	ARG
14	Nordin Wooter	NED
15	Srdjan Andric	CRO
21	Constantinos Charalambides	CYP
22	Alexandros Tziolis	GRE
25	Igor Biscan	CRO
27	Sotirios Leontiou	GRE
28	Georgios Theodoridis	GRE
29	Mikael Nilsson	SWE
45	Vladimir Gadjev	BUL

Forwards
7	Theofanis Gekas	GRE
9	Emmanuel Olisadebe	POL
11	Dimitrios Papadopoulos	GRE
26	Evagelos Mantzios	GRE
34	Stylianos Kritikos	GRE
40	Sándor Torghelle	HUN

PORTO

Goalkeepers
1	Helton	BRA
31	Paulo Ribeiro	POR
99	Vitor Baía	POR

Defenders
2	Jorge Costa	POR
3	Ricardo Costa	POR
4	Pedro Emanuel	POR
6	Ibson	BRA
13	Bruno Alves	POR
14	Pepe	BRA
22	Fatih Sonkaya	TUR
35	Marek Cech	SVK
46	Jorge Lopes	POR

Midfielders
8	Lucho González	ARG
12	Bosingwa	POR
16	Raúl Meireles	POR
18	Paulo Assunção	BRA
20	Diego	BRA
27	Alan	BRA
42	Márcio Sousa	POR
50	Diogo	BRA
59	Fábio	POR
60	Duarte	POR

Forwards
7	Ricardo Quaresma	POR
9	Benni McCarthy	RSA
10	Hélder Postiga	POR
11	Lisandro López	ITA
17	Jorginho	BRA
19	Tomislav Sokota	CRO
21	César Peixoto	POR
25	Ivanildo Cassamá	POR
39	Hugo Almeida	POR

PSV

Goalkeepers
1	Heurelho Gomes	BRA
21	Edwin Zoetebier	NED
23	Nathan Coe	AUS
38	Tom Muijters	BEL

Defenders
2	André Ooijer	NED
3	Michael Reiziger	NED
4	Alex	BRA
18	Eric Addo	GHA
39	Olivier Ter Horst	NED

Midfielders
6	Timmy Simons	BEL
7	Mika Väyrynen	FIN
8	Phillip Cocu	NED
14	Osmar Ferreyra	ARG
16	Theo Lucius	NED
19	Michael Lamey	NED
20	Ibrahim Afellay	NED
25	John de Jong	NED
32	Guy Dufour	BEL
36	Lindsay Wilson	AUS
37	Ismail Aisatti	NED

Forwards
9	Jan Vennegoor of Hesselink	NED
11	DaMarcus Beasley	USA
12	Jefferson Farfán	PER
29	Robert	BRA
33	Roy Beerens	NED
35	Gerald Sibon	NED
40	Fitim Kacik	GER
41	Quincy Allee	NED

RANGERS

Goalkeepers
1	Stefan Klos	GER
25	Ronald Waterreus	NED
41	Lee Robinson	ENG
48	Callum Reidford	SCO

Defenders
2	Fernando Ricksen	NED
3	Olivier Bernard	FRA
5	Marvin Andrews	TRI
12	Robert Malcolm	SCO
14	Sotirios Kyrgiakos	GRE
16	Julien Rodriguez	FRA
18	José Pierre-Fanfan	FRA
20	Alan Hutton	SCO
24	Ian Murray	SCO

Midfielders
6	Barry Ferguson	SCO
7	Brahim Hemdani	FRA
8	Alex Rae	SCO
17	Chris Burke	SCO
31	Hamed Namouchi	TUN
38	Charles Adam	SCO
47	Brian Gilmour	SCO
49	Scott Agnew	SCO
50	Dany N'guessan	FRA

Forwards
4	Thomas Buffel	BEL
9	Dado Prso	CRO
10	Nacho Novo	ESP
19	Steven Thompson	SCO
21	Francis Jeffers	ENG
23	Federico Nieto	ARG
26	Peter Løvenkrands	DEN
39	Robert Davidson	SCO
44	Ross McCormack	SCO

RAPID WIEN

Goalkeepers
1	Raimund Hedl	AUT
24	Helge Payer	AUT
30	Andreas Lukse	AUT

Defenders
2	Marcin Adamski	POL
3	Vladimír Labant	SVK
4	Martin Hiden	AUT
13	Markus Katzer	AUT
14	Thomas Burgstaller	AUT
18	Markus Hiden	AUT
22	Radek Bejbl	CZE
23	Andreas Dober	AUT
26	Jozef Valachovic	SVK
33	Daniel Schreiner	AUT

Midfielders
6	György Korsós	HUN
7	Peter Hlinka	SVK
8	Andreas Ivanschitz	AUT
11	Steffen Hofmann	GER
12	György Garics	AUT
15	Stefan Kulovits	AUT
16	Sebastian Martínez	AUT
17	Veli Kavlak	AUT
19	Matthias Dollinger	AUT
27	Helmut Prenner	AUT
28	Cemil Tosun	AUT
29	Friedrich Breitenfelder	AUT
32	Said Gutic	AUT

Forwards
9	Axel Lawaree	BEL
10	Muhammet Akagündüz	AUT
20	Roman Kienast	AUT
25	Marek Kincl	CZE
31	Mensur Kurtisi	MKD

REAL MADRID

Goalkeepers
1	Iker Casillas	ESP
13	Diego López	ESP
30	Jordi Codina	ESP

Defenders
2	Míchel Salgado	ESP
3	Roberto Carlos	BRA
4	Sergio Ramos	ESP
6	Iván Helguera	ESP
15	Raúl Bravo	ESP
18	Jonathan Woodgate	ENG
21	Carlos Diogo	URU
22	Francisco Pavón	ESP
24	Álvaro Mejía	ESP
26	Álvaro Arbeloa	ESP

Midfielders
5	Zinedine Zidane	FRA
8	Julio César Baptista	BRA
12	Pablo García	URU
14	Guti	ESP
16	Thomas Gravesen	DEN
23	David Beckham	ENG
28	Rubén de la Red	ESP
29	José Manuel Jurado	ESP
40	Adrián Martín Cardona	ESP

Forwards
7	Raúl González	ESP
9	Ronaldo	BRA
10	Robinho	BRA
27	Roberto Soldado	ESP
31	David Barral	ESP
34	Javi García	ESP
35	Javier Ángel Balboa	ESP
36	Ernesto Gómez	ESP
41	Álvaro Negredo	ESP

ROSENBORG

Goalkeepers
1	Espen Johnsen	NOR
12	Roar Husby	NOR
30	Ivar Rønningen	NOR

Defenders
2	Miika Koppinen	FIN
5	Christer Basma	NOR
8	Robbie Russell	USA
10	Vidar Riseth	NOR
18	Alejandro Lago	URU
21	Ståle Stensaas	NOR
26	Bjørn Tore Kvarme	NOR
33	Mikael Dorsin	SWE

Midfielders
4	Fredrik Winsnes	NOR
6	Roar Strand	NOR
7	Ørjan Berg	NOR
11	Jan Gunnar Solli	NOR
14	Sebastián Eguren	URU
15	Per Ciljan Skjelbred	NOR
19	Alexander Tettey	NOR

Forwards
9	Frode Johnsen	NOR
13	Alexander Ødegaard	NOR
17	Øyvind Storflor	NOR
20	Thorstein Helstad	NOR
23	Michael Kleppe Jamtfall	NOR
25	Daniel Braaten	NOR

SCHALKE

Goalkeepers
1	Frank Rost	GER
13	Christofer Heimeroth	GER
29	Manuel Neuer	GER

Defenders
4	Thomas Kläsener	GER
5	Marcelo Bordon	BRA
15	Tomasz Waldoch	POL
16	Dario Rodríguez	URU
18	Rafinha	BRA
20	Mladen Krstajic	SCG
24	Christian Pander	GER
26	Niko Bungert	GER
27	Tim Hoogland	GER
31	Sebastian Boenisch	GER
34	Mario Klinger	GER

Midfielders
2	Christian Poulsen	DEN
3	Levan Kobiashvili	GEO
6	Hamit Altintop	TUR
7	Mimoun Azaouagh	GER
8	Fabian Ernst	GER
10	Lincoln	BRA
19	Gustavo Varela	URU
21	Alexander Baumjohann	GER
23	Simon Cziommer	GER
25	Zlatan Bajramovic	BIH
28	Markus Heppke	GER
36	Aziz Bilal	LIB

Forwards
9	Søren Larsen	DEN
11	Ebbe Sand	DEN
14	Gerald Asamoah	GER
22	Kevin Kuranyi	GER
33	Joseph Laumann	GER

SPARTA PRAHA

Goalkeepers
29	Jaromír Blazek	CZE
30	David Bicík	CZE
31	Tomás Grigar	CZE

Defenders
4	Pavel Pergl	CZE
11	Adam Petrous	CZE
14	Lubos Loucka	CZE
15	Petr Lukás	CZE
19	Martin Petrás	SVK
20	Zdenek Pospech	CZE
22	Stepán Kucera	CZE
23	Michal Kadlec	CZE
27	Jan Simunek	CZE

Midfielders
2	Martin Hasek	CZE
3	Ladislav Volesák	CZE
6	Tomás Sivok	CZE
7	Lukás Zelenka	CZE
13	Ondrej Sedlácek	CZE
16	Jan Simák	CZE
18	Karol Kisel	SVK
21	Tomás Polácek	CZE
24	Zdenek Volek	CZE
25	Miroslav Král	CZE

Forwards
5	Ondrej Honka	CZE
9	Libor Dosek	CZE
10	Miroslav Slepicka	CZE
12	Ondrej Herzán	CZE
17	Ondrej Bíro	CZE
26	Jirí Jeslínek	CZE
28	Miroslav Matusovic	CZE

THUN

Goalkeepers
1	Eldin Jakupovic	SUI
18	Alain Portmann	SUI

Defenders
2	Leandro Vieira	BRA
3	José Gonçalves	SUI
4	Sehid Sinani	SUI
5	Ljubo Milicevic	AUS
7	Grégory Duruz	SUI
10	Adriano Luis Spadoto	BRA
12	Armand Deumi	CMR
17	Alen Orman	AUT
26	Selver Hodzic	SUI

Midfielders
6	Tiago Bernardini	BRA
9	Adriano Pimenta	BRA
11	Andres Gerber	SUI
14	Nenad Savic	SUI
19	Silvan Aegerter	SUI
21	Nelson Ferreira	SUI

Forwards
8	Gelson Rodrigues	LUX
13	Pape Omar	SEN
15	Eren Sen	GER
20	Mauro Lustrinelli	SUI

UDINESE

Goalkeepers
1	Morgan De Sanctis	ITA
12	Gabriele Paoletti	ITA
58	Carlo Sciarrone	ITA

Defenders
2	Cristian Zapata Valencia	COL
4	Valerio Bertotto	ITA
6	Roberto Sensini	ARG
14	Cesare Natali	ITA
19	Felipe	BRA
32	Vincent Candela	FRA
39	Juarez	BRA
41	Emanuele Politti	ITA

Midfielders
5	Christian Obodo	NGA
7	Damiano Zenoni	ITA
8	Vidigal	POR
13	Giampiero Pinzi	ITA
16	Fernando Tissone	ITA
18	Sulley Ali Muntari	GHA
23	Stefano Mauri	ITA
25	Piermario Morosini	ITA
26	Mirko Pieri	ITA
27	Marco Motta	ITA
33	Flavio Lazzari	ITA

Forwards
9	Vincenzo Iaquinta	ITA
10	Antonio Di Natale	ITA
11	Saadi Al Gaddafi	LBY
17	David Di Michele	ITA
20	Fausto Rossini	ITA
31	Paulo Barreto	BRA
42	Alessandro Armellino	ITA

VILLARREAL

Goalkeepers
1	Javier López Vallejo	ESP
13	Sebastián Viera	URU
25	Mariano Barbosa	ARG
27	Juan Carlos Sánchez	ESP
31	Iván Pascual	ESP
32	Vicente Flor Bustos	ESP

Defenders
2	Gonzalo Rodríguez	ARG
3	Rodolfo Arruabarrena	ARG
15	Jan Kromkamp	NED
16	Quique Álvarez	ESP
17	Javi Venta	ESP
22	Juan Manuel Peña	BOL
23	Edu	ESP
29	Samuel Álvarez	ESP
30	Carlos Alcántara	ESP

Midfielders
4	César Arzo	ESP
6	Josico	ESP
8	Juan Román Riquelme	ARG
10	Roger García	ESP
11	Javier Calleja	ESP
12	Juan Pablo Sorín	ARG
14	Héctor Font	ESP
18	Alessio Tacchinardi	ITA
19	Marcos Senna	BRA
20	Luis Valencia	ECU
21	Santiago Cazorla	ESP

Forwards
5	Diego Forlán	URU
7	Antonio Guayre	ESP
9	Luciano Figueroa	ARG
23	José María Romero	ESP
26	Xisco Nadal	ESP

WERDER

Goalkeepers
1	Andreas Reinke	GER
18	Tim Wiese	GER
30	Kasper Jensen	DEN
31	Michael Jürgen	GER
33	Christian Vander	GER

Defenders
2	Frank Fahrenhorst	GER
3	Petri Pasanen	FIN
4	Naldo	BRA
5	Ümit Davala	TUR
6	Frank Baumann	GER
15	Patrick Owomoyela	GER
16	Leon Andreasen	DEN
23	Jelle Van Damme	BEL
27	Christian Schulz	GER
28	Francis Banecki	GER

Midfielders
7	Jurica Vranjes	CRO
10	Johan Micoud	FRA
19	Pekka Lagerblom	FIN
20	Daniel Jensen	DEN
22	Torsten Frings	GER
24	Tim Borowski	GER
26	Florian Mohr	GER

Forwards
9	Nelson Valdez	PAR
11	Miroslav Klose	GER
14	Aaron Hunt	GER
17	Ivan Klasnic	CRO
35	Marco Stier	GER

UEFA CUP 2005–06

UEFA CUP 2005-06 EARLY ROUNDS FOR TEAMS IN GROUPS A TO D

First Qualifying Round   Second Qualifying Round   First Round   Group Stage

Group A

First Qualifying Round				Second Qualifying Round				First Round				Group Stage		
								AS Monaco	FRA	2	3			
								Willem II Tilburg	NED	0	1			
Longford Town	IRL	2	1	FC København	DEN	2	2	Hamburger SV	GER	1	1	Group A		Pts
Carmarthen Town	WAL	0	5	Carmarthen Town	WAL	0	0	FC København	DEN	1	0	AS Monaco	FRA	9
Ekranas	LTU	0	1	Djurgårdens IF	SWE	1	0	Slavia Praha	CZE	2	2	Hamburger SV	GER	9
Cork City	IRL	2	0	Cork City	IRL	1	0	Cork City	IRL	0	1	Slavia Praha	CZE	4
Rhyl	WAL	2	2	Rhyl	WAL	0	1	Viking SK	NOR	1	1	Viking SK Stavanger	NOR	4
Atlantas Klaipeda	LTU	1	3	Viking Stavanger	NOR	1	2	FK Austria	AUT	0	2	CSKA Sofia	BUL	3
Portadown	NIR	1	0	MSK Zilina	SVK	1	2	Bayer Leverkusen	GER	0	0			
Viking Stavanger	NOR	2	1	FK Austria	AUT	2	2	CSKA Sofia	BUL	1	1			
FK Baku	AZE	1	1											
MSK Zilina	SVK	0	3											

Group B

First Qualifying Round				Second Qualifying Round				First Round				Group Stage		
								Palermo	ITA	2	4			
								Anorthosis F'gusta	CYP	1	0			
Ferencváros	HUN	0	2	MTZ-RIPO Minsk	BLR	1	1	SK Teplice	CZE	1	0	Group B		Pts
MTZ-RIPO Minsk	BLR	2	1	SK Teplice	CZE	1	2	Espanyol	ESP	1	2	Palermo	ITA	8
Allianssi Vantaa	FIN	3	1	SK Brann Bergen	NOR	0	2	SK Brann Bergen	NOR	1	2	Espanyol	ESP	8
Pétange	LUX	0	1	Allianssi Vantaa	FIN	0	0	Lok. Moskva	RUS	2	3	Lokomotiv Moskva	RUS	7
				Legia Warszawa	POL	0	1	Brøndby IF	DEN	2	1	Brøndby IF	DEN	4
				FC Zürich	SUI	1	4	FC Zürich	SUI	0	2	Maccabi Petah Tikva	ISR	0
Baskimi	MKD	3	1	Baskimi	MKD	0	0	Maccabi Petah-T	ISR	0	5			
Zepce	BIH	0	1	Maccabi Petah-T	ISR	5	6	Partizan Beograd	SCG	2	2			

Group C

First Qualifying Round				Second Qualifying Round				First Round				Group Stage		
								Vålerenga IF	NOR	0	1			
								Steaua Bucuresti	ROU	3	3			
				Groclin Grodzisk	POL	4	0	RC Lens	FRA	1	4	Group C		Pts
				Dukla B. Bystrica	SVK	1	0	Groclin Grodzisk	POL	1	2	Steaua Bucuresti	ROU	8
Birkirkara	MLT	0	0	APOEL Nicosia	CYP	1	2	APOEL Nicosia	CYP	0	1	RC Lens	FRA	7
APOEL Nicosia	CYP	2	4	Maccabi Tel Aviv	ISR	0	2	Hertha BSC	GER	1	3	Hertha BSC Berlin	GER	6
								Vitória Setúbal	POR	1	0	Sampdoria	ITA	5
								Sampdoria	ITA	1	1	Halmstads BK	SWE	0
Linfield	NIR	1	1	Halmstads BK	SWE	1	4	Halmstads BK	SWE	1	3			
Ventspils	LVA	0	2	Linfield	IRL	1	2	Sporting CP	POR	2	2			

Group D

First Qualifying Round				Second Qualifying Round				First Round				Group Stage		
Torpedo Kutaisi	GEO	0	0	Krylya Sovetov	RUS	2	2	Middlesbrough	ENG	2	0			
BATE Borisov	BLR	1	5	BATE Borisov	BLR	0	0	Xánthi	GRE	0	0			
				Litex Lovech	BUL	1	1	Krylya Sovetov	RUS	5	1	Group D		Pts
				Rijeka	CRO	0	2	AZ Alkmaar	NED	3	3	Middlesbrough	ENG	10
NSI Runavik	FRO	0	0	Liep. Metalurgs	LVA	2	0	Litex Lovech	BUL	2	1	AZ Alkmaar	NED	10
Liep. Metalurgs	LVA	3	3	KRC Genk	BEL	3	3	KRC Genk	BEL	2	0	Litex Lovech	BUL	6
Banants Yerevan	ARM	2	2	Banants Yerevan	ARM	2	0	Hibernian	SCO	0	1	Dnipro Dnipropetrovsk	UKR	3
Lokomotiv Tbilisi	GEO	3	0	D. Dnipropetrovsk	UKR	4	4	D. Dnipropetrovsk	UKR	1	5	Grasshopper-Club	SUI	0
				Grasshopper-Club	SUI	1	2	Grasshopper-Club	SUI	1	3			
				Wisla Plock	POL	0	3	MyPa-47	FIN	1	0			
TVMK Tallinn	EST	1	0	MyPa-47	FIN	0	2							
MyPa-47	FIN	1	1	Dundee United	SCO	0	2							

In each preliminary and first round tie the home team in the first leg is listed above their opponents

UEFA CUP 2005-06 EARLY ROUNDS FOR TEAMS IN GROUPS E TO H

First Qualifying Round				Second Qualifying Round				First Round				Group Stage		
Nistru Otaci	MDA	3	2	Nistru Otaci	MDA	0	0	Grazer AK	AUT	0	0			
Kazar Lenkoran	AZE	1	1	Grazer AK	AUT	2	1	RC Strasbourg	FRA	2	5			
								AS Roma	ITA	5	0	**Group E**		**Pts**
								Aris Thessaloníki	GRE	1	0	**RC Strasbourg**	FRA	8
Teuta Durrës	ALB	3	0	Zeta Golubovci	SCG	0	2	FC Basel	SUI	5	1	**AS Roma**	ITA	7
Siroki Brijeg	BIH	1	3	Siroki Brijeg	BIH	1	4	Siroki Brijeg	BIH	0	0	**FC Basel**	SUI	6
				Inter Zapresic	CRO	1	0	Crvena Zvezda	SCG	0	1	Crvena Zvezda Beograd	SCG	4
				Crvena Zvezda	SCG	3	4	Sporting Braga	POR	0	1	Tromsø IL	NOR	3
Esbjerg FB	DEN	1	6	Esbjerg FB	DEN	0 1	2p	Tromsø IL	NOR	1	1			
Flora Tallinn	EST	2	0	Tromsø IL	NOR	1 0	3p	Galatasaray	TUR	0	1			
								Germinal B'schott	BEL	0 0	1p			
								Oly. Marseille	FRA	0 0	4p			
				Publikum Celje	SVN	1	0	AJ Auxerre	FRA	2	0	**Group F**		**Pts**
				Levski Sofia	BUL	0	3	Levski Sofia	BUL	1	1	**Oly. Marseille**	FRA	9
								Baník Ostrava	CZE	2	0	**Levski Sofia**	BUL	6
								SC Heerenveen	NED	0	5	**SC Heerenveen**	NED	5
IBV Vestm'næyjar	ISL	1	1	FC Midtjylland	DEN	2	2	CSKA Moskva	RUS	3	3	CSKA Moskva	RUS	4
B'36 Tórshavn	FRO	1	2	B'36 Tórshavn	FRO	1	2	FC Midtjylland	DEN	1	1	Dinamo Bucuresti	ROU	4
Omonia Nicosia	CYP	3	3	Dinamo Bucuresti	ROU	3	1	Dinamo Bucuresti	ROU	5	0			
Hibernians	MLT	0	0	Omonia Nicosia	CYP	1	2	Everton	ENG	1	1			
Sant Julià	AND	0	0	Rapid Bucuresti	ROU	3	1	Feyenoord	NED	1	0			
Rapid Bucuresti	ROU	5	5	Vardar Skopje	MKD	0	1	Rapid Bucuresti	ROU	1	1			
Elbasani	ALB	1	0					Shakhtar Donetsk	UKR	4	2	**Group G**		**Pts**
Vardar Skopje	MKD	1	0					Debreceni VSC	HUN	1	0	**Rapid Bucuresti**	ROU	9
Domagnano	SMR	0	0	MS Ashdod	ISR	2	2	VfB Stuttgart	GER	2	0	**Shakhtar Donetsk**	UKR	9
Domzale	SVN	5	3	Domzale	SVN	2	1	Domzale	SVN	0	1	**VfB Stuttgart**	GER	9
				Matáv Sopron	HUN	0	1	PAOK	GRE	1	2	PAOK Thessaloníki	GRE	3
				Metalurh Donetsk	UKR	3	2	Metalurh Donetsk	UKR	1	2	Stade Rennais	FRA	0
								Stade Rennais	FRA	3	0			
								Osasuna	ESP	1	0			
1.FSV Mainz	GER	4	0	1.FSV Mainz	GER	2	2	Sevilla	ESP	0	2			
MIKA Ashtarak	ARM	0	0	Keflavík	ISL	0	0	1. FSV Mainz	GER	0	0			
Etzella Ettelbruck	LUX	0	0	SV Pasching	AUT	2	1	Zenit S Peterburg	RUS	0	1	**Group H**		**Pts**
Keflavík	ISL	4	2	Zenit S Peterburg	RUS	2	1	AEK Athens	GRE	0	0	**Sevilla**	ESP	7
				OFK Beograd	SCG	2	0	Bolton Wanderers	ENG	2	2	**Zenit St Peterburg**	RUS	7
				Lok. Plovdiv	BUL	1	1	Lok. Plovdiv	BUL	1	1	**Bolton Wanderers**	ENG	6
Vaduz	LIE	2	0	Vaduz	LIE	0	1	Besiktas	TUR	0	4	Besiktas	TUR	5
Dacia Chisinau	MDA	0	1	Besiktas	TUR	1	5	Malmö FF	SWE	1	1	Vitória SC Guimarães	POR	1
								Vitória Guimarães	POR	3	1			
								Wisla Kraków	POL	0	0			

In each preliminary and first round tie the home team in the first leg is listed above their opponents

UEFA CUP 2005–06 FINAL ROUNDS

Round of Thirty-two	Round of Sixteen	Quarter-Final	Semi-Final	Final

Sevilla 1 2
Lok. Moskva * 0 0

    Sevilla 0 2
    Lille OSC * 1 0

Shakhtar Don'sk 2 0
Lille OSC 3 0

        Sevilla * 4 1
        Zenit St P'burg 1 1

Oly. Marseille 0 2
Bolton Wand. * 0 1

    Oly. Marseille * 0 1
    Zenit St P'burg 1 1

Rosenborg BK * 0 1
Zenit St P'burg 2 2

            Sevilla 0 1
            Schalke 04 * 0 0

Levski Sofia 1 2
Artmedia * 0 0

    Levski Sofia 0 2
    Udinese * 0 1

RC Lens 0 1
Udinese * 3 0

        Levski Sofia * 1 1
        Schalke 04 3 1

Palermo 1 1
Slavia Praha * 2 0

    Palermo * 1 0
    Schalke 04 0 3

Espanyol 1 0
Schalke 04 * 2 3

                Sevilla 4
                Middlesbrough 0

Steaua Buç'esti 3 0
Heerenveen * 1 1

    Steaua Buç'sti * 0 3
    Real Betis 0 0

AZ Alkmaar 0 2
Real Betis * 2 1

        Steaua Buç'esti 1 0
        Rapid Buç'esti * 1 0

Hamburger SV 0 2
FC Thun * 1 0

    Hamburger SV 0 3
    Rapid Buç'esti * 2 1

Hertha BSC * 0 0
Rapid Buç'esti 1 2

            Steaua Buç'sti * 1 2
            Middlesbrough 0 4

FC Basel * 1 1
AS Monaco 0 1

    FC Basel * 2 2
    RC Strasbourg 0 2

Litex Lovech * 0 0
RC Strasbourg 2 0

        FC Basel * 2 1
        Middlesbrough 0 4

AS Roma 2 2
Club Brugge * 1 1

    AS Roma 0 2
    Middlesbrough * 1 1

VfB Stuttgart * 1 1
Middlesbrough 2 0

* Home team in the first leg

FIRST QUALIFYING ROUND

Flancare Park, Longford, 14-07-2005, 19:30, 2 614, Olsiak SVK
Longford Town 2 Paisley [35], Ferguson [54]
Carmathen Town 0
Latham Park, Newtown, 28-07-2005, 19:30, 850, Prades AND
Carmathen Town 5 Thomas 2 [15] [75], Lloyd 2 [49] [54p], Cotterrall [80]
Longford Town 1
Aukstaitija, Panevezys, 14-07-2005, 18:00, 3 000, Vuorela FIN
Ekranas Panevezys 0
Cork City 2 O'Donovan [25], O'Callaghan [90]
Turner's Cross, Cork, 28-07-2005, 19:30, 5 200, Wildhaber SUI
Cork City 0
Ekranas Panevezys 1 Klimavicius [60]
Belle Vue, Rhyl, 14-07-2005, 19:30, 1 570, Papila TUR
Rhyl 2 Hunt 2 [11] [70]
Atlantas Kleipeda 1 Zvingilas [77]
Centrinis, Klaipeda, 28-07-2005, 18:30, 1 800, Silagava GEO
Atlantas Kleipeda 3 Laurisas 2 [14p] [68], Petreikis [78]
Rhyl 2 Stones [33], Powell.G [62]
Shamrock Park, Portadown, 14-07-2005, 19:00, 675, Zakharov RUS
Portadown 1 Arkins [92+p]
Viking Stavanger 2 Østenstad [53p], Kopteff [79]
Viking, Stavanger, 28-07-2005, 19:00, 4 372, Circhetta SUI
Viking Stavanger 1 Nhleko [57]
Portadown 0
Tofikh Bakhramov, 14-07-2005, 19:00, 3 400, Aydogan TUR
FK Baku 1 Sultanov [78]
MSK Zilina 0
Pod Dubnon, Zilina, 28-07-2005, 20:00, 5 126, Tsachilidis GRE
MSK Zilina 3 Straka [7], Cisovsky [38], Labant [85]
FK Baku 1 Stolcers [68]
Ullöi úti, Budapest, 14-07-2005, 20:00, 4 926, Panic BIH
Ferencváros 0
MTZ-RIPO Minsk 2 Mkhitaryan [38], Tarashchik [93+]
Traktor, Minsk, 28-07-2005, 17:00, 12 000, Havrilla SVK
MTZ-RIPO Minsk 1 Kontsevoi [48]
Ferencváros 2 Lipcsei [45], Dénes Rósa [90]
Pohjola, Vantaa, 14-07-2005, 18:30, 1 709, Rabrenovic SCG
Allianssi Vantaa 3 Vajanne [34], Cleaver [42], Poulsen [85]
Pétange 0
La Frontière, Esch-sur-Alzette, 28-07-2005, 18:30, 717, Kholmatov KAZ
Pétange 1 Kefert [55]
Allianssi Vantaa 1 Poulsen [63]
Gradski, Skopje, 14-07-2005, 18:00, 1 500, Sapi HUN
Baskimi 3 Baskimi awarded match 3-0
Zepce 0
Bilino Polje, Zenica, 28-07-2005, 20:00, 1 243, Mikolajewski POL
Zepce 1 Mesic [80]
Baskimi 1 Gjurcevski [49]
Ta'Qali, Ta'Qali, 28-07-2005, 21:00, 651, Murray SCO
Birkirkara 0
APOEL Nicosia 2 Georgiou [72], Jovanovic [79]
GSP, Nicosia, 28-07-2005, 20:00, 6 300, Kralovec CZE
APOEL Nicosia 4 Kaklamanos 2 [38 58], Neophytou [52], Georgiu [93+]
Birkirkara 0
Windsor Park, Belfast, 14-07-2005, 19:45, 1 600, Curin CZE
Linfield 1 Mouncey [6]
Ventspils 0
Ventspils Pilsetas, Ventspils, 28-07-2005, 18:00, 1 900, Ristoskov BUL
Ventspils 2 Rekhviashvili [39], Rimkus [91+]
Linfield 1
Lokomotivi, Tbilisi, 14-07-2005, 19:00, 800, Moen NOR
Torpedo Kutaisi 0
BATE Borisov 1 Baga [26p]

Gradski, Borisov, 28-07-2005, 20:00, 3 900, Moskalev BUL
BATE Borisov 5 Molosh [10], Lebedev 2 [21 36], Rubnenko 2 [38 43]
Torpedo Kutaisi 0
Toftir, Toftir, 14-07-2005, 18:00, 200, Hietala FIN
NSI Runavík 0
Liepajas Metalurgs 3 Petersen.J OG [23], Karlsons.G [67], Grebis [77]
Daugava, Liepaja, 28-07-2005, 19:00, 2 100, McKeon IRL
Liepajas Metalurgs 3 Dobrecovs 2 [4 35], Klava [81]
NSI Runavík 0
Republican, Yerevan, 14-07-2005, 19:00, 2 150, Megyebiro HUN
Banants Yerevan 2 Aram Hakobyan [82], Gharabaghtsyan [89]
Lokomotiv Tbilisi 3 Alaverdashvili [41], Kebadze [48], Oniani.G [53p]
Lokomotivi, Tbilisi, 28-07-2005, 19:00, 1 200, Strahonja CRO
Lokomotiv Tbilisi 0
Banants Yerevan 2 Aram Hakobyan [22], Khachatryan [81]
Kadriorg, Tallinn, 14-07-2005, 18:30, 410, Valgeirsson ISL
TVMK Tallinn 1 Teever [37]
MyPa-47 1 Kuparinen [77]
Jalkapallokenttä, Anjalankoski, 28-07-2005, 18:00, 1 624, Whitby WAL
MyPa-47 1 Rimas OG [57]
TVMK Tallinn 0
Republika, Chisinau, 14-07-2005, 19:00, 3 000, Arzuman TUR
Nistru Otaci 3 Pancovici [12], Matiura [69p], Blajco [88]
Kazar Lenkoran 1 Ramazanov [25]
Tofikh Bakhramov, 28-07-2005, 20:00, 10 000, Deaconu ROU
Kazar Lenkoran 1 Aliyev [72]
Nistru Otaci 2 Lichioiu 2 [19 40]
Niko Dovana, Durrës, 14-07-2005, 17:30, 1 100, Lautier MLT
Teuta Durrës 3 Mancaku 2 [32 58], Xhafaj [48]
Siroki Brijeg 1 Abramovic [82]
Pecara, Siroki Brijeg, 28-07-2005, 20:15, 3 000, Banari MDA
Siroki Brijeg 3 Medvid [33], Erceg [43], Wagner [70]
Teuta Durrës 0
Idrætspark, Esbjerg, 14-07-2005, 19:00, 4 253, Einwaller AUT
Esbjerg FB 1 Berglund [90]
Flora Tallinn 2 Sirevicius [57], Sidorenkov [60]
Le Coq Arena, Tallinn, 28-07-2005, 18:45, 1 000, Blom NED
Flora Tallinn 0 Andreasen [41], Murcy 2 [55 86]
Esbjerg FB 6 Polsen [15], Kristiansen [16], Berglund [23],
Hásteinsvöllur, Vestmannæyjar, 14-07-2005, 18:00, 390, McCourt NIR
IBV Vestmannæyjar 1 Sigurdsson.P [25]
B'36 Tórshavn 1 Midjord [7]
Tórsvøllur, Tórshavn, 28-07-2005, 4 100, Wilmes LUX
B'36 Tórshavn 2 Mørkøre [1], Midjord [59]
IBV Vestmannæyjar 1 Jeffs [41]
GSP, Nicosia, 14-07-2005, 20:00, 11 073, Kenan ISR
Omonia Nicosia 3 Mguni [30], Kozlej [47], Vakouftsis [85p]
Hibernians 0
Ta'Qali, Ta'Qali, 28-07-2005, 21:00, 369, Podeschi SMR
Hibernians 0
Omonia Nicosia 3 Grozdanovski 2 [5 63], Vakouftsis [43p]
Comunal, Andorra La Vella, 14-07-2005, 18:45, 900, Buttimer IRL
Sant Julià 0
Rapid Bucuresti 5 Niculae 3 [10 34 66], Alvarez OG [62], Vasilache [76]
Giulesti, Bucharest, 28-07-2005, 20:15, 2 585, Lawlor WAL
Rapid Bucuresti 5 Buga 4 [1 14 20 29], Maldarasanu [80]
Sant Julià 0
Ruzhdi Bizhuta, Elbasan, 14-07-2005, 17:30, 7 150, Krajnc SVN
Elbasani 1 Dalipi.K [28]
Vardar Skopje 1 Trickovski [66]
Gradski, Skopje, 28-07-2005, 4 000, Ishchenko UKR
Vardar Skopje 0
Elbasani 0
Olimpico, Serravalle, 14-07-2005, 20:45, 1 000, Gadiyev AZE
Domagnano 0 Kacicnik [81]
Domzale 5 Stevanovic [15], Zavri [48], Nikezic 2 [69 86],

Sportni Park, Domzale, 28-07-2005, 20:45, 652, Jareci ALB
Domzale 3 Juninho [25], Nikezic [46], Zeljkovic [88p]
Domagnano 0
Commerzbank Arena, Mainz, 14-07-2005, 20:30, 22 000, Staberg NOR
1.FSV Mainz 4 Ruman [8], Auer 2 [36] [67], Noveski [58]
MIKA Ashtarak 0
Republican, Yerevan, 28-07-2008, 19:30, 8 000, Tanovic SCG
MIKA Ashtarak 0
1.FSV Mainz 0
Deich, Ettelbruck, 14-07-2005, 18:30, 839, Kailis CYP
Etzella Ettelbruck 0
Keflavík 4 Sveinsson 4 [17] [59] [76] [80]
Laugardalsvöllur, Reykjavík, 28-07-2005, 19:15, 835, Malzinskas LTU
Keflavík 2 Sveinsson [76], Kristinsson [84]
Etzella Ettelbruck 0
Rheinpark, Vaduz, 14-07-2005, 19:30, 850, Isaksen FRO
Vaduz 2 Gohouri [53], Gaspar [71]
Dacia Chisinau 0
Republika, Chisinau, 28-07-2005, 18:30, 4 000, Laursen DEN
Dacia Chisinau 1 Japalau [63]
Vaduz 0

SECOND QUALIFYING
ROUND

Parken, Copenhagen, 11-08-2005, 20:15, 11 399, Attard MLT
FC København 2 Santos [48], Gravgaard [55]
Carmarthen Town 0
Ninian Park, Cardiff, 25-08-2005, 19:30, 882, Orlic MDA
Carmarthen Town 0
FC København 2 Møller 2 [38] [40]
Råsunda, Stockholm, 11-08-2005, 19:00, 4 854, Oriekhov UKR
Djurgårdens IF 1 Murphy OG [81]
Cork City 1 Fenn [8]
Turner's Cross, Cork, 25-08-2005, 19:30, 5 400, Wilmes LUX
Cork City 0
Djurgårdens IF 0
Belle Vue, Rhyl, 11-08-2005, 19:00, 1 540, Valgeirsson ISL
Rhyl 0
Viking Stavanger 1 Kopteff [19]
Viking, Stavanger, 25-08-2005, 19:00, 3 867, Chykun BLR
Viking Stavanger 2 Nhleko 2 [8] [26]
Rhyl 1 Adamson [36]
Pod Dubnon, Zilina, 11-08-2005, 20:15, 5 483, Kari FIN
MSK Zilina 1 Bartos [40]
FK Austria 2 Sebo [91+], Linz [93+]
Franz Horr, Vienna, 25-08-2005, 20:15, 5 600, Kaldma EST
FK Austria 2 Linz 2 [65] [70]
MSK Zilina 2 Cisovsky [26], Gottwald [31]
Traktor, Minsk, 11-08-2005, 18:00, 8 500, Kenan ISR
MTZ-RIPO Minsk 1 Kontsevoi [70]
SK Teplice 1 Rilke [34]
Na Stínadlech, Teplice, 25-08-2005, 17:00, 4 025, Johannesson SWE
SK Teplice 2 Rilke [55], Masek [92+]
MTZ-RIPO Minsk 1 Mkhitaryan [70]
Brann, Bergen, 11-08-2005, 19:00, 2 597, Ishchenko UKR
SK Brann Bergen 0
Allianssi Vantaa 0
Pohjola, Vantaa, 25-08-2005, 21:00, 1 372, Malcolm NIR
Allianssi Vantaa 0
SK Brann Bergen 2 Ludvigsen [58], Miller [88]
Wojska Polskiego, Warsaw, 11-08-2005, 20:00, 6 000, Rodomonti ITA
Legia Warszawa 0
FC Zürich 1 Rafael [91+]

Letzigrund, Zurich, 25-08-2005, 20:00, 9 600, Webb ENG
FC Zürich 4 Keita 2 [25] [64], Dzemaili [29], Clederson [78p]
Legia Warszawa 1 Szalachowski [18]
Gradski, Skopje, 11-08-2005, 20:00, 1 500, Krajnc SVN
Baskimi 0 Ederi [70], Sarsour [90]
Maccabi Petah-T 5 Magomedov [5], Toema [13], Mashiach [22p],
Ramat Gan, Tel Aviv, 25-08-2005, 18:00, 1 000, Salomir ROU
Maccabi Petah-T 6 Golan 3 [9] [40] [89], Ganon [42], Sarsour 2 [63] [67]
Baskimi 0
Dyskobolia, Grodzisk Wielkopols, 11-08-2005, 18:00, 2 100, Kos SVN
Groclin Grodzisk 4 Rocki [46], Wozniak OG [56], Porázik [68], Slusarski [83]
Dukla B. Bystrica 1 Bazík [72]
Stiavnicky, Banská Bystrica, 25-08-2005, 18:00, Brines SCO
Dukla B. Bystrica 0
Groclin Grodzisk 0
GSP, Nicosia, 11-08-2005, 20:45, 10 573, Zrnic BIH
APOEL Nicosia 1 Neophytou [65]
Maccabi Tel Aviv 0
Bloomfield, Tel Aviv, 25-08-2005, 20:00, 7 200, Rogalla SUI
Maccabi Tel Aviv 2 Nimny [63], Mesika [117]
APOEL Nicosia 2 Makridis [93], Neophytou [96]
Orjans Vall, Halmstad, 11-08-2005, 19:00, 1 197, Shmolik BLR
Halmstads BK 1 Johansson.A [32]
Linfield 1 Kearney [73]
Windsor Park, Belfast, 25-08-2005, 19:45, 4 052, Supraha CRO
Linfield 2 Mouncey [54], Gerguson [82]
Halmstads BK 4 Thorvaldsson [9], Jönsson [33], Preko [45], Djuric [74]
Metallurg, Samara, 11-08-2005, 19:00, 15 065, Bertolini SUI
Krylya Sovetov 2 Adamu [8], Husin [76p]
BATE Borisov 0
Gradski, Borisov, 25-08-2005, 21:00, 4 960, Lazarevski MKD
BATE Borisov 0
Krylya Sovetov 2 Bulyga [5], Vinogradov [50]
Gradski, Lovech, 11-08-2005, 20:30, 1 660, Van de Velde BEL
Litex Lovech 1 Zhelev [83]
Rijeka 0
Kantrida, Rijeka, 25-08-2005, 18:00, 4 876, Svendsen DEN
Rijeka 2 Krpan [64], Rendulic [93+]
Litex Lovech 1 Caillet [44p]
Daugava, Liepaja, 11-08-2005, 19:00, 1 899, Staberg NOR
Liep. Metalurgs 2 Kalonas [16], Dobrecovs [83p]
KRC Genk 3 Vandenbergh [47], Daerden [59], Stojanovic [81]
Fenix, Genk, 25-08-2005, 20:45, 6 000, Drabek AUT
KRC Genk 3 Vandenbergh [6], Daerden [18], Stojanovic [28]
Liep. Metalurgs 0
Republican, Yerevan, 11-08-2005, 19:00, 9 000, Panic BIH
Banants Yerevan 2 Aram Hakobyan 2 [24] [43]
D. Dnipropetrovsk 4 Yezerskiy [49], Kornilenko 2 [82] [83], Balabanov [85]
Meteor, Dnipropetrovsk, 25-08-2005, 19:00, 5 000, Sedivy CZE
D. Dnipropetrovsk 4 Shelayev 2 [10p] [45], Rykun [32], Balabanov [70]
Banants Yerevan 0
Hardturm, Zurich, 11-08-2005, 19:30, 3 600, Pereira Gomes POR
Grasshopper-Club 1 Eduardo [68]
Wisla Plock 0
Wisly, Plock, 25-08-2005, 18:00, 6 000, Markusson ISL
Wisla Plock 3 Gesior 2 [35] [38], Zilic [69]
Grasshopper-Club 2 Antonio [30], Eduardo [83]
Jalkapallokenttä, Anjalankoski, 11-08-2005, 20:30, 3 000, Tanovic SCG
MyPa-47 0
Dundee United 0
Tannadice, Dundee, 25-08-2005, 19:45, 9 400, Gonzalez Vazquez ESP
Dundee United 2 Kerr [14], Samuel [28]
MyPa-47 2 Adriano 2 [72p] [80]
Republika, Chisinau, 11-08-2005, 18:30, 4 000, Ryszka POL
Nistru Otaci 0
Grazer AK 2 Schrott [54], Ehmann [57]

Arnold Schwarzenegger, Graz, 25-08-2005, 4 859, Janku ALB

Grazer AK	1	Junuzovic [33]
Nistru Otaci	0	

Pod Goricom, Podgorica, 11-08-2005, 20:00, 3 500, Corpodean ROU

Zeta Golubovci	0	
Siroki Brijeg	1	Erceg [92+]

Pecara, Siroki Brijeg, 25-08-2005, 20:15, 5 000, Levi ISR

Siroki Brijeg	4	Lukacevic [16], Jurcic [18], Ronelle [26], Bubalo [64]
Zeta Golubovci	2	Vukovic 2 [4 44]

Inter Zapresic, Zapresic, 11-08-2005, 17:30, 3 050, Gomes POR

Inter Zapresic	1	Pecelj [41]
Crvena Zvezda	3	Zigic 2 [20 49], Pantelic [80]

Crvena Zvezda, Belgrade, 25-08-2005, 20:15, 28 901, Piccirillo FRA

Crvena Zvezda	4	Jankovic [6], Pantelic 2 [41 85], Zigic [45]
Inter Zapresic	0	

Idrætspark, Esbjerg, 11-08-2005, 19:00, 3 749, Vervecken BEL

Esbjerg FB	0	
Tromsø IL	1	Strand [10]

Altheim, Tromsø, 25-08-2005, 19:00, 4 380, Kircher GER

Tromsø IL		Tromsø W 3-2p
Esbjerg FB	1	Lucena [17]

Arena Petrol, Celje, 11-08-2005, 20:30, 1 500, Mammadov AZE

Publikum Celje	1	Bersnjak [68]
Levski Sofia	0	

Georgi Asparuhov, Sofia, 25-08-2005, 20:15, 7 958, Theodotou CYP

Levski Sofia	3	Yovov 2 [41 64], Domovchiyski [69]
Publikum Celje	0	

Messecentret, Herning, 11-08-2005, 3 819, Lawlor WAL

FC Midtjylland	2	Kristensen 2 [39 71]
B'36 Tórshavn	1	Hojsted [79]

Tórsvøllur, Tórshavn, 25-08-2005, 18:00, 1 300, Kari FIN

B'36 Tórshavn	2	Midjord [4], Mørkøre [85]
FC Midtjylland	2	Pimpong [17], Sørensen [35]

Dinamo, Bucharest, 11-08-2005, 21:45, 7 000, Perez ESP

Dinamo Bucureşti	3	Munteanu [12p], Zicu 2 [25 44]
Omonia Nicosia	1	Konnafis [4]

GSP, Nicosia, 25-08-2005, 20:30, 12 000, Zakaraov RUS

Omonia Nicosia	2	Kaifas [29], Christou.S [31]
Dinamo Bucureşti	1	Niculescu [55]

Giulesti, Bucharest, 11-08-2005, 20:00, 8 000, Sandmoen NOR

Rapid Bucureşti	3	Niculae 2 [44 50], Maldarasanu [67]
Vardar Skopje	0	

Gradski, Skopje, 25-08-2005, 19:00, 1 500, Megyebiro HUN

Vardar Skopje	1	Naumov [40]
Rapid Bucureşti	1	Vasilache [59]

Bloomfield, Tel Aviv, 11-08-2005, 19:00, 2 242, Stanisic SCG

MS Ashdod	2	Rajovic [18], Dika Dika [34]
Domzale	2	Stevanovic [2], De Souza [25]

Sportni Park, Domzale, 25-08-2005, 17:00, 2 788, Tsachilidis GRE

Domzale	1	Nikezic [93+]
MS Ashdod	1	Ebiede [70]

Városi, Soporon, 11-08-2005, 20:30, 4 000, Nalbandyan ARM

Matáv Sopron	0	
Metalurh Donetsk	3	Shyshchenko 52, Oleksienko 2 87 90

Shakhtyor, Donetsk, 25-08-2005, 19:00, 12 000, Ross NIR

Metalurh Donetsk	2	Zotov [56], Oleksienko [90p]
Matáv Sopron	1	Florea OG [88]

Commerzbank Arena, Frankfurt, 11-08-2005, 20:30, 18 100, Culcu TUR

1.FSV Mainz	2	Auer [10], Babatz [70p]
Keflavík	0	

Laugardalsvöllur, Reykjavík, 25-08-2005, 19:15, 880, Derrien FRA

Keflavík	0	
1.FSV Mainz	2	Thurk [26], Geissler [85]

Waldstadion, Pasching, 11-08-2005, 20:45, 4 200, Vink NED

SV Pasching	2	Chaile [33], Wislo [87]
Zenit St Peterburg	2	Kerzhakov [15], Arshavin [73]

Petrovsky, St Petersburg, 25-08-2005, 20:00, 21 750, Dean ENG

Zenit St Peterburg	1	Spivak [11p]
SV Pasching	1	Gilewicz [88]

Omladinski, Belgrade, 11-08-2005, 17:30, 800, Dondarini ITA

OFK Beograd	2	Kirovski [32], Ivanovic [39]
Lokomotiv Plovdiv	1	Kamburov.M 55

Naftex, Burgas, 25-08-2005, 21:00, 8 100, Papila TUR

Lokomotiv Plovdiv	1	Stoynev [76]
OFK Beograd	0	

Rheinpark, Vaduz, 11-08-2005, 19:30, 2 650, Bebek CRO

Vaduz	0	
Besiktas	1	Okan [12]

Inönü, Istanbul, 25-08-2005, 21:00, 15 120, Egorov RUS

Besiktas	5	Ailton [35], Hassan [61], Ahmet [83p], Adem [89], Pancu [92+]
Vaduz	1	Gaspar [28]

FIRST ROUND

Stade Louis II, Monaco, 15-09-2005, 21:00, 9 118, Tudoe ROU

AS Monaco	2	Kapo [24], Adebayor [47]
Willem II Tilburg	0	

Willem II, Tilburg, 29-09-2005, 18:00, 11 600, Iturralde ESP

Willem II Tilburg	1	Hadouir [84]
AS Monaco	3	Maicon [47], Adebayor [54], Chevantón [89]

AOL Arena, Hamburg, 15-09-2005, 20:30, 43 085, Braamhaar NED

Hamburger SV	1	Van der Vaart [37]
FC København	1	Van Heerden [40]

Parken, Copenhagen, 29-09-2005, 21:00, 34 446, Messias ENG

FC København	0	
Hamburger SV	1	Van der Vaart [89p]

Evzena Rosického, Prague, 15-09-2005, 20:00, 4 694, Siric CRO

Slavia Praha	2	Hrdlicka [62], Piták [79]
Cork City	0	

Turner's Cross, Cork, 29-09-2005, 18:30, 5 648, Leuba SUI

Cork City	1	O'Callaghan [73p]
Slavia Praha	2	Piták [28], Vlcek [59]

Viking, Stavanger, 15-09-2005, 18:45, 4 716, Shebek UKR

Viking Stavanger	1	Mumba [71]
FK Austria	0	

Franz Horr, Vienna, 29-09-2005, 20:45, 5 600, Bozinovski MKD

FK Austria	2	Rushfeldt [21], Lasnik [47]
Viking Stavanger	1	Nygaard [12]

BayArena, Leverkusen, 15-09-2005, 18:15, 18 000, Gumienny BEL

Bayer Leverkusen	0	
CSKA Sofia	1	Todorov [15]

Balgarska Armia, Sofia, 29-09-2005, 17:15, 16 693, Berntsen NOR

CSKA Sofia	1	Hdiouad [67]
Bayer Leverkusen	0	

Renzo Barbera, Palermo, 15-09-2005, 21:00, 13 500, Gomes Costa POR

Palermo	2	Corini [5], Brienza [30p]
Anorthosis F'gusta	1	Ketsbaia [76]

GSP, Nicosia, 29-09-2005, 18:00, 8 122, Halsey ENG

Anorthosis F'gusta	0	
Palermo	4	Caracciolo [5], Makinwa 2 [46 69], Santana [53]

Na Stínadlech, Teplice, 15-09-2005, 18:30, 14 620, Delevic SCG

SK Teplice	1	Jirsák [48]
Espanyol	2	Luis García [82]

Montjuïc, Barcelona, 29-09-2005, 21:45, 9 134, Dereli TUR

Espanyol	2	Fredson [80], Jofre [89]
SK Teplice	0	

Brann, Bergen, 15-09-2005, 19:00, 5 113, Van Egmond NED

SK Brann Bergen	1	Winters [45]
Lokomotiv Moskva	2	Ruopolo [71], Lebedenko [77]

Lokomotiv, Moskva, 29-09-2005, 20:00, 13 223, Nobs SUI
Lokomotiv Moskva 3 Loskov [61], Asatiani [77], Bilyaletdinov [91+]
SK Brann Bergen 2 Mcallister [47], Miller [74]

Brøndby Stadion, Brøndby, 15-09-2005, 20:15, 13 614, Lajuks LVA
Brøndby IF 2 Skoubo [46], Johansen [72]
FC Zürich 0

Letzigrund, Zurich, 29-09-2005, 20:15, 8 600, Colombo FRA
FC Zürich 2 Rafael 2 [15 80]
Brøndby IF 1 Elmander [42]

Ramat Gan, Tel Aviv, 15-09-2005, 19:305 500, Kapitanis CYP
Maccabi Petah-T 0
Partizan Beograd 2 Vukcevic [33], Radonjic [46]

Partizan, Belgrade, 29-09-2005, 19:15, 8 500, Megia Davila ESP
Partizan Beograd 2 Radonjic 2 [13p 41]
Maccabi Petah-T 5 Mashiach [4p], Golan 3 [21 44 48], Ederi [88]

Ullevål, Oslo, 15-09-2005, 19:30, 4 192, Richards WAL
Vålerenga IF 0
Steaua Bucureşti 3 Radoi [24], Iacob [35], Goian [74]

Gheorghe Hagi, Constanta, 29-09-2005, 20:00, 8 114, Lopes POR
Steaua Bucureşti 3 Dica [30], Bostina [41], Iacob [48]
Vålerenga IF 1 Hulsker [55]

Félix-Bollaert, Lens, 15-09-2005, 20:00, 20 294, Kelly IRL
RC Lens 1 Hilton [13]
Groclin Grodzisk 1 Lachor OG [14]

Dyskobolia, Grodzisk Wielkopols, 29-09-2005, 18:30, 3 620, Jakobsson ISL
Groclin Grodzisk 2 Sedlácek [57p], Sábik [78]
RC Lens 4 Cousin 2 [23 54], Aruna [30], Lachor [91+]

GSP, Nicosia, 29-09-2005, 21:00, 6 326, Kassai HUN
APOEL Nicosia 0
Hertha Berlin 1 Marcelinho [92+]

Olympiastadion, Berlin, 29-09-2005, 18:30, 22 612, Vollquartz DEN
Hertha Berlin 3 Marcelinho [15], Rafael [25], Cairo [52]
APOEL Nicosia 1 Makridis [76]

0 Bonfim, Setúbal, 15-09-2005, 17:00, 4 152, Piccirillo FRA
Vitória Setúbal 1 Fábio [46]
Sampdoria 1 Flachi [14]

Luigi Ferraris, Genoa, 29-09-2005, 20:45, 21 000, Webb ENG
Sampdoria 1 Gasbarroni [7]
Vitória Setúbal 0

Orjans Vall, Halmstad, 15-09-2005, 20:45, 3 262, Mikulski POL
Halmstads BK 1 Thorvaldsson [42p]
Sporting CP 2 Wender [44], Deivid [47]

José Alvalade, Lisbon, 29-09-2005, 21:15, 14 490, Verbist BEL
Sporting CP 2 Wender [34], Zvirgzdauskas OG [103]
Halmstads BK 3 Thorvaldsson [15], Zvirgzdauskas [89], Ingelsten [113]

Riverside, Middlesbrough, 29-09-2005, 20:00, 14 190, Messner AUT
Middlesbrough 2 Boateng [28], Viduka [83]
Xánthi 0

Xánthis, Xánthi, 29-09-2005, 21:00, 5 013, Kircher GER
Xánthi 0
Middlesbrough 0

Metallurg, Samara, 15-09-2005, 19:00, 25 000, Briakos GRE
Krylya Sovetov 5 Leilton [11], Adamu [44], Kovba [49], Husin [63], Bober [92]
AZ Alkmaar 3 Vlaar [18], Perez [56], Van Galen [85]

Alkmaarderhout, Alkmaar, 29-09-2005, 20:15, 8 000, Clark SCO
AZ Alkmaar 3 Van Galen [44], Koevermans [79], Landzaat [84p]
Krylya Sovetov 1 Adamu [15]

Gradski, Lovech, 29-09-2005, 20:30, 1 800, Hanacsek HUN
Litex Lovech 2 Venkov [65], Novakovic [91+]
KRC Genk 1 Daerden [53], Stojanovic [85]

Fenix, Genk, 29-09-2005, 20:45, 6 343, Paniashvili GEO
KRC Genk 0
Litex Lovech 1 Sandrinho [56]

Easter Road, Edinburgh, 15-09-2005, 19:45, 16 861, Fisker DEN
Hibernian 0
D. Dnipropetrovsk 0

Meteor, Dnipropetrovsk, 29-09-2005, 21:00, 17 000, Stuchlik AUT
D. Dnipropetrovsk 5 Nazarenko [1], Shershun [26], Shelayev [39p],
Hibernian 1 Riordan [10] Melashenko 2 [86 94+]

Hardturm, Zurich, 15-09-2005, 19:30, 3 200, McDonald SCO
Grasshopper-Club 1 Salatic [1]
MyPa-47 1 Manso [19]

Pohjola Vantaa, 29-09-2005, 18:30, 4 101 Godulyan UKR
MyPa-47 0
Grasshopper-Club 3 Touré [75], Salatic [80], Rogerio [86]

Arnold Schwarzenegger, Graz, 15-09-2005, 20:45, 6 274, Jara CZE
Grazer AK 0
RC Strasbourg 2 Pagis [1], Lacour [45]

La Meinau, Strasbourg, 29-09-2005, 18:15, 12 184, Messina ITA
RC Strasbourg 5 Haggui [5], Farnerud.A [40], Farnerud.P [50],
Grazer AK 0 Le Pen [59], Ebrahim [68]

Olimpico, Rome, 15-09-2005, 21:00, 11 620, Oliveira POR
AS Roma 5 Aquilani [1], Panucci 2 [22 43], Montella [27],
Aris Thessaloníki 1 Sanjurjo [39] Totti [53]

Kleanthis Vikelidis, Thessalonica, 29-09-2005, 22:00, 6 350, Yefet ISR
Aris Thessaloníki 0
AS Roma 0

St Jakob-Park, Basel, 15-09-2005, 19:30, 14 448, Szabo HUN
FC Basel 5 Delgado 3 [10 78 88], Ergic [70], Eduardo [85]
Siroki Brijeg 0

Pecara, Siroki, Brijeg, 29-09-2005, 19:30, 4 000, Asumaa FIN
Siroki Brijeg 0
FC Basel 1 Petric [8]

Crvena Zvezda, Belgrade, 15-09-2005, 20:15, 32 786, Bossen NED
Crvena Zvezda 0
Sporting Braga 0

Municipal, Braga, 29-09-2005, 19:30, 12 000, Wack GER
Sporting Braga 1 Jaime Júnior [86]
Crvena Zvezda 1 Purovic [11]

Alfheim, Trømso, 15-09-2005, 20:30, 4 764, Lehner AUT
Tromsø IL 1 Szekeres [77]
Galatasaray 0

Ali Sami Yen, Istanbul, 19:45, 21 751, Almeida Costa POR
Galatasaray 1 Hakan Sükür [79]
Tromsø IL 1 Ademulo [32]

Olympisch, Antwerp, 29-09-2005, 20:30, 11 500, Undiano ESP
Germinal B'schott 0
Oly. Marseille 0

Vélodrome, Marseille, 29-09-2005, 21:00, 22 068, Weiner GER
Oly. Marseille 0 Marseille W 4-1p
Germinal B'schott 0

Abbé-Deschamps, Auxerre, 15-09-2005, 20:30, 3 401, Fleischer GER
AJ Auxerre 2 Poyet [55], Pieroni [84]
Levski Sofia 1 Bardon [34]

Georgi Asparuhov, Sofia, 29-09-2005, 19:30, 15 850, Ingvarsson SWE
Levski Sofia 1 Koprivarov [28]
AJ Auxerre 0

Bazaly, Ostrava, 15-09-2005, 21:00, 10 337, Ivanov.N RUS
Baník Ostrava 2 Klimpi [28], Magera [45p]
SC Heerenveen 0

Abe Lenstra, Heerenveen, 29-09-2005, 21:15, 17 000, D'Urso ENG
SC Heerenveen 5 Samaras [3], Nilsson [45], Huntelaar 2 [60 67],
Baník Ostrava 0 Yildirim [66]

Dinamo, Moscow, 15-09-2005, 19:00, Brugger AUT
CSKA Moskva 3 Gusev [21], Carvalho 2 [76 79]
FC Midtjylland 1 Pimpong [24]

Messecentret, Herning, 29-09-2005, 20:00, 7 022, Trivkovic CRO
FC Midtjylland 1 Nielsen.D [14]
CSKA Moskva 3 Carvalho 2 [61 77], Samodin [76]

Dinamo, Bucharest, 15-09-2005, 21:45, 11 100, Paparesta ITA
Dinamo Bucureşti 5 Niculescu [27], Zicu [51], Petre [74], Bratu 2 [76 92+]
Everton 1 Yobo [30]

Goodison Park, Liverpool, 29-09-2005, 20:00, 21 843, Duhamel FRA
Everton   1   Cahill [28]
Dinamo Bucuresti 0
De Kuip, Rotterdam, 15-09-2005, 19:00, Hrinak SVK
Feyenoord   1   Kuijt [40]
Rapid Bucuresti 1   Vasilache [74p]
Giulesti, Bucharest, 29-09-2005, 19:00, 8 250, Cardoso POR
Rapid Bucuresti 1   Buga [12]
Feyenoord   0
Shakhter, Donetsk, 15-09-2005, 19:00, 24 106, Van de Velde BEL
Shakhter Donetsk 4   Elano [1], Brandão 2 [36 45p], Vorobey [72]
Debreceni VSC   1   Sidibe [88]
Oláh Gábor, Debrecen, 29-09-2005, 20:00, 6 500, Eriksson SWE
Debreceni VSC   0
Shakhter Donetsk 2   Brandão [18], Elano [24]
Gottlieb-Daimler, Stuttgart, 15-09-2005, 16:30, 10 000, Bertini ITA
VfB Stuttgart   2   Tomasson [6], Gentner [88]
Domzale   0
Sportni Park, Domzale, 29-09-2006, 14:15, 2 700, Granat POL
Domzale   1   Stevanovic [16]
VfB Stuttgart   0
Toumba, Thessalonica, 15-09-2005, 20:30, 7 963, Rodriguez ESP
PAOK   1   Salpingidis [25]
Metalurh Donetsk 1   Shyshchenko [66]
Shakhter, Donetsk, 29-09-2005, 19:00, 16 000, Vink NED
Metalurh Donetsk 2   Kosyrin [39], Shyshchenko [57]
PAOK   2   Salpingidis [42], Konstantinidis [46]
Route de Lorient, Rennes, 15-09-2005, 19:00, 19 286, Balaj ROU
Stade Rennais   3   Frei 2 [27 74], Hadji [84]
Osasuna   1   Milosevic [52]
El Sadar, Pamplona, 29-09-2005, 20:30, 17 227, Kaznaferis GRE
Osasuna   0
Stade Rennais   0
Sánchez-Pizjuan, Seville, 15-09-2005, 21:30, 34 160, Styles ENG
Sevilla   0
1.FSV Mainz   0
Commerzbank Arena, Frankfurt, 29-09-2005, 20:30, 33 400, Trefoloni ITA
1.FSV Mainz   0
Sevilla   2   Kanouté 2 [9 40]
Petrovsky, St Petersburg, 15-09-2005, 19:00, 21 000, Skjerven NOR
Zenit St Peterburg 0
AEK Athens   0
Spyros Louis, Athens, 29-09-2005, 21:45, 23 121, Meyer GER
AEK Athens   0
Zenit St Peterburg 1   Arshavin [89]
Reebok Stadium, Bolton, 15-09-2005, 20:10, 19 273, Ceferin SVN
Bolton Wanderers 2   Diouf [72], Borgetti [91+]
Lokomotiv Plovdiv 1   Jancevski [27]
Naftex Burgas, 29-09-2005, 17:55, 8 340, Hyttiä FIN
Lokomotiv Plovdiv 1   Iliev.G [52]
Bolton Wanderers 2   Tunchev OG [79], Nolan [86]
Inönü, Istanbul, 15-09-2005, 20:00, 18 931Allaerts BEL
Besiktas   0
Malmö FF   1   Alves [70]
Malmö Stadion, Malmö, 29-09-2005, 20:30, 8 070, Sippel GER
Malmö FF   1   Alves [61]
Besiktas   4   Youla 2 [28 53], Günes [34], Tümer [94+]
Alfonso Henriques, Guimarães, 15-09-2005, 20:30, 8 300, Bebek CRO
Vitória Guimarães 3 Cléber [24p], Sérgio [70], Benachour [72]
Wisla Kraków   0
Wisly, Kraków, 29-09-2005, 20:30, 13 758, Genov BUL
Wisla Kraków   0
Vitória Guimarães 1 Saganowski [82]

GROUP A

Viking, Stavanger, 20-10-2005, 18:00, 9 684, Lehner AUT
Viking Stavanger 1   Nhleko [18]
AS Monaco   0
Balgarska Armia, Sofia, 20-10-2005, 21:15, 17 585, Oliveira POR
CSKA Sofia   0
Hamburger SV   1   Van der Vaart [57]
AOL Arena, Hamburg, 3-11-2005, 18:30, 37 521, Lajuks LVA
Hamburger SV   2   Van der Vaart [21], Lauth [66]
Viking Stavanger 0
Evzena Rosického, Prague, 3-11-2005, 20:00, 7 171, Shebek UKR
Slavia Praha   4   Fort 2 [5 75], Vlcek [36], Piták [56]
CSKA Sofia   2   Gargorov [10], Sakaliev [58]
Viking, Stavanger, 24-11-2005, 18:00, 7 941, Hanacsek HUN
Viking Stavanger 2   Nhleko [26], Gaarde [55]
Slavia Praha   2   Vlcek [51], Piták [83]
Stade Louis II, Monaco, 24-11-2005, 21:00, 8 954, Rosetti ITA
AS Monaco   2   Adebayor [44], Veigneau [92+]
Hamburger SV   0
Evzena Rosického, Prague, 30-11-2005, 20:45, 12 543, Corpodean ROU
Slavia Praha   0
AS Monaco   2   Maoulida 2 [12 72]
Balgarska Armia, Sofia, 30-11-2005, 21:45, 5 500, Kapitanis CYP
CSKA Sofia   2   Yanev [34p], Zadi [46]
Viking Stavanger 0
Stade Louis II, Monaco, 15-12-2005, 18:30, 13 221, McDonald SCO
AS Monaco   2   Kapo [49], Squillaci [74]
CSKA Sofia   1   Dimitrov.V [83]
AOL Arena, Hamburg, 15-12-2005, 18:30, 46 235, Gonzalez ESP
Hamburger SV   2   Barbarez [9], Mpenza.E [56]
Slavia Praha   0

Group A	Pl	W	D	L	F	A	Pts
AS Monaco	4	3	0	1	6	2	9
Hamburger SV	4	3	0	1	5	2	9
Slavia Praha	4	1	1	2	6	8	4
Viking SK Stavanger	4	1	1	2	3	6	4
CSKA Sofia	4	1	0	3	5	7	3

GROUP B

Lokomotiv, Moscow, 19-10-2005, 19:30, 13 719, Eriksson SWE
Lokomotiv Moskva 0
Espanyol   1   Tamudo [53]
Ramat Gan, Tel Aviv, 20-10-2005, 17:00, 4 512, Tudor ROU
Maccabi Petah-T 1   Golan [45]
Palermo   2   Brienza [11], Terlizzi [77]
Brøndby Stadion, Brøndby, 3-11-2005, 20:45, 14 188, Gomes Costa POR
Brøndby IF   2   Lantz [67], Absalonsen [83]
Maccabi Petah-T 0
Renzo Barbera, Palermo, 3-11-2005, 21:00, 15 833, Garibian FRA
Palermo   0
Lokomotiv Moskva 0
Lokomotiv, Moscow, 23-11-2005, 19:00, 8 700, Wack GER
Lokomotiv Moskva 4   Loskov 2 [60 64 84], Lebedenko [63]
Brøndby IF   2   Retov [12], Skoubo [28]
Montjuïc, Barcelona, 24-11-2005, 21:15, 9 114, Messner AUT
Espanyol   1   Moisés [91+]
Palermo   1   Gonzalez [45]
Brøndby Stadion, Brøndby, 30-11-2005, 20:45, 21 399, Wegereef NED
Brøndby IF   1   Skoubo [65]
Espanyol   1   Tamudo [42]

Ramat Gan, Tel Aviv, 30-11-2005, 21:45, 3 600, Kassai HUN
Maccabi Petah-T 0
Lokomotiv Moskva 4 Loskov [27], Lebedenko 2 [46][47], Ruopolo [52]
Montjuïc, Barcelona, 15-12-2005, 20:45, 5 150, Genov BUL
Espanyol 1 Pochettino [83]
Maccabi Petah-T 0
Renzo Barbera, Palermo, 15-12-2005, 20:45, 4 521, Dougal SCO
Palermo 3 Makinwa [26], Rinaudo 2 [44][88]
Brøndby IF 0

Group B	Pl	W	D	L	F	A	Pts
Palermo	4	2	2	0	6	2	8
Espanyol	4	2	2	0	4	2	8
Lokomotiv Moskva	4	2	1	1	8	3	7
Brøndby IF	4	1	1	2	5	8	4
Maccabi Petah-Tikva	4	0	0	4	1	9	0

GROUP C

Ullevi, Gothenburg, 20-10-2005, 16:15, 2 136, Van de Velde BEL
Halmstads BK 0
Hertha Berlin 1 Neuendorf [67]
Ghencea, Bucharest, 20-10-2005, 20:00, 19 500, Briakos GRE
Steaua Bucuresti 4 Iacob [13], Goian [16], Dica 2 [43][63]
RC Lens 0
Félix-Bollaert, Lens, 3-11-2005, 20:30, 16 189, Siric CRO
RC Lens 5 Cousin 3 [16][23][47], Jemaa [73], Lachor [90]
Halmstads BK 0
Luigi Ferraris, Genoa, 3-11-2005, 20:45, 17 104, Gilewski POL
Sampdoria 0
Steaua Bucuresti 0
Olympiastadion, Berlin, 24-11-2005, 19:00, 18 600, Webb ENG
Hertha Berlin 0
RC Lens 0
Ullevi, Gothenburg, 24-11-2005, 19:00, 3 126, Halsey ENG
Halmstads BK 1 Djuric [17]
Sampdoria 3 Volpi [31], Diana [66], Bonazzoli [86]
Luigi Ferraris, Genoa, 30-11-2005, 20:45, 16 507, Bartolo POR
Sampdoria 0
Hertha Berlin 0
Ghencea, Bucharest, 30-11-2005, 21:45, 22 654, Bozinovski MKD
Steaua Bucuresti 3 Radoi [9], Goian [63], Iacob [73]
Halmstads BK 0
Olympiastadion, Berlin, 15-12-2005, 20:45, 13 600, Vink NED
Hertha Berlin 0
Steaua Bucuresti 0
Félix-Bollaert, Lens, 15-12-2005, 20:45, 31 473, Ovrebo NOR
RC Lens 2 Thomert [10], Jemaa [90]
Sampdoria 1 Flachi [24]

Group C	Pl	W	D	L	F	A	Pts
Steaua Bucuresti	4	2	2	0	7	0	8
Racing Club Lens	4	2	1	1	7	5	7
Hertha BSC Berlin	4	1	3	0	1	0	6
Sampdoria	4	1	2	1	4	3	5
Halmstads BK	4	0	0	4	1	12	0

GROUP D

Hardturm, Zurich, 20-10-2005, 21:00, 8 500, Berntsen NOR
Grasshopper-Club 0
Middlesbrough 1 Hasselbaink [10]

Meteor, Dnipropetrovsk, 20-10-2005, 21:00, 12 300, Mikulski POL
D. Dnipropetrovsk 1 Matiukhin [70]
AZ Alkmaar 2 Arveladze [14], Sektioui [52]
Gradski, Lovech, 3-11-2005, 17:00, 4 175, Kaznaferis GRE
Litex Lovech 2 Novakovic [13], Sandrinho [81]
Grasshopper-Club 1 Antonio [90]
Riverside, Middlesbrough, 3-11-2005, 20:05, 12 953, Layec FRA
Middlesbrough 3 Yakubu [36], Viduka 2 [50][56]
D. Dnipropetrovsk 0
Alkmaarderhout, Alkmaar, 24-11-2005, 18:30, 8 700, Paparesta ITA
AZ Alkmaar 0
Middlesbrough 0
Meteor, Dnipropetrovsk, 24-11-2005, 20:45, 3 000, Hyytiä FIN
D. Dnipropetrovsk 0
Litex Lovech 2 Novakovic [72], Nazarenko OG [92+]
Hardturm, Zurich, 30-11-2005, 20:45, 1 800, Trivcovic CRO
Grasshopper-Club 2 Touré [85], Renggli [90]
D. Dnipropetrovsk 3 Nazarenko [39], Kravchenko [61], Mykhaylenko [84]
Gradski, Lovech, 30-11-2005, 21:45, 4 601, Brugger AUT
Litex Lovech 0
AZ Alkmaar 2 Van Galen [10], Sektioui [83]
Riverside, Middlesbrough, 15-12-2005, 19:45, 9 436, Gumienny BEL
Middlesbrough 2 Maccarone 2 [79][86]
Litex Lovech 0
Alkmaarderhout, Alkmaar, 15-12-2005, 20:45, 8 321, Piccirillo FRA
AZ Alkmaar 1 Koevermans [70]
Grasshopper-Club 0

Group D	Pl	W	D	L	F	A	Pts
Middlesbrough	4	3	1	0	6	0	10
AZ Alkmaar	4	3	1	0	5	1	10
Litex Lovech	4	2	0	2	4	5	6
Dnipro Dnipropetrovsk	4	1	0	3	4	9	3
Grasshopper-Club	4	0	0	4	3	7	0

GROUP E

St Jakob-Park, Basel, 20-10-2005, 19:30, 16 623, Halsey ENG
FC Basel 0
RC Strasbourg 2 Diané [15], Boka [25]
Alfheim, Tromsø, 20-10-2005, 20:45, 5 982, Sippel GER
Tromsø IL 1 Arst [42]
Roma 2 Kuffour [35], Cufré [84]
Crvena Zvezda, Belgrade, 3-11-2005, 17:00, Fisker DEN
Crvena Zvezda 1 Purovic [25]
FC Basel 2 Delgado [30p], Rossi [88]
La Meinau, Strasbourg, 3-11-2005, 20:45, 8 472, Paniashvili GEO
RC Strasbourg 2 Pagis [38], Arrache [66]
Tromsø IL 0
Alfheim, Tromsø, 24-11-2005, 20:00, 4 289, Van Egmond NED
Tromsø IL 3 Kibebe [22], Arst 2 [37][74p]
Crvena Zvezda 1 Zigic [24]
Olimpico, Rome, 24-11-2005, 21:00, 8 109, Undiano ESP
Roma 1 Cassano [72]
RC Strasbourg 1 Bellaid [51]
Crvena Zvezda, Belgrade, 1-12-2005, 20:45, 35 186, Hansson SWE
Crvena Zvezda 3 Zigic 2 [37][86], Purovic [77]
Roma 1 Nonda [23]
St Jakob-Park, Basel, 1-12-2005, 20:45, 14 718, Slupik POL
FC Basel 4 Petric [17], Delgado [61], Chipperfield [67], Degen [75]
Tromsø IL 3 Strand 2 [2][29], Arst [19]
Olimpico, Rome, 14-12-2005, 20:45, 14 000, Fleischer GER
Roma 3 Rodrigo Taddei [12], Totti [45], Nonda [49]
FC Basel 1 Petric [78]

La Meinau, Strasbourg, 14-12-2005, 20:45, 13 410, Messner AUT

RC Strasbourg 2 Gameiro 2 [78] [94+]
Crvena Zvezda 2 Basta [34], Djokaj [63]

Group E	Pl	W	D	L	F	A	Pts
Racing Club Strasbourg	4	2	2	0	7	3	8
Roma	4	2	1	1	7	6	7
FC Basel	4	2	0	2	7	9	6
Crvena Zvezda Beograd	4	1	1	2	7	8	4
Tromsø IL	4	1	0	3	7	9	3

GROUP F

Dinamo, Moscow, 20-10-2005, 19:30, 12 000, Jakobsson ISL

CSKA Moskva 1 Vágner Love [80]
Oly. Marseille 2 Lamouchi [23], Niang [38]

Dinamo, Bucharest, 20-10-2005, 21:45, 11 890, Granat POL

Dinamo Bucuresti 0
SC Heerenveen 0

Georghi Asparuhov, Sofia, 3-11-2005, 19:00, 17 322, Ivanov.N RUS

Levski Sofia 1 Angelov.E [90]
Dinamo Bucuresti 0

Abe Lenstra, Heerenveen, 3-11-2005, 20:30, 20 200, Ingvarsson SWE

SC Heerenveen 0
CSKA Moskva 0

Dinamo, Moscow, 24-11-2005, 18:30, 5 900, Clark SCO

CSKA Moskva 2 Vágner Love 2 [49] [73]
Levski Sofia 1 Domovchiyski [90]

Vélodrome, Marseille, 24-11-2005, 20:45, 11 777, Lopes POR

Oly. Marseille 1 Ismailia [88p]
SC Heerenveen 0

Georghi Asparuhov, Sofia, 1-12-2005, 19:30, 16 616, Vollquartz DEN

Levski Sofia 1 Yovov [54]
Oly. Marseille 0

Dinamo, Bucharest, 1-12-2005, 19:30, 7 000, Stuchlik AUT

Dinamo Bucuresti 1 Munteanu [73]
CSKA Moskva 0

Vélodrome, Marseille, 14-12-2005, 20:45, 15 909, Rodriguez ESP

Oly. Marseille 2 Cesar [38], Delfim [45]
Dinamo Bucuresti 1 Niculescu [51]

Abe Lenstra, Heerenveen, 14-12-2005, 20:45, 20 200, Szabo HUN

SC Heerenveen 2 Samaras [55], Hanssen.A [90]
Levski Sofia 1 Ivanov.M [53]

Group F	Pl	W	D	L	F	A	Pts
Olympique Marseille	4	3	0	1	5	3	9
Levski Sofia	4	2	0	2	4	4	6
SC Heerenveen	4	1	2	1	2	2	5
Dinamo Bucuresti	4	1	1	2	2	3	4
CSKA Moskva	4	1	1	2	3	4	4

GROUP G

Route de Lorient, Rennes, 20-10-2005, 18:15, 23 800, Dean ENG

Stade Rennais 0
VfB Stuttgart 2 Tomasson [87], Ljuboja [90p]

Olimpiyskiy, Donetsk, 20-10-2005, 19:00, 24 650, Kelly IRL

Shakhtar Donetsk 1 Brandão [68p]
PAOK 0

Giulesti, Bucharest, 3-11-2005, 20:00, 7 120, Asumaa FIN

Rapid Bucuresti 2 Niculae [42], Buga [67]
Stade Rennais 0

Gottlieb-Daimler, Stuttgart, 3-11-2005, 20:45, 15 704, Skjerven NOR

VfB Stuttgart 0
Shakhtar Donestk 2 Fernandinho [31], Marica [88]

Toumba, Thessalonica, 24-11-2005, 18:00, 21 479, Megia Davila ESP

PAOK 1 Karipidis [48]
VfB Stuttgart 2 Ljuboja 2 [85] [91+]

Olimpiyskiy, Donetsk, 24-11-2005, 19:30, 17 728, Richards WAL

Shakhtar Donetsk 0
Rapid Bucuresti 1 Maldarasanu [87]

Route de Lorient, Rennes, 1-12-2005, 20:45, 18 727, Dereli TUR

Stade Rennais 0
Shakhtar Donetsk 1 Elano [38p]

Giulesti, Bucharest, 1-12-2005, 21:45, 12 100, Nobs SUI

Rapid Bucuresti 1 Maldarasanu [45]
PAOK 0

Gottlieb-Daimler, Stuttgart, 14-12-2005, 20:45, 14 000, Messina ITA

VfB Stuttgart 2 Gómez 2 [20] [37]
Rapid Bucuresti 1 Burdujan [80]

Toumba, Thessalonica, 14-12-2005, 21:45, 1 012, Almeida Costa POR

PAOK 5 OG [3], Hristodoulopoulos [38], Yiasoumis 2 [79] [89],
Stade Rennais 1 Briand [70]   Salpingidis [83p]

Group G	Pl	W	D	L	F	A	Pts
Rapid Bucuresti	4	3	0	1	5	2	9
Shakhtar Donetsk	4	3	0	1	4	1	9
VfB Stuttgart	4	3	0	1	6	4	9
PAOK Thessaloníki	4	1	0	3	6	5	3
Stade Rennais	4	0	0	4	1	10	0

GROUP H

Petrovsky, St Petersburg, 20-10-2005, 20:00,

Zenit St Peterburg 2 Spivak [39p], Arshavin [54]
Vitória Guimarães 1 Neca [59]

Inönü, Istanbul, 20-10-2005, 21:45,

Besiktas 1 Ailton [7]
Bolton Wanderers 1 Borgetti [29]

Reebok Stadium, Bolton, 3-11-2005, 20:00,

Bolton Wanderers 1 Nolan [24]
Zenit St Peterburg 0

Sánchez-Pizjuán, Seville, 3-11-2005, 21:30,

Sevilla 3 Saviola [64], Kanouté 2 [65] [89]
Besiktas 0

Afonso Henriques, Guimarães, 24-11-2005, 20:00,

Vitória Guimarães 1 Saganowski [84]
Bolton Wanderers 1 Vaz Té [87]

Petrovsky, St Petersburg, 24-11-2005, 20:30,

Zenit St Peterburg 2 Kerzhakov 2 [11] [88]
Sevilla 1 Saviola [93+]

Sánchez-Pizjuán, Seville, 1-12-2005, 20:45,

Sevilla 3 Saviola 2 [10] [28]
Vitória Guimarães 1 Benachour [44]

Inönü, Istanbul, 1-12-2005, 21:45,

Besiktas 1 Akin [23]
Zenit St Peterburg 1 Gorshkov [29]

Afonso Henriques, Guimarães, 14-12-2005, 20:00,

Vitória Guimarães 1 Saganowski [11]
Besiktas 3 Toraman 2 [7] [60], Youla [17]

Reebok Stadium, Bolton, 14-12-2005, 19:45,

Bolton Wanderers 1 N'gotty [66]
Sevilla 1 Adriano [74]

Group H	Pl	W	D	L	F	A	Pts
Sevilla	4	2	1	1	8	4	7
Zenit Sankt Peterburg	4	2	1	1	5	4	7
Bolton Wanderers	4	1	3	0	4	3	6
Besiktas	4	1	2	1	5	6	5
Vitória SC Guimarães	4	0	1	3	4	9	1

ROUND OF THIRTY-TWO

Lokomotiv, Moscow, 15-02-2006, 19:30, 10 223, Bennett ENG
Lokomotiv Moskva 0
Sevilla 1 Jordi [75]
Sánchez-Pizjuán, Seville, 23-02-2006, 21:30, 19 970, Sars FRA
Sevilla 2 Maresca [34], Puerta [90]
Lokomotiv Moskva 0

Métropole, Lille, 15-02-2006, 19:00, 13 644, Paparesta ITA
Lille OSC 3 Fauvergue [19], Dernis [57], Odemwingie [77]
Shakhtar Donetsk 2 Brandão [89], Marica [91+]
Olimpiyskiy, Donetsk, 23-02-2006, 23 250, Vollquartz DEN
Shakhtar Donetsk 0
Lille OSC 0

Reebok, Bolton, 15-02-2006, 19:45, 19 288, Benquerenca POR
Bolton Wanderers 0
Olymp. Marseille 0
Vélodrome, Marseille, 23-02-2006, 20:45, 38 851, Busacca SUI
Olymp. Marseille 2 Ribéry [47+], Ben Haim OG [68]
Bolton Wanderers 1 Giannakopoulos [25]

Lerkendal, Trondheim, 15-02-2006, 19:30, 11 062, Cardoso POR
Rosenborg BK 0
Zenit St Peterburg 2 Arshavin [22], Aleksandr Kerzhakov [32]
Petrovsky, St Petersburg, 23-02-2006, 20:00, 19 133, Hrinak SVK
Zenit St Peterburg 2 Aleksandr Kerzhakov [55], Denisov [86]
Rosenborg BK 1 Riseth [45]

Malatinského, Trnava, 15-02-2006, 17:30, 5 297, Duhamel FRA
Artmedia Bratislava 0
Levski Sofia 1 Emil Angelov [9]
Vassil Levski, Sofia, 23-02-2006, 18:00, 23 422, Lehner AUT
Levski Sofia 2 Emil Angelov [14 27]
Artmedia Bratislava 0

Friuli, Udine, 15-02-2006, 20:45, 6 928, Mejuto ESP
Udinese 3 Di Natale [35], Barreto 2 [61 82]
RC Lens 0
Félix-Bollaert, Lens, 23-02-2006, 20:45, 26 282, Fandel GER
RC Lens 1 Frau [55]
Udinese 0

Evzena Rosického, Prague, 16-02-2006, 20:45, 6 706, Genov BUL
Slavia Praha 2 Jarolím [28], Piták [48]
Palermo 1 Conteh [40]
Renzo Barbara, Palermo, 23-02-2006, 16:00, 8 063, Allaerts BEL
Palermo 1 Godeas [51]
Slavia Praha 0

AufSchalke, Gelsenkirchen, 15-02-2006, 20:00, 54 000, Rosetti ITA
Schalke 04 2 Bordon [67], Ernst [88]
Espanyol 1 Luis Garcia [34]
Montjuïc, Barcelona, 23-02-2006, 21:45, 18 100, Ovrebo NOR
Espanyol 0
Schalke 04 3 Kuranyi [54], Sand [70], Lincoln [73]

Abe Lenstra, Heerenveen, 15-02-2006, 19:15, 20 500, Dougal SCO
SC Heerenveen 1 Bruggink [24]
Steaua Bucuresti 3 Dica [29], Goian [76], Paraschiv [78]
Lia Manoliu, Bucharest, 23-02-2006, 19:00, 46 697, Jara CZE
Steaua Bucuresti 0
SC Heerenveen 1 Bruggink [85]

Ruiz de Lopera, Seville, 15-02-2006, 21:30, 11 112, Ivanov.N RUS
Real Betis 2 Tardelli [70], Robert [79]
AZ Alkmaar 0
Alkmaarderhout, Alkmaar, 23-02-2006, 20:45, 8 073, Meyer GER
AZ Alkmaar 2 Arveladze [26], Jaliens [35]
Real Betis 1 Melli [94]

Stade de Suisse, Bern, 16-02-2006, 18:30, 18 354, Hansson SWE
FC Thun 1 Adriano [30]
Hamburger SV 0
AOL Arena, Hamburg, 23-02-2006, 18:30, 40 254, Yefet ISR
Hamburger SV 2 Van Buyten 2 [2 33]
FC Thun 0

Olympiastadion, Berlin, 15-02-2006, 18:00, 14 430, Iturralde ESP
Hertha BSC Berlin 0
Rapid Bucuresti 1 Negru [68p]
Giulesti, Bucharest, 23-02-2006, 17:15, 13 400, Layec FRA
Rapid Bucuresti 2 Daniel Niculae [50], Buga [79]
Hertha BSC Berlin 0

St Jakob-Park, Basel, 15-02-2006, 18:00, 14 143, Vink NED
FC Basel 1 David Deggen [78]
AS Monaco 0
Stade Louis II, Monaco, 23-02-2006, 20:45, 12 055, Kapitanis CYP
AS Monaco 1 Vieri [21p]
FC Basel 1 Majstorovic [56]

Gradski, Lovech, 15-02-2006, 16:30, 3 546, Gilewski POL
Litex Lovech 0
RC Strasbourg 2 Le Pen [2], Diané [82]
La Meinau, Strasbourg, 23-02-2006, 19:00, 9 760, Ceferin SVN
RC Strasbourg 0
Litex Lovech 0

Jan Breydel, Brugge, 15-02-2006, 20:45, 27 138, Baskakov RUS
Club Brugge 1 Portillo [61]
Roma 2 Vanaudenaerde OG [44], Perrotta [74]
Olimpico, Rome, 23-02-2006, 21:00, 15 209, Larsen DEN
Roma 2 Mancini [55], Bovo [71]
Club Brugge 1 Verheyen [60]

Gottlieb-Daimler, Stuttgart, 16-02-2006, 20:45, 18 638, Hamer LUX
VfB Stuttgart 1 Ljuboja [86]
Middlesbrough 2 Hasselbaink [20], Parnaby [46]
Riverside, Middlesbrough, 23-02-2006, 19:45, 24 018
Middlesbrough 0
VfB Stuttgart 1 Tiffert [13]

ROUND OF SIXTEEN

Métropole, Lille, 9-03-2006, 19:00, 11 009, Stark GER
Lille OSC 1 Dernis [24]
Sevilla 0
Sánchez-Pizjuán, Seville, 15-03-2006, 21:00, 33 660, Riley ENG
Sevilla 2 Kanouté [29], Luis Fabiano [47+]
Lille OSC 0

Vélodrome, Marseille, 9-03-2006, 20:45, 21 500, Cantalejo ESP
Olym. Marseille 0
Zenit St Peterburg 1 Arshavin [51]
Petrovsky, St Petersburg, 16-03-2006, 19:00, 18 902, Fandel GER
Zenit St Peterburg 2 Aleksandr Kerzhakov [69]
Olym. Marseille 1 Déhu [74]

Friuli, Udine, 9-03-2006, 20:45, 7 650, De Bleeckere BEL
Udinese 0
Levski Sofia 0
Vassil Levski, Sofia, 16-03-2006, 18:30, 33 218, Bennett ENG
Levski Sofia 2 Borimirov [51], Tomasis [63]
Udinese 1 Tissone [22]

Renzo Barbera, Palermo, 9-03-2006, 18:00, 10 500, Braamhaar NED

Palermo	1	Brienza [15]
Schalke 04	0	

AufSchalke, Gelsenkirchen, 16-03-2006, 20:30, 52 151, Poll ENG

Schalke 04	3	Kobiashvili [44p], Larsen [72], Azaouagh [80]
Palermo	0	

Lia Manoliu, Bucharest, 9-03-2006, 19:00, 45 023, Baskakov RUS

Steaua Bucuresti	0	
Real Betis	0	

Ruiz de Lopera, Seville, 16-03-2006, 21:30, 16 861, De Santis ITA

Real Betis	0	
Steaua Bucuresti	3	Nicolita 2 [54 82], Iacob [78]

Giulesti, Bucharest, 9-03-2006, 17:00, 16 200, Vassaras GRE

Rapid Bucuresti	2	Daniel Niculae [47+], Buga [88]
Hamburger SV	0	

AOL Arena, Hamburg, 15-03-2006, 19:00, 37 866, Larsen DEN

Hamburger SV	3	Lauth [24], Barbarez [36], Van der Vaart [62]
Rapid Bucuresti	1	Buga [51]

St Jakob-Park, Basel, 9-03-2006, 20:15, 14 243, Farina ITA

FC Basel	2	Delgado [8], Kuzmanovic [89]
RC Strasbourg	0	

La Meinau, Strasbourg, 16-03-2006, 18:00, Benquerenca POR

RC Strasbourg	2	Carlier [11], Kanté [78]
FC Basel	2	Eduardo 2 [3 26]

Riverside, Middlesbrough, 9-03-2006, 20:00, 25 354, Sars FRA

Middlesbrough	1	Ayegbeni [12p]
Roma	0	

Olimpico, Rome, 15-03-2006, 21:00, 32 642, Ovrebo NOR

Roma	2	Mancini 2 [43 66p]
Middlesbrough	1	Hasselbaink [32]

QUARTER-FINALS

1st Leg. Sánchez Pizjuán, Seville
30-03-2006, 21:00, 28 633, Hamer LUX

Sevilla	4
	Saviola 2 [14 80], Martí [56p], Adriano [93+]

Palop•; Martí• (Maresca 75), Navarro, Escudé, Castedo, Sales (Puerta 63), Jordi López (Blanco 81), Renato, Adriano Correia, Saviola, Kanouté•.
Tr: Ramos

Zenit Sankt Peterburg	1
	Kerzhakov [45]

Malafeev; Anyukov, Krizanac, Hagen•53, Skrtel, Siri (Mares 76), Sumulikoski• (Gorshkov• 88), Radimov, Denisov (Spivak 29), Arshavin••90, Kerzhakov.
Tr: Petrzela

2nd leg. Petrovsky, St Petersburg
6-04-2006, 20:00, 17 028, Farina ITA

Zenit Sankt Peterburg	1
	Hyun [50]

Malafeev; Anyukov•, Krizanac•68, Skrtel, Mares, Hyun Young Min (Kozhanov 58), Siri (Trifonov 79), Radimov•, Vlasov, Poskus, Kerzhakov. Tr: Petrzela

Sevilla	1
	Kepa [66]

Palop; Martí, Navarro, Escudé, Daniel• (≠73), Castedo, Navas, Maresca (Renato 70), Ocio, Adriano Correia (Sales 56), Luis Fabiano• (Kepa Blanco 62•67).
Tr: Ramos

1st leg. Vassil Levski, Sofia
30-03-2006, 20:00, 39 000, Riley ENG

Levski Sofia	1
	Borimov [6]

Petkov; Milanov, Topuzakov, Tomasic, Wagner•, Borimirov, Stanislav Angelov, Telkiyski (Bukarev 75), Bardon•••35, Yovov (Koprivarov 70), Domovchiyski (Emil Angelov 58). Tr: Stoilov

Schalke 04	3
	Varela [48], Lincoln [69], Asamoah [79]

Rost; Altintop•, Bordon, Krstajic (Rodríguez 83), Kobiashvili, Poulsen, Ernst•, Lincoln, Larsen• (Varela 45), Asamoah, Kuranyi (Sand 74). Tr: Slomka

2nd leg. Arena AufSchalke, Gelsenkirchen
6-04-2006, 20:30, 52 973, Busacca SUI

Schalke 04	1
	Lincoln [58]

Rost; Rafinha, Bordon, Rodríguez, Poulsen, Kobiashvili, Lincoln (Azaouagh 85), Bajramovic•, Asamoah (Altintop 73), Kuranyi (Sand 78), Larsen. Tr: Slomka

Levski Sofia	1
	Emil Angelov [24]

Petkov; Hristov (Bukarev• 5), Milanov, Tomasic, Borimirov, Domovchiyski•, Ivanov (Telkiyski 65), Stanislav Angelov, Koprivarov• (Yovov 62), Wagner, Emil Angelov. Tr: Stoilov

1st leg. Giulesti, Bucharest
30-03-2006, 20:45, 15 000, Stark GER

Rapid Bucuresti	1
	Moldovan [50]

Coman; Constantin, Maftei, Rada, Badoi, Dica (Negru 79), Constantin Stancu, Ionut Stancu (Grigore• 45), Niculae, Moldovan (Burdujan 65), Buga. Tr: Lucescu

Steaua Bucuresti	1
	Nicolita [5]

Fernandes; Ogararu•, Goian, Ghionea, Marin, Nicolita• (Nesu 91+), Radoi•, Paraschiv (Cristocea 67), Dica, Oprita, Cristea (Lovin 60). Tr: Olaroiu

2nd leg. Lia Manoliu, Bucharest
6-04-2006, 20:30, 39 750, Medina ESP

Steaua Bucuresti	0

Fernandes; Goian, Ghionea, Marin (Lovin 78), Ogararu, Paraschiv, Radoi•, Dica, Oprita (Nesu 67), Nicolita, Cristea (Balan 90). Tr: Olaroiu

Rapid Bucuresti	0

Coman; Ionut Stancu••, Rada, Maftei, Constantin, Badoi, Grigore•, Constantin Stancu (Dica 64), Niculae•, Moldovan (Burdujan 70), Buga (Vasilache 76). Tr: Lucescu

1st Leg. St Jakob-Park, Basel
30-03-2006, 20:45, 23 639, Rosetti ITA

FC Basel	2
	Delgado [43], Degen [45]

Zuberbühler; Majstorovic•, Berner, Smiljanic, Sterjovski (Chipperfield 64), Malick Ba, Delgado, Degen•, Zanni, Eduardo, Petric (Ergic 85). Tr: Gross

Middlesbrough	0

Schwarzer; Parnaby, Riggott•, Pogatetz (Ehiogu 68), Quedrue, Mendieta (Rochemback 74), Parlour, Doriva, Downing•, Hasselbaink (Yakubu 74), Viduka. Tr: McClaren

2nd Leg. Riverside, Middlesbrough
6-04-2006, 20:00, 24 521, Baskakov RUS

Middlesbrough	4
	Viduka 2 [33 57], Hasselbaink [79], Maccarone [90]

Schwarzer; Parnaby•, Southgate, Quedrue (Maccarone• 67), Morrison (Hasselbaink 45), Boateng, Rochemback (Taylor 92+), Downing, Viduka, Yakubu. Tr: McClaren

FC Basel	1
	Eduardo [23]

Zuberbühler•; Majstorovic••73, Berner, Smiljanic, Sterjovski (Quennoz 85), Malick Ba, Delgado (Ergic 70), Degen• (Chipperfield 61), Zanni, Eduardo, Petric. Tr: Gross

SEMI-FINALS

1st Leg. Arena AufSchalke, Gelsenkirchen
20-04-2006, 20:30, Ovrebo NOR

Schalke 04 0

Rost; Krstajic●80, Bordon, Altintop (Lincoln 45), Rafinha, Poulsen, Kobiashvili, Ernst● (Bajramovic 74), Varela (Kuranyi 65), Larsen, Asamoah. Tr: Slomka

Sevilla 0

Palop; Navarro●, Castedo, Daniel, Escudé, Martí, Maresca, Puerta (Adriano Correia 82), Navas, Saviola (Luis Fabiano 61), Kanouté (Renato 32). Tr: Ramos

2nd Leg. Sánchez Pizjuán, Seville
27-04-2006, 21:30, De Santis ITA

Sevilla 1

Puerta [101]

Palop; Daniel, Ocio●, Escudé, Castedo, Navas, Martí, Maresca, Adriano Correia (Puerta● 77), Luis Fabiano (Renato 99), Saviola (Makukula● 107). Tr: Ramos

Schalke 04 0

Rost; Rafinha, Bordon, Rodríguez● (Larsen 82), Poulsen, Kobiashvili, Ernst●, Asamoah (Sand 90), Lincoln, Bajramovic (Varela● 62), Kuranyi●. Tr: Slomka

1st Leg. Lia Manoliu, Bucharest
20-04-2006, 20:45, Hamer LUX

Steaua Bucuresti 1

Dica [30]

Fernandes; Ograraru, Ghionea, Goian●, Marin●, Dica●, Radoi, Bostina, Paraschiv● (Lovin 86), Nicolita●, Oprita (Cristea 89). Tr: Olaroiu

Middlesbrough 0

Schwarzer●; Parnaby, Ehiogu, Bates, Quedrue, Boateng, Rochemback, Downing, Morrison (Parlour● 70), Yakubu (Maccarone 70), Hasselbaink. Tr: McClaren

2nd Leg. Riverside, Middlesbrough
27-04-2006, 20:00, Michel SVK

Middlesbrough 4

Maccarone 2 [33 89], Viduka [64], Riggott [73]

Jones; Riggott, Southgate (Maccarone 26), Quedrue, Parnaby, Boateng●, Rochemback, Downing, Taylor (Yakubu 55), Hasselbaink● (Ehiogu 90), Viduka. Tr: McClaren

Steaua Bucuresti 2

Dica [16], Goian [24]

Fernandes; Ograraru, Ghionea, Goian, Marin, Oprita (Baciu 81), Radoi, Lovin● (Nesu 86), Bostina, Dica●, Iacob (Balan● 65). Tr: Olaroiu

FINAL

Philips Stadion, Eindhoven
10-05-2006, 20:45, 28 000, Fandel GER

SEVILLA 4 0 MIDDLESBROUGH

Luis Fabiano [27], Maresca 2 [78 84], Kanouté [89]

		SEVILLA			MIDDLESBROUGH		
1	GK	Andrés PALOP			SCHWARZER Mark	GK	1
4	DF	DANIEL			PARNABY Stuart	DF	21
2	DF	Javi NAVARRO			RIGGOTT Chris	DF	5
6	DF	Julien ESCUDE			SOUTHGATE Gareth	DF	6
3	DF	David CASTEDO		70	QUEUDRUE Franck	DF	3
15	MF	Jesús NAVAS		46	MORRISON James	MF	25
25	MF	Vicenzo MARESCA			BOATENG George	MF	7
18	MF	José Luis MARTI			ROCHEMBACK Fabio	MF	10
16	MF	ADRIANO CORREA	86		DOWNING Stewart	MF	19
10	FW	LUIS FABIANO	72	86	VIDUKA Mark	FW	36
7	FW	Javier SOVIOLA	46		HASSELBAINK Jimmy	FW	9
		Tr: RAMOS Juande			Tr: McCLAREN Steve		
13	GK	Antonio NOTARIO			JONES Bradley	GK	22
20	DF	Aitor OCIO			EHIOGU Ugo	DF	4
22	DF	Fernando SALES			BATES Matthew	DF	26
23	DF	Pablo RUIZ		86	CATTERMOLE Lee	MF	39
27	DF	Antonio PUERTA	86		PARLOUR Ray	MF	15
30	FW	Kepa BLANCO		46	MACCARONE Massimo	FW	18
12	FW	Frédéric KANOUTE	46	70	Yakubu AYEGBENI	FW	20

UEFA WOMEN'S CUP 2005–06

SEMI-FINALS

1st Leg, Karl Liebknecht, Potsdam
20-11-2005, 15:00, 1 616, Brohet BEL

1.FFC Turbine Potsdam   2
Sousa Silva [11], Pohlers [26]

Angerer - Carlson, Omilade, Becher, Pohlers, Zietz,
Hingst, Sousa Silva (Kerschowski 56), Wimbersky,
Kuznik, Mittag

Djurgården/Alvsjö   3
Fagerström.L [78], Kalmari [86], Svensson [90]

Aström - Helen Fagerström, Ekblom (Johansson 65),
Thunebro, Bengtsson, Linda Fagerström, Hall,
Svensson, Curtsdotter, Norlin (Kalmari 71), Brogårde

2nd Leg, Råsunda, Stockholm
27-11-2005, 12:00, 150, De Toni ITA

Djurgården/Alvsjö   2
Svensson [35], Norlin [56]

Aström - Helen Fagerström, Thunebro, Bengtsson•,
Johansson, Hall, Svensson, Curtsdotter, Norlin
(Ekblom 57), Brogårde, Kalmari

1.FFC Turbine Potsdam   5
Podvorica [5], Zietz [22], Hingst [37], Pohlers [56],
Mittag [87]

Angerer - Carlson (Omilade 57), Becher, Pohlers,
Zietz, Podvorica• (Kerschowski 76), Hingst,
Wimbersky, Kuznik, Thomas•, Mittag

1st Leg, Am Brentano Bad, Frankfurt
20-11-2005, 14:30, 4 300, Ionescu ROU

1.FFC Frankfurt   0

Wissink - Hansen (Bartusiak 68), Pia Wunderlich•,
Tina Wunderlich, Prinz, Lingor, Kliehm, Affeld,
Garefrekes, Jones, Simisek (Künzer 79)

Montpellier HSC   1
Diguelman [50]

Deville - Rigal, Lepailleur, Bompastor•, Faisandier
(Calvié 59), Diguelman• (Ramos 87), Podence•,
Thomis, Lattaf, Soyer, Abily•

2nd Leg, Joseph Blanc, Villeneuve-les-Mag
26-11-2005, 14:30, 1 200, Gall HUN

Montpellier HSC   2
Diguelman 2 [16 84]

Deville• - Rigal•, Lizzano (Ramos 54), Lepailleur,
Calvié (Oumeur 88), Faisandier•••71, Diguelman,
Podence, Thomis•, Lattaf (Lacaze 68), Soyer

1.FFC Frankfurt   3
Smisek 2 [10 49], Lingor [37]

Wissink•71 - Künzer•, Pia Wunderlich (Weber 90),
Prinz, Lingor, Kliehm, Affeld, Garefrekes•, Jones,
Bartusiak (Tina Wunderlich 88), Simisek (Holl 74)

Karl Liebknecht, Potsdam
20-05-2006, 16:00, 4 431, Oedlund SWE

1.FFC POTSDAM   0   4 1.FFC FRANKFURT

Lingor 2 [7 84], Albertz [64]
Garefrekes [77]

	POTSDAM			FRANKFURT	
25	ANGERER Nadine			HOLL Ursula	24
4	CARLSON Britta	83		HANSEN Louise	3
5	PETER Babett			KUNZER Nia	4
6	OMILADE Navina	60	81	WUNDERLICH Tina	8
8	BECHER Inken		96	PRINZ Birgit	9
9	POHLERS Conny			LINGOR Renate	10
17	ZIETZ Jennifer			KLIEHM Katrin	11
17	HINGST Ariane			GAREFREKES Kerstin	18
20	WIMBERSKY Petra	65		ALBERTZ Sandra	21
21	KUZNIK Peggy			JONES Stephanie	22
31	MITTAG Anja			SMISEK Sandra	28
	Tr: SCHRODER Bernd			Tr: TRITSCHOKS Jürgen	
23	ULLRICH Stephanie			JANISCHEWSKI Nicole	29
12	KERSCHOWSKI Isabel	81		WEBER Meike	12
19	SOUSA SILVA Cristiane	96		BARUCHA Patrizia	20
3	KERSCHOWSKI Monique	65		BARTUSIAK Saskia	25
11	SCHIEWE Carolin			GUNTER Sarah	13
13	HOFLER Juliane			ZERBE Christina	14
18	SCHLANKE Josephine			AFFELD Judith	17

Bornheimer Hang, Frankfurt
27-05-2005, 14:15, 13 200, Damkova CZE

1.FFC FRANKFURT 3   2   1.FFC POTSDAM

Jones [23], Lingor [72p], Prinz [93+]   Pohlers 2 [8 35]

	FRANKFURT			POTSDAM	
24	HOLL Ursula			ANGERER Nadine	25
3	HANSEN Louise		46	CARLSON Britta	4
4	KUNZER Nia		64	PETER Babett	5
8	WUNDERLICH Tina			OMILADE Navina	6
9	PRINZ Birgit		46	BECHER Inken	8
10	LINGOR Renate			POHLERS Conny	9
11	KLIEHM Katrin			ZIETZ Jennifer	14
18	GAREFREKES Kerstin			HINGST Ariane	17
21	ALBERTZ Sandra	88	79	WIMBERSKY Petra	20
22	JONES Stephanie			KUZNIK Peggy	21
28	SMISEK Sandra	88		MITTAG Anja	31
	Tr: TRITSCHOKS Jürgen			Tr: SCHRODER Bernd	
1	WISSINK Marleen			ULLRICH Stephanie	23
12	WEBER Meike	88	79	KERSCHOWSKI Monique	3
20	BARUCHA Patrizia	88	46	KERSCHOWSKI Isabel	12
13	GUNTER Sarah		46	SOUSA SILVA Cristiane	19
14	ZERBE Christina			SCHIEWE Carolin	11
17	AFFELD Judith			PODVORICA Aferdita	15
25	BARTUSIAK Saskia			SCHLANKE Josephine	18

UEFA WOMEN'S CUP 2005-06

First round Groups

		Pl	W	D	L	F	A	Pts	POR	WAL	NIR
Montpellier	FRA	3	3	0	0	11	0	9	1-0	2-0	8-0
1. Dezembro	POR	3	2	1	0	10	1	6		3-0	7-0
Cardiff	WAL	3	1	0	2	3	5	3			3-0
Glentoran	NIR	3	0	0	3	0	18	0			

		Pl	W	D	L	F	A	Pts	ITA	IRL	CRO
Neulengbach	AUT	3	2	1	0	10	2	7	0-0	5-1	5-1
Bardolino	ITA	3	2	1	0	5	0	7		2-0	3-0
UCD	IRL	3	1	0	2	3	7	3			2-0
Maksimir	CRO	3	0	0	3	1	10	0			

		Pl	W	D	L	F	A	Pts	ESP	BEL	SCO
Saestum	NED	3	2	1	0	10	2	7	1-1	2-1	7-0
Athletic Bilboko	ESP	3	2	1	0	10	3	7		3-0	6-2
Wezemaal	BEL	3	1	0	2	6	6	3			5-1
Glasgow City	SCO	3	0	0	3	3	18	0			

		Pl	W	D	L	F	A	Pts	NOR	FIN	EST
Valur	ISL	3	3	0	0	14	3	9	4-1	2-1	8-1
Idrettslag	NOR	3	2	0	1	13	7	6		3-2	9-1
United Pietarsaari	FIN	3	1	0	2	5	5	3			2-0
Pärnu	EST	3	0	0	3	2	19	0			

		Pl	W	D	L	F	A	Pts	MDA	FRO	MKD
LUwin.ch	SUI	3	3	0	0	16	1	9	4-0	5-1	7-0
Codru	MDA	3	2	0	1	8	6	6		4-1	4-1
Ki Klaksvik	FRO	3	0	1	2	3	10	1			1-1
Shkiponjat	MKD	3	0	1	2	2	12	1			

		Pl	W	D	L	F	A	Pts	BLR	ROU	LTU
Sparta Praha	CZE	3	2	1	0	12	1	7	3-0	1-1	8-0
Vitebsk	BLR	3	2	0	1	4	4	6		2-1	2-0
Clujana	ROU	3	0	2	1	4	5	2			2-2
Gintra	LTU	3	0	1	2	2	12	1			

		Pl	W	D	L	F	A	Pts	UKR	ISR	CYP
Wroclaw	POL	3	3	0	0	17	0	9	5-0	1-0	11-0
Arsenal Kharkiv	UKR	3	2	0	1	28	6	6		8-1	20-0
M. Holon	ISR	3	1	0	2	7	9	3			6-0
Kokkinochorion	CYP	3	0	0	3	0	37	0			

		Pl	W	D	L	F	A	Pts	BIH	SVK	SVN
Toliatti	RUS	3	3	0	0	14	0	9	3-0	6-0	5-0
Sarajevo	BIH	3	2	0	1	5	4	6		1-0	4-1
Bratislava	SVK	3	1	0	2	3	8	3			3-1
Novo Mesto	SVN	3	0	0	3	2	12	0			

		Pl	W	D	L	F	A	Pts	BUL	GRE	HUN
Alma	KAZ	3	2	1	0	10	3	6	5-0	2-3	3-0
Sofia	BUL	3	1	1	1	4	7	4		3-1	1-1
Aegina	GRE	3	1	1	1	6	7	4			2-2
MTK Budapest	HUN	3	0	2	1	3	6	2			

Second Round Groups

		Pl	W	D	L	F	A	Pts	FRA	NED	AUT
1.FFC Turbine Potsdam	GER	3	2	1	0	14	1	7	0-0	2-0	12-1
Montpellier	FRA	3	2	1	0	6	1	7		2-1	4-0
Saestum	NED	3	1	0	2	5	7	3			4-3
Neulengbach	AUT	3	0	0	3	4	20	0			

		Pl	W	D	L	F	A	Pts	ISL	KAZ	SCG
Djurgården/Älvsjö	SWE	3	3	0	0	12	1	9	2-1	3-0	7-0
Valur	ISL	3	2	0	1	12	2	6		8-0	3-0
Alma	KAZ	3	1	0	2	5	14	3			5-3
Nis	SCG	3	0	0	3	3	15	0			

		Pl	W	D	L	F	A	Pts	CZE	SUI	AZE
1.FFC Frankfurt	GER	3	2	1	0	16	2	7	1-1	4-0	11-1
Sparta Praha	CZE	3	2	1	0	5	1	7		1-0	3-0
LUwin.ch	SUI	3	1	0	2	5	5	3			5-0
Gömrükçü Baku	AZE	3	0	0	3	1	19	0			

		Pl	W	D	L	F	A	Pts	ENG	RUS	POL
Brøndby	DEN	3	3	0	0	6	1	9	1-0	2-0	3-1
Arsenal	ENG	3	2	0	1	4	2	6		1-0	3-1
Toliatti	RUS	3	0	1	2	3	6	1			3-3
Wroclaw	POL	3	0	1	2	5	9	1			

Quarter-finals

	Leg 1	Leg 2
1.FFC Frankfurt	1	3
Arsenal *	1	1
Brøndby	0	1
Montpellier *	3	3
Djurgården/Älvsjö	2	0
Sparta Praha *	0	0
Valur *	1	1
1.FFC Turb. Potsdam	8	11

Semi-finals

	Leg 1	Leg 2
1.FFC Frankfurt *	0	3
Montpellier	1	2
Djurgården/Älvsjö	3	2
1.FFC Turb. Potsdam *	2	5

Final

	Leg 1	Leg 2
1.FFC Frankfurt	4	3
1.FFC Turb. Potsdam *	0	2

Seven clubs received byes to the second round • * Home team in the first leg

UEFA EUROPEAN WOMEN'S U–19 CHAMPIONSHIP 2006

First Qualifying Round Group 1

	Pl	W	D	L	F	A	Pts	HUN	GRE	BUL
Belgium	3	3	0	0	19	2	**9**	4-0	4-0	11-2
Hungary	3	2	0	1	6	5	**6**		1-0	5-1
Greece	3	1	0	2	2	6	**3**			2-1
Bulgaria	3	0	0	3	4	18	**0**			

First Qualifying Round Group 2

	Pl	W	D	L	F	A	Pts	AUT	ISR	ARM
Italy	3	3	0	0	19	0	**9**	3-0	1-0	15-0
Austria	3	2	0	1	22	4	**6**		4-0	18-1
Israel	3	1	0	2	10	5	**3**			10-0
Armenia	3	0	0	3	1	43	**0**			

First Qualifying Round Group 3

	Pl	W	D	L	F	A	Pts	SWE	NIR	LTU
Denmark	3	2	1	0	18	1	**7**	1-1	7-0	10-0
Sweden	3	2	1	0	9	1	**7**		4-0	4-0
Northern Ireland	3	1	0	2	6	11	**3**			6-0
Lithuania	3	0	0	3	0	20	**0**			

First Qualifying Round Group 4

	Pl	W	D	L	F	A	Pts	SCO	FRO	CRO
England	3	3	0	0	17	0	**9**	3-0	11-0	3-0
Scotland	3	2	0	1	8	3	**6**		5-0	3-0
Faroe Islands	3	1	0	2	2	16	**3**			2-0
Croatia	3	0	0	3	0	8	**0**			

First Qualifying Round Group 5

	Pl	W	D	L	F	A	Pts	CZE	SVN	AZE
Poland	3	2	1	0	10	0	**7**	0-0	3-0	7-0
Czech Republic	3	2	1	0	5	0	**7**		2-0	3-0
Slovenia	3	1	0	2	1	5	**3**			1-0
Azerbaijan	3	0	0	3	0	11	**0**			

First Qualifying Round Group 6

	Pl	W	D	L	F	A	Pts	ISL	BIH	GEO
Russia	3	3	0	0	32	1	**9**	5-1	6-0	21-0
Iceland	3	2	0	1	13	5	**6**		5-0	7-0
Bosnia-Herzegov.	3	1	0	2	12	11	**3**			12-0
Georgia	3	0	0	3	0	40	**0**			

First Qualifying Round Group 7

	Pl	W	D	L	F	A	Pts	POR	WAL	KAZ
Slovakia	3	2	0	1	6	3	**6**	2-3	2-0	2-0
Portugal	3	2	0	1	10	4	**6**		1-2	6-0
Wales	3	2	0	1	4	3	**6**			2-0
Kazakhstan	3	0	0	3	0	10	**0**			

First Qualifying Round Group 8

	Pl	W	D	L	F	A	Pts	SCG	ROU	MKD
Netherlands	3	3	0	0	14	1	**9**	2-0	5-1	7-0
Serbia/Montenegro	3	2	0	1	4	2	**6**		1-0	3-0
Romania	3	0	1	2	2	7	**1**			1-1
FYR Makedonia	3	0	1	2	1	11	**1**			

First Qualifying Round Group 9

	Pl	W	D	L	F	A	Pts	UKR	BLR	MDA
Finland	3	3	0	0	17	0	**9**	1-0	14-0	2-0
Ukraine	3	2	0	1	6	4	**6**		3-2	3-1
Belarus	3	1	0	2	5	17	**3**			3-0
Moldova	3	0	0	3	1	8	**0**			

First Qualifying Round Group 10

	Pl	W	D	L	F	A	Pts	NOR	EST	LVA
Republic Ireland	3	3	0	0	13	1	**9**	2-1	7-0	4-0
Norway	3	2	0	1	20	2	**6**		9-0	10-0
Estonia	3	1	0	2	3	17	**3**			3-1
Latvia	3	0	0	3	1	17	**0**			

Second Qualifying Round Group 1

	Pl	W	D	L	F	A	Pts	NOR	POL	SCG
France	3	3	0	0	14	1	**9**	3-1	2-0	9-0
Norway	3	2	0	1	12	5	**6**		4-2	7-0
Poland	3	1	0	2	4	6	**3**			2-0
Serbia/Montenegro	3	0	0	3	0	18	**0**			

Second Qualifying Round Group 2

	Pl	W	D	L	F	A	Pts	POR	FIN	ISR
Russia	3	3	0	0	10	2	**9**	4-1	2-1	4-0
Portugal	3	2	0	1	5	4	**6**		2-0	2-0
Finland	3	1	0	2	3	4	**3**			2-0
Israel	3	0	0	3	0	8	**0**			

Second Qualifying Round Group 3

	Pl	W	D	L	F	A	Pts	ITA	HUN	SVK
Netherlands	3	2	0	1	5	2	**6**	1-0	1-2	3-0
Italy	3	2	0	1	5	1	**6**		2-0	3-0
Hungary	3	1	1	1	2	3	**4**			0-0
Slovakia	3	0	1	2	0	6	**1**			

Second Qualifying Round Group 4

	Pl	W	D	L	F	A	Pts	ENG	ISL	ROM
Denmark	3	3	0	0	11	2	**9**	2-1	2-1	7-0
England	3	2	0	1	16	5	**6**		7-1	8-2
Iceland	3	1	0	2	6	9	**3**			4-0
Romania	3	0	0	3	2	19	**0**			

Second Qualifying Round Group 5

	Pl	W	D	L	F	A	Pts	SCO	IRL	SVN
Germany	3	3	0	0	18	0	**9**	7-0	3-0	8-0
Scotland	3	2	0	1	5	7	**6**		2-0	3-0
Republic of Ireland	3	1	0	2	2	5	**3**			2-0
Slovenia	3	0	0	3	0	13	**0**			

Second Qualifying Round Group 6

	Pl	W	D	L	F	A	Pts	ESP	AUT	GRE
Sweden	3	3	0	0	12	1	**9**	3-1	4-0	5-0
Spain	3	2	0	1	12	5	**6**		4-2	7-0
Austria	3	1	0	2	6	9	**3**			4-1
Greece	3	0	0	3	1	16	**0**			

Second Qualifying Round Group 7

	Pl	W	D	L	F	A	Pts	WAL	CZE	UKR
Belgium	3	3	0	0	8	3	**9**	4-1	2-1	2-1
Wales	3	2	0	1	5	6	**6**		2-1	1-0
Czech Republic	3	1	0	2	5	5	**3**			3-1
Ukraine	3	0	0	3	2	6	**0**			

UEFA EUROPEAN WOMEN'S U–19 CHAMPIONSHIP 2006

First Round Group Stage

Group A	Pl	W	D	L	F	A	Pts	DEN	SWE	BEL
Germany	3	2	1	0	7	1	7	2-0	1-1	4-0
Denmark	3	1	1	1	2	3	4		0-0	2-1
Sweden	3	0	3	0	1	1	3			0-0
Belgium	3	0	1	2	1	6	1			

Semi-finals

Germany	4
Russia	0

Final

Germany	3
France	0

Group B	Pl	W	D	L	F	A	Pts	RUS	SUI	NED
France	3	3	0	0	8	1	9	4-1	3-0	1-0
Russia	3	2	0	1	8	6	6		2-1	5-1
Switzerland	3	1	0	2	3	5	3			2-0
Netherlands	3	0	0	3	1	8	0			

Denmark	0
France	1

Finals held in Switzerland from 11-07-2006 to 22-07-2006

UEFA EUROPEAN U–17 CHAMPIONSHIP 2006

First Qualifying Round Group 1

	Pl	W	D	L	F	A	Pts	NIR	LTU	MLT
Serbia/Montenegro	3	3	0	0	9	1	9	3-1	4-0	2-0
Northern Ireland	3	2	0	1	5	4	6		1-0	3-1
Lithuania	3	1	0	2	2	5	3			2-0
Malta	3	0	0	3	1	7	0			

First Qualifying Round Group 2

	Pl	W	D	L	F	A	Pts	ITA	UKR	LVA
Republic Ireland	3	2	1	0	6	3	7	2-2	2-1	2-0
Italy	3	1	2	0	6	5	5		2-2	2-1
Ukraine	3	1	1	1	4	4	4			1-0
Latvia	3	0	0	3	1	5	0			

First Qualifying Round Group 3

	Pl	W	D	L	F	A	Pts	BUL	AUT	GEO
Belgium	3	1	2	0	5	4	5	1-0	2-2	2-2
Bulgaria	3	1	1	1	5	2	4		4-0	1-1
Austria	3	1	1	1	4	6	4			2-0
Georgia	3	0	2	1	3	5	2			

First Qualifying Round Group 4

	Pl	W	D	L	F	A	Pts	ISR	AZE	ARM
Russia	3	2	1	0	6	1	7	1-0	1-1	4-0
Israel	3	2	0	1	12	4	6		5-1	7-2
Azerbaijan	3	1	1	1	5	6	4			3-0
Armenia	3	0	0	3	2	14	0			

First Qualifying Round Group 5

	Pl	W	D	L	F	A	Pts	POR	FRO	SMR
Germany	3	3	0	0	16	0	9	2-0	4-0	10-0
Portugal	3	2	0	1	9	2	6		4-0	5-0
Faroe Islands	3	0	1	2	3	11	1			3-3
San Marino	3	0	1	2	3	18	1			

First Qualifying Round Group 6

	Pl	W	D	L	F	A	Pts	CZE	ISL	AND
Sweden	3	2	1	0	10	3	7	3-1	2-2	5-0
Czech Republic	3	2	0	1	10	4	6		4-1	5-0
Iceland	3	1	1	1	9	6	4			6-0
Andorra	3	0	0	3	0	16	0			

First Qualifying Round Group 7

	Pl	W	D	L	F	A	Pts	SVK	GRE	BIH
Finland	3	2	1	0	5	2	7	3-1	1-0	1-1
Slovakia	3	2	0	1	12	4	6		7-0	4-1
Greece	3	1	0	2	3	10	3			3-2
Bosnia-Herzegov.	3	0	1	2	4	8	1			

First Qualifying Round Group 8

	Pl	W	D	L	F	A	Pts	MDA	NOR	LIE
Poland	3	2	1	0	4	0	7	0-0	2-0	2-0
Moldova	3	2	1	0	6	2	7		2-0	4-2
Norway	3	1	0	2	3	5	3			3-1
Liechtenstein	3	0	0	3	3	9	0			

First Qualifying Round Group 9

	Pl	W	D	L	F	A	Pts	ROU	CRO	MKD
Turkey	3	3	0	0	6	1	9	1-0	1-0	4-1
Romania	3	1	1	1	4	1	4		0-0	4-0
Croatia	3	1	1	1	2	1	4			2-0
FYR Macedonia	3	0	0	3	1	10	0			

First Qualifying Round Group 10

	Pl	W	D	L	F	A	Pts	CYP	SCO	ALB
Hungary	3	3	0	0	9	1	9	2-0	2-0	5-1
Cyprus	3	2	0	1	3	2	6		1-0	2-0
Scotland	3	1	0	2	3	3	3			3-0
Albania	3	0	0	3	1	10	0			

First Qualifying Round Group 11

	Pl	W	D	L	F	A	Pts	NED	BLR	SVN
Denmark	3	1	2	0	2	1	5	1-1	0-0	1-0
Netherlands	3	1	2	0	3	2	5		1-0	1-1
Belarus	3	1	1	1	1	1	4			1-0
Slovenia	3	0	1	2	1	3	1			

First Qualifying Round Group 12

	Pl	W	D	L	F	A	Pts	WAL	EST	KAZ
Switzerland	3	3	0	0	12	2	9	3-0	5-1	4-1
Wales	3	1	1	1	4	5	4		2-0	2-2
Estonia	3	1	0	2	3	8	3			2-1
Kazakhstan	3	0	1	2	4	8	1			

Elite Round Group 1

	Pl	W	D	L	F	A	Pts	NED	NIR	FIN
Germany	3	2	1	0	9	1	7	1-1	4-0	4-0
Netherlands	3	2	1	0	5	2	7		3-1	1-0
Northern Ireland	3	1	0	2	4	9	3			3-2
Finland	3	0	0	3	2	8	0			

Elite Round Group 2

	Pl	W	D	L	F	A	Pts	POR	UKR	SWE
Hungary	3	2	1	0	9	1	7	1-1	4-0	4-0
Portugal	3	1	2	0	5	4	5		2-2	2-1
Ukraine	3	0	2	1	3	7	2			1-1
Sweden	3	0	1	2	2	7	1			

Elite Round Group 3

	Pl	W	D	L	F	A	Pts	FRA	DEN	TUR
Czech Republic	3	2	0	1	4	3	6	1-3	2-0	1-0
France	3	1	2	0	4	2	5		0-0	1-1
Denmark	3	1	1	1	1	2	4			1-0
Turkey	3	0	1	2	1	3	1			

Elite Round Group 4

	Pl	W	D	L	F	A	Pts	POL	SUI	SVK
Belgium	3	2	1	0	9	3	7	2-0	3-3	4-5
Poland	3	2	0	1	5	3	6		1-0	4-1
Switzerland	3	1	1	1	6	4	4			3-0
Slovakia	3	0	0	3	1	11	0			

Elite Round Group 5

	Pl	W	D	L	F	A	Pts	WAL	CYP	MDA
Spain	3	2	1	0	6	1	7	2-0	1-1	3-0
Wales	3	1	1	1	5	5	4		2-0	3-3
Cyprus	3	1	1	1	3	3	4			2-0
Moldova	3	0	1	2	3	8	1			

Elite Round Group 6

	Pl	W	D	L	F	A	Pts	IRL	ISR	ROM
Serbia/Mont'gro	3	2	0	1	5	2	6	3-0	1-2	1-0
Republic of Ireland	3	1	1	1	5	4	4		1-1	4-0
Israel	3	1	1	1	4	5	4			1-3
Romania	3	1	0	2	3	6	3			

Elite Round Group 7

	Pl	W	D	L	F	A	Pts	ITA	ENG	BUL
Russia	3	2	1	0	7	1	7	0-0	2-1	5-0
Italy	3	1	2	0	5	2	5		2-2	3-0
England	3	0	2	1	3	4	2			0-0
Bulgaria	3	0	1	2	0	8	1			

UEFA EUROPEAN U-17 CHAMPIONSHIP 2006

First Round Group Stage

Group A	Pl	W	D	L	F	A	Pts	RUS	HUN	LUX
Spain	3	3	0	0	12	1	9	3-0	2-0	7-1
Russia	3	2	0	1	3	3	6		1-0	2-0
Hungary	3	1	0	2	4	3	3			4-0
Luxembourg	3	0	0	3	1	13	0			

Group B	Pl	W	D	L	F	A	Pts	CZE	SCG	BEL
Germany	3	2	1	0	8	0	7	0-0	4-0	4-0
Czech Republic	3	2	1	0	5	2	7		2-1	3-1
Serbia/Montenegro	3	0	1	2	2	7	1			1-1
Belgium	3	0	1	2	2	8	1			

Semi-finals

Russia	1
Germany	0

Spain	0
Czech Republic	2

Final

Russia	2	5p
Czech Republic	2	3p

3rd place play-off

Spain	1	3p
Germany	1	2p

Finals held in Luxembourg from 3-05-2006 to 14-05-2006

UEFA EUROPEAN U–19 CHAMPIONSHIP 2006

First Qualifying Round Group 1

	Pl	W	D	L	F	A	Pts	SVN	LTU	EST
Georgia	3	2	1	0	6	2	7	1-1	3-1	2-0
Slovenia	3	2	1	0	7	4	7		2-1	4-2
Lithuania	3	1	0	2	3	5	3			1-0
Estonia	3	0	0	3	2	7	0			

First Qualifying Round Group 2

	Pl	W	D	L	F	A	Pts	SVK	LIE	KAZ
Denmark	3	2	1	0	3	0	7	0-0	2-0	1-0
Slovakia	3	2	1	0	3	1	7		2-1	1-0
Liechtenstein	3	1	0	2	2	4	3			1-0
Kazakhstan	3	0	0	3	0	3	0			

First Qualifying Round Group 3

	Pl	W	D	L	F	A	Pts	CYP	NOR	MLT
Israel	3	3	0	0	10	1	9	3-0	4-1	3-0
Cyprus	3	2	0	1	3	4	6		1-0	2-1
Norway	3	1	0	2	7	5	3			6-0
Malta	3	0	0	3	1	11	0			

First Qualifying Round Group 4

	Pl	W	D	L	F	A	Pts	POR	LUX	AZE
Russia	3	3	0	0	7	0	9	1-0	3-0	3-0
Portugal	3	2	0	1	8	2	6		3-0	5-1
Luxembourg	3	1	0	2	3	7	3			3-1
Azerbaijan	3	0	0	3	2	11	0			

First Qualifying Round Group 5

	Pl	W	D	L	F	A	Pts	SWE	HUN	FRO
Belgium	3	2	0	1	8	2	6	1-0	0-1	7-1
Sweden	3	2	0	1	7	3	6		3-1	4-1
Hungary	3	2	0	1	5	3	6			3-0
Faroe Islands	3	0	0	3	2	14	0			

First Qualifying Round Group 6

	Pl	W	D	L	F	A	Pts	NIR	ITA	MDA
Republic Ireland	3	3	0	0	9	2	9	2-1	4-1	3-0
Northern Ireland	3	1	1	1	3	3	4		0-0	2-1
Italy	3	1	1	1	3	4	4			2-0
Moldova	3	0	0	3	1	7	0			

First Qualifying Round Group 7

	Pl	W	D	L	F	A	Pts	AUT	WAL	SMR
France	3	3	0	0	8	1	**9**	2-0	3-1	3-0
Austria	3	1	1	1	8	2	**4**		0-0	8-0
Wales	3	1	1	1	6	4	4			5-1
San Marino	3	0	0	3	1	16	**0**			

First Qualifying Round Group 8

	Pl	W	D	L	F	A	Pts	SCO	FIN	AND
Switzerland	3	2	1	0	14	0	**7**	0-0	2-0	12-0
Scotland	3	2	1	0	6	0	**7**		1-0	5-0
Finland	3	1	0	2	6	3	**3**			6-0
Andorra	3	0	0	3	0	23	**0**			

First Qualifying Round Group 9

	Pl	W	D	L	F	A	Pts	TUR	MKD	ALB
Romania	3	1	2	0	3	1	**5**	1-1	0-0	2-0
Turkey	3	1	2	0	5	3	**5**		2-2	2-0
FYR Macedonia	3	1	2	0	6	4	**5**			4-2
Albania	3	0	0	3	2	8	**0**			

First Qualifying Round Group 10

	Pl	W	D	L	F	A	Pts	BLR	GRE	NED
Germany	3	2	1	0	11	6	**7**	6-2	3-2	2-2
Belarus	3	1	1	1	4	7	**4**		2-1	0-0
Greece	3	1	0	2	6	7	**3**			3-2
Netherlands	3	0	2	1	4	5	**2**			

First Qualifying Round Group 11

	Pl	W	D	L	F	A	Pts	BUL	ISL	BIH
Croatia	3	2	1	0	8	2	**7**	0-0	3-2	5-0
Bulgaria	3	2	1	0	3	0	**7**		1-0	2-0
Iceland	3	1	0	2	4	4	**3**			2-0
Bosnia-Herzegov.	3	0	0	3	0	9	**0**			

First Qualifying Round Group 12

	Pl	W	D	L	F	A	Pts	UKR	LVA	ARM
Serbia/Montenegro	3	2	1	0	3	0	**7**	2-0	0-0	1-0
Ukraine	3	2	0	1	3	3	**6**		1-0	2-1
Latvia	3	0	2	1	0	1	**2**			0-0
Armenia	3	0	1	2	1	3	1			

Elite Round Group 1

	Pl	W	D	L	F	A	Pts	HUN	RUS	SVN
Austria	3	3	0	0	4	1	**9**	1-0	1-0	2-1
Hungary	3	1	1	1	4	3	**4**		1-1	3-1
Russia	3	1	1	1	2	2	**4**			1-0
Slovenia	3	0	0	3	2	6	**0**			

Elite Round Group 2

	Pl	W	D	L	F	A	Pts	SVK	GEO	IRL
Turkey	3	3	0	0	11	2	**9**	2-1	6-0	3-1
Slovakia	3	2	0	1	8	5	**6**		4-1	3-2
Georgia	3	1	0	2	4	12	**3**			3-2
Republic of Ireland	3	0	0	3	5	9	**0**			

Elite Round Group 3

	Pl	W	D	L	F	A	Pts	FRA	BLR	BUL
Scotland	3	2	1	0	5	3	**7**	1-1	2-1	2-1
France	3	1	2	0	5	1	**5**		0-0	4-0
Belarus	3	1	1	1	3	2	**4**			2-0
Bulgaria	3	0	0	3	1	8	**0**			

Elite Round Group 4

	Pl	W	D	L	F	A	Pts	SUI	UKR	DEN
Czech Republic	3	2	0	1	5	1	**6**	0-1	3-0	2-0
Switzerland	3	2	0	1	4	2	**6**		1-2	2-0
Ukraine	3	2	0	1	5	4	**6**			3-0
Denmark	3	0	0	3	0	7	**0**			

Elite Round Group 5

	Pl	W	D	L	F	A	Pts	CRO	ISR	MKD
Portugal	3	2	0	1	5	3	**6**	2-1	0-1	3-1
Croatia	3	1	1	1	5	4	**4**		2-0	2-2
Israel	3	1	1	1	1	2	**4**			0-0
FYR Macedonia	3	0	2	1	3	5	**2**			

Elite Round Group 6

	Pl	W	D	L	F	A	Pts	SCG	NIR	ENG
Belgium	3	2	1	0	6	4	**7**	1-1	3-2	2-1
Serbia/Montenegro	3	1	1	1	3	5	**4**		1-4	1-0
Northern Ireland	3	1	0	2	7	6	**3**			1-2
England	3	1	0	2	3	4	**3**			

Elite Round Group 7

	Pl	W	D	L	F	A	Pts	GER	SWE	CYP
Spain	3	3	0	0	15	2	**9**	3-1	4-0	8-1
Germany	3	2	0	1	9	4	**6**		2-1	6-0
Sweden	3	1	0	2	4	7	**3**			3-1
Cyprus	3	0	0	3	2	17	**0**			

UEFA EUROPEAN U–19 CHAMPIONSHIP 2006

First Round Group Stage

Group A	Pl	W	D	L	F	A	Pts	AUT	POL	BEL
Czech Republic	3	2	0	1	7	5	**6**	3-1	2-0	2-4
Austria	3	2	0	1	6	4	**6**		1-0	4-1
Poland	3	1	0	2	4	4	**3**			4-1
Belgium	3	1	0	2	6	10	**3**			

Group B	Pl	W	D	L	F	A	Pts	SCO	POR	TUR
Spain	3	2	1	0	10	4	**7**	4-0	1-1	5-3
Scotland	3	1	1	1	5	8	**4**		2-2	3-2
Portugal	3	0	3	0	7	7	**3**			4-4
Turkey	3	0	1	2	9	12	**1**			

Semi-finals

Spain	5
Austria	0
Czech Republic	0
Scotland	1

Final

Spain	2
Scotland	1

Finals held in Poland from 18-07-2006 to 29-07-2006

UEFA EUROPEAN U–21 CHAMPIONSHIP 2004–06

Qualifying Round Group 1

	Pl	W	D	L	F	A	Pts	NED	CZE	ROU	MKD	FIN	ARM
Netherlands	10	7	2	1	21	7	23		0-0	2-0	4-0	4-1	0-0
Czech Republic	10	6	3	1	26	8	21	2-4		4-1	2-0	3-0	6-0
Romania	10	6	1	3	17	8	19	2-0	0-0		5-1	1-0	2-0
FYR Macedonia	10	2	3	5	9	18	9	0-2	2-2	1-0		1-1	4-0
Finland	10	2	1	7	7	16	7	1-2	1-3	0-1	2-0		0-1
Armenia	10	1	2	7	2	25	5	1-3	0-4	0-5	0-0	0-1	

Qualifying Round Group 2

	Pl	W	D	L	F	A	Pts	DEN	UKR	GRE	TUR	GEO	ALB	KAZ
Denmark	12	9	2	1	30	12	29		3-2	2-1	1-1	1-0	7-0	5-1
Ukraine	12	7	2	3	22	7	23	0-1		1-0	0-0	6-0	5-0	2-1
Greece	12	6	2	4	18	9	20	0-1	0-1		2-1	3-0	2-0	5-0
Turkey	12	5	4	3	15	9	19	3-2	1-0	0-1		0-0	4-0	1-0
Georgia	12	3	2	7	7	22	11	2-4	0-3	1-1	0-2		2-1	0-1
Albania	12	2	3	7	9	27	9	1-2	1-1	1-1	1-1	0-1		3-1
Kazakhstan	12	2	1	9	8	23	7	1-1	0-1	1-2	2-1	0-1	0-1	

Qualifying Round Group 3

	Pl	W	D	L	F	A	Pts	POR	RUS	SVK	LVA	EST	LUX
Portugal	10	10	0	0	29	3	30		2-0	2-1	3-0	3-0	4-0
Russia	10	6	1	3	24	6	19	0-1		4-0	1-1	3-0	3-0
Slovakia	10	6	1	3	12	9	19	0-1	1-0		3-1	2-1	1-0
Latvia	10	3	3	4	10	16	12	1-2	0-4	0-0		0-0	2-1
Estonia	10	0	3	7	4	24	3	0-5	1-5	0-2	1-3		0-0
Luxembourg	10	0	2	8	4	25	2	1-6	0-4	0-2	1-2	1-1	

Qualifying Round Group 4

	Pl	W	D	L	F	A	Pts	FRA	SUI	ISR	IRL	CYP
France	8	6	1	1	13	5	19		1-1	1-0	1-0	2-0
Switzerland	8	4	3	1	15	8	15	0-3		0-0	4-2	3-0
Israel	8	4	3	1	11	7	15	3-2	1-1		3-1	1-0
Rep. of Ireland	8	1	2	5	10	14	5	1-2	0-1	2-2		1-1
Cyprus	8	0	1	7	2	17	1	0-1	1-5	0-1	1-1	

Qualifying Round Group 5

	Pl	W	D	L	F	A	Pts	ITA	SVN	NOR	BLR	MDA	SCO
Italy	10	8	1	1	16	3	25		1-0	2-0	2-1	1-0	2-0
Slovenia	10	4	3	3	13	13	15	0-3		2-2	1-4	1-0	3-0
Norway	10	4	2	4	14	13	14	1-0	0-0		2-3	1-2	0-1
Belarus	10	4	1	5	20	19	13	1-1	1-2	2-3		2-3	3-2
Moldova	10	3	2	5	8	12	11	0-1	1-3	1-3	1-0		0-0
Scotland	10	1	3	6	6	17	6	0-3	1-1	0-2	2-3	0-0	

Qualifying Round Group 6

	Pl	W	D	L	F	A	Pts	GER	ENG	POL	AUT	WAL	AZE
Germany	10	7	3	0	24	5	24		1-1	1-2	0-0	4-0	2-0
England	10	6	3	1	21	7	21	2-2		4-1	1-2	2-0	2-0
Poland	10	3	4	3	18	18	13	1-3	1-3		2-2	3-2	3-0
Austria	10	3	2	5	9	14	11	0-3	0-2	0-3		2-0	3-0
Wales	10	3	1	6	9	21	10	0-4	0-4	2-2	1-0		3-0
Azerbaijan	10	0	3	7	1	17	3	0-2	0-0	1-1	0-0	0-1	

Qualifying Round Group 7

	Pl	W	D	L	F	A	Pts	BEL	SCG	ESP	BIH	LTU	SMR
Belgium	10	7	3	0	25	6	24		4-0	1-0	2-1	3-0	5-0
Serbia/Monteneg.	10	7	1	2	29	11	22	1-1		1-0	5-1	3-2	9-0
Spain	10	6	2	2	37	8	20	2-2	2-0		4-2	2-0	14-0
Bosnia-Herzeg.	10	3	1	6	17	20	10	1-1	1-3	0-2		2-0	5-1
Lithuania	10	3	1	6	9	16	10	1-2	0-2	1-1	1-0		2-0
San Marino	10	0	0	10	4	60	0	0-4	0-5	1-10	1-4	1-2	

Qualifying Round Group 8

	Pl	W	D	L	F	A	Pts	CRO	HUN	SWE	ISL	BUL	MLT
Croatia	10	8	1	1	14	6	25		1-0	1-0	2-1	1-0	1-0
Hungary	10	6	1	3	12	7	19	2-2		2-2	0-1	1-0	2-0
Sweden	10	6	0	4	16	12	18	0-2	2-1		1-4	2-0	6-0
Iceland	10	4	1	5	15	11	13	1-2	0-1	3-1		3-1	0-0
Bulgaria	10	2	1	7	9	17	7	2-1	1-2	1-2	1-3		2-1
Malta	10	1	2	7	3	16	5	0-1	0-2	0-1	1-0	1-1	

Play-offs

Home team first leg	Score	Home team second leg
England	1-1 1-2	France
Hungary	1-1 0-1	Italy
Czech Republic	0-2 0-1	Germany
Russia	0-1 1-3	Denmark
Ukraine	2-3 3-1	Belgium
Serbia and Montenegro	3-1 2-1	Croatia
Switzerland	1-1 1-2	Portugal
Slovenia	0-0 0-2	Netherlands

UEFA EUROPEAN UNDER 21 CHAMPIONSHIP 2004-06

First Round Group Stage

Group A	Pl	W	D	L	F	A	Pts	SCG	GER	POR
France	3	3	0	0	6	0	9	2-0	3-0	1-0
Serbia/Montenegro	3	1	0	2	2	3	3		0-1	2-0
Germany	3	1	0	2	1	4	3			0-1
Portugal	3	1	0	2	1	3	3			

Group B	Pl	W	D	L	F	A	Pts	NED	ITA	DEN
Ukraine	3	2	0	1	4	3	6	2-1	0-1	2-1
Netherlands	3	1	1	1	3	3	4		1-0	1-1
Italy	3	1	1	1	4	4	4			3-3
Denmark	3	0	2	1	5	6	2			

Semi-finals

Netherlands	3
France	2

Serbia/Montenegro	0	4p
Ukraine	0	5p

Final

Netherlands	3
Ukraine	0

Tournament held in Portugal from 23-05-2006 to 4-06-2006

REGIONAL CLUB TOURNAMENTS IN EUROPE

ROYAL LEAGUE 2005-06

First round groups

Group A

		Pl	W	D	L	F	A	Pts	DEN	SWE	NOR	NOR
FC Midtjylland	DEN	6	3	3	0	13	5	12		4-1	4-0	1-1
Hammarby IF	SWE	6	2	2	2	12	10	8	2-2		0-0	4-0
Vålerenga IF	NOR	6	2	2	2	8	10	8	0-1	2-1		3-1
IK Start	NOR	6	0	3	3	8	16	3	1-1	2-4	3-3	

Group B

		Pl	W	D	L	F	A	Pts	NOR	DEN	DEN	SWE
Lillestrøm SK	NOR	6	2	4	0	6	3	10		0-0	2-2	0-0
FC København	DEN	6	1	4	1	5	5	7	1-1		1-1	1-1
Brøndby IF	DEN	6	1	3	2	7	7	6	0-1	1-2		2-0
Kalmar FF	SWE	6	1	3	2	3	6	6	0-2	1-0	1-1	

Group C

		Pl	W	D	L	F	A	Pts	SWE	NOR	SWE	DEN
Djurgårdens IF	SWE	6	3	1	2	8	7	10		1-1	0-1	2-1
Lyn Oslo	NOR	6	2	2	2	7	6	8	1-2		1-0	0-0
IFK Göteborg	SWE	6	2	2	2	7	7	8	2-0	1-3		3-3
AaB Aalborg	DEN	6	1	3	2	7	9	6	1-3	2-1	0-0	

The tournament took place from 10-11-2005 to 6-04-2006 • * Home team in the first leg

Quarter-finals

FC København*	2 0 2p
Hammarby IF	0 2 0p

Lyn Oslo*	1 0
FC Midtjylland	3 1

Djurgårdens IF*	2 3
Vålerenga IF	1 1

IFK Göteborg*	0 0
Lillestrøm SK	0 2

Semi-finals

FC København*	3 4
FC Midtjylland	1 0

Djurgårdens IF*	1 0
Lillestrøm SK	3 1

Final

FC København	1
Lillestrøm SK	0

FINAL

Parken, Copenhagen
6-04-2006, Att: 13 617
Ref: Frojfeldt SWE
Scorer - Razak Pimpong 90 for FC København

APPENDIX 1 – MISCELLANEOUS

ITALY 2005-06

SERIE A — ORIGINAL TABLE

	Pl	W	D	L	F	A	Pts	Juve	Milan	Inter	Fiorentina	Roma	Lazio	Chievo	Palermo	Livorno	Empoli	Parma	Ascoli	Udinese	Sampdoria	Reggina	Cagliari	Siena	Messina	Lecce	Treviso
Juventus	38	27	10	1	71	24	91		0-0	2-0	1-1	1-1	1-1	1-0	2-1	3-0	2-1	1-1	2-1	1-0	2-0	1-0	4-0	2-0	1-0	3-1	3-1
Milan	38	28	4	6	85	31	88	3-1		1-0	3-1	2-1	2-0	4-1	2-1	2-0	3-0	4-3	1-0	5-1	1-1	2-1	1-0	3-1	4-0	2-1	5-0
Internazionale	38	23	7	8	68	30	76	1-2	3-2		1-0	2-3	3-1	1-0	3-0	5-0	4-1	2-0	1-0	3-1	1-0	4-0	3-2	1-1	3-0	3-0	3-0
Fiorentina	38	22	8	8	66	41	74	1-2	3-1	2-1		1-1	1-2	2-1	1-0	3-2	2-1	4-1	3-1	4-2	2-1	5-2	2-1	2-1	2-0	1-0	1-0
Roma	38	19	12	7	70	42	69	1-4	1-0	1-1	1-1		1-1	4-0	1-2	3-0	2-1	1-0	0-0	3-1	4-3	2-3	2-1	3-1	1-1	3-1	1-1
Lazio	38	16	14	8	57	47	62	1-1	0-0	0-0	1-0	0-2		2-2	4-2	3-1	3-3	1-0	4-1	1-2	0-0	3-1	1-3	3-2	1-0	1-0	3-1
Chievo Verona	38	13	15	10	54	49	54	1-1	2-1	0-1	0-2	4-4	2-2		0-0	2-1	2-2	1-0	1-1	2-0	1-1	4-0	2-1	4-1	2-0	3-1	0-0
Palermo	38	13	13	12	50	52	52	1-2	0-2	3-0	3-3	3-1	2-2	0-2		2-2	4-2	1-2	0-0	2-1	0-2	1-0	2-2	1-3	1-0	3-0	1-0
Livorno	38	12	13	13	37	44	49	1-3	0-3	0-0	2-0	0-0	2-1	0-0	3-1		2-0	2-0	2-0	0-0	1-0	0-1	1-2	2-2	2-2	2-1	1-1
Empoli	38	13	6	19	47	61	45	0-4	1-3	1-0	1-1	1-0	2-3	2-1	0-1	2-1		1-2	1-2	1-2	1-0	3-0	3-1	2-1	1-3	1-0	1-1
Parma	38	12	9	17	46	60	45	1-2	2-3	1-0	2-4	0-3	1-1	2-1	1-1	2-1	1-0		0-0	1-2	1-1	4-0	1-0	1-1	1-1	2-0	1-1
Ascoli	38	9	16	13	43	53	43	1-3	1-1	1-2	0-2	3-2	4-2	1-1	0-0	3-1	3-1	1-1		1-2	1-1	1-2	2-1	1-0	2-0	1-1	2-2
Udinese	38	11	10	17	40	54	43	0-1	0-4	0-1	0-0	1-4	3-0	1-1	0-0	0-2	1-0	2-0	1-1		2-0	1-2	2-0	1-2	1-0	1-2	2-2
Sampdoria	38	10	11	17	47	51	41	0-1	2-1	2-2	3-1	1-1	2-0	1-2	0-2	0-2	2-0	1-2	1-2	1-1		3-2	1-3	3-4	2-1	3-1	1-1
Reggina	38	11	8	19	39	65	41	0-2	1-4	0-4	1-0	3-1	0-1	3-2	1-1	0-2	2-1	2-0	2-0	2-1			3-1	1-1	3-0	2-0	1-2
Cagliari	38	8	15	15	42	55	39	1-1	0-2	2-2	0-0	0-0	1-1	2-1	1-1	4-1	3-1	2-1	2-1	2-0	0-2			1-0	1-1	0-0	0-2
Siena	38	9	12	17	42	60	39	0-3	0-3	0-0	0-2	0-2	2-3	0-1	1-2	0-0	1-0	2-2	1-1	2-3	1-0	0-0	2-1		4-2	1-2	1-0
Messina	38	6	13	19	33	59	31	2-2	1-3	1-2	2-2	0-2	1-1	2-0	0-0	0-0	1-2	0-1	1-1	1-1	1-4	1-1	1-0	0-0		2-1	3-1
Lecce	38	7	8	23	30	57	29	0-3	1-0	0-2	1-3	2-2	0-0	0-0	2-0	0-0	1-2	1-2	0-0	1-2	0-3	0-0	3-0	3-0	0-2		1-1
Treviso	38	3	12	23	24	56	21	0-0	0-2	0-1	1-3	0-1	0-1	1-2	2-2	0-1	1-2	0-1	2-2	2-1	0-2	0-1	1-2	0-1	0-0	2-1	

ROMANIA 2005-06 DIVIZIA B SERIA 3

	Pl	W	D	L	F	A	Pts
Liberty Salonta	28	17	7	4	37	16	58
Bihor Oradea	28	17	4	7	53	27	55
Universitatea Cluj	28	15	9	4	43	16	54
Gaz Metan Medias	28	15	6	7	39	21	51
FCM Resita	28	11	7	10	26	29	40
Corvinul Hunedoara	28	10	8	10	33	35	38
CFR Timisoara	28	10	6	12	33	40	36
Gloria II Bistrita	28	10	6	12	25	34	36
Industria SC Turzii	28	8	10	10	30	29	34
Minerul Lupeni	28	9	7	12	26	31	34
Olimpia Satu Mare	28	9	5	14	24	36	32
Unirea Dej	28	9	5	14	29	37	32
Apulum Alba Iulia	28	6	10	12	21	31	28
UT Arad	28	6	9	13	25	35	27
Unirea Sanicolau Mare	28	6	5	17	21	48	23
Armatura Zalau				Excluded			

20/08/2005 - 3/06/2006

APPENDIX 2 – MAJOR WORLD RECORDS

NATIONAL CAPS – MEN

		First	Last	Caps
AL DEAYEA Mohamed	KSA	1990	2006	181
SUAREZ Claudio	MEX	1992	2006	178
HASSAN Hossam	EGY	1985	2006	170
JONES Cobi	USA	1992	2004	164
AL TALYANI Adnan	UAE	1984	1997	164
AL JABER Sami	KSA	1992	2006	163
MATTHAUS Lothar	GER	1980	2000	150
DAEI Ali	IRN	1993	2006	149
REIM Martin	EST	1992	2006	147
AL KHILAIWI Mohamed	KSA	1990	2001	143
KRISTAL Marko	EST	1992	2005	143
RAVELLI Thomas	SWE	1981	1997	143
CAFU	BRA	1990	2006	142
ABDULLAH Majed	KSA	1978	1994	139
HONG Myung Bo	KOR	1990	2002	135
AGOOS Jeff	USA	1988	2003	134
HURTADO Ivan	ECU	1992	2006	125
ABDULAZIZ Bashar	KUW	1996	2005	132
CAMPOS Jorge	MEX	1991	2003	130
MUNTEANU Dorinel	ROU	1991	2006	130
PARDO Pavel	MEX	1996	2006	129
BALBOA Marcelo	USA	1988	2000	128
FIGO Luis	POR	1991	2006	127
MALDINI Paolo	ITA	1988	2002	126
SAEED Hussein	IRQ	1977	1990	126
ZUBIZARRETA Andoni	ESP	1985	1998	126

NATIONAL GOALS – MEN

		First	Last	Goals
DAEI Ali	IRN	1993	2006	109
PUSKAS Ferenc	HUN	1945	1956	84
PELE	BRA	1957	1971	77
KOCSIS Sandor	HUN	1948	1956	75
ABDULAZIZ Bashar	KUW	1996	2005	74
WOODWARD Vivian	ENG	1903	1914	73
HASSAN Hossam	EGY	1985	2006	69
MULLER Gerd	GER	1966	1974	68
ABDULLAH Majed	KSA	1978	1994	67
JOHN Stern	TRI	1995	2006	65
SENAMUANG Kiatisuk	THA	1993	2004	64
Al HOUWAIDI Jassem	KUW	1992	2002	63
RONALDO	BRA	1994	2006	62
SAEED Hussein	IRQ	1977	1990	61
SCHLOSSER Imre	HUN	1906	1927	59
BATISTUTA Gabriel	ARG	1991	2002	56
MIURA Kazuyoshi	JPN	1990	2000	56
CHA Bum Kun	KOR	1972	1986	55
KAMAMOTO Kunishige	JPN	1964	1977	55
ROMARIO	BRA	1987	2005	55
STREICH Joachim	GDR	1969	1984	53
AL TALYANI Adnan	UAE	1984	1997	53
NIELSEN Poul	DEN	1910	1925	52
ZICO	BRA	1976	1986	52
TICHY Lajos	HUN	1955	1964	51
HWANG Seong Hong	KOR	1993	2003	50

NATIONAL COACHES

	First	Last	Games
MILUTINOVIC Bora	1983	2004	276
ZAGALLO Mario	1967	1992	204
PARREIRA Carlos Alberto	1976	2006	199
MATURANA Francisco	1987	2003	172
HERBERGER Sepp	1936	1964	167
MEISL Hugo	1912	1937	155
MICHEL Henri	1984	2006	152
SCHON Helmut	1953	1978	148
VOGTS Berti	1990	2004	144
PIONTEK Sepp	1979	1993	143
WINTERBOTTOM Walter	1946	1962	139
PETTERSSON John	1921	1936	138
BAROTI Lajos	1957	1978	132
TIRNANIC Alexander	1946	1966	128
PIECHNICZEK Antoni	1981	1997	127
STABILE Guillermo	1939	1960	127

NATIONAL CAPS – WOMEN

		First	Last	Caps
LILLY Kristine	USA	1987	2006	309
HAMM Mia	USA	1987	2004	275
FOUDY Julie	USA	1988	2004	271
FAWCETT Joy	USA	1987	2004	239
MILBRETT Tiffeny	USA	1991	2006	204
CHASTAIN Brandi	USA	1988	2005	192
FAN Yunjie	CHN	1992	2004	192
RIISE Hege	NOR	1990	2004	188
ZHAO Lihong	CHN	1992	2003	182
MACMILLAN Shannon	USA	1993	2006	175
AILING Liu	CHN	1987	2001	173
OVERBECK Carla	USA	1988	2000	168
SUN Wen	CHN	1973	2006	166
WEN Lirong	CHN	1987	2001	163
WANG Liping	CHN	1992	2004	162
NORDBY Bente	NOR	1994	2006	159

UNBEATEN RUN – NATIONAL TEAM

	Years	Games
Brazil	1993-1995	36
Argentina	1991-1993	31
Spain	1994-1998	31
Hungary	1950-1954	30
France	1994-1996	30
Brazil	1970-1973	29
Colombia	1992-1994	27
Italy	2004-2006	25
Brazil	1975-1978	24
Ghana	1981-1983	23
Czechoslovakia	1974-1976	23
Germany	1978-1980	23
Brazil	1981-1982	23
Brazil	1997-1998	23

UNBEATEN RUN – CLUBS

	Years	Games
ASEC Abidjan	1989-1994	108
Steaua Bucuresti	1986-1989	104
Espérance Tunis	1997-2001	85
Celtic	1915-1917	62
Union Saint-Gilloise	1933-1935	60
Boca Juniors	1924-1927	59
Pyunik Yerevan	2002-2004	59
Milan	1991-1993	58
Olympiacos	1972-1974	58
Skonto Riga	1993-1996	58
Benfica	1976-1978	56
Peñarol	1966-1969	56
Shakhtar Donetsk	2000-2002	55
Dalian Wanda	1995-1997	55

CONSECUTIVE WINS – NATIONAL TEAM

	Years	Games
England (amateurs)	1906-1909	17
Australia	1996-1997	14
Brazil	1997	14
France	2003-2004	14
Scotland	1879-1885	13
Brazil	1960-1962	13
Germany DR	1973-1974	12
Germany FR	1979-1980	12
France	1984-1985	12
Mexico	1987-1990	12

The 2002 FIFA World Cup™ qualifier between Australia and American Samoa on 11 April 2001, set two major records. The 31-0 victory recorded by the Australians is the highest ever win in an international match. 13 of the goals were scored by Archie Thompson, the largest haul by a single player in a match. Records results in international matches for all 207 associations can be found in part two of the Almanack listed under each country. Record victories and defeats are shown for each country along with record sequences. Once FIFA has published the official list of every game ever played, it is our intention to expand this section of the Almanack to reflect the findings of that research.

APPENDIX 3 – HOW TO USE THE ALMANACK

①⇨
Estadio Centenario, Montevideo
7-09-2003, 16:00, 39 253, Zamora PER   ⇦②

URU   5 0   BOL ⇦③

④⇨ Forlan [17], Chevanton 2 [40 61] ⇦⑤
Abeijon [83], Bueno [88]

① Stadium and city/town where the match was played.
② *From left to right:* Date, kick-off time, attendance, name and nationality of referee. Assistant referees are included for FIFA tournaments.
③ Teams (using FIFA abbreviations) and scores.

④ Name of goal scorer and the time that the goal was scored.
⑤ Indicates that 2 goals were scored by Chevanton followed by the times of the goals.

⇕

	BOLIVIA	
①⇨	FERNANDEZ Leonardo	21 ⇦②
	PENA Juan Manuel	2 ⇦③
	HOYOS Miguel	4
	SANCHEZ Oscar	5
	ROJAS Richard	6
	CRISTALDO Luis	7
	MENDEZ Limberg	9
	CASTILLO Jose	11
④⇨ 67	RICALDI Alvaro	15 ⇦⑤
46	RIBEIRO Luis	17
⑥⇨ 46	MOREJON Limber	19
	Tr: ACOSTA Nelson	⇦⑦
46	BALDIVIESO Julio	10
46	JUSTINIANO Raul	16 ⇦⑧

⇔

Estadio Centenario, Montevideo
7-09-2003, 16:00, 39 253, Zamora PER

URU   5 0   BOL

Forlan [17], Chevanton 2 [40 61]
Abeijon [83], Bueno [88]

URUGUAY		BOLIVIA	
1 MUNUA Gustavo		FERNANDEZ Leonardo	21
5 SOSA Marcelo	69	PENA Juan Manuel	2
6 LOPEZ Diego		HOYOS Miguel	4
9 BUENO Carlos		SANCHEZ Oscar	5
10 LIGUERA Martin	77	ROJAS Richard	6
11 NUNEZ Richard		CRISTALDO Luis	7
14 GONZALEZ Cristian		MENDEZ Limberg	9
17 LAGO Eduardo		CASTILLO Jose	11
19 CHEVANTON Ernesto		67 RICALDI Alvaro	15
20 RECOBA Alvaro		46 RIBEIRO Luis	17
21 FORLAN Diego	76	46 MOREJON Limber	19
Tr: CARRASCO Juan Ramon		Tr: ACOSTA Nelson	
8 ABEIJON Nelson	69	46 BALDIVIESO Julio	10
15 SANCHEZ Vicente	76	46 JUSTINIANO Raul	16
16 OLIVERA Ruben	77		

① Family name in capitals, followed by the player's given name.
② Shirt number.
③ A shaded box indicates that the player was cautioned.
④ A shaded box next to a player who has been sent off (see below), indicates a dismissal for two yellow cards.
A blacked-out box indicates a straight red card.

⑤ A blacked-out box indicates the player was dismissed at the time shown in the centre column.
⑥ Substitution time.
⑦ Team coach/trainer.
⑧ Substitute. The time of the substitution corresponds with the player listed in the starting line-up.

CLUB DIRECTORY

	Club	Town/City		Stadium	Capacity	www.	②	③ Lge	④ Cup	⑤ CL
	Borussia Mönchengladbach	Mönchengladbach	①	Borussia-Park	53 148	borussia.de		5	3	0
	Bayern München	Munich		Allianz-Arena	66 000	fcbayern.de		20	13	4
	1.FC Nürnberg	Nuremburg		Frankenstadion	44 833	fcn.de		9	3	0

⑥

① Indicates that Bayern play at the Allianz-Arena, which has a capacity of 66, 000.
② Official club website at http://www(given name).
③ National League Championship.
④ National Cup.

⑤ CL = Champions League of relevant Confederation.
⑥ Indicates that Bayern have won the National League Championship on 20 occasions.

CHINA PR 2004

① SUPER LEAGUE	② Pl	③ W	④ D	⑤ L	⑥ F	⑦ A	⑧ Pts	Shenzhen	Shandong	Shanghai I	Liaoning	Dalian	Tianjin	Beijing	Shenyang	Sichuan	Shanghai S	Qingdao	Chongqing
Shenzhen Jianlibao †	22	11	9	2	30	13	42		2-1		3-0	2-2	0-1	2-0		1-1	3-1	1-0	0-0
Shandong Luneng Tai.	22	10	6	6	44	29	36	1-1		4-2	3-1	2-3	3-1	5-2	4-1	1-2	2-1	1-1	4-1
Shanghai International	22	8	8	6	39	31	32	2-2	2-1		2-1	4-0	3-0	1-1	3-1	3-2	1-1	1-0	1-2
Liaoning Zhongyu	22	10	2	10	39	40	32	1-2	2-3	2-1		1-5	1-5	1-1	1-0	0-0	5-2	3-1	3-0

⇐⑨

15/05/2004 - 5/12/2004 • † Teams qualifying for the AFC Champions League

① Chinese champions of 2004.
All champions are listed in bold. If the club at the top of the table is not listed in bold it means that the table shown represents only part of a season. Relegated clubs are also shown in bold.
② Number of games played.
③ Number of wins.
④ Number of draws.
⑤ Number of losses.
⑥ Number of goals scored.

⑦ Number of goals conceded.
⑧ Number of points gained in the season.
⑨ This result represents the match between Liaoning Zhongyu at home and Chongqing, the away club. The home team score is listed first so Liaoning Zhongyu won 3-0 at home to Chongqing.
⑩ Dates for the season.

BRAZIL NATIONAL TEAM RECORDS AND RECORD SEQUENCES

Records			Sequence records					
Victory	10-1	BOL 1949	① Wins	14	1997	⑤ Clean sheets	8	1989
Defeat	0-6	URU 1920	② Defeats	4	2001	⑥ Goals scored	47	1994-1997
Player Caps	126	CAFU	③ Undefeated	43	1993-1997	⑦ Without goal	5	1990
Player Goals	77	PELE	④ Without win	7	1983-84, 1990-91	⑧ Goals against	24	1937-1944

① Number of consecutive wins.
② Number of consecutive defeats.
③ Number of consecutive games played without defeat.
④ Number of consecutive games played without a win.
⑤ Number of consecutive games played without conceding a goal.
⑥ Number of consecutive games played in which Brazil scored.
⑦ Number of consecutive games played without scoring.
⑧ Number of consecutive games played with opponent scoring.

EXPLANATION OF OTHER TERMS USED IN THE ALMANACK

In the national team record box for each country the % column is worked out by awarding two points for a win and one for a draw
In the Champions League match reports:
 • indicates a booking.

•85 indicates a player was sent off (with minute).
≠90 indicates a player missed a penalty.
2✖ indicates the second penalty in a penalty shoot-out was missed (or scored 2✓)

CALENDAR FOR THE 2006-07 SEASON

Week starting

	Week	Events
September 2006	Sat 1	2-09 & 6-09 FIFA International matchdays; 05-09 to 21-09 AFC U-17 Championship Singapore
	Sat 9	13-09 AFC CL/AFC Cup QF1; 8/9/10-09 CAF CL group; 12/13-09 UEFA CL group matchday 1; 14-09 UEFA Cup R1
	Sat 16	20-09 AFC CL/AFC Cup QF2;
	Sat 23	27-09 AFC CL/AFC Cup SF1; CONMEBOL SA R2; 26/27-09 UEFA CL group matchday 2; 28-09 UEFA Cup R1
	Sat 30	30-09 CAF CL SF1
October 2006	Sat 7	7-10 & 11-10 FIFA International matchdays; CONMEBOL SA R2
	Sat 14	18-10 AFC CL/AFC Cup SF2; 14-10 CAF CL SF2; 18-10 CONMEBOL SA QF1; 17/18-10 UEFA CL group matchday 3 19-10 UEFA Cup group matchday 1
	Sat 21	21-10 COSAFA Cup F; 27-10 AFC Cup F1
	Sat 28	29-10 to 12-11 AFC Youth Championship; 1-11 AFC CL F1; 3-11 AFC Cup F2; 28-10 CAF CL F1; 1-11 CONMEBOL SA QF2; 31-10/1-11 UEFA CL group matchday 4; 2-11 UEFA Cup group matchday 2
November 2006	Sat 4	2-11 to 12-11 FIFA Beach Soccer World Cup Rio de Janeiro; 8-11 CONMEBOL SA SF1
	Sat 11	8-11 AFC CL F2; 15-11 FIFA International matchday; 11-11 CAF CL F2
	Sat 18	18-11 CAF CC F1; CONMEBOL SA SF2; 21/22-11 UEFA CL group matchday 5; 23-11 UEFA Cup group matchday 3
	Sat 25	29-11 AFC awards ceremony; 29-11 CONMEBOL SA F1
December 2006	Sat 2	2-12 CAF CC F2; 6-12 CONMEBOL SA F2; 5/6-12 UEFA CL group matchday 6; 7-12 UEFA Cup group matchday 4
	Sat 9	10-12 to 17-12 FIFA Club World Cup Japan 2006; 14-11 UEFA Cup Group matchday 5
	Sat 16	18-12 FIFA World Player Gala 2006
	Sat 23	
	Sat 30	
January 2007	Sat 6	
	Sat 13	
	Sat 20	
	Sat 27	
February 2007	Sat 3	7-02 FIFA International matchday
	Sat 10	14-02 UEFA Cup R2
	Sat 17	20-02 UEFA CL R2; 22-02 UEFA Cup R2
	Sat 24	
March 2007	Sat 3	7-03 UEFA CL R2; 8-03 UEFA Cup R3
	Sat 10	15-03 UEFA Cup R3
	Sat 17	
	Sat 24	24-03 & 28-03 FIFA International matchdays
	Sat 31	3-04 UEFA CL QF1; 5-04 UEFA Cup QF1
April 2007	Sat 7	11-04 UEFA CL QF2; 12-04 UEFA Cup QF2
	Sat 14	
	Sat 21	24-04 UEFA CL SF1; 26-04 UEFA Cup SF1
	Sat 28	2-05 UEFA CL SF1; 3-05 UEFA Cup SF2
May 2007	Sat 5	
	Sat 12	16-05 UEFA Cup F
	Sat 19	23-05 UEFA CL F
	Sat 26	
June 2007	Sat 2	2-06 & 6-06 FIFA International matchdays; 7-07 to 29-07 AFC Asian Cup 2007 Indonesia, Malaysia, Thailand, Vietnam
	Sat 9	
	Sat 16	
	Sat 23	26-06 to 15-07 Copa America Venezuela
	Sat 30	30-06 to 22-07 FIFA U-20 World Cup Canada
July 2007	Sat 7	
	Sat 14	
	Sat 21	
	Sat 28	

CL = Champions League (according to the confederation indicated) • SA = Copa Sudamericana • CC = Confederation Cup
r1 = first round • r2 = second round • r3 = third round • qf = quarter-final • sf = semi-final • f = final
1L - first leg • 2L = second leg • m/w = mid-week after the week-end indicated • TBC = dates to be confirmed